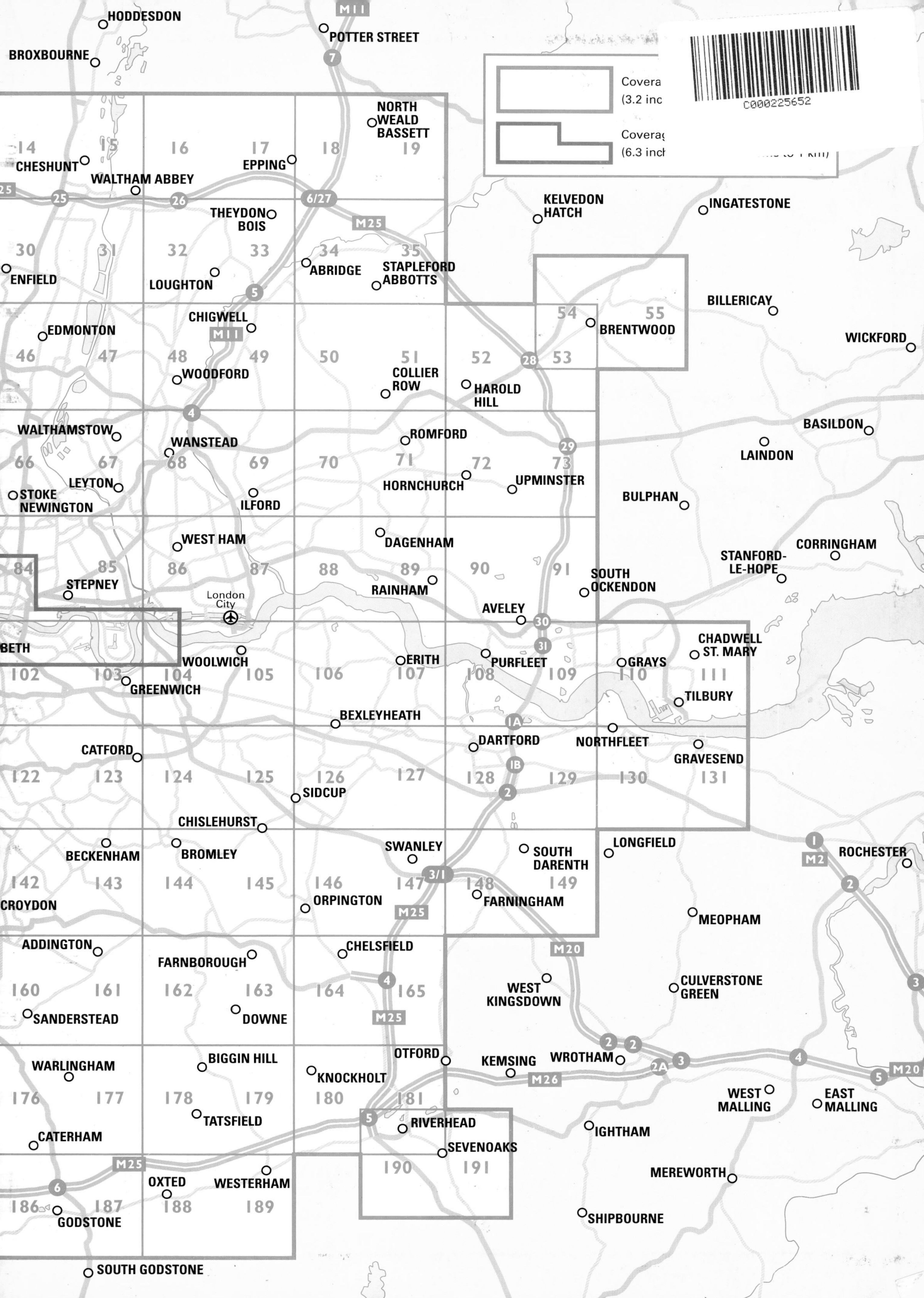

HODDESDON

BROXBOURNE

M11

POTTER STREET

7

NORTH
WEALD
BASSETT

14 CHESHUNT 15 16 17 18 19
EPPING

25

25 25 WALTHAM ABBEY 26 THEYDON
BOIS 6/27

M25

30 ENFIELD 31 32 LOUGHTON 33 34 ABRIDGE 35 STAPLEFORD
ABBOTTS

5

KELVEDON
HATCH INGATESTONE

CHIGWELL

M11

46 EDMONTON 47 48 WOODFORD 49 50 51 COLLIER
ROW 52 53 54 BRENTWOOD 55 BILLERICAY

28 WICKFORD

4

53

WALTHAMSTOW HAROLD
HILL BASILDON

66 67 LEYTON 68 WANSTEAD 69 70 71 ROMFORD 72 73 LAINDON

STOKE
NEWINGTON ILFORD HORNCHURCH UPMINSTER 29

BULPHAN

WEST HAM DAGENHAM CORRINGHAM

84 85 STEPNEY 86 87 88 89 RAINHAM 90 91 SOUTH
OCKENDON STANFORD-
LE-HOPE

AVELEY 30

London
City 31

BETH WOOLWICH PURFLEET CHADWELL
ST. MARY

102 103 104 105 ERITH 106 107 108 109 110 GRAYS 111

GREENWICH TILBURY

BEXLEYHEATH 1A

DARTFORD NORTHFLEET

CATFORD 1B GRAVESEND

122 123 124 125 126 127 128 129 130 131

SIDCUP 2

CHISLEHURST

BECKENHAM BROMLEY SWANLEY SOUTH
DARENTH LONGFIELD

ROCHESTER

142 143 144 145 146 147 148 149 M2

CROYDON ORPINGTON 3/1 FARNINGHAM 2

M25

ADDINGTON CHELSFIELD M20 MEOPHAM

FARNBOROUGH CULVERSTONE
GREEN

160 161 162 163 164 4 165 3

SANDERSTEAD DOWNE WEST
KINGSDOWN

M25

BIGGIN HILL OTFORD WROTHAM 4 M20

WARLINGHAM KNOCKHOLT KEMSING 2 2

176 177 178 179 180 181 2A 3 5

TATSFIELD M26 WEST
MALLING EAST
MALLING

CATERHAM RIVERHEAD IGHTHAM

M25 5 SEVENOAKS

6 OXTED WESTERHAM 190 191 MEREWORTH

186 187 188 189

GODSTONE SHIPBOURNE

SOUTH GODSTONE

LONDON

M25 Master

CONTENTS

MAIN LONDON MAPS

Key to main London maps	ii-iii
Key to map symbols	iii
M25 route planning map	2-3
Main London maps	4-191

CENTRAL LONDON MAPS

London Congestion Charging Zone map	192
Key to Central London maps	193
Key to map symbols	193
Central London maps	194-205

INDEX

Index to places, streets, railway stations, hospitals and places of interest	206-350

Published by Collins
An imprint of HarperCollins*Publishers*
77-85 Fulham Palace Road, Hammersmith, London W6 8JB
www.collins.co.uk

Mapping generated from Collins/Bartholomew digital databases

London Underground Map by permission of Transport Trading Limited
Registered User No. 02/3682

The grid on this map is the National Grid taken from the Ordnance Survey map with the permission of the Controller of Her Majesty's Stationery Office.

ISBN 0 00 715534 4 Paperback imp 001 QM11429
ISBN 0 00 715533 6 Hardback imp 001 QM11428

Printed in China UDM

e-mail: roadcheck@harpercollins.co.uk

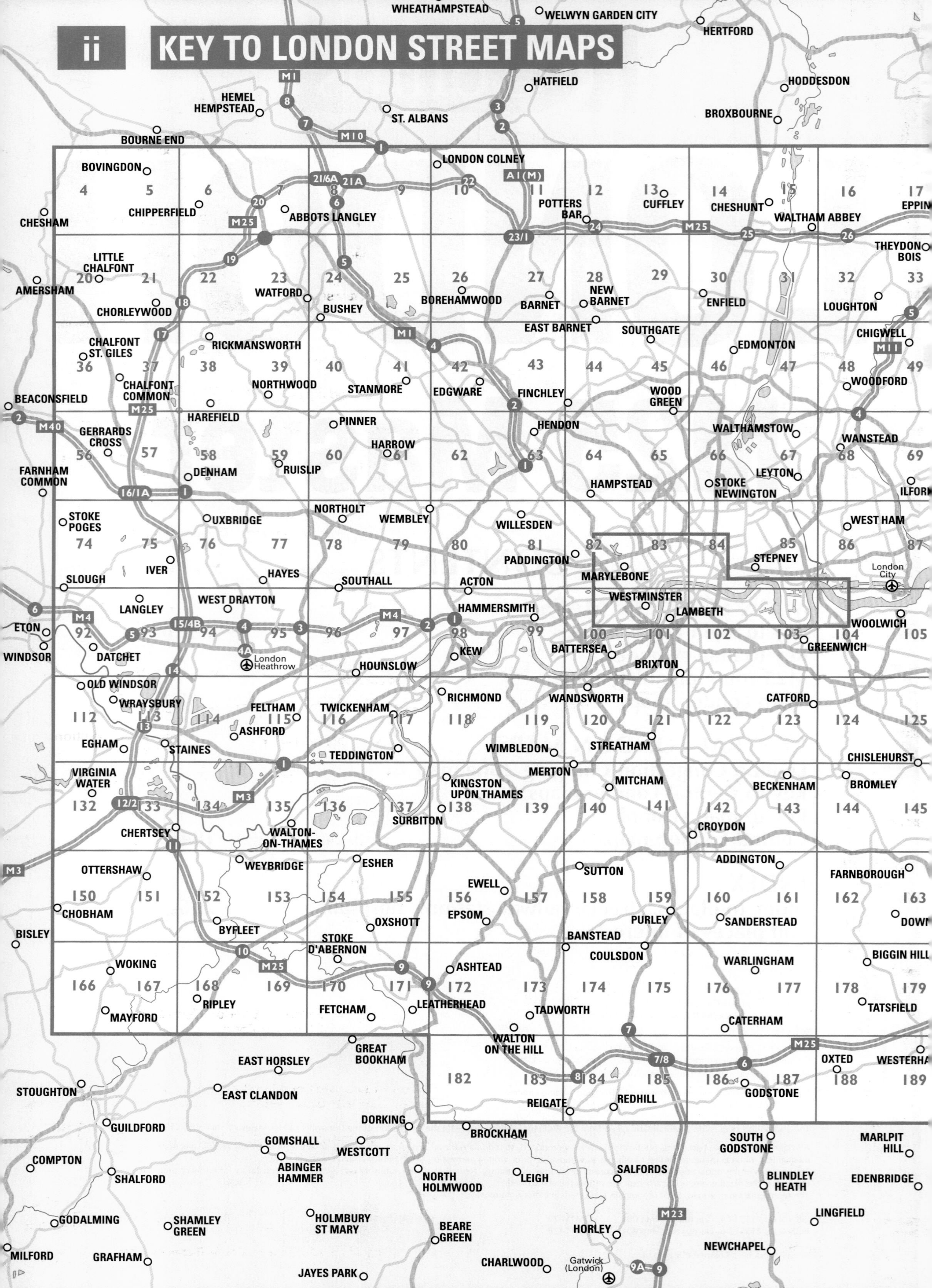

WHEATHAMPSTEAD WELWYN GARDEN CITY HERTFORD

HODDESDON

HATFIELD BROXBOURNE

HEMEL HEMPSTEAD ST. ALBANS

BOURNE END

BOVINGDON LONDON COLNEY

4 5 6 7 21/6A 21A 9 10 22 11 POTTERS BAR 12 CUFFLEY 13 CHESHUNT 14 15 16 17 EPPIN

CHIPPERFIELD ABBOTS LANGLEY WALTHAM ABBEY

CHESHAM 23/1 24 25 26

THEYDON BOIS

LITTLE CHALFONT NEW BARNET

AMERSHAM 20 21 22 23 24 25 26 BARNET 27 28 29 30 31 32 33 LOUGHTON

WATFORD BOREHAMWOOD ENFIELD

CHORLEYWOOD BUSHEY

EAST BARNET SOUTHGATE CHIGWELL

CHALFONT ST. GILES RICKMANSWORTH EDMONTON WOODFORD

36 37 38 39 40 41 42 43 44 45 46 47 48 49

CHALFONT COMMON NORTHWOOD STANMORE EDGWARE FINCHLEY WOOD GREEN WALTHAMSTOW

BEACONSFIELD HAREFIELD PINNER HENDON WANSTEAD

GERRARDS CROSS HARROW LEYTON

56 57 58 59 60 61 62 63 64 65 66 67 68 69

FARNHAM COMMON DENHAM RUISLIP HAMPSTEAD STOKE NEWINGTON ILFOR

STOKE POGES NORTHOLT WEMBLEY WILLESDEN WEST HAM

74 75 76 77 78 79 80 81 82 83 84 85 86 87

SLOUGH IVER UXBRIDGE PADDINGTON MARYLEBONE STEPNEY London City

HAYES ACTON WESTMINSTER

LANGLEY WEST DRAYTON SOUTHALL HAMMERSMITH LAMBETH

ETON 92 5 93 94 95 3 96 97 2 98 99 100 101 102 103 104 105 WOOLWICH

WINDSOR DATCHET 4A London Heathrow KEW BATTERSEA GREENWICH

OLD WINDSOR BRIXTON

WRAYSBURY HOUNSLOW

FELTHAM RICHMOND WANDSWORTH CATFORD

112 113 114 115 116 117 118 119 120 121 122 123 124 125

EGHAM ASHFORD TWICKENHAM CHISLEHURST

VIRGINIA WATER STAINES TEDDINGTON WIMBLEDON STREATHAM

132 133 134 135 136 137 138 139 140 141 142 143 144 145

MERTON MITCHAM BECKENHAM BROMLEY

CHERTSEY KINGSTON UPON THAMES CROYDON

WALTON-ON-THAMES SURBITON

OTTERSHAW WEYBRIDGE ESHER SUTTON ADDINGTON FARNBOROUGH

150 151 152 153 154 155 156 157 158 159 160 161 162 163

CHOBHAM EWELL PURLEY SANDERSTEAD DOW

BISLEY BYFLEET EPSOM BANSTEAD

STOKE D'ABERNON OXSHOTT COULSDON WARLINGHAM BIGGIN HILL

WOKING ASHTEAD

166 167 168 169 170 171 172 173 174 175 176 177 178 179

RIPLEY FETCHAM LEATHERHEAD TADWORTH CATERHAM TATSFIELD

MAYFORD WALTON ON THE HILL OXTED WESTERHA

EAST HORSLEY GREAT BOOKHAM 182 183 184 185 186 187 188 189

STOUGHTON EAST CLANDON REIGATE REDHILL GODSTONE

GUILDFORD DORKING BROCKHAM SOUTH GODSTONE MARLPIT HILL

COMPTON GOMSHALL WESTCOTT BLINDLEY HEATH EDENBRIDGE

SHALFORD ABINGER HAMMER NORTH HOLMWOOD LEIGH SALFORDS LINGFIELD

GODALMING SHAMLEY GREEN HOLMBURY ST MARY BEARE GREEN HORLEY NEWCHAPEL

MILFORD GRAFHAM JAYES PARK CHARLWOOD Gatwick (London)

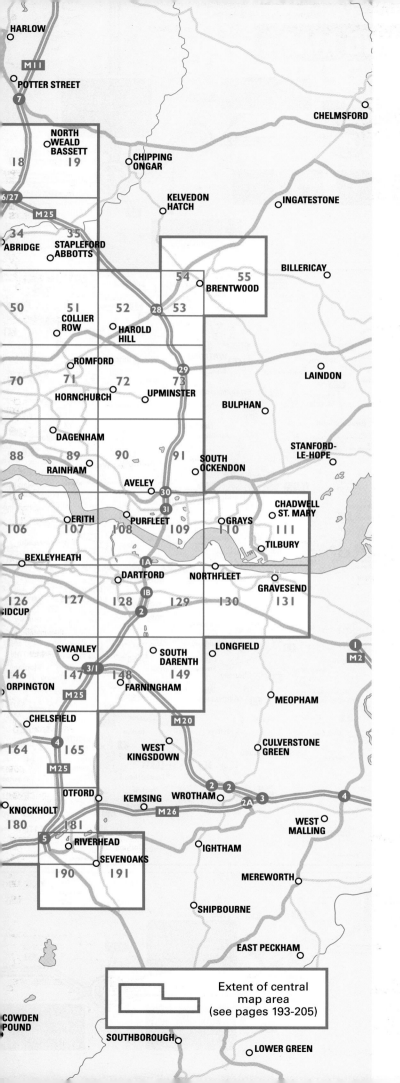

KEY TO MAIN MAP SYMBOLS

M4	Motorway
Dual A4	Primary route
Dual A40	'A' road
B504	'B' road
—	Other road/One way street
—	Toll
—	Street market
—	Restricted access road
—	Pedestrian street
—	Cycle path
-----	Track/Footpath
- - -	Long distance footpath
LC	Level crossing
---P---	Pedestrian ferry
--ᵛ--	Vehicle ferry
—	County/Borough boundary
—	Postal district boundary
Main railway station
Other railway station
London Underground station
DLR	Docklands Light Railway station
Tramlink station
P	Car park
Bus/Coach station

	Leisure & tourism
	Shopping
	Administration & law
	Health & welfare
	Education
	Industry & commerce
	Cemetery
	Golf course
	Public open space/Allotments
	Park/Garden/Sports ground
	Wood/Forest
	Orchard
USA	Embassy
Pol	Police station
Fire Sta	Fire station
PO	Post Office
Lib	Library
i	Tourist information centre
▲	Youth hostel
☐	Tower block
⊕	Heliport
+	Church
☾	Mosque
✡	Synagogue

Extent of London Congestion Charging Zone

The reference grid on this atlas coincides with the Ordnance Survey National Grid System. The grid interval is 500 metres.

🏠 Page Continuation Number   **AT** Grid Reference   **03** OS National Grid Kilometre Square

SCALE

| 0 | ¼ | ½ | ¾ | 1 mile |

| 0 | 0.25 | 0.5 | 0.75 | 1 | 1.25 | 1.5 kilometres |

1:20,000 3.2 inches to 1 mile/5 cms to 1 km

Extent of central map area (see pages 193-205)

M1
The North
Luton ✈   13
21

A405
St Albans   3¼
London (North West)
(M1 South)
21ᴬ

A1081
St Albans   3
22

A1(M)
A1081
London (North West)   3
Barnet
Hatfield   6
Services
23

21

21ᴬ

A1081

22

A1(M)

23

● SOUTH MIMMS
SERVICES

A41
Hemel Hempstead   5
Aylesbury   20
20

A41
Hemel Hempstead   5
Aylesbury   20
20

20

M1
The North
Luton ✈   13
21

A405
Watford   4¼
Harrow (M1)
21ᴬ

A1081
St Albans   3¾
22

A1(M)
A1081
Hatfield   6
Barnet   3
London (North West)
Services
23

A41
Watford   3½
19

19

A404
Rickmansworth   2
Chorleywood   2½
Amersham   7
18

A404
Chorleywood   ½
Amersham   7
18

18

A412
Maple Cross   1
17

17

A412
Maple Cross   1
Rickmansworth   2
17

M40 (East)
Uxbridge   3
London (West)

M40 (West)
Birmingham   100
Oxford   38
16

M40

M40 (West)
Birmingham   100
Oxford (A40)   38

M40 (East)
Uxbridge   3
London (West)
16

16

M4
Heathrow ✈ Terminals
1, 2 & 3   3½
London (West)
Slough   5
The West
15

M4
The West
Slough   5
Reading   25
London (West)
Heathrow ✈ Terminals
1, 2 & 3   3½
15

15

A3113
Heathrow ✈
Terminal 4   3½
& Cargo   3
14

A3113
Heathrow ✈
Terminal 4   3½
& Cargo
14

14

A30
Staines   2
13

13

A30
London (West)
Staines   2
13

M3
Sunbury   6
Southampton   56
Basingstoke   27
12

12

M3
Basingstoke   27
Southampton   56
Sunbury   6
12

A317
A320
Chertsey   2
Woking   5
11

11

A317
A320
Woking   5
Chertsey   2
11

A3
London (South West)
Guildford   8
Kingston   12
10

A243
A24
Leatherhead   2
Dorking   6½
9

A217
Sutton   8
Reigate   2
Redhill (A25)   3½
8

10

A3
London (South West)
Guildford   8
10

9

A243
A24
Leatherhead   2
Dorking   6½
9

8

A217
Reigate
Sutton
Kingston (A240)
8

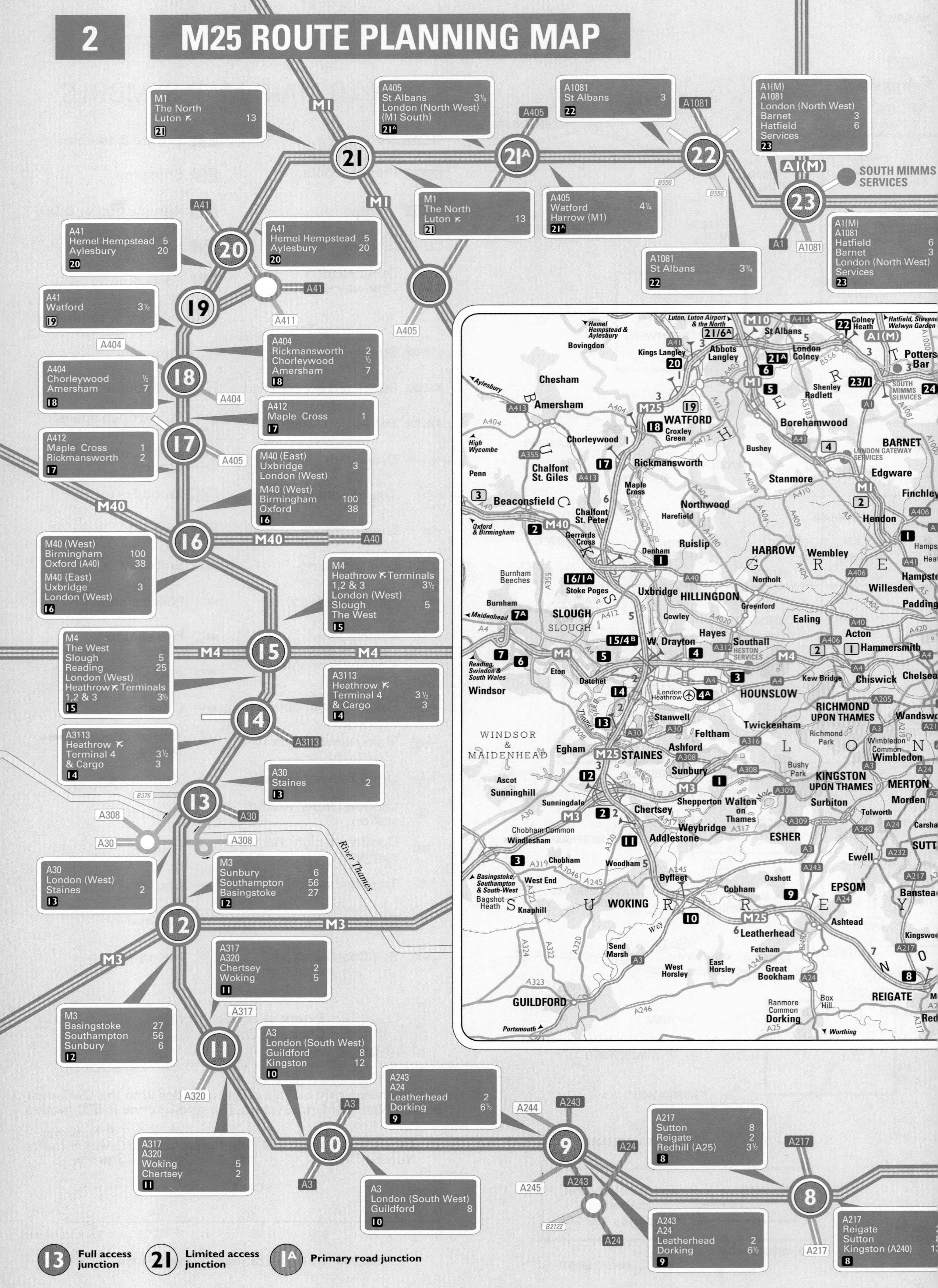

River Thames

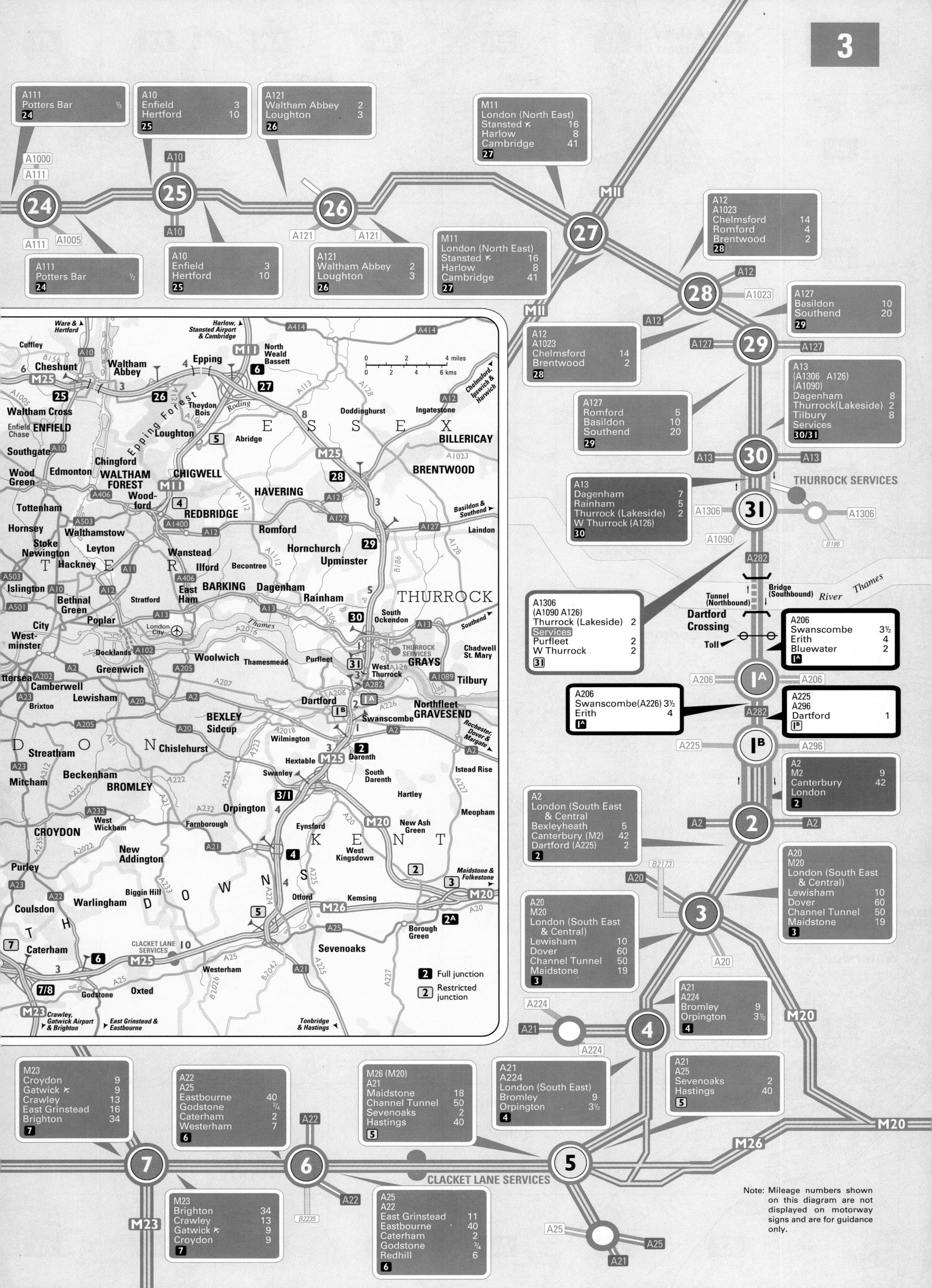

3
A111
Potters Bar ½
24
A10
Enfield 3
Hertford 10
25
A121
Waltham Abbey 2
Loughton 3
26
M11
London (North East)
Stansted 16
Harlow 8
Cambridge 41
27
A1000
A111
A10
24
25
26
A121
A1005
M11
27
A111
Potters Bar ½
24
A10
Enfield 3
Hertford 10
25
A121
Waltham Abbey 2
Loughton 3
26
M11
London (North East)
Stansted 16
Harlow 8
Cambridge 41
27
A12
A1023
Chelmsford 14
Romford 4
Brentwood 2
28
A1023
A127
Basildon 10
Southend 20
29
A12
A1023
Chelmsford 14
Brentwood 2
28
A127
A13
(A1306 A126)
(A1090)
Dagenham 8
Thurrock(Lakeside) 2
Tilbury 8
Services
30/31
A127
Romford 5
Basildon 10
Southend 20
29
30
THURROCK SERVICES
A13
Dagenham 7
Rainham 5
Thurrock (Lakeside) 2
W Thurrock (A126)
30
31
A1306
A1090
B186
A282
Tunnel (Northbound)
Bridge (Southbound)
River Thames
Dartford Crossing
Toll
A1306
(A1090 A126)
Thurrock (Lakeside) 2
Services
Purfleet 2
W Thurrock 2
31
A206
Swanscombe 3½
Erith 4
Bluewater 2
1A
A206
Swanscombe(A226) 3½
Erith 4
1A
A225
A296
Dartford 1
1B
A2
M2
Canterbury 9
London 42
2
A2
London (South East & Central)
Bexleyheath 5
Canterbury (M2) 42
Dartford (A225) 2
2
B2173
A20
M20
London (South East & Central)
Lewisham 10
Dover 60
Channel Tunnel 50
Maidstone 19
3
A20
M20
London (South East & Central)
Lewisham 10
Dover 60
Channel Tunnel 50
Maidstone 19
3
A21
A224
Bromley 9
Orpington 3½
4
A224
M20
A21
A224
London (South East)
Bromley 9
Orpington 3½
4
A21
A25
Sevenoaks 2
Hastings 40
5
M26
M20
M23
Croydon 9
Gatwick 9
Crawley 13
East Grinstead 16
Brighton 34
7
A22
A25
Eastbourne 40
Godstone ¾
Caterham 2
Westerham 7
6
M26 (M20)
A21
Maidstone 18
Channel Tunnel 50
Sevenoaks 2
Hastings 40
5
7
6
5
CLACKET LANE SERVICES
A22
B2235
M23
M23
Brighton 34
Crawley 13
Gatwick 9
Croydon 9
7
A25
A22
East Grinstead 11
Eastbourne 40
Caterham 2
Godstone ¾
Redhill 6
6
A25
A21
Note: Mileage numbers shown on this diagram are not displayed on motorway signs and are for guidance only.
0 2 4 miles
0 2 4 6 kms
Cheshunt
Waltham Abbey
Epping
North Weald Bassett
Waltham Cross
ENFIELD
Epping Forest
Loughton
Theydon Bois
Abridge
ESSEX
BILLERICAY
BRENTWOOD
Doddinghurst
Ingatestone
Southgate
Chingford
WALTHAM FOREST
CHIGWELL
Wood Green
Edmonton
HAVERING
Tottenham
Woodford
REDBRIDGE
Romford
Hornsey
Walthamstow
Hornchurch
Upminster
Laindon
Stoke Newington
Leyton
Wanstead
Ilford
Becontree
Hackney
BARKING
Dagenham
Rainham
THURROCK
Islington
Bethnal Green
Stratford
East Ham
South Ockendon
City
Poplar
London City
West-minster
Docklands
Woolwich
Thamesmead
Purfleet
West Thurrock
GRAYS
Chadwell St. Mary
Tilbury
Greenwich
Camberwell
Lewisham
Dartford
Northfleet
GRAVESEND
Swanscombe
Brixton
BEXLEY
Sidcup
Wilmington
Streatham
Chislehurst
Hextable
Darenth
Beckenham
Swanley
South Darenth
Istead Rise
Mitcham
BROMLEY
Hartley
Orpington
Meopham
CROYDON
West Wickham
Farnborough
Eynsford
New Ash Green
KENT
West Kingsdown
New Addington
Purley
Biggin Hill
NORTH DOWNS
Kemsing
Otford
Coulsdon
Warlingham
Borough Green
Sevenoaks
Caterham
CLACKET LANE SERVICES
Westerham
Godstone
Oxted
Crawley, Gatwick Airport & Brighton
East Grinstead & Eastbourne
Tonbridge & Hastings
Maidstone & Folkestone
Rochester, Dover & Margate
Chelmsford, Ipswich & Harwich
Basildon & Southend
Southend
Ware & Hertford
Harlow, Stansted Airport & Cambridge
Full junction
Restricted junction

4
AS
AT
AU
AV
AW
AX
AY
98
99
00
HP4
HP5
HP6
25
26
27
28
29
30
31
32
33
34
04
03
02
01
20
Ashley Green
Old Oak Farm
Brickies
Sewage Works
Flamstead Farm
Hall
SHORT WOOD
Thorne Barton Farm
Thorne Barton Hall
SPORTS GRD
The Warren
Sunnyside Cottages
Woodside
DEAN'S WOOD
LITTLE GROVE WOOD
FELMOOR WOOD
Little Pressmore Farm
Pressmore Farm
FRANCIS WOOD
Nashleigh Farm
Whitethorn's Farm
Coll
ASHLEY GREEN ROAD
A416
CHILTERN HERTFORDSHIRE
BUCKINGHAMSHIRE
Whelpley Hill Farm
Kenmore Farm
Sale's Farm
Spencer's Farm
Hemming's Farm
Berry Farm
WHELPLEY HILL PARK
Whelpley Hill
GREAT WOOD
Grove Farm
BUSH WOOD
Earthworks
Little Grove
Torrington Farm
Moors Farm
Lye Green
Sch
Electricity Station
The Black Cat PH
Orchard Leigh
RUSHMERE LANE
B4505
Whelpley Ash Farm
LYECROME WOOD
Lyegreen Farm
GEE'S SPRING
Hilltop
Sec Sch
REC GRD
NASHLEIGH HILL
New House Farm
POCKETSDELL LANE
Jasonhill Farm
Brockhurst Farm
CHILTERN LANE
DACORUM
Manchant's Farm
Codmore
SPORTS GROUND
Hall
Crab Tree Farm
Prim Sch
Botley
BOTLEY ROAD
SHANTOCK HILL
CHESHAM AND LEY HILL GOLF COURSE
Cricket Grd
LITTLE WOOD
Game Farm
Clubhouse
Flaunden End Farm
Ashridge Farm
SIMON DEAN'S WOOD
HESHAM
Leisure Centre
SPORTS GROUND
Tennis Courts
HOLLYBUSH WOOD
MAPLE TREE WOOD
Cowcroft Farm
COWCROFT WOOD
BIG ROUND GREEN LANE
Dungrove Farm
LONG KNOTTS
HILL FARM PLANTATION
Barns
Brickworks
HORSEHILL SPRING
Works
Waterside
FURZEFIELD WOOD
PINNER GREEN
KNOTTS SPRING
Hockley Farm
Hill Farm
Youth Cen
Chessmount
HILL FARM SPRING
Cattle Shed
White End Park Farm
CHALK DELL
CODMORE WOOD
CHESHAM MOOR
Lower Bois
QUARRY
Works
WYCHFIELD SPRING
FRITH WOOD
Weir Ho
CHESS VALLEY WALK
REC GRD
Prim Sch
BOIS WOOD
Blackwell Hall
Blackwell Farm
NETHER DITCH
FOUR ACRES
WESTLAND SPRING
JACK OF WADLEY'S SPRING
STAR

5
HP1
HP3
WD3
WD4
Bovingdon
Hogpits Bottom
Flaunden
Belsize
Chipper
Sarratt
H.M. THE MOUNT PRISON
Disused Airfield
COLESHILL WOOD
HANGING WOOD
GORSEFIELD WOOD
RAMACRE WOOD
BURY WOOD
SHEETHANGER COMMON
RAINHILL SPRING
RAINHILL DELL
KINGSHILL DELL
SHORTRIDGE WOOD
OLD DEAN
HOMEFIELD SPRING
BAKER'S WOOD
WOODMAN'S WOOD
LOWER PLANTATION
FLAUNDEN SPRING
LIMEDELL SPRING
HANGING CROFT
DEBARDINE WOOD
ROSEHALL WOOD
PLOUGH WOOD
HILLMEADS SPRING
TOP SPRING
OLDCROFT WOOD
HANGINGLANE WOOD
BRAMBLE CROFT
DAFFODIL SPRING
PENMAN'S GREEN
BOVINGDON GREEN
COVERED RESERVOIR
Bryants Nurseries
Wyevale Garden Centre
Stoney Lane Nursery
Bovingdon FC
R.A.F. Chenies
The Boot PH
Two Brewers PH
The Plough PH
Bricklayer's Arms PH
Bobsleigh Inn PH
Cross Farm
Cottingham Farm
Bulstrode Farm
Longcroft Farm
Nuffield Farm
Tenements Farm
Tufts Farm
Frenches Farm
Woodman's Farm
Olleberrie Farm
Dale Farm
Whitedell Farm
Newhouse Farm
Rose Hall Farm
Moonshine Farm
Great Sarratt Hall Farm
Great Sarratt Hall
Hillmeads Farm
Martin Top Farm
Sharlowe's Farm
Crumlin Farm
Venus Hill Dairy Farm
Chiltern Farm
Long Lane Farm
Meadow Way Farm
Shantock Farm
Bell Farm
Green Farm
Rent Street Farm
Bury Farm
Random Farm
Felden Lodge
Felden Manor
Tower Farm
Cherry Tree Farm
Springview Farm
Dellfield
BOX LANE
HEMPSTEAD ROAD
CHESHAM ROAD
SHOTHANGER WAY
LONGCROFT LANE
FLAUNDEN LANE
BULSTRODE LANE
TOWER HILL
VENUS HILL
HOGPITS BOTTOM
HOG PITS
FLAUNDEN HILL
BRAGMANS LANE
CHENIES HILL
DUNNY LANE
OLLEBERRIE LANE
HOLLY HEDGES LANE
WATER LANE
CHIPPERFIELD ROAD
RED LION LANE
PLOUGH LANE
WINDMILL HILL
DACORUM
THREE RIVERS
01
02
03
04
25
26
27
28
29
30
31
32
33
34
6
21
AZ
BA
BB
BC
BD
BE
BF

6
Felden
Apsley
HP3
WD4
Chipperfield
Kings Langley
Belsize
Commonwood
Bucks Hill
Sarratt
SHEETHANGER COMMON
GREAT WOOD
PHASELS WOOD
Phasels Wood Activity Centre
SHENDISH MANOR GOLF COURSE
SHENDISH HOUSE CONFERENCE & LEISURE CENTRE
SPORTS GROUND
COCK'S HEAD WOOD
HEN'S HEAD WOOD
SCATTERDELLS WOOD
THE GROVE
THE WINGS
RUCKLERS WOOD
DARK WOOD
THE HANGINGS
MERCEYS WOOD
THE NUCKET
OLD DEAN
KING LANGLEY COMMON
Whippendell Bottom
Whippendell Hill
ROOKERY WOOD
CHIPPERFIELD COMMON
PENMAN'S GREEN
DACORUM
THREE RIVERS
BERRYBUSHES WOOD
DEBARDINE WOOD
PLOUGH WOOD
HILLMEADS SPRING
COMMONWOOD COMMON
HAWK SPRING
SHEEPCOTE SPRING
DELLSHOT SPRING
BEECHEN BOTTOM
HIGH SPRING
KINGS LANGLEY BYPASS
A41
A4251
LONDON ROAD
HEMPSTEAD ROAD
HIGH STREET
WATFORD
GRAND UNION CANAL
5
22
BG
BH
BJ
BK
BL
BM
BN
25
26
27
28
29
30
31
32
33
34

7
BP
BQ
BR
BS
BT
BU
BV
08
09
10
HP3
WD5
WD25
POTTERS CROUCH PLANTATION
Bedmond
ABBOTS LANGLEY
Hunton Bridge
Langleybury
Woodside
Leavesden Green
Kingswood
Garston
Junction 20
Junction 21 M25
Junction 6A M1
M25
M1
25
26
27
28
29
30
31
32
33
34
8
23
KINGS LANGLEY
LONG DEANS
NEW PLANTATION
HYDE LANE SPRING
HIGH VIEW CARAVAN PARK
MOOR WOOD
LONG SPRING
BEDMOND PLAYING FIELDS
WELLFIELD SPRING
DEADMAN WOOD
BEDMOND WOOD
PIECORNER WOOD
HANGING WOOD
FURZEFIELD WOOD
JOB'S WOOD
GREAT NOTLEY
STOWES WOOD
LITTLE NOTLEY
LONG WOOD
ROUND WOOD
BLOOM WOOD
MANOR HOUSE GROUNDS
TANNERS WOOD
LEAVESDEN COUNTRY PARK
SOUTH WAY PLAYING FLD
ALBAN WOOD
WOODSIDE STADIUM
WOODSIDE PLAYING FIELDS
JUNCTION PARK
THE ROOKERY
SPORTS GROUND
HILL FARM IND EST
NORTH WATFORD CEMETERY
STANBOROUGH PARK
Leavesden Studios
GRAND UNION CANAL
NORTH ORBITAL ROAD
KINGSWAY
NORTH WESTERN AVENUE
WATFORD ROAD
A41
A405
ST. ALBANS THREE RIVERS

BW
BX
BY
BZ
CA
CB
CC
12
13
14
25
26
27
28
29
30
31
32
33
34
04
03
02
01
7
24
APPSPOND WOOD
PARK WOOD
Holly Bush PH
Potters Crouch East Farm
Potters Crouch Farm
SQUARE WOOD
SCRUBBS WOOD
Westfields Farm
Cuckman's Farm
RAGGED HALL LANE
BEDMOND LANE
BEDMOND ROAD
Potters Crouch
WELLFIELD SPRING
CHISWELL GREEN LANE
FURZEBUSHES LANE
Plaistowes Farm
BLUNTS LANE
NOKE LANE
Bone Hill
THE GDNS OF THE ROSE
Chiswellgreen Farm
The Three Hammers PH
AL2
Chiswell Green
WHITEHOUSE LANE
Whitehouse Farm
HANGING WOOD
FURZEFIELD WOOD
JOB'S WOOD
Millhouse Farm
SEARCHES LANE
Searches Farm
HOLT WOOD
Holt Farm
Moat
Noke Farm
Noke Lane Business Centre
Thistle
M1
M25
WD5
Tenements Farm
Junction 21A
Junction 21 M25
Junction 6A M1
WINCH HILL WOOD
NORTH ORBITAL ROAD
A405
WATFORD ROAD
GREENWOOD PARK
ST. JULIAN'S WOOD
WATLING STREET CARAVAN SITE (TRAVELLERS)
Burston Manor Farm
Burston Nursery
Garden Cen
How Wood
BIRCH WOOD
Birchwood Farm
Lido
Tennis Courts
SUNFOLKS
Kettlewell Farm
Lye House
Clubhouse
Cricket Ground
BLACKGREEN WOOD
GRAVEL PIT
Bricket Wood
BLACKGREEN WOOD
SMUG OAK GREEN BUSINESS CENTRE
Social Club
SMUG OAK GREEN
The Gate PH
SPORTS GROUND
THE LAKES
Sports Centre
BRICKET WOOD
ST. ALBANS
THREE RIVERS
CHEQUERS LANE
CEM
Fortunes Farm
Junction 6
BLOOM WOOD
HIGH ROAD
Garston Manor Rehab. Cen
Sports Centre
BENSKINS SPORTS GRD
Depot
Brookdell Farm
ST. ALBANS ROAD
PENFOLD PARK GOLF COURSE
NOTTLERS WOOD
Nottlers House
Pumping Sta
BRICKET WOOD COMMON
BUILDING RESEARCH ESTABLISHMENT
JACK WILLIAM'S WOOD
NEW PLANTATION
WD25
Garston Manor
WOODSIDE STADIUM
Leisure Cen
WOODSIDE PLAYING FIELDS
MUTCHETTS WOOD
Little Munden Farm
FOUR ACRE PLANTATION
River Colne
COMMONMEADOW LANE
KYTES ESTATE
Three Horseshoes PH
COLDHARBOUR PLANTATION
GARSTON PARK
KINGSWAY
PEARTREE WOOD
CRAB WOOD
Ford
ST. ALBANS
HERTSMERE
WATFORD
MUNDEN SPRING
Munden House
Kingswood
Garston
A412
NORTH WATFORD CEMETERY
STANBOROUGH PARK
Meriden
SCHOOL LANE

9
CD
CE
CF
CG
CH
CJ
CK
15
16
17
AL1
AL2
AL4
WD7
VERULAM GOLF COURSE
NORTH ORBITAL ROAD
A414
Park Street
PARK STREET
Frogmore
Colney Street
Radlett Aerodrome (Disused)
GRAVEL PIT
PARK INDUSTRIAL ESTATE
FROGMORE HOME PARK
CHALKDELL WOOD
Hedges Farm
Napsbury Farm
SPORTS GROUND
LONDON COLNEY
BROAD COLNEY LAKES NATURE RESERVE
Broad Colney Bridge
River Colne
Fir Tree Farm
Superstores
ALL SAINTS PASTORAL CENTRE
M25
QUARRY
COLNEY PARK
Arsenal F.C. Training Grounds
10
VENTURA PARK
Travel Inn
The Red Cow PH
Old Parkbury
HARPERBURY HOSPITAL
Harper Lane Rail Depot
RADLETT GOLF RANGE
HOUND'S WOOD
NINE ACRES
Houndswood Farm
Netherwylde Farm
Hill Farm
Wild Farm
Moat
PORTERS PARK GOLF COURSE
SAND PLANTATION
Clubhouse
SHENLEY PARK
COW BANKS
SHENLEY MANOR
Oakridge Lane Sewage Treatment Works
WATLING STREET
RADLETT
25
26
27
28
29
30
31
32
33
34

CL
CM
CN
CP
CQ
CR
CS
19
20
21
25
26
27
28
29
30
31
32
33
34
04
03
02
01
SAND AND
GRAVEL PIT
Highfield Hall
THE WARREN
Warren Farm
FREDERICK'S WOOD
WELWYN HATFIELD
HERTSMERE
ST. ALBANS
NORTH A414
LONDON COLNEY BYPASS A1081
COPPICE WOOD
(SITE OF SPECIAL SCIENTIFIC INTEREST)
Tyttenhanger Farm
Tyttenhanger House
GARDEN WOOD
THE NEW PLANTATION
Coursers Farm
COURSERS ROAD
River Colne
BIG MAYFIELD WOOD
Bowmansgreen Farm
LONDON COLNEY
MORRIS PLAYING FLD
Works
Prim Sch
Rec Cen
Lib
Comm Cen
ALLOT
AL4
AL2
WALSINGHAM WOOD
Junction 22
The Bull PH
RIDGEVIEW LODGE
BROAD COLNEY LAKES NATURE RESERVE
Broad Colney Bridge
Superstores
BELL LANE
ST. ALBANS ROAD
COBS ASH
ROUND WOOD
Salisbury Hall
Salisbury Hall Farm
MOAT
DE HAVILLAND MOSQUITO AIRCRAFT MUSEUM
Gordon Hall Building
Tennis Courts
UNIVERSITY COLLEGE LONDON SPORTS GROUNDS
Arsenal F.C. Training Grounds
M25
B556
Redwell Wood Farm
REDWELL WOOD
Ridgehill
Sch
SHENLEYBURY
SHENLEYBURY COTTS
DELL GROVE
Southridge Animal Centre R.S.P.C.A.
PACKHORSE LANE
WD7
B5378
RECTORY LANE
Rectory Farm
Shenley Hill Stud Farm
Shenley Hill
COMBE WOOD
COW BANKS
Rabley Park Farm
Rabley Park
Wild Farm
St. Catherine's Farm
Catherine Bourne
MIMMS LANE
Ravenscroft Court
DEEVES HALL LANE
SHENLEY PARK
The Black Lion PH
BLACK LION HILL
LONDON ROAD
Shenley
SPORTS GRD
LITTLERIDGE WOOD
BIG PURSLEY WOOD
SAND PLANTATION
Cricket Ground
WALLED GDN
The Garden Nursery
Tokonoma Bonsai
Ridge Farm
CROSSOAKS LANE
Ridge
WD6
Pursley Farm
LITTLE PURSLEY WOOD
Crossoaks
RADLETT LANE
THE GORSE
GREEN STREET
Cricket Ground
CROSS OAKS WOOD
Auriol Farm
WOODHALL LANE
Wood Hall
SUMMERHOUSE LANE

9
26

11
CT
CU
CV
CW
CX
CY
CZ
22
23
24
WOOD
NORTH MYMMS
PARK
North Mymms Park Training Centre
Cricket Club
Cricket Ground
Home Farm
Water End
DIXONS HILL ROAD
SWANLAND ROAD
WARRENGATE ROAD
BRADMORE LANE
WISE'S LANE
BRICK KILN WOOD
Pumping Sta
Potterells
Potterells Farm
Med Cen
Comm Cen
REC GRD
STATION ROAD
Sibthorpe Arms PH
Hall
WELHAM MANOR
PELPIN'S WOOD
ROUND WOOD
THE LEGG
BROOKMANS PARK GOLF COURSE
BROOKMANS PARK
Prim Sch
PO
Lib
BROOKMANS AVENUE
MOFFATS LANE
BLUEBRIDGE ROAD
WESTLAND DRIVE
OAKLANDS AVENUE
THE GARDENS
GOBIONS OPEN SPACE
GOBIONS GARDEN
GOBIONS POND
AL9
Blue Bridge
Deep Bottom
SWALLOW HOLE
Royal Veterinary College (Hawkshead House)
HAWKSHEAD LANE
Hawkshead Bridge
Royal Veterinary College (Boltons Park Farm)
CANGSLEY WOOD
HAWKSHEAD WOOD
MYMMSHALL WOOD
WELWYN HATFIELD
HERTSMERE
SPORTS GROUND
Pav
Tennis Courts
PILVAGE WOOD
Site of Motte & Baileys
Mimmshall Brook
POTTERS BAR GOLF COURSE
12
25
26
27
28
29
30
31
32
33
34
03
04
02
01
Depot
Works
FURZEFIELD WOOD
KING GEORGE V PLAYING FLDS
Sports Cen
SPORTS GRD
Clubho
CRANBORNE INDUSTRIAL ESTATE
CRANBORNE ROAD
Warrengate Farm
Mimms Hall Farm
A1(M)
MUTTON LANE
B556
Widmore Hall
DEEPDENE
WROXHAM GARDENS
Prim Sch
TEMPLE COURT
MIMMS HALL ROAD
EN6
Theatre
Superstore
POTTERS BAR
Clubhouse
RITZ COURT
DARKES LANE
Comm Cen
Town Farm
CECIL ROAD
Catherine Bourne
South Mimms
BLANCHE LANE
ST. ALBANS ROAD
GREYHOUND LANE
M25
Bignell's Corner
Depot
Holiday Inn South Mimms
South Mimms Services
Days Inn
Works
Nat Inst for Biological Standards & Control
Blanche Farm
Bridgefoot House
BRIDGEFOOT LANE
Dugdale Hill
Sec Sch
Rydal Mount
Rydal Mount Stables
BAKER STREET
SAWYERS LANE
BENTLEY HEATH LANE
Elm Farm
Bentley Heath Farm
Bentley Heath
Garden Centre
27
Junction 23 (M25)
Junction 1 A1(M)

12
DA
DB
DC
DD
DE
DF
DG
26
27
28
BROOKMANS PARK
BROOKMANS PARK GOLF COURSE
ROUND WOOD
GEORGE'S WOOD
THE LEGG
Brookmans Park Transmitting Station
COLDHARBOUR PLANTATION
BROOMBARNS WOOD
Rowbourne Hill
GREAT
GOBIONS OPEN SPACE
GOBIONS GARDEN
GOBIONS POND
GOBIONS WOOD
SWALLOW HOLE
Deep Bottom
AL9
SPORTS GROUND
Queenswood Sch
LEGGATTS WOOD
Leggatts Park
WELL WOOD
NYN POND
THE VINEYARD
Royal Veterinary College (Boltons Park Farm)
POTTERS BAR
COURSE
11
Northaw
NORTHAW PLACE
SPORTS GROUND
EN6
HOOK WOOD
FISH POND
FIVE ACRE WOOD
FIR WOOD
POTTERS BAR
PARKFIELD OPEN SPACE
OAKMERE PARK
Foxhole Hill
POND WOOD
Hooke Hill
POTTERS BAR COMMUNITY HOSP
Junction 24
28
Fenny Shade Hill
New Cottage Farm
Bentley Heath
Ganwick Corner
Elm Farm
Bentley Heath Farm
Chase Farm
FIR WOOD
Plumridge Hill
North Lodge Farm
25
26
27
28
29
30
31
32
33
34
04
03
02
01
GREAT NORTH ROAD
A1000
M25
A1005
B156
B157
B556
A111
SOUTHGATE ROAD
HIGH STREET
BARNET ROAD
THE RIDGEWAY

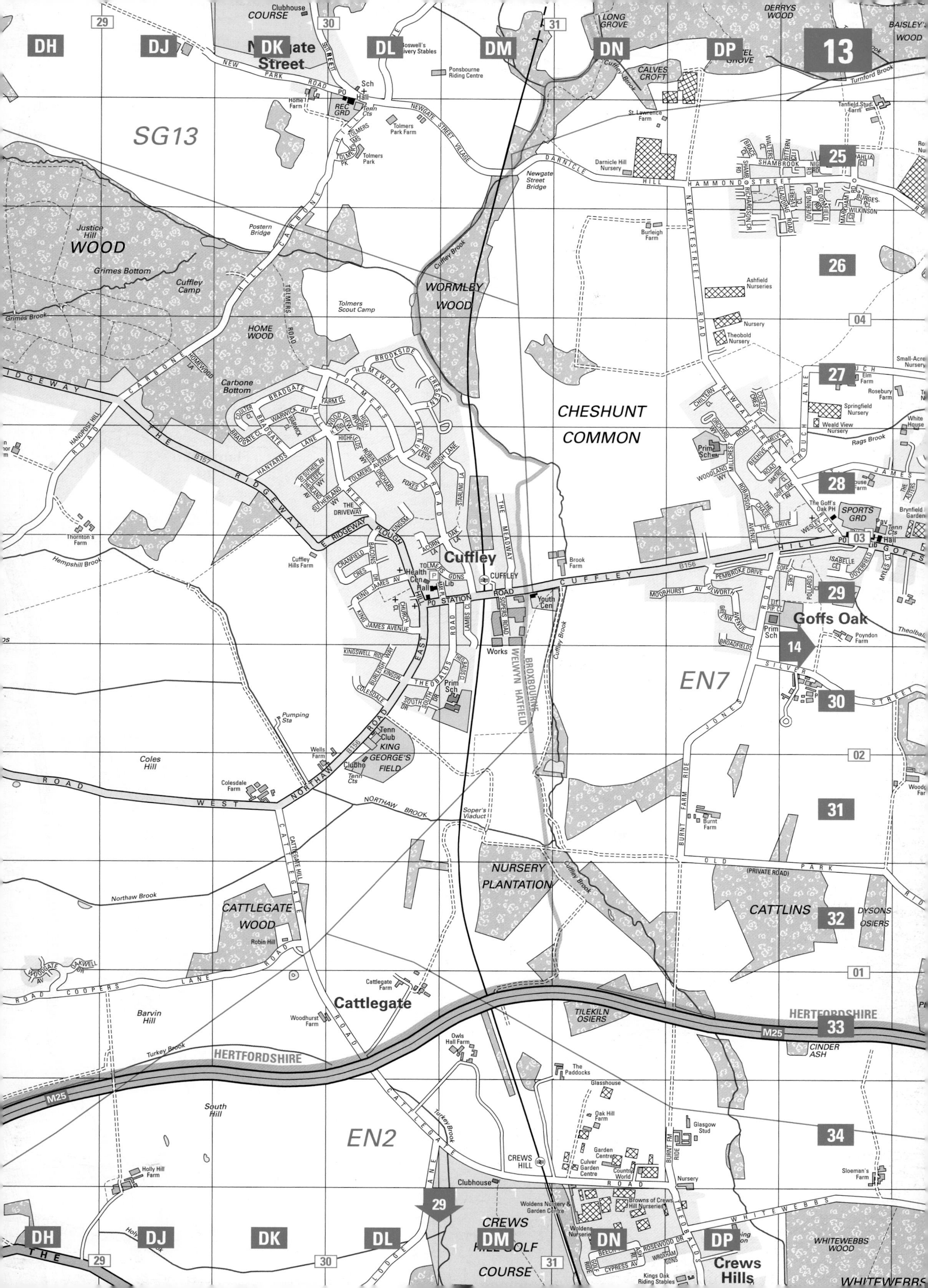
13
DH
DJ
DK
DL
DM
DN
DP
29
30
31
Clubhouse
COURSE
Newgate Street
Boswell's Livery Stables
Ponsbourne Riding Centre
LONG GROVE
DERRYS WOOD
BAISLEY'S WOOD
CALVES CROFT
Turnford Brook
Cuffley Brook
NEW PARK ROAD
Sch
Hall
PO
Home Farm
REC GRD
Tenn Cts
NEWGATE STREET VILLAGE
Tolmers Park Farm
Tolmers Park
TOLMERS MS
TOLMERS PK
St. Lawrence Farm
Tanfield Stud Farm
SG13
Darnicle Hill Nursery
DARNICLE HILL
Newgate Street Bridge
HAMMOND STREET
SHAMBROOK
25
26
27
28
29
30
31
32
33
34
04
03
02
01
CARBONE HILL
Postern Bridge
Justice Hill
WOOD
Grimes Bottom
Grimes Brook
Cuffley Camp
TOLMERS ROAD
Tolmers Scout Camp
HOME WOOD
WORMLEY WOOD
Burleigh Farm
Ashfield Nurseries
Nursery
Theobold Nursery
NEWGATE STREET ROAD
Small-Acre Nursery
Elm Farm
Rosebury Farm
Springfield Nursery
Weald View Nursery
Rags Brook
CROUCH LANE
RIDGEWAY
THE RIDGEWAY
HANDPOST HILL ROAD
Carbone Bottom
BROOKSIDE
HOMEWOOD
CRESCENT
BRADGATE
FARM CL
WARWICK AV
HANYARDS LANE
TOLMERS AVENUE
FOXES LA
THRUSH LANE
STARLING LA
THE MEADWAY
CHESHUNT COMMON
Prim Sch
WOODLAND WY
MILLCREST
ROBINSON AVENUE
THE CHASE
THE DRIVE
The Goff's Oak PH
SPORTS GRD
Pav
Tenn Cts
Hall
Brynfield Gardens
B157
Thornton's Farm
Hempshill Brook
Cuffley Hills Farm
THE DRIVEWAY
PLOUGH HILL
Cuffley
Health Cen
Hall
Lib
CUFFLEY
STATION ROAD
CUFFLEY ROAD
B156
Brook Farm
Youth Cen
Works
SOPERS ROAD
KING JAMES AV
JAMES AVENUE
CHURCH CL
EAST RIDGEWAY
PEMBROKE DRIVE
MOORHURST AV
LULWORTH AVENUE
ISABELLE CL
DOVERFIELD
Goffs Oak
Prim Sch
BROADFIELDS
Poyndon Farm
Theobalds
14
SILVER STREET
EN7
JONES ROAD
KINGSWELL RIDE
BURLEIGH WAY
COLESDALE
THEOBALDS ROAD
Prim Sch
SOUTH DR
Pumping Sta
Tenn Club
KING GEORGE'S FIELD
Clubhouse
Tenn Cts
Wells Farm
NORTHAW ROAD
Coles Hill
Colesdale Farm
WEST ROAD
NORTHAW BROOK
Soper's Viaduct
BROXBOURNE
WELWYN HATFIELD
Cuffley Brook
BURNT FARM RIDE
Burnt Farm
OLD PARK RIDE
(PRIVATE ROAD)
NURSERY PLANTATION
Northaw Brook
CATTLEGATE HILL
CATTLEGATE WOOD
Robin Hill
CATTLINS
DYSONS OSIERS
WOODGATE AV
OAKWELL DR
COOPERS LANE ROAD
THE RIDGEWAY
Cattlegate Farm
Cattlegate
Barvin Hill
Woodhurst Farm
TILEKILN OSIERS
HERTFORDSHIRE
M25
CINDER ASH
Turkey Brook
Owls Hall Farm
The Paddocks
Glasshouse
Oak Hill Farm
Glasgow Stud
South Hill
EN2
CATTLEGATE ROAD
Turkey Brook
CREWS HILL
Garden Centre
Culver Garden Centre
Country World
Nursery
Sloeman's Farm
Holly Hill Farm
Clubhouse
LODGE LANE
Woldens Nursery & Garden Centre
Browns of Crews Hill Nurseries
WHITEWEBBS ROAD
WHITEWEBBS WOOD
CREWS HILL GOLF COURSE
BEECH HILL
ROSEWOOD DR
CYPRESS AV
THEOBALDS
Kings Oak Riding Stables
Crews Hills

DQ
DR
DS
DT
DU
DV
DW
25
26
27
28
29
30
31
32
33
34
13
30
Hammond Street
Goffs Oak
EN7
Flamstead End
Bury Green
EN8
Bulls Cross
Crews Hill
CHESHUNT PARK
CHESHUNT GOLF COURSE
CATTLINS
HOME WOOD
HOME PLANTATION
HANGING PLANTATION
BURYGREEN PLANTATION
BROOM HILLS
THEOBALDS PARK
BULLSCROSS RIDE CEMETERY (JEWISH)
ADATH YISROEL CEMETERY
ROSEDALE SPORTS GROUND
HERTFORDSHIRE
M25
BROXBOURNE
Junction 25
GREAT CAMBRIDGE ROAD
A10
LIEUTENANT ELLIS WAY
GOFFS LANE
SILVER STREET
OLD PARK RIDE
WHITEWEBBS LANE
Capel Manor Horticultural & Environmental Centre

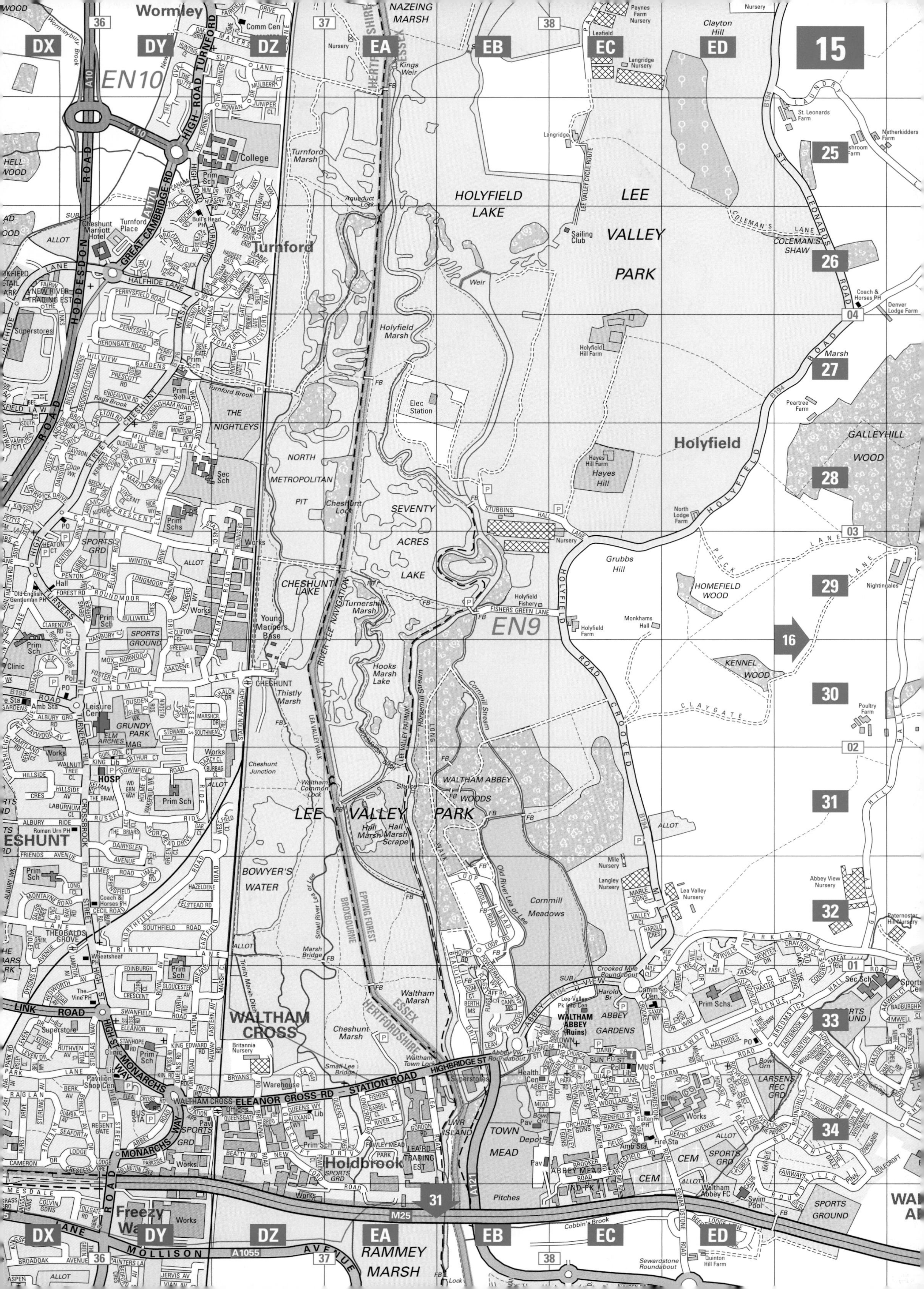

15
DX
DY
DZ
EA
EB
EC
ED
36
37
38
Wormley
EN10
Turnford
Holyfield
EN9
LEE VALLEY PARK
HOLYFIELD LAKE
NAZEING MARSH
Kings Weir
Turnford Marsh
Holyfield Marsh
Holyfield Hill Farm
Hayes Hill Farm
Hayes Hill
Sailing Club
Elec Station
THE NIGHTLEYS
NORTH METROPOLITAN PIT
SEVENTY ACRES LAKE
CHESHUNT LAKE
Cheshunt Lock
Turnershill Marsh
Young Mariners Base
Hooks Marsh Lake
Thistly Marsh
River Lee Navigation
LEA VALLEY WALK
LEE VALLEY PATHWAY
Horsemill Stream
Cornmill Stream
WALTHAM ABBEY WOODS
Cheshunt Junction
Waltham Common Lock
Hall Marsh
Hall Marsh Scrape
BOWYER'S WATER
Small River Lea or Lee
Old River Lea or Lee
Cornmill Meadows
EPPING FOREST
BROXBOURNE
HERTFORDSHIRE
ESSEX
Marsh Bridge
Waltham Marsh
Cheshunt Marsh
Waltham Town Lock
WALTHAM CROSS
Holdbrook
TOWN MEAD
LWR ISLAND
ABBEY GARDENS
WALTHAM ABBEY (Ruins)
Crooked Mile Roundabout
CROOKED MILE
HOLYFIELD ROAD
FISHERS GREEN LANE
STUBBINS HALL LANE
Grubbs Hill
HOMEFIELD WOOD
KENNEL WOOD
Monkhams Hall
Holyfield Farm
GALLEYHILL WOOD
North Lodge Farm
Peartree Farm
Nightingales
Poultry Farm
St. Leonards Farm
Netherkidders Farm
COLEMAN'S SHAW
Coach & Horses PH
Denver Lodge Farm
Clayton Hill
Paynes Farm Nursery
Leafield
Langridge Nursery
Langridge
LEE VALLEY CYCLE ROUTE
Mile Nursery
Langley Nursery
Lea Valley Nursery
Abbey View Nursery
Paternoster Hill Nursery
PARKLANDS
Prim Schs
LARSENS REC GRD
CEM
SPORTS GROUND
Waltham Abbey FC
Swim Pool
Sewardstone Roundabout
Quinton Hill Farm
Cobbin's Brook
RAMMEY MARSH
MOLLISON AVENUE
Freezy Water
M25
A121
A1055
A10
A1170
B194
B198
B176
ESHUNT
HODDESDON ROAD
GREAT CAMBRIDGE RD
HIGH ROAD TURNFORD
HALFHIDE LANE
Cheshunt Marriott Hotel
Turnford Place
College
NEW RIVER TRADING EST
Superstores
HELL WOOD
STATION APPROACH
CHESHUNT
GRUNDY PARK
ELM ARCHES
Leisure Cen
HOSP
LINK ROAD
ELEANOR CROSS RD
STATION ROAD
HIGHBRIDGE ST
MONARCHS WAY
Britannia Nursery
LEA RD TRADING EST
Wheatsheaf
Old English Gentleman PH
Roman Urn PH
Coach & Horses PH
THEOBALDS GROVE
16
31
25
26
27
28
29
30
32
33
34
01
02
03
04

16
EE
EF
EG
EH
EJ
EK
EL
Bumble's Green
Nazeing Gate
NAZEINGWOOD COMMON
COPY WOOD
LONGFIELD SHAW
GALLEYHILL GREEN
DEERPARK WOOD
THE SPRINGS
GALLEYHILL WOOD
BROADGATE SPRINGS
BRAYSHILL SPRING
Aimes Green
Holyfield
LONGCROFT GROVE
STOCKING GROVE
EN9
MAPLE SPRINGS
KENNEL WOOD
FERNHALL WOOD
BROOKMEADOW WOOD
COBBIN POND
COPPED HALL GREEN
WARLIES PARK
Upshire
Copthall Green
OXLEYS WOOD
POTKILN WOOD
BRAMBLY SHAW
CONYBURY WOOD
STABLES SHAW
WALTHAM ABBEY
SPORTS GROUND
LARSENS REC GRD
CLAY PIGEON RANGE
M25
HONEY LANE
15
32
25
26
27
28
29
30
31
32
33
34
40
41
42
04
03
02
01

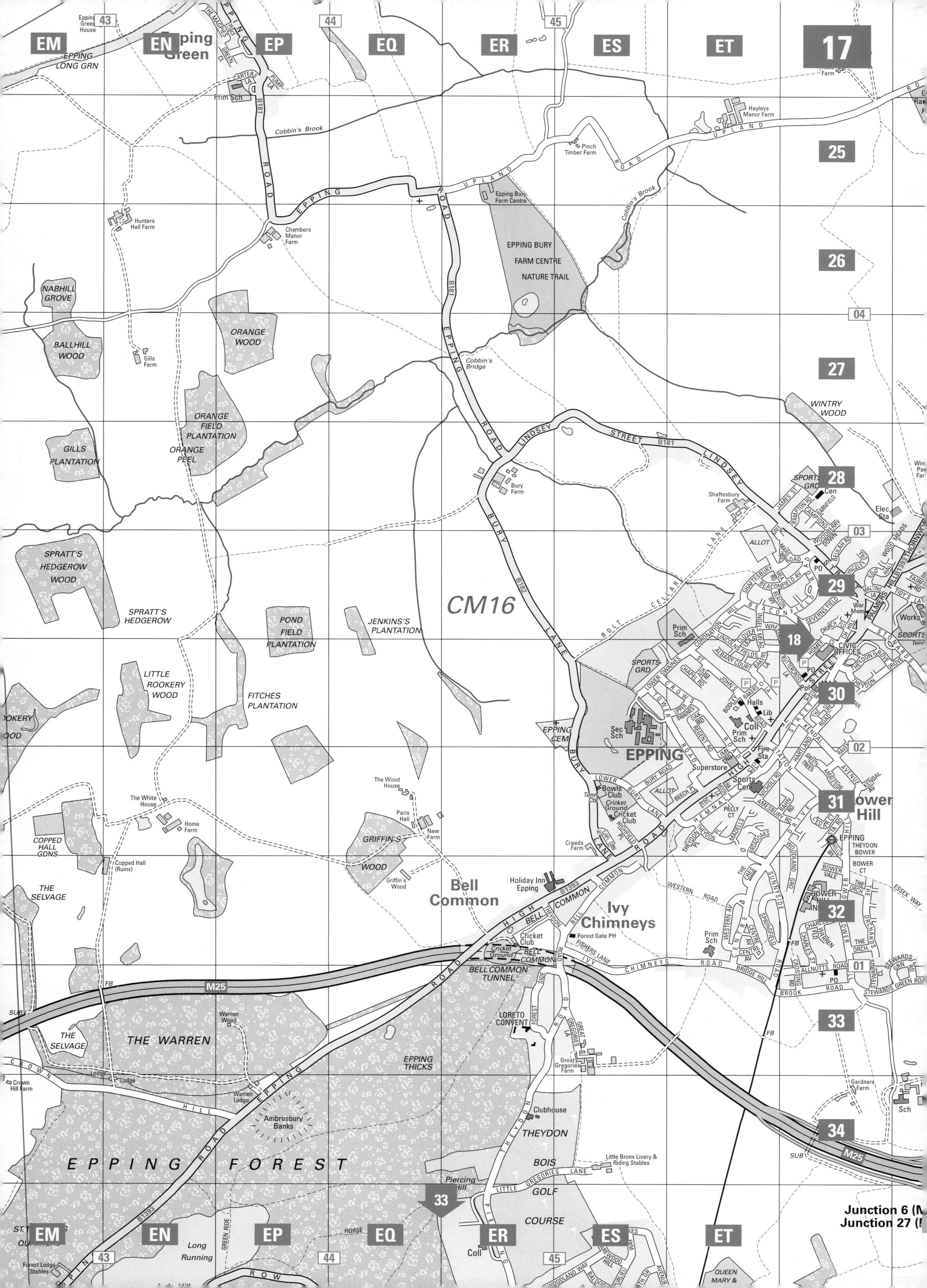

17
EM
EN
EP
EQ
ER
ES
ET
43
44
45
Epping Green
EPPING LONG GRN
Prim Sch
Cobbin's Brook
Hayleys Manor Farm
UPLAND ROAD
Pinch Timber Farm
25
EPPING ROAD
Epping Bury Farm Centre
Hunters Hall Farm
Chambers Manor Farm
EPPING BURY FARM CENTRE NATURE TRAIL
26
NABHILL GROVE
BALLHILL WOOD
ORANGE WOOD
Gills Farm
Cobbin's Bridge
04
27
WINTRY WOOD
ORANGE FIELD PLANTATION
ORANGE PEEL
GILLS PLANTATION
LINDSEY STREET
B181
Bury Farm
Shaftesbury Farm
28
03
ALLOT
SPRATT'S HEDGEROW WOOD
SPRATT'S HEDGEROW
POND FIELD PLANTATION
JENKINS'S PLANTATION
CM16
BURY LANE
BOLT CELLAR LANE
29
18
LITTLE ROOKERY WOOD
FITCHES PLANTATION
EPPING CEM
Sec Sch
EPPING
Superstore
30
02
The Wood House
The White House
Home Farm
Paris Hall
New Farm
COPPED HALL GDNS
Copped Hall (Ruins)
GRIFFIN'S WOOD
Griffin's Wood
31
Lower Hill
EPPING
THEYDON BOWER
Holiday Inn Epping
Bell Common
Ivy Chimneys
THE SELVAGE
Cricket Club
Forest Gate PH
IVY CHIMNEYS ROAD
32
01
BELL COMMON TUNNEL
M25
THE WARREN
Warren Wood
LORETO CONVENT
33
EPPING THICKS
Great Gregories Farm
Crown Hill Farm
Lodge
Warren Lodge
Ambresbury Banks
Clubhouse
THEYDON BOIS
Gardners Farm
Sch
34
EPPING FOREST
Little Bronx Livery & Riding Stables
GOLF COURSE
Piercing Hill
B1393
Long Running
Coll
Forest Lodge Stables
QUEEN MARY &
Junction 6 (M
Junction 27 (M

18
EU
EV
EW
EX
EY
EZ
FA
Thornwood
NORTH WEALD AIRFIELD
WEALD HALL LANE SEWAGE WORKS
Thames Water Sewage Treatment Plant
Hayleys Manor Farm
Golf Range
Rugby Ground
Bird Centre
Garden Centre
Rose Farm
Weald Hall
Weald Hall Farm
DRIVING RANGE
Pitch 'n' Putt
Gliding Club
Hangar
WOODSIDE COMMERCIAL ESTATE
Warehouse
Superstore
WINTRY WOOD
THE LOWER FOREST
NORTH WEALD GOLF COURSE
Clubhouse
Norway House
Piggery
ROUGHTALLEY'S WOOD
Carisbrook Farm
EPPING PLAIN
Wintry Park Farm
Elec Sta
Shaftesbury Farm
ST. MARGARET'S HOSPITAL
SPENCER CLOSE HOSPITAL
GERNON BUSHES
Coopersale
Cricket Club
CM16
POSTERNIANE SPRING
HAWKSHILL WOOD
BIRCHING
COPPICE
FORTY ACRES
REDYN'S WOOD
Coopersale Farm
Coopersale House
Stonards Farm
Gaynes Park House
Gaynes Park
MOUNT QUARTER
ONGAR DOWN
GRAVEL PIT WOOD
High Warren
EPPING
Bower Hill
Theydon Oak PH
Mount End
Fiddlers Hamlet
Home Farm
Merry Fiddlers PH
Masons Bridge Farm
Hornes Farm
Searles Hall
Sawkins Farm
BEACHET WOOD
Little Thorn Hall Farm
Gardners Farm
Hobbs Cross Road Sewage Works
HOBBS CROSS GOLF CENTRE
North House
Mount Hill Farm
THE ROUGH PATCH
Theydon Mount
Junction 6 (M11)
Junction 27 (M25)
34
LONG PLANTATION
ICEHOUSE PLANTATION
BARBER'S WOOD
Garnish Hall
M11
M25
25
26
27
28
29
30
31
32
33
34
17
47
48
49
04
03
02
01

19
North Weald Bassett
Toot Hill
Clatterford End
Greensted Green
CM5
RM4
HIGH ROAD
EPPING ROAD
A414
LANE
Talbot Roundabout
Cricket Ground
Pav
Comm Cen
Sch
Skips Corner
Pol
PO
Lib
Queens Head PH
Kings Head PH
Hall
Bowling Green
Clubhouse
Ongar Park Hall
Chase Farm
Redricks Nursery
New House Farm
Sayers Farm
PEWLEY WOOD
MILLER'S GROVE
DOLMAN'S SPRING
Works
Greensted House
Hardings Farm
PENSONS LANE
GREENSTED WOOD
GREENSTED ROAD
Cold Hall Farm
Elite Gardens Nursery
HIGH WOOD
ONGAR PARK WOOD
ESSEX WAY
Clunes House
Water Tower
MILL LANE
Wealds Farm
BARN MEAD
THE MOAT
Steers Farm
TOOT HILL ROAD
Does Farm
Freemans Farm
EPPING ROAD
MOAT
Moat House
Mount Farm
Willows Farm
Batt Livery Stable
Burrows Farm
COLEMANS LANE
Coleman's Farm
Newhouse
Clark's Farm
Clubhouse
TOOT HILL GOLF COURSE
SCHOOL ROAD
Stewart's Farm
TAWNEY COMMON
Mole Trap PH
STAPLEFORD ROAD
Woodhatch Farm
NORTHLANDS WOOD
KNIGHTSLAND WOOD
BERWICK LANE
Cessland's Farm
Crumps Farm
Stanford Rivers
MUTTON ROW
OLD RECTORY ROAD
CHURCH
LONG SPRING
HANGING SPRING
ROUND SPRING
WELL EAVES
ICEHOUSE WOOD
Berwick Farm
35
TWENTYACRE WOOD
BERWICK HAM
White Bear PH
The Woodman PH
Murrells Farm
Traceys Farm
River Roding
A113
LONDON ROAD
FB FC FD FE FF FG FH
50 51 52
25 26 27 28 29 30 31 32 33 34
04 03 02 01

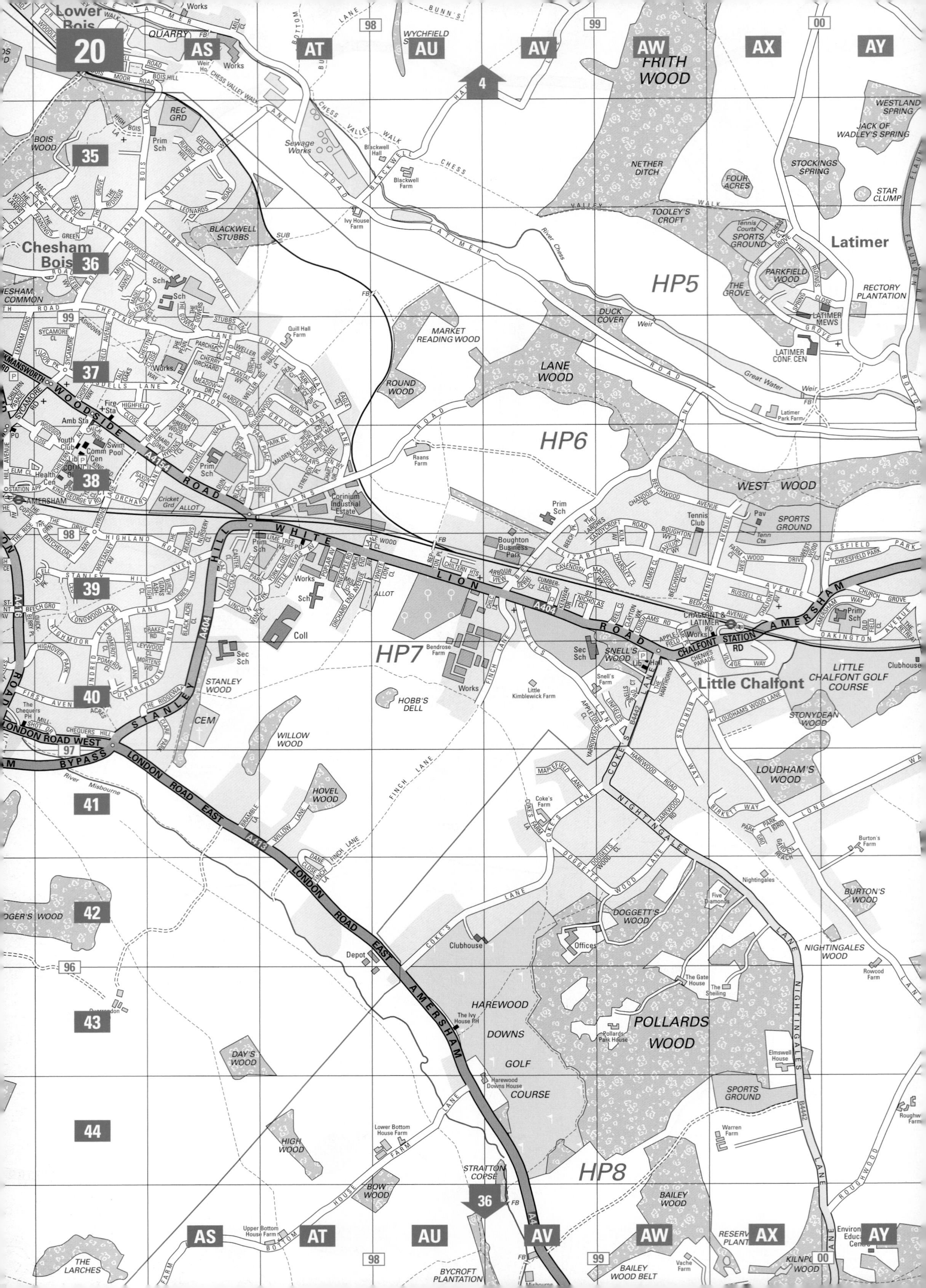

20
4
36
AS
AT
AU
AV
AW
AX
AY
98
99
00
35
36
37
38
39
40
41
42
43
44
97
96
Lower Bois
Chesham Bois
Latimer
Little Chalfont
AMERSHAM
HP5
HP6
HP7
HP8
FRITH WOOD
WESTLAND SPRING
JACK OF WADLEY'S SPRING
STOCKINGS SPRING
STAR CLUMP
FOUR ACRES
NETHER DITCH
TOOLEY'S CROFT
PARKFIELD WOOD
RECTORY PLANTATION
DUCK COVER
LATIMER MEWS
LATIMER CONF. CEN
LANE WOOD
MARKET READING WOOD
ROUND WOOD
BLACKWELL STUBBS
BOIS WOOD
WEST WOOD
SPORTS GROUND
LITTLE CHALFONT GOLF COURSE
STONYDEAN WOOD
LOUDHAM'S WOOD
BURTON'S WOOD
NIGHTINGALES WOOD
DOGGETT'S WOOD
POLLARDS WOOD
HAREWOOD DOWNS GOLF COURSE
HOBB'S DELL
WILLOW WOOD
HOVEL WOOD
STANLEY WOOD
DAY'S WOOD
HIGH WOOD
BOW WOOD
STRATTON COPSE
BAILEY WOOD
BAILEY WOOD BELT
BYCROFT PLANTATION
THE LARCHES
KILNPOND WOOD
CHESS VALLEY WALK
LATIMER ROAD
WHITE LION ROAD
A404
A4154
A413
A416
LONDON ROAD EAST
LONDON ROAD WEST
AMERSHAM ROAD
STANLEY HILL
CHALFONT STATION RD
NIGHTINGALES LANE
B4442
COKE'S LANE
FINCH LANE

HP3
WD3
HANGING CROFT
LONG WOOD
FLAUNDEN GROVE
BALDWIN'S WOOD
R.A.F. Chenies
Martin Top Farm
OLDFIELD SPRING
WALLACE'S WOOD
Moonshine Farm
DACORUM
THREE RIVERS
TOP SPRING
OLDCROFT WOOD
BRAMBLE CROFT
HANGINGLANE WOOD
LIMESHILL WOOD
Valley Farm
Watercress Beds
MOUNT WOOD
Mill Farm
River Chess
Chenies Place
PLACEHOUSE COPSE
CONEY WOOD
WALK WOOD
Greathouse Farm
Manor House
Bedford Arms PH
Chenies
Chenies Garden Centre
Cricket Ground
Football Ground
WYBURN WOOD
NICHOLAS SPRING
TURVEYLANE WOOD
CHILTON'S WOOD
Mountwood Farm
Great Sarratt Hall Farm
Great Sarratt Hall
DAFFODIL SPRING
Sarratt
The Boot PH
Cricketers Inn PH
DAWES COMMON
SANDFIELD WOOD
Ward's Nurseries
Moor Cottage
Adams Nurseries
End Farm
Sarratt Bottom Cottages
Goldingtons
Model Farm
SCRUBBS WOOD
BLUNTS WOOD
Sarrattmill Bridge
Water Works
MEAD SPRING
AMERSHAM ROAD
A404
OLD HANGING WOOD
NEW HANGING WOOD
LODGE COPSE
Lodge Farm
HALSEY'S WOOD
Great Greenstreet Farm
Little Greenstreet Farm
Stubbs Farm
BUCKINGHAMSHIRE
HERTFORDSHIRE
CHILTERN
THREE RIVERS
Sec Sch
Field Study Centre
Tennis Club
DELL WOOD
MILLFIELD PLANTATION
Highlands Water Gardens
Solesbridge Mill Water Gardens
LITTLE LADY'S WOOD
Junction 18
WHITELANDS WOOD
HILLAS WOOD
CARPENTER'S WOOD
CHENIES ROAD
RICKMANSWORTH ROAD
Cricket Ground
Prim Sch
White Horse PH
CHORLEYWOOD COMMON
CHORLEYWOOD GOLF COURSE
Arts Centre
Clubhouse
CHORLEYWOOD
Newhouse Farm
Prim Sch
Black Horse PH
The Cedars
HOMEWOOD
Chorleywood
CROSSLANE WOOD
Fairfield Farm & Livery Stables
Roughwood Park
Lib
Berry Farm
THE SCREEN
SOLOMON'S WOOD
West Herts Riding School
PHEASANTS WOOD
The Hall Farm
Penn Farm
Hill Farm
Prim Sch
Chorleywood Bottom
The Swillet
ALLOT
Bullsland Farm
GROVELAND WOOD
PHILIPSHILL WOOD
Heronsgate
M25
AZ BA BB BC BD BE BF
01 02 03
96 97 98 99
35 36 37 38 39 40 41 42 43 44
5
22
37

Commonwood
Bucks Hill
6
Sarratt
WD4
WD3
Junction 19
Junction 18
Loudwater
Croxley Green
21
38
BG
BH
BJ
BK
BL
BM
BN
05
06
07
35
36
37
38
39
40
41
42
43
44
99
98
97
96
HILLMEADS SPRING
COMMONWOOD COMMON
Great Sarratt Hall
Bucks Hill Farm
CONFERENCE CENTRE
Little Westwood Farm
Great Westwood Farm
BEECHEN BOTTOM
JUNIPER HILL
HIGH SPRING
The Boot PH
SPORTS GROUND
Poultry Houses
Newhall Farm
Buckshill Bottom
TEMPLEPAN WOOD
TEMPLEPAN LANE
Cricketers Inn PH
Prim Sch
Hall
Ward's Nurseries
SANDFIELD WOOD
Adams Nurseries
Green End Farm
Sarratt Bottom Cottages
White House
Yew Court Farm
Potten's Farm
BIRCH SPRING
DARTPATH WOOD
Mickleford Green Farm
GREAT WOOD
SHEEPYARD SPRING
M25
WHITE SHACK LANE
Stevens Nurseries
The Grove Lodge
Chandler's Farm
Clarendon Arms PH
Country Place
New Model Farm
SAWPIT SPRING
Coltspring Riding Stables
Coltyard Farm
Cottage Farm
Blacketts Nursery
SCRUBBS WOOD
BLUNTS WOOD
WILLOW WOOD
HARROCKS WOOD
Sarrattmill Bridge
Water Works
MEAD SPRING
Redhall Farm
WELLING GROVE
MERLIN'S WOOD
MERLIN'S SPRING
Micklefield Hall Farm
Micklefield Hall
Beechen Hill
BEECHENGROVE WOOD
MILLFIELD PLANTATION
LONG SPRING
UPPER PLANTATION
ROUND SPRING
Model Farm
York Ho Sch
WATERDELL SPRING
Highlands Water Gardens
Solesbridge Mill Water Gardens
River Chess
Waterdell House
Thurlwood House
Croxley House
Killingdown Farm
Cricket Ground
Prim Sch
LITTLE LADY'S WOOD
Walden Lodge
Whitestocks Farm
PARROT'S DELL
White Horse PH
Loudwater House
Mont Au Source
Glen Chess
Loudwater Farm
The Cedars
HOME WOOD
Black Horse PH
COPTHORNE WOOD
BALDWINS LANE RECREATION GROUND
CHORLEYWOOD ROAD
SPORTS GROUND
Watercress Beds
ROUND SPRING
Coach & Horses PH
Prim Sch
SPORTS GROUND
Berry Farm
THE SCREEN
SOLOMON'S WOOD
Artichoke PH
West Herts Riding School
PHEASANTS WOOD
Rickmansworth Masonic Sch
HOCKEY GRD
PLAYING FIELD
CRICKET GRD
Clubhouse
FORTUNE COMMON
SPORTS GROUND
CROXLEY HALL WOOD
CHORLEYWOOD ROAD CEMETERY
RICKMANSWORTH PARK
SCOTS HILL
WATFORD ROAD
A404
RICKMANSWORTH ROAD

23
BP
BQ
BR
BS
BT
BU
BV
08
09
10
7
Langleybury
THE ROOKERY
Leavesden Green
Kingswood
Garston
35
36
37
38
39
40
41
42
43
44
24
99
98
97
96
Hunton Bridge Interchange
THREE RIVERS
WATFORD
NORTH WESTERN AVENUE
A41
M25 LINK ROAD
HEMPSTEAD ROAD
A411
KINGSWAY (NORTH ORBITAL ROAD)
A405
ST ALBANS ROAD
A412
PLAYING FIELD
HEATH WOOD
GROVE
PARK
Management & Conference Centre
The Grove
WHIPPENDELL WOOD
WEST HERTFORDSHIRE GOLF COURSE
CHARLOTTE'S VALE
ROUGH WOOD
SPORTS GROUND
CASSIOBURY PARK
PADDLING POOLS
GRAND UNION CANAL
River Gade
WD24
WD17
WD18
NORTH WATFORD
NORTH WATFORD CEMETERY
STANBOROUGH PARK
GOODWOOD REC GRD
CALLOWLAND REC GRD
CHESLYN GDNS
West Herts College
Sports Complex
Watford Tunnels
WATFORD
THE COLOSSEUM
TOWN HALL
Harlequin Centre
Charter Place
WEST WATFORD
VICARAGE RD CEMETERY
WATFORD GENERAL HOSP
VICARAGE ROAD WATFORD FC & SARACENS RFC
WATFORD STADIUM HALT (MATCH DAYS ONLY) (Closed)
WATFORD JUNCTION
WATFORD HIGH STREET
WATFORD NORTH
MOWAT INDUSTRIAL EST
TRIDENT CENTRE
IMPERIAL PARK
RICKMANSWORTH ROAD
WATFORD ROAD
CROXLEY GREEN (Closed)
CROXLEY
CROXLEY BUSINESS PARK
WATFORD BUSINESS PARK
Holywell
HOLYWELL IND EST
KING GEORGE V PLAYING FIELDS
LONG VALLEY WOOD
COMMON MOOR
DURRANTS SPORTS GROUND
WOLSEY BUSINESS PARK
MOOR PARK INDUSTRIAL ESTATE
TOLPITS LANE
EBURY WAY CYCLE PATH
Electricity Transmission Station
OXHEY PARK
DEACONS HILL
A4125
A4178
BEECHEN GROVE
EXCHANGE RD
HAGDEN LANE
WIGGENHALL ROAD
LWR HIGH STREET

24
BW
BX
BY
BZ
CA
CB
CC
8
Garston
NORTH WATFORD CEMETERY
STANBOROUGH PARK
Meriden
University of Hertfordshire
ALDENHAM GOLF COURSE & COUNTRY CLUB
Aldenham
Round Bush
Junction 5
Berrygrove Interchange
TOP GOLF GAME CENTRE
NORTH WATFORD
WD24
WD25
WD17
WD23
WATFORD NORTH
WATFORD JUNCTION
WATFORD HIGH STREET
BUSHEY HALL GOLF COURSE
METROPOLITAN POLICE BUSHEY SPORTS GROUND
BUSHEY JEWISH CEMETERY
The U.S. International University-Europe
The Purcell School
The Lincolnsfields Centre
Hartspring Leisure Cen
The David Lloyd Club
Hilton Watford
SCOTTS WOOD
RADLETT ROAD PLAYING FIELDS
ICEDALE WOODS
Harlequin Centre
WATFORD GENERAL HOSPL
OXHEY
BUSHEY
BUSHEY GOLF COURSE & COUNTRY CLUB
KING GEORGE REC GROUND
WESTERN AVENUE A41
COLNE WAY (NORTH WESTERN AVENUE)
ELTON WAY (NORTH WESTERN AVENUE)
OTTERSPOOL WAY
ST. ALBANS ROAD
STEPHENSON WAY
LONDON ROAD
HIGH STREET
EASTBURY ROAD
M1
23
40
35
36
37
38
39
40
41
42
43
44
12
13
14
97
98
99
96

Oakridge Lane Sewage Treatment Works
CD
CE
CF
CG
CH
CJ
CK
15
16
17
9
26
41
35
36
37
38
39
40
41
42
43
44
99
98
97
96
PARK
SAND PLANTATION
GOLF COURSE
Cricket Ground
Pav
SPORTS GRD
Clubhouse
Sewage Works
Starveacres
Blackbirds Farm
Blackbirds Country Fare (Garden Centre)
Kemprow Farm
High Cross House
RADLETT
THE GORSE
Auriol Farm
Wood Hall Farm
Wood Hall
Catherine
Pol
Fire Sta
Lib
PO
SN
Prim Sch
Tenn & Squash Club
CEM
SCRUBBITTS WOOD
SPORTS GRD
FIR SPRING
ALLOT
Tenn Cts
Bowl Grn
WD7
Tykes Water
Tabard R.F.C.
Radlett Cricket Club
Cricket Ground
Cat & Fiddle PH
Cobden Hill
WELLHOUSE DELL
COBDENHILL DELL
MOSES DELL
Battlers Green Farm
Home Farm
KENDAL WOOD
FISH POND
Lido
Kendal Hall Farm
Little Kendals Farm
LITTLE KENDALS WOOD
Organ Hall Farm
Letchmore Heath
The Fruit Farm
PLAYING FIELD
Aldenham Grange
Aldenham Cottage
Three Horseshoes PH
War Meml.
Bhaktivedanta Manor
SPORTS GROUND
Boydens Hill
Sports Cen
Aldenham Sch
Medburn Cottages
PLAYING FIELD
ELSTREE
DRIVING RANGE
Clubhouse
GOLF
COURSE
North Medburn Farm
North Medburn Stables
Slades Farm
Electricity Transfer Station
Letchmore Lodge
Battle Axes PH
ALDENHAM PARK WOODLAND
MOATS
The Haberdasher's Aske's Sch for Boys
Waggon & Horses PH
Medburn Bridge
South Medburn Farm
ELSTREE AERODROME
Hilfield Farm
Flying Club
Hangars
The Haberdasher's Aske's Sch for Girls
Hilfield Castle
Boathouse
DAM
Pages Farm
WD6
ALDENHAM
Home Farm
ALLOT
HILFIELD PARK RESERVOIR
Pumping Sta
Sewage Works
Works
Hart's Farm Stables
Lister Institute
DAM
Boathouse
PARK
Elli Dani Farm (Stables)
CEMETERY
ALDENHAM COUNTRY PARK
ALDENHAM RESERVOIR
Sailing Club
ELSTREE
SPORTS GROUND
Prim Sch
TYLERS WAY (NORTH WESTERN AV)
M1
Caldecote Farm
Berkeley Cottage
ELSTREE HILL OPEN SPACE
Comm Cen
Works
CONVENT
Coll
Gas Pumping Sta
CENTENNIAL PARK
ELSTREE OPEN SPACE
Edgwarebury Hotel
Tennis Courts
The Leys
Sparrows Herne
Heath House
A5183
A411
B462
A409
WATLING STREET
COBDEN HILL
ELSTREE HILL NORTH
ELSTREE HILL SOUTH
BARNET LANE
ELSTREE ROAD
WATFORD ROAD
ALDENHAM ROAD
HILFIELD LANE
BUTTERFLY LANE
HOGG LANE
DAGGER LANE
ALLUM LANE
THEOBALD STREET
SHENLEY HILL
NEWBERRIES AVENUE

26
CL
CM
CN
CP
CQ
CR
CS
10
19
20
21
SAND PLANTATION
BIG PURSLEY WOOD
LITTLE PURSLEY WOOD
CROSS OAKS WOOD
BIRCH WOOD
WD7
Green Street
Well End
35
36
37
38
39
40
41
42
43
44
99
98
97
96
25
ELSTREE
DRIVING RANGE
GOLF
WD6
COURSE
ALDENHAM
PARK
HERTSMERE BOROUGH COUNCIL CEMETERY
ELSTREE
BOREHAMWOOD
AYCLIFFE ROAD PITCHES
ABERFORD PARK
SPORTS GROUND
MEADOW PARK
B.B.C. Elstree Studios
Imperial Studios
Oaklands College
BOREHAMWOOD IND PARK
MAXWELL PK
KING GEORGES PLAYING FLD
RIPON PARK
G.E.C. SPORTS GROUND
ARKLEY GOLF DRIVING RANGE
LAINGS PLAYING FIELD
ARKLEY GOLF COURSE
Furze Hill
Stirling Corner
FROGHALL WOOD
SCRATCH WOOD
DEACONS HILL OPEN SPACE
42
BOYS HILL WOOD
THISTLE WOOD
GRAVEL PIT WOOD
ELSTREE OPEN SPACE
Elstree Manor
Deacons Hill
ELSTREE & BOREHAMWOOD
A411
A5135
A1
BARNET BYPASS
ELSTREE HILL NORTH
ELSTREE HILL SOUTH
BARNET LANE
SHENLEY ROAD
THEOBALD STREET
WATLING STREET
ALLUM LANE
ROWLEY LANE

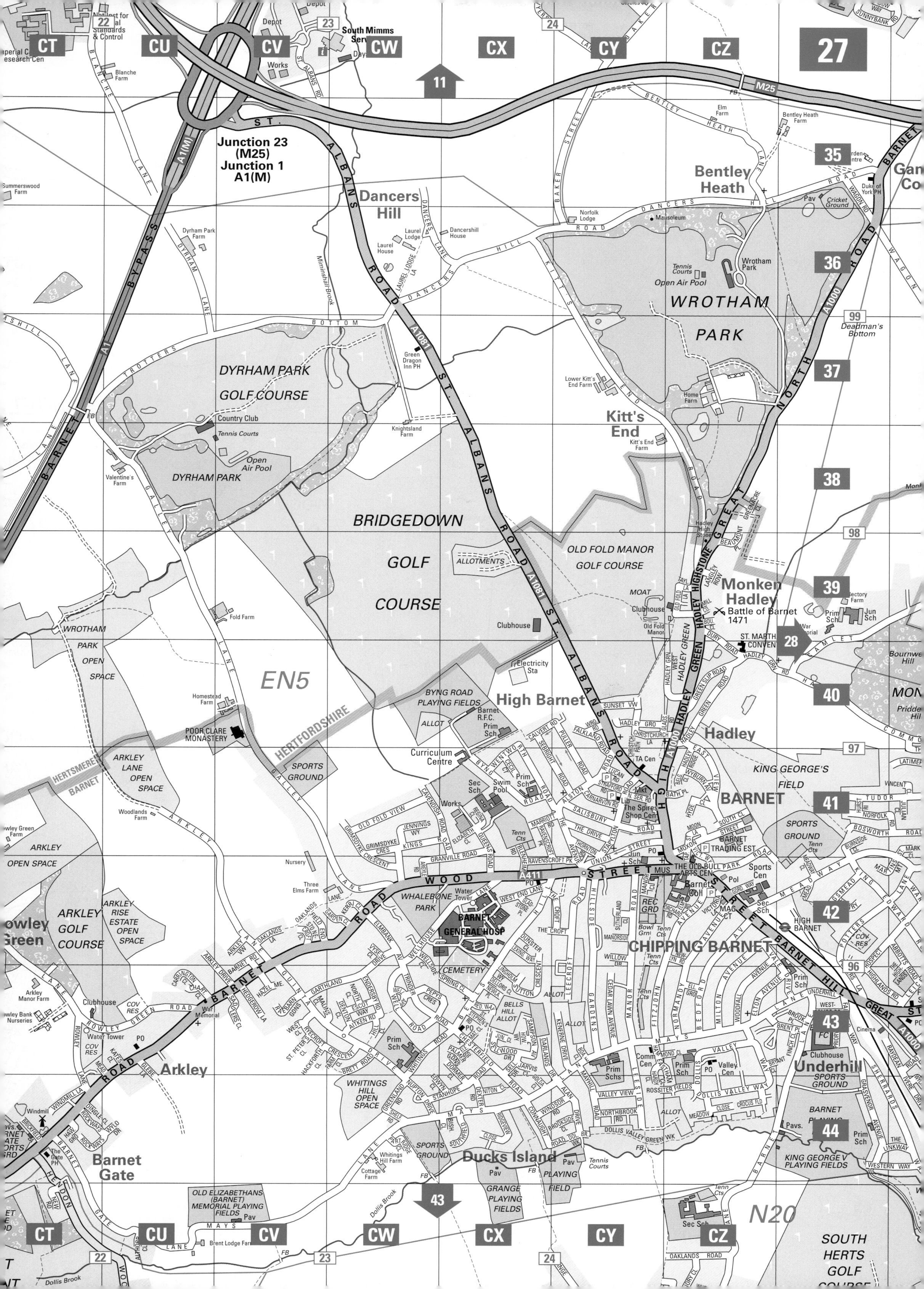

27
CT
CU
CV
CW
CX
CY
CZ
11
Junction 23 (M25) Junction 1 A1(M)
M25
A1(M)
BARNET BY PASS
Dancers Hill
Bentley Heath
WROTHAM PARK
DYRHAM PARK GOLF COURSE
DYRHAM PARK
BRIDGEDOWN GOLF COURSE
OLD FOLD MANOR GOLF COURSE
Kitt's End
Monken Hadley
Battle of Barnet 1471
High Barnet
Hadley
BARNET
CHIPPING BARNET
Arkley
Barnet Gate
Ducks Island
Underhill
EN5
N20
HERTFORDSHIRE
BARNET GENERAL HOSP
KING GEORGE'S FIELD
SOUTH HERTS GOLF COURSE
35
36
37
38
39
40
41
42
43
44
28
43

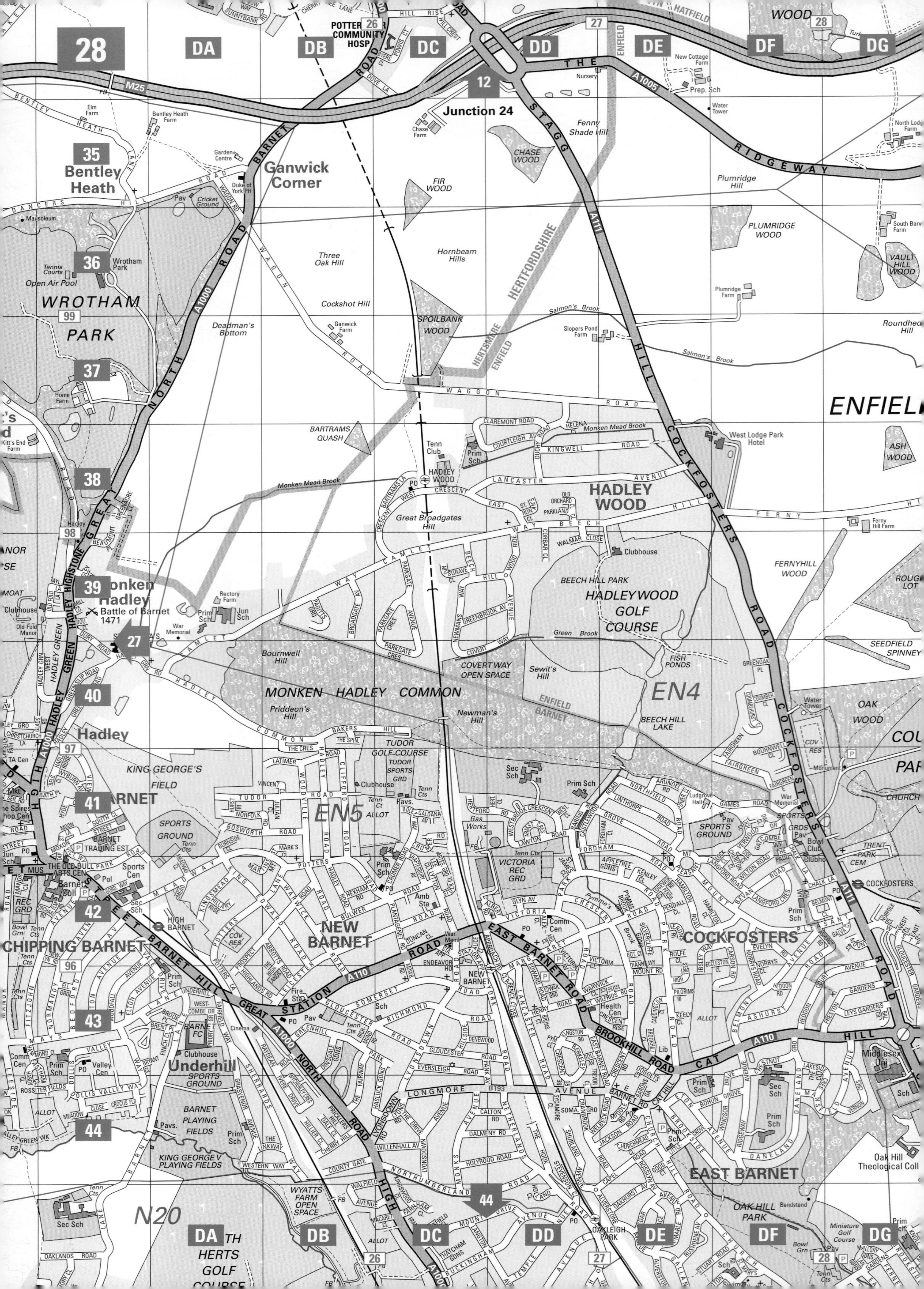
28
DA
DB
DC
DD
DE
DF
DG
POTTERS BAR COMMUNITY HOSP
M25
12
Junction 24
THE RIDGEWAY
A1005
Bentley Heath
Ganwick Corner
WROTHAM PARK
Wrotham Park
Open Air Pool
BARNET ROAD
WAGON ROAD
GREAT NORTH ROAD
A1000
STAGG HILL
A111
COCKFOSTERS ROAD
Chase Farm
CHASE WOOD
Fenny Shade Hill
FIR WOOD
Three Oak Hill
Hornbeam Hills
Cockshot Hill
SPOILBANK WOOD
HERTFORDSHIRE
HERTSMERE
ENFIELD
Deadman's Bottom
Ganwick Farm
Plumridge Hill
PLUMRIDGE WOOD
VAULT HILL WOOD
Plumridge Farm
Salmon's Brook
Slopers Pond Farm
WAGGON ROAD
BARTRAMS QUASH
West Lodge Park Hotel
ENFIELD
ASH WOOD
HADLEY WOOD
Great Broadgates Hill
Monken Mead Brook
FERNY HILL
Ferny Hill Farm
FERNYHILL WOOD
BEECH HILL PARK
HADLEY WOOD GOLF COURSE
Clubhouse
Monken Hadley
Battle of Barnet 1471
Rectory Farm
CAMLET WAY
Bournwell Hill
MONKEN HADLEY COMMON
Priddeon's Hill
Newman's Hill
COVERT WAY OPEN SPACE
Sewit's Hill
FISH PONDS
EN4
BEECH HILL LAKE
SEEDFIELD SPINNEY
OAK WOOD
Hadley
TUDOR GOLF COURSE
KING GEORGE'S FIELD
BARNET
SPORTS GROUND
EN5
VICTORIA REC GRD
SPORTS GROUND
TRENT PARK CEM
COCKFOSTERS
NEW BARNET
HIGH BARNET
CHIPPING BARNET
EAST BARNET ROAD
STATION ROAD
A110
BARNET HILL
CAT HILL
BROOKHILL ROAD
Underhill SPORTS GROUND
BARNET FC
BARNET PLAYING FIELDS
KING GEORGE V PLAYING FIELDS
WYATTS FARM OPEN SPACE
N20
SOUTH HERTS GOLF COURSE
EAST BARNET
OAK HILL PARK
Middlesex Uni
Oak Hill Theological Coll
OAKLEIGH PARK
27
44
26
35
36
37
38
39
40
41
42
43
44
96
97
98
99

29
CREWS HILL GOLF COURSE
Crews Hills
Botany Bay
CHASE
WHITEWEBBS PARK
Clay Hill
HILLY FIELDS PARK
EN2
KING'S OAK PRIVATE HOSPITAL
CHASE FARM HOSPITAL
LAVENDER HILL CEMETERY
Middlesex University
TRENT PARK GOLF COURSE
World's End
ENFIELD GOLF COURSE
GRANGE PARK
BUSH HILL PARK GOLF COURSE
N21
OAKWOOD
OAKWOOD PARK
THE RIDGEWAY
HADLEY ROAD
ENFIELD ROAD
SLADES HILL
WINDMILL HILL

30
DQ
DR
DS
DT
DU
DV
DW
33
34
35
M25
14
Junction 25
BULLSCROSS RIDE
CEMETERY (JEWISH)
COUNTY BROOK PLANTATION
Theobalds Park Camping and Caravan Site
Bulls Cross
Capel Manor Horticultural & Environmental Centre
CAPEL HOUSE
BULLSMOOR
35
Crews Hill
WHITEWEBBS WOOD
WHITEWEBBS PARK
WHITEWEBBS GOLF COURSE
White Webbs House
Sloeman's Farm
Whitewebbs Farm
WHITEWEBBS LANE
SPORTS GROUND
Myddelton House
New River (Old Course)
Turkey Brook
Cuffley Brook
36
WILDWOOD
EN2
Brayside Farm
Clubhouse
FORTY HALL COUNTRY PARK
Forty Hill
FORTY HALL & MUSEUM
Maiden's Bridge
Bullsmoor
CEMETERY
Crematorium
37
Clay Hill
Kingswood
Rendlesham Viaduct
HILLY FIELDS PARK
ALLOTMENTS
38
CEMETERY
98
39
GORDON HILL
29
ENFIELD CEMETERY (JEWISH)
Recycling Cen
QUEEN ELIZABETH STADIUM
David Lloyd Leisure Cen
EN1
40
97
ENFIELD TOWN
CIVIC CENTRE
ENFIELD
ENFIELD PLAYING FIELDS
BASEBALL GROUND
41
WINDMILL HILL
A110
ENFIELD CHASE
SOUTHBURY ROAD
ENFIELD RETAIL PK
Enfield Coll
HERTFORD ROAD
42
TOWN PARK
96
GRANGE PARK
43
BUSH HILL PARK GOLF COURSE
BUSH HILL PARK
MARTINBRIDGE TRADING ESTATE
Middlesex University
GREAT CAMBRIDGE ROAD
A10
44
Salmon's Brook
N21
46
JUBILEE PARK
A1010
A105
LONDON ROAD
DQ
DR
DS
DT
DU
DV
DW
33
34
35

DX
DY
DZ
EA
EB
EC
ED
Holdbrook
Freezy Water
RAMMEY MARSH
INNOVA BUSINESS PARK
Enfield Lock
Enfield Wash
ALBANY PARK
EN3
EN9
SEWARDSTONE MARSH
LEE VALLEY PARK
Sewardstone
KING GEORGE'S RESERVOIR
BRIMSDOWN INDUSTRIAL ESTATE
BRIMSDOWN SPORTS GROUND
Brimsdown
DURANTS PARK
ALMA ROAD OPEN SPACE
CENTENARY ESTATE
PONDERS END IND EST
VALLEY LINK IND EST
RIVERSIDE IND EST
GILWELL PARK
BANCHET FIELD
THE QUICK
THE ROUGH
CARP LAKES
Yardley Hill
THE HAWK WOOD
CHINGFORD GOLF COURSE
CHINGFORD PLAIN
WEST ESSEX GOLF COURSE
E4
POLE HILL
Barn Hill
THOMPSON'S WOOD
FERNHILL WOOD
MOLLISON AVENUE
SEWARDSTONE ROAD
A112
A1055
A110
A121
M25
LEA VALLEY ROAD
MERIDIAN WAY
HERTFORD ROAD
ELEANOR CROSS RD
River Lee Navigation
Small River Lee or Lea
Cattlegate Flood Relief Channel
Overflow Channel
Cobbin's Brook
Quinton Hill Brook
Sewardstone Roundabout
DAWS HILL
AVEY LANE
GILWELL LANE
BURY ROAD
15
35
36
37
38
39
40
41
42
43
44
47
32
99
98
97
96
LEE VALLEY

32
EE
EF
EG
EH
EJ
EK
EL
40
41
42
16
WALTHAM ABBEY
Junction 26
M25
HONEY LANE
A121
WOODRIDDEN HILL
SPORTS GROUND
Waltham Abbey FC
Swim Pool
LODGE LANE
Sewardstone Roundabout
Quinton Hill Farm
CLAY PIGEON RANGE
Southend Farm
SOUTHEND LANE
Upshire Hall
Sudbury Farm
WOODGREEN ROAD
WOODBINE CLOSE
Woodbine Inn PH
SKILLET HILL
Volunteer PH
HONEY LANE PLAIN
CONYBURY WOOD
Woodredon Farm
Woodredon House
STABLES SHAW
Woodredon Riding School
BRAMBLY SHAW
POTKILN WOOD
Works
Marriott Hotel
Prim Sch
The Lodge
Skillet Hill Farm
EN9
35
36
37
38
39
40
41
42
43
44
99
98
97
96
LORD PADGETTS WOOD
POPLARS SHAW
Inner Lodge
WALTHAM ABBEY CEMETERY (JEWISH)
HONEY LANE QUARTERS
SUNSHINE PLAIN
THREE FORESTS WAY
Round Hills
Beech Hill Park
Tile Hill Farm
Darrens Nursery
Beechview Nursery
AVEY LANE
Felicia Nursery
Providence Nursery
Normandy Nursery
BEECH HILL PARK
HIGH BEECH GOLF COURSE
Hanbury Riding School
Avey Lane Farm
PYNEST GRN
Pynest Green
High Beech Nursery
Avey Cottages
High Beech Riding School
Clubho
Duke of Wellington PH
Bowl Club
Y.H.A.
Earthworks
Tumulus
RATS LANE
WAKE ROAD
CLAYPIT HILL
King's Oak PH
Epping Forest Field Cen
LITTLE MONK WOOD
Mount Pleasant
Wake Valley
Grange Hill Nursery
Sewardstone Nursery
SEWARDSTONE ROAD
Plough PH
A112
THOMPSON'S WOOD
Mott Street Nursery
Brookfield Nursery
Netherhouse Farm
MOTT STREET
GRAVEL HILL
THOMPSON'S LANE
Prim Sch
Oak Farm
Manor House
MANOR ROAD
Paul's Nursery
EPPING FOREST
BLACKWEIR POND
Broom Hill
Loughton Camp
Kate's Cellar
Shelley's Hill
Robin Hood PH
IG10
ALDERGROVE WOOD
PEPPER ALLEY
Cricket Ground
Cricket Club
High Beach
Wallsgrove House
CHURCH ROAD
NURSERY ROAD
Sewardstone
31
Barn Hill
BLIND LANE
GREEN LANE
LIPPITTS HILL
Day's Farm
HILL WOOD
CENTENARY WALK
CROSS ROADS
EPPING NEW ROAD
A104
EARL'S PATH
Staples Hill
Loughton Brook
GREEN RIDE
FERNHILL WOOD
Police Training Centre
OWL PARK
Pipers Farm
Owl PH
Suntrap Field Study Centre
Strawberry Hill
NEW-FIELD
GILWELL PARK
BANCHET FIELD
Carrolls Farm
WEST ESSEX GOLF COURSE
Clubhouse
Springfield Farm
Piggeries
WHITEHOUSE PLAIN
ROUND THICKET
FAIRMEAD POND
Fairmead Bottom
STRAWBERRY HILL PONDS
The Scout Association
GILWELL LANE
ALMHOUSE PLAIN
North Long Hills
Long Hills
HORSE RIDE
FAIRMEAD ROAD
E4
Sewardstonebury
Bury Farm
Glasshouses
Tenn Cts
Obelisk
Oaklands Sch
Fire Sta
Sec Sch
SPORTS GRD
Health Cen
WOODMAN'S GLADE
BURY WOOD
BURY ROAD
Cuckoo Pits
Grimston's Oak
Magpie Hill
CONNAUGHT WATER
Warren Hill House
Warren Hill
North Farm House
Holmhurst
MANOR ROAD
HIGH ROAD
CHINGFORD GOLF COURSE
CHINGFORD PLAIN
RANGERS ROAD
A1069
48
Royal Forest Hotel
QUEEN ELIZABETH'S HUNTING LODGE
Clubhouse
THE WARREN
WARREN POND
Tenn & Bowl Club
Buckhurst Hill
Warren Wood PH
Oak Hall
Cricket Ground
FOREST VIEW
CONNAUGHT AVENUE
POLE HILL
CHINGFORD

33
EM
EN
EP
EQ
ER
ES
ET
43
44
45
17
34
49
35
36
37
38
39
40
41
42
43
44
99
98
97
96
EPPING FOREST
THEYDON BOIS
Theydon Bois
THEYDON BOIS GOLF COURSE
Warren Lodge
Ambresbury
Little Bronx Livery & Riding Stables
Junction 6 (M
Junction 27 (M
ST. THOMAS'S QUARTERS
Long Running
Forest Lodge Stables
Jacks Hill
Oak Hill
COPPICE ROW
B172
B1393
EPPING ROAD
HORSE RIDE
GREEN RIDE
Dulsmead Hollow
COPLEY PLAIN
SHELTER PLAIN
FURZE GROUND
THE DITCHES RIDE
GREAT MONK WOOD
BROADSTROOD PLAIN
GOLDINGS HILL
A121
Sixteen Spring Jack PH
Oak Hill Farm
Birch Hall
Birch Hall Farm
THEYDON PLAIN
THE COPPICE
BIRCH WOOD
RED OAK WOOD
GAUNT'S WOOD
Ripley Grange
Debden Green
QUEEN MARY & WESTFIELD COLLEGE SPORTS GROUND
Pav
Prim Sch
Hall
PO
Tenn Club SPORTS GRD
Cricket Club
ALLOTS
Youth Cen
Pol
THEYDON GREEN
ABRIDGE ROAD
Parsonage Farm
Blunts Farm
Depot
Thrifts Hall Farm
CM16
THEYDON BOIS CEMETERY
Theydon Hall Farm
Theydon Hall
LOUGHTON LANE
GREGSON'S RIDE
GOLDING'S HILL PONDS
LOUGHTON GOLF COURSE
Clubhouse
CLAY'S LANE
Sec Sch
WILLINGALE ROAD
Prim Sch
THEYDON PARK ROAD
LONG SHAW
BROADFIELD SHAW
M11
FB
RM4
THEYDON MEAD
HILLYFIELDS OPEN SPACE
RECTORY LANE
A1168
CEM
Debden
SPORTS GROUND
Printing Works
Tenn Cts
Clubhouse
Bowl Grn
PROSPECT BUSINESS PARK
DEBDEN
St. Lukes Sch
Old Golden Lion PH
Coll
Sports Cen
Sir Winston Churchill PH
Plume of Feathers PH
Amb Sta
Clinic
Thea
LOUGHTON
Prim Schs
OAKWOOD HILL INDUSTRIAL ESTATE
LORRY PK
Loughton Bridge
CHIGWELL LANE
Junction 5
River Roding
RIVERSIDE WALK
Woolston Hall
Open Air Pool
DRIVING RANGE
IG7
EPPING FOREST GOLF COURSE
ABRIDGE ROAD
A113
LONDON ROAD
GRAVEL LANE
A1112
ABRIDGE PARK
Great Downs Farm
Turnours Hall
Marchings
Marchings Farm
Taylor May's Farm
Pettits Hall
Home Farm
Rolls Park
Rolls Park Farm
PUDDING LANE

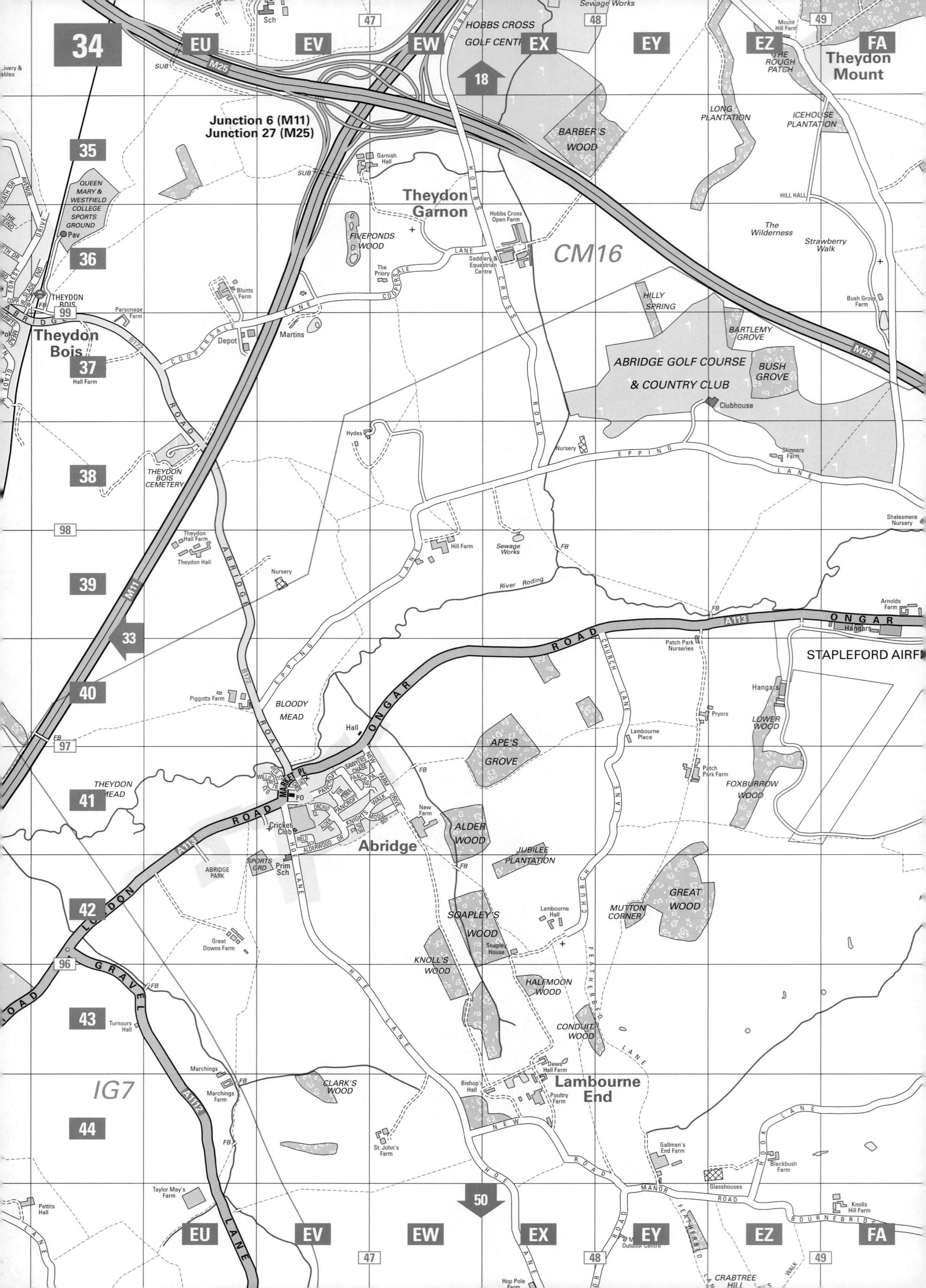
EU
EV
EW
EX
EY
EZ
FA
47
48
49
Sch
Sewage Works
HOBBS CROSS
GOLF CENTR
18
Mount Hill Farm
THE ROUGH PATCH
Theydon Mount
Livery & ables
SUB
M25
Junction 6 (M11)
Junction 27 (M25)
LONG PLANTATION
ICEHOUSE PLANTATION
BARBER'S WOOD
35
QUEEN MARY & WESTFIELD COLLEGE SPORTS GROUND
Pav
Garnish Hall
HILL HALL
Theydon Garnon
Hobbs Cross Open Farm
The Wilderness
Strawberry Walk
FIVEPONDS WOOD
36
LANE
Saddlery & Equestrian Centre
CM16
The Priory
COOPERSALE
Blunts Farm
THEYDON BOIS
HILLY SPRING
Bush Grove Farm
99
Parsonage Farm
Theydon Bois
Depot
Martins
BARTLEMY GROVE
ABRIDGE GOLF COURSE & COUNTRY CLUB
BUSH GROVE
37
Hall Farm
ROAD
Clubhouse
Hydes
Nursery
EPPING
Skinners Farm
LANE
38
THEYDON BOIS CEMETERY
98
Theydon Hall Farm
Theydon Hall
Hill Farm
Sewage Works
FB
Shalesmere Nursery
39
Nursery
M11
River Roding
Arnolds Farm
ONGAR
A113
Hangars
33
Patch Park Nurseries
CHURCH
STAPLEFORD AIRF
40
Piggotts Farm
B172
BLOODY MEAD
Hangars
Pryors
Lambourne Place
LOWER WOOD
Hall
97
APE'S GROVE
Patch Park Farm
THEYDON MEAD
41
MARKET PL
PO
New Farm
FOXBURROW WOOD
Cricket Club
ALDER WOOD
Abridge
JUBILEE PLANTATION
ABRIDGE PARK
SPORTS GRD
Prim Sch
FB
GREAT WOOD
MUTTON CORNER
42
LONDON
SOAPLEY'S WOOD
Lambourne Hall
Great Downs Farm
Soapley House
96
GRAVEL
KNOLL'S WOOD
HALFMOON WOOD
43
Turnours Hall
CONDUIT WOOD
FEATHERBED
Marchings
Dews Hall Farm
IG7
CLARK'S WOOD
Marchings Farm
Bishop's Hall
Lambourne End
Poultry Farm
44
A1112
NEW
HOOK LANE
St. John's Farm
Gallman's End Farm
Blackbush Farm
Glasshouses
Taylor May's Farm
50
MANOR
ROAD
Knolls Hill Farm
Pettits Hall
BOURNEBRIDGE
HOE LANE
Outdoor Centre
Hop Pole Farm
CRABTREE HILL
WALK

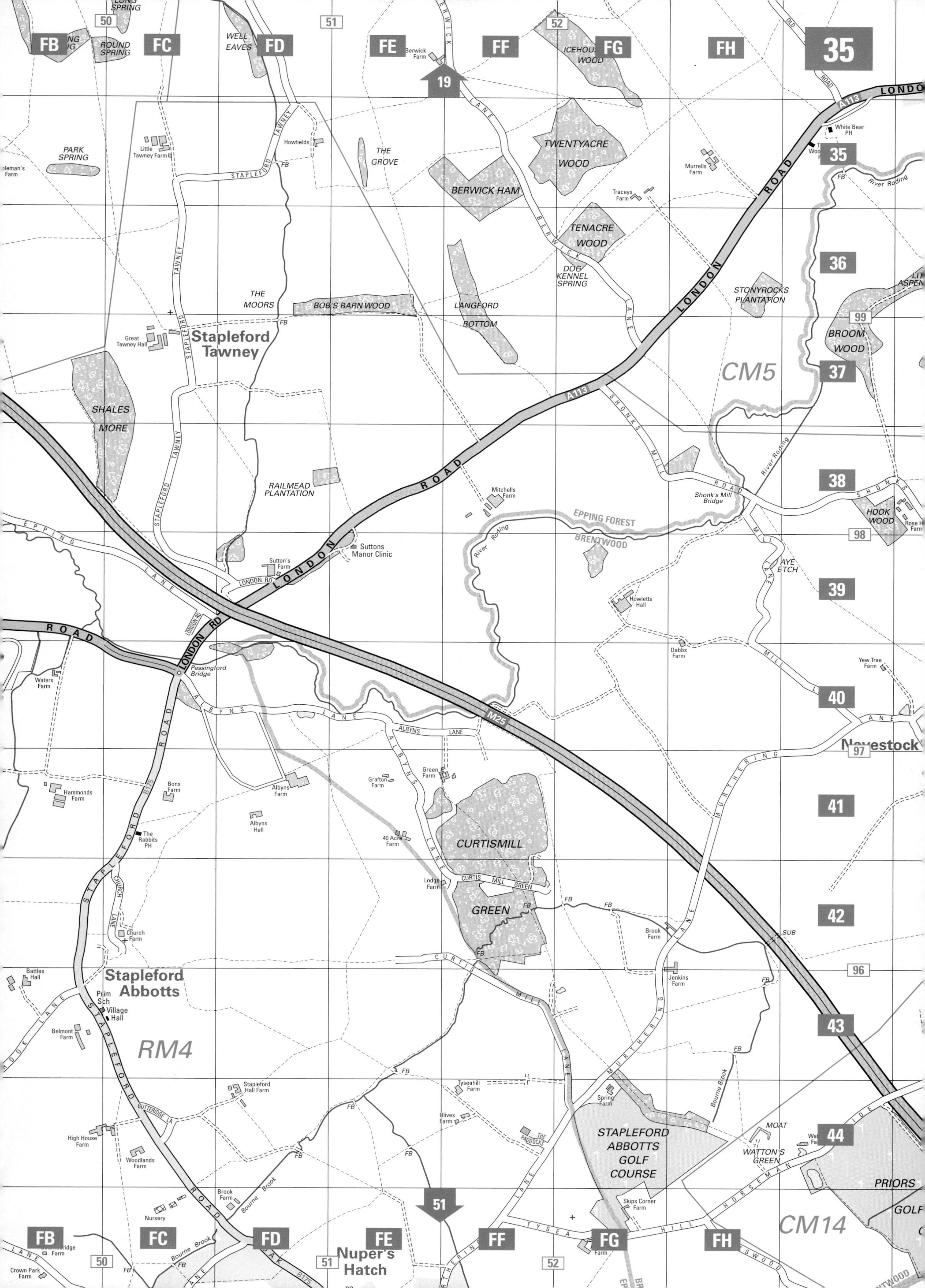
35
FB
FC
FD
FE
FF
FG
FH
19
51
50
52
WELL EAVES
ROUND SPRING
PARK SPRING
ICEHOUSE WOOD
TWENTYACRE WOOD
BERWICK HAM
TENACRE WOOD
DOG KENNEL SPRING
THE GROVE
THE MOORS
BOB'S BARN WOOD
LANGFORD BOTTOM
Stapleford Tawney
SHALES MORE
RAILMEAD PLANTATION
STONYROCKS PLANTATION
BROOM WOOD
CM5
Suttons Manor Clinic
EPPING FOREST
BRENTWOOD
River Roding
HOOK WOOD
Howletts Hall
Passingford Bridge
CURTISMILL GREEN
Navestock
Stapleford Abbotts
RM4
STAPLEFORD ABBOTTS GOLF COURSE
WATTON'S GREEN
MOAT
PRIORS
CM14
Nuper's Hatch
LONDON ROAD
A113
M25
36
37
38
39
40
41
42
43
44
96
97
98
99

AS
AT
AU
AV
AW
AX
AY
20
56
HP7
HP8
HP9
Chalfont St. Giles
Butlers Cross
Seer Green
Jordans
Layter's Green
HODGEMOOR WOODS
CHALFONT PARK GOLF COURSE
LONDON ROAD
AMERSHAM ROAD
GRAVEL HILL
BAILEY WOOD
RESERVOIR PLANTATION
KILNPOND WOOD
SHORTENILLS WOOD
OAK PLANTATION
DELLGARDEN PLANTATION
BAILEY WOOD BELT
BYCROFT PLANTATION
PERRYFIELD PLANTATION
RUSHCROFT WOOD
WELPLEY'S WOOD
HALES WOOD
THE LARCHES
BOW WOOD
HIGH WOOD
MILLFIELD PLANTATION
MILTON'S COTTAGE
TURNER'S WOOD
FOXDELL WOOD
PLAYING FIELD
Dibden Hill
RAWLINGS DELL
BIG COPSE
LITTLE COPSE
LONG WOOD
FARM WOOD
ROUND WOOD
MIDDLE WOOD
OUTFIELD PLANTATION
POND WARREN WOOD
GROVE WOOD
BIRCH PLANTATION
MONTAGUE'S DELL
GREEN WOOD
CRUTCHES WOOD
WELDERS WOOD
SPRING WOOD
WEEDONS DELL
MOUNTHILL WOOD
THE ASH BEDS
WHEATSHEAF WOOD
DEAN WOOD
THIRTY ACRE KNOLL
GREAT LEGS WOOD
MALMS WOOD
PITLANDS WOOD
BIRCHLAND WOOD
HIGH WOOD
BEECH WOOD
BIRCH WOOD
GOLDHILL COMMON
SPORTS GROUND
Greyhound Track
Quaker Conference Centre
Mayflower Barn
Coll
Leisure Centre
HOSP

37
Chorleywood Bottom
The Swillet
Heronsgate
Mill End
Junction 17
NEWLAND PARK
Brunel University Buckinghamshire College
CHILTERN OPEN AIR MUSEUM
SPORTS GROUND
BOTTOM WOOD
LADYWALK WOOD
WD3
FIVE PLANTATIONS
POLLARDSHILL WOOD
Maple Cross
MAPLE CROSS INDUSTRIAL ESTATE
BEECHEN WOOD
Maple Lodge Sewage Treatment Works
PLAYING FIELDS
FRANKLINS SPRING
Chalfont Common
KILN WOOD
ROBERT'S WOOD
SL9
ROUND ROCKET PLANTATION
QUARRY & LANDFILL SITE
MIDDLE WOOD
BLOOM WOOD
LYNSTERS LAKE
PYNESFIELD LAKE
CHALFONT ST. PETER
GRAVEL PIT
HOGTROUGH WOOD
GERRARDS CROSS GOLF COURSE
UB9
SPRINGWELL CHALK PIT
MOUNT PLEASANT SPORTS GRD
NOCKHILL WOOD
JUNIPER WOOD
TRAINING CENTRE DURDENT COURT
THREE RIVERS
SOUTH BUCKS
HERTFORDSHIRE
BUCKINGHAMSHIRE
NORTH ORBITAL ROAD
M25
A412
A405
21
38
57

38
22
58
37
BG
BH
BJ
BK
BL
BM
BN
45
46
47
48
49
50
51
52
53
54
RICKMANSWORTH
Moneyhill
Mill End
Batchworth
Batchworth Heath
HAREFIELD
Hill End
WD3
UB9
MOOR PARK GOLF COURSE
BATCHWORTH PARK GOLF COURSE
BATCHWORTH LAKE
BURY LAKE
STOCKER'S LAKE (NATURE RESERVE)
SPRINGWELL LAKE
LYNSTERS LAKE
PYNESFIELD LAKE
BISHOP'S WOOD
PARK WOOD
HARFIELD HOSPITAL
GRAND UNION CANAL
HERTFORDSHIRE
THREE RIVERS
HILLINGDON
CROXLEY HALL WOOD
Maple Lodge Sewage Treatment Works
MAPLE CROSS INDUSTRIAL ESTATE
HAREFIELD ROAD INDUSTRIAL ESTATE
WOODCOCK HILL CEMETERY
CHORLEYWOOD ROAD CEMETERY
WILLIAM PENN MULTISPORTS ARENA

BP
BQ
BR
BS
BT
BU
BV
39
Holywell
WATFORD BUSINESS PARK
WATFORD STADIUM HALT (MATCH DAYS ONLY)
LONG VALLEY WOOD
COMMON MOOR
HOLYWELL IND EST
23
KING GEORGE V PLAYING FIELDS
Electricity Transmission Station
SPORTS GROUND
WD18
TOLPITS LANE
WOLSEY BUSINESS PARK
MOOR PARK INDUSTRIAL ESTATE
VALE INDUSTRIAL ESTATE
THE EBURY WAY CYCLE PATH
River Gade
River Colne
EASTBURY ROAD
45
46
47
48
49
50
51
52
53
54
40
59
Brightwells Spring
HAMPERMILL LAKE
RUNNING TRACK
Merchant Taylor's Sch
Tolpits Plantation
The Withey Bed Wood
HAMPERMILL LANE
WD19
HAMPERMILL WOOD
BIG WOOD
Ox Pasture Spring
SOUTH OXHEY PLAYING FIELDS
OXHEY PARK GOLF COURSE
SANDY LODGE ROAD
GOLF COURSE
SANDY LODGE GOLF COURSE
MOOR PARK
Hampermill Spring
Round Spring
OLD FURZE FIELD
YOUNG HANGINGS
OLD HANGINGS
SOUTH OXHEY
OXHEY
THE PLANTATION
BECK MASON'S WOOD
OXHEY WOOD
H.M.S. Warrior
Moor Park
MOOR PARK ESTATE
Eastbury
BATHEND CLUMP
BATCHWORTH LANE
THREE RIVERS
WILD WOODS
NANSCOT WOOD
NORTHWOOD
MOUNT VERNON HOSPITAL
FRITHWOOD PARK
St. Helen's Sch
St. John's C of E Boys Sch
PINNER WOOD
PINNER HILL GOLF COURSE
PINNERWOOD PARK
HILLINGDON
HARROW
HA6
THE GRAVEL PITS
HIGH STREET
WATFORD ROAD
RICKMANSWORTH ROAD
GREEN LANE
HOGS BACK OPEN SPACE
NORTHWOOD GOLF COURSE
NORTHWOOD & PINNER COMMUNITY HOSP
Sports Centre
HA5
MONTESOLE PLAYING FIELDS
Northwood Hills
NORTHWOOD CEMETERY
HASTE HILL GOLF COURSE
RUISLIP NATURE RESERVE
COPSE WOOD
DUCKS HILL
YOUNG WOOD
POOR'S FIELD
ST. VINCENT'S ORTHOPAEDIC HOSPITAL
08
09
10
91
92
93
94

40
BW
BX
BY
BZ
CA
CB
CC
24
12
13
14
45
46
47
48
49
50
51
52
53
54
39
60
94
93
92
91
WATFORD HEATH
SHERWOODS WOOD
MARGEHOLES WOOD
GOLF DRIVING RANGE
SPOILBANKS
GROVE BANK
WD19
OXHEY PARK GOLF COURSE
Ox Pasture Spring
SOUTH OXHEY PLAYING FIELDS
Warren Dell
SOUTH OXHEY
OXHEY
POND WOOD
CARPENDERS PARK
CARPENDERS PARK CEMETERY
WOODWALKS
SANDPIT WOOD
MUTTON WOOD
SPORTS GROUND
NANSCOT WOOD
HERTFORDSHIRE
HARROW
HERTSMERE
THREE RIVERS
HILLINGDON
BUSHEY
BUSHEY GOLF COURSE & COUNTRY CLUB
BURIAL GRD
KING GEORGE REC GROUND
MERRY HILL
WD23
HILL MEAD NATURE PARK
HARTSBOURNE GOLF COURSE & COUNTRY CLUB
LEVELS WOOD
GRIM'S DYKE GOLF COURSE
Grim's Dyke Hotel
WEALD WOOD
STONY WOOD
GRIMSTONE LAKE
SADDLERS MEAD REC GROUND
HATCH END
SHAFTESBURY PLAYING FIELDS
PINNER HILL GOLF COURSE
HA5
PINNERWOOD PARK
PINNER WOOD
PINNER GREEN
MONTESOLE PLAYING FIELDS
LITTLE COMMON
PINNER PARK
RAGHUVANSHI CHARITABLE TRUST SPORTS GROUND
HATCH END PLAYING FIELD
SPORTS GROUND
BANNISTER ATHLETICS STADIUM
THE CEDARS
HEADSTONE MANOR
RECREATION
HA2
OXHEY LANE
UXBRIDGE ROAD
PINNER ROAD
EASTBURY ROAD
PRESTWICK ROAD
ST. THOMAS' DRIVE
RICKMANSWORTH RD
A4125
A4008
A411
A410
A404
B4542

41
CD
CE
CF
CG
CH
CJ
CK
15
16
17
25
42
45
46
47
48
49
50
51
52
53
54
61
91
92
93
94
M1
A411
A41
A5
A5183
A409
A4140
A410
ELSTREE ROAD
WATFORD BY PASS
BARNET ROAD
ELSTREE HILL OPEN SPACE
ELSTREE OPEN SPACE
WD6
HERTSMERE
HARROW
Junction 4
Site of Sulloniacae Roman Settlement
ROYAL NATIONAL ORTHOPAEDIC HOSP
Mike Heaffey Sports & Rehabilitation Centre
Aspire Centre
HELIPAD
Brockley Grange
Edgwarebury Hotel
CENTENNIAL PARK
Gas Pumping Sta
Caldecote Farm
Berkeley Cottage
CONVENT
B.U.P.A. HOSPITAL
BUSHEY HEATH
STANMORE COMMON
PEAR WOOD
FISH POND
BROCKLEY HILL GOLF COURSE
GROVE FIELDS
LITTLE COMMON
CLOISTERS WOOD
STANMORE HALL
BENTLEY PRIORY
BENTLEY PRIORY OPEN SPACE
BENTLEY PRIORY NATURE RESERVE
HERIOTS WOOD
DEER PARK
HA7
HARROW WEALD COMMON
HA3
HARROW WEALD CEMETERY
HARROW WEALD LAKE
Weald College
STANMORE
Stanmore College
TEMPLE POND
STANMORE GOLF COURSE
GOVT OFFICES
Canons Corner
N London Collegiate Sch
HA8
KING GEORGE V MEML GDNS
CANONS PARK
CANONS PARK SPORTS GROUND
PLAYING FIELD
SPORTS GROUND
PRINCE EDWARD PLAYING FIELD
RECREATION GROUND
HARROW WEALD
BELMONT
BELMONT CIRCLE
CENTENARY PARK
QUEENSBURY
WEALDSTONE
BYRON REC GRD
UXBRIDGE ROAD
LONDON ROAD
HONEYPOT LANE
BROCKLEY HILL
HIGH ROAD
COMMON ROAD
BROOKSHILL
HIGH STREET
STONEGROVE
SPUR ROAD
MARSH LANE
CHURCH RD
THE BDY
WATLING STREET (ROMAN ROAD)

42
CL
CM
CN
CP
CQ
CR
CS
19
20
21
26
BARNET LANE
Stirling Corner
BARNET
A411
FROGHALL WOOD
Deacons Hill
Woodcock Hill Farm
DEACONS HILL OPEN SPACE
SCRATCH WOOD
BOYS HILL WOOD
THISTLE WOOD
GRAVEL PIT WOOD
Hyver Hall
ELSTREE HILL SOUTH
Elstree Manor
Penniwells Farm
Edgwarebury Hotel
45
ELSTREE OPEN SPACE
A5183
WD6
HERTSMERE
M1
BARNET
CLUMP OF TREES WOOD
TARGET WOOD
LEG OF MUTTON POND
MILL HILL GOLF COURSE
NUT WOOD
A1
London Gateway Services
Depot
46
Junction 4
Brockley Grange
Site of Sulloniacae Roman Settlement
94
Bury Farm
EDGWAREBURY CEMETERY
REC GRD
SPORTS GRD
HEMMINGS WOOD
STONEY WOOD LAKE
STONEY WOOD
Welcome Lodge
47
FISH POND
A41 (WATFORD BYPASS)
BROCKLEY
EDGWARE WAY
BROCKLEY HILL GOLF COURSE
48
EDGWAREBURY PARK
EDGWAREBURY GOLF COURSE
93
GOVT OFFICES
SPORTS GROUND Canons Corner
SPUR ROAD
EDGWARE WAY (WATFORD BYPASS)
Apex Corner
WATFORD WAY
49
A410
SPUR RD ESTATE
STONEGROVE EST
STONEGROVE
CONVENT
A5100
41
STANMORE
50
N London Collegiate Sch
THE LAKE
STONEGROVE PARK
EDGWARE
HALE LANE
SELVAGE LANE
92
Sports Hall
KING GEORGE V MEML GDNS
CANONS PARK
THE SPINNEY
HIGH STREET
STATION ROAD
Broadwalk Shopping Centre
BUS DEPOT
HA8
ALLOTMENTS
DEANS LANE
LYNDHURST PARK
51
A4140
Gas Works
CANONS PARK SPORTS GROUND
DEANSBROOK ROAD
Hendon Coll
SPORTS GROUND
WATLING PARK
PLAYING FIELD
STANMORE MARSH
52
WHITCHURCH LANE
GOVT BUILDINGS
CHANDOS RECREATION GROUND
BURNT OAK
EDGWARE COMMUNITY HOSPITAL
HONEYPOT LANE
91
HA7
PRINCE EDWARD PLAYING FIELD
53
SPORTS GROUND
BURNT OAK BROADWAY
A5
ADASTRAL ESTATE
54
Pitch 'n' Putt
MOLLISON WAY
BRIXTON EST
MONTROSE PLAYING FIELDS
COLINDALE HOSP
BLOOD TRANSFUSION CENTRE
PUBLIC HEALTH LAB.
COLINDALE BUSINESS PK
CAPITOL IND PK
62
QUEENSBURY
Yaohan Plaza
BRIT. LIB NEWSPAPER COLLECTION
COLINDALE
EDGWARE ROAD

43
44
45
46
47
48
49
50
51
52
53
54
27
63
CT
CU
CV
CW
CX
CY
CZ
22
23
24
91
92
93
94
Barnet Gate
Ducks Island
N20
TOTTERIDGE
Highwood Hill
NW7
N12
MILL HILL
N3
CHURCH END
NW4
NW9
HOLDERS HILL
HENDON GOLF COURSE
FINCHLEY GOLF COURSE
KING GEORGE V PLAYING FIELDS
SOUTH HERTS GOLF COURSE
GRANGE PLAYING FIELDS
OLD ELIZABETHANS (BARNET) MEMORIAL PLAYING FIELDS
OLD CHOLMELEIAN SPORTS GROUND
TOTTERIDGE FIELDS NATURE RESERVE
DARLANDS LAKE NATURE RESERVE
ARRANDENE OPEN SPACE
MILL HILL PARK
BITTACY HILL PARK
COPTHALL STADIUM
COPTHALL PLAYING FIELDS
CHASE LODGE PLAYING FIELD
METRO GOLF
HENDON CEMETERY
SUNNY HILL PARK
WINDSOR OPEN SPACE
RAF MUSEUMS
Junction 2
Five Ways Corner
TOTTERIDGE COMMON
TOTTERIDGE VILLAGE
THE RIDGEWAY
WATFORD WAY
GREAT NORTH WAY
DOLLIS ROAD
REGENTS PARK ROAD
EAST END ROAD
BALLARDS LANE
A5109
A1
M1
A41
B552
A504

44
DA
DB
DC
DD
DE
DF
DG
28
26
27
45
46
47
48
49
50
51
52
53
54
43
64
94
93
92
91
KING GEORGE V PLAYING FIELDS
WYATTS FARM OPEN SPACE
SOUTH HERTS GOLF COURSE
BROOK FARM OPEN SPACE
N20
EAST BARNET
Oak Hill Theological Coll
OAK HILL PARK
EN4
OAKLEIGH PARK
DAME ALICE OWEN'S GRD
TOTTERIDGE LANE
TOTTERIDGE & WHETSTONE
TOTTERIDGE GREEN
WHETSTONE
SWAN LANE OPEN SPACE
NORTH MIDDLESEX GOLF COURSE
BRUNSWICK PARK
BETHUNE GOLF COURSE
RECREATION GROUND
FRIARY PARK
FRIERN BARNET
Consolata Missionary Coll
N12
WOODSIDE PARK
NORTH FINCHLEY
COPPETTS WOOD
FINCHLEY
FINCHLEY MEMORIAL HOSP
GLEBELANDS OPEN SPACE
VICTORIA PARK
MUSWELL HILL SPORTS GROUND
COPPETTS WOOD HOSP
ST. PANCRAS & ISLINGTON CEMETERY
COLDFALL WOOD
N2
N3
CHURCH END
FINCHLEY CENTRAL
WEST FINCHLEY
AVENUE HOUSE GRDS
NORTH CIRCULAR ROAD
EAST END ROAD
REGENTS PARK ROAD
BALLARDS LANE
HIGH ROAD
A1000
A5109
A109
A1003
A598
A406
A504

45
DH
DJ
DK
DL
DM
DN
DP
29
30
31
OAKWOOD PARK
WINCHMORE HILL
GROVELANDS PARK
BOATING LAKE
N14
N21
N13
N11
N22
OSIDGE
SOUTHGATE
SOUTHGATE CEMETERY
PALMERS GREEN
ARNOS PARK
NEW SOUTHGATE
BROOMFIELD PARK
BOWES PARK
MUSWELL HILL GOLF COURSE
WOOD GREEN
NOEL PARK
ALEXANDRA PALACE
ALEXANDRA PARK
HORNSEY
MUSWELL HILL
TOTTENHALL SPORTS GROUND
NEW RIVER SPORTS CENTRE
LORDSHIP RECREATION GROUND
THE PAULIN GROUND
CLOWES SPORTS GROUND
HAZELWOOD SPORTS GROUND
TATEM PARK REC GRD
BELMONT REC GRD
WOODCROFT SPORTS GROUND
BOUNDARY PLAYING FIELDS
46
47
48
49
50
51
52
53
54
65
A111
A1004
A1003
A1110
A406
A109
A105
A10
A1080
NORTH CIRCULAR ROAD
BOWES ROAD
GREEN LANES
HIGH ROAD
LORDSHIP LANE
ALDERMANS HILL
THE BOURNE
CHASE SIDE
WATERFALL ROAD
BOUNDS GREEN ROAD
ALEXANDRA PARK ROAD
WESTBURY AVENUE
THE BROADWAY
TURNPIKE LANE

46
DQ
DR
DS
DT
DU
DV
DW
33
34
35
30
45
47
48
49
50
51
52
53
54
66
94
93
92
91
N21
N13
N9
N18
N17
N22
LOWER EDMONTON
EDMONTON
UPPER EDMONTON
TOTTENHAM
TOTTENHAM HALE
NOEL PARK
EDMONTON CEMETERY
FIRS FARM PLAYING FIELDS
CLOWES SPORTS GROUND
THE PAULIN GROUND
CHURCH STREET REC GRD
CHURCHFIELD REC GRD
JUBILEE PARK
PYMMES PARK
TATEM PARK REC.GRD
HOLLY-WOOD GDNS
HAZELWOOD
TOTTENHALL SPORTS GROUND
BOUNDARY PLAYING FIELDS
NEW RIVER SPORTS CENTRE
TOTTENHAM CEMETERY
BRUCE CASTLE PARK
LORDSHIP RECREATION GROUND
TOWER GDNS
BELMONT REC GRD
DOWN LANE REC GRD
CRAIG PARK
EDMONTON FEDERATION CEMETERY (JEWISH)
WESTERN SYNAGOGUE CEMETERY
TOTTENHAM PARK CEMETERY
MONTAGU RECREATION GROUND
MONTAGU RD INDUSTRIAL EST
NORTH MIDDLESEX HOSPITAL
THE ROYAL LONDON ESTATE
WINGATE TRADING EST
MOWLEM TRADING ESTATE
MILMEAD INDUSTRIAL CENTRE
LEE VALLEY TECHNOPARK
TOTTENHAM MARSHES
LOCKWOOD RESERVOIR
LEE VALLEY PARK
NORTHUMBERLAND PARK
WHITE HART LANE
TOTTENHAM HOTSPUR F.C.
GREAT CAMBRIDGE ROAD
NORTH CIRCULAR ROAD
STERLING WAY
ANGEL ROAD
HERTFORD ROAD
FORE STREET
HIGH ROAD
THE ROUNDWAY
LORDSHIP LANE
BRUCE GROVE
MERIDIAN WAY
WATERMEAD WAY
RIDGE AVENUE
GREEN LANES
HEDGE LANE
A10
A406
A1010
A109
A105
A1080
A111
A1055
B154

47
DX
DY
DZ
EA
EB
EC
ED
36
37
38
31
45
46
47
48
49
50
51
52
53
54
67
94
93
92
91
CHINGFORD GOLF COURSE
CHINGFORD PLAIN
THE HAWK WOOD
POLE HILL
LEE VALLEY GOLF COURSE
WILLIAM GIRLING RESERVOIR
CLAVERINGS INDUSTRIAL ESTATE
DEEPHAMS SEWAGE TREATMENT WORKS
LEE VALLEY PARK
LEA VALLEY PLAYING FIELDS
MANSFIELD PARK
CHINGFORD
E4
FRIDAY HILL
RIDGEWAY PARK
CHINGFORD MOUNT CEMETERY
PIMP HALL PARK
CHINGFORD HATCH
LARKSWOOD PLAYING FIELDS
LARKS WOOD
CHINGFORD HALL PARK
SOUTH CHINGFORD
JUBILEE SPORTS GRD
HIGHAMS PARK
THE HIGHAMS PARK
WOODFORD GOLF COURSE
LEA VALLEY VIADUCT
HASTINGWOOD TRADING ESTATE
BANBURY RESERVOIR
HIGHAMS IND EST
HALE END
WOODFORD R.F.C.
EPPING FOREST
WALTHAMSTOW STADIUM
THE LONDON HOSPITAL SPORTS GRD
BRITANNIA SPORTS GROUND
FAIRWAY GOLF RANGE
WADHAM LODGE SPORTS GRD
HIGHAM HILL REC GRD
E17
LLOYD PARK
HIGHAM HILL
WALTHAMSTOW
WALTHAM FOREST ATHLETICS GRD
CHESTNUTS SHOWGROUND
WALTHAMSTOW FOREST
UPLANDS BUSINESS PARK
HIGHAMS LODGE BUSINESS CEN
SOUTHEND RD
NORTH CIRCULAR RD
A110
A112
A1009
A1037
A406
A503
A104
A1055
B160
B169
B179
Crooked Billet Roundabout

48
EE
EF
EG
EH
EJ
EK
EL
40
41
42
32
68
CHINGFORD PLAIN
CHINGFORD GREEN
WHITEHALL PLAIN
HATCH FOREST
BLUEHOUSE GROVE
HATCH GROVE
REED'S FOREST
Buckhurst Hill
LORD'S BUSHES
Knighton Wood
Woodford Wells
WOODFORD GOLF COURSE
WOODFORD GREEN
FRIDAY HILL
HIGHAMS PARK
HALE END
WOODFORD
SOUTH WOODFORD
E4
E18
IG8
IG9
RAY PARK
ASHTON PLAYING FIELD
RODING VALLEY PARK
EPPING FOREST
WALTHAMSTOW FOREST
QUEEN ELIZABETH'S HUNTING LODGE
HOLLY HOUSE HOSP
LUXBOROUGH LANE TREATMENT WORKS
DARTNALLS PLAYING FLD
OLD MONOVIANS SPORTS GRD
WANSTEAD Clubhouse R.F.C.
WOODFORD R.F.C.
SOUTHEND ROAD
NORTH CIRCULAR RD
CHIGWELL ROAD
HIGH ROAD
EPPING NEW ROAD
WOODFORD NEW ROAD
A1069
A110
A104
A121
A1009
A113
A406
A503
A11
Junction 4

49
EM
EN
EP
EQ
ER
ES
ET
33
69
43
44
45
FOREST GOLF
SPORTS GROUND
River Roding
LOUGHTON FC
The David Lloyd Club
ROLLS PARK
Chigwell House
SPORTS GROUND
METROPOLITAN POLICE SPORTS GRD
Chigwell
IG7
CHIGWELL ROW WATER WORKS
RESERVOIR
Chigwell Row
CHIGWELL
CHIGWELL CEMETERY
CHIGWELL GOLF COURSE
CONVENT OF THE SACRED HEART
Grange Hill
HAINAULT
FOREST ROAD PLAYING FIELD
HAINAULT RECREATION GROUND
FAIRLOP OAK PLAYING FIELD
ILFORD WANDERERS R.F.C.
Woodford Bridge
HOSPITAL HILL WOOD
Claybury Woods
COCKED HAT PLANTATION
SPORTS GROUND
FAIRLOP WATER
Fullwell Cross
IG6
FAIRLOP WATER GOLF COURSE
IG5
CLAYHALL
GARDEN OF REST
BARKINGSIDE CEM
BARKINGSIDE
IG2
ALDBOROUGH HATCH
HIGH ROAD
HAINAULT ROAD
FENCEPIECE ROAD
MANOR ROAD
ROMFORD ROAD
GRAVEL LANE
ABRIDGE ROAD
VICARAGE LANE
PUDDING LANE
FOREST ROAD
CHIGWELL LANE
M11
A113
A123
A1112
B173
45
46
47
48
49
50
51
52
53
54
91
92
93
94

50
EU
EV
EW
EX
EY
EZ
FA
34
70
49
Chigwell Row
IG7
HAINAULT FOREST COUNTRY PARK
HAINAULT FOREST GOLF COURSE
Havering Park
Collier Row
Mark's Gate
RM6
RM7
IG6
FAIRLOP WATER
HAINAULT INDUSTRIAL ESTATE
FOREST ROAD PLAYING FIELD
HAINAULT RECREATION GROUND
FAIRLOP OAK PLAYING FIELD
ROMFORD ROAD
WHALEBONE LANE NORTH
GRAVEL LANE
MANOR ROAD
LAMBOURNE ROAD
FOXBURROW ROAD
FIVE OAKS LANE
HOG HILL RD
ROMFORD ROAD
PAINTERS ROAD
BILLET ROAD
THREE CORNERS PLAIN
SPURGATE PLAIN
TAYLOR'S PLAIN
WEDDRELL'S PLAIN
CABIN PLAIN
Cabin Hill
THE LAKE
Dog Kennel Hill
MILE PLANTATION
SANDHILLS
LOWER SANDHILLS
CRABTREE HILL
Willoughby's Hill
Spurgate Brook
Seven Kings Water
EPPING FOREST
REDBRIDGE
ESSEX
HAVERING
BARKING & DAGENHAM
Romford FC
NORTHGATE IND PK
Youth Cen
SPORTS GROUND
MARKS GATE CEM
World War II Gun Emplacements

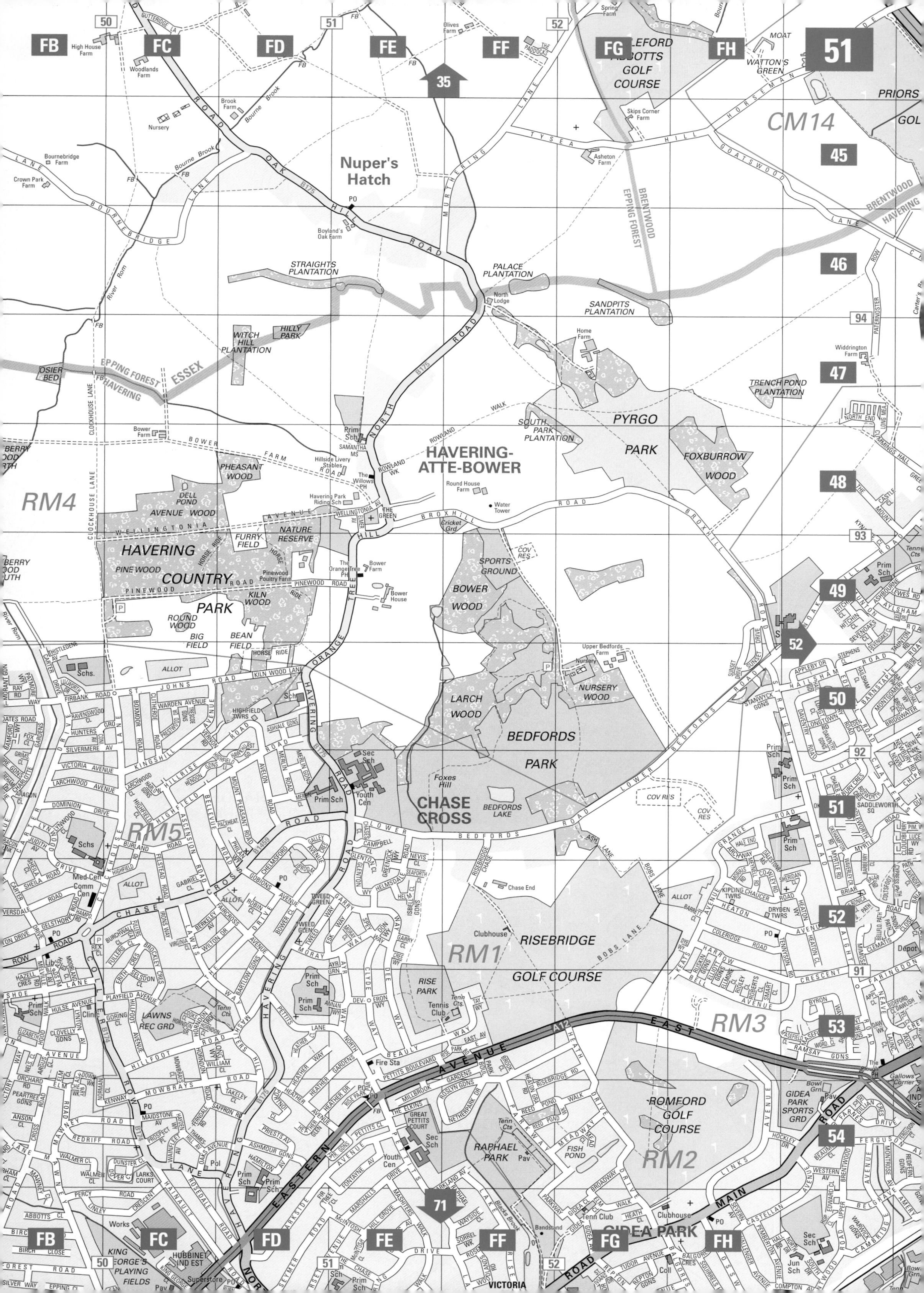

51
FB
FC
FD
FE
FF
FG
FH
35
71
52
CM14
45
46
47
48
49
50
51
52
53
54
High House Farm
Woodlands Farm
Brook Farm
Nursery
Bournebridge Farm
Crown Park Farm
Nuper's Hatch
Boyland's Oak Farm
Olives Farm
THE PADDOCKS
Spring Farm
STAPLEFORD ABBOTTS GOLF COURSE
MOAT
WATTON'S GREEN
PRIORS
Skips Corner Farm
Asheton Farm
EPPING FOREST
BRENTWOOD
HAVERING
ESSEX
STRAIGHTS PLANTATION
PALACE PLANTATION
North Lodge
SANDPITS PLANTATION
WITCH HILL PLANTATION
HILLY PARK
OSIER BED
Home Farm
Widdrington Farm
TRENCH POND PLANTATION
Bower Farm
PHEASANT WOOD
DELL POND
AVENUE WOOD
HAVERING-ATTE-BOWER
SOUTH PARK PLANTATION
PYRGO PARK
FOXBURROW WOOD
Round House Farm
Water Tower
Cricket Grd
RM4
HAVERING COUNTRY PARK
PINE WOOD
FURRY FIELD
NATURE RESERVE
KILN WOOD
ROUND WOOD
BIG FIELD
BEAN FIELD
SPORTS GROUND
BOWER WOOD
COV RES
Bower House
Upper Bedfords Farm
NURSERY WOOD
LARCH WOOD
BEDFORDS PARK
Foxes Hill
CHASE CROSS
BEDFORDS LAKE
RM5
RM1
RISEBRIDGE GOLF COURSE
RISE PARK
Tennis Club
RM3
ROMFORD GOLF COURSE
RM2
RAPHAEL PARK
GIDEA PARK
GIDEA PARK SPORTS GRD
FISH POND
KING GEORGE'S PLAYING FIELDS
HUBBINET IND EST
LAWNS REC GRD
Chase End
Clubhouse
Fire Sta
Superstore
VICTORIA

FJ
FK
FL
FM
FN
FP
FQ
54
55
56
45
46
47
48
49
50
51
52
53
54
94
93
92
91
PRIORS
GOLF
COURSE
ESSEX
BRENTWOOD
HAVERING
CURTIS PLANTATION
WABBING'S PLANTATION
SEVENACRE PLANTATION
CM14
LOCKSMITH WOOD
GOLDSMITH WOOD
Frieze Hall
The Chequers PH
Weald Bridge
Weald Brook
Hou Hatch
Wright's Bridge
Old Macdonalds Farm
Wrightsbridge Farm
Wealdside
Rochetts Farm
St. Vincent's Hamlet
M25
RM4
Pentowan Farm
SPICE PITS WOOD
Spice Pits Farm
NOAK HILL SPORTS GRD
Hill Farm
Hall
Widdrington Farm
Noak Hill
TRENCH POND PLANTATION
FOXBURROW
THE OSIERS
BURNT WOOD
The Bear PH
Manor Farm
DAGNAM PARK
FIR WOOD
COCK WOOD
MAYLANDS
GOLF
COURSE
ALDER WOOD
HATTER'S WOOD
Coll
Sec Sch
Prim Sch
DUCK WOOD NATURE RESERVE
CENTRAL PARK
HAROLD HILL
LONG WOOD
SALE WOOD
Swim Pool
Health Cen
Youth Club
Comm Cen
Pol
Youth Centre
Cricket Ground
SPORTS GRD
Clubhouse
Maylands
Putwell Bridge
SHOULDER OF MUTTON WOOD
RM3
The Saxon King PH
HAROLD PARK
COLCHESTER ROAD
A12
PLAYING FIELD
HALL TERRACE
Paine's Bridge
BATES INDUSTRIAL EST
Ingrebourne River
Sludge Beds
NAGS
HAROLD HILL INDUSTRIAL ESTATE
Depot
Superstore
Harold Court
Roots & Shoots Nursery
King Harold PH
HAROLD WOOD HOSPITAL
Ivy Lodge Farm
The Shepherd & Dog PH
Cockabourne Bridge
RM2
The Plough PH
Gallows Corner
AVENUE INDUSTRIAL ESTATE
GIDEA PARK SPORTS GRD
ROMFORD GOLF COURSE
HAROLD WOOD
Clinic
Comm Cen
Pages Farm
Riding Stables
RM14
HAROLD WOOD PARK
72
Sec Sch
Prim Sch
SOUTHEND ROAD
MAIN ROAD
Clubhouse
Prospect Farm
Ingrebourne Farm
Tyes Farm
Abattoir
Jun Sch
Coll
Works

53
BRENTWOOD
South Weald
WEALD COUNTRY PARK
BROOK STREET
WARLEY
Great Warley
CM15
CM13
Junction 28
WARLEY HOSPITAL
MARILLAC HOSPITAL
B.U.P.A. HARTSWOOD HOSP
LITTLE HIGHWOOD HOSP
HIGHWOOD HOSP
BRENTWOOD COMM HOSP
ESSEX NUFFIELD HOSP
Anglia Polytechnic Uni
CONVENT OF MERCY
BRENTWOOD BYPASS
HIGH STREET
LONDON ROAD
ONGAR ROAD
SHENFIELD ROAD
INGRAVE ROAD
WARLEY HILL
BRENTWOOD
HAVERING
ESSEX
M25
A12
A128
A1023
B186
GOLF COURSE
LITTLE WARLEY COMMON
HOLDEN'S WOOD
CLEMENT'S WOOD
BARRACK WOOD
KENT'S WOOD
HART'S WOOD
FR
FS
FT
FU
FV
FW
FX
57
58
59
45
46
47
48
49
50
51
52
53
54
73
91
92
93
94

FS
FT
FU
FV
FW
FX
FY
58
59
60
41
42
43
44
45
46
47
48
49
50
96
95
94
93
52
53
Bentley
BENTLEY GOLF COURSE
Crow Green
PILGRIM'S HATCH
CM15
CM14
WEALD COUNTRY PARK
South Weald
BRENTWOOD
BROOK STREET
WARLEY
WARLEY HOSPITAL
Junction 28
ONGAR ROAD
BRENTWOOD BYPASS
BRENTWOOD BY PASS
LONDON ROAD
HIGH STREET
SHENFIELD ROAD
INGRAVE ROAD
WEALD ROAD
HIGH WOOD
LITTLE HIGHWOOD HOSP
HIGHWOOD HOSP
Anglia Polytechnic Uni
ESSEX NUFFIELD HOSP
SHENFIELD COMMON
HART'S WOOD
DONKEY LANE PLANTATION
CLEMENT'S WOOD
LOWER BELT
MARILLAC HOSPITAL
CONVENT OF MERCY
BRICK HOUSE WOOD
CANTERBURY TYE SPRING
HALL WOOD
LARCH WOOD
FOX WOOD
BROOM WOOD
TOWER PLANTATION
LANGTONS WOOD
FOXDOWN WOOD
THE FOREST
LAKE FIELD
NURSERY FIELD
SOUTH WEALD LAKE
BELVEDERE FIELD
THE PARK
FRONT PARK
VICARAGE WOOD
THE OAKS
LOWER VICARAGE WOOD
THE GROVE
MORES PLANTATION
PUBLIC TIP
LARKINS PLAYING FIELDS
WARLEY PLAYING FIELDS
SPORTS GROUND
BISHOP'S HALL PARK

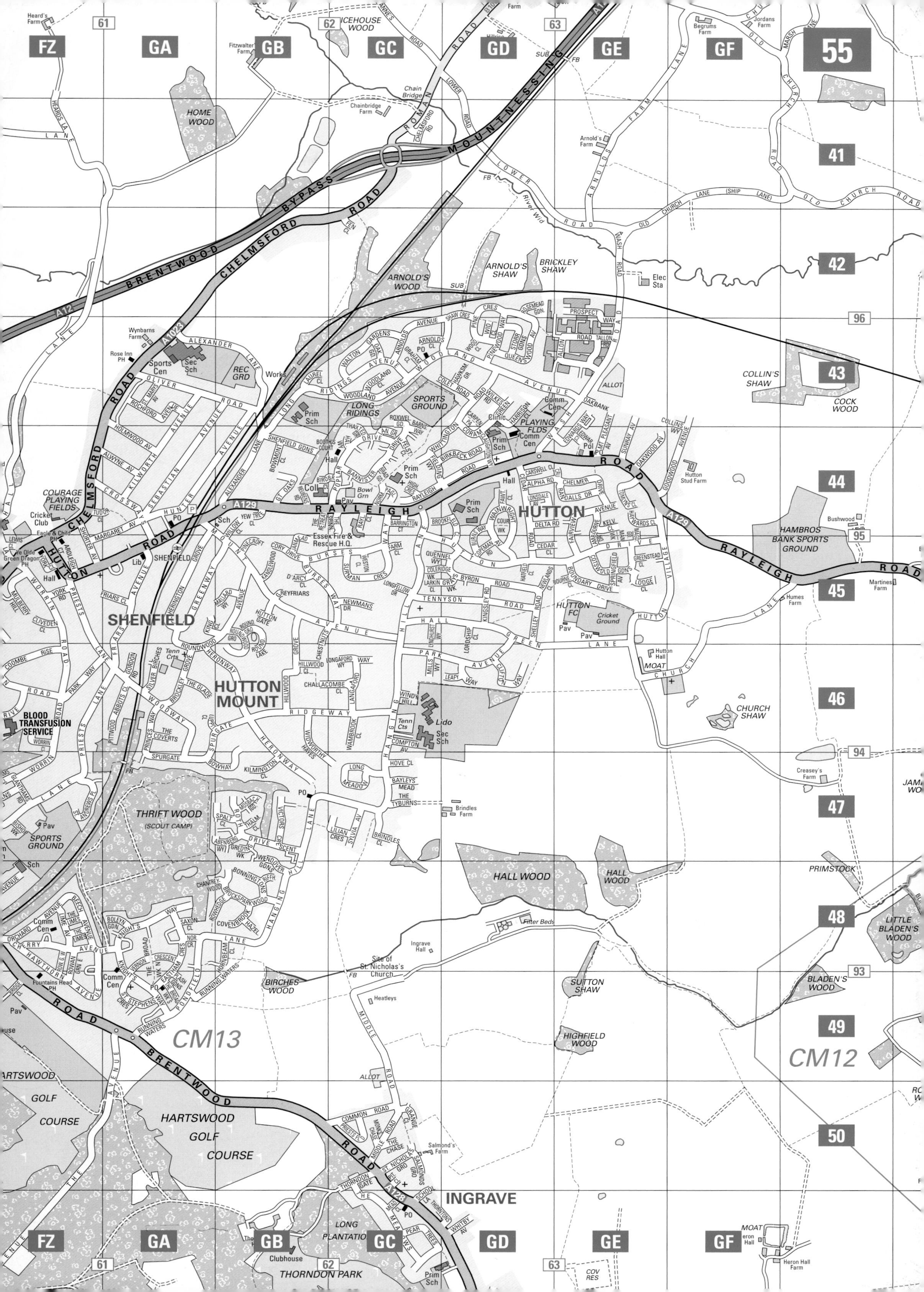

55
FZ
GA
GB
GC
GD
GE
GF
61
62
63
41
42
43
44
45
46
47
48
49
50
96
95
94
93
Heard's Farm
Fitzwalter Farm
ICEHOUSE WOOD
Begrums Farm
Jordans Farm
HOME WOOD
Chain Bridge
Chainbridge Farm
MOUNTNESSING
BYPASS
BRENTWOOD
CHELMSFORD ROAD
A12
A1023
Arnold's Farm
River Wid
OLD CHURCH LANE (SHIP LANE)
ARNOLD'S WOOD
ARNOLD'S SHAW
BRICKLEY SHAW
Elec Sta
PROSPECT WAY
COLLIN'S SHAW
COCK WOOD
Wynbarns Farm
Rose Inn PH
Sports Cen
Sec Sch
REC GRD
Works
LONG RIDINGS
SPORTS GROUND
Prim Sch
Clinic
Comm Cen
PLAYING FLDS
ALLOT
Hutton Stud Farm
COURAGE PLAYING FIELDS
Cricket Club
Eagle & Child PH
Ye Olde Green Dragon PH
RAYLEIGH ROAD
A129
HUTTON
Essex Fire & Rescue H.Q.
Bowl Grn
Pav
Coll
Lib
SHENFIELD
Bushwood
HAMBROS BANK SPORTS GROUND
Martines Farm
Humes Farm
HUTTON FC
Cricket Ground
Hutton Hall
MOAT
HUTTON MOUNT
BLOOD TRANSFUSION SERVICE
Tenn Crts
Lido
Sec Sch
CHURCH SHAW
Creasey's Farm
Brindles Farm
THRIFT WOOD (SCOUT CAMP)
SPORTS GROUND
HALL WOOD
PRIMSTOCK
LITTLE BLADEN'S WOOD
Filter Beds
Ingrave Hall
Site of St. Nicholas's Church
BIRCHES WOOD
SUTTON SHAW
BLADEN'S WOOD
Heatleys
Fountains Head PH
HIGHFIELD WOOD
CM13
CM12
HARTSWOOD GOLF COURSE
Salmond's Farm
A128
INGRAVE
LONG PLANTATION
Clubhouse
THORNDON PARK
Prim Sch
COV RES
MOAT
Heron Hall
Heron Hall Farm

AS
AT
AU
AV
AW
AX
AY
36
74
Green
Hedgerley
GERRARDS CROSS
Fulmer
Farnham Common
BIRCHLAND WOOD
HIGH WOOD
BEECH WOOD
BIRCH WOOD
SIBLET'S WOOD
Bell House Hotel
OXFORD ROAD
Wapsey's Wood Landfill Site
SAND AND GRAVEL PIT
FURTHER WARREN WOOD
WEST PLANTATION
SL9
BULSTRODE PARK
Bulstrode
MENAGERIE WOOD
GROVE PLANTATION
HEDGERLEY LANE
HEDGERLEY GREEN
WAPSEYS LANE
SUTTON'S WOOD
LEITH GROVE
RSPB NATURE RESERVE
CHURCH WOOD
KILN WOOD
HANGING WOOD
HEDGERLEY PARK
MOUNTHILL WOOD
BLACK GROVE
FOOTPATH WOOD
DUKE'S ORCHARD
PARKSIDE CEMETERY
PICKERIDGE WOOD
GRAVEL PIT
TIMBER WOOD
STOKE WOOD
SL2
BROCKHURST WOOD
INGRAM'S COPSE
STOKE COMMON
FRAME WOOD
SL3
HAY WOOD
FISH POND
PENN WOOD
Fulmer Hall (Research Laboratories)
STOKE COMMON ROAD
WINDSOR ROAD
M40
A40
B416
CHILTERN
SOUTH BUCKS
AUSTENWOOD COMMON
GERRARDS CROSS COMMON
CHANTRY WOOD
The Bull Hotel
Crab Hill
SPORTS GRD
Sec Sch
Prim Sch
FULMER COMMON
PARSON'S WOOD

57
AZ
BA
BB
BC
BD
BE
BF
01
02
03
37
HOGTROUGH WOOD
GERRARDS CROSS GOLF COURSE
CHALFONT PARK
SQUARE COPSE
ROUND COPSE
NOCKHILL WOOD
JUNIPER WOOD
GREAT HALINGS WOOD
QUARTERS WOOD
OAKEND WOOD
DENHAM MARSH WOOD
DENHAM AERODROME
NORTHMOOR HILL (NATURE RESERVE)
TRAINING CENTRE DURDENT COURT
THREE RIVERS
SOUTH BUCKS
55
56
BATTLESFORD WOOD
RANSTON COVERT
57
WADLEY COVERT
HOLLY HILL WOOD
NIGHTINGALE WOOD
Rank Film Laboratories
Denham Green
NEWSTEAD WOOD
58
DENHAM GOLF COURSE
COLLSELS WOOD
DENHAM GOLF CLUB
Higher Denham
UB9
88
59
MARTINSFIELD SPORTS GRD
GALLOWS WOOD
MILL WOOD
LITTLE GALLOWS WOOD
THE RANCHO
TOM WILLIAM'S WOOD
BRADBURY'S ISLAND
CAPS WOOD
MISBOURNE MEADOWS
BAKER'S WOOD
58
60
BUCKINGHAMS
87
Tatling End
61
Denham
62
NABOTH
GALDWINS WOOD
BROADSPRING WOOD
HAWKS WOOD
FURZENEY WOOD
Holly Bush
Junction 16 (M25)
86
63
M40
Junction 1a (M40)
BROADSPRING WOOD
GOSSAMS WOOD
BROWN'S WOOD
OLDHOUSE WOOD
64
PARKSPRING WOOD
MOUNT FIDGET WOOD
SL0
75
LONG COPPICE
AZ
BA
BB
BC
BD
BE
BF
01
02
03
LANGLEY COMMON
STRAWBERRY
AMERSHAM ROAD
OXFORD ROAD
NORTH ORBITAL ROAD
DENHAM AVENUE
A412
A413
A40
M25

58
BG
BH
BJ
BK
BL
BM
BN
38
SOUTH HAREFIELD
UB9
BAYHURSTWOOD COUNTRY PARK
Newyears Green
Denham Green
BUCKINGHAMSHIRE GOLF COURSE
DENHAM COUNTRY PARK
UXBRIDGE GOLF COURSE
Denham
Junction 1
WESTERN AVENUE
RIVERSIDE WALK
HILLINGDON HOUSE FARM
UXBRIDGE COMMON
UB10
76
05
06
07
89
88
87
86

59
BP
BQ
BR
BS
BT
BU
BV
08
09
10
39
77
Northwood Hills
COPSE WOOD
YOUNG WOOD
MAD BESS WOOD
HA6
HA5
HA4
RUISLIP NATURE RESERVE
POOR'S FIELD
ST. VINCENT'S ORTHOPAEDIC HOSPITAL
RUISLIP LIDO
PARK WOOD
RUISLIP COMMON
Breakspear Crematorium
Hillingdon Borough FC
EASTCOTE VILLAGE
EASTCOTE HO GRD
EASTCOTE
Eastcote Hockey & Badminton Club
KINGS COLLEGE PLAYING FIELDS
GOVERNMENT OFFICES
RUISLIP
WARRENDER PARK
RUISLIP GOLF COURSE
DRIVING RANGE
WEST RUISLIP
RUISLIP MANOR
RUISLIP GARDENS
ICKENHAM
KING GEORGE V PLAYING FIELD
MAD FIELD COVERT
Compass Theatre
Ickenham Marsh
NORTHOLT AERODROME
NEW POND FARM FIELDS
BESSINGBY FIELD
CAVENDISH REC GRD
PINE GDNS
SOUTH RUISLIP
BRAINTREE INDUSTRIAL ESTATE
ODYSSEY BUSINESS PARK
FREEZELAND COVERT
Master Brewer Hotel
WESTERN AVENUE
WEST END ROAD
HIGH STREET
BURY STREET
DUCKS HILL ROAD
A4180
A404

60
BW
BX
BY
BZ
CA
CB
CC
12
13
14
40
55
56
57
58
59
60
61
62
63
64
78
86
87
88
89
PINNER GREEN
PINNER
MONTESOLE PLAYING FIELDS
LITTLE COMMON
PINNER MEMORIAL PARK
PINNER NEW CEMETERY
PINNER VILLAGE GARDENS
CUCKOO HILL
EASTCOTE VILLAGE
EASTCOTE
HA5
HA2
HA4
UB5
THE CROFT PLAYING FIELD
WARRENDER PARK
CAVENDISH REC GRD
PINE GDNS
BESSINGBY FIELD
ROXBOURNE PARK
Streamside Reservation
RECREATION GROUND
HEADSTONE MANOR
RECREATION GROUND
SPORTS GROUND
HEADSTONE
NORTH HARROW
WEST HARROW
WEST HARROW REC GRD
RAYNERS LANE
SPORTS GRD
NEWTON PARK WEST
NEWTON FM ECOLOGY PK
SOUTH HARROW
ALEXANDRA PARK
SOUTH RUISLIP
PLAYING FIELD
DEANE PARK
BRAINTREE INDUSTRIAL ESTATE
ODYSSEY BUSINESS PARK
VICTORIA RETAIL PARK
FROGMORE ESTATE
SOLID WASTE TRANSFER STATION
NORTHOLT RECREATION GRD
PLAYING FIELD
LORD HALSBURY MEMORIAL GRD
SPORTS GROUND
HILLINGDON
EALING
GEORGE V AVENUE
PINNER ROAD
IMPERIAL DRIVE
ALEXANDRA AVENUE
NORTHOLT ROAD
WEST END ROAD
VICTORIA ROAD
UXBRIDGE ROAD
A404
A4090
A4180
A312
Old Lyonian Sports Club
Fire Training Cen
Yeading Brook
River Pinn

CD
CE
CF
CG
CH
CJ
CK
61
15
16
17
41
BELMONT
HA7
QUEENSBURY
55
56
57
58
59
60
61
62
63
64
WEALDSTONE
BYRON REC GRD
WAVERLEY INDUSTRIAL ESTATE
HARROW & WEALDSTONE
CIVIC CENTRE
CIVIC AMENITY SITE
HAWTHORN CENTRE
HA3
KENTON RECREATION GROUND
KENTON
KENTON ROAD
A4006
WOODCOCK PARK
HARROW REC GROUND
St. Ann's Centre
College
HARROW ON THE HILL
University of Westminster
NORTHWICK PARK HOSPITAL
NORTHWICK PARK
Northwick Park Pavilion
HA1
HARROW SCHOOL PLAYING FIELDS
MINIATURE RIFLE RANGE
THE GROVE OPEN SPACE
HARROW SCHOOL GOLF COURSE
HARROW HILL GOLF COURSE
JOHN BILLAM SPORTS GRD
PRESTON
PRESTON PARK
ROXETH
ST. ANDREW'S AT HARROW HOSP
CLEMENTINE CHURCHILL HOSPITAL
CHASEWOOD PARK
NORTH WEMBLEY
WEMBLEY COMMERCIAL CENTRE
G.E.C. ESTATE
HA9
FORTY FARM SPORTS GROUND
VALE FARM SPORTS GROUND
VALE FARM SPORTS GROUND
WEMBLEY FC
KING EDWARD VII PARK
SPORTS GROUND
SPORTS GRD
EALING NORTHERN SPORTS GRD
REC GRD
Sudbury Tower
UB6
SUDBURY
BARHAM PARK
HA0
WEMBLEY CENTRAL
SUDBURY TOWN
SUDBURY HILL HARROW
SUDBURY & HARROW ROAD
BUTLER'S GRN
PLAYING FIELDS
A404
A4005
A4088
A4090
A4140
A409
A312
79
86
87
88
89

62
CL
CM
CN
CP
CQ
CR
CS
19
20
21
42
61
80
HA7
HA8
HA3
HA9
NW9
NW10
QUEENSBURY
KENTON ROAD
HONEYPOT LANE
A4140
A4006
KINGSBURY ROAD
EDGWARE ROAD
COLINDALE
COLINDALE HOSP
BLOOD TRANSFUSION CENTRE
PUBLIC HEALTH LAB.
BRIT. LIB NEWSPAPER COLLECTION
COLINDALE BUSINESS PK
CAPITOL IND PK
Yaohan Plaza
MONTROSE PLAYING FIELDS
BRIXTON EST
ETON GROVE OPEN SPACE
QUEENSBURY PARK
KINGSBURY COMMUNITY HOSPITAL
ROE GREEN PARK
KINGSBURY SPORTS GRD
KINGSBURY
FRYENT COUNTRY PARK
FRYENT WAY
BARDHILL SPORTS GRD
WOODCOCK PARK
PRESTON
JOHN BILLAM SPORTS GRD
PRESTON PARK
BARN HILL OPEN SPACE
SILVER JUBILEE PARK
CHURCH LANE REC GRD
WEST HENDON PLAYING FIELDS
WEST HENDON
WOODFIELD PARK
WELSH HARP OPEN SPACE
Welsh Harp Day Field Centre
Wembley Sailing Club
Stanmore Junction
WEMBLEY PARK
FORTY FARM SPORTS GROUND
FORTY AVENUE
FORTY LANE
A4088
BLACKBIRD HILL
NEASDEN LANE NORTH
SALMON STREET
BRENT TOWN HALL
WEMBLEY COMMERCIAL CENTRE
G.E.C. ESTATE
WEMBLEY PARK DRIVE
Palace of Industry
WEMBLEY ARENA
Sunday Market
CANNON TRADING EST
CONFERENCE CEN
EXHIB CEN
WEMBLEY STADIUM (Under Redevelopment)
NEASDEN RAIL DEPOT
KING EDWARD VII PARK
WEMBLEY
WEMBLEY STADIUM
WEMBLEY CENTRAL
SHERRINS FARM OPEN SPACE
TOKYNGTON REC GRD
DRURY WAY IND EST
BRENT PARK
IKEA TWR
NORTH CIRCULAR ROAD
CHURCH END
GIBBONS REC GRD
Swaminarayan Hindu Mission Temple
HIGH ROAD
HARROW ROAD
GREAT CENTRAL WAY
B4557
A404
A4089
EALING ROAD
PLAYING FIELDS
DEPOTS
TOKYNGTON

CT
CU
CV
CW
CX
CY
CZ
63
22
23
24
HOLDERS HILL
RAF MUSEUM
SUNNY HILL PARK
43
Thistle Hendon Hall
GARDEN HOSP
N3
55
Peel Cen
Metropolitan Pol
Riding & Driving School
SPORTS GRD
CHURCH FARM HOUSE MUS
Middlesex Uni
A5150
CHURCH ROAD
FINCHLEY
HENDON LANE
NORTH CIRCULAR ROAD
A406
56
THE HYDE
HENDON
WATFORD WAY
THE BURROUGHS
Uni of London
THE DECOY
CARMELITE MONASTERY
BRENT STREET
A502
HENDON CENTRAL
QUEENS ROAD
NW4
HENDON PARK
57
BIG WOOD
MALCOLM PARK
HENDON WAY
PRINCES PARK
NW11
58
HOOP LANE CEMETERY (JEWISH)
Welsh Harp
YORK PARK
BRENT CROSS
Brent Cross Shopping Centre
GOLDERS GREEN ROAD
FINCHLEY ROAD
GARDEN OF REMEMBRANCE
88
GOLDERS GREEN
59
M1
A5
Junction 1
Superstores
Sports Cen
Holiday Inn
A41
64
GOLDERS GREEN DEPOT
Golders Green Hippodrome
NORTH END
BRENT RESERVOIR
AQUARIUS BUSINESS PARK
STAPLES CORNER BUSINESS PK
Refuse Disposal Works
Staples Corner
CLITTERHOUSE PLAYING FIELDS
Hoot Stadium Hendon FC
TRAIN DEPOT
BASING HILL PK
CHILDS HILL PK
60
87
SPORTS GRD
WELLINGTON PARK EST
A406
EDGWARE ROAD
BROADWAY
COLES GREEN COURT
CHILDS HILL
61
DOLLIS HILL EST
BUS GARAGE
A407
HENDON WAY
62
86
DOLLIS HILL
CRICKLEWOOD
CRICKLEWOOD BROADWAY
GLADSTONE PARK
UNIVERSITY COLLEGE SCHOOL SPORTS GRD
HAMPSTEAD CEMETERY
BARNET
CAMDEN
Uni of London King's Coll
63
Open Uni Regional Cen
NW2
A407
CHICHELE ROAD
SHOOT UP HILL
A5
64
Coll of North West London
A4088
DOLLIS HILL
WILLESDEN LANE
81
KILBURN
WEST HAMPSTEAD
A4003
WILLESDEN

64
DA
DB
DC
DD
DE
DF
DG
26
27
28
44
N3
N2
N6
NW11
NW3
EAST FINCHLEY
FORTIS GREEN
HAMPSTEAD GARDEN SUBURB
GOLDERS GREEN
CHILDS HILL
HAMPSTEAD
WEST HAMPSTEAD
HAMPSTEAD HEATH
HAMPSTEAD HEATH EXTENSION
EAST FINCHLEY CEMETERY
HIGHGATE WOOD
HIGHGATE GOLF COURSE
HAMPSTEAD GOLF CLUB
PARLIAMENT HILL
KENWOOD
GOLDERS HILL PARK
NORTH CIRCULAR ROAD
FALLODEN WAY
LYTTELTON ROAD
AYLMER ROAD
ARCHWAY ROAD
FINCHLEY ROAD
NORTH END ROAD
NORTH END WAY
HEATH STREET
SPANIARDS ROAD
HAMPSTEAD LANE
GREAT NORTH ROAD
EAST END ROAD
HAVERSTOCK HILL
ROSSLYN HILL
HAMPSTEAD HIGH ST
HENDON WAY
QUEEN MARY'S HOSP
ROYAL FREE HOSP
NAT HOSP FOR NEUROLOGY & NEUROSURGERY
ATHLONE HOUSE
KEATS HOUSE
THE IVEAGH BEQUEST - KENWOOD HOUSE
55
56
57
58
59
60
61
62
63
64
82
86
87
88
89

DH
DJ
DK
DL
DM
DN
DP
65
29
30
31
45
NOEL PARK
LORDSHIP RECREATION GROUND
ALEXANDRA PALACE
ALEXANDRA PARK
N22
MUSWELL HILL
THE GROVE
SPORTS GROUND
HORNSEY WATER TREATMENT WORKS
HORNSEY
WEST GREEN
BELMONT REC GRD
DOWNHILLS PARK
TURNPIKE LANE
55
56
57
58
59
60
61
62
63
64
66
83
86
87
88
89
PRIORY ROAD
HIGH STREET
PRIORY PARK
N8
QUEEN'S WOOD
CROUCH END PLAYING FIELDS
HARRINGAY
ST. ANN'S HOSPITAL
CHESTNUTS REC GRD
CROUCH END
STROUD GREEN
HARRINGAY GREEN LANES
STATIONERS PARK
HIGHGATE
FINSBURY PARK
N4
AMERICAN GDNS
WEST RESERVOIR
N19
ELTHORNE PARK
HILLSIDE PK
WHITTINGTON HOSPITAL
WATERLOW PARK
HIGHGATE CEMETERY
ARCHWAY
UPPER HOLLOWAY
WHITTINGTON PARK
DARTMOUTH PARK
SIX ACRES EST
ARSENAL
ARSENAL STADIUM
CLISSOLD PARK
SPORTS GROUND
TUFNELL PARK
HOLLOWAY
H.M. PRISON HOLLOWAY
LOWER HOLLOWAY
N7
HIGHBURY
N5
KENTISH TOWN
NW5
CANONBURY
PENTONVILLE PRISON
CALEDONIAN ROAD
HOLLOWAY ROAD
SEVEN SISTERS ROAD
GREEN LANES

NOEL PARK
DQ
DR
DS
DT
DU
DV
DW
33
34
35
46
LORDSHIP RECREATION GROUND
N17
N22
TOTTENHAM MARSHES
RESERVOIR
BRUCE GROVE
DOWN LANE REC GRD
LEE VALLEY TECHNOPARK
MILMEAD INDUSTRIAL CENTRE
TOTTENHAM HALE
LOCKWOOD INDUSTRIAL PARK
LOW MAYNARD RESERVOIR
TOTTENHAM HALE
FERRY LANE
MONUMENT WAY
55
56
57
58
59
60
61
62
63
64
65
84
86
87
88
89
BELMONT REC GRD
TURNPIKE LANE
DOWNHILLS PARK
WEST GREEN
WEST GREEN ROAD
A504
TOWN HALL
HIGH CROSS CENTRE
RESERVOIR NUMBER FOUR
RESERVOIR NUMBER TWO
RESERVOIR NUMBER ONE
RESERVOIR NUMBER THREE
RESERVOIR NUMBER FIVE
CHESTNUTS REC GRD
N15
SEVEN SISTERS
MARKFIELD REC GRD
ST. ANN'S HOSPITAL
SOUTH TOTTENHAM
WARWICK RESERVOIR EAST
WARWICK RESERVOIR WEST
HARRINGAY GREEN LANES
RAILWAY FLDS
A503
SEVEN SISTERS ROAD
AMHURST ROAD
A107
STAMFORD HILL
COPPERMILL PLAYING FIELD
SPRINGHILL SPORTS GRD
AMERICAN GDNS
FINSBURY PARK
N4
EAST RESERVOIR
CLAPTON COMMON
SPRINGFIELD PARK
Walthamstow Marsh Nature Reserve
WEST RESERVOIR
STAMFORD HILL ESTATE
STAMFORD HILL
UPPER CLAPTON
FINSBURY PARK
ABNEY PARK CEMETERY
STOKE NEWINGTON
N16
NORTHWOLD
NORTH MILLFIELDS RECREATION GROUND
E5
CLISSOLD PARK
SPORTS GROUND
ARSENAL
SHACKLEWELL
HACKNEY DOWNS
BUTTERFIELD GREEN
N5
HIGHBURY
E8
DALSTON LANE
A104
A1199
A1207
A10
A105
A1201
KINGSLAND
CANONBURY
HACKNEY
HIGHBURY & ISLINGTON
HACKNEY CENTRAL

67
DX
DY
DZ
EA
EB
EC
ED
36
37
38
47
55
56
57
58
59
60
61
62
63
64
68
85
86
87
88
89
HIGHAM HILL
LLOYD PARK
WALTHAMSTOW
CHESTNUTS SHOWGROUND
TOWN HALL
ASSEMBLY HALL
THORPE COOMBE HOSP
EPPING FOREST
SNARESBROOK
UPPER WALTHAMSTOW
E17
WALTHAMSTOW CENTRAL
WALTHAMSTOW QUEENS ROAD
WALTHAMSTOW CEM
DOUGLAS EYRE PLAYING FIELDS
UPLANDS BUSINESS PARK
HIGHAMS LODGE BUSINESS CEN
ST. JAMES'S PARK
LOW HALL SPORTS GROUND
CIVIC AMENITY TIP
LEYTON IND VILLAGE
FOREST BUSINESS PK
BOXWELL TRADING PK
DORMA TRADING PK
CROMWELL IND EST
BURWELL IND EST
ALLOTMENTS
WHIPPS CROSS HOSPITAL
LEYTONSTONE
E10
LEYTON
LEYTON MARSHES
SEYMOUR ROAD PLAYING FIELD
MARSH LANE PLAYING FIELD
LEE VALLEY PITCH & PUTT GOLF COURSE
NATURE RESERVE
LEA BRIDGE
LEE VALLEY PARK
HACKNEY MARSH
SIDMOUTH PARK
LEYTON ORIENT FC
ST. PATRICK'S RC CEMETERY
New Spitalfields Market
RECREATION GROUND
ETON MANOR SPORTS GROUND
Lea Valley Sports Centre
CLAPTON PARK
LOWER CLAPTON
E9
WICK COMMUNITY WOODLAND
LEE VALLEY PARK
LEE VALLEY CYCLE CIRCUIT
DRAPERS FIELD REC. GRD
HOMERTON
MABLEY GREEN
HACKNEY WICK
STADIUM (CLOSED)
EASTWAY COMMERCIAL CENTRE
EAST CROSS CENTRE
LONDON INTERNATIONAL FREIGHT TERMINAL
E15
STRATFORD
JEWISH CEMETERY
JOHN HOWARD CEN
HOMERTON HOSPITAL
LEA BRIDGE ROAD
FOREST ROAD
HOE STREET
CHURCH ROAD
HIGH ROAD
EAST CROSS ROUTE
RUCKHOLT ROAD
LEYTONSTONE ROAD
WHIPPS CROSS ROAD

68
EE
EF
EG
EH
EJ
EK
EL
40
41
42
48
WOODFORD
E18
NORTH CIRCULAR ROAD
SOUTHEND ROAD
Junction 4
EPPING FOREST
SPORTS GROUND
RODING HOSP
RECREATION GROUND
IG4
55
56
57
58
59
60
61
62
63
64
67
86
87
88
89
SNARESBROOK
SNARESBROOK CROWN COURT
HOLLOW POND
EAGLE POND
WHIPPS CROSS HOSPITAL
WHIPPS CROSS ROAD
EASTERN AVENUE
RUGBY FOOTBALL GROUND
WANSTEAD
WANSTEAD GOLF COURSE
WANSTEAD PARK
WANSTEAD FLATS
THE BASIN
BUSH WOOD
LEYTONSTONE
E11
ALDERSBROOK
CITY OF LONDON CEMETERY
MANOR PARK
MANOR PARK CEMETERY
WEST HAM CEMETERY
JEWISH CEMETERY
FOREST GATE
E7
WOODGRANGE PARK CEMETERY
PLASHET JEWISH CEMETERY
E15
STRATFORD
ROMFORD ROAD

69
EM
EN
EP
EQ
ER
ES
ET
43
44
45
49
55
56
57
58
59
60
61
62
63
64
70
86
87
88
89
CLAYHALL
FAIRLOP WATER GOLF COURSE
IG6
IG5
GARDEN OF REST
BARKINGSIDE CEM
BARKINGSIDE
BARKINGSIDE REC GRD
BARNARDOS VILLAGE
ALDBOROUGH HATCH
CLAYHALL PARK
GANTS HILL
NEWBURY PARK
KING GEORGE HOSPITAL
MAYES HOSPITAL
FORD'S SPORTS GROUND
SEVEN KINGS PARK
SPORTS GROUND
IG2
REDBRIDGE
PORT OF LONDON AUTH. REC GRD
VALENTINES PARK
VALENTINES LAKE
MELBOURNE FIELD
SEVEN KINGS
CRANBROOK
IG1
IG3
REDBRIDGE ENTERPRISE CEN
ILFORD CEMETERY
CRICKLEFIELD ATHLETIC GRD
ILFORD
SOUTH PARK
GOODMAYES PARK REC GRD
KNOX SPORTS FIELD
LITTLE ILFORD PARK
LOXFORD PARK
LOXFORD
BARKING PARK REC GRD
BARKING PARK
MAYESBROOK PARK
BARKING FC Clubhouse
BARRINGTON PLAYING FLDS
SPORTS GROUND
BOATING LAKE
EASTERN AVENUE
CRANBROOK ROAD
HIGH ROAD
GREEN LANE
ILFORD LANE
LONGBRIDGE ROAD
WOODFORD AVENUE
A12
A123
A118
A1083
A124
A406
A1400
SOUTH WOODFORD TO BARKING

70
EU
EV
EW
EX
EY
EZ
FA
47
48
49
50
Mark's Gate
REDBRIDGE
BARKING & DAGENHAM
55
56
57
58
59
60
61
62
63
64
69
86
87
88
89
IG2
IG3
RM6
RM8
RM9
PAINTERS ROAD
HAINAULT ROAD
BILLET ROAD
EASTERN AVENUE
A12
KING GEORGE HOSPITAL
GOODMAYES HOSPITAL
Redbridge College
SPORTS GROUND
PLAYING FIELD
KINGS PARK
SEVEN KINGS
CHADWELL HEATH
ST. CHADS PARK
HIGH ROAD
A118
WHALEBONE LANE NORTH
WHALEBONE LANE SOUTH
A112
LONDON ROAD
GOLF DRIVING RANGE
WESTLANDS PLAYING FIELDS
WEST HAM UNITED FC TRAINING GROUND
MIRRAVALE TRADING ESTATE
Becontree Heath
GOODMAYES
GREEN LANE
A1083
GOODMAYES PARK
GOODMAYES PARK REC GRD
BECONTREE
VALENCE PARK
VALENCE HO MUS
VALENCE MOAT
LONGBRIDGE ROAD
WOOD LANE
A124
HEATHWAY
A1240
Univ of East London
MAYESBROOK PARK
BARKING FC Clubhouse
BOATING LAKE
PARSLOES PARK
Barking Coll
Leisure Centre
PORTERS AVENUE
A1153
DAGENHAM HEATHWAY
MARKS GATE CEM
World War II Gun Emplacements
Warren Farm
Crown Farm

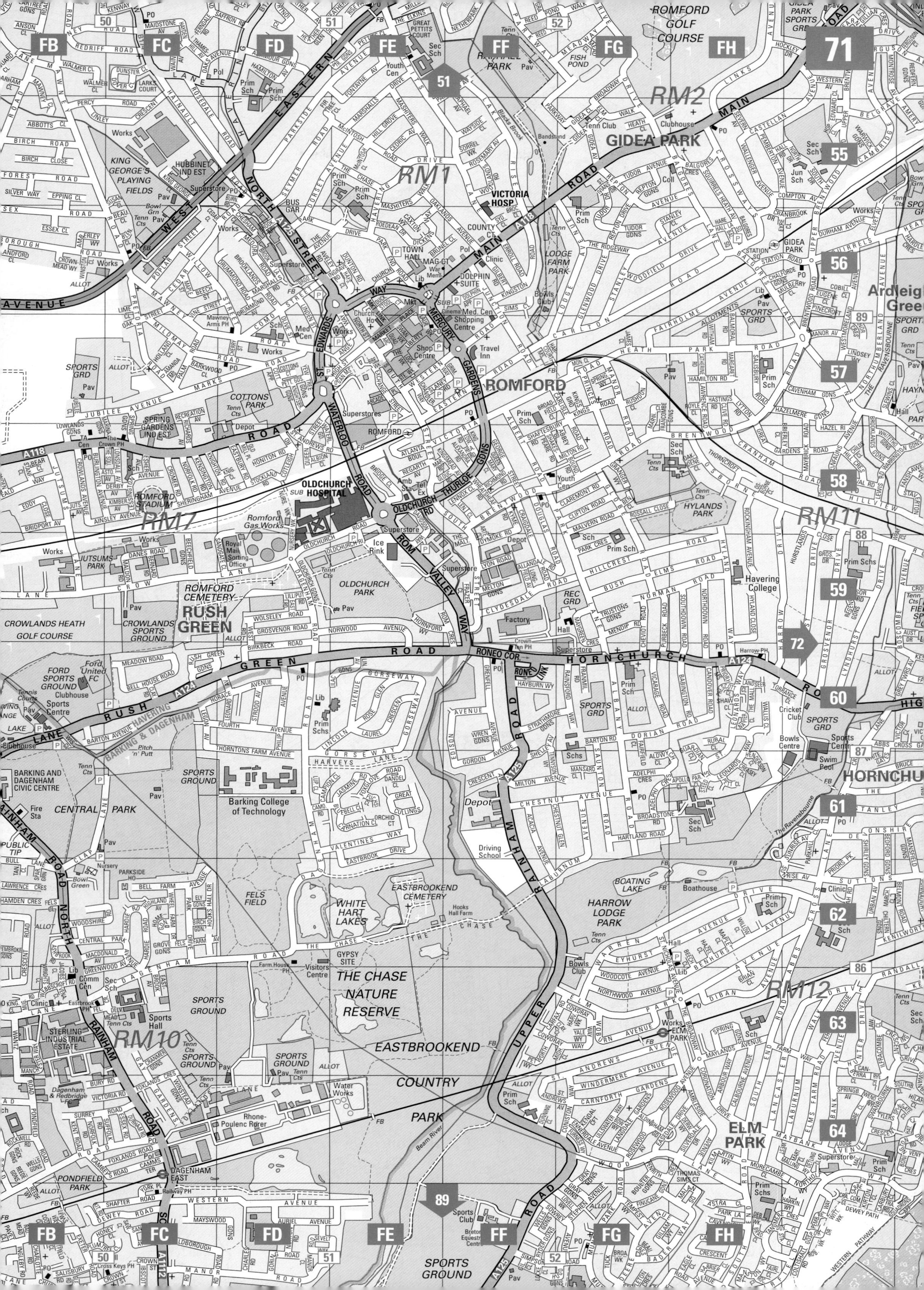

FB
FC
FD
FE
FF
FG
FH
71
50
51
52
ROMFORD GOLF COURSE
RAPHAEL PARK
FISH POND
RM2
GIDEA PARK
RM1
VICTORIA HOSP
KING GEORGE'S PLAYING FIELDS
HUBBINET IND EST
NORTH STREET
EASTERN AVENUE
WEST AVENUE
MAIN ROAD
A118
A125
TOWN HALL
DOLPHIN SUITE
LODGE FARM PARK
55
56
57
58
59
60
61
62
63
64
72
86
87
88
89
Ardleigh Green
ROMFORD
COTTONS PARK
SPRING GARDENS IND EST
ROMFORD STADIUM
OLDCHURCH HOSPITAL
RM7
Romford Gas Works
JUTSUMS PARK
WATERLOO ROAD
ROM VALLEY WAY
OLDCHURCH PARK
HYLANDS PARK
RM11
Havering College
ROMFORD CEMETERY
RUSH GREEN
CROWLANDS HEATH GOLF COURSE
CROWLANDS SPORTS GROUND
RUSH GREEN ROAD
HORNCHURCH ROAD
A124
RONEO COR.
FORD SPORTS GROUND
Ford United FC
BARKING AND DAGENHAM CIVIC CENTRE
CENTRAL PARK
Barking College of Technology
HORNCHURCH
FELS FIELD
WHITE HART LAKES
EASTBROOKEND CEMETERY
HARROW LODGE PARK
BOATING LAKE
RAINHAM ROAD
THE CHASE NATURE RESERVE
EASTBROOKEND COUNTRY PARK
RM10
RM12
STERLING INDUSTRIAL ESTATE
UPPER RAINHAM ROAD
Rhone-Poulenc Rorer
ELM PARK
DAGENHAM EAST
PONDFIELD PARK
SPORTS GROUND
A112
A125

72
FJ
FK
FL
FM
FN
FP
FQ
52
HAROLD WOOD
RM2
RM3
RM11
RM12
ROMFORD GOLF COURSE
GIDEA PARK
HAROLD WOOD PARK
SOUTHEND ARTERIAL ROAD
A127
MAIN ROAD
Havering College of Further Educ
Ardleigh Green
EMERSON PARK
HORNCHURCH
HIGH STREET
UPMINSTER ROAD
A124
ST. MARY'S LANE
UPMINSTER
UPMINSTER GOLF COURSE
UPMINSTER PARK
HORNCHURCH STADIUM
HORNCHURCH CEM
ST. ANDREW'S PARK
ELLIOT PLAYING FIELDS
HYLANDS PARK
Havering College
GAYNES PARKWAY
ST. GEORGES HOSPITAL
ELM PARK
Hacton
PARKLANDS OPEN SPACE
Corbets
Palms Hotel
Mount Pleasant Farm
Prospect Farm
Ingrebourne Farm
Tyes Farm
Chapmans Farm
Lillyputts Farm
Pages Farm
Riding Stables
Abattoir
Hacton House
Park Corner Farm
Lodge Farm
Rainham Lodge Farm
Gardners Cor Hall
Central Farm
Harwood Hall
Poultry Farm
Huntsman & Hounds PH
White Hart PH
Stables
The Optimist PH
Boathouse
ST. MARY'S CONVENT
Ingrebourne River
The Ravensbourne
55
56
57
58
59
60
61
62
63
64
71
86
87
88
89
90
54

73
FR
FS
FT
FU
FV
FW
FX
53
91
55
56
57
58
59
60
61
62
63
64
CM13
RM14
CRANHAM
North Ockendon
Junction 29
M25
ESSEX
BRENTWOOD
HAVERING
SOUTHEND ARTERIAL ROAD
A127
FOXBURROW WOOD
COOMBE WOOD
PARKER'S SHAW
CODHAM HALL WOOD
LATCHET'S SHAW
WARLEY HALL WOOD
GOLF COURSE
CRANHAM PLAYING FIELDS
FRANKS WOOD
CLAY TYE WOOD
UPMINSTER HALL PLAYING FIELDS
UPMINSTER TRADING PARK
Electricity Station
SPRING WOOD
NATURE RESERVE
MIDDLE WOOD
BONUS WOOD
UPMINSTER CEMETERY
TOP MEADOW GOLF COURSE
RUSSELLS LAKE
WARLEY STREET
CLAY TYE ROAD
OCKENDON ROAD
ST MARY'S LANE
PIKE LANE
FEN LANE
Warley Street Flyover
Sewage Works

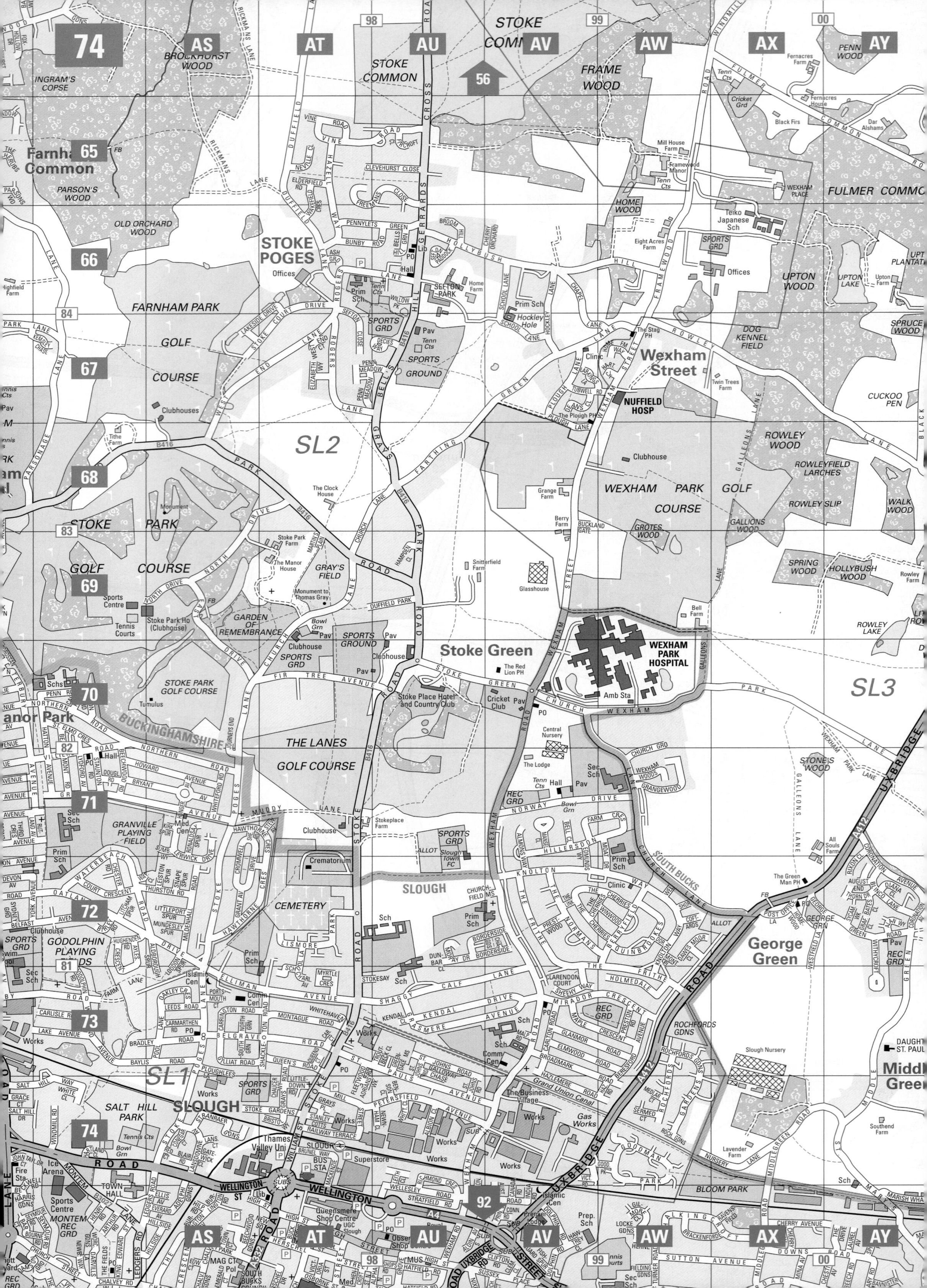
74
AS
AT
AU
AV
AW
AX
AY
98
99
00
56
STOKE COMMON
BROCKHURST WOOD
INGRAM'S COPSE
FRAME WOOD
PENN WOOD
Farnham Common
PARSON'S WOOD
OLD ORCHARD WOOD
STOKE POGES
FULMER COMMON
UPTON WOOD
FARNHAM PARK
GOLF COURSE
Wexham Street
NUFFIELD HOSP
DOG KENNEL FIELD
SPRUCE WOOD
CUCKOO PEN
ROWLEY WOOD
SL2
WEXHAM PARK GOLF COURSE
ROWLEYFIELD LARCHES
ROWLEY SLIP
WALK WOOD
GROTES WOOD
GALLIONS WOOD
STOKE PARK GOLF COURSE
GRAY'S FIELD
SPRING WOOD
HOLLYBUSH WOOD
ROWLEY LAKE
GARDEN OF REMEMBRANCE
Stoke Green
WEXHAM PARK HOSPITAL
SL3
STOKE PARK GOLF COURSE
BUCKINGHAMSHIRE
THE LANES GOLF COURSE
STONE'S WOOD
GRANVILLE PLAYING FIELD
Crematorium
SLOUGH
CEMETERY
GODOLPHIN PLAYING FIELDS
George Green
SL1
SLOUGH
SALT HILL PARK
Grand Union Canal
Thames Valley Uni
WELLINGTON
BLOOM PARK
Slough Nursery
Middle Green
Queensmere Shop Centre
92
65
66
67
68
69
70
71
72
73
74
81
82
83
84

75
57
93
76
AZ
BA
BB
BC
BD
BE
BF
01
02
03
84
83
82
81
65
66
67
68
69
70
71
72
73
74
BROWN'S WOOD
OLDHOUSE WOOD
PARKSPRING WOOD
MOUNT FIDGET WOOD
LONG COPPICE
LANGLEY COMMON
STRAWBERRY WOOD
HEATHFIELD PLANTATION
NATURE RESERVE
Pinewood Film Studios
Heatherden Hall
THE CLUMP
BROOM WARREN
BLACK PARK COUNTRY PARK
DIAMOND WOOD
CHESTNUT WOOD
Blackpark Lake
Centenary Lodge Visitors Centre
FOXES GUTTER
COLUMN LARCHES
CHANDLERS HILL
IVER HEATH
SL0
UB9
LANGLEY PARK WOOD
RHODODENDRON GARDENS
LANGLEY PARK COUNTRY PARK
ROUGHGROUND WOOD
ARBORETUM
Environmental Studies Centre
Ashen Cross
Shreding Green
IVER
SPORTS GROUND
Eureham Centre
Sports Centre
IVER GOLF COURSE
Grand Union Canal (Slough Arm)
BUCKINGHAMSHIRE
SOUTH BUCKS
SLOUGH
THE RIDGEWAY ESTATE
FARLOWS LAKE
Sewage Works
THORNEY PARK GOLF COURSE
Chequer Bridge
LANGLEY BUSINESS CENTRE
SEVEN HILLS ROAD
PINEWOOD ROAD
DENHAM ROAD
CHURCH ROAD
SLOUGH ROAD
A412
A4007
M25
B470
BANGORS ROAD NORTH
BANGORS ROAD SOUTH
SOUTH STREET
NORWOOD LANE
LOVE GREEN LANE
HIGH STREET
IVER LANE
LANGLEY PARK ROAD
BILLET LANE
WOOD LANE
MANSION LANE
THORNEY LANE
HOLLYBUSH LANE
BELLSWOOD LANE
TRENCHES LANE
LOVE HILL LANE
PEACE ROAD
QUEEN'S DRIVE
FULMER COMMON ROAD
CHERRY TREE LANE
ALDERBOURNE LANE
PALMERS MOOR LANE
Alder Bourne
Colne Brook
TOWING PATH
CARAVAN SITE
Five Points
Crooked Billet PH
Stag & Hounds PH
Whip & Collar PH
Red Lion PH
Delaford Manor
Delaford Park
Coppins Farm
Lower Delaford
Iver Lodge
Bangors Park Farm
Norwood Grange
Moorwards
Perivale Livery Stables
Woodlands Park
Mansfield Farm
Round Coppice Farm
Southlands Manor
Copse Hill Farm
Dromenagh Farm
Sevenhills Farm
Belle Farm
Cherry Orchard Farm
Alderbourne Farm
Ways Farm
Saul's Farm
Kingcup Farm
Durham House
Cornerfields
Fulmer Plant Park
BRIDGETTINE CONVENT
Langley Park House
Treal Farm
Love Hill House Farm
Moat House
Clubhouse
Glasshouse
Shredding Green Farm
Park Lodge Farm
Brackenwood
Park Lodge
Warren Lodge
Warren House
Warren House Farm
Fernleigh
Nursery
Huntsmoor Park Farm
Filter Beds
Water Treatment Works
Works
Depot

76
BG
BH
BJ
BK
BL
BM
BN
05
06
07
58
65
66
67
68
69
70
71
72
73
74
75
84
83
82
81
94
UB9
UB10
UB8
UB7
SL0
UXBRIDGE
UXBRIDGE MOOR
COWLEY
HILLINGDON
YIEWSLEY
IVER
WEST DRAYTON
DENHAM ROAD
A412
A4020
A4007
A408
A437
M25
B470
B483
OXFORD ROAD
ROCKINGHAM RD
WINDSOR ST
NEW WINDSOR ST
CROSS ST
ST. JOHNS ROAD
COWLEY ROAD
HIGH STREET
COWLEY HIGH ROAD
HILLINGDON ROAD
HILLINGDON HILL
PARK ROAD
IVER LANE
PACKET BOAT LANE
TROUT LANE
FALLING LANE
STOCKLEY RD
DRAYTON ROAD
PIELD HEATH ROAD
ST. ANDREWS ROAD
Grand Union Canal (Slough Arm)
Fray's River
River Pinn
Colne Brook
Alder Bourne
Shire Ditch
BUCKINGHAMSHIRE
SOUTH BUCKS
HILLINGDON
UXBRIDGE COMMON
HILLINGDON HOUSE FARM SPORTS GROUNDS
Uxbridge College
Open Air Pool
Ski Slopes
Hillingdon Ski Centre
UXBRIDGE STADIUM
HIGHBRIDGE INDUSTRIAL ESTATE
The Pavilions
The Chimes
CIVIC OFFICES
Electricity Sub Station
MIDAS INDUSTRIAL ESTATE
SARUM COMPLEX
CHILTERN BUSINESS VILLAGE
COWLEY BUSINESS PARK
ROCKINGHAM REC GRD
R.A.F. Uxbridge
RIFLE RANGE
HILLINGDON GOLF COURSE
HILLINGDON COURT PARK
BIG CLUMP
R.A.F. SPORTS GRD
HILLINGDON & UXBRIDGE CEMETERY
Brunel University
Halls of Residence
UNIVERSITY PLAYING FIELDS
HILLINGDON HOSPITAL
CONEY GREEN
COLHAM GREEN REC GRD
COWLEY HALL REC GRD
HUNTSMOOR PARK
COWLEY LAKE
LITTLE BRITAIN LAKE
FARLOWS LAKE
TOMO INDUSTRIAL EST
RAINBOW INDUSTRIAL ESTATE
West Drayton Coal Depot
Water Treatment Works
Sewage Works
THE RIDGEWAY ESTATE
THORNEY PARK GOLF COURSE
SPORTS GROUND
Uxbridge FC
HORTON IND PARK
Apple Tree Roundabout
Colham Roundabout
PLAYING FIELD
Milton Hulchings Garden Centre

NORTHOLT AERODROME
HA4
59
NORTH HILLINGDON
WESTERN AVENUE
A40
CUTTHROAT WOOD
NATURE RESERVE
GUTTERIDGE WOOD
FREEZELAND COVERT
Master Brewer Hotel
LONG LANE
A437
WEST END ROAD
65
66
67
68
69
70
71
72
73
74
LIME TREE GOLF CO
UB5
WEST LONDON SHOOTING GROUNDS
HILLINGDON
EALING
LANE COVERT
THE GORSE
SPORTS GROUND
HOME COVERT
HARE PLANTATION
POLE HILL OPEN SPACE
Old Abbotsonians R.F.C.
YEADING BROOK MEADOWS NATURE RESERVE
GROSVENOR PLAYING FIELD
CHARVILLE LANE
HAYES SHRUB
HAYES PARK
Mellow Lane Farm
Dalton's Farm
YEADING
78
UB4
BELMORE PLAYING FIELDS
GRANGE PK
HAYES END
RECREATION GROUND
UXBRIDGE ROAD
A4020
ROSEDALE PARK
GRASSY MEADOW
MEMORIAL GDNS
Hayes Cricket Club
HAYES STADIUM
HAYES
BARRA HALL PARK
BELL HOUSE FLD
WARREN PARK
THE PARKWAY
HAYES BYPASS
A312
Lombardy Retail Park
Uxbridge College Hayes Community Campus
STOCKLEY PARK GOLF COURSE
STOCKLEY PARK
DAWLEY ROAD
HARLINGTON ROAD
UB3
UB11
E.M.I. SPORTS GROUND
HAYES TOWN
95
Grand Union Canal
ADLER IND EST
ABERGLEN INDUSTRIAL ESTATE
WARNFORD IND EST
PROVIDENT INDUSTRIAL ESTATE
ELYSTAN BUSINESS CENTRE
HAYES METRO CENTRE
HEATHROW INTERCHANGE
BROOK INDUSTRIAL ESTATE
GRAND UNION CANAL (PADDINGTON BRANCH)
BP
BQ
BR
BS
BT
BU
BV
08
09
10

78
BW
BX
BY
BZ
CA
CB
CC
HA4
12
13
14
60
SOLID WASTE TRANSFER STATION
FROGMORE ESTATE
NORTHOLT RECREATION GRD
PLAYING FIELD
LORD HALSBURY MEMORIAL REC GRD
HILLINGDON
EALING
NORTHOLT
ISLIP MANOR PARK
WESTERN AVENUE
MANDEVILLE ROAD
CHURCH ROAD
A312
A40
65
66
67
68
69
70
71
72
73
74
77
81
82
83
84
SPORTS GROUND
LIME TREES PARK GOLF COURSE
Down Barns Moated Site
UB5
WEST LONDON SHOOTING GROUNDS
LIME TREE PARK
KELVIN INDUSTRIAL ESTATE
THE METROPOLITAN CENTRE
BELVUE PARK
EALING GOLF RANGE
KENSINGTON & CHELSEA PLAYING FIELDS
MARNHAM FIELDS
NORTHOLT GOLF COURSE
RECTORY PARK
SMITHS FARM EST
RUISLIP ROAD
A4180
B455
THE PARKWAY (HAYES BYPASS)
YEADING
UB4
BELMORE PLAYING FIELDS
GREENFORD
RAVENOR PARK
Taylor Woodrow
KING GEORGE'S FIELD
SPORTS GROUND
GREENFORD PARK REC GRD
JUBILEE PARK
GREENFORD PARK CEMETERY
WARREN PARK
BROOKSIDE
HGV Test Sta
WILLOWTREE MARINA
UXBRIDGE ROAD
A4020
THE BROADWAY
HIGH STREET
SOUTHALL
UB1
SOUTHALL PARK
DORMER'S WELLS
WEST MIDDLESEX GOLF COURSE
Lombardy Retail Park
Uxbridge College Hayes Community Campus
ELYSTAN BUSINESS CENTRE
HAYES METRO CENTRE
HEATHROW INTERCHANGE
BROOK INDUSTRIAL ESTATE
BARRATT INDUSTRIAL PARK
SOUTHALL RAILWAY CENTRE
GRAND UNION CANAL (PADDINGTON BRANCH)
SECURE PARKING
A3005
96
GREENFORD ROAD
FEATHERSTONE IND EST

CD
CE
CF
CG
CH
CJ
CK
15
16
17
79
61
65
66
67
68
69
80
70
82
71
72
81
73
74
83
84
97
SUDBURY
HA0
UB6
W7
W13
W5
WEMBLEY
ALPERTON
GREENFORD
PERIVALE
EALING
HANWELL
SUDBURY GOLF COURSE
HORSENDEN HILL GOLF COURSE
HORSENDEN HILL
HORSENDEN WOOD
GREAT BRAMSTONES
BERKELEY FIELDS
SPORTS GROUND
HOME MEAD
GRAND UNION CANAL (PADDINGTON BRANCH)
ALPERTON CEMETERY
ONE TREE HILL REC GRD
PERIVALE WOOD
PERIVALE INDUSTRIAL PARK
PERIVALE NEW BUSINESS CENTRE
WADSWORTH BUSINESS CENTRE
FLEETWAY BUSINESS PARK
SHERATON BUSINESS CEN
METROPOLITAN POLICE TRAFFIC UNIT
ALPERTON SPORTS GROUND
CAPITAL BUSINESS CEN
OLDFIELD REC GRD
EALING CENTRAL SPORTS GRD
WESTERN AVENUE
ATHLETICS STADIUM
PERIVALE PARK SPORTS GROUND
PERIVALE PARK GOLF COURSE
EALING GOLF COURSE
PITSHANGER PARK
GREYSTOKE PARK TERRACE
HANGER HILL PARK
BRENT VALLEY PARK
BRENT VALLEY GOLF COURSE
CUCKOO PARK
CLEVELAND PARK
DRAYTON GREEN
MONTPELIER PARK
BARCLAYS BANK SPORTS GROUND
CHURCHFIELDS RECREATION GROUND
KENSINGTON & CHELSEA CEMETERY
HANWELL CEMETERY
WALPOLE PARK
PITSHANGER MANOR MUS
EALING COMMON
EALING BROADWAY
WEST EALING
THE BROADWAY
UXBRIDGE ROAD
NEW BROADWAY
HANGER LANE
EALING ROAD
BRIDGEWATER ROAD
GREENFORD ROAD
WHITTON AVENUE WEST
EASTCOTE AVENUE
HARROW ROAD
A4090
A4127
A4005
A40
A4020
B452
B455
B456
ST. BERNARD'S HOSPITAL
EALING HOSPITAL N.H.S.TRUST
Wharncliffe Viaduct
LAMMAS PARK

80
WEMBLEY
TOKYNGTON
CHURCH END
HA0
HA9
ALPERTON
STONEBRIDGE
PARK ROYAL
HARLESDEN
NORTH ACTON
WEST ACTON
W3
EALING
ACTON
EAST ACTON
W5
CL
CM
CN
CP
CQ
CR
CS
62
65
66
67
68
69
70
71
72
73
74
79
98
19
20
21
81
82
83
84
NORTH CIRCULAR ROAD
WESTERN AVENUE
HANGER LANE
GUNNERSBURY AVENUE
UXBRIDGE ROAD
HIGH STREET
HORN LANE
VICTORIA ROAD
EALING ROAD
HARROW ROAD
CRAVEN PARK
HILLSIDE
ONE TREE HILL REC GRD
TOKYNGTON RECREATION GROUND
GIBBONS REC GRD
STONEBRIDGE REC GRD
NORTHFIELDS INDUSTRIAL ESTATE
PREMIER PARK
CENTRAL MIDDLESEX HOSPITAL
GUINNESS SPORTS GRD
HANGER HILL PARK
BARCLAYS BANK SPORTS GROUND
NORTH ACTON PLAYING FIELDS
NORTH THAMES GAS BOARD SPORTS GRD
EALING COMMON
ACTON PARK
ACTON CEMETERY
ALPERTON CEMETERY
PLAYING FIELDS
POPEFIELD PLAYING FIELDS
WESTERN TRADING EST
TOWNSEND INDUSTRIAL ESTATE
HANOVER W INDUSTRIAL EST
POWERGATE BUSINESS PARK
FROGMORE INDUSTRIAL ESTATE
BUSH INDUSTRIAL EST
PILOT INDUSTRIAL EST
VICTORIA IND EST
WESTWAY IND EST
ACTON PK IND EST
CAPITAL BUSINESS CEN
METROPOLITAN TRAFFIC UNIT
ROYALE LEISURE PARK
WESTPOINT TRADING EST
TUDOR ESTATE
GRAND UNION IND EST
Grand Union Canal
River Brent
Twyford Abbey
H.J. Heinz
Princess Royal Distribution Centre
Park Royal Guinness Brewery
Ealing Broadway
Thames Valley Uni
Pitshanger Manor Mus
Ealing Studios
Acton Hosp
Acton Main Line
North Ealing
Park Royal
Hanger Lane
Alperton
Stonebridge Park
Wembley Central
Harlesden
Acton Town
Acton Central

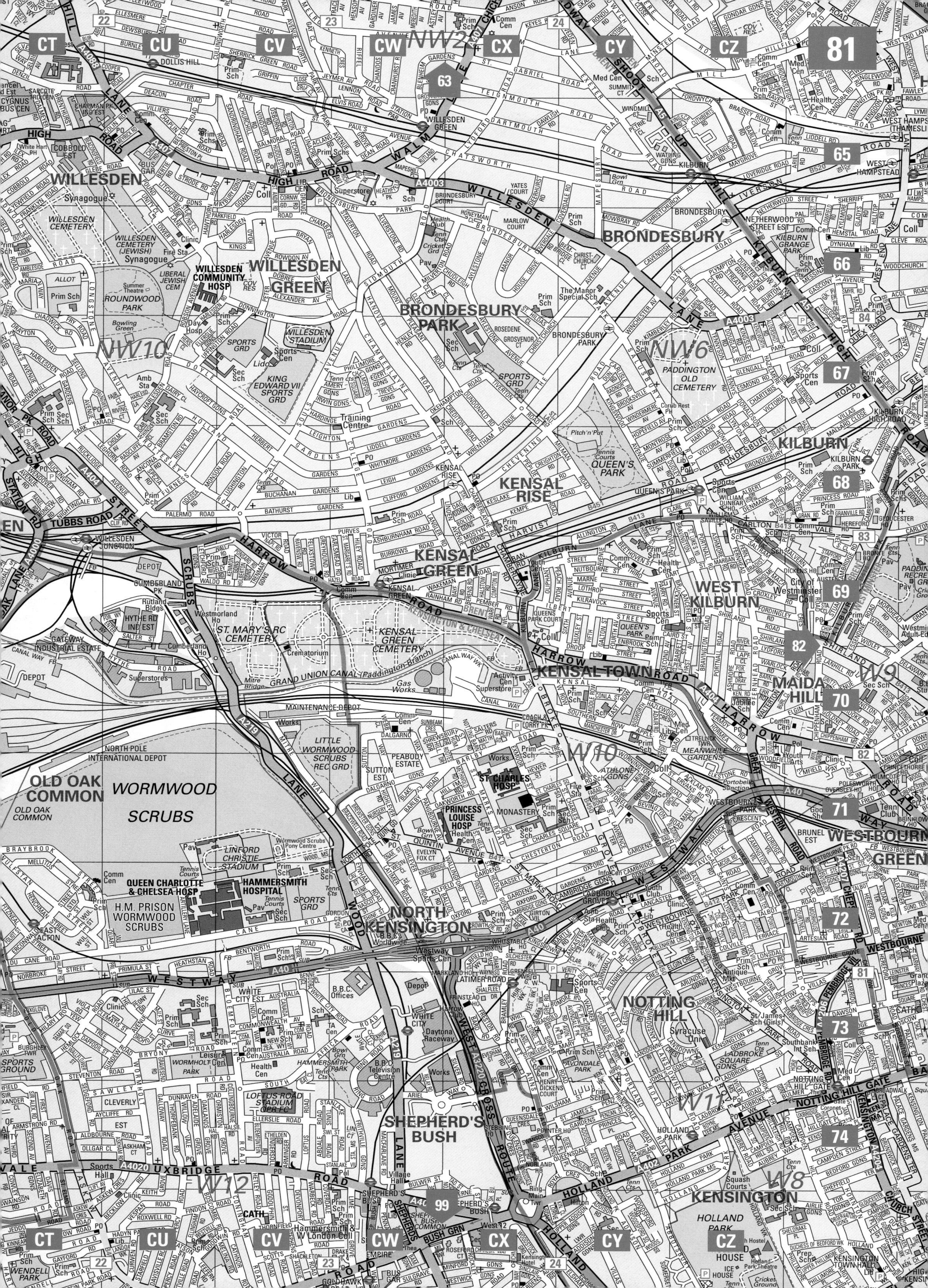

81
CT
CU
CV
CW
CX
CY
CZ
22
23
24
63
65
66
67
68
69
70
71
72
73
74
82
83
84
99
NW2
NW6
NW10
W8
W9
W10
W11
W12
WILLESDEN
WILLESDEN GREEN
BRONDESBURY
BRONDESBURY PARK
KILBURN
KENSAL RISE
KENSAL GREEN
WEST KILBURN
MAIDA HILL
QUEEN'S PARK
KENSAL TOWN
OLD OAK COMMON
WORMWOOD SCRUBS
NORTH KENSINGTON
NOTTING HILL
SHEPHERD'S BUSH
KENSINGTON
WESTBOURNE GREEN
WILLESDEN CEMETERY
ROUNDWOOD PARK
KING EDWARD VII SPORTS GRD
PADDINGTON OLD CEMETERY
ST. MARY'S RC CEMETERY
KENSAL GREEN CEMETERY
GRAND UNION CANAL (Paddington Branch)
LITTLE WORMWOOD SCRUBS REC GRD
ST. CHARLES HOSP
PRINCESS LOUISE HOSP
LINFORD CHRISTIE STADIUM
QUEEN CHARLOTTE & CHELSEA HOSP
HAMMERSMITH HOSPITAL
H.M. PRISON WORMWOOD SCRUBS
WORMHOLT PARK
LOFTUS ROAD STADIUM QPR FC
HOLLAND PARK
WESTWAY

82
DA
DB
DC
DD
DE
DF
DG
26
27
28
64
65
66
67
68
69
70
71
72
73
74
81
83
84
100
WEST HAMPSTEAD
SOUTH HAMPSTEAD
BELSIZE PARK
PRIMROSE HILL
KILBURN
NW6
NW8
NW1
REGENT'S PARK
ST. JOHN'S WOOD
LISSON GROVE
MAIDA VALE
MAIDA HILL
W9
WESTBOURNE GREEN
PADDINGTON
BAYSWATER
W2
MARYLEBONE
NOTTING HILL
W11
KENSINGTON
W8
KENSINGTON GARDENS
HYDE PARK
THE SERPENTINE
ROUND POND
HOLLAND PARK
LONDON ZOO
LORD'S CRICKET GROUND
PADDINGTON RECREATION GROUND
ST. MARY'S HOSP
WELLINGTON HOSP
ROYAL FREE HOSP
TAVISTOCK CEN
FINCHLEY ROAD
MAIDA VALE
EDGWARE ROAD
WESTWAY
BAYSWATER ROAD
OXFORD STREET
KNIGHTSBRIDGE
KENSINGTON ROAD
NOTTING HILL GATE
HAVERSTOCK HILL
ALBERT ROAD
PARK ROAD
MARYLEBONE ROAD
KILBURN HIGH ROAD
PARK LANE
OXFORD STREET where marked is closed to through traffic (except buses & taxis) from 7a.m.-7p.m. Monday - Saturday

NW5
DH
DJ
DK
DL
DM
DN
DP
N7
83
65
29
30
31
LOWER HOLLOWAY
HIGHBURY
KENTISH TOWN
CALEDONIAN PARK
PENTONVILLE PRISON
CANONBURY
BARNSBURY
66
84
67
CAMDEN TOWN
KING'S CROSS
ST. PANCRAS HOSP & HOSP FOR TROPICAL DISEASES
ISLINGTON
N1
CAMLEY ST NATURAL PARK
68
PENTONVILLE
SOMERS TOWN
ST. GEORGE'S CATHEDRAL
83
69
REGENT'S PARK
EUSTON
ST. PANCRAS
FINSBURY
BRITISH LIB
WC1
84
EASTMAN DENTAL HOSP
ST. LUKE'S
EC1
70
CLERKENWELL
CORAM'S FIELDS
82
BLOOMSBURY
BRITISH MUSEUM
MIDDLESEX HOSP
71
BARBICAN
HOLBORN
LINCOLN'S INN FIELDS
ROYAL COURTS OF JUSTICE
72
ST. PAUL'S CATH
SOHO
OXFORD CIRCUS
W1
STRAND
EC4
81
VICTORIA EMBANKMENT
73
RIVER
MAYFAIR
WC2
PICCADILLY CIRCUS
SHAKESPEARE GLOBE THEATRE
TATE MODERN
CHARING CROSS
SOUTHWARK
74
SE1
ST. JAMES'S
SW1
GREEN PARK
ST. JAMES'S PARK
101
WATERLOO
THE BOROUGH
BUCKINGHAM PALACE
WESTMINSTER BR

84
DQ
DR
DS
DT
DU
DV
DW
33
34
35
66
65
67
68
69
70
71
72
73
74
83
82
81
102
HIGHBURY
CANONBURY
KINGSLAND
DALSTON
HACKNEY
LONDON FIELDS
DE BEAUVOIR TOWN
SOUTH HACKNEY
N1
E8
HOXTON
HAGGERSTON
E2
BETHNAL GREEN
ST. LUKE'S
EC1
CLERKENWELL
SHOREDITCH
BROADGATE
BARBICAN
STEPNEY
E1
EC2
WHITECHAPEL
EC4
EC3
RIVER THAMES
SHADWELL
WAPPING
SE1
SOUTHWARK
THE BOROUGH
TOWER OF LONDON
REGENT'S CANAL

85
DX
DY
DZ
EA
EB
EC
ED
36
37
38
67
HOMERTON
E9
HACKNEY WICK
E15
STRATFORD
VICTORIA PARK
OLD FORD
BOW
MILE END
E3
BROMLEY
LIMEHOUSE
E14
POPLAR
ISLE
WEST INDIA DOCKS
SE16
SE10
RIVER THAMES
THE DOME
65
66
67
68
69
70
71
72
73
74
86
103
84
83
82
81
TOWER HAMLETS CEMETERY PARK
MILE END PARK
LEE VALLEY PARK
THREE MILLS GREEN
MEMORIAL RECREATION GROUND
ROYAL LONDON HOSP (MILE END)
ROYAL LON. HOSP (ST. CLEMENTS)
CANARY WHARF
NORTH GREENWICH
CANNING TOWN
WEST HAM
DEVONS RD
BOW CHURCH
BOW RD
MILE END
PUDDING MILL LANE
LIMEHOUSE
WESTFERRY
WEST INDIA QUAY
HERON QUAYS
SOUTH QUAY
BLACKWALL
EAST INDIA
ALL SAINTS
BROMLEY BY BOW
HACKNEY WICK
LONDON INTERNATIONAL FREIGHT TERMINAL
EAST INDIA DOCK ROAD
COMMERCIAL ROAD
BLACKWALL TUNNEL
LIMEHOUSE REACH
BLACKWALL REACH
BOW CREEK
LIMEHOUSE CUT
HERTFORD UNION CANAL
REGENT'S CANAL

86
EE
EF
EG
EH
EJ
EK
EL
40
41
42
FOREST GATE
E7
WOODGRANGE PARK
GRANGE PARK CEMETERY
68
ROMFORD ROAD
E15
STRATFORD
65
66
67
68
69
70
71
72
73
74
84
83
82
81
85
104
PLASHET JEWISH CEMETERY
CHILDRENS ZOO
PLASHET PARK
EAST HAM MEM HOSP
WEST HAM PARK
WEST HAM
UPTON
UPTON LANE
STOPFORD ROAD
UPTON PARK
PRIORY PARK
BOLEYN GRD WEST HAM UTD F.C.
BARKING ROAD
HIGH STREET NORTH
GREEN STREET
NEW PLAISTOW RD
PLAISTOW ROAD
HIGH STREET
PLAISTOW
PLAISTOW HOSP
EAST LONDON CEMETERY
MEMORIAL RECREATION GROUND
SPORTS GROUND
THREE MILLS GREEN
VALLEY PARK
Three Mills Studios
MANOR ROAD
E13
NEWHAM GENERAL HOSPITAL
E6
EAST HAM JEWISH CEMETERY
BRAMPTON PARK
HERMIT RD REC GRD
TERENCE McMILLAN STADIUM
PLAYING FIELDS
BECKTON DISTRICT PARK
NEWHAM WAY
PRINCE REGENT LANE
CANNING TOWN REC GRD
CANNING TOWN
CUSTOM HOUSE
KING GEORGE V PARK
LIMMO PENINSULA ECOLOGICAL PARK
EAST INDIA DOCK BASIN NATURE RESERVE
LOWER LEA CROSSING
VICTORIA DOCK RD
ROYAL VICTORIA
PRINCE REGENT
ROYAL ALBERT
ExCeL
CONNAUGHT BRIDGE
ROYAL VICTORIA DOCK
SILVERTOWN WAY
E16
Millennium Mills
Pontoon Dock
NORTH WOOLWICH ROAD
THAMES BARRIER PARK
SILVERTOWN
SILVERTOWN & LONDON CITY AIRPORT
THAMESIDE INDUSTRIAL EST
SE10
THE DOME
MERIDIAN GARDENS
NORTH GREENWICH
BLACKWALL TUNNEL
RIVER
WOOLWICH REACH
THAMES FLOOD BARRIER
LONDON

87
EM
EN
EP
EQ
ER
ES
ET
43
44
45
69
105
88
65
66
67
68
69
70
71
72
73
74
84
83
82
81
LOXFORD
LITTLE ILFORD PARK
BARKING PARK
THE LAKE
BARKING PARK REC GRD
SPORTS GROUND
BARKING
BARKING HOSPITAL
UPNEY
RIPPLESIDE BURIAL GROUND
BOATING LAKE
BARKING INDUSTRIAL PARK
ALFREDS WAY IND ESTATE
IG11
E12
GREAT FIELDS PARK
FLANDERS RD PLAYING FLDS
BARKING ROAD REC GRD
ABBEY RETAIL PARK
CUCKOLD'S HAVEN
HAND TROUGH CREEK
ABBEY WHARF INDUSTRIAL ESTATE
KATELLA TRADING EST
LYON BUSINESS PARK
RIVERSIDE INDUSTRIAL ESTATE
RIVER ROAD BUSINESS PARK
TRAFALGAR BUSINESS CENTRE
BUZZARD CREEK INDUSTRIAL ESTATE
CREEKMOUTH
City Farm & Ecology Park
GOOSELEY'S PLAYING FIELDS
BECKTON TRIANGLE RETAIL PARK
GATEWAY RETAIL PARK
Nature Reserve
BECKTON REACH SEWAGE TREATMENT WORKS
Filter Beds
Sludge Beds
BARKING FLOOD BARRIER
ALPINE BUSINESS CEN
BECKTON RETAIL PARK
BECKTON
NEW BECKTON PARK
Gas Works
DLR DEPOT
GALLIONS REACH
MARGARET NESS OR TRIPCOCK POINT
Barking or False Point
THAMESMEAD
SE28
BECKTON PARK
CYPRUS
Uni of East London
ALBERT DOCK
CITY AIRPORT
KING GEORGE V DOCK
ALBERT BASIN
BASIN SOUTH
Newham Coll of Further Ed
Norton Healthcare Ltd
ROYAL VICTORIA GDNS
STANDARD INDUSTRIAL ESTATE
North Woolwich Pier
Woolwich Ferry Pier
WOOLWICH CROWN CT
H.M. PRISON BELMARSH
BIRCHMERE
Thamesmere Lake
ALFREDS WAY (BARKING BYPASS) A13
NEWHAM WAY
ROYAL DOCKS ROAD A1020
WOOLWICH MANOR WAY
ALBERT WAY
EASTERN WAY
CENTRAL WAY
LONGBRIDGE ROAD
RIPPLE ROAD A123
RIVER ROAD
THAMES ROAD
BARKING ROAD
HIGH STREET SOUTH A117
WOOLWICH MANOR WAY A117
NORTHERN RELIEF ROAD A124
A406 BARKING RELIEF ROAD
River Roding
Long Reach
Warpools Reach
Gallions Reach
NEWHAM
BARKING & DAGENHAM

88
EU
EV
EW
EX
EY
EZ
FA
47
48
49
70
PARSLOES PARK
RM9
BOATING LAKE
BARKING HOSPITAL
DAGENHAM HEATHWAY
BECONTREE
RIPPLESIDE BURIAL GROUND
CASTLE GREEN
GORESBROOK SPORTS GROUND
GORESBROOK PARK
DAGENHAM LEISURE PK
BARKING INDUSTRIAL PARK
ALFREDS WAY IND ESTATE
WAYSIDE COMMERCIAL EST
RENWICK IND ESTATE
RIPPLESIDE COMMERCIAL ESTATE
MAYBELLS COMM EST
TRAIN DEPOT
Freight Depot
FORD MOTOR WORKS
DAGENHAM DOCK
RIVERSIDE INDUSTRIAL ESTATE
City Farm & Ecology Park
The Ripple Nature Reserve
IG11
COAL DEPOT
POWER STATION
Power Station
Horse Shoe Corner
CREEKMOUTH
BUZZARD CREEK INDUSTRIAL ESTATE
Oil Storage Depot
BARKING FLOOD BARRIER
BARKING & DAGENHAM
CROSSNESS LIGHTHOUSE
THAMESMEAD NORTH
Ecology Study Area
Crossway Lake
RIVERSIDE GOLF COURSE
SE2
Crossness Pumping Station
COVERED RESERVOIRS
Crossness Sewage Treatment Works
Sludge Incinerator
Thamesmere Lake
THAMESMEAD
MOORINGS
CROSSWAY PARK
SOUTHMERE PARK
ERITH MARSHES
LAKESIDE CENTRE
SOUTHMERE
BIRCHMERE PARK
SE28
DA18
WOODLAND WAY
EASTERN WAY
106
H.M. PRISON

SOUTH HORNCHURCH
RAINHAM
RAINHAM MARSHES
Silt Lagoons
HORNCHURCH MARSHES
HORNCHURCH COUNTRY PARK
WENNINGTON MARSHES
OLD DAGENHAM PARK
RM10
RM12
RM13
DA17
SPORTS GROUND
BRITTONS PLAYING FIELD
MANOR ROAD SPORTS GRD
Riverside Sewage Works
FAIRVIEW INDUSTRIAL PARK
ALBRIGHT INDUSTRIAL ESTATE
DENVER INDUSTRIAL ESTATE
CONTAINER DEPOT
BELVEDERE INDUSTRIAL ESTATE
JENNINGTREE POINT LIGHTHOUSE
Rainham Sunday Market
Old Man's Head
Hornchurch Shoot
CAR COMPOUND
THAMES GATEWAY
NEW ROAD
RAINHAM ROAD
RAINHAM ROAD SOUTH
DAGENHAM ROAD
SOUTH AVENUE
Channel Tunnel Rail Link (Under Construction)
Newtons Corner
Dovers Corner
AIRFIELD WOOD
FLIGHTWAY WOOD
FARMFIELD WOOD
LOWFIELD WOOD
71
90
107
FB
FC
FD
FE
FF
FG
FH
50
51
52
65
66
67
68
69
70
71
72
73
74
81
82
83
84

FJ
FK
FL
FM
FN
FP
FQ
54
55
56
Hacton
72
Park Corner Farm
White Hart PH
PARK FARM ROAD
Lodge Farm
Rainham Lodge Farm
Corbets Tey Sch
PARKLANDS
OPEN SPACE
Huntsman & Hounds PH
Harwood Hall
Poultry Farm
Corbets Tey
Stables
Gardners Cor Hall
Central Farm
AVELEY ROAD
SAND & GRAVEL PIT
REFUSE TRANSFER STATION
Gerpins Farm
LITTLE GERPINS LANE
GERPINS LANE
POND ROAD
BERWICK POND ROAD
Superstore
Prim Sch
Prim Schs
65
66
67
68
69
70
71
72
73
74
RM12
HORNCHURCH
COUNTRY
PARK
AIRFIELD WOOD
PINEWOOD
FLIGHTWAY WOOD
FARMFIELD WOOD
LOWFIELD WOOD
WESTERN PATHWAY
EASTERN PATHWAY
Albyns Farm
ABBEY WOOD
BERWICK POND
Berwick Ponds Farm
SAND AND GRAVEL PIT
WATERMEADOW
ABBEY WOOD LANE
Berwick Manor
Berwick Manor Farm
White Post Corner
WARWICK LANE
INGREBOURNE RIVER
RAINHAM
83
84
PARSONAGE ROAD
Prim Sch
UPMINSTER ROAD NORTH
Saxon Horn PH
CEM
RAINHAM CEMETERY (JEWISH)
SPRING FARM PARK
Tennis Cts
Pav
Works
LAUNDERS LANE
SAND AND GRAVEL PIT
WARWICK WOOD
WHITE POST WOOD
89
NEW ROAD
A1306
Health Cen
ALLOT
BOWL GRN
REC GRD
LAMBS LANE SOUTH
82
Sec Sch
RM13
Swim Pool
Prim Sch
South Hall Farm
MOAT
Bretts Farm
Sir Henry Gurnett PH
Southall Bridge
EAST HALL LANE
East Hall Farm
NEW COTTAGES
WENNINGTON ROAD
CHURCH LANE
Moor Hall
The Mariscoe PH
PO
Prim Sch
Wennington Hall
The Willows
Hall
THE GREEN
Fire Sta
Wennington
81
A13
GATEWAY
Channel Tunnel Rail Link (Under Construction)
Common Watercourse
New Farm
SANDY LANE
B1335
Sandy Lane Farm
RAINHAM MARSHES
Silt Lagoons
Works
108
LONDON ROAD
PURFLEET
Nursery
Clubhouse
SPORTS GROUND
WENNINGTON MARSHES
Lib
Hall

North Ockendon
SOUTH OCKENDON
NORTH STIFFORD
AVELEY
RM14
RM15
BELHUS PARK
BELHUS PARK GOLF COURSE
BELHUS WOODS COUNTRY PARK
RUSSELL'S LAKE
COYS LAKE
SAND AND GRAVEL PIT
FREEMAN'S SHAW
TOP MEADOW GOLF COURSE
THE WILDERNESS
CLAY PIT
HAVERING
THURROCK
M25
FORD AVELEY PLANT
The Ockendon Complex
South Ockendon Centre
BONNYGATE WOOD
DILKES PARK
OAK WOOD
ASH PLANTATION
ROOKERY
LONG POND
MILLARD'S GARDEN
BRANNETT'S WOOD
HANGMAN'S WOOD
LOW WELL WOOD
BRICKBARN WOOD
COMBE WOOD
LITTLE PALMER'S SHAW
GREAT PALMER'S SHAW
WHITEHALL WOOD
LITTLE BRICKKILN WOOD
BRICKKILN WOOD
Junction 30
THURROCK ARTERIAL ROAD NORTH
SOUTH OCKENDON REC GRD
Outdoor Pursuits Centre
Stifford Interchange
LAKESIDE COACH PARK
Thurrock Services
Mar Dyke
FR
FS
FT
FU
FV
FW
FX
57
58
59
65
66
67
68
69
70
71
72
73
74
81
82
83
84
109

92
SLOUGH
SALT HILL PARK
AS
AT
AU
AV
AW
AX
AY
98
99
00
74
Thames Valley Uni
BUS STA
Superstore
Works
Gas Works
The Business Village
Union Canal
Lavender Farm
NURSERY LANE
BLOOM PARK
MIDDLEGREEN ROAD
Ice Arena
Fire Sta
TOWN HALL
Sports Centre
MONTEM REC GR
WELLINGTON ST
WELLINGTON
A4
Queensmere Shop Centre
Royal Mail
Observatory Shop Centre
STRATFIELD ROAD
Islamic Cen
Prep. Sch
Premier Lodge
Superstore
Tennis Courts
CHERRY AVENUE
SUTTON AVENUE
DOWNS ROAD
75
CHALVEY RD
CHALVEY ROAD EAST
SOUTH BUCKS COUNCIL
UPTON HOSP
HIGH STREET
UXBRIDGE ROAD
SUSSEX PLACE
LONDON ROAD
LANGLEY ROAD
SPORTS GROUND
Sports Centre
Prim Sch
76
Chalvey
ALBERT ST
A412 MERE RD
YEW TREE
A412
Upton Park
HERSCHEL PARK
Upton
LASCELLES PLAYING FIELD
Tennis Courts
PARK LANE
TRELAWNEY AVENUE
KEDERMISTER PARK
79
WINDSOR ROAD
SLOUGH RD
SL1
A332
77
Agars Plough
UPTON COURT PARK
COURT ROAD
MOTOCROSS TRACK
SLOUGH
WINDSOR & MAIDENHEAD
Pumping Station
Clubhouse
Cricket Ground
SLOUGH R.F.C.
B.M.X. TRACK
MARLBOROUGH ROAD
ETON GOLF COURSE
AGARS PLOUGH PLAYING FIELDS
Cricket Ground
Open Air Pool
Fifteen Arch Bri
78
POCOCKS LANE
ATHLETICS CENTRE
PLAYING FIELDS
Eton Coll
Eton College
DITTON PARK
M4
Riding Court Farm
KINGS OAK
Computer Associates
DITTON PARK
FISH POND
79
Water Works
Romney Lock
THE HOME PARK RECREATION GROUND
DATCHET GOLF COURSE
CASTLE AVENUE
Victoria Bri
EDWARD VII AVENUE
WINDSOR
CUTLERS AIT
80
Eton Coll Boathouse
FIREWORK AIT
WINDSOR & ETON RIVERSIDE
SUMPTERMEAD AIT
Clubhouse
Sec Sch
MAJORS ROAD
DATCHET CEMETERY
WINDSOR CASTLE
EAST TER LAWN
EAST LAWN
LIME AVENUE
DUTCH ELM AV
RIVER THAMES
DATCHET
Lib
Tenn Cts
Med Cen
DATCHET SPORTS GROUND
The Rising Sun PH
77
WINDSOR & ETON CENTRAL
ROYAL STATION
Royal Mews Riding Sch
South Slopes
81
Victoria Barracks
WINDSOR
GOLF COURSE
Cambridge Gate
Adelaide Lodge
MILL PLACE CARAVAN PARK
QUEEN ELIZABETH WALK
82
Long Walk Gate
THE HOME PARK
SL4
FROGMORE GARDENS
Southlea
Pumping Station
76
PRINCESS MARGARET HOSP
A308
Frogmore House
Royal Mausoleum
Mausoleum
Prince Consort's Home Farm
Southlea Farm
83
Albert Bridge
Sludge Lagoon
SUNNYMEADS
EVERGREEN OAK AV
Windsor Hall
Glasshouses
ROYAL GARDENS
Shaw Farm
ALBERT ROAD
NICKCROFT AIT
HAM ISLAND
Sludge Lagoons
Filter Beds
84
GARRISON SPORTS GROUND
The Lord Nelson PH
NEW CUT
Sludge Beds
Sunnymeads
Sailing Club
Manor Farm
Ham Bridge
Clayhall Farm
112
St. George's Farm
Old Windsor Lock
The Manor
Queen's Cottages
Battle Bourne
GREAT PARK
REMENHAM PARK
Sailing Club
CHURCH ROAD
REVIEW GROUND

93
75
IVER GOLF COURSE
BUCKINGHAMSHIRE
SOUTH BUCKS
SLOUGH
LANGLEY
LANGLEY BUSINESS CENTRE
LANGLEY MEMORIAL GROUND
Richings Park
THORNEY PARK GOLF COURSE
SL0
RICHINGS PARK GOLF COURSE
HOME WOOD
AXIS PARK
HARVEY PARK
Junction 15 (M25)
Junction 4B (M4)
OAK PLANTATION
OLD WOOD
M4
Sewage Works
Junction 5
Brands Hill
COLNBROOK BYPASS
A4
94
Colnbrook
THE QUEEN MOTHER RESERVOIR
SL3
Poyle
GRAVEL PIT
SPORTS GRD
GOLF DRIVING RANGE
BRITANNIA INDUSTRIAL EST
MCKAY TRADING ESTATE
TRIDENT INDUSTRIAL ESTATE
POYLE TECH CEN
Horton
Arthur Jacob Nature Reserve
Junction 14
M25
HILLINGDON
AIRPORT WAY
A3113
TW19
113
WRAYSBURY
SURREY
WINDSOR & MAIDENHEAD
STANWELL MOOR
AZ
BA
BB
BC
BD
BE
BF
01
02
03
76
77
78
79
80
81
82
83
84

94
BG
BH
BJ
BK
BL
BM
BN
05
06
07
76
YIEWSLEY
West Drayton Coal Depot
Water Treatment Works
Horton Ind Park
Providence
Horton Road
Roberts
West Drayton
Station Approach
Health Cen
Works
Horton Bridge
DERA
Tenn Cts
Archie Cl
Rutters Cl
Thorney Farm
Thorney Wier House
Millside Court
THORNEY PARK GOLF COURSE
Fairway Avenue
Colne Avenue
Sunray Av
Lawn Avenue
Frays Avenue
Colham Mill Rd
Warwick Road
Cherry Orchard
Furzeham Rd
Bellclose Road
Ferrers Avenue
Swan Rd
Classon Cl
Drayton Gdns
Holly
Sports Grd
Hawthorne Cres
R.A.F. West Drayton
Kings Cl
Queens
Porters Way
Percy Bush Rd
Allot
Sports Ground
Mulberry
Briar
Lavender
Almond Av
West Road
Walnut Way
Hazel Av
Ash
Tree Av
Crowne Plaza Cour
Iver
Walk
Lib
75
Somerset Way
Tenn Cts
Sports Grd
Clubhouse
Bowl Grn
Richings Way
Tower Arms PH
Thorney Mill Rd
Thorney
Wellesley
Sykeings
76
Richings
SL0
79
77
Poynings
The Ridings
Old Slade Farm
Slade Lane
THORNEY
Mill Road
Works
South Bucks
Hillingdon
Bigley Ditch
Frays Island Nat Res
Mayfield Park
Mayfields Lake
Anglers Retreat PH
West Drayton Cricket Club
Crickfield Rd
Colne Park Caravan Site
Sports Ground
Old Farm Rd
Caroline Cl
Medical Cen
Sch
Church Rd
The Grn
Drayton
The Avenue
Tenn Cts
United Biscuits
Youth Cen
Comm Cen
Pol
Thornton
West Drayton Pk Av
Hall
Prim Sch
Kingston Lane
Bagley Cl
THE CLOSES RECREATION GROUND
SOUTHLANDS ARTS CEN
WEST DRAYTON
Family Cen
Place
The Dell
CEM.
Sipson Road
Maxwell Road
Chapman
North Avenue
Myrtle
Beech
East Road
Blackthorn Av
Tenn Cts
Crowne Plaza Hotel
Laurel Lane
Prim Sch
Comm Cen
UB7
PO
Rosary Cl
Wise Lane
Rowan Road
Great Way
Scott Cl
Keats Way
Cherry Lane
Vine Close
Novotel Heathrow
Coler Wy
Keats Wy
Magnolia St
The Ramblers
Harmondsworth
Wordsworth
Milton
Byron
The Glebe
Junction 15 (M25)
Junction 4B (M4)
Colne Brook
Donkey Lane
The Common
M4
78
Littl Benty
FB
Holloway Close
Sub Sipson
Heathrow Coach Cen
Holiday Inn Heathrow
Plough PH
Heathrow Garden Centre
A3044
Holloway Lane
Hurrans Garden Centre
Sipson Way
Russell Gdns
Wyneham Cl
Berkeley Nurseries
Vine
78
Sewage Works
Filter Beds
79
Warehouses
Road
M25
Bigley Ditch
Warehouses
Saxon Way
Allot
HARMONDSWORTH CEM
Tithe Barn
Mead Cl
Priory Way
Harmondsworth Lane
Prim Sch
Hollycroft Cl
Vincent Cl
Homefarm
Moor Lane
High Street
The Lodge
Home Farm
FB
Scotchlake Farm
Accommodation Lane
Wilt Cl
Cambridge Cl
Summerhouse
Harmondsworth
Sipson
Works
Sipson Cl
A408
93
Depot
Slough
Accommodation
PROSPECT PARK
Tarmac Way
British Airways Waterside
Rec Grd
Comm Cen
Prim Sch
Candover Cl
Tenn Cts
Offices
Sheraton Heathrow Hotel
Immigration Cen
Hatch Lane
Bomer Cl
Ashby Way
Colnbrook
80
Greyhound PH
A4
Speedbird Way
Bypass
Skyport Dr
Zealand Av
Depot
Offices
Pinglestone Cl
Warehouses
Works
SIPSON WAR MEML. REC GRD
Comm Cen
Tenn Cts
SL3
77
Sports Grd
Winchester
The Wy
Horns
Sch
Warehouses
Road
Accommodation Lane
Stanwell Moor Rd
The Island
Buses Only
Offices
White Horse PH
Longford Bridge
Thistle Heathrow Park
Bath Road
PO
Depot
Nor Holt
Arora International Hotel
Blunts Avenue
Holiday Inn
Bath Road
Northwood
Napier
Road
British Airways PLC
Nelson
Newbury Road
Newport Rd
West
Fire Sta
81
Golf Driving Range
Pav
Longford Roundabout
Longford
Perimeter Road
Northern Perimeter Road
Bath Road
Mad Bridge
Moor Bridge
Kings Bridge
Elbow Meadow
Poyle Channel
Wraysbury River
River Colne
Stanwell
Western
Balancing Reservoir
82
Poyle Tech Cen
David Road
Perry
Wessex Road
Wessex
Oaks Drive
Sludge Lagoons
Sludge Lagoons
Settling Tanks
Royal Mail
D'Albiad House
Courtney House
76
Bedfont Court Estate
A3044
Moor
PERRY OAKS SEWAGE TREATMENT WORKS
Settling Tanks
Snow Base
Terminal 3
83
Calder Way
Court
Bedfont Court
Longford River
Burrows Hill Cl
Burrows Hill Lane
Western
TW19
TW
Hillingdon
Airport
Junction 14
A3113
Res
Wessex Road
Sludge Lagoons
Wessex
84
M25
Horton
Leylands La
Spout Lane North
Way
Road
Perimeter
Flintlock Cl
Spout Lane
Minerva Cl
Vine Cl
Sports Ground
114
Southern Perimeter Road
Cargo
Stanwell Moor
Hithermoor
River Colne
BG
BH
BJ
BK
BL
BM
BN
05
06
07
Hillingdon
Southern Perimeter
Spelthorne
Surrey
Vermeulens Garden Centre
Sandringham Rd
Shoreham Road East
Shoreham Road West
Cargo Terminal
British Airways Cargo Centre
Hampton Rd
Works

HAYES TOWN
HARLINGTON
CRANFORD PARK
CRANFORD
HEATHROW AIRPORT (LONDON)
HATTON
UB11
UB3
TW4
TW5
TW14
Junction 4
Junction 3
Junction 4A
Grand Union Canal
THE PARKWAY
BATH ROAD
GREAT SOUTH-WEST ROAD
NORTH HYDE ROAD
HIGH STREET
STATION ROAD
NORTHERN PERIMETER ROAD
IMPERIAL COLLEGE SPORTS GROUND
BRITISH AIRWAYS SPORTS GROUND
HOUNSLOW HEATH GOLF COURSE
TERMINAL 1
TERMINAL 2
HEATHROW TERMINALS 1, 2 & 3
HEATHROW TERMINAL 4

96
BW
BX
BY
BZ
CA
CB
CC
12
13
14
78
SOUTHALL
UB1
BROADWAY
HIGH STREET
UXBRIDGE
HEATHROW INTERCHANGE
BROOK INDUSTRIAL ESTATE
BEACONSFIELD ROAD
SECURE PARKING
Gas Works
GRAND UNION CANAL (PADDINGTON BRANCH)
HILLINGDON
EALING
BARRATT INDUSTRIAL PARK
SOUTHALL RAILWAY CENTRE
MIDDLESEX BUSINESS CENTRE
FEATHERSTONE IND EST
Sunrise Radio
SOUTH RD
MERRICK ROAD
75
76
77
79
80
81
82
83
84
THE PARKWAY
HAYES
TENTELOW LANE SPORTS GROUND
Grand Union Canal
UB2
NORWOOD GREEN
SOUTHALL REC GRD
WESTERN INTERNATIONAL MARKET
HARLEQUIN CENTRE
BULLS BRIDGE IND EST
NORTH HYDE
WOLF FLDS
AIRLINKS
GOLF
COURSE
Junction 3
M4
Heston Services
SPITFIRE ESTATE
AIR LINKS INDUSTRIAL ESTATE
BRITISH AIRWAYS SPORTS GROUND
PARKWAY TRADING ESTATE
Thorncliffe Hotel
HESTON PARK
Travelodge
95
TW5
HESTON
HESTON INDUSTRIAL MALL
SUTTON PLAYING FIELD
OSTERLEY PARK HOUSE
OSTERLE
SPORTS GROUND
LONDON TRANSPORT SPORTS GRD
LAMPTON
LAMPTON PARK
HOUNSLOW CIVIC CENTRE
GREAT WEST ROAD
A4
BATH ROAD
HOUNSLOW WEST
BEAVERSFORD PARK
TW4
HOUNSLOW
HOUNSLOW CENTRAL
HOUNSLOW EAST
TW3
INWOOD PARK
HOUNSLOW BUSINESS PARK
HEATHROW INT TRADING ESTATE
RIFLE RANGE
GREEN LANE OPEN SPACE
BALAM RESERVOIR
HOUNSLOW HEATH
CENTRAL PARK EST
STAINES ROAD
A315
WELLINGTON ROAD N
WELLINGTON ROAD S
SOUTH-WEST
CAUSEWAY
116

HANWELL
HANWELL CEMETERY
EALING HOSPITAL N.H.S. TRUST
W7
BRENT RIVER PARK
ELTHORNE PARK
ELTHORNE PARK EXTENSION
W13
WALPOLE PARK
LAMMAS PARK
SOUTH EALING
W5
SOUTH EALING CEMETERY
LITTLE EALING
BOSTON MANOR
BOSTON MANOR PARK
OSTERLEY PARK NT
WYKE GREEN GOLF COURSE
MACFARLANE SPORT FIELD
WEST CROSS CENTRE
BRENTFORD
BRENTFORD BUSINESS CENTRE
Junction 2
TW7
TW8
TW9
Brunel University (Osterley Campus)
SPRING GROVE
WOODLANDS
ISLEWORTH
SYON PARK
SYON HOUSE
Battles of Brentford 1016 & 1642
ROYAL BOTANIC GARDENS
KEW
KEW PALACE
QUEEN'S COTTAGE GARDENS
WEST MIDDLESEX UNIVERSITY HOSP
ISLEWORTH AIT
RIVER THAMES
ROYAL MID-SURREY GOLF COURSE (OLD DEER PARK)
OBSERVATORY GARDENS
OLD DEER PARK RECREATION GROUND
RICHMOND ATHLETIC GROUND
RICHMOND GREEN
MOGDEN WATER TREATMENT WORKS
WORTON HALL INDUSTRIAL ESTATE
REDLEES PARK
ST MARGARETS
TW1
GREAT WEST ROAD
LONDON ROAD
TWICKENHAM ROAD
BOSTON MANOR ROAD
M4
A4
A315
A310
A3002
CD
CE
CF
CG
CH
CJ
CK
15
16
17
75
76
77
78
79
80
81
82
83
84
98
117

98
CL
CM
CN
CP
CQ
CR
CS
W5
W3
W4
TW8
TW9
SW14
SOUTH ACTON
BEDFORD PARK
ACTON PARK
SOUTHFIELDS PLAYING FIELDS
ACTON TOWN
SOUTH EALING
LITTLE EALING
SOUTH EALING CEMETERY
CLAYPONDS HOSP
GUNNERSBURY PARK
GUNNERSBURY PARK MUSEUM
SMALL MANSION ARTS CEN
BOATING LAKE
POTOMAC (FISH POND)
KENSINGTON CEMETERY
International Sch of London
GUNNERSBURY
GUNNERSBURY TRIANGLE NATURE RESERVE
POPEFIELD PLAYING FIELDS
SPORTS GROUND
Junction 1
Junction 2
CHISWICK HIGH ROAD
GREAT WEST RD
HEATHFIELD TER
KEW BRIDGE STEAM MUS
THE MUSICAL MUS
BRENTFORD FC
BRENTFORD
BRENTFORD AIT
KEW BRIDGE
KEW GREEN
KEW PALACE
KEW
OLIVER'S ISLAND
RIVER THAMES
ROYAL BOTANIC GARDENS
KEW GARDENS GALLERY
The Princess of Wales Conservatory
THE POND
Temple of Arethusa
ARBORETUM
WATER LILY POND
MARIANNE NORTH GALLERY
PAGODA
QUEEN'S COTTAGE GARDENS
Battles of Brentford 1016 & 1642
SYON HOUSE
ROYAL MID-SURREY GOLF COURSE (OLD DEER PARK)
RICHMOND ATHLETIC GROUND
London Welsh R.F.C. & Richmond C.C.
ROYAL HOSP
RICHMOND
RICHMOND GREEN
THE SQUARE
NORTH SHEEN
NORTH SHEEN CEMETERY
HAMMERSMITH CEMETERY
PUBLIC RECORD OFFICE
Sewage Works
CIVIC AMENITY SITE
Crematorium
GROVE PARK
CHISWICK
CHISWICK HOUSE GROUNDS
CHISWICK HOUSE
CHISWICK CEMETERY
CHISWICK COMMON
TURNHAM GREEN
CIVIL SERVICE SPORTS GROUND
RIVERSIDE RECREATION GROUND
DUKE'S MEADOW
DUKE'S MEADOW GOLF COURSE
UNI WEST. SPORTS GRD
STADIUM
Chiswick R.F.C.
BARNES BRIDGE
HOUNSLOW
RICHMOND UPON THAMES
MORTLAKE
MORTLAKE HIGH ST
LOWER RICHMOND RD
LOWER MORTLAKE ROAD
UPPER RICHMOND ROAD WEST
SOUTH CIRCULAR ROAD
CLIFFORD AVENUE
CHISWICK BR
GREAT CHERTSEY ROAD
BURLINGTON LANE
ALEXANDRA AV
EAST SHEEN
EAST SHEEN COMMON (NT)
PESTHOUSE COMMON
MORTLAKE CEM
BARNES HOSP
THE BANK OF ENGLAND'S SPORTS GROUND
PALEWELL COMMON
118

99
CT
CU
CV
CW
CX
CY
CZ
SHEPHERD'S BUSH
KENSINGTON
HOLLAND PARK
HAMMERSMITH
EARLS COURT
CASTELNAU
THE WETLANDS CENTRE
PARSONS GREEN
FULHAM
BARNES
PUTNEY
WANDSWORTH
ROEHAMPTON
W12
W14
W11
W8
W6
SW5
SW6
SW13
SW15
SW18
RIVER THAMES
HAMMERSMITH & FULHAM
WANDSWORTH
UPPER RICHMOND ROAD
KING STREET
HAMMERSMITH FLYOVER
TALGARTH ROAD
FULHAM PALACE ROAD
BARNES COMMON
PUTNEY BRIDGE
OLYMPIA
QUEENS CLUB
FULHAM PALACE GARDENS
HURLINGHAM CLUB GDNS
WANDSWORTH PARK
ROEHAMPTON PRIORY HOSPITAL
81
119
75
76
77
78
79
80
82
83
84
100
22
23
24

KENSINGTON GARDENS
HYDE PARK
DA
DB
DC
DD
DE
DF
DG
26
27
28
82
ROUND POND
THE SERPENTINE
SERPENTINE GALLERY
KENSINGTON PALACE
W8
KENSINGTON
HOLLAND PARK
75
76
77
78
79
80
81
82
83
84
99
120
KENSINGTON ROAD
KENSINGTON GORE
KNIGHTSBRIDGE
SW7
SOUTH KENSINGTON
NATURAL HISTORY MUSEUM
SCIENCE MUSEUM
VICTORIA & ALBERT MUSEUM
CROMWELL ROAD
BROMPTON ROAD
BELGRAVIA
BROMPTON
SW5
EARLS COURT
SW10
SW3
WEST BROMPTON
CHELSEA
ROYAL MARSDEN HOSP
ROYAL BROMPTON HOSP
ROYAL HOSPITAL CHELSEA
CHELSEA EMBANKMENT
CHELSEA REACH
BATTERSEA PARK
FULHAM ROAD
KING'S ROAD
WALHAM GREEN
PARSONS GREEN
SANDS END
SW6
HURLINGHAM PARK
SOUTH PARK
SW11
CLAPHAM JUNCTION
CLAPHAM COMMON
SW15
SW18
WANDSWORTH
HAMMERSMITH & FULHAM
KENSINGTON & CHELSEA
BOLINGBROKE HOSP

101
DH
DJ
DK
DL
DM
DN
DP
29
30
31
83
121
102
GREEN PARK
ST. JAMES'S PARK
ST. JAMES'S
SW1
BUCKINGHAM PALACE
WESTMINSTER
VICTORIA
PIMLICO
LISTER HOSPITAL
HOUSES OF PARLIAMENT
ST. THOMAS' HOSP
WATERLOO
WATERLOO INTERNATIONAL
SOUTHWARK
SE1
THE BOROUGH
LAMBETH
LAMBETH PALACE
IMPERIAL WAR MUSEUM
ELEPHANT & CASTLE
SE11
TATE BRITAIN
VAUXHALL
RIVER THAMES
GROSVENOR
NINE ELMS
Battersea Power Station (Disused)
SW8
New Covent Garden Market
THE OVAL (SURREY C.C.C.)
KENNINGTON
KENNINGTON PARK
CAMBERWELL NEW ROAD
SOUTH LAMBETH
BATTERSEA
SW9
STOCKWELL
CLAPHAM
TRINITY HOSPICE
LAMBETH HOSPITAL
BRIXTON
CLAPHAM COMMON
SW4
SE5
SE24
RUSKIN PARK
MYATT'S FIELDS
ST. MARY'S CATHEDRAL
75
76
77
78
79
80
81
82
83
84

102
DQ
DR
DS
DT
DU
DV
DW
33
34
35
84
75
76
77
78
79
80
81
82
83
84
101
122
SOUTHWARK
THE BOROUGH
WAPPING
THE POOL
GUY'S HOSPITAL
LONDON BRIDGE
TOOLEY
ST. THOMAS ST
BERMONDSEY
JAMAICA ROAD
NEWINGTON
ELEPHANT & CASTLE
NEW KENT ROAD
SE1
SE17
WALWORTH
OLD KENT ROAD
SOUTHWARK PARK ROAD
SOUTHWARK PARK
BURGESS PARK
KENNINGTON PARK
CAMBERWELL
CAMBERWELL ROAD
CAMBERWELL NEW ROAD
NORTH PECKHAM ESTATE
PECKHAM
PECKHAM HIGH ST
QUEENS ROAD
SE5
SE15
KING'S COLLEGE HOSPITAL
THE MAUDSLEY HOSPITAL
DENMARK HILL
RUSKIN PARK
COLDHARBOUR LANE
PECKHAM RYE COMMON
PECKHAM RYE PARK
SE22
SE24
EAST DULWICH
NUNHEAD
ROTHERHITHE NEW ROAD

DX
DY
DZ
EA
EB
EC
ED
36
37
38
85
75
76
77
78
79
80
81
82
83
84
104
123
ISLE
OF
DOGS
WEST INDIA DOCKS
MILLWALL
MILLWALL OUTER DOCK
MUDCHUTE PARK
E14
CUBITT TOWN
SE16
SE10
SE8
SE14
SE4
SE13
THE DOME
NORTH GREENWICH
GREENLAND DOCK
SOUTH DOCK
DEPTFORD
PEPYS PARK
DEPTFORD PARK
GREENWICH
GREENWICH PARK
NATIONAL MARITIME MUSEUM
QUEEN'S HOUSE
FLAMSTEED HOUSE (Old Royal Observatory)
BLACKHEATH
NEW CROSS
NEW CROSS GATE
ST JOHN'S
LEWISHAM
HILLY FIELDS
LADYWELL
BROCKLEY
BROCKLEY CEMETERY
LADYWELL CEMETERY
TELEGRAPH HILL PARK
FORDHAM PARK
ISLAND GARDENS
MILLWALL PARK
GREENWICH REACH
TOWER HAMLETS
SOUTHWARK
LEWISHAM
GREENWICH
THE WILDERNESS (DEER PARK)
MANOR HOUSE GARDENS
MANOR PARK

104
EE
EF
EG
EH
EJ
EK
EL
40
41
42
86
E16
LONDON
THE DOME
NORTH GREENWICH
Millennium Pier
SE10
RIVER THAMES
NEWHAM
GREENWICH
WOOLWICH REACH
THAMES FLOOD BARRIER
THAMES BARRIER PARK
SILVERTOWN
LYLE PARK
NORTH WOOLWICH ROAD
A1020
SILVERTOWN & LONDON CITY AIRPORT
THAMESIDE INDUSTRIAL EST
Tate & Lyle Jetty
Barrier Gardens Pier
Barrier Control Building
Greenwich Yacht Club
Manhattan Wharf
Phoenix Wharf
Gas Works
BLACKWALL TUNNEL APPROACH
A102
BLACKWALL LANE
A203
COUNCIL DEPOT
Holiday Inn Express
Cinema
Superstores
THAMES ANCHORAGE POINT IND EST
MERIDIAN TRADING ESTATE
NEW CHARLTON
GREENWICH INDUSTRIAL ESTATE
CABLE TRADE PARK
Stone Lake Retail Pk
WOOLWICH ROAD
A206
MARYON PARK
MARYON WILSON PARK
CHILDRENS ZOO
THE VALLEY CHARLTON ATHLETIC FC
CHARLTON
SE7
CHARLTON PARK
CHARLTON PARK ROAD
B210
Comm Cen
QUEEN ELIZABETH HOSPITAL
RECTORY FIELD
HORNFAIR PARK
SHOOTER'S HILL
A207
SPORTS GROUND
MELLISH IND EST
75
76
77
78
79
80
81
82
83
84
103
EAST GREENWICH PLEASAUNCE
WESTCOMBE PARK
TRAFALGAR ROAD
ROMNEY RD
Uni of Greenwich
NATIONAL MARITIME MUSEUM
GREENWICH
One Tree Hill
GREENWICH PARK
FLAMSTEED HOUSE
The Gardens
THE WILDERNESS (DEER PARK)
RANGER'S HOUSE
Blackheath Gate
MAZE HILL
SE3
BLACKHEATH
SHOOTER'S HILL ROAD
A2
Christ's Coll for Boys
Morden College
KIDBROOKE PARK ROAD
A2213
ROCHESTER WAY RELIEF RD
SPORTS GRDS
KIDBROOKE
KIDBROOKE GREEN (NAT RES)
BLACKHEATH HOSP
BLACKHEATH HALLS
BLACKHEATH PARK
SPORTS GROUNDS
FOOTBALL PITCHES
SE12
SE13
LEE
LEE HIGH ROAD
A20
MANOR HOUSE GARDENS
MANOR PARK
SUTCLIFFE PARK
ELTHAM ROAD
A210
124
UNI OF GREENWICH ATHLETIC GRD
GREENWICH CEMETERY
WESTHORNE AVENUE
ROCHESTER WAY
OLD COLFEIANS
BURNT ASH
LEWISHAM
Leisure Cen
Clubhouse

105
CITY AIRPORT
KING GEORGE V DOCK
EM
EN
EP
EQ
ER
ES
ET
43
44
45
87
Newham Coll of Further Ed
BASIN SOUTH
SE28
Warehouse
Prim Sch
A112
A117
STANDARD INDUSTRIAL ESTATE
NORTH WOOLWICH
ROYAL VICTORIA GDNS
GALLIONS REACH
North East Wharf
Waldair Wharf
North Woolwich Pier
Woolwich Ferry Pier
NEWHAM
GREENWICH
WOOLWICH FOOT TUNNEL
WOOLWICH FREE FERRY
SE. London Aquatic Cen
South Pontoon
Leisure Cen
BROADWATER
A2016
WOOLWICH CROWN CT
H.M. PRISON BELMARSH
WESTERN WAY
EASTERN WAY
Works
75
West Thamesmead Business Park
Southern Outfall Sewer
THAMESMEAD WEST
Firepower
BROADWATER GRN
PETTMAN CRES
HADDEN ROAD
76
Sec Sch
Sports Cen
CHURCH STREET
WOOLWICH HIGH ST
ST MARY'S GDNS
JOHN WILSON ST
BERESFORD ST
A206
PLUMSTEAD ROAD
Greenwich Comm Coll
POLTHORNE EST
WOOLWICH ARSENAL
REC GRD
SE2
79
PLUMSTEAD GARDENS
77
Uni
Health Cen
Fire Sta
Halls of Res
WOOLWICH NEW ROAD
GRAND DEPOT ROAD
ARTILLERY PLACE
Royal Artillery Barracks
WOOLWICH
BARRACK FIELD
Dry Ski Slope
PLUMSTEAD
PLUMSTEAD HIGH STREET
Fire Sta
Leisure Cen
MINI TOWN HALL
78
BOSTALL
WICKHAM LANE
PLUMSTEAD COMMON
Sec Sch
WINN'S COMMON
Youth Club
SE18
WOOLWICH COMMON
A205
CIRCULAR WAY
Rugby Grd
79
A209
Superstore
106
WOOLWICH CEM
ROCK GDNS
WOOLWICH CEMETERY
80
SPORTS GRD
Royal Military Academy
GREEN CHAIN
SHREWSBURY PARK
EAST WICKHAM
ALLOT
77
EAST WICKHAM OPEN SPACE
SHOOTER'S HILL GOLF COURSE
CLOTHWORKERS WOOD
SPORTS GRD
ROYAL HERBERT PAVILIONS
SHOOTER'S HILL
81
ACADEMY ROAD
CASTLEWOOD THERAPY CENTRE
ELTHAM COMMON
MEMORIAL HOSPITAL
A207
HILLVIEW CEMETERY
Woodlands Farm
Nursery
We Anchor in Hope PH
GREENWICH
BEXLEY
82
BELLEGROVE ROAD
Severndroog Castle
Jackwood House
CASTLE WOOD
JACK WOOD
OXLEAS WOOD
OXLEAS MEADOW
ELTHAM COMMON
SHOULDER OF MUTTON GRN
WELLING
DA16
83
Prim Sch
WELLING WAY
A209
FALCONWOOD FIELD
FALCONWOOD
Elec Sta
SHEPHERDLEAS WOOD
ELTHAM PARK NORTH
LONG POND
84
SE9
A2
ROCHESTER WAY RELIEF ROAD
ELTHAM PARK SOUTH
ELTHAM CEMETERY
Crematorium
ELTHAM WARREN GOLF COURSE
125
DA15
EAST ROCHESTER WAY
ELTHAM
Tennis Courts
Environment Curriculum Service
SPORTS GROUND
CON OF MERCY
Clubhouse
BEXLEY ROAD
A210
BLACKFEN

106
EU
EV
EW
EX
EY
EZ
FA
47
48
49
88
75
76
77
78
79
80
81
82
83
84
105
126
SE28
DA18
SE2
SE18
DA16
DA7
DA6
BIRCHMERE PARK
SOUTHMERE PARK
ERITH MARSHES
LAKESIDE CENTRE
SOUTHMERE
WOODLAND WAY
EASTERN WAY
EASTERN IND EST
H.M. PRISON BELMARSH
West Thamesmead Business Park
ABBEY WOOD PARK
THISTLEBROOK INDUSTRIAL EST
ABBEY WOOD
HARROW MANORWAY
KNEE HILL
A2041
LESNES ABBEY (Ruins)
Leather Bottle PH
PLUMSTEAD GARDENS
PLUMSTEAD HIGH STREET
BOSTALL HEATH
BOSTALL HILL
BOSTALL WOODS
WOOLWICH ROAD
A206
WINN'S COMMON
CLAM FIELD RECREATION GROUND
GOLDIE LEIGH HOSPITAL
GREEN CHAIN WALK
HURST ESTATE
WEST HEATH
BELVEDERE SPORTS GRD
ALBERT ROAD ESTATE
WICKHAM LANE
A209
WOOLWICH CEM
WOOLWICH CEMETERY
PLUMSTEAD CEMETERY
EAST WICKHAM
EAST WICKHAM OPEN SPACE
UPPER WICKHAM LANE
STEVENS PARK
BRAMPTON ROAD
BEDONWELL ROAD
LONG LANE
WELLING
WELLING HIGH STREET
WELLING STATION
A207
BELLEGROVE ROAD
PARK VIEW ROAD
CROOK LOG
BROADWAY
BEXLEYHEATH
BEXLEYHEATH STATION
BEXLEYHEATH CEMETERY
Broadway Shop Centre
ARNSBERG WAY
ALBION ROAD
DANSON PARK
DANSON ROAD
A221
The Mansion
Welling United FC
Westbrooke Sch
SPORTS GRD
ROCHESTER WAY
BLACKFEN ROAD
A2

107
FB
FC
FD
FE
FF
FG
FH
50
51
52
89
108
127
75
76
77
78
79
80
81
82
83
84
JENNINGTREE POINT LIGHTHOUSE
RAINHAM MARSHES
Silt Lagoons
Depots
Jetty
Works
BELVEDERE INDUSTRIAL ESTATE
Pier
Depot
EASTERN WY
ANDERSON WAY
MULBERRY
THAMESMEAD SPINE RD
CHURCH MANORWAY INDUSTRIAL ESTATE
CRABTREE MANORWAY IND EST
BRONZE AGE WAY
Erith Oil Works
ERITH REACH
RIVER THAMES
RM13
WENNINGTON MARSHES
FREIGHTMASTER ESTATE
Warehouse
HELIPAD
Coldharbour Point
HAVERING
BEXLEY
THURROCK
ERITH RANDS
DA17
BELVEDERE
FRANK'S PARK
Erith Coll of Technology
PLAYING FIELD
LESSNESS HEATH
ERITH CEMETERY
EUROPA TRADING ESTATE
Superstore
Swim Pool
Landing Stage
Chalk Fm Wharf
A206
A2016
FRASER ROAD
ERITH
QUEEN'S ROAD
Shop Cen
Health Cen
Squash Club
Concrete Works
Sailing Club
The Saltings
DARENT INDUSTRIAL PARK
Crayford
MANOR ROAD
MANFORD IND EST
ANCHOR BAY IND EST
ERITH & DISTRICT HOSP
Prim Sch
MONASTERY
Sports Centre
ERITH REC GRD
ERITH STADIUM
NORTHUMBERLAND HEATH
DA8
THE CHURCH TRADING EST
SLADE GREEN
POWER IND EST
SPORTS GROUND
MOAT
CRAYFORD MARSHES
Howbury Farm
HOWBURY LANE REC GRDS
RAIL DEPOT
The Grange
NORTHEND TRD EST
NORTHEND ROAD
BEXLEY ROAD
BURSTED WOOD
BARNEHURST
BARNEHURST GOLF COURSE
SPORTS GROUND
Chemical Works
THAMES ROAD
Depot & Civic Amenity Site
UNIVERSITY WAY
SWAN BUSINESS PARK
Perry Street Farm
DA1
BAKERS FIELD
MARTENS GROVE PARK
SHENSTONE PARK
BARNES CRAY
CRAYFORD MARSHES
ACORN INDUSTRIAL PARK
WATLING STREET
A207
A220
A2000
LONDON ROAD
CRAYFORD
Victoria Scott Court

108
RAINHAM MARSHES
Silt Lagoons
FJ
FK
FL
FM
FN
FP
FQ
54
55
56
90
107
128
75
76
77
78
79
80
81
82
83
84
WENNINGTON MARSHES
RM13
AVELEY MARSHES
RIFLE RANGES
PURFLEET IND PARK
LONDON ROAD
A1306
A13
PURFLEET
THAMES
ARTERIAL
Bowling Green
Clubhouse
SPORTS GROUND
Fanns Farm
RM15
COV RES
Depot
Mar Dyke
HELIPAD
Jetty
HAVERING
THURROCK
BEXLEY
Crayford Ness
DA8
Prim Sch
TANK HILL ROAD
A1090
PURFLEET
Oil Depot
Oil Storage Tanks
PURFLEET
CHALK PIT
Beacon Hill
RM19
Channel Tunnel Rail Link
Harrisons Wharf
Works
Mill
The Saltings
Sailing Club
DARENT INDUSTRIAL PARK
Pier
FLOOD BARRIER
MANFORD IND EST
DARTFORD SALT MARSHES
DARTFORD
THURROCK
KENT
Chimney
Oil Depot
Longreach Sewage Treatment Works
DA1
CRAYFORD MARSHES
LAMB WAY
SPORTS GRD
MOAT
Howbury Farm
RAIL DEPOT
Littlebrook Power Station
JOYCE GREEN LANE
Joyce Green Farm
MARSH STREET
Chemical Works
River Darent
UNIVERSITY WAY
A206
Tenn Cts
DARTFORD NORTHERN BYPASS
Depot & Civic Amenity Site
West Kent Main Sewer
CEM
DARTFORD FRESH MARSHES
SWAN BUSINESS PARK
MILLSIDE INDUSTRIAL ESTATE
GLAXOWELLCOME
BURNHAM ROAD
A2026
Jolly Farmers PH
BARNES CRAY
CRAYFORD MARSHES
Stanham River
Stanham Farm
REC GRD
VICTORIA INDUSTRIAL PARK
RIVERSIDE IND EST
Holiday Inn Express
CROSSWAYS BUS PARK
Hilton
Junction 1a
TOLL
B2228

109
FR
FS
FT
FU
FV
FW
FX
57
58
59
91
110
129
75
76
77
78
79
80
81
82
83
84
HANGMAN'S WOOD
GARDEN
BRANNETT'S WOOD
LOW WELL WOOD
LOW WELL WOOD
ICKBARN WOOD
COMBE WOOD
Dyke
Stifford Interchange
The Dog & Partridge PH
Police Dog Training
SPORTS GROUND
STIFFORD
Junction 30
Junction 31
Prim Sch
Clinic
A13
ARENA ESSEX RACEWAY
Pav
SPORTS GRD
LAKESIDE COACH PARK
PILGRIMS LANE CARAVAN PARK
PILGRIMS LANE
Thurrock Services
Travelodge
Causeway Bri
SHIP LANE CARAVAN SITE
Purfleet FC & Dartford FC
Mar Dyke Farm
Thurrock Hotel
ARTERIAL A1306 ROAD
WEST THURROCK ARTERIAL ROAD NORTH
Sports Club
Superstore
Travel Inn
Chafford Hundred PH
BUS & COACH STA
Pol
Cinema
Thurrock Lakeside
ALEXANDRA LAKE
Superstores
Tunnel Estate
Clocktower
WESTON AV
Watersport Centre
THURROCK B186 WAY
PO
CHAFFORD HUNDRED
WARREN GORGE
LION GORGE
Health Cen
Oil Depot
PURFLEET
STONEHOUSE LANE
Warehouse
Superstores
WEST THURROCK
Works
WATERGLADE INDUSTRIAL PK
FROGMORE ESTATE
Sewage Works
MOTHERWELL WAY
WEST THURROCK WAY
RM16
SOUTH STIFFORD
MAGNET ESTATE
Prim Sch
CEM
SPORTS GRD
Bowl Grn
Pavs
Fox & Goose
Hall
LYNDALE ESTATE
Formula 1 Hotel
Ibis Hotel
Depot
ELECTRICITY STA
High House
LONDON RD W THURROCK
BYPASS
(Under Construction)
M25
A282
CANTERBURY WAY
LONDON ROAD
A126
REC GRD
GUMLEY ROAD
HEDLEY AVENUE
Elec Sta
LORRY PARK
Warehouse
SPORTS GRD
Ford Distribution Depot
SPORTS GRD
Pavs.
Tenn Cts
WILDLIFE SANCTUARY
OLIVER ROAD
RM20
WEST THURROCK MARSHES
Chemical Works
Electricity Sub Station
Jetty
Oil Depot
Oil Storage Depot
BURNLEY ROAD
Airshafts
Jetties
THURROCK
DARTFORD
QUEEN ELIZABETH II BRIDGE
TUNNEL
ST. CLEMENT'S OR FIDDLER'S REACH
STONENESS LIGHTHOUSE
RIVER THAMES
Pier
Bell Wharf
SWANSCOMBE MARSHES
Offices
Warehouse
Campanile Hotel
CLIPPER BOULEVARD WEST
THAMES EUROPORT
DA2
DA9
DA10
Johnson's Wharf
NEWTONS COURT
CROSSWAYS BOULEVARD
Superstore
Ingress Abbey
Works
STONE CROSSING
ST. MARY'S
Stone
CHARLES STREET
ELIZABETH STREET
HIGH B255 STREET
LONDON ROAD A226
Lib
Clinic
GREENHITHE
Comm Cen
SPORTS GRD
WAKEFIELD RD
CRAYLANDS
The George & Dragon PH
Leisure
ALLOT
Gas

110
FY
FZ
GA
GB
GC
GD
GE
61
62
63
Stifford Interchange
The Dog & Partridge PH
SPORTS GROUND
Pumping Sta
Hogg Lane Roundabout
THURROCK ARTERIAL ROAD NORTH STIFFORD
A13
A1012
75
76
77
78
79
80
81
82
83
84
PILGRIMS LANE
CHAFFORD HUNDRED
WARREN GORGE
LION GORGE
Oil Depot
ELIZABETH ROAD
HOGG LANE
DEVONSHIRE ROAD
Prim Sch
Comm Cen
Health Cen
Gas Works
Amb Sta
Fire Sta
ALLOT
The Sandmartin PH
Acorn PH
ROCK COMMUNITY HOSPITAL
RM16
RM17
GRAYS
Sec Sch
Treetops Sch
TENNYSON AVENUE
LODGE LANE
Sockett's Heath
Little Thurrock
Thurrock R.F.C.
THURROCK ATHLETICS STADIUM
SPEEDWAY
KING GEORGE'S FIELD
Blackshots Leisure Centre
HANGMAN'S WOOD
STANFORD ROAD
A1013
WOODVIEW
CHADWELL ROAD
GRAYS NEW CEMETERY
Orchard Garden Centre
Rookery Hill
SOUTHEND ROAD
PALMERS AV
HIGH VIEW AVENUE
GLOBE IND ESTATES
ORSETT ROAD
CLAREN. RD
EAST THURROCK RD
BROADWAY
DOCK ROAD
MARS. RD
A1089
SOUTH STIFFORD
MAGNET ESTATE
LONDON ROAD
A126
Superstore
CIVIC OFFICES
GRAYS CEM
MUS Thea Lib
Grays Park
Grays Ath. FC
MANOR WAY IND EST
109
Thurrock Yacht Club
Slipway
Grays Beach Riverside Park
The Beach
LITTLE THURROCK MARSHES
Capstan Centre
Finnish Terminal
Grain Terminal
Warehouses
Works
Jetty
Wharf
RIVER THAMES
THURROCK
DARTFORD
NORTHFLEET HOPE
BROADNESS LIGHTHOUSE
Radar Mast
BROADNESS SALT MARSHES
Pylon
Pier
Bell Wharf
SWANSCOMBE MARSHES
DA10
DA11
BOTANY MARSHES
KENT
GRAVESHAM
TILBURY DOCKS
Lock
Mole
Chimney
LOWER ROAD
MANOR WAY
NORTHFLEET INDUSTRIAL ESTATE
RES
LONDON ROAD
A226
GALLEY HILL ROAD
130
STONEBRIDGE ROAD
The George & Dragon PH
EBBSFLEET INDUSTRIAL ESTATE
ROBINS CREEK
Northfleet Hope
Tanks
Leisure Centre
SPORTS GROUND
Fire Sta

GF
GG
GH
GJ
GK
GL
GM
64
65
66
75
76
77
78
79
80
81
82
83
84
ORSETT GOLF COURSE
Orsett Heath
OLD HOUSE WOOD
CHADWELL ST. MARY
GRAVEL PIT
RAINBOW WOOD
ASHEN SHAW
Works
Linford
SS17
Muckingford
Thurrock Technical College
SPORTS GROUND
Sec Sch
TERRELS HEATH
Prim Sch
ST. MARY'S CEM
Whittakers Nursery
The Fox PH
Whitecroft's Farm
Heath Place
Brook Farm
HIGH HOUSE LANE
BRENTWOOD ROAD
BUCKINGHAM HILL ROAD
MUCKINGFORD ROAD
LINFORD ROAD
RIVER VIEW
CHADWELL BYPASS
A126 ROAD
CHADWELL HILL
A128
High House
Mill House Farm
Mill House
Becksland
Ashlea Farm
Walton's Hall
Sutton's Farm
Merie Loots Farm
George & Dragon PH
PORTS GRD
Chadwell Place
Works
Poultry Farm
SHROVE HILL WOOD
Hutts Hill
Hob Hill
Hobhill Farm
Tally Ho Riding School
Broom Hill
Biggin Farm
BIGGIN LANE
SANDY LANE
TURNPIKE LANE
BLUE ANCHOR LANE
Blue Anchor Cottage
Holford Farm
Hall
The Kings Head PH
Manor Farm
RECTORY ROAD
West Tilbury
West Tilbury Hall
Gunhill Farm
GUN HILL
HALLHILL COMMON
COOPERS SHAW ROAD
CHURCH ROAD
Low Street
LOW STREET LANE
STATION ROAD
TILBURY MARSHES
Tilbury FC
ST. CHAD'S ROAD
PARSONAGE COMMON
RM18
WEST TILBURY MARSHES
WALTHAM COMMON
EAST TILBURY MARSHES
Bowaters Farm
KARTING TRACK
KING GEORGE'S FIELD
TILBURY
SPORTS GROUND
ANCHOR FLDS PK
Electricity Station
Works
Electricity Station
CUSTOM HOUSE
DOCK ROAD
FERRY ROAD
A1089
Warehouses
DRY DOCK
Cold Storage
Riverside Rail Terminal
Tidal Basin
Fortress Distribution Park
London International Cruise Terminal
FORT ROAD
MOAT
Tilbury Fort
The Worlds End PH
Sewage Works
Filter Beds
Mercy Creek
Tilbury Energy & Environmental Centre
Chimney
Conveyor Belt
Tilbury B Power Station
Jetty
Pier
RIVER THAMES
131
THURROCK
GRAVESHAM
GRAVESEND REACH
GRAVESEND
Rosherville

AS
AT
AU
AV
AW
AX
AY
92
85
86
87
88
89
90
91
92
93
94
74
73
72
71
98
99
00
GREAT
PARK
REVIEW GROUND
ALBERT ROAD
A308
ROYAL GARDENS
Glasshouses
Clayhall Farm
Battle Bourne
Manor Farm
Ham Bridge
NEW CUT
ISLAND
Filter Beds
Sludge Beds
HAM LANE
Sunnymeads
Sailing Club
HOLLY DRIVE
THE LONG WALK
GROUND
Queen's Cottages
CLAYHALL LANE
MOAT
Tileplace Farm
LANE
MILLERS
PETERSHILL COPSE
Peter's Hill
NEWMEADOWS PLANTATION
Sec Sch
The Oxford Blue PH
CRIMP HILL ROAD
Mount Place
OLD WINDSOR
Hall
The Wheatsheaf PH
Lib
ALLOT
CHURCH
STRAIGHT ROAD
ST. LUKES ROAD
Med. Cen
Prim Sch
Burfield Lodge
BURFIELD
St. George's Farm
Old Windsor Lock
The Manor
The Priory
Priory Stables
FRIARY ISLAND
RIVER THAMES
THE FRIARY
REMENHAM PARK
OLD FERRY DRIVE
Old Ferry House
MANOR FARM ESTATE
WHARF ROAD
OUSELEY
RIVERSIDE
THE EMBANKMENT
WINDSOR ROAD
B376
Prim Sch
POULCOTT
ST. ANDREW'S CL
MOAT
BEAR'S RAILS
RUSH POND
CEM
Woodside Farm
THE GALLOP
PRINCE OF WALES POND
OLD WINDSOR WOOD
SL4
PELLING HILL
B3021
The Bells of Ouseley PH
Beaumont College Farm
War Memorial
Runnymede House
Priest Hill House
PATS CROFT EYOT
MAGNA CARTA LANE
COOPER'S HILL SLOPES NT
MAGNA CARTA ISLAND
WITHY BED
DUKE OF YORK PLANTATION
LIDDELL PLANTATION
OLD COVERT
WILD BOAR ENCLOSURE
SPORTS GROUND
Pav
Tennis Courts
South Lodge Farm
RUNNYMEDE
WINDSOR & MAIDENHEAD
SURREY
Home Farm
Sch
A328
PRIEST HILL
John F Kennedy Memorial
Magna Carta Monument
Benedictine Nunnery (remains)
Priest Hill Farm
COOPER'S HILL SLOPES NT
MARCHIONESS OF HERTFORD PLANTATION
PRINCESS CHRISTIAN PLANTATION
PRINCE CONSORTS PLANTATION
SULTAN PLANTATION
PRINCE OF WALES PLANTATION
QUEEN VICTORIA'S PLANTATION
Spring Hill
GORE PLANTATION
Cookes Hill
Beech Hill
Park Place
Ridgemead House
RIDGEMEAD ROAD
Brunel University, Runnymede Campus
Cooper's Hill Slopes NT
Main Gate Lodges
Bishops Gate
The Dell
Prep Sch
Pumping Sta
COV RES
BISHOPSGATE ROAD
Fox & Hounds PH
Royal Lodge
Chapel Lodge
Bishopsgate House
Dell Park Farm
Round Oak
Castle Hill
CASTLE HILL RD
COOPERS HILL LANE
COOPER'S HILL COPPICE
Air Forces Memorial
SPORTS GROUND
Brunel University (Hall of Residence)
CONSERVATORY COVERT
OX POND
GREENBROOM COVERT
KING GEORGE VI CORONATION GROVE
Chaplain's Lodge
Tennis Courts
COW POND
Savill court Hotel
HAM LANE
ENGLEFIELD GREEN
Castle Hill Farm
Englefield Green
The Barley Mow PH
BARLEY MOW ROAD
RUNNYMEDE PARK
TW20
Runnymede Park
The Vinery
Prim Sch
CUMBERLAND LODGE
Park Close
PROSPECT LANE
NORTHCROFT GDNS
LAUREL AVENUE
WILLSON ROAD
Prim Sch
BARNWAY
ALDERSIDE
THE RETREAT
CHAPEL WOOD
Cumberland Gate
WILDERNESS
Glasshouse
Parkside House
The Sun PH
KINGS LANE
Meadow Cottage Farm
Health Cen
VICTORIA STREET
Hall
Glasshouses
A30
Ripley Springs
THE SAVILL GARDENS
OBELISK RIDE
WINDSOR
SPORTS GROUND
LARCHWOOD
ASHWOOD
ST. JUDE'S CEMETERY
Prim Sch
Sec Sch
CHERRYWOOD AV
ST. JUDE'S ROAD
EGHAM ROAD
University of London Royal Holloway College
Temple Hill
SL5
SMITH'S LAWN
GREAT PARK
ALDER COVERT
FUZZY CLUMP
CORK CLUMP
Prince Consort's Statue
Cumberland Obelisk
OBELISK POND
Parkwood
RHODODENDRON RIDE
FB
MILL POND
SCARLETOAK PLANTATION
Egham Wick
Lubbock House
LONDON ROAD
ST. DAVID'S DR
ROBERTS WAY
BAKEHAM LANE
PRUNE HILL
SPORTS GROUND
FRANK'S PLANTATION
POLO GROUND
Flying Barn
Pav
Breakheart Hill
WEEDEN'S FIELD
JOHNSON'S POND
HEATHER GARDEN
DARKHOLE CLUMP
OXHED
Eton Bridge
Larch Bri
WICK ROAD
132

WRAYSBURY
RESERVOIR
TW19
SL3
Wraysbury
KING
GEORGE VI
RESERVOIR
STAINES
MOOR
Junction 14
Junction 13
Hythe End
RUNNYMEDE NT
RUNNYMEDE PLEASURE GROUND
QUEENSMEAD LAKE
HERON LAKE
RUBBISH DUMP
Pooley Green
EGHAM
Egham Hythe
TW18
Thorpe Lea
STANWELL MOOR
HILLINGDON
AIRPORT
WINDSOR ROAD
BYPASS
THE CAUSEWAY
STAINES BYPASS
LONDON ROAD
CHERTSEY LANE
AZ
BA
BB
BC
BD
BE
BF
93
133
114
01
02
03
74
73
72
71
85
86
87
88
89
90
91
92
93
94

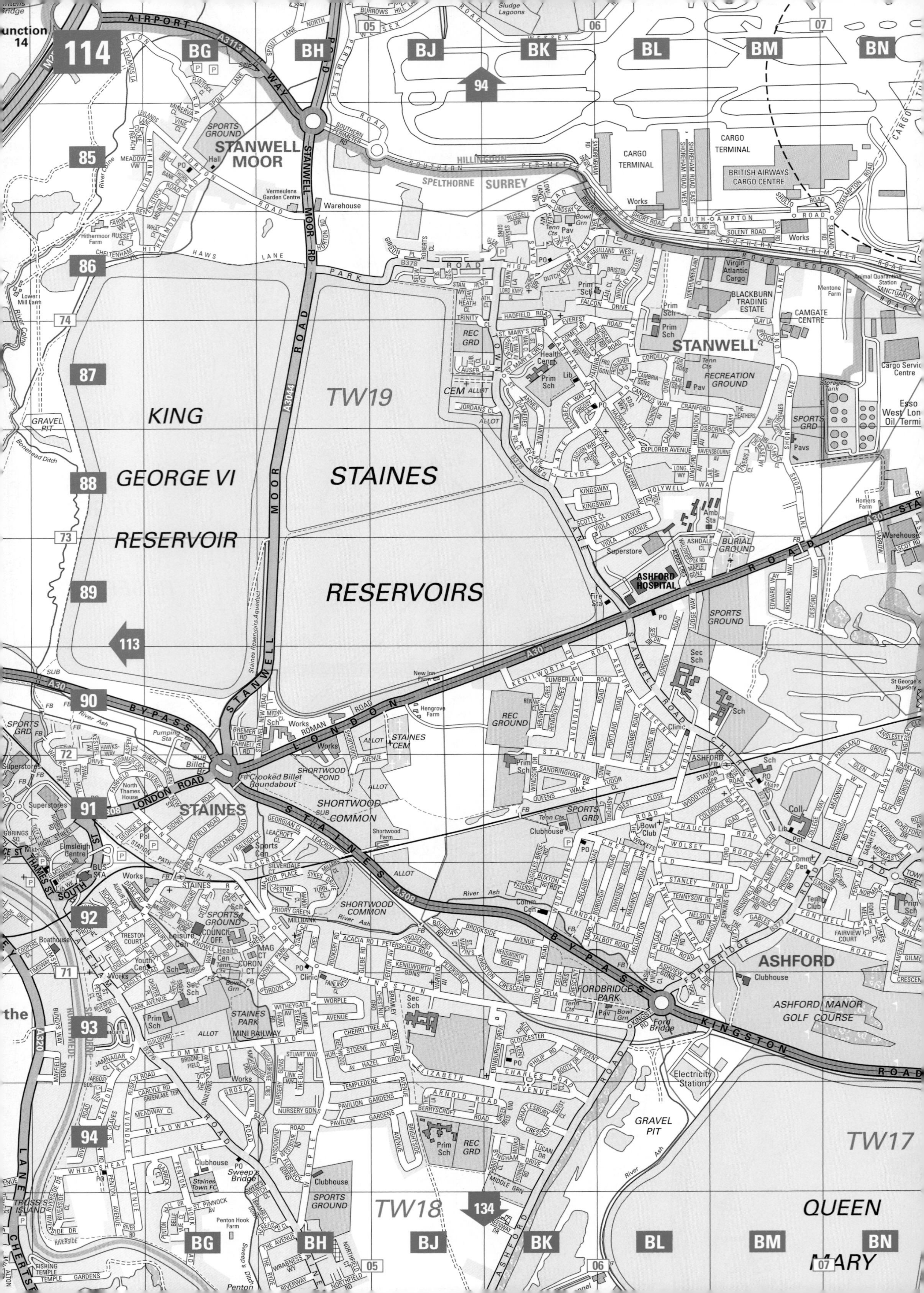
114
Junction 14
AIRPORT WAY
BG
BH
BJ
BK
BL
BM
BN
05
06
07
94
Sludge Lagoons
STANWELL MOOR
SPORTS GROUND
CARGO TERMINAL
BRITISH AIRWAYS CARGO CENTRE
SOUTHERN PERIMETER ROAD
HILLINGDON
SPELTHORNE SURREY
Vermeulens Garden Centre
Warehouse
Works
Hithermoor Farm
HAWS LANE
85
86
87
88
89
90
91
92
93
94
74
73
72
71
Lower Mill Farm
River Colne
GRAVEL PIT
Boneread Ditch
KING GEORGE VI RESERVOIR
STAINES RESERVOIRS
TW19
STANWELL MOOR ROAD
A3044
113
STANWELL
Virgin Atlantic Cargo
BLACKBURN TRADING ESTATE
CAMGATE CENTRE
Mentone Farm
Animal Quarantine Station
Cargo Service Centre
Esso West London Terminal
RECREATION GROUND
SPORTS GRD
Storage Tank
Pavs
Homers Farm
Warehouse
BURIAL GROUND
ASHFORD HOSPITAL
Superstore
SPORTS GROUND
Sec Sch
Clinic
REC GROUND
LONDON ROAD
A30
STAINES BYPASS
STAINES
Crooked Billet Roundabout
SHORTWOOD COMMON
SHORTWOOD POND
STAINES CEM
New Inn Farm
Hengrove Farm
St George's Nursery
SPORTS GRD
River Ash
Elmsleigh Centre
BUS STA
Leisure Cen
STAINES PARK MINI RAILWAY
FORDBRIDGE PARK
Ford Bridge
KINGSTON ROAD
ASHFORD
ASHFORD MANOR GOLF COURSE
Electricity Station
GRAVEL PIT
TW17
TW18
134
QUEEN MARY
Penton Hook Farm
Staines Town FC
Sweep's Bridge
Clubhouse
SPORTS GROUND
CHERTSEY LANE
A320
TRUSS'S ISLAND
the

HATTON
HEATHROW TERMINAL 4
TW6
TW14
TW13
TW15
TW16
EAST BEDFONT
BEDFONT LAKES COUNTRY PARK
H.M. Young Offenders Institution & Remand Centre
LOWER FELTHAM
FELTHAM
FELTHAMHILL
HOUNSLOW HEATH
BEDFONT RECREATION GROUND
HATTON CEM
FELTHAM ARENAS
GLEBELANDS PLAYING FIELDS
BEDFONT LANE REC GRD
GROSVENOR PARK
LAKESIDE SPORTS GROUND
KING GEORGE'S FIELD
ASHFORD COMMON WATER TREATMENT WORKS
KEMPTON PARK
RACECOURSE
SUNBURY
Junction 1
GREAT SOUTH WEST ROAD
STAINES ROAD
HIGH STREET
HARLINGTON ROAD WEST
CHERTSEY ROAD
CADBURY ROAD
STAINES ROAD WEST
DUKE OF NORTHUMBERLAND'S RIVER
Staines Reservoirs Aqueduct
BP BQ BR BS BT BU BV
08 09 10
71 72 73 74
85 86 87 88 89 90 91 92 93 94
95 116 135

116
BW
BX
BY
BZ
CA
CB
CC
TW3
TW4
TW12
TW13
TW14
TW16
12
13
14
96
115
136
85
86
87
88
89
90
91
92
93
94
74
73
72
71
HOUNSLOW
HOUNSLOW HEATH
HOUNSLOW HEATH GOLF COURSE
HOUNSLOW HEATH GOLF COURSE
STAINES ROAD
A315
Metropolitan Police Training Centre
WELLINGTON ROAD SOUTH
HANWORTH ROAD
A314
HOUNSLOW ROAD
HARLINGTON ROAD WEST
HARLINGTON ROAD EAST
UXBRIDGE ROAD
HAMPTON ROAD WEST
A312
GREAT CHERTSEY ROAD
A316
CHERTSEY RD
STAINES RD
TWICKENHAM RD
WHITTON
BOROUGH CEMETERY
HEATHFIELD REC GRD
TWICKENHAM CEMETERY
CRANE PARK
NATURE RESERVE
Crematorium
Recreation Centre
FELTHAM
FELTHAM BUSINESS COMPLEX
HANWORTH PARK
Hanworth Park House
HANWORTH
RECTORY MEADOW
SUNBURY WAY
HANWORTH TRADING ESTATE
HAMPTON FARM IND EST
Apex Retail Park
TWICKENHAM PARK GOLF COURSE
FULWELL PARK
FULWELL GOLF COURSE
Hampton Community Coll
CARLISLE PARK
RESERVOIR
Staines Reservoirs Aqueduct
TWICKENHAM R.F.C. Clubhouse
HALF MOON COVERT
KEMPTON PARK
RACECOURSE
HAMPTON
HYDES FIELD
UPPER SUNBURY ROAD
COUNTRY WAY
PLAYING FIELD
SPORTS GROUND
Feltham R.F.C.
HAMPTON HILL
ST. CLARE BUSINESS PARK
HIGH STREET
A311
A313
A305
B358

117
CD
CE
CF
CG
CH
CJ
CK
MOGDEN WATER TREATMENT WORKS
TW6
TW9
TW1
TW2
TW10
TW11
KT2
ST. MARGARETS
IVYBRIDGE ESTATE
THE RUGBY FOOTBALL UNION TWICKENHAM
Royal Military Sch. of Music
TWICKENHAM TRADING EST
RICHMOND GREEN
RICHMOND
MARBLE HILL
MARBLE HILL HOUSE
MARBLE HILL PARK
RICHMOND UPON THAMES COLLEGE
PETERSHAM MEADOWS
GLOVER'S ISLAND
THAMES
TWICKENHAM
EEL PIE ISLAND
HAM HOUSE (NT)
HAM HOUSE GARDENS
KING GEORGE'S FIELD
PETERSHAM
KING HENRY VIII MOUND
HAM
ST. MICHAEL'S CONVENT
HAM COMMON
THE CASSEL HOSPITAL
STRAWBERRY HILL
STRAWBERRY HILL GOLF COURSE
St. Mary's Uni Coll
Thames Young Mariners Base
Teddington Lock
Teddington Weir
TEDDINGTON CEM
TEDDINGTON
SHELL SPORTS GRD
TROWLOCK ISLAND
NATIONAL PHYSICAL LABORATORY
BUSHY HOUSE
CANAL PLANTATION
ROUND PLANTATION
BUSHY PARK
HALF MOON PLANTATION
OVAL PLANTATION
LEG OF MUTTON POND
HAMPTON WICK
HAMPTON HILL
STEVEN'S EYOT
Kingston Coll
WATERHOUSE WOODLAND GARDEN
97
118
137
85
86
87
88
89
90
91
92
93
94

118
CL
CM
CN
CP
CQ
CR
CS
19
20
21
98
85
86
87
88
89
90
91
92
93
94
117
138
74
73
72
71
RICHMOND
RICHMOND PARK
PETERSHAM
HAM
HAM COMMON
COOMBE
EAST SHEEN
TW1
TW10
SW14
KT2
RICHMOND GREEN
PESTHOUSE COMMON
EAST SHEEN COMMON (NT)
EAST SHEEN CEMETERY
RICHMOND CEMETERY
PALEWELL COMMON
PALEWELL PLAYING FIELDS
THE BANK OF ENGLAND'S SPORTS GROUND
TECK PLANTATION
SHEEN WOOD
ADAM'S POND
The Bog
SHEEN CROSS WOOD
POLO FIELD
CONDUIT WOOD
BISHOP'S PONDS
BARN WOOD POND
SAW PIT PLANTATION
JUBILEE PLANTATION
KIDNEY WOOD
DUCHESS WOOD
WHITE LODGE PLANTATIONS
White Lodge (The Royal Ballet Sch)
SIDMOUTH WOOD
KING HENRY VIII MOUND
QUEEN ELIZABETH'S PLANTATION
LEG OF MUTTON POND
PEN PONDS
DEER PARK
TREEBOX WOOD
KING GEORGE V JUBILEE PLANTATION
SPANKER'S HILL WOOD
LAWN PLANTATION
POND PLANTATION
RICHMOND GOLF COURSE SUDBROOK PARK
The Wilderness
Tercentenary Plantation
MARTIN'S POND
Pond Slade
PRINCE CHARLES'S SPINNEY
HAM CROSS PLANTATION
GIBBET WOOD
ISABELLA PLANTATION
THOMSON'S POND
PEG'S POND
STILL POND
Broomfield Hill
BROOMFIELD HILL PLANTATION
Ham Bottom
Ham Cross
Ham Dip
HIGH WOOD
Deer Fold
Kingston Uni (Dorich House)
Kingston University (Kingston Hill)
Kingston University (Coombehurst)
CORONATION PLANTATION
DANN'S POND
Thatchedhouse Lodge
Ladderstile Gate
GALLOW'S POND
Kings Clump
Dark Hill
COOMBE HILL GOLF COURSE
THE WATERGARDENS
COOMBE WOOD GOLF COURSE
KINGSTON HOSPITAL
RIVER THAMES
PETERSHAM MEADOWS
GLOVER'S ISLAND
TROWLOCK ISLAND
STEVEN'S EYOT
BROOM ROAD REC GRD
UPPER RICHMOND ROAD WEST
UPPER RICHMOND ROAD
SHEEN ROAD
PETERSHAM ROAD
RICHMOND ROAD
KINGSTON HILL
ROBIN HOOD WAY
COOMBE LANE WEST
SAWYER'S HILL
Open During Daylight Hours Only

119
PUTNEY
WANDSWORTH
ROEHAMPTON
ROEHAMPTON GOLF COURSE
ROEHAMPTON PRIORY HOSPITAL
Southlands College
Digby Stuart College
University of Surrey
Froebel College
QUEEN MARY'S UNI HOSP
ROEHAMPTON PLAYING FIELDS
Uni of Greenwich (Downshire House)
Wandsworth Adult Ed Coll
MARYFIELD CONVENT
Uni of Greenwich (Manresa House)
ST.MARY'S CONVENT
SW15
SW18
SW19
SW20
PUTNEY HEATH
Tibbet's Corner
ROYAL HOSPITAL
Uni of Surrey Whitelands Coll
South Thames Coll
EAST PUTNEY
SOUTHFIELDS
WIMBLEDON PARK
ATHLETICS TRACK
GOLF COURSE
ALL ENGLAND LAWN TENNIS & CROQUET CLUB
Kingsfarm Plantation
RICHMOND PARK GOLF COURSE
PUTNEY VALE CEMETERY
Crematorium
Jerry's Hill
WINDMILL MUSEUM
Queen's Mere
King's Mere
Scio Pond
Roehampton Institute of Adult Ed
PARKSIDE CLINIC
PUTNEY VALE
Roehampton Vale Centre
WIMBLEDON
LONDON SCOTTISH GOLF COURSE
BLUEGATE GRAVEL PIT (DISUSED)
HOOKHAMSLADE POND
Queen's Butt (Site off)
Gravelly Hill
COMMON
Farm Bog
Farm Ravine
Caesar's Camp
CANNIZARO PARK
Cannizaro House
RUSHMERE POND
ROYAL WIMBLEDON GOLF COURSE
Fishponds Wood Nature Reserve
Mill Corner
Shadwell Wood
LADY JANE'S WOOD
MUS OF LOCAL HISTORY
King's Coll Sch
WOLFSON MED. REHAB CENTRE
ATKINSON MORLEY'S HOSPITAL
COPSE HILL
OBERON PLAYING FIELD
SPORTS GROUND
DUNDONALD REC GRD
COTTENHAM PARK
MERTON PARK
MERTON
SOUTHFIELDS
Metropolitan Club
KING GEORGE'S PARK
KINGSTON ROAD
WIMBLEDON HILL ROAD
HIGH ST WIMBLEDON
PARKSIDE
WIMBLEDON PARK SIDE
PUTNEY HILL
WEST HILL
UPPER RICHMOND ROAD
KINGSTON BYPASS
A3
A219
A205
A306
A238
CT
CU
CV
CW
CX
CY
CZ
85
86
87
88
89
90
91
92
93
94
99
120
139

WANDSWORTH
SOUTHFIELDS
EARLSFIELD
SUMMERSTOWN
WIMBLEDON PARK
SOUTH WIMBLEDON
UPPER TOOTING
TOOTING GRAVENEY
COLLIER'S WOOD
BALHAM
MERTON
WANDSWORTH COMMON
SW11
SW17
SW18
SW19
H.M. PRISON WANDSWORTH
WANDSWORTH CEMETERY
SPRINGFIELD HOSPITAL
CENTRAL LONDON GOLF CENTRE
STREATHAM CEMETERY
WIMBLEDON STADIUM
WIMBLEDON CEMETERY
LAMBETH CEMETERY
ST. GEORGE'S HOSPITAL
BOLINGBROKE HOSP
KING GEORGE'S PARK
SPENCER PARK
GARRATT PARK
GARRATT GREEN
WANDLE PARK
LONDON ROAD CEMETERY
FIGGE'S MARSH
DA
DB
DC
DD
DE
DF
DG
85
86
87
88
89
90
91
92
93
94
100
119
140

121
DH
DJ
DK
DL
DM
DN
DP
29
30
31
101
141
122
85
86
87
88
89
90
91
92
93
94
74
73
72
71
CLAPHAM COMMON
SW4
CLAPHAM PARK
BRIXTON
SW2
SE24
BROCKWELL PARK
HERNE HILL
STREATHAM HILL
SE21
TULSE HILL
TOOTING BEC COMMON
STREATHAM
SE27
WEST NORWOOD
WEST NORWOOD CEMETERY
STREATHAM PARK
TOOTING GRAVENEY COMMON
STREATHAM COMMON
SW16
NORWOOD GROVE RECREATION GROUND
NORWOOD NEW TOWN
SE19
STREATHAM VALE
NORBURY
NORBURY PARK
BIGGIN WOOD
TRINITY HOSPICE
H.M. PRISON BRIXTON
ST. MICHAEL'S CONVENT
STREATHAM HIGH ROAD
CHRISTCHURCH ROAD
SOUTH CIRCULAR ROAD
POYNDERS ROAD
BRIXTON HILL
TULSE HILL
NORWOOD ROAD
KNIGHTS HILL
CLAPHAM PARK ROAD
BALHAM HILL
CAVENDISH ROAD
BEC ROAD
MITCHAM LANE
STREATHAM COMMON NORTH
CROWN LANE
BEULAH HILL
THURLOW PARK ROAD
DULWICH ROAD
HALF MOON LANE

122
DQ
DR
DS
DT
DU
DV
DW
SE24
SE22
SE21
SE27
SE26
SE19
SE20
HERNE HILL
BROCKWELL PARK
TULSE HILL
DULWICH
EAST DULWICH
WEST DULWICH
WEST NORWOOD
DULWICH PARK
PECKHAM RYE PARK
PECKHAM RYE COMMON
CAMBERWELL OLD CEMETERY
DULWICH & SYDENHAM HILL GOLF COURSE
SYDENHAM HILL WOOD (NATURE RESERVE)
DULWICH WOOD
UPPER SYDENHAM
SYDENHAM
CRYSTAL PALACE PARK
CRYSTAL PALACE ATHLETICS STADIUM
National Sports Cen
NORWOOD
NORWOOD NEW TOWN
UPPER NORWOOD
WEST NORWOOD CEMETERY
NORWOOD PARK
PENGE
ANERLEY
HERNE HILL STADIUM
SOUTH BANK UNIVERSITY SPORTS GROUND
DULWICH PICTURE GALL
KING'S COLL HOSP
HORNIMAN MUS
HORNIMAN GDNS
DAWSON HEIGHTS ESTATE
SYDENHAM HILL ESTATE
WESTOW PARK
BEAULIEU HEIGHTS
SOUTH NORWOOD
ORCHARD
HALF MOON LANE
DULWICH COMMON
LORDSHIP LANE
CROXTED ROAD
THURLOW PARK ROAD
NORWOOD ROAD
WESTWOOD HILL
CRYSTAL PALACE PARADE
BEULAH HILL
CENTRAL HILL
WESTOW HILL
ANERLEY HILL
ANERLEY ROAD
CRYSTAL PALACE PARK ROAD
KIRKDALE
DARTMOUTH ROAD
LONDON ROAD
SYDENHAM HILL
CROWN DALE
KNIGHTS HILL
HERNE HILL
85
86
87
88
89
90
91
92
93
94
121
142
102
33
34
35
71
72
73
74

DX
DY
DZ
EA
EB
EC
ED
123
103
143
124
36
37
38
85
86
87
88
89
90
91
92
93
94
74
73
72
71
LEWISHAM
HILLY FIELDS
BROCKLEY
SE4
LADYWELL CEMETERY
BROCKLEY CEMETERY
LADYWELL
UNIVERSITY LEWISHAM HOSP
LEWISHAM PARK
SE13
MANOR PARK
MANOR HOUSE GARDENS
HITHER GREEN
HONOR OAK SPORTS GRD
CAMBERWELL NEW CEMETERY
HONOR OAK
HONOR OAK PARK
CATFORD GREYHOUND STADIUM
LADYWELL FIELDS
BLYTHE HILL FIELDS
BROCKLEY HILL PARK
SE23
MOUNTFIELD PARK PLAYING FIELDS
BROWNHILL ROAD
A205
S CIRCULAR
CATFORD
CATFORD BRIDGE
TOWN HALL
PRIVATE BANKS SPORTS GRD
FOREST HILL
STANSTEAD ROAD
SOUTH CIRCULAR
SE6
BROMLEY ROAD
A21
BELLINGHAM
BELL GREEN
SPORTS GROUND
FORSTER MEMORIAL PARK
SOUTHEND
SOUTHEND LANE
SOUTHEND PARK
LOWER SYDENHAM
MAYOW PARK
HOME PARK
NATWEST BANK SPORTS GRD
LLOYDS BANK SPORTS GRD
NEW BECKENHAM
BR3
C.G.U. CUACO SPORTS GRD
H.S.B.C. GROUP SPORTS GRD
BECKENHAM PLACE PARK
GOLF COURSE
ASH PLANTATION
SUMMERHOUSE HILL WOOD
LEWISHAM BOROUGH SPORTS GROUND
MIDLAND BANK SPORTS GROUND
WARREN AVE PLAYING FIELDS
BR2
ALEXANDRA REC GRD
CATOR PARK
BECKENHAM
BECKENHAM HILL
BECKENHAM JUNCTION
SHORTLANDS GOLF COURSE
THE SLOANE HOSPITAL
BROMLEY PARK
DOWNHAM
LEWISHAM
BROMLEY

124
EE
EF
EG
EH
EJ
EK
EL
40
41
42
104
85
86
87
88
89
90
91
92
93
94
123
144
73
74
71
72
SE13
SE12
SE6
BR1
BR2
HITHER GREEN
GROVE PARK
MOTTINGHAM
ELTHAM
DOWNHAM
PLAISTOW
SUNDRIDGE
ELMSTEAD
BROMLEY PARK
Widmore Green
HITHER GREEN CEMETERY
Crematorium
NORTHBROOK PARK
MANOR HOUSE GARDENS
MANOR PARK
SUTCLIFFE PARK
OLD COLFEIANS SPORTS GROUND
MIDDLE PARK FIELD
QUEENSCROFT REC GRD
CIVIL SERVICE SPORTS GROUNDS
KING JOHN PLAYING FIELDS
UNI OF WESTMINSTER SPORTS GROUND
MOTTINGHAM SPORTS GROUND
LOWER MARVELS WOOD
MARVELS WOOD
GROVE PARK CEMETERY
CHINBROOK MEADOWS
ELMSTEAD WOOD
SUNDRIDGE PARK GOLF COURSE
Sundridge Park Management Cen
ELMSTEAD WOODS
ROCKPIT WOOD
LOGSHILL WOOD
KING'S MEADOW PLAYING FIELDS
DOWNHAM PLAYING FIELDS
DOWNHAM FIELDS
SHAFTESBURY PARK REC GRD
LEWISHAM BOROUGH SPORTS GROUND
MIDLAND BANK SPORTS GROUND
WARREN AVE PLAYING FIELDS
SHORTLANDS GOLF CO
THE SLOANE HOSPITAL
UNI OF GREENWICH ATHLETIC GRD
FOOTBALL PITCHES
SPORTS GROUNDS
ELTHAM ROAD
SIDCUP ROAD
WESTHORNE AVENUE
S CIRCULAR ROAD
BARING ROAD
BURNT ASH HILL
BURNT ASH LANE
BURNT ASH ROAD
LONDON ROAD
BROMLEY HILL
BROMLEY ROAD
COLLEGE RD
KIDBROOKE PARK
ROCHESTER WAY
A20
A21
A205
A210
A2212
A2213
B226
Quaggy River
Ravensbourne River
LEWISHAM
GREENWICH
BROMLEY

125
EM
EN
EP
EQ
ER
ES
ET
DA16
105
85
86
87
88
89
90
91
92
93
94
126
145
43
44
45
74
73
72
71
ELTHAM PARK SOUTH
ELTHAM WARREN GOLF COURSE
ELTHAM CEMETERY
Crematorium
FALCONWOOD
ROCHESTER WAY RELIEF ROAD
EAST ROCHESTER WAY
BEXLEY ROAD
BLACKFEN ROAD
ELTHAM HIGH ST
Environment Curriculum Service
SPORTS GROUND
AVERY HILL
AVERY HILL PARK
University of Greenwich Avery Hill Campus
Winter Garden
CAMBRIDGE MISSION SPORTS GROUND
CHARLTON ATHLETIC FC TRAINING GRD
FOOTSCRAY PLAYING FIELDS
MILLWALL FC TRAINING GRD
GAELIC ATH. ASSOC. SPORTS GRD
ROYAL BLACKHEATH GOLF COURSE
TARN BIRD SANCTUARY
THE TARN
SE9
FAIRY HILL REC GRD
NEW ELTHAM
St. Olave's Prep. Sch
BLACKFEN
DA15
HOLLY OAK WOOD PK
PARISH WOOD
LAMORBEY
OLD FARM PARK
KING GEORGE'S REC GRD
SIDCUP
DA14
Sidcup Arts Ctr
LONGLANDS
JACK NICKLAUS GOLF CENTRE
FLAMINGO PK SPORTS GRD
LONGLANDS REC GRD
BELMONT LANE OPEN SPACE
Kemnal Manor Stables
DOG RACING TRACK
Beaver's Wood
CHISLEHURST CEMETERY
Hoblands Wood
SIDCUP BYPASS
SIDCUP PLACE
QUEEN MARY'S HOSP
Sch of Nursing & Midwifery
Frognal Corner
CHISLEHURST WEST
Ravensbourne Coll
WHYTES WOODLAND
Bird Sanctuary
BR7
OLD ELTHAMIANS SPORTS GRD
UNIVERSITY COLLEGE LONDON SPORTS GRD
SCADBURY PARK
NATURE RESERVE
LITTLE WOOD
Spring Shaw
Bank's Shaw
BLACK CLUMP
CHISLEHURST
CAMDEN PARK
CHISLEHURST GOLF COURSE
CHISLEHURST COMMON
Perry Street Shaw
Bushy Clump
Icehouse Wood
PARK WOOD
Scadbury Moated Manor House Site
Holbrook Wood
The Larches
Field Study Centre
CHALKPIT WOOD
BANSOME
A208
A20
A210
A211
A222
A2
B2214
B263
B264

EU
EV
EW
EX
EY
EZ
FA
DANSON PARK
DA16
THE LAKE
DA6
BEXLEYHEATH
BEXLEYHEATH GOLF COURSE
BEXLEY
BLACKFEN
DA15
SIDCUP GOLF COURSE
PENHILL PARK
BEXLEY PARK WOOD
RIVERSIDE WALK
LAMORBEY PARK
DA5
GOLDSMITH COLLEGE SPORTS GRD
NORTH CRAY
DA14
FOOTS CRAY MEADOWS
SIDCUP
FOOTS CRAY
SCADBURY PARK
NATURE RESERVE
RUXLEY WOOD
BR5
RUXLEY PARK GOLF COURSE
CRAY VALLEY
106
125
146
47
48
49

127
FB
FC
FD
FE
FF
FG
FH
107
85
86
87
88
89
90
91
92
93
94
128
147
50
51
52
73
74
72
71
CRAYFORD
BARNES CRAY
CRAYFORD MARSHES
DA1
OLD BEXLEY
DARTFORD
DARTFORD HEATH
DARTFORD GOLF COURSE
University of Greenwich
North West Kent College of Technology
HOSPITAL (closed)
Bracton Centre
Coldblow
JOYDEN'S WOOD
Joydens Wood
DA2
Hook Green
ROWHILL WOOD
Rowhill Grange Hotel
THE BIRCHWOOD PARK GOLF COURSE
Hextable
BR8
Swanley Village
HALL PLACE GARDENS
CRAYFORD STADIUM
KENT
DARTFORD
SEVENOAKS
WATLING STREET
LONDON ROAD
DARTFORD ROAD
EAST ROCHESTER WAY
DARTFORD BYPASS
SHEPHERDS LANE
OLD BEXLEY LANE
HOOK GREEN LANE
BROAD LANE
PUDDLEDOCK LANE
COLLEGE ROAD
BARN END LANE

128
CRAYFORD MARSHES
BURNHAM ROAD
SWAN BUSINESS PARK
MILLSIDE INDUSTRIAL ESTATE
FRESH MARSHES
GLAXOWELLCOME
108
VICTORIA INDUSTRIAL PARK
RIVERSIDE IND EST
GlaxoWellcome
VICTORIA ROAD
Junction 1a
BOW ARROW LANE CEM
Indoor Bowls Club
ARCHERY HOUSE
Uni of Greenwich
STONE HOUSE HOSPITAL
CROSSWAYS BUS PARK
DARTFORD
CIVIC CEN
COUNTY CT
Orchards Shop Cen
Priory Shop Centre
WEST HILL
EAST HILL (WATLING STREET)
New Town
EAST HILL CEM
LIVINGSTONE HOSP
THE BRENT
LONDON ROAD
WATLING STREET CEM
North West Kent College of Technology
DARTFORD
CENTRAL PARK
WELLCOME SPORTS GROUND
DA1
PRINCES ROAD
BROOKLANDS LAKE
DARTFORD GOLF COURSE
Leigh City Tech. Coll
University of Greenwich
OAKFIELD PARK
DARTFORD TRADE PARK
GRAVEL PIT
127
DARTFORD BYPASS
Junction 2
DA2
Darenth
Wilmington
Hawley
Hawley Mill
GRAVEL PIT
BR8
ST. JOHN'S JERUSALEM
DEER PARK
THE ALDERS
148
Sutton at Hone
Swanley Village
FJ
FK
FL
FM
FN
FP
FQ
85
86
87
88
89
90
91
92
93
94
54
55
56

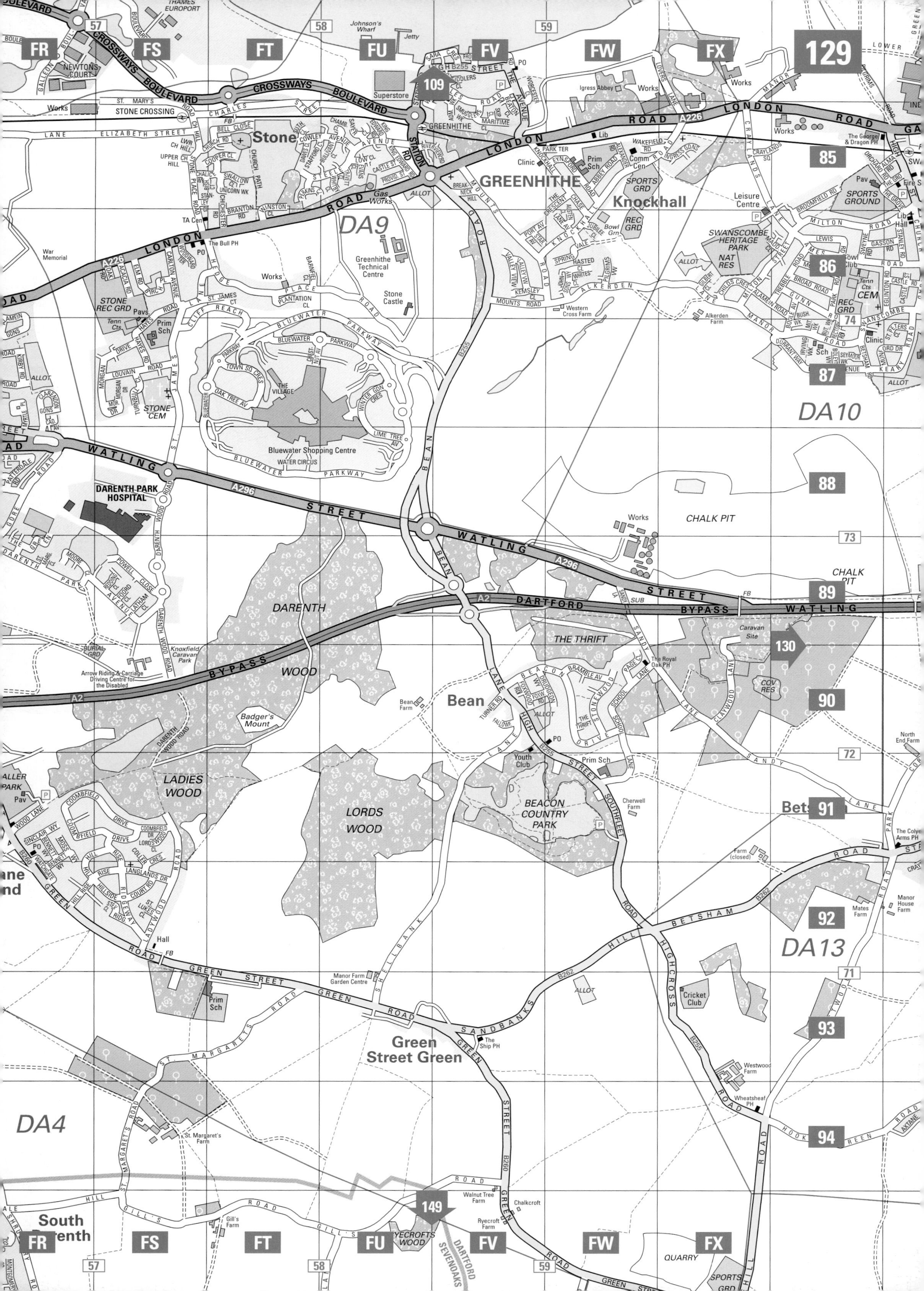

129
FR
FS
FT
FU
FV
FW
FX
57
58
59
109
Stone
GREENHITHE
Knockhall
DA9
DA10
DA13
DA4
85
86
87
88
89
90
91
92
93
94
73
72
71
74
130
149
CROSSWAYS BOULEVARD
STONE CROSSING
LONDON ROAD
A226
WATLING STREET
A296
DARTFORD BYPASS
A2
B255
B260
B262
Bluewater Shopping Centre
BLUEWATER PARKWAY
THE VILLAGE
WATER CIRCUS
Greenhithe Technical Centre
Stone Castle
STONE REC GRD
STONE CEM
DARENTH PARK HOSPITAL
DARENTH WOOD
LADIES WOOD
LORDS WOOD
Badger's Mount
Bean
Bean Farm
THE THRIFT
BEACON COUNTRY PARK
Youth Club
Prim Sch
Caravan Site
COV RES
CHALK PIT
Works
SWANSCOMBE HERITAGE PARK
NAT RES
SPORTS GROUND
SPORTS GRD
REC GRD
Leisure Centre
Clinic
Comm Cen
Bowl Grn
Igress Abbey
Superstore
Johnson's Wharf
Jetty
THAMES EUROPORT
NEWTONS COURT
War Memorial
The Bull PH
Knoxfield Caravan Park
Arrow Riding & Carriage Driving Centre for the Disabled
BURIAL GRD
Western Cross Farm
Alkerden Farm
The Royal Oak PH
Cherwell Farm
North End Farm
The Colyer Arms PH
Farm (closed)
Mates Farm
Manor House Farm
Cricket Club
Westwood Farm
Wheatsheaf PH
Manor Farm Garden Centre
The Ship PH
Green Street Green
St. Margaret's Farm
Walnut Tree Farm
Chalkcroft
Ryecroft Farm
Gill's Farm
YECROFTS WOOD
South Darenth
QUARRY
DARTFORD
SEVENOAKS
The George & Dragon PH
ALLOT
Hall
HIGHCROSS
SANDBANKS
BETSHAM

130
MARSHES
61
62
63
TILBURY DOCKS
FY
FZ
GA
GB
GC
GD
GE
110
85
86
87
88
89
90
91
92
93
94
74
73
72
71
129
LONDON ROAD
A226
GALLEY HILL ROAD
NORTHFLEET INDUSTRIAL ESTATE
EBBSFLEET INDUSTRIAL ESTATE
RIFLE RANGE
SPORTS GROUND
SWANSCOMBE
SWANSCOMBE HERITAGE PARK
Leisure Centre
nockhall
STONEBRIDGE ROAD
HIGH STREET
THE HILL
NORTHFLEET
BLUE CIRCLE SPORTS GRD
Channel Tunnel Rail Link (Under Construction)
SOUTHFLEET ROAD
B259
DA10
DA11
DA2
DA13
Filter Beds
Sewage Works
NORTHFLEET URBAN COUNTRY PARK
SPRINGHEAD ENTERPRISE PARK
THAMES WAY
A2260
Perry Street
SPRINGFIELD REC GRD
NORTHFLEET CEMETRY
WOMBWELL PARK
Superstore
Springhead Nurseries
Electricity Sub Station
CHALK PIT
WATLING STREET
BYPASS
A2
RECYCLING CENTRE
PARK CORNER ROAD
FOXHOUNDS LANE
STATION ROAD
B262
North End Farm
Betsham
The Colyer Arms PH
Cherwell Farm
Mates Farm
Manor House Farm
HIGHCROSS ROAD
B255
Cricket Club
Westwood Farm
Wheatsheaf PH
WESTWOOD
DALE ROAD
BARN END
DARTFORD
GRAVESHAM
Scadbury Manor
Northfleet Green
Northfleet Green Farm
Southfleet
The Ship Inn PH
Court Lodge Farm
Chapter Farm
Manor Farm
Black Lion PH
Redstreet
MADAM WOOD
Hook Green
Hook Green Farm
Hook Place Farm
BANBURY VILLAS
Brakefield House
HOOK GREEN ROAD
DOWNS ROAD
Istead Rise
COURT WOOD
QUARRY
Works
Jetty
Wharf
Pier
Northfleet Hope
Water Tower
Mill
Tanks
Chimneys

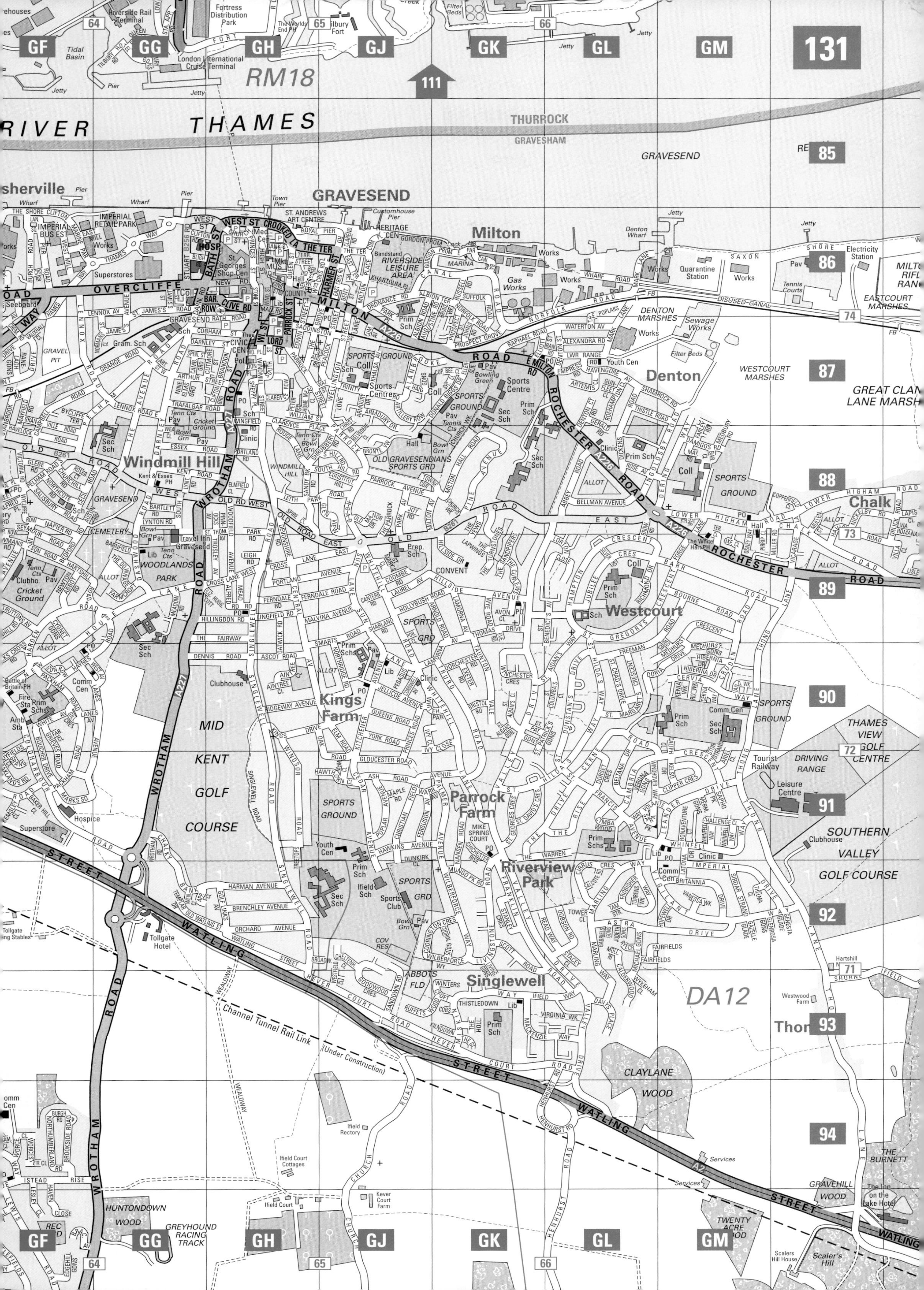

131
GF
GG
GH
GJ
GK
GL
GM
64
65
66
111
RM18
RIVER THAMES
THURROCK
GRAVESHAM
GRAVESEND
85
86
87
88
89
90
91
92
93
94
Tidal Basin
Riverside Rail Terminal
Fortress Distribution Park
Tilbury Fort
London International Cruise Terminal
Gravesend
Milton
Denton
Denton Marshes
Westcourt Marshes
Eastcourt Marshes
Great Clane Lane Marsh
Chalk
Windmill Hill
Westcourt
Kings Farm
Parrock Farm
Riverview Park
Singlewell
Thong
Woodlands Park
Mid Kent Golf Course
Thames View Golf Centre
Driving Range
Southern Valley Golf Course
Claylane Wood
Gravehill Wood
Twenty Acre Wood
Huntondown Wood
Greyhound Racing Track
Scaler's Hill
The Burnett
Riverside Leisure Area
Old Gravesendians Sports Grd
Imperial Retail Park
Imperial Bus Est
Channel Tunnel Rail Link (Under Construction)
Overcliffe
Milton Road
Rochester Road
Old Road West
Old Road East
Wrotham Road
Watling Street
Singlewell Road
Higham Road
A2
A226
A227
B261
71
72
73
74
DA12

132
AS
AT
AU
AV
AW
AX
AY
Egham Wick
112
95
96
97
98
99
100
101
102
103
104
POLO GROUND
VIRGINIA WATER
BLACKNEST ROAD
LONDON ROAD
A30
A329
SL5
GU25
GU24
BELVEDERE WOOD
WENTWORTH
Wentworth
GOLF COURSE
VIRGINIA WATER
CHRISTCHURCH ROAD
WELLINGTON AVENUE
KING GEORGE V PLAYING FIELD
Royal Holloway College
The American Comm Sch
THE VALLEY GARDENS
VIRGINIA WATER PLANTATION
WICK POND
Clubhouse
LONGCROSS
Defence Science & Technology Laboratory
Longcross
M3
CHOBHAM LANE
MILITARY GOLF COURSE
CHERTSEY COMMON
BARROWHILLS
CHOBHAM COMMON NATIONAL NATURE RESERVE
150
The Klondyke Piggeries
KNOWLE GROVE
GREAT WOOD
BEECH WOOD
Knowle Hill
CHERTSEY ROAD
B386
B383
B389
Little Arm
Ship Hill
Long Arm
Oystershell Hill
Rushy Pond
Burnt Hill
Flutters Hill
BOG WOOD
DICKEN'S WOOD
BLUEBELLE WOOD
Trumps Farm
Fairview Farm
Hersham Farm
Grangewood
Lily Pond Farm
Glasshouse
Longcross House
Works

133
TW18
TW20
Thorpe
Stroude
Thorpe Green
Lyne
KT16
KT15
CHERTSEY
ADDLESTONE MOOR
THORPE PARK
Junction 2 (M3), Junction 12 (M25)
Junction 11
113
134
151

BG
BH
BJ
BK
BL
BM
BN
05
06
07
114
QUEEN
MARY
RESERVOIR
TW18
95
96
97
98
99
100
101
102
103
104
69
68
67
66
133
LALEHAM
PENTON HOOK ISLAND
PENTON HOOK
PENTON HOOK MARINA
MANOR LAKE
Abbey Lake
LALEHAM GOLF COURSE
LALEHAM BURWAY
RESERVOIR
Water Works
LALEHAM PARK
LALEHAM PARK SPORTS GROUND
ROUND COPSE
Shepperton Studios
KT16
M3
CHERTSEY
Chertsey Lock
Dumsey Eyot
RECREATION GROUND
CHERTSEY MEADS
Dockett Eddy
PHARAOH'S ISLAND
HAMHAUGH ISLAND
ADDLESTONE MOOR
ADDLESTONE CEMETERY
ABBEY MOOR GOLF COURSE
KT15
WOBURN PARK
St. George's College
M25
Junction 11
152
ADDLESTONE
WEYBRIDGE TRADING ESTATE
WEYBRIDGE BUSINESS PARK
Weybridge Lock
A317
A318
A320
B375
B376
CHERTSEY ROAD
STAINES ROAD
SHEPPERTON ROAD
LALEHAM ROAD
WOBURN HILL
WEYBRIDGE ROAD
ST. PETER'S WAY
EASTWORTH ROAD
CHERTSEY BRIDGE ROAD
THAMES SIDE

BP
BQ
BR
BS
BT
BU
BV
115
Junction 1
ASHFORD COMMON
WATER TREATMENT
WORKS
DOLPHIN EST
TRADING ESTATE
M3
A308
STAINES ROAD WEST
95
96
97
98
99
100
101
102
103
104
136
153
LITTLETON
TW17
TW16
SUNBURY
SUNBURY PARK
KT12
KT13
UPPER HALLIFORD
HAZELWOOD GOLF COURSE
SUNBURY GOLF COURSE
DRIVING RANGE
SUNBURY CEM
LONDON IRISH RUGBY GROUND
GAFLAC SPORTS GROUND
CEDARS REC GRD
SHEPPERTON BUSINESS PARK
LONGWOOD BUSINESS PARK
SHEPPERTON
Shepperton Moat House
Shepperton Marina
BISHOP DUPPA'S REC GRD
LAS PALMAS ESTATE
DESBOROUGH ISLAND
D'OYLY CARTE ISLAND
THAMES MEADOW
COWAY SALE
Bridge Marina
RIVER ASH EST
Sunbury Locks
SUNBURY LOCK AIT
WHEATLEY'S AIT
GRAVEL PIT
APPLE COURT GREEN
ELM GROVE REC GRD
GEORGE FROUDE PK
WALTON-ON THAMES
WALTON & HERSHAM FC
ASHLEY PARK
BROAD WATER
PLAYING FIELDS
Oatlands Park Hotel
OATLANDS PARK
RYDENS
08
09
10
66
67
68
69

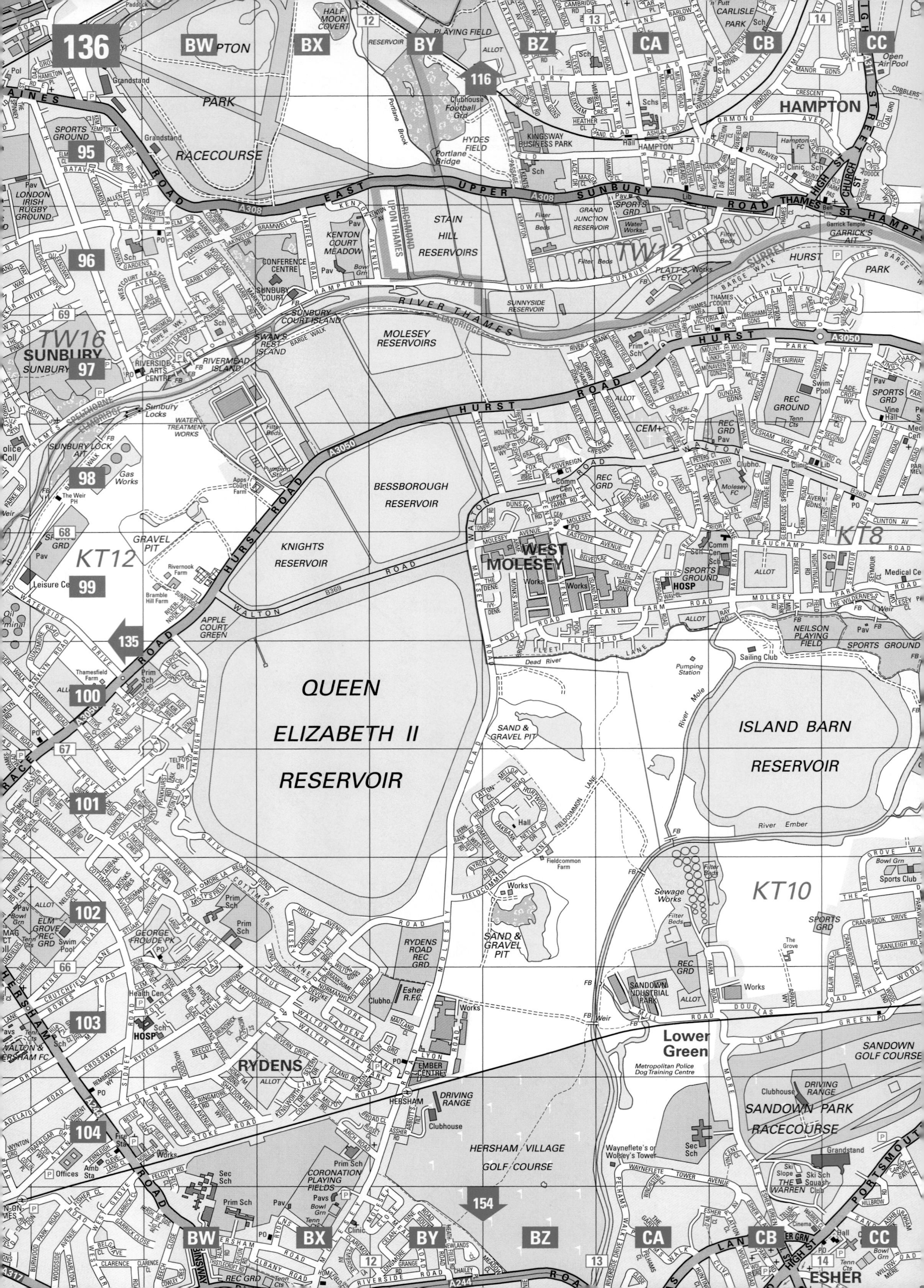

BW
BX
BY
BZ
CA
CB
CC
116
HALF MOON COVERT
PLAYING FIELD
RESERVOIR
Portlane Brook
Clubhouse Football Grd
HYDES FIELD
Portlane Bridge
KINGSWAY BUSINESS PARK
CARLISLE PARK
Open Air Pool
HAMPTON
Hampton FC
Clinic
Garrick Temple
GARRICK'S AIT
PARK
RACECOURSE
Grandstand
SPORTS GROUND
95
LONDON IRISH RUGBY GROUND
96
97
98
99
100
101
102
103
104
69
68
67
66
TW16
SUNBURY
TW12
KT12
KT8
KT10
EAST UPPER SUNBURY ROAD
A308
UPPER THAMES
RICHMOND
STAIN HILL RESERVOIRS
GRAND JUNCTION RESERVOIR
Filter Beds
KENTON COURT MEADOW
CONFERENCE CENTRE
SUNBURY COURT
SUNBURY COURT ISLAND
RIVER THAMES
SURREY
ELMBRIDGE
SPELTHORNE
PLATT'S EYOT
HURST PARK
SUNNYSIDE RESERVOIR
MOLESEY RESERVOIRS
SWAN'S REST ISLAND
RIVERMEAD ISLAND
RIVERSIDE ARTS CENTRE
Sunbury Locks
SUNBURY LOCK AIT
WATER TREATMENT WORKS
Gas Works
Pumping Stn
Apps Court Farm
HURST ROAD
A3050
BESSBOROUGH RESERVOIR
KNIGHTS RESERVOIR
GRAVEL PIT
Rivernook Farm
Bramble Hill Farm
APPLE COURT GREEN
WALTON ROAD
B369
135
Thamesfield Farm
Leisure Cen
The Weir PH
REC GROUND
SPORTS GRD
CEM
REC GRD
Molesey FC
WEST MOLESEY
SPORTS GROUND
HOSP
ALLOT
NEILSON PLAYING FIELD
SPORTS GROUND
Sailing Club
Dead River
Pumping Station
River Mole
QUEEN ELIZABETH II RESERVOIR
SAND & GRAVEL PIT
ISLAND BARN RESERVOIR
River Ember
Fieldcommon Farm
Sewage Works
Filter Beds
SPORTS GRD
The Grove
REC GRD
SANDOWN INDUSTRIAL PARK
Works
Weir
Lower Green
Metropolitan Police Dog Training Centre
SANDOWN GOLF COURSE
DRIVING RANGE
Clubhouse
SANDOWN PARK RACECOURSE
Grandstand
Ski Slope
Ski Sch
Squash Club
THE WARREN
GEORGE FROUDE PK
ELM GROVE REC GRD
Swim Pool
Health Cen
WALTON & HERSHAM FC
RYDENS
RYDENS ROAD REC GRD
Esher R.F.C.
EMBER CENTRE
HERSHAM
DRIVING RANGE
Clubhouse
HERSHAM VILLAGE GOLF COURSE
CORONATION PLAYING FIELDS
Wayneflete's or Wolsey's Tower
Sec Sch
Prim Sch
154
A244
A317
12
13
14
ESHER

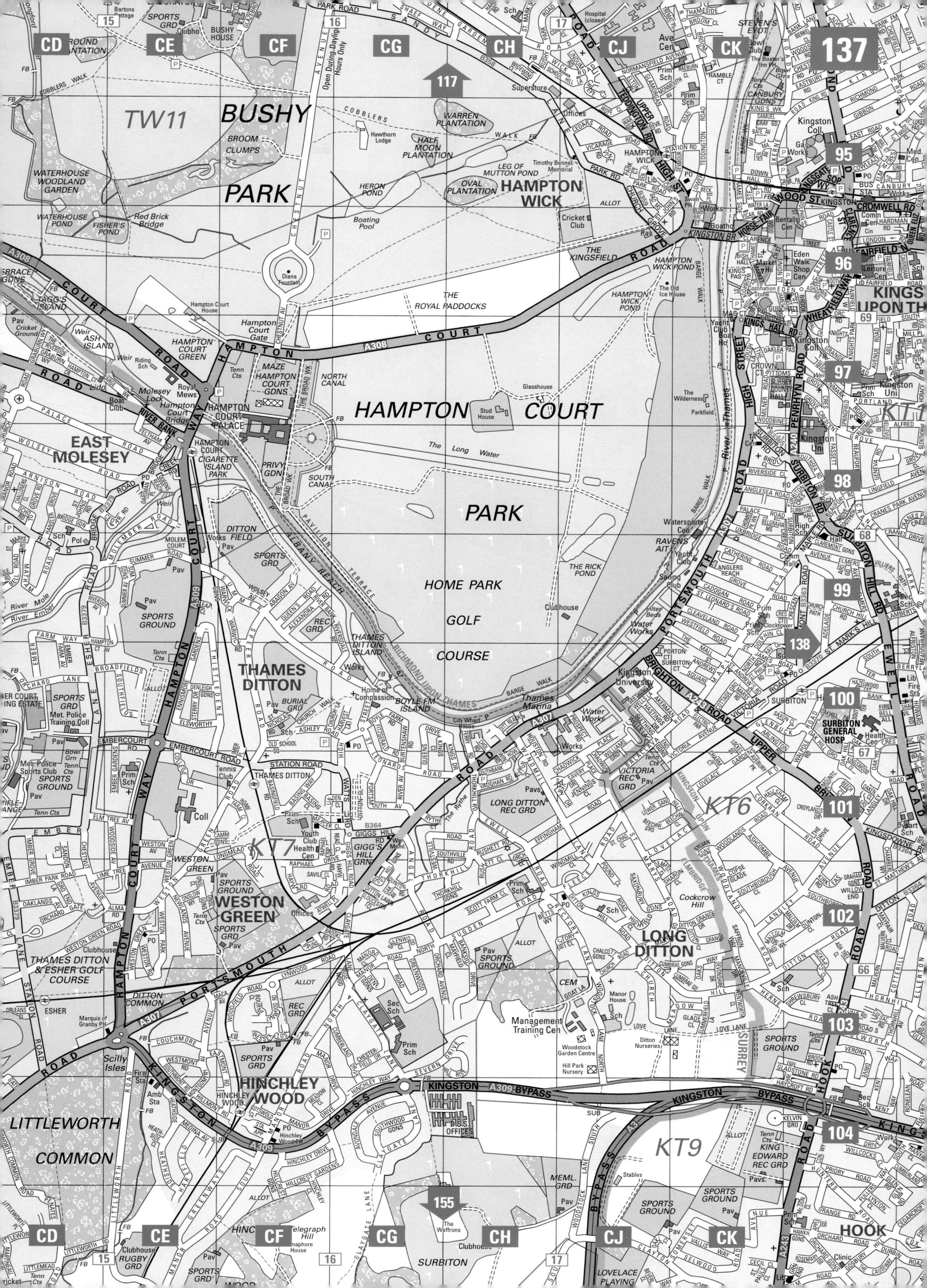
CD
CE
CF
CG
CH
CJ
CK
15
16
17
117
TW11
BUSHY
PARK
BROOM CLUMPS
WATERHOUSE WOODLAND GARDEN
WATERHOUSE POND
FISHER'S POND
Red Brick Bridge
COBBLERS WALK
CHESTNUT AVENUE
Open During Daylight Hours Only
WARREN PLANTATION
HALF MOON PLANTATION
Hawthorn Lodge
HERON POND
LEG OF MUTTON POND
OVAL PLANTATION
Boating Pool
Diana Fountain
HAMPTON WICK
Timothy Bennet Memorial
Superstore
Offices
Cricket Club
THE KINGSFIELD
HAMPTON WICK POND
The Old Ice House
THE ROYAL PADDOCKS
KINGSTON BR
HORSE FAIR
WOOD ST
CROMWELL RD
KINGSTON UPON THAMES
Kingston Coll
95
96
97
98
99
100
101
102
103
104
138
Eden Walk Shop Cen
Bentalls Cen
HIGH ST
UPPER TEDDINGTON RD
TEDDINGTON ROAD
A308
COURT
HAMPTON COURT ROAD
Hampton Court House
Hampton Court Gate
HAMPTON COURT GREEN
TAGG'S ISLAND
ASH ISLAND
Weir
Molesey Lock
Hampton Court Bridge
Royal Mews
MAZE
HAMPTON COURT GDNS
NORTH CANAL
THE BROAD WK
HAMPTON COURT PALACE
HAMPTON
COURT
Stud House
Glasshouse
The Long Water
PRIVY GDN
SOUTH CANAL
PARK
HOME PARK
GOLF
COURSE
THE RICK POND
Clubhouse
The Wilderness
Parkfield
River Thames
BARGE WALK
Watersports Cen
RAVENS AIT
Yacht Club
Sailing Club
Filter Beds
Water Works
PORTSMOUTH ROAD
A307
EAST MOLESEY
RIVER BANK
PALACE
WOLSEY
CIGARETTE ISLAND PARK
DITTON FIELD
SPORTS GRD
SPORTS GROUND
River Mole
River Ember
ALBANY REACH
PAVILION TERRACE
THAMES DITTON ISLAND
RICHMOND UPON THAMES
BOYLE FM ISLAND
Home of Compassion
Thames Marina
City Wharf House
Kingston University
BRIGHTON ROAD
A243
VICTORIA REC GRD
Water Works
HAMPTON COURT WAY
A309
THAMES DITTON
BURIAL GRD
THAMES DITTON
EMBERCOURT ROAD
STATION ROAD
Met. Police Training Coll
Met. Police Sports Club
SPORTS GROUND
Coll
Prim Sch
KT7
GIGG'S HILL GRN
Youth Club
Health Cen
WESTON GREEN
LONG DITTON REC GRD
KT6
Cockcrow Hill
LONG DITTON
SURBITON
SURBITON GENERAL HOSP
SURREY
THAMES DITTON & ESHER GOLF COURSE
DITTON COMMON
ESHER
Marquis of Granby PH
Scilly Isles
LITTLEWORTH COMMON
HINCHLEY WOOD
KINGSTON BYPASS
A309
D.S.S. OFFICES
Management Training Cen
Woodstock Garden Centre
Hill Park Nursery
Ditton Nurseries
KT9
MEML. GRD
SPORTS GROUND
Stables
KING EDWARD REC GRD
HOOK
155
The Waffrons
Telegraph Hill
RUGBY GRD
SURBITON
LOVELACE PLAYING

138
CL
CM
CN
CP
CQ
CR
CS
19
20
21
118
COOMBE
COOMBE WOOD GOLF COURSE
KT2
KINGSTON HOSPITAL
Kingston Coll
95
96
97
98
99
100
101
102
103
104
69
68
67
66
137
156
NORBITON
KINGSTON UPON THAMES
KINGSTON CEMETERY
KT1
Crematorium
NEW MALDEN
KT8
River Thames
HAMPTON WICK POND
The Old Ice House
The Wilderness
Parkfield
SURBITON CEMETERY
Sewage Works
Filter Beds
BERRYLANDS
GREEN LANE REC GRD
HOGSMILL PUBLIC OPEN SPACE
KT3
KT5
SURBITON GENERAL HOSP
SURBITON
FISHPONDS OPEN SPACE
KT6
ALEXANDRA REC GRD
HOGSMILL OPEN SPACE
OLD MALDEN
MAORI SPORTS GROUND
TOLWORTH HOSPITAL
TOLWORTH
Cockcrow Hill
LONG DITTON
KINGSTON UNIVERSITY SPORTS GRD
RIVERHILL SPORTS GRD
Surbiton Raceway
WANDGAS ATHLETIC GROUND
KING GEORGES FIELD
KING EDWARD REC GRD
KT9
HOOK
KING GEORGE'S TRADING EST
KING GEORGE'S FIELD AURIOL PARK
Tolworth Ct Farm
Tolworth Court Bridge
SURREY
KINGSTON BYPASS
A3
A308
A238
A240
A243
A2043
COOMBE LANE WEST
CAMBRIDGE ROAD
KINGSTON ROAD
LONDON ROAD
EWELL ROAD
HOOK ROAD
PORTSMOUTH ROAD
MALDEN WAY
BRIGHTON ROAD
UPPER BRIGHTON ROAD
PENRHYN ROAD
HIGH STREET
RICHMOND ROAD

139
CT
CU
CV
CW
CX
CY
CZ
22
23
24
119
157
140
95
96
97
98
99
100
101
102
103
104
69
68
67
66
WOLFSON MED. REHAB CENTRE
COPSE HILL
ATKINSON MORLEY'S HOSPITAL
SW20
OBERON PLAYING FIELD
COTTENHAM PARK
COTTENHAM PK REC GRD
DUNDONALD REC GRD
MERTON
NELSON HOSP
WIMBLEDON CHASE
JOHN INNES REC GRD
MERTON PARK
SW19
PLAYING FIELDS
GOLF COURSE
SPORTS GROUND
RAYNES PARK SPORTS GRD
RAYNES PARK
KINGSTON BYPASS
COOMBE LANE
KINGSTON ROAD
BUSHEY ROAD
WORPLE ROAD
PRINCE GEORGE'S PLAYING FIELD
The David Lloyd Club
JOSEPH HOOD RECREATION GROUND
MESSINES PLAYING FLD
BUSHEY MEAD
CANNON HILL COMMON
SOUTH MERTON
MORDEN
MOSTYN GARDENS
BEVERLEY PARK
KINGSTON UPON THAMES
MERTON
Wyvern Estate
WEST BARNES
MOTSPUR PARK
RAYNES PARK PLAYING FIELDS
MORDEN PLAYING FIELDS
MORDEN PARK
MORDEN PARK SPORTS GROUND
Merton Coll
MORDEN SOUTH
UNIVERSITY OF LONDON ATHLETIC GROUND
B.B.C. SPORTS GRD
OLD BLUES R.F.C.
THE SIR JOSEPH HOOD MEMORIAL PLAYING FIELDS
Crematorium
MORDEN CEMETERY
MERTON & SUTTON JOINT CEMETERY
KING GEORGE'S FIELD
SM4
MANOR PARK REC GRD
Sewage Treatment Works
GARTH ROAD IND CEN
ST. ANTHONY'S HOSP
St. Raphael's Hospice
MALDEN GRN
WORCESTER PARK
SHADBOLT PK
SM3
SUTTON CEMETERY
KIMPTON TRADE BUSINESS CENTRE
REIGATE AVENUE REC GRD
ST HELIER
EPSOM ROAD
STONECOT HILL
LONDON ROAD
CENTRAL ROAD
CHEAM COMMON ROAD
MALDEN ROAD
KT4
CUDDINGTON REC GRD
EPSOM & EWELL
SUTTON
NORTH CHEAM
Oldfields Trading Est
SM1
COLLINGWOOD PARK
Sutton Utd. FC
A3
A24
A217
A238
A298
A2043
B279
B282
B286

140
DA
DB
DC
DD
DE
DF
DG
26
27
28
SOUTH WIMBLEDON
COLLIER'S WOOD
120
MERTON
NELSON HOSP
MERTON PARK
SW19
MORDEN
MORDEN HALL PARK
MITCHAM
CR4
MORDEN PARK SPORTS GROUND
139
SM4
ST. HELIER
SM5
ROSEHILL
SM3
SUTTON CEMETERY
BENHILTON
THE WRYTHE
SM1
158
95
96
97
98
99
100
101
102
103
104
66
67
68
69
DUNDONALD REC GRD
JOHN INNES REC GRD
ABBEY REC GRD
NURSERY ROAD PLAYING FIELDS
MERTON INDUSTRIAL PARK
LOMBARD BUSINESS PARK
LONDON ROAD CEMETERY
FIGGE'S MARSH
GREENLEA PARK
ROCK TERRACE REC GRD
BURIAL GROUND
RAVENSBURY PARK
MORDEN PLAYING FIELDS
MORDEN REC GRD
MITCHAM GOLF COURSE
MITCHAM JUNCTION
GRACE BUSINESS CENTRE
ABBEY IND EST
WATERMEADS NT
POULTER PARK
SPORTS GROUND
THOMAS WALL PARK
CARSHALTON SPORTS ARENA
ST. HELIER OPEN SPACE
ROSEHILL PARK EAST
GREENSHAW WOOD
ROSEHILL RECREATION GROUND
ST. HELIER HOSP
QUEEN MARY'S HOSP FOR CHILDREN
REIGATE AVENUE REC GRD
ROYSTON PARK
THE WRYTHE REC GRD
DALE PARK
WILDERNESS ISLAND
FELNEX TRADING ESTATE
COLLINGWOOD PARK
LIMES GRN
MILL GREEN
CARSHALTON
A24
A217
A236
A237
A238
A239
A297
MORDEN ROAD
LONDON ROAD
ST. HELIER AVENUE
BISHOPSFORD ROAD
REIGATE AVENUE
CENTRAL ROAD
EPSOM ROAD
OLDFIELDS ROAD
WESTERN ROAD
MERANTUN WAY
HIGH STREET
KINGSTON ROAD
CARSHALTON ROAD

141
DH
DJ
DK
DL
DM
DN
DP
29
30
31
121
159
STREATHAM VALE
NORBURY
NORBURY PARK
SE19
SW16
CR7
CR0
SM6
MITCHAM
COMMON
STREATHAM PARK CEMETERY
NATIONAL WESTMINSTER BANK SPORTS GROUND
GREEN LANE SPORTS GROUND
POLLARDS HILL
SHERWOOD PK
THORNTON HEATH
CROYDON CEMETERY
MAYDAY HOSPITAL
BROAD GREEN
QUEEN'S ROAD CEMETERY
THORNTON ROAD RETAIL PK
HACKBRIDGE
BEDDINGTON
BEDDINGTON PARK
THE GRANGE GARDENS
WADDON
WANDLE PARK
CROYDON SUB STATION
MILL LANE TRADING ESTATE
PROGRESS BUSINESS PK
BEDDINGTON TRADING PARK WEST
PIONEERS INDUSTRIAL PARK
AMPERE WAY
WADDON MARSH
RESERVOIR
Sewage Works
RIFLE RANGE
PLAYING FIELDS
PLAYING FIELD
MERTON
SUTTON
CROYDON
LONDON ROAD
MITCHAM ROAD
PURLEY WAY
CROYDON ROAD
DUPPAS HILL RD
DUPPAS HILL
Tertiary Centre
Croydon Flyover
95
96
97
98
99
100
101
102
103
104
142
66
67
68
69
A23
A236
A232
A235
A212
A213
A215
B272

UPPER NORWOOD
DQ
DR
DS
DT
DU
DV
DW
33
34
35
122
PENGE
SE19
SE20
SE25
CR7
CR0
BEULAH HILL
THE LAWNS
BEAULIEU HEIGHTS
SOUTH NORWOOD GROUNDS
SYLVAN ESTATE
SPORTS GROUND
SOUTH NORWOOD LAKE
ORCHARD SCHOOL SPORTS CENTRE
ANERLEY
BETTS PARK
SOUTH PENGE PARK EST
GREEN LANE SPORTS GROUND
GRANGEWOOD PARK
SOUTH NORWOOD
BECKENHAM CEMETERY
SOUTH NORWOOD COUNTRY PARK
THORNTON HEATH
SELHURST PARK
SOUTH NORWOOD REC GRD
CROYDON AND RYLANDS FIELDS
CROYDON SPORTS ARENA
Croydon FC
ARENA GOLF DRIVING RANGE
QUEEN'S ROAD CEMETERY
MAYDAY HOSPITAL
141
SELHURST
RAIL DEPOT
WOODSIDE
ASHBURTON PARK
SHIRLEY OAKS HOSPITAL
BROAD GREEN
ADDISCOMBE
CROYDON
WANDLE PARK
WHITGIFT PLAYING FIELDS
SHIRLEY PARK GOLF COURSE
HOCKEY PITCH
LLOYD PARK
SPORTS GROUND
DUPPAS HILL
COOMBE ROAD
160
95
96
97
98
99
100
101
102
103
104

143
DX
DY
DZ
EA
EB
EC
ED
36
37
38
123
BECKENHAM
BR2
SHORTLANDS GOLF COURSE
BROMLEY PARK
THE SLOANE HOSPITAL
95
96
97
98
99
100
101
102
103
104
144
BR3
BECKENHAM HOSPITAL
CROYDON RD REC GROUND
ELMERS END
KELSEY PARK
EDEN PARK
HARVINGTON PLAYING FIELD
PARK LANGLEY
UPPER ELMERS END
CROUCH OAK WOOD
MONKS ORCHARD
BETHLEM ROYAL HOSPITAL
HIGH BROOM WOOD
LANGLEY PARK SPORTS GRD
LANGLEY PARK GOLF COURSE
THE ROOKERY
BLAKE REC GRD
WEST WICKHAM
CR0
SHIRLEY
SPRING PARK WOOD
FOXES WOOD
KENNEL WOOD
SPRING PARK
SPARROWS DEN PLAYING FIELDS
BR4
Schiller International University
161

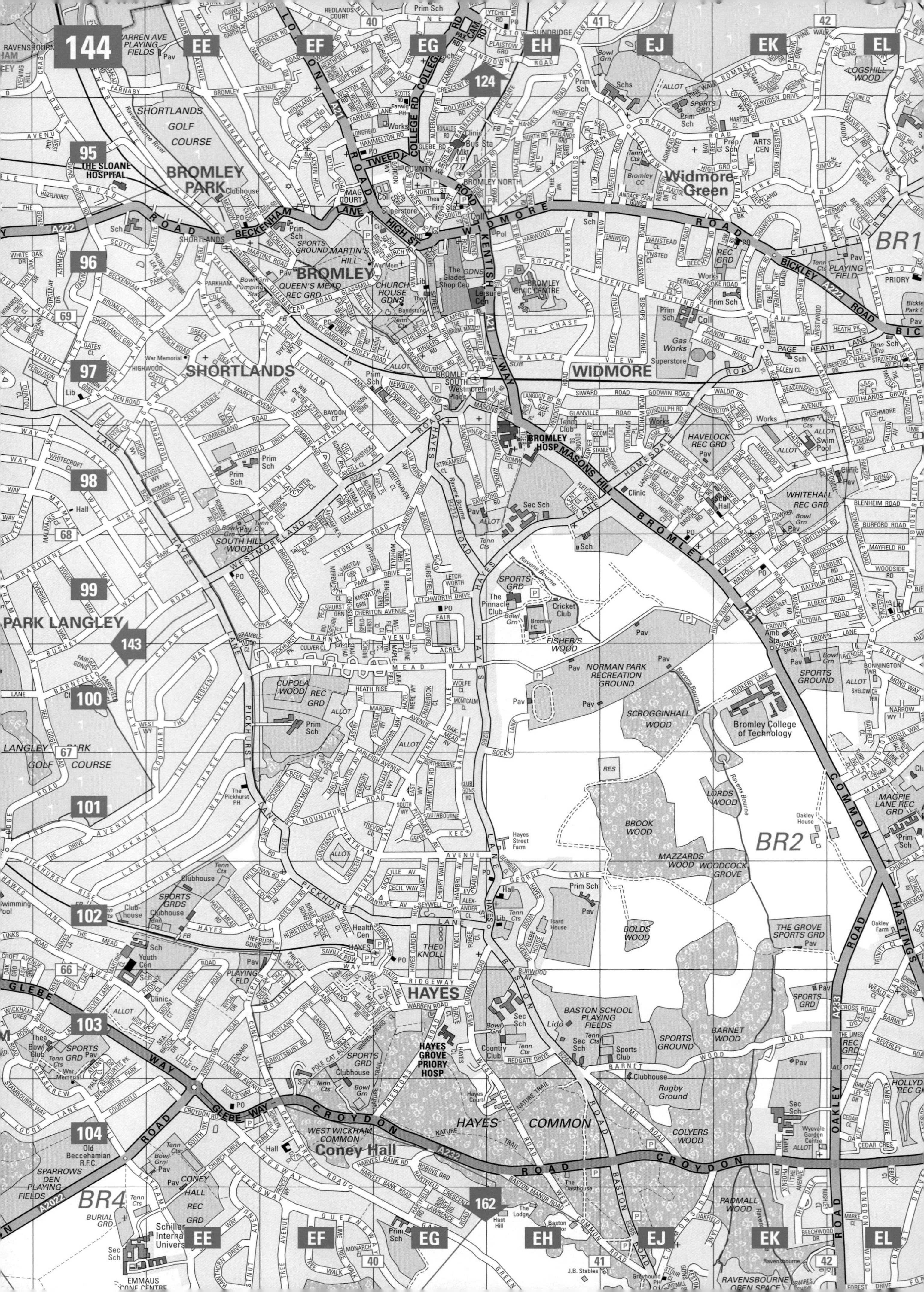

144
EE
EF
EG
EH
EJ
EK
EL
124
95
96
97
98
99
100
101
102
103
104
143
162
40
41
42
66
67
68
69
BROMLEY
BROMLEY PARK
SHORTLANDS
WIDMORE
Widmore Green
PARK LANGLEY
HAYES
Coney Hall
BR1
BR2
BR4
SHORTLANDS GOLF COURSE
THE SLOANE HOSPITAL
BROMLEY NORTH
BROMLEY SOUTH
BROMLEY HOSP
BROMLEY CIVIC CENTRE
The Glades Shop Cen
QUEEN'S MEAD REC GRD
CHURCH HOUSE GDNS
MARTIN'S HILL
SOUTH HILL WOOD
HAVELOCK REC GRD
WHITEHALL REC GRD
NORMAN PARK RECREATION GROUND
SCROGGINHALL WOOD
Bromley College of Technology
LORDS WOOD
BROOK WOOD
MAZZARDS WOOD
WOODCOCK GROVE
BOLDS WOOD
THE GROVE SPORTS GRD
MAGPIE LANE REC GRD
CUPOLA WOOD
FISHER'S WOOD
THE KNOLL
BASTON SCHOOL PLAYING FIELDS
BARNET WOOD
HAYES GROVE PRIORY HOSP
HAYES COMMON
WEST WICKHAM COMMON
COLYERS WOOD
PADMALL WOOD
LANGLEY PARK GOLF COURSE
SPARROWS DEN PLAYING FIELDS
CONEY HALL REC GRD
LOGSHILL WOOD
HOLLYDALE REC GRD
Old Beccehamian R.F.C.
WIDMORE ROAD
BICKLEY ROAD
MASONS HILL
BROMLEY COMMON
HASTINGS ROAD
CROYDON ROAD
GLEBE WAY
HAYES LANE
PICKHURST LANE
WESTMORELAND ROAD
BECKENHAM LANE
KENTISH WAY
HIGH ST
WICKHAM WAY
OAKLEY ROAD
BARNET WOOD ROAD
BASTON ROAD
A21
A222
A232
A233
A2022
B228
B265
Ravensbourne River
Ravens Bourne

145
EM
EN
EP
EQ
ER
ES
ET
43
44
45
125
163
146
95
96
97
98
99
100
101
102
103
104
69
68
67
66
CAMDEN PARK
CHISLEHURST GOLF COURSE
CHISLEHURST COMMON
NATURE RESERVE
PARK WOOD
Perry Street Shaw
Bushy Clump
Icehouse Wood
Scadbury Moated Manor House Site
Field Study Centre
Holbrook Wood
The Larches
BROMLEY LANE
WATTS LANE
MANOR PARK RD
ST. PAUL'S CRAY COMMON
CHALKPIT WOOD
BANSOME WOOD
Marjorie McClure Sch
CHISLEHURST
BIRCH WOOD
GOSHILL WOOD
POND WOOD
BR7
HAWKWOOD ESTATE NT
WALK WOOD
PETTS WOOD NT
Edlmann Memorial Wood
Willett Memorial Wood
HOBLINGWELL WOOD
HOBLINGWELL WOOD REC GRD
ST. PAUL'S CRAY
BICKLEY
Bickley Junction
Chislehurst Junction
GREAT THRIFT
Kyd Brook
Piggeries
M.O.D.
Bickley Manor Hotel
BLACKBROOK WOOD
Bromley High Sch
THORNET WOOD
JUBILEE COUNTRY PARK
Southborough Lane Stables
Petts Wood Junction
PETTS WOOD
BR5
ORPINGTON ROAD
CHISLEHURST ROAD
POVEREST
Sovereign of the Seas PH
Crooked Billet PH
SOUTHBOROUGH OPEN SPACE
COVET WOOD
POVEREST REC GRD
ST. LUKE'S CEM
PARKFIELD
SOUTHBOROUGH RECREATION GROUND
BROMLEY GOLF COURSE
Bromley Common
SPARROW WOOD
PETTS WOOD REC GRD
SPARROW COMMON
ROUNDABOUT WOOD
PLAYING FIELD
CROFTON HEATH
ORPINGTON
Walnuts Shop Cen
Mkt Leisure Cen
BR6
GUMPING COMMON
CLAY WOOD
NOBODY'S WOOD
KNOWLEHILL WOOD
POKERIDDEN WOOD
Knowlehill Farm
CROFTON ROAD
STATION ROAD
SPUR A232
PERRY HALL ROAD A208
NEWSTEAD WOOD
DARRICK COMMON
FARNBOROUGH REC GRD
DARRICK WOOD
FARNBOROUGH HOSPITAL
FARNBOROUGH ROAD
ORPINGTON HOSPITAL
Nursery
Scrubs Farm

146
NATURE RESERVE
EU
EV
EW
EX
EY
EZ
FA
EDGINGTON
SIDCUP BYPASS
DA14
A20
126
RUXLEY WOOD
Ruxley Manor Nursery
BROMLEY
Scadbury Moated Manor House Site
Field-Study Centre
Youth Cen
SEVENOAKS WAY
A224
RUXLEY PARK GOLF COURSE
CRAY VALLEY GOLF COURSE
Ski Centre
Sports Club
DRIVING RANGE
Clubhouse
Superstore
CRAYFIELD IND PARK
Barnfield Bank
Pilgrim Hill
CHAPMANS LANE
95
96
97
98
99
100
101
102
103
104
HOBLINGWELL WOOD REC GRD
ST. PAUL'S CRAY
Simon's Field Shaw
Lower Hockenden Farm
PAULS CRAY HILL PARK
HIGHLANDS WOOD
BR5
BR7
CLARENDON WAY
MURRAY BUSINESS CEN
SPRINGVALE RETAIL PARK
HOCKENDEN WOOD
Hogspring Cottages
KEVINGTON DRIVE
ST MARY CRAY
STAR LANE
SANDWAY PK
WOTTON GREEN
THE WARREN
Sheepcote Farm
BLACKSMITHS LANE
NUGENT IND PARK
CROCKENHILL ROAD
Ringland Farm
CHILD'S WOOD
POVEREST
145
ST. MARY CRAY REC GRD
Shawcroft Sch
B258
Blueberry Farm
Kevington Farm
Derry Downs
KYNASTON WOOD
Waldens Farm
Crouch Farm
POVEREST REC GRD
CRAY AVENUE
GRIGG'S CROSS
PERRY HALL ROAD
A208
COCKMANNINGS ROAD
Walden Manor
Depot
Heather's Holdings
Bleak House Farm
PRIORY GARDENS
BROMLEY MUS
GRASSMEADE RECREATION GROUND
ORPINGTON
COURT ROAD (ORPINGTON BYPASS)
HIGH STREET
Eastwood Farm
GRIFF'S WOOD
RAMSDEN
HOLLINGBOURNE TWR
BEKESBOURNE TWR
Piggery
ORPINGTON
SPUR ROAD
A232
SKEET HILL LANE
SAGE WENTS
Byways Nurseries
PLAYING FIELD
BR6
Crownwood Farm
Cookham Hill Farm
Cookham Farm
Goddington
GODDINGTON PARK
ROUNDS SMALLAMS
Goddington House
Bowling Green
LILLY'S WOOD
BLACK BUSH WOOD
164
A223
ORPINGTON HOSPITAL
Tennis Courts
47
48
49

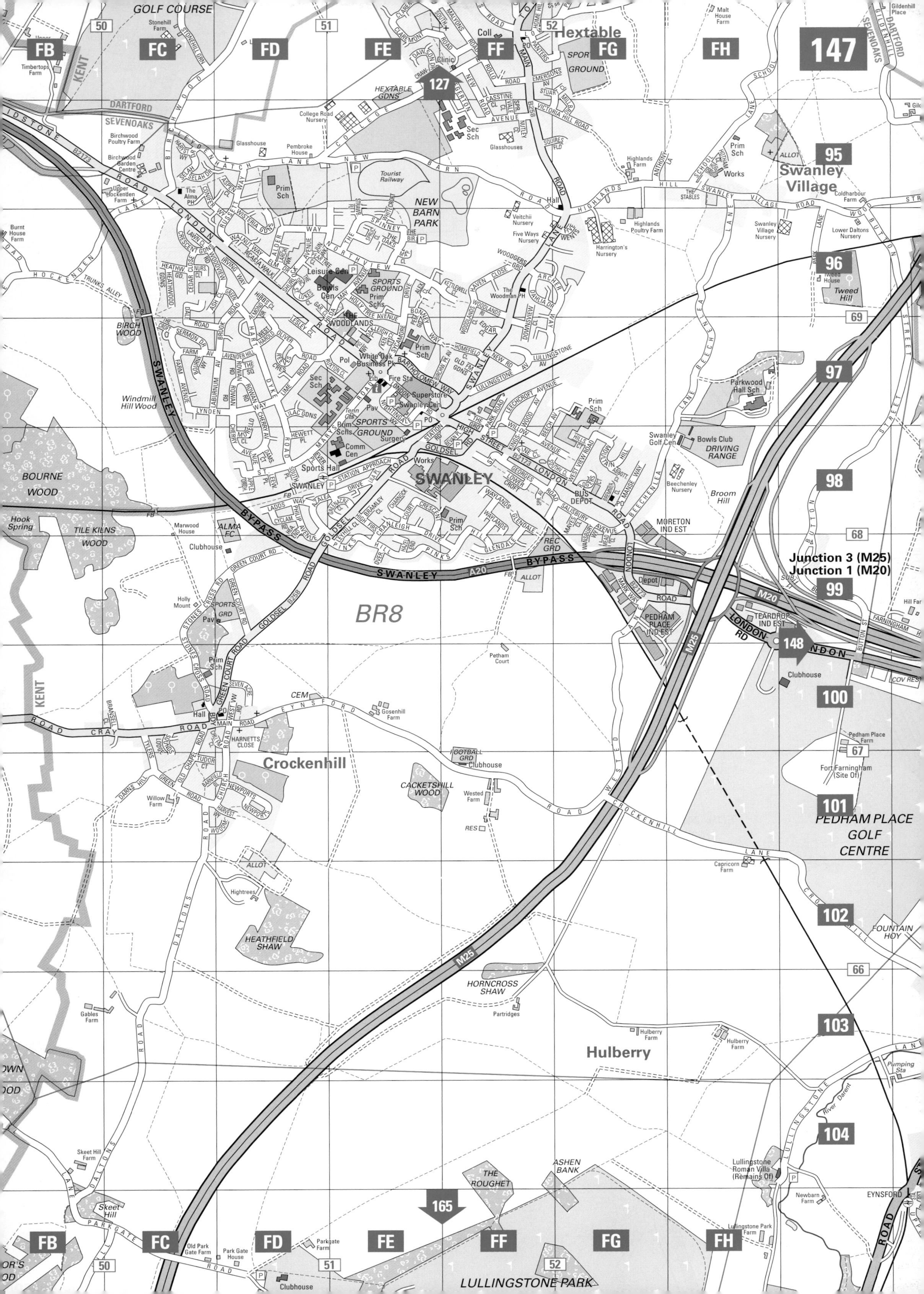

147
GOLF COURSE
FB
FC
FD
FE
FF
FG
FH
50
51
52
Hextable
Swanley Village
SWANLEY
Crockenhill
Hulberry
BR8
KENT
DARTFORD
SEVENOAKS
NEW BARN PARK
Tourist Railway
SPORTS GROUND
THE WOODLANDS
White Oak Business Pk
Swanley Cen
Superstore
Fire Sta
Lib
Sports Hall
Comm Cen
Leisure Cen
Bowls Cen
Prim Sch
Sec Sch
Glasshouses
Swanley Golf Cen
Bowls Club
DRIVING RANGE
Broom Hill
MORETON IND EST
PEDHAM PLACE IND EST
TEARDROP IND EST
BUS DEPOT
REC GRD
ALLOT
Junction 3 (M25)
Junction 1 (M20)
M25
M20
A20
B2173
B258
SWANLEY BY-PASS
LONDON ROAD
GOLDSEL ROAD
HIGH STREET
EYNSFORD ROAD
CRAY ROAD
DALTONS ROAD
CROCKENHILL LANE
WESTED ROAD
BIRCH WOOD
BOURNE WOOD
TILE KILNS WOOD
Windmill Hill Wood
Hook Spring
ALMA FC
Holly Mount
CACKETSHILL WOOD
HEATHFIELD SHAW
HORNCROSS SHAW
THE ROUGHET
ASHEN BANK
LULLINGSTONE PARK
PEDHAM PLACE GOLF CENTRE
Fort Farningham (Site Of)
Pedham Place Farm
Lullingstone Roman Villa (Remains Of)
Lullingstone Park Farm
Newbarn Farm
EYNSFORD
River Darent
Pumping Sta
FOUNTAIN HOY
Skeet Hill
Skeet Hill Farm
Gables Farm
Old Park Gate Farm
Park Gate House
Parkgate Farm
Clubhouse
Partridges
Hulberry Farm
Capricorn Farm
Wested Farm
Gosenhill Farm
Petham Court
Willow Farm
Hightrees
Tweed Hill
Tweed House
Parkwood Hall Sch
Beechenley Nursery
Coldharbour Farm
Lower Daltons Nursery
Swanley Village Nursery
Highlands Farm
Highlands Poultry Farm
Harrington's Nursery
Veitchii Nursery
Five Ways Nursery
The Woodman PH
Birchwood Poultry Farm
Birchwood Garden Centre
Upper Hockenden Farm
Burnt House Farm
Timbertops Farm
Stonehill Farm
College Road Nursery
Pembroke House
Malt House Farm
Marwood House
127
148
165
95
96
97
98
99
100
101
102
103
104
66
67
68
69

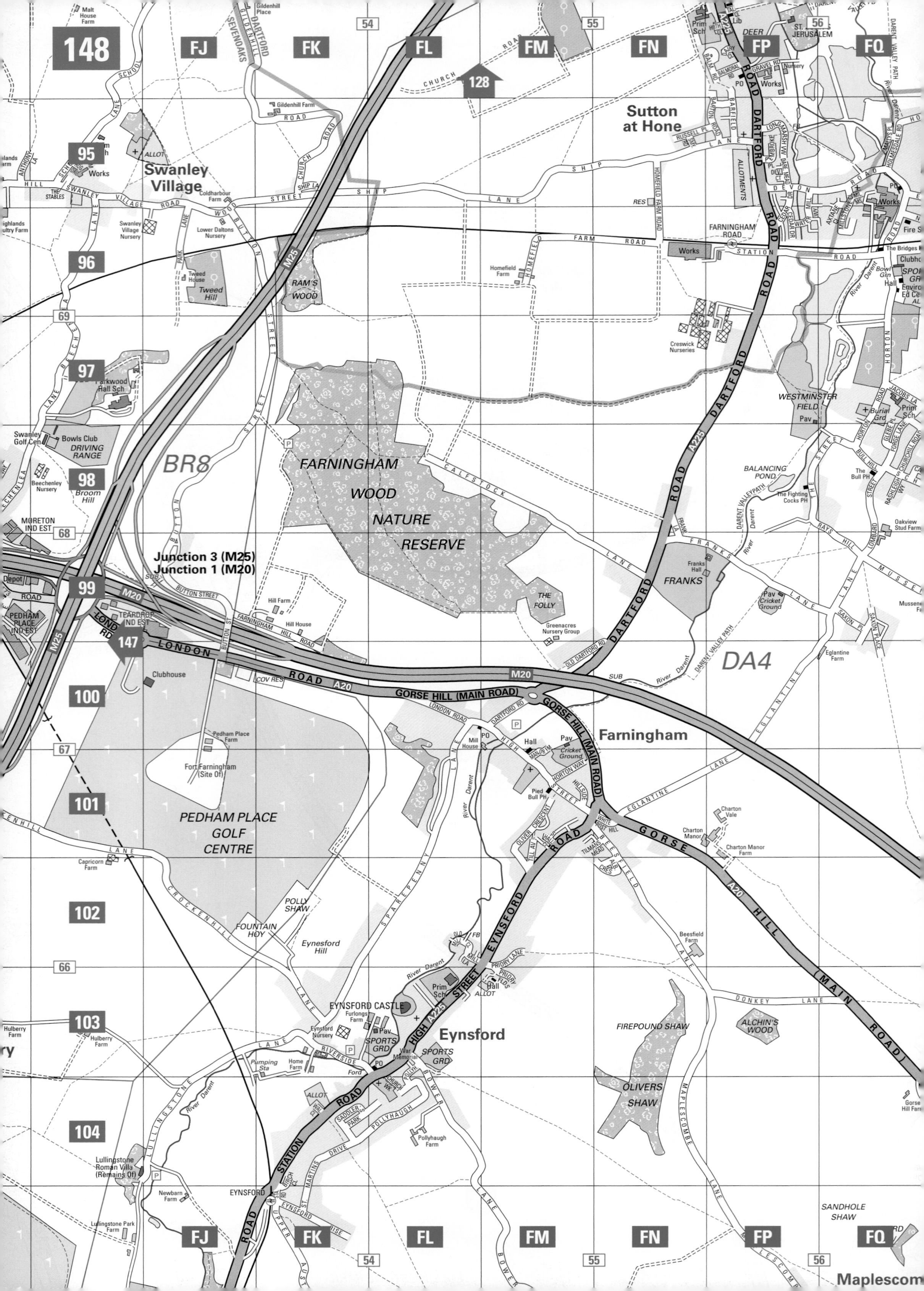

148
FJ
FK
FL
FM
FN
FP
FQ
54
55
56
128
95
96
97
98
99
100
101
102
103
104
147
69
68
67
66
Swanley Village
Sutton at Hone
Farningham
Eynsford
BR8
DA4
FARNINGHAM WOOD NATURE RESERVE
PEDHAM PLACE GOLF CENTRE
Junction 3 (M25)
Junction 1 (M20)
Tweed Hill
RAM'S WOOD
FRANKS
THE FOLLY
WESTMINSTER FIELD
BALANCING POND
FIREPOUND SHAW
OLIVERS SHAW
ALCHIN'S WOOD
POLLY SHAW
FOUNTAIN HOY
Eynesford Hill
EYNSFORD CASTLE
SANDHOLE SHAW
Maplescom
Broom Hill
Swanley Golf Cen
Bowls Club
DRIVING RANGE
MORETON IND EST
PEDHAM PLACE IND EST
TEARDROP IND EST
Clubhouse
Pedham Place Farm
Fort Farningham (Site Of)
Capricorn Farm
Hulberry Farm
Lullingstone Roman Villa (Remains Of)
Newbarn Farm
Lullingstone Park Farm
Pollyhaugh Farm
Beesfield Farm
Charton Vale
Charton Manor
Charton Manor Farm
Eglantine Farm
Oakview Stud Farm
Franks Hall
Greenacres Nursery Group
Hill Farm
Hill House
Homefield Farm
Creswick Nurseries
Gildenhill Farm
Coldharbour Farm
Lower Daltons Nursery
Swanley Village Nursery
Tweed House
Parkwood Hall Sch
Beechenley Nursery
Eynsford Nursery
Furlongs Farm
Home Farm
Pumping Sta
Mill House
Pied Bull PH
The Bull PH
The Fighting Cocks PH
Farningham Road
Works
M25
M20
A20
A225
LONDON ROAD
GORSE HILL (MAIN ROAD)
DARTFORD ROAD
EYNSFORD ROAD
HIGH STREET
STATION ROAD
SHIP LANE
FARM ROAD
CALFSTOCK LANE
FRANKS LANE
EGLANTINE LANE
DONKEY LANE
MAPLESCOMBE LANE
SPAREPENNY LANE
CROCKENHILL LANE
LULLINGSTONE LANE
BUTTON STREET
FARNINGHAM HILL ROAD
SWANLEY VILLAGE ROAD
DARENT VALLEY PATH
River Darent

149
FR
FS
FT
FU
FV
FW
FX
57
58
59
129
South Darenth
St. Margaret's Farm
Gill's Farm
GILL'S ROAD
HILL ROAD
SHRUBBERY ROAD
MONTGOMERY RD
ST. MARGARET'S ROAD
RYECROFTS WOOD
Orchard View
Walnut Tree Farm
Ryecroft Farm
Chalkcroft
GREEN STREET
B260
DARTFORD
SEVENOAKS
DA2
QUARRY
SPORTS GRD
ALLOT
Works
Pinden
Pinden End Farm
Mile End Green
GREEN STREET GREEN ROAD
WHITEHILL ROAD
NORTHDOWN
MAIN ROAD
FOOTBALL PITCH
Pav
Hall
Lib
Longfield
WEST SHAW
ESSEX ROAD
KENT ROAD
ROWANS CL
PO
STATION ROAD
HARTLEY RD
LONGFIELD
CAVENDISH SQ
BRAMBLEFIELD
OAKWOOD RISE
DENE WK
ST MARY'S WAY
Sec Sch
95
96
97
98
99
100
101
102
103
104
69
68
67
66
RABBITS ROAD
GORRINGE AV
VICTORIA DR
PRINCE CHARLES AV
ALLOT
SOUTHDOWNS
Tuppence Farm
WILSON LANE
Rabbits Farm
CANADA FARM ROAD
Dean Bottom Farm
FAWKHAM ROAD
Dean Bottom
CHURCHDOWN WOOD
Horton Kirby
STACK ROAD
Northdown Country Riding Club
HOTTSFIELD
QUAKERS CLOSE
MERTON AV
ASH ROAD
Churchdown Farm
Hartley
PARKFIELD
LARKS
OLD DOWNS
CHURCH
CASTLE HILL
Beeches Farm
Canada Farm
Hill Barn Farm
Hartley Green
GREEN WAY
STACK
Country Club
Bowl Grn
SPORTS GRD
CULVEY
Tenn Cts
Pav
Prim Sch
Lib
CORINTHIAN
PENNIS LANE
Sports Ground
Sports Cen
Gay Dawn Farm
Pennis Farm
Clubho
SPORTS GRD
GOLF
COURSE
FAIRBY LANE
SCUDDERS HILL
VALLEY ROAD
SCHOOL LANE
Lone Oak Farm
Kentdown Mushroom Farm
Nursery
GATES ROAD
Elec Sta
DA3
MUSSENDEN LANE
GROVE WOOD
Grove Farm
MANOR LANE
PENNIS WOOD
YEWFIELD SHAW
ALLOT
The Black Lion PH
HORTON WOOD
Hall
Prim Sch
REDLIBBETS
Clubhouse
GOLF
COURSE
Milestone Sch
Radio Mast
HOPKINS SPRING WOOD
THREE GATES ROAD
FAWKHAM MANOR HOSPITAL
HATCHFIELD WOOD
Fawkham Manor Farm
FB
The Rookery Pig Farm
M20
Speedgate Farm
SPEEDGATE HILL
White House Farm
WOOD ROAD
CHAPEL WOOD
AYELANDS
MILLFIELD
GABRIEL SPRING ROAD
GABRIEL SPRING WOOD
CHOAKS WOOD
ST MICHAELS LANE
WEST YOKE
New Ash Green
BUTCHERS LANE
The Royal Oak PH
COLT STEAD
FOXBURY
Comm Cen
Lib
SCRATCHERS LANE
SUN HILL
The Rising Sun PH
PO
War Memorial
Fawkham Green
SMALL GRAINS
Greyhound Schooling Establishment
Westyoke Farm
Eaglesfield Equestrian Centre
Beechcroft Farm Industries
PUNCH CROFT
Bovis Offices
Woodhall Farm
Works
HATCH ROAD
FAWKHAM GREEN ROAD
TN15
Sports Cen
SPORTS GROUND
REDHILL ROAD
BRANDS HATCH KARTING
Leisure Cen
Brandshatch Place Hotel
SAXTEN'S WOOD
Landway Farm
Stewart Cen
SHETLEY SHAWS
Thistle Brands Hatch
BRANDS HATCH MOTOR RACING CIRCUIT
WEST HILL (MAIN ROAD)
BRANDS HATCH RD
ROGERS WOOD LANE
BILL HILL
The White Swan PH
Ash Place Farm

150
AS
AT
AU
AV
AW
AX
AY
Longcross
132
CHOBHAM COMMON
NATIONAL NATURE
RESERVE
105
106
107
108
109
110
111
112
113
114
Burrowhill
GU24
CHOBHAM
Mimbridge
GU21
HORSELL
COMMON
Stonehill
166
NUFFIELD
HOSPITAL
CHOBHAM
GOLF
COURSE

151
133
167
152
AZ
BA
BB
BC
BD
BE
BF
01
02
03
61
62
63
64
105
106
107
108
109
110
111
112
113
114
MOOR GOLF COURSE
GOLF COURSE
Clubhouse
Foxhills Country Club
Foxhills
Dower House
Tennis Courts
STONEHILL
Kitchenride Corner
Ten Acre Farm
KT16
Nursery
Ether Hill
OTTERSHAW MEMORIAL FIELDS
Youth Club
Queenwood Farm
Coach House
CROSS LANE
CHOBHAM ROAD
A319
RUNNYMEDE
SURREY HEATH
Tusk House
The Mansion
Timber Hill
LONG COPSE
OTTERSHAW PARK
SAMSON'S WOOD
LITTLE BLACKMOLE POND
GREAT BLACKMOLE POND
SANDPIT PLANTATION
DECOY PLANTATION
The Bourne
Bonsey's Bridge
BONSEYS LANE
Tag McLaren HQ
Dunford Bridge
Silverlands Farm
HOLLOW
HOSP
ST PETER'S HOSP
133
Botleys Mansion
HOME WOOD
HOMEWOOD PARK
Hillswood Business Park
HILLSWOOD
FISH POND
Church Farm
Offices
GUILDFORD ROAD
A320
BITTAMS LANE
ST. PETER'S WAY
A320
Junction 11
Woodside Farm
Tenn Cts
OTTERSHAW
Amb Sta
The Otter Nursery
Great Grove Farm
MURRAY ROAD
B3121
SPINNEY HILL
Prim Sch
Sch
PO
Timber Hill
THE COMMON
BOUSLEY RISE
Bousley Farm
Bousley End Stables
Brox Road Nursery
BROX COPSE
BROX LANE
ROW TOWN
KT15
Southern Wood Farm
Glasshouses
Rodwell Farm
Hall's Farm
Glasshouse
ROSE PARK
Holme Farm
Fallow Farm
WOODHAM PARK ROAD
GREAT WOOD
WOODLANDS CL
THE WARREN
Anningsley Park Farm
Anningsley Park
WARE COPSE
BIRCH WOOD
HOYT WOOD
Coomelands Farm
Grange Farm
Sharwood Farm
QUEEN MARYS DRIVE
Lib
WOODHAM
Scotland Lock
PLAYING FIELD
Sec Sch
Sports Club
Tenn Cts
MARTYRS LANE
NEW ZEALAND GOLF COURSE
Clubhouse
WOODHAM LANE
A245
SHEERWATER
Sheerwater Bridge
BASINGSTOKE CANAL
Electricity Station
WEST BYFLEET
ANTHONYS
Danewell Hill
Bleak House PH
HORSELL COMMON
CHERTSEY ROAD
A320
WOODHAM ROAD
Six Cross Roads
SHEERWATER REC GRD
Athletic Club
Prim Sch
Comm Cen
Youth Club
Woodlands
TOWING PATH
KINGSWEY BUSINESS CENTRE
RIVER COURT
GENESIS BUSINESS
WOKING BUSINESS PARK
Monument Bridge
MONUMENT
KT14
Clubhouse
WEST BYFLEET GOLF COURSE
Pyrford
GU22
OLD WOKING ROAD
Superstore
Health Cen
Nursery
Lees Farm
RIDGWAY
COLDHARBOUR
OAKCROFT
WOKING

BG
BH
BJ
BK
BL
BM
BN
05
06
07
MOOR GOLF COURSE
Junction 11
105
106
107
108
109
110
111
112
113
114
134
151
168
A317 ST. PETER'S WAY
ADDLESTONE
St. George's College
WEYBRIDGE ROAD
WEYBRIDGE TRADING ESTATE
WEYBRIDGE BUSINESS PARK
Black Boy Bridge
Weybridge Lock
HOSP
BALFOUR RD
CHURCH ST
Coxes Lock
MILL POND
Crockford Bridge
Crockford Bridge Farm
SAYES COURT PUBLIC OPEN SPACE
KT15
ROW TOWN
NEW HAW
SURREY GOLF AND FITNESS
DRIVING RANGE
CENTRAL VETERINARY LABORATORY
Electricity Station
Addlestone Junction
Nine Arches Bridge
Seven Arches Bridge
Brooklands College
Crickets Hill
PLAYING FIELDS
BROOKLANDS MUSEUM
BROOKLANDS
BROOKLANDS BUSINESS PARK
AIRFIELD (DISUSED)
BROOKLANDS INDUSTRIAL PARK
Paddocks Retail Pk
BARNES WALLIS DR
BYFLEET & NEW HAW
Byfleet Junction
M25
WOODHAM
CAMPHILL INDUSTRIAL ESTATE
HEATHERVALE REC GRD
Botton Lock
BASINGSTOKE CANAL
DARTNELL PARK
PARVIS ROAD
A245
KT14
BYFLEET
BYFLEET TECHNICAL CENTRE
WEST BYFLEET
BROADOAKS GOVERNMENT OFFICES
DODD'S WOOD
TINS WOOD
OLD WOOD
OLDWOOD POND
Murray's Bridge
Dodd's Bridge
GU22
GU23
Pyrford
Sheerwater Bridge
Plough Bridge
Manor Farm
COMMON MEADOWS
THE ISLAND
BUXTON
Sewage Works
Lees Farm

BP
BQ
BR
BS
BT
BU
BV
08
09
10
135
ASHLEY PARK
OATLANDS PARK
BURWOOD PARK
WALTON-ON-THAMES
Oatlands Park Hotel
OATLANDS
QUEENS ROAD
A3050
A317
MONUMENT HILL
Pitch 'n' Putt
Haine's Bridge
105
106
107
108
109
110
111
112
113
114
HERSHAM ROAD
BYPASS
KT12
KT13
KT11
THE HEATH
The Heath
WALTON COMMON
UPPER COMMON
Rabbit Lane House
Squire's Garden Centre
CEM
Burhill Kennels
WARREN POND
SPORTS GROUND
HAWKS HOCKEY CLUB
OLD BURHILL GOLF COURSE
NEW BURHILL GOLF COURSE
154
ST. GEORGE'S HILL
ST. GEORGE'S HILL GOLF COURSE
COVERED RESERVOIRS
FLAGSTAFF HOUSE CONFERENCE CENTRE
WHITELEY VILLAGE
Strawberry Hill
WALTON COMMON
Beards Hill
NOTRE DAME CONVENT
Seven Hills Estate
Dick Turpin's Cottage
River Mole
Norwood Farm
ELVEDON
Hook's Corner
Chestnut Lodge Farm
Chestnut Lodge
West Gate Lodge
DRIVING RANGE
Fairmile Hotel
Chippings Farm
Southwood Manor Farm
Riverside Farm
63
62
61
64
OLD COMMON
A3
ESHER ROAD
FOXHOLM COVERT
COBHAM BUS MUS
SILVER MERE
SILVERMERE GOLF COURSE
Driving Range
BYFLEET ROAD
A245
Walton Firs Scout Camp
MANOR POND
PORTSMOUTH ROAD
Hilton Cobham
PAINSHILL PARK
THE BROOM
Heyswood Girl Guide Camp
Gothic Temple
GROTTO
169
THE LAKE
WHEEL ISLAND
BELL WOOD
Long Orchard Farm
Bramble Hedge Farm
Foxwarren Park
The Tower
Red Hill
Oak Pollard
GUILDFORD
COBHAM COTTAGE HOSP
COBHAM
BETWEEN STREETS
HIGH ST
RIVER HL
MILL RD
STOKE ROAD
R. Mole
ROSE LODGE WOOD
Cobham FC
Visitors Centre
Wood Hill
The Running Mare PH
Superstore
Cricket Club

BW
BX
BY
BZ
CA
CB
CC
136
HERSHAM VILLAGE
DRIVING RANGE
SANDOWN PARK RACE COURSE
Grandstand
Waynefleté's or Wolsey's Tower
CORONATION PLAYING FIELDS
105
106
107
108
109
110
111
112
113
114
HERSHAM
HERSHAM RIVERSIDE PARK
HERSHAM ROAD
HERSHAM BYPASS
ESHER ROAD
River Mole
Albany Bridge
LAMMAS LANE
PRINCESS ALICE HOSPICE
WEST END REC GRD
MOORE PLACE GOLF COURSE
Hawks Hill
ESHER
CIVIC CEN
WEST END
KT12
Garson Farm
Garson Farm Stables
Winterhouse Farm
Nursery
CLARE HILL GOLF COURSE
WEST END COMMON
The Mount
Belvedere Tower
CLAREMONT LANDSCAPE GARDEN
CLAREMONT LAKE
Claremont Park
STABLE POND
ARBROOK COMMON
Southwood Manor Farm
Willow Tree Farm
Riverside Farm
HORSESHOE CLUMP
The Ledges
WINTERDOWN WOOD
BLACKHILLS
Burhill
Clubhouse
153
NEW BURHILL GOLF COURSE
American Community School
SPORTS GROUND
Winterdown
Spa Bottom
Homewood
ESHER COMMON
Upper Court
The Firs
BLACK POND
Round Hill
Norwood Farm
SCHOOL GOLF COURSE
ESHER BYPASS
PORTSMOUTH ROAD
MIDDLE POND
FAIRMILE COMMON
SPRING POND
West Gate Lodge
DRIVING RANGE
Fairmile Hotel
COBHAM R.F.C.
Hook's Corner
Chippings Farm
Chestnut Lodge
OXSHOTT HEATH
War Memorial
Fairmile
COPSEM LANE
WARREN LANE
OXSHOTT
COBHAM COTTAGE HOSP
KT11
LITTLE HEATH COMMON
Knowle Hill
WATERCUT COPSE
CLAY PLANTATION
170
COBHAM
ROSE LODGE WOOD
KNOWLE HILL PARK
THE FURZE
The Running Mare PH
STOKE ROAD
A3
A307
A244
A245
A317
12
13
14
61
62
63
64

155
137
156
171
CD
CE
CF
CG
CH
CJ
CK
LITTLEWORTH COMMON
HINCHLEY WOOD
HINCHLEY WOOD
SURBITON GOLF COURSE
KINGSTON BYPASS
HOOK
CHESSINGTON
CLAYGATE
KT10
KT9
KT22
KT21
CLAYGATE COMMON
LOVELACE PLAYING FIELD
CHESSINGTON SOUTH
CHESSINGTON GOLF CENTRE
BARWELL BUSINESS PARK
CHESSINGTON WORLD OF ADVENTURE
SIXTY ACRE WOOD
HOLROYDS PLANTATION
MILBOURNEHOLD PLANTATION
BIRCH WOOD
LIMEKILN WOOD
OLD CARPENTERS PLANTATION
JUBILEE WOOD
CHESSINGTON WOOD
Malden Rushett
SILVERGLADE BUSINESS PARK
MILBOURNEHOLD WOOD
BRICKYARD PLANTATION
NEW WOOD
STOKE WOOD
PRINCE'S COVERTS
OXSHOTT
THE FOREST
NEWTON WOOD
LEATHERHEAD GOLF COURSE
ASHTEAD COMMON
ESHER BYPASS
LEATHERHEAD ROAD
FAIROAK LANE
RUSHETT LANE
BARWELL LAKE
Winey Hill
Bunkers Hill
Telegraph Hill
STEW POND
GREAT POND
POND WOOD

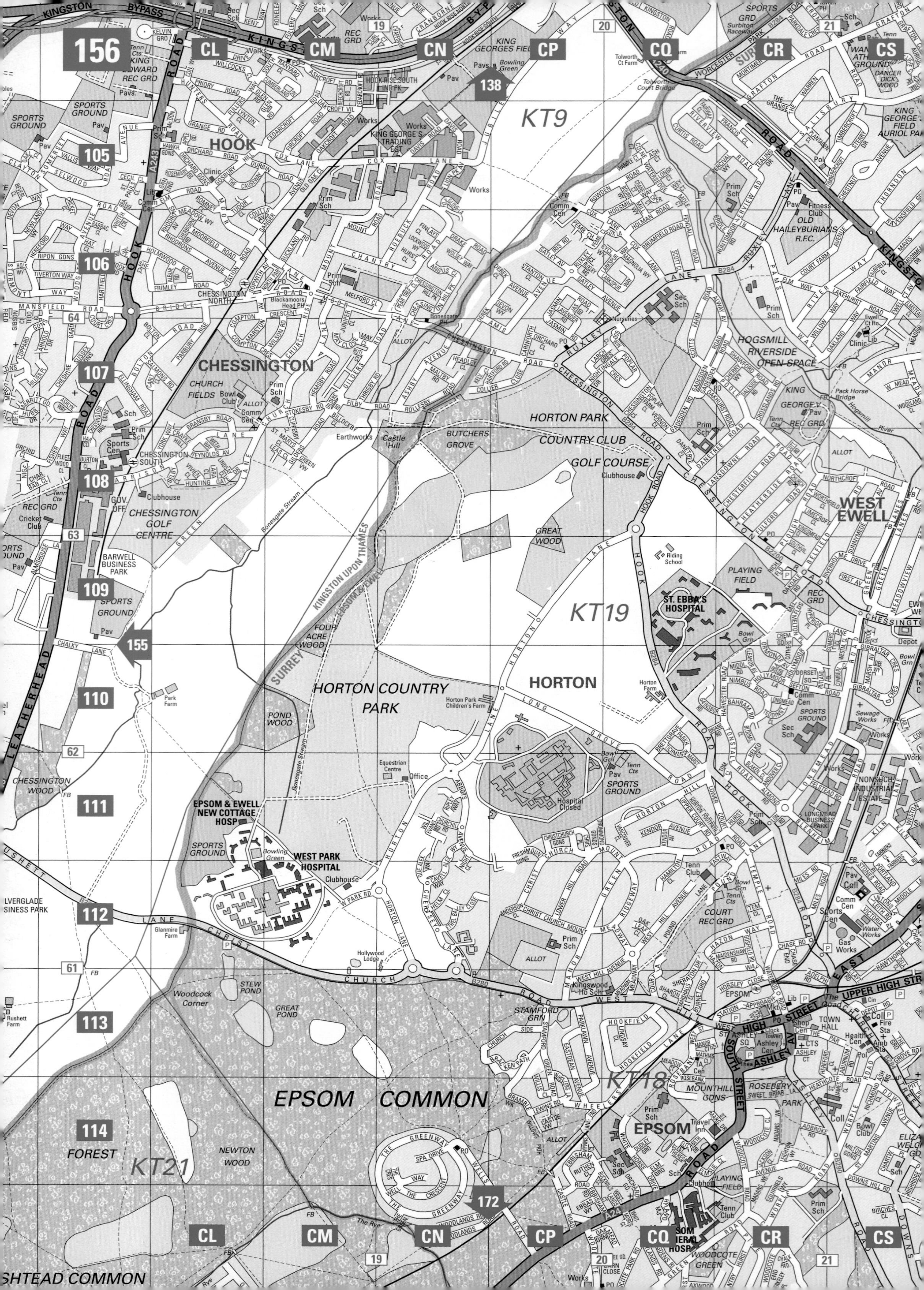
156
CL
CM
CN
CP
CQ
CR
CS
KINGSTON BYPASS
138
KING GEORGES FIELD
KT9
HOOK
KING GEORGE'S TRADING EST
SPORTS GROUND
105
106
107
108
109
110
111
112
113
114
64
63
62
61
19
20
21
CHESSINGTON
CHESSINGTON NORTH
CHESSINGTON SOUTH
CHURCH FIELDS
CHESSINGTON GOLF CENTRE
BARWELL BUSINESS PARK
155
CHALKY LANE
LEATHERHEAD ROAD
HOOK ROAD
CHESSINGTON ROAD
HORTON PARK COUNTRY CLUB GOLF COURSE
BUTCHERS GROVE
Castle Hill
Earthworks
HOGSMILL RIVERSIDE OPEN SPACE
KING GEORGE V REC GRD
OLD HAILEYBURIANS R.F.C.
WEST EWELL
GREAT WOOD
KT19
ST. EBBA'S HOSPITAL
PLAYING FIELD
HORTON
HORTON COUNTRY PARK
FOUR ACRE WOOD
KINGSTON UPON THAMES
SURREY
EPSOM & EWELL
POND WOOD
CHESSINGTON WOOD
EPSOM & EWELL NEW COTTAGE HOSP
WEST PARK HOSPITAL
SPORTS GROUND
Hospital Closed
NONSUCH INDUSTRIAL ESTATE
COURT REC GRD
STEW POND
GREAT POND
Woodcock Corner
EPSOM COMMON
KT18
KT21
FOREST
NEWTON WOOD
EPSOM
ROSEBERY PARK
TOWN HALL
172
The Rye
ASHTEAD COMMON
WOODCOTE GREEN
EPSOM GENERAL HOSP

157
CT
CU
CV
CW
CX
CY
CZ
KT4
CUDDINGTON REC GRD
NORTH CHEAM
SM1
COLLINGWOOD PARK
STONELEIGH
SM3
CHEAM REC GRD
NONSUCH PARK
OAK PLANTATION
Nonsuch Mansion House
THE WOOD
Diana's Dyke
CHEAM PARK
CHEAM
WEST SUTTON
PERRETS FIELD
SEARS PARK
SUTTON
PLAYING FIELDS
Cuddington Church (Site of)
Hatch Furlong
EWELL
EAST EWELL
SM2
OVERTON PARK REC GRD
Sutton & Epsom R.F.C.
EWELL BYPASS
LONDON ROAD
REIGATE ROAD
CHEAM ROAD
BELMONT RISE
BRIGHTON ROAD
ST DUNSTAN'S HILL
Nescot
Glyn Old Boys FC
SPORTS GROUND
KT17
CUDDINGTON GOLF COURSE
BANSTEAD DOWNS GOLF COURSE
SURREY
SM7
EPSOM & EWELL
SUTTON
NORTH LOOE
RIFLE RANGE
BANSTEAD
ALEXANDRA REC GRD
Epsom College
EPSOM DOWNS
COLLEGE ROAD
FIR TREE ROAD
Drift Bridge
NORK
105
106
107
108
109
110
111
112
113
114
139
158
173
22
23
24
61
62
63
64
A24
A217
A232
A240
A2022
A2043

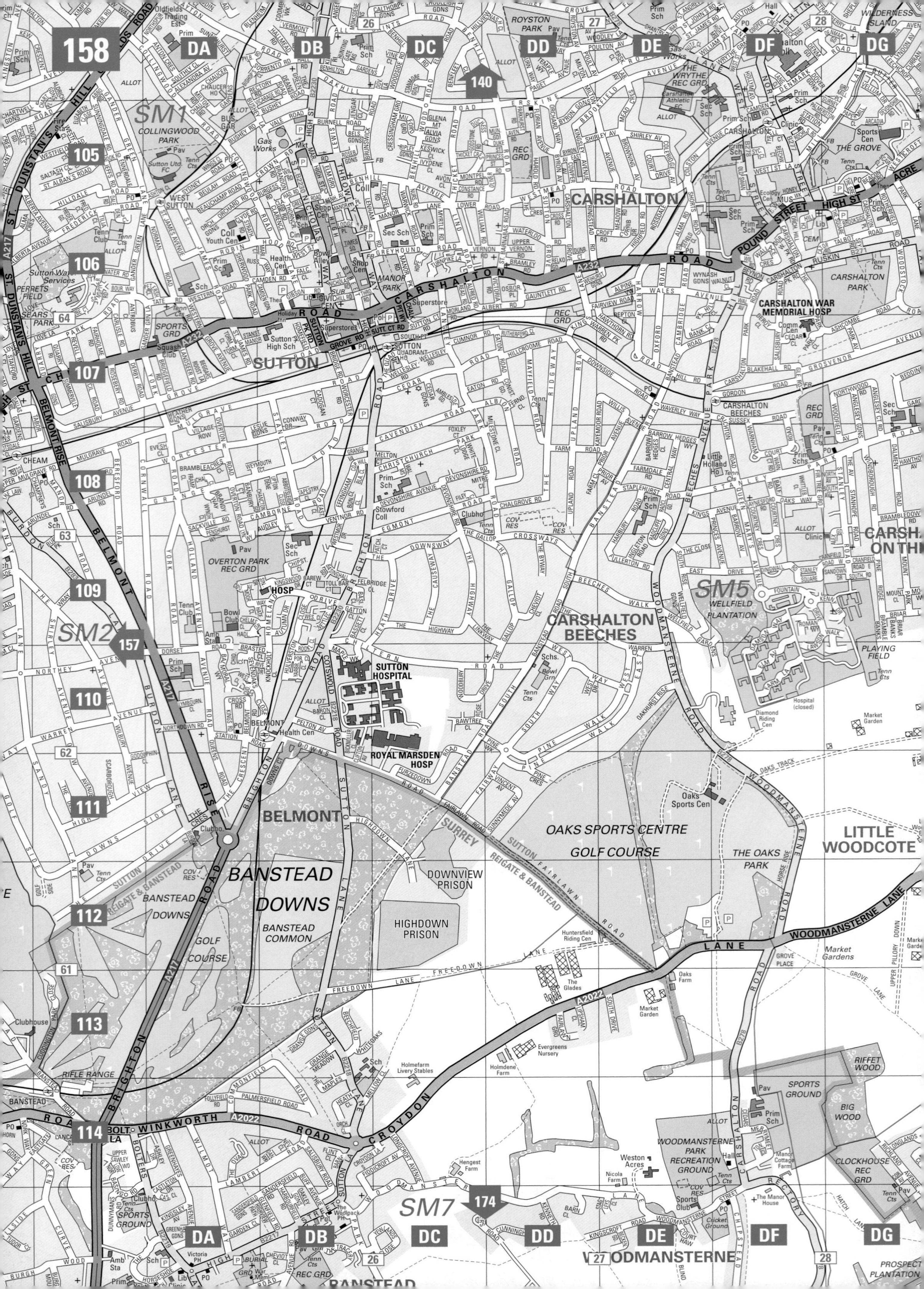
158
DA
DB
DC
DD
DE
DF
DG
140
157
174
26
27
28
105
106
107
108
109
110
111
112
113
114
64
63
62
61
SM1
SM2
SM5
SM7
CARSHALTON
SUTTON
CARSHALTON BEECHES
BELMONT
BANSTEAD DOWNS
LITTLE WOODCOTE
WOODMANSTERNE
BANSTEAD
CARSHALTON ON THE HILL
COLLINGWOOD PARK
ROYSTON PARK
WEST SUTTON
CHEAM
OVERTON PARK REC GRD
CARSHALTON PARK
CARSHALTON WAR MEMORIAL HOSP
CARSHALTON BEECHES
SUTTON HOSPITAL
ROYAL MARSDEN HOSP
WELLFIELD PLANTATION
PLAYING FIELD
OAKS SPORTS CENTRE GOLF COURSE
THE OAKS PARK
DOWNVIEW PRISON
HIGHDOWN PRISON
BANSTEAD DOWNS GOLF COURSE
BANSTEAD COMMON
SPORTS GROUND
RIFFET WOOD
BIG WOOD
WOODMANSTERNE PARK RECREATION GROUND
CLOCKHOUSE REC GRD
THE GROVE
WILDERNESS ISLAND
THE WRYTHE REC GRD
SPORTS GRD
PERRETS FIELD
SEARS PARK
CARSHALTON ROAD
HIGH ST
POUND STREET
ST. DUNSTAN'S HILL
BELMONT RISE
BRIGHTON ROAD
BANSTEAD ROAD
WOODMANSTERNE ROAD
WOODMANSTERNE LANE
CROYDON ROAD
WINKWORTH ROAD
SUTTON LANE
A217
A232
A2022
B278
RIFLE RANGE
PROSPECT PLANTATION

159
141
175
160
DH
DJ
DK
DL
DM
DN
DP
29
30
31
105
106
107
108
109
110
111
112
113
114
64
63
62
61
BEDDINGTON PARK
WALLINGTON
SM6
SOUTH BEDDINGTON
BANDON HILL CEMETERY
ROUNDSHAW PLAYING FIELD
ROUNDSHAW OPEN SPACE
ROUNDSHAW PARK
PURLEY WAY PLAYING FIELDS
CR0
CR2
CR8
CR5
DUPPAS HILL
SOUTH CROYDON
HALING PARK
WADDON
WOODCOTE
PURLEY
PURLEY HOSP
REEDHAM
KENLEY
WOODCOTE PARK GOLF COURSE
WOODCOTE GROVE REC GRD
HIGHER DRIVE REC GRD
FOXLEY WOOD
RIDDLESDOWN WOOD
SOUTH CROYDON REC GRD
PURLEY OAKS
SUTTON
CROYDON
COULSDON COURT
HARTLEY BUSHES
CROYDON ROAD
A232
A237
A23
A235
A22
A2022
B271
B272
B2030
PURLEY WAY
BRIGHTON ROAD
WOODCOTE ROAD
FOXLEY LANE
SMITHAM BOTTOM LANE
DOWNS COURT ROAD
MITCHLEY
GODSTONE RD
STAFFORD ROAD
DUPPAS HILL RD
LITTLE WOODCOTE LANE
WOODCOTE GROVE ROAD
SMITHAM
MANOR ROAD
LONDON ROAD

160
DQ
DR
DS
DT
DU
DV
DW
33
34
35
142
105
106
107
108
109
110
111
112
113
114
159
176
64
63
62
61
WHITGIFT PLAYING FIELDS
GOLF COURSE
LLOYD PARK
DUPPAS HILL RD
DUPPAS HILL
Croydon Flyover
HIGH ST
PARK LANE
COOMBE ROAD
A212
A2039
PARK HILL
COOMBE PARK
SPORTS GROUND
PLAYING FIELD
Coombe Farm
Oaks Farm
OAKS ROAD
ADDINGTON H
COOMBE WOOD
COOMBE LANE
Travel Inn
Central Nursery
SPORTS GROUND
Open Air Pool
BALLARDS PLANTATION
Cottage in the Woods
CONDUIT LANE
BALLARDS WAY
BALLARDS FARM ROAD
CROHAM VALLEY ROAD
HOLLINGSWORTH ROAD
Heathfield Farm
BRAMLEY BANK NATURE RESERVE
THE RUFFET
CHAPEL VIEW
LITTLEHEATH WOODS
SELSDON
SELSDON ROAD
SOUTH CROYDON
BRIGHTON ROAD
A235
HALING PARK
CR0
PURLEY WAY PLAYING FIELDS
SPORTS GROUND
HALING GROVE
SOUTH CROYDON REC GRD
CROHAM HURST
CROHAM HURST GOLF COURSE
Breakneck Hill
Tumulus
THRIFT WOOD
REC GRD
Clubhouse
UPPER SELSDON ROAD
B275
B269
SANDERSTEAD
SANDERSTEAD ROAD
SANDERSTEAD PLANTATION
PURLEY OAKS
Royal Oak Ho
PURLEY BEECHES
ALLOT
PURLEY HOSP
PURLEY
ROTARY FIELD
PURLEY DOWNS GOLF COURSE
PURLEY DOWNS ROAD
CR2
SELSDON PARK HOTEL GOLF COURSE
Selsdon Park Hotel
SPORTS GRD
ADDINGTON ROAD
NEWLANDS WOOD
SPORTS GROUND
RECTORY PARK
A2022
MITCHLEY AVENUE
MITCHLEY WOOD
KINGS WOOD
DOWNS COURT ROAD
GODSTONE ROAD
RIDDLESDOWN
RIDDLESDOWN WOOD
COOMBES WOOD
Keepers Cottage
CR8
FOXLEY WOOD
HIGHER DRIVE REC GRD
RAGGED WOOD
AINSLEY BERRY SHAW
LIMPSFIELD ROAD
KENLEY
LONDON
TANDRIDGE
DISPLEY WOOD
BOURNE

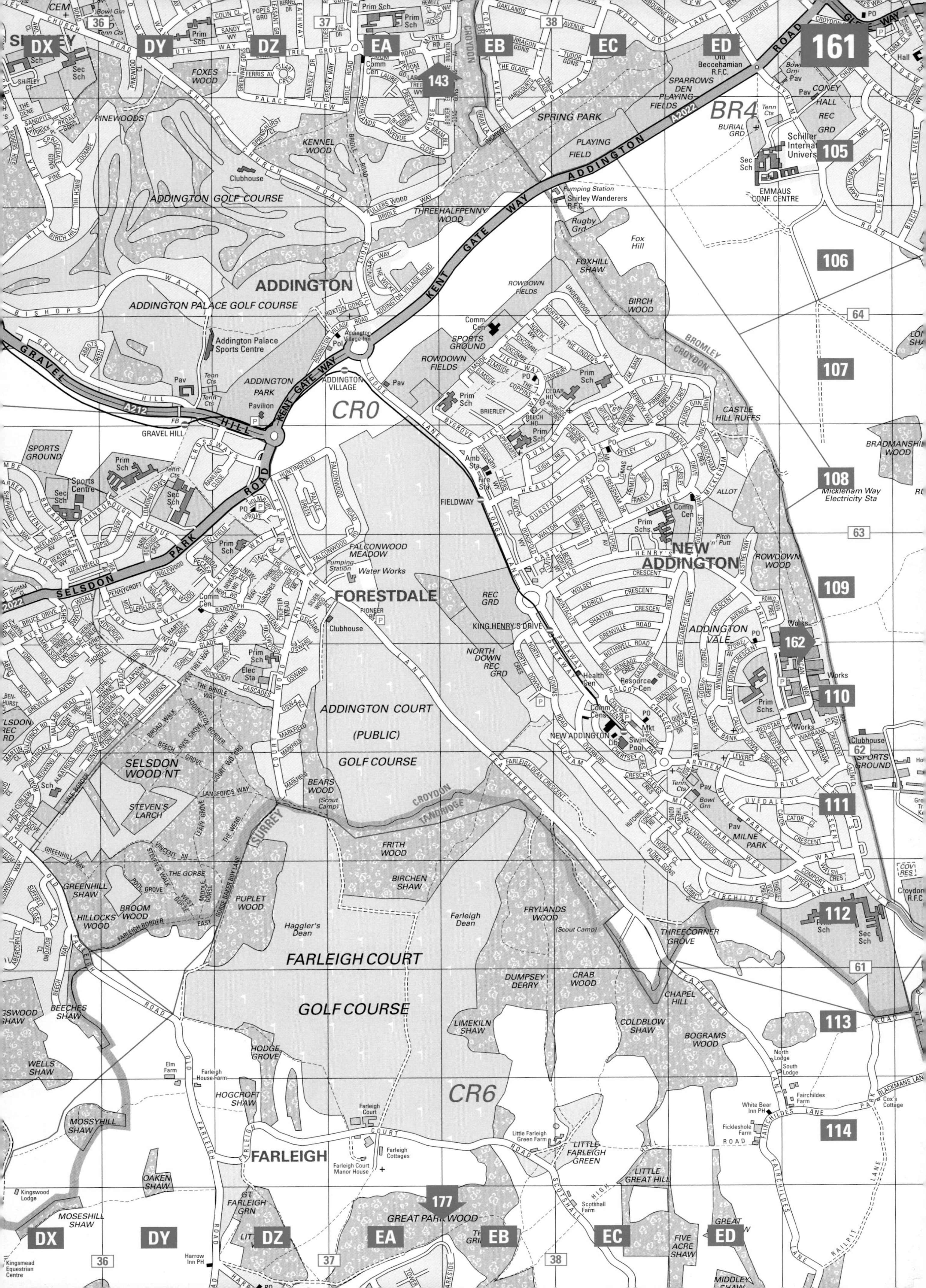
DX
DY
DZ
EA
EB
EC
ED
36
37
38
143
CROYDON
FOXES WOOD
PINEWOODS
KENNEL WOOD
SPRING PARK
PLAYING FIELD
SPARROWS DEN PLAYING FIELDS
Old Beccehamian R.F.C.
BR4
A2022
ADDINGTON ROAD
CONEY HALL REC GRD
BURIAL GRD
Schiller Internat Univers
EMMAUS CONF. CENTRE
105
106
107
108
109
110
111
112
113
114
64
63
62
61
Clubhouse
ADDINGTON GOLF COURSE
THREEHALFPENNY WOOD
Pumping Station
Shirley Wanderers R.F.C.
Rugby Grd
Fox Hill
FOXHILL SHAW
ROWDOWN FIELDS
BIRCH WOOD
ADDINGTON
ADDINGTON PALACE GOLF COURSE
KENT GATE WAY
Addington Palace Sports Centre
ADDINGTON PARK
Pavilion
ADDINGTON VILLAGE
CR0
SPORTS GROUND
BROMLEY
CROYDON
CASTLE HILL RUFFS
BRADMANSHILL WOOD
Mickleham Way Electricity Sta
GRAVEL HILL
A212
SELSDON PARK ROAD
FIELDWAY
NEW ADDINGTON
ROWDOWN WOOD
FALCONWOOD MEADOW
Water Works
FORESTDALE
REC GRD
KING HENRY'S DRIVE
NORTH DOWN REC GRD
ADDINGTON VALE
162
Works
ADDINGTON COURT (PUBLIC) GOLF COURSE
SELSDON WOOD NT
STEVEN'S LARCH
BEARS WOOD (Scout Camp)
SURREY
TANDRIDGE
FRITH WOOD
BIRCHEN SHAW
MILNE PARK
Clubhouse
SPORTS GROUND
Croydon R.F.C.
GREENHILL SHAW
BROOM WOOD
HILLOCKS WOOD
PUPLET WOOD
Haggler's Dean
Farleigh Dean
FRYLANDS WOOD (Scout Camp)
THREECORNER GROVE
FARLEIGH COURT GOLF COURSE
DUMPSEY DERRY
CRAB WOOD
CHAPEL HILL
BEECHES SHAW
LIMEKILN SHAW
COLDBLOW SHAW
BOGRAMS WOOD
WELLS SHAW
HODGE GROVE
Elm Farm
Farleigh House Farm
HOGCROFT SHAW
CR6
MOSSYHILL SHAW
Farleigh Court
Farleigh Cottages
Farleigh Court Manor House
FARLEIGH
Little Farleigh Green Farm
LITTLE FARLEIGH GREEN
LITTLE GREAT HILL
White Bear Inn PH
Fickleshole Farm
Fairchildes Farm
North Lodge
South Lodge
Cox's Cottage
OAKEN SHAW
Kingswood Lodge
MOSESHILL SHAW
GT FARLEIGH GRN
177
GREAT PARK WOOD
Scotshall Farm
FIVE ACRE SHAW
Harrow Inn PH
Kingsmead Equestrian Centre
MIDDLEY SHAW

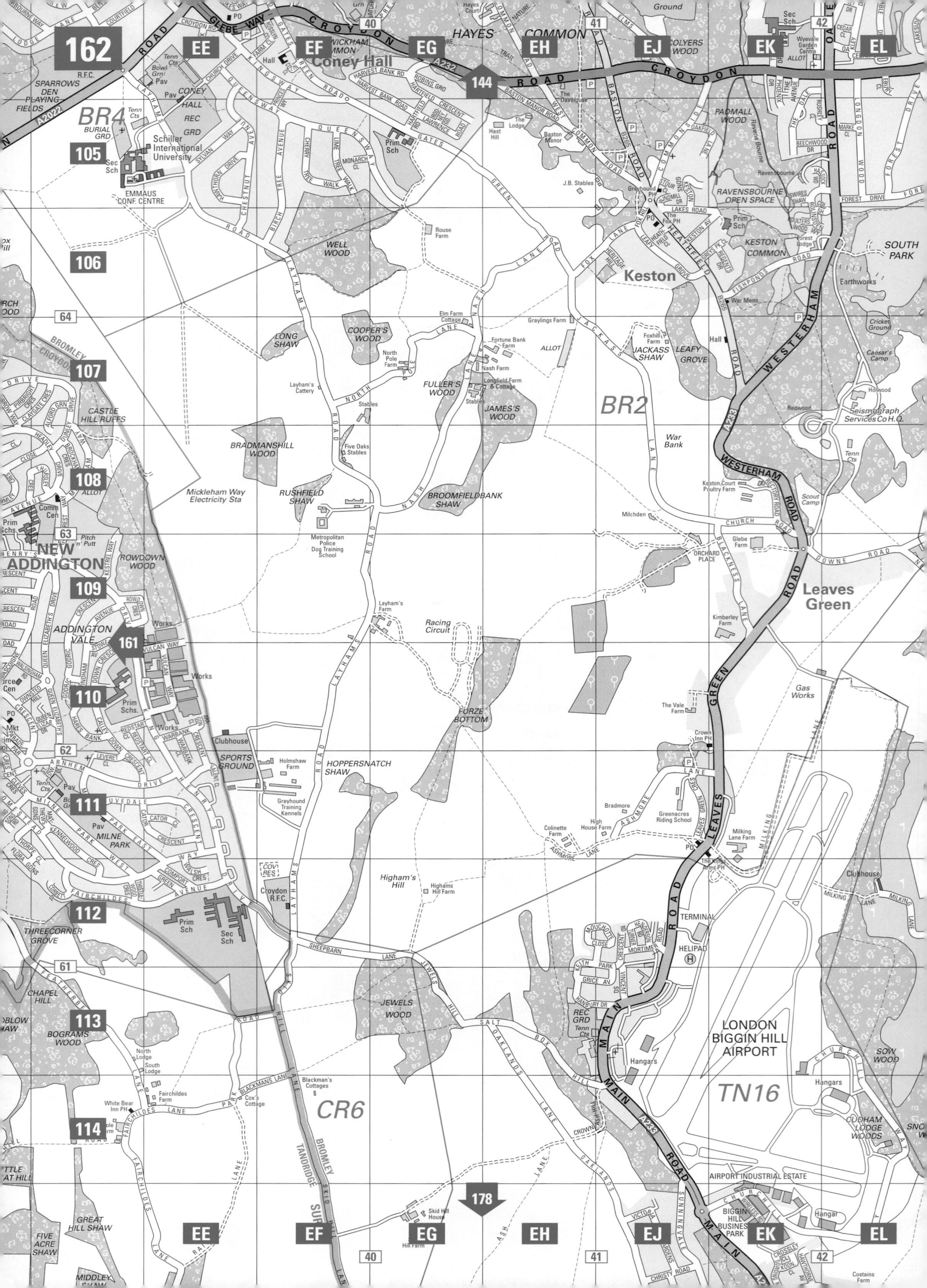

162
EE
EF
EG
EH
EJ
EK
EL
144
Coney Hall
HAYES COMMON
CROYDON ROAD
Keston
KESTON COMMON
SOUTH PARK
RAVENSBOURNE OPEN SPACE
BR4
BR2
NEW ADDINGTON
ADDINGTON VALE
161
MILNE PARK
Leaves Green
LONDON BIGGIN HILL AIRPORT
TN16
CR6
BIGGIN HILL BUSINESS PARK
AIRPORT INDUSTRIAL ESTATE
WESTERHAM ROAD
LEAVES GREEN ROAD
MAIN ROAD
LAYHAMS ROAD
NASH LANE
JACKASS LANE
WAR BANK LANE
FURZE BOTTOM
HOPPERSNATCH SHAW
JEWELS WOOD
178
105
106
107
108
109
110
111
112
113
114
40
41
42
61
62
63
64

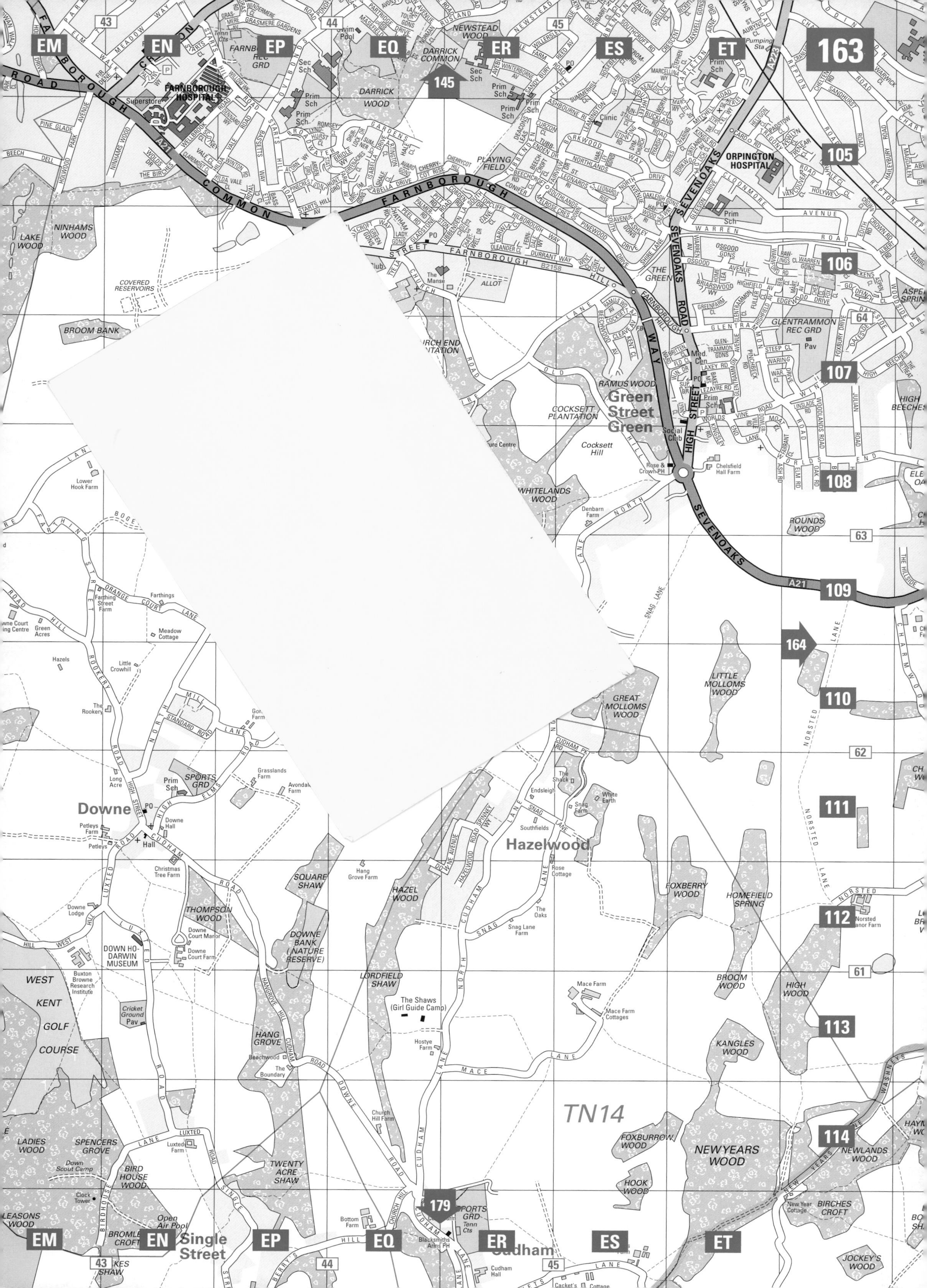163
EM
EN
EP
EQ
ER
ES
ET
43
44
45
145
FARNBOROUGH HOSPITAL
Superstore
FARNBOROUGH COMMON
DARRICK COMMON
DARRICK WOOD
NEWSTEAD WOOD
PLAYING FIELD
ORPINGTON HOSPITAL
SEVENOAKS ROAD
SEVENOAKS WAY
FARNBOROUGH HILL
FARNBOROUGH WAY
HIGH STREET
B2158
A21
A223
LAKE WOOD
NINHAMS WOOD
COVERED RESERVOIRS
BROOM BANK
THE GREEN
GLENTRAMMON REC GRD
RAMUS WOOD
Green Street Green
COCKSETT PLANTATION
Cocksett Hill
WHITELANDS WOOD
Chelsfield Hall Farm
Denbarn Farm
ROUNDS WOOD
105
106
107
108
109
110
111
112
113
114
164
179
63
62
61
64
SNAG LANE
LITTLE MOLLOMS WOOD
GREAT MOLLOMS WOOD
NORSTED LANE
Lower Hook Farm
Farthings
Farthing Street Farm
Meadow Cottage
Hazels
Little Crowhill
The Rookery
Grasslands Farm
Avondale Farm
Downe
Petleys Farm
Downe Hall
Hall
Christmas Tree Farm
Hazelwood
SQUARE SHAW
Hang Grove Farm
HAZEL WOOD
FOXBERRY WOOD
HOMEFIELD SPRING
THOMPSON WOOD
DOWNE BANK (NATURE RESERVE)
Downe Court Manor
Downe Court Farm
DOWN HO- DARWIN MUSEUM
Downe Lodge
Buxton Browne Research Institute
WEST KENT GOLF COURSE
Cricket Ground Pav
LORDFIELD SHAW
The Shaws (Girl Guide Camp)
Mace Farm
Mace Farm Cottages
BROOM WOOD
HIGH WOOD
Norsted Manor Farm
HANG GROVE
Hostye Farm
KANGLES WOOD
MACE LANE
TN14
Church Hill Farm
LADIES WOOD
SPENCERS GROVE
Luxted Farm
Down Scout Camp
BIRD HOUSE WOOD
Clock Tower
Open Air Pool
TWENTY ACRE SHAW
FOXBURROW WOOD
HOOK WOOD
NEWYEARS WOOD
NEWLANDS WOOD
New Year Cottage
BIRCHES CROFT
Bottom Farm
SPORTS GRD
Blacksmiths Arms PH
Single Street
Cudham
Cudham Hall
JOCKEY'S WOOD

164
EU
EV
EW
EX
EY
EZ
FA
146
Goddington
GODDINGTON PARK
BR6
CHELSFIELD
CHELSFIELD PARK HOSPITAL
Maypole
CHELSFIELD LAKES GOLF COURSE
BROKE HILL GOLF COURSE
Pratt's Bottom
163
180
Halstead
Knockholt Pound
105
106
107
108
109
110
111
112
113
114

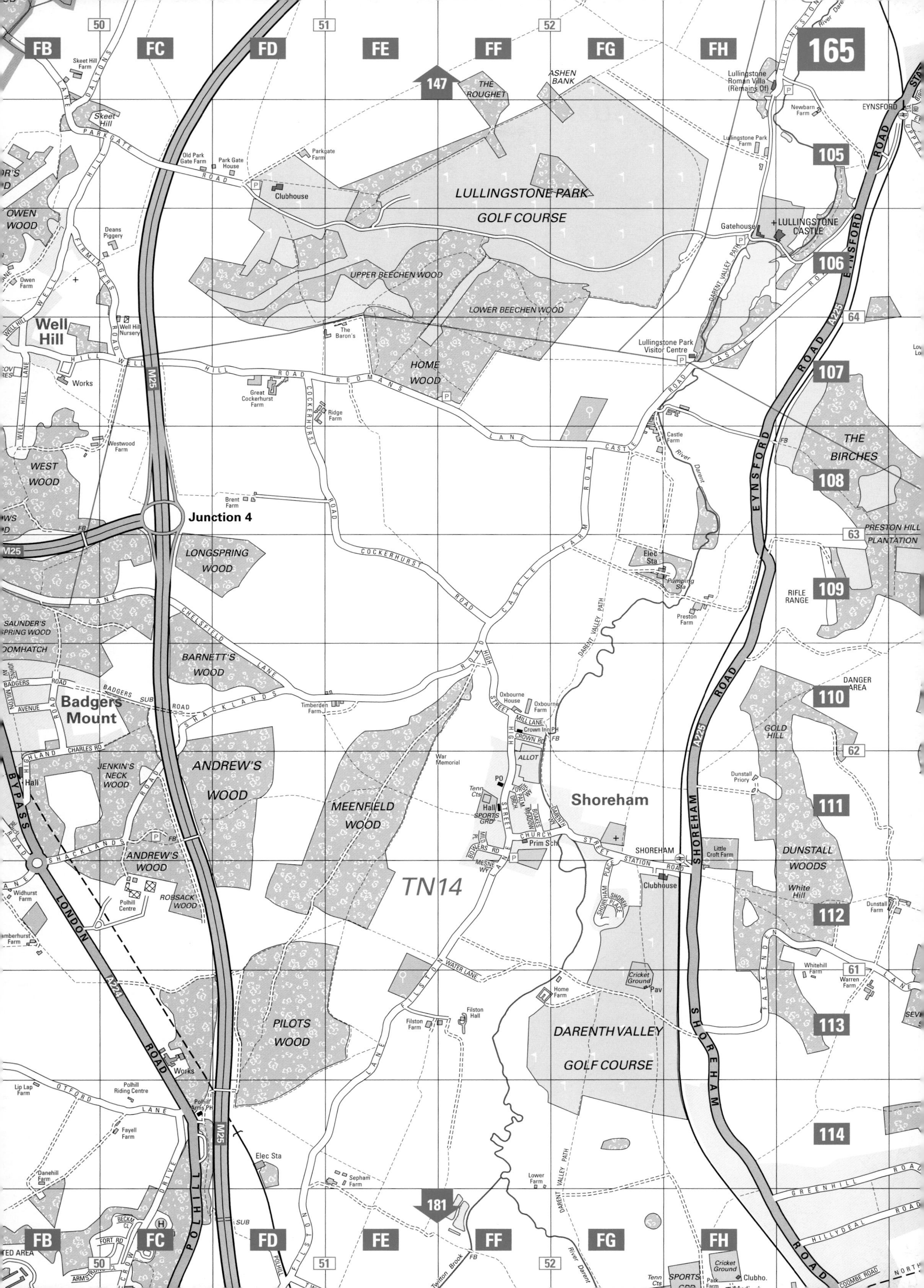
FB
FC
FD
FE
FF
FG
FH
50
51
52
147
181
LULLINGSTONE PARK GOLF COURSE
UPPER BEECHEN WOOD
LOWER BEECHEN WOOD
HOME WOOD
THE ROUGHET
ASHEN BANK
Lullingstone Roman Villa (Remains Of)
LULLINGSTONE CASTLE
Gatehouse
Lullingstone Park Visitor Centre
Lullingstone Park Farm
Newbarn Farm
EYNSFORD
EYNSFORD ROAD
A225
Well Hill
Skeet Hill
Skeet Hill Farm
Old Park Gate Farm
Park Gate House
Parkgate Farm
PARKGATE ROAD
Clubhouse
OWEN WOOD
Owen Farm
Deans Piggery
Well Hill Nursery
The Baron's
Works
Great Cockerhurst Farm
Ridge Farm
Westwood Farm
WEST WOOD
REDMANS LANE
CASTLE ROAD
COCKERHURST ROAD
CASTLE FARM ROAD
Castle Farm
River Darent
THE BIRCHES
PRESTON HILL PLANTATION
Brent Farm
Junction 4
M25
LONGSPRING WOOD
Elec Sta
Pumping Sta
Preston Farm
RIFLE RANGE
SAUNDER'S SPRING WOOD
CHELSFIELD LANE
BARNETT'S WOOD
Badgers Mount
BADGERS ROAD
SHACKLANDS ROAD
Timberden Farm
Oxbourne House
Oxbourne Farm
MILL LANE
Crown Inn PH
CROWN RD
ALLOT
HIGH STREET
DANGER AREA
GOLD HILL
ANDREW'S WOOD
MEENFIELD WOOD
War Memorial
JENKIN'S NECK WOOD
Shoreham
PO
Hall
SPORTS GRD
Prim Sch
CHURCH STREET
STATION ROAD
SHOREHAM
Clubhouse
Little Croft Farm
Dunstall Priory
DUNSTALL WOODS
White Hill
Dunstall Farm
TN14
ROBSACK WOOD
Polhill Centre
Widhurst Farm
LONDON ROAD
A224
SHOREHAM ROAD
SHOREHAM PLACE
FACKENDEN LANE
Whitehill Farm
Warren Farm
WATER LANE
Home Farm
Cricket Ground
Pav
PILOTS WOOD
Filston Farm
Filston Hall
FILSTON LANE
DARENTH VALLEY GOLF COURSE
DARENT VALLEY PATH
Works
Lip Lap Farm
Polhill Riding Centre
OTFORD LANE
Polhill Arms PH
Fayell Farm
Elec Sta
Danehill Farm
Sepham Farm
Lower Farm
POLHILL
GREENHILL ROAD
HILLYDEAL ROAD
Twitton Brook
Cricket Ground
Clubho.
COOMBE ROAD
105
106
107
108
109
110
111
112
113
114
64
63
62
61

166
AS
AT
AU
AV
AW
AX
AY
150
98
99
00
GU21
GU24
GU3
115
116
117
118
119
120
121
122
123
124
59
58
57
56
CHOBHAM GOLF COURSE
Clubhouse
LITTLEWICK COMMON
HORSELL COMMON
HORSELL BIRCH
TRACIOVS COPSE
GOLDSWORTH PARK REC GRD
GOLDSWORTH PARK TRADING ESTATE
Goldsworth Park
Knaphill
WATERERS PARK
Horsell
HORSELL MOOR
Mount Hermon
St. John's
Hook Heath
WOKING GOLF COURSE
WOKING CEMETERY
Crematorium
WEST HILL GOLF COURSE
WORPLESDON GOLF COURSE
Mayford
HOE VALLEY LINEAR PARK
SUTTON GREEN GOLF COURSE
SMART'S HEATH
PREY HEATH
Fisher's Hill
Burdenshot Hill
BRIDLEY COPSE
WORPLESDON
WHITMOOR
Beech Hill
Pye Hill
Brookwood Lye
LOCKFIELD DRIVE
A324
A320
A3046
B380
AMSTEL WAY
CARTHOUSE LANE
LITTLEWICK ROAD
HOOK HEATH ROAD
SAUNDERS LANE
SMARTS HEATH LANE
PREY HEATH ROAD
EGLEY ROAD
GUILDFORD ROAD
BLACKHORSE ROAD
HERMITAGE ROAD
WYCH HILL LANE
Basingstoke Canal
WOKING GUILDFORD

AZ
BA
BB
BC
BD
BE
BF
01
02
03
151
168
115
116
117
118
119
120
121
122
123
124
59
58
57
56
WEST BYFLEET
GOLF COURSE
Pyrford
KINGSWEY BUSINESS CENTRE
WOKING BUSINESS PARK
GENESIS BUSINESS PARK
RIVER-COURT
CHERTSEY ROAD
A320
A245
Monument Bridge
IND EST
Chertsey Road Bri
Maybury Cen
Holiday Inn
Superstores
PYRFORD COMMON
THE ROUGH
Pyrford Court
The Bothy
Maybury
WOKING
GU22
HOEBRIDGE GOLF CENTRE
Clubhouse
Monument Hill
Fox Hill
Church Farm
Lady Place
Wheelers Farm
Abbey Stream Bridge
Newark Priory (Remains)
Newark New Bridge
Newark Lock
Newark Mill Bridge
Irish Hole
Sewage Works
Filter Beds
Pumping Sta
Roundbridge Farm
Hoebridge Farm
Hoe Bridge
Hoe Stream
Woking Park Farm
OLDHILL COPSE
WOKING PARK
Leisure Cen
Swim Pool
SPORTS GRD
Sec Sch
Coll
LOOP ROAD SPORTS FIELD
Clubhouse
Tenn Club
CAPITAL PARK
HIGH STREET
A247
Old Woking
BURIAL GRD
Riverdale Farm
River Wey
WOKING GUILDFORD
Papercourt Lock
Papercourt Farm
GARLICK'S ARCH COPSE
Homewood Farm
Devonia Farm
Sailing Club
Westfield
Moorlane Farm
Nursery
Cartbridge House
Weir
Cart Bridge
River Wey Navigation NT
Broadmead Cut
BROADMEAD ROAD
Mill
SAND PIT
Prews Farm
GU23
ALLOT
Depot
Works
Fisher's Farm
New Inn PH
Hall
Christian Centre
SEND ROAD
SPORTS GRD
Send
Send Marsh
MARSH ROAD
B368
Aldertons
Boughton Farm
Oxenham Mill Stream
GU4
Lower Westfield Farm
Runtley Wood Farm
Cricketshill Farm
Cricket Ground
Pav
Triggs Lock
Triggs Lock Bridge
Prim Sch
Tudor Barn Farm
Stables
SEND BARNS LANE
PORTSMOUTH ROAD
CEM
Sutton Green
Fareham's Farm

168
152
167
BG
BH
BJ
BK
BL
BM
BN
05
06
07
59
58
57
56
KT14
GU22
GU23
Pyrford
Pyrford Green
Pyrford Village
Wisley
WISLEY COMMON
THE WISLEY GOLF COURSE
PYRFORD GOLF COURSE
ROYAL HORTICULTURAL SOCIETY WISLEY GARDENS
OCKHAM COMMON
Elm Corner
OCKHAM PARK
Ockham
Ripley
RIPLEY GREEN
Send Marsh
PARK WOOD
WALSHAM MEADOW
WALSHAM PLANTATION
LOVELAND'S COPSE
ROBOROW WOOD
BRAMBLERIDE COPSE
BACHELOR'S COPSE
GARLICK'S ARCH COPSE
BUXTON WOOD
WOOLGER'S WOOD
PEATMOOR WOOD
COMMON MEADOWS
River Wey
M25
PORTSMOUTH ROAD
RIPLEY BY-PASS
A3
NEWARK LANE
ROSE LANE
OCKHAM ROAD NORTH
115
116
117
118
119
120
121
122
123
124

PAINSHILL PARK
KT11
KT24
Ockham Common
Martyr's Green
May's Green
Downside
Cobham
Effingham Junction
Effingham Common
The Drift Golf Course
Hook Wood
Stumps Grove
Barnsthorns Wood
Chatley Heath
Hatchford Park
Junction 10
M25
A3
Portsmouth Road
Old Lane
Ockham Lane
Horsley Road
Downside Road
Plough Lane
Pointers Road
Chilbrook Road
Elmbridge
Guildford
Old Oak Common
The New Preserve
Peaked Rough
Roundabout
Hurst Hill
Chaffers Copse
Tanners Copse
Trulliber Copse
Norton Wood
Bramble Wood
Brickfield Copse
Little Brickfield Copse
Hatchford Wood
Hunt's Copse
Curries Clump
Chatley Wood
Wheel Island
The Lake
Gallows Grove
Clamp Rough
Bushy Thicket
Thicket Copse
Little Mornshill Wood
New Barn Wood
Beaumont Plantation
Downside Common
Ockham Road North
Drift Road
Forest Road
Effingham Common Road
Lower Farm Road
Pikes Pool
Mallards Mere
Bolder Mere

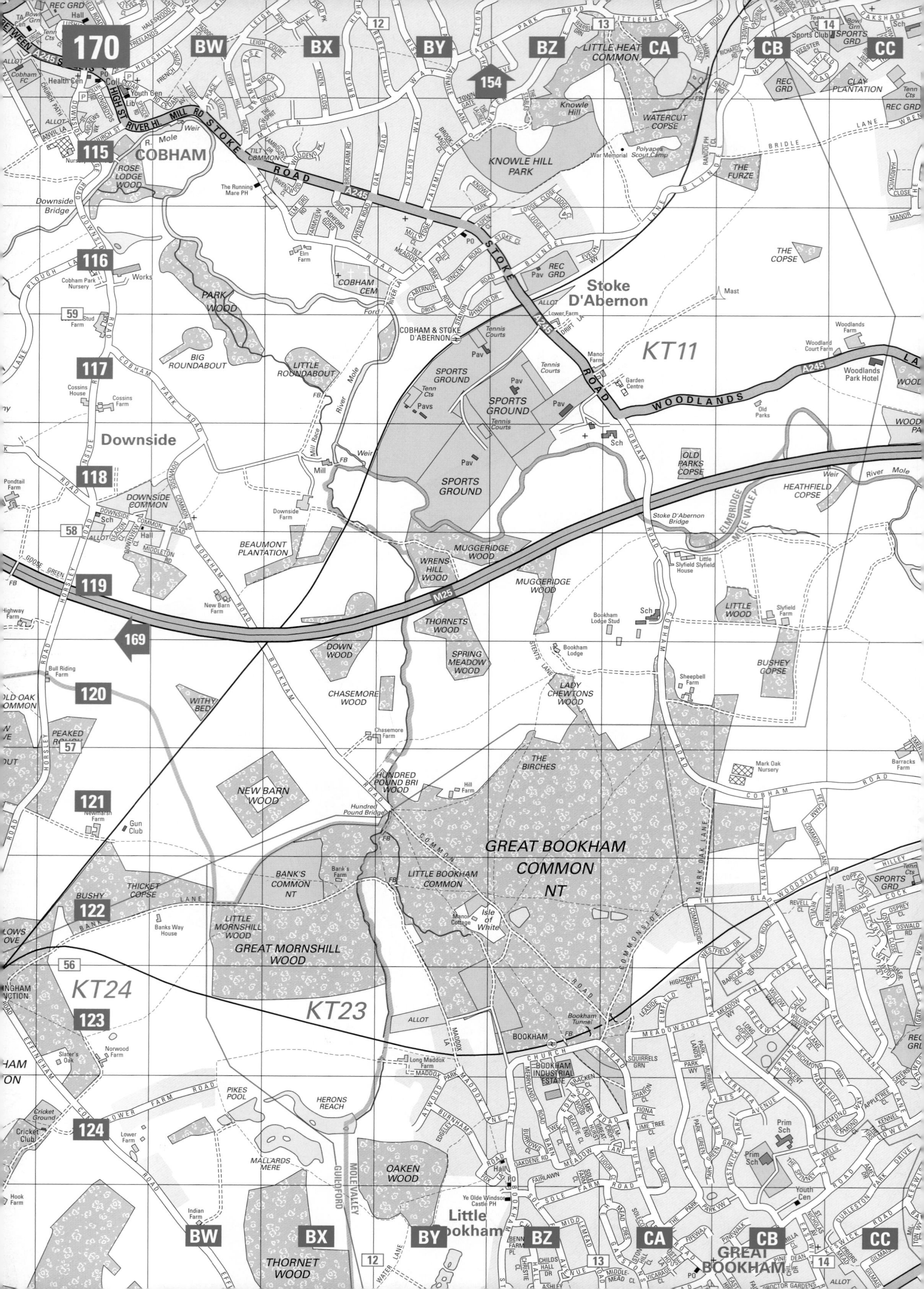

170
154
169
BW
BX
BY
BZ
CA
CB
CC
115
116
117
118
119
120
121
122
123
124
59
58
57
56
12
13
14
COBHAM
R. Mole
ROSE LODGE WOOD
Downside Bridge
The Running Mare PH
STOKE ROAD
A245
KNOWLE HILL PARK
Knowle Hill
LITTLE HEATH COMMON
WATERCUT COPSE
War Memorial
Polyapes Scout Camp
THE FURZE
CLAY PLANTATION
REC GRD
THE COPSE
Elm Farm
COBHAM CEM
Cobham Park Nursery
Works
PARK WOOD
BIG ROUNDABOUT
LITTLE ROUNDABOUT
Stoke D'Abernon
COBHAM & STOKE D'ABERNON
Mast
KT11
Woodlands Farm
Woodland Court Farm
Woodlands Park Hotel
WOODLANDS
SPORTS GROUND
Tennis Courts
Manor Farm
Garden Centre
Old Parks
Downside
Cossins House
Cossins Farm
Mill
Weir
River Mole
OLD PARKS COPSE
HEATHFIELD COPSE
Stoke D'Abernon Bridge
ELMBRIDGE
MOLE VALLEY
DOWNSIDE COMMON
Pondtail Farm
Downside Farm
BEAUMONT PLANTATION
MUGGERIDGE WOOD
WRENS HILL WOOD
M25
New Barn Farm
Highway Farm
THORNETS WOOD
DOWN WOOD
SPRING MEADOW WOOD
Bookham Lodge Stud
Bookham Lodge
Slyfield House
Slyfield Farm
LITTLE WOOD
BUSHEY COPSE
Sheepbell Farm
LADY CHEWTONS WOOD
Bull Riding Farm
OLD OAK COMMON
WITHY BED
CHASEMORE WOOD
Chasemore Farm
PEAKED ROUGH
THE BIRCHES
Mark Oak Nursery
Barracks Farm
NEW BARN WOOD
HUNDRED POUND BRI WOOD
Hundred Pound Bridge
Hill Farm
Newmarsh Farm
Gun Club
GREAT BOOKHAM COMMON NT
BANK'S COMMON NT
Bank's Farm
LITTLE BOOKHAM COMMON
THICKET COPSE
BUSHY
Banks Way House
LITTLE MORNSHILL WOOD
GREAT MORNSHILL WOOD
Manor Cottage
Isle of White
KT24
KT23
ALLOT
Bookham Tunnel
BOOKHAM
Norwood Farm
Slater's Oak
Long Maddox Farm
BOOKHAM INDUSTRIAL ESTATE
PIKES POOL
HERONS REACH
Cricket Ground
Cricket Club
Lower Farm
MALLARDS MERE
OAKEN WOOD
GUILDFORD
MOLE VALLEY
Prim Sch
Youth Cen
Hook Farm
Indian Farm
Ye Olde Windsor Castle PH
Little Bookham
THORNET WOOD
GREAT BOOKHAM

171
CD
CE
CF
CG
CH
CJ
CK
15
16
17
KT9
155
FOREST
LEATHERHEAD GOLF COURSE
ASHTEAD COMMON
Horns Hill
EPSOM GAP
PACHESHAM LAKE
Pachesham Park
Clubhouse
WOODLANDS PARK
Prince's Coverts
Clouds Hill Farm
Crab Apple Court
Pachesham Manor
Tyrwhitt House
OXSHOTT ROAD
KINGSTON ROAD
A243
A244
M25
Junction 9
KT21
ASHTEAD
Lower Ashtead
WOOD FIELD
Paddocks Lodge Stables
Ashtead Court
TEAZLE WOOD
Clubhouse DRIVING RANGE
PACHESHAM GOLF CENTRE
Leatherhead Common
THE MOUNTS
BUSHY PLATT
Earthworks
Tower
Mast
Sewage Works
Composting Plant
Filter Beds
Brook Willow Farm
Pachesham Equestrian Centre
FETCHAM PARK UTD. FC
SPRING POND
National Grid
KT22
RANDALLS ROAD
A245
Crematorium
RANDALLS PARK CEMETERY
Cannon Grove Nursery
LEATHERHEAD
MOLE BUSINESS PARK
River Mole
STATION RD
BULL HILL
LEATHERHEAD BYPASS ROAD
SPORTS FLD
SPORTS GRD
SPORTS GROUND
Barnettwood Farm
ALLOT
Junction 9
ASHTEAD HOSP
172
Esso House
HOSP
Fetcham
Leatherhead Bridge
Leatherhead FC
Hockey & Cricket Club
Athletics Club
Leisure Centre
WATER PARK
Thorncroft Manor
Rifle Range
Water Works
MILL POND
Hawk's Hill
COV RES
Beaverbrook Roundabout
SHEPHERDS CLOSE
Downside Farm
Bocketts Farm
YOUNG STREET
A246
LEATHERHEAD BYPASS
GUILDFORD ROAD
REIGATE ROAD
B2033
B2450
B2122
HEADLEY ROAD
COVERED RESERVOIR
Highlands Farm
115
116
117
118
119
120
121
122
123
124
59
58
57
56
TYRI

172
EPSOM COMMON
NEWTON WOOD
ASHTEAD COMMON
WOOD FIELD
ASHTEAD
Lower Ashtead
ASHTEAD PARK
Ashtead Park
City of London Freemen's School
ASHTEAD HOSP
EPSOM GENERAL HOSP
WOODCOTE GREEN
Woodcote
HALFMOON CLUMP
WORLDS END
FISH POND
WOODCOTE PARK GOLF COURSE
Woodcote Park Country Club
THE GROVE
Langley Vale
LANGLEY BOTTOM WOOD
THE WARREN
KT21
KT18
KT22
EPSOM & EWELL
MOLE VALLEY
ADDLESTEAD WOOD
LITTLE HURST WOOD
Tyrrell's Wood
TYRRELL'S WOOD
HAMBLETON WOOD
HEADLEY COURT
HOOK WOOD
GREAT HURST WOOD
PIGNUT WOOD
OYSTER HILL NT
NOWER WOOD
TYRRELL'S WOOD GOLF COURSE
COSTAL WOOD
Headley
Beaverbrook Roundabout
COVERED RESERVOIR
Esso House
Chase Farm Stud
Highlands Farm
Addlestead Farm
Court Farm
Larchfield
Langley Bottom Farm
Woodcote Stud Farm
Marsden Nursery
Ashtead House
Farm Lane Nurseries
Cottage in the Park
Clubhouse
Sports Hall
BURIAL GRD
SPORTS GRD
ASHTEAD REC GRD
M25
A24
B2033
EPSOM ROAD
DORKING ROAD
THE STREET
LEATHERHEAD ROAD
LEATHERHEAD BYPASS
REIGATE ROAD
HEADLEY ROAD
PEBBLE LANE
ROMAN ROAD
WALTON ROAD
LANGLEY VALE ROAD
SHEPHERDS WALK
GRAY'S LANE
PARK LANE
FARM LANE
WIMBERHATCH
CHALK LANE
ROSEBERY ROAD
GROSVENOR ROAD
CONSFIELD
156
171
182
115
116
117
118
119
120
121
122
123
124
CL
CM
CN
CP
CQ
CR
CS
19
20
21
56
57
58
59

173
CT
CU
CV
CW
CX
CY
CZ
157
115
116
117
118
119
174
120
121
122
123
124
183
22
23
24
59
58
57
56
KT17
SM7
KT20
NORK
NORK PARK
PARK WOOD
Tattenham Corner
Burgh Heath
BURGH HEATH
TADWORTH
KINGSWOOD
Walton on the Hill
BANSTEAD
BANSTEAD HEATH
EPSOM DOWNS
EPSOM RACE COURSE
EPSOM DOWNS GOLF COURSE
WALTON DOWNS
LANGLEY VALE
SANDHILL WOOD
CANONS WOOD
RUFFETT WOOD
PAGES ACRE
BEECHEN COPSE
MILLFIELD WOOD
TATTENHAM WAY RECREATION GROUND
SPORTS GROUND
THE CHILDRENS TRUST
Epsom College
Toyota
Superstore
COVERED RESERVOIR
Premier Lodge
Legal & General House
Kingswood Warren
Police Training School
Clubhouse
Grandstand
Buckle's Gap
Cricket Ground
WORKHOUSE POND
MERE POND
The Clock Tower Riding Centre
REIGATE ROAD
BRIGHTON ROAD
A217
A240
A2022
B290
B2032
B2220
B2221
B284

174
DA
DB
DC
DD
DE
DF
DG
158
26
27
28
A2022
WINKWORTH
CROYDON
BANSTEAD
SM7
WOODMANSTERNE
SPORTS GROUND
REC GRD
Cricket Club
THE SHRUBBERY
Banstead Place
Place Farm
SCRATCH WOOD
Courtlands Farm
Mint Farm
The Mint PH
Tall Trees
New Place
Little Haugh
GREAT SOLOM'S WOOD
SOLOM'S COURT ROAD
CHALK WORKS
How Hills
CLOCKHOUSE REC GRD
PROSPECT PLANTATION
ALLOT
Prim Sch
115
116
117
118
119
120
121
122
123
124
59
58
57
56
PAGES ACRE
RUFFETT WOOD
CANONS WOOD
HOLLY LANE
PARK DOWNS
PARK LANE
B2219
DEPOT
NATURE RESERVE
BANSTEAD WOOD
CHIPSTEAD GOLF COURSE
Chipstead
Clubhouse
COVERED RESERVOIR
HOLLYMEAD
Canons Farm
173
Perrotts Farm
LUNCH WOOD
FAMES ROUGH
CHIPSTEAD BOTTOM
CHIPHOUSE WOOD
WELL COPSE
OUTWOOD LANE
B2032
Chipstead Bottom
CASTLE ROAD
Longshaw
STARROCK SHAW
CHIPSTEAD MEADS REC GRD
SPORTS GROUND
Legal & General House
St Monica's
KT20
Tenn Club
KINGSWOOD
WATERHOUSE
OUTWOOD SHAW
POORFIELD WOOD
Elmore
Chipstead R.F.C.
Bowl Club
EMBERS SHAW
War Memorial
OUTWOOD
SPORTS GRD
Chipstead FC
Cricket Ground
THE GROVE
Hooley
FOURTEEN ACRE SHAW
Noke Farm Barns
Shabden Park
THE BELT
THE LONG PLANTATION
Eyhurst Farm
Eyhurst Park
THE RUFFETT
ROUND WOOD
RUFFETTS WOOD
Kingswood Warren
KINGSWOOD
KINGSWOOD GOLF COURSE AND COUNTRY CLUB
WHITE HILL
Pigeonhouse Farm
Manor Park
South Lodge
Clubhouse
SMUGGLERS PIT PLANTATION
TOP SHAW
ROUND WOOD
HEDGELAND SHAW
CHIPSTEAD LANE
Well House PH
WELLFIELD SHAW
HOMEFIELD SHAWS
Reeves Rest
MONKSWELL
184
RECTORY ROAD
BEECHEN
SPORTS
COPSE
MILLFIELD WOOD
Mugswell
Park Farm
HARPS OAK SHAW
BOARS GREEN SHAW
LONG WOOD
LITTLE WOOD
HIGH ROAD
MARKEDGE LANE
BRIGHTON ROAD

175
DH
DJ
DK
DL
DM
DN
DP
29
30
31
159
WOODCOTE PARK GOLF COURSE
COULSDON
SMITHAM
COULSDON SOUTH
ULLSWATER BUSINESS PARK
COULSDON COURT PUBLIC GOLF COURSE
HARTLEY BUSHES
COULSDON MANOR GOLF COURSE
STONYFIELD SHAW
GRANGE PARK
CR8
KENLEY
HIGHER DRIVE REC GRD
RIDDLESDOWN WOOD
115
116
117
118
119
120
121
122
123
124
176
185
59
58
57
56
BETTS MEAD RECREATION GROUND
Wattenden Arms PH
TWINERS WOOD
DUNSTAN'S WOOD
POSTERN WOOD
MARLFIELD SHAW
Cane Hill S.A.S.S. Unit
FARTHING OR FAIRDEAN DOWNS
INWOOD
Old Coulsdon
Coulsdon Coll
CR5
STAR SHAW
THREE CORNERED SHAW
SPORTS GRD
BOXERS WOOD
DITCHES SHAW
DEVILS DEN WOOD
THE DEVILS DEN
SPARKLIE WOOD
HAPPY VALLEY PARK
SPORTS GROUND
COULSDON COMMON
Purley John Fisher R.F.C.
Youth Club
SURREY
CROYDON
TANDRIDGE
REIGATE & BANSTEAD
RIFLE RANGES
PETERSHOLE SHAW
NETHERNE WOOD
HOSPITAL (closed)
GRASSCUTS SHAW
LORD'S WOOD
THE GULLET
FIGGS WOOD
BROAD WOOD
PILES WOOD
CHURCH GREEN
HAPPY VALLEY GOLF COURSE
Clubhouse
ALDERSTEAD HEATH CARAVAN CLUB SITE
FURZEFIELD WOOD
ALDERSTEAD HEATH
RH1
SPARTICLES WOOD
Airshafts
Merstham Tunnel
Dean Farm
Court Farm
FRYERN BROOM WOOD
Fryern Farm
Chaldon
CR3
Rook Hill
WILLEY BROOM WOOD
BROTHERS FIELD
COVERED RESERVOIR
Alderstead Farm
Uplands Farm
Junction 7
BRIGHTON ROAD
A23
WOODCOTE GROVE
A237
B2030
B2031
B2032
B276

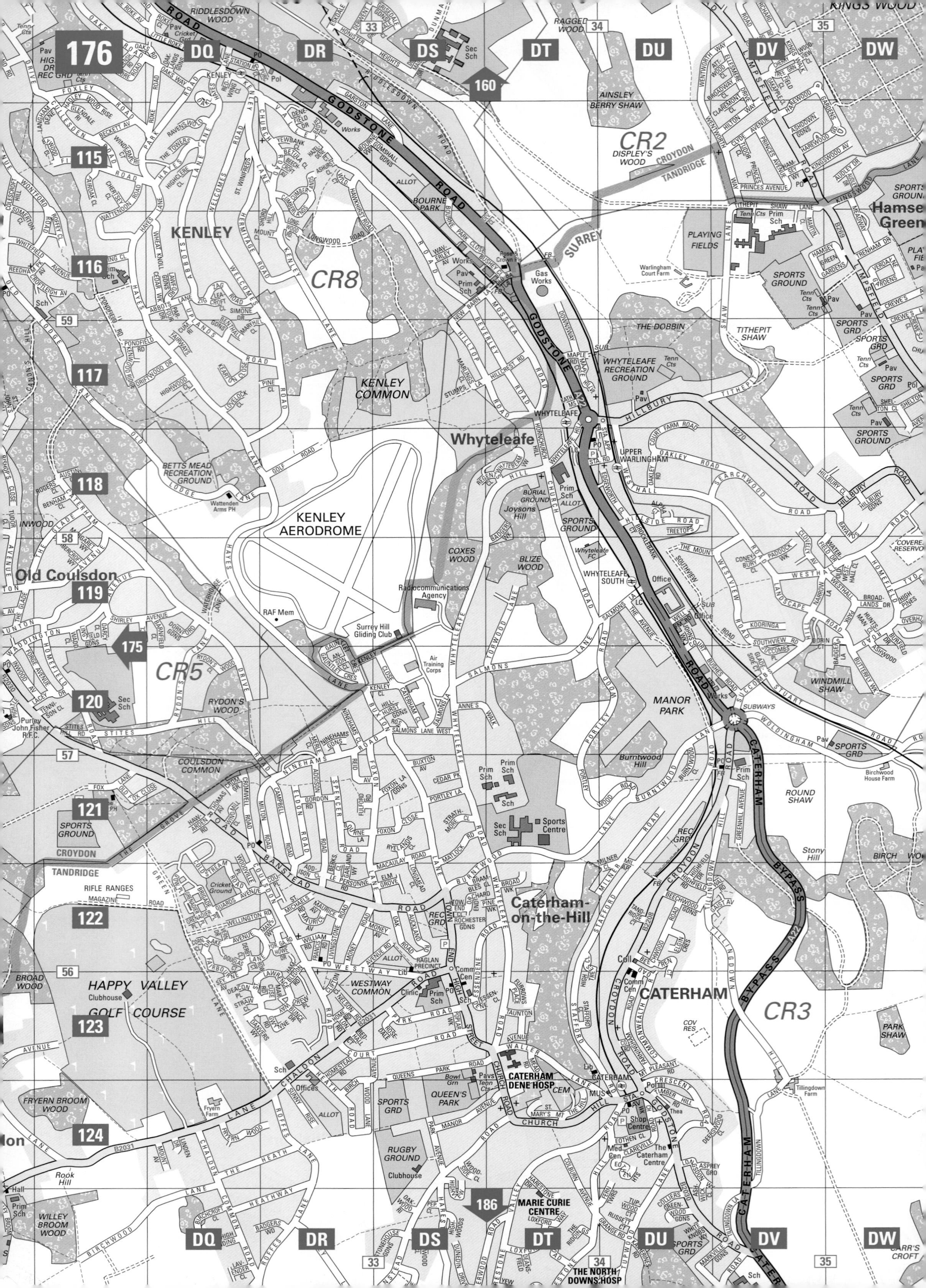

176
DQ
DR
DS
DT
DU
DV
DW
33
34
35
160
RIDDLESDOWN WOOD
RAGGED WOOD
KINGS WOOD
KENLEY
AINSLEY BERRY SHAW
CR2
DISPLEY'S WOOD
CROYDON
TANDRIDGE
SURREY
115
116
117
118
119
120
121
122
123
124
59
58
57
56
CR8
KENLEY COMMON
BOURNE PARK
GODSTONE ROAD
Gas Works
PLAYING FIELDS
Hamsey Green
SPORTS GROUND
THE DOBBIN
TITHEPIT SHAW
WHYTELEAFE RECREATION GROUND
Whyteleafe
UPPER WARLINGHAM
BETTS MEAD RECREATION GROUND
KENLEY AERODROME
COXES WOOD
BLIZE WOOD
Joysons Hill
WHYTELEAFE SOUTH
Old Coulsdon
175
CR5
RYDON'S WOOD
Radiocommunications Agency
RAF Mem
Surrey Hill Gliding Club
Air Training Corps
MANOR PARK
Burntwood Hill
WINDMILL SHAW
ROUND SHAW
Stony Hill
COULSDON COMMON
Purley John Fisher R.F.C.
CROYDON
TANDRIDGE
RIFLE RANGES
Caterham-on-the-Hill
CATERHAM
CATERHAM BYPASS
A22
CR3
BROAD WOOD
HAPPY VALLEY GOLF COURSE
Clubhouse
WESTWAY COMMON
CATERHAM DENE HOSP
QUEEN'S PARK
PARK SHAW
FRYERN BROOM WOOD
Rook Hill
WILLEY BROOM WOOD
RUGBY GROUND
186
MARIE CURIE CENTRE
The Caterham Centre
THE NORTH DOWNS HOSP
CARR'S CROFT

177
DX
DY
DZ
EA
EB
EC
ED
36
37
38
161
187
178
115
116
117
118
119
120
121
122
123
124
59
58
57
56
FARLEIGH
HOGCROFT SHAW
MOSSYHILL SHAW
OAKEN SHAW
MOSESHILL SHAW
Kingswood Lodge
Farleigh Court
Farleigh Cottages
Farleigh Court Manor House
Little Farleigh Green Farm
LITTLE FARLEIGH GREEN
White Bear Inn PH
Fairchildes Farm
Cox's Cottage
LITTLE GREAT HILL
FIVE ACRE SHAW
GREAT HILL SHAW
MIDDLEY SHAW
HONEYOAK WOOD
Scotshall Farm
GT FARLEIGH GRN
LITTLEPARK WOOD
GREAT PARK WOOD
THE GRIPES
Harrow Inn PH
Kingsmead Equestrian Centre
CREWE'S WOOD
MOUNT HOPPER
Pinel House
SPORTS GROUND
SPORTS GRD
HOLT WOOD
Smuggler's Hole
Slades Farm
BURIAL GRD
Sec Sch
SPORTS GROUND
The Bull PH
CHELSHAM COMMON
BULL GREEN
Kennel Farm
Ledgers Farm
CR6
Chelsham
Prim Sch
MILL COMMON
HENLEY WOOD
WASHPOND SHAW
OLDBURY SHAW
Chelsham Court Farm
Chelsham Court
Broom Lodge Farm
GREENLAWN MEMORIAL PARK
Chelsham Place Farm
Superstore
Amb Sta
Hare & Hounds PH
Knights Garden Centre
COV RES
BIRCHEN SHAW
CONY CROOK
WARLINGHAM
REC GRD
Highlands Farm
WORMS HEATH
Radio Sta
Masts
SLINES GREEN
SLINES OAK
HALLILOO PLANTATION
DUKE'S DENE GOLF COURSE
Clubhouse
COTTERSHILL SHAW
Dukes Hill House
LUMBERDINE WOOD
ASHEN SHAW
High Breach
Beech Farm
Warren Barn Farm
Hovings Hole
Woldingham Garden Village
Knights Garden Centre
Chevere Farm
WOLDINGHAM
THE BUSHES
Woldingham
Prim Sch
Clubhouse
SPORTS GRD
Woldingham Equestrian Centre
Hall
Marden Park Farm
GREENHILL SHAW
Botley Hill Farmhouse PH
Botley Hill Farm
Mast
Marden Hillboxes Farm
LITTLE CHURCH WOOD
Whistlers Wood Farm
Water Tower
Masts
WHISTLERS WOOD
HELL SHAW
TITSEY PLANTATION
TEMPLEHILL PLANTATION
GREAT CHURCH WOOD NATURE RESERVE
NORTH DOWNS GOLF COURSE
Whistlers Court
CHALK PITS
MARDEN
Sch
Tennis
Airshaft
CROYDON ROAD
LIMPSFIELD ROAD
CHURCH LANE
CHELSHAM ROAD
HALLILOO VALLEY ROAD
BUTLERS DENE ROAD
SLINES OAK ROAD
STATION ROAD
PARK VIEW ROAD
CHURCH ROAD
SOUTHFIELDS
NORTHDOWN ROAD
WASHPOND LANE
FARM ROAD
HARROW ROAD
FARLEIGH ROAD
SUNNY BANK
RIDGE
B269

178
EE
EF
EG
EH
EJ
EK
EL
40
41
42
162
177
188
115
116
117
118
119
120
121
122
123
124
59
58
57
56
White Bear Inn PH
Fairchildes Farm
Cox's Cottage
Cottages
Hangars
FAIRCHILDES LANE
PARK
BLACKNESS
FAIRCHILDES
LANE
RAILPIT
LANE
FAIRCHILDES
LITTLE HEAT HILL
GREAT HEAT SHAW
FIVE ACRE SHAW
MIDDLEY SHAW
HONEYOAK WOOD
TANDRIDGE
BROMLEY
SURREY
SKID HILL
LANE
Skid Hill House
Skid Hill Farm
ASH
LANE
CROWN
OAKLANDS
MAIN ROAD
A233
CUDHAM
AIRPORT INDUSTRIAL ESTATE
CHURCHILL WAY
BIGGIN HILL BUSINESS PARK
Hangar
VICTORIA
GARDENS
SUNNINGVALE
CHRISTY ROAD
ARTHUR
CROSSLEY CL
AV
Costains Farm
JAIL LANE
MAGNOLIA DRIVE
ACER
SPRUCE RD
BIGGIN HILL CEM
Tenn Cts
Pav
REC GRD
Fire Sta
Clinic
Lib
The Spitfire Centre
ALLOT
CHURCH ROAD
THE RIDINGS
NELSON CL
VILLAGE GREEN AVENUE
MALAN CL
HAIG RD
DOUGLAS CL
Prim Schs
BIGGIN HILL
CAMELOT CL
MELROSE RD
AVENUE
KINGS
NORHEADS LANE
STOCK HILL
CREST ROAD
Norheads Farm
CHALLOCK CL
GRAND VW
CHURCH
Flying Machine PH
DAWELL DR
SUNNINGVALE
MT PLEASANT
RUSH DENE WK
PLEASANT
Hall
LEBANON GDNS
PO
SUTHERLAND
STEEPLE HEIGHTS DR
CHARLTON DR
ROSEHILL RD
SUNNINGVALE AVENUE
Comm Cen & Clinic
HILLINGDALE
HIGHFIELD
ROAD
JERRY REDDINGS SHAW
NORHEADS
MOLLARDS WOOD
CROWN
HESIERS ROAD
CHURCH
LANE
BURIAL GRD
HESIERS HILL
ROAD
COURT
OLDBURY SHAW
Chelsham Court Farm
Broom Lodge Farm
Chelsham Court
CHELSHAM
CR6
OWLS WOOD
BEDDLESTEAD
WHITE BANK
LONG COPPICE
TIMBERTOP RD
ST MARYS
VALLEY VW
LILLIE RD
MEWS END
RICKETTS
EAGLES DR
SURREY
GROVE
CONY CROOK
COWYARD SHAW
SPRING HOLM CL
UPPER WOOD RD
WAKELEY CL
GREENOAK RI
KINGS
MELODY
SCARBOROUGH CL
SWIEVELANDS
ALEXANDRA RD
PARSONS SHAW
HALL
Kingscote
Masts
FARM LANE
ROUND WOOD
NORHEADS
LANE
Beddlestead Farm
HOME WOOD
Lusted Hall Farm
ISLE SHAW
KEMSLEY ROAD
BEECH
AVENUE
PAYNESFIELD
LUMBERDINE WOOD
CHERRY TREE SHAW
CUDHAM
Manor House
ASHEN SHAW
MANOR
BEECH
Beech Farm
B269
ASHEN SHAW
SHEPHERDS SHAW
LUSTED
GOATSFIELD
GREENWAY
JOHNS ROAD
GEORGES RD
CROSSWAYS
Tatsfield
LONGLANDS SHAW
LUSTED HALL LA
GROVE RD
REDHOUSE RD
WESTMORE
WESTMORE GREEN
LIMEHOUSE BOTTOM
Works
Park Farm
SHIP
Hall
Old Ship PH
SHIPFIELD CL
NINEHAMS
MAESMAUR
EDGAR ROAD
BOROUGH RD
OLD HILL
RAG HILL
TANDRIDGE
BROMLEY
ROAD
CROYDON
Cheverells Farm
SPORTS GROUND
Pav
APPROACH
Prim Sch
BEAVER WATER WORLD
PARK WOOD GOLF COURSE
Clubhouse
Church Farm
CHURCH HILL
CLARKS LANE SHAW
PITCHERS WOOD
Masts
Clarks Lane Farm
CHESTNUT
LANE
CLARKS
B2024
TATSFIELD
Mast
RECTORY LANE
COLDHARBOUR BEECHES
HIGH TREES
CLARKS
ROAD
Botley Hill
TITSEY
WHITE LANE
Botley Hill Farmhouse PH
Botley Hill Farm
Mast
RIDGE
PITCHFONT
CR3
Masts
RH8
Pilgrims Farm
CLACKET LANE
HELL SHAW
TITSEY PLANTATION
TITSEY PARK
Titsey Place
TITSEY PLACE GDNS
Titsey
PILGRIMS
BROOMLANDS
FB
CHURCH WOOD
CLACKET WOOD
SQUARE WOOD
Whistlers Court
Flint House
THE RIDGE
PITS
DOWNS
Pitchfont Farm
BARTON SHAW

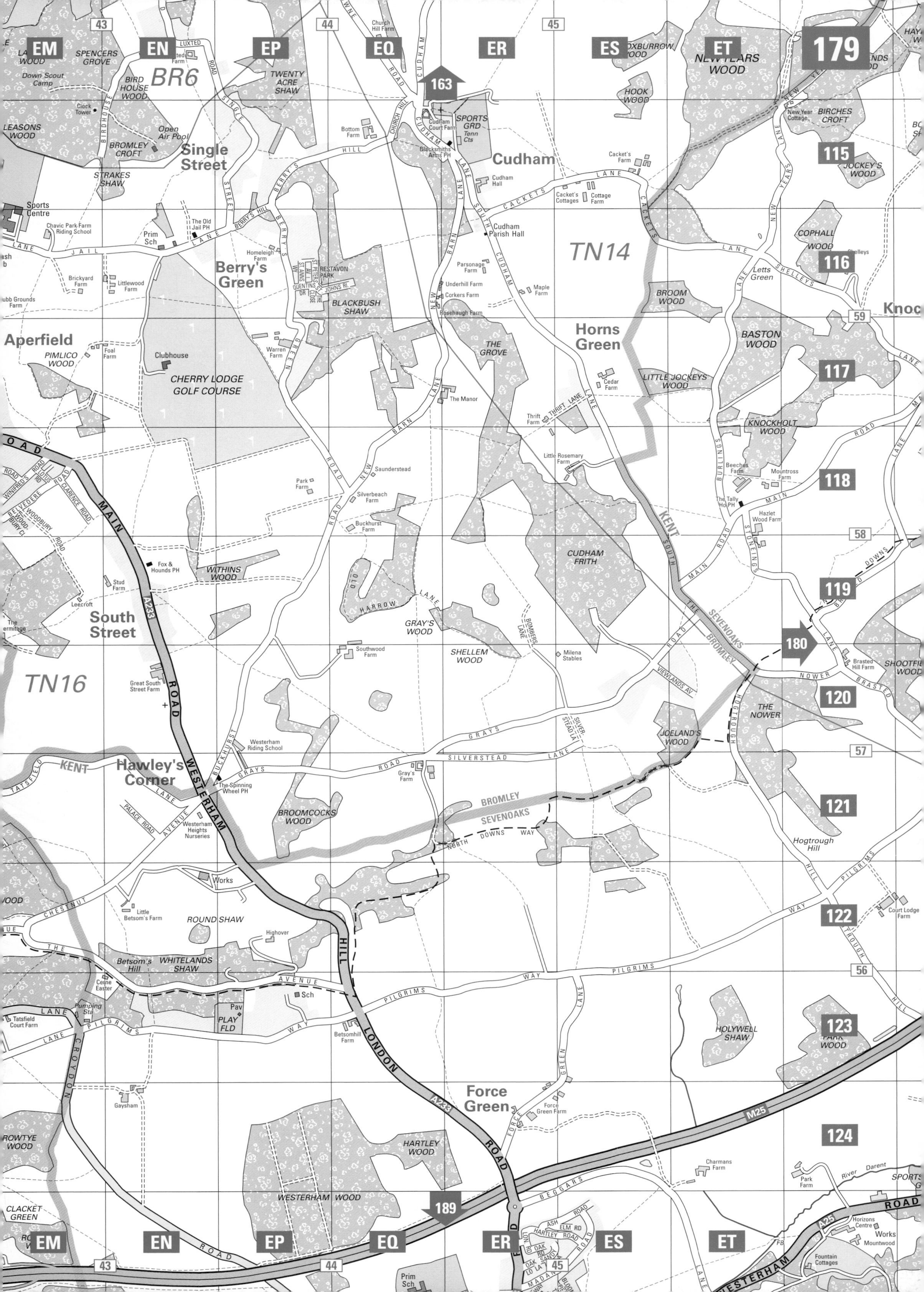

EM
EN
EP
EQ
ER
ES
ET
43
44
45
163
BR6
TN14
TN16
Single Street
Berry's Green
Cudham
Horns Green
Aperfield
South Street
Hawley's Corner
Force Green
Letts Green
SPENCERS GROVE
BIRD HOUSE WOOD
Down Scout Camp
Clock Tower
LEASONS WOOD
Open Air Pool
BROMLEY CROFT
STRAKES SHAW
TWENTY ACRE SHAW
Sports Centre
Chavic Park Farm Riding School
The Old Jail PH
Prim Sch
JAIL LANE
BERRY'S HILL
Brickyard Farm
Littlewood Farm
Homeleigh Farm
RESTAVON PARK
BLACKBUSH SHAW
Warren Farm
PIMLICO WOOD
Foal Farm
Clubhouse
CHERRY LODGE GOLF COURSE
Church Hill Farm
Bottom Farm
Cudham Court Farm
SPORTS GRD
Tenn Cts
Blacksmiths Arms PH
Cudham Hall
Cudham Parish Hall
CACKETS LANE
Cacket's Farm
Cacket's Cottages
Cottage Farm
OXBURROW WOOD
NEWYEARS WOOD
HOOK WOOD
New Year Cottage
BIRCHES CROFT
JOCKEY'S WOOD
COPHALL WOOD
Shelleys
SHELLEYS LANE
NEW YEARS LANE
BROOM WOOD
BASTON WOOD
LITTLE JOCKEYS WOOD
KNOCKHOLT WOOD
Parsonage Farm
Underhill Farm
Corkers Farm
Rosehaugh Farm
Maple Farm
THE GROVE
Cedar Farm
The Manor
Thrift Farm
THRIFT LANE
Little Rosemary Farm
NEW BARN LANE
SOUTH CUDHAM LANE
Saunderstead
Park Farm
Silverbeach Farm
Buckhurst Farm
BURLINGS LANE
Beeches Farm
Mountross Farm
The Tally Ho PH
Hazlet Wood Farm
MAIN ROAD
STONINGS
DOWNS
CUDHAM FRITH
KENT
SOUTH
THE SEVENOAKS BROMLEY
OLD HARROW LANE
GRAY'S WOOD
SHELLEM WOOD
BOMBERS LANE
Milena Stables
VIEWLANDS AV
180
Brasted Hill Farm
SHOOTFIELD WOOD
NOWER
BRASTED
THE NOWER
HOGTROUGH
JOELAND'S WOOD
MAIN ROAD
WINIFRED'S RD
LOTUS RD
CLARENCE ROAD
BELVEDERE ROAD
WOODBURY CL
Fox & Hounds PH
WITHINS WOOD
Stud Farm
Leecroft
The Hermitage
A233
Southwood Farm
Great South Street Farm
GRAYS ROAD
SILVERSTEAD LANE
Westerham Riding School
BUCKHURST
Gray's Farm
TATSFIELD
LANE
The Spinning Wheel PH
PALACE ROAD
AVENUE
Westerham Heights Nurseries
BROOMCOCKS WOOD
BROMLEY
SEVENOAKS
NORTH DOWNS WAY
WESTERHAM ROAD
Hogtrough Hill
Court Lodge Farm
PILGRIMS WAY
Works
CHESTNUT
Little Betsom's Farm
ROUND SHAW
Highover
Betsom's Hill
WHITELANDS SHAW
THE AVENUE
Cerne Easter
Sch
Pumping Sta
Pav
PLAY FLD
Tatsfield Court Farm
CROYDON
Betsomhill Farm
LONDON ROAD
HOLYWELL SHAW
PARK WOOD
Force Green Farm
FORCE GREEN LANE
M25
Gaysham
CROWTYE WOOD
HARTLEY WOOD
Charmans Farm
Park Farm
River Darent
SPORTS
WESTERHAM WOOD
189
BEGGARS
CLACKET GREEN
ASH
ELM RD
HARTLEY ROAD
OAK RD
OAK LA
SANDY
MADAN
Prim Sch
Horizons Centre
Works
Mountwood
Fountain Cottages
A25
WESTERHAM ROAD
115
116
117
118
119
120
121
122
123
124
59
58
57
56

180
EU
EV
EW
EX
EY
EZ
FA
47
48
49
164
179
115
116
117
118
119
120
121
122
123
124
59
58
57
56
Knockholt Pound
Knockholt
Chevening
Sundridge
Brasted
TN16
Junction 5
M25
A25
B2211
KENT
BROMLEY
SEVENOAKS
NEWLANDS WOOD
HAYMAN'S WOOD
BIRCHES CROFT
LONG BOTTOM SHAW
HAWFIELD WOOD
JOCKEY'S WOOD
COPHALL WOOD
BROOM WOOD
BASTON WOOD
LITTLE JOCKEYS WOOD
KNOCKHOLT WOOD
KNOCKHOLT BEECHES
COOPER'S WOOD
ASHPLATT
SAND BANKS
PARK WOOD
SUMMERHOUSE WOOD
HAGBUSH WOOD
ROUGHFIELDS WOOD
SHOOTFIELD WOOD
THE NOWER
JOELAND'S WOOD
CHAPEL CROFT
LEES WOOD
DUTCHMORE WOOD
BROOMFIELD WOOD
ASHFIELD WOOD
STAR HILL WOOD
MINNY WOOD
CHEVENING PARK
THE SPINNEY
HOME WOOD
CLAYPIT SHAW
COMBEBANK WOOD
COMBE WOOD
THE ROOKERIES
THE WARREN
SPORTS GROUND
New Stables Farm
Curry Farm
Warehouses
Singles Cross
Blueberry Farm
The Spinney Nurseries
Works
Harrow Inn PH
Aldwyn House
Meadow Farm
Warren Farm
Rose Cottage Farm
Comm Cen
Clinic
Ivy Farm
The Grange
Bowl Grn
Mast
Football Pitch
The Mill House
Whitelegg's Garden Centre
Chine Farm
Homefield
Shelleys
Letts Green
Court Lodge
War Meml
Sec Sch
The Crown PH
Masts
COV RES
Keepers Cottage
Sundridge Hill
Beeches
Mountross Farm
The Tally Ho PH
Hazlet Wood Farm
Shootfield
Home Farm
Well
Chevening House
BURIAL GRD
Brasted Hill Farm
Chevening Cross
Grove House
Oveny Green Farm
Combe Bank Farm
Farm
Ovenden Lodge
Hogtrough Hill
Court Lodge Farm
Combe Bank Wood
Pumping Station
ST. MARTINS MEADOW
Tanners
Stanhope Arms PH
Mill Farm
The Old Rectory
PYM ORCHARD
Sch
Pav
Little Coombe Bank
Offices
Council Depot
Pumping Sta
Warren Farm
Bowling Green
The Lamb PH
White Horse PH
Hall
The Old Rectory
Mill
Depot
THE OLD YARD
Tennis Courts
Bull Inn PH
White Hart Inn PH
Orchard Farm
Brasted Place
Brasted Place Farm
Charmans Farm
Park Farm
River Darent
Horizons Centre
Works
Mountwood
Fountain Cottages
Prim Sch
Long Barn
NEW YEARS LANE
SINGLES CROSS LANE
RANDLES LANE
POUND LANE
HALSTEAD ROAD
MAIN ROAD
OLD LONDON ROAD
HARROW ROAD
BIRCHWOOD LA
STAR HILL
CHEVENING LANE
IVY LA
BOND CL
WAYLANDS CL
BLUEBERRY LANE
NORTH DOWNS WAY
CHATHAM'S RIDE
LORD
SUNDRIDGE LANE
SHELLEYS LANE
CACKETS LANE
PILGRIMS WAY
STONEINGS
BRASTED LANE
NOWER
OVENDEN ROAD
COMBE BANK DRIVE
BRASTED HILL
HOGTROUGH HILL
STATION ROAD
COLES LANE
RECTORY LANE
GLEBE COTTS
THORNS MEADOW
CHURCH ROAD
HIGH STREET
WILKINS WAY
ELLIOTTS LA
THE CARRIAGEWAY
CHART LANE
WEST END
CHAPMANS ROAD
MANOR RD
WOODSIDE ROAD
NEW ROAD
GREYSTONE PK
CHURCH ROAD
ST. MARY'S CH RD
CHEVENING ROAD
VIEWLANDS AV

FB
FC
FD
FE
FF
FG
FH
165
50
51
52
Twitton
Otford
TN14
Dunton Green
Longford
Chipstead
Riverhead
Bessels Green
TN13
SEVENOAKS WILDFOWL RESERVE
EAST LAKE
WEST LAKE
CHIPSTEAD LAKE
GRAVEL PIT
OTFORD CEMETERY
ORCHARD HEY
BLUEBELL WOOD
RYE WOOD
HOME WOOD
ALDER SHAW
EDWARD SHAW
RAKEFIELD WOOD
OLD GROVE
CHALK PIT
DEFENCE SCIENCE & TECHNOLOGY LABORATORY FORT HALSTEAD
MONTREAL PARK
ANT WOOD
ASH PLAT WOOD
OBELISK WOOD
COLD ARBOR WOOD
LITTLE BRITAIN'S WOOD
MIDDLINGS WOOD
KNOLE PADDOCK
KNOLE ENVIRONMENTAL PARK
THE MOORS
SEVENOAKS HOSP
Morants Court Cross
Donnington Manor Hotel
West Kent Cold Storage
Riverside Retail Park
DUNTON GREEN
SEVENOAKS
Otford Junction
M25
M26
A25
A224
A225
A21
POLHILL
LONDON ROAD
STATION ROAD
OTFORD ROAD
WESTERHAM ROAD
BRADBOURNE VALE ROAD
SEAL ROAD
DARTFORD ROAD
MORANTS COURT ROAD
115
116
117
118
119
120
121
122
123
124
191
190
59
58
57
56

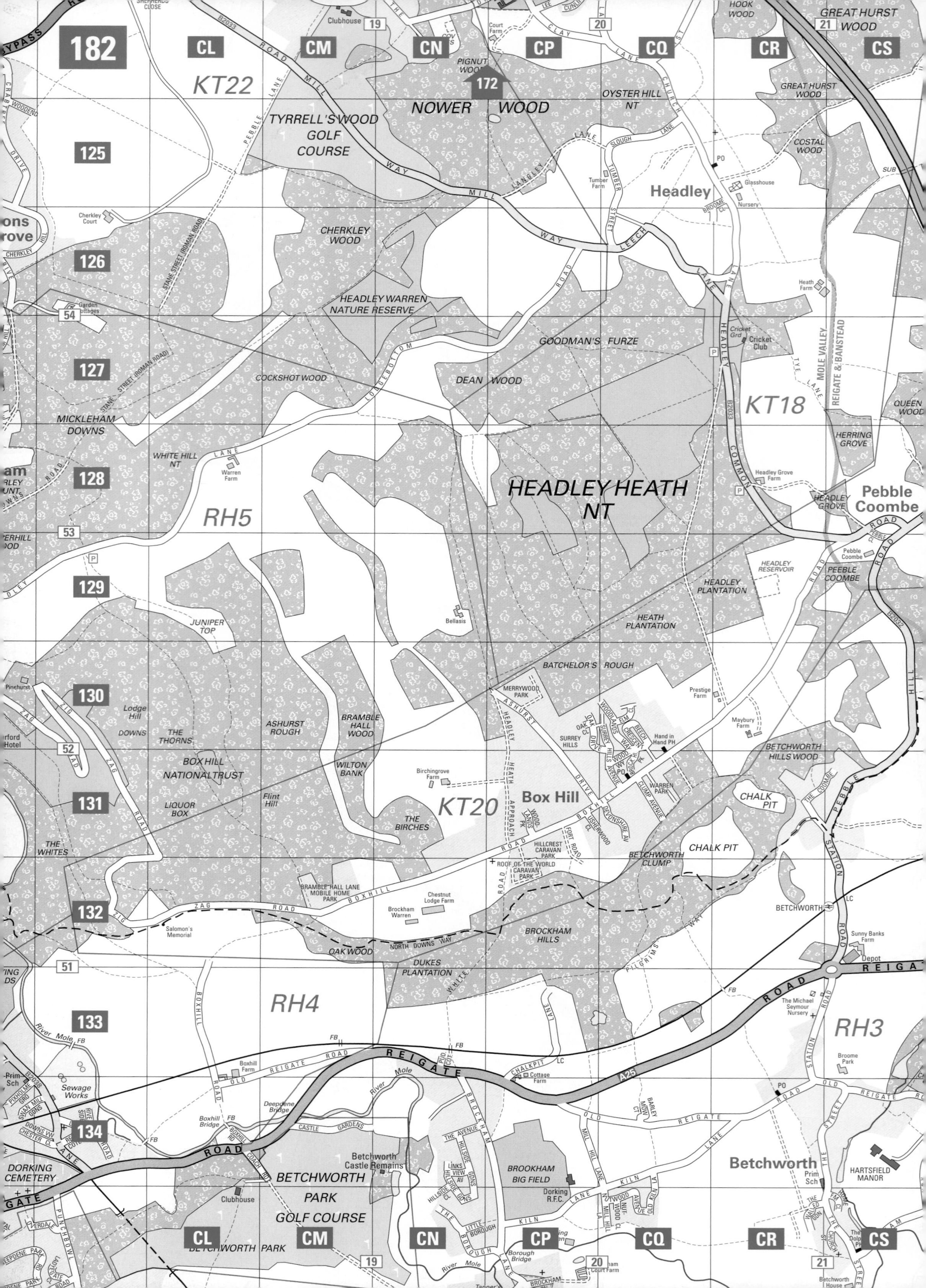

182
CL
CM
CN
CP
CQ
CR
CS
172
KT22
NOWER WOOD
TYRRELL'S WOOD GOLF COURSE
OYSTER HILL NT
Headley
GREAT HURST WOOD
COSTAL WOOD
CHERKLEY WOOD
HEADLEY WARREN NATURE RESERVE
GOODMAN'S FURZE
COCKSHOT WOOD
DEAN WOOD
MICKLEHAM DOWNS
KT18
HERRING GROVE
WHITE HILL NT
HEADLEY HEATH NT
Pebble Coombe
RH5
HEADLEY PLANTATION
HEATH PLANTATION
JUNIPER TOP
BATCHELOR'S ROUGH
ASHURST ROUGH
BRAMBLE HALL WOOD
BOX HILL NATIONAL TRUST
Box Hill
KT20
BETCHWORTH HILLS WOOD
CHALK PIT
THE BIRCHES
BETCHWORTH CLUMP
BROCKHAM HILLS
OAK WOOD
DUKES PLANTATION
RH4
RH3
DORKING CEMETERY
BETCHWORTH PARK GOLF COURSE
BROOKHAM BIG FIELD
Betchworth
HARTSFIELD MANOR
125
126
127
128
129
130
131
132
133
134

173
184
Walton on the Hill
BANSTEAD HEATH
KT20
WALTON HEATH GOLF COURSE
WALTON HEATH
CHUSSEX PLAIN
LITTLE HEATH
Pfizer
Lower Kingswood
Mogador
MARGERY WOOD NT
Colley Hill
THE HORSESHOE
THE SADDLE KNOB
QUEEN'S PARK
FOUR ACRE UPPER WOODS
THE BEECHES
Juniper Hill
Mount Hill
Conybury Hill
Thistle Hill
Lady Hill
Buckland Hills
DEWRIDING PLANTATION
ROUND WOOD
NORTH DOWNS WAY
PILGRIMS' WAY
NORTHLAND SHAW
BUSHY SHAW
COLLEYLAND SHAW
BUSHFIELD COPPICE
COLLEY COPSE
COLLEY WOOD
Buckland
RH2
SAND AND GRAVEL PIT
TAP WOOD
ROUND ALDERS
THE ALDERS
REIGATE HEATH GOLF COURSE
REIGATE HEATH
REIGATE
PRIORY POND
SPORTS GROUND
BUCKLAND ROAD
A25
WEST STREET
HIGH STREET
BRIGHTON ROAD
A217
M25
MOLE VALLEY
REIGATE & BANSTEAD
CT CU CV CW CX CY CZ
22 23 24
51 52 53 54
125 126 127 128 129 130 131 132 133 134

DA
DB
DC
DD
DE
DF
DG
26
27
28
174
183
125
126
127
128
129
130
131
132
133
134
54
53
52
51
Mugswell
CR5
Lower Kingswood
KT20
Margery
Junction 8
RH2
Gatton
REIGATE
GOLF COU
Coles Meads
REIGATE
REDHILL
UPPER GATTON WOOD
UPPER GATTON PARK
GATTON PARK
THE LAKE
TEMPLE WOOD
NUTWOOD NT
REIGATE HILL NT
COLLEY COPSE
COLL WOOD
QUEEN'S PARK
FOUR ACRE UPPER WOODS
THE BEECHES
MARGERY WOOD NT
Colley Hill
GATWICK WOOD
COLTS BUSHES
FURZEFIELD COPSE
GRUB WOOD
MILLFIELD WOOD
BEECHEN COPSE
JUBILEE PLANTATIONS
PARK SHAW
GATTON BOTTOM
HALFMOON CLUMP
GREAT BUCK WOOD
WINGATE HILL
GREENCLUMP HILL
SERPENTINE WOOD
HIGH BEECHES
TOWER WOOD
Ashtead Hill
FURZEFIELD SHAW
DELL WOOD
HEDGEL SHAW
HARPS OAK SHAW
BOARS GREEN SHAW
WRAY COMMON
HILL COMMON
REIGATE CEMETERY
East Surrey Coll
MEML PARK
BRIGHTON ROAD
A217
M25
A25
A23
A242
B2034
REIGATE HILL
CROYDON ROAD
GATTON ROAD
PARK ROAD
LONDON ROAD
HIGH STREET
CHURCH STREET
STATION RD
HATCHLANDS RD
QUEENSWAY

Merstham
South Merstham
Holmethorpe
Warwick Wold
Nutfield
Bletchingley
Junction 7
Junction 8 (M23),
Junction 7 (M25)
CR3
RH1
M23
M25
MERCERS
PARK
COUNTRY
PARK
SAND & SILICON WORKS
SAND PIT
SAND AND GRAVEL PIT
PUBLIC TIP
NUTFIELD CEMETERY
NUTFIELD PRIORY LAKE
QUARRYSIDE BUSINESS PARK
HOLMETHORPE IND EST
COCKLEY PLANTATION
COOMBES COPPICE
STANLEY'S WOOD
PARK WOOD
NORTH PARK
175
186
REDSTONE CEMETERY

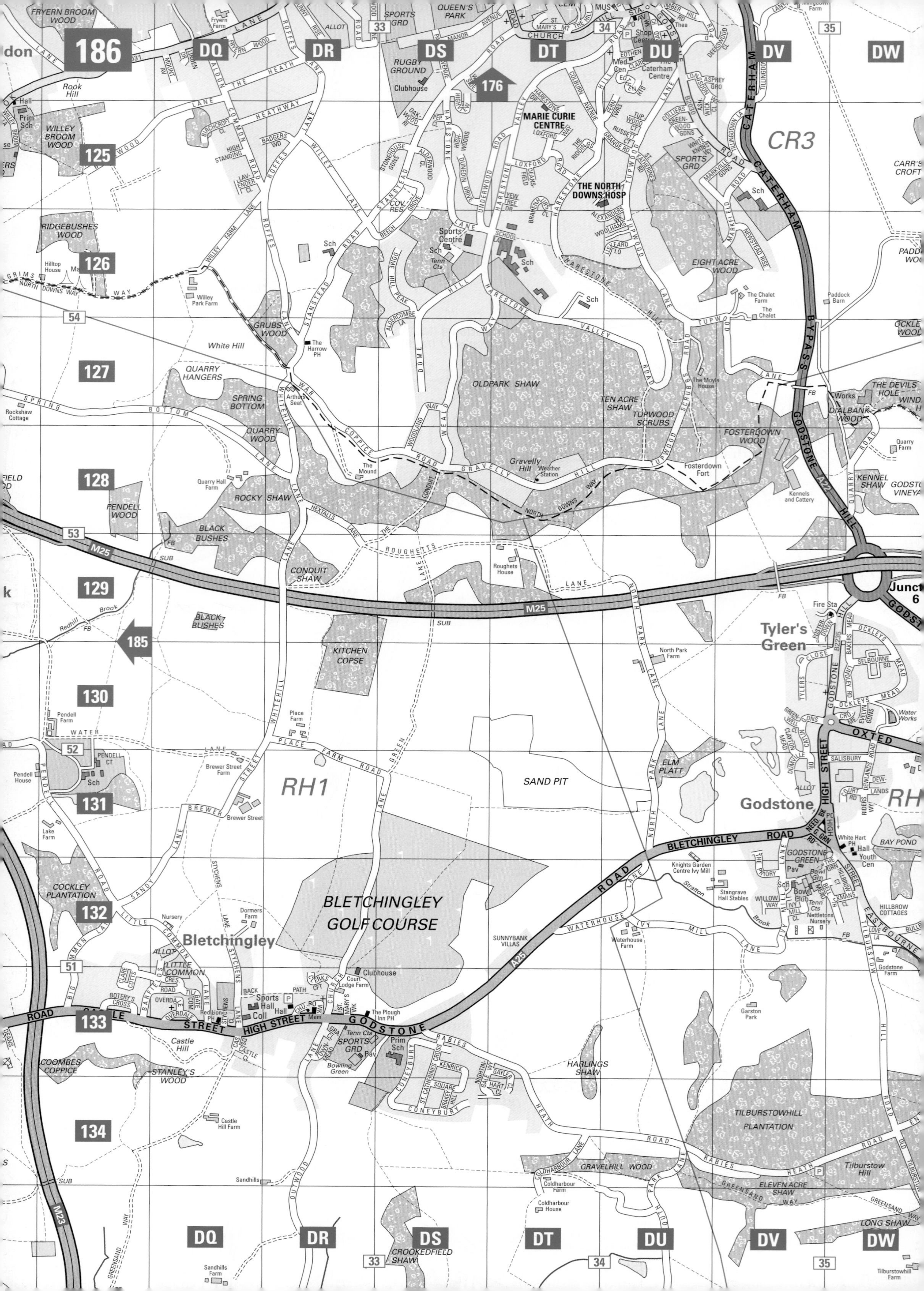
186
176
185
DQ
DR
DS
DT
DU
DV
DW
33
34
35
125
126
127
128
129
130
131
132
133
134
54
53
52
51
CR3
RH1
FRYERN BROOM WOOD
WILLEY BROOM WOOD
Rook Hill
RIDGEBUSHES WOOD
Hilltop House
NORTH DOWNS WAY
GRIMS
Willey Park Farm
White Hill
QUARRY HANGERS
SPRING BOTTOM
QUARRY WOOD
Rockshaw Cottage
Quarry Hall Farm
ROCKY SHAW
PENDELL WOOD
BLACK BUSHES
CONDUIT SHAW
KITCHEN COPSE
Arthur's Seat
The Harrow PH
GRUBS WOOD
SPORTS GRD
QUEEN'S PARK
RUGBY GROUND
Clubhouse
MARIE CURIE CENTRE
THE NORTH DOWNS HOSP
Caterham Centre
Sports Centre
Sch
Tenn Cts
OLDPARK SHAW
TEN ACRE SHAW
TUPWOOD SCRUBS
FOSTERDOWN WOOD
Fosterdown Fort
Gravelly Hill
Weather Station
The Mound
EIGHT ACRE WOOD
The Chalet Farm
The Chalet
The Moyle House
Paddock Barn
THE DEVILS HOLE
DIALBANK WOOD
Quarry Farm
KENNEL SHAW
Kennels and Cattery
CATERHAM BYPASS
GODSTONE HILL
A22
M25
M23
Roughets House
North Park Farm
Fire Sta
Tyler's Green
Godstone
ELM PLATT
SAND PIT
Water Works
OXTED ROAD
HIGH STREET
BLETCHINGLEY ROAD
A25
White Hart PH
Hall
Youth Cen
BAY POND
GODSTONE GREEN
Knights Garden Centre Ivy Mill
Stangrave Hall Stables
HILLBROW COTTAGES
Godstone Farm
Garston Park
Pendell Farm
Pendell House
Place Farm
Brewer Street Farm
Brewer Street
Lake Farm
COCKLEY PLANTATION
Dormers Farm
Nursery
Bletchingley
BLETCHINGLEY GOLF COURSE
Clubhouse
Court Lodge Farm
SUNNYBANK VILLAS
Waterhouse Farm
The Plough Inn PH
Prim Sch
Bowling Green
Castle Hill
COOMBES COPPICE
STANLEY'S WOOD
Castle Hill Farm
HARLINGS SHAW
TILBURSTOWHILL PLANTATION
GRAVELHILL WOOD
Coldharbour Farm
Coldharbour House
ELEVEN ACRE SHAW
Tilburstow Hill
LONG SHAW
Sandhills
Sandhills Farm
CROOKEDFIELD SHAW
Tilburstowhill Farm
GREENSAND WAY

DX
DY
DZ
EA
EB
EC
ED
36
37
38
177
125
126
127
128
129
130
131
132
133
134
188
54
53
52
51
ROOKERY
Sch
Tennis Courts
TEMPLEHILL PLANTATION
Airshaft
Oxted Tunnel
LITTLE CHURCH WOOD
GREAT CHURCH WOOD NATURE RESERVE
MARDEN PARK
Clubhouse
NORTH DOWNS GOLF COURSE
SOUTHFIELDS ROAD
SOUTHVIEW ROAD
WHISTLERS WOOD
Whistlers Court
Flint House
Masts
HELL SHAW
TITSEY PLANTATION
THE RIDGE
CHALK PITS
CHALKPIT LANE
OXTED QUARRY
CHALK PIT
Works
BEECH PLANTATION NT
OXTED DOWNS NT
NORTH DOWNS
STUBBS COPSE
SPORTS GROUND
THE RUMPS
WHITFIELD PLANTATION
SOUTH HAWKE
NT
HAZEL SHAW
HORSE SHAW
Chaldens Farm
GANGERS HILL
NORTH DOWNS WAY
HANGING WOOD
HOGTROUGH LANE
RYE SHAW
LODGE WOOD
ARMITAGE WOOD
HAMFIELD SHAW
FIVE ACRE SHAW
RYE WOOD
CHALKPIT WOOD
HOSP (closed)
BARNETT'S SHAW
Prim Schs
GORDONS WAY
Flint Hall Farm
Tandridge Hill Farm
M25
ROBINS GROVE WOOD
Barrow Green Court
BARROW GREEN ROAD
Blunt House
Barrow Green Farm
THE ABBEYS
SANDY LANE
RH8
THE MOUNT
THE BOGS
MASTER PARK
OXTED
Clubhouse
Superstore
Swim Pool
Gas Holder
Pol
EAST HILL RD
STATION ROAD EAST
STATION ROAD WEST
BLUEHOUSE
BURIAL GRD
PALMERS WOOD OILFIELD
FLOWER WOOD
FLOWER LANE
Works
Flower Farm
SPORTS GROUND
TANDRIDGE HILL LANE
SAND PIT
Tandridge Priory
Riding Centre
MEADOWBROOK
HIGH STREET
WEST HILL BANK
WOODHURST LANE
QUARRY ROAD
A22
A25
BYPASS
OXTED ROAD
GODSTONE ROAD
Round Lodge
Knights Garden Centre
JACKASS LANE
BUSHEY CROFT REC GRD
ST CLAIR CL
NED LANE
Mill Barn
SPRING LANE
TANDRIDGE GOLF COURSE
MOORE'S SHAW
GLEBE WATER
The Glebe House
Leigh Place
LEIGH PLACE LANE
B2236
CASTLEHILL WOOD
Leigh Mill House
THE BIRCHES
Beechwood Hill
NEW BUSTONS WOOD
BUSTONS WOOD
Little Court Farm
Tandridge Court
Oxted Place
BROADHAM GREEN
TANHOUSE ROAD
Haycutter PH
Health Centre
Stonehall Farm
River Eden
OLDPARK WOOD
ROUND WOOD
STONEPIT SHAW
Southlands
Tandridge Court Farm
MAIZENHALL SHAW
REDDINGS WOOD
Perrysfield Farm
Perrysfield
Tandridge
Hall
Barley Mow PH
DEAN SHAW
Prim Sch
Tandridge Hall
SOUTHLANDS SHAWS
Stockett's Manor
HOPGARDEN WOOD
Sewage Works
Filter Beds
Gibbs Brook
EASTBOURNE ROAD
GODSTONE BYPASS
Southlands Lodge
SOUTHLANDS WOOD
SOUTHLANDS LANE
Rose Farm
BROOK LANE
POPES LANE
STOW COPPICE
TANDRIDGE LANE
Newhouse Farm
B2239
Hollybush

188
EE
EF
EG
EH
EJ
EK
EL
178
CR3
RH8
HELL SHAW
TITSEY PLANTATION
TITSEY PARK
TITSEY PLACE GDNS
Titsey
CHURCH WOOD
ROUGHFIELD SHAW
SQUARE WOOD
BARTON SHAW
Pitchfont Farm
Limpsfield Lodge Farm
Park Farm
OXTED DOWNS NT
BEECH PLANTATION NT
TITSEY WOOD
Travel Inn
M25
CHALKPIT WOOD
ASHEN COPPICE
Broomlands Farm
SAND PIT
GRUBSTREET SHAW
GRUBSTREET COPSE
HOSP (closed)
BARNETT'S SHAW
Prim Schs
Tennis Courts
Sports Hall
Sec Sch
SPORTS GROUND
Limpsfield
OXTED
MASTER PARK
Health Cen
COUNCIL OFF.
Swim Pool
Gas Holder
Superstore
Fire Sta
LIMPSFIELD CHART
Cricket Club
Clubhouse
GOLF COURSE
LIMPSFIELD COMMON
ANDREWS WOOD
WEST HEATH
Wildshaw
Swallowfield
Woodhurst Bridge
Limpsfield Tunnel
Mill Barn
Stonehall Farm
Stonehamme
Health Centre
Haycutter PH
THE ALDERS
Boulthurst Farm
TENCHLEY'S WOOD
LITTLE HEATH NT
Chartfield House
Tenchley's Park
LOAMPIT WOOD
Whitegates Farm
Crabbett Wood
Crabbett Wood Farm
CRABBETT WOOD
Tenchleys Manor
Hurst Green
Comm Cen
Prim Sch
RUNNING TRACK
REC GRD
Doghurst
ITCHINGWOOD COMMON
Red Lane Farm
FAIRVIEW IND EST
PARISHCROFT WOOD
Parishcroft Wood Farm
Holland
Coltsford Mill
Perrysfield
Stockett's Manor
Sewage Works
Filter Beds
Depot
POWDERDICK SHAW
The Diamond PH
Connerton Stables
Clubhouse
Oxted R.F.C.
HONESLAND WOOD
Stockenden Farm
COLLESTERS WOOD
MOLLSTONES WOOD
Upper Gincox Farm
Rose Farm
Hollybush
Oxted Place
Whistlers Court
Blunt House
40
41
42
54
53
52
51
125
126
127
128
129
130
131
132
133
134
187

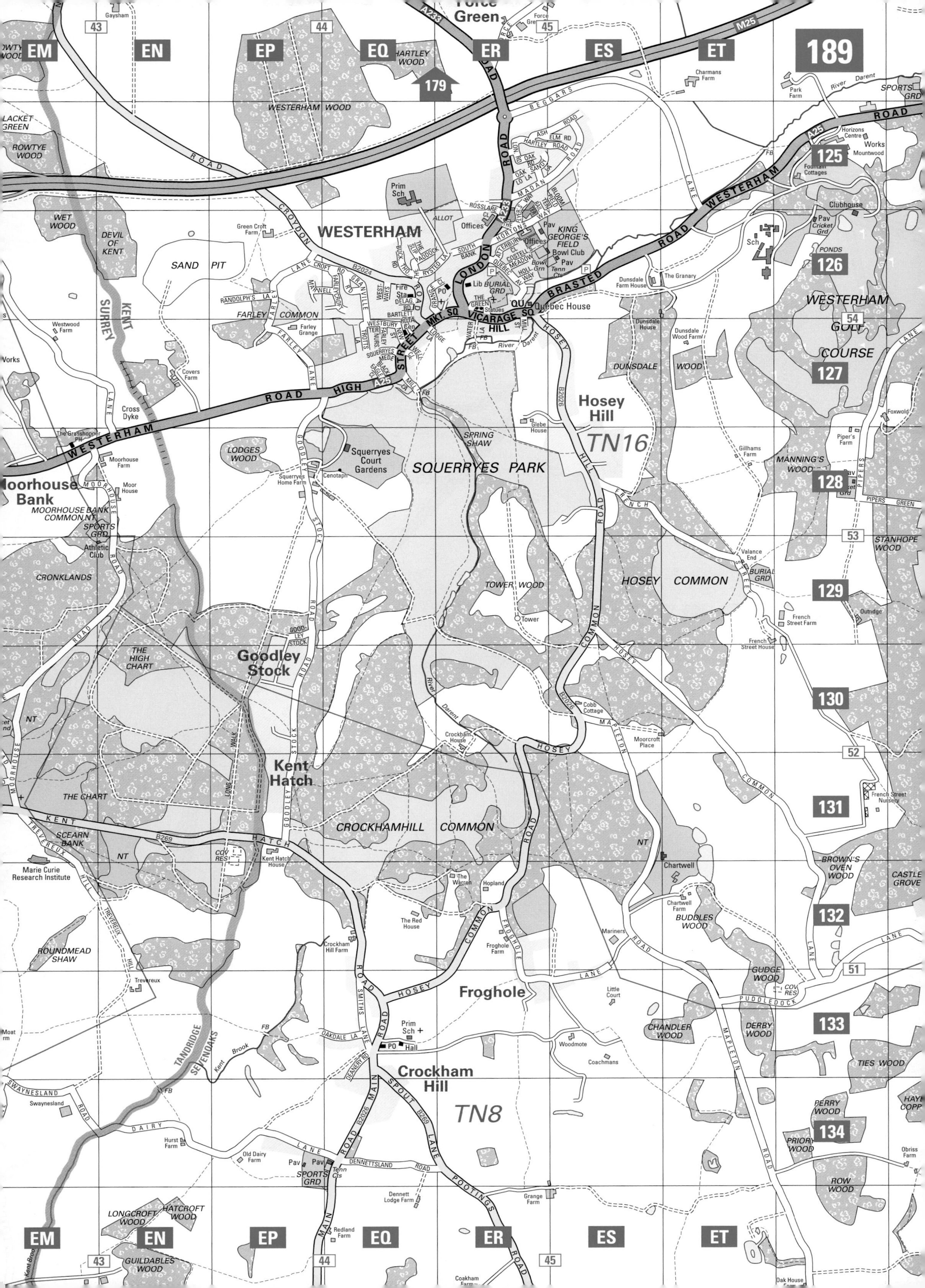
WESTERHAM
Hosey Hill
TN16
SQUERRYES PARK
Squerryes Court Gardens
Goodley Stock
Kent Hatch
CROCKHAMHILL COMMON
Froghole
Crockham Hill
TN8
Moorhouse Bank
HOSEY COMMON
WESTERHAM GOLF COURSE
Chartwell
Marie Curie Research Institute
WESTERHAM WOOD
TOWER WOOD
DUNSDALE
SAND PIT
FARLEY COMMON
THE HIGH CHART
THE CHART
CRONKLANDS
LODGES WOOD
SPRING SHAW
MANNING'S WOOD
STANHOPE WOOD
BROWN'S OVEN WOOD
CASTLE GROVE
BUDDLES WOOD
GUDGE WOOD
DERBY WOOD
CHANDLER WOOD
TIES WOOD
PERRY WOOD
PRIORY WOOD
ROW WOOD
ROUNDMEAD SHAW
LONGCROFT WOOD
HATCROFT WOOD
GUILDABLES WOOD
WET WOOD
DEVIL OF KENT
ROWTYE WOOD
HARTLEY WOOD
SURREY
KENT
TANDRIDGE
SEVENOAKS
M25
A25
A233
B2026
B2024
B269
179
125
126
127
128
129
130
131
132
133
134
EM
EN
EP
EQ
ER
ES
ET
43
44
45
51
52
53
54

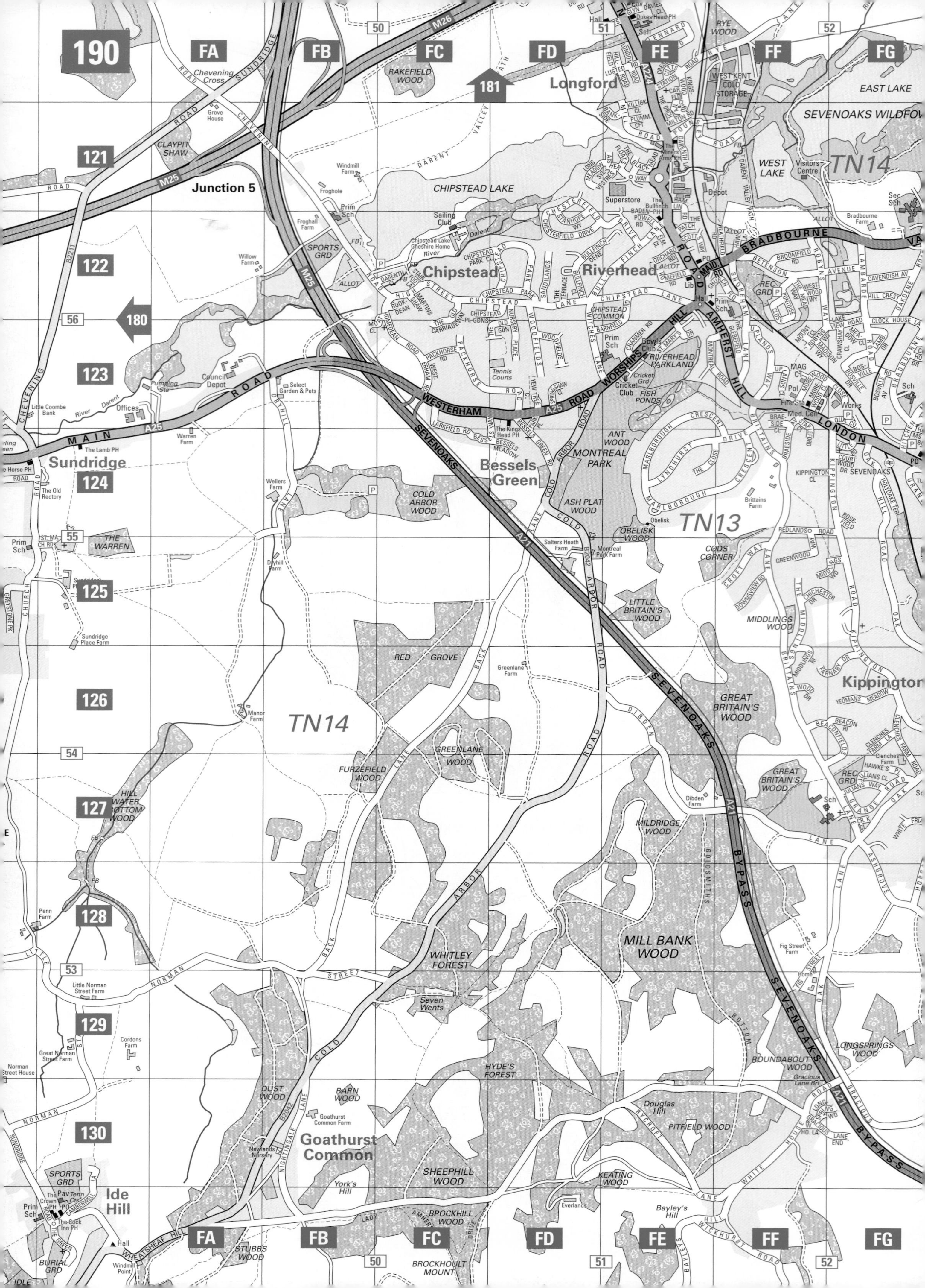
FA
FB
FC
FD
FE
FF
FG
181
180
TN14
TN13
Longford
Chipstead
Riverhead
Sundridge
Bessels Green
Kippington
Goathurst Common
Ide Hill
Junction 5
CHIPSTEAD LAKE
SEVENOAKS WILDFOWL
EAST LAKE
WEST LAKE
RAKEFIELD WOOD
CLAYPIT SHAW
COLD ARBOR WOOD
THE WARREN
ANT WOOD
MONTREAL PARK
ASH PLAT WOOD
OBELISK WOOD
LITTLE BRITAIN'S WOOD
MIDDLINGS WOOD
RED GROVE
GREAT BRITAIN'S WOOD
GREENLANE WOOD
FURZEFIELD WOOD
HILL WATER BOTTOM WOOD
MILDRIDGE WOOD
MILL BANK WOOD
WHITLEY FOREST
Seven Wents
HYDE'S FOREST
DUST WOOD
BARN WOOD
PITFIELD WOOD
SHEEPHILL WOOD
KEATING WOOD
BROCKHILL WOOD
STUBBS WOOD
BROCKHOULT MOUNT
LONGSPRINGS WOOD
ROUNDABOUT WOOD
CODS CORNER
RIVERHEAD PARKLAND
FISH PONDS
M25
M26
A21
A25
A224
B2042
B2211
SEVENOAKS BY-PASS
WESTERHAM ROAD
MAIN ROAD
SUNDRIDGE ROAD
CHEVENING ROAD
COLD ARBOR ROAD
BACK LANE
DIBDEN LANE
NORMAN STREET
WHITE HOUSE LANE
WICKHURST ROAD
BRADBOURNE VALE
LONDON ROAD
AMHERST HILL
WORSHIPS HILL
CHIPSTEAD LANE
GRACIOUS LANE
50
51
52
53
54
55
56
121
122
123
124
125
126
127
128
129
130

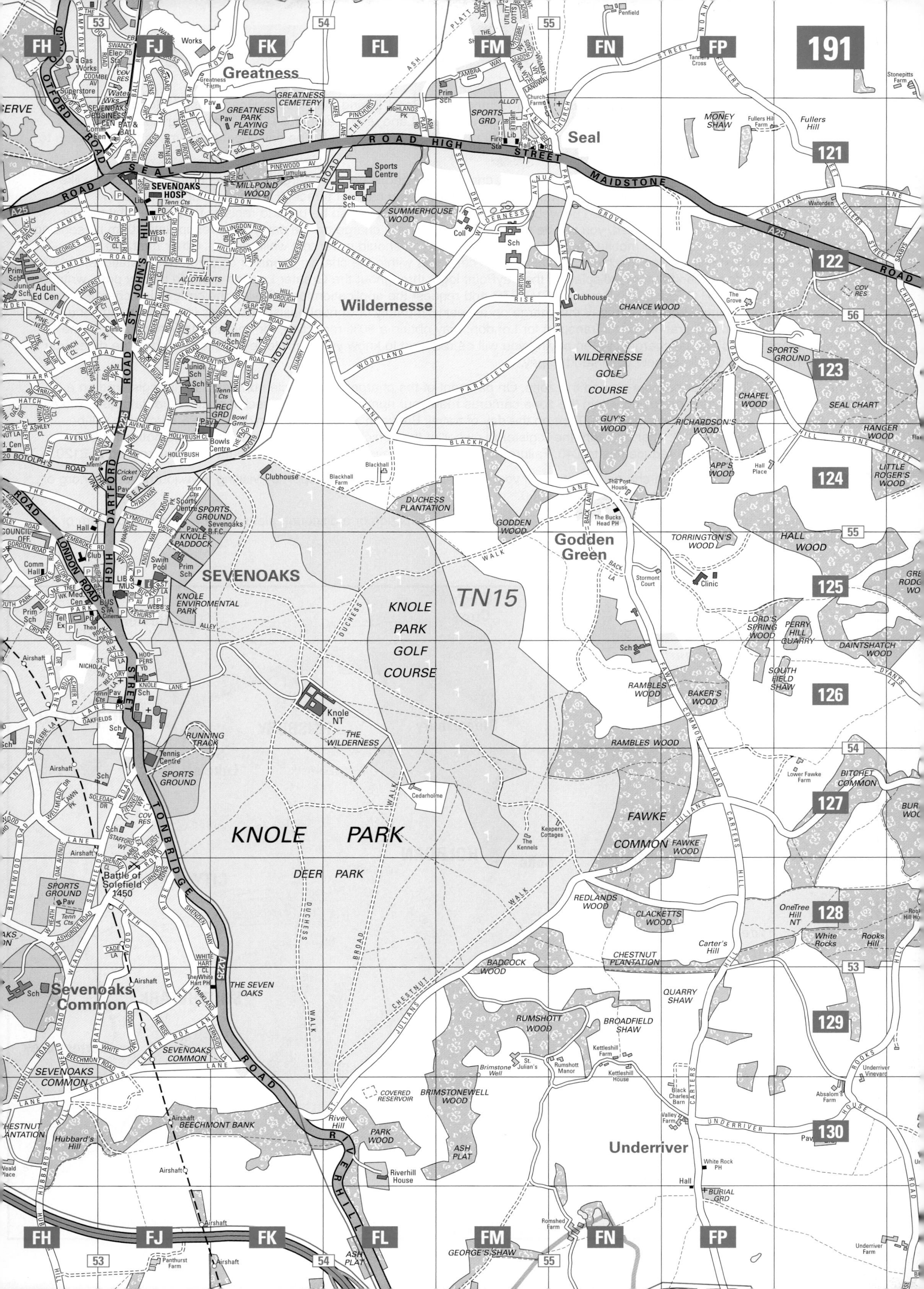

FH
FJ
FK
FL
FM
FN
FP
53
54
55
56
Greatness
Seal
Wilderness
SEVENOAKS
Godden Green
TN15
KNOLE PARK
DEER PARK
KNOLE PARK GOLF COURSE
WILDERNESSE GOLF COURSE
Sevenoaks Common
SEVENOAKS COMMON
Underriver
FAWKE COMMON
SEAL CHART
GREATNESS CEMETERY
GREATNESS PARK PLAYING FIELDS
SEVENOAKS HOSP
MILLPOND WOOD
SUMMERHOUSE WOOD
CHANCE WOOD
GUY'S WOOD
RICHARDSON'S WOOD
CHAPEL WOOD
APP'S WOOD
HANGER WOOD
LITTLE ROGER'S WOOD
DUCHESS PLANTATION
GODDEN WOOD
TORRINGTON'S WOOD
HALL WOOD
LORD'S SPRING WOOD
PERRY HILL QUARRY
DAINTSHATCH WOOD
SOUTH FIELD SHAW
RAMBLES WOOD
BAKER'S WOOD
BITCHET COMMON
FAWKE WOOD
REDLANDS WOOD
CLACKETTS WOOD
CHESTNUT PLANTATION
BADCOCK WOOD
QUARRY SHAW
RUMSHOTT WOOD
BROADFIELD SHAW
BRIMSTONEWELL WOOD
PARK WOOD
ASH PLAT
BEECHMONT BANK
THE SEVEN OAKS
KNOLE ENVIRONMENTAL PARK
RUNNING TRACK
SPORTS GROUND
Battle of Solefield 1450
Knole NT
THE WILDERNESS
Cedarholme
Keepers Cottages
The Kennels
Riverhill House
River Hill
COVERED RESERVOIR
MONEY SHAW
Fullers Hill
Stonepitts Farm
Penfield
Tanners Cross
White Rocks
Rooks Hill
Carter's Hill
OneTree Hill NT
Absalom's Farm
Underriver Vineyard
Underriver Farm
Romshed Farm
GEORGE'S SHAW
Panthurst Farm
Hubbard's Hill
Kettleshill Farm
Kettleshill House
Rumshott Manor
St. Julian's
Brimstone Well
Black Charles Barn
Valley Farm
White Rock PH
BURIAL GRD
Lower Fawke Farm
The Bucks Head PH
The Post House
Stormont Court
Blackhall Farm
Hall Place
The Grove
Waterden
Clubhouse
MAIDSTONE ROAD
HIGH STREET
SEAL ROAD
TONBRIDGE ROAD
RIVERHILL
DARTFORD ROAD
ST. JOHN'S HILL
LONDON ROAD
OTFORD ROAD
A25
A225
121
122
123
124
125
126
127
128
129
130

● London's congestion charging zone operates inside the 'Inner Ring Road' linking Marylebone Road, Euston Road, Pentonville Road, Tower Bridge, Elephant and Castle, Vauxhall Bridge and Park Lane (see map below). The 'Inner Ring Road' provides a route around the charging zone and charges do not apply to vehicles travelling on it. The daily operating time is from 7.00 am to 6.30 pm, Monday to Friday, excluding public holidays.

● Payment of a £5 congestion charge allows you to enter, drive around and leave the charging zone as many times as you like that day. Payments can be made online at www.cclondon.com where you can get a receipt if required, or by phone on 0845 900 1234 charged at the local rate. The web site or phone number may also be used to register for payment by mobile phone text message. Once registered, you will be able to pay the £5 daily charge on the day you travel up until 10pm by sending a simple text message from your mobile phone. Please remember you should never text while driving. Other methods of payment are at most self service machines in major public car parks within the charging zone or selected petrol stations, newsagents and convenience stores, displaying the PayPoint logo, throughout the Greater London area. To pay by post, write to: Congestion charging, P O Box 2985, Coventry CV7 8ZR and request the application form 'Paying the congestion charge'. Regular drivers in central London can pay the charge on a weekly, monthly or annual basis. Residents in the charging zone, by paying a £10 annual registration fee to Transport for London, may obtain a 90% reduction, for one private vehicle only, in the weekly, monthly and annual charges. When paying you will be required to know your vehicle registration number, the dates you want to pay for and details of how you intend to pay.

● There are no tollbooths or barriers around the zone. On payment of the charge your vehicle number plate is registered on a database and on entering or driving within the zone cameras read your number plate and check it against the database. You can pay the charge, without penalty, until 10.00 pm on the day of travel. Between 10.00 pm and midnight a £5 surcharge will be made, making a total of £10; after midnight the registered owner of the vehicle will be sent a penalty charge notice for £80, payment within 14 days will reduce this to £40. Failure to pay within 28 days will result in the penalty being increased to £120.

● To avoid paying the congestion charge you can find your easiest route by public transport by visiting www.journeyplanner.org or calling London Travel Information on 020 7918 4300.

For any further information, including a list of vehicles eligible for exemption or a discount, please visit www.cclondon.com or call 0845 900 1234.

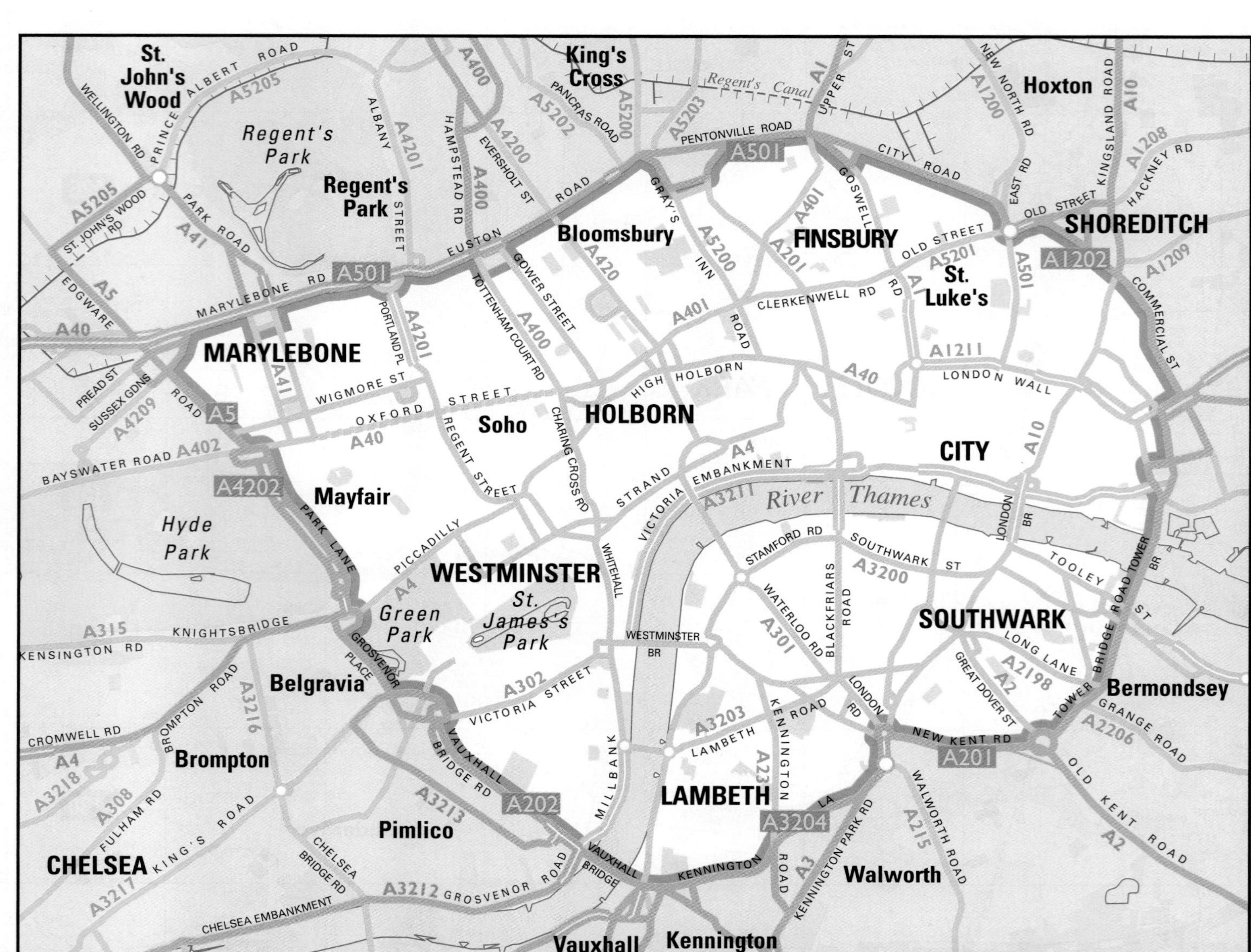

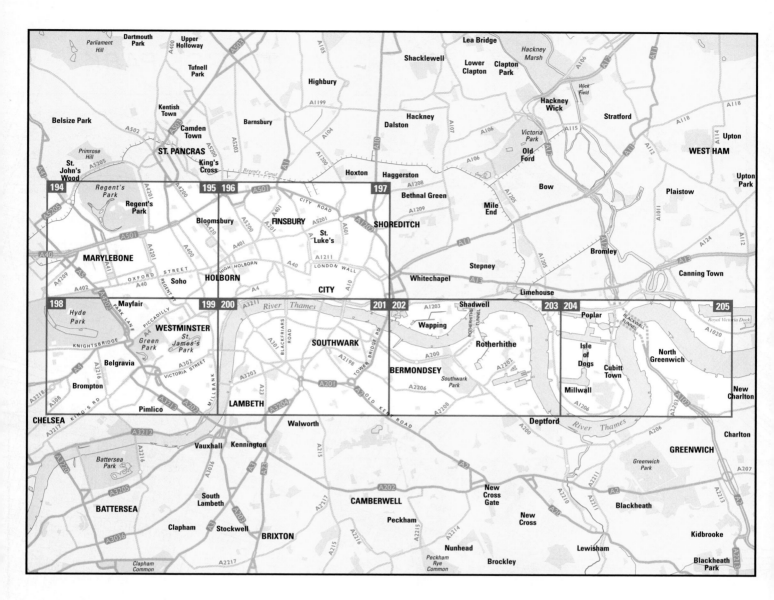

KEY TO MAP SYMBOLS

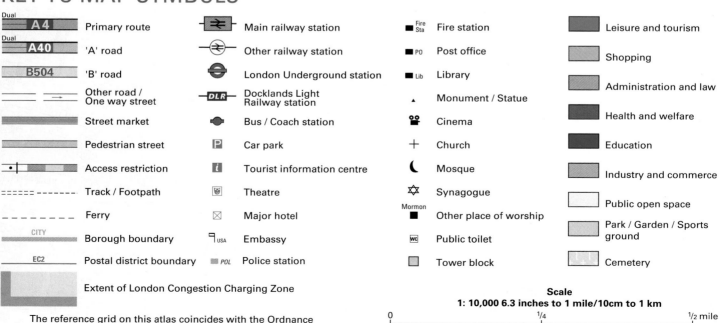

Dual **A4**	Primary route	
Dual **A40**	'A' road	
B504	'B' road	
Other road / One way street		
Street market		
Pedestrian street		
Access restriction		
Track / Footpath		
Ferry		
CITY Borough boundary		
EC2 Postal district boundary		
Extent of London Congestion Charging Zone		

Main railway station	
Other railway station	
London Underground station	
DLR Docklands Light Railway station	
Bus / Coach station	
P Car park	
i Tourist information centre	
Theatre	
Major hotel	
USA Embassy	
POL Police station	

Fire Sta Fire station	
PO Post office	
Lib Library	
▲ Monument / Statue	
Cinema	
✝ Church	
☽ Mosque	
✡ Synagogue	
Mormon Other place of worship	
WC Public toilet	
Tower block	

Leisure and tourism	
Shopping	
Administration and law	
Health and welfare	
Education	
Industry and commerce	
Public open space	
Park / Garden / Sports ground	
Cemetery	

Scale
1: 10,000 6.3 inches to 1 mile/10cm to 1 km

0	1/4	1/2 mile
0	0.25	0.5	0.75 kilometre

The reference grid on this atlas coincides with the Ordnance Survey National Grid System. The grid interval is 250 metres.

10 Grid reference **200** Page continuation number

194
A
B
C
D
E
F
G
1
2
3
4
5
6
7
8
9
10
REGENT'S PARK
NW1
NW8
ST. JOHN'S WOOD
LORD'S CRICKET GROUND
M.C.C. MUSEUM
LORD'S TAVERN PH
LISSON GROVE
LISSON GREEN ESTATE
LILESTONE ESTATE
CHURCH STREET ESTATE
PADDINGTON GREEN
St. Marys Mans
CITY OF WESTMINSTER COLL
Paddington Basin
ST. MARY'S HOSP
PADDINGTON
Hilton
Norfolk Towers
MARYLEBONE
W1
W2
SELFRIDGES
WALLACE COLLECTION
Speaker's Corner
MARBLE ARCH
LANCASTER GATE
Marlborough Gate
The Fountains
Royal Lancaster
Victoria Gate
THE (NORTH CARRIAGE DRIVE) RING
BAYSWATER ROAD
A402
A5
A41
A40
A501
A4205
A4209
A5205
B507
EDGWARE ROAD
PRINCE ALBERT ROAD
WELLINGTON ROAD
ST. JOHN'S WOOD ROAD
PARK ROAD
GLOUCESTER PLACE
BAKER ST
MARYLEBONE ROAD
OXFORD STREET
PARK LANE
SEYMOUR PL
PRAED ST
SUSSEX GARDENS
WIGMORE
PORTMAN SQUARE
London Central Mosque
HANOVER GATE
BOATING LAKE
QUEEN MARY'S GARDENS
OPEN AIR THEATRE
THE HOLME
REGENT'S COLLEGE
Clarence Gate
D.E.T.R. Parks Dept
LONDON BUSINESS SCH
LONDON ZOO
RUNNING TRACK
WINFIELD HOUSE
MADAME TUSSAUD'S
PLANETARIUM
ROYAL ACADEMY OF MUSIC
UNIV OF WESTMINSTER
Sherlock Holmes
BAKER STREET
MARYLEBONE
Landmark
Westminster Council Ho
CHARTER NIGHTINGALE HOSP
Ramada Jarvis
Metropole
EDGWARE ROAD
Roosevelt Memorial
Le Meridien Grosvenor House
Thistle Marble Arch
Cumberland
82
198
OXFORD ST where marked is closed to through traffic (except buses & taxis) from 7a.m. - 7p.m. Monday - Saturday

195
H
J
K
L
M
N
P
MORNINGTON CRESCENT
83
REGENT'S PARK
SOMERS TOWN
BRITISH LIBRARY
ST. PANCRAS
KING'S CROSS
KING'S CROSS & ST. PANCRAS
EUSTON
EUSTON SQUARE
EUSTON ROAD
ST. GEORGE'S CATHEDRAL
ST PANCRAS
WARREN ST.
GT. PORTLAND ST.
REGENT'S PARK
UNIVERSITY OF LONDON - U.C.L.
RUSSELL SQUARE GARDENS
196
WC1
BLOOMSBURY
THE BRITISH MUSEUM
GOODGE ST.
TOTTENHAM COURT RD
OXFORD CIRCUS
OXFORD ST
NEW OXFORD ST
HOLBORN
WC2
COVENT GARDEN
ROYAL OPERA HOUSE
SOHO
LEICESTER SQ.
STRAND
199
PICCADILLY CIR.
MAYFAIR
NATIONAL GALLERY
1
2
3
4
5
6
7
8
9
10

196
A
B
C
D
E
F
G
1
2
3
4
5
6
7
8
9
10
83
195
200
KING'S CROSS
KING'S CROSS & ST. PANCRAS
KING'S CROSS THAMESLINK
ST. PANCRAS
BRITISH LIBRARY
CAMDEN TOWN HALL
PENTONVILLE
PENTONVILLE ROAD
A501
ANGEL
The Angel Cen
CITY ROAD
GOSWELL ROAD
ST. JOHN ST
FINSBURY
SADLER'S WELLS THEATRE
NEW RIVER HEAD
CLERKENWELL
EC1
CLERKENWELL ROAD
A5201
FARRINGDON ROAD
FARRINGDON
MOUNT PLEASANT MAIL CENTRE
ROSEBERY AV
A401
KING'S CROSS RD
GRAY'S INN RD
EUSTON RD
ST. PANCRAS
WC1
CORAM'S FIELDS
RUSSELL SQUARE GARDENS
GUILFORD STREET
B502
THE NAT HOSP
HOSP FOR CHILDREN
GRAY'S INN GARDENS
THEOBALD'S ROAD
BOURNE ESTATE
HATTON GARDEN
BLOOMSBURY
THE BRITISH MUSEUM
HOLBORN
HOLBORN VIADUCT
CHANCERY LANE
LINCOLN'S INN FIELDS
KINGSWAY
ROYAL COURTS OF JUSTICE
FLEET STREET
NEW OXFORD ST
HIGH HOLBORN
SHAFTESBURY AV
WC2
COVENT GARDEN
ROYAL OPERA HOUSE
STRAND
ALDWYCH
SOMERSET HOUSE
TEMPLE
EC4
VICTORIA EMBANKMENT
BLACKFRIARS
CITY THAMESLINK
CENTRAL CRIMINAL COURT (Old Bailey)
ST. BARTHOLOMEW'S HOSPITAL
Central Markets (Smithfield)
RIVER THAMES
H.M.S. PRESIDENT
WELLINGTON MASTER MARINERS'
KING'S REACH
LEICESTER SQ
NATIONAL GALLERY

197
H
J
K
L
M
N
P
84
84
201
1
2
3
4
5
6
7
8
9
10
HOXTON
SHOREDITCH
BROADGATE
BARBICAN
ST. LUKE'S
CITY
N1
E2
E1
EC2
EC3
REGENT'S CANAL
CITY ROAD BASIN
WENLOCK BASIN
CITY ROAD
OLD STREET
GREAT EASTERN STREET
COMMERCIAL STREET
BISHOPSGATE
HOUNDSDITCH
SHOREDITCH HIGH STREET
KINGSLAND
HACKNEY ROAD
COLUMBIA RD
BETHNAL GREEN
MIDDLESEX STREET
WHITECHAPEL HIGH ST
MINORIES
MANSELL ST
LEMAN
PRESCOT ST
ROYAL MINT
LONDON WALL
CHISWELL STREET
MOORGATE
FINSBURY SQ
FINSBURY CIRCUS
LIVERPOOL STREET
CHEAPSIDE
POULTRY
THREADNEEDLE ST
CORNHILL
LEADENHALL
FENCHURCH
GRACECHURCH ST
EASTCHEAP
CANNON STREET
QUEEN VICTORIA
LOWER THAMES ST
SOUTHWARK BRIDGE
MILLENNIUM BRIDGE
BANKSIDE
ALDERSGATE ST
GOSWELL RD
ST. PAUL'S CATHEDRAL
MANSION HOUSE
BANK
MONUMENT
ALDGATE
TOWER HILL
TOWER GATEWAY
TOWER OF LONDON
BUNHILL FIELDS
MOORFIELDS EYE HOSP
OLD SPITALFIELDS MARKET
Bank of England
Stock Exch
Lloyds of London
Tower 42
Guildhall
Swan Lane Pier
SHAKESPEARE'S GLOBE THEATRE
HACKNEY COMM COLL
PITFIELD ESTATE
PROVOST ESTATE
ARDEN ESTATE
CRANSTON ESTATE
DORSET EST
SHOREDITCH PARK

198
A
B
C
D
E
F
G
1
2
3
4
5
6
7
8
9
10
194
W2
82
100
OXFORD STREET where marked is closed to through traffic (except buses & taxis) from 7a.m. - 7p.m. Monday - Saturday
HYDE PARK
KENSINGTON GARDENS
BAYSWATER ROAD
HYDE PARK GARDENS
HYDE PK GARDENS
CUMBERLAND GATE
Speakers Corner
Marble Arch
Victoria Gate
LANCASTER GATE
Royal Lancaster
Marlborough Gate
The Fountains
THE (NORTH CARRIAGE DRIVE) RING
THE (WEST CARRIAGE DRIVE) RING
BUCK HILL WALK
NORTH RIDE
THE LONG WATER
Speke's Monument
Peter Pan
Bird Sanctuary
POL
BROOK GATE
GROSVENOR GATE
Centre Fountain
BROAD WALK
LOVER'S WALK
Queens Temple
LANCASTER WALK
SERPENTINE ROAD
THE SERPENTINE
The Lido
Pier
SERPENTINE GALLERY
Bandstand
War Memorial
Holocaust Memorial
STANHOPE GATE
CURZON GATE
ACHILLES WAY
Achilles Statue
Queen Elizabeth Gate
APSLEY HOUSE WELLINGTON MUS
HYDE PARK CORNER
ROTTEN ROW
Gates
PUTTING GREEN
Prince of Wales Gate
Rutland Gate
Edinburgh Gate
Albert Gate
NEW RIDE
Albert Memorial
Coalbrookdale Gate
Alexandra Gate
SOUTH CARRIAGE DRIVE
HYDE PARK BARRACKS
Mandarin Oriental Hyde Park
KENSINGTON RD
A315
KNIGHTSBRIDGE
KENSINGTON GORE
Royal Geographical Society
ROYAL COLL OF ART
ALBERT HALL
SW7
IMPERIAL COLL
BOLNEY GATE
RUSSIAN ORTH CATH
ENNISMORE GDNS
PRINCES GATE
PRINCE CONSORT RD
ROYAL COLL OF MUSIC
IMPERIAL COLL
GOETHE INSTITUT
Holy Trinity
EXHIBITION RD
IMPERIAL COLLEGE ROAD
SCIENCE MUSEUM
BROMPTON
Brompton Oratory
VICTORIA & ALBERT MUSEUM
NATURAL HISTORY MUSEUM
CROMWELL ROAD
CROMWELL GDNS
THURLOE PL
THURLOE SQ
SOUTH KENSINGTON
Lycee Sch
PELHAM STREET
ONSLOW SQ
SYDNEY PL
HARRODS
BROMPTON ROAD
A4
BEAUCHAMP PL
HANS ROAD
HANS CRESCENT
SLOANE STREET
A3216
PONT STREET
B319
CADOGAN PLACE
CADOGAN SQUARE
LOWNDES SQUARE
BELGRAVE SQUARE
BELGRAVIA
CHESHAM PL
EATON PLACE
EATON SQUARE
A3217
KENSINGTON & CHELSEA
HARVEY NICHOLS
MINEMA
Lanesborough
GROSVENOR CRES
WILTON CRES
PARK LANE
A4202
UPPER BROOK ST
UPPER GROSVENOR ST
Le Meridien Grosvenor House
The Dorchester
SW3
SLOANE SQ
PETER JONES
ROYAL COURT
LOWER SLOANE ST
KING'S ROAD
DUKE OF YORK'S HEADQUARTERS
FULHAM ROAD
A308
A3218
ROYAL MARSDEN HOSP
ROYAL BROMPTON HOSP
SYDNEY STREET
B304
SAMUEL LEWIS TRUST DWELLINGS
SUTTON EST
GUINNESS TRUST BLDGS
CHELSEA COLL OF ART & DESIGN
ROYAL HOSPITAL CHELSEA
BURTON'S COURT
ROYAL HOSPITAL ROAD
B302
CHELSEA BRIDGE ROAD
PIMLICO ROAD
A3214
CHELSEA BARRACKS
RANELAGH GARDENS
MUSEUM
INCHBALD SCH OF DESIGN
Francis Holland Sch
St. Barnabas

199
H
J
K
L
M
N
P
SOHO
MAYFAIR
W1
STRAND
PICCADILLY CIR.
ROYAL ACAD. OF ARTS
NATIONAL GALLERY
TRAFALGAR SQUARE
CHARING CROSS
LEICESTER SQ.
HAYMARKET
REGENT ST
PICCADILLY
GREEN PARK
ST. JAMES'S
ST. JAMES'S PARK
PALL MALL
THE MALL
CONSTITUTION HILL
BIRDCAGE WALK
BUCKINGHAM PALACE GARDENS
BUCKINGHAM PALACE
THE QUEEN'S GALLERY
THE ROYAL MEWS
WELLINGTON BARRACKS
HORSE GUARDS
WHITEHALL
MINISTRY OF DEFENCE
DOWNING ST
FOREIGN & COMMONWEALTH OFFICE
H.M. TREASURY
WESTMINSTER
PARLIAMENT SQUARE
HOUSES OF PARLIAMENT
200
WESTMINSTER ABBEY
VICTORIA TOWER GARDENS
VICTORIA EMBANKMENT
LONDON EYE
ST. THOMAS' HOSP
WESTMINSTER
SW1
VICTORIA
VICTORIA ST
BUCKINGHAM PALACE RD
VAUXHALL BRIDGE RD
HORSEFERRY RD
MILLBANK
LAMBETH BRI
TATE BRITAIN
MILLBANK TOWER
PLAYING FIELDS
GORDON HOSP
LILLINGTON GARDENS EST
PIMLICO
BELGRAVE ROAD
WARWICK WAY
RIVERSIDE GARDENS
VAUXHALL BRIDGE
ALBERT EMBANKMENT
TACHBROOK EST
CHURCHILL GARDENS
DOLPHIN SQUARE
101
195
1
2
3
4
5
6
7
8
9
10

200
A
B
C
D
E
F
G
1
2
3
4
5
6
7
8
9
10
196
199
101
STRAND
EMBANKMENT
VICTORIA EMBANKMENT
RIVER THAMES
BLACKFRIARS
H.M.S. PRESIDENT
H.Q.S. WELLINGTON MASTER MARINERS'
ST. KATHERINE
WESTMINSTER
LAMBETH
SOUTHWARK
KING'S REACH
H.M. CUSTOMS AND EXCISE
QUEENS WALK
BANKSIDE GALLERY
T.S. QUEEN MARY
Cleopatra's Needle
Charing Cross Pier
CHARING CROSS
NATIONAL GALLERY
TRAFALGAR SQ
SOMERSET HOUSE
SAVOY
ADELPHI
COLISEUM
QUEEN ELIZABETH HALL & PURCELL ROOM
Festival Pier
ROYAL FESTIVAL HALL
HAYWARD GALLERY
ROYAL NATIONAL
NAT FILM THEA
IBM
The London Television Centre
GABRIELS WHARF
OXO TWR WHARF
KING'S COLL UNI OF LON
IMAX
Shell Centre
JUBILEE GDNS
LONDON EYE
County Hall
London Aquarium
Travel Inn
Marriott
FORUM MAGNUM SQ
WATERLOO
WATERLOO INTERNATIONAL
WATERLOO EAST
St. John the Evangelist
St. Patrick (RC)
THE YOUNG VIC
THE OLD VIC
SOUTHWARK COLL (Waterloo Cen)
St. Andrew with St. Thomas
PEABODY ESTATE
PEABODY SQUARE
TANSWELL EST
LAMBETH NORTH
ST. GEORGE'S CIRCUS
ST. GEORGE'S CATH (RC)
MORLEY COLL
SOUTH BANK UNIVERSITY
Notre Dame High Sch
GAYWOOD EST
SOUTHWARK COLL
St. George's Centre
LON. COLL OF PRINTING & DIST. TRADES
Rec Cen
London Park
NEWINGTON BUTTS
ELEPHANT & CASTLE
IMPERIAL WAR MUS
GERALDINE MARY HARMSWORTH PARK
WESTMINSTER BRIDGE RD
WESTMINSTER BRI
LAMBETH BRI
LAMBETH PALACE RD
LAMBETH RD
KENNINGTON RD
KENNINGTON LANE
KENNINGTON PARK RD
BOROUGH RD
LONDON RD
BLACKFRIARS RD
WATERLOO RD
STAMFORD STREET
UPPER GROUND
THE CUT
SOUTHWARK UNION
YORK ROAD
BAYLIS ROAD
ST. GEORGES ROAD
BROOK DRIVE
LAMBETH WALK
BLACK PRINCE RD
VAUXHALL WALK
ALBERT EMBANKMENT
MILLBANK
HOUSES OF PARLIAMENT
St. Stephen's Tower (Big Ben)
Victoria Tower
VICTORIA TOWER GARDENS
Burghers of Calais Mon.
WESTMINSTER ABBEY
ABBEY MUS
PARLIAMENT SQUARE
ST. THOMAS' HOSP
FLORENCE NIGHTINGALE MUS
ST. THOMAS' MEDICAL SCH & THE NIGHTINGALE SCH
LAMBETH
LAMBETH PALACE GDNS
Lambeth Palace
MUS OF GARDEN HISTORY
ARCHBISHOP'S PARK
SPORTS GRD
Lambeth Pier
Westminster Pier
H.M. TREASURY
MINISTRY OF DEFENCE
FOREIGN & COMMONWEALTH OFFICE
DEPT OF HEALTH & DWP
CABINET OFFICE
DOWNING ST
RICHMOND TER
WHITEHALL
PARLIAMENTARY COUNSEL OFFICE
DEPT FOR ENVIR. FOOD & RURAL AFFAIRS
Royal Horseguards Thistle
PS TATTERSHALL CASTLE
HISPANIOLA
HUNGERFORD BRI
WESTMINSTER
EMBANKMENT
THAMES HOUSE
DEFRA
TATE BRITAIN
MILLBANK TOWER
MILLBANK BARRACKS
RIVERSIDE GARDENS
GOVT OFF. FOR LONDON
SW1
SE11
INT MARITIME ORG.
PARLIAMENT VIEW APARTS
Novotel Waterloo
LAMBETH REC GRD
LAMBETH WK OPEN SPACE
Lilian Baylis Sec Sch
Lilian Baylis Sch (Annexe)
PEDLARS PARK
DRAW DOCK
VAUXHALL
VAUXHALL GDNS EST
St. Peter
St. Anselm
St. Philip
COUNTY COURT
CITY & GUILDS LONDON ART SCH
KENNINGTON
St. Mary
GUINNESS TRUST BUILDINGS
ALBERTA
WALWORTH
HURLEY HO
EBENEZER HO
FAIRFORD HO
DRYDEN COURT
ST. GEORGE WHARF

H
J
K
L
M
N
P
197
202
102
1
2
3
4
5
6
7
8
9
10
FENCHURCH ST
MONUMENT
EASTCHEAP
TOWER HILL
ROYAL MINT ST
MINORIES
PRESCOT
CITY
CANNON ST
Southwark Bridge Steps
Bankside Jetty
SHAKESPEARE'S GLOBE THEATRE
MILLENNIUM BRIDGE
Swan Lane Pier
Site of Old Billingsgate Mkt
Custom House
LOWER THAMES ST
TOWER OF LONDON
Tower Pier
ST. KATHARINE'S DOCK
Ivory Ho
St. Katharine's Pier
Alderman Stairs
London Commodity Ex
LONDON BRIDGE HOSPITAL
London Bridge City Pier
H.M.S. BELFAST
TOWER HAMLETS
SOUTHWARK
SOUTHWARK CATHEDRAL
CLINK PRISON MUS
GOLDEN HINDE
Financial Times
Lloyds TSB
VINOPOLIS
Offices
Hay's Galleria
SOUTHWARK CROWN COURT
CITY HALL (Greater London Authority)
POTTERS FIELDS PARK
TOWER BRIDGE
TOWER BRIDGE EXPERIENCE
TOWER BRIDGE RD
Butler's Wharf
George's Stairs
DESIGN MUSEUM
SHAD THAMES
A3200
A200
A2198
A100
A2
A201
A2206
B202
B203
A215
B240
A300
SOUTHWARK BRIDGE ROAD
SOUTHWARK STREET
PEABODY TRUST
BRAMAH MUS
Borough Mkt
LONDON DUNGEON
BRITAIN AT WAR
LONDON BRIDGE
TOOLEY STREET
ST. THOMAS STREET
BOROUGH HIGH ST.
OLD OPERATING THEATRE MUS
GUY'S HOSP
SNOWSFIELDS
BERMONDSEY STREET
CRUCIFIX LA
DRUID ST
LAMBETH COLL
ST. OLAVE'S EST
UNION ST
MARSHALSEA RD
Prim Schs
LON. FIRE BRIGADE MUS
A.C.A.S.
LOCKYER EST
LEATHERMARKET GARDENS
St. George the Martyr
BOROUGH
THE BOROUGH
LONG LANE
TABARD GARDENS
TABARD GARDEN ESTATE
KIPLING EST
Leather Mkt
Travel Inn London Tower Bri
PURBROOK ESTATE
ST. SAVIOUR'S EST
ST. JOHN'S ESTATE
MILLENNIUM SQ
JAMAICA RD
TANNER ST
ABBEY ST
ARNOLD EST
NECKINGER EST
BERMONDSEY
Town Hall
GRANGE RD
BERMONDSEY SPA
VAUBAN ESTATE
ELIM ESTATE
CLUNY EST
SE1
MEAKIN EST
GRANGE CENTRE
HAROLD ESTATE
CREASY EST
KING'S COLL
SPORTS GROUND
INNER LONDON CROWN COURT
NEWINGTON GDNS
ROCKINGHAM
ROCKINGHAM ESTATE
LAWSON EST
Geoffrey Chaucer Sch
Brotherhood of the Cross & Star
St. Saviour's & St. Olave's Sch
OLD KENT RD
NEW KENT ROAD
ELEPHANT & CASTLE
NEWINGTON
Driscoll House
DEACON WAY
HEYGATE ST
BRANDON ST
Royal Mail
Offices
Bricklayer's Arms Distribution Centre
LONGFIELD ESTATE
Aylwin Sch
ENGLISH MARTYRS (RC)
DAWES HOUSE
ALVEY EST
LORRY PARK
CUMING MUS
WALWORTH
WALWORTH ROAD
EAST STREET
Walworth Lower Sch
LULWORTH
STUDLAND
TRAFALGAR ST
SE17
KINGLAKE EST
SURREY SQUARE PARK
Superstores
ROLLS RD
DUNTON RD
FARADAY GARDENS
WOODSFORD
MICHAEL FARADAY HO
AYLESBURY EST
PENROSE HOUSE
DEPOT
St. Peter
Walworth Sch
OLD CANAL MEWS

202
84
201
102
A
B
C
D
E
F
G
1
2
3
4
5
6
7
8
9
10
FENCHURCH ST
TOWER HILL
TOWER OF LONDON
Tower Pier
TOWER BRIDGE
TOWER BRIDGE APP
MINORIES
MANSELL ST
ROYAL MINT ST
CABLE STREET
PRESCOT ST
LEMAN ST
DOCK ST
THE HIGHWAY
A1203
EAST SMITHFIELD
THOMAS MORE ST
B107
VAUGHAN WAY
PENNINGTON STREET
News International
Tobacco Dock
SHADWELL
SHADWELL BASIN
St. Paul
WAPPING
WAPPING LANE
WAPPING HIGH STREET
WAPPING WALL
E1
ST. KATHARINE'S DOCK
EAST DOCK
Ivory Ho
St. Katharine's Pier
Alderman Stairs
John Orwell (Wapping) Sports Cen
TOWER HAMLETS
SOUTHWARK
Wapping Dock Stairs
New Crane Stairs
Wapping Old Stairs
Wapping New Stairs
UPPER POOL
THE POOL
LOWER POOL
Cherry Garden Pier
King's Stairs
East Lane Stairs
Mill Stairs
Princes Stairs
TOWER BRIDGE EXPERIENCE
POTTERS FIELDS
BUTLER'S WHARF
George's Stairs
DESIGN MUSEUM
SHAD THAMES
MAYFLOWER PH
BRUNEL ENGINE HOUSE
ROTHERHITHE
ROTHERHITHE STREET
BRUNEL RD
ROTHERHITHE TUNNEL APP.
St. Mary with All Saints
KING'S STAIRS GARDENS
BERMONDSEY WALL EAST
BERMONDSEY WALL WEST
CHAMBERS ST
JAMAICA ROAD
A200
BERMONDSEY
DICKENS ESTATE
ARNOLD EST
MILLPOND EST
St. Peter (RC)
ST. SAVIOUR'S EST
NECKINGER EST
BERMONDSEY
Town Hall
SPA ROAD
A220
BERMONDSEY SPA
VAUBAN ESTATE
EVELINE LOWE EST
KIRBY ESTATE
SOUTHWARK COLL
LOCKWOOD SQUARE
MARDEN SQUARE
Africa House
SOUTHWARK PARK
Works
Lido
SE16
Seven Islands Leisure Cen
LOWER ROAD
CANADA ESTATE
HOWLAND ESTATE
SOUTHWARK PARK ROAD
RAYMOUTH RD
LONGFIELD ESTATE
MANOR ESTATE
TRADING ESTATE
RENNIE ESTATE
LYNTON ROAD
LYNTON EST
PATERSON PARK
SE1
ROLLS ROAD
B204
DUNTON ROAD
B203
CATLIN STREET
ROTHERHITHE NEW ROAD
A2208
SOUTH BERMONDSEY
OLD KENT ROAD
Superstores
Offices
St. Augustine
St. Philip & St. Mark
ILDERTON ROAD
Lewisham Lions Cen

203
LIMEHOUSE
H
J
K
L
M
N
P
JARDINE ROAD
NARROW
Stone Stairs
Ratcliffe Cross Stairs
FREE TRADE WHARF
Pier
Victoria Wharf
Blyth's Wharf
Free Trade Wharf
THE GRAPES PH
Duke Shore Wharf
85
A1203
HORSEFERRY RD
MEDLAND HO
BREWSTER HO
LIMEHOUSE CAUSEWAY
NARROW ST
MILLIGAN ST
WESTFERRY
PENNYFIELDS
MING ST
B123
DINGLE GDNS
LINK
ASPEN
GARFORD ST
CANNON WORKSHOPS
CANNON DRIVE
HERTSMERE
MUSEUM IN DOCKLANDS
1
RIVER THAMES
Lavender Wharf
Limehouse Hole Stairs
LIMEHOUSE
E14
Four Seasons
BELGRAVE CT
Health Club
ONTARIO WAY
WEST INDIA AVE
CABOT
COLONNADE
Cabot Place
CANARY WHARF
SOUTH COLONNADE
Offices
MACKENZIE WK
2
WESTFERRY CIRCUS
ABERDEEN SQ
PARK PL
HERON QUAY
3
HERON QUAYS
BANK
WEST INDIA
MARSH
ROTHERHITHE STREET
SPORTS GROUND
Prim Sch
LAVENDER RD
HERITAGE MUS
Lavender Pond Nature Pk
Sunderland Wharf
Ordnance Wharf
Lawrence Wharf
Columbia Wharf
BLACKSMITHS ARMS PH
Jetty
Hilton Docklands
MERMAID CT
CHRISTIAN CT
TIVOLI CT
SALTER ROAD
B205
FISHER ATHLETIC FC
MELLISH SPORTS GROUND
STAPLES CLO
FARRINS RENTS
SALTER ROAD
CAPSTAN WAY
RUSSIA DOCK RD
TIMBRELL PL
FILIGREE CT
SURREY WATER
Bacon's Coll
ECOLOGICAL PARK
Stave Hill
DOCK HILL AVENUE
WATERMANS WALK
ROAD
HOLYOAKE CT
DURANDS WK
Holy Trinity
STANTON HO
LIMEHOUSE REACH
West India Dock Pier
TOWER HAMLETS
SOUTHWARK
Express Wharf
ANCHORAGE POINT
CUBA ST
MILLENNIUM HARBOUR
MANILLA ST
BYNG STREET
A1206
STRAFFORD STREET
St. Luke
TOPMAST POINT
HAVANNAH ST
MIDSHIP POINT
MALABAR ST
Comm Cen
4
5
Guardian Newspaper Print Works
LIGHTERMAN RD
INDESCON COURT
Tate & Lyle Sugar Works
LANTERNS COURT
MASTMAKER RD
ALPHA GROVE
Prim Sch
Our Lady (RC)
RUSSIA DOCK WOODLAND
DOWNTOWN ROAD
HOWLAND WAY
Surrey Docks Farm
VAUGHAN ST
WYATT CLO
ROTHERHITH. ST
Comm Cen
Mail Newspapers Printing Works
MULBERRY BUSINESS CENTRE
QUEBEC WAY
ROTHERHITHE
Superstores
CANADA WATER
Works
SHIPWRIGHT RD
CUSTOM HOUSE REACH
REDRIFF ESTATE
ODESSA STREET
ELGAR STREET
NEW CALEDONIAN WHARF
KING FREDERIK IX TOWER
QUEEN OF DENMARK COURT
OCEAN WHARF
KNIGHTHEAD PT
SIR JOHN MCDOUGAL GDNS
204
BOWSPRIT PT
MELLISH STREET
6
TILLER ROAD
CLAIRE PL
STARBOARD WAY
GLENGALL CAUSEWAY
ARNHEM PL
DOCK RD
MILLWALL
16
Bowling Alley
MAST LEISURE PK
Surrey Quays Retail Centre
REDRIFF ROAD
A2202
TEREDO STREET
BRUNSWICK QUAY
NORWAY DOCK
FINLAND STREET
HELSINKI SQ
TAVISTOCK TOWER
GREENLAND DOCK
PRINCES COURT
Greenland Pier
South Lock
St. George's Stairs
RAINBOW QUAY
New Atlas Wharf
Telegraph & Express Print Works
7
OLD BELLGATE PL
Docklands Watersport Cen
MILLWALL OUTER
Surrey Docks Water Sports Cen
ROPE STREET
SOUTH DOCK
GREENLAND QUAY
CALYPSO WAY
PLOUGH WAY
SURREY QUAYS
LOWER ROAD
A200
B206
LIGHTER CLO
CAPSTAN RD
TARIFF CRES
DEPTFORD WF
JODANE ST
ARAGON TWR
WESTFERRY
SEVERNAKE CL
8
ARDEN CRES
St. Edmund (RC)
Works
CHILTON GROVE
Depot
Pump. Sta
PLOUGH
ROTHERHITHE NEW ROAD
ROTHERHITHE OLD RD
BUSH RD
OLDFIELD GROVE
ST. HELENA RD
BESTWOOD ST
CANNON WHARF BUSINESS CENTRE
CROFT STREET
Medical Cen
WINDLASS PL
LONGSHORE
DEPTFORD STRAND
LEWISHAM
MAST HOUSE TER
FERGUSON CLOSE
9
Youth Comm Cen
CULVER ROAD
SKETCHLEY GDNS
TRUNDLEYS
EVELYN
RAINSBOROUGH AVE
EDDYSTONE TWR
DAUBENEY TWR
FORESHORE
BOWDITCH
SE8
Landing Stage
MARITIME QUAY
NAPIER AVE
BLASKER WALK
10
Pier
Palmer's Wharf
OXESTALLS ROAD
PEPYS PARK
LEEWAY
DEPTFORD PARK
Tenn Cts
SPORTS GROUND
SCAWEN RD
B207
103
DRAGOON ROAD
DEPTFORD
Royal Naval Yd
Payne's Wharf
Borthwick Wharf
Power Station
Chimney
SAYES COURT PARK
GRINSTEAD ROAD
INWEN COURT
Fire Sta

A
B
C
D
E
F
G
1
2
3
4
5
6
7
8
9
10
POPLAR
POPLAR HIGH STREET
B123
ASPEN WAY
A1261
WEST INDIA QUAY
Tower Hamlets Coll
Train Depot
Poplar
Museum in Docklands
Billingsgate Fish Mkt
E14
Poplar Dock
Blackwall Basin
Blackwall
Poplar Business Park
Council Offices
East India
Reuters
Blackwall Tunnel
A102
Meridian Gardens
Airy's Point
Blackwall Reach
West India Circus
Westferry Road
Canary Wharf
Cabot Place
HSBC
Canada Square
Citygroup
Jubilee Pk
Heron Quays
South Quay
South Quay Plaza
Thames Quay (L.D.D.C.)
Admirals Way
Marsh Wall
West India Docks
The International Hotel
Cartier Circle
Trafalgar Way
Preston's Road
Cold Harbour
The Gun PH
Works
Manchester Road
A1206
ISLE OF DOGS
Millwall Inner Dock
Millwall Outer Dock
Guardian Newspaper Print Works
Tate & Lyle Sugar Works
Great Eastern Enterprise Cen
London Arena
Crossharbour & London Arena
Skylines Village
Meridian Gate
Cubitt Town
Telegraph & Express Print Works
Superstore
Mudchute
Mudchute Park
Mudchute Farm
Allot
Millwall Park
Island Gardens
Dockland Sailing & Watersport Cen
MILLWALL
Sir John McDougal Gdns
New Atlas Wharf
Ocean Wharf
St. Edmund (RC)
Globe Rope Walk
Christ & St. John
Leisure Cen
George Green's Sch
Newcastle Draw Dock
Ferry House PH
Rowing Club
Greenwich Foot Tunnel
Tower Hamlets
Greenwich
Lewisham
Royal Naval Yd
Palmer's Wharf
Payne's Wharf
Landing Stage
Lovell's Wharf
High Bridge Wharf
Delta Wharf
85
103
203

LOWER LEA CROSSING
H
J
K
L
M
N
P
86
ROYAL VICTORIA
CUSTOM HOUSE
ExCel
E16
ROYAL VICTORIA DOCK
1
2
3
4
5
6
7
8
9
10
SILVERTOWN WAY
NORTH WOOLWICH ROAD
A1020
Thames Wharf
Blackwall Beach
Blackwall Pier
Trinity Buoy Wharf
London City Airport Pier
Millennium Pier
THE DOME
NORTH GREENWICH
COACH STA
SKYSCAPE
Phoenix Wharf
Manhattan Wharf
RIVER THAMES
NEWHAM
GREENWICH
GREENSHIELDS INDUSTRIAL ESTATE
LYLE PARK
MILLENNIUM MILLS
Works
Jetty
Slipway
Pontoon
Greenwich Yacht Club
THAMES PATH
SE10
JOHN HARRISON WAY
PARKSIDE
TUNNEL APPROACH
A102
BLACKWALL LANE
A2203
BUGSBY'S WAY
MERIDIAN TRADING ESTATE
GREENWICH INDUSTRIAL ESTATE
STONE LAKE RETAIL PARK
Superstores
Holiday Inn Express Greenwich
WOOLWICH ROAD
A206
104
EAST GREENWICH PLEASAUNCE
WESTCOMBE PARK
Warehouses
CHARLTON

The index starting on page 208 combines entries for street names, place names, places of interest, stations and hospitals.

Place names are shown in capital letters,
e.g.**ACTON**, W3 . . . .**80**   CN74
These include towns, villages and other localities within the area covered by this atlas.

Places of interest are shown with a star symbol,
e.g. **★British Mus**, WC1 . . .**195**   P7
These include parks, museums, galleries, other important buildings and tourist attractions.

Hospitals and types of station are shown by symbols as listed :-

    Ⓗ   Hospital
    ≷   Railway station
    ⊖   London Underground station
    DLR   Docklands Light Railway station
    ⬦   Tramlink station

All other entries are for street names. When there is more than one street with exactly the same name then that name is shown only once in the index. It is then followed by a list of entries for each postal district that contains a street with that same name. For example, there are three streets called **Ardley Close** in this atlas and the index entry shows that one of these is in London postal district NW10, one is in London postal district SE6 and one is in Ruislip HA4.
e.g.**Ardley Cl**, NW10 . . .**62**   CS62
      SE6 . . . .**123**   DY90
      Ruislip HA4 . . . . . .**59**   BQ59
All entries are followed by the page number and grid reference on which the name will be found. So, in the example above, **Ardley Close**, NW10 will be found on page **62** in square CS62.
All entries are indexed to the largest scale map on which they are shown.

The index also contains some streets which are not actually named on the maps because there is not enough space. In these cases the adjoining or nearest named thoroughfare to such a street is shown in *italic*. The reference indicates where the unnamed street is located *off* the named thoroughfare.
e.g.**Bacton St**, E2
     off Roman Rd **84**   DW69
This means that **Bacton Street** is not named on the map, but it is located *off Roman Road* on page **84** in square DW69.

A strict letter-by-letter alphabetical order is followed in this index. All non-alphabetic characters such as spaces, hyphens or apostrophes have not been included in the index order. For example **Belle Vue Road** and **Bellevue Road** will be found listed together.

Standard terms such as **Avenue, Close, Rise** and **Road** are abbreviated in the index but are ordered alphabetically as if given in full. So, for example, **Abbots Ri** comes before **Abbots Rd.**

Names beginning with a definite article (i.e. **The**) are indexed from their second word onwards with the definite article being placed at the end of the name.
e.g. **Avenue, The**, E4 . . .**47** ED51
The alphabetical order extends to include postal information so that where two or more streets have exactly the same name, London postal district references are given first in alpha-numeric order and are followed by non-London post town references in alphabetical order, e.g. **Ardley Close**, NW10 is followed by **Ardley Close**, SE6 and then **Ardley Close**, Ruislip HA4.

In cases where there are two or more streets of the same name in the same postal area, extra information is given in brackets to aid location. For example, **High St**, Orpington BR6 (Farnborough), and **High St**, Orpington BR6 (Green St Grn), distinguishes between two streets called **High Street** which are both in the post town of Orpington and within the same postal district of BR6.

Extra locational information is also given for some localities within large post towns. This is also to aid location.
e.g.**Adrian Cl**, Uxb. (Hare.) UB9. . .**38** BK53
This street is within the locality of Harefield which is part of the post town of Uxbridge, and it is within postal district UB9.

A full list of locality and post town abbreviations used in this atlas is given on the following page.

All	Alley	Ct	Court	Hosp	Hospital	Rd	Road
Allot	Allotments	Cts	Courts	Hts	Heights	Rds	Roads
Amb	Ambulance	Ctyd	Courtyard	Ind	Industrial	Rec	Recreation
App	Approach	Dep	Depot	Int	International	Res	Reservoir
Arc	Arcade	Dev	Development	Junct	Junction	Ri	Rise
Av	Avenue	Dr	Drive	La	Lane	S	South
Bdy	Broadway	Dws	Dwellings	Las	Lanes	Sch	School
Bk	Bank	E	East	Lib	Library	Sec	Secondary
Bldgs	Buildings	Ed	Education	Lo	Lodge	Shop	Shopping
Boul	Boulevard	Elec	Electricity	Lwr	Lower	Sq	Square
Bowl	Bowling	Embk	Embankment	Mag	Magistrates	St.	Saint
Br	Bridge	Est	Estate	Mans	Mansions	St	Street
C of E	Church of	Ex	Exchange	Mem	Memorial	Sta	Station
England		Exhib	Exhibition	Mkt	Market	Sts	Streets
Cath	Cathedral	FB	Footbridge	Mkts	Markets	Sub	Subway
Cem	Cemetery	FC	Football Club	Ms	Mews	Swim	Swimming
Cen	Central, Centre	Fld	Field	Mt	Mount	TA	Territorial Army
Cft	Croft	Flds	Fields	Mus	Museum	TH	Town Hall
Cfts	Crofts	Fm	Farm	N	North	Tenn	Tennis
Ch	Church	Gall	Gallery	NT	National Trust	Ter	Terrace
Chyd	Churchyard	Gar	Garage	Nat	National	Thea	Theatre
Cin	Cinema	Gdn	Garden	PH	Public House	Trd	Trading
Circ	Circus	Gdns	Gardens	PO	Post Office	Twr	Tower
Cl	Close	Gen	General	Par	Parade	Twrs	Towers
Co	County	Govt	Government	Pas	Passage	Uni	University
Coll	College	Gra	Grange	Pav	Pavilion	Vil	Villas
Comm	Community	Grd	Ground	Pk	Park	Vil	Villa
Conv	Convent	Grds	Grounds	Pl	Place	Vw	View
Cor	Corner	Grn	Green	Pol	Police	W	West
Coron	Coroners	Grns	Greens	Prec	Precinct	Wd	Wood
Cors	Corners	Gro	Grove	Prim	Primary	Wds	Woods
Cotts	Cottages	Gros	Groves	Prom	Promenade	Wf	Wharf
Cov	Covered	Gt	Great	Pt	Point	Wk	Walk
Crem	Crematorium	Ho	House	Quad	Quadrant	Wks	Works
Cres	Crescent	Hos	Houses	RC	Roman Catholic	Yd	Yard

Locality & post town abbreviations

Note: In the list of abbreviations shown below Post Towns are in bold type.

Abbreviation	Locality / Post Town
Abb.L.	Abbots Langley
Add.	**Addlestone**
Ald.	Aldenham
Amer.	**Amersham**
Ashf.	**Ashford**
Ashtd.	**Ashtead**
Bad.Dene	Badgers Dene
Bad.Mt.	Badgers Mount
Bans.	**Banstead**
Bark.	**Barking**
Barn.	**Barnet**
Barne.	Barnehurst
Beac.	**Beaconsfield**
Beck.	**Beckenham**
Bedd.	Beddington
Bedd.Cor.	Beddington Corner
Belv.	**Belvedere**
Berry's Grn.	Berry's Green
Bet.	**Betchworth**
Bex.	**Bexley**
Bexh.	**Bexleyheath**
Bigg.H.	Biggin Hill
Bkhm.	Bookham
Bletch.	Bletchingley
Borwd.	**Borehamwood**
Bov.	Bovingdon
Brent.	**Brentford**
Brick.Wd.	Bricket Wood
Brock.	Brockham
Brom.	**Bromley**
Brook.Pk.	Brookmans Park
Brox.	**Broxbourne**
Brwd.	**Brentwood**
Buck.H.	**Buckhurst Hill**
Burgh Hth.	Burgh Heath
Bushey Hth.	Bushey Heath
Carp.Pk.	Carpenders Park
Cars.	**Carshalton**
Cat.	**Caterham**
Ch.End	Church End
Ch.St.G.	**Chalfont St. Giles**
Chad.Hth.	Chadwell Heath
Chad.St.M	Chadwell St. Mary
Chaff.Hun.	Chafford Hundred
Chal.St.P.	Chalfont St. Peter
Chel.	Chelsham
Chels.	Chelsfield
Cher.	**Chertsey**
Chesh.	**Chesham**
Chess.	**Chessington**
Chev.	Chevening
Chig.	**Chigwell**
Chipper.	Chipperfield
Chis.	**Chislehurst**
Chob.Com.	Chobham Common
Chorl.	Chorleywood
Chsht.	Cheshunt
Clay.	Claygate
Cob.	**Cobham**
Cockfos.	Cockfosters
Coll.Row	Collier Row
Coln.Hth.	Colney Heath
Coln.St.	Colney Street
Colnbr.	Colnbrook
Cooper.	Coopersale
Couls.	**Coulsdon**
Cran.	Cranford
Cray.	Crayford
Crock.	Crockenhill
Crock.H.	Crockham Hill
Crox.Grn.	Croxley Green
Croy.	**Croydon**
Dag.	**Dagenham**
Dance.H.	Dancers Hill
Dart.	**Dartford**
Denh.	Denham
Dor.	**Dorking**
Down.	Downside
Dunt.Grn.	Dunton Green
E.Bed.	East Bedfont
E.Croy.	East Croydon
E.Ewell	East Ewell
E.Hors.	East Horsley
E.Mol.	**East Molesey**
E.Til.	East Tilbury
Eastcote Vill.	Eastcote Village
Eden.	**Edenbridge**
Edg.	**Edgware**
Eff.	Effingham
Eff.Junct.	Effingham Junction
Egh.	**Egham**
Egh. & Wind.	**Egham & Windsor**
Egh.H.	Egham Hythe
Elm Pk.	Elm Park
Elm.Wds.	Elmstead Woods
Enf.	**Enfield**
Eng.Grn.	Englefield Green
Epp.	**Epping**
Epp. & Loug.	**Epping & Loughton**
Epp.Grn.	Epping Green
Ewell E.	Ewell East
Ewell W.	Ewell West
Eyns.	Eynsford
Farnboro.	Farnborough
Fawk.	Fawkham
Fawk.Grn.	Fawkham Green
Felt.	**Feltham**
Fetch.	Fetcham
Flam.	Flamstead
Flaun.	Flaunden
Fnghm.	Farningham
Frog.	Frogmore
Gdse.	**Godstone**
Geo.Grn.	George Green
Ger.Cr.	**Gerrards Cross**
Gidea Pk.	Gidea Park
Godden Grn.	Godden Green
Grav.	**Gravesend**
Green.	**Greenhithe**
Grn.St.Grn.	Green Street Green
Grnf.	**Greenford**
Gt.Warley	Great Warley
Guil.	**Guildford**
Hackbr.	Hackbridge
Had.Wd.	Hadley Wood
Halst.	Halstead
Han.	Hanworth
Har.	**Harrow**
Har.Hill	Harrow on the Hill
Har.Wld.	Harrow Weald
Hare.	Harefield
Harm.	Harmondsworth
Harold Wd.	Harold Wood
Hat.	**Hatfield**
Hatt.Cr.	Hatton Cross
Hav.at.Bow.	Havering-atte-Bower
Hedg.	Hedgerley
Hem.H.	**Hemel Hempstead**
Herons.	Heronsgate
Hert.	**Hertford**
Hext.	Hextable
High Barn.	High Barnet
Highams Pk.	Highams Park
Hinch.Wd.	Hinchley Wood
Hlgdn.	Hillingdon
Hmptn.	**Hampton**
Hmptn.H.	Hampton Hill
Hmptn.W.	Hampton Wick
Hook Grn.	Hook Green
Horn.	**Hornchurch**
Hort.Kir.	Horton Kirby
Houns.	**Hounslow**
Houns.W.	Hounslow West
Hthrw.Air.	Heathrow Airport
Hthrw.Air.N.	Heathrow Airport North
Ickhm.	Ickenham
Ilf.	**Ilford**
Islw.	**Isleworth**
Ken.	**Kenley**
Kes.	**Keston**
Kgfld.	Kingfield
Kgswd.	Kingswood
Kings L.	**Kings Langley**
Kings.T.	**Kingston upon Thames**
Knap.	Knaphill
Knock.	Knockholt
Knock.P.	Knockholt Pound
Lamb.End	Lambourne End
Let.Hth.	Letchmore Heath
Lmpfld.	Limpsfield
Lmpfld.Ch.	Limpsfield Chart
Lon.Col.	London Colney
Long Dit.	Long Ditton
Long.	**Longfield**
Longcr.	Longcross
Loud.	Loudwater
Loug.	**Loughton**
Lt.Chal.	Little Chalfont
Lt.Hth.	Little Heath
Lt.Warley	Little Warley
Lthd.	**Leatherhead**
Lwr.Kgswd.	Lower Kingswood
Lwr.Sydenham	Lower Sydenham
Lyon Pk Av	Lyon Park Avenue
Map.Cr.	Maple Cross
Mdgrn.	Middlegreen
Merst.	Merstham
Mick.	Mickleham
Mimbr.	Mimbridge
Mitch.	**Mitcham**
Mord.	**Morden**
Mots.Pk.	Motspur Park
Mtnsg.	Mountnessing
N.Finchley	North Finchley
N.Har.	North Harrow
N.Mal.	**New Malden**
N.Mymms	North Mymms
N.Ock.	North Ockendon
N.Stfd.	North Stifford
N.Wld.	North Weald
N.Wld.Bas.	North Weald Bassett
Nave.	Navestock
Nave.S.	Navestock Side
New Adgtn.	New Addington
New Barn.	New Barnet
Newgate St.	Newgate Street
Northumb.Hth.	Northumberland Heath
Norwood Junct.	Norwood Junction
Nthflt.	Northfleet
Nthlt.	**Northolt**
Nthwd.	**Northwood**
Nutfld.	Nutfield
Old Wind.	Old Windsor
Old Wok.	Old Woking
Ong.	**Ongar**
Orch.L.	Orchard Leigh
Orp.	**Orpington**
Ott.	Ottershaw
Oxt.	**Oxted**
Park St.	Park Street
Perry St.	Perry Street
Petts Wd	Petts Wood
Pilg.Hat.	Pilgrim's Hatch
Pnr.	**Pinner**
Pond.End	Ponders End
Pot.B.	**Potters Bar**
Pr.Bot.	Pratt's Bottom
Pur.	**Purley**
Purf.	**Purfleet**
Rad.	**Radlett**
Rain.	**Rainham**
Red.	**Redhill**
Reig.	**Reigate**
Rich.	**Richmond**
Rick.	**Rickmansworth**
Rod.Val.	Roding Valley
Rom.	**Romford**
Rosh.	Rosherville
Ruis.	**Ruislip**
Runny.	Runnymede
Rush Grn.	Rush Green
Russ.Hill	Russell Hill
Rvrhd.	Riverhead
S.Croy.	**South Croydon**
S.Darenth	South Darenth
S.Har.	South Harrow
S.Merst.	South Merstham
S.Mimms	South Mimms
S.Norwood	South Norwood
S.Nutfld.	South Nutfield
S.Ock.	**South Ockendon**
S.Oxhey	South Oxhey
S.Ruis.	South Ruislip
S.Stfd.	South Stifford
S.le H.	**Stanford-le-Hope**
Scad.Pk.	Scadbury Park
Send M.	Send Marsh
Sev.	**Sevenoaks**
Sev.Wld.	Sevenoaks Weald
Sheer.	Sheerwater
Shenf.	Shenfield
Shep.	**Shepperton**
Shore.	Shoreham
Short.	Shortlands
Sid.	**Sidcup**
Slade Grn.	Slade Green
Slou.	**Slough**
St.Alb.	**St. Albans**
St.Geo.H.	St. George's Hill
St.M.Cray	St. Mary Cray
St.P.Cray	St. Paul's Cray
Stai.	**Staines**
Stan.	**Stanmore**
Stanw.	Stanwell
Stap.Abb.	Stapleford Abbotts
Stap.Taw.	Stapleford Tawney
Sthflt.	Southfleet
Sthl.	**Southall**
Sthl.Grn.	Southall Green
Stoke D'Ab.	Stoke D'Abernon
Stoke P.	Stoke Poges
Sun.	**Sunbury-on-Thames**
Sund.	Sundridge
Surb.	**Surbiton**
Sutt.	**Sutton**
Sutt.Grn.	Sutton Green
Sutt.H.	Sutton at Hone
Swan.	**Swanley**
Swans.	**Swanscombe**
T.Ditt.	**Thames Ditton**
Tad.	**Tadworth**
Tand.	Tandridge
Tats.	Tatsfield
Tedd.	**Teddington**
Th.Hth.	**Thornton Heath**
They.B.	Theydon Bois
Thnwd.	Thornwood
Til.	**Tilbury**
Tkgtn.	Tokyngton
Turnf.	Turnford
Twick.	**Twickenham**
Tyr.Wd.	Tyrrell's Wood
Undrvr.	Underriver
Upmin.	**Upminster**
Uxb.	**Uxbridge**
Vir.W.	**Virginia Water**
W.Byf.	**West Byfleet**
W.Croy.	West Croydon
W.Ewell	West Ewell
W.Hors.	West Horsley
W.Mol.	**West Molesey**
W.Thur.	West Thurrock
W.Til.	West Tilbury
W.Wick.	**West Wickham**
Wal.Abb.	**Waltham Abbey**
Wal.Cr.	**Waltham Cross**
Wall.	**Wallington**
Walt.	**Walton-on-Thames**
Warl.	**Warlingham**
Wat.	**Watford**
Wdf.Grn.	**Woodford Green**
Well.	**Welling**
Wem.	**Wembley**
Wenn.	Wennington
West Dr.	**West Drayton**
West.	**Westerham**
Wey.	**Weybridge**
Whel.Hill	Whelpley Hill
Whyt.	**Whyteleafe**
Wilm.	Wilmington
Wind.	**Windsor**
Wldste.	Wealdstone
Wok.	**Woking**
Wold.	Woldingham
Woodside Pk.	Woodside Park
Wor.Pk.	**Worcester Park**
Wrays.	Wraysbury
Yiew.	Yiewsley

02 Shop Cen, NW3 *off Finchley Rd* 82 DC65

A

Aaron Hill Rd, E6 87 EN71
Abberley Ms, SW4 *off Cedars Rd* 101 DH83
Abberton Wk, Rain. RM13 *off Ongar Way* 89 FE66
Abbess Cl, E6 *off Oliver Gdns* 86 EL71
SW2 121 DP88
Abbeville Rd, N8 *off Barrington Rd* 65 DK56
SW4 121 DJ86
Abbey Av, Wem. HA0 80 CL68
Abbey Business Cen, SW8 *off Ingate Pl* 101 DH81
Abbey Cl, Hayes UB3 77 BV74
Northolt UB5 *off Invicta Gro* 78 BZ69
Pinner HA5 59 BV55
Romford RM1 71 FG58
Woking GU22 167 BE116
Abbey Ct, Wal.Abb. EN9 15 EB34
Abbey Cres, Belv. DA17 106 FA77
Abbeydale Rd, Wem. HA0 80 CN67
Abbey Dr, SW17 *off Church La* 120 DG92
Abbots Langley WD5 7 BU32
Staines TW18 134 BJ98
Abbeyfield Rd, SE16 202 F8
Abbeyfields Cl, NW10 80 CN68
Abbeyfields Mobile Home Pk, Cher. KT16 134 BK101
Abbey Gdns, NW8 82 DC68
SE16 202 C8
W6 99 CY79
Chertsey KT16 134 BG100
Chislehurst BR7 145 EN95
Waltham Abbey EN9 15 EC33
Abbey Grn, Cher. KT16 134 BG100
Abbey Gro, SE2 106 EV77
Abbeyhill Rd, Sid. DA15 126 EW89
Abbey Ind Est, Mitch. CR4 140 DF99
Wembley HA0 80 CM67
Abbey La, E15 85 EC68
Beckenham BR3 123 EA94
Abbey Mead Ind Pk, Wal.Abb. EN9 15 EC34
Abbey Ms, E17 *off Leamington Av* 67 EA57
Abbey Orchard St, SW1 199 N6
Abbey Par, SW19 *off Merton High St* 120 DC94
W5 *off Hanger La* 80 CM69
Abbey Pk, Beck. BR3 123 EA94
Abbey Pl, Dart. DA1 *off Priory Rd N* 128 FK85
Abbey Retail Pk, Bark. IG11 87 EP67
Abbey Rd, E15 86 EE68
NW6 82 DB66
NW8 82 DC68
NW10 80 CP68
SE2 106 EX77
SW19 120 DC94
Barking IG11 87 EP66
Belvedere DA17 106 EX77
Bexleyheath DA7 106 EY84
Chertsey KT16 134 BH101
Croydon CR0 141 DP104
Enfield EN1 30 DS43
Gravesend DA12 131 GL88
Greenhithe DA9 129 FW85
Ilford IG2 69 ER57
Shepperton TW17 134 BN102
South Croydon CR2 161 DX110
Virginia Water GU25 132 AX99
Waltham Cross EN8 15 DY34
Woking GU21 166 AW117
Abbey Rd Est, NW8 82 DB67
Abbey St, E13 86 EG70
SE1 201 N6
Abbey Ter, SE2 106 EW77
Abbey Vw, NW7 43 CT48
Radlett WD7 25 CF35
Waltham Abbey EN9 15 EB33
Watford WD25 24 BX36
Abbey Vw Roundabout, Wal.Abb. EN9 15 EB33
Abbey Wk, W.Mol. KT8 136 CB97
Abbey Way, SE2 106 EX76
Abbey Wf Ind Est, Bark. IG11 87 ER68
ABBEY WOOD, SE2 106 EV76
⇌ **Abbey Wood** 106 EW76
Abbey Wd La, Rain. RM13 90 FK68
Abbey Wd Rd, SE2 106 EV77
Abbot Cl, Stai. TW18 114 BK94
West Byfleet (Byfleet) KT14 152 BK110
Abbots Av, Epsom KT19 156 CN111
Abbotsbury Cl, E15 85 EC68
W14 *off Abbotsbury Rd* 99 CZ75
Abbotsbury Gdns, Pnr. HA5 60 BW58
Abbotsbury Ms, SE15 102 DW83
Abbotsbury Rd, W14 99 CY75
Bromley BR2 144 EF103
Morden SM4 140 DB99
Abbots Cl, N1 *off Alwyne Rd* 84 DQ65
Brentwood CM15 55 GA46
Orpington BR5 145 EQ102
Rainham RM13 90 FJ68
Ruislip HA4 60 BX62
Abbots Dr, Har. HA2 60 CA61
Virginia Water GU25 132 AW98
Abbots Fld, Grav. DA12 *off Ruffets Wd* 131 GJ93
Abbotsford Av, N15 66 DQ56
Abbotsford Cl, Wok. GU22 *off Onslow Cres* 167 BA117
Abbotsford Gdns, Wdf.Grn. IG8 48 EG52
Abbotsford Lo, Nthwd. HA6 39 BS50
Abbotsford Rd, Ilf. IG3 70 EU61
Abbots Gdns, N2 64 DD56
W8 *off St. Mary's Pl* 100 DB76
Abbots Grn, Croy. CR0 161 DX107
Abbotshade Rd, SE16 203 J2
Abbotshall Av, N14 45 DJ48
Abbotshall Rd, SE6 123 ED88
Abbots La, SE1 201 N3
Kenley CR8 176 DQ116
ABBOTS LANGLEY 7 BR31
Abbotsleigh Cl, Sutt. SM2 158 DB108
Abbotsleigh Rd, SW16 121 DJ91
Abbots Manor Est, SW1 199 H9
Abbotsmede Cl, Twick. TW1 117 CF89
Abbots Pk, SW2 121 DN88
Abbot's Pl, NW6 82 DB67
Abbots Ri, Kings L. WD4 6 BM26
Redhill RH1 184 DG132
Abbot's Rd, E6 86 EK67
Abbots Rd, Abb.L. WD5 7 BS30
Edgware HA8 42 CQ52
Abbots Ter, N8 65 DL58
Abbotstone Rd, SW15 99 CW83
Abbot St, E8 84 DT65
Abbots Vw, Kings L. WD4 6 BM27
Abbots Wk, W8 *off St. Mary's Pl* 100 DB76
Caterham CR3 *off Tillingdown Hill* 176 DU122
Abbots Way, Beck. BR3 143 DY99
Chertsey KT16 133 BF101
Abbotswell Rd, SE4 123 DZ85
Abbotswood Cl, Belv. DA17 *off Coptefield Dr* 106 EY76
Abbotswood Dr, Wey. KT13 153 BR110
Abbotswood Gdns, Ilf. IG5 69 EM55
Abbotswood Rd, SE22 102 DS84
SW16 121 DK90
Abbotswood Way, Hayes UB3 77 BV74
Abbott Av, SW20 139 CX96
Abbott Cl, Hmptn. TW12 116 BY93
Northolt UB5 78 BZ65
Abbott Rd, E14 85 EC71
Abbotts Cl, SE28 88 EW73
Romford RM7 71 FB55
Swanley BR8 147 FG98
Uxbridge UB8 76 BK71
Abbotts Cres, E4 47 ED49
Enfield EN2 29 DP40
Abbotts Dr, Wal.Abb. EN9 16 EG34
Wembley HA0 61 CH61
Abbotts Pk Rd, E10 67 EC59
Abbotts Rd, Barn. EN5 28 DB42
Mitcham CR4 141 DJ98
Southall UB1 78 BY74
Sutton SM3 139 CZ104
Abbott's Tilt, Walt. KT12 136 BY104
Abbotts Wk, Bexh. DA7 106 EX80
Abbs Cross Gdns, Horn. RM12 72 FJ60
Abbs Cross La, Horn. RM12 72 FJ63
Abchurch La, EC4 197 L10
Abchurch Yd, EC4 197 K10
Abdale Rd, W12 81 CV74
Abenberg Way, Brwd. (Hutton) CM13 55 GB47
Aberavon Rd, E3 85 DY69
Abercairn Rd, SW16 121 DJ94
Aberconway Rd, Mord. SM4 140 DB97
Abercorn Cl, NW7 43 CY52
NW8 82 DC69
South Croydon CR2 161 DX112
Abercorn Cres, Har. HA2 60 CB60
Abercorn Gdns, Har. HA3 61 CK59
Romford RM6 70 EV58
Abercorn Gro, Ruis. HA4 59 BR56
Abercorn Pl, NW8 82 DC69
Abercorn Rd, NW7 43 CY52
Stanmore HA7 41 CJ52
Abercorn Way, SE1 202 B10
Woking GU21 166 AU118
Abercrombie Dr, Enf. EN1 *off Linwood Cres* 30 DU39
Abercrombie St, SW11 100 DE82
Aberdale Ct, SE16 *off Poolmans St* 103 DX75
Aberdale Gdns, Pot.B. EN6 11 CZ33
Aberdare Cl, W.Wick. BR4 143 EC103
Aberdare Gdns, NW6 82 DB66
NW7 43 CX52
Aberdare Rd, Enf. EN3 30 DW42
Aberdeen La, N5 65 DP64
Aberdeen Par, N18 *off Angel Rd* 46 DV50
Aberdeen Pk, N5 65 DP64
Aberdeen Pk Ms, N5 66 DQ63
Aberdeen Pl, NW8 82 DD70
Aberdeen Rd, N5 66 DQ63
N18 46 DV50
NW10 63 CT64
Croydon CR0 160 DQ105
Harrow HA3 41 CF54
Aberdeen Sq, E14 203 P2
Aberdeen Ter, SE3 103 ED82
Aberdour Rd, Ilf. IG3 70 EV62
Aberdour St, SE1 201 M8
Aberfeldy St, E14 85 EC72
Aberford Gdns, SE18 104 EL81
Aberford Rd, Borwd. WD6 26 CN40
Aberfoyle Rd, SW16 121 DK93
Abergeldie Rd, SE12 124 EH86
Aberglen Ind Est, Hayes UB3 95 BR75
Abernethy Rd, SE13 104 EE84
Abersham Rd, E8 66 DT64
Abery St, SE18 105 ES77
Abigail Ms, Rom. RM3 *off King Alfred Rd* 52 FM54
Abingdon Cl, NW1 *off Camden Sq* 83 DK65
SE1 202 A10
SW19 120 DC93
Uxbridge UB10 76 BM67
Woking GU21 166 AV118
Abingdon Pl, Pot.B. EN6 12 DB32
Abingdon Rd, N3 44 DC54
SW16 141 DL96
W8 100 DA76
Abingdon St, SW1 199 P6
Abingdon Vil, W8 100 DA76
Abingdon Way, Orp. BR6 164 EV105
Abinger Av, Sutt. SM2 157 CW109
Abinger Cl, Bark. IG11 70 EU63
Bromley BR1 144 EL97
Croydon CR0 161 EC107
Wallington SM6 159 DL106
Abinger Gdns, Islw. TW7 97 CE83
Abinger Gro, SE8 103 DZ79
Abinger Ms, W9 *off Warlock Rd* 82 DA70
Abinger Rd, W4 98 CS76
Ablett St, SE16 102 DW78
Abney Gdns, N16 *off Stoke Newington High St* 66 DT61
Aboyne Dr, SW20 139 CU96
Aboyne Est, SW17 120 DD90
Aboyne Rd, NW10 62 CS62
SW17 120 DD90
Abraham Cl, Wat. WD19 *off Muirfield Rd* 39 BV49
ABRIDGE, Rom. 34 EV41
Abridge Cl, Wal.Cr. EN8 31 DX35
Abridge Gdns, Rom. RM5 50 FA51
Abridge Pk, Rom. (Abridge) RM4 34 EU42
Abridge Rd, Chig. IG7 33 ER44
Epping (They.B.) CM16 33 ES36
Romford (Abridge) RM4 34 EU39
Abridge Way, Bark. IG11 88 EV68
Abyssinia Cl, SW11 *off Cairns Rd* 100 DE84
Abyssinia Rd, SW11 *off Auckland Rd* 100 DE84
Acacia Av, N17 46 DR52
Brentford TW8 97 CH80
Hayes UB3 77 BT72
Hornchurch RM12 71 FF61
Mitcham CR4 *off Acacia Rd* 141 DH96
Ruislip HA4 59 BU60
Shepperton TW17 134 BN99
Staines (Wrays.) TW19 92 AY84
Wembley HA9 62 CL64
West Drayton UB7 76 BM73
Woking GU22 166 AX120
Acacia Cl, SE8 203 K9
SE20 *off Selby Rd* 142 DU96
Addlestone (Woodham) KT15 151 BF110
Orpington BR5 145 ER99
Stanmore HA7 41 CE51
Waltham Cross EN7 14 DS27
Acacia Ct, Wal.Abb. EN9 *off Farthingale La* 16 EG34
Acacia Dr, Add. (Woodham) KT15 151 BF110
Banstead SM7 157 CX114
Sutton SM3 139 CZ102
Upminster RM14 72 FN63
Acacia Gdns, NW8 *off Acacia Rd* 82 DD68
Upminster RM14 73 FT59
West Wickham BR4 143 EC103
Acacia Gro, SE21 122 DR89
New Malden KT3 138 CR97
Acacia Ms, West Dr. UB7 94 BK79
Acacia Pl, NW8 82 DD68
Acacia Rd, E11 68 EE61
E17 67 DY58
N22 45 DN53
NW8 82 DD68
SW16 141 DL95
W3 80 CQ73
Beckenham BR3 143 DZ97
Dartford DA1 128 FK88
Enfield EN2 30 DR39
Greenhithe DA9 129 FS86
Hampton TW12 116 CA93
Mitcham CR4 141 DH96
Staines TW18 114 BH92
Acacia Wk, Swan. BR8 147 FD96
Acacia Way, Sid. DA15 125 ET88
Academy Gdns, Croy. CR0 142 DT102
Northolt UB5 78 BX68
Academy Pl, SE18 105 EM81
Academy Rd, SE18 105 EM81
Acanthus Dr, SE1 202 B10
Acanthus Rd, SW11 100 DG83
Accommodation La, West Dr. UB7 94 BJ79
Accommodation Rd, NW11 63 CZ59
Chertsey (Longcr.) KT16 132 AX104
A.C. Ct, T.Ditt. KT7 *off Harvest La* 137 CG100
Acer Av, Hayes UB4 78 BY71
Rainham RM13 90 FK69
Acer Rd, West. (Bigg.H.) TN16 178 EK116
Acers, St.Alb. (Park St.) AL2 8 CC28
Acfold Rd, SW6 100 DB81
Achilles Cl, SE1 202 C10
Achilles Pl, Wok. GU21 166 AW117
Achilles Rd, NW6 64 DA64
Achilles St, SE14 103 DY80
Achilles Way, W1 198 G3
Acklam Rd, W10 81 CZ71
Acklington Dr, NW9 42 CS53
Ackmar Rd, SW6 100 DA81
Ackroyd Dr, E3 85 DZ71
Ackroyd Rd, SE23 123 DX87
Acland Cl, SE18 *off Clothworkers Rd* 105 ER80
Acland Cres, SE5 102 DR84
Acland Rd, NW2 81 CV65
Acme Rd, Wat. WD24 23 BU38
Acock Gro, Nthlt. UB5 60 CB63
Acol Cres, Ruis. HA4 59 BV64
Acol Rd, NW6 82 DA66
Aconbury Rd, Dag. RM9 88 EV67
Acorn Cl, E4 47 EA50
Chislehurst BR7 125 EQ92
Enfield EN2 29 DP39
Acorn Cl, Hmptn. TW12 116 CB93
Stanmore HA7 41 CH52
Acorn Ct, Ilf. IG2 69 ES58
Acorn Gdns, SE19 142 DT95
W3 80 CR71
Acorn Gro, Hayes UB3 95 BT80
Ruislip HA4 59 BT63
Tadworth KT20 173 CY124
Woking GU22 *off Old Sch Pl* 166 AY121
Acorn Ind Pk, Dart. DA1 127 FG85
Acorn La, Pot.B. (Cuffley) EN6 13 DL29
Acorn Par, SE15 *off Carlton Gro* 102 DV80
Acorn Pl, Wat. WD24 23 BU37
Acorn Rd, Dart. DA1 127 FF85
Acorns, The, Chig. IG7 49 ES49
Acorns Way, Esher KT10 154 CC106
Acorn Wk, SE16 203 L2
Acorn Way, SE23 123 DX90
Beckenham BR3 143 EC99
Orpington BR6 163 EP105
Acre Dr, SE22 102 DU84
Acrefield Rd, Ger.Cr. (Chal.St.P.) SL9 56 AX55
Acre La, SW2 101 DL84
Carshalton SM5 158 DG105
Wallington SM6 158 DG105
Acre Path, Nthlt. UB5 *off Arnold Rd* 78 BY65
Acre Rd, SW19 120 DD93
Dagenham RM10 89 FB66
Kingston upon Thames KT2 138 CL95
Acres End, Amer. HP7 20 AS39
Acres Gdns, Tad. KT20 173 CX119
Acre Vw, Horn. RM11 72 FL56
Acre Way, Nthwd. HA6 39 BT53
Acris St, SW18 120 DC85
ACTON, W3 80 CN74
⇌ **Acton Central** 80 CR74
Acton Cl, N9 46 DU47
Waltham Cross (Chsht.) EN8 15 DY31
Acton Hill Ms, W3 *off Uxbridge Rd* 80 CP74
H **Acton Hosp**, W3 98 CN75
Acton La, NW10 80 CS68
W3 98 CQ75
W4 98 CR76
⇌ **Acton Main Line** 80 CQ72
Acton Ms, E8 84 DT67
Acton Pk Ind Est, W3 98 CR75
Acton St, WC1 196 B3
⊖ **Acton Town** 98 CN75
Acuba Rd, SW18 120 DB89
Acworth Cl, N9 *off Turin Rd* 46 DW45
Ada Gdns, E14 85 ED72
E15 86 EF67
Adair Cl, SE25 142 DV97
Adair Rd, W10 81 CY70
Adair Twr, W10 *off Appleford Rd* 81 CY70
Adam & Eve Ct, W1 195 L8
Adam & Eve Ms, W8 100 DA76
Adam Cl, SE6 123 DZ91
Adam Ct, SW7 *off Gloucester Rd* 100 DC77
Adam Pl, N16 *off Stoke Newington High St* 66 DT61
Adam Rd, E4 47 DZ51
Adams Cl, N3 *off Falkland Av* 44 DA52
NW9 62 CP61
Surbiton KT5 138 CM100
Adams Ct, EC2 197 L8
Adamsfield, Wal.Cr. EN7 14 DU27
Adams Gdns Est, SE16 202 F4
Adamson Rd, E16 86 EG72
NW3 82 DD66
Adams Pl, N7 *off George's Rd* 65 DM64
Adamsrill Cl, Enf. EN1 30 DR44
Adamsrill Rd, SE26 123 DY91
Adams Rd, N17 46 DS54
Beckenham BR3 143 DY99
Adams Row, W1 198 G1
Adams Sq, Bexh. DA6 *off Regency Way* 106 EY83
Adam St, WC2 200 A1
Adams Wk, Kings.T. KT1 138 CL96
Adams Way, Croy. CR0 142 DT100
Adam Wk, SW6 99 CW80
Ada Pl, E2 84 DU67
Adare Wk, SW16 121 DM90
Ada Rd, SE5 102 DS80
Wembley HA0 61 CK62
Adastral Est, NW9 42 CS53
Ada St, E8 84 DV67
Adcock Wk, Orp. BR6 *off Borkwood Pk* 163 ET105
Adderley Gdns, SE9 125 EN91
Adderley Gro, SW11 *off Culmstock Rd* 120 DG85
Adderley Rd, Har. HA3 41 CF53
Adderley St, E14 85 EC72
ADDINGTON, Croy. 161 DZ106
Addington Border, Croy. CR0 161 DY110
Addington Ct, SW14 98 CR83
Addington Dr, N12 44 DC51
Addington Gro, SE26 123 DY91
Addington Rd, E3 85 EA69
E16 86 EE70
N4 65 DN58
Croydon CR0 141 DN102
South Croydon CR2 160 DU111
West Wickham BR4 144 EE103
Addington Sq, SE5 102 DQ80
Addington St, SE1 200 C5
Tramlink **Addington Village** 161 EA107
Addington Village Rd, Croy. CR0 161 EA106
Addis Cl, Enf. EN3 31 DX39
ADDISCOMBE, Croy. 142 DT102
Tramlink **Addiscombe** 142 DU102
Addiscombe Av, Croy. CR0 142 DU101
Addiscombe Cl, Har. HA3 61 CJ57
Addiscombe Ct Rd, Croy. CR0 142 DS102
Addiscombe Gro, Croy. CR0 142 DR103
Addiscombe Rd, Croy. CR0 142 DS103
Watford WD18 23 BV42
Addison Av, N14 29 DH44
W11 81 CY74
Hounslow TW3 96 CC81
Addison Br Pl, W14 99 CZ77
Addison Cl, Cat. CR3 176 DR122
Northwood HA6 39 BU53
Orpington BR5 145 EQ100
Addison Ct, Epp. CM16 *off Centre Dr* 18 EU31
Addison Cres, W14 99 CY76
Addison Dr, SE12 *off Eltham Rd* 124 EH85
Addison Gdns, W14 99 CX76
Grays RM17 *off Palmers Dr* 110 GC77
Surbiton KT5 138 CM98
Addison Gro, W4 98 CS76
Addison Pl, W11 81 CY74
Southall UB1 *off Longford Av* 78 CA73
Addison Rd, E11 68 EG58
E17 67 EB57
SE25 142 DU98
W14 99 CZ76
Bromley BR2 144 EJ99
Caterham CR3 176 DR121
Enfield EN3 30 DW39
Ilford IG6 49 EQ53
Teddington TW11 117 CH93
Woking GU21 *off Chertsey Rd* 167 AZ117
Addison's Cl, Croy. CR0 143 DZ103
Addison Way, NW11 63 CZ56
Hayes UB3 77 BU72
Northwood HA6 39 BT53
Addle Hill, EC4 196 G10
ADDLESTONE 152 BJ106
⇌ **Addlestone** 152 BK105
ADDLESTONE MOOR, Add. 134 BG103
Addlestone Moor, Add. KT15 134 BJ103
Addlestone Pk, Add. KT15 152 BH106
Addlestone Rd, Add. KT15 152 BL105
Addle St, EC2 197 J7
Adecroft Way, W.Mol. KT8 136 CC97
Adela Av, N.Mal. KT3 139 CV99
Adelaide Av, SE4 103 DZ84
Adelaide Cl, Enf. EN1 30 DT38
Stanmore HA7 41 CG49
Adelaide Cotts, W7 97 CF75
Adelaide Gdns, Rom. RM6 70 EY57
Adelaide Gro, W12 81 CU74
Adelaide Pl, Wey. KT13 153 BR105
Adelaide Rd, E10 67 EB62
NW3 82 DD66
SW18 *off Putney Br Rd* 120 DA85
W13 79 CG74
Ashford TW15 114 BK92
Chislehurst BR7 125 EP92
Hounslow TW5 96 BY81
Ilford IG1 69 EP61
Richmond TW9 98 CM84
Southall UB2 96 BY77
Surbiton KT6 138 CL99
Teddington TW11 117 CF93
Tilbury RM18 111 GF81
Walton-on-Thames KT12 135 BU104
Adelaide St, WC2 199 P1
Adelaide Ter, Brent. TW8 97 CK78
Adelaide Wk, SW9 *off Sussex Wk* 101 DN84
Adela St, W10 *off Kensal Rd* 81 CY70
Adelina Gro, E1 84 DW71
Adelina Ms, SW12 *off King's Av* 121 DK88
Adeline Pl, WC1 195 N7
Adeliza Cl, Bark. IG11 *off North St* 87 EP66
Adelphi Ct, SE16 *off Poolmans St* 103 DX75
Adelphi Cres, Hayes UB4 77 BT69
Hornchurch RM12 71 FG61
Adelphi Gdns, Slou. SL1 92 AS75
Adelphi Rd, Epsom KT17 156 CR113
Adelphi Ter, WC2 200 A1
Adelphi Way, Hayes UB4 77 BT69
Adeney Cl, W6 99 CX79
Aden Gro, N16 66 DR63
Adenmore Rd, SE6 123 EA87
Aden Rd, Enf. EN3 31 DY42
Ilford IG1 69 EP59
Aden Ter, N16 66 DR63
Adie Rd, W6 99 CW76
Adine Rd, E13 86 EH70
Adler Ind Est, Hayes UB3 95 BR75
Adler St, E1 84 DU72
Adley St, E5 67 DY64
Adlington Cl, N18 46 DR50
Admaston Rd, SE18 105 EQ80
Admiral Cl, Orp. BR5 146 EX98
Admiral Ct, NW4 *off Barton Cl* 63 CU57
Admiral Ho, Tedd. TW11 *off Twickenham Rd* 117 CG91
Admiral Pl, SE16 203 L2
Admirals Cl, E18 68 EH56
Admiral Seymour Rd, SE9 105 EM84
Admiral Sq, SW10 100 DD81
Admiral Stirling Ct, Wey. KT13 *off Weybridge Rd* 152 BM105
Admiral St, SE8 103 EA82
Admirals Wk, NW3 64 DC62
Coulsdon CR5 175 DM120
Greenhithe DA9 129 FV85
Admirals Way, E14 204 A4
★ **Admiralty Arch**, SW1 199 N2
Admiralty Cl, SE8 *off Reginald Sq* 103 EA80
Admiralty Rd, Tedd. TW11 117 CF93
Admiral Wk, W9 82 DA71
Adnams Wk, Rain. RM13 *off Lovell Wk* 89 FF65

★ Place of interest ⇌ Railway station ⊖ London Underground station DLR Docklands Light Railway station Tramlink Tramlink station H Hospital

Adolf St, SE6 123 EB91
Adolphus Rd, N4 65 DP61
Adolphus St, SE8 103 DZ80
Adomar Rd, Dag. RM8 70 EX62
Adpar St, W2 82 DD70
Adrian Av, NW2 off North Circular Rd 63 CV60
Adrian Cl, Uxb. (Hare.) UB9 38 BK53
Adrian Ms, SW10 100 DB79
Adrian Rd, Abb.L. WD5 7 BS31
Adrians Wk, Slou. SL2 74 AT74
Adrienne Av, Sthl. UB1 78 BZ70
Adstock Ms, Ger.Cr. (Chal.St.P.) SL9 off Church La 36 AX53
Adstock Way, Grays (Bad.Dene) RM17 110 FZ77
Advance Rd, SE27 122 DQ91
Advent Ct, Wdf.Grn. IG8 off Wood La 48 EF50
Advent Way, N18 47 DX50
Advice Av, Grays RM16 110 GA75
Adys Rd, SE15 102 DT83
Aerodrome Rd, NW4 63 CT55
NW9 43 CT54
Aerodrome Way, Houns. TW5 96 BW79
Aeroville, NW9 42 CS54
Affleck St, N1 196 C1
Afghan Rd, SW11 100 DE82
★ Africa Cen, WC2 off King St 195 P10
Africa Ho, SE16 202 E6
Afton Dr, S.Ock. RM15 91 FV72
Agamemnon Rd, NW6 63 CZ64
Agar Cl, Surb. KT6 138 CM103
Agar Gro, NW1 83 DJ66
Agar Gro Est, NW1 83 DK66
Agar Pl, NW1 83 DJ66
Agars Plough, Slou. (Datchet) SL3 92 AU79
Agar St, WC2 199 P1
Agate Cl, E16 86 EK72
Agate Rd, W6 99 CW76
Agates La, Ashtd. KT21 171 CK118
Agatha Cl, E1 202 E2
Agaton Rd, SE9 125 EQ89
Agave Rd, NW2 63 CW63
Agdon St, EC1 196 F4
Agincourt Rd, NW3 64 DF63
Agister Rd, Chig. IG7 50 EU50
Agnes Av, Ilf. IG1 69 EP63
Agnes Cl, E6 87 EN73
Agnesfield Cl, N12 44 DE51
Agnes Gdns, Dag. RM8 70 EX63
Agnes Rd, W3 81 CT74
Agnes Scott Ct, Wey. KT13 off Palace Dr 135 BP104
Agnes St, E14 85 DZ72
Agnew Rd, SE23 123 DX87
Agricola Ct, E3 off Parnell Rd 85 DZ67
Agricola Pl, Enf. EN1 30 DT43
Aidan Cl, Dag. RM8 70 EY63
Aileen Wk, E15 86 EF66
Ailsa Av, Twick. TW1 117 CG85
Ailsa Rd, Twick. TW1 117 CH85
Ailsa St, E14 85 EC71
AIMES GREEN, Wal.Abb. 16 EF28
Ainger Ms, NW3 off Ainger Rd 82 DF66
Ainger Rd, NW3 82 DF66
Ainsdale Cl, Orp. BR6 145 ER102
Ainsdale Cres, Pnr. HA5 60 CA55
Ainsdale Dr, SE1 102 DU78
Ainsdale Rd, W5 79 CK70
Watford WD19 40 BW48
Ainsdale Way, Wok. GU21 166 AU118
Ainsley Av, Rom. RM7 71 FB58
Ainsley Cl, N9 46 DS46
Ainsley St, E2 84 DV69
Ainslie Wk, SW12 121 DH87
Ainslie Wd Cres, E4 47 EB50
Ainslie Wd Gdns, E4 47 EB49
Ainslie Wd Rd, E4 47 EA50
Ainsty Est, SE16 203 H5
Ainsworth Cl, NW2 63 CU62
SE15 off Lyndhurst Gro 102 DS82
Ainsworth Rd, E9 84 DW66
Croydon CR0 141 DP103
Ainsworth Way, NW8 82 DC67
Aintree Av, E6 86 EL67
Aintree Cl, Grav. DA12 131 GH90
Slough (Colnbr.) SL3 93 BE81
Uxbridge UB8 off Craig Dr 77 BP72
Aintree Cres, Ilf. IG6 49 EQ54
Aintree Est, SW6 off Dawes Rd 99 CY80
Aintree Gro, Upmin. RM14 72 FM62
Aintree Rd, Grnf. UB6 79 CH68
Aintree St, SW6 99 CY80
Aird Ct, Hmptn. TW12 off Oldfield Rd 136 BZ95
Airdrie Cl, N1 83 DM66
Hayes UB4 off Glencoe Rd 78 BY71
Airedale Av, W4 99 CT77
Airedale Av S, W4 off Netheravon Rd S 99 CT78
Airedale Cl, Dart. DA2 128 FQ88
Airedale Rd, SW12 120 DF87
W5 97 CJ76
Aire Dr, S.Ock. RM15 91 FV70
Airey Neave Ct, Grays RM17 110 GA75
Airfield Way, Horn. RM12 89 FH65
Watford WD25 off Ashfields 7 BU32
★ Air Forces Mem, Egh. (Runny.) TW20 112 AX91
Airlie Gdns, W8 100 DA75
Ilford IG1 69 EP60
Air Links Ind Est, Houns. TW5 96 BW78
Air Pk Way, Felt. TW13 115 BV89
Airport Ind Est, West. TN16 162 EK114
Airport Roundabout, E16 off Connaught Br 86 EK74
Airport Way, Stai. TW19 93 BF84
Air St, W1 199 L1
Airthrie Rd, Ilf. IG3 70 EV61
Aisgill Av, W14 99 CZ78
Aisher Rd, SE28 88 EW73
Aisher Way, Sev. (Rvrhd.) TN13 190 FE121
Aislibie Rd, SE12 104 EE84
Aiten Pl, W6 off Standish Rd 99 CU77
Aitken Cl, E8 off Pownall Rd 84 DU67
Mitcham CR4 140 DF101
Aitken Rd, SE6 123 EB89
Barnet EN5 27 CW43
Ajax Av, NW9 62 CS55
Ajax Rd, NW6 64 DA64
Akabusi Cl, Croy. CR0 142 DU100
Akehurst La, Sev. TN13 191 FJ125
Akehurst St, SW15 119 CU86
Akenside Rd, NW3 64 DD64
Akerman Rd, SW9 101 DP82
Surbiton KT6 137 CJ100
Akers Way, Rick. (Chorl.) WD3 21 BD44
Alabama St, SE18 105 ER80
Alacross Rd, W5 97 CJ75
Alamein Gdns, Dart. DA2 129 FR87
Alamein Rd, Swans. DA10 129 FX86
Alanbrooke, Grav. DA12 131 GJ87
Alan Cl, Dart. DA1 108 FJ84
Alandale Dr, Pnr. HA5 39 BV54
Aland Ct, SE16 203 L6
Alander Ms, E17 67 EC56
Alan Dr, Barn. EN5 27 CY44
Alan Gdns, Rom. RM7 70 FA59
Alan Hocken Way, E15 86 EE68
Alan Rd, SW19 119 CY92
Alanthus Cl, SE12 124 EF86
Alan Way, Slou. (Geo.Grn.) SL3 74 AY72
Alaska St, SE1 200 D3
Alba Cl, Hayes UB4 off Ramulis Dr 78 BX70
Albacore Cres, SE13 123 EB86
Alba Gdns, NW11 63 CY58
Albain Cres, Ashf. TW15 114 BL89
Alban Cres, Borwd. WD6 26 CP39
Dartford (Fnghm.) DA4 148 FN102
Alban Highwalk, EC2 off London Wall 84 DQ71
Albans Vw, Wat. WD25 7 BV33
Albany, W1 199 K1
Albany, The, Wdf.Grn. IG8 48 EF49
Albany Cl, N15 65 DP56
SW14 98 CP84
Bexley DA5 126 EW87
Bushey WD23 25 CD44
Esher KT10 154 CA109
Reigate RH2 184 DA132
Uxbridge UB10 58 BN64
Albany Ct, E4 off Chelwood Cl 31 EB44
Epping CM16 17 ET30
Albany Ctyd, W1 199 L1
Albany Cres, Edg. HA8 42 CN52
Esher (Clay.) KT10 155 CE107
Albany Mans, SW11 100 DE80
Albany Ms, N1 off Barnsbury Pk 83 DN66
SE5 off Albany Rd 102 DQ79
Bromley BR1 124 EG93
Kingston upon Thames KT2 off Albany Pk Rd 117 CK93
St. Albans AL2 off North Orbital Rd 8 CA27
Sutton SM1 off Camden Rd 158 DB106
⇌ Albany Park 126 EX89
Albany Pk, Slou. (Colnbr.) SL3 93 BD81
Albany Pk Av, Enf. EN3 30 DW39
Albany Pk Rd, Kings.T. KT2 118 CL93
Leatherhead KT22 171 CG119
Albany Pas, Rich. TW10 118 CM85
Albany Pl, N7 off Benwell Rd 65 DN63
Brentford TW8 off Albany Rd 98 CL79
Egham TW20 113 BA91
Albany Rd, E10 67 EA59
E12 68 EK63
E17 67 DY58
N4 65 DM58
N18 46 DV50
SE5 102 DR79
SW19 120 DB92
W13 79 CH73
Belvedere DA17 106 EZ79
Bexley DA5 126 EW87
Brentford TW8 97 CK79
Brentwood CM15 54 FV44
Chislehurst BR7 125 EP92
Enfield EN3 31 DX37
Hornchurch RM12 71 FG60
New Malden KT3 138 CR98
Richmond TW10 off Albert Rd 118 CM85
Romford RM6 70 EZ58
Walton-on-Thames KT12 154 BX105
Windsor (Old Wind.) SL4 112 AU85
Albanys, The, Reig. RH2 184 DA131
Albany St, NW1 83 DH68
Albany Ter, NW1 off Marylebone Rd 83 DH70
Albany Vw, Buck.H. IG9 48 EG46
Alba Pl, W11 off Portobello Rd 81 CZ72
Albatross Gdns, S.Croy. CR2 161 DX111
Albatross St, SE18 105 ES80
Albatross Way, SE16 103 DX75
Albemarle, SW19 119 CX89
Albemarle App, Ilf. IG2 69 EP58
Albemarle Av, Pot.B. EN6 12 DB33
Twickenham TW2 116 BZ88
Waltham Cross (Chsht.) EN8 14 DW28
Albemarle Cl, Grays RM17 110 GA75
Albemarle Gdns, Ilf. IG2 69 EP58
New Malden KT3 138 CR98
Albemarle Pk, Stan. HA7 off Marsh La 41 CJ50
Albemarle Rd, Barn. EN4 44 DE45
Beckenham BR3 143 EB95
Albemarle St, W1 199 J1
Albemarle Way, EC1 196 F5
Alberon Gdns, NW11 63 CZ56
Alberta Av, Sutt. SM1 157 CY105
Alberta Est, SE17 200 G10
Alberta Rd, Enf. EN1 30 DT44
Erith DA8 107 FC81
Alberta St, SE17 200 F10
Albert Av, E4 47 EA49
SW8 101 DM80
Chertsey KT16 134 BG97
Albert Br, SW3 100 DE79
SW11 100 DE79
Albert Br Rd, SW11 100 DE80
Albert Carr Gdns, SW16 121 DL92
Albert Cl, E9 off Northiam St 84 DV67
N22 45 DK53
Grays RM16 110 GC76
Slough SL1 off Albert St 92 AT76
Albert Ct, SW7 off Prince Consort Rd 100 DD75
Albert Cres, E4 47 EA49
Albert Dr, SW19 119 CY89
Woking GU21 151 BD114
Albert Embk, SE1 101 DL78
Albert Gdns, E1 85 DX72
Albert Gate, SW1 198 E4
Albert Gro, SW20 139 CX95
Albert Hall Mans, SW7 off Kensington Gore 100 DD75
Albertine Cl, Epsom KT17 173 CV116
Albert Mans, SW11 off Albert Br Rd 100 DF81
★ Albert Mem, SW7 100 DD75
Albert Ms, E14 off Narrow St 85 DY73
W8 off Victoria Gro 100 DC76
Albert Murray Cl, Grav. DA12 off Armoury Dr 131 GJ87
Albert Pl, N3 44 DA53
N17 off High Rd 66 DT55
W8 100 DB75
Albert Rd, E10 67 EC61
E16 86 EL74
E17 67 EA57
E18 68 EH55
N4 65 DM60
N15 66 DS58
N22 45 DJ53
NW4 63 CX56
NW6 81 CZ68
NW7 43 CT50
SE9 124 EL90
SE20 123 DX94
SE25 142 DU98
W5 79 CH70
Addlestone KT15 134 BK104
Ashford TW15 114 BM92
Ashtead KT21 172 CM118
Barnet EN4 28 DC42
Belvedere DA17 106 EZ78
Bexley DA5 126 FA86
Bromley BR2 144 EK99
Buckhurst Hill IG9 48 EK47
Dagenham RM8 70 FA60
Dartford DA2 128 FJ90
Egham (Eng.Grn.) TW20 112 AX93
Epsom KT17 157 CT113
Hampton (Hmptn.H.) TW12 116 CC92
Harrow HA2 60 CC55
Hayes UB3 95 BS76
Hounslow TW3 96 CA84
Ilford IG1 69 EP62
Kingston upon Thames KT1 138 CM96
Mitcham CR4 140 DF97
New Malden KT3 139 CT98
Orpington (Chels.) BR6 164 EU106
Orpington (St.M.Cray) BR5 146 EV100
Redhill RH1 185 DJ129
Richmond TW10 118 CL85
Romford RM1 71 FF57
Southall UB2 96 BX76
Sutton SM1 158 DD106
Swanscombe DA10 130 FZ86
Teddington TW11 117 CF93
Twickenham TW1 117 CF88
Warlingham CR6 177 DZ117
West Drayton UB7 76 BL74
Albert Rd Est, Belv. DA17 106 EZ78
Albert Rd N, Reig. RH2 183 CZ133
Watford WD17 23 BV41
Albert Rd S, Wat. WD17 23 BV41
Albert Sq, E15 68 EE64
SW8 101 DM80
Albert St, N12 44 DC50
NW1 83 DH67
Brentwood CM14 54 FW50
Slough SL1 92 AT76
Albert Ter, NW1 82 DG67
NW10 80 CR67
Buckhurst Hill IG9 48 EK47
Albert Ter Ms, NW1 off Regents Pk Rd 82 DG67
Albert Way, SE15 102 DV80
Albion Av, N10 44 DG53
SW8 101 DK82
Albion Bldgs, EC1 off Bartholomew Cl 84 DQ71
Albion Cl, W2 194 C10
Romford RM7 71 FD58
Slough SL2 74 AU74
Albion Cres, Ch.St.G. HP8 36 AV48
Albion Dr, E8 84 DT66
Albion Est, SE16 203 H5
Albion Gdns, W6 99 CV77
Albion Gro, N16 66 DS63
Albion Hill, SE13 103 EB82
Loughton IG10 32 EJ43
Albion Ho, Slou. SL3 93 BB78
Woking GU21 167 AZ117
Albion Ms, N1 83 DN67
NW6 off Kilburn High Rd 81 CZ66
W2 194 C9
W6 off Galena Rd 99 CV77
Albion Par, N16 off Albion Rd 66 DR63
Gravesend DA12 131 GK86
Albion Pk, Loug. IG10 32 EK43
Albion Pl, EC1 196 F6
Albion Pl, SE25 off High St 142 DU97
W6 99 CV77
Albion Rd, E17 67 EC55
N16 66 DR63
N17 46 DT54
Bexleyheath DA6 106 EZ84
Chalfont St. Giles HP8 36 AV47
Gravesend DA12 131 GJ87
Hayes UB3 77 BS72
Hounslow TW3 96 CA84
Kingston upon Thames KT2 138 CQ95
Sutton SM2 158 DD107
Twickenham TW2 117 CE88
Albion Sq, E8 84 DT66
Albion St, SE16 202 G5
W2 194 C9
Croydon CR0 141 DP102
Albion Ter, E8 84 DT66
Gravesend DA12 131 GJ86
Albion Vil Rd, SE26 122 DW90
Albion Way, EC1 197 H7
SE13 103 EC84
Wembley HA9 off North End Rd 62 CP62
Albright Ind Est, Rain. RM13 89 FF71
Albrighton Rd, SE22 102 DS83
Albuhera Cl, Enf. EN2 29 DN39
Albury Av, Bexh. DA7 106 EY82
Isleworth TW7 97 CF80
Sutton SM2 157 CW109
Albury Cl, Cher. (Longcr.) KT16 132 AU104
Hampton TW12 116 CA93
Albury Ct, Sutt. SM1 off Ripley Gdns 158 DC105
Albury Dr, Pnr. HA5 40 BX52
Albury Gro Rd, Wal.Cr. (Chsht.) EN8 15 DX30
Albury Ms, E12 68 EJ60
Albury Ride, Wal.Cr. (Chsht.) EN8 15 DX31
Albury Rd, Chess. KT9 156 CL106
Redhill RH1 185 DJ129
Walton-on-Thames KT12 153 BS107
Albury St, SE8 103 EA79
Albury Wk, Wal.Cr. (Chsht.) EN8 15 DX32
Albyfield, Brom. BR1 145 EM97
Albyn Rd, SE8 103 EA81
Albyns Cl, Rain. RM13 89 FG66
Albyns La, Rom. RM4 35 FC40
Alcester Cres, E5 66 DV61
Alcester Rd, Wall. SM6 159 DH105
Alcock Cl, Wall. SM6 159 DK108
Alcock Rd, Houns. TW5 96 BX80
Alcocks Cl, Tad. KT20 173 CY120
Alcocks La, Tad. (Kgswd.) KT20 173 CY120
Alconbury Rd, E5 66 DU61
Alcorn Cl, Sutt. SM3 140 DA103
Alcott Cl, W7 off Westcott Cres 79 CF71
Alcuin Ct, Stan. HA7 off Old Ch La 41 CJ52
ALDBOROUGH HATCH, Ilf. 69 ES55
Aldborough Rd, Dag. RM10 89 FC65
Upminster RM14 72 FM61
Aldborough Rd N, Ilf. IG2 69 ET57
Aldborough Rd S, Ilf. IG3 69 ES60
Aldborough Spur, Slou. SL1 74 AS72
Aldbourne Rd, W12 81 CT74
Aldbridge St, SE17 201 N10
Aldburgh Ms, W1 194 G8
Aldbury Av, Wem. HA9 80 CP66
Aldbury Cl, Wat. WD25 24 BX36
Aldbury Ms, N9 46 DR45
Aldbury Rd, Rick. (Mill End) WD3 37 BF45
Aldebert Ter, SW8 101 DL80
Aldeburgh Cl, E5 off Southwold Rd 66 DV61
Aldeburgh Pl, SE10 205 N9
Woodford Green IG8 48 EG49
Aldeburgh St, SE10 205 M10
Alden Av, E15 86 EF69
ALDENHAM, Wat. 24 CB38
Aldenham Av, Rad. WD7 25 CG36
★ Aldenham Country Pk, Borwd. (Elstree) WD6 25 CH43
Aldenham Dr, Uxb. UB8 77 BP70
Aldenham Gro, Rad. WD7 9 CH34
Aldenham Rd, Borwd. (Elstree) WD6 25 CH42
Bushey WD23 24 BZ42
Radlett WD7 25 CG35
Watford WD19 24 BX44
Watford (Let.Hth.) WD25 25 CE39
Aldenham St, NW1 195 L1
Aldenholme, Wey. KT13 153 BS107
Aldensley Rd, W6 99 CV76
Alder Av, Upmin. RM14 72 FM63
Alderbourne La, Iver SL0 57 BA64
Slough (Fulmer) SL3 56 AX63
Alderbrook Rd, SW12 121 DH86
Alderbury Rd, SW13 99 CU79
Slough SL3 93 AZ75
Alderbury Rd W, Slou. SL3 93 AZ75
Alder Cl, SE15 102 DT79
Egham (Eng.Grn.) TW20 112 AY92
St. Albans (Park St.) AL2 8 CB28
Aldercombe La, Cat. CR3 186 DS127
Aldercroft, Couls. CR5 175 DM116
Alder Dr, S.Ock. RM15 off Laburnum Gro 91 FW70
Alder Gro, NW2 63 CV61
Aldergrove Gdns, Houns. TW3 off Bath Rd 96 BY82
Aldergrove Wk, Horn. RM12 off Airfield Way 90 FJ65
Alderholt Way, SE15 off Daniel Gdns 102 DT80
Alderman Av, Bark. IG11 88 EU69
Aldermanbury, EC2 197 J8
Aldermanbury Sq, EC2 197 J7
Alderman Cl, Dart. DA1 off Lower Sta Rd 127 FE86
Alderman Judge Mall, Kings.T. KT1 off Eden St 138 CL96
Aldermans Hill, N13 45 DL49
Alderman's Wk, EC2 197 M7
Aldermary Rd, Brom. BR1 144 EG95
Alder Ms, N19 off Bredgar Rd 65 DJ61
Aldermoor Rd, SE6 123 DZ90
Alderney Av, Houns. TW5 96 CB80
Alderney Gdns, Nthlt. UB5 78 BZ66
Alderney Ms, SE1 201 K6
Alderney Rd, E1 85 DX70
Erith DA8 107 FG80
Alderney St, SW1 199 J10
Alder Rd, SW14 98 CR83
Iver SL0 75 BC68
Sidcup DA14 125 ET90
Uxbridge (Denh.) UB9 76 BJ65
Alders, The, N21 29 DN44
Feltham TW13 116 BY91
Hounslow TW5 96 BZ79
West Byfleet KT14 152 BJ112
West Wickham BR4 143 EB102
Alders Av, Wdf.Grn. IG8 48 EE51
ALDERSBROOK, E12 68 EH61
Aldersbrook Av, Enf. EN1 30 DS40
Aldersbrook Dr, Kings.T. KT2 118 CM93
Aldersbrook La, E12 69 EM62
Aldersbrook Rd, E11 68 EH61
E12 68 EK62
Alders Cl, E11 off Aldersbrook Rd 68 EH61
W5 97 CK76
Edgware HA8 42 CQ50
Aldersey Gdns, Bark. IG11 87 ER65
Aldersford Cl, SE4 123 DX85
Aldersgate St, EC1 197 H8
Alders Gro, E.Mol. KT8 off Esher Rd 137 CD99
Aldersgrove, Wal.Abb. EN9 off Roundhills 16 EE34
Aldersgrove Av, SE9 124 EJ90
Aldershot Rd, NW6 81 CZ67
Alderside Wk, Egh. (Eng.Grn.) TW20 112 AY92
Aldersmead Av, Croy. CR0 143 DX100
Aldersmead Rd, Beck. BR3 123 DY94
Alderson Pl, Sthl. UB2 78 CC74
Alderson St, W10 off Kensal Rd 81 CY70
Alders Rd, Edg. HA8 42 CQ50
Reigate RH2 184 DB132
Alderstead Heath, Red. RH1 175 DK124
Alderstead Heath Caravan Club, Red. RH1 175 DK123
Alderstead La, Red. RH1 185 DK126
Alderton Cl, NW10 62 CR62
Brentwood CM15 54 FV43
Loughton IG10 33 EN42
Alderton Cres, NW4 63 CV57
Alderton Hall La, Loug. IG10 33 EN42
Alderton Hill, Loug. IG10 32 EL43
Alderton Ms, Loug. IG10 off Alderton Hall La 33 EN42
Alderton Ri, Loug. IG10 33 EN42
Alderton Rd, SE24 102 DQ83
Croydon CR0 142 DT101
Alderton Way, NW4 63 CV57
Loughton IG10 33 EM43
Alderville Rd, SW6 99 CZ82
Alder Wk, Ilf. IG1 69 EQ64
Watford WD25 off Aspen Pk Dr 23 BV35
Alder Way, Swan. BR8 147 FD96
Alderwick Dr, Houns. TW3 97 CD83
Alderwood Cl, Cat. CR3 186 DS125
Romford (Abridge) RM4 34 EV41
Alderwood Dr, Rom. (Abridge) RM4 34 EV41
Alderwood Rd, SE9 125 ER86
Aldford St, W1 198 F2
⊖ Aldgate 197 P8
Aldgate, EC3 197 P9
Aldgate Av, E1 197 P8
Aldgate Barrs Shop Cen, E1 off Whitechapel High St 84 DT72
⊖ Aldgate East 84 DT72
Aldgate High St, EC3 197 P9
Aldham Dr, S.Ock. RM15 91 FW71
Aldin Av N, Slou. SL1 92 AV75
Aldin Av S, Slou. SL1 92 AU75
Aldine Ct, W12 off Aldine St 81 CW74
Aldine Pl, W12 off Uxbridge Rd 81 CW74
Aldine St, W12 99 CW75
Aldingham Ct, Horn. RM12 off Easedale Dr 71 FG64
Aldingham Gdns, Horn. RM12 71 FG64
Aldington Cl, Dag. RM8 70 EW59
Aldington Rd, SE18 104 EK76
Aldis Ms, SW17 off Aldis St 120 DE92
Enfield EN3 off Government Row 31 EA37
Aldis St, SW17 120 DE92
Aldred Rd, NW6 64 DA64
Aldren Rd, SW17 120 DC90
Aldrich Cres, Croy. (New Adgtn.) CR0 161 EC109
Aldriche Way, E4 47 EC51
Aldrich Gdns, Sutt. SM3 139 CZ104
Aldrich Ter, SW18 off Lidiard Rd 120 DC89
Aldridge Av, Edg. HA8 42 CP48
Enfield EN3 31 EA38
Ruislip HA4 60 BX61
Stanmore HA7 42 CL53
Aldridge Ri, N.Mal. KT3 138 CS101
Aldridge Rd Vil, W11 81 CZ71
Aldridge Wk, N14 45 DL45
Aldrington Rd, SW16 121 DJ92
Aldsworth Cl, W9 82 DB70
Aldwick Cl, SE9 125 ER90
Aldwick Rd, Croy. CR0 141 DM104
Aldworth Gro, SE13 123 EC86
Aldworth Rd, E15 86 EE66

Ald - Amb

Aldwych, WC2 196 B10
Aldwych Av, Ilf. IG6 69 EQ56
Aldwych Cl, Horn. RM12 71 FG61
Aldwych Underpass, WC2
off Kingsway 83 DM72
Alers Rd, Bexh. DA6 126 EX85
Alesia Cl, N22
off Nightingale Rd 45 DL52
Alestan Beck Rd, E16 86 EK71
Alexa Ct, W8
off Lexham Gdns 100 DA77
Sutton SM2
off Mulgrave Rd 158 DA107
Alexander Av, NW10 81 CV66
Alexander Cl, Barn. EN4 28 DD42
Bromley BR2 144 EG102
Sidcup DA15 125 ES85
Southall UB2 78 CC74
Twickenham TW2 117 CF89
Alexander Ct, Wal.Cr. (Chsht.)
EN8 15 DX30
Alexander Cres, Cat. CR3
off Coulsdon Rd 176 DQ122
Alexander Evans Ms, SE23
off Sunderland Rd 123 DX88
★ Alexander Fleming Laboratory
Mus, W2 off Praed St 194 A8
Alexander Godley Cl, Ashtd.
KT21 172 CM119
Alexander La, Brwd. CM13,
CM15 55 GB44
Alexander Ms, W2
off Alexander St 82 DB72
Alexander Pl, SW7 198 B8
Alexander Rd, N19 65 DL62
Bexleyheath DA7 106 EX82
Chislehurst BR7 125 EP92
Coulsdon CR5 175 DH115
Egham TW20 113 BB92
Greenhithe DA9 129 FW85
St. Albans (Lon.Col.) AL2 9 CJ25
Alexander Sq, SW3 198 B8
Alexander St, W2 82 DA72
Alexanders Wk, Cat. CR3 186 DT126
Alexandra Av, N22 45 DK53
SW11 100 DG81
W4 98 CR80
Harrow HA2 60 BZ60
Southall UB1 78 BZ73
Sutton SM1 140 DA104
Warlingham CR6 177 DZ117
Alexandra Cl, SE8 103 DZ79
Ashford TW15
off Alexandra Rd 115 BR94
Grays RM16 111 GH75
Harrow HA2
off Alexandra Av 60 CA62
Staines TW18 114 BK93
Swanley BR8 147 FE96
Walton-on-Thames KT12 135 BU103
Alexandra Cotts, SE14 103 DZ81
Alexandra Ct, N14 29 DJ43
N16 off Belgrade Rd 66 DT63
Ashford TW15
off Alexandra Rd 115 BR93
Wembley HA9 62 CM63
Alexandra Cres, Brom. BR1 124 EF93
Alexandra Dr, SE19 122 DS92
Surbiton KT5 138 CN101
Alexandra Gdns, N10 65 DH56
W4 98 CR80
Carshalton SM5 158 DG109
Hounslow TW3 96 CB82
Alexandra Gro, N4 65 DP60
N12 44 DB50
Alexandra Ms, N2
off Fortis Grn 64 DF55
SW19 off Alexandra Rd 120 DA93
★ Alexandra Palace, N22 45 DK54
⇌ Alexandra Palace 45 DL54
Alexandra Palace, N22 45 DK54
Alexandra Palace Way, N22 65 DJ55
Alexandra Pk Rd, N10 45 DH54
N22 45 DK54
Alexandra Pl, NW8 82 DC67
SE25 142 DR99
Croydon CR0
off Alexandra Rd 142 DS102
Alexandra Rd, E6 87 EN69
E10 67 EC62
E17 67 DZ58
E18 68 EH55
N8 65 DN55
N9 46 DV45
N10 45 DH51
N15 66 DR57
NW4 63 CX56
NW8 82 DC66
SE26 123 DX93
SW14 98 CR83
SW19 119 CZ93
W4 98 CR75
Addlestone KT15 152 BK105
Ashford TW15 115 BR94
Borehamwood WD6 26 CR38
Brentford TW8 97 CK79
Brentwood CM14 54 FW48
Croydon CR0 142 DS102
Egham (Eng.Grn.) TW20 112 AW93
Enfield EN3 31 DX42
Epsom KT17 157 CT113
Erith DA8 107 FF79
Gravesend DA12 131 GL87
Hounslow TW3 96 CB82
Kings Langley WD4 6 BN29
Kings Langley (Chipper.)
WD4 6 BG30
Kingston upon Thames
KT2 118 CN94
Mitcham CR4 120 DE94
Rainham RM13 89 FF67
Richmond TW9 98 CM82
Rickmansworth (Sarratt)
WD3 22 BG36
Alexandra Rd, Rom. RM1 71 FF58
Romford (Chad.Hth.) RM6 70 EX58
Thames Ditton KT7 137 CF99
Tilbury RM18 111 GF82
Twickenham TW1 117 CJ86
Uxbridge UB8 76 BK68
Warlingham CR6 177 DY117
Watford WD17 23 BU40
Westerham (Bigg.H.) TN16 178 EH119
Alexandra Sq, Mord. SM4 140 DA99
Alexandra St, E16 86 EG71
SE14 103 DY80
Alexandra Wk, SE19 122 DS92
Alexandra Way, Epsom KT19 156 CN112
Waltham Cross EN8 15 DZ34
Alexandria Rd, W13 79 CG73
Alexis St, SE16 202 B8
Alfan La, Dart. DA2 127 FD92
Alfearn Rd, E5 66 DW63
Alford Grn, Croy. (New Adgtn.)
CR0 161 ED107
Alford Pl, N1 197 J1
Alford Rd, SW8 101 DK81
Erith DA8 107 FD78
Alfoxton Av, N15 65 DP56
Alfreda St, SW11 101 DH81
Alfred Cl, W4 off Belmont Rd 98 CR77
Alfred Gdns, Sthl. UB1 78 BY73
Alfred Ms, W1 195 M6
Alfred Pl, WC1 195 M6
Gravesend (Nthflt.) DA11 131 GF88
Alfred Prior Ho, E12 69 EN63
Alfred Rd, E15 68 EF64
SE25 142 DU99
W2 82 DA71
W3 80 CQ74
Belvedere DA17 106 EZ78
Brentwood CM14 54 FX47
Buckhurst Hill IG9 48 EK47
Dartford (Hawley) DA2 128 FL91
Feltham TW13 116 BW89
Gravesend DA11 131 GH89
Kingston upon Thames
KT1 138 CL97
South Ockendon (Aveley)
RM15 90 FQ74
Sutton SM1 158 DC106
Alfred's Gdns, Bark. IG11 87 ES68
Alfred St, E3 85 DZ69
Grays RM17 110 GC79
Alfreds Way, Bark. IG11 87 EQ69
Alfreds Way Ind Est, Bark.
IG11 88 EU67
Alfreton Cl, SW19 119 CX90
Alfriston Av, Croy. CR0 141 DL101
Harrow HA2 60 CA58
Alfriston Cl, Dart. DA1
off Lower Sta Rd 127 FE86
Surbiton KT5 138 CM99
Alfriston Rd, SW11 120 DF85
Algar Cl, Islw. TW7
off Algar Rd 97 CG83
Stanmore HA7 41 CF50
Algar Rd, Islw. TW7 97 CG83
Algarve Rd, SW18 120 DB88
Algernon Rd, NW4 63 CU58
NW6 82 DA67
SE13 103 EB84
Algers Cl, Loug. IG10 32 EK43
Algers Mead, Loug. IG10 32 EK43
Algers Rd, Loug. IG10 32 EK43
Algiers Rd, SE13 103 EA84
Alibon Gdns, Dag. RM10 70 FA64
Alibon Rd, Dag. RM9, RM10 70 EZ64
Alice Cl, Barn. EN5 28 DC42
Alice Ct, SW15 off Deodar Rd 99 CZ84
Alice Gilliatt Ct, W14 99 CZ79
Alice La, E3 85 DZ67
Alice Ms, Tedd. TW11
off Luther Rd 117 CF92
Alice Ruston Pl, Wok. GU22 166 AW119
Alice St, SE1 201 M7
Alice Thompson Cl, SE12 124 EJ89
Alice Walker Cl, SE24
off Shakespeare Rd 101 DP84
Alice Way, Houns. TW3 96 CB84
Alicia Av, Har. HA3 61 CH56
Alicia Cl, Har. HA3 61 CJ56
Alicia Gdns, Har. HA3 61 CH56
Alie St, E1 84 DT72
Alington Cres, NW9 62 CQ60
Alington Gro, Wall. SM6 159 DJ109
Alison Cl, E6 87 EN72
Croydon CR0
off Shirley Oaks Rd 143 DX102
Woking GU21 166 AY115
Aliwal Rd, SW11 100 DE84
Alkerden La, Green. DA9 129 FW86
Swanscombe DA10 129 FW86
Alkerden Rd, W4 98 CS78
Alkham Rd, N16 66 DT61
Allan Barclay Cl, N15
off High Rd 66 DT58
Allan Cl, N.Mal. KT3 138 CR99
Allandale Av, N3 63 CY55
Allandale Cres, Pot.B. EN6 11 CY32
Allandale Pl, Orp. BR6 146 EX104
Allandale Rd, Enf. EN3 31 DX36
Hornchurch RM11 71 FF59
Allan Way, W3 80 CQ71
Allard Cl, Orp. BR5 146 EW101
Waltham Cross (Chsht.)
EN7 14 DT27
Allard Cres, Bushey (Bushey Hth.)
WD23 40 CC46
Allard Gdns, SW4 121 DK85
Allardyce St, SW4 101 DM84
Allbrook Cl, Tedd. TW11 117 CE92
Allcot Cl, Felt. TW14 115 BT88
Allcroft Rd, NW5 64 DG64
Allenby Av, S.Croy. CR2 160 DQ109
Allenby Cl, Grnf. UB6 78 CA69
Allenby Cres, Grays RM17 110 GB78
Allenby Dr, Horn. RM11 72 FL60
Allenby Rd, SE23 123 DY90
Southall UB1 78 CA72
Westerham (Bigg.H.) TN16 178 EL117
Allen Cl, Mitch. CR4 141 DH95
Radlett (Shenley) WD7
off Russet Dr 10 CL32
Sunbury-on-Thames
TW16 135 BV95
Allen Ct, Grnf. UB6 61 CF64
Allendale Av, Sthl. UB1 78 CA72
Allendale Cl, SE5
off Daneville Rd 102 DR81
SE26 123 DX92
Dartford DA2
off Princes Rd 129 FR88
Allendale Rd, Grnf. UB6 79 CH65
Allen Edwards Dr, SW8 101 DL81
Allenford Ho, SW15
off Tunworth Cres 119 CT86
Allen Ho Pk, Wok. GU22 166 AW120
Allen Pl, Twick. TW1
off Church St 117 CG88
Allen Rd, E3 85 DZ68
N16 66 DS63
Beckenham BR3 143 DX96
Croydon CR0 141 DM101
Rainham RM13 90 FJ69
Sunbury-on-Thames
TW16 135 BV95
Allensbury Pl, NW1 83 DK66
Allens Rd, Enf. EN3 30 DW43
Allen St, W8 100 DA76
Allenswood Rd, SE9 104 EL83
Allerford Ct, Har. HA2 60 CB57
Allerford Rd, SE6 123 EB91
Allerton Cl, Borwd. WD6 26 CM38
Allerton Ct, NW4
off Holders Hill Rd 43 CX54
Allerton Rd, N16 66 DQ61
Borehamwood WD6 26 CL38
Allerton Wk, N7
off Durham Rd 65 DM61
Allestree Rd, SW6 99 CY80
Alleyn Cres, SE21 122 DR89
Alleyndale Rd, Dag. RM8 70 EW61
Alleyn Pk, SE21 122 DR89
Southall UB2 96 BZ77
Alleyn Rd, SE21 122 DR90
Allfarthing La, SW18 120 DB86
Allgood Cl, Mord. SM4 139 CX100
Allgood St, E2
off Hackney Rd 84 DT68
Allhallows La, EC4 201 K1
★ All Hallows-on-the-Wall C of E
Church, EC2
off London Wall 197 L7
Allhallows Rd, E6 86 EL71
All Hallows Rd, N17 46 DS53
Allhusen Gdns, Slou. (Fulmer)
SL3 off Alderbourne La 56 AY63
Alliance Cl, Wem. HA0 61 CK63
Alliance Ct, W3
off Alliance Rd 80 CP70
Alliance Rd, E13 86 EJ70
SE18 106 EU79
W3 80 CP70
Allied Way, W3 off Larden Rd 98 CS75
Allingham Cl, W7 79 CF73
Allingham Ms, N1
off Allingham St 84 DQ68
Allingham St, N1 84 DQ68
Allington Av, N17 46 DS51
Allington Cl, SW19
off High St Wimbledon 119 CX92
Gravesend DA12
off Farley Rd 131 GM88
Greenford UB6 78 CC66
Allington Ct, Enf. EN3 31 DX43
Slough SL2 off Myrtle Cres 74 AT73
Allington Rd, NW4 63 CV57
W10 81 CY68
Harrow HA2 60 CC57
Orpington BR6 145 ER103
Allington St, SW1 199 K7
Allison Cl, SE10
off Dartmouth Hill 103 EC81
Waltham Abbey EN9 16 EG33
Allison Gro, SE21 122 DS88
Allison Rd, N8 65 DN57
W3 80 CQ72
Allitsen Rd, NW8 194 B1
Allmains Cl, Wal.Abb. EN9 16 EH25
Allnutts Rd, Epp. CM16 18 EU33
Allnutt Way, SW4 121 DK85
Alloa Rd, SE8 203 J10
Ilford IG3 70 EU61
Allonby Dr, Ruis. HA4 59 BP59
Allonby Gdns, Wem. HA9 61 CJ60
Allotment La, Sev. TN13 191 FJ122
Allotment Way, NW2
off Midland Ter 63 CX62
Alloway Cl, Wok. GU21
off Inglewood 166 AV118
Alloway Rd, E3 85 DY69
Allports Ms, E1
off Stepney Grn 84 DW70
DLR All Saints 85 EB73
All Saints Cl, N9 46 DT47
SW8 off Lansdowne Way 101 DL81
Chigwell IG7 50 EU48
Swanscombe DA10
off High St 130 FZ85
All Saints Cres, Wat. WD25 8 BX33
All Saints Dr, SE3 104 EE82
South Croydon CR2 160 DT112
All Saints La, Rick. (Crox.Grn.)
WD3 22 BN44
All Saints Ms, Har. HA3 41 CE51
All Saints Pas, SW18
off Wandsworth High St 120 DB85
All Saints Rd, SW19 120 DC94
W3 98 CQ76
W11 81 CZ71
Gravesend (Nthflt.) DA11 131 GF88
Sutton SM1 140 DB104
All Saints St, N1 83 DM68
All Saints Twr, E10 67 EB59
Allsop Pl, NW1 194 E5
All Souls Av, NW10 81 CV68
All Souls Pl, W1 195 J7
Allum Cl, Borwd. (Elstree)
WD6 26 CL42
Allum Gro, Tad. KT20
off Preston La 173 CV121
Allum La, Borwd. (Elstree)
WD6 26 CM42
Allum Way, N20 44 DC46
Allwood Cl, SE26 123 DX91
Allwood Rd, Wal.Cr. EN7 14 DT27
Allyn Cl, Stai. TW18
off Penton Rd 113 BF93
Alma Av, E4 47 EC52
Hornchurch RM12 72 FL63
Almack Rd, E5 66 DW63
Alma Cl, Wok. (Knap.) GU21 166 AS118
Alma Cres, Sutt. SM1 157 CY106
Alma Gro, SE1 202 A9
Alma Pl, NW10 off Harrow Rd 81 CV69
SE19 122 DT94
Thornton Heath CR7 141 DN99
Alma Rd, N10 44 DG52
SW18 120 DC85
Carshalton SM5 158 DE106
Enfield EN3 31 DY43
Esher KT10 137 CE102
Orpington BR5 146 EX103
Reigate RH2 184 DB133
Sidcup DA14 126 EU90
Southall UB1 78 BY73
Swanscombe DA10 130 FZ85
Alma Row, Har. HA3 41 CD53
Alma Sq, NW8 82 DC69
Alma St, E15 85 ED65
NW5 83 DH65
Alma Ter, SW18 120 DD87
W8 off Allen St 100 DA76
Almeida St, N1 83 DP66
Almeric Rd, SW11 100 DF84
Almer Rd, SW20 119 CU94
Almington St, N4 65 DM60
Almners Rd, Cher. (Lyne)
KT16 133 BC100
Almond Av, W5 98 CL76
Carshalton SM5 140 DF103
Uxbridge UB10 59 BP62
West Drayton UB7 94 BN76
Woking GU22 166 AX121
Almond Cl, SE15 102 DU82
Bromley BR2 145 EN101
Egham (Eng.Grn.) TW20 112 AV93
Feltham TW13
off Highfield Rd 115 BU88
Grays RM16 111 GG76
Hayes UB3 77 BS73
Ruislip HA4 off Roundways 59 BT62
Shepperton TW17 135 BQ96
Almond Dr, Swan. BR8 147 FD96
Almond Gro, Brent. TW8 97 CH80
Almond Rd, N17 46 DU52
SE16 202 E8
Dartford DA2 128 FQ87
Epsom KT19 156 CR111
Almonds Av, Buck.H. IG9 48 EG47
Almond Way, Borwd. WD6 26 CP42
Bromley BR2 145 EN101
Harrow HA2 40 CB54
Mitcham CR4 141 DK99
Almons Way, Slou. SL2 74 AV71
Almorah Rd, N1 84 DR66
Hounslow TW5 96 BX81
Alms Heath, Wok. (Ockham)
GU23 169 BP121
Almshouse La, Chess. KT9 155 CJ109
Enfield EN1 30 DV37
Alnwick Gro, Mord. SM4
off Bordesley Rd 140 DB98
Alnwick Rd, E16 86 EJ72
SE12 124 EH87
ALPERTON, Wem. 80 CM67
⊖ Alperton 80 CL67
Alperton La, Grnf. UB6 79 CK69
Wembley HA0 79 CK69
Alperton St, W10 81 CZ70
Alphabet Gdns, Cars. SM5 140 DD100
Alphabet Sq, E3
off Hawgood St 85 EA71
Alpha Cl, NW1 194 C3
Alpha Ct, Whyt. CR3 176 DU118
Alpha Gro, E14 204 A5
Alpha Pl, NW6 82 DA68
SW3 100 DE79
Alpha Rd, E4 47 EB48
N18 46 DU51
SE14 103 DZ81
Brentwood CM13 55 GD44
Croydon CR0 142 DS102
Enfield EN3 31 DY42
Surbiton KT5 138 CM100
Teddington TW11 117 CD92
Uxbridge UB10 77 BP70
Woking GU22 167 BB116
Woking (Chobham) GU24 150 AT110
Alpha St, SE15 102 DU82
Alpha St N, Slou. SL1 92 AU75
Alpha St S, Slou. SL1 92 AT76
Alpha Way, Egh. TW20 133 BC95
Alphea Cl, SW19
off Courtney Rd 120 DE94
Alpine Av, Surb. KT5 138 CQ103
Alpine Business Cen, E6 87 EN71
Alpine Cl, Croy. CR0 142 DS104
Alpine Copse, Brom. BR1 145 EN96
Alpine Gro, E9 84 DW66
Alpine Rd, E10 67 EB61
SE16 203 H10
Redhill RH1 184 DG131
Walton-on-Thames KT12 135 BU101
Alpine Vw, Cars. SM5 158 DE106
Alpine Wk, Stan. HA7 41 CE47
Alpine Way, E6 87 EN71
Alric Av, NW10 80 CR66
New Malden KT3 138 CS97
Alroy Rd, N4 65 DN59
Alsace Rd, SE17 201 M10
Alscot Rd, SE1 202 A8
Alscot Way, SE1 201 P8
Alsike Rd, SE2 106 EX76
Alsike Rd, Erith DA18 106 EY76
Alsom Av, Wor.Pk. KT4 157 CU105
Alsop Cl, St.Alb. (Lon.Col.)
AL2 10 CL27
Alston Cl, Surb. KT6 137 CH101
Alston Rd, N18 46 DV50
SW17 120 DD91
Barnet EN5 27 CY41
Altair Cl, N17 46 DT51
Altair Way, Nthwd. HA6 39 BT49
Altash Way, SE9 125 EM89
Altenburg Av, W13 97 CH76
Altenburg Gdns, SW11 100 DF84
Alterton Cl, Wok. GU21 166 AU117
Alt Gro, SW19
off St. George's Rd 119 CZ94
Altham Rd, Pnr. HA5 40 BY52
Althea St, SW6 100 DB83
Althorne Gdns, E18 68 EF56
Althorne Way, Dag. RM10 70 FA61
Althorp Cl, Barn. EN5 43 CU45
Althorpe Gro, SW11
off Westbridge Rd 100 DD81
Althorpe Ms, SW11
off Westbridge Rd 100 DD81
Althorpe Rd, Har. HA1 60 CC57
Althorp Rd, SW17 120 DF88
Altmore Av, E6 87 EM66
Alton Av, Stan. HA7 41 CF52
Alton Cl, Bex. DA5 126 EY88
Isleworth TW7 97 CF82
Alton Ct, Stai. TW18 133 BE95
Alton Gdns, Beck. BR3 123 EA94
Twickenham TW2 117 CD87
Alton Rd, N17 66 DR55
SW15 119 CU88
Croydon CR0 141 DN104
Richmond TW9 98 CL84
Alton St, E14 85 EB71
Altyre Cl, Beck. BR3 143 DZ99
Altyre Rd, Croy. CR0 142 DR103
Altyre Way, Beck. BR3 143 DZ99
Aluric Cl, Grays RM16 111 GH77
Alvanley Gdns, NW6 64 DB64
Alva Way, Wat. WD19 40 BX47
Alverstoke Rd, Rom. RM3 52 FL52
Alverstone Av, SW19 120 DA89
Barnet EN4 44 DE45
Alverstone Gdns, SE9 125 EQ88
Alverstone Rd, E12 69 EN63
NW2 81 CW66
New Malden KT3 139 CT98
Wembley HA9 62 CM60
Alverston Gdns, SE25 142 DS99
Alverton St, SE8 103 DZ78
Alveston Av, Har. HA3 61 CH55
Alvey Est, SE17 201 M9
Alvey St, SE17 201 M10
Alvia Gdns, Sutt. SM1 158 DC105
Alvington Cres, E8 66 DT64
Alway Av, Epsom KT19 156 CQ106
Alwen Gro, S.Ock. RM15 91 FV71
Alwold Cres, SE12 124 EH86
Alwyn Av, W4 98 CR78
Alwyn Cl, Borwd. (Elstree)
WD6 26 CM44
Croydon (New Adgtn.)
CR0 161 EB108
Alwyne Av, Brwd. CM15 55 GA44
Alwyne Ct, Wok. GU21 166 AY116
Alwyne La, N1
off Alwyne Vil 83 DP66
Alwyne Pl, N1 84 DQ65
Alwyne Rd, N1 84 DQ66
SW19 119 CZ93
W7 79 CE73
Alwyne Sq, N1 84 DQ65
Alwyne Vil, N1 83 DP66
Alwyn Gdns, NW4 63 CU56
W3 80 CP72
Alwyns Cl, Cher. KT16
off Alwyns La 134 BG100
Alwyns La, Cher. KT16 133 BF100
Alyth Gdns, NW11 64 DA58
Alzette Ho, E2 85 DX69
Amalgamated Dr, Brent. TW8 97 CG79
Amanda Cl, Chig. IG7 49 ER51
Amanda Ct, Slou. SL3 92 AX76
Amanda Ms, Rom. RM7 71 FC57
Amazon St, E1 off Hessel St 84 DV72
Ambassador Cl, Houns. TW3 96 BY82
Ambassador Gdns, E6 87 EM71
Ambassador's Ct, SW1 199 L3
Ambassador Sq, E14 204 B9
Amber Av, E17 47 DY53
Amber Ct, SW17
off Brudenell Rd 120 DG91
Staines TW18
off Laleham Rd 113 BF92
Ambercroft Way, Couls. CR5 175 DP119
Amberden Av, N3 64 DA55
Ambergate St, SE17 200 G10
Amber Gro, NW2
off Prayle Gro 63 CX60
Amberley Cl, Orp. BR6
off Warnford Rd 163 ET106
Pinner HA5 60 BZ55
Amberley Ct, Sid. DA14 126 EW92
Amberley Dr, Add. (Woodham)
KT15 151 BF110
Amberley Gdns, Enf. EN1 46 DS45
Epsom KT19 157 CT105
Amberley Gro, SE26 122 DV91
Croydon CR0 142 DT101
Amberley Rd, E10 67 EB59
N13 45 DM47
SE2 106 EX79
W9 82 DA71
Buckhurst Hill IG9 48 EJ46
Enfield EN1 46 DT45
Amberley Way, Houns. TW4 116 BW85
Morden SM4 139 CZ101
Romford RM7 71 FB56
Uxbridge UB10 76 BL69
Amber Ms, N22
off Brampton Pk Rd 65 DN55
Amberside Cl, Islw. TW7 117 CD86

★ Place of interest ⇌ Railway station ⊖ London Underground station DLR Docklands Light Railway station Tramlink station H Hospital

211

Amb - Aqu

Amber St, E15
off Great Eastern Rd 85 ED65
Amberwood Cl, Wall. SM6
off The Chase 159 DL106
Amberwood Ri, N.Mal. KT3 ..138 CS100
Amblecote, Cob. KT11 .....154 BY111
Amblecote Cl, SE12 .....124 EH90
Amblecote Meadows, SE12 .124 EH90
Amblecote Rd, SE12 .....124 EH90
Ambler Rd, N4 .....65 DP62
Ambleside, Brom. BR1 .....123 ED93
Epping CM16 .....18 EU31
Ambleside Av, SW16 .....121 DK91
Beckenham BR3 .....143 DY99
Hornchurch RM12 .....71 FH64
Walton-on-Thames KT12 ..136 BW102
Ambleside Cl, E9
off Churchill Wk 66 DW64
E10 .....67 EB59
Ambleside Cres, Enf. EN3 ....31 DX41
Ambleside Dr, Felt. TW14 ....115 BT88
Ambleside Gdns, SW16 .....121 DK92
Ilford IG4 .....68 EL56
South Croydon CR2 .....161 DX109
Sutton SM2 .....158 DC107
Wembley HA9 .....61 CK60
Ambleside Pt, SE15
off Ilderton Rd 102 DW80
Ambleside Rd, NW10 .....81 CT66
Bexleyheath DA7 .....106 FA82
Ambleside Wk, Uxb. UB8
off High St 76 BK67
Ambleside Way, Egh. TW20 ..113 BB94
Ambrey Way, Wall. SM6 ....159 DK109
Ambrooke Rd, Belv. DA17 ...106 FA76
Ambrosden Av, SW1 .....199 L7
Ambrose Av, NW11 .....63 CY59
Ambrose Cl, E6
off Lovage App 86 EL71
Dartford (Cray.) DA1 .....107 FF84
Orpington BR6
off Stapleton Rd 145 ET104
Ambrose Ms, SW11 .....100 DE82
Ambrose St, SE16 .....202 D8
Ambrose Wk, E3
off Malmesbury Rd 85 EA68
Amelia Cl, W3 .....80 CP74
Amelia St, SE17 .....200 G10
Amen Cor, EC4 .....196 G9
SW17 .....120 DF93
Amen Ct, EC4 .....196 G8
Amenity Way, Mord. SM4 ...139 CW101
America Sq, EC3 .....197 P10
America St, SE1 .....201 H3
Amerland Rd, SW18 .....119 CZ86
Amersham Av, N18 .....46 DR51
Amersham Cl, Rom. RM3 ....52 FM51
Amersham Dr, Rom. RM3 ....52 FL51
Amersham Gro, SE14 .....103 DZ80
Amersham Pl, Amer. HP7 ....20 AW39
Amersham Rd, SE14 .....103 DZ80
Amersham (Lt.Chal.) HP6 ..20 AX39
Chalfont St. Giles HP8 .....20 AU43
Croydon CR0 .....142 DQ100
Gerrards Cross SL9 .....57 BB59
Gerrards Cross (Chal.St.P.)
SL9 .....56 AY55
Rickmansworth WD3 .....21 BB39
Romford RM3 .....52 FM51
Amersham Vale, SE14 .....103 DZ80
Amersham Wk, Rom. RM3
off Amersham Rd 52 FM51
Amersham Way, Amer. HP6 ..20 AX39
Amery Gdns, NW10 .....81 CV67
Romford RM2 .....72 FK55
Amery Rd, Har. HA1 .....61 CG61
Amesbury, Wal.Abb. EN9 ....16 EG32
Amesbury Av, SW2 .....121 DL89
Amesbury Cl, Epp. CM16
off Amesbury Rd 17 ET31
Worcester Park KT4 .....139 CW102
Amesbury Dr, E4 .....31 EB44
Amesbury Rd, Brom. BR1 ...144 EK97
Dagenham RM9 .....88 EX66
Epping CM16 .....17 ET31
Feltham TW13 .....116 BX89
Amesbury Twr, SW8
off Westbury St 101 DJ82
Ames Rd, Swans. DA10 .....130 FY86
Amethyst Rd, E15 .....67 ED63
Amey Dr, Lthd. (Bkhm.)
KT23 .....170 CC124
Amherst Av, W13 .....79 CJ72
Amherst Cl, Orp. BR5 .....146 EU98
Amherst Dr, Orp. BR5 .....145 ET98
Amherst Hill, Sev. TN13 ....190 FE122
Amherst Rd, W13 .....79 CJ72
Sevenoaks TN13 .....191 FH122
Amhurst Gdns, Islw. TW7 ....97 CF81
Amhurst Par, N16
off Amhurst Pk 66 DT59
Amhurst Pk, N16 .....66 DR59
Amhurst Pas, E8 .....66 DU64
Amhurst Rd, E8 .....66 DV64
N16 .....66 DT63
Amhurst Ter, E8 .....66 DU63
Amhurst Wk, SE28
off Pitfield Cres 88 EU74
Amidas Gdns, Dag. RM8 .....70 EV63
Amiel St, E1 .....84 DW70
Amies St, SW11 .....100 DF83
Amina Way, SE16 .....202 B7
Amis Av, Add. (New Haw)
KT15 .....152 BG111
Epsom KT19 .....156 CP107
Amis Rd, Wok. GU21 .....166 AS119
Amity Gro, SW20 .....139 CW95
Amity Rd, E15 .....86 EF67
Ammanford Grn, NW9
off Ruthin Cl 62 CS58
Amner Rd, SW11 .....120 DG86
Amor Rd, W6 .....99 CW76
Amott Rd, SE15 .....102 DU83
Amoy Pl, E14 .....85 EA72
-o- Ampere Way 141 DM101
Ampere Way, Croy. CR0 ....141 DL101
Ampleforth Rd, SE2 .....106 EV75
Ampthill Sq Est, NW1 .....195 L1
Ampton Pl, WC1 .....196 B3
Ampton St, WC1 .....196 B3
Amroth Cl, SE23 .....122 DV88
Amroth Grn, NW9
off Fryent Gro 62 CS58
Amstel Way, Wok. GU21 ....166 AT118
Amsterdam Rd, E14 .....204 E7
Amundsen Ct, E14
off Napier Av 103 EA78
Amwell Cl, Enf. EN2 .....30 DR43
Watford WD25
off Phillipers 24 BY35
Amwell Ct, Wal.Abb. EN9 ....16 EF33
Amwell Ct Est, N4 .....66 DQ60
Amwell St, EC1 .....196 D2
Amyand Cotts, Twick. TW1
off Amyand Pk Rd 117 CH86
Amyand La, Twick. TW1
off Marble Hill Gdns 117 CH87
Amyand Pk Gdns, Twick. TW1
off Amyand Pk Rd 117 CH87
Amyand Pk Rd, Twick. TW1 ...117 CG87
Amy Cl, Wall. SM6
off Mollison Dr 159 DL108
Amy Rd, Oxt. RH8 .....188 EE129
Amyruth Rd, SE4 .....123 EA85
Amy Warne Cl, E6
off Evelyn Denington Rd ..86 EL70
Anatola Rd, N19
off Dartmouth Pk Hill 65 DH61
Ancaster Cres, N.Mal. KT3 ...139 CU100
Ancaster Ms, Beck. BR3 .....143 DX97
Ancaster Rd, Beck. BR3 .....143 DX97
Ancaster St, SE18 .....105 ES80
Anchorage Cl, SW19 .....120 DA92
Anchorage Pt, E14 .....203 P4
Anchorage Pt Ind Est, SE7 ...104 EJ76
Anchor & Hope La, SE7 .....104 EH76
Anchor Bay Ind Est, Erith
DA8 .....107 FG79
Anchor Boul, Dart. DA2 .....108 FQ84
Anchor Cl, Bark. IG11 .....88 EV69
Waltham Cross (Chsht.)
EN8 .....15 DX28
Anchor Dr, Rain. RM13 .....89 FH69
Anchor Ms, SW12
off Hazelbourne Rd 121 DH86
Anchor Retail Pk, E1 .....84 DW70
Anchor St, SE16 .....202 D8
Anchor Ter, E1 off Cephas Av ..84 DW70
Anchor Wf, E3 off Watts Gro ..85 EB71
Anchor Yd, EC1 .....197 J4
Ancill Cl, W6 .....99 CY79
Ancona Rd, NW10 .....81 CU68
SE18 .....105 ER78
Andace Pk Gdns, Brom. BR1 .144 EJ95
Andalus Rd, SW9 .....101 DL83
Ander Cl, Wem. HA0 .....61 CK63
Anderson Cl, N21 .....29 DM43
W3 .....80 CR72
Epsom KT19 .....156 CP112
Sutton SM3 .....140 DA102
Uxbridge (Hare.) UB9 .....38 BG53
Anderson Dr, Ashf. TW15 ....115 BQ91
Anderson Ho, Bark. IG11
off The Coverdales 87 ER68
Anderson Pl, Houns. TW3 .....96 CB84
Anderson Rd, E9 .....85 DX65
Radlett (Shenley) WD7 .....10 CN33
Weybridge KT13 .....135 BR104
Woodford Green IG8 .....68 EK55
Andersons Sq, N1
off Gaskin St 83 DP67
Anderson St, SW3 .....198 D10
Anderson Way, Belv. DA17 ...107 FB75
Anderton Cl, SE5 .....102 DR83
Andmark Ct, Sthl. UB1
off Herbert Rd 78 BZ74
Andover Av, E16
off King George Av 86 EK72
Andover Cl, Epsom KT19 .....156 CR111
Feltham TW14 .....115 BT88
Greenford UB6
off Ruislip Rd 78 CB70
Uxbridge UB8 .....76 BH68
Andover Pl, NW6 .....82 DB68
Andover Rd, N7 .....65 DM61
Orpington BR6 .....145 ER102
Twickenham TW2 .....117 CD88
Andrea Av, Grays RM16 .....110 GA75
Andre St, E8 .....66 DU64
Andrew Borde St, WC2 .....195 N8
Andrew Cl, Dart. DA1 .....127 FD85
Ilford IG6 .....49 ER51
Radlett (Shenley) WD7 .....10 CM33
Andrewes Gdns, E6 .....86 EL72
Andrewes Ho, EC2 .....197 J7
Andrew Pl, SW8
off Cowthorpe Rd 101 DK81
Andrew Reed Ho, SW18
off Linstead Way 119 CY87
Andrews Cl, E6
off Linton Gdns 86 EL72
Buckhurst Hill IG9 .....48 EJ47
Epsom KT17 .....157 CT114
Harrow HA1
off Bessborough Rd 61 CD59
Orpington BR5 .....146 EX96
Worcester Park KT4 .....139 CX103
Andrews Crosse, WC2 .....196 D9
Andrews La, Wal.Cr. (Chsht.)
EN7 .....14 DU28
Andrews Pl, SE9 .....125 EP86
Andrew's Rd, E8 .....84 DV67
Andrew St, E14 .....85 EC72
Andrews Wk, SE17
off Dale Rd 101 DP79
Andwell Cl, SE2 .....106 EV75
ANERLEY, SE20 .....142 DV95
⇌ Anerley 122 DV94
Anerley Gro, SE19 .....122 DT94
Anerley Hill, SE19 .....122 DT93
Anerley Pk, SE20 .....122 DU94
Anerley Pk Rd, SE20 .....122 DV94
Anerley Rd, SE19 .....122 DU94
SE20 .....122 DU94
Anerley Sta Rd, SE20 .....142 DV95
Anerley St, SW11 .....100 DF82
Anerley Vale, SE19 .....122 DT94
Anfield Cl, SW12
off Belthorn Cres 121 DJ87
Angas Ct, Wey. KT13 .....153 BQ106
⊖ Angel 83 DN68
Angel All, E1
off Whitechapel Rd 84 DU72
Angel Cl, N18 .....46 DT49
Angel Cor Par, N18
off Fore St 46 DU50
Angel Ct, EC2 .....197 L8
SW1 .....199 L3
SW17 .....120 DF91
Angelfield, Houns. TW3 .....96 CB84
Angel Gate, EC1 .....196 G2
Angel Hill, Sutt. SM1
off Sutton Common Rd ..140 DB104
Angel Hill Dr, Sutt. SM1 ...140 DB104
Angelica Cl, West Dr. UB7
off Lovibonds Av 76 BL72
Angelica Dr, E6 .....87 EN71
Angelica Gdns, Croy. CR0 ..143 DX102
Angel La, E15 .....85 ED65
Hayes UB3 .....77 BR71
Angell Pk Gdns, SW9 .....101 DN83
Angell Rd, SW9 .....101 DN83
Angell Town Est, SW9 .....101 DN82
Angel Ms, E1 off Cable St ...84 DU73
N1 .....196 E1
SW15
off Roehampton High St .119 CU87
Angel Pas, EC4 .....201 K1
Angel Pl, N18 .....46 DU50
SE1 .....201 K4
⇌ Angel Road 46 DW50
Angel Rd, N18 .....46 DV50
Harrow HA1 .....61 CE58
Thames Ditton KT7 .....137 CG101
Angel Rd Wks, N18 .....46 DW50
Angel Sq, EC1 .....196 E1
Angel St, EC1 .....197 H8
Angel Wk, W6 .....99 CW77
Angel Way, Rom. RM1 .....71 FE57
Angerstein La, SE3 .....104 EF80
Angle Cl, Uxb. UB10 .....76 BN67
Angle Grn, Dag. RM8 .....70 EW60
Angle Rd, Grays RM20 .....109 FX79
Anglers Cl, Rich. TW10
off Locksmeade Rd 117 CJ91
Angler's La, NW5 .....83 DH65
Anglers Reach, Surb. KT6 ...137 CK99
Anglesea Av, SE18 .....105 EP77
Anglesea Cen, Grav. DA11
off New Rd 131 GH86
Anglesea Ms, SE18
off Anglesea Av 105 EP77
Anglesea Pl, Grav. DA11
off Clive Rd 131 GH86
Anglesea Rd, SE18 .....105 EP77
Kingston upon Thames
KT1 .....137 CK98
Orpington BR5 .....146 EW100
Anglesea Ter, W6
off Wellesley Av 99 CV76
Anglesey Cl, Ashf. TW15 ....114 BN90
Anglesey Ct Rd, Cars. SM5 ..158 DG107
Anglesey Dr, Rain. RM13 .....89 FG71
Anglesey Gdns, Cars. SM5 ..158 DG107
Anglesey Rd, Enf. EN3 .....30 DV42
Watford WD19 .....40 BW50
Anglesmede Cres, Pnr. HA5 ..60 CA55
Anglesmede Way, Pnr. HA5 ..60 BZ55
Angles Rd, SW16 .....121 DL91
Anglia Cl, N17 off Park La 46 DV52
Anglia Ct, Dag. RM8
off Spring Cl 70 EX60
Anglia Ho, E14 .....85 DY72
Anglian Cl, Wat. WD24 .....24 BW40
Anglian Rd, E11 .....67 ED62
Anglia Wk, E6 .....87 EM67
Anglo Rd, E3 .....85 DZ68
Anglo Way, Red. RH1 .....184 DG132
Angrave Ct, E8 .....84 DT67
Angrave Pas, E8
off Haggerston Rd 84 DT67
Angus Cl, Chess. KT9 .....156 CN106
Angus Dr, Ruis. HA4 .....60 BW63
Angus Gdns, NW9 .....42 CR53
Angus Rd, E13 .....86 EJ69
Angus St, SE14 .....103 DY80
Anhalt Rd, SW11 .....100 DE80
Ankerdine Cres, SE18 .....105 EN80
Ankerwycke Priory, Stai. (Wrays.)
TW19 .....113 AZ89
Anlaby Rd, Tedd. TW11 .....117 CE92
Anley Rd, W14 .....99 CX75
Anmersh Gro, Stan. HA7 .....41 CK53
Annabel Cl, E14 .....85 EB72
Anna Cl, E8 .....84 DT67
Annalee Gdns, S.Ock. RM15 ..91 FV71
Annalee Rd, S.Ock. RM15 .....91 FV71
Annandale Gro, Uxb. UB10
off Thorpland Av 59 BQ62
Annandale Rd, SE10 .....104 EF79
W4 .....98 CS77
Croydon CR0 .....142 DU103
Sidcup DA15 .....125 ES87
Annan Dr, Cars. SM5
off Kenny Dr 158 DG109
Anna Neagle Cl, E7
off Dames Rd 68 EG63
Annan Way, Rom. RM1 .....51 FD53
Anne Boleyn's Wk, Kings.T.
KT2 .....118 CL92
Sutton SM3 .....157 CX108
Anne Case Ms, N.Mal. KT3
off Sycamore Gro 138 CR97
Anne Compton Ms, SE12 ....124 EF87
Anne of Cleves Rd, Dart.
DA1 .....128 FK85
Anners Cl, Egh. TW20 .....133 BC97
Annesley Av, NW9 .....62 CR55
Annesley Cl, NW10 .....62 CS62
Annesley Dr, Croy. CR0 .....143 DZ104
Annesley Rd, SE3 .....104 EH81
Annesley Wk, N19 .....65 DJ61
Anne St, E13 .....86 EG70
Anne's Wk, Cat. CR3 .....176 DS120
Anne Taylor Ho, E12
off Walton Rd 69 EN63
Annett Cl, Shep. TW17 .....135 BS98
Annette Cl, Har. HA3
off Spencer Rd 41 CE54
Annette Cres, N1
off Essex Rd 84 DQ66
Annette Rd, N7 .....65 DM63
Annett Rd, Walt. KT12 .....135 BU101
Anne Way, Ilf. IG6 .....49 EQ51
West Molesey KT8 .....136 CB98
Annie Besant Cl, E3 .....85 DZ67
Annie Brookes Cl, Stai. TW18 .113 BD90
Annifer Way, S.Ock. RM15 ....91 FV71
Anning St, EC2 .....197 N4
Annington Rd, N2 .....64 DF55
Annis Rd, E9 .....85 DY65
Ann La, SW10 .....100 DD80
Ann Moss Way, SE16 .....202 F6
Ann's Cl, SW1 .....198 E5
Ann's Pl, E1 .....197 P7
Ann St, SE18 .....105 ER77
Annsworthy Av, Th.Hth. CR7
off Grange Pk Rd 142 DR97
Annsworthy Cres, SE25
off Grange Rd 142 DR96
Ansdell Rd, SE15 .....102 DW82
Ansdell St, W8 .....100 DB76
Ansdell Ter, W8
off Ansdell St 100 DB76
Ansell Gro, Cars. SM5 .....140 DG102
Ansell Rd, SW17 .....120 DE90
Anselm Cl, Croy. CR0
off Park Hill Ri 142 DT104
Anselm Rd, SW6 .....100 DA79
Pinner HA5 .....40 BZ52
Ansford Rd, Brom. BR1 .....123 EC92
Ansleigh Pl, W11 .....81 CX73
Ansley Cl, S.Croy. CR2 .....160 DV114
Anslow Gdns, Iver SL0 .....75 BD68
Anson Cl, Hem.H. (Bov.) HP3 ..5 AZ27
Kenley CR8 .....176 DR120
Romford RM7 .....51 FB54
Anson Pl, SE28 .....105 ER75
Anson Rd, N7 .....65 DJ63
NW2 .....63 CX64
Anson Ter, Nthlt. UB5 .....78 CB65
Anson Wk, Nthwd. HA6 .....39 BQ49
Anstead Dr, Rain. RM13 .....89 FG68
Anstey Rd, SE15 .....102 DU83
Anstey Wk, N15 .....65 DP56
Anstice Cl, W4 .....98 CS80
Anstridge Path, SE9 .....125 ER86
Anstridge Rd, SE9 .....125 ER86
Antelope Av, Grays RM16
off Hogg La 110 GA76
Antelope Rd, SE18 .....105 EM76
Anthony Cl, NW7 .....42 CS49
Sevenoaks (Dunt.Grn.)
TN13 .....181 FE120
Watford WD19 .....40 BW46
★ Anthony d'Offay Gall, W1 .195 J9
Anthony La, Swan. BR8 .....147 FG95
Anthony Rd, SE25 .....142 DU100
Borehamwood WD6 .....26 CM40
Greenford UB6 .....79 CE68
Welling DA16 .....106 EU81
Anthonys, Wok. GU21 .....151 BB112
Anthony St, E1
off Commercial Rd 84 DV72
Anthorne Cl, Pot.B. EN6 .....12 DB31
Anthus Ms, Nthwd. HA6 .....39 BS52
Antigua Cl, SE19
off Salters Hill 122 DR92
Antigua Wk, SE19 .....122 DR92
Antill Rd, E3 .....85 DY69
N15 .....66 DT56
Antill Ter, E1 .....85 DX72
Antlers Hill, E4 .....31 EB43
Antoinette Ct, Abb.L. WD5
off Dairy Way 7 BT29
Anton Cres, Sutt. SM1 .....140 DA104
Antoneys Cl, Pnr. HA5 .....40 BX54
Anton Pl, Wem. HA9 .....62 CP62
Anton Rd, S.Ock. RM15 .....91 FV70
Anton St, E8 .....66 DU64
Antrim Gro, NW3 .....82 DF65
Antrim Mans, NW3 .....82 DE65
Antrim Rd, NW3 .....82 DF65
Antrobus Cl, Sutt. SM1 .....157 CZ106
Antrobus Rd, W4 .....98 CQ77
Anvil Cl, SW16 .....121 DJ94
Hemel Hempstead (Bov.) HP3
off Yew Tree Dr 5 BB28
Anvil Ct, Slou. (Langley) SL3
off Blacksmith Row 93 BA77
Anvil La, Cob. KT11 .....153 BU114
Anvil Pl, St.Alb. AL2 .....8 CA26
Anvil Rd, Sun. TW16 .....135 BU97
Anworth Cl, Wdf.Grn. IG8 .....48 EH51
Anyards Rd, Cob. KT11 .....153 BV113
Apeldoorn Dr, Wall. SM6 ....159 DL109
Aperdele Rd, Lthd. KT22 ....171 CG118
APERFIELD, West. 179 EM117
Aperfield Rd, Erith DA8 .....107 FF79
Westerham (Bigg.H.) TN16 .178 EL117
Apers Av, Wok. GU22 .....167 AZ121
Apex Cl, Beck. BR3 .....143 EB95
Weybridge KT13 .....135 BR104
Apex Cor, NW7 .....42 CR49
Apex Ind Est, NW10
off Hythe Rd 81 CU69
Apex Retail Pk, Felt. TW13 ..116 BZ90
Apex Twr, N.Mal. KT3 .....138 CS97
Aplin Way, Islw. TW7 .....97 CE81
Apollo Av, Brom. BR1
off Rodway Rd 144 EH95
Northwood HA6 .....39 BU50
Apollo Cl, Horn. RM12 .....71 FH61
★ Apollo Hammersmith, W6 ..99 CW78
Apollo Pl, E11 .....68 EE62
SW10 .....100 DD80
Woking (St. John's) GU21
off Church Rd 166 AU119
★ Apollo Thea, W1
off Shaftesbury Av 195 M10
★ Apollo Victoria Thea,
SW1 .....199 K7
Apollo Way, SE28
off Broadwater Rd 105 ER76
Apostle Way, Th.Hth. CR7 ...141 DP96
Apothecary St, EC4 .....196 F9
Appach Rd, SW2 .....121 DN86
Apple Blossom Ct, SW8
off Pascal St 101 DK80
Appleby Cl, E4 .....47 EC51
N15 .....66 DR57
Twickenham TW2 .....117 CD89
Appleby Dr, Rom. RM3 .....52 FJ50
Appleby Gdns, Felt. TW14 ...115 BT88
Appleby Grn, Rom. RM3
off Appleby Dr 52 FJ50
Appleby Rd, E8 .....84 DU66
E16 .....86 EF72
Appleby St, E2 .....84 DT68
Waltham Cross (Chsht.)
EN7 .....14 DT26
Apple Cotts, Hem.H. (Bov.)
HP3 .....5 BA27
Applecroft, St.Alb. (Park St.)
AL2 .....8 CB28
Appledore Av, Bexh. DA7 ....107 FC81
Ruislip HA4 .....59 BV62
Appledore Cl, SW17 .....120 DF89
Bromley BR2 .....144 EF99
Edgware HA8 .....42 CN53
Romford RM3 .....52 FJ53
Appledore Cres, Sid. DA14 ..125 ES90
Appledore Way, NW7
off Bittacy Hill 43 CY52
Appledown Ri, Couls. CR5 ...175 DJ115
Applefield, Amer. HP7 .....20 AW39
Appleford Rd, W10 .....81 CY70
Apple Garth, Brent. TW8 .....97 CK77
Applegarth, Croy. (New Adgtn.)
CR0 .....161 EB108
Esher (Clay.) KT10 .....155 CF106
Applegarth Dr, Dart. DA1 ....128 FL89
Ilford IG2 .....69 ET56
Applegarth Ho, Erith DA8 ...107 FF82
Applegarth Rd, SE28 .....88 EV74
W14 .....99 CX76
Applegate, Brwd. CM14 .....54 FT43
Apple Gro, Chess. KT9 .....156 CL105
Enfield EN1 .....30 DS41
Apple Mkt, Kings.T. KT1
off Eden St 137 CK96
Apple Orchard, Swan. BR8 ..147 FD98
Apple Rd, E11 .....68 EE62
Appleshaw Cl, Grav. DA11 ...131 GG92
Appleton Cl, Amer. HP7 .....20 AV40
Appleton Dr, Dart. DA2 .....127 FH90
Appleton Gdns, N.Mal. KT3 .139 CU100
Appleton Rd, SE9 .....104 EL83
Loughton IG10 .....33 EP41
Appleton Sq, Mitch. CR4
off Silbury Av 140 DE95
Appleton Way, Horn. RM12 ...72 FK60
Appletree Av, Uxb. UB8 .....76 BM71
West Drayton UB7 .....76 BM71
Appletree Cl, SE20
off Jasmine Gro 142 DV95
Leatherhead KT22 .....170 CC124
Appletree Gdns, Barn. EN4 ...28 DE42
Appletree La, Slou. SL3 .....92 AW76
Apple Tree Roundabout, West Dr.
UB7 .....76 BM73
Appletree Wk, Wat. WD25 .....7 BV34
Apple Tree Yd, SW1 .....199 L2
Applewood Cl, N20 .....44 DE46
NW2 .....63 CV62
Applewood Dr, E13 .....86 EH70
Appold St, EC2 .....197 M6
Erith DA8 .....107 FF79
Apprentice Way, E5
off Clarence Rd 66 DV63
Approach, The, NW4 .....63 CX57
W3 .....80 CR72
Enfield EN1 .....30 DV40
Orpington BR6 .....145 ET103
Potters Bar EN6 .....11 CZ32
Upminster RM14 .....72 FP62
Approach Cl, N16
off Cowper Rd 66 DS64
Approach Rd, E2 .....84 DW68
SW20 .....139 CW96
Ashford TW15 .....115 BQ93
Barnet EN4 .....28 DD42
Purley CR8 .....159 DP112
West Molesey KT8 .....136 CA99
Aprey Gdns, NW4 .....63 CW56
April Cl, W7 .....79 CE73
Ashtead KT21 .....172 CM117
Feltham TW13 .....115 BU90
Orpington BR6
off Briarswood Way 163 ET106
April Glen, SE23 .....123 DX90
April St, E8 .....66 DT63
Aprilwood Cl, Add. (Woodham)
KT15 .....151 BF111
Apsledene, Grav. DA12
off Miskin Way 131 GK93
APSLEY, Hem.H. 6 BK25
⇌ Apsley 6 BL25
Apsley Cl, Har. HA2 .....60 CC57
★ Apsley Ho, Wellington Mus,
W1 .....198 F4
Apsley Rd, SE25 .....142 DV98
New Malden KT3 .....138 CQ97
Apsley Way, NW2 .....63 CU61
W1 .....198 G4
Aquarius Business Pk, NW2 ..63 CU60
Aquarius Way, Nthwd. HA6 ...39 BU50
★ Aquatic Experience, Brent.
TW8 .....97 CH81
Aquila Cl, Lthd. KT22 .....172 CL121
Aquila St, NW8 .....82 DD68
Aquinas St, SE1 .....200 E3

★ Place of interest ⇌ Railway station ⊖ London Underground station DLR Docklands Light Railway station -o- Tramlink station H Hospital

Ara - Ash

Arabella Dr, SW15 ... 98 CS84
Arabia Cl, E4 ... 47 ED45
Arabin Rd, SE4 ... 103 DY84
Araglen Av, S.Ock. RM15 ... 91 FV71
Aragon Av, Epsom KT17 ... 157 CV109
Thames Ditton KT7 ... 137 CF99
Aragon Cl, Brom. BR2 ... 145 EM102
Croydon (New Adgtn.) CR0 ... 162 EE110
Enfield EN2 ... 29 DM38
Loughton IG10 ... 32 EL44
Romford RM5 ... 51 FB51
Sunbury-on-Thames TW16 ... 115 BT94
Aragon Dr, Ilf. IG6 ... 49 EQ52
Ruislip HA4 ... 60 BX60
Aragon Rd, Kings.T. KT2 ... 118 CL92
Morden SM4 ... 139 CX100
Aragon Twr, SE8 ... 103 DZ77
Aragon Wk, W.Byf. (Byfleet) KT14 ... 152 BM113
Aran Ct, Wey. KT13 *off Mallards Reach* ... 135 BR103
Arandora Cres, Rom. RM6 ... 70 EV59
Aran Dr, Stan. HA7 ... 41 CJ49
Aran Hts, Ch.St.G. HP8 ... 36 AV49
Arbery Rd, E3 ... 85 DY69
Arbor Cl, Beck. BR3 ... 143 EB96
Arbor Ct, N16 *off Lordship Rd* ... 66 DR61
Arborfield Cl, SW2 ... 121 DM88
Slough SL1 ... 92 AS76
Arbor Rd, E4 ... 47 ED48
Arbour Cl, Brwd. CM14 ... 54 FW50
Leatherhead (Fetch.) KT22 ... 171 CF123
Arbour Rd, Enf. EN3 ... 31 DX42
Arbour Sq, E1 ... 85 DX72
Arbour Vw, Amer. HP7 ... 20 AV39
Arbour Way, Horn. RM12 ... 71 FH64
Arbroath Grn, Wat. WD19 ... 39 BU48
Arbroath Rd, SE9 ... 104 EL83
Arbrook Chase, Esher KT10 ... 154 CC107
Arbrook Cl, Orp. BR5 ... 146 EU97
Arbrook La, Esher KT10 ... 154 CC107
Arbury Ter, SE26 *off Oaksford Av* ... 122 DV90
Arbuthnot La, Bex. DA5 ... 126 EY86
Arbuthnot Rd, SE14 ... 103 DX82
Arbutus St, E8 ... 84 DS67
Arcade, The, EC2 ... 197 M7
Croydon CR0 *off High St* ... 142 DQ104
Arcade Pl, Rom. RM1 ... 71 FE57
Arcadia Av, N3 ... 44 DA53
Arcadia Caravans, Stai. TW18 ... 134 BH95
Arcadia Cl, Cars. SM5 ... 158 DG105
Arcadian Av, Bex. DA5 ... 126 EY86
Arcadian Cl, Bex. DA5 ... 126 EY86
Arcadian Gdns, N22 ... 45 DM52
Arcadian Rd, Bex. DA5 ... 126 EY86
Arcadia Shop Cen, W5 ... 79 CK73
Arcadia St, E14 ... 85 EA72
Arcany Rd, S.Ock. RM15 ... 91 FV70
Archangel St, SE16 ... 203 J5
Archates Av, Grays RM16 ... 110 GA76
Archbishops Pl, SW2 ... 121 DM86
Archdale Pl, N.Mal. KT3 ... 138 CP97
Archdale Rd, SE22 ... 122 DT85
Archel Rd, W14 ... 99 CZ79
Archer Cl, Kings L. WD4 ... 6 BM29
Kingston upon Thames KT2 ... 118 CL94
Archer Ho, SW11 *off Vicarage Cres* ... 100 DD81
Archer Ms, Hmptn. (Hmptn.H.) TW12 *off Windmill Rd* ... 116 CC93
Archer Rd, SE25 ... 142 DV98
Orpington BR5 ... 146 EU99
Archers Ct, S.Ock. RM15 ... 91 FV71
Archers Dr, Enf. EN3 ... 30 DW40
Archer Sq, SE14 *off Chubworthy St* ... 103 DY79
Archer St, W1 ... 195 M10
Archer Ter, West Dr. UB7 *off Yew Av* ... 76 BL73
Archer Way, Swan. BR8 ... 147 FF96
Archery Cl, W2 ... 194 C9
Harrow HA3 ... 61 CF55
Archery Rd, SE9 ... 125 EM85
Arches, The, SW6 *off Munster Rd* ... 99 CZ82
WC2 ... 200 A2
Harrow HA2 ... 60 CB61
Archibald Ms, W1 ... 198 G2
Archibald Rd, N7 ... 65 DK63
Romford RM3 ... 52 FN53
Archibald St, E3 ... 85 EA69
Archie Cl, West Dr. UB7 ... 94 BN75
Archie St, SE1 ... 201 N5
Arch Rd, Walt. KT12 ... 136 BX104
Arch St, SE1 ... 201 H7
⊖ **Archway** ... 65 DJ61
Archway, Rom. RM3 ... 51 FH51
Archway Cl, N19 *off St. Johns Way* ... 65 DJ61
SW19 ... 120 DB91
W10 ... 81 CX71
Wallington SM6 ... 141 DK104
Archway Mall, N19 *off Magdala Av* ... 65 DJ61
Archway Ms, SW15 *off Putney Br Rd* ... 99 CY84
Archway Rd, N6 ... 64 DG58
N19 ... 65 DJ60
Archway St, SW13 ... 98 CS83
Arcola St, E8 ... 66 DT64
Arctic St, NW5 *off Gillies St* ... 64 DG64
Arcus Rd, Brom. BR1 ... 124 EE93
Ardbeg Rd, SE24 ... 122 DR86
Arden Cl, Bushey (Bushey Hth.) WD23 ... 41 CF45
Harrow HA1 ... 61 CD62
Hemel Hempstead (Bov.) HP3 ... 5 BA28
Arden Ct Gdns, N2 ... 64 DD58
Arden Cres, E14 ... 204 A8
Arden Cres, Dag. RM9 ... 88 EW66
Arden Est, N1 ... 197 M1
Arden Gro, Orp. BR6 ... 163 EP105
Arden Ho, SW9 *off Grantham Rd* ... 101 DL82
Arden Ms, E17 ... 67 EB57
Arden Mhor, Pnr. HA5 ... 59 BV56
Arden Rd, N3 ... 63 CY55
W13 ... 79 CJ73
Ardent Cl, SE25 ... 142 DS97
Ardesley Wd, Wey. KT13 ... 153 BS105
Ardfern Av, SW16 ... 141 DN97
Ardfillan Rd, SE6 ... 123 ED88
Ardgowan Rd, SE6 ... 124 EE87
Ardilaun Rd, N5 ... 66 DQ63
Ardingly Cl, Croy. CR0 ... 143 DX104
Ardleigh Cl, Horn. RM11 ... 72 FK55
Ardleigh Ct, Brwd. CM15 ... 55 FZ45
Ardleigh Gdns, Brwd. CM13 *off Fairview Av* ... 55 GE44
Sutton SM3 ... 140 DA101
ARDLEIGH GREEN, Horn. ... 72 FJ56
Ardleigh Grn Rd, Horn. RM11 ... 72 FK57
Ardleigh Ho, Bark. IG11 *off St. Ann's* ... 87 EQ67
Ardleigh Ms, Ilf. IG1 *off Bengal Rd* ... 69 EP62
Ardleigh Rd, E17 ... 47 DZ53
N1 ... 84 DR65
Ardleigh Ter, E17 ... 47 DZ53
Ardley Cl, NW10 ... 62 CS62
SE6 ... 123 DY90
Ruislip HA4 ... 59 BQ59
Ardlui Rd, SE27 ... 122 DQ89
Ardmay Gdns, Surb. KT6 ... 138 CL99
Ardmere Rd, SE13 ... 123 ED86
Ardmore La, Buck.H. IG9 ... 48 EH45
Ardmore Pl, Buck.H. IG9 ... 48 EH45
Ardmore Rd, S.Ock. RM15 ... 91 FV70
Ardoch Rd, SE6 ... 123 ED89
Ardra Rd, N9 ... 47 DX48
Ardrossan Gdns, Wor.Pk. KT4 ... 139 CU104
Ardross Av, Nthwd. HA6 ... 39 BS50
Ardshiel Cl, SW15 *off Bemish Rd* ... 99 CX83
Ardwell Av, Ilf. IG6 ... 69 EQ57
Ardwell Rd, SW2 ... 121 DL89
Ardwick Rd, NW2 ... 64 DA63
Tramlink **Arena** ... 142 DW99
Arena, The, Enf. EN3 ... 31 DZ38
Arewater Grn, Loug. IG10 ... 33 EM39
Argali Ho, Erith DA18 *off Kale Rd* ... 106 EY76
Argall Av, E10 ... 67 DX59
Argall Way, E10 ... 67 DX60
Argenta Way, NW10 ... 80 CP66
Argent Cl, Egh. TW20 *off Holbrook Meadow* ... 113 BC93
Argent St, SE1 ... 200 G4
Grays RM17 ... 110 FY79
Argent Way, Wal.Cr. (Chsht.) EN7 ... 14 DR26
Argles Cl, Green. DA9 *off Cowley Av* ... 129 FU85
Argon Ms, SW6 ... 100 DA80
Argon Rd, N18 ... 46 DW50
Argosy Gdns, Stai. TW18 ... 113 BF93
Argosy La, Stai. (Stanw.) TW19 ... 114 BK87
Argus Cl, Rom. RM7 ... 51 FB53
Argus Way, W3 ... 98 CP76
Northolt UB5 ... 78 BY69
Argyle Av, Houns. TW3 ... 116 CA86
Argyle Cl, W13 ... 79 CG70
Argyle Gdns, Upmin. RM14 ... 73 FR61
Argyle Pas, N17 ... 46 DT53
Argyle Pl, W6 ... 99 CV77
Argyle Rd, E1 ... 85 DX70
E15 ... 68 EE63
E16 ... 86 EJ72
N12 ... 44 DA50
N17 ... 46 DU53
N18 ... 46 DU49
W13 ... 79 CG71
Barnet EN5 ... 27 CW42
Greenford UB6 ... 79 CF69
Harrow HA2 ... 60 CB58
Hounslow TW3 ... 116 CB85
Ilford IG1 ... 69 EN61
Sevenoaks TN13 ... 191 FH125
Teddington TW11 ... 117 CE92
Argyle Sq, WC1 ... 196 A2
Argyle St, WC1 ... 195 P2
Argyle Wk, WC1 ... 196 A3
Argyle Way, SE16 ... 102 DU78
Argyll Av, Sthl. UB1 ... 78 CB74
Argyll Cl, SW9 *off Dalyell Rd* ... 101 DM83
Argyll Gdns, Edg. HA8 ... 42 CP54
Argyll Rd, W8 ... 100 DA75
Grays RM17 ... 110 GA78
Argyll St, W1 ... 195 K9
Arica Rd, SE4 ... 103 DY84
Ariel Cl, Grav. DA12 ... 131 GM91
Ariel Rd, NW6 ... 82 DA65
Ariel Way, W12 ... 81 CW74
Hounslow TW4 ... 95 BV83
Arisdale Av, S.Ock. RM15 ... 91 FV71
Aristotle Rd, SW4 ... 101 DK83
Ark Av, Grays RM16 ... 110 GA76
Arkell Gro, SE19 ... 121 DP94
Arkindale Rd, SE6 ... 123 EC90
ARKLEY, Barn. ... 27 CU43
Arkley Cres, E17 ... 67 DZ57
Arkley Dr, Barn. EN5 ... 27 CU42
Arkley La, Barn. EN5 ... 27 CU41
Arkley Pk, Barn. EN5 ... 26 CR44
Arkley Rd, E17 ... 67 DZ57
Arkley Vw, Barn. EN5 ... 27 CV42
Arklow Ct, Rick. (Chorl.) WD3 *off Station App* ... 21 BC42
Arklow Ms, Surb. KT6 *off Vale Rd S* ... 138 CL103
Arklow Rd, SE14 ... 103 DZ79
Arkwright Rd, NW3 ... 64 DC64
Slough (Colnbr.) SL3 ... 93 BE82
South Croydon CR2 ... 160 DT110
Arkwright Rd, Til. RM18 ... 111 GG82
Arlesey Cl, SW15 *off Lytton Gro* ... 119 CY86
Arlesford Rd, SW9 ... 101 DL83
Arlingford Rd, SW2 ... 121 DN85
Arlingham Ms, Wal.Abb. EN9 *off Sun St* ... 15 EC33
Arlington, N12 ... 44 DA48
Arlington Av, N1 ... 84 DQ68
Arlington Cl, SE13 ... 123 ED86
Sidcup DA15 ... 125 ES87
Sutton SM1 ... 140 DA103
Twickenham TW1 ... 117 CJ86
Arlington Ct, Hayes UB3 *off Shepiston La* ... 95 BR78
Reigate RH2 *off Oakfield Dr* ... 184 DB132
Arlington Cres, Wal.Cr. EN8 ... 15 DY34
Arlington Dr, Cars. SM5 ... 140 DF103
Ruislip HA4 ... 59 BR58
Arlington Gdns, W4 ... 98 CQ78
Ilford IG1 ... 69 EN60
Romford RM3 ... 52 FL53
Arlington Grn, NW7 *off Bittacy Hill* ... 43 CY52
Arlington Lo, SW2 ... 101 DM84
Weybridge KT13 ... 153 BP105
Arlington Ms, Twick. TW1 *off Arlington Rd* ... 117 CJ86
Arlington Pl, SE10 *off Greenwich S St* ... 103 EC80
Arlington Rd, N14 ... 45 DH47
NW1 ... 83 DH67
W13 ... 79 CH72
Ashford TW15 ... 114 BM92
Richmond TW10 ... 117 CK89
Surbiton KT6 ... 137 CK100
Teddington TW11 ... 117 CF91
Twickenham TW1 ... 117 CJ86
Woodford Green IG8 ... 48 EG53
Arlington Sq, N1 ... 84 DQ67
Arlington St, SW1 ... 199 K2
Arlington Way, EC1 ... 196 E2
Arliss Way, Nthlt. UB5 ... 78 BW67
Arlow Rd, N21 ... 45 DN46
Armada Ct, SE8 *off Watergate St* ... 103 EA79
Grays RM16 *off Hogg La* ... 110 GA76
Armadale Cl, N17 ... 66 DV56
Armadale Rd, SW6 ... 100 DA80
Feltham TW14 ... 115 BU85
Woking GU21 ... 166 AU117
Armada St, SE8 ... 103 EA79
Armada Way, E6 ... 87 EQ73
Armagh Rd, E3 ... 85 DZ67
Armand Cl, Wat. WD17 ... 23 BT38
Armfield Cl, W.Mol. KT8 ... 136 BZ99
Armfield Cres, Mitch. CR4 ... 140 DF96
Armfield Rd, Enf. EN2 ... 30 DR39
Arminger Rd, W12 ... 81 CV74
Armistice Gdns, SE25 *off Penge Rd* ... 142 DU97
Armitage Cl, Rick. (Loud.) WD3 ... 22 BK42
Armitage Rd, NW11 ... 63 CZ60
SE10 ... 205 K10
Armor Rd, Purf. RM19 ... 109 FR77
Armour Cl, N7 *off Roman Way* ... 83 DM65
Armoury Dr, Grav. DA12 ... 131 GJ87
Armoury Rd, SE8 ... 103 EB82
Armoury Way, SW18 ... 120 DA85
Armstead Wk, Dag. RM10 ... 88 FA66
Armstrong Av, Wdf.Grn. IG8 ... 48 EE51
Armstrong Cl, E6 *off Porter Rd* ... 87 EM72
Borehamwood WD6 *off Manor Way* ... 26 CQ41
Dagenham RM8 *off Palmer Rd* ... 70 EX60
Pinner HA5 ... 59 BU58
St. Albans (Lon.Col.) AL2 *off Willowside* ... 10 CL27
Sevenoaks (Halst.) TN14 ... 181 FB115
Walton-on-Thames KT12 *off Sunbury La* ... 135 BU100
Armstrong Cres, Barn. EN4 ... 28 DD41
Armstrong Gdns, Rad. (Shenley) WD7 ... 10 CL32
Armstrong Rd, SW7 ... 100 DD76
W3 ... 81 CT74
Egham (Eng.Grn.) TW20 ... 112 AW93
Feltham TW13 ... 116 BY92
Armstrong Way, Sthl. UB2 ... 96 CB75
Armytage Rd, Houns. TW5 ... 96 BX80
Arnal Cres, SW18 ... 119 CY87
Arncliffe Cl, N11 *off Kettlewell Cl* ... 44 DG51
Arncroft Ct, Bark. IG11 *off Renwick Rd* ... 88 EV69
Arndale Wk, SW18 *off Garratt La* ... 120 DB85
Arndale Way, Egh. TW20 *off Church Rd* ... 113 BA92
Arne Gro, Orp. BR6 ... 145 ET104
Arne St, WC2 ... 196 A9
Arnett Cl, Rick. WD3 ... 22 BG44
Arnett Sq, E4 *off Burnside Av* ... 47 DZ51
Arnett Way, Rick. WD3 ... 22 BG44
Arne Wk, SE3 ... 104 EF84
Arneways Av, Rom. RM6 ... 70 EX55
Arneway St, SW1 ... 199 N7
Arnewood Cl, SW15 ... 119 CU88
Leatherhead (Oxshott) KT22 ... 154 CB113
Arney's La, Mitch. CR4 ... 140 DG100
Arngask Rd, SE6 ... 123 ED87
Arnhem Av, S.Ock. (Aveley) RM15 ... 90 FQ74
Arnhem Dr, Croy. (New Adgtn.) CR0 ... 161 ED111
Arnhem Pl, E14 ... 203 P7
Arnhem Way, SE22 *off East Dulwich Gro* ... 122 DS85
Arnhem Wf, E14 *off Arnhem Pl* ... 103 EA76
Arnison Rd, E.Mol. KT8 ... 137 CD98
Arnold Av E, Enf. EN3 ... 31 EA38
Arnold Av W, Enf. EN3 ... 31 DZ38
Arnold Circ, E2 ... 197 P3
Arnold Cl, Har. HA3 ... 62 CM59
Arnold Cres, Islw. TW7 ... 117 CD85
Arnold Dr, Chess. KT9 ... 155 CK107
Arnold Est, SE1 ... 202 A5
Arnold Gdns, N13 ... 45 DP50
Arnold Pl, Til. RM18 *off Kipling Av* ... 111 GJ81
Arnold Rd, E3 ... 85 EA69
N15 ... 66 DT55
SW17 ... 120 DF94
Dagenham RM9, RM10 ... 88 EZ66
Gravesend DA12 ... 131 GJ89
Northolt UB5 ... 78 BX65
Staines TW18 ... 114 BJ94
Waltham Abbey EN9 ... 31 EC35
Woking GU21 ... 167 BB116
Arnolds Av, Brwd. CM13 ... 55 GC43
Arnolds Cl, Brwd. CM13 ... 55 GC43
Arnolds Fm La, Brwd. CM13 ... 55 GE41
Arnolds La, Dart. (Sutt.H.) DA4 ... 128 FM93
⊖ **Arnos Grove** ... 45 DJ49
Arnos Gro, N14 ... 45 DK49
Arnos Rd, N11 ... 45 DJ50
Arnott Cl, SE28 *off Applegarth Rd* ... 88 EW73
W4 *off Fishers La* ... 98 CR77
Arnould Av, SE5 ... 102 DR84
Arnsberg Way, Bexh. DA7 ... 106 FA84
Arnside Gdns, Wem. HA9 ... 61 CK60
Arnside Rd, Bexh. DA7 ... 106 FA81
Arnside St, SE17 ... 102 DQ79
Arnulf St, SE6 ... 123 EB91
Arnulls Rd, SW16 ... 121 DN93
Arodene Rd, SW2 ... 121 DM86
Arosa Rd, Twick. TW1 ... 117 CK86
Arpley Sq, SE20 *off High St* ... 122 DW94
Arragon Gdns, SW16 ... 121 DL94
West Wickham BR4 ... 143 EB104
Arragon Rd, E6 ... 86 EK67
SW18 ... 120 DB88
Twickenham TW1 ... 117 CG87
Arran Cl, Erith DA8 ... 107 FD79
Wallington SM6 ... 159 DH105
Arran Dr, E12 ... 68 EK60
Arran Grn, Wat. WD19 *off Prestwick Rd* ... 40 BW46
Arran Ms, W5 ... 80 CM74
Arranmore Ct, Bushey WD23 *off Bushey Hall Rd* ... 24 BY42
Arran Rd, SE6 ... 123 EB89
Arran Wk, N1 ... 84 DQ66
Arran Way, Esher KT10 ... 136 CB103
Arras Av, Mord. SM4 ... 140 DC99
Arreton Mead, Wok. (Horsell) GU21 ... 150 AY114
Arrol Rd, Beck. BR3 ... 142 DW97
Arrow Rd, E3 ... 85 EB69
Arrowscout Wk, Nthlt. UB5 *off Argus Way* ... 78 BY69
Arrowsmith Cl, Chig. IG7 ... 49 ET50
Arrowsmith Path, Chig. IG7 ... 49 ET50
Arrowsmith Rd, Chig. IG7 ... 49 ES50
Loughton IG10 ... 32 EL41
⊖ **Arsenal** ... 65 DN62
★ **Arsenal FC**, N5 ... 65 DP62
Arsenal Rd, SE9 ... 105 EM82
Artemis Cl, Grav. DA12 ... 131 GL87
Arterberry Rd, SW20 ... 119 CW94
Arterial Av, Rain. RM13 ... 89 FH70
Arterial Rd N Stifford, Grays RM17 ... 110 FY75
Arterial Rd Purfleet, Purf. RM19 ... 108 FN76
Arterial Rd W Thurrock, Grays RM16, RM20 ... 109 FU76
Artesian Cl, NW10 ... 80 CR66
Hornchurch RM11 ... 71 FF58
Artesian Gro, Barn. EN5 ... 28 DC42
Artesian Rd, W2 ... 82 DA72
Artesian Wk, E11 ... 68 EE62
Arthingworth St, E15 ... 86 EE67
Arthur Ct, W2 *off Queensway* ... 82 DB72
Arthurdon Rd, SE4 ... 123 EA85
Arthur Gro, SE18 ... 105 EQ77
Arthur Henderson Ho, SW6 ... 99 CZ82
Arthur Horsley Wk, E7 *off Magpie Cl* ... 68 EF64
★ **Arthur Jacob Nature Reserve**, Slou. SL3 ... 93 BC83
Arthur Rd, E6 ... 87 EM68
N7 ... 65 DM63
N9 ... 46 DT47
SW19 ... 120 DA90
Kingston upon Thames KT2 ... 118 CN94
New Malden KT3 ... 139 CV99
Romford RM6 ... 70 EW59
Westerham (Bigg.H.) TN16 ... 178 EJ115
Arthur's Br Rd, Wok. GU21 ... 166 AW117
Arthur St, EC4 ... 201 L1
Bushey WD23 ... 24 BX42
Erith DA8 ... 107 FF80
Gravesend DA11 ... 131 GG87
Grays RM17 ... 110 GC79
Arthur St W, Grav. DA11 ... 131 GG87
Arthur Toft Ho, Grays RM17 *off New Rd* ... 110 GB79
Artichoke Dell, Rick. (Chorl.) WD3 ... 21 BE43
Artichoke Hill, E1 ... 202 D1
Artichoke Pl, SE5 *off Camberwell Ch St* ... 102 DR81
Artillery Cl, Ilf. IG2 *off Horns Rd* ... 69 EQ58
Artillery La, E1 ... 197 N7
W12 ... 81 CU72
Artillery Pas, E1 ... 197 N7
Artillery Pl, SE18 ... 105 EM77
SW1 ... 199 M7
Harrow HA3 *off Chicheley Rd* ... 40 CC52
Artillery Row, SW1 ... 199 M7
Artillery Row, Grav. DA12 ... 131 GJ87
Artington Cl, Orp. BR6 ... 163 EQ105
Artisan Cl, E6 *off Ferndale St* ... 87 EP72
Artizan St, E1 ... 197 N8
Arundel Av, Epsom KT17 ... 157 CV110
Morden SM4 ... 139 CZ98
South Croydon CR2 ... 160 DU110
Arundel Cl, E15 ... 68 EE63
SW11 *off Chivalry Rd* ... 120 DE85
Bexley DA5 ... 126 EZ86
Croydon CR0 ... 141 DP104
Hampton (Hmptn.H.) TW12 ... 116 CB92
Waltham Cross (Chsht.) EN8 ... 14 DW29
Arundel Ct, N12 ... 44 DE51
Harrow HA2 ... 60 CA63
Slough SL3 ... 92 AX77
Arundel Dr, Borwd. WD6 ... 26 CQ43
Harrow HA2 ... 60 BZ63
Orpington BR6 ... 164 EV106
Woodford Green IG8 ... 48 EG52
Arundel Gdns, N21 ... 45 DN46
W11 ... 81 CZ73
Edgware HA8 ... 42 CR52
Ilford IG3 ... 70 EU61
Arundel Gt Ct, WC2 ... 196 C10
Arundel Gro, N16 ... 66 DS64
Arundel Pl, N1 ... 83 DN65
Arundel Rd, Abb.L. WD5 ... 7 BU32
Barnet EN4 ... 28 DE41
Croydon CR0 ... 142 DR100
Dartford DA1 ... 108 FJ84
Hounslow TW4 ... 96 BW83
Kingston upon Thames KT1 ... 138 CP96
Romford RM3 ... 52 FM53
Sutton SM2 ... 157 CZ108
Uxbridge UB8 ... 76 BH68
Arundel Sq, N7 ... 83 DN65
Arundel St, WC2 ... 196 C10
Arundel Ter, SW13 ... 99 CV79
Arvon Rd, N5 ... 65 DN64
Asbaston Ter, Ilf. IG1 *off Buttsbury Rd* ... 69 EQ64
Ascalon St, SW8 ... 101 DJ80
Ascension Rd, Rom. RM5 ... 51 FC51
Ascham Dr, E4 *off Rushcroft Rd* ... 47 EB52
Ascham End, E17 ... 47 DY53
Ascham St, NW5 ... 65 DJ64
Aschurch Rd, Croy. CR0 ... 142 DT101
Ascot Cl, Borwd. (Elstree) WD6 ... 26 CN43
Ilford IG6 ... 49 ES51
Northolt UB5 ... 60 CA64
Ascot Gdns, Enf. EN3 ... 30 DW37
Hornchurch RM12 ... 72 FL63
Southall UB1 ... 78 BZ71
Ascot Ms, Wall. SM6 ... 159 DJ109
Ascot Rd, E6 ... 87 EM69
N15 ... 66 DR57
N18 ... 46 DU49
SW17 ... 120 DG93
Feltham TW14 ... 114 BN88
Gravesend DA12 ... 131 GH90
Orpington BR5 ... 145 ET98
Watford WD18 ... 23 BS43
Ascott Av, W5 ... 98 CL75
Ashbeam Cl, Brwd. CM13 *off Canterbury Way* ... 53 FW51
Ashbourne Av, E18 ... 68 EH56
N20 ... 44 DF47
NW11 ... 63 CZ57
Bexleyheath DA7 ... 106 EY80
Harrow HA2 ... 61 CD61
Ashbourne Cl, N12 ... 44 DB49
W5 ... 80 CN71
Coulsdon CR5 ... 175 DJ118
Ashbourne Ct, E5 *off Daubeney Rd* ... 67 DY63
Ashbourne Gro, NW7 ... 42 CR50
SE22 ... 122 DT85
W4 ... 98 CS78
Ashbourne Par, W5 *off Ashbourne Rd* ... 80 CM70
Ashbourne Ri, Orp. BR6 ... 163 ER105
Ashbourne Rd, W5 ... 80 CM71
Mitcham CR4 ... 120 DG93
Romford RM3 ... 52 FJ49
Ashbourne Sq, Nthwd. HA6 ... 39 BS51
Ashbourne Ter, SW19 ... 120 DA94
Ashbourne Way, NW11 *off Ashbourne Av* ... 63 CZ57
Ashbridge Rd, E11 ... 68 EF59
Ashbridge St, NW8 ... 194 B5
Ashbrook Rd, N19 ... 65 DK60
Dagenham RM10 ... 71 FB62
Windsor (Old Wind.) SL4 ... 112 AV87
Ashburn Gdns, SW7 ... 100 DC77
Ashburnham Av, Har. HA1 ... 61 CF58
Ashburnham Cl, N2 ... 64 DD55
Sevenoaks TN13 *off Fiennes Way* ... 191 FJ127
Watford WD19 *off Ashburnham Dr* ... 39 BU48
Ashburnham Dr, Wat. WD19 ... 39 BU48
Ashburnham Gdns, Har. HA1 ... 61 CF58
Upminster RM14 ... 72 FP60
Ashburnham Gro, SE10 ... 103 EB80
Ashburnham Pk, Esher KT10 ... 154 CC105
Ashburnham Pl, SE10 ... 103 EB80
Ashburnham Retreat, SE10 ... 103 EB80
Ashburnham Rd, NW10 ... 81 CW69
SW10 ... 100 DC80
Belvedere DA17 ... 107 FC77
Richmond TW10 ... 117 CH90
Ashburn Pl, SW7 ... 100 DC77
Ashburton Av, Croy. CR0 ... 142 DV102
Ilford IG3 ... 69 ES63
Ashburton Cl, Croy. CR0 ... 142 DU102
Ashburton Ct, Pnr. HA5 ... 60 BX55
Ashburton Gdns, Croy. CR0 ... 142 DU103
Ashburton Gro, N7 ... 65 DN63
Ashburton Rd, E16 ... 86 EG72
Croydon CR0 ... 142 DU102

★ Place of interest | ≠ Railway station | ⊖ London Underground station | DLR Docklands Light Railway station | Tramlink station | H Hospital

213

Ash - Aub

Ashburton Rd, Ruis. HA4 . . . . .59 BU61
Ashburton Ter, E13
off Grasmere Rd 86 EG68
Ashbury Dr, Uxb. UB10 . . . . . .59 BP61
Ashbury Gdns, Rom. RM6 . . . .70 EX57
Ashbury Pl, SW19 . . . . .120 DC93
Ashbury Rd, SW11 . . . . .100 DF83
Ashby Av, Chess. KT9 . . . . . .156 CN107
Ashby Cl, Horn. RM11
off Holme Rd 72 FN60
Ashby Gro, N1 . . . . .84 DQ66
Ashby Ms, SE4 . . . . .103 DZ82
Ashby Rd, N15 . . . . .66 DU57
SE4 . . . . .103 DZ82
Watford WD24 . . . . .23 BU38
Ashby St, EC1 . . . . .196 G3
Ashby Wk, Croy. CR0 . . . . . . .142 DQ100
Ashby Way, West Dr. UB7 . . . .94 BN80
Ashchurch Gro, W12 . . . . .99 CU75
Ashchurch Pk Vil, W12 . . . . . .99 CU76
Ashchurch Ter, W12 . . . . .99 CU76
Ash Cl, SE20 . . . . .142 DW96
Abbots Langley WD5 . . . . . . .7 BR32
Brentwood CM15 . . . . .54 FT43
Carshalton SM5 . . . . .140 DF103
Edgware HA8 . . . . .42 CQ49
Hatfield AL9 . . . . .12 DA25
New Malden KT3 . . . . .138 CR96
Orpington BR5 . . . . .145 ER99
Redhill RH1 . . . . .185 DJ130
Romford RM5 . . . . .51 FB52
Sidcup DA14 . . . . .126 EV90
Slough SL3 . . . . .93 BB76
Stanmore HA7 . . . . .41 CG51
Swanley BR8 . . . . .147 FC96
Uxbridge (Hare.) UB9 . . . . .38 BK53
Watford WD25 . . . . .23 BV35
Woking GU22 . . . . .166 AY120
Woking (Pyrford) GU22 . . .168 BG115
Ashcombe Av, Surb. KT6 . . . .137 CK101
Ashcombe Gdns, Edg. HA8 . . .42 CN49
Ashcombe Ho, Enf. EN3 . . . . .31 DX41
Ashcombe Pk, NW2 . . . . .62 CS62
Ashcombe Rd, SW19 . . . . . . .120 DA92
Carshalton SM5 . . . . .158 DG107
Redhill RH1 . . . . .185 DJ127
Ashcombe Sq, N.Mal. KT3 . .138 CQ97
Ashcombe St, SW6 . . . . .100 DB82
Ashcombe Ter, Tad. KT20 . . . .173 CV120
Ash Copse, St.Alb. (Brick.Wd.)
AL2 .8 BZ31
Ash Ct, Epsom KT19 . . . . . . .156 CQ105
Ashcroft, Pnr. HA5 . . . . .40 CA51
Ashcroft Av, Sid. DA15 . . . . .126 EU86
Ashcroft Ct, N20
off Oakleigh Rd N 44 DD47
Ashcroft Cres, Sid. DA15 . . . .126 EU86
Ashcroft Dr, Uxb. (Denh.)
UB9 . . . . .57 BF58
Ashcroft Pk, Cob. KT11 . . . . .154 BY112
Ashcroft Ri, Couls. CR5 . . . . .175 DL116
Ashcroft Rd, E3 . . . . .85 DY69
Chessington KT9 . . . . .138 CM104
Ashcroft Sq, W6 off King St . . .99 CW77
Ashdale Cl, Stai. TW19 . . . . . .114 BL89
Twickenham TW2 . . . . .116 CC87
Ashdale Gro, Stan. HA7 . . . . . .41 CF51
Ashdale Rd, SE12 . . . . .124 EH88
Ashdale Way, Twick. TW2
off Ashdale Cl 116 CC87
Ashdene, SE15 . . . . .102 DV81
Pinner HA5 . . . . .60 BW55
Ashdene Cl, Ashf. TW15 . . . . .115 BQ94
Ashdon Cl, Brwd. CM13
off Poplar Dr 55 GC44
South Ockendon RM15
off Afton Dr 91 FV72
Woodford Green IG8 . . . . . .48 EH51
Ashdon Rd, NW10 . . . . .80 CS67
Bushey WD23 . . . . .24 BX41
Ashdown Cl, Beck. BR3 . . . . .143 EB96
Bexley DA5 . . . . .127 FC87
Ashdown Cres, NW5
off Queen's Cres 64 DG64
Waltham Cross (Chsht.)
EN8 . . . . .15 DY28
Ashdown Dr, Borwd. WD6 . . . .26 CM40
Ashdown Est, E11
off High Rd Leytonstone . .68 EE63
Ashdown Gdns, S.Croy. CR2 .176 DV115
Ashdown Rd, Enf. EN3 . . . . . .30 DW41
Epsom KT17 . . . . .157 CT113
Kingston upon Thames
KT1 . . . . .138 CL96
Uxbridge UB10 . . . . .76 BN68
Ashdown Wk, E14 . . . . .204 A8
Romford RM7 . . . . .51 FB54
Ashdown Way, SW17 . . . . . . .120 DG89
Ashen, E6 off Downings 87 EN72
Ashen Cross, Slou. SL3 . . . . . .75 BB71
Ashenden Rd, E5 . . . . .67 DX64
Ashen Dr, Dart. DA1 . . . . . . .127 FG86
Ashen Gro, SW19 . . . . .120 DA90
Ashentree Ct, EC4 . . . . .196 E9
Ashen Vale, S.Croy. CR2 . . . .161 DX109
Asher Loftus Way, N11 . . . . . .44 DF51
Asher Way, E1 . . . . .202 C2
Ashfield Av, Bushey WD23 . . .24 CB44
Feltham TW13 . . . . .115 BV88
Ashfield Cl, Beck. BR3 . . . . . .123 EA94
Richmond TW10 . . . . .118 CL88
Ashfield La, Chis. BR7 . . . . . .125 EQ93
Ashfield Par, N14 . . . . .45 DK46
Ashfield Rd, N4 . . . . .66 DQ58
N14 .45 DJ48
W3 .81 CT74
Ashfields, Loug. IG10 . . . . . . .33 EM40
Reigate RH2 . . . . .184 DB132
Watford WD25 . . . . .23 BT35
Ashfield St, E1 . . . . .84 DV71
Ashfield Yd, E1 off Ashfield St .84 DV71
ASHFORD 114 BM92
⇌ **Ashford** 114 BL91
Ashford Av, N8 . . . . .65 DL56
Ashford TW15 . . . . .115 BP93
Brentwood CM14 . . . . .54 FV48
Hayes UB4 . . . . .78 BX72
Ashford Cl, E17 . . . . .67 DZ58
Ashford Cl, Ashf. TW15 . . . . . .114 BL91
Ashford Cres, Ashf. TW15 . . . .114 BL90
Enfield EN3 . . . . .30 DW40
Ashford Gdns, Cob. KT11 . . . .170 BX116
Ashford Grn, Wat. WD19 . . . . .40 BX50
H **Ashford Hosp**, Ashf.
TW15 . . . . .114 BL89
Ashford Ind Est, Ashf. TW15 . .115 BQ91
Ashford Ms, N17
off Vicarage Rd 46 DU53
Ashford Rd, E6 . . . . .87 EN65
E18 .48 EH54
NW2 . . . . .63 CX63
Ashford TW15 . . . . .115 BQ94
Feltham TW13 . . . . .115 BT90
Iver SL0 . . . . .75 BC66
Staines TW18 . . . . .134 BK95
Ashford St, N1 . . . . .197 M2
Ash Grn, Uxb. (Denh.) UB9 . . .76 BH65
Ash Gro, E8 . . . . .84 DV67
N13 .46 DQ48
NW2 . . . . .63 CX63
SE20 . . . . .142 DW96
W5 .98 CL75
Enfield EN1 . . . . .46 DS45
Feltham TW14 . . . . .115 BS88
Hayes UB3 . . . . .77 BR73
Hounslow TW5 . . . . .96 BX81
Slough (Stoke P.) SL2 . . . . . .74 AT66
Southall UB1 . . . . .78 CA71
Staines TW18 . . . . .114 BJ93
Uxbridge (Hare.) UB9 . . . . .38 BK53
Wembley HA0 . . . . .61 CG63
West Drayton UB7 . . . . .76 BM73
West Wickham BR4 . . . . . .143 EC103
Ashgrove Rd, Ashf. TW15 . . . .115 BQ92
Bromley BR1 . . . . .123 ED93
Ilford IG3 . . . . .69 ET60
Sevenoaks TN13 . . . . .190 FG127
Ash Hill Cl, Bushey WD23 . . . .40 CB46
Ash Hill Dr, Pnr. HA5 . . . . .60 BW55
Ashingdon Cl, E4 . . . . .47 EC48
Ashington Rd, SW6 . . . . .99 CZ82
Ash Island, E.Mol. KT8 . . . . . .137 CD97
Ashlake Rd, SW16 . . . . .121 DL91
Ashland Pl, W1 . . . . .194 F6
Ash La, Horn. RM11
off Southend Arterial Rd . .72 FN56
Romford RM1 . . . . .51 FG51
Ashlar Pl, SE18
off Masons Hill 105 EP77
Ashlea Rd, Ger.Cr. (Chal.St.P.)
SL9 . . . . .36 AX54
Ashleigh Av, Egh. TW20 . . . . .113 BC94
Ashleigh Cl, Amer. HP7 . . . . . .20 AS39
Ashleigh Ct, Wal.Abb. EN9
off Lamplighters Cl 16 EG34
Ashleigh Gdns, Sutt. SM1 . . .140 DB103
Upminster RM14 . . . . .73 FR62
Ashleigh Pt, SE23
off Dacres Rd 123 DX90
Ashleigh Rd, SE20 . . . . .142 DV97
SW14 . . . . .98 CS83
Ashley Av, Epsom KT18 . . . . .156 CR113
Ilford IG6 . . . . .49 EP54
Morden SM4
off Chalgrove Av 140 DA99
Ashley Cen, Epsom KT18 . . . .156 CR113
Ashley Cl, NW4 . . . . .43 CW54
Pinner HA5 . . . . .39 BV54
Sevenoaks TN13 . . . . .191 FH124
Walton-on-Thames KT12 . . .135 BT102
Ashley Ct, Epsom KT18 . . . . .156 CR113
Woking GU21 . . . . .166 AT118
Ashley Cres, N22 . . . . .45 DN54
SW11 . . . . .100 DG83
Ashley Dr, Bans. SM7 . . . . . .158 DA114
Borehamwood WD6 . . . . .26 CQ43
Isleworth TW7 . . . . .97 CE79
Twickenham TW2 . . . . .116 CB87
Walton-on-Thames KT12 . .135 BU104
Ashley Gdns, N13 . . . . .46 DQ49
SW1 . . . . .199 L7
Orpington BR6 . . . . .163 ES106
Richmond TW10 . . . . .117 CK90
Wembley HA9 . . . . .62 CL61
Ashley Gro, Loug. IG10
off Staples Rd 32 EL41
Ashley La, NW4 . . . . .43 CW54
Croydon CR0 . . . . .159 DP105
ASHLEY PARK, Walt. 135 BT104
Ashley Pk Av, Walt. KT12 . . . .135 BT103
Ashley Pk Cres, Walt. KT12 . . .135 BT102
Ashley Pk Rd, Walt. KT12 . . . .135 BU103
Ashley Pl, SW1 . . . . .199 K7
Ashley Ri, Walt. KT12 . . . . . . .153 BU105
Ashley Rd, E4 . . . . .47 EA50
E7 . . . . .86 EJ66
N17 .66 DU55
N19 .65 DL60
SW19 . . . . .120 DB93
Enfield EN3 . . . . .30 DW40
Epsom KT18 . . . . .156 CR114
Hampton TW12 . . . . .136 CA95
Richmond TW9
off Jocelyn Rd 98 CL83
Sevenoaks TN13 . . . . .191 FH123
Thames Ditton KT7 . . . . . . .137 CF100
Thornton Heath CR7 . . . . . .141 DM98
Uxbridge UB8 . . . . .76 BH68
Walton-on-Thames KT12 . .135 BU102
Woking GU21 . . . . .166 AT118
Ashleys, Rick. WD3 . . . . .37 BF45
Ashley Sq, Epsom KT18 . . . . .156 CR113
Ashley Wk, NW7 . . . . .43 CW52
Ashling Rd, Croy. CR0 . . . . . .142 DU102
Ashlin Rd, E15 . . . . .67 ED63
Ashlone Rd, SW15 . . . . .99 CW83
Ashlyn Cl, Bushey WD23 . . . . .24 BY42
Ashlyn Gro, Horn. RM11 . . . . . .72 FK55
Ashlyns Pk, Cob. KT11 . . . . . .154 BY113
Ashlyns Rd, Epp. CM16 . . . . . .17 ET30
Ashlyns Way, Chess. KT9 . . . .155 CK107
Ashmead, N14 . . . . .29 DJ43
Ashmead Dr, Uxb. (Denh.)
UB9 . . . . .58 BG61
Ashmead Gate, Brom. BR1 . .144 EJ95
Ashmead La, Uxb. (Denh.) UB9 .58 BG61
Ashmead Rd, SE8 . . . . .103 EA82
Feltham TW14 . . . . .115 BU88
Ashmeads Ct, Rad. (Shenley)
WD7 off Porters Pk Dr 9 CK33
Ashmere Av, Beck. BR3 . . . . .143 ED96
Ashmere Cl, Sutt. SM3 . . . . .157 CW106
Ashmere Gro, SW2 . . . . .101 DL84
Ash Ms, Epsom KT18 . . . . . . .156 CS113
Ashmill St, NW1 . . . . .194 B6
Ashmole Pl, SW8 . . . . .101 DM79
Ashmole St, SW8 . . . . .101 DM79
Ashmore Ct, Houns. TW5
off Wheatlands 96 CA79
Ashmore Gdns, Grav. (Nthflt.)
DA11 . . . . .130 GD91
Ashmore Gro, Well. DA16 . . . .105 ER83
Ashmore La, Kes. BR2 . . . . . .162 EH111
Ashmore Rd, W9 . . . . .81 CZ70
Ashmount Est, N19
off Ashmount Rd 65 DK59
Ashmount Rd, N15 . . . . .66 DT57
N19 .65 DJ59
Ashmount Ter, W5
off Murray Rd 97 CK77
Ashmour Gdns, Rom. RM1 . . . .51 FD54
Ashneal Gdns, Har. HA1 . . . . .61 CD62
Ashness Gdns, Grnf. UB6 . . . .79 CH65
Ashness Rd, SW11 . . . . .120 DF85
Ash Platt, The, Sev. (Seal)
TN14 . . . . .191 FL121
Ash Platt Rd, Sev. (Seal)
TN15 . . . . .191 FL121
Ash Ride, Enf. EN2 . . . . .29 DN35
Ashridge Cl, Har. HA3 . . . . . . .61 CJ58
Hemel Hempstead (Bov.)
HP3 .5 BA28
Ashridge Cres, SE18 . . . . . . .105 EQ80
Ashridge Dr, St.Alb. (Brick.Wd.)
AL2 .8 BY30
Watford WD19 . . . . .40 BW50
Ashridge Gdns, N13 . . . . .45 DK50
Pinner HA5 . . . . .60 BY56
Ashridge Rd, Chesh. HP5 . . . . . .4 AW31
Ashridge Way, Mord. SM4 . . .139 CZ97
Sunbury-on-Thames TW16 .115 BU93
Ash Rd, E15 . . . . .68 EE64
Croydon CR0 . . . . .143 EA103
Dartford DA1 . . . . .128 FK88
Dartford (Hawley) DA2 . . . .128 FM91
Gravesend DA12 . . . . .131 GJ91
Orpington BR6 . . . . .163 ET108
Shepperton TW17 . . . . .134 BN98
Sutton SM3 . . . . .139 CY101
Westerham TN16 . . . . .189 ER125
Woking GU22 . . . . .166 AX120
Ash Row, Brom. BR2 . . . . . . .145 EN101
ASHTEAD 172 CL118
⇌ **Ashtead** 171 CK117
Ashtead Gap, Lthd. KT22 . . . .171 CH116
H **Ashtead Hosp**, Ashtd.
KT21 . . . . .172 CL119
ASHTEAD PARK, Ashtd. 172 CN118
Ashtead Rd, E5 . . . . .66 DU59
Ashtead Wds Rd, Ashtd.
KT21 . . . . .171 CJ117
Ashton Cl, Sutt. SM1 . . . . . . .158 DA105
Walton-on-Thames KT12 . .153 BV107
Ashton Gdns, Houns. TW4 . . . .96 BZ84
Romford RM6 . . . . .70 EY58
Ashton Rd, E15 . . . . .67 ED64
Enfield EN3 . . . . .31 DY36
Romford RM3 . . . . .52 FK52
Woking GU21 . . . . .166 AT117
Ashton St, E14 . . . . .85 EC73
Ashtree Av, Mitch. CR4 . . . . .140 DE96
Ash Tree Cl, Croy. CR0 . . . . . .143 DY100
Ashtree Cl, Orp. BR6
off Broadwater Gdns 163 EP105
Ash Tree Cl, Surb. KT6 . . . . . .138 CL102
Ashtree Ct, Wal.Abb. EN9
off Farthingale La 16 EG34
Ash Tree Dell, NW9 . . . . .62 CQ57
Ash Tree Rd, Wat. WD24 . . . . . .23 BV36
Ash Tree Way, Croy. CR0 . . . . .143 DY99
Ashurst Cl, SE20 . . . . .142 DV95
Dartford DA1 . . . . .107 FF83
Kenley CR8 . . . . .176 DR115
Northwood HA6 . . . . .39 BS52
Ashurst Dr, Ilf. IG2, IG6 . . . . . .69 EP58
Shepperton TW17 . . . . .134 BL99
Tadworth KT20 . . . . .182 CP130
Ashurst Rd, N12 . . . . .44 DE50
Barnet EN4 . . . . .28 DF43
Tadworth KT20 . . . . .173 CV121
Ashurst Wk, Croy. CR0 . . . . . .142 DV103
Ash Vale, Rick. (Map.Cr.) WD3 .37 BD50
Ashvale Dr, Upmin. RM14 . . . . .73 FS61
Ashvale Gdns, Rom. RM5 . . . . .51 FD50
Upminster RM14 . . . . .73 FS61
Ashvale Rd, SW17 . . . . .120 DF92
Ashview Cl, Ashf. TW15 . . . . .114 BL93
Ashview Gdns, Ashf. TW15 . . .114 BL92
Ashville Rd, E11 . . . . .67 ED61
Ash Wk, SW2 . . . . .121 DM88
South Ockendon RM15 . . . . .91 FX69
Wembley HA0 . . . . .61 CJ63
Ashwater Rd, SE12 . . . . .124 EG88
Ashwell Cl, E6
off Northumberland Rd . . .86 EL72
Ashwells Rd, Brwd. CM15 . . . . .54 FS41
Ashwells Way, Ch.St.G. HP8 . .36 AW47
Ashwick Cl, Cat. CR3 . . . . . . .186 DU125
Ashwindham Ct, Wok. GU21 .166 AS118
Ashwin St, E8 . . . . .84 DT65
Ashwood, Warl. CR6 . . . . . . .176 DW120
Ashwood Av, Rain. RM13 . . . . .89 FH70
Uxbridge UB8 . . . . .76 BN72
Ashwood Gdns, Croy.
(New Adgtn.) CR0 . . . . . . .161 EB107
Hayes UB3 off Cranford Dr .95 BT77
Ashwood Pk, Lthd. (Fetch.)
KT22 . . . . .170 CC124
Woking GU22 . . . . .167 BA118
Ashwood Pl, Dart. (Bean) DA2
off Bean La 129 FV90
Ashwood Rd, E4 . . . . .47 ED48
Ashwood Rd, Egh. (Eng.Grn.)
TW20 . . . . .112 AV93
Potters Bar EN6 . . . . .12 DB33
Woking GU22 . . . . .167 AZ118
Ashworth Cl, SE5
off Love Wk 102 DR82
Ashworth Rd, W9 . . . . .82 DB69
Askern Cl, Bexh. DA6 . . . . . . .106 EX84
Aske St, N1 . . . . .197 M2
Askew Cres, W12 . . . . .99 CT75
Askew Fm La, Grays RM17 . . .110 FY78
Askew Rd, W12 . . . . .81 CT74
Northwood HA6 . . . . .39 BR47
Askham Ct, W12 . . . . .81 CU74
Askham Rd, W12 . . . . .81 CU74
Askill Dr, SW15
off Keswick Rd 119 CY85
Askwith Rd, Rain. RM13 . . . . . .89 FD69
Asland Rd, E15 . . . . .86 EE67
Aslett St, SW18 . . . . .120 DB87
Asmara Rd, NW2 . . . . .63 CY64
Asmar Cl, Couls. CR5 . . . . . .175 DL115
Asmuns Hill, NW11 . . . . .64 DA57
Asmuns Pl, NW11 . . . . .63 CZ57
Asolando Dr, SE17 . . . . .201 J9
Aspdin Rd, Grav. (Nthflt.)
DA11 . . . . .130 GD90
Aspen Cl, N19
off Hargrave Pk 65 DJ61
W5 .98 CM75
Cobham (Stoke D'Ab.)
KT11 . . . . .170 BY116
Orpington BR6 . . . . .164 EU106
St. Albans (Brick.Wd.) AL2 . . .8 BY30
Staines TW18 . . . . .113 BF90
Swanley BR8 . . . . .147 FD95
West Drayton UB7 . . . . .76 BM74
Aspen Copse, Brom. BR1 . . . .145 EM96
Aspen Ct, Hayes UB3 . . . . .95 BS77
Virginia Water GU25 . . . . .132 AY98
Aspen Dr, Wem. HA0 . . . . .61 CG63
Aspen Gdns, W6 . . . . .99 CV78
Ashford TW15 . . . . .115 BQ92
Mitcham CR4 . . . . .140 DG99
Aspen Grn, Erith DA18 . . . . . .106 EZ76
Aspen Gro, Upmin. RM14 . . . . .72 FN63
Aspen La, Nthlt. UB5 . . . . .78 BY69
Aspenlea Rd, W6 . . . . .99 CX79
Aspen Pk Dr, Wat. WD25 . . . . . .23 BV35
Aspen Sq, Wey. KT13
off Oatlands Dr 135 BR104
Aspen Vale, Whyt. CR3
off Whyteleafe Hill 176 DT118
Aspen Way, E14 . . . . .204 A1
Banstead SM7 . . . . .157 CX114
Enfield EN3 . . . . .31 DX35
Feltham TW13 . . . . .115 BV90
South Ockendon RM15 . . . . .91 FX69
Aspern Gro, NW3 . . . . .64 DE64
Aspinall Rd, SE4 . . . . .103 DX83
Aspinden Rd, SE16 . . . . .202 E8
Aspley Rd, SW18 . . . . .120 DB85
Asplins Rd, N17 . . . . .46 DU53
Asprey Gro, Cat. CR3 . . . . . . .176 DU124
Asprey Pl, Brom. BR1
off Chislehurst Rd 144 EK96
Asquith Cl, Dag. RM8 . . . . .70 EW60
Assam St, E1
off White Ch La 84 DU72
Assata Ms, N1
off St. Paul's Rd 83 DP65
Assembly Pas, E1 . . . . .84 DW71
Assembly Wk, Cars. SM5 . . . . .140 DE101
Assher Rd, Walt. KT12 . . . . . .136 BY104
Ass Ho La, Har. HA3 . . . . .40 CB49
Assurance Cotts, Belv. DA17
off Heron Hill 106 EZ78
Astall Cl, Har. HA3 . . . . .41 CE53
Astbury Rd, SE15 . . . . .102 DW81
Astede Pl, Ashtd. KT21 . . . . . .172 CM118
Astell St, SW3 . . . . .198 C10
Asters, The, Wal.Cr. EN7 . . . . .14 DR28
Aste St, E14 . . . . .204 D5
Asteys Row, N1 off River Pl . .83 DP66
Asthall Gdns, Ilf. IG6 . . . . .69 EQ56
Astleham Rd, Shep. TW17 . . . .134 BL97
Astle St, SW11 . . . . .100 DG82
Astley, Grays RM17 . . . . .110 FZ79
Astley Av, NW2 . . . . .63 CW64
Aston Av, Har. HA3 . . . . .61 CJ59
Aston Cl, Ashtd. KT21 . . . . . . .171 CJ118
Bushey WD23 . . . . .24 CC44
Sidcup DA14 . . . . .126 EU90
Watford WD24 . . . . .24 BW40
Aston Grn, Houns. TW4 . . . . . .96 BW82
Aston Ms, Rom. RM6 . . . . .70 EW59
Aston Pl, SW16
off Averil Gro 121 DP93
Aston Rd, SW20 . . . . .139 CW96
W5 .79 CK72
Esher (Clay.) KT10 . . . . . . .155 CE106
Astons Rd, Nthwd. HA6 . . . . . .39 BQ48
Aston St, E14 . . . . .85 DY72
Aston Ter, SW12
off Cathles Rd 121 DH86
Astonville St, SW18 . . . . .120 DA88
Aston Way, Epsom KT18 . . . . .173 CT116
Potters Bar EN6 . . . . .12 DD32
Astor Av, Rom. RM7 . . . . .71 FC58
Astor Cl, Add. KT15 . . . . .152 BK105
Kingston upon Thames
KT2 . . . . .118 CP93
Astoria Wk, SW9 . . . . .101 DN83
Astra Cl, Horn. RM12 . . . . .89 FH65
Astra Dr, Grav. DA12 . . . . . . .131 GL92
Astrop Ms, W6 . . . . .99 CW76
Astrop Ter, W6 . . . . .99 CW76
Astwood Ms, SW7 . . . . .100 DB77
Asylum Rd, SE15 . . . . .102 DV80
Atalanta Cl, Pur. CR8 . . . . . . .159 DN110
Atalanta St, SW6 . . . . .99 CX81
Atbara Ct, Tedd. TW11 . . . . . .117 CH93
Atbara Rd, Tedd. TW11 . . . . . .117 CH93
Atcham Rd, Houns. TW3 . . . . . .96 CC84
Atcost Rd, Bark. IG11 . . . . .88 EU71
Atheldene Rd, SW18 . . . . . . .120 DB88
Athelney St, SE6 . . . . .123 EA90
Athelstan Cl, Rom. RM3
off Athelstan Rd 52 FM54
Athelstane Gro, E3 . . . . .85 DZ68
Athelstane Ms, N4
off Stroud Grn Rd 65 DN60
Athelstan Rd, Kings.T. KT1 . .138 CM98
Romford RM3 . . . . .52 FM53
Athelstan Way, Orp. BR5 . . . .146 EU95
Athelstone Rd, Har. HA3 . . . . .41 CD54
Athena Cl, Har. HA2
off Byron Hill Rd 61 CE61
Kingston upon Thames
KT1 . . . . .138 CM97
Athenaeum Pl, N10
off Fortis Grn Rd 65 DH55
Athenaeum Rd, N20 . . . . .44 DC46
Athena Pl, Nthwd. HA6
off The Drive 39 BT53
Athenia Cl, Wal.Cr. EN7
off Cuffley Hill 13 DP29
Athenlay Rd, SE15 . . . . .123 DX85
Athens Gdns, W9
off Harrow Rd 82 DA70
Atherden Rd, E5 . . . . .66 DW63
Atherfold Rd, SW9 . . . . .101 DL83
Atherley Way, Houns. TW4 . . .116 BZ87
Atherstone Ct, W2
off Delamere Ter 82 DB71
Atherstone Ms, SW7 . . . . . . .100 DC77
Atherton Cl, Stai. (Stanw.)
TW19 . . . . .114 BK86
Atherton Dr, SW19 . . . . .119 CX91
Atherton Gdns, Grays RM16 .111 GJ77
Atherton Hts, Wem. HA0 . . . . .79 CJ65
Atherton Ms, E7 . . . . .86 EF65
Atherton Pl, Har. HA2 . . . . . . .61 CD55
Southall UB1
off Longford Av 78 CB73
Atherton Rd, E7 . . . . .68 EF64
SW13 . . . . .99 CU80
Ilford IG5 . . . . .48 EL54
Atherton St, SW11 . . . . .100 DE82
Athlone, Esher (Clay.) KT10 . .155 CE107
Athlone Cl, E5 off Goulton Rd .66 DV63
Radlett WD7 . . . . .25 CH36
H **Athlone Ho**, N6 . . . . .64 DF60
Athlone Rd, SW2 . . . . .121 DM87
Athlone St, NW5 . . . . .82 DG65
Athlon Rd, Wem. HA0 . . . . . . .79 CK68
Athol Cl, Pnr. HA5 . . . . .39 BV53
Athole Gdns, Enf. EN1 . . . . . . .30 DS43
Athol Gdns, Pnr. HA5 . . . . .39 BV53
Atholl Rd, Ilf. IG3 . . . . .70 EU59
Athol Rd, Erith DA8 . . . . .107 FC78
Athol Sq, E14 . . . . .85 EC72
Athol Way, Uxb. UB10 . . . . . . .76 BN69
Atkins Cl, Wok. GU21
off Greythorne Rd 166 AU118
Atkins Dr, W.Wick. BR4 . . . . .143 ED103
Atkinson Cl, Orp. BR6
off Martindale Av 164 EU106
H **Atkinson Morley's Hosp**,
SW20 . . . . .119 CV94
Atkinson Rd, E16 . . . . .86 EJ71
Atkins Rd, E10 . . . . .67 EB58
SW12 . . . . .121 DK87
Atlanta Boul, Rom. RM1 . . . . . .71 FE58
Atlantic Rd, SW9 . . . . .101 DN84
Atlantis Cl, Bark. IG11 . . . . . . .88 EV69
Atlas Gdns, SE7 . . . . .104 EJ77
Atlas Ms, E8 off Tyssen St 84 DT65
N7 . . . . .83 DM65
Atlas Rd, E13 . . . . .86 EG68
N11 .45 DH51
NW10 . . . . .80 CS69
Dartford DA1
off Cornwall Rd 108 FM83
Wembley HA9 . . . . .62 CQ63
Atley Rd, E3 . . . . .85 EA67
Atlip Rd, Wem. HA0 . . . . .80 CL67
Atney Rd, SW15 . . . . .99 CY84
Atria Rd, Nthwd. HA6 . . . . .39 BU50
Attenborough Cl, Wat. WD19
off Harrow Way 40 BY48
Atterbury Cl, West. TN16 . . . .189 ER126
Atterbury Rd, N4 . . . . .65 DN58
Atterbury St, SW1 . . . . .199 N9
Attewood Av, NW10 . . . . .62 CS62
Attewood Rd, Nthlt. UB5 . . . . .78 BY65
Attfield Cl, N20 . . . . .44 DD47
Attle Cl, Uxb. UB10 . . . . .76 BN68
Attlee Cl, Hayes UB4 . . . . .77 BV69
Thornton Heath CR7 . . . . .142 DQ100
Attlee Ct, Grays RM17 . . . . . .110 GA76
Attlee Dr, Dart. DA1 . . . . .128 FN85
Attlee Rd, SE28 . . . . .88 EV73
Hayes UB4 . . . . .77 BU69
Attlee Ter, E17 . . . . .67 EB56
Attneave St, WC1 . . . . .196 D3
Attwood Cl, S.Croy. CR2 . . . . .160 DV114
Atwater Cl, SW2 . . . . .121 DN88
Atwell Cl, E10
off Belmont Pk Rd 67 EB58
Atwell Pl, T.Ditt. KT7 . . . . . . .137 CF102
Atwell Rd, SE15
off Rye La 102 DU82
Atwood, Lthd. (Bkhm.) KT23 .170 BY124
Atwood Av, Rich. TW9 . . . . . . .98 CN82
Atwood Rd, W6 . . . . .99 CV77
Atwoods All, Rich. TW9
off Leyborne Pk 98 CN81
Aubert Pk, N5 . . . . .65 DP63
Aubert Rd, N5 . . . . .65 DP63
Aubretia Cl, Rom. RM3 . . . . . . .52 FL53
Aubrey Av, St.Alb. (Lon.Col.)
AL2 .9 CJ26
Aubrey Pl, NW8 off Violet Hill .82 DC68
Aubrey Rd, E17 . . . . .67 EA55
N8 . . . . .65 DL57
W8 . . . . .81 CZ74
Aubrey Wk, W8 . . . . .81 CZ74
Auburn Cl, SE14 . . . . .103 DY80
Aubyn Hill, SE27 . . . . .122 DQ91

★ Place of interest ⇌ Railway station ⊖ London Underground station DLR Docklands Light Railway station Tramlink station H Hospital

Aub - Bad

Aubyn Sq, SW15 99 CU84
Auckland Av, Rain. RM13 89 FF69
Auckland Cl, SE19 142 DT95
 Enfield EN1 30 DV37
 Tilbury RM18 111 GG82
Auckland Gdns, SE19 142 DS95
Auckland Hill, SE27 122 DQ91
Auckland Ri, SE19 142 DS95
Auckland Rd, E10 67 EB62
 SE19 142 DT95
 SW11 100 DE84
 Caterham CR3 176 DS122
 Ilford IG1 69 EP60
 Kingston upon Thames
 KT1 138 CM98
 Potters Bar EN6 11 CY32
Auckland St, SE11
 off Kennington La 101 DM78
Auden Pl, NW1 82 DG67
 Sutton SM3
 off Wordsworth Dr 157 CW105
Audleigh Pl, Chig. IG7 49 EN51
Audley Cl, N10 45 DH52
 SW11 100 DG83
 Addlestone KT15 152 BH106
 Borehamwood WD6 26 CN41
Audley Ct, E18 68 EF56
 Pinner HA5
 off Rickmansworth Rd 40 BW54
Audley Dr, E16 205 P2
 Warlingham CR6 176 DW115
Audley Firs, Walt. KT12 154 BW105
Audley Gdns, Ilf. IG3 69 ET61
 Loughton IG10 33 EQ40
 Waltham Abbey EN9 15 EC34
Audley Pl, Sutt. SM2 158 DA108
Audley Rd, NW4 63 CV58
 W5 80 CM71
 Enfield EN2 29 DP40
 Richmond TW10 118 CM85
Audley Sq, W1 198 G2
Audley Wk, Orp. BR5 146 EW100
Audrey Cl, Beck. BR3 143 EB100
Audrey Gdns, Wem. HA0 61 CH61
Audrey Rd, Ilf. IG1 69 EP62
Audrey St, E2 84 DU68
Audric Cl, Kings.T. KT2 138 CN95
Audwick Cl, Wal.Cr. (Chsht.)
 EN8 15 DX28
Augur Cl, Stai. TW18 113 BF92
Augurs La, E13 86 EH69
Augusta Cl, W.Mol. KT8
 off Freeman Dr 136 BZ97
Augusta Rd, Twick. TW2 116 CC89
Augusta St, E14 85 EB72
August End, Slou. (Geo.Grn.)
 SL3 74 AY72
Augustine Cl, Slou. (Colnbr.)
 SL3 93 BE83
Augustine Ct, Wal.Abb. EN9
 off Beaulieu Dr 15 EB33
Augustine Rd, W14 99 CX76
 Gravesend DA12 131 GJ87
 Harrow HA3 40 CB53
 Orpington BR5 146 EX97
Augustus Cl, Brent. TW8 97 CJ80
Augustus La, Orp. BR6 146 EU103
Augustus Rd, SW19 119 CY88
Augustus St, NW1 195 J1
Aultone Way, Cars. SM5 140 DF104
 Sutton SM1 140 DB103
Aulton Pl, SE11 101 DN78
Aurelia Gdns, Croy. CR0 141 DM99
Aurelia Rd, Croy. CR0 141 DL100
Auriel Av, Dag. RM10 89 FD65
Auriga Ms, N16 66 DR64
Auriol Cl, Wor.Pk. KT4
 off Auriol Pk Rd 138 CS104
Auriol Dr, Grnf. UB6 79 CD66
 Uxbridge UB10 76 BN65
Auriol Pk Rd, Wor.Pk. KT4 138 CS104
Auriol Rd, W14 99 CY77
Austell Gdns, NW7 42 CS48
Austen Cl, SE28 88 EV74
 Greenhithe DA9 129 FW85
 Loughton IG10 33 ER41
 Tilbury RM18
 off Coleridge Rd 111 GJ82
Austen Gdns, Dart. DA1 108 FM84
Austen Ho, NW6 82 DA69
Austen Rd, Erith DA8 107 FB80
 Harrow HA2 60 CB61
Austenway, Ger.Cr. (Chal.St.P.)
 SL9 56 AX55
Austenwood Cl, Ger.Cr. (Chal.St.P.)
 SL9 36 AX54
Austenwood La, Ger.Cr. (Chal.St.P.)
 SL9 36 AX54
Austin Av, Brom. BR2 144 EL99
Austin Cl, SE23 123 DZ87
 Coulsdon CR5 175 DP118
 Twickenham TW1 117 CJ85
Austin Ct, E6 off Kings Rd 86 EJ67
Austin Friars, EC2 197 L8
Austin Friars Pas, EC2 197 L8
Austin Friars Sq, EC2 197 L8
Austin Rd, SW11 100 DG81
 Gravesend (Nthflt.) DA11 131 GF88
 Hayes UB3 95 BT75
 Orpington BR5 146 EU100
Austin's La, Uxb. UB10 59 BR63
Austins Mead, Hem.H. (Bov.)
 HP3 5 BB28
Austin St, E2 197 P3
Austin Waye, Uxb. UB8 76 BJ67
Austral Cl, Sid. DA15 125 ET90
Austral Dr, Horn. RM11 72 FK59
Australia Rd, W12 81 CV73
 Slough SL1 92 AV75
Austral St, SE11 200 F8
Austyn Gdns, Surb. KT5 138 CP102
Autumn Cl, SW19 120 DC93
 Enfield EN1 30 DU39
Autumn Dr, Sutt. SM2 158 DB109
Autumn St, E3 85 EA67
Auxiliaries Way, Uxb. UB9 57 BF57
Avalon Cl, SW20 139 CY96
 W13 79 CG71
 Enfield EN2 29 DN40
 Orpington BR6 146 EX104
 Watford WD25 8 BY32
Avalon Rd, SW6 100 DB81
 W13 79 CG70
 Orpington BR6 146 EW103
Avard Gdns, Orp. BR6 163 EQ105
Avarn Rd, SW17 120 DF93
Avebury Ct, N1 off Poole St 84 DR67
Avebury Pk, Surb. KT6 137 CK101
Avebury Rd, E11
 off Southwest Rd 67 ED60
 SW19 139 CZ95
 Orpington BR6 145 ER104
Avebury St, N1 off Poole St 84 DR67
AVELEY, S.Ock. 91 FR73
Aveley Bypass, S.Ock. RM15 90 FQ73
Aveley Cl, Erith DA8 107 FF79
 South Ockendon (Aveley)
 RM15 91 FR74
Aveley Rd, Rom. RM1 71 FD56
 Upminster RM14 90 FP65
Aveline St, SE11 200 D10
Aveling Cl, Pur. CR8 159 DM113
Aveling Pk Rd, E17 47 EA54
Avelon Rd, Rain. RM13 89 FG67
 Romford RM5 51 FD51
Ave Maria La, EC4 196 G9
Avenell Rd, N5 65 DP62
Avening Rd, SW18
 off Brathway Rd 120 DA87
Avening Ter, SW18 120 DA86
Avenons Rd, E13 86 EG70
Avenue, The, E4 47 ED51
 E11 (Leytonstone) 68 EF61
 E11 (Wanstead) 68 EH58
 N3 44 DA54
 N8 65 DN55
 N10 45 DJ54
 N11 45 DH49
 N17 46 DS54
 NW6 81 CX67
 SE7 104 EJ80
 SE10 103 ED80
 SW4 120 DG85
 SW11 120 DE87
 SW18 120 DE87
 W4 98 CS76
 W13 79 CH73
 Addlestone (New Haw)
 KT15 152 BG110
 Barnet EN5 27 CY41
 Beckenham BR3 143 EB95
 Betchworth (Brock.) RH3 182 CN134
 Bexley DA5 126 EX87
 Brentwood CM13 53 FX51
 Bromley BR1 144 EK97
 Bushey WD23 24 BZ42
 Carshalton SM5 158 DG108
 Coulsdon CR5 175 DK115
 Croydon CR0 142 DS104
 Egham TW20 113 BB91
 Epsom KT17 157 CV108
 Esher (Clay.) KT10 155 CE107
 Gravesend DA11 131 GG88
 Greenhithe DA9 109 FV84
 Hampton TW12 116 BZ93
 Harrow HA3 41 CF53
 Hornchurch RM12 72 FJ61
 Hounslow TW3 116 CB85
 Hounslow (Cran.) TW5 95 BU81
 Isleworth TW7 97 CD79
 Keston BR2 144 EK104
 Leatherhead KT22 155 CF112
 Loughton IG10 32 EK44
 Northwood HA6 39 BQ51
 Orpington BR6 145 ET103
 Orpington (St.P.Cray) BR5 126 EV94
 Pinner HA5 60 BZ58
 Pinner (Hatch End) HA5 40 CA52
 Potters Bar EN6 11 CZ30
 Radlett WD7 9 CG33
 Richmond TW9 98 CM82
 Romford RM1 71 FD56
 Slough (Datchet) SL3 92 AV81
 Staines TW18 134 BH95
 Staines (Wrays.) TW19 92 AX83
 Sunbury-on-Thames
 TW16 135 BV95
 Surbiton KT5 138 CM100
 Sutton SM2 157 CZ109
 Sutton (Cheam) SM3 157 CW108
 Tadworth KT20 173 CV122
 Twickenham TW1 117 CJ85
 Uxbridge (Cowley) UB8 76 BK70
 Uxbridge (Ickhm.) UB10 58 BN63
 Waltham Abbey (Nazeing)
 EN9 16 EJ25
 Watford WD17 23 BU40
 Wembley HA9 62 CM61
 West Drayton UB7 94 BL76
 West Wickham BR4 143 EC101
 Westerham TN16 179 EP123
 Whyteleafe CR3 176 DU119
 Windsor (Old Wind.) SL4 112 AV85
 Woking (Chobham) GU24 150 AT109
 Worcester Park KT4 139 CT103
Avenue App, Kings L. WD4 6 BN30
Avenue Cl, N14 29 DJ44
 NW8 82 DE67
 Hounslow TW5
 off The Avenue 95 BU81
 Romford RM3 52 FM52
 Tadworth KT20 173 CV122
 West Drayton UB7 94 BK76
Avenue Ct, Tad. KT20
 off The Avenue 173 CV123
Avenue Cres, W3 98 CP75
 Hounslow TW5 95 BV80
Avenue Dr, Slou. SL3 75 AZ71
Avenue Elmers, Surb. KT6 138 CL99
Avenue Gdns, SE25 142 DU97
 SW14 98 CS83
Avenue Gdns, W3 98 CP75
 Hounslow TW5
 off The Avenue 95 BU80
 Teddington TW11 117 CF94
Avenue Gate, Loug. IG10 32 EJ44
Avenue Ind Est, E4 47 DZ51
 Romford RM3 52 FK54
Avenue Ms, N10 65 DH55
Avenue Pk Rd, SE27 121 DP89
Avenue Ri, Bushey WD23 24 CA43
Avenue Road (Tramlink) 143 DX96
Avenue Rd, E7 68 EH64
 N6 65 DJ59
 N12 44 DC49
 N14 45 DH45
 N15 66 DR57
 NW3 82 DD66
 NW8 82 DD66
 NW10 81 CT68
 SE20 142 DW95
 SE25 142 DU96
 SW16 141 DK96
 SW20 139 CV96
 W3 98 CP75
 Banstead SM7 174 DB115
 Beckenham BR3 142 DW95
 Belvedere DA17 107 FC77
 Bexleyheath DA7 106 EY83
 Brentford TW8 97 CJ78
 Brentwood CM14 54 FW49
 Caterham CR3 176 DR122
 Cobham KT11 170 BX116
 Epping (They.B.) CM16 33 ER36
 Epsom KT18 156 CR114
 Erith DA8 107 FC80
 Feltham TW13 115 BT90
 Hampton TW12 136 CB95
 Isleworth TW7 97 CF81
 Kingston upon Thames
 KT1 138 CL97
 New Malden KT3 138 CS98
 Pinner HA5 60 BY55
 Romford (Chad.Hth.) RM6 70 EV59
 Romford (Harold Wd.) RM3 52 FM52
 Sevenoaks TN13 191 FJ123
 Southall UB1 96 BZ75
 Staines TW18 113 BD92
 Sutton SM2 158 DA110
 Teddington TW11 117 CG94
 Wallington SM6 159 DJ108
 Westerham (Tats.) TN16 178 EL120
 Woodford Green IG8 48 EJ51
Avenue S, Surb. KT5 138 CM101
Avenue Ter, N.Mal. KT3
 off Kingston Rd 138 CQ97
 Watford WD19 24 BY44
Averil Gro, SW16 121 DP93
Averill St, W6 99 CX79
Avern Gdns, W.Mol. KT8 136 CB98
Avern Rd, W.Mol. KT8 136 CB99
Avery Fm Row, SW1 198 G9
Avery Gdns, Ilf. IG2 69 EM57
AVERY HILL, SE9 125 EQ86
★ Avery Hill Pk, SE9
 (Eltham) 125 EQ86
Avery Hill Rd, SE9 125 ER86
Avery Row, W1 195 H10
Avey La, Loug. IG10 32 EH39
 Waltham Abbey EN9 31 ED36
Aviary Cl, E16 86 EF71
Aviary Rd, Wok. GU22 168 BG116
Aviemore Cl, Beck. BR3 143 DZ99
Aviemore Way, Beck. BR3 143 DY99
Avignon Rd, SE4 103 DX83
Avington Ct, SE1
 off Old Kent Rd 102 DS77
Avington Gro, SE20 122 DW94
Avington Way, SE15
 off Daniel Gdns 102 DT80
Avion Cres, NW9 43 CU53
Avior Dr, Nthwd. HA6 39 BT49
Avis Gro, Croy. CR0 161 DY110
Avis Sq, E1 85 DX72
Avoca Rd, SW17 120 DG91
Avocet Ms, SE28 105 ER76
Avon Cl, Add. KT15 152 BG107
 Gravesend DA12 131 GK89
 Hayes UB4 78 BW70
 Sutton SM1 158 DC105
 Watford WD25 8 BW34
 Worcester Park KT4 139 CU103
Avon Ct, Grnf. UB6
 off Braund Av 78 CB70
Avondale Av, N12 44 DB50
 NW2 62 CS62
 Barnet EN4 44 DF46
 Esher KT10 137 CG104
 Staines TW18 113 BF94
 Worcester Park KT4 139 CT102
Avondale Cl, Loug. IG10 49 EM45
 Walton-on-Thames KT12
 off Pleasant Pl 154 BW106
Avondale Ct, E11 68 EE60
 E16 off Avondale Rd 86 EE71
 E18 48 EH53
Avondale Cres, Enf. EN3 31 DY41
 Ilford IG4 68 EK57
Avondale Dr, Hayes UB3 77 BU74
 Loughton IG10 49 EM45
Avondale Gdns, Houns. TW4 116 BZ85
Avondale Ms, Brom. BR1
 off Avondale Rd 124 EG93
Avondale Pk Gdns, W11 81 CY73
Avondale Pk Rd, W11 81 CY73
Avondale Pavement, SE1
 off Avondale Sq 102 DU78
Avondale Ri, SE15 102 DT83
Avondale Rd, E16 86 EE71
 E17 67 EA59
 N3 44 DC53
 N13 45 DN47
 N15 65 DP57
 SE9 124 EL89
 SW14 98 CR83
 SW19 120 DB92
 Ashford TW15 114 BK90
 Bromley BR1 124 EE93
Avondale Rd, Harrow HA3 61 CF55
 South Croydon CR2 160 DQ107
 Welling DA16 106 EW82
Avondale Sq, SE1 102 DU78
Avon Grn, S.Ock. RM15 91 FV72
Avonley Rd, SE14 102 DW80
Avonmead, Wok. GU21
 off Silversmiths Way 166 AW118
Avon Ms, Pnr. HA5 40 BZ53
Avonmore Gdns, W14
 off Avonmore Rd 99 CY77
Avonmore Pl, W14
 off Avonmore Rd 99 CY77
Avonmore Rd, W14 99 CZ77
Avonmouth Rd, Dart. DA1 128 FK85
Avonmouth St, SE1 201 H6
Avon Path, S.Croy. CR2 160 DQ107
Avon Pl, SE1 201 J5
Avon Rd, E17 67 ED55
 SE4 103 EA83
 Greenford UB6 78 CA70
 Sunbury-on-Thames
 TW16 115 BT94
 Upminster RM14 73 FR58
Avonstowe Cl, Orp. BR6 145 EQ104
Avontar Rd, S.Ock. RM15 91 FV70
Avon Way, E18 68 EG55
Avonwick Rd, Houns. TW3 96 CB82
Avril Way, E4 47 EC50
Avro Way, Wall. SM6 159 DL108
 Weybridge KT13 152 BL110
Awlfield Av, N17 46 DR53
Awliscombe Rd, Well. DA16 105 ET82
Axe St, Bark. IG11 87 EQ67
Axholme Av, Edg. HA8 42 CN53
Axis Pk, Slou. (Langley) SL3 93 BB78
Axminster Cres, Well. DA16 106 EW81
Axminster Rd, N7 65 DL62
Axtaine Rd, Orp. BR5 146 EX101
Axtane, Grav. (Sthflt.) DA13 130 FZ94
Axtane Cl, Dart. (Sutt.H.)
 DA4 148 FQ96
Axwood, Epsom KT18 172 CQ115
Aybrook St, W1 194 F7
Aycliffe Cl, Brom. BR1 145 EM98
Aycliffe Rd, W12 81 CT74
 Borehamwood WD6 26 CL39
Ayebridges Av, Egh. TW20 113 BC94
Aylands Cl, Wem. HA9
 off Preston Rd 62 CL61
Aylands Rd, Enf. EN3 30 DW36
Aylesbury Cl, E7
 off Atherton Rd 86 EF65
Aylesbury Ct, Sutt. SM1
 off Benhill Wd Rd 140 DC104
Aylesbury Est, SE17
 off Villa St 102 DR78
Aylesbury Rd, SE17 102 DR78
 Bromley BR2 144 EG97
Aylesbury St, EC1 196 F5
 NW10 62 CR62
Aylesford Av, Beck. BR3 143 DY99
Aylesford St, SW1 199 M10
Aylesham Cen, The, SE15 102 DU81
Aylesham Cl, NW7 43 CU52
Aylesham Rd, Orp. BR6 145 ET101
Ayles Rd, Hayes UB4 77 BV69
Aylestone Av, NW6 81 CX67
Aylesworth Spur, Wind.
 (Old Wind.) SL4 112 AV87
Aylett Rd, SE25 142 DV98
 Isleworth TW7 97 CE82
 Upminster RM14 72 FQ61
Ayley Cft, Enf. EN1 30 DU43
Ayliffe Cl, Kings.T. KT1
 off Cambridge Gdns 138 CN96
Aylmer Cl, Stan. HA7 41 CG49
Aylmer Dr, Stan. HA7 41 CG49
Aylmer Par, N2 64 DF57
Aylmer Rd, E11 68 EF60
 N2 64 DE57
 W12 99 CT75
 Dagenham RM8 70 EY62
Ayloffe Rd, Dag. RM9 88 EZ65
Ayloffs Cl, Horn. RM11 72 FL57
Ayloffs Wk, Horn. RM11 72 FK57
Aylsham Dr, Uxb. UB10 59 BR62
Aylsham La, Rom. RM3 52 FJ49
Aylton Est, SE16 202 G5
Aylward Rd, SE23 123 DX89
 SW20 139 CZ96
Aylwards Ri, Stan. HA7 41 CG49
Aylward St, E1 84 DW72
Aylwyn Est, SE1 201 P6
Aymer Cl, Stai. TW18 133 BE95
Aymer Dr, Stai. TW18 133 BE95
Aynhoe Rd, W14 99 CX77
Aynho St, Wat. WD18 23 BV43
Aynscombe Angle, Orp. BR6 146 EV101
Aynscombe La, SW14 98 CQ83
Aynscombe Path, SW14
 off Thames Bk 98 CQ82
Ayot Path, Borwd. WD6 26 CN37
Ayr Ct, W3 off Monks Dr 80 CN71
Ayres Cl, E13 86 EG69
Ayres Cres, NW10 80 CR66
Ayres St, SE1 201 J4
Ayr Grn, Rom. RM1 51 FE52
Ayron Rd, S.Ock. RM15 91 FV70
Ayrsome Rd, N16 66 DS62
Ayrton Rd, SW7
 off Wells Way 100 DD76
Ayr Way, Rom. RM1 51 FE52
Aysgarth Ct, Sutt. SM1
 off Sutton Common Rd 140 DB104
Aysgarth Rd, SE21 122 DS86
Aytoun Pl, SW9 101 DM82
Aytoun Rd, SW9 101 DM82
Azalea Cl, W7 79 CF74
 Ilford IG1 69 EP64
Azalea Ct, Wok. GU22 166 AX119
 Woodford Green IG8
 off The Bridle Path 48 EE52
Azalea Dr, Swan. BR8 147 FD98
Azalea Wk, Pnr. HA5 59 BV57
 Southall UB2
 off Navigator Dr 96 CC75
Azalea Way, Slou. (Geo.Grn.) SL3
 off Blinco La 74 AY72
Azania Ms, NW5
 off Cathcart St 83 DH65
Azenby Rd, SE15 102 DT82
Azile Everitt Ho, SE18
 off Vicarage Pk 105 EQ78
Azof St, SE10 205 J9

B

Baalbec Rd, N5 65 DP64
Babbacombe Cl, Chess. KT9 155 CK106
Babbacombe Gdns, Ilf. IG4 68 EL56
Babbacombe Rd, Brom. BR1 144 EG95
Baber Dr, Felt. TW14 116 BW86
Babington Ri, Wem. HA9 80 CN65
Babington Rd, NW4 63 CV56
 SW16 121 DK92
 Dagenham RM8 70 EW64
 Hornchurch RM12 71 FH60
Babmaes St, SW1 199 L1
Babylon La, Tad. (Lwr.Kgswd.)
 KT20 184 DA127
Bacchus Wk, N1 197 M1
Bachelor's La, Wok. GU23 168 BN124
Baches St, N1 197 L3
Back Ch La, E1 84 DU73
Back Grn, Walt. KT12 154 BW107
Back Hill, EC1 196 D5
Backhouse Pl, SE17 201 N9
Back La, N8 65 DL57
 NW3 off Heath St 64 DC63
 Bexley DA5 126 FA87
 Brentford TW8 97 CK79
 Chalfont St. Giles HP8 36 AU48
 Edgware HA8 42 CQ53
 Grays (N.Stfd.) RM16 91 FW74
 Purfleet RM19 109 FS76
 Richmond TW10 117 CJ90
 Rickmansworth (Chenies)
 WD3 21 BB38
 Romford RM6
 off St. Chad's Rd 70 EY59
 Sevenoaks (Godden Grn.)
 TN15 191 FN124
 Sevenoaks (Ide Hill) TN14 190 FC126
 Watford (Let.Hth.) WD25 25 CE39
Backley Gdns, SE25 142 DU100
Back Path, Red. RH1 186 DQ133
Back Rd, Sid. DA14 126 EU91
Bacon Gro, SE1 201 P7
Bacon La, NW9 62 CP56
 Edgware HA8 42 CN53
Bacon Link, Rom. RM5 51 FB51
Bacons Dr, Pot.B. (Cuffley)
 EN6 13 DL29
Bacons La, N6 64 DG60
Bacons Mead, Uxb. (Denh.)
 UB9 58 BG61
Bacon St, E1 84 DT70
 E2 84 DT70
Bacon Ter, Dag. RM8
 off Fitzstephen Rd 70 EV64
Bacton, NW5 64 DG64
Bacton St, E2 off Roman Rd 84 DW69
Badburgham Ct, Wal.Abb. EN9 16 EF33
Baddeley Cl, Enf. EN3
 off Government Row 31 EA38
Baddow Cl, Dag. RM10 88 FA67
 Woodford Green IG8 48 EK51
Baddow Wk, N1 84 DQ67
Baden Cl, Stai. TW18 114 BG94
Baden Pl, SE1 201 K4
Baden Powell Cl, Dag. RM9 88 EY67
 Surbiton KT6 138 CM103
Baden Powell Rd, Sev. TN13 190 FE121
Baden Rd, N8 65 DK56
 Ilford IG1 69 EP64
Bader Cl, Ken. CR8 176 DR115
Bader Wk, Grav. (Nthflt.)
 DA11 130 GE90
Bader Way, Rain. RM13 89 FG65
Badger Cl, Felt. TW13
 off Sycamore Cl 115 BU90
 Hounslow TW4 96 BW83
 Ilford IG2 69 EQ59
Badgers Cl, Ashf. TW15
 off Fordbridge Rd 114 BM92
 Borehamwood WD6
 off Kingsley Av 26 CM40
 Enfield EN2 29 DP41
 Harrow HA1 61 CD58
 Hayes UB3 77 BS73
 Woking GU21 166 AW118
Badgers Copse, Orp. BR6 145 ET103
 Worcester Park KT4 139 CT103
Badgers Cft, N20 43 CY46
 SE9 125 EN90
Badgers Hill, Vir.W. GU25 132 AW99
Badgers Hole, Croy. CR0 161 DX105
Badgers La, Warl. CR6 176 DW120
BADGERS MOUNT, Sev. 165 FB110
Badgers Mt, Grays (Orsett)
 RM16 111 GF75
Badgers Ri, Sev. (Bad.Mt.)
 TN14 164 FA110
Badgers Rd, Sev. (Bad.Mt.)
 TN14 165 FB110
Badgers Wk, N.Mal. KT3 138 CS96
 Purley CR8 159 DK111
 Rickmansworth (Chorl.)
 WD3 21 BF42
 Whyteleafe CR3 176 DT119
Badgers Wd, Cat. CR3 186 DQ125
Badingham Dr, Lthd. (Fetch.)
 KT22 171 CE123
Badlis Rd, E17 47 EA54
Badlow Cl, Erith DA8 107 FE80
Badminton Cl, Borwd. WD6 26 CN40
 Harrow HA1 61 CE56
 Northolt UB5 78 CA65
Badminton Ms, E16 205 N2
Badminton Rd, SW12 120 DG86

Badric Ct, SW11
off Yelverton Rd 100 DD82
Badsworth Rd, SE5 102 DQ80
Baffin Way, E14
off Prestons Rd 85 EC73
Bagley Cl, West Dr. UB7 94 BL75
Bagley's La, SW6 100 DB81
Bagleys Spring, Rom. RM6 70 EY56
Bagot Cl, Ashtd. KT21 172 CM116
Bagshot Ct, SE18
off Prince Imperial Rd 105 EN81
Bagshot Rd, Egh. (Eng.Grn.)
TW20 112 AW94
Enfield EN1 46 DT45
Bagshot St, SE17 102 DS78
Bahram Rd, Epsom KT19 156 CR110
Baildon St, SE8 103 DZ80
Bailey Cl, E4 47 EC49
N11 45 DK52
Purfleet RM19
off Gabion Av 109 FR77
Bailey Pl, SE26 123 DX93
Baillie Cl, Rain. RM13 89 FH70
Baillies Wk, W5
off Liverpool Rd 97 CK75
Bainbridge Cl, Rich. TW10
off Latchmere Cl 118 CL92
Bainbridge Rd, Dag. RM9 70 EZ63
Bainbridge St, WC1 195 N8
Baines Cl, S.Croy. CR2
off Brighton Rd 160 DQ106
Bainton Mead, Wok. GU21 166 AU117
Baird Av, Sthl. UB1 78 CB73
Baird Cl, E10 off Marconi Rd 67 EA60
NW9 62 CQ58
Bushey WD23
off Ashfield Av 24 CB44
Baird Gdns, SE19 122 DS91
Baird Rd, Enf. EN1 30 DV42
Baird St, EC1 197 J4
Bairstow Cl, Borwd. WD6 26 CL39
Baizdon Rd, SE3 104 EE82
Bakeham La, Egh. (Eng.Grn.)
TW20 112 AW94
Baker Boy La, Croy. CR0 161 DZ112
Baker Hill Cl, Grav. (Nthflt.)
DA11 131 GF91
Baker La, Mitch. CR4 140 DG96
Baker Pas, NW10 off Acton La 80 CS67
Baker Rd, NW10 80 CS67
SE18 104 EL80
Bakers Av, E17 67 EB58
Bakers Cl, Ken. CR8
off Park Rd 160 DQ114
Bakers Ct, SE25 142 DS97
Bakers End, SW20 139 CY96
Bakers Fld, N7
off Crayford Rd 65 DK63
Bakers Gdns, Cars. SM5 140 DE103
Bakers Hill, E5 66 DW60
Barnet EN5 28 DB40
Bakers La, N6 64 DF57
Epping CM16 17 ET30
Bakers Mead, Gdse. RH9 186 DW130
Baker's Ms, W1 194 F8
Bakers Ms, Orp. BR6 163 ET107
Bakers Pas, NW3 off Heath St 64 DC63
Baker's Rents, E2 197 P3
Bakers Rd, Uxb. UB8 76 BK66
Waltham Cross (Chsht.)
EN7 14 DV30
Bakers Row, E15 86 EE68
Baker's Row, EC1 196 D5
⊖ Baker Street 194 E5
Baker St, NW1 194 E5
W1 194 E6
Enfield EN1 30 DR41
Potters Bar EN6 27 CY35
Weybridge KT13 152 BN105
Bakers Wd, Uxb. (Denh.) UB9 57 BD60
Baker's Yd, EC1
off Baker's Row 83 DN70
Uxbridge UB8
off Bakers Rd 76 BK66
Bakery Cl, SW9 101 DM81
Bakery Path, Edg. HA8
off Station Rd 42 CP51
Bakery Pl, SW11
off Altenburg Gdns 100 DF84
Bakewell Way, N.Mal. KT3 138 CS96
Balaams La, N14 45 DK47
Balaam St, E13 86 EG69
Balaclava Rd, SE1 202 A9
Surbiton KT6 137 CJ101
Bala Grn, NW9
off Snowdon Dr 62 CS58
Balcaskie Rd, SE9 125 EM85
Balchen Rd, SE3 104 EK82
Balchier Rd, SE22 122 DV86
Balcombe Cl, Bexh. DA6 106 EX84
Balcombe St, NW1 194 D4
Balcon Ct, W5 off Boileau Rd 80 CM72
Balcon Way, Borwd. WD6 26 CQ39
Balcorne St, E9 84 DW66
Balder Ri, SE12 124 EH89
Balderton St, W1 194 G9
Baldocks Rd, Epp. (They.B.)
CM16 33 ES35
Baldock St, E3 85 EB68
Baldock Way, Borwd. WD6 26 CM39
Baldry Gdns, SW16 121 DL93
Baldwin Cres, SE5 102 DQ81
Baldwin Gdns, Houns. TW3
off Chamberlain Gdns 96 CC81
Baldwin's Gdns, EC1 196 D6
Baldwins Hill, Loug. IG10 33 EM40
Baldwins La, Rick. (Crox.Grn.)
WD3 22 BN42
Baldwin St, EC1 197 K3
Baldwin Ter, N1 84 DQ68
Baldwyn Gdns, W3 80 CR73
Baldwyns Pk, Bex. DA5 127 FD89
Baldwyns Rd, Bex. DA5 127 FD89
Bale Rd, E1 85 DY71
Balfern Gro, W4 98 CS78
Balfern St, SW11 100 DE81
Balfe St, N1 196 A1
Balfont Cl, S.Croy. CR2 160 DU113
Balfour Av, W7 79 CF74
Balfour Av, Wok. GU22 166 AY122
Balfour Business Cen, Sthl.
UB2 96 BX76
Balfour Gro, N20 44 DF48
Balfour Ho, W10
off St. Charles Sq 81 CX71
Balfour Ms, N9
off The Broadway 46 DU48
W1 198 G2
Balfour Pl, SW15 99 CV84
W1 198 G1
Balfour Rd, N5 66 DQ63
SE25 142 DU98
SW19 120 DB94
W3 80 CQ71
W13 97 CG75
Bromley BR2 144 EK99
Carshalton SM5 158 DF108
Grays RM17 110 GC77
Harrow HA1 61 CD57
Hounslow TW3 96 CB83
Ilford IG1 69 EP61
Southall UB2 96 BX76
Weybridge KT13 152 BN105
Balfour St, SE17 201 K8
Balfron Twr, E14
off St. Leonards Rd 85 EC72
Balgonie Rd, E4 47 ED46
Balgores Cres, Rom. RM2 71 FH55
Balgores La, Rom. RM2 71 FH55
Balgores Sq, Rom. RM2 71 FH56
Balgowan Cl, N.Mal. KT3 138 CS99
Balgowan Rd, Beck. BR3 143 DY97
Balgowan St, SE18 105 ET77
BALHAM, SW12 120 DF88
⇌ Balham 121 DH88
⊖ Balham 121 DH88
Balham Continental Mkt,
SW12 off Shipka Rd 121 DH88
Balham Gro, SW12 120 DG87
Balham High Rd, SW12 120 DG88
SW17 120 DG89
Balham Hill, SW12 121 DH87
Balham New Rd, SW12 121 DH87
Balham Pk Rd, SW12 120 DF88
Balham Rd, N9 46 DU47
Balham Sta Rd, SW12 121 DH88
Balkan Wk, E1 202 D1
Balladier Wk, E14 85 EB71
Ballamore Rd, Brom. BR1 124 EG90
Ballance Rd, E9 85 DX65
Ballands N, The, Lthd. KT22 171 CE122
Ballands S, The, Lthd. KT22 171 CE123
Ballantine St, SW18 100 DC84
Ballantyne Dr, Tad. (Kgswd.)
KT20 173 CZ121
Ballard Cl, Kings.T. KT2 118 CR94
Ballards Cl, Dag. RM10 89 FB67
Ballards Fm Rd, Croy. CR0 160 DU107
South Croydon CR2 160 DU107
Ballards Grn, Tad. KT20 173 CY119
Ballards La, N3 44 DA53
N12 44 DA53
Oxted RH8 188 EJ129
Ballards Ms, Edg. HA8 42 CN51
Ballards Ri, S.Croy. CR2 160 DU107
Ballards Rd, NW2 63 CU61
Dagenham RM10 89 FB67
Ballards Way, Croy. CR0 160 DV107
South Croydon CR2 160 DU107
Ballast Quay, SE10 204 G10
Ballater Cl, Wat. WD19 40 BW49
Ballater Rd, SW2 101 DL84
South Croydon CR2 160 DT106
Ballenger Ct, Wat. WD18 23 BV41
Ballina St, SE23 123 DX86
Ballingdon Rd, SW11 120 DG86
Ballinger Pt, E3
off Bromley High St 85 EB69
Balliol Av, E4 47 ED49
Balliol Rd, N17 46 DS53
W10 81 CW72
Welling DA16 106 EV82
Balloch Rd, SE6 123 ED88
Ballogie Av, NW10 62 CS63
Ballow Cl, SE5 off Harris St 102 DS80
Balls Pond Pl, N1
off Balls Pond Rd 84 DR65
Balls Pond Rd, N1 84 DR65
Balmain Cl, W5 79 CK74
Balmer Rd, E3 85 DZ68
Balmes Rd, N1 84 DR67
Balmoral Av, N11 44 DG50
Beckenham BR3 143 DY98
Balmoral Cl, SW15
off Westleigh Av 119 CX86
St. Albans (Park St.) AL2 8 CC28
Balmoral Ct, Wor.Pk. KT4 139 CV103
Balmoral Cres, W.Mol. KT8 136 CA97
Balmoral Dr, Borwd. WD6 26 CR43
Hayes UB4 77 BT71
Southall UB1 78 BZ70
Woking GU22 167 BC116
Balmoral Gdns, W13 97 CG76
Bexley DA5 126 EZ87
Ilford IG3 69 ET60
South Croydon CR2 160 DR110
Balmoral Gro, N7 83 DM65
Balmoral Ms, W12 99 CT75
Balmoral Rd, E7 68 EJ63
E10 67 EB61
NW2 81 CV65
Abbots Langley WD5 7 BU32
Brentwood CM15 54 FV44
Dartford (Sutt.H.) DA4 128 FP94
Enfield EN3 31 DX36
Harrow HA2 60 CA63
Hornchurch RM12 72 FK62
Kingston upon Thames
KT1 138 CM98
Romford RM2 71 FH56
Watford WD24 24 BW38
Worcester Park KT4 139 CV104
Balmoral Way, Sutt. SM2 158 DA110
Balmore Cl, E14 85 EC72
Balmore Cres, Barn. EN4 28 DG43
Balmore St, N19 65 DH61
Balmuir Gdns, SW15 99 CW84
Balnacraig Av, NW10 62 CS63
Balniel Gate, SW1 199 N10
Balquhain Cl, Ashtd. KT21 171 CK117
Baltic Cl, SW19 120 DD94
Baltic Ct, SE16 203 J4
Baltic Pl, N1
off Kingsland Rd 84 DS67
Baltic St E, EC1 197 H5
Baltic St W, EC1 197 H5
Baltimore Pl, Well. DA16 105 ET82
Balvaird Pl, SW1 101 DK78
Balvernie Gro, SW18 119 CZ87
Bamber Ho, Bark. IG11
off St. Margarets 87 EQ67
Bamborough Gdns, W12 99 CW75
Bamford Av, Wem. HA0 80 CM67
Bamford Ct, E15 off Clays La 67 EB64
Bamford Rd, Bark. IG11 87 EQ65
Bromley BR1 123 EC92
Bamford Way, Rom. RM5 51 FB50
Bampfylde Cl, Wall. SM6 141 DJ104
Bampton Dr, NW7 43 CU52
Bampton Rd, SE23 123 DX90
Romford RM3 52 FL53
Bampton Way, Wok. GU21 166 AU118
Banavie Gdns, Beck. BR3 143 EC95
Banbury Cl, Enf. EN2
off Holtwhites Hill 29 DP39
Banbury Ct, WC2 195 P10
Sutton SM2 158 DA108
Banbury Enterprise Cen, Croy.
CR0 off Factory La 141 DP103
Banbury Rd, E9 85 DX66
E17 47 DX52
Banbury St, SW11 100 DE82
Watford WD18 23 BU43
Banbury Vil, Grav. DA13 130 FZ94
Banbury Wk, Nthlt. UB5
off Brabazon Rd 78 CA68
Banchory Rd, SE3 104 EH80
Bancroft Av, N2 64 DE57
Buckhurst Hill IG9 48 EG47
Bancroft Cl, Ashf. TW15
off Feltham Hill Rd 114 BN92
Bancroft Ct, Nthlt. UB5 78 BW67
Reigate RH2 184 DB134
Bancroft Gdns, Har. HA3 40 CC53
Orpington BR6 145 ET102
Bancroft Rd, E1 84 DW69
Harrow HA3 40 CC54
Reigate RH2 184 DA134
Band La, Egh. TW20 113 AZ92
Bandon Cl, Uxb. UB10 76 BM67
Bandon Ri, Wall. SM6 159 DK106
Banfield Rd, SE15 102 DV84
Bangalore St, SW15 99 CW83
Bangor Cl, Nthlt. UB5 60 CB64
Bangors Cl, Iver SL0 75 BE72
Bangors Rd N, Iver SL0 75 BD67
Bangors Rd S, Iver SL0 75 BE71
Banim St, W6 99 CV76
Banister Rd, W10 81 CX69
⊖ Bank 197 K9
DLR Bank 197 K9
Bank, The, N6
off Cholmeley Pk 65 DH60
Bank Av, Mitch. CR4 140 DD96
Bank Ct, Dart. DA1
off High St 128 FL86
Bank End, SE1 201 J2
Bankfoot, Grays (Bad.Dene)
RM17 110 FZ77
Bankfoot Rd, Brom. BR1 124 EE91
Bankhurst Rd, SE6 123 DZ87
Bank La, SW15 118 CS85
Kingston upon Thames
KT2 118 CL94
Bank Ms, Sutt. SM1
off Sutton Ct Rd 158 DC107
★ Bank of England, EC2 197 K9
★ Bank of England Mus,
EC2 197 L9
Bank Pl, Brwd. CM14
off High St 54 FW47
Banksian Wk, Islw. TW7 97 CE81
Banksia Rd, N18 46 DW50
Bankside, SE1 201 H1
Enfield EN2 29 DP39
Gravesend (Nthflt.) DA11 130 GC86
Sevenoaks (Dunt.Grn.)
TN13 190 FE121
South Croydon CR2 160 DT107
Southall UB1 78 BX74
Woking GU21
off Wyndham Rd 166 AV118
Bankside Av, Nthlt. UB5
off Townson Av 77 BU68
Bankside Cl, Bex. DA5 127 FD91
Carshalton SM5 158 DE107
Isleworth TW7 97 CF84
Westerham (Bigg.H.) TN16 178 EJ118
Bankside Dr, T.Ditt. KT7 137 CH102
★ Bankside Gall, SE1
off Hopton St 200 G1
Bankside Rd, Ilf. IG1 69 EQ64
Bankside Way, SE19
off Lunham Rd 122 DS93
Banks La, Bexh. DA6 106 EZ84
Epping CM16 18 EY32
Bank's La, Lthd. KT24 169 BV122
Banks Rd, Borwd. WD6 26 CQ40
Bank St, E14 204 A3
Gravesend DA12 131 GH86
Sevenoaks TN13 191 FH125
Banks Way, E12
off Grantham Rd 69 EN63
Bankton Rd, SW2 101 DN84
Bankwell Rd, SE13 104 EE84
Bann Cl, S.Ock. RM15 91 FV73
Banner Cl, Purf. RM19
off Brimfield Rd 109 FR77
Bannerman Ho, SW8 101 DM79
Banner St, EC1 197 J5
Banning St, SE10 104 EE78
Bannister Cl, SW2
off Ewen Cres 121 DN88
Bannister Cl, Grnf. UB6 61 CD64
Slough SL3 92 AY75
Bannister Dr, Brwd. CM13 55 GC44
Bannister Gdns, Orp. BR5
off Main Rd 146 EW97
Bannister Ho, E9
off Homerton High St 67 DX64
Bannockburn Rd, SE18 105 ES77
★ Banqueting Ho, SW1 199 P3
BANSTEAD 174 DB115
⇌ Banstead 157 CY114
Banstead Gdns, N9 46 DS48
Banstead Pl, Bans. SM7 174 DC116
Banstead Rd, Bans. SM7 157 CX112
Carshalton SM5 158 DE107
Caterham CR3 176 DR121
Epsom KT17 157 CV110
Purley CR8 159 DN111
Banstead Rd S, Sutt. SM2 158 DD110
Banstead St, SE15 102 DW83
Banstead Way, Wall. SM6 159 DL106
Banstock Rd, Edg. HA8 42 CP51
Banting Dr, N21 29 DM43
Banton Cl, Enf. EN1
off Central Av 30 DV40
Bantry St, SE5 102 DR80
Banwell Rd, Bex. DA5
off Woodside La 126 EX86
Banyard Rd, SE16 202 E7
Banyards, Horn. RM11 72 FL56
Bapchild Pl, Orp. BR5 146 EW98
Baptist Gdns, NW5
off Queen's Cres 82 DG65
Barandon Wk, W11 81 CX73
Barbara Brosnan Ct, NW8
off Grove End Rd 82 DD68
Barbara Cl, Shep. TW17 135 BP99
Barbara Hucklesby Cl, N22
off The Sandlings 45 DP54
Barbauld Rd, N16 66 DS62
Barbel Cl, Wal.Cr. EN8 15 EA34
Barber Cl, N21 45 DN45
Barberry Cl, Rom. RM3 52 FJ52
Barber's All, E13 86 EH69
Barbers Rd, E15 85 EB68
BARBICAN, EC2 197 H7
⇌ Barbican 196 G6
⊖ Barbican 196 G6
Barbican, The, EC2 197 H6
★ Barbican Arts & Conf Cen,
EC2 197 J6
Barbican Rd, Grnf. UB6 78 CB72
Barb Ms, W6 99 CW76
Barbon Cl, WC1 196 B6
Barbot Cl, N9 46 DU48
Barchard St, SW18 120 DB85
Barchester Cl, W7 79 CF74
Uxbridge UB8 76 BJ70
Barchester Rd, Har. HA3 41 CD54
Slough SL3 93 AZ75
Barchester St, E14 85 EB71
Barclay Cl, SW6 100 DA80
Leatherhead (Fetch.) KT22 170 CB123
Watford WD18 23 BU44
Barclay Oval, Wdf.Grn. IG8 48 EG49
Barclay Path, E17 67 EC57
Barclay Rd, E11 68 EE60
E13 86 EJ70
E17 67 EC57
N18 46 DR51
SW6 100 DA80
Croydon CR0 142 DR104
Barclay Way, SE22
off Lordship La 122 DU87
Grays (W.Thur.) RM20 109 FT78
Barcombe Av, SW2 121 DL89
Barcombe Cl, Orp. BR5 145 ET97
Barden Cl, Uxb. (Hare.) UB9 38 BJ52
Barden St, SE18 105 ES80
Bardeswell Cl, Brwd. CM14 54 FW47
Bardfield Av, Rom. RM6 70 EX55
Bardney Rd, Mord. SM4 140 DB98
Bardolph Av, Croy. CR0 161 DZ109
Bardolph Rd, N7 65 DL63
Richmond TW9
off St. Georges Rd 98 CM83
Bardon Wk, Wok. GU21
off Bampton Way 166 AV117
Bard Rd, W10 81 CX73
Bardsey Pl, E1
off Mile End Rd 84 DW71
Bardsey Wk, N1
off Clephane Rd 84 DQ65
Bardsley Cl, Croy. CR0 142 DT104
Bardsley La, SE10 103 EC79
Barfett St, W10 81 CZ70
Barfield, Dart. (Sutt.H.) DA4 148 FP95
Barfield Av, N20 44 DE47
Barfield Rd, E11 68 EF60
Bromley BR1 145 EN97
Barfields, Loug. IG10 33 EN42
Redhill (Bletch.) RH1 185 DP133
Barfields Gdns, Loug. IG10
off Barfields 33 EN42
Barfields Path, Loug. IG10 33 EN42
Barford Cl, NW4 43 CU53
Barford St, N1 83 DN67
Barforth Rd, SE15 102 DV83
Barfreston Way, SE20 142 DV95
Bargate Cl, SE18 105 ET78
New Malden KT3 139 CU100
Barge Ho Rd, E16 87 EP74
Barge Ho St, SE1 200 E2
Bargery Rd, SE6 123 EB88
Barge Wk, E.Mol. KT8 137 CK96
Kingston upon Thames
KT1 137 CK95
Walton-on-Thames KT12 136 CC96
Bargrove Cl, SE20 122 DU94
Bargrove Cres, SE6
off Elm La 123 DZ89
Barham Av, Borwd. (Elstree)
WD6 26 CM41
Barham Cl, Brom. BR2 144 EL102
Chislehurst BR7 125 EP92
Barham Cl, Grav. DA12 131 GM88
Romford RM7 51 FB54
Wembley HA0 79 CH65
Weybridge KT13 153 BQ105
Barham Rd, SW20 119 CU94
Chislehurst BR7 125 EP92
Dartford DA1 128 FN87
South Croydon CR2 160 DQ106
Baring Cl, SE12 124 EG89
Baring Rd, SE12 124 EG87
Barnet EN4 28 DD41
Croydon CR0 142 DU102
Baring St, N1 84 DR67
Barkantine Shop Par, The, E14
off The Quarterdeck 103 EA75
Bark Burr Rd, Grays RM16 110 FZ75
Barker Cl, N.Mal. KT3 138 CP98
Northwood HA6 39 BT52
Barker Dr, NW1 83 DJ66
Barker Ms, SW4 101 DH84
Barker Rd, Cher. KT16 133 BE101
Barker St, SW10 100 DC79
Barker Wk, SW16 121 DK90
Barker Way, SE22
off Dulwich Common 122 DU88
Barkham Rd, N17 46 DR52
Barkham Ter, SE1 200 E6
Bark Hart Rd, Orp. BR6 146 EV102
BARKING 87 EP67
⇌ Barking 87 EQ66
⊖ Barking 87 EQ66
Barking Ind Pk, Bark. IG11 87 ET67
Barking Rd, E6 86 EK68
E13 86 EH70
E16 86 EF71
BARKINGSIDE, Ilf. 69 EP55
⊖ Barkingside 69 ER56
Bark Pl, W2 82 DB73
Barkston Gdns, SW5 100 DB77
Barkston Path, Borwd. WD6 26 CN37
Barkwood Cl, Rom. RM7 71 FC57
Barkworth Rd, SE16 102 DV78
Barlborough St, SE14 102 DW80
Barlby Gdns, W10 81 CX70
Barlby Rd, W10 81 CX71
Barlee Cres, Uxb. UB8 76 BJ71
Barle Gdns, S.Ock. RM15 91 FV72
Barley Brow, Wat. WD25
off High Elms La 8 BW31
Barley Cl, Bushey WD23 24 CB43
Barleycorn Way, E14 85 DZ73
Hornchurch RM11 72 FM58
Barleyfields Cl, Rom. RM6 70 EV59
Barley La, Ilf. IG3 70 EU60
Romford RM6 70 EV58
Barley Mow Ct, Bet. RH3 182 CQ134
Barley Mow Pas, EC1 196 G7
W4 98 CR78
Barley Mow Rd, Egh. (Eng.Grn.)
TW20 112 AW92
Barley Mow Way, Shep.
TW17 134 BN98
Barley Shotts Business Pk, W10
off St. Ervans Rd 81 CZ71
Barlow Cl, Wall. SM6 159 DL108
Barlow Dr, SE18 104 EL81
Barlow Pl, W1 199 J1
Barlow Rd, NW6 81 CZ65
W3 80 CP74
Hampton TW12 116 CA94
Barlow St, SE17 201 L9
Barlow Way, Rain. RM13 89 FD71
Barmeston Rd, SE6 123 EB89
Barmor Cl, Har. HA2 40 CB54
Barmouth Av, Grnf. UB6 79 CF68
Barmouth Rd, SW18 120 DC86
Croydon CR0 143 DX103
Barnabas Ct, N21
off Cheyne Wk 29 DN43
Barnabas Rd, E9 67 DX64
Barnaby Cl, Har. HA2 60 CC61
Barnaby Pl, SW7 100 DD77
Barnaby Way, Chig. IG7 49 EP48
Barnacre Cl, Uxb. UB8
off New Peachey La 76 BK72
Barnacres Rd, Hem.H. HP3 6 BM25
Barnard Cl, SE18 105 EN77
Chislehurst BR7 145 ER95
Sunbury-on-Thames TW16
off Oak Gro 115 BV94
Wallington SM6 159 DK108
Barnard Ct, Wok. GU21
off Raglan Rd 166 AS118
Barnard Gdns, Hayes UB4 77 BV70
New Malden KT3 139 CU98
Barnard Gro, E15
off Vicarage La 86 EF66
Barnard Hill, N10 44 DG54
Barnard Ms, SW11 100 DE84
Barnardo Dr, Ilf. IG6 69 EQ56
Barnardo Gdns, E1
off Devonport St 85 DX73
Barnardo St, E1
off Devonport St 85 DX72
Barnardos Village, Ilf. IG6 69 EQ55
Barnard Rd, SW11 100 DE84
Enfield EN1 30 DV40
Mitcham CR4 140 DG97
Warlingham CR6 177 EB119
Barnard's Inn, EC1 196 E8
Barnards Pl, S.Croy. CR2 159 DP109
Barnato Cl, W.Byf. KT14
off Viscount Gdns 152 BL112
Barnby Sq, E15 off Barnby St 86 EE67
Barnby St, E15 86 EE67
NW1 195 L1
Barn Cl, Ashf. TW15 115 BP92
Banstead SM7 174 DD115
Epsom KT18 172 CQ115
Northolt UB5 78 BW68
Radlett WD7 25 CG35
Barn Cres, Pur. CR8 160 DR113
Stanmore HA7 41 CJ51
Barncroft Cl, Loug. IG10 33 EN43

★ Place of interest ⇌ Railway station ⊖ London Underground station DLR Docklands Light Railway station Tramlink station H Hospital

Bar - Bay

Barncroft Cl, Uxb. UB8 ... 77 BP71
Barncroft Grn, Loug. IG10 ... 33 EN43
Barncroft Rd, Loug. IG10 ... 33 EN43
BARNEHURST, Bexh. ... 107 FD83
⇌ **Barnehurst** ... 107 FC82
Barnehurst Av, Bexh. DA7 ... 107 FC81
Erith DA8 ... 107 FC81
Barnehurst Cl, Erith DA8 ... 107 FC81
Barnehurst Rd, Bexh. DA7 ... 107 FC82
Barn Elms Pk, SW15 ... 99 CW82
Barn End Dr, Dart. DA2 ... 128 FJ90
Barn End La, Dart. DA2 ... 128 FJ92
BARNES, SW13 ... 99 CU82
⇌ **Barnes** ... 99 CU83
Barnes All, Hmptn. TW12 *off Hampton Ct Rd* ... 136 CC96
Barnes Av, SW13 ... 99 CU80
Southall UB2 ... 96 BZ77
⇌ **Barnes Bridge** ... 98 CS82
Barnes Br, SW13 ... 98 CS82
W4 ... 98 CS82
Barnesbury Ho, SW4 ... 121 DK85
Barnes Cl, E12 ... 68 EK63
★ **Barnes Common**, SW13 ... 99 CU83
Barnes Ct, E16 *off Ridgwell Rd* ... 86 EJ71
Woodford Green IG8 ... 48 EK50
BARNES CRAY, Dart. ... 107 FH84
Barnes Cray Cotts, Dart. DA1 *off Maiden La* ... 127 FG85
Barnes Cray Rd, Dart. DA1 ... 107 FG84
Barnesdale Cres, Orp. BR5 ... 146 EU100
Barnes End, N.Mal. KT3 ... 139 CU99
Barnes High St, SW13 ... 99 CT82
H **Barnes Hosp**, SW14 ... 98 CS83
Barnes Ho, Bark. IG11 *off St. Marys* ... 87 ER67
Barnes La, Kings L. WD4 ... 6 BH27
Barnes Pikle, W5 ... 79 CK73
Barnes Ri, Kings L. WD4 ... 6 BM27
Barnes Rd, N18 ... 46 DW49
Ilford IG1 ... 69 EQ64
Barnes St, E14 ... 85 DY72
Barnes Ter, SE8 ... 103 DZ78
Barnes Wallis Dr, Wey. KT13 ... 152 BL111
Barnes Way, Iver SL0 ... 75 BF73
BARNET ... 27 CZ41
Barnet Bypass, Barn. EN5 ... 26 CS41
Barnet Dr, Brom. BR2 ... 144 EL103
BARNET GATE, Barn. ... 27 CT44
Barnet Gate La, Barn. EN5 ... 27 CT44
H **Barnet Gen Hosp**, Barn. EN5 ... 27 CX42
Barnet Gro, E2 ... 84 DU69
Barnet Hill, Barn. EN5 ... 28 DA42
Barnet Ho, N20 ... 44 DC47
Barnet La, N20 ... 43 CZ46
Barnet EN5 ... 27 CZ44
Borehamwood WD6 ... 25 CK44
★ **Barnet Mus**, Barn. EN5 *off Wood St* ... 27 CY42
Barnet Rd, Barn. EN5 ... 27 CV43
Potters Bar EN6 ... 28 DA35
St. Albans (Lon.Col.) AL2 ... 10 CL27
Barnett Cl, Erith DA8 ... 107 FF82
Leatherhead KT22 ... 171 CH119
Barnet Trd Est, Barn. EN5 ... 27 CZ41
Barnetts Shaw, Oxt. RH8 ... 187 ED127
Barnett St, E1 *off Cannon St Rd* ... 84 DV72
Barnett Wd La, Ashtd. KT21 ... 171 CJ119
Leatherhead KT22 ... 171 CH120
Barnet Way, NW7 ... 42 CR45
Barnet Wd Rd, Brom. BR2 ... 144 EJ103
Barney Cl, SE7 ... 104 EJ78
Barnfield, Bans. SM7 ... 158 DB114
Epping CM16 ... 18 EU28
Gravesend DA11 ... 131 GG89
Iver SL0 ... 75 BE72
New Malden KT3 ... 138 CS100
Barnfield Av, Croy. CR0 ... 142 DW103
Kingston upon Thames KT2 ... 118 CL92
Mitcham CR4 ... 141 DH98
Barnfield Cl, N4 *off Crouch Hill* ... 65 DL59
SW17 ... 120 DC90
Coulsdon CR5 ... 176 DQ119
Greenhithe DA9 ... 129 FT86
Swanley BR8 ... 147 FC101
Barnfield Gdns, SE18 *off Plumstead Common Rd* ... 105 EP79
Kingston upon Thames KT2 ... 118 CL91
Barnfield Pl, E14 ... 204 A9
Barnfield Rd, SE18 ... 105 EP79
W5 ... 79 CJ70
Belvedere DA17 ... 106 EZ79
Edgware HA8 ... 42 CQ53
Orpington BR5 ... 146 EX97
Sevenoaks TN13 ... 190 FD123
South Croydon CR2 ... 160 DS109
Westerham (Tats.) TN16 ... 178 EK120
Barnfield Way, Oxt. RH8 ... 188 EG133
Barnfield Wd Cl, Beck. BR3 ... 143 ED100
Barnfield Wd Rd, Beck. BR3 ... 143 ED100
Barnham Dr, SE28 ... 87 ET74
Barnham Rd, Grnf. UB6 ... 78 CC69
Barnham St, SE1 ... 201 N4
Barnhill, Pnr. HA5 ... 60 BW57
Barn Hill, Wem. HA9 ... 62 CP61
Barnhill Av, Brom. BR2 ... 144 EF99
Barnhill La, Hayes UB4 ... 77 BV69
Barnhill Rd, Hayes UB4 ... 77 BV70
Wembley HA9 ... 62 CQ62
Barnhurst Path, Wat. WD19 ... 40 BW50
Barningham Way, NW9 ... 62 CR58
Barn Lea, Rick. (Mill End) WD3 ... 38 BG46
Barnlea Cl, Felt. TW13 ... 116 BY89
Barn Mead, Epp. (They.B.) CM16 ... 33 ES36
Ongar CM5 ... 19 FE29
Barnmead, Wok. (Chobham) GU24 ... 150 AT110
Barnmead Gdns, Dag. RM9 ... 70 EZ64
Barn Meadow, Epp. CM16 *off Upland Rd* ... 17 ET25
Barn Meadow La, Lthd. (Bkhm.) KT23 ... 170 BZ124
Barnmead Rd, Beck. BR3 ... 143 DY95
Dagenham RM9 ... 70 EZ64
Barn Ms, Har. HA2 ... 60 CA62
Barnock Cl, Dart. DA1 *off Lower Sta Rd* ... 127 FE86
Barn Ri, Wem. HA9 ... 62 CN60
BARNSBURY, N1 ... 83 DM66
Barnsbury Cl, N.Mal. KT3 ... 138 CQ98
Barnsbury Cres, Surb. KT5 ... 138 CQ102
Barnsbury Est, N1 *off Barnsbury Rd* ... 83 DN67
Barnsbury Gro, N7 ... 83 DM66
Barnsbury La, Surb. KT5 ... 138 CP103
Barnsbury Pk, N1 ... 83 DN66
Barnsbury Rd, N1 ... 83 DN68
Barnsbury Sq, N1 ... 83 DN66
Barnsbury St, N1 ... 83 DN66
Barnsbury Ter, N1 ... 83 DM66
Barnscroft, SW20 ... 139 CV97
Barnsdale Av, E14 ... 204 A8
Barnsdale Cl, Borwd. WD6 ... 26 CM39
Barnsdale Rd, W9 ... 81 CZ70
Barnsfield Pl, Uxb. UB8 ... 76 BJ66
Barnsley Rd, Rom. RM3 ... 52 FM52
Barnsley St, E1 ... 84 DV70
Barnstaple Path, Rom. RM3 ... 52 FJ50
Barnstaple Rd, Rom. RM3 ... 52 FJ50
Ruislip HA4 ... 60 BW62
Barnston Wk, N1 *off Popham St* ... 84 DQ67
Barnston Way, Brwd. CM13 ... 55 GC43
Barn St, N16 *off Stoke Newington Ch St* ... 66 DS62
Barnsway, Kings L. WD4 ... 6 BL28
Barnway, Egh. (Eng.Grn.) TW20 ... 112 AW92
Barn Way, Wem. HA9 ... 62 CN60
Barnwell Rd, SW2 ... 121 DN85
Dartford DA1 ... 108 FM83
Barnwood Cl, W9 ... 82 DB70
Ruislip HA4 *off Lysander Rd* ... 59 BR61
Barnyard, The, Tad. KT20 ... 173 CU124
Baron Cl, N11 *off Balmoral Av* ... 44 DG50
Sutton SM2 ... 158 DB110
Baroness Rd, E2 *off Diss St* ... 84 DT69
Baronet Gro, N17 *off St. Paul's Rd* ... 46 DU53
Baronet Rd, N17 ... 46 DU53
Baron Gdns, Ilf. IG6 ... 69 EQ55
Baron Gro, Mitch. CR4 ... 140 DE98
Baron Rd, Dag. RM8 ... 70 EX60
Barons, The, Twick. TW1 ... 117 CH86
⊖ **Barons Court** ... 99 CY78
Barons Ct, Wall. SM6 *off Whelan Way* ... 141 DK104
Barons Ct Rd, W14 ... 99 CY78
Baronsfield Rd, Twick. TW1 ... 117 CH86
Barons Gate, Barn. EN4 ... 28 DE44
Barons Hurst, Epsom KT18 ... 172 CQ116
Barons Keep, W14 ... 99 CY78
Barons Mead, Har. HA1 ... 61 CE56
Baronsmead Rd, SW13 ... 99 CU81
Baronsmede, W5 ... 98 CM75
Baronsmere Rd, N2 ... 64 DE56
Barons Pl, SE1 ... 200 E5
Baron St, N1 ... 83 DN68
Barons Wk, Croy. CR0 ... 143 DY100
Barons Way, Egh. TW20 ... 113 BD93
Baron Wk, E16 ... 86 EF71
Mitcham CR4 ... 140 DE98
Barque Ms, SE8 *off Watergate St* ... 103 EA79
Barrack Path, Wok. GU21 ... 166 AT118
Barrack Rd, Houns. TW4 ... 96 BX84
Barrack Row, Grav. DA11 ... 131 GH86
Barracks, The, Add. KT15 ... 134 BH104
Barracks La, Barn. EN5 *off High St* ... 27 CY41
Barra Hall Circ, Hayes UB3 ... 77 BS72
Barra Hall Rd, Hayes UB3 ... 77 BS73
Barras Cl, Enf. EN3 *off Government Row* ... 31 EA38
Barratt Av, N22 ... 45 DM54
Barratt Ind Pk, Sthl. UB1 ... 96 CA75
Barratt Way, Har. HA3 *off Tudor Rd* ... 61 CD55
Barrenger Rd, N10 ... 44 DF53
Barrens Brae, Wok. GU22 ... 167 BA118
Barrens Cl, Wok. GU22 ... 167 BA118
Barrens Pk, Wok. GU22 ... 167 BA118
Barrett Cl, Rom. RM3 ... 51 FH52
Barrett Rd, E17 ... 67 EC56
Leatherhead (Fetch.) KT22 ... 170 CC124
Barretts Grn Rd, NW10 ... 80 CQ68
Barretts Gro, N16 ... 66 DS64
Barretts Rd, Sev. (Dunt.Grn.) TN13 ... 181 FD120
Barrett St, W1 ... 194 G9
Barrhill Rd, SW2 ... 121 DL89
Barricane, Wok. GU21 ... 166 AV119
Barrie Cl, Couls. CR5 ... 175 DJ115
Barriedale, SE14 ... 103 DY81
Barrie Est, W2 *off Craven Ter* ... 82 DD73
Barrie Ho, W3 ... 98 CQ75
Barrier App, SE7 ... 104 EK76
Barrier Pt Rd, E16 ... 86 EJ74
Barringer Sq, SW17 ... 120 DG91
Barrington Cl, NW5 ... 64 DG64
Ilford IG5 ... 49 EM53
Loughton IG10 *off Barrington Rd* ... 33 EQ42
Barrington Ct, Brwd. CM13 ... 55 GC44
Barrington Dr, Uxb. (Hare.) UB9 ... 38 BG52
Barrington Grn, Loug. IG10 ... 33 EQ42
Barrington Lo, Wey. KT13 ... 153 BQ106
Barrington Pk Gdns, Ch.St.G. HP8 ... 36 AX46
Barrington Rd, E12 ... 87 EN65
N8 ... 65 DK57
SW9 ... 101 DP83
Bexleyheath DA7 ... 106 EX82
Loughton IG10 ... 33 EQ41
Purley CR8 ... 159 DJ112
Sutton SM3 ... 140 DA102
Barrington Vil, SE18 ... 105 EN81
Barrow Av, Cars. SM5 ... 158 DF108
Barrow Cl, N21 ... 45 DP48
Barrowdene Cl, Pnr. HA5 *off Paines La* ... 40 BY54
Barrowell Grn, N21 ... 45 DP47
Barrowfield Cl, N9 ... 46 DV48
Barrowgate Rd, W4 ... 98 CQ78
Barrow Grn Rd, Oxt. RH8 ... 187 EC128
Barrow Hedges Cl, Cars. SM5 ... 158 DE108
Barrow Hedges Way, Cars. SM5 ... 158 DE108
Barrow Hill, Wor.Pk. KT4 ... 138 CS103
Barrow Hill Cl, Wor.Pk. KT4 *off Barrow Hill* ... 138 CS103
Barrow Hill Est, NW8 *off Barrow Hill Rd* ... 82 DE68
Barrow Hill Rd, NW8 ... 194 B1
Barrow La, Wal.Cr. (Chsht.) EN7 ... 14 DT30
Barrow Pt Av, Pnr. HA5 ... 40 BY54
Barrow Pt La, Pnr. HA5 ... 40 BY54
Barrow Rd, SW16 ... 121 DK93
Croydon CR0 ... 159 DN106
Barrowsfield, S.Croy. CR2 ... 160 DT112
Barrow Wk, Brent. TW8 *off Glenhurst Rd* ... 97 CJ78
Barr Rd, Grav. DA12 ... 131 GM89
Potters Bar EN6 ... 12 DC33
Barrs Rd, NW10 ... 80 CR66
Barry Av, N15 *off Craven Pk Rd* ... 66 DT58
Bexleyheath DA7 ... 106 EY80
Barry Cl, Grays RM16 ... 111 GG75
Orpington BR6 ... 145 ES104
St. Albans AL2 ... 8 CB25
Barry Rd, E6 ... 86 EL72
NW10 ... 80 CQ66
SE22 ... 122 DU86
Barset Rd, SE15 ... 102 DW83
Barson Cl, SE20 ... 122 DW94
Barston Rd, SE27 ... 122 DQ90
Barstow Cres, SW2 ... 121 DM88
Barter St, WC1 ... 196 A7
Barters Wk, Pnr. HA5 *off High St* ... 60 BY55
Bartholomew Cl, EC1 ... 197 H7
SW18 ... 100 DC84
Bartholomew Dr, Rom. (Harold Wd.) RM3 ... 52 FK54
Bartholomew La, EC2 ... 197 L9
Bartholomew Pl, EC1 ... 197 H7
Bartholomew Rd, NW5 ... 83 DJ65
Bartholomew Sq, E1 *off Coventry Rd* ... 84 DV70
EC1 ... 197 J4
Bartholomew St, SE1 ... 201 K7
Bartholomew Vil, NW5 ... 83 DJ65
Bartholomew Way, Swan. BR8 ... 147 FE97
Barth Rd, SE18 ... 105 ES77
Bartle Av, E6 ... 86 EL68
Bartle Rd, W11 ... 81 CY72
Bartlett Cl, E14 ... 85 EA72
Bartlett Ct, EC4 ... 196 E8
Bartlett Rd, Grav. DA11 ... 131 GG88
Westerham TN16 ... 189 EQ126
Bartletts Pas, EC4 ... 196 E8
Bartlett St, S.Croy. CR2 ... 160 DR106
Bartlow Gdns, Rom. RM5 ... 51 FD53
Barton, The, Cob. KT11 ... 154 BX112
Barton Av, Rom. RM7 ... 71 FB60
Barton Cl, E6 ... 87 EM72
E9 *off Churchill Wk* ... 66 DW64
NW4 ... 63 CU56
SE15 *off Kirkwood Rd* ... 102 DV83
Addlestone KT15 ... 152 BG107
Bexleyheath DA6 ... 126 EY85
Chigwell IG7 ... 49 EQ47
Shepperton TW17 ... 135 BP100
Barton Grn, N.Mal. KT3 ... 138 CR96
Barton Meadows, Ilf. IG6 ... 69 EQ56
Barton Rd, W14 ... 99 CY78
Dartford (Sutt.H.) DA4 ... 148 FP95
Hornchurch RM12 ... 71 FG60
Sidcup DA14 ... 126 EY93
Slough SL3 ... 93 AZ75
Bartons, The, Borwd. (Elstree) WD6 ... 25 CK44
Barton St, SW1 ... 199 P6
Bartonway, NW8 *off Queen's Ter* ... 82 DD68
Barton Way, Borwd. WD6 ... 26 CN40
Rickmansworth (Crox.Grn.) WD3 ... 23 BP43
Bartram Cl, Uxb. UB8 *off Lees Rd* ... 77 BP70
Bartram Rd, SE4 ... 123 DY85
Bartrams La, Barn. EN4 ... 28 DC38
Bartrop Cl, Wal.Cr. EN7 *off Poppy Wk* ... 14 DR28
Barts Cl, Beck. BR3 ... 143 EA99
Barville Cl, SE4 *off St. Norbert Rd* ... 103 DY84
Barwell Business Pk, Chess. KT9 ... 155 CK109
Barwick Dr, Uxb. UB8 *off Harlington Rd* ... 77 BP71
Barwick Rd, E7 ... 68 EH63
Barwood Av, W.Wick. BR4 ... 143 EB102
Bascombe Gro, Dart. DA1 *off Lower Sta Rd* ... 127 FE86
Bascombe St, SW2 ... 121 DN86
Basden Gro, Felt. TW13 ... 116 CA89
Basedale Rd, Dag. RM9 ... 88 EV66
Baseing Cl, E6 ... 87 EN73
Basevi Way, SE8 ... 103 EB79
Bashley Rd, NW10 ... 80 CR70
Basil Av, E6 ... 86 EL68
Basildene Rd, Houns. TW4 ... 96 BX82
Basildon Av, Ilf. IG5 ... 49 EN53
Basildon Cl, Sutt. SM2 ... 158 DB109
Watford WD18 ... 23 BQ44
Basildon Rd, SE2 ... 106 EU78
Basil Gdns, SE27 ... 122 DQ92
Croydon CR0 *off Primrose La* ... 143 DX102
Basilon Rd, Bexh. DA7 ... 106 EY82
Basil St, SW3 ... 198 D6
Basin App, E14 *off Commercial Rd* ... 85 DY72
Basing Cl, T.Ditt. KT7 ... 137 CF101
Basing Ct, SE15 ... 102 DT81
Basingdon Way, SE5 ... 102 DR84
Basing Dr, Bex. DA5 ... 126 EZ86
Basingfield Rd, T.Ditt. KT7 ... 137 CF101
Basinghall Av, EC2 ... 197 K7
Basinghall Gdns, Sutt. SM2 ... 158 DB109
Basinghall St, EC2 ... 197 K8
Basing Hill, NW11 ... 63 CZ60
Wembley HA9 ... 62 CM61
Basing Ho, Bark. IG11 *off St. Margarets* ... 87 ER67
Basing Ho Yd, E2 ... 197 N2
Basing Pl, E2 ... 197 N2
Basing Rd, Bans. SM7 ... 157 CZ114
Rickmansworth (Mill End) WD3 ... 37 BF46
Basing St, W11 ... 81 CZ72
Basing Way, N3 ... 64 DA55
Thames Ditton KT7 ... 137 CF101
Basire St, N1 ... 84 DQ67
Baskerville Rd, SW18 ... 120 DE87
Basket Gdns, SE9 ... 124 EL85
Baslow Cl, Har. HA3 ... 41 CD53
Baslow Wk, E5 *off Overbury St* ... 67 DX63
Basnett Rd, SW11 ... 100 DG83
Basque Ct, SE16 ... 203 H5
Bassano St, SE22 ... 122 DT85
Bassant Rd, SE18 ... 105 ET79
Bassein Pk Rd, W12 ... 99 CT75
Basset Cl, Add. (New Haw) KT15 ... 152 BH110
Bassett Cl, Sutt. SM2 ... 158 DB109
Bassett Dr, Reig. RH2 ... 184 DA133
Bassett Flds, Epp. (N.Wld.) CM16 *off High Rd* ... 19 FD25
Bassett Gdns, Epp. (N.Wld.Bas.) CM16 ... 19 FB26
Isleworth TW7 ... 96 CC80
Bassett Ho, Dag. RM9 ... 88 EV67
Bassett Rd, W10 ... 81 CX72
Uxbridge UB8 *off New Windsor St* ... 76 BJ66
Woking GU22 ... 167 BC116
Bassetts Cl, Orp. BR6 ... 163 EP105
Bassett St, NW5 ... 82 DG65
Bassetts Way, Orp. BR6 ... 163 EP105
Bassett Way, Grnf. UB6 ... 78 CB72
Bassingham Rd, SW18 ... 120 DC87
Wembley HA0 ... 79 CK65
Bassishaw Highwalk, EC2 *off London Wall* ... 84 DQ71
Basswood Cl, SE15 *off Linden Gro* ... 102 DV83
Bastable Av, Bark. IG11 ... 87 ES68
Bastion Highwalk, EC2 *off London Wall* ... 84 DQ71
Bastion Ho, EC2 *off London Wall* ... 84 DQ71
Bastion Rd, SE2 ... 106 EU78
Baston Manor Rd, Brom. BR2 ... 144 EH104
Baston Rd, Brom. BR2 ... 144 EH102
Bastwick St, EC1 ... 197 H4
Basuto Rd, SW6 ... 100 DA81
⇌ **Bat & Ball** ... 191 FJ121
Bat & Ball Rd, Sev. TN14 ... 191 FJ121
Batavia Cl, Sun. TW16 ... 136 BW95
Batavia Ms, SE14 *off Goodwood Rd* ... 103 DY80
Batavia Rd, SE14 ... 103 DY80
Sunbury-on-Thames TW16 ... 135 BV95
Batchelor St, N1 ... 83 DN68
Batchwood Grn, Orp. BR5 ... 146 EU97
BATCHWORTH, Rick. ... 38 BM47
BATCHWORTH HEATH, Rick. ... 38 BN49
Batchworth Heath Hill, Rick. WD3 ... 38 BN49
Batchworth Hill, Rick. WD3 ... 38 BM48
Batchworth La, Nthwd. HA6 ... 39 BS50
Batchworth Roundabout, Rick. WD3 ... 38 BK46
Bateman Cl, Bark. IG11 *off Glenny Rd* ... 87 EQ65
Bateman Ho, SE17 *off Otto St* ... 101 DP79
Bateman Rd, E4 ... 47 EA51
Rickmansworth (Crox.Grn.) WD3 ... 22 BN44
Bateman's Bldgs, W1 ... 195 M9
Bateman's Row, EC2 ... 197 N4
Bateman St, W1 ... 195 M9
Bates Cl, Slou. (Geo.Grn.) SL3 ... 74 AY72
Bates Cres, SW16 ... 121 DJ94
Croydon CR0 ... 159 DN106
Bates Ind Est, Rom. (Harold Wd.) RM3 ... 52 FP52
Bateson St, SE18 ... 105 ES77
Bateson Way, Wok. GU21 ... 151 BC114
Bates Pt, E13 *off Pelly Rd* ... 86 EG67
Bates Rd, Rom. RM3 ... 52 FN52
Bate St, E14 *off Three Colt St* ... 85 DZ73
Bates Wk, Add. KT15 ... 152 BJ108
B.A.T. Export Ho, Wok. GU21 ... 166 AY117
Bath Cl, SE15 *off Asylum Rd* ... 102 DV80
Bath Ct, EC1 ... 196 D5
Bathgate Rd, SW19 ... 119 CX90
Bath Ho Rd, Croy. CR0 ... 141 DL102
Bath Pas, Kings.T. KT1 *off St. James Rd* ... 137 CK96
Bath Pl, EC2 ... 197 M3
Barnet EN5 ... 27 CZ41
Bath Rd, E7 ... 86 EK65
N9 ... 46 DV47
W4 ... 98 CS77
Dartford DA1 ... 127 FH87
Hayes UB3 ... 95 BQ81
Hounslow TW3, TW4, TW5, TW6 ... 96 BX82
Mitcham CR4 ... 140 DD97
Romford RM6 ... 70 EY58
Slough (Colnbr.) SL3 ... 93 BB79
West Drayton UB7 ... 94 BK81
Baths Rd, Brom. BR2 ... 144 EK98
Bath St, EC1 ... 197 J3
Gravesend DA11 ... 131 GH86
Bath Ter, SE1 ... 201 H7
Bathurst Av, SW19 *off Brisbane Av* ... 140 DB95
Bathurst Cl, Iver SL0 ... 93 BF75
Bathurst Gdns, NW10 ... 81 CV68
Bathurst Ms, W2 *off Sussex Pl* ... 82 DD73
Bathurst Rd, Ilf. IG1 ... 69 EP60
Bathurst St, W2 ... 82 DD73
Bathurst Wk, Iver SL0 ... 93 BE75
Bathway, SE18 ... 105 EN77
Batley Cl, Mitch. CR4 ... 140 DF101
Batley Pl, N16 ... 66 DT62
Batley Rd, N16 *off Stoke Newington High St* ... 66 DT62
Enfield EN2 ... 30 DQ39
Batman Cl, W12 ... 81 CV74
Baton Cl, Purf. RM19 *off Brimfield Rd* ... 109 FR77
Batoum Gdns, W6 ... 99 CW76
Batson St, W12 ... 99 CU75
Batsworth Rd, Mitch. CR4 ... 140 DD97
Batten Av, Wok. GU21 ... 166 AS119
Battenburg Wk, SE19 *off Brabourne Cl* ... 122 DS92
Batten Cl, E6 *off Savage Gdns* ... 87 EM72
Batten St, SW11 ... 100 DE83
Battersby Rd, SE6 ... 123 ED89
BATTERSEA, SW11 ... 101 DH81
Battersea Br, SW3 ... 100 DD80
SW11 ... 100 DD80
Battersea Br Rd, SW11 ... 100 DE80
Battersea Ch Rd, SW11 ... 100 DD81
★ **Battersea Dogs Home**, SW8 ... 101 DH80
Battersea High St, SW11 ... 100 DD81
★ **Battersea Park**, SW11 ... 100 DF80
⇌ **Battersea Park** ... 101 DH80
Battersea Pk, SW11 ... 100 DF80
Battersea Pk Rd, SW8 ... 101 DH81
SW11 ... 100 DE82
Battersea Ri, SW11 ... 120 DE85
Battersea Sq, SW11 *off Battersea High St* ... 100 DD81
Battery Rd, SE28 ... 105 ES75
Battis, The, Rom. RM1 *off Waterloo Rd* ... 71 FE58
Battishill Gdns, N1 *off Waterloo Ter* ... 83 DP66
Battishill St, N1 *off Waterloo Ter* ... 83 DP66
Battlebridge Ct, N1 *off Wharfdale Rd* ... 83 DL68
Battle Br La, SE1 ... 201 M3
Battlebridge La, Red. RH1 ... 185 DH130
Battle Br Rd, NW1 ... 195 P1
Battle Cl, SW19 *off North Rd* ... 120 DC93
Battledean Rd, N5 ... 65 DP64
Battle Rd, Belv. DA17 ... 107 FC77
Erith DA8 ... 107 FC77
Battlers Grn Dr, Rad. WD7 ... 25 CE37
Batts Hill, Red. RH1 ... 184 DE132
Reigate RH2 ... 184 DD132
Batty St, E1 ... 84 DU72
Baudwin Rd, SE6 ... 124 EE89
Baugh Rd, Sid. DA14 ... 126 EW92
Baulk, The, SW18 ... 120 DA87
Bavant Rd, SW16 ... 141 DL96
Bavaria Rd, N19 ... 65 DL61
Bavdene Ms, NW4 *off The Burroughs* ... 63 CV56
Bavent Rd, SE5 ... 102 DQ82
Bawdale Rd, SE22 ... 122 DT85
Bawdsey Av, Ilf. IG2 ... 69 ET56
Bawtree Cl, Sutt. SM2 ... 158 DC110
Bawtree Rd, SE14 ... 103 DY80
Uxbridge UB8 ... 76 BK65
Bawtry Rd, N20 ... 44 DF48
Baxendale, N20 ... 44 DC47
Baxendale St, E2 ... 84 DU69
Baxter Av, Red. RH1 ... 184 DE134
Baxter Cl, Slou. SL1 ... 92 AS76
Southall UB2 ... 96 CB75
Uxbridge UB10 ... 77 BP69
Baxter Gdns, Rom. (Noak Hill) RM3 *off Cummings Hall La* ... 52 FJ48
Baxter Rd, E16 ... 86 EJ72
N1 ... 84 DR65
N18 ... 46 DV49
NW10 ... 80 CS70
Ilford IG1 ... 69 EP64
Bayards, Warl. CR6 ... 176 DW118
Bay Ct, W5 *off Popes La* ... 98 CL76
Baycroft Cl, Pnr. HA5 ... 60 BW55
Baydon Ct, Brom. BR2 ... 144 EF97
Bayes Cl, SE26 ... 122 DW92
Bayeux, Tad. KT20 ... 173 CX122
Bayfield Rd, SE9 ... 104 EK84
Bayford Ms, E8 *off Bayford St* ... 84 DV66
Bayford Rd, NW10 ... 81 CX69
Bayford St, E8 ... 84 DV66
Bayham Pl, NW1 ... 83 DJ67
Bayham Rd, W4 ... 98 CR76
W13 ... 79 CH73
Morden SM4 ... 140 DB98
Sevenoaks TN13 ... 191 FJ123
Bayham St, NW1 ... 83 DJ67
Bayhurst Dr, Nthwd. HA6 ... 39 BT51
★ **Bayhurst Wood Country Pk**, Uxb. (Hare.) UB9 ... 58 BM56

Bay - Bee

Bayleys Mead, Brwd. CM13 ... 55 GC47
Bayley St, WC1 ... 195 M7
Bayley Wk, SE2
off Woolwich Rd ... 106 EY78
Baylin Rd, SW18
off Garratt La ... 120 DB86
Baylis Rd, SE1 ... 200 D5
Bayliss Av, SE28 ... 88 EX73
Bayliss Cl, N21 ... 29 DL43
Bayly Rd, Dart. DA1 ... 128 FN86
Bay Manor La, Grays RM20 ... 109 FT79
Baymans Wd, Brwd. CM15 ... 54 FY47
Bayne Cl, E6 off Savage Gdns ... 87 EM72
Baynes Cl, Enf. EN1 ... 30 DU40
Baynes Ms, NW3
off Belsize La ... 82 DD65
Baynes St, NW1 ... 83 DJ66
Baynham Cl, Bex. DA5 ... 126 EZ86
Bayonne Rd, W6 ... 99 CY79
Bayshill Ri, Nthlt. UB5 ... 78 CB65
Bayston Rd, N16 ... 66 DT62
BAYSWATER, W2 ... 82 DC72
⊖ Bayswater ... 82 DB73
Bayswater Rd, W2 ... 194 A10
Baythorne St, E3 ... 85 DZ71
Bay Tree Av, Lthd. KT22 ... 171 CG120
Bay Tree Cl, Brom. BR1 ... 144 EJ95
Baytree Cl, St.Alb. (Park St.)
AL2 ... 8 CB27
Sidcup DA15 ... 125 ET88
Waltham Cross EN7 ... 14 DT27
Baytree Ho, E4 off Dells Cl ... 47 EB45
Baytree Rd, SW2 ... 101 DM84
Baytree Wk, Wat. WD17 ... 23 BT38
Baywood Sq, Chig. IG7 ... 50 EV49
Bazalgette Cl, N.Mal. KT3 ... 138 CR99
Bazalgette Gdns, N.Mal. KT3 ... 138 CR99
Bazely St, E14 ... 85 EC73
Bazile Rd, N21 ... 29 DN44
Beacham Cl, SE7 ... 104 EK78
Beachborough Rd, Brom.
BR1 ... 123 EC91
Beachcroft Rd, E11 ... 68 EE62
Beachcroft Way, N19 ... 65 DK60
Beach Gro, Felt. TW13 ... 116 CA89
Beachy Rd, E3 ... 85 EA66
Beacon Cl, Bans. SM7 ... 173 CX116
Gerrards Cross (Chal.St.P.)
SL9 ... 36 AY52
Uxbridge UB8 ... 58 BK64
★ Beacon Country Pk, Dart.
(Bean) DA2 ... 129 FV91
Beacon Dr, Dart. (Bean) DA2 ... 129 FV90
Beaconfield Av, Epp. CM16 ... 17 ET29
Beaconfield Rd, Epp. CM16 ... 17 ET29
Beaconfields, Sev. TN13 ... 190 FF126
Beaconfield Way, Epp. CM16 ... 17 ET29
Beacon Gate, SE14 ... 103 DX83
Beacon Gro, Cars. SM5 ... 158 DG105
Beacon Hill, N7 ... 65 DL64
Purfleet RM19 ... 108 FP78
Woking GU21 ... 166 AW118
Beacon Ri, Sev. TN13 ... 190 FG126
Beacon Rd, SE13 ... 123 ED86
Erith DA8 ... 107 FH80
Hounslow (Hthrw.Air.)
TW6 ... 114 BN86
Beacon Rd Roundabout, Houns.
(Hthrw.Air.) TW6 ... 115 BP86
Beacons, The, Loug. IG10 ... 33 EN38
Beacons Cl, E6
off Oliver Gdns ... 86 EL71
Beaconsfield Cl, N11 ... 44 DG49
SE3 ... 104 EG79
W4 ... 98 CQ78
Beaconsfield Par, SE9
off Beaconsfield Rd ... 124 EL91
Beaconsfield Pl, Epsom
KT17 ... 156 CS112
Beaconsfield Rd, E10 ... 67 EC61
E16 ... 86 EF70
E17 ... 67 DZ58
N9 ... 46 DU49
N11 ... 44 DG48
N15 ... 66 DS56
NW10 ... 81 CT65
SE3 ... 104 EF80
SE9 ... 124 EL89
SE17 ... 102 DR78
W4 ... 98 CR76
W5 ... 97 CJ75
Bexley DA5 ... 127 FE88
Bromley BR1 ... 144 EK97
Croydon CR0 ... 142 DR100
Enfield EN3 ... 31 DX37
Epsom KT18 ... 172 CR119
Esher (Clay.) KT10 ... 155 CE108
Hayes UB4 ... 78 BW74
New Malden KT3 ... 138 CR96
Southall UB1 ... 78 BX74
Surbiton KT5 ... 138 CM101
Twickenham TW1 ... 117 CH86
Woking GU22 ... 167 AZ120
Beaconsfield Ter, Rom. RM6 ... 70 EX58
Beaconsfield Ter Rd, W14 ... 99 CY76
Beaconsfield Wk, E6
off East Ham Manor Way ... 87 EN72
SW6 ... 99 CZ81
Beacontree Av, E17 ... 47 ED53
Beacontree Rd, E11 ... 68 EF59
Beacon Way, Bans. SM7 ... 173 CX116
Rickmansworth WD3 ... 38 BG45
Beadles La, Oxt. RH8 ... 187 ED130
Beadlow Cl, Cars. SM5
off Olveston Wk ... 140 DD100
Beadman Pl, SE27
off Norwood High St ... 121 DP91
Beadman St, SE27 ... 121 DP91
Beadnell Rd, SE23 ... 123 DX88
Beadon Rd, W6 ... 99 CW77
Bromley BR2 ... 144 EG98
Beads Hall La, Brwd. CM15 ... 54 FV42
Beaford Gro, SW20 ... 139 CY97
Beagle Cl, Felt. TW13 ... 115 BV91
Radlett WD7 ... 25 CF37
Beagles Cl, Orp. BR5 ... 146 EX103
Beak St, W1 ... 195 L10
Beal Cl, Well. DA16 ... 106 EU81
Beale Cl, N13 ... 45 DP50
Beale Pl, E3 ... 85 DZ68
Beale Rd, E3 ... 85 DZ67
Beales La, Wey. KT13 ... 134 BN104
Beal Rd, Ilf. IG1 ... 69 EN61
Beam Av, Dag. RM10 ... 89 FB67
Beaminster Gdns, Ilf. IG6 ... 49 EP54
Beamish Cl, Epp. (N.Wld.Bas.)
CM16 ... 19 FC25
Beamish Dr, Bushey (Bushey Hth.)
WD23 ... 40 CC46
Beamish Rd, N9 ... 46 DU46
Orpington BR5 ... 146 EW101
Beam Way, Dag. RM10 ... 89 FD66
BEAN, Dart. ... 129 FV90
Beanacre Cl, E9 ... 85 DZ65
Beane Cft, Grav. DA12
off Damigos Rd ... 131 GM88
Bean La, Dart. (Bean) DA2 ... 129 FV89
Bean Rd, Bexh. DA6 ... 106 EX84
Greenhithe DA9 ... 129 FU88
Beanshaw, SE9 ... 125 EN91
Beansland Gro, Rom. RM6 ... 50 EY54
Bear All, EC4 ... 196 F8
Bear Cl, Rom. RM7 ... 71 FB58
Beardell St, SE19 ... 122 DT93
Beardow Gro, N14 ... 29 DJ44
Beard Rd, Kings.T. KT2 ... 118 CM92
Beardsfield, E13
off Valetta Gro ... 86 EG67
Beard's Hill, Hmptn. TW12 ... 136 CA95
Beard's Hill Cl, Hmptn. TW12
off Beard's Hill ... 136 CA95
Beardsley Ter, Dag. RM8
off Fitzstephen Rd ... 70 EV64
Beardsley Way, W3 ... 98 CR75
Beards Rd, Ashf. TW15 ... 115 BS93
Bearfield Rd, Kings.T. KT2 ... 118 CL94
Bear Gdns, SE1 ... 201 H2
Bearing Cl, Chig. IG7 ... 50 EU49
Bearing Way, Chig. IG7 ... 50 EU49
Bear La, SE1 ... 200 G2
Bear Rd, Felt. TW13 ... 116 BX92
Bears Den, Tad. (Kgswd.)
KT20 ... 173 CZ122
Bears Rails Pk, Wind. (Old Wind.)
SL4 ... 112 AT87
Bearstead Ri, SE4 ... 123 DZ85
Bearsted Ter, Beck. BR3 ... 143 EA95
Bear St, WC2 ... 195 N10
Bearwood Cl, Add. KT15
off Ongar Pl ... 152 BG107
Potters Bar EN6 ... 12 DD31
Beasley's Ait La, Sun. TW16 ... 135 BT100
Beasleys Yd, Uxb. UB8
off Warwick Pl ... 76 BJ66
Beaton Cl, SE15 off Kelly Av ... 102 DT80
Greenhithe DA9 ... 109 FV84
Beatrice Av, SW16 ... 141 DM97
Wembley HA9 ... 62 CL64
Beatrice Cl, E13
off Chargeable La ... 86 EG70
Pinner HA5 off Reid Cl ... 59 BU56
Beatrice Ct, Buck.H. IG9 ... 48 EK47
Beatrice Gdns, Grav. (Nthflt.)
DA11 ... 130 GE89
Beatrice Pl, W8 ... 100 DB76
Beatrice Rd, E17 ... 67 EA57
N4 ... 65 DN59
N9 ... 46 DW45
SE1 ... 202 C9
Oxted RH8 ... 188 EE129
Richmond TW10
off Albert Rd ... 118 CM85
Southall UB1 ... 78 BZ74
Beatson Wk, SE16 ... 203 K2
Beattie Cl, Felt. TW14 ... 115 BT88
Leatherhead (Bkhm.)
KT23 ... 170 BZ124
Beattock Ri, N10 ... 65 DH56
Beatty Rd, N16 ... 66 DS63
Stanmore HA7 ... 41 CJ51
Waltham Cross EN8 ... 15 DZ34
Beatty St, NW1 ... 83 DJ68
Beattyville Gdns, Ilf. IG6 ... 69 EN55
Beauchamp Cl, W4
off Church Path ... 98 CQ76
Beauchamp Ct, Stan. HA7
off Hardwick Cl ... 41 CJ50
Beauchamp Gdns, Rick. (Mill End)
WD3 ... 38 BG46
Beauchamp Pl, SW3 ... 198 C6
Beauchamp Rd, E7 ... 86 EH66
SE19 ... 142 DR95
SW11 ... 100 DE84
East Molesey KT8 ... 136 CB99
Sutton SM1 ... 158 DA106
Twickenham TW1 ... 117 CG87
West Molesey KT8 ... 136 CB99
Beauchamp St, EC1 ... 196 D7
Beauchamp Ter, SW15
off Dryburgh Rd ... 99 CV83
Beauclare Cl, Lthd. KT22
off Hatherwood ... 171 CK121
Beauclerc Rd, W6 ... 99 CV76
Beauclerk Cl, Felt. TW13
off Florence Rd ... 115 BV88
Beaudesert Ms, West Dr. UB7 ... 94 BL75
Beaufort, E6
off Newark Knok ... 87 EN71
Beaufort Av, Har. HA3 ... 61 CG56
Beaufort Cl, E4
off Higham Sta Av ... 47 EB51
SW15 ... 119 CV87
W5 ... 80 CM71
Epping (N.Wld.Bas.) CM16 ... 18 FA27
Grays (Chaff.Hun.) RM16
off Clifford Rd ... 110 FZ76
Reigate RH2 ... 183 CZ133
Romford RM7 ... 71 FC56
Woking GU22 ... 167 BC116
Beaufort Ct, Rich. TW10
off Beaufort Rd ... 117 CJ91
Beaufort Dr, NW11 ... 64 DA56
Beaufort Gdns, NW4 ... 63 CW58
SW3 ... 198 C6
Beaufort Gdns, SW16 ... 121 DM94
Hounslow TW5 ... 96 BY81
Ilford IG1 ... 69 EN60
Beaufort Ms, SW6
off Lillie Rd ... 99 CZ79
Beaufort Pk, NW11 ... 64 DA56
Beaufort Rd, W5 ... 80 CM71
Kingston upon Thames
KT1 ... 138 CL98
Reigate RH2 ... 183 CZ133
Richmond TW10 ... 117 CJ91
Ruislip HA4
off Lysander Rd ... 59 BR61
Twickenham TW1 ... 117 CJ87
Woking GU22 ... 167 BC116
Beauforts, Egh. (Eng.Grn.)
TW20 ... 112 AW92
Beaufort St, SW3 ... 100 DD79
Beaufort Way, Epsom KT17 ... 157 CU108
Beaufoy Rd, N17 ... 46 DS52
Beaufoy Wk, SE11 ... 200 C9
Beaulieu Av, E16 ... 205 P2
SE26 ... 122 DV91
Beaulieu Cl, NW9 ... 62 CS56
SE5 ... 102 DR83
Hounslow TW4 ... 116 BZ85
Mitcham CR4 ... 140 DG95
Slough (Datchet) SL3 ... 92 AV82
Twickenham TW1 ... 117 CK87
Watford WD19 ... 40 BW46
Beaulieu Dr, Pnr. HA5 ... 60 BX58
Waltham Abbey EN9 ... 15 EB32
Beaulieu Gdns, N21 ... 46 DQ45
Beaulieu Pl, W4
off Rothschild Rd ... 98 CQ76
Beauly Way, Rom. RM1 ... 51 FE53
Beaumanor Gdns, SE9 ... 125 EN91
Beaumaris Dr, Wdf.Grn. IG8 ... 48 EK52
Beaumaris Grn, NW9
off Goldsmith Av ... 62 CS58
Beaumont Av, W14 ... 99 CZ78
Harrow HA2 ... 60 CB58
Richmond TW9 ... 98 CM83
Wembley HA0 ... 61 CJ64
Beaumont Cl, Kings.T. KT2 ... 118 CN94
Romford RM2 ... 52 FJ54
Beaumont Cres, W14 ... 99 CZ78
Rainham RM13 ... 89 FG65
Beaumont Dr, Ashf. TW15 ... 115 BR92
Gravesend (Nthflt.) DA11 ... 130 GE87
Beaumont Gdns, NW3 ... 64 DA62
Brentwood CM13
off Bannister Dr ... 55 GC44
Beaumont Gate, Rad. WD7
off Shenley Hill ... 25 CH35
Beaumont Gro, E1 ... 85 DX70
Beaumont Ms, W1 ... 194 G6
Beaumont Pl, W1 ... 195 L4
Barnet EN5 ... 27 CZ39
Isleworth TW7 ... 117 CF85
Beaumont Ri, N19 ... 65 DK60
Beaumont Rd, E10 ... 67 EB59
E13 ... 86 EH69
SE19 ... 122 DQ93
SW19 ... 119 CY87
W4 ... 98 CQ76
Orpington BR5 ... 145 ER100
Purley CR8 ... 159 DN113
Beaumont Sq, E1 ... 85 DX70
Beaumont St, W1 ... 194 G6
Beaumont Vw, Wal.Cr. (Chsht.)
EN7 ... 14 DR26
Beaumont Wk, NW3 ... 82 DF66
Beauvais Ter, Nthlt. UB5 ... 78 BX69
Beauval Rd, SE22 ... 122 DT86
Beaverbank Rd, SE9 ... 125 ER88
Beaverbrook Roundabout, Lthd.
KT22 ... 172 CL123
Beaver Cl, SE20
off Lullington Rd ... 122 DU94
Hampton TW12 ... 136 CB95
Beaver Gro, Nthlt. UB5
off Jetstar Way ... 78 BY69
Beaver Rd, Ilf. IG6 ... 50 EW50
Beavers Cres, Houns. TW4 ... 96 BW84
Beavers La, Houns. TW4 ... 96 BW83
Beavers La Camp, Houns. TW4
off Beavers La ... 96 BW83
Beaverwood Rd, Chis. BR7 ... 125 ES93
Beavor Gro, W6 off Beavor La ... 99 CU77
Beavor La, W6 ... 99 CU77
Bebbington Rd, SE18 ... 105 ES77
Beblets Cl, Orp. BR6 ... 163 ET106
Beccles Dr, Bark. IG11 ... 87 ES65
Beccles St, E14 ... 85 DZ73
Bec Cl, Ruis. HA4 ... 60 BX62
Beck Cl, SE13 ... 103 EB81
Beck Ct, Beck. BR3 ... 143 DX97
BECKENHAM ... 143 EA95
Beckenham Business Cen, Beck.
BR3 ... 123 DY93
Beckenham Gdns, N9 ... 46 DS48
Beckenham Gro, Brom. BR2 ... 143 ED96
⇌ Beckenham Hill ... 123 EC92
Beckenham Hill Rd, SE6 ... 123 EB92
Beckenham BR3 ... 123 EB92
H Beckenham Hosp, Beck.
BR3 ... 143 DZ96
⇌ Beckenham Junction ... 143 EA95
⊝ Beckenham Junction ... 143 EA95
⊝ Beckenham Road ... 143 DY95
Beckenham Rd, Beck. BR3 ... 143 DX95
West Wickham BR4 ... 143 EB101
Beckenshaw Gdns, Bans.
SM7 ... 174 DE115
Beckers, The, N16
off Rectory Rd ... 66 DU62
Becket Av, E6 ... 87 EN69
Becket Cl, SE25 ... 142 DU100
Brentwood CM13 ... 53 FW51
Becket Fold, Har. HA1
off Courtfield Cres ... 61 CF57
Becket Rd, N18 ... 46 DW49
Becket St, SE1 ... 201 K6
Beckett Av, Ken. CR8 ... 175 DP115
Beckett Cl, NW10 ... 80 CR65
SW16 ... 121 DK89
Belvedere DA17
off Tunstock Way ... 106 EY76
Becketts Cl, Felt. TW14 ... 115 BV86
Orpington BR6 ... 145 ET104
Becketts Pl, Kings.T. KT1 ... 137 CK95
Beckett Wk, Beck. BR3 ... 123 DY93
Beckford Dr, Orp. BR5 ... 145 ER101
Beckford Pl, SE17
off Walworth Rd ... 102 DQ78
Beckford Rd, Croy. CR0 ... 142 DT100
Beck La, Beck. BR3 ... 143 DX97
Becklow Gdns, W12
off Becklow Rd ... 99 CU75
Becklow Ms, W12
off Becklow Rd ... 99 CT75
Becklow Rd, W12 ... 99 CU75
Beckman Cl, Sev. (Halst.)
TN14 ... 181 FC115
Beck River Pk, Beck. BR3 ... 143 DZ95
Beck Rd, E8 ... 84 DV67
Becks Rd, Sid. DA14 ... 126 EU90
BECKTON, E6 ... 87 EN71
DLR Beckton ... 87 EN71
DLR Beckton Park ... 87 EM73
Beckton Pk Roundabout, E16
off Royal Albert Way ... 87 EM73
Beckton Retail Pk, E6 ... 87 EN71
Beckton Rd, E16 ... 86 EF71
Beckton Triangle Retail Pk, E6 ... 87 EN70
Beck Way, Beck. BR3 ... 143 DZ97
Beckway Rd, SW16 ... 141 DK96
Beckway St, SE17 ... 201 L9
Beckwith Rd, SE24 ... 122 DR86
Beclands Rd, SW17 ... 120 DG93
Becmead Av, SW16 ... 121 DK91
Harrow HA3 ... 61 CH57
Becondale Rd, SE19 ... 122 DS92
BECONTREE, Dag. ... 70 EY62
⊖ Becontree ... 88 EW66
Becontree Av, Dag. RM8 ... 70 EV63
BECONTREE HEATH, Dag. ... 70 FA60
Bective Pl, SW15
off Bective Rd ... 99 CZ84
Bective Rd, E7 ... 68 EG63
SW15 ... 99 CZ84
Becton Pl, Erith DA8 ... 107 FB80
Bedale Rd, Enf. EN2 ... 30 DQ38
Romford RM3 ... 52 FN50
Bedale St, SE1 ... 201 K3
Bedale Wk, Dart. DA2 ... 128 FP88
BEDDINGTON, Wall. ... 141 DK103
BEDDINGTON CORNER,
Mitch. ... 140 DG101
Beddington Cross, Croy.
CR0 ... 141 DK102
Beddington Fm Rd, Croy.
CR0 ... 141 DL102
Beddington Gdns, Cars.
SM5 ... 158 DG107
Wallington SM6 ... 159 DH107
Beddington Grn, Orp. BR5 ... 145 ET95
Beddington Gro, Wall. SM6 ... 159 DK106
⊝ Beddington Lane ... 141 DJ100
Beddington La, Croy. CR0 ... 141 DJ99
Beddington Path, Orp. BR5 ... 145 ET95
Beddington Rd, Ilf. IG3 ... 69 ET59
Orpington BR5 ... 145 ES96
Beddington Trd Pk W, Croy.
CR0 ... 141 DL102
Beddlestead La, Warl. CR6 ... 178 EF117
Bede Cl, Pnr. HA5 ... 40 BX53
Bedenham Way, SE15
off Daniel Gdns ... 102 DT80
Bedens Rd, Sid. DA14 ... 126 EY93
Bede Rd, Rom. RM6 ... 70 EW58
Bedfont Cl, Felt. TW14 ... 115 BQ86
Mitcham CR4 ... 140 DG96
Bedfont Ct, Stai. TW19 ... 94 BH84
Bedfont Ct Est, Stai. TW19 ... 94 BG83
Bedfont Grn Cl, Felt. TW14 ... 115 BQ88
Bedfont La, Felt. TW13, TW14 ... 115 BT87
Bedfont Rd, Felt. TW13,
TW14 ... 115 BS89
Staines (Stanw.) TW19 ... 114 BL86
Bedford Av, WC1 ... 195 N7
Amersham HP6 ... 20 AW39
Barnet EN5 ... 27 CZ43
Hayes UB4 ... 77 BV72
Bedfordbury, WC2 ... 195 P10
Bedford Cl, N10 ... 44 DG52
W4 ... 98 CS79
Rickmansworth (Chenies)
WD3 ... 21 BB38
Woking GU21 ... 166 AW115
Bedford Cor, W4
off The Avenue ... 98 CS77
Bedford Ct, WC2 ... 199 P1
Bedford Cres, Enf. EN3 ... 31 DY35
Bedford Gdns, W8 ... 82 DA74
Hornchurch RM12 ... 72 FJ61
Bedford Hill, SW12 ... 121 DH88
SW16 ... 121 DH88
★ Bedford Hill Gall, SW12 ... 121 DH88
Bedford Ho, SW4 ... 101 DL84
Bedford Ms, N2
off Bedford Rd ... 64 DE55
BEDFORD PARK, W4 ... 98 CR76
Bedford Pk, Croy. CR0 ... 142 DQ102
Bedford Pk Cor, W4
off Bath Rd ... 98 CS77
Bedford Pas, SW6
off Dawes Rd ... 99 CY80
Bedford Pl, WC1 ... 195 P6
Croydon CR0 ... 142 DR102
Bedford Rd, E6 ... 87 EN67
E17 ... 47 EA54
E18 ... 48 EG54
N2 ... 64 DE55
N8 ... 65 DK58
N9 ... 46 DV45
N15 ... 66 DS56
N22 ... 45 DL53
NW7 ... 42 CS48
SW4 ... 101 DL83
W4 ... 98 CR76
Bedford Rd, W13 ... 79 CH73
Dartford DA1 ... 128 FN87
Bedford Rd, Grav. (Nthflt.)
DA11 ... 131 GF89
Grays RM17 ... 110 GB78
Harrow HA1 ... 60 CC58
Ilford IG1 ... 69 EP62
Northwood HA6 ... 39 BQ48
Orpington BR6 ... 146 EV103
Ruislip HA4 ... 59 BT63
Sidcup DA15 ... 125 ES90
Twickenham TW2 ... 117 CD90
Worcester Park KT4 ... 139 CW103
Bedford Row, WC1 ... 196 C6
Bedford Sq, WC1 ... 195 N7
Bedford St, WC2 ... 195 P10
Watford WD24 ... 23 BV39
Bedford Ter, SW2
off Lyham Rd ... 121 DL85
Bedford Way, WC1 ... 195 N5
Bedgebury Gdns, SW19 ... 119 CY89
Bedgebury Rd, SE9 ... 104 EK84
Bedivere Rd, Brom. BR1 ... 124 EG90
Bedlam Ms, SE11 ... 200 C8
Bedlow Way, Croy. CR0 ... 159 DM105
BEDMOND, Abb.L. ... 7 BS27
Bedmond La, Abb.L. WD5 ... 7 BV25
Bedmond Rd, Abb.L. WD5 ... 7 BT29
Bedonwell Rd, SE2 ... 106 EY79
Belvedere DA17 ... 106 FA79
Bexleyheath DA7 ... 106 FA79
Bedser Cl, SE11
off Harleyford Rd ... 101 DM79
Thornton Heath CR7 ... 142 DQ97
Woking GU21 ... 167 BA116
Bedser Dr, Grnf. UB6 ... 61 CD64
Bedster Gdns, W.Mol. KT8 ... 136 CB96
Bedwardine Rd, SE19 ... 122 DS94
Bedwell Gdns, Hayes UB3 ... 95 BS78
Bedwell Rd, N17 ... 46 DS53
Belvedere DA17 ... 106 FA78
Beeby Rd, E16 ... 86 EH71
Beech Av, N20 ... 44 DE46
W3 ... 80 CS74
Brentford TW8 ... 97 CH80
Brentwood CM13 ... 55 FZ48
Buckhurst Hill IG9 ... 48 EH47
Enfield EN2 ... 29 DN35
Radlett WD7 ... 9 CG33
Ruislip HA4 ... 59 BV60
Sidcup DA15 ... 126 EU87
South Croydon CR2 ... 160 DR111
Swanley BR8 ... 147 FF98
Upminster RM14 ... 72 FP62
Westerham (Tats.) TN16 ... 178 EK119
Beech Cl, N9 ... 30 DU44
SE8 off Clyde St ... 103 DZ79
SW15 ... 119 CU87
SW19 ... 119 CW93
Ashford TW15 ... 115 BR92
Carshalton SM5 ... 140 DF103
Cobham KT11 ... 154 CA112
Hornchurch RM12 ... 71 FH62
Loughton IG10 off Cedar Dr ... 33 EP40
Staines (Stanw.) TW19
off St. Mary's Cres ... 114 BK87
Sunbury-on-Thames TW16
off Harfield Rd ... 136 BX96
Walton-on-Thames KT12 ... 154 BW105
West Byfleet (Byfleet)
KT14 ... 152 BL112
West Drayton UB7 ... 94 BN76
Beech Cl Ct, Cob. KT11 ... 154 BZ111
Beech Copse, Brom. BR1 ... 145 EM96
South Croydon CR2 ... 160 DS106
Beech Ct, E17 ... 67 ED55
SE9 ... 124 EL86
Ilford IG1 off Riverdene Rd ... 69 EN62
Surbiton KT6 ... 138 CL101
Beech Cres, Tad. KT20 ... 182 CQ130
Beechcroft, Ashtd. KT21 ... 172 CM119
Chislehurst BR7 ... 125 EN94
Beechcroft Av, NW11 ... 63 CZ59
Bexleyheath DA7 ... 107 FD81
Harrow HA2 ... 60 CA59
Kenley CR8 ... 176 DR115
New Malden KT3 ... 138 CQ95
Rickmansworth (Crox.Grn.)
WD3 ... 23 BQ44
Southall UB1 ... 78 BZ74
Beechcroft Cl, Houns. TW5 ... 96 BY80
Orpington BR6 ... 163 ER105
Beechcroft Gdns, Wem. HA9 ... 62 CM62
Beechcroft Lo, Sutt. SM2
off Devonshire Rd ... 158 DC108
Beechcroft Manor, Wey.
KT13 ... 135 BR104
Beechcroft Rd, E18 ... 48 EH54
SW14 off Elm Rd ... 98 CQ83
SW17 ... 120 DE89
Bushey WD23 ... 24 BY43
Chessington KT9 ... 138 CM104
Orpington BR6 ... 163 ER105
Beechdale, N21 ... 45 DM47
Beechdale Rd, SW2 ... 121 DM86
Beech Dell, Kes. BR2 ... 163 EM105
Beechdene, Tad. KT20 ... 173 CV122
Beech Dr, N2 ... 64 DF55
Borehamwood WD6 ... 26 CM40
Reigate RH2 ... 184 DD134
Tadworth (Kgswd.) KT20 ... 173 CZ122
Woking (Ripley) GU23 ... 168 BG124
Beechen Cliff Way, Islw. TW7
off Henley Cl ... 97 CF81
Beechen Gro, Pnr. HA5 ... 60 BZ55
Watford WD17 ... 24 BW42
Beechen La, Tad. KT20 ... 183 CZ125
Beechenlea La, Swan. BR8 ... 147 FH97
Beeches, The, Bans. SM7 ... 174 DB116
Brentwood CM14 ... 54 FV48
Hounslow TW3 ... 96 CB81
Leatherhead (Fetch.) KT22 ... 171 CE124
Rickmansworth (Chorl.)
WD3 ... 21 BF43

★ Place of interest ⇌ Railway station ⊖ London Underground station DLR Docklands Light Railway station ⊝ Tramlink station H Hospital

Bee - Ben

Bengeworth Rd, SE5 ... 102 DQ83
Harrow HA1 ... 61 CG61
Ben Hale Cl, Stan. HA7 ... 41 CH49
Benham Cl, SW11 ... 100 DD83
Chessington KT9
off Merritt Gdns ... 155 CJ107
Coulsdon CR5 ... 175 DP118
Benham Gdns, Houns. TW4 ... 116 BZ85
Benham Rd, W7 ... 79 CE71
Benhams Pl, NW3
off Holly Wk ... 64 DC63
Benhill Av, Sutt. SM1 ... 158 DB105
Benhill Rd, SE5 ... 102 DR80
Sutton SM1 ... 140 DC104
Benhill Wd Rd, Sutt. SM1 ... 140 DC104
BENHILTON, Sutt. ... 140 DB103
Benhilton Gdns, Sutt. SM1 ... 140 DB104
Benhurst Av, Horn. RM12 ... 71 FH62
Benhurst Cl, S.Croy. CR2 ... 161 DX110
Benhurst Ct, SW16 ... 121 DN92
Benhurst Gdns, S.Croy. CR2 ... 160 DW110
Benhurst La, SW16 ... 121 DN92
Benin St, SE13 ... 123 ED87
Benison Ct, Slou. SL1
off Osborne St ... 92 AT76
Benjafield Cl, N18
off Brettenham Rd ... 46 DV49
Benjamin Cl, E8 ... 84 DU67
Hornchurch RM11 ... 71 FG58
Benjamin St, EC1 ... 196 F6
Ben Jonson Rd, E1 ... 85 DY71
Benledi St, E14 ... 85 ED72
Benn Cl, Oxt. RH8 ... 188 EG134
Bennelong Cl, W12 ... 81 CV73
Bennerley Rd, SW11 ... 120 DE85
Bennetsfield Rd, Uxb. UB11 ... 77 BP74
Bennet's Hill, EC4 ... 196 G10
Bennett Cl, Cob. KT11 ... 153 BU113
Kingston upon Thames
KT1 ... 137 CJ95
Northwood HA6 ... 39 BT52
Welling DA16 ... 106 EU82
Bennett Gro, SE13 ... 103 EB81
Bennett Pk, SE3 ... 104 EF83
Bennett Rd, E13 ... 86 EJ70
N16 ... 66 DS63
Romford RM6 ... 70 EY58
Bennetts Av, Croy. CR0 ... 143 DY103
Greenford UB6 ... 79 CE67
Bennetts Castle La, Dag. RM8 ... 70 EW63
Bennetts Cl, N17 ... 46 DT51
Mitcham CR4 ... 141 DH95
Bennetts Copse, Chis. BR7 ... 124 EL93
Bennett St, SW1 ... 199 K2
W4 ... 98 CS79
Bennetts Way, Croy. CR0 ... 143 DY103
Bennetts Yd, SW1 ... 199 N7
Uxbridge UB8 off High St ... 76 BJ66
Bennett Way, Dart. (Lane End)
DA2 ... 129 FR91
Benningholme Rd, Edg. HA8 ... 42 CS51
Bennington Rd, N17 ... 46 DS53
Woodford Green IG8 ... 48 EE52
Bennions Cl, Horn. RM12
off Franklin Rd ... 90 FK65
Bennison Dr, Rom. (Harold Wd.)
RM3 ... 52 FK54
Benn St, E9 ... 85 DY65
Benn's Wk, Rich. TW9
off Rosedale Rd ... 98 CL84
Benrek Cl, Ilf. IG6 ... 49 EQ53
Bensbury Cl, SW15 ... 119 CV87
Bensham Cl, Th.Hth. CR7 ... 142 DQ98
Bensham Gro, Th.Hth. CR7 ... 142 DQ96
Bensham La, Croy. CR0 ... 141 DP101
Thornton Heath CR7 ... 141 DP98
Bensham Manor Rd, Th.Hth.
CR7 ... 142 DQ98
Bensington Ct, Felt. TW14 ... 115 BR86
Benskin Rd, Wat. WD18 ... 23 BU43
Benskins La, Rom. (Noak Hill)
RM4 ... 52 FK46
Bensley Cl, N11 ... 44 DF50
Ben Smith Way, SE16 ... 202 C6
Benson Av, E6 ... 86 EJ68
Benson Cl, Houns. TW3 ... 96 CA84
Slough SL2 ... 74 AU74
Uxbridge UB8 ... 76 BL71
Benson Quay, E1 ... 202 F1
Benson Rd, SE23 ... 122 DW88
Croydon CR0 ... 141 DN104
Grays RM17 ... 110 GB79
Bentalls Cen, Kings.T. KT1 ... 138 CL96
Bentfield Gdns, SE9
off Aldersgrove Av ... 124 EJ90
Benthall Gdns, Ken. CR8 ... 176 DQ116
Benthal Rd, N16 ... 66 DU61
Bentham Av, Wok. GU21 ... 167 BC115
Bentham Ct, N1
off Rotherfield St ... 84 DQ66
Bentham Rd, E9 ... 85 DX65
SE28 ... 88 EV73
Bentham Wk, NW10 ... 62 CQ64
Ben Tillet Cl, Bark. IG11 ... 88 EU66
Ben Tillett Cl, E16
off Newland St ... 87 EM74
Bentinck Cl, Ger.Cr. SL9 ... 56 AX57
Bentinck Ms, W1 ... 194 G8
Bentinck Pl, NW8 ... 194 B1
Bentinck Rd, West Dr. UB7 ... 76 BK74
Bentinck St, W1 ... 194 G8
Bentley Dr, NW2 ... 63 CZ62
Ilford IG2 ... 69 EQ58
Weybridge KT13 ... 152 BN109
BENTLEY HEATH, Barn. ... 27 CZ35
Bentley Heath La, Barn. EN5 ... 11 CY34
Bentley Ms, Enf. EN1 ... 30 DR44
★ Bentley Priory, Stan. HA7 ... 41 CE48
Bentley Rd, N1
off Tottenham Rd ... 84 DS65
Bentley St, Grav. DA12 ... 131 GJ86
Bentley Way, Stan. HA7 ... 41 CG50
Woodford Green IG8 ... 48 EG48
Benton Rd, Ilf. IG1 ... 69 ER60
Watford WD19 ... 40 BX50
Bentons La, SE27 ... 122 DQ91
Bentons Ri, SE27 ... 122 DR92
Bentry Cl, Dag. RM8 ... 70 EY61
Bentry Rd, Dag. RM8 ... 70 EY61
Bentworth Rd, W12 ... 81 CV72
Benwell Ct, Sun. TW16 ... 135 BU95
Benwell Rd, N7 ... 65 DN63
Benwick Cl, SE16 ... 202 E8
Benworth St, E3 ... 85 DZ69
Benyon Path, S.Ock. RM15
off Tyssen Pl ... 91 FW68
Benyon Rd, N1
off Southgate Rd ... 84 DR67
Beomonds Row, Cher. KT16
off Heriot Rd ... 134 BG101
Berberis Wk, West Dr. UB7 ... 94 BL77
Berber Pl, E14
off Birchfield St ... 85 EA73
Berber Rd, SW11 ... 120 DF85
Berberry Cl, Edg. HA8
off Larkspur Gro ... 42 CQ49
Berceau Wk, Wat. WD17 ... 23 BS39
Bercta Rd, SE9 ... 125 EQ89
Beredens La, Brwd. CM13 ... 73 FT55
Berenger Wk, SW10
off Blantyre St ... 100 DD80
Berens Rd, NW10 ... 81 CX69
Orpington BR5 ... 146 EX99
Berens Way, Chis. BR7 ... 145 ET98
Beresford Av, N20 ... 44 DF47
W7 ... 79 CD71
Slough SL2 ... 74 AW74
Surbiton KT5 ... 138 CP102
Twickenham TW1 ... 117 CJ86
Wembley HA0 ... 80 CM67
Beresford Dr, Brom. BR1 ... 144 EK97
Woodford Green IG8 ... 48 EJ49
Beresford Gdns, Enf. EN1 ... 30 DS42
Hounslow TW4 ... 116 BZ85
Romford RM6 ... 70 EY57
Beresford Rd, E4 ... 48 EE46
E17 ... 47 EB53
N2 ... 64 DE55
N5 ... 66 DQ64
N8 ... 65 DN57
Gravesend (Nthflt.) DA11 ... 130 GE87
Harrow HA1 ... 61 CD57
Kingston upon Thames
KT2 ... 138 CM95
New Malden KT3 ... 138 CQ98
Rickmansworth (Mill End)
WD3 ... 37 BF46
Southall UB1 ... 78 BX74
Sutton SM2 ... 157 CZ108
Beresford Sq, SE18 ... 105 EP77
Beresford St, SE18 ... 105 EP76
Beresford Ter, N5 ... 66 DQ64
Berestede Rd, W6 ... 99 CT78
Bere St, E1 off Cranford St ... 85 DX73
Bergen Sq, SE16 ... 203 L6
Berger Cl, Orp. BR5 ... 145 ER100
Berger Rd, E9 ... 85 DX65
Berghem Ms, W14
off Blythe Rd ... 99 CX76
Bergholt Av, Ilf. IG4 ... 68 EL57
Bergholt Cres, N16 ... 66 DS59
Bergholt Ms, NW1
off Rossendale Way ... 83 DJ66
Berglen Ct, E14 off Branch Rd ... 85 DY72
Bering Sq, E14 off Napier Av ... 103 EA78
Bering Wk, E16 ... 86 EK72
Berisford Ms, SW18 ... 120 DC86
Berkeley Av, Bexh. DA7 ... 106 EX81
Greenford UB6 ... 79 CE65
Hounslow TW4 ... 95 BU82
Ilford IG5 ... 49 EN54
Romford RM5 ... 51 FC52
Berkeley Cl, Abb.L. WD5 ... 7 BT32
Borehamwood (Elstree)
WD6 ... 26 CN43
Hornchurch RM11 ... 72 FP61
Kingston upon Thames
KT2 ... 118 CL94
Orpington BR5 ... 145 ES101
Potters Bar EN6 ... 11 CY32
Ruislip HA4 ... 59 BU62
Staines TW19 ... 113 BD89
Berkeley Ct, N14 ... 29 DJ44
Rickmansworth (Crox.Grn.)
WD3 off Mayfare ... 23 BR43
Wallington SM6 ... 141 DJ104
Weybridge KT13 ... 135 BR103
Berkeley Cres, Barn. EN4 ... 28 DD43
Dartford DA1 ... 128 FM88
Berkeley Dr, Horn. RM11 ... 72 FN60
West Molesey KT8 ... 136 BZ97
Berkeley Gdns, N21 ... 46 DR45
W8 off Brunswick Gdns ... 82 DA74
Esher (Clay.) KT10 ... 155 CG107
Walton-on-Thames KT12 ... 135 BT101
West Byfleet KT14 ... 151 BF114
Berkeley Ho, E3 ... 85 EA70
Berkeley Ms, W1 ... 194 E8
Berkeley Pl, SW19 ... 119 CX93
Epsom KT18 ... 172 CR115
Berkeley Rd, E12 ... 68 EL64
N8 ... 65 DK57
N15 ... 66 DR58
NW9 ... 62 CN56
SW13 ... 99 CU81
Uxbridge UB10 ... 77 BQ66
Berkeleys, The, Lthd. (Fetch.)
KT22 ... 171 CE124
Berkeley Sq, W1 ... 199 J1
Berkeley St, W1 ... 199 J1
Berkeley Wk, N7
off Durham Rd ... 65 DM61
Berkeley Waye, Houns. TW5 ... 96 BX80
Berkhampstead Rd, Belv.
DA17 ... 106 FA78
Berkhamsted Av, Wem. HA9 ... 80 CM65
Berkley Av, Wal.Cr. EN8 ... 15 DX34
Berkley Cres, Grav. DA12
off Milton Rd ... 131 GJ86
Berkley Gro, NW1
off Berkley Rd ... 82 DF66
Berkley Rd, NW1 ... 82 DF66
Gravesend DA12 ... 131 GH86
Berks Hill, Rick. (Chorl.) WD3 ... 21 BC43
Berkshire Cl, Cat. CR3 ... 176 DR122
Berkshire Gdns, N13 ... 45 DN51
N18 ... 46 DV50
Berkshire Rd, E9 ... 85 DZ65
Berkshire Sq, Mitch. CR4
off Berkshire Way ... 141 DL98
Berkshire Way, Horn. RM11 ... 72 FN57
Mitcham CR4 ... 141 DL98
Bermans Cl, Brwd. CM13
off Hanging Hill La ... 55 GB47
Bermans Way, NW10 ... 63 CS63
BERMONDSEY, SE1 ... 201 P7
⊖ Bermondsey ... 202 C6
★ Bermondsey Leather Mkt,
SE1 ... 201 M5
Bermondsey Sq, SE1 ... 201 N6
Bermondsey St, SE1 ... 201 M3
Bermondsey Wall E, SE16 ... 202 C5
Bermondsey Wall W, SE16 ... 202 B4
Bermuda Rd, Til. RM18 ... 111 GG82
Bernal Cl, SE28
off Haldane Rd ... 88 EX73
Bernard Ashley Dr, SE7 ... 104 EH78
Bernard Av, W13 ... 97 CH76
Bernard Cassidy St, E16 ... 86 EF71
Bernard Gdns, SW19 ... 119 CZ92
Bernard Gro, Wal.Abb. EN9
off Beaulieu Dr ... 15 EB33
Bernard Rd, N15 ... 66 DT57
Romford RM7 ... 71 FC59
Wallington SM6 ... 159 DH105
Bernards Cl, Ilf. IG6 ... 49 EQ51
Bernard St, WC1 ... 195 P5
Gravesend DA12 ... 131 GH86
Bernato Cl, W.Byf. KT14
off Viscount Gdns ... 152 BL112
Bernays Cl, Stan. HA7 ... 41 CJ51
Bernays Gro, SW9 ... 101 DM84
Bernel Dr, Croy. CR0 ... 143 DZ104
Berne Rd, Th.Hth. CR7 ... 142 DQ99
Berners Dr, W13 ... 79 CG72
Bernersmede, SE3
off Blackheath Pk ... 104 EG83
Berners Ms, W1 ... 195 L7
Berners Pl, W1 ... 195 L8
Berners Rd, N1 ... 83 DN67
N22 ... 45 DN53
Berners St, W1 ... 195 L7
Berney Rd, Croy. CR0 ... 142 DR101
Bernhardt Cres, NW8 ... 194 B4
Bernhart Cl, Edg. HA8 ... 42 CQ52
Bernice Cl, Rain. RM13 ... 90 FJ70
Bernville Way, Har. HA3
off Kenton Rd ... 62 CM57
Bernwell Rd, E4 ... 48 EE48
Berridge Grn, Edg. HA8 ... 42 CN52
Berridge Ms, NW6
off Hillfield Rd ... 64 DA64
Berridge Rd, SE19 ... 122 DR92
Berriman Rd, N7 ... 65 DM62
Berrington Dr, Lthd. (E.Hors.)
KT24 ... 169 BT124
Berriton Rd, Har. HA2 ... 60 BZ60
Berry Av, Wat. WD24 ... 23 BU36
Berrybank Cl, E4
off Greenbank Cl ... 47 EC47
Berry Cl, N21 ... 45 DP46
NW10 ... 80 CS66
Dagenham RM10 ... 70 FA64
Hornchurch RM12
off Airfield Way ... 72 FJ64
Rickmansworth WD3 ... 38 BH45
Berry Ct, Houns. TW4 ... 116 BZ85
Berrydale Rd, Hayes UB4 ... 78 BY70
Berryfield, Slou. SL2 ... 74 AW72
Berryfield Cl, E17 ... 67 EB56
Bromley BR1 ... 144 EL95
Berryfield Rd, SE17 ... 200 G10
Berry Gro La, Wat. WD25 ... 24 CA39
Berryhill, SE9 ... 105 EP84
Berry Hill, Stan. HA7 ... 41 CK49
Berryhill Gdns, SE9 ... 105 EP84
BERRYLANDS, Surb. ... 138 CM99
⇌ Berrylands ... 138 CN98
Berrylands, SW20 ... 139 CW97
Orpington BR6 ... 146 EW104
Surbiton KT5 ... 138 CN99
Berrylands Rd, Surb. KT5 ... 138 CM100
Berry La, SE21 ... 122 DR91
Rickmansworth WD3 ... 38 BH46
Walton-on-Thames KT12
off Burwood Rd ... 154 BX106
Berryman Cl, Dag. RM8
off Bennetts Castle La ... 70 EW62
Berrymans La, SE26 ... 123 DX91
Berry Meade, Ashtd. KT21 ... 172 CM117
Berry Meade Cl, Ashtd. KT21
off Berry Meade ... 172 CM117
Berrymead Gdns, W3 ... 80 CQ74
Berrymede Rd, W4 ... 98 CR76
Berry Pl, EC1 ... 196 G3
Berryscroft Ct, Stai. TW18
off Berryscroft Rd ... 114 BJ94
Berryscroft Rd, Stai. TW18 ... 114 BJ94
BERRY'S GREEN, West. ... 179 EP116
Berry's Grn Rd, West.
(Berry's Grn.) TN16 ... 179 EP116
Berry's Hill, West. (Berry's Grn.)
TN16 ... 179 EP115
Berrys La, W.Byf. (Byfleet)
KT14 ... 152 BK111
Berry St, EC1 ... 196 G4
Berry Wk, Ashtd. KT21 ... 172 CM119
Berry Way, W5 ... 98 CL76
Rickmansworth WD3 ... 38 BH45
Bersham La, Grays (Bad.Dene)
RM17 ... 110 FZ77
Bertal Rd, SW17 ... 120 DD91
Berther Rd, Horn. RM11 ... 72 FK59
Berthold Ms, Wal.Abb. EN9 ... 15 EB33
Berthon St, SE8 ... 103 EA80
Bertie Rd, NW10 ... 81 CU65
SE26 ... 123 DX93
Bertram Cotts, SW19
off Hartfield Rd ... 120 DA94
Bertram Rd, NW4 ... 63 CU58
Enfield EN1 ... 30 DU42
Bertram Rd, Kings.T. KT2 ... 118 CN94
Bertram St, N19 ... 65 DH61
Bertram Way, Enf. EN1 ... 30 DT42
Bertrand St, SE13 ... 103 EB83
Bertrand Way, SE28 ... 88 EV73
Bert Rd, Th.Hth. CR7 ... 142 DQ99
Bert Way, Enf. EN1
off Percival Rd ... 30 DT42
Berwick Av, Hayes UB4 ... 78 BX72
Berwick Cl, Stan. HA7
off Gordon Av ... 41 CF52
Waltham Cross EN8 ... 15 EA34
Berwick Cres, Sid. DA15 ... 125 ES86
Berwick La, Ong. CM5 ... 35 FF36
Berwick Pond Cl, Rain. RM13 ... 90 FK68
Berwick Pond Rd, Rain. RM13 ... 90 FL68
Upminster RM14 ... 90 FM66
Berwick Rd, E16 ... 86 EH72
N22 ... 45 DP53
Borehamwood WD6 ... 26 CM38
Rainham RM13 ... 90 FK68
Welling DA16 ... 106 EV81
Berwick St, W1 ... 195 M9
Berwick Way, Orp. BR6 ... 146 EU102
Sevenoaks TN14 ... 191 FH121
Berwyn Av, Houns. TW3 ... 96 CB81
Berwyn Rd, SE24 ... 121 DP88
Richmond TW10 ... 98 CP84
Beryl Av, E6 ... 86 EL71
Beryl Ho, SE18 off Spinel Cl ... 105 ET78
Beryl Rd, W6 ... 99 CX78
Berystede, Kings.T. KT2 ... 118 CP94
Besant Ct, N1
off Newington Grn Rd ... 66 DR64
Besant Rd, NW2 ... 63 CY63
Besant Wk, N7 off Newington
Barrow Way ... 65 DM61
Besant Way, NW10 ... 62 CQ64
Besley St, SW16 ... 121 DJ93
Bessant Dr, Rich. TW9 ... 98 CP81
Bessborough Gdns, SW1 ... 199 N10
Bessborough Pl, SW1 ... 199 M10
Bessborough Rd, SW15 ... 119 CU88
Harrow HA1 ... 61 CD60
Bessborough St, SW1 ... 199 M10
BESSELS GREEN, Sev. ... 190 FC124
Bessels Grn Rd, Sev. TN13 ... 190 FD123
Bessels Meadow, Sev. TN13 ... 190 FD124
Bessels Way, Sev. TN13 ... 190 FC124
Bessemer Rd, SE5 ... 102 DQ82
Bessie Lansbury Cl, E6 ... 87 EN72
Bessingby Rd, Ruis. HA4 ... 59 BU61
Bessingham Wk, SE4
off Frendsbury Rd ... 103 DX84
Besson St, SE14 ... 102 DW81
Bessy St, E2 off Roman Rd ... 84 DW69
Bestwood St, SE8 ... 203 J9
Beswick Ms, NW6
off Lymington Rd ... 82 DB65
Betam Rd, Hayes UB3 ... 95 BR75
Beta Pl, SW4 off Santley St ... 101 DL84
Beta Rd, Wok. GU22 ... 167 BB116
Woking (Chobham) GU24 ... 150 AT110
Beta Way, Egh. TW20 ... 133 BC95
BETCHWORTH ... 182 CR134
⇌ Betchworth ... 182 CR132
Betchworth Cl, Sutt. SM1
off Turnpike La ... 158 DD106
Betchworth Rd, Ilf. IG3 ... 69 ES61
Betchworth Way, Croy.
(New Adgtn.) CR0 ... 161 EC109
Betenson Av, Sev. TN13 ... 190 FF122
Betham Rd, Grnf. UB6 ... 79 CD69
Bethany Waye, Felt. TW14 ... 115 BS87
Bethecar Rd, Har. HA1 ... 61 CE57
Bethell Av, E16 ... 86 EF70
Ilford IG1 ... 69 EN59
Bethel Rd, Sev. TN13 ... 191 FJ123
Welling DA16 ... 106 EW83
Bethersden Cl, Beck. BR3 ... 123 DZ94
H Bethlem Royal Hosp, Beck.
BR3 ... 143 EA101
BETHNAL GREEN, E2 ... 84 DU68
⇌ Bethnal Green ... 84 DV70
⊖ Bethnal Green ... 84 DW69
Bethnal Grn Est, E2 ... 84 DW69
★ Bethnal Green Mus of
Childhood, E2 ... 84 DV69
Bethnal Grn Rd, E1 ... 197 P4
E2 ... 197 P4
Bethune Av, N11 ... 44 DF49
Bethune Rd, N16 ... 66 DR59
NW10 ... 80 CR70
Bethwin Rd, SE5 ... 101 DP80
Betjeman Cl, Couls. CR5 ... 175 DM117
Pinner HA5 ... 60 CA56
Waltham Cross EN7
off Rosedale Way ... 14 DU28
Betley Ct, Walt. KT12 ... 135 BV104
Betony Cl, Croy. CR0
off Primrose La ... 143 DX102
Betony Rd, Rom. RM3
off Cloudberry Rd ... 52 FK51
Betoyne Av, E4 ... 48 EE49
BETSHAM, Dart. ... 130 FY91
BETSHAM, Grav. ... 130 FY91
Betsham Rd, Erith DA8 ... 107 FF80
Gravesend (Sthflt.) DA13 ... 129 FX92
Swanscombe DA10 ... 130 FY87
Betstyle Rd, N11 ... 45 DH49
Betterton Dr, Sid. DA14 ... 126 EY89
Betterton Rd, Rain. RM13 ... 89 FE69
Betterton St, WC2 ... 195 P9
Bettles Cl, Uxb. UB8
off Wescott Way ... 76 BJ68
Bettons Pk, E15 ... 86 EE67
Bettridge Rd, SW6 ... 99 CZ82
Betts Cl, Beck. BR3
off Kendall Rd ... 143 DY96
Betts Ms, E17 off Queen's Rd ... 67 DZ58
Betts Rd, E16
off Victoria Dock Rd ... 86 EH73
Betts St, E1 ... 202 D1
Betts Way, SE20 ... 142 DV95
Surbiton KT6 ... 137 CH102
Betula Cl, Ken. CR8 ... 176 DR115
Betula Wk, Rain. RM13 ... 90 FK69
Between Sts, Cob. KT11 ... 153 BU114
Beulah Av, Th.Hth. CR7
off Beulah Rd ... 141 DM98
Beulah Cl, Edg. HA8 ... 42 CP48
Beulah Cres, Th.Hth. CR7 ... 142 DQ96
Beulah Gro, Croy. CR0 ... 142 DQ100
Beulah Hill, SE19 ... 121 DP93
Beulah Path, E17
off Addison Rd ... 67 EB57
Beulah Rd, E17 ... 67 EB57
SW19 ... 119 CZ94
Epping CM16 ... 18 EU29
Hornchurch RM12 ... 72 FJ62
Sutton SM1 ... 158 DA105
Thornton Heath CR7 ... 142 DQ97
Beulah Wk, Cat. (Wold.) CR3 ... 177 DY120
Beult Rd, Dart. DA1 ... 107 FG83
Bevan Av, Bark. IG11 ... 88 EU66
Bevan Ct, Croy. CR0 ... 159 DN106
Bevan Ho, Grays RM16
off Laird Av ... 110 GD75
Bevan Pl, Swan. BR8 ... 147 FF98
Bevan Rd, SE2 ... 106 EV78
Barnet EN4 ... 28 DF42
Bevans Cl, Green. DA9
off Johnsons Way ... 129 FW86
Bevan St, N1 ... 84 DQ67
Bevan Way, Horn. RM12 ... 72 FM63
Bev Callender Cl, SW8
off Daley Thompson Way ... 101 DH83
Bevenden St, N1 ... 197 L2
Bevercote Wk, Belv. DA17
off Osborne Rd ... 106 EZ79
Beveridge Rd, NW10
off Curzon Cres ... 80 CS66
Beverley Av, SW20 ... 139 CT95
Hounslow TW4 ... 96 BZ84
Sidcup DA15 ... 125 ET87
Beverley Cl, N21 ... 46 DQ46
SW11 off Maysoule Rd ... 100 DD84
SW13 ... 99 CT82
Addlestone KT15 ... 152 BK106
Chessington KT9 ... 155 CJ105
Enfield EN1 ... 30 DS42
Epsom KT17 ... 157 CW111
Hornchurch RM11 ... 72 FM59
Weybridge KT13 ... 135 BS103
Beverley Cotts, SW15
off Kingston Vale ... 118 CR91
Beverley Ct, N14 ... 45 DJ45
N20 off Farnham Cl ... 44 DC45
SE4 ... 103 DZ83
Slough SL1 off Dolphin Rd ... 92 AV75
Beverley Cres, Wdf.Grn. IG8 ... 48 EH53
Beverley Dr, Edg. HA8 ... 62 CP55
Beverley Gdns, NW11 ... 63 CY59
SW13 ... 99 CT83
Hornchurch RM11 ... 72 FM59
Stanmore HA7 ... 41 CG53
Waltham Cross (Chsht.)
EN7 ... 14 DT30
Wembley HA9 ... 62 CM60
Worcester Park KT4
off Green La ... 139 CU102
Beverley Hts, Reig. RH2 ... 184 DB132
Beverley Ho, NW8 ... 194 B3
Beverley La, SW15 ... 119 CT90
Kingston upon Thames
KT2 ... 118 CS94
Beverley Ms, E4
off Beverley Rd ... 47 ED51
Beverley Path, SW13 ... 99 CT82
Beverley Rd, E4 ... 47 ED51
E6 ... 86 EK69
SE20 off Wadhurst Cl ... 142 DV96
SW13 ... 99 CT83
W4 ... 99 CT78
Bexleyheath DA7 ... 107 FC82
Bromley BR2 ... 144 EL103
Dagenham RM9 ... 70 EY63
Kingston upon Thames
KT1 ... 137 CJ95
Mitcham CR4 ... 141 DK98
New Malden KT3 ... 139 CU98
Ruislip HA4 ... 59 BU61
Southall UB2 ... 96 BY76
Sunbury-on-Thames
TW16 ... 135 BT95
Whyteleafe CR3 ... 176 DS116
Worcester Park KT4 ... 139 CW103
Beverley Trd Est, Mord. SM4
off Garth Rd ... 139 CX101
Beverley Way, SW20 ... 139 CT95
New Malden KT3 ... 139 CT95
Beversbrook Rd, N19 ... 65 DK62
Beverstone Rd, SW2 ... 121 DM85
Thornton Heath CR7 ... 141 DN98
Beverston Ms, W1 ... 194 D7
Bevill Allen Cl, SW17 ... 120 DF92
Bevill Cl, SE25 ... 142 DU97
Bevin Cl, SE16 ... 203 K2
Bevin Ct, WC1 off Holford St ... 83 DN69
Bevington Path, SE1
off Tanner St ... 102 DT75
Bevington Rd, W10 ... 81 CY71
Beckenham BR3 ... 143 EB96
Bevington St, SE16 ... 202 C5
Bevin Rd, Hayes UB4 ... 77 BU69
Bevin Sq, SW17 ... 120 DF90
Bevin Way, WC1 ... 196 D2
Bevis Cl, Dart. DA2 ... 128 FQ87
Bevis Marks, EC3 ... 197 N8
Bewcastle Gdns, Enf. EN2 ... 29 DL42
Bewdley St, N1 ... 83 DN66
Bewick St, SW8 ... 101 DH82
Bewley Cl, Wal.Cr. (Chsht.)
EN8 ... 15 DX31
Bewley St, E1 off Dellow St ... 84 DV73
Bewley St, SW19
off East Rd ... 120 DC93
Bewlys Rd, SE27 ... 121 DP92
Bexhill Cl, Felt. TW13 ... 116 BY89
Bexhill Rd, N11 ... 45 DK50
SE4 ... 123 DZ87

★ Place of interest ⇌ Railway station ⊖ London Underground station DLR Docklands Light Railway station Tramlink station H Hospital

Bex - Bla

Bexhill Rd, SW14 98 CQ83
Bexhill Wk, E15 *off Mitre Rd* 86 EE68
BEXLEY 126 FA86
⇌ Bexley 126 FA88
Bexley Cl, Dart. DA1 127 FE85
Bexley Gdns, N9 46 DR48
Romford (Chad.Hth.) RM6 70 EV57
BEXLEYHEATH 126 EZ85
⇌ Bexleyheath 106 EY82
Bexley High St, Bex. DA5 126 FA87
Bexley La, Dart. DA1 127 FE85
Sidcup DA14 126 EW90
Bexley Rd, SE9 125 EP85
Erith DA8 107 FC80
Beynon Rd, Cars. SM5 158 DF106
Bianca Ho, N1 *off Crondall St* 84 DS68
Bianca Rd, SE15 102 DT79
Bibsworth Rd, N3 43 CZ54
Bibury Cl, SE15 102 DS79
Bicester Rd, Rich. TW9 98 CN83
Bickenhall St, W1 194 E6
Bickersteth Rd, SW17 120 DF93
Bickerton Rd, N19 65 DJ61
BICKLEY, Brom. 145 EM97
⇌ Bickley 144 EL97
Bickley Cres, Brom. BR1 144 EL98
Bickley Pk Rd, Brom. BR1 144 EL97
Bickley Rd, E10 67 EB59
Bromley BR1 144 EK96
Bickley St, SW17 120 DE92
Bicknell Rd, SE5 102 DQ83
Bickney Way, Lthd. (Fetch.)
KT22 170 CC122
Bicknoller Cl, Sutt. SM2 158 DB110
Bicknoller Rd, Enf. EN1 30 DT39
Bicknor Rd, Orp. BR6 145 ES101
Bidborough Cl, Brom. BR2 144 EF99
Bidborough St, WC1 195 P3
Biddenden Way, SE9 125 EN91
Gravesend (Istead Rise)
DA13 130 GE94
Biddenham Turn, Wat. WD25 24 BW35
Bidder St, E16 86 EE71
Biddestone Rd, N7 65 DM63
Biddulph Rd, W9 82 DB69
South Croydon CR2 160 DQ109
Bideford Av, Grnf. UB6 79 CH68
Bideford Cl, Edg. HA8 42 CN53
Feltham TW13 116 BZ90
Romford RM3 52 FJ53
Bideford Gdns, Enf. EN1 46 DS45
Bideford Rd, Brom. BR1 124 EF90
Enfield EN3 31 DZ38
Ruislip HA4 59 BV62
Welling DA16 106 EV80
Bidhams Cres, Tad. KT20 173 CW121
Bidwell Gdns, N11 45 DJ52
Bidwell St, SE15 102 DV81
★ Big Ben (St. Stephens Twr),
SW1 200 A5
Bigbury Cl, N17
off Weir Hall Rd 46 DR52
Bigbury Rd, N17
off Barkham Rd 46 DS52
Big Common La, Red. (Bletch.)
RH1 185 DP133
Biggerstaff Rd, E15 85 EC67
Biggerstaff St, N4 65 DN61
Biggin Av, Mitch. CR4 140 DF95
BIGGIN HILL, West. 178 EH116
Biggin Hill, SE19 121 DP94
Biggin Hill Business Pk, West.
TN16 178 EK115
Biggin Hill Cl, Kings.T. KT2 117 CJ92
Biggin La, Grays RM16 111 GH79
Biggin Way, SE19 121 DP94
Bigginwood Rd, SW16 121 DP94
Biggs Gro Rd, Wal.Cr. (Chsht.)
EN7 14 DR27
Biggs Row, SW15
off Felsham Rd 99 CX83
Big Hill, E5 66 DV60
Bigland St, E1 84 DV72
Bignell Rd, SE18 105 EP78
Bignold Rd, E7 68 EG63
Bigwood Rd, NW11 64 DB57
Biko Cl, Uxb. UB8
off Sefton Way 76 BJ72
Billet Cl, Rom. RM6 70 EX55
Billet La, Horn. RM11 72 FK60
Iver SL0 75 BB69
Slough SL3 75 BB73
Billet Rd, E17 47 DX54
Romford RM6 70 EV55
Staines TW18
off Farnell Rd 114 BG90
Billets Hart Cl, W7 97 CE75
Billet Wks, E17 47 DZ53
Bill Hamling Cl, SE9 125 EM89
Billingford Cl, SE4 103 DX84
Billing Pl, SW10 100 DB80
Billing Rd, SW10 100 DB80
Billings Cl, Dag. RM9
off Ellerton Rd 88 EW66
★ Billingsgate Fish Mkt,
E14 204 C2
Billing St, SW10 100 DB80
Billington Rd, SE14 103 DX80
Billiter Sq, EC3 197 N10
Billiter St, EC3 197 N9
Bill Nicholson Way, N17
off High Rd 46 DT52
Billockby Cl, Chess. KT9 156 CM107
Billson St, E14 204 E9
Billy Lows La, Pot.B. EN6 12 DA31
Bilsby Gro, SE9 124 EK91
Bilton Cl, Slou. (Poyle) SL3 93 BE82
Bilton Rd, Erith DA8 107 FG80
Greenford UB6 79 CH67
Bilton Way, Enf. EN3 31 DY39
Hayes UB3 95 BV75
Bina Gdns, SW5 100 DC77
Bincote Rd, Enf. EN2 29 DM41
Binden Rd, W12 99 CT76
Bindon Grn, Mord. SM4 140 DB98
Binfield Rd, SW4 101 DL81
South Croydon CR2 160 DT106
West Byfleet (Byfleet)
KT14 152 BL112
Bingfield St, N1 83 DL67
Bingham Cl, S.Ock. RM15 91 FV72
Bingham Ct, N1
off Halton Rd 83 DP66
Bingham Dr, Stai. TW18 114 BK94
Woking GU21 166 AT118
Bingham Pl, W1 194 F6
Bingham Pt, SE18
off Whitworth Pl 105 EP77
Bingham Rd, Croy. CR0 142 DU102
Bingham St, N1 84 DR65
Bingley Rd, E16 86 EJ72
Greenford UB6 78 CC71
Sunbury-on-Thames TW16 115 BU94
Binley Ho, SW15
off Highcliffe Dr 119 CU86
Binney St, W1 194 G10
Binns Rd, W4 98 CS78
Binns Ter, W4 *off Binns Rd* 98 CS78
Binsey Wk, SE2 88 EW74
Binyon Cres, Stan. HA7 41 CF50
Birbetts Rd, SE9 125 EM89
Bircham Path, SE4
off St. Norbert Rd 103 DX84
Birchanger Rd, SE25 142 DU99
Birch Av, N13 46 DQ48
Caterham CR3 176 DR124
Leatherhead KT22 171 CF120
West Drayton UB7 76 BM72
Birch Cl, E16 86 EE71
N19 *off Hargrave Pk* 65 DJ61
SE15 *off Bournemouth Rd* 102 DU82
Addlestone (New Haw)
KT15 152 BK109
Amersham HP6 20 AS37
Brentford TW8 97 CH80
Buckhurst Hill IG9 48 EK48
Dartford (Eyns.) DA4 148 FK104
Hounslow TW3 97 CD83
Iver SL0 75 BD68
Romford RM7 71 FB55
Sevenoaks TN13 191 FH123
South Ockendon RM15 91 FX69
Teddington TW11 117 CG92
Woking GU21 166 AW119
Birch Copse, St.Alb. (Brick.Wd.)
AL2 8 BY30
Birch Ct, Nthwd. HA6
off Rickmansworth Rd 39 BQ51
Birch Cres, Horn. RM11 72 FL56
South Ockendon RM15 91 FX69
Uxbridge UB10 76 BM67
Birchcroft Cl, Cat. CR3 186 DQ125
Birchdale, Ger.Cr. SL9 56 AX60
Birchdale Cl, W.Byf. KT14 152 BJ111
Birchdale Gdns, Rom. RM6 70 EX59
Birchdale Rd, E7 68 EJ64
Birchdene Dr, SE28 106 EU75
Birch Dr, Rick. (Map.Cr.) WD3 37 BD50
Birchen Cl, NW9 62 CR61
Birchend Cl, S.Croy. CR2 160 DR107
Birchen Gro, NW9 62 CR61
Birches, The, N21 29 DM44
SE7 104 EH79
Brentwood CM13 54 FY48
Bushey WD23 24 CC43
Epping (N.Wld.Bas.) CM16 19 FB26
Orpington BR6 163 EN105
Swanley BR8 147 FE96
Woking GU22
off Heathside Rd 167 AZ118
Birches Cl, Epsom KT18 172 CS115
Mitcham CR4 140 DF97
Pinner HA5 60 BY57
Birches, The, Wal.Abb. EN9
off Honey La 16 EF34
Birchfield Cl, Add. KT15 152 BH105
Coulsdon CR5 175 DM116
Birchfield Gro, Epsom KT17 157 CW110
Birchfield Rd, Wal.Cr. (Chsht.)
EN8 14 DV29
Birchfield St, E14 85 EA73
Birch Gdns, Amer. HP7 20 AS39
Dagenham RM10 71 FC62
Birchgate Ms, Tad. KT20
off Bidhams Cres 173 CW121
Birch Grn, NW9
off Clayton Fld 42 CS52
Staines TW18 114 BG91
Birch Gro, E11 68 EE62
SE12 124 EF87
W3 80 CN74
Cobham KT11 154 BW114
Potters Bar EN6 12 DA32
Shepperton TW17 135 BS96
Tadworth KT20 173 CY124
Welling DA16 106 EU84
Woking GU22 167 BD115
★ Birch Hall, Epp. (They.B.)
CM16 33 EQ36
Birch Hill, Croy. CR0 161 DX106
Birchington Cl, Bexh. DA7 107 FB81
Orpington BR5
off Hart Dyke Rd 146 EW102
Birchington Rd, N8 65 DK58
NW6 82 DA67
Surbiton KT5 138 CM101
Birchin La, EC3 197 L9
Birchlands Av, SW12 120 DF87
Birch La, Hem.H. (Flaun.) HP3 5 BB33
Purley CR8 159 DL111
Birch Mead, Orp. BR6 145 EN103
Birchmead, Wat. WD17 23 BT38
Birchmead Av, Pnr. HA5 60 BW56
Birchmere Row, SE3 104 EF82
Birchmore Wk, N5 66 DQ62
Birch Pk, Har. HA3 40 CC52
Birch Pl, Green. DA9 129 FS86
Birch Rd, Felt. TW13 116 BX92
Romford RM7 71 FB55
Birch Row, Brom. BR2 145 EN101
Birch Tree Av, W.Wick. BR4 162 EF106
Birch Tree Gro, Chesh. (Ley Hill)
HP5 4 AV30
Birch Tree Wk, Wat. WD17 23 BT37
Birch Tree Way, Croy. CR0 142 DV103
Birch Vale, Cob. KT11 154 CA112
Birch Vw, Epp. CM16 18 EV29
Birchville Ct, Bushey (Bushey Hth.)
WD23 *off Heathbourne Rd* 41 CE46
Birch Wk, Borwd. WD6 26 CN39
Erith DA8 107 FC79
Mitcham CR4 141 DH95
West Byfleet KT14 152 BG112
Birchway, Hayes UB3 77 BU74
Birch Way, St.Alb. (Lon.Col.)
AL2 9 CK27
Warlingham CR6 177 DY118
Birch Wd, Rad. (Shenley) WD7 10 CN34
Birchwood, Wal.Abb. EN9
off Roundhills 16 EE34
Birchwood Av, N10 64 DG55
Beckenham BR3 143 DZ98
Sidcup DA14 126 EV89
Wallington SM6 140 DG104
Birchwood Cl, Brwd. CM13
off Canterbury Way 53 FW51
Morden SM4 140 DB98
Birchwood Ct, N13 45 DP50
Edgware HA8 42 CQ54
Birchwood Dr, NW3 64 DB62
Dartford DA2 127 FE91
West Byfleet KT14 152 BG112
Birchwood Gro, Hmptn.
TW12 116 CA93
Birchwood La, Cat. CR3 185 DP125
Esher KT10 155 CD110
Leatherhead KT22 155 CD110
Sevenoaks (Knock.) TN14 180 EZ115
Birchwood Pk Av, Swan.
BR8 147 FE97
Birchwood Rd, SW17 121 DH92
Dartford DA2 127 FE92
Orpington BR5 145 ER98
Swanley BR8 147 FC95
West Byfleet KT14 152 BG112
Birchwood Ter, Swan. BR8
off Birchwood Rd 147 FC95
Birchwood Way, St.Alb. (Park St.)
AL2 8 CB28
Birdbrook Cl, Brwd. CM13 55 GB44
Dagenham RM10 89 FC66
Birdbrook Rd, SE3 104 EJ83
Birdcage Wk, SW1 199 L5
Birdham Cl, Brom. BR1 144 EL99
Birdhouse La, Orp. BR6 179 EN115
Birdhurst Av, S.Croy. CR2 160 DR105
Birdhurst Gdns, S.Croy. CR2 160 DR105
Birdhurst Ri, S.Croy. CR2 160 DS106
Birdhurst Rd, SW18 100 DC84
SW19 120 DE93
South Croydon CR2 160 DS106
Bird in Bush Rd, SE15 102 DU80
Bird-in-Hand La, Brom. BR1 144 EK96
Bird-in-Hand Pas, SE23
off Dartmouth Rd 122 DW89
Bird La, Brwd. CM13 73 FX55
Upminster RM14 73 FR57
Uxbridge (Hare.) UB9 38 BJ54
Birds Fm Av, Rom. RM5 51 FB53
Birdsfield La, E3 85 DZ67
Birds Hill Dr, Lthd. (Oxshott)
KT22 155 CD113
Birds Hill Ri, Lthd. (Oxshott)
KT22 155 CD113
Birds Hill Rd, Lthd. (Oxshott)
KT22 155 CD112
Bird St, W1 194 G9
Birdswood Dr, Wok. GU21 166 AS119
Bird Wk, Twick. TW2 116 BZ88
Birdwood Cl, S.Croy. CR2 161 DX111
Teddington TW11 117 CE91
⇌ Birkbeck 142 DW97
⊕ Birkbeck 142 DW97
Birkbeck Av, W3 80 CQ73
Greenford UB6 78 CC67
Birkbeck Gdns, Wdf.Grn. IG8 48 EF47
Birkbeck Gro, W3 98 CR75
Birkbeck Hill, SE21 121 DP89
Birkbeck Ms, E8
off Sandringham Rd 66 DT64
Birkbeck Pl, SE21 122 DQ88
Birkbeck Rd, E8 66 DT64
N8 65 DL56
N12 44 DC50
N17 46 DT53
NW7 43 CT50
SW19 120 DB92
W3 80 CR74
W5 97 CJ77
Beckenham BR3 142 DW96
Brentwood CM13 55 GD44
Enfield EN2 30 DR39
Ilford IG2 69 ER57
Romford RM7 71 FD60
Sidcup DA14 126 EU90
Birkbeck St, E2 84 DV69
Birkbeck Way, Grnf. UB6 78 CC67
Birkdale Av, Pnr. HA5 60 CA55
Romford RM3 52 FM52
Birkdale Cl, SE16
off Masters Dr 102 DV78
Orpington BR6 145 ER101
Birkdale Gdns, Croy. CR0 161 DX105
Watford WD19 40 BX48
Birkdale Rd, SE2 106 EU77
W5 80 CL70
Birkenhead Av, Kings.T. KT2 138 CM96
Birkenhead St, WC1 196 A2
Birken Ms, Nthwd. HA6 39 BP50
Birkett Way, Ch.St.G. HP8 20 AX41
Birkhall Rd, SE6 123 ED88
Birkheads Rd, Reig. RH2 184 DA133
Birklands La, St.Alb. AL1 9 CH25
Birkwood Cl, SW12 121 DK87
Birley Rd, N20 44 DC47
Birley St, SW11 100 DG82
Birling Rd, Erith DA8 107 FD80
Birnam Rd, N4 65 DM61
Birnham Cl, Wok. (Send M.)
GU23 168 BG123
Birrell Ho, SW9
off Stockwell Rd 101 DM82
Birse Cres, NW10 62 CS63
Birstall Grn, Wat. WD19 40 BX49
Birstall Rd, N15 66 DS57
Birtley Path, Borwd. WD6 26 CL39
Biscay Rd, W6 99 CX78
Biscoe Cl, Houns. TW5 96 CA79
Biscoe Way, SE13 103 ED83
Bisenden Rd, Croy. CR0 142 DS103
Bisham Cl, Cars. SM5 140 DF102
Bisham Gdns, N6 64 DG60
Bishop Butt Cl, Orp. BR6
off Stapleton Rd 145 ET104
Bishop Cl, W4 98 CQ78
Bishop Duppa's Pk, Shep.
TW17 135 BR101
Bishop Fox Way, W.Mol. KT8 136 BZ98
Bishop Ken Rd, Har. HA3 41 CF54
Bishop Kings Rd, W14 99 CY77
Bishop Rd, N14 45 DH45
Bishop's Av, E13 86 EH67
SW6 99 CX82
Bishops Av, Borwd. (Elstree)
WD6 26 CM43
Bromley BR1 144 EJ96
Northwood HA6 39 BS49
Romford RM6 70 EW58
Bishops Av, The, N2 64 DD59
Bishops Br, W2 82 DC71
Bishops Br Rd, W2 82 DC72
Bishops Cl, E17 67 EB56
N19 *off Wyndham Cres* 65 DJ62
SE9 125 EQ89
Barnet EN5 27 CX44
Bishop's Cl, Couls. CR5 175 DN118
Bishops Cl, Enf. EN1
off Central Av 30 DV40
Richmond TW10 117 CK90
Bishop's Cl, Sutt. SM1 140 DA104
Bishops Cl, Uxb. UB10 76 BN68
Bishop's Ct, EC4 196 F8
WC2 196 D8
Bishops Ct, Green. DA9 129 FS85
Waltham Cross EN8
off Churchgate 14 DV30
Bishops Dr, Felt. TW14 115 BR86
Northolt UB5 78 BY67
Bishopsford Rd, Mord. SM4 140 DC101
Bishopsgate, EC2 197 M9
Bishopsgate Arc, EC2 197 N7
Bishopsgate Chyd, EC2 197 M8
Bishopsgate Rd, Egh. (Eng.Grn.)
TW20 112 AT90
Bishops Gro, N2 64 DD58
Hampton TW12 116 BZ91
Bishop's Hall, Kings.T. KT1 137 CK96
Bishops Hall Rd, Brwd. CM15 54 FV44
Bishops Hill, Walt. KT12 135 BU101
Bishop's Pk, SW6 99 CX82
Bishop's Pk Rd, SW6 99 CX82
Bishops Pk Rd, SW16 141 DL95
Bishops Pl, Sutt. SM1
off Lind Rd 158 DC106
Bishops Rd, N6 64 DG58
SW6 99 CZ81
W7 97 CE75
Croydon CR0 141 DP101
Hayes UB3 77 BQ71
Slough SL1 92 AU75
Bishops Ter, SE11 200 E8
Bishopsthorpe Rd, SE26 123 DX91
Bishop St, N1 84 DQ67
Bishops Wk, Chis. BR7 145 EQ95
Croydon CR0 161 DX106
Bishop's Wk, Pnr. HA5
off High St 60 BY55
Bishops Way, E2 84 DV68
Egham TW20 113 BD93
Bishops Wd, Wok. GU21 166 AT117
H Bishopswood Private Hosp,
Nthwd. HA6 39 BP51
Bishopswood Rd, N6 64 DF59
Bishop Wk, Brwd. (Shenf.)
CM15 55 FZ47
Bishop Way, NW10 80 CS66
Bishop Wilfred Wd Cl, SE15
off Moncrieff St 102 DU82
Biskra, Wat. WD17 23 BU39
Bisley Cl, Wal.Cr. EN8 15 DX33
Worcester Park KT4 139 CW102
Bisley Ho, SW19 119 CX89
Bispham Rd, NW10 80 CM69
Bisson Rd, E15 85 EC68
Bisterne Av, E17 67 ED55
Bittacy Cl, NW7 43 CX51
Bittacy Hill, NW7 43 CX51
Bittacy Pk Av, NW7 43 CX51
Bittacy Ri, NW7 43 CW51
Bittacy Rd, NW7 43 CX51
Bittams La, Cher. KT16 151 BE105
Bittern Cl, Hayes UB4 78 BX71
Hemel Hempstead HP3
off Belswains La 6 BM25
Waltham Cross (Chsht.)
EN7 14 DQ25
Bitterne Dr, Wok. GU21 166 AT117
Bittern St, SE1 201 H5
Bittoms, The, Kings.T. KT1 137 CK97
Bixley Cl, Sthl. UB2 96 BZ77
Black Acre Cl, Amer. HP7 20 AS39
Blackacre Rd, Epp. (They.B.)
CM16 33 ES37
Blackall St, EC2 197 M4
Blackberry Cl, Shep. TW17
off Cherry Way 135 BS98
Blackberry Fm Cl, Houns.
TW5 96 BY80
Blackberry Fld, Orp. BR5 146 EU95
Blackbird Hill, NW9 62 CQ61
Blackbirds La, Wat. (Ald.)
WD25 25 CD35
Blackbird Yd, E2
off Ravenscroft St 84 DT69
Blackborne Rd, Dag. RM10 88 FA65
Blackborough Cl, Reig. RH2 184 DC134
Black Boy La, N15 66 DQ57
Black Boy Wd, St.Alb. (Brick.Wd.)
AL2 8 CA30
Blackbridge Rd, Wok. GU22 166 AX119
Blackbrook La, Brom. BR1,
BR2 145 EN97
Blackburn, The, Lthd. (Bkhm.) KT23
off Little Bookham St 170 BZ124
Blackburne's Ms, W1 194 F10
Blackburn Rd, NW6 82 DB65
Blackburn Trd Est, Stai. (Stanw.)
TW19 114 BM86
Blackbury Cl, Pot.B. EN6 12 DC31
Blackbush Av, Rom. RM6 70 EX57
Blackbush Cl, Sutt. SM2 158 DB108
Blackdale, Wal.Cr. (Chsht.)
EN7 14 DU27
Blackdown Av, Wok. GU22 167 BE115
Blackdown Cl, N2 44 DC54
Woking GU22 167 BC116
Blackdown Ter, SE18
off Prince Imperial Rd 105 EN80
Black Eagle Cl, West. TN16 189 EQ127
Blackett Cl, Stai. TW18 133 BE96
Blackett St, SW15 99 CX83
Blacketts Wd Dr, Rick. (Chorl.)
WD3 21 BB43
Black Fan Cl, Enf. EN2 30 DQ39
BLACKFEN, Sid. 125 ET87
Blackfen Rd, Sid. DA15 125 ES85
Blackford Cl, S.Croy. CR2 159 DP109
Blackford Rd, Wat. WD19 40 BX50
Blackford's Path, SW15
off Roehampton High St 119 CU87
⇌ Blackfriars 196 G10
⊖ Blackfriars 196 G10
Blackfriars Br, EC4 196 F10
SE1 196 F10
Black Friars Ct, EC4 196 F10
Black Friars La, EC4 196 F10
Blackfriars Pas, EC4 196 F10
Blackfriars Rd, SE1 200 F5
Black Gates, Pnr. HA5
off Church La 60 BZ55
Blackhall La, Sev. TN15 191 FK123
Blackhall Pl, Sev. TN15
off Blackhall La 191 FL124
BLACKHEATH, SE3 104 EE81
★ Blackheath, SE3 103 ED81
⇌ Blackheath 104 EE83
Blackheath Av, SE10 103 ED80
Blackheath Gro, SE3 104 EF82
Blackheath Hill, SE10 103 EC81
H Blackheath Hosp, The,
SE3 104 EF83
BLACKHEATH PARK, SE3 104 EF84
Blackheath Pk, SE3 104 EF83
Blackheath Ri, SE13 103 EC82
Blackheath Rd, SE10 103 EB81
Blackheath Vale, SE3 104 EE82
Blackheath Village, SE3 104 EF82
Blackhills, Esher KT10 154 CA109
Blackhorse Cl, Amer. HP6 20 AS38
Black Horse Ct, SE1 201 L6
Blackhorse Cres, Amer. HP6 20 AS38
⊕ Blackhorse Lane 142 DU101
Blackhorse La, E17 67 DX56
Croydon CR0 142 DU101
Epping (N.Wld.Bas.) CM16 19 FD25
Potters Bar EN6 10 CS30
Reigate RH2 184 DB129
Blackhorse Ms, E17
off Blackhorse La 67 DX55
Black Horse Pl, Uxb. UB8
off Waterloo Rd 76 BJ67
⇌ Blackhorse Road 67 DX56
⊖ Blackhorse Road 67 DX56
Blackhorse Rd, E17 67 DX56
SE8 103 DY78
Sidcup DA14 126 EU91
Woking GU22 166 AS122
Black Lake Cl, Egh. TW20 133 BA95
Blacklands Dr, Hayes UB4 77 BQ70
Blacklands Meadow, Red.
(Nutfld.) RH1 185 DL133
Blacklands Rd, SE6 123 EC91
Blacklands Ter, SW3 198 D9
Blackley Cl, Wat. WD17 23 BT37
Black Lion Hill, Rad. (Shenley)
WD7 10 CL32
Black Lion La, W6 99 CU77
Black Lion Ms, W6
off Black Lion La 99 CU77
Blackmans Cl, Dart. DA1 128 FJ88
Blackmans La, Warl. CR6 162 EE114
Blackmans Yd, E2
off Cheshire St 84 DU70
Blackmead, Sev. (Rvrhd.)
TN13 190 FE121
Blackmoor La, Wat. WD18 23 BR43
Blackmore Av, Sthl. UB1 79 CD74
Blackmore Cl, Grays RM17 110 GC78
Blackmore Ct, Wal.Abb. EN9 16 EG33
Blackmore Cres, Wok. GU21 167 BB115
Blackmore Rd, Buck.H. IG9 48 EL45
Blackmores Gro, Tedd. TW11 117 CG93
Blackmore Way, Uxb. UB8 76 BK65
Blackness La, Kes. BR2 162 EK109
Woking GU22 166 AY119
★ Black Park Country Pk, Slou.
SL3 75 AZ67
Black Pk Rd, Slou. SL3 75 AZ68
Black Path, E10 67 DX59
Blackpool Gdns, Hayes UB4 77 BS70
Blackpool Rd, SE15 102 DV82
Black Prince Cl, W.Byf. (Byfleet)
KT14 152 BM114
Black Prince Rd, SE1 200 B9
SE11 200 C9
Black Rod Cl, Hayes UB3 95 BT76
Blackshaw Pl, N1
off Hertford Rd 84 DS66
Blackshaw Rd, SW17 120 DC91
Blackshots La, Grays RM16 110 GD75
Blacksmith Cl, Ashtd. KT21
off Rectory La 172 CM119

★ Place of interest ⇌ Railway station ⊖ London Underground station DLR Docklands Light Railway station ⊕ Tramlink station H Hospital

Blacksmith Row, Slou. SL3 . . .93 BA77
Blacksmiths Cl, Rom. RM6 . . .70 EW58
Blacksmiths Hill, S.Croy.
CR2 . . . . .160 DU113
Blacksmiths La, Cher. KT16 . .134 BG101
Orpington BR5 . . . . .146 EW99
Rainham RM13 . . . . .89 FF67
Staines TW18 . . . . .134 BH97
Uxbridge (Denh.) UB9 . . . . .57 BC61
Blacks Rd, W6
off Queen Caroline St 99 CW77
Blackstock Ms, N4
off Blackstock Rd 65 DP61
Blackstock Rd, N4 . . . . .65 DP61
N5 .65 DP61
Blackstone Est, E8 . . . . .84 DV66
Blackstone Hill, Red. RH1 . . .184 DE134
Blackstone Rd, NW2 . . . . . . .63 CW64
Black Swan Yd, SE1 . . . . .201 N4
Black's Yd, Sev. TN13
off Bank St 191 FJ125
Blackthorn Av, West Dr. UB7 . .94 BN77
Blackthorn Cl, Wat. WD25 . . . . .7 BV32
Blackthorn Ct, Houns. TW5 . . .96 BY80
Blackthorn Dell, Slou. SL3 . . .92 AW76
Blackthorne Av, Croy. CR0 . . .142 DW101
Blackthorne Cres, Slou. (Colnbr.)
SL3 . . . . .93 BE83
Blackthorne Dr, E4 . . . . .47 ED49
Blackthorne Rd, Slou. (Colnbr.)
SL3 . . . . .93 BE83
Westerham (Bigg.H.) TN16 .178 EK116
Blackthorn Gro, Bexh. DA7 . .106 EX83
Blackthorn St, E3 . . . . .85 EA70
Blackthorn Way, Brwd. CM14 .54 FX50
Blacktree Ms, SW9 . . . . .101 DN83
DLR Blackwall 204 E1
Blackwall La, SE10 . . . . .205 J10
Blackwall Pier, E14 . . . . .205 H1
Blackwall Trd Est, E14 . . . . . . .85 ED71
Blackwall Tunnel, E14 . . . . . .204 F1
Blackwall Tunnel App, SE10 . .205 H5
Blackwall Tunnel Northern App,
E3 .85 EA68
E14 . . . . .85 EA68
Blackwall Way, E14 . . . . .204 E1
Blackwater Cl, E7 . . . . .68 EF63
Rainham RM13 . . . . .89 FF71
Blackwater Rd, Sutt. SM1
off High St 158 DB105
Blackwater St, SE22 . . . . . . .122 DT85
Blackwell Cl, E5 . . . . .67 DX63
Harrow HA3 . . . . .41 CD52
Blackwell Dr, Wat. WD19 . . . .24 BW44
Blackwell Gdns, Edg. HA8 . . . .42 CN48
Blackwell Hall La, Chesh. HP5 . .4 AW33
Blackwell Rd, Kings L. WD4 . . . .6 BN29
Blackwood Cl, W.Byf. KT14 . .152 BJ112
Blackwood Ct, Brox. EN10
off Groom Rd 15 DZ26
Blackwood St, SE17 . . . . .201 K10
Blade Ms, SW15
off Deodar Rd 99 CZ84
Bladen Cl, Wey. KT13 . . . . . . .153 BR107
Blades Cl, Lthd. KT22 . . . . . . .171 CK120
Blades Ct, SW15
off Deodar Rd 99 CZ84
Bladindon Dr, Bex. DA5 . . . . .126 EW87
Bladon Gdns, Har. HA2 . . . . . .60 CB58
Blagdens Cl, N14 . . . . .45 DJ47
Blagdens La, N14 . . . . .45 DK47
Blagdon Rd, SE13 . . . . .123 EB86
New Malden KT3 . . . . .139 CT98
Blagdon Wk, Tedd. TW11 . . . .117 CJ93
Blagrove Rd, W10 . . . . .81 CY71
Blair Av, NW9 . . . . .62 CS59
Esher KT10 . . . . .136 CC103
Blair Cl, N1 . . . . .84 DQ65
Hayes UB3 . . . . .95 BU77
Sidcup DA15 . . . . .125 ES85
Blairderry Rd, SW2 . . . . .121 DL89
Blair Dr, Sev. TN13 . . . . .191 FH123
Blairhead Dr, Wat. WD19 . . . .39 BV48
Blair Rd, Slou. SL1 . . . . .74 AS74
Blair St, E14 . . . . .85 EC72
Blake Av, Bark. IG11 . . . . .87 ES67
Blakeborough Dr, Rom.
(Harold Wd.) RM3 . . . . . . .52 FL54
Blake Cl, W10 . . . . .81 CW71
Carshalton SM5 . . . . .140 DE101
Rainham RM13 . . . . .89 FF67
Welling DA16 . . . . .105 ES81
Blakeden Dr, Esher (Clay.)
KT10 . . . . .155 CF107
Blake Gdns, SW6 . . . . .100 DB81
Dartford DA1 . . . . .108 FM84
Blake Hall Cres, E11 . . . . .68 EG60
Blake Hall Rd, E11 . . . . .68 EG59
Blakehall Rd, Cars. SM5 . . . .158 DF107
Blake Hall Rd, Ong. CM5 . . . . .19 FG25
Blake Ho, Beck. BR3 . . . . . . .123 EA93
Blakeley Cotts, SE10
off Tunnel Av 103 ED75
Blakemore Rd, SW16 . . . . . . .121 DL90
Thornton Heath CR7 . . . . . .141 DM99
Blakemore Way, Belv. DA17 . .106 EY76
Blakeney Av, Beck. BR3 . . . . .143 DZ95
Blakeney Cl, E8
off Ferncliff Rd 66 DU64
N20 . . . . .44 DC46
NW1
off Rossendale Way 83 DK66
Epsom KT19 . . . . .156 CR111
Blakeney Rd, Beck. BR3 . . . . .123 DZ94
Blakenham Rd, SW17 . . . . . . .120 DF91
Blaker Ct, SE7 off Fairlawn . . .104 EJ80
Blake Rd, E16 . . . . .86 EF70
N11 . . . . .45 DJ52
Croydon CR0 . . . . .142 DS103
Mitcham CR4 . . . . .140 DE97
Blaker Rd, E15 . . . . .85 EC67
Blakes Av, N.Mal. KT3 . . . . . .139 CT99
Blake's Grn, W.Wick. BR4 . . . .143 EC102
Blakes La, N.Mal. KT3 . . . . . .139 CT99
Blakesley Av, W5 . . . . .79 CJ72
Blakesley Wk, SW20
off Kingston Rd 139 CZ96
Blakes Rd, SE15 . . . . .102 DS80
Blakes Ter, N.Mal. KT3 . . . . . .139 CU99
Blake St, SE8
off Watergate St 103 EA79
Blakesware Gdns, N9 . . . . . . .46 DR45
Blakes Way, Til. RM18
off Coleridge Rd 111 GJ82
Blakewood Cl, Felt. TW13 . . . .116 BW91
Blanchard Chase, Horn. RM12
off Upper Rainham Rd 71 FF61
Blanchard Cl, SE9 . . . . .124 EL90
Blanchard Gro, Enf. EN3
off Government Row 31 EA37
Blanchard Way, E8 . . . . .84 DU65
Blanch Cl, SE15
off Culmore Rd 102 DW80
Blanchedowne, SE5 . . . . .102 DR84
Blanche La, Pot.B. EN6 . . . . . .11 CT34
Blanche St, E16 . . . . .86 EF70
Blanchland Rd, Mord. SM4 . .140 DB99
Blanchmans Rd, Warl. CR6 . .177 DY118
Blandfield Rd, SW12 . . . . . . .120 DG86
Blandford Av, Beck. BR3 . . . .143 DY96
Twickenham TW2 . . . . .116 CB88
Blandford Cl, N2 . . . . .64 DC56
Croydon CR0 . . . . .141 DL104
Romford RM7 . . . . .71 FB56
Slough SL3 . . . . .92 AX76
Woking GU22 . . . . .167 BB117
Blandford Ct, Slou. SL3
off Blandford Rd S 92 AX76
Blandford Cres, E4 . . . . .47 EC45
Blandford Rd, W4 . . . . .98 CS76
W5 .97 CK75
Beckenham BR3 . . . . .142 DW96
Southall UB2 . . . . .96 CA77
Teddington TW11 . . . . .117 CD92
Blandford Rd N, Slou. SL3 . . . .92 AX76
Blandford Rd S, Slou. SL3 . . . .92 AX76
Blandford Sq, NW1 . . . . .194 C5
Blandford St, W1 . . . . .194 E8
Blandford Waye, Hayes UB4 . .78 BW72
Bland St, SE9 . . . . .104 EK84
Blaney Cres, E6 . . . . .87 EP69
Blanmerle Rd, SE9 . . . . .125 EP88
Blann Cl, SE9 . . . . .124 EK86
Blantyre St, SW10 . . . . .100 DD80
Blantyre Wk, SW10
off Blantyre St 100 DD80
Blashford, NW3 . . . . .82 DF66
Blashford St, SE13 . . . . .123 ED87
Blasker Wk, E14 . . . . .204 A10
Blattner Cl, Borwd. (Elstree)
WD6 . . . . .26 CL42
Blawith Rd, Har. HA1 . . . . .61 CE56
Blaxland Ter, Wal.Cr. (Chsht.)
EN8 off Davison Dr 15 DX28
Blaydon Cl, N17 . . . . .46 DV52
Ruislip HA4 . . . . .59 BS59
Blaydon Wk, N17 . . . . .46 DV52
Blays Cl, Egh. (Eng.Grn.)
TW20 . . . . .112 AW93
Blays La, Egh. (Eng.Grn.)
TW20 . . . . .112 AV94
Bleak Hill La, SE18 . . . . .105 ET79
Blean Gro, SE20 . . . . .122 DW94
Bleasdale Av, Grnf. UB6 . . . . .79 CG68
Blechynden St, W10
off Bramley Rd 81 CX73
Bleddyn Cl, Sid. DA15 . . . . . .126 EW86
Bledlow Cl, SE28 . . . . .88 EW73
Bledlow Ri, Grnf. UB6 . . . . . . .78 CC68
Bleeding Heart Yd, EC1 . . . . .196 E7
Blegborough Rd, SW16 . . . . .121 DJ93
Blencarn Cl, Wok. GU21 . . . .166 AT116
Blendon Dr, Bex. DA5 . . . . . .126 EX86
Blendon Path, Brom. BR1 . . .124 EF94
Blendon Rd, Bex. DA5 . . . . . .126 EX86
Blendon Ter, SE18 . . . . .105 EQ78
Blendworth Pt, SW15
off Wanborough Dr 119 CV88
Blendworth Way, SE15
off Daniel Gdns 102 DS80
Blenheim Av, Ilf. IG2 . . . . . . .69 EN58
Blenheim Cl, N21
off Elm Pk Rd 46 DQ46
SE12 off Guibal Rd 124 EH88
SW20 . . . . .139 CW97
Dartford DA1 . . . . .128 FJ86
Greenford UB6
off Leaver Gdns 79 CD68
Romford RM7 . . . . .71 FC56
Slough SL3 . . . . .75 AZ74
Upminster RM14 . . . . .73 FS60
Wallington SM6 . . . . .159 DJ108
Watford WD19 . . . . .24 BX45
West Byfleet KT14
off Madeira Rd 151 BF113
Blenheim Ct, N19
off Marlborough Rd 65 DL61
Sidcup DA14 . . . . .125 ER90
Sutton SM2
off Wellesley Rd 158 DC107
Woodford Green IG8
off Navestock Cres 48 EJ52
Blenheim Cres, W11 . . . . .81 CY72
Ruislip HA4 . . . . .59 BR61
South Croydon CR2 . . . . . .160 DQ108
Blenheim Dr, Well. DA16 . . . .105 ET81
Blenheim Gdns, NW2 . . . . . . .63 CW64
SW2 . . . . .121 DM86
Kingston upon Thames
KT2 . . . . .118 CP94
South Croydon CR2 . . . . . .160 DU112
South Ockendon (Aveley)
RM15 . . . . .90 FP74
Wallington SM6 . . . . .159 DJ107
Wembley HA9 . . . . .62 CL62
Woking GU22 . . . . .166 AV119
Blenheim Gro, SE15 . . . . . . .102 DU82
Blenheim Pk Rd, S.Croy.
CR2 . . . . .160 DQ109
Blenheim Pas, NW8
off Blenheim Ter 82 DC68
Blenheim Ri, N15
off Talbot Rd 66 DT56
Blenheim Rd, E6 . . . . .86 EK69
Blenheim Rd, E15 . . . . .68 EE63
E17 . . . . .67 DX55
NW8 . . . . .82 DC68
SE20 off Maple Rd 122 DW94
SW20 . . . . .139 CW97
W4 . . . . .98 CS76
Abbots Langley WD5 . . . . . . .7 BU33
Barnet EN5 . . . . .27 CX41
Brentwood CM15 . . . . .54 FU44
Bromley BR1 . . . . .144 EL98
Dartford DA1 . . . . .128 FJ86
Epsom KT19 . . . . .156 CR111
Harrow HA2 . . . . .60 CB58
Northolt UB5 . . . . .78 CB65
Orpington BR6 . . . . .146 EW103
Sidcup DA15 . . . . .126 EW88
Slough SL3 . . . . .92 AX77
Sutton SM1 . . . . .140 DA104
Blenheim Shop Cen, SE20 . . .122 DW94
Blenheim St, W1 . . . . .195 H9
Blenheim Ter, NW8 . . . . .82 DC68
Blenheim Way, Epp. (N.Wld.Bas.)
CM16 . . . . .18 FA27
Isleworth TW7 . . . . .97 CG81
Blenkarne Rd, SW11 . . . . . . .120 DF86
Bleriot Rd, Houns. TW5 . . . . . .96 BW80
Blessbury Rd, Edg. HA8 . . . . . .42 CQ53
Blessington Cl, SE13 . . . . . . .103 ED83
Blessington Rd, SE13 . . . . . . .103 ED83
Blessing Way, Bark. IG11 . . . . .88 EW69
BLETCHINGLEY, Red. 186 DQ132
Bletchingley Cl, Red. RH1 . . .185 DJ129
Thornton Heath CR7 . . . . .141 DP98
Bletchingley Rd, Gdse. RH9 . .186 DU131
Redhill (Bletch.) RH1 . . . . .185 DN133
Redhill (S.Merst.) RH1 . . . .185 DJ129
Bletchley Ct, N1 . . . . .197 K1
Bletchley St, N1 . . . . .197 J1
Bletchmore Cl, Hayes UB3 . . . .95 BR78
Bletsoe Wk, N1 off Cropley St . .84 DQ68
Blewbury Ho, SE2
off Yarnton Way 106 EX75
Bligh Rd, Grav. DA11 . . . . . . .131 GG86
Bligh's Rd, Sev. TN13 . . . . . . .191 FH125
Blincoe Cl, SW19 . . . . .119 CX89
Blinco La, Slou. (Geo.Grn.)
SL3 . . . . .74 AY72
Blind La, Bans. SM7 . . . . .174 DE115
Loughton (High Beach)
IG10 . . . . .32 EE40
Waltham Abbey EN9 . . . . . . .16 EJ33
Blindman's La, Wal.Cr. (Chsht.)
EN8 . . . . .15 DX30
Bliss Cres, SE13
off Coldbath St 103 EB82
Blissett St, SE10 . . . . .103 EC81
Bliss Ms, W10 off Third Av 81 CY69
Blisworth Cl, Hayes UB4
off Braunston Dr 78 BY70
Blithbury Rd, Dag. RM9 . . . . . .88 EV65
Blithdale Rd, SE2 . . . . .106 EU77
Blithfield St, W8 . . . . .100 DB76
Blockhouse Rd, Grays RM17 . .110 GC79
Blockley Rd, Wem. HA0 . . . . . .61 CH61
Bloemfontein Av, W12 . . . . . . .81 CV74
Bloemfontein Rd, W12 . . . . . .81 CV73
Blomfield Rd, W9 . . . . .82 DC71
Blomfield St, EC2 . . . . .197 L7
Blomfield Vil, W2 . . . . .82 DB71
Blomville Rd, Dag. RM8 . . . . . .70 EY62
Blondell Cl, West Dr. UB7 . . . .94 BK79
Blondel St, SW11 . . . . .100 DG82
Blondin Av, W5 . . . . .97 CJ77
Blondin St, E3 . . . . .85 EA68
Bloomburg St, SW1 . . . . .199 L9
Bloomfield Cl, Wok. (Knap.)
GU21 . . . . .166 AS118
Bloomfield Cres, Ilf. IG2 . . . . .69 EP58
Bloomfield Pl, W1 . . . . .195 J10
Bloomfield Rd, N6 . . . . .64 DG58
SE18 . . . . .105 EP78
Bromley BR2 . . . . .144 EK99
Kingston upon Thames
KT1 . . . . .138 CL98
Waltham Cross (Chsht.)
EN7 . . . . .14 DQ25
Bloomfield Ter, SW1 . . . . . . .198 G10
Westerham TN16 . . . . .189 ES125
Bloom Gro, SE27 . . . . .121 DP90
Bloomhall Rd, SE19 . . . . .122 DR92
Bloom Pk Rd, SW6 . . . . .99 CZ80
BLOOMSBURY, WC1 . . . . . . .195 N7
Bloomsbury Cl, W5 . . . . .80 CM73
Epsom KT19 . . . . .156 CR110
Bloomsbury Ct, WC1 . . . . . . .196 A7
Pinner HA5 . . . . .60 BZ55
Bloomsbury Ho, SW4 . . . . . . .121 DK86
Bloomsbury Pl, SW18
off Fullerton Rd 120 DC85
WC1 . . . . .196 A6
Bloomsbury Sq, WC1 . . . . . . .196 A7
Bloomsbury St, WC1 . . . . . . .195 N7
Bloomsbury Way, WC1 . . . . . .195 P8
Blore Cl, SW8
off Thessaly Rd 101 DK81
Blore Ct, W1 . . . . .195 M9
Blossom Cl, W5
off Almond Av 98 CL75
Dagenham RM9 . . . . .88 EZ67
South Croydon CR2 . . . . . .160 DT106
Blossom La, Enf. EN2 . . . . . . .30 DQ39
Blossom Pl, E1 . . . . .197 N5
Blossom St, E1 . . . . .197 N6
Blossom Way, Uxb. UB10 . . . . .76 BM66
West Drayton UB7 . . . . .94 BN77
Blossom Waye, Houns. TW5 . . .96 BY80
Blount St, E14 . . . . .85 DY72
Bloxam Gdns, SE9 . . . . .124 EL85
Bloxhall Rd, E10 . . . . .67 DZ60
Bloxham Cres, Hmptn. TW12 .116 BZ94
Bloxworth Cl, Wall. SM6 . . . .141 DJ104
Blucher Rd, SE5 . . . . .102 DQ80
Blue Anchor All, Rich. TW9
off Kew Rd 98 CL84
Blue Anchor La, SE16 . . . . . .202 C8
Tilbury (W.Til.) RM18 . . . . .111 GL77
Blue Anchor Yd, E1 . . . . .84 DU73
Blue Ball La, Egh. TW20 . . . . .113 AZ92
Blue Ball Yd, SW1 . . . . .199 K3
Blue Barn La, Wey. KT13 . . . .152 BN111
Bluebell Av, E12 . . . . .68 EK64
Bluebell Cl, E9 off Moulins Rd .84 DW67
SE26 . . . . .122 DT91
Orpington BR6 . . . . .145 EQ103
Romford (Rush Grn.) RM7 . .71 FE61
Wallington SM6 . . . . .141 DH102
Bluebell Ct, Wok. GU22 . . . . .166 AX119
Bluebell Dr, Abb.L. (Bedmond)
WD5 . . . . .7 BT27
Waltham Cross EN7 . . . . . . .14 DR28
Bluebell Way, Ilf. IG1 . . . . . . .87 EP65
Blueberry Cl, Wdf.Grn. IG8 . . .48 EG51
Blueberry Gdns, Couls. CR5 .175 DM116
Blueberry La, Sev. (Knock.)
TN14 . . . . .180 EW116
Bluebird La, Dag. RM10 . . . . . .88 FA66
Bluebird Way, SE28 . . . . .105 ER75
St. Albans AL2 . . . . .8 BY30
Bluebridge Av, Hat. AL9 . . . . . .11 CZ27
Bluebridge Rd, Hat. AL9 . . . . . .11 CY26
Blue Cedars, Bans. SM7 . . . .157 CX114
Blue Cedars Pl, Cob. KT11 . . .154 BX112
Bluefield Cl, Hmptn. TW12 . . .116 CA92
Bluegates, Epsom (Ewell)
KT17 . . . . .157 CU108
Bluehouse Gdns, Oxt. RH8 . .188 EG128
Bluehouse La, Oxt. RH8 . . . .188 EG127
Bluehouse Rd, E4 . . . . .48 EE48
Blue Leaves Av, Couls. CR5
off Netherne La 175 DK122
Bluelion Pl, SE1 . . . . .201 M6
Bluett Rd, St.Alb. (Lon.Col.)
AL2 .9 CK27
Bluewater Ho, SW18
off Smugglers Way 100 DB84
Bluewater Parkway, Green.
(Bluewater) DA9 . . . . .129 FS87
Bluewater Shop Cen, Green.
DA9 . . . . .129 FT88
Blundel La, Cob. (Stoke D'Ab.)
KT11 . . . . .154 CB114
Blundell Rd, Edg. HA8 . . . . . . .42 CR53
Blundell St, N7 . . . . .83 DL66
Blunden Cl, Dag. RM8 . . . . . . .70 EW60
Blunden Dr, Slou. SL3 . . . . . . .93 BB77
Blunesfield, Pot.B. EN6 . . . . . .12 DD31
Blunt Rd, S.Croy. CR2 . . . . . .160 DR106
Blunts Av, West Dr. UB7 . . . . .94 BN80
Blunts La, St.Alb. AL2 . . . . .8 BW27
Blunts Rd, SE9 . . . . .125 EN85
Blurton Rd, E5 . . . . .66 DW63
Blyth Cl, E14 . . . . .204 F8
Borehamwood WD6 . . . . . . .26 CM39
Twickenham TW1
off Grimwood Rd 117 CF86
Blythe Cl, SE6 . . . . .123 DZ87
Iver SL0 . . . . .75 BF72
Blythe Hill, SE6 . . . . .123 DZ87
Orpington BR5 . . . . .145 ET95
Blythe Hill La, SE6 . . . . .123 DZ87
Blythe Rd, W14 . . . . .99 CX76
Blythe St, E2 . . . . .84 DV69
Blythe Vale, SE6 . . . . .123 DZ88
Blyth Rd, E17 . . . . .67 DZ59
SE28 . . . . .88 EW73
Bromley BR1 . . . . .144 EF95
Hayes UB3 . . . . .95 BS75
Blyth's Wf, E14 . . . . .203 L1
Blythswood Rd, Ilf. IG3 . . . . . .70 EU60
Blyth Wk, Upmin. RM14 . . . . . .73 FS58
Blyth Wd Pk, Brom. BR1
off Blyth Rd 144 EF95
Blythwood Rd, N4 . . . . .65 DL59
Pinner HA5 . . . . .40 BX53
Boades Ms, NW3
off New End 64 DD63
Boadicea St, N1
off Copenhagen St 83 DM67
Boakes Cl, NW9 . . . . .62 CQ56
Boakes Meadow, Sev. (Shore.)
TN14 . . . . .165 FF111
Boar Cl, Chig. IG7 . . . . .50 EU50
Boardman Av, E4 . . . . .31 EB43
Boardman Cl, Barn. EN5 . . . . .27 CY43
Board Sch Rd, Wok. GU21 . . .167 AZ116
Boardwalk Pl, E14 . . . . .204 D2
Boar's Head Yd, Brent. TW8
off Brent Way 97 CK80
Boathouse Wk, SE15 . . . . . . .102 DT80
Richmond TW9 . . . . .98 CL81
Boat Lifter Way, SE16 . . . . . .203 L8
Bob Anker Cl, E13
off Chesterton Rd 86 EG69
Bobbin Cl, SW4 . . . . .101 DJ83
Bobby Moore Way, N10 . . . . . .44 DF52
Bob Marley Way, SE24
off Mayall Rd 101 DN84
Bobs La, Rom. RM1 . . . . .51 FG52
Bocketts La, Lthd. KT22 . . . . .171 CF124
Bockhampton Rd, Kings.T.
KT2 . . . . .118 CM94
Bocking St, E8 . . . . .84 DV67
Boddicott Cl, SW19 . . . . .119 CY89
Bodell Cl, Grays RM16 . . . . . .110 GB76
Bodiam Cl, Enf. EN1 . . . . .30 DR40
Bodiam Rd, SW16 . . . . .121 DK94
Bodicea Ms, Houns. TW4 . . . .116 BZ87
Bodle Av, Swans. DA10 . . . . . .130 FY87
Bodley Cl, Epp. CM16 . . . . . . .17 ET30
New Malden KT3 . . . . .138 CS99
Bodley Manor Way, SW2
off Papworth Way 121 DN87
Bodley Rd, N.Mal. KT3 . . . . . .138 CR100
Bodmin Cl, Har. HA2 . . . . .60 BZ62
Orpington BR5 . . . . .146 EW102
Bodmin Gro, Mord. SM4 . . . .140 DB99
Bodmin St, SW18 . . . . .120 DA88
Bodnant Gdns, SW20 . . . . . . .139 CU97
Bodney Rd, E8 . . . . .66 DV64
Boeing Way, Sthl. UB2 . . . . . .95 BV76
Boevey Path, Belv. DA17 . . . .106 EZ79
Bogey La, Orp. BR6 . . . . .163 EN108
Bognor Gdns, Wat. WD19
off Bowring Grn 40 BW50
Bognor Rd, Well. DA16 . . . . . .106 EX81
Bohemia Pl, E8 . . . . .84 DV65
Bohn Rd, E1 . . . . .85 DY71
Bohun Gro, Barn. EN4 . . . . . . .28 DE44
Boileau Par, W5
off Boileau Rd 80 CM72
Boileau Rd, SW13 . . . . .99 CU80
W5 .80 CM72
Bois Hall Rd, Add. KT15 . . . . .152 BK105
Bois Hill, Chesh. HP5 . . . . .4 AS34
Bolden St, SE8 . . . . .103 EB82
Bolderwood Way, W.Wick.
BR4 . . . . .143 EB103
Boldmere Rd, Pnr. HA5 . . . . . .60 BW59
Boleyn Av, Enf. EN1 . . . . .30 DV39
Epsom KT17 . . . . .157 CV110
Boleyn Cl, E17 . . . . .67 EA56
Grays (Chaff.Hun.) RM16
off Clifford Rd 110 FZ76
Loughton IG10
off Roding Gdns 32 EL44
Staines TW18
off Chertsey La 113 BE92
Boleyn Ct, Buck.H. IG9 . . . . . . .48 EG46
Boleyn Dr, Ruis. HA4 . . . . .60 BX61
West Molesey KT8 . . . . . . .136 BZ97
Boleyn Gdns, Brwd. CM13 . . .55 GA48
Dagenham RM10 . . . . .89 FC66
West Wickham BR4 . . . . . .143 EB103
Boleyn Gro, W.Wick. BR4 . . .143 EC103
Boleyn Rd, E6 . . . . .86 EK68
E7 .86 EG66
N16 . . . . .66 DS64
Boleyn Wk, Lthd. KT22 . . . . .171 CF120
Boleyn Way, Barn. EN5 . . . . . .28 DC41
Ilford IG6 . . . . .49 EQ51
Swanscombe DA10 . . . . . . .130 FY87
Bolina Rd, SE16 . . . . .202 G10
Bolingbroke Gro, SW11 . . . . .100 DE84
H Bolingbroke Hosp, SW11 .120 DE85
Bolingbroke Rd, W14 . . . . .99 CX76
Bolingbroke Wk, SW11 . . . . . .100 DD80
Bolingbroke Way, Hayes UB3 . .77 BR74
Bolliger Ct, NW10
off Park Royal Rd 80 CQ70
Bollo Br Rd, W3 . . . . .98 CP76
Bollo La, W3 . . . . .98 CP75
W4 .98 CQ77
Bolney Gate, SW7 . . . . .198 B5
Bolney St, SW8 . . . . .101 DM80
Bolney Way, Felt. TW13 . . . . .116 BY90
Bolsover Gro, Red. RH1 . . . . .185 DL129
Bolsover St, W1 . . . . .195 J5
Bolstead Rd, Mitch. CR4 . . . .141 DH95
Bolt Cellar La, Epp. CM16 . . . .17 ES29
Bolt Ct, EC4 . . . . .196 E9
Bolters La, Bans. SM7 . . . . . .157 CZ114
Boltmore Cl, NW4 . . . . .63 CX55
Bolton Cl, SE20
off Selby Rd 142 DU96
Chessington KT9 . . . . .155 CK107
Bolton Cres, SE5 . . . . .101 DP79
Bolton Gdns, NW10 . . . . .81 CX68
SW5 . . . . .100 DB78
Bromley BR1 . . . . .124 EF93
Teddington TW11 . . . . .117 CG93
Bolton Gdns Ms, SW10 . . . . .100 DB78
Bolton Rd, E15 . . . . .86 EF65
N18 . . . . .46 DT50
NW8 . . . . .82 DB67
NW10 . . . . .80 CS67
W4 .98 CQ80
Chessington KT9 . . . . .155 CK107
Harrow HA1 . . . . .60 CC56
Boltons, The, SW10 . . . . . . .100 DC78
Wembley HA0 . . . . .61 CF63
Woodford Green IG8 . . . . . . .48 EG49
Boltons Cl, Wok. GU22 . . . . .168 BG116
Boltons La, Hayes UB3 . . . . . .95 BQ80
Woking GU22 . . . . .168 BG116
Boltons Pl, SW5 . . . . .100 DC78
Bolton St, W1 . . . . .199 J2
Bolton Wk, N7 off Durham Rd .65 DM61
Bombay St, SE16 . . . . .202 D8
Bombers La, West. TN16 . . . .179 ER119
Bomer Cl, West Dr. UB7 . . . . . .94 BN80
Bomore Rd, W11 . . . . .81 CX73
Bonar Pl, Chis. BR7 . . . . .124 EL94
Bonar Rd, SE15 . . . . .102 DU80
Bonaventure Ct, Grav. DA12 .131 GM91
Bonchester Cl, Chis. BR7 . . . .125 EN94
Bonchurch Cl, Sutt. SM2 . . . .158 DB108
Bonchurch Rd, W10 . . . . .81 CY71
W13 . . . . .79 CH74
Bond Cl, Sev. (Knock.) TN14 . .180 EX115
West Drayton UB7 . . . . .76 BM72
Bond Ct, EC4 . . . . .197 K9
Bondfield Av, Hayes UB4 . . . . .77 BU69
Bondfield Rd, E6
off Lovage App 86 EL71
Bondfield Wk, Dart. DA1 . . . .108 FM84
Bond Gdns, Wall. SM6 . . . . . .159 DJ105
Bonding Yd Wk, SE16 . . . . . .203 L5
Bond Rd, Mitch. CR4 . . . . . . .140 DE96
Surbiton KT6 . . . . .138 CM103
Warlingham CR6 . . . . .177 DX118
⊖ Bond Street 194 G9
Bond St, E15 . . . . .68 EE64
W4 .98 CS77
W5 .79 CK73
Egham (Eng.Grn.) TW20 . . .112 AV92
Grays RM17 . . . . .110 GC79
Bondway, SW8 . . . . .101 DL79
Bone Mill La, Gdse. RH9
off Eastbourne Rd 187 DY134
Boneta Rd, SE18 . . . . .105 EM76
Bonfield Rd, SE13 . . . . .103 EC84
Bonham Gdns, Dag. RM8 . . . . .70 EX61
Bonham Rd, SW2 . . . . .121 DM85
Dagenham RM8 . . . . .70 EX61
Bonheur Rd, W4 . . . . .98 CR75
Bonhill St, EC2 . . . . .197 L5
Boniface Gdns, Har. HA3 . . . . .40 CB52
Boniface Rd, Uxb. UB10 . . . . .59 BP62

Bon - Bra

Boniface Wk, Har. HA3 ....40 CB52
Bonington Ho, Enf. EN1
off Ayley Cft 30 DU43
Bonington Rd, Horn. RM12 ....72 FK64
Bon Marche Ter Ms, SE27
off Gipsy Rd 122 DS91
Bonner Hill Rd, Kings.T. KT1 ....138 CM97
Bonner Rd, E2 ....84 DW68
Bonners Cl, Wok. GU22 ....166 AY122
Bonnersfield Cl, Har. HA1 ....61 CF58
Bonnersfield La, Har. HA1 ....61 CG58
Bonner St, E2 ....84 DW68
Bonner Wk, Grays RM16
off Clifford Rd 110 FZ76
Bonnett Ms, Horn. RM11 ....72 FL60
Bonneville Gdns, SW4 ....121 DJ86
Bonney Gro, Wal.Cr. (Chsht.)
EN7 ....14 DU30
Bonney Way, Swan. BR8 ....147 FE96
Bonningtons, Brwd. CM13 ....55 GB48
Bonnington Sq, SW8 ....101 DM79
Bonnington Twr, Brom. BR2 ....144 EL100
Bonny St, NW1 ....83 DJ66
Bonser Rd, Twick. TW1 ....117 CF89
Bonsey Cl, Wok. GU22 ....166 AY121
Bonsey La, Wok. GU22 ....166 AY121
Bonseys La, Wok. (Chobham)
GU24 ....151 AZ110
Bonsor Dr, Tad. KT20 ....173 CY122
Bonsor St, SE5 ....102 DS80
Bonville Gdns, NW4
off Handowe Cl 63 CU56
Bonville Rd, Brom. BR1 ....124 EF92
Bookbinders' Cotts, N20
off Manor Dr 44 DF48
Booker Cl, E14
off Wallwood St 85 DZ71
Booker Rd, N18 ....46 DU50
⇌ Bookham 170 BZ123
Bookham Ct, Lthd. KT23
off Church Rd 170 BZ123
Bookham Ind Est, Lthd. (Bkhm.)
KT23 ....170 BZ123
Bookham Rd, Cob. (Down.)
KT11 ....170 BW119
Book Ms, WC2 ....195 N9
Boone Ct, N9 ....46 DW48
Boones Rd, SE13 ....104 EE84
Boone St, SE13 ....104 EE84
Boord St, SE10 ....205 J6
Boothby Rd, N19 ....65 DK61
Booth Cl, E9
off Victoria Pk Rd 84 DV67
SE28 ....88 EV73
Booth Dr, Stai. TW18 ....114 BK93
Booth Rd, NW9 ....42 CS54
Croydon CR0
off Waddon New Rd 141 DP103
Booth's Ct, Brwd. (Hutton)
CM13 ....55 GB44
Booth's Pl, W1 ....195 L7
Boot St, N1 ....197 M3
Bordars Rd, W7 ....79 CE71
Bordars Wk, W7 ....79 CE71
Borden Av, Enf. EN1 ....30 DR44
Border Cres, SE26 ....122 DV92
Border Gdns, Croy. CR0 ....161 EB105
Bordergate, Mitch. CR4 ....140 DE95
Border Rd, SE26 ....122 DV92
Borderside, Slou. SL2 ....74 AU72
Borders La, Loug. IG10 ....33 EN42
Bordesley Rd, Mord. SM4 ....140 DB98
Bordon Wk, SW15 ....119 CU87
Boreas Wk, N1 ....196 G1
Boreham Av, E16 ....86 EG72
Boreham Cl, E11
off Hainault Rd 67 EC60
Boreham Holt, Borwd. (Elstree)
WD6 ....26 CM42
Boreham Rd, N22 ....46 DQ54
BOREHAMWOOD 26 CP41
Borehamwood Ind Pk, Borwd.
WD6 ....26 CR40
Borgard Rd, SE18 ....105 EM77
Borkwood Pk, Orp. BR6 ....163 ET105
Borkwood Way, Orp. BR6 ....163 ES105
Borland Cl, Green. DA9
off Steele Av 129 FU85
Borland Rd, SE15 ....102 DW84
Teddington TW11 ....117 CH93
Bornedene, Pot.B. EN6 ....11 CY31
Borneo St, SW15 ....99 CW83
⊖ Borough 201 J5
BOROUGH, THE, SE1 ....201 H5
Borough High St, SE1 ....201 H5
Borough Hill, Croy. CR0 ....141 DP104
★ Borough Mkt, SE1 ....201 K3
Borough Rd, SE1 ....200 F6
Isleworth TW7 ....97 CE81
Kingston upon Thames
KT2 ....138 CN95
Mitcham CR4 ....140 DE96
Westerham (Tats.) TN16 ....178 EK121
Borough Sq, SE1 ....201 H5
Borough Way, Pot.B. EN6 ....11 CY32
Borrett Cl, SE17
off Penrose St 102 DQ78
Borrodaile Rd, SW18 ....120 DB86
Borrowdale Av, Har. HA3 ....41 CG54
Borrowdale Cl, Egh. TW20
off Derwent Rd 113 BB94
Ilford IG4 ....68 EL56
South Croydon CR2 ....160 DT113
Borrowdale Ct, Enf. EN2 ....30 DQ39
Borrowdale Dr, S.Croy. CR2 ....160 DT112
Borthwick Ms, E15
off Borthwick Rd 68 EE63
Borthwick Rd, E15 ....68 EE63
NW9 off West Hendon Bdy 63 CT58
Borthwick St, SE8 ....103 EA78
Borwick Av, E17 ....67 DZ55
Bosanquet Cl, Uxb. UB8 ....76 BK70
Bosbury Rd, SE6 ....123 EC90
Boscastle Rd, NW5 ....65 DH62
Boscobel Pl, SW1 ....198 G8
Boscobel St, NW8 ....194 A5
Bosco Cl, Orp. BR6
off Strickland Way 163 ET105
Boscombe Av, E10 ....67 ED59
Grays RM17 ....110 GD77
Hornchurch RM11 ....72 FK60
Boscombe Cl, E5 ....67 DY64
Egham TW20 ....133 BC95
Boscombe Gdns, SW16 ....121 DL93
Boscombe Rd, SW17 ....120 DG93
SW19 ....140 DB95
W12 ....99 CU75
Worcester Park KT4 ....139 CW102
Bose Cl, N3 off Claremont Pk 43 CY53
Bosgrove, E4 ....47 EC46
Boshers Gdns, Egh. TW20 ....113 AZ93
Boss St, SE1 ....201 P4
Bostall Heath, SE2 ....106 EW78
Bostall Hill, SE2 ....106 EU78
Bostall La, SE2 ....106 EV78
Bostall Manorway, SE2 ....106 EV77
Bostall Pk Av, Bexh. DA7 ....106 EY80
Bostall Rd, Orp. BR5 ....126 EV94
Bostal Row, Bexh. DA7
off Harlington Rd 106 EZ83
Boston Gdns, W4 ....98 CS79
W7 ....97 CG77
Brentford TW8 ....97 CG77
Boston Gro, Ruis. HA4 ....59 BQ58
★ Boston Manor, Brent.
TW8 ....97 CH78
⊖ Boston Manor 97 CG77
Boston Manor Rd, Brent. TW8 ....97 CH77
Boston Pk Rd, Brent. TW8 ....97 CJ78
Boston Pl, NW1 ....194 D5
Boston Rd, E6 ....86 EL69
E17 ....67 EA58
W7 ....79 CE74
Croydon CR0 ....141 DM100
Edgware HA8 ....42 CQ52
Boston St, E2 off Audrey St 84 DU68
Bostonthorpe Rd, W7 ....97 CE75
Boston Vale, W7 ....97 CG77
Bosun Cl, E14 ....204 A4
Bosville Av, Sev. TN13 ....190 FG123
Bosville Dr, Sev. TN13 ....190 FG123
Bosville Rd, Sev. TN13 ....190 FG123
Boswell Cl, Orp. BR5
off Killewarren Way 146 EW100
Radlett (Shenley) WD7 ....10 CL32
Boswell Ct, WC1 ....196 A6
Boswell Path, Hayes UB3
off Croyde Av 95 BT77
Boswell Rd, Th.Hth. CR7 ....142 DQ98
Boswell St, WC1 ....196 A6
Bosworth Cl, E17 ....47 DZ53
Bosworth Cres, Rom. RM3 ....52 FJ51
Bosworth Rd, N11 ....45 DK51
W10 ....81 CY70
Barnet EN5 ....28 DA41
Dagenham RM10 ....70 FA63
BOTANY BAY, Enf. 29 DK36
Botany Bay La, Chis. BR7 ....145 EQ97
Botany Cl, Barn. EN4 ....28 DE42
Botany Rd, Grav. (Nthflt.)
DA11 ....110 GA83
Botany Way, Purf. RM19 ....108 FP78
Boteley Cl, E4 ....47 ED47
Botery's Cross, Red. RH1 ....185 DP133
Botham Cl, Edg. HA8
off Pavilion Way 42 CQ52
Botham Dr, Slou. SL1 ....92 AS76
Botha Rd, E13 ....86 EH71
Bothwell Cl, E16 ....86 EF71
Bothwell Rd, Croy. (New Adgtn.)
CR0 ....161 EC110
Bothwell St, W6
off Delorme St 99 CX79
BOTLEY, Chesh. 4 AV30
Botley La, Chesh. HP5 ....4 AU30
Botley Rd, Chesh. HP5 ....4 AT30
Botolph All, EC3 ....197 M10
Botolph La, EC3 ....197 M10
Botsford Rd, SW20 ....139 CY96
Bottom Ho Fm La, Ch.St.G.
HP8 ....36 AT45
Bottom La, Chesh. HP5 ....4 AT34
Kings Langley WD4 ....22 BH35
Bottrells Cl, Ch.St.G. HP8 ....36 AT47
Bottrells La, Ch.St.G. HP8 ....36 AT47
Bott Rd, Dart. (Hawley) DA2 ....128 FM91
Botts Ms, W2
off Chepstow Rd 82 DA72
Botts Pas, W2
off Chepstow Rd 82 DA72
Botwell Common Rd, Hayes
UB3 ....77 BR73
Botwell Cres, Hayes UB3 ....77 BS72
Botwell La, Hayes UB3 ....77 BS74
Boucher Cl, Tedd. TW11 ....117 CF92
Boucher Dr, Grav. (Nthflt.)
DA11 ....131 GF90
Bouchier Wk, Rain. RM13
off Deere Av 89 FG65
Boughton Av, Brom. BR2 ....144 EF101
Boughton Business Pk, Amer.
HP6 ....20 AV39
Boughton Hall Av, Wok. (Send)
GU23 ....167 BF124
Boughton Rd, SE28 ....105 ES76
Boughton Way, Amer. HP6 ....20 AW38
Boulcott St, E1 ....85 DX72
Boulevard, The, SW6 ....100 DC81
SW17 off Balham High Rd 120 DG89
Pinner HA5
off Pinner Rd 60 CA56
Watford WD18 ....23 BR43
Woodford Green IG8 ....49 EN52
Boulevard 25 Retail Pk, Borwd.
WD6 ....26 CN41
Boulmer Rd, Uxb. UB8 ....76 BJ69
Boulogne Rd, Croy. CR0 ....142 DQ100
Boulter Gdns, Rain. RM13 ....89 FG65
Boulthurst Way, Oxt. RH8 ....188 EH132
Boulton Ho, Brent. TW8
off Green Dragon La 98 CL78
Boulton Rd, Dag. RM8 ....70 EY62
Boultwood Rd, E6 ....86 EL72
Bounce Hill, Rom. (Nave.) RM4
off Mill La 35 FH38
Bounces La, N9 ....46 DV47
Bounces Rd, N9 ....46 DV46
Boundaries Rd, SW12 ....120 DF89
Feltham TW13 ....116 BW88
Boundary Av, E17 ....67 DZ59
Boundary Cl, SE20
off Haysleigh Gdns 142 DU96
Barnet EN5 ....27 CZ39
Ilford IG3 off Loxford La 69 ES63
Kingston upon Thames
KT1 ....138 CP97
Southall UB2 ....96 CA78
Boundary Dr, Brwd. CM13 ....55 GE45
Boundary La, E13 ....86 EK69
SE17 ....102 DQ79
Boundary Pas, E2 ....197 P4
Boundary Rd, E13 ....86 EJ68
E17 ....67 DZ59
N9 ....30 DW44
N22 ....65 DP55
NW8 ....82 DB67
SW19 ....120 DD93
Ashford TW15 ....114 BJ92
Barking IG11 ....87 EQ68
Carshalton SM5 ....159 DH107
Gerrards Cross (Chal.St.P.)
SL9 ....36 AX52
Pinner HA5 ....60 BX58
Romford RM1 ....71 FG58
Sidcup DA15 ....125 ES85
Upminster RM14 ....72 FN62
Wallington SM6 ....159 DH107
Wembley HA9 ....62 CL62
Woking GU21 ....167 BA116
Boundary Row, SE1 ....200 F4
Boundary St, E2 ....197 P3
Erith DA8 ....107 FF80
Boundary Way, Croy. CR0 ....161 EA106
Watford WD25 ....7 BV32
Woking GU21 ....167 BA115
Boundary Yd, Wok. GU21
off Boundary Rd 167 BA116
Boundfield Rd, SE6 ....124 EE90
⊖ Bounds Green 45 DK51
Bounds Grn Rd, N11 ....45 DJ51
N22 ....45 DJ51
Bourchier Cl, Sev. TN13 ....191 FH126
Bourchier St, W1 ....195 M10
Bourdon Pl, W1 ....195 J10
Bourdon Rd, SE20 ....142 DW96
Bourdon St, W1 ....195 J10
Bourke Cl, NW10 off Mayo Rd 80 CS65
SW4 ....121 DL86
Bourke Hill, Couls. CR5 ....174 DF118
Bourlet Cl, W1 ....195 K7
Bourn Av, N15 ....66 DR56
Barnet EN4 ....28 DD43
Uxbridge UB8 ....76 BN70
Bournbrook Rd, SE3 ....104 EK83
Bourne, The, N14 ....45 DK46
Hemel Hempstead (Bov.)
HP3 ....5 BA27
Bourne Av, N14 ....45 DL47
Chertsey KT16 ....134 BG97
Hayes UB3 ....95 BQ76
Ruislip HA4 ....60 BW64
Bournebridge Cl, Brwd. CM13 ....55 GE45
Bournebridge La, Rom. (Stap.Abb.)
RM4 ....50 EZ45
Bourne Cl, T.Ditt. KT7 ....137 CF103
West Byfleet KT14 ....152 BH113
Bourne Ct, Ruis. HA4 ....59 BV64
Bourne Dr, Mitch. CR4 ....140 DD96
Bourne End, Horn. RM11 ....72 FN59
Bourne End Rd, Nthwd. HA6 ....39 BS49
Bourne Est, EC1 ....196 D6
Bournefield Rd, Whyt. CR3
off Godstone Rd 176 DT118
Bourne Gdns, E4 ....47 EB49
Bourne Gro, Ashtd. KT21 ....171 CK119
Bournehall Av, Bushey WD23 ....24 CA43
Bournehall La, Bushey WD23 ....24 CA44
★ Bourne Hall Mus, Epsom
(Ewell) KT17 ....157 CT109
Bournehall Rd, Bushey WD23 ....24 CA44
Bourne Hill, N13 ....45 DL46
Bourne Ind Pk, Dart. DA1
off Bourne Rd 127 FE85
Bourne La, Cat. CR3 ....176 DR121
Bourne Mead, Bex. DA5 ....127 FD85
Bournemead Av, Nthlt. UB5 ....77 BU68
Bournemead Cl, Nthlt. UB5 ....77 BU68
Bourne Meadow, Egh. TW20 ....133 BB98
Bournemead Way, Nthlt. UB5 ....77 BV68
Bournemouth Cl, SE15 ....102 DU82
Bournemouth Rd, SE15 ....102 DU82
SW19 ....140 DA95
Bourne Pk Cl, Ken. CR8 ....176 DS115
Bourne Pl, W4 off Dukes Av 98 CR78
Bourne Rd, E7 ....68 EF62
N8 ....65 DL58
Bexley DA5 ....127 FB86
Bromley BR2 ....144 EK98
Bushey WD23 ....24 CA43
Dartford DA1 ....127 FC86
Gravesend DA12 ....131 GM89
Redhill RH1 ....185 DJ130
Virginia Water GU25 ....132 AX99
Bourneside, Vir.W. GU25 ....132 AU101
Bourneside Cres, N14 ....45 DK46
Bourneside Gdns, SE6 ....123 EC92
Bourneside Rd, Add. KT15 ....152 BK105
Bourne St, SW1 ....198 F9
Croydon CR0
off Waddon New Rd 141 DP103
Bourne Ter, W2 ....82 DB71
Bourne Vale, Brom. BR2 ....144 EG101
Bournevale Rd, SW16 ....121 DL91
Bourne Vw, Grnf. UB6 ....79 CF65
Kenley CR8 ....176 DR115
Bourne Way, Add. KT15 ....152 BJ106
Bromley BR2 ....144 EF103
Epsom KT19 ....156 CQ105
Bourne Way, Sutt. SM1 ....157 CZ106
Swanley BR8 ....147 FC97
Woking GU22 ....166 AX122
Bournewood Rd, SE18 ....106 EU80
Orpington BR5 ....146 EV101
Bournville Rd, SE6 ....123 EA87
Bournwell Cl, Barn. EN4 ....28 DF41
Bourton Cl, Hayes UB3
off Avondale Dr 77 BU74
Bousfield Rd, SE14 ....103 DX82
Bousley Ri, Cher. (Ott.) KT16 ....151 BD108
Boutflower Rd, SW11 ....100 DE84
Bouverie Gdns, Har. HA3 ....61 CK58
Purley CR8 ....159 DL114
Bouverie Ms, N16
off Bouverie Rd 66 DS61
Bouverie Pl, W2 ....194 A8
Bouverie Rd, N16 ....66 DS61
Coulsdon CR5 ....174 DG118
Harrow HA1 ....60 CC59
Bouverie St, EC4 ....196 E9
Bouverie Way, Slou. SL3 ....92 AY78
Bouvier Rd, Enf. EN3 ....30 DW38
Boveney Rd, SE23 ....123 DX87
Bovey Way, S.Ock. RM15 ....91 FV71
Bovill Rd, SE23 ....123 DX87
BOVINGDON, Hem.H. 5 BA28
Bovingdon Av, Wem. HA9 ....80 CN65
Bovingdon Cl, N19
off Brookside Rd 65 DJ61
Bovingdon Cres, Wat. WD25 ....8 BX34
Bovingdon La, NW9 ....42 CS53
Bovingdon Rd, SW6 ....100 DB81
Bovingdon Sq, Mitch. CR4
off Leicester Av 141 DL98
BOW, E3 ....85 DZ68
Bow Arrow La, Dart.
DA1, DA2 ....128 FN86
Bowater Cl, NW9 ....62 CR57
SW2 ....121 DL86
Bowater Gdns, Sun. TW16 ....135 BV96
Bowater Pl, SE3 ....104 EH80
Bowater Ridge, Wey. KT13 ....153 BR110
Bowater Rd, SE18 ....104 EK76
Bow Br Est, E3 ....85 EB69
DLR Bow Church 85 EA69
Bow Chyd, EC4 ....197 J9
Bow Common La, E3 ....85 DZ70
Bowden Cl, Felt. TW14 ....115 BS88
Bowden Dr, Horn. RM11 ....72 FL60
Bowden St, SE11 ....101 DN78
Bowditch, SE8 ....203 M10
Bowdon Rd, E17 ....67 EA59
Bowen Dr, SE21 ....122 DS90
Bowen Rd, Har. HA1 ....60 CC59
Bowen St, E14 ....85 EB72
Bowens Wd, Croy. CR0 ....161 DZ109
Bower Av, SE10 ....104 EE81
Bower Cl, Nthlt. UB5 ....78 BW68
Romford RM5 ....51 FD52
Bower Ct, Epp. CM16 ....18 EU32
Woking GU22
off Princess Rd 167 BB116
Bowerdean St, SW6 ....100 DB81
Bower Fm Rd, Rom. (Hav.at.Bow.)
RM4 ....51 FC48
BOWER HILL, Epp. 18 EU31
Bower Hill, Epp. CM16 ....18 EU32
Bower Hill Ind Est, Epp.
CM16 ....18 EU32
Bower La, Dart. (Eyns.) DA4 ....148 FL103
Bowerman Av, SE14 ....103 DY79
Bowerman Rd, Grays RM16 ....111 GG77
Bower Rd, Swan. BR8 ....127 FG94
Bowers Av, Grav. (Nthflt.)
DA11 ....131 GF91
Bowers Rd, Sev. (Shore.)
TN14 ....165 FF111
Bower St, E1 ....85 DX72
Bowers Wk, E6 ....86 EL72
Bower Ter, Epp. CM16
off Bower Hill 18 EU32
Bower Vale, Epp. CM16 ....18 EU32
Bowes Cl, Sid. DA15 ....126 EV86
BOWES PARK, N22 ....45 DL51
⇌ Bowes Park 45 DL51
Bowes Rd, N11 ....45 DH50
N13 ....45 DL50
W3 ....80 CS73
Dagenham RM8 ....70 EW63
Staines TW18 ....113 BE92
Walton-on-Thames KT12 ....135 BV103
Bowfell Rd, W6 ....99 CW79
Bowford Av, Bexh. DA7 ....106 EY81
Bowhay, Brwd. CM13 ....55 GA47
Bowhill Cl, SW9 ....101 DN80
Bowie Cl, SW4 ....121 DK87
Bow Ind Pk, E15 ....85 EA66
Bowland Rd, SW4 ....101 DK84
Woodford Green IG8 ....48 EJ51
Bowland Yd, SW1 ....198 E5
Bow La, EC4 ....197 J9
N12 ....44 DC53
Morden SM4 ....139 CY100
Bowl Ct, EC2 ....197 N5
Bowlers Orchard, Ch.St.G.
HP8 ....36 AU48
Bowles Grn, Enf. EN1 ....30 DV36
Bowles Rd, SE1
off Old Kent Rd 102 DU79
Bowley Cl, SE19 ....122 DT93
Bowley La, SE19 ....122 DT92
Bowling Cl, Uxb. UB10
off Birch Cres 76 BM67
Bowling Ct, Wat. WD18 ....23 BU42
Bowling Grn Cl, SW15 ....119 CV87
Bowling Grn La, EC1 ....196 E4
Bowling Grn Pl, SE1 ....201 K4
Bowling Grn Rd, Wok. (Chobham)
GU24 ....150 AS109
Bowling Grn Row, SE18
off Samuel St 105 EM76
Bowling Grn St, SE11 ....101 DN79
Bowling Grn Wk, N1 ....197 M2
Bowls, The, Chig. IG7 ....49 ES49
Bowls Cl, Stan. HA7 ....41 CH50
Bowman Av, E16 ....86 EF73
Bowman Ms, SW18 ....119 CZ88
Bowmans Cl, W13 ....79 CH74
Potters Bar EN6 ....12 DD32
Bowmans Grn, Wat. WD25 ....24 BX36
Bowmans Lea, SE23 ....122 DW87
Bowmans Meadow, Wall.
SM6 ....141 DH104
Bowmans Ms, E1
off Hooper St 84 DU72
N7 off Seven Sisters Rd 65 DL62
Bowmans Pl, N7
off Holloway Rd 65 DL62
Bowmans Rd, Dart. DA1 ....127 FF87
Bowman's Trd Est, NW9
off Westmoreland Rd 62 CM55
Bowmead, SE9 ....125 EM89
Bowmont Cl, Brwd. CM13 ....55 GB44
Bowmore Wk, NW1
off St. Paul's Cres 83 DK66
Bown Cl, Til. RM18 ....111 GH82
Bowness Cl, E8
off Beechwood Rd 84 DT65
Bowness Cres, SW15 ....118 CS92
Bowness Dr, Houns. TW4 ....96 BY84
Bowness Rd, SE6 ....123 EB87
Bexleyheath DA7 ....107 FB82
Bowness Way, Horn. RM12 ....71 FG64
Bowood Rd, SW11 ....100 DG84
Enfield EN3 ....31 DX40
Bowring Grn, Wat. WD19 ....40 BW50
⊖ Bow Road 85 DZ69
Bow Rd, E3 ....85 DZ69
Bowrons Av, Wem. HA0 ....79 CK66
Bowry Dr, Stai. (Wrays.)
TW19 ....113 AZ86
Bowsley Ct, Felt. TW13
off Highfield Rd 115 BU88
Bowsprit, The, Cob. KT11 ....170 BW115
Bowsprit Pt, E14 ....103 EA76
Bow St, E15 ....68 EE64
WC2 ....196 A9
Bowstridge La, Ch.St.G. HP8 ....36 AW51
Bowyer Cl, E6 ....87 EM71
Bowyer Cres, Uxb. (Denh.)
UB9 ....57 BF58
Bowyer Pl, SE5 ....102 DR80
Bowyers Cl, Ashtd. KT21 ....172 CM118
Bowyer St, SE5 ....102 DQ80
Boxall Rd, SE21 ....122 DS86
Boxford Cl, S.Croy. CR2 ....161 DX112
Boxgrove Rd, SE2 ....106 EW76
BOX HILL, Tad. 182 CP131
Boxhill Dr, Grays RM20 ....110 FY79
Boxhill Rd, Dor. RH4 ....182 CL133
Tadworth KT20 ....182 CP131
Box La, Bark. IG11 ....88 EV68
Boxley Rd, Mord. SM4 ....140 DC98
Boxley St, E16 ....205 P3
Boxmoor Rd, Har. HA3 ....61 CH56
Romford RM5 ....51 FC50
Boxoll Rd, Dag. RM9 ....70 EZ63
Box Ridge Av, Pur. CR8 ....159 DM112
Boxted Cl, Buck.H. IG9 ....48 EL46
Boxtree La, Har. HA3 ....40 CC53
Boxtree Rd, Har. HA3 ....41 CD52
Boxtree Wk, Orp. BR5 ....146 EX102
Boxwood Cl, West Dr. UB7
off Hawthorne Cres 94 BM75
Boxwood Way, Warl. CR6 ....177 DX117
Boxworth Cl, N12 ....44 DD50
Boxworth Gro, N1
off Richmond Av 83 DM67
Boyard Rd, SE18 ....105 EP78
Boyce Cl, Borwd. WD6 ....26 CL39
Boyce St, SE1 ....200 C3
Boyce Way, E13 ....86 EG70
Boycroft Av, NW9 ....62 CQ58
Boyd Av, Sthl. UB1 ....78 BZ74
Boyd Cl, Kings.T. KT2
off Crescent Rd 118 CN94
Boydell Ct, NW8
off St. John's Wd Pk 82 DD66
Boyd Rd, SW19 ....120 DD93
Boyd St, E1 ....84 DU72
Boyfield St, SE1 ....200 G5
Boyland Rd, Brom. BR1 ....124 EF92
Boyle Av, Stan. HA7 ....41 CG51
Boyle Cl, Uxb. UB10 ....76 BM68
Boyle Fm Island, T.Ditt. KT7 ....137 CG100
Boyle Fm Rd, T.Ditt. KT7 ....137 CG100
Boyle St, W1 ....195 K10
Boyne Av, NW4 ....63 CX56
Boyne Rd, SE13 ....103 EC83
Dagenham RM10 ....70 FA62
Boyne Ter Ms, W11 ....81 CZ74
Boyseland Ct, Edg. HA8 ....42 CQ47
Boyson Rd, SE17 ....102 DR79
Boyton Cl, E1
off Stayner's Rd 85 DX70
N8 ....65 DL55
Boyton Rd, N8 ....65 DL55
Brabant Ct, EC3 ....197 M10
Brabant Rd, N22 ....45 DM54
Brabazon Av, Wall. SM6 ....159 DL108
Brabazon Rd, Houns. TW5 ....96 BW80
Northolt UB5 ....78 CA68
Brabazon St, E14 ....85 EB72
Brabourne Cl, SE19 ....122 DS92
Brabourne Cres, Bexh. DA7 ....106 EZ79
Brabourne Hts, NW7 ....42 CS48
Brabourne Ri, Beck. BR3 ....143 EC99
Brabourn Gro, SE15 ....102 DW82
Brace Cl, Wal.Cr. (Chsht.) EN7 ....13 DP25
Bracewell Av, Grnf. UB6 ....61 CF64
Bracewell Rd, W10 ....81 CW71
Bracewood Gdns, Croy. CR0 ....142 DT104
Bracey Ms, N4
off Bracey St 65 DL61
Bracey St, N4 ....65 DL61
Bracken, The, E4
off Hortus Rd 47 EC47
Bracken Av, SW12 ....120 DG86
Croydon CR0 ....143 EB104
Brackenbridge Dr, Ruis. HA4 ....60 BX62
Brackenbury Gdns, W6 ....99 CV76
Brackenbury Rd, N2 ....64 DC55
W6 ....99 CV76

★ Place of interest ⇌ Railway station ⊖ London Underground station DLR Docklands Light Railway station Tramlink station H Hospital

Bracken Cl, E6 87 EM71
Borehamwood WD6 26 CP39
Leatherhead (Bkhm.)
KT23 170 BZ124
Sunbury-on-Thames TW16
off Cavendish Rd 115 BT93
Twickenham TW2
off Hedley Rd 116 CA87
Woking GU22 167 AZ118
Brackendale, N21 45 DM47
Potters Bar EN6 12 DA33
Brackendale Cl, Houns. TW3 96 CB81
Brackendale Gdns, Upmin.
RM14 72 FQ63
Brackendene, Dart. DA2 127 FE91
St. Albans (Brick.Wd.) AL2 8 BZ30
Brackendene Cl, Wok. GU21 167 BA115
Bracken Dr, Chig. IG7 49 EP51
Bracken End, Islw. TW7 117 CD85
Brackenfield Cl, E5
off Tiger Way 66 DV63
Brackenforde, Slou. SL3 92 AW75
Bracken Gdns, SW13 99 CU82
Brackenhill, Cob. KT11 154 CA111
Bracken Hill Cl, Brom. BR1
off Bracken Hill La 144 EF95
Bracken Hill La, Brom. BR1 144 EF95
Bracken Ind Est, Ilf. IG6 49 ET52
Bracken Ms, E4
off Hortus Rd 47 EC47
Romford RM7 70 FA58
Bracken Path, Epsom KT18 156 CP113
Brackens, The, Enf. EN1 46 DS45
Orpington BR6 164 EU106
Brackens Dr, Brwd. CM14 54 FW50
Bracken Way, Wok. (Chobham)
GU24 150 AT110
Brackenwood, Sun. TW16 135 BU95
Brackley, Wey. KT13 153 BR106
Brackley Cl, Wall. SM6 159 DL108
Brackley Rd, W4 98 CS78
Beckenham BR3 123 DZ94
Brackley Sq, Wdf.Grn. IG8 48 EK52
Brackley St, EC1 197 H6
Brackley Ter, W4 98 CS78
Bracklyn Cl, N1 *off Parr St* 84 DR68
Bracklyn Ct, N1
off Wimbourne St 84 DR68
Bracklyn St, N1 84 DR68
Bracknell Cl, N22 45 DN53
Bracknell Gdns, NW3 64 DB63
Bracknell Gate, NW3 64 DB64
Bracknell Way, NW3 64 DB63
Bracondale, Esher KT10 154 CC107
Bracondale Rd, SE2 106 EU77
Bradbery, Rick. (Map.Cr.)
WD3 37 BD50
Bradbourne Pk Rd, Sev.
TN13 190 FG123
Bradbourne Rd, Bex. DA5 126 FA87
Grays RM17 110 GB79
Sevenoaks TN13 191 FH122
Bradbourne St, SW6 100 DA82
Bradbourne Vale Rd, Sev.
TN13 190 FF122
Bradbury Cl, Borwd. WD6 26 CP39
Southall UB2 96 BZ77
Bradbury Gdns, Slou. (Fulmer)
SL3 56 AX63
Bradbury Ms, N16
off Bradbury St 66 DS64
Bradbury St, N16 66 DS64
Bradd Cl, S.Ock. RM15
off Brandon Gros Av 91 FW69
Braddock Cl, Islw. TW7 97 CF83
Braddon Rd, Rich. TW9 98 CM83
Braddyll St, SE10 104 EE78
Bradenham Av, Well. DA16 106 EU84
Bradenham Cl, SE17 102 DR79
Bradenham Rd, Har. HA3 61 CH56
Hayes UB4 77 BS69
Bradenhurst Cl, Cat. CR3 186 DT126
Braden St, W9
off Shirland Rd 82 DB70
Bradfield Cl, Wok. GU22 166 AY118
Bradfield Dr, Bark. IG11 70 EU64
Bradfield Rd, E16 205 N4
Ruislip HA4 60 BY64
Bradford Cl, N17
off Commercial Rd 46 DS51
SE26 *off Coombe Rd* 122 DV91
Bromley BR2 145 EM102
Bradford Dr, Epsom KT19 157 CT107
Bradford Rd, W3
off Warple Way 98 CS75
Ilford IG1 69 ER60
Rickmansworth (Herons.)
WD3 37 BC45
Bradgate, Pot.B. (Cuffley) EN6 13 DK27
Bradgate Cl, Pot.B. (Cuffley)
EN6 13 DK28
Bradgate Rd, SE6 123 EA86
Brading Cres, E11 68 EH61
Brading Rd, SW2 121 DM87
Croydon CR0 141 DM100
Bradiston Rd, W9 81 CZ69
Bradleigh Av, Grays RM17 110 GC77
Bradley Cl, N7
off Sutterton St 83 DM65
Sutton (Belmont) SM2
off Station Rd 158 DA110
Bradley Gdns, W13 79 CH72
Bradley Ms, SW17
off Bellevue Rd 120 DF88
Bradley Rd, N22 45 DM54
SE19 122 DQ93
Enfield EN3 31 DY38
Waltham Abbey EN9 31 EC35
Bradley's Cl, N1
off White Lion St 83 DN68
Bradley Stone Rd, E6 87 EM71
Bradman Row, Edg. HA8
off Pavilion Way 42 CQ52
Bradmead, SW8 101 DH80
Bradmore Grn, Couls. CR5
off Coulsdon Rd 175 DM118
Hatfield AL9 11 CY26
Bradmore La, Hat. AL9 11 CW27
Bradmore Pk Rd, W6 99 CV76
Bradmore Way, Couls. CR5 175 DL117
Hatfield AL9 11 CY26
Bradshaw Cl, SW19 120 DA93
Bradshaw Dr, NW7
off Bittacy Hill 43 CY52
Bradshawe Waye, Uxb. UB8 76 BL71
Bradshaw Rd, Wat. WD24 24 BW39
Bradshaws Cl, SE25 142 DU97
Bradstock Rd, E9 85 DX65
Epsom KT17 157 CU106
Brad St, SE1 200 E3
Bradwell Av, Dag. RM10 70 FA61
Bradwell Cl, E18 68 EF56
Hornchurch RM12 89 FH65
Bradwell Grn, Brwd. CM13 55 GC44
Bradwell Ms, N18
off Lyndhurst Rd 46 DU49
Bradwell Rd, Buck.H. IG9 48 EL46
Bradwell St, E1 85 DX69
Brady Av, Loug. IG10 33 EQ40
Bradymead, E6 87 EN72
Brady St, E1 84 DV70
Braemar Av, N22 45 DL53
NW10 62 CR62
SW19 120 DA89
Bexleyheath DA7 107 FC84
South Croydon CR2 160 DQ109
Thornton Heath CR7 141 DN97
Wembley HA0 79 CK66
Braemar Gdns, NW9 42 CR53
Hornchurch RM11 72 FN58
Sidcup DA15 125 ER90
West Wickham BR4 143 EC102
Braemar Rd, E13 86 EF70
N15 66 DS57
Brentford TW8 97 CL79
Worcester Park KT4 139 CV104
Braeside, Add. (New Haw)
KT15 152 BH111
Beckenham BR3 123 EA92
Braeside Av, SW19 139 CY95
Sevenoaks TN13 190 FF124
Braeside Cl, Pnr. HA5
off The Avenue 40 CA52
Sevenoaks TN13 190 FF123
Braeside Cres, Bexh. DA7 107 FC84
Braeside Rd, SW16 121 DJ94
Braes St, N1 83 DP66
Braesyde Cl, Belv. DA17 106 EZ77
Brafferton Rd, Croy. CR0 160 DQ105
Braganza St, SE17 200 F10
Bragg Cl, Dag. RM8
off Porters Av 88 EV65
Bragmans La, Hem.H. (Flaun.)
HP3 5 BB34
Rickmansworth (Sarratt)
WD3 5 BE33
Braham St, E1 84 DT72
Braid, The, Chesh. HP5 4 AS30
Braid Av, W3 80 CS72
Braid Cl, Felt. TW13 116 BZ89
Braid Ct, W4 *off Lawford Rd* 98 CQ80
Braidwood Pas, EC1
off Aldersgate St 84 DQ71
Braidwood Rd, SE6 123 ED88
Braidwood St, SE1 201 M3
Brailsford Cl, Mitch. CR4 120 DE94
Brailsford Rd, SW2 121 DN85
Brainton Av, Felt. TW14 115 BV87
Braintree Av, Ilf. IG4 68 EL56
Braintree Ind Est, Ruis. HA4 59 BV63
Braintree Rd, Dag. RM10 70 FA62
Ruislip HA4 59 BV63
Braintree St, E2 84 DW69
Braithwaite Av, Rom. RM7 70 FA59
Braithwaite Gdns, Stan. HA7 41 CJ53
Braithwaite Rd, Enf. EN3 31 DZ41
Braithwaite Twr, W2 82 DD71
Brakefield Rd, Grav. (Sthflt.)
DA13 130 GB93
Brakey Hill, Red. (Bletch.)
RH1 186 DS134
Bramah Grn, SW9 101 DN81
★ **Bramah Mus**, SE1 202 A4
Bramalea Cl, N6 64 DG58
Bramall Cl, E15
off Idmiston Rd 68 EF64
Bramber Ct, Brent. TW8
off Sterling Pl 98 CL77
Bramber Rd, N12 44 DE50
W14 99 CZ79
Brambleacres Cl, Sutt. SM2 158 DA108
Bramble Av, Dart. (Bean)
DA2 129 FW90
Bramble Banks, Cars. SM5 158 DG109
Bramblebury Rd, SE18 105 EQ78
Bramble Cl, Beck. BR3 143 EC99
Croydon CR0 161 EA105
Shepperton TW17
off Halliford Cl 135 BR98
Stanmore HA7 41 CK52
Uxbridge UB8 76 BM71
Watford WD25 7 BU34
Bramble Cft, Erith DA8 107 FC77
Brambledene Cl, Wok. GU21 166 AW118
Brambledown, Stai. TW18 134 BG95
Brambledown Cl, W.Wick.
BR4 144 EE99
Brambledown Rd, Cars.
SM5 158 DG108
South Croydon CR2 160 DS108
Wallington SM6 159 DH108
Bramblefield Cl, Long. DA3 149 FX97
Bramble Gdns, W12
off Wallflower St 81 CT73
Bramble Hall La Mobile
Home Pk, Tad. KT20 182 CM132
Bramble La, Amer. HP7 20 AS41
Hampton TW12 116 BZ93
Sevenoaks TN13 191 FH128
Upminster RM14 90 FQ67
Bramble Mead, Ch.St.G. HP8 36 AU48
Bramble Ri, Cob. KT11 170 BW115
Brambles, The, Chig. IG7
off Clayside 49 EQ50
Brambles, The, Wal.Cr. EN8 15 DX31
West Drayton UB7 94 BL77
Brambles Cl, Cat. CR3 176 DS122
Isleworth TW7 97 CH80
Brambles Fm Dr, Uxb. UB10 76 BN69
Bramble Wk, Epsom KT18 156 CP114
Bramble Way, Wok. (Ripley)
GU23 167 BF124
Bramblewood, Red. RH1 185 DH129
Bramblewood Cl, Cars. SM5 140 DE102
Brambling Cl, Bushey WD23 24 BY42
Bramblings, The, E4 47 ED49
Bramcote Av, Mitch. CR4 140 DF98
Bramcote Ct, Mitch. CR4
off Bramcote Av 140 DF98
Bramcote Gro, SE16 202 F10
Bramcote Rd, SW15 99 CV84
Bramdean Cres, SE12 124 EG88
Bramdean Gdns, SE12 124 EG88
Bramerton Rd, Beck. BR3 143 DZ97
Bramerton St, SW3 100 DE79
Bramfield, Wat. WD25
off Garston La 8 BY34
Bramfield Ct, N4
off Queens Dr 66 DQ61
Bramfield Rd, SW11 120 DE86
Bramford Ct, N14 45 DK47
Bramford Rd, SW18 100 DC84
Bramham Gdns, SW5 100 DB78
Chessington KT9 155 CK105
Bramhope La, SE7 104 EH79
Bramlands Cl, SW11 100 DE83
Bramleas, Wat. WD18 23 BT42
Bramley Av, Couls. CR5 175 DJ115
Bramley Cl, E17 47 DY54
N14 29 DH43
Chertsey KT16 134 BH102
Gravesend (Istead Rise)
DA13 131 GF94
Hayes UB3 *off Orchard Rd* 77 BU73
Orpington BR6 145 EP102
Pinner HA5 *off Wiltshire La* 59 BT55
South Croydon CR2 159 DP106
Staines TW18 114 BJ93
Swanley BR8 147 FE98
Twickenham TW2 116 CC86
Bramley Ct, Wat. WD25
off Orchard Av 7 BV31
Welling DA16 106 EV81
Bramley Cres, SW8
off Pascal St 101 DK80
Ilford IG2 69 EN58
Bramley Gdns, Wat. WD19 40 BW50
Bramley Hill, S.Croy. CR2 159 DP106
Bramley Ho, SW15
off Tunworth Cres 119 CT86
Bramley Pl, Dart. DA1 107 FG84
Bramley Rd, N14 29 DH43
W5 97 CJ76
W10 81 CX73
Sutton SM1 158 DD106
Sutton (Cheam) SM2 157 CX109
Bramley Shaw, Wal.Abb. EN9 16 EF33
Bramley Way, Ashtd. KT21 172 CM117
Hounslow TW4 116 BZ85
West Wickham BR4 143 EB103
Brampton Cl, E5 66 DV61
Waltham Cross (Chsht.)
EN7 14 DU28
Brampton Gdns, N15
off Brampton Rd 66 DQ57
Walton-on-Thames KT12 154 BW106
Brampton Gro, NW4 63 CV56
Harrow HA3 61 CG56
Wembley HA9 62 CN60
Brampton La, NW4 63 CW56
Brampton Pk Rd, N22 65 DN55
Brampton Rd, E6 86 EK69
N15 66 DQ57
NW9 62 CN56
SE2 106 EW79
Bexleyheath DA7 106 EX80
Croydon CR0 142 DT101
Uxbridge UB10 77 BP68
Watford WD19 39 BU48
Brampton Ter, Borwd. WD6 26 CN38
Bramshaw Gdns, Wat. WD19 40 BX50
Bramshaw Ri, N.Mal. KT3 138 CS100
Bramshaw Rd, E9 85 DX65
Bramshill Cl, Chig. IG7
off Tine Rd 49 ES50
Bramshill Gdns, NW5 65 DH62
Bramshill Rd, NW10 81 CT68
Bramshot Av, SE7 104 EG79
Bramshot Way, Wat. WD19 39 BU47
Bramston Cl, Ilf. IG6 49 ET51
Bramston Rd, NW10 81 CU68
SW17 120 DC90
Bramwell Cl, Sun. TW16 136 BX96
Bramwell Ms, N1 83 DM67
Brancaster Dr, NW7 43 CT52
Brancaster La, Pur. CR8 160 DQ112
Brancaster Pl, Loug. IG10 33 EM41
Brancaster Rd, E12 69 EM63
SW16 121 DL90
Ilford IG2 69 ER58
Brancepeth Gdns, Buck.H.
IG9 48 EG47
Branch Hill, NW3 64 DC62
Branch Pl, N1 84 DR67
Branch Rd, E14 85 DY73
Ilford IG6 50 EV50
St. Albans (Park St.) AL2 9 CD27
Branch St, SE15 102 DS80
Brancker Cl, Wall. SM6
off Brown Cl 159 DL108
Brancker Rd, Har. HA3 61 CK55
Brancroft Way, Enf. EN3 31 DY39
Brand Cl, N4 65 DP60
Brandesbury Sq, Wdf.Grn.
IG8 49 EN52
Brandlehow Rd, SW15 99 CZ84
Brandon Cl, Grays (Chaff.Hun.)
RM16 110 FZ75
Waltham Cross (Chsht.)
EN7 14 DS26
Brandon Est, SE17 101 DP79
Brandon Gros Av, S.Ock.
RM15 91 FW69
Brandon Ms, EC2
off The Barbican 84 DQ71
Brandon Rd, E17 67 EC55
N7 83 DL66
Dartford DA1 128 FN87
Southall UB2 96 BZ78
Sutton SM1 158 DB105
Brandon St, SE17 201 J9
Gravesend DA11 131 GH87
Brandram Ms, SE13
off Brandram Rd 104 EE83
Brandram Rd, SE13 104 EE83
Brandreth Rd, E6 87 EM72
SW17 121 DH89
Brandries, The, Wall. SM6 141 DK104
BRANDS HILL, Slou. 93 BB79
Brands Rd, Slou. SL3 93 BB79
Brand St, SE10 103 EC80
Brandville Gdns, Ilf. IG6 69 EP56
Brandville Rd, West Dr. UB7 94 BL75
Brandy Way, Sutt. SM2 158 DA108
Branfill Rd, Upmin. RM14 72 FP61
Brangbourne Rd, Brom.
BR1 123 EC92
Brangton Rd, SE11 101 DM78
Brangwyn Cres, SW19 140 DD95
Branksea St, SW6 99 CY80
Branksome Av, N18 46 DT50
Branksome Cl, Tedd. TW11 117 CD91
Walton-on-Thames KT12 136 BX103
Branksome Rd, SW2 121 DL85
SW19 140 DA95
Branksome Way, Har. HA3 62 CL58
New Malden KT3 138 CQ95
Bransby Rd, Chess. KT9 156 CL107
Branscombe Gdns, N21 45 DN45
Branscombe St, SE13 103 EB83
Bransdale Cl, NW6
off West End La 82 DB67
Bransell Cl, Swan. BR8 147 FC100
Bransgrove Rd, Edg. HA8 42 CM53
Branston Cres, Orp. BR5 145 ER102
Branstone Rd, Rich. TW9 98 CM81
Branton Rd, Green. DA9 129 FT86
Brants Wk, W7 79 CE70
Brantwood Av, Erith DA8 107 FC80
Isleworth TW7 97 CG84
Brantwood Cl, E17 67 EB55
West Byfleet KT14
off Brantwood Gdns 152 BG113
Brantwood Ct, W.Byf. KT14
off Brantwood Dr 151 BF113
Brantwood Dr, W.Byf. KT14 151 BF113
Brantwood Gdns, Enf. EN2 29 DL42
Ilford IG4 68 EL56
West Byfleet KT14 151 BF113
Brantwood Rd, N17 46 DT51
SE24 122 DQ85
Bexleyheath DA7 107 FB82
South Croydon CR2 160 DQ109
Brantwood Way, Orp. BR5 146 EW97
Brasenose Dr, SW13 99 CW79
Brasher Cl, Grnf. UB6 61 CD64
Brassett Pt, E15 86 EE67
Brassey Cl, Felt. TW14 115 BU88
Oxted RH8
off Westerham Rd 188 EG129
Brassey Hill, Oxt. RH8 188 EG130
Brassey Rd, NW6 81 CZ65
Oxted RH8 188 EF130
Brassey Sq, SW11 100 DG83
Brassie Av, W3 80 CS72
Brass Tally All, SE16 203 J5
BRASTED, West. 180 EW124
Brasted Cl, SE26 122 DW91
Bexleyheath DA6 126 EX85
Orpington BR6 146 EU103
Sutton SM2 158 DA110
Brasted Hill, Sev. (Knock.)
TN14 180 EU120
Brasted Hill Rd, West. (Brasted)
TN16 180 EV121
Brasted La, Sev. (Knock.)
TN14 180 EU119
Brasted Rd, Erith DA8 107 FE80
Westerham TN16 189 ES126
Brathway Rd, SW18 120 DA87
Bratley St, E1 *off Weaver St* 84 DU70
Brattle Wd, Sev. TN13 191 FH129
Braund Av, Grnf. UB6 78 CB70
Braundton Av, Sid. DA15 125 ET88
Braunston Dr, Hayes UB4 78 BY70
Bravington Cl, Shep. TW17 134 BM99
Bravington Pl, W9
off Bravington Rd 81 CZ70
Bravington Rd, W9 81 CZ68
Brawlings La, Ger.Cr. (Chal.St.P.)
SL9 37 BA49
Brawne Ho, SE17
off Hillingdon St 101 DP79
Braxfield Rd, SE4 103 DY84
Braxted Pk, SW16 121 DM93
Bray, NW3 82 DE66
Brayards Rd, SE15 102 DV82
Braybourne Cl, Uxb. UB8 76 BJ65
Braybourne Dr, Islw. TW7 97 CF80
Braybrooke Gdns, SE19
off Fox Hill 122 DT94
Braybrook St, W12 81 CT71
Brayburne Av, SW4 101 DJ82
Bray Cl, Borwd. WD6 26 CQ39
Braycourt Av, Walt. KT12 135 BV101
Bray Cres, SE16 203 H4
Braydon Rd, N16 66 DT60
Bray Dr, E16 86 EF73
Brayfield Ter, N1
off Lofting Rd 83 DN66
Brayford Sq, E1
off Summercourt Rd 84 DW72
Bray Gdns, Wok. GU22 167 BE116
Bray Pas, E16 86 EG73
Bray Pl, SW3 198 D9
Bray Rd, NW7 43 CX51
Cobham (Stoke D'Ab.)
KT11 170 BY116
Bray Springs, Wal.Abb. EN9
off Roundhills 16 EE34
Brayton Gdns, Enf. EN2 29 DK42
Braywood Av, Egh. TW20 113 AZ93
Braywood Rd, SE9 105 ER84
Brazil Cl, Croy. (Bedd.) CR0 141 DL101
Breach Barn Mobile Home Pk,
Wal.Abb. EN9 16 EH29
Breach Barns La, Wal.Abb. EN9
off Galley Hill 16 EF30
Breach La, Dag. RM9 88 FA69
Breach Rd, Grays RM20 109 FT79
Bread & Cheese La, Wal.Cr.
(Chsht.) EN7 14 DR25
Bread St, EC4 197 J9
Breakfield, Couls. CR5 175 DL116
Breakneck Hill, Green. DA9 129 FV85
Breakspeare Cl, Abb.L. WD5 7 BT30
Breakspeare Cl, Wat. WD24 23 BV38
Breakspeare Rd, Abb.L. WD5 7 BS31
Breakspear Path, Uxb. (Hare.)
UB9 58 BJ55
Breakspear Rd, Ruis. HA4 59 BP59
Breakspear Rd N, Uxb. (Hare.)
UB9 58 BN57
Breakspear Rd S, Uxb. (Ickhm.)
UB9, UB10 58 BM62
Breakspears Dr, Orp. BR5 146 EU95
Breakspears Ms, SE4
off Breakspears Rd 103 EA82
Breakspears Rd, SE4 103 DZ83
Bream Cl, N17 66 DV56
Bream Gdns, E6 87 EN69
Breamore Cl, SW15 119 CU88
Breamore Rd, Ilf. IG3 69 ET61
Bream's Bldgs, EC4 196 D8
Bream St, E3 85 EA66
Breamwater Gdns, Rich.
TW10 117 CH90
Brearley Cl, Edg. HA8
off Pavilion Way 42 CQ52
Uxbridge UB8 76 BL65
Breasley Cl, SW15 99 CV84
Brechin Pl, SW7
off Rosary Gdns 100 DC77
Brecknock Rd, N7 65 DJ63
N19 65 DJ63
Brecknock Rd Est, N7 65 DJ63
Breckonmead, Brom. BR1
off Wanstead Rd 144 EJ96
Brecon Cl, Mitch. CR4 141 DL97
Worcester Park KT4 139 CW103
Brecon Grn, NW9
off Goldsmith Av 62 CS58
Brecon Rd, W6 99 CY79
Enfield EN3 30 DW42
Brede Cl, E6 87 EN69
Bredgar, SE13 123 EC85
Bredgar Rd, N19 65 DJ61
Bredhurst Cl, SE20 122 DW93
Bredon Rd, SE5 102 DQ83
Croydon CR0 142 DT101
Bredune, Ken. CR8 176 DR115
Breech La, Tad. KT20 173 CU124
Breer St, SW6 100 DB83
Breezers Hill, E1 202 C1
Breeze Ter, Wal.Cr. (Chsht.)
EN8 *off Collet Cl* 15 DX28
Brember Rd, Har. HA2 60 CC61
Bremer Ms, E17
off Church La 67 EB56
Bremer Rd, Stai. TW18 114 BG90
Bremner Cl, Swan. BR8 147 FG98
Bremner Rd, SW7 100 DC75
Brenchley Av, Grav. DA11 131 GH92
Brenchley Cl, Brom. BR2 144 EF100
Chislehurst BR7 145 EN95
Brenchley Gdns, SE23 122 DW86
Brenchley Rd, Orp. BR5 145 ET95
Brendans Cl, Horn. RM11 72 FL60
Brenda Rd, SW17 120 DF89
Brenda Ter, Swans. DA10
off Manor Rd 130 FY87
Brende Gdns, W.Mol. KT8 136 CB98
Brendon Av, NW10 62 CS63
Brendon Cl, Erith DA8 107 FE81
Esher KT10 154 CC107
Hayes UB3 95 BQ80
Brendon Ct, Rad. WD7
off The Avenue 9 CH34
Brendon Dr, Esher KT10 154 CC107
Brendon Gdns, Har. HA2 60 CB63
Ilford IG2 69 ES57
Brendon Gro, N2 44 DC54
Brendon Rd, SE9 125 ER89
Dagenham RM8 70 EZ60
Brendon St, W1 194 C8
Brendon Way, Enf. EN1 46 DS45
Brenley Cl, Mitch. CR4 140 DG97
Brenley Gdns, SE9 104 EK84
Brennan Rd, Til. RM18 111 GH82
Brent, The, Dart. DA1, DA2 128 FN87
Brent Cl, Bex. DA5 126 EY88
Dartford DA2 128 FP86
Brentcot Cl, W13 79 CH70
Brent Cres, NW10 80 CM68
⊖ **Brent Cross** 63 CX59
Brent Cross Gdns, NW4
off Haley Rd 63 CX58
Brent Cross Shop Cen, NW4 63 CW59
Brentfield, NW10 80 CP66
Brentfield Cl, NW10
off Normans Mead 80 CR65
Brentfield Gdns, NW2
off Hendon Way 63 CX59
Brentfield Rd, NW10 80 CR65
Dartford DA1 128 FN86
BRENTFORD 97 CK79
⇌ **Brentford** 97 CJ79
Brentford Business Cen, Brent.
TW8 97 CJ80
Brentford Cl, Hayes UB4 78 BX70
★ **Brentford FC**, Brent. TW8 97 CK79
Brent Grn, NW4 63 CW57

★ Place of interest ⇌ Railway station ⊖ London Underground station DLR Docklands Light Railway station Tramlink station H Hospital

Bre - Bro

Brent Grn Wk, Wem. HA9 .62 CQ62
Brentham Way, W5 .79 CK70
Brenthouse Rd, E9 .84 DV66
Brenthurst Rd, NW10 .81 CT65
Brentlands Dr, Dart. DA1 .128 FN88
Brent La, Dart. DA1 .128 FM87
Brent Lea, Brent. TW8 .97 CJ80
Brentmead Cl, W7 .79 CE73
Brentmead Gdns, NW10 .80 CM68
Brentmead Pl, NW11
off North Circular Rd .63 CX58
Brenton St, E14 .85 DY72
Brent Pk, NW10 .62 CR64
Brent Pk Rd, NW4 .63 CV59
NW9 .63 CU60
Brent Pl, Barn. EN5 .28 DA43
Brent Rd, E16 .86 EG71
SE18 .105 EP80
Brentford TW8 .97 CJ79
South Croydon CR2 .160 DV109
Southall UB2 .96 BW76
Brent Side, Brent. TW8 .97 CJ79
Brentside Cl, W13 .79 CG70
Brentside Executive Cen, Brent. TW8 .97 CH79
Brent St, NW4 .63 CW56
Brent Ter, NW2 .63 CW61
Brentvale Av, Sthl. UB1 .79 CD74
Wembley HA0 .80 CM67
Brent Vw Rd, NW9 .63 CU59
Brent Way, N3 .44 DA51
Brentford TW8 .97 CK80
Dartford DA2 .128 FP86
Wembley HA9 .80 CP65
Brentwick Gdns, Brent. TW8 .98 CL77
BRENTWOOD .54 FV47
≠ Brentwood .54 FW48
Brentwood Bypass, Brwd. CM14, CM15 .53 FR49
Brentwood Cl, SE9 .125 EQ88
H Brentwood Comm Hosp & Minor Injuries Unit, Brwd. CM15 .54 FY46
Brentwood Ct, Add. KT15 .152 BH105
Brentwood Ho, SE18
off Shooter's Hill Rd .104 EK80
★ Brentwood Mus, Brwd. CM14 .54 FW49
Brentwood Pl, Brwd. CM15 .54 FX46
Brentwood Rd, Brwd. CM13 .55 GA49
Grays RM16 .111 GH77
Romford RM1, RM2 .71 FF58
Brereton Rd, N17 .46 DT52
Bressenden Pl, SW1 .199 J6
Bressey Av, Enf. EN1 .30 DU39
Bressey Gro, E18 .48 EF54
Bretlands Rd, Cher. KT16 .133 BE103
Brett Cl, N16 off Yoakley Rd .66 DS61
Northolt UB5
off Broomcroft Av .78 BX69
Brett Ct, N9 .46 DW47
Brett Cres, NW10 .80 CR66
Brettell St, SE17
off Merrow St .102 DR78
Brettenham Av, E17 .47 EA53
Brettenham Rd, E17 .47 EA54
N18 .46 DV49
Brett Gdns, Dag. RM9 .88 EY66
Brettgrave, Epsom KT19 .156 CQ110
Brett Ho Cl, SW15
off Putney Heath La .119 CX86
Brett Pas, E8 off Kenmure Rd .66 DV64
Brett Pl, Wat. WD24
off The Harebreaks .23 BU37
Brett Rd, E8 .66 DV64
Barnet EN5 .27 CW43
Brevet Cl, Purf. RM19 .109 FR77
Brewer's Fld, Dart. DA2 .128 FJ91
Brewer's Grn, SW1 .199 M6
Brewers Hall Gdns, EC2 .197 J7
Brewers La, Rich. TW9 .117 CK85
Brewer St, W1 .195 L10
Redhill (Bletch.) RH1 .186 DQ131
Brewery Cl, Wem. HA0 .61 CG64
Brewery La, Sev. TN13
off High St .191 FJ125
Twickenham TW1 .117 CF87
West Byfleet (Byfleet) KT14 .152 BL113
Brewery Rd, N7 .83 DL66
SE18 .105 ER78
Bromley BR2 .144 EL102
Woking GU21 .166 AX117
Brewery Sq, SE1
off Horselydown La .84 DT74
Brewery Wk, Rom. RM1 .71 FE57
Brewhouse La, E1 .202 E3
Brewhouse Rd, SE18 .105 EM77
Brewhouse St, SW15 .99 CY83
Brewhouse Wk, SE16 .203 K3
Brewhouse Yd, EC1 .196 F4
Gravesend DA12
off Queen St .131 GH86
Brewood Rd, Dag. RM8 .88 EV65
Brewster Gdns, W10 .81 CW71
Brewster Ho, E14 .85 DZ73
Brewster Rd, E10 .67 EB60
Brian Av, S.Croy. CR2 .160 DS112
Brian Cl, Horn. RM12 .71 FH63
Briane Rd, Epsom KT19 .156 CQ110
Brian Rd, Rom. RM6 .70 EW57
Briants Cl, Pnr. HA5 .40 BZ54
Briant St, SE14 .103 DX81
Briar Av, SW16 .121 DM94
Briarbank Rd, W13 .79 CG72
Briar Banks, Cars. SM5 .158 DG109
Briar Cl, N2 .64 DB55
N13 .46 DQ48
Buckhurst Hill IG9 .48 EK47
Hampton TW12 .116 BZ92
Isleworth TW7 .117 CF85
Waltham Cross (Chsht.) EN8 .14 DW29
Warlingham CR6 .177 EA116
West Byfleet KT14 .152 BJ111
Briar Ct, Sutt. SM3 .157 CW105
Briar Cres, Nthlt. UB5 .78 CB65
Briardale Gdns, NW3 .64 DA62
Briarfield Av, N3 .44 DB54
Briar Gdns, Brom. BR2 .144 EF102
Briar Gro, S.Croy. CR2 .160 DU113
Briar Hill, Pur. CR8 .159 DL111
Briaris Cl, N17 .46 DV52
Briar La, Cars. SM5 .158 DG109
Croydon CR0 .161 EB105
Briarleas Gdns, Upmin. RM14 .73 FS59
Briar Pas, SW16 .141 DL97
Briar Pl, SW16 .141 DM97
Briar Rd, NW2 .63 CW63
SW16 .141 DL97
Bexley DA5 .127 FD90
Harrow HA3 .61 CJ57
Romford RM3 .52 FJ52
Shepperton TW17 .134 BM99
Twickenham TW2 .117 CE88
Watford WD25 .7 BU34
Woking (Send) GU23 .167 BB123
Briars, The, Bushey (Bushey Hth.) WD23 .41 CE45
Rickmansworth (Sarratt) WD3 .22 BH36
Slough SL3 .93 AZ78
Waltham Cross (Chsht.) EN8 .15 DY31
Briars Ct, Lthd. KT22 .155 CD114
Briars Wk, Rom. RM3 .52 FL54
Briarswood, Wal.Cr. EN7 .14 DS28
Briarswood Way, Orp. BR6 .163 ET106
Briar Wk, SW15 .99 CV84
W10 off Droop St .81 CY70
Edgware HA8 .42 CQ52
West Byfleet KT14 .152 BG112
Briar Way, West Dr. UB7 .94 BN75
Briarwood, Bans. SM7
off High St .174 DA115
Briarwood Cl, NW9 .62 CQ58
Feltham TW13 .115 BS90
Briarwood Dr, Nthwd. HA6 .39 BU54
Briarwood Rd, SW4 .121 DK85
Epsom KT17 .157 CU107
Briary Cl, NW3 off Fellows Rd .82 DE66
Briary Ct, Sid. DA14 .126 EV92
Briary Gdns, Brom. BR1 .124 EH92
Briary Gro, Edg. HA8 .42 CP54
Briary La, N9 .46 DT48
Brick Ct, EC4 .196 D9
Grays RM17
off Columbia Wf Rd .110 GA79
Brickcroft, Brox. EN10 .15 DY26
Brickenden Ct, Wal.Abb. EN9 .16 EF33
Brickett Cl, Ruis. HA4 .59 BQ57
BRICKET WOOD, St.Alb. .8 BZ29
≠ Bricket Wood .8 CA30
Brick Fm Cl, Rich. TW9 .98 CP81
Brickfield Cl, Brent. TW8 .97 CJ80
Brickfield Cotts, SE18 .105 ET79
Brickfield Fm Gdns, Orp. BR6 .163 EQ105
Brickfield La, Barn. EN5 .27 CT44
Hayes UB3 .95 BR79
Brickfield Rd, SW19 .120 DB91
Epping CM16 .18 EX29
Thornton Heath CR7 .141 DP95
Brickfields, Har. HA2 .61 CD61
Brickfields La, Epp. CM16
off Brickfield Rd .18 EX29
Brickfields Way, West Dr. UB7 .94 BM76
Brick Kiln Cl, Wat. WD19 .24 BY44
Brick Kiln La, Oxt. RH8 .188 EJ131
Brick La, E1 .84 DT71
E2 .84 DT69
Enfield EN1, EN3 .30 DV40
Stanmore HA7
off Honeypot La .41 CK52
Bricklayer's Arms Distribution Cen, SE1 .201 N9
Bricklayer's Arms Roundabout, SE1 off Old Kent Rd .102 DR76
Brick St, W1 .199 H3
Brickwall La, Ruis. HA4 .59 BS60
Brickwood Cl, SE26 .122 DV90
Brickwood Rd, Croy. CR0 .142 DS103
Brideale Cl, SE15
off Colegrove Rd .102 DT80
Bride Ct, EC4 .196 F9
Bride La, EC4 .196 F9
Bridel Ms, N1
off Colebrooke Row .83 DP67
Bride St, N7 .83 DM65
Bridewain St, SE1 .201 P6
Bridewell Pl, E1 .202 E3
EC4 .196 F9
Bridford Ms, W1 .195 J6
Bridge, The, Har. HA3 .61 CE55
Bridge App, NW1 .82 DG66
Bridge Av, W6 .99 CW78
W7 .79 CD71
Upminster RM14 .72 FN61
Bridge Barn La, Wok. GU21 .166 AW117
Bridge Cl, W10
off Kingsdown Cl .81 CX72
Brentwood CM13 .55 FZ49
Dartford DA2 .109 FR83
Enfield EN1 .30 DV40
Romford RM7 .71 FE58
Staines TW18 .113 BE91
Teddington TW11
off Shacklegate La .117 CF91
Walton-on-Thames KT12 .135 BT101
West Byfleet (Byfleet) KT14 .152 BM112
Woking GU21 .166 AW117
Bridge Cotts, Upmin. RM14 .73 FU64
Bridge Ct, Wok. GU21 .166 AX117
Bridge Dr, N13 .45 DM49
Bridge End, E17 .47 EC53
Bridgefield Cl, Bans. SM7 .173 CW115
Bridgefield Rd, Sutt. SM1 .158 DA107
Bridgefoot, SE1 .101 DL78
Bridgefoot La, Pot.B. EN6 .11 CX33
Bridge Gdns, Ashf. TW15 .115 BQ94
East Molesey KT8 .137 CD98
Bridge Gate, N21 off Ridge Av .46 DQ45
Bridgeham Cl, Wey. KT13
off Mayfield Rd .152 BN106
Bridge Hill, Epp. CM16 .17 ET33
Bridge Ho Quay, E14 .204 E3
Bridgeland Rd, E16 .86 EG73
Bridge La, NW11 .63 CY57
SW11 .100 DE81
Virginia Water GU25 .132 AY99
Bridgeman Rd, N1 .83 DM66
Teddington TW11 .117 CG93
Bridgeman St, NW8 .194 B1
Bridge Meadows, SE14 .103 DX79
Bridge Ms, Wok. GU21
off Bridge Barn La .166 AX117
Bridgend Rd, SW18 .100 DC84
Enfield EN1 .30 DW35
Bridgenhall Rd, Enf. EN1 .30 DT39
Bridgen Rd, Bex. DA5 .126 EY86
Bridge Pk, SW18 .120 DA85
Bridge Pl, SW1 .199 J8
Amersham HP6 .20 AT38
Croydon CR0 .142 DR101
Watford WD17 .24 BX43
Bridgeport Pl, E1 .202 C2
Bridger Cl, Wat. WD25 .8 BX33
Bridge Rd, E6 .87 EM66
E15 .85 ED66
E17 .67 DZ59
N9 off The Broadway .46 DU48
N22 .45 DL53
NW10 .80 CS65
Beckenham BR3 .123 DZ94
Bexleyheath DA7 .106 EY82
Chertsey KT16 .134 BH101
Chessington KT9 .156 CL106
East Molesey KT8 .137 CE98
Epsom KT17 .157 CT112
Erith DA8 .107 FF81
Grays RM17 .110 GB78
Hounslow TW3 .97 CD82
Isleworth TW7 .97 CD83
Kings Langley WD4 .7 BQ33
Orpington BR5 .146 EV100
Rainham RM13 .89 FF70
Southall UB2 .96 BZ75
Sutton SM2 .158 DB107
Twickenham TW1 .117 CH86
Uxbridge UB8 .76 BJ68
Wallington SM6 .159 DJ106
Wembley HA9 .62 CN62
Weybridge KT13 .152 BM105
Bridge Row, Croy. CR0
off Cross Rd .142 DR102
Bridges Ct, SW11 .100 DD83
Bridges Dr, Dart. DA1 .128 FP85
Bridges La, Croy. CR0 .159 DL105
Bridges Pl, SW6 .99 CZ81
Bridges Rd, SW19 .120 DB93
Stanmore HA7 .41 CF50
Bridges Rd Ms, SW19
off Bridges Rd .120 DB93
Bridge St, SW1 .199 P5
W4 .98 CR77
Leatherhead KT22 .171 CG122
Pinner HA5 .60 BX55
Richmond TW9 .117 CK85
Slough (Colnbr.) SL3 .93 BD80
Staines TW18 .113 BE91
Walton-on-Thames KT12 .135 BT102
Bridge Ter, E15 off Bridge Rd .85 ED66
Bridgetown Cl, SE19
off St. Kitts Ter .122 DS92
Bridge Vw, W6 .99 CW78
Bridgeview Ct, Ilf. IG6 .49 ER51
Bridgewater Cl, Chis. BR7 .145 ES97
Bridgewater Ct, Slou. SL3 .93 BA78
Bridgewater Gdns, Edg. HA8 .42 CM54
Bridgewater Rd, Ruis. HA4 .59 BU63
Wembley HA0 .79 CJ66
Weybridge KT13 .153 BR107
Bridgewater Sq, EC2 .197 H6
Bridgewater St, EC2 .197 H6
Bridgewater Way, Bushey WD23 .24 CB44
Bridge Way, N11
off Pymmes Grn Rd .45 DJ48
NW11 .63 CZ57
Bridgeway, Bark. IG11 .87 ET66
Bridge Way, Cob. KT11 .153 BT113
Coulsdon CR5 .174 DE119
Twickenham TW2 .116 CC87
Uxbridge UB10 .59 BP64
Bridgeway, Wem. HA0 .80 CL66
Bridgeway St, NW1 .195 M1
Bridge Wf, Cher. KT16 .134 BJ102
Bridge Wf Rd, Islw. TW7
off Church St .97 CH83
Bridgewood Cl, SE20 .122 DV94
Bridgewood Rd, SW16 .121 DK94
Worcester Park KT4 .157 CU105
Bridge Wks, Uxb. UB8 .76 BJ70
Bridge Yd, SE1 .201 L2
Bridgford St, SW18 .120 DC90
Bridgman Rd, W4 .98 CQ76
Bridgwater Cl, Rom. RM3 .52 FK50
Bridgwater Rd, E15 .85 EC67
Romford RM3 .52 FJ50
Bridgwater Wk, Rom. RM3 .52 FK50
Bridle Cl, Enf. EN3 .31 DZ37
Epsom KT19 .156 CR106
Kingston upon Thames KT1 .137 CK98
Sunbury-on-Thames TW16
off Forge La .135 BU97
Bridle End, Epsom KT17 .157 CT114
Bridle La, W1 .195 L10
Cobham KT11 .170 CB115
Leatherhead KT22 .170 CB115
Rickmansworth (Loud.) WD3 .22 BK41
Twickenham TW1
off Crown Rd .117 CH86
Bridle Path, Croy. CR0 .141 DM104
Watford WD17 .23 BV40
Bridle Path, The, Epsom KT17 .157 CV110
Bridle Path, The, Wdf.Grn. IG8 .48 EE52
Bridlepath Way, Felt. TW14 .115 BS88
Bridle Rd, Croy. CR0 .143 EA104
Epsom KT17 .157 CT113
Esher (Clay.) KT10 .155 CH107
Pinner HA5 .60 BW58
Bridle Rd, The, Pur. CR8 .159 DL110
Bridle Way, Croy. CR0 .161 EA106
Orpington BR6 .163 EQ105
Bridle Way, The, Croy. CR0 .161 DY110
Bridleway, The, Wall. SM6 .159 DJ105
Bridleway Cl, Epsom KT17 .157 CW110
Bridlington Cl, West. (Bigg.H.) TN16 .178 EH119
Bridlington Rd, N9 .46 DV45
Watford WD19 .40 BX48
Bridport Av, Rom. RM7 .71 FB58
Bridport Pl, N1 .84 DR68
Bridport Rd, N18 .46 DS50
Greenford UB6 .78 CB67
Thornton Heath CR7 .141 DN97
Bridport Ter, SW8
off Wandsworth Rd .101 DK81
Bridstow Pl, W2 off Talbot Rd .82 DA72
Brief St, SE5 .101 DP81
Brier Lea, Tad. (Lwr.Kgswd.) KT20 .183 CZ126
Brierley, Croy. (New Adgtn.) CR0 .161 EB107
Brierley Av, N9 .46 DW46
Brierley Cl, SE25 .142 DU98
Hornchurch RM11 .72 FJ58
Brierley Rd, E11 .67 ED63
SW12 .121 DJ89
Brierly Gdns, E2
off Royston St .84 DW68
Brier Rd, Tad. KT20 .173 CV119
Briery Ct, Rick. (Chorl.) WD3 .22 BG42
Briery Fld, Rick. (Chorl.) WD3 .22 BG42
Briery Way, Amer. HP6 .20 AS37
Brigade Cl, Har. HA2 .61 CD61
Brigade Pl, Cat. CR3 .176 DQ122
Brigade St, SE3
off Royal Par .104 EF82
Brigadier Av, Enf. EN2 .30 DQ39
Brigadier Hill, Enf. EN2 .30 DQ38
Briggeford Cl, E5
off Geldeston Rd .66 DU61
Briggs Cl, Mitch. CR4 .141 DH95
Bright Cl, Belv. DA17 .106 EX77
Brightfield Rd, SE12 .124 EF85
Brightlands, Grav. (Nthflt.) DA11 .130 GE91
Brightlands Rd, Reig. RH2 .184 DC132
Brightling Rd, SE4 .123 DZ86
Brightlingsea Pl, E14 .85 DZ73
Brightman Rd, SW18 .120 DD88
Brighton Av, E17 .67 DZ57
Brighton Cl, Add. KT15 .152 BJ106
Uxbridge UB10 .77 BP66
Brighton Dr, Nthlt. UB5 .78 CA65
Brighton Rd, E6 .87 EN69
N2 .44 DC54
N16 .66 DS63
Addlestone KT15 .152 BJ105
Banstead SM7 .157 CZ114
Coulsdon CR5 .175 DJ119
Purley CR8 .160 DQ110
South Croydon CR2 .160 DQ106
Surbiton KT6 .137 CJ100
Sutton SM2 .158 DB109
Tadworth KT20 .173 CY119
Watford WD24 .23 BU38
Brighton Ter, SW9 .101 DM84
Brights Av, Rain. RM13 .89 FH70
Brightside, The, Enf. EN3 .31 DX39
Brightside Av, Stai. TW18 .114 BJ94
Brightside Rd, SE13 .123 ED86
Bright St, E14 .85 EB72
Brightview Cl, St.Alb. (Brick.Wd.) AL2 .8 BY29
Brightwell Cl, Croy. CR0
off Sumner Rd .141 DN102
Brightwell Cres, SW17 .120 DF92
Brightwell Rd, Wat. WD18 .23 BU43
Brig Ms, SE8
off Watergate St .103 EA79
Brigstock Rd, Belv. DA17 .107 FB77
Coulsdon CR5 .175 DH115
Thornton Heath CR7 .141 DN99
Brill Pl, NW1 .195 N1
Brimfield Rd, Purf. RM19 .109 FR77
Brim Hill, N2 .64 DC56
Brimpsfield Cl, SE2 .106 EV76
BRIMSDOWN, Enf. .31 DY41
≠ Brimsdown .31 DY41
Brimsdown Av, Enf. EN3 .31 DY40
Brimsdown Ind Est, Enf. EN3 .31 DZ40
Brimshot La, Wok. (Chobham) GU24 .150 AS109
Brimstone Cl, Orp. BR6 .164 EW108
Brindle Gate, Sid. DA15 .125 ES88
Brindles, Horn. RM11 .72 FL56
Brindles, The, Bans. SM7 .173 CZ117
Brindles Cl, Brwd. CM13 .55 GC47
Brindley Cl, Bexh. DA7 .107 FB83
Wembley HA0 .79 CJ67
Brindley Ho, SW2
off New Pk Rd .121 DL87
Brindley St, SE14 .103 DZ81
Brindley Way, Brom. BR1 .124 EG92
Southall UB1 .78 CB73
Brindwood Rd, E4 .47 DZ48
Brinkburn Cl, SE2 .106 EU77
Edgware HA8 .42 CP54
Brinkburn Gdns, Edg. HA8 .62 CN55
Brinkley, Kings.T. KT1
off Burritt Rd .138 CN96
Brinkley Rd, Wor.Pk. KT4 .139 CV103
Brinklow Cres, SE18 .105 EP80
Brinklow Ho, W2 .82 DB71
Brinkworth Rd, Ilf. IG5 .68 EL55
Brinkworth Way, E9 .85 DZ65
Brinley Cl, Wal.Cr. (Chsht.) EN8 .15 DX31
Brinsdale Rd, NW4 .63 CX56
Brinsley Rd, Har. HA3 .41 CD54
Brinsley St, E1
off Watney St .84 DV72
Brinsmead, St.Alb. (Park St.) AL2 .9 CD27
Brinsmead Rd, Rom. RM3 .52 FN54
Brinsworth Cl, Twick. TW2 .117 CD89
Brinton Wk, SE1 .200 F3
Brion Pl, E14 .85 EC71
Brisbane Av, SW19 .140 DB95
Brisbane Ct, N10
off Sydney Rd .45 DH52
Brisbane Ho, Til. RM18
off Leicester Rd .111 GF81
Brisbane Rd, E10 .67 EB61
W13 .97 CG75
Ilford IG1 .69 EP59
Brisbane St, SE5 .102 DR80
Briscoe Cl, E11 .68 EF61
Briscoe Rd, SW19 .120 DD93
Rainham RM13 .90 FJ68
Briset Rd, SE9 .104 EK83
Briset St, EC1 .196 F6
Briset Way, N7 .65 DM61
Brisson Cl, Esher KT10 .154 BZ107
Bristol Cl, Stai. (Stanw.) TW19 .114 BL86
Bristol Gdns, SW15
off Portsmouth Rd .119 CW87
W9 .82 DB70
Bristol Ms, W9
off Bristol Gdns .82 DB70
Bristol Pk Rd, E17 .67 DY56
Bristol Rd, E7 .86 EJ65
Gravesend DA12 .131 GK90
Greenford UB6 .78 CB67
Morden SM4 .140 DC99
Bristol Way, Slou. SL1 .74 AT74
Briston Gro, N8 .65 DL58
Briston Ms, NW7 .43 CU52
Bristow Rd, SE19 .122 DS92
Bexleyheath DA7 .106 EY81
Croydon CR0 .159 DL105
Hounslow TW3 .96 CC83
★ Britain at War Experience, SE1 .201 M3
Britannia Cl, SW4
off Bowland Rd .101 DK84
Erith DA8 off Manor Rd .107 FF79
Northolt UB5 .78 BX69
Britannia Dr, Grav. DA12 .131 GM92
Britannia Gate, E16 .205 N2
Britannia Ind Est, Slou. (Colnbr.) SL3 .93 BE82
Britannia La, Twick. TW2 .116 CC87
Britannia Rd, E14 .204 A9
N12 .44 DC48
SW6 .100 DB80
Brentwood CM14 .54 FW50
Ilford IG1 .69 EP62
Surbiton KT5 .138 CM101
Waltham Cross EN8 .15 DZ34
Britannia Row, N1 .83 DP67
Britannia St, WC1 .196 B2
Britannia Wk, N1 .197 K2
Britannia Way, NW10 .80 CP70
SW6 off Britannia Rd .100 DB81
Staines (Stanw.) TW19 .114 BK87
★ British Dental Association Mus, W1 off Wimpole St .195 H7
British Gro, W4 .99 CT78
British Gro Pas, W4 .99 CT78
British Gro S, W4
off British Gro Pas .99 CT78
British Legion Rd, E4 .48 EF47
★ British Lib, NW1 .195 N2
★ British Lib Newspaper Collection, NW9 .62 CS55
★ British Medical Association, WC1 .195 N4
★ British Mus, WC1 .195 P7
British St, E3 .85 DZ69
Briton Cl, S.Croy. CR2 .160 DS111
Briton Cres, S.Croy. CR2 .160 DS111
Briton Hill Rd, S.Croy. CR2 .160 DS110
Brittain Rd, Dag. RM8 .70 EY62
Walton-on-Thames KT12 .154 BX106
Brittains La, Sev. TN13 .190 FF123
Britten Cl, NW11 .64 DB60
Borehamwood (Elstree) WD6
off Rodgers Cl .25 CK44
Brittenden Cl, Orp. BR6 .163 ES107
Britten Dr, Sthl. UB1 .78 CA72
Britten St, SW3 .100 DE78
Britton Cl, SE6
off Brownhill Rd .123 ED87
Britton St, EC1 .196 F5
Brixham Cres, Ruis. HA4 .59 BU60
Brixham Gdns, Ilf. IG3 .69 ES64
Brixham Rd, Well. DA16 .106 EX81
Brixham St, E16 .87 EM74
BRIXTON, SW2 .101 DL84
≠ Brixton .101 DN84
⊖ Brixton .101 DN84
★ Brixton Academy, The, SW9 .101 DM83
Brixton Est, Edg. HA8 .42 CP54
Brixton Hill, SW2 .121 DL87
Brixton Hill Pl, SW2
off Brixton Hill .121 DL87
Brixton Oval, SW2 .101 DN84
Brixton Rd, SW9 .101 DN82
Watford WD24 .23 BV39
Brixton Sta Rd, SW9 .101 DN84
Brixton Water La, SW2 .121 DM85
Broad Acre, St.Alb. (Brick.Wd.) AL2 .8 BY30
Broadacre, Stai. TW18 .114 BG92
Broadacre Cl, Uxb. UB10 .59 BP62
Broadbent Cl, N6 .65 DH60
Broadbent St, W1 .195 H10
Broadberry Ct, N18 .46 DV50
Broadbridge Cl, SE3 .104 EG80
Broad Cl, Walt. KT12 .136 BX104
Broadcoombe, S.Croy. CR2 .160 DW108
Broad Ct, WC2 .196 A9
Broadcroft Av, Stan. HA7 .41 CK54
Broadcroft Rd, Orp. BR5 .145 ER101

225

Bro - Bro

Broad Ditch Rd, Grav. (Sthflt.) DA13 130 GC94
Broadeaves Cl, S.Croy. CR2 160 DS106
Broadfield Cl, NW2 63 CW62
Croydon CR0 off Progress Way 141 DM103
Romford RM1 71 FF57
Tadworth KT20 173 CW120
Broadfield Ct, Bushey (Bushey Hth.) WD23 41 CE47
Broadfield La, NW1 83 DL66
Broadfield Rd, SE6 124 EE87
Broadfields, E.Mol. KT8 137 CD100
Harrow HA2 40 CB54
Waltham Cross (Chsht.) EN7 13 DP29
Broadfields Av, N21 45 DN45
Edgware HA8 42 CP49
Broadfields Hts, Edg. HA8 42 CP49
Broadfields La, Wat. WD19 39 BV46
Broadfield Sq, Enf. EN1 30 DV40
Broadfields Way, NW10 63 CT64
Broadfield Way, Buck.H. IG9 48 EJ48
Broadford La, Wok. (Chobham) GU24 150 AT112
BROADGATE, EC2 197 L6
Broadgate, E13 86 EJ68
EC2 off Liverpool St 84 DS71
Waltham Abbey EN9 16 EF33
Broadgate Circle, EC2 197 M6
Broadgate Rd, E16 86 EK72
Broadgates Av, Barn. EN4 28 DB39
Broadgates Rd, SW18 off Ellerton Rd 120 DD88
BROAD GREEN, Croy. 141 DN100
Broad Grn Av, Croy. CR0 141 DP101
Broadgreen Rd, Wal.Cr. (Chsht.) EN7 14 DR26
Broadham Grn Rd, Oxt. RH8 187 ED132
Broadham Pl, Oxt. RH8 187 ED131
Broadhead Strand, NW9 43 CT53
Broadheath Dr, Chis. BR7 125 EM92
Broad Highway, Cob. KT11 154 BX114
Broadhinton Rd, SW4 101 DH83
Broadhurst, Ashtd. KT21 172 CL116
Broadhurst Av, Edg. HA8 42 CP49
Ilford IG3 69 ET63
Broadhurst Cl, NW6 off Broadhurst Gdns 82 DC65
Richmond TW10 off Lower Gro Rd 118 CM85
Broadhurst Gdns, NW6 82 DB65
Chigwell IG7 49 EQ49
Ruislip HA4 60 BW61
Broadhurst Wk, Rain. RM13 89 FG65
Broadlake Cl, St.Alb. (Lon.Col.) AL2 9 CK27
Broadlands, Felt. TW13 116 BZ90
Grays (Bad.Dene) RM17 off Bankfoot 110 FZ78
Broadlands Av, SW16 121 DL89
Enfield EN3 30 DV41
Shepperton TW17 135 BQ100
Broadlands Cl, N6 64 DG59
SW16 121 DL89
Enfield EN3 30 DV41
Waltham Cross EN8 15 DX34
Broadlands Dr, Warl. CR6 176 DW119
Broadlands Rd, N6 64 DF59
Bromley BR1 124 EH91
Broadlands Way, N.Mal. KT3 139 CT100
Broad La, EC2 197 M6
N8 off Tottenham La 65 DM57
N15 66 DT56
Dartford DA2 127 FG91
Hampton TW12 116 CA93
Broad Lawn, SE9 125 EN89
Broadlawns Ct, Har. HA3 41 CF53
Broadley Gdns, Rad. (Shenley) WD7 off Queens Way 10 CL32
Broadley St, NW8 194 A6
Broadley Ter, NW1 194 C5
Broadmark Rd, Slou. SL2 74 AV73
Broadmayne, SE17 201 K10
Broadmead, SE6 123 EA90
Broad Mead, Ashtd. KT21 172 CM117
Broadmead Av, Wor.Pk. KT4 139 CU101
Broadmead Cl, Hmptn. TW12 116 CA93
Pinner HA5 40 BY52
Broadmead Est, Wdf.Grn. IG8 48 EJ52
Broadmead Rd, Hayes UB4 78 BY70
Northolt UB5 78 BY70
Woking (Old Wok.) GU22, GU23 167 BB122
Woodford Green IG8 48 EG51
Broadmeads, Wok. (Send) GU23 off Broadmead Rd 167 BB122
Broad Oak, Sun. TW16 115 BT93
Woodford Green IG8 48 EH50
Broadoak Av, Enf. EN3 31 DX35
Broad Oak Cl, E4 off Royston Av 47 EA50
Broadoak Cl, Dart. (Sutt.H.) DA4 128 FN93
Broad Oak Cl, Orp. BR5 146 EU96
Broadoak Rd, Erith DA8 107 FD80
Broadoaks, Epp. CM16 17 ET31
Surbiton KT6 138 CP102
Broadoaks Cres, W.Byf. KT14 152 BH114
Broadoaks Way, Brom. BR2 144 EF99
Broad Platts, Slou. SL3 92 AX76
Broad Ride, Egh. TW20 132 AU96
Virginia Water GU25 132 AU96
Broad Rd, Swans. DA10 130 FY86
Broad Sanctuary, SW1 199 N5
Broadstone Pl, W1 194 F7
Broadstone Rd, Horn. RM12 71 FG61
Broad St, Dag. RM10 88 FA66
Teddington TW11 117 CF93
Broad St Av, EC2 197 M7
Broad St Pl, EC2 197 L7
Broadstrood, Loug. IG10 33 EN38
Broad Vw, NW9 62 CN58
Broadview Av, Grays RM16 110 GD75
Broadview Rd, SW16 121 DK94
Broadwalk, E18 68 EF55
Broad Wk, N21 45 DM47
Broad Wk, NW1 195 H3
SE3 104 EJ83
W1 198 F2
Caterham CR3 176 DT122
Coulsdon CR5 174 DG123
Croydon CR0 161 DY110
Epsom KT18 off Chalk La 172 CS117
Epsom (Burgh Hth.) KT18 173 CX119
Broadwalk, Har. HA2 60 CA57
Broad Wk, Houns. TW5 96 BX81
Orpington BR6 146 EX104
Richmond TW9 98 CM80
Sevenoaks TN15 191 FL128
Broad Wk, The, W8 82 DB74
East Molesey KT8 137 CF97
Broadwalk, The, Nthwd. HA6 39 BQ54
Broadwalk Ct, W8 82 DA74
Broad Wk La, NW11 63 CZ59
Broad Wk N, The, Brwd. CM13 55 GA49
Broadwalk Shop Cen, Edg. HA8 42 CP51
Broad Wk S, The, Brwd. CM13 55 GA49
Broadwall, SE1 200 E2
Broadwater, Pot.B. EN6 12 DB30
Broadwater Cl, Stai. (Wrays.) TW19 113 AZ87
Walton-on-Thames KT12 153 BU106
Woking GU21 151 BD112
Broad Water Cres, Wey. KT13 off Churchill Dr 135 BQ104
Broadwater Gdns, Orp. BR6 163 EP105
Uxbridge (Hare.) UB9 58 BH56
Broadwater La, Uxb. (Hare.) UB9 58 BH56
Broadwater Pk, Uxb. (Denh.) UB9 58 BG58
Broadwater Pl, Wey. KT13 off Oatlands Dr 135 BS103
Broadwater Rd, N17 46 DS53
SE28 105 ER76
SW17 120 DE91
Broadwater Rd N, Walt. KT12 153 BT106
Broadwater Rd S, Walt. KT12 153 BT106
Broadway, E15 85 ED66
SW1 199 M6
W13 79 CG74
Barking IG11 87 EQ66
Bexleyheath DA6 106 EY84
Grays RM17 110 GC79
Rainham RM13 89 FG70
Romford RM2 71 FG55
Staines TW18 off Kingston Rd 114 BH92
Surbiton KT6 138 CP102
Swanley BR8 147 FC100
Tilbury RM18 111 GF82
Broadway, The, E4 47 EC51
E13 86 EH68
N8 65 DL58
N9 46 DU48
N14 off Winchmore Hill Rd 45 DK46
N22 45 DN54
NW7 42 CS50
SW13 off The Terrace 98 CS82
SW19 119 CZ93
W5 79 CK73
W7 79 CE74
Addlestone (New Haw) KT15 152 BG110
Croydon CR0 off Croydon Rd 159 DL105
Dagenham RM8 70 EZ61
Greenford UB6 78 CC70
Harrow HA2 41 CE54
Hornchurch RM12 71 FH63
Loughton IG10 33 EQ42
Pinner HA5 40 BZ52
Southall UB1 78 BX73
Staines (Laleham) TW18 134 BJ97
Stanmore HA7 41 CJ50
Sutton (Cheam) SM3 157 CY107
Thames Ditton KT7 off Hampton Ct Way 137 CE102
Watford WD17 24 BW41
Wembley HA9 off East La 62 CL62
Woking GU21 167 AZ117
Woodford Green IG8 48 EH51
Broadway Av, Croy. CR0 142 DR99
Twickenham TW1 117 CH86
Broadway Cl, S.Croy. CR2 160 DV114
Woodford Green IG8 48 EH51
Broadway Ct, SW19 off The Broadway 120 DA93
Broadway E, Uxb. (Denh.) UB9 58 BG58
Broadway Gdns, Mitch. CR4 140 DE98
Broadway Ho, Brom. BR1 off Elmfield Pk 144 EG97
Broadway Mkt, E8 84 DV67
Broadway Mkt Ms, E8 off Brougham Rd 84 DU67
Broadway Ms, E5 66 DT59
N13 off Elmdale Rd 45 DM50
N21 off Compton Rd 45 DP46
Broadway Par, N8 65 DL58
Hayes UB3 off Coldharbour La 77 BU74
Hornchurch RM12 off The Broadway 71 FH63
Broadway Pl, SW19 off Hartfield Rd 119 CZ93
Broadway Shop Cen, W6 off Hammersmith Bdy 99 CW77
Bexleyheath DA6 106 FA84
Broadwick St, W1 195 L10
Broadwood, Grav. DA11 131 GH92
Broadwood Av, Ruis. HA4 59 BS58
Broadwood Ter, W8 off Pembroke Rd 99 CZ77
Broad Yd, EC1 196 F5
Brocas Cl, NW3 off Fellows Rd 82 DE66
Brockbridge Ho, SW15 off Tangley Gro 119 CT86
Brockdish Av, Bark. IG11 69 ET64
Brockenhurst, W.Mol. KT8 136 BZ100
Brockenhurst Av, Wor.Pk. KT4 138 CS102
Brockenhurst Cl, Wok. GU21 151 AZ114
Brockenhurst Gdns, NW7 42 CS50
Ilford IG1 69 EQ64
Brockenhurst Ms, N18 off Lyndhurst Rd 46 DU49
Brockenhurst Rd, Croy. CR0 142 DV101
Brockenhurst Way, SW16 141 DK96
Brocket Cl, Chig. IG7 off Burrow Rd 49 ET50
Brocket Rd, Grays RM16 111 GG76
Brocket Way, Chig. IG7 49 ES50
Brock Grn, S.Ock. RM15 off Cam Grn 91 FV72
Brockham Cl, SW19 119 CZ92
Brockham Cres, Croy. (New Adgtn.) CR0 161 ED108
Brockham Dr, SW2 off Fairview Pl 121 DM87
Ilford IG2 69 EP58
Brockham Hill Pk, Tad. KT20 182 CQ131
Brockham La, Bet. (Brock.) RH3 182 CN134
Brockham St, SE1 201 J6
Brockhurst Cl, Stan. HA7 41 CF51
Brockill Cres, SE4 103 DY84
Brocklebank Ct, Whyt. CR3 176 DU118
Brocklebank Rd, SE7 205 P9
SW18 120 DC87
Brocklehurst St, SE14 103 DX80
Brocklesbury Cl, Wat. WD24 24 BW41
Brocklesby Rd, SE25 142 DV98
BROCKLEY, SE4 123 DY85
⇌ Brockley 103 DY83
Brockley Av, Stan. HA7 42 CL48
Brockley Cl, Stan. HA7 42 CL49
Brockley Combe, Wey. KT13 153 BR105
Brockley Cres, Rom. RM5 51 FC52
Brockley Cross, SE4 off Endwell Rd 103 DY83
Brockley Footpath, SE15 102 DW84
Brockley Gdns, SE4 103 DZ82
Brockley Gro, SE4 123 DZ85
Brentwood CM13 55 GA46
Brockley Hall Rd, SE4 123 DY86
Brockley Hill, Stan. HA7 41 CJ46
Brockley Ms, SE4 123 DY85
Brockley Pk, SE23 123 DY87
Brockley Ri, SE23 123 DY86
Brockley Rd, SE4 103 DZ83
Brockleyside, Stan. HA7 41 CK49
Brockley Vw, SE23 123 DY87
Brockley Way, SE4 123 DX85
Brockman Ri, Brom. BR1 123 ED91
Brock Pl, E3 85 EB70
Brock Rd, E13 86 EH71
Brocks Dr, Sutt. SM3 139 CY104
Brockshot Cl, Brent. TW8 97 CK79
Brocksparkwood, Brwd. CM13 55 GB48
Brock St, SE15 off Evelina Rd 102 DW83
Brockton Cl, Rom. RM1 71 FF56
Brock Way, Vir.W. GU25 132 AW99
Brockway Cl, E11 68 EE60
Brockway Ho, Slou. SL3 93 BB78
Brockwell Cl, Orp. BR5 145 ET99
★ Brockwell Park, SE24 121 DP86
Brockwell Pk Gdns, SE24 121 DN87
Brockwell Pk Row, SW2 121 DN86
Brodewater Rd, Borwd. WD6 26 CP40
Brodia Rd, N16 66 DS62
Brodie Rd, E4 47 EC46
Enfield EN2 30 DQ38
Brodie St, SE1 202 A10
Brodlove La, E1 85 DX73
Brodrick Gro, SE2 106 EV77
Brodrick Rd, SW17 120 DE89
Brograve Gdns, Beck. BR3 143 EB96
Broke Fm Dr, Orp. BR6 164 EW109
Brokengate La, Uxb. (Denh.) UB9 57 BC60
Broken Wf, EC4 197 H10
Brokes Cres, Reig. RH2 184 DA132
Brokesley St, E3 85 DZ70
Brokes Rd, Reig. RH2 184 DA132
Broke Wk, E8 84 DU67
Bromar Rd, SE5 102 DS83
Bromborough Grn, Wat. WD19 40 BW50
Bromefield, Stan. HA7 41 CJ53
Bromefield Ct, Wal.Abb. EN9 16 EG33
Bromehead Rd, E1 84 DW72
Bromehead St, E1 off Commercial Rd 84 DW72
Bromell's Rd, SW4 101 DJ84
Brome Rd, SE9 105 EM83
Bromet Cl, Wat. WD17 off Hempstead Rd 23 BT38
Bromfelde Rd, SW4 101 DK82
Bromfelde Wk, SW4 101 DK82
Bromfield St, N1 83 DN68
Bromford Cl, Oxt. RH8 188 EG133
Bromhall Rd, Dag. RM8, RM9 88 EV65
Bromhedge, SE9 125 EM90
Bromholm Rd, SE2 106 EV76
Bromleigh Cl, Wal.Cr. (Chsht.) EN8 off Martins Dr 15 DY28
Bromleigh Ct, SE23 off Lapse Wd Wk 122 DV89
BROMLEY, E3 85 EB70
BROMLEY 144 EF96
Bromley, Grays RM17 110 FZ79
Bromley Av, Brom. BR1 124 EE94
⊖ Bromley-by-Bow 85 EB69
BROMLEY COMMON, Brom. 145 EM101
Bromley Common, Brom. BR2 144 EJ98
Bromley Cres, Brom. BR2 144 EF97
Ruislip HA4 59 BT63
Bromley Gdns, Brom. BR2 144 EF97
Bromley Gro, Brom. BR2 143 ED96
Bromley Hall Rd, E14 85 EC71
Bromley High St, E3 85 EB69
Bromley Hill, Brom. BR1 124 EE92
H Bromley Hosp, Brom. BR2 144 EH98
Bromley La, Chis. BR7 125 EQ94
Bromley Mall, The, Brom. BR1 144 EG97
★ Bromley Mus, Orp. BR6 146 EV101
⇌ Bromley North 144 EG95
BROMLEY PARK, Brom. 144 EE95
Bromley Pk, Brom. BR1 off London Rd 144 EF95
Bromley Pl, W1 195 K6
Bromley Rd, E10 67 EB58
E17 47 EA54
N17 46 DR48
N18 46 DT53
SE6 123 EB88
Beckenham BR3 143 EB95
Bromley (Downham) BR1 123 EC91
Bromley (Short.) BR2 143 EC96
Chislehurst BR7 145 EP95
⇌ Bromley South 144 EG97
Bromley St, E1 85 DX71
BROMPTON, SW3 198 B7
Brompton Arc, SW3 198 D5
Brompton Cl, SE20 off Selby Rd 142 DU96
Hounslow TW4 116 BZ85
Brompton Dr, Erith DA8 107 FH80
Brompton Gro, N2 64 DE56
★ Brompton Oratory, SW7 off Brompton Rd 198 B7
Brompton Pk Cres, SW6 100 DB79
Brompton Pl, SW3 198 C6
Brompton Rd, SW1 198 C6
SW3 198 B8
SW7 198 C6
Brompton Sq, SW3 198 B6
Brompton Ter, SE18 off Prince Imperial Rd 105 EN81
Bromwich Av, N6 64 DG61
Bromyard Av, W3 80 CS74
Bromyard Ho, SE15 102 DV80
BRONDESBURY, NW2 81 CY66
⇌ Brondesbury 81 CZ66
Brondesbury Ct, NW2 81 CW65
Brondesbury Ms, NW6 off Willesden La 82 DA66
BRONDESBURY PARK, NW6 81 CW66
⇌ Brondesbury Park 81 CX67
Brondesbury Pk, NW2 81 CV65
NW6 81 CX66
Brondesbury Rd, NW6 81 CZ68
Brondesbury Vil, NW6 81 CZ68
Bronsart Rd, SW6 99 CY80
Bronsdon Way, Uxb. (Denh.) UB9 57 BF61
Bronson Rd, SW20 139 CX96
Bronte Cl, E7 off Bective Rd 68 EG63
Erith DA8 107 FB80
Ilford IG2 69 EN57
Tilbury RM18 111 GJ82
Bronte Gro, Dart. DA1 108 FM84
Bronte Ho, NW6 82 DA69
Bronte Vw, Grav. DA12 131 GJ88
Bronti Cl, SE17 102 DQ78
Bronze Age Way, Belv. DA17 107 FC76
Erith DA8 107 FC76
Bronze St, SE8 103 EA80
Brook Av, Dag. RM10 89 FB66
Edgware HA8 42 CP51
Wembley HA9 62 CN62
Brookbank Av, W7 79 CD71
Brookbank Rd, SE13 103 EA83
Brook Cl, NW7 off Frith Ct 43 CY52
SW17 120 DG89
SW20 139 CV97
W3 off West Lo Av 80 CN74
Borehamwood WD6 26 CP41
Epsom KT19 156 CS109
Romford RM2 51 FF53
Ruislip HA4 59 BS59
Staines (Stanw.) TW19 114 BM87
Brook Ct, Buck.H. IG9 48 EH46
Brook Cres, E4 47 EA49
N9 46 DV49
Brookdale, N11 45 DJ49
Brookdale Av, Upmin. RM14 72 FN62
Brookdale Cl, Upmin. RM14 72 FP62
Brookdale Rd, E17 67 EA55
SE6 123 EB86
Bexley DA5 126 EY86
Brookdene Av, Wat. WD19 39 BV45
Brookdene Dr, Nthwd. HA6 39 BT52
Brookdene Rd, SE18 105 ET77
Brook Dr, SE11 200 E7
Harrow HA1 60 CC56
Radlett WD7 9 CF33
Ruislip HA4 59 BS58
Sunbury-on-Thames TW16 off Chertsey Rd 115 BS92
Brooke Av, Har. HA2 60 CC62
Brooke Cl, Bushey WD23 40 CC45
Brookehowse Rd, SE6 123 EB90
Brookend Rd, Sid. DA15 125 ES88
Brooke Rd, E5 66 DU62
E17 67 EC56
N16 66 DT62
Grays RM17 110 GA78
Brooker Rd, Wal.Abb. EN9 15 EC34
Brookers Cl, Ashtd. KT21 171 CJ117
Brooke's Ct, EC1 196 D6
Brookes Mkt, EC1 196 E6
Brooke St, EC1 196 D7
Brooke Way, Bushey WD23 off Richfield Rd 40 CC45
Brook Fm Rd, Cob. KT11 170 BX115
Brookfield, N6 64 DG62
Epping (Thnwd.) CM16 18 EW25
Woking GU21 166 AV116
Brookfield Av, E17 67 EC56
NW7 43 CV51
W5 79 CK70
Sutton SM1 158 DD105
Brookfield Cen, Wal.Cr. (Chsht.) EN8 off Halfhide La 15 DX27
Brookfield Cl, NW7 43 CV51
Brookfield Cl, Brent. CM13 55 GC44
Chertsey (Ott.) KT16 151 BD107
Brookfield Ct, Grnf. UB6 78 CC69
Harrow HA3 61 CK57
Brookfield Cres, NW7 43 CV51
Harrow HA3 62 CL57
Brookfield Gdns, Esher (Clay.) KT10 155 CF107
Waltham Cross (Chsht.) EN8 15 DX27
Brookfield La, Wal.Cr. (Chsht.) EN8 15 DX27
Brookfield La W, Wal.Cr. (Chsht.) EN8 14 DV28
Brookfield Pk, NW5 65 DH62
Brookfield Path, Wdf.Grn. IG8 48 EE51
Brookfield Retail Pk, Wal.Cr. (Chsht.) EN8 15 DX26
Brookfield Rd, E9 85 DY65
N9 46 DU48
W4 98 CR75
Brookfields, Enf. EN3 31 DX42
Brookfields Av, Mitch. CR4 140 DE99
Brook Gdns, E4 47 EB49
SW13 99 CT83
Kingston upon Thames KT2 138 CQ95
Brook Gate, W1 198 E1
Brook Grn, W6 99 CX77
Woking (Chobham) GU24 off Brookleys 150 AT110
Brook Hill, Oxt. RH8 187 EC130
Brookhill Cl, SE18 105 EP78
Barnet EN4 28 DE43
Brookhill Rd, SE18 105 EP78
Barnet EN4 28 DE43
Brookhouse Gdns, E4 48 EE49
Brookhurst Rd, Add. KT15 152 BH107
Brook Ind Est, Hayes UB4 78 BX74
Brooking Rd, E7 68 EG64
Brookland Cl, NW11 64 DA56
Brookland Garth, NW11 64 DB56
Brookland Hill, NW11 64 DA56
Brookland Ri, NW11 64 DA56
BROOKLANDS, Wey. 152 BM109
Brooklands, Dart. DA1 128 FL88
Brooklands App, Rom. RM1 71 FD56
Brooklands Av, SW19 120 DB89
Sidcup DA15 125 ER89
Brooklands Business Pk, Wey. KT13 152 BN110
Brooklands Cl, Cob. KT11 170 BY115
Romford RM7 off Marshalls Rd 71 FD56
Sunbury-on-Thames TW16 135 BS95
Brooklands Ct, Add. (New Haw) KT15 152 BK110
Brooklands Dr, Grnf. UB6 79 CK67
Brooklands Gdns, Horn. RM11 72 FJ57
Potters Bar EN6 11 CY32
Brooklands Ind Pk, Wey. KT13 152 BL110
Brooklands La, Rom. RM7 71 FD56
Weybridge KT13 152 BM107
★ Brooklands Mus, Wey. KT13 152 BN109
Brooklands Pk, SE3 104 EG83
Brooklands Rd, Rom. RM7 71 FD56
Thames Ditton KT7 137 CF102
Weybridge KT13 153 BP107
Brooklands Way, Red. RH1 184 DE132
Brook La, SE3 104 EH82
Bexley DA5 126 EX86
Bromley BR1 124 EG93
Woking (Send) GU23 167 BE122
Brook La N, Brent. TW8 97 CK78
Brooklea Cl, NW9 42 CS53
Brookleys, Wok. (Chobham) GU24 150 AT110
Brooklyn Av, SE25 142 DV98
Loughton IG10 32 EL42
Brooklyn Cl, Cars. SM5 140 DE103
Woking GU22 166 AY119
Brooklyn Ct, Wok. GU22 off Brooklyn Rd 166 AY119
Brooklyn Gro, SE25 142 DV98
Brooklyn Rd, SE25 142 DV98
Bromley BR2 144 EK99
Woking GU22 166 AY118
Brooklyn Way, West Dr. UB7 94 BK76
Brookmans Av, Hat. AL9 11 CY26
Brookmans Cl, Upmin. RM14 73 FS59
BROOKMANS PARK, Hat. 11 CY26
⇌ Brookmans Park 11 CX27
Brookmarsh Ind Est, SE10 off Norman Rd 103 EB80
Brook Mead, Epsom KT19 156 CS107
Brookmead Av, Brom. BR1 145 EM99
Brookmead Cl, Orp. BR5 146 EV101
Brook Meadow, N12 44 DB49
Brook Meadow Cl, Wdf.Grn. IG8 48 EE51
Brookmeadow Way, Wal.Abb. EN9 off Breach Barn Mobile Home Pk 16 EH30
Brookmead Rd, Croy. CR0 141 DJ100
Brookmeads Est, Mitch. CR4 140 DE99
Brookmead Way, Orp. BR5 146 EV100
Brook Ms N, W2 off Craven Ter 82 DD73
Brookmill Cl, Wat. WD19 off Brookside Rd 39 BV45
Brookmill Rd, SE8 103 EA81
Brook Par, Chig. IG7 off High Rd 49 EP48
Brook Pk Cl, N21 29 DP44
Brook Path, Loug. IG10 32 EL42
Brook Pl, Barn. EN5 28 DA43
Brook Ri, Chig. IG7 49 EN48
Brook Rd, N8 65 DL56
N22 65 DM55

Bro - Buf

Brook Rd, NW2 .63 CU61
Borehamwood WD6 .26 CN40
Brentwood CM14 .54 FT48
Buckhurst Hill IG9 .48 EG47
Epping CM16 .18 EU33
Gravesend (Nthflt.) DA11 .130 GE88
Ilford IG2 .69 ES58
Loughton IG10 .32 EL43
Redhill (Merst.) RH1 .185 DJ129
Romford RM2 .51 FF53
Surbiton KT6 .138 CL103
Swanley BR8 .147 FD97
Thornton Heath CR7 .142 DQ98
Twickenham TW1 .117 CG86
Waltham Cross EN8 .15 DZ34
Brook Rd S, Brent. TW8 .97 CK79
Brooks Av, E6 .87 EM70
Brooksbank St, E9 .85 DX65
Brooksby Ms, N1
off Brooksby St .83 DN66
Brooksby St, N1 .83 DN66
Brooksby's Wk, E9 .67 DX64
Brooks Cl, SE9 .125 EN89
Weybridge KT13 .152 BN110
Brooks Ct, E15
off Clays La .67 EB64
Brookscroft, Croy. CR0 .161 DY110
Brookscroft Rd, E17 .47 EB53
Brookshill, Har. HA3 .41 CD50
Brookshill Av, Har. HA3 .41 CD50
Brookshill Dr, Har. HA3 .41 CD50
Brookside, N21 .29 DM44
Barnet EN4 .28 DE44
Carshalton SM5 .158 DG106
Chertsey KT16 .133 BE101
Hornchurch RM11 .72 FL57
Ilford IG6 .49 EQ51
Orpington BR6 .145 ET101
Potters Bar EN6 .11 CU32
Slough (Colnbr.) SL3 .93 BC80
Uxbridge UB10 .76 BM66
Waltham Abbey EN9
off Broomstick Hall Rd .16 EE33
Brookside Av, Ashf. TW15 .114 BJ92
Staines (Wrays.) TW19 .92 AY83
Brookside Cl, Barn. EN5 .27 CY44
Feltham TW13
off Sycamore Cl .115 BU90
Harrow (Kenton) HA2 .61 CK57
Harrow (S.Har.) HA3 .60 BY63
Brookside Cres, Pot.B. (Cuffley)
EN6 .13 DL27
Worcester Park KT4
off Green La .139 CU102
Brookside Gdns, Enf. EN1 .30 DV37
Brookside Rd, N9 .46 DV49
N19 .65 DJ61
NW11 .63 CY58
Gravesend (Istead Rise)
DA13 .131 GF94
Hayes UB4 .78 BW73
Watford WD19 .39 BV45
Brookside S, Barn. EN4 .44 DG45
Brookside Wk, N3 .43 CY54
N12 .44 DA51
NW4 .63 CY56
NW11 .63 CY56
Brookside Way, Croy. CR0 .143 DX100
Brooks La, W4 .98 CN79
Brook's Ms, W1 .195 H10
Brook Sq, SE18
off Shooter's Hill Rd .104 EL81
Brooks Rd, E13 .86 EG67
W4 .98 CN78
BROOK STREET, Brwd. .54 FS49
Brook St, N17 off High Rd .46 DT54
W1 .194 G10
W2 .194 A10
Belvedere DA17 .107 FB78
Brentwood CM14 .54 FS50
Erith DA8 .107 FB79
Kingston upon Thames
KT1 .138 CL96
Brooksville Av, NW6 .81 CY67
Brooks Way, Orp. BR5 .146 EW96
Brook Vale, Erith DA8 .107 FB81
Brookview Rd, SW16 .121 DJ92
Brookville Rd, SW6 .99 CZ80
Brook Wk, N2 .44 DD53
Edgware HA8 .42 CR51
Brookway, SE3 .104 EG83
Brook Way, Chig. IG7 .49 EN48
Leatherhead KT22 .171 CG118
Rainham RM13 .89 FH71
Brookwood Av, SW13 .99 CT82
Brookwood Cl, Brom. BR2 .144 EF98
Brookwood Rd, SW18 .119 CZ88
Hounslow TW3 .96 CB81
Broom Av, Orp. BR5 .146 EV96
Broom Cl, Brom. BR2 .144 EL100
Esher KT10 .154 CB106
Teddington TW11 .117 CK94
Waltham Cross (Chsht.)
EN7 .14 DU27
Broomcroft Av, Nthlt. UB5 .78 BW69
Broomcroft Cl, Wok. GU22 .167 BD116
Broomcroft Dr, Wok. GU22 .167 BD115
Broome Cl, Epsom (Headley)
KT18 .182 CQ126
Broome Pl, S.Ock. (Aveley)
RM15 .91 FR74
Broome Rd, Hmptn. TW12 .116 BZ94
Broomer Pl, Wal.Cr. EN8 .14 DW29
Broome Way, SE5 .102 DQ80
Broomfield, E17 .67 DZ59
St. Albans (Park St.) AL2 .8 CC27
Staines TW18 .114 BG93
Sunbury-on-Thames
TW16 .135 BU95
Broomfield Av, N13 .45 DM50
Broxbourne EN10 .15 DY26
Loughton IG10 .33 EM44
Broomfield Cl, Rom. RM5 .51 FD52
Broomfield Ct, Wey. KT13 .153 BP107
Broomfield La, N13 .45 DM49
Broomfield Pl, W13
off Broomfield Rd .79 CH74
Broomfield Ride, Lthd. (Oxshott)
KT22 .155 CD112
Broomfield Ri, Abb.L. WD5 .7 BR32
Broomfield Rd, N13 .45 DL50
W13 .79 CH74
Addlestone (New Haw)
KT15 .152 BH111
Beckenham BR3 .143 DY97
Bexleyheath DA6 .126 FA85
Richmond TW9 .98 CM81
Romford RM6 .70 EX59
Sevenoaks TN13 .190 FF122
Surbiton KT5 .138 CM102
Swanscombe DA10 .130 FY86
Teddington TW11
off Melbourne Rd .117 CJ93
Broomfields, Esher KT10 .154 CC106
Broomfield St, E14 .85 EA71
Broom Gdns, Croy. CR0 .143 EA104
Broom Gro, Wat. WD17 .23 BU38
Broomgrove Gdns, Edg. HA8 .42 CN53
Broomgrove Rd, SW9 .101 DM82
Broom Hall, Lthd. (Oxshott)
KT22 .155 CD114
Broomhall End, Wok. GU21
off Broomhall La .166 AY116
Broomhall La, Wok. GU21 .166 AY116
Broomhall Rd, S.Croy. CR2 .160 DR109
Woking GU21 .166 AY116
Broom Hill, Slou. (Stoke P.)
SL2 .74 AU66
Broomhill Ct, Wdf.Grn. IG8
off Broomhill Rd .48 EG51
Broomhill Ri, Bexh. DA6 .126 FA85
Broomhill Rd, SW18 .120 DA85
Dartford DA1 .127 FH86
Ilford IG3 .70 EU61
Orpington BR6 .146 EU101
Woodford Green IG8 .48 EG51
Broomhills, Grav. (Sthflt.)
DA13 off Betsham Rd .130 FY91
Broomhill Wk, Wdf.Grn. IG8 .48 EF52
Broomhouse La, SW6 .100 DA82
Broomhouse Rd, SW6 .100 DA82
Broomlands La, Oxt. RH8 .188 EJ125
Broom La, Wok. (Chobham)
GU24 .150 AS109
Broomloan La, Sutt. SM1 .140 DA103
Broom Lock, Tedd. TW11 .117 CJ93
Broom Mead, Bexh. DA6 .126 FA85
Broom Pk, Tedd. TW11 .117 CK94
Broom Rd, Croy. CR0 .143 EA104
Teddington TW11 .117 CJ93
Broomsleigh St, NW6 .63 CZ64
Broomstick Hall Rd, Wal.Abb.
EN9 .16 EE33
Broomstick La, Chesh. HP5 .4 AU30
Broom Water, Tedd. TW11 .117 CJ93
Broom Water W, Tedd. TW11 .117 CJ92
Broom Way, Wey. KT13 .153 BS105
Broomwood Cl, Croy. CR0 .143 DX99
Broomwood Gdns, Brwd.
CM15 .54 FU44
Broomwood Rd, SW11 .120 DF86
Orpington BR5 .146 EV96
Broseley Gdns, Rom. RM3 .52 FL49
Broseley Gro, SE26 .123 DY92
Broseley Rd, Rom. RM3 .52 FL49
Broster Gdns, SE25 .142 DT97
Brougham Rd, E8 .84 DU67
W3 .80 CQ72
Brougham St, SW11 .100 DF82
Brough Cl, SW8
off Kenchester Cl .101 DL80
Kingston upon Thames
KT2 .117 CK92
Broughinge Rd, Borwd. WD6 .26 CP40
Broughton Av, N3 .63 CY55
Richmond TW10 .117 CH90
Broughton Dr, SW9 .101 DN84
Broughton Gdns, N6 .65 DJ58
Broughton Rd, SW6 .100 DB82
W13 .79 CH73
Orpington BR6 .145 ER103
Sevenoaks (Otford) TN14 .181 FG116
Thornton Heath CR7 .141 DN100
Broughton Rd App, SW6
off Wandsworth Br Rd .100 DB82
Broughton St, SW8 .100 DG82
Broughton Way, Rick. WD3 .38 BG45
Brouncker Rd, W3 .98 CQ75
Brow, The, Ch.St.G. HP8 .36 AX48
Watford WD25 .7 BV33
Brow Cl, Orp. BR5
off Brow Cres .146 EX101
Brow Cres, Orp. BR5 .146 EW102
Browells La, Felt. TW13 .115 BV89
Brownacres Towpath, Wey.
KT13 .135 BP102
Brown Cl, Wall. SM6 .159 DL108
Browne Cl, Brwd. CM14 .54 FV46
Romford RM5
off Bamford Way .51 FB50
Brownfield St, E14 .85 EB72
Browngraves Rd, Hayes
UB3 .95 BQ80
Brown Hart Gdns, W1 .194 G10
Brownhill Rd, SE6 .123 EB87
Browning Av, W7 .79 CF72
Sutton SM1 .158 DE105
Worcester Park KT4 .139 CV102
Browning Cl, E17 .67 EC56
W9 off Randolph Av .82 DC70
Hampton TW12 .116 BZ91
Romford (Coll.Row) RM5 .50 EZ52
Welling DA16 .105 ES81
Browning Ho, W12
off Wood La .81 CW72
Browning Ms, W1 .195 H7
Browning Rd, E11 .68 EF59
E12 .87 EM65
Dartford DA1 .108 FM84
Enfield EN2 .30 DR38
Browning St, SE17 .201 J10
Browning Wk, Til. RM18
off Coleridge Rd .111 GJ82
Browning Way, Houns. TW5 .96 BX81
Brownlea Gdns, Ilf. IG3 .70 EU61
Brownlow Ms, WC1 .196 C5
Brownlow Rd, E7
off Woodford Rd .68 EH63
E8 .84 DT67
N3 .44 DB52
N11 .45 DL51
NW10 .80 CS66
W13 .79 CG74
Borehamwood WD6 .26 CN42
Croydon CR0 .160 DS105
Redhill RH1 .184 DE134
Brownlow St, WC1 .196 C7
Brownrigg Rd, Ashf. TW15 .114 BN91
Brown Rd, Grav. DA12 .131 GL88
Brown's Bldgs, EC3 .197 N9
Brownsea Wk, NW7
off Sanders La .43 CX51
Browns La, NW5 .65 DH64
Brownspring Dr, SE9 .125 EP91
Browns Rd, E17 .67 EA55
Surbiton KT5 .138 CM101
Brown St, W1 .194 D8
Brownswell Rd, N2 .44 DD54
Brownswood Rd, N4 .65 DP62
Broxash Rd, SW11 .120 DG86
Broxbourne Av, E18 .68 EH56
Broxbourne Rd, E7 .68 EG62
Orpington BR6 .145 ET101
Broxburn Dr, S.Ock. RM15 .91 FV73
Broxburn Par, S.Ock. RM15
off Broxburn Dr .91 FV73
Broxhill Rd, Rom. (Hav.at.Bow.)
RM4 .51 FH48
Broxholm Rd, SE27 .121 DN90
Brox La, Cher. (Ott.) KT16 .151 BD109
Brox Rd, Cher. (Ott.) KT16 .151 BC107
Broxted Ms, Brwd. CM13
off Bannister Dr .55 GC44
Broxted Rd, SE6 .123 DZ89
Broxwood Way, NW8 .82 DE67
Bruce Av, Horn. RM12 .72 FK61
Shepperton TW17 .135 BQ100
★ Bruce Castle Mus, N17
(Tottenham) .46 DS53
Bruce Castle Rd, N17 .46 DT53
Bruce Cl, W10
off Ladbroke Gro .81 CY71
Welling DA16 .106 EV81
West Byfleet (Byfleet)
KT14 .152 BK113
Bruce Dr, S.Croy. CR2 .161 DX109
Bruce Gdns, N20
off Balfour Gro .44 DF48
⇌ Bruce Grove .46 DT54
Bruce Gro, N17 .46 DS53
Orpington BR6 .146 EU102
Watford WD24 .24 BW38
Bruce Hall Ms, SW17
off Brudenell Rd .120 DG91
Bruce Rd, E3 .85 EB69
NW10 .80 CR66
SE25 .142 DR98
Barnet EN5
off St. Albans Rd .27 CY41
Harrow HA3 .41 CE54
Mitcham CR4 .120 DG94
Bruce's Wf Rd, Grays RM17 .110 GA79
Bruce Way, Wal.Cr. EN8 .15 DX33
Bruckner St, W10 .81 CZ69
Brudenell Rd, SW17 .120 DF90
Bruffs Meadow, Nthlt. UB5 .78 BY65
Bruges Pl, NW1
off Randolph St .83 DJ66
Brumana Cl, Wey. KT13
off Elgin Rd .153 BP106
Brumfield Rd, Epsom KT19 .156 CQ106
Brummel Cl, Bexh. DA7 .107 FC83
★ Brunei Gall, WC1
off Russell Sq .195 N5
Brunel Cl, SE19 .122 DT93
Hounslow TW5 .95 BV80
Northolt UB5 .78 BZ69
Romford RM1 .71 FE56
Tilbury RM18 .111 GH83
★ Brunel Engine Ho, SE16 .202 F4
Brunel Est, W2 .82 DA71
Brunel Pl, Sthl. UB1 .78 CB72
Brunel Rd, E17 .67 DY58
SE16 .202 F5
W3 .80 CS71
Woodford Green IG8 .49 EM50
Brunel St, E16
off Victoria Dock Rd .86 EF72
Brunel Wk, N15 .66 DS56
Twickenham TW2
off Stephenson Rd .116 CA87
Brunel Way, Slou. SL1 .74 AT74
Brune St, E1 .197 P7
Brunner Cl, NW11 .64 DC57
Brunner Ct, Cher. (Ott.) KT16 .151 BC106
Brunner Rd, E17 .67 DZ57
W5 .79 CK70
Bruno Pl, NW9 .62 CQ61
Brunswick Av, N11 .44 DG48
Upminster RM14 .73 FS59
Brunswick Cl, Bexh. DA6 .106 EX84
Pinner HA5 .60 BY58
Thames Ditton KT7 .137 CF102
Twickenham TW2 .117 CD90
Walton-on-Thames KT12 .136 BW103
Brunswick Ct, EC1
off Northampton Sq .83 DP69
SE1 .201 N5
Barnet EN4 .28 DD43
Upminster RM14
off Waycross Rd .73 FS59
Brunswick Cres, N11 .44 DG48
Brunswick Gdns, W5 .80 CL69
W8 .82 DA74
Ilford IG6 .49 EQ52
Brunswick Gro, N11 .44 DG48
Cobham KT11 .154 BW113
Brunswick Ind Pk, N11 .45 DH49
Brunswick Ms, SW16
off Potters La .121 DK93
W1 .194 E8
BRUNSWICK PARK, N11 .44 DF47
Brunswick Pk, SE5 .102 DR81
Brunswick Pk Gdns, N11 .44 DG47
Brunswick Pk Rd, N11 .44 DG47
Brunswick Pl, N1 .197 L3
NW1 .194 G4
SE19 .122 DU94
Brunswick Quay, SE16 .203 J7
Brunswick Rd, E10 .67 EC60
E14 off Blackwall Tunnel
Northern App .85 EC72
N15 .66 DS57
W5 .79 CK70
Bexleyheath DA6 .106 EX84
Enfield EN3 .31 EA38
Kingston upon Thames
KT2 .138 CN95
Sutton SM1 .158 DB105
Brunswick Shop Cen, WC1 .195 P4
Brunswick Sq, N17 .46 DT51
WC1 .196 A5
Brunswick St, E17 .67 EC57
Brunswick Vil, SE5 .102 DS81
Brunswick Wk, Grav. DA12 .131 GK87
Brunswick Way, N11 .45 DH49
Brunton Pl, E14 .85 DY72
Brushfield St, E1 .197 N7
Brushrise, Wat. WD24 .23 BU36
Brushwood Dr, Rick. (Chorl.)
WD3 .21 BC42
Brussels Rd, SW11 .100 DD84
Bruton Cl, Chis. BR7 .125 EM94
Bruton La, W1 .199 J1
Bruton Pl, W1 .199 J1
Bruton Rd, Mord. SM4 .140 DC99
Bruton St, W1 .199 J1
Bruton Way, W13 .79 CG71
Bryan Av, NW10 .81 CV66
Bryan Cl, Sun. TW16 .115 BU94
Bryan Rd, SE16 .203 M4
Bryan's All, SW6
off Wandsworth Br Rd .100 DB82
Bryanston Av, Twick. TW2 .116 CB88
Bryanston Cl, Sthl. UB2 .96 BZ77
Bryanstone Ct, Sutt. SM1
off Oakhill Rd .158 DC105
Bryanstone Rd, N8 .65 DK57
Waltham Cross EN8 .15 DZ34
Bryanston Ms E, W1 .194 D7
Bryanston Ms W, W1 .194 D7
Bryanston Pl, W1 .194 D7
Bryanston Rd, Til. RM18 .111 GJ82
Bryanston Sq, W1 .194 D7
Bryanston St, W1 .194 D9
Bryant Av, Rom. RM3 .52 FK53
Bryant Cl, Barn. EN5 .27 CZ43
Bryant Ct, E2 .84 DT68
Bryant Rd, Nthlt. UB5 .78 BW69
Bryant Row, Rom. (Noak Hill)
RM3 off Cummings Hall La .52 FJ48
Bryant St, E15 .85 ED66
Bryantwood Rd, N7 .65 DN64
Brycedale Cres, N14 .45 DK49
Bryce Rd, Dag. RM8 .70 EW63
Bryden Cl, SE26 .123 DY92
Brydges Pl, WC2 .199 P1
Brydges Rd, E15 .67 ED64
Brydon Wk, N1
off Outram Pl .83 DL67
Bryer Ct, EC2
off Aldersgate St .84 DQ71
Bryett Rd, N7 .65 DL62
Brymay Cl, E3 .85 EA68
Brynford Cl, Wok. GU21 .166 AY115
Brynmaer Rd, SW11 .100 DF81
Bryn-y-Mawr Rd, Enf. EN1 .30 DT42
Bryony Cl, Loug. IG10 .33 EP42
Uxbridge UB8 .76 BM71
Bryony Rd, W12 .81 CU73
Bryony Way, Sun. TW16 .115 BT93
Bubblestone Rd, Sev. (Otford)
TN14 .181 FH116
Buccleuch Rd, Slou. (Datchet)
SL3 .92 AU80
Buchanan Cl, N21 .29 DM43
South Ockendon (Aveley)
RM15 .90 FQ74
Buchanan Ct, Borwd. WD6 .26 CQ40
Buchanan Gdns, NW10 .81 CV68
Buchan Cl, Uxb. UB8 .76 BJ69
Buchan Rd, SE15 .102 DW83
Bucharest Rd, SW18 .120 DC87
Buckbean Path, Rom. RM3
off Clematis Cl .52 FJ52
Buckden Cl, N2
off Southern Rd .64 DF56
SE12 off Upwood Rd .124 EF86
Buckettsland La, Borwd. WD6 .26 CR38
Buckfast Rd, Mord. SM4 .140 DB98
Buckfast St, E2 .84 DU69
Buckham Thorns Rd, West.
TN16 .189 EQ126
Buck Hill Wk, W2 .198 A1
Buckhold Rd, SW18 .120 DA86
Buckhurst Av, Cars. SM5 .140 DE102
Sevenoaks TN13 .191 FJ125
Buckhurst Cl, Red. RH1 .184 DE132
BUCKHURST HILL .48 EH45
⊖ Buckhurst Hill .48 EK47
Buckhurst La, Sev. TN13 .191 FJ125
Buckhurst Rd, West. TN16 .179 EN121
Buckhurst St, E1 .84 DV70
Buckhurst Way, Buck.H. IG9 .48 EK49
Buckingham Arc, WC2 .200 A1
Buckingham Av, N20 .44 DC45
Feltham TW14 .115 BV86
Greenford UB6 .79 CG67
Thornton Heath CR7 .141 DN95
Welling DA16 .105 ES84
West Molesey KT8 .136 CB97
Buckingham Cl, W5 .79 CJ71
Enfield EN1 .30 DS40
Hampton TW12 .116 BZ92
Hornchurch RM11 .72 FK58
Buckingham Cl, Orp. BR5 .145 ES101
Buckingham Ct, NW4 .63 CU55
Loughton IG10
off Rectory La .33 EN40
Buckingham Dr, Chis. BR7 .125 EP92
Buckingham Gdns, Edg. HA8 .42 CM52
Slough SL1 .92 AT75
Thornton Heath CR7 .141 DN96
West Molesey KT8
off Buckingham Av .136 CB96
Buckingham Gate, SW1 .199 K5
Buckingham Gro, Uxb. UB10 .76 BN68
Buckingham La, SE23 .123 DY87
Buckingham Ms, N1
off Buckingham Rd .84 DS65
NW10 off Buckingham Rd .81 CT68
SW1 .199 K6
★ Buckingham Palace, SW1 199 J5
Buckingham Palace Rd, SW1 .199 H9
Buckingham Pl, SW1 .199 K6
Buckingham Rd, E10 .67 EB62
E11 .68 EJ57
E15 .68 EF64
E18 .48 EF53
N1 .84 DS65
N22 .45 DL53
NW10 .81 CT68
Borehamwood WD6 .26 CR42
Edgware HA8 .42 CM52
Gravesend DA11
off Dover Rd .130 GD87
Hampton TW12 .116 BZ91
Harrow HA1 .61 CD57
Ilford IG1 .69 ER61
Kingston upon Thames
KT1 .138 CM98
Mitcham CR4 .141 DL99
Richmond TW10 .117 CK89
Watford WD24 .24 BW37
Buckingham St, WC2 .200 A1
Buckingham Way, Wall. SM6 .159 DJ109
BUCKLAND, Bet. .183 CU133
Buckland Av, Slou. SL3 .92 AV77
Buckland Ct Gdns, Bet. RH3 .183 CU133
Buckland Cres, NW3 .82 DD66
Buckland Gate, Slou. (Wexham)
SL2 .74 AV68
Buckland La, Bet. RH3 .183 CT129
Tadworth KT20 .183 CT129
Buckland Ri, Pnr. HA5 .40 BW53
Buckland Rd, E10 .67 EC61
Chessington KT9 .156 CM106
Orpington BR6 .163 ES105
Reigate RH2 .183 CX133
Sutton SM2 .157 CW110
Tadworth (Lwr.Kgswd.)
KT20 .183 CZ128
Bucklands, The, Rick. WD3 .38 BG45
Bucklands Rd, Tedd. TW11 .117 CJ93
Buckland St, N1 .197 L1
Buckland Wk, W3 .98 CQ75
Morden SM4 .140 DC98
Buckland Way, Wor.Pk. KT4 .139 CW102
Buck La, NW9 .62 CR57
Buckleigh Av, SW20 .139 CY97
Buckleigh Rd, SW16 .121 DK93
Buckleigh Way, SE19 .142 DT95
Buckler Gdns, SE9
off Southold Ri .125 EM90
Bucklers All, SW6 .99 CZ79
Bucklersbury, EC4 .197 K9
Bucklersbury Pas, EC4 .197 K9
Bucklers Ct, Brwd. CM14 .54 FW50
Bucklers Way, Cars. SM5 .140 DF104
Buckles Ct, Belv. DA17
off Fendyke Rd .106 EX76
Buckles La, S.Ock. RM15 .91 FW71
Buckle St, E1
off Leman St .84 DT72
Buckles Way, Bans. SM7 .173 CY116
Buckley Cl, Dart. DA1 .107 FF82
Buckley Rd, NW6 .81 CZ66
Buckley St, SE1 .200 D3
Buckmaster Cl, SW9
off Stockwell Pk Rd .101 DM83
Buckmaster Rd, SW11 .100 DE84
Bucknalls Cl, Wat. WD25 .8 BY32
Bucknalls Dr, St.Alb. (Brick.Wd.)
AL2 .8 BZ31
Bucknalls La, Wat. WD25 .8 BX32
Bucknall St, WC2 .195 N8
Bucknall Way, Beck. BR3 .143 EB98
Bucknell Cl, SW2 .101 DM84
Buckner Rd, SW2 .101 DM84
Bucknills Cl, Epsom KT18 .156 CP114
Buckrell Rd, E4 .47 ED47
Bucks Av, Wat. WD19 .40 BY45
Bucks Cl, W.Byf. KT14 .152 BH114
Bucks Cross Rd, Grav. (Nthflt.)
DA11 .131 GF90
Orpington BR6 .164 EY106
BUCKS HILL, Kings L. .6 BK34
Bucks Hill, Kings L. WD4 .6 BK34
Buckstone Cl, SE23 .122 DW86
Buckstone Rd, N18 .46 DU51
Buck St, NW1 .83 DH66
Buckters Rents, SE16 .203 K3
Buckthorne Ho, Chig. IG7 .50 EV49
Buckthorne Rd, SE4 .123 DY86
Buckton Rd, Borwd. WD6 .26 CM38
Buck Wk, E17 off Wood St .67 ED56
Budd Cl, N12 .44 DB49
Buddings Circle, Wem. HA9 .62 CQ62
Budd's All, Twick. TW1
off Arlington Cl .117 CJ85
Budebury Rd, Stai. TW18 .114 BG92
Bude Cl, E17 .67 DZ57
Budge La, Mitch. CR4 .140 DF101
Budgen Dr, Red. RH1 .184 DG131
Budge Row, EC4 .197 K10
Budge's Wk, W2 .82 DC73
Budgin's Hill, Orp. BR6 .164 EW112
Budleigh Cres, Well. DA16 .106 EW81
Budoch Ct, Ilf. IG3 .70 EU61
Budoch Dr, Ilf. IG3 .70 EU61
Buer Rd, SW6 .99 CY82
Buff Av, Bans. SM7 .158 DB114

Buffers La, Lthd. KT22
off Kingston Rd 171 CG119
Bug Hill, Cat. (Wold.) CR3 177 DX120
Bugsby's Way, SE7 104 EG77
SE10 205 K8
Bulganak Rd, Th.Hth. CR7 142 DQ98
Bulinga St, SW1 199 N9
Bulkeley Cl, Egh. (Eng.Grn.)
TW20 112 AW91
Bullace La, Dart. DA1
off High St 128 FL86
Bullace Row, SE5 102 DR80
Bull All, Well. DA16
off Welling High St 106 EV83
Bullards Pl, E2 85 DX69
Bullbanks Rd, Belv. DA17 107 FC77
Bullbeggars La, Gdse. RH9 186 DW132
Woking GU21 166 AV116
Bull Cl, Grays RM16 110 FZ75
Bullen St, SW11 100 DE82
Buller Cl, SE15 102 DU80
Buller Rd, N17 46 DU54
N22 45 DN54
NW10
off Chamberlayne Rd 81 CX69
Barking IG11 87 ES66
Thornton Heath CR7 142 DR96
Bullers Cl, Sid. DA14 126 EY92
Bullers Wd Dr, Chis. BR7 124 EL94
Bullescroft Rd, Edg. HA8 42 CN48
Bullfinch Cl, Sev. TN13 190 FD122
Bullfinch Dene, Sev. TN13 190 FD122
Bullfinch La, Sev. TN13 190 FD122
Bullfinch Rd, S.Croy. CR2 161 DX110
Bullhead Rd, Borwd. WD6 26 CQ41
Bull Hill, Dart. (Hort.Kir.)
DA4 148 FQ98
Leatherhead KT22 171 CG121
Bullied Way, SW1 199 J9
Bull Inn Ct, WC2 200 A1
Bullivant Cl, Green. DA9 129 FU85
Bullivant St, E14 85 EC73
Bull La, N18 46 DS50
Chislehurst BR7 125 ER94
Dagenham RM10 71 FB62
Gerrards Cross (Chal.St.P.)
SL9 56 AX55
Bull Rd, E15 86 EF68
Bullrush Cl, Croy. CR0 142 DS100
Bullrush Gro, Uxb. UB8 76 BJ70
Bull's All, SW14 98 CR82
Bulls Br Ind Est, Sthl. UB2 95 BV77
Bulls Br Rd, Sthl. UB2 95 BV76
Bullsbrook Rd, Hayes UB4 78 BW74
BULLS CROSS, Wal.Cr. 30 DT35
Bulls Cross, Enf. EN2 30 DU37
Bulls Cross Ride, Wal.Cr. EN7 30 DU35
Bulls Gdns, SW3 198 C8
Bull's Head Pas, EC3 197 M9
Bullsland Gdns, Rick. (Chorl.)
WD3 21 BB44
Bullsland La, Ger.Cr. SL9 37 BB45
Rickmansworth (Chorl.)
WD3 21 BB44
BULLSMOOR, Enf. 30 DV37
Bullsmoor Cl, Wal.Cr. EN8 30 DW35
Bullsmoor Gdns, Wal.Cr. EN8 30 DV35
Bullsmoor La, Enf. EN1, EN3 30 DW35
Waltham Cross EN7 30 DU35
Bullsmoor Ride, Wal.Cr. EN8 30 DW35
Bullsmoor Way, Wal.Cr. EN8 30 DV35
Bullwell Cres, Wal.Cr. (Chsht.)
EN8 15 DY29
Bull Wf La, EC4 197 J10
Bull Yd, Grav. DA12
off High St 131 GH86
Bulmer Gdns, Har. HA3 61 CK59
Bulmer Ms, W11
off Ladbroke Rd 82 DA73
Bulmer Pl, W11 82 DA74
Bulmer Wk, Rain. RM13 90 FJ68
Bulow Est, SW6
off Broughton Rd 100 DB82
Bulrush Cl, Cars. SM5
off Fellowes Rd 140 DE103
Bulstrode Av, Houns. TW3 96 BZ82
Bulstrode Ct, Ger.Cr. SL9 56 AX58
Bulstrode Gdns, Houns. TW3 96 BZ83
Bulstrode La, Hem.H. (Felden)
HP3 6 BG27
Kings Langley (Chipper.)
WD4 5 BE29
Bulstrode Pl, W1 194 G7
Slough SL1 92 AT76
Bulstrode Rd, Houns. TW3 96 CA83
Bulstrode St, W1 194 G8
Bulstrode Way, Ger.Cr. SL9 56 AX57
Bulwer Ct Rd, E11 67 ED60
Bulwer Gdns, Barn. EN5
off Bulwer Rd 28 DC42
Bulwer Rd, E11 67 ED59
N18 46 DS49
Barnet EN5 28 DB42
Bulwer St, W12 81 CW74
Bumbles Grn La, Wal.Abb.
EN9 16 EH25
Bunbury Way, Epsom KT17 173 CV116
Bunby Rd, Slou. (Stoke P.)
SL2 74 AT66
Bunce Dr, Cat. CR3 176 DR123
Bunces La, Wdf.Grn. IG8 48 EF52
Bundys Way, Stai. TW18 113 BF93
Bungalow Rd, SE25 142 DS98
Woking GU23 169 BQ124
Bungalows, The, SW16 121 DH94
Wallington SM6 159 DH106
Bunhill Row, EC1 197 K4
Bunhouse Pl, SW1 198 F10
Bunkers Hill, NW11 64 DC59
Belvedere DA17 106 FA77
Sidcup DA14 126 EZ90
Bunning Way, N7 83 DL66
Bunns La, NW7 43 CT51
Bunn's La, Chesh. HP5 4 AU34
Bunsen St, E3
off Kenilworth Rd 85 DY68
Buntingbridge Rd, Ilf. IG2 69 ER57
Bunting Cl, N9
off Dunnock Cl 47 DX46
Mitcham CR4 140 DF99
Bunton St, SE18 105 EN76
Bunyan Ct, EC2
off Beech St 84 DQ71
Bunyan Rd, E17 67 DY55
Bunyard Dr, Wok. GU21 151 BC114
Bunyons Cl, Brwd. CM13
off Essex Way 53 FW51
Buonaparte Ms, SW1 199 M10
H BUPA Bushey Hosp, Bushey
WD23 41 CF46
H BUPA Hartswood Hosp, Brwd.
CM13 53 FV51
Burbage Cl, SE1 201 K7
Hayes UB3 77 BR72
Waltham Cross (Chsht.)
EN8 15 DZ31
Burbage Rd, SE21 122 DR86
SE24 122 DQ86
Burberry Cl, N.Mal. KT3 138 CS96
Burbidge Rd, Shep. TW17 134 BN98
Burbridge Way, N17 46 DT54
Burcham St, E14 85 EB72
Burcharbro Rd, SE2 106 EX79
Burchell Ct, Bushey WD23
off Catsey La 40 CC45
Burchell Rd, E10 67 EB60
SE15 102 DV81
Burchetts Way, Shep. TW17 135 BP100
Burchett Way, Rom. RM6 70 EZ58
Burch Rd, Grav. (Nthflt.)
DA11 131 GF86
Burchwall Cl, Rom. RM5 51 FC52
Burcote, Wey. KT13 153 BR107
Burcote Rd, SW18 120 DD88
Burcott Gdns, Add. KT15 152 BJ107
Burcott Rd, Pur. CR8 159 DN114
Burden Cl, Brent. TW8 97 CJ78
Burdenshott Av, Rich. TW10 98 CP84
Burdenshott Rd, Wok. GU22 166 AU124
Burden Way, E11
off Brading Cres 68 EH61
Burder Cl, N1 84 DS65
Burder Rd, N1
off Balls Pond Rd 84 DS65
Burdett Av, SW20 139 CU95
Burdett Cl, W7
off Cherington Rd 97 CF75
Sidcup DA14 126 EY92
Burdett Ms, NW3
off Belsize Cres 82 DD65
W2
off Hatherley Gro 82 DB72
Burdett Rd, E3 85 DZ70
E14 85 DZ70
Croydon CR0 142 DR100
Richmond TW9 98 CM83
Burdetts Rd, Dag. RM9 88 EZ67
Burdett St, SE1 200 D6
Burdock Cl, Croy. CR0 143 DX102
Burdock Rd, N17 66 DU55
Burdon La, Sutt. SM2 157 CY108
Burdon Pk, Sutt. SM2 157 CZ109
Burfield Cl, SW17 120 DD91
Burfield Dr, Warl. CR6 176 DW119
Burfield Rd, Rick. (Chorl.)
WD3 21 BB43
Windsor (Old Wind.) SL4 112 AU86
Burford Cl, Dag. RM8 70 EW62
Ilford IG6 69 EQ56
Uxbridge UB10 58 BL63
Burford Gdns, N13 45 DM48
Burford La, Epsom KT17 157 CW111
Burford Rd, E6 86 EL69
E15 85 ED66
SE6 123 DZ89
Brentford TW8 98 CL78
Bromley BR1 144 EL98
Sutton SM1 140 DA103
Worcester Park KT4 139 CT101
Burford Wk, SW6
off Cambria St 100 DB80
Burford Way, Croy. (New Adgtn.)
CR0 161 EC107
Burgate Cl, Dart. DA1 107 FF83
Burges Cl, Horn. RM11 72 FM58
Burges Ct, E6 87 EN66
Burges Gro, SW13 99 CV80
Burges Rd, E6 86 EL66
Burgess Av, NW9 62 CR58
Burgess Cl, Felt. TW13 116 BY91
Waltham Cross (Chsht.)
EN7 14 DQ25
Burgess Ct, Borwd. WD6
off Belford Rd 26 CM38
Burgess Hill, NW2 64 DA63
Burgess Rd, E15 68 EE63
Sutton SM1 158 DB105
Burgess St, E14 85 EA71
Burge St, SE1 201 L7
Burges Way, Stai. TW18 114 BG92
Burghfield, Epsom KT17 173 CT115
Burghfield Rd, Grav. (Istead Rise)
DA13 131 GF94
BURGH HEATH, Tad. 173 CX119
Burgh Heath Rd, Epsom
KT17 156 CS114
★ Burgh Ho (Hampstead Mus),
NW3 64 DD63
Burghill Rd, SE26 123 DY91
Burghley Av, Borwd. WD6 26 CQ43
New Malden KT3 138 CR95
Burghley Hall Cl, SW19 119 CY87
Burghley Ho, SW19 119 CY90
Burghley Pl, Mitch. CR4 140 DG99
Burghley Rd, E11 68 EE60
N8 65 DN55
NW5 65 DH64
SW19 119 CX91
Grays (Chaff.Hun.) RM16 109 FW76
Burghley Twr, W3 81 CT73
Burgh Mt, Bans. SM7 173 CZ115
Burgh St, N1 83 DP68
Burgh Wd, Bans. SM7 173 CY115
Burgon St, EC4 196 G9
Burgos Cl, Croy. CR0 159 DN107
Burgos Gro, SE10 103 EB81
Burgoyne Rd, N4 65 DP58
SE25 142 DT98
SW9 101 DM83
Sunbury-on-Thames TW16 115 BT93
Burham Cl, SE20
off Maple Rd 122 DW94
Burhill Gro, Pnr. HA5 40 BY54
Burhill Rd, Walt. KT12 154 BW107
Burke Cl, SW15 98 CS84
Burke St, E16 86 EF72
Burket Cl, Sthl. UB2
off Kingsbridge Rd 96 BZ77
Burland Rd, SW11 120 DF85
Brentwood CM15 54 FX46
Romford RM5 51 FC51
Burlea Cl, Walt. KT12 153 BV106
Burleigh Av, Sid. DA15 125 ET85
Wallington SM6 140 DG104
Burleigh Cl, Add. KT15 152 BH106
Burleigh Gdns, N14 45 DJ46
Ashford TW15 115 BQ92
Burleigh Ho, W10
off St. Charles Sq 81 CX71
Burleigh Pk, Cob. KT11 154 BY112
Burleigh Pl, SW15 119 CX85
Burleigh Rd, Add. KT15 152 BH105
Enfield EN1 30 DS42
Sutton SM3 139 CY102
Uxbridge UB10 77 BP67
Waltham Cross (Chsht.)
EN8 15 DY32
Burleigh St, WC2 196 B10
Burleigh Wk, SE6
off Muirkirk Rd 123 EC88
Burleigh Way, Enf. EN2
off Church St 30 DR41
Potters Bar (Cuffley) EN6 13 DL30
Burley Cl, E4 47 EA50
SW16 141 DK96
Burley Orchard, Cher. KT16 134 BG100
Burley Rd, E16 86 EJ72
Burlings La, Sev. (Knock.)
TN14 179 ET118
Burlington Arc, W1 199 K1
Burlington Av, Rich. TW9 98 CN81
Romford RM7 71 FB58
Slough SL1 92 AS75
Burlington Cl, E6
off Northumberland Rd 86 EL72
W9 81 CZ70
Feltham TW14 115 BR87
Orpington BR6 145 EP103
Pinner HA5 59 BV55
Burlington Gdns, W1 199 K1
W3 80 CQ74
W4 98 CQ78
Romford RM6 70 EY59
Burlington La, W4 98 CS80
Burlington Ms, SW15 119 CZ85
W3 80 CQ74
Burlington Pl, SW6
off Burlington Rd 99 CY82
Reigate RH2 184 DA134
Woodford Green IG8 48 EG48
Burlington Ri, Barn. EN4 44 DE46
Burlington Rd, N10
off Tetherdown 44 DG54
N17 46 DU53
SW6 99 CY82
W4 98 CQ78
Enfield EN2 30 DR39
Isleworth TW7 97 CD81
New Malden KT3 139 CU98
Slough SL1 92 AS75
Thornton Heath CR7 142 DQ96
Burman Cl, Dart. DA2 128 FQ87
Burma Rd, N16 66 DR63
Chertsey (Longcr.) KT16 132 AT104
Burmester Rd, SW17 120 DC90
Burnaby Cres, W4 98 CP79
Burnaby Gdns, W4 98 CQ79
Burnaby Rd, Grav. (Nthflt.)
DA11 130 GE87
Burnaby St, SW10 100 DC80
Burnbrae Cl, N12 44 DB51
Burnbury Rd, SW12 121 DJ88
Burn Cl, Add. KT15 152 BK105
Leatherhead (Oxshott)
KT22 170 CC115
Burncroft Av, Enf. EN3 30 DW40
Burne Jones Ho, W14 99 CZ77
Burnell Av, Rich. TW10 117 CJ92
Welling DA16 106 EU82
Burnell Gdns, Stan. HA7 41 CK53
Burnell Rd, Sutt. SM1 158 DB105
Burnell Wk, SE1 202 A10
Brentwood CM13 53 FW51
Burnels Av, E6 87 EN69
Burness Cl, N7
off Roman Way 83 DM65
Uxbridge UB8
off Whitehall Rd 76 BK68
Burne St, NW1 194 B6
Burnet Gro, Epsom KT19 156 CQ113
Burnett Cl, E9 66 DW64
Burnett Rd, Erith DA8 108 FK79
Burney Av, Surb. KT5 138 CM99
Burney Dr, Loug. IG10 33 EP40
Burney St, SE10 103 EC80
Burnfoot Av, SW6 99 CY81
Burnfoot Ct, SE22 122 DV88
Burnham, NW3 82 DE66
Burnham Av, Uxb. UB10 59 BQ63
Burnham Cl, NW7 43 CU52
SE1 202 A9
Enfield EN1 30 DS38
Harrow (Wldste.) HA3 61 CG56
Burnham Ct, NW4 63 CW56
Burnham Cres, E11 68 EJ56
Dartford DA1 108 FJ84
Burnham Dr, Reig. RH2 184 DA133
Worcester Park KT4 139 CX103
Burnham Gdns, Croy. CR0 142 DT101
Hayes UB3 95 BR76
Hounslow TW4 95 BV81
Burnham Rd, E4 47 DZ50
Dagenham RM9 88 EV66
Dartford DA1 108 FJ84
Morden SM4 140 DB99
Romford RM7 71 FD55
Sidcup DA14 126 EY89
Burnhams Rd, Lthd. (Bkhm.)
KT23 170 BY124
Burnham St, E2 84 DW69
Kingston upon Thames
KT2 138 CN95
Burnham Way, SE26 123 DZ92
W13 97 CH77
Burnhill Rd, Beck. BR3 143 EA96
Burnley Cl, Wat. WD19 40 BW50
Burnley Rd, NW10 63 CU64
SW9 101 DM82
Grays RM20 109 FT81
Burnsall St, SW3 198 C10
Burns Av, Felt. TW14 115 BU86
Romford (Chad.Hth.) RM6 70 EW59
Sidcup DA15 126 EV86
Southall UB1 78 CA73
Burns Cl, E17 67 EC56
SW19 120 DD93
Carshalton SM5
off Kenny Dr 158 DG109
Erith DA8 107 FF81
Hayes UB4 77 BT71
Welling DA16 105 ET81
Burns Dr, Bans. SM7 157 CY114
Burn Side, N9 46 DW48
Burnside, Ashtd. KT21 172 CM118
Burnside Av, E4 47 DZ51
Burnside Cl, SE16 203 J2
Barnet EN5 28 DA41
Twickenham TW1 117 CG86
Burnside Cres, Wem. HA0 79 CK67
Burnside Rd, Dag. RM8 70 EW61
Burns Pl, Til. RM18 111 GH81
Burns Rd, NW10 81 CT67
SW11 100 DF82
W13 97 CH75
Wembley HA0 79 CK68
Burns Way, Brwd. CM13 55 GD45
Hounslow TW5 96 BX82
Burnt Ash Hill, SE12 124 EF86
Burnt Ash La, Brom. BR1 124 EG93
Burnt Ash Rd, SE12 124 EF85
Burnt Fm Ride, Enf. EN2 13 DP34
Waltham Cross EN7 13 DP31
Burnt Ho La, Dart. (Hawley)
DA2 128 FL91
Burnthwaite Rd, SW6 100 DA80
BURNT OAK, Edg. 42 CQ52
⊖ Burnt Oak 42 CQ53
Burnt Oak Bdy, Edg. HA8 42 CP52
Burnt Oak Flds, Edg. HA8 42 CQ53
Burnt Oak La, Sid. DA15 126 EU86
Burntwood, Brwd. CM14 54 FW48
Burntwood Av, Horn. RM11 72 FK58
Burntwood Cl, SW18 120 DD88
Caterham CR3 176 DU121
Burntwood Gra Rd, SW18 120 DD88
Burntwood Gro, Sev. TN13 191 FH127
Burntwood La, SW17 120 DE89
Caterham CR3 176 DU121
Burntwood Rd, Sev. TN13 191 FH128
Burntwood Vw, SE19
off Bowley La 122 DT92
Burnway, Horn. RM11 72 FL59
Buross St, E1
off Commercial Rd 84 DV72
Burrage Gro, SE18 105 EQ77
Burrage Pl, SE18 105 EP78
Burrage Rd, SE18 105 EQ79
Burrard Rd, E16 86 EH72
NW6 64 DA64
Burr Cl, E1 202 B2
Bexleyheath DA7 106 EZ83
St. Albans (Lon.Col.) AL2 10 CL27
Burrell Cl, Croy. CR0 143 DY100
Edgware HA8 42 CP47
Burrell Row, Beck. BR3
off High St 143 EA96
Burrell St, SE1 200 F2
Burrells Wf Sq, E14 204 B10
Burrell Twr, E10 67 EA59
Burrfield Dr, Orp. BR5 146 EX99
Burr Hill La, Wok. (Chobham)
GU24 150 AS109
Burritt Rd, Kings.T. KT1 138 CN96
Burroughs, The, NW4 63 CV57
Burroughs Gdns, NW4 63 CV56
Burroughs Par, NW4
off The Burroughs 63 CV56
Burroway Rd, Slou. SL3 93 BB76
Burrow Cl, Chig. IG7
off Burrow Rd 49 ET50
Burrow Grn, Chig. IG7 49 ET50
BURROWHILL, Wok. 150 AS108
Burrow Rd, SE22 102 DS84
Chigwell IG7 49 ET50
Burrows Chase, Wal.Abb.
EN9 31 ED36
Burrows Cl, Lthd. (Bkhm.)
KT23 170 BZ124
Burrows Hill Cl, Houns.
(Hthrw.Air.) TW6 94 BJ84
Burrows Hill La, Houns.
(Hthrw.Air.) TW6 94 BH84
Burrows Ms, SE1 200 F4
Burrows Rd, NW10 81 CW69
Burrow Wk, SE21
off Rosendale Rd 122 DQ87
Burr Rd, SW18 120 DA87
Bursar St, SE1 201 M3
Bursdon Cl, Sid. DA15 125 ET89
Burses Way, Brwd. CM13 55 GB45
Bursland Rd, Enf. EN3 31 DX42
Burslem Av, Ilf. IG6 50 EU51
Burslem St, E1 84 DU72
Burstead Cl, Cob. KT11 154 BX113
Burstock Rd, SW15 99 CY84
Burston Dr, St.Alb. (Park St.)
AL2 8 CC28
Burston Rd, SW15 119 CX85
Burston Vil, SW15
off St. John's Av 119 CX85
Burstow Rd, SW20 139 CY95
Burtenshaw Rd, T.Ditt. KT7 137 CG101
Burtley Cl, N4 66 DQ60
Burton Av, Wat. WD18 23 BU42
Burton Cl, Chess. KT9 155 CK108
Thornton Heath CR7 142 DR97
Burton Ct, SW3
off Franklin's Row 100 DF78
Burton Dr, Enf. EN3
off Government Row 31 EA37
Burton Gdns, Houns. TW5 96 BZ81
Burton Gro, SE17
off Portland St 102 DR78
Burtonhole Cl, NW7 43 CX49
Burtonhole La, NW7 43 CY49
Burton La, SW9 101 DN82
Waltham Cross (Chsht.)
EN7 14 DS29
Burton Ms, SW1 198 G9
Burton Pl, WC1 195 N3
Burton Rd, E18 68 EH55
NW6 81 CZ66
SW9 101 DP82
Kingston upon Thames
KT2 118 CL94
Loughton IG10 33 EQ42
Burtons La, Ch.St.G. HP8 21 AZ43
Rickmansworth WD3 21 AZ43
Burtons Rd, Hmptn. (Hmptn.H.)
TW12 116 CB91
Burton St, WC1 195 N3
Burtons Way, Ch.St.G. HP8 20 AW40
Burt Rd, E16 86 EJ74
Burtwell La, SE27 122 DR91
Burwash Ct, Orp. BR5
off Rookery Gdns 146 EW99
Burwash Ho, SE1 201 L5
Burwash Rd, SE18 105 ER78
Burway Cres, Cher. KT16 134 BG97
Burwell Av, Grnf. UB6 79 CE65
Burwell Cl, E1 off Bigland St 84 DV72
Burwell Ind Est, E10 67 DY60
Burwell Rd, E10 67 DY60
Burwell Wk, E3 85 EA70
Burwood Av, Brom. BR2 144 EH103
Kenley CR8 159 DP114
Pinner HA5 60 BW57
Burwood Cl, Reig. RH2 184 DD134
Surbiton KT6 138 CN102
Walton-on-Thames KT12 154 BW107
Burwood Gdns, Rain. RM13 89 FF69
BURWOOD PARK, Walt. 153 BT106
Burwood Pk Rd, Walt. KT12 153 BV105
Burwood Pl, W2 194 C8
Burwood Rd, Walt. KT12 153 BV107
Bury Av, Hayes UB4 77 BS68
Ruislip HA4 59 BQ58
Bury Cl, SE16 203 J2
Woking GU21 166 AX116
Bury Ct, EC3 197 N8
Burydell La, St.Alb. (Park St.)
AL2 9 CD27
BURY GREEN, Wal.Cr. 14 DV31
Bury Grn Rd, Wal.Cr. (Chsht.)
EN7 14 DU31
Bury Gro, Mord. SM4 140 DB99
Bury La, Epp. CM16 17 ES31
Rickmansworth WD3 38 BK46
Woking GU21 166 AW116
Bury Meadows, Rick. WD3 38 BK46
Bury Pl, WC1 195 P7
Bury Ri, Hem.H. HP3 5 BD25
Bury Rd, E4 32 EE43
N22 65 DN55
Dagenham RM10 71 FB64
Epping CM16 17 ES31
Bury St, EC3 197 N9
N9 46 DU46
SW1 199 K2
Ruislip HA4 59 BQ57
Bury St W, N9 46 DR45
Bury Wk, SW3 198 B9
Busbridge Ho, E14
off Brabazon St 85 EA71
Busby Ms, NW5
off Torriano Av 83 DK65
Busby Pl, NW5 83 DK65
Busby St, E2 off Chilton St 84 DT70
Bushbaby Cl, SE1 201 M7
Bushbarns, Wal.Cr. (Chsht.)
EN7 14 DU29
Bushberry Rd, E9 85 DY65
Bush Cl, Add. KT15 152 BJ106
Ilford IG2 69 ER57
Bush Cotts, SW18
off Putney Br Rd 120 DA85
Bush Ct, W12
off Shepherds Bush Grn 99 CX75
Bushell Cl, SW2 121 DM89
Bushell Grn, Bushey (Bushey Hth.)
WD23 41 CD47
Bushell St, E1 202 C3
Bushell Way, Chis. BR7 125 EN92
Bush Elms Rd, Horn. RM11 71 FG59
Bushetts Gro, Red. RH1 185 DH129
BUSHEY 40 CA45
⇌ Bushey 24 BX44
Bushey Av, E18 68 EF55
Orpington BR5 145 ER101
Bushey Cl, E4 47 EC48
Kenley CR8 176 DS116
Uxbridge UB10 59 BP61
Bushey Ct, SW20 139 CV96
Bushey Cft, Oxt. RH8 187 EC130
Bushey Down, SW12
off Bedford Hill 121 DH89
Bushey Gro Rd, Bushey
WD23 24 BX42
Bushey Hall Dr, Bushey
WD23 24 BY42
Bushey Hall Rd, Bushey
WD23 24 BX42

Bus - Cam

BUSHEY HEATH, Bushey 41 CE46
Bushey Hill Rd, SE5 . . . . .102 DS81
Bushey La, Sutt. SM1 . . . . . .158 DA105
Bushey Lees, Sid. DA15
off Fen Gro 125 ET86
BUSHEY MEAD, SW20 . . . . .139 CX97
Bushey Mill Cres, Wat. WD24 . .24 BW37
Bushey Mill La, Bushey WD23 .24 BZ40
Watford WD24 . . . . .24 BW37
Bushey Rd, E13 . . . . .86 EJ68
N15 . . . . .66 DS58
SW20 . . . . .139 CV97
Croydon CR0 . . . . .143 EA103
Hayes UB3 . . . . .95 BS77
Sutton SM1 . . . . .158 DB105
Uxbridge UB10 . . . . .58 BN61
Bushey Shaw, Ashtd. KT21 . .171 CH117
Bushey Vw Wk, Wat. WD24 . . .24 BX40
Bushey Way, Beck. BR3 . . . .143 ED100
Bushfield Cl, Edg. HA8 . . . . . .42 CP47
Bushfield Cres, Edg. HA8 . . . . .42 CP47
Bushfield Rd, Hem.H. (Bov.)
HP3 .5 BC25
Bushfields, Loug. IG10 . . . . . .33 EN43
Bushfield Wk, Swans. DA10 . .130 FY86
Bush Gro, NW9 . . . . .62 CQ59
Stanmore HA7 . . . . .41 CK53
Bushgrove Rd, Dag. RM8 . . . .70 EX63
Bush Hill, N21 . . . . .46 DQ45
BUSH HILL PARK, Enf. 30 DS43
⇌ **Bush Hill Park** 30 DT44
Bush Hill Rd, N21 . . . . .30 DR44
Harrow HA3 . . . . .62 CM58
Bush Ind Est, NW10 . . . . .80 CR70
Bush La, EC4 . . . . .197 K10
Woking (Send) GU23 . . . . . .167 BD124
Bushmead Cl, N15
off Copperfield Dr 66 DT56
Bushmoor Cres, SE18 . . . . . .105 EQ80
Bushnell Rd, SW17 . . . . .121 DH89
Bush Rd, E8 . . . . .84 DV67
E11 . . . . .68 EF59
SE8 . . . . .203 J8
Buckhurst Hill IG9 . . . . .48 EK49
Richmond TW9 . . . . .98 CM79
Shepperton TW17 . . . . .134 BM99
Bushway, Dag. RM8 . . . . .70 EX63
Bushwood, E11 . . . . .68 EF60
Bushwood Dr, SE1 . . . . .202 A9
Bushwood Rd, Rich. TW9 . . . . .98 CN79
★ **Bushy Park**, Tedd. TW11 . .137 CF95
Bushy Pk, Hmptn. (Hmptn.H.)
TW12 . . . . .137 CF95
Teddington TW11 . . . . .137 CF95
Bushy Pk Gdns, Tedd. TW11 . .117 CD92
Bushy Pk Rd, Tedd. TW11 . . .117 CH94
Bushy Rd, Lthd. (Fetch.)
KT22 . . . . .170 CB122
Teddington TW11 . . . . .117 CF93
★ **Business Design Cen**, N1 . .83 DN67
Business Village, The, Slou.
SL2 . . . . .74 AV74
Butcher Row, E1 . . . . .85 DX73
E14 . . . . .85 DX73
Butchers La, Sev. TN15 . . . . .149 FX103
Butchers Rd, E16 . . . . .86 EG72
Butcher Wk, Swans. DA10 . . .130 FY87
Bute Av, Rich. TW10 . . . . . . .118 CL89
Bute Ct, Wall. SM6
off Bute Rd 159 DJ106
Bute Gdns, W6 . . . . .99 CX77
Wallington SM6 . . . . .159 DJ106
Bute Gdns W, Wall. SM6 . . . .159 DJ106
Bute Ms, NW11 *off Northway* .64 DC56
Bute Rd, Croy. CR0 . . . . .141 DN102
Ilford IG6 . . . . .69 EP57
Wallington SM6 . . . . .159 DJ105
Bute St, SW7 . . . . .100 DD77
Bute Wk, N1
off Marquess Rd 84 DR65
Butler Av, Har. HA1 . . . . .61 CD59
Butler Ct, Wem. HA0
off Harrow Rd 61 CG63
Butler Ho, Grays RM17
off Argent St 110 GA79
Butler Pl, SW1 . . . . .199 M6
Butler Rd, NW10
off Curzon Cres 81 CT66
Dagenham RM8 . . . . .70 EV63
Harrow HA1 . . . . .60 CC59
Butlers Ct, Wal.Cr. EN8
off Trinity La 15 DY32
BUTLERS CROSS, Beac. 36 AT49
Butlers Dene Rd, Cat. (Wold.)
CR3 . . . . .177 DZ120
Butlers Dr, E4 . . . . .31 EC38
Butler St, E2
off Knottisford St 84 DW69
Uxbridge UB10 . . . . .77 BP70
Butlers Wf, SE1 . . . . .202 A3
Butler Wk, Grays RM17
off Palmers Dr 110 GD77
Buttell Cl, Grays RM17 . . . . .110 GD78
Buttercross La, Epp. CM16 . . .18 EU30
Buttercup Cl, Rom. RM3
off Copperfields Way 52 FK53
Buttercup Sq, Stai. (Stanw.)
TW19 *off Diamedes Av* . .114 BK88
Butterfield Cl, N17
off Devonshire Rd 46 DQ51
SE16 . . . . .202 D5
Twickenham TW1
off Rugby Rd 117 CF86
Butterfields, E17 . . . . .67 EC57
Butterfield Sq, E6
off Harper Rd 87 EM72
Butterfly La, SE9 . . . . .125 EP86
Borehamwood (Elstree)
WD6 . . . . .25 CG41
Butterfly Wk, SE5
off Denmark Hill 102 DR81
Warlingham CR6 . . . . .176 DW120
Butter Hill, Cars. SM5 . . . . . .140 DG104
Wallington SM6 . . . . .140 DG104
Butteridges Cl, Dag. RM9 . . . .88 EZ67
Butterly Av, Dart. DA1 . . . . . .128 FM89
Buttermere Cl, E15 . . . . .67 ED63
SE1 . . . . .201 P8
Feltham TW14 . . . . .115 BT88
Morden SM4 . . . . .139 CX100
Buttermere Dr, SW15 . . . . . . .119 CY85
Buttermere Gdns, Pur. CR8 . .160 DR113
Buttermere Rd, Orp. BR5 . . . .146 EX98
Buttermere Wk, E8 . . . . .84 DT65
Buttermere Way, Egh. TW20
off Keswick Rd 113 BB94
Butterwick, W6 . . . . .99 CW77
Watford WD25 . . . . .24 BY36
Butterworth Gdns, Wdf.Grn.
IG8 . . . . .48 EG51
Buttesland St, N1 . . . . .197 L2
Buttfield Cl, Dag. RM10 . . . . .89 FB65
Buttlehide, Rick. (Map.Cr.)
WD3 . . . . .37 BD50
Buttmarsh Cl, SE18 . . . . .105 EP78
Button Rd, Grays RM17 . . . . .110 FZ77
Button St, Swan. BR8 . . . . . .148 FJ96
Butts, The, Brent. TW8 . . . . . .97 CK79
Sevenoaks (Otford) TN14 . .181 FH116
Sunbury-on-Thames TW16
off Elizabeth Gdns 136 BW97
Buttsbury Rd, Ilf. IG1 . . . . . . .69 EQ64
Butts Cotts, Felt. TW13 . . . . .116 BZ90
Butts Cres, Felt. TW13 . . . . . .116 CA90
Butts Grn Rd, Horn. RM11 . . . .72 FK58
Buttsmead, Nthwd. HA6 . . . . . .39 BQ52
Butts Piece, Nthlt. UB5
off Longhook Gdns 77 BV68
Butts Rd, Brom. BR1 . . . . . . .124 EE92
Woking GU21 . . . . .166 AY117
Buxhall Cres, E9 . . . . .85 DZ65
Buxted Rd, E8 . . . . .84 DT66
N12 . . . . .44 DE50
SE22 . . . . .102 DS84
Buxton Av, Cat. CR3 . . . . . . .176 DS121
Buxton Cl, Wdf.Grn. IG8 . . . . .48 EK51
Buxton Ct, N1 . . . . .197 J2
Buxton Cres, Sutt. SM3 . . . . .157 CY105
Buxton Dr, E11 . . . . .68 EE56
New Malden KT3 . . . . .138 CR96
Buxton Gdns, W3 . . . . .80 CP73
Buxton La, Cat. CR3 . . . . . . .176 DR120
Buxton Path, Wat. WD19 . . . . .40 BW48
Buxton Rd, E4 . . . . .47 ED45
E6 .86 EL69
E15 . . . . .68 EE64
E17 . . . . .67 DY56
N19 . . . . .65 DK60
NW2 . . . . .81 CV65
SW14 . . . . .98 CS83
Ashford TW15 . . . . .114 BK92
Epping (They.B.) CM16 . . . . .33 ES36
Erith DA8 . . . . .107 FD80
Grays RM16 . . . . .110 GE75
Ilford IG2 . . . . .69 ES58
Thornton Heath CR7 . . . . . .141 DP99
Waltham Abbey EN9 . . . . . . .16 EG32
Buxton St, E1 . . . . .84 DT70
Buzzard Creek Ind Est, Bark.
IG11 . . . . .87 ET71
Byam St, SW6 . . . . .100 DC82
Byards Cft, SW16 . . . . .141 DK95
Byatt Wk, Hmptn. TW12
off Victors Dr 116 BY93
Bychurch End, Tedd. TW11
off Church Rd 117 CF92
Bycliffe Ter, Grav. DA11 . . . . .131 GF87
Bycroft Rd, Sthl. UB1 . . . . .78 CA70
Bycroft St, SE20
off Parish La 123 DX94
Bycullah Av, Enf. EN2 . . . . . . .29 DP41
Bycullah Rd, Enf. EN2 . . . . . . .29 DP41
Bye, The, W3 . . . . .80 CS72
Byegrove Rd, SW19 . . . . .120 DD93
Byers Cl, Pot.B. EN6 . . . . .12 DC34
Byewaters, Wat. WD18 . . . . . .23 BQ44
Byeway, The, SW14 . . . . .98 CQ83
Bye Way, The, Har. HA3 . . . . . .41 CE53
Byeway, The, Rick. WD3 . . . . . .38 BL47
Byeways, Twick. TW2 . . . . . . .116 CB90
Byeways, The, Ashtd. KT21
off Skinners La 171 CK118
Surbiton KT5 . . . . .138 CN99
Byfeld Gdns, SW13 . . . . .99 CU81
Byfield Cl, SE16 . . . . .203 L4
Byfield Pas, Islw. TW7 . . . . . . .97 CG83
Byfield Rd, Islw. TW7 . . . . .97 CG83
BYFLEET, W.Byf. 152 BM113
⇌ **Byfleet & New Haw** 152 BK110
Byfleet Rd, Add. (New Haw)
KT15 . . . . .152 BK108
Cobham KT11 . . . . .153 BS113
West Byfleet (Byfleet)
KT14 . . . . .152 BN112
Byfleet Technical Cen, W.Byf.
(Byfleet) KT14 . . . . .152 BK111
Byford Cl, E15 . . . . .86 EE66
Bygrove, Croy. (New Adgtn.)
CR0 . . . . .161 EB107
Bygrove St, E14 . . . . .85 EB72
Byland Cl, N21 . . . . .45 DM45
Bylands, Wok. GU22 . . . . .167 BA119
Bylands Cl, SE2
off Finchale Rd 106 EV76
SE16 . . . . .203 J2
Byne Rd, SE26 . . . . .122 DW93
Carshalton SM5 . . . . .140 DE103
Bynes Rd, S.Croy. CR2 . . . . . .160 DR108
Byng Dr, Pot.B. EN6 . . . . .12 DA31
Byng Pl, WC1 . . . . .195 M5
Byng Rd, Barn. EN5 . . . . .27 CX41
Byng St, E14 . . . . .203 P4
Bynon Av, Bexh. DA7 . . . . . . .106 EY83
Byre, The, N14
off Farm La 29 DH44
Byre Rd, N14
off Farm La 28 DG44
Byrne Rd, SW12 . . . . .121 DH88
Byron Av, E12 . . . . .86 EL65
E18 . . . . .68 EF55
NW9 . . . . .62 CP56
Byron Av, Borwd. WD6 . . . . . .26 CN43
Coulsdon CR5 . . . . .175 DL115
Hounslow TW4 . . . . .95 BU82
New Malden KT3 . . . . .139 CU99
Sutton SM1 . . . . .158 DD105
Watford WD24 . . . . .24 BX39
Byron Av E, Sutt. SM1 . . . . . .158 DD105
Byron Cl, E8 . . . . .84 DU67
SE26 *off Porthcawe Rd* 123 DY91
SE28 . . . . .88 EW74
Hampton TW12 . . . . .116 BZ91
Waltham Cross EN7
off Allard Cl 14 DT27
Walton-on-Thames KT12 . .136 BY102
Woking (Knap.) GU21 . . . .166 AS117
Byron Ct, W9 *off Lanhill Rd* . . .82 DA70
Enfield EN2
off Bycullah Rd 29 DP40
Harrow HA1 . . . . .61 CE58
Byron Dr, N2 . . . . .64 DD58
Erith DA8 . . . . .107 FB80
Byron Gdns, Sutt. SM1 . . . . .158 DD105
Tilbury RM18 . . . . .111 GJ81
Byron Hill Rd, Har. HA2 . . . . . .61 CD60
Byron Ho, Beck. BR3 . . . . . . .123 EA93
Slough SL3 . . . . .93 BB78
Byron Ms, NW3 . . . . .64 DE64
W9 *off Shirland Rd* 82 DA70
Byron Pl, Lthd. KT22 . . . . . . .171 CH122
Byron Rd, E10 . . . . .67 EB60
E17 . . . . .67 EA55
NW2 . . . . .63 CV61
NW7 . . . . .43 CU50
W5 . . . . .80 CM74
Addlestone KT15 . . . . .152 BL105
Brentwood CM13 . . . . .55 GD45
Dartford DA1 . . . . .108 FP84
Harrow HA1 . . . . .61 CE58
Harrow (Wldste.) HA3 . . . . . .41 CF54
South Croydon CR2 . . . . . .160 DV110
Wembley HA0 . . . . .61 CJ62
Byron St, E14
off St. Leonards Rd 85 EC72
Byron Ter, N9 . . . . .46 DW45
Byron Way, Hayes UB4 . . . . . .77 BT70
Northolt UB5 . . . . .78 BY69
Romford RM3 . . . . .52 FJ53
West Drayton UB7 . . . . .94 BM77
Bysouth Cl, N15 . . . . .66 DR56
Ilford IG5 . . . . .49 EP53
By the Wd, Wat. WD19 . . . . . . .40 BX47
Bythorn St, SW9 . . . . .101 DM83
Byton Rd, SW17 . . . . .120 DF93
Byward Av, Felt. TW14 . . . . . .116 BW86
Byward St, EC3 . . . . .201 N1
Bywater Pl, SE16 . . . . .203 L2
Bywater St, SW3 . . . . .198 D10
Byway, The, Epsom KT19 . . . .157 CT105
Potters Bar EN6 . . . . .12 DA33
Sutton SM2 . . . . .158 DD109
Bywell Pl, W1 . . . . .195 K7
Bywood Av, Croy. CR0 . . . . . .142 DW100
Bywood Cl, Ken. CR8 . . . . . . .175 DP115
By-Wood End, Ger.Cr. (Chal.St.P.)
SL9 . . . . .37 AZ50
Byworth Wk, N19
off Courtauld Rd 65 DK60

C

Cabbell Pl, Add. KT15 . . . . . .152 BJ105
Cabbell St, NW1 . . . . .194 B7
Caberfeigh Pl, Red. RH1 . . . .184 DE134
★ **Cabinet War Rooms**,
SW1 . . . . .199 N4
Cabinet Way, E4 . . . . .47 DZ51
Cable Pl, SE10
off Diamond Ter 103 EC81
Cable St, E1 . . . . .84 DU73
Cable Trade Pk, SE7 . . . . . . .104 EJ77
Cabot Pl, E14 . . . . .204 A2
Cabot Sq, E14 . . . . .204 A2
Cabot Way, E6 *off Parr Rd* 86 EK67
Cabrera Av, Vir.W. GU25 . . . .132 AW100
Cabrera Cl, Vir.W. GU25 . . . . .132 AX100
Cabul Rd, SW11 . . . . .100 DE82
Cacket's Cotts, Sev. TN14
off Cackets La 179 ES115
Cackets La, Sev. (Cudham)
TN14 . . . . .179 ER115
Cactus Cl, SE15
off Lyndhurst Gro 102 DS82
Cactus Wk, W12
off Du Cane Rd 81 CT72
Cadbury Cl, Islw. TW7 . . . . . . .97 CG81
Sunbury-on-Thames TW16 .115 BS94
Cadbury Rd, Sun. TW16 . . . . .115 BS94
Cadbury Way, SE16 . . . . .202 A7
Caddington Cl, Barn. EN4 . . . . .28 DE43
Caddington Rd, NW2 . . . . .63 CY62
Caddis Cl, Stan. HA7
off Daventer Dr 41 CF52
Caddy Cl, Egh. TW20 . . . . . . .113 BA92
Cade La, Sev. TN13 . . . . .191 FJ128
Cadell Cl, E2
off Shipton St 84 DT69
Cade Rd, SE10 . . . . .103 ED81
Cader Rd, SW18 . . . . .120 DC86
Cadet Dr, SE1 . . . . .202 A10
Cadet Pl, SE10 . . . . .205 H10
Cadiz Ct, Dag. RM10
off Rainham Rd S 89 FD66
Cadiz Rd, Dag. RM10 . . . . .89 FC66
Cadiz St, SE17 . . . . .102 DQ78
Cadley Ter, SE23 . . . . .122 DW89
Cadlocks Hill, Sev. (Halst.)
TN14 . . . . .164 EZ110
Cadman Cl, SW9
off Langton Rd 101 DP80
Cadmer Cl, N.Mal. KT3 . . . . . .138 CS98
Cadmore La, Wal.Cr. (Chsht.)
EN8 . . . . .15 DX28
Cadmus Cl, SW4
off Aristotle Rd 101 DK83
Cadnam Pt, SW15
off Dilton Gdns 119 CV88
Cadogan Av, Dart. DA2 . . . . .129 FR87
Cadogan Cl, E9
off Cadogan Ter 85 DZ66
Beckenham BR3
off Albemarle Rd 143 ED95
Harrow HA2 . . . . .60 CB63
Teddington TW11 . . . . .117 CE92
Cadogan Ct, Sutt. SM2 . . . . .158 DB107
Cadogan Gdns, E18 . . . . .68 EH55
N3 .44 DB53
N21 . . . . .29 DN43
SW3 . . . . .198 E8
Cadogan Gate, SW1 . . . . .198 E8
Cadogan La, SW1 . . . . .198 F7
Cadogan Pl, SW1 . . . . .198 E6
Cadogan Rd, Surb. KT6 . . . . .137 CK99
Cadogan Sq, SW1 . . . . .198 E7
Cadogan St, SW3 . . . . .198 D9
Cadogan Ter, E9 . . . . .85 DZ65
Cadoxton Av, N15 . . . . .66 DT58
Cadwallon Rd, SE9 . . . . .125 EP89
Caedmon Rd, N7 . . . . .65 DM63
Caenshill Rd, Wey. KT13 . . . .152 BN108
Caenwood Cl, Wey. KT13 . . . .152 BN107
Caen Wd Rd, Ashtd. KT21 . . .171 CJ118
Caerleon Cl, Sid. DA14 . . . . .126 EW92
Caerleon Ter, SE2
off Blithdale Rd 106 EV77
Caernarvon Cl, Horn. RM11 . . .72 FN60
Mitcham CR4 . . . . .141 DL97
Caernarvon Dr, Ilf. IG5 . . . . . .49 EN53
Caesars Wk, Mitch. CR4 . . . . .140 DF99
Caesars Way, Shep. TW17 . . .135 BR100
Cage Pond Rd, Rad. (Shenley)
WD7 . . . . .10 CM33
Cage Yd, Reig. RH2
off High St 184 DA134
Cahill St, EC1 . . . . .197 J5
Cahir St, E14 . . . . .204 B9
Caillard Rd, W.Byf. (Byfleet)
KT14 . . . . .152 BL111
Cains La, Felt. TW14 . . . . . . .115 BS85
Caird St, W10 . . . . .81 CY69
Cairn Av, W5 . . . . .79 CK74
Cairndale Cl, Brom. BR1 . . . . .124 EF94
Cairnes Ms, SE18
off Shooter's Hill Rd 104 EL81
Cairnfield Av, NW2 . . . . .62 CS62
Cairngorm Cl, Tedd. TW11
off Vicarage Rd 117 CG92
Cairns Av, Wdf.Grn. IG8 . . . . .48 EL51
Cairns Cl, Dart. DA1 . . . . .128 FK85
Cairns Rd, SW11 . . . . .120 DE85
Cairn Way, Stan. HA7 . . . . . . .41 CF51
Cairo New Rd, Croy. CR0 . . . .141 DP103
Cairo Rd, E17 . . . . .67 EA56
Caishowe Rd, Borwd. WD6 . . .26 CP39
Caistor Ms, SW12
off Caistor Rd 121 DH87
Caistor Pk Rd, E15 . . . . .86 EF67
Caistor Rd, SW12 . . . . .121 DH87
Caithness Gdns, Sid. DA15 . .125 ET86
Caithness Rd, W14 . . . . .99 CX77
Mitcham CR4 . . . . .121 DH94
Calabria Rd, N5 . . . . .83 DP65
Calais Cl, Wal.Cr. EN7
off Argent Way 14 DR26
Calais Gate, SE5
off Calais St 101 DP81
Calais St, SE5 . . . . .101 DP81
Calbourne Av, Horn. RM12 . . . .71 FH64
Calbourne Rd, SW12 . . . . .120 DF87
Calcott Cl, Brwd. CM14 . . . . . .54 FV46
Calcott Wk, SE9 . . . . .124 EK91
Calcutta Rd, Til. RM18 . . . . . .111 GF82
Caldbeck, Wal.Abb. EN9 . . . . . .15 ED34
Caldbeck Av, Wor.Pk. KT4 . . .139 CU103
Caldecot Av, Wal.Cr. EN7 . . . . .14 DT29
Caldecote Gdns, Bushey
WD23 . . . . .25 CE44
Caldecote La, Bushey WD23 . .41 CF45
Caldecot Rd, SE5 . . . . .102 DQ82
Caldecott Way, E5 . . . . .67 DX62
Calder Av, Grnf. UB6 . . . . .79 CF68
Hatfield AL9 . . . . .12 DB26
Calder Cl, Enf. EN1 . . . . .30 DS41
Calder Ct, Slou. SL3 . . . . .93 AZ78
Calder Gdns, Edg. HA8 . . . . . .62 CN55
Calderon Pl, W10
off St. Quintin Gdns 81 CW71
Calderon Rd, E11 . . . . .67 EC63
Calder Rd, Mord. SM4 . . . . . .140 DC99
Caldervale Rd, SW4 . . . . .121 DK85
Calder Way, Slou. (Colnbr.)
SL3 . . . . .93 BF83
Calderwood, Grav. DA12 . . . . .131 GL92
Calderwood St, SE18 . . . . . . .105 EN77
Caldicot Grn, NW9
off Snowdon Dr 62 CS58
Caldwell Rd, Wat. WD19 . . . . . .40 BX49
Caldwell St, SW9 . . . . .101 DM80
Caldwell Yd, EC4
off Upper Thames St 84 DQ73
Caldy Rd, Belv. DA17 . . . . . . .107 FB76
Caldy Wk, N1
off Clephane Rd 84 DQ65
Caleb St, SE1 . . . . .201 H4
Caledonian Cl, Ilf. IG3 . . . . . . .70 EV60
⊖ **Caledonian Road** 83 DL65
Caledonian Rd, N1 . . . . .196 A1
N7 .65 DM64
⇌ **Caledonian Road &
Barnsbury** 83 DM66
Caledonian Wf, E14 . . . . .204 F9
Caledonia Rd, Stai. TW19 . . . .114 BL88
Caledonia St, N1 . . . . .196 A1
Caledon Rd, E6 . . . . .86 EL67
St. Albans (Lon.Col.) AL2 . . . .9 CK26
Wallington SM6 . . . . .158 DG105
Cale St, SW3 . . . . .198 B10
Caletock Way, SE10 . . . . .205 K10
Calfstock La, Dart. (S.Darenth)
DA4 . . . . .148 FL98
Calico Row, SW11
off York Pl 100 DC83
Calidore Cl, SW2
off Endymion Rd 121 DM86
California La, Bushey (Bushey Hth.)
WD23 . . . . .41 CD46
California Rd, N.Mal. KT3 . . . .138 CQ98
Caliph Cl, Grav. DA12 . . . . . .131 GM90
Callaby Ter, N1
off Wakeham St 84 DR65
Callaghan Cl, SE13
off Glenton Rd 104 EE84
Callander Rd, SE6 . . . . .123 EB89
Callan Gro, S.Ock. RM15 . . . . .91 FV73
Callard Av, N13 . . . . .45 DP50
Callcott Rd, NW6 . . . . .81 CZ66
Callcott St, W8
off Hillgate Pl 82 DA74
Callendar Rd, SW7 . . . . .100 DD76
Calley Down Cres, Croy.
(New Adgtn.) CR0 . . . . . . .161 ED110
Callingham Cl, E14
off Wallwood St 85 DZ71
Callis Fm Cl, Stai. (Stanw.)
TW19 *off Bedfont Rd* 114 BL86
Callis Rd, E17 . . . . .67 DZ58
Callow Fld, Pur. CR8 . . . . . . .159 DN113
Callow Hill, Vir.W. GU25 . . . . .132 AW97
Callowland Cl, Wat. WD24 . . . .23 BV38
Callow St, SW3 . . . . .100 DD79
Calluna Ct, Wok. GU22
off Heathside Rd 167 AZ118
Calmont Rd, Brom. BR1 . . . . .123 ED93
Calmore Cl, Horn. RM12 . . . . . .72 FJ64
Calne Av, Ilf. IG5 . . . . .49 EP53
Calonne Rd, SW19 . . . . .119 CX91
Calshot Av, Grays (Chaff.Hun.)
RM16 . . . . .110 FZ75
Calshot Rd, Houns. (Hthrw.Air.)
TW6 . . . . .94 BN82
Calshot St, N1 . . . . .83 DM68
Calshot Way, Enf. EN2 . . . . . . .29 DP41
Hounslow (Hthrw.Air.) TW6
off Calshot Rd 95 BP82
Calthorpe Gdns, Edg. HA8
off Jesmond Way 42 CL50
Sutton SM1 . . . . .140 DC104
Calthorpe St, WC1 . . . . .196 C4
Calton Av, SE21 . . . . .122 DS85
Calton Rd, Barn. EN5 . . . . .28 DC44
Calverley Cl, Beck. BR3 . . . . .123 EB93
Calverley Cres, Dag. RM10 . . . .70 FA61
Calverley Gdns, Har. HA3 . . . . .61 CK59
Calverley Gro, N19 . . . . .65 DK60
Calverley Rd, Epsom KT17 . . .157 CU107
Calvert Av, E2 . . . . .197 N3
Calvert Cl, Belv. DA17 . . . . . . .106 FA77
Sidcup DA14 . . . . .126 EY93
Calverton, SE5 . . . . .102 DS79
Calverton Rd, E6 . . . . .87 EN67
Calvert Rd, SE10 . . . . .104 EF78
Barnet EN5 . . . . .27 CX40
Calvert's Bldgs, SE1 . . . . .201 K3
Calvert St, NW1
off Chalcot Rd 82 DG67
Calvin Cl, Orp. BR5 . . . . .146 EX97
Calvin St, E1 . . . . .197 P5
Calydon Rd, SE7 . . . . .104 EH78
Calypso Way, SE16 . . . . .203 M7
Camac Rd, Twick. TW2 . . . . . .117 CD88
Cambalt Rd, SW15 . . . . .119 CX85
Camberley Av, SW20 . . . . . . .139 CV96
Enfield EN1 . . . . .30 DS42
Camberley Cl, Sutt. SM3 . . . .139 CX104
Camberley Rd, Houns. (Hthrw.Air.)
TW6 . . . . .94 BN83
Cambert Way, SE3 . . . . .104 EH84
CAMBERWELL, SE5 . . . . .102 DQ80
Camberwell Ch St, SE5 . . . . . .102 DR81
Camberwell Glebe, SE5 . . . . .102 DR81
Camberwell Grn, SE5 . . . . . . .102 DR81
Camberwell Gro, SE5 . . . . . . .102 DR81
Camberwell New Rd, SE5 . . . .101 DN80
Camberwell Pas, SE5
off Camberwell Grn 102 DQ81
Camberwell Rd, SE5 . . . . .102 DQ79
Camberwell Sta Rd, SE5 . . . .102 DQ81
Cambeys Rd, Dag. RM10 . . . . .71 FB64
Camborne Av, W13 . . . . .97 CH75
Romford RM3 . . . . .52 FL52
Camborne Cl, Houns. (Hthrw.Air.)
TW6 *off Camborne Rd S* . .94 BN83
Camborne Ms, W11
off St. Marks Rd 81 CY72
Camborne Rd, SW18 . . . . .120 DA87
Croydon CR0 . . . . .142 DU101
Morden SM4 . . . . .139 CX99
Sidcup DA14 . . . . .126 EW90
Sutton SM2 . . . . .158 DA108
Welling DA16 . . . . .105 ET82
Camborne Rd N, Houns. (Hthrw.Air.)
TW6 *off Camborne Rd S* . .94 BN83
Camborne Rd S, Houns. (Hthrw.Air.)
TW6 . . . . .94 BN83
Camborne Way, Houns. TW5 . .96 CA81
Hounslow (Hthrw.Air.) TW6
off Camborne Rd S 94 BN83
Romford RM3 . . . . .52 FL52
Cambourne Av, N9 . . . . .47 DX45
Cambray Rd, SW12 . . . . .121 DJ88
Orpington BR6 . . . . .145 ET101
Cambria Cl, Houns. TW3 . . . . . .96 CA84
Sidcup DA15 . . . . .125 ER88
Cambria Ct, Felt. TW14
off Hounslow Rd 115 BV87
Slough SL3 *off Turner Rd* . . .92 AW75
Cambria Cres, Grav. DA12 . . . .131 GL91
Cambria Gdns, Stai. TW19 . . .114 BL87
Cambrian Av, Ilf. IG2 . . . . .69 ES57
Cambrian Cl, SE27 . . . . .121 DP90
Cambrian Grn, NW9
off Snowdon Dr 62 CS57
Cambrian Gro, Grav. DA11 . . .131 GG87
Cambrian Rd, E10 . . . . .67 EA59
Richmond TW10 . . . . .118 CM86
Cambria Rd, SE5 . . . . .102 DQ83
Cambria St, SW6 . . . . .100 DB80
Cambridge Av, NW6 . . . . .82 DA68
Greenford UB6 . . . . .61 CF64

★ Place of interest ⇌ Railway station ⊖ London Underground station DLR Docklands Light Railway station Tramlink station H Hospital

Cambridge Av, N.Mal. KT3 139 CT96
Romford RM2 72 FJ55
Welling DA16 105 ET84
Cambridge Barracks Rd, SE18 105 EM77
Cambridge Circ, WC2 195 N9
Cambridge Cl, E17 67 DZ58
N22 *off Pellatt Gro* 45 DN53
NW10 *off Lawrence Way* 62 CQ62
SW20 139 CV95
Hounslow TW4 96 BY84
Waltham Cross (Chsht.) EN8 14 DW29
West Drayton UB7 94 BK79
Woking GU21 *off Bingham Dr* 166 AT118
Cambridge Cotts, Rich. TW9 98 CN79
Cambridge Cres, E2 84 DV68
Teddington TW11 117 CG92
Cambridge Dr, SE12 124 EG85
Potters Bar EN6 11 CX31
Ruislip HA4 60 BW61
Cambridge Gdns, N10 45 DH53
N13 45 DN50
N17 *off Gt. Cambridge Rd* 46 DR52
N21 46 DR45
NW6 82 DA68
W10 81 CY72
Enfield EN1 30 DU40
Grays RM16 111 GG77
Kingston upon Thames KT1 138 CN96
Cambridge Gate, NW1 195 J3
Cambridge Gate Ms, NW1 195 J3
Cambridge Grn, SE9 125 EP88
Cambridge Gro, SE20 142 DV95
W6 99 CV77
Cambridge Gro Rd, Kings.T. KT1 138 CN96
⇌ Cambridge Heath 84 DV68
Cambridge Heath Rd, E1 84 DV68
E2 84 DV68
Cambridge Mans, SW11 *off Cambridge Rd* 100 DF81
Cambridge Par, Enf. EN1 *off Great Cambridge Rd* 30 DU39
Cambridge Pk, E11 68 EG59
Twickenham TW1 117 CK87
Cambridge Pk Rd, E11 *off Cambridge Pk* 68 EF59
Cambridge Pl, W8 100 DB75
Cambridge Rd, E4 47 ED46
E11 68 EF58
NW6 82 DA69
SE20 142 DV97
SW11 100 DF81
SW13 99 CT82
SW20 139 CU95
W7 97 CF75
Ashford TW15 115 BQ94
Barking IG11 87 EQ66
Bromley BR1 124 EG94
Carshalton SM5 158 DE107
Hampton TW12 116 BZ94
Harrow HA2 60 CA57
Hounslow TW4 96 BY84
Ilford IG3 69 ES60
Kingston upon Thames KT1 138 CM96
Mitcham CR4 141 DJ97
New Malden KT3 138 CS98
Richmond TW9 98 CN80
Sidcup DA14 125 ES91
Southall UB1 78 BZ74
Teddington TW11 117 CF91
Twickenham TW1 117 CK86
Uxbridge UB8 76 BK65
Walton-on-Thames KT12 135 BV100
Watford WD18 24 BW42
West Molesey KT8 136 BZ98
Cambridge Rd N, W4 98 CP78
Cambridge Rd S, W4 98 CP78
Cambridge Row, SE18 105 EP78
Cambridge Sq, W2 194 B8
Cambridge St, SW1 199 J9
Cambridge Ter, N13 45 DN50
NW1 195 J3
Cambridge Ter Ms, NW1 195 J3
Cambstone Cl, N11 44 DG47
Cambus Cl, Hayes UB4 78 BY71
Cambus Rd, E16 86 EG71
Camdale Rd, SE18 105 ET80
★ Camden Arts Cen, NW3 64 DC64
Camden Av, Felt. TW13 116 BW89
Hayes UB4 78 BW73
Camden Cl, Chis. BR7 125 EQ94
Gravesend DA11 130 GC88
Grays RM16 111 GH77
Camden Gdns, NW1 *off Kentish Town Rd* 83 DH66
Sutton SM1 158 DB106
Thornton Heath CR7 141 DP97
Camden Gro, Chis. BR7 125 EP93
Camden High St, NW1 83 DH67
Camden Hill Rd, SE19 122 DS93
Camdenhurst St, E14 85 DY72
Camden La, N7 *off Rowstock Gdns* 83 DK65
★ Camden Lock Mkt & Waterbuses, NW1 83 DH66
Camden Lock Pl, NW1 *off Chalk Fm Rd* 83 DH66
Camden Ms, NW1 83 DK65
Camden Pk Rd, NW1 83 DK65
Chislehurst BR7 125 EM94
Camden Pas, N1 83 DP67
⇌ Camden Road 83 DJ66
Camden Rd, E11 68 EH58
E17 67 DZ58
N7 65 DK64
NW1 83 DJ66
Bexley DA5 126 EZ88
Carshalton SM5 158 DF105
Grays RM16 110 FY76
Sevenoaks TN13 191 FH122
Sutton SM1 158 DA106
Camden Row, SE3 104 EE82
Camden Sq, NW1 83 DK65
SE15 *off Watts St* 102 DT81
Camden St, NW1 83 DJ66
Camden Ter, NW1 *off North Vil* 83 DK65
CAMDEN TOWN, NW1 83 DJ67
⊖ Camden Town 83 DH67
Camden Wk, N1 83 DP67
Camden Way, Chis. BR7 125 EM94
Thornton Heath CR7 141 DP97
Camelford Wk, W11 *off Lancaster Rd* 81 CY72
Camel Gro, Kings.T. KT2 117 CK92
Camellia Cl, Rom. RM3 *off Columbine Way* 52 FL53
Camellia Ct, Wdf.Grn. IG8 *off The Bridle Path* 48 EE52
Camellia Pl, Twick. TW2 116 CB87
Camellia St, SW8 101 DL80
Camelot Cl, SE28 105 ER75
SW19 120 DA91
Westerham (Bigg.H.) TN16 178 EJ116
Camelot Ho, N9 *off Salisbury Rd* 46 DU48
Camelot St, SE15 *off Bird in Bush Rd* 102 DV80
Camel Rd, E16 86 EK74
Camera Pl, SW10 100 DD79
Cameron Cl, N18 46 DV49
N20 *off Myddelton Pk* 44 DE47
Bexley DA5 127 FD90
Brentwood CM14 54 FW49
Cameron Dr, Wal.Cr. EN8 15 DX34
Cameron Pl, E1 *off Varden St* 84 DV72
Cameron Rd, SE6 123 DZ89
Bromley BR2 144 EG98
Croydon CR0 141 DP100
Ilford IG3 69 ES60
Cameron Sq, Mitch. CR4 140 DE95
Camerton Cl, E8 *off Buttermere Wk* 84 DT65
Camgate Cen, Stai. (Stanw.) TW19 114 BM86
Cam Grn, S.Ock. RM15 91 FV72
Camilla Cl, Sun. TW16 115 BS93
Camilla Rd, SE16 202 D9
Camille Cl, SE25 142 DU97
Camlan Rd, Brom. BR1 124 EF91
Camlet St, E2 197 P4
Camlet Way, Barn. EN4 28 DA40
Camley St, NW1 83 DK66
★ Camley St Natural Pk, NW1 83 DL68
Camm Gdns, Kings.T. KT1 *off Church Rd* 138 CM96
Thames Ditton KT7 137 CE101
Camms Ter, Dag. RM10 71 FC64
Camomile Av, Mitch. CR4 140 DF95
Camomile Rd, Rom. (Rush Grn.) RM7 71 FD61
Camomile St, EC3 197 M8
Camomile Way, West Dr. UB7 76 BL72
Campana Rd, SW6 100 DA81
Campbell Av, Ilf. IG6 69 EQ56
Woking GU22 167 AZ121
Campbell Cl, SE18 *off Moordown* 105 EN81
SW16 121 DK91
Romford (Hav.at.Bow.) RM1 51 FE51
Ruislip HA4 59 BU58
Twickenham TW2 117 CD89
Campbell Ct, N17 46 DT53
Campbell Cft, Edg. HA8 42 CN50
Campbell Gordon Way, NW2 63 CV63
Campbell Rd, E3 85 EA69
E6 86 EL67
E15 *off Trevelyan Rd* 68 EF63
E17 67 DZ56
N17 46 DU53
W7 79 CE73
Caterham CR3 176 DR121
Croydon CR0 141 DP101
East Molesey KT8 *off Hampton Ct Rd* 137 CF97
Gravesend DA11 131 GF88
Twickenham TW2 117 CD89
Weybridge KT13 152 BN108
Campbell Wk, N1 *off Outram Pl* 83 DL67
Campdale Rd, N7 65 DK62
Campden Cres, Dag. RM8 70 EV63
Wembley HA0 61 CH61
Campden Gro, W8 100 DA75
Campden Hill Ct, W8 *off Campden Hill Rd* 100 DA75
Campden Hill Gdns, W8 82 DA74
Campden Hill Gate, W8 *off Duchess of Bedford's Wk* 100 DA75
Campden Hill Pl, W11 *off Holland Pk Av* 81 CZ74
Campden Hill Rd, W8 82 DA74
Campden Hill Sq, W8 81 CZ74
Campden Hill Twrs, W11 *off Notting Hill Gate* 82 DA74
Campden Ho Cl, W8 *off Hornton St* 100 DA75
Campden Rd, S.Croy. CR2 160 DS106
Uxbridge UB10 58 BM62
Campden St, W8 82 DA74
Campen Cl, SW19 *off Queensmere Rd* 119 CY89
Camp End Rd, Wey. KT13 153 BR110
Camperdown St, E1 *off Leman St* 84 DT72
Campfield Rd, SE9 124 EK87
Camphill Ct, W.Byf. KT14 152 BG112
Camphill Ind Est, W.Byf. KT14 152 BH111
Camphill Rd, W.Byf. KT14 152 BG112
Campine Cl, Wal.Cr. (Chsht.) EN8 *off Welsummer Way* 15 DX28
Campion Cl, E6 87 EM73
Croydon CR0 160 DS105
Gravesend (Nthflt.) DA11 130 GE91
Harrow HA3 62 CM58
Campion Cl, Rom. (Rush Grn.) RM7 71 FD61
Uxbridge (Denh.) UB9 *off Lindsey Rd* 58 BG62
Uxbridge (Hlgdn.) UB8 76 BM71
Watford WD25 7 BU33
Campion Ct, Grays RM17 110 GD79
Campion Dr, Tad. KT20 173 CV120
Campion Gdns, Wdf.Grn. IG8 48 EG50
Campion Pl, SE28 88 EV74
Campion Rd, SW15 99 CW84
Isleworth TW7 97 CF81
Campions, Epp. CM16 18 EU28
Loughton IG10 33 EN38
Campions, The, Borwd. WD6 26 CN38
Campions Cl, Borwd. WD6 26 CP37
Campion Ter, NW2 63 CX62
Campion Way, Edg. HA8 42 CQ49
Cample La, S.Ock. RM15 91 FU73
Camplin Rd, Har. HA3 62 CL57
Camplin St, SE14 103 DX80
Camp Rd, SW19 119 CW92
Caterham (Wold.) CR3 177 DY120
Gerrards Cross SL9 56 AX59
Campsbourne, The, N8 *off High St* 65 DL56
Campsbourne Rd, N8 65 DL55
Campsey Gdns, Dag. RM9 88 EV66
Campsey Rd, Dag. RM9 88 EV66
Campsfield Rd, N8 *off Campsbourne Rd* 65 DL55
Campshill Pl, SE13 *off Campshill Rd* 123 EC85
Campshill Rd, SE13 123 EC85
Campus Rd, E17 67 DZ58
Campus Way, NW4 *off Greyhound Hill* 63 CV55
Camp Vw, SW19 119 CV92
Cam Rd, E15 85 ED67
Camrose Av, Edg. HA8 42 CM53
Erith DA8 107 FB79
Feltham TW13 115 BV91
Camrose Cl, Croy. CR0 143 DY101
Morden SM4 140 DA98
Camrose St, SE2 106 EU78
Canada Av, N18 45 DQ51
Canada Cres, W3 80 CQ71
Canada Est, SE16 202 G6
Canada Fm Rd, Dart. (S.Darenth) DA4 149 FU98
Longfield DA3 149 FU99
Canada Gdns, SE13 123 EC85
Canada La, Brox. EN10 15 DY25
Canada Rd, W3 80 CQ70
Cobham KT11 154 BW113
Erith DA8 107 FH80
Slough SL1 92 AV75
West Byfleet (Byfleet) KT14 152 BK111
Canadas, The, Brox. EN10 15 DY25
Canada Sq, E14 204 B2
Canada St, SE16 203 H5
⊖ Canada Water 202 G5
Canada Way, W12 81 CV73
Canadian Av, SE6 123 EB88
Canadian Memorial Av, Egh. TW20 132 AT96
Canal App, SE8 103 DY79
Canal Basin, Grav. DA12 131 GK86
Canal Cl, E1 85 DY70
W10 81 CX70
Canal Est, Slou. (Langley) SL3 93 BA75
Canal Gro, SE15 102 DU79
Canal Path, E2 84 DT67
Canal Rd, Grav. DA12 131 GJ86
Canal Side, Uxb. (Hare.) UB9 *off Summerhouse La* 38 BG51
Canal St, SE5 102 DR79
Canal Wk, N1 84 DR67
SE26 122 DW92
Croydon CR0 142 DS100
Canal Way, N1 *off Packington Sq* 84 DQ68
NW1 194 B3
NW8 194 A4
NW10 81 CT70
W10 81 CX70
Canal Way Wk, W10 81 CX70
Canal Wf, Slou. SL3 93 BA75
⊖ Canary Wharf 204 A2
DLR Canary Wharf 204 A2
Canberra Cl, NW4 63 CU55
Dagenham RM10 89 FD66
Hornchurch RM12 72 FJ63
Canberra Cres, Dag. RM10 89 FD66
Canberra Dr, Hayes UB4 78 BW69
Northolt UB5 78 BW69
Canberra Rd, E6 *off Barking Rd* 87 EM67
SE7 104 EJ79
W13 79 CG74
Bexleyheath DA7 106 EX79
Hounslow (Hthrw.Air.) TW6 94 BN83
Canberra Sq, Til. RM18 111 GG82
Canbury Av, Kings.T. KT2 138 CM95
Canbury Ms, SE26 *off Wells Pk Rd* 122 DU90
Canbury Pk Rd, Kings.T. KT2 138 CL95
Canbury Pas, Kings.T. KT2 137 CK95
Canbury Path, Orp. BR5 146 EU98
Cancell Rd, SW9 101 DN81
Candahar Rd, SW11 100 DE82
Cander Way, S.Ock. RM15 91 FV73
Candler St, N15 66 DR58
Candlerush Cl, Wok. GU22 167 BB117
Candlestick La, Wal.Cr. EN7 *off Park La* 14 DV27
Candover Cl, West Dr. UB7 94 BK80
Candover Rd, Horn. RM12 71 FH60
Candover St, W1 195 K7
Candy St, E3 85 DZ67
Cane Cl, Wall. SM6 159 DL108
Cane Hill, Rom. (Harold Wd.) RM3 *off Bennison Dr* 52 FK54
Caneland Ct, Wal.Abb. EN9 16 EF34
Canewdon Cl, Wok. GU22 *off Guildford Rd* 166 AY119
Caney Ms, NW2 *off Claremont Rd* 63 CX61
Canfield Dr, Ruis. HA4 59 BV64
Canfield Gdns, NW6 82 DC66
Canfield Pl, NW6 *off Canfield Gdns* 82 DC65
Canfield Rd, Rain. RM13 89 FF67
Woodford Green IG8 48 EL52
Canford Av, Nthlt. UB5 78 BY67
Canford Cl, Enf. EN2 29 DN40
Canford Dr, Add. KT15 134 BH103
Canford Gdns, N.Mal. KT3 138 CR100
Canford Pl, Tedd. TW11 117 CH93
Canford Rd, SW11 120 DG85
Canham Rd, SE25 142 DS97
W3 98 CS75
Can Hatch, Tad. KT20 173 CY118
Canmore Gdns, SW16 121 DJ94
Cann Hall Rd, E11 68 EE63
Canning Cres, N22 45 DM53
Canning Cross, SE5 102 DS82
Canning Pas, W8 100 DC76
Canning Pl, W8 100 DC76
Canning Pl Ms, W8 *off Canning Pl* 100 DC76
Canning Rd, E15 86 EE68
E17 67 DY56
N5 65 DP62
Croydon CR0 142 DT103
Harrow HA3 61 CF55
Cannington Rd, Dag. RM9 88 EW65
CANNING TOWN, E16 86 EG72
⇌ Canning Town 86 EE72
⊖ Canning Town 86 EE72
DLR Canning Town 86 EE72
Cannizaro Rd, SW19 119 CW93
Cannonbury Av, Pnr. HA5 60 BX58
Cannon Cl, SW20 139 CW97
Hampton TW12 *off Hanworth Rd* 116 CB93
Cannon Cres, Wok. (Chobham) GU24 150 AS111
Cannon Dr, E14 203 P1
Cannon Gro, Lthd. (Fetch.) KT22 171 CE121
Cannon Hill, N14 45 DK48
NW6 64 DA64
Cannon Hill La, SW20 139 CY97
Cannon La, NW3 64 DD62
Pinner HA5 60 BY60
Cannon Ms, Wal.Abb. EN9 15 EB33
Cannon Pl, NW3 64 DD62
SE7 104 EL78
Cannon Rd, N14 45 DL48
Bexleyheath DA7 106 EY81
Watford WD18 24 BW43
Cannonside, Lthd. (Fetch.) KT22 171 CE122
⇌ Cannon Street 201 K1
⊖ Cannon Street 201 K1
Cannon St, EC4 197 H9
Cannon St Rd, E1 84 DV72
Cannon Trd Est, Wem. HA9 62 CP63
Cannon Way, Lthd. (Fetch.) KT22 171 CE121
West Molesey KT8 136 CA98
Cannon Wf Business Cen, SE8 103 DY77
Cannon Workshops, E14 203 P1
Canon Av, Rom. RM6 70 EW57
Canon Beck Rd, SE16 202 G4
Canonbie Rd, SE23 122 DW87
CANONBURY, N1 84 DQ65
⇌ Canonbury 66 DQ64
Canonbury Cres, N1 84 DQ66
Canonbury Gro, N1 84 DQ66
Canonbury La, N1 83 DP66
Canonbury Pk N, N1 84 DQ65
Canonbury Pk S, N1 84 DQ65
Canonbury Pl, N1 83 DP65
Canonbury Rd, N1 83 DP65
Enfield EN1 30 DS39
Canonbury Sq, N1 83 DP66
Canonbury St, N1 84 DQ66
Canonbury Vil, N1 83 DP66
Canonbury Yd, N1 *off New N Rd* 84 DQ67
Canonbury Yd W, N1 *off Compton Rd* 83 DP65
Canon Mohan Cl, N14 *off Farm La* 29 DH44
Canon Rd, Brom. BR1 144 EJ97
Canon Row, SW1 199 P5
Canons Cl, N2 64 DD59
Edgware HA8 42 CM51
Radlett WD7 25 CH35
Reigate RH2 183 CZ133
Canons Cor, Edg. HA8 42 CL49
Canons Dr, Edg. HA8 42 CL51
Canons Gate, Wal.Cr. (Chsht.) EN8 15 DZ26
Canon's Hill, Couls. CR5 175 DN117
Canons La, Tad. KT20 173 CY118
Canonsleigh Rd, Dag. RM9 88 EV66
CANONS PARK, Edg. 42 CL52
⊖ Canons Park 42 CL52
Canons Pk Cl, Edg. HA8 *off Donnefield Av* 42 CL52
Canon St, N1 84 DQ67
Canons Wk, Croy. CR0 143 DX104
Canopus Way, Nthwd. HA6 39 BU49
Staines TW19 114 BL87
Canrobert St, E2 84 DV69
Cantelowes Rd, NW1 83 DK65
Canterbury Av, Ilf. IG1 68 EL59
Sidcup DA15 126 EW89
Upminster RM14 73 FT60
Canterbury Cl, E6 *off Harper Rd* 87 EM72
Amersham HP7 20 AS39
Beckenham BR3 143 EB95
Chigwell IG7 49 ET48
Dartford DA1 128 FN87
Greenford UB6 78 CB72
Northwood HA6 39 BT51
Canterbury Cres, SW9 101 DN83
Canterbury Gro, SE27 121 DP90
Canterbury Ho, Borwd. WD6 26 CN40
Canterbury Ms, Lthd. (Oxshott) KT22 *off Steels La* 154 CC113
Canterbury Par, S.Ock. RM15 91 FW69
Canterbury Pl, SE17 200 G9
Canterbury Rd, E10 67 EC59
NW6 82 DA68
Borehamwood WD6 26 CN40
Croydon CR0 141 DM101
Feltham TW13 116 BY90
Gravesend DA12 131 GJ89
Harrow HA1, HA2 60 CB57
Morden SM4 140 DC99
Watford WD17 23 BV40
Canterbury Ter, NW6 82 DA68
Canterbury Way, Brwd. CM13 53 FW51
Purfleet RM19 109 FS80
Rickmansworth (Crox.Grn.) WD3 23 BQ41
Cantley Gdns, SE19 142 DT95
Ilford IG2 69 EQ58
Cantley Rd, W7 97 CG76
Canton St, E14 85 EA72
Cantrell Rd, E3 85 DZ70
Cantwell Rd, SE18 105 EP80
Canute Gdns, SE16 203 H8
Canvey St, SE1 200 G2
Cape Cl, Bark. IG11 *off North St* 87 EQ65
Capel Av, Wall. SM6 159 DM106
Capel Cl, N20 44 DC48
Bromley BR2 144 EL102
Capel Ct, EC2 197 L9
SE20 *off Melvin Rd* 142 DW95
Capel Gdns, Ilf. IG3 69 ET63
Pinner HA5 60 BZ56
Capella Rd, Nthwd. HA6 39 BT50
Capell Av, Rick. (Chorl.) WD3 21 BC43
Capell Rd, Rick. (Chorl.) WD3 21 BC43
Capell Way, Rick. (Chorl.) WD3 21 BD43
Capel Pl, Dart. DA2 128 FJ91
Capel Pt, E7 68 EH63
Capel Rd, E7 68 EH63
E12 68 EJ63
Barnet EN4 28 DE44
Enfield EN1 30 DV36
Watford WD19 24 BY44
Capel Vere Wk, Wat. WD17 23 BS39
Capener's Cl, SW1 198 F5
Capern Rd, SW18 *off Cargill Rd* 120 DC88
Cape Rd, N17 *off High Cross Rd* 66 DU55
Cape Yd, E1 202 C2
Capital Business Cen, Wem. HA0 79 CK68
Capital Ind Est, Mitch. CR4 *off Willow La* 140 DF99
Capital Interchange Way, Brent. TW8 98 CN78
Capital Pk, Wok. (Old Wok.) GU22 167 BB121
Capitol Ind Pk, NW9 62 CQ55
Capitol Way, NW9 62 CQ55
Capland St, NW8 194 A4
Caple Par, NW10 *off Harley Rd* 80 CS68
Caple Rd, NW10 81 CT68
Capon Cl, Brwd. CM14 54 FV46
Capper St, WC1 195 L5
Caprea Cl, Hayes UB4 *off Triandra Way* 78 BX71
Capri Rd, Croy. CR0 142 DT102
Capstan Cen, Til. RM18 110 GD80
Capstan Cl, Rom. RM6 70 EV58
Capstan Ct, Dart. DA2 108 FQ84
Capstan Ms, Grav. DA11 *off Rosherville Way* 130 GE87
Capstan Ride, Enf. EN2 29 DN40
Capstan Rd, SE8 203 M8
Capstan Sq, E14 204 E5
Capstan's Wf, Wok. (St. John's) GU21 166 AT118
Capstan Way, SE16 203 L3
Capstone Rd, Brom. BR1 124 EF91
Captain Cook Cl, Ch.St.G. HP8 36 AU49
Capthorne Av, Har. HA2 60 BY60
Capuchin Cl, Stan. HA7 41 CH51
Capulet Ms, E16 205 N2
Capworth St, E10 67 EA60
Caractacus Cottage Vw, Wat. WD18 39 BU45
Caractacus Grn, Wat. WD18 23 BT44
Caradoc Cl, W2 82 DA72
Caradoc St, SE10 205 H10
Caradon Cl, E11 *off Brockway Cl* 68 EE61
Woking GU21 166 AV118
Caradon Way, N15 66 DR56
Caravan La, Rick. WD3 38 BL45
Caravel Cl, E14 *off Tiller Rd* 103 EA76
Grays RM16 110 FZ76
Caravelle Gdns, Nthlt. UB5 *off Javelin Way* 78 BX69
Caravel Ms, SE8 *off Watergate St* 103 EA79
Caraway Cl, E13 86 EH71
Caraway Pl, Wall. SM6 141 DH104
Carberry Rd, SE19 122 DS93
Carbery Av, W3 98 CM75
Carbis Cl, E4 47 ED46
Carbis Rd, E14 85 DZ72
Carbone Hill, Hert. (Newgate St.) SG13 13 DK26
Potters Bar (Cuffley) EN6 13 DJ27
Carbuncle Pas Way, N17 46 DU54
Carburton St, W1 195 J6
Carbury Cl, Horn. RM12 90 FJ65
Cardale St, E14 204 D6

Car - Cas

Carden Rd, SE15 102 DV83
Cardiff Rd, W7 97 CG76
Enfield EN3 30 DV42
Watford WD18 23 BV44
Cardiff St, SE18 105 ES80
Cardiff Way, Abb.L. WD5 7 BU32
Cardigan Cl, Wok. GU21
off Bingham Dr 166 AS118
Cardigan Gdns, Ilf. IG3 70 EU61
Cardigan Rd, E3 85 DZ68
SW13 99 CU82
SW19 off Haydons Rd 120 DC93
Richmond TW10 118 CL86
Cardigan St, SE11 200 D10
Cardigan Wk, N1
off Ashby Gro 84 DQ66
Cardinal Av, Borwd. WD6 26 CP41
Kingston upon Thames
KT2 118 CL92
Morden SM4 139 CY100
Cardinal Bourne St, SE1 201 L7
Cardinal Cl, Chis. BR7 145 ER95
Edgware HA8
off Abbots Rd 42 CR52
Morden SM4 139 CY101
South Croydon CR2 160 DU113
Waltham Cross (Chsht.) EN7
off Adamsfield 14 DT26
Worcester Park KT4 157 CU105
Cardinal Ct, Borwd. WD6
off Cardinal Av 26 CP41
Cardinal Cres, N.Mal. KT3 138 CQ96
Cardinal Dr, Ilf. IG6 49 EQ51
Walton-on-Thames KT12 136 BX102
Cardinal Hinsley Cl, NW10 81 CU68
Cardinal Pl, SW15 99 CX84
Cardinal Rd, Felt. TW13 115 BV88
Ruislip HA4 60 BX60
Cardinals Wk, Hmptn. TW12 116 CC94
Sunbury-on-Thames TW16 115 BS93
Cardinals Way, N19 65 DK60
Cardinal Way, Har. HA3
off Wolseley Rd 61 CE55
Rainham RM13 90 FK68
Cardine Ms, SE15 102 DV80
Cardingham, Wok. GU21 166 AU117
Cardington Sq, Houns. TW4 96 BX84
Cardington St, NW1 195 K2
Cardinham Rd, Orp. BR6 163 ET105
Cardozo Rd, N7 65 DL64
Cardrew Av, N12 44 DD50
Cardrew Cl, N12 44 DE50
Cardross St, W6 99 CV76
Cardwell Rd, N7 65 DL63
Carew Cl, N7 65 DM61
Coulsdon CR5 175 DP119
Carew Ct, Sutt. SM2 158 DB109
Carew Rd, N17 46 DU54
W13 97 CJ75
Ashford TW15 115 BQ93
Mitcham CR4 140 DG96
Northwood HA6 39 BS51
Thornton Heath CR7 141 DP97
Wallington SM6 159 DJ107
Carew St, SE5 102 DQ82
Carew Way, Wat. WD19 40 BZ48
Carey Ct, Bexh. DA6 127 FB85
Carey Gdns, SW8 101 DJ81
Carey La, EC2 197 H8
Carey Pl, SW1 199 M9
Carey Rd, Dag. RM9 70 EY63
Carey's Fld, Sev. (Dunt.Grn.)
TN13 181 FE120
Carey St, WC2 196 C9
Carey Way, Wem. HA9 62 CP63
Carfax Pl, SW4
off Holwood Pl 101 DK84
Carfax Rd, Hayes UB3 95 BT78
Hornchurch RM12 71 FF63
Carfree Cl, N1 off Bewdley St 83 DN66
Cargill Rd, SW18 120 DB88
Cargreen Pl, SE25
off Cargreen Rd 142 DT98
Cargreen Rd, SE25 142 DT98
Carholme Rd, SE23 123 DZ88
Carisbrooke Av, Bex. DA5 126 EX88
Watford WD24 24 BX39
Carisbrooke Cl, Enf. EN1 30 DT39
Hornchurch RM11 72 FN60
Stanmore HA7 41 CK54
Carisbrooke Ct, Slou. SL1 74 AT73
Carisbrooke Gdns, SE15
off Commercial Way 102 DT80
Carisbrooke Rd, E17 67 DY56
Bromley BR2 144 EJ98
Mitcham CR4 141 DK98
St. Albans AL2 8 CB26
Carisbrook Rd, Brwd. CM15 54 FV44
Carker's La, NW5 65 DH64
Carl Ekman Ho, Grav. DA11 130 GD87
Carleton Av, Wall. SM6 159 DK109
Carleton Cl, Esher KT10 137 CD102
Carleton Pl, Dart. (Hort.Kir.)
DA4 148 FQ98
Carleton Rd, N7 65 DK64
Dartford DA1 128 FN87
Waltham Cross (Chsht.)
EN8 15 DX28
Carleton Vil, NW5
off Leighton Gro 65 DJ64
Carlile Cl, E3 85 DZ68
Carlina Gdns, Wdf.Grn. IG8 48 EH50
Carlingford Gdns, Mitch.
CR4 120 DF94
Carlingford Rd, N15 65 DP55
NW3 64 DD63
Morden SM4 139 CX100
Carlisle Av, EC3 197 N9
W3 80 CS72
Carlisle Cl, Kings.T. KT2 138 CN95
Pinner HA5 60 BY59
Carlisle Gdns, Har. HA3 61 CK59
Ilford IG1 68 EL58
Carlisle La, SE1 200 C7
Carlisle Ms, NW8 194 A6
Carlisle Pl, N11 45 DH49
SW1 199 K7
Carlisle Rd, E10 67 EA60
N4 65 DN59
NW6 81 CY67
NW9 62 CQ55
Dartford DA1 128 FN86
Hampton TW12 116 CB94
Romford RM1 71 FG57
Sutton SM1 157 CZ106
Carlisle St, W1 195 M9
Carlisle Wk, E8 off Laurel St 84 DT65
Carlisle Way, SW17 120 DG92
Carlos Pl, W1 198 G1
Carlow St, NW1
off Arlington Rd 83 DJ68
Carlton Av, N14 29 DK43
Feltham TW14 116 BW86
Greenhithe DA9 129 FS86
Harrow HA3 61 CH57
Hayes UB3 95 BS77
South Croydon CR2 160 DS108
Carlton Av E, Wem. HA9 62 CL60
Carlton Av W, Wem. HA0 61 CH61
Carlton Cl, NW3 64 DA61
Borehamwood WD6 26 CR42
Chessington KT9 155 CK107
Edgware HA8 42 CN50
Northolt UB5
off Whitton Av W 60 CC64
Upminster RM14 72 FP61
Woking GU21 151 AZ114
Carlton Ct, SW9 101 DP81
Ilford IG6 69 ER55
Uxbridge UB8 76 BK71
Carlton Cres, Sutt. SM3 157 CY105
Carlton Dr, SW15 119 CY85
Ilford IG6 69 ER55
Carlton Gdns, SW1 199 M3
W5 79 CJ72
Carlton Grn, Red. RH1 184 DE131
Carlton Gro, SE15 102 DV81
Carlton Hill, NW8 82 DB68
Carlton Ho, Felt. TW14 115 BT87
Carlton Ho Ter, SW1 199 M3
Carlton Par, Orp. BR6 146 EV101
Sevenoaks TN13
off St. John's Hill 191 FJ122
Carlton Pk Av, SW20 139 CW96
Carlton Pl, Nthwd. HA6 39 BP50
Weybridge KT13
off Castle Vw Rd 153 BP105
Carlton Rd, E11 68 EF60
E12 68 EK63
E17 47 DY53
N4 65 DN59
N11 44 DG50
SW14 98 CQ83
W4 98 CR75
W5 79 CJ73
Erith DA8 107 FB79
Grays RM16 111 GF75
New Malden KT3 138 CS96
Redhill RH1 184 DF131
Reigate RH2 184 DD132
Romford RM2 71 FG57
Sidcup DA14 125 ET92
Slough SL2 74 AV73
South Croydon CR2 160 DR107
Sunbury-on-Thames TW16 115 BT94
Walton-on-Thames KT12 135 BV101
Welling DA16 106 EV83
Woking GU21 151 BA114
Carlton Sq, E1 off Argyle Rd 85 DX70
Carlton St, SW1 199 M1
Carlton Ter, E11 68 EH57
N18 46 DR48
SE26 122 DW90
Carlton Twr Pl, SW1 198 E6
Carlton Vale, NW6 82 DB68
Carlton Vil, SW15
off St. John's Av 119 CW85
Carlwell St, SW17 120 DE92
Carlyle Av, Brom. BR1 144 EK97
Southall UB1 78 BZ73
Carlyle Cl, N2 64 DC58
NW10 80 CR67
West Molesey KT8 136 CB96
Carlyle Gdns, Sthl. UB1 78 BZ73
Carlyle Lo, Barn. (New Barn.)
EN5 off Richmond Rd 28 DC43
Carlyle Ms, E1
off Alderney Rd 85 DX70
Carlyle Pl, SW15 99 CX84
Carlyle Rd, E12 68 EL63
SE28 88 EV73
W5 97 CJ78
Croydon CR0 142 DU103
Staines TW18 113 BF94
★ Carlyle's Ho, SW3 100 DE79
Carlyle Sq, SW3 100 DD78
Carlyon Av, Har. HA2 60 BZ63
Carlyon Cl, Wem. HA0 80 CL67
Carlyon Rd, Hayes UB4 78 BW72
Wembley HA0 80 CL68
Carmalt Gdns, SW15 99 CW84
Walton-on-Thames KT12 154 BW106
Carmarthen Grn, NW9
off Snowdon Dr 62 CS58
Carmarthen Rd, Slou. SL1 74 AS73
Carmel Cl, Wok. GU22 166 AY118
Carmel Ct, W8 off Holland St 100 DB75
Wembley HA9 62 CP61
Carmelite Cl, Har. HA3 40 CC53
Carmelite Rd, Har. HA3 40 CC53
Carmelite St, EC4 196 E10
Carmelite Wk, Har. HA3 40 CC53
Carmelite Way, Har. HA3 40 CC54
Carmen Ct, Borwd. WD6
off Belford Rd 26 CM38
Carmen St, E14 85 EB72
Carmichael Cl, SW11
off Darien Rd 100 DD83
Ruislip HA4 59 BU63
Carmichael Ms, SW18 120 DD87
Carmichael Rd, SE25 142 DU99
Carminia Rd, SW17 121 DH89
Carnaby St, W1 195 K9
Carnach Grn, S.Ock. RM15 91 FV73
Carnac St, SE27 122 DR91
Carnanton Rd, E17 47 ED53
Carnarvon Av, Enf. EN1 30 DT41
Carnarvon Dr, Hayes UB3 95 BQ76
Carnarvon Rd, E10 67 EC58
E15 86 EF65
E18 48 EF53
Barnet EN5 27 CY41
Carnation Cl, Rom. (Rush Grn.)
RM7 71 FE61
Carnation St, SE2 106 EV78
Carnbrook Rd, SE3 104 EK83
Carnecke Gdns, SE9 124 EL85
Carnegie Cl, Enf. EN3
off Government Row 31 EA37
Surbiton KT6
off Fullers Av 138 CM103
Carnegie Pl, SW19 119 CX90
Carnegie St, N1 83 DM67
Carnet Cl, Dart. DA1
off Lower Sta Rd 127 FE86
Carnforth Cl, Epsom KT19 156 CP107
Carnforth Gdns, Horn. RM12 71 FG64
Carnforth Rd, SW16 121 DK94
Carnie Lo, SW17
off Manville Rd 121 DH90
Carnoustie Dr, N1 83 DM66
Carnwath Rd, SW6 100 DA83
Carol Cl, NW4 63 CX56
Carolina Cl, E15 68 EE64
Carolina Rd, Th.Hth. CR7 141 DP96
Caroline Cl, N10
off Alexandra Pk Rd 45 DH54
SW16 121 DM91
W2 off Bayswater Rd 82 DB73
Croydon CR0
off Brownlow Rd 160 DS105
Isleworth TW7 97 CD80
West Drayton UB7 94 BK75
Caroline Ct, Ashf. TW15 115 BP93
Stanmore HA7
off The Chase 41 CG51
Caroline Gdns, SE15 102 DV80
Caroline Pl, SW11 100 DG82
W2 82 DB73
Hayes UB3 95 BS80
Watford WD19 24 BY44
Caroline Pl Ms, W2
off Orme La 82 DB73
Caroline Rd, SW19 119 CZ94
Caroline St, E1 85 DX72
Caroline Ter, SW1 198 F9
Caroline Wk, W6 99 CY79
Carol St, NW1 83 DJ67
Carolyn Cl, Wok. GU21 166 AT119
Carolyn Dr, Orp. BR6 146 EU104
Caroon Dr, Rick. (Sarratt)
WD3 22 BH36
Carpenders Av, Wat. WD19 40 BY48
CARPENDERS PARK, Wat. 40 BZ47
⇌ Carpenders Park 40 BX48
Carpenders Pk, Wat. WD19 40 BY47
Carpenter Cl, Epsom KT17
off West St 157 CT109
Carpenter Gdns, N21 45 DP47
Carpenter Path, Brwd. CM13 55 GD43
Carpenters Arms La, Epp. (Thnwd.)
CM16 18 EV25
Carpenters Arms Path, SE9
off Eltham High St 125 EM86
Carpenters Ct, Twick. TW2 117 CE89
Carpenters Pl, SW4 101 DK84
Carpenters Rd, E15 85 EB65
Enfield EN1 30 DW36
Carpenter St, W1 199 H1
Carpenters Wd Dr, Rick. (Chorl.)
WD3 21 BB42
Carpenter Way, Pot.B. EN6 12 DC33
Carrara Wk, SW9 101 DP84
Carrara Wf, SW6 99 CY83
Carr Gro, SE18 104 EL77
Carriage Dr E, SW11 100 DG80
Carriage Dr N, SW11 100 DG79
Carriage Dr S, SW11 100 DF81
Carriage Dr W, SW11 100 DF80
Carriage Ms, Ilf. IG1 69 EQ61
Carriage Pl, N16 66 DR62
SW16 off Eardley Rd 121 DJ92
Carriageway, The, West.
TN16 180 EX124
Carrick Cl, Islw. TW7 97 CG83
Carrick Dr, Ilf. IG6 49 EQ53
Sevenoaks TN13 191 FH123
Carrick Gdns, N17
off Flexmere Rd 46 DS52
Carrick Gate, Esher KT10 136 CC104
Carrick Ms, SE8
off Watergate St 103 EA79
Carrill Way, Belv. DA17 106 EX77
Carrington Av, Borwd. WD6 26 CP43
Hounslow TW3 116 CB85
Carrington Cl, Barn. EN5 27 CU43
Borehamwood WD6 26 CQ43
Croydon CR0 143 DY101
Kingston upon Thames
KT2 118 CQ92
Redhill RH1 184 DF133
Carrington Gdns, E7
off Woodford Rd 68 EH63
Carrington Pl, Esher KT10 154 CC105
Carrington Rd, Dart. DA1 128 FM86
Richmond TW10 98 CN84
Slough SL1 74 AS73
Carrington Sq, Har. HA3 40 CC52
Carrington St, W1 199 H3
Carrol Cl, NW5 65 DH63
Carroll Cl, E15 68 EF64
Carroll Hill, Loug. IG10 33 EM41
Carronade Pl, SE28 105 EQ76
Carron Cl, E14 85 EB72
Carroun Rd, SW8 101 DM80
Carroway La, Grnf. UB6
off Cowgate Rd 79 CD69
Carrow Rd, Dag. RM9 88 EV66
Carrow Rd, Walt. KT12
off Kenilworth Dr 136 BX104
Carr Rd, E17 47 DZ54
Northolt UB5 78 CA65
Carrs La, N21 30 DQ43
Carr St, E14 85 DY71
CARSHALTON 158 DD105
⇌ Carshalton 158 DF105
CARSHALTON BEECHES,
Cars. 158 DD109
⇌ Carshalton Beeches 158 DF107
Carshalton Gro, Sutt. SM1 158 DD105
CARSHALTON ON THE HILL,
Cars. 158 DG109
Carshalton Pk Rd, Cars.
SM5 158 DF106
Carshalton Pl, Cars. SM5 158 DG105
Carshalton Rd, Bans. SM7 158 DF114
Carshalton SM5 158 DC106
Mitcham CR4 140 DG98
Sutton SM1 158 DC106
H Carshalton War Mem Hosp,
Cars. SM5 158 DF107
Carsington Gdns, Dart. DA1 128 FK89
Carslake Rd, SW15 119 CW86
Carson Rd, E16 86 EG70
SE21 122 DR89
Barnet EN4 28 DF42
Carstairs Rd, SE6 123 EC90
Carston Cl, SE12 124 EF85
Carswell Cl, Brwd. CM13 55 GD44
Ilford IG4
off Roding La S 68 EK56
Carswell Rd, SE6 123 EC87
Cartbridge Cl, Wok. (Send)
GU23 off Send Rd 167 BB123
Cartel Cl, Purf. RM19 109 FR77
Carter Cl, Rom. RM5 51 FB52
Wallington SM6 159 DK108
Carter Ct, EC4
off Carter La 83 DP72
Carter Dr, Rom. RM5 51 FB52
Carteret St, SW1 199 M5
Carteret Way, SE8 203 L9
Carterhatch La, Enf. EN1 30 DU40
Carterhatch Rd, Enf. EN3 30 DW40
Carter La, EC4 196 G9
Carter Pl, SE17 102 DQ78
Carter Rd, E13 86 EH67
SW19 120 DD93
Carters Cl, Wor.Pk. KT4 139 CX103
Cartersfield Rd, Wal.Abb. EN9 15 EC34
Carters Hill, Sev. (Undrvr.)
TN15 191 FP127
Carters Hill Cl, SE9 124 EJ88
Carters La, SE23 123 DY89
Woking GU22 167 BC120
Carters Rd, Epsom KT17 173 CT115
Carters Row, Grav. (Nthflt.)
DA11 131 GF88
Carter St, SE17 102 DQ79
Carters Yd, SW18
off Wandsworth High St 120 DA85
Carthew Rd, W6 99 CV76
Carthew Vil, W6 99 CV76
Carthouse La, Wok. GU21 150 AS114
Carthusian St, EC1 197 H6
Cartier Circle, E14 204 C3
Carting La, WC2 200 A1
Cart La, E4 47 ED45
Cartmel Cl, N17
off Heybourne Rd 46 DV52
Reigate RH2 184 DE133
Cartmel Gdns, Mord. SM4 140 DC99
Cartmel Rd, Bexh. DA7 106 FA81
Carton St, W1 194 E8
Cart Path, Wat. WD25 8 BW33
Cartwright Gdns, WC1 195 P3
Cartwright Rd, Dag. RM9 88 EZ66
Cartwright St, E1 84 DT73
Cartwright Way, SW13 99 CV80
Carver Cl, W4 98 CQ76
Carver Rd, SE24 122 DQ86
Carville Cres, Brent. TW8 98 CL77
Cary Rd, E11 68 EE63
Carysfort Rd, N8 65 DK57
N16 66 DR62
Cary Wk, Rad. WD7 9 CH34
Cascade Av, N10 65 DJ56
Cascade Cl, Buck.H. IG9
off Cascade Rd 48 EK47
Orpington BR5 146 EW97
Cascade Rd, Buck.H. IG9 48 EK47
Cascades, Croy. CR0 161 DZ110
Caselden Cl, Add. KT15 152 BJ106
Casella Rd, SE14 103 DX80
Casewick Rd, SE27 121 DP91
Casey Cl, NW8 194 B3
Casimir Rd, E5 66 DV62
Casino Av, SE24 122 DQ85
Caspian St, SE5 102 DR80
Caspian Wk, E16 86 EK72
Caspian Wf, E3 off Violet Rd 85 EB71
Cassandra Cl, Nthlt. UB5 61 CD63
Cassandra Gate, Wal.Cr. EN8 15 DZ27
Casselden Rd, NW10 80 CR66
H Cassel Hosp, The, Rich.
TW10 117 CK91
Cassidy Rd, SW6 100 DA80
Cassilda Rd, SE2 106 EU77
Cassilis Rd, Twick. TW1 117 CH85
Cassiobridge, Wat. WD18 23 BR42
Cassiobridge Rd, Wat. WD18 23 BS42
Cassiobury Av, Felt. TW14 115 BT86
Cassiobury Ct, Wat. WD17 23 BT40
Cassiobury Dr, Wat. WD17 23 BT40
★ Cassiobury Park, Wat.
WD18 23 BS41
Cassiobury Pk, Wat. WD18 23 BS41
Cassiobury Pk Av, Wat. WD18 23 BS41
Cassiobury Rd, E17 67 DX57
Cassio Rd, Wat. WD18 23 BV41
Cassis Ct, Loug. IG10 33 EQ42
Cassland Rd, E9 84 DW66
Thornton Heath CR7 142 DR98
Casslee Rd, SE6 123 DZ87
Cassocks Sq, Shep. TW17 135 BR100
Casson St, E1 84 DU71
Casstine Cl, Swan. BR8 127 FF94
Castalia Sq, E14
off Roserton St 103 EC75
Castalia St, E14
off Plevna St 103 EC75
Castano Ct, Abb.L. WD5 7 BS31
Castellain Rd, W9 82 DB70
Castellan Av, Rom. RM2 71 FH55
Castellane Cl, Stan. HA7
off Daventer Dr 41 CF52
Castello Av, SW15 119 CW85
Castell Rd, Loug. IG10 33 EQ39
CASTELNAU, SW13 99 CU79
Castelnau, SW13 99 CV79
Castelnau Gdns, SW13
off Arundel Ter 99 CV79
Castelnau Pl, SW13
off Castelnau 99 CV79
Castelnau Row, SW13
off Lonsdale Rd 99 CV79
Casterbridge, NW6 82 DB67
Casterbridge Rd, SE3 104 EG83
Casterton St, E8
off Wilton Way 84 DV65
Castile Rd, SE18 105 EN77
Castillon Rd, SE6 124 EE89
Castlands Rd, SE6 123 DZ89
Castle Av, E4 47 ED50
Epsom KT17 157 CU109
Rainham RM13 89 FE66
Slough (Datchet) SL3 92 AU79
West Drayton UB7 76 BL73
Castlebar Hill, W5 79 CH71
Castlebar Ms, W5 79 CJ71
⇌ Castle Bar Park 79 CF71
Castlebar Pk, W5 79 CH70
Castlebar Rd, W5 79 CJ71
Castle Baynard St, EC4 196 G10
Castlebrook Cl, SE11 200 F8
Castle Cl, E9
off Swinnerton St 67 DY64
SW19 119 CX90
W3 98 CP75
Bromley BR2 144 EE97
Bushey WD23 24 CB44
Redhill (Bletch.) RH1 186 DQ133
Romford RM3 52 FJ48
Sunbury-on-Thames TW16
off Mill Fm Av 115 BS94
Castlecombe Dr, SW19 119 CX87
Castlecombe Rd, SE9 124 EL91
Castle Ct, EC3 197 L9
SE26 off Champion Rd 123 DY91
Castledine Rd, SE20 122 DV94
Castle Dr, Ilf. IG4 68 EL58
Castle Fm Rd, Sev. (Shore.)
TN14 165 FF109
Castlefield Rd, Reig. RH2 184 DA133
Castleford Av, SE9 125 EP88
Castleford Cl, N17 46 DT51
Castle Gdns, Dor. RH4 182 CM134
Castlegate, Rich. TW9 98 CM83
Castle Grn, Wey. KT13 135 BS104
Castle Gro Rd, Wok. (Chobham)
GU24 150 AS113
Castlehaven Rd, NW1 83 DH66
Castle Hill, Long. (Fawk.)
DA3 149 FX99
Castle Hill Av, Croy. (New Adgtn.)
CR0 161 EB109
Castle Hill Rd, Egh. TW20 112 AV91
Castle La, SW1 199 L6
Castleleigh Ct, Enf. EN2 30 DR43
Castlemaine Av, Epsom
KT17 157 CV109
South Croydon CR2 160 DT106
Castlemaine Twr, SW11 100 DF81
Castle Ms, N12
off Castle Rd 44 DC50
NW1 off Castle Rd 83 DH65
Castle Par, Epsom KT17
off Ewell Bypass 157 CU108
Castle Pl, NW1 83 DH65
W4 off Windmill Rd 98 CS77
Castle Pt, E13 86 EJ68
Castlereagh St, W1 194 D8
Castle Rd, N12 44 DC50
NW1 83 DH65
Coulsdon CR5 174 DE120
Dagenham RM9 88 EV67
Dartford (Eyns.) DA4 165 FH107
Enfield EN3 31 DY39
Epsom KT18 172 CP115
Grays RM17 110 FZ79
Isleworth TW7 97 CF82
Northolt UB5 78 CB65
Sevenoaks (Shore.) TN14 165 FG108
Southall UB2 96 BZ76
Swanscombe DA10 130 FZ86
Weybridge KT13 135 BS104
Woking GU21 151 AZ114
Castle Sq, Red. (Bletch.) RH1 186 DQ133
Castle St, E6 86 EJ68
Greenhithe DA9 129 FU85
Kingston upon Thames
KT1 138 CL96
Redhill (Bletch.) RH1 185 DP133
Slough SL1 92 AT76
Swanscombe DA10 130 FZ86
Castleton Av, Bexh. DA7 107 FD81
Wembley HA9 62 CL63
Castleton Cl, Bans. SM7 174 DA115
Croydon CR0 143 DY100
Castleton Dr, Bans. SM7 174 DA115
Castleton Gdns, Wem. HA9 62 CL62
Castleton Rd, E17 47 ED54
SE9 124 EK91
Ilford IG3 70 EU60
Mitcham CR4 141 DK98
Ruislip HA4 60 BX60
Castletown Rd, W14 99 CY78
Castle Vw, Epsom KT18 156 CP114
Castleview Cl, N4 66 DQ60
Castleview Gdns, Ilf. IG1 68 EL58
Castleview Rd, Slou. SL3 92 AW77
Castle Vw Rd, Wey. KT13 153 BP105

★ Place of interest ⇌ Railway station ⊖ London Underground station DLR Docklands Light Railway station Tramlink station H Hospital

A B C D E F G H I J K L M N O P Q R S T U V W X Y Z

Castle Wk, Reig. RH2
off High St .184 DA134
Sunbury-on-Thames TW16
off Elizabeth Gdns .136 BW97
Castle Way, SW19 .119 CX90
Epsom KT17
off Castle Av .157 CU109
Feltham TW13 .116 BW91
Castlewood Dr, SE9 .105 EM82
Castlewood Rd, N15 .66 DU58
N16 .66 DU59
Barnet EN4 .28 DD41
H Castlewood Therapy Cen,
SE18 .105 EN81
Castle Yd, N6 off North Rd .64 DG59
SE1 .200 G2
Richmond TW10 off Hill St .117 CK85
Castor La, E14 .204 B1
Catalina Av, Grays (Chaff.Hun.)
RM16 .110 FZ75
Catalin Ct, Wal.Abb. EN9
off Howard Cl .15 ED33
CATERHAM .176 DU123
⇌ Caterham .176 DU124
Caterham Av, Ilf. IG5 .49 EM54
Caterham Bypass, Cat. CR3 .176 DV120
Caterham Cl, Cat. CR3 .176 DS120
Caterham Ct, Wal.Abb. EN9 .16 EF34
H Caterham Dene Hosp, Cat.
CR3 .176 DT123
Caterham Dr, Couls. CR5 .175 DP118
CATERHAM-ON-THE-HILL,
Cat. .176 DT122
Caterham Rd, SE13 .103 EC83
Catesby St, SE17 .201 L9
CATFORD, SE6 .123 EB88
⇌ Catford .123 EA87
⇌ Catford Bridge .123 EA87
Catford Bdy, SE6 .123 EB87
Catford Hill, SE6 .123 DZ89
Catford Ms, SE6
off Holbeach Rd .123 EB87
Catford Rd, SE6 .123 EA87
Cathall Rd, E11 .67 ED62
Cathay St, SE16 .202 E5
Cathay Wk, Nthlt. UB5
off Brabazon Rd .78 CA68
Cathcart Dr, Orp. BR6 .145 ES103
Cathcart Hill, N19 .65 DJ62
Cathcart Rd, SW10 .100 DC79
Cathcart St, NW5 .83 DH65
Cathedral Piazza, SW1 .199 K7
Cathedral Pl, EC4 .197 H8
Cathedral St, SE1 .201 K2
Catherall Rd, N5 .66 DQ62
Catherine Cl, Brwd. CM15 .54 FU43
Grays RM16 .110 FZ75
Loughton IG10
off Roding Gdns .33 EM44
West Byfleet (Byfleet)
KT14 .152 BL114
Catherine Ct, N14
off Conisbee Ct .29 DJ43
Catherine Dr, Rich. TW9 .98 CL84
Sunbury-on-Thames TW16 .115 BT93
Catherine Gdns, Houns. TW3 .97 CD84
Catherine Griffiths Ct, EC1 .196 E4
Catherine Gro, SE10 .103 EB81
Catherine Howard Ct, Wey.
KT13 off Old Palace Rd .135 BP104
Catherine Pl, SW1 .199 K6
Harrow HA1 .61 CF57
Catherine Rd, Enf. EN3 .31 DY36
Romford RM2 .71 FH57
Surbiton KT6 .137 CK99
Catherine's Cl, West Dr. UB7
off Money La .94 BK76
Catherine St, WC2 .196 B10
Catherine Wheel All, E1 .197 N7
Catherine Wheel Rd, Brent.
TW8 .97 CK80
Catherine Wheel Yd, SW1 .199 K3
Cat Hill, Barn. EN4 .28 DE44
Cathles Rd, SW12 .121 DH86
Cathnor Rd, W12 .99 CV75
Catisfield Rd, Enf. EN3 .31 DY37
Catlin Cres, Shep. TW17 .135 BR99
Catlin Gdns, Gdse. RH9 .186 DV130
Catling Cl, SE23 .122 DW90
Catlins La, Pnr. HA5 .59 BV55
Catlin St, SE16 .202 C10
Cator Cl, Croy. (New Adgtn.)
CR0 .162 EE111
Cator Cres, Croy. (New Adgtn.)
CR0 .161 ED111
Cator La, Beck. BR3 .143 DZ96
Cato Rd, SW4 .101 DK83
Cator Rd, SE26 .123 DX93
Carshalton SM5 .158 DF106
Cator St, SE15 .102 DT79
Cato St, W1 .194 C7
Catsey La, Bushey WD23 .40 CC45
Catsey Wds, Bushey WD23 .40 CC45
Catterick Cl, N11 .44 DG51
Catterick Way, Borwd. WD6 .26 CM39
Cattistock Rd, SE9 .124 EL92
CATTLEGATE, Enf. .13 DL33
Cattlegate Hill, Pot.B. (Northaw)
EN6 .13 DK31
Cattlegate Rd, Enf. EN2 .13 DL34
Potters Bar EN6 .13 DK31
Cattley Cl, Barn. EN5
off Wood St .27 CY42
Cattlins Cl, Wal.Cr. EN7 .14 DT29
Catton St, WC1 .196 B7
Caulfield Rd, E6 .87 EM66
SE15 .102 DV82
Causeway, The, N2 .64 DE56
SW18 .100 DB84
SW19 .119 CX92
Carshalton SM5 .140 DG104
Chessington KT9 .156 CL105
Esher (Clay.) KT10 .155 CF108
Feltham TW14 .95 BU84
Hounslow TW4 .95 BU84
Potters Bar EN6 .12 DC31
Staines TW18 .113 BC91
Causeway, The, Sutt. SM2 .158 DC109
Teddington TW11
off Broad St .117 CF93
Causeway Cl, Pot.B. EN6 .12 DD31
Causeway Ct, Wok. GU21
off Bingham Dr .166 AT118
Causeyware Rd, N9 .46 DV45
Causton Rd, N6 .65 DH59
Causton Sq, Dag. RM10 .88 FA66
Causton St, SW1 .199 N9
Cautley Av, SW4 .121 DJ85
Cavalier Cl, Rom. RM6 .70 EX56
Cavalier Gdns, Hayes UB3
off Hanover Circle .77 BR72
Cavalry Barracks, Houns. TW4 .96 BX83
Cavalry Cres, Houns. TW4 .96 BX84
Cavalry Gdns, SW15 .119 CY85
Cavaye Pl, SW10
off Fulham Rd .100 DC78
Cavell Cres, Dart. DA1 .108 FN84
Romford (Harold Wd.) RM3 .52 FL54
Cavell Dr, Enf. EN2 .29 DN40
Cavell Rd, N17 .46 DR52
Waltham Cross (Chsht.)
EN7 .14 DT27
Cavell St, E1 .84 DV71
Cavell Way, Epsom KT19 .156 CN112
Cavendish Av, N3 .44 DA54
NW8 .194 A1
W13 .79 CG71
Erith DA8 .107 FC79
Harrow HA1 .61 CD63
Hornchurch RM12 .89 FH65
New Malden KT3 .139 CV99
Ruislip HA4 .59 BV64
Sevenoaks TN13 .190 FG122
Sidcup DA15 .126 EU87
Welling DA16 .105 ET83
Woodford Green IG8 .48 EH53
Cavendish Cl, N18 .46 DV50
NW6 off Cavendish Rd .81 CZ66
NW8 .194 A2
Amersham HP6 .20 AV39
Hayes UB4
off Westacott .77 BS71
Sunbury-on-Thames TW16 .115 BT93
Cavendish Ct, EC3 .197 N8
Rickmansworth (Crox.Grn.)
WD3 off Mayfare .23 BR43
Sunbury-on-Thames TW16 .115 BT93
Cavendish Cres, Borwd. (Elstree)
WD6 .26 CN42
Hornchurch RM12 .89 FH65
Cavendish Dr, E11 .67 ED60
Edgware HA8 .42 CM51
Esher (Clay.) KT10 .155 CE106
Cavendish Gdns, Bark. IG11 .69 ES64
Ilford IG1 .69 EN60
Redhill RH1 .184 DG133
Romford RM6 .70 EY57
Cavendish Ms N, W1 .195 J6
Cavendish Ms S, W1 .195 J7
Cavendish Par, Houns. TW4
off Bath Rd .96 BY82
Cavendish Pl, W1 .195 J8
Cavendish Rd, E4 .47 EC51
N4 .65 DN58
N18 .46 DV50
NW6 .81 CY66
SW12 .121 DH86
SW19 .120 DD94
W4 .98 CQ81
Barnet EN5 .27 CW41
Croydon CR0 .141 DP102
New Malden KT3 .139 CT99
Redhill RH1 .184 DG134
Sunbury-on-Thames TW16 .115 BT93
Sutton SM2 .158 DC108
Weybridge KT13 .153 BQ108
Woking GU22 .166 AX119
Cavendish Sq, W1 .195 J8
Longfield DA3 .149 FX97
Cavendish St, N1 .197 K1
Cavendish Ter, Felt. TW13
off High St .115 BU89
Cavendish Way, W.Wick. BR4 .143 EB102
Cavenham Cl, Wok. GU22 .166 AY119
Cavenham Gdns, Horn. RM11 .72 FJ57
Ilford IG1 .69 ER62
Caverleigh Way, Wor.Pk. KT4 .139 CU102
Cave Rd, E13 .86 EH68
Richmond TW10 .117 CJ91
Caversham Av, N13 .45 DN48
Sutton SM3 .139 CY103
Caversham Ct, N11 .44 DG48
Caversham Flats, SW3
off Caversham St .100 DF79
Caversham Rd, N15 .66 DQ56
NW5 .83 DJ65
Kingston upon Thames
KT1 .138 CM96
Caversham St, SW3 .100 DF79
Caverswall St, W12 .81 CW72
Caveside Cl, Chis. BR7 .145 EN95
Cave St, N1 off Carnegie St .83 DM68
Cavill's Wk, Chig. IG7 .50 EW47
Romford RM4 .50 EX47
Cawdor Av, S.Ock. RM15 .91 FU73
Cawdor Cres, W7 .97 CG77
Cawnpore St, SE19 .122 DS92
Cawsey Way, Wok. GU21 .166 AY117
Caxton Av, Add. KT15 .152 BG107
Caxton Dr, Uxb. UB8
off Chiltern Vw Rd .76 BK68
Caxton Gro, E3 .85 EA69
★ Caxton Hall, SW1 .199 L6
Caxton La, Oxt. RH8 .188 EL131
Caxton Ms, Brent. TW8
off The Butts .97 CK79
Caxton Ri, Red. RH1 .184 DG133
Caxton Rd, N22 .45 DM54
SW19 .120 DC92
W12 .99 CX75
Southall UB2 .96 BX76
Caxton St, SW1 .199 L6
Caxton St N, E16
off Victoria Dock Rd .86 EF73
Caxton Way, Rom. RM1 .71 FE56
Watford WD18 .23 BR44
Cayenne Ct, SE1 .202 A3
Caygill Cl, Brom. BR2 .144 EF98
Cayley Cl, Wall. SM6 .159 DL108
Cayley Rd, Sthl. UB2
off McNair Rd .96 CB76
Cayton Pl, EC1 .197 K3
Cayton Rd, Couls. CR5 .175 DJ122
Greenford UB6 .79 CE68
Cayton St, EC1 .197 K3
Cazenove Rd, E17 .47 EA53
N16 .66 DT61
Cearns Ho, E6 .86 EK67
Cearn Way, Couls. CR5 .175 DM115
Cecil Av, Bark. IG11 .87 ER66
Enfield EN1 .30 DT42
Grays RM16 .110 FZ75
Hornchurch RM11 .72 FL55
Wembley HA9 .62 CM64
Cecil Cl, W5 off Helena Rd .79 CK71
Ashford TW15 .115 BQ93
Chessington KT9 .155 CK105
Cecil Ct, WC2 .199 N1
Barnet EN5 .27 CX41
Cecile Pk, N8 .65 DL58
Cecilia Cl, N2 .64 DC55
★ Cecilia Coleman Gall, NW8
off St. John's Wd High St .82 DD68
Cecilia Rd, E8 .66 DU64
Cecil Pk, Pnr. HA5 .60 BY56
Cecil Pl, Mitch. CR4 .140 DF99
Cecil Rd, E11 .68 EE62
E13 .86 EG67
E17 .47 EA53
N10 .45 DH54
N14 .45 DJ46
NW9 .62 CS55
NW10 .80 CS67
SW19 .120 DB94
W3 .80 CQ71
Ashford TW15 .115 BQ94
Croydon CR0 .141 DM100
Enfield EN2 .30 DR42
Gravesend DA11 .131 GF88
Harrow HA3 .61 CE55
Hounslow TW3 .96 CC82
Ilford IG1 .69 EP63
Iver SL0 .75 BE72
Potters Bar EN6 .11 CU32
Romford RM6 .70 EX59
Sutton SM1 .157 CZ107
Waltham Cross (Chsht.)
EN8 .15 DX32
★ Cecil Sharp Ho, NW1 .82 DG67
Cecil St, Wat. WD24 .23 BV38
Cecil Way, Brom. BR2 .144 EG102
Cedar Av, Barn. EN4 .44 DE45
Cobham KT11 .170 BW115
Enfield EN3 .30 DW40
Gravesend DA12 .131 GJ91
Hayes UB3 .77 BU72
Romford RM6 .70 EY57
Ruislip HA4 .78 BW65
Sidcup DA15 .126 EU87
Twickenham TW2 .116 CB86
Upminster RM14 .72 FN63
Waltham Cross EN8 .15 DX33
West Drayton UB7 .76 BM74
Cedar Cl, SE21 .122 DQ88
SW15 .118 CR91
Borehamwood WD6 .26 CP42
Brentwood CM13 .55 GD45
Bromley BR2 .144 EL104
Buckhurst Hill IG9 .48 EK47
Carshalton SM5 .158 DF107
East Molesey KT8
off Cedar Rd .137 CE98
Epsom KT17 .157 CT114
Esher KT10 .154 BZ108
Iver SL0 off Thornbridge Rd .75 BC66
Potters Bar EN6 .12 DA30
Romford RM7 .71 FC56
Staines TW18 .134 BJ97
Swanley BR8 .147 FC96
Warlingham CR6 .177 DY118
Cedar Copse, Brom. BR1 .145 EM96
Cedar Ct, E11
off Grosvenor Rd .68 EH57
N1 off Essex Rd .84 DQ66
SE9 .124 EL86
SW19 .119 CX90
Egham TW20 .113 BA91
Epping CM16 .18 EU31
Cedar Cres, Brom. BR2 .144 EL104
Cedarcroft Rd, Chess. KT9 .156 CM105
Cedar Dr, N2 .64 DE56
Dartford (Sutt.H.) DA4 .148 FP96
Leatherhead (Fetch.) KT22 .171 CE123
Loughton IG10 .33 EP40
Pinner HA5 .40 CA51
Cedar Gdns, Sutt. SM2 .158 DC107
Upminster RM14 .72 FQ62
Woking GU21
off St. John's Rd .166 AV118
Cedar Gro, W5 .98 CL76
Bexley DA5 .126 EW86
Southall UB1 .78 CA71
Weybridge KT13 .153 BQ105
Cedar Hts, Rich. TW10 .118 CL88
Cedar Hill, Epsom KT18 .172 CQ116
Cedar Ho, Croy. CR0 .161 EB107
Sunbury-on-Thames TW16 .115 BT94
Cedarhurst, Brom. BR1
off Elstree Hill .124 EE94
Cedarhurst Dr, SE9 .124 EJ85
Cedar Lawn Av, Barn. EN5 .27 CY43
Cedar Mt, SE9 .124 EK88
Cedarne Rd, SW6 .100 DB80
Cedar Pk, Cat. CR3 .176 DS121
Chigwell IG7
off High Rd .49 EP49
Cedar Pk Gdns, Rom. RM6 .70 EX59
Cedar Pk Rd, Enf. EN2 .30 DQ38
Cedar Pl, SE7 off Floyd Rd .104 EJ78
Northwood HA6 .39 BQ51
Cedar Ri, N14 .44 DG45
Cedar Ri, S.Ock. RM15
off Sycamore Way .91 FX70
Cedar Rd, N17 .46 DT53
NW2 .63 CW63
Brentwood CM13 .55 GD44
Bromley BR1 .144 EJ96
Cobham KT11 .153 BV114
Croydon CR0 .142 DS103
Dartford DA1 .128 FK88
East Molesey KT8 .137 CE98
Enfield EN2 .29 DP38
Erith DA8 .107 FG81
Feltham TW14 .115 BR88
Grays RM16 .111 GG76
Hornchurch RM12 .72 FJ62
Hounslow TW4 .96 BW82
Romford RM7 .71 FC56
Sutton SM2 .158 DC107
Teddington TW11 .117 CG92
Watford WD19 .24 BW44
Weybridge KT13 .152 BN105
Woking GU22 .166 AV120
Cedars, Bans. SM7 .158 DF114
Cedars, The, E15 off Portway .86 EF67
W13 off Heronsforde .79 CJ72
Buckhurst Hill IG9 .48 EG46
Leatherhead KT22 .172 CL121
Reigate RH2 .184 DD134
Teddington TW11
off Adelaide Rd .117 CF93
West Byfleet (Byfleet)
KT14 .152 BM112
Cedars Av, E17 .67 EA57
Mitcham CR4 .140 DG98
Rickmansworth WD3 .38 BJ46
Cedars Cl, NW4 .63 CX55
Gerrards Cross (Chal.St.P.)
SL9 .36 AY50
Cedars Ct, N9 off Church St .46 DS47
Cedars Dr, Uxb. UB10 .76 BM68
Cedars Ms, SW4
off Cedars Rd .101 DH84
Cedars Rd, E15 .86 EE65
N9 off Church St .46 DU47
N21 .45 DP47
SW4 .101 DH83
SW13 .99 CT82
W4 .98 CQ78
Beckenham BR3 .143 DY96
Croydon CR0 .141 DL104
Kingston upon Thames
KT1 .137 CJ95
Morden SM4 .140 DA98
Cedars Wk, Rick. (Chorl.) WD3 .21 BF42
Cedar Ter, Rich. TW9 .98 CL84
Cedar Ter Rd, Sev. TN13 .191 FJ123
Cedar Tree Gro, SE27 .121 DP92
Cedarville Gdns, SW16 .121 DM93
Cedar Vista, Rich. TW9
off Kew Rd .98 CL81
Cedar Wk, Esher (Clay.)
KT10 .155 CF107
Kenley CR8 .176 DQ116
Tadworth (Kgswd.) KT20 .173 CY120
Waltham Abbey EN9 .15 ED34
Cedar Way, NW1 .83 DK66
Slough SL3 .92 AY78
Sunbury-on-Thames TW16 .115 BS94
Cedar Wd Dr, Wat. WD25 .23 BV35
Cedra Ct, N16 .66 DU60
Cedric Av, Rom. RM1 .71 FE55
Cedric Rd, SE9 .125 EQ90
Celadon Cl, Enf. EN3 .31 DY41
Celandine Cl, E14 .85 EA71
South Ockendon RM15 .91 FW70
Celandine Dr, E8 .84 DT66
SE28 .88 EV74
Celandine Rd, Walt. KT12 .154 BY105
Celandine Way, E15 .86 EE69
Celbridge Ms, W2
off Porchester Rd .82 DB72
Celedon Cl, Grays RM16 .110 FY75
Celestial Gdns, SE13 .103 ED84
Celia Cres, Ashf. TW15 .114 BK93
Celia Rd, N19 .65 DJ63
Cell Fm Av, Wind. (Old Wind.)
SL4 .112 AV85
Celtic Av, Brom. BR2 .144 EE97
Celtic Rd, W.Byf. (Byfleet)
KT14 .152 BL114
Celtic St, E14 .85 EB71
Cement Block Cotts, Grays
RM17 .110 GC79
Cemetery La, SE7 .104 EL79
Shepperton TW17 .135 BP101
Waltham Abbey EN9 .16 EF25
Cemetery Rd, E7 .68 EF63
N17 .46 DS52
SE2 .106 EV80
Cenacle Cl, NW3 .64 DA62
★ Cenotaph, The, SW1 .199 P4
Centaurs Business Cen, Islw.
TW7 .97 CG79
Centaur St, SE1 .200 C6
Centaury Ct, Grays RM17 .110 GD79
Centenary Est, Enf. EN3 .31 DZ42
Centenary Rd, Enf. EN3 .31 DZ42
Centenary Wk, Loug. IG10 .32 EH41
Centenary Way, Amer. HP6 .20 AT38
Centennial Av, Borwd. (Elstree)
WD6 .41 CH45
Centennial Pk, Borwd. (Elstree)
WD6 .41 CJ45
Central Av, E11 .67 ED61
N2 .44 DD54
N9 .46 DS48
SW11 .100 DF80
Enfield EN1 .30 DV40
Gravesend DA12 .131 GH89
Grays RM20 .109 FT77
Hayes UB3 .77 BU73
Hounslow TW3 .96 CC84
Pinner HA5 .60 BZ58
South Ockendon (Aveley)
RM15 .108 FQ75
Tilbury RM18 .111 GG81
Wallington SM6 .159 DL106
Central Av, Wal.Cr. EN8 .15 DY33
Welling DA16 .105 ET82
West Molesey KT8 .136 BZ98
Central Circ, NW4
off Hendon Way .63 CV57
★ Central Criminal Ct
(Old Bailey), EC4 .196 G8
Central Dr, Horn. RM12 .72 FL62
Central Gdns, Mord. SM4
off Central Rd .140 DB99
Central Hill, SE19 .122 DR92
Central Mkts, EC1 .196 G7
H Central Middlesex Hosp,
NW10 .80 CQ69
Central Par, Croy. (New Adgtn.)
CR0 .161 EC110
Feltham TW14 .116 BW87
Greenford UB6 .79 CG69
Hounslow TW5
off Heston Rd .96 CA80
Surbiton KT6
off St. Mark's Hill .138 CL100
Central Pk Av, Dag. RM10 .71 FB62
Central Pk Est, Houns. TW4 .116 BX85
Central Pk Rd, E6 .86 EK68
Central Pl, SE25
off Portland Rd .142 DV98
Central Rd, Dart. DA1 .128 FL85
Morden SM4 .140 DA99
Wembley HA0 .61 CH64
Worcester Park KT4 .139 CU103
Central Sch Footpath, SW14 .98 CQ83
Central Sq, NW11 .64 DB58
Wembley HA9
off Station Gro .62 CL64
West Molesey KT8 .136 BZ98
Central St, EC1 .197 H3
Central Way, NW10 .80 CQ69
SE28 .88 EU73
Carshalton SM5 .158 DE108
Feltham TW14 .115 BV85
Oxted RH8 .187 ED127
Centre, The, Felt. TW13 .115 BU89
Walton-on-Thames KT12 .135 BT102
Centre at the Circ, W1 .199 L1
Centre Av, W3 .80 CR74
W10 off Harrow Rd .81 CW69
Epping CM16 .17 ET32
Centre Cl, Epp. CM16
off Centre Av .17 ET32
Centre Common Rd, Chis.
BR7 .125 EQ93
Centre Ct Shop Cen, SW19 .119 CZ93
Centre Dr, Epp. CM16 .17 ET32
Centre Grn, Epp. CM16
off Centre Av .17 ET32
Centrepoint, WC1 .195 N8
Centre Rd, E7 .68 EG61
E11 .68 EG61
Dagenham RM10 .89 FB68
Centre St, E2 .84 DV68
Centre Way, E17 .47 EC52
N9 .46 DW47
Centreway, Ilf. IG1 .69 EQ61
Centric Cl, NW1
off Oval Rd .83 DH67
Centurion Cl, N7 .83 DM66
Centurion Ct, Wall. SM6
off Wandle Rd .141 DH103
Centurion La, E3
off Libra Rd .85 DZ68
Centurion Way, Erith DA18 .106 FA76
Purfleet RM19 .108 FM77
Century Cl, NW4 .63 CX57
Century Ct, Wok. GU21 .167 AZ116
Century Ms, E5
off Lower Clapton Rd .66 DW63
Century Pk, Wat. WD17 .24 BW43
Century Rd, E17 .67 DY55
Staines TW18 .113 BC92
Cephas Av, E1 .84 DW70
Cephas St, E1 .84 DW70
Ceres Rd, SE18 .105 ET77
Cerise Rd, SE15 .102 DU81
Cerne Cl, Hayes UB4 .78 BX73
Cerne Rd, Grav. DA12 .131 GL91
Morden SM4 .140 DC100
Cerney Ms, W2
off Gloucester Ter .82 DD73
Cerotus Pl, Cher. KT16 .133 BF101
Cervantes Ct, W2
off Inverness Ter .82 DB72
Northwood HA6
off Green La .39 BT52
Cervia Way, Grav. DA12 .131 GM90
Cester St, E2 off Whiston Rd .84 DU67
Ceylon Rd, W14 .99 CX76
Chace Av, Pot.B. EN6 .12 DD32
Chadacre Av, Ilf. IG5 .69 EM55
Chadacre Rd, Epsom KT17 .157 CV107
Chadbourn St, E14 .85 EB71
Chadd Dr, Brom. BR1 .144 EL97
Chadd Grn, E13 .86 EG67
Chadfields, Til. RM18 .111 GG80
Chadview Ct, Rom. (Chad.Hth.)
RM6 .70 EX59
Chadville Gdns, Rom. RM6 .70 EX57
Chadway, Dag. RM8 .70 EW60
Chadwell Av, Rom. RM6 .70 EV59
Waltham Cross (Chsht.)
EN8 .14 DW28
Chadwell Bypass, Grays
RM16 .111 GF78
CHADWELL HEATH, Rom. .70 EX58
⇌ Chadwell Heath .70 EX59
Chadwell Heath La, Rom.
RM6 .70 EV57
Chadwell Hill, Grays RM16 .111 GH78
Chadwell Rd, Grays RM17 .110 GC77
CHADWELL ST. MARY, Grays .111 GJ76
Chadwell St, EC1 .196 E2
Chadwick Av, E4 .47 ED49
N21 .29 DM43
SW19 .120 DA93

Cha - Cha

Chadwick Cl, SW15 ... 119 CT87
W7 off Westcott Cres ... 79 CF71
Gravesend (Nthflt.) DA11 ... 130 GE89
Teddington TW11 ... 117 CG93
Chadwick Dr, Rom. (Harold Wd.)
RM3 ... 52 FK54
Chadwick Pl, Surb. KT6 ... 137 CJ101
Chadwick Rd, E11 ... 68 EE59
NW10 ... 81 CT67
SE15 ... 102 DT82
Ilford IG1 ... 69 EP62
Chadwick St, SW1 ... 199 N7
Chadwick Way, SE28 ... 88 EX73
Chadwin Rd, E13 ... 86 EH71
Chadworth Way, Esher (Clay.)
KT10 ... 155 CD106
Chaffers Mead, Ashtd. KT21 ... 172 CM116
Chaffinch Av, Croy. CR0 ... 143 DX100
Chaffinch Cl, N9 ... 47 DX46
Croydon CR0 ... 143 DX100
Surbiton KT6 ... 138 CN104
Chaffinch La, Wat. WD18 ... 39 BT45
Chaffinch Rd, Beck. BR3 ... 143 DY95
CHAFFORD HUNDRED,
Grays ... 110 FY76
⇌ Chafford Hundred ... 109 FV77
Chafford Wk, Rain. RM13 ... 90 FJ68
Chafford Way, Rom. RM6 ... 70 EW56
Chagford St, NW1 ... 194 D5
Chailey Av, Enf. EN1 ... 30 DT40
Chailey Cl, Houns. TW5
off Springwell Rd ... 96 BX81
Chailey Pl, Walt. KT12 ... 154 BY105
Chailey St, E5 ... 66 DW62
Chairmans Av, Uxb. (Denh.)
UB9 ... 57 BF58
Chalbury Wk, N1 ... 83 DM68
Chalcombe Rd, SE2 ... 106 EV76
Chalcot Cl, Sutt. SM2 ... 158 DA108
Chalcot Cres, NW1 ... 82 DF67
Chalcot Gdns, NW3 ... 82 DF65
Chalcot Ms, SW16 ... 121 DL90
Chalcot Rd, NW1 ... 82 DG66
Chalcot Sq, NW1 ... 82 DG66
Chalcott Gdns, Surb. KT6 ... 137 CJ102
Chalcroft Rd, SE13 ... 124 EE85
CHALDON, Cat. ... 175 DN124
Chaldon Common Rd, Cat.
CR3 ... 176 DQ124
Chaldon Path, Th.Hth. CR7 ... 141 DP98
Chaldon Rd, SW6 ... 99 CY80
Caterham CR3 ... 176 DR124
Chaldon Way, Couls. CR5 ... 175 DL117
Chale Rd, SW2 ... 121 DL86
Chalet Cl, Bex. DA5 ... 127 FD91
Chalet Est, NW7 ... 43 CU49
Chale Wk, Sutt. SM2
off Hulverston Cl ... 158 DB109
⇌ Chalfont & Latimer ... 20 AW39
⊖ Chalfont & Latimer ... 20 AW39
Chalfont Av, Amer. HP6 ... 20 AX39
Wembley HA9 ... 80 CP65
CHALFONT COMMON, Ger.Cr. 37 AZ49
Chalfont Ct, NW9 ... 63 CT55
Chalfont Grn, N9 ... 46 DS48
Chalfont La, Ger.Cr. SL9 ... 37 BC51
Rickmansworth (Chorl.)
WD3 ... 21 BB43
Rickmansworth (Map.Cr.)
WD3 ... 37 BC51
Chalfont Pk, Ger.Cr. (Chal.St.P.)
SL9 ... 57 AZ55
Chalfont Rd, N9 ... 46 DS48
SE25 ... 142 DT97
Gerrards Cross SL9 ... 37 BB48
Hayes UB3 ... 95 BU75
Rickmansworth (Map.Cr.)
WD3 ... 37 BD49
CHALFONT ST. GILES ... 36 AV47
CHALFONT ST. PETER, Ger.Cr. 37 AZ53
🅗 Chalfonts & Gerrards Cross
Hosp, Ger.Cr. SL9 ... 36 AX53
Chalfont Sta Rd, Amer. HP7 ... 20 AW40
Chalfont Wk, Pnr. HA5
off Willows Cl ... 40 BW54
Chalfont Way, W13 ... 97 CH76
Chalford Cl, W.Mol. KT8 ... 136 CA98
Chalforde Gdns, Rom. RM2 ... 71 FH56
Chalford Rd, SE21 ... 122 DR91
Chalford Wk, Wdf.Grn. IG8 ... 48 EK53
Chalgrove Av, Mord. SM4 ... 140 DA99
Chalgrove Cres, Ilf. IG5 ... 48 EL54
Chalgrove Gdns, N3 ... 63 CY55
Chalgrove Rd, N17 ... 46 DV53
Sutton SM2 ... 158 DD108
Chalice Cl, Wall. SM6
off Lavender Vale ... 159 DK107
Chalice Way, Green. DA9 ... 129 FS85
Chalkenden Cl, SE20 ... 122 DV94
⊖ Chalk Farm ... 82 DG66
Chalk Fm Rd, NW1 ... 82 DG66
Chalk Hill, Wat. WD19 ... 24 BX44
Chalk Hill Rd, W6
off Shortlands ... 99 CX77
Chalkhill Rd, Wem. HA9 ... 62 CP62
Chalklands, Wem. HA9 ... 62 CQ62
Chalk La, Ashtd. KT21 ... 172 CM119
Barnet EN4 ... 28 DF42
Epsom KT18 ... 172 CR115
Chalkley Cl, Mitch. CR4 ... 140 DF96
Chalkmill Dr, Enf. EN1 ... 30 DV41
Chalk Paddock, Epsom KT18 .172 CR115
Chalk Pit Av, Orp. BR5 ... 146 EW97
Chalkpit La, Bet. RH3 ... 182 CP133
Oxted RH8 ... 187 EC125
Chalk Pit Rd, Bans. SM7 ... 174 DA117
Epsom KT18 ... 172 CQ119
Chalk Pit Way, Sutt. SM1 ... 158 DC106
Chalkpit Wd, Oxt. RH8 ... 187 ED127
Chalk Rd, E13 ... 86 EH71
Chalkstone Cl, Well. DA16 ... 106 EU81
Chalkwell Pk Av, Enf. EN1 ... 30 DS42
Chalky Bk, Grav. DA11 ... 131 GG91
Chalky La, Chess. KT9 ... 155 CK109
Challacombe Cl, Brwd. CM13 .55 GB46
Challenge Cl, Grav. DA12 ... 131 GM91
Challenge Ct, Lthd. KT22 ... 171 CH119
Challenge Rd, Ashf. TW15 ... 115 BQ90
Challice Way, SW2 ... 121 DM88
Challin St, SE20 ... 142 DW95
Challis Rd, Brent. TW8 ... 97 CK78
Challock Cl, West. (Bigg.H.)
TN16 ... 178 EJ116
Challoner Cl, N2 ... 44 DD54
Challoner Cres, W14
off Challoner St ... 99 CZ78
Challoners Cl, E.Mol. KT8 ... 137 CD98
Challoner St, W14 ... 99 CZ78
Chalmers Ct, Rick. (Crox.Grn.)
WD3 ... 22 BM44
Chalmers Rd, Ashf. TW15 ... 115 BP91
Banstead SM7 ... 174 DD115
Chalmers Rd E, Ashf. TW15 ... 115 BP91
Chalmers Wk, SE17
off Hillingdon St ... 101 DP79
Chalmers Way, Felt. TW14 ... 115 BU85
Chaloner Ct, SE1 ... 201 K4
Chalsey Rd, SE4 ... 103 DZ84
Chalton Dr, N2 ... 64 DC58
Chalton St, NW1 ... 195 N2
Chalvey Gdns, Slou. SL1 ... 92 AS75
Chalvey Pk, Slou. SL1 ... 92 AS75
Chalvey Rd E, Slou. SL1 ... 92 AS75
Chalvey Rd W, Slou. SL1 ... 92 AS75
Chamberlain Cl, SE28
off Broadwater Rd ... 105 ER76
Chamberlain Cotts, SE5
off Camberwell Gro ... 102 DR81
Chamberlain Cres, W.Wick.
BR4 ... 143 EB102
Chamberlain Gdns, Houns.
TW3 ... 96 CC81
Chamberlain La, Pnr. HA5 ... 59 BU56
Chamberlain Pl, E17 ... 67 DY55
Chamberlain Rd, N2 ... 44 DC54
N9 ... 46 DU48
W13 off Midhurst Rd ... 97 CG75
Chamberlain St, NW1
off Regents Pk Rd ... 82 DF66
Chamberlain Wk, Felt. TW13
off Burgess Cl ... 116 BY91
Chamberlain Way, Pnr. HA5 ... 59 BV55
Surbiton KT6 ... 138 CL101
Chamberlayne Av, Wem. HA9 .62 CL61
Chamberlayne Rd, NW10 ... 81 CX69
Chambersbury La, Hem.H. HP3 .6 BN25
Chambers Cl, Green. DA9 ... 129 FU85
Chambers Gdns, N2 ... 44 DD53
Chambers La, NW10 ... 81 CV66
Chambers Pl, S.Croy. CR2
off Rolleston Rd ... 160 DR108
Chambers Rd, N7 ... 65 DL63
Chambers St, SE16 ... 202 B4
Chamber St, E1 ... 84 DT73
Chambon Pl, W6
off Beavor La ... 99 CU77
Chambord St, E2 ... 84 DT69
Champion Cres, SE26 ... 123 DY91
Champion Gro, SE5 ... 102 DR83
Champion Hill, SE5 ... 102 DR83
Champion Hill Est, SE5 ... 102 DS83
Champion Pk, SE5 ... 102 DR82
Champion Pk Est, SE5
off Denmark Hill ... 102 DR83
Champion Rd, SE26 ... 123 DY91
Upminster RM14 ... 72 FP61
Champness Cl, SE27
off Rommany Rd ... 122 DR91
Champness Rd, Bark. IG11 ... 87 ET65
Champneys Cl, Sutt. SM2 ... 157 CZ108
Chance Cl, Grays RM16 ... 110 FZ76
Chancellor Gdns, S.Croy.
CR2 ... 159 DP109
Chancellor Gro, SE21 ... 122 DQ89
Chancellor Pas, E14 ... 204 A3
Chancellor Pl, NW9 ... 43 CT54
Chancellors Rd, W6 ... 99 CW78
Chancellors St, W6 ... 99 CW78
Chancellor Way, Sev. TN13 ... 190 FG122
Chancelot Rd, SE2 ... 106 EV77
Chancel St, SE1 ... 200 F2
Chancery Ct, Dart. DA1
off Downs Av ... 128 FN87
⊖ Chancery Lane ... 196 D7
Chancery La, WC2 ... 196 D8
Beckenham BR3 ... 143 EB96
Chancery Ms, SW17 ... 120 DE89
Chance St, E1 ... 197 P4
E2 ... 197 P4
Chanctonbury Chase, Red.
RH1 ... 185 DH134
Chanctonbury Cl, SE9 ... 125 EP90
Chanctonbury Gdns, Sutt.
SM2 ... 158 DB108
Chanctonbury Way, N12 ... 43 CZ49
Chandler Av, E16 ... 86 EG71
Chandler Cl, Hmptn. TW12 ... 136 CA95
Chandler Rd, Loug. IG10 ... 33 EP39
Chandlers Cl, Felt. TW14 ... 115 BT87
Chandlers Dr, Erith DA8 ... 107 FD77
Chandler's La, Rick. WD3 ... 22 BL37
Chandlers Ms, E14 ... 203 P4
Chandler St, E1 ... 202 E2
Chandlers Way, SW2 ... 121 DN87
Romford RM1 ... 71 FE57
Chandler Way, SE15 ... 102 DT80
Chandon Lo, Sutt. SM2
off Devonshire Rd ... 158 DC108
Chandos Av, E17 ... 47 EA54
N14 ... 45 DJ48
N20 ... 44 DC46
W5 ... 97 CJ77
Chandos Cl, Amer. HP6 ... 20 AW38
Buckhurst Hill IG9 ... 48 EH47
Chandos Cres, Edg. HA8 ... 42 CM52
Chandos Mall, Slou. SL1
off High St ... 92 AT75
Chandos Par, Edg. HA8
off Chandos Cres ... 42 CM52
Chandos Pl, WC2 ... 199 P1
Chandos Rd, E15 ... 67 ED64
Chandos Rd, N2 ... 44 DD54
N17 ... 46 DS54
NW2 ... 63 CW64
NW10 ... 80 CS70
Borehamwood WD6 ... 26 CM40
Harrow HA1 ... 60 CC57
Pinner HA5 ... 60 BW59
Staines TW18 ... 113 BD92
Chandos St, W1 ... 195 J7
Chandos Way, NW11 ... 64 DB60
Change All, EC3 ... 197 L9
Chanlock Path, S.Ock. RM15
off Carnach Grn ... 91 FV73
Channel Cl, Houns. TW5 ... 96 CA81
Channel Gate Rd, NW10
off Old Oak La ... 81 CT69
Channelsea Rd, E15 ... 85 ED67
Channing Cl, Horn. RM11 ... 72 FM59
Channings, Wok. (Horsell)
GU21 ... 166 AY115
Chanton Dr, Epsom KT17 ... 157 CW110
Sutton SM2 ... 157 CW110
Chantress Cl, Dag. RM10 ... 89 FC67
Chantrey Cl, Ashtd. KT21 ... 171 CJ119
Chantrey Rd, SW9 ... 101 DM83
Chantreywood, Brwd. CM13 ... 55 GA48
Chantry, The, Uxb. UB8 ... 76 BM69
Chantry Cl, NW7
off Hendon Wd La ... 27 CT44
W9 off Elgin Av ... 81 CZ70
Enfield EN2 off Bedale Rd ... 30 DQ38
Harrow HA3 ... 62 CM57
Kings Langley WD4 ... 6 BN29
Sidcup DA14
off Ellenborough Rd ... 126 EY92
Sunbury-on-Thames TW16 ... 115 BU94
West Drayton UB7 ... 76 BK73
Chantry Ct, Cars. SM5 ... 140 DE104
Chantry Ho, Rain. RM13
off Chantry Way ... 89 FD68
Chantry Hurst, Epsom KT18 ... 172 CR115
Chantry La, Brom. BR2
off Bromley Common ... 144 EK99
St. Albans (Lon.Col.) AL2 ... 9 CK26
Chantry Pl, Har. HA3 ... 40 CB53
Chantry Rd, Cher. KT16 ... 134 BJ101
Chessington KT9 ... 156 CM106
Harrow HA3 ... 40 CB53
Chantry Sq, W8
off St. Mary's Pl ... 100 DB76
Chantry St, N1 ... 83 DP67
Chantry Way, Mitch. CR4 ... 140 DD97
Rainham RM13 ... 89 FD68
Chant Sq, E15 ... 85 ED66
Chant St, E15 ... 85 ED66
Chapel Av, Add. KT15 ... 152 BH105
Chapel Cl, Dart. DA1 ... 127 FE85
Grays RM20 ... 109 FV79
Hatfield AL9 ... 12 DD27
Watford WD25 ... 7 BT34
Chapel Ct, N2 ... 64 DE55
SE1 ... 201 K4
Chapel Cft, Kings L. (Chipper.)
WD4 ... 6 BG31
Chapel End, Ger.Cr. (Chal.St.P.)
SL9 off Austenwood La ... 36 AX54
Chapel Fm Rd, SE9 ... 125 EM90
Chapel Gro, Add. KT15 ... 152 BH105
Epsom KT18 ... 173 CW119
Chapel High Shop Prec, Brwd.
CM14 ... 54 FW47
Chapel Hill, Dart. DA1 ... 127 FE85
Chapel Ho St, E14 ... 204 C10
Chapel La, Chig. IG7 ... 49 ET48
Pinner HA5 ... 60 BX55
Romford RM6 ... 70 EX59
Slough (Stoke P.) SL2 ... 74 AV66
Uxbridge UB8 ... 76 BN72
Chapel Mkt, N1 ... 83 DN68
Chapel Ms, Wdf.Grn. IG8 ... 49 EN51
Chapelmount Rd, Wdf.Grn.
IG8 ... 49 EM51
Chapel Pk Rd, Add. KT15 ... 152 BH105
Chapel Path, E11 ... 68 EG58
Chapel Pl, EC2 ... 197 M3
N1 off Chapel Mkt ... 83 DN68
N17 off White Hart La ... 46 DT52
W1 ... 195 H9
Chapel Rd, SE27 ... 121 DP91
W13 ... 79 CH74
Bexleyheath DA7 ... 106 FA84
Epping CM16 ... 17 ET30
Hounslow TW3 ... 96 CB83
Ilford IG1 ... 69 EN62
Oxted RH8 ... 188 EJ130
Redhill RH1 ... 184 DF134
Tadworth KT20 ... 173 CW123
Twickenham TW1 ... 117 CH87
Warlingham CR6 ... 177 DX118
Chapel Row, Uxb. (Hare.)
UB9 ... 38 BJ53
Chapel Side, W2 ... 82 DB73
Chapel Sq, Vir.W. GU25 ... 132 AY98
Chapel Stones, N17 ... 46 DT53
Chapel St, NW1 ... 194 B7
SW1 ... 198 G6
Enfield EN2 ... 30 DQ41
Slough SL1 ... 92 AT75
Uxbridge UB8
off Trumper Way ... 76 BJ67
Woking GU21 ... 167 AZ117
Chapel Ter, Loug. IG10
off Forest Rd ... 32 EL42
Chapel Vw, S.Croy. CR2 ... 160 DV107
Chapel Wk, NW4 ... 63 CV56
Croydon CR0
off Wellesley Rd ... 142 DQ103
Chapel Way, N7
off Sussex Way ... 65 DM62
Abbots Langley (Bedmond)
WD5 ... 7 BT27
Epsom KT18 ... 173 CW119
Chapel Yd, SW18
off Wandsworth High St ... 120 DA85
Chaplaincy Gdns, Horn. RM11 .72 FL60
Chaplin Cl, SE1 ... 200 E4
Chaplin Cres, Sun. TW16 ... 115 BS93
Chaplin Rd, E15 ... 86 EE68
N17 ... 66 DT55
NW2 ... 81 CU65
Dagenham RM9 ... 88 EZ66
Wembley HA0 ... 79 CJ65
Chaplin Sq, N12 ... 44 DD52
Chapman Cl, West Dr. UB7 ... 94 BM76
Chapman Cres, Har. HA3 ... 62 CL57
Chapman Pk Ind Est, NW10 ... 81 CT65
Chapman Pl, N4 ... 65 DP61
Chapman Rd, E9 ... 85 DZ65
Belvedere DA17 ... 106 FA78
Croydon CR0 ... 141 DN102
Chapman's La, SE2 ... 106 EW77
Belvedere DA17 ... 106 EX77
Chapmans La, Orp. BR5 ... 146 EX96
Chapman Sq, SW19 ... 119 CX89
Chapmans Rd, Sev. (Sund.)
TN14 ... 180 EY124
Chapman St, E1 ... 84 DV73
Chapmans Yd, Wat. WD25
off New Rd ... 24 BW42
Chapone Pl, W1 ... 195 M9
Chapter Cl, W4
off Beaumont Rd ... 98 CQ76
Uxbridge UB10 ... 76 BM66
Chapter Ho Ct, EC4 ... 197 H9
Chapter Rd, NW2 ... 63 CU64
SE17 ... 101 DP78
Chapter St, SW1 ... 199 M9
Chapter Way, Hmptn. TW12 ... 116 CA91
Chara Pl, W4 ... 98 CR79
Charcot Ho, SW15
off Highcliffe Dr ... 119 CT86
Charcroft Gdns, Enf. EN3 ... 31 DX42
Chardin Rd, W4
off Elliott Rd ... 98 CS77
Chardmore Rd, N16 ... 66 DU60
Chard Rd, Houns. (Hthrw.Air.) TW6
off Heathrow Tunnel App ... 94 BN83
Chardwell Cl, E6
off Northumberland Rd ... 86 EL72
Charecroft Way, W12 ... 99 CX75
Charfield Ct, W9
off Shirland Rd ... 82 DB70
Charford Rd, E16 ... 86 EH71
Chargate Cl, Walt. KT12 ... 153 BT107
Chargeable La, E13 ... 86 EF70
Chargeable St, E16 ... 86 EF70
Chargrove Cl, SE16 ... 203 J4
Charing Cl, Orp. BR6 ... 163 ET105
⇌ Charing Cross ... 199 P2
⊖ Charing Cross ... 199 P2
Charing Cross, SW1 ... 199 P2
🅗 Charing Cross Hosp, W6 ... 99 CX79
Charing Cross Rd, WC2 ... 195 N8
Charlbert St, NW8 ... 82 DE68
Charlbury Av, Stan. HA7 ... 41 CK50
Charlbury Cl, Rom. RM3 ... 52 FJ51
Charlbury Cres, Rom. RM3 ... 52 FJ51
Charlbury Gdns, Ilf. IG3 ... 69 ET61
Charlbury Gro, W5 ... 79 CJ72
Charlbury Rd, Uxb. UB10 ... 58 BM62
Charldane Rd, SE9 ... 125 EP90
Charlecote Gro, SE26 ... 122 DV90
Charlecote Rd, Dag. RM8 ... 70 EY62
Charlemont Rd, E6 ... 87 EM69
Charles Babbage Cl, Chess.
KT9 ... 155 CJ108
Charles Barry Cl, SW4 ... 101 DJ83
Charles Burton Ct, E5
off Ashenden Rd ... 67 DY64
Charles Cl, Sid. DA14 ... 126 EV91
Charles Cobb Gdns, Croy.
CR0 ... 159 DN106
Charles Coveney Rd, SE15 ... 102 DT81
Charles Cres, Har. HA1 ... 61 CD59
Charles Dickens Ho, E2 ... 84 DV69
Charles Dickens Ter, SE20
off Maple Rd ... 122 DW94
Charlesfield, SE9 ... 124 EJ90
Charles Flemwell Ms, E16 ... 205 N3
Charles Gdns, Slou. SL2 ... 74 AV72
Charles Grinling Wk, SE18 ... 105 EN77
Charles Haller St, SW2
off Tulse Hill ... 121 DN87
Charles Ho, N17 off Love La ... 46 DT52
Charles La, NW8 ... 194 A1
Charles Pl, NW1 ... 195 L3
Charles Rd, E7 off Lens Rd ... 86 EJ66
SW19 ... 140 DA95
W13 ... 79 CG72
Dagenham RM10 ... 89 FD65
Romford RM6 ... 70 EX59
Sevenoaks (Bad.Mt.) TN14 ... 165 FB110
Staines TW18 ... 114 BK93
Charles II Pl, SW3
off King's Rd ... 100 DF78
Charles II St, SW1 ... 199 M2
Charles Sevright Dr, NW7 ... 43 CX50
Charles Sq, N1 ... 197 L3
Charles Sq Est, N1
off Pitfield St ... 84 DR69
Charles St, E16 ... 86 EK74
SW13 ... 98 CS82
W1 ... 199 H2
Chertsey KT16 ... 133 BF102
Croydon CR0 ... 142 DQ104
Enfield EN1 ... 30 DT43
Epping CM16 ... 18 EU32
Grays RM17 ... 110 GB79
Greenhithe DA9 ... 129 FT85
Hounslow TW3 ... 96 BZ82
Uxbridge UB10 ... 77 BP70
Charleston Cl, Felt. TW13
off Vineyard Rd ... 115 BU90
Charleston St, SE17 ... 201 J9
Charles Townsend Ho, EC1 ... 196 E3
Charles Whincup Rd, E16 ... 205 P2
Charleville Circ, SE26 ... 122 DU92
Charleville Rd, W14 ... 99 CY78
Charlie Chaplin Wk, SE1
off Waterloo Rd ... 83 DN74
Charlieville Rd, Erith DA8
off Northumberland Pk ... 107 FC80
Charlmont Rd, SW17 ... 120 DF93
Charlock Way, Wat. WD18 ... 23 BT44
Charlotte Av, Slou. SL2 ... 74 AT73
Charlotte Cl, Bexh. DA6 ... 126 EY85
Ilford IG6 off Connor Cl ... 49 EQ53
Charlotte Despard Av, SW11 .100 DG81
Charlotte Gdns, Rom. RM5 ... 51 FB51
Charlotte Ms, W1 ... 195 L6
W10 ... 81 CX72
W14 off Munden St ... 99 CY77
Charlotte Pl, NW9
off Uphill Dr ... 62 CQ57
SW1 ... 199 K9
W1 ... 195 L7
Grays RM20 ... 109 FV79
Charlotte Rd, EC2 ... 197 M4
SW13 ... 99 CT81
Dagenham RM10 ... 89 FB65
Wallington SM6 ... 159 DJ107
Charlotte Row, SW4 ... 101 DJ83
Charlotte Sq, Rich. TW10
off Greville Rd ... 118 CM86
Charlotte St, W1 ... 195 L6
Charlotte Ter, N1 ... 83 DM67
Charlow Cl, SW6
off Townmead Rd ... 100 DC82
CHARLTON, SE7 ... 104 EJ79
⇌ Charlton ... 104 EH78
★ Charlton Athletic FC, SE7 .104 EJ78
Charlton Av, Walt. KT12 ... 153 BV105
Charlton Ch La, SE7 ... 104 EJ78
Charlton Cl, Uxb. UB10 ... 59 BP61
Charlton Cres, Bark. IG11 ... 87 ET68
Charlton Dene, SE7 ... 104 EJ80
Charlton Dr, West. (Bigg.H.)
TN16 ... 178 EK117
Charlton Gdns, Couls. CR5 ... 175 DJ118
Charlton Kings, Wey. KT13 ... 135 BS104
Charlton Kings Rd, NW5 ... 65 DK64
Charlton La, SE7 ... 104 EK78
Shepperton TW17 ... 135 BS98
Charlton Pk La, SE7 ... 104 EK80
Charlton Pk Rd, SE7 ... 104 EK79
Charlton Pl, N1 ... 83 DP68
Charlton Rd, N9 ... 47 DX46
NW10 ... 80 CS67
SE3 ... 104 EG80
SE7 ... 104 EH80
Harrow HA3 ... 61 CK56
Shepperton TW17 ... 135 BQ97
Wembley HA9 ... 62 CM60
Charlton St, Grays RM20 ... 109 FX79
Charlton Way, SE3 ... 104 EE81
Charlwood, Croy. CR0 ... 161 DZ109
Charlwood Cl, Har. HA3
off Kelvin Cres ... 41 CE52
Charlwood Dr, Lthd. (Oxshott)
KT22 ... 171 CD115
Charlwood Pl, SW1 ... 199 L9
Charlwood Rd, SW15 ... 99 CX83
Charlwood Sq, Mitch. CR4 ... 140 DD97
Charlwood St, SW1 ... 199 L9
Charlwood Ter, SW15
off Cardinal Pl ... 99 CX84
Charman Rd, Red. RH1 ... 184 DE134
Charmian Av, Stan. HA7 ... 61 CK55
Charminster Av, SW19 ... 140 DB96
Charminster Ct, Surb. KT6 ... 137 CK101
Charminster Rd, SE9 ... 124 EK91
Worcester Park KT4 ... 139 CX102
Charmouth Rd, Well. DA16 ... 106 EW81
Charmwood La, Orp. BR6 ... 164 EV109
Charne, The, Sev. (Otford)
TN14 ... 181 FG117
Charnock, Swan. BR8 ... 147 FE98
Charnock Rd, E5 ... 66 DV62
Charnwood Av, SW19 ... 140 DA96
Charnwood Cl, N.Mal. KT3 ... 138 CS98
Charnwood Dr, E18 ... 68 EH55
Charnwood Gdns, E14 ... 204 A8
Charnwood Pl, N20 ... 44 DC48
Charnwood Rd, SE25 ... 142 DR99
Enfield EN1 ... 30 DV36
Uxbridge UB10 ... 76 BN68
Charnwood St, E5 ... 66 DU61
Charrington Rd, Croy. CR0
off Drayton Rd ... 141 DP103
Charrington St, NW1 ... 83 DK68
Charsley Cl, Amer. HP6 ... 20 AW39
Charsley Rd, SE6 ... 123 EB89
Charta Rd, Egh. TW20 ... 113 BC92
Chart Cl, Brom. BR2 ... 144 EE95
Croydon CR0
off Stockbury Rd ... 142 DW100
Charter Av, Ilf. IG2 ... 69 ER60
Charter Cl, Slou. SL1
off Osborne St ... 92 AT76
Charter Ct, N.Mal. KT3 ... 138 CS97
Charter Cres, Houns. TW4 ... 96 BY84
Charter Dr, Amer. HP6 ... 20 AT38
Bexley DA5 ... 126 EY87
★ Chartered Insurance
Institutes Mus,
EC2 off Aldermanbury ... 197 J8
★ Charterhouse, EC1 ... 196 G6
Charterhouse Av, Wem. HA0 ... 61 CJ63
Charterhouse Bldgs, EC1 ... 196 G5
Charterhouse Dr, Sev. TN13 ... 190 FG123
Charterhouse Ms, EC1 ... 196 G6
Charterhouse Rd, Orp. BR6 ... 146 EU104
Charterhouse Sq, EC1 ... 196 G6
Charterhouse St, EC1 ... 196 E7
Charteris Rd, N4 ... 65 DN60
NW6 ... 81 CZ67
Woodford Green IG8 ... 48 EH52
🅗 Charter Nightingale Hosp,
NW1 ... 194 C6
Charter Pl, Stai. TW18 ... 114 BG93
Uxbridge UB8 ... 76 BK66
Watford WD17 ... 24 BW41
Charter Rd, Kings.T. KT1 ... 138 CP97
Charter Rd, The, Wdf.Grn. IG8 .48 EE51
Charters Cl, SE19 ... 122 DS92
Charter Sq, Kings.T. KT1 ... 138 CP96
Charter Way, N3 ... 63 CZ56
N14 ... 29 DJ44
Chartfield Av, SW15 ... 119 CV85
Chartfield Pl, Wey. KT13
off Hanger Hill ... 153 BP106

★ Place of interest ⇌ Railway station ⊖ London Underground station DLR Docklands Light Railway station Tramlink station 🅗 Hospital

233

Cha - Che

Chartfield Sq, SW15 119 CX85
Chartham Gro, SE27
off Royal Circ 121 DN90
Chartham Rd, SE25 142 DV97
Chart Hills Cl, SE28
off Fairway Dr 88 EY72
Chart La, Reig. RH2 184 DB134
Chartley Av, NW2 62 CS62
Stanmore HA7 41 CF51
Charton Cl, Belv. DA17
off Nuxley Rd 106 EZ79
Chartridge Cl, Barn. EN5 27 CU43
Bushey WD23 24 CC44
Chart St, N1 197 L2
Chartway, Reig. RH2 184 DB133
Sevenoaks TN13 191 FJ124
★ **Chartwell**, West. TN16 189 ET131
Chartwell Cl, SE9 125 EQ89
Croydon CR0 142 DR102
Greenford UB6 78 CB67
Waltham Abbey EN9 16 EE33
Chartwell Dr, Orp. BR6 163 ER106
Chartwell Gdns, Sutt. SM3 157 CY105
Chartwell Pl, Epsom KT18 156 CS114
Harrow HA2 61 CD61
Sutton SM3 157 CZ105
Chartwell Rd, Nthwd. HA6 39 BT51
Chartwell Way, SE20 142 DV95
Charville La, Hayes UB4 77 BS68
Charville La W, Uxb. UB10 77 BP69
Charwood, SW16 121 DN91
Charwood Cl, Rad. (Shenley)
WD7 10 CL33
Chase, The, E12 68 EK63
SW4 101 DH83
SW16 121 DM94
SW20 139 CY95
Ashtead KT21 171 CJ118
Bexleyheath DA7 107 FB83
Brentwood (Cromwell Rd)
CM14 54 FV49
Brentwood (Ingrave) CM13 55 GC50
Brentwood (Seven Arches Rd)
CM14 54 FX48
Brentwood (Woodman Rd)
CM14 54 FX50
Bromley BR1 144 EH97
Chigwell IG7 49 EQ49
Coulsdon CR5 159 DJ114
Edgware HA8 42 CP53
Grays RM20 109 FX79
Hornchurch RM12 71 FE62
Leatherhead (Oxshott)
KT22 170 CC115
Loughton IG10 48 EJ45
Pinner HA5 60 BZ56
Pinner (Eastcote) HA5 60 BW58
Radlett WD7 25 CF35
Reigate RH2 184 DD134
Romford RM1 71 FE55
Romford (Chad.Hth.) RM6 70 EY58
Romford (Rush Grn.) RM7 71 FD62
Stanmore HA7 41 CG50
Sunbury-on-Thames TW16 135 BV95
Tadworth (Kgswd.) KT20 174 DA122
Upminster RM14 73 FS62
Uxbridge UB10 58 BN64
Wallington SM6 159 DL106
Waltham Cross (Goffs Oak)
EN7 13 DP28
Watford WD18 23 BS42
Chase Ct Gdns, Enf. EN2 30 DQ41
CHASE CROSS, Rom. 51 FE51
Chase Cross Rd, Rom. RM5 51 FC52
Chase End, Epsom KT19 156 CR112
H **Chase Farm Hosp**, Enf.
EN2 29 DN38
Chasefield Rd, SW17 120 DF91
Chase Gdns, E4 47 EA49
Twickenham TW2 117 CD86
Chase Grn, Enf. EN2 30 DQ41
Chase Grn Av, Enf. EN2 29 DP40
Chase Hill, Enf. EN2 30 DQ41
Chase Ho Gdns, Horn. RM11
off Great Nelmes Chase 72 FM57
Chase La, Chig. IG7 50 EU48
Ilford IG6 69 ER57
Chaseley Dr, W4
off Wellesley Rd 98 CP81
South Croydon CR2 160 DR110
Chaseley St, E14 85 DY72
Chasemore Cl, Mitch. CR4 140 DF101
Chasemore Gdns, Croy. CR0
off Thorneloe Gdns 159 DP106
Chase Ridings, Enf. EN2 29 DN40
Chase Rd, N14 29 DJ44
NW10 80 CR70
W3 80 CR70
Brentwood CM14 54 FW48
Epsom KT19 156 CR112
Chase Side, N14 28 DG44
Enfield EN2 30 DQ41
Chase Side Av, SW20 139 CY95
Enfield EN2 30 DQ40
Chaseside Cl, Rom. RM1 51 FE51
Chase Side Cres, Enf. EN2 30 DQ39
Chaseside Gdns, Cher. KT16 134 BH101
Chase Side Pl, Enf. EN2
off Chase Side 30 DQ40
Chase Sq, Grav. DA11
off High St 131 GH86
Chaseville Pk Rd, N21 29 DL43
Chase Way, N14 45 DH47
Chasewood Av, Enf. EN2 29 DP40
Chasewood Pk, Har. HA1 61 CF62
Chastilian Rd, Dart. DA1 127 FF87
Chatfield Ct, Cat. CR3
off Yorke Gate Rd 176 DR122
Chatfield Rd, SW11 100 DC83
Croydon CR0 141 DP102
Chatham Av, Brom. BR2 144 EF101
Chatham Cl, NW11 64 DA57
Sutton SM3 139 CZ101
Chatham Hill Rd, Sev. TN14 191 FJ121
Chatham Pl, E9 84 DW65
Chatham Rd, E17 67 DY55
E18 *off Grove Hill* 48 EF54
Chatham Rd, SW11 120 DF86
Kingston upon Thames
KT1 138 CN96
Orpington BR6 163 EQ106
Chatham St, SE17 201 K8
Chatsfield, Epsom KT17 157 CU110
Chatsfield Pl, W5 80 CL72
Chatsworth Av, NW4 43 CW54
SW20 139 CY95
Bromley BR1 124 EH91
Sidcup DA15 126 EU88
Wembley HA9 62 CM64
Chatsworth Cl, NW4 43 CW54
Borehamwood WD6 26 CN41
West Wickham BR4 144 EF103
Chatsworth Ct, W8 100 DA77
Stanmore HA7
off Marsh La 41 CJ50
Chatsworth Cres, Houns. TW3 97 CD84
Chatsworth Dr, Enf. EN1 46 DU45
Chatsworth Est, E5
off Elderfield Rd 67 DX63
Chatsworth Gdns, W3 80 CP73
Harrow HA2 60 CB60
New Malden KT3 139 CT99
Chatsworth Par, Orp. BR5
off Queensway 145 EQ99
Chatsworth Pl, Lthd. (Oxshott)
KT22 155 CD112
Mitcham CR4 140 DF97
Teddington TW11 117 CG91
Chatsworth Ri, W5 80 CM70
Chatsworth Rd, E5 66 DW62
E15 68 EF64
NW2 81 CX65
W4 98 CQ79
W5 80 CM70
Croydon CR0 160 DR105
Dartford DA1 128 FJ85
Hayes UB4 77 BV70
Sutton SM3 157 CX106
Chatsworth Way, SE27 121 DP90
Chatteris Av, Rom. RM3 52 FJ51
Chattern Hill, Ashf. TW15 115 BP91
Chattern Rd, Ashf. TW15 115 BQ91
Chatterton Ms, N4
off Chatterton Rd 65 DP62
Chatterton Rd, N4 65 DP62
Bromley BR2 144 EK98
Chatto Rd, SW11 120 DF85
Chaucer Av, Hayes UB4 77 BU71
Hounslow TW4 95 BV82
Richmond TW9 98 CN82
Weybridge KT13 152 BN108
Chaucer Cl, N11 45 DJ50
Banstead SM7 157 CY114
Tilbury RM18 111 GJ82
Chaucer Ct, N16 66 DS63
Chaucer Dr, SE1 202 A9
Chaucer Gdns, Sutt. SM1 140 DA104
Chaucer Grn, Croy. CR0 142 DV101
Chaucer Ho, Sutt. SM1 140 DA104
Chaucer Pk, Dart. DA1 128 FM87
Chaucer Rd, E7 86 EG65
E11 68 EG58
E17 47 EC54
SE24 121 DN85
W3 80 CQ74
Ashford TW15 114 BL91
Gravesend (Nthflt.) DA11 130 GD90
Romford RM3 51 FH52
Sidcup DA15 126 EW88
Sutton SM1 158 DA105
Welling DA16 105 ES81
Chaucer Way, SW19 120 DD93
Addlestone KT15 152 BG107
Dartford DA1 108 FN84
Slough SL1 74 AT74
Chauncey Cl, N9 46 DU48
Chauncy Av, Pot.B. EN6 12 DC33
Chaundrye Cl, SE9 124 EL86
Chauntler Cl, E16 86 EH72
Chavecroft Ter, Epsom KT18 173 CW119
Chave Rd, Dart. DA2 128 FL90
Chaworth Cl, Cher. KT16 151 BC107
Chaworth Rd, Cher. (Ott.)
KT16 151 BC107
CHEAM, Sutt. 157 CX107
⇌ **Cheam** 157 CY108
Cheam Cl, Tad. KT20
off Waterfield 173 CV121
Cheam Common Rd, Wor.Pk.
KT4 139 CV103
Cheam Mans, Sutt. SM3 157 CY108
Cheam Pk Way, Sutt. SM3 157 CY107
Cheam Rd, Epsom KT17 157 CU109
Sutton SM1 157 CZ107
Sutton (E.Ewell) SM2 157 CX110
Cheam St, SE15
off Evelina Rd 102 DV83
Cheapside, EC2 197 J9
N13 *off Taplow Rd* 46 DQ49
Woking GU21 150 AX114
Cheapside La, Uxb. (Denh.)
UB9 57 BF61
Cheddar Cl, N11
off Martock Gdns 44 DG51
Cheddar Rd, Houns. (Hthrw.Air.)
TW6 *off Cromer Rd* 94 BN82
Cheddar Waye, Hayes UB4 77 BV72
Cheddington Rd, N18 46 DS48
Chedworth Cl, E16
off Hallsville Rd 86 EF72
Cheelson Rd, S.Ock. RM15 91 FW68
Cheeseman Cl, Hmptn.
TW12 116 BY93
Cheesemans Ter, W14 99 CZ78
Cheldon Av, NW7
off Bittacy Hill 43 CY52
Chelford Rd, Brom. BR1 123 ED92
Chelmer Cres, Bark. IG11 88 EV68
Chelmer Dr, Brwd. CM13 55 GE44
South Ockendon RM15 91 FW73
Chelmer Rd, E9 67 DX64
Grays RM16 111 GG78
Upminster RM14 73 FR58
Chelmsford Av, Rom. RM5 51 FD52
Chelmsford Cl, E6
off Guildford Rd 87 EM72
W6 99 CX79
Sutton SM2 158 DA109
Chelmsford Dr, Upmin. RM14 72 FM62
Chelmsford Gdns, Ilf. IG1 68 EL59
Chelmsford Rd, E11 67 ED60
E17 67 EA58
E18 48 EF53
N14 45 DJ45
Brentwood CM15 55 FZ44
Chelmsford Sq, NW10 81 CW67
CHELSEA, SW3 100 DD79
H **Chelsea & Westminster
Hosp**, SW10 100 DC79
★ **Chelsea Antique Mkt**,
SW3 100 DD79
Chelsea Br, SW1 101 DH79
SW8 101 DH79
Chelsea Br Rd, SW1 198 F10
Chelsea Cloisters, SW3
off Lucan Pl 100 DE77
Chelsea Cl, NW10
off Winchelsea Rd 80 CR67
Edgware HA8 42 CN54
Hampton (Hmptn.H.)
TW12 116 CC92
Worcester Park KT4 139 CU101
Chelsea Cres, SW10
off Harbour Av 100 DC81
Chelsea Embk, SW3 100 DE79
★ **Chelsea FC**, SW6 100 DB80
Chelsea Gdns, W13
off Hathaway Gdns 79 CF71
Sutton SM3 157 CY105
Chelsea Harbour, SW10 100 DC81
Chelsea Harbour Dr, SW10 100 DC81
Chelsea Manor Ct, SW3
off Chelsea Manor St 100 DE79
Chelsea Manor Gdns, SW3 100 DE79
Chelsea Manor St, SW3 100 DE78
Chelsea Ms, Horn. RM11
off St. Leonards Way 71 FH60
Chelsea Pk Gdns, SW3 100 DD79
★ **Chelsea Physic Gdn**,
SW3 100 DF79
Chelsea Sq, SW3 198 A10
Chelsea Wf, SW10 100 DD80
CHELSFIELD, Orp. 164 EW106
⇌ **Chelsfield** 164 EV106
Chelsfield Av, N9 47 DX45
Chelsfield Gdns, SE26 122 DW90
Chelsfield Grn, N9
off Chelsfield Av 47 DX45
Chelsfield Hill, Orp. BR6 164 EW109
Chelsfield La, Orp. BR5, BR6 146 EX101
Orpington (Maypole) BR6 164 FA108
Sevenoaks TN14 165 FC109
H **Chelsfield Park Hosp**, Orp.
BR6 164 EZ106
Chelsfield Rd, Orp. BR5 146 EW100
CHELSHAM, Warl. 177 EA117
Chelsham Cl, Warl. CR6 177 DY118
Chelsham Common Rd, Warl.
CR6 177 EA116
Chelsham Ct Rd, Warl. CR6 177 ED118
Chelsham Rd, SW4 101 DK83
South Croydon CR2 160 DR107
Warlingham CR6 177 EA117
Chelston App, Ruis. HA4 59 BU61
Chelston Rd, Ruis. HA4 59 BU60
Chelsworth Cl, Rom. RM3
off Chelsworth Dr 52 FM53
Chelsworth Dr, SE18 105 ER79
Romford RM3 52 FL53
Cheltenham Av, Twick. TW1 117 CG87
Cheltenham Cl, Grav. DA12 131 GJ92
New Malden KT3
off Northcote Rd 138 CQ97
Northolt UB5 78 CB65
Cheltenham Gdns, E6 86 EL68
Loughton IG10 32 EL44
Cheltenham Pl, W3 80 CP74
Harrow HA3 62 CL56
Cheltenham Rd, E10 67 EC58
SE15 102 DW84
Orpington BR6 146 EU104
Cheltenham Ter, SW3 198 E10
Cheltenham Vil, Stai. TW19 113 BF86
Chelverton Rd, SW15 99 CX84
Chelwood, N20
off Oakleigh Rd N 44 DD47
Chelwood Cl, E4 31 EB44
Coulsdon CR5
off Starrock Rd 175 DJ119
Epsom KT17 157 CT112
Northwood HA6 39 BQ52
Chelwood Gdns, Rich. TW9 98 CN82
Chelwood Gdns Pas, Rich. TW9
off Chelwood Gdns 98 CN82
Chelwood Wk, SE4 103 DY84
Chenappa Cl, E13 86 EG69
Chenduit Way, Stan. HA7 41 CF50
Cheney Rd, NW1 195 P1
Cheney Row, E17 47 DZ53
Cheneys Rd, E11 68 EE62
Cheney St, Pnr. HA5 60 BW57
CHENIES, Rick. 21 BB38
Chenies, The, Dart. DA2 127 FE91
Orpington BR6 145 ES100
Chenies Av, Amer. HP6 20 AW39
Chenies Hill, Hem.H. (Flaun.)
HP3 5 BB34
★ **Chenies Manor**, Rick. WD3 21 BA38
Chenies Ms, WC1 195 M5
Chenies Par, Amer. HP7 20 AW40
Chenies Pl, NW1 83 DK68
Chenies Rd, Rick. (Chorl.)
WD3 21 BD40
Chenies St, WC1 195 M6
Chenies Way, Wat. WD18 39 BS45
Cheniston Cl, W.Byf. KT14 152 BG113
Cheniston Gdns, W8 100 DB76
Chepstow Av, Horn. RM12 72 FL62
Chepstow Cl, SW15
off Lytton Gro 119 CY86
Chepstow Cres, W11 82 DA73
Chepstow Cres, Ilf. IG3 69 ES58
Chepstow Gdns, Sthl. UB1 78 BZ72
Chepstow Pl, W2 82 DA72
Chepstow Ri, Croy. CR0 142 DS104
Chepstow Rd, W2 82 DA72
W7 97 CG76
Croydon CR0 142 DS104
Chepstow Vil, W11 81 CZ73
Chepstow Way, SE15 102 DT80
Chequers, Buck.H. IG9
off Hills Rd 48 EH46
Chequers Cl, NW9 62 CS55
Orpington BR5 145 ET98
Tadworth KT20 183 CU125
Chequers Gdns, N13 45 DP50
Chequers La, Dag. RM9 88 EZ70
Tadworth KT20 183 CU125
Watford WD25 8 BW30
Chequers Orchard, Iver SL0 75 BF72
Chequers Par, SE9
off Eltham High St 125 EM86
Chequers Rd, Brwd. CM14 52 FM46
Loughton IG10 33 EN43
Romford RM3 52 FL47
Chequers Sq, Uxb. UB8
off High St 76 BJ66
Chequer St, EC1 197 J5
Chequers Wk, Wal.Abb. EN9 16 EF33
Chequers Way, N13 46 DQ50
Chequer Tree Cl, Wok. (Knap.)
GU21 166 AS116
Cherbury Cl, SE28 88 EX72
Cherbury Ct, N1 197 L1
Cherbury St, N1 197 L1
Cherchefelle Ms, Stan. HA7 41 CH50
Cherimoya Gdns, W.Mol. KT8
off Kelvinbrook 136 CB97
Cherington Rd, W7 79 CF74
Cheriton Av, Brom. BR2 144 EF99
Ilford IG5 49 EM54
Cheriton Cl, W5 79 CJ71
Barnet EN4 28 DF41
Cheriton Ct, Walt. KT12
off St. Johns Dr 136 BW102
Cheriton Dr, SE18 105 ER80
Cheriton Sq, SW17 120 DG89
Cherries, The, Slou. SL2 74 AV72
Cherry Acre, Ger.Cr. (Chal.St.P.)
SL9 36 AX49
Cherry Av, Brwd. CM13 55 FZ48
Slough SL3 92 AX75
Southall UB1 78 BX74
Swanley BR8 147 FD97
Cherry Blossom Cl, N13 45 DP50
Cherry Cl, E17
off Eden Rd 67 EB56
NW9 42 CS54
SW2 *off Tulse Hill* 121 DN87
W5 97 CK76
Banstead SM7 157 CX114
Carshalton SM5 140 DF103
Morden SM4 139 CY98
Ruislip HA4
off Roundways 59 BT62
Cherrycot Hill, Orp. BR6 163 ER105
Cherrycot Ri, Orp. BR6 163 EQ105
Cherry Cres, Brent. TW8 97 CH80
Cherry Cft, Rick. (Crox.Grn.)
WD3 22 BN44
Cherrycroft Gdns, Pnr. HA5
off Westfield Pk 40 BZ52
Cherrydale, Wat. WD18 23 BT42
Cherrydown Av, E4 47 DZ48
Cherrydown Cl, E4 47 DZ48
Cherrydown Rd, Sid. DA14 126 EX89
Cherrydown Wk, Rom. RM7 51 FB54
Cherry Gdns, Dag. RM9 70 EZ64
Northolt UB5 78 CB66
Cherry Gdn St, SE16 202 D5
Cherry Garth, Brent. TW8 97 CK77
Cherry Gro, Hayes UB3 77 BV74
Uxbridge UB8 77 BP71
Cherry Hill, Barn. EN5 28 DB44
Harrow HA3 41 CE51
Rickmansworth (Loud.)
WD3 22 BH41
St. Albans AL2 8 CA25
Cherry Hill Gdns, Croy. CR0 159 DM105
Cherry Hills, Wat. WD19 40 BY50
Cherry Hollow, Abb.L. WD5 7 BT31
Cherrylands Cl, NW9 62 CQ61
Cherry La, West Dr. UB7 94 BM77
Cherry La Roundabout, West Dr.
UB7 95 BP77
Cherry Laurel Wk, SW2
off Beechdale Rd 121 DM86
Cherry Orchard, Amer. HP6 20 AS37
Ashtead KT21 172 CP118
Slough (Stoke P.) SL2 74 AV66
Staines TW18 114 BG92
West Drayton UB7 94 BL75
Cherry Orchard Cl, Orp. BR5 146 EW99
Cherry Orchard Gdns, Croy.
CR0 *off Oval Rd* 142 DR103
West Molesey KT8 136 BZ97
Cherry Orchard Rd, Brom.
BR2 144 EL103
Croydon CR0 142 DR103
West Molesey KT8 136 CA97
Cherry Ri, Ch.St.G. HP8 36 AX47
Cherry Rd, Enf. EN3 30 DW38
Cherry St, Rom. RM7 71 FD57
Woking GU21 166 AY118
Cherry Tree Av, St.Alb. (Lon.Col.)
AL2 9 CK26
Staines TW18 114 BH93
West Drayton UB7 76 BM72
Cherry Tree Cl, E9
off Moulins Rd 84 DW67
Grays RM17 110 GC79
Rainham RM13 89 FG68
Wembley HA0 61 CF63
Cherry Tree Ct, NW9 62 CQ56
Coulsdon CR5 175 DM117
Cherry Tree Dr, SW16 121 DL90
South Ockendon RM15 91 FX70
Cherry Tree Grn, S.Croy. CR2 160 DV114
Cherry Tree La, Dart. DA2 127 FF90
Epsom KT19
off Christ Ch Rd 156 CN112
Cherrytree La, Ger.Cr. (Chal.St.P.)
SL9 36 AX54
Cherry Tree La, Iver SL0 76 BG67
Potters Bar EN6 12 DB34
Rainham RM13 89 FE69
Rickmansworth (Herons.)
WD3 37 BC46
Slough (Fulmer) SL3 75 AZ65
Cherry Tree Ri, Buck.H. IG9 48 EJ49
Cherry Tree Rd, E15
off Wingfield Rd 68 EE63
N2 64 DF56
Watford WD24 23 BV36
Cherry Tree Wk, EC1 197 J5
Beckenham BR3 143 DZ98
West Wickham BR4 162 EF105
Cherry Tree Way, Stan. HA7 41 CH51
Cherry Wk, Brom. BR2 144 EG102
Grays RM16 111 GG76
Rainham RM13 89 FF68
Rickmansworth (Loud.)
WD3 22 BJ40
Cherry Way, Epsom KT19 156 CR107
Shepperton TW17 135 BR98
Slough (Horton) SL3 93 BC83
Cherrywood Av, Egh. (Eng.Grn.)
TW20 112 AV93
Cherrywood Cl, E3 85 DY69
Kingston upon Thames
KT2 118 CN94
Cherrywood Dr, SW15 119 CX85
Gravesend (Nthflt.) DA11 130 GE90
Cherrywood La, Mord. SM4 139 CY98
Cherry Wd Way, W5
off Hanger Vale La 80 CN71
Cherston Gdns, Loug. IG10
off Cherston Rd 33 EN42
Cherston Rd, Loug. IG10 33 EN42
CHERTSEY 134 BG102
⇌ **Chertsey** 133 BF102
Chertsey Br Rd, Cher. KT16 134 BK101
Chertsey Cl, Ken. CR8 175 DP115
Chertsey Cres, Croy. (New Adgtn.)
CR0 161 EC110
Chertsey Dr, Sutt. SM3 139 CY103
Chertsey La, Cher. KT16 133 BE95
Epsom KT19 156 CN112
Staines TW18 113 BE92
★ **Chertsey Mus**, Cher. KT16
off Windsor St 134 BG100
Chertsey Rd, E11 67 ED61
Addlestone KT15 134 BH103
Ashford TW15 115 BR94
Feltham TW13 115 BS92
Ilford IG1 69 ER63
Shepperton TW17 134 BN101
Sunbury-on-Thames TW16 115 BR94
Twickenham TW1, TW2 117 CF86
West Byfleet (Byfleet)
KT14 152 BK111
Woking GU21 151 BA113
Woking (Chobham) GU24 150 AY110
Chertsey St, SW17 120 DG92
Chervil Cl, Felt. TW13 115 BU90
Chervil Ms, SE28 88 EV74
Cherwell Cl, Rick. (Crox.Grn.)
WD3 22 BN43
Slough SL3 *off Tweed Rd* 93 BB79
Cherwell Ct, Epsom KT19 156 CQ105
Cherwell Gro, S.Ock. RM15 91 FV73
Cherwell Way, Ruis. HA4 59 BQ58
Cheryls Cl, SW6 100 DB81
Cheseman St, SE26 122 DV90
Chesfield Rd, Kings.T. KT2 118 CL94
Chesham Av, Orp. BR5 145 EP100
Chesham Cl, SW1 198 F7
Romford RM7 71 FD56
Sutton SM2 157 CY110
Chesham Ct, Nthwd. HA6
off Frithwood Av 39 BT51
Chesham Cres, SE20 142 DW96
Chesham La, Ch.St.G. HP8 36 AY48
Gerrards Cross (Chal.St.P.)
SL9 36 AY49
Chesham Ms, SW1 198 F6
Chesham Pl, SW1 198 F7
Chesham Rd, SE20 142 DW96
SW19 120 DD92
Hemel Hempstead (Bov.)
HP3 4 AY27
Kingston upon Thames
KT1 138 CN95
Chesham St, NW10 62 CR62
SW1 198 F7
Chesham Ter, W13 97 CH75
Chesham Way, Wat. WD18 23 BS44
Cheshire Cl, E17 47 EB53
SE4 103 DZ82
Chertsey (Ott.) KT16 151 BC107
Hornchurch RM11 72 FN57
Mitcham CR4 141 DL97
Cheshire Ct, EC4 196 E9
Slough SL1
off Clements Cl 92 AV75
Cheshire Dr, Wat. WD25
off Ashfields 7 BT34
Cheshire Gdns, Chess. KT9 155 CK107
Cheshire Ho, N18 46 DV49
Cheshire Rd, N22 45 DM52
Cheshire St, E2 84 DT70
Chesholm Rd, N16 66 DS62
CHESHUNT, Wal.Cr. 15 DX31
⇌ **Cheshunt** 15 DZ30
H **Cheshunt Comm Hosp**,
Wal.Cr. EN8 15 DY31
Cheshunt Link Rd, Wal.Cr. (Chsht.)
EN8 14 DW33
Cheshunt Pk, Wal.Cr. (Chsht.)
EN7 14 DV26
Cheshunt Rd, E7 86 EH65
Belvedere DA17 106 FA78

Che - Chi

Cheshunt Wash, Wal.Cr. (Chsht.) EN8 15 DY27
Chesil Ct, E2 84 DW68
Chesilton Rd, SW6 99 CZ81
Chesil Way, Hayes UB4 77 BT69
Chesley Gdns, E6 86 EK68
Cheslyn Gdns, Wat. WD17 23 BT37
Chesney Cres, Croy. (New Adgtn.) CR0 161 EC108
Chesney St, SW11 100 DG81
Chesnut Est, N17 66 DT55
Chesnut Gro, N17
off Chesnut Rd 66 DT55
Chesnut Rd, N17 66 DT55
Chess Cl, Chesh. (Latimer) HP5 20 AX36
Rickmansworth (Loud.) WD3 22 BK42
Chessfield Pk, Amer. HP6 20 AY39
Chess Hill, Rick. (Loud.) WD3 22 BK42
Chessholme Ct, Sun. TW16
off Scotts Av 115 BS94
Chessholme Rd, Ashf. TW15 115 BQ93
CHESSINGTON 156 CL107
Chessington Av, N3 63 CY55
Bexleyheath DA7 106 EY80
Chessington Cl, Epsom KT19 156 CQ107
Chessington Ct, Pnr. HA5 60 BZ56
Chessington Hall Gdns, Chess. KT9 155 CK108
Chessington Hill Pk, Chess. KT9 156 CN106
Chessington Lo, N3 63 CZ55
⇌ **Chessington North** 156 CL106
Chessington Rd, Epsom KT17, KT19 157 CT109
⇌ **Chessington South** 155 CK108
Chessington Way, W.Wick. BR4 143 EB103
★ **Chessington World of Adventure**, Chess. KT9 155 CJ110
Chess La, Rick. (Loud.) WD3 22 BK42
Chesson Rd, W14 99 CZ79
Chess Vale Ri, Rick. (Crox.Grn.) WD3 22 BM44
Chess Valley Wk, Chesh. HP5 20 AU35
Rickmansworth WD3 22 BL44
Chess Way, Rick. (Chorl.) WD3 22 BG41
Chesswood Way, Pnr. HA5 40 BX54
Chester Av, Rich. TW10 118 CM85
Twickenham TW2 116 BZ88
Upminster RM14 73 FS61
Chester Cl, SW1 198 G5
SW13 99 CV83
Ashford TW15 115 BR92
Loughton IG10 33 EQ39
Potters Bar EN6 12 DB29
Sutton SM1 140 DA103
Uxbridge UB8
off Dawley Av 77 BP72
Chester Cl N, NW1 195 J2
Chester Cl S, NW1 195 J3
Chester Cotts, SW1 198 F9
Chester Ct, NW1 195 J2
SE5 102 DR80
Chester Cres, E8
off Ridley Rd 84 DT65
Chester Dr, Har. HA2 60 BZ58
Chesterfield Cl, Orp. BR5 146 EX98
Chesterfield Dr, Dart. DA1 127 FH85
Esher KT10 137 CG103
Sevenoaks TN13 190 FD122
Chesterfield Gdns, N4 65 DP57
SE10 *off Crooms Hill* 103 ED80
W1 199 H2
Chesterfield Gro, SE22 122 DT85
Chesterfield Hill, W1 199 H1
Chesterfield Ms, N4
off Chesterfield Gdns 65 DP57
Ashford TW15
off Chesterfield Rd 114 BL91
Chesterfield Rd, E10 67 EC58
N3 44 DA51
W4 98 CQ79
Ashford TW15 114 BL91
Barnet EN5 27 CX43
Enfield EN3 31 DY37
Epsom KT19 156 CR108
Chesterfield St, W1 199 H2
Chesterfield Wk, SE10 103 ED81
Chesterfield Way, SE15 102 DW80
Hayes UB3 95 BU75
Chesterford Gdns, NW3 64 DB63
Chesterford Ho, SE18
off Shooter's Hill Rd 104 EK80
Chesterford Rd, E12 69 EM64
Chester Gdns, W13 79 CG72
Enfield EN3 30 DV44
Morden SM4 140 DC100
Chester Gate, NW1 195 H3
Chester Gibbons Grn, St.Alb. AL2 *off High St* 9 CK26
Chester Grn, Loug. IG10 33 EQ39
Chester Ms, SW1 199 H6
Chester Path, Loug. IG10 33 EQ39
Chester Pl, NW1 195 J2
Chester Rd, E7 86 EK66
E11 68 EH58
E16 86 EE70
E17 67 DX57
N9 46 DV46
N17 66 DR55
N19 65 DH61
NW1 194 G3
SW19 119 CW93
Borehamwood WD6 26 CQ41
Chigwell IG7 49 EN48
Hounslow TW4 95 BV83
Hounslow (Hthrw.Air.) TW6 94 BN83
Ilford IG3 69 ET60
Loughton IG10 33 EP40
Northwood HA6 39 BS52
Sidcup DA15 125 ES85
Chester Rd, Wat. WD18 23 BU43
Chester Row, SW1 198 F9
Chesters, The, N.Mal. KT3 138 CS95
Chester Sq, SW1 199 H8
Chester Sq Ms, SW1 199 H7
Chester St, E2 84 DU70
SW1 198 G6
Chester Ter, NW1 195 H2
Chesterton Cl, SW18
off Ericcson Cl 120 DA85
Greenford UB6 78 CB68
Chesterton Dr, Red. RH1 185 DL128
Staines TW19 114 BM88
Chesterton Rd, E13 86 EG69
W10 81 CX71
Chesterton Sq, W8
off Pembroke Rd 99 CZ77
Chesterton Ter, E13 86 EG69
Kingston upon Thames KT1 138 CN96
Chesterton Way, Til. RM18 111 GJ82
Chester Way, SE11 200 E9
Chesthunte Rd, N17 46 DQ53
Chestnut All, SW6
off Lillie Rd 99 CZ79
Chestnut Av, E7 68 EH63
N8 65 DL57
SW14 *off Thornton Rd* 98 CR83
Brentford TW8 97 CK77
Brentwood CM14 54 FS45
Buckhurst Hill IG9 48 EK48
East Molesey KT8 137 CF97
Edgware HA8 42 CL51
Epsom KT19 156 CS105
Esher KT10 137 CD101
Grays RM16 110 GB75
Greenhithe (Bluewater) DA9 129 FT87
Hampton TW12 116 CA94
Hornchurch RM12 71 FF61
Northwood HA6 39 BT54
Rickmansworth WD3 22 BG43
Slough SL3 92 AX75
Teddington TW11 137 CF96
Virginia Water GU25 132 AT98
Walton-on-Thames KT12 153 BS109
Wembley HA0 61 CH64
West Drayton UB7 76 BM73
West Wickham BR4 162 EE106
Westerham TN16 178 EK122
Weybridge KT13 153 BQ108
Chestnut Av N, E17 67 EC56
Chestnut Av S, E17 67 EC56
Chestnut Cl, N14 29 DJ43
N16 *off Lordship Gro* 66 DR61
SE6 123 EC92
SE14 *off Shardeloes Rd* 103 DZ83
SW16 121 DN91
Addlestone KT15 152 BK106
Ashford TW15 115 BP91
Buckhurst Hill IG9 48 EK47
Carshalton SM5 140 DF102
Egham (Eng.Grn.) TW20 112 AW93
Gerrards Cross (Chal.St.P.) SL9 37 AZ52
Gravesend (Nthflt.) DA11
off Burch Rd 131 GF86
Hayes UB3 77 BS73
Hornchurch RM12
off Lancaster Dr 72 FJ63
Orpington BR6 164 EU106
Sidcup DA15 126 EU88
Sunbury-on-Thames TW16 115 BT93
Tadworth KT20 174 DA123
West Drayton UB7 95 BP80
Woking (Ripley) GU23 168 BG124
Chestnut Copse, Oxt. RH8 188 EG132
Chestnut Ct, SW6
off North End Rd 99 CZ79
Amersham HP6 20 AS37
Surbiton KT6
off Penners Gdns 138 CL101
Chestnut Cres, Walt. KT12
off Chestnut Av 153 BS109
Chestnut Dr, E11 68 EG58
Bexleyheath DA7 106 EX83
Egham (Eng.Grn.) TW20 112 AX93
Harrow HA3 41 CF52
Pinner HA5 60 BX58
Chestnut Glen, Horn. RM12 71 FF61
Chestnut Gro, SE20 122 DW94
SW12 120 DG87
W5 97 CK76
Barnet EN4 28 DF43
Brentwood CM14 54 FW47
Dartford DA2 127 FD91
Ilford IG6 49 ES51
Isleworth TW7 97 CG84
Mitcham CR4 141 DK98
New Malden KT3 138 CR97
South Croydon CR2 160 DV108
Staines TW18 114 BJ93
Wembley HA0 61 CH64
Woking GU22 166 AY120
Chestnut La, N20 43 CY46
Sevenoaks TN13 191 FH124
Weybridge KT13 153 BP106
Chestnut Manor Cl, Stai. TW18 114 BH92
Chestnut Mead, Red. RH1
off Oxford Rd 184 DE133
Chestnut Pl, Ashtd. KT21 172 CL119
Epsom KT17 157 CU111
Chestnut Ri, SE18 105 ER79
Bushey WD23 40 CB45
Chestnut Rd, SE27 121 DP90
SW20 139 CX96
Ashford TW15 115 BP91
Dartford DA1 128 FK88
Enfield EN3 31 DY36
Kingston upon Thames KT2 118 CL94
Twickenham TW2 117 CE89
Chestnut Row, N3
off Nether St 44 DA52
Chestnuts, Brwd. CM13 55 GB46
Chestnuts, The, SE14 103 DZ81
Chestnuts, The, Rom. (Abridge) RM4 34 EV41
Walton-on-Thames KT12 135 BU102
Chestnut Wk, Ger.Cr. (Chal.St.P.) SL9 36 AY52
Sevenoaks TN15 191 FL129
Shepperton TW17 135 BS99
Walton-on-Thames KT12
off Octagon Rd 153 BS109
Watford WD24 23 BU37
West Byfleet (Byfleet) KT14
off Royston Rd 152 BL112
Woodford Green IG8 48 EG50
Chestnut Way, Felt. TW13 115 BV90
Cheston Av, Croy. CR0 143 DY103
Chestwood Gro, Uxb. UB10 76 BM66
Cheswick Cl, Dart. DA1 107 FF84
Chesworth Cl, Erith DA8 107 FE81
Chettle Cl, SE1 201 K6
Chettle Ct, N8 65 DN58
Chetwode Dr, Epsom KT18 173 CX118
Chetwode Rd, SW17 120 DF90
Tadworth KT20 173 CW119
Chetwood Wk, E6 86 EL72
Chetwynd Av, Barn. EN4 44 DF46
Chetwynd Dr, Uxb. UB10 76 BM68
Chetwynd Rd, NW5 65 DH63
Chevalier Cl, Stan. HA7 42 CL49
Cheval Pl, SW7 198 C6
Cheval St, E14 203 P6
Cheveley Cl, Rom. RM3
off Chelsworth Dr 52 FM53
Chevely Cl, Epp. CM16 18 EX29
Cheveney Wk, Brom. BR2
off Marina Cl 144 EG97
CHEVENING, Sev. 180 EZ119
Chevening Cross, Sev. (Chev.) TN14 180 FA120
Chevening La, Sev. (Knock. TN14 180 EY115
Chevening Rd, NW6 81 CX68
SE10 104 EF78
SE19 122 DR93
Sevenoaks (Chev.) TN14 180 EZ119
Sevenoaks (Sund.) TN14 180 EY123
Chevenings, The, Sid. DA14 126 EW90
Cheverton Rd, N19 65 DK60
Chevet St, E9
off Kenworthy Rd 67 DY64
Chevington Way, Horn. RM12 72 FK63
Cheviot Cl, Bans. SM7 174 DB115
Bexleyheath DA7 107 FE82
Bushey WD23 24 CC44
Enfield EN1 30 DR40
Hayes UB3 95 BR80
Sutton SM2 158 DD109
Cheviot Gdns, NW2 63 CX61
SE27 121 DP91
Cheviot Gate, NW2 63 CY61
Cheviot Rd, SE27 121 DN92
Hornchurch RM11 71 FG60
Slough SL3 93 BA78
Cheviot Way, Ilf. IG2 69 ES56
Chevron Cl, E16 86 EG72
Chevy Rd, Sthl. UB2 96 CC75
Chewton Rd, E17 67 DY56
Cheyham Gdns, Sutt. SM2 157 CX110
Cheyham Way, Sutt. SM2 157 CY110
Cheyne Av, E18 68 EF55
Twickenham TW2 116 BZ88
Cheyne Cl, NW4 63 CW57
Bromley BR2
off Cedar Cres 144 EL104
Gerrards Cross SL9 56 AY60
Cheyne Ct, SW3
off Flood St 100 DF79
Banstead SM7
off Park Rd 174 DB115
Cheyne Gdns, SW3 100 DE79
Cheyne Hill, Surb. KT5 138 CM98
Cheyne Ms, SW3 100 DE79
Cheyne Path, W7 79 CF71
Cheyne Pl, SW3 100 DF79
Cheyne Rd, Ashf. TW15 115 BR93
Cheyne Row, SW3 100 DE79
Cheyne Wk, N21 29 DP43
NW4 63 CW58
SW3 100 DE79
SW10 100 DD80
Croydon CR0 142 DU103
Longfield DA3
off Cavendish Sq 149 FX97
Cheyneys Av, Edg. HA8 41 CK51
Chichele Gdns, Croy. CR0
off Brownlow Rd 160 DT105
Chichele Rd, NW2 63 CX64
Oxted RH8 188 EE128
Chicheley Gdns, Har. HA3 40 CC52
Chicheley Rd, Har. HA3 40 CC52
Chicheley St, SE1 200 C4
Chichester Av, Ruis. HA4 59 BR61
Chichester Cl, E6 86 EL72
SE3 104 EJ81
Hampton TW12
off Maple Cl 116 BZ93
South Ockendon (Aveley) RM15 90 FQ74
Chichester Ct, Epsom KT17 157 CT109
Slough SL1 92 AU75
Stanmore HA7 62 CL55
Chichester Dr, Pur. CR8 159 DM112
Sevenoaks TN13 190 FF125
Chichester Gdns, Ilf. IG1 68 EL59
Chichester Ms, SE27 121 DN91
Chichester Rents, WC2 196 D8
Chichester Ri, Grav. DA12 131 GK91
Chichester Rd, E11 68 EE62
N9 46 DU46
NW6 82 DA68
W2 82 DB71
Croydon CR0 142 DS104
Greenhithe DA9 129 FT85
Chichester St, SW1 101 DJ78
Chichester Way, E14 204 F8
Feltham TW14 115 BV87
Watford WD25 8 BY33
Chicksand St, E1 84 DT71
Chiddingfold, N12 44 DA48
Chiddingstone Av, Bexh. DA7 106 EZ80
Chiddingstone Cl, Sutt. SM2 158 DA110
Chiddingstone St, SW6 100 DA82
Chieftan Dr, Purf. RM19 108 FM77
Chieveley Rd, Bexh. DA7 107 FB84
Chiffinch Gdns, Grav. (Nthflt.) DA11 130 GE90
Chignell Pl, W13
off Broadway 79 CG74
CHIGWELL 49 EP48
⊖ **Chigwell** 49 EP49
Chigwell Hill, E1 202 D1
Chigwell Hurst Ct, Pnr. HA5 60 BX55
Chigwell La, Loug. IG10 33 EQ43
Chigwell Pk, Chig. IG7 49 EP49
Chigwell Pk Dr, Chig. IG7 49 EN48
Chigwell Ri, Chig. IG7 49 EN47
Chigwell Rd, E18 68 EH55
Woodford Green IG8 48 EJ54
CHIGWELL ROW, Chig. 50 EU47
Chigwell Vw, Rom. RM5
off Lodge La 50 FA51
Chilberton Dr, Red. RH1 185 DJ130
Chilbrook Rd, Cob. (Down.) KT11 169 BU118
Chilcombe Ho, SW15
off Fontley Way 119 CU87
Chilcot Cl, E14
off Grundy St 85 EB72
Chilcote La, Amer. (Lt.Chal.) HP7 20 AV39
Chilcott Rd, Wat. WD24 23 BS36
Childebert Rd, SW17 121 DH89
Childeric Rd, SE14 103 DY80
Childerley, Kings.T. KT1
off Burritt Rd 138 CN97
Childerley St, SW6
off Fulham Palace Rd 99 CX81
Childers, The, Wdf.Grn. IG8 49 EM50
Childers St, SE8 103 DY79
Child La, SE10 205 L7
H **Childrens Trust, The**, Tad. KT20 173 CX121
Childs Av, Uxb. (Hare.) UB9 38 BJ54
Childs Cl, Horn. RM11 72 FJ58
Childs Cres, Swans. DA10 129 FX86
CHILDS HILL, NW2 64 DA61
Childs Hill Wk, NW2 63 CZ62
Childs La, SE19
off Westow St 122 DS93
Child's Ms, SW5
off Child's Pl 100 DA77
Child's Pl, SW5 100 DA77
Child's St, SW5 100 DA77
Child's Wk, SW5
off Child's St 100 DA77
Childs Way, NW11 63 CZ57
Chilham Cl, Bex. DA5 126 EZ87
Greenford UB6 79 CG68
Chilham Rd, SE9 124 EL91
Chilham Way, Brom. BR2 144 EG101
Chillerton Rd, SW17 120 DG92
Chillingworth Gdns, Twick. TW1 *off Tower Rd* 117 CF90
Chillingworth Rd, N7 65 DM64
Chilmark Gdns, N.Mal. KT3 139 CT101
Redhill RH1 185 DL129
Chilmark Rd, SW16 141 DK96
Chilmead La, Red. (Nutfld.) RH1 185 DK132
Chilsey Grn Rd, Cher. KT16 133 BE100
Chiltern Av, Bushey WD23 24 CC44
Twickenham TW2 116 CA88
Chiltern Business Village, Uxb. UB8 76 BH68
Chiltern Cl, Bexh. DA7
off Cumbrian Av 107 FE81
Borehamwood WD6 26 CM40
Bushey WD23 24 CB44
Croydon CR0 142 DS104
Uxbridge (Ickhm.) UB10 59 BP61
Waltham Cross (Chsht.) EN7 13 DP27
Woking GU22 166 AW122
Worcester Park KT4
off Cotswold Way 139 CW103
Chiltern Dene, Enf. EN2 29 DM42
Chiltern Dr, Rick. (Mill End) WD3 37 BF45
Surbiton KT5 138 CP99
Chiltern Gdns, NW2 63 CX62
Bromley BR2 144 EF98
Hornchurch RM12 72 FJ62
Chiltern Hts, Amer. HP7 20 AU39
Chiltern Hill, Ger.Cr. (Chal.St.P.) SL9 36 AY53
★ **Chiltern Open Air Mus**, Ch.St.G. HP8 37 AZ47
Chiltern Rd, E3 85 EA70
Gravesend (Nthflt.) DA11 130 GE90
Ilford IG2 69 ES56
Pinner HA5 60 BW57
Sutton SM2 158 DB109
Chilterns, The, Sutt. SM2
off Gatton Cl 158 DB109
Chiltern St, W1 194 F6
Chiltern Vw Rd, Uxb. UB8 76 BJ68
Chiltern Way, Wdf.Grn. IG8 48 EG48
Chilthorne Cl, SE6
off Ravensbourne Pk Cres 123 DZ87
Chilton Av, W5 97 CK77
Chilton Ct, Walt. KT12 153 BU105
Chilton Gro, SE8 203 J9
Chiltonian Ind Est, SE12 124 EF86
Chilton Rd, Edg. HA8
off Manor Pk Cres 42 CN51
Grays RM16 111 GG76
Richmond TW9 98 CN83
Chiltons, The, E18
off Grove Hill 48 EG54
Chiltons Cl, Bans. SM7
off High St 174 DB115
Chilton St, E2 84 DT70
Chilver St, SE10 205 L10
Chilwell Gdns, Wat. WD19 40 BW49
Chilworth Ct, SW19
off Windlesham Gro 119 CX88
Chilworth Gdns, Sutt. SM1 140 DC104
Chilworth Ms, W2 82 DC72
Chilworth St, W2 82 DC72
Chimes Av, N13 45 DN50
Chimes Shop Cen, The, Uxb. UB8 76 BK66
China Ms, SW2 *off Craster Rd* 121 DM87
★ **Chinatown**, W1
off Gerrard St 195 M10
Chinbrook Cres, SE12 124 EH90
Chinbrook Est, SE9 124 EK90
Chinbrook Rd, SE12 124 EH90
Chinchilla Dr, Houns. TW4 96 BW82
Chindits La, Brwd. CM14 54 FW50
Chine, The, N10 65 DJ56
N21 29 DP44
Wembley HA0 61 CH64
Ching Ct, WC2 195 P9
Chingdale Rd, E4 48 EE48
CHINGFORD, E4 48 EF46
⇌ **Chingford** 48 EE45
Chingford Av, E4 47 EB48
CHINGFORD GREEN, E4 48 EF46
CHINGFORD HATCH, E4 48 EC49
Chingford Ind Cen, E4 47 DY50
Chingford La, Wdf.Grn. IG8 48 EE49
Chingford Mt Rd, E4 47 EA49
Chingford Rd, E4 47 EA51
E17 47 EB53
Chingley Cl, Brom. BR1 124 EE93
Ching Way, E4 47 DZ51
Chinnery Cl, Enf. EN1
off Garnault Rd 30 DT39
Chinnor Cres, Grnf. UB6 78 CB68
Chipka St, E14 204 D5
Chipley St, SE14 103 DY79
Chipmunk Gro, Nthlt. UB5
off Argus Way 78 BY69
Chippendale All, Uxb. UB8
off Chippendale Waye 76 BK66
Chippendale St, E5 67 DX62
Chippendale Waye, Uxb. UB8 76 BK66
Chippenham Av, Wem. HA9 62 CP64
Chippenham Cl, Pnr. HA5 59 BT56
Romford RM3
off Chippenham Rd 52 FK50
Chippenham Gdns, NW6 82 DA69
Romford RM3 52 FK50
Chippenham Ms, W9 82 DA70
Chippenham Rd, W9 82 DA70
Romford RM3 52 FK51
Chippenham Wk, Rom. RM3
off Chippenham Rd 52 FK51
CHIPPERFIELD, Kings L. 6 BG31
Chipperfield Cl, Upmin. RM14 73 FS60
Chipperfield Rd, Hem.H. (Bov.) HP3 5 BB27
Kings Langley WD4 6 BK30
Orpington BR5 146 EU95
CHIPPING BARNET, Barn. 27 CY42
Chipping Cl, Barn. EN5
off St. Albans Rd 27 CY41
CHIPSTEAD, Couls. 174 DG119
CHIPSTEAD, Sev. 190 FC122
⇌ **Chipstead** 174 DF118
Chipstead, Ger.Cr. (Chal.St.P.) SL9 36 AW53
Chipstead Av, Th.Hth. CR7 141 DP98
CHIPSTEAD BOTTOM, Couls. 174 DE121
Chipstead Cl, SE19 122 DT94
Coulsdon CR5 174 DG116
Sutton SM2 158 DB109
Chipstead Ct, Wok. (Knap.) GU21 *off Creston Av* 166 AS117
Chipstead Gdns, NW2 63 CV61
Chipstead Gate, Couls. CR5
off Woodfield Cl 175 DJ119
Chipstead La, Couls. CR5 174 DB124
Sevenoaks TN13 190 FC122
Tadworth KT20 183 CZ125
Chipstead Pk, Sev. TN13 190 FD122
Chipstead Pk Cl, Sev. TN13 190 FC122
Chipstead Pl Gdns, Sev. TN13 190 FC122
Chipstead Rd, Bans. SM7 173 CZ117
Erith DA8 107 FE80
Chipstead Sta Par, Couls. (Chipstead) CR5
off Station App 174 DF118
Chipstead St, SW6 100 DA81
Chipstead Valley Rd, Couls. CR5 175 DH116
Chipstead Way, Bans. SM7 174 DF115
Chip St, SW4 101 DK83
Chirk Cl, Hayes UB4
off Braunston Dr 78 BY70
Chirton Wk, Wok. GU21
off Shilburn Way 166 AU118
Chisenhale Rd, E3 85 DY68
Chisholm Rd, Croy. CR0 142 DS103
Richmond TW10 118 CM86
CHISLEHURST 125 EN94
⇌ **Chislehurst** 145 EN96
Chislehurst Av, N12 44 DC52
★ **Chislehurst Caves**, Chis. BR7 *off Caveside Cl* 145 EN95
Chislehurst Rd, Brom. BR1 144 EK96
Chislehurst BR7 144 EK96
Orpington BR5, BR6 145 ES98
Richmond TW10 118 CL86
Sidcup DA14 126 EU92
CHISLEHURST WEST, Chis. 125 EM92
Chislet Cl, Beck. BR3
off Abbey La 123 EA94
Chisley Rd, N15 66 DS58
Chiswell Ct, Wat. WD24 24 BW38
CHISWELL GREEN, St.Alb. 8 CA26
Chiswell Grn La, St.Alb. AL2 8 BX25
Chiswell Sq, SE3
off Brook La 104 EH82
Chiswell St, EC1 197 J6
CHISWICK, W4 98 CR79
⇌ **Chiswick** 98 CQ80
Chiswick Br, SW14 98 CQ82
W4 98 CQ82
Chiswick Cl, Croy. CR0 141 DM104

235

Chi - Chu

Chiswick Common Rd, W4 **98** CR77
Chiswick Ct, Pnr. HA5 **60** BZ55
Chiswick Grn Studios, W4 *off Evershed Wk* **98** CQ77
Chiswick High Rd, W4 **98** CR77
Brentford TW8 **98** CM78
★ **Chiswick Ho**, W4 **98** CS79
Chiswick Ho Grds, W4 **98** CR79
Chiswick La, W4 **98** CS78
Chiswick La S, W4 **99** CT78
H **Chiswick Lo Hosp**, W4 **99** CT78
Chiswick Mall, W4 **99** CT79
W6 **99** CT79
⊖ **Chiswick Park** **98** CQ77
Chiswick Quay, W4 **98** CQ81
Chiswick Rd, N9 **46** DU47
W4 **98** CQ77
Chiswick Roundabout, W4 *off Chiswick High Rd* **98** CN78
Chiswick Sq, W4 *off Hogarth Roundabout* **98** CS79
Chiswick Staithe, W4 **98** CQ81
Chiswick Ter, W4 *off Acton La* **98** CQ77
Chiswick Village, W4 **98** CP78
Chiswick Wf, W4 **99** CT79
Chittenden Cotts, Wok. (Wisley) GU23 **168** BL116
Chitterfield Gate, West Dr. UB7 **94** BN80
Chitty's La, Dag. RM8 **70** EX61
Chitty St, W1 **195** L6
Chivalry Rd, SW11 **120** DE85
Chivenor Gro, Kings.T. KT2 **117** CK92
Chivers Rd, E4 **47** EB48
Choats Manor Way, Bark. IG11 **88** EW70
Choats Rd, Bark. IG11 **88** EW68
Dagenham RM9 **88** EW68
CHOBHAM, Wok. **150** AT111
Chobham Cl, Cher. (Ott.) KT16 **151** BB107
★ **Chobham Common NNR**, Wok. GU24 **150** AS105
Chobham Gdns, SW19 **119** CX89
Chobham La, Cher. (Longcr.) KT16 **132** AV102
Chobham Pk La, Wok. (Chobham) GU24 **150** AU110
Chobham Rd, E15 **67** ED64
Chertsey (Ott.) KT16 **151** BA108
Woking GU21 **166** AY116
Woking (Horsell) GU21 **150** AW113
Choir Grn, Wok. (Knap.) GU21 *off Semper Cl* **166** AS117
Cholmeley Cres, N6 **65** DH59
Cholmeley Pk, N6 **65** DH60
Cholmley Gdns, NW6 *off Fortune Grn Rd* **64** DA64
Cholmley Rd, T.Ditt. KT7 **137** CH100
Cholmondeley Av, NW10 **81** CU68
Cholmondeley Wk, Rich. TW9 **117** CJ85
Choppins Ct, E1 **202** E2
Chopwell Cl, E15 *off Bryant St* **85** ED66
CHORLEYWOOD, Rick. **21** BE43
⇌ **Chorleywood** **21** BD42
⊖ **Chorleywood** **21** BD42
CHORLEYWOOD BOTTOM, Rick. **21** BD44
Chorleywood Bottom, Rick. (Chorl.) WD3 **21** BD43
Chorleywood Cl, Rick. WD3 *off Nightingale Rd* **38** BK45
Chorleywood Common, Rick. (Chorl.) WD3 **21** BE42
Chorleywood Cres, Orp. BR5 **145** ET96
Chorleywood Ho Dr, Rick. (Chorl.) WD3 **21** BE41
Chorleywood Lo La, Rick. (Chorl.) WD3 *off Rickmansworth Rd* **21** BF41
Chorleywood Rd, Rick. WD3 **21** BG42
Choumert Gro, SE15 **102** DU82
Choumert Rd, SE15 **102** DT83
Choumert Sq, SE15 **102** DU82
Chow Sq, E8 *off Arcola St* **66** DT64
Chrislaine Cl, Stai. (Stanw.) TW19 *off High St* **114** BK86
Chrisp St, E14 **85** EB71
Christchurch Av, N12 **44** DC51
NW6 **81** CY66
Erith DA8 **107** FD79
Harrow HA3 **61** CH56
Rainham RM13 **89** FF68
Teddington TW11 **117** CG92
Wembley HA0 **80** CL65
Christchurch Cl, SW19 **120** DD94
Enfield EN2 **30** DQ40
Christchurch Ct, NW6 **81** CY66
Christchurch Cres, Grav. DA12 *off Christchurch Rd* **131** GJ87
Radlett WD7 **25** CG36
Christchurch Gdns, Epsom KT19 **156** CP111
Harrow HA3 **61** CG56
Christchurch Grn, Wem. HA0 **80** CL65
Christchurch Hill, NW3 **64** DD62
Christchurch La, Barn. EN5 **27** CY40
Christ Ch Mt, Epsom KT19 **156** CP112
Christchurch Pk, Sutt. SM2 **158** DC108
Christ Ch Pas, EC1 **196** G8
Christchurch Pas, NW3 **64** DC62
Barnet EN5 **27** CY41
Christ Ch Path, Hayes UB3 **95** BQ76
Christchurch Pl, Epsom KT19 **156** CP111
Christchurch Rd, N8 **65** DL58
SW2 **121** DM88
SW14 **118** CP85
SW19 **140** DD95
Christ Ch Rd, Beck. BR3 *off Fairfield Rd* **143** EA96
Christchurch Rd, Dart. DA1 **128** FJ87
Christ Ch Rd, Epsom KT19 **156** CL112
Christchurch Rd, Grav. DA12 **131** GJ88
Hounslow (Hthrw.Air.) TW6 *off Courtney Rd* **94** BN83
Christchurch Rd, Ilf. IG1 **69** EP60
Purley CR8 **159** DP110
Sidcup DA15 **125** ET91
Christ Ch Rd, Surb. KT5 **138** CM100
Christchurch Rd, Til. RM18 **111** GG81
Virginia Water GU25 **132** AU97
Christchurch Sq, E9 *off Victoria Pk Rd* **84** DW67
Christchurch St, SW3 **100** DF79
Christchurch Ter, SW3 *off Christchurch St* **100** DF79
Christchurch Way, SE10 **205** J9
Woking GU21 *off Church St E* **167** AZ117
Christian Ct, SE16 **203** M3
Christian Flds, SW16 **121** DN94
Christian Flds Av, Grav. DA12 **131** GJ91
Christian St, E1 **84** DU72
Christie Dr, Croy. CR0 **142** DU99
Christie Gdns, Rom. RM6 **70** EV58
Christie Rd, E9 **85** DY65
Waltham Abbey EN9 *off Deer Pk Way* **31** EB36
Christies Av, Sev. (Bad.Mt.) TN14 **164** FA110
Christie Wk, Cat. CR3 *off Hambledon Rd* **176** DR122
Christina Sq, N4 *off Adolphus Rd* **65** DP60
Christina St, EC2 **197** M4
Christine Worsley Cl, N21 *off Highfield Rd* **45** DP47
Christopher Av, W7 **97** CG76
Christopher Cl, SE16 **203** H4
Hornchurch RM12 *off Chevington Way* **72** FK63
Sidcup DA15 **125** ET85
Christopher Ct, Tad. KT20 *off High St* **173** CW123
Christopher Gdns, Dag. RM9 *off Wren Rd* **70** EX64
Christopher Pl, NW1 **195** N3
Christopher Rd, Sthl. UB2 **95** BV77
Christopher's Ms, W11 *off Penzance St* **81** CY74
Christopher St, EC2 **197** L5
Christy Rd, West. (Bigg.H.) TN16 **178** EJ115
Chryssell Rd, SW9 **101** DN80
Chubworthy St, SE14 **103** DY79
Chucks La, Tad. KT20 **173** CV124
Chudleigh Cres, Ilf. IG3 **69** ES63
Chudleigh Gdns, Sutt. SM1 **140** DC104
Chudleigh Rd, NW6 **81** CX66
SE4 **123** DZ85
Romford RM3 **52** FL49
Twickenham TW2 **117** CF87
Chudleigh St, E1 **85** DX72
Chudleigh Way, Ruis. HA4 **59** BU60
Chulsa Rd, SE26 **122** DV92
Chumleigh St, SE5 **102** DS79
Chumleigh Wk, Surb. KT5 **138** CM98
Church All, Croy. CR0 **141** DN102
Gravesend DA11 *off High St* **131** GH86
Watford (Ald.) WD25 **24** CC38
Church App, SE21 **122** DR90
Egham TW20 **133** BC97
Sevenoaks (Cudham) TN14 *off Cudham La S* **179** EQ115
Staines (Stanw.) TW19 **114** BK86
Church Av, E4 **47** ED51
NW1 *off Kentish Town Rd* **83** DH65
SW14 **98** CR83
Beckenham BR3 **143** EA95
Northolt UB5 **78** BZ66
Pinner HA5 **60** BY58
Ruislip HA4 **59** BR60
Sidcup DA14 **126** EU92
Southall UB2 **96** BY76
Churchbury Cl, Enf. EN1 **30** DS40
Churchbury La, Enf. EN1 **30** DR41
Churchbury Rd, SE9 **124** EK87
Enfield EN1 **30** DR40
Church Cl, N20 **44** DE48
W8 *off Kensington Ch St* **100** DB75
Addlestone KT15 **152** BH105
Edgware HA8 **42** CQ50
Hayes UB4 **77** BR71
Leatherhead (Fetch.) KT22 **171** CD124
Loughton IG10 **33** EM40
Northwood HA6 **39** BT52
Potters Bar (Cuffley) EN6 **13** DL29
Radlett WD7 **25** CG36
Staines TW18 *off The Broadway* **134** BJ97
Tadworth KT20 *off Buckland Rd* **183** CZ127
Uxbridge UB8 **76** BH68
West Drayton UB7 **94** BL76
Woking (Horsell) GU21 **166** AX116
Church Ct, Reig. RH2 **184** DB134
Richmond TW9 *off George St* **117** CK85
Church Cres, E9 **85** DX66
N3 **43** CZ53
N10 **65** DH56
N20 **44** DE48
South Ockendon RM15 **91** FW69
Churchcroft Cl, SW12 *off Endlesham Rd* **120** DG87
Churchdown, Brom. BR1 **124** EE91
Church Dr, NW9 **62** CR60
Harrow HA2 **60** BZ58
West Wickham BR4 **144** EE104
Church Elm La, Dag. RM10 **88** FA65
CHURCH END, N3 **43** CZ53
CHURCH END, NW10 **80** CS65
Church End, E17 **67** EB56
NW4 **63** CV55
Church Entry, EC4 **196** G9
Church Fm Cl, Swan. BR8 **147** FC100
★ **Church Farm Ho Mus**, NW4 (Hendon) **63** CV55
Church Fm La, Sutt. SM3 **157** CY107
Church Fm Way, Wat. (Ald.) WD25 **24** CB38
Church Fld, Dart. DA2 **128** FK89
Epping CM16 **18** EU29
Radlett WD7 **25** CG36
Sevenoaks TN13 **190** FE122
Churchfield Av, N12 **44** DC51
Churchfield Cl, Har. HA2 **60** CC56
Hayes UB3 *off West Av* **77** BT73
Churchfield Ms, Slou. SL2 **74** AU72
Churchfield Path, Wal.Cr. (Chsht.) EN8 **14** DW29
Churchfield Rd, W3 **80** CQ74
W7 **97** CE75
W13 **79** CH74
Gerrards Cross (Chal.St.P.) SL9 **36** AX53
Reigate RH2 **183** CZ133
Walton-on-Thames KT12 **135** BU102
Welling DA16 **106** EU83
Weybridge KT13 **152** BN105
Churchfields, E18 **48** EG53
SE10 *off Roan St* **103** EC79
Loughton IG10 **32** EL42
West Molesey KT8 **136** CA97
Woking (Horsell) GU21 **166** AY116
Churchfields Av, Felt. TW13 **116** BZ90
Weybridge KT13 **153** BP105
Churchfields Rd, Beck. BR3 **143** DX96
Watford WD24 **23** BT36
Church Gdns, W5 **97** CK75
Wembley HA0 **61** CG63
Church Gate, SW6 **99** CY83
Churchgate, Wal.Cr. (Chsht.) EN8 **14** DV30
Churchgate Rd, Wal.Cr. (Chsht.) EN8 **14** DV29
Church Grn, Hayes UB3 **77** BT72
Walton-on-Thames KT12 **154** BW107
Church Gro, SE13 **103** EB84
Amersham HP6 **20** AY39
Kingston upon Thames KT1 **137** CJ95
Slough (Wexham) SL3 **74** AW71
Church Hill, E17 **67** EA56
N21 **45** DM45
SE18 **105** EM76
SW19 **119** CZ92
Abbots Langley (Bedmond) WD5 **7** BT26
Carshalton SM5 **158** DF106
Caterham CR3 **176** DT124
Dartford DA2 **128** FK90
Dartford (Cray.) DA2 **107** FE84
Epping CM16 **18** EU29
Greenhithe DA9 **129** FS85
Harrow HA1 **61** CE60
Loughton IG10 **32** EL41
Orpington BR6 **146** EU101
Purley CR8 **159** DL110
Redhill (Merst.) RH1 **185** DH126
Redhill (Nutfld.) RH1 **185** DM133
Sevenoaks (Plaxtol) TN15 **179** EQ115
Uxbridge (Hare.) UB9 **58** BJ55
Westerham (Tats.) TN16 **178** EK122
Woking (Horsell) GU21 **166** AX116
Woking (Pyrford) GU22 **167** BF117
Church Hill Rd, E17 **67** EB56
Barnet EN4 **44** DF45
Surbiton KT6 **138** CL99
Sutton SM3 **157** CX105
Church Hill Wd, Orp. BR5 **145** ET99
Church Hollow, Purf. RM19 **108** FN78
Church Hyde, SE18 *off Old Mill Rd* **105** ES79
Churchill Av, Har. HA3 **61** CH58
Uxbridge UB10 **77** BP69
Churchill Cl, Dart. DA1 **128** FP88
Feltham TW14 **115** BT88
Leatherhead (Fetch.) KT22 **171** CE123
Uxbridge UB10 **77** BP69
Warlingham CR6 **176** DW117
Churchill Ct, W5 **80** CM70
Northolt UB5 **60** CA64
Staines TW18 *off Chestnut Gro* **114** BJ93
Churchill Dr, Wey. KT13 **135** BQ104
Churchill Gdns, SW1 **101** DJ78
W3 **80** CN72
Churchill Gdns Rd, SW1 **101** DH78
Churchill Ms, Wdf.Grn. IG8 *off High Rd Woodford Grn* **48** EF51
Churchill Pl, E14 **204** C2
Harrow HA1 *off Sandridge Cl* **61** CE56
Churchill Rd, E16 **86** EJ72
NW2 **81** CV65
NW5 **65** DH63
Dartford (Hort.Kir.) DA4 **148** FQ98
Edgware HA8 **42** CM51
Epsom KT19 **156** CN111
Gravesend DA11 **131** GF88
Grays RM17 **110** GD79
Slough SL3 **93** AZ77
South Croydon CR2 **160** DQ109
Churchill Ter, E4 **47** EA49
Churchill Wk, E9 **66** DW64
Churchill Way, Brom. BR1 *off Ethelbert Rd* **144** EG97
Sunbury-on-Thames TW16 **115** BU92
Westerham (Bigg.H.) TN16 **162** EK113
Church Island, Stai. TW18 **113** BD91
Church La, E11 **68** EE60
E17 **67** EB56
N2 **64** DD55
N8 **65** DM56
N9 **46** DU47
N17 **46** DS53
NW9 **62** CQ61
SW17 **121** DH91
SW19 **139** CZ95
W5 **97** CJ75
Banstead (Nork) SM7 **173** CX117
Brentwood (Gt.Warley) CM13 **73** FW58
Brentwood (Hutton) CM13 **55** GE46
Bromley BR2 **144** EL102
Church La, Caterham CR3 **175** DN123
Chessington KT9 **156** CM107
Chislehurst BR7 **145** EQ95
Coulsdon CR5 **174** DG122
Dagenham RM10 **89** FB65
Enfield EN1 **30** DR41
Epping (N.Wld.Bas.) CM16 **19** FB26
Epsom (Headley) KT18 **172** CQ124
Gerrards Cross (Chal.St.P.) SL9 **36** AX53
Godstone RH9 **187** DX132
Harrow HA3 **41** CF53
Hemel Hempstead (Bov.) HP3 **5** BB27
Kings Langley WD4 **6** BN29
Loughton IG10 **33** EM41
Oxted RH8 **188** EE129
Pinner HA5 **60** BY55
Potters Bar (Northaw) EN6 **12** DG30
Purfleet RM19 *off London Rd Purfleet* **108** FN78
Rainham (Wenn.) RM13 **90** FK72
Redhill (Bletch.) RH1 **186** DR133
Richmond TW10 **118** CL88
Rickmansworth (Mill End) WD3 **38** BG46
Rickmansworth (Sarratt) WD3 **21** BF38
Romford RM1 **71** FE56
Romford (Abridge) RM4 **34** EY40
Romford (Stap.Abb.) RM4 **35** FC42
Slough (Stoke P.) SL2 **74** AT69
Slough (Wexham) SL3 **74** AW71
Teddington TW11 **117** CF92
Thames Ditton KT7 **137** CF100
Twickenham TW1 **117** CG88
Upminster (N.Ock.) RM14 **73** FV64
Uxbridge UB8 **76** BH68
Wallington SM6 **141** DK104
Waltham Cross (Chsht.) EN8 **14** DV29
Warlingham CR6 **177** DX117
Warlingham (Chel.) CR6 **177** EC116
Watford (Ald.) WD25 **24** CB38
Westerham TN16 **178** EK122
Weybridge KT13 **152** BN105
Church La Av, Couls. CR5 **175** DH122
Church La Dr, Couls. CR5 **175** DH122
Churchley Rd, SE26 **122** DV91
Church Manor Est, SW9 *off Vassall Rd* **101** DN80
Church Manorway, SE2 **105** ET77
Erith DA8 **107** FD76
Church Manorway Ind Est, Erith DA8 **107** FC76
Churchmead Cl, Barn. EN4 **28** DE44
Church Meadow, Surb. KT6 **137** CJ103
Churchmead Rd, NW10 **81** CU65
Church Ms, Add. KT15 **152** BJ105
Churchmore Rd, SW16 **141** DJ95
Church Mt, N2 **64** DD57
Church Paddock Ct, Wall. SM6 **141** DK104
Church Pas, EC2 *off Gresham St* **84** DQ72
Barnet EN5 *off Wood St* **27** CZ42
Surbiton KT6 **138** CL99
Church Path, E11 **68** EG57
E17 *off St. Mary Rd* **67** EB56
N12 **44** DC50
N17 *off White Hart La* **46** DS52
N20 **44** DC49
NW10 **80** CS66
SW14 **98** CR83
SW19 **140** DA96
W4 **98** CQ76
W7 **79** CE74
Cobham KT11 **153** BV114
Coulsdon CR5 **175** DN118
Gravesend (Nthflt.) DA11 **130** GC86
Grays RM17 **110** GA79
Greenhithe DA9 **129** FT85
Mitcham CR4 **140** DE97
Southall UB1 **78** CA74
Southall (Sthl.Grn.) UB2 **96** BZ76
Woking GU21 *off High St* **167** AZ117
Church Pl, SW1 **199** L1
W5 *off Church Gdns* **97** CK75
Mitcham CR4 **140** DE97
Twickenham TW1 *off Church St* **117** CH88
Uxbridge (Ickhm.) UB10 **59** BQ62
Church Ri, SE23 **123** DX88
Chessington KT9 **156** CM107
Church Rd, E10 **67** EB61
E12 **68** EL64
E17 **47** DY54
N6 **64** DG58
N17 **46** DS53
NW4 **63** CV56
NW10 **80** CS65
SE19 **142** DS95
SW13 **99** CT82
SW19 (Wimbledon) **119** CY91
W3 **98** CQ75
W7 **79** CF74
Addlestone KT15 **152** BG106
Ashford TW15 **114** BM90
Ashtead KT21 **171** CK117
Barking IG11 **87** EQ65
Bexleyheath DA7 **106** EZ82
Bromley BR2 **144** EG96
Bromley (Short.) BR2 **144** EE97
Buckhurst Hill IG9 **48** EH46
Caterham CR3 **176** DT123
Caterham (Wold.) CR3 **177** DX122
Croydon CR0 **141** DP104
Dartford (Sutt.H.) DA4 **128** FL94
East Molesey KT8 **137** CD98
Egham TW20 **113** BA92
Enfield EN3 **30** DW44
Epsom KT17 **156** CS112
Epsom (W.Ewell) KT19 **156** CR108
Erith DA8 **107** FD78
Esher (Clay.) KT10 **155** CF107
Feltham TW13 **116** BX92
Gravesend (Cobham) DA12, DA13 **131** GJ94
Church Rd, Green. DA9 **129** FS85
Hayes UB3 **77** BT72
Hounslow (Cran.) TW5 **95** BV78
Hounslow (Heston) TW5 **96** CA80
Ilford IG2 **69** ER58
Isleworth TW7 **97** CD81
Iver SL0 **75** BC69
Kenley CR8 **176** DR115
Keston BR2 **162** EK108
Kingston upon Thames KT1 **138** CM96
Leatherhead KT22 **171** CH122
Leatherhead (Bkhm.) KT23 **170** BZ123
Loughton (High Beach) IG10 **32** EH40
Mitcham CR4 **140** DD96
Northolt UB5 **78** BZ66
Northwood HA6 **39** BT52
Orpington (Chels.) BR6 **164** EY106
Orpington (Farnboro.) BR6 **163** EQ106
Potters Bar EN6 **12** DB30
Purley CR8 **159** DL110
Richmond TW9, TW10 **118** CL85
Richmond (Ham) TW10 **118** CM92
Romford (Harold Wd.) RM3 **52** FN53
Romford (Noak Hill) RM4 **52** FK46
Sevenoaks (Halst.) TN14 **164** EY111
Sevenoaks (Seal) TN15 **191** FM121
Shepperton TW17 **135** BP101
Sidcup DA14 **126** EU91
Southall UB2 **96** BZ76
Stanmore HA7 **41** CH50
Surbiton KT6 **137** CJ103
Sutton SM3 **157** CY107
Swanley BR8 **148** FK95
Swanley (Crock.) BR8 **147** FD101
Swanscombe DA10 **130** FZ86
Teddington TW11 **117** CE91
Tilbury RM18 **111** GF81
Tilbury (W.Til.) RM18 **111** GL79
Uxbridge (Cowley) UB8 **76** BK70
Uxbridge (Hare.) UB9 **58** BJ55
Wallington SM6 **141** DJ104
Warlingham CR6 **176** DW117
Watford WD17 **23** BU39
Welling DA16 **106** EV82
West Byfleet (Byfleet) KT14 **152** BM113
West Drayton UB7 **94** BK76
Westerham (Bigg.H.) TN16 **178** EK117
Westerham (Brasted) TN16 **180** EV124
Whyteleafe CR3 **176** DT118
Windsor (Old Wind.) SL4 **112** AV85
Woking (Horsell) GU21 **166** AY116
Woking (St. John's) GU21 **166** AU119
Worcester Park KT4 **138** CS102
Church Rd Merton, SW19 **140** DD95
Church Rd Twr Block, Stan. HA7 *off Church Rd* **41** CJ50
Church Row, NW3 **64** DC63
Chislehurst BR7 **125** EQ94
Church Side, Epsom KT18 **156** CP113
Churchside Cl, West. (Bigg.H.) TN16 **178** EJ117
Church Sq, Shep. TW17 **135** BP101
Church Street **141** DP103
Church St, E15 **86** EE67
E16 **87** EP74
N9 **46** DS47
NW8 **194** A6
W2 **194** A6
W4 **98** CS79
Cobham KT11 **169** BV115
Croydon CR0 **142** DQ103
Dagenham RM10 **89** FB65
Enfield EN2 **30** DR41
Epsom KT17 **156** CS113
Epsom (Ewell) KT17 **157** CU109
Esher KT10 **154** CB105
Gravesend DA11 **131** GH86
Gravesend (Sthflt.) DA13 **130** GA92
Grays RM17 **110** GC79
Hampton TW12 **136** CC95
Hemel Hempstead (Bov.) HP3 **5** BB27
Isleworth TW7 **97** CH83
Kingston upon Thames KT1 **137** CK96
Leatherhead KT22 **171** CH122
Reigate RH2 **184** DA134
Rickmansworth WD3 **38** BL46
Sevenoaks (Seal) TN15 **191** FN121
Sevenoaks (Shore.) TN14 **165** FF111
Slough SL1 **92** AT76
Staines TW18 **113** BE91
Sunbury-on-Thames TW16 **135** BV97
Sutton SM1 *off High St* **158** DB106
Twickenham TW1 **117** CG88
Waltham Abbey EN9 **15** EC33
Walton-on-Thames KT12 **135** BU102
Watford WD18 **24** BW42
Weybridge KT13 **152** BN105
Woking (Old Wok.) GU22 **167** BC121
Church St E, Wok. GU21 **167** AZ117
Church St Est, NW8 **194** A5
Church St N, E15 **86** EE67
Church St Pas, E15 *off Church St* **86** EE67
Church St W, Wok. GU21 **166** AY117
Church Stretton Rd, Houns. TW3 **116** CC85
Church Ter, NW4 **63** CV55
SE13 **104** EE83
SW8 **101** DK82
Richmond TW10 **117** CK85
CHURCH TOWN, Gdse. **187** DX131
Church Trd Est, The, Erith DA8 **107** FG80
Church Vale, N2 **64** DF55
SE23 **122** DW89

Chu - Cle

Church Vw, S.Ock. (Aveley) RM15 108 FQ75
Swanley BR8 off Lime Rd 147 FD97
Upminster RM14 72 FN61
Churchview Rd, Twick. TW2 117 CD88
Church Vil, Sev. TN13 off Church Fld 190 FE122
Church Wk, N6 off Swains La 64 DG62
N16 66 DR63
NW2 63 CZ62
NW4 63 CW55
NW9 62 CR61
SW13 99 CU81
SW15 119 CV85
SW16 141 DJ96
SW20 139 CW97
Brentford TW8 97 CJ79
Bushey WD23 off High St 24 CA44
Caterham CR3 176 DU124
Chertsey KT16 134 BG101
Dartford DA2 128 FK90
Dartford (Eyns.) DA4 148 FL104
Enfield EN2 off Church La 30 DR41
Gravesend DA12 131 GK88
Hayes UB3 77 BT72
Leatherhead KT22 off The Crescent 171 CH122
Redhill (Bletch.) RH1 186 DR133
Reigate RH2 off Reigate Rd 184 DC134
Richmond TW9 off Red Lion St 117 CK85
Thames Ditton KT7 137 CF100
Walton-on-Thames KT12 135 BU102
Weybridge KT13 off Beales La 135 BP103
Church Wk Shop Cen, Cat. CR3 off Church Wk 176 DU124
Church Way, N20 44 DD48
Churchway, NW1 195 N2
Church Way, Barn. EN4 28 DF42
Edgware HA8 42 CN51
Oxted RH8 188 EF132
South Croydon CR2 160 DT110
Churchwell Path, E9 66 DW64
Churchwood Gdns, Wdf.Grn. IG8 48 EG49
Churchyard Row, SE11 200 G8
Church Yd Wk, W2 off St. Marys Sq 82 DD71
Churston Av, E13 86 EH67
Churston Cl, SW2 off Tulse Hill 121 DP88
Churston Dr, Mord. SM4 139 CX99
Churston Gdns, N11 45 DJ51
Churton Pl, SW1 199 L9
Churton St, SW1 199 L9
Chusan Pl, E14 off Commercial Rd 85 DZ72
Chuters Cl, W.Byf. (Byfleet) KT14 152 BL112
Chuters Gro, Epsom KT17 157 CT112
Chyne, The, Ger.Cr. SL9 57 AZ57
Chyngton Cl, Sid. DA15 125 ET90
Cibber Rd, SE23 123 DX89
Cicada Rd, SW18 120 DC85
Cicely Rd, SE15 102 DU81
Cimba Wd, Grav. DA12 131 GL91
Cinderella Path, NW11 off North End Rd 64 DB60
Cinderford Way, Brom. BR1 124 EE91
Cinder Path, Wok. GU22 166 AW119
Cinema Par, W5 off Ashbourne Rd 80 CM70
Cinnabar Wf, E1 202 C3
Cinnamon Cl, Croy. CR0 141 DL101
Cinnamon Row, SW11 100 DC83
Cinnamon St, E1 202 E3
Cintra Pk, SE19 122 DT94
Circle, The, NW2 62 CS62
NW7 42 CR50
SE1 201 P4
Tilbury RM18 off Toronto Rd 111 GG81
Circle Gdns, SW19 140 DA96
West Byfleet (Byfleet) KT14 off High Rd 152 BM112
Circle Rd, Walt. KT12 153 BS110
Circuits, The, Pnr. HA5 60 BW56
Circular Rd, N17 66 DT55
Circular Way, SE18 105 EM79
Circus Ms, W1 194 D6
Circus Pl, EC2 197 L7
Circus Rd, NW8 82 DD69
Circus St, SE10 103 EC80
Cirencester St, W2 82 DB71
Cirrus Cres, Grav. DA12 131 GL92
Cissbury Ring N, N12 43 CZ50
Cissbury Ring S, N12 43 CZ50
Cissbury Rd, N15 66 DR57
Citadel Pl, SE11 200 B10
Citizen Ho, N7 off Harvist Est 65 DN63
Citizen Rd, N7 65 DN63
C.I. Twr, N.Mal. KT3 138 CS97
Citron Ter, SE15 off Nunhead La 102 DV83
City Forum, EC1 197 H2
City Gdn Row, N1 196 G1
City Gate Ho, Ilf. IG2 69 EP58
City Ho, Croy. CR0 141 DP101
★ City of Westminster Archives Cen, SW1 off St. Ann's St 199 N6
City Pt, EC2 197 K7
City Rd, EC1 196 F1
⇌ City Thameslink 196 F9
★ City Uni, EC1 196 F3
Civic Sq, Til. RM18 111 GG82
Civic Way, Ilf. IG6 69 EQ56
Ruislip HA4 60 BX64
Clabon Ms, SW1 198 D7
Clacket La, West. TN16 178 EL124
Clack La, Ruis. HA4 59 BQ60
Clack St, SE16 202 G5
Clacton Rd, E6 86 EK69
E17 67 DY58
N17 off Sperling Rd 46 DT54
Claigmar Gdns, N3 44 DB53
Claire Ct, N12 44 DC48
Bushey (Bushey Hth.) WD23 41 CD46
Pinner HA5 off Westfield Pk 40 BZ52
Claire Gdns, Stan. HA7 41 CJ50
Claire Pl, E14 204 A6
Clairvale, Horn. RM11 72 FL59
Clairvale Rd, Houns. TW5 96 BX81
Clairview Rd, SW16 121 DH92
Clairville Ct, Reig. RH2 184 DD134
Clairville Gdns, W7 79 CF74
Clairville Pt, SE23 123 DX90
Clammas Way, Uxb. UB8 76 BJ71
Clamp Hill, Stan. HA7 41 CD49
Clancarty Rd, SW6 100 DA82
Clandon Av, Egh. TW20 113 BC94
Clandon Cl, W3 off Avenue Rd 98 CP75
Epsom KT17 157 CT107
Clandon Gdns, N3 64 DA55
Clandon Rd, Ilf. IG3 69 ES61
Clandon St, SE8 103 EA82
Clanfield Way, SE15 off Diamond St 102 DS80
Clanricarde Gdns, W2 82 DA73
Clapgate Rd, Bushey WD23 24 CB44
CLAPHAM, SW4 101 DH83
★ Clapham Common, SW4 100 DG84
⊖ Clapham Common 101 DJ84
Clapham Common N Side, SW4 101 DH84
Clapham Common S Side, SW4 121 DH85
Clapham Common W Side, SW4 100 DG84
Clapham Cres, SW4 101 DK84
Clapham Est, SW11 100 DE84
⇌ Clapham High Street 101 DK83
Clapham High St, SW4 101 DK84
⇌ Clapham Junction 100 DD84
Clapham Manor St, SW4 101 DJ83
⊖ Clapham North 101 DL83
CLAPHAM PARK, SW4 121 DK86
Clapham Pk Est, SW4 121 DK86
Clapham Pk Rd, SW4 101 DK84
Clapham Rd, SW9 101 DL83
Clapham Rd Est, SW4 101 DK83
⊖ Clapham South 121 DH86
Clap La, Dag. RM10 71 FB62
Claps Gate La, E6 87 EP70
⇌ Clapton 66 DV61
Clapton Common, E5 66 DT59
CLAPTON PARK, E5 67 DY63
Clapton Pk Est, E5 off Blackwell Cl 67 DY63
Clapton Pas, E5 66 DW64
Clapton Sq, E5 66 DW64
Clapton Ter, N16 off Oldhill St 66 DU60
Clapton Way, E5 66 DU63
Clara Pl, SE18 105 EN77
Clare Cl, N2 off Thomas More Way 64 DC55
Borehamwood (Elstree) WD6 26 CM44
West Byfleet KT14 152 BG113
Clare Cor, SE9 125 EP87
Clare Cotts, Red. (Bletch.) RH1 185 DP133
Clare Ct, Cat. (Wold.) CR3 177 EA123
Northwood HA6 39 BS50
Clare Cres, Lthd. KT22 171 CG118
Claredale, Wok. GU22 off Claremont Av 166 AY119
Claredale St, E2 84 DU68
Clare Gdns, E7 68 EG63
W11 off Westbourne Pk Rd 81 CY72
Barking IG11 87 ET65
Egham TW20 off Mowbray Cres 113 BA92
Clare Hill, Esher KT10 154 CB107
Clare Ho, E3 85 DZ67
Clare La, N1 84 DQ66
Clare Lawn Av, SW14 118 CR85
Clare Mkt, WC2 196 B9
Clare Ms, SW6 off Waterford Rd 100 DB80
Claremont, St.Alb. (Brick.Wd.) AL2 8 CA31
Waltham Cross (Chsht.) EN7 14 DT29
Claremont Av, Esher KT10 154 BZ107
Harrow HA3 62 CL57
New Malden KT3 139 CU99
Sunbury-on-Thames TW16 135 BV95
Walton-on-Thames KT12 154 BX105
Woking GU22 166 AY119
Claremont Cl, E16 87 EN74
N1 196 E1
SW2 off Streatham Hill 121 DL88
Grays RM16 off Premier Av 110 GC76
Orpington BR6 163 EN105
South Croydon CR2 176 DV115
Walton-on-Thames KT12 154 BW106
Claremont Ct, Surb. KT6 off St. James Rd 137 CK100
Claremont Cres, Dart. DA1 107 FE84
Rickmansworth (Crox.Grn.) WD3 23 BQ43
Claremont Dr, Esher KT10 154 CB108
Shepperton TW17 135 BP100
Woking GU22 166 AY119
Claremont End, Esher KT10 154 CB107
Claremont Gdns, Ilf. IG3 69 ES61
Surbiton KT6 138 CL99
Upminster RM14 73 FR60
Claremont Gro, W4 off Edensor Gdns 98 CS80
Woodford Green IG8 48 EJ51
★ Claremont Landscape Gdns, Esher KT10 154 BZ108
Claremont La, Esher KT10 154 CB105
CLAREMONT PARK, Esher 154 CB108
Claremont Pk, N3 43 CY53
Claremont Pk Rd, Esher KT10 154 CB107
Claremont Pl, Grav. DA11 off Cutmore St 131 GH87
Claremont Rd, E7 68 EH64
E17 47 DY54
N6 65 DJ59
NW2 63 CX62
W9 81 CY68
W13 79 CG71
Barnet EN4 28 DD37
Bromley BR1 144 EL98
Croydon CR0 142 DU102
Esher (Clay.) KT10 155 CE108
Harrow HA3 41 CE54
Hornchurch RM11 71 FG58
Redhill RH1 184 DG131
Staines TW18 113 BD92
Surbiton KT6 138 CL100
Swanley BR8 127 FE94
Teddington TW11 117 CF92
Twickenham TW1 117 CJ86
West Byfleet KT14 152 BG112
Claremont Sq, N1 196 D1
Claremont St, E16 87 EN74
N18 46 DU51
SE10 103 EB79
Claremont Way, NW2 63 CW60
Claremount Cl, Epsom KT18 173 CW117
Claremount Gdns, Epsom KT18 173 CW117
Clarence Av, SW4 121 DK86
Bromley BR1 144 EL98
Ilford IG2 69 EN58
New Malden KT3 138 CQ96
Upminster RM14 72 FN61
Clarence Cl, Barn. EN4 28 DD43
Bushey (Bushey Hth.) WD23 41 CF45
Walton-on-Thames KT12 154 BW105
Clarence Ct, Egh. TW20 off Clarence St 113 AZ93
Clarence Cres, SW4 121 DK86
Sidcup DA14 126 EV90
Clarence Dr, Egh. (Eng.Grn.) TW20 112 AW91
Clarence Gdns, NW1 195 J3
Clarence Gate, Wdf.Grn. IG8 49 EN51
Clarence Gate Gdns, NW1 off Glentworth St 82 DF70
★ Clarence Ho, SW1 199 L4
Clarence La, SW15 118 CS86
Clarence Ms, E5 66 DV64
SE16 203 H3
SW12 121 DH87
Clarence Pas, NW1 195 P1
Clarence Pl, E5 66 DV64
Gravesend DA12 131 GH87
Clarence Rd, E5 66 DV63
E12 68 EK64
E16 86 EE70
E17 47 DX54
N15 66 DQ57
N22 45 DL52
NW6 81 CZ66
SE9 124 EL89
SW19 120 DB93
W4 98 CN78
Bexleyheath DA6 106 EY84
Brentwood CM15 54 FV44
Bromley BR1 144 EK97
Croydon CR0 142 DR101
Enfield EN3 30 DV43
Grays RM17 110 GA79
Richmond TW9 98 CM81
Sidcup DA14 126 EV90
Sutton SM1 158 DB105
Teddington TW11 117 CF93
Wallington SM6 159 DH106
Walton-on-Thames KT12 153 BV105
Westerham (Bigg.H.) TN16 179 EM118
Clarence Row, Grav. DA12 131 GH87
Clarence St, Egh. TW20 113 AZ93
Kingston upon Thames KT1 138 CL96
Richmond TW9 98 CL84
Southall UB2 96 BX76
Staines TW18 113 BE91
Clarence Ter, NW1 194 E4
Hounslow TW3 96 CB84
Clarence Wk, SW4 101 DL82
Clarence Way, NW1 83 DH66
Clarence Way Est, NW1 83 DH66
Clarenden Pl, Dart. DA2 127 FD92
Clarendon Cl, E9 84 DW66
W2 194 B10
Orpington BR5 146 EU97
Clarendon Ct, Slou. SL2 74 AV73
Clarendon Cres, Twick. TW2 117 CD90
Clarendon Cross, W11 off Portland Rd 81 CY73
Clarendon Dr, SW15 99 CW84
Clarendon Gdns, NW4 63 CV55
W9 82 DC70
Dartford DA2 129 FR87
Ilford IG1 69 EM60
Wembley HA9 62 CL63
Clarendon Gate, Cher. (Ott.) KT16 151 BD107
Clarendon Grn, Orp. BR5 146 EU98
Clarendon Gro, NW1 195 M2
Mitcham CR4 140 DF97
Orpington BR5 146 EU97
Clarendon Ms, W2 194 B9
Ashtead KT21 172 CL119
Bexley DA5 127 FB88
Borehamwood WD6 off Clarendon Rd 26 CN41
Clarendon Path, Orp. BR5 146 EU97
Clarendon Pl, W2 194 B10
Sevenoaks TN13 off Clarendon Rd 190 FG125
Clarendon Ri, SE13 103 EC83
Clarendon Rd, E11 67 ED60
Clarendon Rd, E17 67 EB58
E18 68 EG55
N8 65 DM55
N15 65 DP56
N18 46 DU51
N22 45 DM54
SW19 120 DE94
W5 80 CL70
W11 81 CY73
Ashford TW15 114 BM91
Borehamwood WD6 26 CN41
Croydon CR0 141 DP103
Gravesend DA12 131 GJ86
Harrow HA1 61 CE58
Hayes UB3 95 BT75
Redhill RH1 184 DF133
Sevenoaks TN13 190 FG124
Wallington SM6 159 DJ107
Waltham Cross (Chsht.) EN8 15 DX29
Watford WD17 23 BV40
Clarendon St, SW1 101 DH78
Clarendon Ter, W9 off Lanark Pl 82 DC70
Clarendon Wk, W11 81 CY72
Clarendon Way, N21 30 DQ44
Chislehurst BR7 145 ET97
Orpington BR5 145 ET97
Clarens St, SE6 123 DZ89
Clare Pk, Amer. HP7 20 AS40
Clare Pl, SW15 off Minstead Gdns 119 CT87
Clare Pt, NW2 off Claremont Rd 63 CX60
Clare Rd, E11 67 ED58
NW10 81 CU66
SE14 103 DZ81
Greenford UB6 79 CD65
Hounslow TW4 96 BZ83
Staines (Stanw.) TW19 114 BL87
Clare St, E2 84 DV68
Claret Gdns, SE25 142 DS98
Clareville Gro, SW7 100 DC77
Clareville Rd, Cat. CR3 176 DU124
Orpington BR5 145 EQ103
Clareville St, SW7 100 DC77
Clare Way, Bexh. DA7 106 EY81
Sevenoaks TN13 191 FJ127
Clare Wd, Lthd. KT22 171 CH118
Clarewood Wk, SW9 off Somerleyton Rd 101 DN84
Clarges Ms, W1 199 H2
Clarges St, W1 199 J2
Claribel Rd, SW9 101 DP82
Clarice Way, Wall. SM6 159 DL109
Claridge Rd, Dag. RM8 70 EX60
Clarina Rd, SE20 off Evelina Rd 123 DX94
Clarissa Rd, Rom. RM6 70 EX59
Clarissa St, E8 84 DT67
Clark Cl, Erith DA8 off Forest Rd 107 FG81
Clarkebourne Dr, Grays RM17 110 GD79
Clarke Grn, Wat. WD25 23 BU35
Clarke Ms, N9 off Plevna Rd 46 DV48
Clarke Path, N16 66 DU60
Clarkes Av, Wor.Pk. KT4 139 CX102
Clarkes Dr, Uxb. UB8 76 BL71
Clarke's Ms, W1 194 G6
Clarke Way, Wat. WD25 23 BU35
Clarkfield, Rick. (Mill End) WD3 38 BH46
Clark Lawrence Ct, SW11 off Winstanley Rd 100 DD83
Clarks La, Epp. CM16 17 ET31
Sevenoaks (Halst.) TN14 164 EZ112
Warlingham CR6 178 EF123
Westerham TN16 178 EK123
Clarks Mead, Bushey WD23 40 CC45
Clarkson Rd, E16 86 EF72
Clarkson Row, NW1 195 J1
Clarksons, The, Bark. IG11 87 EQ68
Clarkson St, E2 84 DV69
Clarks Pl, EC2 197 M8
Clarks Rd, Ilf. IG1 69 ER61
Clark St, E1 84 DV71
Clark Way, Houns. TW5 96 BX80
Classon Cl, West Dr. UB7 94 BL75
Claston Cl, Dart. DA1 off Iron Mill La 107 FE84
CLATTERFORD END, Ong. 19 FG30
Claude Rd, E10 67 EC61
E13 86 EH67
SE15 102 DV82
Claude St, E14 203 P8
Claudia Jones Way, SW2 121 DL86
Claudian Way, Grays RM16 111 GH76
Claudia Pl, SW19 119 CY88
Claughton Rd, E13 86 EJ68
Claughton Way, Brwd. CM13 55 GD44
Clauson Av, Nthlt. UB5 60 CB64
Clavell St, SE10 103 EC79
Claverdale Rd, SW2 121 DM87
Claverhambury Rd, Wal.Abb. EN9 16 EF29
Clavering Av, SW13 99 CV79
Clavering Cl, Twick. TW1 117 CG91
Clavering Rd, E12 68 EK60
Claverings Ind Est, N9 47 DX47
Clavering Way, Brwd. CM13 off Poplar Dr 55 GC44
Claverley Gro, N3 44 DA52
Claverley Vil, N3 off Claverley Gro 44 DB52
Claverton Cl, Hem.H. (Bov.) HP3 5 BA28
Claverton St, SW1 101 DJ78
Clave St, E1 202 F3
Claxton Gro, W6 99 CX78
Clay Av, Mitch. CR4 141 DH96
Claybank Gro, SE13 off Algernon Rd 103 EB83
Claybourne Ms, SE19 off Church Rd 122 DS94
Claybridge Rd, SE12 124 EJ91
Claybrook Cl, N2 64 DD55
Claybrook Rd, W6 99 CX79
Clayburn Gdns, S.Ock. RM15 91 FV73
Claybury, Bushey WD23 40 CB45
Claybury Bdy, Ilf. IG5 68 EL55
Claybury Rd, Wdf.Grn. IG8 48 EL52
Claydon Dr, Croy. CR0 159 DL105
Claydon End, Ger.Cr. (Chal.St.P.) SL9 56 AY55
Claydon La, Ger.Cr. (Chal.St.P.) SL9 56 AY55
Claydon Rd, Wok. GU21 166 AU116
Claydown Ms, SE18 off Woolwich New Rd 105 EN78
Clayfarm Rd, SE9 125 EQ89
CLAYGATE, Esher 155 CE108
⇌ Claygate 155 CD107
Claygate Cl, Horn. RM12 71 FG63
Claygate Cres, Croy. (New Adgtn.) CR0 161 EC107
Claygate La, Esher KT10 137 CG103
Thames Ditton KT7 137 CG102
Waltham Abbey EN9 15 ED30
Claygate Lo Cl, Esher (Clay.) KT10 155 CE108
Claygate Rd, W13 97 CH76
CLAYHALL, Ilf. 49 EM54
Clayhall Av, Ilf. IG5 68 EL55
Clayhall La, Wind. (Old Wind.) SL4 112 AT85
CLAY HILL, Enf. 30 DQ37
Clay Hill, Enf. EN2 30 DQ37
Clayhill, Surb. KT5 138 CN99
Clayhill Cres, SE9 124 EK91
Claylands Pl, SW8 101 DN80
Claylands Rd, SW8 101 DM79
Clay La, Bushey (Bushey Hth.) WD23 41 CE45
Edgware HA8 42 CN46
Epsom (Headley) KT18 172 CP124
Staines (Stanw.) TW19 114 BM87
Claymill Ho, SE18 105 EQ78
Claymore Cl, Mord. SM4 140 DA101
Claymore Ct, E17 off Billet Rd 47 DY53
Claypit Hill, Wal.Abb. EN9 32 EJ36
Claypole Dr, Houns. TW5 96 BY81
Claypole Rd, E15 85 EC68
Clayponds Av, Brent. TW8 98 CL77
Clayponds Gdns, W5 97 CK77
H Clayponds Hosp, W5 98 CL77
Clayponds La, Brent. TW8 98 CL78
Clay Rd, The, Loug. IG10 32 EL39
Clayside, Chig. IG7 49 EQ51
Clays La, E15 67 EB64
Clay's La, Loug. IG10 33 EN39
Clays La Cl, E15 67 EB64
Clay St, W1 194 E7
Clayton Av, Upmin. RM14 72 FP64
Wembley HA0 80 CL66
Clayton Cl, E6 off Brandreth Rd 87 EM72
Clayton Cres, N1 off Havelock St 83 DL67
Brentford TW8 97 CK78
Clayton Cft Rd, Dart. DA2 127 FG89
Clayton Fld, NW9 42 CS52
Clayton Mead, Gdse. RH9 186 DV130
Clayton Ms, SE10 103 ED81
Clayton Rd, SE15 102 DU81
Chessington KT9 155 CJ105
Epsom KT17 156 CS113
Hayes UB3 95 BS75
Isleworth TW7 97 CE83
Romford RM7 71 FC60
Clayton St, SE11 101 DN79
Clayton Ter, Hayes UB4 off Jollys La 78 BX71
Clayton Wk, Amer. HP7 20 AW39
Clayton Way, Uxb. UB8 76 BK70
Clay Tye Rd, Upmin. RM14 73 FW63
Claywood Cl, Orp. BR6 145 ES101
Claywood La, Dart. (Bean) DA2 129 FX90
Clayworth Cl, Sid. DA15 126 EV86
Cleall Av, Wal.Abb. EN9 off Quaker La 15 EC34
Cleanthus Cl, SE18 off Cleanthus Rd 105 EP81
Cleanthus Rd, SE18 105 EP81
Clearbrook Way, E1 off West Arbour St 85 DX72
Cleardown, Wok. GU22 167 BB118
Clearmount, Wok. (Chobham) GU24 150 AS107
Clears, The, Reig. RH2 183 CY132
Clearwater Ter, W11 off Lorne Gdns 99 CX75
Clearwell Dr, W9 82 DB70
Cleave Av, Hayes UB3 95 BS77
Orpington BR6 163 ES107
Cleaveland Rd, Surb. KT6 137 CK99
Cleave Prior, Couls. CR5 174 DE119
Cleaverholme Cl, SE25 142 DV100
Cleaver Sq, SE11 200 E10
Cleaver St, SE11 200 E10
Cleeve Ct, Felt. TW14 off Kilross Rd 115 BS88
Cleeve Hill, SE23 122 DV88
Cleeve Pk Gdns, Sid. DA14 126 EV89
Cleeve Rd, Lthd. KT22 171 CF120
Cleeve Way, SW15 off Danebury Av 119 CT87
Clegg Ho, SE3 off Pinto Way 104 EH84
Clegg St, E1 202 E2
E13 86 EG68
Cleland Path, Loug. IG10 33 EP39
Cleland Rd, Ger.Cr. (Chal.St.P.) SL9 36 AX54
Clematis Cl, Rom. RM3 52 FJ52
Clematis Gdns, Wdf.Grn. IG8 48 EG50
Clematis St, W12 81 CT73
Clem Attlee Ct, SW6 99 CZ79
Clem Attlee Est, SW6 off Lillie Rd 99 CZ79
Clem Attlee Par, SW6 off Clem Attlee Ct 99 CZ79

★ Place of interest ⇌ Railway station ⊖ London Underground station DLR Docklands Light Railway station Tramlink station H Hospital

Clemence Rd, Dag. RM10 89 FC67
Clemence St, E14 85 DZ71
Clement Av, SW4 101 DK84
Clement Cl, NW6 81 CW66
W4 *off Acton La* 98 CR77
Purley CR8
off Croftleigh Av 175 DP116
Clement Gdns, Hayes UB3 95 BS77
Clementhorpe Rd, Dag. RM9 88 EW65
Clementina Rd, E10 67 DZ60
🅷 **Clementine Churchill Hosp**,
Har. HA1 61 CF62
Clementine Cl, W13
off Balfour Rd 97 CH75
Clement Rd, SW19 119 CY92
Beckenham BR3 143 DX96
Waltham Cross (Chsht.)
EN8 15 DY27
Clements Av, E16 86 EG73
Clements Cl, Slou. SL1 92 AV75
Clements Ct, Houns. TW4 96 BX84
Ilford IG1 *off Clements La* 69 EP62
Clement's Inn, WC2 196 C9
Clement's Inn Pas, WC2 196 C9
Clements La, EC4 197 L10
Ilford IG1 69 EP62
Clements Mead, Lthd. KT22 171 CG119
Clements Pl, Brent. TW8 97 CK78
Clements Rd, E6 87 EM66
SE16 202 C7
Ilford IG1 69 EP62
Rickmansworth (Chorl.)
WD3 21 BD43
Walton-on-Thames KT12 135 BV103
Clement St, Swan. BR8 128 FK93
Clement Way, Upmin. RM14 72 FM62
Clenches Fm La, Sev. TN13 190 FG126
Clenches Fm Rd, Sev. TN13 190 FG126
Clendon Way, SE18
off Polthorne Gro 105 ER77
Clennam St, SE1 201 J4
Clensham Ct, Sutt. SM1
off Sutton Common Rd 140 DA103
Clensham La, Sutt. SM1 140 DA103
Clenston Ms, W1 194 D8
★ **Cleopatra's Needle**, WC2 200 B1
Clephane Rd, N1 84 DQ65
Clere St, EC2 197 L4
Clerics Wk, Shep. TW17
off Gordon Rd 135 BR100
CLERKENWELL, EC1 196 F5
Clerkenwell Cl, EC1 196 E4
Clerkenwell Grn, EC1 196 E5
Clerkenwell Rd, EC1 196 D5
Clerks Cft, Red. (Bletch.) RH1 186 DR133
Clerks Piece, Loug. IG10 33 EM41
Clermont Rd, E9 84 DW67
Clevedon, Wey. KT13 153 BQ106
Clevedon Cl, N16
off Smalley Cl 66 DT62
Clevedon Gdns, Hayes UB3 95 BR76
Hounslow TW5 95 BV81
Clevedon Rd, SE20 143 DX95
Kingston upon Thames
KT1 138 CN96
Twickenham TW1 117 CK86
Clevehurst Cl, Slou. (Stoke P.)
SL2 74 AT65
Cleveland Av, SW20 139 CZ96
W4 99 CT77
Hampton TW12 116 BZ94
Cleveland Cl, Walt. KT12 135 BV104
Cleveland Cres, Borwd. WD6 26 CQ43
Cleveland Dr, Stai. TW18 134 BH96
Cleveland Gdns, N4 66 DQ57
NW2 63 CX61
SW13 99 CT82
W2 82 DC72
Worcester Park KT4 138 CS103
Cleveland Gro, E1
off Cleveland Way 84 DW70
Cleveland Ms, W1 195 K6
Cleveland Pk, Stai. TW19
off Northumberland Cl 114 BL86
Cleveland Pk Av, E17 67 EA56
Cleveland Pk Cres, E17 67 EA56
Cleveland Pl, SW1 199 L2
Cleveland Ri, Mord. SM4 139 CX101
Cleveland Rd, E18 68 EG55
N1 84 DR66
N9 46 DV45
SW13 99 CT82
W4 *off Antrobus Rd* 98 CQ76
W13 79 CH71
Ilford IG1 69 EP62
Isleworth TW7 97 CG84
New Malden KT3 138 CS98
Uxbridge UB8 76 BK68
Welling DA16 105 ET82
Worcester Park KT4 138 CS103
Cleveland Row, SW1 199 K3
Cleveland Sq, W2 82 DC72
Cleveland St, W1 195 K5
Cleveland Ter, W2 82 DC72
Cleveland Way, E1 84 DW70
Cleveley Cl, SE7 104 EK77
Cleveley Cres, W5 80 CL68
Cleveleys Rd, E5 66 DV62
Cleverly Est, W12 81 CU74
Cleve Rd, NW6 82 DA66
Sidcup DA14 126 EX90
Cleves Av, Brwd. CM14 54 FV46
Epsom KT17 157 CV109
Cleves Cl, Cob. KT11 153 BV114
Loughton IG10 32 EL44
Cleves Cres, Croy. (New Adgtn.)
CR0 161 EC111
Cleves Rd, E6 86 EK67
Richmond TW10 117 CJ90
Cleves Wk, Ilf. IG6 49 EQ52
Cleves Way, Hmptn. TW12 116 BZ94
Ruislip HA4 60 BX60
Sunbury-on-Thames TW16 115 BT93
Cleves Wd, Wey. KT13 153 BS105
Clewer Cres, Har. HA3 41 CD53
Clewer Ho, SE2
off Wolvercote Rd 106 EX75
Clichy Est, E1 84 DW71
Clifden Rd, E5 66 DW64
Brentford TW8 97 CK79
Twickenham TW1 117 CF88
Cliff End, Pur. CR8 159 DP112
Cliffe Rd, S.Croy. CR2 160 DR106
Cliffe Wk, Sutt. SM1
off Turnpike La 158 DC106
Clifford Av, SW14 98 CP83
Chislehurst BR7 125 EM93
Ilford IG5 49 EP53
Wallington SM6 159 DJ105
Clifford Cl, Nthlt. UB5 78 BY67
Clifford Dr, SW9 101 DP84
Clifford Gdns, NW10 81 CW68
Hayes UB3 95 BR77
Clifford Gro, Ashf. TW15 114 BN91
Clifford Rd, E16 86 EF70
E17 47 EC54
N9 30 DW44
SE25 142 DU98
Barnet EN5 28 DB41
Grays (Chaff.Hun.) RM16 110 FZ75
Hounslow TW4 96 BX83
Richmond TW10 117 CK89
Wembley HA0 79 CK67
Clifford's Inn Pas, EC4 196 D9
Clifford St, W1 199 K1
Clifford Way, NW10 63 CT63
Cliff Pl, S.Ock. RM15 91 FX69
Cliff Reach, Green. (Bluewater)
DA9 129 FS87
Cliff Rd, NW1 83 DK65
Cliff Ter, SE8 103 EA82
Cliffview Rd, SE13 103 EA83
Cliff Vil, NW1 83 DK65
Cliff Wk, E16 86 EF71
Clifton Av, E17 67 DX55
N3 43 CZ53
W12 81 CT74
Feltham TW13 116 BW90
Stanmore HA7 41 CH54
Sutton SM2 158 DB111
Wembley HA9 80 CM65
Clifton Cl, Add. KT15 134 BH103
Caterham CR3 176 DR123
Orpington BR6 163 EQ106
Waltham Cross (Chsht.)
EN8 15 DY29
Clifton Ct, N4 *off Playford Rd* 65 DN61
NW8 *off Edgware Rd* 82 DD70
Woodford Green IG8
off Snakes La W 48 EG51
Clifton Cres, SE15 102 DV80
Clifton Est, SE15
off Consort Rd 102 DV81
Clifton Gdns, N15 66 DT58
NW11 63 CZ58
W4 *off Dolman Rd* 98 CR77
W9 82 DC70
Enfield EN2 29 DL42
Uxbridge UB10 77 BP68
Clifton Gro, E8 84 DU65
Gravesend DA11 131 GH87
Clifton Hill, NW8 82 DB68
Clifton Marine Par, Grav.
DA11 131 GF86
Clifton Pk Av, SW20 139 CW96
Clifton Pl, SE16 202 G4
W2 194 A10
Banstead SM7
off Court Rd 174 DA116
Clifton Ri, SE14 103 DY80
Clifton Rd, E7 86 EK65
E16 86 EE71
N3 44 DC53
N8 65 DK58
N22 45 DJ53
NW10 81 CU68
SE25 142 DS98
SW19 119 CX93
W9 82 DC70
Coulsdon CR5 175 DH115
Gravesend DA11 131 GG86
Greenford UB6 78 CC70
Harrow HA3 62 CM57
Hornchurch RM11 71 FG58
Hounslow (Hthrw.Air.) TW6
off Inner Ring E 95 BP83
Ilford IG2 69 ER58
Isleworth TW7 97 CD82
Kingston upon Thames
KT2 118 CM94
Loughton IG10 32 EL42
Sidcup DA14 125 ES91
Slough SL1 92 AV75
Southall UB2 96 BY77
Teddington TW11 117 CE91
Wallington SM6 159 DH106
Watford WD18 23 BV43
Welling DA16 106 EW83
Cliftons La, Reig. RH2 183 CX131
Clifton St, EC2 197 M6
Clifton Ter, N4 65 DN61
Clifton Vil, W9 82 DB71
Clifton Wk, E6 86 EL72
W6 *off King St* 99 CV77
Dartford DA2
off Osbourne Rd 128 FP86
Clifton Way, SE15 102 DV80
Borehamwood WD6 26 CN39
Brentwood CM13 55 GD46
Wembley HA0 80 CL67
Woking GU21 166 AT117
Climb, The, Rick. WD3 22 BH44
Clinch Ct, E16 86 EG71
Cline Rd, N11 45 DJ51
Clinger Ct, N1 *off Pitfield St* 84 DS67
★ **Clink Prison Mus**, SE1 201 K2
Clink St, SE1 201 J2
Clinton Av, E.Mol. KT8 136 CC98
Welling DA16 105 ET84
Clinton Cres, Ilf. IG6 49 ES51
Clinton Rd, E3 85 DY69
E7 68 EG63
N15 66 DR56
Leatherhead KT22 171 CJ123
Clinton Ter, Sutt. SM1
off Manor La 158 DC105
Clipper Boul, Dart. DA2 109 FS83
Clipper Boul W, Dart. DA2 109 FR83
Clipper Cl, SE16 203 H4
Clipper Cres, Grav. DA12 131 GM91
Clipper Way, SE13 103 EC84
Clippesby Cl, Chess. KT9 156 CM108
Clipstone Ms, W1 195 K5
Clipstone Rd, Houns. TW3 96 CA83
Clipstone St, W1 195 J6
Clissold Cl, N2 64 DF55
Clissold Ct, N4 66 DQ61
Clissold Cres, N16 66 DR62
Clissold Rd, N16 66 DR62
Clitheroe Av, Har. HA2 60 CA60
Clitheroe Gdns, Wat. WD19 40 BX48
Clitheroe Rd, SW9 101 DL82
Romford RM5 51 FC50
Clitherow Av, W7 97 CG76
Clitherow Pas, Brent. TW8 97 CJ78
Clitherow Rd, Brent. TW8 97 CJ78
Clitterhouse Cres, NW2 63 CW60
Clitterhouse Rd, NW2 63 CW60
Clive Av, N18
off Claremont St 46 DU51
Dartford DA1 127 FF86
Clive Cl, Pot.B. EN6 11 CZ31
Clive Ct, W9 *off Maida Vale* 82 DC70
Cliveden Cl, N12
off Woodside Av 44 DC49
Brentwood CM15 55 FZ45
Cliveden Pl, SW1 198 F8
Shepperton TW17 135 BP100
Cliveden Rd, SW19 139 CZ95
Clivedon Ct, W13 79 CH71
Clivedon Rd, E4 48 EE50
Clive Par, Nthwd. HA6
off Maxwell Rd 39 BS52
Clive Pas, SE21 *off Clive Rd* 122 DR90
Clive Rd, SE21 122 DR90
SW19 120 DE93
Belvedere DA17 106 FA77
Brentwood CM13 53 FW52
Enfield EN1 30 DU42
Esher KT10 154 CB105
Feltham TW14 115 BU86
Gravesend DA11 131 GH86
Romford RM2 71 FH57
Twickenham TW1 117 CF91
Clivesdale Dr, Hayes UB3 77 BV74
Clive Way, Enf. EN1 30 DU42
Watford WD24 24 BW39
Cloak La, EC4 197 J10
⇌ **Clock House** 143 DY96
Clockhouse Av, Bark. IG11 87 EQ67
Clockhouse Cl, SW19 119 CW90
Clock Ho Cl, W.Byf. (Byfleet)
KT14 152 BM112
Clockhouse La, Ashf. TW15 114 BN91
Feltham TW14 115 BP89
Grays RM16 91 FX74
Romford RM5 51 FB52
Clock Ho La, Sev. TN13 190 FG123
Clockhouse La E, Egh. TW20 113 BB94
Clockhouse La W, Egh. TW20 113 BA94
Clock Ho Mead, Lthd. (Oxshott)
KT22 154 CB114
Clockhouse Ms, Rick. (Chorl.) WD3
off Chorleywood Ho Dr 21 BE41
Clockhouse Pl, SW15 119 CY85
Feltham TW14 115 BQ88
Clock Ho Rd, Beck. BR3 143 DY97
Clockhouse Roundabout, Felt.
TW14 115 BP88
★ **Clockmakers Company Collection, Guildhall Lib**, EC2 197 J8
Clock Twr Ms, N1
off Arlington Av 84 DQ67
SE28 88 EV73
Clock Twr Pl, N7 83 DL65
Clock Twr Rd, Islw. TW7 97 CF83
Cloister Cl, Rain. RM13 89 FH70
Teddington TW11 117 CH92
Cloister Gdns, SE25 142 DV100
Edgware HA8 42 CQ50
Cloister Rd, NW2 63 CZ62
W3 80 CQ71
Cloisters, The, Bushey WD23 24 CB44
Rickmansworth WD3 38 BL45
Woking GU22 167 BB121
Cloisters Av, Brom. BR2 145 EM99
Cloisters Business Cen, SW8
off Battersea Pk Rd 101 DH80
Cloisters Mall, Kings.T. KT1
off Union St 137 CK96
Clonard Way, Pnr. HA5 40 CA51
Clonbrock Rd, N16 66 DS63
Cloncurry St, SW6 99 CX82
Clonmel Cl, Har. HA2 61 CD60
Clonmell Rd, N17 66 DR55
Clonmel Rd, SW6 99 CZ80
Teddington TW11 117 CD91
Clonmore St, SW18 119 CZ88
Cloonmore Av, Orp. BR6 163 ET105
Clorane Gdns, NW3 64 DA62
Close, The, E4
off Beech Hall Rd 47 EC52
N14 45 DK47
N20 43 CZ47
SE3 *off Heath La* 103 ED82
Barnet EN4 28 DF44
Beckenham BR3 143 DY98
Bexley DA5 126 FA86
Brentwood CM14 54 FW48
Bushey WD23 24 CB43
Carshalton SM5 158 DE109
Dartford DA2 128 FJ90
Grays RM16 110 GC75
Harrow HA2 40 CC54
Hatfield AL9 11 CY26
Isleworth TW7 97 CD82
Iver SL0 75 BC69
Mitcham CR4 140 DF98
New Malden KT3 138 CQ96
Orpington BR5 145 ES100
Pinner (Eastcote) HA5 60 BW59
Close, The, Pnr. (Rayners La)
HA5 60 BZ59
Potters Bar EN6 12 DA32
Purley (Pampisford Rd)
CR8 159 DP110
Purley (Russ.Hill) CR8 159 DM110
Radlett WD7 9 CF33
Richmond TW9 98 CP83
Rickmansworth WD3 38 BJ46
Romford RM6 70 EY58
Sevenoaks TN13 190 FE124
Sidcup DA14 126 EV92
Sutton SM3 139 CZ101
Uxbridge UB10 76 BL66
Uxbridge (Hlgdn.) UB10 76 BN67
Virginia Water GU25 132 AW99
Wembley (Barnhill Rd) HA9 62 CQ62
Wembley (Lyon Pk Av) HA0 80 CL65
West Byfleet KT14 152 BG113
Westerham (Berry's Grn.)
TN16 179 EP116
Closemead Cl, Nthwd. HA6 39 BQ51
Cloth Ct, EC1 196 G7
Cloth Fair, EC1 196 G7
Clothier St, E1 197 N8
Cloth St, EC1 197 H6
Clothworkers Rd, SE18 105 ER80
Cloudberry Rd, Rom. RM3 52 FK51
Cloudesdale Rd, SW17 121 DH89
Cloudesley Pl, N1 83 DN67
Cloudesley Rd, N1 83 DN67
Bexleyheath DA7 106 EZ81
Erith DA8 107 FF81
Cloudesley Sq, N1 83 DN67
Cloudesley St, N1 83 DN67
Clouston Cl, Wall. SM6 159 DL106
Clova Rd, E7 86 EF65
Clove Cres, E14 85 ED73
Clove Hitch Quay, SW11 100 DC83
Clovelly Av, NW9 63 CT56
Uxbridge UB10 59 BQ63
Warlingham CR6 176 DV118
Clovelly Cl, Pnr. HA5 59 BV55
Uxbridge UB10 59 BQ63
Clovelly Ct, Horn. RM11 72 FN61
Clovelly Gdns, SE19 142 DT95
Enfield EN1 46 DS45
Romford RM7 51 FB53
Clovelly Rd, N8 65 DK56
W4 98 CQ75
W5 97 CJ75
Bexleyheath DA7 106 EY79
Hounslow TW3 96 CA82
Clovelly Way, E1
off Jamaica St 84 DW72
Harrow HA2 60 BZ61
Orpington BR6 145 ET100
Clover Cl, E11 *off Norman Rd* 67 ED61
Clover Ct, Grays RM17
off Churchill Rd 110 GD79
Woking GU22 166 AX118
Cloverdale Gdns, Sid. DA15 125 ET86
Clover Fld, The, Bushey WD23 24 BZ44
Clover Hill, Couls. CR5 175 DH121
Clover Leas, Epp. CM16 17 ET30
Cloverleys, Loug. IG10 32 EK43
Clover Ms, SW3 *off Dilke St* 100 DF79
Clovers, The, Grav. (Nthflt.)
DA11 130 GE91
Clover Way, Wall. SM6 140 DG102
Clove St, E13 *off Barking Rd* 86 EG70
Clowders Rd, SE6 123 DZ90
Clowser Cl, Sutt. SM1
off Turnpike La 158 DC106
Cloysters Grn, E1 202 B2
Cloyster Wd, Edg. HA8 41 CK52
Club Gdns Rd, Brom. BR2 144 EG101
Club Row, E1 197 P4
E2 197 P4
Clump, The, Rick. WD3 22 BG43
Clump Av, Tad. KT20 182 CQ131
Clumps, The, Ashf. TW15 115 BR91
Clunas Gdns, Rom. RM2 72 FK55
Clunbury Av, Sthl. UB2 96 BZ78
Clunbury St, N1 197 L1
Cluny Est, SE1 201 M6
Cluny Ms, SW5 100 DA77
Cluny Pl, SE1 201 M6
Cluse Ct, N1 *off Dame St* 84 DQ68
Clutterbucks, Rick. (Sarratt)
WD3 22 BG36
Clutton St, E14 85 EB71
Clydach Rd, Enf. EN1 30 DT42
Clyde Av, S.Croy. CR2 176 DV115
Clyde Circ, N15 66 DS56
Clyde Cl, Red. RH1 184 DG133
Clyde Ct, Red. RH1
off Clyde Cl 184 DG133
Clyde Cres, Upmin. RM14 73 FS58
Clyde Pl, E10 67 EB59
Clyde Rd, N15 66 DS56
N22 45 DK53
Croydon CR0 142 DT102
Staines (Stanw.) TW19 114 BK88
Sutton SM1 158 DA106
Wallington SM6 159 DJ106
Clydesdale, Enf. EN3 31 DX42
Clydesdale Av, Stan. HA7 61 CK55
Clydesdale Cl, Borwd. WD6 26 CR43
Isleworth TW7 97 CF83
Clydesdale Gdns, Rich. TW10 98 CP84
Clydesdale Ho, Erith DA18
off Kale Rd 106 EY75
Clydesdale Rd, W11 81 CZ72
Hornchurch RM11 71 FF59
Clydesdale Wk, Brox. EN10
off Tarpan Way 15 DZ25
Clyde St, SE8 103 DZ79
Clyde Ter, SE23 122 DW89
Clyde Vale, SE23 122 DW89
Clyde Way, Rom. RM1 51 FE53
Clydon Cl, Erith DA8 107 FE79
Clyfford Rd, Ruis. HA4 59 BT63
Clymping Dene, Felt. TW14 115 BV87
Clyston Rd, Wat. WD18 23 BT44
Clyston St, SW8 101 DJ82
Clyve Way, Stai. TW18 133 BE95
Coach & Horses Yd, W1 195 J10
Coach Ho La, N5
off Highbury Hill 65 DP63
SW19 119 CX91
Coach Ho Ms, SE14
off Waller Rd 103 DX82
Coachhouse Ms, SE20 122 DV94
Coach Ho Ms, SE23 123 DX86
Coach Ho Yd, SW18
off Ebner St 100 DB84
Coachmaker Ms, SW4
off Fenwick Pl 101 DL83
Coach Rd, Bet. (Brock.) RH3 182 CL134
Chertsey (Ott.) KT16 151 BC107
Coach Yd Ms, N19
off Trinder Rd 65 DL60
Coal Ct, Grays RM17
off Columbia Wf Rd 110 GA79
Coaldale Wk, SE21
off Lairdale Cl 122 DQ87
Coalecroft Rd, SW15 99 CW84
Coal Rd, Til. RM18 111 GL77
Coal Wf Rd, W12
off Sterne St 99 CX75
Coates Av, SW18 120 DE86
Coates Dell, Wat. WD25 8 BY33
Coates Hill Rd, Brom. BR1 145 EN96
Coates Rd, Borwd. (Elstree)
WD6 41 CK45
Coate St, E2 84 DU68
Coates Wk, Brent. TW8 98 CL78
Coates Way, Wat. WD25 8 BX33
Cobb Cl, Borwd. WD6 26 CQ43
Slough (Datchet) SL3 92 AX81
Cobbett Cl, Enf. EN3 30 DW36
Cobbett Rd, SE9 104 EL83
Twickenham TW2 116 CA88
Cobbetts Av, Ilf. IG4 68 EK57
Cobbetts Cl, Wok. GU21 166 AV117
Cobbetts Hill, Wey. KT13 153 BP107
Cobbett St, SW8 101 DM80
Cobb Grn, Wat. WD25 7 BV32
Cobbins, The, Wal.Abb. EN9 16 EE33
Cobbinsend Rd, Wal.Abb.
EN9 16 EK29
Cobble La, N1
off Edwards Ms 83 DP66
Cobble Ms, N5 66 DQ62
Cobblers Wk, E.Mol. KT8 137 CG95
Hampton TW12 116 CC94
Kingston upon Thames
KT2 137 CG95
Teddington TW11 137 CG95
Cobbles, The, Brwd. CM15 54 FY47
Upminster RM14 73 FT59
Cobblestone Pl, Croy. CR0
off Oakfield Rd 142 DQ102
Cobbold Est, NW10 81 CT65
Cobbold Ms, W12
off Cobbold Rd 99 CT75
Cobbold Rd, E11 68 EF62
NW10 81 CT65
W12 98 CS75
Cobb's Ct, EC4
off Carter La 83 DP72
Cobb's Rd, Houns. TW4 96 BZ84
Cobb St, E1 197 P7
Cobden Cl, Uxb. UB8 76 BJ67
Cobden Hill, Rad. WD7 25 CH36
Cobden Rd, E11 68 EE62
SE25 142 DU99
Orpington BR6 163 ER105
Sevenoaks TN13 191 FJ123
COBHAM 169 BV115
Cobham, Grays RM16 110 GB75
⇌ **Cobham & Stoke D'Abernon** 170 BY117
Cobham Av, N.Mal. KT3 139 CU99
★ **Cobham Bus Mus**, Cob.
KT11 153 BQ112
Cobham Cl, SW11 120 DE86
Bromley BR2 144 EL101
Edgware HA8 42 CP54
Enfield EN1 30 DU41
Sidcup DA15
off Park Mead 126 EV86
Wallington SM6 159 DL107
Cobham Gate, Cob. KT11 153 BV114
🅷 **Cobham Hosp**, Cob.
KT11 153 BV113
Cobham Ho, Bark. IG11
off St. Margarets 87 EQ67
Cobham Ms, NW1
off Agar Gro 83 DK66
Cobham Pk Rd, Cob. KT11 169 BV117
Cobham Pl, Bexh. DA6 126 EX85
Cobham Rd, E17 47 EC53
N22 65 DP55
Cobham (Stoke D'Ab.)
KT11 170 CA118
Hounslow TW5 96 BW80
Ilford IG3 69 ES61
Kingston upon Thames
KT1 138 CN95
Leatherhead (Fetch.) KT22 171 CE122
Cobham St, Grav. DA11 131 GG87
Cobill Cl, Horn. RM11 72 FJ56
Cobland Rd, SE12 124 EJ91
Coborn Rd, E3 85 DZ69
Coborn St, E3 85 DZ69
Cobourg Rd, SE5 102 DT79
Cobourg St, NW1 195 L3
Cobsdene, Grav. DA12 131 GK93
Cobs Way, Add. (New Haw)
KT15 152 BJ110
Coburg Cl, SW1 199 L8
Coburg Cres, SW2 121 DM88
Coburg Gdns, Ilf. IG5 48 EK54
Coburg Rd, N22 65 DM55
Cochrane Ms, NW8 194 A1
Cochrane Rd, SW19 119 CZ94
Cochrane St, NW8 194 A1
Cockayne Way, SE8 203 L10
Cockerell Rd, E17 67 DY59

Coc - Com

Cockerhurst Rd, Sev. (Shore.) TN14 ...165 FD107
Cocker Rd, Enf. EN1 ...30 DV36
Cockett Rd, Slou. SL3 ...92 AY76
COCKFOSTERS, Barn. ...28 DE42
⊖ Cockfosters ...28 DG42
Cockfosters Rd, Barn. EN4 ...28 DF40
Cock Hill, E1 ...197 N7
Cock La, EC1 ...196 F7
Leatherhead (Fetch.) KT22 ...170 CC122
Cockle Way, Rad. (Shenley) WD7 ...10 CL33
Cockmannings La, Orp. BR5 .146 EX102
Cockmannings Rd, Orp. BR5 .146 EX101
Cockpit Steps, SW1 ...199 N5
Cockpit Yd, WC1 ...196 C6
Cocks Cres, N.Mal. KT3 ...139 CT98
Cocksett Av, Orp. BR6 ...163 ES107
Cockspur Ct, SW1 ...199 N2
Cockspur St, SW1 ...199 N2
Cocksure La, Sid. DA14 ...126 FA90
Cock's Yd, Uxb. UB8 off Bakers Rd ...76 BJ66
Code St, E1 ...84 DT70
Codham Hall La, Brwd. CM13 .73 FV56
Codicote Dr, Wat. WD25 ...8 BX34
Codicote Ter, N4 off Green Las ...66 DQ61
Codling Cl, E1 ...202 C2
Codling Way, Wem. HA0 ...61 CK63
CODMORE, Chesh. ...4 AS29
Codmore Cres, Chesh. HP5 ...4 AS30
Codmore Wd Rd, Chesh. HP5 ..4 AW33
Codrington Ct, Wok. GU21 off Raglan Rd ...166 AS118
Codrington Cres, Grav. DA12 ...131 GJ92
Codrington Gdns, Grav. DA12 ...131 GK92
Codrington Hill, SE23 ...123 DY87
Codrington Ms, W11 off Blenheim Cres ...81 CY72
Cody Cl, Har. HA3 ...61 CK55
Wallington SM6 off Alcock Cl ...159 DK108
Cody Rd, E16 ...85 ED70
Cody Rd Business Cen, E16 ...85 ED70
Coe Av, SE25 ...142 DU100
Coe's All, Barn. EN5 off Wood St ...27 CY42
Coftards, Slou. SL2 ...74 AW72
Cogan Av, E17 ...47 DY53
Cohen Cl, Wal.Cr. EN8 ...15 DY31
Coin St, SE1 ...200 D2
Coity Rd, NW5 ...82 DG65
Cokers La, SE21 off Perifield .122 DR88
Coke's Fm La, Ch.St.G. HP8 ...20 AV41
Coke's La, Amer. HP7 ...20 AW41
Chalfont St. Giles HP8 ...20 AU42
Coke St, E1 ...84 DU72
Colas Ms, NW6 off Birchington Rd ...82 DA67
Colbeck Ms, SW7 ...100 DB77
Colbeck Rd, Har. HA1 ...60 CC59
Colberg Pl, N16 ...66 DS59
Colborne Way, Wor.Pk. KT4 .139 CW104
Colbrook Av, Hayes UB3 ...95 BR76
Colbrook Cl, Hayes UB3 ...95 BR76
Colburn Av, Cat. CR3 ...176 DT124
Pinner HA5 ...40 BY51
Colburn Way, Sutt. SM1 ...140 DD104
Colby Ms, SE19 off Gipsy Hill ...122 DS92
Colby Rd, SE19 ...122 DS92
Walton-on-Thames KT12 off Winchester Rd ...135 BU102
Colchester Av, E12 ...69 EM62
Colchester Dr, Pnr. HA5 ...60 BX57
Colchester Rd, E10 ...67 EC59
E17 ...67 EA58
Edgware HA8 ...42 CQ52
Northwood HA6 ...39 BU54
Romford RM3 ...52 FK53
Colchester St, E1 off Braham St ...84 DT72
Colcokes Rd, Bans. SM7 ...174 DA116
Cold Arbor Rd, Sev. TN13 ...190 FD124
Coldbath Sq, EC1 ...196 D4
Coldbath St, SE13 ...103 EB81
COLDBLOW, Bex. ...127 FC89
Cold Blow Cres, Bex. DA5 ...127 FD88
Cold Blow La, SE14 ...103 DX80
Cold Blows, Mitch. CR4 ...140 DG97
Coldershaw Rd, W13 ...79 CG74
Coldfall Av, N10 ...44 DF54
Coldham Gro, Enf. EN3 ...31 DY37
Cold Harbour, E14 ...204 E3
Coldharbour Cl, Egh. TW20 ...133 BC97
Coldharbour Crest, SE9 off Great Harry Dr ...125 EN90
Coldharbour La, SE5 ...101 DN84
SW9 ...101 DN84
Bushey WD23 ...24 CB44
Egham TW20 ...133 BC97
Hayes UB3 ...77 BU73
Purley CR8 ...159 DN110
Rainham RM13 ...89 FE72
Redhill (Bletch.) RH1 ...186 DT134
Woking GU22 ...167 BF115
Coldharbour Pl, SE5 off Denmark Hill ...102 DQ82
Coldharbour Rd, Croy. CR0 ...159 DN106
Gravesend (Nthflt.) DA11 ...130 GE89
West Byfleet KT14 ...151 BF114
Woking GU22 ...167 BF115
Coldharbour Way, Croy. CR0 .159 DN106
Coldshott, Oxt. RH8 ...188 EG133
Coldstream Gdns, SW18 ...119 CZ86
Coldstream Rd, Cat. CR3 ...176 DQ121
Cole Av, Grays RM16 ...111 GJ77
Colebeck Ms, N1 ...83 DP65
Colebert Av, E1 ...84 DW70
Colebrook, Cher. (Ott.) KT16 .151 BD107
Colebrook Cl, NW7 off Bittacy Hill ...43 CY52
SW15 off West Hill ...119 CX87
Colebrooke Av, W13 ...79 CH72
Colebrooke Dr, E11 ...68 EH59
Colebrooke Pl, N1 off St. Peters St ...83 DP67
Colebrooke Ri, Brom. BR2 ...144 EE96
Colebrooke Rd, Red. RH1 ...184 DE132
Colebrooke Row, N1 ...196 F1
Colebrook Gdns, Loug. IG10 ...33 EP40
Colebrook Ho, E14 off Brabazon St ...85 EB72
Colebrook La, Loug. IG10 ...33 EP40
Colebrook Path, Loug. IG10 ...33 EP40
Colebrook Pl, Cher. (Ott.) KT16 ...151 BB108
Colebrook Rd, SW16 ...141 DL95
Colebrook Way, N11 ...45 DH50
Coleby Path, SE5 off Harris St ...102 DR80
Cole Cl, SE28 ...88 EV74
Coledale Dr, Stan. HA7 ...41 CJ53
Coleford Rd, SW18 ...120 DC85
Cole Gdns, Houns. TW5 ...95 BU80
Colegrave Rd, E15 ...67 ED64
Colegrove Rd, SE15 ...102 DT80
Coleherne Ct, SW5 ...100 DB78
Coleherne Ms, SW10 ...100 DB78
Coleherne Rd, SW10 ...100 DB78
Colehill Gdns, SW6 off Fulham Palace Rd ...99 CY82
Colehill La, SW6 ...99 CY81
Coleman Cl, SE25 ...142 DU96
Coleman Flds, N1 ...84 DQ67
Coleman Rd, SE5 ...102 DS80
Belvedere DA17 ...106 FA77
Dagenham RM9 ...88 EY65
Colemans Heath, SE9 ...125 EP90
Colemans La, Ong. CM5 ...19 FH30
Coleman's La, Wal.Abb. EN9 ..15 ED26
Coleman St, EC2 ...197 K8
Colenso Dr, NW7 ...43 CU52
Colenso Rd, E5 ...66 DW63
Ilford IG2 ...69 ES60
Cole Pk Gdns, Twick. TW1 ...117 CG86
Cole Pk Rd, Twick. TW1 ...117 CG86
Cole Pk Vw, Twick. TW1 off Hill Vw Rd ...117 CG86
Colepits Wd Rd, SE9 ...125 EQ85
Coleraine Rd, N8 ...65 DN55
SE3 ...104 EF79
Coleridge Av, E12 ...86 EL65
Sutton SM1 ...158 DE105
Coleridge Cl, SW8 ...101 DH82
Waltham Cross (Chsht.) EN7 off Peakes La ...14 DT27
Coleridge Cres, Slou. (Colnbr.) SL3 ...93 BE81
Coleridge Gdns, NW6 off Fairhazel Gdns ...82 DC66
Coleridge La, N8 off Coleridge Rd ...65 DL58
Coleridge Rd, E17 ...67 DZ56
N4 ...65 DN61
N8 ...65 DK58
N12 ...44 DC50
Ashford TW15 ...114 BL91
Croydon CR0 ...142 DW101
Dartford DA1 ...108 FN84
Romford RM3 ...51 FH52
Tilbury RM18 ...111 GJ82
Coleridge Sq, W13 off Berners Dr ...79 CG72
Coleridge Wk, NW11 ...64 DA56
Brentwood CM13 ...55 GC45
Coleridge Way, Hayes UB4 ...77 BU72
Orpington BR6 ...146 EU100
West Drayton UB7 ...94 BM77
Cole Rd, Twick. TW1 ...117 CG86
Watford WD17 off Stamford Rd ...23 BV39
Colesburg Rd, Beck. BR3 ...143 DZ97
Coles Cres, Har. HA2 ...60 CB61
Colescroft Hill, Pur. CR8 ...175 DN115
Colesdale, Pot.B. (Cuffley) EN6 ...13 DL30
Coles Grn, Bushey (Bushey Hth.) WD23 ...40 CC46
Loughton IG10 ...33 EN39
Coles Grn Ct, NW2 ...63 CU61
Coles Grn Rd, NW2 ...63 CU60
Coleshill Rd, Tedd. TW11 ...117 CE93
Coles La, West. (Brasted) TN16 ...180 EW123
Colesmead Rd, Red. RH1 ...184 DF131
COLES MEADS, Red. ...184 DF131
Colestown St, SW11 ...100 DE82
Cole St, SE1 ...201 J5
Colet Cl, N13 ...45 DP51
Colet Gdns, W14 ...99 CX77
Colet Rd, Brwd. CM13 ...55 GC43
Colets Orchard, Sev. (Otford) TN14 ...181 FH116
Coley Av, Wok. GU22 ...167 BA118
Coley St, WC1 ...196 C5
Colfe Rd, SE23 ...123 DY88
Colgate Pl, Enf. EN3 off Government Row ...31 EA38
Colham Av, West Dr. UB7 ...76 BL74
Colham Grn Rd, Uxb. UB8 ...76 BN71
Colham Mill Rd, West Dr. UB7 .94 BK75
Colham Rd, Uxb. UB8 ...76 BM70
Colham Roundabout, Uxb. UB8 ...76 BN73
Colina Ms, N15 off Harringay Rd ...65 DP57
Colina Rd, N15 ...65 DP57
Colin Cl, NW9 ...62 CS56
Croydon CR0 ...143 DZ104
Dartford DA2 ...128 FP86
West Wickham BR4 ...144 EF104
Colin Cres, NW9 ...63 CT56
⊖ Colindale ...62 CS55
Colindale Av, NW9 ...62 CR55
Colindale Business Pk, NW9 ..62 CQ55
H Colindale Hosp, NW9 ...42 CS54
Colindeep Gdns, NW4 ...63 CU57
Colindeep La, NW4 ...62 CS55
NW9 ...62 CS55
Colin Dr, NW9 ...63 CT57
Colinette Rd, SW15 ...99 CW84
Colin Gdns, NW9 ...63 CT57
Colin Par, NW9 off Edgware Rd ...62 CS56
Colin Pk Rd, NW9 ...62 CS56
Colin Rd, NW10 ...81 CU65
Caterham CR3 ...176 DU123
Colinton Rd, Ilf. IG3 ...70 EV61
★ Coliseum, The, WC2 ...199 P1
Coliston Pas, SW18 off Coliston Rd ...120 DA87
Coliston Rd, SW18 ...120 DA87
Collamore Av, SW18 ...120 DE88
Collapit Cl, Har. HA1 ...60 CB57
Collard Av, Loug. IG10 ...33 EQ40
Collard Grn, Loug. IG10 off Collard Av ...33 EQ40
Collard Pl, NW1 off Harmood St ...83 DH66
College App, SE10 ...103 EC79
College Av, Egh. TW20 ...113 BB93
Epsom KT17 ...157 CT114
Grays RM17 ...110 GB77
Harrow HA3 ...41 CE53
Slough SL1 ...92 AS76
College Cl, E9 off Median Rd ..66 DW64
N18 ...46 DT50
Addlestone KT15 ...134 BK104
Grays RM17 ...110 GC77
Harrow HA3 ...41 CE52
Twickenham TW2 off Meadway ...117 CD88
College Ct, Wal.Cr. (Chsht.) EN8 ...14 DW30
College Cres, NW3 ...82 DD65
Redhill RH1 ...184 DG131
College Cross, N1 ...83 DN66
College Dr, Ruis. HA4 ...59 BU59
Thames Ditton KT7 ...137 CE101
College Gdns, E4 ...47 EB45
N18 ...46 DT50
SE21 ...122 DS88
SW17 ...120 DE89
Enfield EN2 ...30 DR39
Ilford IG4 ...68 EL57
New Malden KT3 ...139 CT99
College Grn, SE19 ...122 DS94
College Gro, NW1 off St. Pancras Way ...83 DK67
College Hill, EC4 ...197 J10
College Hill Rd, Har. HA3 ...41 CF53
College La, NW5 ...65 DH63
Woking GU22 ...166 AW119
College Ms, SW1 ...199 P6
SW18 off St. Ann's Hill ...120 DB85
★ College of Arms, EC4 ...196 G10
College Pk Cl, SE13 ...103 ED84
College Pk Rd, N17 off College Rd ...46 DT51
College Pl, E17 ...68 EE56
NW1 ...83 DJ67
SW10 off Hortensia Rd ...100 DC80
College Pt, E15 ...86 EF65
College Rd, E17 ...67 EC57
N17 ...46 DT51
N21 ...45 DN47
NW10 ...81 CW68
SE19 ...122 DT92
SE21 ...122 DS87
SW19 ...120 DD93
W13 ...79 CH72
Abbots Langley WD5 ...7 BT31
Bromley BR1 ...124 EG94
Croydon CR0 ...142 DR103
Enfield EN2 ...30 DR40
Epsom KT17 ...157 CU114
Gravesend (Nthflt.) DA11 ...130 GB85
Grays RM17 ...110 GC77
Harrow (Har.Hill) HA1 ...61 CE58
Harrow (Har.Wld.) HA3 ...41 CE53
Isleworth TW7 ...97 CF81
Swanley BR8 ...147 FE95
Waltham Cross (Chsht.) EN8 ...14 DV30
Wembley HA9 ...61 CK60
Woking GU22 ...167 BB116
College Row, E9 ...67 DX64
College Slip, Brom. BR1 ...144 EG95
College St, EC4 ...197 J10
College Ter, E3 ...85 DZ69
N3 off Hendon La ...43 CZ54
College Vw, SE9 ...124 EK88
College Wk, Kings.T. KT1 off Grange Rd ...138 CL96
College Way, Ashf. TW15 ...114 BM91
Hayes UB3 ...77 BU73
Northwood HA6 ...39 BR51
College Yd, NW5 off College La ...65 DH63
Collent St, E9 ...84 DW65
Coller Cres, Dart. (Lane End) DA2 ...129 FS91
Colless Rd, N15 ...66 DT57
Collet Cl, Wal.Cr. (Chsht.) EN8 .15 DX28
Collet Gdns, Wal.Cr. (Chsht.) EN8 off Collet Cl ...15 DX28
Collett Rd, SE16 ...202 C7
Collett Way, Sthl. UB2 ...78 CB74
Colley Hill La, Slou. (Hedg.) SL2 ...56 AT62
Colleyland, Rick. (Chorl.) WD3 .21 BD42
Colley La, Reig. RH2 ...183 CY132
Colley Manor Dr, Reig. RH2 ..183 CX133
Colley Way, Reig. RH2 ...183 CY131
Collier Cl, E6 off Trader Rd ...87 EP72
Epsom KT19 ...156 CN107
Collier Dr, Edg. HA8 ...42 CN54
COLLIER ROW, Rom. ...50 FA53
Collier Row La, Rom. RM5 ...51 FB52
Collier Row Rd, Rom. RM5 ...50 EZ53
Colliers, Cat. CR3 ...186 DU125
Colliers Cl, Wok. GU21 ...166 AV117
Colliers Shaw, Kes. BR2 ...162 EK105
Collier St, N1 ...196 B1
Colliers Water La, Th.Hth. CR7 ...141 DN99
COLLIER'S WOOD, SW19 ...120 DD94
⊖ Colliers Wood ...120 DD94
Collindale Av, Erith DA8 ...107 FB79
Sidcup DA15 ...126 EU88
Collingbourne Rd, W12 ...81 CV74
Collingham Gdns, SW5 ...100 DB77
H Collingham Gardens Hosp, SW5 ...100 DB77
Collingham Pl, SW5 ...100 DB77
Collingham Rd, SW5 ...100 DB77
Collings Cl, N22 off Whittington Rd ...45 DM51
Collington Cl, Grav. (Nthflt.) DA11 off Beresford Rd ...130 GE87
Collingtree Rd, SE26 ...122 DW91
Collingwood Av, N10 ...64 DG55
Surbiton KT5 ...138 CQ102
Collingwood Cl, SE20 ...142 DV95
Twickenham TW2 ...116 CA86
Collingwood Dr, St.Alb. (Lon.Col.) AL2 ...9 CK25
Collingwood Pl, Walt. KT12 ..135 BU104
Collingwood Rd, E17 ...67 EA58
N15 ...66 DS56
Mitcham CR4 ...140 DE96
Sutton SM1 ...140 DA104
Uxbridge UB8 ...77 BP70
Collingwood St, E1 ...84 DV70
Collins Av, Stan. HA7 ...42 CL54
Collins Dr, Ruis. HA4 ...60 BW61
Collinson St, SE1 ...201 H5
Collinson Wk, SE1 ...201 H5
Collins Rd, N5 ...66 DQ63
Collins Sq, SE3 off Tranquil Vale ...104 EF82
Collins St, SE3 ...104 EE82
Collins Way, Brwd. CM13 ...55 GE43
Collin's Yd, N1 off Islington Grn ...83 DP67
Collinwood Av, Enf. EN3 ...30 DW41
Collinwood Gdns, Ilf. IG5 ...69 EM57
Collis All, Twick. TW2 off The Green ...117 CE88
Colls Rd, SE15 ...102 DW81
Collyer Av, Croy. CR0 ...159 DL105
Collyer Pl, SE15 off Peckham High St ...102 DU81
Collyer Rd, Croy. CR0 ...159 DL105
St. Albans (Lon.Col.) AL2 ...9 CJ27
Colman Cl, Epsom KT18 ...173 CW117
Colman Rd, E16 ...86 EJ71
Colman Way, Red. RH1 ...184 DE132
Colmar Cl, E1 off Alderney Rd .85 DX70
Colmer Pl, Har. HA3 ...41 CD52
Colmer Rd, SW16 ...141 DL95
Colmore Ms, SE15 ...102 DV81
Colmore Rd, Enf. EN3 ...30 DW42
COLNBROOK, Slou. ...93 BD80
Colnbrook Bypass, Slou. SL3 .93 BF80
West Drayton UB7 ...93 BF80
Colnbrook Cl, St.Alb. (Lon.Col.) AL2 ...10 CL28
Colnbrook Ct, Slou. SL3 ...93 BF81
Colnbrook St, SE1 ...200 F7
Colndale Rd, Slou. (Colnbr.) SL3 ...93 BE82
Colne Av, Rick. (Mill End) WD3 ...38 BG47
Watford WD19 ...23 BV44
West Drayton UB7 ...94 BJ75
Colne Bk, Slou. (Horton) SL3 ..93 BC83
Colnebridge Cl, Stai. TW18 off Clarence St ...113 BE91
Colne Br Retail Pk, Wat. WD17 off Lower High St ...24 BX44
Colne Cl, S.Ock. RM15 ...91 FW73
Colne Ct, Epsom KT19 ...156 CQ105
Colnedale Rd, Uxb. UB8 ...58 BK64
Colne Dr, Rom. RM3 ...52 FM51
Walton-on-Thames KT12 ..136 BX104
Colne Gdns, St.Alb. (Lon.Col.) AL2 ...10 CL27
Colne Ho, Bark. IG11 ...87 EP65
Colne Mead, Rick. (Mill End) WD3 off Uxbridge Rd ...38 BG47
Colne Orchard, Iver SL0 ...75 BF72
Colne Pk Caravan Site, West Dr. UB7 ...94 BJ77
Colne Reach, Stai. TW19 ...113 BF85
Colne Rd, E5 ...67 DY63
N21 ...46 DR45
Twickenham TW1, TW2 ...117 CE88
Colne St, E13 off Grange Rd ...86 EG69
Colne Valley, Upmin. RM14 ...73 FS58
Colne Way, Stai. TW19 ...113 BB90
Watford WD24, WD25 ...24 BY37
Colney Hatch La, N10 ...44 DG52
N11 ...44 DF51
Colney Rd, Dart. DA1 ...128 FM86
COLNEY STREET, St.Alb. ...9 CE31
Cologne Rd, SW11 ...100 DD84
Colombo Rd, Ilf. IG1 ...69 EQ60
Colombo St, SE1 ...200 F3
Colomb St, SE10 ...104 EE78
Colonels La, Cher. KT16 ...134 BG100
Colonels Wk, Enf. EN2 ...29 DP41
Colonial Av, Twick. TW2 ...116 CC85
Colonial Rd, Felt. TW14 ...115 BS87
Slough SL1 ...92 AU75
Colonial Way, Wat. WD24 ...24 BX39
Colonnade, WC1 ...195 P5
Colonnades, The, W2 ...82 DB72
Colonnade Wk, SW1 ...199 H9
Colosseum Ter, NW1 off Albany St ...83 DH70
Colson Gdns, Loug. IG10 off Colson Rd ...33 EP42
Colson Path, Loug. IG10 ...33 EN42
Colson Rd, Croy. CR0 ...142 DS103
Loughton IG10 ...33 EP42
Colson Way, SW16 ...121 DJ91
Colsterworth Rd, N15 ...66 DT56
Colston Av, Cars. SM5 ...158 DE105
Colston Cl, Cars. SM5 off West St ...158 DF105
Colston Cres, Wal.Cr. (Chsht.) EN7 ...13 DP27
Colston Rd, E7 ...86 EK65
SW14 ...98 CQ84
Colthurst Cres, N4 ...66 DQ61
Colthurst Dr, N9 off Plevna Rd ...46 DV48
Coltishall Rd, Horn. RM12 ...90 FJ65
Colt Ms, Enf. EN3 off Government Row ...31 EA37
Coltness Cres, SE2 ...106 EV78
Colton Gdns, N17 ...66 DQ55
Colton Rd, Har. HA1 ...61 CE57
Coltsfoot Ct, Grays RM17 ...110 GD79
Coltsfoot Dr, West Dr. UB7 ...76 BL72
Coltsfoot La, Oxt. RH8 ...188 EF133
Coltsfoot Path, Rom. RM3 ...52 FJ52
Columbia Av, Edg. HA8 ...42 CP53
Ruislip HA4 ...59 BV60
Worcester Park KT4 ...139 CT101
Columbia Pt, SE16 ...202 G6
Columbia Rd, E2 ...197 P2
E13 ...86 EF70
Columbia Sq, SW14 off Upper Richmond Rd W .98 CQ84
Columbia Wf Rd, Grays RM17 ...110 GA79
Columbine Av, E6 ...86 EL71
South Croydon CR2 ...159 DP108
Columbine Way, SE13 ...103 EC82
Romford RM3 ...52 FL53
Columbus Ct, SE16 off Rotherhithe St ...84 DW74
Columbus Ctyd, E14 ...203 P2
Columbus Gdns, Nthwd. HA6 .39 BU53
Columbus Sq, Erith DA8 ...107 FF79
Colva Wk, N19 off Chester Rd ...65 DH61
Colvestone Cres, E8 ...66 DT64
Colview Ct, SE9 off Mottingham La ...124 EK88
Colville Est, N1 ...84 DS67
Colville Gdns, W11 ...81 CZ72
Colville Hos, W11 ...81 CZ72
Colville Ms, W11 off Lonsdale Rd ...81 CZ72
Colville Pl, W1 ...195 L7
Colville Rd, E11 ...67 EC62
E17 ...47 DY54
N9 ...46 DV46
W3 ...98 CP76
W11 ...81 CZ72
Colville Sq, W11 ...81 CZ72
Colville Ter, W11 ...81 CZ72
Colvin Cl, SE26 ...122 DW92
Colvin Gdns, E4 ...47 EC48
E11 ...68 EH56
Ilford IG6 ...49 EQ53
Waltham Cross EN8 ...31 DX35
Colvin Rd, E6 ...86 EL66
Thornton Heath CR7 ...141 DN99
Colwall Gdns, Wdf.Grn. IG8 ...48 EG50
Colwell Rd, SE22 ...122 DT85
Colwick Cl, N6 ...65 DK59
Colwith Rd, W6 ...99 CW79
Colwood Gdns, SW19 ...120 DD94
Colworth Gro, SE17 ...201 J9
Colworth Rd, E11 ...68 EE58
Croydon CR0 ...142 DU102
Colwyn Av, Grnf. UB6 ...79 CF68
Colwyn Cl, SW16 ...121 DJ92
Colwyn Cres, Houns. TW3 ...96 CC81
Colwyn Grn, NW9 off Snowdon Dr ...62 CS58
Colwyn Rd, NW2 ...63 CV62
Colyer Cl, N1 ...83 DM68
SE9 ...125 EP89
Colyer Rd, Grav. (Nthflt.) DA11 ...130 GC89
Colyers Cl, Erith DA8 ...107 FD81
Colyers La, Erith DA8 ...107 FC81
Colyers Wk, Erith DA8 off Colyers La ...107 FE81
Colyton Cl, Well. DA16 ...106 EX81
Wembley HA0 off Bridgewater Rd ...79 CJ65
Woking GU21 ...166 AW118
Colyton Rd, SE22 ...122 DV85
Colyton Way, N18 ...46 DU50
Combe Av, SE3 ...104 EF80
Combe Bk Dr, Sev. (Sund.) TN14 ...180 EY122
Combedale Rd, SE10 ...205 M10
Combe La, Walt. KT12 ...153 BT109
Combe Lo, SE7 off Elliscombe Rd ...104 EJ79
Combe Martin, Kings.T. KT2 .118 CQ92
Combemartin Rd, SW18 ...119 CY87
Combe Ms, SE3 ...104 EF80
Comber Cl, NW2 ...63 CV62
Comber Gro, SE5 ...102 DQ81
Combermere Rd, SW9 ...101 DM83
Morden SM4 ...140 DB100
Combe Rd, Wat. WD18 ...23 BT44
Comberton Rd, E5 ...66 DV61
Combeside, SE18 ...105 ET80
Combwell Cres, SE2 ...106 EU76
Comely Bk Rd, E17 ...67 EC57
Comeragh Cl, Wok. GU22 ...166 AU120
Comeragh Ms, W14 ...99 CY78
Comeragh Rd, W14 ...99 CY78
Comer Cres, Sthl. UB2 off Windmill Av ...96 CC75
Comerford Rd, SE4 ...103 DY84
Comet Cl, E12 ...68 EK63
Purfleet RM19 ...108 FN77
Watford WD25 ...7 BT34
Comet Pl, SE8 ...103 EA80
Comet Rd, Stai. (Stanw.) TW19 ...114 BK87
Comet St, SE8 ...103 EA80
Comforts Fm Av, Oxt. RH8 ...188 EF133
Comfort St, SE15 off St. Georges Way ...102 DT79
Comfrey Ct, Grays RM17 ...110 GD79

★ Place of interest ⇌ Railway station ⊖ London Underground station DLR Docklands Light Railway station Tramlink station H Hospital

239

Com - Cop

Commerce Rd, N22 45 DM53
Brentford TW8 97 CJ80
Commerce Way, Croy. CR0 141 DM103
Commercial Pl, Grav. DA12 131 GJ86
Commercial Rd, E1 84 DU72
E14 84 DW72
N17 46 DS51
N18 46 DS50
Staines TW18 114 BG93
Commercial St, E1 197 P5
Commercial Way, NW10 80 CP68
SE15 102 DT80
Woking GU21 167 AZ117
Commerell St, SE10 205 J10
Commodity Quay, E1 202 A1
Commodore St, E1 85 DY70
Common, The, E15 86 EE65
W5 80 CL73
Kings Langley (Chipper.)
WD4 6 BG32
Richmond TW10 117 CK90
Southall UB2 96 BW77
Stanmore HA7 41 CE47
West Drayton UB7 94 BJ77
Common Cl, Wok. GU21 150 AX114
Commondale, SW15 99 CW83
Commonfield La, SW17
off Tooting Gro 120 DE92
Commonfield Rd, Bans. SM7 158 DA114
Common Gate Rd, Rick. (Chorl.)
WD3 21 BD43
Common La, Add. (New Haw)
KT15 152 BJ109
Dartford DA2 127 FG89
Esher (Clay.) KT10 155 CG108
Kings Langley WD4 6 BM28
Radlett WD7 25 CE39
Watford (Let.Hth.) WD25 25 CE39
Commonmeadow La, Wat. (Ald.)
WD25 8 CB33
Common Mile Cl, SE4
off Crescent La 121 DK85
Common Rd, SW13 99 CU83
Brentwood CM13 55 GC50
Esher (Clay.) KT10 155 CG107
Leatherhead KT23 170 BY121
Rickmansworth (Chorl.)
WD3 21 BD42
Slough (Langley) SL3 93 BA77
Stanmore HA7 41 CD49
Commonside, Epsom KT18 172 CN115
Keston BR2 162 EJ105
Leatherhead (Bkhm.) KT23 170 CA122
Commonside Cl, Couls. CR5
off Coulsdon Rd 175 DP120
Sutton SM2 off Downs Rd 158 DB110
Commonside E, Mitch. CR4 140 DF97
Commonside W, Mitch. CR4 140 DF97
Commonwealth Av, W12 81 CV73
Hayes UB3 77 BR72
★ Commonwealth Institute,
W8 99 CZ76
Commonwealth Rd, N17 46 DU52
Caterham CR3 176 DU123
Commonwealth Way, SE2 106 EV78
COMMONWOOD, Kings L. 6 BH34
Commonwood La, Kings L.
WD4 22 BH35
Community Cl, Houns. TW5 95 BV81
Uxbridge UB10 59 BQ62
Community La, N7 65 DK64
Community Rd, E15 67 ED64
Greenford UB6 78 CC67
Community Wk, Esher KT10
off High St 154 CC105
Community Way, Rick. (Crox.Grn.)
WD3 off Barton Way 23 BP43
Como Rd, SE23 123 DY89
Como St, Rom. RM7 71 FD57
Compass Hill, Rich. TW10 117 CK86
Compass Ho, SW18
off Smugglers Way 100 DB84
Compayne Gdns, NW6 82 DB66
Comport Grn, Croy. (New Adgtn.)
CR0 162 EE112
Compton Av, E6 86 EK68
N1 83 DP65
N6 64 DE59
Brentwood CM13 55 GC46
Romford RM2 71 FH55
Compton Cl, E3 85 EA71
NW1 195 J3
NW11 off The Vale 63 CX62
W13 79 CG72
Edgware HA8
off Pavilion Way 42 CQ52
Esher KT10 154 CC106
Compton Ct, SE19
off Victoria Cres 122 DS92
Compton Cres, N17 46 DQ52
W4 98 CQ79
Chessington KT9 156 CL107
Northolt UB5 78 BX67
Compton Gdns, Add. KT15
off Monks Cres 152 BH106
St. Albans AL2 8 CB26
Compton Pas, EC1 196 G4
Compton Pl, WC1 195 P4
Erith DA8 107 FF79
Watford WD19 40 BY48
Compton Ri, Pnr. HA5 60 BY57
Compton Rd, N1 83 DP65
N21 45 DN46
NW10 81 CX69
SW19 119 CZ93
Croydon CR0 142 DV102
Hayes UB3 77 BS73
Compton St, EC1 196 F4
Compton Ter, N1 83 DP65
Computer Ho, Brent. TW8 97 CJ79
Comreddy Cl, Enf. EN2 29 DP39
Comus Pl, SE17 201 M9
Comyne Rd, Wat. WD24 23 BT36
Comyn Rd, SW11 100 DE84
Comyns, The, Bushey (Bushey Hth.)
WD23 40 CC46
Comyns Cl, E16 86 EF71
Comyns Rd, Dag. RM9 88 FA66
Conant Ms, E1 off Back Ch La 84 DU73
Conaways Cl, Epsom KT17 157 CU110
Concanon Rd, SW2 101 DM84
Concert Hall App, SE1 200 C3
Concord Cl, Nthlt. UB5
off Britannia Cl 78 BX69
Concorde Cl, Houns. TW3
off Lampton Rd 96 CB82
Uxbridge UB10 76 BL68
Concorde Dr, E6 87 EM71
Concord Rd, W3 80 CP70
Enfield EN3 30 DW43
Concourse, The, N9
off New Rd 46 DU47
NW9 43 CT53
Concrete Cotts, Wok. (Wisley)
GU23 off Wisley La 168 BL116
Condell Rd, SW8 101 DJ81
Conder St, E14 off Salmon La 85 DY72
Conderton Rd, SE5 102 DQ83
Condor Path, Nthlt. UB5
off Brabazon Rd 78 CA68
Condor Rd, Stai. TW18 134 BH97
Condor Wk, Horn. RM12
off Heron Flight Av 89 FH66
Condover Cres, SE18 105 EP80
Condray Pl, SW11 100 DE80
Conduit, The, Red. (Bletch.)
RH1 186 DS129
Conduit Av, SE10
off Crooms Hill 103 ED81
Conduit Ct, WC2 195 P10
Conduit La, N18 46 DW50
Croydon CR0 160 DU106
Enfield EN3 off Morson Rd 31 DY44
South Croydon CR2 160 DU106
Conduit Ms, SE18 105 EP78
W2 82 DD72
Conduit Pas, W2
off Conduit Pl 82 DD72
Conduit Pl, W2 82 DD72
Conduit Rd, SE18 105 EP78
Slough SL3 92 AY78
Conduit St, W1 195 J10
Conduit Way, NW10 80 CQ66
Conegar Ct, Slou. SL1 74 AS74
Conewood St, N5 65 DP62
Coney Acre, SE21 122 DQ88
Coney Burrows, E4
off Wyemead Cres 48 EE47
Coneybury, Red. (Bletch.)
RH1 186 DS134
Coneybury Cl, Warl. CR6 176 DV119
Coney Gro, Uxb. UB8 76 BN69
Coneygrove Path, Nthlt. UB5
off Arnold Rd 78 BY65
CONEY HALL, W.Wick. 144 EF104
Coney Hill Rd, W.Wick. BR4 144 EE103
Coney Way, SW8 101 DM79
Conference Cl, E4
off Greenbank Cl 47 EC47
★ Conference Forum, The,
E1 84 DU72
Conference Rd, SE2 106 EW77
Congleton Gro, SE18 105 EQ78
Congo Rd, SE18 105 ER78
Congress Rd, SE2 106 EW77
Congreve Rd, SE9 105 EM83
Waltham Abbey EN9 16 EE33
Congreve St, SE17 201 M8
Congreve Wk, E16 86 EK71
Conical Cor, Enf. EN2 30 DQ40
Conifer Av, Rom. RM5 51 FB50
Conifer Cl, Orp. BR6 163 ER105
Reigate RH2 184 DA132
Waltham Cross EN7 14 DT29
Conifer Dr, Brwd. CM14 54 FX50
Conifer Gdns, SW16 121 DL90
Enfield EN1 30 DS44
Sutton SM1 140 DB103
Conifer La, Egh. TW20 113 BC92
Conifers, Wey. KT13 153 BS105
Conifers, The, Wat. WD25 24 BW35
Conifers Cl, Tedd. TW11 117 CH94
Conifer Way, Hayes UB3
off Longmead Rd 77 BU73
Swanley BR8 147 FC95
Wembley HA0 61 CJ62
Coniger Rd, SW6 100 DA82
Coningesby Dr, Wat. WD17 23 BS39
Coningham Ms, W12
off Percy Rd 81 CU74
Coningham Rd, W12 99 CV75
Coningsby Cotts, W5
off Coningsby Rd 97 CK75
Coningsby Dr, Pot.B. EN6 12 DD33
Coningsby Gdns, E4 47 EB51
Coningsby Rd, N4 65 DP59
W5 97 CJ75
South Croydon CR2 160 DQ109
Conington Rd, SE13 103 EB82
Conisbee Ct, N14 29 DJ43
Conisborough Cres, SE6 123 EC90
Coniscliffe Cl, Chis. BR7 145 EN95
Coniscliffe Rd, N13 46 DQ48
Conista Ct, Wok. GU21
off Roundthorn Way 166 AT116
Coniston Av, Bark. IG11 87 ES66
Greenford UB6 79 CH69
Upminster RM14 72 FQ63
Welling DA16 105 ES83
Coniston Cl, N20 44 DC48
SW13 off Lonsdale Rd 99 CT80
SW20 139 CX100
W4 98 CQ81
Barking IG11
off Coniston Av 87 ES66
Bexleyheath DA7 107 FC81
Dartford DA1 127 FH88
Erith DA8 107 FE80
Conistone Way, N7 83 DL66
Coniston Gdns, N9 46 DW46
NW9 62 CR57
Ilford IG4 68 EL56
Pinner HA5 59 BU56
Sutton SM2 158 DD107
Coniston Gdns, Wem. HA9 61 CJ60
Coniston Ho, SE5 102 DQ80
Coniston Rd, N10 45 DH54
N17 46 DU51
Bexleyheath DA7 107 FC81
Bromley BR1 124 EE93
Coulsdon CR5 175 DJ116
Croydon CR0 142 DU101
Kings Langley WD4 6 BM28
Twickenham TW2 116 CB86
Woking GU22 167 BB120
Coniston Wk, E9
off Clifden Rd 66 DW64
Coniston Way, Chess. KT9 138 CL104
Egham TW20 113 BB94
Hornchurch RM12 71 FG64
Reigate RH2 184 DE133
Conlan St, W10 81 CY70
Conley Rd, NW10 80 CS65
Conley St, SE10 205 J10
Connaught Av, E4 47 ED45
SW14 98 CQ83
Ashford TW15 114 BL91
Barnet EN4 44 DF46
Enfield EN1 30 DS40
Grays RM16 110 GB75
Hounslow TW4 116 BY85
Loughton IG10 32 EK42
Connaught Br, E16 86 EK74
Connaught Business Cen, Mitch.
CR4 off Wandle Way 140 DF99
Connaught Cl, E10 67 DY61
W2 194 B9
Enfield EN1 30 DS40
Sutton SM1 140 DD103
Uxbridge UB8 off New Rd 77 BQ70
Connaught Ct, E17
off Orford Rd 67 EB56
Buckhurst Hill IG9 48 EH46
Connaught Dr, NW11 64 DA56
Weybridge KT13 152 BN111
Connaught Gdns, N10 65 DH57
N13 45 DP49
Morden SM4 140 DC98
Connaught Hill, Loug. IG10 32 EK42
Connaught La, Ilf. IG1
off Connaught Rd 69 ER61
Connaught Ms, SE18 105 EN78
Ilford IG1
off Connaught Rd 69 ER61
Connaught Pl, W2 194 D10
Connaught Rd, E4 48 EE45
E11 67 ED60
E16 86 EK74
E17 67 EA57
N4 65 DN59
NW10 80 CS67
SE18 105 EN78
W13 79 CH73
Barnet EN5 27 CX44
Harrow HA3 41 CF53
Hornchurch RM12 72 FK62
Ilford IG1 69 ER61
New Malden KT3 138 CS98
Richmond TW10
off Albert Rd 118 CM85
Slough SL1 92 AV75
Sutton SM1 140 DD103
Teddington TW11 117 CD92
Connaught Roundabout, E16
off Connaught Br 86 EK73
Connaught Sq, W2 194 D9
Connaught St, W2 194 B9
Connaught Way, N13 45 DP49
Connell Cres, W5 80 CM70
Connemara Cl, Borwd. WD6
off Percheron Rd 26 CR44
Connington Cres, E4 47 ED48
Connop Rd, Enf. EN3 31 DX38
Connor Cl, E11 68 EE59
Ilford IG6 49 EP53
Connor Rd, Dag. RM9 70 EZ63
Connor St, E9
off Lauriston Rd 85 DX67
Conolly Rd, W7 79 CE74
Conquest Rd, Add. KT15 152 BG106
Conrad Cl, Grays RM16 110 GB75
Conrad Dr, Wor.Pk. KT4 139 CW102
Conrad Gdns, Grays RM16 110 GA75
Conrad Ho, N16 66 DS64
Consfield Av, N.Mal. KT3 139 CU98
Consort Cl, Brwd. CM14 54 FW50
Consort Ms, Islw. TW7 117 CD85
Consort Rd, SE15 102 DV81
Consort Way, Uxb. (Denh.) UB9
off Knowland Way 57 BF58
Cons St, SE1 200 E4
Constable Av, E16 205 P2
Constable Cl, NW11 64 DB58
Hayes UB4
off Charville La 77 BQ69
Constable Cres, N15 66 DU57
Constable Gdns, Edg. HA8 42 CN53
Isleworth TW7 117 CD85
Constable Ms, Dag. RM8
off Stonard Rd 70 EV63
Constable Rd, Grav. (Nthflt.)
DA11 130 GE90
Constable Wk, SE21 122 DT90
Constance Cres, Brom. BR2 144 EF101
Constance Rd, Croy. CR0 141 DP101
Enfield EN1 30 DS44
Sutton SM1 158 DC105
Twickenham TW2 116 CB87
Constance St, E16
off Albert Rd 86 EL74
Constantine Pl, Uxb. (Hlgdn.)
UB10 76 BM67
Constantine Rd, NW3 64 DE63
Constitution Hill, SW1 199 H4
Gravesend DA12 131 GJ88
Woking GU22 166 AY119
Constitution Ri, SE18 105 EN81
Consul Av, Dag. RM9 89 FC69
Consul Gdns, Swan. BR8 127 FG94
Content St, SE17 201 J9
Contessa Cl, Orp. BR6 163 ES106
Control Twr Rd, Houns. (Hthrw.Air.)
TW6 94 BN83
Convair Wk, Nthlt. UB5
off Kittiwake Rd 78 BX69
Convent Cl, Beck. BR3 123 EC94
Convent Gdns, W5 97 CJ77
W11 off Kensington Pk Rd 81 CZ72
Convent Hill, SE19 122 DQ93
Convent La, Cob. KT11
off Seven Hills Rd 153 BS111
Convent Rd, Ashf. TW15 114 BN92
Convent Way, Sthl. UB2 96 BW77
Conway Cl, Rain. RM13 89 FG66
Stanmore HA7 41 CG51
Conway Cres, Grnf. UB6 79 CE68
Romford RM6 70 EW59
Conway Dr, Ashf. TW15 115 BQ93
Hayes UB3 95 BQ76
Sutton SM2 158 DB107
Conway Gdns, Enf. EN2 30 DS38
Grays RM17 110 GB80
Mitcham CR4 141 DK98
Wembley HA9 61 CJ59
Conway Gro, W3 80 CR71
Conway Ms, W1 195 K5
Conway Rd, N14 45 DL48
N15 66 DP57
NW2 63 CW61
SE18 105 ER77
SW20 139 CW95
Feltham TW13 116 BX92
Hounslow TW4 116 BZ87
Hounslow (Hthrw.Air.) TW6
off Inner Ring E 95 BP83
Conway St, E13 86 EG70
W1 195 K5
Conway Wk, Hmptn. TW12
off Fearnley Cres 116 BZ93
Conybeare, NW3
off King Henry's Rd 82 DE66
Conybury Cl, Wal.Abb. EN9 16 EG32
Cony Cl, Wal.Cr. (Chsht.) EN7 14 DS26
Conyers Cl, Walt. KT12 154 BX106
Woodford Green IG8 48 EE51
Conyers Rd, SW16 121 DK92
Conyer St, E3 85 DY68
Conyers Way, Loug. IG10 33 EP41
Cooden Cl, Brom. BR1
off Plaistow La 124 EH94
Cook Ct, SE16
off Rotherhithe St 84 DW74
Cooke Cl, E14 off Cabot Sq 85 EA74
Cookes Cl, E11 68 EF61
Cookes La, Sutt. SM3 157 CY107
Cookham Cl, Sthl. UB2 96 CB75
Cookham Cres, SE16 203 H4
Cookham Dene Cl, Chis.
BR7 145 ER95
Cookham Hill, Orp. BR6 146 FA104
Cookham Rd, Sid. DA14 126 FA94
Swanley BR8 146 FA95
Cookhill Rd, SE2 106 EV75
Cook Rd, Dag. RM9 88 EY67
Cooks Cl, Rom. RM5 51 FC53
Cook's Hole Rd, Enf. EN2 29 DP38
Cooks Mead, Bushey WD23 24 CB44
Cookson Gro, Erith DA8 107 FB80
Cook Sq, Erith DA8 107 FF80
Cook's Rd, E15 85 EB68
Cooks Rd, SE17 101 DP79
Coolfin Rd, E16 86 EG72
Coolgardie Av, E4 47 EC50
Chigwell IG7 49 EN48
Coolgardie Rd, Ashf. TW15 115 BQ92
Coolhurst Rd, N8 65 DK58
Cool Oak La, NW9 62 CS59
Coomassie Rd, W9
off Bravington Rd 81 CZ70
COOMBE, Kings.T. 118 CQ94
Coombe, The, Bet. RH3 182 CR131
Coombe Av, Croy. CR0 160 DS105
Sevenoaks TN14 181 FH120
Coombe Bk, Kings.T. KT2 138 CS95
Coombe Cl, Edg. HA8 42 CM54
Hounslow TW3 96 CA84
Coombe Cor, N21 45 DP46
Coombe Cres, Hmptn. TW12 116 BY94
Coombe Dr, Add. KT15 151 BF107
Kingston upon Thames
KT2 118 CR94
Ruislip HA4 59 BV60
Coombe End, Kings.T. KT2 118 CR94
Coombefield Cl, N.Mal. KT3 138 CS99
Coombe Gdns, SW20 139 CU96
New Malden KT3 139 CT98
Coombe Hts, Kings.T. KT2 118 CS94
Coombe Hill Glade, Kings.T.
KT2 118 CS94
Coombe Hill Rd, Kings.T.
KT2 118 CS94
Rickmansworth (Mill End)
WD3 38 BG45
Coombe Ho Chase, N.Mal.
KT3 138 CR95
Coombehurst Cl, Barn. EN4 28 DF40
Coombelands La, Add. KT15 152 BG107
Coombe Lane 160 DW106
Coombe La, SW20 139 CU95
Croydon CR0 160 DV106
Coombe La W, Kings.T. KT2 118 CS94
Coombe Lea, Brom. BR1 144 EL97
Coombe Neville, Kings.T.
KT2 118 CR94
Coombe Pk, Kings.T. KT2 118 CR92
Coombe Ridings, Kings.T.
KT2 118 CQ92
Coombe Ri, Brwd. CM15 55 FZ46
Kingston upon Thames
KT2 138 CQ95
Coombe Rd, N22 45 DN53
NW10 62 CR62
SE26 122 DV91
W4 98 CS78
W13 off Northcroft Rd 97 CH76
Bushey WD23 40 CC45
Croydon CR0 160 DR105
Gravesend DA12 131 GJ89
Coombe Rd, Hmptn. TW12 116 BZ93
Kings.T KT2 138 CN95
New Malden KT3 138 CS96
Romford RM3 72 FM55
Coomber Way, Croy. CR0 141 DK101
Coombes Rd, Dag. RM9 88 EZ67
St. Albans (Lon.Col.) AL2 9 CH26
Coombe Vale, Ger.Cr. SL9 56 AY60
Coombe Wk, Sutt. SM1 140 DB104
Coombe Way, W.Byf. (Byfleet)
KT14 152 BM112
Coombewood Dr, Rom. RM6 70 EZ58
Coombe Wd Hill, Pur. CR8 160 DQ112
Coombe Wd Rd, Kings.T.
KT2 118 CQ92
Coombfield Dr, Dart. (Lane End)
DA2 129 FR91
Coombs St, N1 196 G1
Coomer Ms, SW6
off Coomer Pl 99 CZ79
Coomer Pl, SW6 99 CZ79
Coomer Rd, SW6
off Coomer Pl 99 CZ79
Cooms Wk, Edg. HA8
off East Rd 42 CQ53
Cooperage Cl, N17
off Brantwood Rd 46 DT51
Cooper Av, E17 47 DX53
Cooper Cl, SE1 200 E5
Greenhithe DA9 129 FT85
Cooper Ct, E15 off Clays La 67 EB64
Cooper Cres, Cars. SM5 140 DF104
Cooper Rd, NW4 63 CX58
NW10 63 CU64
Croydon CR0 159 DN105
COOPERSALE, Epp. 18 EX29
Coopersale Common, Epp.
CM16 18 EX28
Coopersale La, Epp. CM16 34 EU37
Coopersale Rd, E9 67 DX64
Coopersale St, Epp. CM16 18 EW32
Coopersall Cl, Wdf.Grn. IG8
off Navestock Cres 48 EJ52
Coopers Cl, E1 84 DW70
Chigwell IG7 50 EV47
Dagenham RM10 89 FB65
Dartford (S.Darenth) DA4 148 FQ95
Staines TW18 113 BE92
Coopers Cres, Borwd. WD6 26 CQ39
Coopers Hill La, Egh. TW20 112 AY91
Coopers Hill Rd, Red. (Nutfld.)
RH1 185 DM133
Coopers La, E10 67 EB60
NW1 83 DK68
Cooper's La, SE12 124 EH89
Coopers La, Pot.B. EN6 12 DD31
Coopers La Rd, Pot.B. EN6 12 DE31
Coopers Ms, Wat. WD25
off High Elms La 8 BW31
Coopers Rd, SE1 102 DT78
Gravesend (Nthflt.) DA11 130 GE88
Potters Bar EN6 12 DC30
Cooper's Row, EC3 197 P10
Coopers Row, Iver SL0 75 BC70
Coopers Shaw Rd, Til. RM18 111 GK80
Cooper St, E16
off Lawrence St 86 EF71
Coopers Wk, E15
off Maryland St 67 ED64
Waltham Cross (Chsht.)
EN8 15 DX28
Cooper's Yd, SE19
off Westow Hill 122 DS93
Coote Gdns, Dag. RM8 70 EZ62
Coote Rd, Bexh. DA7 106 EZ81
Dagenham RM8 70 EZ62
Copeland Dr, E14 204 A8
Copeland Rd, E17 67 EB57
SE15 102 DU82
Copeman Cl, SE26 122 DW92
Copeman Rd, Brwd. CM13 55 GD45
Copenhagen Gdns, W4 98 CQ75
Copenhagen Pl, E14 85 DZ72
Copenhagen St, N1 83 DL67
Copenhagen Way, Walt.
KT12 135 BV104
Cope Pl, W8 100 DA76
Copers Cope Rd, Beck. BR3 123 DZ93
Cope St, SE16 203 H8
Copford Cl, Wdf.Grn. IG8 48 EL51
Copford Wk, N1
off Popham St 84 DQ67
Copgate Path, SW16 121 DM93
Copinger Wk, Edg. HA8
off North Rd 42 CP53
Copland Av, Wem. HA0 61 CK64
Copland Cl, Wem. HA0 61 CJ64
Copland Ms, Wem. HA0
off Copland Rd 80 CL65
Copland Rd, Wem. HA0 80 CL65
Copleigh Dr, Tad. KT20 173 CY120
Copleston Ms, SE15
off Copleston Rd 102 DT82
Copleston Pas, SE15 102 DT83
Copleston Rd, SE15 102 DT83
Copley Cl, SE17
off Hillingdon St 101 DP79
W7 79 CF71
Redhill RH1 184 DE132
Woking GU21 166 AS119
Copley Dene, Brom. BR1 144 EK95
Copley Pk, SW16 121 DM93
Copley Rd, Stan. HA7 41 CJ50
Copley St, E1 85 DX71
Copley Way, Tad. KT20 173 CX120
Copmans Wick, Rick. (Chorl.)
WD3 21 BD43
Copnor Way, SE15
off Diamond St 102 DS80
Coppard Gdns, Chess. KT9 155 CJ107
Copped Hall, SE21
off Glazebrook Cl 122 DR89
Coppelia Rd, SE3 104 EF84
Coppen Rd, Dag. RM8 70 EZ59

Cop - Cou

Copperas St, SE8 ...103 EB79
Copperbeech Cl, NW3
off Akenside Rd ...64 DD64
Copper Beech Cl, NW3
off Daleham Ms ...82 DD65
Gravesend DA12 ...131 GK87
Ilford IG5 ...49 EN53
Orpington BR5
off Rookery Gdns ...146 EW99
Woking GU22 ...166 AV121
Copper Beech Ct, Loug. IG10 ...33 EN39
Copper Beeches, Islw. TW7
off Eversley Cres ...97 CD81
Copper Beech Rd, S.Ock.
RM15 ...91 FW69
Copper Cl, SE19
off Auckland Rd ...122 DT94
Copperdale Rd, Hayes UB3 ...95 BU75
Copperfield, Chig. IG7 ...49 ER51
Copperfield App, Chig. IG7 ...49 ER51
Copperfield Av, Uxb. UB8 ...76 BN71
Copperfield Cl, S.Croy. CR2 ...160 DQ111
Copperfield Ct, Lthd. KT22
off Kingston Rd ...171 CG121
Pinner HA5
off Copperfield Way ...60 BZ56
Copperfield Dr, N15 ...66 DT56
Copperfield Gdns, Brwd.
CM14 ...54 FV46
Copperfield Ms, N18 ...46 DS50
Copperfield Ri, Add. KT15 ...151 BF106
Copperfield Rd, E3 ...85 DY70
SE28 ...88 EW72
Copperfields, Dart. DA1
off Spital St ...128 FL86
Leatherhead (Fetch.) KT22 ...170 CC122
Copperfield St, SE1 ...200 G4
Copperfields Way, Rom.
RM3 ...52 FK53
Copperfield Ter, Slou. SL2
off Mirador Cres ...74 AV73
Copperfield Way, Chis. BR7 ...125 EQ93
Pinner HA5 ...60 BZ56
Coppergate Cl, Brom. BR1 ...144 EH95
Coppergate Ct, Wal.Abb. EN9
off Farthingale La ...16 EG34
Copper Mead Cl, NW2 ...63 CW62
Copper Mill Dr, Islw. TW7 ...97 CF82
Coppermill La, E17 ...66 DW58
Copper Mill La, SW17 ...120 DC91
Coppermill La, Rick. WD3 ...37 BE52
Uxbridge (Hare.) UB9 ...37 BE52
Coppermill Rd, Stai. (Wrays.)
TW19 ...113 BA86
Copper Ridge, Ger.Cr. (Chal.St.P.)
SL9 ...37 AZ50
Copper Row, SE1 ...201 P3
Coppetts Cl, N12 ...44 DE52
Coppetts Rd, N10 ...44 DG54
H Coppetts Wood Hosp, N10 ...44 DF53
Coppice, The, Ashf. TW15
off School Rd ...115 BP93
Enfield EN2 ...29 DP42
Watford WD19 ...24 BW44
West Drayton UB7 ...76 BL72
Coppice Cl, SW20 ...139 CW97
Beckenham BR3 ...143 EB98
Ruislip HA4 ...59 BR58
Stanmore HA7 ...41 CF51
Coppice Dr, SW15 ...119 CV86
Staines (Wrays.) TW19 ...112 AX87
Coppice End, Wok. GU22 ...167 BE116
Coppice La, Reig. RH2 ...183 CZ132
Coppice Path, Chig. IG7 ...50 EV49
Coppice Row, Epp. (They.B.)
CM16 ...33 EM36
Coppice Wk, N20 ...44 DA48
Coppice Way, E18 ...68 EF56
Coppies Gro, N11 ...44 DG49
Copping Cl, Croy. CR0
off Tipton Dr ...160 DS105
Coppins, The, Croy. (New Adgtn.)
CR0 ...161 EB107
Harrow HA3 ...41 CE51
Coppins La, Iver SL0 ...75 BF71
Coppock Cl, SW11 ...100 DE82
Coppsfield, W.Mol. KT8
off Hurst Rd ...136 CA97
Copse, The, E4 ...48 EF46
Caterham CR3
off Tupwood La ...186 DU126
Leatherhead (Fetch.) KT22 ...170 CB123
Copse Av, W.Wick. BR4 ...143 EB104
Copse Cl, SE7 ...104 EH79
Northwood HA6 ...39 BQ54
West Drayton UB7 ...94 BK76
Copse Edge Av, Epsom KT17 ...157 CT113
Copse Glade, Surb. KT6 ...137 CK102
COPSE HILL, SW20 ...119 CU94
Copse Hill, SW20 ...119 CV94
Purley CR8 ...159 DL113
Sutton SM2 ...158 DB108
Copse La, Beac. (Jordans)
HP9 ...36 AS52
Copsem Dr, Esher KT10 ...154 CB107
Copsem La, Esher KT10 ...154 CB107
Leatherhead (Oxshott)
KT22 ...154 CC111
Copsem Way, Esher KT10 ...154 CC107
Copsen Wd, Lthd. KT22 ...154 CC111
Copse Rd, Cob. KT11 ...153 BV113
Woking GU21 ...166 AT118
Copse Vw, S.Croy. CR2 ...161 DX109
Copse Wd, Iver SL0 ...75 BD67
Copsewood Cl, Sid. DA15 ...125 ES86
Copse Wd Ct, Reig. RH2
off Green La ...184 DE132
Copsewood Rd, Wat. WD24 ...23 BV39
Copse Wd Way, Nthwd. HA6 ...39 BQ52
Coptefield Dr, Belv. DA17 ...106 EX76
Coptfold Rd, Brwd. CM14 ...54 FW47
Copthall Av, EC2 ...197 L8
Copthall Bldgs, EC2 ...197 K8
Copthall Cl, EC2 ...197 K8
Copthall Cl, Ger.Cr. (Chal.St.P.)
SL9 ...37 AZ52
Copthall Cor, Ger.Cr. (Chal.St.P.)
SL9 ...36 AY52
Copthall Ct, EC2 ...84 DR72
Copthall Dr, NW7 ...43 CU52
Copthall Gdns, NW7 ...43 CU52
Twickenham TW1 ...117 CF88
COPTHALL GREEN, Wal.Abb. ...16 EK33
Copthall La, Ger.Cr. (Chal.St.P.)
SL9 ...36 AY52
Copthall Rd E, Uxb. UB10 ...58 BN61
Copthall Rd W, Uxb. UB10 ...58 BN61
Copthall Way, Add. (New Haw)
KT15 ...151 BF110
Copt Hill La, Tad. KT20 ...173 CY120
Copthorne Av, SW12 ...121 DK87
Bromley BR2 ...145 EM103
Ilford IG6 ...49 EP51
Copthorne Chase, Ashf. TW15
off Ford Rd ...114 BM91
Copthorne Cl, Rick. (Crox.Grn.)
WD3 ...22 BM43
Shepperton TW17 ...135 BQ100
Copthorne Gdns, Horn.
RM11 ...72 FN57
Copthorne Ms, Hayes UB3 ...95 BS77
Copthorne Ri, S.Croy. CR2 ...160 DR113
Copthorne Rd, Lthd. KT22 ...171 CH120
Rickmansworth (Crox.Grn.)
WD3 ...22 BM44
Coptic St, WC1 ...195 P7
Copwood Cl, N12 ...44 DD49
Coral Cl, Rom. RM6 ...70 EW56
Coraline Cl, Sthl. UB1 ...78 BZ69
Coralline Wk, SE2 ...106 EW75
Coral Row, SW11
off Gartons Way ...100 DC83
Coral St, SE1 ...200 E5
Coram Grn, Brwd. CM13 ...55 GD44
Coram St, WC1 ...195 P5
Coran Cl, N9 ...47 DX45
Corban Rd, Houns. TW3 ...96 CA83
Corbar Cl, Barn. EN4 ...28 DD38
Corbden Cl, SE15 ...102 DT81
Corbet Cl, Wall. SM6 ...140 DG102
Corbet Ct, EC3 ...197 L9
Corbet Pl, E1 ...197 P6
Corbet Rd, Epsom KT17 ...156 CS110
Corbets Av, Upmin. RM14 ...72 FP64
CORBETS TEY, Upmin. ...90 FQ65
Corbets Tey Rd, Upmin. RM14 ...72 FP63
Corbett Cl, Croy. CR0 ...161 ED112
Corbett Gro, N22 ...45 DL52
Corbett Ho, Wat. WD19 ...40 BW48
Corbett Rd, E11 ...68 EJ58
E17 ...67 EC55
Corbetts La, SE16 ...202 F9
Corbetts Pas, SE16 ...202 F9
Corbicum, E11 ...68 EE59
Corbiere Ct, SW19
off Thornton Rd ...119 CX93
Corbiere Ho, N1 ...84 DS67
Corbins La, Har. HA2 ...60 CB62
Corbridge Cres, E2 ...84 DV68
Corby Cl, Egh. (Eng.Grn.)
TW20 ...112 AW93
St. Albans AL2 ...8 CA25
Corby Cres, Enf. EN2 ...29 DL42
Corby Dr, Egh. (Eng.Grn.)
TW20 ...112 AV93
Corbylands Rd, Sid. DA15 ...125 ES87
Corbyn St, N4 ...65 DL60
Corby Rd, NW10 ...80 CR68
Corby Way, E3 off Knapp Rd ...85 EA70
Corcorans, Brwd. CM15 ...54 FV44
Cordelia Cl, SE24 ...101 DP84
Cordelia Gdns, Stai. TW19 ...114 BL87
Cordelia Rd, Stai. TW19 ...114 BL87
Cordelia St, E14 ...85 EB72
Cordell Cl, Wal.Cr. (Chsht.)
EN8 ...15 DY28
Cordell Ho, N15
off Newton Rd ...66 DT57
Corderoy Pl, Cher. KT16 ...133 BE100
Cordingley Rd, Ruis. HA4 ...59 BR61
Cording St, E14 off Chrisp St ...85 EB71
Cordons Cl, Ger.Cr. (Chal.St.P.)
SL9 ...36 AX53
Cordova Rd, E3 ...85 DY69
Cordrey Gdns, Couls. CR5 ...175 DL115
Cordwainers Wk, E13
off Clegg St ...86 EG68
Cord Way, E14 ...204 A6
Cordwell Rd, SE13 ...124 EE85
Corefield Cl, N11
off Benfleet Way ...44 DG47
Corelli Rd, SE3 ...104 EL82
Corfe Av, Har. HA2 ...60 CA63
Corfe Cl, Ashtd. KT21 ...171 CJ118
Borehamwood WD6
off Chester Rd ...26 CR41
Hayes UB4 ...78 BW72
Corfe Twr, W3 ...98 CP75
Corfield Rd, N21 ...29 DM43
Corfield St, E2 ...84 DV69
Corfton Rd, W5 ...80 CL72
Coriander Av, E14 ...85 ED72
Cories Cl, Dag. RM8 ...70 EX61
Corinium Cl, Wem. HA9 ...62 CM63
Corinium Ind Est, Amer. HP6 ...20 AT38
Corinne Rd, N19 ...65 DJ63
Corinthian Manorway, Erith
DA8 ...107 FD77
Corinthian Rd, Erith DA8 ...107 FD77
Corinthian Way, Stai. (Stanw.)
TW19 off Clare Rd ...114 BK87
Corker Wk, N7 ...65 DM61
Corkran Rd, Surb. KT6 ...137 CK101
Corkscrew Hill, W.Wick. BR4 ...143 ED103
Cork Sq, E1 ...202 D2
Cork St, W1 ...199 K1
Cork St Ms, W1 ...199 K1
Cork Tree Way, E4 ...47 DY50
Corlett St, NW1 ...194 B6
Cormongers La, Red. (Nutfld.)
RH1 ...185 DK131
Cormont Rd, SE5 ...101 DP81
Cormorant Cl, E17
off Banbury Rd ...47 DX53
Cormorant Ho, Enf. EN3
off Alma Rd ...31 DX43
Cormorant Pl, Sutt. SM1
off Sandpiper Rd ...157 CZ106
Cormorant Rd, E7 ...68 EF63
Cormorant Wk, Horn. RM12
off Heron Flight Av ...89 FH65
Cornbury Rd, Edg. HA8 ...41 CK52
Cornelia Pl, Erith DA8
off Queen St ...107 FE79
Cornelia St, N7 ...83 DM65
Cornell Cl, Sid. DA14 ...126 EY93
Cornell Way, Rom. RM5 ...50 FA50
Corner, The, W.Byf. KT14 ...152 BG113
Corner Fm Cl, Tad. KT20 ...173 CW122
Corner Grn, SE3 ...104 EG82
Corner Ho St, WC2 ...199 P2
Corner Mead, NW9 ...43 CT52
Cornerside, Ashf. TW15 ...115 BQ94
Corney Reach Way, W4 ...98 CS80
Corney Rd, W4 ...98 CS79
Cornfield Cl, Uxb. UB8
off The Greenway ...76 BK68
Cornfield Rd, Bushey WD23 ...24 CB42
Cornflower La, Croy. CR0 ...143 DX102
Cornflower Ter, SE22 ...122 DV86
Cornflower Way, Rom. RM3 ...52 FL53
Cornford Cl, Brom. BR2 ...144 EG99
Cornford Gro, SW12 ...121 DH89
Cornhill, EC3 ...197 L9
Cornhill Cl, Add. KT15 ...134 BH103
Cornhill Dr, Enf. EN3
off Ordnance Rd ...31 DY37
Cornish Ct, N9 ...46 DV45
Cornish Gro, SE20 ...122 DV94
Cornish Ho, SE17
off Otto St ...101 DP79
Brentford TW8
off Green Dragon La ...98 CM78
Cornmill, Wal.Abb. EN9 ...15 EB33
Corn Mill Dr, Orp. BR6 ...145 ET101
Cornmill La, SE13 ...103 EB83
Cornmill Ms, Wal.Abb. EN9
off Highbridge St ...15 EB33
Cornmow Dr, NW10 ...63 CT64
Cornshaw Rd, Dag. RM8 ...70 EX60
Cornsland, Brwd. CM14 ...54 FX48
Cornsland Ct, Brwd. CM14 ...54 FW48
Cornthwaite Rd, E5 ...66 DW62
Cornwall Av, E2 ...84 DW69
N3 ...44 DA52
N22 ...45 DL53
Esher (Clay.) KT10
off The Causeway ...155 CF108
Southall UB1 ...78 BZ71
Welling DA16 ...105 ES83
West Byfleet (Byfleet)
KT14 ...152 BM114
Cornwall Cl, Bark. IG11 ...87 ET65
Hornchurch RM11 ...72 FN56
Waltham Cross EN8 ...15 DY33
Cornwall Cres, W11 ...81 CY73
Cornwall Dr, Orp. BR5 ...126 EW94
Cornwall Gdns, NW10 ...81 CV65
SW7 ...100 DB76
Cornwall Gdns Wk, SW7
off Cornwall Gdns ...100 DB76
Cornwall Gate, Purf. RM19
off Fanns Ri ...108 FN77
Cornwall Gro, W4 ...98 CS78
Cornwallis Av, N9 ...46 DV47
SE9 ...125 ER89
Cornwallis Cl, Cat. CR3 ...176 DQ122
Erith DA8 ...107 FF79
Cornwallis Gro, N9 ...46 DV47
Cornwallis Rd, E17 ...67 DX56
N9 ...46 DV47
N19 ...65 DL61
Dagenham RM9 ...70 EX63
Cornwallis Sq, N19 ...65 DL61
Cornwallis Wk, SE9 ...105 EM83
Cornwall Ms S, SW7 ...100 DC76
Cornwall Ms W, SW7
off Cornwall Gdns ...100 DB76
Cornwall Rd, N4 ...65 DN59
N15 ...66 DR57
N18 off Fairfield Rd ...46 DU50
SE1 ...200 D2
Brentwood CM15 ...54 FV43
Croydon CR0 ...141 DP103
Dartford DA1 ...108 FM83
Esher (Clay.) KT10 ...155 CG108
Harrow HA1 ...60 CC58
Pinner HA5 ...40 BZ52
Ruislip HA4 ...59 BT62
Sutton SM2 ...157 CZ108
Twickenham TW1 ...117 CG88
Uxbridge UB8 ...76 BK65
Windsor SL4 ...112 AU86
Cornwall Sq, SE11 ...200 F10
Cornwall St, E1 off Watney St ...84 DV73
Cornwall Ter, NW1 ...194 E5
Cornwall Ter Ms, NW1 ...194 E5
Cornwall Way, Stai. TW18 ...113 BE93
Corn Way, E11 ...67 ED62
Cornwell Av, Grav. DA12 ...131 GJ90
Cornwood Cl, N2 ...64 DD57
Cornwood Dr, E1 ...84 DW72
Cornworthy Rd, Dag. RM8 ...70 EW64
Corona Rd, SE12 ...124 EG87
Coronation Av, N16
off Victorian Rd ...66 DT62
Slough (Geo.Grn.) SL3 ...74 AY72
Windsor SL4 ...92 AT81
Coronation Cl, Bex. DA5 ...126 EX86
Ilford IG6 ...69 EQ56
Coronation Dr, Horn. RM12 ...71 FH63
Coronation Hill, Epp. CM16 ...17 ET30
Coronation Rd, E13 ...86 EJ69
NW10 ...80 CM69
Hayes UB3 ...95 BT77
Coronation Wk, Twick. TW2 ...116 BZ88
Coronet St, N1 ...197 M3
Corporation Av, Houns. TW4 ...96 BY84
Corporation Row, EC1 ...196 E4
Corporation St, E15 ...86 EE68
N7 ...65 DL64
Corrance Rd, SW2 ...101 DL84
Corran Way, S.Ock. RM15 ...91 FV73
Corri Av, N14 ...45 DK49
Corrib Dr, Sutt. SM1 ...158 DE106
Corrie Gdns, Vir.W. GU25 ...132 AW101
Corrie Rd, Add. KT15 ...152 BK105
Woking GU22 ...167 BC120
Corrigan Av, Couls. CR5 ...158 DG114
Corrigan Cl, NW4 ...63 CW55
Corringham Ct, NW11
off Corringham Rd ...64 DB59
Corringham Rd, NW11 ...64 DA59
Wembley HA9 ...62 CN61
Corringway, NW11 ...64 DB59
W5 ...80 CN70
Corris Grn, NW9
off Snowdon Dr ...62 CS58
Corsair Cl, Stai. TW19 ...114 BK87
Corsair Rd, Stai. TW19 ...114 BL87
Corscombe Cl, Kings.T. KT2 ...118 CQ92
Corsehill St, SW16 ...121 DJ93
Corsham St, N1 ...197 L3
Corsica St, N5 ...83 DP65
Cortayne Rd, SW6 ...99 CZ82
Cortis Rd, SW15 ...119 CV86
Cortis Ter, SW15 ...119 CV86
Cortland Cl, Dart. DA1
off Lower Sta Rd ...127 FE86
Corunna Rd, SW8 ...101 DJ81
Corunna Ter, SW8 ...101 DJ81
Corve La, S.Ock. RM15 ...91 FV73
Corvette Sq, SE10
off Feathers Pl ...103 ED79
Corwell Gdns, Uxb. UB8 ...77 BQ72
Corwell La, Uxb. UB8 ...77 BQ72
Cory Dr, Brwd. CM13 ...55 GB45
Coryton Path, W9
off Ashmore Rd ...81 CZ70
Cosbycote Av, SE24 ...122 DQ85
Cosdach Av, Wall. SM6 ...159 DK108
Cosedge Cres, Croy. CR0 ...159 DN106
Cosgrove Cl, N21 ...46 DQ47
Hayes UB4
off Kingsash Dr ...78 BY70
Cosmo Pl, WC1 ...196 A6
Cosmur Cl, W12 ...99 CT76
Cossall Wk, SE15 ...102 DV81
Cossar Ms, SW2
off Tulse Hill ...121 DN86
Cosser St, SE1 ...200 D6
Costa St, SE15 ...102 DU82
Costead Manor Rd, Brwd.
CM14 ...54 FV46
Costell's Meadow, West.
TN16 ...189 ER126
Costons Av, Grnf. UB6 ...79 CD69
Costons La, Grnf. UB6 ...79 CD69
Coston Wk, SE4
off Frendsbury Rd ...103 DX84
Cosway St, NW1 ...194 C6
Cotall St, E14 ...85 EA72
Coteford Cl, Loug. IG10 ...33 EP40
Pinner HA5 ...59 BU57
Coteford St, SW17 ...120 DF91
Cotelands, Croy. CR0 ...142 DS104
Cotesbach Rd, E5 ...66 DW62
Cotesmore Gdns, Dag. RM8 ...70 EW63
Cotford Rd, Th.Hth. CR7 ...142 DQ98
Cotham St, SE17 ...201 J9
Cotherstone, Epsom KT19 ...156 CR110
Cotherstone Rd, SW2 ...121 DM88
Cotlandswick, St.Alb. (Lon.Col.)
AL2 ...9 CJ26
Cotleigh Av, Bex. DA5 ...126 EX89
Cotleigh Rd, NW6 ...82 DA66
Romford RM7 ...71 FD58
Cotman Cl, NW11 ...64 DC58
SW15 off Westleigh Av ...119 CX86
Cotmandene Cres, Orp. BR5 ...146 EU96
Cotman Gdns, Edg. HA8 ...42 CN54
Cotman Ms, Dag. RM8
off Highgrove Rd ...70 EW64
Cotmans Cl, Hayes UB3 ...77 BU74
Coton Rd, Well. DA16 ...106 EU83
Cotsford Av, N.Mal. KT3 ...138 CQ99
Cotswold Av, Bushey WD23 ...24 CC44
Cotswold Cl, Bexh. DA7 ...107 FE82
Esher KT10 ...137 CF104
Kingston upon Thames
KT2 ...118 CP93
Staines TW18 ...114 BG92
Uxbridge UB8 ...76 BJ67
Cotswold Ct, EC1 ...197 H4
N11 ...44 DG49
Cotswold Gdns, E6 ...86 EK69
NW2 ...63 CX61
Brentwood CM13 ...55 GE45
Ilford IG2 ...69 ER59
Cotswold Gate, NW2
off Cotswold Gdns ...63 CY60
Cotswold Grn, Enf. EN2
off Cotswold Way ...29 DM42
Cotswold Ms, SW11
off Battersea High St ...100 DD81
Cotswold Ri, Orp. BR6 ...145 ET100
Cotswold Rd, Grav. (Nthflt.)
DA11 ...130 GE90
Hampton TW12 ...116 CA93
Romford RM3 ...52 FM54
Sutton SM2 ...158 DB110
Cotswold St, SE27
off Norwood High St ...121 DP91
Cotswold Way, Enf. EN2 ...29 DM42
Worcester Park KT4 ...139 CW103
Cottage Av, Brom. BR2 ...144 EL102
Cottage Cl, Cher. (Ott.) KT16 ...151 BC107
Rickmansworth (Crox.Grn.)
WD3 off Scots Hill ...22 BM44
Ruislip HA4 ...59 BR60
Watford WD17 ...23 BT40
Cottage Fm Way, Egh. TW20
off Green Rd ...133 BC97
Cottage Fld Cl, Sid. DA14 ...126 EW88
Cottage Gdns, Wal.Cr. EN8 ...14 DW29
Cottage Grn, SE5 ...102 DR80
Cottage Gro, SW9 ...101 DL83
Surbiton KT6 ...137 CK100
Cottage Homes, NW7 ...43 CU49
Cottage Pl, SW3 ...198 B6
Cottage Rd, Epsom KT19 ...156 CR108
Cottage St, E14 ...85 EB73
Cottage Wk, N16
off Smalley Cl ...66 DT62
Cottenham Dr, NW9 ...63 CT55
SW20 ...119 CV94
Cottenham Par, SW20
off Durham Rd ...139 CV96
COTTENHAM PARK, SW20 ...139 CV95
Cottenham Pk Rd, SW20 ...119 CV94
Cottenham Pl, SW20 ...119 CV94
Cottenham Rd, E17 ...67 DZ56
Cotterill Rd, Surb. KT6 ...138 CL103
Cottesbrooke Cl, Slou. (Colnbr.)
SL3 ...93 BD81
Cottesbrook St, SE14
off Nynehead St ...103 DY80
Cottesloe Ms, SE1 ...200 E6
Cottesmore Av, Ilf. IG5 ...49 EN54
Cottesmore Gdns, W8 ...100 DB76
Cottimore Av, Walt. KT12 ...135 BV102
Cottimore Cres, Walt. KT12 ...135 BV101
Cottimore La, Walt. KT12 ...136 BW102
Cottimore Ter, Walt. KT12 ...135 BV101
Cottingham Chase, Ruis. HA4 ...59 BU62
Cottingham Rd, SE20 ...123 DX94
SW8 ...101 DM80
Cottington Rd, Felt. TW13 ...116 BX91
Cottington St, SE11 ...200 E10
Cottle Way, SE16 ...202 F5
Cotton Av, W3 ...80 CR72
Cotton Cl, Dag. RM9
off Flamstead Rd ...88 EW66
Cottongrass Cl, Croy. CR0
off Cornflower La ...143 DX102
Cotton Hill, Brom. BR1 ...123 ED91
Cotton La, Dart. DA2 ...128 FQ86
Greenhithe DA9 ...128 FQ85
Cotton Rd, Pot.B. EN6 ...12 DC31
Cotton Row, SW11 ...100 DC83
Cottons App, Rom. RM7 ...71 FD57
Cottons Ct, Rom. RM7 ...71 FD57
Cottons Gdns, E2 ...197 N2
Cottons La, SE1 ...201 L2
Cotton St, E14 ...85 EC73
Cottrell Ct, SE10
off Greenroof Way ...104 EF76
Cotts Cl, W7
off Westcott Cres ...79 CF71
Couchmore Av, Esher KT10 ...137 CE103
Ilford IG5 ...49 EM54
Coulgate St, SE4 ...103 DY83
COULSDON ...175 DJ116
Coulsdon Common, Cat.
CR3 ...176 DQ121
Coulsdon Ct Rd, Couls. CR5 ...175 DM116
Coulsdon La, Couls. CR5 ...174 DF119
Coulsdon Pl, Cat. CR3 ...176 DR122
Coulsdon Ri, Couls. CR5 ...175 DL117
Coulsdon Rd, Cat. CR3 ...176 DQ122
Coulsdon CR5 ...175 DM115
≠ Coulsdon South ...175 DK116
Coulson Cl, Dag. RM8 ...70 EW59
Coulson St, SW3 ...198 D10
Coulter Cl, Hayes UB4
off Berrydale Rd ...78 BY70
Potters Bar (Cuffley) EN6 ...13 DK27
Coulter Rd, W6 ...99 CV76
Coulton Av, Grav. (Nthflt.)
DA11 ...130 GE87
Council Av, Grav. (Nthflt.)
DA11 ...130 GC86
Council Cotts, Wok. (Wisley)
GU23 off Wisley La ...168 BK115
Councillor St, SE5 ...102 DQ80
Counter Ct, SE1
off Southwark St ...84 DR74
Counter St, SE1 ...201 M3
Countess Cl, Uxb. (Hare.)
UB9 ...38 BJ54
Countess Rd, NW5 ...65 DJ64
Countisbury Av, Enf. EN1 ...46 DT45
Countisbury Gdns, Add. KT15
off Addlestone Pk ...152 BH106
Country Way, Felt. TW13 ...115 BV94
Sunbury-on-Thames TW16 ...115 BV94
County Gate, SE9 ...125 EQ90
Barnet EN5 ...28 DB44
County Gro, SE5 ...102 DQ81
★ County Hall, SE1 ...200 B4
County Rd, E6 ...87 EP71
Thornton Heath CR7 ...141 DP96
County St, SE1 ...201 J7
Coupland Pl, SE18 ...105 EQ78
Courage Cl, Horn. RM11 ...72 FJ58
Courage Wk, Brwd. CM13 ...55 GD44
Courcy Rd, N8 ...65 DN55
Courier Rd, Dag. RM9 ...89 FC70
Courland Gro, SW8 ...101 DK81
Courland Rd, Add. KT15 ...134 BH104
Courland St, SW8 ...101 DK81
Course, The, SE9 ...125 EN90
Coursers Rd, St.Alb. (Coln.Hth.)
AL4 ...10 CN27
Court, The, Ruis. HA4 ...60 BY63
Warlingham CR6 ...177 DY118
Courtauld Cl, SE28
off Pitfield Cres ...88 EU74
★ Courtauld Gall, WC2 ...196 B10
Courtauld Rd, N19 ...65 DK60
Courtaulds, Kings L. (Chipper.)
WD4 ...6 BH30
Court Av, Belv. DA17 ...106 EZ78
Coulsdon CR5 ...175 DN118
Romford RM3 ...52 FN52
Court Bushes Rd, Whyt. CR3 ...176 DU120
Court Cl, Har. HA3 ...62 CL55
Twickenham TW2 ...116 CB90
Wallington SM6 ...159 DK108
Court Cl Av, Twick. TW2 ...116 CB90
Court Cres, Chess. KT9 ...155 CK106
Swanley BR8 ...147 FE98

Court Downs Rd, Beck. BR3 . 143 EB96
★ Court Dress Collection, Kensington Palace, W8 . . 100 DB75
Court Dr, Croy. CR0 . 159 DM105
Stanmore HA7 . 42 CL49
Sutton SM1 . 158 DE105
Uxbridge UB10 . 76 BM67
Courtenay Av, N6 . 64 DE59
Harrow HA3 . 40 CC53
Sutton SM2 . 158 DA109
Courtenay Dr, Beck. BR3 . 143 ED96
Grays (Chaff.Hun.) RM16 *off Clifford Rd* . 110 FZ76
Courtenay Gdns, Har. HA3 . . 40 CC54
Upminster RM14 . 72 FQ60
Courtenay Ms, E17 *off Cranbrook Ms* . 67 DY57
Courtenay Pl, E17 . 67 DY57
Courtenay Rd, E11 . 68 EF62
E17 . 67 DX56
SE20 . 123 DX94
Wembley HA9 . 61 CK62
Woking GU21 . 167 BA116
Worcester Park KT4 . 139 CW104
Courtenay Sq, SE11 *off Courtenay St* . 101 DN78
Courtenay St, SE11 . 200 D10
Courtens Ms, Stan. HA7 . 41 CJ52
Court Fm Av, Epsom KT19 . . 156 CR106
Court Fm Rd, SE9 . 124 EK89
Northolt UB5 . 78 CA66
Warlingham CR6 . 176 DU118
Courtfield, W5 *off Castlebar Hill* . 79 CJ71
Courtfield Av, Har. HA1 . 61 CF57
Courtfield Cres, Har. HA1 . 61 CF57
Courtfield Gdns, SW5 . 100 DB77
W13 . 79 CG72
Ruislip HA4 . 59 BT61
Uxbridge (Denh.) UB9 . 58 BG62
Courtfield Ms, SW5 *off Courtfield Gdns* . 100 DB77
Courtfield Ri, W.Wick. BR4 . . 143 ED104
Courtfield Rd, SW7 . 100 DB77
Ashford TW15 . 115 BP93
Court Gdns, N7 . 83 DN65
Court Grn Hts, Wok. GU22 . . 166 AW120
Court Haw, Bans. SM7 . 174 DE115
Court Hill, Couls. CR5 . 174 DE118
South Croydon CR2 . 160 DS112
Courthill Rd, SE13 . 103 EC84
Courthope Rd, NW3 . 64 DF63
SW19 . 119 CY92
Greenford UB6 . 79 CD68
Courthope Vil, SW19 . 119 CY94
Court Ho Gdns, N3 . 44 DA51
Courthouse Rd, N12 . 44 DB51
Courtland Av, E4 . 48 EF47
NW7 . 42 CR48
SW16 . 121 DM94
Ilford IG1 . 69 EM61
Courtland Dr, Chig. IG7 . 49 EP48
Courtland Gro, SE28 . 88 EX73
Courtland Rd, E6 *off Harrow Rd* . 86 EL67
Courtlands, Rich. TW10 . 98 CN84
Courtlands Av, SE12 . 124 EH85
Bromley BR2 . 144 EF102
Esher KT10 . 154 BZ107
Hampton TW12 . 116 BZ93
Richmond TW9 . 98 CP82
Slough SL3 . 92 AX77
Courtlands Cl, Ruis. HA4 . 59 BT59
South Croydon CR2 . 160 DT110
Watford WD24 . 23 BS35
Courtlands Cres, Bans. SM7 . 174 DA116
Courtlands Dr, Epsom KT19 . 156 CS107
Watford WD17, WD24 . 23 BS37
Courtlands Rd, Surb. KT5 . . 138 CN101
Court La, SE21 . 122 DS86
Epsom KT19 . 156 CQ113
Iver SL0 . 76 BG74
Court La Gdns, SE21 . 122 DS87
Courtleas, Cob. KT11 . 154 CA113
Courtleet Dr, Erith DA8 . 107 FB81
Courtleigh Av, Barn. EN4 . 28 DD38
Courtleigh Gdns, NW11 . 63 CY56
Courtman Rd, N17 . 46 DQ52
Court Mead, Nthlt. UB5 . 78 BZ69
Courtmead Cl, SE24 . 122 DQ86
Courtnell St, W2 . 82 DA72
Courtney Cl, SE19 . 122 DS93
Courtney Cres, Cars. SM5 . . 158 DF108
Courtney Pl, Cob. KT11 . 154 BZ112
Croydon CR0 . 141 DN104
Courtney Rd, N7 *off Bryantwood Rd* . 65 DN64
SW19 . 120 DE94
Croydon CR0 . 141 DN104
Grays RM16 . 111 GJ75
Hounslow (Hthrw.Air.) TW6 . 94 BN83
Courtney Way, Houns. (Hthrw.Air.) TW6 *off Courtney Rd* . 94 BN82
Court Par, Wem. HA0 . 61 CH62
Courtrai Rd, SE23 . 123 DY86
Court Rd, SE9 . 124 EL89
SE25 . 142 DT96
Banstead SM7 . 174 DA116
Caterham CR3 . 176 DR123
Dartford (Lane End) DA2 . . 129 FS92
Godstone RH9 . 186 DW131
Orpington BR6 . 146 EV101
Southall UB2 . 96 BZ77
Uxbridge UB10 . 59 BP64
Courtside, N8 . 65 DK58
Court St, E1 *off Durward St* . . 84 DV71
Bromley BR1 . 144 EG96
Court Way, NW9 . 62 CS56
W3 . 80 CQ71
Ilford IG6 . 69 EQ55
Romford RM3 . 52 FL54
Twickenham TW2 . 117 CF87
Courtway, Wdf.Grn. IG8 . 48 EJ50
Courtway, The, Wat. WD19 . 40 BY47
Court Wd Dr, Sev. TN13 . 190 FG124
Court Wd Gro, Croy. CR0 . 161 DZ111
Court Wd La, Croy. CR0 . 161 DZ111
Court Yd, SE9 . 124 EL86
Courtyard, The, N1 . 83 DM66
Courtyards, The, Slou. SL3 *off Waterside Dr* . 93 BA75
Cousin La, EC4 . 201 K1
Cousins Cl, West Dr. UB7 . 76 BL73
Couthurst Rd, SE3 . 104 EH79
Coutts Av, Chess. KT9 . 156 CL106
Coutts Cres, NW5 . 64 DG62
Coval Gdns, SW14 . 98 CP84
Coval La, SW14 . 98 CP84
Coval Rd, SW14 . 98 CP84
Coveham Cres, Cob. KT11 . . 153 BU113
Covelees Wall, E6 . 87 EN72
Covell Ct, SE8 *off Reginald Sq* . 103 EA80
Covenbrook, Brwd. CM13 . 55 GB48
★ Covent Garden, WC2 . 196 A10
⊖ Covent Garden . 195 P10
Covent Gdn, WC2 . 196 A10
Coventry Cl, E6 *off Harper Rd* . 87 EM72
NW6 *off Kilburn High Rd* . . 82 DA67
Coventry Cross, E3 *off Gillender St* . 85 EC70
Coventry Rd, E1 . 84 DV70
E2 . 84 DV70
SE25 . 142 DU98
Ilford IG1 . 69 EP60
Coventry St, W1 . 199 M1
Coverack Cl, N14 . 29 DJ44
Croydon CR0 . 143 DY101
Coverdale Cl, Stan. HA7 . 41 CH50
Coverdale Ct, Enf. EN3 *off Raynton Rd* . 31 DY37
Coverdale Gdns, Croy. CR0 *off Park Hill Ri* . 142 DT104
Coverdale Rd, N11 . 44 DG51
NW2 . 81 CX66
W12 . 81 CV74
Coverdales, The, Bark. IG11 . . 87 ER68
Coverley Cl, E1 . 84 DU71
Brentwood CM13 *off Wilmot Grn* . 53 FW51
Covert, The, Nthwd. HA6 . 39 BQ53
Orpington BR6 . 145 ES100
Coverton Rd, SW17 . 120 DE92
Covert Rd, Ilf. IG6 . 49 ET51
Coverts, The, Brwd. CM13 . 55 GA46
Coverts Rd, Esher (Clay.) KT10 . 155 CF109
Covert Way, Barn. EN4 . 28 DC40
Covet Wd Cl, Orp. BR5 *off Lockesley Dr* . 145 ET100
Covey Cl, SW19 . 140 DB96
Covington Gdns, SW16 . 121 DP94
Covington Way, SW16 . 121 DM93
Cowan Cl, E6 *off Oliver Gdns* . 86 EL71
Cowbridge La, Bark. IG11 . 87 EP66
Cowbridge Rd, Har. HA3 . 62 CM56
Cowcross St, EC1 . 196 F6
Cowdenbeath Path, N1 . 83 DM67
Cowden Rd, Orp. BR6 . 145 ET101
Cowden St, SE6 . 123 EA91
Cowdray Rd, Uxb. UB10 . 77 BQ67
Cowdray Way, Horn. RM12 . 71 FF63
Cowdrey Cl, Enf. EN1 . 30 DS40
Cowdrey Ct, Dart. DA1 . 127 FH87
Cowdrey Rd, SW19 . 120 DB92
Cowdry Rd, E9 *off Wick Rd* . 85 DY65
Cowen Av, Har. HA2 . 60 CC61
Cowgate Rd, Grnf. UB6 . 79 CD68
Cowick Rd, SW17 . 120 DF91
Cowings Mead, Nthlt. UB5 . . 78 BY66
Cowland Av, Enf. EN3 . 30 DW42
Cow La, Grnf. UB6 . 79 CD68
Watford WD25 . 24 BW36
Cow Leaze, E6 . 87 EN72
Cowleaze Rd, Kings.T. KT2 . . 138 CL95
Cowles, Wal.Cr. (Chsht.) EN7 . . 14 DT27
COWLEY, Uxb. . 76 BJ70
Cowley Av, Cher. KT16 . 133 BF101
Greenhithe DA9 . 129 FT85
Cowley Business Pk, Uxb. UB8 . 76 BJ69
Cowley Cl, S.Croy. CR2 . 160 DW109
Cowley Cres, Uxb. UB8 . 76 BJ71
Walton-on-Thames KT12 . . 154 BW105
Cowley Hill, Borwd. WD6 . 26 CP37
Cowley La, E11 *off Cathall Rd* . 68 EE62
Chertsey KT16 . 133 BF101
Cowley Mill Rd, Uxb. UB8 . 76 BH68
Cowley Pl, NW4 . 63 CW57
Cowley Rd, E11 . 68 EH57
SW9 . 101 DN81
SW14 . 98 CS83
W3 . 81 CT74
Ilford IG1 . 69 EM59
Romford RM3 . 51 FH52
Uxbridge UB8 . 76 BJ68
Cowley St, SW1 . 199 P6
Cowling Cl, W11 *off Wilsham St* . 81 CY74
Cowper Av, E6 . 86 EL66
Sutton SM1 . 158 DD105
Tilbury RM18 . 111 GH81
Cowper Cl, Brom. BR2 . 144 EK98
Chertsey KT16 . 133 BF100
Welling DA16 . 126 EU85
Cowper Ct, Wat. WD24 . 23 BU37
Cowper Gdns, N14 . 29 DJ44
Wallington SM6 . 159 DJ107
Cowper Rd, N14 . 45 DH46
N16 . 66 DS64
N18 . 46 DU50
SW19 . 120 DC93
W3 . 80 CR74
W7 . 79 CF73
Belvedere DA17 . 106 FA77
Bromley BR2 . 144 EK98
Kingston upon Thames KT2 . 118 CM92
Rainham RM13 . 89 FG70
Cowper St, EC2 . 197 L4
Cowper Ter, W10 *off St. Marks Rd* . 81 CX71
Cowslip Cl, Uxb. UB10 . 76 BL66
Cowslip La, Wok. GU21 . 166 AV115
Cowslip Rd, E18 . 48 EH54
Cowthorpe Rd, SW8 . 101 DK81
Cox Cl, Rad. (Shenley) WD7 . . 10 CM32
Coxdean, Epsom KT18 . 173 CW119
Coxe Pl, Har. (Wldste.) HA3 . . 61 CG56
Cox La, Chess. KT9 . 156 CM105
Epsom KT19 . 156 CP106
Coxley Ri, Pur. CR8 . 160 DQ113
Coxmount Rd, SE7 . 104 EK78
Coxson Way, SE1 . 201 P5
Cox's Wk, SE21 . 122 DU88
Coxwell Rd, SE18 . 105 ER78
SE19 . 122 DS94
Coxwold Path, Chess. KT9 *off Garrison La* . 156 CL108
Crabbs Cft Cl, Orp. BR6 *off Ladycroft Way* . 163 EQ106
Crab Hill, Beck. BR3 . 123 ED94
Crab La, Wat. (Ald.) WD25 . 24 CB35
Crabtree Av, Rom. RM6 . 70 EX56
Wembley HA0 . 80 CL68
Crabtree Cl, E2 . 197 P1
Bushey WD23 . 24 CB43
Crabtree Cor, Egh. TW20 . 133 BB95
Crabtree Ct, E15 *off Clays La* . 67 EB64
Crabtree Dr, Lthd. KT22 . 171 CJ124
Crabtree Hill, Rom. (Abridge) RM4 . 50 EZ45
Crabtree La, SW6 . 99 CX80
Crabtree Manorway Ind Est, Belv. DA17 . 107 FB76
Crabtree Manorway N, Belv. DA17 . 107 FC75
Crabtree Manorway S, Belv. DA17 . 107 FC76
Crabtree Rd, Egh. TW20 . 133 BC96
Crace St, NW1 . 195 M2
Craddock Rd, Enf. EN1 . 30 DT41
Craddocks Av, Ashtd. KT21 . . 172 CL117
Craddocks Par, Ashtd. KT21 . . 172 CL117
Craddock St, NW5 *off Prince of Wales Rd* . 82 DG65
Cradley Rd, SE9 . 125 ER88
★ Crafts Council, N1 . 196 E1
Cragg Av, Rad. WD7 . 25 CF36
Craigdale Rd, Horn. RM11 . 71 FF58
Craig Dr, Uxb. UB8 . 77 BP72
Craigen Av, Croy. CR0 . 142 DV102
Craigerne Rd, SE3 . 104 EH80
Craig Gdns, E18 . 48 EF54
Craigholm, SE18 . 105 EN82
Craigmore Twr, Wok. GU22 *off Guildford Rd* . 166 AY119
Craig Mt, Rad. WD7 . 25 CH35
Craigmuir Pk, Wem. HA0 . 80 CM67
Craignair Rd, SW2 . 121 DN87
Craignish Av, SW16 . 141 DM96
Craig Pk Rd, N18 . 46 DV50
Craig Rd, Rich. TW10 . 117 CJ91
Craigs Ct, SW1 . 199 P2
Craigs Wk, Wal.Cr. (Chsht.) EN8 *off Davison Dr* . 15 DX28
Craigton Rd, SE9 . 105 EM84
Craigweil Av, Rad. WD7 . 25 CH35
Craigweil Cl, Stan. HA7 . 41 CK50
Craigweil Dr, Stan. HA7 . 41 CK50
Craigwell Av, Felt. TW13 . 115 BU90
Craigwell Cl, Stai. TW18 . 133 BE95
Craik Ct, NW6 *off Carlton Vale* . 81 CZ68
Crail Row, SE17 . 201 L9
Cramer Ct, N.Mal. KT3 *off Warwick Rd* . 138 CQ97
Cramer St, W1 . 194 G7
Crammerville Wk, Rain. RM13 . 89 FH70
Cramond Cl, W6 . 99 CY79
Cramond Ct, Felt. TW14 *off Kilross Rd* . 115 BR88
Crampshaw La, Ashtd. KT21 . 172 CM119
Crampton Rd, SE20 . 122 DW93
Cramptons Rd, Sev. TN14 . . 181 FH120
Crampton St, SE17 . 201 H9
Cranberry Cl, Nthlt. UB5 *off Parkfield Av* . 78 BX68
Cranberry La, E16 . 86 EE70
Cranborne Av, Sthl. UB2 . 96 CA77
Surbiton KT6 . 138 CN104
Cranborne Cl, Pot.B. EN6 . 11 CY31
Cranborne Cres, Pot.B. EN6 . . 11 CY31
Cranborne Gdns, Upmin. RM14 . 72 FP61
Cranborne Ind Est, Pot.B. EN6 . 11 CY30
Cranborne Rd, Bark. IG11 . 87 ER67
Potters Bar EN6 . 11 CY30
Waltham Cross (Chsht.) EN8 . 15 DX32
Cranborne Waye, Hayes UB4 . 78 BW73
Cranbourn All, WC2 . 195 N10
Cranbourne Av, E11 . 68 EH56
Cranbourne Cl, SW16 . 141 DL97
Cranbourne Dr, Pnr. HA5 . 60 BX57
Cranbourne Gdns, NW11 . 63 CY57
Ilford IG6 . 69 EQ55
Cranbourne Rd, E12 *off High St N* . 68 EL64
E15 . 67 EC63
N10 . 45 DH54
Northwood HA6 . 59 BT55
Cranbourn Pas, SE16 *off Marigold St* . 102 DV75
Cranbourn St, WC2 . 195 N10
CRANBROOK, Ilf. . 69 EM60
Cranbrook Cl, Brom. BR2 . 144 EG100
Cranbrook Dr, Esher KT10 . . 136 CC102
Romford RM2 . 71 FH56
Twickenham TW2 . 116 CB88
Cranbrook Ms, E17 . 67 DY57
Cranbrook Pk, N22 . 45 DM53
Cranbrook Ri, Ilf. IG1 . 69 EM59
Cranbrook Rd, SE8 . 103 EA81
SW19 . 119 CY94
W4 . 98 CS78
Barnet EN4 . 28 DD44
Bexleyheath DA7 . 106 EZ81
Hounslow TW4 . 96 BZ84
Ilford IG1, IG2, IG6 . 69 EN59
Cranbrook Rd, Th.Hth. CR7 . . 142 DQ96
Cranbrook St, E2 *off Mace St* . 85 DX68
Cranbury Rd, SW6 . 100 DB82
Crane Av, W3 . 80 CQ73
Isleworth TW7 . 117 CG85
Cranebrook, Twick. TW2 *off Manor Rd* . 116 CC89
Crane Cl, Dag. RM10 . 88 FA65
Harrow HA2 . 60 CC62
Crane Ct, EC4 . 196 E9
Epsom KT19 . 156 CQ105
Cranefield Dr, Wat. WD25 . 8 BY32
Craneford Cl, Twick. TW2 . 117 CF87
Craneford Way, Twick. TW2 . . 117 CE87
Crane Gdns, Hayes UB3 . 95 BT77
Crane Gro, N7 . 83 DN65
Cranell Grn, S.Ock. RM15 . 91 FV74
Crane Lo Rd, Houns. TW5 . 95 BV79
Crane Mead, SE16 . 203 H9
Crane Pk Rd, Twick. TW2 . 116 CB89
Crane Rd, Twick. TW2 . 117 CE88
Cranesbill Cl, NW9 *off Colindale Av* . 62 CR55
Cranes Dr, Surb. KT5 . 138 CL98
Cranes Pk, Surb. KT5 . 138 CL98
Cranes Pk Av, Surb. KT5 . 138 CL98
Cranes Pk Cres, Surb. KT5 . . 138 CM98
Crane St, SE10 . 103 ED78
SE15 . 102 DT81
Craneswater, Hayes UB3 . 95 BT80
Craneswater Pk, Sthl. UB2 . . 96 BZ78
Cranes Way, Borwd. WD6 . 26 CQ43
Crane Way, Twick. TW2 . 116 CC87
Cranfield Cl, SE27 *off Dunelm Gro* . 122 DQ90
Cranfield Ct, Wok. GU21 *off Martindale Rd* . 166 AU118
Cranfield Cres, Pot.B. (Cuffley) EN6 . 13 DL29
Cranfield Dr, NW9 . 42 CS52
Cranfield Rd, SE4 . 103 DZ83
Cranfield Rd E, Cars. SM5 . . 158 DG109
Cranfield Rd W, Cars. SM5 . . 158 DF109
Cranfield Row, SE1 . 200 E6
CRANFORD, Houns. . 95 BU80
Cranford Av, N13 . 45 DL50
Staines TW19 . 114 BL87
Cranford Cl, SW20 . 139 CV95
Purley CR8 . 160 DQ113
Staines TW19 *off Canopus Way* . 114 BL87
Cranford Cotts, E1 *off Cranford St* . 85 DX73
Cranford Dr, Hayes UB3 . 95 BT77
Cranford La, Hayes UB3 . 95 BR79
Hounslow (Hthrw.Air.) TW6 . 95 BT83
Hounslow (Hthrw.Air.N.) TW6 . 95 BT81
Hounslow (Heston) TW5 . . . 96 BX80
Cranford Pk Rd, Hayes UB3 . . 95 BT77
Cranford Ri, Esher KT10 . 154 CC106
Cranford Rd, Dart. DA1 . 128 FL88
Cranford St, E1 . 85 DX73
Cranford Way, N8 . 65 DM57
CRANHAM, Upmin. . 73 FS59
Cranham Gdns, Upmin. RM14 . 73 FS60
Cranham Rd, Horn. RM11 . 71 FH58
Cranhurst Rd, NW2 . 63 CW64
Cranleigh Cl, SE20 . 142 DV96
Bexley DA5 . 127 FB86
Orpington BR6 . 146 EU104
South Croydon CR2 . 160 DU112
Waltham Cross (Chsht.) EN7 . 14 DU28
Cranleigh Dr, Swan. BR8 . 147 FE98
Cranleigh Gdns, N21 . 29 DN43
SE25 . 142 DS97
Barking IG11 . 87 ER66
Harrow HA3 . 62 CL57
Kingston upon Thames KT2 . 118 CM93
Loughton IG10 . 33 EM44
South Croydon CR2 . 160 DU112
Southall UB1 . 78 BZ72
Sutton SM1 . 140 DB103
Cranleigh Gdns Ind Est, Sthl. UB1 *off Cranleigh Gdns* . . 78 BZ72
Cranleigh Ms, SW11 . 100 DE82
Cranleigh Rd, N15 . 66 DQ57
SW19 . 140 DA97
Esher KT10 . 136 CC102
Feltham TW13 . 115 BT91
Cranleigh St, NW1 . 195 L1
Cranley Dene Ct, N10 . 65 DH56
Cranley Dr, Ilf. IG2 . 69 EQ59
Ruislip HA4 . 59 BT61
Cranley Gdns, N10 . 65 DJ56
N13 . 45 DM48
SW7 . 100 DC78
Wallington SM6 . 159 DJ108
Cranley Ms, SW7 . 100 DC78
Cranley Par, SE9 *off Beaconsfield Rd* . 124 EL91
Cranley Pl, SW7 . 100 DD77
Cranley Rd, E13 . 86 EH71
Ilford IG2 . 69 EQ58
Walton-on-Thames KT12 . . 153 BS106
Cranmer Av, W13 . 97 CH76
Cranmer Cl, Mord. SM4 . 139 CX100
Potters Bar EN6 . 12 DB30
Ruislip HA4 . 60 BX60
Stanmore HA7 . 41 CJ52
Warlingham CR6 . 177 DY117
Weybridge KT13 . 152 BN108
Cranmer Ct, SW3 . 198 C9
SW4 . 101 DK83
Hampton (Hmptn.H.) TW12 *off Cranmer Rd* . 116 CB92
Cranmer Fm Cl, Mitch. CR4 . . 140 DF98
Cranmer Gdns, Dag. RM10 . 71 FC63
Warlingham CR6 . 177 DY117
Cranmer Rd, E7 . 68 EH63
SW9 . 101 DN80
Croydon CR0 . 141 DP104
Edgware HA8 . 42 CP48
Cranmer Rd, Hmptn. (Hmptn.H.) TW12 . 116 CB92
Hayes UB3 . 77 BR72
Kingston upon Thames KT2 . 118 CL92
Mitcham CR4 . 140 DF98
Sevenoaks TN13 . 190 FE123
Cranmer Ter, SW17 . 120 DD92
Cranmore Av, Islw. TW7 . 96 CC80
Cranmore Rd, Brom. BR1 . 124 EE90
Chislehurst BR7 . 125 EM92
Cranmore Way, N10 . 65 DJ56
Cranston Cl, Houns. TW3 . 96 BY82
Uxbridge UB10 . 59 BR61
Cranston Est, N1 . 197 L1
Cranston Gdns, E4 . 47 EB50
Cranston Pk Av, Upmin. RM14 . 72 FP63
Cranston Rd, SE23 . 123 DY88
Cranswick Rd, SE16 . 202 E10
Crantock Rd, SE6 . 123 EB89
Cranwell Cl, E3 . 85 EB70
Cranwell Gro, Shep. TW17 . . 134 BM98
Cranwich Av, N21 . 46 DR45
Cranwich Rd, N16 . 66 DR59
Cranwood St, EC1 . 197 K3
Cranworth Cres, E4 . 47 ED46
Cranworth Gdns, SW9 . 101 DN81
Craster Rd, SW2 . 121 DM87
Crathie Rd, SE12 . 124 EH86
Cravan Av, Felt. TW13 . 115 BU89
Craven Av, W5 . 79 CJ73
Southall UB1 . 78 BZ71
Craven Cl, Hayes UB4 . 77 BU72
Craven Gdns, SW19 . 120 DA92
Barking IG11 . 87 ES68
Ilford IG6 . 49 ER54
Romford (Coll.Row) RM5 . . 50 FA50
Romford (Harold Wd.) RM3 . 52 FQ51
Craven Hill, W2 . 82 DC73
Craven Hill Gdns, W2 . 82 DC73
Craven Hill Ms, W2 . 82 DC73
Craven Ms, SW11 *off Taybridge Rd* . 100 DG83
Craven Pk, NW10 . 80 CS67
Craven Pk Ms, NW10 . 80 CS67
Craven Pk Rd, N15 . 66 DT58
NW10 . 80 CS67
Craven Pas, WC2 . 199 P2
Craven Rd, NW10 . 80 CR67
W2 . 82 DC73
W5 . 79 CJ73
Croydon CR0 . 142 DV102
Kingston upon Thames KT2 . 138 CM95
Orpington BR6 . 146 EX104
Craven St, WC2 . 199 P2
Craven Ter, W2 . 82 DC73
Craven Wk, N16 . 66 DU59
Crawford Av, Wem. HA0 . 61 CK64
Crawford Cl, Islw. TW7 . 97 CE82
Crawford Compton Cl, Horn. RM12 . 90 FJ65
Crawford Est, SE5 . 102 DQ82
Crawford Gdns, N13 . 45 DP48
Northolt UB5 . 78 BZ69
Crawford Ms, W1 . 194 D7
Crawford Pas, EC1 . 196 D5
Crawford Pl, W1 . 194 C8
Crawford Rd, SE5 . 102 DQ81
Crawfords, Swan. BR8 . 127 FE94
Crawford St, NW10 *off Fawood Av* . 80 CR66
W1 . 194 D7
Crawley Rd, E10 . 67 EB60
N22 . 46 DQ54
Enfield EN1 . 46 DS45
Crawshaw Rd, Cher. (Ott.) KT16 . 151 BD107
Crawshay Cl, Sev. TN13 . 190 FG123
Crawshay Ct, SW9 *off Eythorne Rd* . 101 DN81
Crawthew Gro, SE22 . 102 DT84
Cray Av, Ashtd. KT21 . 172 CL116
Orpington BR5 . 146 EV99
Craybrooke Rd, Sid. DA14 . . 126 EV91
Crayburne, Grav. (Sthflt.) DA13 . 130 FZ92
Craybury End, SE9 . 125 EQ89
Cray Cl, Dart. DA1 . 107 FG84
Craydene Rd, Erith DA8 . 107 FF81
Crayfield Ind Pk, Orp. BR5 . . 146 EW96
CRAYFORD, Dart. . 127 FD85
⇌ Crayford . 127 FE86
Crayford Cl, E6 *off Neatscourt Rd* . 86 EL71
Crayford High St, Dart. DA1 . . 107 FE84
Crayford Rd, N7 . 65 DK63
Dartford DA1 . 127 FF85
Crayford Way, Dart. DA1 . 127 FF85
Crayke Hill, Chess. KT9 . 156 CL108
Craylands, Orp. BR5 . 146 EW97
Craylands La, Swans. DA10 . . 129 FX85
Craylands Sq, Swans. DA10 . 129 FX85
Craymill Sq, Dart. DA1 . 107 FF82
Crayonne Cl, Sun. TW16 . 135 BS95
Cray Riverway, Dart. DA1 . 127 FG85
Cray Rd, Belv. DA17 . 106 FA79
Sidcup DA14 . 126 EW94
Swanley BR8 . 147 FB100
Crayside Ind Est, Dart. DA1 *off Thames Rd* . 107 FH84
Cray Valley Rd, Orp. BR5 . 146 EU99
Crealock Gro, Wdf.Grn. IG8 . . 48 EF50
Crealock St, SW18 . 120 DB86
Creasey Cl, Horn. RM11 . 71 FH61
Creasy Cl, Abb.L. WD5 . 7 BT31
Creasy Est, SE1 . 201 M7
Crebor St, SE22 . 122 DU86
Credenhall Dr, Brom. BR2 . . 145 EM102
Credenhill St, SW16 . 121 DJ93
Crediton Hill, NW6 . 64 DB64

A B C D E F G H I J K L M N O P Q R S T U V W X Y Z

★ Place of interest ⇌ Railway station ⊖ London Underground station DLR Docklands Light Railway station Tramlink station H Hospital

Cre - Cro

Crediton Rd, E16
off Pacific Rd 86 EG72
NW10 81 CX67
Crediton Way, Esher (Clay.)
KT10 155 CG106
Credon Rd, E13 86 EJ68
SE16 202 E10
Credo Way, Grays RM20 109 FV79
Creechurch La, EC3 197 N9
Creechurch Pl, EC3 197 N9
Creed Ct, EC4
off Ludgate Hill 83 DP72
Creed La, EC4 196 G9
Creek, The, Grav. DA11 130 GB85
Sunbury-on-Thames
TW16 135 BU99
CREEKMOUTH, Bark. 88 EU70
Creek Rd, SE8 103 EA79
SE10 103 EA79
Barking IG11 87 ET69
East Molesey KT8 137 CE98
Creekside, SE8 103 EB80
Rainham RM13 89 FE70
Creeland Gro, SE6
off Catford Hill 123 DZ88
Cree Way, Rom. RM1 51 FE52
Crefeld Cl, W6 99 CX79
Creffield Rd, W3 80 CM73
W5 80 CM73
Creighton Av, E6 86 EK68
N2 64 DE55
N10 64 DE55
Creighton Cl, W12
off Bloemfontein Rd 81 CV73
Creighton Rd, N17 46 DS52
NW6 81 CX68
W5 97 CK76
Cremer St, E2 197 P1
Cremorne Est, SW10
off Milman's St 100 DD79
Cremorne Gdns, Epsom
KT19 156 CR109
Cremorne Rd, SW10 100 DC80
Gravesend (Nthflt.) DA11 131 GF87
Crescent, EC3 197 P10
Crescent, The, E17 67 DY57
N11 44 DF49
NW2 63 CV62
SW13 99 CT82
SW19 120 DA90
W3 80 CS72
Abbots Langley WD5 7 BT30
Ashford TW15 114 BM92
Barnet EN5 28 DB41
Beckenham BR3 143 EA95
Bexley DA5 126 EW87
Caterham CR3 177 EA123
Chertsey KT16
off Western Av 134 BG97
Croydon CR0 142 DR99
Egham TW20 112 AY93
Epping CM16 17 ET32
Epsom KT18 156 CN114
Gravesend (Nthflt.) DA11 131 GF89
Greenhithe DA9 129 FW85
Harrow HA2 61 CD60
Hayes UB3 95 BQ80
Ilford IG2 69 EN58
Leatherhead KT22 171 CH122
Loughton IG10 32 EK43
New Malden KT3 138 CQ96
Reigate RH2 off Chartway 184 DB134
Rickmansworth (Crox.Grn.)
WD3 23 BP44
St. Albans (Brick.Wd.) AL2 8 CA30
Sevenoaks TN13 191 FK121
Shepperton TW17 135 BT101
Sidcup DA14 125 ET91
Slough SL1 92 AS75
Southall UB1 96 BZ75
Surbiton KT6 138 CL99
Sutton SM1 158 DD105
Sutton (Belmont) SM2 158 DA111
Upminster RM14 73 FS59
Watford WD18 24 BW42
Watford (Ald.) WD25 24 CB37
Wembley HA0 61 CH61
West Molesey KT8 136 CA98
West Wickham BR4 144 EE100
Weybridge KT13 134 BN104
Crescent Av, Grays RM17 110 GD78
Hornchurch RM12 71 FF61
Crescent Cotts, Sev. TN13 181 FE120
Crescent Ct, Surb. KT6 137 CK99
Crescent Dr, Brwd. CM15 54 FY46
Orpington BR5 145 EP100
Crescent E, Barn. EN4 28 DC38
Crescent Gdns, SW19 120 DA90
Ruislip HA4 59 BV58
Swanley BR8 147 FC96
Crescent Gro, SW4 101 DJ84
Mitcham CR4 140 DE98
Crescent Ho, SE13
off Ravensbourne Pl 103 EB82
Crescent La, SW4 121 DK85
Crescent Ms, N22
off Palace Gates Rd 45 DL53
Crescent Pl, SW3 198 B8
Crescent Ri, N22 45 DK53
Barnet EN4 28 DE43
Crescent Rd, E4 48 EE45
E6 86 EJ67
E10 67 EB61
E13 86 EG67
E18 48 EJ54
N3 43 CZ53
N8 65 DK59
N9 46 DU46
N11 44 DF49
N15 off Carlingford Rd 65 DP55
N22 45 DK53
SE18 105 EP78
SW20 139 CX95
Barnet EN4 28 DE43
Crescent Rd, Beck. BR3 143 EB96
Brentwood CM14 54 FV49
Bromley BR1 124 EG94
Caterham CR3 176 DU124
Dagenham RM10 71 FB63
Enfield EN2 29 DP41
Erith DA8 107 FF79
Kingston upon Thames
KT2 118 CN94
Redhill (Bletch.) RH1 186 DQ133
Shepperton TW17 135 BQ99
Sidcup DA15 125 ET90
South Ockendon (Aveley)
RM15 108 FQ75
Crescent Row, EC1 197 H5
Crescent Stables, SW15
off Upper Richmond Rd 99 CY84
Crescent St, N1 83 DM66
Crescent Vw, Loug. IG10 32 EK44
Crescent Wk, S.Ock. (Aveley)
RM15 108 FQ75
Crescent Way, N12 44 DE51
SE4 103 EA83
SW16 121 DM94
Orpington BR6 163 ES106
South Ockendon (Aveley)
RM15 91 FR74
Crescent W, Barn. EN4 28 DC38
Crescent Wd Rd, SE26 122 DU90
Cresford Rd, SW6 100 DB81
Crespigny Rd, NW4 63 CV58
Cressage Cl, Sthl. UB1 78 CA70
Cressall Cl, Lthd. KT22 171 CH120
Cressall Mead, Lthd. KT22 171 CH120
Cress End, Rick. WD3
off Springwell Av 38 BG46
Cresset Rd, E9 84 DW65
Cresset St, SW4 101 DK83
Cressfield Cl, NW5 64 DG64
Cressida Rd, N19 65 DJ60
Cressingham Gro, Sutt.
SM1 158 DC105
Cressingham Rd, SE13 103 EC83
Edgware HA8 42 CR51
Cressington Cl, N16
off Wordsworth Rd 66 DS64
Cresswell Gdns, SW5 100 DC78
Cresswell Pk, SE3 104 EF83
Cresswell Pl, SW10 100 DC78
Cresswell Rd, SE25 142 DU98
Feltham TW13 116 BY91
Twickenham TW1 117 CK86
Cresswell Way, N21 45 DN45
Cressy Ct, E1 off Cressy Pl 84 DW71
W6 99 CV76
Cressy Pl, E1 84 DW71
Cressy Rd, NW3 64 DF64
Crest, The, N13 45 DN49
NW4 63 CW57
Surbiton KT5 138 CN99
Waltham Cross (Chsht.) EN7
off Orchard Way 13 DP27
Cresta Dr, Add. (Woodham)
KT15 151 BF110
Crest Av, Grays RM17 110 GB80
Crestbrook Av, N13 45 DP48
Crestbrook Pl, N13 45 DP48
Crest Cl, Sev. (Bad.Mt.) TN14 165 FB111
Crest Dr, Enf. EN3 30 DW38
Crestfield St, WC1 196 A2
Crest Gdns, Ruis. HA4 60 BW62
Cresthill Av, Grays RM17 110 GC77
Creston Av, Wok. (Knap.)
GU21 166 AS116
Creston Way, Wor.Pk. KT4 139 CX102
Crest Rd, NW2 63 CT62
Bromley BR2 144 EF101
South Croydon CR2 160 DV108
Crest Vw, Green. DA9
off Woodland Way 109 FU84
Pinner HA5 60 BX56
Crest Vw Dr, Orp. BR5 145 EP99
Crestway, SW15 119 CV86
Crestwood Way, Houns. TW4 116 BZ85
Creswick Rd, W3 80 CP73
Creswick Wk, E3
off Malmesbury Rd 85 EA69
NW11 63 CZ56
Crete Hall Rd, Grav. DA11 130 GD86
Creton St, SE18 105 EN76
Crewdson Rd, SW9 101 DN80
Crewe Pl, NW10 81 CT69
Crewe's Av, Warl. CR6 176 DW116
Crewe's Cl, Warl. CR6 176 DW116
Crewe's Fm La, Warl. CR6 177 DX116
Crewe's La, Warl. CR6 177 DX116
CREWS HILL, Enf. 29 DP35
⇌ Crews Hill 13 DM34
Crews St, E14 203 P8
Crewys Rd, NW2 63 CZ61
SE15 102 DV82
Crichton Av, Wall. SM6 159 DK106
Crichton Rd, Cars. SM5 158 DF107
Crichton St, SW8
off Westbury St 101 DJ82
Cricketers Arms Rd, Enf. EN2 30 DQ40
Cricketers Cl, N14 45 DJ45
Chessington KT9 155 CK105
Erith DA8 107 FE78
Cricketers Ct, SE11 200 F9
Cricketers Ms, SW18
off East Hill 120 DB85
Cricketers Ter, Cars. SM5
off Wrythe La 140 DE104
Cricketfield Rd, E5 66 DV63
Cricket Fld Rd, Uxb. UB8 76 BK67
Cricketfield Rd, West Dr. UB7 94 BJ77
Cricket Grn, Mitch. CR4 140 DF97
Cricket Grd Rd, Chis. BR7 145 EP95
Cricket La, Beck. BR3 123 DY93
Cricket Way, Wey. KT13 135 BS103
Cricklade Av, SW2 121 DL89
Romford RM3 52 FK51
CRICKLEWOOD, NW2 63 CX62
⇌ Cricklewood 63 CX63
Cricklewood Bdy, NW2 63 CX62
Cricklewood La, NW2 63 CX63
Cridland St, E15 off Church St 86 EF67
Crieff Ct, Tedd. TW11 117 CJ94
Crieff Rd, SW18 120 DC86
Criffel Av, SW2 121 DK89
Crimp Hill, Egh. (Eng.Grn.)
TW20 112 AU90
Crimp Hill Rd, Wind. (Old Wind.)
SL4 112 AT87
Crimscott St, SE1 201 N7
Crimsworth Rd, SW8 101 DK81
Crinan St, N1 83 DL68
Cringle St, SW8 101 DJ80
Cripplegate St, EC2 197 H6
Cripps Grn, Hayes UB4
off Stratford Rd 77 BV70
Crispe Ho, Bark. IG11
off Dovehouse Mead 87 ER68
Crispen Rd, Felt. TW13 116 BY91
Crispian Cl, NW10 62 CS63
Crispin Cl, Ashtd. KT21 172 CM118
Croydon CR0
off Harrington Cl 141 DL103
Crispin Cres, Croy. CR0 141 DK104
Crispin Rd, Edg. HA8 42 CQ51
Crispin St, E1 197 P7
Crisp Rd, W6 99 CW78
Criss Cres, Ger.Cr. (Chal.St.P.)
SL9 36 AW54
Criss Gro, Ger.Cr. (Chal.St.P.)
SL9 36 AW54
Cristowe Rd, SW6 99 CZ82
Criterion Ms, N19 65 DK61
Crittall's Cor, Sid. DA14 126 EW94
Crockenhall Way, Grav.
(Istead Rise) DA13 130 GE94
CROCKENHILL, Swan. 147 FD101
Crockenhill La, Dart. (Eyns.)
DA4 148 FJ102
Swanley BR8 147 FG101
Crockenhill Rd, Orp. BR5 146 EX99
Swanley BR8 146 EZ100
Crockerton Rd, SW17 120 DF89
Crockford Cl, Add. KT15 152 BJ105
Crockford Pk Rd, Add. KT15 152 BJ106
CROCKHAM HILL, Eden. 189 EQ133
Crockham Way, SE9 125 EN91
Crocus Cl, Croy. CR0
off Cornflower La 143 DX102
Crocus Fld, Barn. EN5 27 CZ44
Croffets, Tad. KT20 173 CX121
Croft, The, E4 48 EE47
NW10 81 CT68
W5 80 CL71
Barnet EN5 27 CX42
Hounslow TW5 96 BY79
Loughton IG10 33 EN40
Pinner HA5 off Rayners La 60 BZ59
Ruislip HA4 60 BW63
St. Albans AL2 8 CA25
Swanley BR8 147 FC97
Wembley HA0 61 CJ64
Croft Av, W.Wick. BR4 143 EC102
Croft Cl, NW7 42 CS48
Belvedere DA17 106 EZ78
Chislehurst BR7 125 EM91
Hayes UB3 95 BQ80
Kings Langley (Chipper.)
WD4 6 BG30
Uxbridge UB10 76 BN66
Croft Ct, Borwd. WD6
off Kensington Way 26 CR41
Croftdown Rd, NW5 64 DG62
Croft End Cl, Chess. KT9
off Ashcroft Rd 138 CM104
Croft End Rd, Kings L. (Chipper.)
WD4 6 BG30
Crofters, The, Wind. SL4 112 AU86
Crofters Cl, Islw. TW7
off Ploughmans End 117 CD85
Crofters Ct, SE8
off Croft St 103 DY77
Crofters Mead, Croy. CR0 161 DZ109
Crofters Rd, Nthwd. HA6 39 BS49
Crofters Way, NW1 83 DK67
Croft Fld, Kings L. (Chipper.)
WD4 6 BG30
Croft Gdns, W7 97 CG75
Ruislip HA4 59 BT60
Croft La, Kings L. (Chipper.)
WD4 6 BG30
Croftleigh Av, Pur. CR8 175 DN116
Croft Lo Cl, Wdf.Grn. IG8 48 EH51
Croft Meadow, Kings L. (Chipper.)
WD4 6 BG30
Croft Ms, N12 44 DC48
Crofton, Ashtd. KT21 172 CL118
Crofton Av, W4 98 CR80
Bexley DA5 126 EX87
Orpington BR6 145 EQ103
Walton-on-Thames KT12 136 BW104
Crofton Cl, Cher. (Ott.) KT16 151 BC108
Croftongate Way, SE4 123 DY85
Crofton Gro, E4 47 ED49
Crofton La, Orp. BR5, BR6 145 ER101
⇌ Crofton Park 123 DZ85
Crofton Pk Rd, SE4 123 DZ86
Crofton Rd, E13 86 EH70
SE5 102 DS81
Grays RM16 110 GE76
Orpington BR6 145 EN104
Crofton Ter, E5 off Studley Cl 67 DY64
Richmond TW9 98 CM84
Crofton Way, Barn. EN5
off Wycherley Cres 28 DB44
Enfield EN2 29 DN40
Croft Rd, SW16 141 DN95
SW19 120 DC94
Bromley BR1 124 EG93
Caterham (Wold.) CR3 177 DZ122
Enfield EN3 31 DY39
Gerrards Cross (Chal.St.P.)
SL9 36 AY54
Sutton SM1 158 DE106
Westerham TN16 189 EP126
Crofts, The, Shep. TW17 135 BS98
Croftside, SE25
off Sunny Bk 142 DU97
Crofts La, N22
off Glendale Av 45 DN52
Crofts Rd, Har. HA1 61 CG58
Crofts St, E1 202 B1
Croft St, SE8 203 K9
Croftway, NW3 64 DA63
Richmond TW10 117 CH90
Croft Way, Sev. TN13 190 FF125
Sidcup DA15 125 ES90
Crogsland Rd, NW1 82 DG66
Croham Cl, S.Croy. CR2 160 DS107
Croham Manor Rd, S.Croy.
CR2 160 DS106
Croham Mt, S.Croy. CR2 160 DS108
Croham Pk Av, S.Croy. CR2 160 DT106
Croham Rd, S.Croy. CR2 160 DR106
Croham Valley Rd, S.Croy.
CR2 160 DT107
Croindene Rd, SW16 141 DL95
Cromartie Rd, N19 65 DK59
Cromarty Rd, Edg. HA8 42 CP47
Crombie Cl, Ilf. IG4 69 EM57
Crombie Rd, Sid. DA15 125 ER88
Cromer Cl, Uxb. UB8
off Dawley Av 77 BQ72
Cromer Pl, Orp. BR6
off Andover Rd 145 ER102
Cromer Rd, E10
off James La 67 ED58
N17 46 DU54
SE25 142 DV97
SW17 120 DG93
Barnet EN5 28 DC42
Hornchurch RM11 72 FK59
Hounslow (Hthrw.Air.) TW6 94 BN83
Romford RM7 71 FC58
Romford (Chad.Hth.) RM6 70 EY58
Watford WD24 24 BW38
Woodford Green IG8 48 EG49
Cromer Rd W, Houns. (Hthrw.Air.)
TW6 94 BN83
Cromer St, WC1 196 A3
Cromer Ter, E8 off Ferncliff Rd 66 DU64
Cromer Vil Rd, SW18 119 CZ86
Cromford Cl, Orp. BR6 145 ES104
Cromford Path, E5
off Overbury St 67 DX63
Cromford Rd, SW18 120 DA85
Cromford Way, N.Mal. KT3 138 CR95
Cromlix Cl, Chis. BR7 145 EP96
Crompton Pl, Enf. EN3
off Government Row 31 EA37
Crompton St, W2 82 DD70
Cromwell Av, N6 65 DH60
W6 99 CV78
Bromley BR2 144 EH98
New Malden KT3 139 CT99
Waltham Cross (Chsht.)
EN7 14 DU30
Cromwell Cl, E1
off Vaughan Way 84 DU74
N2 64 DD56
W3 off High St 80 CQ74
Bromley BR2 144 EH98
Chalfont St. Giles HP8 36 AW48
Walton-on-Thames KT12 135 BV102
Cromwell Cres, SW5 100 DA77
Cromwell Dr, Slou. SL1 74 AS72
Cromwell Gdns, SW7 198 A7
Cromwell Gro, W6 99 CW76
Caterham CR3 176 DQ121
Cromwell Highwalk, EC2
off Beech St 84 DQ71
H Cromwell Hosp, The,
SW5 100 DB77
Cromwell Ind Est, E10 67 DY60
Cromwell Ms, SW7 198 A8
Cromwell Pl, N6 65 DH60
SW7 198 A8
SW14 98 CQ83
W3 off Grove Pl 80 CQ74
Cromwell Rd, E7 86 EJ66
E17 67 EC57
N3 44 DC53
N10 44 DG52
SW5 100 DB77
SW7 100 DB77
SW9 101 DP81
SW19 120 DA92
Beckenham BR3 143 DY96
Borehamwood WD6 26 CL39
Brentwood CM14 54 FV49
Caterham CR3 176 DQ121
Croydon CR0 142 DR101
Feltham TW13 115 BV88
Grays RM17 110 GA77
Hayes UB3 77 BR72
Hounslow TW3 96 CA84
Kingston upon Thames
KT2 138 CL95
Redhill RH1 184 DF133
Teddington TW11 117 CG93
Waltham Cross (Chsht.)
EN7 14 DV28
Walton-on-Thames KT12 135 BV102
Wembley HA0 80 CL68
Worcester Park KT4 138 CR104
Cromwells Mere, Rom. RM1
off Havering Rd 51 FD51
Cromwell St, Houns. TW3 96 CA84
Cromwell Twr, EC2 197 J6
Cromwell Wk, Red. RH1 184 DF134
Crondace Rd, SW6 100 DA81
Crondall Ct, N1 197 M1
Crondall Ho, SW15
off Fontley Way 119 CU88
Crondall St, N1 197 L1
Cronin St, SE15 102 DT80
Crooked Billet, SW19
off Woodhayes Rd 119 CW93
Crooked Billet Roundabout,
E17 47 EA52
Staines TW18 114 BG91
Crooked Billet Yd, E2
off Kingsland Rd 84 DS69
Crooked La, Grav. DA12 131 GH86
Crooked Mile, Wal.Abb. EN9 15 EC33
Crooked Mile Roundabout,
Wal.Abb. EN9 15 EC33
Crooked Usage, N3 63 CY55
Crooke Rd, SE8 203 K10
Crookham Rd, SW6 99 CZ81
Crook Log, Bexh. DA6 106 EX83
Crookston Rd, SE9 105 EN83
Croombs Rd, E16 86 EJ71
Crooms Hill, SE10 103 ED80
Crooms Hill Gro, SE10 103 EC80
Cropley Ct, N1 off Cropley St 84 DR68
Cropley St, N1 84 DR68
Croppath Rd, Dag. RM10 70 FA63
Cropthorne Ct, W9
off Maida Vale 82 DC69
Crosby Cl, Felt. TW13 116 BY91
Crosby Ct, SE1 201 K4
Crosby Rd, E7 86 EG65
Dagenham RM10 89 FB68
Crosby Row, SE1 201 K5
Crosby Sq, EC3 197 M9
Crosby Wk, E8 off Laurel St 84 DT65
SW2 121 DN87
Crosier Cl, SE3 104 EL81
Crosier Rd, Uxb. (Ickhm.)
UB10 59 BQ63
Crosier Way, Ruis. HA4 59 BS62
Crosland Pl, SW11
off Taybridge Rd 100 DG83
Crossacres, Wok. GU22 167 BE115
Cross Av, SE10 103 ED79
Crossbow Rd, Chig. IG7 49 ET50
Crossbrook Rd, SE3 104 EL82
Crossbrook St, Wal.Cr. (Chsht.)
EN8 15 DX31
Cross Cl, SE15
off Gordon Rd 102 DV81
Cross Deep, Twick. TW1 117 CF89
Cross Deep Gdns, Twick. TW1 117 CF89
Crossfield Pl, Wey. KT13 153 BP108
Crossfield Rd, N17 66 DQ55
NW3 82 DD66
Crossfields, Loug. IG10 33 EP43
Crossfield St, SE8 103 EA80
Crossford St, SW9 101 DM82
Crossgate, Edg. HA8 42 CN48
Greenford UB6 79 CH65
DLR Crossharbour & London
Arena 204 C6
Crossing Rd, Epp. CM16 18 EU32
Cross Keys Cl, N9
off Balham Rd 46 DU47
W1 194 G7
Sevenoaks TN13 190 FG127
Cross Keys Sq, EC1 197 H7
Cross Lances Rd, Houns. TW3 96 CB84
Crossland Rd, Red. RH1 184 DG134
Thornton Heath CR7 141 DP100
Crosslands, Cher. KT16 133 BE104
Crosslands Av, W5 80 CM74
Southall UB2 96 BZ78
Crosslands Rd, Epsom KT19 156 CR107
Cross La, EC3 201 M1
N8 65 DM56
Bexley DA5 126 EZ87
Chertsey (Ott.) KT16 151 BB107
Cross La E, Grav. DA12 131 GH89
Cross Las, Ger.Cr. (Chal.St.P.)
SL9 36 AY50
Cross Las Cl, Ger.Cr. (Chal.St.P.)
SL9 off Cross Las 37 AZ50
Cross La W, Grav. DA11 131 GH89
Crosslet St, SE17 201 L8
Crosslet Vale, SE10 103 EB81
Crossley Cl, West. (Bigg.H.)
TN16 178 EK115
Crossleys, Ch.St.G. HP8 36 AW49
Crossley St, N7 83 DN65
Crossmead, SE9 125 EM88
Watford WD19 23 BV44
Crossmead Av, Grnf. UB6 78 CA69
Crossmount Ho, SE5 102 DQ80
Crossness La, SE28 88 EX73
★ Crossness Pumping Sta,
SE2 88 EY72
Crossness Rd, Bark. IG11 87 ET69
Crossoaks La, Borwd. WD6 26 CR35
Potters Bar (S.Mimms)
EN6 10 CS34
Crosspath, The, Rad. WD7 25 CG35
Cross Rd, E4 48 EE46
N11 45 DH50
N22 45 DN52
SE5 102 DS82
SW19 120 DA94
Bromley BR2 144 EL103
Croydon CR0 142 DR102
Dartford DA1 128 FJ86
Dartford (Hawley) DA2 128 FM91
Enfield EN1 30 DS42
Feltham TW13 116 BY91
Gravesend (Nthflt.) DA11 131 GF86
Harrow HA1 61 CD56
Harrow (S.Har.) HA2 60 CB62
Harrow (Wldste.) HA3 41 CG54
Kingston upon Thames
KT2 118 CM94
Orpington BR5 146 EV99
Purley CR8 159 DP113
Romford RM7 70 FA55
Romford (Chad.Hth.) RM6 70 EW59
Sidcup DA14
off Sidcup Hill 126 EV91
Sutton SM2 158 DD106
Sutton (Belmont) SM2 158 DA110
Tadworth KT20 173 CW122
Uxbridge UB8
off New Windsor St 76 BJ66
Waltham Cross EN8 15 DY33
Watford WD19 24 BY44
Weybridge KT13 135 BR104
Woodford Green IG8 49 EM51
Cross Rds, Loug. (High Beach)
IG10 32 EH40
Cross St, N1 83 DP67
SW13 98 CS82
Erith DA8 off Bexley Rd 107 FE78

243

Cro - Cyp

Cross St, Hmptn. (Hmptn.H.)
TW12 116 CC92
Uxbridge UB8 76 BJ66
Watford WD17 24 BW41
Cross Ter, Wal.Abb. EN9
off Stonyshotts 16 EE34
Crossthwaite Av, SE5 102 DR84
Crosswall, EC3 197 P10
Crossway, N12 44 DD51
N16 66 DS64
NW9 63 CT56
SE28 88 EW72
SW20 139 CW98
W13 79 CG70
Chesham HP5 4 AS30
Dagenham RM8 70 EW62
Enfield EN1 46 DS45
Hayes UB3 77 BU74
Orpington BR5 145 ER98
Pinner HA5 39 BV54
Ruislip HA4 60 BW63
Walton-on-Thames KT12 135 BV103
Woodford Green IG8 48 EJ49
Crossway, The, N22 45 DP52
SE9 124 EK89
Cross Way, The, Har. HA3 41 CE54
Crossway, The, Uxb. UB10 76 BM68
Crossways, N21 30 DQ44
Brentwood CM15 55 GA44
Egham TW20 113 BD93
Romford RM2 71 FH55
South Croydon CR2 161 DY108
Sunbury-on-Thames TW16 115 BT94
Sutton SM2 158 DD109
Westerham (Tats.) TN16 178 EJ120
Crossways, The, Couls. CR5 175 DM119
Hounslow TW5 96 BZ80
Redhill RH1 185 DJ130
Wembley HA9 62 CN61
Crossways Boul, Dart. DA2 108 FQ84
Greenhithe DA9 109 FT84
Crossways Business Pk, Dart.
DA2 108 FQ84
Crossways La, Reig. RH2 184 DC128
Crossways Rd, Beck. BR3 143 EA98
Mitcham CR4 141 DH97
Crosswell Cl, Shep. TW17 135 BQ96
Croston St, E8 84 DU67
Crothall Cl, N13 45 DM48
Crouch Av, Bark. IG11 88 EV68
Crouch Cl, Beck. BR3
off Abbey La 123 EA93
Crouch Cft, SE9 125 EN90
CROUCH END, N8 65 DJ58
Crouch End Hill, N8 65 DK59
Crouch Hall Rd, N8 65 DK58
⇌ **Crouch Hill** 65 DM59
Crouch Hill, N4 65 DL58
N8 65 DL58
Crouch La, Wal.Cr. (Chsht.)
EN7 14 DQ28
Crouchman's Cl, SE26 122 DT90
Crouch Oak La, Add. KT15 152 BJ105
Crouch Rd, NW10 80 CR66
Grays RM16 111 GG78
Crouch Valley, Upmin. RM14 73 FS59
Crowborough Cl, Warl. CR6 177 DY117
Crowborough Dr, Warl. CR6 177 DY118
Crowborough Path, Wat. WD19
off Prestwick Rd 40 BX49
Crowborough Rd, SW17 120 DG93
Crowden Way, SE28 88 EW73
Crowder St, E1 84 DV73
Crow Dr, Sev. (Halst.) TN14 181 FC115
Crowfoot Cl, E9
off Lee Conservancy Rd 67 DZ64
CROW GREEN, Brwd. 54 FT41
Crow Grn La, Brwd. CM15 54 FU43
Crow Grn Rd, Brwd. CM15 54 FT43
Crowhurst Cl, SW9 101 DN82
Crowhurst Mead, Gdse. RH9 186 DW130
Crowhurst Way, Orp. BR5 146 EW99
Crowland Av, Hayes UB3 95 BS77
Crowland Gdns, N14 45 DL45
Crowland Rd, N15 66 DT57
Thornton Heath CR7 142 DR98
Crowlands Av, Rom. RM7 71 FB58
Crowland Ter, N1 84 DR66
Crowland Wk, Mord. SM4 140 DB100
Crow La, Rom. RM7 70 EZ59
Crowley Cres, Croy. CR0 159 DN106
Crowline Wk, N1
off Clephane Rd 84 DR65
Crowmarsh Gdns, SE23
off Tyson Rd 122 DW87
Crown Arc, Kings.T. KT1
off Union St 137 CK96
Crown Ash Hill, West. TN16 162 EH114
Crown Ash La, Warl. CR6 178 EG116
Westerham TN16 178 EG116
Crown Cl, E3 85 EA67
NW6 82 DB65
NW7 43 CT47
Hayes UB3 95 BT75
Orpington BR6 164 EU105
Slough (Colnbr.) SL3 93 BC80
Walton-on-Thames KT12 136 BW101
Crown Ct, EC2 197 J9
SE12 124 EH86
WC2 196 A9
Bromley BR2
off Victoria Rd 144 EK99
Crown Dale, SE19 121 DP93
Crowndale Rd, NW1 83 DJ68
Crownfield Av, Ilf. IG2 69 ES57
Crownfield Rd, E15 67 ED64
Crownfields, Sev. TN13 191 FH125
Crown Hill, Croy. CR0
off Church St 142 DQ103
Epping CM16 17 EM33
Waltham Abbey EN9 17 EM33
Crownhill Rd, NW10 81 CT67
Woodford Green IG8 48 EL52
Crown Ho, Bark. IG11
off Linton Rd 87 EQ66
Crown La, N14 45 DJ46
SW16 121 DN92
Crown La, Brom. BR2 144 EK99
Chislehurst BR7 145 EQ95
Morden SM4 140 DB97
Virginia Water GU25 132 AX100
Crown La Gdns, SW16
off Crown La 121 DN92
Crown La Spur, Brom. BR2 144 EK100
Crown Meadow, Slou. (Colnbr.)
SL3 93 BB80
Crownmead Way, Rom. RM7 71 FB56
Crown Ms, E13
off Waghorn Rd 86 EJ67
W6 99 CU77
Crown Office Row, EC4 196 D10
Crown Pas, SW1 199 L3
Kingston upon Thames KT1
off Church St 137 CK96
Watford WD18
off The Crescent 24 BW42
Crown Pl, EC2 197 M6
NW5 *off Kentish Town Rd* 83 DH65
Crown Pt Par, SE19
off Beulah Hill 121 DP93
Crown Ri, Cher. KT16 133 BF102
Watford WD25 8 BW34
Crown Rd, N10 44 DG52
Borehamwood WD6 26 CN39
Enfield EN1 30 DV42
Grays RM17 110 GA79
Ilford IG6 69 ER56
Morden SM4 140 DB98
New Malden KT3 138 CQ95
Orpington BR6 164 EU106
Ruislip HA4 60 BX64
Sevenoaks (Shore.) TN14 165 FF110
Sutton SM1 158 DB105
Twickenham TW1 117 CH86
Virginia Water GU25 132 AW100
Crown Sq, Wok. GU21
off Commercial Way 167 AZ117
Crownstone Rd, SW2 121 DN85
Crown St, SE5 102 DQ80
W3 80 CP74
Brentwood CM14 54 FW47
Dagenham RM10 89 FC65
Egham TW20 113 BA92
Harrow HA2 61 CD60
Crown Ter, Rich. TW9 98 CM84
Crowntree Cl, Islw. TW7 97 CF79
Crown Wk, Uxb. UB8
off Oxford Rd 76 BJ66
Wembley HA9 62 CM62
Crown Way, West Dr. UB7 76 BM74
Crown Wds La, SE9 105 EP82
SE18 105 EP82
Crown Wds Way, SE9 125 ER85
Crown Wks, E2
off Temple St 84 DV68
Crown Yd, Houns. TW3
off High St 96 CC83
Crowshott Av, Stan. HA7 41 CJ53
Crows Rd, E15 85 ED69
Barking IG11 87 EP65
Epping CM16 17 ET30
Crowstone Rd, Grays RM16 110 GC75
Crowther Av, Brent. TW8 98 CL77
Crowther Rd, SE25 142 DU98
Crowthorne Cl, SW18 119 CZ88
Crowthorne Rd, W10 81 CX72
Croxdale Rd, Borwd. WD6 26 CM40
Croxden Cl, Edg. HA8 62 CM55
Croxden Wk, Mord. SM4 140 DC100
Croxford Gdns, N22 45 DP52
Croxford Way, Rom. RM7
off Horace Av 71 FD60
⊖ **Croxley** 23 BP44
Croxley Business Pk, Wat.
WD18 23 BR43
Croxley Cl, Orp. BR5 146 EV96
CROXLEY GREEN, Rick. 22 BN43
⇌ **Croxley Green (closed)** 23 BR43
Croxley Grn, Orp. BR5 146 EV95
Croxley Rd, W9 81 CZ69
Croxley Vw, Wat. WD18 23 BS44
Croxted Cl, SE21 122 DQ87
Croxted Rd, SE21 122 DQ87
SE24 122 DQ87
Croyde Av, Grnf. UB6 78 CC69
Hayes UB3 95 BS77
Croyde Cl, Sid. DA15 125 ER87
CROYDON 142 DR103
Croydon Flyover, Croy. CR0 159 DP105
Croydon Gro, Croy. CR0 141 DP102
Croydon La, Bans. SM7 158 DB114
Croydon La S, Bans. SM7 158 DB114
★ **Croydon Mus**, Croy. CR0 142 DQ104
Croydon Rd, E13 86 EF70
SE20 142 DV96
Beckenham BR3 143 DY98
Bromley BR2 144 EF104
Caterham CR3 176 DU122
Croydon (Bedd.) CR0 159 DL105
Hounslow (Hthrw.Air.) TW6 95 BP82
Keston BR2 144 EJ104
Mitcham CR4 140 DG98
Reigate RH2 184 DB134
Wallington SM6 159 DH105
Warlingham CR6 177 ED122
West Wickham BR4 144 EE104
Westerham TN16 179 EM123
Croyland Rd, N9 46 DU46
Croylands Dr, Surb. KT6 138 CL101
Croysdale Av, Sun. TW16 135 BU97
Crozier Dr, S.Croy. CR2 160 DV110
Crozier Ho, SE3
off Ebdon Way 104 EH83
Crozier Ter, E9 67 DX64
Crucible Cl, Rom. RM6 70 EV58
Crucifix La, SE1 201 M4
Cruden Ho, SE17
off Hillingdon St 101 DP79
Cruden Rd, Grav. DA12 131 GM90
Cruden St, N1 83 DP67
Cruick Av, S.Ock. RM15 91 FW73
Cruikshank Rd, E15 68 EE63
Cruikshank St, WC1 196 D2
Crummock Gdns, NW9 62 CS57
Crumpsall St, SE2 106 EW77
Crundale Av, NW9 62 CN57
Crundal Twr, Orp. BR5 146 EW102
Crunden Rd, S.Croy. CR2 160 DR108
Crusader Cl, Purf. RM19
off Centurion Way 108 FN77
Crusader Gdns, Croy. CR0
off Cotelands 142 DS104
Crusader Way, Wat. WD18 23 BT44
Crushes Cl, Brwd. CM13 55 GE44
Crusoe Ms, N16 66 DR61
Crusoe Rd, Erith DA8 107 FD78
Mitcham CR4 120 DF94
Crutched Friars, EC3 197 N10
Crutches La, Beac. (Jordans)
HP9 36 AS51
Crutchfield La, Walt. KT12 135 BV103
Crutchley Rd, SE6 124 EE89
Crystal Av, Horn. RM12 72 FL63
Crystal Ct, SE19
off College Rd 122 DT92
Crystal Ho, SE18
off Spinel Cl 105 ET78
⇌ **Crystal Palace** 122 DU93
★ **Crystal Palace FC**, SE25 142 DS98
★ **Crystal Palace National
Sport Cen**, SE19 122 DU93
Crystal Palace Par, SE19 122 DT93
★ **Crystal Palace Pk**, SE19 122 DT92
Crystal Palace Pk Rd, SE26 122 DU92
Crystal Palace Rd, SE22 102 DU84
Crystal Palace Sta Rd, SE19
off Anerley Hill 122 DU93
Crystal Ter, SE19 122 DR93
Crystal Vw Ct, Brom. BR1
off Winlaton Rd 123 ED91
Crystal Way, Dag. RM8 70 EW60
Harrow HA1 61 CF57
Cuba Dr, Enf. EN3 30 DW40
Cuba St, E14 203 P4
Cubitt Sq, Sthl. UB2
off Windmill Av 78 CC74
Cubitt Steps, E14 204 A2
Cubitt St, WC1 196 B3
Croydon CR0 159 DM106
Cubitts Yd, WC2 196 A10
Cubitt Ter, SW4 101 DJ83
CUBITT TOWN, E14 204 E6
Cuckmans Dr, St.Alb. AL2 8 CA25
Cuckoo Av, W7 79 CE70
Cuckoo Dene, W7 79 CD71
Cuckoo Hall La, N9 46 DW45
Cuckoo Hill, Pnr. HA5 60 BW55
Cuckoo Hill Dr, Pnr. HA5 60 BW55
Cuckoo Hill Rd, Pnr. HA5 60 BW56
Cuckoo La, W7 79 CE73
Cuckoo Pound, Shep. TW17 135 BS99
Cudas Cl, Epsom KT19 157 CT105
Cuddington Av, Wor.Pk. KT4 139 CT104
Cuddington Cl, Tad. KT20 173 CW120
Cuddington Pk Cl, Bans.
SM7 157 CZ113
Cuddington Way, Sutt. SM2 157 CX112
CUDHAM, Sev. 179 ER115
Cudham Cl, Sutt. (Belmont)
SM2 158 DA110
Cudham Dr, Croy. (New Adgtn.)
CR0 161 EC110
Cudham La N, Orp. BR6 163 ES110
Sevenoaks (Cudham)
TN14 163 ER112
Cudham La S, Sev. (Cudham)
TN14 179 EQ115
Cudham Pk Rd, Sev. (Cudham)
TN14 163 ES110
Cudham Rd, Orp. BR6 163 EN111
Westerham (Tats.) TN16 178 EL120
Cudham St, SE6 123 EC87
Cudworth St, E1 84 DV70
Cuff Cres, SE9 124 EK86
CUFFLEY, Pot.B. 13 DM29
⇌ **Cuffley** 13 DM29
Cuffley Av, Wat. WD25 8 BX34
Cuffley Hill, Wal.Cr. (Chsht.)
EN7 13 DN29
Cuff Pt, E2 197 P2
Cugley Rd, Dart. DA2 128 FQ87
Culford Gdns, SW3 198 E9
Culford Gro, N1 84 DS65
Culford Ms, N1 *off Culford Rd* 84 DS65
Culford Rd, N1 84 DS66
Grays RM16 110 GC75
Culgaith Gdns, Enf. EN2 29 DL42
Cullen Sq, S.Ock. RM15 91 FW73
Cullen Way, NW10 80 CQ70
Cullera Cl, Nthwd. HA6 39 BT51
Cullerne Cl, Epsom (Ewell)
KT17 157 CT110
Cullesden Rd, Ken. CR8 175 DP115
Culling Rd, SE16 202 F6
Cullings Ct, Wal.Abb. EN9 16 EF33
Cullington Cl, Har. HA3 61 CG56
Cullingworth Rd, NW10 63 CU64
Culloden Cl, SE16 102 DU78
Culloden Rd, Enf. EN2 29 DP40
Culloden St, E14 85 EC72
Cullum St, EC3 197 M10
Culmington Rd, W13 97 CJ75
South Croydon CR2 160 DQ109
Culmore Cross, SW12 121 DH88
Culmore Rd, SE15 102 DV80
Culmstock Rd, SW11 120 DG85
Culpeper Cl, Ilf. IG6 49 EP51
Culross Cl, N15 66 DQ56
Culross St, W1 198 F1
Culsac Rd, Surb. KT6 138 CL103
Culverden Rd, SW12 121 DJ89
Watford WD19 39 BV48
Culver Dr, Oxt. RH8 188 EE130
Culver Gro, Stan. HA7 41 CJ54
Culverhay, Ashtd. KT21 172 CL116
Culverhouse Gdns, SW16 121 DM90
Culverlands Cl, Stan. HA7 41 CH49
Culverley Rd, SE6 123 EB88
Culvers Av, Cars. SM5 140 DF103
Culvers Retreat, Cars. SM5 140 DF102
Culverstone Cl, Brom. BR2 144 EF100
Culvers Way, Cars. SM5 140 DF103
Culvert La, Uxb. UB8 76 BH68
Culvert Pl, SW11 100 DG82
Culvert Rd, N15 66 DS57
Culvert Rd, SW11 100 DF82
Culworth St, NW8 194 B1
Cumberland Av, NW10 80 CP69
Gravesend DA12 131 GJ87
Hornchurch RM12 72 FL62
Welling DA16 105 ES83
Cumberland Cl, E8 84 DT65
SW20 *off Lansdowne Rd* 119 CX94
Amersham HP7 20 AV39
Epsom KT19 156 CS110
Hornchurch RM12 72 FL62
Ilford IG6 *off Carrick Dr* 49 EQ53
Twickenham TW1
off Westmorland Cl 117 CH86
Cumberland Cres, W14 99 CY77
Cumberland Dr, Bexh. DA7 106 EY80
Chessington KT9 138 CM104
Dartford DA1 128 FM87
Esher KT10 137 CG103
Cumberland Gdns, NW4 43 CY54
WC1 196 C2
Cumberland Gate, W1 194 D10
Cumberland Mkt, NW1 195 J2
Cumberland Mkt Est, NW1 195 J2
Cumberland Mills Sq, E14 204 F10
Cumberland Pk, NW10 81 CU69
W3 80 CQ73
Cumberland Pl, NW1 195 H2
SE6 124 EF88
Sunbury-on-Thames
TW16 135 BU98
Cumberland Rd, E12 68 EK63
E13 86 EH71
E17 47 DY54
N9 46 DW46
N22 45 DM54
SE25 142 DV100
SW13 99 CT81
W3 80 CQ73
W7 97 CF75
Ashford TW15 114 BK90
Bromley BR2 144 EE98
Grays (Chaff.Hun.) RM16 110 FY75
Harrow HA1 60 CB57
Richmond TW9 98 CN80
Stanmore HA7 62 CM55
Cumberlands, Ken. CR8 176 DR115
Cumberland St, SW1 199 J10
Staines TW18 113 BD92
Cumberland Ter, NW1 195 H2
Cumberland Ter Ms, NW1 195 H1
Cumberland Vil, W3
off Cumberland Rd 80 CQ73
Cumberlow Av, SE25 142 DT97
Cumbernauld Gdns, Sun.
TW16 115 BT92
Cumberton Rd, N17 46 DR53
Cumbrae Cl, Slou. SL2
off St. Pauls Av 74 AU74
Cumbrae Gdns, Surb. KT6 137 CK103
Cumbria Ho, SE26
off High Level Dr 122 DU91
Cumbrian Av, Bexh. DA7 107 FE81
Cumbrian Gdns, NW2 63 CX61
Cumbrian Way, Uxb. UB8
off Chippendale Waye 76 BK66
★ **Cuming Mus**, SE17 201 H9
Cumley Rd, Ong. CM5 19 FE30
Cummings Hall La, Rom.
(Noak Hill) RM3 52 FJ48
Cumming St, N1 196 B1
Cumnor Gdns, Epsom KT17 157 CU107
Cumnor Ri, Ken. CR8 176 DQ117
Cumnor Rd, Sutt. SM2 158 DC107
Cunard Cres, N21 30 DR44
Cunard Pl, EC3 197 N9
Cunard Rd, NW10 80 CR69
Cunard St, SE5
off Albany Rd 102 DS79
Cunard Wk, SE16 203 J8
Cundy Rd, E16 86 EJ72
Cundy St, SW1 198 G9
Cundy St Est, SW1 198 G9
Cunliffe Cl, Epsom (Headley)
KT18 172 CP124
Cunliffe Rd, Epsom KT19 157 CT105
Cunliffe St, SW16 121 DJ93
Cunningham Av, Enf. EN3 31 DY36
Cunningham Cl, Rom. RM6 70 EW57
West Wickham BR4 143 EB103
Cunningham Pk, Har. HA1 60 CC57
Cunningham Pl, NW8 82 DD70
Cunningham Ri, Epp. (N.Wld.Bas.)
CM16 19 FC25
Cunningham Rd, N15 66 DU56
Banstead SM7 174 DD115
Waltham Cross (Chsht.)
EN8 15 DY27
Cunnington St, W4 98 CQ76
Cupar Rd, SW11 100 DG81
Cupola Cl, Brom. BR1 124 EH92
Curates Wk, Dart. DA1 128 FK90
Cureton St, SW1 199 N9
Curfew Bell Rd, Cher. KT16 133 BF101
Curfew Ho, Bark. IG11
off St. Ann's 87 EQ67
Curie Gdns, NW9
off Pasteur Cl 42 CS54
Curlew Cl, SE28 88 EX73
South Croydon CR2 161 DX111
Curlew Ct, Surb. KT6 138 CM104
Curlew Ho, Enf. EN3
off Allington Ct 31 DX43
Curlews, The, Grav. DA12 131 GK89
Curlew St, SE1 201 P4
Curlew Ter, Ilf. IG5
off Tiptree Cres 69 EN55
Curlew Way, Hayes UB4 78 BX71
Curling Cl, Couls. CR5 175 DM120
Curling La, Grays (Bad.Dene)
RM17 110 FZ78
Curnick's La, SE27
off Chapel Rd 122 DQ91
Curnock Est, NW1
off Plender St 83 DJ67
Curran Av, Sid. DA15 125 ET85
Wallington SM6 140 DG104
Curran Cl, Uxb. UB8 76 BJ70
Currey Rd, Grnf. UB6 79 CD65
Curricle St, W3 80 CS74
Currie Hill Cl, SW19 119 CZ91
Curry Ri, NW7 43 CX51
Cursitor St, EC4 196 D8
Curtain Pl, EC2
off Curtain Rd 84 DS69
Curtain Rd, EC2 197 M5
Curthwaite Gdns, Enf. EN2 29 DK42
Curtis Cl, Rick. (Mill End)
WD3 38 BG46
Curtis Dr, W3 80 CR72
Watford WD25 *off Ashfields* 7 BT34
Curtis Fld Rd, SW16 121 DM91
Curtis La, Wem. HA0
off Montrose Cres 80 CL65
Curtismill Cl, Orp. BR5 146 EV97
Curtis Mill Grn, Rom. (Nave.)
RM4 35 FF42
Curtis Mill La, Rom. (Nave.)
RM4 35 FF42
Curtismill Way, Orp. BR5 146 EV97
Curtis Rd, Epsom KT19 156 CQ105
Hornchurch RM11 72 FM60
Hounslow TW4 116 BZ87
Curtis St, SE1 201 P8
Curtis Way, SE1 201 P8
SE28 *off Tawney Rd* 88 EV73
Curvan Cl, Epsom KT17 157 CT110
Curve, The, W12 81 CU73
Curwen Av, E7
off Woodford Rd 68 EH63
Curwen Rd, W12 99 CU75
Curzon Av, Enf. EN3 31 DX43
Stanmore HA7 41 CG53
Curzon Cl, Orp. BR6 163 ER105
Weybridge KT13
off Curzon Rd 152 BN105
Curzon Cres, NW10 81 CT66
Barking IG11 87 ET68
Curzon Dr, Grays RM17 110 GC80
Curzon Gate, W1 198 G3
Curzon Mall, Slou. SL1
off High St 92 AT75
Curzon Pl, Pnr. HA5 60 BW57
Curzon Rd, N10 45 DH54
W5 79 CH70
Thornton Heath CR7 141 DN100
Weybridge KT13 152 BN105
Curzon Sq, W1 198 G3
Curzon St, W1 198 G3
Cusack Cl, Twick. TW1
off Waldegrave Rd 117 CF91
Cussons Cl, Wal.Cr. (Chsht.)
EN7 14 DU29
CUSTOM HOUSE, E16 86 EK72
★ **Custom House**, EC3 201 M1
⇌ **Custom House** 86 EH73
DLR **Custom House** 86 EH73
Custom Ho Quay, EC3
off Lower Thames St 84 DS73
Custom Ho Reach, SE16 203 M5
Custom Ho Wk, EC3 201 M1
Cut, The, SE1 200 E4
Cutcombe Rd, SE5 102 DQ82
Cuthberga Cl, Bark. IG11
off George St 87 EQ66
Cuthbert Gdns, SE25 142 DS97
Cuthbert Rd, E17 67 EC55
N18 *off Fairfield Rd* 46 DU50
Croydon CR0 141 DP103
Cuthberts Cl, Wal.Cr. EN7 14 DT29
Cuthbert St, W2 82 DD70
Cut Hills, Egh. TW20 132 AV95
Virginia Water GU25 132 AV95
Cuthill Wk, SE5 102 DR81
Cutlers Gdns, E1 197 N8
Cutlers Gdns Arc, EC2
off Cutler St 84 DS72
Cutlers Sq, E14 204 A9
Cutlers Ter, N1
off Balls Pond Rd 84 DR65
Cutler St, E1 197 N8
Cutmore St, Grav. DA11 131 GH87
Cutthroat All, Rich. TW10
off Ham St 117 CJ89
★ **Cutty Sark**, SE10 103 EC79
DLR **Cutty Sark** 103 EC79
Cutty Sark Ct, Green. DA9
off Low Cl 129 FU85
Cutty Sark Gdns, SE10
off King William Wk 103 EC79
Cuxton Cl, Bexh. DA6 126 EY85
Cyclamen Cl, Hmptn. TW12
off Gresham Rd 116 CA93
Cyclamen Rd, Swan. BR8 147 FD98
Cyclamen Way, Epsom KT19 156 CP106
Cyclops Ms, E14 203 P8
Cygnet Av, Felt. TW14 116 BW87
Cygnet Cl, NW10 62 CR64
Borehamwood WD6 26 CQ39
Northwood HA6 39 BQ52
Woking GU21 166 AV116
Cygnet Gdns, Grav. (Nthflt.)
DA11 131 GF89
Cygnets, The, Felt. TW13 116 BY91
Staines TW18
off Edgell Rd 113 BF92
Cygnets Cl, Red. RH1 184 DG132
Cygnet St, E1
off Sclater St 84 DT70
Cygnet Vw, Grays RM20 109 FT77
Cygnet Way, Hayes UB4 78 BX71
Cygnus Business Cen, NW10 81 CT65
Cymbeline Ct, Har. HA1 61 CF58
Cynthia St, N1 196 C1
Cyntra Pl, E8 84 DV66
Cypress Av, Enf. EN2 29 DN35
Twickenham TW2 116 CC87

★ Place of interest ⇌ Railway station ⊖ London Underground station DLR Docklands Light Railway station Tramlink station H Hospital

Cyp - Dau

Cypress CI, Wal.Abb. EN9 . . . . .15 ED34
Cypress Ct, Vir.W. GU25 . . . .132 AY98
Cypress Gro, Ilf. IG6 . . . . .49 ES51
Cypress Path, Rom. RM3 . . . . .52 FK52
Cypress PI, W1 . . . . .195 L5
Cypress Rd, SE25 . . . . .142 DS96
  Harrow HA3 . . . . .41 CD54
Cypress Tree CI, Sid. DA15
  off White Oak Gdns 125 ET87
Cypress Wk, Egh. (Eng.Grn.)
  TW20 . . . . .112 AV93
  Watford WD25
  off Cedar Wd Dr 23 BV35
Cypress Way, Bans. SM7 . . . .157 CX114
DLR Cyprus 87 EN73
Cyprus Av, N3 . . . . .43 CY54
Cyprus CI, N4
  off Atterbury Rd 65 DP58
Cyprus Gdns, N3 . . . . .43 CY54
Cyprus PI, E2 . . . . .84 DW68
  E6 . . . . .87 EN73
Cyprus Rd, N3 . . . . .43 CZ54
  N9 . . . . .46 DT47
Cyprus Roundabout, E16
  off Royal Albert Way 87 EN73
Cyprus St, E2 . . . . .84 DW68
Cyrena Rd, SE22 . . . . .122 DT86
Cyril Mans, SW11 . . . . .100 DF81
Cyril Rd, Bexh. DA7 . . . . . . .106 EY82
  Orpington BR6 . . . . .146 EU101
Cyrus St, EC1 . . . . .196 G4
Czar St, SE8 . . . . .103 EA79

D

Dabbling CI, Erith DA8 . . . . . .107 FH80
Dabbs Hill La, Nthlt. UB5 . . . . .60 CB64
D'Abernon CI, Esher KT10 . . .154 CA105
D'Abernon Dr, Cob. (Stoke d'Ab.)
  KT11 . . . . .170 BY116
Dabin Cres, SE10 . . . . .103 EC81
Dacca St, SE8 . . . . .103 DZ79
Dace Rd, E3 . . . . .85 EA66
Dacre Av, Ilf. IG5 . . . . .49 EN54
  South Ockendon (Aveley)
  RM15 . . . . .91 FR74
Dacre CI, Chig. IG7 . . . . .49 EQ49
  Greenford UB6 . . . . .78 CB68
Dacre Cres, S.Ock. (Aveley)
  RM15 . . . . .91 FR74
Dacre Gdns, SE13 . . . . .104 EE84
  Borehamwood WD6 . . . . . .26 CR43
  Chigwell IG7 . . . . .49 EQ49
Dacre Pk, SE13 . . . . .104 EE83
Dacre PI, SE13 . . . . .104 EE83
Dacre Rd, E11 . . . . .68 EF60
  E13 . . . . .86 EH67
  Croydon CR0 . . . . .141 DL101
Dacres Rd, SE23 . . . . .123 DX90
Dacre St, SW1 . . . . .199 M6
Dade Way, Sthl. UB2 . . . . .96 BZ78
Daerwood CI, Brom. BR2 . . . .145 EM102
Daffodil CI, Croy. CR0
  off Primrose La 143 DX102
Daffodil Gdns, Ilf. IG1 . . . . . . .69 EP64
Daffodil CI, Hmptn. TW12
  off Gresham Rd 116 CA93
Daffodil St, W12 . . . . .81 CT73
Dafforne Rd, SW17 . . . . .120 DG90
DAGENHAM 88 FA65
Dagenham Av, Dag. RM9 . . . . .88 EY67
 ≢ Dagenham Dock 88 EZ68
 ⊖ Dagenham East 71 FC64
 ⊖ Dagenham Heathway 88 EZ65
Dagenham Rd, E10 . . . . .67 DZ60
  Dagenham RM10 . . . . .71 FC63
  Rainham RM13 . . . . .89 FD66
  Romford RM7 . . . . .71 FD62
Dagger La, Borwd. (Elstree)
  WD6 . . . . .25 CG44
Dagmar Av, Wem. HA9 . . . . . .62 CM63
Dagmar Gdns, NW10 . . . . .81 CX68
Dagmar Ms, Sthl. UB2
  off Dagmar Rd 96 BY76
Dagmar Pas, N1
  off Cross St 83 DP67
Dagmar Rd, N4 . . . . .65 DN59
  N15 off Cornwall Rd 66 DR56
  N22 . . . . .45 DK53
  SE5 . . . . .102 DS81
  SE25 . . . . .142 DS99
  Dagenham RM10 . . . . .89 FC66
  Kingston upon Thames
  KT2 . . . . .138 CM95
  Southall UB2 . . . . .96 BY76
Dagmar Ter, N1 . . . . .83 DP67
Dagnall Pk, SE25 . . . . .142 DS100
Dagnall Rd, SE25 . . . . .142 DS99
Dagnall St, SW11 . . . . .100 DF82
Dagnam Pk CI, Rom. RM3 . . . .52 FN50
Dagnam Pk Dr, Rom. RM3 . . . .52 FL50
Dagnam Pk Gdns, Rom.
  RM3 . . . . .52 FN51
Dagnam Pk Sq, Rom. RM3 . . . .52 FP51
Dagnan Rd, SW12 . . . . .121 DH87
Dagonet Gdns, Brom. BR1 . . .124 EG90
Dagonet Rd, Brom. BR1 . . . . .124 EG90
Dahlia CI, Wal.Cr. (Chsht.)
  EN7 . . . . .14 DQ25
Dahlia Dr, Swan. BR8 . . . . . . .147 FF96
Dahlia Gdns, Ilf. IG1 . . . . .87 EP65
  Mitcham CR4 . . . . .141 DK98
Dahlia Rd, SE2 . . . . .106 EV77
Dahomey Rd, SW16 . . . . .121 DJ93
Daiglen Dr, S.Ock. RM15 . . . . .91 FU73
Daimler Way, Wall. SM6 . . . . .159 DL108
Daines CI, E12
  off Colchester Av 69 EM62
  South Ockendon RM15 . . . .91 FU70

Dainford CI, Brom. BR1 . . . . .123 ED92
Dainton CI, Brom. BR1 . . . . . .144 EH95
Daintry CI, Har. HA3 . . . . .61 CG56
Daintry Lo, Nthwd. HA6 . . . . . .39 BT52
Daintry Way, E9
  off Osborne Rd 85 DZ65
Dairsie Rd, SE9 . . . . .105 EN85
Dairy CI, NW10 . . . . .81 CU67
  Dartford (Sutt.H.) DA4 . . .128 FP94
  Thornton Heath CR7 . . . . .142 DQ96
Dairyglen Av, Wal.Cr. EN8 . . . .15 DY31
Dairy La, SE18 . . . . .105 EM77
  Edenbridge (Crock.H.) TN8 .189 EN134
Dairyman CI, NW2
  off Claremont Rd 63 CY62
Dairy Ms, SW9 . . . . .101 DL83
Dairy Wk, SW19 . . . . .119 CY91
Dairy Way, Abb.L. WD5 . . . . . . .7 BT29
Daisy CI, Croy. CR0
  off Primrose La 143 DX102
Daisy Dobbins Wk, N19
  off Hillrise Rd 65 DL59
Daisy La, SW6 . . . . .100 DA83
Daisy Rd, E16
  off Cranberry La 86 EE70
  E18 . . . . .48 EH54
Dakota CI, Wall. SM6
  off Handley Page Rd 159 DM108
Dakota Gdns, E6 . . . . .86 EL70
  Northolt UB5
  off Argus Way 78 BY69
Dalberg Rd, SW2 . . . . .121 DN85
Dalberg Way, SE2
  off Lanridge Rd 106 EX76
Dalby Rd, SW18 . . . . .100 DC84
Dalby St, NW5 . . . . .83 DH65
Dalcross Rd, Houns. TW4 . . . . .96 BY82
Dale, The, Kes. BR2 . . . . .162 EK105
  Waltham Abbey EN9 . . . . .16 EE34
  Hounslow TW4 . . . . .96 BY83
Dalebury Rd, SW17 . . . . .120 DE89
Dale CI, SE3 . . . . .104 EG83
  Addlestone KT15 . . . . . . .152 BH106
  Barnet EN5 . . . . .28 DB44
  Dartford DA1 . . . . .127 FF86
  Pinner HA5 . . . . .39 BV53
  South Ockendon RM15 . . . .91 FU72
Dale Dr, Hayes UB4 . . . . .77 BT70
Dale End, Dart. DA1
  off Dale Rd 127 FF86
Dale Gdns, Wdf.Grn. IG8 . . . . .48 EH49
Dalegarth Gdns, Pur. CR8 . . .160 DR113
Dale Grn Rd, N11 . . . . .45 DH48
Dale Gro, N12 . . . . .44 DC50
Daleham Av, Egh. TW20 . . . . .113 BA93
Daleham Dr, Uxb. UB8 . . . . . . .77 BP72
Daleham Gdns, NW3 . . . . .64 DD64
Daleham Ms, NW3 . . . . .82 DD65
Dalehead, NW1 . . . . .195 K1
Dalemain Ms, E16 . . . . .205 N2
Dale Pk Av, Cars. SM5 . . . . . .140 DF104
Dale Pk Rd, SE19 . . . . .142 DQ95
Dale Rd, NW5 off Grafton Rd .64 DG64
  SE17 . . . . .101 DP79
  Dartford DA1 . . . . .127 FF86
  Gravesend (Sthflt.) DA13 .130 GA91
  Greenford UB6 . . . . .78 CB71
  Purley CR8 . . . . .159 DN112
  Sunbury-on-Thames TW16 .115 BT94
  Sutton SM1 . . . . .157 CZ105
  Swanley BR8 . . . . .147 FC96
  Walton-on-Thames KT12 . .135 BT101
Dale Row, W11
  off St. Marks Rd 81 CY72
Daleside, Ger.Cr. SL9 . . . . . . .56 AY60
  Orpington BR6 . . . . .164 EU106
Daleside CI, Orp. BR6 . . . . . .164 EU107
Daleside Dr, Pot.B. EN6 . . . . . .11 CZ32
Daleside Gdns, Chig. IG7 . . . . .49 EQ48
Daleside Rd, SW16 . . . . .121 DH92
  Epsom KT19 . . . . .156 CR107
Dales Path, Borwd. WD6
  off Farriers Way 26 CR43
Dales Rd, Borwd. WD6 . . . . . .26 CR43
Dalestone Ms, Rom. RM3 . . . . .51 FH51
Dale St, W4 . . . . .98 CS78
Dale Vw, Epsom (Headley)
  KT18 . . . . .172 CP123
  Erith DA8 . . . . .107 FF82
  Woking GU21 . . . . .166 AU118
Dale Vw Cres, E4 . . . . .47 EC47
Dale Vw Gdns, E4 . . . . .47 ED48
Daleview Rd, N15 . . . . .66 DS58
Dale Wk, Dart. DA2 . . . . .128 FQ88
Dalewood CI, Horn. RM11 . . . . .72 FM59
Dalewood Gdns, Wor.Pk.
  KT4 . . . . .139 CV103
Dale Wd Rd, Orp. BR6 . . . . . .145 ES101
Daley St, E9 . . . . .85 DX65
Daley Thompson Way, SW8 . .101 DH82
Dalgarno Gdns, W10 . . . . .81 CW71
Dalgarno Way, W10 . . . . .81 CW70
Dalgleish St, E14 . . . . .85 DY72
Daling Way, E3 . . . . .85 DY67
Dalkeith Gro, Stan. HA7 . . . . . .41 CK50
Dalkeith Rd, SE21 . . . . .122 DQ88
  Ilford IG1 . . . . .69 EQ62
Dallas Rd, NW4 . . . . .63 CU59
  SE26 . . . . .122 DV91
  W5 . . . . .80 CM71
  Sutton SM3 . . . . .157 CY107
Dallas Ter, Hayes UB3 . . . . . . .95 BT76
Dallega CI, Hayes UB3
  off Dawley Rd 77 BR73
Dallinger Rd, SE12 . . . . .124 EF86
Dalling Rd, W6 . . . . .99 CV76
Dallington CI, Walt. KT12 . . . .154 BW107
Dallington Sq, EC1
  off Dallington St 83 DP70
Dallington St, EC1 . . . . .196 G4
Dallin Rd, SE18 . . . . .105 EP80
  Bexleyheath DA6 . . . . . . .106 EX84
Dalmain Rd, SE23 . . . . .123 DX88
Dalmally Rd, Croy. CR0 . . . . .142 DT101
Dalmeny Av, N7 . . . . .65 DK63

Dalmeny Av, SW16 . . . . .141 DN96
Dalmeny CI, Wem. HA0 . . . . . .79 CJ65
Dalmeny Cres, Houns. TW3 . . .97 CD84
Dalmeny Rd, N7 . . . . .65 DK62
  Barnet EN5 . . . . .28 DC44
  Carshalton SM5 . . . . . . .158 DG108
  Erith DA8 . . . . .107 FB81
  Worcester Park KT4 . . . . .139 CV104
Dalmeyer Rd, NW10 . . . . .81 CT65
Dalmore Av, Esher (Clay.)
  KT10 . . . . .155 CF107
Dalmore Rd, SE21 . . . . .122 DQ89
Dalroy CI, S.Ock. RM15 . . . . . .91 FU72
Dalrymple CI, N14 . . . . .45 DK45
Dalrymple Rd, SE4 . . . . .103 DY84
DALSTON, E8 . . . . .84 DU66
Dalston Cross Shop Cen, E8 . .84 DT65
Dalston Gdns, Stan. HA7 . . . . .42 CL53
 ≢ Dalston Kingsland 84 DS65
Dalston La, E8 . . . . .84 DT65
Dalton Av, Mitch. CR4 . . . . . .140 DE96
Dalton CI, Hayes UB4 . . . . . . .77 BR70
  Orpington BR6 . . . . .145 ES104
  Purley CR8 . . . . .160 DQ112
Daltons Rd, Orp. BR6 . . . . . . .147 FB104
  Swanley BR8 . . . . .147 FC102
Dalton St, SE27 . . . . .121 DP89
Dalton Way, Wat. WD17 . . . . . .24 BX43
Dalwood St, SE5 . . . . .102 DS81
Daly Ct, E15
  off Clays La 67 EC64
Dalyell Rd, SW9 . . . . .101 DM83
Damascene Wk, SE21
  off Lovelace Rd 122 DQ88
Damask Cres, E16
  off Cranberry La 86 EE70
Damer Ter, SW10
  off Tadema Rd 100 DC80
Dames Rd, E7 . . . . .68 EG62
Dame St, N1 . . . . .84 DQ68
Dameswick Vw, St.Alb. AL2 . . . .8 CA27
Damien CI, E1 . . . . .84 DV72
Damigos Rd, Grav. DA12 . . . .131 GM88
Damon CI, Sid. DA14 . . . . . . .126 EV90
Damson Ct, Swan. BR8 . . . . . .147 FD98
Damson Dr, Hayes UB3 . . . . . .77 BU73
Damson Way, Cars. SM5 . . . .158 DF110
Damsonwood Rd, Sthl. UB2 . . .96 CA76
Danbrook Rd, SW16 . . . . .141 DL95
Danbury CI, Brwd. CM15 . . . . .54 FT43
  Romford RM6 . . . . .70 EX55
Danbury Cres, S.Ock. RM15 . . .91 FV72
Danbury Gdns, Rom. RM6 . . . .70 EX55
Danbury Ms, Wall. SM6 . . . . .159 DH105
Danbury Rd, Loug. IG10 . . . . . .48 EL45
  Rainham RM13 . . . . .89 FF67
Danbury St, N1 . . . . .83 DP68
Danbury Way, Wdf.Grn. IG8 . . .48 EJ51
Danby St, SE15 . . . . .102 DT83
Dancer Rd, SW6 . . . . .99 CZ81
  Richmond TW9 . . . . .98 CN83
DANCERS HILL, Barn. 27 CW35
Dancers Hill Rd, Barn. EN5 . . .27 CY36
Dancers La, Barn. EN5 . . . . . .27 CW35
Dandelion CI, Rom. (Rush Grn.)
  RM7 . . . . .71 FE61
Dando Cres, SE3 . . . . .104 EH83
Dandridge CI, SE10 . . . . .205 L10
  Slough SL3 . . . . .92 AX76
Danebury, Croy. (New Adgtn.)
  CR0 . . . . .161 EB107
Danebury Av, SW15 . . . . .118 CS86
Daneby Rd, SE6 . . . . .123 EB90
Dane CI, Amer. HP7 . . . . .20 AT41
  Bexley DA5 . . . . .126 FA87
  Orpington BR6 . . . . .163 ER106
Dane Ct, Wok. GU22 . . . . .167 BF115
Danecourt Gdns, Croy. CR0 . .142 DT104
Danecroft Rd, SE24 . . . . .122 DQ85
Danehill Wk, Sid. DA14
  off Hatherley Rd 126 EU90
Danehurst, Egh. TW20 . . . . . .112 AY93
Danehurst Gdns, Ilf. IG4 . . . . .68 EL57
Danehurst St, SW6 . . . . .99 CY81
Daneland, Barn. EN4 . . . . .28 DF44
Danemead Gro, Nthlt. UB5 . . . .60 CB64
Danemere St, SW15 . . . . .99 CW83
Dane PI, E3 off Roman Rd 85 DY68
Dane Rd, N18 . . . . .46 DW48
  SW19 . . . . .140 DC95
  W13 . . . . .79 CJ74
  Ashford TW15 . . . . .115 BQ93
  Ilford IG1 . . . . .69 EQ64
  Sevenoaks (Otford) TN14 .181 FE117
  Southall UB1 . . . . .78 BY73
  Warlingham CR6 . . . . . . .177 DX117
Danes, The, St.Alb. (Park St.)
  AL2 . . . . .8 CC28
Danesbury Rd, Felt. TW13 . . .115 BV88
Danes CI, Grav. (Nthflt.)
  DA11 . . . . .130 GC90
  Leatherhead (Oxshott)
  KT22 . . . . .154 CC114
Danescombe, SE12
  off Winn Rd 124 EG88
Danes Ct, Wem. HA9 . . . . .62 CP62
Danescourt Cres, Sutt. SM1 . .140 DC103
Danescroft, NW4 . . . . .63 CX57
Danescroft Av, NW4 . . . . .63 CX57
Danescroft Gdns, NW4 . . . . . .63 CX57
Danesdale Rd, E9 . . . . .85 DY65
Danesfield, SE5 . . . . .102 DS79
  Woking GU23
  off Polesden La 167 BF123
Danesfield CI, Walt. KT12 . . . .135 BV101
Danes Gate, Har. HA1 . . . . . . .61 CE55
Daneshill, Red. RH1 . . . . .184 DE133
Danes Hill, Wok. GU22 . . . . . .167 BA118
Daneshill CI, Red. RH1 . . . . . .184 DE133
Danes Rd, Rom. RM7 . . . . . . .71 FC59
Dane St, WC1 . . . . .196 B7
Danes Way, Brwd. CM15 . . . . .54 FU43
  Leatherhead (Oxshott)
  KT22 . . . . .155 CD114
Daneswood Av, SE6 . . . . .123 EC90
Daneswood CI, Wey. KT13 . . .153 BP106

Danethorpe Rd, Wem. HA0 . . .79 CK65
Danetree CI, Epsom KT19 . . . .156 CQ108
Danetree Rd, Epsom KT19 . . .156 CQ108
Danette Gdns, Dag. RM10 . . . .70 EZ61
Daneville Rd, SE5 . . . . .102 DR81
Dangan Rd, E11 . . . . .68 EG58
Daniel Bolt CI, E14
  off Uamvar St 85 EB71
Daniel CI, N18 . . . . .46 DW49
  SW17 . . . . .120 DE93
  Grays RM16 . . . . .111 GH76
  Grays (Chaff.Hun.) RM16 . .110 FY75
  Hounslow TW4
  off Harvey Rd 116 BZ87
Daniel Gdns, SE15 . . . . .102 DT80
Daniell Way, Croy. CR0 . . . . . .141 DL102
Daniel PI, NW4 . . . . .63 CV58
Daniel Rd, W5 . . . . .80 CM73
Daniels La, Warl. CR6 . . . . . . .177 DZ116
Daniels Ms, SE4 . . . . .103 DZ84
Daniels Rd, SE15 . . . . .102 DW83
Daniel Way, Bans. SM7 . . . . . .158 DB114
Dan Leno Wk, SW6
  off Britannia Rd 100 DB80
Dansey PI, W1 . . . . .195 M10
Dansington Rd, Well. DA16 . . .106 EU84
Danson Cres, Well. DA16 . . . .106 EV83
Danson La, Well. DA16 . . . . . .106 EV84
Danson Mead, Well. DA16 . . .106 EW83
 ★ Danson Park, Well. DA16 . .106 EW84
Danson Pk, Bexh. DA6 . . . . . .106 EW84
Danson Rd, Bex. DA5 . . . . . . .126 EX85
  Bexleyheath DA6 . . . . . . .126 EX85
Danson Underpass, Sid. DA15
  off Danson Rd 126 EW86
Dante PI, SE11 . . . . .200 G8
Dante Rd, SE11 . . . . .200 F8
Danube St, SW3 . . . . .198 C10
Danvers Rd, N8 . . . . .65 DK56
Danvers St, SW3 . . . . .100 DD79
Danvers Way, Cat. CR3 . . . . . .176 DQ123
Danyon CI, Rain. RM13 . . . . . . .90 FJ68
Danziger Way, Borwd. WD6 . . .26 CQ39
Daphne Gdns, E4
  off Gunners Gro 47 EC48
Daphne Rd, SW18 . . . . .120 DC86
Daplyn St, E1
  off Hanbury St 84 DU71
D'Arblay St, W1 . . . . .195 L9
Darby CI, Cat. CR3
  off Fairbourne La 176 DQ122
Darby Cres, Sun. TW16 . . . . . .136 BW96
Darby Dr, Wal.Abb. EN9 . . . . . .15 EC33
Darby Gdns, Sun. TW16 . . . . .136 BW96
D'Arcy Av, Wall. SM6 . . . . . . .159 DJ105
Darcy CI, N20 . . . . .44 DD47
D'Arcy CI, Brwd. CM13 . . . . . .55 GB45
D'Arcy CI, Couls. CR5 . . . . . . .175 DP119
  Waltham Cross (Chsht.)
  EN8 . . . . .15 DY31
D'Arcy Dr, Har. HA3 . . . . .61 CK56
Darcy Gdns, Dag. RM9 . . . . . .88 EZ67
D'Arcy Gdns, Har. HA3 . . . . . . .62 CL56
D'Arcy PI, Ashtd. KT21 . . . . . .172 CM117
  Bromley BR2 . . . . .144 EG98
Darcy Rd, SW16 . . . . .141 DL96
D'Arcy Rd, Ashtd. KT21 . . . . .172 CM117
  Isleworth TW7
  off London Rd 97 CG81
  Sutton SM3 . . . . .157 CX105
Dare Gdns, Dag. RM8
  off Grafton Rd 70 EY62
Darell Rd, Rich. TW9 . . . . .98 CN83
Darenth CI, Sev. TN13 . . . . . .190 FC122
Darenth Gdns, West. TN16
  off Quebec Av 189 ER126
Darenth Hill, Dart. (Darenth)
  DA2 . . . . .128 FQ92
Darenth La, Sev. (Dunt.Grn.)
  TN13 . . . . .190 FE121
  South Ockendon RM15 . . . .91 FU72
Darenth Pk Av, Dart. DA2 . . . .129 FR89
Darenth Rd, N16 . . . . .66 DT59
  Dartford DA1 . . . . .128 FM87
  Dartford (Darenth) DA2 . .128 FP91
  Welling DA16 . . . . .106 EU81
Darenth Way, Sev. (Shore.)
  TN14 . . . . .165 FG111
Darenth Wd Rd, Dart. DA2 . . .129 FS89
Darent Ind Pk, Erith DA8 . . . .108 FJ79
Darent Mead, Dart. (Sutt.H.)
  DA4 . . . . .148 FP95
Darent Valley Path, Dart. DA1,
  DA2, DA4 . . . . .128 FM89
  Sevenoaks TN13, TN14 . . .181 FG115
Darfield Rd, SE4 . . . . .123 DZ85
Darfield Way, W10 . . . . .81 CX72
Darfur St, SW15 . . . . .99 CX83
Dargate CI, SE19
  off Chipstead CI 122 DT94
Darien Rd, SW11 . . . . .100 DD83
Darkes La, Pot.B. EN6 . . . . . . .12 DA32
Dark Ho Wk, EC3
  off King William St 84 DS73
Dark La, Brwd. CM14 . . . . .53 FU52
  Waltham Cross (Chsht.)
  EN7 . . . . .14 DU31
Darlands Dr, Barn. EN5 . . . . . .27 CX43
Darlan Rd, SW6 . . . . .99 CZ80
Darlaston Rd, SW19 . . . . .119 CX94
Darley CI, Add. KT15 . . . . . . .152 BJ106
  Croydon CR0 . . . . .143 DY100
Darley Dr, N.Mal. KT3 . . . . . . .138 CR96
Darley Gdns, Mord. SM4 . . . .140 DB100
Darley Rd, N9 . . . . .46 DT46
  SW11 . . . . .120 DF86
Darling Rd, SE4 . . . . .103 EA83
Darling Row, E1 . . . . .84 DV70
Darlington Gdns, Rom. RM3 . . .52 FK50
Darlington Path, Rom. RM3
  off Darlington Gdns 52 FK50
Darlington Rd, SE27 . . . . .121 DP92
Darlton CI, Dart. DA1 . . . . . . .107 FF83
Darmaine CI, S.Croy. CR2
  off Churchill Rd 160 DQ108

Darnaway PI, E14
  off Abbott Rd 85 EC72
Darndale CI, E17 . . . . .47 DZ54
Darnets Fld, Sev. (Otford)
  TN14 . . . . .181 FF117
Darnhills, Rad. WD7 . . . . .25 CG35
Darnicle Hill, Wal.Cr. (Chsht.)
  EN7 . . . . .13 DM25
Darnley Ho, E14 . . . . .85 DY72
Darnley Pk, Wey. KT13 . . . . . .135 BP104
Darnley Rd, E9 . . . . .84 DV65
  Gravesend DA11 . . . . . . .131 GG88
  Grays RM17
  off Stanley Rd 110 GB79
  Woodford Green IG8 . . . . .48 EG53
Darnley St, Grav. DA11 . . . . . .131 GG87
Darnley Ter, W11
  off St. James's Gdns 81 CY74
Darns Hill, Swan. BR8 . . . . . .147 FC101
Darrell CI, Slou. SL3 . . . . .93 AZ77
Darrell Rd, SE22 . . . . .122 DU85
Darren CI, N4 . . . . .65 DM59
Darrick Wd Rd, Orp. BR6 . . . .145 ER103
Darrington Rd, Borwd. WD6 . . .26 CL39
Darris CI, Hayes UB4 . . . . .78 BY70
Darsley Dr, SW8 . . . . .101 DL81
Dart CI, Slou. SL3 . . . . .93 BB78
  Upminster RM14 . . . . .73 FR58
Dartfields, Rom. RM3 . . . . . . .52 FK51
DARTFORD 128 FJ87
 ≢ Dartford 128 FL86
Dartford Av, N9 . . . . .30 DW44
Dartford Bypass, Dart. DA2 . . .127 FE88
Dartford Bypass, Dart. (Chad.Hth.)
  RM6 off Heathfield Pk Dr . .70 EV58
 ★ Dartford Heath, Dart. DA1 . .127 FG88
Dartford Mus, Dart. DA1 . . . . .128 FL87
Dartford Northern Bypass, Dart.
  DA1 . . . . .108 FN83
Dartford Rd, Bex. DA5 . . . . . .127 FC88
  Dartford DA1 . . . . .127 FG86
  Dartford (Fnghm.) DA4 . . .148 FP95
  Sevenoaks TN13 . . . . . . .191 FJ124
Dartford St, SE17 . . . . .102 DQ79
Dartford Trade Pk, Dart. DA1 .128 FL89
Dartford Tunnel, Dart. DA1 . . .109 FR83
  Purfleet RM19 . . . . .109 FR83
Dartford Tunnel App Rd, Dart.
  DA1 . . . . .128 FN86
Dart Grn, S.Ock. RM15 . . . . . .91 FV71
Dartmoor Wk, E14 . . . . .204 A8
Dartmouth Av, Wok. GU21 . . .151 BC114
Dartmouth CI, W11 . . . . .81 CZ72
Dartmouth Grn, Wok. GU21 . .151 BD114
Dartmouth Gro, SE10 . . . . . .103 EC81
Dartmouth Hill, SE10 . . . . . . .103 EC81
DARTMOUTH PARK, NW5 . . . .65 DH62
Dartmouth Pk Av, NW5 . . . . . .65 DH62
Dartmouth Pk Hill, N19 . . . . . .65 DH60
  NW5 . . . . .65 DH60
Dartmouth Pk Rd, NW5 . . . . . .65 DH63
Dartmouth Path, Wok.
  GU21 . . . . .151 BD114
Dartmouth PI, SE23
  off Dartmouth Rd 122 DW89
  W4 . . . . .98 CS79
Dartmouth Rd, E16
  off Fords Pk Rd 86 EG72
  NW2 . . . . .81 CX65
  NW4 . . . . .63 CU58
  SE23 . . . . .122 DW90
  SE26 . . . . .122 DW90
  Bromley BR2 . . . . .144 EG101
  Ruislip HA4 . . . . .59 BU62
Dartmouth Row, SE10 . . . . . .103 EC82
Dartmouth St, SW1 . . . . .199 M5
Dartmouth Ter, SE10 . . . . . . .103 ED81
Dartnell Av, W.Byf. KT14 . . . .152 BH112
Dartnell CI, W.Byf. KT14 . . . . .152 BH112
Dartnell Ct, W.Byf. KT14 . . . . .152 BJ112
Dartnell Cres, W.Byf. KT14 . . .152 BH112
DARTNELL PARK, W.Byf. 152 BJ112
Dartnell Pk Rd, W.Byf.
  KT14 . . . . .152 BJ111
Dartnell PI, W.Byf. KT14 . . . . .152 BH112
Dartnell Rd, Croy. CR0 . . . . . .142 DT101
Dartrey Wk, SW10
  off World's End Est 100 DD80
Dart St, W10 . . . . .81 CY69
Dartview CI, Grays RM17 . . . .110 GF77
Darvel CI, Wok. GU21 . . . . . . .166 AU116
Darville Rd, N16 . . . . .66 DT62
Darwell CI, E6 . . . . .87 EN68
Darwin CI, N11 . . . . .45 DH48
  Orpington BR6 . . . . .163 ER106
Darwin Dr, Sthl. UB1 . . . . .78 CB72
Darwin Gdns, Wat. WD19
  off Barnhurst Path 40 BW50
Darwin Rd, N22 . . . . .45 DP53
  W5 . . . . .97 CJ78
  Slough SL3 . . . . .93 AZ75
  Tilbury RM18 . . . . .111 GF81
  Welling DA16 . . . . .105 ET83
Darwin St, SE17 . . . . .201 L8
Daryngton Dr, Grnf. UB6 . . . . .79 CD68
Dashwood CI, Bexh. DA6 . . . .126 FA85
  Slough SL3 . . . . .92 AW77
  West Byfleet KT14 . . . . . .152 BJ112
Dashwood Rd, N8 . . . . .65 DM58
  Gravesend DA11 . . . . . . .131 GG89
Dassett Rd, SE27 . . . . .121 DP92
Datchelor PI, SE5 . . . . .102 DR81
DATCHET, Slou. 92 AV81
 ≢ Datchet 92 AV81
Datchet PI, Slou. (Datchet)
  SL3 . . . . .92 AV81
Datchet Rd, SE6 . . . . .123 DZ90
  Slough SL3 . . . . .92 AT76
  Slough (Horton) SL3 . . . . .93 AZ83
  Windsor (Old Wind.) SL4 . .92 AU84
Datchworth Ct, N4
  off Queens Dr 66 DQ62
Date St, SE17 . . . . .102 DQ78
Daubeney Gdns, N17 . . . . .46 DQ52
Daubeney Rd, E5 . . . . .67 DY63
  N17 . . . . .46 DQ52
Daubeney Twr, SE8 . . . . .203 M9
Dault Rd, SW18 . . . . .120 DC86

Davall Ho, Grays RM17
off Argent St **110** GA79
Davema Cl, Chis. BR7
off Brenchley Cl **145** EN95
Davenant Rd, N19 . . . .**65** DK61
Croydon CR0
off Duppas Hill Rd **159** DP105
Davenant St, E1 . . . .**84** DU71
Davenham Av, Nthwd. HA6 . . .**39** BT49
Davenport Cl, Tedd. TW11 . . . .**117** CG93
Davenport Rd, SE6 . . . .**123** EB86
Sidcup DA14 . . . .**126** EX89
Daventer Dr, Stan. HA7 . . . . . .**41** CF52
Daventry Av, E17 . . . .**67** EA57
Daventry Cl, Slou. (Colnbr.)
SL3 . . . .**93** BF81
Daventry Gdns, Rom. RM3 . . .**52** FJ50
Daventry Grn, Rom. RM3
off Hailsham Rd **52** FJ50
Daventry Rd, Rom. RM3 . . . . .**52** FJ50
Daventry St, NW1 . . . .**194** B6
Davern Cl, SE10 . . . .**205** K9
Davey Cl, N7 . . . .**83** DM65
Davey Rd, E9 . . . .**85** EA66
Davey St, SE15 . . . .**102** DT79
David Av, Grnf. UB6 . . . .**79** CE69
David Cl, Hayes UB3 . . . .**95** BR80
David Dr, Rom. RM3 . . . .**52** FN51
Davidge St, SE1 . . . .**200** F5
David Lee Pt, E15 . . . .**86** EE67
David Ms, W1 . . . .**194** E6
David Rd, Dag. RM8 . . . .**70** EY61
Slough (Colnbr.) SL3 . . . . . .**93** BF82
Davidson Gdns, SW8 . . . .**101** DL80
Davidson La, Har. HA1
off Grove Hill **61** CF59
Davidson Rd, Croy. CR0 . . . . .**142** DT100
Davidson Way, Rom. RM7 . . . .**71** FE58
Davids Rd, SE23 . . . .**122** DW88
David St, E15 . . . .**85** ED65
David's Way, Ilf. IG6 . . . .**49** ES52
David Twigg Cl, Kings.T. KT2 .**138** CL95
Davies Cl, Croy. CR0 . . . .**142** DU100
Rainham RM13 . . . .**90** FJ69
Davies La, E11 . . . .**68** EE61
Davies Ms, W1 . . . .**195** H10
Davies St, W1 . . . .**195** H10
Davington Gdns, Dag. RM8 . . .**70** EV64
Davington Rd, Dag. RM8 . . . . .**88** EV65
Davinia Cl, Wdf.Grn. IG8
off Deacon Way **49** EM51
Davis Av, Grav. (Nthflt.)
DA11 . . . .**130** GE88
Davis Cl, Sev. TN13 . . . .**191** FJ122
Davison Cl, Wal.Cr. EN8 . . . . . .**15** DX28
Davison Dr, Wal.Cr. (Chsht.)
EN8 . . . .**15** DX28
Davis Rd, W3 . . . .**81** CT74
Chessington KT9 . . . .**156** CN105
Grays (Chaff.Hun.) RM16 . .**110** FZ76
South Ockendon (Aveley)
RM15 . . . .**91** FR74
Weybridge KT13 . . . .**152** BM110
Davis St, E13 . . . .**86** EH68
Davisville Rd, W12 . . . .**99** CU75
Davos Cl, Wok. GU22 . . . .**166** AY119
Davys Pl, Grav. DA12 . . . .**131** GL93
Dawell Dr, West. (Bigg.H.)
TN16 . . . .**178** EJ117
Dawes Av, Horn. RM12 . . . . . .**72** FK62
Isleworth TW7 . . . .**117** CG85
Dawes Cl, Green. DA9 . . . .**129** FT85
Dawes Ct, Esher KT10 . . . . . .**154** CB105
Dawes Ho, SE17 . . . .**201** L9
Dawes La, Rick. (Sarratt) WD3 .**21** BE37
Dawes Moor Cl, Slou. SL2 . . . .**74** AW72
Dawes Rd, SW6 . . . .**99** CY80
Uxbridge UB10 . . . .**76** BL68
Dawes St, SE17 . . . .**201** L10
Dawley Av, Uxb. UB8 . . . .**77** BQ71
Dawley Grn, S.Ock. RM15 . . . .**91** FU72
Dawley Par, Hayes UB3
off Dawley Rd **77** BQ73
Dawley Ride, Slou. (Colnbr.)
SL3 . . . .**93** BE81
Dawley Rd, Hayes UB3 . . . . . .**95** BS76
Dawlish Av, N13 . . . .**45** DL49
SW18 . . . .**120** DB89
Greenford UB6 . . . .**79** CG68
Dawlish Dr, Ilf. IG3 . . . .**69** ES63
Pinner HA5 . . . .**60** BY57
Ruislip HA4 . . . .**59** BU61
Dawlish Rd, E10 . . . .**67** EC61
N17 . . . .**66** DU55
NW2 . . . .**81** CX65
Dawlish Wk, Rom. RM3 . . . . . .**52** FJ53
Dawnay Gdns, SW18 . . . .**120** DD89
Dawnay Rd, SW18 . . . .**120** DC89
Dawn Cl, Houns. TW4 . . . .**96** BY83
Dawn Cres, E15
off Bridge Rd **85** ED67
Dawn Redwood Cl, Slou. (Horton)
SL3 . . . .**93** BA83
Dawpool Rd, NW2 . . . .**63** CT61
Daws Hill, E4 . . . .**31** EC41
Daws La, NW7 . . . .**43** CT50
Dawson Av, Bark. IG11 . . . .**87** ES66
Orpington BR5 . . . .**146** EV96
Dawson Cl, SE18 . . . .**105** EQ77
Hayes UB3 . . . .**77** BR71
Dawson Dr, Rain. RM13 . . . . . .**89** FH66
Swanley BR8 . . . .**127** FE94
Dawson Gdns, Bark. IG11
off Dawson Av **87** ET66
Dawson Hts Est, SE22 . . . . . .**122** DU87
Dawson Pl, W2 . . . .**82** DA73
Dawson Rd, NW2 . . . .**63** CW64
Kingston upon Thames
KT1 . . . .**138** CM97
West Byfleet (Byfleet)
KT14 . . . .**152** BK111
Dawson St, E2 . . . .**84** DT68
Dax Ct, Sun. TW16
off Thames St **136** BW97
Daybrook Rd, SW19 . . . .**140** DB96
Daylesford Av, SW15 . . . .**99** CU84
Daylop Dr, Chig. IG7 . . . .**50** EV48
Daymer Gdns, Pnr. HA5 . . . . . .**59** BV56
Daymerslea Ridge, Lthd.
KT22 . . . .**171** CJ121
Days Acre, S.Croy. CR2 . . . . .**160** DT110
Daysbrook Rd, SW2 . . . .**121** DM88
Days La, Brwd. CM15 . . . .**54** FU42
Sidcup DA15 . . . .**125** ES87
Dayton Dr, Erith DA8 . . . .**108** FK78
Dayton Gro, SE15 . . . .**102** DW81
Deacon Cl, Cob. (Down.)
KT11 . . . .**169** BV119
Purley CR8 . . . .**159** DL109
Deacon Ms, N1 . . . .**84** DR66
Deacon Pl, Cat. CR3 . . . .**176** DQ123
Deacon Rd, NW2 . . . .**63** CU64
Kingston upon Thames
KT2 . . . .**138** CM95
Deacons Cl, Borwd. (Elstree)
WD6 . . . .**26** CN42
Pinner HA5 . . . .**39** BV54
Deacons Hill, Wat. WD19 . . . . .**24** BW44
Deacon's Hill Rd, Borwd. (Elstree)
WD6 . . . .**26** CM42
Deacons Leas, Orp. BR6 . . . . .**163** ER105
Deacons Ri, N2 . . . .**64** DD57
Deacons Wk, Hmptn. TW12
off Bishops Gro **116** BZ91
Deacon Way, SE17 . . . .**201** H8
Woodford Green IG8 . . . .**49** EM52
Deadhearn La, Ch.St.G. HP8 . .**36** AY46
Deadman's Ash La, Rick. (Sarratt)
WD3 . . . .**22** BH36
Deakin Cl, Wat. WD18
off Chenies Way **39** BS45
Deal Ms, W5
off Darwin Rd **97** CK77
Deal Porters Way, SE16 . . . . .**202** G6
Deal Rd, SW17 . . . .**120** DG93
Deal's Gateway, SE10
off Blackheath Rd **103** EB81
Deal St, E1 . . . .**84** DU71
Dealtry Rd, SW15 . . . .**99** CW84
Deal Wk, SW9
off Mandela St **101** DN80
Deanacre Cl, Ger.Cr. (Chal.St.P.)
SL9 . . . .**36** AY51
DEAN BOTTOM, Dart. **149** FV97
Dean Bradley St, SW1 . . . . . .**199** P7
Dean Cl, E9 *off Churchill Wk* . .**66** DW64
SE16 . . . .**203** J3
Uxbridge UB10 . . . .**76** BM66
Woking GU22 . . . .**167** BE115
Dean Ct, Wem. HA0 . . . .**61** CH62
Deancroft Rd, Ger.Cr. (Chal.St.P.)
SL9 . . . .**36** AY51
Deancross St, E1 . . . .**84** DW72
Dean Dr, Stan. HA7 . . . .**42** CL54
Deane Av, Ruis. HA4 . . . .**60** BW64
Deane Cft Rd, Pnr. HA5 . . . . . .**59** BV58
Deanery Cl, N2 . . . .**64** DE56
Deanery Ms, W1 . . . .**198** G2
Deanery Rd, E15 . . . .**86** EE65
Edenbridge (Crock.H.) TN8 .**189** EQ134
Deanery St, W1 . . . .**198** G2
Deane Way, Ruis. HA4 . . . .**59** BV58
Dean Farrar St, SW1 . . . .**199** M6
Dean Fld, Hem.H. (Bov.) HP3 . . .**5** BA27
Dean Gdns, E17 . . . .**67** ED56
W13 *off Northfield Av* **79** CH74
Deanhill Rd, SW14 . . . .**98** CP84
Dean La, Red. RH1 . . . .**175** DH123
Dean Rd, NW2 . . . .**81** CW65
SE28 . . . .**88** EU73
Croydon CR0 . . . .**160** DR105
Hampton TW12 . . . .**116** CA92
Hounslow TW3 . . . .**116** CB85
Dean Ryle St, SW1 . . . .**199** P8
Deansbrook Cl, Edg. HA8 . . . . .**42** CQ52
Deansbrook Rd, Edg. HA8 . . . .**42** CQ51
Deans Bldgs, SE17 . . . .**201** K9
Deans Cl, W4 . . . .**98** CP79
Abbots Langley WD5 . . . .**7** BR32
Amersham HP6 . . . .**20** AT37
Dean's Cl, Croy. CR0 . . . .**142** DT104
Deans Cl, Edg. HA8 . . . .**42** CQ51
Slough (Stoke P.) SL2 . . . . . .**74** AV67
Tadworth KT20
off Deans La **173** CV124
Deans Ct, EC4 . . . .**196** G9
Deanscroft Av, NW9 . . . .**62** CQ61
Deans Dr, N13 . . . .**45** DP51
Edgware HA8 . . . .**42** CR50
Deansfield, Cat. CR3 . . . .**186** DT125
Dean's Gate Cl, SE23 . . . .**123** DX90
Deans La, W4 . . . .**98** CP79
Edgware HA8 . . . .**42** CQ51
Redhill (Nutfld.) RH1 . . . . . .**185** DN133
Tadworth KT20 . . . .**173** CV124
Deans Ms, W1 . . . .**195** J8
Dean's Pl, SW1 . . . .**199** M10
Deans Rd, W7 . . . .**79** CF74
Brentwood CM14 . . . .**54** FV49
Redhill RH1 . . . .**185** DJ130
Sutton SM1 . . . .**140** DB104
Dean Stanley St, SW1 . . . . . .**199** P7
Dean St, E7 . . . .**68** EG64
W1 . . . .**195** M8
Deans Wk, Couls. CR5 . . . . . .**175** DN118
Deansway, N2 . . . .**64** DD56
N9 . . . .**46** DS48
Deans Way, Edg. HA8 . . . .**42** CQ50
Dean's Yd, SW1 . . . .**199** N6
Dean Trench St, SW1 . . . .**199** P7
Dean Wk, Edg. HA8
off Deansbrook Rd **42** CQ51
Deanway, Ch.St.G. HP8 . . . . . .**36** AU48
Dean Way, Sthl. UB2 . . . .**96** CB75
Dearne Cl, Stan. HA7 . . . .**41** CG50
De'Arn Gdns, Mitch. CR4 . . . .**140** DE97
Dearsley Ho, Rain. RM13 . . . . .**89** FD68
Dearsley Rd, Enf. EN1 . . . .**30** DU41
Deason St, E15
off High St **85** EC67
De Barowe Ms, N5
off Leigh Rd **65** DP63
DEBDEN, Loug. **33** ER41
⊖ **Debden** **33** EQ42
Debden Cl, Kings.T. KT2 . . . . .**117** CK92
Woodford Green IG8 . . . .**48** EJ52
DEBDEN GREEN, Loug. **33** EQ38
Debden Grn, Loug. IG10 . . . . .**33** EP38
Debden La, Loug. IG10 . . . . . .**33** EP38
Debden Rd, Loug. IG10 . . . . . .**33** EP38
Debden Wk, Horn. RM12 . . . . . .**89** FH65
De Beauvoir Cres, N1 . . . .**84** DS67
De Beauvoir Est, N1 . . . .**84** DR67
De Beauvoir Rd, N1 . . . .**84** DS67
De Beauvoir Sq, N1 . . . .**84** DS66
DE BEAUVOIR TOWN, N1 . . . . .**84** DR67
Debenham Rd, Wal.Cr. (Chsht.)
EN7 . . . .**14** DV27
Debnams Rd, SE16 . . . .**202** F9
De Bohun Av, N14 . . . .**29** DH44
Deborah Cl, Islw. TW7 . . . .**97** CE81
Deborah Cres, Ruis. HA4 . . . . .**59** BR59
Debrabant Cl, Erith DA8 . . . . .**107** FD79
De Brome Rd, Felt. TW13 . . . .**116** BW88
De Burgh Gdns, Tad. KT20 . . .**173** CX119
De Burgh Pk, Bans. SM7 . . . .**174** DB115
Deburgh Rd, SW19 . . . .**120** DC94
Decies Way, Slou. (Stoke P.)
SL2 . . . .**74** AU67
Decima St, SE1 . . . .**201** M6
Deck Cl, SE16 . . . .**203** J4
Decoy Av, NW11 . . . .**63** CY57
De Crespigny Pk, SE5 . . . . . .**102** DR82
Dee Cl, Upmin. RM14 . . . .**73** FS58
Deeley Rd, SW8 . . . .**101** DK81
Deena Cl, W3 . . . .**80** CM72
Deepdale, SW19 . . . .**119** CX91
Deepdale Av, Brom. BR2 . . . . .**144** EF98
Deepdale Cl, N11
off Ribblesdale Av **44** DG51
Deepdene, W5 . . . .**80** CM70
Potters Bar EN6 . . . .**11** CX31
Deepdene Av, Croy. CR0 . . . .**142** DT104
Deepdene Cl, E11 . . . .**68** EG56
Deepdene Ct, N21 . . . .**29** DP44
Deepdene Gdns, SW2 . . . . . .**121** DM87
Deepdene Path, Loug. IG10 . . .**33** EN42
Deepdene Pt, SE23
off Dacres Rd **123** DX90
Deepdene Rd, SE5 . . . .**102** DR84
Loughton IG10 . . . .**33** EN42
Welling DA16 . . . .**106** EU83
Deep Fld, Slou. (Datchet) SL3 .**92** AV80
Deepfield Way, Couls. CR5 . . .**175** DL116
Deep Pool La, Wok. (Chobham)
GU24 . . . .**150** AV114
Deepwell Cl, Islw. TW7 . . . .**97** CG81
Deepwood La, Grnf. UB6
off Cowgate Rd **79** CD69
Deerbrook Rd, SE24 . . . .**121** DP88
Deerdale Rd, SE24 . . . .**102** DQ84
Deere Av, Rain. RM13 . . . .**89** FG65
Deerhurst Cl, Felt. TW13 . . . . .**115** BU91
Deerhurst Cres, Hmptn. (Hmptn.H.)
TW12 . . . .**116** CC92
Deerhurst Rd, NW2 . . . .**81** CX65
SW16 . . . .**121** DM92
Deerings Dr, Pnr. HA5 . . . .**59** BU57
Deerings Rd, Reig. RH2 . . . . .**184** DB134
Deerleap Gro, E4 . . . .**31** EB43
Deerleap La, Sev. TN14 . . . . .**164** EX113
Dee Rd, Rich. TW9 . . . .**98** CM84
Deer Pk Cl, Kings.T. KT2 . . . . .**118** CP94
Deer Pk Gdns, Mitch. CR4 . . . .**140** DD97
Deer Pk Rd, SW19 . . . .**140** DB96
Deer Pk Wk, Chesh. HP5 . . . .**4** AS28
Deer Pk Way, Wal.Abb. EN9 . . .**31** EC36
West Wickham BR4 . . . .**144** EF103
Deers Fm Cl, Wok. (Wisley)
GU23 . . . .**168** BL116
Deerswood Cl, Cat. CR3 . . . . .**176** DU124
Deeside Rd, SW17 . . . .**120** DD90
Dee St, E14 . . . .**85** EC72
Deeves Hall La, Pot.B. EN6 . . . .**10** CS33
Dee Way, Epsom KT19 . . . . . .**156** CS110
Romford RM1 . . . .**51** FE53
Defiance Wk, SE18 . . . .**105** EM76
Defiant Way, Wall. SM6 . . . . .**159** DL108
Defoe Av, Rich. TW9 . . . .**98** CN80
Defoe Cl, SE16 . . . .**203** M5
SW17 . . . .**120** DE93
Erith DA8 *off Selkirk Dr* **107** FE81
Defoe Ho, EC2 . . . .**197** J6
Defoe Par, Grays RM16 . . . . .**111** GH76
Defoe Pl, EC2 *off Beech St* **84** DQ71
SW17 *off Lessingham Av* . .**120** DF91
Defoe Rd, N16 . . . .**66** DS61
Defoe Way, Rom. RM5 . . . .**51** FB51
De Frene Rd, SE26 . . . .**123** DX91
De Gama Pl, E14
off Maritime Quay **103** EA78
Degema Rd, Chis. BR7 . . . . . .**125** EP92
Dehar Cres, NW9 . . . .**63** CT59
Dehavilland Cl, Nthlt. UB5 . . . .**78** BX69
De Havilland Ct, Rad. (Shenley)
WD7 *off Armstrong Gdns* . .**10** CL32
De Havilland Dr, Wey. KT13 . .**152** BL111
★ **De Havilland Mosquito
Aircraft Mus**, St.Alb.
(Lon.Col.) AL2 . . . .**10** CP29
De Havilland Rd, Edg. HA8 . . . .**42** CP54
Hounslow TW5 . . . .**96** BW80
Wallington SM6 . . . .**159** DL108
De Havilland Way, Abb.L. WD5 . .**7** BT32
Staines (Stanw.) TW19 . . . . .**114** BK86
Dekker Rd, SE21 . . . .**122** DS86
Delabole Rd, Red. RH1 . . . . . .**185** DL129
Delacourt Rd, SE3
off Old Dover Rd **104** EH80
Delafield Rd, SE7 . . . .**104** EH78
Grays RM17 . . . .**110** GD78
Delaford Cl, Iver SL0 . . . .**75** BF72
Delaford Rd, SE16 . . . .**202** E10
Delaford St, SW6 . . . .**99** CY80
Delagarde Rd, West. TN16 . . . .**189** EQ126
Delamare Cres, Croy. CR0 . . .**142** DW100
Delamare Rd, Wal.Cr. (Chsht.)
EN8 . . . .**15** DZ30
Delamere Gdns, NW7 . . . .**42** CR51
Delamere Rd, SW20 . . . .**139** CX95
W5 . . . .**80** CL74
Delamere Rd, Borwd. WD6 . . . .**26** CP39
Hayes UB4 . . . .**78** BX73
Delamere Ter, W2 . . . .**82** DB71
Delancey Pas, NW1
off Delancey St **83** DH67
Delancey St, NW1 . . . .**83** DH67
Delaporte Cl, Epsom KT17 . . .**156** CS112
De Lapre Cl, Orp. BR5 . . . . . .**146** EX101
De Lara Way, Wok. GU21 . . . . .**166** AX118
Delargy Cl, Grays RM16 . . . . .**111** GH76
De Laune St, SE17 . . . .**101** DP78
Delaware Rd, W9 . . . .**82** DB70
Delawyk Cres, SE24 . . . .**122** DQ86
Delcombe Av, Wor.Pk. KT4 . . .**139** CW102
Delderfield, Lthd. KT22 . . . . .**171** CK120
Delft Way, SE22
off East Dulwich Gro **122** DS85
Delhi Rd, Enf. EN1 . . . .**46** DT45
Delhi St, N1 . . . .**83** DL67
Delia St, SW18 . . . .**120** DB87
Delisle Rd, SE28 . . . .**87** ES74
Delius Cl, Borwd. (Elstree)
WD6 . . . .**25** CJ44
Delius Gro, E15 . . . .**85** ED68
Dell, The, SE2 . . . .**106** EU78
SE19 . . . .**142** DT95
Bexley DA5 . . . .**127** FE88
Brentford TW8 . . . .**97** CJ79
Brentwood (Gt.Warley)
CM13 . . . .**53** FV51
Feltham TW14
off Harlington Rd W **115** BV87
Gerrards Cross (Chal.St.P.)
SL9 . . . .**36** AY51
Northwood HA6 . . . .**39** BS47
Pinner HA5 . . . .**40** BX54
Radlett WD7 . . . .**25** CG36
Reigate RH2 . . . .**184** DA133
Tadworth KT20 . . . .**173** CW121
Waltham Abbey EN9
off Greenwich Way **31** EC36
Wembley HA0 . . . .**61** CH64
Woking GU21 . . . .**166** AW118
Woodford Green IG8 . . . .**48** EH48
Della Path, E5
off Napoleon Rd **66** DV62
Dellbow Rd, Felt. TW14
off Central Way **115** BV85
Dell Cl, E15 . . . .**85** ED67
Leatherhead (Fetch.) KT22 .**171** CE123
Wallington SM6 . . . .**159** DK105
Woodford Green IG8 . . . .**48** EH48
Dell Fm Rd, Ruis. HA4 . . . .**59** BR57
Dellfield Cl, Beck. BR3
off Foxgrove Rd **123** EC94
Radlett WD7 . . . .**25** CE35
Watford WD17 . . . .**23** BU40
Dellfield Cres, Uxb. UB8 . . . . .**76** BJ70
Dellfield Par, Uxb. (Cowley) UB8
off High St **76** BJ70
Dell La, Epsom KT17 . . . .**157** CU106
Dellmeadow, Abb.L. WD5 . . . . .**7** BS30
Dellors Cl, Barn. EN5 . . . .**27** CX43
Dellow Cl, Ilf. IG2 . . . .**69** ER59
Dellow St, E1 . . . .**84** DV73
Dell Ri, St.Alb. (Park St.) AL2 . . .**8** CB26
Dell Rd, Enf. EN3 . . . .**30** DW38
Epsom KT17 . . . .**157** CU107
Grays RM17 . . . .**110** GB77
Watford WD24 . . . .**23** BU37
West Drayton UB7 . . . .**94** BM76
Dells Cl, E4 . . . .**47** EB45
Teddington TW11
off Middle La **117** CF93
Dellside, Uxb. (Hare.) UB9 . . . .**58** BJ57
Dell Side, Wat. WD24
off The Harebreaks **23** BU37
Dell's Ms, SW1 . . . .**199** L9
Dell Wk, N.Mal. KT3 . . . .**138** CS96
Dell Way, W13 . . . .**79** CJ72
Dellwood, Rick. WD3 . . . .**38** BH46
Dellwood Gdns, Ilf. IG5 . . . .**69** EN55
Delmare Cl, SW9
off Brighton Ter **101** DM84
Delme Cres, SE3 . . . .**104** EH82
Delmey Cl, Croy. CR0
off Radcliffe Rd **142** DT104
Deloraine St, SE8 . . . .**103** EA81
Delorme St, W6 . . . .**99** CX79
Delta Cl, Wok. (Chobham)
GU24 . . . .**150** AT110
Worcester Park KT4 . . . .**139** CT104
Delta Ct, NW2 . . . .**63** CU61
Delta Gain, Wat. WD19 . . . .**40** BX47
Delta Gro, Nthlt. UB5 . . . .**78** BX69
Delta Rd, Brwd. CM13 . . . .**55** GD44
Woking GU21 . . . .**167** BA116
Woking (Chobham) GU24 .**150** AT110
Worcester Park KT4 . . . .**138** CS104
Delta St, E2
off Wellington Row **84** DU69
Delta Way, Egh. TW20 . . . . . .**133** BC95
De Luci Rd, Erith DA8 . . . .**107** FC78
De Lucy St, SE2 . . . .**106** EV77
Delvan Cl, SE18
off Ordnance Rd **105** EN80
Delvers Mead, Dag. RM10 . . . . .**71** FC63
Delverton Rd, SE17 . . . .**101** DP78
Delves, Tad. KT20
off Heathcote **173** CX121
Delvino Rd, SW6 . . . .**100** DA81
De Mandeville Gate, Enf. EN1
off Southbury Rd **30** DU42
De Mel Cl, Epsom KT19
off Abbots Av **156** CN112
Demesne Rd, Wall. SM6 . . . . .**159** DK106
Demeta Cl, Wem. HA9 . . . .**62** CQ62
De Montfort Par, SW16
off Streatham High Rd **121** DL90
De Montfort Rd, SW16 . . . . . .**121** DL90
De Morgan Rd, SW6 . . . .**100** DB83
Dempster Cl, Surb. KT6 . . . . . .**137** CJ102
Dempster Rd, SW18 . . . .**120** DC85
Denbar Par, Rom. RM7
off Mawney Rd **71** FC56
Denberry Dr, Sid. DA14 . . . . . .**126** EV90
Denbigh Cl, NW10 . . . .**80** CS66
Denbigh Cl, W11 . . . .**81** CZ73
Chislehurst BR7 . . . .**125** EM93
Hornchurch RM11 . . . .**72** FN56
Ruislip HA4 . . . .**59** BT61
Southall UB1 . . . .**78** BZ72
Sutton SM1 . . . .**157** CZ106
Denbigh Dr, Hayes UB3 . . . . . .**95** BQ75
Denbigh Gdns, Rich. TW10 . . .**118** CM85
Denbigh Ms, SW1 . . . .**199** K9
Denbigh Pl, SW1 . . . .**199** K10
Denbigh Rd, E6 . . . .**86** EK69
W11 . . . .**81** CZ73
W13 . . . .**79** CH73
Hounslow TW3 . . . .**96** CB82
Southall UB1 . . . .**78** BZ72
Denbigh St, SW1 . . . .**199** K9
Denbigh Ter, W11 . . . .**81** CZ73
Denbridge Rd, Brom. BR1 . . . .**145** EM96
Denby Rd, Cob. KT11 . . . .**154** BW113
Den Cl, Beck. BR3 . . . .**143** ED97
Dendridge Cl, Enf. EN1 . . . .**30** DV37
Dene, The, W13 . . . .**79** CH71
Croydon CR0 . . . .**161** DX105
Sevenoaks TN13 . . . .**191** FH126
Sutton SM2 . . . .**157** CZ111
Wembley HA9 . . . .**62** CL63
West Molesey KT8 . . . .**136** BZ99
Dene Av, Houns. TW3 . . . .**96** BZ83
Sidcup DA15 . . . .**126** EV87
Dene Cl, SE4 . . . .**103** DY83
Bromley BR2 . . . .**144** EF102
Coulsdon CR5 . . . .**174** DE119
Dartford DA2 . . . .**127** FE91
Worcester Park KT4 . . . .**139** CT103
Dene Ct, Stan. HA7
off Marsh La **41** CJ50
Denecroft Cres, Uxb. UB10 . . . .**77** BP67
Denecroft Gdns, Grays RM17 .**110** GD76
Dene Dr, Orp. BR6 . . . .**146** EV104
Denefield Dr, Ken. CR8 . . . . . .**176** DR115
Dene Gdns, Stan. HA7 . . . .**41** CJ50
Thames Ditton KT7 . . . .**137** CG103
Dene Holm Rd, Grav. (Nthflt.)
DA11 . . . .**130** GD90
Denehurst Gdns, NW4 . . . .**63** CW58
W3 . . . .**80** CP74
Richmond TW10 . . . .**98** CN84
Twickenham TW2 . . . .**117** CD87
Woodford Green IG8 . . . .**48** EH49
Dene Path, S.Ock. RM15 . . . . . .**91** FU72
Dene Pl, Wok. GU21 . . . .**166** AV118
Dene Rd, N11 . . . .**44** DF46
Ashtead KT21 . . . .**172** CM119
Buckhurst Hill IG9 . . . .**48** EK46
Dartford DA1 . . . .**128** FM87
Northwood HA6 . . . .**39** BS51
Denewood, Barn. EN5 . . . .**28** DC43
Denewood Cl, Wat. WD17 . . . . .**23** BT37
Denewood Rd, N6 . . . .**64** DF58
Dengie Wk, N1 *off Basire St* . .**84** DQ67
DENHAM, Uxb. **58** BG62
⇌ **Denham** **58** BG59
★ **Denham Aerodrome**, Uxb.
UB9 . . . .**57** BD57
Denham Av, Uxb. (Denh.)
UB9 . . . .**57** BF61
Denham Cl, Uxb. (Denh.) UB9 .**58** BG62
Welling DA16
off Park Vw Rd **106** EW83
Denham Ct Dr, Uxb. (Denh.)
UB9 . . . .**58** BH63
Denham Cres, Mitch. CR4 . . .**140** DF98
Denham Dr, Ilf. IG2 . . . .**69** EQ58
Denham Gdn Village, Uxb. UB9
off Denham Grn La **57** BF58
⇌ **Denham Golf Club** **57** BD59
DENHAM GREEN, Uxb. **57** BE58
Denham Grn Cl, Uxb. (Denh.)
UB9 . . . .**58** BG59
Denham Grn La, Uxb. (Denh.)
UB9 . . . .**57** BE57
Denham La, Ger.Cr. (Chal.St.P.)
SL9 . . . .**37** BA53
Denham Lo, Uxb. UB9 . . . .**76** BJ65
Denham Rd, N20 . . . .**44** DF48
Egham TW20 . . . .**113** BA91
Epsom KT17 . . . .**157** CT112
Feltham TW14 . . . .**116** BW86
Iver SL0 . . . .**75** BE65
Uxbridge (Denh.) UB9 . . . . . .**75** BE65
Denham St, SE10 . . . .**205** M10
Denham Wk, Ger.Cr. (Chal.St.P.)
SL9 . . . .**37** AZ51
Denham Way, Bark. IG11 . . . . . .**87** ES67
Borehamwood WD6 . . . .**26** CR39
Rickmansworth (Map.Cr.)
WD3 . . . .**37** BE52
Uxbridge (Denh.) UB9 . . . . . .**58** BG62
Denholme Rd, W9 . . . .**81** CZ69
Denholme Wk, Rain. RM13
off Ryder Gdns **89** FF65
Denison Cl, N2 . . . .**64** DC55
Denison Rd, SW19 . . . .**120** DD93
W5 . . . .**79** CJ70
Feltham TW13 . . . .**115** BT91
Deniston Av, Bex. DA5 . . . .**126** EY88
Denleigh Gdns, N21 . . . .**45** DN46
Thames Ditton KT7 . . . .**137** CE100
Denman Dr, NW11 . . . .**64** DA57
Ashford TW15 . . . .**115** BP93
Esher (Clay.) KT10 . . . .**155** CG106
Denman Dr N, NW11 . . . .**64** DA57
Denman Dr S, NW11 . . . .**64** DA57
Denman Pl, W1
off Great Windmill St **83** DK73
Denman Rd, SE15 . . . .**102** DT81
Denman St, W1 . . . .**199** M1
Denmark Av, SW19 . . . .**119** CY94
Denmark Ct, Mord. SM4 . . . . .**140** DA99
Denmark Gdns, Cars. SM5 . . .**140** DG104
Denmark Gro, N1 . . . .**83** DN68
⇌ **Denmark Hill** **102** DR82
Denmark Hill, SE5 . . . .**102** DR81
Denmark Hill Dr, NW9 . . . .**63** CT56

★ Place of interest ⇌ Railway station ⊖ London Underground station DLR Docklands Light Railway station Tramlink station H Hospital

Den - Dit

Denmark Hill Est, SE5 102 DR84
Denmark Pl, WC2 195 N8
Denmark Rd, N8 65 DM56
NW6 81 CZ68
SE5 102 DQ81
SE25 142 DU99
SW19 119 CX93
W13 79 CH73
Bromley BR1 144 EH95
Carshalton SM5 140 DF104
Kingston upon Thames KT1 138 CL97
Twickenham TW2 117 CD90
Denmark St, E11
off High Rd Leytonstone 68 EE62
E13 86 EH71
N17 46 DV53
WC2 195 N9
Watford WD17 23 BV40
Denmark Wk, SE27 122 DQ91
Denmead Cl, Ger.Cr. SL9 56 AY59
Denmead Ho, SW15
off Highcliffe Dr 119 CT86
Denmead Rd, Croy. CR0 141 DP102
Denmead Way, SE15
off Pentridge St 102 DT80
Dennan Rd, Surb. KT6 138 CM102
Dennard Way, Orp. BR6 163 EP105
Denner Rd, E4 47 EA47
Denne Ter, E8 84 DT67
Dennett Rd, Croy. CR0 141 DN102
Dennetts Gro, SE14
off Dennetts Rd 103 DX82
Dennettsland Rd, Eden. (Crock.H.) TN8 189 EQ134
Dennetts Rd, SE14 102 DW81
Denning Av, Croy. CR0 159 DN105
Denning Cl, NW8 82 DC69
Hampton TW12 116 BZ93
Denning Rd, NW3 64 DD63
Dennington Cl, E5
off Detmold Rd 66 DV61
Dennington Pk Rd, NW6 82 DA65
Denningtons, The, Wor.Pk. KT4 138 CS103
Dennis Av, Wem. HA9 62 CM64
Dennis Cl, Ashf. TW15 115 BR93
Redhill RH1 184 DE132
Dennises La, Upmin. RM14 91 FS67
Dennis Gdns, Stan. HA7 41 CJ50
Dennis La, Stan. HA7 41 CH48
Dennison Pt, E15 85 EC66
Dennis Pk Cres, SW20 139 CY95
Dennis Reeve Cl, Mitch. CR4 140 DF95
Dennis Rd, E.Mol. KT8 136 CC98
Gravesend DA11 131 GG90
South Ockendon RM15 91 FU66
Dennis Way, SW4
off Gauden Rd 101 DK83
Denny Av, Wal.Abb. EN9 15 ED34
Denny Cl, E6 *off Linton Gdns* 86 EL71
Denny Cres, SE11 200 E9
Denny Gdns, Dag. RM9
off Canonsleigh Rd 88 EV66
Denny Gate, Wal.Cr. EN8 15 DZ27
Denny Rd, N9 46 DV46
Slough SL3 93 AZ77
Denny St, SE11 200 E10
Den Rd, Brom. BR2 143 ED97
Densham Dr, Pur. CR8 159 DN114
Densham Rd, E15 86 EE67
Densole Cl, Beck. BR3
off Kings Hall Rd 143 DY95
Densworth Gro, N9 46 DW47
Dent Cl, S.Ock. RM15 91 FU72
DENTON, Grav. 131 GL87
Denton Cl, Barn. EN5 27 CW43
Denton Ct Rd, Grav. DA12 131 GL87
Denton Gro, Walt. KT12 136 BX103
Denton Rd, N8 65 DM57
N18 46 DS49
Bexley DA5 127 FE89
Dartford DA1 127 FE88
Twickenham TW1 117 CK86
Welling DA16 106 EW80
Denton St, SW18 120 DB86
Gravesend DA12 131 GL87
Denton Ter, Bex. DA5
off Denton Rd 127 FE89
Denton Way, E5 67 DX62
Woking GU21 166 AT118
Dents Gro, Tad. KT20 183 CZ128
Dents Rd, SW11 120 DF86
Denvale Wk, Wok. GU21 166 AU118
Denver Cl, Orp. BR6 145 ES100
Denver Ind Est, Rain. RM13 89 FF71
Denver Rd, N16 66 DS59
Dartford DA1 127 FG87
Denyer St, SW3 198 C9
Denziloe Av, Uxb. UB10 77 BP69
Denzil Rd, NW10 63 CT64
Deodara Cl, N20 44 DE48
Deodar Rd, SW15 99 CY84
★ Department for Environment, Food & Rural Affairs (DEFRA), SW1 199 P2
★ Department for Transport, Local Government & Regions (DTLR), SW1 199 K6
★ Department of Health & Department for Work & Pensions (DWP), SW1 199 P4
Depot App, NW2 63 CX63
Depot Rd, Epsom KT17 156 CS113
Hounslow TW3 97 CD83
DEPTFORD, SE8 103 DZ78
⇌ Deptford 103 DZ80
DLR Deptford Bridge 103 EA81
Deptford Br, SE8 103 EA81
Deptford Bdy, SE8 103 EA81
Deptford Ch St, SE8 103 EA79
Deptford Ferry Rd, E14 204 A9
Deptford Grn, SE8 103 EA79
Deptford High St, SE8 103 EA79
Deptford Strand, SE8 203 N9
Deptford Wf, SE8 203 M8
De Quincey Ms, E16 205 N2
De Quincey Rd, N17 46 DR53
Derby Arms Rd, Epsom KT18 173 CT117
Derby Av, N12 44 DC50
Harrow HA3 41 CD53
Romford RM7 71 FC58
Upminster RM14 72 FM62
Derby Cl, Epsom KT18 173 CV119
Derby Ct, E5
off Overbury St 67 DX63
Derby Gate, SW1 199 P4
Derby Hill, SE23 122 DW89
Derby Hill Cres, SE23 122 DW89
Derby Rd, E7 86 EJ66
E9 85 DX67
E18 48 EF53
N18 46 DW50
SW14 98 CP84
SW19 *off Russell Rd* 120 DA94
Croydon CR0 141 DP103
Enfield EN3 30 DV43
Grays RM17 110 GB78
Greenford UB6 78 CB67
Hounslow TW3 96 CB84
Surbiton KT5 138 CN102
Sutton SM1 157 CZ107
Uxbridge UB8 76 BJ68
Watford WD17 24 BW41
Derby Rd Br, Grays RM17 110 GB79
Derbyshire St, E2 84 DU69
Derby Stables Rd, Epsom KT18 172 CS117
Derby St, W1 198 G3
Dereham Pl, EC2 197 N3
Romford RM5 51 FB51
Dereham Rd, Bark. IG11 87 ET65
Derek Av, Epsom KT19 156 CN106
Wallington SM6 159 DH105
Wembley HA9 80 CP66
Derek Cl, Epsom (Ewell) KT19 156 CP106
Derek Walcott Cl, SE24
off Shakespeare Rd 121 DP85
Derham Gdns, Upmin. RM14 72 FQ62
Deri Av, Rain. RM13 89 FH70
Dericote St, E8 84 DU67
Deridene Cl, Stai. (Stanw.) TW19
off Bedfont Rd 114 BL86
Derifall Cl, E6 87 EM71
Dering Pl, Croy. CR0 160 DQ105
Dering Rd, Croy. CR0 160 DQ105
Dering St, W1 195 H9
Dering Way, Grav. DA12 131 GM88
Derinton Rd, SW17 120 DF91
Derley Rd, Sthl. UB2 96 BW76
Dermody Gdns, SE13 123 ED85
Dermody Rd, SE13 123 ED85
Deronda Rd, SE24 121 DP88
De Ros Pl, Egh. TW20 113 BA93
Deroy Cl, Cars. SM5 158 DF107
Derrick Av, S.Croy. CR2 160 DQ110
Derrick Gdns, SE7
off Anchor & Hope La 104 EJ77
Derrick Rd, Beck. BR3 143 DZ97
Derry Av, S.Ock. RM15 91 FU72
Derrydown, Wok. GU22 166 AW121
DERRY DOWNS, Orp. 146 EX100
Derry Downs, Orp. BR5 146 EW100
Derry Rd, Croy. CR0 141 DL104
Derry St, W8 100 DB75
Dersingham Av, E12 69 EN64
Dersingham Rd, NW2 63 CY62
Derwent Av, N18 46 DR50
NW7 42 CR50
SW15 118 CS91
Barnet EN4 44 DF46
Pinner HA5 40 BY51
Uxbridge UB10 58 BN62
Derwent Cl, Add. KT15 152 BK106
Amersham HP7 20 AV39
Dartford DA1 127 FH88
Esher (Clay.) KT10 155 CE107
Feltham TW14 115 BT88
Derwent Cres, N20 44 DC48
Bexleyheath DA7 106 FA82
Stanmore HA7 41 CJ54
Derwent Dr, NW9 62 CS57
Hayes UB4 77 BS71
Orpington BR5 145 ER101
Purley CR8 160 DR113
Derwent Gdns, Ilf. IG4 68 EL56
Wembley HA9 61 CJ59
Derwent Gro, SE22 102 DT84
Derwent Par, S.Ock. RM15 91 FV72
Derwent Ri, NW9 62 CS58
Derwent Rd, N13 45 DM49
SE20 142 DU96
SW20 139 CX100
W5 97 CJ76
Egham TW20 113 BB94
Southall UB1 78 CA72
Twickenham TW2 116 CB86
Derwent St, SE10 205 H10
Derwent Wk, Wall. SM6 159 DH108
Derwentwater Rd, W3 80 CQ74
Derwent Way, Horn. RM12 71 FH64
Derwent Yd, W5
off Northfield Av 97 CJ76
De Salis Rd, Uxb. UB10 77 BQ70
Desborough Cl, W2 82 DB71
Shepperton TW17 134 BN101
Desborough St, W2
off Cirencester St 82 DB71
Desenfans Rd, SE21 122 DS86
Desford Ct, Ashf. TW15
off Desford Way 114 BM89
Desford Ms, E16
off Desford Rd 86 EE70
Desford Rd, E16 86 EE70
Desford Way, Ashf. TW15 114 BM89
★ Design Mus, SE1 202 A3
Desmond Rd, Wat. WD24 23 BT36
Desmond St, SE14 103 DY79
Despard Rd, N19 65 DJ60
Detillens La, Oxt. RH8 188 EG129
Detling Cl, Horn. RM12 72 FJ64
Detling Rd, Brom. BR1 124 EG92
Erith DA8 107 FD80
Gravesend (Nthflt.) DA11 130 GD88
Detmold Rd, E5 66 DW61
Devalls Cl, E6 87 EN73
Devana End, Cars. SM5 140 DF104
Devas Rd, SW20 139 CW95
Devas St, E3 85 EB70
Devenay Rd, E15 86 EF66
Devenish Rd, SE2 106 EU75
Deventer Cres, SE22 122 DS85
De Vere Cotts, W8
off Canning Pl 100 DC76
De Vere Gdns, W8 100 DC75
Ilford IG1 69 EM61
Deverell St, SE1 201 K7
De Vere Ms, W8
off Canning Pl 100 DC76
Devereux Ct, WC2 196 D9
Devereux Dr, Wat. WD17 23 BS38
Devereux La, SW13 99 CV80
Devereux Rd, SW11 120 DF86
Grays RM16 110 FZ76
De Vere Wk, Wat. WD17 23 BS40
Deverill Ct, SE20 142 DW95
Deverills Way, Slou. SL3 93 BC77
Deveron Gdns, S.Ock. RM15 91 FU71
Deveron Way, Rom. RM1 51 FE53
Devey Cl, Kings.T. KT2 118 CS94
Devils La, Egh. TW20 113 BD94
Devitt Cl, Ashtd. KT21 172 CN116
Devizes St, N1 *off Poole St* 84 DR67
Devoke Way, Walt. KT12 136 BX103
Devon Av, Twick. TW2 116 CC88
Devon Cl, N17 66 DT55
Buckhurst Hill IG9 48 EH47
Greenford UB6 79 CJ67
Kenley CR8 176 DT116
Devon Ct, Buck.H. IG9 48 EH46
Dartford (Sutt.H.) DA4 148 FP95
Devon Cres, Red. RH1 184 DD134
Devoncroft Gdns, Twick. TW1 117 CG87
Devon Gdns, N4 65 DP58
Devonhurst Pl, W4
off Heathfield Ter 98 CR78
Devonia Gdns, N18 46 DQ51
Devonia Rd, N1 83 DP68
Devonport Gdns, Ilf. IG1 69 EM58
Devonport Ms, W12
off Devonport Rd 81 CV74
Devonport Rd, W12 99 CV75
Devonport St, E1 84 DW72
Devon Ri, N2 64 DD56
Devon Rd, Bark. IG11 87 ES67
Dartford (Sutt.H.) DA4 148 FP95
Redhill RH1 185 DJ130
Sutton SM2 157 CY109
Walton-on-Thames KT12 154 BW105
Watford WD24 24 BX39
Devons Est, E3 85 EB69
Devonshire Av, Dart. DA1 127 FH86
Sutton SM2 158 DC108
Tadworth KT20 182 CQ131
Woking GU21 151 BC114
Devonshire Cl, E15 68 EE63
N13 45 DN49
W1 195 H6
Devonshire Cres, NW7 43 CX52
Devonshire Dr, SE10 103 EB80
Surbiton KT6 137 CK102
Devonshire Gdns, N17 46 DQ51
N21 46 DQ45
W4 98 CQ80
Devonshire Gro, SE15 102 DV79
Devonshire Hill La, N17 46 DQ51
Devonshire Ho, Sutt. SM2
off Devonshire Av 158 DC108
Devonshire Ms, SW10
off Park Wk 100 DD79
W4 *off Glebe St* 98 CS78
Devonshire Ms N, W1 195 H6
Devonshire Ms S, W1 195 H6
Devonshire Ms W, W1 195 H5
Devonshire Pas, W4 98 CS78
Devonshire Pl, NW2 64 DA62
W1 194 G5
W4 98 CS78
W8 *off St. Mary's Pl* 100 DB76
Devonshire Pl Ms, W1 194 G5
Devonshire Rd, E16 86 EH72
E17 67 EA58
N9 46 DW46
N13 45 DM49
N17 46 DQ51
NW7 43 CX52
SE9 124 EL89
SE23 122 DW88
SW19 120 DE94
W4 98 CS78
W5 97 CJ76
Bexleyheath DA6 106 EY84
Carshalton SM5 158 DG105
Croydon CR0 142 DR101
Feltham TW13 116 BY90
Gravesend DA12 131 GH88
Grays RM16 110 FY77
Harrow HA1 61 CD58
Hornchurch RM12 72 FJ61
Ilford IG2 69 ER59
Orpington BR6 146 EU101
Pinner (Eastcote) HA5 60 BW58
Pinner (Hatch End) HA5 40 BZ53
Southall UB1 78 CA71
Sutton SM2 158 DC108
Weybridge KT13 152 BN105
Devonshire Row, EC2 197 N7
Devonshire Row Ms, W1 195 J5
Devonshire Sq, EC2 197 N8
Bromley BR2 144 EH98
Devonshire St, W1 194 G6
W4 98 CS78
Devonshire Ter, W2 82 DC72
Devonshire Way, Croy. CR0 143 DY103
Hayes UB4 77 BV72
DLR Devons Road 85 EB70
Devons Rd, E3 85 EA71
Devon St, SE15 102 DV79
Devon Way, Chess. KT9 155 CJ106
Epsom KT19 156 CP106
Uxbridge UB10 76 BM68
Devon Waye, Houns. TW5 96 BZ80
De Walden St, W1 194 G7
Dewar St, SE15 102 DU83
Dewberry Gdns, E6 86 EL71
Dewberry St, E14 85 EC71
Dewey Path, Horn. RM12 90 FJ65
Dewey Rd, N1 83 DN68
Dagenham RM10 89 FB65
Dewey St, SW17 120 DF92
Dewgrass Gro, Wal.Cr. EN8 33 DX35
Dewhurst Rd, W14 99 CX76
Waltham Cross (Chsht.) EN8 14 DW29
Dewlands, Gdse. RH9 186 DW131
Dewlands Av, Dart. DA2 128 FP87
Dewlands Ct, NW4
off Holders Hill Rd 43 CX54
Dewsbury Cl, Pnr. HA5 60 BZ58
Romford RM3 52 FL51
Dewsbury Ct, W4
off Chiswick Rd 98 CQ77
Dewsbury Gdns, Rom. RM3 52 FK51
Worcester Park KT4 139 CU104
Dewsbury Rd, NW10 63 CU64
Romford RM3 52 FK51
Dewsbury Ter, NW1
off Camden High St 83 DH67
Dexter Cl, Grays RM17 110 GA76
Dexter Ho, Erith DA18
off Kale Rd 106 EY76
Dexter Rd, Barn. EN5 27 CX44
Uxbridge (Hare.) UB9 38 BJ54
Deyncourt Gdns, Upmin. RM14 72 FQ61
Deyncourt Rd, N17 46 DQ53
Deynecourt Gdns, E11 68 EJ56
D'Eynsford Rd, SE5 102 DR81
Diadem Ct, W1 195 M9
Dial Cl, Green. DA9
off Knockhall Rd 129 FX85
Dialmead, Pot.B. EN6
off Crossoaks La 11 CT34
Dial Wk, The, W8 100 DB75
Diamedes Av, Stai. (Stanw.) TW19 114 BK87
Diameter Rd, Orp. BR5 145 EP101
Diamond Cl, Dag. RM8 70 EW60
Grays RM16 110 FZ76
Diamond Rd, Ruis. HA4 60 BX63
Slough SL1 92 AU75
Watford WD24 23 BU38
Diamond St, NW10
off Fawood Av 80 CR66
SE15 102 DS80
Diamond Ter, SE10 103 EC81
Diamond Way, SE8
off Deptford High St 103 EA80
Diana Cl, E18 48 EH53
SE8 *off Staunton St* 103 DZ79
Grays (Chaff.Hun.) RM16 110 FZ76
Slough (Geo.Grn.) SL3 74 AY72
Diana Gdns, Surb. KT6 138 CM103
Diana Ho, SW13 99 CT81
Diana Pl, NW1 195 J4
Diana Rd, E17 67 DZ55
Dianne Way, Barn. EN4 28 DE43
Dianthus Cl, SE2
off Carnation St 106 EV78
Chertsey KT16 133 BE101
Dianthus Ct, Wok. GU22 166 AX118
Diban Av, Horn. RM12 71 FH63
Dibden Hill, Ch.St.G. HP8 36 AW49
Dibden La, Sev. (Ide Hill) TN14 190 FE126
Dibden Row, SE1
off Gerridge St 101 DN76
Dibden St, N1 83 DP67
Dibdin Cl, Sutt. SM1 140 DA104
Dibdin Rd, Sutt. SM1 140 DA104
Diceland Rd, Bans. SM7 173 CZ116
Dicey Av, NW2 63 CW64
Dickens Av, N3 44 DC53
Dartford DA1 108 FN84
Tilbury RM18 111 GH81
Uxbridge UB8 77 BP72
Dickens Cl, Erith DA8 107 FB80
Hayes UB3 *off Croyde Av* 95 BS77
Richmond TW10 118 CL89
Waltham Cross EN7 14 DU26
Dickens Dr, Add. KT15 151 BF107
Chislehurst BR7 125 EQ93
Dickens Est, SE1 202 B5
SE16 202 B5
★ Dickens Ho, WC1 196 C5
Dickens Ho, NW6 82 DA69
Dickens La, N18 46 DS50
Dickenson Cl, N9
off Croyland Rd 46 DU46
Dickenson Rd, N8 65 DL59
Feltham TW13 116 BW92
Dickensons La, SE25 142 DU99
Dickensons Pl, SE25 142 DU100
Dickenson St, NW5
off Dalby St 83 DH65
Dickens Ri, Chig. IG7 49 EN48
Dickens Rd, E6 86 EK68
Gravesend DA12 131 GL88
Dickens Sq, SE1 201 J6
Dickens St, SW8 101 DH82
Dickens Way, Rom. RM1 71 FE56
Dickenswood Cl, SE19 121 DP94
Dickerage La, N.Mal. KT3 138 CQ97
Dickerage Rd, Kings.T. KT1 138 CQ95
New Malden KT3 138 CQ95
Dickinson Av, Rick. (Crox.Grn.) WD3 22 BN44
Dickinson Sq, Rick. (Crox.Grn.) WD3 22 BN44
Dickson, Wal.Cr. (Chsht.) EN7 14 DT27
Dickson Fold, Pnr. HA5 60 BX56
Dickson Rd, SE9 104 EL83
Dick Turpin Way, Felt. TW14 95 BT84
Didsbury Cl, E6
off Barking Rd 87 EM67
Digby Cres, N4 66 DQ61
Digby Gdns, Dag. RM10 88 FA67
Digby Pl, Croy. CR0 142 DT104
Digby Rd, E9 85 DX65
Barking IG11 87 ET66
Digby St, E2 84 DW69
Digby Wk, Horn. RM12
off Pembrey Way 90 FJ65
Digby Way, W.Byf. (Byfleet) KT14
off High Rd 152 BM112
Dig Dag Hill, Wal.Cr. (Chsht.) EN7 14 DT27
Digdens Ri, Epsom KT18 172 CQ115
Diggon St, E1
off Stepney Way 85 DX71
Dighton Ct, SE5 102 DQ79
Dighton Rd, SW18 120 DC85
Dignum St, N1
off Cloudesley Rd 83 DN68
Digswell Cl, Borwd. WD6 26 CN38
Digswell St, N7
off Holloway Rd 83 DN65
Dilhorne Cl, SE12 124 EH90
Dilke St, SW3 100 DF79
Dilloway Yd, Sthl. UB2
off The Green 96 BY75
Dillwyn Cl, SE26 123 DY91
Dilston Cl, Nthlt. UB5
off Yeading La 78 BW69
Dilston Gro, SE16 202 F8
Dilston Rd, Lthd. KT22 171 CG119
Dilton Gdns, SW15 119 CU88
Dilwyn Ct, E17 *off Hillyfield* 67 DY55
Dimes Pl, W6 *off King St* 99 CV77
Dimmock Dr, Grnf. UB6 61 CD64
Dimmocks La, Rick. (Sarratt) WD3 22 BH36
Dimond Cl, E7 68 EG63
Dimsdale Dr, NW9 62 CQ60
Enfield EN1 30 DU44
Dimsdale Wk, E13
off Stratford Rd 86 EG67
Dimson Cres, E3 85 EA70
Dingle, The, Uxb. UB10 77 BP68
Dingle Cl, Barn. EN5 27 CT44
Dingle Gdns, E14 204 A1
Dingle Rd, Ashf. TW15 115 BP92
Dingley La, SW16 121 DK89
Dingley Pl, EC1 197 J3
Dingley Rd, EC1 197 H3
Dingwall Av, Croy. CR0 142 DQ103
Dingwall Gdns, NW11 64 DA58
Dingwall Rd, SW18 120 DC87
Carshalton SM5 158 DF109
Croydon CR0 142 DR103
Dinmont St, E2
off Coate St 84 DV68
Dinmore, Hem.H. (Bov.) HP3 5 AZ28
Dinsdale Cl, Wok. GU22 167 BA118
Dinsdale Gdns, SE25 142 DS99
Barnet EN5 28 DB43
Dinsdale Rd, SE3 104 EF79
Dinsmore Rd, SW12 121 DH87
Dinton Rd, SW19 120 DD93
Kingston upon Thames KT2 118 CM94
Diploma Av, N2 64 DE56
Diploma Ct, N2
off Diploma Av 64 DE56
Dirdene Cl, Epsom KT17 157 CT112
Dirdene Gdns, Epsom KT17 157 CT112
Dirdene Gro, Epsom KT17 156 CS112
Dirleton Rd, E15 86 EF67
Disbrowe Rd, W6 99 CY79
Discovery Business Pk, SE16
off St. James's Rd 102 DU76
Discovery Wk, E1 202 D1
Dishforth La, NW9 42 CS53
Disney Ms, N4
off Chesterfield Gdns 65 DP57
Disney Pl, SE1 201 J4
Disney St, SE1 201 J4
Dison Cl, Enf. EN3 31 DX39
Disraeli Cl, SE28 88 EW74
W4 *off Acton La* 98 CR77
Disraeli Ct, Slou. SL3
off Sutton Pl 93 BB79
Disraeli Gdns, SW15
off Fawe Pk Rd 99 CZ84
Disraeli Rd, E7 86 EG65
NW10 80 CQ68
SW15 99 CY84
W5 79 CK74
Diss St, E2 197 P2
Distaff La, EC4 197 H10
Distillery La, W6
off Fulham Palace Rd 99 CW78
Distillery Rd, W6 99 CW78
Distillery Wk, Brent. TW8 98 CL79
Distin St, SE11 200 D9
District Rd, Wem. HA0 61 CH64
Ditch All, SE10 103 EB81
Ditchburn St, E14 204 E1
Ditches La, Cat. CR3 175 DM122
Coulsdon CR5 175 DL120
Ditches Ride, The, Loug. IG10 33 EN37
Ditchfield Rd, Hayes UB4 78 BY70
Dittisham Rd, SE9 124 EL91
Ditton Cl, T.Ditt. KT7 137 CG101
Dittoncroft Cl, Croy. CR0 160 DS105
Ditton Gra Cl, Surb. KT6 137 CK102
Ditton Gra Dr, Surb. KT6 137 CK102
Ditton Hill, Surb. KT6 137 CJ102
Ditton Hill Rd, Surb. KT6 137 CJ102
Ditton Lawn, T.Ditt. KT7 137 CG102
Ditton Pk, Slou. SL3 92 AX78
Ditton Pk Rd, Slou. SL3 92 AY79
Ditton Pl, SE20 142 DV95
Ditton Reach, T.Ditt. KT7 137 CH100
Ditton Rd, Bexh. DA6 126 EX85
Slough SL3 93 AZ79
Slough (Datchet) SL3 92 AX81
Southall UB2 96 BZ77

A B C D E F G H I J K L M N O P Q R S T U V W X Y Z

Ditton Rd, Surb. KT6 138 CL102
Divis Way, SW15 119 CV86
Dixon Clark Ct, N1
off Canonbury Rd 83 DP65
Dixon Cl, E6 off Brandreth Rd 87 EM72
Dixon Dr, Wey. KT13 152 BM110
Dixon Ho, W10 81 CX72
Dixon Pl, W.Wick. BR4 143 EB102
Dixon Rd, SE14 103 DY81
SE25 142 DS97
Dixon's All, SE16 202 D5
Dixons Hill Cl, Hat. (N.Mymms)
AL9 11 CV25
Dixons Hill Rd, Hat. (N.Mymms)
AL9 11 CU25
Dobbin Cl, Har. HA3 41 CG54
Dobell Rd, SE9 125 EM85
Dobree Av, NW10 81 CV66
Dobson Cl, NW6 82 DD66
Dobson Rd, Grav. DA12 131 GL92
Dockers Tanner Rd, E14 203 P7
Dockett Eddy La, Shep.
TW17 134 BM102
Dockhead, SE1 202 A5
Dock Hill Av, SE16 203 J4
Dockland St, E16 87 EN74
Dockley Rd, SE16 202 B7
Dock Rd, E16 205 L1
Brentford TW8 97 CK80
Grays RM17 110 GD79
Tilbury RM18 111 GF82
Dock St, E1 84 DU73
Dockwell Cl, Felt. TW14 95 BU84
Dockyard Ind Est, SE18
off Woolwich Ch St 104 EL76
Doctor Johnson Av, SW17 121 DH90
★ Doctor Johnson's Ho,
EC4 196 E9
Doctors Cl, SE26 122 DW92
Doctors La, Cat. CR3 175 DN123
Docwra's Bldgs, N1 84 DS65
Dodbrooke Rd, SE27 121 DN90
Doddinghurst Rd, Brwd.
CM15 54 FW44
Doddington Gro, SE17 101 DP79
Doddington Pl, SE17 101 DP79
Dodd's Cres, W.Byf. KT14 152 BH114
Dodds La, Ch.St.G. HP8 36 AU47
Dodd's La, Wok. GU22 152 BG114
Dodsley Pl, N9 46 DV48
Dodson St, SE1 200 E5
Dod St, E14 85 DZ72
Doebury Wk, SE18
off Prestwood Cl 106 EU79
Doel Cl, SW19 120 DC94
Doggetts Ct, Barn. EN4 28 DE43
Doggett Rd, SE6 123 EA87
Doggetts Fm Rd, Uxb. (Denh.)
UB9 57 BC59
Doggetts Wd Cl, Ch.St.G. HP8 20 AV42
Doggetts Wd La, Ch.St.G.
HP8 20 AV41
Doghurst Av, Hayes UB3 95 BP80
Doghurst Dr, West Dr. UB7 95 BP80
Doghurst La, Couls. CR5 174 DF120
Dog Kennel Hill, SE22 102 DS83
Dog Kennel Hill Est, SE22 102 DS83
Dog Kennel La, Rick. (Chorl.)
WD3 21 BF42
Dog La, NW10 62 CS63
Dogwood Cl, Grav. (Nthflt.)
DA11 130 GE91
Doherty Rd, E13 86 EG70
Dokal Ind Est, Sthl. UB2
off Hartington Rd 96 BY76
Dolben St, SE1 200 F3
Dolby Ct, EC4 197 J10
Dolby Rd, SW6 99 CZ82
Dolland St, SE11 101 DM78
Dollis Av, N3 43 CZ53
Dollis Brook Wk, Barn. EN5 27 CY44
Dollis Cres, Ruis. HA4 60 BW60
DOLLIS HILL, NW2 63 CV62
⊖ Dollis Hill 63 CU64
Dollis Hill Av, NW2 63 CV62
Dollis Hill Est, NW2 63 CU62
Dollis Hill La, NW2 63 CV62
Dollis Ms, N3 off Dollis Pk 43 CZ53
Dollis Pk, N3 43 CZ53
Dollis Rd, N3 43 CY52
NW7 43 CY52
Dollis Valley Grn Wk, N20
off Totteridge La 44 DC47
Barnet EN5 27 CY44
Dollis Valley Way, Barn. EN5 27 CZ44
Dolman Cl, N3
off Avondale Rd 44 DC54
Dolman Rd, W4 98 CR77
Dolman St, SW4 101 DM84
Dolphin App, Rom. RM1 71 FF56
Dolphin Cl, SE16 203 H4
SE28 88 EX72
Surbiton KT6 137 CK100
Dolphin Ct, NW11 63 CY58
Slough SL1 off Dolphin Rd 92 AV75
Staines TW18
off Bremer Rd 114 BG90
Dolphin Ct N, Stai. TW18
off Bremer Rd 114 BG90
Dolphin Est, Sun. TW16 135 BS95
Dolphin Ho, SW18
off Smugglers Way 100 DB84
Dolphin La, E14 204 B1
Dolphin Rd, Nthlt. UB5 78 BZ68
Slough SL1 92 AV75
Sunbury-on-Thames
TW16 135 BS95
Dolphin Rd N, Sun. TW16 135 BS95
Dolphin Rd S, Sun. TW16 135 BR95
Dolphin Rd W, Sun. TW16 135 BR95
Dolphin Sq, SW1 101 DJ78
W4 98 CS80
Dolphin St, Kings.T. KT1 138 CL95
Dolphin Twr, SE8
off Abinger Gro 103 DZ79
Dolphin Way, Purf. RM19 109 FS78
Dombey St, WC1 196 B6
★ Dome, The, SE10 205 H3
Dome Hill, Cat. CR3 186 DS127
Dome Hill Pk, SE26 122 DT91
Dome Hill Peak, Cat. CR3 186 DS126
Domett Cl, SE5 102 DR84
Dome Way, Red. RH1 184 DF133
Domfe Pl, E5
off Rushmore Rd 66 DW63
Domingo St, EC1 197 H4
Dominica Cl, E13 86 EJ68
Dominic Ct, Wal.Abb. EN9 15 EB33
Dominion Dr, Rom. RM5 51 FB51
Dominion Rd, Croy. CR0 142 DT101
Southall UB2 96 BY76
Dominion St, EC2 197 L6
★ Dominion Thea, W1 195 N8
Dominion Way, Rain. RM13 89 FG69
Domonic Dr, SE9 125 EP91
Domville Cl, N20 44 DD47
Donald Biggs Dr, Grav.
DA12 131 GK87
Donald Dr, Rom. RM6 70 EW57
Donald Rd, E13 86 EH67
Croydon CR0 141 DM100
Donaldson Rd, NW6 81 CZ67
SE18 105 EN81
Donald Wds Gdns, Surb.
KT5 138 CP103
Doncaster Dr, Nthlt. UB5 60 BZ64
Doncaster Gdns, N4
off Stanhope Gdns 66 DQ58
Northolt UB5 60 BZ64
Doncaster Grn, Wat. WD19 40 BW50
Doncaster Rd, N9 46 DV45
Doncaster Way, Upmin. RM14 72 FM62
Doncel Ct, E4 47 ED45
Donegal St, N1 196 C1
Doneraile St, SW6 99 CX82
Dongola Rd, E1 85 DY71
E13 86 EH69
N17 66 DS55
Dongola Rd W, E13
off Balaam St 86 EH69
Donington Av, Ilf. IG6 69 EQ57
Donkey All, SE22 122 DU87
Donkey La, Dart. (Fnghm.)
DA4 148 FP103
Enfield EN1 30 DU40
West Drayton UB7 94 BJ77
Donnay Cl, Ger.Cr. SL9 56 AX58
Donne Ct, SE24 122 DQ86
Donnefield Av, Edg. HA8 42 CL52
Donne Gdns, Wok. GU22 167 BE115
Donne Pl, SW3 198 C8
Mitcham CR4 141 DH98
Donne Rd, Dag. RM8 70 EW61
Donnington Rd, NW10 81 CV66
Harrow HA3 61 CK57
Sevenoaks (Dunt.Grn.)
TN13 181 FD120
Worcester Park KT4 139 CU103
Donnybrook Rd, SW16 121 DJ94
Donovan Av, N10 45 DH54
Donovan Cl, Epsom KT19
off Nimbus Rd 156 CR110
Don Phelan Cl, SE5 102 DR81
Don Way, Rom. RM1 51 FE52
Doods Pk Rd, Reig. RH2 184 DC133
Doods Rd, Reig. RH2 184 DC133
Doods Way, Reig. RH2 184 DD133
Doone Cl, Tedd. TW11 117 CG93
Doon St, SE1 200 D3
Dorado Gdns, Orp. BR6 146 EX104
Doral Way, Cars. SM5 158 DF106
Dorando Cl, W12 81 CV73
Doran Dr, Red. RH1 184 DD134
Doran Gdns, Red. RH1 184 DD134
Doran Gro, SE18 105 ES80
Doran Wk, E15 85 EC66
Dora Rd, SW19 120 DA92
Dora St, E14 85 DZ72
Dorchester Av, N13 46 DQ49
Bexley DA5 126 EX88
Harrow HA2 60 CC58
Dorchester Cl, Dart. DA1 128 FM87
Northolt UB5 60 CB64
Orpington BR5
off Grovelands Rd 126 EU94
Dorchester Ct, N14 45 DH45
SE24 122 DQ85
Rickmansworth (Crox.Grn.) WD3
off Mayfare 23 BR43
Woking GU22 167 BA116
Dorchester Dr, SE24 122 DQ85
Feltham TW14 115 BS86
Dorchester Gdns, E4 47 EA49
NW11 64 DA56
Dorchester Gro, W4 98 CS78
Dorchester Ms, N.Mal. KT3
off Elm Rd 138 CR98
Twickenham TW1 117 CJ87
Dorchester Rd, Grav. DA12 131 GK90
Morden SM4 140 DB101
Northolt UB5 60 CB64
Weybridge KT13 135 BP104
Worcester Park KT4 139 CW102
Dorchester Way, Har. HA3 62 CM58
Dorchester Waye, Hayes UB4 78 BW72
Dorcis Av, Bexh. DA7 106 EY82
Dordrecht Rd, W3 80 CS74
Dore Av, E12 69 EN64
Doreen Av, NW9 62 CR60
Dore Gdns, Mord. SM4 140 DB101
Dorell Cl, Sthl. UB1 78 BZ71
Doria Dr, Grav. DA12 131 GL90
Dorian Rd, Horn. RM12 71 FG60
Doria Rd, SW6 99 CZ82
Doric Dr, Tad. KT20 173 CZ120
Doric Way, NW1 195 M2
Dorien Rd, SW20 139 CX96
Dorin Ct, Warl. CR6 176 DV119
Dorincourt, Wok. GU22 167 BE115
Doris Av, Erith DA8 107 FC81
Doris Rd, E7 86 EG66
Ashford TW15 115 BR93
Dorking Cl, SE8 103 DZ79
Worcester Park KT4 139 CX103
Dorking Gdns, Rom. RM3 52 FK50
Dorking Glen, Rom. RM3 52 FK49
Dorking Ri, Rom. RM3 52 FK49
Dorking Rd, Epsom KT18 172 CN116
Leatherhead KT22 171 CH122
Romford RM3 52 FK49
Tadworth KT20 173 CX123
Dorking Wk, Rom. RM3 52 FK49
Dorkins Way, Upmin. RM14 73 FS59
Dorlcote Rd, SW18 120 DE87
Dorling Dr, Epsom KT17 157 CT112
Dorly Cl, Shep. TW17 135 BS99
Dorman Pl, N9 off Balham Rd 46 DU47
Dormans Cl, Nthwd. HA6 39 BR52
Dorman Wk, NW10
off Garden Way 62 CR64
Dorman Way, NW8 82 DD67
Dorma Trd Pk, E10 67 DX60
Dormay St, SW18 120 DB85
Dormer Cl, E15 86 EF65
Barnet EN5 27 CX43
Dormers Av, Sthl. UB1 78 CA72
Dormers Ri, Sthl. UB1 78 CB72
DORMER'S WELLS, Sthl. 78 CB73
Dormers Wells La, Sthl. UB1 78 CA72
Dormywood, Ruis. HA4 59 BT57
Dornberg Cl, SE3 104 EG80
Dornberg Rd, SE3
off Banchory Rd 104 EH80
Dorncliffe Rd, SW6 99 CY82
Dornels, Slou. SL2 74 AW72
Dorney, NW3 82 DE66
Dorney Gro, Wey. KT13 135 BP103
Dorney Ri, Orp. BR5 145 ET98
Dorney Way, Houns. TW4 116 BY85
Dornfell St, NW6 63 CZ64
Dornford Gdns, Couls. CR5 176 DQ119
Dornton Rd, SW12 121 DH89
South Croydon CR2 160 DR106
Dorothy Av, Wem. HA0 80 CL66
Dorothy Evans Cl, Bexh.
DA7 107 FB84
Dorothy Gdns, Dag. RM8 70 EV63
Dorothy Rd, SW11 100 DF83
Dorrell Pl, SW9
off Brixton Rd 101 DN84
Dorrien Wk, SW16 121 DK89
Dorrington Ct, SE25 142 DS96
Dorrington Gdns, Horn.
RM12 72 FK60
Dorrington Pt, E3
off Bromley High St 85 EB69
Dorrington St, EC1 196 D6
Dorrit Ms, N18 46 DS49
Dorrit Way, Chis. BR7 125 EQ93
Dorrofield Cl, Rick. (Crox.Grn.)
WD3 23 BQ43
Dors Cl, NW9 62 CR60
Dorset Av, Hayes UB4 77 BS69
Romford RM1 71 FD55
Southall UB2 96 CA77
Welling DA16 105 ET84
Dorset Bldgs, EC4 196 F9
Dorset Cl, NW1 194 D6
Hayes UB4 77 BS69
Dorset Cres, Grav. DA12 131 GL91
Dorset Dr, Edg. HA8 42 CM51
Woking GU22 167 BB117
Dorset Est, E2 84 DT69
Dorset Gdns, Mitch. CR4 141 DM98
Dorset Ho, Enf. EN3 31 DX37
Dorset Ms, N3 44 DA53
SW1 199 H6
Dorset Pl, E15 85 ED65
SW1 199 M10
Dorset Ri, EC4 196 F9
Dorset Rd, E7 86 EJ66
N15 66 DR56
N22 45 DL53
SE9 124 EL89
SW8 101 DM80
SW19 140 DA95
W5 97 CJ76
Ashford TW15 114 BK90
Beckenham BR3 143 DX97
Harrow HA1 60 CC58
Mitcham CR4 140 DE96
Sutton SM2 158 DA110
Dorset Sq, NW1 194 D5
Epsom KT19 156 CR110
Dorset St, W1 194 E7
Sevenoaks TN13
off High St 191 FH125
Dorset Way, Twick. TW2 117 CD88
Uxbridge UB10 76 BM68
West Byfleet (Byfleet)
KT14 152 BK110
Dorset Waye, Houns. TW5 96 BZ80
Dorton Cl, SE15
off Chandler Way 102 DT80
Dorton Dr, Sev. TN15 191 FM122
Dorton Way, Wok. (Ripley)
GU23 168 BH121
Dorville Cres, W6 99 CV76
Dorville Rd, SE12 124 EF85
Dothill Rd, SE18 105 ER80
Douai Gro, Hmptn. TW12 136 CC95
Doubleday Rd, Loug. IG10 33 EQ41
Doughty Ms, WC1 196 B5
Doughty St, WC1 196 B4
Douglas Av, E17 47 EA53
New Malden KT3 139 CV98
Romford RM3 52 FL54
Watford WD24 24 BX37
Wembley HA0 80 CL66
Douglas Cl, Grays (Chaff.Hun.)
RM16 110 FY76
Stanmore HA7 41 CG50
Wallington SM6 159 DL108
Douglas Ct, Cat. CR3 176 DQ122
Westerham TN16 178 EL117
Douglas Cres, Hayes UB4 78 BW70
Douglas Dr, Croy. CR0 143 EA104
Douglas Est, N1 84 DQ65
Douglas La, Stai. (Wrays.)
TW19 113 AZ85
Douglas Ms, NW2 63 CY62
Douglas Ms, Bans. SM7
off North Acre 173 CZ116
Douglas Rd, E4 48 EE45
E16 86 EG71
N1 84 DQ66
N22 45 DN53
NW6 81 CZ67
Addlestone KT15 134 BH104
Esher KT10 136 CB103
Hornchurch RM11 71 FF58
Hounslow TW3 96 CB83
Ilford IG3 70 EU58
Kingston upon Thames
KT1 138 CP96
Reigate RH2 184 DA133
Staines (Stanw.) TW19 114 BK86
Surbiton KT6 138 CM103
Welling DA16 106 EV81
Douglas Sq, Mord. SM4 140 DA100
Douglas St, SW1 199 M9
Douglas Ter, E17
off Douglas Av 47 EA53
Douglas Way, SE8 103 DZ80
Doug Siddons Ct, Grays RM17
off Elm Rd 110 GC79
Doulton Ms, NW6
off Lymington Rd 82 DB65
Doultons, The, Stai. TW18 114 BG94
Dounesforth Gdns, SW18 120 DB88
Dounsell Ct, Brwd. CM15
off Ongar Rd 54 FU44
Douro Pl, W8 100 DB76
Douro St, E3 85 EA68
Douthwaite Sq, E1 202 C2
Dove App, E6 86 EL71
Dove Cl, NW7 off Bunns La 43 CT52
Northolt UB5
off Wayfarer Rd 78 BX70
South Croydon CR2 161 DX111
Wallington SM6
off Hurricane Rd 159 DM108
Dovecot Cl, Pnr. HA5 59 BV57
Dovecote Av, N22 65 DN55
Dovecote Cl, Wey. KT13 135 BP104
Dovecote Gdns, SW14
off Avondale Rd 98 CR83
Dove Ct, EC2 197 K9
Dovedale Av, Har. HA3 61 CJ58
Ilford IG5 49 EN54
Dovedale Cl, Uxb. (Hare.)
UB9 38 BJ54
Welling DA16 106 EU82
Dovedale Ri, Mitch. CR4 120 DF94
Dovedale Rd, SE22 122 DV85
Dartford DA2 128 FQ88
Dovedon Cl, N14 45 DL47
Dove Ho Gdns, E4 47 EA47
Dovehouse Grn, Wey. KT13
off Rosslyn Pk 153 BR105
Dovehouse Mead, Bark. IG11 87 ER68
Dovehouse St, SW3 198 B10
Dove La, Pot.B. EN6 12 DB34
Dove Ms, SW5 100 DC77
Doveney Cl, Orp. BR5 146 EW97
Dove Pk, Pnr. HA5 40 CA52
Rickmansworth (Chorl.)
WD3 21 BB44
Dover Cl, NW2 off Brent Ter 63 CX61
Romford RM5 51 FC54
Dovercourt Av, Th.Hth. CR7 141 DN98
Dovercourt Est, N1 84 DR65
Dovercourt Gdns, Stan. HA7 42 CL50
Dovercourt La, Sutt. SM1 140 DC104
Dovercourt Rd, SE22 122 DS86
Doverfield, Wal.Cr. EN7 14 DQ29
Doverfield Rd, SW2 121 DL86
Dover Flats, SE1
off Old Kent Rd 102 DS77
Dover Gdns, Cars. SM5 140 DF104
Dover Ho Rd, SW15 99 CU84
Doveridge Gdns, N13 45 DP49
Dove Rd, N1 84 DR65
Dove Row, E2 84 DU67
Dover Pk Dr, SW15 119 CV86
Dover Patrol, SE3
off Kidbrooke Way 104 EH82
Dover Rd, E12 68 EJ61
N9 46 DW47
SE19 122 DR93
Gravesend (Nthflt.) DA11 130 GD87
Romford RM6 70 EY58
Dover Rd E, Grav. DA11 130 GE87
Doversmead, Wok. (Knap.)
GU21 166 AS116
Dover St, W1 199 J1
Dover Way, Rick. (Crox.Grn.)
WD3 23 BQ42
Dover Yd, W1 199 K2
Doves Cl, Brom. BR2 144 EL103
Doves Yd, N1 83 DN67
Doveton Rd, S.Croy. CR2 160 DR106
Doveton St, E1
off Malcolm Rd 84 DW70
Dove Wk, SW1 198 F10
Hornchurch RM12
off Heron Flight Av 89 FH65
Dowanhill Rd, SE6 123 ED88
Dowdeswell Cl, SW15 98 CS84
Dowding Pl, Stan. HA7 41 CG51
Dowding Rd, Uxb. UB10 76 BM66
Westerham (Bigg.H.) TN16 178 EK115
Dowding Wk, Grav. (Nthflt.)
DA11 130 GE90
Dowding Way, Horn. RM12 89 FH66
Watford WD25 off Ashfields 7 BT34
Dowdney Cl, NW5 65 DJ64
Dower Av, Wall. SM6 159 DH109
Dowgate Hill, EC4 197 K10
Dowland St, W10 81 CY68
Dowlas Est, SE5
off Dowlas St 102 DS80
Dowlas St, SE5 102 DS80
Dowlerville Rd, Orp. BR6 163 ET107
Dowman Cl, SW19
off Nelson Gro Rd 140 DB95
Downage, NW4 63 CW55
Downage, The, Grav. DA11 131 GG89
Downalong, Bushey (Bushey Hth.)
WD23 41 CD46
Downbank Av, Bexh. DA7 107 FD81
Downbarns Rd, Ruis. HA4 60 BX62
Downbury Ms, SW18
off Merton Rd 120 DA86
Down Cl, Nthlt. UB5 77 BV68
Downderry Rd, Brom. BR1 123 ED90
DOWNE, Orp. 163 EM111
Downe Av, Sev. (Cudham)
TN14 163 EQ112
Downe Cl, Well. DA16 106 EW80
Downend, SE18
off Moordown 105 EP80
Downer Dr, Rick. (Sarratt)
WD3 22 BG36
Downe Rd, Kes. BR2 162 EK109
Mitcham CR4 140 DF96
Sevenoaks (Cudham)
TN14 163 EQ114
Downers Cotts, SW4
off The Pavement 101 DJ84
Downes Cl, Twick. TW1
off St. Margarets Rd 117 CH86
Downes Ct, N21 45 DN46
Downfield, Wor.Pk. KT4 139 CT102
Downfield Cl, W9 82 DB70
Downfield Rd, Wal.Cr. (Chsht.)
EN8 15 DY31
Down Hall Rd, Kings.T. KT2 137 CK95
DOWNHAM, Brom. 124 EF92
Downham Cl, Rom. RM5 50 FA52
Downham La, Brom. BR1
off Downham Way 123 ED92
Downham Rd, N1 84 DR66
Downham Way, Brom. BR1 123 ED92
Downhills Av, N17 66 DR55
Downhills Pk Rd, N17 66 DQ55
Downhills Way, N17 66 DQ55
★ Down Ho - Darwin Mus, Orp.
BR6 163 EN112
Downhurst Av, NW7 42 CR50
Downing Cl, Har. HA2 60 CC55
Downing Dr, Grnf. UB6 79 CD67
Downing Rd, Dag. RM9 88 EZ67
Downings, E6 87 EN72
Downing St, SW1 199 P4
Downings Wd, Rick. (Map.Cr.)
WD3 37 BD50
Downland Cl, N20 44 DC46
Coulsdon CR5 159 DH114
Epsom KT18 173 CV118
Downland Gdns, Epsom
KT18 173 CV118
Downlands, Wal.Abb. EN9 16 EE34
Downlands Rd, Pur. CR8 159 DL113
Downland Way, Epsom KT18 173 CV118
Downleys Cl, SE9 124 EL89
Downman Rd, SE9 104 EL83
Down Pl, W6 99 CV77
Down Rd, Tedd. TW11 117 CH93
Downs, The, SW20 119 CX94
Downs Av, Chis. BR7 125 EM92
Dartford DA1 128 FN87
Epsom KT18 156 CS114
Pinner HA5 60 BZ58
Downs Br Rd, Beck. BR3 143 ED95
Downsbury Ms, SW18
off Merton Rd 120 DA85
Downs Ct, Sutt. SM2 158 DB111
Downs Ct Rd, Pur. CR8 159 DP112
Downsell Rd, E15 67 EC63
Downsfield Rd, E17 67 DY58
Downshall Av, Ilf. IG3 69 ES58
Downs Hill, Beck. BR3 123 ED94
Gravesend (Sthflt.) DA13 130 GC94
Downs Hill Rd, Epsom KT18 156 CS114
Downshire Hill, NW3 64 DD63
Downs Ho Rd, Epsom KT18 173 CT118
DOWNSIDE, Cob. 169 BV118
Downside, Cher. KT16 133 BF102
Epsom KT18 156 CS114
Sunbury-on-Thames
TW16 135 BU95
Twickenham TW1 117 CF90
Downside Br Rd, Cob. KT11 169 BV115
Downside Cl, SW19 120 DC93
Downside Common, Cob. (Down.)
KT11 169 BV118
Downside Common Rd, Cob.
(Down.) KT11 169 BV118
Downside Cres, NW3 64 DE64
W13 79 CG70
Downside Orchard, Wok. GU22
off Park Rd 167 BA117
Downside Rd, Cob. (Down.)
KT11 169 BV116
Sutton SM2 158 DD107
Downside Wk, Nthlt. UB5 78 BZ69
Downsland Dr, Brwd. CM14 54 FW48
Downs La, E5
off Downs Rd 66 DV63
Leatherhead KT22 171 CH123
Downs Pk Rd, E5 66 DU64
E8 66 DT64
Downs Rd, E5 66 DU63
Beckenham BR3 143 EB96
Coulsdon CR5 175 DK118
Enfield EN1 30 DS42
Epsom KT18 172 CS115
Gravesend (Istead Rise)
DA13 130 GD91
Purley CR8 159 DP111
Slough SL3 92 AX75
Sutton SM2 158 DB110
Thornton Heath CR7 142 DQ95
Downs Side, Sutt. SM2 157 CZ111
Down St, W1 199 H3
West Molesey KT8 136 CA99
Down St Ms, W1 199 H3
Downs Vw, Islw. TW7 97 CF80
Tadworth KT20 173 CV121
Downsview Av, Wok. GU22 167 AZ121
Downsview Cl, Orp. BR6 164 EW110

Dow - Dun

Downsview Cl, Swan. BR8 . . .147 FF97
Downsview Gdns, SE19 . . . .121 DP94
Downsview Rd, SE19 . . . . . .122 DQ94
Sevenoaks TN13 . . . . .190 FF125
Downs Way, Epsom KT18 . . .173 CT116
Downsway, Orp. BR6 . . . . . .163 ES106
Downs Way, Oxt. RH8 . . . . .188 EE127
Downsway, S.Croy. CR2 . . . .160 DS111
Downs Way, Tad. KT20 . . . . .173 CV121
Downsway, Whyt. CR3 . . . . .176 DT116
Downsway, The, Sutt. SM2 . .158 DC109
Downs Way Cl, Tad. KT20 . . .173 CU121
Downs Wd, Epsom KT18 . . . .173 CV117
Downswood, Reig. RH2 . . . . .184 DE131
Downton Av, SW2 . . . . .121 DL89
Downtown Rd, SE16 . . . . . . .203 L4
Downview Cl, Cob. KT11 . . . .169 BV119
Downway, N12 . . . . .44 DE52
Down Way, Nthlt. UB5 . . . . . .77 BV69
Dowrey St, N1
off Richmond Av 83 DN67
Dowry Wk, Wat. WD17 . . . . . .23 BT38
Dowsett Rd, N17 . . . . .46 DT54
Dowson Cl, SE5 . . . . .102 DR84
Doyce St, SE1 . . . . .201 H4
Doyle Cl, Erith DA8 . . . . . . .107 FE81
Doyle Gdns, NW10 . . . . .81 CU67
Doyle Rd, SE25 . . . . .142 DU98
Doyle Way, Til. RM18
off Coleridge Rd 111 GJ82
D'Oyley St, SW1 . . . . .198 F8
D'Oyly Carte Island, Wey.
KT13 . . . . .135 BP102
Doynton St, N19 . . . . .65 DH61
Draco St, SE17 . . . . .102 DQ79
Dragonfly Cl, E13
off Hollybush St 86 EH69
Dragon La, Wey. KT13 . . . . .152 BN110
Dragon Rd, SE15 . . . . .102 DS79
Dragoon Rd, SE8 . . . . .103 DZ78
Dragor Rd, NW10 . . . . .80 CQ70
Drake Av, Cat. CR3 . . . . . . .176 DQ122
Slough SL3 . . . . .92 AX77
Staines TW18 . . . . .113 BF92
Drake Cl, SE16 . . . . .203 J4
Brentwood CM14 . . . . .54 FX50
Drake Ct, SE19 . . . . .122 DT92
W12 . . . . .99 CW75
Harrow HA2 . . . . .60 BZ60
Drake Cres, SE28 . . . . .88 EW72
Drakefell Rd, SE4 . . . . .103 DX82
SE14 . . . . .103 DX82
Drakefield Rd, SW17 . . . . . .120 DG90
Drakeley Ct, N5
off Highbury Hill 65 DP63
Drake Ms, Horn. RM12
off Fulmar Rd 89 FG66
Drake Rd, SE4 . . . . .103 EA83
Chessington KT9 . . . . .156 CN106
Croydon CR0 . . . . .141 DM101
Grays (Chaff.Hun.) RM16 . .110 FY75
Harrow HA2 . . . . .60 BZ61
Mitcham CR4 . . . . .140 DG100
Drakes Cl, Esher KT10 . . . . .154 CA106
Waltham Cross (Chsht.)
EN8 . . . . .15 DX28
Drakes Ctyd, NW6 . . . . .81 CZ66
Drakes Dr, Nthwd. HA6 . . . . .39 BP53
Drakes Rd, Amer. HP7 . . . . . .20 AS39
Drake St, WC1 . . . . .196 B7
Enfield EN2 . . . . .30 DR39
Drakes Wk, E6 . . . . .87 EM67
Drakes Way, Wok. GU22 . . . .166 AX122
Drakewood Rd, SW16 . . . . . .121 DK94
Draper Cl, Belv. DA17 . . . . .106 EZ77
Isleworth TW7 . . . . .97 CD82
Draper Pl, N1 off Dagmar Ter .83 DP67
Drapers Gdns, EC2
off Copthall Av 84 DR72
Drapers Rd, E15 . . . . .67 ED63
N17 . . . . .66 DT55
Enfield EN2 . . . . .29 DP40
Drappers Way, SE16 . . . . . . .202 C8
Draven Cl, Brom. BR2 . . . . .144 EF101
Drawdock Rd, SE10 . . . . . . .204 G3
Drawell Cl, SE18 . . . . .105 ES78
Drax Av, SW20 . . . . .119 CV94
Draxmont, SW19 . . . . .119 CY93
Draycot Rd, E11 . . . . .68 EH58
Surbiton KT6 . . . . .138 CN102
Draycott Av, SW3 . . . . .198 C8
Harrow HA3 . . . . .61 CH58
Draycott Cl, NW2 . . . . .63 CX62
Harrow HA3 . . . . .61 CH58
Draycott Ms, SW6
off New Kings Rd 99 CZ82
Draycott Pl, SW3 . . . . .198 D9
Draycott Ter, SW3 . . . . .198 E8
Drayford Cl, W9 . . . . .81 CZ70
Dray Gdns, SW2 . . . . .121 DM85
Draymans Way, Islw. TW7 . . . .97 CF83
Drayside Ms, Sthl. UB2
off Kingston Rd 96 BZ75
Drayson Cl, Wal.Abb. EN9 . . . .16 EE32
Drayson Ms, W8 . . . . .100 DA75
Drayton Av, W13 . . . . .79 CG73
Loughton IG10 . . . . .33 EM44
Orpington BR6 . . . . .145 EP102
Potters Bar EN6 . . . . .11 CY32
Drayton Br Rd, W7 . . . . .79 CF73
W13 . . . . .79 CF73
Drayton Cl, Houns. TW4
off Bramley Way 116 BZ85
Ilford IG1 . . . . .69 ER60
Leatherhead (Fetch.) KT22 .171 CE124
Drayton Ford, Rick. WD3 . . . .38 BG48
Drayton Gdns, N21 . . . . .45 DP45
SW10 . . . . .100 DC78
W13 . . . . .79 CG73
West Drayton UB7 . . . . .94 BL75
⇌ Drayton Green 79 CF72
Drayton Grn, W13 . . . . .79 CG73
Drayton Grn Rd, W13 . . . . . . .79 CH73
Drayton Gro, W13 . . . . .79 CG73
⇌ Drayton Park 65 DN63
Drayton Pk, N5 . . . . .65 DN64
Drayton Pk Ms, N5
off Drayton Pk 65 DN64
Drayton Rd, E11 . . . . .67 ED60
N17 . . . . .46 DS54
NW10 . . . . .81 CT67
W13 . . . . .79 CG73
Borehamwood WD6 . . . . . . .26 CN42
Croydon CR0 . . . . .141 DP103
Drayton Waye, Har. HA3 . . . . .61 CH58
Drenon Sq, Hayes UB3 . . . . . .77 BT73
Dresden Cl, NW6 . . . . .82 DB65
Dresden Rd, N19 . . . . .65 DK60
Dresden Way, Wey. KT13 . . . .153 BQ106
Dressington Av, SE4 . . . . . . .123 EA86
Drew Av, NW7 . . . . .43 CY51
Drew Gdns, Grnf. UB6 . . . . . .79 CF65
Drew Pl, Cat. CR3 . . . . .176 DR123
Drew Rd, E16 . . . . .86 EL74
Drewstead Rd, SW16 . . . . . .121 DK89
Drey, The, Ger.Cr. (Chal.St.P.)
SL9 . . . . .36 AY50
Driffield Rd, E3 . . . . .85 DY68
Drift, The, Brom. BR2 . . . . . .144 EK104
Drift La, Cob. KT11 . . . . . . .170 BZ117
Drift Rd, Lthd. KT24 . . . . . .169 BT124
Drift Way, Rich. TW10 . . . . . .118 CM88
Slough (Colnbr.) SL3 . . . . . . .93 BC81
Driftway, The, Bans. SM7 . . . .173 CW115
Leatherhead KT22
off Downs La 171 CH123
Mitcham CR4 . . . . .140 DG95
Driftwood Av, St.Alb. AL2 . . . . .8 CA26
Driftwood Dr, Ken. CR8 . . . . .175 DP117
Drill Hall Rd, Cher. KT16 . . . .134 BG101
Drinkwater Rd, Har. HA2 . . . . .60 CB61
Drive, The, E4 . . . . .47 ED45
E17 . . . . .67 EB56
E18 . . . . .68 EG56
N3 . . . . .44 DA52
N6 . . . . .64 DF57
N11 . . . . .45 DJ51
NW10 off Longstone Av 81 CT67
NW11 . . . . .63 CY59
SW6 off Fulham Rd 99 CY82
SW16 . . . . .141 DM97
SW20 . . . . .119 CW94
W3 . . . . .80 CQ72
Ashford TW15 . . . . .115 BR94
Banstead SM7 . . . . .173 CY117
Barking IG11 . . . . .87 ET66
Barnet (High Barn.) EN5 . . . .27 CY41
Barnet (New Barn.) EN5 . . . .28 DC44
Beckenham BR3 . . . . .143 EA96
Bexley DA5 . . . . .126 EW86
Brentwood CM13 . . . . .54 FW50
Buckhurst Hill IG9 . . . . .48 EJ45
Chislehurst BR7 . . . . .145 ET97
Chislehurst (Scad.Pk.)
BR7 . . . . .145 ES95
Cobham KT11 . . . . .154 BY114
Coulsdon CR5 . . . . .159 DL114
Edgware HA8 . . . . .42 CN50
Enfield EN2 . . . . .30 DR39
Epsom KT19 . . . . .157 CT107
Epsom (Headley) KT18 . . . .172 CN124
Erith DA8 . . . . .107 FB80
Esher KT10 . . . . .136 CC102
Feltham TW14 . . . . .116 BW87
Gerrards Cross (Chal.St.P.)
SL9 . . . . .36 AY52
Gravesend DA12 . . . . .131 GK91
Harrow HA2 . . . . .60 CA59
Hatfield (Brook.Pk.) AL9 . . . .12 DA25
Hounslow TW3 . . . . .97 CD82
Ilford IG1 . . . . .69 EM60
Isleworth TW7 . . . . .97 CD82
Kingston upon Thames
KT2 . . . . .118 CQ94
Leatherhead (Fetch.) KT22 .171 CE122
Leatherhead (Tyr.Wd.)
KT22 . . . . .172 CN124
Loughton IG10 . . . . .32 EL41
Morden SM4 . . . . .140 DD99
Northwood HA6 . . . . .39 BS54
Orpington BR6 . . . . .145 ET103
Potters Bar EN6 . . . . .11 CZ33
Radlett WD7 . . . . .9 CG34
Rickmansworth WD3 . . . . . . .22 BJ44
Romford (Coll.Row) RM5 . . .51 FC53
Romford (Harold Wd.) RM3 .52 FL53
St. Albans (Lon.Col.) AL2 . . . .9 CG26
Sevenoaks TN13 . . . . .191 FH124
Sidcup DA14 . . . . .126 EV90
Slough SL3 . . . . .92 AY75
Slough (Datchet) SL3 . . . . . .92 AV81
Staines (Wrays.) TW19 . . . .112 AX85
Surbiton KT6 . . . . .138 CL101
Sutton SM2 . . . . .157 CZ112
Thornton Heath CR7 . . . . . .142 DR98
Uxbridge UB10 . . . . .58 BL63
Virginia Water GU25 . . . . . .133 AZ99
Wallington SM6 . . . . .159 DJ110
Waltham Cross (Chsht.)
EN7 . . . . .13 DP28
Watford WD17 . . . . .23 BR37
Wembley HA9 . . . . .62 CQ61
West Wickham BR4 . . . . . . .143 ED101
Woking GU22 . . . . .166 AV120
Drive Mead, Couls. CR5 . . . . .159 DL114
Drive Rd, Couls. CR5 . . . . . .175 DM119
Drive Spur, Tad. KT20 . . . . .174 DB121
Driveway, The, E17
off Hoe St 67 EB58
Potters Bar (Cuffley) EN6 . . .13 DL28
Droitwich Cl, SE26 . . . . .122 DU90
Dromey Gdns, Har. HA3 . . . . .41 CF52
Dromore Rd, SW15 . . . . .119 CY86
Dronfield Gdns, Dag. RM8 . . . .70 EW64
Droop St, W10 . . . . .81 CY70
Drop La, St.Alb. (Brick.Wd.)
AL2 . . . . .8 CB30
Drover La, SE15 . . . . .102 DV80
Drovers Pl, SE15 . . . . .102 DV80
Drovers Rd, S.Croy. CR2 . . . .160 DR106
Droveway, Loug. IG10 . . . . . . .33 EP40
Drove Way, The, Grav. (Istead Rise)
DA13 . . . . .130 GE94
Druce Rd, SE21 . . . . .122 DS86
Drudgeon Way, Dart. (Bean)
DA2 . . . . .129 FV90
Druids Cl, Ashtd. KT21 . . . . .172 CM120
Druid St, SE1 . . . . .201 N4
Druids Way, Brom. BR2 . . . . .143 ED98
Drumaline Ridge, Wor.Pk.
KT4 . . . . .138 CS103
Drummond Av, Rom. RM7 . . . .71 FD56
Drummond Cen, Croy. CR0 . .142 DQ103
Drummond Cl, Erith DA8 . . . .107 FE81
Drummond Cres, NW1 . . . . . .195 M2
Drummond Dr, Stan. HA7 . . . .41 CF52
Drummond Gdns, Epsom
KT19 . . . . .156 CP111
Drummond Gate, SW1 . . . . . .199 N10
Drummond Pl, Rich. TW9 . . . . .98 CL84
Twickenham TW1 . . . . .117 CH86
Drummond Rd, E11 . . . . .68 EJ58
SE16 . . . . .202 D6
Croydon CR0 . . . . .142 DQ103
Romford RM7 . . . . .71 FD56
Drummonds, The, Buck.H. IG9 .48 EH47
Epping CM16 . . . . .18 EU30
Drummond St, NW1 . . . . . . .195 K4
Drum St, E1
off Whitechapel High St . . .84 DT72
Drury Cres, Croy. CR0 . . . . .141 DN103
Drury La, WC2 . . . . .196 A9
Drury Rd, Har. HA1 . . . . .60 CC59
Drury Way, NW10 . . . . .62 CR64
Drury Way Ind Est, NW10 . . . .62 CQ64
Dryad St, SW15 . . . . .99 CX83
Dryburgh Gdns, NW9 . . . . . . .62 CN55
Dryburgh Rd, SW15 . . . . .99 CV83
Dryden Av, W7 . . . . .79 CF72
Dryden Cl, Ilf. IG6 . . . . .49 ET51
Dryden Ct, SE11 . . . . .200 E9
Dryden Pl, Til. RM18
off Fielding Av 111 GH81
Dryden Rd, SW19 . . . . .120 DC93
Enfield EN1 . . . . .30 DS44
Harrow HA3 . . . . .41 CF53
Welling DA16 . . . . .105 ES81
Dryden St, WC2 . . . . .196 A9
Dryden Twrs, Rom. RM3 . . . . .51 FH52
Dryden Way, Orp. BR6 . . . . .146 EU102
Dryfield Cl, NW10 . . . . .80 CQ65
Dryfield Rd, Edg. HA8 . . . . . . .42 CQ51
Dryfield Wk, SE8
off New King St 103 EA79
Dryhill La, Sev. (Sund.) TN14 .190 FB123
Dryhill Rd, Belv. DA17 . . . . . .106 EZ79
Dryland Av, Orp. BR6 . . . . . .163 ET105
Drylands Rd, N8 . . . . .65 DL58
Drynham Pk, Wey. KT13 . . . .135 BS104
Drysdale Av, E4 . . . . .47 EB45
Drysdale Cl, Nthwd. HA6
off Northbrook Dr 39 BS52
Drysdale Pl, N1 . . . . .197 N2
Drysdale St, N1 . . . . .197 N2
Duarte Pl, Grays RM16 . . . . .110 FZ76
Dublin Av, E8 . . . . .84 DU67
Du Burstow Ter, W7 . . . . .97 CE75
Ducal St, E2 off Brick La 84 DT69
Du Cane Cl, W12 . . . . .81 CW72
Du Cane Ct, SW17 . . . . .120 DG88
Du Cane Rd, W12 . . . . .81 CT72
Duchess Cl, N11 . . . . .45 DH50
Sutton SM1 . . . . .158 DC105
Duchess Gro, Buck.H. IG9 . . . .48 EH47
Duchess Ms, W1 . . . . .195 J7
Duchess of Bedford's Wk,
W8 . . . . .100 DA75
Duchess St, W1 . . . . .195 J7
Duchess Wk, Sev. TN15 . . . .191 FL125
Duchy Rd, Barn. EN4 . . . . . . .28 DD38
Duchy St, SE1 . . . . .200 E2
Ducie St, SW4 . . . . .101 DM84
Duckett Ms, N4
off Duckett Rd 65 DP58
Duckett Rd, N4 . . . . .65 DP58
Ducketts Rd, Dart. DA1 . . . . .127 FF85
Duckett St, E1 . . . . .85 DX70
Ducking Stool Ct, Rom. RM1 . .71 FE56
Duck La, W1 . . . . .195 M9
Epping (Thnwd.) CM16 . . . . .18 EW26
Duck Lees La, Enf. EN3 . . . . . .31 DY42
Ducks Hill, Nthwd. HA6 . . . . . .39 BP54
Ducks Hill Rd, Nthwd. HA6 . . . .39 BP54
Ruislip HA4 . . . . .39 BP54
DUCKS ISLAND, Barn. 27 CX44
Ducks Wk, Twick. TW1 . . . . . .117 CJ85
Du Cros Dr, Stan. HA7 . . . . . .41 CK51
Du Cros Rd, W3 off The Vale . .80 CS74
Dudden Hill La, NW10 . . . . . . .63 CT63
Duddington Cl, SE9 . . . . .124 EK91
Dudley Av, Har. HA3 . . . . .61 CJ55
Waltham Cross EN8 . . . . .15 DX32
Dudley Cl, Add. KT15 . . . . . .134 BJ104
Grays (Chaff.Hun.) RM16 . .110 FY75
Hemel Hempstead (Bov.)
HP3 . . . . .5 BA27
Dudley Ct, NW11 . . . . .63 CZ56
Slough SL1 off Upton Rd 92 AU76
Dudley Dr, Mord. SM4 . . . . . .139 CY101
Ruislip HA4 . . . . .59 BV64
Dudley Gdns, W13 . . . . .97 CH75
Harrow HA2 . . . . .61 CD60
Romford RM3
off Dudley Rd 52 FK51
Dudley Gro, Epsom KT18 . . .156 CQ114
Dudley Ms, SW2
off Bascombe St 121 DN86
Dudley Rd, E17 . . . . .47 EA54
N3 . . . . .44 DB54
NW6 . . . . .81 CY68
SW19 . . . . .120 DA93
Ashford TW15 . . . . .114 BM92
Feltham TW14 . . . . .115 BQ88
Gravesend (Nthflt.) DA11 . . .130 GE87
Harrow HA2 . . . . .60 CC61
Ilford IG1 . . . . .69 EP63
Kingston upon Thames
KT1 . . . . .138 CM97
Dudley Rd, Rich. TW9 . . . . . . .98 CM82
Romford RM3 . . . . .52 FK51
Southall UB2 . . . . .96 BX75
Walton-on-Thames KT12 . .135 BU100
Dudley St, W2 . . . . .82 DD71
Dudlington Rd, E5 . . . . .66 DW61
Dudmaston Ms, SW3 . . . . . . .198 A10
Dudsbury Rd, Dart. DA1 . . . .127 FG86
Sidcup DA14 . . . . .126 EV93
Dudset La, Houns. TW5 . . . . . .95 BU81
Dufferin Av, EC1 . . . . .197 K5
Dufferin St, EC1 . . . . .197 J5
Duffield Cl, Grays (Daniel Cl)
RM16 . . . . .110 FY75
Grays (Davis Rd) RM16 . . .110 FZ76
Harrow HA1 . . . . .61 CF57
Duffield Dr, N15
off Copperfield Dr 66 DT56
Duffield La, Slou. (Stoke P.)
SL2 . . . . .74 AT65
Duffield Pk, Slou. (Stoke P.)
SL2 . . . . .74 AT69
Duffield Rd, Tad. KT20 . . . . .173 CV124
Duffins Orchard, Cher. (Ott.)
KT16 . . . . .151 BC108
Duff St, E14 . . . . .85 EB72
Dufour's Pl, W1 . . . . .195 L9
Dugard Way, SE11 . . . . .200 F8
Dugdale Hill La, Pot.B. EN6 . . .11 CY33
Dugdales, Rick. (Crox.Grn.)
WD3 . . . . .22 BN42
Duke Gdns, Ilf. IG6
off Duke Rd 69 ER56
Duke Humphrey Rd, SE3 . . . .104 EE81
Duke of Cambridge Cl, Twick.
TW2 . . . . .117 CD86
Duke of Edinburgh Rd, Sutt.
SM1 . . . . .140 DD103
Duke of Wellington Pl, SW1 . .198 G4
Duke of York St, SW1 . . . . . .199 L2
Duke Rd, W4 . . . . .98 CR78
Ilford IG6 . . . . .69 ER56
Dukes Av, N3 . . . . .44 DB53
N10 . . . . .65 DJ55
W4 . . . . .98 CR78
Edgware HA8 . . . . .42 CM51
Epping (They.B.) CM16 . . . . .33 ES35
Grays RM17 . . . . .110 GA75
Harrow HA1 . . . . .61 CE56
Harrow (N.Har.) HA2 . . . . . . .60 BZ58
Hounslow TW4 . . . . .96 BY84
Kingston upon Thames
KT2 . . . . .117 CJ91
New Malden KT3 . . . . .139 CT97
Northolt UB5 . . . . .78 BY66
Richmond TW10 . . . . .117 CJ91
Dukes Cl, Ashf. TW15 . . . . . .115 BQ91
Epping (N.Wld.Bas.) CM16 . .19 FB27
Gerrards Cross SL9 . . . . . . .56 AX60
Hampton TW12 . . . . .116 BZ92
Dukes Ct, E6 . . . . .87 EN67
Woking GU21 . . . . .167 AZ117
Dukes Grn Av, Felt. TW14 . . . .115 BU85
Dukes Head Yd, N6
off Highgate High St 65 DH60
Dukes Hill, Cat. (Wold.) CR3 . .177 DY120
Duke Shore Pl, E14 . . . . .203 M1
Duke Shore Wf, E14
off Narrow St 85 DZ73
Dukes Kiln Dr, Ger.Cr. SL9 . . . .56 AW60
Dukes La, W8 . . . . .100 DA75
Gerrards Cross SL9 . . . . . . .56 AY59
Dukes Lo, Nthwd. HA6
off Eastbury Av 39 BS50
Duke's Meadows, W4
off Great Chertsey Rd 98 CQ82
Dukes Ms, N10 off Dukes Av . .65 DH55
Duke's Ms, W1 . . . . .194 G8
Dukes Orchard, Bex. DA5 . . . .127 FC88
Duke's Pas, E17 . . . . .67 EC56
Dukes Pl, EC3 . . . . .197 N9
Dukes Ride, Ger.Cr. SL9 . . . . .56 AY60
Uxbridge UB10 . . . . .58 BL63
Dukes Rd, E6 . . . . .87 EN67
W3 . . . . .80 CN71
Duke's Rd, WC1 . . . . .195 N3
Dukes Rd, Walt. KT12 . . . . . .154 BX106
Dukesthorpe Rd, SE26 . . . . . .123 DX91
Duke St, SW1 . . . . .199 L2
W1 . . . . .194 G8
Richmond TW9 . . . . .97 CK84
Sutton SM1 . . . . .158 DD105
Watford WD17 . . . . .24 BW41
Woking GU21 . . . . .167 AZ117
Duke St Hill, SE1 . . . . .201 L2
Dukes Valley, Ger.Cr. SL9 . . . . .56 AV61
Dukes Way, Uxb. UB8
off Waterloo Rd 76 BJ67
West Wickham BR4 . . . . . . .144 EE104
Dukes Wd Av, Ger.Cr. SL9 . . . .56 AY60
Dukes Wd Dr, Ger.Cr. SL9 . . . .56 AW60
Duke's Yd, W1 . . . . .194 G10
Dulas St, N4 off Everleigh St . .65 DM60
Dulford St, W11 . . . . .81 CY73
Dulka Rd, SW11 . . . . .120 DF85
Dulverton Rd, SE9 . . . . .125 EQ89
Romford RM3 . . . . .52 FK51
Ruislip HA4 . . . . .59 BU60
South Croydon CR2 . . . . . .160 DW110
DULWICH, SE21 . . . . .122 DS87
★ Dulwich Coll Picture Gall,
SE21 . . . . .122 DS87
Dulwich Common, SE21 . . . . .122 DS88
SE22 . . . . .122 DS88
Dulwich Lawn Cl, SE22
off Colwell Rd 122 DT85
Dulwich Oaks, The, SE21 . . . .122 DS90
Dulwich Rd, SE24 . . . . .121 DN85
Dulwich Village, SE21 . . . . . .122 DS86
Dulwich Way, Rick. (Crox.Grn.)
WD3 . . . . .22 BN43
Dulwich Wd Av, SE19 . . . . . .122 DS91
Dulwich Wd Pk, SE19 . . . . . .122 DS91
Dumbarton Av, Wal.Cr. EN8 . . .15 DX34
Dumbarton Rd, SW2 . . . . . . .121 DL86
Dumbleton Cl, Kings.T. KT1
off Gloucester Rd 138 CP95
Dumbletons, The, Rick. (Map.Cr.)
WD3 . . . . .37 BE49
Dumbreck Rd, SE9 . . . . .105 EM84
Dumfries Cl, Wat. WD19 . . . . .39 BT48
Dumont Rd, N16 . . . . .66 DS62
Dumpton Pl, NW1
off Gloucester Av 82 DG66
Dumville Dr, Gdse. RH9 . . . . .186 DV131
Dunally Pk, Shep. TW17 . . . . .135 BR101
Dunbar Av, SW16 . . . . .141 DN96
Beckenham BR3 . . . . .143 DY98
Dagenham RM10 . . . . .70 FA62
Dunbar Cl, Hayes UB4 . . . . . .77 BU71
Dunbar Cl, Slou. SL2 . . . . . . .74 AU72
Dunbar Ct, Sutt. SM1 . . . . . .158 DD106
Walton-on-Thames KT12 . .136 BW103
Dunbar Gdns, Dag. RM10 . . . .70 FA64
Dunbar Rd, E7 . . . . .86 EG65
N22 . . . . .45 DN53
New Malden KT3 . . . . .138 CQ98
Dunbar St, SE27 . . . . .122 DQ90
Dunblane Cl, Edg. HA8
off Tayside Dr 42 CP47
Dunblane Rd, SE9 . . . . .104 EL83
Dunboe Pl, Shep. TW17 . . . . .135 BQ101
Dunboyne Rd, NW3 . . . . .64 DF64
Dunbridge Ho, SW15
off Highcliffe Dr 119 CT86
Dunbridge St, E2 . . . . .84 DU70
Duncan Cl, Barn. EN5 . . . . . . .28 DC42
Duncan Gdns, Stai. TW18
off Burges Way 114 BG92
Duncan Gro, W3 . . . . .80 CS72
Duncannon St, WC2 . . . . . . .199 P1
Duncan Rd, E8 . . . . .84 DV67
Richmond TW9 . . . . .98 CL84
Tadworth KT20 . . . . .173 CY119
Duncan St, N1 . . . . .83 DP68
Duncan Ter, N1 . . . . .196 F1
Duncan Way, Bushey WD23 . . .24 BZ40
Dunch St, E1 off Watney St . . .84 DV72
Duncombe Cl, Amer. HP6 . . . .20 AS38
Duncombe Ct, Stai. TW18 . . . .113 BF94
Duncombe Hill, SE23 . . . . . .123 DY87
Duncombe Rd, N19 . . . . .65 DK60
Duncrievie Rd, SE13 . . . . . . .123 ED86
Duncroft, SE18 . . . . .105 ES80
Duncroft Cl, Reig. RH2 . . . . .183 CZ133
Dundalk Rd, SE4 . . . . .103 DY83
Dundas Gdns, W.Mol. KT8 . . .136 CB97
Dundas Ms, Enf. EN3
off Government Row 31 EA37
Dundas Rd, SE15 . . . . .102 DW82
Dundee Rd, E13 . . . . .86 EH68
SE25 . . . . .142 DV99
Dundee St, E1 . . . . .202 D3
Dundee Way, Enf. EN3 . . . . . .31 DY41
Dundela Gdns, Wor.Pk. KT4 . .157 CV105
Dundonald Cl, E6
off Northumberland Rd 86 EL72
Dundonald Road 119 CZ94
Dundonald Rd, NW10 . . . . . . .81 CX67
SW19 . . . . .119 CY94
Dundrey Cres, Red. RH1 . . . .185 DL129
Dunedin Dr, Cat. CR3 . . . . . .186 DS125
Dunedin Ho, E16
off Manwood St 87 EM74
Dunedin Rd, E10 . . . . .67 EB62
Ilford IG1 . . . . .69 EQ60
Rainham RM13 . . . . .89 FF69
Dunedin Way, Hayes UB4 . . . .78 BW70
Dunelm Gro, SE27 . . . . .122 DQ91
Dunelm St, E1 . . . . .85 DX72
Dunfee Way, W.Byf. KT14 . . . .152 BL112
Dunfield Gdns, SE6 . . . . . . .123 EB91
Dunfield Rd, SE6 . . . . .123 EB92
Dunford Rd, N7 . . . . .65 DM63
Dungarvan Av, SW15 . . . . . . .99 CU84
Dungates La, Bet. (Buckland)
RH3 . . . . .183 CU133
Dunheved Cl, Th.Hth. CR7 . . .141 DN100
Dunheved Rd N, Th.Hth. CR7 .141 DN100
Dunheved Rd S, Th.Hth. CR7 .141 DN100
Dunheved Rd W, Th.Hth.
CR7 . . . . .141 DN100
Dunhill Pt, SW15
off Dilton Gdns 119 CV88
Dunholme Grn, N9 . . . . .46 DT48
Dunholme La, N9
off Dunholme Rd 46 DT48
Dunholme Rd, N9 . . . . .46 DT48
Dunkeld Rd, SE25 . . . . .142 DR98
Dagenham RM8 . . . . .70 EV61
Dunkellin Gro, S.Ock. RM15
off Dunkellin Way 91 FU72
Dunkellin Way, S.Ock. RM15 . .91 FU72
Dunkery Rd, SE9 . . . . .124 EK91
Dunkin Rd, Dart. DA1 . . . . . .108 FN84
Dunkirk Cl, Grav. DA12 . . . . .131 GJ92
Dunkirk St, SE27
off Waring St 122 DQ91
Dunlace Rd, E5 . . . . .66 DW63
Dunleary Cl, Houns. TW4 . . . .116 BZ87
Dunley Dr, Croy. (New Adgtn.)
CR0 . . . . .161 EB108
Dunlin Ho, W13 . . . . .79 CF70
Dunloe Av, N17 . . . . .66 DR55
Dunloe St, E2 . . . . .197 P1
Dunlop Pl, SE16 . . . . .202 A7
Dunlop Rd, Til. RM18 . . . . . .111 GF81
Dunmail Dr, Pur. CR8 . . . . . .160 DS114
Dunmore Pt, E2 . . . . .197 P3
Dunmore Rd, NW6 . . . . .81 CY67
SW20 . . . . .139 CW95
Dunmow Cl, Felt. TW13 . . . . .116 BY91
Loughton IG10 . . . . .32 EL44
Romford RM6 . . . . .70 EW57
Dunmow Dr, Rain. RM13 . . . . .89 FF67
Dunmow Ho, Dag. RM9 . . . . . .88 EV67
Dunmow Rd, E15 . . . . .67 ED63
Dunmow Wk, N1
off Popham St 84 DQ67
Dunnage Cres, SE16 . . . . . . .203 L8
Dunnets, Wok. (Knap.) GU21 .166 AS117
Dunning Cl, S.Ock. RM15
off Dent Cl 91 FU72
Dunningford Cl, Horn. RM12 . .71 FF64

A B C D E F G H I J K L M N O P Q R S T U V W X Y Z

Dunn Mead, NW9
off Field Mead 43 CT52
Dunnock Cl, N9 47 DX46
Borehamwood WD6 26 CN42
Dunnock Rd, E6 86 EL72
Dunns Pas, WC1 196 A8
Dunn St, E8 66 DT64
Dunny La, Kings L. (Chipper.)
WD4 5 BE32
Dunnymans Rd, Bans. SM7 173 CZ115
Dunollie Pl, NW5
off Dunollie Rd 65 DJ64
Dunollie Rd, NW5 65 DJ64
Dunoon Rd, SE23 122 DW87
Dunraven Dr, Enf. EN2 29 DN40
Dunraven Rd, W12 81 CU74
Dunraven St, W1 194 E10
Dunsany Rd, W14 99 CX76
Dunsborough Pk, Wok. (Ripley)
GU23 168 BJ120
Dunsbury Cl, Sutt. SM2
off Nettlecombe Cl 158 DB109
Dunsfold Ri, Couls. CR5 159 DK113
Dunsfold Way, Croy. (New Adgtn.)
CR0 161 EB108
SW15 off Dover Pk Dr 119 CV86
Dunsmore Cl, Bushey WD23 25 CD44
Hayes UB4
off Kingsash Dr 78 BY70
Dunsmore Rd, Walt. KT12 135 BV100
Dunsmore Way, Bushey
WD23 25 CD44
Dunsmure Rd, N16 66 DS60
Dunspring La, Ilf. IG5 49 EP54
Dunstable Cl, Rom. RM3
off Dunstable Rd 52 FK51
Dunstable Ms, W1 194 G6
Dunstable Rd, Rich. TW9 98 CL84
Romford RM3 52 FK51
West Molesey KT8 136 BZ98
Dunstall Grn, Wok. (Chobham)
GU24 150 AW109
Dunstall Rd, SW20 119 CV93
Dunstall Way, W.Mol. KT8 136 CB97
Dunstan Cl, N2
off Thomas More Way 64 DC55
Dunstan Rd, NW11 63 CZ60
Coulsdon CR5 175 DK117
Dunstans Gro, SE22 122 DV86
Dunstans Rd, SE22 122 DU87
Dunster Av, Mord. SM4 139 CX102
Dunster Cl, Barn. EN5 27 CX42
Romford RM5 51 FC54
Uxbridge (Hare.) UB9 38 BH53
Dunster Ct, EC3 197 M10
Borehamwood WD6
off Kensington Way 26 CR41
Dunster Cres, Horn. RM11 72 FN61
Dunster Dr, NW9 62 CQ60
Dunster Gdns, NW6 81 CZ66
Dunsterville Way, SE1 201 L5
Dunster Way, Har. HA2 60 BY62
Wallington SM6
off London Rd 140 DG102
Dunston Rd, E8 84 DT67
SW11 100 DG82
Dunston St, E8 84 DT67
Dunton Cl, Surb. KT6 138 CL102
DUNTON GREEN, Sev. 181 FC119
⇌ Dunton Green 181 FE119
Dunton Rd, E10 67 EB59
SE1 201 P10
Romford RM1 71 FE56
Duntshill Rd, SW18 120 DB88
Dunvegan Cl, W.Mol. KT8 136 CB98
Dunvegan Rd, SE9 105 EM84
Dunwich Rd, Bexh. DA7 106 EZ81
Dunworth Ms, W11
off Portobello Rd 81 CZ72
Duplex Ride, SW1 198 E5
Dupont Rd, SW20 139 CX96
Duppas Av, Croy. CR0
off Violet La 159 DP105
Duppas Cl, Shep. TW17
off Green La 135 BR99
Duppas Hill La, Croy. CR0
off Duppas Hill Rd 159 DP105
Duppas Hill Rd, Croy. CR0 159 DP105
Duppas Hill Ter, Croy. CR0 141 DP104
Duppas Rd, Croy. CR0 141 DN104
Dupre Cl, Grays (Chaff.Hun.)
RM16 110 FY76
Dupree Rd, SE7 205 P10
Dura Den Cl, Beck. BR3 123 EB94
Durand Cl, Cars. SM5 140 DF102
Durand Gdns, SW9 101 DM81
Durands Wk, SE16 203 L4
Durand Way, NW10 80 CQ66
Durant Rd, Swan. BR8 127 FG93
Durants Pk Av, Enf. EN3 31 DX42
Durants Rd, Enf. EN3 30 DW42
Durant St, E2 84 DU68
Durban Gdns, Dag. RM10 89 FC66
Durban Rd, E15 86 EE69
E17 47 DZ53
N17 46 DS51
SE27 122 DQ91
Beckenham BR3 143 DZ96
Ilford IG2 69 ES60
Durban Rd E, Wat. WD18 23 BU42
Durban Rd W, Wat. WD18 23 BU42
Durbin Rd, Chess. KT9 156 CL105
Durdans Rd, Sthl. UB1 78 BZ72
Durell Gdns, Dag. RM9 70 EX64
Durell Rd, Dag. RM9 70 EX64
Durfold Dr, Reig. RH2 184 DC134
Durford Cres, SW15 119 CV88
Durham Av, Brom. BR2 144 EF98
Hounslow TW5 96 BZ78
Romford RM2 72 FJ56
Woodford Green IG8 48 EK50
Durham Cl, SW20
off Durham Rd 139 CV96
Durham Hill, Brom. BR1 124 EF91
Durham Ho St, WC2 200 A1
Durham Pl, SW3
off Smith St 100 DF78
Durham Pl, Ilf. IG1
off Eton Rd 69 EQ63
Durham Ri, SE18 105 EQ78
Durham Rd, E12 68 EK63
E16 86 EE70
N2 64 DE55
N7 65 DM61
N9 46 DU47
SW20 139 CV95
W5 97 CK76
Borehamwood WD6 26 CQ41
Bromley BR2 144 EF97
Dagenham RM10 71 FC64
Feltham TW14 116 BW87
Durham Rd, Har. HA1 60 CB57
Sidcup DA14 126 EV92
Durham Row, E1 85 DY71
Durham St, SE11 101 DM78
Durham Ter, W2 82 DB72
Durham Wf, Brent. TW8
off London Rd 97 CJ80
Durham Yd, E2
off Teesdale St 84 DV69
Duriun Way, Erith DA8 107 FH80
Durley Av, Pnr. HA5 60 BY59
Durley Gdns, Orp. BR6 164 EV105
Durley Rd, N16 66 DS59
Durlston Rd, E5 66 DU61
Kingston upon Thames
KT2 118 CL93
Durndale La, Grav. (Nthflt.)
DA11 131 GF91
Durnell Way, Loug. IG10 33 EN41
Durnford St, N15 66 DS57
SE10 off Greenwich Ch St 103 EC79
Durning Rd, SE19 122 DR92
Durnsford Av, SW19 120 DA89
Durnsford Rd, N11 45 DK53
SW19 120 DA89
Durrants Cl, Rain. RM13 90 FJ68
Durrants Dr, Rick. (Crox.Grn.)
WD3 23 BQ42
Durrant Way, Orp. BR6 163 ER106
Swanscombe DA10 130 FY87
Durrell Rd, SW6 99 CZ81
Durrell Way, Shep. TW17 135 BR100
Durrington Av, SW20 139 CW95
Durrington Pk Rd, SW20 119 CW94
Durrington Rd, E5 67 DY63
Durrington Twr, SW8
off Westbury St 101 DJ82
Dursley Cl, SE3 104 EJ82
Dursley Gdns, SE3 104 EK81
Dursley Rd, SE3 104 EJ82
Durward St, E1 84 DV71
Durweston Ms, W1 194 E6
Durweston St, W1 194 E6
Dury Falls Cl, Horn. RM11 72 FM60
Dury Rd, Barn. EN5 27 CZ39
Dutch Barn Cl, Stai. (Stanw.)
TW19 114 BK86
Dutch Elm Av, Wind. SL4 92 AT80
Dutch Gdns, Kings.T. KT2
off Windmill Ri 118 CP93
Dutch Yd, SW18
off Wandsworth High St 120 DA85
Duthie St, E14 204 E1
Dutton St, SE10 103 EC81
Dutton Way, Iver SL0 75 BE72
Duxberry Cl, Brom. BR2
off Southborough La 144 EL99
Duxford Cl, Horn. RM12 89 FH65
Duxford Ho, SE2
off Wolvercote Rd 106 EX75
Dwight Ct, SW6
off Burlington Rd 99 CY82
Dwight Rd, Wat. WD18 39 BR45
Dye Ho La, E3 85 EA67
Dyer's Bldgs, EC1 196 D7
Dyers Hall Rd, E11 68 EE60
Dyers La, SW15 99 CV84
Dyers Way, Rom. RM3 51 FH52
Dyke Dr, Orp. BR5 146 EW102
Dykes Path, Wok. GU21
off Bentham Av 167 BC115
Dykes Way, Brom. BR2 144 EF97
Dykewood Cl, Bex. DA5 127 FE90
Dylan Cl, Borwd. (Elstree) WD6
off Coates Rd 41 CK45
Dylan Rd, SE24 101 DP84
Belvedere DA17 106 FA76
Dylan Thomas Ho, N8 65 DM56
Dylways, SE5 102 DR84
Dymchurch Cl, Ilf. IG5 49 EN54
Orpington BR6 163 ES105
Dymes Path, SW19
off Queensmere Rd 119 CX89
Dymock St, SW6 100 DB83
Dymoke Rd, Horn. RM11 71 FF59
Dymond Est, SW17
off Glenburnie Rd 120 DE90
Dyneley Rd, SE12 124 EJ91
Dyne Rd, NW6 81 CZ66
Dynevor Rd, N16 66 DS62
Richmond TW10 118 CL85
Dynham Rd, NW6 82 DA66
Dyott St, WC1 195 P8
Dyrham La, Barn. EN5 27 CU36
Dysart Av, Kings.T. KT2 117 CJ92
Dysart St, EC2 197 M5
Dyson Rd, E11 68 EE58
E15 86 EF65
Dysons Cl, Wal.Cr. EN8 15 DX33
Dysons Rd, N18 46 DV50

E

Eade Rd, N4 66 DQ59
Eagans Cl, N2 off Market Pl 64 DE55
Eagle Av, Rom. RM6 70 EY58
Eagle Cl, SE16 off Varcoe Rd 102 DW78
Amersham HP6 20 AT37
Enfield EN3 30 DW42
Hornchurch RM12 89 FH65
Eagle Cl, Wall. SM6 159 DL107
Waltham Abbey EN9 16 EG34
Eagle Ct, EC1 196 F6
Eagle Dr, NW9 42 CS54
Eagle Hill, SE19 122 DR93
Eagle La, E11 68 EG56
Eagle Ms, N1
off Tottenham Rd 84 DS65
Eagle Pl, SW1 199 L1
SW7 off Old Brompton Rd 100 DC78
Eagle Rd, Wem. HA0 79 CK66
Eagles Dr, West. (Tats.) TN16 178 EK118
Eaglesfield Rd, SE18 105 EP80
Eagles Rd, Green. DA9 109 FV84
Eagle St, WC1 196 B7
Eagle Ter, Wdf.Grn. IG8 48 EH52
Eagle Trd Est, Mitch. CR4
off Willow La 140 DF100
Eagle Way, Brwd. CM13 53 FV51
Gravesend (Nthflt.) DA11 130 GA85
Eagle Wf, E14
off Broomfield St 85 EB71
Eagle Wf Rd, N1 84 DQ68
Ealdham Sq, SE9 104 EJ84
EALING, W5 79 CJ73
⇌ Ealing Broadway 79 CK73
⊖ Ealing Broadway 79 CK73
Ealing Bdy Shop Cen, W5 79 CK73
Ealing Cl, Borwd. WD6 26 CR39
★ Ealing Common, W5 80 CL74
⊖ Ealing Common 80 CM74
Ealing Downs Ct, Grnf. UB6
off Perivale La 79 CG69
Ealing Grn, W5 79 CK74
H Ealing Hosp NHS Trust, Sthl.
UB1 79 CD74
Ealing Pk Gdns, W5 97 CJ77
Ealing Rd, Brent. TW8 97 CK78
Northolt UB5 78 CA66
Wembley HA0 80 CL67
Ealing Village, W5 80 CL72
Eamont Cl, Ruis. HA4
off Allonby Dr 59 BP59
Eamont St, NW8 82 DE68
Eardemont Cl, Dart. DA1 107 FF84
Eardley Cres, SW5 100 DA78
Eardley Pt, SE18
off Wilmount St 105 EP77
Eardley Rd, SW16 121 DJ92
Belvedere DA17 106 FA78
Sevenoaks TN13 191 FH124
Earl Cl, N11 45 DH50
Earldom Rd, SW15 99 CW84
Earle Gdns, Kings.T. KT2 118 CL93
Earleswood, Cob. KT11 154 BX112
Earlham Gro, E7 68 EF64
N22 45 DM52
Earlham St, WC2 195 N9
Earl Ri, SE18 105 ER77
Earl Rd, SW14 off Elm Rd 98 CQ84
Gravesend (Nthflt.) DA11 130 GE89
EARLS COURT, SW5 99 CZ78
⊖ Earls Court 100 DA78
★ Earls Court Exhibition Cen,
SW5 100 DA78
Earls Ct Gdns, SW5 100 DB77
Earls Ct Rd, SW5 100 DA77
W8 100 DA76
Earls Ct Sq, SW5 100 DB78
Earls Cres, Har. HA1 61 CE56
Earlsdown Ho, Bark. IG11
off Wheelers Cross 87 ER68
Earlsferry Way, N1 83 DM66
EARLSFIELD, SW18 120 DC88
⇌ Earlsfield 120 DC88
Earlsfield Rd, SW18 120 DC88
Earlshall Rd, SE9 105 EM84
Earls La, Pot.B. EN6 10 CS32
Earlsmead, Har. HA2 60 BZ63
Earlsmead Rd, N15 66 DT57
NW10 81 CW68
Earl's Path, Loug. IG10 32 EJ40
Earls Ter, W8 99 CZ76
Earlsthorpe Ms, SW12 120 DG86
Earlsthorpe Rd, SE26 123 DX91
Earlstoke St, EC1 196 F2
Earlston Gro, E9 84 DV67
Earl St, EC2 197 M6
Watford WD17 24 BW41
Earls Wk, W8 100 DA76
Dagenham RM8 70 EV63
Earls Way, Orp. BR6
off Station Rd 145 ET103
Earlswood Av, Th.Hth. CR7 141 DN99
Earlswood Cl, SE10
off Earlswood St 104 EE78
Earlswood Gdns, Ilf. IG5 69 EN55
Earlswood St, SE10 104 EE78
Early Ms, NW1
off Arlington Rd 83 DH67
Earnshaw St, WC2 195 N8
Earsby St, W14 99 CY77
Easby Cres, Mord. SM4 140 DB100
Easebourne Rd, Dag. RM8 70 EW64
Easedale Dr, Horn. RM12 71 FG64
Easedale Ho, Islw. TW7
off Summerwood Rd 117 CF85
Eashing Pt, SW15
off Wanborough Dr 119 CV88
Easington Way, S.Ock. RM15 91 FU71
Easley's Ms, W1 194 G8
EAST ACTON, W3 80 CR74
⊖ East Acton 81 CT72
East Acton La, W3 80 CS73
East Arbour St, E1 85 DX72
East Av, E12 86 EL66
E17 67 EB56
Hayes UB3 95 BT75
Southall UB1 78 BZ73
Wallington SM6 159 DM106
Walton-on-Thames KT12
off Octagon Rd 153 BT110
East Bk, N16 66 DS59
Eastbank Rd, Hmptn. (Hmptn.H.)
TW12 116 CC92
EAST BARNET, Barn. 28 DE44
East Barnet Rd, Barn. EN4 28 DE44
EAST BEDFONT, Felt. 115 BS88
Eastbourne Av, W3 80 CR72
Eastbourne Gdns, SW14 98 CQ83
Eastbourne Ms, W2 82 DC72
Eastbourne Rd, E6 87 EN69
E15 86 EE67
N15 66 DS58
SW17 120 DG93
W4 98 CQ79
Brentford TW8 97 CJ78
Feltham TW13 116 BX89
Godstone RH9 186 DW132
Eastbourne Ter, W2 82 DC72
Eastbournia Av, N9 46 DV48
Eastbridge, Slou. SL2
off Victoria Rd 74 AV74
Eastbrook Av, N9 46 DW45
Dagenham RM10 71 FC63
Eastbrook Cl, Wok. GU21 167 BA116
Eastbrook Dr, Rom. RM7 71 FE62
Eastbrook Rd, SE3 104 EH80
Waltham Abbey EN9 16 EE33
EASTBURY, Nthwd. 39 BS49
Eastbury Av, Bark. IG11 87 ES67
Enfield EN1 30 DS39
Northwood HA6 39 BS50
Eastbury Ct, Bark. IG11 87 ES67
Eastbury Gro, W4 98 CS78
Eastbury Ho, Bark. IG11 87 ET67
★ Eastbury Ho, Bark. IG11 87 ET67
Eastbury Pl, Nthwd. HA6
off Eastbury Av 39 BT50
Eastbury Rd, E6 87 EN70
Kingston upon Thames
KT2 118 CL94
Northwood HA6 39 BS51
Orpington BR5 145 ER100
Romford RM7 71 FD58
Watford WD19 39 BV45
Eastbury Sq, Bark. IG11 87 ET67
Eastbury Ter, E1 85 DX70
Eastcastle St, W1 195 K8
Eastcheap, EC3 197 L10
East Churchfield Rd, W3 80 CR74
Eastchurch Rd, Houns. (Hthrw.Air.)
TW6 95 BS82
East Cl, W5 80 CN70
Barnet EN4 28 DG42
Greenford UB6 78 CC68
Rainham RM13 89 FH70
St. Albans AL2 8 CB25
Eastcombe Av, SE7 104 EH79
East Common, Ger.Cr. SL9 56 AY59
EASTCOTE, Pnr. 60 BW58
⊖ Eastcote 60 BW59
Eastcote, Orp. BR6 145 ET102
Eastcote Av, Grnf. UB6 61 CG64
Harrow HA2 60 CB61
West Molesey KT8 136 BZ99
Eastcote La, Har. HA2 60 CA62
Northolt UB5 78 CA66
Eastcote La N, Nthlt. UB5 78 BZ65
Eastcote Pl, Pnr. HA5 59 BV58
Eastcote Rd, Har. HA2 60 CC62
Pinner HA5 60 BX57
Pinner (Eastcote Vill.) HA5 59 BU58
Ruislip HA4 59 BS59
Welling DA16 105 ER82
Eastcote St, SW9 101 DM82
Eastcote Vw, Pnr. HA5 60 BW56
EASTCOTE VILLAGE, Pnr. 59 BV57
Eastcourt, Sun. TW16 136 BW96
East Ct, Wem. HA0 61 CJ61
East Cres, N11 44 DF49
Enfield EN1 30 DT43
East Cres Rd, Grav. DA12 131 GJ86
Eastcroft Rd, Epsom KT19 156 CS108
East Cross Cen, E15 85 EA65
East Cross Route, E3 85 DZ66
E9 85 DZ65
⇌ East Croydon 142 DR103
⬦ East Croydon 142 DR103
Eastdean Av, Epsom KT18 156 CP113
East Dene Dr, Rom. (Harold Hill)
RM3 52 FK50
Eastdown Pk, SE13 103 ED84
East Dr, Cars. SM5 158 DE109
Northwood HA6 39 BS47
Orpington BR5 146 EV100
Slough (Stoke P.) SL2 74 AS69
Virginia Water GU25 132 AU101
Watford WD25 23 BV35
East Duck Lees La, Enf. EN3 31 DY42
EAST DULWICH, SE22 122 DU86
⇌ East Dulwich 102 DS84
East Dulwich Gro, SE22 122 DS86
East Dulwich Rd, SE15 102 DT84
SE22 102 DT84
East End Rd, N2 64 DC55
N3 44 DA54
East End Way, Pnr. HA5 60 BY55
East Entrance, Dag. RM10 89 FB68
Eastern Av, E11 68 EJ58
Chertsey KT16 134 BG97
Grays (W.Thur.) RM20 109 FT78
Ilford IG2, IG4 68 EL58
Pinner HA5 60 BX59
Romford RM6 70 EW56
South Ockendon (Aveley)
RM15 90 FQ74
Waltham Cross EN8 15 DY33
Eastern Av E, Rom. RM1,
RM2, RM3 71 FD55
Eastern Av W, Rom. RM1,
RM5, RM6, RM7 70 EY56
Eastern Ind Est, Erith DA18 106 FA75
Eastern Pathway, Horn.
RM12 90 FJ67
Eastern Perimeter Rd Houns.
(Hthrw.Air.) TW6 95 BT83
Eastern Rd, E13 86 EH68
E17 67 EC57
N2 64 DF55
N22 45 DL53
SE4 103 EA84
Grays RM17 110 GD77
Romford RM1 71 FE57
Eastern Vw, West. (Bigg.H.)
TN16 178 EJ117
Easternville Gdns, Ilf. IG2 69 EQ58
Eastern Way, SE2 88 EX74
SE28 106 EU75
Belvedere DA17 107 FB75
Erith DA18 88 EX74
Grays RM17 110 GA79
EAST EWELL, Sutt. 157 CX110
East Ferry Rd, E14 204 C8
Eastfield Av, Wat. WD24 24 BX39
Eastfield Cl, Slou. SL1
off St. Laurence Way 92 AU76
Eastfield Cotts, Hayes UB3 95 BS78
Eastfield Gdns, Dag. RM10 70 FA63
Eastfield Par, Pot.B. EN6 12 DD32
Eastfield Rd, E17 67 EA56
N8 65 DL55
Brentwood CM14 54 FX47
Dagenham RM9, RM10 70 FA63
Enfield EN3 31 DX38
Waltham Cross EN8 15 DY32
Eastfields, Pnr. HA5 60 BW57
Eastfields Rd, W3 80 CQ71
Mitcham CR4 140 DG96
Eastfield St, E14 85 DY71
EAST FINCHLEY, N2 64 DD56
⊖ East Finchley 64 DE56
East Gdns, SW17 120 DE93
Woking GU22 167 BC117
Eastgate, Bans. SM7 157 CY114
Eastgate Cl, SE28 88 EX72
Eastglade, Nthwd. HA6 39 BS50
Pinner HA5 60 BY55
East Gorse, Croy. CR0 161 DY112
East Grn, Hem.H. HP3 6 BM25
East Hall La, Rain. (Wenn.)
RM13 90 FK72
East Hall Rd, Orp. BR5 146 EY101
EAST HAM, E6 86 EL68
⊖ East Ham 86 EL66
Eastham Cl, Barn. EN5 27 CY43
Eastham Cres, Brwd. CM13 55 GA49
East Ham Ind Est, E6 86 EL70
East Ham Manor Way, E6 87 EN72
H East Ham Mem Hosp, E7 86 EK66
East Ham Shop Hall, E6
off Myrtle Rd 86 EL67
East Harding St, EC4 196 E8
East Heath Rd, NW3 64 DD62
East Hill, SW18 120 DB85
Dartford DA1 128 FM87
Dartford (S.Darenth) DA4 148 FQ95
Oxted RH8 188 EE129
South Croydon CR2 160 DS110
Wembley HA9 62 CN61
Westerham (Bigg.H.) TN16 178 EH118
Woking GU22 167 BC116
East Hill Dr, Dart. DA1 128 FM87
East Hill Rd, Oxt. RH8 188 EE129
Eastholm, NW11 64 DB56
East Holme, Erith DA8 107 FD81
Eastholme, Hayes UB3 77 BU74
DLR East India 85 ED73
East India Dock Rd, E14 85 EA72
East Kent Av, Grav. (Nthflt.)
DA11 130 GC86
Eastlake Rd, SE5 101 DP82
Eastlands Cl, Oxt. RH8
off Eastlands Way 187 ED127
Eastlands Cres, SE21 122 DT86
Eastlands Way, Oxt. RH8 187 ED127
East La, SE16 202 B5
Abbots Langley WD5 7 BU29
Dartford (S.Darenth) DA4 149 FR96
Kingston upon Thames KT1
off High St 137 CK97
Wembley HA0, HA9 61 CK62
Eastlea Av, Wat. WD25 24 BY37
Eastlea Ms, E16
off Desford Rd 86 EE70
Eastleigh Av, Har. HA2 60 CB61
Eastleigh Cl, NW2 62 CS62
Sutton SM2 158 DB108
Eastleigh Rd, E17 47 DZ54
Bexleyheath DA7 107 FC82
Hounslow (Hthrw.Air.) TW6
off Cranford La 95 BT83
Eastleigh Wk, SW15 119 CU87
Eastleigh Way, Felt. TW14 115 BU88
East Lo La, Enf. EN2 29 DK36
H Eastman Dental Hosp,
WC1 196 B4
Eastman Rd, W3 80 CR74
East Mascalls, SE7
off Mascalls Rd 104 EJ79
East Mead, Ruis. HA4 60 BX62
Eastmead, Wok. GU21 166 AV117
Eastmead Av, Grnf. UB6 78 CB69
Eastmead Cl, Brom. BR1 144 EL96
Eastmearn Rd, SE21 122 DQ89
East Mill, Grav. DA11 131 GF86
East Milton Rd, Grav. DA12 131 GK87
EAST MOLESEY 137 CD98
Eastmont Rd, Esher KT10 137 CE103
Eastmoor Pl, SE7
off Eastmoor St 104 EK76
Eastmoor St, SE7 104 EK76
East Mt St, E1 84 DV71
Eastney Rd, Croy. CR0 141 DP102
Eastney St, SE10 103 ED78
Eastnor, Hem.H. (Bov.) HP3 5 BA28
Eastnor Rd, SE9 125 EQ88
Easton Gdns, Borwd. WD6 26 CR42
Easton St, WC1 196 D3
East Pk Cl, Rom. RM6 70 EX57
East Parkside, SE10 205 K5
Warlingham CR6 177 EA116
East Pas, EC1 196 G6
East Pier, E1 202 D3
East Pl, SE27 off Pilgrim Hill 122 DQ91
East Poultry Av, EC1 196 F7
⊖ East Putney 119 CY85
East Ramp, Houns. (Hthrw.Air.)
TW6 95 BP81

★ Place of interest ⇌ Railway station ⊖ London Underground station DLR Docklands Light Railway station ⬦ Tramlink station H Hospital

Eas - Eld

Elderberry Gro, SE27
off Linton Gro 122 DQ92
Elderberry Rd, W5 .....98 CL75
Elderberry Way, Wat. WD25 ...23 BV35
Elder Cl, N20 .....44 DB47
Sidcup DA15 .....125 ET88
West Drayton UB7
off Yew Av 76 BL73
Elder Ct, Bushey (Bushey Hth.)
WD23 .....41 CE47
Elderfield Pl, SW17 .....121 DH91
Elderfield Rd, E5 .....66 DW63
Slough (Stoke P.) SL2 .....74 AT65
Elderfield Wk, E11 .....68 EH57
Elderflower Way, E15 .....86 EE66
Elder Gdns, SE27
off Gladstone Ter 122 DQ91
Elder Oak Cl, SE20 .....142 DV95
Elder Rd, SE27 .....122 DQ92
Eldersley Cl, Red. RH1 .....184 DF132
Elderslie Cl, Beck. BR3 .....143 EB99
Elderslie Rd, SE9 .....125 EN85
Elder St, E1 .....197 P6
Elderton Rd, SE26 .....123 DY91
Eldertree Pl, Mitch. CR4
off Eldertree Way 141 DJ95
Eldertree Way, Mitch. CR4 ...141 DH95
Elder Wk, N1
off Essex Rd 83 DP67
Elder Way, Rain. RM13 .....90 FK69
Slough (Langley) SL3 .....93 AZ75
Elderwood Pl, SE27
off Elder Rd 122 DQ92
Eldon Av, Borwd. WD6 .....26 CN40
Croydon CR0 .....142 DW103
Hounslow TW5 .....96 CA80
Eldon Gro, NW3 .....64 DD64
Eldon Pk, SE25 .....142 DV98
Eldon Rd, E17 .....67 DZ56
N9 .....46 DW47
N22 .....45 DP53
W8 .....100 DB76
Caterham CR3 .....176 DR121
Eldon St, EC2 .....197 L7
Eldon Way, NW10 .....80 CP68
Eldred Dr, Orp. BR5 .....146 EW103
Eldred Gdns, Upmin. RM14 ...73 FS59
Eldred Rd, Bark. IG11 .....87 ES67
Eldrick Ct, Felt. TW14
off Kilross Rd 115 BR88
Eldridge Cl, Felt. TW14 .....115 BU88
Eleanor Av, Epsom KT19 .....156 CR110
Eleanor Cl, N15 off Arnold Rd .66 DT55
SE16 .....203 H4
Eleanor Cres, NW7 .....43 CX49
Eleanor Cross Rd, Wal.Cr.
EN8 .....15 DY34
Eleanor Gdns, Barn. EN5 .....27 CX43
Dagenham RM8 .....70 EZ62
Eleanor Gro, SW13 .....98 CS83
Uxbridge (Ickhm.) UB10 .....59 BP62
Eleanor Rd, E8 .....84 DV66
E15 .....86 EF65
N11 .....45 DL51
Gerrards Cross (Chal.St.P.)
SL9 .....36 AW53
Waltham Cross EN8 .....15 DY33
Eleanor St, E3 .....85 EA69
Eleanor Wk, SE18
off Samuel St 105 EM77
Eleanor Way, Brwd. CM14 .....54 FX50
Waltham Cross EN8 .....15 DZ34
Electric Av, SW9 .....101 DN84
Enfield EN3 .....31 DZ36
Electric La, SW9 .....101 DN84
Electric Par, E18
off George La 48 EG54
Surbiton KT6 .....137 CK100
⇌ **Elephant & Castle** 201 H8
⊖ **Elephant & Castle** 200 G8
Elephant & Castle, SE1 .....200 G7
Elephant & Castle Shop Cen, SE1
off Elephant & Castle 102 DQ77
Elephant La, SE16 .....202 F4
Elephant Rd, SE17 .....201 H8
Elers Rd, W13 .....97 CJ75
Hayes UB3 .....95 BR77
Eleven Acre Ri, Loug. IG10 .....33 EM41
Eley Est, N18 .....46 DW50
Eley Rd, N18 .....47 DX50
Elfindale Rd, SE24 .....122 DQ85
Elfin Gro, Tedd. TW11
off Broad St 117 CF92
Elford Cl, SE3 .....104 EH84
Elfort Rd, N5 .....65 DN63
Elfrida Cres, SE6 .....123 EA91
Elfrida Rd, Wat. WD18 .....24 BW43
Elf Row, E1 .....84 DW73
Elfwine Rd, W7 .....79 CE71
Elgal Cl, Orp. BR6
off Orchard Rd 163 EP106
Elgar Av, NW10
off Mitchellbrook Way 80 CR65
SW16 .....141 DL97
W5 .....98 CL75
Surbiton KT5 .....138 CP101
Elgar Cl, E13 off Bushey Rd ...86 EJ68
SE8 off Comet St 103 EA80
Borehamwood (Elstree)
WD6 .....41 CK45
Buckhurst Hill IG9 .....48 EK47
Uxbridge UB10 .....58 BN61
Elgar Gdns, Til. RM18 .....111 GH81
Elgar St, SE16 .....203 L6
Elgin Av, W9 .....82 DB69
Ashford TW15 .....115 BQ93
Harrow HA3 .....41 CH54
Romford RM3 .....52 FP52
Elgin Cres, W11 .....81 CZ72
Caterham CR3 .....176 DU122
Hounslow (Hthrw.Air.) TW6
off Eastern Perimeter Rd ..95 BS82
Elgin Dr, Nthwd. HA6 .....39 BS52
Elgin Ms, W11
off Ladbroke Gro 81 CY72
Elgin Ms N, W9
off Randolph Av 82 DB69
Elgin Ms S, W9
off Randolph Av 82 DB69
Elgin Rd, N22 .....45 DJ54
Croydon CR0 .....142 DT102
Ilford IG3 .....69 ES60
Sutton SM1 .....140 DC104
Wallington SM6 .....159 DJ107
Waltham Cross (Chsht.)
EN8 .....14 DW30
Weybridge KT13 .....152 BN106
Elgood Av, Nthwd. HA6 .....39 BU51
Elgood Cl, W11
off Avondale Pk Rd 81 CY73
Elham Cl, Brom. BR1 .....124 EK94
Elia Ms, N1 .....196 F1
Elias Pl, SW8 .....101 DN79
Elia St, N1 .....196 F1
Elibank Rd, SE9 .....105 EN84
Elim Est, SE1 .....201 M6
Elim Way, E13 .....86 EF69
Eliot Bk, SE23 .....122 DV89
Eliot Cotts, SE3 off Eliot Pl ...104 EE82
Eliot Ct, N15
off Tynemouth Rd 66 DT56
Eliot Dr, Har. HA2 .....60 CB61
Eliot Gdns, SW15 .....99 CU84
Eliot Hill, SE13 .....103 EC82
Eliot Ms, NW8 .....82 DC68
Eliot Pk, SE13 .....103 EC83
Eliot Pl, SE3 .....104 EE82
Eliot Rd, Dag. RM9 .....70 EX63
Dartford DA1 .....128 FP85
Eliot Vale, SE3 .....103 ED82
Elizabethan Cl, Stai. (Stanw.) TW19
off Elizabethan Way 114 BK87
Elizabethan Way, Stai. (Stanw.)
TW19 .....114 BK87
Elizabeth Av, N1 .....84 DQ66
Amersham HP6 .....20 AV39
Enfield EN2 .....29 DP41
Ilford IG1 .....69 ER61
Staines TW18 .....114 BJ93
Elizabeth Blackwell Ho, N22
off Progress Way 45 DN53
Elizabeth Br, SW1 .....199 H9
Elizabeth Cl, E14
off Grundy St 85 EB72
W9 off Randolph Av 82 DC70
Barnet EN5 .....27 CX41
Romford RM7 .....51 FB53
Sutton SM1 .....157 CZ105
Tilbury RM18 .....111 GH82
Elizabeth Clyde Cl, N15 .....66 DS56
Elizabeth Cotts, Rich. TW9 .....98 CM81
Elizabeth Ct, SW1 .....199 N7
Gravesend DA11
off St. James's Rd 131 GG86
Watford WD17 .....23 BT38
Woodford Green IG8
off Navestock Cres 48 EJ52
Elizabeth Dr, Epp. (They.B.)
CM16 .....33 ES36
Elizabeth Est, SE17 .....102 DR79
Elizabeth Fry Cl, SE18 .....104 EL81
Elizabeth Fry Rd, E8
off Lamb La 84 DV66
Elizabeth Gdns, W3 .....81 CT74
Stanmore HA7 .....41 CJ51
Sunbury-on-Thames
TW16 .....136 BW97
Elizabeth Huggins Cotts, Grav.
DA11 .....131 GG89
Elizabeth Ms, NW3 .....82 DE65
Elizabeth Pl, N15 .....66 DR56
Elizabeth Ride, N9 .....46 DV45
Elizabeth Rd, E6 .....86 EK67
N15 .....66 DS57
Brentwood CM15 .....54 FV44
Grays RM16 .....110 FZ76
Rainham RM13 .....89 FH71
Elizabeth Sq, SE16 .....203 K1
Elizabeth St, SW1 .....198 G8
Greenhithe DA9 .....129 FS85
Elizabeth Ter, SE9 .....125 EM86
Elizabeth Way, SE19 .....122 DR94
Feltham TW13 .....116 BW91
Orpington BR5 .....146 EW99
Slough (Stoke P.) SL2 .....74 AT67
Elkanette Ms, N20
off Ridgeview Rd 44 DC47
Elkington Rd, E13 .....86 EH70
Elkins, The, Rom. RM1 .....51 FE54
Elkins Rd, Slou. (Hedg.) SL2 ..56 AS61
Elkstone Rd, W10 .....81 CZ71
Ellaline Rd, W6 .....99 CX79
Ellanby Cres, N18 .....46 DV50
Elland Rd, SE15 .....102 DW84
Walton-on-Thames KT12 ..136 BX103
Ella Rd, N8 .....65 DL59
Ellement Cl, Pnr. HA5 .....60 BX57
Ellenborough Pl, SW15 .....99 CU84
Ellenborough Rd, N22 .....46 DQ53
Sidcup DA14 .....126 EX92
Ellenbridge Way, S.Croy.
CR2 .....160 DS109
Ellenbrook Cl, Wat. WD24
off Hatfield Rd 23 BV39
Ellen Cl, Brom. BR1 .....144 EK97
Ellen Ct, N9
off Densworth Gro 46 DW47
Ellen St, E1 .....84 DU72
Ellen Webb Dr, Har. (Wldste.)
HA3 .....61 CE55
Elleray Rd, Tedd. TW11 .....117 CF93
Ellerby St, SW6 .....99 CX81
Ellerdale Cl, NW3
off Ellerdale Rd 64 DC63
Ellerdale Rd, NW3 .....64 DC64
Ellerdale St, SE13 .....103 EB84
Ellerdine Rd, Houns. TW3 .....96 CC84
Ellerker Gdns, Rich. TW10 .....118 CL86
Ellerman Av, Twick. TW2 .....116 BZ88
Ellerman Rd, Til. RM18 .....111 GF82
Ellerslie, Grav. DA12 .....131 GK87
Ellerslie Gdns, NW10 .....81 CU67
Ellerslie Rd, W12 .....81 CV74
Ellerslie Sq Ind Est, SW2 .....121 DL85
Ellerton Gdns, Dag. RM9 .....88 EW66
Ellerton Rd, SW13 .....99 CU81
SW18 .....120 DD88
SW20 .....119 CU94
Dagenham RM9 .....88 EW66
Surbiton KT6 .....138 CM103
Ellery Rd, SE19 .....122 DR94
Ellery St, SE15 .....102 DV82
Ellesborough Cl, Wat. WD19 ..40 BW50
Ellesmere Av, NW7 .....42 CR48
Beckenham BR3 .....143 EB96
Ellesmere Cl, E11 .....68 EF57
Ruislip HA4 .....59 BQ59
Ellesmere Dr, S.Croy. CR2 ...160 DV114
Ellesmere Gdns, Ilf. IG4 .....68 EL57
Ellesmere Gro, Barn. EN5 .....27 CZ43
Ellesmere Pl, Walt. KT12 .....153 BS106
Ellesmere Rd, E3 .....85 DY68
NW10 .....63 CU64
W4 .....98 CR79
Greenford UB6 .....78 CC70
Twickenham TW1 .....117 CJ86
Weybridge KT13 .....153 BR107
Ellesmere St, E14 .....85 EB72
Ellice Rd, Oxt. RH8 .....188 EF129
Elliman Av, Slou. SL2 .....74 AS73
Ellingfort Rd, E8 .....84 DV66
Ellingham Rd, E15 .....67 ED63
W12 .....99 CU75
Chessington KT9 .....155 CK107
Ellington Rd, N10 .....65 DH56
Feltham TW13 .....115 BT91
Hounslow TW3 .....96 CB82
Ellington St, N7 .....83 DN65
Ellington Way, Epsom KT18 ..173 CV117
Elliot Cl, E15 .....86 EE66
Elliot Rd, NW4 .....63 CV58
Stanmore HA7 .....41 CG51
Elliott Av, Ruis. HA4 .....59 BV61
Elliott Cl, Wem. HA9 .....62 CM62
Elliott Gdns, Rom. RM3 .....51 FH53
Shepperton TW17 .....134 BN98
Elliott Rd, SW9 .....101 DP80
W4 .....98 CS77
Bromley BR2 .....144 EK98
Thornton Heath CR7 .....141 DP98
Elliotts Cl, Uxb. (Cowley) UB8 .76 BJ71
Elliotts La, West. (Brasted)
TN16 .....180 EW124
Elliott's Pl, N1
off St. Peters St 83 DP67
Elliott Sq, NW3 .....82 DE66
Elliotts Row, SE11 .....200 F8
Elliott St, Grav. DA12 .....131 GK87
Ellis Av, Ger.Cr. (Chal.St.P.)
SL9 .....37 AZ53
Rainham RM13 .....89 FG71
Slough SL1 .....92 AS75
Ellis Cl, NW10
off High Rd 81 CV65
SE9 .....125 EQ89
Coulsdon CR5 .....175 DM120
Elliscombe Rd, SE7 .....104 EJ78
Ellis Ct, W7 .....79 CF71
Ellis Fm Cl, Wok. GU22 .....166 AX122
Ellisfield Dr, SW15 .....119 CT87
Ellis Ms, SE7 .....104 EJ79
Ellison Gdns, Sthl. UB2 .....96 BZ77
Ellison Ho, SE13
off Lewisham Rd 103 EC82
Ellison Rd, SW13 .....99 CT82
SW16 .....121 DK94
Sidcup DA15 .....125 ER88
Ellis Rd, Couls. CR5 .....175 DM120
Mitcham CR4 .....140 DF100
Southall UB2 .....78 CC74
Ellis St, SW1 .....198 E8
Elliston Ho, SE18 .....105 EN77
Ellis Way, Dart. DA1 .....128 FM89
Ellmore Cl, Rom. RM3 .....51 FH53
Ellora Rd, SW16 .....121 DK92
Ellsworth St, E2 .....84 DV69
Ellwood Ct, W9
off Clearwell Dr 82 DB70
Ellwood Gdns, Wat. WD25 .....7 BV34
Ellwood Ri, Ch.St.G. HP8 .....36 AW47
Elmar Rd, N15 .....66 DR56
Elm Av, W5 .....80 CL74
Carshalton SM5 .....158 DF110
Ruislip HA4 .....59 BU60
Upminster RM14 .....72 FP62
Watford WD19 .....40 BY45
Elmbank, N14 .....45 DL45
Elm Bk, Brom. BR1 .....144 EK96
Elmbank Av, Barn. EN5 .....27 CW42
Egham (Eng.Grn.) TW20 ...112 AV93
Elm Bk Gdns, SW13 .....98 CS82
Elmbank Way, W7 .....79 CD71
Elmbourne Dr, Belv. DA17 .....107 FB77
Elmbourne Rd, SW17 .....120 DG90
Elmbridge Av, Surb. KT5 .....138 CP99
Elmbridge Cl, Ruis. HA4 .....59 BU58
Elmbridge Dr, Ruis. HA4 .....59 BT57
Elmbridge La, Wok. GU22 .....167 AZ119
★ **Elmbridge Mus**, Wey.
KT13 .....152 BN105
Elmbridge Rd, Ilf. IG6 .....50 EU51
Elmbridge Wk, E8
off Wilman Gro 84 DU66
Elmbrook Cl, Sun. TW16 .....135 BV95
Elmbrook Gdns, SE9 .....104 EL84
Elmbrook Rd, Sutt. SM1 .....157 CZ105
Elm Cl, E11 .....68 EH58
N19 off Hargrave Pk 65 DJ61
NW4 .....63 CX57
SW20 off Grand Dr 139 CW98
Buckhurst Hill IG9 .....48 EK47
Carshalton SM5 .....140 DF102
Dartford DA1 .....128 FJ88
Harrow HA2 .....60 CB58
Hayes UB3 .....77 BU72
Leatherhead KT22 .....171 CH122
Romford RM7 .....51 FB54
South Croydon CR2 .....160 DS107
Staines (Stanw.) TW19 .....114 BK88
Surbiton KT5 .....138 CQ101
Tadworth KT20 .....182 CQ130
Elm Cl, Twick. TW2 .....116 CB89
Waltham Abbey EN9 .....15 ED34
Warlingham CR6 .....177 DX117
Woking GU21 .....166 AX115
Woking (Send M.) GU23 ..168 BG124
ELM CORNER, Wok. 168 BN119
Elmcote Way, Rick. (Crox.Grn.)
WD3 .....22 BM44
Elm Ct, EC4 .....196 D10
Mitcham CR4
off Armfield Cres 140 DF96
Sunbury-on-Thames TW16 .115 BT94
Elmcourt Rd, SE27 .....121 DP89
Elm Cres, W5 .....80 CL74
Kingston upon Thames
KT2 .....138 CL95
Elmcroft, N8 .....65 DM57
Leatherhead KT23 .....170 CA124
Elm Cft, Slou. (Datchet) SL3 ..92 AW81
Elmcroft Av, E11 .....68 EH57
N9 .....30 DV44
NW11 .....63 CZ59
Sidcup DA15 .....125 ET86
Elmcroft Cl, E11 .....68 EH56
W5 .....79 CK72
Chessington KT9 .....138 CL104
Feltham TW14 .....115 BT86
Elmcroft Cres, NW11 .....63 CY59
Harrow HA2 .....60 CA55
Elmcroft Dr, Ashf. TW15 .....114 BN92
Chessington KT9 .....138 CL104
Elmcroft Gdns, NW9 .....62 CN57
Elmcroft Rd, Orp. BR6 .....146 EU101
Elmcroft St, E5 .....66 DW63
Elmdale Rd, N13 .....45 DM50
Elmdene, Surb. KT5 .....138 CQ102
Elmdene Av, Horn. RM11 .....72 FM57
Elmdene Cl, Beck. BR3 .....143 DZ99
Elmdene Ct, Wok. GU22
off Constitution Hill 166 AY118
Elmdene Rd, SE18 .....105 EP78
Elmdon Rd, Houns. TW4 .....96 BX82
Hounslow (Hatt.Cr.) TW6 ...95 BT83
Elm Dr, Har. HA2 .....60 CB58
Leatherhead KT22 .....171 CH122
Sunbury-on-Thames
TW16 .....136 BW96
Swanley BR8 .....147 FD96
Waltham Cross (Chsht.)
EN8 .....15 DY28
Woking (Chobham) GU24 .150 AT110
Elmer Av, Rom. (Hav.at.Bow.)
RM4 .....51 FE48
Elmer Cl, Enf. EN2 .....29 DM41
Rainham RM13 .....89 FG66
Elmer Cotts, Lthd. KT22 .....171 CG123
Elmer Gdns, Edg. HA8 .....42 CP52
Isleworth TW7 .....97 CD83
Rainham RM13 .....89 FG66
Elmer Ms, Lthd. (Fetch.)
KT22 .....171 CG123
Elmer Rd, SE6 .....123 EC87
Elmers Dr, Tedd. TW11
off Kingston Rd 117 CH93
ELMERS END, Beck. 143 DY97
⇌ **Elmers End** 143 DX98
Tramlink **Elmers End** 143 DX98
Elmers End Rd, SE20 .....142 DW96
Beckenham BR3 .....142 DW96
Elmerside Rd, Beck. BR3 .....143 DY98
Elmers Rd, SE25 .....142 DU101
Elm Fm Caravan Pk, Cher. (Lyne)
KT16 .....133 BC101
Elmfield, Lthd. (Bkhm.) KT23 .170 CA123
Elmfield Av, N8 .....65 DL57
Mitcham CR4 .....140 DG95
Teddington TW11 .....117 CF92
Elmfield Cl, Grav. DA11 .....131 GH88
Harrow HA1 .....61 CE61
Potters Bar EN6 .....11 CY33
Elmfield Pk, Brom. BR1 .....144 EG97
Elmfield Rd, E4 .....47 EC47
E17 .....67 DX58
N2 .....64 DD55
SW17 .....120 DG89
Bromley BR1 .....144 EG97
Potters Bar EN6 .....11 CY33
Southall UB2 .....96 BY76
Elmfield Way, W9 .....82 DA71
South Croydon CR2 .....160 DT109
Elm Friars Wk, NW1 .....83 DK66
Elm Gdns, N2 .....64 DC55
Enfield EN2 .....30 DR38
Epping (N.Wld.Bas.) CM16 .19 FB26
Epsom KT18 .....173 CW119
Esher (Clay.) KT10 .....155 CF107
Mitcham CR4 .....141 DK98
Elmgate Av, Felt. TW13 .....115 BV90
Elmgate Gdns, Edg. HA8 .....42 CR50
Elm Grn, W3 .....80 CS72
Elmgreen Cl, E15
off Church St N 86 EE67
Elm Gro, N8 .....65 DL58
NW2 .....63 CX63
SE15 .....102 DT82
SW19 .....119 CY94
Caterham CR3 .....176 DS122
Epsom KT18 .....156 CQ114
Erith DA8 .....107 FD80
Harrow HA2 .....60 CA59
Hornchurch RM11 .....72 FL58
Kingston upon Thames
KT2 .....138 CL95
Orpington BR6 .....145 ET102
Sutton SM1 .....158 DB105
Watford WD24 .....23 BU37
West Drayton UB7
off Willow Av 76 BM73
Woodford Green IG8 .....48 EF50
Elmgrove Cres, Har. HA1 .....61 CF57
Elmgrove Gdns, Har. HA1 .....61 CG57
Elm Gro Par, Wall. SM6
off Butter Hill 140 DG104
Elm Gro Rd, SW13 .....99 CU82
W5 .....98 CL75
Cobham KT11 .....170 BX116
Elmgrove Rd, Croy. CR0 .....142 DV101
Elmgrove Rd, Har. HA1 .....61 CF57
Weybridge KT13 .....152 BN105
Elm Hall Gdns, E11 .....68 EH57
Elmhurst, Belv. DA17 .....106 EY79
Elmhurst Av, N2 .....64 DD55
Mitcham CR4 .....121 DH94
Elmhurst Dr, E18 .....48 EG54
Hornchurch RM11 .....72 FJ60
Elmhurst Gdns, E18
off Elmhurst Dr 48 EH53
Elmhurst Rd, E7 .....86 EH66
N17 .....46 DT54
SE9 .....124 EL89
Enfield EN3 .....30 DW37
Slough SL3 .....93 BA76
Elmhurst St, SW4 .....101 DK83
Elmhurst Vil, SE15
off Cheltenham Rd 102 DW84
Elmhurst Way, Loug. IG10 .....49 EM45
Elmington Cl, Bex. DA5 .....127 FB86
Elmington Est, SE5 .....102 DR80
Elmington Rd, SE5 .....102 DR81
Elmira St, SE13 .....103 EB83
Elm La, SE6 .....123 DZ89
Woking GU23 .....169 BP118
Elm Lawn Cl, Uxb. UB8
off Park Rd 76 BL66
Elmlea Dr, Hayes UB3
off Grange Rd 77 BS71
Elmlee Cl, Chis. BR7 .....125 EM93
Elmley Cl, E6
off Northumberland Rd ...86 EL71
Elmley St, SE18 .....105 ER77
Elm Ms, Rich. TW10
off Grove Rd 118 CM86
Elmore Cl, Wem. HA0 .....80 CL68
Elmore Rd, E11 .....67 EC62
Coulsdon CR5 .....174 DF121
Enfield EN3 .....31 DX39
Elmores, Loug. IG10 .....33 EN41
Elmore St, N1 .....84 DQ66
Elm Par, Horn. RM12
off St. Nicholas Av 71 FH63
ELM PARK, Horn. 71 FH64
⊖ **Elm Park** 71 FH63
Elm Pk, SW2 .....121 DM86
Stanmore HA7 .....41 CH50
Elm Pk Av, N15 .....66 DT57
Hornchurch RM12 .....71 FG63
Elm Pk Ct, Pnr. HA5 .....60 BW55
Elm Pk Gdns, NW4 .....63 CX57
SW10 .....100 DD78
Elmpark Gdns, S.Croy. CR2 ..160 DW110
Elm Pk La, SW3 .....100 DD78
Elm Pk Mans, SW10
off Park Wk 100 DC79
Elm Pk Rd, E10 .....67 DY60
N3 .....43 CZ52
N21 .....46 DQ45
SE25 .....142 DT97
SW3 .....100 DD79
Pinner HA5 .....40 BW54
Elm Pl, SW7 .....100 DD78
Elm Quay Ct, SW8 .....101 DK79
Elm Rd, E7 .....86 EF65
E11 .....67 ED61
E17 .....67 EC57
N22 off Granville Rd 45 DP53
SW14 .....98 CQ83
Barnet EN5 .....27 CZ42
Beckenham BR3 .....143 DZ96
Chessington KT9 .....156 CL105
Dartford DA1 .....128 FK88
Epsom KT17 .....157 CT107
Erith DA8 .....107 FG81
Esher (Clay.) KT10 .....155 CF107
Feltham TW14 .....115 BR88
Gravesend DA12 .....131 GJ90
Grays RM17 .....110 GC79
Greenhithe DA9 .....129 FS86
Kingston upon Thames
KT2 .....138 CM95
Leatherhead KT22 .....171 CH122
New Malden KT3 .....138 CR98
Orpington BR6 .....164 EU108
Purley CR8 .....159 DP113
Redhill RH1 .....184 DE134
Romford RM7 .....51 FB54
Sidcup DA14 .....126 EU91
South Ockendon (Aveley)
RM15 .....90 FQ74
Thornton Heath CR7 .....142 DR98
Wallington SM6 .....140 DG102
Warlingham CR6 .....177 DX117
Wembley HA9 .....62 CL64
Westerham TN16 .....189 ES125
Woking GU21 .....166 AX118
Woking (Horsell) GU21 ...167 AZ115
Elm Rd W, Sutt. SM3 .....139 CZ101
Elm Row, NW3 .....64 DC62
Elmroyd Av, Pot.B. EN6 .....11 CZ33
Elmroyd Cl, Pot.B. EN6 .....11 CZ33
Elms, The, SW13 .....99 CT83
Elms Av, N10 .....65 DH55
NW4 .....63 CX57
Elmscott Gdns, N21 .....30 DQ44
Elmscott Rd, Brom. BR1 .....124 EF92
Elms Ct, Wem. HA0 .....61 CF63
Elms Cres, SW4 .....121 DJ86
Elmscroft Gdns, Pot.B. EN6 ...11 CY32
Elmsdale Rd, E17 .....67 DZ56
Elms Fm Rd, Horn. RM12 .....72 FJ64
Elms Gdns, Dag. RM9 .....70 EZ63
Wembley HA0 .....61 CG63
Elmshaw Rd, SW15 .....119 CU85
Elmshorn, Epsom KT17 .....173 CW116
Elmshurst Cres, N2 .....64 DD56
Elmside, Croy. (New Adgtn.)
CR0 .....161 EB107
Elmside Rd, Wem. HA9 .....62 CN62
Elms La, Wem. HA0 .....61 CG63
Elmsleigh Av, Har. HA3 .....61 CH56
Elmsleigh Cen, The, Stai.
TW18 .....113 BF91

Elm - Esh

Elmsleigh Ct, Sutt. SM1 ....140 DB104
Elmsleigh Rd, Stai. TW18 ....113 BF92
Twickenham TW2 ....117 CD89
Elmslie Cl, Epsom KT18 ....156 CQ114
Woodford Green IG8 ....49 EM51
Elmslie Pt, E3 ....85 DZ71
Elms Ms, W2 ....82 DD73
Elms Pk Av, Wem. HA0 ....61 CG63
Elms Rd, SW4 ....121 DJ85
Gerrards Cross (Chal.St.P.)
SL9 ....36 AY52
Harrow HA3 ....41 CE52
ELMSTEAD, Chis. 124 EK92
Elmstead Av, Chis. BR7 ....125 EM92
Wembley HA9 ....62 CL60
Elmstead Cl, N20 ....44 DA47
Epsom KT19 ....156 CS106
Sevenoaks TN13 ....190 FE122
Elmstead Cres, Well. DA16 ....106 EW79
Elmstead Gdns, Wor.Pk.
KT4 ....139 CU104
Elmstead Glade, Chis. BR7 ....125 EM93
Elmstead La, Chis. BR7 ....125 EM92
Elmstead Rd, Erith DA8 ....107 FE81
Ilford IG3 ....69 ES61
West Byfleet KT14 ....152 BG113
⇌ Elmstead Woods 124 EL93
Elmstone Rd, SW6 ....100 DA81
Elm St, WC1 ....196 C5
Elmsway, Ashf. TW15 ....114 BM92
Elmswood, Lthd. (Bkhm.)
KT23 ....170 BZ124
Elmsworth Av, Houns. TW3 ....96 CB82
Elm Ter, NW2 ....64 DA62
NW3
off Constantine Rd 64 DE63
SE9 ....125 EN86
Grays RM20 ....109 FV79
Harrow HA3 ....41 CD52
Elmton Way, E5
off Rendlesham Rd 66 DU62
Elm Tree Av, Esher KT10 ....137 CD101
Elm Tree Cl, NW8 ....82 DD69
Ashford TW15
off Convent Rd 115 BP92
Chertsey KT16 ....133 BE103
Northolt UB5 ....78 BZ68
Elmtree Cl, W.Byf. (Byfleet)
KT14 ....152 BL113
Elm Tree Rd, NW8 ....82 DD69
Elmtree Rd, Tedd. TW11 ....117 CE91
Elm Tree Wk, Rick. (Chorl.)
WD3 ....21 BF42
Elm Wk, NW3 ....64 DA61
SW20 ....139 CW98
Orpington BR6 ....145 EM104
Radlett WD7 ....25 CF36
Romford RM2 ....71 FG55
Elm Way, N11 ....44 DG51
NW10 ....62 CS63
Brentwood CM14 ....54 FU48
Epsom KT19 ....156 CR106
Rickmansworth WD3 ....38 BH46
Worcester Park KT4 ....139 CW104
Elmwood Av, N13 ....45 DL50
Borehamwood WD6 ....26 CP42
Feltham TW13 ....115 BU89
Harrow HA3 ....61 CG57
Elmwood Cl, Ashtd. KT21 ....171 CK117
Epsom KT17 ....157 CU108
Wallington SM6 ....140 DG103
Elmwood Ct, SW11 ....101 DH81
Ashtead KT21
off Elmwood Cl 171 CK117
Wembley HA0 ....61 CG62
Elmwood Cres, NW9 ....62 CQ56
Elmwood Dr, Bex. DA5 ....126 EY87
Epsom KT17 ....157 CU107
Elmwood Gdns, W7 ....79 CE72
Elmwood Pk, Ger.Cr. SL9 ....56 AY60
Elmwood Rd, SE24 ....122 DR85
W4 ....98 CQ79
Croydon CR0 ....141 DP101
Mitcham CR4 ....140 DF97
Redhill RH1 ....184 DG130
Slough SL2 ....74 AV73
Elmworth Gro, SE21 ....122 DR89
Elnathan Ms, W9
off Shirland Rd 82 DB70
Elphinstone Rd, E17 ....47 DZ54
Elphinstone St, N5
off Avenell Rd 65 DP63
Elrick Cl, Erith DA8
off Queen St 107 FE79
Elrington Rd, E8 ....84 DU65
Woodford Green IG8 ....48 EG50
Elruge Cl, West Dr. UB7 ....94 BK76
Elsa Rd, Well. DA16 ....106 EV82
Elsa St, E1 ....85 DY71
Elsdale St, E9 ....84 DW65
Elsden Ms, E2
off Old Ford Rd 84 DW68
Elsden Rd, N17 ....46 DT53
Elsdon Rd, Wok. GU21 ....166 AU117
Elsenham Rd, E12 ....69 EN64
Elsenham St, SW18 ....119 CZ88
Elsham Rd, E11 ....68 EE62
W14 ....99 CY75
Elsham Ter, W14 ....99 CY76
Elsiedene Rd, N21 ....46 DQ45
Elsiemaud Rd, SE4 ....123 DZ85
Elsie Rd, SE22 ....102 DT84
Elsinge Rd, Enf. EN1 ....30 DV36
Elsinore Av, Stai. TW19 ....114 BL87
Elsinore Gdns, NW2 ....63 CY62
Elsinore Rd, SE23 ....123 DY88
Elsinore Way, Rich. TW9
off Lower Richmond Rd 98 CP83
Elsley Rd, SW11 ....100 DF83
Elspeth Rd, SW11 ....100 DF84
Wembley HA0 ....62 CL64
Elsrick Av, Mord. SM4
off Chalgrove Av 140 DA99
Elstan Way, Croy. CR0 ....143 DY101
Elstead Ct, Sutt. SM3
off Stonecot Hill 139 CY102
Elsted St, SE17 ....201 L9
Elstow Cl, SE9 ....125 EN85
Ruislip HA4 ....60 BX59
Elstow Gdns, Dag. RM9 ....88 EY67
Elstow Rd, Dag. RM9 ....88 EY66
ELSTREE, Borwd. 25 CK43
★ Elstree Aerodrome, Borwd.
WD6 ....25 CF41
⇌ Elstree & Borehamwood 26 CM42
Elstree Gdns, N9 ....46 DV46
Belvedere DA17 ....106 EY77
Ilford IG1 ....69 EQ64
Elstree Hill, Brom. BR1 ....124 EE94
Elstree Hill N, Borwd. (Elstree)
WD6 ....25 CK44
Elstree Hill S, Borwd. (Elstree)
WD6 ....41 CJ45
Elstree Pk, Borwd. WD6 ....26 CR44
Elstree Rd, Borwd. (Elstree)
WD6 ....25 CG44
Bushey (Bushey Hth.)
WD23 ....41 CD45
Elstree Way, Borwd. WD6 ....26 CP41
Elswick Rd, SE13 ....103 EB82
Elswick St, SW6 ....100 DC82
Elsworth Cl, Felt. TW14 ....115 BS88
Elsworthy, T.Ditt. KT7 ....137 CE100
Elsworthy Ri, NW3 ....82 DE66
Elsworthy Rd, NW3 ....82 DE67
Elsworthy Ter, NW3 ....82 DE66
Elsynge Rd, SW18 ....120 DD85
ELTHAM, SE9 ....124 EK86
⇌ Eltham 125 EM85
Eltham Grn, SE9 ....124 EJ85
Eltham Grn Rd, SE9 ....104 EJ84
Eltham High St, SE9 ....125 EM86
Eltham Hill, SE9 ....124 EK85
★ Eltham Palace, SE9 ....124 EL87
Eltham Palace Rd, SE9 ....124 EJ86
Eltham Pk Gdns, SE9 ....105 EN84
Eltham Rd, SE9 ....124 EJ85
SE12 ....124 EF85
Elthiron Rd, SW6 ....100 DA81
Elthorne Av, W7 ....97 CF75
Elthorne Ct, Felt. TW13 ....116 BW88
Elthorne Pk Rd, W7 ....97 CF75
Elthorne Rd, N19 ....65 DK61
NW9 ....62 CR59
Uxbridge UB8 ....76 BK68
Elthorne Way, NW9 ....62 CR58
Elthruda Rd, SE13 ....123 ED86
Eltisley Rd, Ilf. IG1 ....69 EP63
Elton Av, Barn. EN5 ....27 CZ43
Greenford UB6 ....79 CF65
Wembley HA0 ....61 CH64
Elton Cl, Kings.T. KT1 ....117 CJ94
Elton Ho, E3 ....85 DZ67
Elton Pk, Wat. WD17 ....23 BV40
Elton Pl, N16 ....66 DS64
Elton Rd, Kings.T. KT2 ....138 CM95
Purley CR8 ....159 DJ112
Elton Way, Wat. WD25 ....24 CB40
Eltringham St, SW18 ....100 DC84
Elvaston Ms, SW7 ....100 DC76
Elvaston Pl, SW7 ....100 DC76
Elveden Cl, Wok. GU22 ....168 BH117
Elveden Pl, NW10 ....80 CN68
Elveden Rd, NW10 ....80 CN68
Elvedon Rd, Cob. KT11 ....153 BV111
Elvendon Rd, N13 ....45 DL51
Elver Gdns, E2
off St. Peter's Cl 84 DU68
DLR Elverson Road 103 EB82
Elverson Rd, SE8 ....103 EB82
Elverton St, SW1 ....199 M8
Elvet Av, Rom. RM2 ....72 FJ56
Elvington Grn, Brom. BR2 ....144 EF99
Elvington La, NW9 ....42 CS53
Elvino Rd, SE26 ....123 DY92
Elvis Rd, NW2 ....81 CW65
Elwell Cl, Egh. TW20
off Mowbray Cres 113 BA92
Elwick Rd, S.Ock. RM15 ....91 FW72
Elwill Way, Beck. BR3 ....143 EC98
Elwin St, E2 ....84 DU69
Elwood St, N5 ....65 DP62
Elwyn Gdns, SE12 ....124 EG87
Ely Cl, Amer. HP7 ....20 AS39
Erith DA8 ....107 FF82
New Malden KT3 ....139 CT96
Ely Ct, EC1 ....196 E7
Ely Gdns, Borwd. WD6 ....26 CR43
Dagenham RM10 ....71 FC62
Ilford IG1
off Canterbury Av 68 EL59
Elyne Rd, N4 ....65 DN58
Ely Pl, EC1 ....196 E7
Woodford Green IG8 ....49 EN51
Ely Rd, E10 ....67 EC58
Croydon CR0 ....142 DR99
Hounslow (Hthrw.Air.) TW6
off Eastern Perimeter Rd 95 BT82
Hounslow (Houns.W.) TW4 ....96 BW83
Elysian Av, Orp. BR5 ....145 ET100
Elysium Pl, SW6
off Fulham Pk Gdns 99 CZ82
Elysium St, SW6
off Fulham Pk Gdns 99 CZ82
Elystan Business Cen, Hayes
UB4 ....78 BW73
Elystan Cl, Wall. SM6 ....159 DH109
Elystan Pl, SW3 ....198 C10
Elystan St, SW3 ....198 B9
Elystan Wk, N1
off Cloudesley Rd 83 DN67
Emanuel Av, W3 ....80 CQ72
Emanuel Dr, Hmptn. TW12 ....116 BZ92
⊖ Embankment 200 A2
Embankment, SW15 ....99 CX82
Embankment, The, Stai. (Wrays.)
TW19 ....112 AW87
Twickenham TW1 ....117 CG88
Embankment Gdns, SW3 ....100 DF79
Embankment Pl, WC2 ....200 A2
Embassy Ct, Sid. DA14 ....126 EV90
Embassy Ct, Well. DA16
off Welling High St 106 EV83
Embassy Gdns, Beck. BR3
off Blakeney Rd 143 DZ95
Emba St, SE16 ....202 C5
Ember Cen, Walt. KT12 ....136 BY103
Ember Cl, Add. KT15 ....152 BK106
Orpington BR5 ....145 EQ101
Embercourt Rd, T.Ditt. KT7 ....137 CE100
Ember Fm Av, E.Mol. KT8 ....137 CD100
Ember Fm Way, E.Mol. KT8 ....137 CD100
Ember Gdns, T.Ditt. KT7 ....137 CE101
Ember La, E.Mol. KT8 ....137 CD101
Esher KT10 ....137 CD101
Ember Rd, Slou. SL3 ....93 BB76
Emberson Way, Epp. (N.Wld.Bas.)
CM16 ....19 FC26
Emberton, SE5 ....102 DS79
Embleton Rd, SE13 ....103 EB83
Watford WD19 ....39 BU48
Embleton Wk, Hmptn. TW12
off Fearnley Cres 116 BZ93
Embry Cl, Stan. HA7 ....41 CG49
Embry Dr, Stan. HA7 ....41 CG51
Embry Way, Stan. HA7 ....41 CG50
Emden Cl, West Dr. UB7 ....94 BN75
Emden St, SW6 ....100 DB81
Emerald Cl, E16 ....86 EL72
Emerald Ct, Slou. SL1 ....92 AS75
Emerald Gdns, Dag. RM8 ....70 FA60
Emerald Sq, Sthl. UB2 ....96 BX76
Emerald St, WC1 ....196 B6
Emerson Dr, Horn. RM11 ....72 FK59
Emerson Gdns, Har. HA3 ....62 CM58
EMERSON PARK, Horn. 72 FL58
⇌ Emerson Park 72 FL59
Emerson Rd, Ilf. IG1 ....69 EN59
Emersons Av, Swan. BR8 ....127 FF94
Emerson St, SE1 ....201 H2
Emerton Cl, Bexh. DA6 ....106 EY84
Emerton Rd, Lthd. KT22 ....170 CC120
Emery Hill St, SW1 ....199 L7
Emery St, SE1 ....200 E6
Emes Rd, Erith DA8 ....107 FC80
Emilia Cl, Enf. EN3 ....30 DV43
Emily Davidson Dr, Epsom
KT18 ....173 CV118
Emily Jackson Cl, Sev. TN13 ....191 FH124
Emily Pl, N7 ....65 DN63
Emley Rd, Add. KT15 ....134 BG104
Emlyn Gdns, W12 ....98 CS75
Emlyn La, Lthd. KT22 ....171 CG122
Emlyn Rd, W12 ....98 CS75
Emmanuel Lo, Wal.Cr. (Chsht.)
EN8 off College Rd 14 DW30
Emmanuel Rd, SW12 ....121 DJ88
Northwood HA6 ....39 BT52
Emma Rd, E13 ....86 EF68
Emma St, E2 ....84 DV68
Emmaus Way, Chig. IG7 ....49 EN50
Emmett Cl, Rad. (Shenley)
WD7 ....10 CL33
Emmetts Cl, Wok. GU21 ....166 AW117
Emmott Av, Ilf. IG6 ....69 EQ57
Emmott Cl, E1 ....85 DY70
NW11 ....64 DC58
Emms Pas, Kings.T. KT1
off High St 137 CK96
Emperor's Gate, SW7 ....100 DB76
Empire Av, N18 ....46 DQ50
Empire Ct, Wem. HA9 ....62 CP62
Empire Rd, Grnf. UB6 ....79 CJ67
Empire Sq, N7 ....65 DL62
SE20 off High St 123 DX94
Empire Way, Wem. HA9 ....62 CM63
Empire Wf Rd, E14 ....204 F9
Empress Av, E4 ....47 EA52
E12 ....68 EJ61
Ilford IG1 ....69 EM61
Woodford Green IG8 ....48 EF52
Empress Dr, Chis. BR7 ....125 EP93
Empress Pl, SW6 ....100 DA78
Empress Rd, Grav. DA12 ....131 GL87
Empress St, SE17 ....102 DQ79
Empson St, E3 ....85 EB70
Emsworth Cl, N9 ....46 DW46
Emsworth Rd, Ilf. IG6 ....49 EP54
Emsworth St, SW2 ....121 DM89
Emu Rd, SW8 ....101 DH82
Ena Rd, SW16 ....141 DL97
Enborne Grn, S.Ock. RM15
off Elan Rd 91 FU71
Enbrook St, W10 ....81 CY69
Endale Cl, Cars. SM5 ....140 DF103
Endeavour Ho, Barn. EN5 ....28 DC42
Endeavour Rd, Wal.Cr. (Chsht.)
EN8 ....15 DY27
Endeavour Way, SW19 ....120 DB91
Barking IG11 ....88 EU68
Croydon CR0 ....141 DK101
Endell St, WC2 ....195 P8
Enderby St, SE10 ....205 H10
Enderley Cl, Har. HA3
off Enderley Rd 41 CE53
Enderley Rd, Har. HA3 ....41 CE53
Endersby Rd, Barn. EN5 ....27 CW43
Endersleigh Gdns, NW4 ....63 CU56
Endlebury Rd, E4 ....47 EB47
Endlesham Rd, SW12 ....120 DG87
Endsleigh Cl, S.Croy. CR2 ....160 DW110
Endsleigh Gdns, WC1 ....195 M4
Ilford IG1 ....69 EM61
Surbiton KT6 ....137 CJ100
Walton-on-Thames
KT12 ....154 BW106
Endsleigh Pl, WC1 ....195 N4
Endsleigh Rd, W13 ....79 CG73
Redhill RH1 ....185 DJ129
Southall UB2 ....96 BY77
Endsleigh St, WC1 ....195 M4
Endway, Surb. KT5 ....138 CN101
Endwell Rd, SE4 ....103 DY82
Endymion Rd, N4 ....65 DN59
SW2 ....121 DM86
Energen Cl, NW10 ....80 CS65
ENFIELD 30 DT41
⇌ Enfield Chase 30 DQ41
Enfield Cl, Uxb. UB8
off Villier St 76 BK68
ENFIELD HIGHWAY, Enf. 30 DW41
ENFIELD LOCK, Enf. 31 DZ37
⇌ Enfield Lock 31 DY37
Enfield Retail Pk, Enf. EN1 ....30 DV41
Enfield Rd, N1 ....84 DS66
W3 ....98 CP75
Brentford TW8 ....97 CK78
Enfield EN2 ....29 DK42
Hounslow (Hthrw.Air.) TW6
off Eastern Perimeter Rd 95 BS82
ENFIELD TOWN, Enf. 30 DR40
⇌ Enfield Town 30 DS42
Enfield Wk, Brent. TW8 ....97 CK78
ENFIELD WASH, Enf. 31 DX38
Enford St, W1 ....194 D6
Engadine Cl, Croy. CR0 ....142 DT104
Engadine St, SW18 ....119 CZ88
Engate St, SE13 ....103 EC84
Engayne Gdns, Upmin. RM14 ....72 FP60
Engel Pk, NW7 ....43 CW51
Engineer Cl, SE18 ....105 EN79
Engineers Way, Wem. HA9 ....62 CN63
Englands La, NW3 ....82 DF65
Loughton IG10 ....33 EN40
England Way, N.Mal. KT3 ....138 CP98
Englefield Cl, Croy. CR0
off Queen's Rd 142 DQ100
Egham (Eng.Grn.) TW20
off Alexandra Rd 112 AW93
Enfield EN2 ....29 DN40
Orpington BR5 ....145 ET98
Englefield Cres, Orp. BR5 ....145 ET98
ENGLEFIELD GREEN, Egh. 112 AV92
Englefield Grn, Egh. (Eng.Grn.)
TW20 ....112 AW91
Englefield Path, Orp. BR5 ....145 ET98
Englefield Rd, N1 ....84 DR65
Orpington BR5 ....146 EU98
Engleheart Dr, Felt. TW14 ....115 BT86
Engleheart Rd, SE6 ....123 EB87
Englehurst, Egh. (Eng.Grn.)
TW20 ....112 AW93
Englemere Pk, Lthd. (Oxshott)
KT22 ....154 CB114
Englewood Rd, SW12 ....121 DH86
Engliff La, Wok. GU22 ....167 BF116
English Gdns, Stai. (Wrays.)
TW19 ....92 AX84
English Grds, SE1 ....201 M3
English St, E3 ....85 DZ70
Enid Cl, St.Alb. (Brick.Wd.)
AL2 ....8 BZ31
Enid St, SE16 ....202 A6
Enmore Av, SE25 ....142 DU99
Enmore Gdns, SW14 ....118 CR85
Enmore Rd, SE25 ....142 DU99
SW15 ....99 CW84
Southall UB1 ....78 CA70
Ennerdale Av, Horn. RM12 ....71 FG64
Stanmore HA7 ....61 CJ55
Ennerdale Cl, Felt. TW14 ....115 BT88
Sutton (Cheam) SM1 ....157 CZ105
Ennerdale Dr, NW9 ....62 CS57
Ennerdale Gdns, Wem. HA9 ....61 CK60
Ennerdale Ho, E3 ....85 DZ70
Ennerdale Rd, Bexh. DA7 ....106 FA81
Richmond TW9 ....98 CM82
Ennersdale Rd, SE13 ....123 ED85
Ennismore Av, W4 ....99 CT77
Greenford UB6 ....79 CE65
Ennismore Gdns, SW7 ....198 B5
Thames Ditton KT7 ....137 CE100
Ennismore Gdns Ms, SW7 ....198 B6
Ennismore Ms, SW7 ....198 B5
Ennismore St, SW7 ....198 B6
Ennis Rd, N4 ....65 DN60
SE18 ....105 EQ79
Ensign Cl, Pur. CR8 ....159 DN110
Staines (Stanw.) TW19 ....114 BK88
Ensign Dr, N13 ....46 DQ48
Ensign St, E1 ....84 DU73
Ensign Way, Stai. (Stanw.)
TW19 ....114 BK88
Enslin Rd, SE9 ....125 EN86
Ensor Ms, SW7
off Cranley Gdns 100 DD78
Enstone Rd, Enf. EN3 ....31 DY41
Uxbridge UB10 ....58 BM62
Enterdent Rd, Gdse. RH9 ....186 DW134
Enterprise Cl, Croy. CR0 ....141 DN102
Enterprise Way, NW10 ....81 CU69
SW18 ....100 DA84
Teddington TW11 ....117 CF92
Enterprize Way, SE8 ....203 M8
Eothen Cl, Cat. CR3 ....176 DU124
Eothen Hts, Cat. CR3 ....176 DU124
Epirus Ms, SW6 ....100 DA80
Epirus Rd, SW6 ....99 CZ80
EPPING 17 ES31
⊖ Epping 18 EU31
Epping Cl, E14 ....204 A8
Romford RM7 ....71 FB55
★ Epping Forest,
Epp. & Loug. 32 EJ39
★ Epping Forest District Mus,
Wal.Abb. EN9 off Sun St 15 EC33
Epping Glade, E4 ....31 EC44
Epping La, Rom. (Stap.Taw.)
RM4 ....34 EV40
Epping New Rd, Buck.H. IG9 ....48 EH47
Loughton IG10 ....32 EH43
Epping Pl, N1
off Liverpool Rd 83 DN65
Epping Rd, Epp. CM16 ....33 EM36
Epping (Epp.Grn.) CM16 ....17 ER27
Epping (N.Wld.Bas.) CM16 ....18 EW28
Ongar (Toot Hill) CM5 ....19 FC30
Epping Way, E4 ....31 EB44
Epple Rd, SW6 ....99 CZ81
EPSOM 156 CQ114
⇌ Epsom 156 CR113
[H] Epsom & Ewell New Cottage
Hosp, Epsom KT19 ....156 CL111
Epsom Cl, Bexh. DA7 ....107 FB83
Northolt UB5 ....60 BZ64
⇌ Epsom Downs 173 CV115
Epsom Downs, Epsom
KT18 ....173 CU118
Epsom Downs Metro Cen, Tad.
KT20 off Waterfield 173 CV120
Epsom Gap, Lthd. KT22 ....171 CH115
[H] Epsom Gen Hosp, Epsom
KT18 ....172 CQ115
Epsom La N, Epsom KT18 ....173 CV118
Tadworth KT20 ....173 CV118
Epsom La S, Tad. KT20 ....173 CW121
★ Epsom Racecourse, Epsom
KT18 ....173 CT118
Epsom Rd, E10 ....67 EC58
Ashtead KT21 ....172 CM118
Croydon CR0 ....159 DN105
Epsom KT17 ....157 CT110
Ilford IG3 ....69 ET58
Leatherhead KT22 ....171 CH121
Morden SM4 ....139 CZ101
Sutton SM3 ....139 CZ101
Epsom Sq, Houns. (Hthrw.Air.) TW6
off Eastern Perimeter Rd 95 BT82
Epsom Way, Horn. RM12 ....72 FM63
Epstein Rd, SE28 ....88 EU74
Epworth Rd, Islw. TW7 ....97 CH80
Epworth St, EC2 ....197 L5
Equity Sq, E2
off Shacklewell St 84 DT69
Erasmus St, SW1 ....199 N9
Erconwald St, W12 ....81 CT72
Eresby Dr, Beck. BR3 ....143 EA102
Eresby Pl, NW6 ....82 DA66
Erica Ct, Swan. BR8
off Azalea Dr 147 FE98
Woking GU22 ....166 AX118
Erica Gdns, Croy. CR0 ....161 EB105
Erica St, W12 ....81 CU73
Eric Clarke La, Bark. IG11 ....87 EP70
Eric Cl, E7 ....68 EG63
Ericcson Cl, SW18 ....120 DA85
Eric Rd, E7 ....68 EG63
NW10 off Church Rd 81 CT65
Romford RM6 ....70 EX59
Eric Steele Ho, St.Alb. AL2 ....8 CB27
Eric St, E3 ....85 DZ70
Eridge Grn Cl, Orp. BR5
off Petten Gro 146 EW102
Eridge Rd, W4 ....98 CR76
Erin Cl, Brom. BR1 ....124 EE94
Ilford IG3 ....70 EU58
Erindale, SE18 ....105 ER79
Erindale Ter, SE18 ....105 ER79
Eriswell Cres, Walt. KT12 ....153 BS107
Eriswell Rd, Walt. KT12 ....153 BT105
ERITH 107 FD79
⇌ Erith 107 FE78
[H] Erith & District Hosp, Erith
DA8 ....107 FD79
Erith Ct, Purf. RM19
off Thamley 108 FN77
Erith Cres, Rom. RM5 ....51 FC53
Erith High St, Erith DA8 ....107 FE78
★ Erith Lib & Mus, Erith DA8
off Walnut Tree Rd 107 FE78
Erith Rd, Belv. DA17 ....106 FA78
Bexleyheath DA7 ....107 FB84
Erith DA8 ....107 FB84
Erkenwald Cl, Cher. KT16 ....133 BE101
Erlanger Rd, SE14 ....103 DX81
Erlesmere Gdns, W13 ....97 CG76
Ermine Cl, Houns. TW4 ....96 BW82
Waltham Cross (Chsht.)
EN7 ....14 DV31
Ermine Ho, N17
off Moselle St 46 DT52
Ermine Rd, N15 ....66 DT58
SE13 ....103 EB83
Ermine Side, Enf. EN1 ....30 DU43
Ermington Rd, SE9 ....125 EQ89
Ermyn Cl, Lthd. KT22 ....171 CK121
Ermyn Way, Lthd. KT22 ....171 CK121
Ernald Av, E6 ....86 EL68
Ernan Cl, S.Ock. RM15 ....91 FU71
Ernan Rd, S.Ock. RM15 ....91 FU71
Erncroft Way, Twick. TW1 ....117 CF86
Ernest Av, SE27 ....121 DP91
Ernest Cl, Beck. BR3 ....143 EA99
Ernest Gdns, W4 ....98 CP79
Ernest Gro, Beck. BR3 ....143 DZ99
Ernest Rd, Horn. RM11 ....72 FL58
Kingston upon Thames
KT1 ....138 CP96
Ernest Sq, Kings.T. KT1 ....138 CP96
Ernest St, E1 ....85 DX70
Ernle Rd, SW20 ....119 CV94
Ernshaw Pl, SW15
off Carlton Dr 119 CY85
★ Eros, W1 ....199 M1
Erpingham Rd, SW15 ....99 CW83
Erridge Rd, SW19 ....140 DA96
Erriff Dr, S.Ock. RM15 ....91 FT71
Errington Cl, Grays RM16
off Cedar Rd 111 GH76
Errington Rd, W9 ....81 CZ70
Errol Gdns, Hayes UB4 ....77 BV70
New Malden KT3 ....139 CU98
Erroll Rd, Rom. RM1 ....71 FF56
Errol St, EC1 ....197 J5
Erskine Cl, Sutt. SM1 ....140 DE104
Erskine Cres, N17 ....66 DV56
Erskine Hill, NW11 ....64 DA57
Erskine Ms, NW3
off Erskine Rd 82 DF66
Erskine Rd, E17 ....67 DZ56
NW3 ....82 DF66
Sutton SM1 ....158 DD105
Watford WD19 ....40 BW48
Erwood Rd, SE7 ....104 EL78
Esam Way, SW16 ....121 DN92
Escott Gdns, SE9 ....124 EL91
Escott Pl, Cher. (Ott.) KT16 ....151 BC107
Escot Way, Barn. EN5 ....27 CW43
Escreet Gro, SE18 ....105 EN77
Esdaile Gdns, Upmin. RM14 ....73 FR59
ESHER 154 CB105
⇌ Esher 137 CD103

Esher Av, Rom. RM7 71 FC58
Sutton SM3 139 CX104
Walton-on-Thames KT12 135 BU101
Esher Bypass, Chess. KT9 155 CH108
Cobham KT11 153 BU112
Esher KT10 155 CH108
Esher Cl, Bex. DA5 126 EY88
Esher KT10 154 CB106
Esher Cres, Houns. (Hthrw.Air.) TW6
off Eastern Perimeter Rd 95 BS82
Esher Gdns, SW19 119 CX89
Esher Grn, Esher KT10 154 CB105
Esher Ms, Mitch. CR4 140 DF97
Esher Pk Av, Esher KT10 154 CC105
Esher Pl Av, Esher KT10 154 CB105
Esher Rd, E.Mol. KT8 137 CD100
Ilford IG3 69 ES62
Walton-on-Thames KT12 154 BX106
Eskdale, St.Alb. (Lon.Col.)
AL2 10 CM27
Eskdale Av, Nthlt. UB5 78 BZ67
Eskdale Cl, Dart. DA2 128 FQ89
Wembley HA9 61 CK61
Eskdale Gdns, Pur. CR8 160 DR114
Eskdale Rd, Bexh. DA7 106 FA82
Uxbridge UB8 76 BH68
Eskley Gdns, S.Ock. RM15 91 FV70
Eskmont Ridge, SE19 122 DS94
Esk Rd, E13 86 EG70
Esk Way, Rom. RM1 51 FD52
Esmar Cres, NW9 63 CU59
Esme Ho, SW15 99 CT84
Esmeralda Rd, SE1 202 C9
Esmond Cl, Rain. RM13
off Dawson Dr 89 FH66
Esmond Rd, NW6 81 CZ67
W4 98 CR77
Esmond St, SW15 99 CY84
Esparto St, SW18 120 DB87
Essendene Cl, Cat. CR3 176 DS123
Essendene Rd, Cat. CR3 176 DS123
Essenden Rd, Belv. DA17 106 FA78
South Croydon CR2 160 DS108
Essendine Rd, W9 82 DA70
Essex Av, Islw. TW7 97 CE83
Essex Cl, E17 67 DY56
Addlestone KT15 152 BJ105
Morden SM4 139 CX101
Romford RM7 71 FB56
Ruislip HA4 60 BX60
Essex Ct, EC4 196 D9
SW13 99 CT82
Essex Gdns, N4 65 DP58
Hornchurch RM11 72 FM57
Essex Gro, SE19 122 DR93
Essex Ho, E14 *off Giraud St* 85 EB72
Essex La, Kings L. WD4 7 BS33
H **Essex Nuffield Hosp**, Brwd.
CM15 54 FY46
Essex Pk, N3 44 DB51
Essex Pk Ms, W3 80 CS74
Essex Pl, W4 98 CQ77
Essex Pl Sq, W4
off Chiswick High Rd 98 CR77
≠ **Essex Road** 84 DQ66
Essex Rd, E4 48 EE46
E10 67 EC58
E12 68 EL64
E17 67 DY58
E18 48 EH54
N1 83 DP67
NW10 80 CS66
W3 80 CQ73
W4 *off Belmont Rd* 98 CR77
Barking IG11 87 ER66
Borehamwood WD6 26 CN41
Dagenham RM10 71 FC64
Dartford DA1 128 FK86
Enfield EN2 30 DR42
Gravesend DA11 131 GG88
Grays RM20 109 FU79
Longfield DA3 149 FX96
Romford RM7 71 FB56
Romford (Chad.Hth.) RM6 70 EW59
Watford WD17 23 BU40
Essex Rd S, E11 67 ED59
Essex St, E7 68 EG64
WC2 196 D10
Essex Twr, SE20 142 DV95
Essex Vil, W8 100 DA75
Essex Way, Brwd. CM13 53 FW51
Epping CM16 18 EV32
Ongar CM5 19 FF29
Essex Wf, E5 66 DW61
Essian St, E1 85 DY71
Essoldo Way, Edg. HA8 62 CM55
Estate Way, E10 67 DZ60
Estcourt Rd, SE25 142 DV100
SW6 99 CZ80
Watford WD17 24 BW41
Estella Av, N.Mal. KT3 139 CV98
Estelle Rd, NW3 64 DF63
Esterbrooke St, SW1 199 M9
Este Rd, SW11 100 DE83
Esther Cl, N21 45 DN45
Esther Rd, E11 68 EE59
Estoria Cl, SW2 121 DN87
★ **Estorick Collection of Modern Italian Art**, N1 83 DP65
Estreham Rd, SW16 121 DK93
Estridge Cl, Houns. TW3 96 CA84
Estuary Cl, Bark. IG11 88 EV69
Eswyn Rd, SW17 120 DF91
Etchingham Pk Rd, N3 44 DB52
Etchingham Rd, E15 67 EC63
Eternit Wk, SW6 99 CW81
Etfield Gro, Sid. DA14 126 EV92
Ethel Bailey Cl, Epsom KT19 156 CN112
Ethelbert Cl, Brom. BR1 144 EG97
Ethelbert Gdns, Ilf. IG2 69 EM57
Ethelbert Rd, SW20 139 CX95
Bromley BR1 144 EG97
Dartford (Hawley) DA2 128 FL91
Erith DA8 107 FC80
Orpington BR5 146 EX97
Ethelbert St, SW12
off Fernlea Rd 121 DH88
Ethelburga Rd, Rom. RM3 52 FM53
Ethelburga St, SW11 100 DE81
Etheldene Av, N10 65 DJ56
Ethelden Rd, W12 81 CV74
Ethel Rd, E16 86 EH72
Ashford TW15 114 BL92
Ethel St, SE17 201 H9
Ethel Ter, Orp. BR6 164 EW109
Ethelwine Pl, Abb.L. WD5
off The Crescent 7 BT30
Etheridge Grn, Loug. IG10
off Etheridge Rd 33 EQ41
Etheridge Rd, NW2 63 CW59
Loughton IG10 33 EP40
Etherley Rd, N15 66 DQ57
Etherow St, SE22 122 DU86
Etherstone Grn, SW16 121 DN91
Etherstone Rd, SW16 121 DN91
Ethnard Rd, SE15 102 DV79
Ethorpe Cl, Ger.Cr. SL9 56 AY57
Ethorpe Cres, Ger.Cr. SL9 56 AY57
Ethronvi Rd, Bexh. DA7 106 EY83
Etloe Rd, E10 67 EA61
Eton Av, N12 44 DC52
NW3 82 DD66
Barnet EN4 28 DE44
Hounslow TW5 96 BZ79
New Malden KT3 138 CR99
Wembley HA0 61 CH63
Eton Cl, SW18 120 DB87
Slough (Datchet) SL3 92 AU79
Eton Coll Rd, NW3 82 DF65
Eton Ct, NW3 *off Eton Av* 82 DD66
Staines TW18
off Richmond Rd 113 BF92
Wembley HA0
off Eton Av 61 CJ63
Eton Garages, NW3
off Lambolle Pl 82 DE65
Eton Gro, NW9 62 CN55
SE13 104 EE83
Eton Hall, NW3
off Eton Coll Rd 82 DF65
Eton Pl, NW3
off Haverstock Hill 82 DG66
Eton Ri, NW3
off Eton Coll Rd 82 DF65
Eton Rd, NW3 82 DF66
Hayes UB3 95 BT80
Ilford IG1 69 EQ64
Orpington BR6 164 EV105
Slough (Datchet) SL3 92 AT78
Eton St, Rich. TW9 118 CL85
Eton Vil, NW3 82 DF65
Eton Way, Dart. DA1 108 FJ84
Etta St, SE8 103 DY79
Etton Cl, Horn. RM12 72 FL61
Ettrick St, E14 85 EC72
Etwell Pl, Surb. KT5 138 CM100
Euclid Way, Grays RM20 109 FU78
Euesden Cl, N9
off Plevna Rd 46 DV48
Eugene Cl, Rom. RM2 72 FJ56
Eugenia Rd, SE16 202 G9
Eureka Rd, Kings.T. KT1
off Washington Rd 138 CN96
Europa Pl, EC1 197 H3
Europa Trd Est, Erith DA8 107 FD78
Europe Rd, SE18 105 EM76
Eustace Rd, E6 86 EL69
SW6 100 DA80
Romford RM6 70 EX59
≠ **Euston** 195 L2
⊖ **Euston** 199 L2
Euston Av, Wat. WD18 23 BT43
Euston Cen, NW1
off Triton Sq 83 DJ70
Euston Gro, NW1 195 M3
Euston Rd, N1 195 P2
NW1 195 J5
Croydon CR0 141 DN102
⊖ **Euston Square** 195 L4
Euston Sq, NW1 195 M3
Euston Sta Colonnade, NW1 195 M3
Euston St, NW1 195 L4
Euston Twr, NW1 83 DJ70
Evandale Rd, SW9 101 DN82
Evangelist Rd, NW5 65 DH63
Evans Av, Wat. WD25 23 BT35
Evans Cl, E8
off Buttermere Wk 84 DT65
Greenhithe DA9 129 FU85
Rickmansworth (Crox.Grn.) WD3
off New Rd 22 BN43
Evansdale, Rain. RM13
off New Zealand Way 89 FF69
Evans Gro, Felt. TW13 116 CA89
Evans Rd, SE6 124 EE89
Evanston Av, E4 47 EC52
Evanston Gdns, Ilf. IG4 68 EL58
Eva Rd, Rom. RM6 70 EW59
Evelina Rd, SE15 102 DW83
SE20 123 DX94
Eveline Lowe Est, SE16 202 B7
Eveline Rd, Mitch. CR4 140 DF95
Evelyn Av, NW9 62 CR56
Ruislip HA4 59 BT58
Evelyn Cl, Twick. TW2 116 CB87
Woking GU22 166 AX120
Evelyn Ct, N1 197 K1
Evelyn Cres, Sun. TW16 135 BT95
Evelyn Denington Rd, E6 86 EL70
Evelyn Dr, Pnr. HA5 40 BX52
Evelyn Fox Ct, W10 81 CW71
Evelyn Gdns, SW7 100 DD78
Godstone RH9 186 DW130
Richmond TW9
off Kew Rd 98 CL84
Evelyn Gro, W5 80 CM74
Southall UB1 78 BZ72
Evelyn Rd, E16 205 P2
E17 67 EC56
SW19 120 DB92
W4 98 CR76
Barnet EN4 28 DF42
Richmond TW9 98 CL83
Richmond (Ham) TW10 117 CJ90
Evelyns Cl, Uxb. UB8 76 BN72
Evelyn Sharp Cl, Rom. RM2
off Amery Gdns 72 FK55
Evelyn St, SE8 203 K9
Evelyn Ter, Rich. TW9 98 CL83
Evelyn Wk, N1 197 K1
Brentwood CM13 53 FW51
Evelyn Way, Cob. (Stoke D'Ab.)
KT11 170 BZ116
Epsom KT19 *off Queen Alexandra's Way* 156 CN111
Sunbury-on-Thames
TW16 135 BT95
Wallington SM6 159 DK105
Evelyn Yd, W1 195 M8
Evening Hill, Beck. BR3 123 EC94
Evensyde, Wat. WD18 23 BR44
Evenwood Cl, SW15 119 CY85
Everard Av, Brom. BR2 144 EG102
Slough SL1 92 AS75
Everard La, Cat. CR3
off Tillingdown Hill 176 DU122
Everard Way, Wem. HA9 62 CL62
Everatt Cl, SW18
off Amerland Rd 119 CZ86
Everdon Rd, SW13 99 CU79
Everest Cl, Grav. (Nthflt.)
DA11 130 GE90
Everest Ct, Wok. GU21
off Langmans Way 166 AS116
Everest Pl, E14 85 EC71
Swanley BR8 147 FD98
Everest Rd, SE9 125 EM85
Staines (Stanw.) TW19 114 BK87
Everett Cl, Bushey (Bushey Hth.)
WD23 41 CE46
Pinner HA5 59 BT55
Waltham Cross (Chsht.)
EN7 14 DQ25
Everett Wk, Belv. DA17
off Osborne Rd 106 EZ78
Everglade, West. (Bigg.H.)
TN16 178 EK118
Everglade Strand, NW9 43 CT53
Evergreen Ct, Stai. (Stanw.) TW19
off Evergreen Way 114 BK87
Evergreen Oak Av, Wind. SL4 92 AU83
Evergreen Sq, E8 84 DT66
Evergreen Way, Hayes UB3 77 BT73
Staines (Stanw.) TW19 114 BK87
Everilda St, N1 83 DM67
Evering Rd, E5 66 DT62
N16 66 DT62
Everington Rd, N10 44 DF54
Everington St, W6 99 CX79
Everitt Rd, NW10 80 CR69
Everlands Cl, Wok. GU22 166 AY118
Everleigh St, N4 65 DM60
Eve Rd, E11 68 EE63
E15 86 EE68
N17 66 DS55
Isleworth TW7 97 CG84
Woking GU21 167 BB115
Eversfield Gdns, NW7 42 CS52
Eversfield Rd, Reig. RH2 184 DB134
Richmond TW9 98 CM82
Evershed Wk, W4 98 CR77
Eversholt St, NW1 83 DJ68
Evershot Rd, N4 65 DM60
Eversleigh Gdns, Upmin.
RM14 73 FR60
Eversleigh Rd, E6 86 EK67
N3 43 CZ52
SW11 100 DF83
Barnet EN5 28 DC43
Eversley Av, Bexh. DA7 107 FD82
Wembley HA9 62 CN61
Eversley Cl, N21 29 DM44
Loughton IG10
off The Broadway 33 EQ41
Eversley Cres, N21 29 DM44
Isleworth TW7 97 CD81
Ruislip HA4 59 BS61
Eversley Cross, Bexh. DA7 107 FE82
Eversley Mt, N21 29 DM44
Eversley Pk, SW19 119 CV92
Eversley Pk Rd, N21 29 DM44
Eversley Rd, SE7 104 EH79
SE19 122 DR94
Surbiton KT5 138 CM98
Eversley Way, Croy. CR0 161 EA105
Egham TW20 133 BC96
Everthorpe Rd, SE15 102 DT83
Everton Bldgs, NW1 195 K3
Everton Dr, Stan. HA7 62 CM55
Everton Rd, Croy. CR0 142 DU102
Evesham Av, E17 47 EA54
Evesham Cl, Grnf. UB6 78 CB68
Reigate RH2 183 CZ133
Sutton SM2 158 DA108
Evesham Grn, Mord. SM4 140 DB100
Evesham Rd, E15 86 EF67
N11 45 DJ50
Gravesend DA12 131 GK89
Morden SM4 140 DB100
Reigate RH2 183 CZ134
Evesham Rd N, Reig. RH2 183 CZ133
Evesham St, W11 81 CX73
Evesham Wk, SE5
off Love Wk 102 DR82
SW9 101 DN82
Evesham Way, SW11 100 DG83
Ilford IG5 69 EN55
Evreham Rd, Iver SL0 75 BE72
Evry Rd, Sid. DA14 126 EW93
Ewald Rd, SW6 99 CZ82
Ewanrigg Ter, Wdf.Grn. IG8 48 EJ50
Ewan Rd, Rom. (Harold Wd.)
RM3 52 FK54
Ewart Gro, N22 45 DN53
Ewart Pl, E3
off Roman Rd 85 DZ68
Ewart Rd, SE23 123 DX87
Ewe Cl, N7 83 DL65
EWELL, Epsom 157 CU110
Ewell Bypass, Epsom KT17 157 CU108
Ewell Ct Av, Epsom KT19 156 CS106
Ewell Downs Rd, Epsom
KT17 157 CU111
≠ **Ewell East** 157 CV110
Ewell Ho Gro, Epsom KT17 157 CT110
Ewellhurst Rd, Ilf. IG5 48 EL54
Ewell Pk Gdns, Epsom KT17 157 CU108
Ewell Pk Way, Epsom (Ewell)
KT17 157 CU107
Ewell Rd, Surb. KT6 138 CL100
Surbiton (Long Dit.) KT6 137 CH101
Sutton SM3 157 CY107
≠ **Ewell West** 156 CS109
Ewelme Rd, SE23 122 DW88
Ewen Cres, SW2 121 DN87
Ewer St, SE1 201 H3
Ewhurst Av, S.Croy. CR2 160 DT109
Ewhurst Cl, E1 84 DW71
Sutton SM2 157 CW109
Ewhurst Rd, SE4 123 DZ86
Exbury Rd, SE6 123 EA89
★ **ExCeL**, E16 86 EH73
Excel Ct, WC2 199 N1
Excelsior Cl, Kings.T. KT1
off Washington Rd 138 CN96
Excelsior Gdns, SE13 103 EC82
Exchange Arc, EC2 197 N6
Exchange Bldgs, E1
off Cutler St 84 DS72
Exchange Cl, N11
off Benfleet Way 44 DG47
Exchange Ct, WC2 200 A1
Exchange Pl, EC2 197 M6
Exchange Rd, Wat. WD18 23 BV42
Exchange Sq, EC2 197 M6
Exchange St, Rom. RM1 71 FE57
Exchange Ill Shop Cen, The, Ilf.
IG1 69 EP61
Exeforde Av, Ashf. TW15 114 BN91
Exeter Cl, E6
off Harper Rd 87 EM72
Watford WD24 24 BW40
Exeter Gdns, Ilf. IG1 68 EL60
Exeter Ho, SW15
off Putney Heath 119 CW86
Exeter Ms, NW6
off West Hampstead Ms 82 DB65
SW6 *off Farm La* 100 DA80
Exeter Rd, E16 86 EG71
E17 67 EA57
N9 46 DW47
N14 45 DH46
NW2 63 CY64
Croydon CR0 142 DS101
Dagenham RM10 89 FB65
Enfield EN3 31 DX41
Feltham TW13 116 BZ90
Gravesend DA12 131 GK90
Harrow HA2 60 BY61
Hounslow (Hthrw.Air.) TW6 95 BS82
Welling DA16 105 ET82
Exeter St, WC2 196 A10
Exeter Way, SE14 103 DZ80
Hounslow (Hthrw.Air.) TW6 95 BS83
Exford Gdns, SE12 124 EH88
Exford Rd, SE12 124 EH89
Exhibition Cl, W12 81 CW73
Exhibition Rd, SW7 198 A5
Exmoor Cl, Ilf. IG6 49 EQ53
Exmoor St, W10 81 CX70
Exmouth Mkt, EC1 196 D4
Exmouth Ms, NW1 195 L3
Exmouth Pl, E8 84 DV66
Exmouth Rd, E17 67 DZ57
Bromley BR2 144 EH97
Grays RM17 110 GB79
Hayes UB4 77 BS69
Ruislip HA4 60 BW62
Welling DA16 106 EW81
Exmouth St, E1
off Commercial Rd 84 DW72
Exning Rd, E16 86 EF70
Exon St, SE17 201 M10
Explorer Av, Stai. TW19 114 BL88
Explorer Dr, Wat. WD18 23 BT44
Express Dr, Ilf. IG3 70 EV60
Exton Cres, NW10 80 CQ66
Exton Gdns, Dag. RM8 70 EW64
Exton St, SE1 200 D3
Eyebright Cl, Croy. CR0
off Primrose La 143 DX102
Eyhurst Av, Horn. RM12 71 FG62
Eyhurst Cl, NW2 63 CU61
Tadworth (Kgswd.) KT20 173 CZ123
Eyhurst Pk, Tad. KT20 174 DC123
Eyhurst Spur, Tad. KT20 173 CZ124
Eylewood Rd, SE27 122 DQ92
Eynella Rd, SE22 122 DT87
Eynham Rd, W12 81 CW72
EYNSFORD, Dart. 148 FL103
★ **Eynsford Castle**, Dart.
DA4 148 FK103
Eynsford Cl, Orp. BR5 145 EQ101
Eynsford Cres, Bex. DA5 126 EW88
Eynsford Rd, Dart. (Fnghm.)
DA4 148 FM102
Greenhithe DA9 129 FW85
Ilford IG3 69 ES61
Sevenoaks TN14 165 FH108
Swanley BR8 147 FD100
Eynsham Dr, SE2 106 EU77
Eynswood Dr, Sid. DA14 126 EV92
Eyot Gdns, W6 99 CT78
Eyot Grn, W4
off Chiswick Mall 99 CT79
Eyre Cl, Rom. RM2 71 FH56
Eyre Ct, NW8 *off Finchley Rd* 82 DD68
Eyre St Hill, EC1 196 D5
Eyston Dr, Wey. KT13 152 BN110
Eythorne Rd, SW9 101 DN81
Ezra St, E2 84 DT69

F

Faber Gdns, NW4 63 CU57
Fabian Rd, SW6 99 CZ80
Fabian St, E6 87 EM70
Fackenden La, Sev. (Shore.)
TN14 165 FH113
Factory La, N17 46 DT54
Croydon CR0 141 DN102
Factory Rd, E16 86 EL74
Gravesend (Nthflt.) DA11 130 GC86
Factory Sq, SW16 121 DL93
Factory Yd, W7
off Uxbridge Rd 79 CE74
Faesten Way, Bex. DA5 127 FE90
Faggotts Cl, Rad. WD7 25 CJ35
Faggs Rd, Felt. TW14 115 BU85
Fagus Av, Rain. RM13 90 FK69
Faints Cl, Wal.Cr. EN7 14 DT29
Fairacre, N.Mal. KT3 138 CS97
Fairacres, SW15 99 CU84
Fair Acres, Brom. BR2 144 EG99
Fairacres, Cob. KT11 154 BX112
Croydon CR0 161 DZ109
Ruislip HA4 59 BT59
Tadworth KT20 173 CW121
Fairacres Cl, Pot.B. EN6 11 CZ33
Fairbairn Cl, Pur. CR8 159 DN113
Fairbairn Grn, SW9 101 DN81
Fairbank Av, Orp. BR6 145 EP103
Fairbank Est, N1 *off East Rd* 84 DR68
Fairbanks Rd, N17 66 DT55
Fairbourne, Cob. KT11 154 BX113
Fairbourne Cl, Wok. GU21
off Abercorn Way 166 AU118
Fairbourne La, Cat. CR3 176 DQ122
Fairbourne Rd, N17 66 DS55
Fairbridge Rd, N19 65 DK61
Fairbrook Cl, N13 45 DN50
Fairbrook Rd, N13 45 DN51
Fairburn Cl, Borwd. WD6 26 CN39
Fairburn Ct, SW15
off Mercier Rd 119 CY85
Fairby Rd, SE12 124 EH85
Faircharm Trd Est, SE8 103 EB80
Fairchild Cl, SW11 *off Wye St* 100 DD82
Fairchildes Av, Croy. (New Adgtn.)
CR0 161 ED112
Fairchildes La, Warl. CR6 161 ED114
Fairchild Pl, EC2 197 N5
Fairchild St, EC2 197 N5
Fair Cl, Bushey WD23
off Claybury 40 CB45
Fairclough St, E1 84 DU72
Faircross Av, Bark. IG11 87 EQ65
Romford RM5 51 FD52
Fairdale Gdns, SW15 99 CV84
Hayes UB3 77 BU74
Fairdene Rd, Couls. CR5 175 DK117
Fairey Av, Hayes UB3 95 BT77
Fairfax Av, Epsom KT17 157 CV109
Redhill RH1 184 DE133
Fairfax Cl, Walt. KT12 135 BV102
Fairfax Gdns, SE3 104 EK81
Fairfax Ms, E16 205 P2
SW15 99 CW84
Fairfax Pl, NW6 82 DC66
W14 *off Holland Rd* 99 CY76
Fairfax Rd, N8 65 DN56
NW6 82 DC66
W4 98 CS76
Grays RM17 110 GB78
Teddington TW11 117 CG93
Tilbury RM18 111 GF81
Woking GU22 167 BB120
Fairfax Way, N10
off Cromwell Rd 44 DG52
Fairfield App, Stai. (Wrays.)
TW19 112 AX86
Fairfield Av, NW4 63 CV58
Edgware HA8 42 CP51
Ruislip HA4 59 BQ59
Slough (Datchet) SL3 92 AW80
Staines TW18 113 BF91
Twickenham TW2 116 CB88
Upminster RM14 72 FQ62
Watford WD19 40 BW48
Fairfield Cl, N12 44 DC49
Enfield EN3
off Scotland Grn Rd N 31 DY42
Epsom (Ewell) KT19 156 CS106
Hornchurch RM12 71 FG60
Mitcham CR4 120 DE94
Northwood HA6
off Thirlmere Gdns 39 BP50
Radlett WD7 25 CE37
Sidcup DA15 125 ET86
Slough (Datchet) SL3 92 AX80
Fairfield Ct, NW10 81 CU67
Northwood HA6
off Windsor Cl 39 BU54
Fairfield Cres, Edg. HA8 42 CP51
Fairfield Dr, SW18 120 DB85
Greenford UB6 79 CJ67
Harrow HA2 60 CC55
Fairfield E, Kings.T. KT1 138 CL96
Fairfield Gdns, N8
off Elder Av 65 DL57
Fairfield Gro, SE7 104 EK78
★ **Fairfield Halls**, Croy. CR0 142 DR104
Fairfield Ind Est, Kings.T.
KT1 138 CM97
Fairfield N, Kings.T. KT1 138 CL96
Fairfield Pk, Cob. KT11 154 BX114
Fairfield Path, Croy. CR0 142 DR104
Fairfield Pathway, Horn.
RM12 90 FJ66
Fairfield Pl, Kings.T. KT1 138 CL97
Fairfield Rd, E3 85 EA68
E17 47 DY54
N8 65 DL57
N18 46 DU49
W7 97 CG76
Beckenham BR3 143 EA96
Bexleyheath DA7 106 EZ82
Brentwood CM14 54 FW48
Bromley BR1 124 EG94

★ Place of interest ≠ Railway station ⊖ London Underground station DLR Docklands Light Railway station Tramlink station H Hospital

Fai - Far

Fairfield Rd, Croy. CR0 142 DS104
Epping CM16 18 EV29
Ilford IG1 87 EP65
Kingston upon Thames KT1 138 CL96
Leatherhead KT22 171 CH121
Orpington BR5 145 ER100
Southall UB1 78 BZ72
Staines (Wrays.) TW19 112 AX86
Uxbridge UB8 76 BK65
West Drayton UB7 76 BL74
Woodford Green IG8 48 EG51
Fairfields, Cher. KT16 134 BG102
Gravesend DA12 131 GL92
Fairfields Cl, NW9 62 CQ57
Fairfields Cres, NW9 62 CQ56
Fairfield S, Kings.T. KT1 138 CL96
Fairfields Rd, Houns. TW3 96 CC83
Fairfield St, SW18 120 DB85
Fairfield Wk, Lthd. KT22 *off Fairfield Rd* 171 CH121
Waltham Cross (Chsht.) EN8 15 DY28
Fairfield Way, Barn. EN5 28 DA43
Coulsdon CR5 159 DK114
Epsom KT19 156 CS106
Fairfield W, Kings.T. KT1 138 CL96
Fairfolds, Wat. WD25 24 BY36
Fairfoot Rd, E3 85 EA70
Fairford Av, Bexh. DA7 107 FD81
Croydon CR0 143 DX99
Fairford Cl, Croy. CR0 143 DY99
Reigate RH2 184 DC132
Romford RM3 *off Fairford Way* 52 FP51
West Byfleet KT14 151 BF114
Fairford Ct, Sutt. SM2 *off Grange Rd* 158 DB108
Fairford Gdns, Wor.Pk. KT4 139 CT104
Fairford Ho, SE11 200 E9
Fairford Way, Rom. RM3 52 FP51
Fairgreen, Barn. EN4 28 DF41
Fairgreen E, Barn. EN4 28 DF41
Fairgreen Par, Mitch. CR4 *off London Rd* 140 DF97
Fairgreen Rd, Th.Hth. CR7 141 DP99
Fairham Av, S.Ock. RM15 91 FU73
Fairhaven, Egh. TW20 113 AZ92
Fairhaven Av, Croy. CR0 143 DX100
Fairhaven Cres, Wat. WD19 39 BU48
Fairhaven Rd, Red. RH1 184 DG130
Fairhazel Gdns, NW6 82 DB65
Fairholme, Felt. TW14 115 BR87
Fairholme Av, Rom. RM2 71 FG57
Fairholme Cl, N3 63 CY56
Fairholme Cres, Ashtd. KT21 171 CJ117
Hayes UB4 77 BT70
Fairholme Gdns, N3 63 CY55
Upminster RM14 73 FT59
Fairholme Rd, W14 99 CY78
Ashford TW15 114 BL92
Croydon CR0 141 DN101
Harrow HA1 61 CF57
Ilford IG1 69 EM59
Sutton SM1 157 CZ107
Fairholt Cl, N16 66 DS60
Fairholt Rd, N16 66 DR60
Fairholt St, SW7 198 C6
Fairkytes Av, Horn. RM11 72 FK60
Fairland Rd, E15 86 EF65
Fairlands Av, Buck.H. IG9 48 EG47
Sutton SM1 140 DA103
Thornton Heath CR7 141 DM98
Fairlands Ct, SE9 *off North Pk* 125 EN86
Fair La, Couls. CR5 184 DC125
Fairlawn, SE7 104 EJ79
Leatherhead (Bkhm.) KT23 170 BZ124
Fairlawn Av, N2 64 DE56
W4 98 CQ77
Bexleyheath DA7 106 EX82
Fairlawn Cl, N14 29 DJ44
Esher (Clay.) KT10 155 CF107
Feltham TW13 116 BZ91
Kingston upon Thames KT2 118 CQ93
Fairlawn Dr, Wdf.Grn. IG8 48 EG52
Fairlawnes, Wall. SM6 *off Maldon Rd* 159 DH106
Fairlawn Gdns, Sthl. UB1 78 BZ73
Fairlawn Gro, W4 98 CQ77
Banstead SM7 158 DD113
Fairlawn Pk, SE26 123 DY92
Woking GU21 150 AY114
Fairlawn Rd, SW19 119 CZ94
Banstead SM7 158 DD112
Carshalton SM5 158 DC111
Fairlawns, Add. (Woodham) KT15 151 BF111
Brentwood CM14 54 FU48
Pinner HA5 40 BW54
Sunbury-on-Thames TW16 135 BU97
Twickenham TW1 117 CJ86
Watford WD17 *off Langley Rd* 23 BT38
Weybridge KT13 153 BS106
Fairlawns Cl, Horn. RM11 72 FM59
Staines TW18 114 BH93
Fairlea Pl, W5 79 CK70
Fairley Way, Wal.Cr. (Chsht.) EN7 14 DV28
Fairlie Gdns, SE23 122 DW87
Fairlight Av, E4 47 ED47
NW10 80 CS68
Woodford Green IG8 48 EG51
Fairlight Cl, E4 47 ED47
Worcester Park KT4 157 CW105
Fairlight Dr, Uxb. UB8 76 BK65
Fairlight Rd, SW17 120 DD91
⊖ **Fairlop** 49 ER53
Fairlop Cl, Horn. RM12 89 FH65
Fairlop Gdns, Ilf. IG6 49 EQ52
Fairlop Rd, E11 67 ED59
Ilford IG6 49 EQ54
Fairmark Dr, Uxb. UB10 76 BN65
Fairmead, Brom. BR1 145 EM98
Surbiton KT5 138 CP102
Woking GU21 166 AW118
Fairmead Cl, Brom. BR1 145 EM98
Hounslow TW5 96 BX80
New Malden KT3 138 CR97
Fairmead Cres, Edg. HA8 42 CQ48
Fairmead Gdns, Ilf. IG4 68 EL57
Fairmead Rd, N19 65 DK62
Croydon CR0 141 DM102
Loughton IG10 32 EH42
Fairmeads, Cob. KT11 154 BZ113
Loughton IG10 33 EP40
Fairmead Side, Loug. IG10 32 EJ43
FAIRMILE, Cob. 154 BZ112
Fairmile Av, SW16 121 DK92
Cobham KT11 154 BY114
Fairmile Ho, Tedd. TW11 *off Twickenham Rd* 117 CG91
Fairmile La, Cob. KT11 154 BX112
Fairmile Pk Copse, Cob. KT11 154 BZ112
Fairmile Pk Rd, Cob. KT11 154 BZ113
Fairmont Cl, Belv. DA17 *off Lullingstone Rd* 106 EZ78
Fairmount Rd, SW2 121 DM86
Fairoak Cl, Ken. CR8 175 DP115
Leatherhead (Oxshott) KT22 155 CD112
Orpington BR5 145 EP101
Fairoak Dr, SE9 125 ER85
Fairoak Gdns, Rom. RM1 51 FE54
Fairoak La, Chess. KT9 155 CF111
Leatherhead (Oxshott) KT22 155 CF111
Fairseat Cl, Bushey (Bushey Hth.) WD23 *off Hive Rd* 41 CE47
Fairs Rd, Lthd. KT22 171 CG119
Fairstead Wk, N1 *off Popham Rd* 84 DQ67
Fair St, SE1 201 N4
Hounslow TW3 *off High St* 96 CC83
Fairthorn Rd, SE7 205 N10
Fairtrough Rd, Orp. BR6 164 EV112
Fairview, Epsom KT17 157 CW111
Erith DA8 *off Guild Rd* 107 FF80
Potters Bar EN6 *off Hawkshead Rd* 12 DB29
Fairview Av, Brwd. CM13 55 GE45
Rainham RM13 90 FK68
Wembley HA0 79 CK65
Woking GU22 166 AY118
Fairview Cl, E17 47 DY53
Chigwell IG7 49 ES49
Woking GU22 *off Fairview Av* 167 AZ118
Fairview Ct, Ashf. TW15 114 BN92
Fairview Cres, Har. HA2 60 CA60
Fairview Dr, Chig. IG7 49 ES49
Orpington BR6 163 ER105
Shepperton TW17 134 BM99
Watford WD17 23 BS36
Fairview Gdns, Wdf.Grn. IG8 48 EH53
Fairview Ind Est, Oxt. RH8 188 EG133
Fairview Ind Pk, Rain. RM13 89 FE71
Fairview Pl, SW2 121 DM87
Fairview Rd, N15 66 DT57
SW16 141 DM95
Chigwell IG7 49 ES49
Enfield EN2 29 DN39
Epsom KT17 157 CT111
Gravesend (Istead Rise) DA13 130 GD94
Sutton SM1 158 DD106
Fairview Way, Edg. HA8 42 CN49
Fairwater Av, Well. DA16 106 EU84
Fairwater Dr, Add. (New Haw) KT15 152 BK109
Fairway, SW20 139 CW97
Bexleyheath DA6 126 EY85
Carshalton SM5 158 DC111
Chertsey KT16 134 BH102
Orpington BR5 145 ER99
Virginia Water GU25 132 AV100
Woodford Green IG8 48 EJ50
Fairway, The, N13 46 DQ48
N14 29 DH44
NW7 42 CR48
W3 80 CS72
Abbots Langley WD5 7 BR32
Barnet EN5 28 DB44
Bromley BR1 145 EM99
Gravesend DA11 131 GG89
Leatherhead KT22 171 CG118
New Malden KT3 138 CR95
Northolt UB5 78 CC65
Northwood HA6 39 BS49
Ruislip HA4 60 BX62
Upminster RM14 72 FQ59
Uxbridge UB10 76 BM68
Wembley HA0 61 CH62
West Molesey KT8 136 CB97
Weybridge KT13 152 BN111
Fairway Av, NW9 62 CP55
Borehamwood WD6 26 CP40
West Drayton UB7 76 BJ74
Fairway Cl, NW11 64 DC59
Croydon CR0 143 DY99
Epsom KT19 156 CQ105
Hounslow TW4 116 BW85
St. Albans (Park St.) AL2 8 CC27
West Drayton UB7 *off Fairway Av* 76 BK74
Woking GU22 166 AU119
Fairway Ct, NW7 *off The Fairway* 42 CR48
Fairway Dr, SE28 88 EX72
Dartford DA2 128 FP87
Greenford UB6 78 CB66
Fairway Gdns, Beck. BR3 143 ED100
Ilford IG1 69 EQ64
Fairways, Ashf. TW15 115 BP93
Kenley CR8 176 DQ117
Fairways, Stan. HA7 42 CL54
Teddington TW11 117 CK94
Waltham Abbey EN9 16 EE34
Waltham Cross (Chsht.) EN8 15 DX26
Fairweather Cl, N15 66 DS56
Fairweather Rd, N16 66 DU58
Fairwyn Rd, SE26 123 DY91
Fakenham Cl, NW7 43 CU52
Northolt UB5 *off Goodwood Dr* 78 CA65
Fakruddin St, E1 84 DU70
Falaise, Egh. TW20 112 AY92
Falcon Av, Brom. BR1 144 EL98
Grays RM17 110 GB79
Falconberg Ct, W1 195 N8
Falconberg Ms, W1 195 M8
Falcon Cl, SE1 200 G2
W4 *off Sutton La S* 98 CQ79
Dartford DA1 128 FM85
Northwood HA6 39 BS52
Waltham Abbey EN9 *off Kestrel Rd* 16 EG34
Falcon Ct, EC4 196 D9
Woking GU21 151 BC113
Falcon Cres, Enf. EN3 31 DX43
Falcon Dr, Stai. (Stanw.) TW19 114 BK86
Falconer Rd, Bushey WD23 24 BZ44
Ilford IG6 50 EV50
Falconer Wk, N7 *off Newington Barrow Way* 65 DM61
Falcon Gro, SW11 100 DE83
Falcon Ho, W13 79 CF70
Falconhurst, Lthd. (Oxshott) KT22 171 CD115
Falcon La, SW11 100 DE83
Falcon Ms, Grav. DA11 130 GE88
Falcon Pk Ind Est, NW10 63 CT64
Falcon Rd, SW11 100 DE82
Enfield EN3 31 DX43
Hampton TW12 116 BZ94
Falcons Cl, West. (Bigg.H.) TN16 178 EK117
Falcon St, E13 86 EG70
Falcon Ter, SW11 100 DE83
Falcon Way, E11 68 EG56
E14 204 C8
NW9 42 CS54
Feltham TW14 115 BV85
Harrow HA3 62 CL57
Hornchurch RM12 89 FG66
Sunbury-on-Thames TW16 135 BS96
Watford WD25 8 BY34
FALCONWOOD, Well. 105 ER83
⇌ **Falconwood** 105 EQ84
Falconwood, Egh. TW20 112 AY92
Leatherhead (E.Hors.) KT24 171 CF120
Falconwood Av, Well. DA16 105 ER82
Falconwood Par, Well. DA16 105 ES84
Falconwood Rd, Croy. CR0 161 EA108
Falcourt Cl, Sutt. SM1 158 DB106
Falkirk Cl, Horn. RM11 72 FN60
Falkirk Gdns, Wat. WD19 *off Blackford Rd* 40 BX50
Falkirk Ho, W9 82 DB69
Falkirk St, N1 197 N1
Falkland Av, N3 44 DA52
N11 44 DG49
Falkland Pk Av, SE25 142 DS97
Falkland Pl, NW5 *off Falkland Rd* 65 DJ64
Falkland Rd, N8 65 DN56
NW5 65 DJ64
Barnet EN5 27 CY40
Fallaize Av, Ilf. IG1 *off Riverdene Rd* 69 EP63
Falling La, West Dr. UB7 76 BL73
Falloden Way, NW11 64 DA56
Fallow Cl, Chig. IG7 49 ET50
Fallow Ct, SE16 *off Argyle Way* 102 DU78
Fallow Ct Av, N12 44 DC52
Fallowfield, Dart. (Bean) DA2 129 FV90
Stanmore HA7 41 CG48
Fallowfield Cl, Uxb. (Hare.) UB9 38 BJ53
Fallowfield Ct, Stan. HA7 41 CG48
Fallow Flds, Loug. IG10 48 EJ45
Fallowfields Dr, N12 44 DE51
Fallows Cl, N2 44 DC54
Fallsbrook Rd, SW16 121 DJ94
Falman Cl, N9 *off Croyland Rd* 46 DU46
Falmer Rd, E17 67 EB55
N15 66 DQ57
Enfield EN1 30 DS42
Falmouth Av, E4 47 ED50
Falmouth Cl, N22 *off Truro Rd* 45 DM52
SE12 124 EF85
Falmouth Gdns, Ilf. IG4 68 EL57
Falmouth Rd, SE1 201 J6
Walton-on-Thames KT12 154 BW105
Falmouth St, E15 67 ED64
Falmouth Way, E17 *off Gosport Rd* 67 DZ57
Falstaff Cl, Dart. DA1 *off Lower Sta Rd* 127 FE86
Falstaff Ms, Hmptn. (Hmptn.H.) TW12 *off Hampton Rd* 117 CD92
Falstone, Wok. GU21 166 AV118
Fambridge Cl, SE26 123 DZ91
Fambridge Rd, Dag. RM8 70 FA60
Famet Av, Pur. CR8 160 DQ113
Famet Cl, Pur. CR8 160 DQ113
Famet Wk, Pur. CR8 160 DQ113
★ **Family Records Cen, Public Record Office**, EC1 196 E3
Fane St, W14 *off North End Rd* 99 CZ79
Fangrove Pk, Cher. (Lyne) KT16 133 BB102
★ **Fan Mus**, SE10 103 EC80
Fanns Ri, Purf. RM19 108 FN77
Fann St, EC1 197 H5
EC2 197 H5
Fanshawe Av, Bark. IG11 87 EQ65
Fanshawe Cres, Dag. RM9 70 EY64
Hornchurch RM11 72 FK58
Fanshawe Rd, Grays RM16 111 GG76
Richmond TW10 117 CJ91
Fanshaw St, N1 197 M2
Fanthorpe St, SW15 99 CW83
Faraday Av, Sid. DA14 126 EU89
Faraday Cl, N7 *off Bride St* 83 DM65
Watford WD18 23 BR44
★ **Faraday Mus**, W1 *off Albermarle St* 199 K1
Faraday Rd, E15 86 EF65
SW19 120 DA93
W3 80 CQ73
W10 81 CY71
Southall UB1 78 CB73
Welling DA16 106 EU83
West Molesey KT8 136 CA98
Faraday Way, SE18 104 EK76
Croydon CR0 *off Ampere Way* 141 DM102
Orpington BR5 146 EV98
Fareham Rd, Felt. TW14 116 BW87
Fareham St, W1 195 M8
Farewell Pl, Mitch. CR4 140 DE95
Faringdon Av, Brom. BR2 145 EP100
Romford RM3 52 FJ53
Faringford Cl, Pot.B. EN6 12 DD31
Faringford Rd, E15 86 EE66
Farington Acres, Wey. KT13 *35 BR104
Faris Barn Dr, Add. (Woodham) KT15 151 BF112
Faris La, Add. (Woodham) KT15 151 BF111
Farjeon Rd, SE3 104 EK81
FARLEIGH, Warl. 161 DZ114
Farleigh Av, Brom. BR2 144 EF100
Farleigh Border, Croy. CR0 161 DY112
Farleigh Ct Rd, Warl. CR6 161 DZ114
Farleigh Dean Cres, Croy. CR0 161 EB111
Farleigh Pl, N16 *off Farleigh Rd* 66 DT63
Farleigh Rd, N16 66 DT63
Addlestone (New Haw) KT15 152 BG111
Warlingham CR6 177 DX118
Farleton Cl, Wey. KT13 153 BR107
Farley Common, West. TN16 189 EP126
Farleycroft, West. TN16 189 EQ126
Farley Dr, Ilf. IG3 69 ES60
Farley La, West. TN16 189 EP127
Farley Ms, SE6 123 EC87
Farley Nursery, West. TN16 189 EQ127
Farley Pk, Oxt. RH8 187 ED130
Farley Pl, SE25 142 DU98
Farley Rd, SE6 123 EB87
Gravesend DA12 131 GM88
South Croydon CR2 160 DV108
Farlington Pl, SW15 *off Roehampton La* 119 CV87
Farlow Cl, Grav. (Nthflt.) DA11 131 GF90
Farlow Rd, SW15 99 CX83
Farlton Rd, SW18 120 DB87
Farman Gro, Nthlt. UB5 *off Wayfarer Rd* 78 BX69
Farm Av, NW2 63 CY62
SW16 121 DL91
Harrow HA2 60 BZ59
Swanley BR8 147 FC97
Wembley HA0 79 CJ65
Farmborough Cl, Har. HA1 *off Pool Rd* 61 CD59
Farm Cl, SW6 *off Farm La* 100 DA80
Amersham HP6 20 AX39
Barnet EN5 27 CW43
Borehamwood WD6 25 CK38
Brentwood CM13 55 GC45
Buckhurst Hill IG9 48 EJ48
Chertsey (Lyne) KT16 133 BA100
Coulsdon CR5 174 DF120
Dagenham RM10 89 FC66
Leatherhead (Fetch.) KT22 171 CD124
Potters Bar (Cuffley) EN6 13 DK27
Radlett WD7 10 CL30
Shepperton TW17 134 BN101
Southall UB1 78 CB73
Staines TW18 113 BE92
Sutton SM2 158 DD108
Uxbridge UB10 59 BP61
Wallington SM6 159 DJ110
Waltham Cross (Chsht.) EN8 14 DW30
West Byfleet (Byfleet) KT14 152 BM112
West Wickham BR4 144 EE104
Farmcote Rd, SE12 124 EG88
Farm Ct, NW4 63 CU55
Farm Cres, Slou. SL2 74 AV71
Farmcroft, Grav. DA11 131 GG89
Farmdale Rd, SE10 205 N10
Carshalton SM5 158 DE108
Farm Dr, Croy. CR0 143 DZ103
Purley CR8 159 DK112
Farm End, E4 32 EE43
Northwood HA6 *off Drakes Dr* 39 BP53
Farmer Rd, E10 67 EB60
Farmers Cl, Wat. WD25 7 BV33
Farmers Ct, Wal.Abb. EN9 *off Winters Way* 16 EG33
Farmers Rd, SE5 101 DP80
Staines TW18 113 BE92
Farmer St, W8 *off Uxbridge St* 82 DA74
Farm Fld, Wat. WD17 23 BS38
Farmfield Rd, Brom. BR1 124 EE92
Farm Flds, S.Croy. CR2 160 DS111
Farm Hill Rd, Wal.Abb. EN9 15 EC34
Farm Ho Cl, Brox. EN10 15 DZ25
Farmhouse Cl, Wok. GU22 167 BD115
Farmhouse Rd, SW16 121 DJ94
Farmilo Rd, E17 67 DZ59
Farmington Av, Sutt. SM1 140 DD104
Farmlands, Enf. EN2 29 DN39
Pinner HA5 59 BU56
Farmlands, The, Nthlt. UB5 78 BZ65
Farmland Wk, Chis. BR7 125 EP92
Farm La, N14 28 DG44
SW6 100 DA79
Addlestone KT15 152 BG107
Ashtead KT21 172 CN116
Carshalton SM5 158 DF110
Croydon CR0 143 DZ103
Epsom KT18 172 CP119
Purley CR8 159 DJ110
Rickmansworth (Loud.) WD3 22 BH41
Woking (Send) GU23 167 BC124
Farmleigh, N14 45 DJ45
Farmleigh Gro, Walt. KT12 153 BT106
Farm Pl, W8 *off Uxbridge St* 82 DA74
Dartford DA1 107 FG84
Farm Rd, N21 45 DP46
NW10 *off Mordaunt Rd* 80 CR67
Edgware HA8 42 CP51
Esher KT10 136 CB102
Grays (Orsett) RM16 111 GF75
Hounslow TW4 116 BY88
Morden SM4 140 DB99
Northwood HA6 39 BQ50
Rainham RM13 90 FJ69
Rickmansworth (Chorl.) WD3 21 BA42
Sevenoaks TN14 191 FJ121
Staines TW18 114 BH93
Sutton SM2 158 DD108
Warlingham CR6 177 DY119
Woking GU22 167 BB120
Farmstead Rd, SE6 123 EB91
Harrow HA3 41 CD53
Farm St, W1 199 H1
Farm Vale, Bex. DA5 127 FB86
Farmview, Cob. KT11 170 BX116
Farm Vw, Tad. (Lwr.Kgswd.) KT20 183 CZ127
Farm Wk, NW11 63 CZ57
Farm Way, Buck.H. IG9 48 EJ49
Bushey WD23 24 CB42
Farmway, Dag. RM8 70 EW63
Farm Way, Horn. RM12 71 FH63
Northwood HA6 39 BS49
Staines TW19 113 BF86
Worcester Park KT4 139 CW104
Farnaby Dr, Sev. TN13 190 FF126
Farnaby Rd, SE9 104 EJ84
Bromley BR1, BR2 123 ED94
Farnan Av, E17 47 EA54
Farnan Rd, SW16 121 DL92
FARNBOROUGH, Orp. 163 EP106
Farnborough Av, E17 67 DY55
South Croydon CR2 161 DX108
Farnborough Cl, Wem. HA9 *off Chalkhill Rd* 62 CP61
Farnborough Common, Orp. BR6 145 EM104
Farnborough Cres, Brom. BR2 *off Saville Row* 144 EF102
South Croydon CR2 161 DY109
Farnborough Hill, Orp. BR6 163 ER106
[H] **Farnborough Hosp**, Orp. BR6 145 EN104
Farnborough Ho, SW15 *off Fontley Way* 119 CU88
Farnborough Way, SE15 *off Chandler Way* 102 DT80
Orpington BR6 163 EQ105
Farncombe St, SE16 202 C5
Farndale Av, N13 45 DP48
Farndale Cres, Grnf. UB6 78 CC69
Farnell Ms, SW5 *off Earls Ct Sq* 100 DB78
Farnell Rd, Islw. TW7 97 CD83
Staines TW18 114 BG90
Farnes Dr, Rom. RM2 52 FJ54
Farnham Cl, N20 44 DC45
Hemel Hempstead (Bov.) HP3 5 BA28
Farnham Gdns, SW20 139 CV96
Farnham Pl, SE1 200 G3
Farnham Rd, Ilf. IG3 69 ET59
Romford RM3 52 FK50
Welling DA16 106 EW82
Farnham Royal, SE11 101 DM78
FARNINGHAM, Dart. 148 FN100
Farningham Cres, Cat. CR3 *off Commonwealth Rd* 176 DU123
Farningham Hill Rd, Dart. (Fnghm.) DA4 148 FJ99
⇌ **Farningham Road** 148 FP96
Farningham Rd, N17 46 DU52
Caterham CR3 176 DU123
Farnley, Wok. GU21 166 AT117
Farnley Rd, E4 48 EE45
SE25 142 DR98
Farnol Rd, Dart. DA1 108 FN84
Faro Cl, Brom. BR1 145 EN96
Faroe Rd, W14 99 CX76
Farorna Wk, Enf. EN2 29 DN39
Farquhar Rd, SE19 122 DT92
SW19 120 DA90
Farquharson Rd, Croy. CR0 142 DQ102
Farraline Rd, Wat. WD18 23 BV42
Farrance Rd, Rom. RM6 70 EY58
Farrance St, E14 85 DZ72
Farrans Ct, Har. HA3 61 CH59
Farrant Av, N22 45 DN54
Farrant Cl, Orp. BR6 164 EU108
Farrant Way, Borwd. WD6 26 CL39
Farr Av, Bark. IG11 88 EU68
Farrell Ho, E1 84 DW72
Farren Rd, SE23 123 DY89
Farrer Ms, N8 *off Farrer Rd* 65 DJ56
Farrer Rd, N8 65 DJ56
Harrow HA3 62 CL57
Farrer's Pl, Croy. CR0 161 DX105
Farrier Cl, Sun. TW16 135 BU98
Uxbridge UB8 *off Horseshoe Dr* 76 BN72

★ Place of interest ⇌ Railway station ⊖ London Underground station DLR Docklands Light Railway station Tramlink station [H] Hospital

255

Far - Fil

Farrier Rd, Nthlt. UB5 ....78 CA68
Farriers Cl, Epsom KT17 ....156 CS111
Gravesend DA12 ....131 GM88
Hemel Hempstead (Bov.) HP3
off Chipperfield Rd 5 BB28
Farriers Ct, Sutt. SM3
off Forge La 157 CY108
Watford WD25 ....7 BV32
Farriers End, Brox. EN10 ....15 DZ26
Farriers Rd, Epsom KT17 ....156 CS112
Farrier St, NW1 ....83 DH66
Farriers Way, Borwd. WD6 ....26 CQ44
Farrier Wk, SW10 ....100 DC79
⇌ Farringdon 196 E6
⊖ Farringdon 196 E6
Farringdon La, EC1 ....196 E5
Farringdon Rd, EC1 ....196 D4
Farringdon St, EC4 ....196 F8
Farringford Cl, St.Alb. AL2 ....8 CA26
Farrington Av, Orp. BR5 ....146 EV97
Farrington Pl, Chis. BR7 ....125 ER94
Northwood HA6 ....39 BT49
Farrins Rents, SE16 ....203 K3
Farrow La, SE14 ....102 DW80
Farrow Pl, SE16 ....203 K6
Farr Rd, Enf. EN2 ....30 DR39
Farthingale Ct, Wal.Abb. EN9 ....16 EG34
Farthingale La, Wal.Abb. EN9 ....16 EG34
Farthingale Wk, E15 ....85 ED66
Farthing All, SE1 ....202 B5
Farthing Cl, Dart. DA1 ....108 FM84
Farthing Flds, E1 ....202 E2
Farthing Grn La, Slou. (Stoke P.)
SL2 ....74 AU68
Farthings, Wok. (Knap.)
GU21 ....166 AS116
Farthings, The, Kings.T. KT2
off Brunswick Rd 138 CN95
Farthings Cl, E4 ....48 EE48
Pinner HA5 ....59 BV58
Farthing St, Orp. BR6 ....163 EM108
Farwell Rd, Sid. DA14 ....126 EV90
Farwig La, Brom. BR1 ....144 EF95
Fashion St, E1 ....197 P7
Fashoda Rd, Brom. BR2 ....144 EK98
Fassett Rd, E8 ....84 DU65
Kingston upon Thames
KT1 ....138 CL98
Fassett Sq, E8 ....84 DU65
Fassnidge Way, Uxb. UB8
off Oxford Rd 76 BJ66
Fauconberg Rd, W4 ....98 CQ79
Faulkner Cl, Dag. RM8 ....70 EX59
Faulkner's All, EC1 ....196 F6
Faulkners Rd, Walt. KT12 ....154 BW106
Faulkner St, SE14 ....102 DW81
Fauna Cl, Rom. RM6 ....70 EW59
Faunce St, SE17
off Harmsworth St 101 DP78
Favart Rd, SW6 ....100 DA81
Faverolle Grn, Wal.Cr. EN8 ....15 DX28
Faversham Av, E4 ....48 EE46
Enfield EN1 ....30 DR44
Faversham Cl, Chig. IG7 ....50 EV47
Faversham Rd, SE6 ....123 DZ87
Beckenham BR3 ....143 DZ96
Morden SM4 ....140 DB100
Fawcett Cl, SW11 ....100 DD82
SW16 ....121 DN91
Fawcett Est, E5 ....66 DU60
Fawcett Rd, NW10 ....81 CT67
Croydon CR0 ....142 DQ104
Fawcett St, SW10 ....100 DC79
Fawcus Cl, Esher (Clay.) KT10
off Dalmore Av 155 CF107
Fawe Pk Rd, SW15 ....99 CZ84
Fawe St, E14 ....85 EB71
Fawke Common, Sev. (Undrvr.)
TN15 ....191 FP127
Fawke Common Rd, Sev.
TN15 ....191 FP126
Fawkes Av, Dart. DA1 ....128 FM89
FAWKHAM GREEN, Long. 149 FV104
Fawkham Grn Rd, Long.
(Fawk.Grn.) DA3 ....149 FV104
H Fawkham Manor Hosp,
Long. DA3 ....149 FW102
Fawkham Rd, Long. DA3 ....149 FX97
Fawley Rd, NW6 ....64 DB64
Fawnbrake Av, SE24 ....121 DP85
Fawn Rd, E13 ....86 EJ68
Chigwell IG7 ....49 ET50
Fawns Manor Cl, Felt. TW14 ....115 BQ88
Fawns Manor Rd, Felt. TW14 ....115 BR88
Fawood Av, NW10 ....80 CR66
Fawsley Cl, Slou. (Colnbr.)
SL3 ....93 BE80
Fawters Cl, Brwd. CM13 ....55 GD44
Fayerfield, Pot.B. EN6 ....12 DD31
Faygate Cres, Bexh. DA6 ....126 FA85
Faygate Rd, SW2 ....121 DM89
Fay Grn, Abb.L. WD5 ....7 BR33
Fayland Av, SW16 ....121 DJ92
Faymore Gdns, S.Ock. RM15 ....91 FU72
Fearney Mead, Rick. (Mill End)
WD3 ....38 BG46
Fearnley Cres, Hmptn. TW12 ....116 BY92
Fearnley St, Wat. WD18 ....23 BV42
Fearns Mead, Brwd. CM14
off Bucklers Ct 54 FW50
Fearon St, SE10 ....205 M10
Featherbed La, Abb.L. (Bedmond)
WD5 off Sergehill La 7 BV26
Croydon CR0 ....161 DZ108
Romford RM4 ....50 EY45
Warlingham CR6 ....161 ED113
Feathers La, Stai. (Wrays.)
TW19 ....113 BA89
Feathers Pl, SE10 ....103 ED79
Featherstone Av, SE23 ....122 DV89
Featherstone Gdns, Borwd.
WD6 ....26 CQ42
Featherstone Ind Est, Sthl.
UB2 ....96 BY75
Featherstone Rd, NW7 ....43 CV51
Southall UB2 ....96 BY76
Featherstone St, EC1 ....197 K4
Featherstone Ter, Sthl. UB2 ....96 BY76
Featley Rd, SW9 ....101 DP83
Federal Rd, Grnf. UB6 ....79 CJ68
Federal Way, Wat. WD24 ....24 BW38
Federation Rd, SE2 ....106 EV77
Fee Fm Rd, Esher (Clay.)
KT10 ....155 CF108
Feenan Highway, Til. RM18 ....111 GH80
Felbridge Av, Stan. HA7 ....41 CG53
Felbridge Cl, SW16 ....121 DN91
Sutton SM2 ....158 DC109
Felbrigge Rd, Ilf. IG3 ....69 ET61
Felcott Cl, Walt. KT12 ....136 BW104
Felcott Rd, Walt. KT12 ....136 BW104
Felday Rd, SE13 ....123 EB86
Felden Cl, Pnr. HA5 ....40 BY52
Watford WD25 ....8 BX34
Felden St, SW6 ....99 CZ81
Feldman Cl, N16 ....66 DU60
Felgate Ms, W6 ....99 CV77
Felhampton Rd, SE9 ....125 EP89
Felhurst Cres, Dag. RM10 ....71 FB63
Felicia Way, Grays RM16 ....111 GH77
Felipe Rd, Grays (Chaff.Hun.)
RM16 ....109 FW76
Felix Av, N8 ....65 DL58
Felix La, Shep. TW17 ....135 BS100
Felix Rd, W13 ....79 CG73
Walton-on-Thames KT12 ....135 BU100
Felixstowe Ct, E16
off Fishguard Way 105 EP75
Felixstowe Rd, N9 ....46 DU49
N17 ....66 DT55
NW10 ....81 CV69
SE2 ....106 EV76
Fellbrigg Rd, SE22 ....122 DT85
Fellbrigg St, E1
off Headlam St 84 DV70
Fellbrook, Rich. TW10 ....117 CH90
Fellmongers Path, SE1 ....201 N5
Fellmongers Yd, Croy. CR0
off Surrey St 142 DQ103
Fellowes Cl, Hayes UB4
off Paddington Cl 78 BX70
Fellowes Rd, Cars. SM5 ....140 DE104
Fellows Ct, E2 ....197 P1
Fellows Rd, NW3 ....82 DD66
Fell Rd, Croy. CR0 ....142 DQ104
Felltram Way, SE7 ....205 N10
Fell Wk, Edg. HA8
off East Rd 42 CP53
Felmersham Cl, SW4
off Haselrigge Rd 101 DK84
Felmingham Rd, SE20 ....142 DW96
Felnex Trd Est, Wall. SM6 ....140 DG103
Felsberg Rd, SW2 ....121 DL86
Fels Cl, Dag. RM10 ....71 FB62
Fels Fm Av, Dag. RM10 ....71 FC62
Felsham Rd, SW15 ....99 CX83
Felspar Cl, SE18 ....105 ET78
Felstead Av, Ilf. IG5 ....49 EN53
Felstead Cl, Brwd. CM13 ....55 GC44
Felstead Gdns, E14
off Ferry St 103 EC78
Felstead Rd, E11 ....68 EG59
Epsom KT19 ....156 CR111
Loughton IG10 ....48 EL45
Orpington BR6 ....146 EU103
Romford RM5 ....51 FC51
Waltham Cross EN8 ....15 DY32
Felstead St, E9 ....85 DZ65
Felsted Rd, E16 ....86 EK72
FELTHAM 115 BU89
⇌ Feltham 115 BV88
Feltham Av, E.Mol. KT8 ....137 CE98
Felthambrook Way, Felt.
TW13 ....115 BV90
Feltham Business Complex, Felt.
TW13 ....115 BV89
FELTHAMHILL, Felt. 115 BT92
Feltham Hill Rd, Ashf. TW15 ....115 BP92
Feltham TW13 ....115 BU91
Feltham Rd, Ashf. TW15 ....115 BP91
Mitcham CR4 ....140 DF96
Felton Cl, Borwd. WD6 ....26 CL38
Broxbourne EN10 ....15 DZ25
Orpington BR5 ....145 EP100
Felton Gdns, Bark. IG11
off Sutton Rd 87 ES67
Felton Ho, SE3
off Ryan Cl 104 EH84
Felton Lea, Sid. DA14 ....125 ET92
Felton Rd, W13
off Camborne Av 97 CJ75
Barking IG11
off Sutton Rd 87 ES68
Felton St, N1 ....84 DR67
Fencepiece Rd, Chig. IG7 ....49 EQ50
Ilford IG6 ....49 EQ50
Fenchurch Av, EC3 ....197 M9
Fenchurch Bldgs, EC3 ....197 N9
Fenchurch Pl, EC3 ....197 N10
⇌ Fenchurch Street 197 N10
Fenchurch St, EC3 ....197 M10
Fen Cl, Brwd. CM15 ....55 GC42
Fen Ct, EC3 ....197 M10
Fendall Rd, Epsom KT19 ....156 CQ106
Fendall St, SE1 ....201 N7
Fendt Cl, E16
off Bowman Av 86 EF73
Fendyke Rd, Belv. DA17 ....106 EX76
Fenelon Pl, W14 ....99 CZ77
Fengates Rd, Red. RH1 ....184 DE134
Fen Gro, Sid. DA15 ....125 ET86
Fenham Rd, SE15 ....102 DU80
Fen La, Upmin. (N.Ock.)
RM14 ....73 FW64
Fenman Ct, N17
off Shelbourne Rd 46 DV53
Fenman Gdns, Ilf. IG3 ....70 EV60
Fenn Cl, Brom. BR1 ....124 EG93
Fennel Cl, E16
off Cranberry La 86 EE70
Croydon CR0
off Primrose La 143 DX102
Fennells Mead, Epsom KT17 ....157 CT109
Fennel St, SE18 ....105 EN79
Fenner Cl, SE16 ....202 E8
Fenner Ho, Walt. KT12 ....153 BU105
Fenner Rd, Grays RM16 ....109 FW77
Fenner Sq, SW11
off Thomas Baines Rd 100 DD83
Fenning St, SE1 ....201 M4
Fenn St, E9 ....66 DW64
Fenns Way, Wok. GU21 ....166 AY115
Fenstanton Av, N12 ....44 DD50
Fen St, E16
off Victoria Dock Rd 86 EF73
Fens Way, Swan. BR8 ....127 FG93
Fenswood Cl, Bex. DA5 ....126 FA85
Fentiman Rd, SW8 ....101 DL79
Fentiman Way, Horn. RM11 ....72 FL60
Fenton Av, Stai. TW18 ....114 BJ93
Fenton Cl, E8 off Laurel St 84 DT65
SW9 ....101 DM82
Chislehurst BR7 ....125 EM92
Redhill RH1 ....184 DG134
★ Fenton Ho, NW3
(Hampstead) 64 DC62
Fenton Rd, N17 ....46 DQ52
Grays (Chaff.Hun.) RM16 ....110 FY75
Redhill RH1 ....184 DG134
Fentons Av, E13 ....86 EH68
Fenwick Cl, SE18 off Ritter St 105 EN79
Woking GU21 ....166 AV118
Fenwick Gro, SE15 ....102 DU83
Fenwick Path, Borwd. WD6 ....26 CM38
Fenwick Pl, SW9 ....101 DL83
South Croydon CR2
off Columbine Av 159 DP108
Fenwick Rd, SE15 ....102 DU83
Ferdinand Pl, NW1
off Ferdinand St 82 DG66
Ferdinand St, NW1 ....82 DG65
Ferguson Av, Grav. DA12 ....131 GJ91
Romford RM2 ....52 FJ54
Surbiton KT5 ....138 CM99
Ferguson Cl, E14 ....203 P9
Bromley BR2 ....143 EC97
Ferguson Ct, Rom. RM2 ....52 FK54
Ferguson Dr, W3 ....80 CR72
Fergus Rd, N5
off Calabria Rd 65 DP64
Ferme Pk Rd, N4 ....65 DL57
N8 ....65 DL57
Fermor Rd, SE23 ....123 DY88
Fermoy Rd, W9 ....81 CZ70
Greenford UB6 ....78 CB70
Fern Av, Mitch. CR4 ....141 DK98
Fernbank, Buck.H. IG9 ....48 EH46
Fernbank Av, Horn. RM12 ....72 FJ63
Walton-on-Thames KT12 ....136 BY101
Wembley HA0 ....61 CF63
Fernbank Ms, SW12 ....121 DJ86
Fernbank Rd, Add. KT15 ....152 BG106
Fernbrook Av, Sid. DA15
off Blackfen Rd 125 ES85
Fernbrook Cres, SE13 ....124 EE86
Fernbrook Dr, Har. HA2 ....60 CB59
Fernbrook Rd, SE13 ....124 EE86
Ferncliff Rd, E8 ....66 DU64
Fern Cl, Erith DA8
off Hollywood Way 107 FH81
Warlingham CR6 ....177 DY118
Ferncroft Av, N12 ....44 DE51
NW3 ....64 DA62
Ruislip HA4 ....60 BW61
Ferndale, Brom. BR1 ....144 EJ96
Ferndale Av, E17 ....67 ED57
Chertsey KT16 ....133 BE104
Hounslow TW4 ....96 BY83
Ferndale Cl, Bexh. DA7 ....106 EY81
Ferndale Ct, SE3 ....104 EF80
Ferndale Cres, Uxb. UB8 ....76 BJ69
Ferndale Rd, E7 ....86 EH66
E11 ....68 EE61
N15 ....66 DT58
SE25 ....142 DV99
SW4 ....101 DL84
SW9 ....101 DM83
Ashford TW15 ....114 BK92
Banstead SM7 ....173 CZ116
Enfield EN3 ....31 DY37
Gravesend DA12 ....131 GH89
Romford RM5 ....51 FC54
Woking GU21 ....167 AZ116
Ferndale St, E6 ....87 EP73
Ferndale Ter, Har. HA1 ....61 CF56
Ferndale Way, Orp. BR6 ....163 ER106
Ferndell Av, Bex. DA5 ....127 FD90
Fern Dene, W13
off Templewood 79 CH71
Ferndene, St.Alb. (Brick.Wd.)
AL2 ....8 BZ31
Ferndene Rd, SE24 ....102 DQ84
Fernden Way, Rom. RM7 ....71 FB58
Ferndown, Horn. RM11 ....72 FM58
Northwood HA6 ....39 BU54
Ferndown Av, Orp. BR6 ....145 ER102
Ferndown Cl, Pnr. HA5 ....40 BY52
Sutton SM2 ....158 DD107
Ferndown Gdns, Cob. KT11 ....154 BW113
Ferndown Rd, SE9 ....124 EK87
Watford WD19 ....40 BW48
Fernery, The, Stai. TW18 ....113 BE92
Fernes Cl, Uxb. UB8 ....76 BJ72
Ferney Ct, W.Byf. (Byfleet) KT14
off Ferney Rd 152 BK112
Ferney Meade Way, Islw. TW7 ....97 CG82
Ferney Rd, Barn. EN4 ....44 DG45
Waltham Cross (Chsht.)
EN7 ....14 DR26
West Byfleet (Byfleet)
KT14 ....152 BK112
Fern Gro, Felt. TW14 ....115 BV87
Ferngrove Cl, Lthd. (Fetch.)
KT22 ....171 CE122
Fernhall Dr, Ilf. IG4 ....68 EK57
Fernhall La, Wal.Abb. EN9 ....16 EK31
Fernham Rd, Th.Hth. CR7 ....142 DQ97
Fernhead Rd, W9 ....81 CZ70
Fernheath Way, Dart. DA2 ....127 FD92
Fernhill, Lthd. (Oxshott)
KT22 ....155 CD114
Fernhill Cl, Wok. GU22 ....166 AW120
Fernhill Ct, E17 ....47 ED54
Fernhill Gdns, Kings.T. KT2 ....117 CK92
Fernhill La, Wok. GU22 ....166 AW120
Fernhill Pk, Wok. GU22 ....166 AW120
Fernhills, Kings L. WD4 ....7 BR33
Fernhill St, E16 ....87 EM74
Fernholme Rd, SE15 ....123 DX85
Fernhurst Gdns, Edg. HA8 ....42 CN51
Fernhurst Rd, SW6 ....99 CY81
Ashford TW15 ....115 BQ91
Croydon CR0 ....142 DU101
Fernie Cl, Chig. IG7 ....50 EU50
Fernihough Cl, Wey. KT13 ....152 BN111
Fernlands Cl, Cher. KT16 ....133 BE104
Fern La, Houns. TW5 ....96 BZ78
Fernlea, Lthd. (Bkhm.) KT23 ....170 CB123
Fernlea Rd, SW12 ....121 DH88
Mitcham CR4 ....140 DG96
Fernleigh Cl, W9 ....81 CZ69
Croydon CR0
off Stafford Rd 159 DN105
Walton-on-Thames KT12 ....135 BV104
Fernleigh Ct, Har. HA2 ....40 CB54
Wembley HA9 ....62 CL61
Fernleigh Rd, N21 ....45 DN47
Fernsbury St, WC1 ....196 D3
Ferns Cl, Enf. EN3 ....31 DY36
South Croydon CR2 ....160 DV110
Fernshaw Rd, SW10 ....100 DC79
Fernside, NW11
off Finchley Rd 64 DA61
Buckhurst Hill IG9 ....48 EH46
Fernside Av, NW7 ....42 CR48
Feltham TW13 ....115 BV91
Fernside La, Sev. TN13 ....191 FJ129
Fernside Rd, SW12 ....120 DF88
Fernsleigh Cl, Ger.Cr. (Chal.St.P.)
SL9 ....36 AY51
Ferns Rd, E15 ....86 EF65
Fern St, E3 ....85 EA70
Fernthorpe Rd, SW16 ....121 DJ93
Ferntower Rd, N5 ....66 DR64
Fern Twrs, Cat. CR3 ....186 DU125
Fern Wk, SE16
off Argyle Way 102 DU78
Ashford TW15
off Ferndale Rd 114 BK92
Fern Way, Wat. WD25 ....23 BU35
Fernways, Ilf. IG1
off Cecil Rd 69 EP63
Fernwood Av, SW16 ....121 DK91
Wembley HA0
off Bridgewater Rd 61 CJ64
Fernwood Cl, Brom. BR1 ....144 EJ96
Fernwood Cres, N20 ....44 DF48
Ferny Hill, Barn. EN4 ....28 DF38
Ferranti Cl, SE18 ....104 EK76
Ferraro Cl, Houns. TW5 ....96 CA79
Ferrers Av, Wall. SM6 ....159 DK105
West Drayton UB7 ....94 BK75
Ferrers Rd, SW16 ....121 DK92
Ferrestone Rd, N8 ....65 DM56
Ferrey Ms, SW9 ....101 DN82
Ferriby Cl, N1
off Bewdley St 83 DN66
Ferrier Pt, E16
off Forty Acre La 86 EH71
Ferrier St, SW18 ....100 DB84
Ferriers Way, Epsom KT18 ....173 CW119
Ferring Cl, Har. HA2 ....60 CC60
Ferrings, SE21 ....122 DS89
Ferris Av, Croy. CR0 ....143 DZ104
Ferris Rd, SE22 ....102 DU84
Ferron Rd, E5 ....66 DV62
Ferro Rd, Rain. RM13 ....89 FG70
Ferrour Ct, N2 ....64 DD55
Ferry Av, Stai. TW18 ....113 BE94
Ferryhills Cl, Wat. WD19 ....40 BW48
Ferry La, N17 ....66 DU56
SW13 ....99 CT79
Brentford TW8 ....98 CL79
Chertsey KT16 ....134 BH98
Rainham RM13 ....89 FE72
Richmond TW9 ....98 CM79
Shepperton TW17 ....134 BN102
Staines (Laleham) TW18 ....134 BJ97
Staines (Wrays.) TW19 ....113 BB89
Ferryman's Quay, SW6 ....100 DC82
Ferrymead Av, Grnf. UB6 ....78 CA69
Ferrymead Dr, Grnf. UB6 ....78 CA68
Ferrymead Gdns, Grnf. UB6 ....78 CC68
Ferrymoor, Rich. TW10 ....117 CH90
Ferry Pl, SE18
off Woolwich High St 105 EN76
Ferry Rd, SW13 ....99 CU80
Teddington TW11 ....117 CH92
Thames Ditton KT7 ....137 CH100
Tilbury RM18 ....111 GG83
Twickenham TW1 ....117 CH88
West Molesey KT8 ....136 CA97
Ferry Sq, Brent. TW8 ....98 CL79
Shepperton TW17 ....135 BP101
Ferry St, E14 ....204 D10
Feryby Rd, Grays RM16 ....111 GH76
Festing Rd, SW15 ....99 CX83
Festival Cl, Bex. DA5 ....126 EX88
Erith DA8 off Betsham Rd 107 FF80
Uxbridge UB10 ....77 BP67
Festival Path, Wok. GU21 ....166 AT119
Festival Wk, Cars. SM5 ....158 DF106
FETCHAM, Lthd. 171 CD123
Fetcham Common La, Lthd.
(Fetch.) KT22 ....170 CB121
Fetcham Pk Dr, Lthd. (Fetch.)
KT22 ....171 CE123
Fetherstone Cl, Pot.B. EN6 ....12 DD32
Fetter La, EC4 ....196 E9
Ffinch St, SE8 ....103 EA80
Fiddicroft Av, Bans. SM7 ....158 DB114
Fiddlers Cl, Green. DA9 ....109 FV84
FIDDLERS HAMLET, Epp. 18 EW32
Fidler Pl, Bushey WD23
off Ashfield Av 24 CB44
Field Cl, E4 ....47 EB51
NW2 ....63 CU61
Bromley BR1 ....144 EJ96
Field Cl, Buck.H. IG9 ....48 EJ48
Chesham HP5 ....4 AS28
Chessington KT9 ....155 CJ106
Hayes UB3 ....95 BQ80
Hounslow TW4 ....95 BV81
Romford (Abridge) RM4 ....34 EV41
Ruislip HA4 off Field Way 59 BQ60
South Croydon CR2 ....160 DV114
West Molesey KT8 ....136 CB99
Fieldcommon La, Walt. KT12 ....136 BZ101
Field Ct, WC1 ....196 C7
Oxted RH8
off Silkham Rd 188 EE127
Field End, Barn. EN5 ....27 CV42
Coulsdon CR5 ....159 DK114
Northolt UB5 ....78 BX65
Ruislip HA4 ....78 BW65
Twickenham TW1 ....117 CF91
Field End Cl, Wat. WD19 ....40 BY45
Fieldend Rd, SW16 ....141 DJ95
Field End Rd, Pnr. HA5 ....59 BV58
Ruislip HA4 ....60 BY63
Fielders Cl, Enf. EN1
off Woodfield Cl 30 DS42
Harrow HA2 ....60 CC60
Fielders Way, Rad. (Shenley)
WD7 ....10 CL33
Fieldfare Rd, SE28 ....88 EW73
Fieldgate La, Mitch. CR4 ....140 DE97
Fieldgate St, E1 ....84 DU71
Fieldhouse Cl, E18 ....48 EG53
Fieldhouse Rd, SW12 ....121 DJ88
Fieldhurst, Slou. SL3 ....93 AZ78
Fieldhurst Cl, Add. KT15 ....152 BH106
Fielding Av, Til. RM18 ....111 GH81
Twickenham TW2 ....116 CC90
Fielding Gdns, Slou. SL3 ....92 AW75
Fielding Ho, NW6 ....82 DA69
Fielding Ms, SW13
off Castelnau 99 CV79
Fielding Rd, W4 ....98 CR76
W14 ....99 CX76
Fieldings, The, SE23 ....122 DW88
Banstead SM7 ....173 CZ117
Woking GU21 ....166 AT116
Fieldings Rd, Wal.Cr. (Chsht.)
EN8 ....15 DZ29
Fielding St, SE17 ....102 DQ79
Fielding Wk, W13 ....97 CH76
Fielding Way, Brwd. CM13 ....55 GC44
Field La, Brent. TW8 ....97 CJ80
Teddington TW11 ....117 CG92
Field Mead, NW7 ....42 CS52
NW9 ....42 CS52
Field Pl, N.Mal. KT3 ....139 CT100
Field Rd, E7 ....68 EF63
N17 ....66 DR55
W6 ....99 CY78
Feltham TW14 ....115 BV86
South Ockendon (Aveley)
RM15 ....90 FQ74
Uxbridge (Denh.) UB9 ....57 BE63
Watford WD19 ....24 BY44
Fields Ct, Pot.B. EN6 ....12 DD33
Fieldsend Rd, Sutt. SM3 ....157 CY106
Fields Est, E8 ....84 DU66
Fieldside Cl, Orp. BR6
off State Fm Av 163 EQ105
Fieldside Rd, Brom. BR1 ....123 ED92
Fields Pk Cres, Rom. RM6 ....70 EX57
Field St, WC1 ....196 B2
Fieldview, SW18 ....120 DD88
Field Vw, Egh. TW20 ....113 BC92
Feltham TW13 ....115 BR91
Fieldview Ct, Stai. TW18
off Burges Way 114 BG93
Field Vw Ri, St.Alb. (Brick.Wd.)
AL2 ....8 BY29
Field Vw Rd, Pot.B. EN6 ....12 DA33
Fieldway 161 EB108
Field Way, NW10
off Twybridge Way 80 CQ66
Croydon CR0 ....161 EB107
Fieldway, Dag. RM8 ....70 EV63
Field Way, Ger.Cr. (Chal.St.P.)
SL9 ....36 AX52
Greenford UB6 ....78 CB67
Hemel Hempstead (Bov.)
HP3 ....5 BA27
Fieldway, Orp. BR5 ....145 ER100
Field Way, Rick. WD3 ....38 BH46
Ruislip HA4 ....59 BQ60
Uxbridge UB8 ....76 BK70
Fieldway Cres, N5 ....65 DN64
Fiennes Cl, Dag. RM8 ....70 EW60
Fiennes Way, Sev. TN13 ....191 FJ127
Fiesta Dr, Dag. RM9 ....89 FC70
Fifehead Cl, Ashf. TW15 ....114 BL93
Fife Rd, E16 ....86 EG71
N22 ....45 DP52
SW14 ....118 CQ85
Kingston upon Thames
KT1 ....138 CL96
Fife Ter, N1 ....83 DM68
Fifield Path, SE23
off Bampton Rd 123 DX90
Fifth Av, E12 ....69 EM63
W10 ....81 CY69
Grays RM20 ....109 FU79
Hayes UB3 ....77 BT74
Watford WD25 ....24 BX35
Fifth Cross Rd, Twick. TW2 ....117 CD89
Fifth Way, Wem. HA9 ....62 CP63
Figges Rd, Mitch. CR4 ....120 DG94
Fig St, Sev. TN14 ....190 FF129
Fig Tree Cl, NW10
off Craven Pk 80 CS67
Filby Rd, Chess. KT9 ....156 CM107
Filey Av, N16 ....66 DU60
Filey Cl, Sutt. SM2 ....158 DC108
Westerham (Bigg.H.) TN16 ....178 EH119
Filey Waye, Ruis. HA4 ....59 BU61
Filigree Ct, SE16 ....203 L3
Fillebrook Av, Enf. EN1 ....30 DS40

Fil - Fol

Fillebrook Rd, E11 67 ED60
Filmer La, Sev.TN14 191 FL121
Filmer Rd, SW6 99 CY81
Filston La, Sev.TN14 165 FE113
Filston Rd, Erith DA8 off Riverdale Rd 107 FB78
Finborough Rd, SW10 100 DB78
SW17 120 DF93
Finchale Rd, SE2 106 EU76
Fincham Cl, Uxb. UB10 off Aylsham Dr 59 BQ61
Finch Av, SE27 122 DR91
Finch Cl, NW10 62 CR64
Barnet EN5 28 DA43
Finchdean Ho, SW15 off Tangley Gro 119 CT87
Finch Dr, Felt. TW14 116 BX87
Finch Gdns, E4 47 EA50
Finch Grn, Rick. (Chorl.) WD3 21 BF42
Finchingfield Av, Wdf.Grn. IG8 48 EJ52
Finch La, EC3 197 L9
Amersham HP7 20 AV40
Bushey WD23 24 CA43
FINCHLEY, N3 44 DB53
⊖ Finchley Central 44 DA53
Finchley Cl, Dart. DA1 128 FN86
Finchley Ct, N3 44 DB51
Finchley La, NW4 63 CW56
H Finchley Mem Hosp, N12 44 DC52
Finchley Pk, N12 44 DC49
Finchley Pl, NW8 82 DD68
⊖ Finchley Road 82 DC65
Finchley Rd, NW2 64 DA62
NW3 82 DC65
NW8 82 DD67
NW11 63 CZ58
Grays RM17 110 GB79
⇌ Finchley Road & Frognal 64 DC64
Finchley Way, N3 44 DA52
Finch Ms, SE15 102 DT80
Finck St, SE1 200 C5
Finden Rd, E7 68 EH64
Findhorn Av, Hayes UB4 77 BV71
Findhorn St, E14 85 EC72
Findon Cl, SW18 off Wimbledon Pk Rd 120 DA86
Harrow HA2 60 CB62
Findon Ct, Add. KT15 off Spinney Hill 151 BF106
Findon Gdns, Rain. RM13 89 FG71
Findon Rd, N9 46 DV46
W12 99 CU75
Fine Bush La, Uxb. (Hare.) UB9 59 BP58
Fingal St, SE10 205 L10
Finglesham Cl, Orp. BR5 off Westwell Cl 146 EX102
Finians Cl, Uxb. UB10 76 BM66
Finland Quay, SE16 203 L7
Finland Rd, SE4 103 DY83
Finland St, SE16 203 L7
Finlay Gdns, Add. KT15 152 BJ105
Finlays Cl, Chess. KT9 156 CN106
Finlay St, SW6 99 CX81
Finnart Cl, Wey. KT13 153 BQ105
Finnart Ho Dr, Wey. KT13 off Vaillant Rd 153 BQ105
Finney La, Islw. TW7 97 CG81
Finnis St, E2 84 DV69
Finnymore Rd, Dag. RM9 88 EY66
FINSBURY, EC1 196 E2
Finsbury Av, EC2 197 L7
Finsbury Circ, EC2 197 L7
Finsbury Cotts, N22 off Clarence Rd 45 DL52
Finsbury Ct, Wal.Cr. EN8 off Parkside 15 DY34
Finsbury Est, EC1 196 F3
Finsbury Ho, N22 45 DL53
Finsbury Mkt, EC2 197 M5
FINSBURY PARK, N4 65 DN60
★ Finsbury Park, N4 65 DP59
⇌ Finsbury Park 65 DN61
⊖ Finsbury Park 65 DN61
Finsbury Pk Av, N4 66 DQ58
Finsbury Pk Rd, N4 65 DP61
Finsbury Pavement, EC2 197 L6
Finsbury Rd, N22 45 DM53
Finsbury Sq, EC2 197 L6
Finsbury St, EC2 197 K6
Finsbury Twr, EC1 197 K5
Finsbury Way, Bex. DA5 126 EZ86
Finsen Rd, SE5 102 DQ83
Finstock Rd, W10 81 CX72
Finucane Dr, Orp. BR5 146 EW101
Finucane Gdns, Rain. RM13 89 FG65
Finucane Ri, Bushey (Bushey Hth.) WD23 40 CC47
Finway Ct, Wat. WD18 off Whippendell Rd 23 BT43
Fiona Cl, Lthd. (Bkhm.) KT23 170 CA124
Firbank Cl, E16 86 EK71
Enfield EN2 off Gladbeck Way 30 DQ42
Firbank Dr, Wat. WD19 40 BY45
Woking GU21 166 AV119
Firbank La, Wok. GU21 166 AV119
Firbank Pl, Egh. (Eng.Grn.) TW20 112 AV93
Firbank Rd, SE15 102 DV82
Romford RM5 51 FB50
Fir Cl, Walt. KT12 135 BU101
Fircroft Cl, Slou. (Stoke P.) SL2 74 AU65
Woking GU22 167 AZ118
Fircroft Ct, Wok. GU22 off Fircroft Cl 167 AZ118
Fircroft Gdns, Har. HA1 61 CE62
Fircroft Rd, SW17 120 DF89
Chessington KT9 156 CM105
Fir Dene, Orp. BR6 145 EM104
Firdene, Surb. KT5 138 CQ102
Fire Bell All, Surb. KT6 138 CL100
Firecrest Dr, NW3 64 DB62
Firefly Cl, Wall. SM6 159 DL108
Firefly Gdns, E6 off Jack Dash Way 86 EL70
★ Firepower, SE18 105 EP76
Fire Sta All, Barn. EN5 off Christchurch La 27 CZ40
Firethorn Cl, Edg. HA8 off Larkspur Gro 42 CQ49
Firfield Rd, Add. KT15 152 BG105
Firfields, Wey. KT13 153 BP107
Fir Gra Av, Wey. KT13 153 BP106
Fir Gro, N.Mal. KT3 139 CT100
Woking GU21 166 AU119
Firham Pk Av, Rom. RM3 52 FN52
Firhill Rd, SE6 123 EA91
Firlands, Wey. KT13 153 BS107
Firmingers Rd, Orp. BR6 165 FB106
Firmin Rd, Dart. DA1 128 FJ85
Fir Rd, Felt. TW13 116 BX92
Sutton SM3 139 CZ102
Firs, The, E17 off Leucha Rd 67 DY57
N20 44 DD46
W5 79 CK71
Bexley DA5 off Dartford Rd 127 FD88
Brentwood (Pilg.Hat.) CM15 54 FU44
Caterham CR3 off Yorke Gate Rd 176 DR122
Leatherhead (Bkhm.) KT23 170 CC124
Tadworth KT20 off Brighton Rd 183 CZ126
Waltham Cross (Chsht.) EN7 14 DS27
Firs Av, N10 64 DG55
N11 44 DG51
SW14 98 CQ84
Firsby Av, Croy. CR0 143 DX102
Firsby Rd, N16 66 DT60
Firs Cl, N10 off Firs Av 64 DG55
SE23 123 DX87
Esher (Clay.) KT10 155 CE107
Iver SL0 off Thornbridge Rd 75 BC67
Mitcham CR4 141 DH96
Firscroft, N13 46 DQ48
Firsdene Cl, Cher. (Ott.) KT16 off Slade Rd 151 BD107
Firs Dr, Houns. TW5 95 BV80
Loughton IG10 33 EN39
Slough SL3 75 AZ74
Firs End, Ger.Cr. (Chal.St.P.) SL9 56 AY55
Firsgrove Cres, Brwd. CM14 54 FV49
Firsgrove Rd, Brwd. CM14 54 FV49
Firside Gro, Sid. DA15 125 ET88
Firs La, N13 46 DQ48
N21 46 DQ47
Potters Bar EN6 12 DB33
Firs Pk Av, N21 46 DR46
Firs Pk Gdns, N21 46 DQ46
Firs Rd, Ken. CR8 175 DP115
First Av, E12 68 EL63
E13 86 EG69
E17 67 EA57
N18 46 DW49
NW4 63 CW56
SW14 98 CS83
W3 81 CT74
W10 81 CZ70
Bexleyheath DA7 106 EW80
Dagenham RM10 89 FB68
Enfield EN1 30 DT44
Epsom KT19 156 CS109
Gravesend (Nthflt.) DA11 130 GE88
Grays RM20 109 FU79
Greenford UB6 79 CD66
Hayes UB3 77 BT74
Romford RM6 70 EW57
Tadworth (Lwr.Kgswd.) KT20 183 CY125
Waltham Abbey EN9 off Breach Barn Mobile Home Pk 16 EH30
Walton-on-Thames KT12 135 BV100
Watford WD25 24 BW35
Wembley HA9 61 CK61
West Molesey KT8 136 BZ98
First Cl, W.Mol. KT8 136 CC97
First Cross Rd, Twick. TW2 117 CE89
First Dr, NW10 80 CQ66
First Slip, Lthd. KT22 171 CG118
First St, SW3 198 C8
Firstway, SW20 139 CW96
First Way, Wem. HA9 62 CP63
Firs Wk, Nthwd. HA6 39 BR51
Woodford Green IG8 48 EG50
Firswood Av, Epsom KT19 157 CT106
Firs Wd Cl, Pot.B. EN6 12 DF32
Firth Gdns, SW6 99 CY81
Fir Tree Av, Mitch. CR4 140 DG96
Slough (Stoke P.) SL2 74 AT70
West Drayton UB7 94 BN76
Fir Tree Cl, SW16 121 DJ92
W5 80 CL72
Epsom KT17 173 CW115
Epsom (Ewell) KT19 157 CT105
Esher KT10 154 CC106
Grays RM17 110 GD79
Leatherhead KT22 171 CJ123
Orpington BR6 off Highfield Av 163 ET106
Romford RM1 71 FD55
Firtree Ct, Borwd. (Elstree) WD6 26 CM42
Fir Tree Gdns, Croy. CR0 161 EA105
Fir Tree Gro, Cars. SM5 158 DF108
Fir Tree Hill, Rick. WD3 22 BM38
Fir Tree Pl, Ashf. TW15 off Percy Av 114 BN92
Fir Tree Rd, Bans. SM7 157 CW114
Epsom KT17 173 CV116
Hounslow TW4 96 BY84
Leatherhead KT22 171 CJ123
Fir Trees, Rom. (Abridge) RM4 34 EV41
Fir Trees Cl, SE16 203 L3
Fir Tree Wk, Dag. RM10 off Wheel Fm Dr 71 FC62
Enfield EN1 30 DR41
Reigate RH2 184 DD134
Firwood Cl, Wok. GU21 166 AS119
Firwood Rd, Vir.W. GU25 132 AS100
Fisher Cl, Croy. CR0 off Grant Rd 142 DT102
Enfield EN3 off Government Row 31 EA37
Greenford UB6 off Gosling Cl 78 CA69
Kings Langley WD4 6 BN29
Walton-on-Thames KT12 153 BV105
Fisherman Cl, Rich. TW10 off Locksmeade Rd 117 CJ91
Fishermans Dr, SE16 203 J4
Fishermans Hill, Grav. DA11 130 GB85
Fisherman's Wk, E14 203 P2
Fishermans Wk, SE28 off Tugboat St 105 ES75
Fisher Rd, Har. HA3 41 CF54
Fishers Cl, SW16 off Garrad's Rd 121 DK90
Bushey WD23 24 BY41
Waltham Cross EN8 15 EA34
Fishers Ct, SE14 off Besson St 103 DX81
Fishersdene, Esher (Clay.) KT10 155 CG108
Fishers Grn La, Wal.Abb. EN9 15 EB29
Fishers La, W4 98 CR77
Epping CM16 17 ES32
Fisher St, E16 86 EG71
WC1 196 A7
Fishers Way, Belv. DA17 89 FC74
Fisherton St, NW8 82 DD70
Fishguard Spur, Slou. SL1 92 AV75
Fishguard Way, E16 105 EP75
Fishing Temple, Stai. TW18 133 BF95
Fishponds Rd, SW17 120 DE91
Keston BR2 162 EK106
Fish St Hill, EC3 197 L10
Fitzalan Rd, N3 63 CY55
Esher (Clay.) KT10 155 CE108
Fitzalan St, SE11 200 C8
Fitzgeorge Av, W14 99 CY77
New Malden KT3 138 CR95
Fitzgerald Av, SW14 98 CS83
Fitzgerald Cl, E11 off Fitzgerald Rd 68 EG57
Fitzgerald Ho, E14 85 EB72
Hayes UB3 77 BV74
Fitzgerald Rd, E11 68 EG57
SW14 98 CR83
Thames Ditton KT7 137 CG100
Fitzhardinge St, W1 194 F8
Fitzherbert Ho, Rich. TW10 off Kingsmead 118 CM86
Fitzhugh Gro, SW18 120 DD86
Fitzilian Av, Rom. RM3 52 FM53
Fitzjames Av, W14 99 CY77
Croydon CR0 142 DU103
Fitzjohn Av, Barn. EN5 27 CY43
Fitzjohn's Av, NW3 64 DD64
Fitzmaurice Pl, W1 199 J2
Fitzneal St, W12 81 CT72
Fitzrobert Pl, Egh. TW20 113 BA93
Fitzroy Cl, N6 64 DF60
Fitzroy Ct, W1 195 L5
Fitzroy Cres, W4 98 CR80
Fitzroy Gdns, SE19 122 DS94
Fitzroy Ms, W1 195 K5
Fitzroy Pk, N6 64 DF60
Fitzroy Rd, NW1 82 DG67
Fitzroy Sq, W1 195 K5
Fitzroy St, W1 195 K5
Fitzroy Yd, NW1 off Fitzroy Rd 82 DG67
Fitzstephen Rd, Dag. RM8 70 EV64
Fitzwarren Gdns, N19 65 DJ60
Fitzwilliam Av, Rich. TW9 98 CM82
Fitzwilliam Ms, E16 205 M2
Fitzwilliam Rd, SW4 101 DJ83
Fitzwygram Cl, Hmptn. (Hmptn.H.) TW12 116 CC92
Five Acre, NW9 43 CT53
Fiveacre Cl, Th.Hth. CR7 141 DN100
Five Acres, Kings L. WD4 6 BM29
St. Albans (Lon.Col.) AL2 9 CK25
Five Acres Av, St.Alb. (Brick.Wd.) AL2 8 BZ29
Fiveash Rd, Grav. DA11 131 GF87
Five Bell All, E14 off Three Colt St 85 DZ73
Five Elms Rd, Brom. BR2 144 EH104
Dagenham RM9 70 EZ62
Five Flds Cl, Wat. WD19 40 BZ48
Five Oaks, Add. KT15 151 BF107
Five Oaks La, Chig. IG7 50 EY51
Five Points, Iver SL0 75 BC69
Fives Ct, SE11 200 F8
Five Ways Cor, NW4 43 CV53
Fiveways Rd, SW9 101 DN82
Five Wents, Swan. BR8 147 FG96
Fladbury Rd, N15 66 DR58
Fladgate Rd, E11 68 EE58
Flag Cl, Croy. CR0 143 DX102
Flagstaff Cl, Wal.Abb. EN9 15 EB33
Flagstaff Rd, Wal.Abb. EN9 15 EB33
Flag Wk, Pnr. HA5 off Eastcote Rd 59 BU58
Flambard Rd, Har. HA1 61 CG58
Flamborough Cl, West. (Bigg.H.) TN16 178 EH119
Flamborough Rd, Ruis. HA4 59 BU62
Flamborough St, E14 85 DY72
Flamborough Wk, E14 off Flamborough St 85 DY72
Flamingo Gdns, Nthlt. UB5 off Jetstar Way 78 BY69
Flamingo Wk, Horn. RM12 89 FG65
FLAMSTEAD END, Wal.Cr. EN7 14 DU28
Flamstead End Rd, Wal.Cr. (Chsht.) EN8 14 DV28
Flamstead Gdns, Dag. RM9 off Flamstead Rd 88 EW66
Flamstead Rd, Dag. RM9 88 EW66
Flamsted Av, Wem. HA9 80 CN65
★ Flamsteed House Mus, SE10 103 ED80
Flamsteed Rd, SE7 104 EL78
Flanchford Rd, W12 99 CT76
Reigate RH2 183 CX134
Flanders Ct, Egh. TW20 113 BC92
Flanders Cres, SW17 120 DF94
Flanders Rd, E6 87 EM68
W4 98 CS77
Flanders Way, E9 85 DX65
Flank St, E1 off Dock St 84 DU73
Flash La, Enf. EN2 29 DP37
Flask Cotts, NW3 off New End Sq 64 DD63
Flask Wk, NW3 64 DD63
Flat Iron Sq, SE1 off Union St 84 DQ74
FLAUNDEN, Hem.H. 5 BB33
Flaunden Bottom, Chesh. HP5 20 AY36
Hemel Hempstead (Flaun.) HP3 20 AY35
Flaunden Hill, Hem.H. (Flaun.) HP3 5 AZ33
Flaunden La, Hem.H. (Bov.) HP3 5 BB32
Rickmansworth WD3 5 BD33
Flaunden Pk, Hem.H. (Flaun.) HP3 5 BA32
Flavell Ms, SE10 205 J10
Flaxen Cl, E4 off Flaxen Rd 47 EB48
Flaxen Rd, E4 47 EB48
Flaxley Rd, Mord. SM4 140 DB100
Flaxman Ct, W1 195 M9
Flaxman Rd, SE5 101 DP82
Flaxman Ter, WC1 195 N3
Flaxton Rd, SE18 105 ER81
Flecker Cl, Stan. HA7 41 CF50
Fleece Dr, N9 46 DU49
Fleece Rd, Surb. KT6 137 CJ102
Fleece Wk, N7 off Manger Rd 83 DL65
Fleeming Cl, E17 off Pennant Ter 47 DZ54
Fleeming Rd, E17 47 DZ54
Fleet Av, Dart. DA2 128 FQ88
Upminster RM14 73 FR58
Fleet Cl, Ruis. HA4 59 BQ58
Upminster RM14 73 FR58
West Molesey KT8 136 BZ99
Fleetdale Par, Dart. DA2 off Fleet Av 128 FQ88
Fleet La, W.Mol. KT8 136 BZ100
Fleet Pl, EC4 off Farringdon St 83 DN72
Fleet Rd, NW3 64 DE64
Dartford DA2 128 FQ88
Gravesend (Nthflt.) DA11 130 GC90
Fleetside, W.Mol. KT8 136 BZ100
Fleet Sq, WC1 196 B3
Fleet St, EC4 196 D9
Fleet St Hill, E1 off Weaver St 84 DU70
Fleetway, Egh. TW20 133 BC97
Fleetway Business Pk, Grnf. UB6 79 CH68
Fleetwood Cl, E16 86 EK71
Chalfont St. Giles HP8 36 AU49
Chessington KT9 155 CK108
Croydon CR0 142 DT104
Tadworth KT20 173 CW120
Fleetwood Ct, E6 off Evelyn Denington Rd 87 EM71
West Byfleet KT14 152 BG113
Fleetwood Gro, W3 off East Acton La 80 CS73
Fleetwood Rd, NW10 63 CU64
Kingston upon Thames KT1 138 CP97
Slough SL2 74 AT74
Fleetwood Sq, Kings.T. KT1 138 CP97
Fleetwood St, N16 off Stoke Newington Ch St 66 DS61
Fleetwood Way, Wat. WD19 40 BW49
Fleming Cl, W9 off Chippenham Rd 82 DA70
Waltham Cross (Chsht.) EN7 14 DU26
Fleming Ct, W2 off St. Marys Ter 82 DD71
Croydon CR0 159 DN106
Fleming Dr, N21 29 DM43
Fleming Gdns, Rom. (Harold Wd.) RM3 off Bartholomew Dr 52 FK54
Tilbury RM18 off Fielding Av 111 GJ81
Fleming Mead, Mitch. CR4 120 DE94
Fleming Rd, SE17 101 DP79
Grays (Chaff.Hun.) RM16 109 FW77
Southall UB1 78 CB72
Waltham Abbey EN9 off Sewardstone Rd 31 ED35
Flemings, Brwd. CM13 53 FW51
Fleming Wk, NW9 off Pasteur Cl 42 CS54
Fleming Way, SE28 88 EX73
Isleworth TW7 97 CF83
Flemish Flds, Cher. KT16 134 BG101
Flemming Av, Ruis. HA4 59 BV60
Flempton Rd, E10 67 DY60
Fletcher Cl, E6 off Trader Rd 87 EP72
Chertsey (Ott.) KT16 151 BE107
Fletcher La, E10 67 EC59
Fletcher Path, SE8 off New Butt La 103 EA80
Fletcher Rd, W4 98 CQ76
Chertsey (Ott.) KT16 151 BD107
Chigwell IG7 49 ET50
Fletchers Cl, Brom. BR2 144 EH98
Fletcher St, E1 off Cable St 84 DU73
Fletching Rd, E5 66 DW62
SE7 104 EJ79
Fletton Rd, N11 45 DL52
Fleur de Lis St, E1 197 N5
Fleur Gates, SW19 off Princes Way 119 CX87
Flexmere Gdns, N17 off Flexmere Rd 46 DR53
Flexmere Rd, N17 46 DR53
Flight App, NW9 43 CT54
Flimwell Cl, Brom. BR1 124 EE92
Flint Cl, Bans. SM7 158 DB114
Redhill RH1 184 DF133
Flint Down Cl, Orp. BR5 146 EU95
Flintlock Cl, Stai. TW19 94 BG84
Flintmill Cres, SE3 104 EL82
Flinton St, SE17 201 N10
Flint St, SE17 201 L9
Grays RM20 109 FV79
Flitcroft St, WC2 195 N8
Floats, The, Sev. (Rvrhd.) TN13 190 FE121
Flock Mill Pl, SW18 120 DB88
Flockton St, SE16 202 B5
Flodden Rd, SE5 102 DQ81
Flood La, Twick. TW1 off Church La 117 CG88
Flood Pas, SE18 off Samuel St 105 EM77
Flood St, SW3 100 DE78
Flood Wk, SW3 100 DE79
Flora Cl, E14 85 EB72
Flora Gdns, W6 off Ravenscourt Rd 99 CV77
Croydon CR0 161 EC111
Romford RM6 70 EW58
Floral Ct, Ashtd. KT21 off Rosedale 171 CJ118
Floral Dr, St.Alb. (Lon.Col.) AL2 9 CK26
Floral St, WC2 195 P10
Flora St, Belv. DA17 off Victoria St 106 EZ78
Florence Av, Add. (New Haw) KT15 152 BG111
Enfield EN2 30 DQ41
Morden SM4 140 DC99
Florence Cantwell Wk, N19 off Hillrise Rd 65 DL59
Florence Cl, Grays RM20 110 FY79
Hornchurch RM12 72 FL61
Walton-on-Thames KT12 off Florence Rd 135 BV101
Watford WD25 23 BU35
Florence Dr, Enf. EN2 30 DQ41
Florence Elson Cl, E12 off Grantham Rd 69 EN63
Florence Gdns, W4 98 CQ79
Romford RM6 off Roxy Av 70 EW59
Staines TW18 114 BH94
Florence Nightingale Ho, N1 off Clephane Rd 84 DR65
★ Florence Nightingale Mus, SE1 200 B5
Florence Rd, E6 86 EJ67
E13 86 EF68
N4 65 DN60
SE2 106 EW76
SE14 103 DZ81
SW19 120 DB93
W4 98 CR76
W5 80 CL73
Beckenham BR3 143 DX96
Bromley BR1 144 EG95
Feltham TW13 115 BV88
Kingston upon Thames KT2 118 CM94
South Croydon CR2 160 DR109
Southall UB2 96 BX77
Walton-on-Thames KT12 135 BV101
Florence St, E16 86 EF70
N1 83 DP66
NW4 63 CW56
Florence Ter, SE14 103 DZ81
Florence Way, SW12 120 DF88
Uxbridge UB8 off Wyvern Way 76 BJ67
Florfield Pas, E8 off Reading La 84 DV65
Florfield Rd, E8 off Reading La 84 DV65
Florian Av, Sutt. SM1 158 DD105
Florian Rd, SW15 99 CY84
Florida Cl, Bushey (Bushey Hth.) WD23 41 CD47
Florida Rd, Th.Hth. CR7 141 DP95
Florida St, E2 84 DU69
Florin Ct, SE1 off Tanner St 102 DT75
Floris Pl, SW4 off Fitzwilliam Rd 101 DJ83
Floriston Av, Uxb. UB10 77 BQ66
Floriston Cl, Stan. HA7 41 CH53
Floriston Ct, Nthlt. UB5 60 CB64
Floriston Gdns, Stan. HA7 41 CH53
Floss St, SW15 99 CW82
Flower & Dean Wk, E1 off Thrawl St 84 DT71
Flower Cres, Cher. (Ott.) KT16 151 BB107
Flowerfield, Sev. (Otford) TN14 181 FF117
Flowerhill Way, Grav. (Istead Rise) DA13 130 GE94
Flower La, NW7 43 CT50
Godstone RH9 187 DY128
★ Flower Mkt, New Covent Garden Mkt, SW8 101 DK79
Flower Ms, NW11 63 CY58
Flower Pot Cl, N15 off St. Ann's Rd 66 DT58
Flowers Cl, NW2 63 CU62
Flowersmead, SW17 120 DG89
Flowers Ms, N19 off Archway Rd 65 DJ61
Flower Wk, The, SW7 100 DC75
Floyd Rd, SE7 104 EJ78
Floyds La, Wok. GU22 168 BG116
Fludyer St, SE13 104 EE84
Flux's La, Epp. CM16 18 EU33
Flyer's Way, The, West. TN16 189 ER126
Fogerty Cl, Enf. EN3 off Government Row 31 EA37
Foley Ms, Esher (Clay.) KT10 155 CE108

★ Place of interest ⇌ Railway station ⊖ London Underground station DLR Docklands Light Railway station Tramlink station H Hospital

257

Fol - Fox

Foley Rd, Esher (Clay.) KT10 155 CE108
Westerham (Bigg.H.) TN16 178 EK118
Foley St, W1 195 K7
Folgate St, E1 197 N6
Foliot St, W12 81 CT72
Folkes La, Upmin. RM14 73 FT57
Folkestone Ct, Slou. SL3 93 BA78
Folkestone Rd, E6 87 EN68
E17 67 EB56
N18 46 DU49
Folkingham La, NW9 42 CR53
Folkington Cor, N12 43 CZ50
Follet Dr, Abb.L. WD5 7 BT31
Follett Cl, Wind. (Old Wind.) SL4 112 AV86
Follett St, E14 85 EC72
Folly Cl, Rad. WD7 25 CF36
Follyfield Rd, Bans. SM7 158 DA114
Folly La, E4 47 DZ52
E17 47 DY53
Folly Ms, W11 off Portobello Rd 81 CZ72
Folly Pathway, Rad. WD7 25 CF35
Folly Wall, E14 204 E5
Fontaine Rd, SW16 121 DM94
Fontarabia Rd, SW11 100 DG84
Fontayne Av, Chig. IG7 49 EQ49
Rainham RM13 89 FE66
Romford RM1 51 FE54
Fontenoy Rd, SW12 121 DH89
Fonteyne Gdns, Wdf.Grn. IG8 off Lechmere Av 48 EK54
Fonthill Cl, SE20 off Selby Rd 142 DU96
Fonthill Ms, N4 off Lennox Rd 65 DN61
Fonthill Rd, N4 65 DM60
Font Hills, N2 44 DC54
Fontley Way, SW15 119 CU87
Fontmell Cl, Ashf. TW15 114 BN92
Fontmell Pk, Ashf. TW15 114 BM92
Fontwell Cl, Har. HA3 41 CE52
Northolt UB5 78 CA65
Fontwell Dr, Brom. BR2 145 EN99
Fontwell Pk Gdns, Horn. RM12 72 FL63
Foord Cl, Dart. DA2 129 FS89
Football La, Har. HA1 61 CE60
Footbury Hill Rd, Orp. BR6 146 EU101
Footpath, The, SW15 119 CU85
FOOTS CRAY, Sid. 126 EV93
Foots Cray High St, Sid. DA14 126 EW93
Foots Cray La, Sid. DA14 126 EW88
Footscray Rd, SE9 125 EN86
Footway, The, SE9 125 EQ87
Forbench Cl, Wok. (Ripley) GU23 168 BH122
Forbes Av, Pot.B. EN6 12 DD33
Forbes Cl, NW2 63 CU62
Hornchurch RM11 off St. Leonards Way 71 FH60
Forbes Ct, SE19 122 DS92
Forbes St, E1 off Ellen St 84 DU72
Forbes Way, Ruis. HA4 59 BV61
Forburg Rd, N16 66 DU60
FORCE GREEN, West. 179 ER124
Force Grn La, West. TN16 179 ER124
Fordbridge Cl, Cher. KT16 134 BH102
Fordbridge Rd, Ashf. TW15 114 BL93
Shepperton TW17 135 BS100
Sunbury-on-Thames TW16 135 BS100
Ford Cl, E3 off Roman Rd 85 DY68
Ashford TW15 114 BL93
Bushey WD23 24 CC42
Harrow HA1 61 CD59
Rainham RM13 89 FF66
Shepperton TW17 134 BN98
Thornton Heath CR7 141 DP100
Fordcroft Rd, Orp. BR5 146 EV99
Forde Av, Brom. BR1 144 EJ97
Fordel Rd, SE6 123 ED88
Ford End, Uxb. (Denh.) UB9 57 BF61
Woodford Green IG8 48 EH51
Fordham Cl, Barn. EN4 28 DE41
Hornchurch RM11 72 FN59
Fordham Rd, Barn. EN4 28 DD41
Fordham St, E1 84 DU72
Fordhook Av, W5 80 CM73
Fordingley Rd, W9 81 CZ69
Fordington Rd, N6 64 DF57
Ford La, Iver SL0 76 BG72
Rainham RM13 89 FF66
Fordmill Rd, SE6 123 EA89
Ford Rd, E3 85 DY67
Ashford TW15 114 BM91
Chertsey KT16 134 BH102
Dagenham RM9, RM10 88 EZ66
Gravesend (Nthflt.) DA11 130 GB85
Woking (Old Wok.) GU22 167 BB120
Fords Gro, N21 46 DQ46
Fords Pk Rd, E16 86 EG72
Ford Sq, E1 84 DV71
Ford St, E3 85 DY67
E16 86 EF72
Fordwater Rd, Cher. KT16 134 BH102
Fordwater Trd Est, Cher. KT16 134 BJ102
Fordwich Cl, Orp. BR6 145 ET101
Fordwych Rd, NW2 63 CY64
Fordyce Cl, Horn. RM11 72 FM59
Fordyce Ho, SW16 off Colson Way 121 DJ91
Fordyce Rd, SE13 123 EC86
Fordyke Rd, Dag. RM8 70 EZ61
Forefield, St.Alb. AL2 8 CA27
★ Foreign & Commonwealth Office, SW1 199 P4
Foreland Ct, NW4 43 CY53
Foreland St, SE18 off Plumstead Rd 105 ER77
Foreman Ct, W6 off Hammersmith Bdy 99 CW77
Foremark Cl, Ilf. IG6 49 ET50
Foreshore, SE8 203 N9
Forest, The, E11 68 EE56
Forest App, E4 48 EE45
Woodford Green IG8 48 EF52
Forest Av, E4 48 EE45
Chigwell IG7 49 EN50
Forest Business Pk, E17 67 DX59
Forest Cl, E11 68 EF57
Chislehurst BR7 145 EN95
Waltham Abbey EN9 32 EH37
Woking GU22 167 BD115
Woodford Green IG8 48 EH48
Forest Ct, E4 48 EF46
E11 68 EE56
Forest Cres, Ashtd. KT21 172 CN116
Forest Cft, SE23 122 DV89
FORESTDALE, Croy. 161 EA109
Forestdale, N14 45 DK49
Forest Dr, E12 68 EK62
Epping (They.B.) CM16 33 ES36
Keston BR2 162 EL105
Sunbury-on-Thames TW16 115 BT94
Tadworth (Kgswd.) KT20 173 CZ121
Woodford Green IG8 47 ED52
Forest Dr E, E11 67 ED59
Forest Dr W, E11 67 EC59
Forest Edge, Buck.H. IG9 48 EJ49
Forester Rd, SE15 102 DV84
Foresters Cl, Wall. SM6 159 DK108
Waltham Cross EN7 14 DS27
Woking GU21 166 AT118
Foresters Cres, Bexh. DA7 107 FB84
Foresters Dr, E17 67 ED56
Wallington SM6 159 DK108
Forest Gdns, N17 46 DT54
FOREST GATE, E7 68 EG64
⇌ Forest Gate 68 EG64
Forest Gate, NW9 62 CS57
Forest Glade, E4 48 EE49
E11 68 EE58
Epping (N.Wld.Bas.) CM16 18 EY27
Forest Gro, E8 84 DT66
Forest Hts, Buck.H. IG9 48 EG47
FOREST HILL, SE23 123 DX88
⇌ Forest Hill 122 DW89
Forest Hill Business Cen, SE23 122 DW89
Forest Hill Ind Est, SE23 off Perry Vale 122 DW89
Forest Hill Rd, SE22 122 DV85
SE23 122 DV85
Forestholme Cl, SE23 122 DW89
Forest Ind Pk, Ilf. IG6 49 ES53
Forest La, E7 68 EE64
E15 68 EE64
Chigwell IG7 49 EN50
Leatherhead (E.Hors.) KT24 169 BT124
Forest Mt Rd, Wdf.Grn. IG8 47 ED52
Fore St, EC2 197 J7
N9 46 DU50
N18 46 DT51
Pinner HA5 59 BU57
Fore St Av, EC2 197 K7
Forest Ridge, Beck. BR3 143 EA97
Keston BR2 162 EL105
Forest Ri, E17 67 ED57
Forest Rd, E7 68 EG63
E8 84 DT65
E11 67 ED59
E17 66 DW56
N9 46 DV46
N17 66 DW56
Enfield EN3 31 DY36
Erith DA8 107 FG81
Feltham TW13 116 BW89
Ilford IG6 49 ES53
Leatherhead (E.Hors.) KT24 169 BU123
Loughton IG10 32 EK41
Richmond TW9 98 CN80
Romford RM7 71 FB55
Sutton SM3 140 DA102
Waltham Cross (Chsht.) EN8 15 DX29
Watford WD25 7 BV33
Woking GU22 167 BD115
Woodford Green IG8 48 EG48
Forest Side, E4 48 EF45
E7 off Capel Rd 68 EH63
Buckhurst Hill IG9 48 EJ46
Epping CM16 17 ER33
Waltham Abbey EN9 32 EJ36
Worcester Park KT4 139 CT102
Forest St, E7 68 EG64
Forest Vw, E4 47 ED45
E11 off High Rd Leytonstone 68 EF59
Forest Vw Av, E10 67 ED57
Forest Vw Rd, E12 68 EL63
E17 47 EC53
Loughton IG10 32 EK42
Forest Wk, Bushey WD23 off Millbrook Rd 24 BZ39
Forest Way, N19 off Hargrave Pk 65 DJ61
Ashtead KT21 172 CM117
Loughton IG10 32 EL41
Orpington BR5 145 ET99
Sidcup DA15 125 ER87
Waltham Abbey EN9 32 EK35
Woodford Green IG8 48 EH49
Forfar Rd, N22 45 DP53
SW11 100 DG81
Forge Av, Couls. CR5 175 DN120
Forge Br La, Couls. CR5 175 DH121
Forge Cl, Brom. BR2 144 EG102
Hayes UB3 off High St 95 BR79
Kings Langley (Chipper.) WD4 6 BG31
Forge Cotts, W5 off Ealing Grn 79 CK74
Forge Dr, Esher (Clay.) KT10 155 CG108
Forge End, St.Alb. AL2 8 CA26
Woking GU21 166 AY117
Forgefield, West. (Bigg.H.) TN16 off Main Rd 178 EK116
Forge La, Dart. (Hort.Kir.) DA4 148 FQ98
Feltham TW13 116 BY92
Gravesend DA12 131 GM89
Northwood HA6 39 BS52
Sunbury-on-Thames TW16 135 BU97
Sutton SM3 157 CY108
Forge Ms, Sun. TW16 off Forge La 135 BU97
Forge Pl, NW1 off Malden Cres 82 DG65
Forge Way, Sev. (Shore.) TN14 165 FF111
Forlong Path, Nthlt. UB5 off Arnold Rd 78 BY65
Forman Pl, N16 off Farleigh Rd 66 DT63
Formation, The, E16 off Woolwich Manor Way 105 EP75
Formby Av, Stan. HA7 61 CJ55
Formby Cl, Slou. SL3 93 BC77
Formosa St, W9 82 DB70
Formunt Cl, E16 off Vincent St 86 EF71
Forres Gdns, NW11 64 DA58
Forrester Path, SE26 123 DX91
Forrest Gdns, SW16 141 DM97
Forris Av, Hayes UB3 77 BT74
Forset St, W1 194 C8
Forstal Cl, Brom. BR2 off Ridley Rd 144 EG97
Forster Cl, E17 47 ED52
Forster Rd, E17 67 DY58
N17 66 DT55
SW2 121 DL87
Beckenham BR3 143 DY97
Croydon CR0 off Windmill Rd 142 DQ101
Forsters Cl, Rom. RM6 70 EZ58
Forster's Way, SW18 120 DB88
Forsters Way, Hayes UB4 77 BV72
Forston St, N1 off Cropley St 84 DR68
Forsyte Cres, SE19 142 DS95
Forsyth Gdns, SE17 101 DP79
Forsythia Cl, Ilf. IG1 69 EP64
Forsythia Gdns, Slou. SL3 92 AY76
Forsyth Path, Wok. GU21 151 BD113
Forsyth Pl, Enf. EN1 30 DS43
Forsyth Rd, Wok. GU21 151 BC114
Forterie Gdns, Ilf. IG3 70 EU62
Fortescue Av, E8 off Mentmore Ter 84 DV66
Twickenham TW2 116 CC90
Fortescue Rd, SW19 120 DD94
Edgware HA8 42 CR53
Weybridge KT13 152 BM105
Fortess Gro, NW5 off Fortess Rd 65 DH64
Fortess Rd, NW5 65 DH64
Fortess Wk, NW5 off Fortess Rd 65 DH64
Forthbridge Rd, SW11 100 DG84
Forth Rd, Upmin. RM14 73 FR58
Fortin Cl, S.Ock. RM15 91 FU73
Fortin Path, S.Ock. RM15 91 FU73
Fortin Way, S.Ock. RM15 91 FU73
Fortis Cl, E16 86 EJ72
FORTIS GREEN, N2 64 DF56
Fortis Grn, N2 64 DE56
N10 64 DE56
Fortis Grn Av, N2 64 DF55
Fortis Grn Rd, N10 64 DG55
Fortismere Av, N10 64 DG55
Fort La, Reig. RH2 184 DB130
Fortnam Rd, N19 65 DK61
★ Fortnum & Mason, W1 199 K2
Fortnums Acre, Stan. HA7 41 CF51
Fortress Distribution Pk, Til. RM18 111 GH84
Fort Rd, SE1 202 A9
Northolt UB5 78 CA66
Sevenoaks (Halst.) TN14 181 FC115
Tadworth KT20 182 CP131
Tilbury RM18 111 GH84
Fortrose Gdns, SW2 off New Pk Rd 121 DK88
Fortrye Cl, Grav. (Nthflt.) DA11 130 GE89
Fort St, E1 197 N7
E16 86 EH74
Fortuna Cl, N7 off Vulcan Way 83 DM65
Fortune Gate Rd, NW10 80 CS67
Fortune Grn Rd, NW6 64 DA63
Fortune La, Borwd. (Elstree) WD6 25 CK44
Fortunes Mead, Nthlt. UB5 78 BY65
Fortune St, EC1 197 J5
Fortune Wk, SE28 off Broadwater Rd 105 ER76
Fortune Way, NW10 81 CU69
Forty Acre La, E16 86 EG71
Forty Av, Wem. HA9 62 CM62
Forty Cl, Wem. HA9 62 CM61
Forty Footpath, SW14 98 CQ83
Fortyfoot Rd, Lthd. KT22 171 CJ121
★ Forty Hall & Mus, Enf. EN2 30 DT38
FORTY HILL, Enf. 30 DS37
Forty Hill, Enf. EN2 30 DT38
Forty La, Wem. HA9 62 CP61
Forum, The, W.Mol. KT8 136 CB98
★ Forum Club, NW5 65 DH64
Forum Magnum Sq, SE1 200 B4
Forumside, Edg. HA8 off High St 42 CN51
Forum Way, Edg. HA8 off High St 42 CN51
Forval Cl, Mitch. CR4 140 DF99
Forward Dr, Har. HA3 61 CF56
Fosbury Ms, W2 off Inverness Ter 82 DB73
Foscote Ms, W9 off Amberley Rd 82 DA71
Foscote Rd, NW4 63 CV58
Foskett Rd, SW6 99 CZ82
Foss Av, Croy. CR0 159 DN106
Fossdene Rd, SE7 104 EH78
Fossdyke Cl, Hayes UB4 78 BY71
Fosse Way, W13 79 CG71
West Byfleet KT14 off Brantwood Dr 151 BF113
Fossil Rd, SE13 103 EA83
Fossington Rd, Belv. DA17 106 EX77
Foss Rd, SW17 120 DD91
Fossway, Dag. RM8 70 EW61
Foster Cl, Wal.Cr. (Chsht.) EN8 15 DX30
Fosterdown, Gdse. RH9 186 DV129
Foster La, EC2 197 H8
Foster Rd, E13 86 EG70
W3 80 CS73
W4 98 CR78
Fosters Cl, E18 48 EH53
Chislehurst BR7 125 EM92
Foster St, NW4 63 CW56
Foster Wk, NW4 off New Brent St 63 CW56
Fothergill Cl, E13 86 EG68
Fothergill Dr, N21 29 DL43
Fotheringham Rd, Enf. EN1 30 DT42
Fotherley Rd, Rick. (Mill End) WD3 37 BF47
Foubert's Pl, W1 195 K9
Foulden Rd, N16 66 DT63
Foulden Ter, N16 off Foulden Rd 66 DT63
Foulis Ter, SW7 198 A10
Foulser Rd, SW17 120 DF90
Foulsham Rd, Th.Hth. CR7 142 DQ97
Founder Cl, E6 off Trader Rd 87 EP72
Founders Ct, EC2 197 K8
Founders Dr, Uxb. (Denh.) UB9 57 BF58
Founders Gdns, SE19 122 DQ94
Foundry Cl, SE16 203 K2
Foundry La, Slou. (Horton) SL3 93 BB83
Foundry Ms, NW1 195 L4
Fountain Cl, Uxb. UB8 off New Rd 77 BQ71
Fountain Ct, EC4 196 D10
Fountain Dr, SE19 122 DT91
Carshalton SM5 158 DF109
Fountain Grn Sq, SE16 202 C4
Fountain La, Sev. TN15 191 FP122
Fountain Ms, N5 off Kelross Rd 66 DQ63
NW3 off Haverstock Hill 82 DF65
Fountain Pl, SW9 101 DN81
Waltham Abbey EN9 15 EC34
Fountain Rd, SW17 120 DD92
Thornton Heath CR7 142 DQ96
Fountains, The, Loug. IG10 off Fallow Flds 48 EK45
Fountains Av, Felt. TW13 116 BZ90
Fountains Cl, Felt. TW13 116 BZ89
Fountains Cres, N14 45 DL45
Fountain Sq, SW1 199 H8
Fountain St, E2 off Columbia Rd 84 DT69
Fountain Wk, Grav. (Nthflt.) DA11 130 GE86
Fountayne Rd, N15 66 DU56
N16 66 DU61
Fount St, SW8 101 DK80
Fouracres, SW12 off Little Dimocks 121 DH89
Four Acres, Cob. KT11 154 BY113
Fouracres, Enf. EN3 31 DY39
Fourland Wk, Edg. HA8 42 CQ51
Fournier St, E1 197 P6
Four Seasons Cl, E3 85 EA68
Fourth Av, E12 69 EM63
W10 81 CY70
Grays RM20 109 FU79
Hayes UB3 77 BT74
Romford RM7 71 FD60
Watford WD25 24 BX35
Fourth Cross Rd, Twick. TW2 117 CD89
Fourth Dr, Couls. CR5 175 DK116
Fourth Way, Wem. HA9 62 CQ63
Four Tubs, The, Bushey WD23 41 CD45
Four Wents, Cob. KT11 153 BV113
Four Wents, The, E4 off Kings Rd 47 ED47
Fowey Av, Ilf. IG4 68 EK57
Fowey Cl, E1 202 D2
Fowler Cl, SW11 100 DD83
Fowler Rd, E7 68 EG63
N1 off Halton Rd 83 DP66
Ilford IG6 50 EV51
Mitcham CR4 140 DG96
Fowlers Cl, Sid. DA14 off Thursland Rd 126 EY92
Fowlers Mead, Wok. (Chobham) GU24 off Windsor Rd 150 AS109
Fowlers Wk, W5 79 CK70
Fowley Cl, Wal.Cr. EN8 15 DZ34
Fowley Mead Pk, Wal.Cr. EN8 15 EA34
Fownes St, SW11 100 DE83
Foxacre, Cat. CR3 off Town End Cl 176 DS122
Fox & Knot St, EC1 196 G6
Foxberry Rd, SE4 103 DY83
Foxberry Wk, Grav. (Nthflt.) DA11 off Rowmarsh Cl 130 GD91
Foxborough Cl, Slou. SL3 93 AZ78
Foxborough Gdns, SE4 123 EA86
Foxbourne Rd, SW17 120 DG89
Foxburrow Rd, Chig. IG7 50 EX50
Foxbury Av, Chis. BR7 125 ER93
Foxbury Cl, Brom. BR1 124 EH93
Orpington BR6 off Foxbury Dr 164 EU106
Foxbury Dr, Orp. BR6 164 EU107
Foxbury Rd, Brom. BR1 124 EG93
Fox Cl, E1 84 DW70
E16 86 EG71
Borehamwood (Elstree) WD6 off Rodgers Cl 25 CK44
Bushey WD23 24 CB42
Orpington BR6 164 EU106
Romford RM5 51 FB50
Fox Cl, Wey. KT13 153 BR106
Woking GU22 167 BD115
Foxcombe, Croy. (New Adgtn.) CR0 161 EB107
Foxcombe Cl, E6 off Boleyn Rd 86 EK68
Foxcombe Rd, SW15 off Alton Rd 119 CU88
Foxcote, SE5 102 DS78
Fox Covert, Lthd. (Fetch.) KT22 171 CD124
Foxcroft Rd, SE18 105 EP81
Foxdell, Nthwd. HA6 39 BR51
Foxdell Way, Ger.Cr. (Chal.St.P.) SL9 36 AY50
Foxearth Cl, West. (Bigg.H.) TN16 178 EL118
Foxearth Rd, S.Croy. CR2 160 DW110
Foxearth Spur, S.Croy. CR2 160 DW109
Foxes Dale, SE3 104 EG83
Bromley BR2 143 ED97
Foxes Dr, Wal.Cr. EN7 14 DU29
Foxes Grn, Grays (Orsett) RM16 111 GG75
Foxes La, Pot.B. (Cuffley) EN6 13 DL28
Foxfield Cl, Nthwd. HA6 39 BT51
Foxfield Rd, Orp. BR6 145 ER103
Foxglove Cl, Sthl. UB1 78 BY73
Staines (Stanw.) TW19 114 BK88
Foxglove Gdns, E11 68 EJ56
Purley CR8 159 DL111
Foxglove La, Chess. KT9 156 CN105
Foxglove Rd, Rom. (Rush Grn.) RM7 71 FE61
South Ockendon RM15 91 FW71
Foxglove St, W12 81 CT73
Foxglove Way, Wall. SM6 141 DH102
Foxgrove, N14 45 DL48
Fox Gro, Walt. KT12 135 BV101
Foxgrove Av, Beck. BR3 123 EB94
Foxgrove Dr, Wok. GU21 167 BA115
Foxgrove Path, Wat. WD19 40 BX50
Foxgrove Rd, Beck. BR3 123 EB94
Foxhall Rd, Upmin. RM14 72 FQ64
Foxham Rd, N19 65 DK62
Foxhanger Gdns, Wok. GU22 off Oriental Rd 167 BA116
Foxherne, Slou. SL3 92 AW75
Fox Hill, SE19 122 DT94
Keston BR2 162 EJ106
Foxhill, Wat. WD24 23 BU36
Fox Hill Gdns, SE19 122 DT94
Foxhills, Wok. GU21 166 AW117
Foxhills Cl, Cher. (Ott.) KT16 151 BB107
Foxhills Ms, Cher. KT16 133 BB104
Foxhills Rd, Cher. (Ott.) KT16 151 BA105
Foxhole Rd, SE9 124 EL85
Foxholes, Wey. KT13 153 BR106
Fox Hollow Cl, SE18 105 ES78
Fox Hollow Dr, Bexh. DA7 106 EX83
Foxholt Gdns, NW10 80 CQ66
Foxhome Cl, Chis. BR7 125 EN93
Foxhounds La, Grav. DA13 130 GA90
Fox Ho Rd, Belv. DA17 107 FB77
Foxlake Rd, W.Byf. (Byfleet) KT14 152 BM112
Foxlands Cl, Wat. WD25 7 BU34
Foxlands Cres, Dag. RM10 71 FC64
Foxlands La, Dag. RM10 71 FC64
Foxlands Rd, Dag. RM10 71 FC64
Fox La, N13 45 DM48
W5 80 CL70
Caterham CR3 175 DP121
Keston BR2 162 EH106
Leatherhead (Bkhm.) KT23 170 BY124
Reigate RH2 184 DB131
Fox La N, Cher. KT16 133 BF102
Fox La S, Cher. KT16 off Guildford St 133 BF102
Foxlees, Wem. HA0 61 CG63
Foxley Cl, E8 off Ferncliff Rd 66 DU64
Loughton IG10 33 EP40
Foxley Ct, Sutt. SM2 158 DC108
Foxley Gdns, Pur. CR8 159 DP113
Foxley Hill Rd, Pur. CR8 159 DN112
Foxley La, Pur. CR8 159 DK111
Foxley Rd, SW9 101 DN80
Kenley CR8 159 DP114
Thornton Heath CR7 141 DP98
Foxleys, Wat. WD19 40 BY48
Foxley Sq, SW9 off Cancell Rd 101 DP80
Fox Manor Way, Grays RM20 109 FV79
Foxmead Cl, Enf. EN2 29 DM41
Foxmoor Ct, Uxb. (Denh.) UB9 off North Orbital Rd 58 BG58
Foxmore St, SW11 100 DF81
Foxon Cl, Cat. CR3 176 DS121
Foxon La, Cat. CR3 176 DR121
Foxon La Gdns, Cat. CR3 176 DS121
Fox Rd, E16 86 EF71
Slough SL3 92 AX77
Fox's Path, Mitch. CR4 140 DE96
Foxton Gro, Mitch. CR4 140 DD96
Foxton Rd, Grays RM20 109 FX79
Foxwarren, Esher (Clay.) KT10 155 CF109
Foxwell Ms, SE4 off Foxwell St 103 DY83
Foxwell St, SE4 103 DY83
Foxwood Chase, Wal.Abb. EN9 31 ED35
Foxwood Cl, NW7 42 CS49
Feltham TW13 115 BV90
Foxwood Grn Cl, Enf. EN1 30 DS44
Foxwood Gro, Grav. (Nthflt.) DA11 130 GE88
Orpington BR6 164 EW110
Foxwood Rd, SE3 104 EF84
Dartford (Bean) DA2 129 FV90

★ Place of interest ⇌ Railway station London Underground station DLR Docklands Light Railway station Tramlink station H Hospital

Foy - Fur

Foyle Dr, S.Ock. RM15 .91 FU71
Foyle Rd, N17 .46 DU53
SE3 .104 EF79
Frailey Cl, Wok. GU22 .167 BB116
Frailey Hill, Wok. GU22 .167 BB116
Framewood Rd, Slou. SL2,
SL3 .74 AW66
Framfield Cl, N12 .44 DA48
Framfield Ct, Enf. EN1 .30 DS44
Framfield Rd, N5 .65 DP64
W7 .79 CE72
Mitcham CR4 .120 DG94
Framlingham Cl, E5
off Detmold Rd .66 DW61
Framlingham Cres, SE9 .124 EL91
Frampton Cl, Sutt. SM2 .158 DA108
Frampton Pk Rd, E9 .84 DW65
Frampton Rd, Epp. CM16 .18 EU28
Hounslow TW4 .116 BY85
Potters Bar EN6 .12 DC30
Frampton St, NW8 .82 DD70
Francemary Rd, SE4 .123 EA85
Frances Av, Grays (Chaff.Hun.)
RM16 .109 FW77
Frances Gdns, S.Ock. RM15 .91 FT72
Frances Rd, E4 .47 EA51
Frances St, SE18 .105 EM77
Franche Ct Rd, SW17 .120 DC90
Francis Av, Bexh. DA7 .106 FA82
Feltham TW13 .115 BU90
Ilford IG1 .69 ER61
Francis Barber Cl, SW16
off Well Cl .121 DM91
Franciscan Rd, SW17 .120 DF92
Francis Chichester Way,
SW11 .100 DG81
Francis Cl, E14 .204 F8
Epsom KT19 .156 CR105
Shepperton TW17 .134 BN98
Francisco Cl, Grays (Chaff.Hun.)
RM16 .109 FW76
Francis Gro, SW19 .119 CZ93
Francis Rd, E10 .67 EC60
N2 *off Lynmouth Rd* .64 DF56
Caterham CR3 .176 DR122
Croydon CR0 .141 DP101
Dartford DA1 .128 FK85
Greenford UB6 .79 CJ67
Harrow HA1 .61 CG57
Hounslow TW4 .96 BX82
Ilford IG1 .69 ER61
Orpington BR5 .146 EX97
Pinner HA5 .60 BW57
Wallington SM6 .159 DJ107
Watford WD18 .23 BV42
Francis St, E15 .68 EE64
SW1 .199 K8
Ilford IG1 .69 ER61
Francis Ter, N19
off Junction Rd .65 DJ62
Francis Wk, N1
off Bingfield St .83 DM67
Francklyn Gdns, Edg. HA8 .42 CN48
Francombe Gdns, Rom. RM1 .71 FG58
Franconia Rd, SW4 .121 DJ85
Frank Bailey Wk, E12
off Gainsborough Av .69 EN64
Frank Burton Cl, SE7
off Victoria Way .104 EH78
Frank Dixon Cl, SE21 .122 DS88
Frank Dixon Way, SE21 .122 DS88
Frankfurt Rd, SE24 .122 DQ85
Frankham St, SE8 .103 EA80
Frankland Cl, SE16 .202 E7
Rickmansworth (Crox.Grn.)
WD3 .38 BN45
Woodford Green IG8 .48 EJ50
Frankland Rd, E4 .47 EA50
SW7 *off Armstrong Rd* .100 DD76
Rickmansworth (Crox.Grn.)
WD3 .23 BP44
Franklands Dr, Add. KT15 .151 BF108
Franklin Av, Wal.Cr. (Chsht.)
EN7 .14 DV30
Franklin Cl, N20 .44 DC45
SE13 .103 EB81
SE27 .121 DP90
Kingston upon Thames
KT1 .138 CN97
Franklin Cres, Mitch. CR4 .141 DJ98
Franklin Ho, NW9 .63 CT59
Franklin Pas, SE9 .104 EL83
Franklin Rd, SE20 .122 DW94
Bexleyheath DA7 .106 EY81
Gravesend DA12 .131 GK92
Hornchurch RM12 .90 FJ65
Watford WD17 .23 BV40
Franklins Ms, Har. HA2 .60 CC61
Franklin Sq, W14
off Marchbank Rd .99 CZ78
Franklin's Row, SW3 .198 E10
Franklin St, E3
off St. Leonards St .85 EB69
N15 .66 DS58
Franklin Way, Croy. CR0 .141 DL101
Franklyn Gdns, Ilf. IG6 .49 ER51
Franklyn Rd, NW10 .81 CT66
Walton-on-Thames KT12 .135 BU100
Frank Martin Ct, Wal.Cr.
EN7 .14 DU30
Franks Av, N.Mal. KT3 .138 CQ98
Franks La, Dart. (Hort.Kir.)
DA4 .148 FN98
Frank St, E13 .86 EG70
Frankswood Av, Orp. BR5 .145 EP99
West Drayton UB7 .76 BM72
Frank Towell Ct, Felt. TW14 .115 BU88
Franlaw Cres, N13 .46 DQ49
Franmil Rd, Horn. RM12 .71 FG60
Fransfield Gro, SE26 .122 DV90
Frant Cl, SE20 .122 DW94
Franthorne Way, SE6 .123 EB89
Frant Rd, Th.Hth. CR7 .141 DP99
Fraser Cl, E6 *off Linton Gdns* .86 EL72
Fraser Cl, Bex. DA5
off Dartford Rd .127 FC88
Fraser Ho, Brent. TW8
off Green Dragon La .98 CM78
Fraser Rd, E17 .67 EB57
N9 .46 DV48
Erith DA8 .107 FC78
Greenford UB6 .79 CH67
Waltham Cross (Chsht.)
EN8 .15 DY28
Fraser St, W4 .98 CS78
Frating Cres, Wdf.Grn. IG8 .48 EG51
Frays Av, West Dr. UB7 .94 BK75
Frays Cl, West Dr. UB7 .94 BK76
Frays Lea, Uxb. UB8 .76 BJ68
Frays Waye, Uxb. UB8 .76 BJ67
Frazer Av, Ruis. HA4 .60 BW64
Frazer Cl, Rom. RM1 .71 FF59
Frazier St, SE1 .200 D5
Frean St, SE16 .202 B6
Freda Corbett Cl, SE15
off Bird in Bush Rd .102 DU80
Frederica Rd, E4 .47 ED45
Frederica St, N7
off Caledonian Rd .83 DM66
Frederick Andrews Ct, Grays
RM17 .110 GD79
Frederick Cl, W2 .194 D10
Sutton SM1 .157 CZ105
Frederick Ct, NW2
off Douglas Ms .63 CY62
Frederick Cres, SW9 .101 DP80
Enfield EN3 .30 DW40
Frederick Gdns, Sutt. SM1 .157 CZ106
Frederick Pl, SE18 .105 EP78
Frederick Rd, SE17
off Chapter Rd .101 DP78
Rainham RM13 .89 FD68
Sutton SM1 .157 CZ106
Frederick's Pl, EC2 .197 K9
Fredericks Pl, N12 .44 DC49
Frederick Sq, SE16 .203 K1
Frederick's Row, EC1 .196 F2
Frederick St, WC1 .196 B3
Frederick Ter, E8
off Haggerston Rd .84 DT67
Frederick Vil, W7
off Lower Boston Rd .79 CE74
Frederic Ms, SW1 .198 E5
Frederic St, E17 .67 DY57
Fredora Av, Hayes UB4 .77 BT70
Fred White Wk, N7
off Market Rd .83 DL65
Fred Wigg Twr, E11 .68 EF61
Freeborne Gdns, Rain. RM13
off Mungo Pk Rd .89 FG65
Freedom Cl, E17 .67 DY56
Freedom Rd, N17 .46 DR54
Freedom St, SW11 .100 DF82
Freedown La, Sutt. SM2 .158 DC113
Freegrove Rd, N7 .65 DL64
Freeland Pk, NW4 .43 CY54
Freeland Rd, W5 .80 CM73
Freelands Av, S.Croy. CR2 .161 DX109
Freelands Gro, Brom. BR1 .144 EH95
Freelands Rd, Brom. BR1 .144 EH95
Cobham KT11 .153 BV114
Freeland Way, Erith DA8
off Slade Grn Rd .107 FG81
Freeling St, N1
off Caledonian Rd .83 DM66
Freeman Cl, Nthlt. UB5 .78 BY66
Shepperton TW17 .135 BS98
Freeman Ct, N7
off Tollington Way .65 DL62
Freeman Dr, W.Mol. KT8 .136 BZ97
Freeman Rd, Grav. DA12 .131 GL90
Morden SM4 .140 DD99
Freemans Cl, Slou. (Stoke P.)
SL2 .74 AT65
Freemans La, Hayes UB3 .77 BS73
Freemantle Av, Enf. EN3 .31 DX43
Freemantle St, SE17 .201 M10
Freeman Way, Horn. RM11 .72 FL58
★ **Freemason's Hall (United Grand Lodge of England)**,
WC2 .196 A8
Freemasons Rd, E16 .86 EH71
Croydon CR0 .142 DS102
Free Prae Rd, Cher. KT16 .134 BG102
Freesia Cl, Orp. BR6
off Briarswood Way .163 ET106
Freethorpe Cl, SE19 .142 DR95
Free Trade Wf, E1
off The Highway .86 EF73
Freezeland Way, Uxb. UB10
off Western Av .76 BN65
FREEZY WATER, Wal.Cr. .31 DY35
★ **Freightliners City Fm**,
N7 .83 DM65
Freightmaster Est, Rain.
RM13 .107 FG76
Freke Rd, SW11 .100 DG83
Fremantle Ho, Til. RM18
off Leicester Rd .111 GF81
Fremantle Rd, Belv. DA17 .106 FA77
Ilford IG6 .49 EQ54
Fremont St, E9 .84 DW67
French Apartments, The, Pur. CR8
off Lansdowne Rd .159 DN112
Frenchaye, Add. KT15 .152 BJ106
Frenches, The, Red. RH1 .184 DG132
Frenches Ct, Red. RH1
off Frenches Rd .184 DG132
Frenches Dr, Red. RH1
off The Frenches .184 DG132
Frenches Rd, Red. RH1 .184 DG132
French Gdns, Cob. KT11 .154 BW114
French Ordinary Ct, EC3 .197 N10
French Pl, E1 .197 N3
French St, Sun. TW16 .136 BW96
Westerham TN16 .189 ES128
French's Wells, Wok. GU21 .166 AV117
Frendsbury Rd, SE4 .103 DY84
Frensham, Wal.Cr. (Chsht.)
EN7 .14 DT27
Frensham Cl, Sthl. UB1 .78 BZ70
Frensham Ct, Mitch. CR4
off Phipps Br Rd .140 DD97
Frensham Dr, SW15 .119 CU89
Croydon (New Adgtn.)
CR0 .161 EC108
Frensham Rd, SE9 .125 ER89
Kenley CR8 .159 DP114
Frensham St, SE15 .102 DU79
Frensham Way, Epsom KT17 .173 CW116
Frere St, SW11 .100 DE82
Freshfield Av, E8 .84 DT66
Freshfield Cl, SE13
off Marischal Rd .103 ED84
Freshfield Dr, N14 .45 DH45
Freshfields, Croy. CR0 .143 DZ101
Freshfields Av, Upmin.
RM14 .72 FP64
Freshford St, SW18 .120 DC90
Freshmount Gdns, Epsom
KT19 .156 CP111
Freshwater Cl, SW17 .120 DG93
Freshwater Rd, SW17 .120 DG93
Dagenham RM8 .70 EX60
Freshwell Av, Rom. RM6 .70 EW56
Fresh Wf Rd, Bark. IG11 .87 EP67
Freshwood Cl, Beck. BR3 .143 EB95
Freshwood Way, Wall. SM6 .159 DH109
Freston Gdns, Barn. EN4 .28 DG43
Freston Pk, N3 .43 CZ54
Freston Rd, W10 .81 CX73
W11 .81 CX73
Freta Rd, Bexh. DA6 .126 EZ85
★ **Freud Mus**, NW3 .82 DC65
Frewin Rd, SW18 .120 DD88
Friar Ms, SE27
off Prioress Rd .121 DP90
Friar Rd, Hayes UB4 .78 BX70
Orpington BR5 .146 EU99
Friars, The, Chig. IG7 .49 ES49
Friars Av, N20 .44 DE48
SW15 .119 CT90
Brentwood CM15 .55 GA46
Friars Cl, E4 .47 EC48
N2 .64 DD56
SE1 *off Bear La* .83 DP74
Brentwood (Shenf.) CM15 .55 FZ45
Ilford IG1 *off Leeds Rd* .69 ER60
Northolt UB5
off Broomcroft Av .78 BX69
Friars Gdns, W3
off St. Dunstans Av .80 CR72
Friars Gate Cl, Wdf.Grn. IG8 .48 EG49
Friars La, Rich. TW9 .117 CK85
Friars Mead, E14 .204 D7
Friars Ms, SE9 .125 EN85
Friars Orchard, Lthd. (Fetch.)
KT22 .171 CD121
Friars Pl La, W3 .80 CR73
Friars Ri, Wok. GU22 .167 BA118
Friars Rd, E6 .86 EK67
Virginia Water GU25 .132 AX98
Friars Stile Pl, Rich. TW10
off Friars Stile Rd .118 CL86
Friars Stile Rd, Rich. TW10 .118 CL86
Friar St, EC4 .196 G9
Friars Wk, N14 .45 DH46
SE2 .106 EX78
Friars Way, W3 .80 CR72
Bushey WD23 .24 BZ39
Chertsey KT16 .134 BG100
Kings Langley WD4 .6 BN30
Friars Wd, Croy. CR0 .161 DY109
Friary, The, Wind. (Old Wind.)
SL4 .112 AV86
Friary Cl, N12 .44 DE50
Friary Ct, SW1 .199 L3
Woking GU21 .166 AT118
Friary Est, SE15 .102 DU79
Friary Island, Stai. (Wrays.)
TW19 .112 AW86
Friary La, Wdf.Grn. IG8 .48 EG49
Friary Rd, N12 .44 DD49
SE15 .102 DU80
W3 .80 CR72
Staines (Wrays.) TW19 .112 AW86
Friary Way, N12 .44 DE49
FRIDAY HILL, E4 .47 ED47
Friday Hill, E4 .48 EE47
Friday Hill E, E4 .48 EE48
Friday Hill W, E4 .48 EE47
Friday Rd, Erith DA8 .107 FD78
Mitcham CR4 .120 DF94
Friday St, EC4 .197 H9
Frideswide Pl, NW5
off Islip St .65 DJ64
Friendly Pl, SE13
off Lewisham Rd .103 EB81
Friendly St, SE8 .103 EA81
Friendly St Ms, SE8
off Friendly St .103 EA82
Friends Av, Wal.Cr. EN8 .15 DX31
Friendship Wk, Nthlt. UB5
off Wayfarer Rd .78 BX69
Friends Rd, Croy. CR0 .142 DR104
Purley CR8 .159 DP112
Friend St, EC1 .196 F2
Friends Wk, Stai. TW18 .113 BF92
Uxbridge UB8
off Bakers Rd .76 BK66
FRIERN BARNET, N11 .44 DE49
Friern Barnet La, N11 .44 DE49
N20 .44 DE49
Friern Barnet Rd, N11 .44 DF50
Friern Br Retail Pk, N11 .45 DH51
Friern Ct, N20 .44 DD48
Friern Mt Dr, N20 .44 DC45
Friern Pk, N12 .44 DC50
Friern Rd, SE22 .122 DU86
Friern Watch Av, N12 .44 DC49
Frigate Ms, SE8
off Watergate St .103 EA79
Frimley Av, Horn. RM11 .72 FN60
Wallington SM6 .159 DL106
Frimley Cl, SW19 .119 CY89
Croydon (New Adgtn.)
CR0 .161 EC108
Frimley Ct, Sid. DA14 .126 EV92
Frimley Cres, Croy. (New Adgtn.)
CR0 .161 EC108
Frimley Gdns, Mitch. CR4 .140 DE97
Frimley Rd, Chess. KT9 .156 CL106
Ilford IG3 .69 ES62
Frimley Way, E1 .85 DX70
Fringewood Cl, Nthwd. HA6 .39 BP53
Frinstead Ho, W10 .81 CX73
Frinsted Cl, Orp. BR5 .146 EX98
Frinsted Rd, Erith DA8 .107 FD80
Frinton Cl, Wat. WD19 .39 BV47
Frinton Dr, Wdf.Grn. IG8 .47 ED52
Frinton Ms, Ilf. IG2
off Bramley Cres .69 EN58
Frinton Rd, E6 .86 EK69
N15 .66 DS58
SW17 .120 DG93
Romford RM5 .50 EZ52
Sidcup DA14 .126 EY89
Friston Path, Chig. IG7 .49 ES50
Friston St, SW6 .100 DB82
Friswell Pl, Bexh. DA6 .106 FA84
Fritham Cl, N.Mal. KT3 .138 CS100
Frith Ct, NW7 .43 CY52
Frithe, The, Slou. SL2 .74 AV72
Frith Knowle, Walt. KT12 .153 BV106
Frith La, NW7 .43 CY52
Frith Rd, E11 .67 EC63
Croydon CR0 .142 DQ103
Friths Dr, Reig. RH2 .184 DB131
Frith St, W1 .195 M9
Frithville Gdns, W12 .81 CW74
Frithwald Rd, Cher. KT16 .133 BF101
Frithwood Av, Nthwd. HA6 .39 BS51
Frizlands La, Dag. RM10 .71 FB63
Frobisher Cl, Bushey WD23 .24 CA44
Kenley CR8 *off Hayes La* .176 DR117
Pinner HA5 .60 BX59
Frobisher Cres, EC2
off Beech St .84 DQ71
Staines TW19 .114 BL87
Frobisher Gdns, Stai. TW19 .114 BL87
Frobisher Pas, E14 .204 A2
Frobisher Rd, E6 .87 EM72
N8 .65 DN56
Erith DA8 .107 FF80
Frobisher St, SE10 .104 EE79
Frobisher Way, Grav. DA12 .131 GL92
Greenhithe DA9 .109 FV84
Froggy La, Uxb. (Denh.) UB9 .57 BD62
Froghall La, Chig. IG7 .49 ER49
FROGHOLE, Eden. .189 ER133
Froghole La, Eden. TN8 .189 ER132
Frogley Rd, SE22 .102 DT84
Frogmoor La, Rick. WD3 .38 BK47
FROGMORE, St.Alb. .9 CE28
Frogmore, SW18 .120 DA85
St. Albans AL2 .9 CD27
Frogmore Av, Hayes UB4 .77 BS69
Frogmore Cl, Sutt. SM3 .139 CX104
Frogmore Dr, Wind. SL4 .92 AS81
Frogmore Est, Ruis. HA4 .60 BX64
Frogmore Gdns, Hayes UB4 .77 BS70
Sutton SM3 .157 CY105
Frogmore Home Pk, St.Alb.
AL2 .9 CD28
Frogmore Ind Est, NW10 .80 CQ69
Frognal, NW3 .64 DC64
Frognal Av, Har. HA1 .61 CF56
Sidcup DA14 .126 EU92
Frognal Cl, NW3 .64 DC64
Frognal Ct, NW3 .82 DC65
Frognal Gdns, NW3 .64 DC63
Frognal La, NW3 .64 DB64
Frognal Par, NW3
off Frognal Ct .82 DC65
Frognal Pl, Sid. DA14 .126 EU93
Frognal Ri, NW3 .64 DC63
Frognal Way, NW3 .64 DC63
Froissart Rd, SE9 .124 EK85
Frome Rd, N22
off Westbury Av .65 DP55
Frome St, N1 .84 DQ68
Fromondes Rd, Sutt. SM3 .157 CY106
Front La, Upmin. RM14 .73 FS59
Frostic Wk, E1 .84 DT71
Froude St, SW8 .101 DH82
Frowyke Cres, Pot.B. EN6 .11 CU32
Fruen Rd, Felt. TW14 .115 BT87
Fruiterers Pas, EC4
off Southwark Br .84 DQ73
Fryatt Rd, N17 .46 DR52
Fry Cl, Rom. RM5 .50 FA50
Fryent Cl, NW9 .62 CN58
Fryent Cres, NW9 .62 CS58
Fryent Flds, NW9 .62 CS58
Fryent Gro, NW9 .62 CS58
Fryent Way, NW9 .62 CN57
Fryern Wd, Cat. CR3 .176 DQ124
Frye's Bldgs, N1 *off Upper St* .83 DN68
Frying Pan All, E1 .197 P7
Fry Rd, E6 .86 EK66
NW10 .81 CT67
Fryston Av, Couls. CR5 .159 DH114
Croydon CR0 .142 DU103
Fuchsia Cl, Rom. (Rush Grn.)
RM7 .71 FE61
Fuchsia St, SE2 .106 EV78
Fulbeck Dr, NW9 .42 CS53
Fulbeck Wk, Edg. HA8
off Knightswood Cl .42 CP47
Fulbeck Way, Har. HA2 .40 CC54
Fulbourne Cl, Red. RH1
off Dennis Cl .184 DE132
Fulbourne Rd, E17 .47 EC53
Fulbourne St, E1
off Durward St .84 DV71
Fulbrook Av, Add. (New Haw)
KT15 .152 BG111
Fulbrook La, S.Ock. RM15 .91 FT73
Fulbrook Rd, N19
off Junction Rd .65 DJ63
Fulford Gro, Wat. WD19 .39 BV47
Fulford Rd, Cat. CR3 .176 DR121
Epsom KT19 .156 CR108
Fulford St, SE16 .202 E5
FULHAM, SW6 .99 CY82
⊖ **Fulham Broadway** .100 DA80
Fulham Bdy, SW6 .100 DA80
Fulham Cl, Uxb. UB10
off Uxbridge Rd .77 BQ70
Fulham Ct, SW6
off Shottendane Rd .100 DA80
★ **Fulham FC (share Loftus Rd Stadium with QPR FC)**SW6 .99 CX81
Fulham High St, SW6 .99 CY82
★ **Fulham Palace Mus**, SW6 .99 CX82
Fulham Palace Rd, SW6 .99 CX80
W6 .99 CW78
Fulham Pk Gdns, SW6 .99 CZ82
Fulham Pk Rd, SW6 .99 CZ82
Fulham Rd, SW3 .100 DC79
SW6 .99 CY82
SW10 .100 DB80
Fullarton Cres, S.Ock. RM15 .91 FT72
Fullbrooks Av, Wor.Pk. KT4 .139 CT102
Fuller Cl, E2
off St. Matthew's Row .84 DU70
Orpington BR6 .163 ET106
Fuller Gdns, Wat. WD24
off Fuller Rd .23 BV37
Fuller Rd, Dag. RM8 .70 EV62
Watford WD24 .23 BV37
Fullers Av, Surb. KT6 .138 CM103
Woodford Green IG8 .48 EF52
Fullers Cl, Rom. RM5 .51 FC52
Waltham Abbey EN9 .16 EG33
★ **Fuller's Griffin Brewery**,
W4 .99 CT79
Fullers Hill, West. TN16
off High St .189 ER126
Fullers La, Rom. RM5 .51 FC52
Fullers Rd, E18 .48 EF53
Fuller St, NW4 .63 CW56
Fullers Way N, Surb. KT6 .138 CM104
Fullers Way S, Chess. KT9 .156 CL105
Fullers Wd, Croy. CR0 .161 EA106
Fullers Wd La, Red. (S.Nutfld.)
RH1 .185 DJ134
Fuller Ter, Ilf. IG1
off Oaktree Gro .69 EQ64
Fullerton Cl, W.Byf. (Byfleet)
KT14 .152 BM114
Fullerton Dr, W.Byf. (Byfleet)
KT14 .152 BL114
Fullerton Rd, SW18 .120 DC85
Carshalton SM5 .158 DE109
Croydon CR0 .142 DT101
West Byfleet (Byfleet)
KT14 .152 BM114
Fullerton Way, W.Byf. (Byfleet)
KT14 .152 BL114
Fuller Way, Hayes UB3 .95 BT78
Rickmansworth (Crox.Grn.)
WD3 .22 BN43
Fullmer Way, Add. (Woodham)
KT15 .151 BF110
Fullwell Av, Ilf. IG5, IG6 .49 EM53
FULLWELL CROSS, Ilf. .49 ER53
Fullwell Cross Roundabout, Ilf. IG6
off Fencepiece Rd .49 ER54
Fullwoods Ms, N1 .197 L2
Fulmar Cl, Surb. KT5 .138 CM100
Fulmar Rd, Horn. RM12 .89 FG66
Fulmead St, SW6 .100 DB81
FULMER, Slou. .56 AX63
Fulmer Cl, Hmptn. TW12 .116 BY92
Fulmer Common Rd, Iver SL0 .75 AZ65
Slough (Fulmer) SL3 .75 AZ65
Fulmer Dr, Ger.Cr. SL9 .56 AW60
Fulmer La, Ger.Cr. SL9 .57 BB60
Slough (Fulmer) SL3 .56 AY62
Fulmer Ri Est, Slou. SL3 .75 AZ65
Fulmer Rd, E16 .86 EK71
Gerrards Cross SL9 .56 AY62
Slough (Fulmer) SL3 .56 AY63
Fulmer Way, W13 .97 CH76
Gerrards Cross SL9 .56 AY58
Fulready Rd, E10 .67 ED57
Fulstone Cl, Houns. TW4 .96 BZ84
Fulthorp Rd, SE3 .104 EF82
Fulton Ms, W2
off Porchester Ter .82 DC73
Fulton Rd, Wem. HA9 .62 CN62
⇌ **Fulwell** .117 CD91
Fulwell Pk Av, Twick. TW2 .116 CB89
Fulwell Rd, Tedd. TW11 .117 CD91
Fulwich Rd, Dart. DA1 .128 FM86
Fulwood Av, Wem. HA0 .80 CM67
Fulwood Cl, Hayes UB3 .77 BT72
Fulwood Gdns, Twick. TW1 .117 CF86
Fulwood Pl, WC1 .196 C7
Fulwood Wk, SW19 .119 CY88
Furber St, W6 .99 CV76
Furham Feild, Pnr. HA5 .40 CA52
Furley Rd, SE15 .102 DU80
Furlong Cl, Wall. SM6 .140 DG102
Furlong Rd, N7 .83 DN65
Furlough, The, Wok. GU22
off Pembroke Rd .167 BA117
Furmage St, SW18 .120 DB87
Furneaux Av, SE27 .121 DP92
Furner Cl, Dart. DA1 .107 FF83
Furness Cl, Grays RM16 .111 GH78
Furness Rd, NW10 .81 CU68
SW6 .100 DB82
Harrow HA2 .60 CB59
Morden SM4 .140 DB101
Furness Way, Horn. RM12 .71 FG64
Furnival Cl, Vir.W. GU25 .132 AX100
Furnival St, EC4 .196 D8
Furrow La, E9 .66 DW64
Furrows, The, Uxb. (Hare.)
UB9 .58 BJ57
Walton-on-Thames KT12 .136 BW103
Furrows Pl, Cat. CR3 .176 DT123
Fursby Av, N3 .44 DA51
Further Acre, NW9 .43 CT54
Furtherfield, Abb.L. WD5 .7 BS32
Furtherfield Cl, Croy. CR0 .141 DN100
Further Grn Rd, SE6 .124 EE87
Furzebushes La, St.Alb. AL2 .8 BY25
Furze Cl, Red. RH1 .184 DF133
Watford WD19 .40 BW50

★ Place of interest ⇌ Railway station ⊖ London Underground station DLR Docklands Light Railway station Tramlink station H Hospital

FURZEDOWN, SW17 ... 120 DG92
Furzedown Cl, Egh. TW20 ... 112 AY93
Furzedown Dr, SW17 ... 121 DH92
Furzedown Rd, SW17 ... 121 DH92
Sutton SM2 ... 158 DC111
Furze Fm Cl, Rom. RM6 ... 50 EY54
Furze Fld, Lthd. (Oxshott)
KT22 ... 155 CD113
Furzefield, Wal.Cr. (Chsht.)
EN8 ... 14 DV28
Furzefield Cl, Chis. BR7 ... 125 EP93
Furzefield Rd, SE3 ... 104 EH79
Furzeground Way, Uxb. UB11 ... 77 BQ74
Furze Gro, Tad. KT20 ... 173 CZ121
Furzeham Rd, West Dr. UB7 ... 94 BL75
Furze Hill, Pur. CR8 ... 159 DL111
Redhill RH1
off Linkfield La ... 184 DE133
Tadworth (Kgswd.) KT20 ... 173 CZ120
Furzehill Rd, Borwd. WD6 ... 26 CN42
Furzehill Sq, Orp. (St.M.Cray)
BR5 ... 146 EV98
Furze La, Pur. CR8 ... 159 DL111
Furze Rd, Add. KT15 ... 151 BF107
Thornton Heath CR7 ... 142 DQ97
Furze St, E3 ... 85 EA71
Furze Vw, Rick. (Chorl.) WD3 ... 21 BC44
Furzewood, Sun. TW16 ... 135 BU95
Fuschia Ct, Wdf.Grn. IG8
off The Bridle Path ... 48 EE52
Fusedale Way, S.Ock. RM15 ... 91 FT73
Fyfe Way, Brom. BR1
off Widmore Rd ... 144 EG96
Fyfield Cl, Brom. BR2 ... 143 ED98
Fyfield Ct, E7 ... 86 EG65
Fyfield Rd, E17 ... 67 ED55
SW9 ... 101 DN83
Enfield EN1 ... 30 DS41
Rainham RM13 ... 89 FF67
Woodford Green IG8 ... 48 EJ52
Fynes St, SW1 ... 199 M8

G

Gabion Av, Purf. RM19 ... 109 FR77
Gable Cl, Abb.L. WD5 ... 7 BS32
Dartford DA1 ... 127 FG85
Pinner HA5 ... 40 CA52
Gable Ct, SE26
off Lawrie Pk Av ... 122 DV92
Gables, The, Bans. SM7 ... 173 CZ117
Leatherhead (Oxshott)
KT22 ... 154 CC112
Wembley HA9 ... 62 CM62
Gables Av, Ashf. TW15 ... 114 BM92
Borehamwood WD6 ... 26 CM41
Gables Cl, SE5 ... 102 DS81
SE12 ... 124 EG88
Gerrards Cross (Chal.St.P.)
SL9 ... 36 AY49
Slough (Datchet) SL3 ... 92 AU79
Woking (Kgfld.) GU22
off Kingfield Rd ... 167 AZ120
Gables Ct, Wok. (Kgfld.) GU22
off Kingfield Rd ... 167 AZ120
Gables Way, Bans. SM7 ... 173 CZ117
Gabriel Cl, Felt. TW13 ... 116 BX91
Grays (Chaff.Hun.) RM16 ... 109 FW76
Romford RM5 ... 51 FC52
Gabrielle Cl, Wem. HA9 ... 62 CM62
Gabrielle Ct, NW3 ... 82 DD65
Gabriels Gdns, Grav. DA12 ... 131 GL92
Gabriel Spring Rd, Long.
(Fawk.Grn.) DA3 ... 149 FR103
Gabriel Spring Rd (East), Long.
(Fawk.Grn.) DA3 ... 149 FS103
Gabriel St, SE23 ... 123 DX87
Gabriel's Wf, SE1 ... 200 D2
Gad Cl, E13 ... 86 EH69
Gaddesden Av, Wem. HA9 ... 80 CM65
Gaddesden Cres, Wat. WD25 ... 8 BX34
Gade Av, Wat. WD18 ... 23 BS42
Gade Bk, Rick. (Crox.Grn.)
WD3 ... 23 BR42
Gade Cl, Hayes UB3 ... 77 BV74
Watford WD18 ... 23 BS42
Gadesden Rd, Epsom KT19 ... 156 CQ107
Gadeside, Wat. WD25
off North Western Av ... 23 BS35
Gade Twr, Hem.H. HP3 ... 6 BN25
Gade Valley Cl, Kings L. WD4 ... 6 BN28
Gade Vw Gdns, Kings L. WD4 ... 7 BQ32
Gadsbury Cl, NW9 ... 63 CT58
Gadsden Cl, Upmin. RM14 ... 73 FS58
Gadswell Cl, Wat. WD25 ... 24 BX36
Gadwall Cl, E16
off Freemasons Rd ... 86 EH72
Gadwall Way, SE28 ... 105 ER75
Gage Rd, E16
off Malmesbury Rd ... 86 EE71
Gage St, WC1 ... 196 A6
Gainford St, N1
off Richmond Av ... 83 DN67
Gainsboro Gdns, Grnf. UB6 ... 61 CE64
Gainsborough Av, E12 ... 69 EN64
Dartford DA1 ... 128 FJ85
Tilbury RM18 ... 111 GG81
Gainsborough Cl, Beck. BR3 ... 123 EA94
Esher KT10
off Lime Tree Av ... 137 CE102
Gainsborough Ct, N12 ... 44 DB50
W12
off Lime Gro ... 99 CW75
Walton-on-Thames
KT12 ... 153 BU105
Gainsborough Dr, Grav. (Nthflt.)
DA11 ... 130 GD90
South Croydon CR2 ... 160 DU113
Gainsborough Gdns, NW3 ... 64 DD62
NW11 ... 63 CZ59
Edgware HA8 ... 42 CM54
Isleworth TW7 ... 117 CD85
Gainsborough Ho, Enf. EN1
off Ayley Cft ... 30 DU43
Gainsborough Ms, SE26
off Panmure Rd ... 122 DV90
Gainsborough Pl, Chig. IG7 ... 49 ET48
Gainsborough Rd, E11 ... 68 EE59
E15 ... 86 EE69
N12 ... 44 DB50
W4 ... 99 CT77
Dagenham RM8 ... 70 EV63
Epsom KT19 ... 156 CQ110
Hayes UB4 ... 77 BQ68
New Malden KT3 ... 138 CR101
Rainham RM13 ... 89 FG67
Richmond TW9 ... 98 CM83
Woodford Green IG8 ... 48 EL51
Gainsborough Sq, Bexh. DA6
off Regency Way ... 106 EX83
Gainsford Rd, E17 ... 67 DZ56
Gainsford St, SE1 ... 201 P4
Gairloch Rd, SE5 ... 102 DS82
Gaisford St, NW5 ... 83 DJ65
Gaist Av, Cat. CR3 ... 176 DU122
Gaitskell Ct, SW11 ... 100 DE82
Gaitskell Rd, SE9 ... 125 EQ88
Galahad Rd, Brom. BR1 ... 124 EG90
Galata Rd, SW13 ... 99 CU80
Galatea Sq, SE15
off Scylla Rd ... 102 DV83
Galbraith St, E14 ... 204 D6
Galdana Av, Barn. EN5 ... 28 DC41
Galeborough Av, Wdf.Grn.
IG8 ... 47 ED52
Gale Cl, Hmptn. TW12
off Stewart Cl ... 116 BY93
Mitcham CR4 ... 140 DD97
Gale Cres, Bans. SM7 ... 174 DA117
Galena Ho, SE18
off Grosmont Rd ... 105 ET78
Galena Rd, W6 ... 99 CV77
Galen Cl, Epsom KT19
off Williams Evans Rd ... 156 CN111
Galen Pl, WC1 ... 196 A7
Galesbury Rd, SW18 ... 120 DC86
Gales Gdns, E2 ... 84 DV69
Gale St, E3 ... 85 EA71
Dagenham RM9 ... 88 EX67
Gales Way, Wdf.Grn. IG8 ... 48 EL52
Galey Grn, S.Ock. RM15
off Bovey Way ... 91 FV71
Galgate Cl, SW19 ... 119 CY88
Gallants Fm Rd, Barn. EN4 ... 44 DE45
Galleon Boul, Dart. DA2 ... 109 FR84
Galleon Cl, SE16 ... 202 G4
Erith DA8 ... 107 FD77
Galleon Ms, Grav. DA11
off Rosherville Way ... 130 GE87
Galleon Rd, Grays (Chaff.Hun.)
RM16 ... 109 FW77
Galleons Dr, Bark. IG11 ... 88 EU69
Galleons La, Slou. (Geo.Grn.)
SL3 ... 74 AX71
Gallery Gdns, Nthlt. UB5 ... 78 BX68
Gallery Rd, SE21 ... 122 DR88
Galley Hill, Wal.Abb. EN9 ... 16 EF30
Galley Hill Rd, Grav. (Nthflt.)
DA11 ... 130 FZ85
Swanscombe DA10 ... 130 FZ85
Galley La, Barn. EN5 ... 27 CV41
Galleymead Rd, Slou. (Colnbr.)
SL3 ... 93 BF81
Galleywall Rd, SE16 ... 202 D9
Galleywood Cres, Rom. RM5 ... 51 FD51
Galliard Cl, N9 ... 30 DW44
Galliard Rd, N9 ... 46 DU46
Gallia Rd, N5 ... 65 DP64
Gallions Cl, Bark. IG11 ... 88 EU69
DLR Gallions Reach ... 87 EP72
Gallions Rd, SE7 ... 104 EH77
Gallions Roundabout, E16 ... 87 EP73
Gallions Vw Rd, SE28
off Goldfinch Rd ... 105 ES75
Gallon Cl, SE7 ... 104 EJ77
Gallop, The, S.Croy. CR2 ... 160 DV108
Sutton SM2 ... 158 DC108
Gallops, The, Tad. KT20 ... 183 CV126
Gallosson Rd, SE18 ... 105 ES77
Galloway Chase, Slou. SL2 ... 74 AU73
Galloway Cl, Brox. EN10 ... 15 DZ26
Galloway Dr, Dart. DA1
off Lower Sta Rd ... 127 FE86
Galloway Path, Croy. CR0 ... 160 DR105
Galloway Rd, W12 ... 81 CU74
Gallows Cor, Rom. (Harold Wd.)
RM3 ... 52 FK53
Gallows Hill, Kings L. WD4 ... 7 BQ31
Gallows Hill La, Abb.L. WD5 ... 7 BQ32
Gallus Cl, N21 ... 29 DM44
Gallus Sq, SE3 ... 104 EH83
Galpins Rd, Th.Hth. CR7 ... 141 DM98
Galsworthy Av, E14 ... 85 DY71
Romford RM6 ... 70 EV59
Galsworthy Cl, SE28 ... 88 EV74
Galsworthy Cres, SE3
off Merriman Rd ... 104 EJ81
Galsworthy Rd, NW2 ... 63 CY63
Chertsey KT16 ... 134 BG101
Kingston upon Thames
KT2 ... 118 CP94
Tilbury RM18 ... 111 GJ81
Galsworthy Ter, N16
off Hawksley Rd ... 66 DS62
Galton St, W10 ... 81 CY70
Galva Cl, Barn. EN4 ... 28 DG42
Galvani Way, Croy. CR0
off Ampere Way ... 141 DM102
Galveston Rd, SW15 ... 119 CZ85
Galway Cl, SE16
off Masters Dr ... 102 DV78
Galway St, EC1 ... 197 J3
Gambetta St, SW8 ... 101 DH82
Gambia St, SE1 ... 200 G3
Gambles La, Wok. (Ripley)
GU23 ... 168 BJ124
Gambole Rd, SW17 ... 120 DE91
Games Rd, Barn. EN4 ... 28 DF41
Gamlen Rd, SW15 ... 99 CX84
Gammons Fm Cl, Wat. WD24 ... 23 BT36
Gammons La, Brox. EN10 ... 14 DT25
Gammons La, Wat. WD24 ... 23 BV38
Gamuel Cl, E17 ... 67 EA58
Gander Grn Cres, Hmptn.
TW12 ... 136 CA95
Gander Grn La, Sutt. SM1,
SM3 ... 139 CY103
Ganders Ash, Wat. WD25 ... 7 BU33
Gandhi Cl, E17 ... 67 EA58
Gandolfi St, SE15
off St. Georges Way ... 102 DS
Gangers Hill, Cat. (Wold.)
CR3 ... 187 EA127
Godstone RH9 ... 187 EA127
Gant Ct, Wal.Abb. EN9 ... 16 EF34
Ganton St, W1 ... 195 K10
Ganton Wk, Wat. WD19
off Woodhall La ... 40 BY49
GANTS HILL, Ilf. ... 69 EN57
⊖ Gants Hill ... 69 EN58
Gants Hill, Ilf. IG2
off Eastern Av ... 69 EN58
Gantshill Cres, Ilf. IG2 ... 69 EN57
GANWICK CORNER, Barn. ... 28 DB35
Gap Rd, SW19 ... 120 DA92
Garage Rd, W3 ... 80 CN72
Garbrand Wk, Epsom KT17 ... 157 CT109
Garbutt Pl, W1 ... 194 G6
Garbutt Rd, Upmin. RM14 ... 72 FQ61
Garden Av, Bexh. DA7 ... 106 FA83
Mitcham CR4 ... 121 DH94
Garden City, Edg. HA8 ... 42 CN51
Garden Cl, E4 ... 47 EA50
SE12 ... 124 EH90
SW15 ... 119 CV87
Addlestone KT15 ... 152 BK105
Ashford TW15 ... 115 BQ93
Banstead SM7 ... 174 DA115
Barnet EN5 ... 27 CW42
Hampton TW12 ... 116 BZ92
Leatherhead KT22 ... 171 CJ124
Northolt UB5 ... 78 BY67
Ruislip HA4 ... 59 BS61
Wallington SM6 ... 159 DL106
Watford WD17 ... 23 BT40
Garden Cotts, Orp. BR5
off Main Rd ... 146 EW96
Garden Ct, EC4 ... 196 D10
N12 off Holden Rd ... 44 DB50
Richmond TW9
off Lichfield Rd ... 98 CM81
Stanmore HA7
off Marsh La ... 41 CJ50
West Molesey KT8
off Avern Rd ... 136 CB98
Garden End, Amer. HP6 ... 20 AS37
Gardeners Cl, N11 ... 44 DG47
Gardeners Rd, Croy. CR0 ... 141 DP102
H Garden Hosp, The, NW4 ... 63 CW55
Gardenia Rd, Enf. EN1 ... 30 DS44
Gardenia Way, Wdf.Grn. IG8 ... 48 EG50
Garden La, SW2
off Christchurch Rd ... 121 DM88
Bromley BR1 ... 124 EH93
Garden Ms, W2
off Linden Gdns ... 82 DA73
Slough SL1
off Littledown Rd ... 74 AT74
Garden Pl, Dart. DA2 ... 128 FK90
Garden Reach, Ch.St.G. HP8 ... 20 AX41
Garden Rd, NW8 ... 82 DC69
SE20 ... 142 DW95
Abbots Langley WD5 ... 7 BS31
Bromley BR1 ... 124 EH94
Richmond TW9 ... 98 CN83
Sevenoaks TN13 ... 191 FK122
Walton-on-Thames KT12 ... 135 BV100
Garden Row, SE1 ... 200 F7
Gravesend (Nthflt.) DA11 ... 131 GF90
Gardens, The, SE22 ... 102 DU84
Beckenham BR3 ... 143 EC96
Esher KT10 ... 154 CA105
Feltham TW14 ... 115 BR85
Harrow HA1 ... 60 CC58
Hatfield AL9 ... 11 CY27
Pinner HA5 ... 60 BZ58
Watford WD17 ... 23 BT40
★ Gardens of the Rose, St.Alb.
AL2 ... 8 BY26
Garden St, E1 ... 85 DX71
Garden Ter, SW1 ... 199 M10
Garden Wk, EC2 ... 197 M3
Beckenham BR3
off Hayne Rd ... 143 DZ95
Coulsdon CR5 ... 175 DH123
Garden Way, NW10 ... 80 CQ65
Loughton IG10 ... 33 EN38
Gardiner Av, NW2 ... 63 CW64
Gardiner Cl, Dag. RM8 ... 70 EX63
Enfield EN3 ... 31 DX44
Orpington BR5 ... 146 EW96
Gardner Cl, E11 ... 68 EH58
Gardner Gro, Felt. TW13 ... 116 BZ89
Gardner Pl, Felt. TW14 ... 115 BV86
Gardner Rd, E13 ... 86 EH70
Gardners La, EC4 ... 197 H10
Gardnor Rd, NW3
off Flask Wk ... 64 DD63
Gard St, EC1 ... 196 G2
Garendon Gdns, Mord. SM4 ... 140 DB101
Garendon Rd, Mord. SM4 ... 140 DB101
Gareth Cl, Wor.Pk. KT4
off Burnham Dr ... 139 CX103
Gareth Gro, Brom. BR1 ... 124 EG91
Garfield Ms, SW11
off Garfield Rd ... 100 DG83
Garfield Rd, E4 ... 47 ED46
E13 ... 86 EF70
SW11 ... 100 DG83
SW19 ... 120 DC92
Addlestone KT15 ... 152 BJ106
Enfield EN3 ... 30 DW42
Twickenham TW1 ... 117 CG88
Garfield St, Wat. WD24 ... 23 BV38
Garford St, E14 ... 203 P1
Garganey Wk, SE28 ... 88 EX73
Gargery Cl, Grav. DA12
off Damigos Rd ... 131 GM88
Garibaldi St, SE18 ... 105 ES77
Garland Cl, Wal.Cr. EN8 ... 15 DY31
Garland Rd, SE18 ... 105 ER80
Stanmore HA7 ... 42 CL53
Garlands Ct, Croy. CR0
off Chatsworth Rd ... 160 DR105
Garlands Rd, Lthd. KT22 ... 171 CH121
Garland Way, Cat. CR3 ... 176 DR122
Hornchurch RM11 ... 72 FL56
Garlichill Rd, Epsom KT18 ... 173 CV117
Garlick Hill, EC4 ... 197 J10
Garlies Rd, SE23 ... 123 DY90
Garlinge Rd, NW2 ... 82 CZ65
Garman Cl, N18 ... 46 DR50
Garman Rd, N17 ... 46 DW52
Garnault Ms, EC1 ... 196 E3
Garnault Pl, EC1 ... 196 E3
Garnault Rd, Enf. EN1 ... 30 DT38
Garner Cl, Dag. RM8 ... 70 EX60
Garner Dr, Brox. EN10 ... 15 DY26
Garner Rd, E17 ... 47 EC53
Garners Cl, Ger.Cr. (Chal.St.P.)
SL9 ... 36 AY51
Garners End, Ger.Cr. (Chal.St.P.)
SL9 ... 36 AY51
Garners Rd, Ger.Cr. (Chal.St.P.)
SL9 ... 36 AY51
Garner St, E2 off Coate St ... 84 DU68
Garnet Rd, NW10 ... 80 CS65
Thornton Heath CR7 ... 142 DR98
Garnet St, E1 ... 202 F1
Garnett Cl, SE9 ... 105 EM83
Watford WD24 ... 24 BX37
Garnett Dr, St.Alb. (Brick.Wd.)
AL2 ... 8 BZ29
Garnett Rd, NW3 ... 64 DF64
Garnett Way, E17
off McEntee Av ... 47 DY53
Garnet Wk, E6
off Kingfisher St ... 86 EL71
Garnham Cl, N16
off Garnham St ... 66 DT61
Garnham St, N16 ... 66 DT61
Garnies Cl, SE15 ... 102 DT80
Garnon Mead, Epp. CM16 ... 18 EX28
Garrad's Rd, SW16 ... 121 DK90
Garrard Cl, Bexh. DA7 ... 106 FA83
Chislehurst BR7 ... 125 EP92
Garrard Rd, Bans. SM7 ... 174 DA116
Garrard Wk, NW10
off Garnet Rd ... 80 CS65
Garratt Cl, Croy. CR0 ... 159 DL105
Garratt La, SW17 ... 120 DD91
SW18 ... 120 DB85
Garratt Rd, Edg. HA8 ... 42 CN52
Garratts La, Bans. SM7 ... 173 CZ116
Garratts Rd, Bushey WD23 ... 40 CC45
Garratt Ter, SW17 ... 120 DE91
Garrett Cl, W3
off Jenner Av ... 80 CR71
Garrett St, EC1 ... 197 J4
Garrick Av, NW11 ... 63 CY58
Garrick Cl, SW18 ... 100 DC84
W5 ... 80 CL70
Richmond TW9
off The Green ... 117 CK85
Staines TW18 ... 114 BG94
Walton-on-Thames KT12 ... 153 BV105
Garrick Cres, Croy. CR0 ... 142 DS103
Garrick Dr, NW4 ... 43 CW54
SE28 off Broadwater Rd ... 105 ER76
Garrick Gdns, W.Mol. KT8 ... 136 CA97
Garrick Pk, NW4 ... 43 CX54
Garrick Rd, NW9 ... 63 CT58
Greenford UB6 ... 78 CB70
Richmond TW9 ... 98 CN82
Garrick St, WC2 ... 195 P10
Gravesend DA11
off Barrack Row ... 131 GH86
Garrick Way, NW4 ... 63 CX56
Garrison Cl, SE18
off Red Lion La ... 105 EN80
Hounslow TW4 ... 116 BZ85
Garrison La, Chess. KT9 ... 155 CK108
Garrison Par, Purf. RM19
off Comet Cl ... 108 FN77
Garrolds Cl, Swan. BR8 ... 147 FD96
Garron La, S.Ock. RM15 ... 91 FT72
Garry Cl, Rom. RM1 ... 51 FE52
Garry Way, Rom. RM1 ... 51 FE52
Garsdale Cl, N11 ... 44 DG51
Garside Cl, SE28
off Goosander Way ... 105 ER76
Hampton TW12 ... 116 CB93
Garsington Ms, SE4 ... 103 DZ83
Garsmouth Way, Wat. WD25 ... 24 BX36
Garson Cl, Esher KT10
off Garson Rd ... 154 BZ107
Garson La, Stai. (Wrays.)
TW19 ... 112 AX87
Garson Mead, Esher KT10 ... 154 BZ106
Garson Rd, Esher KT10 ... 154 BZ107
GARSTON, Wat. ... 24 BW35
⇌ Garston ... 24 BX35
Garston Cres, Wat. WD25 ... 8 BW34
Garston Dr, Wat. WD25 ... 8 BW34
Garston Gdns, Ken. CR8
off Godstone Rd ... 176 DR115
Garston La, Ken. CR8 ... 160 DR114
Watford WD25 ... 8 BX34
Garston Pk Par, Wat. WD25 ... 8 BX34
Garter Way, SE16 ... 203 H5
Garth, The, N12
off Holden Rd ... 44 DB50
Abbots Langley WD5 ... 7 BR33
Cobham KT11 ... 154 BY113
Hampton (Hmptn.H.) TW12
off Uxbridge Rd ... 116 CB93
Harrow HA3 ... 62 CM58
Garth Cl, W4 ... 98 CR78
Kingston upon Thames
KT2 ... 118 CM92
Morden SM4 ... 139 CX101
Ruislip HA4 ... 60 BX60
Garth Ct, W4
off Garth Rd ... 98 CR78
Garthland Dr, Barn. EN5 ... 27 CV43
Garth Ms, W5
off Greystoke Gdns ... 80 CL70
Garthorne Rd, SE23 ... 123 DX87
Garth Rd, NW2 ... 63 CZ61
W4 ... 98 CR79
Kingston upon Thames
KT2 ... 118 CM92
Morden SM4 ... 139 CW100
Sevenoaks TN13 ... 191 FJ128
South Ockendon RM15 ... 91 FW70
Garth Rd Ind Cen, Mord.
SM4 ... 139 CX101
Garthside, Rich. TW10 ... 118 CL92
Garthway, N12 ... 44 DE51
Gartlett Rd, Wat. WD17 ... 24 BW41
Gartmoor Gdns, SW19 ... 119 CZ88
Gartmore Rd, Ilf. IG3 ... 69 ET60
Garton Pl, SW18 ... 120 DC86
Gartons Cl, Enf. EN3 ... 30 DW43
Gartons Way, SW11 ... 100 DC83
Garvary Rd, E16 ... 86 EH72
Garvock Dr, Sev. TN13 ... 190 FG126
Garway Rd, W2 ... 82 DB72
Gascoigne Gdns, Wdf.Grn.
IG8 ... 48 EE52
Gascoigne Pl, E2 ... 197 P3
Gascoigne Rd, Bark. IG11 ... 87 EQ67
Croydon (New Adgtn.)
CR0 ... 161 EC110
Weybridge KT13 ... 135 BP104
Gascony Av, NW6 ... 82 DA66
Gascoyne Cl, Pot.B. EN6 ... 11 CU32
Romford RM3 ... 52 FK52
Gascoyne Dr, Dart. DA1 ... 107 FF82
Gascoyne Rd, E9 ... 85 DX66
Gaselee St, E14 ... 204 E1
Gasholder Pl, SE11
off Kennington La ... 101 DM78
Gaskarth Rd, SW12 ... 121 DH86
Edgware HA8 ... 42 CQ53
Gaskell Rd, N6 ... 64 DF58
Gaskell St, SW4 ... 101 DL82
Gaskin St, N1 ... 83 DP67
Gaspar Cl, SW5
off Courtfield Gdns ... 100 DB77
Gaspar Ms, SW5
off Courtfield Gdns ... 100 DB77
Gassiot Rd, SW17 ... 120 DF91
Gassiot Way, Sutt. SM1 ... 140 DD104
Gasson Rd, Swans. DA10 ... 130 FY86
Gastein Rd, W6 ... 99 CX79
Gaston Bell Cl, Rich. TW9 ... 98 CM83
Gaston Br Rd, Shep. TW17 ... 135 BS99
Gaston Rd, Mitch. CR4 ... 140 DG97
Gaston Way, Shep. TW17 ... 135 BR99
Gataker St, SE16 ... 202 E6
Gatcombe Ms, W5 ... 80 CM73
Gatcombe Rd, E16 ... 205 N2
N19 ... 65 DK62
Gatcombe Way, Barn. EN4 ... 28 DF41
Gate Cl, Borwd. WD6 ... 26 CQ39
Gate End, Nthwd. HA6 ... 39 BU52
Gateforth St, NW8 ... 194 B5
Gatehill Rd, Nthwd. HA6 ... 39 BT52
Gatehope Dr, S.Ock. RM15 ... 91 FT72
Gatehouse Cl, Kings.T. KT2 ... 118 CQ94
Gatehouse Sq, SE1
off Southwark Br Rd ... 84 DQ74
Gateley Rd, SW9 ... 101 DM83
Gate Ms, SW7 ... 198 C5
Gater Dr, Enf. EN2 ... 30 DR39
Gatesborough St, EC2 ... 197 M4
Gatesden Cl, Lthd. (Fetch.)
KT22 ... 170 CC123
Gatesden Rd, Lthd. (Fetch.)
KT22 ... 170 CC123
Gates Grn Rd, Kes. BR2 ... 162 EG105
West Wickham BR4 ... 144 EF104
Gateshead Rd, Borwd. WD6 ... 26 CM39
Gateside Rd, SW17 ... 120 DF90
Gatestone Rd, SE19 ... 122 DS93
Gate St, WC2 ... 196 B8
Gateway, SE17 ... 102 DQ79
Weybridge KT13
off Palace Dr ... 135 BP104
Gateway, The, Wok. GU21 ... 151 BB114
Gateway Arc, N1
off Islington High St ... 83 DP68
Gateway Cl, Nthwd. HA6 ... 39 BQ51
Gateway Ho, Bark. IG11
off St. Ann's ... 87 EQ67
Gateway Ind Est, NW10 ... 81 CT69
Gateway Ms, E8
off Shacklewell La ... 66 DT64
Gateway Retail Pk, E6 ... 87 EP70
Gateway Rd, E10 ... 67 EB62
Gateways, The, SW3 ... 198 C9
Waltham Cross EN7 ... 14 DR28
Gatewick Cl, Slou. SL1 ... 74 AS74
Gatfield Gro, Felt. TW13 ... 116 CA89
Gathorne Rd, N22 ... 45 DN54
Gathorne St, E2 off Mace St ... 85 DX68
Gatley Av, Epsom KT19 ... 156 CP106
Gatliff Rd, SW1 ... 101 DH78
Gatling Rd, SE2 ... 106 EU78
Gatonby St, SE15
off Kelly Av ... 102 DT80
Gatting Cl, Edg. HA8
off Pavilion Way ... 42 CQ52
Gatting Way, Uxb. UB8 ... 76 BL65
GATTON, Reig. ... 184 DF128
Gatton Bottom, Red. RH1 ... 185 DH127
Reigate RH2 ... 184 DE128
Gatton Cl, Reig. RH2 ... 184 DC131
Sutton SM2 ... 158 DB109
Gatton Pk, Reig. RH2 ... 184 DF129
Gatton Pk Rd, Red. RH1 ... 184 DD132
Reigate RH2 ... 184 DD132
Gatton Rd, SW17 ... 120 DE91
Reigate RH2 ... 184 DC131
Gattons Way, Sid. DA14 ... 126 EZ91
Gatward Cl, N21 ... 29 DP44
Gatward Grn, N9 ... 46 DS47
Gatwick Rd, SW18 ... 119 CZ87

★ Place of interest ⇌ Railway station ⊖ London Underground station DLR Docklands Light Railway station Tramlink station H Hospital

Gat - Gla

Gatwick Rd, Grav. DA12 131 GH90
Gatwick Way, Horn. RM12
off Haydock Cl 72 FM63
Gauden Cl, SW4 101 DK83
Gauden Rd, SW4 101 DK82
Gaumont App, Wat. WD17 23 BV41
Gaumont Ter, W12
off Lime Gro 99 CW75
Gauntlet Cl, Nthlt. UB5 78 BY66
Gauntlet Cres, Ken. CR8 176 DR120
Gauntlett Ct, Wem. HA0 61 CH64
Gauntlett Rd, Sutt. SM1 158 DD106
Gaunt St, SE1 200 G6
Gautrey Rd, SE15 102 DW82
Gautrey Sq, E6 87 EM72
Gavell Rd, Cob. KT11 153 BU113
Gavel St, SE17 201 L8
Gavenny Path, S.Ock. RM15 91 FT72
Gaveston Cl, W.Byf. (Byfleet)
KT14 152 BM113
Gavestone Cres, SE12 124 EH87
Gavestone Rd, SE12 124 EH87
Gaveston Rd, Lthd. KT22 171 CG120
Gaviller Pl, E5 *off Clarence Rd* 66 DV63
Gavina Cl, Mord. SM4 140 DE99
Gavin St, SE18 105 ES77
Gaviots Cl, Ger.Cr. SL9 57 AZ60
Gaviots Grn, Ger.Cr. SL9 56 AY60
Gaviots Way, Ger.Cr. SL9 56 AY59
Gawber St, E2 84 DW69
Gawsworth Cl, E15
off Ash Rd 68 EE64
Gawthorne Av, NW7
off Lane App 43 CY50
Gawthorne Ct, E3
off Mostyn Gro 85 EA68
Gay Cl, NW2 63 CV64
Gaydon Ho, W2 82 DB71
Gaydon La, NW9 42 CS53
Gayfere Rd, Epsom KT17 157 CU106
Ilford IG5 69 EM55
Gayfere St, SW1 199 P7
Gayford Rd, W12 99 CT75
Gay Gdns, Dag. RM10 71 FC63
Gayhurst, SE17
off Hopwood Rd 102 DR79
Gayhurst Rd, E8 84 DU66
Gayler Cl, Red. (Bletch.) RH1 186 DT133
Gaylor Rd, Nthlt. UB5 60 BZ64
Tilbury RM18 110 GE81
Gaynes Ct, Upmin. RM14 72 FP63
Gaynesford Rd, SE23 123 DX89
Carshalton SM5 158 DF108
Gaynes Hill Rd, Wdf.Grn. IG8 48 EL51
Gaynes Pk, Epp. CM16 18 EY31
Gaynes Pk Rd, Upmin. RM14 72 FN63
Gaynes Rd, Upmin. RM14 72 FP61
Gay Rd, E15 85 ED68
Gaysham Av, Ilf. IG2 69 EN57
Gaysham Hall, Ilf. IG5 69 EP55
Gay St, SW15 99 CX83
Gayton Cl, Amer. HP6 20 AS35
Ashtead KT21 172 CL118
Gayton Ct, Har. HA1 61 CF58
Gayton Cres, NW3 64 DD63
Gayton Rd, NW3 64 DD63
SE2 *off Florence Rd* 106 EW76
Harrow HA1 61 CF58
Gayville Rd, SW11 120 DF86
Gaywood Av, Wal.Cr. (Chsht.)
EN8 15 DX30
Gaywood Cl, SW2 121 DM88
Gaywood Est, SE1 200 G7
Gaywood Rd, E17 67 EA55
Ashtead KT21 172 CM118
Gaywood St, SE1 200 G7
Gaza St, SE17
off Braganza St 101 DP78
Gazelle Glade, Grav. DA12 131 GM92
Geariesville Gdns, Ilf. IG6 69 EP56
Geary Dr, Brwd. CM14 54 FW46
Geary Rd, NW10 63 CU64
Geary St, N7 65 DM64
G.E.C. Est, Wem. HA9 61 CK62
Geddes Pl, Bexh. DA6
off Market Pl 106 FA84
Geddes Rd, Bushey WD23 24 CC42
Gedeney Rd, N17 46 DQ53
Gedling Pl, SE1 202 A6
Geere Rd, E15 86 EF67
Gees Ct, W1 194 G9
Gee St, EC1 197 H4
Geffrye Ct, N1 197 N1
Geffrye Est, N1
off Stanway St 84 DS68
★ Geffrye Mus, E2 197 N1
Geffrye St, E2 84 DT68
Geisthorp Ct, Wal.Abb. EN9
off Winters Way 16 EG33
Geldart Rd, SE15 102 DV80
Geldeston Rd, E5 66 DU61
Gellatly Rd, SE14 102 DW82
Gell Cl, Uxb. UB10 58 BM62
Gelsthorpe Rd, Rom. RM5 51 FB52
Gemini Gro, Nthlt. UB5
off Javelin Way 78 BY69
General Gordon Pl, SE18 105 EP77
Generals Wk, The, Enf. EN3 31 DY37
General Wolfe Rd, SE10 103 ED81
Genesis Business Pk, Wok.
GU21 167 BC115
Genesis Cl, Stai. (Stanw.)
TW19 114 BM88
Genesta Rd, SE18 105 EP79
Geneva Cl, Shep. TW17 135 BS96
Geneva Dr, SW9 101 DN84
Geneva Gdns, Rom. RM6 70 EY57
Geneva Rd, Kings.T. KT1 138 CL98
Thornton Heath CR7 142 DQ99
Genever Cl, E4 47 EA50
Genista Rd, N18 46 DV50
Genoa Av, SW15 119 CW85
Genoa Rd, SE20 142 DW95
Genotin Rd, Enf. EN1 30 DR41
Genotin Ter, Enf. EN1
off Genotin Rd 30 DR41
Gentian Row, SE13
off Sparta St 103 EC81
Gentlemans Row, Enf. EN2 30 DQ41
Gentry Gdns, E13
off Whitwell Rd 86 EG70
Geoffrey Av, Rom. RM3 52 FN51
Geoffrey Cl, SE5 102 DQ82
Geoffrey Gdns, E6 86 EL68
Geoffrey Rd, SE4 103 DZ83
George Avey Cft, Epp. (N.Wld.Bas.)
CM16 19 FB26
George Beard Rd, SE8 203 M9
George Comberton Wk, E12
off Gainsborough Av 69 EN64
George Ct, WC2 200 A1
George Cres, N10 44 DG52
George Crook's Ho, Grays RM17
off New Rd 110 GB79
George Downing Est, N16
off Cazenove Rd 66 DT61
George V Av, Pnr. HA5 60 CA55
George V Cl, Pnr. HA5
off George V Av 60 CA55
George V Way, Grnf. UB6 79 CH67
Rickmansworth (Sarratt)
WD3 22 BG36
George Gange Way, Har. (Wldste.)
HA3 61 CE55
GEORGE GREEN, Slou. 74 AX72
George Grn Dr, Slou. (Geo.Grn.)
SL3 75 AZ71
George Grn Rd, Slou. (Geo.Grn.)
SL3 74 AX72
George Gro Rd, SE20 142 DU95
★ George Inn, SE1
off Borough High St 201 K3
George Inn Yd, SE1 201 K3
Georgelands, Wok. (Ripley)
GU23 168 BH121
George La, E18 48 EG54
SE13 123 EC86
Bromley BR2 144 EH102
George Lansbury Ho, N22
off Progress Way 45 DN53
George Loveless Ho, E2
off Diss St 84 DT69
George Lovell Dr, Enf. EN3
off Government Row 31 EA37
George Lowe Ct, W2
off Bourne Ter 82 DB71
George Mathers Rd, SE11 200 F8
George Ms, NW1 195 K3
Enfield EN2 *off Sydney Rd* 30 DR41
George Pl, N17
off Dongola Rd 66 DS55
George Rd, E4 47 EA51
Kingston upon Thames
KT2 118 CP94
New Malden KT3 139 CT98
George Row, SE16 202 B5
Georges Cl, Orp. BR5 146 EW97
Georges Dr, Brwd. CM15 54 FT43
Georges Mead, Borwd. (Elstree)
WD6 25 CK44
George Sq, SW19
off Mostyn Rd 139 CZ97
George's Rd, N7 65 DM64
Georges Rd, West. (Tats.)
TN16 178 EK120
Georges Sq, SW6
off North End Rd 99 CZ79
Georges Ter, Cat. CR3
off Coulsdon Rd 176 DQ122
(Tramlink) George Street 142 DQ103
George St, E16 86 EF72
W1 194 E8
W7 *off The Broadway* 79 CE74
Barking IG11 87 EQ66
Croydon CR0 142 DR103
Grays RM17 110 GA79
Hounslow TW3 96 BZ82
Richmond TW9 117 CK85
Romford RM1 71 FF58
Southall UB2 96 BY77
Staines TW18 113 BF91
Uxbridge UB8 76 BK66
Watford WD18 24 BW42
George's Wd Rd, Hat. AL9 12 DA26
George Tilbury Ho, Grays
RM16 111 GH75
Georgetown Cl, SE19
off St. Kitts Ter 122 DR92
Georgette Pl, SE10
off King George St 103 EC80
Georgeville Gdns, Ilf. IG6 69 EP56
Georgewood Rd, Hem.H. HP3 6 BM25
George Wyver Cl, SW19
off Beaumont Rd 119 CY87
George Yd, EC3 197 L9
W1 194 G10
Georgiana St, NW1 83 DJ67
Georgian Cl, Brom. BR2 144 EH101
Staines TW18 114 BH91
Stanmore HA7 41 CG52
Uxbridge UB10 58 BL63
Georgian Ct, SW16
off Gleneldon Rd 121 DL91
Wembley HA9 80 CN65
Georgian Way, Har. HA1 61 CD61
Georgia Rd, N.Mal. KT3 138 CQ98
Thornton Heath CR7 141 DP95
Georgina Gdns, E2
off Columbia Rd 84 DT69
Geraint Rd, Brom. BR1 124 EG91
Geraldine Rd, SW18 120 DC85
W4 98 CN79
Geraldine St, SE11 200 F7
Gerald Ms, SW1 198 G8
Gerald Rd, E16 86 EF70
SW1 198 G8
Dagenham RM8 70 EZ61
Gravesend DA12 131 GL87
Geralds Gro, Bans. SM7 157 CX114
Gerard Av, Houns. TW4
off Redfern Av 116 CA87
Gerard Gdns, Rain. RM13 89 FE68
Gerard Rd, SW13 99 CT81
Harrow HA1 61 CG58
Gerards Cl, SE16 102 DW78
Gerda Rd, SE9 125 EQ89
Gerdview Dr, Dart. DA2 128 FJ91
Germander Way, E15 86 EE69
Gernigan Ho, SW18
off Fitzhugh Gro 120 DD86
Gernon Cl, Rain. RM13
off Jordans Way 90 FK68
Gernon Rd, E3 85 DY68
Geron Way, NW2 63 CV60
Gerpins La, Upmin. RM14 90 FM68
Gerrard Cres, Brwd. CM14 54 FV48
Gerrard Gdns, Pnr. HA5 59 BU57
Gerrard Pl, W1 195 N10
Gerrard Rd, N1 83 DP68
Gerrards Cl, N14 29 DJ43
GERRARDS CROSS 56 AX58
⇌ Gerrards Cross 56 AY57
Gerrards Cross Rd, Slou. (Stoke P.)
SL2 74 AU66
Gerrards Mead, Bans. SM7
off Garratts La 173 CZ117
Gerrard St, W1 195 M10
Gerridge St, SE1 200 E5
Gerry Raffles Sq, E15
off Great Eastern Rd 85 ED65
Gertrude Rd, Belv. DA17 106 FA77
Gertrude St, SW10 100 DC79
Gervase Cl, Wem. HA9 62 CQ62
Gervase Rd, Edg. HA8 42 CQ53
Gervase St, SE15 102 DV80
Gews Cor, Wal.Cr. (Chsht.)
EN8 15 DX29
Ghent St, SE6 123 EA89
Ghent Way, E8 *off Tyssen St* 84 DT65
Giant Arches Rd, SE24 122 DQ87
Giant Tree Hill, Bushey (Bushey Hth.)
WD23 41 CD46
Gibbard Ms, SW19 119 CX92
Gibbfield Cl, Rom. RM6 70 EY55
Gibbins Rd, E15 85 EC66
Gibbon Rd, SE15 102 DW82
W3 80 CS73
Kingston upon Thames
KT2 138 CL95
Gibbons Cl, Borwd. WD6 26 CL39
Gibbons Rents, SE1
off Magdalen St 84 DS74
Gibbons Rd, NW10 80 CR65
Gibbon Wk, SW15
off Swinburne Rd 99 CU84
Gibbs Av, SE19 122 DR92
Gibbs Cl, SE19 122 DR92
Waltham Cross (Chsht.)
EN8 15 DX29
Gibbs Couch, Wat. WD19 40 BX48
Gibbs Grn, W14 99 CZ78
Edgware HA8 42 CQ50
Gibbs Rd, N18 46 DW49
Gibbs Sq, SE19 122 DR92
Gibraltar Cl, Brwd. CM13
off Essex Way 53 FW51
Gibraltar Cres, Epsom KT19 156 CS110
Gibraltar Ho, Brwd. CM13 53 FW51
Gibraltar Wk, E2 84 DT69
Gibson Cl, E1 *off Colebert Av* 84 DW70
N21 29 DN44
Chessington KT9 155 CJ107
Epping (N.Wld.Bas.) CM16
off Beamish Cl 19 FC25
Gravesend (Nthflt.) DA11 131 GF90
Isleworth TW7 97 CD83
Gibson Ct, Slou. SL3 93 AZ78
Gibson Gdns, N16
off Northwold Rd 66 DT61
Gibson Pl, Stai. (Stanw.)
TW19 114 BJ86
Gibson Rd, SE11 200 C9
Dagenham RM8 70 EW60
Sutton SM1 158 DB106
Uxbridge UB10 58 BM63
Gibson's Hill, SW16 121 DN93
Gibson Sq, N1 83 DN67
Gibson St, SE10 104 EE78
Gidd Hill, Couls. CR5 174 DG116
Gidea Av, Rom. RM2 71 FG55
Gidea Cl, Rom. RM2 71 FG55
South Ockendon RM15
off Tyssen Pl 91 FW69
GIDEA PARK, Rom. 71 FG55
⇌ Gidea Park 72 FJ56
Gideon Cl, Belv. DA17 107 FB77
Gideon Ms, W5 97 CK75
Gideon Rd, SW11 100 DG83
Gidian Ct, St.Alb. AL2 9 CD27
Giesbach Rd, N19 65 DJ61
Giffard Rd, N18 46 DS50
Giffin St, SE8 103 EA80
Gifford Gdns, W7 79 CD71
Gifford Pl, Brwd. CM14
off Blackthorn Way 54 FX50
Giffordside, Grays RM16 111 GH78
Gifford St, N1 83 DL66
Gift La, E15 86 EE67
Giggs Hill, Orp. BR5 146 EU96
Giggs Hill Gdns, T.Ditt. KT7 137 CG102
Giggs Hill Rd, T.Ditt. KT7 137 CG101
Gilbert Cl, SE18 105 EM81
Swanscombe DA10 129 FX86
Gilbert Gro, Edg. HA8 42 CR53
Gilbert Ho, EC2
off The Barbican 84 DQ71
SE8 *off McMillan St* 103 EA79
Gilbert Pl, WC1 195 P7
Gilbert Rd, SE11 200 E9
SW19 120 DC94
Belvedere DA17 106 FA76
Bromley BR1 124 EG94
Grays (Chaff.Hun.) RM16 109 FW76
Pinner HA5 60 BX56
Romford RM1 71 FF56
Uxbridge (Hare.) UB9 38 BK54
Gilbert St, E15 68 EE63
W1 194 G9
Gilbert St, Enf. EN3 30 DW37
Hounslow TW3
off High St 96 CC83
Gilbert Way, Croy. CR0
off Beddington Fm Rd 141 DL102
Gilbey Cl, Uxb. UB10 59 BP63
Gilbey Rd, SW17 120 DE91
Gilbeys Yd, NW1 82 DG66
Gilbourne Rd, SE18 105 ET79
Gilda Av, Enf. EN3 31 DY43
Gilda Cres, N16 66 DU60
Gildea Cl, Pnr. HA5 40 CA52
Gildea St, W1 195 J7
Gilden Cres, NW5 64 DG64
Gildenhill Rd, Swan. BR8 128 FJ94
Gildersome St, SE18
off Nightingale Vale 105 EN79
Gilders Rd, Chess. KT9 156 CM107
Giles Cl, Rain. RM13 90 FK68
Giles Coppice, SE19 122 DT91
Giles Travers Cl, Egh. TW20 133 BC97
Gilfrid Cl, Uxb. UB8
off Craig Dr 77 BP72
Gilhams Av, Bans. SM7 157 CY112
Gilkes Cres, SE21 122 DS86
Gilkes Pl, SE21 122 DS86
Gillam Way, Rain. RM13 89 FG65
Gillan Grn, Bushey (Bushey Hth.)
WD23 40 CC47
Gillards Ms, E17
off Gillards Way 67 EA56
Gillards Way, E17 67 EA56
Gill Av, E16 86 EG72
Gill Cl, Wat. WD18 23 BQ44
Gill Cres, Grav. (Nthflt.)
DA11 131 GF90
Gillender St, E3 85 EC70
E14 85 EC70
Gillespie Rd, N5 65 DN62
Gillett Av, E6 86 EL68
Gillette Cor, Islw. TW7 97 CG80
Gillett Pl, N16 *off Gillett St* 66 DS64
Gillett Rd, Th.Hth. CR7 142 DR98
Gillett St, N16 66 DS64
Gillfoot, NW1 195 L1
Gillham Ter, N17 46 DU51
Gilliam Gro, Pur. CR8 159 DN110
Gillian Cres, Rom. RM2 52 FJ54
Gillian Pk Rd, Sutt. SM3 139 CZ102
Gillian St, SE13 123 EB85
Gilliat Cl, Iver SL0
off Dutton Way 75 BE72
Gilliat Rd, Slou. SL1 74 AS73
Gilliat's Grn, Rick. (Chorl.)
WD3 21 BD42
Gillies St, NW5 64 DG64
Gilling Ct, NW3 82 DE65
Gillingham Ms, SW1 199 K8
Gillingham Rd, NW2 63 CY62
Gillingham Row, SW1 199 K8
Gillingham St, SW1 199 K8
Gillison Wk, SE16 202 C6
Gillman Dr, E15 86 EF67
Gillmans Rd, Orp. BR5 146 EV102
Gills Hill, Rad. WD7 25 CF35
Gills Hill La, Rad. WD7 25 CF36
Gills Hollow, Rad. WD7 25 CF36
Gill's Rd, Dart. (S.Darenth)
DA2, DA4 149 FS95
Gill St, E14 85 DZ72
Gillum Cl, Barn. EN4 44 DF46
Gilmore Cl, Slou. SL3 92 AW75
Uxbridge UB10 58 BN62
Gilmore Cres, Ashf. TW15 114 BN92
Gilmore Rd, SE13 103 ED84
Gilmour Cl, Wal.Cr. EN7 30 DU35
Gilpin Av, SW14 98 CR84
Gilpin Cl, W2 *off Porteus Rd* 82 DC71
Mitcham CR4 140 DE96
Gilpin Cres, N18 46 DT50
Twickenham TW2 116 CB87
Gilpin Rd, E5 67 DY63
Gilpin Way, Hayes UB3 95 BR80
Gilroy Cl, Rain. RM13 89 FF65
Gilroy Way, Orp. BR5 146 EV101
Gilsland, Wal.Abb. EN9 32 EE35
Gilsland Rd, Th.Hth. CR7 142 DR98
Gilstead Ho, Bark. IG11 88 EV68
Gilstead Rd, SW6 100 DB82
Gilston Rd, SW10 100 DC78
Gilton Rd, SE6 124 EE90
Giltspur St, EC1 196 G8
Gilwell Cl, E4 *off Antlers Hill* 31 EB42
Gilwell La, E4 31 EC42
Gilwell Pk, E4 31 EC41
Gimcrack Hill, Lthd. KT22
off Dorking Rd 171 CH123
Gippeswyck Cl, Pnr. HA5
off Uxbridge Rd 40 BX53
⇌ Gipsy Hill 122 DS92
Gipsy Hill, SE19 122 DS91
Gipsy La, SW15 99 CU83
Grays RM17 110 GC79
★ Gipsy Moth IV, SE10 103 EC79
Gipsy Rd, SE27 122 DQ91
Welling DA16 106 EX81
Gipsy Rd Gdns, SE27 122 DQ91
Giralda Cl, E16 *off Fulmer Rd* 86 EK71
Giraud St, E14 85 EB72
Girdlers Rd, W14 99 CX77
Girdlestone Wk, N19 65 DJ61
Girdwood Rd, SW18 119 CY87
Girling Way, Felt. TW14 95 BU83
Girona Cl, Grays (Chaff.Hun.)
RM16 109 FW76
Gironde Rd, SW6 99 CZ80
Girtin Rd, Bushey WD23 24 CB43
Girton Av, NW9 62 CN55
Girton Cl, Nthlt. UB5 78 CC65
Girton Ct, Wal.Cr. EN8 15 DY30
Girton Gdns, Croy. CR0 143 EA104
Girton Rd, SE26 123 DX92
Northolt UB5 78 CC65
Girton Vil, W10 81 CX72
Girton Way, Rick. (Crox.Grn.)
WD3 23 BQ43
Gisborne Gdns, Rain. RM13 89 FF69
Gisbourne Cl, Wall. SM6 141 DK104
Gisburne Way, Wat. WD24 23 BU37
Gisburn Rd, N8 65 DM56
Gissing Wk, N1 *off Lofting Rd* 83 DN66
Gittens Cl, Brom. BR1 124 EF91
Given Wilson Wk, E13 86 EF68
Glacier Way, Wem. HA0 79 CK68
Gladbeck Way, Enf. EN2 29 DP42
Gladding Rd, E12 68 EK63
Waltham Cross (Chsht.)
EN7 13 DP25
Glade, The, N21 29 DM44
SE7 104 EJ80
Brentwood CM13 55 GA46
Bromley BR1 144 EK96
Coulsdon CR5 175 DN119
Croydon CR0 143 DX99
Enfield EN2 29 DN41
Epsom KT17 157 CU106
Gerrards Cross SL9 56 AX60
Ilford IG5 49 EM53
Leatherhead (Fetch.) KT22 170 CA122
Sevenoaks TN13 191 FH123
Staines TW18 114 BH94
Sutton SM2 157 CY109
Tadworth KT20 174 DA121
Upminster RM14 72 FQ64
West Byfleet KT14 151 BE113
West Wickham BR4 143 EB104
Woodford Green IG8 48 EH48
Glade Cl, Surb. KT6 137 CK103
Glade Ct, Ilf. IG5
off The Glade 49 EM53
Glade Gdns, Croy. CR0 143 DY101
Glade La, Sthl. UB2 96 CB75
Glades, The, Grav. DA12 131 GK93
Gladeside, N21 29 DM44
Croydon CR0 143 DX100
Gladeside Cl, Chess. KT9
off Leatherhead Rd 155 CK108
Gladeside Ct, Warl. CR6 176 DV120
Gladesmore Rd, N15 66 DT58
Glade Spur, Tad. KT20 174 DB121
Glades Shop Cen, The, Brom.
BR1 144 EG96
Gladeswood Rd, Belv. DA17 107 FB77
Gladeway, The, Wal.Abb. EN9 15 ED33
Gladiator St, SE23 123 DY86
Glading Ter, N16 66 DT62
Gladioli Cl, Hmptn. TW12
off Gresham Rd 116 CA93
Gladsdale Dr, Pnr. HA5 59 BU56
Gladsmuir Cl, Walt. KT12 136 BW103
Gladsmuir Rd, N19 65 DJ60
Barnet EN5 27 CY40
Gladstone Av, E12 86 EL66
N22 45 DN54
Feltham TW14 115 BU86
Twickenham TW2 117 CD87
Gladstone Ct, SW19
off Gladstone Rd 120 DA94
Gladstone Gdns, Houns. TW3
off Palmerston Rd 96 CC81
Gladstone Ms, N22
off Pelham Rd 45 DN54
NW6 *off Cavendish Rd* 81 CZ66
SE20 122 DW94
Gladstone Par, NW2
off Edgware Rd 63 CV60
Gladstone Pk Gdns, NW2 63 CV62
Gladstone Pl, E3
off Roman Rd 85 DZ68
Barnet EN5 27 CX42
Gladstone Rd, SW19 120 DA94
W4 *off Acton La* 98 CR76
Ashtead KT21 171 CK118
Buckhurst Hill IG9 48 EH46
Croydon CR0 142 DR101
Dartford DA1 128 FM86
Kingston upon Thames
KT1 138 CN97
Orpington BR6 163 EQ106
Southall UB2 96 BY76
Surbiton KT6 137 CK103
Watford WD17 24 BW41
Gladstone St, SE1 200 F6
Gladstone Ter, SE27 122 DQ91
SW8 101 DH81
Gladstone Way, Har. (Wldste.)
HA3 61 CE55
Gladwell Rd, N8 65 DM58
Bromley BR1 124 EG93
Gladwyn Rd, SW15 99 CX83
Gladys Rd, NW6 82 DA66
Glaisher St, SE8 103 EB79
Glaisyer Way, Iver SL0 75 BC68
Glamis Cl, Wal.Cr. (Chsht.)
EN7 14 DU29
Glamis Cres, Hayes UB3 95 BQ76
Glamis Dr, Horn. RM11 72 FL60
Glamis Pl, E1 84 DW73
Glamis Rd, E1 84 DW73
Glamis Way, Nthlt. UB5 78 CC65
Glamorgan Cl, Mitch. CR4 141 DL97
Glamorgan Rd, Kings.T. KT1 117 CJ94
Glanfield Rd, Beck. BR3 143 DZ98
Glanleam Rd, Stan. HA7 41 CK49
Glanmead, Brwd. CM15 54 FY46
Glanmor Rd, Slou. SL2 74 AV73
Glanthams Cl, Brwd. CM15 54 FY47
Glanthams Rd, Brwd. CM15 55 FZ47
Glanty, The, Egh. TW20 113 BB91
Glanville Dr, Horn. RM11 72 FM60
Glanville Rd, SW2 121 DL85
Bromley BR2 144 EH97
Glasbrook Av, Twick. TW2 116 BZ88
Glasbrook Rd, SE9 124 EK87
Glaserton Rd, N16 66 DS59
Glasford St, SW17 120 DF93
Glasgow Ho, W9 82 DB68
Glasgow Rd, E13 86 EH68
N18 *off Aberdeen Rd* 46 DV50
Glasgow Ter, SW1 101 DJ78
Glasse Cl, W13 79 CG73
Glasshill St, SE1 200 G4
Glasshouse Cl, Uxb. UB8
off Harlington Rd 77 BP71

Gla - Gol

Glasshouse Flds, E1 85 DX73
Glasshouse St, W1 199 L1
Glasshouse Wk, SE11 200 A10
Glasshouse Yd, EC1 197 H6
Glasslyn Rd, N8 65 DK57
Glassmill La, Brom. BR2 144 EF96
Glass St, E2 off Coventry Rd 84 DV70
Glass Yd, SE18
off Woolwich High St 105 EN76
Glastonbury Av, Wdf.Grn. IG8 48 EK52
Glastonbury Cl, Orp. BR5 146 EW102
Glastonbury Pl, E1
off Sutton St 84 DW72
Glastonbury Rd, N9 46 DU46
Morden SM4 140 DA101
Glastonbury St, NW6 63 CZ64
Glaucus St, E3 85 EB71
Glazbury Rd, W14 99 CY77
Glazebrook Cl, SE21 122 DR89
Glazebrook Rd, Tedd. TW11 117 CF94
Glebe, The, SE3 104 EE83
SW16 121 DK91
Chislehurst BR7 145 EQ95
Kings Langley WD4 6 BN29
Watford WD25 8 BW33
West Drayton UB7 94 BM77
Worcester Park KT4 139 CT102
Glebe Av, Enf. EN2 29 DP41
Harrow HA3 62 CL55
Mitcham CR4 140 DE96
Ruislip HA4 77 BV65
Uxbridge UB10 59 BQ63
Woodford Green IG8 48 EG51
Glebe Cl, W4 off Glebe St 98 CS78
Gerrards Cross (Chal.St.P.)
SL9 36 AX52
South Croydon CR2 160 DT111
Uxbridge UB10 59 BQ63
Glebe Cotts, Sutt. SM1
off Vale Rd 158 DB105
Westerham (Brasted)
TN16 180 EV123
Glebe Ct, W7 79 CD73
Coulsdon CR5
off Whitethorn Av 175 DH115
Mitcham CR4 140 DF97
Sevenoaks TN13
off Oak La 191 FH126
Stanmore HA7
off Glebe Rd 41 CJ50
Glebe Cres, NW4 63 CW56
Harrow HA3 62 CL55
Glebefield, The, Sev. TN13 190 FF123
Glebe Gdns, N.Mal. KT3 138 CS101
West Byfleet (Byfleet)
KT14 152 BK114
Glebe Ho Dr, Brom. BR2 144 EH102
Glebe Hyrst, SE19
off Giles Coppice 122 DT91
South Croydon CR2 160 DT112
Glebeland Gdns, Shep.
TW17 135 BQ100
Glebelands, Chig. IG7 50 EV48
Dartford DA1 107 FF84
Esher (Clay.) KT10 155 CF109
West Molesey KT8 136 CB99
Glebelands Av, E18 48 EG54
Ilford IG2 69 ER59
Glebelands Cl, SE5
off Grove Hill Rd 102 DS83
Glebelands Rd, Felt. TW14 115 BU87
Glebe La, Barn. EN5 27 CU43
Harrow HA3 62 CL56
Sevenoaks TN13 191 FH126
Glebe Path, Mitch. CR4 140 DE97
Glebe Pl, SW3 100 DE79
Dartford (Hort.Kir.) DA4 148 FQ98
Glebe Rd, E8
off Middleton Rd 84 DT66
N3 44 DC53
N8 65 DM56
NW10 81 CT65
SW13 99 CU82
Ashtead KT21 171 CK118
Bromley BR1 144 EG95
Carshalton SM5 158 DF107
Dagenham RM10 89 FB65
Egham TW20 113 BC93
Gerrards Cross (Chal.St.P.)
SL9 36 AW53
Gravesend DA11 131 GF88
Hayes UB3 77 BT74
Rainham RM13 90 FJ69
Redhill RH1 175 DH124
Staines TW18 114 BH93
Stanmore HA7 41 CJ50
Sutton SM2 157 CY109
Uxbridge UB8 76 BJ68
Warlingham CR6 177 DX117
Windsor (Old Wind.) SL4 112 AV85
Glebe Side, Twick. TW1 117 CF86
Glebe St, W4 98 CS78
Glebe Ter, E3 off Bow Rd 85 EA69
Glebe Way, Erith DA8 107 FE79
Feltham TW13 116 CA90
Hornchurch RM11 72 FL59
South Croydon CR2 160 DT111
West Wickham BR4 143 EC103
Glebeway, Wdf.Grn. IG8 48 EJ50
Gledhow Gdns, SW5 100 DC77
Gledhow Wd, Tad. KT20 174 DB121
Gledstanes Rd, W14 99 CY78
Gledwood Av, Hayes UB4 77 BT71
Gledwood Cres, Hayes UB4 77 BT71
Gledwood Dr, Hayes UB4 77 BT71
Gledwood Gdns, Hayes UB4 77 BT71
Gleed Av, Bushey (Bushey Hth.)
WD23 41 CD47
Gleeson Dr, Orp. BR6 163 ET106
Gleeson Ms, Add. KT15 152 BJ105
Glegg Pl, SW15 99 CX84
Glen, The, Add. KT15 151 BF106
Bromley BR2 144 EE96
Croydon CR0 143 DX103
Enfield EN2 29 DP42
Northwood HA6 39 BR52
Orpington BR6 145 EM104
Glen, The, Pnr. HA5 60 BY59
Pinner (Eastcote) HA5 59 BV57
Rainham RM13 90 FJ70
Slough SL3 92 AW77
Southall UB2 96 BZ78
Wembley HA9 61 CK63
Glenaffric Av, E14 204 F9
Glen Albyn Rd, SW19 119 CX89
Glenalla Rd, Ruis. HA4 59 BT59
Glenalmond Rd, Har. HA3 62 CL56
Glenalvon Way, SE18 104 EL77
Glena Mt, Sutt. SM1 158 DC105
Glenarm Rd, E5 66 DW64
Glen Av, Ashf. TW15 114 BN91
Glenavon Cl, Esher (Clay.)
KT10 155 CG108
Glenavon Gdns, Slou. SL3 92 AW77
Glenavon Rd, E15 86 EE66
Glenbarr Cl, SE9
off Dumbreck Rd 105 EP83
Glenbow Rd, Brom. BR1 124 EE93
Glenbrook N, Enf. EN2 29 DM42
Glenbrook Rd, NW6 64 DA64
Glenbrook S, Enf. EN2 29 DM42
Glenbuck Ct, Surb. KT6
off Glenbuck Rd 137 CK100
Glenbuck Rd, Surb. KT6 137 CK100
Glenburnie Rd, SW17 120 DF90
Glencairn Dr, W5 79 CH70
Glencairne Cl, E16 86 EK71
Glencairn Rd, SW16 141 DL95
Glen Cl, Shep. TW17 134 BN98
Tadworth (Kgswd.) KT20 173 CY123
Glencoe Av, Ilf. IG2 69 ER59
Glencoe Dr, Dag. RM10 70 FA63
Glencoe Rd, Bushey WD23 24 CA44
Hayes UB4 78 BX71
Weybridge KT13 134 BN104
Glencorse Grn, Wat. WD19
off Caldwell Rd 40 BX49
Glen Ct, Stai. TW18
off Riverside Dr 113 BF94
Glen Cres, Wdf.Grn. IG8 48 EH51
Glendale, Swan. BR8 147 FF99
Glendale Av, N22 45 DN52
Edgware HA8 42 CM49
Romford RM6 70 EW59
Glendale Cl, SE9
off Dumbreck Rd 105 EN83
Brentwood CM15 54 FY45
Woking GU21 166 AW118
Glendale Dr, SW19 119 CZ92
Glendale Gdns, Wem. HA9 61 CK60
Glendale Ms, Beck. BR3 143 EB95
Glendale Ri, Ken. CR8 175 DP115
Glendale Rd, Erith DA8 107 FC77
Gravesend (Nthflt.) DA11 130 GE91
Glendale Wk, Wal.Cr. (Chsht.)
EN8 15 DY30
Glendale Way, SE28 88 EW73
Glendall St, SW9 101 DM84
Glendarvon St, SW15 99 CX83
Glendevon Cl, Edg. HA8
off Tayside Dr 42 CP48
Glendish Rd, N17 46 DU53
Glendor Gdns, NW7 42 CR49
Glendower Cres, Orp. BR6 146 EU100
Glendower Gdns, SW14
off Glendower Rd 98 CR83
Glendower Pl, SW7 100 DD77
Glendower Rd, E4 47 ED46
SW14 98 CR83
Glendown Rd, SE2 106 EU78
Glendun Rd, W3 80 CS73
Gleneagle Ms, SW16
off Ambleside Av 121 DK92
Gleneagle Rd, SW16 121 DK92
Gleneagles, Stan. HA7 41 CH51
Gleneagles Cl, SE16
off Ryder Dr 102 DV78
Orpington BR6 145 ER102
Romford RM3 52 FM52
Staines (Stanw.) TW19 114 BK86
Watford WD19 40 BX49
Gleneagles Grn, Orp. BR6
off Tandridge Dr 145 ER102
Gleneagles Twr, Sthl. UB1 78 CC72
Gleneldon Ms, SW16 121 DL91
Gleneldon Rd, SW16 121 DL91
Glenelg Rd, SW2 121 DL85
Glenesk Rd, SE9 105 EN83
Glenfarg Rd, SE6 123 ED88
Glenfield Cres, Ruis. HA4 59 BR59
Glenfield Rd, SW12 121 DJ88
W13 97 CH75
Ashford TW15 115 BP93
Banstead SM7 174 DB115
Glenfield Ter, W13 97 CH75
Glenfinlas Way, SE5 101 DP80
Glenforth St, SE10 205 L10
Glengall Causeway, E14 203 P6
Glengall Gro, E14 204 D6
Glengall Rd, NW6 81 CZ67
SE15 102 DT79
Bexleyheath DA7 106 EY83
Edgware HA8 42 CP48
Woodford Green IG8 48 EG51
Glengall Ter, SE15 102 DT79
Glen Gdns, Croy. CR0 141 DN104
Glengarnock Av, E14 204 E9
Glengarry Rd, SE22 122 DS85
Glenham Dr, Ilf. IG2 69 EP57
Glenhaven Av, Borwd. WD6 26 CN41
Glenhead Cl, SE9
off Dumbreck Rd 105 EP83
Glenheadon Cl, Lthd. KT22
off Glenheadon Ri 171 CK123
Glenheadon Ri, Lthd. KT22 171 CK123
Glenhill Cl, N3 44 DA54
Glenhouse Rd, SE9 125 EN85
Glenhurst Av, NW5 64 DG63
Bexley DA5 126 EZ88
Ruislip HA4 59 BQ59
Glenhurst Ct, SE19 122 DT92
Glenhurst Ri, SE19 122 DQ94
Glenhurst Rd, N12 44 DD50
Brentford TW8 97 CJ79
Glenilla Rd, NW3 82 DE65
Glenister Ho, Hayes UB3 77 BV74
Glenister Pk Rd, SW16 121 DK94
Glenister Rd, SE10 205 K10
Glenister St, E16 87 EN74
Glenkerry Ho, E14
off Burcham St 85 EC72
Glenlea Rd, SE9 125 EM85
Glenlion Ct, Wey. KT13 135 BS104
Glenloch Rd, NW3 82 DE65
Enfield EN3 30 DW40
Glenluce Rd, SE3 104 EG80
Glenlyon Rd, SE9 125 EN85
Glenmere Av, NW7 43 CU52
Glen Ms, E17 off Glen Rd 67 DZ57
Glenmill, Hmptn. TW12 116 BZ92
Glenmore Cl, Add. KT15 134 BH104
Glenmore Gdns, Abb.L. WD5
off Stewart Cl 7 BU32
Glenmore Rd, NW3 82 DE65
Welling DA16 105 ET81
Glenmore Way, Bark. IG11 88 EU69
Glenmount Path, SE18
off Raglan Rd 105 EQ78
Glenn Av, Pur. CR8 159 DP111
Glennie Rd, SE27 121 DN90
Glenny Rd, Bark. IG11 87 EQ65
Glenorchy Cl, Hayes UB4 78 BY71
Glenparke Rd, E7 86 EH65
Glen Ri, Wdf.Grn. IG8 48 EH51
Glen Rd, E13 86 EJ70
E17 67 DZ57
Chessington KT9 138 CL104
Glen Rd End, Wall. SM6 159 DH109
Glenrosa Gdns, Grav. DA12 131 GM92
Glenrosa St, SW6 100 DC82
Glenrose Ct, Sid. DA14 126 EV92
Glenroy St, W12 81 CW72
Glensdale Rd, SE4 103 DZ83
Glenshee Cl, Nthwd. HA6
off Rickmansworth Rd 39 BQ51
Glenshiel Rd, SE9 125 EN85
Glenside, Chig. IG7 49 EP51
Glenside Cotts, Slou. SL1 92 AT76
Glentanner Way, SW17
off Aboyne Rd 120 DD90
Glen Ter, E14 204 E4
Glentham Gdns, SW13
off Glentham Rd 99 CV79
Glentham Rd, SW13 99 CU79
Glenthorne Av, Croy. CR0 142 DV102
Glenthorne Cl, Sutt. SM3 140 DA102
Uxbridge UB10
off Uxbridge Rd 76 BN69
Glenthorne Gdns, Ilf. IG6 69 EN55
Sutton SM3 140 DA102
Glenthorne Ms, W6
off Glenthorne Rd 99 CV77
Glenthorne Rd, E17 67 DY57
N11 44 DF50
W6 99 CW77
Kingston upon Thames
KT1 138 CM98
Glenthorpe Rd, Mord. SM4 139 CX99
Glenton Cl, Rom. RM1 51 FE51
Glenton Rd, SE13 104 EE84
Glenton Way, Rom. RM1 51 FE52
Glentrammon Av, Orp. BR6 163 ET107
Glentrammon Cl, Orp. BR6 163 ET107
Glentrammon Gdns, Orp.
BR6 163 ET107
Glentrammon Rd, Orp. BR6 163 ET107
Glentworth St, NW1 194 E5
Glenure Rd, SE9 125 EN85
Glenview, SE2 106 EX79
Glen Vw, Grav. DA12 131 GJ88
Glenview Rd, Brom. BR1 144 EK96
Glenville Av, Enf. EN2 30 DQ38
Glenville Ct, SE19
off Lymer Av 122 DT92
Glenville Gro, SE8 103 DZ80
Glenville Ms, SW18 120 DB87
Glenville Rd, Kings.T. KT2 138 CN95
Glen Wk, Islw. TW7 117 CD85
Glen Way, Wat. WD17 23 BS38
Glenwood Av, NW9 62 CS60
Rainham RM13 89 FH70
Glenwood Cl, Har. HA1 61 CF57
Glenwood Ct, E18
off Clarendon Rd 68 EG55
Glenwood Dr, Rom. RM2 71 FG56
Glenwood Gdns, Ilf. IG2 69 EN57
Glenwood Gro, NW9 62 CQ60
Glenwood Rd, N15 65 DP57
NW7 42 CS48
SE6 123 DZ88
Epsom KT17 157 CU107
Hounslow TW3 97 CD83
Glenwood Way, Croy. CR0 143 DX100
Glenworth Av, E14 204 F9
Gliddon Rd, W14 99 CY77
Glimpsing Grn, Erith DA18 106 EY76
Glisson Rd, Uxb. UB10 76 BN68
Gload Cres, Orp. BR5 146 EX103
Global App, E3
off Hancock Rd 85 EB68
Globe Ind Estates, Grays
RM17 110 GC78
Globe Pond Rd, SE16 203 K3
Globe Rd, E1 84 DW69
E2 84 DW69
E15 68 EF64
Hornchurch RM11 71 FG58
Woodford Green IG8 48 EJ51
Globe Rope Wk, E14 204 D9
Globe St, SE1 201 J6
Globe Ter, E2 off Globe Rd 84 DW69
Globe Yd, W1 195 H9
Glossop Rd, S.Croy. CR2 160 DR109
Gloster Rd, N.Mal. KT3 138 CS98
Woking GU22 167 BA120
Gloucester Arc, SW7
off Gloucester Rd 100 DC77
Gloucester Av, NW1 82 DG66
Grays RM16 110 GC75
Hornchurch RM11 72 FN56
Sidcup DA15 125 ES89
Gloucester Av, Wal.Cr. EN8 15 DY33
Welling DA16 105 ET84
Gloucester Circ, SE10 103 EC80
Gloucester Cl, NW10 80 CR66
Thames Ditton KT7 137 CG102
Gloucester Ct, EC3 201 N1
Richmond TW9 98 CN80
Tilbury RM18
off Dock Rd 111 GF82
Uxbridge (Denh.) UB9
off Moorfield Rd 58 BG58
Gloucester Cres, NW1 83 DH67
Staines TW18 114 BK93
Gloucester Dr, N4 65 DP61
NW11 64 DA56
Staines TW18 113 BC90
Gloucester Gdns, NW11 63 CZ59
W2 off Bishops Br Rd 82 DC72
Barnet EN4 28 DG42
Ilford IG1 68 EL59
Sutton SM1 140 DB103
Gloucester Gate, NW1 83 DH68
Gloucester Gate Ms, NW1
off Gloucester Gate 83 DH68
Gloucester Gro, Edg. HA8 42 CR53
Gloucester Gro Est, SE15 102 DS79
Gloucester Ho, NW6 82 DA68
Gloucester Ms, E10
off Gloucester Rd 67 EA59
W2 82 DC72
Gloucester Ms W, W2
off Cleveland Ter 82 DC72
Gloucester Par, Sid. DA15 126 EU85
Gloucester Pk, SW7
off Courtfield Rd 100 DC77
Gloucester Pl, NW1 194 D4
W1 194 E6
Enfield EN2
off Chase Side 30 DQ40
Gloucester Pl Ms, W1 194 E7
⊖ Gloucester Road 100 DC77
Gloucester Rd, E10 67 EA59
E11 68 EH57
E12 69 EM62
E17 47 DX54
N17 46 DR54
N18 46 DT50
SW7 100 DC76
W3 98 CQ75
W5 97 CJ75
Barnet EN5 28 DC43
Belvedere DA17 106 EZ78
Brentwood (Pilg.Hat.)
CM15 54 FV43
Croydon CR0 142 DR100
Dartford DA1 127 FH87
Enfield EN2 30 DQ38
Feltham TW13 116 BW88
Gravesend DA12 131 GJ91
Hampton TW12 116 CB94
Harrow HA1 60 CB57
Hounslow TW4 96 BY84
Kingston upon Thames
KT1 138 CP96
Redhill RH1 184 DF133
Richmond TW9 98 CN80
Romford RM1 71 FE58
Teddington TW11 117 CE92
Twickenham TW2 116 CC88
Gloucester Sq, E2
off Whiston Rd 84 DU67
W2 194 A9
Woking GU21
off Church St E 166 AY117
Gloucester St, SW1 101 DJ78
Gloucester Ter, W2 82 DD73
Gloucester Wk, W8 100 DA75
Woking GU21 167 AZ117
Gloucester Way, EC1 196 E3
Glover Cl, SE2 106 EW77
Waltham Cross EN7
off Allwood Rd 14 DT27
Glover Dr, N18 46 DW51
Glover Rd, Pnr. HA5 60 BX58
Glovers Gro, Ruis. HA4 59 BP59
Gloxinia Rd, Grav. (Sthflt.)
DA13 130 GB93
Gloxinia Wk, Hmptn. TW12 116 CA93
Glycena Rd, SW11 100 DF83
Glyn Av, Barn. EN4 28 DD42
Glyn Cl, SE25 142 DS96
Epsom KT17 157 CU109
Glyn Ct, SW16 121 DN90
Glyn Davies Cl, Sev. (Dunt.Grn.)
TN13 181 FE120
Glyndebourne Pk, Orp. BR6 145 EP103
Glynde Ms, SW3 198 C7
Glynde Rd, Bexh. DA7 106 EX83
Glynde St, SE4 123 DZ86
Glyndon Rd, SE18 105 EQ77
Glyn Dr, Sid. DA14 126 EV91
Glynfield Rd, NW10 80 CS66
Glynne Rd, N22 45 DN54
Glyn Rd, E5 67 DX62
Enfield EN3 30 DW42
Worcester Park KT4 139 CX103
Glyn St, SE11
off Kennington La 101 DM78
Glynswood, Ger.Cr. (Chal.St.P.)
SL9 37 AZ52
Glynwood Ct, SE23 122 DW89
Goaters All, SW6 99 CZ80
GOATHURST COMMON, Sev. 190 FB130
Goat La, Enf. EN1 30 DT38
Surbiton KT6 137 CJ103
Goat Rd, Mitch. CR4 140 DG101
Goatsfield Rd, West. (Tats.)
TN16 178 EJ120
Goat St, SE1 201 P4
Goatswood La, Rom. (Nave.)
RM4 51 FH45
Goat Wf, Brent. TW8 98 CL79
Gobions Av, Rom. RM5 51 FD52
Gobions Way, Pot.B. EN6
off Swanley Bar La 12 DB28
Godalming Av, Wall. SM6 159 DL106
Godalming Rd, E14 85 EB71
Godbold Rd, E15 86 EE69
Goddard Cl, Shep. TW17
off Magdalene Rd 134 BM97
Goddard Pl, N19 65 DJ62
Goddard Rd, Beck. BR3 143 DX98
Goddards Way, Ilf. IG1 69 ER60
GODDEN GREEN, Sev. 191 FN125
H Godden Green Clinic, Sev.
TN15 191 FP125
GODDINGTON, Orp. 146 EW104
Goddington Chase, Orp.
BR6 164 EV105
Goddington La, Orp. BR6 146 EU104
Godfrey Av, Nthlt. UB5 78 BY67
Twickenham TW2 117 CD87
Godfrey Hill, SE18 104 EL77
Godfrey Rd, SE18 105 EM77
Godfrey St, E15 85 EC68
SW3 198 C10
Godfrey Way, Houns. TW4 116 BZ87
Goding St, SE11 101 DL78
Godley Rd, SW18 120 DD88
West Byfleet (Byfleet)
KT14 152 BM113
Godliman St, EC4 197 H9
Godman Rd, SE15 102 DV82
Grays RM16 111 GG76
Godolphin Cl, N13 45 DP51
Sutton SM2 157 CZ111
Godolphin Pl, W3
off Vyner Rd 80 CR73
Godolphin Rd, W12 99 CV75
Weybridge KT13 153 BR107
Godric Cres, Croy. (New Adgtn.)
CR0 161 ED110
Godson Rd, Croy. CR0 141 DN104
Godson St, N1 83 DN68
GODSTONE 186 DV131
Godstone Bypass, Gdse.
RH9 186 DW129
Godstone Grn, Gdse. RH9 186 DV131
Godstone Grn Rd, Gdse.
RH9 186 DV131
Godstone Hill, Gdse. RH9 186 DV127
Godstone Rd, Cat. CR3 176 DU124
Kenley CR8 159 DN112
Oxted RH8 187 EA131
Purley CR8 159 DN112
Redhill (Bletch.) RH1 186 DR133
Sutton SM1 158 DC105
Twickenham TW1 117 CG86
Whyteleafe CR3 176 DT116
Godstow Rd, SE2 106 EW75
Godwin Cl, E4 31 EC38
N1 off Napier Gro 84 DQ68
Epsom KT19 156 CQ107
Godwin Ct, NW1
off Crowndale Rd 83 DJ68
Godwin Rd, E7 68 EH63
Bromley BR2 144 EJ97
Goffers Rd, SE3 103 ED81
Goffs Cres, Wal.Cr. (Chsht.)
EN7 13 DP29
Goffs La, Wal.Cr. (Chsht.) EN7 14 DU29
GOFFS OAK, Wal.Cr. 14 DQ29
Goffs Oak Av, Wal.Cr. (Chsht.)
EN7 13 DP28
Goffs Rd, Ashf. TW15 115 BR93
Gogmore Fm Cl, Cher. KT16 133 BF101
Gogmore La, Cher. KT16 134 BG101
Goidel Cl, Wall. SM6 159 DK105
Golborne Gdns, W10
off Golborne Rd 81 CZ70
Golborne Ms, W10
off Portobello Rd 81 CY71
Golborne Rd, W10 81 CY71
Goldace, Grays RM17 110 FZ79
Golda Cl, Barn. EN5 27 CX44
Goldbeaters Gro, Edg. HA8 42 CS51
Goldcliff Cl, Mord. SM4 140 DA100
Goldcrest Cl, E16
off Sheerwater Rd 86 EK71
SE28 88 EW73
Goldcrest Ms, W5
off Montpelier Av 79 CK71
Goldcrest Way, Bushey WD23 40 CC46
Croydon (New Adgtn.)
CR0 161 ED109
Purley CR8 159 DK110
Golden Ct, Rich. TW9
off George St 117 CK85
Golden Cres, Hayes UB3 77 BT74
Golden Cross Ms, W11
off Basing St 81 CZ72
★ Golden Hinde, SE1
off Cathedral St 201 K2
Golden La, EC1 197 H5
Golden La Est, EC1 197 H5
Golden Manor, W7 79 CE73
Golden Plover Cl, E16
off Maplin Rd 86 EH72
Golden Sq, W1 195 L10
Golden Yd, NW3
off Heath St 64 DC63
Golders Cl, Edg. HA8 42 CP50
Golders Gdns, NW11 63 CY59
GOLDERS GREEN, NW11 64 DA59
⊖ Golders Green 64 DA59
Golders Grn Cres, NW11 63 CZ59
Golders Grn Rd, NW11 63 CY58
Golders Manor Dr, NW11 63 CX58
Golders Pk Cl, NW11 64 DB60
Golders Ri, NW4 63 CX57
Golders Way, NW11 63 CZ59
Goldfinch Cl, Orp. BR6 164 EU106
Goldfinch Rd, SE28 105 ER76
South Croydon CR2 161 DY110
Goldfinch Way, Borwd. WD6 26 CN42
Goldfort Wk, Wok. GU21
off Langmans Way 166 AS116
Goldhawk Ms, W12
off Devonport Rd 99 CV75
⊖ Goldhawk Road 99 CV75
Goldhawk Rd, W6 99 CT77

★ Place of interest ⇌ Railway station ⊖ London Underground station DLR Docklands Light Railway station Tramlink station H Hospital

Gol - Gra

Goldhawk Rd, W12 99 CU76
Goldhaze Cl, Wdf.Grn. IG8 48 EK52
Gold Hill, Edg. HA8 42 CR51
Gold Hill E, Ger.Cr. (Chal.St.P.)
SL9 36 AX54
Gold Hill N, Ger.Cr. (Chal.St.P.)
SL9 36 AW53
Gold Hill W, Ger.Cr. (Chal.St.P.)
SL9 36 AW53
Goldhurst Ter, NW6 82 DB66
H Goldie Leigh Hosp, SE2 106 EW79
Golding Cl, Chess. KT9
off Coppard Gdns 155 CJ107
Goldingham Av, Loug. IG10 33 EQ40
Golding Rd, Sev. TN13 191 FJ122
Goldings, The, Wok. GU21 166 AT116
Goldings Hill, Loug. IG10 33 EN39
Goldings Ri, Loug. IG10 33 EN39
Goldings Rd, Loug. IG10 33 EN39
Golding St, E1 84 DU72
Golding Ter, SW11
off Longhedge St 100 DG82
Goldington Cres, NW1 83 DK68
Goldington St, NW1 83 DK68
Gold La, Edg. HA8 42 CR51
Goldman Cl, E2 84 DU70
Goldmark Ho, SE3
off Lebrun Sq 104 EH83
Goldney Rd, W9 82 DA70
Goldrill Dr, N11 44 DG47
Goldrings Rd, Lthd. (Oxshott)
KT22 154 CC113
Goldsboro Rd, SW8 101 DK81
Goldsborough Cres, E4 47 EC47
Goldsdown Cl, Enf. EN3 31 DY40
Goldsdown Rd, Enf. EN3 31 DX40
Goldsel Rd, Swan. BR8 147 FD99
Goldsmid St, SE18
off Sladedale Rd 105 ES78
Goldsmith, Grays RM17 110 FZ79
Goldsmith Av, E12 86 EL65
NW9 63 CT58
W3 80 CR73
Romford RM7 70 FA59
Goldsmith Cl, W3
off East Acton La 80 CS74
Harrow HA2 60 CB60
Goldsmith La, NW9 62 CP56
Goldsmith Rd, E10 67 EA60
E17 47 DX54
N11 44 DF50
SE15 102 DU81
W3 80 CR74
Goldsmiths Bottom, Sev.
TN14 190 FE127
Goldsmiths Cl, Wok. GU21 166 AW118
★ Goldsmiths' Hall, EC2 197 J8
Goldsmith's Row, E2 84 DU68
Goldsmith's Sq, E2 84 DU68
Goldsmith St, EC2 197 J8
Goldsworth Orchard, Wok. GU21
off St. John's Rd 166 AU118
GOLDSWORTH PARK, Wok. 166 AU117
Goldsworth Pk Trd Est, Wok.
GU21 166 AV116
Goldsworth Rd, Wok. GU21 166 AW118
Goldsworthy Gdns, SE16 202 G9
Goldwell Rd, Th.Hth. CR7 141 DM98
Goldwin Cl, SE14 102 DW81
Goldwing Cl, E16 86 EG72
Golf Cl, Bushey WD23 24 BX41
Stanmore HA7 41 CJ52
Thornton Heath CR7
off Kensington Av 141 DN95
Woking GU22 151 BE114
Golf Club Dr, Kings.T. KT2 118 CR94
Golf Club Rd, Hat. AL9 12 DA26
Weybridge KT13 153 BP109
Woking GU22 166 AU120
Golfe Rd, Ilf. IG1 69 ER62
Golf Ho Rd, Oxt. RH8 188 EJ129
Golf Links Av, Grav. DA11 131 GH92
Golf Ride, Enf. EN2 29 DN35
Golf Rd, W5 *off Boileau Rd* 80 CM72
Bromley BR1 145 EN97
Kenley CR8 176 DR118
Golf Side, Sutt. SM2 157 CY111
Twickenham TW2 117 CD90
Golfside Cl, N20 44 DE48
New Malden KT3 138 CS96
Goliath Cl, Wall. SM6 159 DL108
Gollogly Ter, SE7 104 EJ78
Gomer Gdns, Tedd. TW11 117 CG93
Gomer Pl, Tedd. TW11 117 CG93
Gomm Rd, SE16 202 F7
Gomshall Av, Wall. SM6 159 DL106
Gomshall Gdns, Ken. CR8 176 DS115
Gomshall Rd, Sutt. SM2 157 CW110
Gondar Gdns, NW6 63 CZ64
Gonson Pl, SE8 103 EA79
Gonson St, SE8 103 EB79
Gonston Cl, SW19
off Boddicott Cl 119 CY89
Gonville Av, Rick. (Crox.Grn.)
WD3 23 BP44
Gonville Cres, Nthlt. UB5 78 CB65
Gonville Rd, Th.Hth. CR7 141 DM99
Gonville St, SW6
off Putney Br App 99 CY83
Goodall Rd, E11 67 EC62
Gooden Ct, Har. HA1 61 CE62
Goodenough Cl, Couls. CR5 175 DN120
Goodenough Rd, SW19 119 CZ94
Goodenough Way, Couls.
CR5 175 DM120
Gooderham Ho, Grays RM16 111 GH75
Goodge Pl, W1 195 L7
⊖ Goodge Street 195 L6
Goodge St, W1 195 L7
Goodhall St, NW10 80 CS69
Goodhart Pl, E14 85 DY73
Goodhart Way, W.Wick. BR4 144 EE101
Goodhew Rd, Croy. CR0 142 DU100
Gooding Cl, N.Mal. KT3 138 CQ98
Goodinge Cl, N7 83 DL65
Goodlake Ct, Uxb. (Denh.)
UB9 57 BF59
GOODLEY STOCK, West. 189 EP130
Goodley Stock, West. TN16 189 EP129
Goodley Stock Rd, Eden. (Crock.H.)
TN8 189 EP131
Westerham TN16 189 EP128
Goodman Cres, SW2 121 DK89
Goodman Pk, Slou. SL2 74 AW74
Goodman Pl, Stai. TW18 113 BF91
Goodman Rd, E10 67 EC59
Goodmans Ct, E1 197 P10
Wembley HA0 61 CK63
Goodman's Stile, E1 84 DU72
Goodmans Yd, E1 197 P10
GOODMAYES, Ilf. 70 EV61
⇌ Goodmayes 70 EU60
Goodmayes Av, Ilf. IG3 70 EU60
H Goodmayes Hosp, Ilf. IG3 70 EU57
Goodmayes La, Ilf. IG3 70 EU63
Goodmayes Rd, Ilf. IG3 70 EU60
Goodmead Rd, Orp. BR6 146 EU101
Goodrich Cl, Wat. WD25 23 BU35
Goodrich Rd, SE22 122 DT86
Goodson Rd, NW10 80 CS66
Goods Way, NW1 83 DL68
Goodway Gdns, E14 85 ED72
Goodwin Cl, SE16 202 A7
Mitcham CR4 140 DD97
Goodwin Ct, Barn. EN4 28 DE44
Waltham Cross EN8 15 DY28
Goodwin Dr, Sid. DA14 126 EX90
Goodwin Gdns, Croy. CR0 159 DP107
Goodwin Rd, N9 46 DW46
W12 99 CU75
Croydon CR0 159 DP106
Goodwins Ct, WC2 195 P10
Goodwin St, N4
off Fonthill Rd 65 DN61
Goodwood Av, Brwd. CM13 55 GE44
Enfield EN3 30 DW37
Hornchurch RM12 72 FL63
Watford WD24 23 BS35
Goodwood Cl, Mord. SM4 140 DA98
Stanmore HA7 41 CJ50
Goodwood Cres, Grav. DA12 131 GJ93
Goodwood Dr, Nthlt. UB5 78 CA65
Goodwood Path, Borwd. WD6
off Stratfield Rd 26 CN41
Goodwood Rd, SE14 103 DY80
Redhill RH1 184 DF132
Goodwyn Av, NW7 42 CS50
Goodwyns Vale, N10 44 DG53
Goodyers Av, Rad. WD7 9 CF33
Goodyers Gdns, NW4 63 CX57
Goosander Way, SE28 105 ER76
Goose Acre, Chesh. HP5 4 AT30
Gooseacre La, Har. HA3 61 CK57
Goosefields, Rick. WD3 22 BJ44
Goose Grn, Cob. KT11 169 BU119
Goose Grn Cl, Orp. BR5 146 EU96
Goose La, Wok. GU22 166 AV122
Gooseley La, E6 87 EN69
Goosens Cl, Sutt. SM1
off Turnpike La 158 DC106
Goose Sq, E6 *off Harper Rd* 87 EM72
Gooshays Dr, Rom. RM3 52 FL50
Gooshays Gdns, Rom. RM3 52 FL51
Gophir La, EC4 197 K10
Gopsall St, N1 84 DR67
Goral Mead, Rick. WD3 38 BK46
Gordon Av, E4 48 EE51
SW14 98 CS84
Hornchurch RM12 71 FF61
South Croydon CR2 160 DQ110
Stanmore HA7 41 CH51
Twickenham TW1 117 CG85
Gordonbrock Rd, SE4 123 EA85
Gordon Cl, E17 67 EA58
N19 *off Highgate Hill* 65 DJ60
Chertsey KT16 133 BE104
Staines TW18 114 BH93
Gordon Ct, W12 81 CW72
Gordon Cres, Croy. CR0 142 DS102
Hayes UB3 95 BU76
Gordondale Rd, SW19 120 DA89
Gordon Dr, Cher. KT16 133 BE104
Shepperton TW17 135 BR100
Gordon Gdns, Edg. HA8 42 CP54
Gordon Gro, SE5 101 DP82
⇌ Gordon Hill 29 DP39
Gordon Hill, Enf. EN2 30 DQ39
H Gordon Hosp, SW1 199 M9
Gordon Ho, E1 *off Glamis Rd* 84 DW73
Gordon Ho Rd, NW5 64 DG63
Gordon Pl, W8 100 DA75
Gravesend DA12
off East Ter 131 GJ86
Gordon Prom, Grav. DA12 131 GJ86
Gordon Prom E, Grav. DA12 131 GJ86
Gordon Rd, E4 48 EE45
E11 68 EG58
E15 67 EC63
E18 48 EH53
N3 43 CZ52
N9 46 DV47
N11 45 DK52
SE15 102 DV82
W4 98 CP79
W5 79 CJ73
W13 79 CH73
Ashford TW15 114 BL90
Barking IG11 87 ES67
Beckenham BR3 143 DZ97
Belvedere DA17 107 FC77
Brentwood CM15 55 GA46
Carshalton SM5 158 DF107
Caterham CR3 176 DR121
Dartford DA1 128 FK87
Enfield EN2 30 DQ39
Esher (Clay.) KT10 155 CE107
Gravesend (Nthflt.) DA11 130 GE87
Grays RM16 111 GF75
Harrow HA3 61 CE55
Hounslow TW3 96 CC84
Ilford IG1 69 ER62
Gordon Rd, Kings.T. KT2 138 CM95
Redhill RH1 184 DG131
Richmond TW9 98 CM82
Romford RM6 70 EZ58
Sevenoaks TN13 191 FH125
Shepperton TW17 135 BR100
Sidcup DA15 125 ES85
Southall UB2 96 BY77
Staines TW18 113 BC91
Surbiton KT5 138 CM101
Waltham Abbey EN9 15 EA34
West Drayton UB7 76 BL73
Gordon Sq, WC1 195 N5
Gordon St, E13
off Grange Rd 86 EG69
WC1 195 M4
Gordons Way, Oxt. RH8 187 ED128
Gordon Way, Barn. EN5 27 CZ42
Bromley BR1 144 EG95
Chalfont St. Giles HP8 36 AV48
Gore Cl, Uxb. (Hare.) UB9 58 BH56
Gore Ct, NW9 62 CN57
Gorefield Pl, NW6 82 DA68
Gorelands La, Ch.St.G. HP8 37 AZ47
Gore Rd, E9 84 DW67
SW20 139 CW96
Dartford DA2 128 FQ90
Goresbrook Rd, Dag. RM9 88 EV67
Goresbrook Village, Dag. RM9
off Goresbrook Rd 88 EV67
Gore St, SW7 100 DC76
Gorham Pl, W11 *off Mary Pl* 81 CY73
Goring Cl, Rom. RM5 51 FC53
Goring Gdns, Dag. RM8 70 EW63
Goring Rd, N11 45 DL51
Dagenham RM10 89 FD65
Staines TW18 113 BD92
Gorings Sq, Stai. TW18 113 BE91
Goring St, EC3 197 N8
Goring Way, Grnf. UB6 78 CC68
Gorle Cl, Wat. WD25 7 BU34
Gorleston Rd, N15 66 DR57
Gorleston St, W14 99 CY77
Gorman Rd, SE18 105 EM77
Gorringe Av, Dart. (S.Darenth)
DA4 149 FR96
Gorringe Pk Av, Mitch. CR4 120 DF94
Gorse Cl, E16 86 EG72
Tadworth KT20 173 CV120
Gorse Hill, Dart. (Fnghm.)
DA4 148 FL100
Gorse Hill La, Vir.W. GU25 132 AX98
Gorse Hill Rd, Vir.W. GU25 132 AX98
Gorselands Cl, W.Byf. KT14 152 BJ111
Gorse La, Wok. (Chobham)
GU24 150 AS108
Gorse Ri, SW17 120 DG92
Gorse Rd, Croy. CR0 161 EA105
Orpington BR5 146 FA103
Gorse Wk, West Dr. UB7 76 BL72
Gorseway, Rom. RM7 71 FD61
Gorst Rd, NW10 80 CQ70
SW11 120 DF86
Gorsuch Pl, E2 197 P2
Gorsuch St, E2 197 P2
Gosberton Rd, SW12 120 DG88
Gosbury Hill, Chess. KT9 156 CL105
Gosfield Rd, Dag. RM8 70 FA61
Epsom KT19 156 CR112
Gosfield St, W1 195 K6
Gosford Gdns, Ilf. IG4 69 EM57
Gosforth La, Wat. WD19 40 BW48
Gosforth Path, Wat. WD19 39 BU48
Goshawk Gdns, Hayes UB4 77 BS69
Goslett Ct, Bushey WD23
off Bournehall Av 24 CA43
Goslett Yd, WC2 195 N9
Gosling Cl, Grnf. UB6 78 CA69
Gosling Grn, Slou. SL3 92 AY76
Gosling Rd, Slou. SL3 92 AY76
Gosling Way, SW9 101 DN81
Gospatrick Rd, N17 46 DQ52
GOSPEL OAK, NW5 64 DG63
⇌ Gospel Oak 64 DG63
Gospel Oak Est, NW5 64 DF64
Gosport Dr, Horn. RM12 90 FJ65
Gosport Rd, E17 67 DZ57
Gosport Wk, N17
off Yarmouth Cres 66 DV57
Gosport Way, SE15
off Pentridge St 102 DT80
Gossage Rd, SE18
off Ancona Rd 105 ER78
Uxbridge UB10 76 BM66
Gossamers, The, Wat. WD25 24 BY36
Gosset St, E2 84 DT69
Goss Hill, Dart. DA2 128 FJ93
Swanley BR8 128 FJ93
Gosshill Rd, Chis. BR7 145 EN96
Gossington Cl, Chis. BR7
off Beechwood Ri 125 EP91
Gosterwood St, SE8 103 DY79
Gostling Rd, Twick. TW2 116 CA88
Goston Gdns, Th.Hth. CR7 141 DN97
Goswell Rd, EC1 197 H5
Gothic Cl, Dart. DA1 128 FK90
Gothic Ct, Hayes UB3
off Sipson La 95 BR79
Gothic Rd, Twick. TW2 117 CD89
Gottfried Ms, NW5
off Fortess Rd 65 DJ63
Gouch Ho, E5 66 DV62
Goudhurst Rd, Brom. BR1 124 EE92
Gouge Av, Grav. (Nthflt.)
DA11 130 GE88
Gough Rd, E15 68 EF63
Enfield EN1 30 DV40
Gough Sq, EC4 196 E8
Gough St, WC1 196 C4
Gough Wk, E14
off Saracen St 85 EA72
Gould Ct, SE19 122 DT92
Goulden Ho App, SW11 100 DE82
Goulding Gdns, Th.Hth. CR7 141 DP96
Gould Rd, Felt. TW14 115 BS87
Twickenham TW2 117 CE88
Goulds Grn, Uxb. UB8 77 BP72
Gould Ter, E8 *off Kenmure Rd* 66 DV64
Goulston St, E1 197 P8
Goulton Rd, E5 66 DV63
Gourley Pl, N15
off Gourley St 66 DS57
Gourley St, N15 66 DS57
Gourock Rd, SE9 125 EN85
Govan St, E2 *off Whiston Rd* 84 DU67
Government Row, Enf. EN3 31 EA38
Governors Av, Uxb. (Denh.)
UB9 57 BF57
Governors Cl, Amer. HP6 20 AT37
Govett Av, Shep. TW17 135 BQ99
Govier Cl, E15 86 EE66
Gowan Av, SW6 99 CY81
Gowan Rd, NW10 81 CV65
Gowar Fld, Pot.B. EN6 11 CU32
Gower, The, Egh. TW20 133 BB97
Gower Cl, SW4 121 DJ86
Gower Ct, WC1 195 M4
Gower Ms, WC1 195 M7
Gower Pl, WC1 195 L4
Gower Rd, E7 86 EG65
Isleworth TW7 97 CF79
Weybridge KT13 153 BR107
Gowers, The, Amer. HP6 20 AS36
Gowers La, Grays (Orsett)
RM16 111 GF75
Gower St, WC1 195 M5
Gower's Wk, E1 84 DU72
Gowland Pl, Beck. BR3 143 DZ96
Gowlett Rd, SE15 102 DU83
Gowrie Pl, Cat. CR3 176 DQ122
Gowrie Rd, SW11 100 DG83
Graburn Way, E.Mol. KT8 137 CD97
Grace Av, Bexh. DA7 106 EZ82
Radlett (Shenley) WD7 9 CK33
Grace Business Cen, Mitch.
CR4 140 DF99
Gracechurch St, EC3 197 L10
Grace Cl, SE9 124 EK90
Borehamwood WD6 26 CR39
Edgware HA8
off Pavilion Way 42 CQ52
Ilford IG6 49 ET51
Gracedale Rd, SW16 121 DH92
Gracefield Gdns, SW16 121 DL90
Grace Jones Cl, E8
off Parkholme Rd 84 DU65
Grace Path, SE26 122 DW91
Grace Pl, E3
off St. Leonards St 85 EB69
Grace Rd, Croy. CR0 142 DQ100
Grace's All, E1 84 DU73
Graces Ms, SE5 102 DS82
Graces Rd, SE5 102 DS82
Grace St, E3 85 EB69
Gracious La, Sev. TN13 190 FG130
Gracious La End, Sev. TN14 190 FF130
Gracious Pond Rd, Wok.
(Chobham) GU24 150 AT108
Gradient, The, SE26 122 DU91
Graduate Pl, SE1 *off Long La* 102 DS76
Graeme Rd, Enf. EN1 30 DR40
Graemesdyke Av, SW14 98 CP83
Grafton Cl, W13 79 CG72
Hounslow TW4 116 BY88
Slough (Geo.Grn.) SL3 74 AY72
West Byfleet KT14
off Madeira Rd 151 BF113
Worcester Park KT4 138 CS104
Grafton Ct, Felt. TW14
off Loxwood Cl 115 BR88
Grafton Cres, NW1 83 DH65
Grafton Gdns, N4 66 DQ58
Dagenham RM8 70 EY61
Grafton Ho, E3 85 EA69
Grafton Ms, W1 195 K5
Grafton Pk Rd, Wor.Pk. KT4 138 CS103
Grafton Pl, NW1 195 M3
Grafton Rd, NW5 64 DG64
W3 80 CQ73
Croydon CR0 141 DN102
Dagenham RM8 70 EY61
Enfield EN2 29 DM41
Harrow HA1 60 CC57
New Malden KT3 138 CS97
Worcester Park KT4 138 CR104
Graftons, The, NW2
off Hermitage La 64 DA62
Grafton Sq, SW4 101 DJ83
Grafton St, W1 199 J1
Grafton Ter, NW5 64 DF64
Grafton Way, W1 195 K5
WC1 195 K5
West Molesey KT8 136 BZ98
Grafton Yd, NW5
off Prince of Wales Rd 83 DH65
Graham Av, W13 97 CH75
Mitcham CR4 140 DG95
Graham Cl, Brwd. CM13 55 GC43
Croydon CR0 143 EA103
Grahame Pk Est, NW9 42 CS53
Grahame Pk Way, NW7 43 CT52
NW9 43 CT54
Graham Gdns, Surb. KT6 138 CL102
Graham Rd, E8 84 DU65
E13 86 EG70
N15 65 DP55
NW4 63 CV58
SW19 119 CZ94
W4 98 CR76
Bexleyheath DA6 106 FA84
Hampton TW12 116 CA91
Harrow HA3 61 CE55
Mitcham CR4 140 DG95
Purley CR8 159 DN113
Graham St, N1 196 G1
Graham Ter, SW1 198 F9
Grainger Cl, Nthlt. UB5
off Lancaster Rd 60 CC64
Grainger Rd, N22 46 DQ53
Isleworth TW7 97 CF82
Grainge's Yd, Uxb. UB8
off Cross St 76 BJ66
Gramer Cl, E11
off Norman Rd 67 ED61
Grampian Cl, Hayes UB3 95 BR80
Orpington BR6
off Cotswold Ri 145 ET100
Sutton SM2
off Devonshire Rd 158 DC108
Grampian Gdns, NW2 63 CY60
Grampian Ho, N9
off Plevna Rd 46 DV47
Grampian Way, Slou. SL3 93 BA78
Granard Av, SW15 119 CV85
Granard Rd, SW12 120 DF87
Granaries, The, Wal.Abb. EN9 16 EE34
Granary Cl, N9 *off Turin Rd* 46 DW45
Granary Rd, E1 84 DV70
Granary St, NW1 83 DK67
Granby Pk Rd, Wal.Cr. (Chsht.)
EN7 14 DT28
Granby Pl, SE1 200 D5
Granby Rd, SE9 105 EM82
Gravesend DA11 130 GC86
Granby St, E2 84 DT70
Granby Ter, NW1 195 K1
Grand Arc, N12
off Ballards La 44 DC50
Grand Av, EC1 196 G6
N10 64 DG56
Surbiton KT5 138 CP99
Wembley HA9 62 CN64
Grand Av E, Wem. HA9 62 CP64
Grand Depot Rd, SE18 105 EN78
Grand Dr, SW20 139 CW96
Southall UB2 96 CC75
Granden Rd, SW16 141 DL96
Grandfield Av, Wat. WD17 23 BT39
Grandis Cotts, Wok. (Ripley)
GU23 168 BH122
Grandison Rd, SW11 120 DF85
Worcester Park KT4 139 CW103
Grand Junct Wf, N1 197 H1
Grand Par Ms, SW15
off Upper Richmond Rd 119 CY85
Grand Stand Rd, Epsom
KT18 173 CT117
Grand Union Canal Wk, W7 97 CE76
Grand Union Cl, W9
off Woodfield Rd 81 CZ71
Grand Union Cres, E8 84 DU66
Grand Union Ind Est, NW10 80 CP68
Grand Union Wk, NW1 83 DH66
Grand Vw Av, West. (Bigg.H.)
TN16 178 EJ117
Grand Wk, E1 *off Solebay St* 85 DY70
Granfield St, SW11 100 DD81
Grange, The, N2
off Central Av 44 DD54
N20 44 DC46
SE1 201 P6
SW19 119 CX93
Croydon CR0 143 DZ103
Dartford (S.Darenth) DA4 149 FR95
Walton-on-Thames KT12 135 BV103
Wembley HA0 80 CN66
Windsor (Old Wind.) SL4 112 AV85
Woking (Chobham) GU24 150 AS110
Worcester Park KT4 138 CR104
Grange Av, N12 44 DC50
N20 43 CY45
SE25 142 DS96
Barnet EN4 44 DE46
Stanmore HA7 41 CH54
Twickenham TW2 117 CE89
Woodford Green IG8 48 EG51
Grangecliffe Gdns, SE25 142 DS96
Grange Cl, Brwd. CM13 55 GC50
Edgware HA8 42 CQ50
Gerrards Cross (Chal.St.P.)
SL9 36 AY53
Hayes UB3 77 BS71
Hounslow TW5 96 BZ79
Leatherhead KT22 171 CK120
Redhill (Bletch.) RH1 186 DR133
Redhill (Merst.) RH1 185 DH128
Sidcup DA15 126 EU90
Staines (Wrays.) TW19 112 AY86
Watford WD17 23 BU39
West Molesey KT8 136 CB98
Westerham TN16 189 EQ126
Woodford Green IG8 48 EG52
Grange Ct, WC2 196 C9
Chigwell IG7 49 EQ47
Loughton IG10 32 EK43
Northolt UB5 78 BW68
Staines TW18 114 BG92
Waltham Abbey EN9 15 EC34
Walton-on-Thames KT12 135 BU103
Grangecourt Rd, N16 66 DS60
Grange Cres, SE28 88 EW72
Chigwell IG7 49 ER50
Dartford DA2 128 FP86
Grangedale Cl, Nthwd. HA6 39 BS53
Grange Dr, Chis. BR7 124 EL93
Orpington BR6
off Rushmore Hill 164 EW109
Redhill (Merst.) RH1
off London Rd S 185 DH128
Woking GU21 150 AY114
Grange Fm Cl, Har. HA2 60 CC61
Grange Flds, Ger.Cr. (Chal.St.P.)
SL9 *off Lower Rd* 36 AY53
Grange Gdns, N14 45 DK46
NW3 64 DB62
SE25 142 DS96
Banstead SM7 158 DB113
Pinner HA5 60 BZ56
Grange Gro, N1 83 DP65
GRANGE HILL, Chig. 49 ER51
⊖ Grange Hill 49 ER49
Grange Hill, SE25 142 DS96
Edgware HA8 42 CQ50
Grangehill Pl, SE9
off Westmount Rd 105 EM83
Grangehill Rd, SE9 105 EM83
Grange Ho, Bark. IG11
off St. Margarets 87 ER67
Erith DA8 107 FG82
Grange La, SE21 122 DT89
Watford (Let.Hth.) WD25 25 CD39

★ Place of interest ⇌ Railway station ⊖ London Underground station DLR Docklands Light Railway station Tramlink station H Hospital

Grange Mans, Epsom KT17 . .157 CT108
Grange Meadow, Bans. SM7 .158 DB113
Grange Ms, SE10
off Crooms Hill 103 ED80
Grangemill Rd, SE6 . . . . .123 EA90
Grangemill Way, SE6 . . . . . . .123 EA89
Grangemount, Lthd. KT22 . . .171 CK120
★ **Grange Mus of Comm History**,
NW10 *off Neasden La* 62 CS63
GRANGE PARK, N21 . . . . .29 DP43
⇌ **Grange Park** 29 DP43
Grange Pk, W5 . . . . .80 CL74
Woking GU21 . . . . .166 AY115
Grange Pk Av, N21 . . . . .29 DP44
Grange Pk Pl, SW20 . . . . .119 CV94
Grange Pk Rd, E10 . . . . .67 EB60
Thornton Heath CR7 . . . . . . .142 DR98
Grange Pl, NW6 . . . . .82 DA66
Staines TW18 . . . . .134 BJ96
Walton-on-Thames KT12 . .135 BU103
Grange Rd, E10 . . . . .67 EA60
E13 .86 EF69
E17 .67 DY57
N6 . . . . .64 DG58
N17 .46 DU51
N18 .46 DU51
NW10 . . . . .81 CV65
SE1 . . . . .201 N6
SE19 . . . . .142 DR98
SE25 . . . . .142 DR98
SW13 . . . . .99 CU81
W4 . . . . .98 CP78
W5 . . . . .79 CK74
Addlestone (New Haw)
KT15 . . . . .152 BG110
Borehamwood (Elstree)
WD6 . . . . .26 CM43
Bushey WD23 . . . . .24 BY43
Caterham CR3 . . . . .186 DU125
Chessington KT9 . . . . .156 CL105
Edgware HA8 . . . . .42 CR51
Egham TW20 . . . . .113 AZ92
Gerrards Cross (Chal.St.P.)
SL9 .36 AY53
Gravesend DA11 . . . . .131 GG87
Grays RM17 . . . . .110 GB79
Harrow HA1 . . . . .61 CG58
Harrow (S.Har.) HA2 . . . . . .61 CD61
Hayes UB3 . . . . .77 BS72
Ilford IG1 . . . . .69 EP63
Kingston upon Thames
KT1 . . . . .138 CL97
Leatherhead KT22 . . . . . . .171 CK120
Orpington BR6 . . . . .145 EQ103
Romford RM3 . . . . .51 FH51
Sevenoaks TN13 . . . . .190 FG127
South Croydon CR2 . . . . . .160 DQ110
South Ockendon (Aveley)
RM15 . . . . .90 FQ74
Southall UB1 . . . . .96 BY75
Sutton SM2 . . . . .158 DA108
Thornton Heath CR7 . . . . . .142 DR98
Walton-on-Thames KT12 . .154 BY105
West Molesey KT8 . . . . . . .136 CB98
Woking GU21 . . . . .150 AY114
Granger Way, Rom. RM1 . . . . .71 FG58
Grange St, N1 . . . . .84 DR67
Grange Vale, Sutt. SM2 . . . . .158 DB108
Grange Vw Rd, N20 . . . . .44 DC46
Grange Wk, SE1 . . . . .201 N6
Grangeway, N12 . . . . .44 DB49
NW6 *off Messina Av* 82 DA66
Grange Way, Erith DA8 . . . . .107 FH80
Iver SL0 . . . . .75 BF72
Grangeway, Wdf.Grn. IG8 . . . .48 EJ49
Grangeway, The, N21 . . . . .29 DP44
Grangeway Gdns, Ilf. IG4 . . . .68 EL57
Grangeways Cl, Grav. (Nthflt.)
DA11 . . . . .131 GF91
Grangewood, Bex. DA5
off Hurst Rd 126 EZ88
Potters Bar EN6 . . . . .12 DB30
Slough (Wexham) SL3 . . . . .74 AW71
Grangewood Av, Grays
RM16 . . . . .110 GE76
Rainham RM13 . . . . .90 FJ70
Grangewood Cl, Brwd. CM13
off Knight's Way 55 GA48
Pinner HA5 . . . . .59 BU57
Grangewood Dr, Sun. TW16
off Forest Dr 115 BT94
Grangewood La, Beck. BR3 . .123 DZ93
Grangewood St, E6 . . . . .86 EJ67
Grangewood Ter, SE25
off Grange Rd 142 DR97
Grange Yd, SE1 . . . . .201 P7
Granham Gdns, N9 . . . . .46 DT47
Granite St, SE18 . . . . .105 ET78
Granleigh Rd, E11 . . . . .68 EE61
Gransden Av, E8 . . . . .84 DV66
Gransden Rd, W12
off Wendell Rd 99 CT75
Grant Av, Slou. SL1 . . . . .74 AS72
Grantbridge St, N1 . . . . .83 DP68
Grantchester Cl, Har. HA1 . . . .61 CF62
Grant Cl, N14 . . . . .45 DJ45
Shepperton TW17 . . . . .135 BP100
Grantham Cl, Edg. HA8 . . . . . .42 CL48
Grantham Gdns, Rom. RM6 . . .70 EZ58
Grantham Grn, Borwd. WD6 . .26 CQ43
Grantham Pl, W1 . . . . .199 H3
Grantham Rd, E12 . . . . .69 EN63
SW9 . . . . .101 DL82
W4 . . . . .98 CS80
Grantley Pl, Esher KT10 . . . . .154 CB106
Grantley Rd, Houns. TW4 . . . .96 BW82
Grantley St, E1 . . . . .85 DX69
Grantock Rd, E17 . . . . .47 ED53
Granton Av, Upmin. RM14 . . . .72 FM61
Granton Rd, SW16 . . . . .141 DJ95
Ilford IG3 . . . . .70 EU60
Sidcup DA14 . . . . .126 EW93
Grant Pl, Croy. CR0 . . . . .142 DT102
Grant Rd, SW11 . . . . .100 DD84
Croydon CR0 . . . . .142 DT102
Harrow HA3 . . . . .61 CE55
Grants Cl, NW7 . . . . .43 CW52
Grants La, Oxt. RH8 . . . . .188 EJ132
Grant's Quay Wf, EC3 . . . . . . .201 L1
Grant St, E13 . . . . .86 EG69
N1 *off Chapel Mkt* 83 DN68
Grantully Rd, W9 . . . . .82 DB69
Grant Way, Islw. TW7 . . . . .97 CG79
Granville Av, N9 . . . . .46 DW48
Feltham TW13 . . . . .115 BU89
Hounslow TW3 . . . . .116 CA85
Granville Cl, Croy. CR0 . . . . .142 DS103
West Byfleet (Byfleet) KT14
off Church Rd 152 BM113
Weybridge KT13 . . . . .153 BQ107
Granville Ct, N1 . . . . .84 DR67
Granville Dene, Hem.H. (Bov.)
HP3 . . . . .5 BA27
Granville Gdns, SW16 . . . . . .141 DM95
W5 . . . . .80 CM74
Granville Gro, SE13 . . . . .103 EC83
Granville Ms, Sid. DA14 . . . . .126 EU91
Granville Pk, SE13 . . . . .103 EC83
Granville Pl, N12 (N.Finchley)
off High Rd 44 DC52
SW6 *off Maxwell Rd* 100 DB80
W1 .194 F9
Pinner HA5 . . . . .60 BX55
Granville Rd, E17 . . . . .67 EB58
E18 . . . . .48 EH54
N4 . . . . .65 DM58
N12 .44 DB52
N13 *off Russell Rd* 45 DM51
N22 .45 DP53
NW2 .63 CZ61
NW6 .82 DA68
SW18 . . . . .120 DA87
SW19 *off Russell Rd* 120 DA94
Barnet EN5 . . . . .27 CW42
Epping CM16 . . . . .18 EV29
Gravesend DA11 . . . . .131 GF87
Hayes UB3 . . . . .95 BT77
Ilford IG1 . . . . .69 EP60
Oxted RH8 . . . . .188 EF129
Sevenoaks TN13 . . . . .190 FG124
Sidcup DA14 . . . . .126 EU91
Uxbridge UB10 . . . . .77 BP65
Watford WD18 . . . . .24 BW42
Welling DA16 . . . . .106 EW83
Westerham TN16 . . . . .189 EQ126
Weybridge KT13 . . . . .153 BQ107
Woking GU22 . . . . .167 AZ120
Granville Sq, SE15 . . . . .102 DS80
WC1 . . . . .196 C3
Granville St, WC1 . . . . .196 C3
Grape St, WC2 . . . . .195 P8
Graphite Sq, SE11 . . . . .200 B10
Grapsome Cl, Chess. KT9
off Nigel Fisher Way 155 CJ108
Grasdene Rd, SE18 . . . . .106 EU80
Grasholm Way, Slou. SL3 . . . .93 BC77
Grasmere Av, SW15 . . . . .118 CR91
SW19 . . . . .140 DA97
W3 . . . . .80 CQ73
Hounslow TW3 . . . . .116 CB86
Orpington BR6 . . . . .145 EP104
Ruislip HA4 . . . . .59 BQ59
Slough SL2 . . . . .74 AU73
Wembley HA9 . . . . .61 CK59
Grasmere Cl, Egh. TW20
off Keswick Rd 113 BB94
Feltham TW14 . . . . .115 BT88
Loughton IG10 . . . . .33 EM40
Watford WD25 . . . . .7 BV32
Grasmere Ct, N22
off Palmerston Rd 45 DM51
Grasmere Gdns, Har. HA3 . . . .41 CG54
Ilford IG4 . . . . .69 EM57
Orpington BR6 . . . . .145 EP104
Grasmere Pt, SE15
off Ilderton Rd 102 DW80
Grasmere Rd, E13 . . . . .86 EG68
N10 .45 DH53
N17 .46 DU51
SE25 . . . . .142 DV100
SW16 . . . . .121 DM92
Bexleyheath DA7 . . . . .107 FC81
Bromley BR1 . . . . .144 EF95
Orpington BR6 . . . . .145 EP104
Purley CR8 . . . . .159 DP111
Grasmere Way, W.Byf. (Byfleet)
KT14 . . . . .152 BM112
Grassfield Cl, Couls. CR5 . . . .175 DH119
Grasshaven Way, SE28 . . . . . . .87 ET74
Grassingham End, Ger.Cr.
(Chal.St.P.) SL9 . . . . .36 AY52
Grassingham Rd, Ger.Cr.
(Chal.St.P.) SL9 . . . . .36 AY52
Grassington Cl, N11
off Ribblesdale Av 44 DG51
St. Albans (Brick.Wd.) AL2 . . .8 CA30
Grassington Rd, Sid. DA14 . . .126 EU91
Grassmere Rd, Horn. RM11 . . .72 FM56
Grassmount, SE23 . . . . .122 DV89
Purley CR8 . . . . .159 DJ110
Grass Pk, N3 . . . . .43 CZ53
Grassway, Wall. SM6 . . . . . . .159 DJ105
Grassy La, Sev. TN13 . . . . . . .191 FH126
Grasvenor Av, Barn. EN5 . . . . .28 DA44
Grately Way, SE15
off Daniel Gdns 102 DT80
Gratton Rd, W14 . . . . .99 CY76
Gratton Ter, NW2 . . . . .63 CX62
Gravel Cl, Chig. IG7 . . . . .50 EU47
Graveley, Kings.T. KT1
off Willingham Way 138 CN96
Graveley Av, Borwd. WD6 . . . .26 CQ42
⇔ **Gravel Hill** 161 DY108
Gravel Hill, N3 . . . . .43 CZ54
Bexleyheath DA6 . . . . .127 FB85
Croydon CR0 . . . . .161 DX107
Gerrards Cross (Chal.St.P.)
SL9 .36 AY53
Leatherhead KT22
off North St 171 CH121
Loughton (High Beach)
IG10 . . . . .32 EG38
Uxbridge UB8 . . . . .58 BK64
Gravel Hill Cl, Bexh. DA6 . . . .127 FB85
Gravel La, E1 . . . . .197 P8
Chigwell IG7 . . . . .50 EU46
Gravelly Hill, Cat. CR3 . . . . . .186 DS128
Gravelly Ride, SW19 . . . . .119 CV91
Gravel Pit La, SE9 . . . . .125 EQ85
Gravel Pit Way, Orp. BR6 . . . .146 EU103
Gravel Rd, Brom. BR2 . . . . . .144 EL103
Dartford (Sutt.H.) DA4 . . . . .128 FP94
Twickenham TW2 . . . . .117 CE88
Gravelwood Cl, Chis. BR7 . . . .125 EQ90
Graveney Gro, SE20 . . . . .122 DW94
Graveney Rd, SW17 . . . . .120 DE91
GRAVESEND 131 GJ85
⇌ **Gravesend** 131 GG87
🅷 **Gravesend & North Kent
Hosp**, Grav. DA11 . . . . . . .131 GG86
Gravesend Rd, W12 . . . . .81 CU73
Gravesham Ct, Grav. DA12
off Clarence Row 131 GH87
★ **Gravesham Mus**, Grav.
DA11 . . . . .131 GH86
Gray Av, Dag. RM8 . . . . .70 EZ60
Grayburn Cl, Ch.St.G. HP8 . . . .36 AU47
Gray Gdns, Rain. RM13 . . . . . .89 FG65
Grayham Cres, N.Mal. KT3 . . .138 CR98
Grayham Rd, N.Mal. KT3 . . . .138 CR98
Grayland Cl, Brom. BR1 . . . . .144 EK95
Graylands, Epp. (They.B.)
CM16 . . . . .33 ER37
Woking GU21 . . . . .166 AY116
Graylands Cl, Wok. GU21 . . . .166 AY116
Grayling Cl, E16
off Cranberry La 86 EE70
Grayling Rd, N16 . . . . .66 DR61
Graylings, The, Abb.L. WD5 . . . .7 BR33
Grayling Sq, E2 . . . . .84 DU69
Gray Pl, Cher. KT16
off Murray Rd 151 BD106
Chertsey (Ott.) KT16
off Clarendon Gate 151 BC107
GRAYS 110 GA78
⇌ **Grays** 110 GA79
Grayscroft Rd, SW16 . . . . . . .121 DK94
Grays End Cl, Grays RM17 . . .110 GA76
Grays Fm Rd, Orp. BR5 . . . . .146 EV95
Grayshott Rd, SW11 . . . . .100 DG82
★ **Gray's Inn**, WC1 . . . . .196 C6
Gray's Inn, WC1 . . . . .196 C6
Gray's Inn Pl, WC1 . . . . .196 C7
Gray's Inn Rd, WC1 . . . . .196 B3
Gray's Inn Sq, WC1 . . . . .196 D6
Grays La, Ashf. TW15 . . . . . . .115 BP91
Gray's La, Ashtd. KT21 . . . . .172 CM119
Epsom KT18
off Shepherds' Wk 172 CP121
Grays Pk Rd, Slou. (Stoke P.)
SL2 .74 AU68
Grays Pl, Slou. SL2 . . . . .74 AT74
Grays Rd, Slou. SL1 . . . . .74 AT74
Uxbridge UB10 . . . . .76 BL67
Westerham TN16 . . . . .179 EP121
Gray St, SE1 . . . . .200 E5
Grays Wk, Brwd. CM13 . . . . . .55 GD45
Grayswood Gdns, SW20
off Farnham Gdns 139 CV96
Grayswood Pt, SW15
off Norley Vale 119 CU88
Gray's Yd, W1 . . . . .194 G9
Graywood Ct, N12 . . . . .44 DC52
Grazebrook Rd, N16 . . . . .66 DR61
Grazeley Cl, Bexh. DA6 . . . . .127 FC85
Grazeley Ct, SE19
off Gipsy Hill 122 DS91
Great Acre Ct, SW4
off St. Alphonsus Rd 101 DK84
Great Bell All, EC2 . . . . .197 K8
Great Benty, West Dr. UB7 . . .94 BL77
★ **Great Bookham Common**,
Lthd. KT23 . . . . .170 BZ121
Great Brownings, SE21 . . . . .122 DT91
Great Bushey Dr, N20 . . . . . . .44 DB46
Great Cambridge Rd, N9 . . . . .46 DS46
N17 .46 DR50
N18 .46 DR50
Broxbourne EN10 . . . . .15 DY26
Enfield EN1 . . . . .30 DU42
Waltham Cross (Chsht.)
EN8 .14 DW34
Great Castle St, W1 . . . . .195 J8
Great Cen Av, Ruis. HA4 . . . . .60 BW64
Great Cen St, NW1 . . . . .194 D6
Great Cen Way, NW10 . . . . . . .62 CS64
Wembley HA9 . . . . .62 CQ63
Great Chapel St, W1 . . . . .195 M8
Great Chertsey Rd, W4 . . . . . .98 CQ82
Feltham TW13 . . . . .116 CA90
Great Ch La, W6 . . . . .99 CX78
Great Coll St, SW1 . . . . .199 P6
Great Cross Av, SE10 . . . . . .104 EE80
Great Cullings, Rom. RM7 . . . .71 FE61
Great Cumberland Ms, W1 . .194 D9
Great Cumberland Pl, W1 . . .194 D8
Great Dover St, SE1 . . . . .201 J5
Greatdown Rd, W7 . . . . .79 CF70
Great Eastern Rd, E15 . . . . . . .85 ED66
Brentwood CM14 . . . . .54 FW49
Great Eastern St, EC2 . . . . . .197 M3
Great Eastern Wk, EC2 . . . . . .197 N7
Great Ellshams, Bans. SM7 . .174 DA116
Great Elms Rd, Brom. BR2 . . .144 EJ98
Great Fld, NW9 . . . . .42 CS53
Greatfield Av, E6 . . . . .87 EM70
Greatfield Cl, N19
off Warrender Rd 65 DJ63
SE4 .103 EA84
Greatfields Dr, Uxb. UB8 . . . . .76 BN71
Greatfields Rd, Bark. IG11 . . . .87 ER67
Great Fleete Way, Bark. IG11
off Choats Rd 88 EW68
Great Galley Cl, Bark. IG11 . . .88 EV69
Great Gdns Rd, Horn. RM11 . . .71 FH58
Great Gatton Cl, Croy. CR0 . . .143 DY101
Great George St, SW1 . . . . . .199 N5
Great Gregories La, Epp.
CM16 . . . . .17 ES33
Great Gro, Bushey WD23 . . . . .24 CB42
Great Gros, Wal.Cr. EN7 . . . . .14 DS28
Great Guildford St, SE1 . . . . .201 H2
Greatham Rd, Bushey WD23 . .24 BX41
Greatham Wk, SW15 . . . . .119 CU88
Great Harry Dr, SE9 . . . . .125 EN90
Greathurst End, Lthd. (Bkhm.)
KT23 . . . . .170 BZ124
Great James St, WC1 . . . . . . .196 B5
Great Julians, Rick. WD3
off Grove Cres 22 BN42
Great Marlborough St, W1 . . .195 K9
Great Maze Pond, SE1 . . . . . .201 L4
Great Nelmes Chase, Horn.
RM11 . . . . .72 FM57
Greatness La, Sev. TN14 . . . .191 FJ121
Greatness Rd, Sev. TN14 . . . .191 FJ121
Great Newport St, WC2
off Cranbourn St 83 DK73
Great New St, EC4 . . . . .196 E8
Great N Rd, N2 . . . . .64 DE56
N6 . . . . .64 DE56
Barnet EN5 . . . . .27 CZ38
Barnet (New Barn.) EN5 . . . .28 DA43
Hatfield AL9 . . . . .12 DB27
Potters Bar EN6 . . . . .12 DB27
Great N Way, NW4 . . . . .43 CW54
Great Oaks, Brwd. CM13 . . . . .55 GB44
Chigwell IG7 . . . . .49 EQ49
Greatorex St, E1 . . . . .84 DU71
Great Ormond St, WC1 . . . . .196 A6
🅷 **Great Ormond St Hosp for
Children**, WC1 . . . . .196 A5
Great Owl Rd, Chig. IG7 . . . . .49 EN48
Great Pk, Kings L. WD4 . . . . . .6 BM30
Great Percy St, WC1 . . . . . . .196 C2
Great Peter St, SW1 . . . . .199 M7
Great Pettits Ct, Rom. RM1 . . .51 FE54
⊖ **Great Portland Street** 195 J5
Great Portland St, W1 . . . . . .195 J6
Great Pulteney St, W1 . . . . . .195 L10
Great Queen St, WC2 . . . . . . .196 A9
Dartford DA1 . . . . .128 FM87
Great Ropers La, Brwd. CM13 .53 FU51
Great Russell St, WC1 . . . . . .195 N8
Great St. Helens, EC3 . . . . . .197 M8
Great St. Thomas Apostle,
EC4 . . . . .197 J10
Great Scotland Yd, SW1 . . . .199 P3
Great Slades, Pot.B. EN6 . . . . .11 CZ33
Great Smith St, SW1 . . . . . . .199 N6
Great South-West Rd, Felt.
TW14 . . . . .115 BQ87
Hounslow TW4 . . . . .95 BT84
Great Spilmans, SE22 . . . . . .122 DS85
Great Stockwood Rd, Wal.Cr.
(Chsht.) EN7 . . . . .14 DR26
Great Strand, NW9 . . . . .43 CT53
Great Suffolk St, SE1 . . . . . .200 G3
Great Sutton St, EC1 . . . . . . .196 G5
Great Swan All, EC2 . . . . .197 K8
Great Tattenhams, Epsom
KT18 . . . . .173 CV118
Great Thrift, Orp. BR5 . . . . . .145 EQ98
Great Till Cl, Sev. (Otford)
TN14 . . . . .181 FE116
Great Titchfield St, W1 . . . . .195 K8
Great Twr St, EC3 . . . . .197 M10
Great Trinity La, EC4 . . . . . . .197 J10
Great Turnstile, WC1 . . . . . . .196 C7
GREAT WARLEY, Brwd. 53 FV53
Great Warley St, Brwd. CM13 .53 FU53
Great Western Rd, W2 . . . . . . .81 CZ71
W9 . . . . .81 CZ71
W11 .81 CZ71
Great W Rd, W4 . . . . .98 CP78
W6 . . . . .99 CT78
Brentford TW8 . . . . .98 CP78
Hounslow TW5 . . . . .96 BX82
Isleworth TW7 . . . . .97 CE80
Great Wf Rd, E14
off Churchill Pl 85 EB74
Great Winchester St, EC2 . . .197 L8
Great Windmill St, W1 . . . . . .195 M10
Greatwood, Chis. BR7 . . . . . .125 EN94
Greatwood Cl, Cher. (Ott.)
KT16 . . . . .151 BC109
Great Woodcote Dr, Pur.
CR8 . . . . .159 DK110
Great Woodcote Pk, Pur.
CR8 . . . . .159 DK110
Great Yd, SE1 . . . . .201 N4
Greaves Cl, Bark. IG11
off Norfolk Rd 87 ES66
Greaves Pl, SW17 . . . . .120 DE91
Grebe Av, Hayes UB4
off Cygnet Way 78 BX72
Grebe Cl, E7
off Cormorant Rd 68 EF64
E17 .47 DY52
Barking IG11 . . . . .88 EU70
Grebe Ct, Sutt. SM1 . . . . .157 CZ106
Grebe Crest, Grays RM20 . . . .109 FU77
Grecian Cres, SE19 . . . . .121 DP93
Greding Wk, Brwd. CM13 . . . . .55 GB47
Gredo Ho, Bark. IG11 . . . . .88 EV69
Greek Ct, W1 . . . . .195 N9
Greek St, W1 . . . . .195 N9
Greek Yd, WC2 . . . . .195 P10
Green, The, E4 . . . . .47 EC46
E11 .68 EH58
E15 .86 EE65
N9 . . . . .46 DU47
N14 .45 DK48
N21 .45 DN45
SW14 . . . . .98 CQ83
SW19 . . . . .119 CX92
W3 . . . . .80 CS72
W5 *off High St* 79 CK74
Bexleyheath DA7 . . . . .106 FA81
Bromley BR1
off Downham Way 124 EG90
Bromley (Hayes) BR2 . . . . .144 EG101
Carshalton SM5 . . . . .158 DG105
Caterham (Wold.) CR3 . . . .177 EA123
Chalfont St. Giles HP8
off High St 36 AW47
Croydon CR0 . . . . .161 DZ109
Dartford DA2 . . . . .129 FR89
Green, The, Epp. (They.B.)
CM16 . . . . .33 ES37
Epsom KT17 . . . . .157 CU111
Esher (Clay.) KT10 . . . . . . .155 CF107
Feltham TW13 . . . . .115 BV89
Hayes UB3
off Wood End 77 BS72
Hemel Hempstead (Bov.)
HP3 . . . . .5 BA29
Hounslow TW5
off Heston Rd 96 CA79
Leatherhead (Fetch.) KT22 .171 CD124
Morden SM4 . . . . .139 CY98
New Malden KT3 . . . . .138 CQ97
Orpington (Pr.Bot.) BR6
off Rushmore Hill 164 EW110
Orpington (St.P.Cray) BR5
off The Avenue 126 EV94
Rainham (Wenn.) RM13 . . . .90 FL73
Richmond TW9 . . . . .117 CK85
Rickmansworth (Crox.Grn.)
WD3 . . . . .22 BN44
Rickmansworth (Sarratt)
WD3 . . . . .22 BG35
Romford (Hav.at.Bow.)
RM4 . . . . .51 FE48
Sevenoaks TN13 . . . . .191 FK122
Shepperton TW17 . . . . .135 BS98
Sidcup DA14 . . . . .126 EU91
Slough (Datchet) SL3 . . . . . .92 AV80
South Ockendon RM15 . . . . .91 FW69
Southall UB2 . . . . .96 BY76
Staines (Wrays.) TW19 . . . .112 AY86
Sutton SM1 . . . . .140 DB104
Tadworth (Burgh Hth.)
KT20 . . . . .173 CY119
Tilbury (W.Til.) RM18 . . . . .111 GL79
Twickenham TW2 . . . . .117 CE88
Uxbridge (Hare.) UB9 . . . . . .38 BJ53
Uxbridge (Ickhm.) UB10 . . . .59 BQ61
Waltham Abbey EN9
off Sewardstone Rd 15 EC34
Waltham Cross (Chsht.)
EN8 .14 DW28
Walton-on-Thames KT12
off Octagon Rd 153 BS110
Warlingham CR6 . . . . .177 DX117
Watford (Let.Hth.) WD25 . . .25 CE39
Welling DA16 . . . . .105 ES84
Wembley HA0 . . . . .61 CG61
West Drayton UB7 . . . . .94 BK76
Westerham TN16 . . . . .189 ER126
Woking (Ripley) GU23 . . . .168 BH121
Woodford Green IG8 . . . . . .48 EG50
Greenacre, Dart. DA1
off Oakfield La 128 FL89
Woking (Knap.) GU21
off Mead Ct 166 AS116
Greenacre Cl, Barn. EN5 . . . . .27 CZ38
Northolt UB5 . . . . .60 BZ64
Swanley BR8 . . . . .147 FE98
Greenacre Ct, Egh. (Eng.Grn.)
TW20 . . . . .112 AW93
Greenacre Gdns, E17 . . . . .67 EC56
Greenacre Pl, Wall. (Hackbr.) SM6
off Park Rd 141 DH103
Greenacres, N3 . . . . .43 CY54
SE9 . . . . .125 EN86
Bushey (Bushey Hth.)
WD23 . . . . .41 CD47
Green Acres, Croy. CR0 . . . . .142 DT104
Greenacres, Epp. CM16 . . . . . .17 ET29
Leatherhead (Bkhm.)
KT23 . . . . .170 CB124
Oxted RH8 . . . . .188 EE127
Greenacres Av, Uxb. UB10 . . . .58 BM62
Greenacres Cl, Orp. BR6 . . . .163 EQ105
Rainham RM13 . . . . .90 FL69
Greenacres Dr, Stan. HA7 . . . .41 CH52
Greenacre Sq, SE16 . . . . .203 J4
Greenacre Wk, N14 . . . . .45 DL48
Greenall Cl, Wal.Cr. (Chsht.)
EN8 .15 DY30
Green Arbour Ct, EC1 . . . . . .196 F8
Green Av, NW7 . . . . .42 CR49
W13 .97 CH76
Greenaway Gdns, NW3 . . . . . .64 DB63
Green Bk, E1 . . . . .202 D3
N12 .44 DB49
Greenbank, Wal.Cr. (Chsht.)
EN8 .14 DV28
Greenbank Av, Wem. HA0 . . . .61 CG64
Greenbank Cl, E4 . . . . .47 EC47
Romford RM3 . . . . .52 FK48
Greenbank Cres, NW4 . . . . . . .63 CY56
Greenbank Rd, Wat. WD17 . . . .23 BR36
Greenbanks, Dart. DA1 . . . . . .128 FL89
Upminster RM14 . . . . .73 FS60
Greenbay Rd, SE7 . . . . .104 EK80
Greenberry St, NW8 . . . . .194 B1
Greenbrook Av, Barn. EN4 . . . .28 DC39
Greenbury Cl, Rick. (Chorl.)
WD3 . . . . .21 BC41
Green Cl, NW9 . . . . .62 CQ58
NW11 . . . . .64 DC59
Bromley BR2 . . . . .144 EE97
Carshalton SM5 . . . . .140 DF103
Feltham TW13 . . . . .116 BY92
Hatfield AL9
off Station Rd 11 CY26
Waltham Cross (Chsht.)
EN8 .15 DY32
Greencoat Pl, SW1 . . . . .199 L8
Greencoat Row, SW1 . . . . . . .199 L7
Greencourt Av, Croy. CR0 . . .142 DV103
Edgware HA8 . . . . .42 CP53
Greencourt Gdns, Croy. CR0 .142 DV102
Greencourt Rd, Orp. BR5 . . . .145 ER99
Green Ct Rd, Swan. BR8 . . . . .147 FD99
Greencrest Pl, NW2
off Dollis Hill La 63 CU62
Green Cft, Edg. HA8
off Deans La 42 CQ50
Greencroft Av, Ruis. HA4 . . . . .60 BW61

Gre - Gri

Greencroft Cl, E6
off Neatscourt Rd 86 EL71
Greencroft Gdns, NW6 . . . . . .82 DB66
Enfield EN1 . . . . .30 DS41
Greencroft Rd, Houns. TW5 . . .96 BZ81
Green Curve, Bans. SM7 . . . .157 CZ114
Green Dale, SE5 . . . . .102 DR84
SE22 . . . . .122 DS85
Green Dale Cl, SE22
off Green Dale 122 DS85
Greendale Ms, Slou. SL2 . . . . .74 AU73
Greendale Wk, Grav. (Nthflt.)
DA11 . . . . .130 GE90
Green Dragon Ct, SE1 . . . . . .201 K2
Green Dragon La, N21 . . . . . . .29 DP44
Brentford TW8 . . . . .98 CL78
Green Dragon Yd, E1
off Old Montague St 84 DU71
Green Dr, Slou. SL3 . . . . .92 AY77
Southall UB1 . . . . .78 CA74
Woking (Ripley) GU23 . . . .167 BF123
Green E Rd, Beac. (Jordans)
HP9 . . . . .36 AS52
Green Edge, Wat. WD25
off Clarke Grn 23 BU35
Greene Fielde End, Stai.
TW18 . . . . .114 BK94
Green End, N21 . . . . .45 DP47
Chessington KT9 . . . . . . .156 CL105
Green End Business Cen, Rick.
WD3 off Church La 22 BG37
Greenend Rd, W4 . . . . .98 CS75
Greenfarm Cl, Orp. BR6 . . . . .163 ET106
Greenfield Av, Surb. KT5 . . . .138 CP101
Watford WD19 . . . . .40 BX47
Greenfield End, Ger.Cr. (Chal.St.P.)
SL9 . . . . .36 AY51
Greenfield Gdns, NW2 . . . . . . .63 CY61
Dagenham RM9 . . . . .88 EX67
Orpington BR5 . . . . .145 ER101
Greenfield Link, Couls. CR5 . .175 DL115
Greenfield Rd, E1 . . . . .84 DU71
N15 . . . . .66 DS57
Dagenham RM9 . . . . .88 EW67
Dartford DA2 . . . . .127 FD92
Greenfields, Loug. IG10 . . . . . .33 EN42
Potters Bar (Cuffley) EN6
off South Dr 13 DL30
Greenfields Cl, Brwd. CM13
off Essex Way 53 FW51
Loughton IG10 . . . . .33 EN42
Greenfield St, Wal.Abb. EN9 . . .15 EC34
Greenfield Way, Har. HA2 . . . .60 CB55
GREENFORD 78 CB69
⇌ Greenford 79 CD67
⊖ Greenford 79 CD67
Greenford Av, W7 . . . . .79 CE70
Southall UB1 . . . . .78 BZ73
Greenford Gdns, Grnf. UB6 . . . .78 CB69
Greenford Rd, Grnf. UB6 . . . .78 CC71
Harrow HA1 . . . . .61 CE64
Southall UB1 . . . . .78 CC74
Sutton SM1 . . . . .158 DB105
Green Gdns, Orp. BR6 . . . . . .163 EQ106
Greengate, Grnf. UB6 . . . . . . .79 CH65
Greengate St, E13 . . . . .86 EH68
Green Glade, Epp. (They.B.)
CM16 . . . . .33 ES37
Green Glades, Horn. RM11 . . . .72 FM58
Greenhalgh Wk, N2 . . . . .64 DC56
Greenham Cl, SE1 . . . . .200 D5
Greenham Cres, E4 . . . . .47 DZ51
Greenham Rd, N10 . . . . .44 DG54
Greenham Wk, Wok. GU21 . . .166 AW118
Greenhaven Dr, SE28 . . . . .88 EV72
Greenhayes Av, Bans. SM7 . .158 DA114
Greenhayes Cl, Reig. RH2 . . .184 DC134
Greenhayes Gdns, Bans.
SM7 . . . . .174 DA115
Greenheys Cl, Nthwd. HA6 . . . .39 BS53
Greenheys Dr, E18 . . . . .68 EF55
Greenheys Pl, Wok. GU22
off White Rose La 167 AZ118
Greenhill, NW3
off Hampstead High St 64 DD63
SE18 . . . . .105 EM78
Green Hill, Buck.H. IG9 . . . . . .48 EJ46
Orpington BR6 . . . . .162 EL112
Greenhill, Sutt. SM1 . . . . . . .140 DC103
Wembley HA9 . . . . .62 CP61
Greenhill Av, Cat. CR3 . . . . . .176 DV121
Greenhill Cres, Wat. WD18 . . . .23 BS44
Greenhill Gdns, Nthlt. UB5 . . . .78 BZ68
Greenhill Gro, E12 . . . . .68 EL63
Green Hill La, Warl. CR6 . . . . .177 DY117
Greenhill Pk, NW10 . . . . .80 CS67
Barnet EN5 . . . . .28 DB43
Greenhill Rd, NW10 . . . . .80 CS67
Gravesend (Nthflt.) DA11 . . .131 GF89
Harrow HA1 . . . . .61 CE58
Greenhills Cl, Rick. WD3 . . . . .22 BH43
Greenhill's Rents, EC1 . . . . . .196 G6
Greenhills Ter, N1
off Baxter Rd 84 DR65
Greenhill Ter, SE18 . . . . .105 EM78
Northolt UB5 . . . . .78 BZ68
Greenhill Way, Croy. CR0 . . . .161 DX111
Harrow HA1 . . . . .61 CE58
Wembley HA9 . . . . .62 CP61
GREENHITHE 129 FV85
⇌ Greenhithe 129 FU85
Greenhithe Cl, Sid. DA15 . . . .125 ES87
Greenholm Rd, SE9 . . . . .125 EP85
Green Hundred Rd, SE15 . . . .102 DU79
Greenhurst La, Oxt. RH8 . . . .188 EG132
Greenhurst Rd, SE27 . . . . . . .121 DN92
Greening St, SE2 . . . . .106 EW77
Greenlake Ter, Stai. TW18 . . . .113 BF94
Greenland Cres, Sthl. UB2 . . . .96 BW76
Greenland Ms, SE8
off Trundleys Rd 103 DX78
Greenland Pl, NW1
off Greenland Rd 83 DH67
Greenland Quay, SE16 . . . . . .203 J8
Greenland Rd, NW1 . . . . .83 DJ67
Barnet EN5 . . . . .27 CW44
Greenlands, Cher. KT16 . . . . .133 BC104
Greenlands Rd, Stai. TW18 . . .114 BG91
Weybridge KT13 . . . . .135 BP104
Greenland St, NW1
off Camden High St 83 DH67
Green La, E4 . . . . .32 EE41
NW4 . . . . .63 CX57
SE9 . . . . .125 EN89
SE20 . . . . .123 DX94
SW16 . . . . .121 DM94
W7 .97 CE75
Addlestone KT15 . . . . .134 BG104
Amersham HP6 . . . . .20 AS38
Ashtead KT21 . . . . .171 CJ117
Brentwood (Pilg.Hat.)
CM15 . . . . .54 FV43
Brentwood (Warley) CM14 . .53 FU52
Caterham CR3 . . . . .176 DQ122
Chertsey KT16 . . . . .133 BE103
Chesham HP5 . . . . .4 AV33
Chessington KT9 . . . . .156 CL109
Chigwell IG7 . . . . .49 ER47
Chislehurst BR7 . . . . .125 EP91
Cobham KT11 . . . . .154 BY112
Coulsdon CR5 . . . . .184 DA125
Dagenham RM8 . . . . .70 EU60
Edgware HA8 . . . . .42 CN50
Egham TW20 . . . . .113 BB91
Egham (Thorpe) TW20 . . . .133 BD95
Feltham TW13 . . . . .116 BY92
Harrow HA1 . . . . .61 CE62
Hemel Hempstead (Bov.)
HP3 . . . . .5 AZ28
Hounslow TW4 . . . . .95 BV83
Ilford IG1, IG3 . . . . .69 EQ61
Leatherhead KT22 . . . . . . .171 CK121
Morden SM4 . . . . .140 DB100
New Malden KT3 . . . . .138 CQ99
Northwood HA6 . . . . .39 BT52
Purley CR8 . . . . .159 DJ111
Redhill RH1 . . . . .184 DE132
Redhill (Bletch.) RH1 . . . . .186 DS131
Reigate RH2 . . . . .183 CZ134
Rickmansworth (Crox.Grn.)
WD3 . . . . .22 BM43
Shepperton TW17 . . . . . . .135 BQ100
Slough (Datchet) SL3 . . . . . .92 AV81
South Ockendon RM15 . . . . .91 FR69
Staines TW18 . . . . .133 BE95
Stanmore HA7 . . . . .41 CH49
Sunbury-on-Thames TW16 .115 BT94
Tadworth KT20 . . . . .183 CZ126
Thornton Heath CR7 . . . . . .141 DN95
Upminster RM14 . . . . .91 FR68
Uxbridge UB8 . . . . .77 BQ71
Waltham Abbey EN9 . . . . . . .16 EJ34
Walton-on-Thames KT12 . . .153 BV107
Warlingham CR6 . . . . .177 DY116
Watford WD19 . . . . .40 BW46
West Byfleet (Byfleet)
KT14 . . . . .152 BM112
West Molesey KT8 . . . . . . .136 CB99
Woking (Chobham) GU24 .150 AT110
Woking (Mayford) GU24
off Copper Beech Cl 166 AV121
Woking (Ockham) GU23 . .169 BP124
Worcester Park KT4 . . . . . .139 CU102
Green La Av, Walt. KT12 . . . . .154 BW106
Green La Cl, Cher. KT16 . . . . .133 BE103
West Byfleet (Byfleet)
KT14 . . . . .152 BM112
Green La Gdns, Th.Hth. CR7 . .142 DQ96
Green Las, N4 . . . . .66 DQ60
N8 .65 DP55
N13 . . . . .45 DM51
N15 . . . . .65 DP55
N16 . . . . .66 DQ62
N21 . . . . .45 DP46
Epsom KT19 . . . . .156 CS109
Greenlaw Gdns, N.Mal. KT3 . .139 CT101
Green Lawns, Ruis. HA4 . . . . . .60 BW60
Greenlaw St, SE18 . . . . .105 EN76
Green Leaf Av, Wall. SM6 . . . .159 DK105
Greenleaf Cl, SW2
off Tulse Hill 121 DN87
Greenleafe Dr, Ilf. IG6 . . . . . . .69 EP56
Greenleaf Rd, E6
off Redclyffe Rd 86 EJ67
E17 . . . . .67 DZ55
Greenlea Pk, SW19 . . . . .140 DD95
Green Leas, Sun. TW16 . . . . . .115 BT93
Waltham Abbey EN9
off Roundhills 15 ED34
Green Leas Cl, Sun. TW16
off Green Leas 115 BT93
Greenleaves Ct, Ashf. TW15
off Redleaves Av 115 BP93
Greenleigh Av, Orp. BR5 . . . .146 EV98
Green Man Gdns, W13 . . . . . . .79 CG73
Green Man La, W13 . . . . .79 CG74
Feltham TW14 . . . . .95 BU84
Green Manor Way, Grav.
DA11 . . . . .110 FZ84
Green Man Pas, W13 . . . . .79 CG73
Green Man Roundabout, E11 . .68 EF59
Greenman St, N1 . . . . .84 DQ66
Green Mead, Esher KT10
off Winterdown Gdns 154 BZ107
Greenmead Cl, SE25 . . . . . . .142 DU99
Green Meadow, Pot.B. EN6 . . . .12 DA30
Greenmeads, Wok. GU22 . . . .166 AY122
Green Moor Link, N21 . . . . . . .45 DP45
Greenmoor Rd, Enf. EN3 . . . . .30 DW40
Green N Rd, Beac. (Jordans)
HP9 . . . . .36 AS51
Greenoak Pl, Barn. EN4 . . . . . .28 DF40
Greenoak Ri, West. (Bigg.H.)
TN16 . . . . .178 EJ118
Greenoak Way, SW19 . . . . . . .119 CX91
Greenock Rd, SW16 . . . . .141 DK95
W3 .98 CP76
Greenock Way, Rom. RM1 . . . . .51 FE51
Greeno Cres, Shep. TW17 . . . .134 BN99
★ Green Park, SW1 . . . . .199 J4
⊖ Green Park 199 K3
Green Pk, Stai. TW18 . . . . . . .113 BE90
Greenpark Ct, Wem. HA0 . . . . .79 CJ66
Green Pk Way, Grnf. UB6 . . . . .79 CE67
Green Pl, Dart. DA1 . . . . .127 FE85
Green Pt, E15 . . . . .86 EE65
Green Pond Cl, E17 . . . . .67 DZ55
Green Pond Rd, E17 . . . . .67 DY55
Green Ride, Epp. CM16 . . . . . .33 EP35
Loughton IG10 . . . . .32 EG43
Green Rd, N14 . . . . .29 DH44
N20 . . . . .44 DC48
Egham (Thorpe) TW20 . . . .133 BB98
Greenroof Way, SE10 . . . . . . .205 L7
Greensand Cl, Red. (S.Merst.)
RH1 . . . . .185 DK128
Green Sand Rd, Red. RH1 . . . .184 DG133
Greens Cl, The, Loug. IG10 . . .33 EN40
Green's Ct, W1 . . . . .195 M10
Green's End, SE18 . . . . .105 EP77
Greenshank Cl, E17
off Banbury Rd 47 DY52
Greenshaw, Brwd. CM14 . . . . .54 FV46
Greenshields Ind Est, E16 . . .205 P3
Greenside, Bex. DA5 . . . . . . .126 EY88
Borehamwood WD6 . . . . . . .26 CN38
Dagenham RM8 . . . . .70 EW60
Swanley BR8 . . . . .147 FD96
Greenside Cl, N20 . . . . .44 DD47
SE6 . . . . .123 ED89
Greenside Dr, Ashtd. KT21 . . .171 CH118
Greenside Rd, W12 . . . . .99 CU76
Croydon CR0 . . . . .141 DN101
Weybridge KT13 . . . . .135 BP104
Greenside Wk, West. (Bigg.H.)
TN16 off Kings Rd 178 EH118
Greenslade Av, Ashtd. KT21 . .172 CP119
Greenslade Rd, Bark. IG11 . . . .87 ER66
Green Slip Rd, Barn. EN5 . . . . .27 CZ40
Greenstead Av, Wdf.Grn.
IG8 . . . . .48 EJ52
Greenstead Cl, Brwd. CM13 . . .55 GE45
Woodford Green IG8
off Greenstead Gdns 48 EJ51
Greenstead Gdns, SW15 . . . . .119 CU85
Woodford Green IG8 . . . . . .48 EJ51
GREENSTEAD GREEN, Ong. 19 FH28
Greensted Rd, Loug. IG10 . . . . .48 EL45
Ongar CM5 . . . . .19 FG28
Greenstone Ms, E11 . . . . .68 EG58
GREEN STREET, Borwd. 26 CP37
Green St, E7 . . . . .86 EH65
E13 . . . . .86 EJ67
W1 . . . . .194 E10
Borehamwood WD6 . . . . . . .26 CN36
Enfield EN3 . . . . .30 DW40
Radlett (Shenley) WD7 . . . . .26 CN36
Rickmansworth (Chorl.)
WD3 . . . . .21 BC40
Sunbury-on-Thames
TW16 . . . . .135 BU95
GREEN STREET GREEN,
Dart. 129 FU93
GREEN STREET GREEN,
Orp. 163 ES107
Green St Grn Rd, Dart.
DA1, DA2 . . . . .128 FP88
Greensward, Bushey WD23 . . . .24 CB44
Green Ter, EC1 . . . . .196 E3
Green Tiles La, Uxb. (Denh.)
UB9 . . . . .57 BF58
Greentrees, Epp. CM16 . . . . . .18 EU31
Green Vale, W5 . . . . .80 CM72
Bexleyheath DA6 . . . . .126 EX85
Greenvale Rd, SE9 . . . . .105 EM84
Green Verges, Stan. HA7 . . . . .41 CK52
Green Vw, Chess. KT9 . . . . . .156 CM108
Greenview Av, Beck. BR3 . . . .143 DY100
Croydon CR0 . . . . .143 DY100
Greenview Cl, W3 . . . . .80 CS74
Green Vw Cl, Hem.H. (Bov.)
HP3 . . . . .5 BA29
Greenview Ct, Ashf. TW15
off Village Way 114 BM91
Green Wk, NW4 . . . . .63 CX57
SE1 . . . . .201 M7
Buckhurst Hill IG9 . . . . .48 EL45
Dartford DA1 . . . . .107 FF84
Hampton TW12
off Orpwood Cl 116 BZ93
Ruislip HA4 . . . . .59 BT60
Southall UB2 . . . . .96 CA78
Woodford Green IG8 . . . . . . .48 EL51
Green Wk, The, E4 . . . . .47 EC46
Greenway, N14 . . . . .45 DL47
N20 . . . . .44 DA47
Green Way, SE9 . . . . .124 EK85
Greenway, SW20 . . . . .139 CW98
Brentwood CM13 . . . . .55 GA45
Green Way, Brom. BR2 . . . . . .144 EL100
Greenway, Chis. BR7 . . . . . . .125 EN92
Dagenham RM8 . . . . .70 EW61
Harrow HA3 . . . . .62 CL57
Hayes UB4 . . . . .77 BV70
Leatherhead KT23 . . . . . . .170 CB123
Pinner HA5 . . . . .39 BV54
Green Way, Red. RH1 . . . . . . .184 DE132
Greenway, Rom. RM3 . . . . .52 FP51
Green Way, Sun. TW16 . . . . . .135 BU98
Greenway, Wall. SM6 . . . . . . .159 DJ105
Westerham (Tats.) TN16 . . .178 EJ120
Woodford Green IG8 . . . . . . .48 EJ50
Greenway, The, NW9 . . . . .42 CR54
Enfield EN3 . . . . .31 DX35
Epsom KT18 . . . . .172 CN115
Gerrards Cross (Chal.St.P.)
SL9 . . . . .56 AX55
Harrow HA3 . . . . .41 CE53
Hounslow TW4 . . . . .96 BZ84
Orpington BR5 . . . . .146 EV100
Oxted RH8 . . . . .188 EH133
Pinner HA5 . . . . .60 BZ58
Potters Bar EN6 . . . . .12 DA33
Rickmansworth (Mill End)
WD3 . . . . .38 BG45
Uxbridge UB8 . . . . .76 BJ68
Uxbridge (Ickhm.) UB10 . . . .59 BQ61
Greenway Av, E17 . . . . .67 ED56
Greenway Cl, N4 . . . . .66 DQ61
N11 . . . . .44 DG51
N15 off Copperfield Dr 66 DT56
N20 . . . . .44 DA47
NW9 . . . . .42 CR54
West Byfleet KT14 . . . . . . .152 BG113
Greenway Dr, Stai. TW18 . . . .134 BK95
Greenway Gdns, NW9 . . . . . . .42 CR54
Croydon CR0 . . . . .143 DZ104
Greenford UB6 . . . . .78 CA69
Harrow HA3 . . . . .41 CE54
Greenways, Abb.L. WD5 . . . . . .7 BS32
Beckenham BR3 . . . . .143 EA96
Egham TW20 . . . . .112 AY93
Esher KT10 . . . . .155 CE105
Tadworth KT20 . . . . .183 CV125
Waltham Cross (Chsht.)
EN7 . . . . .13 DP29
Woking GU22
off Pembroke Rd 167 BA117
Greenways, The, Twick. TW1
off South Western Rd 117 CG86
Greenwell Cl, Gdse. RH9 . . . .186 DV130
Greenwell St, W1 . . . . .195 J5
Green W Rd, Beac. (Jordans)
HP9 . . . . .36 AS52
GREENWICH, SE10 . . . . .103 ED79
⇌ Greenwich 103 EB80
DLR Greenwich 103 EB80
★ Greenwich Borough Mus, SE18
off Plumstead High St . . .105 ET78
Greenwich Ch St, SE10 . . . . . .103 EC79
Greenwich Ct, Wal.Cr. EN8
off Parkside 15 DY34
Greenwich Cres, E6
off Swan App 86 EL71
Greenwich Foot Tunnel, E14 . .103 EC78
SE10 . . . . .103 EC78
Greenwich High Rd, SE10 . . . .103 EB81
Greenwich Ind Est, SE7 . . . . .205 P9
Greenwich Mkt, SE10
off King William Wk 103 EC79
★ Greenwich Park, SE10 . . . .103 ED80
Greenwich Pk, SE10 . . . . .104 EE80
Greenwich Pk St, SE10 . . . . . .103 ED78
★ Greenwich Pier, SE10 . . . . .103 EC79
Greenwich S St, SE10 . . . . . .103 EB81
Greenwich Vw Pl, E14 . . . . . .204 B7
Greenwich Way, Wal.Abb.
EN9 . . . . .31 EC36
Greenwood Av, Dag. RM10 . . . .71 FB63
Enfield EN3 . . . . .31 DY40
Waltham Cross (Chsht.)
EN7 . . . . .14 DV31
Greenwood Cl, Add. (Woodham)
KT15 . . . . .151 BF111
Amersham HP6 . . . . .20 AS37
Bushey (Bushey Hth.) WD23
off Langmead Dr 41 CE45
Morden SM4 . . . . .139 CY98
Orpington BR5 . . . . .145 ES100
Sidcup DA15
off Hurst Rd 126 EU89
Thames Ditton KT7 . . . . . .137 CG102
Waltham Cross (Chsht.) EN7
off Greenwood Av 14 DV31
Greenwood Ct, SW1 . . . . .199 K10
Greenwood Dr, E4
off Avril Way 47 EC50
Watford WD25 . . . . .7 BV34
Greenwood Gdns, N13 . . . . . . .45 DP48
Caterham CR3 . . . . .186 DU125
Ilford IG6 . . . . .49 EQ52
Oxted RH8 . . . . .188 EG134
Radlett (Shenley) WD7 . . . . .10 CL33
Greenwood Ho, Grays RM17
off Argent St 110 GA79
Greenwood La, Hmptn. (Hmptn.H.)
TW12 . . . . .116 CB92
Greenwood Pk, Kings.T. KT2 . .118 CS94
Greenwood Pl, NW5
off Highgate Rd 65 DH64
Greenwood Rd, E8 . . . . .84 DU65
E13 off Maud Rd 86 EF68
Bexley DA5 . . . . .127 FD91
Chigwell IG7 . . . . .50 EV49
Croydon CR0 . . . . .141 DP101
Isleworth TW7 . . . . .97 CE83
Mitcham CR4 . . . . .141 DK97
Thames Ditton KT7 . . . . . .137 CG102
Woking GU21 . . . . .166 AS120
Greenwoods, The, Har. (S.Har.)
HA2 . . . . .60 CC61
Greenwood Ter, NW10 . . . . . . .80 CR67
Greenwood Way, Sev. TN13 . .190 FF125
Green Wrythe Cres, Cars.
SM5 . . . . .140 DE102
Green Wrythe La, Cars. SM5 .140 DD100
Greenyard, Wal.Abb. EN9 . . . . .15 EC33
Greer Rd, Har. HA3 . . . . .40 CC53
Greet St, SE1 . . . . .200 E3
Greg Cl, E10 . . . . .67 EC58
Gregor Ms, SE3 . . . . .104 EG80
Gregory Av, Pot.B. EN6 . . . . . .12 DC33
Gregory Cl, Wok. GU21 . . . . .166 AW117
Gregory Cres, SE9 . . . . .124 EK87
Gregory Dr, Wind. (Old Wind.)
SL4 . . . . .112 AV86
Gregory Ms, Wal.Abb. EN9
off Beaulieu Dr 15 EB33
Gregory Pl, W8 . . . . .100 DB75
Gregory Rd, Rom. RM6 . . . . . . .70 EX56
Southall UB2 . . . . .96 CA76
Gregson Cl, Borwd. WD6 . . . . .26 CQ39
Gregson's Ride, Loug. IG10 . . .33 EN38
Greig Cl, N8 . . . . .65 DL57
Greig Ter, SE17
off Lorrimore Sq 101 DP79
Grenaby Av, Croy. CR0 . . . . . .142 DR101
Grenaby Rd, Croy. CR0 . . . . . .142 DR101
Grenada Rd, SE7 . . . . .104 EJ80
Grenade St, E14 . . . . .85 DZ73
Grenadier Pl, Cat. CR3 . . . . . .176 DQ122
Grenadier St, E16 . . . . .87 EN74
Grenadine Cl, Wal.Cr. EN7
off Allwood Rd 14 DT27
Grena Gdns, Rich. TW9 . . . . . .98 CM84
Grena Rd, Rich. TW9 . . . . .98 CM84
Grendon Gdns, Wem. HA9 . . .62 CN61
Grendon St, NW8 . . . . .194 B4
Grenfell Av, Horn. RM12 . . . . .71 FF60
Grenfell Cl, Borwd. WD6 . . . . .26 CQ39
Grenfell Gdns, Har. HA3 . . . . .62 CL59
Grenfell Rd, W11 . . . . .81 CX73
Mitcham CR4 . . . . .120 DF93
Grenfell Twr, W11 . . . . .81 CX73
Grenfell Wk, W11 . . . . .81 CX73
Grennell Cl, Sutt. SM1 . . . . . .140 DD103
Grennell Rd, Sutt. SM1 . . . . .140 DC103
Grenoble Gdns, N13 . . . . .45 DN51
Grenville Cl, N3 . . . . .43 CZ53
Cobham KT11 . . . . .154 BX113
Surbiton KT5 . . . . .138 CQ102
Waltham Cross EN8 . . . . . . .15 DX32
Grenville Gdns, Wdf.Grn. IG8 . .48 EJ53
Grenville Ms, SW7 . . . . .100 DC77
Hampton TW12 . . . . .116 CB92
Grenville Pl, NW7 . . . . .42 CR50
SW7 . . . . .100 DC76
Grenville Rd, N19 . . . . .65 DL60
Croydon (New Adgtn.)
CR0 . . . . .161 EC109
Grays (Chaff.Hun.) RM16 . .109 FV78
Grenville St, WC1 . . . . .196 A5
Gresham Av, N20 . . . . .44 DF49
Warlingham CR6 . . . . .177 DY118
Gresham Cl, Bex. DA5 . . . . . .126 EY86
Brentwood CM14 . . . . .54 FW48
Enfield EN2 . . . . .30 DQ41
Oxted RH8 . . . . .188 EF128
Gresham Dr, Rom. RM6 . . . . . .70 EV57
Gresham Gdns, NW11 . . . . . . .63 CY60
Gresham Rd, E6 . . . . .87 EM68
E16 . . . . .86 EH72
NW10 . . . . .62 CR64
SE25 . . . . .142 DU98
SW9 . . . . .101 DN83
Beckenham BR3 . . . . .143 DY96
Brentwood CM14 . . . . .54 FW48
Edgware HA8 . . . . .42 CM51
Hampton TW12 . . . . .116 CA93
Hounslow TW3 . . . . .96 CC81
Oxted RH8 . . . . .188 EF128
Staines TW18 . . . . .113 BF92
Uxbridge UB10 . . . . .76 BN68
Gresham St, EC2 . . . . .197 H8
Gresham Way, SW19 . . . . . . .120 DA90
Gresley Cl, E17 . . . . .67 DY58
N15 off Clinton Rd 66 DR56
Gresley Ct, Pot.B. EN6 . . . . . . .12 DC29
Gresley Rd, N19 . . . . .65 DJ60
Gressenhall Rd, SW18 . . . . . .119 CZ86
Gresse St, W1 . . . . .195 M7
Gresswell Cl, Sid. DA14 . . . . .126 EU90
Greswell St, SW6 . . . . .99 CX81
Gretton Rd, N17 . . . . .46 DS52
Greville Av, S.Croy. CR2 . . . . .161 DX110
Greville Cl, Ashtd. KT21 . . . .172 CL119
Twickenham TW1 . . . . .117 CH87
Greville Hall, NW6 . . . . .82 DB68
Greville Ms, NW6
off Greville Rd 82 DB68
Greville Pk Av, Ashtd. KT21 . .172 CL118
Greville Pk Rd, Ashtd. KT21 . .172 CL118
Greville Pl, NW6 . . . . .82 DB68
Greville Rd, E17 . . . . .67 EC56
NW6 . . . . .82 DB67
Richmond TW10 . . . . .118 CM86
Greville St, EC1 . . . . .196 E7
Grey Alders, Bans. SM7
off High Beeches 157 CW114
Greycaine Rd, Wat. WD24 . . . .24 BX37
Grey Cl, NW11 . . . . .64 DC58
Greycoat Pl, SW1 . . . . .199 M7
Greycoat St, SW1 . . . . .199 M7
Greycot Rd, Beck. BR3 . . . . . .123 EA92
Grey Eagle St, E1 . . . . .197 P6
Greyfell Cl, Stan. HA7
off Coverdale Cl 41 CH50
Greyfields Cl, Pur. CR8 . . . . .159 DP113
Greyfriars, Brwd. CM13 . . . . . .55 GB45
Greyfriars Pas, EC1 . . . . .196 G8
Greyfriars Rd, Wok. (Ripley)
GU23 . . . . .168 BG124
Greyhound Hill, NW4 . . . . .63 CU55
Greyhound La, SW16 . . . . . . .121 DK93
Grays (Orsett) RM16 . . . . . .111 GG75
Potters Bar EN6 . . . . .11 CU33
Greyhound Rd, N17 . . . . .66 DS55
NW10 . . . . .81 CV69
W6 .99 CX79
W14 . . . . .99 CY79
Sutton SM1 . . . . .158 DC106
Greyhound Ter, SW16 . . . . . . .141 DJ95
Greyhound Way, Dart. DA1 . . .127 FE86
Greys Pk Cl, Kes. BR2 . . . . . .162 EJ106
Greystead Rd, SE23 . . . . .122 DW87
Greystoke Av, Pnr. HA5 . . . . . .60 CA55
Greystoke Dr, Ruis. HA4 . . . . .59 BP58
Greystoke Gdns, W5 . . . . .80 CL70
Enfield EN2 . . . . .29 DK42
Greystoke Pk Ter, W5 . . . . . . .79 CK69
Greystoke Pl, EC4 . . . . .196 D8
Greystone Cl, S.Croy. CR2 . . .160 DW111
Greystone Gdns, Har. HA3 . . . .61 CJ58
Ilford IG6 . . . . .49 EQ54
Greystone Path, E11
off Grove Rd 68 EF59
Greystones Dr, Reig. RH2 . . .184 DC132
Greyswood St, SW16 . . . . . . .121 DH93
Greythorne Rd, Wok. GU21 . . .166 AU118
Grey Twrs Av, Horn. RM11 . . . .72 FK60
Grey Twrs Gdns, Horn. RM11
off Grey Twrs Av 72 FK60
Grice Av, West. (Bigg.H.)
TN16 . . . . .162 EH113
Gridiron Pl, Upmin. RM14 . . . . .72 FP62
Grierson Rd, SE23 . . . . .123 DX87
Grieves Rd, Grav. (Nthflt.)
DA11 . . . . .131 GF90
Griffin Av, Upmin. RM14 . . . . .73 FS58
Griffin Cen, The, Felt. TW14 . .115 BV85
Griffin Cl, NW10 . . . . .63 CV64
Griffin Manor Way, SE28 . . . .105 ER76

★ Place of interest ⇌ Railway station ⊖ London Underground station DLR Docklands Light Railway station Tramlink station H Hospital

Griffin Rd, N17 .46 DS54
SE18 .105 ER78
Griffins, The, Grays RM16 .110 GB75
Griffin Wk, Green. DA9
off Church Rd .129 FT85
Griffin Way, Sun.TW16 .135 BU96
Griffith Cl, Dag. RM8
off Gibson Rd .70 EW60
Griffiths Cl, Wor.Pk. KT4 .139 CV103
Griffiths Rd, SW19 .120 DA94
Griffon Way, Wat. WD25
off Ashfields .7 BT34
Grifon Rd, Grays (Chaff.Hun.)
RM16 .109 FW76
Griggs App, Ilf. IG1 .69 EQ61
Griggs Gdns, Horn. RM12
off Tylers Cres .72 FJ64
Griggs Pl, SE1 .201 N7
Griggs Rd, E10 .67 EC58
Grilse Cl, N9 .46 DV49
Grimsby Gro, E16 .87 EP74
Grimsby St, E2
off Cheshire St .84 DU70
Grimsdyke Cres, Barn. EN5 .27 CW41
Grimsdyke Rd, Pnr. HA5 .40 BY52
Grimsel Path, SE5
off Laxley Cl .101 DP80
Grimshaw Cl, N6 .64 DG59
Grimshaw Way, Rom. RM1 .71 FF57
Grimstone Cl, Rom. RM5 .51 FB51
Grimston Rd, SW6 .99 CZ82
Grimwade Av, Croy. CR0 .142 DU104
Grimwade Cl, SE15 .102 DW83
Grimwood Rd, Twick. TW1 .117 CF87
Grindall Cl, Croy. CR0
off Hillside Rd .159 DP105
Grindal St, SE1 .200 D5
Grindleford Av, N11 .44 DG47
Grindley Gdns, Croy. CR0 .142 DT100
Grinling Pl, SE8 .103 EA79
Grinstead Rd, SE8 .103 DY78
Grisedale Cl, Pur. CR8 .160 DS114
Grisedale Gdns, Pur. CR8 .160 DS114
Grittleton Av, Wem. HA9 .80 CP65
Grittleton Rd, W9 .82 DA70
Grizedale Ter, SE23 .122 DV89
Grobars Av, Wok. GU21 .166 AW115
Grocer's Hall Ct, EC2 .197 K9
Grogan Cl, Hmptn. TW12 .116 BZ93
Groombridge Cl, Walt. KT12 .153 BV106
Welling DA16 .126 EU85
Groombridge Rd, E9 .85 DX66
Groom Cl, Brom. BR2 .144 EH98
Groom Cres, SW18 .120 DD87
Groomfield Cl, SW17 .120 DG91
Groom Pl, SW1 .198 G6
Groom Rd, Brox. EN10 .15 DZ26
Grooms Cotts, Chesh. HP5 .4 AV30
Grooms Dr, Pnr. HA5 .59 BU57
Grosmont Rd, SE18 .105 ET78
Grosse Way, SW15 .119 CV86
Grosvenor Av, N5 .66 DQ64
SW14 .98 CS83
Carshalton SM5 .158 DF107
Harrow HA2 .60 CB58
Hayes UB4 .77 BS68
Kings Langley WD4 .7 BQ28
Richmond TW10
off Grosvenor Rd .118 CL85
Grosvenor Cl, Iver SL0 .75 BD69
Loughton IG10 .33 EP39
Grosvenor Cotts, SW1 .198 F8
Grosvenor Ct, N14 .45 DJ45
NW6 .81 CX67
Rickmansworth (Crox.Grn.) WD3
off Mayfare .23 BR43
Slough SL1
off Stoke Poges La .74 AS72
Grosvenor Cres, NW9 .62 CN56
SW1 .198 G5
Dartford DA1 .128 FK85
Uxbridge UB10 .77 BP66
Grosvenor Cres Ms, SW1 .198 F5
Grosvenor Dr, Horn. RM11 .72 FJ60
Loughton IG10 .33 EP39
Grosvenor Est, SW1 .199 N8
Grosvenor Gdns, E6 .86 EK69
N10 .65 DJ55
N14 .29 DK43
NW2 .63 CW64
NW11 .63 CZ58
SW1 .199 H6
SW14 .98 CS83
Kingston upon Thames
KT2 .117 CK93
Upminster RM14 .73 FR60
Wallington SM6 .159 DJ108
Woodford Green IG8 .48 EG51
Grosvenor Gdns Ms E, SW1 .199 J6
Grosvenor Gdns Ms N, SW1 .199 H7
Grosvenor Gdns Ms S, SW1 .199 J7
Grosvenor Gate, W1 .198 E1
Grosvenor Hill, SW19 .119 CY93
W1 .195 H10
Grosvenor Pk, SE5 .102 DQ79
Grosvenor Pk Rd, E17 .67 EA57
Grosvenor Path, Loug. IG10 .33 EP39
Grosvenor Pl, SW1 .198 G5
Weybridge KT13
off Vale Rd .135 BR104
Grosvenor Ri E, E17 .67 EB57
Grosvenor Rd, E6 .86 EK67
E7 .86 EH65
E10 .67 EC60
E11 .68 EG57
N3 .43 CZ52
N9 .46 DV46
N10 .45 DH53
SE25 .142 DU98
SW1 .101 DH79
W4 .98 CP78
W7 .79 CG74
Belvedere DA17 .106 FA79
Bexleyheath DA6 .126 EX85
Borehamwood WD6 .26 CN41
Brentford TW8 .97 CK79
Dagenham RM8 .70 EZ60
Grosvenor Rd, Epsom KT18 .172 CR119
Hounslow TW3 .96 BZ83
Ilford IG1 .69 EQ62
Northwood HA6 .39 BT50
Orpington BR5 .145 ES100
Richmond TW10 .118 CL85
Romford RM7 .71 FD59
Southall UB2 .96 BZ76
Staines TW18 .114 BG94
Twickenham TW1 .117 CG87
Wallington SM6 .159 DH107
Watford WD17 .24 BW42
West Wickham BR4 .143 EB102
Grosvenor Sq, W1 .194 G10
Kings Langley WD4
off Grosvenor Av .7 BQ28
Grosvenor St, W1 .195 H10
Grosvenor Ter, SE5 .101 DP80
Grosvenor Vale, Ruis. HA4 .59 BT61
Grosvenor Way, E5 .66 DW61
Grosvenor Wf Rd, E14 .204 F9
Grote's Bldgs, SE3 .104 EE82
Grote's Pl, SE3 .104 EE82
Groton Rd, SW18 .120 DB89
Grotto Pas, W1 .194 G6
Grotto Rd, Twick. TW1 .117 CF89
Weybridge KT13 .135 BP104
Grove, The, E15 .86 EE65
N3 .44 DA53
N4 .65 DM59
N6 .64 DG60
N8 .65 DK57
N13 .45 DN50
N14 .29 DJ43
NW9 .62 CR57
NW11 .63 CY59
W5 .79 CK74
Addlestone KT15 .152 BH106
Bexleyheath DA6 .106 EX84
Brentwood CM14 .54 FT49
Caterham CR3 .175 DP121
Chesham HP5 .20 AX36
Coulsdon CR5 .175 DK115
Edgware HA8 .42 CP49
Egham TW20 .113 BA92
Enfield EN2 .29 DN40
Epsom KT17 .156 CS113
Epsom (Ewell) KT17 .157 CT110
Esher KT10 .136 CB102
Gravesend DA12 .131 GH87
Greenford UB6 .78 CC72
Hatfield AL9 .12 DA27
Isleworth TW7 .97 CE81
Potters Bar EN6 .12 DC32
Radlett WD7 .9 CG34
Sidcup DA14 .126 EY91
Slough SL1 .92 AU75
Stanmore HA7 .41 CG47
Swanley BR8 .147 FF97
Swanscombe DA10 .130 FZ85
Teddington TW11 .117 CG91
Twickenham TW1
off Bridge Rd .117 CH86
Upminster RM14 .72 FP63
Uxbridge UB10 .58 BN64
Walton-on-Thames KT12 .135 BV101
Watford WD17 .23 BQ37
West Wickham BR4 .143 EB104
Westerham (Bigg.H.) TN16 .178 EK118
Woking GU21 .167 AZ116
Grove Av, N3 .44 DA52
N10 .45 DJ54
W7 .79 CE72
Epsom KT17 .156 CS113
Pinner HA5 .60 BY56
Sutton SM1 .158 DA107
Twickenham TW1 .117 CF88
Grove Bk, Wat. WD19 .40 BX46
Grovebarns, Stai. TW18 .114 BG93
Grovebury Cl, Erith DA8 .107 FD79
Grovebury Gdns, St.Alb. (Park St.)
AL2 .8 CC27
Grovebury Rd, SE2 .106 EV75
Grove Cl, N14 *off Avenue Rd* .45 DH45
SE23 .123 DX88
Bromley BR2 .144 EG103
Feltham TW13 .116 BY91
Gerrards Cross (Chal.St.P.) SL9
off Grove La .36 AW53
Kingston upon Thames
KT1 .138 CM98
Slough SL1 *off Alpha St S* .92 AU76
Uxbridge UB10 .58 BN64
Windsor (Old Wind.) SL4 .112 AV87
Grove Cotts, SW3 .100 DE79
Grove Ct, SE3 .104 EG81
Barnet EN5 *off High St* .27 CZ41
East Molesey KT8
off Walton Rd .137 CD99
Waltham Abbey EN9
off Highbridge St .15 EB33
Grove Cres, E18 .48 EF54
NW9 .62 CQ56
SE5 .102 DS82
Feltham TW13 .116 BY91
Kingston upon Thames
KT1 .138 CL97
Rickmansworth (Crox.Grn.)
WD3 .22 BN42
Walton-on-Thames KT12 .135 BV101
Grove Cres Rd, E15 .85 ED65
Grovedale Cl, Wal.Cr. (Chsht.)
EN7 .14 DT30
Grovedale Rd, N19 .65 DK61
Grove End, E18
off Grove Hill .48 EF54
NW5 *off Chetwynd Rd* .65 DH63
Gerrards Cross (Chal.St.P.)
SL9 .36 AW53
Grove End Gdns, NW8
off Grove End Rd .82 DD68
Grove End La, Esher KT10 .137 CD102
Grove End Rd, NW8 .82 DD69
Grove Fm Ct, Mitch. CR4
off Brookfields Av .140 DF98
Grove Fm Pk, Nthwd. HA6 .39 BR50
Grove Footpath, Surb. KT5 .138 CL98
Grove Gdns, NW4 .63 CU56
NW8 .194 C3
Dagenham RM10 .71 FC62
Enfield EN3 .31 DX39
Teddington TW11 .117 CG91
Grove Grn Rd, E11 .67 EC62
Grove Hall Ct, NW8
off Hall Rd .82 DC69
Grove Hall Rd, Bushey WD23 .24 BY42
Grove Heath, Wok. (Ripley)
GU23 .168 BJ124
Grove Heath Ct, Wok. (Ripley)
GU23 .168 BJ124
Grove Heath N, Wok. (Ripley)
GU23 .168 BH122
Grove Heath Rd, Wok. (Ripley)
GU23 .168 BJ123
Groveherst Rd, Dart. DA1 .108 FM83
Grove Hill, E18 .48 EF54
Gerrards Cross (Chal.St.P.)
SL9 .36 AW52
Harrow HA1 .61 CE59
Grove Hill Rd, SE5 .102 DS83
Harrow HA1 .61 CE59
Grovehill Rd, Red. RH1 .184 DE134
Grove Ho Rd, N8 .65 DL56
Groveland Av, SW16 .121 DM94
Groveland Ct, EC4 .197 J9
Groveland Rd, Beck. BR3 .143 DZ97
Grovelands, St.Alb. (Park St.)
AL2 .8 CB27
West Molesey KT8 .136 CA98
Grovelands Cl, SE5 .102 DS82
Harrow HA2 .60 CB62
Grovelands Ct, N14 .45 DK45
Grovelands Rd, N13 .45 DM49
N15 .66 DU58
Orpington BR5 .126 EU94
Purley CR8 .159 DL112
Grovelands Way, Grays
RM17 .110 FZ78
Groveland Way, N.Mal. KT3 .138 CQ99
Grove La, SE5 .102 DR81
Chesham HP5 .4 AV27
Chigwell IG7 .49 ET48
Coulsdon CR5 .158 DG113
Epping CM16 *off High St* .18 EU30
Gerrards Cross (Chal.St.P.)
SL9 .36 AW53
Kingston upon Thames
KT1 .138 CL98
Uxbridge UB8 .76 BM70
Grove La Ter, SE5
off Grove La .102 DS83
Groveley Rd, Sun. TW16 .115 BT92
Grove Mkt Pl, SE9 .125 EM86
Grove Ms, W6 .99 CW76
W11 *off Portobello Rd* .81 CZ72
Grove Mill La, Wat. WD17 .23 BP37
Grove Mill Pl, Cars. SM5 .140 DG104
GROVE PARK, SE12 .124 EG89
GROVE PARK, W4 .98 CP80
⇌ **Grove Park** .124 EG90
Grove Pk, E11 .68 EH58
NW9 .62 CQ56
SE5 .102 DS82
Grove Pk Av, E4 .47 EB52
Grove Pk Br, W4 .98 CQ80
Grove Pk Gdns, W4 .98 CP79
Grove Pk Ms, W4 .98 CQ80
Grove Pk Rd, N15 .66 DS56
SE9 .124 EJ90
W4 .98 CP80
Rainham RM13 .89 FG67
Grove Pk Ter, W4 .98 CP79
Grove Pas, E2 .84 DV68
Teddington TW11 .117 CG92
Grove Path, Wal.Cr. (Chsht.)
EN7 .14 DU31
Grove Pl, NW3
off Christchurch Hill .64 DD63
SW12 *off Cathles Rd* .121 DH86
W3 .80 CQ74
W5 *off The Grove* .79 CK74
Banstead SM7 .158 DF112
Barking IG11
off Clockhouse Av .87 EQ67
Watford WD25 .24 CB39
Weybridge KT13
off Princes Rd .153 BQ106
Grove Rd, E3 .85 DX67
E4 .47 EB49
E11 .68 EF59
E17 .67 EB58
E18 .48 EF54
N11 .45 DH50
N12 .44 DD50
N15 .66 DS57
NW2 .81 CW65
SW13 .99 CT82
SW19 .120 DC94
W3 .80 CQ74
W5 .79 CK73
Amersham HP6 .20 AT37
Ashtead KT21 .172 CM118
Barnet EN4 .28 DE41
Belvedere DA17 .106 EZ79
Bexleyheath DA7 .107 FC84
Borehamwood WD6 .26 CN39
Brentford TW8 .97 CJ78
Chertsey KT16 .133 BF100
East Molesey KT8 .137 CD98
Edgware HA8 .42 CN51
Epsom KT17 .156 CS113
Gravesend (Nthflt.) DA11 .130 GB85
Grays RM17 .110 GC79
Hounslow TW3 .96 CB84
Isleworth TW7 .97 CE81
Mitcham CR4 .141 DH96
Northwood HA6 .39 BR50
Oxted RH8
off Southlands La .187 EC134
Pinner HA5 .60 BZ57
Richmond TW10 .118 CM86
Rickmansworth (Mill End)
WD3 .38 BG47
Romford RM6 .70 EV59
Grove Rd, Sev. TN14 .191 FJ121
Sevenoaks (Seal) TN15 .191 FN122
Shepperton TW17 .135 BQ100
Surbiton KT6 .137 CK99
Sutton SM1 .158 DB107
Thornton Heath CR7 .141 DN98
Twickenham TW2 .117 CD90
Uxbridge UB8 .76 BK66
Westerham (Tats.) TN16 .178 EJ120
Woking GU21 .167 AZ116
Grove Rd W, Enf. EN3 .30 DW37
Grover Rd, Wat. WD19 .40 BX45
Grove Shaw, Tad. (Kgswd.)
KT20 .173 CY124
Groveside Cl, W3 .80 CN72
Carshalton SM5 .140 DE103
Groveside Rd, E4 .48 EE47
Grovestile Waye, Felt. TW14 .115 BR87
Grove St, N18 .46 DT51
SE8 .203 M8
Grove Ter, NW5 .65 DH62
Teddington TW11 .117 CG91
Grove Ter Ms, NW5
off Grove Ter .65 DH62
Grove Vale, SE22 .102 DS84
Chislehurst BR7 .125 EN93
Grove Vil, E14 .85 EB73
Groveway, SW9 .101 DM81
Dagenham RM8 .70 EX63
Grove Way, Esher KT10 .136 CC101
Rickmansworth (Chorl.)
WD3 .21 BB42
Uxbridge UB8 .76 BK66
Wembley HA9 .62 CP64
Grovewood, Rich. TW9
off Sandycombe Rd .98 CN81
Grovewood Cl, Rick. (Chorl.)
WD3 .21 BB43
Grove Wd Hill, Couls. CR5 .159 DK114
Grovewood Pl, Wdf.Grn. IG8 .49 EM51
Grubb St, Oxt. RH8 .188 EJ128
Grummant Rd, SE15 .102 DT81
Grundy St, E14 .85 EB72
Gruneisen Rd, N3 .44 DB52
Guardian Cl, Horn. RM11 .71 FH60
Guards Av, Cat. CR3 .176 DQ122
Guardsman Cl, Brwd. CM14 .54 FX50
★ **Guards Mus**, SW1 .199 L5
Gubbins La, Rom. RM3 .52 FM52
Gubyon Av, SE24 .121 DP85
Guerin Sq, E3 .85 DZ69
Guernsey Cl, Houns. TW5 .96 CA81
Guernsey Fm Dr, Wok. GU21 .166 AX115
Guernsey Gro, SE24 .122 DQ87
Guernsey Ho, Enf. EN3
off Eastfield Rd .31 DX38
Guernsey Rd, E11 .67 ED60
Guibal Rd, SE12 .124 EH87
Guildersfield Rd, SW16 .121 DL94
Guildford Av, Felt. TW13 .115 BT89
Guildford Gdns, Rom. RM3 .52 FL51
Guildford Gro, SE10 .103 EB81
Guildford La, Wok. GU22 .166 AX120
Guildford Rd, E6 .86 EL72
E17 .47 EC53
SW8 .101 DL81
Chertsey KT16 .133 BE102
Croydon CR0 .142 DR100
Ilford IG3 .69 ES61
Leatherhead (Fetch.) KT22 .171 CG122
Romford RM3 .52 FL51
Woking GU22 .166 AY119
Woking (Mayford) GU22 .166 AX122
Guildford St, Cher. KT16 .134 BG101
Staines TW18 .114 BG93
Guildford Way, Wall. SM6 .159 DL106
★ **Guildhall, The**, EC2 .197 K8
★ **Guildhall Art Gall,**
Guildhall Lib, EC2 .197 J8
Guildhall Bldgs, EC2
off Basinghall St .84 DR72
Guildhall Yd, EC2 .197 K8
Guildhouse St, SW1 .199 K9
Guildown Av, N12 .44 DB49
Guild Rd, SE7 .104 EK78
Erith DA8 .107 FF80
Guildsway, E17 .47 DZ53
Guileshill La, Wok. (Ockham)
GU23 .168 BL123
Guilford Av, Surb. KT5 .138 CM99
Guilford Pl, WC1 .196 B5
Guilford St, WC1 .195 P5
Guilford Vil, Surb. KT5
off Alpha Rd .138 CM100
Guilsborough Cl, NW10 .80 CS66
Guinevere Gdns, Wal.Cr. EN8 .15 DY31
Guinness Cl, E9 .85 DY66
Hayes UB3 .95 BR76
Guinness Ct, Wok. GU21
off Iveagh Rd .166 AT118
Guinness Sq, SE1 .201 M8
Guinness Trust Bldgs, SE1
off Snowsfields .102 DS75
SE11 .200 G10
SW3 .198 D9
SW9 .101 DP84
Guinness Trust Est, N16
off Holmleigh Rd .66 DS60
Guion Rd, SW6 .99 CZ82
Gulland Cl, Bushey WD23 .24 CC43
Gulland Wk, N1
off Clephane Rd .84 DQ65
Gull Cl, Wall. SM6 .159 DL108
Gullet Wd Rd, Wat. WD25 .23 BU35
Gulliver Cl, Nthlt. UB5 .78 BZ67
Gulliver Rd, Sid. DA15 .125 ES89
Gulliver St, SE16 .203 M6
Gull Wk, Horn. RM12
off Heron Flight Av .89 FH66
Gulston Wk, SW3 .198 E9
Gumleigh Rd, W5 .97 CJ77
Gumley Gdns, Islw. TW7 .97 CG83
Gumley Rd, Grays RM20 .109 FX79
Gumping Rd, Orp. BR5 .145 EQ103
Gundulph Rd, Brom. BR2 .144 EJ97
Gunfleet Cl, Grav. DA12 .131 GL87
Gun Hill, Til. (W.Til.) RM18 .111 GK79

Gunmakers La, E3 .85 DY67
Gunnell Cl, SE26 .122 DU92
Croydon CR0 .142 DU100
Gunner Dr, Enf. EN3
off Government Row .31 EA37
Gunner La, SE18 .105 EN78
GUNNERSBURY, W4 .98 CP77
⇌ **Gunnersbury** .98 CP78
⊖ **Gunnersbury** .98 CP78
Gunnersbury Av, W3 .98 CN76
W4 .98 CN76
W5 .80 CM74
Gunnersbury Cl, W4
off Grange Rd .98 CP78
Gunnersbury Ct, W3
off Bollo La .98 CP75
Gunnersbury Cres, W3 .98 CN75
Gunnersbury Dr, W5 .98 CM75
Gunnersbury Gdns, W3 .98 CN75
Gunnersbury La, W3 .98 CN76
Gunnersbury Ms, W4
off Chiswick High Rd .98 CP78
★ **Gunnersbury Park**, W3
(Ealing) .98 CM77
Gunnersbury Pk, W3 .98 CM77
W5 .98 CM77
★ **Gunnersbury Park Mus &**
Art Cen, W3 .98 CN76
Gunners Gro, E4 .47 EC48
Gunners Rd, SW18 .120 DD89
Gunning Rd, Grays RM17 .110 GD78
Gunning St, SE18 .105 ES77
Gunn Rd, Swans. DA10 .130 FY86
Gunpowder Sq, EC4 .196 E8
Gunstor Rd, N16 .66 DS63
Gun St, E1 .197 P7
Gunter Gro, SW10 .100 DC79
Edgware HA8 .42 CR53
Gunterstone Rd, W14 .99 CY77
Gunthorpe St, E1 .84 DT71
Gunton Rd, E5 .66 DV62
SW17 .120 DG93
Gunwhale Cl, SE16 .203 J3
Gurdon Rd, SE7 .104 EG78
Gurnard Cl, West Dr. UB7
off Trout Rd .76 BK73
Gurnell Gro, W13 .79 CF70
Gurney Cl, E15
off Gurney Rd .68 EE64
E17 .47 DX53
Barking IG11 .87 EP65
Gurney Cres, Croy. CR0 .141 DM102
Gurney Dr, N2 .64 DC57
Gurney Rd, E15 .68 EE64
Carshalton SM5 .158 DG105
Northolt UB5 .77 BV69
Guthrie St, SW3 .198 B10
Gutteridge La, Rom. (Stap.Abb.)
RM4 .35 FC44
Gutter La, EC2 .197 J8
Guyatt Gdns, Mitch. CR4
off Ormerod Gdns .140 DG96
Guy Barnett Gro, SE3
off Casterbridge Rd .104 EG83
Guy Rd, Wall. SM6 .141 DK104
Guyscliff Rd, SE13 .123 EC85
Guysfield Cl, Rain. RM13 .89 FG67
Guysfield Dr, Rain. RM13 .89 FG67
H **Guy's Hosp**, SE1 .201 L4
Guy St, SE1 .201 L4
Gwalior Rd, SW15
off Felsham Rd .99 CX83
Gwendolen Av, SW15 .119 CX85
Gwendolen Cl, SW15 .119 CX85
Gwendoline Av, E13 .86 EH67
Gwendwr Rd, W14 .99 CY78
Gwent Cl, Wat. WD25 .8 BX34
Gwillim Cl, Sid. DA15 .126 EU85
Gwydor Rd, Beck. BR3 .143 DX98
Gwydyr Rd, Brom. BR2 .144 EF97
Gwyn Cl, SW6 .100 DC80
Gwynne Av, Croy. CR0 .143 DX101
Gwynne Cl, W4
off Pumping Sta Rd .99 CT79
Gwynne Pk Av, Wdf.Grn. IG8 .49 EM51
Gwynne Pl, WC1 .196 C3
Gwynne Rd, SW11 .100 DD82
Caterham CR3 .176 DR123
Gwynn Rd, Grav. (Nthflt.)
DA11 .130 GC89
Gyfford Wk, Wal.Cr. EN7 .14 DV31
Gylcote Cl, SE5 .102 DR84
Gyles Pk, Stan. HA7 .41 CJ53
Gyllyngdune Gdns, Ilf. IG3 .69 ET61
Gypsy La, Kings L. WD4 .23 BR35
Slough (Stoke P.) SL2 .56 AS63

H

Haarlem Rd, W14 .99 CX76
Haberdasher Est, N1
off Haberdasher St .84 DR69
Haberdasher Pl, N1 .197 L2
Haberdasher St, N1 .197 L2
Habgood Rd, Loug. IG10 .32 EL41
Haccombe Rd, SW19
off Haydons Rd .120 DC93
HACKBRIDGE, Wall. .141 DH103
⇌ **Hackbridge** .141 DH103
Hackbridge Grn, Wall. SM6 .140 DG103
Hackbridge Pk Gdns, Cars.
SM5 .140 DG103
Hackbridge Rd, Wall. SM6 .140 DG103
Hacketts La, Wok. GU22 .151 BF114
Hackford Rd, SW9 .101 DM81
Hackforth Cl, Barn. EN5 .27 CV43
Hackington Cres, Beck. BR3 .123 EA93
HACKNEY, E8 .84 DV65
⇌ **Hackney Central** .84 DV65
★ **Hackney City Fm**, E2 .84 DU68
Hackney Cl, Borwd. WD6 .26 CR43

Hac - Ham

≠ Hackney Downs ..66 DV64
Hackney Gro, E8
off Reading La ..84 DV65
★ Hackney Marsh, E9 ..67 DY62
★ Hackney Mus, E8 ..84 DV65
Hackney Rd, E2 ..197 P3
HACKNEY WICK, E9 ..67 EA64
≠ Hackney Wick ..85 EA65
Hackworth Pt, E3
off Rainhill Way ..85 EB69
HACTON, Rain. ..72 FM64
Hacton Dr, Horn. RM12 ..72 FK63
Hacton La, Horn. RM12 ..72 FM62
Upminster RM14 ..72 FM64
Hadden Rd, SE28 ..105 ES76
Hadden Way, Grnf. UB6 ..79 CD65
Haddestoke Gate, Wal.Cr. (Chsht.)
EN8 ..15 DZ26
Haddington Rd, Brom. BR1 ..123 ED90
Haddon Cl, Borwd. WD6 ..26 CN41
Enfield EN1 ..30 DU44
New Malden KT3 ..139 CT99
Weybridge KT13 ..135 BR104
Haddonfield, SE8 ..203 J9
Haddon Gro, Sid. DA15 ..126 EU87
Haddon Rd, Orp. BR5 ..146 EW99
Rickmansworth (Chorl.)
WD3 ..21 BC43
Sutton SM1 ..158 DB105
Haddo St, SE10 ..103 EB79
Hadfield Cl, Sthl. UB1
off Adrienne Av ..78 BZ69
Hadfield Rd, Stai. (Stanw.)
TW19 ..114 BK86
Hadlands Cl, Hem.H. (Bov.)
HP3 ..5 AZ26
Hadleigh Cl, E1
off Mantus Rd ..84 DW70
SW20 ..139 CZ96
Hadleigh Dr, Sutt. SM2 ..158 DA109
Hadleigh Rd, N9 ..46 DV45
Hadleigh St, E2 ..84 DW70
Hadleigh Wk, E6 ..86 EL72
HADLEY, Barn. ..27 CZ40
Hadley Cl, N21 ..29 DN44
Borehamwood (Elstree)
WD6 ..26 CM44
Hadley Common, Barn. EN5 ..28 DA40
Hadley Gdns, W4 ..98 CR78
Southall UB2 ..96 BZ78
Hadley Grn, Barn. EN5 ..27 CZ40
Hadley Grn Rd, Barn. EN5 ..27 CZ40
Hadley Grn W, Barn. EN5 ..27 CZ40
Hadley Gro, Barn. EN5 ..27 CY40
Hadley Highstone, Barn.
EN5 ..27 CZ39
Hadley Pl, Wey. KT13 ..152 BN108
Hadley Ridge, Barn. EN5 ..27 CZ41
Hadley Rd, Barn. (Had.Wd.)
EN4 ..29 DH38
Barnet (New Barn.) EN5 ..28 DB42
Belvedere DA17 ..106 EZ77
Enfield EN2 ..29 DL38
Mitcham CR4 ..141 DK98
Hadley St, NW1 ..83 DH65
Hadley Way, N21 ..29 DN44
HADLEY WOOD, Barn. ..28 DD38
≠ Hadley Wood ..28 DC38
Hadley Wd Ri, Ken. CR8 ..175 DP115
Hadlow Pl, SE19 ..122 DU94
Hadlow Rd, Sid. DA14 ..126 EU91
Welling DA16 ..106 EW80
Hadlow Way, Grav. (Istead Rise)
DA13 ..130 GE94
Hadrian Cl, Stai. TW19
off Hadrian Way ..114 BL88
Wallington SM6 ..159 DL108
Hadrian Ct, Sutt. SM2
off Stanley Rd ..158 DB108
Hadrian Est, E2 ..84 DU68
Hadrian Ms, N7
off Roman Way ..83 DM66
Hadrians Ride, Enf. EN1 ..30 DT43
Hadrian St, SE10 ..104 EE78
Hadrian Way, Stai. (Stanw.)
TW19 ..114 BL87
Hadyn Pk Rd, W12 ..99 CU75
Hafer Rd, SW11 ..100 DF84
Hafton Rd, SE6 ..124 EE88
Hagden La, Wat. WD18 ..23 BT43
Haggard Rd, Twick. TW1 ..117 CH87
HAGGERSTON, E2 ..84 DT68
Haggerston Rd, E8 ..84 DT66
Borehamwood WD6 ..26 CL38
Hague St, E2
off Derbyshire St ..84 DU69
Ha-Ha Rd, SE18 ..105 EM79
Haig Gdns, Grav. DA12 ..131 GJ87
Haig Pl, Mord. SM4
off Green La ..140 DA100
Haig Rd, Grays RM16 ..111 GG76
Stanmore HA7 ..41 CJ50
Uxbridge UB8 ..77 BP71
Westerham (Bigg.H.) TN16 ..178 EL117
Haig Rd E, E13 ..86 EJ69
Haig Rd W, E13 ..86 EJ69
Haigville Gdns, Ilf. IG6 ..69 EP56
Hailes Cl, SW19
off North Rd ..120 DC93
Haileybury Av, Enf. EN1 ..30 DT44
Haileybury Rd, Orp. BR6 ..164 EU105
Hailey Rd, Erith DA18 ..106 FA75
Hailsham Av, SW2 ..121 DM89
Hailsham Cl, Rom. RM3 ..52 FJ50
Surbiton KT6 ..137 CK101
Hailsham Dr, Har. HA1 ..61 CD55
Hailsham Gdns, Rom. RM3 ..52 FJ50
Hailsham Rd, SW17 ..120 DG93
Romford RM3 ..52 FJ50
Hailsham Ter, N18 ..46 DQ50
Haimo Rd, SE9 ..124 EK85
HAINAULT, Ilf. ..49 ES52
⊖ Hainault ..49 ES52
Hainault Ct, E17 ..67 ED56
★ Hainault Forest Country Pk,
Chig. IG7 ..50 EW47
Hainault Gore, Rom. RM6 ..70 EY57
Hainault Gro, Chig. IG7 ..49 EQ49
Hainault Ind Est, Ilf. IG6 ..50 EW50
Hainault Rd, E11 ..67 EC60
Chigwell IG7 ..49 EP48
Romford RM5 ..51 FC54
Romford (Chad.Hth.) RM6 ..70 EZ58
Romford (Lt.Hth.) RM6 ..70 EV55
Hainault St, SE9 ..125 EP88
Ilford IG1 ..69 EP61
Haines Ct, Wey. KT13
off St. George's Lo ..153 BR106
Haines Wk, Mord. SM4
off Dorchester Rd ..140 DB101
Haines Way, Wat. WD25 ..7 BU34
Hainford Cl, SE4 ..103 DX84
Haining Cl, W4
off Wellesley Rd ..98 CN78
Hainthorpe Rd, SE27 ..121 DP90
Hainton Cl, E1 ..84 DV72
Halberd Ms, E5
off Knightland Rd ..66 DV61
Halbutt Gdns, Dag. RM9 ..70 EZ62
Halbutt St, Dag. RM9 ..70 EZ63
Halcomb St, N1 ..84 DS67
Halcot Av, Bexh. DA6 ..127 FB85
Halcrow St, E1
off Newark St ..84 DV71
Halcyon Way, Horn. RM11 ..72 FM60
Haldane Cl, N10 ..45 DH52
Enfield EN3
off Government Row ..31 EA37
Haldane Gdns, Grav. DA11 ..130 GC88
Haldane Pl, SW18 ..120 DB88
Haldane Rd, E6 ..86 EK69
SE28 ..88 EX73
SW6 ..99 CZ80
Southall UB1 ..78 CC72
Haldan Rd, E4 ..47 EC51
Haldon Cl, Chig. IG7
off Arrowsmith Rd ..49 ES50
Haldon Rd, SW18 ..119 CZ85
Hale, The, E4 ..47 ED52
N17 ..66 DU56
Hale Cl, E4 ..47 EC48
Edgware HA8 ..42 CQ50
Orpington BR6 ..163 EQ105
Hale Dr, NW7 ..42 CQ51
HALE END, E4 ..47 ED51
Hale End, Rom. RM3 ..51 FH51
Woking GU22 ..166 AV121
Hale End Cl, Ruis. HA4 ..59 BU58
Hale End Rd, E4 ..47 ED51
E17 ..47 ED53
Woodford Green IG8 ..47 ED52
Halefield Rd, N17 ..46 DU53
Hale Gdns, N17 ..66 DU55
W3 ..80 CN74
Hale Gro Gdns, NW7 ..42 CR50
Hale La, NW7 ..42 CR50
Edgware HA8 ..42 CP50
Sevenoaks (Otford) TN14 ..181 FE117
Hale Path, SE27 ..121 DP91
Hale Rd, E6 ..86 EL70
N17 ..66 DU55
Halesowen Rd, Mord. SM4 ..140 DB101
Hales St, SE8
off Deptford High St ..103 EA80
Hale St, E14 ..85 EB73
Staines TW18 ..113 BE91
Haleswood, Cob. KT11 ..153 BV114
Halesworth Cl, E5
off Theydon Rd ..66 DW61
Romford RM3 ..52 FL52
Halesworth Rd, SE13 ..103 EB83
Romford RM3 ..52 FL51
Hale Wk, W7 ..79 CE71
Haley Rd, NW4 ..63 CW58
Half Acre, Brent. TW8 ..97 CK79
Halfacre Hill, Ger.Cr. (Chal.St.P.)
SL9 ..36 AY53
Half Acre Rd, W7 ..79 CE74
Halfhide La, Brox. (Turnf.)
EN10 ..15 DY26
Waltham Cross (Chsht.)
EN8 ..15 DX27
Halfhides, Wal.Abb. EN9 ..15 ED33
Half Moon Ct, EC1 ..197 H7
Half Moon Cres, N1 ..83 DM68
Half Moon La, SE24 ..122 DQ86
Epping CM16 ..17 ET31
Half Moon Pas, E1
off Braham St ..84 DT72
Half Moon St, W1 ..199 J2
Halford Cl, Edg. HA8 ..42 CP54
Halford Rd, E10 ..67 ED57
SW6 ..100 DA79
Richmond TW10 ..118 CL85
Uxbridge UB10 ..58 BN64
Halfway Ct, Purf. RM19
off Thamley ..108 FN77
Halfway Grn, Walt. KT12 ..135 BV104
Halfway St, Sid. DA15 ..125 ER87
Haliburton Rd, Twick. TW1 ..117 CG85
Haliday Wk, N1
off Balls Pond Rd ..84 DR65
Halidon Cl, E9 *off Urswick Rd* ..66 DW64
Halidon Ri, Rom. RM3 ..52 FP51
Halifax Cl, St.Alb. AL2 ..8 BZ30
Watford WD25 *off Ashfields* ..7 BT34
Halifax Rd, Enf. EN2 ..30 DQ40
Greenford UB6 ..78 CB67
Rickmansworth (Herons.)
WD3 ..37 BC45
Halifax St, SE26 ..122 DV91
Halifield Dr, Belv. DA17 ..106 EY76
Haling Down Pas, S.Croy.
CR2 ..160 DQ109
Haling Gro, S.Croy. CR2 ..160 DQ108
Haling Pk, S.Croy. CR2 ..160 DQ107
Haling Pk Gdns, S.Croy. CR2 ..159 DP107
Haling Pk Rd, S.Croy. CR2 ..159 DP106
Haling Rd, S.Croy. CR2 ..160 DR107
Halings La, Uxb. (Denh.) UB9 ..57 BE56
Halkin Arc, SW1 ..198 F6
Halkingcroft, Slou. SL3 ..92 AW75
Halkin Ms, SW1 ..198 F6
Halkin Pl, SW1 ..198 F6
Halkin St, SW1 ..198 G5
Hall, The, SE3 ..104 EG83
Hallam Cl, Chis. BR7 ..125 EM92
Watford WD24 ..24 BW40
Hallam Gdns, Pnr. HA5 ..40 BY52
Hallam Ms, W1 ..195 J6
Hallam Rd, N15 ..65 DP56
SW13 ..99 CV83
Hallam St, W1 ..195 J5
Halland Way, Nthwd. HA6 ..39 BR51
Hall Av, N18
off Weir Hall Av ..46 DR51
South Ockendon (Aveley)
RM15 ..90 FQ74
Hall Cl, W5 ..80 CL71
Rickmansworth (Mill End)
WD3 ..38 BG46
Hall Ct, Slou. (Datchet) SL3 ..92 AV80
Teddington TW11
off Teddington Pk ..117 CF92
Hall Cres, S.Ock. (Aveley)
RM15 ..108 FQ75
Hall Dr, SE26 ..122 DW92
W7 ..79 CE72
Uxbridge (Hare.) UB9 ..38 BJ53
Halley Gdns, SE13 ..103 ED84
Halley Rd, E7 ..86 EJ65
E12 ..86 EK65
Waltham Abbey EN9 ..31 EB36
Halleys App, Wok. GU21 ..166 AU118
Halleys Ct, Wok. GU21
off Halleys App ..166 AU118
Halley St, E14 ..85 DY71
Halleys Wk, Add. KT15 ..152 BJ108
Hall Fm Cl, Stan. HA7 ..41 CH49
Hall Fm Dr, Twick. TW2 ..117 CD87
Hallfield Est, W2 ..82 DC72
Hallford Way, Dart. DA1 ..128 FJ85
Hall Gdns, E4 ..47 DZ49
Hall Gate, NW8 *off Hall Rd* ..82 DC69
Hall Grn La, Brwd. CM13 ..55 GC45
Hall Hill, Oxt. RH8 ..187 ED131
Sevenoaks (Seal) TN15 ..191 FP123
Halliards, The, Walt. KT12
off Felix Rd ..135 BU100
Halliday Cl, Rad. (Shenley)
WD7 ..10 CL32
Halliday Sq, Sthl. UB2 ..79 CD74
Halliford Cl, Shep. TW17 ..135 BR98
Halliford Rd, Shep. TW17 ..135 BS99
Sunbury-on-Thames
TW16 ..135 BS99
Halliford St, N1 ..84 DQ66
Halliloo Valley Rd, Cat. (Wold.)
CR3 ..177 DZ119
Hallingbury Ct, E17 ..67 EB55
Hallington Cl, Wok. GU21 ..166 AV117
Halliwell Rd, SW2 ..121 DM86
Halliwick Rd, N10 ..44 DG53
Hall La, E4 ..47 DY50
NW4 ..43 CU53
Brentwood (Shenf.) CM15 ..55 FZ44
Hayes UB3 ..95 BR80
South Ockendon RM15 ..91 FX68
Upminster RM14 ..72 FQ60
Hallmark Trd Est, NW10
off Great Cen Way ..62 CQ63
Hallmead Rd, Sutt. SM1 ..140 DB104
Hall Oak Wk, NW6
off Barlow Rd ..81 CZ65
Hallowell Av, Croy. CR0 ..159 DL105
Hallowell Cl, Mitch. CR4 ..140 DG97
Hallowell Rd, Nthwd. HA6 ..39 BS52
Hallowes Cres, Wat. WD19
off Hayling Rd ..39 BU48
Hallowfield Way, Mitch. CR4 ..140 DD98
Hall Pk Rd, Upmin. RM14 ..72 FQ64
★ Hall Pl, Bex. DA5 ..127 FC86
Hall Pl, W2 ..82 DD70
Woking GU21 ..167 BA116
Hall Pl Cres, Bex. DA5 ..127 FC85
Hall Pl Dr, Wey. KT13 ..153 BS106
Hall Rd, E6 ..87 EM67
E15 ..67 ED63
NW8 ..82 DC69
Dartford DA1 ..108 FM84
Gravesend (Nthflt.) DA11 ..130 GC90
Isleworth TW7 ..117 CD85
Romford (Chad.Hth.) RM6 ..70 EW58
Romford (Gidea Pk.) RM2 ..71 FH55
South Ockendon (Aveley)
RM15 ..108 FQ75
Wallington SM6 ..159 DH109
Hallside Rd, Enf. EN1 ..30 DT38
Hallsland Way, Oxt. RH8 ..188 EF133
Hall St, EC1 ..196 G2
N12 ..44 DC50
Hallsville Rd, E16 ..86 EF72
Hallswelle Rd, NW11 ..63 CZ57
Hall Ter, Rom. RM3 ..52 FN52
South Ockendon (Aveley)
RM15 ..109 FR75
Hall Twr, W2 ..194 A6
Hall Vw, SE9 ..124 EK89
Hall Way, Pur. CR8 ..159 DP113
Hallwood Cres, Brwd. CM15 ..54 FY45
Hallywell Cres, E6 ..87 EM71
Halons Rd, SE9 ..125 EN87
Halpin Pl, SE17 ..201 L9
Halsbrook Rd, SE3 ..104 EK83
Halsbury Cl, Stan. HA7 ..41 CH49
Halsbury Rd, W12 ..81 CV74
Halsbury Rd E, Nthlt. UB5 ..60 CC63
Halsbury Rd W, Nthlt. UB5 ..60 CB64
Halsend, Hayes UB3 ..77 BV74
Halsey Ms, SW3 ..198 D8
Halsey Pk, St.Alb. (Lon.Col.)
AL2 ..10 CM27
Halsey Pl, Wat. WD24 ..23 BV38
Halsey Rd, Wat. WD18 ..23 BV41
Halsey St, SW3 ..198 D8
Halsham Cres, Bark. IG11 ..87 ET65
Halsmere Rd, SE5 ..101 DP81
HALSTEAD, Sev. ..164 EZ113
Halstead Cl, Croy. CR0
off Charles St ..142 DQ104
Halstead Ct, N1 ..197 L1
Halstead Gdns, N21 ..46 DR46
Halstead Hill, Wal.Cr. (Chsht.)
EN7 ..14 DS29
Halstead La, Sev. (Knock.)
TN14 ..164 EZ114
Halstead Rd, E11 ..68 EG57
N21 ..46 DQ46
Enfield EN1 ..30 DS42
Erith DA8 ..107 FE81
Halstead Way, Brwd. CM13 ..55 GC44
Halston Cl, SW11 ..120 DF86
Halstow Rd, NW10 ..81 CX69
SE10 ..205 M10
Halsway, Hayes UB3 ..77 BU74
Halter Cl, Borwd. WD6
off Clydesdale Cl ..26 CR43
Halton Cl, N11
off Colney Hatch La ..44 DF51
Halton Cross St, N1 ..83 DP67
Halton Pl, N1 *off Dibden St* ..84 DQ67
Halton Rd, N1 ..83 DP66
Grays RM16 ..111 GJ76
Halt Robin La, Belv. DA17
off Halt Robin Rd ..107 FB77
Halt Robin Rd, Belv. DA17 ..106 FA77
HAM, Rich. ..117 CK90
Ham, The, Brent. TW8 ..97 CJ80
Hambalt Rd, SW4 ..121 DJ85
Hamble Cl, Ruis. HA4
off Chichester Av ..59 BS61
Woking GU21 ..166 AU117
Hamble Ct, Kings.T. KT1 ..117 CK94
Hambledon Cl, Uxb. UB8
off Aldenham Dr ..77 BP71
Hambledon Gdns, SE25 ..142 DT97
Hambledon Hill, Epsom
KT18 ..172 CQ116
Hambledon Pl, SE21 ..122 DS88
Hambledon Rd, SW18 ..119 CZ87
Caterham CR3 ..176 DR123
Hambledon Vale, Epsom
KT18 ..172 CQ116
Hambledown Rd, Sid. DA15 ..125 ER87
Hamble La, S.Ock. RM15 ..91 FT71
Hamble St, SW6 ..100 DB83
Hambleton Cl, Wor.Pk. KT4
off Cotswold Way ..139 CW103
Hamble Wk, Nthlt. UB5
off Brabazon Rd ..78 CA68
Woking GU21 ..166 AU118
Hamblings Cl, Rad. (Shenley)
WD7 ..9 CK33
Hambridge Way, SW2 ..121 DN87
Hambro Av, Brom. BR2 ..144 EG102
Hambrook Rd, SE25 ..142 DV97
Hambro Rd, SW16 ..121 DK93
Brentwood CM14 ..54 FX47
Hambrough Rd, Sthl. UB1 ..78 BY74
Hamburgh Ct, Wal.Cr. EN8 ..15 DX28
Ham Cl, Rich. TW10 ..117 CJ90
Ham Common, Rich. TW10 ..118 CM91
Hamden Cres, Dag. RM10 ..71 FB62
Hamel Cl, Har. HA3 ..61 CK55
Hamelin St, E14
off St. Leonards Rd ..85 EC72
Hamer Cl, Hem.H. (Bov.) HP3 ..5 BA28
Hamerton Rd, Grav. (Nthflt.)
DA11 ..130 GB85
Hameway, E6 ..87 EN70
Ham Fm Rd, Rich. TW10 ..117 CK91
Hamfield Cl, Oxt. RH8 ..187 EC127
Hamfrith Rd, E15 ..86 EF65
Ham Gate Av, Rich. TW10 ..117 CK90
Hamhaugh Island, Shep.
TW17 ..134 BN103
★ Ham Ho, Rich. TW10 ..117 CJ88
Hamilton Av, N9 ..46 DU45
Cobham KT11 ..153 BU113
Ilford IG6 ..69 EP56
Romford RM1 ..51 FD54
Surbiton KT6 ..138 CP102
Sutton SM3 ..139 CY103
Woking GU22 ..167 BE115
Hamilton Cl, N17 ..66 DT55
NW8 ..82 DD69
SE16 ..203 L5
Barnet EN4 ..28 DE42
Chertsey KT16 ..133 BF102
Epsom KT19 ..156 CQ112
Feltham TW13 ..115 BT92
Potters Bar EN6 ..11 CU33
Purley CR8 ..159 DP112
St. Albans (Brick.Wd.) AL2 ..8 CA30
Stanmore HA7 ..41 CF47
Hamilton Ct, W5 ..80 CM73
W9 *off Maida Vale* ..82 DC69
Hamilton Cres, N13 ..45 DN49
Brentwood CM14 ..54 FW49
Harrow HA2 ..60 BZ62
Hounslow TW3 ..116 CB85
Hamilton Dr, Rom. RM3 ..52 FL54
Hamilton Gdns, NW8 ..82 DC69
Hamilton La, N5
off Hamilton Pk ..65 DP63
Hamilton Mead, Hem.H. (Bov.)
HP3 ..5 BA27
Hamilton Ms, SW18
off Merton Rd ..120 DA88
W1 ..199 H4
Hamilton Pk, N5 ..65 DP63
Hamilton Pk W, N5 ..65 DP63
Hamilton Pl, N19
off Wedmore St ..65 DK62
W1 ..198 G3
Sunbury-on-Thames TW16 ..115 BV94
Tadworth (Kgswd.) KT20 ..173 CZ122
Hamilton Rd, E15 ..86 EE69
E17 ..47 DY54
N2 ..64 DC55
N9 ..46 DU45
NW10 ..63 CU64
NW11 ..63 CX59
SE27 ..122 DR91
SW19 ..120 DB94
Hamilton Rd, W4 ..98 CS75
W5 ..80 CL73
Barnet EN4 ..28 DE42
Bexleyheath DA7 ..106 EY82
Brentford TW8 ..97 CK79
Feltham TW13 ..115 BT91
Harrow HA1 ..61 CE57
Hayes UB3 ..77 BV73
Ilford IG1 ..69 EP63
Kings Langley WD4 ..7 BQ33
Romford RM2 ..71 FH57
Sidcup DA15 ..126 EU91
Southall UB1 ..78 BZ74
Thornton Heath CR7 ..142 DR97
Twickenham TW2 ..117 CE88
Uxbridge UB8 ..76 BK71
Watford WD19 ..39 BV48
Hamilton Rd Ind Est, SE27 ..122 DR91
Hamilton Sq, N12
off Sandringham Gdns ..44 DD51
SE1 ..201 L4
Hamilton St, SE8
off Deptford High St ..103 EA79
Watford WD18 ..24 BW43
Hamilton Ter, NW8 ..82 DB68
Hamilton Wk, Erith DA8 ..107 FF80
Hamilton Way, N3 ..44 DA51
N13 ..45 DP49
Wallington SM6 ..159 DK109
Ham Island, Wind. (Old Wind.)
SL4 ..92 AX84
Ham La, Egh. (Eng.Grn.)
TW20 ..112 AV91
Windsor (Old Wind.) SL4 ..92 AX84
Hamlea Cl, SE12 ..124 EF85
Hamlet, The, SE5 ..102 DR83
Hamlet Cl, SE13 *off Old Rd* ..104 EE84
Romford RM5 ..50 FA52
St. Albans AL2 ..8 BZ30
Hamlet Gdns, W6 ..99 CU77
Hamlet Rd, SE19 ..122 DT94
Romford RM5 ..50 FA52
Hamlet Sq, NW2 ..63 CY62
Hamlets Way, E3 ..85 DZ70
Hamlet Way, SE1 ..201 L4
★ Hamleys, W1 ..195 K10
Hamlin Cres, Pnr. HA5 ..60 BW57
Hamlin Rd, Sev. TN13 ..190 FE121
Hamlyn Cl, Edg. HA8 ..42 CL48
Hamlyn Gdns, SE19 ..122 DS94
Hamm Ct, Wey. KT13 ..134 BL103
Hammelton Grn, SW9
off Cromwell Rd ..101 DP81
Hammelton Rd, Brom. BR1 ..144 EF95
Hammer Par, Wat. WD25 ..7 BU33
Hammers Gate, St.Alb. AL2 ..8 CA25
Hammers La, NW7 ..43 CU50
HAMMERSMITH, W6 ..99 CW78
⊖ Hammersmith ..99 CW77
Hammersmith Br, SW13 ..99 CV78
W6 ..99 CV78
Hammersmith Br Rd, W6 ..99 CW78
Hammersmith Bdy, W6 ..99 CW77
Hammersmith Flyover, W6 ..99 CW78
Hammersmith Gro, W6 ..99 CW76
H Hammersmith Hosp, W12 ..81 CV72
Hammersmith Rd, W6 ..99 CX77
W14 ..99 CX77
Hammersmith Ter, W6 ..99 CU78
Hammet Cl, Hayes UB4
off Willow Tree La ..78 BX71
Hammett St, EC3 ..197 P10
Hamm Moor La, Add. KT15 ..152 BL106
Hammond Av, Mitch. CR4 ..141 DH96
Hammond Cl, Barn. EN5 ..27 CY43
Greenford UB6
off Lilian Board Way ..61 CD64
Hampton TW12 ..136 CA95
Waltham Cross (Chsht.)
EN7 ..14 DS26
Woking GU21 ..166 AW115
Hammond Rd, Enf. EN1 ..30 DV40
Southall UB2 ..96 BY76
Woking GU21 ..166 AW115
Hammonds Cl, Dag. RM8 ..70 EW62
Hammonds La, Brwd. CM13 ..53 FV51
HAMMOND STREET, Wal.Cr. ..14 DR26
Hammond St, NW5 ..83 DJ65
Hammondstreet Rd, Wal.Cr.
(Chsht.) EN7 ..14 DR26
Hammond Way, SE28
off Oriole Way ..88 EV73
Hamond Cl, S.Croy. CR2 ..159 DP109
Hamonde Cl, Edg. HA8 ..42 CP47
Ham Pk Rd, E7 ..86 EF66
E15 ..86 EF66
Hampden Av, Beck. BR3 ..143 DY96
Hampden Cl, NW1 ..195 N1
Epping (N.Wld.Bas.) CM16 ..18 FA27
Slough (Stoke P.) SL2 ..74 AU69
Hampden Cres, Brwd. CM14 ..54 FW49
Waltham Cross (Chsht.)
EN7 ..14 DV31
Hampden Gurney St, W1 ..194 D9
Hampden La, N17 ..46 DT53
Hampden Pl, St.Alb. (Frog.)
AL2 ..9 CE29
Hampden Rd, N8 ..65 DN56
N10 ..44 DG52
N17 ..46 DU53
N19 *off Holloway Rd* ..65 DK61
Beckenham BR3 ..143 DY96
Gerrards Cross (Chal.St.P.)
SL9 ..36 AX53
Grays RM17 ..110 GB78
Harrow HA3 ..40 CC53
Kingston upon Thames
KT1 ..138 CN97
Romford RM5 ..51 FB52
Slough SL3 ..93 AZ76
Hampden Sq, N14
off Osidge La ..45 DH46
Hampden Way, N14 ..45 DH47
Watford WD17 ..23 BS36
Hampermill La, Wat. WD19 ..39 BT47
Hampshire Cl, N18
off Berkshire Gdns ..46 DV50

★ Place of interest ≠ Railway station ⊖ London Underground station DLR Docklands Light Railway station Tramlink station H Hospital

Hampshire Hog La, W6
off King St 99 CV77
Hampshire Rd, N22 45 DM52
Hornchurch RM11 72 FN56
Hampshire St, NW5
off Torriano Av 83 DK65
Hampson Way, SW8 101 DM81
HAMPSTEAD, NW3 64 DD63
⊖ Hampstead 64 DC63
Hampstead Cl, SE28 88 EV74
Hampstead Gdns, NW11 64 DA58
Romford (Chad.Hth.) RM6 70 EV57
HAMPSTEAD GARDEN SUBURB, N2 64 DC57
Hampstead Grn, NW3 64 DE64
Hampstead Gro, NW3 64 DC62
★ Hampstead Heath, NW3 64 DD61
⇌ Hampstead Heath 64 DE63
Hampstead Hts, N2 64 DC56
Hampstead High St, NW3 64 DC63
Hampstead Hill Gdns, NW3 64 DD63
Hampstead La, N6 64 DD59
NW3 64 DD59
Hampstead Rd, NW1 195 K1
Hampstead Sq, NW3 64 DC62
Hampstead Wk, E3
off Parnell Rd 85 DZ67
Hampstead Way, NW11 64 DC60
HAMPTON 136 CB95
⇌ Hampton 136 CA95
Hampton Cl, N11
off Balmoral Av 45 DH50
NW6 82 DA69
SW20 119 CW94
⇌ Hampton Court 137 CE98
Hampton Ct, N1 *off Upper St* 83 DP65
Hampton Ct Av, E.Mol. KT8 137 CD99
Hampton Ct Cres, E.Mol. KT8 137 CD97
Hampton Ct Palace, E.Mol. KT8 137 CF97
★ Hampton Court Palace & Pk, E.Mol. KT8 137 CE97
Hampton Ct Par, E.Mol. KT8
off Creek Rd 137 CE98
Hampton Ct Rd, E.Mol. KT8 137 CF97
Hampton TW12 136 CC96
Kingston upon Thames KT1 137 CF97
Hampton Ct Way, E.Mol. KT8 137 CE100
Thames Ditton KT7 137 CE103
Hampton Cres, Grav. DA12 131 GL89
Hampton Fm Ind Est, Felt. TW13 116 BZ90
Hampton Gro, Epsom KT17 157 CT111
HAMPTON HILL, Hmptn. 116 CC93
Hampton Hill Business Pk, Hmptn. TW12 *off Wellington Rd* 116 CC92
Hampton La, Felt. TW13 116 BY91
Hampton Mead, Loug. IG10 33 EP41
Hampton Ms, NW10
off Minerva Rd 80 CR69
Hampton Ri, Har. HA3 62 CL58
Hampton Rd, E4 47 DZ50
E7 68 EH64
E11 67 ED60
Croydon CR0 142 DQ100
Hampton (Hmptn.H.) TW12 117 CD92
Ilford IG1 69 EP63
Teddington TW11 117 CD92
Twickenham TW2 117 CD90
Worcester Park KT4 139 CU103
Hampton Rd E, Felt. TW13 116 BZ90
Hampton Rd W, Felt. TW13 116 BY89
Hampton St, SE1 200 G9
SE17 200 G9
HAMPTON WICK, Kings.T. 137 CH95
⇌ Hampton Wick 137 CJ95
Ham Ridings, Rich. TW10 118 CM92
HAMSEY GREEN, Warl. 176 DW116
Hamsey Grn Gdns, Warl. CR6 176 DV116
Hamsey Way, S.Croy. CR2 176 DV115
Hamshades Cl, Sid. DA15 125 ET90
Ham St, Rich. TW10 117 CJ89
Ham Vw, Croy. CR0 143 DY100
Ham Yd, W1 195 M10
Hanah Ct, SW19 119 CX94
Hanameel St, E16 205 N2
Hanbury Cl, NW4 63 CW55
Waltham Cross (Chsht.) EN8 15 DX29
Hanbury Dr, N21 29 DM43
Westerham (Bigg.H.) TN16 162 EH113
Hanbury Ms, N1 *off Mary St* 84 DQ67
Hanbury Path, Wok. GU21 151 BD114
Hanbury Rd, N17 46 DV54
W3 98 CP75
Hanbury St, E1 197 P6
Hanbury Wk, Bex. DA5 127 FE90
Hancock Ct, Borwd. WD6 26 CQ39
Hancock Rd, E3 85 EC69
SE19 122 DR93
Handa Wk, N1
off Clephane Rd 84 DR65
Hand Ct, WC1 196 C7
Handcroft Rd, Croy. CR0 141 DP101
Handel Cl, Edg. HA8 42 CM51
Handel Cres, Til. RM18 111 GG80
Handel Pl, NW10
off Mitchellbrook Way 80 CR65
Handel St, WC1 195 P4
Handel Way, Edg. HA8 42 CN52
Handen Rd, SE12 124 EE85
Handforth Rd, SW9 101 DN80
Ilford IG1 *off Winston Way* 69 EP62
Handley Gro, NW2 63 CX62
Handley Page Rd, Wall. SM6 159 DM108
Handley Rd, E9 84 DW66
Handowe Cl, NW4 63 CU56
Handpost Hill, Pot.B. (Northaw) EN6 13 DH28
Handside Cl, Wor.Pk. KT4
off Carters Cl 139 CX102
Hands Wk, E16 86 EG72
Handsworth Av, E4 47 ED51
Handsworth Rd, N17 66 DR55
Handsworth Way, Wat. WD19
off Hayling Rd 39 BU48
Handtrough Way, Bark. IG11
off Fresh Wf Rd 87 EP68
Hanford Cl, SW18 120 DA88
Hanford Rd, S.Ock. (Aveley) RM15 90 FQ74
Hanford Row, SW19 119 CW93
Hangar Ruding, Wat. WD19 40 BZ48
Hanger Grn, W5 80 CN70
Hanger Hill, Wey. KT13 153 BP107
⊖ Hanger Lane 80 CM69
Hanger La, W5 80 CM70
Hanger Vale La, W5 80 CM72
Hanger Vw Way, W3 80 CN72
Hanging Hill La, Brwd. CM13 55 GB48
Hanging Sword All, EC4
off Salisbury Ct 83 DN72
Hangrove Hill, Orp. BR6 163 EP113
Hankey Pl, SE1 201 L5
Hankins La, NW7 42 CS48
Hanley Pl, Beck. BR3 123 EA94
Hanley Rd, N4 65 DL60
Hanmer Wk, N7 *off Newington Barrow Way* 65 DM62
Hannah Cl, NW10 62 CQ63
Beckenham BR3 143 EC97
Hannah Mary Way, SE1 202 C9
Hannah Ms, Wall. SM6 159 DJ108
Hannards Way, Ilf. IG6 50 EV50
Hannay La, N8 65 DK59
Hannay Wk, SW16 121 DK89
Hannell Rd, SW6 99 CY80
Hannen Rd, SE27
off Norwood High St 121 DP90
Hannibal Rd, E1 84 DW71
Staines (Stanw.) TW19 114 BK87
Hannibal Way, Croy. CR0 159 DM106
Hannington Rd, SW4 101 DH83
Hanover Av, E16 205 M2
Feltham TW13 115 BU88
Hanover Circle, Hayes UB3 77 BQ72
Hanover Cl, Egh. (Eng.Grn.) TW20 112 AV93
Redhill RH1 185 DJ128
Richmond TW9 98 CN80
Slough SL1 92 AU76
Sutton SM3 157 CZ105
Hanover Ct, SE19
off Anerley Rd 122 DU94
W12 *off Uxbridge Rd* 81 CU74
Woking GU22
off Midhope Rd 166 AY119
Hanover Dr, Chis. BR7 125 EQ91
Hanover Gdns, SE11 101 DN79
Abbots Langley WD5 7 BT30
Ilford IG6 49 EQ52
Hanover Gate, NW1 194 C3
Hanover Gate Mans, NW1 194 C4
Hanover Ho, Surb. KT6
off Lenelby Rd 138 CN102
Hanover Pk, SE15 102 DU81
Hanover Pl, E3
off Brokesley St 85 DZ69
WC2 196 A9
Hanover Rd, N15 66 DT56
NW10 81 CW66
SW19 120 DC94
Hanover Sq, W1 195 J9
Hanover St, W1 195 J9
Croydon CR0
off Abbey Rd 141 DP104
Hanover Ter, NW1 194 D3
Hanover Ter Ms, NW1 194 C3
Hanover Wk, Wey. KT13 135 BS104
Hanover Way, Bexh. DA6 106 EX83
Hanover W Ind Est, NW10 80 CR68
Hanover Yd, N1 *off Noel Rd* 83 DP68
Hansard Ms, W14
off Holland Rd 99 CX75
Hansart Way, Enf. EN2
off The Ridgeway 29 DN39
Hans Cres, SW1 198 D6
Hanselin Cl, Stan. HA7
off Chenduit Way 41 CF50
Hansen Dr, N21 29 DM43
Hansha Dr, Edg. HA8 42 CR53
Hansler Gro, E.Mol. KT8 137 CD98
Hansler Rd, SE22 122 DT85
Hansol Rd, Bexh. DA6 126 EY85
Hanson Cl, SW12 121 DH87
SW14 98 CQ83
Beckenham BR3 123 EB93
Loughton IG10
off Hanson Dr 33 EQ40
West Drayton UB7 94 BM76
Hanson Dr, Loug. IG10 33 EQ40
Hanson Gdns, Sthl. UB1 96 BY75
Hanson Grn, Loug. IG10
off Hanson Dr 33 EQ40
Hanson St, W1 195 K6
Hans Pl, SW1 198 E6
Hans Rd, SW3 198 D6
Hans St, SW1 198 E7
Hanway Pl, W1 195 M8
Hanway Rd, W7 79 CD72
Hanway St, W1 195 M8
HANWELL, W7 79 CF74
⇌ Hanwell 79 CE73
HANWORTH, Felt. 116 BX91
Hanworth La, Cher. KT16 133 BF102
Hanworth Rd, Felt. TW13 115 BV88
Hampton TW12 116 CB93
Hounslow TW3, TW4 96 CB83
Sunbury-on-Thames TW16 115 BU94
Hanworth Ter, Houns. TW3 96 CB84
Hanworth Trd Est, Felt. TW13 116 BY90
Hanyards End, Pot.B. (Cuffley) EN6 13 DL28
Hanyards La, Pot.B. (Cuffley) EN6 13 DK28
Hapgood Cl, Grnf. UB6 61 CD64
Harads Pl, E1 202 B1
Harben Rd, NW6 82 DC66
Harberson Rd, E15 86 EF67
Harberson Rd, SW12 121 DH88
Harberton Rd, N19 65 DJ60
Harbet Rd, E4 47 DX50
N18 47 DX50
W2 194 A7
Harbex Cl, Bex. DA5 127 FB87
Harbinger Rd, E14 204 B9
Harbledown Pl, Orp. BR5 146 EW98
Harbledown Rd, SW6 100 DA81
South Croydon CR2 160 DU111
Harbord Cl, SE5
off De Crespigny Pk 102 DR82
Harbord St, SW6 99 CX81
Harborne Cl, Wat. WD19 40 BW50
Harborough Av, Sid. DA15 125 ES87
Harborough Rd, SW16 121 DM91
Harbour Av, SW10 100 DC81
Harbourer Cl, Ilf. IG6 50 EV50
Harbourer Rd, Ilf. IG6 50 EV50
Harbour Ex Sq, E14 204 C5
Harbourfield Rd, Bans. SM7 174 DB115
Harbour Rd, SE5 102 DQ83
Harbour Yd, SW10
off Harbour Av 100 DC81
Harbridge Av, SW15 119 CT87
Harbury Rd, Cars. SM5 158 DE109
Harbut Rd, SW11 100 DD84
Harcombe Rd, N16 66 DS62
Harcourt, Stai. (Wrays.) TW19 112 AY86
Harcourt Av, E12 69 EM63
Edgware HA8 42 CQ48
Sidcup DA15 126 EW86
Wallington SM6 159 DH105
Harcourt Cl, Egh. TW20 113 BC93
Isleworth TW7 97 CG83
Harcourt Fld, Wall. SM6 159 DH105
Harcourt Lo, Wall. SM6
off Croydon Rd 159 DH105
Harcourt Ms, Rom. RM2 71 FF57
Harcourt Rd, E15 86 EF68
N22 45 DK53
SE4 103 DY84
SW19 *off Russell Rd* 120 DA94
Bexleyheath DA6 106 EY84
Bushey WD23 24 CC43
Thornton Heath CR7 141 DM100
Wallington SM6 159 DH105
Harcourt St, W1 194 C7
Harcourt Ter, SW10 100 DB78
Hardcastle Cl, Croy. CR0 142 DU100
Hardcourts Cl, W.Wick. BR4 143 EB104
Hardell Cl, Egh. TW20 113 BA92
Hardel Ri, SW2 121 DP89
Hardel Wk, SW2
off Papworth Way 121 DN87
Harden Fm Cl, Couls. CR5 175 DJ121
Harden Rd, Grav. (Nthflt.) DA11 131 GF90
Hardens Manorway, SE7 104 EK76
Harders Rd, SE15 102 DV82
Hardess St, SE24
off Herne Hill Rd 102 DQ83
Hardie Cl, NW10 62 CR64
Hardie Rd, Dag. RM10 71 FC62
Harding Cl, SE17
off Hillingdon St 102 DQ79
Croydon CR0 142 DT104
Watford WD25 8 BW33
Hardinge Cl, Uxb. UB8
off Dawley Av 77 BP72
Hardinge Rd, N18 46 DS50
NW10 81 CV67
Hardinge St, E1 84 DW72
Harding Ho, Hayes UB3 77 BV72
Harding Rd, Bexh. DA7 106 EZ82
Epsom KT18 172 CS119
Grays RM16 111 GG76
Hardings Cl, Iver SL0 75 BD69
Harding's Cl, Kings.T. KT2 138 CM95
Hardings La, SE20 123 DX93
Hardings Row, Iver SL0 75 BC69
Hardley Cres, Horn. RM11 72 FK56
Hardman Rd, SE7 205 P10
Kingston upon Thames KT2 138 CL96
Hardwick Cl, Lthd. (Oxshott) KT22 170 CC115
Stanmore HA7 41 CJ50
Hardwick Cres, Dart. DA2 128 FP86
Hardwicke Av, Houns. TW5 96 CA81
Hardwicke Gdns, Amer. HP6 20 AS38
Hardwicke Ms, WC1 196 C3
Hardwicke Pl, St.Alb. (Lon.Col.) AL2 9 CK27
Hardwicke Rd, N13 45 DL51
W4 98 CR77
Reigate RH2 184 DA133
Richmond TW10 117 CJ91
Hardwicke St, Bark. IG11 87 EQ67
Hardwick Grn, W13 79 CH71
Hardwick La, Cher. (Lyne) KT16 133 BC101
Hardwick St, EC1 196 E3
Hardwicks Way, SW18
off Buckhold Rd 120 DA85
Hardwidge St, SE1 201 M4
Hardy Av, E16 205 N2
Gravesend (Nthflt.) DA11 130 GE89
Ruislip HA4 59 BV64
Hardy Cl, SE16 203 J5
Barnet EN5 27 CY44
Pinner HA5 60 BX59
Hardy Gro, Dart. DA1 108 FN84
Hardy Rd, E4 47 DZ51
SE3 104 EF80
SW19 120 DB94
Hardy Way, Enf. EN2 29 DN39
Hare & Billet Rd, SE3 103 ED81
Harebell Dr, E6 87 EN71
Harebell Hill, Cob. KT11 154 BX114
Harebell Way, Rom. RM3 52 FK52
Harebreaks, The, Wat. WD24 23 BV38
Harecastle Cl, Hayes UB4
off Braunston Dr 78 BY70
Hare Ct, EC4 196 D9
Harecourt Rd, N1 84 DQ65
Hare Cres, Wat. WD25 7 BU32
Harecroft, Lthd. (Fetch.) KT22 170 CB123
Haredale Rd, SE24 102 DQ84
Haredon Cl, SE23 122 DW87
HAREFIELD, Uxb. 38 BL53
Harefield, Esher KT10 155 CE105
Harefield Av, Sutt. SM2 157 CY109
Harefield Cl, Enf. EN2 29 DN39
H Harefield Hosp, Uxb. UB9 38 BJ53
Harefield Ms, SE4 103 DZ83
Harefield Rd, N8 65 DK57
SE4 103 DZ83
SW16 121 DM94
Rickmansworth WD3 38 BK50
Sidcup DA14 126 EX89
Uxbridge UB8 76 BK65
Harefield Rd Ind Est, Rick. WD3 38 BL49
Hare Hall La, Rom. RM2 71 FH56
Hare Hill, Add. KT15 151 BF107
Hare Hill Cl, Wok. (Pyrford) GU22 168 BG115
Harelands Cl, Wok. GU21 166 AW117
Harelands La, Wok. GU21 166 AW117
Hare La, Esher (Clay.) KT10 155 CE107
Hare Marsh, E2
off Cheshire St 84 DU70
Harendon, Tad. KT20 173 CW121
Hare Pl, EC4 196 E9
Hare Row, E2 84 DV68
Hares Bk, Croy. (New Adgtn.) CR0 161 ED110
Haresfield Rd, Dag. RM10 88 FA65
Harestone Dr, Cat. CR3 176 DT124
Harestone Hill, Cat. CR3 186 DT126
Harestone La, Cat. CR3 186 DS125
Harestone Valley Rd, Cat. CR3 186 DT126
Hare St, SE18 105 EN76
Hare Ter, Grays RM20
off Mill La 109 FX78
Hare Wk, N1 197 N1
Harewood, Rick. WD3 22 BH43
Harewood Av, NW1 194 C5
Northolt UB5 78 BY66
Harewood Cl, Nthlt. UB5 78 BZ66
Reigate RH2 184 DC132
Harewood Dr, Ilf. IG5 49 EM54
Harewood Gdns, S.Croy. CR2 176 DV115
Harewood Hill, Epp. (They.B.) CM16 33 ES35
Harewood Pl, W1 195 J9
Slough SL1 92 AU76
Harewood Rd, SW19 120 DE93
Brentwood CM15 54 FV44
Chalfont St. Giles HP8 20 AW41
Isleworth TW7 97 CF80
South Croydon CR2 160 DS107
Watford WD19 39 BV48
Harewood Row, NW1 194 C6
Harewood Ter, Sthl. UB2 96 BZ77
Harfield Gdns, SE5 102 DS83
Harfield Rd, Sun. TW16 136 BX96
Harford Cl, E4 47 EB45
Harford Dr, Wat. WD17 23 BS38
Harford Ms, N19
off Wedmore St 65 DK62
Harford Rd, E4 47 EB45
Harford St, E1 85 DY70
Harford Wk, N2 64 DD57
Harfst Way, Swan. BR8 147 FC95
Hargood Cl, Har. HA3 62 CL58
Hargood Rd, SE3 104 EJ81
Hargrave Pk, N19 65 DJ61
Hargrave Pl, N7
off Brecknock Rd 65 DK64
Hargrave Rd, N19 65 DJ61
Hargreaves Av, Wal.Cr. (Chsht.) EN7 14 DV30
Hargreaves Cl, Wal.Cr. (Chsht.) EN7 14 DV31
Hargwyne St, SW9 101 DM83
Haringey Pk, N8 65 DL58
Haringey Pas, N4 65 DP58
N8 65 DN56
Haringey Rd, N8 65 DL56
Harington Ter, N9 46 DR48
N18 46 DR48
Harkett Cl, Har. HA3
off Byron Rd 41 CF54
Harkett Ct, Har. HA3 41 CF54
Harkness, Wal.Cr. (Chsht.) EN7 14 DU29
Harkness Cl, Epsom KT17 173 CW116
Romford RM3 52 FM50
Harland Av, Croy. CR0 142 DT104
Sidcup DA15 125 ER90
Harland Cl, SW19 140 DB97
Harland Rd, SE12 124 EG88
Harlands Gro, Orp. BR6
off Pinecrest Gdns 163 EP105
Harlech Gdns, Houns. TW5 96 BW79
Pinner HA5 60 BX59
Harlech Rd, N14 45 DL48
Abbots Langley WD5 7 BU31
Harlech Twr, W3 98 CP75
Harlequin Av, Brent. TW8 97 CG79
Harlequin Cen, Wat. WD17 24 BW42
Harlequin Cl, Hayes UB4
off Cygnet Way 78 BX71
Isleworth TW7 117 CE85
Harlequin Ho, Erith DA18
off Kale Rd 106 EY76
Harlequin Rd, Tedd. TW11 117 CH94
★ Harlequins FC (Rugby), Twick. TW2 117 CE87
Harlescott Rd, SE15 103 DX84
HARLESDEN, NW10 80 CS68
⇌ Harlesden 80 CR68
⊖ Harlesden 80 CR68
Harlesden Cl, Rom. RM3 52 FM52
Harlesden Gdns, NW10 81 CT67
Harlesden La, NW10 81 CU67
Harlesden Rd, NW10 81 CU67
Romford RM3 52 FM51
Harlesden Wk, Rom. RM3
off Harlesden Rd 52 FM52
Harleston Cl, E5
off Theydon Rd 66 DW61
Harley Cl, Wem. HA0 79 CK65
Harley Ct, E11
off Blake Hall Rd 68 EG59
Harley Cres, Har. HA1 61 CD56
Harleyford, Brom. BR1 144 EH95
Harleyford Rd, SE11 101 DM79
Harleyford St, SE11 101 DN79
Harley Gdns, SW10 100 DC78
Orpington BR6 163 ES105
Harley Gro, E3 85 DZ69
Harley Pl, W1 195 H7
Harley Rd, NW3 82 DD66
NW10 80 CS68
Harrow HA1 61 CD56
Harley St, W1 195 H7
Harling Ct, SW11
off Latchmere Rd 100 DF82
Harlinger St, SE18 104 EL76
HARLINGTON, Hayes 95 BQ79
Harlington Cl, Hayes UB3
off New Rd 95 BQ80
Harlington Rd, Bexh. DA7 106 EY83
Hounslow (Hthrw.Air.) TW6 95 BT84
Uxbridge UB8 77 BP71
Harlington Rd E, Felt. TW13, TW14 115 BV87
Harlington Rd W, Felt. TW14 115 BV86
Harlow Gdns, Rom. RM5 51 FC51
Harlow Rd, N13 46 DR48
Rainham RM13 89 FF67
Harlton Ct, Wal.Abb. EN9 16 EF34
Harlyn Dr, Pnr. HA5 59 BV55
Harman Av, Grav. DA11 131 GH92
Woodford Green IG8 48 EF52
Harman Cl, E4 47 ED49
NW2 63 CY62
Harman Dr, NW2 63 CY62
Sidcup DA15 125 ET86
Harman Pl, Pur. CR8 159 DP111
Harman Rd, Enf. EN1 30 DT43
Harmer Rd, Swans. DA10 130 FZ86
Harmer St, Grav. DA12 131 GJ86
HARMONDSWORTH, West Dr. 94 BK79
Harmondsworth La, West Dr. UB7 94 BL79
Harmondsworth Rd, West Dr. UB7 94 BL78
Harmony Cl, NW11 63 CY57
Wallington SM6 159 DL109
Harmony Way, NW4
off Victoria Rd 63 CW56
Harmood Gro, NW1
off Clarence Way 83 DH66
Harmood Pl, NW1
off Harmood St 83 DH66
Harmood St, NW1 83 DH66
Harmsworth Ms, SE11 200 F7
Harmsworth St, SE17 101 DP78
Harmsworth Way, N20 43 CZ46
Harness Rd, SE28 106 EU75
Harnetts Cl, Swan. BR8 147 FD100
Harold Av, Belv. DA17 106 EZ78
Hayes UB3 95 BT76
Harold Ct Rd, Rom. RM3 52 FP51
Harold Cres, Wal.Abb. EN9 15 EC32
Harold Est, SE1 201 N7
Harold Gibbons Ct, SE7
off Victoria Way 104 EJ79
HAROLD HILL, Rom. 52 FL50
Harold Hill Ind Est, Rom. RM3 52 FK52
Harold Laski Ho, EC1 196 F3
HAROLD PARK, Rom. 52 FN51
Harold Pl, SE11 101 DN78
Harold Rd, E4 47 EC49
E11 68 EE60
E13 86 EH67
N8 65 DM57
N15 66 DT57
NW10 80 CR69
SE19 122 DS93
Dartford (Hawley) DA2 128 FM91
Sutton SM1 158 DD105
Woodford Green IG8 48 EG53
Haroldstone Rd, E17 67 DX57
Harold Vw, Rom. RM3 52 FM54
HAROLD WOOD, Rom. 52 FL54
⇌ Harold Wood 52 FM53
H Harold Wood Hosp, Rom. RM3 52 FL54
Harp All, EC4 196 F8
Harpenden Rd, E12 68 EJ61
SE27 121 DP90
Harpenmead Pt, NW2
off Granville Rd 63 CZ61
H Harperbury Hosp, Rad. WD7 9 CJ31
Harper Cl, N14
off Alexandra Ct 29 DJ43
Harper La, Rad. WD7 9 CG32
Harper Ms, SW17 120 DC90
Harper Rd, E6 87 EM72
SE1 201 H6
Harpers Yd, N17
off Ruskin Rd 46 DT53
Harpesford Av, Vir.W. GU25 132 AV99
Harp Island Cl, NW10 62 CR61
Harp La, EC3 201 M1
Harpley Sq, E1 84 DW69
Harpour Rd, Bark. IG11 87 EQ65
Harp Rd, W7 79 CF70
Harpsden St, SW11 100 DG81
Harps Oak La, Red. RH1 184 DF125
Harpur Ms, WC1 196 B6
Harpurs, Tad. KT20 173 CX122
Harpur St, WC1 196 B6
Harraden Rd, SE3 104 EJ81
Harrap Chase, Grays (Bad.Dene) RM17 110 FZ78
Harrap St, E14 85 EC73

Har - Haw

Harrier Av, E11
off Eastern Av 68 EH58
Harrier Cl, Horn. RM12 89 FH65
Harrier Ms, SE28 105 ER76
Harrier Rd, NW9 42 CS54
Harriers Cl, W5 80 CL73
Harrier Way, E6 87 EM71
Waltham Abbey EN9 16 EG34
Harriescourt, Wal.Abb. EN9 16 EG32
Harries Rd, Hayes UB4 78 BW70
Harriet Cl, E8 84 DU67
Harriet Gdns, Croy. CR0 142 DU103
Harriet St, SW1 198 E5
Harriet Tubman Cl, SW2 121 DN87
Harriet Wk, SW1 198 E5
Harriet Walker Way, Rick. WD3
off Thellusson Way 37 BF45
Harriet Way, Bushey WD23 41 CD45
HARRINGAY, N8 65 DN57
⇌ **Harringay** 65 DN58
Harringay Gdns, N8 65 DP56
⇌ **Harringay Green Lanes** 65 DP58
Harringay Rd, N15 65 DP57
Harrington Cl, NW10 62 CR62
Croydon CR0 141 DL103
Harrington Ct, W10
off Dart St 81 CZ69
Harrington Gdns, SW7 100 DB77
Harrington Hill, E5 66 DV60
⇔ **Harrington Road** 142 DW97
Harrington Rd, E11 68 EE60
SE25 142 DU98
SW7 100 DD77
Harrington Sq, NW1 195 K1
Harrington St, NW1 195 K2
Harrington Way, SE18 104 EK76
Harriott Cl, SE10 205 K9
Harriotts Cl, Ashtd. KT21
off Harriotts La 171 CJ120
Harriotts La, Ashtd. KT21 171 CJ119
Harris Cl, Enf. EN2 29 DP39
Gravesend (Nthflt.) DA11 130 GE90
Hounslow TW3 96 CA81
Romford RM3 52 FL52
Harris La, Rad. (Shenley) WD7 10 CN34
Harrison Cl, N20 44 DE46
Brentwood CM13 55 GD43
Northwood HA6 39 BQ51
Harrison Ct, Shep. TW17
off Greeno Cres 135 BP99
Harrison Dr, Epp. (N.Wld.Bas.)
CM16 19 FB26
Harrison Rd, Dag. RM10 89 FB65
Harrisons Ri, Croy. CR0 141 DP104
Harrison St, WC1 196 A3
Harrisons Wf, Purf. RM19 108 FN78
Harrison Wk, Wal.Cr. (Chsht.)
EN8 15 DX30
Harrison Way, Sev. TN13 190 FG122
Waltham Abbey EN9
off Greenwich Way 31 EC36
Harris Rd, Bexh. DA7 106 EY81
Dagenham RM9 70 EZ64
Watford WD25 23 BU35
Harris St, E17 67 DZ59
SE5 102 DR80
Harris Way, Sun. TW16 135 BS95
★ **Harrods**, SW1 198 D6
Harrogate Ct, N11
off Coverdale Rd 44 DG51
Slough SL3 93 BA78
Harrogate Rd, Wat. WD19 40 BW48
Harrold Rd, Dag. RM8 70 EV64
HARROW 61 CD59
⇌ **Harrow & Wealdstone** 61 CE56
⊖ **Harrow & Wealdstone** 61 CE56
★ **Harrow Arts Cen**, Pnr.
HA5 40 CB52
Harrow Av, Enf. EN1 30 DT44
Harroway Rd, SW11 100 DD82
Harrow Bottom Rd, Vir.W.
GU25 133 AZ100
Harrowby Gdns, Grav. (Nthflt.)
DA11 130 GE89
Harrowby St, W1 194 C8
Harrow Cl, Add. KT15 134 BH103
Chessington KT9 155 CK108
Harrow Cres, Rom. RM3 51 FH52
Harrowdene Cl, Wem. HA0 61 CK63
Harrowdene Gdns, Tedd.
TW11 117 CG93
Harrowdene Rd, Wem. HA0 61 CK62
Harrow Dr, N9 46 DT46
Hornchurch RM11 71 FH60
Harrowes Meade, Edg. HA8 42 CN48
Harrow Flds Gdns, Har. HA1 61 CE62
Harrow Gdns, Orp. BR6 164 EV105
Warlingham CR6 177 DZ115
Harrowgate Rd, E9 85 DY65
Harrow Grn, E11
off Harrow Rd 68 EE62
Harrow La, E14 204 D1
Harrow Manorway, SE2 88 EW74
Harrow Mkt, Slou. SL3 93 BA76
★ **Harrow Mus & Heritage Cen**,
Har. HA2 60 CC55
HARROW ON THE HILL, Har. 61 CE61
⇌ **Harrow on the Hill** 61 CE58
⊖ **Harrow on the Hill** 61 CE58
Harrow Pk, Har. HA1 61 CE61
Harrow Pas, Kings.T. KT1
off Market Pl 137 CK96
Harrow Pl, E1 197 N8
Harrow Rd, E6 86 EL67
E11 68 EE62
NW10 81 CV69
W2 81 CZ70
W9 81 CZ70
W10 81 CX70
Barking IG11 87 ES67
Carshalton SM5 158 DE106
Feltham TW14 114 BN88
Ilford IG1 69 EQ63
Sevenoaks (Knock.) TN14 180 EY115
Harrow Rd, Slou. SL3 93 AZ76
Warlingham CR6 177 DZ115
Wembley HA0 61 CJ64
Wembley (Tkgtn.) HA9 62 CM64
★ **Harrow Sch**, Har. HA1 61 CE60
Harrow Vw, Har. HA1, HA2 61 CD56
Hayes UB3 77 BU72
Uxbridge UB10 77 BQ69
Harrow Vw Rd, W5 79 CH70
Harrow Way, Shep. TW17 135 BQ96
Watford WD19 40 BY48
HARROW WEALD, Har. 41 CD53
Harrow Weald Pk, Har. HA3 41 CD51
Harston Dr, Enf. EN3 31 EA38
Hart Cl, Red. (Bletch.) RH1 186 DT134
Hart Cor, Grays RM20 109 FX78
Hart Cres, Chig. IG7 49 ET50
Hart Dyke Cres, Swan. BR8
off Hart Dyke Rd 147 FD97
Hart Dyke Rd, Orp. BR5 146 EW102
Swanley BR8 147 FD97
Harte Rd, Houns. TW3 96 BZ82
Hartfield Av, Borwd. (Elstree)
WD6 26 CN43
Northolt UB5 77 BV68
Hartfield Cl, Borwd. (Elstree)
WD6 26 CN43
Hartfield Cres, SW19 119 CZ94
West Wickham BR4 144 EG104
Hartfield Gro, SE20 142 DV95
Hartfield Pl, Grav. (Nthflt.)
DA11 130 GD87
Hartfield Rd, SW19 119 CZ94
Chessington KT9 155 CK106
West Wickham BR4 162 EG105
Hartfield Ter, E3 85 EA68
Hartford Av, Har. HA3 61 CG55
Hartforde Rd, Borwd. WD6 26 CN40
Hartford Rd, Bex. DA5 126 FA86
Epsom KT19 156 CN107
Hart Gro, W5 80 CN74
Southall UB1 78 CA71
Harthall La, Hem.H. HP3 7 BS26
Kings Langley WD4 7 BP28
Hartham Cl, N7 65 DL64
Isleworth TW7 97 CG81
Hartham Rd, N7 65 DL64
N17 46 DT54
Isleworth TW7 97 CF81
Harting Rd, SE9 124 EL91
Hartington Cl, Har. HA1 61 CE63
Hartington Ct, W4 98 CP80
Hartington Pl, Reig. RH2 184 DA132
Hartington Rd, E16 86 EH72
E17 67 DY58
SW8 101 DL81
W4 98 CP80
W13 79 CH73
Southall UB2 96 BY75
Twickenham TW1 117 CH87
Hartismere Rd, SW6 99 CZ80
Hartlake Rd, E9 85 DX65
Hartland Cl, N21
off Elmscott Gdns 30 DQ44
Addlestone (New Haw)
KT15 152 BJ110
Edgware HA8 42 CN47
Hartland Dr, Edg. HA8 42 CN47
Ruislip HA4 59 BV62
Hartland Rd, E15 86 EF66
N11 44 DF50
NW1 83 DH66
NW6 81 CZ68
Addlestone KT15 152 BG108
Epping CM16 18 EU31
Hampton (Hmptn.H.)
TW12 116 CB91
Hornchurch RM12 71 FG61
Isleworth TW7 97 CG83
Morden SM4 140 DA101
Waltham Cross (Chsht.)
EN8 15 DX30
Hartlands Cl, Bex. DA5 126 EZ86
Hartland Way, Croy. CR0 143 DY103
Morden SM4 139 CZ101
Hartlepool Ct, E16
off Fishguard Way 105 EP75
Hartley Av, E6 86 EL67
NW7 43 CT50
Hartley Cl, NW7 43 CT50
Bromley BR1 145 EM96
Slough (Stoke P.) SL3 74 AW67
Hartley Copse, Wind. (Old Wind.)
SL4 112 AU86
Hartley Down, Pur. CR8 159 DM113
Hartley Fm Est, Pur. CR8 175 DM115
HARTLEY GREEN, Long. 149 FX99
Hartley Hill, Pur. CR8 175 DM115
Hartley Old Rd, Pur. CR8 159 DM114
Hartley Rd, E11 68 EF60
Croydon CR0 141 DP101
Welling DA16 106 EW80
Westerham TN16 189 ER125
Hartley St, E2 84 DW69
Hartley Way, Pur. CR8 175 DM115
Hartmann Rd, E16 86 EK74
Hartmoor Ms, Enf. EN3 31 DX37
Hartnoll St, N7 *off Eden Gro* 65 DM64
Harton Cl, Brom. BR1 144 EK95
Harton Rd, N9 46 DV47
Harton St, SE8 103 EA81
Hart Rd, W.Byf. (Byfleet)
KT14 152 BL113
Hartsbourne Av, Bushey
(Bushey Hth.) WD23 40 CC47
Hartsbourne Cl, Bushey
(Bushey Hth.) WD23 41 CD47
Hartsbourne Rd, Bushey
(Bushey Hth.) WD23 41 CD47
Harts Cl, Bushey WD23 24 CA40
Hartscroft, Croy. CR0 161 DY109
Harts Gro, Wdf.Grn. IG8 48 EG50
Hartshill Cl, Uxb. UB10 76 BN65
Hartshill Rd, Grav. (Nthflt.)
DA11 131 GF89
Hartshill Wk, Wok. GU21 166 AV116
Hartshorn All, EC3 197 N9
Hartshorn Gdns, E6 87 EN70
Hartslands Rd, Sev. TN13 191 FJ123
Harts La, SE14 103 DY80
Barking IG11 87 EP65
Hartslock Dr, SE2 106 EX75
Hartsmead Rd, SE9 125 EM89
Hartspring La, Bushey WD23 24 CA39
Watford WD25 24 CA39
Hart St, EC3 197 N10
Brentwood CM14 54 FW47
Hartsway, Enf. EN3 30 DW42
Hartswood Cl, Brwd. CM14 54 FY49
Hartswood Gdns, W12 99 CT76
Hartswood Grn, Bushey
(Bushey Hth.) WD23 41 CD47
Hartswood Rd, W12 99 CT75
Brentwood CM14 54 FY49
Hartsworth Cl, E13 86 EF68
Hartville Rd, SE18 105 ES77
Hartwell Dr, E4 47 EC51
Hartwell St, E8 *off Dalston La* 84 DT65
Harvard Hill, W4 98 CP79
Harvard La, W4 98 CP78
Harvard Rd, SE13 123 EC85
W4 98 CP78
Isleworth TW7 97 CE81
Harvard Wk, Horn. RM12 71 FG63
Harvel Cl, Orp. BR5 146 EU97
Harvel Cres, SE2 106 EX78
Harvest Bk Rd, W.Wick. BR4 144 EF104
Harvest Ct, Shep. TW17 134 BN98
Harvest End, Wat. WD25 24 BX36
Harvester Rd, Epsom KT19 156 CR110
Harvesters Cl, Islw. TW7 117 CD85
Harvest La, Loug. IG10 48 EK45
Thames Ditton KT7 137 CG100
Harvest Rd, Bushey WD23 24 CB42
Egham (Eng.Grn.) TW20 112 AX92
Feltham TW13 115 BU91
Harvest Way, Swan. BR8 147 FD101
Harvey, Grays RM16 110 GB75
Harvey Dr, Hmptn. TW12 136 CB95
Harveyfields, Wal.Abb. EN9 15 EC34
Harvey Gdns, E11
off Harvey Rd 68 EF60
SE7 104 EK77
Loughton IG10 33 EP41
Harvey Ho, Brent. TW8
off Green Dragon La 98 CL78
Harvey Pt, E16 *off Fife Rd* 86 EH71
Harvey Rd, E11 68 EE60
N8 65 DM57
SE5 102 DR81
Hounslow TW4 116 BZ87
Ilford IG1 69 EP64
Northolt UB5 78 BW66
Rickmansworth (Crox.Grn.)
WD3 22 BN44
St. Albans (Lon.Col.) AL2 9 CJ26
Slough SL3 93 BB76
Uxbridge UB10 76 BN68
Walton-on-Thames KT12 135 BU101
Harveys La, Rom. RM7 71 FD61
Harvey St, N1 84 DR67
Harvill Rd, Sid. DA14 126 EX92
Harvil Rd, Uxb. (Hare.) UB9 58 BK58
Uxbridge (Ickhm.) UB10 58 BL60
Harvington Wk, E8
off Wilman Gro 84 DU66
Harvist Est, N7 65 DN63
Harvist Rd, NW6 81 CX68
Harwater Dr, Loug. IG10 33 EM40
Harwell Cl, Ruis. HA4 59 BR60
Harwell Pas, N2 64 DF56
Harwich La, EC2 197 N6
Harwood Av, Brom. BR1 144 EH96
Hornchurch RM11 72 FL55
Mitcham CR4 140 DE97
Harwood Cl, N12
off Summerfields Av 44 DE51
Wembley HA0
off Harrowdene Rd 61 CK63
Harwood Dr, Uxb. UB10 76 BM67
Harwood Gdns, Wind. (Old Wind.)
SL4 112 AV87
Harwood Hall La, Upmin.
RM14 90 FP65
Harwood Rd, SW6 100 DA80
Harwoods Rd, Wat. WD18 23 BU42
Harwoods Yd, N21
off Wades Hill 45 DN45
Harwood Ter, SW6 100 DB81
Hascombe Ter, SE5
off Love Wk 102 DR82
Haselbury Rd, N9 46 DS49
N18 46 DS49
Haseldine Rd, St.Alb. (Lon.Col.)
AL2 9 CK26
Haseley End, SE23
off Tyson Rd 122 DW87
Haselrigge Rd, SW4 101 DK84
Haseltine Rd, SE26 123 DZ91
Haselwood Dr, Enf. EN2 29 DP42
Haskard Rd, Dag. RM9 70 EX63
Haskell Ho, NW10 80 CR67
Hasker St, SW3 198 C8
Haslam Av, Sutt. SM3 139 CY102
Haslam Cl, N1 83 DN66
Uxbridge UB10 59 BQ61
Haslam St, SE15 102 DT80
Haslemere Av, NW4 63 CX58
SW18 120 DB89
W7 97 CG76
W13 97 CG76
Barnet EN4 44 DF46
Hounslow TW5 96 BW82
Mitcham CR4 140 DD96
Haslemere Cl, Hmptn. TW12 116 BZ92
Wallington SM6
off Stafford Rd 159 DL106
Haslemere Gdns, N3 63 CZ55
Haslemere Heathrow Est, Houns.
TW4 95 BV82
Haslemere Rd, N8 65 DK59
N21 45 DP47
Bexleyheath DA7 106 EZ82
Ilford IG3 69 ET61
Haslemere Rd, Th.Hth. CR7 141 DP99
Hasler Cl, SE28 88 EV73
Haslett Rd, Shep. TW17 135 BS96
Hasluck Gdns, Barn. EN5 28 DC44
Hassard St, E2
off Hackney Rd 84 DT68
Hassendean Rd, SE3 104 EH79
Hassett Rd, E9 85 DX65
Hassocks Cl, SE26 122 DV90
Hassocks Rd, SW16 141 DK95
Hassock Wd, Kes. BR2 162 EK105
Hassop Rd, NW2 63 CX63
Hassop Wk, SE9 124 EL91
Hasted Cl, Green. DA9 129 FW86
Hasted Rd, SE7 104 EK78
Hastings Av, Ilf. IG6 69 EQ56
Hastings Cl, SE15 102 DU80
Barnet EN5 *off Leicester Rd* 28 DC42
Grays RM17 110 FY79
Hastings Dr, Surb. KT6 137 CJ100
Hastings Ho, SE18 105 EM77
Hastings Rd, N11 45 DJ50
N17 66 DR55
W13 79 CH73
Bromley BR2 144 EL102
Croydon CR0 142 DT102
Romford RM2 71 FH57
Hastings St, WC1 195 P3
Hastings Way, Bushey WD23 24 BY42
Rickmansworth (Crox.Grn.)
WD3 23 BP42
Hastingwood Trd Est, N18 47 DX51
Hastoe Cl, Hayes UB4
off Kingsash Dr 78 BY70
Hat & Mitre Ct, EC1 196 G5
Hatch, The, Enf. EN3 31 DX39
Hatcham Pk Ms, SE14
off Hatcham Pk Rd 103 DX81
Hatcham Pk Rd, SE14 103 DX81
Hatcham Rd, SE15 102 DW79
Hatchard Rd, N19 65 DK61
Hatch Cl, Add. KT15 134 BH104
Hatchcroft, NW4 63 CV55
HATCH END, Pnr. 40 BY51
⇌ **Hatch End** 40 BZ52
Hatchers Ms, SE1 201 N5
Hatchett Rd, Felt. TW14 115 BQ88
Hatch Gdns, Tad. KT20 173 CX120
Hatch Gro, Rom. RM6 70 EY56
Hatchlands Rd, Red. RH1 184 DE134
Hatch La, E4 47 ED49
Cobham KT11 169 BP119
Coulsdon CR5 174 DG115
West Drayton UB7 94 BK80
Woking (Ockham) GU23 169 BP120
Hatch Pl, Kings.T. KT2 118 CM92
Hatch Rd, SW16 141 DL96
Brentwood CM15 54 FU43
Hatch Side, Chig. IG7 49 EN50
Hatchwood Cl, Wdf.Grn. IG8
off Sunset Av 48 EF49
Hatcliffe Cl, SE3 104 EF83
Hatcliffe St, SE10 205 K10
Hatfield Cl, SE14
off Reaston St 103 DX80
Brentwood CM13 55 GD45
Hornchurch RM12 72 FK64
Ilford IG6 69 EP55
Mitcham CR4 140 DD98
Sutton SM2 158 DA109
West Byfleet KT14 152 BH112
Hatfield Mead, Mord. SM4
off Central Rd 140 DA99
Hatfield Rd, E15 68 EE64
W4 98 CR75
W13 79 CG74
Ashtead KT21 172 CM119
Dagenham RM9 88 EY65
Grays (Chaff.Hun.) RM16 109 FX77
Potters Bar EN6 12 DC30
Slough SL1 92 AU75
Watford WD24 23 BV39
Hatfields, SE1 200 E2
Loughton IG10 33 EP41
Hathaway Cl, Brom. BR2 145 EM102
Ruislip HA4 *off Stafford Rd* 59 BT63
Stanmore HA7 41 CG50
Hathaway Cres, E12 87 EM65
Hathaway Gdns, W13 79 CF71
Grays RM17
off Hathaway Rd 110 GB76
Romford RM6 70 EX57
Hathaway Rd, Croy. CR0 141 DP101
Grays RM17 110 GB77
Hatherleigh Cl, NW7
off Bittacy Hill 43 CY52
Chessington KT9 155 CK106
Morden SM4 140 DA98
Hatherleigh Gdns, Pot.B. EN6 12 DD32
Hatherleigh Rd, Ruis. HA4 59 BU61
Hatherleigh Way, Rom. RM3 52 FK53
Hatherley Cres, Sid. DA14 126 EU89
Hatherley Gdns, E6 86 EK68
N8 65 DL58
Hatherley Gro, W2 82 DB72
Hatherley Ms, E17 67 EA56
Hatherley Rd, E17 67 DZ56
Richmond TW9 98 CM82
Sidcup DA14 126 EU91
Hatherley St, SW1 199 L8
Hathern Gdns, SE9 125 EN91
Hatherop Rd, Hmptn. TW12 116 BZ94
Hatherwood, Lthd. KT22 171 CK121
Hathorne Cl, SE15 102 DV82
Hathway St, SE15
off Gibbon Rd 102 DW82
Hathway Ter, SE14
off Kitto Rd 102 DW82
Hatley Av, Ilf. IG6 69 EQ56
Hatley Cl, N11 44 DF50
Hatley Rd, N4 65 DM61
Hatteraick St, SE16 202 G4
Hattersfield Cl, Belv. DA17 106 EZ77
Hatters La, Wat. WD18 23 BR44
HATTON, Felt. 95 BT84
Hatton Cl, SE18 105 ER80
Gravesend (Nthflt.) DA11 130 GE90
Hatton Cl, Grays (Chaff.Hun.)
RM16 109 FX76
Hatton Ct, E5 *off Gilpin Rd* 67 DY63
⊖ **Hatton Cross** 95 BT84
Hatton Gdn, EC1 196 E6
Hatton Gdns, Mitch. CR4 140 DF99
Hatton Grn, Felt. TW14 95 BU84
Hatton Gro, West Dr. UB7 94 BK75
Hatton Ho, E1
off Wellclose Sq 84 DU73
Hatton Pl, EC1 196 E5
Hatton Rd, Croy. CR0 141 DN102
Feltham TW14 115 BS85
Waltham Cross (Chsht.)
EN8 15 DX29
Hatton Row, NW8 194 A5
Hatton St, NW8 194 A5
Hatton Wall, EC1 196 D6
Haunch of Venison Yd, W1 195 H9
Havana Cl, Rom. RM1
off Exchange St 71 FE57
Havana Rd, SW19 120 DA89
Havannah St, E14 204 A5
Havant Rd, E17 67 EC55
Havant Way, SE15
off Daniel Gdns 102 DT80
Havelock Pl, Har. HA1 61 CE58
Havelock Rd, N17 46 DU54
SW19 120 DC92
Belvedere DA17 106 EZ77
Bromley BR2 144 EJ98
Croydon CR0 142 DT102
Dartford DA1 127 FH87
Gravesend DA11 131 GF88
Harrow HA3 61 CE55
Kings Langley WD4 6 BN28
Southall UB2 96 BZ76
Havelock St, N1 83 DL67
Ilford IG1 69 EP61
Havelock Ter, SW8 101 DH80
Havelock Wk, SE23 122 DW88
Haven, The, SE26
off Springfield Rd 122 DV92
Grays RM16 111 GF78
Richmond TW9 98 CN83
Sunbury-on-Thames TW16 115 BU94
Haven Cl, SE9 125 EM90
SW19 119 CX90
Gravesend (Istead Rise)
DA13 131 GF94
Hayes UB4 77 BS71
Sidcup DA14 126 EW93
Swanley BR8 147 FF96
Havengore Av, Grav. DA12 131 GL87
Haven Grn, W5 79 CK72
Haven Grn Ct, W5
off Haven Grn 79 CK72
Havenhurst Ri, Enf. EN2 29 DN40
Haven La, W5 80 CL72
Haven Ms, E3
off St. Pauls Way 85 DZ71
Haven Pl, W5
off The Broadway 79 CK73
Grays RM16 110 GC75
Haven Rd, Ashf. TW15 115 BP91
Havensfield, Kings L. (Chipper.)
WD4 6 BH31
Haven St, NW1
off Castlehaven Rd 83 DH66
Haven Ter, W5
off The Broadway 79 CK73
Havenwood, Wem. HA9 62 CP62
Havenwood Cl, Brwd. CM13
off Wilmot Grn 53 FW51
Haverfield Gdns, Rich. TW9 98 CN80
Haverfield Rd, E3 85 DY69
Haverford Way, Edg. HA8 42 CM53
Haverhill Rd, E4 47 EC46
SW12 121 DJ88
HAVERING-ATTE-BOWER,
Rom. 51 FE48
Havering Dr, Rom. RM1 71 FE56
Havering Gdns, Rom. RM6 70 EW57
HAVERING PARK, Rom. 50 FA50
Havering Rd, Rom. RM1 71 FD55
Havering St, E1
off Devonport St 85 DX72
Havering Way, Bark. IG11 88 EV69
Havers Av, Walt. KT12 154 BX106
Haversfield Est, Brent. TW8 98 CL78
Haversham Cl, Twick. TW1 117 CK86
Haversham Pl, N6 64 DF61
Haverstock Ct, Orp. BR5 146 EU96
Haverstock Hill, NW3 64 DE64
Haverstock Pl, N1
off Haverstock St 83 DP68
Haverstock Rd, NW5 64 DG64
Haverstock St, N1 196 G1
Haverthwaite Rd, Orp. BR6 145 ER103
Havil St, SE5 102 DS80
Havisham Pl, SE19 121 DP93
Hawarden Gro, SE24 122 DQ87
Hawarden Hill, NW2 63 CU62
Hawarden Rd, E17 67 DX56
Caterham CR3 176 DQ121
Hawbridge Rd, E11 67 ED60
Hawes Cl, Nthwd. HA6 39 BT52
Hawes La, E4 31 EC38
West Wickham BR4 143 ED102
Hawes Rd, N18 46 DV51
Bromley BR1 144 EH95
Tadworth KT20
off Hatch Gdns 173 CX120
Hawes St, N1 83 DP66
Haweswater Dr, Wat. WD25 8 BW33
Haweswater Ho, Islw. TW7
off Summerwood Rd 117 CF85
Hawfield Bk, Orp. BR6 146 EX104
Hawfield Gdns, St.Alb. (Park St.)
AL2 9 CD26
Hawgood St, E3 85 EA71
Hawk Cl, Wal.Abb. EN9 16 EG34
Hawkdene, E4 31 EB44
Hawke Pk Rd, N22 65 DP55
Hawke Pl, SE16 203 J4
Hawker Cl, Wall. SM6 159 DL108
Hawke Rd, SE19 122 DS93

★ Place of interest ⇌ Railway station ⊖ London Underground station DLR Docklands Light Railway station ⇔ Tramlink station H Hospital

Hawkesbury Rd, SW15 119 CV85
Hawkes Cl, Grays RM17
off New Rd 110 GB79
Hawkesfield Rd, SE23 123 DY89
Hawkesley Cl, Twick. TW1 117 CG91
Hawke's Pl, Sev. TN13 190 FG127
Hawkes Rd, Felt. TW14 115 BU87
Mitcham CR4 140 DE95
Hawkesworth Cl, Nthwd. HA6 39 BS52
Hawke Twr, SE14
off Nynehead St 103 DY79
Hawkewood Rd, Sun. TW16 135 BU97
Hawkhirst Rd, Ken. CR8 176 DR115
Hawkhurst, Cob. KT11 154 CA114
Hawkhurst Gdns, Chess.
KT9 156 CL105
Romford RM5 51 FD51
Hawkhurst Rd, SW16 141 DK95
Hawkhurst Way, N.Mal. KT3 138 CR99
West Wickham BR4 143 EB103
Hawkinge Wk, Orp. BR5 146 EV97
Hawkinge Way, Horn. RM12 90 FJ65
Hawkins Av, Grav. DA12 131 GJ91
Hawkins Cl, NW7 off Hale La 42 CR50
Borehamwood WD6
off Banks Rd 26 CQ40
Harrow HA1 61 CD59
Hawkins Dr, Grays (Chaff.Hun.)
RM16 109 FX75
Hawkins Rd, Tedd. TW11 117 CH93
Hawkins Way, SE6 123 EA92
Hemel Hempstead (Bov.)
HP3 5 BA26
Hawkley Gdns, SE27 121 DP89
Hawkridge Cl, Rom. RM6 70 EW59
Hawkridge Dr, Grays RM17 110 GD78
Hawksbrook La, Beck. BR3 143 EB100
Hawkshaw Cl, SW2
off Tierney Rd 121 DL87
Hawkshead Cl, Brom. BR1 124 EE94
Hawkshead La, Hat. AL9 11 CW28
Hawkshead Rd, NW10 81 CT66
W4 98 CS75
Potters Bar EN6 12 DB29
Hawks Hill, Epp. (N.Wld.Bas.)
CM16 18 FA27
Hawk's Hill, Lthd. KT22 171 CF123
Hawkshill Cl, Esher KT10 154 CA107
Hawks Hill Cl, Lthd. (Fetch.)
KT22 171 CF122
Hawkshill Way, Esher KT10 154 BZ107
Hawkslade Rd, SE15 123 DX85
Hawksley Rd, N16 66 DS62
Hawksmead Cl, Enf. EN3 31 DX35
Hawks Ms, SE10 off Luton Pl 103 EC80
Hawksmoor, Rad. (Shenley)
WD7 10 CN33
Hawksmoor Cl, E6
off Allhallows Rd 86 EL72
SE18 105 ES78
Hawksmoor Grn, Brwd. CM13 55 GD43
Hawksmoor Ms, E1
off Cable St 84 DV73
Hawksmoor St, W6 99 CX79
Hawksmouth, E4 47 EB45
Hawks Rd, Kings.T. KT1 138 CM96
Hawkstone Rd, SE16 202 G9
Hawksview, Cob. KT11 154 BZ113
Hawksway, Stai. TW18 113 BF90
Hawkswell Cl, Wok. GU21 166 AT117
Hawkswell Wk, Wok. GU21
off Lockfield Dr 166 AS117
Hawkswood Gro, Slou. (Fulmer)
SL3 75 AZ65
Hawkswood La, Ger.Cr. SL9 57 AZ64
Hawk Ter, Ilf. IG5
off Tiptree Cres 69 EN55
Hawkwell Ct, E4
off Colvin Gdns 47 EC48
Hawkwell Ho, Dag. RM8 70 FA60
Hawkwell Wk, N1
off Basire St 84 DQ67
Hawkwood Cres, E4 31 EB44
Hawkwood La, Chis. BR7 145 EQ95
Hawkwood Mt, E5 66 DV60
Hawlands Dr, Pnr. HA5 60 BY59
HAWLEY, Dart. 128 FM92
Hawley Cl, Hmptn. TW12 116 BZ93
Hawley Cres, NW1 83 DH66
Hawley Ms, NW1
off Hawley St 83 DH66
Hawley Mill, Dart. DA2 128 FN91
Hawley Rd, N18 47 DX50
NW1 83 DH66
Dartford DA1, DA2 128 FL89
HAWLEY'S CORNER, West. 179 EN121
Hawley St, NW1 83 DH66
Hawley Ter, Dart. DA2
off Hawley Rd 128 FN92
Hawley Vale, Dart. DA2 128 FN92
Hawley Way, Ashf. TW15 114 BN92
Haws La, Stai. TW19 114 BG86
Hawstead La, Orp. BR6 164 EZ106
Hawstead Rd, SE6 123 EB86
Hawsted, Buck.H. IG9 48 EH45
Hawthorn Av, E3 85 DZ67
N13 45 DL50
Brentwood CM13 55 FZ48
Carshalton SM5 158 DG108
Rainham RM13 89 FH70
Richmond TW9
off Kew Rd 98 CL82
Thornton Heath CR7 141 DP95
Hawthorn Cen, Har. HA1 61 CF56
Hawthorn Cl, Abb.L. WD5 7 BU32
Banstead SM7 157 CY114
Gravesend DA12 131 GH91
Hampton TW12 116 CA92
Hounslow TW5 95 BV80
Iver SL0 75 BD68
Orpington BR5 145 ER100
Watford WD17 23 BT38
Woking GU22 166 AY120
Hawthorn Cotts, Well. DA16
off Hook La 106 EU83
Hawthorn Ct, Rich. TW9
off West Hall Rd 98 CP81
Hawthorn Cres, SW17 120 DG92
South Croydon CR2 160 DW111
Hawthornden Cl, N12
off Fallowfields Dr 44 DE51
Hawthorndene Cl, Brom.
BR2 144 EF103
Hawthorndene Rd, Brom.
BR2 144 EF103
Hawthorn Dr, Har. HA2 60 BZ58
Uxbridge (Denh.) UB9 76 BJ65
West Wickham BR4 162 EE105
Hawthorne Av, Har. HA3 61 CG58
Mitcham CR4 140 DD96
Ruislip HA4 59 BV58
Waltham Cross (Chsht.)
EN7 14 DV31
Westerham (Bigg.H.) TN16 178 EK115
Hawthorne Cl, N1 84 DS65
Bromley BR1 145 EM97
Sutton SM1
off Aultone Way 140 DB103
Waltham Cross (Chsht.)
EN7 14 DV31
Hawthorne Ct, Nthwd. HA6
off Ryefield Cres 39 BU54
Walton-on-Thames KT12
off Ambleside Av 136 BX103
Hawthorne Cres, Slou. SL1 74 AS71
West Drayton UB7 94 BM75
Hawthorne Fm Av, Nthlt. UB5 78 BY67
Hawthorne Gro, NW9 62 CQ59
Hawthorne Ms, Grnf. UB6
off Greenford Rd 78 CC72
Hawthorne Pl, Epsom KT17 156 CS112
Hayes UB3 77 BT73
Hawthorne Rd, E17 67 EA55
Bromley BR1 144 EL97
Radlett WD7 9 CG34
Staines TW18 113 BC92
Hawthorne Way, N9 46 DS47
Staines (Stanw.) TW19 114 BK87
Hawthorn Gdns, W5 97 CK76
Hawthorn Gro, SE20 122 DV94
Barnet EN5 27 CT44
Enfield EN2 30 DR38
Hawthorn Hatch, Brent. TW8 97 CH80
Hawthorn La, Sev. TN13 190 FF122
Hawthorn Ms, NW7
off Holders Hill Rd 43 CY53
Hawthorn Pl, Erith DA8 107 FC78
Hawthorn Rd, N8 65 DK55
N18 46 DT50
NW10 81 CU66
Bexleyheath DA6 106 EZ84
Brentford TW8 97 CH80
Buckhurst Hill IG9 48 EK49
Dartford DA1 128 FK88
Sutton SM1 158 DE107
Wallington SM6 159 DH108
Woking GU22 166 AX120
Woking (Send M.) GU23 168 BG124
Hawthorns, Wdf.Grn. IG8 48 EG48
Hawthorns, The, Ch.St.G.
HP8 20 AW40
Epsom KT17
off Ewell Bypass 157 CT107
Loughton IG10 33 EN42
Oxted RH8 188 EG133
Rickmansworth (Map.Cr.)
WD3 37 BD50
Slough (Colnbr.) SL3 93 BF81
Hawthorn Wk, W10
off Droop St 81 CY70
Hawthorn Way, Add. (New Haw)
KT15 152 BJ110
Shepperton TW17 135 BR98
Hawtrees, Rad. WD7 25 CF35
Hawtrey Av, Nthlt. UB5 78 BX68
Hawtrey Cl, Slou. SL1 92 AV75
Hawtrey Dr, Ruis. HA4 59 BU59
Hawtrey Rd, NW3 82 DE66
Haxted Rd, Brom. BR1
off North Rd 144 EH95
Hayburn Way, Horn. RM12 71 FF60
Hay Cl, E15 86 EE66
Borehamwood WD6 26 CQ40
Haycroft Cl, Couls. CR5
off Caterham Dr 175 DP118
Haycroft Gdns, NW10 81 CU67
Haycroft Rd, SW2 121 DL85
Surbiton KT6 138 CL104
Hay Currie St, E14 85 EB72
Hayday Rd, E16 86 EG71
Hayden Ct, Add. (New Haw)
KT15 152 BH111
Hayden Rd, Wal.Abb. EN9 31 EC35
Haydens Cl, Orp. BR5 146 EV100
Haydens Pl, W11
off Portobello Rd 81 CZ72
Hayden Way, Rom. RM5 51 FC54
Haydn Av, Pur. CR8 159 DN114
Haydns Ms, W3
off Emanuel Av 80 CQ72
Haydock Av, Nthlt. UB5 78 CA65
Haydock Cl, Horn. RM12 72 FM63
Haydock Grn, Nthlt. UB5
off Haydock Av 78 CA65
Haydon Cl, NW9 62 CQ56
Enfield EN1
off Mortimer Dr 30 DS44
Haydon Dr, Pnr. HA5 59 BU56
Haydon Pk Rd, SW19 120 DB92
Haydon Rd, Dag. RM8 70 EW61
Watford WD19 24 BY44
⇌ Haydons Road 120 DC92
Haydons Rd, SW19 120 DB92
Haydon St, EC3 197 P10
Haydon Wk, E1 off Mansell St 84 DT73
Haydon Way, SW11 100 DD84
HAYES, Brom. 144 EG103
HAYES 77 BS72
⇌ Hayes 144 EF102
Hayes, The, Epsom KT18 172 CR119
⇌ Hayes & Harlington 95 BT76
Hayes Barton, Wok. GU22 167 BD116
Hayes Bypass, Hayes UB3,
UB4 78 BX70
Hayes Chase, W.Wick. BR4 144 EE99
Hayes Cl, Brom. BR2 144 EG103
Grays RM20 109 FW79
Hayes Ct, SW2 121 DL88
Hayes Cres, NW11 63 CZ57
Sutton SM3 157 CX105
Hayes Dr, Rain. RM13 89 FH66
HAYES END, Hayes 77 BQ71
Hayes End Cl, Hayes UB4 77 BR70
Hayes End Dr, Hayes UB4 77 BR70
Hayes End Rd, Hayes UB4 77 BR70
Hayesford Pk Dr, Brom. BR2 144 EF99
Hayes Gdn, Brom. BR2 144 EG103
H Hayes Grove Priory Hosp,
Brom. BR2 144 EG103
Hayes Hill, Brom. BR2 144 EE102
Hayes Hill Rd, Brom. BR2 144 EF102
Hayes La, Beck. BR3 143 EC97
Bromley BR2 144 EG99
Kenley CR8 160 DQ114
Hayes Mead Rd, Brom. BR2 144 EE102
Hayes Metro Cen, Hayes UB4 78 BW73
Hayes Pk, Hayes UB4 77 BS70
Hayes Pl, NW1 194 C5
Hayes Rd, Brom. BR2 144 EG98
Greenhithe DA9 129 FS87
Southall UB2 95 BV77
Hayes St, Brom. BR2 144 EH102
HAYES TOWN, Hayes 95 BS75
Hayes Wk, Brox. EN10
off Landau Way 15 DZ25
Potters Bar EN6
off Hyde Av 12 DB33
Hayes Way, Beck. BR3 143 EC98
Hayes Wd Av, Brom. BR2 144 EH102
Hayfield Cl, Bushey WD23 24 CB42
Hayfield Pas, E1
off Stepney Grn 84 DW70
Hayfield Rd, Orp. BR5 146 EU99
Hayfield Yd, E1
off Mile End Rd 84 DW70
Haygarth Pl, SW19 119 CX92
Haygreen Cl, Kings.T. KT2 118 CP93
Hay Hill, W1 199 J1
Hayland Cl, NW9 62 CR56
Hay La, NW9 62 CR56
Slough (Fulmer) SL3 56 AX63
Hayles St, SE11 200 F8
Haylett Gdns, Kings.T. KT1
off Anglesea Rd 137 CK98
Hayling Av, Felt. TW13 115 BU90
Hayling Cl, N16
off Pellerin Rd 66 DS64
Hayling Rd, Wat. WD19 39 BV47
Haymaker Cl, Uxb. UB10
off Honey Hill 76 BM66
Hayman Cres, Hayes UB4 77 BR68
Hayman St, N1 off Cross St 83 DP66
Haymarket, SW1 199 M1
Haymarket Arc, SW1 199 M1
Haymeads Dr, Esher KT10 154 CC107
Haymer Gdns, Wor.Pk. KT4 139 CU104
Haymerle Rd, SE15 102 DU79
Haymill Cl, Grnf. UB6 79 CF69
Hayne Rd, Beck. BR3 143 DZ96
Haynes Cl, N11 44 DG48
N17 46 DV52
SE3 104 EE83
Slough SL3 93 AZ78
Woking (Ripley) GU23 168 BH122
Haynes Dr, N9 off Plevna Rd 46 DV48
Haynes La, SE19 122 DS93
Haynes Rd, Grav. (Nthflt.)
DA11 131 GF90
Hornchurch RM11 72 FK57
Wembley HA0 80 CL66
Hayne St, EC1 196 G6
Haynt Wk, SW20 139 CY97
★ Hay's Galleria, SE1 201 M2
Hay's Galleria, SE1 201 M2
Hay's La, SE1 201 M3
Haysleigh Gdns, SE20 142 DU96
Hay's Ms, W1 199 H1
Haysoms Cl, Rom. RM1 71 FE56
Haystall Cl, Hayes UB4 77 BS68
Hay St, E2 84 DU67
Hays Wk, Sutt. SM2 157 CX110
Hayter Ct, E11 68 EH61
Hayter Rd, SW2 121 DL85
Hayton Cl, E8
off Buttermere Wk 84 DT65
Haywain, Oxt. RH8 187 ED130
Hayward Cl, SW19 140 DB95
Dartford DA1 127 FD85
Hayward Dr, Dart. DA1 128 FM89
★ Hayward Gall, SE1 200 C2
Hayward Gdns, SW15 119 CW86
Hayward Rd, N20 44 DC47
Thames Ditton KT7 137 CG102
Haywards Cl, Brwd. CM13 55 GE44
Romford (Chad.Hth.) RM6 70 EV57
Hayward's Pl, EC1 196 F5
Haywood Cl, Pnr. HA5 40 BX54
Haywood Ct, Wal.Abb. EN9 16 EF34
Haywood Dr, Rick. WD3
off Haywood Pk 21 BF43
Haywood Pk, Rick. (Chorl.)
WD3 21 BF43
Haywood Ri, Orp. BR6 163 ES105
Haywood Rd, Brom. BR2 144 EK98
Hayworth Cl, Enf. EN3
off Green St 31 DY40
Hazel Av, West Dr. UB7 94 BN76
Hazelbank, Surb. KT5 138 CQ102
Hazelbank Ct, Cher. KT16 134 BJ102
Hazelbank Rd, SE6 123 ED89
Chertsey KT16 134 BJ102
Hazelbourne Rd, SW12 121 DH86
Hazelbrouck Gdns, Ilf. IG6 49 ER52
Hazelbury Av, Abb.L. WD5 7 BQ32
Hazelbury Cl, SW19 140 DA96
Hazelbury Grn, N9 46 DS48
Hazelbury La, N9 46 DS48
Hazel Cl, N13 46 DR48
N19 off Hargrave Pk 65 DJ61
SE15 102 DU82
Brentford TW8 97 CH80
Hazel Cl, Croy. CR0 143 DX101
Egham (Eng.Grn.) TW20 112 AV93
Hornchurch RM12 71 FH62
Mitcham CR4 141 DK98
Twickenham TW2 116 CC87
Waltham Cross EN7
off The Laurels 14 DS26
Hazelcroft, Pnr. HA5 40 CA51
Hazelcroft Cl, Uxb. UB10 76 BM66
Hazeldean Rd, NW10 80 CR66
Hazeldene, Add. KT15 152 BJ106
Waltham Cross EN8 15 DY32
Hazeldene Ct, Ken. CR8 176 DR115
Hazeldene Dr, Pnr. HA5 60 BW55
Hazeldene Gdns, Uxb. UB10 77 BQ67
Hazeldene Rd, Ilf. IG3 70 EV61
Welling DA16 106 EW82
Hazeldon Rd, SE4 123 DY85
Hazel Dr, Erith DA8 107 FH81
South Ockendon RM15 91 FW69
Hazeleigh, Brwd. CM13 55 GB48
Hazeleigh Gdns, Wdf.Grn. IG8 48 EL50
Hazel End, Swan. BR8 147 FE99
Hazel Gdns, Edg. HA8 42 CP49
Grays RM16 110 GE76
Hazelgreen Cl, N21 45 DP46
Hazel Gro, SE26 123 DX91
Enfield EN1
off Dimsdale Dr 30 DU44
Orpington BR6 145 EP103
Romford RM6 70 EY55
Staines TW18 114 BH93
Watford WD25
off Cedar Wd Dr 23 BV35
Wembley HA0
off Carlyon Rd 80 CL67
Hazel Gro Est, SE26 123 DX91
Hazelhurst, Beck. BR3 143 ED95
Hazelhurst Rd, SW17 120 DC91
Hazel La, Rich. TW10 118 CL89
Hazell Cres, Rom. RM5 51 FB53
Hazells Rd, Grav. DA13 130 GD92
Hazellville Rd, N19 65 DK59
Hazell Way, Slou. (Stoke P.)
SL2 74 AT65
Hazel Mead, Barn. EN5 27 CV43
Epsom KT17 157 CU110
Hazelmere Cl, Felt. TW14 115 BR86
Leatherhead KT22 171 CH119
Northolt UB5 78 BZ68
Hazelmere Dr, Nthlt. UB5 78 BZ68
Hazelmere Gdns, Horn. RM11 71 FH57
Hazelmere Rd, NW6 82 DA67
Northolt UB5 78 BZ68
Orpington BR5 145 EQ98
Hazelmere Wk, Nthlt. UB5 78 BZ68
Hazelmere Way, Brom. BR2 144 EG100
Hazel Ms, N22
off Alexandra Rd 65 DN55
Hazel Ri, Horn. RM11 72 FJ58
Hazel Rd, E15
off Wingfield Rd 68 EE64
NW10 81 CW69
Dartford DA1 128 FK89
Erith DA8 107 FG81
St. Albans (Park St.) AL2 8 CB28
West Byfleet KT14 152 BG114
Hazeltree La, Nthlt. UB5 78 BY69
Hazel Tree Rd, Wat. WD24 23 BV37
Hazel Wk, Brom. BR2 145 EN100
Hazel Way, E4 47 DZ51
SE1 201 P8
Coulsdon CR5 174 DF119
Leatherhead (Fetch.) KT22 170 CC122
HAZELWOOD, Sev. 163 ER111
Hazelwood, Loug. IG10 32 EK43
Hazelwood Av, Mord. SM4 140 DB98
Hazelwood Cl, W5 98 CL75
Harrow HA2 60 CB56
Hazelwood Ct, NW10
off Neasden La N 62 CS62
Hazelwood Cres, N13 45 DN49
Hazelwood Cft, Surb. KT6 138 CL100
Hazelwood Dr, Pnr. HA5 39 BV54
Hazelwood Gdns, Brwd.
CM15 54 FU44
Hazelwood Gro, S.Croy. CR2 160 DV113
Hazelwood Hts, Oxt. RH8 188 EG131
Hazelwood La, N13 45 DN49
Abbots Langley WD5 7 BQ32
Coulsdon CR5 174 DF119
Hazelwood Pk Cl, Chig. IG7 49 ES50
Hazelwood Rd, E17 67 DY57
Enfield EN1 30 DT44
Oxted RH8 188 EH132
Rickmansworth (Crox.Grn.)
WD3 23 BQ44
Sevenoaks (Cudham)
TN14 163 ER112
Woking (Knap.) GU21 166 AS118
Hazlebury Rd, SW6 100 DB82
Hazledean Rd, Croy. CR0 142 DR103
Hazledene Rd, W4 98 CQ79
Hazlemere Gdns, Wor.Pk.
KT4 139 CV102
Hazlemere Rd, Slou. SL2 74 AW74
Hazlewell Rd, SW15 119 CV85
Hazlewood Cl, E5
off Mandeville St 67 DY62
Hazlewood Cres, W10 81 CY70
Hazlitt Cl, Felt. TW13 116 BY91
Hazlitt Ms, W14 off Hazlitt Rd 99 CY76
Hazlitt Rd, W14 99 CY76
Hazon Way, Epsom KT19 156 CR112
Heacham Av, Uxb. UB10 59 BQ62
Headcorn Pl, Th.Hth. CR7
off Headcorn Rd 141 DM98
Headcorn Rd, N17 46 DT52
Bromley BR1 124 EF92
Thornton Heath CR7 141 DM98
Headfort Pl, SW1 198 G5
Headingley Cl, Ilf. IG6 49 ET51
Radlett (Shenley) WD7 10 CL32
Waltham Cross (Chsht.)
EN7 14 DT26
Headington Rd, SW18 120 DC89
Headlam Rd, SW4 121 DK86
Headlam St, E1 84 DV70
HEADLEY, Epsom 182 CQ125
Headley App, Ilf. IG2 69 EN57
Headley Av, Wall. SM6 159 DM106
Headley Chase, Brwd. CM14 54 FW49
Headley Cl, Epsom KT19 156 CN107
Headley Common, Brwd. CM13
off Warley Gap 53 FV52
Headley Common Rd, Epsom
(Headley) KT18 182 CR127
Tadworth KT20 182 CR127
Headley Ct, SE26 122 DV92
Headley Dr, Croy. (New Adgtn.)
CR0 161 EB108
Epsom KT18 173 CV119
Ilford IG2 69 EP58
Headley Gro, Tad. KT20 173 CV120
★ Headley Heath, Epsom
KT18 182 CP128
Headley Heath App, Dor. (Mick.)
RH5 off Ashurst Dr 182 CP130
Tadworth KT20 182 CP130
Headley Rd, Epsom (Tyr.Wd.)
KT18 172 CN123
Epsom (Woodcote) KT18 172 CP118
Leatherhead KT22 171 CK123
Head's Ms, W11
off Artesian Rd 82 DA72
HEADSTONE, Har. 60 CC56
Headstone Dr, Har. HA1, HA3 61 CE55
Headstone Gdns, Har. HA2 60 CC56
⇌ Headstone Lane 40 CB53
Headstone La, Har. HA2, HA3 60 CB56
Headstone Rd, Har. HA1 61 CE57
Head St, E1 85 DX72
Headway, The, Epsom KT17 157 CT109
Headway Cl, Rich. TW10
off Locksmeade Rd 117 CJ91
Heald St, SE14 103 DZ81
Healey Dr, Orp. BR6 163 ET105
Healey Rd, Wat. WD18 23 BT44
Healey St, NW1 83 DH65
Heanor Ct, E5 off Pedro St 67 DX62
Heards La, Brwd. CM15 55 FZ41
Hearne Ct, Ch.St.G. HP8
off Gordon Way 36 AV48
Hearne Rd, W4 98 CN79
Hearn Ri, Nthlt. UB5 78 BX67
Hearn Rd, Rom. RM1 71 FF58
Hearn's Bldgs, SE17 201 L9
Hearn's Rd, Orp. BR5 146 EW98
Hearn St, EC2 197 N5
Hearnville Rd, SW12 120 DG88
H Heart Hosp, The, W1 194 G7
Heath, The, W7
off Lower Boston Rd 79 CE74
Caterham CR3 176 DQ124
Radlett WD7 9 CG33
Heathacre, Slou. (Colnbr.) SL3
off Park St 93 BE81
Heatham Pk, Twick. TW2 117 CF87
Heath Av, Bexh. DA7 106 EX79
Heathbourne Rd, Bushey
(Bushey Hth.) WD23 41 CE47
Stanmore HA7 41 CE47
Heathbridge, Wey. KT13 152 BN108
Heath Brow, NW3
off North End Way 64 DC62
Heath Cl, NW11 64 DB59
W5 80 CM70
Banstead SM7 158 DB114
Hayes UB3 95 BR80
Orpington BR5
off Sussex Rd 146 EW100
Potters Bar EN6 12 DB30
Romford RM2 71 FG55
Staines (Stanw.) TW19 114 BJ86
Virginia Water GU25 132 AX98
Heathclose Av, Dart. DA1 127 FH87
Heathclose Rd, Dart. DA1 127 FG88
Heathcock Ct, WC2
off Strand 83 DL73
Heathcote, Tad. KT20 173 CX121
Heathcote Av, Ilf. IG5 49 EM54
Heathcote Ct, Ilf. IG5
off Heathcote Av 49 EM54
Heathcote Gro, E4 47 EC48
Heathcote Pt, E9
off Wick Rd 85 DX65
Heathcote Rd, Epsom KT18 156 CR114
Twickenham TW1 117 CH86
Heathcote St, WC1 196 B4
Heathcote Way, West Dr. UB7
off Tavistock Rd 76 BK74
Heath Cotts, Pot.B. EN6
off Heath Rd 12 DB30
Heath Ct, Houns. TW4 96 BZ84
Uxbridge UB8 76 BL66
Heathcroft, NW11 64 DB60
W5 80 CM70
Heathcroft Av, Sun. TW16 115 BT94
Heathcroft Gdns, E17 47 ED53
Heathdale Av, Houns. TW4 96 BY83
Heathdene, Tad. KT20
off Canons La 173 CY119
Heathdene Dr, Belv. DA17 107 FB77
Heathdene Rd, SW16 121 DM94
Wallington SM6 159 DH108
Heathdown Rd, Wok. GU22 167 BD115
Heath Dr, NW3 64 DB63
SW20 139 CW98
Epping (They.B.) CM16 33 ES35
Potters Bar EN6 12 DA30
Romford RM2 51 FG53
Sutton SM2 158 DC109
Tadworth KT20 183 CU125
Woking (Send) GU23 167 BB122
Heathedge, SE26 122 DV89
Heath End Rd, Bex. DA5 127 FE88
Heather Av, Rom. RM1 51 FD54
Heatherbank, SE9 105 EM82
Chislehurst BR7 145 EN96
Heatherbank Cl, Dart. DA1 127 FE86
Heather Cl, E6 87 EP72

Hea - Her

Heather Cl, N7 off Newington Barrow Way .65 DM62
SE13 .123 ED87
SW8 .101 DH83
Abbots Langley WD5 .7 BU32
Addlestone (New Haw) KT15 .152 BH110
Brentwood CM15 .54 FV43
Hampton TW12 .136 BZ95
Isleworth TW7 off Harvesters Cl .117 CD85
Redhill RH1 .185 DH130
Romford RM1 .51 FD53
Tadworth KT20 .173 CY122
Uxbridge UB8 off Violet Av .76 BM71
Woking GU21 .166 AW115
Heatherdale Cl, Kings.T. KT2 .118 CN93
Heatherdene Cl, N12 off Bow La .44 DC53
Mitcham CR4 .140 DE98
Heatherden Grn, Iver SL0 .75 BC67
Heather Dr, Dart. DA1 .127 FG87
Enfield EN2 off Chasewood Av .29 DP40
Romford RM1 .51 FD54
Heather End, Swan. BR8 .147 FD98
Heatherfields, Add. (New Haw) KT15 .152 BH110
Heatherfold Way, Pnr. HA5 .59 BT55
Heather Gdns, NW11 .63 CY58
Romford RM1 .51 FD54
Sutton SM2 .158 DA107
Waltham Abbey EN9 .31 EC36
Heather Glen, Rom. RM1 .51 FD54
Heatherlands, Sun. TW16 .115 BU93
Heather La, Wat. WD24 .23 BT35
West Drayton UB7 .76 BL72
Heatherley Dr, Ilf. IG5 .68 EL55
Heather Pk Dr, Wem. HA0 .80 CN66
Heather Pl, Esher KT10 off Park Rd .154 CB105
Heather Ri, Bushey WD23 .24 BZ40
Heather Rd, E4 .47 DZ51
NW2 .63 CT61
SE12 .124 EG89
Heathers, The, Stai. TW19 .114 BM87
Heatherset Cl, Esher KT10 .154 CC106
Heatherset Gdns, SW16 .121 DM94
Heatherside Dr, Vir.W. GU25 .132 AU100
Heatherside Rd, Epsom KT19 .156 CR108
Sidcup DA14 off Wren Rd .126 EX90
Heatherton Ter, N3 .44 DB54
Heathervale Caravan Pk, Add. (New Haw) KT15 .152 BJ110
Heathervale Rd, Add. (New Haw) KT15 .152 BH110
Heather Wk, W10 off Droop St .81 CY70
Edgware HA8 .42 CP50
Twickenham TW2 off Stephenson Rd .116 CA87
Walton-on-Thames KT12 off Octagon Rd .153 BT110
Heather Way, Pot.B. EN6 .11 CZ32
Romford RM1 .51 FD54
South Croydon CR2 .161 DX109
Stanmore HA7 .41 CF51
Woking (Chobham) GU24 .150 AS108
Heatherwood Cl, E12 .68 EJ61
Heatherwood Dr, Hayes UB4 off Charville La .77 BR68
Heath Fm Ct, Wat. WD17 off Grove Mill La .23 BR37
Heathfield, E4 .47 EC48
Chislehurst BR7 .125 EQ93
Cobham KT11 .154 CA114
Heathfield Av, SW18 off Heathfield Rd .120 DD87
South Croydon CR2 .161 DY109
Heathfield Cl, E16 .86 EK71
Keston BR2 .162 EJ106
Potters Bar EN6 .12 DB30
Watford WD19 .40 BW45
Woking GU22 .167 BA118
Heathfield Dr, Mitch. CR4 .140 DE95
Heathfield Gdns, NW11 .63 CX58
SE3 .104 EE82
SW18 off Heathfield Rd .120 DD86
W4 .98 CQ78
Croydon CR0 off Coombe Rd .160 DR105
Heathfield La, Chis. BR7 .125 EP93
Heathfield N, Twick. TW2 .117 CF87
Heathfield Pk, NW2 .81 CW65
Heathfield Pk Dr, Rom. (Chad.Hth.) RM6 .70 EV57
Heathfield Ri, Ruis. HA4 .59 BQ59
Heathfield Rd, SW18 .120 DC86
W3 .98 CP75
Bexleyheath DA6 .106 EZ84
Bromley BR1 .124 EF94
Bushey WD23 .24 BY42
Croydon CR0 .160 DR105
Keston BR2 .162 EJ106
Sevenoaks TN13 .190 FF122
Walton-on-Thames KT12 .154 BY105
Woking GU22 .167 BA118
Heathfields Cl, Ashtd. KT21 .171 CJ118
Heathfields Ct, Houns. TW4 off Frampton Rd .116 BY85
Heathfield S, Twick. TW2 .117 CF87
Heathfield Sq, SW18 .120 DD87
Heathfield St, W11 off Portland Rd .81 CY73
Heathfield Ter, SE18 .105 ET79
W4 .98 CQ78
Heathfield Vale, S.Croy. CR2 .161 DX109
Heath Gdns, Twick. TW1 .117 CF88
Heathgate, NW11 .64 DB58
Heathgate Pl, NW3 off Agincourt Rd .64 DF64
Heath Gro, SE20 off Maple Rd .122 DW94
Heath Gro, Sun. TW16 .115 BT94
Heath Hurst Rd, NW3 .64 DE63
Heathhurst Rd, S.Croy. CR2 .160 DS109
Heathland Rd, N16 .66 DS60
Heathlands, Tad. KT20 .173 CX122
Heathlands Cl, Sun. TW16 .135 BU96
Twickenham TW1 .117 CF89
Woking GU21 .150 AY114
Heathlands Ri, Dart. DA1 .127 FH86
Heathlands Way, Houns. TW4 .116 BY85
Heath La, SE3 .103 ED82
Dartford (Lower) DA1 .128 FJ88
Dartford (Upper) DA1 .127 FG89
Heathlee Rd, SE3 .104 EF84
Dartford DA1 .127 FE86
Heathley End, Chis. BR7 .125 EQ93
Heathmans Rd, SW6 .99 CZ81
Heath Mead, SW19 .119 CX90
Heath Pk Ct, Rom. RM2 off Heath Pk Rd .71 FG57
Heath Pk Dr, Brom. BR1 .144 EL97
Heath Pk Rd, Rom. RM2 .71 FG57
Heath Pas, NW3 .64 DB61
Heath Ridge Grn, Cob. KT11 .154 CA113
Heath Ri, SW15 .119 CX86
Bromley BR2 .144 EF100
Virginia Water GU25 .132 AX98
Woking (Ripley) GU23 .168 BH123
Heath Rd, SW8 .101 DH82
Bexley DA5 .127 FC88
Caterham CR3 .176 DR123
Dartford DA1 .127 FF86
Grays RM16 .111 GG75
Harrow HA1 .60 CC59
Hounslow TW3 .96 CB84
Leatherhead (Oxshott) KT22 .154 CC112
Potters Bar EN6 .12 DA30
Romford RM6 .70 EX59
Thornton Heath CR7 .142 DQ97
Twickenham TW1, TW2 .117 CF88
Uxbridge UB10 .77 BQ70
Watford WD19 .40 BX45
Weybridge KT13 .152 BN106
Woking GU21 .167 AZ115
★ Heathrow Airport (London), Houns. TW6 .95 BP81
Heathrow Cl, West Dr. UB7 .94 BH81
Heathrow Interchange, Hayes UB4 .78 BW74
Heathrow Int Trd Est, Houns. TW4 .95 BV83
⇌ Heathrow Terminal 4 .115 BP85
⊖ Heathrow Terminal 4 .115 BP85
⇌ Heathrow Terminals 1,2,3 .95 BP83
⊖ Heathrow Terminals 1,2,3 .95 BP83
Heathrow Tunnel App, Houns. (Hthrw.Air.) TW6 .95 BP83
Heathrow Vehicle Tunnel, Houns. (Hthrw.Air.) TW6 .95 BP81
Heaths Cl, Enf. EN1 .30 DS40
Heath Side, NW3 .64 DD63
Heathside, Esher KT10 .137 CE104
Hounslow TW4 .116 BZ87
Heath Side, Orp. BR5 .145 EQ102
Heathside, Wey. KT13 .153 BP106
Heathside Av, Bexh. DA7 .106 EY81
Heathside Cl, Esher KT10 .137 CE104
Ilford IG2 .69 ER57
Northwood HA6 .39 BR50
Heathside Ct, Tad. KT20 .173 CV123
Heathside Cres, Wok. GU22 .167 AZ117
Heathside Gdns, Wok. GU22 .167 BA117
Heathside Pk Rd, Wok. GU22 .167 AZ118
Heathside Pl, Epsom KT18 .173 CX118
Heathside Rd, Nthwd. HA6 .39 BR49
Woking GU22 .167 AZ118
Heathstan Rd, W12 .81 CU72
Heath St, NW3 .64 DC63
Dartford DA1 .128 FK87
Heath Vw, N2 .64 DC56
Heathview Av, Dart. DA1 .127 FE86
Heath Vw Cl, N2 .64 DC56
Heathview Ct, SW19 .119 CX89
Heathview Cres, Dart. DA1 .127 FG88
Heathview Dr, SE2 .106 EX79
Heathview Gdns, SW15 .119 CW87
Heath Vw Gdns, Grays RM16 .110 GC75
Heath Vw Rd, Grays RM16 .110 GC75
Heathview Rd, Th.Hth. CR7 .141 DN98
Heath Vil, SE18 .105 ET78
SW18 off Cargill Rd .120 DC88
Heathville Rd, N19 .65 DL59
Heathwall St, SW11 .100 DF83
Heathway, SE3 .104 EF80
Caterham CR3 .186 DQ125
Croydon CR0 .143 DZ104
Dagenham RM9, RM10 .88 FA66
Heath Way, Erith DA8 .107 FC81
Heathway, Iver SL0 .75 BD68
Leatherhead (E.Hors.) KT24 .169 BT124
Woodford Green IG8 .48 EJ49
Heathway Ind Est, Dag. RM10 off Manchester Way .71 FB63
Heathwood Gdns, SE7 .104 EL77
Swanley BR8 .147 FC96
Heathwood Pt, SE23 off Dacres Rd .123 DX90
Heathwood Wk, Bex. DA5 .127 FE88
Heaton Av, Rom. RM3 .51 FH52
Heaton Cl, E4 .47 EC48
Romford RM3 .52 FJ52
Heaton Ct, Wal.Cr. (Chsht.) EN8 .15 DX29
Heaton Gra Rd, Rom. RM2 .51 FF54
Heaton Rd, SE15 .102 DU83
Mitcham CR4 .120 DG94
Heaton Way, Rom. RM3 .52 FJ52
Heaver Rd, SW11 off Wye St .100 DD83
Heavitree Cl, SE18 .105 ER78
Heavitree Rd, SE18 .105 ER78
Hebden Ct, E2 off Laburnum St .84 DT67
Hebden Ter, N17 off Commercial Rd .46 DS51
Hebdon Rd, SW17 .120 DE90
Heber Rd, NW2 .63 CX64
SE22 .122 DT86
Hebron Rd, W6 .99 CV76
Hecham Cl, E17 .47 DY54
Heckfield Pl, SW6 off Fulham Rd .100 DA80
Heckford Cl, Wat. WD18 .23 BQ44
Heckford St, E1 off The Highway .85 DX73
Hector St, SE18 .105 ES77
Heddington Gro, N7 .65 DM64
Heddon Cl, Islw. TW7 .97 CG84
Heddon Ct Av, Barn. EN4 .28 DF43
Heddon Rd, Barn. EN4 .28 DF43
Heddon St, W1 .195 K10
Hedge Hill, Enf. EN2 .29 DP39
Hedge La, N13 .45 DP48
Hedgeley, Ilf. IG4 .69 EM56
Hedgemans Rd, Dag. RM9 .88 EX66
Hedgemans Way, Dag. RM9 .88 EY65
Hedge Pl Rd, Green. DA9 .129 FT86
Hedgerley Ct, Wok. GU21 .166 AW117
Hedgerley Gdns, Grnf. UB6 .78 CC68
Hedgerley Grn, Slou. (Hedg.) SL2 .56 AT58
Hedgerley La, Ger.Cr. SL9 .56 AV59
Slough SL2 .56 AS58
Hedgerow, Ger.Cr. (Chal.St.P.) SL9 .36 AY51
Hedgerow La, Barn. EN5 .27 CV43
Hedgerows, The, Grav. (Nthflt.) DA11 .130 GE89
Hedgerow Wk, Wal.Cr. EN8 .15 DX30
Hedgers Cl, Loug. IG10 off Newmans La .33 EN42
Hedgers Gro, E9 .85 DY65
Hedger St, SE11 .200 F8
Hedgeside Rd, Nthwd. HA6 .39 BQ50
Hedge Wk, SE6 .123 EB91
Hedgewood Gdns, Ilf. IG5 .69 EN57
Hedgley St, SE12 .124 EF85
Hedingham Cl, N1 off Popham Rd .84 DQ66
Hedingham Rd, Dag. RM8 .70 EV64
Grays (Chaff.Hun.) RM16 .109 FW78
Hornchurch RM11 .72 FN60
Hedley Av, Grays RM20 .109 FW80
Hedley Cl, Rom. RM1 off High St .71 FE57
Hedley Rd, Twick. TW2 .116 CA87
Hedley Row, N5 off Poets Rd .66 DR64
Hedworth Av, Wal.Cr. EN8 .15 DX33
Heenan Cl, Bark. IG11 off Glenny Rd .87 EQ65
Heene Rd, Enf. EN2 .30 DR39
Heideck Gdns, Brwd. CM13 off Victors Cres .55 GB47
Heidegger Cres, SW13 off Trinity Ch Rd .99 CV79
Heigham Rd, E6 .86 EK66
Heighton Gdns, Croy. CR0 .159 DP106
Heights, The, SE7 .104 EJ78
Beckenham BR3 .123 EC94
Loughton IG10 .33 EM40
Northolt UB5 .60 BZ64
Waltham Abbey (Nazeing) EN9 .16 EH25
Weybridge KT13 .152 BN110
Heights Cl, SW20 .119 CV94
Banstead SM7 .173 CY116
★ Heinz Gall, RIBA, W1 .194 F8
Heiron St, SE17 .101 DP79
Helby Rd, SW4 .121 DK86
Helder Gro, SE12 .124 EF87
Helder St, S.Croy. CR2 .160 DR107
Heldmann Cl, Houns. TW3 .97 CD84
Helegon Cl, Orp. BR6 .163 ET105
Helena Cl, Barn. EN4 .28 DD38
Wallington SM6 off Kingsford Av .159 DL108
Helena Pl, E9 off Fremont St .84 DW67
Helena Rd, E13 .86 EF68
E17 .67 EA57
NW10 .63 CV64
W5 .79 CK71
Helena Sq, SE16 .203 K1
Helen Av, Felt. TW14 .115 BV87
Helen Cl, N2 off Thomas More Way .64 DC55
Dartford DA1 .127 FH87
West Molesey KT8 .136 CB98
Helen Rd, Horn. RM11 .72 FK55
Helens Gate, Wal.Cr. EN8 .15 DZ26
Helenslea Av, NW11 .63 CZ60
Helen's Pl, E2 off Roman Rd .84 DW69
Helen St, SE18 off Wilmount St .105 EP77
Helford Cl, Ruis. HA4 off Chichester Av .59 BS61
Helford Wk, Wok. GU21 .166 AU118
Helford Way, Upmin. RM14 .73 FR58
Helgiford Gdns, Sun. TW16 .115 BS94
Helios Rd, Wall. SM6 off London Rd .140 DG102
Helix Gdns, SW2 off Helix Rd .121 DM86
Helix Rd, SW2 .121 DM86
Helleborine, Grays (Bad.Dene) RM17 .110 FZ78
Hellings St, E1 .202 C3
Helm Cl, Epsom KT19 .156 CN112
Helme Cl, SW19 .119 CZ92
Helmet Row, EC1 .197 J4
Helmore Rd, Bark. IG11 .87 ET66
Helmsdale, Wok. GU21 off Winnington Way .166 AV118
Helmsdale Cl, Hayes UB4 .78 BY70
Romford RM1 .51 FE52
Helmsdale Rd, SW16 .141 DJ95
Romford RM1 .51 FE52
Helmsley Pl, E8 .84 DV66
Helsinki Sq, SE16 .203 L6
Helston Cl, Pnr. HA5 .40 BZ52
Helston Pl, Abb.L. WD5 off Shirley Rd .7 BT32
Helvellyn Cl, Egh. TW20 .113 BB94
Helvetia St, SE6 .123 DZ89
Hemans St, SW8 .101 DK80
Hemberton Rd, SW9 .101 DL83
Hemery Rd, Grnf. UB6 .61 CD64
Hemingford Cl, N12 .44 DD50
Hemingford Rd, N1 .83 DM67
Sutton SM3 .157 CW105
Watford WD17 .23 BS36
Heming Rd, Edg. HA8 .42 CP52
Hemington Av, N11 .44 DF50
Hemlock Cl, Tad. (Kgswd.) KT20 .173 CY123
Hemlock Rd, W12 .81 CT73
Hemmen La, Hayes UB3 .77 BT72
Hemming Cl, Hmptn. TW12 off Chandler Cl .136 CA95
Hemmings Cl, Sid. DA14 .126 EV89
Hemming St, E1 .84 DU70
Hemming Way, Wat. WD25 .23 BU35
Hemnall St, Epp. CM16 .17 ET31
Hempshaw Av, Bans. SM7 .174 DF116
Hempson Av, Slou. SL3 .92 AW76
Hempstead Cl, Buck.H. IG9 .48 EG47
Hempstead Rd, E17 .47 ED54
Hemel Hempstead HP3 .5 BA27
Kings Langley WD4 .6 BM26
Watford WD17 .23 BT39
Hemp Wk, SE17 .201 L8
Hemsby Rd, Chess. KT9 .156 CM107
Hemstal Rd, NW6 .82 DA66
Hemsted Rd, Erith DA8 .107 FE80
Hemswell Dr, NW9 .42 CS53
Hemsworth Ct, N1 off Hemsworth St .84 DS68
Hemsworth St, N1 .84 DS68
Hemus Pl, SW3 off Chelsea Manor St .100 DE78
Hen & Chicken Ct, EC4 off Fleet St .83 DN72
Henbane Path, Rom. RM3 off Clematis Cl .52 FK52
Henbit Cl, Tad. KT20 .173 CV119
Henbury Way, Wat. WD19 .40 BX48
Henchman St, W12 .81 CT72
Hencroft St N, Slou. SL1 .92 AT75
Hencroft St S, Slou. SL1 .92 AT76
Hendale Av, NW4 .63 CU55
Henderson Cl, NW10 .80 CQ65
Hornchurch RM11 .71 FH61
Henderson Dr, NW8 off Cunningham Pl .82 DD70
Dartford DA1 .108 FM84
H Henderson Hosp, Sutt. SM2 .158 DB109
Henderson Pl, Abb.L. (Bedmond) WD5 .7 BT27
Henderson Rd, E7 .86 EJ65
N9 .46 DV46
SW18 .120 DE87
Croydon CR0 .142 DR100
Hayes UB4 .77 BU69
Westerham (Bigg.H.) TN16 .162 EJ112
Hendham Rd, SW17 .120 DE89
HENDON, NW4 .63 CV56
⇌ Hendon .63 CU58
Hendon Av, N3 .43 CY53
⊖ Hendon Central .63 CW57
Hendon Gdns, Rom. RM5 .51 FC51
Hendon Hall Ct, NW4 off Parson St .63 CX55
Hendon La, N3 .63 CY55
Hendon Pk Row, NW11 .63 CZ58
Hendon Rd, N9 .46 DU47
Hendon Way, NW2 .63 CZ62
NW4 .63 CV58
Staines (Stanw.) TW19 .114 BK86
Hendon Wd La, NW7 .27 CT44
Hendren Cl, Grnf. UB6 off Dimmock Dr .61 CD64
Hendre Rd, SE1 .201 N9
Hendrick Av, SW12 .120 DF86
Heneage Cres, Croy. (New Adgtn.) CR0 .161 EC110
Heneage La, EC3 .197 N9
Heneage St, E1 .84 DT71
Henfield Cl, N19 .65 DJ60
Bexley DA5 .126 FA86
Henfield Rd, SW19 .139 CZ95
Hengelo Gdns, Mitch. CR4 .140 DD98
Hengist Rd, SE12 .124 EH87
Erith DA8 .107 FB80
Hengist Way, Brom. BR2 .144 EE98
Hengrave Rd, SE23 .123 DX87
Hengrove Ct, Bex. DA5 off Hurst Rd .126 EY88
Hengrove Cres, Ashf. TW15 .114 BK90
Henhurst Rd, Grav. (Cobham) DA12 .131 GK94
Henley Av, Sutt. SM3 .139 CY104
Henley Cl, Grnf. UB6 .78 CC68
Isleworth TW7 .97 CF81
Henley Ct, N14 .45 DJ45
Woking GU22 .167 BB120
Henley Cross, SE3 .104 EH83
Henley Deane, Grav. (Nthflt.) DA11 .130 GE91
Henley Dr, SE1 .202 A8
Kingston upon Thames KT2 .119 CT94
Henley Gdns, Pnr. HA5 .59 BV55
Romford RM6 .70 EY57
Henley Rd, E16 .105 EM75
N18 .46 DS49
NW10 .81 CW67
Ilford IG1 .69 EQ63
Henley St, SW11 .100 DG82
Henley Way, Felt. TW13 .116 BX92
Henlow Pl, Rich. TW10 off Sandpits Rd .117 CK89
Hennel Cl, SE23 .122 DW90
Hennessy Ct, Wok. GU21 .151 BC113
Henniker Gdns, E6 .86 EK69
Henniker Ms, SW3 off Callow St .100 DD79
Henniker Pt, E15 .68 EE64
Henniker Rd, E15 .67 ED64
Henningham Rd, N17 .46 DR53
Henning St, SW11 .100 DE81
Henrietta Cl, SE8 .103 EA79
Henrietta Ms, WC1 .196 A4
Henrietta Pl, W1 .195 H9
Henrietta St, E15 .67 EC64
WC2 .196 A10
Henriques St, E1 .84 DU72
Henry Addlington Cl, E6 .87 EP71
Henry Cl, Enf. EN2 .30 DS38
Henry Cooper Way, SE9 .124 EK90
Henry Darlot Dr, NW7 .43 CX50
Henry De Gray Cl, Grays RM17 .110 FZ77
Henry Dickens Ct, W11 .81 CX74
Henry Doulton Dr, SW17 .121 DH91
Henry Jackson Rd, SW15 .99 CX83
Henry Macaulay Av, Kings.T. KT2 .137 CK95
Henry Rd, E6 .86 EL68
N4 .66 DQ60
Barnet EN4 .28 DD43
Henry's Av, Wdf.Grn. IG8 .48 EF50
Henryson Rd, SE4 .123 EA85
Henry St, Brom. BR1 .144 EH95
Grays RM17 off East Thurrock Rd .110 GC79
Henry's Wk, Ilf. IG6 .49 ER52
Hensford Gdns, SE26 off Wells Pk Rd .122 DV91
Henshall St, N1 .84 DR65
Henshawe Rd, Dag. RM8 .70 EX62
Henshaw St, SE17 .201 K8
Henshill Pt, E3 off Bromley High St .85 EB69
Hensley Pt, E9 off Wick Rd .85 DX65
Henslowe Rd, SE22 .122 DU85
Henslow Way, Wok. GU21 .151 BD114
Henson Av, NW2 .63 CW64
Henson Cl, Orp. BR6 .145 EP103
Henson Path, Har. HA3 .61 CK55
Henson Pl, Nthlt. UB5 .78 BW67
Henstridge Pl, NW8 .82 DE68
Hensworth Rd, Ashf. TW15 .114 BK93
Henty Cl, SW11 .100 DE80
Henty Wk, SW15 .119 CV85
Henville Rd, Brom. BR1 .144 EH95
Henwick Rd, SE9 .104 EK83
Henwood Side, Wdf.Grn. IG8 off Love La .49 EM51
Hepburn Cl, Grays (Chaff.Hun.) RM16 .109 FX77
Hepburn Gdns, Brom. BR2 .144 EE102
Hepburn Ms, SW11 off Webbs Rd .120 DF85
Hepple Cl, Islw. TW7 .97 CH82
Hepplestone Cl, SW15 off Dover Pk Dr .119 CV86
Hepscott Rd, E9 .85 EA66
Hepworth Ct, Bark. IG11 .70 EU64
Hepworth Gdns, Bark. IG11 .70 EU64
Hepworth Rd, SW16 .121 DL94
Hepworth Wk, NW3 off Haverstock Hill .64 DE64
Hepworth Way, Walt. KT12 .135 BT102
Heracles Cl, Wall. SM6 .159 DL108
Herald Gdns, Wall. SM6 .141 DH104
Herald's Ct, SE11 .200 F9
Herald's Pl, SE11 .200 E8
Herald St, E2 off Three Colts La .84 DV70
Herald Wk, Dart. DA1 off Temple Hill Sq .128 FM85
Herbal Hill, EC1 .196 E5
Herbert Cres, SW1 .198 E6
Woking (Knap.) GU21 .166 AS117
Herbert Gdns, NW10 .81 CV68
W4 off Magnolia Rd .98 CP79
Romford RM6 .70 EX59
St. Albans AL2 .8 CB29
Herbert Ms, SW2 off Bascombe St .121 DN86
Herbert Morrison Ho, SW6 off Clem Attlee Ct .99 CZ79
Herbert Pl, SE18 off Plumstead Common Rd .105 EP79
Herbert Rd, E12 .68 EL63
E17 .67 DZ59
N11 .45 DL52
N15 .66 DT57
NW9 .63 CU58
SE18 .105 EN80
SW19 .119 CZ94
Bexleyheath DA7 .106 EY82
Bromley BR2 .144 EK99
Hornchurch RM11 .72 FL59
Ilford IG3 .69 ES61
Kingston upon Thames KT1 .138 CM97
Southall UB1 .78 BZ74
Swanley BR8 .127 FH93
Swanscombe DA10 .130 FZ86
Herbert St, E13 .86 EG68
NW5 .82 DG65
Herbert Ter, SE18 off Herbert Rd .105 EP79
Herbrand St, WC1 .195 P4
Hercies Rd, Uxb. UB10 .76 BM66
Hercules Pl, N7 off Hercules St .65 DL62
Hercules Rd, SE1 .200 C7
Hercules St, N7 .65 DL62
Hereford Av, Barn. EN4 .44 DF46
Hereford Cl, Epsom KT18 .156 CR113
Staines TW18 .134 BH95
Hereford Copse, Wok. GU22 .166 AV119
Hereford Ct, Sutt. SM2 off Worcester Rd .158 DA108
Hereford Gdns, SE13 off Longhurst Rd .124 EE85
Ilford IG1 .68 EL59
Pinner HA5 .60 BY57
Twickenham TW2 .116 CC88
Hereford Ho, NW6 .82 DA68

★ Place of interest ⇌ Railway station ⊖ London Underground station DLR Docklands Light Railway station Tramlink station H Hospital

271
Her - Hig

Hereford Ms, W2
off Hereford Rd 82 DA72
Hereford Pl, SE14 103 DZ80
Hereford Retreat, SE15
off Bird in Bush Rd 102 DU80
Hereford Rd, E11 68 EH57
W2 82 DA72
W3 80 CP73
W5 97 CJ76
Feltham TW13 116 BW88
Hereford Sq, SW7 100 DC77
Hereford St, E2 84 DU70
Hereford Way, Chess. KT9 155 CJ106
Herent Dr, Ilf. IG5 69 EM55
Hereward Av, Pur. CR8 159 DN111
Hereward Cl, Wal.Abb. EN9 15 ED32
Hereward Gdns, N13 45 DN50
Hereward Grn, Loug. IG10 33 EQ39
Hereward Rd, SW17 120 DF91
Herga Ct, Har. HA1 61 CE62
Watford WD17 23 BU40
Herga Rd, Har. HA3 61 CF56
Herington Gro, Brwd. CM13 55 GA45
Heriot Av, E4 47 EA47
Heriot Rd, NW4 63 CW57
Chertsey KT16 134 BG101
Heriots Cl, Stan. HA7 41 CG49
Heritage Cl, SW9 101 DP83
Uxbridge UB8 76 BJ70
Heritage Hill, Kes. BR2 162 EJ106
Heritage Pl, SW18
off Earlsfield Rd 120 DC88
Heritage Vw, Har. HA1 61 CF62
Heritage Wk, Rick. (Chorl.) WD3
off Chenies Rd 21 BE41
Herkomer Cl, Bushey WD23 24 CB44
Herkomer Rd, Bushey WD23 24 CA43
Herlwyn Av, Ruis. HA4 59 BS62
Herlwyn Gdns, SW17 120 DF91
Hermes Cl, W9
off Chippenham Rd 82 DA70
Hermes St, N1 196 D1
Hermes Wk, Nthlt. UB5
off Hotspur Rd 78 CA68
Hermes Way, Wall. SM6 159 DK108
Herm Ho, Enf. EN3
off Eastfield Rd 31 DX38
Hermiston Av, N8 65 DL57
Hermitage, The, SE23 122 DW88
SW13 99 CT81
Feltham TW13 115 BT90
Richmond TW10 117 CK85
Uxbridge UB8 76 BL65
Hermitage Cl, E18 68 EF56
Enfield EN2 29 DP40
Esher (Clay.) KT10 155 CG107
Shepperton TW17 134 BN98
Slough SL3 92 AW76
Hermitage Ct, E18 68 EG56
NW2 off Hermitage La 64 DA62
Potters Bar EN6
off Southgate Rd 12 DC33
Hermitage Gdns, NW2 64 DA62
SE19 122 DQ93
Hermitage La, N18 46 DR50
NW2 64 DA62
SE25 142 DU100
SW16 121 DM94
Croydon CR0 142 DU100
Hermitage Path, SW16 141 DL95
Hermitage Rd, N4 65 DP59
N15 65 DP59
SE19 122 DQ94
Kenley CR8 176 DQ116
Woking GU21 166 AT119
Hermitage Row, E8 66 DU64
Hermitage St, W2 82 DD71
Hermitage Wk, E18 68 EF56
Hermitage Wall, E1 202 C3
Hermitage Waterside, E1 202 B2
Hermitage Way, Stan. HA7 41 CG53
Hermitage Wds Cres, Wok.
GU21 166 AS119
Hermit Pl, NW6
off Belsize Rd 82 DB67
Hermit Rd, E16 86 EF71
Hermit St, EC1 196 F2
Hermon Gro, Hayes UB3 77 BU74
Hermon Hill, E11 68 EG57
E18 68 EG57
Herndon Cl, Egh. TW20 113 BA91
Herndon Rd, SW18 120 DC85
Herne Cl, NW10
off North Circular Rd 62 CR64
HERNE HILL, SE24 122 DQ85
⇌ Herne Hill 121 DP86
Herne Hill, SE24 122 DQ86
Herne Hill Ho, SE24
off Railton Rd 121 DP86
Herne Hill Rd, SE24 102 DQ83
Herne Ms, N18
off Lyndhurst Rd 46 DU49
Herne Pl, SE24 121 DP85
Herne Rd, Bushey WD23 24 CB44
Surbiton KT6 137 CK103
Heron Cl, E17 47 DZ54
NW10 80 CS65
Buckhurst Hill IG9 48 EG46
Hemel Hempstead HP3
off Belswains La 6 BM25
Rickmansworth WD3 38 BK47
Sutton SM1
off Sandpiper Rd 157 CZ106
Uxbridge UB8 76 BK65
Heron Ct, Brom. BR2 144 EJ98
Heron Cres, Sid. DA14 125 ES90
Heron Dale, Add. KT15 152 BK106
Herondale, S.Croy. CR2 161 DX109
Herondale Av, SW18 120 DD88
Heron Dr, N4 66 DQ61
Slough SL3 93 BB77
Heronfield, Egh. (Eng.Grn.)
TW20 112 AV93
Potters Bar EN6 12 DC30
Heron Flight Av, Horn. RM12 89 FG66
Herongate Rd, E12 68 EJ61
Swanley BR8 127 FE93
Herongate Rd, Wal.Cr. (Chsht.)
EN8 15 DY27
Heron Hill, Belv. DA17 106 EZ77
Heron Ms, Ilf. IG1
off Balfour Rd 69 EP61
Heron Pl, SE16 203 L2
Heron Quay, E14 203 P3
DLR Heron Quays 204 A3
Heron Rd, SE24 102 DQ84
Croydon CR0
off Tunstall Rd 142 DS103
Twickenham TW1 97 CG84
Heronry, The, Walt. KT12 153 BU107
Herons, The, E11 68 EF58
Herons Cft, Wey. KT13 153 BR107
Heronsforde, W13 79 CJ72
HERONSGATE, Rick. 37 BD45
Heronsgate, Edg. HA8 42 CN50
Heronsgate Rd, Rick. (Chorl.)
WD3 21 BB44
Heronslea, Wat. WD25 24 BW36
Heronslea Dr, Stan. HA7 42 CL50
Heron's Pl, Islw. TW7 97 CH83
Heron Sq, Rich. TW9
off Bridge St 117 CK85
Herons Ri, Barn. EN4 28 DE42
Heronswood, Wal.Abb. EN9
off Roundhills 16 EE34
Heron Trd Est, W3
off Alliance Rd 80 CP70
Heron Wk, Nthwd. HA6 39 BS49
Woking GU21
off Blackmore Cres 151 BC114
Heronway, Brwd. CM13 55 GA46
Heron Way, Felt. TW14
off The Causeway 95 BU84
Grays RM20 109 FV78
Upminster RM14 73 FS60
Heronway, Wdf.Grn. IG8 48 EJ49
Herrick Rd, N5 66 DQ62
Herrick St, SW1 199 N8
Herries St, W10 81 CY68
Herringham Rd, SE7 104 EJ76
Herrings La, Cher. KT16 134 BG100
Herrongate Cl, Enf. EN1 30 DT40
Hersant Cl, NW10 81 CU67
Herschell Rd, SE23 123 DY87
Herschel Pk Dr, Slou. SL1 92 AT75
Herschel St, Slou. SL1 92 AT75
HERSHAM, Walt. 154 BX107
⇌ Hersham 136 BY104
Hersham Bypass, Walt. KT12 153 BV106
Hersham Cl, SW15 119 CU87
Hersham Gdns, Walt. KT12 154 BW105
Hersham Rd, Walt. KT12 154 BW105
Hertford Av, SW14 118 CS85
Hertford Cl, Barn. EN4 28 DD41
Hertford Pl, W1 195 K5
Hertford Rd, N1 84 DS67
N2 64 DE55
N9 46 DV47
Barking IG11 87 EP66
Barnet EN4 28 DC41
Enfield EN3 30 DW41
Ilford IG2 69 ES58
Waltham Cross EN8 31 DX37
Hertford Sq, Mitch. CR4
off Hertford Way 141 DL98
Hertford St, W1 199 H2
Hertford Wk, Belv. DA17
off Hoddesdon Rd 106 FA78
Hertford Way, Mitch. CR4 141 DL98
Hertslet Rd, N7 65 DM62
Hertsmere Rd, E14 203 P1
Hervey Cl, N3 44 DA53
Hervey Pk Rd, E17 67 DY56
Hervey Rd, SE3 104 EH81
Hesa Rd, Hayes UB3 77 BU72
Hesewall Cl, SW4
off Brayburne Av 101 DJ82
Hesiers Hill, Warl. CR6 178 EE117
Hesiers Rd, Warl. CR6 178 EE117
Hesketh Av, Dart. DA2 128 FP88
Hesketh Pl, W11 81 CY73
Hesketh Rd, E7 68 EG62
Heslop Rd, SW12 120 DF88
Hesper Ms, SW5 100 DB78
Hesperus Cres, E14 204 B9
Hessel Rd, W13 97 CG75
Hessel St, E1 84 DV72
Hesselyn Dr, Rain. RM13 89 FH66
Hessle Gro, Epsom KT17 157 CT111
Hestercombe Av, SW6 99 CY82
Hesterman Way, Croy. CR0 141 DL102
Hester Rd, N18 46 DU50
SW11 100 DE80
Hester Ter, Rich. TW9
off Chilton Rd 98 CN83
HESTON, Houns. 96 BZ80
Heston Av, Houns. TW5 96 BY80
Heston Gra La, Houns. TW5 96 BZ79
Heston Ind Mall, Houns. TW5 96 BZ80
Heston Rd, Houns. TW5 96 CA80
Heston St, SE14 103 DZ81
Heswell Grn, Wat. WD19
off Fairhaven Cres 39 BU48
Hetherington Rd, SW4 101 DL84
Shepperton TW17 135 BQ96
Hetherington Way, Uxb. UB10 58 BL63
Hethersett Cl, Reig. RH2 184 DC131
Hetley Gdns, SE19
off Fox Hill 122 DT94
Hetley Rd, W12 81 CV74
Heton Gdns, NW4 63 CU56
Heusden Way, Ger.Cr. SL9 57 AZ60
Hevelius Cl, SE10 205 K10
Hever Ct Rd, Grav. DA12 131 GK93
Hever Cft, SE9 125 EN91
Hever Gdns, Brom. BR1 145 EN97
Heverham Rd, SE18 105 ES77
Heversham Rd, Bexh. DA7 106 FA82
Hewens Rd, Hayes UB4 77 BQ70
Uxbridge UB10 77 BQ70
Hewer St, W10 81 CX71
Hewers Way, Tad. KT20 173 CV120
Hewett Cl, Stan. HA7 41 CH49
Hewett Pl, Swan. BR8 147 FD98
Hewett Rd, Dag. RM8 70 EX64
Hewett St, EC2 197 N5
Hewins Cl, Wal.Abb. EN9
off Broomstick Hall Rd 16 EE33
Hewish Rd, N18 46 DS49
Hewison St, E3 85 DZ68
Hewitt Av, N22 45 DP54
Hewitt Cl, Croy. CR0 143 EA104
Hewitt Rd, N8 65 DN57
Hewitts Rd, Orp. BR6 164 EZ108
Hewlett Rd, E3 85 DY68
Hexagon, The, N6 64 DF60
Hexal Rd, SE6 124 EE90
Hexham Gdns, Islw. TW7 97 CG80
Hexham Rd, SE27 122 DQ89
Barnet EN5 28 DB42
Morden SM4 140 DB102
HEXTABLE, Swan. 127 FG94
Hextalls La, Red. (Bletch.)
RH1 186 DR128
Heybourne Rd, N17 46 DV52
Heybridge Av, SW16 121 DL94
Heybridge Dr, Ilf. IG6 49 ER54
Heybridge Way, E10 67 DY59
Heyford Av, SW8 101 DL80
SW20 139 CZ97
Heyford Rd, Mitch. CR4 140 DE96
Radlett WD7 25 CF37
Heyford Ter, SW8
off Heyford Av 101 DL80
Heygate St, SE17 201 H9
Heylyn Sq, E3
off Malmesbury Rd 85 DZ69
Heymede, Lthd. KT22 171 CJ123
Heynes Rd, Dag. RM8 70 EW63
Heysham Dr, Wat. WD19 40 BW50
Heysham La, NW3 64 DB62
Heysham Rd, N15 66 DR58
Heythorp Cl, Wok. GU21 166 AT117
Heythorp St, SW18 119 CZ88
Heythrop Dr, Uxb. (Ickhm.)
UB10 58 BM63
Heywood Av, NW9 42 CS53
Heyworth Rd, E5 66 DV63
E15 68 EF64
Hibbert Av, Wat. WD24 24 BX38
Hibbert Lo, Ger.Cr. (Chal.St.P.) SL9
off Gold Hill E 36 AX54
Hibbert Rd, E17 67 DZ59
Harrow HA3 41 CF54
Hibbert St, SW11 100 DC83
Hibberts Way, Ger.Cr. SL9
off North Pk 56 AY56
Hibbs Cl, Swan. BR8 147 FD96
Hibernia Dr, Grav. DA12 131 GM90
Hibernia Gdns, Houns. TW3 96 CA84
Hibernia Pt, SE2
off Wolvercote Rd 106 EX75
Hibernia Rd, Houns. TW3 96 CA84
Hibiscus Cl, Edg. HA8
off Campion Way 42 CQ49
Hichisson Rd, SE15 122 DW85
Hickin Cl, SE7 104 EK77
Hickin St, E14 204 D6
Hickling Rd, Ilf. IG1 69 EP64
Hickman Av, E4 47 EC51
Hickman Cl, E16 86 EK71
Hickman Rd, Rom. RM6 70 EW59
Hickmans Cl, Gdse. RH9 186 DW132
Hickmore Wk, SW4 101 DJ83
Hickory Cl, N9 46 DU45
Hicks Av, Grnf. UB6 79 CD68
Hicks Cl, SW11 100 DE83
Hicks St, SE8 203 K10
Hidcote Cl, Wok. GU22 167 BB116
Hidcote Gdns, SW20 139 CV97
Hide, E6 off Downings 87 EN72
Hideaway, The, Abb.L. WD5 7 BU31
Hide Pl, SW1 199 M9
Hide Rd, Har. HA1 61 CD56
Hides St, N7
off Sheringham Rd 83 DM65
Hide Twr, SW1 199 M9
Higgins Rd, Wal.Cr. (Chsht.)
EN7 14 DR27
Higgins Wk, Hmptn. TW12
off Abbott Cl 116 BY93
High Acres, Abb.L. WD5 7 BR32
Enfield EN2 off Old Pk Vw 29 DP41
HIGHAM HILL, E17 47 DY54
Higham Hill Rd, E17 47 DY54
Higham Pl, E17 67 DY55
Higham Rd, N17 66 DR55
Woodford Green IG8 48 EG51
Highams Ct, E4 off Friars Cl 47 ED48
Highams Lo Business Cen,
E17 67 DY55
HIGHAMS PARK, E4 47 ED50
⇌ Highams Park 47 ED51
Highams Pk Ind Est, E4 47 EC51
Higham Sta Av, E4 47 EB51
Higham St, E17 67 DY55
Higham Vw, Epp. (N.Wld.Bas.)
CM16 19 FB26
Highbanks Cl, Well. DA16 106 EV80
Highbanks Rd, Pnr. HA5 40 CB50
Highbank Way, N8 65 DN58
HIGH BARNET, Barn. 27 CX40
⊖ High Barnet 28 DA42
Highbarns, Hem.H. HP3 6 BN25
Highbarrow Rd, Croy. CR0 142 DU101
HIGH BEACH, Loug. 32 EG39
High Beech, S.Croy. CR2 160 DS108
High Beeches, Bans. SM7 157 CX114
Gerrards Cross SL9 56 AX60
Orpington BR6 164 EU107
Sidcup DA14 126 EY92
High Beeches Cl, Pur. CR8 159 DK110
High Beech Rd, Loug. IG10 32 EK42
High Br, SE10 103 ED78
Highbridge Ind Est, Uxb. UB8 76 BJ66
Highbridge Rd, Bark. IG11 87 EP67
Highbridge St, Wal.Abb. EN9 15 EA33
High Br Wf, SE10 103 ED78
Highbrook Rd, SE3 104 EK83
High Broom Cres, W.Wick.
BR4 143 EB101
HIGHBURY, N5 65 DP64
⇌ Highbury & Islington 83 DP65
⊖ Highbury & Islington 83 DP65
Highbury Av, Th.Hth. CR7 141 DN96
Highbury Cl, N.Mal. KT3 138 CQ98
West Wickham BR4 143 EB103
Highbury Cor, N5 83 DN65
Highbury Cres, N5 65 DN64
Highbury Est, N5 66 DQ64
Highbury Gdns, Ilf. IG3 69 ES61
Highbury Gra, N5 65 DP63
Highbury Gro, N5 83 DP65
Highbury Hill, N5 65 DN62
Highbury Ms, N7
off Holloway Rd 83 DN65
Highbury New Pk, N5 66 DQ64
Highbury Pk, N5 65 DP62
Highbury Pk Ms, N5
off Highbury Gra 66 DQ63
Highbury Pl, N5 83 DP65
Highbury Quad, N5 66 DQ62
Highbury Rd, SW19 119 CY92
Highbury Sta Rd, N1 83 DN65
Highbury Ter, N5 65 DP64
Highbury Ter Ms, N5 65 DP64
High Canons, Borwd. WD6 26 CQ37
High Cedar Dr, SW20 119 CV94
Highclere Cl, Ken. CR8 176 DQ115
Highclere Rd, N.Mal. KT3 138 CR97
Highclere St, SE26 123 DY91
Highcliffe Dr, SW15 119 CT86
Highcliffe Gdns, Ilf. IG4 68 EL57
High Cl, Rick. WD3 22 BJ43
Highcombe, SE7 104 EH79
Highcombe Cl, SE9 124 EK88
High Coombe Pl, Kings.T.
KT2 118 CR94
Highcroft, NW9 62 CR57
Highcroft Av, Wem. HA0 80 CN67
Highcroft Ct, Lthd. (Bkhm.)
KT23 170 CA123
Highcroft Gdns, NW11 63 CZ58
Highcroft Rd, N19 65 DL59
Hemel Hempstead (Felden)
HP3 6 BG25
High Cross, Wat. (Ald.) WD25 25 CD37
High Cross Cen, N15 66 DU56
High Cross Rd, N17 66 DU55
Highcross Rd, Grav. (Sthflt.)
DA13 129 FX92
Highcross Way, SW15 119 CU88
Highdaun Dr, SW16 141 DM98
Highdown, Wor.Pk. KT4 138 CS103
Highdown La, Sutt. SM2 158 DB111
Highdown Rd, SW15 119 CV86
High Dr, Cat. (Wold.) CR3 177 DZ122
Leatherhead (Oxshott)
KT22 155 CD114
New Malden KT3 138 CQ95
High Elms, Chig. IG7 49 ES49
Upminster RM14 73 FS60
Woodford Green IG8 48 EG50
High Elms Cl, Nthwd. HA6 39 BR51
High Elms La, Wat. WD25 7 BV31
High Elms Rd, Orp. BR6 163 EP110
HIGHER DENHAM, Uxb. 57 BB59
Higher Dr, Bans. SM7 157 CX112
Purley CR8 159 DN113
Higher Grn, Epsom KT17 157 CU113
Highfield, Bans. SM7 174 DE117
Bushey (Bushey Hth.) WD23
off High Rd 41 CE47
Chalfont St. Giles HP8 36 AX47
Feltham TW13 115 BU88
Kings Langley WD4 6 BL28
Watford WD19 40 BZ48
Highfield Av, NW9 62 CQ57
NW11 63 CX59
Erith DA8 107 FB79
Greenford UB6 61 CE64
Orpington BR6 163 ET106
Pinner HA5 60 BZ57
Wembley HA9 62 CM62
Highfield Cl, N22 45 DN53
NW9 62 CQ57
SE13 123 ED87
Egham (Eng.Grn.) TW20 112 AW93
Leatherhead (Oxshott)
KT22 155 CD111
Northwood HA6 39 BS53
Romford RM5 51 FC51
Surbiton KT6 137 CJ102
West Byfleet KT14 152 BG113
Highfield Ct, N14 29 DJ44
Highfield Cres, Horn. RM12 72 FM61
Northwood HA6 39 BS53
Highfield Dr, Brom. BR2 144 EE98
Caterham CR3 176 DU122
Epsom KT19 157 CT108
Uxbridge (Ickhm.) UB10 58 BL63
West Wickham BR4 143 EB103
Highfield Gdns, NW11 63 CY58
Grays RM16 110 GD75
Highfield Grn, Epp. CM16 17 ES31
Highfield Hill, SE19 122 DR94
Highfield Link, Rom. RM5 51 FC51
Highfield Ms, NW6
off Compayne Gdns 82 DB66
Highfield Pl, Epp. CM16 17 ES31
Highfield Rd, N21 45 DP47
NW11 63 CY58
W3 80 CP71
Bexleyheath DA6 126 EZ85
Bromley BR1 145 EM98
Bushey WD23 24 BY43
Caterham CR3 176 DU122
Chertsey KT16 134 BG102
Chislehurst BR7 145 ET97
Dartford DA1 128 FK87
Feltham TW13 115 BU89
Hornchurch RM12 72 FM61
Isleworth TW7 97 CF81
Northwood HA6 39 BS53
Purley CR8 159 DM110
Romford RM5 51 FC52
Sunbury-on-Thames
TW16 135 BT98
Highfield Rd, Surb. KT5 138 CQ101
Sutton SM1 158 DE106
Waltham Cross (Chsht.)
EN7 14 DS26
Walton-on-Thames KT12 135 BU102
West Byfleet KT14 152 BG113
Westerham (Bigg.H.) TN16 178 EJ117
Woodford Green IG8 48 EL52
Highfield Rd S, Dart. DA1 128 FK87
Highfields, Ashtd. KT21 171 CK119
Leatherhead (Fetch.) KT22 171 CD124
Potters Bar (Cuffley) EN6 13 DL28
Radlett WD7 25 CF35
Highfields Gro, N6 64 DF60
Highfield Twr, Rom. RM5 51 FD50
Highfield Way, Horn. RM12 72 FM61
Potters Bar EN6 12 DB32
Rickmansworth WD3 22 BH44
High Firs, Rad. WD7 25 CF35
Swanley BR8 147 FE98
High Foleys, Esher (Clay.)
KT10 155 CH108
High Gables, Loug. IG10 32 EK43
High Garth, Esher KT10 154 CC107
HIGHGATE, N6 64 DG61
⊖ Highgate 65 DH58
Highgate Av, N6 65 DH58
★ Highgate Cem, N6 64 DG60
Highgate Cl, N6 64 DG59
Highgate High St, N6 64 DG60
Highgate Hill, N6 65 DH60
N19 65 DH60
Highgate Rd, NW5 65 DH63
Highgate Wk, SE23 122 DW89
Highgate W Hill, N6 64 DG61
High Gro, SE18 105 ER80
Highgrove, Brwd. CM15 54 FV44
High Gro, Brom. BR1 144 EJ95
Highgrove Cl, N11
off Balmoral Av 44 DG50
Chislehurst BR7 144 EL95
Highgrove Ms, Cars. SM5 140 DF104
Grays RM17 110 GC78
Highgrove Rd, Dag. RM8 70 EW64
Highgrove Way, Ruis. HA4 59 BU58
High Hill Est, E5
off Mount Pleasant La 66 DV60
High Hill Ferry, E5 66 DV60
High Hill Rd, Warl. CR6 177 EC115
High Holborn, WC1 196 A8
High Ho La, Grays (Orsett)
RM16 111 GJ75
Tilbury (W.Til.) RM18 111 GK77
Highland Av, W7 79 CE72
Brentwood CM15 54 FW46
Dagenham RM10 71 FC62
Loughton IG10 32 EL44
Highland Cotts, Wall. SM6 159 DH105
Highland Ct, E18 48 EH53
Highland Cft, Beck. BR3 123 EB92
Highland Dr, Bushey WD23 40 CC45
Highland Pk, Felt. TW13 115 BT91
Highland Rd, SE19 122 DS93
Bexleyheath DA6 126 FA85
Bromley BR1, BR2 144 EF95
Northwood HA6 39 BT54
Purley CR8 159 DN114
Sevenoaks (Bad.Mt.) TN14 165 FB111
Highlands, Ashtd. KT21 171 CJ119
Watford WD19 40 BW46
Highlands, The, Edg. HA8 42 CP54
Potters Bar EN6 28 DB43
Rickmansworth WD3 38 BH45
Highlands Av, N21 29 DM43
W3 80 CQ73
Leatherhead KT22 171 CJ122
Highlands Cl, N4
off Mount Vw Rd 65 DL59
Gerrards Cross (Chal.St.P.)
SL9 37 AZ52
Hounslow TW3 96 CB81
Leatherhead KT22 171 CH122
Highlands End, Ger.Cr. (Chal.St.P.)
SL9 36 AY52
Highlands Gdns, Ilf. IG1 69 EM60
Highlands Heath, SW15 119 CW87
Highlands Hill, Swan. BR8 147 FG96
Highlands La, Ger.Cr. (Chal.St.P.)
SL9 37 AZ51
Woking GU22 166 AY122
Highlands Pk, Lthd. KT22 171 CK123
Sevenoaks (Seal) TN15 191 FL121
Highlands Rd, Barn. EN5 28 DA43
Leatherhead KT22 171 CH122
Orpington BR5 146 EV101
Reigate RH2 184 DD133
High La, W7 79 CD72
Caterham CR3 177 DZ119
Warlingham CR6 177 DZ118
High Lawns, Har. HA1 61 CE62
Highlea Cl, NW9 42 CS53
High Level Dr, SE26 122 DU91
Highlever Rd, W10 81 CW71
Highmead, SE18 105 ET80
High Mead, Chig. IG7 49 EQ47
Harrow HA1 61 CE57
West Wickham BR4 143 ED103
Highmead Cres, Wem. HA0 80 CM66
High Meadow Cl, Pnr. HA5
off Daymer Gdns 59 BV56
High Meadow Cres, NW9 62 CR57
High Meadow Pl, Cher. KT16 133 BF100
High Meadows, Chig. IG7 49 ER50
High Meads Rd, E16 86 EK72
Highmore Rd, SE3 104 EE80
High Mt, NW4 63 CU58
High Oaks, Enf. EN2 29 DM38
High Pk Av, Rich. TW9 98 CN81
High Pk Rd, Rich. TW9 98 CN81
High Path, SW19 140 DB95
High Pine Cl, Wey. KT13 153 BQ106
High Pines, Warl. CR6 176 DW119
High Pt, N6 64 DG59
SE9 125 EP90

★ Place of interest ⇌ Railway station ⊖ London Underground station DLR Docklands Light Railway station Tramlink station H Hospital

Hig - Hil

High Pt, Wey. KT13 . . . . .152 BN106
High Ridge, Pot.B. (Cuffley)
EN6 . . . . .13 DL27
Highridge Cl, Epsom KT18 . . .172 CS115
High Ridge Cl, Hem.H. HP3 . . .6 BK25
High Ridge Rd, Hem.H. HP3 . . .6 BK25
High Rd, N2 . . . . .44 DD53
N11 . . . . .45 DH50
N12 . . . . .44 DC51
N15 . . . . .66 DT58
N17 . . . . .46 DT53
N20 . . . . .44 DC45
N22 . . . . .65 DN55
NW10 (Willesden) 81 CV65
Buckhurst Hill IG9 . . . . .48 EH47
Bushey (Bushey Hth.)
WD23 . . . . .41 CD46
Chigwell IG7 . . . . .49 EM50
Coulsdon CR5 . . . . .174 DF121
Dartford (Wilm.) DA2 . . . . .128 FJ90
Epping CM16 . . . . .17 ER32
Epping (N.Wld.Bas.) CM16 . .19 FB27
Epping (Thnwd.) CM16 . . . . .18 EV28
Harrow (Har.Wld.) HA3 . . . .41 CE52
Ilford IG1 . . . . .69 EP62
Ilford (Seven Kings) IG3 . . . .69 ET60
Loughton IG10 . . . . .48 EJ45
Pinner HA5 . . . . .59 BV56
Reigate RH2 . . . . .184 DD126
Romford (Chad.Hth.) RM6 . .70 EV60
Uxbridge UB8 . . . . .76 BJ71
Watford WD25 . . . . .23 BT35
Wembley HA0, HA9 . . . . . . .61 CK64
West Byfleet (Byfleet)
KT14 . . . . .152 BM112
High Rd Ickenham, Uxb.
UB10 . . . . .59 BP62
High Rd Leyton, E10 . . . . .67 EB60
E15 . . . . .67 EC62
High Rd Leytonstone, E11 . . .68 EE63
E15 . . . . .68 EE63
High Rd Turnford, Brox.
EN10 . . . . .15 DY25
High Rd Woodford Grn, E18 . .48 EF52
Woodford Green IG8 . . . . . .48 EF52
Highshore Rd, SE15 . . . . . . .102 DT82
High Silver, Loug. IG10 . . . . . .32 EK42
High Standing, Cat. CR3 . . . .186 DQ125
Highstead Cres, Erith DA8 . . .107 FE81
Highstone Av, E11 . . . . .68 EG58
High St, E11 . . . . .68 EG57
E13 . . . . .86 EG68
E15 . . . . .85 EC68
E17 . . . . .67 DZ57
N8 .65 DL56
N14 . . . . .45 DK46
NW7 . . . . .43 CV49
NW10 (Harlesden) 81 CT68
SE20 . . . . .122 DV93
SE25 (S.Norwood) 142 DT98
W3 .80 CP74
W5 .79 CK73
Abbots Langley WD5 . . . . . . .6 BN29
Abbots Langley (Bedmond)
WD5 . . . . .7 BS31
Addlestone KT15 . . . . .152 BH105
Banstead SM7 . . . . .174 DA115
Barnet EN5 . . . . .27 CY41
Beckenham BR3 . . . . .143 EA96
Borehamwood (Elstree)
WD6 . . . . .25 CK44
Brentford TW8 . . . . .97 CK79
Brentwood CM14 . . . . .54 FV47
Bromley BR1 . . . . .144 EG96
Bushey WD23 . . . . .24 CA44
Carshalton SM5 . . . . .158 DG105
Caterham CR3 . . . . .176 DS123
Chalfont St. Giles HP8 . . . . .36 AW48
Chislehurst BR7 . . . . .125 EP93
Cobham KT11 . . . . .153 BV114
Croydon CR0 . . . . .142 DQ103
Dartford DA1 . . . . .128 FL86
Dartford (Bean) DA2 . . . . . .129 FV90
Dartford (Eyns.) DA4 . . . . .148 FL103
Dartford (Fnghm.) DA4 . . . .148 FM100
Edgware HA8 . . . . .42 CN51
Egham TW20 . . . . .113 BA92
Enfield (Pond.End) EN3 . . . .30 DW42
Epping CM16 . . . . .17 ET31
Epsom KT19 . . . . .156 CR113
Epsom (Ewell) KT17 . . . . . .157 CT109
Esher KT10 . . . . .154 CB105
Esher (Clay.) KT10 . . . . . . .155 CF107
Feltham TW13 . . . . .115 BT90
Gerrards Cross (Chal.St.P.)
SL9 . . . . .36 AY53
Godstone RH9 . . . . .186 DV131
Gravesend DA11 . . . . .131 GH86
Gravesend (Nthflt.) DA11 . .130 GB86
Grays RM17 . . . . .110 GA79
Greenhithe DA9 . . . . .109 FV84
Hampton TW12 . . . . .116 CC93
Harrow HA1, HA2 . . . . .61 CE60
Harrow (Wldste.) HA3 . . . . .61 CE55
Hayes UB3 . . . . .95 BS78
Hemel Hempstead (Bov.)
HP3 . . . . .5 BA27
Hornchurch RM11, RM12 . . .72 FK60
Hounslow TW3 . . . . .96 CC83
Hounslow (Cran.) TW5 . . . . .95 BV80
Ilford (Barkingside) IG6 . . . .49 EQ54
Iver SL0 . . . . .75 BE72
Kings Langley WD4 . . . . .7 BT27
Kingston upon Thames
KT1 . . . . .137 CK96
Kingston upon Thames
(Hmptn.W.) KT1 . . . . .137 CJ95
Leatherhead KT22 . . . . . . .171 CH122
Leatherhead (Oxshott)
KT22- 155 CD113
New Malden KT3 . . . . .138 CS97
Northwood HA6 . . . . .39 BT53
Orpington BR6 . . . . .146 EU102
Orpington (Downe) BR6 . . .163 EN111
High St, Orp. (Farnboro.)
BR6 . . . . .163 EP106
Orpington (Grn.St.Grn.)
BR6 . . . . .163 ET108
Orpington (St.M.Cray)
BR5 . . . . .146 EW98
Oxted RH8 . . . . .187 ED130
Oxted (Lmpfld.) RH8 . . . . .188 EG128
Pinner HA5 . . . . .60 BY55
Potters Bar EN6 . . . . .12 DC33
Purfleet RM19
off London Rd Purfleet . . .108 FN78
Purley CR8 . . . . .159 DN111
Redhill RH1 . . . . .184 DF134
Redhill (Bletch.) RH1 . . . . .186 DQ133
Redhill (Merst.) RH1 . . . . .185 DH128
Redhill (Nutfld.) RH1 . . . . .185 DM133
Reigate RH2 . . . . .184 DA134
Rickmansworth WD3 . . . . . .38 BK46
Romford RM1 . . . . .71 FE57
Ruislip HA4 . . . . .59 BS59
St. Albans (Lon.Col.) AL2 . . . .9 CJ25
Sevenoaks TN13 . . . . .191 FJ125
Sevenoaks (Chipstead)
TN13 . . . . .190 FC122
Sevenoaks (Otford) TN14 . .181 FF116
Sevenoaks (Seal) TN15 . . . .191 FL121
Sevenoaks (Shore.) TN14 . .165 FF110
Shepperton TW17 . . . . .135 BP100
Slough SL1 . . . . .92 AU75
Slough (Colnbr.) SL3 . . . . . .93 BC80
Slough (Datchet) SL3 . . . . . .92 AV81
Slough (Langley) SL3 . . . . . .93 AZ78
South Ockendon (Aveley)
RM15 . . . . .91 FR74
Southall UB1 . . . . .78 BZ74
Staines TW18 . . . . .113 BF91
Staines (Stanw.) TW19 . . . .114 BK86
Staines (Wrays.) TW19 . . . .112 AY86
Sutton SM1 . . . . .158 DB105
Sutton (Cheam) SM3 . . . . .157 CY107
Swanley BR8 . . . . .147 FF98
Swanscombe DA10 . . . . . . .130 FZ85
Tadworth KT20 . . . . .173 CW123
Teddington TW11 . . . . .117 CG92
Thames Ditton KT7 . . . . . . .137 CG101
Thornton Heath CR7 . . . . . .142 DQ98
Twickenham (Whitton)
TW2 . . . . .116 CC87
Uxbridge UB8 . . . . .76 BK67
Uxbridge (Cowley) UB8 . . . .76 BJ70
Uxbridge (Hare.) UB9 . . . . .38 BJ54
Waltham Cross EN8 . . . . . . .15 DY34
Waltham Cross (Chsht.)
EN8 . . . . .15 DX29
Walton-on-Thames KT12 . .135 BU102
Watford WD17 . . . . .23 BV41
Wembley HA9 . . . . .62 CM63
West Drayton (Harm.) UB7 .94 BK79
West Drayton (Yiew.) UB7 . .76 BK74
West Molesey KT8 . . . . . . .136 CA98
West Wickham BR4 . . . . . .143 EB102
Westerham TN16 . . . . .189 EQ127
Westerham (Brasted)
TN16 . . . . .180 EV124
Weybridge KT13 . . . . .152 BN105
Woking GU21 . . . . .166 AY117
Woking (Chobham) GU24 .150 AS111
Woking (Horsell) GU21 . . .166 AV115
Woking (Old Wok.) GU22 . .167 BB121
Woking (Ripley) GU23 . . . .168 BJ121
High St Colliers Wd, SW19 . .120 DD94
⊖ High Street Kensington . .100 DB75
High St Ms, SW19 . . . . .119 CY92
High St N, E6 . . . . .86 EL67
E12 . . . . .68 EL64
High St S, E6 . . . . .87 EM68
High St Wimbledon, SW19 . . .119 CX92
High Timber St, EC4 . . . . . . .197 H10
High Tor Cl, Brom. BR1
off Babbacombe Rd 124 EH94
High Tree Cl, Add. KT15 . . . .151 BF106
High Tree Ct, W7 . . . . .79 CE73
High Trees, SW2 . . . . .121 DN88
Barnet EN4 . . . . .28 DE43
Croydon CR0 . . . . .143 DY102
High Trees Cl, Cat. CR3 . . . .176 DT123
High Trees Ct, Brwd. CM14
off Warley Mt 54 FW49
Highview, Cat. CR3 . . . . . . .176 DS124
High Vw, Ch.St.G. HP8 . . . . . .36 AX47
Highview, Nthlt. UB5 . . . . . . .78 BY69
High Vw, Pnr. HA5 . . . . .60 BW56
Rickmansworth (Chorl.)
WD3 . . . . .22 BG42
Sutton SM2 . . . . .157 CZ111
Watford WD18 . . . . .23 BT44
Highview, Wok. (Knap.) GU21
off Mulgrave Way 166 AS117
Highview Av, Edg. HA8 . . . . . .42 CQ49
High Vw Av, Grays RM17 . . . .110 GC78
Highview Av, Wall. SM6 . . . .159 DM106
High Vw Caravan Pk, Kings L.
WD4 . . . . .7 BR28
High Vw Cl, SE19 . . . . .142 DT96
Loughton IG10 . . . . .32 EJ43
Highview Cl, Pot.B. EN6 . . . . .12 DC33
Highview Cres, Brwd. CM13 . .55 GC44
Highview Gdns, N3 . . . . .63 CY55
N11 . . . . .45 DJ50
Edgware HA8 . . . . .42 CQ49
High Vw Gdns, Grays RM17 . .110 GC78
Highview Gdns, Pot.B. EN6 . . .12 DC33
Upminster RM14 . . . . .72 FP61
Highview Ho, Rom. RM6 . . . . .70 EY56
Highview Path, Bans. SM7 . .174 DA115
High Vw Rd, E18 . . . . .68 EF55
Highview Rd, SE19 . . . . .122 DR93
W13 . . . . .79 CG71
Sidcup DA14 . . . . .126 EV91
Highway, The, E1 . . . . .202 C1
E14 . . . . .202 C1
Orpington BR6 . . . . .164 EW106
Stanmore HA7 . . . . .41 CF53
Sutton SM2 . . . . .158 DC109
Highwold, Couls. CR5 . . . . . .174 DG118
Highwood, Brom. BR2 . . . . . .144 EE97
Highwood Av, N12 . . . . .44 DC49
Bushey WD23 . . . . .24 BZ39
Highwood Cl, Brwd. CM14 . . .54 FV45
Kenley CR8 . . . . .176 DQ117
Orpington BR6 . . . . .145 EQ103
Highwood Dr, Orp. BR6 . . . . .145 EQ103
Highwood Gdns, Ilf. IG5 . . . . .69 EM57
Highwood Gro, NW7 . . . . .42 CR50
Highwood Hall La, Hem.H.
HP3 .7 BQ25
HIGHWOOD HILL, NW7 . . . . . .43 CU47
Highwood Hill, NW7 . . . . .43 CT47
H Highwood Hosp, Brwd.
CM15 . . . . .54 FW45
Highwood La, Loug. IG10 . . . .33 EN43
Highwood Rd, N19 . . . . .65 DL62
Highwoods, Cat. CR3 . . . . . .186 DS125
Leatherhead KT22 . . . . . . .171 CJ121
High Worple, Har. HA2 . . . . . .60 BZ59
Highworth Rd, N11 . . . . .45 DK51
Hilary Av, Mitch. CR4 . . . . . .140 DG97
Hilary Cl, SW6 . . . . .100 DB80
Erith DA8 . . . . .107 FC81
Hornchurch RM12 . . . . .72 FK64
Hilary Rd, W12 . . . . .81 CT72
Slough SL3 . . . . .92 AY76
Hilbert Rd, Sutt. SM3 . . . . . .139 CX104
Hilborough Way, Orp. BR6 . . .163 ER106
Hilda May Av, Swan. BR8 . . . .147 FE97
Hilda Rd, E6 . . . . .86 EK66
E16 . . . . .86 EE70
Hilda Ter, SW9 . . . . .101 DN82
Hilda Vale Cl, Orp. BR6 . . . .163 EP105
Hilda Vale Rd, Orp. BR6 . . . .163 EN105
Hildenborough Gdns, Brom.
BR1 . . . . .124 EE93
Hilden Dr, Erith DA8 . . . . . . .107 FH80
Hildenlea Pl, Brom. BR2 . . . .144 EE96
Hildenley Cl, Red. RH1
off Malmstone Av 185 DK128
Hilders, The, Ashtd. KT21 . . .172 CP117
Hildreth St, SW12 . . . . .121 DH88
Hildyard Rd, SW6 . . . . .100 DA79
Hiley Rd, NW10 . . . . .81 CW69
Hilfield La, Wat. (Ald.) WD25 . .25 CD41
Hilfield La S, Bushey WD23 . . .25 CF44
Hilgrove Rd, NW6 . . . . .82 DC66
Hiliary Gdns, Stan. HA7 . . . . . .41 CJ54
Hiljon Cres, Ger.Cr. (Chal.St.P.)
SL9 . . . . .36 AY53
Hill, The, Cat. CR3 . . . . .176 DT124
Gravesend (Nthflt.) DA11 . .130 GC86
Hillars Heath Rd, Couls. CR5 .175 DL115
Hillary Av, Grav. (Nthflt.)
DA11 . . . . .130 GE90
Hillary Cres, Walt. KT12 . . . .136 BW102
Hillary Dr, Islw. TW7 . . . . .97 CF84
Hillary Ri, Barn. EN5 . . . . .28 DA42
Hillary Rd, Sthl. UB2 . . . . .96 CA76
Hill Barn, S.Croy. CR2 . . . . . .160 DS111
Hillbeck Cl, SE15 . . . . .102 DW80
Hillbeck Way, Grnf. UB6 . . . . .79 CD67
Hillborne Cl, Hayes UB3 . . . . .95 BU78
Hillborough Av, Sev. TN13 . . .191 FK122
Hillborough Cl, SW19 . . . . . .120 DC94
Hillbrook Gdns, Wey. KT13 . .152 BN108
Hillbrook Rd, SW17 . . . . .120 DF90
Hill Brow, Brom. BR1 . . . . . . .144 EK95
Dartford DA1 . . . . .127 FF86
Hillbrow, N.Mal. KT3 . . . . . . .139 CT97
Hillbrow Cl, Bex. DA5 . . . . . .127 FD91
Hillbrow Cotts, Gdse. RH9 . . .186 DW132
Hillbrow Ct, Gdse. RH9 . . . . .186 DW132
Hillbrow Rd, Brom. BR1 . . . . .124 EE94
Esher KT10 . . . . .154 CC105
Hillbury Av, Har. HA3 . . . . . . .61 CH57
Hillbury Cl, Warl. CR6 . . . . . .176 DV118
Hillbury Gdns, Warl. CR6 . . .176 DW118
Hillbury Rd, SW17 . . . . .121 DH90
Warlingham CR6 . . . . .176 DU117
Whyteleafe CR3 . . . . .176 DU117
Hill Cl, NW2 . . . . .63 CV62
NW11 . . . . .64 DA58
Barnet EN5 . . . . .27 CW43
Chislehurst BR7 . . . . .125 EP92
Cobham KT11 . . . . .154 CA112
Gravesend (Istead Rise)
DA13 . . . . .130 GE94
Harrow HA1 . . . . .61 CE62
Purley CR8 . . . . .160 DQ113
Stanmore HA7 . . . . .41 CH49
Woking GU21 . . . . .166 AX115
Hillcote Av, SW16 . . . . .121 DN94
Hill Ct, Nthlt. UB5 . . . . .60 CA64
Hillcourt Av, N12 . . . . .44 DB51
Hillcourt Est, N16 . . . . .66 DR60
Hillcourt Rd, SE22 . . . . .122 DV86
Hill Cres, N20 . . . . .44 DB47
Bexley DA5 . . . . .127 FC88
Harrow HA1 . . . . .61 CG57
Hornchurch RM11 . . . . .72 FJ58
Surbiton KT5 . . . . .138 CM99
Worcester Park KT4 . . . . . .139 CW103
Hillcrest, N6 . . . . .64 DG59
N21 . . . . .45 DP45
Hill Crest, Pot.B. EN6 . . . . . . .12 DC34
Sevenoaks TN13 . . . . .190 FG122
Sidcup DA15 . . . . .126 EU87
Hillcrest, Wey. KT13 . . . . . . .153 BP105
Hillcrest Av, NW11 . . . . .63 CY57
Chertsey KT16 . . . . .151 BE105
Edgware HA8 . . . . .42 CP49
Grays RM20 . . . . .109 FU79
Pinner HA5 . . . . .60 BX56
Hillcrest Caravan Pk, Tad.
KT20 . . . . .182 CP131
Hillcrest Cl, SE26 . . . . .122 DU91
Beckenham BR3 . . . . .143 DZ99
Epsom KT18 . . . . .173 CT115
Hillcrest Ct, Sutt. SM2
off Eaton Rd 158 DD107
Hillcrest Dr, Green. DA9
off Riverview Rd 129 FV85
Hillcrest Gdns, N3 . . . . .63 CY56
NW2 . . . . .63 CU62
Esher KT10 . . . . .137 CF104
Hillcrest Par, Couls. CR5 . . . .159 DH114
Hillcrest Rd, E17 . . . . .47 ED54
E18 . . . . .48 EF54
W3 .80 CN74
W5 .80 CL71
Bromley BR1 . . . . .124 EG92
Dartford DA1 . . . . .127 FF87
Hornchurch RM11 . . . . .71 FG59
Loughton IG10 . . . . .32 EK44
Ongar CM5 . . . . .19 FE30
Orpington BR6 . . . . .146 EU103
Purley CR8 . . . . .159 DM110
Radlett (Shenley) WD7 . . . . .10 CN33
Westerham (Bigg.H.) TN16 .178 EK116
Whyteleafe CR3 . . . . .176 DT117
Hillcrest Vw, Beck. BR3 . . . . .143 DZ100
Hillcrest Way, Epp. CM16 . . . . .18 EU31
Hillcrest Waye, Ger.Cr. SL9 . . .57 AZ59
Hillcroft, Loug. IG10 . . . . .33 EN40
Hillcroft Av, Pnr. HA5 . . . . . . .60 BZ58
Purley CR8 . . . . .159 DJ113
Hillcroft Cres, W5 . . . . .80 CL72
Ruislip HA4 . . . . .60 BX62
Watford WD19 . . . . .39 BV46
Wembley HA9 . . . . .62 CM63
Hillcroft Rd, E6 . . . . .87 EP71
Hillcroome Rd, Sutt. SM2 . . .158 DD107
Hillcross Av, Mord. SM4 . . . .139 CZ99
Hilldale Rd, Sutt. SM1 . . . . . .157 CZ105
Hilldeane Rd, Pur. CR8 . . . . .159 DN109
Hilldene Av, Rom. RM3 . . . . . .52 FJ51
Hilldene Cl, Rom. RM3 . . . . . .52 FK50
Hilldown Rd, SW16 . . . . .121 DL94
Bromley BR2 . . . . .144 EE102
Hill Dr, NW9 . . . . .62 CQ60
SW16 . . . . .141 DM97
Hilldrop Cres, N7 . . . . .65 DK64
Hilldrop Est, N7 . . . . .65 DK64
Hilldrop La, N7 . . . . .65 DK64
Hilldrop Rd, N7 . . . . .65 DK64
Bromley BR1 . . . . .124 EG93
HILL END, Uxb. 38 BH51
Hillend, SE18 . . . . .105 EN81
Hill End, Orp. BR6
off The Approach 145 ET103
Hill End Rd, Uxb. (Hare.) UB9 .38 BH51
Hillersdon, Slou. SL2 . . . . .74 AV71
Hillersdon Av, SW13 . . . . .99 CU82
Edgware HA8 . . . . .42 CM50
Hillery Cl, SE17 . . . . .201 L9
Hilley Fld La, Lthd. (Fetch.)
KT22 . . . . .170 CC122
Hill Fm Av, Wat. WD25 . . . . .7 BU33
Hill Fm Cl, Wat. WD25 . . . . .7 BU33
Hill Fm Ind Est, Wat. WD25 . . . .7 BT33
Hill Fm La, Ch.St.G. HP8 . . . . .36 AT46
Hill Fm Rd, W10 . . . . .81 CW71
Gerrards Cross (Chal.St.P.)
SL9 . . . . .36 AY52
Uxbridge UB10
off Austin's La 59 BR63
Hillfield Av, N8 . . . . .65 DL57
NW9 . . . . .62 CS57
Wembley HA0 . . . . .80 CL66
Hillfield Cl, Har. HA2 . . . . .60 CC56
Redhill RH1 . . . . .184 DG134
Hillfield Ct, NW3 . . . . .64 DE64
Hillfield Par, Mord. SM4 . . . .140 DE100
Hillfield Pk, N10 . . . . .65 DH56
N21 . . . . .45 DN47
Hillfield Pk Ms, N10 . . . . .65 DH56
Hillfield Rd, NW6 . . . . .63 CZ64
Gerrards Cross (Chal.St.P.)
SL9 . . . . .36 AY52
Hampton TW12 . . . . .116 BZ94
Redhill RH1 . . . . .184 DG134
Sevenoaks (Dunt.Grn.)
TN13 . . . . .181 FE120
Hillfield Sq, Ger.Cr. (Chal.St.P.)
SL9 . . . . .36 AY52
Hillfoot Av, Rom. RM5 . . . . . . .51 FC53
Hillfoot Rd, Rom. RM5 . . . . . . .51 FC53
Hillgate Pl, SW12 . . . . .121 DH87
W8 .82 DA74
Hillgate St, W8 . . . . .82 DA74
Hill Gro, Felt. TW13
off Watermill Way 116 BZ89
Hillgrove, Ger.Cr. (Chal.St.P.)
SL9 . . . . .37 AZ53
Hill Gro, Rom. RM1 . . . . .71 FE55
Hill Hall, Epp. CM16 . . . . .34 EZ35
Hillhouse, Wal.Abb. EN9 . . . . .16 EF33
Hill Ho Av, Stan. HA7 . . . . . . .41 CF52
Hill Ho Cl, N21 . . . . .45 DN45
Gerrards Cross (Chal.St.P.) SL9
off Rickmansworth La 36 AY52
Hill Ho Dr, Hmptn. TW12 . . . .136 CA95
Weybridge KT13 . . . . .152 BN111
Hill Ho Rd, SW16 . . . . .121 DM92
Hillhouse Rd, Dart. DA2 . . . . .128 FQ87
Hillhurst Gdns, Cat. CR3 . . . .176 DS120
Hilliard Rd, Nthwd. HA6 . . . . .39 BT53
Hilliards Ct, E1 . . . . .202 E2
Hilliards Rd, Uxb. UB8 . . . . . . .76 BK72
Hillier Cl, Barn. EN5 . . . . .28 DB44
Hillier Gdns, Croy. CR0
off Crowley Cres 159 DN106
Hillier Pl, Chess. KT9 . . . . . .155 CJ107
Hillier Rd, SW11 . . . . .120 DF86
Hilliers Av, Uxb. UB8
off Harlington Rd 76 BN69
Hilliers La, Croy. CR0 . . . . . .141 DL104
Hillingdale, West. (Bigg.H.)
TN16 . . . . .178 EH118
HILLINGDON, Uxb. 76 BN69
⊖ Hillingdon 58 BN64
Hillingdon Av, Sev. TN13 . . . .191 FJ121
Staines TW19 . . . . .114 BL88
Hillingdon Hill, Uxb. UB10 . . . .76 BL69
H Hillingdon Hosp, Uxb.
UB8 . . . . .76 BM71
Hillingdon Ri, Sev. TN13 . . . .191 FK122
Hillingdon Rd, Bexh. DA7 . . . .107 FC82
Gravesend DA11 . . . . .131 GG89
Uxbridge UB10 . . . . .76 BL67
Watford WD25 . . . . .7 BU34
Hillingdon St, SE5 . . . . .101 DP79
SE17 . . . . .101 DP79
Hillington Gdns, Wdf.Grn. IG8 .48 EK54
Hill La, Ruis. HA4 . . . . .59 BQ60
Tadworth (Kgswd.) KT20 . . .173 CY121
Hill Leys, Pot.B. (Cuffley)
EN6 . . . . .13 DL28
Hillman Cl, Horn. RM11 . . . . . .72 FK55
Uxbridge UB8 . . . . .58 BL64
Hillman Dr, W10 . . . . .81 CW70
Hillman St, E8 . . . . .84 DV65
Hillmarton Rd, N7 . . . . .65 DL64
Hillmead Dr, SW9 . . . . .101 DP84
Hillmont Rd, Esher KT10 . . . .137 CE104
Hillmore Gro, SE26 . . . . .123 DX92
Hillmount, Wok. GU22
off Constitution Hill 166 AY119
Hill Pk Dr, Lthd. KT22 . . . . . .171 CF119
Hill Path, SW16
off Valley Rd 121 DM92
Hillpoint, Rick. (Loud.) WD3 . . .22 BJ43
Hillreach, SE18 . . . . .105 EM78
Hill Ri, N9 . . . . .30 DV44
NW11 . . . . .64 DB56
SE23 off London Rd 122 DV88
Dartford (Lane End) DA2 . . .129 FR92
Esher KT10 . . . . .137 CH103
Gerrards Cross (Chal.St.P.)
SL9 . . . . .36 AX54
Greenford UB6 . . . . .78 CC66
Potters Bar EN6 . . . . .12 DC34
Potters Bar (Cuffley) EN6 . . .13 DK27
Richmond TW10 . . . . .117 CK85
Rickmansworth WD3 . . . . . . .22 BH44
Ruislip HA4 . . . . .59 BQ60
Slough SL3 . . . . .93 BA79
Upminster RM14 . . . . .72 FN61
Hillrise, Walt. KT12 . . . . .135 BT101
Hillrise Av, Wat. WD24 . . . . . .24 BX38
Hill Ri Cres, Ger.Cr. (Chal.St.P.)
SL9 . . . . .36 AY54
Hillrise Rd, N19 . . . . .65 DL59
Romford RM5 . . . . .51 FC51
Hill Rd, N10 . . . . .44 DF53
NW8 . . . . .82 DC68
Brentwood CM14 . . . . .54 FU48
Carshalton SM5 . . . . .158 DE107
Dartford DA2 . . . . .128 FL89
Epping (They.B.) CM16 . . . . .33 ES37
Harrow HA1 . . . . .61 CG57
Leatherhead (Fetch.) KT22 .170 CB122
Mitcham CR4 . . . . .141 DH95
Northwood HA6 . . . . .39 BR51
Pinner HA5 . . . . .60 BY57
Purley CR8 . . . . .159 DM112
Sutton SM1 . . . . .158 DB106
Wembley HA0 . . . . .61 CH62
Hillsborough Grn, Wat. WD19
off Ashburnham Dr 39 BU48
Hillsborough Rd, SE22 . . . . .122 DS85
Hills Chace, Brwd. CM14 . . . . .54 FW49
Hillsgrove, Well. DA16 . . . . . .106 EW80
Hillside, NW9 . . . . .62 CR56
NW10 . . . . .80 CQ67
SW19 . . . . .119 CX93
Banstead SM7 . . . . .173 CY115
Barnet EN5 . . . . .28 DC43
Dartford (Fnghm.) DA4 . . . .148 FM101
Dartford (Lane End) DA2 . . .129 FS92
Erith DA8 . . . . .107 FD77
Grays RM17 . . . . .110 GD77
Slough SL1 . . . . .92 AS75
Uxbridge (Hare.) UB9 . . . . . .58 BJ57
Virginia Water GU25 . . . . . .132 AW100
Woking GU22 . . . . .166 AX120
Hillside, The, Orp. BR6 . . . . .164 EV109
Hillside Av, N11 . . . . .44 DF51
Borehamwood WD6 . . . . .26 CP42
Gravesend DA12 . . . . .131 GK89
Purley CR8 . . . . .159 DP113
Waltham Cross (Chsht.)
EN8 . . . . .15 DX31
Wembley HA9 . . . . .62 CM63
Woodford Green IG8 . . . . . .48 EJ50
Hillside Cl, NW8 . . . . .82 DB68
Abbots Langley WD5 . . . . . . .7 BS32
Banstead SM7 . . . . .173 CY116
Chalfont St. Giles HP8 . . . . .36 AV48
Gerrards Cross (Chal.St.P.)
SL9 . . . . .36 AY51
Morden SM4 . . . . .139 CY98
Woodford Green IG8 . . . . . .48 EJ50
Hillside Ct, Swan. BR8 . . . . . .147 FG98
Hillside Cres, Enf. EN2 . . . . . .30 DR38
Harrow HA2 . . . . .60 CC60
Northwood HA6 . . . . .39 BU53
Waltham Cross (Chsht.)
EN8 . . . . .15 DX31
Watford WD19 . . . . .24 BY44
Hillside Dr, Edg. HA8 . . . . .42 CN51
Gravesend DA12 . . . . .131 GK89
Hillside Est, N15 . . . . .66 DT58
Hillside Gdns, E17 . . . . .67 ED55
N6 .64 DG58
SW2 . . . . .121 DN89
Addlestone KT15 . . . . .151 BF107
Barnet EN5 . . . . .27 CY42
Betchworth (Brock.) RH3 . . .182 CN134
Edgware HA8 . . . . .42 CM49
Harrow HA3 . . . . .62 CL59
Northwood HA6 . . . . .39 BU52
Wallington SM6 . . . . .159 DJ108
Hillside Gro, N14 . . . . .45 DK45
NW7 . . . . .43 CU52
Hillside La, Brom. BR2 . . . . . .144 EG103
Hillside Pas, SW2 . . . . .121 DM89
Hillside Ri, Nthwd. HA6 . . . . . .39 BU52
Hillside Rd, N15 . . . . .66 DS59
SW2 . . . . .121 DN89
W5 .80 CL71
Ashtead KT21 . . . . .172 CM117
Bromley BR2 . . . . .144 EF97
Bushey WD23 . . . . .24 BY43
Coulsdon CR5 . . . . .175 DM118
Croydon CR0 . . . . .159 DP106
Dartford DA1 . . . . .127 FG86
Epsom KT17 . . . . .157 CW110
Northwood HA6 . . . . .39 BU52
Pinner HA5 . . . . .39 BV52

★ Place of interest   ⇌ Railway station   ⊖ London Underground station   DLR Docklands Light Railway station   ⊖ Tramlink station   H Hospital

273

Hil - Hol

Hillside Rd, Radlett WD7 .....25 CH35
Rickmansworth (Chorl.)
WD3 .....21 BC43
Sevenoaks TN13 .....191 FK123
Southall UB1 .....78 CA70
Surbiton KT5 .....138 CM99
Sutton SM2 .....157 CZ108
Westerham (Tats.) TN16 ...178 EL119
Whyteleafe CR3 .....176 DU118
Hillside Wk, Brwd. CM14 .....54 FU48
Hills La, Nthwd. HA6 .....39 BS53
Hillsleigh Rd, W8 .....81 CZ74
Hillsmead Way, S.Croy. CR2 .160 DU113
Hills Ms, W5 .....80 CL73
Hills Pl, W1 .....195 K9
Hills Rd, Buck.H. IG9 .....48 EH46
Hillstowe St, E5 .....66 DW61
Hill St, W1 .....198 G2
Richmond TW9 .....117 CK85
Hillswood Business Pk, Cher.
KT16 .....151 BC105
Hillswood Dr, Cher. KT16 ...151 BC105
Hill Top, NW11 .....64 DB56
Loughton IG10 .....33 EN40
Morden SM4 .....140 DA100
Sutton SM3 .....139 CZ101
Hilltop Cl, Lthd. KT22 .....171 CJ123
Hill Top Cl, Loug. IG10 .....33 EN41
Hilltop Cl, Wal.Cr. (Chsht.)
EN7 .....14 DT26
Hilltop Gdns, NW4 .....43 CV54
Dartford DA1 .....128 FM85
Orpington BR6 .....145 ES103
Hilltop La, Cat. CR3 .....185 DN126
Redhill RH1 .....185 DN126
Hill Top Pl, Loug. IG10 .....33 EN41
Hilltop Rd, NW6 .....82 DA66
Grays RM20 .....109 FV79
Kings Langley WD4 .....7 BR27
Whyteleafe CR3 .....176 DS117
Hill Top Vw, Wdf.Grn. IG8 ...49 EM51
Hilltop Wk, Cat. CR3 .....177 DY120
Hilltop Way, Stan. HA7 .....41 CG48
Hillview, SW20 .....119 CV94
Mitcham CR4 .....141 DL98
Whyteleafe (Wold.) CR3 ...176 DT117
Hillview Av, Har. HA3 .....62 CL57
Hornchurch RM11 .....72 FJ58
Hillview Cl, Pnr. HA5 .....40 BZ51
Purley CR8 .....159 DP111
Hill Vw Cl, Tad. KT20
off Shelvers Way 173 CW121
Hillview Cl, Wem. HA9 .....62 CM61
Hillview Ct, Wok. GU22 .....167 AZ118
Hillview Cres, Ilf. IG1 .....69 EM58
Hill Vw Cres, Orp. BR6 .....145 ET102
Hill Vw Dr, Well. DA16 .....105 ES82
Hillview Gdns, NW4 .....63 CX56
Hill Vw Gdns, NW9 .....62 CR57
Hillview Gdns, Har. HA2 .....60 CA55
Waltham Cross (Chsht.)
EN8 .....15 DX27
Hillview Rd, NW7 .....43 CX49
Chislehurst BR7 .....125 EN92
Hill Vw Rd, Esher (Clay.)
KT10 .....155 CG108
Orpington BR6 .....145 ET102
Hillview Rd, Pnr. HA5 .....40 BZ52
Hill Vw Rd, Stai. (Wrays.)
TW19 .....112 AX86
Hillview Rd, Sutt. SM1 .....140 DC104
Hill Vw Rd, Twick. TW1 .....117 CG86
Woking GU22 .....167 AZ118
Hillway, N6 .....64 DG61
NW9 .....62 CS60
Hill Waye, Ger.Cr. SL9 .....57 AZ58
Hillwood Cl, Brwd. CM13 .....55 GB46
Hillwood Gro, Brwd. CM13 ...55 GB46
Hillworth Rd, SW2 .....121 DN87
Hillyard Rd, W7 .....79 CE71
Hillyard St, SW9 .....101 DN81
Hillyfield, E17 .....47 DY54
Hillyfields, Loug. IG10 .....33 EN40
Hilly Flds Cres, SE4 .....103 EA83
Hilperton Rd, Slou. SL1 .....92 AS75
Hilsea Pt, SW15
off Wanborough Dr 119 CV88
Hilsea St, E5 .....66 DW63
Hilton Av, N12 .....44 DD50
Hilton Cl, Uxb. UB8 .....76 BH68
Hilton Way, S.Croy. CR2 ...176 DV115
Hilversum Cres, SE22
off East Dulwich Gro 122 DS85
Himalayan Way, Wat. WD18 ...23 BT44
Himley Rd, SW17 .....120 DE92
Hinchcliffe Cl, Wall. SM6 .....159 DM108
Hinchley Cl, Esher KT10 .....137 CF104
Hinchley Dr, Esher KT10 .....137 CF104
Hinchley Way, Esher KT10 ...137 CG104
HINCHLEY WOOD, Esher 137 CF104
⇌ Hinchley Wood 137 CF104
Hinckley Rd, SE15 .....102 DU84
Hind Cl, Chig. IG7 .....49 ET50
Hind Ct, EC4 .....196 E9
Hind Cres, Erith DA8 .....107 FD79
Hinde Ms, W1
off Marylebone La 82 DG72
Hindes Rd, Har. HA1 .....61 CD57
Hinde St, W1 .....194 G8
Hind Gro, E14 .....85 EA72
Hindhead Cl, N16 .....66 DS60
Uxbridge UB8
off Aldenham Dr 77 BP71
Hindhead Gdns, Nthlt. UB5 ...78 BY67
Hindhead Grn, Wat. WD19 ....40 BW50
Hindhead Pt, SW15
off Wanborough Dr 119 CV88
Hindhead Way, Wall. SM6 ...159 DL106
Hind Ho, N7 off Harvist Est ...65 DN63
Hindmans Rd, SE22 .....122 DU85
Hindmans Way, Dag. RM9 ....88 EZ70
Hindmarsh Cl, E1
off Cable St 84 DU73
Hindrey Rd, E5 .....66 DV64
Hindsley's Pl, SE23 .....122 DW89
Hind Ter, Grays RM20
off Mill La 109 FX78
Hine Cl, Couls. CR5 .....175 DJ122
Hinkler Cl, Wall. SM6 .....159 DL108
Hinkler Rd, Har. HA3 .....61 CK55
Hinkley Cl, Uxb. (Hare.) UB9 ..58 BJ56
Hinksey Cl, Slou. SL3 .....93 BB76
Hinksey Path, SE2 .....106 EX76
Hinstock Rd, SE18 .....105 EQ79
Hinton Av, Houns. TW4 .....96 BX84
Hinton Cl, SE9 .....124 EL88
Hinton Rd, N18 .....46 DS49
SE24 .....101 DP83
Uxbridge UB8 .....76 BJ67
Wallington SM6 .....159 DJ107
Hipley St, Wok. GU22 .....167 BB121
Hippodrome Ms, W11
off Portland Rd 81 CY73
Hippodrome Pl, W11 .....81 CY73
Hiscocks Ho, NW10 .....80 CQ66
Hitcham Rd, E17 .....67 DZ59
Hitchcock Cl, Shep. TW17 ...134 BM97
Hitchen Hatch La, Sev. TN13 .190 FG124
Hitchin Cl, Rom. RM3 .....52 FJ49
Hitchin Sq, E3 .....85 DY68
Hitherbroom Rd, Hayes UB3 ..77 BU74
Hither Fm Rd, SE3 .....104 EJ83
Hitherfield Rd, SW16 .....121 DM89
Dagenham RM8 .....70 EY61
HITHER GREEN, SE13 .....124 EE86
⇌ Hither Green 124 EE86
Hither Grn La, SE13 .....123 EC85
Hitherlands, SW12 .....121 DH89
Hither Meadow, Ger.Cr. (Chal.St.P.)
SL9 off Lower Rd 36 AY53
Hithermoor Rd, Stai. TW19 ...114 BG85
Hitherwell Dr, Har. HA3 .....41 CD53
Hitherwood Cl, Horn. RM12
off Swanbourne Dr 72 FK63
Reigate RH2 .....184 DD132
Hitherwood Dr, SE19 .....122 DT91
Hive, The, Grav. (Nthflt.) DA11
off Fishermans Hill 130 GB85
Hive Cl, Brwd. CM14 .....54 FU47
Bushey (Bushey Hth.)
WD23 .....41 CD47
Hive La, Grav. (Nthflt.) DA11 .130 GB86
Hive Rd, Bushey (Bushey Hth.)
WD23 .....41 CD47
★ HMS Belfast, SE1 .....201 N2
★ HMS President, EC4 .....196 E10
★ HM Treasury, SW1 .....199 P4
Hoadly Rd, SW16 .....121 DK90
Hobart Cl, N20
off Oakleigh Rd N 44 DE47
Hayes UB4 .....78 BX70
Hobart Dr, Hayes UB4 .....78 BX70
Hobart Gdns, Th.Hth. CR7 ...142 DR97
Hobart La, Hayes UB4 .....78 BX70
Hobart Pl, SW1 .....199 H6
Richmond TW10
off Chisholm Rd 118 CM86
Hobart Rd, Dag. RM9 .....70 EX63
Hayes UB4 .....78 BX70
Ilford IG6 .....49 EQ54
Tilbury RM18 .....111 GG81
Worcester Park KT4 .....139 CV104
Hobarts Dr, Uxb. (Denh.) UB9 .57 BF58
Hobbayne Rd, W7 .....79 CD72
Hobbes Wk, SW15 .....119 CV85
Hobbs Cl, Wal.Cr. (Chsht.)
EN8 .....15 DX29
West Byfleet KT14 .....152 BH113
Hobbs Cross Rd, Epp. CM16 ..34 EW35
Hobbs Grn, N2 .....64 DC55
Hobbs Ms, Ilf. IG3
off Ripley Rd 69 ET61
Hobbs Pl Est, N1
off Pitfield St 84 DS67
Hobbs Rd, SE27 .....122 DQ91
Hobby Horse Cl, Wal.Cr.
(Chsht.) EN7
off Great Stockwood Rd ...14 DR26
Hobday St, E14 .....85 EB71
Hobill Wk, Surb. KT5 .....138 CM100
Hoblands End, Chis. BR7 ...125 ES93
Hobsons Pl, E1 off Hanbury St .84 DU71
Hobury St, SW10 .....100 DC79
Hockenden La, Swan. BR8 ...147 FB96
Hockering Gdns, Wok. GU22 .167 BA117
Hockering Rd, Wok. GU22 ...167 BA118
Hocker St, E2 .....197 P3
Hockett Cl, SE8 .....203 L8
Hockley Av, E6 .....86 EL68
Hockley Ct, E18
off Churchfields 48 EG53
Hockley Dr, Rom. RM2 .....51 FH54
Hockley La, Slou. (Stoke P.)
SL2 .....74 AV67
Hockley Ms, Bark. IG11 .....87 ES68
Hocroft Av, NW2 .....63 CZ62
Hocroft Rd, NW2 .....63 CZ63
Hocroft Wk, NW2 .....63 CZ62
Hodder Dr, Grnf. UB6 .....79 CF68
Hoddesdon Rd, Belv. DA17 ..106 FA78
Broxbourne EN10 .....15 DX27
Hodford Rd, NW11 .....63 CZ61
Hodgemoor Vw, Ch.St.G.
HP8 .....36 AT48
Hodges Way, Wat. WD18 .....23 BU44
Hodgkin Cl, SE28
off Fleming Way 88 EX73
Hodister Cl, SE5
off Badsworth Rd 102 DQ80
Hodnet Gro, SE16 .....203 H8
Hodsoll Ct, Orp. BR5 .....146 EX100
Hodson Cl, Har. HA2 .....60 BZ62
Hodson Cres, Orp. BR5 .....146 EX100
Hodson Pl, Enf. EN3
off Government Row 31 EA37
Hoe, The, Wat. WD19 .....40 BX47
Hoebrook Cl, Wok. GU22 ...166 AX121
Hoechst, Houns. TW4 .....96 BW83
Hoe La, Enf. EN1, EN3 .....30 DU38
Romford (Abridge) RM4 ...34 EV43
Hoe St, E17 .....67 EA56
Hofland Rd, W14 .....99 CX76
Hogan Ms, W2
off Porteus Rd 82 DD71
Hogan Way, E5
off Geldeston Rd 66 DU61
Hogarth Av, Ashf. TW15 .....115 BQ93
Brentwood CM15 .....54 FY48
Hogarth Business Pk, W4 ...98 CS79
Hogarth Cl, E16 .....86 EK71
W5 .....80 CL71
Hogarth Ct, EC3 .....197 N10
SE19 off Fountain Dr 122 DT91
Bushey WD23
off Steeplands 40 CB45
Hogarth Cres, SW19 .....140 DD95
Croydon CR0 .....142 DQ101
Hogarth Gdns, Houns. TW5 ..96 CA80
Hogarth Hill, NW11 .....63 CZ56
Hogarth La, W4 .....98 CS79
Hogarth Pl, SW5
off Hogarth Rd 100 DB77
Hogarth Reach, Loug. IG10 ...33 EM43
Hogarth Rd, SW5 .....100 DB77
Dagenham RM8 .....70 EV64
Edgware HA8 .....42 CN54
Hogarth Roundabout, W4 ....98 CS79
Hogarth Roundabout Flyover, W4
off Burlington La 98 CS79
★ Hogarth's Ho, W4
off Hogarth La 98 CS79
Hogarth Way, Hmptn. TW12 ..136 CC95
Hogg La, Borwd. (Elstree)
WD6 .....25 CG42
Grays RM16, RM17 .....110 GA76
Hogg La Roundabout, Grays
RM16 .....110 FZ75
Hog Hill Rd, Rom. RM5 .....50 EZ52
Hog Pits, Hem.H. (Flaun.)
HP3 .....5 BB32
HOGPITS BOTTOM, Hem.H. ...5 BA31
Hogpits Bottom, Hem.H. (Flaun.)
HP3 .....5 BA32
Hogscross La, Couls. CR5 ...174 DF123
Hogshead Pas, E1 .....202 E1
Hogshill La, Cob. KT11 .....154 BX112
Hogs La, Grav. DA11 .....130 GD90
Hogsmill Way, Epsom KT19 ..156 CQ106
Hogs Orchard, Swan. BR8 ...147 FH95
Hogtrough Hill, West. (Brasted)
TN16 .....179 ET120
Hogtrough La, Gdse. RH9 ...187 EA128
Oxted RH8 .....187 EB128
Holbeach Gdns, Sid. DA15 ...125 ES86
Holbeach Ms, SW12
off Harberson Rd 121 DH88
Holbeach Rd, SE6 .....123 EA87
Holbeck La, Wal.Cr. (Chsht.)
EN7 .....14 DT26
Holbeck Row, SE15 .....102 DU80
Holbein Gate, Nthwd. HA6 ...39 BS50
Holbein Ms, SW1 .....198 F10
Holbein Pl, SW1 .....198 F9
Holbein Ter, Dag. RM8
off Marlborough Rd 70 EV63
Holberton Gdns, NW10 .....81 CV69
HOLBORN, WC2 .....196 B8
⊖ Holborn 196 A7
Holborn, EC1 .....196 D7
Holborn Circ, EC1 .....196 E7
Holborn Pl, WC1 .....196 B7
Holborn Rd, E13 .....86 EH70
Holborn Viaduct, EC1 .....196 E7
Holborn Way, Mitch. CR4 ...140 DF96
Holbreck Pl, Wok. GU22
off Heathside Rd 167 AZ118
Holbrook Cl, N19
off Dartmouth Pk Hill 65 DH60
Enfield EN1 .....30 DT39
Holbrooke Ct, N7 .....65 DL63
Holbrooke Pl, Rich. TW10
off Hill Ri 117 CK85
Holbrook La, Chis. BR7 .....125 ER94
Holbrook Meadow, Egh.
TW20 .....113 BC93
Holbrook Rd, E15 .....86 EF68
Holbrook Way, Brom. BR2 ...145 EM100
Holburne Cl, SE3 .....104 EJ81
Holburne Gdns, SE3 .....104 EK81
Holburne Rd, SE3 .....104 EJ81
Holcombe Hill, NW7 .....43 CU48
Holcombe Rd, N17 .....66 DT55
Ilford IG1 .....69 EN59
Holcombe St, W6 .....99 CV78
Holcon Ct, Red. RH1 .....184 DG131
Holcote Cl, Belv. DA17
off Blakemore Way 106 EY76
Holcroft Rd, E9 .....84 DW66
HOLDBROOK, Wal.Cr. 15 EA34
Holdbrook N, Wal.Cr. EN8
off Eleanor Way 15 DZ34
Holdbrook S, Wal.Cr. EN8
off Queens Way 15 DZ34
Holdbrook Way, Rom. RM3 ...52 FM54
Holden Av, N12 .....44 DB50
NW9 .....62 CQ60
Holdenby Rd, SE4 .....123 DY85
Holden Cl, Dag. RM8 .....70 EV62
Holden Gdns, Brwd. CM14 ...54 FX50
Holdenhurst Av, N12 .....44 DB52
Holden Pl, Cob. KT11 .....153 BV114
Holden Pt, E15
off Waddington Rd 85 ED65
Holden Rd, N12 .....44 DB50
Holden St, SW11 .....100 DG82
Holden Way, Upmin. RM14 ...73 FR59
Holder Cl, N3 .....44 DB52
Holdernesse Cl, Islw. TW7 ....97 CG81
Holdernesse Rd, SW17 .....120 DF90
Holderness Way, SE27 .....121 DP92
HOLDERS HILL, NW4 .....43 CX54
Holders Hill Av, NW4 .....43 CX54
Holders Hill Circ, NW7
off Dollis Rd 43 CY52
Holders Hill Cres, NW4 .....43 CX54
Holders Hill Dr, NW4 .....63 CX55
Holders Hill Gdns, NW4 .....43 CY54
Holders Hill Rd, NW4 .....43 CX54
NW7 .....43 CX54
Holdgate St, SE7
off Westmoor St 104 EK76
Holecroft, Wal.Abb. EN9 .....16 EE34
Hole Fm La, Brwd. CM13 .....73 FV55
Holford Ms, WC1
off Cruikshank St 83 DN69
Holford Pl, WC1 .....196 C2
Holford Rd, NW3 .....64 DC62
Grays RM16 .....111 GK76
Stanford-le-Hope (Linford)
SS17 .....111 GL75
Tilbury RM18 .....111 GK76
Holford St, WC1 .....196 D2
Holford Yd, WC1
off Cruikshank St 83 DN69
Holgate Av, SW11 .....100 DD83
Holgate Gdns, Dag. RM10 ....70 FA64
Holgate Rd, Dag. RM10 .....70 FA64
HOLLAND, Oxt. 188 EG134
Holland Av, SW20 .....139 CT95
Sutton SM2 .....158 DA109
Holland Cl, Barn. EN5 .....44 DD45
Bromley BR2 .....144 EF103
Redhill RH1 .....184 DF134
Romford RM7 .....71 FC57
Stanmore HA7 .....41 CH50
Holland Ct, E17
off Evelyn Rd 67 EC56
NW7 off Page St 43 CU51
Holland Cres, Oxt. RH8 .....188 EG133
Holland Dr, SE23 .....123 DY90
Holland Gdns, W14 .....99 CY76
Egham TW20 .....133 BF96
Watford WD25 .....24 BW35
Holland Gro, SW9 .....101 DN80
★ Holland Ho & Pk, W8 .....99 CZ75
Holland La, Oxt. RH8 .....188 EG133
⊖ Holland Park 81 CY74
Holland Pk, W8 .....99 CZ75
W11 .....99 CY75
Holland Pk Av, W11 .....99 CY75
Ilford IG3 .....69 ES58
Holland Pk Gdns, W14 .....81 CY74
Holland Pk Ms, W11 .....81 CY74
Holland Pk Rd, W14 .....99 CZ76
Holland Pas, N1 off Basire St .84 DQ67
Holland Pl, W8
off Kensington Ch St 100 DB75
Holland Rd, E6 .....87 EM67
E15 .....86 EE69
NW10 .....81 CU67
SE25 .....142 DU99
W14 .....99 CX75
Oxted RH8 .....188 EG133
Wembley HA0 .....79 CK65
Hollands, The, Felt. TW13 ...116 BX91
Woking GU22
off Montgomery Rd 166 AY118
Worcester Park KT4 .....139 CT102
Holland St, SE1 .....200 G2
W8 .....100 DA75
Holland Vil Rd, W14 .....99 CY75
Holland Wk, N19
off Duncombe Rd 65 DK60
W8 .....99 CZ75
Stanmore HA7 .....41 CG50
Holland Way, Brom. BR2 ...144 EF103
Hollar Rd, N16 off Stoke
Newington High St 66 DT62
Hollen St, W1 .....195 M8
Holles Cl, Hmptn. TW12 .....116 CA93
Holles St, W1 .....195 J8
Holley Rd, W3 .....98 CS75
Hollickwood Av, N12 .....44 DF51
Holliday Sq, SW11
off Fowler Cl 100 DD83
Hollidge Way, Dag. RM10 ....89 FB65
Hollies, The, E11 .....68 EG57
N20 off Oakleigh Pk N 44 DD46
Gravesend DA12 .....131 GK93
Harrow HA3 .....61 CG56
Hemel Hempstead (Bov.)
HP3 .....5 BA29
Hollies Av, Sid. DA15 .....125 ET89
West Byfleet KT14 .....151 BF113
Hollies Cl, SW16 .....121 DN93
Twickenham TW1 .....117 CF89
Hollies Ct, Add. KT15 .....152 BJ106
Hollies End, NW7 .....43 CV50
Hollies Rd, W5 .....97 CJ77
Hollies Way, SW12
off Bracken Av 120 DG87
Potters Bar EN6 .....12 DC31
Holligrave Rd, Brom. BR1 ...144 EG95
Hollingbourne Av, Bexh.
DA7 .....106 EZ80
Hollingbourne Gdns, W13 ....79 CH71
Hollingbourne Rd, SE24 ....122 DQ85
Hollingbourne Twr, Orp. BR5 .146 EX102
Hollingsworth Rd, Croy. CR0 .160 DV107
Hollington Cres, N.Mal. KT3 .139 CT100
Hollington Rd, E6 .....87 EM69
N17 .....46 DU54
Hollingworth Cl, W.Mol. KT8 .136 BZ98
Hollingworth Rd, Orp. BR5 ..145 EP100
Hollingworth Way, West.
TN16 .....189 ER126
Hollis Pl, Grays RM17
off Ward Av 110 GA77
Hollman Gdns, SW16 .....121 DP93
Hollow, The, Wdf.Grn. IG8 ....48 EF49
HOLLOWAY, N7 .....65 DL63
Holloway Cl, West Dr. UB7 ...94 BL78
Holloway Dr, Vir.W. GU25 ...132 AY98
Holloway Hill, Cher. KT16 ...133 BC104
Holloway La, Rick. (Chenies)
WD3 .....21 BD36
West Drayton UB7 .....94 BL79
⊖ Holloway Road 65 DM64
Holloway Rd, E6 .....87 EM69
E11 .....68 EE62
N7 .....65 DM63
N19 .....65 DK61
Holloway St, Houns. TW3 ....96 CB83
Hollow Cotts, Purf. RM19 ...108 FN78
Hollowfield Av, Grays RM17 .110 GD77
Hollowfield Wk, Nthlt. UB5 ...78 BY65
Hollow Hill La, Iver SL0 .....75 BB73
Hollow La, Vir.W. GU25 .....132 AY97
Hollows, The, Brent. TW8
off Kew Br Rd 98 CM79
Hollow Wk, Rich. TW9
off Kew Rd 98 CL80
Hollow Way La, Amer. HP6 ...20 AS35
Chesham HP5 .....20 AS35
Holly Av, Add. (New Haw)
KT15 .....152 BG110
Stanmore HA7 .....42 CL54
Walton-on-Thames KT12 ..136 BX102
Hollybank Cl, Hmptn. TW12 ..116 CA92
Hollybank Rd, W.Byf. KT14 ..152 BG114
Holly Bk Rd, Wok. GU22 ...166 AV121
Hollyberry La, NW3
off Holly Wk 64 DC63
Hollybrake Cl, Chis. BR7 ...125 ER94
Hollybush Cl, E11 .....68 EG57
Harrow HA3 .....41 CE53
Sevenoaks TN13 .....191 FJ124
Watford WD19 .....40 BW45
Hollybush Ct, Sev. TN13 ...191 FJ124
Hollybush Gdns, E2 .....84 DV69
Hollybush Hill, E11 .....68 EF58
Holly Bush Hill, NW3 .....64 DC63
Hollybush Hill, Slou. (Stoke P.)
SL2 .....74 AU66
Holly Bush La, Hmptn. TW12 .116 BZ94
Hollybush La, Iver SL0 .....75 BB72
Orpington BR6 .....164 FA107
Holly Bush La, Sev. TN13 ...191 FJ123
Hollybush La, Uxb. (Denh.)
UB9 .....57 BE63
Woking (Ripley) GU23 ...168 BK119
Hollybush Pl, E2
off Bethnal Grn Rd 84 DV69
Hollybush Rd, Grav. DA12 ...131 GJ89
Kingston upon Thames
KT2 .....118 CL92
Holly Bush Steps, NW3
off Heath St 64 DC63
Hollybush St, E13 .....86 EH69
Holly Bush Vale, NW3
off Heath St 64 DC63
Hollybush Wk, SW9 .....101 DP84
Hollybush Way, Wal.Cr. EN7 ..14 DU28
Holly Cl, NW10 .....80 CS66
Beckenham BR3 .....143 EC98
Buckhurst Hill IG9 .....48 EK48
Chertsey (Longcr.) KT16 ..132 AU104
Egham (Eng.Grn.) TW20 ...112 AV93
Feltham TW13 .....116 BY92
Wallington SM6 .....159 DH108
Woking GU21 .....166 AV119
Hollycombe, Egh. (Eng.Grn.)
TW20 .....112 AW91
Holly Cottage Ms, Uxb. UB8
off Pield Heath Rd 76 BN71
Holly Ct, Sutt. SM2
off Worcester Rd 158 DA108
Holly Cres, Beck. BR3 .....143 DZ99
Woodford Green IG8 .....47 ED52
Hollycroft Av, NW3 .....64 DA62
Wembley HA9 .....62 CM61
Hollycroft Cl, S.Croy. CR2 ..160 DS106
West Drayton UB7 .....94 BN79
Hollycroft Gdns, West Dr. UB7 .94 BN79
Hollydale Cl, Nthlt. UB5
off Dorchester Rd 60 CB63
Hollydale Dr, Brom. BR2 ...145 EM104
Hollydale Rd, SE15 .....102 DW81
Hollydene, SE15 .....102 DV81
Hollydown Way, E11 .....67 ED62
Holly Dr, E4 .....47 EB45
Brentford TW8 .....97 CG79
Potters Bar EN6 .....12 DB33
South Ockendon RM15 ....91 FX70
Windsor SL4 .....112 AS85
Holly Fm Rd, Sthl. UB2 .....96 BY78
Hollyfield Av, N11 .....44 DF50
Hollyfield Rd, Surb. KT5 ...138 CM101
Hollyfields, Brox. EN10 .....15 DY26
Holly Gdns, West Dr. UB7 ...94 BM75
Holly Grn, Wey. KT13 .....135 BR104
Holly Gro, NW9 .....62 CQ59
SE15 .....102 DT82
Bushey WD23 .....41 CD45
Pinner HA5 .....40 BY53
Hollyhedge Rd, Cob. KT11 ...153 BV114
Holly Hedges La, Hem.H. (Bov.)
HP3 .....5 BC30
Rickmansworth WD3 .....5 BC30
Holly Hedge Ter, SE13 .....123 ED85
Holly Hill, N21 .....29 DM44
NW3 .....64 DC63
Holly Hill Dr, Bans. SM7 ...174 DA116
Holly Hill Pk, Bans. SM7 ...174 DA117
Holly Hill Rd, Belv. DA17 ...107 FB78
Erith DA8 .....107 FB78
Holly Ho, Brwd. CM15
off Sawyers Hall La 54 FX46
H Holly House Hosp, Buck.H.
IG9 .....48 EH47
Holly La, Bans. SM7 .....174 DA116
Holly La E, Bans. SM7 .....174 DA116
Holly La W, Bans. SM7 .....174 DA117
Holly Lo Gdns, N6 .....64 DG61
Holly Lo Mobile Home Pk, Tad.
KT20 .....183 CY126
Hollymead, Cars. SM5 .....140 DF104
Hollymead Rd, Couls. CR5 ...174 DG118
Hollymeoak Rd, Couls. CR5 ..175 DH119
Holly Ms, SW10
off Drayton Gdns 100 DC78
Hollymoor La, Epsom KT19 ..156 CR110
Holly Mt, NW3
off Holly Bush Hill 64 DC63
Hollymount Cl, SE10 .....103 EC81
Holly Pk, N3 .....63 CZ55
N4 .....65 DM59
Holly Pk Est, N4
off Blythwood Rd 65 DM59
Holly Pk Gdns, N3 .....64 DA55
Holly Pk Rd, N11 .....44 DG50
W7 .....79 CF74

Hol - Hor

Holly Pl, NW3 off Holly Wk 64 DC63
Holly Rd, E11 68 EF59
W4 off Dolman Rd 98 CR77
Dartford DA1 128 FK88
Enfield EN3 31 DX36
Hampton (Hmptn.H.)
TW12 116 CC93
Hounslow TW3 96 CB84
Orpington BR6 164 EU108
Twickenham TW1 117 CG88
Holly St, E8 84 DT65
Holly Ter, N6
off Highgate W Hill 64 DG60
N20 off Swan La 44 DC47
Holly Tree Av, Swan. BR8 147 FE96
Hollytree Cl, SW19 119 CX88
Holly Tree Cl, Chesh. (Ley Hill)
HP5 4 AV31
Hollytree Cl, Ger.Cr. (Chal.St.P.)
SL9 36 AY50
Holly Tree Rd, Cat. CR3
off Elm Gro 176 DS122
Holly Vw Cl, NW4 63 CU58
Holly Village, N6
off Swains La 65 DH61
Holly Wk, NW3 64 DC63
Enfield EN2 30 DQ41
Richmond TW9 98 CL82
Holly Way, Mitch. CR4 141 DK98
Hollywood Ct, Borwd. (Elstree)
WD6 off Deacon's Hill Rd 26 CM42
Hollywood Gdns, Hayes
UB4 77 BV72
Hollywood Ms, SW10
off Hollywood Rd 100 DC79
Hollywood Rd, E4 47 DY50
SW10 100 DC79
Hollywoods, Croy. CR0 161 DZ109
Hollywood Way, Erith DA8 107 FH81
Woodford Green IG8 47 ED52
Holman Rd, SW11 100 DD82
Epsom KT19 156 CQ106
Holmbank Dr, Shep. TW17 135 BS98
Holmbridge Gdns, Enf. EN3 31 DX42
Holmbrook Dr, NW4 63 CX57
Holmbury Ct, SW17 120 DF90
SW19 off Cavendish Rd 120 DE94
Holmbury Gdns, Hayes UB3
off Church Rd 77 BT74
Holmbury Gro, Croy. CR0 161 DZ108
Holmbury Pk, Brom. BR1 124 EL94
Holmbury Vw, E5 66 DV60
Holmbush Rd, SW15 119 CY86
Holm Cl, Add. (Woodham)
KT15 151 BE112
Holmcote Gdns, N5 66 DQ64
Holmcroft, Tad. KT20 183 CV125
Holmcroft Way, Brom. BR2 145 EM99
Holmdale Cl, Borwd. WD6 26 CM40
Holmdale Gdns, NW4 63 CX57
Holmdale Rd, NW6 64 DA64
Chislehurst BR7 125 EQ92
Holmdale Ter, N15 66 DS59
Holmdene Av, NW7 43 CU51
SE24 122 DQ85
Harrow HA2 60 CB55
Holmdene Cl, Beck. BR3 143 EC96
Holmead Rd, SW6 100 DB80
Holmebury Cl, Bushey
(Bushey Hth.) WD23 41 CE47
Holme Chase, Wey. KT13 153 BQ107
Holme Cl, Wal.Cr. (Chsht.)
EN8 15 DY31
Holmedale, Slou. SL2 74 AW73
Holmefield Ct, NW3 82 DE65
Holme Lacey Rd, SE12 124 EF86
Holme Lea, Wat. WD25
off Kingsway 8 BW34
Holme Pk, Borwd. WD6 26 CM40
Holme Rd, E6 86 EL67
Hornchurch RM11 72 FN60
Holmes Av, E17 67 DZ55
NW7 43 CY50
Holmes Cl, Wok. GU22 167 AZ121
Holmesdale, Wal.Cr. EN8 31 DX35
Holmesdale Av, SW14 98 CP83
Holmesdale Cl, SE25 142 DT97
Holmesdale Hill, Dart. (S.Darenth)
DA4 148 FQ95
Holmesdale Rd, N6 65 DH59
SE25 142 DR99
Bexleyheath DA7 106 EX82
Croydon CR0 142 DR99
Dartford (S.Darenth) DA4 148 FQ95
Reigate RH2 184 DA133
Richmond TW9 98 CM81
Sevenoaks TN13 191 FJ123
Teddington TW11 117 CJ93
Holmesley Rd, SE23 123 DY86
Holmes Pl, SW10
off Fulham Rd 100 DC79
Holmes Rd, NW5 65 DH64
SW19 120 DC94
Twickenham TW1 117 CF89
Holmes Ter, SE1 200 D4
HOLMETHORPE, Red. 185 DH132
Holmethorpe Av, Red. RH1 185 DH131
Holmethorpe Ind Est, Red. RH1
off Holmethorpe Av 185 DH131
Holme Way, Stan. HA7 41 CF51
Holmewood Gdns, SW2 121 DM87
Holmewood Rd, SE25 142 DS97
SW2 121 DL87
Holmfield Av, NW4 63 CX57
Holm Gro, Uxb. UB10 76 BN66
Holmhurst Rd, Belv. DA17 107 FB78
Holmlea Rd, Slou. (Datchet)
SL3 92 AX81
Holmlea Wk, Slou. (Datchet)
SL3 92 AW81
Holmleigh Av, Dart. DA1 108 FJ84
Holmleigh Rd, N16 66 DS60
Holmleigh Rd Est, N16
off Holmleigh Rd 66 DT60
Holm Oak Cl, SW15
off West Hill 119 CZ86
Holm Oak Ms, SW4
off King's Av 121 DL85
Holmsdale Cl, Iver SL0 75 BF72
Holmsdale Gro, Bexh. DA7 107 FE82
Holmshaw Cl, SE26 123 DY91
Holmshill La, Borwd. WD6 26 CS36
Holmside Ri, Wat. WD19 39 BV48
Holmside Rd, SW12 120 DG86
Holmsley Cl, N.Mal. KT3 139 CT100
Holmsley Ho, SW15
off Tangley Gro 119 CT87
Holms St, E2 84 DU68
Holmstall Av, Edg. HA8 62 CQ55
Holm Wk, SE3
off Blackheath Pk 104 EG82
Holmwood Av, Brwd. CM15 55 GA44
South Croydon CR2 160 DT113
Holmwood Cl, Add. KT15 152 BG106
Harrow HA2 60 CC55
Northolt UB5 78 CB65
Sutton SM2 157 CX109
Holmwood Gdns, N3 44 DA54
Wallington SM6 159 DH107
Holmwood Gro, NW7 42 CR50
Holmwood Rd, Chess. KT9 155 CK106
Enfield EN3 31 DX36
Ilford IG3 69 ES61
Sutton SM2 157 CW110
Holmwood Vil, SE7 205 N10
Holne Chase, N2 64 DC58
Morden SM4 139 CZ100
Holness Rd, E15 86 EF65
Holroyd Cl, Esher (Clay.)
KT10 155 CF109
Holroyd Rd, SW15 99 CW84
Esher (Clay.) KT10 155 CF109
Holsart Cl, Tad. KT20 173 CV122
Holstein Av, Wey. KT13 152 BN105
Holstein Way, Erith DA18 106 EY76
Holstock Rd, Ilf. IG1 69 EQ62
Holsworth Cl, Har. HA2 60 CC57
Holsworthy Sq, WC1 196 C5
Holsworthy Way, Chess. KT9 155 CJ106
Holt, The, Ilf. IG6 49 EQ51
Wallington SM6 159 DJ105
Holt Cl, N10 64 DG56
SE28 88 EV73
Borehamwood (Elstree)
WD6 26 CM42
Chigwell IG7 49 ET50
Holt Ct, E15 off Clays La 67 EC64
Holton St, E1 85 DX70
Holt Rd, E16 86 EL74
Romford RM3 52 FL52
Wembley HA0 61 CH62
Holtsmere Cl, Wat. WD25 24 BW35
Holt Way, Chig. IG7 49 ET50
Holtwhite Av, Enf. EN2 30 DQ40
Holtwhites Hill, Enf. EN2 29 DP39
Holtwood Rd, Lthd. (Oxshott)
KT22 154 CC113
Holwell Pl, Pnr. HA5 60 BY56
Holwood Cl, Walt. KT12 136 BW103
Holwood Pk Av, Orp. BR6 163 EM105
Holwood Pl, SW4 101 DK84
Holybourne Av, SW15 119 CU87
HOLYFIELD, Wal.Abb. 15 ED28
Holyfield Rd, Wal.Abb. EN9 15 EC29
Holyhead Cl, E3 85 EA69
E6 off Valiant Way 87 EM71
Holyoake Av, Wok. GU21 166 AW117
Holyoake Ct, SE16 203 L4
Holyoake Cres, Wok. GU21 166 AW117
Holyoake Ter, Sev. TN13 190 FG124
Holyoake Wk, N2 64 DC55
W5 79 CJ70
Holyoak Rd, SE11 200 F8
Holyport Rd, SW6 99 CW80
Holyrood Av, Har. HA2 60 BY63
Holyrood Gdns, Edg. HA8 62 CP55
Grays RM16 111 GJ77
Holyrood Ms, E16 205 N2
Holyrood Rd, Barn. EN5 28 DC44
Holyrood St, SE1 201 M3
HOLYWELL, Wat. 23 BS44
Holywell Cl, SE3 104 EG79
SE16 202 E10
Orpington BR6 164 EU105
Staines TW19 114 BL88
Holywell Ind Est, Wat. WD18 23 BR44
Holywell La, EC2 197 N4
Holywell Rd, Wat. WD18 23 BU43
Holywell Row, EC2 197 M5
Holywell Way, Stai. TW19 114 BL88
Home Cl, Cars. SM5 140 DF103
Leatherhead (Fetch.) KT22 171 CD121
Northolt UB5 78 BZ69
Virginia Water GU25 132 AX100
Home Ct, Felt. TW13 115 BU88
Homecroft Gdns, Loug. IG10 33 EP42
Homecroft Rd, N22 46 DQ53
SE26 122 DW92
Homedean Rd, Sev. (Chipstead)
TN13 190 FC122
Home Fm, Orp. BR6
off Hawstead La 164 EZ106
Home Fm Cl, Cher. (Ott.)
KT16 151 BA108
Esher KT10 154 CB107
Shepperton TW17 135 BS98
Tadworth KT20 173 CX117
Thames Ditton KT7 137 CF101
Home Fm Gdns, Walt. KT12 136 BW103
Homefarm Rd, W7 79 CE72
Home Fm Rd, Rick. WD3 38 BN49
Home Fm Way, Slou. (Stoke P.)
SL3 74 AW67
Homefield, Hem.H. (Bov.) HP3 5 BB28
Waltham Abbey EN9 16 EG32
Walton-on-Thames KT12 154 BX105
Homefield Av, Ilf. IG2 69 ES57
Homefield Cl, NW10 80 CQ65
Addlestone (Woodham)
KT15 151 BE112
Epping CM16 18 EU30
Homefield Cl, Hayes UB4 78 BW70
Leatherhead KT22 171 CJ121
Orpington BR5 146 EV98
Swanley BR8 147 FF97
Homefield Fm Rd, Dart. (Sutt.H.)
DA4 148 FM96
Homefield Gdns, N2 64 DD55
Mitcham CR4 140 DC96
Tadworth KT20 173 CW120
Homefield Ms, Beck. BR3 143 EA95
Homefield Pk, Sutt. SM1 158 DB107
Homefield Ri, Orp. BR6 146 EU102
Homefield Rd, SW19 119 CX93
W4 99 CT77
Bromley BR1 144 EJ95
Bushey WD23 24 CA43
Coulsdon CR5 175 DP119
Edgware HA8 42 CR51
Radlett WD7 25 CF37
Rickmansworth (Chorl.)
WD3 21 BC42
Sevenoaks TN13 190 FE122
Walton-on-Thames KT12 136 BY101
Warlingham CR6 176 DW119
Wembley HA0 61 CG63
Homefield St, N1 197 M1
Home Gdns, Dag. RM10 71 FC62
Dartford DA1 128 FL86
Home Hill, Swan. BR8 127 FF94
Homeland Dr, Sutt. SM2 158 DB109
Homelands, Lthd. KT22 171 CJ121
Homelands Dr, SE19 122 DS94
Home Lea, Orp. BR6 163 ET106
Homeleigh Ct, Wal.Cr. EN8 14 DV29
Homeleigh Rd, SE15 123 DX85
Homemead, SW12 121 DJ89
Gravesend DA12
off Home Mead Cl 131 GH87
Home Mead, Stan. HA7 41 CJ53
Home Mead Cl, Grav. DA12 131 GH87
Home Meadow, Bans. SM7 174 DA116
Homemead Rd, Brom. BR2 145 EM99
Croydon CR0 141 DJ100
★ Home Office, SW1 199 M5
Home Orchard, Dart. DA1 128 FL86
Home Pk, Oxt. RH8 188 EG131
Home Pk Mill Link Rd, Kings L.
WD4 7 BP31
Home Pk Rd, SW19 120 DA90
Home Pk Wk, Kings.T. KT1 137 CK98
Homer Cl, Bexh. DA7 107 FC81
Homer Dr, E14 203 P8
Home Rd, SW11 100 DE82
Homer Rd, E9 85 DY65
Croydon CR0 143 DX100
Homer Row, W1 194 C7
Homersham Rd, Kings.T.
KT1 138 CN96
Homer St, W1 194 C7
HOMERTON, E9 67 DY64
⇌ Homerton 85 DX65
Homerton Gro, E9 67 DX64
Homerton High St, E9 66 DW64
H Homerton Hosp, E9 67 DX64
Homerton Rd, E9 67 DY64
Homerton Row, E9 66 DW64
Homerton Ter, E9
off Morning La 84 DW65
Homesdale Cl, E11 68 EG57
Homesdale Rd, Brom.
BR1, BR2 144 EJ98
Caterham CR3 176 DR123
Orpington BR5 145 ES101
Homesfield, NW11 64 DA57
Homestall Rd, SE22 122 DW85
Homestead, The, N11 45 DH49
Dartford DA1 128 FJ86
Homestead Cl, St.Alb. (Park St.)
AL2 8 CC27
Homestead Gdns, Esher (Clay.)
KT10 155 CE106
Homestead Paddock, N14 29 DH43
Homestead Pk, NW2 63 CT62
Homestead Rd, SW6 99 CZ80
Caterham CR3 176 DR123
Dagenham RM8 70 EZ61
Orpington BR6 164 EV108
Rickmansworth WD3
off Park Rd 38 BK45
Staines TW18 114 BH93
Homestead Way, Croy.
(New Adgtn.) CR0 161 EC111
Homewaters Av, Sun. TW16 135 BT95
Home Way, Rick. (Mill End)
WD3 37 BF46
Homeway, Rom. RM3 52 FP51
Homewillow Cl, N21 29 DP44
Homewood, Slou. (Geo.Grn.)
SL3 74 AX72
Homewood Av, Pot.B. (Cuffley)
EN6 13 DL27
Homewood Cl, Hmptn. TW12
off Fearnley Cres 116 BZ93
Homewood Cres, Chis. BR7 125 ES93
Homewood La, Pot.B. EN6 13 DJ27
Honduras St, EC1 197 H4
Honeybourne Rd, NW6 64 DB64
Honeybourne Way, Orp. BR5 145 ER102
Honey Brook, Wal.Abb. EN9 16 EE33
Honeybrook Rd, SW12 121 DJ87
Honey Cl, Dag. RM10 89 FB65
Honeycroft, Loug. IG10 33 EN42
Honeycroft Hill, Uxb. UB10 76 BL66
Honeyden Rd, Sid. DA14 126 EY93
Honey Hill, Uxb. UB10 76 BM66
Honey La, EC2 197 J9
Waltham Abbey EN9 32 EG35
Honeyman Cl, NW6 81 CX66
Honeypot Cl, NW9 62 CM56
Honeypot La, NW9 62 CM55
Brentwood CM14 54 FU48
Stanmore HA7 62 CM55
Honeypots Rd, Wok. GU22 166 AX122
Honeysett Rd, N17
off Reform Row 46 DT54
Honeysuckle Cl, Brwd. CM15 54 FV43
Iver SL0 75 BC72
Honeysuckle Cl, Rom. RM3
off Cloudberry Rd 52 FK51
Southall UB1 78 BY73
Honeysuckle Gdns, Croy. CR0
off Primrose La 143 DX102
Honeywell Rd, SW11 120 DF86
Honeywood Cl, Pot.B. EN6 12 DE33
Honeywood Rd, NW10 81 CT68
Isleworth TW7 97 CG84
Honeywood Wk, Cars. SM5 158 DF105
Honister Cl, Stan. HA7 41 CH53
Honister Gdns, Stan. HA7 41 CH52
Honister Hts, Pur. CR8 160 DR114
Honister Pl, Stan. HA7 41 CH53
Honiton Gdns, NW7
off Bittacy Hill 43 CY52
Honiton Rd, NW6 81 CZ68
Romford RM7 71 FD58
Welling DA16 105 ET82
Honley Rd, SE6 123 EB87
Honnor Gdns, Islw. TW7 97 CD82
Honnor Rd, Stai. TW18 114 BK94
HONOR OAK, SE23 122 DW86
HONOR OAK PARK, SE4 123 DY86
⇌ Honor Oak Park 123 DX86
Honor Oak Pk, SE23 122 DW86
Honor Oak Ri, SE23 122 DW86
Honor Oak Rd, SE23 122 DW88
Hood Av, N14 29 DH44
SW14 118 CQ85
Orpington BR5 146 EV99
Hood Cl, Croy. CR0
off Parson's Mead 141 DP102
Hoodcote Gdns, N21 45 DP45
Hood Ct, EC4 196 E9
Hood Rd, SW20 119 CT94
Rainham RM13 89 FE67
Hood Wk, Rom. RM7 51 FB53
HOOK, Chess. 156 CL105
Hook, The, Barn. EN5 28 DD44
Hookers Rd, E17 67 DX55
Hook Fm Rd, Brom. BR2 144 EK99
Hookfield, Epsom KT19 156 CQ113
Hookfields, Grav. (Nthflt.)
DA11 130 GE90
Hook Gate, Enf. EN1 30 DV36
HOOK GREEN, Dart. 127 FG91
HOOK GREEN, Grav. 130 FZ93
Hook Grn La, Dart. DA2 127 FF90
Hook Grn Rd, Grav. (Sthflt.)
DA13 130 FY94
HOOK HEATH, Wok. 166 AV120
Hook Heath Av, Wok. GU22 166 AV119
Hook Heath Gdns, Wok.
GU22 166 AT121
Hook Heath Rd, Wok. GU22 166 AW121
Hook Hill, S.Croy. CR2 160 DS110
Hook Hill La, Wok. GU22 166 AV121
Hook Hill Pk, Wok. GU22 166 AV121
Hooking Grn, Har. HA2 60 CB57
Hook La, Pot.B. EN6 12 DF32
Romford RM4 34 EZ44
Welling DA16 125 ET85
Hook Ri N, Surb. KT6 138 CN104
Hook Ri S, Surb. KT6 138 CN104
Hook Ri S Ind Pk, Surb. KT6 138 CM104
Hook Rd, Chess. KT9 155 CK106
Epsom KT19 156 CR111
Surbiton KT6 138 CL104
Hooks Cl, SE15
off Woods Rd 102 DV81
Hooks Hall Dr, Dag. RM10 71 FC62
Hookstone Way, Wdf.Grn. IG8 48 EK52
Hooks Way, SE22
off Dulwich Common 122 DU88
Hook Wk, Edg. HA8 42 CQ51
Hookwood Cor, Oxt. RH8
off Hookwood La 188 EH128
Hookwood La, Oxt. RH8 188 EH128
Hookwood Rd, Orp. BR6 164 EW111
HOOLEY, Couls. 174 DG122
Hooper Rd, E16 86 EG72
Hooper's Ct, SW3 198 D5
Hooper Sq, E1 off Hooper St 84 DU73
Hooper St, E1 84 DU72
Hoopers Yd, Sev. TN13 191 FJ126
Hoop La, NW11 63 CZ59
Hope Cl, N1 off Wallace Rd 84 DQ65
SE12 124 EH90
Brentford TW8
off Burford Rd 98 CL78
Romford (Chad.Hth.) RM6 70 EW56
Sutton SM1 158 DC106
Woodford Green IG8
off West Gro 48 EJ51
Hopedale Rd, SE7 104 EH79
Hopefield Av, NW6 81 CY68
Hope Grn, Wat. WD25 7 BU33
Hope Pk, Brom. BR1 124 EF94
Hope Rd, Swans. DA10 130 FZ86
Hopes Cl, Houns. TW5
off Old Cote Dr 96 CA79
Hope St, SW11 100 DD83
Hope Ter, Grays RM20 109 FX78
Hopetown St, E1
off Brick La 84 DT71
Hopewell Dr, Grav. DA12 131 GM92
Hopewell St, SE5 102 DR80
Hopewell Yd, SE5
off Hopewell St 102 DR80
Hope Wf, SE16
off St. Marychurch St 102 DW75
Hopfield, Wok. (Horsell)
GU21 166 AY116
Hopfield Av, W.Byf. (Byfleet)
KT14 152 BL112
Hopgarden La, Sev. TN13 190 FG128
Hop Gdns, WC2 199 P1
Hop Gdn Way, Wat. WD25
off High Elms La 8 BW31
Hopgood St, W12
off Macfarlane Rd 81 CW74
Hopkins Cl, N10 44 DG52
Romford RM2 72 FJ55
Hopkins Ms, E15 off West Rd 86 EF67
Hopkinsons Pl, NW1
off Fitzroy Rd 82 DG67
Hopkins St, W1 195 L9
Hoppers Rd, N13 45 DN47
N21 45 DN47
Hoppett Rd, E4 48 EE48
Hoppety, The, Tad. KT20 173 CX122
Hopping La, N1
off St. Mary's Gro 83 DP65
Hoppingwood Av, N.Mal.
KT3 138 CS97
Hoppit Rd, Wal.Abb. EN9 15 EB32
Hoppner Rd, Hayes UB4 77 BQ68
Hop St, SE10 205 L8
Hopton Gdns, SE1 200 G2
New Malden KT3 139 CU100
Hopton Rd, SW16 121 DL92
Hopton St, SE1 200 G2
Hopwood Cl, SW17 120 DC90
Watford WD17 23 BR36
Hopwood Rd, SE17 102 DR79
Hopwood Wk, E8
off Wilman Gro 84 DU66
Horace Av, Rom. RM7 71 FC60
Horace Rd, E7 68 EH63
Ilford IG6 69 EQ55
Kingston upon Thames
KT1 138 CM97
Horatio Ct, SE16
off Rotherhithe St 84 DW74
Horatio Pl, E14 204 E4
SW19 off Kingston Rd 120 DA94
Horatio St, E2 84 DT68
Horatius Way, Croy. CR0 159 DM106
Horbury Cres, W11 82 DA73
Horbury Ms, W11
off Ladbroke Rd 81 CZ73
Horder Rd, SW6 99 CY81
Hordle Prom E, SE15
off Daniel Gdns 102 DT80
Hordle Prom N, SE15
off Daniel Gdns 102 DT80
Hordle Prom S, SE15
off Pentridge St 102 DT80
Hordle Prom W, SE15
off Diamond St 102 DS80
Horizon Way, SE7 104 EH77
Horksley Gdns, Brwd. CM13
off Bannister Dr 55 GC44
Horle Wk, SE5 off Lilford Rd 101 DP82
Horley Cl, Bexh. DA6 126 FA85
Horley Rd, SE9 124 EL91
Hormead Rd, W9 81 CZ70
Hornbeam Av, Upmin. RM14 72 FN63
Hornbeam Chase, S.Ock.
RM15 91 FX69
Hornbeam Cl, NW7 43 CT48
SE11 200 D8
Borehamwood WD6 26 CN39
Brentwood CM13 55 GB48
Buckhurst Hill IG9
off Hornbeam Rd 48 EK48
Epping (They.B.) CM16 33 ES37
Ilford IG1 69 ER64
Northolt UB5 60 BZ64
Hornbeam Cres, Brent. TW8 97 CH80
Hornbeam Gdns, Slou. SL1
off Upton Rd 92 AU76
Hornbeam Gro, E4 48 EE48
Hornbeam La, E4 32 EE43
Bexleyheath DA7 107 FC82
Hornbeam Rd, Buck.H. IG9 48 EK48
Epping (They.B.) CM16 33 ER37
Hayes UB4 78 BW71
Hornbeams, St.Alb. (Brick.Wd.)
AL2 8 BZ30
Hornbeams Av, Enf. EN1 30 DW35
Hornbeams Ri, N11 44 DG51
Hornbeam Ter, Cars. SM5 140 DE102
Hornbeam Wk, Rich. TW10 118 CM90
Walton-on-Thames KT12
off Octagon Rd 153 BT109
Hornbeam Way, Brom. BR2 145 EN100
Waltham Cross EN7 14 DT29
Hornbill Cl, Uxb. UB8 76 BK72
Hornblower Cl, SE16 203 K8
Hornbuckle Cl, Har. HA2 61 CD61
Hornby Cl, NW3 82 DD66
Horncastle Cl, SE12 124 EG87
Horncastle Rd, SE12 124 EG87
HORNCHURCH 72 FJ61
⊖ Hornchurch 72 FK62
Hornchurch Cl, Kings.T. KT2 117 CK91
Hornchurch Hill, Whyt. CR3 176 DT117
Hornchurch Rd, Horn.
RM11, RM12 71 FG60
Horndean Cl, SW15
off Bessborough Rd 119 CU88
Horndon Cl, Rom. RM5 51 FC53
Horndon Grn, Rom. RM5 51 FC53
Horndon Rd, Rom. RM5 51 FC53
Horne Rd, Shep. TW17 134 BN98
Hornets, The, Wat. WD18 23 BV42
Horne Way, SW15 99 CW82
Hornfair Rd, SE7 104 EJ79
Hornford Way, Rom. RM7 71 FE59
Hornhill Rd, Ger.Cr. SL9 37 BB50
Rickmansworth (Map.Cr.)
WD3 37 BD50
Horniman Dr, SE23 122 DV88
★ Horniman Mus, SE23 122 DV88
Horning Cl, SE9 124 EL91
Horn La, SE10 205 M9
W3 80 CQ73
Woodford Green IG8 48 EG51
Horn Link Way, SE10 205 M8
Hornminster Glen, Horn.
RM11 72 FN61
Horn Pk Cl, SE12 124 EH85
Horn Pk La, SE12 124 EH85
Hornsby La, Grays (Orsett)
RM16 111 GG75
Horns End Pl, Pnr. HA5 60 BW56
HORNSEY, N8 65 DM55
⇌ Hornsey 65 DM56
H Hornsey Cen Hosp, N8 65 DK57
Hornsey La, N6 65 DH60
N19 65 DJ60

★ Place of interest ⇌ Railway station ⊖ London Underground station DLR Docklands Light Railway station Tramlink station H Hospital

275

Hor - Hur

Hornsey La Est, N19
off Hornsey La 65 DK59
Hornsey La Gdns, N6 65 DJ59
Hornsey Pk Rd, N8 65 DM55
Hornsey Ri, N19 65 DK59
Hornsey Ri Gdns, N19 65 DK59
Hornsey Rd, N7 65 DL61
N19 65 DL61
Hornsey St, N7 65 DM64
HORNS GREEN, Sev. 179 ES117
Hornshay St, SE15 102 DW79
Horns Rd, Ilf. IG2, IG6 69 EQ57
Hornton Pl, W8 100 DA75
Hornton St, W8 100 DA75
Horsa Cl, Wall. SM6 159 DL108
Horsa Rd, SE12 124 EJ87
Erith DA8 107 FC80
Horse & Dolphin Yd, W1 195 N10
Horsebridge Cl, Dag. RM9 88 EY67
Horsecroft, Bans. SM7
off Lyme Regis Rd 173 CZ117
Horsecroft Cl, Orp. BR6 146 EV102
Horsecroft Rd, Edg. HA8 42 CR52
Horse Fair, Kings.T. KT1 137 CK96
Horseferry Pl, SE10 103 EC79
Horseferry Rd, E14 85 DY73
SW1 199 M7
Horse Guards Av, SW1 199 P3
★ Horse Guards Par, SW1 199 N3
Horse Guards Rd, SW1 199 N3
Horse Hill, Chesh. HP5 4 AX32
Horse Leaze, E6 87 EN72
HORSELL, Wok. 166 AY116
Horsell Birch, Wok. GU21 166 AV115
Horsell Common, Wok.
GU21 150 AX114
Horsell Common Rd, Wok.
GU21 150 AW114
Horsell Ct, Cher. KT16
off Stepgates 134 BH101
Horsell Moor, Wok. GU21 166 AX117
Horsell Pk, Wok. GU21 166 AX116
Horsell Pk Cl, Wok. GU21 166 AX116
Horsell Ri, Wok. GU21 166 AX115
Horsell Ri Cl, Wok. GU21 166 AX115
Horsell Rd, N5 65 DN64
Orpington BR5 146 EV95
Horsell Vale, Wok. GU21 166 AY115
Horsell Way, Wok. GU21 166 AW116
Horselydown La, SE1 201 P4
Horselydown Old Stairs,
SE1 201 P3
Horseman Side, Brwd. (Nave.S.)
CM14 51 FH45
Horsemans Ride, St.Alb. AL2 8 CA26
Horsemongers Ms, SE1 201 J5
Horsemoor Cl, Slou. SL3
off Parlaunt Rd 93 BA77
Horsenden Av, Grnf. UB6 61 CE64
Horsenden Cres, Grnf. UB6 61 CF64
Horsenden La N, Grnf. UB6 79 CF65
Horsenden La S, Grnf. UB6 79 CG67
Horse Ride, SW1 199 M3
Tadworth KT20 183 CY125
Horse Rd, E7 *off Centre Rd* 68 EH62
Horseshoe, The, Bans. SM7 173 CZ115
Coulsdon CR5 159 DK113
Horseshoe Cl, E14 204 D10
NW2 63 CV61
Waltham Abbey EN9 16 EG34
Horse Shoe Cres, Nthlt. UB5 78 CA68
Horseshoe Dr, Uxb. UB8 76 BN72
Horse Shoe Grn, Sutt. SM1
off Aultone Way 140 DB103
Horseshoe Hill, Wal.Abb. EN9 16 EJ33
Horseshoe La, N20 43 CX46
Enfield EN2 *off Chase Side* 30 DQ41
Watford WD25 7 BV32
Horseshoe Ridge, Wey. KT13 153 BQ111
Horse Yd, N1 *off Essex Rd* 83 DP67
Horsfeld Gdns, SE9 124 EL85
Horsfeld Rd, SE9 124 EK85
Horsfield Cl, Dart. DA2 128 FQ87
Horsford Rd, SW2 121 DM85
Horsham Av, N12 44 DE50
Horsham Rd, Bexh. DA6 126 FA85
Feltham TW14 115 BQ86
Horsley Cl, Epsom KT19 156 CR113
Horsley Dr, Croy. (New Adgtn.)
CR0 161 EC108
Kingston upon Thames
KT2 117 CK92
Horsley Rd, E4 47 EC47
Bromley BR1
off Palace Rd 144 EH95
Cobham KT11 169 BV119
Horsleys, Rick. (Map.Cr.) WD3 37 BD50
Horsley St, SE17 102 DR79
Horsmonden Cl, Orp. BR6 145 ES101
Horsmonden Rd, SE4 123 DZ85
Hortensia Rd, SW10 100 DC80
Horticultural Pl, W4
off Heathfield Ter 98 CR78
HORTON, Epsom 156 CP110
HORTON, Slou. 93 BA83
Horton Av, NW2 63 CY63
Horton Br Rd, West Dr. UB7 76 BM74
Horton Cl, West Dr. UB7 76 BM74
★ Horton Country Pk, Epsom
KT19 156 CM110
Horton Footpath, Epsom
KT19 156 CQ111
Horton Gdns, Epsom KT19
off Horton Hill 156 CQ111
Horton Hill, Epsom KT19 156 CQ111
Horton Ind Pk, West Dr. UB7 76 BM74
HORTON KIRBY, Dart. 149 FR98
Horton La, Epsom KT19 156 CP110
★ Horton Park Children's Fm,
Epsom KT19 156 CN110
Horton Rd, E8 84 DV65
Dartford (Hort.Kir.) DA4 148 FQ97
Slough (Colnbr.) SL3 93 BA81
Slough (Datchet) SL3 92 AW81
Slough (Poyle) SL3 93 BE83
Staines TW19 114 BG85
West Drayton UB7 76 BN74
Horton St, SE13 103 EB83
Hortons Way, West. TN16 189 ER126
Horton Way, Croy. CR0 143 DX99
Dartford (Fnghm.) DA4 148 FM101
Hortus Rd, E4 47 EC47
Southall UB2 96 BZ75
Horvath Cl, Wey. KT13 153 BR105
Horwood Cl, Rick. WD3
off Thellusson Way 38 BG45
Horwood Ct, Wat. WD24 24 BX37
Hosack Rd, SW17 120 DF89
Hoser Av, SE12 124 EG89
Hosey Common La, West.
TN16 189 ES130
Hosey Common Rd, Eden.
TN8 189 EQ133
Westerham TN16 189 ER130
HOSEY HILL, West. 189 ES127
Hosey Hill, West. TN16 189 ER127
Hosier La, EC1 196 F7
Hoskins Cl, E16 86 EJ72
Hayes UB3
off Cranford Dr 95 BT78
Hoskins Rd, Oxt. RH8 188 EE129
Hoskins St, SE10 103 ED78
Hoskins Wk, Oxt. RH8 188 EE129
Hospital Br Rd, Twick. TW2 116 CB87
H Hospital of St. John & St.
Elizabeth, NW8 82 DD68
Hospital Rd, E9
off Homerton Row 67 DX64
Hounslow TW3 96 CA83
Sevenoaks TN13 191 FJ121
Hotham Cl, Dart. (Sutt.H.)
DA4 128 FP94
Swanley BR8 147 FH95
West Molesey KT8
off Garrick Gdns 136 CA97
Hotham Rd, SW15 99 CW83
SW19 120 DC94
Hotham Rd Ms, SW19
off Haydons Rd 120 DC94
Hotham St, E15 86 EE67
Hothfield Pl, SE16 202 G7
Hotspur Rd, Nthlt. UB5 78 CA68
Hotspur St, SE11 200 D10
Houblon Rd, Rich. TW10 118 CL85
Houblons Hill, Epp. CM16 18 EW31
Houghton Cl, E8
off Buttermere Wk 84 DT65
Hampton TW12 116 BY93
Houghton Rd, N15
off West Grn Rd 66 DT57
Houghton St, WC2 196 C9
Houlder Cres, Croy. CR0 159 DP107
Houndsden Rd, N21 29 DM44
Houndsditch, EC3 197 N8
Houndsfield Rd, N9 46 DV45
HOUNSLOW 96 BZ84
⇌ Hounslow 116 CB85
Hounslow Av, Houns. TW3 116 CB85
Hounslow Business Pk, Houns.
TW3 96 CA84
⊖ Hounslow Central 96 CA83
⊖ Hounslow East 96 CC82
Hounslow Gdns, Houns.
TW3 116 CB85
★ Hounslow Heath, Houns.
TW4 116 BY86
Hounslow Rd, Felt. (Feltham)
TW14 115 BV88
Feltham (Han.) TW13 116 BX91
Twickenham TW2 116 CC86
HOUNSLOW WEST, Houns. 96 BX83
⊖ Hounslow West 96 BY82
Houseman Way, SE5
off Hopewell St 102 DR80
★ Houses of Parliament,
SW1 200 A5
Houston Pl, Esher KT10
off Lime Tree Av 137 CE102
Houston Rd, SE23 123 DY89
Surbiton KT6 137 CH100
Hove Av, E17 67 DZ57
Hove Cl, Brwd. CM13 55 GC47
Grays RM17
off Argent St 110 GA79
Hoveden Rd, NW2 63 CY64
Hove Gdns, Sutt. SM1 140 DB102
Hoveton Rd, SE28 88 EW72
Howard Agne Cl, Hem.H. (Bov.)
HP3 5 BA27
Howard Av, Bex. DA5 126 EW88
Epsom KT17 157 CU110
Howard Business Pk, Wal.Abb.
EN9 *off Howard Cl* 15 ED33
Howard Cl, N11 44 DG47
NW2 63 CY63
W3 80 CP72
Ashtead KT21 172 CM118
Bushey (Bushey Hth.)
WD23 41 CE45
Hampton TW12 116 CC93
Leatherhead KT22 171 CJ123
Loughton IG10 32 EL44
Sunbury-on-Thames TW16
off Catherine Dr 115 BT93
Tadworth KT20 183 CT125
Waltham Abbey EN9 15 ED34
Watford WD24 23 BU37
Howard Ct, Reig. RH2 184 DC133
Howard Dr, Borwd. WD6 26 CR42
Howard Ms, N5
off Hamilton Pk 65 DP63
Slough SL3
off Laburnum Gro 93 BB79
Howard Pl, SW1 199 K7
Reigate RH2 184 DA132
Howard Rd, E6 87 EM68
E11 68 EE62
E17 67 EA55
N15 66 DS58
N16 66 DR63
NW2 63 CX63
SE20 142 DW95
SE25 142 DU99
Barking IG11 87 ER67
Howard Rd, Brom. BR1 124 EG94
Coulsdon CR5 175 DJ115
Dartford DA1 128 FN86
Grays (Chaff.Hun.) RM16 109 FW76
Ilford IG1 69 EP63
Isleworth TW7 97 CF83
Leatherhead (Eff.Junct.)
KT24 169 BU122
New Malden KT3 138 CS97
Southall UB1 78 CB72
Surbiton KT5 138 CM100
Upminster RM14 72 FQ61
Howards Cl, Pnr. HA5 39 BV54
Woking GU22 167 BA120
Howards Crest Cl, Beck. BR3 143 EC96
Howards La, SW15 99 CV84
Addlestone KT15 151 BE107
Howards Rd, E13 86 EG69
Woking GU22 167 AZ120
Howards Thicket, Ger.Cr.
SL9 56 AW61
Howard St, T.Ditt. KT7 137 CH101
Howards Wd Dr, Ger.Cr. SL9 56 AX61
Howard Wk, N2 64 DC56
Howard Way, Barn. EN5 27 CX43
Howarth Ct, E15
off Clays La 67 EC64
Howarth Rd, SE2 106 EU78
Howberry Cl, Edg. HA8 41 CK51
Howberry Rd, Edg. HA8 41 CK51
Stanmore HA7 41 CK51
Thornton Heath CR7 142 DR95
Howbury La, Erith DA8 107 FG82
Howbury Rd, SE15 102 DW83
Howcroft Cres, N3 44 DA52
Howcroft La, Grnf. UB6
off Cowgate Rd 79 CD69
Howden Cl, SE28 88 EX73
Howden Rd, SE25 142 DT96
Howden St, SE15 102 DU83
Howe Cl, Rad. (Shenley) WD7 10 CL32
Romford RM7 50 FA53
Howe Dr, Cat. CR3 176 DR122
Howell Cl, Rom. RM6 70 EX57
Howell Hill Cl, Epsom KT17 157 CW111
Howell Hill Gro, Epsom
KT17 157 CW110
Howell Wk, SE1 200 G9
Howes Cl, N3 64 DA55
Howfield Pl, N17 66 DT55
Howgate Rd, SW14 98 CR83
Howick Pl, SW1 199 L7
Howie St, SW11 100 DE80
Howitt Cl, N16 *off Allen Rd* 66 DS63
NW3 *off Howitt Rd* 82 DE65
Howitt Rd, NW3 82 DE65
Howitts Cl, Esher KT10 154 CA107
Howland Est, SE16 202 G6
Howland Ms E, W1 195 L6
Howland St, W1 195 K6
Howland Way, SE16 203 L5
How La, Couls. CR5 174 DG117
Howletts La, Ruis. HA4 59 BQ57
Howletts Rd, SE24 122 DQ86
Howley Pl, W2 82 DC71
Howley Rd, Croy. CR0 141 DP104
Hows Cl, Uxb. UB8
off Hows Rd 76 BJ67
Howse Rd, Wal.Abb. EN9
off Deer Pk Way 31 EB35
Howsman Rd, SW13 99 CU79
Howson Rd, SE4 103 DY84
Howson Ter, Rich. TW10 118 CL86
Hows Rd, Uxb. UB8 76 BJ67
Hows St, E2 84 DT68
Howton Pl, Bushey (Bushey Hth.)
WD23 41 CD46
HOW WOOD, St.Alb. 8 CC27
⇌ How Wood 8 CC28
How Wd, St.Alb. (Park St.) AL2 8 CB28
HOXTON, N1 197 M1
Hoxton Mkt, N1 197 M3
Hoxton Sq, N1 197 M3
Hoxton St, N1 197 N3
Hoylake Cres, Uxb. (Ickhm.)
UB10 58 BN60
Hoylake Gdns, Mitch. CR4 141 DJ97
Romford RM3 52 FN53
Ruislip HA4 59 BV60
Watford WD19 40 BX49
Hoylake Rd, W3 80 CS72
Hoyland Cl, SE15
off Commercial Way 102 DV80
Hoyle Rd, SW17 120 DE92
Hoy St, E16 86 EF72
Hoy Ter, Grays RM20 109 FX78
★ HQS Wellington, Master
Mariners' Hall, WC2 196 D10
Hubbard Dr, Chess. KT9 155 CJ107
Hubbard Rd, SE27 122 DQ91
Hubbards Chase, Horn. RM11 72 FN57
Hubbards Cl, Horn. RM11 72 FN57
Uxbridge UB8 77 BP72
Hubbard's Hill, Sev. (Sev.Wld.)
TN13 191 FH130
Hubbards Rd, Rick. (Chorl.)
WD3 21 BD43
Hubbard St, E15 86 EE67
Hubbinet Ind Est, Rom. RM7 71 FC55
Hubert Gro, SW9 101 DL83
Hubert Rd, E6 86 EK69
Brentwood CM14 54 FV48
Rainham RM13 89 FF69
Slough SL3 92 AX76
Hucknall Cl, Rom. RM3 52 FM51
Huddart St, E3 85 DZ71
Huddleston Cl, E2 84 DW68
Huddlestone Cres, Red. RH1 185 DK128
Huddlestone Rd, E7 68 EF63
NW2 81 CV65
Huddleston Rd, N7 65 DK63
Hudons Cl, Grays RM20 109 FT78
Hudson Av, Uxb. (Denh.) UB9 57 BF58
Hudson Cl, Wat. WD24 23 BT36
Hudson Ct, E14
off Maritime Quay 103 EA78
SW19 120 DB94
Hudson Gdns, Orp. BR6
off Superior Dr 163 ET107
Hudson Pl, SE18 105 EQ78
Hudson Rd, Bexh. DA7 106 EZ82
Hayes UB3 95 BR79
Hudsons, Tad. KT20 173 CX121
Hudson's Pl, SW1 199 J8
Hudson Way, NW2
off Gratton Ter 63 CX62
Huggin Ct, EC4 197 J10
Huggin Hill, EC4 197 J10
Huggins Pl, SW2
off Roupell Rd 121 DM88
Hughan Rd, E15 67 ED64
Hugh Dalton Av, SW6 99 CZ79
Hughenden Av, Har. HA3 61 CH57
Hughenden Gdns, Nthlt.
UB5 78 BW69
Hughenden Rd, Wor.Pk. KT4 139 CU101
Hughendon Ter, E15
off Westdown Rd 67 EC63
Hughes Cl, N12
off Coleridge Rd 44 DC50
Hughes Rd, Ashf. TW15 115 BQ94
Grays RM16 111 GG76
Hayes UB3 77 BV73
Hughes Wk, Croy. CR0
off St. Saviours Rd 142 DQ101
Hugh Gaitskell Cl, SW6 99 CZ79
Hugh Ms, SW1 199 J9
Hugh Pl, SW1 199 M8
Hugh St, SW1 199 J9
Hugo Gdns, Rain. RM13 89 FF65
Hugo Gryn Way, Rad. (Shenley)
WD7 *off Farm Cl* 10 CL31
Hugon Rd, SW6 100 DB83
Hugo Rd, N19 65 DJ63
Huguenot Pl, E1 84 DT71
SW18 120 DC85
Huguenot Sq, SE15
off Scylla Rd 102 DV83
HULBERRY, Swan. 147 FG103
Hullbridge Ms, N1
off Sherborne St 84 DR67
Hull Cl, SE16 203 J4
Sutton SM2
off Yarbridge Cl 158 DB110
Waltham Cross (Chsht.)
EN7 14 DR26
Hulletts La, Brwd. CM15 54 FT43
Hull Pl, E16
off Fishguard Way 105 EP75
Hull St, EC1 197 H3
Hulme Pl, SE1 201 J5
Hulse Av, Bark. IG11 87 ER65
Romford RM7 51 FB53
Hulse Ter, Ilf. IG1
off Buttsbury Rd 69 EQ64
Hulsewood Cl, Dart. DA2 127 FH90
Hulton Cl, Lthd. KT22 171 CJ123
Hulverston Cl, Sutt. SM2 158 DB110
Humber Av, S.Ock. RM15 91 FT72
Humber Cl, West Dr. UB7 76 BK74
Humber Dr, W10 81 CX70
Upminster RM14 73 FR58
Humber Rd, NW2 63 CV61
SE3 104 EF79
Dartford DA1 128 FK85
Humberstone Rd, E13 86 EJ69
Humberton Cl, E9
off Marsh Hill 67 DY64
Humber Way, Slou. SL3 93 BA77
Humbolt Rd, W6 99 CY79
Hume Av, Til. RM18 111 GG83
Humes Av, W7 97 CE76
Hume Ter, E16
off Prince Regent La 86 EJ72
Hume Way, Ruis. HA4 59 BU58
Hummer Rd, Egh. TW20 113 BA91
Humphrey Cl, Ilf. IG5 49 EM53
Leatherhead (Fetch.) KT22 170 CC122
Humphrey St, SE1 201 P10
Humphries Cl, Dag. RM9 70 EZ63
Hundred Acre, NW9 43 CT54
Hungerdown, E4 47 EC46
Hungerford Av, Slou. SL2 74 AS71
Hungerford Br, SE1 200 A2
WC2 200 A2
Hungerford La, WC2 199 P2
Hungerford Rd, N7 65 DK64
Hungerford Sq, Wey. KT13
off Rosslyn Pk 153 BR105
Hungerford St, E1
off Commercial Rd 84 DV72
Hungry Hill, Wok. (Ripley) GU23
off Hungry Hill La 168 BK124
Hungry Hill La, Wok. (Send)
GU23 168 BK124
Hunsdon Cl, Dag. RM9 88 EY65
Hunsdon Dr, Sev. TN13 191 FH123
Hunsdon Rd, SE14 103 DX79
Hunslett St, E2
off Royston St 84 DW68
Hunstanton Cl, Slou. (Colnbr.)
SL3 93 BC80
Hunston Rd, Mord. SM4 140 DB102
Hunter Av, Brwd. CM15 55 GA44
Hunter Cl, SE1 201 L7
SW12 *off Balham Pk Rd* 120 DG88
Borehamwood WD6 26 CQ43
Potters Bar EN6 12 DB33
Huntercrombe Gdns, Wat.
WD19 40 BW50
Hunter Dr, Horn. RM12 72 FJ63
Hunter Ho, Felt. TW13 115 BU88
Hunter Rd, SW20 139 CW95
Ilford IG1 69 EP64
Thornton Heath CR7 142 DR97
Hunters, The, Beck. BR3 143 EC95
Hunters Cl, Bex. DA5 127 FE90
Epsom KT19
off Marshalls Cl 156 CQ113
Hemel Hempstead (Bov.)
HP3 5 BA29
Hunters Ct, Rich. TW9
off Friars La 117 CK85
Huntersfield Cl, Reig. RH2 184 DB131
Hunters Gate, Wat. WD25
off Hunters La 7 BU33
Hunters Gro, Har. HA3 61 CJ56
Hayes UB3 77 BU74
Orpington BR6 163 EP105
Romford RM5 51 FB50
Hunters Hall Rd, Dag. RM10 70 FA63
Hunters Hill, Ruis. HA4 60 BW62
Hunters La, Wat. WD25 7 BT33
Hunters Meadow, SE19
off Dulwich Wd Av 122 DS91
Hunters Reach, Wal.Cr. EN7 14 DT29
Hunters Ride, St.Alb. (Brick.Wd.)
AL2 8 CA31
Hunters Rd, Chess. KT9 138 CL104
Hunters Sq, Dag. RM10 70 FA63
Hunter St, WC1 196 A4
Hunters Wk, Sev. (Knock.)
TN14 164 EY114
Hunters Way, Croy. CR0
off Brownlow Rd 160 DS105
Enfield EN2 29 DN39
Hunter Wk, E13 86 EG68
Borehamwood WD6
off Hunter Cl 26 CQ43
Hunting Cl, Esher KT10 154 CA105
Huntingdon Cl, Mitch. CR4 141 DL97
Huntingdon Gdns, W4 98 CQ80
Worcester Park KT4 139 CW104
Huntingdon Rd, N2 64 DE55
N9 46 DW46
Redhill RH1 184 DF134
Woking GU21 166 AT117
Huntingdon St, E16 86 EF72
N1 83 DM66
Huntingfield, Croy. CR0 161 DZ108
Huntingfield Rd, SW15 99 CU84
Huntingfield Way, Egh. TW20 113 BD94
Hunting Gate Cl, Enf. EN2 29 DN41
Hunting Gate Dr, Chess.
KT9 156 CL108
Hunting Gate Ms, Sutt. SM1 140 DB104
Twickenham TW2
off Colne Rd 117 CE88
Huntings Rd, Dag. RM10 88 FA65
Huntland Cl, Rain. RM13 89 FH71
Huntley Av, Grav. (Nthflt.)
DA11 130 GB86
H Huntley Cen, WC1 195 M5
Huntley Cl, Stai. (Stanw.) TW19
off Cambria Gdns 114 BL87
Huntley Dr, N3 44 DA51
Huntley St, WC1 195 L5
Huntley Way, SW20 139 CU96
Huntly Rd, SE25 142 DS98
HUNTON BRIDGE, Kings L. 7 BP33
Hunton Br Hill, Kings L. WD4 7 BQ33
Hunton St, E1 84 DU70
Hunt Rd, Grav. (Nthflt.) DA11 130 GE90
Southall UB2 96 CA76
Hunt's Cl, SE3 104 EG82
Hunt's Ct, WC2 199 N1
Hunts La, E15 85 EC68
Huntsman Cl, Warl. CR6 176 DW119
Huntsman Rd, Ilf. IG6 50 EU51
Huntsmans Cl, Felt. TW13 115 BV91
Leatherhead (Fetch.) KT22
off The Green 171 CD124
Huntsmans Dr, Upmin. RM14 72 FQ64
Huntsman St, SE17 201 L9
Hunts Mead, Enf. EN3 31 DX41
Hunts Mead Cl, Chis. BR7 125 EM94
Huntsmoor Rd, Epsom KT19 156 CR106
Huntspill St, SW17 120 DC90
Hunts Slip Rd, SE21 122 DS90
Huntsworth Ms, NW1 194 D5
Hunt Way, SE22
off Dulwich Common 122 DU88
Hurcules Way, Wat. WD25
off Ashfields 7 BT33
Hurdwick Pl, NW1
off Harrington Sq 83 DJ68
Hurley Cl, Walt. KT12 135 BV103
Hurley Cres, SE16 203 J4
Hurley Ho, SE11 200 E9
Hurley Rd, Grnf. UB6 78 CB72
Hurlfield, Dart. DA2 128 FJ90
Hurlford, Wok. GU21 166 AU117
Hurlingham Business Pk,
SW6 100 DA83
Hurlingham Ct, SW6 99 CZ83
Hurlingham Gdns, SW6 99 CZ83
★ Hurlingham Ho, SW6 100 DA83
★ Hurlingham Park, SW6 99 CZ82
Hurlingham Retail Pk, SW6
off Carnwath Rd 100 DB83
Hurlingham Rd, SW6 99 CZ82
Bexleyheath DA7 106 EZ80
Hurlingham Sq, SW6 100 DA83
Hurlock St, N5 65 DP62
Hurlstone Rd, SE25 142 DR99
Hurn Ct Rd, Houns. TW4
off Renfrew Rd 96 BX82
Hurnford Cl, S.Croy. CR2 160 DS110
Huron Cl, Orp. BR6
off Winnipeg Dr 163 ET107
Huron Rd, SW17 120 DG89
Hurren Cl, SE3 104 EE83
Hurricane Rd, Wall. SM6 159 DM108
Hurricane Way, Abb.L. WD5
off Abbey Dr 7 BU32
Epping (N.Wld.Bas.) CM16 18 EZ27
Slough SL3 93 BB78
Hurry Cl, E15 86 EE66
Hursley Rd, Chig. IG7
off Tufter Rd 49 ET50
Hurst Av, E4 47 EA49
N6 65 DJ58
Hurstbourne, Esher (Clay.)
KT10 155 CF107
Hurstbourne Gdns, Bark. IG11 87 ES65
Hurstbourne Ho, SW15
off Tangley Gro 119 CT86
Hurstbourne Rd, SE23 123 DY88

Hur - Isl

Hurst Cl, E4 47 EA48
NW11 64 DB58
Bromley BR2 144 EF102
Chessington KT9 156 CN106
Northolt UB5 78 BZ65
Woking GU22 166 AW120
Hurstcourt Rd, Sutt. SM1 140 DB103
Hurstdene Av, Brom. BR2 144 EF102
Staines TW18 114 BH93
Hurstdene Gdns, N15 66 DS59
Hurst Dr, Tad. KT20 183 CU126
Waltham Cross EN8 15 DX34
Hurst Est, SE2 106 EX78
Hurstfield, Brom. BR2 144 EG99
Hurstfield Cres, Hayes UB4 77 BS70
Hurstfield Rd, W.Mol. KT8 136 CA97
HURST GREEN, Oxt. 188 EG132
⇌ Hurst Green 188 EF132
Hurst Grn Cl, Oxt. RH8 188 EG132
Hurst Grn Rd, Oxt. RH8 188 EF132
Hurst Gro, Walt. KT12 135 BT102
Hurstlands, Oxt. RH8 188 EG132
Hurstlands Cl, Horn. RM11 72 FJ59
Hurst La, SE2 106 EX78
East Molesey KT8 136 CC98
Egham TW20 133 BA96
Epsom (Headley) KT18 172 CQ124
Hurstleigh Cl, Red. RH1 184 DF132
Hurstleigh Dr, Red. RH1 184 DF132
Hurstleigh Gdns, Ilf. IG5 49 EM53
Hurstmead Ct, Edg. HA8 42 CP49
Hurst Pk Av, Horn. RM12
off Newmarket Way 72 FL63
Hurst Pl, Nthwd. HA6 39 BP53
Hurst Ri, Barn. EN5 28 DA41
Hurst Rd, E17 67 EB55
N21 45 DN46
Bexley DA5 126 EX88
Buckhurst Hill IG9 48 EK46
Croydon CR0 160 DR106
East Molesey KT8 136 CA97
Epsom KT19 156 CR111
Epsom (Headley) KT18 172 CR123
Erith DA8 107 FC80
Sidcup DA15 126 EU89
Tadworth KT20 172 CR123
Walton-on-Thames KT12 136 BW99
West Molesey KT8 136 BY97
Hurst Springs, Bex. DA5 126 EY88
Hurst St, SE24 121 DP86
Hurst Vw Rd, S.Croy. CR2 160 DS108
Hurst Way, Sev. TN13 191 FJ127
South Croydon CR2 160 DS107
Woking (Pyrford) GU22 151 BE114
Hurstway Wk, W11 81 CX73
Hurstwood Av, E18 68 EH56
Bexley DA5 126 EY88
Bexleyheath DA7 107 FE81
Brentwood CM15
off Ongar Rd 54 FV45
Erith DA8 107 FE81
Hurstwood Ct, Upmin. RM14 72 FQ60
Hurstwood Dr, Brom. BR1 145 EM97
Hurstwood Rd, NW11 63 CY56
Hurtwood Rd, Walt. KT12 136 BZ101
Hurworth Av, Slou. SL3 92 AW76
Huson Cl, NW3 82 DE66
Hussars Cl, Houns. TW4 96 BY83
Husseywell Cres, Brom. BR2 144 EG102
Hutchingsons Rd, Croy.
(New Adgtn.) CR0 161 EC111
Hutchings St, E14 203 P5
Hutchings Wk, NW11 64 DB56
Hutchins Cl, E15
off Gibbins Rd 85 EC66
Hornchurch RM12 72 FL62
Hutchinson Ter, Wem. HA9 61 CK62
Hutchins Rd, SE28 88 EU73
Hutson Ter, Purf. RM19
off London Rd Purfleet 109 FR78
HUTTON, Brwd. 55 GD44
Hutton Cl, Grnf. UB6
off Mary Peters Dr 61 CD64
Woodford Green IG8 48 EH51
Hutton Dr, Brwd. CM13 55 GD45
Hutton Gdns, Har. HA3 40 CC52
Hutton Gate, Brwd. CM13 55 GB45
Hutton Gro, N12 44 DB50
Hutton La, Har. HA3 40 CC52
HUTTON MOUNT, Brwd. 55 GB46
Hutton Rd, Brwd. CM15 55 FZ45
Hutton Row, Edg. HA8
off Pavilion Way 42 CQ52
Hutton St, EC4 196 E9
Hutton Village, Brwd. CM13 55 GE45
Hutton Wk, Har. HA3 40 CC52
Huxbear St, SE4 123 DZ85
Huxley Cl, Nthlt. UB5 78 BY67
Uxbridge UB8 76 BK70
Huxley Dr, Rom. RM6 70 EV59
Huxley Gdns, NW10 80 CM69
Huxley Par, N18 46 DR50
Huxley Pl, N13 45 DP49
Huxley Rd, E10 67 EC61
N18 46 DR49
Welling DA16 105 ET83
Huxley Sayze, N18 46 DR50
Huxley St, W10 81 CY69
Hyacinth Cl, Hmptn. TW12
off Gresham Rd 116 CA93
Ilford IG1 87 EP65
Hyacinth Ct, Pnr. HA5
off Tulip Ct 60 BW55
Hyacinth Dr, Uxb. UB10 76 BL66
Hyacinth Rd, SW15 119 CU88
Hyburn Cl, St.Alb. (Brick.Wd.)
AL2 8 BZ30
Hycliffe Gdns, Chig. IG7 49 EQ49
HYDE, THE, NW9 63 CT56
Hyde, The, NW9 62 CS57
Hyde Av, Pot.B. EN6 12 DB33
Hyde Cl, E13 86 EG68
Ashford TW15 *off Hyde Ter* 115 BS93
Barnet EN5 27 CZ41
Hyde Cl, Grays (Chaff.Hun.)
RM16 109 FX76
Hyde Ct, N20 44 DD48
Waltham Cross EN8
off Parkside 15 DY34
Hyde Cres, NW9 62 CS57
Hyde Dr, Orp. BR5 146 EV98
Hyde Est Rd, NW9 63 CT57
Hyde Fm Ms, SW12
off Telferscot Rd 121 DK88
Hydefield Cl, N21 46 DR46
Hydefield Ct, N9 46 DS47
Hyde Ho, NW9 62 CS57
Hyde La, SW11
off Battersea Br Rd 100 DE81
Hemel Hempstead HP3 7 BR26
Hemel Hempstead (Bov.)
HP3 5 BA27
St. Albans (Frog.) AL2 9 CE28
Woking (Ockham) GU23 168 BN120
Hyde Meadows, Hem.H. (Bov.)
HP3 5 BA28
★ Hyde Park, W2 198 B2
Hyde Pk, SW7 198 B2
W1 198 B2
W2 198 B2
Hyde Pk Av, N21 46 DQ47
⊖ Hyde Park Corner 198 F4
Hyde Pk Cor, W1 198 G4
Hyde Pk Cres, W2 194 B9
Hyde Pk Gdns, N21 46 DQ46
W2 194 A10
Hyde Pk Gdns Ms, W2 194 A10
Hyde Pk Gate, SW7 100 DC75
Hyde Pk Gate Ms, SW7
off Hyde Pk Gate 100 DC75
Hyde Pk Pl, W2 194 C10
Hyde Pk Sq, W2 194 B9
Hyde Pk Sq Ms, W2 194 B9
Hyde Pk St, W2 194 B9
Hyderabad Way, E15 86 EE66
Hyde Rd, N1 84 DR67
Bexleyheath DA7 106 EZ82
Richmond TW10
off Albert Rd 118 CM85
South Croydon CR2 160 DS113
Watford WD17 23 BU40
Hyder Rd, Grays RM16 111 GJ76
Hydeside Gdns, N9 46 DT47
Hydes Pl, N1
off Compton Av 83 DP66
Hyde St, SE8
off Deptford High St 103 EA79
Hyde Ter, Ashf. TW15 115 BS93
Hydethorpe Av, N9 46 DT47
Hydethorpe Rd, SW12 121 DJ88
Hyde Vale, SE10 103 EC80
Hyde Wk, Mord. SM4 140 DA101
Hyde Way, N9 46 DT47
Hayes UB3 95 BT77
Hyland Cl, Horn. RM11 71 FH59
Hylands Cl, Epsom KT18 172 CQ115
Hylands Ms, Epsom KT18 172 CQ115
Hylands Rd, E17 47 ED54
Epsom KT18 172 CQ115
Hyland Way, Horn. RM11 71 FH59
Hylton St, SE18 105 ET77
Hyndewood, SE23 123 DX90
Hyndman St, SE15 102 DV79
Hynton Rd, Dag. RM8 70 EW61
Hyperion Pl, Epsom KT19 156 CR109
Hyrons Cl, Amer. HP6 20 AS38
Hyrstdene, S.Croy. CR2 159 DP105
Hyson Rd, SE16 202 E10
Hythe, The, Stai. TW18 113 BE92
Hythe Av, Bexh. DA7 106 EZ80
Hythe Cl, N18 46 DU49
Orpington BR5
off Sandway Rd 146 EW98
HYTHE END, Stai. 113 BB90
Hythe End Rd, Stai. (Wrays.)
TW19 113 BA89
Hythe Fld Av, Egh. TW20 113 BD93
Hythe Pk Rd, Egh. TW20 113 BC92
Hythe Path, Th.Hth. CR7 142 DR97
Hythe Rd, NW10 81 CU70
Staines TW18 113 BD92
Thornton Heath CR7 142 DR96
Hythe Rd Ind Est, NW10 81 CU69
Hythe St, Dart. DA1 128 FL86
Hythe St Lwr, Dart. DA1 128 FL85
Hyver Hill, NW7 26 CR44

I

Ian Sq, Enf. EN3
off Lansbury Rd 31 DX39
Ibbetson Path, Loug. IG10 33 EP41
Ibbotson Av, E16 86 EF72
Ibbott St, E1 *off Mantus Rd* 84 DW70
Iberian Av, Wall. SM6 159 DK105
Ibis La, W4 98 CQ81
Ibis Way, Hayes UB4
off Cygnet Way 78 BX72
Ibscott Cl, Dag. RM10 89 FC65
Ibsley Gdns, SW15 119 CU88
Ibsley Way, Barn. EN4 28 DE43
Icehouse Wd, Oxt. RH8 188 EE131
Iceland Rd, E3 85 EA67
Iceni Ct, E3 *off Roman Rd* 85 DZ67
Ice Wf, N1 *off New Wf Rd* 83 DL68
Ice Wf Marina, N1
off New Wf Rd 83 DL68
Ickburgh Est, E5
off Ickburgh Rd 66 DV62
Ickburgh Rd, E5 66 DV62
ICKENHAM, Uxb. 59 BQ62
⊖ Ickenham 59 BQ63
Ickenham Cl, Ruis. HA4 59 BR61
Ickenham Rd, Ruis. HA4 59 BR60
Uxbridge (Ickhm.) UB10 59 BQ61
Ickleton Rd, SE9 124 EL91
Icklingham Gate, Cob. KT11 154 BW112
Icklingham Rd, Cob. KT11 154 BW112
Icknield Dr, Ilf. IG2 69 EP57
Ickworth Pk Rd, E17 67 DY56
Ida Rd, N15 66 DR57
Ida St, E14 85 EC72
Iden Cl, Brom. BR2 144 EE97
Idlecombe Rd, SW17 120 DG93
Idmiston Rd, E15 68 EF64
SE27 122 DQ90
Worcester Park KT4 139 CT101
Idmiston Sq, Wor.Pk. KT4 139 CT101
Idol La, EC3 201 M1
Idonia St, SE8 103 DZ80
Iffley Cl, Uxb. UB8 76 BK66
Iffley Rd, W6 99 CV76
Ifield Rd, SW10 100 DB79
Ifield Way, Grav. DA12 131 GK93
Ifor Evans Pl, E1
off Mile End Rd 85 DX70
Ightham Rd, Erith DA8 106 FA80
Ikea Twr, NW10 62 CR64
Ikona Ct, Wey. KT13 153 BQ106
Ilbert St, W10 81 CX69
Ilchester Gdns, W2 82 DB73
Ilchester Pl, W14 99 CZ76
Ilchester Rd, Dag. RM8 70 EV64
Ildersly Gro, SE21 122 DR89
Ilderton Rd, SE15 102 DW80
SE16 202 E10
Ilex Cl, Egh. (Eng.Grn.) TW20 112 AV94
Sunbury-on-Thames TW16
off Oakington Dr 136 BW96
Ilex Ho, N4 65 DM59
Ilex Rd, NW10 81 CT65
Ilex Way, SW16 121 DN92
ILFORD 69 EQ62
⇌ Ilford 69 EN62
Ilford Hill, Ilf. IG1 69 EN62
Ilford La, Ilf. IG1 69 EP62
Ilfracombe Cres, Horn. RM12 72 FJ63
Ilfracombe Gdns, Rom. RM6 70 EV59
Ilfracombe Rd, Brom. BR1 124 EF90
Iliffe St, SE17 200 G10
Iliffe Yd, SE17 200 G10
Ilkeston Ct, E5
off Overbury St 67 DX63
Ilkley Cl, SE19 122 DR93
Ilkley Rd, E16 86 EJ71
Watford WD19 40 BX50
Illingworth Cl, Mitch. CR4 140 DD97
Illingworth Way, Enf. EN1 30 DS42
Ilmington Rd, Har. HA3 61 CK58
Ilminster Gdns, SW11 100 DE84
Imber Cl, N14 45 DJ45
Esher KT10 *off Ember La* 137 CD102
Imber Ct Trd Est, E.Mol. KT8 137 CD100
Imber Gro, Esher KT10 137 CD101
Imber Pk Rd, Esher KT10 137 CD102
Imber St, N1 84 DR67
Imer Pl, T.Ditt. KT7 137 CF101
Imperial Av, N16
off Victorian Rd 66 DT62
Imperial Business Est, Grav.
DA11 131 GF86
Imperial Cl, Har. HA2 60 CA58
★ Imperial Coll, Uni of
London, SW7 100 DD76
Imperial Coll Rd, SW7 100 DD76
Imperial Cres, Wey. KT13
off Churchill Dr 135 BQ104
Imperial Dr, Grav. DA12 131 GM92
Harrow HA2 60 CA59
Imperial Gdns, Mitch. CR4 141 DH97
Imperial Ms, E6
off Central Pk Rd 86 EJ68
Imperial Pk, Wat. WD24 24 BW39
Imperial Retail Pk, Grav.
DA11 131 GG86
Imperial Rd, N22 45 DL53
SW6 100 DB81
Feltham TW14 115 BS87
Imperial Sq, SW6 100 DB81
Imperial St, E3 85 EC69
★ Imperial War Mus, SE1 200 E7
Imperial Way, Chis. BR7 125 EQ90
Croydon CR0 159 DM107
Harrow HA3 62 CL58
Watford WD24 24 BW39
Imprimo Pk, Loug. IG10
off Lenthall Rd 33 ER42
Imre Cl, W12 *off Ellerslie Rd* 81 CV74
Inca Dr, SE9 125 EP87
Ince Rd, Walt. KT12 153 BS107
Inchmery Rd, SE6 123 EB89
Inchwood, Croy. CR0 161 EB105
Independent Pl, E8
off Downs Pk Rd 66 DT64
Independents Rd, SE3
off Blackheath Village 104 EF83
Inderwick Rd, N8 65 DM57
Indescon Ct, E14 204 A5
India Pl, WC2 196 B10
India Rd, Slou. SL1 92 AV75
India St, EC3 197 P9
India Way, W12 81 CV73
Indigo Ms, E14 *off Ashton St* 85 EC73
N16 66 DR62
Indus Rd, SE7 104 EJ80
Industry Ter, SW9
off Canterbury Cres 101 DN83
Ingal Rd, E13 86 EG70
Ingate Pl, SW8 101 DH81
Ingatestone Rd, E12 68 EJ60
SE25 142 DV98
Woodford Green IG8 48 EG52
Ingelow Rd, SW8 101 DH82
Ingels Mead, Epp. CM16 17 ET29
Ingersoll Rd, W12 81 CV74
Enfield EN3 30 DW38
Ingestre Pl, W1 195 L9
Ingestre Rd, E7 68 EG63
NW5 65 DH63
Ingham Cl, S.Croy. CR2 161 DX109
Ingham Rd, NW6 64 DA63
South Croydon CR2 160 DW109
Inglebert St, EC1 196 D2
Ingleboro Dr, Pur. CR8 160 DR113
Ingleborough St, SW9 101 DN82
Ingleby Dr, Har. HA1 61 CD62
Ingleby Gdns, Chig. IG7 50 EV48
Ingleby Rd, N7 *off Bryett Rd* 65 DL62
Dagenham RM10 89 FB65
Grays RM16 111 GH76
Ilford IG1 69 EP60
Ingleby Way, Chis. BR7 125 EN92
Wallington SM6 159 DK109
Ingle Cl, Pnr. HA5 60 BY55
Ingledew Rd, SE18 105 ER78
Inglefield, Pot.B. EN6 12 DA30
Ingleglen, Horn. RM11 72 FN59
Inglehurst, Add. (New Haw)
KT15 152 BH110
Inglehurst Gdns, Ilf. IG4 69 EM57
Inglemere Rd, SE23 123 DX90
Mitcham CR4 120 DF94
Inglesham Wk, E9 85 DZ65
Ingleside, Slou. (Colnbr.)
SL3 93 BE81
Ingleside Cl, Beck. BR3 123 EA94
Ingleside Gro, SE3 104 EF79
Inglethorpe St, SW6 99 CX81
Ingleton Av, Well. DA16 126 EU85
Ingleton Rd, N18 46 DU51
Carshalton SM5 158 DE109
Ingleton St, SW9 101 DN82
Ingleway, N12 44 DD51
Inglewood, Cher. KT16 133 BF104
Croydon CR0 161 DY109
Woking GU21 166 AV118
Inglewood Cl, E14 204 A8
Hornchurch RM12 72 FK63
Ilford IG6 49 ET51
Inglewood Copse, Brom.
BR1 144 EL96
Inglewood Rd, NW6 64 DA64
Bexleyheath DA7 107 FD84
Inglis Barracks, NW7 43 CX50
Inglis Rd, W5 80 CM73
Croydon CR0 142 DT102
Inglis St, SE5 101 DP81
Ingoldsby Rd, Grav. DA12 131 GL88
Ingram Av, NW11 64 DC59
Ingram Cl, SE11 200 C8
Stanmore HA7 41 CJ50
Ingram Rd, N2 64 DE56
Dartford DA1 128 FL88
Grays RM17 110 GD77
Thornton Heath CR7 142 DQ95
Ingrams Cl, Walt. KT12 154 BW106
Ingram Way, Grnf. UB6 79 CD67
Ingrave Ho, Dag. RM9 88 EV67
Ingrave Rd, Brwd. CM13,
CM15 54 FX47
Romford RM1 71 FD56
Ingrave St, SW11 100 DD83
Ingrebourne Gdns, Upmin.
RM14 72 FQ60
Ingrebourne Rd, Rain. RM13 89 FH70
Ingrebourne Valley Grn Way, Horn.
RM12 72 FK64
Ingress Gdns, Green. DA9 129 FX85
Ingress St, W4
off Devonshire Rd 98 CS78
Ingreway, Rom. RM3 52 FP52
Inigo Jones Rd, SE7 104 EL80
Inigo Pl, WC2 195 P10
Inkerman Rd, NW5 83 DH65
Woking (Knap.) GU21 166 AS118
Inkerman Ter, W8
off Allen St 100 DA76
Inkerman Way, Wok. GU21 166 AS118
Inks Grn, E4 47 EC50
Inman Rd, NW10 80 CS67
SW18 120 DC87
Inmans Row, Wdf.Grn. IG8 48 EG49
Inner Circle, NW1 194 F3
Inner Pk Rd, SW19 119 CX88
Inner Ring E, Houns. (Hthrw.Air.)
TW6 95 BP83
Inner Ring W, Houns. (Hthrw.Air.)
TW6 94 BN83
Inner Temple La, EC4 196 D9
Innes Cl, SW20 139 CY96
Innes Gdns, SW15 119 CV86
Innes Yd, Croy. CR0
off Whitgift St 142 DQ104
Inniskilling Rd, E13 86 EJ68
Innova Pk, Enf. EN3 31 DZ36
Innovation Cl, Wem. HA0 80 CL67
Innova Way, Enf. EN3 31 DZ36
Inskip Cl, E10 67 EB61
Inskip Dr, Horn. RM11 72 FL60
Inskip Rd, Dag. RM8 70 EX60
★ Institute of Contemporary
Arts (ICA), SW1 199 N2
Institute Pl, E8
off Amhurst Rd 66 DV64
Institute Rd, Epp. CM16 18 EX29
Instone Cl, Wall. SM6 159 DL108
Instone Rd, Dart. DA1 128 FK87
Integer Gdns, E11
off Forest Rd 67 ED59
Interchange E Ind Est, E5
off Theydon Rd 66 DW60
International Av, Houns. TW5 96 BW78
International Trd Est, Sthl.
UB2 95 BV76
Inveraray Pl, SE18
off Old Mill Rd 105 ER79
Inver Cl, E5 *off Theydon Rd* 66 DW61
Inverclyde Gdns, Rom. RM6 70 EX56
Inver Ct, W2 *off Inverness Ter* 82 DB72
Inveresk Gdns, Wor.Pk. KT4 139 CT104
Inverforth Cl, NW3
off North End Way 64 DC61
Inverforth Rd, N11 45 DH50
Inverine Rd, SE7 104 EH78
Invermore Pl, SE18 105 EQ77
Inverness Av, Enf. EN1 30 DS39
Inverness Dr, Ilf. IG6 49 ES51
Inverness Gdns, W8
off Vicarage Gate 82 DB74
Inverness Ms, E16 87 EQ74
W2 *off Inverness Ter* 82 DB73
Inverness Pl, W2 82 DB73
Inverness Rd, N18
off Aberdeen Rd 46 DV50
Hounslow TW3 96 BZ84
Southall UB2 96 BY77
Worcester Park KT4 139 CX102
Inverness St, NW1 83 DH67
Inverness Ter, W2 82 DB73
Inverton Rd, SE15 103 DX84
Invicta Cl, Chis. BR7 125 EN92
Feltham TW14
off Westmacott Dr 115 BT88
Invicta Gro, Nthlt. UB5 78 BZ69
Invicta Plaza, SE1 200 F2
Invicta Rd, SE3 104 EG80
Dartford DA2 128 FP86
Inville Rd, SE17 102 DR78
Inwen Ct, SE8 103 DY78
Inwood Av, Couls. CR5 175 DN120
Hounslow TW3 96 CC83
Inwood Cl, Croy. CR0 143 DY103
Inwood Ct, Walt. KT12 136 BW103
Inwood Rd, Houns. TW3 96 CB84
Inworth St, SW11 100 DE82
Inworth Wk, N1
off Popham St 84 DQ67
Iona Cl, SE6 123 EA87
Morden SM4 140 DB101
Ion Sq, E2 *off Hackney Rd* 84 DU68
Ipswich Rd, SW17 120 DG93
Ireland Cl, E6
off Bradley Stone Rd 87 EM71
Ireland Pl, N22
off Whittington Rd 45 DL52
Ireland Yd, EC4 196 G9
Irene Rd, SW6 100 DA81
Cobham (Stoke D'Ab.)
KT11 154 CA114
Orpington BR6 145 ET101
Ireton Av, Walt. KT12 135 BS103
Ireton Cl, N10 44 DG52
Ireton Pl, Grays RM17
off Russell Rd 110 GA77
Ireton St, E3 *off Tidworth Rd* 85 EA70
Iris Av, Bex. DA5 126 EY85
Iris Cl, E6 86 EL70
Brentwood CM15 54 FV43
Croydon CR0 143 DX102
Surbiton KT6 138 CM101
Iris Ct, Pnr. HA5 60 BW55
Iris Cres, Bexh. DA7 106 EZ79
Iris Path, Rom. RM3
off Clematis Cl 52 FJ52
Iris Rd, Epsom (W.Ewell)
KT19 156 CP106
Iris Wk, Edg. HA8 *off Ash Cl* 42 CQ49
Iris Way, E4 47 DZ51
Irkdale Av, Enf. EN1 30 DT39
Iron Br Cl, NW10 62 CS64
Southall UB2 78 CC74
Iron Br Rd, Uxb. UB11 94 BN75
West Drayton UB7 94 BN75
Iron Mill La, Dart. DA1 107 FE84
Iron Mill Pl, SW18
off Garratt La 120 DB86
Dartford DA1 107 FF84
Iron Mill Rd, SW18 120 DB86
Ironmonger La, EC2 197 K9
Ironmonger Pas, EC1 197 J4
Ironmonger Row, EC1 197 J4
Ironmongers Pl, E14 204 A9
Ironside Cl, SE16 203 H4
Irons Way, Rom. RM5 51 FC52
Irvine Av, Har. HA3 61 CG55
Irvine Cl, N20 44 DE47
Irvine Gdns, S.Ock. RM15 91 FT72
Irvine Pl, Vir.W. GU25 132 AY99
Irvine Way, Orp. BR6 145 ET101
Irving Av, Nthlt. UB5 78 BX67
Irving Gro, SW9 101 DM82
Irving Ms, N1 *off Alwyne Rd* 84 DQ65
Irving Rd, W14 99 CX76
Irving St, WC2 195 N10
Irving Wk, Swans. DA10 130 FY87
Irving Way, NW9 63 CT57
Swanley BR8 147 FD96
Irwin Av, SE18 105 ES80
Irwin Cl, Uxb. UB10 58 BN62
Irwin Gdns, NW10 81 CV67
Isabel Gate, Wal.Cr. (Chsht.)
EN8 15 DZ26
Isabel Hill Cl, Hmptn. TW12
off Upper Sunbury Rd 136 CB95
Isabella Cl, N14 45 DJ45
Isabella Ct, Rich. TW10
off Grove Rd 118 CM86
Isabella Dr, Orp. BR6 163 EQ105
Isabella Rd, E9 66 DW64
Isabella St, SE1 200 F3
Isabelle Cl, Wal.Cr. EN7 14 DQ29
Isabel St, SW9 101 DM81
Isambard Cl, Uxb. UB8 76 BK69
Isambard Ms, E14 204 E7
Isambard Pl, SE16 202 G3
Isbell Gdns, Rom. RM1 51 FE52
Isel Way, SE22
off East Dulwich Gro 122 DS85
Isham Rd, SW16 141 DL96
Isis Cl, SW15 99 CW84
Ruislip HA4 59 BQ58
Isis Dr, Upmin. RM14 73 FS58
Isis St, SW18 120 DC89
Island, The, Stai. (Wrays.)
TW19 113 BA90
West Drayton UB7 94 BH81
Island Cl, Stai. TW18 113 BE91
Island Fm Av, W.Mol. KT8 136 BZ99
Island Fm Rd, W.Mol. KT8 136 BZ99
DLR Island Gardens 204 D9
Island Rd, Mitch. CR4 120 DF94
Island Row, E14 85 DZ72
Isla Rd, SE18 105 EQ79
Islay Gdns, Houns. TW4 116 BX85
Islay Wk, N1 *off Douglas Rd* 84 DQ66
Isledon Rd, N7 65 DN62
Islehurst Cl, Chis. BR7 145 EN95
ISLEWORTH 97 CF83
⇌ Isleworth 97 CF82

★ Place of interest ⇌ Railway station ⊖ London Underground station DLR Docklands Light Railway station Tramlink station H Hospital

Isleworth Business Complex, Islw.
TW7 off St. John's Rd ... 97 CF82
Isleworth Prom, Twick. TW1 ... 97 CH84
ISLINGTON, N1 ... 83 DM67
Islington Grn, N1 ... 83 DP67
Islington High St, N1 ... 196 E1
Islington Pk Ms, N1
off Islington Pk St ... 83 DN66
Islington Pk St, N1 ... 83 DN66
Islip Gdns, Edg. HA8 ... 42 CR52
Northolt UB5 ... 78 BY66
Islip Manor Rd, Nthlt. UB5 ... 78 BY66
Islip St, NW5 ... 65 DJ64
Ismailia Rd, E7 ... 86 EH66
★ Ismaili Cen & Zamana Gall,
SW7 ... 198 A8
Ismay Ct, Slou. SL2
off Elliman Av ... 74 AS73
Isom Cl, E13
off Belgrave Rd ... 86 EJ70
ISTEAD RISE, Grav. ... 130 GE94
Istead Ri, Grav. DA13 ... 131 GF94
Itchingwood Common Rd, Oxt.
RH8 ... 188 EJ133
Ivanhoe Cl, Uxb. UB8 ... 76 BK71
Ivanhoe Dr, Har. HA3 ... 61 CG55
Ivanhoe Rd, SE5 ... 102 DT83
Hounslow TW4 ... 96 BX83
Ivatt Pl, W14 ... 99 CZ78
Ivatt Way, N17 ... 65 DP55
Iveagh Av, NW10 ... 80 CN68
Iveagh Cl, E9 ... 85 DX67
NW10 ... 80 CN68
Northwood HA6 ... 39 BP53
Iveagh Rd, Wok. GU21 ... 166 AT118
Iveagh Ter, NW10
off Iveagh Av ... 80 CN68
Ivedon Rd, Well. DA16 ... 106 EW82
Ive Fm Cl, E10 ... 67 EA61
Ive Fm La, E10 ... 67 EA61
Iveley Rd, SW4 ... 101 DJ82
IVER ... 75 BF72
⇌ Iver ... 93 BF75
Iverdale Cl, Iver SL0 ... 75 BC73
Ivere Dr, Barn. EN5 ... 28 DB44
IVER HEATH, Iver ... 75 BD69
Iverhurst Cl, Bexh. DA6 ... 126 EX85
Iver La, Iver SL0 ... 76 BH71
Uxbridge UB8 ... 76 BH71
Iverna Ct, W8 ... 100 DA76
Iverna Gdns, W8 ... 100 DA76
Feltham TW14 ... 115 BR85
Iver Rd, Brwd. CM15 ... 54 FV44
Iver SL0 ... 76 BG72
Iverson Rd, NW6 ... 81 CZ65
Ivers Way, Croy. (New Adgtn.)
CR0 ... 161 EB108
Ives Gdns, Rom. RM1
off Sims Cl ... 71 FF56
Ives Rd, E16 ... 86 EE71
Slough SL3 ... 93 AZ76
Ives St, SW3 ... 198 C8
Ivestor Ter, SE23 ... 122 DW87
Ivimey St, E2 ... 84 DU69
Ivinghoe Cl, Enf. EN1 ... 30 DS40
Watford WD25 ... 24 BX35
Ivinghoe Rd, Bushey WD23 ... 41 CD45
Dagenham RM8 ... 70 EV64
Rickmansworth (Mill End)
WD3 ... 38 BG45
Ivor Gro, SE9 ... 125 EP88
Ivor Pl, NW1 ... 194 D5
Ivor St, NW1 ... 83 DJ66
Ivorydown, Brom. BR1 ... 124 EG91
Ivory Sq, SW11
off Gartons Way ... 100 DC83
Ivy Bower Cl, Green. DA9
off Riverview Rd ... 129 FV85
Ivybridge Cl, Twick. TW1 ... 117 CG86
Uxbridge UB8 ... 76 BL69
Ivybridge Est, Islw. TW7 ... 117 CF85
Ivybridge La, WC2 ... 200 A1
IVY CHIMNEYS, Epp. ... 17 ES32
Ivy Chimneys Rd, Epp. CM16 17 ES32
Ivychurch Cl, SE20 ... 122 DW94
Ivychurch La, SE17 ... 201 P10
Ivy Cl, Dart. DA1 ... 128 FN87
Gravesend DA12 ... 131 GJ90
Harrow HA2 ... 60 BZ63
Pinner HA5 ... 60 BW59
Sunbury-on-Thames
TW16 ... 136 BW96
Ivy Cotts, E14 off Grove Vil ... 85 EB73
Ivy Ct, SE16 off Argyle Way ... 102 DU78
Ivy Cres, W4 ... 98 CQ77
Ivydale Rd, SE15 ... 103 DX83
Carshalton SM5 ... 140 DF103
Ivyday Gro, SW16 ... 121 DM90
Ivydene, W.Mol. KT8 ... 136 BZ99
Ivydene Cl, Sutt. SM1 ... 158 DC105
Ivy Gdns, N8 ... 65 DL58
Mitcham CR4 ... 141 DK97
Ivy Ho La, Sev. TN14 ... 181 FD118
Ivyhouse Rd, Dag. RM9 ... 88 EX65
Ivy Ho Rd, Uxb. UB10 ... 59 BP62
Ivy La, Houns. TW4 ... 96 BZ84
Sevenoaks (Knock.) TN14 . 180 EY116
Woking GU22 ... 167 BB118
Ivy Lea, Rick. WD3
off Springwell Av ... 38 BG46
Ivy Lo La, Rom. RM3 ... 52 FP53
Ivy Mill Cl, Gdse. RH9 ... 186 DV132
Ivy Mill La, Gdse. RH9 ... 186 DU132
Ivymount Rd, SE27 ... 121 DN90
Ivy Pl, Surb. KT5
off Alpha Rd ... 138 CM100
Ivy Rd, E16 off Pacific Rd ... 86 EG72
E17 ... 67 EA58
N14 ... 45 DJ45
NW2 ... 63 CW63
SE4 ... 103 DZ84
SW17 off Tooting High St . 120 DE92
Hounslow TW3 ... 96 CB84
Surbiton KT6 ... 138 CN102
Ivy St, N1 ... 84 DS68
Ivy Wk, Dag. RM9 ... 88 EY65
Ixworth Pl, SW3 ... 198 B10
Izane Rd, Bexh. DA6 ... 106 EZ84

J

Jacaranda Cl, N.Mal. KT3 ... 138 CS97
Jacaranda Gro, E8 ... 84 DT66
Jackass La, Kes. BR2 ... 162 EH107
Oxted (Tand.) RH8 ... 187 DZ131
Jack Barnett Way, N22 ... 45 DM54
Jack Clow Rd, E15 ... 86 EE68
Jack Cornwell St, E12 ... 69 EN63
Jack Dash Way, E6 ... 86 EL70
Jackets La, Nthwd. HA6 ... 39 BP53
Uxbridge (Hare.) UB9 ... 38 BN52
Jacketts Fld, Abb.L. WD5 ... 7 BT31
Jack Goodchild Way, Kings.T. KT1
off Kingston Rd ... 138 CP97
Jacklin Grn, Wdf.Grn. IG8 ... 48 EG49
Jackman Ms, NW10 ... 62 CS62
Jackmans La, Wok. GU21 ... 166 AU119
Jackman St, E8 ... 84 DV67
Jacks La, Uxb. (Hare.) UB9 ... 38 BG53
Jackson Cl, E9 ... 84 DW66
Epsom KT18 ... 156 CR114
Greenhithe DA9
off Cowley Av ... 129 FU85
Hornchurch RM11 ... 72 FM56
Uxbridge UB10
off Jackson Rd ... 76 BL66
Jackson Ct, E11
off Brading Cres ... 68 EH60
Jackson Rd, N7 ... 65 DM63
Barking IG11 ... 87 ER67
Barnet EN4 ... 28 DE44
Bromley BR2 ... 144 EL103
Uxbridge UB10 ... 76 BL66
Jacksons Dr, Wal.Cr. EN7 ... 14 DU28
Jacksons La, N6 ... 64 DG59
Jacksons Pl, Croy. CR0
off Cross Rd ... 142 DR102
Jackson St, SE18 ... 105 EN79
Jacksons Way, Croy. CR0 ... 143 EA104
Jackson Way, Sthl. UB2 ... 96 CB75
Jack Walker Ct, N5 ... 65 DP63
Jacob Ho, Erith DA18
off Kale Rd ... 106 EX75
Jacobs Av, Rom. (Harold Wd.)
RM3 ... 52 FL54
Jacobs Cl, Dag. RM10 ... 71 FB63
Jacobs Ho, E13 ... 86 EJ69
Jacobs La, Dart. (Hort.Kir.)
DA4 ... 148 FQ97
Jacob St, SE1 ... 202 A4
Jacob's Well Ms, W1 ... 194 G8
Jacqueline Cl, Nthlt. UB5
off Canford Av ... 78 BZ67
Jade Cl, E16 ... 86 EK72
NW2 off Marble Dr ... 63 CX59
Dagenham RM8 ... 70 EW60
Jaffe Rd, Ilf. IG1 ... 69 EQ60
Jaffray Pl, SE27
off Chapel Rd ... 121 DP91
Jaffray Rd, Brom. BR2 ... 144 EK98
Jaggard Way, SW12 ... 120 DF87
Jagger Cl, Dart. DA2 ... 128 FQ87
Jago Cl, SE18 ... 105 EQ79
Jago Wk, SE5 ... 102 DR80
Jail La, West. (Bigg.H.) TN16 . 178 EK116
Jamaica Rd, SE1 ... 202 A5
SE16 ... 202 D6
Thornton Heath CR7 ... 141 DP100
Jamaica St, E1 ... 84 DW72
James Av, NW2 ... 63 CW64
Dagenham RM8 ... 70 EZ60
James Bedford Cl, Pnr. HA5 ... 40 BW54
James Boswell Cl, SW16
off Curtis Fld Rd ... 121 DN91
James Cl, E13
off Richmond St ... 86 EG68
NW11 off Woodlands ... 63 CY58
Bushey WD23
off Aldenham Rd ... 24 BY43
Romford RM2 ... 71 FG57
James Collins Cl, W9
off Fermoy Rd ... 81 CZ70
James Ct, N1
off Morton Rd ... 84 DQ66
James Dudson Ct, NW10 ... 80 CQ66
James Gdns, N22 ... 45 DP52
James Hammett Ho, E2
off Ravenscroft St ... 84 DT69
James Joyce Wk, SE24
off Shakespeare Rd ... 101 DP84
James La, E10 ... 67 ED59
E11 ... 67 ED58
James Lee Sq, Enf. EN3
off Government Row ... 31 EA37
James Martin Cl, Uxb. (Denh.)
UB9 ... 58 BG58
James Newman Ct, SE9
off Great Harry Dr ... 125 EN90
Jameson Cl, W3
off Acton La ... 98 CQ75
Jameson Ct, E2 ... 84 DW68
Jameson St, W8 ... 82 DA74
Jameson Wk, Wdf.Grn. IG8
off Baddow Cl ... 48 EK51
James Pl, N17 ... 46 DT53
James Rd, Dart. DA1 ... 127 FG87
James's Cotts, Rich. TW9
off Kew Rd ... 98 CN80
James Sinclair Pt, E13 ... 86 EJ67
James St, W1 ... 194 G8
WC2 ... 196 A10
Barking IG11 ... 87 EQ66
Enfield EN1 ... 30 DT43
Epping CM16 ... 17 ET28
Hounslow TW3 ... 97 CD83
James Ter, SW14
off Mullins Path ... 98 CR83
Jamestown Rd, NW1 ... 83 DH67
Jamestown Way, E14 ... 204 G1
James Watt Way, Erith DA8 ... 107 FF79
James Yd, E4 ... 47 ED51
Jamieson Ho, Houns. TW4 ... 116 BZ87
Jamnagar Cl, Stai. TW18 ... 113 BF93
Jamuna Cl, E14 ... 85 DY71
Jane St, E1
off Commercial Rd ... 84 DV72
Janet St, E14 ... 204 A6
Janeway Pl, SE16 ... 202 D5
Janeway St, SE16 ... 202 C5
Janice Ms, Ilf. IG1
off Oakfield Rd ... 69 EP62
Janmead, Brwd. CM13 ... 55 GB45
Janoway Hill La, Wok. GU21 . 166 AW119
Jansen Wk, SW11
off Hope St ... 100 DD84
Janson Cl, E15 off Janson Rd . 68 EE64
NW10 ... 62 CR62
Janson Rd, E15 ... 68 EE64
Jansons Rd, N15 ... 66 DS55
Japan Cres, N4 ... 65 DM59
Japan Rd, Rom. RM6 ... 70 EX58
Japonica Cl, Wok. GU21 ... 166 AW118
Jardine Rd, E1 ... 85 DX73
Jarrah Cotts, Purf. RM19
off London Rd Purfleet ... 109 FR79
Jarrett Cl, SW2 ... 121 DP88
Jarrow Cl, Mord. SM4 ... 140 DB99
Jarrow Rd, N17 ... 66 DV56
SE16 ... 202 F9
Romford RM6 ... 70 EW58
Jarrow Way, E9 ... 67 DY63
Jarvis Cleys, Wal.Cr. (Chsht.)
EN7 ... 14 DT26
Jarvis Cl, Bark. IG11
off Westbury Rd ... 87 ER67
Barnet EN5 ... 27 CX43
Jarvis Rd, SE22
off Melbourne Gro ... 102 DS84
South Croydon CR2 ... 160 DR107
Jarvis Way, Rom. (Harold Wd.)
RM3 ... 52 FL54
Jasmin Cl, Nthwd. HA6 ... 39 BT53
Jasmine Cl, Ilf. IG1 ... 69 EP64
Orpington BR6 ... 145 EP103
Southall UB1 ... 78 BY73
Woking GU21 ... 166 AT116
Jasmine Gdns, Croy. CR0 ... 143 EB104
Harrow HA2 ... 60 CA61
Jasmine Gro, SE20 ... 142 DV95
Jasmine Rd, Rom. (Rush Grn.)
RM7 ... 71 FE61
Jasmine Ter, West Dr. UB7 ... 94 BN75
Jasmine Way, E.Mol. KT8
off Hampton Ct Way ... 137 CE98
Jasmin Rd, Epsom KT19 ... 156 CP106
Jason Cl, Brwd. CM14 ... 54 FT49
Weybridge KT13 ... 153 BQ106
Jason Ct, W1
off Marylebone La ... 82 DG72
Jasons Hill, Chesh. HP5 ... 4 AV30
Jason Wk, SE9 ... 125 EN91
Jasper Cl, Enf. EN3 ... 30 DW38
Jasper Pas, SE19 ... 122 DT93
Jasper Rd, E16 ... 86 EK72
SE19 ... 122 DT92
Jasper Wk, N1 ... 197 K2
Javelin Way, Nthlt. UB5 ... 78 BX69
Jaycroft, Enf. EN2
off The Ridgeway ... 29 DN39
Jay Gdns, Chis. BR7 ... 125 EM91
Jay Ms, SW7 ... 100 DC75
Jays Covert, Couls. CR5 ... 174 DG119
Jean Batten Cl, Wall. SM6
off Lancastrian Rd ... 159 DM108
Jebb Av, SW2 ... 121 DL86
Jebb St, E3 ... 85 EA68
Jedburgh Rd, E13 ... 86 EJ69
Jedburgh St, SW11 ... 100 DG84
Jeddo Rd, W12 ... 99 CT75
Jefferson Cl, W13 ... 97 CH76
Ilford IG2 ... 69 EP57
Slough SL3 ... 93 BA77
Jefferson Wk, SE18
off Kempt St ... 105 EN79
Jeffreys Pl, NW1
off Jeffreys St ... 83 DJ66
Jeffreys Rd, SW4 ... 101 DL82
Enfield EN3 ... 31 DZ41
Jeffreys St, NW1 ... 83 DH66
Jeffreys Wk, SW4 ... 101 DL82
Jeffries Ho, NW10 ... 80 CR67
Jeffs Cl, Hmptn. TW12
off Uxbridge Rd ... 116 CB93
Jeffs Rd, Sutt. SM1 ... 157 CZ105
Jeger Av, E2 ... 84 DT67
Jeken Rd, SE9 ... 104 EJ84
Jelf Rd, SW2 ... 121 DN85
Jellicoe Av, Grav. DA12 ... 131 GJ90
Jellicoe Av W, Grav. DA12
off Kitchener Av ... 131 GJ90
Jellicoe Gdns, Stan. HA7 ... 41 CF51
Jellicoe Rd, E13
off Jutland Rd ... 86 EG70
N17 ... 46 DR52
Watford WD18 ... 23 BU44
Jemmett Cl, Kings.T. KT2 ... 138 CP95
Jengar Cl, Sutt. SM1 ... 158 DB105
Jenkins Av, St.Alb. (Brick.Wd.)
AL2 ... 8 BY30
Jenkins La, E6 ... 87 EN68
Barking IG11 ... 87 EP68
Jenkins Rd, E13 ... 86 EH70
Jenner Av, W3 ... 80 CR71
Jenner Ho, SE3 ... 104 EE79
Jenner Pl, SW13 ... 99 CV79
Jenner Rd, N16 ... 66 DT61
Jennett Rd, Croy. CR0 ... 141 DN104
Jennifer Rd, Brom. BR1 ... 124 EF90
Jennings Cl, Add. (New Haw)
KT15 off Woodham La ... 152 BJ109
Surbiton KT6 ... 137 CJ101
Jennings Rd, SE22 ... 122 DT86
Jennings Way, Barn. EN5 ... 27 CW41
Jenningtree Rd, Erith DA8 ... 107 FH80
Jenningtree Way, Belv. DA17 . 107 FC75
Jenny Hammond Cl, E11
off Newcomen Rd ... 68 EF62
Jenny Path, Rom. RM3 ... 52 FK52
Jennys Way, Couls. CR5 ... 175 DJ122
Jenson Way, SE19 ... 122 DT94
Jenton Av, Bexh. DA7 ... 106 EY81
Jephson Rd, E7 ... 86 EJ66
Jephson St, SE5
off Grove La ... 102 DR81
Jephtha Rd, SW18 ... 120 DA86
Jeppos La, Mitch. CR4 ... 140 DF98
Jepps Cl, Wal.Cr. EN7
off Little Gro Av ... 14 DS27
Jerdan Pl, SW6 ... 100 DA80
Jeremiah St, E14 ... 85 EB72
Jeremys Grn, N18 ... 46 DV49
Jermyn St, SW1 ... 199 K2
Jerningham Av, Ilf. IG5 ... 49 EP54
Jerningham Rd, SE14 ... 103 DY82
Jerome Cres, NW8 ... 194 B4
Jerome Pl, Kings.T. KT1
off Wadbrook St ... 137 CK96
Jerome St, E1 ... 197 P6
Jerrard St, N1 ... 197 N1
SE13 ... 103 EB83
Jersey Av, Stan. HA7 ... 41 CH54
Jersey Cl, Cher. KT16 ... 133 BF104
Jersey Dr, Orp. BR5 ... 145 ER100
Jersey Ho, Enf. EN3
off Eastfield Rd ... 31 DX38
Jersey Par, Houns. TW5 ... 96 CB81
Jersey Rd, E11 ... 67 ED60
E16 off Prince Regent La ... 86 EJ72
SW17 ... 121 DH93
W7 ... 97 CG75
Hounslow TW3, TW5 ... 96 CB81
Ilford IG1 ... 69 EP63
Isleworth TW7 ... 97 CE79
Rainham RM13 ... 89 FG66
Jersey St, E2
off Bethnal Grn Rd ... 84 DV69
Jerusalem Pas, EC1 ... 196 F5
Jervis Av, Enf. EN3 ... 31 DY35
Jervis Ct, W1 ... 195 J9
Jerviston Gdns, SW16 ... 121 DN93
Jesmond Av, Wem. HA9 ... 80 CM65
Jesmond Cl, Mitch. CR4 ... 141 DH97
Jesmond Rd, Croy. CR0 ... 142 DT101
Jesmond Way, Stan. HA7 ... 42 CL50
Jessam Av, E5 ... 66 DV60
Jessamine Pl, Dart. DA2 ... 128 FQ87
Jessamine Rd, W7 ... 79 CE74
Jessamine Ter, Swan. BR8
off Birchwood Rd ... 147 FC95
Jessamy Rd, Wey. KT13 ... 135 BP103
Jessel Dr, Loug. IG10 ... 33 EQ39
Jesse Rd, E10 ... 67 EC60
Jessett Cl, Erith DA8
off West St ... 107 FD77
Jessica Rd, SW18 ... 120 DC86
Jessie Blythe La, N19 ... 65 DL59
Jessiman Ter, Shep. TW17 ... 134 BN99
Jessop Av, Sthl. UB2 ... 96 BZ77
Jessop Rd, SE24
off Milkwood Rd ... 101 DP84
Jessop Sq, E14
off Heron Quay ... 85 EA74
Jessops Way, Croy. CR0 ... 141 DJ100
Jessup Cl, SE18 ... 105 EQ77
Jetstar Way, Nthlt. UB5 ... 78 BY69
Jetty Wk, Grays RM17 ... 110 GA79
Jevington Way, SE12 ... 124 EH88
Jewel Rd, E17 ... 67 EA55
Jewels Hill, West. (Bigg.H.)
TN16 ... 162 EG112
★ Jewel Twr, Houses of
Parliament, SW1 ... 199 P6
★ Jewish Mus, NW1 ... 83 DH67
Jewry St, EC3 ... 197 P9
Jew's Row, SW18 ... 100 DC84
Jews Wk, SE26 ... 122 DV91
Jeymer Av, NW2 ... 63 CV64
Jeymer Dr, Grnf. UB6 ... 78 CC67
Jeypore Pas, SW18
off Jeypore Rd ... 120 DC86
Jeypore Rd, SW18 ... 120 DC87
Jillian Cl, Hmptn. TW12 ... 116 CA94
Jim Bradley Cl, SE18
off John Wilson St ... 105 EN77
Jim Griffiths Ho, SW6
off Clem Attlee Ct ... 99 CZ79
Joan Cres, SE9 ... 124 EK87
Joan Gdns, Dag. RM8 ... 70 EY61
Joan Rd, Dag. RM8 ... 70 EY61
Joan St, SE1 ... 200 F3
Jocelyn Rd, Rich. TW9 ... 98 CL83
Jocelyn St, SE15 ... 102 DU81
Jockey's Flds, WC1 ... 196 C6
Jodane St, SE8 ... 203 M9
Jodrell Cl, Islw. TW7 ... 97 CG81
Jodrell Rd, E3 ... 85 DZ67
Jodrell Way, Grays (W.Thur.)
RM20 ... 109 FT78
Joel St, Nthwd. HA6 ... 59 BU55
Pinner HA5 ... 59 BU55
Johanna St, SE1 ... 200 D5
John Adam St, WC2 ... 200 A1
John Aird Ct, W2 ... 82 DC71
John Archer Way, SW18 ... 120 DD86
John Ashby Cl, SW2 ... 121 DL86
John Austin Cl, Kings.T. KT2
off Queen Elizabeth Rd ... 138 CM95
John Barnes Wk, E15 ... 86 EF65
John Bradshaw Rd, N14
off High St ... 45 DK46
John Burns Dr, Bark. IG11 ... 87 ES66
Johnby Cl, Enf. EN3
off Manly Dixon Dr ... 31 DY37
John Campbell Rd, N16 ... 66 DS64
John Carpenter St, EC4 ... 196 F10
John Cobb Rd, Wey. KT13 ... 152 BN108
John Cornwell VC Ho, E12 ... 69 EN63
John Drinkwater Cl, E11
off Browning Rd ... 68 EF59
John Felton Rd, SE16 ... 202 B5
John Fisher St, E1 ... 84 DU73
John Gooch Dr, Enf. EN2 ... 29 DP39
John Harrison Way, SE10 ... 205 K7
John Horner Ms, N1
off Frome St ... 84 DQ68
John Islip St, SW1 ... 199 P9
John Keats Ho, N22 ... 45 DM52
John Maurice Cl, SE17 ... 201 K8
John McKenna Wk, SE16 ... 202 C6
John Newton Ct, Well. DA16
off Danson La ... 106 EV83
John Parker Cl, Dag. RM10 ... 89 FB66
John Parker Sq, SW11
off Thomas Baines Rd ... 100 DD83
John Penn St, SE13 ... 103 EB81
John Perrin Pl, Har. HA3 ... 62 CL59
John Princes St, W1 ... 195 J8
John Rennie Wk, E1 ... 202 E2
John Roll Way, SE16 ... 202 C6
John Ruskin St, SE5 ... 101 DP80
Johns Av, NW4 ... 63 CW56
Johns Cl, Ashf. TW15 ... 115 BQ91
Johns Ct, Sutt. SM2
off Mulgrave Rd ... 158 DB107
Johnsdale, Oxt. RH8 ... 188 EF129
John Silkin La, SE8 ... 203 J9
Johns La, Mord. SM4 ... 140 DC99
John's Ms, WC1 ... 196 C5
John Smith Av, SW6 ... 99 CZ80
Johnson Cl, E8 ... 84 DU67
Gravesend (Nthflt.) DA11 ... 130 GD90
Johnson Rd, NW10
off Milton Av ... 80 CR67
Bromley BR2 ... 144 EK99
Croydon CR0 ... 142 DR101
Hounslow TW5 ... 96 BW80
Johnsons Av, Sev. (Bad.Mt.)
TN14 ... 165 FB110
Johnsons Cl, Cars. SM5 ... 140 DF104
Johnson's Ct, EC4
off Fleet St ... 83 DN72
Johnsons Ct, Sev. (Seal) TN15
off School La ... 191 FM121
Johnsons Dr, Hmptn. TW12 ... 136 CC95
Johnson's Pl, SW1 ... 101 DJ78
Johnson St, E1 off Cable St ... 84 DW73
Southall UB2 ... 96 BW76
Johnsons Way, NW10 ... 80 CP70
Greenhithe DA9 ... 129 FW86
Johnsons Yd, Uxb. UB8
off Redford Way ... 76 BJ66
John Spencer Sq, N1 ... 83 DP65
John's Pl, E1
off Damien St ... 84 DV72
Johns Rd, West. (Tats.) TN16 . 178 EK120
John's Ter, Croy. CR0 ... 142 DR102
Romford RM3 ... 52 FP51
Johnston Cl, SW9
off Hackford Rd ... 101 DM81
Johnstone Rd, E6 ... 87 EM69
Johnston Rd, Wdf.Grn. IG8 ... 48 EG50
Johnston Ter, NW2
off Kara Way ... 63 CX62
John St, E15 ... 86 EF67
SE25 ... 142 DU98
WC1 ... 196 C5
Enfield EN1 ... 30 DT43
Grays RM17 ... 110 GC79
Hounslow TW3 ... 96 BY82
Johns Wk, Whyt. CR3 ... 176 DU119
John Trundle Ct, EC2
off The Barbican ... 84 DQ71
John Walsh Twr, E11 ... 68 EF61
John Williams Cl, SE14 ... 103 DX79
Kingston upon Thames KT2
off Henry Macaulay Av ... 137 CK95
John Wilson St, SE18 ... 105 EN76
John Woolley Cl, SE13 ... 104 EE84
Joiner's Arms Yd, SE5
off Denmark Hill ... 102 DR81
Joiners Cl, Chesh. (Ley Hill)
HP5 ... 4 AV30
Gerrards Cross (Chal.St.P.)
SL9 ... 37 AZ52
Joiners La, Ger.Cr. (Chal.St.P.)
SL9 ... 36 AY53
Joiners Pl, N5
off Leconfield Rd ... 66 DR63
Joiner St, SE1 ... 201 L3
Joiners Way, Ger.Cr. (Chal.St.P.)
SL9 ... 36 AY52
Joinville Pl, Add. KT15 ... 152 BK105
Jolliffe Rd, Red. RH1 ... 185 DJ126
Jollys La, Har. HA2 ... 61 CD60
Hayes UB4 ... 78 BX71
Jonathan Ct, W4
off Windmill Rd ... 98 CS77
Jonathan St, SE11 ... 200 B10
Jones Rd, E13
off Holborn Rd ... 86 EH70
Waltham Cross (Chsht.)
EN7 ... 13 DP30
Jones St, W1 ... 199 H1
Jones Wk, Rich. TW10
off Pyrland Rd ... 118 CM86
Jonquil Gdns, Hmptn. TW12
off Partridge Rd ... 116 BZ93
Jonson Cl, Hayes UB4 ... 77 BU71
Mitcham CR4 ... 141 DH98
Jordan Cl, Dag. RM10
off Muggeridge Rd ... 71 FB63
Harrow HA2
off Hamilton Cres ... 60 BZ62
South Croydon CR2 ... 160 DT111
Watford WD25 ... 23 BT35
Jordan Ct, SW15
off Charlwood Rd ... 99 CX84
Jordan Rd, Grnf. UB6 ... 79 CH67
JORDANS, Beac. ... 36 AT52
Jordans Cl, Islw. TW7 ... 97 CE81
Staines (Stanw.) TW19 ... 114 BJ87
Jordans La, Beac. (Jordans)
HP9 ... 36 AS53
Jordans Rd, Rick. WD3 ... 38 BG45
Jordans Way, Beac. (Jordans)
HP9 ... 36 AT51
Rainham RM13 ... 90 FK68
St. Albans (Brick.Wd.) AL2 ... 8 BZ30
Joseph Av, W3 ... 80 CR72
Josephine Av, SW2 ... 121 DM85

Jos - Ken

K

279

Ken - Kin

Kennel La, Lthd. (Fetch.)
KT22 170 CC122
Kennelwood Cres, Croy.
(New Adgtn.) CR0 161 ED111
Kennet Cl, SW11
off Maysoule Rd 100 DD84
Upminster RM14 73 FS58
Kennet Grn, S.Ock. RM15 91 FV73
Kenneth Av, Ilf. IG1 69 EP63
Kenneth Cres, NW2 63 CV64
Kenneth Gdns, Stan. HA7 41 CG51
Kenneth More Rd, Ilf. IG1
off Oakfield Rd 69 EP62
Kenneth Rd, Bans. SM7 174 DD115
Romford RM6 70 EX59
Kenneth Robbins Ho, N17 46 DV52
Kennet Rd, W9 81 CZ70
Dartford DA1 107 FG83
Isleworth TW7 97 CF83
Kennet Sq, Mitch. CR4 140 DE95
Kennet St, E1 202 C2
Kennett Ct, Swan. BR8 147 FE97
Kennett Dr, Hayes UB4 78 BY71
Kennett Rd, Slou. SL3 93 BB76
Kennet Wf La, EC4 197 J10
Kenninghall Rd, E5 66 DU62
N18 46 DW50
Kenning St, SE16 202 G4
Kennings Way, SE11 200 F10
Kenning Ter, N1 84 DS67
KENNINGTON, SE11 101 DN79
⊖ Kennington 200 F10
Kennington Grn, SE11
off Montford Pl 101 DN78
Kennington Gro, SE11
off Oval Way 101 DM79
Kennington La, SE11 200 E10
Kennington Oval, SE11 101 DM79
Kennington Pk Est, SE11
off Harleyford St 101 DN79
Kennington Pk Gdns, SE11 101 DP79
Kennington Pk Pl, SE11 101 DN79
Kennington Pk Rd, SE11 101 DN79
Kennington Rd, SE1 200 D6
SE11 200 D7
Kenny Dr, Cars. SM5 158 DF109
Kenny Rd, NW7 43 CY50
Kenrick Pl, W1 194 F6
Kenrick Sq, Red. (Bletch.)
RH1 186 DS133
KENSAL GREEN, NW10 81 CW69
⇌ Kensal Green 81 CW69
⊖ Kensal Green 81 CW69
★ Kensal Green Cem, W10 81 CW69
KENSAL RISE, NW6 81 CX68
⇌ Kensal Rise 81 CX68
Kensal Rd, W10 81 CY70
KENSAL TOWN, W10 81 CX70
KENSINGTON, W8 99 CZ75
Kensington Av, E12 86 EL65
Thornton Heath CR7 141 DN95
Watford WD18 23 BT42
Kensington Ch Ct, W8 100 DB75
Kensington Ch St, W8 82 DA74
Kensington Ch Wk, W8 100 DB75
Kensington Cl, N11 44 DG51
Kensington Ct, NW7
off Grenville Pl 42 CR50
W8 100 DB75
Kensington Ct Gdns, W8
off Kensington Ct Pl 100 DB76
Kensington Ct Ms, W8
off Kensington Ct Pl 100 DB75
Kensington Ct Pl, W8 100 DB76
Kensington Dr, Wdf.Grn. IG8 48 EK53
★ Kensington Gdns, W2 82 DC74
Kensington Gdns, W2 82 DC74
Ilford IG1 69 EM61
Kingston upon Thames KT1
off Portsmouth Rd 137 CK97
Kensington Gdns Sq, W2 82 DB72
Kensington Gate, W8 100 DC76
Kensington Gore, SW7 100 DD75
Kensington Hall Gdns, W14
off Beaumont Av 99 CZ78
Kensington High St, W8 100 DA76
W14 99 CY77
Kensington Mall, W8 82 DA74
⇌ Kensington (Olympia) 99 CY76
⊖ Kensington (Olympia) 99 CY76
★ Kensington Palace, W8 100 DB75
Kensington Palace Gdns, W8 82 DB74
Kensington Pk Gdns, W11 81 CZ73
Kensington Pk Ms, W11
off Kensington Pk Rd 81 CZ72
Kensington Pk Rd, W11 81 CZ73
Kensington Pl, W8 82 DA74
Kensington Rd, SW7 198 A5
W8 100 DB75
Brentwood CM15 54 FU44
Northolt UB5 78 CA69
Romford RM7 71 FC58
Kensington Sq, W8 100 DB75
Kensington Ter, S.Croy. CR2
off Sanderstead Rd 160 DR108
Kensington Way, Borwd. WD6 26 CR41
Kent Av, W13 79 CH71
Dagenham RM9 88 FA70
Welling DA16 125 ET85
Kent Cl, Borwd. WD6 26 CR38
Mitcham CR4 141 DL98
Orpington BR6 163 ES107
Staines TW18 114 BK93
Uxbridge UB8 76 BJ65
Kent Dr, Barn. EN4 28 DG42
Hornchurch RM12 72 FK63
Teddington TW11 117 CE92
Kentford Way, Nthlt. UB5 78 BY67
Kent Gdns, W13 79 CH71
Ruislip HA4 59 BV58
Kent Gate Way, Croy. CR0 161 EA106
KENT HATCH, Eden. 189 EP131
Kent Hatch Rd, Eden. (Crock.H.)
TN8 189 EM131
Oxted RH8 188 EJ129
⇌ Kent House 143 DY95
Kent Ho La, Beck. BR3 123 DY92
Kent Ho Rd, SE26 143 DX95
Beck. BR3 123 DY92
Kentish Bldgs, SE1 201 K3
Kentish La, Hat. AL9 12 DC25
Kentish Rd, Belv. DA17 106 FA77
KENTISH TOWN, NW5 83 DJ65
⇌ Kentish Town 65 DJ64
⊖ Kentish Town 65 DJ64
Kentish Town Rd, NW1 83 DH66
NW5 83 DH66
⇌ Kentish Town West 82 DG65
Kentish Way, Brom. BR1 144 EG96
Kentlea Rd, SE28 105 ES75
Kentmere Rd, SE18 105 ES77
KENTON, Har. 61 CH57
⇌ Kenton 61 CH58
⊖ Kenton 61 CH58
Kenton Av, Har. HA1 61 CF59
Southall UB1 78 CA73
Sunbury-on-Thames
TW16 136 BY96
Kenton Ct, W14
off Kensington High St 99 CZ76
Kenton Gdns, Har. HA3 61 CJ57
Kenton La, Har. HA3 61 CJ55
Kenton Pk Av, Har. HA3 61 CK56
Kenton Pk Cl, Har. HA3 61 CJ56
Kenton Pk Cres, Har. HA3 61 CK56
Kenton Pk Rd, Har. HA3 61 CJ56
Kenton Rd, E9 85 DX65
Harrow HA1, HA3 61 CK57
Kenton St, WC1 195 P4
Kenton Way, Hayes UB4
off Exmouth Rd 77 BS69
Woking GU21 166 AT117
Kent Pas, NW1 194 D4
Kent Rd, N21 46 DR46
W4 98 CQ76
Dagenham RM10 71 FB64
Dartford DA1 128 FK86
East Molesey KT8 136 CC98
Gravesend DA11 131 GG88
Grays RM17 110 GC79
Kingston upon Thames KT1
off The Bittoms 137 CK97
Longfield DA3 149 FX96
Orpington BR5 146 EV100
Richmond TW9 98 CN80
West Wickham BR4 143 EB102
Woking GU22 167 BB116
Kents Pas, Hmptn. TW12 136 BZ95
Kent St, E2 84 DT68
E13 86 EJ69
Kent Ter, NW1 194 C3
Kent Twr, SE20 122 DV94
Kent Vw, S.Ock. (Aveley)
RM15 108 FQ75
Kent Vw Gdns, Ilf. IG3 69 ES61
Kent Wk, SW9
off Moorland Rd 101 DP84
Kent Way, Surb. KT6 138 CL104
Kentwode Grn, SW13 99 CU80
Kent Yd, SW7 198 C5
Kenver Av, N12 44 DD51
Kenward Rd, SE9 124 EJ85
Kenway, Rain. RM13 90 FJ69
Romford RM5 51 FC54
Ken Way, Wem. HA9 62 CQ61
Kenway Cl, Rain. RM13
off Kenway 90 FJ69
Kenway Dr, Amer. HP7 20 AV39
Kenway Rd, SW5 100 DB77
Kenway Wk, Rain. RM13
off Kenway 90 FK69
Kenwood Av, N14 29 DK43
SE14 off Besson St 103 DX81
Kenwood Cl, NW3 64 DD60
West Drayton UB7 94 BN79
Kenwood Dr, Beck. BR3 143 EC97
Rickmansworth (Mill End)
WD3 37 BF47
Walton-on-Thames KT12 153 BV107
Kenwood Gdns, E18 68 EH55
Ilford IG2 69 EN56
★ Kenwood Ho (The Iveagh
Bequest), NW3 64 DE60
Kenwood Pk, Wey. KT13 153 BR107
Kenwood Ridge, Ken. CR8 175 DP117
Kenwood Rd, N6 64 DF58
N9 46 DU46
Kenworth Cl, Wal.Cr. EN8 15 DX33
Kenworthy Rd, E9 67 DY64
Kenwyn Dr, NW2 62 CS62
Kenwyn Rd, SW4 101 DK84
SW20 139 CW95
Dartford DA1 128 FK85
Kenya Rd, SE7 104 EK80
Kenyngton Dr, Sun. TW16 115 BU92
Kenyngton Pl, Har. HA3 61 CJ57
Kenyon St, SW6 99 CX81
Keogh Rd, E15 86 EE65
Kepler Rd, SW4 101 DL84
Keppel Rd, E6 87 EM66
Dagenham RM9 70 EY63
Keppel Row, SE1 201 H3
Keppel Spur, Wind. (Old Wind.)
SL4 112 AV87
Keppel St, WC1 195 N6
Kerbela St, E2 off Cheshire St 84 DU70
Kerbey St, E14 85 EB72
Kerdistone Cl, Pot.B. EN6 12 DB30
Kerfield Cres, SE5 102 DR81
Kerfield Pl, SE5 102 DR81
Kernow Cl, Horn. RM12 72 FL61
Kerri Cl, Barn. EN5 27 CW42
Kerridge Ct, N1 84 DS65
Kerrill Av, Couls. CR5 175 DN119
Kerrison Pl, W5 79 CK74
Kerrison Rd, E15 85 ED67
SW11 100 DE83
W5 79 CK74
Kerrison Vil, W5
off Kerrison Pl 79 CK74
Kerry Av, S.Ock. (Aveley)
RM15 108 FM75
Stanmore HA7 41 CK49
Kerry Cl, E16 86 EH72
Kerry Cl, N13 45 DM47
Upminster RM14 73 FT59
Kerry Ct, Stan. HA7 41 CK49
Kerry Dr, Upmin. RM14 73 FT59
Kerry Path, SE14
off Kerry Rd 103 DZ79
Kerry Rd, SE14 103 DZ79
Kerry Ter, Wok. GU21 167 BB116
Kersey Dr, S.Croy. CR2 160 DW112
Kersey Gdns, SE9 124 EL91
Romford RM3 52 FL53
Kersfield Rd, SW15 119 CX86
Kershaw Cl, SW18
off Westover Rd 120 DD86
Grays (Chaff.Hun.) RM16 109 FW77
Hornchurch RM11 72 FL59
Kershaw Rd, Dag. RM10 70 FA62
Kersley Ms, SW11 100 DF82
Kersley Rd, N16 66 DS62
Kersley St, SW11 100 DF82
Kerstin Cl, Hayes UB3
off St. Mary's Rd 77 BT73
Kerswell Cl, N15 66 DS57
Kerwick Cl, N7
off Sutterton St 83 DM66
Keslake Rd, NW6 81 CX68
Kessock Cl, N17 66 DV57
Kesteven Cl, Ilf. IG6 49 ET51
Kestlake Rd, Bex. DA5
off East Rochester Way 126 EW86
KESTON 162 EJ106
Keston Av, Add. (New Haw)
KT15 152 BG111
Coulsdon CR5 175 DN119
Keston BR2 162 EJ106
Keston Cl, N18 46 DR48
Welling DA16 106 EW80
Keston Gdns, Kes. BR2 162 EJ105
Keston Ms, Wat. WD17
off Nascot Rd 23 BV40
Keston Pk Cl, Kes. BR2 145 EM104
Keston Rd, N17 66 DR55
SE15 102 DU83
Thornton Heath CR7 141 DN100
Kestral Ct, Wall. SM6
off Carew Rd 159 DJ106
Kestrel Av, E6 off Swan App 86 EL71
SE24 121 DP85
Staines TW18 113 BF90
Kestrel Cl, NW9 42 CS54
NW10 62 CR64
Epsom KT19
off Abbots Av 156 CN111
Hornchurch RM12 89 FH66
Ilford IG6 50 EW49
Kingston upon Thames
KT2 117 CK91
Watford WD25 8 BY34
Kestrel Ho, EC1 197 H2
W13 79 CF70
Enfield EN3 off Alma Rd 31 DX43
Kestrel Pl, SE14
off Milton Ct Rd 103 DY79
Kestrel Rd, Wal.Abb. EN9 16 EG34
Kestrels, The, St.Alb. AL2
off Bucknalls Dr 8 BZ31
Kestrel Way, Croy. (New Adgtn.)
CR0 161 ED109
Hayes UB3 off Betam Rd 95 BR75
Keswick Av, SW15 118 CS92
SW19 140 DA96
Hornchurch RM11 72 FK60
Keswick Bdy, SW15
off Upper Richmond Rd 119 CY85
Keswick Cl, Sutt. SM1 158 DC105
Keswick Ct, Slou. SL2
off Stoke Rd 74 AT73
Keswick Dr, Enf. EN3 30 DW36
Keswick Gdns, Ilf. IG4 68 EL57
Ruislip HA4 59 BR58
Wembley HA9 62 CL63
Keswick Ms, W5 80 CL74
Keswick Rd, SW15 119 CY85
Bexleyheath DA7 106 FA82
Egham TW20 113 BB94
Leatherhead (Fetch.) KT22 170 CC124
Orpington BR6 145 ET102
Twickenham TW2 116 CC86
West Wickham BR4 144 EE103
Kettering Rd, Enf. EN3
off Beaconsfield Rd 31 DX37
Romford RM3 52 FL52
Kettering St, SW16 121 DJ93
Kett Gdns, SW2 121 DM85
Kettlebaston Rd, E10 67 DZ60
Kettlewell Cl, N11 44 DG51
Woking GU21 150 AX114
Kettlewell Ct, Swan. BR8 147 FF96
Kettlewell Dr, Wok. GU21 150 AY114
Kettlewell Hill, Wok. GU21 150 AY114
Ketton Grn, Red. RH1
off Malmstone Av 185 DK128
Kevan Dr, Wok. (Send) GU23 167 BE124
Kevan Ho, SE5 102 DQ80
Kevelioc Rd, N17 46 DQ53
Kevin Cl, Houns. TW4 96 BX82
Kevington Cl, Orp. BR5 145 ET98
Kevington Dr, Chis. BR7 145 ET98
Orpington BR5 145 ET98
KEW, Rich. 98 CN79
⇌ Kew Bridge 98 CM78
Kew Br, Brent. TW8 98 CM79
Richmond TW9 98 CM79
Kew Br Arches, Rich. TW9
off Kew Br 98 CM79
Kew Br Ct, W4 98 CN78
Kew Br Rd, Brent. TW8 98 CM79
★ Kew Bridge Steam Mus,
Brent. TW8 98 CM78
Kew Cres, Sutt. SM3 139 CY104
Kewferry Dr, Nthwd. HA6 39 BP50
Kewferry Rd, Nthwd. HA6 39 BQ51
Kew Foot Rd, Rich. TW9 98 CL84
⇌ Kew Gardens 98 CM81
⊖ Kew Gardens 98 CM81
Kew Gdns Rd, Rich. TW9 98 CM80
Kew Grn, Rich. TW9 98 CN79
Kew Meadow Path, Rich. TW9 98 CN81
★ Kew Observatory,
Rich. TW9 97 CH83
★ Kew Palace, Royal Botanic
Gdns, Rich. TW9 98 CL80
Kew Palace, Rich. TW9 98 CL80
Kew Rd, Rich. TW9 98 CN79
Keybridge Ho, SW8 101 DL79
Key Cl, E1 84 DV70
Keyes Rd, NW2 63 CX64
Dartford DA1 108 FM84
Keymer Cl, West. (Bigg.H.)
TN16 178 EK116
Keymer Rd, SW2 121 DM89
Keynes Cl, N2 64 DF55
Keynsham Av, Wdf.Grn. IG8 48 EE49
Keynsham Gdns, SE9 124 EL85
Keynsham Rd, SE9 124 EK85
Morden SM4 140 DB102
Keynsham Wk, Mord. SM4 140 DB102
Keys, The, Brwd. CM13
off Eagle Way 53 FW51
Keyse Rd, SE1 201 P7
Keysham Av, Houns. TW5
off The Avenue 95 BU81
Keys Ho, Enf. EN3
off Beaconsfield Rd 31 DX37
Keystone Cres, N1 196 A1
Keywood Dr, Sun. TW16 115 BU93
Keyworth Cl, E5 67 DY63
Keyworth St, SE1 200 G6
Kezia St, SE8
off Trundleys Rd 103 DY78
Khalsa Av, Grav. DA12 131 GJ87
Khalsa Ct, N22
off Acacia Rd 45 DP53
Khama Rd, SW17 120 DE91
Khartoum Pl, Grav. DA12 131 GJ86
Khartoum Rd, E13 86 EH69
SW17 120 DD91
Ilford IG1 69 EP64
Khyber Rd, SW11 100 DE82
Kibworth St, SW8 101 DM80
KIDBROOKE, SE3 104 EH83
⇌ Kidbrooke 104 EH83
Kidbrooke Gdns, SE3 104 EG82
Kidbrooke Gro, SE3 104 EG81
Kidbrooke La, SE9 104 EL84
Kidbrooke Pk Cl, SE3 104 EH81
Kidbrooke Pk Rd, SE3 104 EH81
Kidbrooke Way, SE3 104 EH82
Kidderminster Pl, Croy. CR0
off Kidderminster Rd 141 DP102
Kidderminster Rd, Croy. CR0 141 DP102
Kidderpore Av, NW3 64 DA63
Kidderpore Gdns, NW3 64 DA63
Kidd Pl, SE7 104 EL78
Kidlington Way, NW9 42 CS54
Kielder Cl, Ilf. IG6 49 ET51
Kiffen St, EC2 197 L4
Kilberry Cl, Islw. TW7 97 CD81
KILBURN, NW6 82 DA68
⊖ Kilburn 81 CZ65
Kilburn Br, NW6
off Kilburn High Rd 81 CZ66
Kilburn Gate, NW6
off Kilburn Priory 82 DB68
⇌ Kilburn High Road 82 DA67
Kilburn High Rd, NW6 81 CZ66
Kilburn La, W9 81 CX69
W10 81 CX69
⊖ Kilburn Park 82 DA68
Kilburn Pk Rd, NW6 82 DA69
Kilburn Pl, NW6 82 DA67
Kilburn Priory, NW6 82 DB67
Kilburn Sq, NW6
off Kilburn High Rd 82 DA67
Kilburn Vale, NW6
off Belsize Rd 82 DB67
Kilby Cl, Wat. WD25 24 BX35
Kilby Ter, Wdf.Grn. IG8
off Baddow Cl 48 EK51
Kilcorral Cl, Epsom KT17 157 CU114
Kildare Cl, Ruis. HA4 60 BW60
Kildare Gdns, W2 82 DA72
Kildare Rd, E16 86 EG71
Kildare Ter, W2 82 DA72
Kildare Wk, E14
off Farrance St 85 EA72
Kildonan Cl, Wat. WD17 23 BT39
Kildoran Rd, SW2 121 DL85
Kildowan Rd, Ilf. IG3 70 EU60
Kilgour Rd, SE23 123 DY86
Kilkie St, SW6 100 DC82
Killarney Rd, SW18 120 DC86
Killasser Ct, Tad. KT20 173 CW123
Killburns Mill Cl, Wall. SM6
off London Rd 159 DH105
Killearn Rd, SE6 123 ED88
Killester Gdns, Wor.Pk. KT4 157 CV105
Killewarren Way, Orp. BR5 146 EW100
Killick Cl, Sev. (Dunt.Grn.)
TN13 190 FE121
Killick St, N1 83 DM68
Killieser Av, SW2 121 DL89
Killip Cl, E16 86 EF72
Killowen Av, Nthlt. UB5 60 CC64
Killowen Rd, E9 85 DX65
Killy Hill, Wok. (Chobham)
GU24 150 AS108
Killyon Rd, SW8 101 DJ82
Killyon Ter, SW8 101 DJ82
Kilmaine Rd, SW6 99 CY80
Kilmarnock Gdns, Dag. RM8
off Lindsey Rd 70 EW62
Kilmarnock Pk, Reig. RH2 184 DB133
Kilmarnock Rd, Wat. WD19 40 BX49
Kilmarsh Rd, W6 99 CW77
Kilmartin Av, SW16 141 DM97
Kilmartin Rd, Ilf. IG3 70 EU61
Kilmartin Way, Horn. RM12 71 FH64
Kilmeston Way, SE15
off Daniel Gdns 102 DT80
Kilmington Cl, Brwd. CM13 55 GB47
Kilmington Rd, SW13 99 CU79
Kilmiston Av, Shep. TW17 135 BQ100
Kilmorey Gdns, Twick. TW1 117 CH85
Kilmorey Rd, Twick. TW1 97 CH84
Kilmorie Rd, SE23 123 DY88
Kiln Av, Amer. HP6 20 AW38
Kiln Cl, Hayes UB3
off Brickfield La 95 BR79
Kilndown, Grav. DA12 131 GK93
Kilner St, E14 85 EA71
Kiln La, Bet. (Brock.) RH3 182 CQ134
Chesham (Ley Hill) HP5 4 AV31
Epsom KT17 156 CS111
Woking (Ripley) GU23 168 BH124
Kiln Ms, SW17 120 DD92
Kiln Pl, NW5 64 DG64
Kiln Rd, Epp. (N.Wld.Bas.)
CM16 18 FA27
Kilnside, Esher (Clay.) KT10 155 CG108
Kiln Way, Grays (Bad.Dene)
RM17 110 FZ78
Northwood HA6 39 BS51
Kilnwood, Sev. (Halst.) TN14 164 EZ113
Kiln Wd La, Rom. (Hav.at.Bow.)
RM4 51 FD50
Kilpatrick Way, Hayes UB4 78 BY71
Kilravock St, W10 81 CY69
Kilross Rd, Felt. TW14 115 BR88
Kilrue La, Walt. KT12 153 BT105
Kilrush Ter, Wok. GU21 167 BA116
Kilsby Wk, Dag. RM9
off Rugby Rd 88 EV65
Kilsha Rd, Walt. KT12 135 BV100
Kilsmore La, Wal.Cr. (Chsht.)
EN8 15 DX28
Kilvinton Dr, Enf. EN2 30 DR38
Kilworth Av, Brwd. CM15 55 GA44
Kimbell Gdns, SW6 99 CY81
Kimbell Pl, SE3
off Tudway Rd 104 EJ84
Kimberley Av, E6 86 EL68
SE15 102 DV82
Ilford IG2 69 ER59
Romford RM7 71 FC58
Kimberley Cl, Slou. SL3 93 AZ77
Kimberley Dr, Sid. DA14 126 EX89
Kimberley Gdns, N4 65 DP57
Enfield EN1 30 DT41
Kimberley Gate, Brom. BR1
off Oaklands Rd 124 EF94
Kimberley Ind Est, E17 47 DZ53
Kimberley Pl, Pur. CR8
off Brighton Rd 159 DN111
Kimberley Ride, Cob. KT11 154 CB113
Kimberley Rd, E4 48 EE46
E11 67 ED61
E16 86 EF70
E17 47 DZ53
N17 46 DU54
N18 46 DV51
NW6 81 CY67
SW9 101 DL82
Beckenham BR3 143 DX96
Croydon CR0 141 DP100
Kimberley Way, E4 48 EE46
Kimber Rd, SW18 120 DA87
Kimble Cl, Wat. WD18 23 BS44
Kimble Cres, Bushey WD23 40 CC45
Kimble Rd, SW19 120 DD93
Kimbolton Cl, SE12 124 EF86
Kimbolton Grn, Borwd. WD6 26 CQ42
Kimbolton Row, SW3 198 B9
Kimmeridge Gdns, SE9 124 EL91
Kimmeridge Rd, SE9 124 EL91
Kimpton Av, Brwd. CM15 54 FV45
Kimpton Ho, SW15
off Fontley Way 119 CU87
Kimpton Pl, Wat. WD25 8 BX34
Kimpton Rd, SE5 102 DR81
Sutton SM3 139 CZ103
Kimptons Cl, Pot.B. EN6 11 CX33
Kimptons Mead, Pot.B. EN6 11 CX32
Kimpton Trade Business Cen,
Sutt. SM3 139 CZ103
Kinburn Dr, Egh. TW20 112 AY92
Kinburn St, SE16 203 H4
Kincaid Rd, SE15 102 DV80
Kincardine Gdns, W9
off Harrow Rd 81 CZ70
Kinch Gro, Wem. HA9 62 CM59
Kincraig Dr, Sev. TN13 190 FG124
Kinder Cl, SE28 88 EX73
Kindersley Way, Abb.L. WD5 7 BQ31
Kinder St, E1
off Cannon St Rd 84 DV72
Kinetic Cres, Enf. EN3 31 DZ36
Kinfauns Av, Horn. RM11 72 FJ58
Kinfauns Rd, SW2 121 DN89
Ilford IG3 70 EU60
Kingaby Gdns, Rain. RM13 89 FG66
King Acre Ct, Stai. TW18
off Moor La 113 BE90
King Alfred Av, SE6 123 EA90
King Alfred Rd, Rom. RM3 52 FM54
King & Queen Cl, SE9
off St. Keverne Rd 124 EL91
King & Queen St, SE17 201 J9
King Arthur Cl, SE15 102 DW80
King Arthur Ct, Wal.Cr. EN8 15 DX31
King Charles Cres, Surb.
KT5 138 CM101
King Charles Rd, Rad. (Shenley)
WD7 10 CL32
Surbiton KT5 138 CM99
King Charles St, SW1 199 N4
King Charles Ter, E1 202 E1
King Charles Wk, SW19
off Princes Way 119 CY88
Kingcup Cl, Croy. CR0
off Primrose La 143 DX102
King David La, E1 84 DW73
Kingdon Rd, NW6 82 DA65
King Edward Av, Dart. DA1 128 FK86
Rainham RM13 90 FK68
King Edward Dr, Chess. KT9
off Kelvin Gro 138 CL104
Grays RM16 110 GE75

★ Place of interest ⇌ Railway station ⊖ London Underground station DLR Docklands Light Railway station Tramlink station H Hospital

Kin - Kin

King Edward Ms, SW13 ... 99 CU81
King Edward Rd, E10 ... 67 EC60
E17 ... 67 DY55
Barnet EN5 ... 28 DA42
Brentwood CM14 ... 54 FW48
Greenhithe DA9 ... 129 FU85
Radlett (Shenley) WD7 ... 10 CM33
Romford RM1 ... 71 FF58
Waltham Cross EN8 ... 15 DY33
Watford WD19 ... 24 BY44
King Edward VII Av, Wind.
SL4 ... 92 AS80
H King Edward VII Hosp
for Officers, W1 ... 194 G6
King Edwards Gdns, W3 ... 80 CN74
King Edwards Gro, Tedd.
TW11 ... 117 CH93
King Edward's Pl, W3
off King Edward's Gdns ... 80 CN74
King Edwards Rd, E9 ... 84 DV67
N9 ... 46 DV45
Barking IG11 ... 87 ER67
King Edward's Rd, Enf. EN3 ... 31 DX42
King Edwards Rd, Ruis. HA4 ... 59 BR60
King Edward St, EC1 ... 197 H8
King Edward III Ms, SE16 ... 202 E5
King Edward Wk, SE1 ... 200 E6
Kingfield Cl, Wok. GU22 ... 167 AZ120
Kingfield Dr, Wok. GU22 ... 167 AZ120
Kingfield Gdns, Wok. GU22 ... 167 AZ120
Kingfield Grn, Wok. GU22 ... 167 AZ120
Kingfield Rd, W5 ... 79 CK70
Woking GU22 ... 166 AY120
Kingfield St, E14 ... 204 E9
Kingfisher Av, E11
off Eastern Av ... 68 EH58
Kingfisher Cl, SE28 ... 88 EW73
Brentwood CM13 ... 55 GA45
Harrow (Har.Wld.) HA3 ... 41 CF52
Northwood HA6 ... 39 BP53
Orpington BR5 ... 146 EX98
Walton-on-Thames KT12
off Old Esher Rd ... 154 BY106
Kingfisher Ct, SW19
off Queensmere Rd ... 119 CY89
Enfield EN2 *off Mount Vw* ... 29 DM38
Surbiton KT6 *off Ewell Rd* ... 138 CM101
Sutton SM1
off Sandpiper Rd ... 157 CZ106
Woking GU21
off Vale Fm Rd ... 166 AY117
Woking (Sheer.) GU21
off Blackmore Cres ... 151 BC114
Kingfisher Dr, Hem.H. HP3
off Belswains La ... 6 BM25
Redhill RH1 ... 184 DG131
Richmond TW10 ... 117 CH91
Staines TW18 ... 113 BF91
Kingfisher Gdns, S.Croy.
CR2 ... 161 DX111
Kingfisher Lure, Kings L. WD4 ... 7 BP29
Rickmansworth (Loud.)
WD3 ... 22 BH42
Kingfisher Rd, Upmin. RM14 ... 73 FT60
Kingfisher Sq, SE8 ... 103 DZ79
Kingfisher St, E6 ... 86 EL71
Kingfisher Wk, NW9
off Eagle Dr ... 42 CS54
Kingfisher Way, NW10 ... 62 CR64
Beckenham BR3 ... 143 DX99
King Frederik IX Twr, SE16 ... 203 M6
King Gdns, Croy. CR0 ... 159 DP106
King George Av, E16 ... 86 EK72
Bushey WD23 ... 24 CB44
Ilford IG2 ... 69 ER57
Walton-on-Thames KT12 ... 136 BX102
King George Cl, Rom. RM7 ... 71 FC55
Sunbury-on-Thames
TW16 ... 115 BS92
H King George Hosp
(Eastern Av), Ilf. IG2 ... 69 ER58
H King George Hosp
(Barley La), Ilf. IG3 ... 70 EV57
King George Rd, Wal.Abb.
EN9 ... 15 EC34
King Georges Av, Wat. WD18 ... 23 BS43
King Georges Dr, Add. (New Haw)
KT15 ... 152 BG110
Southall UB1 ... 78 BZ71
King George VI Av, Mitch.
CR4 ... 140 DF98
Westerham TN16 ... 178 EK116
King George Sq, Rich. TW10 ... 118 CM86
King Georges Rd, Brwd.
CM15 ... 54 FV44
King George's Trd Est, Chess.
KT9 ... 156 CN105
King George St, SE10 ... 103 EC80
Kingham Cl, SW18 ... 120 DC87
W11 ... 99 CY75
King Harolds Way, Bexh.
DA7 ... 106 EX80
King Henry Ms, Orp. BR6
off Osgood Av ... 163 ET106
King Henry's Ct, Wal.Abb. EN9
off Deer Pk Way ... 31 EC36
⊸ King Henry's Drive ... 161 EB109
King Henry's Dr, Croy.
(New Adgtn.) CR0 ... 161 EC109
King Henry's Ms, Enf. EN3 ... 31 EA37
King Henry's Reach, W6 ... 99 CW79
King Henry's Rd, NW3 ... 82 DE66
Kingston upon Thames
KT1 ... 138 CP97
King Henry St, N16 ... 66 DS64
King Henry's Wk, N1 ... 84 DS65
King Henry Ter, E1 ... 202 E1
Kinghorn St, EC1 ... 197 H7
King James Av, Pot.B. (Cuffley)
EN6 ... 13 DL29
King James Ct, SE1
off Borough Rd ... 101 DP75
King James St, SE1 ... 200 G5
King John Ct, EC2 ... 197 N4
King John's Cl, Stai. (Wrays.)
TW19 ... 112 AW86
King John St, E1 ... 85 DX71
King Johns Wk, SE9 ... 124 EK88
Kinglake Ct, Wok. GU21
off Raglan Rd ... 166 AS118
Kinglake Est, SE17 ... 201 N10
Kinglake St, SE17 ... 102 DS78
Kingly Ct, W1 ... 195 K10
Kingly St, W1 ... 195 K9
Kingsand Rd, SE12 ... 124 EG89
Kings Arbour, Sthl. UB2 ... 96 BY78
Kings Arms Ct, E1
off Old Montague St ... 84 DU71
Kings Arms Yd, EC2 ... 197 K8
Kingsash Dr, Hayes UB4 ... 78 BY70
Kings Av, N10 ... 64 DG55
N21 ... 45 DP46
King's Av, SW4 ... 121 DK87
SW12 ... 121 DK88
Kings Av, W5 ... 79 CK72
Bromley BR1 ... 124 EF93
Buckhurst Hill IG9 ... 48 EK47
Carshalton SM5 ... 158 DE108
Greenford UB6 ... 78 CB72
Hounslow TW3 ... 96 CB81
New Malden KT3 ... 138 CS98
Romford RM6 ... 70 EZ58
Sunbury-on-Thames TW16 ... 115 BT92
Watford WD18 ... 23 BT42
West Byfleet (Byfleet)
KT14 ... 152 BK112
Woodford Green IG8 ... 48 EH51
Kings Bench St, SE1 ... 200 G4
Kings Bench Wk, EC4 ... 196 E9
Kingsbridge Av, W3 ... 98 CM75
Kingsbridge Circ, Rom. RM3 ... 52 FL51
Kingsbridge Cl, Rom. RM3 ... 52 FL51
Kingsbridge Ct, E14
off Dockers Tanner Rd ... 103 EA77
Kingsbridge Cres, Sthl. UB1 ... 78 BZ71
Kingsbridge Dr, NW7
off Bittacy Hill ... 43 CY52
Kingsbridge Rd, W10 ... 81 CW72
Barking IG11 ... 87 ER68
Morden SM4 ... 139 CX101
Romford RM3 ... 52 FL51
Southall UB2 ... 96 BZ77
Walton-on-Thames KT12 ... 135 BV101
Kingsbridge Way, Hayes UB4 ... 77 BS69
Kingsbrook, Lthd. KT22
off Ryebrook Rd ... 171 CG118
KINGSBURY, NW9 ... 62 CP58
⊖ Kingsbury ... 62 CN57
Kingsbury Circle, NW9 ... 62 CN57
Kingsbury Cres, Stai. TW18 ... 113 BD91
Kingsbury Dr, Wind. (Old Wind.)
SL4 ... 112 AV86
H Kingsbury Hosp, NW9 ... 62 CN56
Kingsbury Rd, N1 ... 84 DS65
NW9 ... 62 CP57
Kingsbury Ter, N1 ... 84 DS65
Kingsbury Trd Est, NW9 ... 62 CR58
Kings Chace Vw, Enf. EN2
off Crofton Way ... 29 DN40
Kings Chase, Brwd. CM14 ... 54 FW48
East Molesey KT8 ... 136 CC97
Kingsclere Cl, SW15 ... 119 CU87
Kingsclere Ct, Barn. EN5
off Gloucester Rd ... 28 DC43
Kingsclere Pl, Enf. EN2
off Chase Side ... 30 DQ40
Kingscliffe Gdns, SW19 ... 119 CZ88
Kings Cl, E10 ... 67 EB59
NW4 ... 63 CX56
Chalfont St. Giles HP8 ... 36 AX47
Dartford DA1 ... 107 FE84
Kings Langley (Chipper.)
WD4 ... 6 BH31
Northwood HA6 ... 39 BT51
Staines TW18 ... 114 BK94
Thames Ditton KT7 ... 137 CG100
Walton-on-Thames KT12 ... 135 BV102
King's Cl, Wat. WD18
off Lady's Cl ... 23 BV42
H King's Coll Hosp, SE5 ... 102 DR82
H King's Coll Hosp Dulwich,
SE22 ... 102 DS84
Kings Coll Rd, NW3 ... 82 DE66
Ruislip HA4 ... 59 BT58
Kingscote Rd, W4 ... 98 CR76
Croydon CR0 ... 142 DV101
New Malden KT3 ... 138 CR97
Kingscote St, EC4 ... 196 F10
Kings Ct, E13 ... 86 EH67
W6 *off King St* ... 99 CU77
Tadworth KT20 ... 173 CW122
Wembley HA9 ... 62 CP61
Kingscourt Rd, SW16 ... 121 DK90
Kings Ct S, SW3
off Chelsea Manor Gdns ... 100 DE78
Kings Cres, N4 ... 66 DQ62
Kings Cres Est, N4 ... 66 DQ61
Kingscroft Rd, NW2 ... 81 CZ65
Banstead SM7 ... 174 DD115
Leatherhead KT22 ... 171 CH120
KING'S CROSS, N1 ... 83 DK67
≠ King's Cross ... 195 P1
King's Cross Br, N1 ... 196 A2
King's Cross Rd, WC1 ... 196 C2
⊖ King's Cross St. Pancras ... 196 A1
≠ King's Cross Thameslink ... 196 A1
Kingsdale Ct, Wal.Abb. EN9
off Lamplighters Cl ... 16 EG34
Kingsdale Gdns, W11 ... 81 CX74
Kingsdale Rd, SE18 ... 105 ET80
SE20 ... 123 DX94
Kingsdene, Tad. KT20 ... 173 CV121
Kingsdown Av, W3 ... 80 CS73
W13 ... 97 CH75
South Croydon CR2 ... 159 DP109
Kingsdown Cl, SE16
off Masters Dr ... 102 DV78
W10 ... 81 CX72
Gravesend DA12
off Farley Rd ... 131 GM88
Kingsdowne Rd, Surb. KT6 ... 138 CL101
Kingsdown Rd, E11 ... 68 EE62
N19 ... 65 DL61
Epsom KT17 ... 157 CU113
Sutton SM3 ... 157 CY106
Kingsdown Way, Brom. BR2 ... 144 EG101
Kings Dr, Edg. HA8 ... 42 CM49
Gravesend DA12 ... 131 GH90
Surbiton KT5 ... 138 CN101
Teddington TW11 ... 117 CD92
Thames Ditton KT7 ... 137 CH100
Wembley HA9 ... 62 CP61
Kings Dr, The, Walt. KT12 ... 153 BT110
Kingsend, Ruis. HA4 ... 59 BR60
KINGS FARM, Grav. ... 131 GJ90
Kings Fm Av, Rich. TW10 ... 98 CN84
Kings Fm Rd, Rick. (Chorl.)
WD3 ... 21 BD44
Kingsfield Av, Har. HA2 ... 60 CB56
Kingsfield Ct, Wat. WD19 ... 40 BX45
Kingsfield Dr, Enf. EN3 ... 31 DX35
Kingsfield Ho, SE9 ... 124 EK90
Kingsfield Rd, Har. HA1 ... 61 CD59
Watford WD19 ... 40 BX45
Kingsfield Ter, Dart. DA1
off Priory Rd S ... 128 FK86
Kingsfield Way, Enf. EN3 ... 31 DX35
Kingsford Av, Wall. SM6 ... 159 DL108
Kingsford St, NW5 ... 64 DF64
Kingsford Way, E6 ... 87 EM71
Kings Gdns, NW6
off West End La ... 82 DA66
Ilford IG1 ... 69 ER60
Upminster RM14 ... 73 FS59
King's Garth Ms, SE23
off London Rd ... 122 DW89
Kingsgate, Wem. HA9 ... 62 CQ62
Kingsgate Av, N3 ... 64 DA55
Kingsgate Cl, Bexh. DA7 ... 106 EY81
Orpington BR5
off Main Rd ... 146 EW97
Kingsgate Pl, NW6 ... 82 DA66
Kingsgate Rd, NW6 ... 82 DA66
Kingston upon Thames
KT2 ... 138 CL95
Kings Grn, Loug. IG10 ... 32 EL41
Kingsground, SE9 ... 124 EL87
Kings Gro, SE15 ... 102 DV80
Romford RM1 ... 71 FG57
Kingshall Ms, SE13
off Lewisham Rd ... 103 EC83
Kings Hall Rd, Beck. BR3 ... 123 DY94
Kings Head Hill, E4 ... 47 EB45
Kings Head La, W.Byf. (Byfleet)
KT14 ... 152 BK111
Kings Head Yd, SE1 ... 201 K3
Kings Highway, SE18 ... 105 ES79
Kings Hill, Loug. IG10 ... 32 EL40
Kingshill Av, Har. HA3 ... 61 CH56
Hayes UB4 ... 77 BS69
Northolt UB5 ... 77 BU69
Romford RM5 ... 51 FC51
Worcester Park KT4 ... 139 CU101
Kingshill Dr, Har. HA3 ... 61 CH55
Kingshold Est, E9
off Victoria Pk Rd ... 84 DW67
Kingshold Rd, E9 ... 84 DW66
Kingsholm Gdns, SE9 ... 104 EK84
Kingshurst Rd, SE12 ... 124 EG87
Kingside Business Pk, SE18
off Woolwich Ch St ... 104 EL76
Kings Keep, Kings.T. KT1
off Beaufort Rd ... 138 CL98
KINGSLAND, N1 ... 84 DS65
Kingsland, NW8
off Broxwood Way ... 82 DE67
Potters Bar EN6 ... 11 CZ33
Kingsland Grn, E8 ... 84 DS65
Kingsland High St, E8 ... 66 DT64
Kingsland Pas, E8
off Kingsland Grn ... 84 DS65
Kingsland Rd, E2 ... 197 N2
E8 ... 84 DS68
E13 ... 86 EJ69
Kings La, Egh. (Eng.Grn.)
TW20 ... 112 AU92
Kings Langley (Chipper.)
WD4 ... 6 BG31
Sutton SM1 ... 158 DD107
KINGS LANGLEY ... 6 BM30
≠ Kings Langley ... 7 BQ30
Kings Langley Bypass, Kings L.
WD4 ... 6 BK28
Kingslawn Cl, SW15
off Howards La ... 119 CV85
Kingsleigh Cl, Lthd. KT22 ... 171 CG120
Kingsleigh Pl, Mitch. CR4
off Chatsworth Pl ... 140 DF97
Kingsleigh Wk, Brom. BR2
off Stamford Dr ... 144 EF98
Kingsley Av, W13 ... 79 CG72
Banstead SM7 ... 174 DA115
Borehamwood WD6 ... 26 CM40
Dartford DA1 ... 128 FN85
Egham (Eng.Grn.) TW20 ... 112 AV93
Hounslow TW3 ... 96 CC82
Southall UB1 ... 78 CA73
Sutton SM1 ... 158 DD105
Waltham Cross (Chsht.)
EN8 ... 14 DV29
Kingsley Cl, N2 ... 64 DC57
Dagenham RM10 ... 71 FB63
Kingsley Ct, Edg. HA8 ... 42 CP47
Kingsley Dr, Wor.Pk. KT4
off Badgers Copse ... 139 CT103
Kingsley Flats, SE1
off Old Kent Rd ... 102 DS77
Kingsley Gdns, E4 ... 47 EA50
Hornchurch RM11 ... 72 FK56
Kingsley Ms, E1 ... 202 E1
W8 *off Stanford Rd* ... 100 DB76
Chislehurst BR7 ... 125 EP93
Kingsley Pl, N6 ... 64 DG59
Kingsley Rd, E7 ... 86 EG66
E17 ... 47 EC54
N13 ... 45 DN49
NW6 ... 81 CZ67
SW19 ... 120 DB92
Kingsley Rd, Brwd CM13 ... 55 GD45
Croydon CR0 ... 141 DN102
Harrow HA2 ... 60 CC63
Hounslow TW3 ... 96 CC82
Ilford IG6 ... 49 EQ53
Loughton IG10 ... 33 ER41
Orpington BR6 ... 163 ET108
Pinner HA5 ... 60 BZ56
Kingsley St, SW11 ... 100 DF83
Kingsley Wk, Grays RM16 ... 111 GG77
Kingsley Way, N2 ... 64 DC58
Kingsley Wd Dr, SE9 ... 125 EM90
Kingslyn Cres, SE19 ... 142 DS95
Kings Lynn Cl, Rom. RM3
off Kings Lynn Dr ... 52 FK51
Kings Lynn Dr, Rom. RM3 ... 52 FK51
Kings Lynn Path, Rom. RM3
off Kings Lynn Dr ... 52 FK51
Kings Mall, W6 ... 99 CW77
Kingsman Par, SE18
off Woolwich Ch St ... 105 EM76
Kingsman St, SE18 ... 105 EM76
Kingsmead, Barn. EN5 ... 28 DA42
Potters Bar (Cuffley) EN6 ... 13 DL28
Richmond TW10 ... 118 CM86
Waltham Cross EN8 ... 15 DX28
Westerham (Bigg.H.)
TN16 ... 178 EK116
Kingsmead Av, N9 ... 46 DV46
NW9 ... 62 CR59
Mitcham CR4 ... 141 DJ97
Romford RM1 ... 71 FE58
Sunbury-on-Thames
TW16 ... 136 BW97
Surbiton KT6 ... 138 CN103
Worcester Park KT4 ... 139 CV104
Kingsmead Cl, Epsom KT19 ... 156 CR108
Sidcup DA15 ... 126 EU89
Teddington TW11 ... 117 CG93
Kingsmead Dr, Nthlt. UB5 ... 78 BZ66
Kingsmead Est, E9
off Kingsmead Way ... 67 DY63
Kings Meadow, Kings L. WD4 ... 6 BN28
Kings Mead Pk, Esher (Clay.)
KT10 ... 155 CE108
Kingsmead Rd, SW2 ... 121 DN89
Kingsmead Way, E9 ... 67 DY63
Kingsmere Cl, SW15
off Felsham Rd ... 99 CY83
Kingsmere Pk, NW9 ... 62 CP60
Kingsmere Pl, N16 ... 66 DR60
Kingsmere Rd, SW19 ... 119 CX89
Kings Ms, SW4 *off King's Av* ... 121 DL85
King's Ms, WC1 ... 196 C5
Kings Ms, Chig. IG7 ... 49 EQ47
Kingsmill Gdns, Dag. RM9 ... 70 EZ64
Kingsmill Rd, Dag. RM9 ... 70 EZ64
Kingsmill Ter, NW8 ... 82 DD68
Kingsnympton Pk, Kings.T.
KT2 ... 118 CP93
Kings Oak, Rom. RM7 ... 70 FA55
H King's Oak Private Hosp,
Enf. EN2 ... 29 DN38
King's Orchard, SE9 ... 124 EL86
Kings Paddock, Hmptn.
TW12 ... 136 CC95
Kings Par, Cars. SM5
off Wrythe La ... 140 DE104
Kingspark Ct, E18 ... 68 EG55
King's Pas, E11 ... 68 EE59
Kings Pas, Kings.T. KT1 ... 137 CK96
Kings Pl, SE1 ... 201 H5
W4 ... 98 CQ78
Buckhurst Hill IG9 ... 48 EJ47
Loughton IG10 ... 48 EK45
King Sq, EC1 ... 197 H3
King's Reach Twr, SE1 ... 200 E2
Kings Ride Gate, Rich. TW10 ... 98 CN84
Kingsridge, SW19 ... 119 CY89
Kingsridge Gdns, Dart. DA1 ... 128 FK86
Kings Rd, E4 ... 47 ED46
E6 ... 86 EJ67
E11 ... 68 EE59
King's Rd, N17 ... 46 DT53
Kings Rd, N18 ... 46 DU50
N22 ... 45 DM53
NW10 ... 81 CV66
SE25 ... 142 DU97
King's Rd, SW1 ... 198 C10
SW3 ... 198 C10
SW6 ... 100 DB81
SW10 ... 100 DB81
Kings Rd, SW14 ... 98 CR83
SW19 ... 120 DA93
W5 ... 79 CK71
Addlestone (New Haw)
KT15 ... 152 BH110
Barking IG11 *off North St* ... 87 EQ66
Barnet EN5 ... 27 CW41
Brentwood CM14 ... 54 FW48
Chalfont St. Giles HP8 ... 36 AX47
Egham TW20 ... 113 BA91
Feltham TW13 ... 116 BW88
Harrow HA2 ... 60 BZ61
Kingston upon Thames
KT2 ... 118 CL94
Mitcham CR4 ... 140 DG97
Orpington BR6 ... 163 ET105
Richmond TW10 ... 118 CM85
Romford RM1 ... 71 FG57
St. Albans (Lon.Col.) AL2 ... 9 CJ26
Slough SL1 ... 92 AS76
Surbiton KT6 ... 137 CJ102
Sutton SM2 ... 158 DA110
Teddington TW11 ... 117 CD92
Twickenham TW1 ... 117 CH86
King's Rd, Uxb. UB8 ... 76 BK68
Kings Rd, Wal.Cr. EN8 ... 15 DY34
Walton-on-Thames KT12 ... 135 BV103
West Drayton UB7 ... 94 BM75
Westerham (Bigg.H.) TN16 ... 178 EJ118
Woking GU21 ... 167 BA116
Kings Rd Bungalows, Har. HA2
off Kings Rd ... 60 BZ62
King's Scholars' Pas, SW1 ... 199 K8
King Stairs Cl, SE16 ... 202 E4
King's Ter, NW1 *off Plender St* ... 83 DJ67
Kings Ter, Islw. TW7
off Worple Rd ... 97 CG83
Kingsthorpe Rd, SE26 ... 123 DX91
≠ Kingston ... 138 CL95
Kingston Av, Felt. TW14 ... 115 BS86
Leatherhead KT22 ... 171 CH121
Sutton SM3 ... 139 CY104
West Drayton UB7 ... 76 BM73
Kingston Br, Kings.T. KT1 ... 137 CK96
Kingston Bypass, SW15 ... 118 CS91
SW20 ... 118 CS91
Esher KT10 ... 137 CG104
New Malden KT3 ... 139 CT95
Surbiton KT5, KT6 ... 138 CL104
Kingston Cl, Nthlt. UB5 ... 78 BZ67
Romford RM6 ... 70 EY55
Teddington TW11 ... 117 CH93
Kingston Ct, N4
off Wiltshire Gdns ... 66 DQ58
Gravesend (Nthflt.) DA11 ... 130 GB85
Kingston Cres, Ashf. TW15 ... 114 BJ92
Beckenham BR3 ... 143 DZ95
Kingston Gdns, Croy. CR0
off Wandle Rd ... 141 DL104
Kingston Hall Rd, Kings.T.
KT1 ... 137 CK97
Kingston Hill, Kings.T. KT2 ... 118 CQ93
Kingston Hill Av, Rom. RM6 ... 70 EY55
Kingston Hill Pl, Kings.T. KT2 ... 118 CQ91
H Kingston Hosp, Kings.T.
KT2 ... 138 CP95
Kingston Ho Gdns, Lthd. KT22
off Upper Fairfield Rd ... 171 CG121
Kingston La, Tedd. TW11 ... 117 CG92
Uxbridge UB8 ... 76 BL69
West Drayton UB7 ... 94 BM75
★ Kingston Mus & Heritage
Cen, Kings.T. KT1 ... 138 CL96
Kingston Pk Est, Kings.T.
KT2 ... 118 CP93
Kingston Pl, Har. HA3
off Richmond Gdns ... 41 CF52
Kingston Ri, Add. (New Haw)
KT15 ... 152 BG110
Kingston Rd, N9 ... 46 DU47
SW15 ... 119 CU88
SW19 ... 139 CZ95
SW20 ... 139 CW96
Ashford TW15 ... 114 BL93
Barnet EN4 ... 28 DD43
Epsom KT17, KT19 ... 156 CS106
Ilford IG1 ... 69 EP63
Kingston upon Thames
KT1 ... 138 CP97
Leatherhead KT22 ... 171 CG117
New Malden KT3 ... 138 CR98
Romford RM1 ... 71 FF56
Southall UB2 ... 96 BZ75
Staines TW18 ... 114 BH93
Surbiton KT5 ... 138 CP103
Teddington TW11 ... 117 CH92
Worcester Park KT4 ... 138 CP103
Kingston Sq, SE19 ... 122 DR92
KINGSTON UPON THAMES ... 138 CL96
KINGSTON VALE, SW15 ... 118 CS91
Kingston Vale, SW15 ... 118 CR91
Kingstown St, NW1 ... 82 DG67
King St, E13 ... 86 EG70
EC2 ... 197 J9
N2 ... 64 DD55
N17 ... 46 DT53
SW1 ... 199 L3
W3 ... 80 CP74
W6 ... 99 CU77
WC2 ... 195 P10
Chertsey KT16 ... 134 BG102
Gravesend DA12 ... 131 GH86
Richmond TW9 ... 117 CK85
Southall UB2 ... 96 BY76
Twickenham TW1 ... 117 CG88
Watford WD18 ... 24 BW42
Kings Wk, Grays RM17 ... 110 GA79
King's Wk, Kings.T. KT2 ... 137 CK95
Kings Wk, S.Croy. CR2 ... 160 DV114
Kings Wk Shop Mall, SW3
off King's Rd ... 100 DF78
Kings Warren, Lthd. (Oxshott)
KT22 ... 154 CC111
Kingswater Pl, SW11
off Battersea Ch Rd ... 100 DE80
Kingsway, N12 ... 44 DC51
SW14 ... 98 CP83
WC2 ... 196 B8
Croydon CR0 ... 159 DM106
Enfield EN3 ... 30 DV43
Gerrards Cross (Chal.St.P.)
SL9 ... 56 AY55
Kings Way, Har. HA1 ... 61 CE56
Kingsway, Hayes UB3 ... 77 BQ71
Iver SL0 *off High St* ... 75 BE72
New Malden KT3 ... 139 CW98
Orpington BR5 ... 145 ES99
Potters Bar (Cuffley) EN6 ... 13 DL30
Staines TW19 ... 114 BK88
Watford WD25 ... 8 BW34
Wembley HA9 ... 62 CL63
West Wickham BR4 ... 144 EE104
Woking GU21 ... 166 AX118
Woodford Green IG8 ... 48 EJ50
Kingsway, The, Epsom KT17 ... 157 CT111
Kingsway Av, S.Croy. CR2 ... 160 DW109
Woking GU21 ... 166 AX118
Kingsway Business Pk, Hmptn.
TW12 ... 136 BZ95
Kingsway Cres, Har. HA2 ... 60 CC56
Kingsway Pl, EC1 ... 196 E4
Kingsway Rd, Sutt. SM3 ... 157 CY108
Kingsway Shop Cen, NW3
off Hampstead High St ... 64 DC63
Kingswear Rd, NW5 ... 65 DH62
Ruislip HA4 ... 59 BU61
Kingswell Ride, Pot.B. (Cuffley)
EN6 ... 13 DL30
Kingswey Business Pk, Wok.
GU21 ... 151 BC114
KINGSWOOD, Tad. ... 173 CY123
KINGSWOOD, Wat. ... 7 BV34

★ Place of interest ≠ Railway station ⊖ London Underground station DLR Docklands Light Railway station ⊸ Tramlink station H Hospital

⇌ **Kingswood** 173 CZ121
Kingswood Av, NW6 81 CY67
Belvedere DA17 106 EZ77
Bromley BR2 144 EE97
Hampton TW12 116 CB93
Hounslow TW3 96 BZ81
South Croydon CR2 176 DV115
Swanley BR8 147 FF98
Thornton Heath CR7 141 DN99
Kingswood Cl, N20 28 DC44
SW8 101 DL80
Dartford DA1 128 FJ86
Egham (Eng.Grn.) TW20 112 AX91
Enfield EN1 30 DS43
New Malden KT3
off Motspur Pk 139 CT100
Orpington BR6 145 ER101
Surbiton KT6 138 CL101
Weybridge KT13 153 BP108
Kingswood Creek, Stai. (Wrays.)
TW19 112 AX85
Kingswood Dr, SE19 122 DS91
Carshalton SM5 140 DF102
Sutton SM2 158 DB109
Kingswood Est, SE21
off Bowen Dr 122 DS91
Kingswood La, S.Croy. CR2 160 DW113
Warlingham CR6 176 DW115
Kingswood Ms, N15
off Harringay Rd 65 DP57
Kingswood Pk, N3 43 CZ54
Kingswood Pl, SE13 104 EE84
Kingswood Ri, Egh. (Eng.Grn.)
TW20 112 AX92
Kingswood Rd, E11
off Grove Grn Rd 67 ED61
SE20 122 DW93
SW2 121 DL86
SW19 119 CZ94
W4 98 CQ76
Bromley BR2 143 ED98
Ilford IG3 70 EU60
Sevenoaks (Dunt.Grn.)
TN13 181 FE120
Tadworth KT20 173 CV121
Watford WD25 7 BV34
Wembley HA9 62 CN62
Kingswood Ter, W4
off Kingswood Rd 98 CQ76
Kingswood Way, S.Croy.
CR2 160 DW113
Wallington SM6 159 DL106
Kingsworth Cl, Beck. BR3 143 DY99
Kingsworthy Cl, Kings.T.
KT1 138 CM97
King's Yd, SW15
off Stanbridge Rd 99 CW83
Kingthorpe Rd, NW10 80 CR66
Kingthorpe Ter, NW10 80 CR65
Kingwell Rd, Barn. EN4 28 DD38
Kingweston Cl, NW2
off Windmill Dr 63 CY62
King William Ct, Wal.Abb. EN9
off Deer Pk Way 31 EB36
King William IV Gdns, SE20
off St. John's Rd 122 DW93
King William La, SE10
off Orlop St 104 EE78
King William St, EC4 201 L1
King William Wk, SE10 103 EC79
Kingwood Rd, SW6 99 CX81
Kinlet Rd, SE18 105 EQ81
Kinloch Dr, NW9 62 CS59
Kinloch St, N7
off Hornsey Rd 65 DM62
Kinloss Ct, N3
off Haslemere Gdns 63 CZ56
Kinloss Gdns, N3 63 CZ56
Kinloss Rd, Cars. SM5 140 DC101
Kinnaird Av, W4 98 CQ80
Bromley BR1 124 EF93
Kinnaird Cl, Brom. BR1 124 EF93
Kinnaird Way, Wdf.Grn. IG8 49 EM51
Kinnear Rd, W12 99 CT75
Kinnerton Pl N, SW1 198 E5
Kinnerton Pl S, SW1 198 E5
Kinnerton St, SW1 198 F5
Kinnerton Yd, SW1 198 E5
Kinnoul Rd, W6 99 CY79
Kinross Av, Wor.Pk. KT4 139 CU103
Kinross Cl, Edg. HA8
off Tayside Dr 42 CP47
Harrow HA3 62 CM57
Sunbury-on-Thames TW16 115 BT92
Kinross Dr, Sun. TW16 115 BT92
Kinross Ter, E17 47 DZ54
Kinsale Rd, SE15 102 DU83
Kintore Way, SE1 201 P8
Kintyre Cl, SW16 141 DM97
Kinveachy Gdns, SE7 104 EL78
Kinver Rd, SE26 122 DW91
Kipings, Tad. KT20 173 CX122
Kipling Av, Til. RM18 111 GH81
Kipling Dr, SW19 120 DD93
Kipling Est, SE1 201 L5
Kipling Pl, Stan. HA7
off Uxbridge Rd 41 CF51
Kipling Rd, Bexh. DA7 106 EY81
Dartford DA1 128 FP85
Kipling St, SE1 201 L5
Kipling Ter, N9 46 DR48
Kipling Twrs, Rom. RM3 51 FH52
KIPPINGTON, Sev. 190 FG126
Kippington Cl, Sev. TN13 190 FF124
Kippington Dr, SE9 124 EK88
Kippington Ho, Sev. TN13
off Kippington Rd 190 FG126
Kippington Rd, Sev. TN13 190 FG124
Kirby Cl, Epsom KT19 157 CT106
Ilford IG6 49 ES51
Loughton IG10 48 EL45
Northwood HA6 39 BT51
Romford RM3 52 FN50
Kirby Est, SE16 202 D6
Kirby Gro, SE1 201 M4
Kirby Rd, Dart. DA2 128 FQ87
Woking GU21 166 AW117
Kirby St, EC1 196 E6
Kirby Way, Walt. KT12 136 BW100
Kirchen Rd, W13 79 CH73
Kirkby Cl, N11
off Coverdale Rd 44 DG51
Kirkcaldy Grn, Wat. WD19
off Trevose Way 40 BW48
Kirk Ct, Sev. TN13 190 FG123
Kirkdale, SE26 122 DV89
Kirkdale Rd, E11 68 EE60
Kirkfield Cl, W13
off Broomfield Rd 79 CH74
Kirkham Rd, E6 86 EL72
Kirkham St, SE18 105 ES79
Kirkland Av, Ilf. IG5 49 EN54
Woking GU21 166 AS116
Kirkland Cl, Sid. DA15 125 ES86
Kirkland Dr, Enf. EN2 29 DP39
Kirkland Wk, E8 84 DT65
Kirk La, SE18 105 EQ79
Kirkleas Rd, Surb. KT6 138 CL102
Kirklees Rd, Dag. RM8 70 EW64
Thornton Heath CR7 141 DN99
Kirkley Rd, SW19 140 DA95
Kirkly Cl, S.Croy. CR2 160 DS109
Kirkman Pl, W1 195 M7
Kirkmichael Rd, E14
off Dee St 85 EC72
Kirk Ri, Sutt. SM1 140 DB104
Kirk Rd, E17 67 DZ58
Kirkside Rd, SE3 104 EG79
Kirks Pl, E14
off Rhodeswell Rd 85 DZ71
Kirkstall Av, N17 66 DR56
Kirkstall Gdns, SW2 121 DK88
Kirkstall Rd, SW2 121 DK88
Kirkstead Ct, E5
off Mandeville St 67 DY62
Kirksted Rd, Mord. SM4 140 DB102
Kirkstone Way, Brom. BR1 124 EE94
Kirk St, WC1
off Northington St 83 DM70
Kirkton Rd, N15 66 DS56
Kirkwall Pl, E2 84 DW69
Kirkwall Spur, Slou. SL1 74 AS71
Kirkwood Rd, SE15 102 DV82
Kirn Rd, W13 *off Kirchen Rd* 79 CH73
Kirrane Cl, N.Mal. KT3 139 CT99
Kirtley Rd, SE26 123 DY91
Kirtling St, SW8 101 DJ80
Kirton Cl, W4 *off Dolman Rd* 98 CR77
Hornchurch RM12 90 FJ65
Kirton Gdns, E2
off Chambord St 84 DT69
Kirton Rd, E13 86 EJ68
Kirton Wk, Edg. HA8 42 CQ52
Kirwyn Way, SE5 101 DP80
Kitcat Ter, E3 85 EA69
Kitchener Av, Grav. DA12 131 GJ90
Kitchener Rd, E7 86 EH65
E17 47 EB53
N2 64 DE55
N17 66 DR55
Dagenham RM10 89 FB65
Thornton Heath CR7 142 DR97
Kitchenride Cor, Cher.
KT16 151 BA105
Kite Pl, E2 *off Nelson Gdns* 84 DU69
Kite Yd, SW11
off Cambridge Rd 100 DF81
Kitley Gdns, SE19 142 DT95
Kitsmead La, Cher. (Longcr.)
KT16 132 AX103
Kitson Rd, SE5 102 DR80
SW13 99 CU81
Kitswell Way, Rad. WD7 9 CF33
Kitters Grn, Abb.L. WD5
off High St 7 BS31
Kittiwake Cl, S.Croy. CR2 161 DY110
Kittiwake Pl, Sutt. SM1
off Sandpiper Rd 157 CZ106
Kittiwake Rd, Nthlt. UB5 78 BX69
Kittiwake Way, Hayes UB4 78 BX71
Kitto Rd, SE14 103 DX82
KITT'S END, Barn. 27 CY37
Kitt's End Rd, Barn. EN5 27 CX36
Kiver Rd, N19 65 DK61
Kiwi Cl, Twick. TW1
off Crown Rd 117 CH86
Klea Av, SW4 121 DJ86
Knapdale Cl, SE23 122 DV89
Knapmill Rd, SE6 123 EA89
Knapmill Way, SE6 123 EB89
Knapp Cl, NW10 80 CS65
Knapp Rd, E3 85 EA70
Ashford TW15 114 BM91
Knapton Ms, SW17
off Seely Rd 120 DG93
Knaresborough Dr, SW18 120 DB88
Knaresborough Pl, SW5 100 DB77
Knatchbull Rd, NW10 80 CR67
SE5 102 DQ81
Knebworth Av, E17 47 EA53
Knebworth Path, Borwd.
WD6 26 CR42
Knebworth Rd, N16
off Nevill Rd 66 DS63
Knee Hill, SE2 106 EW77
Knee Hill Cres, SE2 106 EW77
Kneller Gdns, Islw. TW7 117 CD85
Kneller Rd, SE4 103 DY84
New Malden KT3 138 CS101
Twickenham TW2 116 CC86
Knighten St, E1 202 C3
Knighthead Pt, E14 103 EA76
Knightland Rd, E5 66 DV61
Knighton Cl, Rom. RM7 71 FD58
South Croydon CR2 159 DP108
Woodford Green IG8 48 EH49
Knighton Dr, Wdf.Grn. IG8 48 EG49
Knighton Grn, Buck.H. IG9
off High Rd 48 EH47
Knighton La, Buck.H. IG9 48 EH47
Knighton Pk Rd, SE26 123 DX92
Knighton Rd, E7 68 EG62
Romford RM7 71 FC58
Sevenoaks (Otford) TN14 181 FF116
Knighton Way La, Uxb. (Denh.)
UB9 76 BH65
Knightrider Ct, EC4 197 H10
Knightrider St, EC4
off Godliman St 84 DQ73
Knights Arc, SW1 198 D5
Knights Av, W5 98 CL75
⊖ **Knightsbridge** 198 D5
Knightsbridge, SW1 198 E5
SW7 198 C5
Knightsbridge Cl, Slou. (Langley)
SL3 *off High St* 93 BA77
Knightsbridge Cres, Stai.
TW18 114 BH93
Knightsbridge Gdns, Rom.
RM7 71 FD57
Knightsbridge Grn, SW1 198 D5
Knights Cl, E9
off Churchill Wk 66 DW64
Egham TW20 113 BD93
Knights Ct, Kings.T. KT1 138 CL97
Romford RM6 70 EY58
Knights Hill, SE27 121 DP92
Knights Hill Sq, SE27
off Knights Hill 121 DP91
Knights La, N9 46 DU48
Knights Manor Way, Dart.
DA1 128 FM86
Knights Ms, Sutt. SM2
off York Rd 158 DA108
Knights Pk, Kings.T. KT1 138 CL97
Knights Pl, Red. RH1
off Noke Dr 184 DG133
Knights Ridge, Orp. BR6
off Stirling Dr 164 EV106
Knights Rd, E16 205 N4
Stanmore HA7 41 CJ49
Knights Wk, SE11 200 F9
Romford (Abridge) RM4 34 EV41
Knight's Way, Brwd. CM13 55 GA48
Knights Way, Ilf. IG6 49 EQ51
Knightswood, Wok. GU21 166 AT118
Knightswood Cl, Edg. HA8 42 CQ47
Knightwood Cres, N.Mal.
KT3 138 CS100
Knipp Hill, Cob. KT11 154 BZ113
Knivet Rd, SW6 100 DA79
Knobs Hill Rd, E15 85 EB67
KNOCKHALL, Green. 129 FW85
Knockhall Chase, Green.
DA9 129 FV85
Knockhall Rd, Green. DA9 129 FW86
KNOCKHOLT, Sev. 180 EU116
⇌ **Knockholt** 164 EY109
Knockholt Cl, Sutt. SM2 158 DB110
Knockholt Main Rd, Sev. (Knock.)
TN14 180 EY115
KNOCKHOLT POUND, Sev. 180 EX115
Knockholt Rd, SE9 124 EK85
Sevenoaks (Halst.) TN14 164 EZ113
Knole, The, SE9 125 EN91
Gravesend (Istead Rise)
DA13 130 GE94
Knole Cl, Croy. CR0
off Stockbury Rd 142 DW100
Knole Gate, Sid. DA15
off Woodside Cres 125 ES90
★ **Knole Ho & Pk**, Sev.
TN15 191 FL126
Knole La, Sev. TN13, TN15 191 FJ126
Knole Rd, Dart. DA1 127 FG87
Sevenoaks TN13 191 FK123
Knole Way, Sev. TN13 191 FJ125
Knoll, The, W13 79 CJ71
Beckenham BR3 143 EB95
Bromley BR2 144 EG103
Chertsey KT16 133 BF102
Cobham KT11 154 CA113
Leatherhead KT22 171 CJ120
Knoll Ct, SE19 122 DT92
Knoll Cres, Nthwd. HA6 39 BS53
Knoll Dr, N14 44 DG45
Knollmead, Surb. KT5 138 CQ102
Knoll Pk Rd, Cher. KT16 133 BF102
Knoll Ri, Orp. BR6 145 ET102
Knoll Rd, SW18 120 DC85
Bexley DA5 126 FA87
Sidcup DA14 126 EV92
Knolls, The, Epsom KT17 173 CW116
Knolls Cl, Wor.Pk. KT4 139 CV104
Knollys Cl, SW16 121 DN90
Knollys Rd, SW16 121 DN90
Knolton Way, Slou. SL2 74 AW72
Knottisford St, E2 84 DW69
Knotts Grn Ms, E10 67 EB58
Knotts Grn Rd, E10 67 EB58
Knotts Pl, Sev. TN13 190 FG124
Knowland Way, Uxb. (Denh.)
UB9 57 BF58
Knowle, The, Tad. KT20 173 CW121
Knowle Av, Bexh. DA7 106 EY80
Knowle Cl, SW9 101 DN83
Knowle Gdns, W.Byf. KT14
off Madeira Rd 151 BF113
Knowle Grn, Stai. TW18 114 BG92
Knowle Gro, Vir.W. GU25 132 AW101
Knowle Gro Cl, Vir.W. GU25 132 AW101
Knowle Hill, Vir.W. GU25 132 AV101
Knowle Pk, Cob. KT11 170 BY115
Knowle Pk Av, Stai. TW18 114 BH93
Knowle Rd, Brom. BR2 144 EL103
Twickenham TW2 117 CE88
Knowles Cl, West Dr. UB7 76 BL74
Knowles Hill Cres, SE13 123 ED85
Knowles Wk, SW4 101 DJ83
Knowl Hill, Wok. GU22 167 BB119
Knowl Pk, Borwd. (Elstree)
WD6 26 CL43
Knowlton Grn, Brom. BR2 144 EF99
Knowl Way, Borwd. (Elstree)
WD6 26 CL42
Knowsley Av, Sthl. UB1 78 CA74
Knowsley Rd, SW11 100 DF82
Knoxfield Caravan Pk, Dart.
DA2 129 FS90
Knox Rd, E7 86 EF65
Knox St, W1 194 D6
Knoyle St, SE14
off Chubworthy St 103 DY79
Knutsford Av, Wat. WD24 24 BX38
Kohat Rd, SW19 120 DB92
Koh-i-noor Av, Bushey
WD23 24 CA44
Koonowla Cl, West. (Bigg.H.)
TN16 178 EK115
Kooringa, Warl. CR6 176 DV119
Korda Cl, Shep. TW17 134 BM97
Kossuth St, SE10 205 H10
Kotree Way, SE1 202 C9
Kramer Ms, SW5
off Kempsford Gdns 100 DA78
Kreedman Wk, E8 66 DU64
Kreisel Wk, Rich. TW9 98 CM79
Kuala Gdns, SW16 141 DM95
Kuhn Way, E7 *off Forest La* 68 EG64
Kydbrook Cl, Orp. BR5 145 ER101
Kylemore Cl, E6 *off Parr Rd* 86 EK68
Kylemore Rd, NW6 82 DA66
Kymberley Rd, Har. HA1 61 CE58
Kyme Rd, Horn. RM11 71 FF58
Kynance Cl, Rom. RM3 52 FJ48
Kynance Gdns, Stan. HA7 41 CJ53
Kynance Ms, SW7 100 DB76
Kynance Pl, SW7 100 DC76
Kynaston Av, N16
off Dynevor Rd 66 DT62
Thornton Heath CR7 142 DQ99
Kynaston Cl, Har. HA3 41 CD52
Kynaston Cres, Th.Hth. CR7 142 DQ99
Kynaston Rd, N16 66 DS62
Bromley BR1 124 EG92
Enfield EN2 30 DR39
Orpington BR5 146 EV101
Thornton Heath CR7 142 DQ99
Kynaston Wd, Har. HA3 41 CD52
Kynersley Cl, Cars. SM5
off William St 140 DF104
Kynock Rd, N18 46 DW49
Kyrle Rd, SW11 120 DG85
Kytes Dr, Wat. WD25 8 BX33
Kytes Est, Wat. WD25 8 BX33
Kyverdale Rd, N16 66 DT61

L

Laburnham Cl, Upmin. RM14 73 FU59
Wembley HA0
off Highcroft Av 80 CN67
Laburnham Gdns, Upmin.
RM14 73 FT59
Laburnum Av, N9 46 DS47
N17 46 DR52
Dartford DA1 128 FJ88
Hornchurch RM12 71 FF62
Sutton SM1 140 DE104
Swanley BR8 147 FC97
West Drayton UB7 76 BM73
Laburnum Cl, E4 47 DZ51
N11 44 DG51
SE15 *off Clifton Way* 102 DW80
Waltham Cross (Chsht.)
EN8 15 DX31
Laburnum Ct, E2
off Laburnum St 84 DT67
Stanmore HA7 41 CJ49
Laburnum Cres, Sun. TW16
off Batavia Rd 135 BV95
Laburnum Gdns, N21 46 DQ47
Croydon CR0 143 DX101
Laburnum Gro, N21 46 DQ47
NW9 62 CQ59
Gravesend (Nthflt.) DA11 130 GD87
Hounslow TW3 96 BZ84
New Malden KT3 138 CR96
Ruislip HA4 59 BR58
St. Albans AL2 8 CB25
Slough SL3 93 BB79
South Ockendon RM15 91 FW69
Southall UB1 78 BZ70
Laburnum Ho, Dag. RM10
off Bradwell Av 70 FA61
Laburnum Pl, Egh. (Eng.Grn.)
TW20 112 AV93
Laburnum Rd, SW19 120 DC94
Chertsey KT16 134 BG102
Epping CM16 18 EW29
Epsom KT18 156 CS113
Hayes UB3 95 BT77
Mitcham CR4 140 DG96
Woking GU22 166 AX120
Laburnum St, E2 84 DT67
Laburnum Wk, Horn. RM12 72 FJ64
Laburnum Way, Brom. BR2 145 EN101
Staines TW19 114 BM88
Waltham Cross (Chsht.) EN7
off Millcrest Rd 13 DP28
Lacebark Cl, Sid. DA15 125 ET87
Lacey Av, Couls. CR5 175 DN120
Lacey Cl, N9 46 DU47
Egham TW20 113 BD94
Lacey Dr, Couls. CR5 175 DN120
Dagenham RM8 70 EV63
Edgware HA8 42 CL49
Hampton TW12 136 BZ95
Lacey Grn, Couls. CR5 175 DN120
Lacey Wk, E3 85 EA68
Lackford Rd, Couls. CR5 174 DF118
Lackington St, EC2 197 L6
Lackmore Rd, Enf. EN1 30 DW35
Lacock Cl, SW19 120 DC93
Lacon Rd, SE22 102 DU84
Lacy Rd, SW15 99 CX84
Ladas Rd, SE27 122 DQ91
Ladbroke Ct, Red. RH1 184 DG132
Ladbroke Cres, W11
off Ladbroke Gro 81 CY72
Ladbroke Gdns, W11 81 CZ73
⊖ **Ladbroke Grove** 81 CY72
Ladbroke Gro, W10 81 CX70
W11 81 CY72
Redhill RH1 184 DG133
Ladbroke Ms, W11
off Ladbroke Rd 81 CY74
Ladbroke Rd, W11 81 CZ74
Enfield EN1 30 DT44
Epsom KT18 156 CR114
Redhill RH1 184 DG133
Ladbroke Sq, W11 81 CZ73
Ladbroke Ter, W11 81 CZ73
Ladbroke Wk, W11 81 CZ74
Ladbrook Cl, Pnr. HA5 60 BZ57
Ladbrooke Cl, Pot.B. EN6
off Strafford Gate 12 DA32
Ladbrooke Cres, Sid. DA14 126 EX90
Ladbrooke Dr, Pot.B. EN6 12 DA32
Ladbrook Rd, SE25 142 DR97
Ladderstile Ride, Kings.T. KT2 118 CP92
Ladderswood Way, N11 45 DJ50
Ladds Way, Swan. BR8 147 FD98
Lady Booth Rd, Kings.T. KT1 138 CL96
Ladybower Ct, E5
off Gilpin Rd 67 DY63
Ladycroft Gdns, Orp. BR6 163 EQ106
Ladycroft Rd, SE13 103 EB83
Ladycroft Wk, Stan. HA7 41 CK53
Ladycroft Way, Orp. BR6 163 EQ106
Lady Dock Path, SE16 203 K5
Ladyfield Cl, Loug. IG10 33 EP42
Ladyfields, Grav. (Nthflt.)
DA11 131 GF91
Loughton IG10 33 EP42
Ladygate La, Ruis. HA4 59 BP58
Ladygrove, Croy. CR0 161 DY109
Lady Hay, Wor.Pk. KT4 139 CT103
Lady Margaret Rd, N19 65 DJ63
NW5 65 DJ64
Southall UB1 78 BZ71
Ladymeadow, Kings L. WD4 6 BK27
Lady's Cl, Wat. WD18 23 BV42
Ladysmith Av, E6 86 EL68
Ilford IG2 69 ER59
Ladysmith Cl, NW7
off Colenso Dr 43 CU52
Ladysmith Rd, E16 86 EF69
N17 46 DU54
N18 46 DV50
SE9 125 EN86
Enfield EN1 30 DS41
Harrow HA3 41 CE54
Lady Somerset Rd, NW5 65 DH63
Ladythorpe Cl, Add. KT15
off Church Rd 152 BH105
Ladywalk, Rick. (Map.Cr.)
WD3 37 BE50
LADYWELL, SE13 123 EA85
⇌ **Ladywell** 123 EB85
Ladywell Cl, SE4
off Adelaide Av 103 DZ84
Ladywell Hts, SE4 123 DZ86
H **Ladywell Mental Health Unit - Uni Hosp Lewisham**, SE4 123 EA86
Ladywell Rd, SE13 123 EA85
Ladywell St, E15
off Plaistow Gro 86 EF67
Ladywood Av, Orp. BR5 145 ES99
Ladywood Cl, Rick. WD3 22 BH41
Ladywood Rd, Dart. (Lane End)
DA2 129 FS92
Surbiton KT6 138 CN103
Lady Yorke Pk, Iver SL0 75 BD65
Lafone Av, Felt. TW13
off Alfred Rd 116 BW88
Lafone St, SE1 201 P4
Lagado Ms, SE16 203 J3
Lagger, The, Ch.St.G. HP8 36 AV48
Lagger Cl, Ch.St.G. HP8 36 AV48
Laglands Cl, Reig. RH2 184 DC132
Lagonda Av, Ilf. IG6 49 ET51
Lagonda Way, Dart. DA1 108 FJ84
Lagoon Rd, Orp. BR5 146 EV99
Laidlaw Dr, N21 29 DM42
Laing Cl, Ilf. IG6 49 ER51
Laing Dean, Nthlt. UB5 78 BW67
Laings Av, Mitch. CR4 140 DF96
Lainlock Pl, Houns. TW3
off Spring Gro Rd 96 CB81
Lainson St, SW18 120 DA87
Lairdale Cl, SE21 122 DQ88
Laird Av, Grays RM16 110 GD75
Laird Ho, SE5 102 DQ80
Lairs Cl, N7 *off Manger Rd* 83 DL65
Laitwood Rd, SW12 121 DH88
Lake, The, Bushey (Bushey Hth.)
WD23 40 CC46
Lake Av, Brom. BR1 124 EG93
Rainham RM13 90 FK68
Lake Cl, SW19 *off Lake Rd* 119 CZ92
West Byfleet (Byfleet)
KT14 152 BK112
Lakedale Rd, SE18 105 ES79
Lake Dr, Bushey (Bushey Hth.)
WD23 40 CC47
Lakefield Cl, SE20
off Limes Av 122 DV94
Lakefield Rd, N22 45 DP54
Lakefields Cl, Rain. RM13 90 FK68
Lake Gdns, Dag. RM10 70 FA64
Richmond TW10 117 CH89
Wallington SM6 141 DH104
Lakehall Gdns, Th.Hth. CR7 141 DP99
Lakehall Rd, Th.Hth. CR7 141 DP99
Lake Ho Rd, E11 68 EG62
Lakehurst Rd, Epsom KT19 156 CS106
Lakeland Cl, Chig. IG7 50 EV49
Harrow HA3 41 CD51
Lakenheath, N14 29 DK44
Lake Ri, Grays RM20 109 FU77
Romford RM1 71 FF55
Lake Rd, SW19 119 CZ92
Croydon CR0 143 DZ103
Romford RM6 70 EX56
Virginia Water GU25 132 AV98
Laker Pl, SW15 119 CZ86
Lakers Ri, Bans. SM7 174 DE116
Lakeside, N3 44 DB54

282

Lak - Lan

Lakeside, W13 *off Edgehill Rd* .79 CJ72
Beckenham BR3 .143 EB97
Enfield EN2 .29 DK42
Rainham RM13 .90 FL68
Redhill RH1 .184 DG132
Wallington SM6
off Derek Av .141 DH104
Weybridge KT13 .135 BS103
Woking GU21 .166 AS119
Lakeside Av, SE28 .88 EU74
Ilford IG4 .68 EK56
Lakeside Cl, SE25 .142 DU96
Chigwell IG7 .49 ET49
Ruislip HA4 .59 BR56
Sidcup DA15 .126 EW85
Woking GU21 .166 AS119
Lakeside Ct, N4 .65 DP61
Borehamwood (Elstree) WD6
off Cavendish Cres .26 CN43
Lakeside Cres, Barn. EN4 .28 DF43
Brentwood CM14 .54 FX48
Weybridge KT13
off Churchill Dr .135 BQ104
Lakeside Dr, Brom. BR2 .144 EL104
Esher KT10 .154 CC107
Slough (Stoke P.) SL2 .74 AS67
Lakeside Gra, Wey. KT13 .135 BQ104
Lakeside Pl, St.Alb. (Lon.Col.)
AL2 .9 CK27
Lakeside Rd, N13 .45 DM49
W14 .99 CX76
Slough SL3 .93 BF80
Waltham Cross (Chsht.)
EN8 .14 DW28
Lakeside Way, Wem. HA9 .62 CN63
Lakes Rd, Kes. BR2 .162 EJ106
Lakeswood Rd, Orp. BR5 .145 EP100
Lake Vw, Edg. HA8 .42 CM50
Potters Bar EN6 .12 DC33
Lakeview Ct, SW19
off Victoria Dr .119 CY89
Lakeview Rd, SE27 .121 DN92
Lake Vw Rd, Sev. TN13 .190 FG122
Lakeview Rd, Well. DA16 .106 EV84
Lakis Cl, NW3 *off Flask Wk* .64 DC63
LALEHAM, Stai. .134 BJ97
Laleham Av, NW7 .42 CR48
Laleham Cl, Stai. TW18
off Worple Rd .134 BH95
Laleham Ct, Wok. GU21 .166 AY116
★ **Laleham Heritage Cen**, Stai.
TW18 .134 BJ97
Laleham Pk, Stai. TW18 .134 BJ98
Laleham Reach, Cher. KT16 .134 BH96
Laleham Rd, SE6 .123 EC86
Shepperton TW17 .134 BM98
Staines TW18 .113 BF92
Lalor St, SW6 .99 CY82
Lambarde Av, SE9 .125 EN91
Lambarde Dr, Sev. TN13 .190 FG123
Lambarde Rd, Sev. TN13 .190 FG122
Lambardes Cl, Orp. BR6 .164 EW110
Lamb Cl, Til. RM18
off Coleridge Rd .111 GJ82
Watford WD25 .8 BW34
Lamberhurst Cl, Orp. BR5 .146 EX102
Lamberhurst Rd, SE27 .121 DN91
Dagenham RM8 .70 EZ60
Lambert Av, Rich. TW9 .98 CP83
Slough SL3 .92 AY75
Lambert Cl, West. (Bigg.H.)
TN16 .178 EK116
Lambert Ct, Bushey WD23 .24 BX42
Lambert Jones Ms, EC2
off The Barbican .84 DQ71
Lambert Rd, E16 .86 EH72
N12 .44 DD50
SW2 .121 DL85
Banstead SM7 .158 DA114
Lamberts Pl, Croy. CR0 .142 DR102
Lamberts Rd, Surb. KT5 .138 CL99
Lambert St, N1 .83 DN66
Lambert Wk, Wem. HA9 .61 CK62
Lambert Way, N12
off Woodhouse Rd .44 DC50
LAMBETH, SE1 .200 B6
Lambeth Br, SE1 .200 A8
SW1 .200 A8
Lambeth High St, SE1 .200 B9
Lambeth Hill, EC4 .197 H10
⊖ **Lambeth North** .200 D5
★ **Lambeth Palace**, SE1 .200 B7
Lambeth Palace Rd, SE1 .200 B7
Lambeth Rd, SE1 .200 C7
SE11 .200 C7
Croydon CR0 .141 DN101
Lambeth Wk, SE11 .200 C8
Lamb La, E8 .84 DV66
Lamble St, NW5 .64 DG64
Lambley Rd, Dag. RM9 .88 EV65
Lambly Hill, Vir.W. GU25 .132 AY97
Lambolle Pl, NW3 .82 DE65
Lambolle Rd, NW3 .82 DE65
Lambourn Chase, Rad. WD7 .25 CF36
Lambourn Cl, W7 .97 CF75
Lambourne Av, SW19 .119 CZ91
Lambourne Cl, Chig. IG7 .50 EV48
Lambourne Ct, Wdf.Grn. IG8
off Navestock Cres .48 EJ52
Lambourne Cres, Chig. IG7 .50 EV47
Woking GU21 .151 BD113
Lambourne Dr, Brwd. CM13 .55 GE45
Cobham KT11 .170 BX115
LAMBOURNE END, Rom. .34 EX44
Lambourne Gdns, E4 .47 EA47
Barking IG11
off Lambourne Rd .87 ET66
Enfield EN1 .30 DT40
Hornchurch RM12 .72 FK61
Lambourne Gro, Kings.T. KT1
off Kenley Rd .138 CP96
Lambourne Pl, SE3
off Shooter's Hill Rd .104 EH81
Lambourne Rd, E11 .67 EC59
Lambourne Rd, Bark. IG11 .87 ES66
Chigwell IG7 .49 ES49
Ilford IG3 .69 ES61
Lambourn Rd, SW4 .101 DH83
Lambrook Ter, SW6 .99 CY81
Lamb's Bldgs, EC1 .197 K5
Lambs Cl, Pot.B. (Cuffley)
EN6 .13 DM29
Lambs Conduit Pas, WC1 .196 B6
Lamb's Conduit St, WC1 .196 B5
Lambscroft Av, SE9 .124 EJ90
Lambscroft Way, Ger.Cr. (Chal.St.P.)
SL9 .36 AY54
Lambs La N, Rain. RM13 .90 FJ70
Lambs La S, Rain. RM13 .89 FH71
Lambs Meadow, Wdf.Grn.
IG8 .48 EK54
Lambs Ms, N1
off Colebrooke Row .83 DP67
Lamb's Pas, EC1 .197 K5
Lambs Ter, N9 .46 DR47
Lamb St, E1 .197 P6
Lambs Wk, Enf. EN2 .30 DQ40
Lambton Av, Wal.Cr. EN8 .15 DX32
Lambton Pl, W11
off Westbourne Gro .81 CZ72
Lambton Rd, N19 .65 DL60
SW20 .139 CW95
Lamb Wk, SE1 .201 M5
Lamb Yd, Wat. WD17 .24 BX43
Lamerock Rd, Brom. BR1 .124 EF91
Lamerton Rd, Ilf. IG6 .49 EP54
Lamerton St, SE8 .103 EA79
Lamford Cl, N17 .46 DR52
Lamington St, W6 .99 CV77
Lamlash St, SE11 .200 F8
Lammas Av, Mitch. CR4 .140 DG96
Lammas Cl, Stai. TW18 .113 BE90
Lammas Ct, Stai. TW19 .113 BD89
Lammas Dr, Stai. TW18 .113 BD90
Lammas Grn, SE26 .122 DV90
Lammas La, Esher KT10 .154 CA106
Lammas Pk, W5 .97 CJ75
Lammas Pk Gdns, W5 .97 CJ75
Lammas Pk Rd, W5 .79 CJ74
Lammas Rd, E9 .85 DX66
E10 .67 DY61
Richmond TW10 .117 CJ91
Watford WD18 .24 BW43
Lammermoor Rd, SW12 .121 DH87
Lamont Rd, SW10 .100 DC79
Lamont Rd Pas, SW10
off Lamont Rd .100 DD79
LAMORBEY, Sid. .125 ET88
Lamorbey Cl, Sid. DA15 .125 ET88
Lamorna Av, Grav. DA12 .131 GJ90
Lamorna Cl, E17 .47 EC53
Orpington BR6 .146 EU101
Radlett WD7 .9 CH34
Lamorna Gro, Stan. HA7 .41 CK53
Lampard Gro, N16 .66 DT60
Lampern Sq, E2
off Nelson Gdns .84 DU69
Lampeter Cl, NW9 .62 CS58
Woking GU22 .166 AY118
Lampeter Sq, W6
off Humbolt Rd .99 CY79
Lamplighter Cl, E1
off Cleveland Way .84 DW70
Lamplighters Cl, Dart. DA1 .128 FM86
Waltham Abbey EN9 .16 EG34
Lampmead Rd, SE12 .124 EE85
Lamp Office Ct, WC1 .196 B5
Lamport Cl, SE18 .105 EM77
LAMPTON, Houns. .96 CB81
Lampton Av, Houns. TW3 .96 CB81
Lampton Ho Cl, SW19 .119 CX91
Lampton Pk Rd, Houns. TW3 .96 CB82
Lampton Rd, Houns. TW3 .96 CB82
Lamson Rd, Rain. RM13 .89 FF70
Lanacre Av, NW9 .43 CT53
Lanark Cl, W5 .79 CJ71
Lanark Ms, W9 *off Lanark Rd* .82 DC69
Lanark Pl, W9 .82 DC70
Lanark Rd, W9 .82 DB68
Lanark Sq, E14 .204 C6
Lanata Wk, Hayes UB4
off Ramulis Dr .78 BX70
Lanbury Rd, SE15 .103 DX84
Lancashire Ct, W1 .195 J10
Lancaster Av, E18 .68 EH56
SE27 .121 DP89
SW19 .119 CX92
Barking IG11 .87 ES66
Barnet EN4 .28 DD38
Mitcham CR4 .141 DL99
Lancaster Cl, N1
off Hertford Rd .84 DS66
N17 *off Park La* .46 DU52
NW9 .43 CT52
Brentwood CM15 .54 FU43
Bromley BR2 .144 EF98
Egham TW20 .112 AX92
Kingston upon Thames
KT2 .117 CK92
Staines (Stanw.) TW19 .114 BL86
Woking GU21 .167 BA116
Lancaster Cotts, Rich. TW10
off Lancaster Pk .118 CL86
Lancaster Ct, SE27 .121 DP89
SW6 .99 CZ80
W2 *off Lancaster Gate* .82 DC73
Banstead SM7 .157 CZ114
Walton-on-Thames KT12 .135 BU101
Lancaster Dr, E14 .204 E3
NW3 .82 DE65
Hemel Hempstead (Bov.)
HP3 .5 AZ27
Hornchurch RM12 .71 FH64
Loughton IG10 .32 EL44
Lancaster Gdns, SW19 .119 CY92
W13 .97 CH75
Bromley BR1
off Southborough Rd .144 EL99
Kingston upon Thames
KT2 .117 CK92
⊖ **Lancaster Gate** .82 DD73
Lancaster Gate, W2 .82 DC73
Lancaster Gro, NW3 .82 DD65
★ **Lancaster Ho**, SW1 .199 K4
Lancaster Ms, SW18
off East Hill .120 DB85
W2 .82 DC73
Richmond TW10
off Richmond Hill .118 CL86
Lancaster Pk, Rich. TW10 .118 CL85
Lancaster Pl, SW19
off Lancaster Rd .119 CX92
WC2 .196 B10
Hounslow TW4 .96 BW82
Ilford IG1 *off Staines Rd* .69 EQ64
Twickenham TW1 .117 CG86
Lancaster Rd, E7 .86 EG66
E11 .68 EE61
E17 .47 DX54
N4 .65 DN59
N11 .45 DK51
N18 .46 DT50
NW10 .63 CU64
SE25 .142 DT96
SW19 .119 CX92
W11 .81 CY72
Barnet EN4 .28 DD43
Enfield EN2 .30 DR39
Epping (N.Wld.Bas.) CM16 .18 FA26
Grays (Chaff.Hun.) RM16 .109 FX78
Harrow HA2 .60 CA57
Northolt UB5 .78 CC65
Southall UB1 .78 BY73
Uxbridge UB8 .76 BK65
Lancaster St, SE1 .200 G5
Lancaster Ter, W2 .82 DD73
Lancaster Wk, W2 .82 DC74
Hayes UB3 .77 BQ72
Lancaster Way, Abb.L. WD5 .7 BT31
Lancaster W, W11
off Grenfell Rd .81 CX73
Lancastrian Rd, Wall. SM6 .159 DL108
Lancefield St, W10 .81 CZ69
Lancell St, N16 *off Stoke
Newington Ch St* .66 DS61
Lancelot Av, Wem. HA0 .61 CK63
Lancelot Cres, Wem. HA0 .61 CK63
Lancelot Gdns, Barn. EN4 .44 DG45
Lancelot Ho, N9 *off Barbot Cl* .46 DU48
Lancelot Pl, SW7 .198 D5
Lancelot Rd, Ilf. IG6 .49 ES51
Welling DA16 .106 EU84
Wembley HA0 .61 CK64
Lance Rd, Har. HA1 .60 CC59
Lancer Sq, W8 *off Old Ct Pl* .100 DB75
Lancey Cl, SE7
off Cleveley Cl .104 EK77
Lanchester Rd, N6 .64 DF57
Lancing Gdns, N9 .46 DT46
Lancing Rd, W13
off Drayton Grn Rd .79 CH73
Croydon CR0 .141 DM100
Feltham TW13 .115 BT89
Ilford IG2 .69 ER58
Orpington BR6 .146 EU103
Romford RM3 .52 FL52
Lancing St, NW1 .195 M3
Lancing Way, Rick. (Crox.Grn.)
WD3 .23 BP43
Lancresse Cl, Uxb. UB8 .76 BK65
Lancresse Ct, N1 .84 DS67
Landale Gdns, Dart. DA1 .128 FJ87
Landau Way, Brox. EN10 .15 DZ26
Erith DA8 .108 FK78
Landcroft Rd, SE22 .122 DT86
Landells Rd, SE22 .122 DT86
Lander Rd, Grays RM17 .110 GD78
Landford Cl, Rick. WD3 .38 BL47
Landford Rd, SW15 .99 CW83
Landgrove Rd, SW19 .120 DA92
Landmann Way, SE14 .103 DX79
Landmead Rd, Wal.Cr. (Chsht.)
EN8 .15 DY29
Landon Pl, SW1 .198 D6
Landons Cl, E14 .204 E2
Landon Wk, E14
off Cottage St .85 EB73
Landon Way, Ashf. TW15
off Courtfield Rd .115 BP93
Landor Rd, SW9 .101 DL83
H **Landor Rd Unit**, SW9 .101 DL83
Landor Wk, W12 .99 CU75
Landport Way, SE15
off Daniel Gdns .102 DT80
Landra Gdns, N21 .29 DP44
Landridge Dr, Enf. EN1 .30 DV38
Landridge Rd, SW6 .99 CZ82
Landrock Rd, N8 .65 DL58
Landscape Rd, Warl. CR6 .176 DV119
Woodford Green IG8 .48 EH52
Landseer Av, E12 .69 EN64
Gravesend (Nthflt.) DA11 .130 GD90
Landseer Cl, SW19
off Brangwyn Cres .140 DC95
Edgware HA8 .42 CN54
Hornchurch RM11 .71 FH60
Landseer Rd, N19 .65 DL62
Enfield EN1 .30 DU43
New Malden KT3 .138 CR101
Sutton SM1 .158 DA107
Lands End, Borwd. (Elstree)
WD6 .25 CK44
Landstead Rd, SE18 .105 ER80
Landway, The, Orp. BR5 .146 EW97
Lane, The, NW8
off Marlborough Pl .82 DC68
SE3 .104 EG83
Chertsey KT16 .134 BG97
Virginia Water GU25 .132 AY97
Lane App, NW7 .43 CY50
Lane Av, Green. DA9 .129 FW86
Lane Cl, NW2 .63 CV62
Addlestone KT15 .152 BG106
LANE END, Dart. .129 FR92
Lane End, Bexh. DA7 .107 FB83
Epsom KT18 .156 CP114
Lane Gdns, Bushey (Bushey Hth.)
WD23 .41 CE45
Lane Ms, E12
off Colchester Av .69 EM62
Lanercost Cl, SW2 .121 DN89
Lanercost Gdns, N14 .45 DL45
Lanercost Rd, SW2 .121 DN89
Lanes Av, Grav. (Nthflt.)
DA11 .131 GG90
Lanesborough Pl, SW1 .198 F4
Laneside, Chis. BR7 .125 EP92
Edgware HA8 .42 CQ50
Laneside Av, Dag. RM8 .70 EZ59
Laneway, SW15 .119 CV85
Lane Wd Cl, Amer. HP7 .20 AT39
Lanfranc Rd, E3 .85 DY68
Lanfrey Pl, W14
off North End Rd .99 CZ78
Langaller La, Lthd. KT22 .170 CB122
Langbourne Av, N6 .64 DG61
Langbourne Pl, E14 .204 B10
Langbourne Way, Esher (Clay.)
KT10 .155 CG107
Langbrook Rd, SE3 .104 EK83
Lang Cl, Lthd. (Fetch.) KT22 .170 CB123
Langcroft Cl, Cars. SM5 .140 DF104
Langdale Av, Mitch. CR4 .140 DF97
Langdale Cl, SE17 .102 DQ79
SW14 .98 CP84
Dagenham RM8 .70 EW60
Orpington BR6
off Grasmere Rd .145 EP104
Woking GU21 .166 AW116
Langdale Cres, Bexh. DA7 .106 FA80
Langdale Dr, Hayes UB4 .77 BS68
Langdale Gdns, Grnf. UB6 .79 CH69
Hornchurch RM12 .71 FG64
Waltham Cross EN8 .31 DX35
Langdale Rd, SE10 .103 EC80
Thornton Heath CR7 .141 DN98
Langdale St, E1
off Burslem St .84 DV72
Langdale Wk, Grav. (Nthflt.)
DA11 *off Landseer Av* .130 GE90
Langdon Ct, NW10 .80 CS67
Langdon Cres, E6 .87 EN68
Langdon Dr, NW9 .62 CQ60
Langdon Pk Rd, N6 .65 DJ59
Langdon Pl, SW14
off Rosemary La .98 CQ83
Langdon Rd, E6 .87 EN67
Bromley BR2 .144 EH97
Morden SM4 .140 DC99
Langdons Ct, Sthl. UB2 .96 CA76
Langdon Shaw, Sid. DA14 .125 ET92
Langdon Wk, Mord. SM4 .140 DC99
Langdon Way, SE1 .202 C9
Langford Cl, E8 .66 DU64
N15 .66 DS58
NW8 *off Langford Pl* .82 DC68
W3 .98 CP75
Langford Ct, NW8 .82 DC68
Langford Cres, Barn. EN4 .28 DF42
Langford Grn, SE5 .102 DS83
Brentwood CM13 .55 GC44
Langford Pl, NW8 .82 DC68
Sidcup DA14 .126 EU90
Langford Rd, SW6 .100 DB82
Barnet EN4 .28 DE42
Woodford Green IG8 .48 EJ51
Langfords, Buck.H. IG9 .48 EK47
Langfords Way, Croy. CR0 .161 DY111
Langham Cl, N15
off Langham Rd .65 DP55
Langham Ct, Horn. RM11 .72 FK59
Langham Dene, Ken. CR8 .175 DP115
Langham Dr, Rom. RM6 .70 EV58
Langham Gdns, N21 .29 DN43
W13 .79 CH73
Edgware HA8 .42 CQ52
Richmond TW10 .117 CJ91
Wembley HA0 .61 CJ61
Langham Ho Cl, Rich. TW10 .117 CK91
Langham Pk Pl, Brom. BR2 .144 EF98
Langham Pl, N15 .65 DP55
W1 .195 J7
W4
off Hogarth Roundabout .98 CS79
Egham TW20 .113 AZ92
Langham Rd, N15 .65 DP55
SW20 .139 CW95
Edgware HA8 .42 CQ51
Teddington TW11 .117 CH92
Langham St, W1 .195 J7
Langhedge Cl, N18
off Langhedge La .46 DT51
Langhedge La, N18 .46 DT50
Langhedge La Ind Est, N18 .46 DT51
Langholm Cl, SW12
off King's Av .121 DK87
Langholme, Bushey WD23 .40 CC46
Langhorn Dr, Twick. TW2 .117 CE87
Langhorne Rd, Dag. RM10 .88 FA66
Langland Ct, Nthwd. HA6 .39 BQ52
Langland Cres, Stan. HA7 .62 CL55
Langland Dr, Pnr. HA5 .40 BY52
Langland Gdns, NW3 .64 DB64
Croydon CR0 .143 DZ103
Langlands Dr, Dart. (Lane End)
DA2 .129 FS92
Langlands Ri, Epsom KT19
off Burnet Gro .156 CQ113
Langler Rd, NW10 .81 CW68
LANGLEY, Slou. .93 BA76
⇌ **Langley** .93 BA75
Langley Av, Ruis. HA4 .59 BV60
Surbiton KT6 .137 CK102
Worcester Park KT4 .139 CX103
Langley Broom, Slou. SL3 .93 AZ78
LANGLEYBURY, Kings L. .7 BP34
Langleybury La, Kings L. WD4 .23 BP37
Langley Business Cen, Slou.
(Langley) SL3 .93 BA75
Langley Cl, Epsom KT18 .172 CR119
Romford RM3 .52 FK52
Langley Cor, Slou. (Fulmer)
SL3 .75 AZ65
Langley Ct, SE9 .125 EN86
WC2 .195 P10
Langley Ct, Beck. BR3 .143 EB99
Langley Cres, E11 .68 EJ59
Dagenham RM9 .88 EW66
Edgware HA8 .42 CQ48
Hayes UB3 .95 BT80
Kings Langley WD4 .6 BN30
Langley Dr, E11 .68 EH59
W3 .98 CP75
Brentwood CM14 .54 FU48
Langley Gdns, Brom. BR2 .144 EJ98
Dagenham RM9 .88 EW66
Orpington BR5 .145 EP100
Langley Gro, N.Mal. KT3 .138 CS96
Langley Hill, Kings L. WD4 .6 BM29
Langley Hill Cl, Kings L. WD4 .6 BN29
Langley La, SW8 .101 DM79
Abbots Langley WD5 .7 BT31
Epsom (Headley) KT18 .182 CP125
Langley Lo La, Kings L. WD4 .6 BN31
Langley Meadow, Loug. IG10 .33 ER40
Langley Oaks Av, S.Croy.
CR2 .160 DU110
Langley Pk, NW7 .42 CS51
★ **Langley Park Country Pk**,
Slou. SL3 .75 BA70
Langley Pk Rd, Iver SL0 .75 BC72
Slough SL3 .93 BA75
Sutton SM1, SM2 .158 DC106
Langley Quay, Slou. (Langley)
SL3 .93 BA75
Langley Rd, SW19 .139 CZ95
Abbots Langley WD5 .7 BS31
Beckenham BR3 .143 DY98
Isleworth TW7 .97 CF82
Kings Langley (Chipper.)
WD4 .6 BH30
Slough SL3 .92 AW75
South Croydon CR2 .161 DX109
Staines TW18 .113 BF93
Surbiton KT6 .138 CL101
Watford WD17 .23 BU39
Welling DA16 .106 EW79
Langley Row, Barn. EN5 .27 CZ39
Langley St, WC2 .195 P9
LANGLEY VALE, Epsom .172 CR120
Langley Vale Rd, Epsom
KT18 .172 CR118
Langley Wk, Wok. GU22
off Midhope Rd .166 AY119
Langley Way, Wat. WD17 .23 BS40
West Wickham BR4 .143 ED102
Langmans La, Wok. GU21 .166 AV118
Langmans Way, Wok. GU21 .166 AS116
Langmead Dr, Bushey
(Bushey Hth.) WD23 .41 CD46
Langmead St, SE27
off Beadman St .121 DP91
Langmore Ct, Bexh. DA6
off Regency Way .106 EX83
Langport Ct, Walt. KT12 .136 BW102
Langridge Ms, Hmptn. TW12
off Oak Av .116 BZ93
Langroyd Rd, SW17 .120 DF89
Langshott Cl, Add. (Woodham)
KT15 .151 BE111
Langside Av, SW15 .99 CU84
Langside Cres, N14 .45 DK48
Langston Hughes Cl, SE24
off Shakespeare Rd .101 DP84
Langston Rd, Loug. IG10 .33 EQ43
Lang St, E1 .84 DW70
Langthorn Ct, EC2 .197 K8
Langthorne Cres, Grays
RM17 .110 GC77
Langthorne Rd, E11 .67 ED62
Langthorne St, SW6 .99 CX80
Langton Av, E6 .87 EN69
N20 .44 DC45
Epsom KT17 .157 CT111
Langton Cl, WC1 .196 C3
Addlestone KT15 .134 BH104
Woking GU21 .166 AT117
Langton Gro, Nthwd. HA6 .39 BQ50
Langton Ho, SW16
off Colson Way .121 DJ91
Langton Pl, SW18
off Merton Rd .120 DA88
Langton Ri, SE23 .122 DV87
Langton Rd, NW2 .63 CW62
SW9 .101 DP80
Harrow HA3 .40 CC52
West Molesey KT8 .136 CC98
Langton St, SW10 .100 DC79
Langton Way, SE3 .104 EF81
Croydon CR0 .160 DS105
Egham TW20 .113 BC93
Grays RM16 .111 GJ77
Langtry Pl, SW6
off Seagrave Rd .100 DA79
Langtry Rd, NW8 .82 DB67
Northolt UB5 .78 BX68
Langtry Wk, NW8
off Alexandra Pl .82 DC66
Langwood Chase, Tedd.
TW11 .117 CJ93
Langwood Cl, Ashtd. KT21 .172 CN117
Langwood Gdns, Wat. WD17 .23 BU39
Langworth Cl, Dart. DA2 .128 FK90
Langworth Dr, Hayes UB4 .77 BU72
Lanhill Rd, W9 .82 DA70
Lanier Rd, SE13 .123 EC86
Lanigan Dr, Houns. TW3 .116 CB85
Lankaster Gdns, N2 .44 DD53
Lankers Dr, Har. HA2 .60 BZ58
Lankton Cl, Beck. BR3 .143 EC95
Lannock Rd, Hayes UB3 .77 BS74
Lannoy Rd, SE9 .125 EQ88
Lanrick Rd, E14 .85 ED72
Lanridge Rd, SE2 .106 EX76
Lansbury Av, N18 .46 DR50
Barking IG11 .88 EU66
Feltham TW14 .115 BV86
Romford RM6 .70 EY57
Lansbury Cl, NW10 .62 CQ64
Lansbury Cres, Dart. DA1 .128 FN85
Lansbury Dr, Hayes UB4 .77 BT71
Lansbury Est, E14 .85 EB72

★ Place of interest ⇌ Railway station ⊖ London Underground station DLR Docklands Light Railway station Tramlink station H Hospital

Lansbury Gdns, E14 85 ED72
Tilbury RM18 111 GG81
Lansbury Rd, Enf. EN3 31 DX39
Lansbury Way, N18 46 DS50
Lanscombe Wk, SW8 101 DL81
Lansdell Rd, Mitch. CR4 140 DG96
Lansdown Cl, Walt. KT12
off St. Johns Dr 136 BW102
Woking GU21 166 AT119
Lansdowne Av, Bexh. DA7 106 EX80
Orpington BR6 145 EP102
Slough SL1 74 AS74
Lansdowne Cl, SW20 119 CX94
Surbiton KT5
off Kingston Rd 138 CP103
Twickenham TW1
off Lion Rd 117 CF88
Watford WD25 8 BX34
Lansdowne Copse, Wor.Pk. KT4
off The Avenue 139 CU103
Lansdowne Ct, Pur. CR8 159 DP110
Slough SL1 74 AS74
Worcester Park KT4
off The Avenue 139 CU103
Lansdowne Cres, W11 81 CY73
Lansdowne Dr, E8 84 DU65
Lansdowne Gdns, SW8 101 DL81
Lansdowne Grn, SW8
off Hartington Rd 101 DL81
Lansdowne Gro, NW10 62 CS63
Lansdowne Hill, SE27 121 DP90
Lansdowne La, SE7 104 EK79
Lansdowne Ms, SE7 104 EK78
W11 *off Lansdowne Rd* 81 CZ74
Lansdowne Pl, SE1 201 L7
SE19 122 DT94
Lansdowne Ri, W11 81 CY73
Lansdowne Rd, E4 47 EA47
E11 68 EF61
E17 67 EA57
E18 68 EG55
N3 43 CZ52
N10 45 DJ54
N17 46 DT53
SW20 119 CW94
W11 81 CY73
Bromley BR1 124 EG94
Croydon CR0 142 DR103
Epsom KT19 156 CQ108
Harrow HA1 61 CE59
Hounslow TW3 96 CB83
Ilford IG3 69 ET60
Purley CR8 159 DN112
Sevenoaks TN13 191 FK122
Staines TW18 114 BH94
Stanmore HA7 41 CJ51
Tilbury RM18 111 GF82
Uxbridge UB8 77 BP72
Lansdowne Row, W1 199 J2
Lansdowne Sq, Grav. (Nthflt.)
DA11 131 GF86
Lansdowne Ter, WC1 196 A5
Lansdowne Wk, W11 81 CY74
Lansdowne Way, SW8 101 DL81
Lansdowne Wd Cl, SE27 121 DP90
Lansdown Pl, Grav. (Nthflt.)
DA11 131 GF88
Lansdown Rd, E7 86 EJ66
Gerrards Cross (Chal.St.P.)
SL9 36 AX53
Sidcup DA14 126 EV90
Lansfield Av, N18 46 DU49
Lantern Cl, SW15 99 CU84
Wembley HA0 61 CK64
Lanterns Ct, E14 204 A5
Lantern Way, West Dr. UB7 94 BL75
Lant St, SE1 201 H4
Lanvanor Rd, SE15 102 DW82
Lapford Cl, W9 81 CZ70
La Plata Gro, Brwd. CM14 54 FV48
Lapponum Wk, Hayes UB4
off Lochan Cl 78 BX71
Lapse Wd Wk, SE23 122 DV88
Lapstone Gdns, Har. HA3 61 CJ58
Lapwing Cl, Erith DA8 107 FH80
South Croydon CR2 161 DY110
Lapwing Ct, Surb. KT6
off Chaffinch Cl 138 CN104
Lapwings, The, Grav. DA12 131 GK89
Lapwing Twr, SE8
off Abinger Gro 103 DZ79
Lapwing Way, Abb.L. WD5 7 BU31
Hayes UB4 78 BX72
Lapworth Cl, Orp. BR6 146 EW103
Lara Cl, SE13 123 EC86
Chessington KT9 156 CL108
Larbert Rd, SW16 141 DJ95
Larby Pl, Epsom KT17 156 CS110
Larch Av, W3 80 CS74
St. Albans (Brick.Wd.) AL2 8 BY30
Larch Cl, E13 86 EH70
N11 44 DG52
N19 *off Bredgar Rd* 65 DJ61
SE8 *off Clyde St* 103 DZ79
SW12 121 DH89
Tadworth KT20 174 DC121
Waltham Cross EN7
off The Firs 14 DS27
Warlingham CR6 177 DY119
Larch Cres, Epsom KT19 156 CP107
Hayes UB4 78 BW70
Larchdene, Orp. BR6 145 EN103
Larch Dr, W4
off Gunnersbury Av 98 CN78
Larches, The, N13 46 DQ48
Amersham HP6 20 AV38
Bushey WD23 24 BY43
Northwood HA6
off Rickmansworth Rd 39 BQ51
Uxbridge UB10 77 BP69
Woking GU21 166 AY116
Larches Av, SW14 98 CR84
Enfield EN1 30 DW35
Larch Grn, NW9
off Clayton Fld 42 CS53
Larch Gro, Sid. DA15 125 ET88
Larch Rd, E10 *off Walnut Rd* 67 EA61
Larch Rd, NW2 63 CW63
Dartford DA1 128 FK87
Larch Tree Way, Croy. CR0 143 EA104
Larch Wk, Swan. BR8 147 FD96
Larch Way, Brom. BR2 145 EN101
Larchwood Av, Rom. RM5 51 FB51
Larchwood Cl, Bans. SM7 173 CY116
Romford RM5 51 FC51
Larchwood Dr, Egh. (Eng.Grn.)
TW20 112 AV93
Larchwood Gdns, Brwd.
CM15 54 FU44
Larchwood Rd, SE9 125 EP89
Larcombe Cl, Croy. CR0 160 DT105
Larcom St, SE17 201 J9
Larden Rd, W3 80 CS74
Largewood Av, Surb. KT6 138 CN103
Largo Wk, Erith DA8
off Selkirk Dr 107 FE81
Larissa St, SE17 201 L10
Lark Av, Stai. TW18
off Kestrel Av 113 BF90
Larkbere Rd, SE26 123 DY91
Larken Cl, Bushey WD23
off Larken Dr 40 CC46
Larken Dr, Bushey WD23 40 CC46
Larkfield, Cob. KT11 153 BU113
Larkfield Av, Har. HA3 61 CH55
Larkfield Cl, Brom. BR2 144 EF103
Larkfield Rd, Rich. TW9 98 CL84
Sevenoaks TN13 190 FC123
Sidcup DA14 125 ET90
Larkfields, Grav. (Nthflt.)
DA11 130 GE90
Larkhall Cl, Walt. KT12 154 BW107
Larkhall La, SW4 101 DK82
Larkhall Ri, SW4 101 DJ83
Larkham Cl, Felt. TW13 115 BS90
Larkhill Ter, SE18 105 EN81
Larkin Cl, Brwd. CM13 55 GC45
Coulsdon CR5 175 DM117
Larkings La, Slou. (Stoke P.)
SL2 74 AV67
Lark Row, E2 84 DW67
Larksfield, Egh. (Eng.Grn.)
TW20 112 AW94
Larksfield Gro, Enf. EN1 30 DV39
Larks Gro, Bark. IG11 87 ES66
Larkshall Ct, Rom. RM7 51 FC54
Larkshall Cres, E4 47 EC49
Larkshall Rd, E4 47 EC50
Larkspur Cl, E6 86 EL71
N17 *off Fryatt Rd* 46 DR52
NW9 62 CP57
Orpington BR6 146 EW103
Ruislip HA4 59 BQ59
South Ockendon RM15 91 FW69
Larkspur Gro, Edg. HA8 42 CQ49
Larkspur Way, Epsom KT19 156 CQ106
Larkswood Cl, Erith DA8 107 FG81
Larkswood Ct, E4 47 ED50
Larkswood Ri, Pnr. HA5 60 BW56
Larkswood Rd, E4 47 EA49
Lark Way, Cars. SM5 140 DE101
Larkway Cl, NW9 62 CR56
Larmans Rd, Enf. EN3 30 DW36
Larnach Rd, W6 99 CX79
Larne Rd, Ruis. HA4 59 BT59
Larner Rd, Erith DA8 107 FE80
La Roche Cl, Slou. SL3 92 AW76
Larpent Av, SW15 119 CW85
Larsen Dr, Wal.Abb. EN9 15 ED34
Larwood Cl, Grnf. UB6 61 CD64
Lascelles Av, Har. HA1 61 CD59
Lascelles Cl, E11 67 ED61
Brentwood CM15 54 FU43
Lascelles Rd, Slou. SL3 92 AV76
Lascotts Rd, N22 45 DM51
Las Palmas Est, Shep. TW17 135 BQ101
Lassa Rd, SE9 124 EL85
Lassell St, SE10 103 ED78
Lasseter Pl, SE3
off Vanbrugh Hill 104 EF79
Lasswade Rd, Cher. KT16 133 BF101
Latchett Rd, E18 48 EH53
Latchford Pl, Chig. IG7
off Manford Way 50 EV49
Latching Cl, Rom. RM3
off Troopers Dr 52 FK49
Latchingdon Ct, E17 67 DX56
Latchingdon Gdns, Wdf.Grn.
IG8 48 EL51
Latchmere Cl, Rich. TW10 118 CL92
Latchmere La, Kings.T. KT2 118 CM93
Latchmere Pas, SW11
off Cabul Rd 100 DE82
Latchmere Rd, SW11 100 DF82
Kingston upon Thames
KT2 118 CL94
Latchmere St, SW11 100 DF82
Latchmoor Av, Ger.Cr. (Chal.St.P.)
SL9 56 AX56
Latchmoor Gro, Ger.Cr. (Chal.St.P.)
SL9 56 AX56
Latchmoor Way, Ger.Cr. (Chal.St.P.)
SL9 56 AX56
Lateward Rd, Brent. TW8 97 CK79
Latham Cl, E6
off Oliver Gdns 86 EL72
Dartford DA2 129 FS89
Twickenham TW1 117 CG87
Westerham (Bigg.H.) TN16 178 EJ116
Latham Ho, E1 85 DX72
Latham Rd, Bexh. DA6 126 FA85
Twickenham TW1 117 CF87
Lathams Way, Croy. CR0 141 DM102
Lathkill Cl, Enf. EN1 46 DU45
Lathom Rd, E6 87 EM66
LATIMER, Chesh. 20 AY36
Latimer, SE17
off Beaconsfield Rd 102 DS78
Latimer Av, E6 87 EM67
Latimer Cl, Amer. HP6 20 AW39
Pinner HA5 40 BW53
Watford WD18 39 BS45
Woking GU22 167 BB116
Worcester Park KT4 157 CV105
H **Latimer Day Hosp**, W1 195 K6
Latimer Dr, Horn. RM12 72 FK62
Latimer Gdns, Pnr. HA5 40 BW53
Latimer Pl, W10 81 CW72
⊖ **Latimer Road** 81 CX73
Latimer Rd, E7 68 EH63
N15 66 DS58
SW19 120 DB93
W10 81 CW72
Barnet EN5 28 DB41
Chesham HP5 20 AU36
Croydon CR0
off Abbey Rd 141 DP104
Rickmansworth (Chenies)
WD3 21 BB38
Teddington TW11 117 CF92
Latona Dr, Grav. DA12 131 GM92
Latona Rd, SE15 102 DU79
La Tourne Gdns, Orp. BR6 145 EQ104
Lattimer Pl, W4 98 CS79
Latton Cl, Esher KT10 154 CB105
Walton-on-Thames KT12 136 BY101
Latymer Cl, Wey. KT13 153 BQ105
Latymer Ct, W6 99 CX77
Latymer Rd, N9 46 DT46
Latymer Way, N9 46 DR47
Lauder Cl, Nthlt. UB5 78 BX68
Lauderdale Dr, Rich. TW10 117 CK90
Lauderdale Pl, EC2
off Beech St 84 DQ71
Lauderdale Rd, W9 82 DB69
Kings Langley WD4 7 BQ33
Lauderdale Twr, EC2 197 H6
Laud St, SE11 200 B10
Croydon CR0 142 DQ104
Laughton Ct, Borwd. WD6
off Banks Rd 26 CR40
Laughton Rd, Nthlt. UB5 78 BX67
Launcelot Rd, Brom. BR1 124 EG91
Launcelot St, SE1 200 D5
Launceston Cl, Rom. RM3 52 FJ53
Launceston Gdns, Grnf. UB6 79 CJ67
Launceston Pl, W8 100 DC76
Launceston Rd, Grnf. UB6 79 CJ67
Launch St, E14 204 D6
Launders La, Rain. RM13 90 FM69
Laundress La, N16 66 DU62
Laundry La, N1
off Greenman St 84 DQ67
Waltham Abbey EN9 16 EE25
Laundry Rd, W6 99 CY79
Laura Cl, E11 68 EJ57
Enfield EN1 30 DS43
Lauradale Rd, N2 64 DF56
Laura Dr, Swan. BR8 127 FG94
Laura Pl, E5 66 DW63
Laurel Av, Egh. (Eng.Grn.)
TW20 112 AV92
Gravesend DA12 131 GJ89
Potters Bar EN6 11 CZ32
Slough SL3 92 AY75
Twickenham TW1 117 CF88
Laurel Bk Gdns, SW6
off New Kings Rd 99 CZ82
Laurel Bk Rd, Enf. EN2 30 DQ39
Laurel Bk Vil, W7
off Lower Boston Rd 79 CE74
Laurel Cl, N19
off Hargrave Pk 65 DJ61
SW17 120 DE92
Brentwood CM13 55 GB43
Dartford DA1
off Willow Rd 128 FJ88
Ilford IG6 49 EQ51
Sidcup DA14 126 EU90
Slough (Colnbr.) SL3 93 BE80
Woking GU21 151 BD113
Laurel Ct, Pot.B. (Cuffley) EN6
off Station Rd 13 DM29
Laurel Cres, Croy. CR0 143 EA104
Romford RM7 71 FE60
Woking GU21 151 BC113
Laurel Dr, N21 45 DN45
Oxted RH8 188 EF131
South Ockendon RM15 91 FX70
Laurel Flds, Pot.B. EN6 11 CZ31
Laurel Gdns, E4 47 EB45
NW7 42 CR48
W7 79 CE74
Addlestone (New Haw)
KT15 152 BH110
Bromley BR1
off Southborough Rd 144 EL98
Hounslow TW4 96 BY84
Laurel Gro, SE20 122 DV94
SE26 123 DX91
Laurel La, Horn. RM12
off Station La 72 FL61
West Drayton UB7 94 BL77
Laurel Lo La, Barn. EN5 27 CW36
Laurel Manor, Sutt. SM2
off Devonshire Rd 158 DC108
Laurel Pk, Har. HA3 41 CF52
Laurel Rd, SW13 99 CU82
SW20 139 CV95
Gerrards Cross (Chal.St.P.)
SL9 36 AX53
Hampton (Hmptn.H.)
TW12 117 CD92
Laurels, The, Bans. SM7 173 CZ117
Cobham KT11 170 BY115
Dartford DA2 128 FJ90
Waltham Cross EN7 14 DS27
Weybridge KT13 135 BR104
Laurels Rd, Iver SL0 75 BD68
Laurel St, E8 84 DT65
Laurel Vw, N12 44 DB48
Laurel Way, E18 68 EF56
N20 44 DA48
Laurence Ms, W12
off Askew Rd 99 CU75
Laurence Pountney Hill, EC4 197 K10
Laurence Pountney La, EC4 197 K10
Laurie Gro, SE14 103 DY81
Laurie Rd, W7 79 CE71
Laurier Rd, NW5 65 DH62
Croydon CR0 142 DT101
Laurie Wk, Rom. RM1 71 FE57
Laurimel Cl, Stan. HA7
off September Way 41 CH51
Laurino Pl, Bushey (Bushey Hth.)
WD23 40 CC47
Lauriston Rd, E9 85 DX67
SW19 119 CX93
Lausanne Rd, N8 65 DN56
SE15 102 DW81
Lauser Rd, Stai. (Stanw.)
TW19 114 BJ87
Lavell St, N16 66 DR63
Lavender Av, NW9 62 CQ60
Brentwood CM15 54 FV43
Mitcham CR4 140 DE95
Worcester Park KT4 139 CW104
Lavender Cl, SW3
off Danvers St 100 DD79
Bromley BR2 144 EL100
Carshalton SM5 158 DG105
Caterham CR3 186 DQ125
Coulsdon CR5 175 DJ119
Leatherhead KT22 171 CJ123
Romford RM3 52 FK52
Waltham Cross (Chsht.)
EN7 14 DT27
Lavender Ct, W.Mol. KT8
off Molesham Way 136 CB97
Lavender Dr, Uxb. UB8 76 BM71
Lavender Gdns, SW11 100 DF84
Enfield EN2 29 DP39
Harrow HA3
off Uxbridge Rd 41 CE51
Lavender Gate, Lthd. KT22 154 CB113
Lavender Gro, E8 84 DT66
Mitcham CR4 140 DE95
Lavender Hill, SW11 100 DE84
Enfield EN2 29 DN39
Swanley BR8 147 FD97
Lavender Pk Rd, W.Byf. KT14 152 BG112
Lavender Pl, Ilf. IG1 69 EP64
Lavender Ri, West Dr. UB7 94 BN75
Lavender Rd, SE16 203 K2
SW11 100 DD83
Carshalton SM5 158 DG105
Croydon CR0 141 DM100
Enfield EN2 30 DR39
Epsom KT19 156 CP106
Sutton SM1 158 DD105
Uxbridge UB8 76 BM71
Woking GU22 167 BB116
Lavender Sq, E11
off Anglian Rd 67 ED62
Lavender St, E15
off Manbey Gro 86 EE65
Lavender Sweep, SW11 100 DF84
Lavender Ter, SW11
off Falcon Rd 100 DE83
Lavender Vale, Wall. SM6 159 DK107
Lavender Wk, SW11 100 DF84
Mitcham CR4 140 DG97
Lavender Way, Croy. CR0 143 DX100
Lavengro Rd, SE27 122 DQ89
Lavenham Rd, SW18 119 CZ89
Lavernock Rd, Bexh. DA7 106 FA82
Lavers Rd, N16 66 DS62
Laverstoke Gdns, SW15 119 CU87
Laverton Ms, SW5
off Laverton Pl 100 DB77
Laverton Pl, SW5 100 DB77
Lavidge Rd, SE9 124 EL89
Lavina Gro, N1
off Wharfdale Rd 83 DM68
Lavington Cl, E9 85 DZ65
Lavington Rd, W13 79 CH74
Croydon CR0 141 DM104
Lavington St, SE1 200 G3
Lavinia Av, Wat. WD25 8 BX34
Lavinia Rd, Dart. DA1 128 FM86
Lavrock La, Rick. WD3 38 BM45
Lawdons Gdns, Croy. CR0 159 DP105
Lawford Av, Rick. (Chorl.)
WD3 21 BC44
Lawford Cl, Horn. RM12 72 FJ63
Rickmansworth (Chorl.)
WD3 21 BC44
Wallington SM6 159 DL109
Lawford Gdns, Dart. DA1 128 FJ85
Kenley CR8 176 DQ116
Lawford Rd, N1 84 DS66
NW5 83 DJ65
W4 98 CQ80
Law Ho, Bark. IG11 88 EU68
Lawless St, E14 85 EB73
Lawley Rd, N14 45 DH45
Lawley St, E5 66 DW63
Lawn, The, Sthl. UB2 96 CA78
Lawn Av, West Dr. UB7 94 BJ75
Lawn Cl, N9 46 DT45
Bromley BR1 124 EH93
New Malden KT3 138 CS96
Ruislip HA4 59 BT62
Slough (Datchet) SL3 92 AW80
Swanley BR8 147 FC96
Lawn Cres, Rich. TW9 98 CN82
Lawn Fm Gro, Rom. RM6 70 EY56
Lawnfield, NW2
off Coverdale Rd 81 CX66
Lawn Gdns, W7 79 CE74
Lawn Ho Cl, E14 204 D4
Lawn La, SW8 101 DL79
Lawn Pk, Sev. TN13 191 FH127
Lawn Rd, NW3 64 DF64
Beckenham BR3 123 DZ94
Gravesend DA11 130 GC86
Uxbridge UB8
off New Windsor St 76 BJ66
Lawns, The, E4 47 EA50
SE3 *off Lee Ter* 104 EE83
SE19 142 DR95
Pinner HA5 40 CB52
Radlett (Shenley) WD7 10 CL33
Sidcup DA14 126 EV91
Sutton SM2 157 CY108
Lawns Ct, Wem. HA9
off The Avenue 62 CM61
Lawns Cres, Grays RM17 110 GD79
Lawnside, SE3 104 EF84
Lawns Way, Rom. RM5 51 FC52
Lawn Ter, SE3 104 EE83
Lawn Vale, Pnr. HA5 40 BX54
Lawrance Gdns, Wal.Cr. (Chsht.)
EN8 15 DX28
Lawrence Av, E12 69 EN63
E17 47 DX53
N13 45 DP49
NW7 42 CS49
New Malden KT3 138 CR100
Lawrence Bldgs, N16 66 DT62
Lawrence Campe Cl, N20
off Friern Barnet La 44 DD48
Lawrence Cl, E3 85 EA68
N15 *off Lawrence Rd* 66 DS55
Lawrence Ct, NW7 42 CS50
Woodford Green IG8
off Baddow Cl 48 EJ51
Lawrence Cres, Dag. RM10 71 FB62
Edgware HA8 42 CN54
Lawrence Dr, Uxb. UB10 59 BQ63
Lawrence Gdns, NW7 43 CT48
Tilbury RM18 111 GH80
Lawrence Hill, E4 47 EA47
Lawrence Hill Gdns, Dart.
DA1 128 FJ86
Lawrence Hill Rd, Dart. DA1 128 FJ86
Lawrence La, EC2 197 J9
Betchworth (Buckland)
RH3 183 CV131
Lawrence Orchard, Rick. (Chorl.)
WD3 21 BD43
Lawrence Pl, N1 *off Outram Pl* 83 DL67
Lawrence Rd, E6 86 EK67
E13 86 EH67
N15 66 DS56
N18 46 DV49
SE25 142 DT98
W5 97 CK77
Erith DA8 107 FB80
Hampton TW12 116 BZ94
Hayes UB4 77 BQ68
Hounslow TW4 96 BW84
Pinner HA5 60 BX57
Richmond TW10 117 CJ91
Romford RM2 71 FH57
West Wickham BR4 162 EG105
Lawrence Sq, Grav. DA11
off Haynes Rd 131 GF90
Lawrence St, E16 86 EF71
NW7 43 CT49
SW3 100 DE79
Lawrence Way, NW10 62 CQ62
Lawrence Weaver Cl, Mord. SM4
off Green La 140 DB100
Lawrie Pk Av, SE26 122 DV92
Lawrie Pk Cres, SE26 122 DV92
Lawrie Pk Gdns, SE26 122 DV91
Lawrie Pk Rd, SE26 122 DV93
Lawson Cl, E16 86 EJ71
SW19 119 CX90
Lawson Est, SE1 201 K7
Lawson Gdns, Dart. DA1 128 FK85
Pinner HA5 59 BV55
Lawson Rd, Dart. DA1 108 FK84
Enfield EN3 30 DW39
Southall UB1 78 BZ70
Lawson Wk, Cars. SM5 158 DF110
Law St, SE1 201 L6
Lawton Rd, E3 85 DY69
E10 67 EC60
Barnet EN4 28 DD41
Loughton IG10 33 EP41
Laxcon Cl, NW10 62 CQ64
Laxey Rd, Orp. BR6 163 ET107
Laxley Cl, SE5 101 DP80
Laxton Gdns, Rad. (Shenley) WD7
off Porters Pk Dr 10 CL32
Redhill RH1 185 DK128
Laxton Pl, NW1 195 J4
Layard Rd, SE16 202 E8
Enfield EN1 30 DT39
Thornton Heath CR7 142 DR96
Layard Sq, SE16 202 D8
Layborne Av, Rom. RM3
off Cummings Hall La 52 FJ48
Layburn Cres, Slou. SL3 93 BB79
Laycock St, N1 83 DN65
Layer Gdns, W3 80 CN73
Layfield Cl, NW4 63 CV59
Layfield Cres, NW4 63 CV59
Layfield Rd, NW4 63 CV59
Layhams Rd, Kes. BR2 162 EF106
West Wickham BR4 143 ED104
Laymarsh Cl, Belv. DA17 106 EZ76
Laymead Cl, Nthlt. UB5 78 BY65
Laystall St, EC1 196 D5
Layters Av, Ger.Cr. (Chal.St.P.)
SL9 36 AW54
Layters Av S, Ger.Cr. (Chal.St.P.)
SL9 36 AW54
Layters Cl, Ger.Cr. (Chal.St.P.)
SL9 36 AW54
Layters End, Ger.Cr. (Chal.St.P.)
SL9 36 AW54
LAYTER'S GREEN, Ger.Cr. 36 AV54
Layters Grn La, Ger.Cr. (Chal.St.P.)
SL9 56 AU55
Layter's Grn Mobile Home Pk,
Ger.Cr. (Chal.St.P.) SL9
off Layters Grn La 36 AV54
Layters Way, Ger.Cr. SL9 56 AX56
Layton Ct, Wey. KT13
off Castle Vw Rd 153 BP105
Layton Cres, Croy. CR0 159 DN106
Layton Pl, Rich. TW9
off Station Av 98 CN81
Layton Rd, Brent. TW8 97 CK78
Hounslow TW3 96 CB84
Laytons Bldgs, SE1 201 J4
Laytons La, Sun. TW16 135 BT96
Layzell Wk, SE9
off Mottingham La 124 EK88

284

Laz - Lew

Lazar Wk, N7 off Briset Way . .65 DM61
Lea, The, Egh. TW20 . . . . .133 BB95
Leabank Cl, Har. HA1 . . . . .61 CE62
Leabank Sq, E9 . . . . .85 EA65
Leabank Vw, N15 . . . . .66 DU58
Leabourne Rd, N16 . . . . .66 DU58
LEA BRIDGE, E5 . . . . .67 DX62
Lea Br Business Cen, E10
off Burwell Rd 67 DY60
Lea Br Rd, E5 . . . . .66 DW62
E10 . . . . .67 DY60
E17 . . . . .67 ED56
Lea Bushes, Wat. WD25 . . . . . .24 BY35
Leachcroft, Ger.Cr. (Chal.St.P.)
SL9 . . . . .36 AV53
Leach Gro, Lthd. KT22 . . . . . .171 CJ122
Lea Cl, Bushey WD23 . . . . .24 CB43
Twickenham TW2 . . . . .116 BZ87
Lea Cres, Ruis. HA4 . . . . .59 BT63
Leacroft, Stai. TW18 . . . . .114 BH91
Leacroft Av, SW12 . . . . .120 DF87
Leacroft Cl, Ken. CR8 . . . . . . .176 DQ116
Staines TW18 . . . . .114 BH91
West Drayton UB7 . . . . .76 BL72
Leacroft Rd, Iver SL0 . . . . .75 BD72
Leadale Av, E4 . . . . .47 EA47
Leadale Rd, N15 . . . . .66 DU58
N16 . . . . .66 DU58
Leadbeaters Cl, N11
off Goldsmith Rd 44 DF50
★ Leadenhall Mkt, EC3 . . . . . .197 M9
Leadenhall Mkt, EC3 . . . . .197 M9
Leadenhall Pl, EC3 . . . . .197 M9
Leadenhall St, EC3 . . . . .197 M9
Leader Av, E12 . . . . .69 EN64
Leadings, The, Wem. HA9 . . . . .62 CQ62
Leaf Cl, Nthwd. HA6 . . . . .39 BR52
Thames Ditton KT7 . . . . .137 CE99
Leaf Gro, SE27 . . . . .121 DN92
Leafield Cl, SW16 . . . . .121 DP93
Woking GU21
off Winnington Way 166 AV118
Leafield La, Sid. DA14 . . . . . . .126 EZ91
Leafield Rd, SW20 . . . . .139 CZ97
Sutton SM1 . . . . .140 DA103
Leaford Cres, Wat. WD24 . . . . . .23 BT37
Leaforis Rd, Wal.Cr. EN7 . . . . . .14 DU28
Leafy Gro, Croy. CR0 . . . . .161 DY111
Keston BR2 . . . . .162 EJ106
Leafy Oak Rd, SE12 . . . . .124 EJ90
Leafy Way, Brwd. CM13 . . . . . . .55 GD46
Croydon CR0 . . . . .142 DT103
Lea Gdns, Wem. HA9 . . . . .62 CL63
Leagrave St, E5 . . . . .66 DW62
Lea Hall Rd, E10 . . . . .67 EA60
Leaholme Way, Ruis. HA4 . . . . .59 BP58
Leahurst Rd, SE13 . . . . .123 ED85
Leake St, SE1 . . . . .200 C4
Lealand Rd, N15 . . . . .66 DT58
Leamington Av, E17 . . . . .67 EA57
Bromley BR1 . . . . .124 EJ92
Morden SM4 . . . . .139 CZ98
Orpington BR6 . . . . .163 ES105
Leamington Cl, E12 . . . . .68 EL64
Bromley BR1 . . . . .124 EJ92
Hounslow TW3 . . . . .116 CC85
Romford RM3 . . . . .52 FM51
Leamington Cres, Har. HA2 . . . .60 BY62
Leamington Gdns, Ilf. IG3 . . . . .69 ET61
Leamington Pk, W3 . . . . .80 CR71
Leamington Pl, Hayes UB4 . . . .77 BT70
Leamington Rd, Rom. RM3 . . . . .52 FN50
Southall UB2 . . . . .96 BX77
Leamington Rd Vil, W11 . . . . . .81 CZ71
Leamore St, W6 . . . . .99 CV77
Lea Mt, Wal.Cr. EN7 . . . . .14 DS28
Leamouth Rd, E6
off Remington Rd 86 EL72
E14 . . . . .85 ED72
Leander Ct, SE8 . . . . .103 EA81
Leander Dr, Grav. DA12 . . . . . .131 GM91
Leander Gdns, Wat. WD25 . . . . .24 BY37
Leander Rd, SW2 . . . . .121 DM86
Northolt UB5 . . . . .78 CA68
Thornton Heath CR7 . . . . . . .141 DM98
Learner Dr, Har. HA2 . . . . .60 CA61
Lea Rd, Beck. BR3
off Fairfield Rd 143 EA96
Enfield EN2 . . . . .30 DR39
Grays RM16 . . . . .111 GG78
Sevenoaks TN13 . . . . .191 FJ127
Southall UB2 . . . . .96 BY77
Waltham Abbey EN9 . . . . .15 EA34
Learoyd Gdns, E6 . . . . .87 EN73
Leas, The, Bushey WD23 . . . . . .24 BZ39
Staines TW18
off Raleigh Ct 114 BG91
Upminster RM14 . . . . .73 FR59
Leas Cl, Chess. KT9 . . . . .156 CM108
Leas Dale, SE9 . . . . .125 EN90
Leas Dr, Iver SL0 . . . . .75 BE72
Leas Grn, Chis. BR7 . . . . .125 ET93
Leaside, Lthd. (Bkhm.) KT23 . .170 CA123
Leaside Av, N10 . . . . .64 DG55
Leaside Ct, Uxb. UB10
off The Larches 77 BP69
Leaside Rd, E5 . . . . .66 DW60
Leas La, Warl. CR6 . . . . .177 DX118
Leasowes Rd, E10 . . . . .67 EA60
Leas Rd, Warl. CR6 . . . . .177 DX118
Leasway, Brwd. CM14 . . . . .54 FX48
Upminster RM14 . . . . .72 FQ62
Leathart Cl, Horn. RM12
off Dowding Way 89 FH66
Leatherbottle Grn, Erith
DA18 . . . . .106 EZ76
Leather Bottle La, Belv.
DA17 . . . . .106 EY77
Leather Cl, Mitch. CR4 . . . . . .140 DG96
Leatherdale St, E1
off Portelet Rd 85 DX70
Leather Gdns, E15
off Abbey Rd 86 EE67
LEATHERHEAD 171 CF121
⇌ Leatherhead 171 CG121
Leatherhead Bypass Rd, Lthd.
KT22 . . . . .171 CH120
Leatherhead Cl, N16 . . . . .66 DT60
LEATHERHEAD COMMON,
Lthd. 171 CF119
H Leatherhead Hosp, Lthd.
KT22 . . . . .171 CJ122
★ Leatherhead Mus of Local
History, Lthd. KT22 . . . . . .171 CH122
Leatherhead Rd, Ashtd.
KT21 . . . . .171 CK121
Chessington KT9 . . . . .155 CJ111
Leatherhead KT22 . . . . .171 CK121
Leatherhead (Oxshott)
KT22 . . . . .155 CD114
Leather La, EC1 . . . . .196 E7
Hornchurch RM11
off North St 72 FK60
Leathermarket Ct, SE1 . . . . . .201 M5
Leathermarket St, SE1 . . . . . .201 M5
Leathersellers Cl, Barn. EN5
off The Avenue 27 CY42
Leathsail Rd, Har. HA2 . . . . . . .60 CB62
Leathwaite Rd, SW11 . . . . . . .100 DF84
Leathwell Rd, SE8 . . . . .103 EB82
Lea Vale, Dart. DA1 . . . . .107 FD84
Lea Valley Rd, E4 . . . . .31 DX43
Enfield EN3 . . . . .31 DX43
Lea Valley Trd Est, N18 . . . . . . .47 DX50
Lea Valley Viaduct, E4 . . . . . . .47 DX50
N18 . . . . .47 DX50
Lea Valley Wk, E3 . . . . .85 EC70
E5 .67 DY62
E9 .67 DY62
E10 . . . . .67 DY62
E14 . . . . .85 EB71
E15 . . . . .85 EC69
E17 . . . . .46 DW53
N9 .47 DY46
N15 . . . . .66 DU58
N16 . . . . .66 DU58
N17 . . . . .46 DW53
N18 . . . . .46 DW53
Enfield EN3 . . . . .31 DZ41
Waltham Abbey EN9 . . . . .15 DZ30
Waltham Cross EN8 . . . . .15 DZ30
Leaveland Cl, Beck. BR3 . . . . .143 EA98
Leaver Gdns, Grnf. UB6 . . . . . .79 CD68
LEAVESDEN GREEN, Wat. 7 BT34
Leavesden Rd, Stan. HA7 . . . . .41 CG51
Watford WD24 . . . . .23 BV38
Weybridge KT13 . . . . .153 BP106
LEAVES GREEN, Kes. 162 EK109
Leaves Grn Cres, Kes. BR2 . . .162 EJ111
Leaves Grn Rd, Kes. BR2 . . . .162 EK111
Leaview, Wal.Abb. EN9 . . . . . . .15 EB33
Lea Vw Hos, E5
off Springfield 66 DV60
Leaway, E10 . . . . .67 DX60
Leazes Av, Cat. CR3 . . . . .175 DN123
Leazes La, Cat. CR3 . . . . .175 DN123
Lebanon Av, Felt. TW13 . . . . . .116 BX92
Lebanon Cl, Wat. WD17 . . . . . . .23 BR36
Lebanon Ct, Twick. TW1 . . . . . .117 CH87
Lebanon Dr, Cob. KT11 . . . . . .154 CA113
Lebanon Gdns, SW18 . . . . . . .120 DA86
Westerham (Bigg.H.) TN16 .178 EK117
Lebanon Pk, Twick. TW1 . . . . . .117 CH87
Lebanon Road 142 DS103
Lebanon Rd, SW18 . . . . .120 DA85
Croydon CR0 . . . . .142 DS102
Lebrun Sq, SE3 . . . . .104 EH83
Lechmere App, Wdf.Grn. IG8 . .48 EJ54
Lechmere Av, Chig. IG7 . . . . . .49 EQ49
Woodford Green IG8 . . . . .48 EK54
Lechmere Rd, NW2 . . . . .81 CV65
Leckford Rd, SW18 . . . . .120 DC89
Leckwith Av, Bexh. DA7 . . . . .106 EY79
Lecky St, SW7 . . . . .100 DD78
Leclair Ho, SE3 off Gallus Sq .104 EH83
Leconfield Av, SW13 . . . . .99 CT83
Leconfield Rd, N5 . . . . .66 DR63
Leconfield Wk, Horn. RM12
off Airfield Way 90 FJ65
Le Corte Cl, Kings L. WD4 . . . . .6 BM29
Leda Av, Enf. EN3 . . . . .31 DX39
Leda Rd, SE18 . . . . .105 EM76
Ledbury Est, SE15 . . . . .102 DV80
Ledbury Ms N, W11
off Ledbury Rd 82 DA73
Ledbury Ms W, W11
off Ledbury Rd 82 DA73
Ledbury Pl, Croy. CR0
off Ledbury Rd 160 DQ105
Ledbury Rd, W11 . . . . .81 CZ72
Croydon CR0 . . . . .160 DQ105
Reigate RH2 . . . . .183 CZ133
Ledbury St, SE15 . . . . .102 DU80
Ledger Dr, Add. KT15 . . . . . . .151 BF106
Ledgers Rd, Slou. SL1 . . . . .92 AS75
Warlingham CR6 . . . . .177 EB117
Ledrington Rd, SE19
off Anerley Hill 122 DU93
Ledway Dr, Wem. HA9 . . . . .62 CM59
LEE, SE12 . . . . .104 EE84
⇌ Lee 124 EG86
Lee, The, Nthwd. HA6 . . . . .39 BT50
Lee Av, Rom. RM6 . . . . .70 EY58
Lee Br, SE13 . . . . .103 EC83
Leechcroft Av, Sid. DA15 . . . . .125 ET85
Swanley BR8 . . . . .147 FF97
Leechcroft Rd, Wall. SM6 . . . .140 DG104
Leech La, Epsom (Headley)
KT18 . . . . .182 CQ126
Leatherhead KT22 . . . . .182 CQ126
Lee Ch St, SE13 . . . . .104 EE84
Lee Cl, E17 . . . . .47 DX53
Barnet EN5 . . . . .28 DC42
Lee Conservancy Rd, E9 . . . . . .67 DZ64
Leecroft Rd, Barn. EN5 . . . . . . .27 CY43
Leeds Cl, Orp. BR6 . . . . .146 EX103
Leeds Pl, N4 off Tollington Pk . .65 DM61
Leeds Rd, Ilf. IG1 . . . . .69 ER60
Slough SL1 . . . . .74 AS73
Leeds St, N18 . . . . .46 DU50
Lee Fm Cl, Chesh. HP5 . . . . . . .4 AU30
Leefern Rd, W12 . . . . .99 CU75
Leefe Way, Pot.B. EN6 . . . . . . .13 DK28
Lee Gdns Av, Horn. RM11 . . . . .72 FN60
Leegate, SE12 . . . . .124 EF85
Leegate Cl, Wok. GU21
off Sythwood 166 AV116
Lee Grn, SE12
off Lee High Rd 124 EF85
Orpington BR5 . . . . .146 EU99
Lee Grn La, Epsom KT18 . . . . .172 CP124
Lee Gro, Chig. IG7 . . . . .49 EN47
Lee High Rd, SE12 . . . . .103 ED83
SE13 . . . . .103 ED83
Leeke St, WC1 . . . . .196 B2
Leeland Rd, W13 . . . . .79 CG74
Leeland Ter, W13 . . . . .79 CG74
Leeland Way, NW10 . . . . .63 CT63
Leeming Rd, Borwd. WD6 . . . . .26 CM39
Lee Pk, SE3 . . . . .104 EF84
Lee Pk Way, N9 . . . . .47 DX49
N18 . . . . .47 DX49
Leerdam Dr, E14 . . . . .204 E7
Lee Rd, NW7 . . . . .43 CX52
SE3 . . . . .104 EF83
SW19 . . . . .140 DB95
Enfield EN1 . . . . .30 DU44
Greenford UB6 . . . . .79 CJ67
Lees, The, Croy. CR0 . . . . .143 DZ103
Lees Av, Nthwd. HA6 . . . . .39 BT53
Leeside, Barn. EN5 . . . . .27 CY43
Potters Bar EN6
off Wayside 12 DD31
Leeside Ct, SE16 . . . . .203 H2
Leeside Cres, NW11 . . . . .63 CZ58
Leeside Rd, N17 . . . . .46 DV51
Leeson Rd, SE24 . . . . .101 DN84
Leesons Hill, Chis. BR7 . . . . . .145 ES97
Orpington BR5 . . . . .146 EU97
Leesons Way, Orp. BR5 . . . . . .145 ET96
Lees Pl, W1 . . . . .194 F10
Lees Rd, Uxb. UB8 . . . . .77 BP70
Lee St, E8 . . . . .84 DT67
Lee Ter, SE3 . . . . .104 EE83
SE13 . . . . .104 EE83
Lee Valley Cycle Route, Wal.Abb.
EN9 . . . . .15 EC26
★ Lee Valley Pk, E10 . . . . .15 DZ31
Lee Valley Pathway, E9 . . . . . . .67 DZ62
E10 . . . . .66 DW59
E17 . . . . .66 DW59
Waltham Abbey EN9 . . . . .15 EA31
Lee Valley Technopark, N17 . . .66 DU55
Lee Vw, Enf. EN2 . . . . .29 DP39
Leeward Gdns, SW19 . . . . . . .119 CZ93
Leeway, SE8 . . . . .203 M10
Leeway Cl, Pnr. HA5 . . . . .40 BZ52
Leewood Cl, SE12
off Upwood Rd 124 EF86
Leewood Pl, Swan. BR8 . . . . . .147 FD98
Lefevre Wk, E3 . . . . .85 EA67
Lefroy Rd, W12 . . . . .99 CT75
Legard Rd, N5 . . . . .65 DP62
Legatt Rd, SE9 . . . . .124 EK85
Leggatt Rd, E15 . . . . .85 EC68
Leggatts Cl, Wat. WD24 . . . . . .23 BT36
Leggatts Ri, Wat. WD25 . . . . . .23 BU35
Leggatts Way, Wat. WD24 . . . . .23 BT36
Leggatts Wd Av, Wat. WD24 . . .23 BV36
Legge St, SE13 . . . . .123 EC85
Leghorn Rd, NW10 . . . . .81 CT68
SE18 . . . . .105 ER78
Legion Cl, N1 . . . . .83 DN65
Legion Ct, Mord. SM4 . . . . . . .140 DA100
Legion Rd, Grnf. UB6 . . . . .78 CC67
Legion Ter, E3 off Lefevre Wk . .85 DZ67
Legion Way, N12 . . . . .44 DE52
Legon Av, Rom. RM7 . . . . .71 FC60
Legrace Av, Houns. TW4 . . . . . .96 BX82
Leicester Av, Mitch. CR4 . . . . .141 DL98
Leicester Cl, Wor.Pk. KT4 . . . .157 CW105
Leicester Ct, WC2 . . . . .195 N10
Leicester Gdns, Ilf. IG3 . . . . . . .69 ES59
Leicester Ms, N2
off Leicester Rd 64 DE55
Leicester Pl, WC2 . . . . .195 N10
Leicester Rd, E11 . . . . .68 EH57
N2 .64 DE55
Barnet EN5 . . . . .28 DB43
Croydon CR0 . . . . .142 DS101
Tilbury RM18 . . . . .111 GF81
⊖ Leicester Square 195 N10
Leicester Sq, WC2 . . . . .199 N1
Leicester St, WC2 . . . . .195 N10
Leigham Av, SW16 . . . . .121 DL90
Leigham Ct, Wall. SM6
off Stafford Rd 159 DJ107
Leigham Ct Rd, SW16 . . . . . . .121 DL89
Leigham Dr, Islw. TW7 . . . . . . .97 CE80
Leigham Vale, SW2 . . . . .121 DM90
SW16 . . . . .121 DM90
Leigh Av, Ilf. IG4 . . . . .68 EK56
Leigh Cl, Add. KT15 . . . . .151 BF108
New Malden KT3 . . . . .138 CR98
Leigh Cor, Cob. KT11
off Leigh Hill Rd 154 BW114
Leigh Ct, SE4
off Lewisham Way 103 EA82
Borehamwood WD6
off Banks Rd 26 CR40
Harrow HA2 . . . . .61 CE60
Leigh Ct Cl, Cob. KT11 . . . . . .154 BW114
Leigh Cres, Croy. (New Adgtn.)
CR0 . . . . .161 EB108
Leigh Dr, Rom. RM3 . . . . .52 FK49
Leigh Gdns, NW10 . . . . .81 CW68
Leigh Hill Rd, Cob. KT11 . . . . .154 BW114
Leigh Hunt Dr, N14 . . . . .45 DK46
Leigh Hunt St, SE1 . . . . .201 H4
Leigh Orchard Cl, SW16 . . . . .121 DM90
Leigh Pk, Slou. (Datchet) SL3 . .92 AV80
Leigh Pl, EC1 . . . . .196 D6
Cobham KT11 . . . . .170 BW115
Dartford DA2
off Hawley Rd 128 FN92
Welling DA16 . . . . .106 EU82
Leigh Pl La, Gdse. RH9 . . . . . .187 DY132
Leigh Rd, E6 . . . . .87 EN65
Leigh Rd, E10 . . . . .67 EC59
N5 .65 DP63
Cobham KT11 . . . . .153 BV113
Gravesend DA11 . . . . .131 GH89
Hounslow TW3 . . . . .97 CD84
Leigh Rodd, Wat. WD19 . . . . . .40 BZ48
Leigh St, WC1 . . . . .195 P4
Leigh Ter, Orp. BR5
off Saxville Rd 146 EV97
Leighton Av, E12 . . . . .69 EN64
Pinner HA5 . . . . .60 BY55
Leighton Cl, Edg. HA8 . . . . . . .42 CN54
Leighton Cres, NW5
off Leighton Gro 65 DJ64
Leighton Gdns, NW10 . . . . .81 CV68
South Croydon CR2 . . . . . . .160 DV113
Tilbury RM18 . . . . .111 GG80
Leighton Gro, NW5 . . . . .65 DJ64
★ Leighton Ho Mus, W14 . . . . .99 CZ76
Leighton Pl, NW5 . . . . .65 DJ64
Leighton Rd, NW5 . . . . .65 DK64
W13 . . . . .97 CG75
Enfield EN1 . . . . .30 DT43
Harrow (Har.Wld.) HA3 . . . . . .41 CD54
Leighton St, Croy. CR0 . . . . . .141 DP102
Leighton Way, Epsom KT18 . .156 CR114
Leila Parnell Pl, SE7 . . . . .104 EJ79
Leinster Av, SW14 . . . . .98 CQ83
Leinster Gdns, W2 . . . . .82 DC72
Leinster Ms, W2 . . . . .82 DC73
Leinster Pl, W2 . . . . .82 DC72
Leinster Rd, N10 . . . . .65 DH56
Leinster Sq, W2 . . . . .82 DA72
Leinster Ter, W2 . . . . .82 DC73
Leiston Spur, Slou. SL1 . . . . . .74 AS72
Leisure La, W.Byf. KT14 . . . . .152 BH112
Leisure Way, N12 . . . . .44 DD52
Leith Cl, NW9 . . . . .62 CR60
Slough SL1 . . . . .74 AU74
Leithcote Gdns, SW16 . . . . . .121 DM91
Leithcote Path, SW16 . . . . . . .121 DM90
Leith Hill, Orp. BR5 . . . . .146 EU95
Leith Hill Grn, Orp. BR5
off Leith Hill 146 EU95
Leith Pk Rd, Grav. DA12 . . . . .131 GH88
Leith Rd, N22 . . . . .45 DP53
Epsom KT17 . . . . .156 CS112
Leith Yd, NW6 off Quex Rd 82 DA67
Lela Av, Houns. TW4 . . . . .96 BW82
Lelitia Cl, E8 off Pownall Rd . . .84 DU67
Leman St, E1 . . . . .84 DT72
Lemark Cl, Stan. HA7 . . . . .41 CJ50
Le May Av, SE12 . . . . .124 EH90
Lemmon Rd, SE10 . . . . .104 EE79
Lemna Rd, E11 . . . . .68 EE59
Lemonfield Dr, Wat. WD25 . . . . .8 BY32
Lemonwell Ct, SE9
off Lemonwell Dr 125 EQ85
Lemonwell Dr, SE9 . . . . .125 EQ85
Lemsford Cl, N15 . . . . .66 DU57
Lemsford Ct, N4
off Brownswood Rd 66 DQ61
Borehamwood WD6 . . . . .26 CQ42
Lemuel St, SW18 . . . . .120 DB86
Lena Gdns, W6 . . . . .99 CW76
Lena Kennedy Cl, E4 . . . . .47 EB51
Lenanton Steps, E14 . . . . .204 A4
Lendal Ter, SW4 . . . . .101 DK83
Lenelby Rd, Surb. KT6 . . . . . .138 CN102
Len Freeman Pl, SW6
off John Smith Av 99 CZ80
Lenham Rd, SE12 . . . . .104 EF84
Bexleyheath DA7 . . . . .106 EZ79
Sutton SM1 . . . . .158 DB105
Thornton Heath CR7 . . . . . . .142 DR96
Lenmore Av, Grays RM17 . . . . .110 GC76
Lennard Av, W.Wick. BR4 . . . .144 EE103
Lennard Cl, W.Wick. BR4 . . . . .144 EE103
Lennard Rd, SE20 . . . . .122 DW93
Beckenham BR3 . . . . .123 DX93
Bromley BR2 . . . . .145 EM102
Croydon CR0 . . . . .142 DQ102
Sevenoaks (Dunt.Grn.)
TN13 . . . . .181 FE120
Lennard Row, S.Ock. (Aveley)
RM15 . . . . .91 FR74
Lennon Rd, NW2 . . . . .63 CW64
Lennox Av, Grav. DA11 . . . . . .131 GF86
Lennox Cl, Grays (Chaff.Hun.)
RM16 . . . . .109 FW77
Romford RM1 . . . . .71 FF58
Lennox Gdns, NW10 . . . . .63 CT63
SW1 . . . . .198 D7
Croydon CR0 . . . . .159 DP105
Ilford IG1 . . . . .69 EM60
Lennox Gdns Ms, SW1 . . . . . . .198 D7
Lennox Rd, E17 . . . . .67 DZ58
N4 .65 DM61
Gravesend DA11 . . . . .131 GF86
Lennox Rd E, Grav. DA11 . . . . .131 GG87
Lenor Cl, Bexh. DA6 . . . . .106 EY84
Lensbury Cl, Wal.Cr. (Chsht.) EN8
off Ashdown Cres 15 DY28
Lensbury Way, SE2 . . . . .106 EW76
Lens Rd, E7 . . . . .86 EJ66
Lenthall Av, Grays RM17 . . . . .110 GA75
Lenthall Rd, E8 . . . . .84 DU66
Loughton IG10 . . . . .33 ER42
Lenthorp Rd, SE10 . . . . .205 K10
Lentmead Rd, Brom. BR1 . . . .124 EF90
Lenton Path, SE18 . . . . .105 ER79
Lenton Ri, Rich. TW9
off Evelyn Ter 98 CL83
Lenton St, SE18 . . . . .105 ER77
Leof Cres, SE6 . . . . .123 EB92
Leominster Rd, Mord. SM4 . . .140 DC100
Leominster Wk, Mord. SM4 . . .140 DC100
Leonard Av, Mord. SM4 . . . . . .140 DC99
Romford RM7 . . . . .71 FD60
Sevenoaks (Otford) TN14 . . .181 FH116
Swanscombe DA10 . . . . .130 FY87
Leonard Pl, N16 off Allen Rd . . .66 DS63
Leonard Rd, E4 . . . . .47 EA51
E7 . . . . .68 EG63
N9 .46 DT48
SW16 . . . . .141 DJ95
Southall UB2 . . . . .96 BX76
Leonard Robbins Path, SE28
off Tawney Rd 88 EV73
Leonard St, E16 . . . . .86 EL74
EC2 . . . . .197 L4
Leonard Way, Brwd. CM14 . . . . .54 FS49
Leontine Cl, SE15 . . . . .102 DU80
Leopards Ct, EC1 . . . . .196 D6
Leopold Av, SW19 . . . . .119 CZ92
Leopold Ms, E9
off Fremont St 84 DW67
Leopold Rd, E17 . . . . .67 EA57
N2 .64 DD55
N18 . . . . .46 DV50
NW10 . . . . .80 CS66
SW19 . . . . .119 CZ91
W5 .80 CM74
Leopold St, E3 . . . . .85 DZ71
Leopold Ter, SW19
off Dora Rd 120 DA92
Leo St, SE15 . . . . .102 DV80
Leo Yd, EC1 . . . . .196 G5
Le Personne Rd, Cat. CR3 . . .176 DR122
Leppoc Rd, SW4 . . . . .121 DK85
Leret Way, Lthd. KT22 . . . . . .171 CH121
Leroy St, SE1 . . . . .201 M8
Lerwick Dr, Slou. SL1 . . . . .74 AS71
Lescombe Cl, SE23 . . . . .123 DY90
Lescombe Rd, SE23 . . . . .123 DY90
Lesley Cl, Bex. DA5 . . . . .127 FB87
Gravesend (Istead Rise)
DA13 . . . . .131 GF94
Swanley BR8 . . . . .147 FD97
Leslie Gdns, Sutt. SM2 . . . . . .158 DA108
Leslie Gro, Croy. CR0 . . . . . . .142 DS102
Leslie Gro Pl, Croy. CR0
off Leslie Gro 142 DR102
Leslie Pk Rd, Croy. CR0 . . . . .142 DS102
Leslie Rd, E11 . . . . .67 EC63
E16 . . . . .86 EH72
N2 .64 DD55
Woking (Chobham) GU24 . .150 AS110
Leslie Smith Sq, SE18
off Nightingale Vale 105 EN79
★ Lesnes Abbey (ruins), Erith
DA18 . . . . .106 EX77
Lesney Fm Est, Erith DA8 . . . .107 FD80
Lesney Pk, Erith DA8 . . . . . . .107 FD79
Lesney Pk Rd, Erith DA8 . . . . .107 FD79
Lessar Av, SW4 . . . . .121 DJ85
Lessingham Av, SW17 . . . . . .120 DF91
Ilford IG5 . . . . .69 EN55
Lessing St, SE23 . . . . .123 DY87
Lessington Av, Rom. RM7 . . . . .71 FC58
Lessness Av, Bexh. DA7 . . . . .106 EX80
LESSNESS HEATH, Belv. 107 FB78
Lessness Pk, Belv. DA17 . . . . .106 EZ78
Lessness Rd, Belv. DA17
off Stapley Rd 106 FA78
Morden SM4 . . . . .140 DC100
Lester Av, E15 . . . . .86 EE69
Leston Cl, Rain. RM13 . . . . . . .89 FG69
Leswin Pl, N16 off Leswin Rd .66 DT62
Leswin Rd, N16 . . . . .66 DT62
Letchfield, Chesh. (Ley Hill)
HP5 .4 AV31
Letchford Gdns, NW10 . . . . . . .81 CU69
Letchford Ms, NW10
off Letchford Gdns 81 CU69
Letchford Ter, Har. HA3 . . . . . .40 CB53
LETCHMORE HEATH, Wat. 25 CD38
Letchmore Rd, Rad. WD7 . . . . .25 CG36
Letchworth Av, Felt. TW14 . . . .115 BT87
Letchworth Cl, Brom. BR2 . . . .144 EG99
Watford WD19 . . . . .40 BX50
Letchworth Dr, Brom. BR2 . . . .144 EG99
Letchworth St, SW17 . . . . . . .120 DF91
Lethbridge Cl, SE13 . . . . .103 EC81
Letter Box La, Sev. TN13 . . . .191 FJ129
Letterstone Rd, SW6
off Varna Rd 99 CZ80
Lettice St, SW6 . . . . .99 CZ81
Lett Rd, E15 . . . . .85 ED66
Lettsom St, SE5 . . . . .102 DS82
Lettsom Wk, E13 . . . . .86 EG68
Leucha Rd, E17 . . . . .67 DY57
Levana Cl, SW19 . . . . .119 CY88
Levehurst Way, SW4 . . . . . . .101 DL82
Leven Cl, Wal.Cr. EN8 . . . . . . .15 DX33
Watford WD19 . . . . .40 BX50
Levendale Rd, SE23 . . . . .123 DY89
Leven Dr, Wal.Cr. EN8 . . . . . . .15 DX33
Leven Rd, E14 . . . . .85 EC71
Leven Way, Hayes UB3 . . . . . . .77 BS72
Leveret Cl, Croy. (New Adgtn.)
CR0 . . . . .161 ED111
Watford WD25 . . . . .7 BU34
Leverett St, SW3 . . . . .198 C8
Leverholme Gdns, SE9 . . . . . .125 EN90
Leverson St, SW16 . . . . .121 DJ93
Lever Sq, Grays RM16 . . . . . .111 GG77
Lever St, EC1 . . . . .196 G3
Leverton Pl, NW5
off Leverton St 65 DJ64
Leverton St, NW5 . . . . .65 DJ64
Leverton Way, Wal.Abb. EN9 . . .15 EC33
Leveson Rd, Grays RM16 . . . .111 GH76
Levett Gdns, Ilf. IG3 . . . . .69 ET63
Levett Rd, Bark. IG11 . . . . . . .87 ES65
Leatherhead KT22 . . . . .171 CH120
Levine Gdns, Bark. IG11 . . . . .88 EX68
Levison Way, N19
off Grovedale Rd 65 DK61
Lewes Cl, Grays RM17 . . . . . .110 GA79
Northolt UB5 . . . . .78 CA65
Lewesdon Cl, SW19 . . . . .119 CX88
Lewes Rd, N12 . . . . .44 DE50
Bromley BR1 . . . . .144 EK96
Romford RM3 . . . . .52 FJ49
Leweston Pl, N16 . . . . .66 DT59
Lewes Way, Rick. (Crox.Grn.)
WD3 . . . . .23 BQ42
Lewey Ho, E3 . . . . .85 DZ70
Lewgars Av, NW9 . . . . .62 CQ58
Lewin Rd, SW14 . . . . .98 CR83
SW16 . . . . .121 DK93
Bexleyheath DA6 . . . . .106 EY84
Lewins Rd, Epsom KT18 . . . . .156 CP114

★ Place of interest ⇌ Railway station ⊖ London Underground station DLR Docklands Light Railway station Tramlink station H Hospital

Lewins Rd, Ger.Cr. (Chal.St.P.)
SL9 56 AX55
Lewis Av, E17 47 EA53
Lewis Cl, N14 *off Orchid Rd* 45 DJ45
Addlestone KT15 152 BJ105
Brentwood CM15 55 FZ45
Uxbridge (Hare.) UB9 38 BJ54
Lewis Cres, NW10 62 CQ64
Lewis Gdns, N2 44 DD54
Lewis Gro, SE13 103 EC83
LEWISHAM, SE13 103 EB84
⇌ **Lewisham** 103 EC83
DLR **Lewisham** 103 EC83
Lewisham Cen, SE13 103 EC83
Lewisham High St, SE13 103 EC83
Lewisham Hill, SE13 103 EC82
Lewisham Pk, SE13 123 EB86
Lewisham Rd, SE13 103 EB81
Lewisham St, SW1 199 N5
Lewisham Way, SE4 103 DZ81
SE14 103 DZ81
Lewis La, Ger.Cr. (Chal.St.P.)
SL9 36 AY53
Lewis Pl, E8 66 DU64
Lewis Rd, Horn. RM11 72 FJ58
Mitcham CR4 140 DD96
Richmond TW10
off Red Lion St 117 CK85
Sidcup DA14 126 EW90
Southall UB1 96 BY75
Sutton SM1 158 DB105
Swanscombe DA10 130 FY86
Welling DA16 106 EW83
Lewis St, NW1 83 DH65
Lewis Way, Dag. RM10 89 FB65
Lexden Dr, Rom. RM6 70 EV58
Lexden Rd, W3 80 CP73
Mitcham CR4 141 DK98
Lexham Ct, Grnf. UB6 79 CD67
Lexham Gdns, W8 100 DB76
Lexham Gdns Ms, W8 100 DB76
Lexham Ho, Bark. IG11
off St. Margarets 87 ER67
Lexham Ms, W8 100 DA77
Lexham Wk, W8
off Lexham Gdns 100 DB76
Lexington, The, EC1 197 K4
Lexington Cl, Borwd. WD6 26 CM41
Lexington Ct, Pur. CR8 160 DQ110
Lexington St, W1 195 L9
Lexington Way, Barn. EN5 27 CX42
Upminster RM14 73 FT58
Lexton Gdns, SW12 121 DK88
Leybourne Av, W13 97 CH75
Leybourne Pk, Rich. TW9 98 CN81
Leybourne Av, W.Byf. (Byfleet)
KT14 152 BM113
Leybourne Cl, Brom. BR2 144 EG100
West Byfleet (Byfleet) KT14
off Leybourne Av 152 BM113
Leybourne Rd, E11 68 EF60
NW1 83 DH66
NW9 62 CN57
Uxbridge UB10 77 BQ67
Leybourne St, NW1
off Hawley St 83 DH66
Leybridge Ct, SE12 124 EG85
Leyburn Cl, E17 *off Church La* 67 EB56
Leyburn Cres, Rom. RM3 52 FL52
Leyburn Gdns, Croy. CR0 142 DS103
Leyburn Gro, N18 46 DU51
Leyburn Rd, N18 46 DU51
Romford RM3 52 FL52
Leycroft Cl, Loug. IG10 33 EN43
Leycroft Gdns, Erith DA8 107 FH81
Leydenhatch La, Swan. BR8 147 FC95
Leyden St, E1 197 P7
Leydon Cl, SE16 203 J3
Leyfield, Wor.Pk. KT4 138 CS102
Leyhill Cl, Swan. BR8 147 FE99
Ley Hill Rd, Hem.H. (Bov.) HP3 4 AX30
Leyland Av, Enf. EN3 31 DY40
Leyland Cl, Wal.Cr. (Chsht.)
EN8 14 DW28
Leyland Gdns, Wdf.Grn. IG8 48 EJ50
Leyland Rd, SE12 124 EG85
Leylands La, Stai. TW19 113 BF85
Leylang Rd, SE14 103 DX80
Leys, The, N2 64 DC56
Harrow HA3 62 CM58
Leys Av, Dag. RM10 89 FC66
Leys Cl, Dag. RM10 89 FC66
Harrow HA1 61 CD57
Uxbridge (Hare.) UB9 38 BK53
Leysdown Av, Bexh. DA7 107 FC84
Leysdown Rd, SE9 124 EL89
Leysfield Rd, W12 99 CU75
Leys Gdns, Barn. EN4 28 DG43
Leyspring Rd, E11 68 EF60
Leys Rd, Lthd. (Oxshott)
KT22 155 CD112
Leys Rd E, Enf. EN3 31 DY39
Leys Rd W, Enf. EN3 31 DY39
Ley St, Ilf. IG1, IG2 69 EP61
Leyswood Dr, Ilf. IG2 69 ES57
Leythe Rd, W3 98 CQ75
LEYTON, E11 67 EB60
⊖ **Leyton** 67 EC62
Leyton Business Cen, E10 67 EA61
Leyton Cross Rd, Dart. DA2 127 FF90
Leyton Gra, E10
off Goldsmith Rd 67 EB60
Leyton Gra Est, E10 67 EB60
Leyton Grn Rd, E10 67 EC58
Leyton Ind Village, E10 67 DX59
⇌ **Leyton Midland Road** 67 EC60
★ **Leyton Orient FC**, E10 67 EB62
Leyton Pk Rd, E10 67 EC62
Leyton Rd, E15 67 ED64
SW19 120 DC94
LEYTONSTONE, E11 67 ED59
⊖ **Leytonstone** 68 EE60
⇌ **Leytonstone High Road** 68 EE61
Leytonstone Rd, E15 68 EE64
Leyton Way, E11 68 EE59
Leywick St, E15 86 EE68
Lezayre Rd, Orp. BR6 163 ET107
Liardet St, SE14 103 DY79
Liberia Rd, N5 83 DP65
★ **Liberty**, W1 195 K9
Liberty, The, Rom. RM1 71 FE57
Liberty Av, SW19 140 DD95
Liberty Hall Rd, Add. KT15 152 BG106
Liberty La, Add. KT15 152 BG106
Liberty Ms, SW12 121 DH86
Liberty Ri, Add. KT15 152 BG107
Liberty St, SW9 101 DM81
Libra Rd, E3 85 DZ67
E13 86 EG68
Library Hill, Brwd. CM14
off Coptfold Rd 54 FX47
Library Pl, E1 *off Cable St* 84 DV73
Library St, SE1 200 F5
Library Way, Twick. TW2
off Nelson Rd 116 CC87
Licenced Victuallers National Homes, Uxb. (Denh.) UB9
off Denham Grn La 57 BF58
Lichfield Cl, Barn. EN4 28 DF41
Lichfield Ct, Rich. TW9
off Sheen Rd 98 CL84
Lichfield Gdns, Rich. TW9 98 CL84
Lichfield Gro, N3 44 DA53
Lichfield Rd, E3 85 DY69
E6 86 EK69
N9 *off Winchester Rd* 46 DU47
NW2 63 CY63
Dagenham RM8 70 EV63
Hounslow TW4 96 BW83
Northwood HA6 59 BU55
Richmond TW9 98 CM81
Woodford Green IG8 48 EE49
Lichfield Ter, Upmin. RM14 73 FS61
Lichfield Way, S.Croy. CR2 161 DX110
Lichlade Cl, Orp. BR6 163 ET105
Lidbury Rd, NW7 43 CY51
Lidcote Gdns, SW9 101 DN82
Liddall Way, West Dr. UB7 76 BM74
Liddell Cl, Har. HA3 61 CK55
Liddell Gdns, NW10 81 CW68
Liddell Rd, NW6 82 DA65
Lidding Rd, Har. HA3 61 CK57
Liddington Rd, E15 86 EF67
Liddon Rd, E13 86 EH69
Bromley BR1 144 EJ97
Liden Cl, E17 *off Hitcham Rd* 67 DZ60
Lidfield Rd, N16 66 DR63
Lidgate Rd, SE15
off Chandler Way 102 DT80
Lidiard Rd, SW18 120 DC89
Lidlington Pl, NW1 195 K1
Lido Sq, N17 46 DR54
Lidstone Cl, Wok. GU21 166 AV117
Lidyard Rd, N19 65 DJ60
Lieutenant Ellis Way, Wal.Cr.
EN7, EN8 14 DT31
★ **Lifetimes Mus**, Croy.
CR0 142 DQ104
Liffler Rd, SE18 105 ES78
Liffords Pl, SW13 99 CT82
Lifford St, SW15 99 CX84
Lightcliffe Rd, N13 45 DN49
Lighter Cl, SE16 203 L8
Lighterman Ms, E1 85 DX72
Lightermans Rd, E14 204 A5
Lightfoot Rd, N8 65 DL57
Lightley Cl, Wem. HA0
off Stanley Av 80 CM66
Lightswood Cl, Wal.Cr. (Chsht.)
EN7 14 DR27
Ligonier St, E2 197 P4
Lilac Av, Enf. EN1 30 DW36
Woking GU22 166 AX120
Lilac Cl, E4 47 DZ51
Brentwood CM15
off Magnolia Way 54 FV43
Waltham Cross (Chsht.) EN7
off Greenwood Av 14 DV31
Lilac Gdns, W5 97 CK76
Croydon CR0 143 EA104
Hayes UB3 77 BS72
Romford RM7 71 FE60
Swanley BR8 147 FD97
Lilac Ms, N8 *off Courcy Rd* 65 DN55
Lilac Pl, SE11 200 B9
West Drayton UB7
off Cedar Av 76 BM73
Lilac St, W12 81 CU73
Lila Pl, Swan. BR8 147 FE98
Lilburne Gdns, SE9 124 EL85
Lilburne Rd, SE9 124 EL85
Lilburne Wk, NW10 80 CQ65
Lile Cres, W7 79 CE71
Lilestone Est, NW8
off Fisherton St 82 DD70
Lilestone St, NW8 194 B4
Lilford Rd, SE5 101 DP82
Lilian Barker Cl, SE12 124 EG85
Lilian Board Way, Grnf. UB6 61 CD64
Lilian Cl, N16
off Barbauld Rd 66 DS62
Lilian Cres, Brwd. CM13 55 GC47
Lilian Gdns, Wdf.Grn. IG8 48 EH53
Lilian Rd, SW16 141 DJ95
Lillechurch Rd, Dag. RM8 88 EV65
Lilleshall Rd, Mord. SM4 140 DD100
Lilley Cl, E1 202 C3
Brentwood CM14 54 FT49
Lilley Dr, Tad. (Kgswd.) KT20 174 DB122
Lilley La, NW7 42 CR50
Lillian Av, W3 98 CN75
Lillian Rd, SW13 99 CU79
Lillie Rd, SW6 99 CY80
Westerham (Bigg.H.) TN16 178 EK118
Lillieshall Rd, SW4 101 DH83
Lillie Yd, SW6 100 DA79
Lillington Gdns Est, SW1 199 L9
Lillington Ho, N7
off Harvist Est 65 DN63
Lilliots La, Lthd. KT22
off Kingston Rd 171 CG119
Lilliput Av, Nthlt. UB5 78 BZ67
Lilliput Rd, Rom. RM7 71 FD59
Lily Cl, W14 99 CY77
Lily Dr, West Dr. UB7 94 BK77
Lily Gdns, Wem. HA0 79 CJ68
Lily Pl, EC1 196 E6
Lily Rd, E17 67 EA58
Lilyville Rd, SW6 99 CZ81
Limbourne Av, Dag. RM8 70 EZ59
Limburg Rd, SW11 100 DF84
Lime Av, Brwd. CM13 55 FZ48
Gravesend (Nthflt.) DA11 130 GD87
Upminster RM14 72 FN63
West Drayton UB7 76 BM73
Windsor SL4 92 AT80
Limeburner La, EC4 196 F9
Limebush Cl, Add. (New Haw)
KT15 152 BJ109
Lime Cl, E1 202 C2
Bromley BR1 144 EL98
Buckhurst Hill IG9 48 EK48
Carshalton SM5 140 DF103
Harrow HA3 41 CF54
Pinner HA5 59 BT55
Romford RM7 71 FC56
South Ockendon RM15 91 FW69
Watford WD19 40 BX45
Lime Ct, Mitch. CR4
off Lewis Rd 140 DD96
Lime Cres, Sun. TW16 136 BW96
Limecroft Cl, Epsom KT19 156 CR108
Limedene Cl, Pnr. HA5 40 BX53
Lime Gro, E4 *off Burnside Av* 47 DZ51
N20 43 CZ46
W12 99 CW75
Addlestone KT15 152 BG105
Hayes UB3 77 BR73
Ilford IG6 49 ET51
New Malden KT3 138 CR97
Orpington BR6 145 EP103
Ruislip HA4 59 BV59
Sidcup DA15 125 ET86
Twickenham TW1 117 CF86
Warlingham CR6 177 DY118
Woking GU22 166 AY121
Limeharbour, E14 204 C5
LIMEHOUSE, E14 85 DY73
⇌ **Limehouse** 85 DY72
DLR **Limehouse** 85 DY72
Limehouse Causeway, E14 85 DZ73
Limehouse Flds Est, E14 85 DY71
Limehouse Link, E14 85 DY73
Limekiln Dr, SE7 104 EH79
Limekiln Pl, SE19 122 DT94
Lime Meadow Av, S.Croy.
CR2 160 DU113
Lime Pit La, Sev. TN14 181 FC117
Limerick Cl, SW12 121 DJ87
Limerick Gdns, Upmin. RM14 73 FT59
Lime Rd, Epp. CM16 17 ET31
Richmond TW9
off St. Mary's Gro 98 CM84
Swanley BR8 147 FD97
Lime Row, Erith DA18
off Northwood Pl 106 EZ76
Limerston St, SW10 100 DC79
Limes, The, W2
off Linden Gdns 82 DA73
Brentwood CM13 55 FZ48
Bromley BR2 144 EL103
Purfleet RM19
off Tank Hill Rd 108 FN78
Woking GU21 166 AX115
Limes Av, E11 68 EH56
N12 44 DC49
NW7 42 CS51
NW11 63 CY59
SE20 122 DV94
SW13 99 CT82
Carshalton SM5 140 DF102
Chigwell IG7 49 ER51
Croydon CR0 141 DN104
Limes Av, The, N11 45 DH50
Limes Cl, Ashf. TW15 114 BN92
Limes Ct, Brwd. CM15
off Sawyers Hall La 54 FX46
Limesdale Gdns, Edg. HA8 42 CQ54
Limes Fld Rd, SW14
off White Hart La 98 CS83
Limesford Rd, SE15 103 DX84
Limes Gdns, SW18 120 DA86
Limes Gro, SE13 103 EC84
Limes Pl, Croy. CR0 142 DR101
Limes Rd, Beck. BR3 143 EB96
Croydon CR0 142 DR100
Egham TW20 113 AZ92
Waltham Cross (Chsht.)
EN8 15 DX32
Weybridge KT13 152 BN105
Limes Row, Orp. BR6
off Orchard Rd 163 EP106
Limestone Wk, Erith DA18 106 EX76
Lime St, E17 67 DY56
EC3 197 M10
Lime St Pas, EC3 197 M9
Limes Wk, SE15 102 DV84
W5 *off Chestnut Gro* 97 CK75
Lime Ter, W7 *off Manor Ct Rd* 79 CE73
Lime Tree Av, Esher KT10 137 CD102
Greenhithe (Bluewater)
DA9 129 FU88
Thames Ditton KT7 137 CD102
Limetree Cl, SW2 121 DM88
Lime Tree Cl, Lthd. (Bkhm.)
KT23 170 CA124
Lime Tree Gro, Croy. CR0 143 DZ104
Lime Tree Pl, Mitch. CR4 141 DH95
Lime Tree Rd, Houns. TW5 96 CB81
Lime Tree Ter, SE6
off Winterstoke Rd 123 DZ88
Limetree Ter, Well. DA16
off Hook La 106 EU83
Limetree Wk, SW17
off Church La 120 DG92
Lime Tree Wk, Amer. HP7 20 AT39
Bushey (Bushey Hth.)
WD23 41 CE46
Enfield EN2 30 DQ38
Rickmansworth WD3 22 BH43
Sevenoaks TN13 191 FH125
Lime Tree Wk, Vir.W. GU25 132 AY98
West Wickham BR4 162 EF105
Lime Wk, E15 *off Church St N* 86 EE67
Uxbridge (Denh.) UB9 58 BJ64
Limewood Cl, E17 67 DZ56
W13 *off St. Stephens Rd* 79 CH72
Beckenham BR3 143 EC99
Limewood Ct, Ilf. IG4 69 EM57
Limewood Rd, Erith DA8 107 FC80
Lime Wks Rd, Red. (Merst.)
RH1 185 DJ126
LIMPSFIELD, Oxt. 188 EG128
Limpsfield Av, SW19 119 CX89
Thornton Heath CR7 141 DM99
LIMPSFIELD CHART, Oxt. 188 EL130
Limpsfield Rd, S.Croy. CR2 160 DU112
Warlingham CR6 176 DW116
Linacre Ct, W6 99 CX78
Linacre Rd, NW2 81 CV65
Linberry Wk, SE8 203 M9
Linchfield Rd, Slou. (Datchet)
SL3 92 AW81
Linchmere Rd, SE12 124 EF87
Lincoln Av, N14 45 DJ48
SW19 119 CX90
Romford RM7 71 FD60
Twickenham TW2 116 CB89
Lincoln Cl, SE25
off Woodside Grn 142 DU100
Erith DA8 107 FF82
Greenford UB6 78 CC67
Harrow HA2 60 BZ57
Hornchurch RM11 72 FN57
Lincoln Ct, N16 66 DR59
Borehamwood WD6 26 CR43
Lincoln Cres, Enf. EN1 30 DS43
Lincoln Dr, Rick. (Crox.Grn.)
WD3 23 BP42
Watford WD19 40 BW48
Woking GU22 167 BE115
Lincoln Gdns, Ilf. IG1 68 EL59
Lincoln Grn Rd, Orp. BR5 145 ET99
Lincoln Ms, NW6
off Willesden La 81 CZ67
SE21 122 DR88
Lincoln Pk, Amer. HP7 20 AS39
Lincoln Rd, E7 86 EK65
E13 86 EH70
E18 *off Grove Rd* 48 EG53
N2 64 DE55
SE25 142 DV97
Enfield EN1, EN3 30 DU43
Erith DA8 107 FF82
Feltham TW13 116 BZ90
Gerrards Cross (Chal.St.P.)
SL9 36 AY53
Harrow HA2 60 BZ57
Mitcham CR4 141 DL99
New Malden KT3 138 CQ97
Northwood HA6 59 BT55
Sidcup DA14 126 EV92
Wembley HA0 79 CK65
Worcester Park KT4 139 CV102
Lincolns, The, NW7 43 CT48
Lincolns Flds, Epp. CM16 17 ET29
Lincolnshott, Grav. (Sthflt.)
DA13 130 GB92
★ **Lincoln's Inn**, WC2 196 C8
Lincoln's Inn, WC2 196 C8
Lincoln's Inn Flds, WC2 196 B8
Lincoln St, E11 68 EE61
SW3 198 D9
Lincoln Wk, Epsom KT19
off Hollymoor La 156 CR110
Lincoln Way, Enf. EN1 30 DV43
Rickmansworth (Crox.Grn.)
WD3 23 BP42
Sunbury-on-Thames
TW16 135 BS95
Lincombe Rd, Brom. BR1 124 EF90
Lindal Cres, Enf. EN2 29 DL42
Lindale Cl, Vir.W. GU25 132 AT98
Lindales, The, N17
off Brantwood Rd 46 DT51
Lindal Rd, SE4 123 DZ85
Lindbergh Rd, Wall. SM6 159 DL109
Linden Av, NW10 81 CX68
Coulsdon CR5 175 DH116
Dartford DA1 128 FJ88
Enfield EN1 30 DU39
Hounslow TW3 116 CB85
Ruislip HA4 59 BU60
Thornton Heath CR7 141 DP98
Wembley HA9 62 CM64
Linden Chase Rd, Sev. TN13 191 FH122
Linden Cl, N14 29 DJ44
Addlestone (New Haw)
KT15 152 BG111
Orpington BR6 164 EU106
Purfleet RM19 108 FQ79
Ruislip HA4 59 BU60
Stanmore HA7 41 CH50
Tadworth KT20 173 CX120
Thames Ditton KT7 137 CF101
Waltham Cross EN7 14 DV30
Linden Ct, W12 81 CW74
Egham (Eng.Grn.) TW20 112 AV93
Leatherhead KT22 171 CH121
Linden Cres, Grnf. UB6 79 CF65
Kingston upon Thames
KT1 138 CM96
Woodford Green IG8 48 EH51
Linden Dr, Cat. CR3 176 DQ124
Gerrards Cross (Chal.St.P.) SL9
off Woodside Hill 36 AY54
Lindenfield, Chis. BR7 145 EP96
Linden Gdns, W2 82 DA73
W4 98 CR78
Enfield EN1 30 DU39
Leatherhead KT22 171 CJ121
Linden Gro, SE15 102 DV83
SE26 122 DW93
New Malden KT3 138 CS97
Teddington TW11
off Waldegrave Rd 117 CF92
Walton-on-Thames KT12 135 BT103
Warlingham CR6 177 DY118
Linden Ho, Slou. SL3 93 BB78
Linden Lawns, Wem. HA9 62 CM63
Linden Lea, N2 64 DC57
Watford WD25 7 BU33
Linden Leas, W.Wick. BR4 143 ED103
Linden Ms, N1
off Mildmay Gro N 66 DR64
W2 *off Linden Gdns* 82 DA73
Linden Pas, W4
off Linden Gdns 98 CR78
Linden Pit Path, Lthd. KT22 171 CH121
Linden Pl, Epsom KT17
off East St 156 CS112
Mitcham CR4 140 DE98
Linden Ri, Brwd. CM14 54 FX50
Linden Rd, E17 *off High St* 67 DZ57
N10 65 DH56
N11 44 DF47
N15 66 DQ56
Hampton TW12 116 CA94
Leatherhead KT22 171 CH121
Weybridge KT13 153 BQ109
Lindens, The, N12 44 DD50
W4 *off Hartington Rd* 98 CQ81
Croydon (New Adgtn.)
CR0 161 EC107
Loughton IG10 33 EM43
Linden Sq, Sev. TN13
off London Rd 190 FE122
Linden St, Rom. RM7 71 FD56
Linden Wk, N19
off Hargrave Pk 65 DJ61
Linden Way, N14 29 DJ44
Purley CR8 159 DJ110
Shepperton TW17 135 BQ99
Woking GU22 167 AZ121
Woking (Send M.) GU23 167 BF124
Lindeth Cl, Stan. HA7
off Old Ch La 41 CJ51
Lindfield Gdns, NW3 64 DB64
Lindfield Rd, W5 79 CJ70
Croydon CR0 142 DT100
Romford RM3 52 FL50
Lindfield St, E14 85 EA72
Lindhill Cl, Enf. EN3 31 DX39
Lindisfarne Cl, Grav. DA12
off St. Benedict's Av 131 GL89
Lindisfarne Rd, SW20 119 CU94
Dagenham RM8 70 EW62
Lindisfarne Way, E9 67 DY63
Lindley Est, SE15
off Bird in Bush Rd 102 DU80
Lindley Pl, Rich. TW9 98 CN81
Lindley Rd, E10 67 EB61
Godstone RH9 186 DW130
Walton-on-Thames KT12 136 BX104
Lindley St, E1 84 DW71
Lindore Rd, SW11 100 DF84
Lindores Rd, Cars. SM5 140 DC101
Lindo St, SE15
off Selden Rd 102 DW82
Lind Rd, Sutt. SM1 158 DC106
Lindrop St, SW6 100 DC82
Lindsay Cl, Chess. KT9 156 CL108
Epsom KT19 156 CQ113
Staines (Stanw.) TW19 114 BK85
Lindsay Dr, Har. HA3 62 CL58
Shepperton TW17 135 BR100
Lindsay Pl, Wal.Cr. EN7 14 DV30
Lindsay Rd, Add. (New Haw)
KT15 152 BG110
Hampton (Hmptn.H.)
TW12 116 CB91
Worcester Park KT4 139 CV103
Lindsay Sq, SW1 199 N10
Lindsell St, SE10 103 EC81
Lindsey Cl, Brwd. CM14 54 FU49
Bromley BR1 144 EK97
Mitcham CR4 141 DL98
Lindsey Gdns, Felt. TW14 115 BR87
Lindsey Ms, N1 84 DQ66
Lindsey Rd, Dag. RM8 70 EW63
Uxbridge (Denh.) UB9 58 BG62
Lindsey St, EC1 196 G6
Epping CM16 17 ER28
Lindsey Way, Horn. RM11 72 FJ57
Lind St, SE8 103 EB82
Lindum Rd, Tedd. TW11 117 CJ94
Lindvale, Wok. GU21 166 AY115
Lindway, SE27 121 DP92
Lindwood Cl, E6
off Northumberland Rd 86 EL71
Linfield Cl, NW4 63 CW55
Walton-on-Thames KT12 153 BV106
Linfields, Amer. HP7 20 AW40
LINFORD, S.le H. 111 GM75
Linford Rd, E17 67 EC55
Grays RM16 111 GH78
Linford St, SW8 101 DJ81
Lingards Rd, SE13 103 EC84
Lingey Cl, Sid. DA15 125 ET89
Lingfield Av, Dart. DA2 128 FP87
Kingston upon Thames
KT1 138 CL98
Upminster RM14 72 FM62
Lingfield Cl, Enf. EN1 30 DS44
Northwood HA6 39 BS52
Lingfield Cres, SE9 105 ER84
Lingfield Gdns, N9 46 DV45
Coulsdon CR5 175 DP119
Lingfield Rd, SW19 119 CX92
Gravesend DA12 131 GH89
Worcester Park KT4 139 CW104
Lingfield Way, Wat. WD17 23 BT38
Lingham St, SW9 101 DL82
Lingholm Way, Barn. EN5 27 CX43
Lingmere Cl, Chig. IG7 49 EQ47
Lingmoor Dr, Wat. WD25 8 BW33
Ling Rd, E16 86 EG71
Erith DA8 107 FC79
Lingrove Gdns, Buck.H. IG9
off Beech La 48 EH47
Lings Coppice, SE21 122 DR89
Lingwell Rd, SW17 120 DE90

★ Place of interest ⇌ Railway station ⊖ London Underground station DLR Docklands Light Railway station Tramlink station H Hospital

Lin - Lod

Lingwood Gdns, Islw. TW7 . . . 97 CE80
Lingwood Rd, E5 . . . 66 DU59
Linhope St, NW1 . . . 194 D4
Linington Av, Chesh. HP5 . . . 4 AU30
Link, The, SE9 . . . 125 EN90
W3 . . . 80 CP72
Enfield EN3 . . . 31 DY39
Northolt UB5
off Eastcote La . . . 60 BZ64
Pinner HA5 . . . 60 BW59
Slough SL2 . . . 74 AV72
Wembley HA0
off Nathans Rd . . . 61 CJ60
Link Av, Wok. GU22 . . . 167 BD115
Linkfield, Brom. BR2 . . . 144 EG100
West Molesey KT8 . . . 136 CA97
Linkfield Cor, Red. RH1
off Hatchlands Rd . . . 184 DE133
Linkfield Gdns, Red. RH1
off Hatchlands Rd . . . 184 DE134
Linkfield La, Red. RH1 . . . 184 DE133
Linkfield Rd, Islw. TW7 . . . 97 CF82
Linkfield St, Red. RH1 . . . 184 DE134
Link La, Wall. SM6 . . . 159 DK107
Linklea Cl, NW9 . . . 42 CS52
Link Rd, N11 . . . 44 DG49
Addlestone KT15
off Weybridge Rd . . . 152 BL105
Dagenham RM9 . . . 89 FB68
Feltham TW14 . . . 115 BT87
Rickmansworth (Chenies)
WD3 . . . 21 BA37
Slough (Datchet) SL3 . . . 92 AW80
Wallington SM6 . . . 140 DG102
Watford WD24 . . . 24 BX40
Links, The, E17 . . . 67 DY56
Waltham Cross (Chsht.)
EN8 . . . 15 DX26
Walton-on-Thames KT12 . . 135 BU103
Links Av, Mord. SM4 . . . 140 DA98
Romford RM2 . . . 51 FH54
Links Brow, Lthd. (Fetch.)
KT22 . . . 171 CE124
Links Cl, Ashtd. KT21 . . . 171 CJ117
Linkscroft Av, Ashf. TW15 . . . 115 BP93
Links Dr, N20 . . . 44 DA46
Borehamwood (Elstree)
WD6 . . . 26 CM41
Radlett WD7 . . . 9 CF33
Links Gdns, SW16 . . . 121 DN94
Links Grn Way, Cob. KT11 . . . 154 CA114
Linkside, N12 . . . 43 CZ51
Chigwell IG7 . . . 49 EQ50
New Malden KT3 . . . 138 CS96
Linkside Cl, Enf. EN2 . . . 29 DM41
Linkside Gdns, Enf. EN2 . . . 29 DM41
Links Pl, Ashtd. KT21 . . . 171 CK117
Links Rd, NW2 . . . 63 CT61
SW17 . . . 120 DF93
W3 . . . 80 CN72
Ashford TW15 . . . 114 BL92
Ashtead KT21 . . . 171 CJ118
Epsom KT17 . . . 157 CU113
West Wickham BR4 . . . 143 EC102
Woodford Green IG8 . . . 48 EG50
Links Side, Enf. EN2 . . . 29 DN41
Link St, E9 . . . 84 DW65
Links Vw, N3 . . . 43 CZ52
Dartford DA1 . . . 128 FJ88
Links Vw Av, Bet. (Brock.)
RH3 . . . 182 CN134
Links Vw Cl, Stan. HA7 . . . 41 CG51
Links Vw Rd, Croy. CR0 . . . 143 EA104
Hampton (Hmptn.H.)
TW12 . . . 116 CC92
Linksway, NW4 . . . 43 CX54
Links Way, Beck. BR3 . . . 143 EA100
Linksway, Nthwd. HA6 . . . 39 BQ53
Links Way, Rick. (Crox.Grn.)
WD3 . . . 23 BQ41
Links Yd, E *off Spelman St* . . . 84 DU71
Linkway, N4 . . . 66 DQ59
SW20 . . . 139 CV97
Link Way, Brom. BR2 . . . 144 EL101
Linkway, Dag. RM8 . . . 70 EW63
Link Way, Horn. RM11 . . . 72 FL60
Pinner HA5 . . . 40 BX53
Linkway, Rich. TW10 . . . 117 CH89
Link Way, Stai. TW18 . . . 114 BH93
Uxbridge (Denh.) UB9 . . . 58 BG58
Linkway, Wok. GU22 . . . 167 BC117
Linkway, The, Barn. EN5 . . . 28 DB44
Sutton SM2 . . . 158 DC109
Link Way Rd, Brwd. CM14 . . . 54 FT48
Linkwood Wk, NW1
off Maiden La . . . 83 DK66
Linley Cres, Rom. RM7 . . . 71 FB55
Linley Rd, N17 . . . 46 DS54
★ Linley Sambourne Ho,
W8 . . . 100 DA75
Linnell Cl, NW11 . . . 64 DB58
Linnell Dr, NW11 . . . 64 DB58
Linnell Rd, N18
off Fairfield Rd . . . 46 DU50
SE5 . . . 102 DS82
Linnet Cl, N9 . . . 47 DX46
SE28 . . . 88 EW73
Bushey WD23 . . . 40 CC45
South Croydon CR2 . . . 161 DX110
Linnet Ms, SW12 . . . 120 DG87
Linnet Rd, Abb.L. WD5 . . . 7 BU31
Linnett Cl, E4 . . . 47 EC49
Linnet Ter, Ilf. IG5
off Tiptree Cres . . . 69 EN55
Linnet Way, Purf. RM19 . . . 108 FP78
Linom Rd, SW4 . . . 101 DL84
Linscott Rd, E5 . . . 66 DW63
Linsdell Rd, Bark. IG11 . . . 87 EQ67
Linsey St, SE16 . . . 202 B8
Linslade Cl, Houns. TW4
off Frampton Rd . . . 116 BY85
Pinner HA5 . . . 59 BV55
Linslade Rd, Orp. BR6 . . . 164 EU107
Linstead Ct, SE9 . . . 125 ES86
Linstead St, NW6 . . . 82 DA66
Linstead Way, SW18 . . . 119 CY87
Linster Gro, Borwd. WD6 . . . 26 CQ43
Lintaine Cl, W6 *off Moylan Rd* . 99 CY79
Linthorpe Av, Wem. HA0 . . . 79 CJ65
Linthorpe Rd, N16 . . . 66 DS59
Barnet EN4 . . . 28 DE41
Linton Av, Borwd. WD6 . . . 26 CM39
Linton Cl, Mitch. CR4 . . . 140 DF101
Welling DA16
off Anthony Rd . . . 106 EV81
Linton Gdns, E6 . . . 86 EL72
Linton Glade, Croy. CR0 . . . 161 DY109
Linton Gro, SE27 . . . 121 DP92
Linton Rd, Bark. IG11 . . . 87 EQ66
Lintons, The, Bark. IG11 . . . 87 EQ66
Lintons La, Epsom KT17 . . . 156 CS112
Linton St, N1 . . . 84 DQ67
Lintott Ct, Stai. (Stanw.)
TW19 . . . 114 BK86
Linver Rd, SW6 . . . 100 DA82
Linwood Cl, SE5 . . . 102 DT82
Linwood Cres, Enf. EN1 . . . 30 DU39
Linwood Way, SE15
off Daniel Gdns . . . 102 DT80
Linzee Rd, N8 . . . 65 DL56
Lion Av, Twick. TW1
off Lion Rd . . . 117 CF88
Lion Cl, SE4 . . . 123 EA86
Shepperton TW17 . . . 134 BL97
Lion Ct, Borwd. WD6 . . . 26 CQ39
Lionel Gdns, SE9 . . . 124 EK85
Lionel Ms, W10 *off Telford Rd* . 81 CY71
Lionel Oxley Ho, Grays RM17
off New Rd . . . 110 GB79
Lionel Rd, SE9 . . . 124 EK85
Lionel Rd N, Brent. TW8 . . . 98 CL77
Lionel Rd S, Brent. TW8 . . . 98 CM78
Lion Gate Gdns, Rich. TW9 . . . 98 CM83
Lion Grn Rd, Couls. CR5 . . . 175 DK115
Lion La, Red. RH1 . . . 184 DF133
Lion Pk Av, Chess. KT9 . . . 156 CN105
Lion Plaza, EC2
off Threadneedle St . . . 84 DR72
Lion Rd, E6 . . . 87 EM71
N9 . . . 46 DU47
Bexleyheath DA6 . . . 106 EZ84
Croydon CR0 . . . 142 DQ99
Twickenham TW1 . . . 117 CF88
Lions Cl, SE9 . . . 124 EJ90
Lion Way, Brent. TW8 . . . 97 CK80
Lion Wf Rd, Islw. TW7 . . . 97 CH83
Lion Yd, SW4
off Tremadoc Rd . . . 101 DK84
Liphook Cl, Horn. RM12
off Petworth Way . . . 71 FF63
Liphook Cres, SE23 . . . 122 DW87
Liphook Rd, Wat. WD19 . . . 40 BX49
Lippitts Hill, Loug. (High Beach)
IG10 . . . 32 EE39
Lipsham Cl, Bans. SM7 . . . 158 DD113
Lipton Cl, SE28 *off Aisher Rd* . 88 EW73
Lipton Rd, E1 *off Bower St* . . . 85 DX72
Lisbon Av, Twick. TW2 . . . 116 CC89
Lisbon Cl, E17 . . . 47 DZ54
Lisburne Rd, NW3 . . . 64 DF63
Lisford St, SE15 . . . 102 DT81
Lisgar Ter, W14 . . . 99 CZ77
Liskeard Cl, Chis. BR7 . . . 125 EQ93
Liskeard Gdns, SE3 . . . 104 EG81
Liskeard Lo, Cat. CR3 . . . 186 DU126
Lisle Cl, SW17 . . . 121 DH91
Lisle Pl, Grays RM17 . . . 110 GA76
Lisle St, WC2 . . . 195 N10
Lismore Circ, NW5 . . . 64 DG64
Lismore Cl, Islw. TW7 . . . 97 CG82
Lismore Pk, Slou. SL2 . . . 74 AT72
Lismore Rd, N17 . . . 66 DR55
South Croydon CR2 . . . 160 DS107
Lismore Wk, N1
off Clephane Rd . . . 84 DQ65
Lissenden Gdns, NW5 . . . 64 DG63
Lissoms Rd, Couls. CR5 . . . 174 DG118
Lisson Grn Est, NW8 . . . 194 B3
LISSON GROVE, NW8 . . . 194 A5
Lisson Gro, NW1 . . . 194 B4
NW8 . . . 194 A3
Lisson St, NW1 . . . 194 B6
Liss Way, SE15
off Pentridge St . . . 102 DT80
Lister Av, Rom. RM3 . . . 52 FK54
Lister Cl, W3 . . . 80 CR71
Mitcham CR4 . . . 140 DE95
Lister Ct, NW9 *off Pasteur Cl* . 42 CS54
Lister Gdns, N18 . . . 46 DQ50
H Lister Hosp, SW1 . . . 101 DH78
Lister Ho, SE3 . . . 104 EE79
Lister Rd, E11 . . . 68 EE60
Tilbury RM18 . . . 111 GG82
Lister Wk, SE28
off Haldane Rd . . . 88 EX73
Liston Ct, Wdf.Grn. IG8
off Navestock Cres . . . 48 EJ52
Liston Rd, N17 . . . 46 DU53
SW4 . . . 101 DJ83
Liston Way, Wdf.Grn. IG8 . . . 48 EJ52
Listowel Cl, SW9
off Mandela St . . . 101 DN80
Listowel Rd, Dag. RM10 . . . 70 FA62
Listria Pk, N16 . . . 66 DS61
Litchfield Av, E15 . . . 86 EE65
Morden SM4 . . . 139 CZ101
Litchfield Gdns, NW10 . . . 81 CU65
Litchfield Rd, Sutt. SM1 . . . 158 DC105
Litchfield St, WC2 . . . 195 N10
Litchfield Way, NW11 . . . 64 DB57
Lithos Rd, NW3 . . . 82 DB65
Little Acre, Beck. BR3 . . . 143 EA97
Little Albany St, NW1 . . . 195 J4
Little Argyll St, W1 . . . 195 K9
Little Aston Rd, Rom. RM3 . . . 52 FM52
Little Belhus Cl, S.Ock. RM15 . 91 FU70
Little Benty, West Dr. UB7 . . . 94 BK78
Little Birch Cl, Add. (New Haw)
KT15 . . . 152 BK109
Little Birches, Sid. DA15 . . . 125 ES89
Little Boltons, The, SW5 . . . 100 DB78
Little Boltons, The, SW10 . . . 100 DB78
Little Bookham Common, Lthd.
(Bkhm.) KT23 . . . 170 BY122
Little Bookham St, Lthd. (Bkhm.)
KT23 . . . 170 BZ124
Little Bornes, SE21 . . . 122 DS91
Little Britain, EC1 . . . 197 H8
Littlebrook Cl, Croy. CR0 . . . 143 DX100
Littlebrook Gdns, Wal.Cr. (Chsht.)
EN8 . . . 14 DW30
Littlebrook Manor Way, Dart.
DA1 . . . 128 FN85
Little Brownings, SE23 . . . 122 DV89
Littlebury Rd, SW4 . . . 101 DK83
Little Bury St, N9 . . . 46 DR46
Little Bushey La, Bushey
WD23 . . . 25 CD44
Little Bushey La Footpath, Bushey
WD23 *off Little Bushey La* . 41 CD45
Little Cedars, N12
off Woodside Av . . . 44 DC49
LITTLE CHALFONT, Amer. . . . 20 AW40
LITTLE CHALFONT, Ch.St.G. . . 20 AW40
Little Chester St, SW1 . . . 198 G6
Little Cloisters, SW1
off Tufton St . . . 101 DK76
Little Coll La, EC4
off Garlick Hill . . . 84 DR73
Little Coll St, SW1 . . . 199 P6
Littlecombe, SE7 . . . 104 EH79
Littlecombe Cl, SW15 . . . 119 CX86
Little Common, Stan. HA7 . . . 41 CG48
Little Common La, Red. (Bletch.)
RH1 . . . 185 DP132
Littlecote Cl, SW19 . . . 119 CX87
Littlecote Pl, Pnr. HA5 . . . 40 BY53
Little Ct, W.Wick. BR4 . . . 144 EE103
Littlecourt Rd, Sev. TN13 . . . 190 FG124
Littlecroft, SE9 . . . 105 EN83
Gravesend (Istead Rise)
DA13 . . . 130 GE94
Littlecroft Rd, Egh. TW20 . . . 113 AZ92
Littledale, SE2 . . . 106 EU79
Dartford DA2 . . . 128 FQ90
Little Dean's Yd, SW1 . . . 199 P6
Little Dimocks, SW12 . . . 121 DH89
Little Dormers, Ger.Cr. SL9 . . . 57 AZ56
Little Dorrit Ct, SE1 . . . 201 J4
Littledown Rd, Slou. SL1 . . . 74 AT74
Little Dragons, Loug. IG10 . . . 32 EK42
LITTLE EALING, W5 . . . 97 CJ77
Little Ealing La, W5 . . . 97 CJ77
Little Edward St, NW1 . . . 195 J2
Little Elms, Hayes UB3 . . . 95 BR80
Little Essex St, WC2 . . . 196 D10
Little Ferry Rd, Twick. TW1
off Ferry Rd . . . 117 CH88
Littlefield Cl, N19
off Tufnell Pk Rd . . . 65 DJ63
Kingston upon Thames KT1
off Fairfield W . . . 138 CL96
Littlefield Rd, Edg. HA8 . . . 42 CQ52
Little Friday Rd, E4 . . . 48 EE47
Little Gaynes Gdns, Upmin.
RM14 . . . 72 FP63
Little Gaynes La, Upmin.
RM14 . . . 72 FM63
Little Gearies, Ilf. IG6 . . . 69 EP56
Little George St, SW1 . . . 199 P5
Little Gerpins La, Upmin.
RM14 . . . 90 FM67
Little Gra, Grnf. UB6
off Perivale La . . . 79 CG69
Little Graylings, Abb.L. WD5 . . 7 BS33
Little Grn, Rich. TW9 . . . 97 CK84
Little Grn La, Cher. KT16 . . . 133 BE104
Rickmansworth (Crox.Grn.)
WD3 . . . 23 BP41
Little Grn St, NW5
off College La . . . 65 DH63
Little Gregories La, Epp. (They.B.)
CM16 . . . 33 ER35
Littlegrove, Barn. EN4 . . . 28 DE44
Little Gro, Bushey WD23 . . . 24 CB42
Little Gro Av, Wal.Cr. (Chsht.)
EN7 . . . 14 DS27
Little Halliards, Walt. KT12
off Felix Rd . . . 135 BU100
Little Hayes, Kings L. WD4 . . . 6 BN29
Little Heath, SE7 . . . 104 EL79
Romford (Chad.Hth.) RM6 . . 70 EV56
Littleheath La, Cob. KT11 . . . 154 CA114
Little Heath La, Wok. (Chobham)
GU24 . . . 150 AS109
Little Heath Rd, Bexh. DA7 . . . 106 EZ81
Littleheath Rd, S.Croy. CR2 . . 160 DV108
Little Heath Rd, Wok. (Chobham)
GU24 . . . 150 AS109
H Little Highwood Hosp,
Brwd. CM15 . . . 54 FV45
Little Hill, Rick. (Herons.) WD3 . 21 BC44
★ Little Holland Ho, Cars.
SM5 . . . 158 DE108
Little How Cft, Abb.L. WD5 . . . 7 BQ31
LITTLE ILFORD, E12 . . . 68 EL64
Little Ilford La, E12 . . . 69 EM63
Littlejohn Rd, W7 . . . 79 CF72
Orpington BR5 . . . 146 EU100
Little Julians Hill, Sev. TN13 . 190 FG128
Little London Cl, Uxb. UB8
off Harlington Rd . . . 77 BP71
Little Marlborough St, W1 . . . 195 K9
Little Martins, Bushey WD23 . . 24 CB43
Littlemead, Esher KT10 . . . 155 CD105
Little Mead, Wok. GU21 . . . 166 AT116
Littlemede, SE9 . . . 125 EM90
Littlemoor Rd, Ilf. IG1 . . . 69 ER62
Littlemore Rd, SE2 . . . 106 EU75
Little Moreton Cl, W.Byf.
KT14 . . . 152 BH112
Little Moss La, Pnr. HA5 . . . 40 BY54
Little Newport St, WC2 . . . 195 N10
Little New St, EC4 . . . 196 E8
Little Orchard, Add. (Woodham)
KT15 . . . 151 BF111
Woking GU21 . . . 151 BA114
Little Orchard Cl, Abb.L. WD5 . . 7 BR32
Little Orchard Cl, Pin. HA5
off Barrow Pt La . . . 40 BY54
Little Oxhey La, Wat. WD19 . . . 40 BX50
Little Pk, Hem.H. (Bov.) HP3 . . . 5 BA28
Little Pk Dr, Felt. TW13 . . . 116 BX89
Little Pk Gdns, Enf. EN2 . . . 30 DQ41
Little Pipers Cl, Wal.Cr. (Chsht.)
EN7 . . . 13 DP29
Little Pluckets Way, Buck.H.
IG9 . . . 48 EJ46
Little Portland St, W1 . . . 195 K8
Littleport Spur, Slou. SL1 . . . 74 AS72
Little Potters, Bushey WD23 . . 41 CD45
Little Queens Rd, Tedd. TW11 . 117 CF93
Little Queen St, Dart. DA1 . . . 128 FM87
Little Redlands, Brom. BR1 . . . 144 EL96
Little Reeves Av, Amer. HP7 . . 20 AT39
Little Riding, Wok. GU22 . . . 167 BB116
Little Rd, Croy. CR0 *off Lower*
Addiscombe Rd . . . 142 DS102
Hayes UB3 . . . 95 BT75
Little Roke Av, Ken. CR8 . . . 159 DP114
Little Roke Rd, Ken. CR8 . . . 160 DQ114
Littlers Cl, SW19
off Runnymede . . . 140 DD95
Little Russell St, WC1 . . . 195 P7
Little Russets, Brwd. CM13
off Hutton Village . . . 55 GE45
Little St. James's St, SW1 . . . 199 K3
Little St. Leonards, SW14 . . . 98 CQ83
Little Sanctuary, SW1 . . . 199 N5
Little Smith St, SW1 . . . 199 N6
Little Somerset St, E1 . . . 197 P9
Littlestock Rd, Wal.Cr. (Chsht.)
EN7 . . . 14 DR26
Littlestone Cl, Beck. BR3
off Abbey La . . . 123 EA93
Little Strand, NW9 . . . 43 CT54
Little Stream Cl, Nthwd. HA6 . 39 BS50
Little St, Wal.Abb. EN9
off Greenwich Way . . . 31 EB36
Little Sutton La, Slou. SL3 . . . 93 BC78
Little Thrift, Orp. BR5 . . . 145 EQ98
LITTLE THURROCK, Grays . . . 110 GD76
Little Titchfield St, W1 . . . 195 K7
LITTLETON, Shep. . . . 135 BP97
Littleton Av, E4 . . . 48 EF46
Littleton Cres, Har. HA1 . . . 61 CF61
Littleton La, Shep. TW17 . . . 134 BK101
Littleton Rd, Ashf. TW15 . . . 115 BQ94
Harrow HA1 . . . 61 CF61
Littleton St, SW18 . . . 120 DC89
Little Trinity La, EC4 . . . 197 J10
Little Turnstile, WC1 . . . 196 B8
★ Little Venice (Waterbuses),
W2 . . . 82 DC71
Littlewick Rd, Wok. GU21 . . . 150 AW114
Little Windmill Hill, Kings L.
(Chipper.) WD4 . . . 5 BE32
Littlewood, SE13 . . . 123 EC85
Sevenoaks TN13 . . . 191 FJ122
Littlewood Cl, W13 . . . 97 CH76
Little Wd Cl, Orp. BR5 . . . 146 EU95
LITTLE WOODCOTE, Cars. . . . 158 DG111
Little Woodcote Est, Cars. SM5
off Woodmansterne La . . 158 DG111
Wallington SM6
off Woodmansterne La . . 158 DG111
Little Woodcote La, Cars.
SM5 . . . 159 DH112
Purley CR8 . . . 159 DH112
Wallington SM6 . . . 159 DH112
Littleworth Av, Esher KT10 . . 155 CD106
Littleworth Common Rd, Esher
KT10 . . . 137 CD104
Littleworth La, Esher KT10 . . 155 CD105
Littleworth Pl, Esher KT10 . . . 155 CD105
Littleworth Rd, Esher KT10 . . 155 CE105
Livermere Rd, E8 . . . 84 DT67
Liverpool Gro, SE17 . . . 102 DR78
Liverpool Rd, E10 . . . 67 EC58
E16 . . . 86 EE71
N1 . . . 83 DN68
N7 . . . 65 DN64
W5 . . . 97 CK75
Kingston upon Thames
KT2 . . . 118 CN94
Thornton Heath CR7 . . . 142 DQ97
Watford WD18 . . . 23 BV43
⇌ Liverpool Street . . . 197 M7
⊖ Liverpool Street . . . 197 M7
Liverpool St, EC2 . . . 197 M7
Livesey Cl, Kings.T. KT1 . . . 138 CM97
★ Livesey Mus, SE15 . . . 102 DV79
Livesey Pl, SE15
off Peckham Pk Rd . . . 102 DU79
Livingstone Ct, E10
off Matlock Rd . . . 67 EC58
Barnet EN5
off Christchurch La . . . 27 CY40
Livingstone Gdns, Grav.
DA12 . . . 131 GK92
H Livingstone Hosp, Dart.
DA1 . . . 128 FM87
Livingstone Pl, E14
off Ferry St . . . 103 EC78
Livingstone Rd, E15 . . . 85 EC67
E17 . . . 67 EB58
N13 . . . 45 DL51
SW11 *off Winstanley Rd* . . . 100 DD83
Caterham CR3 . . . 176 DR122
Gravesend DA12 . . . 131 GK92
Hounslow TW3 . . . 96 CC84
Southall UB1 . . . 78 BX73
Thornton Heath CR7 . . . 142 DQ96
Livingstone Ter, Rain. RM13 . . 89 FE67
Livingstone Wk, SW11 . . . 100 DD83
Livonia St, W1 . . . 195 L9
Lizard St, EC1 . . . 197 J3
Lizban St, SE3 . . . 104 EH80
Llanbury Cl, Ger.Cr. (Chal.St.P.)
SL9 . . . 36 AY52
Llanelly Rd, NW2 . . . 63 CZ61
Llanover Rd, SE18 . . . 105 EN79
Wembley HA9 . . . 61 CK62
Llanthony Rd, Mord. SM4 . . . 140 DD100
Llanvanor Rd, NW2 . . . 63 CZ61
Llewellyn St, SE16 . . . 202 C5
Lloyd Av, SW16 . . . 141 DL95
Coulsdon CR5 . . . 158 DG114
Lloyd Baker St, WC1 . . . 196 C3
Lloyd Ct, Pnr. HA5 . . . 60 BX57
Lloyd Ms, Enf. EN3
off Government Row . . . 31 EA37
Tramlink Lloyd Park . . . 160 DT105
Lloyd Pk Av, Croy. CR0 . . . 160 DT105
Lloyd Rd, E6 . . . 87 EM67
E17 . . . 67 DX56
Dagenham RM9 . . . 88 EZ65
Worcester Park KT4 . . . 139 CW104
Lloyd's Av, EC3 . . . 197 N9
★ Lloyds of London, EC3 . . . 197 M9
Lloyds Pl, SE3 . . . 104 EE82
Lloyd Sq, WC1 . . . 196 D2
Lloyd's Row, EC1 . . . 196 E3
Lloyd St, WC1 . . . 196 D2
Lloyds Way, Beck. BR3 . . . 143 DY99
Loampit Hill, SE13 . . . 103 EA82
Loampit Vale, SE13 . . . 103 EB83
Loanda Cl, E8 *off Clarissa St* . . 84 DT67
Loates La, Wat. WD17 . . . 24 BW41
Loats Rd, SW2 . . . 121 DL86
Lobelia Cl, E6 *off Sorrel Gdns* . 86 EL71
Local Board Rd, Wat. WD17 . . . 24 BW43
Locarno Rd, W3 *off High St* . . . 80 CQ74
Greenford UB6 . . . 78 CC70
Lochaber Rd, SE13 . . . 104 EE84
Lochaline St, W6 . . . 99 CW79
Lochan Cl, Hayes UB4 . . . 78 BY70
Lochinvar St, SW12 . . . 121 DH87
Lochmere Cl, Erith DA8 . . . 107 FB79
Lochnagar St, E14 . . . 85 EC71
Lock Chase, SE3 . . . 104 EE83
Lock Cl, Add. (Woodham)
KT15 . . . 151 BE113
Southall UB2
off Navigator Dr . . . 96 CC75
Locke Cl, Rain. RM13 . . . 89 FF65
Locke Gdns, Slou. SL3 . . . 92 AW75
Locke King Cl, Wey. KT13 . . . 152 BN108
Locke King Rd, Wey. KT13 . . . 152 BN108
Lockesfield Pl, E14 . . . 204 C10
Lockesley Dr, Orp. BR5 . . . 145 ET100
Lockesley Sq, Surb. KT6 . . . 137 CK100
Locket Rd, Har. HA3 . . . 61 CE55
Locke Way, Wok. GU21
off The Broadway . . . 167 AZ117
Lockfield Av, Enf. EN3 . . . 31 DY40
Lockfield Dr, Wok. GU21 . . . 166 AT118
Lockgate Cl, E9
off Lee Conservancy Rd . . . 67 DZ64
Lockhart Cl, N7 . . . 83 DM65
Enfield EN3 *off Derby Rd* . . . 30 DV43
Lockhart Rd, Cob. KT11 . . . 154 BW113
Lockhart St, E3 . . . 85 DZ70
Lockhurst St, E5 . . . 67 DX63
Lockie Pl, SE25 . . . 142 DU97
Lockier Wk, Wem. HA9 . . . 61 CK62
Lockington Rd, SW8 . . . 101 DH81
Lock Island, Shep. TW17 . . . 134 BN103
Lock La, Wok. GU22 . . . 168 BH116
Lockmead Rd, N15 . . . 66 DU58
SE13 . . . 103 EC83
Lock Rd, Rich. TW10 . . . 117 CJ91
Locks La, Mitch. CR4 . . . 140 DF95
Locksley Dr, Wok. GU21
off Robin Hood Rd . . . 166 AT118
Locksley Est, E14 . . . 85 DZ72
Locksley St, E14 . . . 85 DZ71
Locksmeade Rd, Rich. TW10 . . 117 CJ91
Lockswood Cl, Barn. EN4 . . . 28 DF42
Lockwood Cl, SE26 . . . 123 DX91
Lockwood Ind Pk, N17 . . . 66 DV55
Lockwood Path, Wok. GU21 . . 151 BD113
Lockwood Sq, SE16 . . . 202 D6
Lockwood Wk, Rom. RM1 . . . 71 FE57
Lockwood Way, E17 . . . 47 DX54
Chessington KT9 . . . 156 CN106
Lockyer Est, SE1 . . . 201 L4
Lockyer Rd, Purf. RM19 . . . 108 FQ79
Lockyer St, SE1 . . . 201 L5
Loddiges Rd, E9 . . . 84 DW66
Loddon Spur, Slou. SL1 . . . 74 AS73
Loder Cl, Wok. GU21 . . . 151 BD113
Loder St, SE15 . . . 102 DW81
Lodge Av, SW14 . . . 98 CS83
Borehamwood (Elstree)
WD6 . . . 26 CM43
Croydon CR0 . . . 141 DN104
Dagenham RM8, RM9 . . . 88 EU67
Dartford DA1 . . . 128 FJ86
Harrow HA3 . . . 62 CL56
Romford RM2 . . . 71 FG56
Lodgebottom Rd, Lthd.
KT22 . . . 182 CM127
Lodge Cl, N18 . . . 46 DQ50
Brentwood (Hutton) CM13 . . 55 GE45
Chigwell IG7 . . . 50 EU48
Cobham (Stoke D'Ab.)
KT11 . . . 170 BZ115
Edgware HA8 . . . 42 CM51
Egham (Eng.Grn.) TW20 . . . 112 AX92
Epsom KT17
off Howell Hill Gro . . . 157 CW110
Isleworth TW7 . . . 97 CH81
Leatherhead (Fetch.) KT22 . 171 CD122
Orpington BR6 . . . 146 EV102
Uxbridge UB8 . . . 76 BJ70
Wallington SM6 . . . 140 DG102
Lodge Ct, Horn. RM12 . . . 72 FL61
Wembley HA0 . . . 62 CL64
Lodge Cres, Orp. BR6 . . . 146 EV102
Waltham Cross EN8 . . . 15 DX34
Lodge Dr, N13 . . . 45 DN49
Rickmansworth (Loud.)
WD3 . . . 22 BJ42
Lodge End, Rad. WD7 . . . 9 CH34
Rickmansworth (Crox.Grn.)
WD3 . . . 23 BR42
Lodge Gdns, Beck. BR3 . . . 143 DZ99
Lodge Hill, SE2 . . . 106 EV80
Ilford IG4 . . . 68 EL56
Purley CR8 . . . 175 DN115
Welling DA16 . . . 106 EV80

Lodgehill Pk Cl, Har. HA2 . . . .60 CB61
Lodge La, N12 . . . . .44 DC50
Bexley DA5 . . . . .126 EX86
Chalfont St. Giles HP8 . . . . .21 AZ41
Croydon (New Adgtn.)
CR0 . . . . .161 EA107
Grays RM16, RM17 . . . . . . .110 GA75
Romford RM5 . . . . .50 FA52
Waltham Abbey EN9 . . . . . . .31 ED35
Westerham TN16 . . . . .189 EQ127
Lodge Pl, Sutt. SM1 . . . . .158 DB106
Lodge Rd, NW4 . . . . .63 CW56
NW8 . . . . .194 A3
Bromley BR1 . . . . .124 EH94
Croydon CR0 . . . . .141 DP100
Leatherhead (Fetch.) KT22 .170 CC122
Sutton SM1
off Throwley Way 158 DB106
Wallington SM6 . . . . .159 DH106
Lodge Vil, Wdf.Grn. IG8 . . . . . .48 EF52
Lodge Wk, Warl. CR6 . . . . . . .177 EA116
Lodge Way, Ashf. TW15 . . . . . .114 BL89
Shepperton TW17 . . . . .135 BQ96
Lodore Gdns, NW9 . . . . .62 CS57
Lodore Grn, Uxb. UB10 . . . . . .58 BL62
Lodore St, E14 . . . . .85 EC72
Loewen Rd, Grays RM16 . . . .111 GG76
Lofthouse Pl, Chess. KT9 . . . .155 CJ107
Loftie St, SE16 . . . . .202 C5
Lofting Rd, N1 . . . . .83 DM66
Loftus Rd, W12 . . . . .81 CV74
Logan Cl, Enf. EN3 . . . . .31 DX39
Hounslow TW4 . . . . .96 BZ83
Logan Ct, Rom. RM1
off Logan Ms 71 FE57
Logan Ms, W8 . . . . .100 DA77
Romford RM1 . . . . .71 FE57
Logan Pl, W8 . . . . .100 DA77
Logan Rd, N9 . . . . .46 DV47
Wembley HA9 . . . . .62 CL61
Loggetts, The, SE21 . . . . .122 DS89
Logs Hill, Brom. BR1 . . . . . . .124 EL94
Chislehurst BR7 . . . . .124 EL94
Logs Hill Cl, Chis. BR7 . . . . . .124 EL95
Lois Dr, Shep. TW17 . . . . .135 BP99
Lolesworth Cl, E1
off Commercial St 84 DT71
Lollard St, SE11 . . . . .200 C8
Loman Path, S.Ock. RM15 . . . .91 FT72
Loman St, SE1 . . . . .200 G4
Lomas Cl, Croy. CR0 . . . . . . .161 EC108
Lomas Dr, E8 . . . . .84 DT66
Lomas St, E1 . . . . .84 DU71
Lombard Av, Enf. EN3 . . . . . . .30 DW39
Ilford IG3 . . . . .69 ES60
Lombard Business Pk, SW19 .140 DC96
Lombard Ct, EC3 . . . . .197 L10
W3 off Crown St 80 CP74
Lombard La, EC4 . . . . .196 E9
Lombard Rd, N11 . . . . .45 DH50
SW11 . . . . .100 DD82
SW19 . . . . .140 DB96
Lombards, The, Horn. RM11 . .72 FM59
Lombard St, EC3 . . . . .197 L9
Dartford (Hort.Kir.) DA4 . . .148 FQ99
Lombard Wall, SE7 . . . . .205 P7
Lombardy Cl, Wok. GU21
off Nethercote Av 166 AT117
Lombardy Pl, W2 off Bark Pl . .82 DB73
Lombardy Retail Pk, Hayes
UB3 . . . . .77 BV73
Lombardy Way, Borwd. WD6 . .26 CL39
Lomond Cl, N15 . . . . .66 DS56
Wembley HA0 . . . . .80 CM66
Lomond Gdns, S.Croy. CR2 . .161 DY108
Lomond Gro, SE5 . . . . .102 DR80
Loncin Mead Av, Add. (New Haw)
KT15 . . . . .152 BJ109
Loncroft Rd, SE5 . . . . .102 DS79
Londesborough Rd, N16 . . . . . .66 DS63
★ London Aquarium, SE1 . .200 B4
★ London Arena, E14 . . . . . .204 C6
★ London Biggin Hill Airport,
West. TN16 . . . . .162 EK113
★ London Brass Rubbing Cen, St.
Martin-in-the-Fields Church,
WC2 . . . . .199 P1
⇌ London Bridge 201 M3
⊖ London Bridge 201 M3
London Br, EC4 . . . . .201 L2
SE1 . . . . .201 L2
H London Bridge Hosp,
SE1 . . . . .201 L2
London Br St, SE1 . . . . .201 K3
London Br Wk, SE1 . . . . .201 L2
★ London Broncos RLC (share
Griffin Pk with Brentford FC),
Brent. TW8 . . . . .97 CK79
★ London Butterfly Ho, Syon Pk,
Brent. TW8 . . . . .97 CH81
★ London Canal Mus, The,
N1 . . . . .83 DL68
★ London Cen Mosque,
NW8 . . . . .194 C3
H London Chest Hosp, E2 . . .84 DW68
★ London City Airport, E16 . .86 EL74
London City Airport, E16 . . . . .87 EM74
H London Clinic, The, W1 . . .194 G5
LONDON COLNEY, St.Alb. 10 CL26
London Colney Bypass, St.Alb.
AL2 . . . . .9 CK25
★ London Commodity
Exchange, E1 . . . . .202 A1
★ London Dungeon, SE1 . . .201 L3
★ London Eye, SE1 . . . . . . .200 B4
⇌ London Fields 84 DV66
London Flds, E8 . . . . .84 DV66
London Flds E Side, E8 . . . . . .84 DV66
London Flds W Side, E8 . . . . .84 DU66
★ London Fire Brigade Mus,
SE1 . . . . .201 H4
H London Foot Hosp & Sch of .
Podiatric Medicine, W1 . . .195 K5
★ London Heathrow Airport,
Houns. TW6 . . . . .95 BP81
H London Independent Hosp,
E1 . . . . .85 DX71
London La, E8 . . . . .84 DV66
Bromley BR1 . . . . .124 EF94
★ London Metropolitan
Archives, EC1 . . . . .196 E4
London Ms, W2 . . . . .194 A9
★ London Palladium, W1 . . .195 K9
★ London Peace Pagoda,
SW11 . . . . .100 DF79
★ London Regatta Cen, E16 .86 EK73
London Rd, E13 . . . . .86 EG68
SE1 . . . . .200 F6
SE23 . . . . .122 DU88
SW16 . . . . .141 DM95
SW17 . . . . .140 DF96
Ashford TW15 . . . . .114 BH90
Barking IG11 . . . . .87 EP66
Borehamwood WD6 . . . . . . .10 CN34
Brentford TW8 . . . . .97 CJ80
Brentwood CM14 . . . . .54 FT49
Bromley BR1 . . . . .124 EF94
Bushey WD23 . . . . .24 BY44
Caterham CR3 . . . . .176 DR123
Chalfont St. Giles HP8 . . . . .36 AW47
Croydon CR0 . . . . .141 DP101
Dartford (Cray.) DA1 . . . . . .127 FD85
Dartford (Fnghm.) DA4 . . . .148 FL100
Dartford (Stone) DA2 . . . . .128 FP87
Egham (Eng.Grn.) TW20 . . .132 AV95
Enfield EN2 . . . . .30 DR41
Epsom KT17 . . . . .157 CT109
Feltham TW14 . . . . .114 BH90
Gravesend (Nthflt.) DA11 . .130 GD86
Grays RM17, RM20 . . . . . . .109 FW79
Greenhithe DA9 . . . . .129 FS86
Harrow HA1 . . . . .61 CE61
Hounslow TW3 . . . . .96 CC83
Isleworth TW7 . . . . .97 CF82
Kingston upon Thames
KT2 . . . . .138 CM96
Mitcham CR4 . . . . .140 DF96
Mitcham (Bedd.Cor.) CR4 . .140 DG101
Morden SM4 . . . . .140 DA99
Ongar CM5 . . . . .35 FH36
Radlett (Shenley) WD7 . . . . .10 CM33
Redhill RH1 . . . . .184 DG132
Reigate RH2 . . . . .184 DA134
Rickmansworth WD3 . . . . . .38 BM47
Romford (Abridge) RM4 . . . .33 ET42
Romford (Chad.Hth.)
RM6, RM7 . . . . .70 FA58
Romford (Stap.Taw.) RM4 . .35 FC40
Sevenoaks TN13 . . . . .190 FF123
Sevenoaks (Halst.) TN14 . .165 FB112
Sevenoaks (Longford)
TN13 . . . . .181 FD117
Slough SL3 . . . . .93 AZ78
Slough (Datchet) SL3 . . . . . .92 AX80
South Ockendon (Aveley)
RM15 . . . . .90 FM74
Staines TW18 . . . . .113 BF91
Stanmore HA7 . . . . .41 CJ50
Sutton SM3 . . . . .139 CX104
Swanley BR8 . . . . .147 FC95
Swanscombe DA10 . . . . . . .129 FV85
Thornton Heath CR7 . . . . . .141 DN99
Tilbury RM18 . . . . .111 GH82
Twickenham TW1 . . . . .117 CG85
Virginia Water GU25 . . . . . .132 AV95
Wallington SM6 . . . . .159 DH105
Wembley HA9 . . . . .80 CL65
Westerham TN16 . . . . .189 ER125
London Rd E, Amer. HP7 . . . . .20 AT42
London Rd N, Red. (Merst.)
RH1 . . . . .185 DH125
London Rd Purfleet, Purf.
RM19 . . . . .108 FN78
London Rd S, Red. (Merst.)
RH1 . . . . .184 DG130
London Rd W Thurrock, Grays
RM20 . . . . .109 FS79
Londons Cl, Upmin. RM14 . . . .72 FQ64
London Shop Pavilion, W1 . . .199 M1
★ London Silver Vaults,
WC2 . . . . .196 D7
London Silver Vaults, WC2 . . .196 D7
London Stile, W4
off Wellesley Rd 98 CN78
★ London Stone, EC4 . . . . .197 K10
London St, EC3 . . . . .197 N10
W2 . . . . .82 DD72
Chertsey KT16 . . . . .134 BG101
★ London Transport Mus, WC2
off Covent Gdn 196 A10
London Wall, EC2 . . . . .197 J7
London Wall Bldgs, EC2 . . . . .197 L7
★ London Wildlife Trust,
NW1 . . . . .83 DK67
★ London Zoo, NW1 . . . . . . .82 DG68
Lonesome Way, SW16 . . . . . .141 DH95
Long Acre, WC2 . . . . .195 P10
Orpington BR6 . . . . .146 EX103
Longacre Pl, Cars. SM5
off Beddington Gdns 158 DG107
Longacre Rd, E17 . . . . .47 ED53
Longaford Way, Brwd. CM13 . .55 GB46
Long Barn Cl, Wat. WD25 . . . . . .7 BV32
Longbeach Rd, SW11 . . . . . . .100 DF83
Longberrys, NW2 . . . . .63 CZ62
Longboat Row, Sthl. UB1 . . . . .78 BZ72
Longbourne Way, Cher.
KT16 . . . . .133 BF100
Longboyds, Cob. KT11 . . . . . .153 BV114
Longbridge Rd, Bark. IG11 . . . .87 EQ66
Dagenham RM8 . . . . .70 EU63
Longbridge Way, SE13 . . . . . .123 EC85
Uxbridge UB8 . . . . .76 BH68
Longbury Cl, Orp. BR5 . . . . . .146 EV97
Longbury Dr, Orp. BR5 . . . . . .146 EV97
Longcliffe Path, Wat. WD19
off Gosforth La 39 BU48
Long Copse Cl, Lthd. (Bkhm.)
KT23 . . . . .170 CB123
Long Ct, Purf. RM19
off Thamley 108 FN77
Longcroft, SE9 . . . . .125 EM90
Watford WD19 . . . . .39 BV45
Longcroft Av, Bans. SM7 . . . .158 DC114
Longcroft Dr, Wal.Cr. EN8 . . . .15 DZ34
Longcrofte Rd, Edg. HA8 . . . . .41 CK52
Longcroft La, Hem.H. (Bov.)
HP3 . . . . .5 BC28
Longcroft Ri, Loug. IG10 . . . . .33 EN43
Longcroft Rd, Rick. (Map.Cr.)
WD3 . . . . .37 BD50
Longcrofts, Wal.Abb. EN9
off Roundhills 16 EE34
LONGCROSS, Cher. 132 AU104
⇌ Longcross 132 AT102
Longcross Rd, Cher. (Longcr.)
KT16 . . . . .132 AY104
Long Deacon Rd, E4 . . . . .48 EE46
LONG DITTON, Surb. 137 CJ102
Longdon Wd, Kes. BR2 . . . . .162 EL105
Longdown La N, Epsom
KT17 . . . . .157 CU114
Longdown La S, Epsom
KT17 . . . . .157 CU114
Longdown Rd, SE6 . . . . .123 EA91
Epsom KT17 . . . . .157 CU114
Long Dr, W3 . . . . .80 CS72
Greenford UB6 . . . . .78 CB67
Ruislip HA4 . . . . .60 BX63
Long Elmes, Har. HA3 . . . . . . .40 CB53
Long Elms, Abb.L. WD5 . . . . . . .7 BR33
Long Elms Cl, Abb.L. WD5
off Long Elms 7 BR33
Long Fallow, St.Alb. AL2 . . . . . .8 CA27
Longfellow Dr, Brwd. CM13 . . .55 GC45
Longfellow Rd, E17 . . . . .67 DZ58
Worcester Park KT4 . . . . . .139 CU103
Longfellow Way, SE1 . . . . . . .202 A9
Long Fld, NW9 . . . . .42 CS52
Longfield, Brom. BR1 . . . . . . .144 EF95
Loughton IG10 . . . . .32 EJ43
Longfield Av, E17 . . . . .67 DY56
NW7 . . . . .43 CU52
W5 . . . . .79 CJ73
Enfield EN3 . . . . .30 DW37
Hornchurch RM11 . . . . .71 FF59
Wallington SM6 . . . . .140 DG102
Wembley HA9 . . . . .62 CL60
Longfield Cres, SE26 . . . . . . .122 DW90
Tadworth KT20 . . . . .173 CW120
Longfield Dr, SW14 . . . . .118 CP85
Mitcham CR4 . . . . .120 DE94
Longfield Est, SE1 . . . . .202 A9
Longfield La, Wal.Cr. (Chsht.)
EN7 . . . . .14 DU27
Longfield Rd, W5 . . . . .79 CJ73
Longfield St, SW18 . . . . .120 DA87
Longfield Wk, W5 . . . . .79 CJ72
LONGFORD, Sev. 181 FD120
LONGFORD, West Dr. 94 BH81
Longford Av, Felt. TW14 . . . . .115 BS86
Southall UB1 . . . . .78 CA73
Staines TW19 . . . . .114 BL88
Longford Cl, Hmptn. (Hmptn.H.)
TW12 . . . . .116 CA91
Hayes UB4
off Longford Gdns 78 BX73
Longford Ct, E5 off Pedro St . .67 DX63
NW4 . . . . .63 CX56
Epsom KT19 . . . . .156 CQ105
Longford Gdns, Hayes UB4 . . .78 BX73
Sutton SM1 . . . . .140 DC104
Longford Rd, Twick. TW2 . . . .116 CA88
Longford Roundabout, West Dr.
UB7 . . . . .94 BH81
Longford St, NW1 . . . . .195 J4
Longford Wk, SW2
off Papworth Way 121 DN87
Longford Way, Stai. TW19 . . .114 BL88
Long Grn, Chig. IG7 . . . . .49 ES49
Long Gro, Rom. (Harold Wd.)
RM3 . . . . .52 FL54
Long Gro Rd, Epsom KT19 . .156 CP110
Longhayes Av, Rom. RM6 . . . .70 EX56
Longhayes Ct, Rom. RM6
off Longhayes Av 70 EX56
Longheath Gdns, Croy. CR0 . .142 DW99
Longhedge Ho, SE26 . . . . . . .122 DT91
Long Hedges, Houns. TW3 . . . .96 CA81
Longhedge St, SW11 . . . . . . .100 DG82
Long Hill, Cat. (Wold.) CR3 . .177 DX121
Longhill Rd, SE6 . . . . .123 ED89
Longhook Gdns, Nthlt. UB5 . . .77 BU68
Longhope Cl, SE15 . . . . .102 DS79
Longhouse Rd, Grays RM16 . .111 GH76
Longhurst Rd, SE13 . . . . .123 ED85
Croydon CR0 . . . . .142 DV100
Longland Ct, SE1 . . . . .202 B10
Longland Dr, N20 . . . . .44 DB48
LONGLANDS, Chis. 125 EQ90
Longlands Av, Couls. CR5 . . .158 DG114
Longlands Cl, Wal.Cr. (Chsht.)
EN8 . . . . .15 DX32
Longlands Ct, W11
off Portobello Rd 81 CZ73
Mitcham CR4
off Summerhill Way 140 DG95
Longlands Pk Cres, Sid.
DA15 . . . . .125 ES90
Longlands Rd, Sid. DA15 . . . .125 ES90
Long La, EC1 . . . . .196 G6
N2 . . . . .44 DC54
N3 . . . . .44 DC54
SE1 . . . . .201 K5
Bexleyheath DA7 . . . . .106 EX80
Croydon CR0 . . . . .142 DW99
Grays RM16 . . . . .110 GA75
Hemel Hempstead (Bov.)
HP3 . . . . .5 AZ31
Rickmansworth (Herons.)
WD3 . . . . .21 BC44
Rickmansworth (Mill End)
WD3 . . . . .37 BF47
Staines (Stanw.) TW19 . . . .114 BM87
Uxbridge UB10 . . . . .76 BN69
Longleat Ms, Orp. BR5
off High St 146 EW98
Longleat Rd, Enf. EN1 . . . . . . .30 DS43
Longleat Way, Felt. TW14 . . . .115 BR87
Longlees, Rick. (Map.Cr.) WD3 .37 BC50
Longleigh La, SE2 . . . . .106 EW79
Longleigh La, Bexh. DA7 . . . .106 EW79
Longlents Ho, NW10 . . . . .80 CR67
Longley Av, Wem. HA0 . . . . . .80 CM67
Longley Rd, SW17 . . . . .120 DE93
Croydon CR0 . . . . .141 DP101
Harrow HA1 . . . . .60 CC57
Long Leys, E4 . . . . .47 EB51
Longley St, SE1 . . . . .202 B9
Longley Way, NW2 . . . . .63 CW62
Long Lo Dr, Walt. KT12 . . . . .136 BW104
Longmans Cl, Wat. WD18
off Byewaters 23 BQ44
Long Mark Rd, E16
off Fulmer Rd 86 EK71
Longmarsh Vw, Dart. (Sutt.H.)
DA4 . . . . .148 FP95
Long Mead, NW9 . . . . .43 CT53
Longmead, Chis. BR7 . . . . . .145 EN96
Epsom KT19 . . . . .156 CR110
Longmead Business Pk, Epsom
KT19 . . . . .156 CR111
Longmead Cl, Brwd. CM15 . . .54 FY46
Caterham CR3 . . . . .176 DS122
Longmead Dr, Sid. DA14 . . . .126 EX89
Longmeade, Grav. DA12
off Damigos Rd 131 GM88
Long Meadow, NW5
off Torriano Av 65 DK64
Brentwood CM13 . . . . .55 GC47
Romford (Noak Hill) RM3 . .52 FJ48
Sevenoaks (Rvrhd.) TN13 . .190 FD121
Long Meadow Cl, W.Wick.
BR4 . . . . .143 EC101
Longmeadow Rd, Sid. DA15 .125 ES88
Longmead Rd, SW17 . . . . . . .120 DF92
Epsom KT19 . . . . .156 CR111
Hayes UB3 . . . . .77 BT73
Thames Ditton KT7 . . . . . . .137 CE101
Longmere Gdns, Tad. KT20 . .173 CW119
Longmoor, Wal.Cr. (Chsht.)
EN8 . . . . .15 DY29
Longmoore St, SW1 . . . . . . .199 K9
Longmoor Pt, SW15
off Norley Vale 119 CV88
Longmore Av, Barn. EN4, EN5 .28 DC44
Longmore Cl, Rick. (Map.Cr.)
WD3 . . . . .37 BF49
Longmore Rd, Walt. KT12 . . . .154 BY105
Longnor Rd, E1 . . . . .85 DX69
Long Pond Rd, SE3 . . . . .104 EE81
Longport Cl, Ilf. IG6 . . . . .50 EU51
Long Reach, Wok. (Ockham)
GU23 . . . . .168 BN123
Long Reach Ct, Bark. IG11 . . . .87 ER68
Longreach Rd, Bark. IG11 . . . .87 ET70
Erith DA8 . . . . .107 FH80
Longridge Gro, Wok. GU22
off Old Woking Rd 151 BE114
Longridge La, Sthl. UB1 . . . . . .78 CB73
Longridge Rd, SW5 . . . . .100 DA77
Long Ridings Av, Brwd.
CM13 . . . . .55 GB43
Long Rd, SW4 . . . . .101 DH84
Longs Cl, Wok. GU22 . . . . . . .168 BG116
Long's Ct, WC2 . . . . .195 M10
Longs Ct, Rich. TW9
off Crown Ter 98 CM84
Longsdon Way, Cat. CR3 . . . .176 DU124
Long Shaw, Lthd. KT22 . . . . .171 CG119
Longshaw Rd, E4 . . . . .47 ED48
Longshore, SE8 . . . . .203 M9
Longside Cl, Egh. TW20 . . . . .133 BC95
Longspring, Wat. WD24 . . . . . .23 BV38
Longspring Wd, Sev. TN14 . . .190 FF130
Longstaff Cres, SW18 . . . . . .120 DA86
Longstaff Rd, SW18 . . . . .120 DA86
Longstone Av, NW10 . . . . .81 CT66
Longstone Rd, SW17 . . . . . . .121 DH92
Iver SL0 . . . . .75 BC68
Long St, E2 . . . . .197 P2
Waltham Abbey EN9 . . . . . . .16 EL32
Longthornton Rd, SW16 . . . . .141 DJ96
Longton Av, SE26 . . . . .122 DU91
Longton Gro, SE26 . . . . .122 DV91
Longtown Cl, Rom. RM3 . . . . .52 FJ50
Longtown Rd, Rom. RM3 . . . . .52 FJ50
Longview Way, Rom. RM5 . . . .51 FD53
Longville Rd, SE11 . . . . .200 F8
Long Wk, SE1 . . . . .201 N6
SE18 . . . . .105 EP79
SW13 . . . . .98 CS82
Chalfont St. Giles HP8 . . . . .20 AX41
Epsom KT18 . . . . .173 CX119
New Malden KT3 . . . . .138 CQ97
Waltham Abbey EN9 . . . . . . .15 EA30
West Byfleet KT14 . . . . .152 BJ114
Longwalk Rd, Uxb. UB11 . . . . .77 BP74
Longwood Business Pk, Sun.
TW16 . . . . .135 BT99
Longwood Cl, Upmin. RM14 . .72 FQ64
Longwood Dr, SW15 . . . . .119 CU86
Long Wd Dr, Beac. (Jordans)
HP9 . . . . .36 AT51
Longwood Gdns, Ilf. IG5, IG6 .69 EM56
Longwood Rd, Ken. CR8 . . . .176 DR116
Longworth Cl, SE28 . . . . .88 EX72
Long Yd, WC1 . . . . .196 B5
Loning, The, NW9 . . . . .62 CS56
Enfield EN3 . . . . .30 DW38
Lonsdale Av, E6 . . . . .86 EK69
Brentwood CM13 . . . . .55 GD44
Romford RM7 . . . . .71 FC58
Wembley HA9 . . . . .62 CL64
Lonsdale Cl, E6
off Lonsdale Av 86 EL70
SE9 . . . . .124 EK90
Edgware HA8
off Orchard Dr 42 CM50
Pinner HA5 . . . . .40 BY52
Uxbridge UB8
off Dawley Av 77 BQ71
Lonsdale Cres, Dart. DA2 . . . .128 FQ88
Ilford IG2 . . . . .69 EP58
Lonsdale Dr, Enf. EN2 . . . . . . .29 DL43
Lonsdale Gdns, Th.Hth. CR7 . .141 DM98
Lonsdale Ms, Rich. TW9
off Elizabeth Cotts 98 CN81
Lonsdale Pl, N1
off Barnsbury St 83 DN66
Lonsdale Rd, E11 . . . . .68 EF59
NW6 . . . . .81 CZ68
SE25 . . . . .142 DV98
SW13 . . . . .99 CU79
W4 .99 CT77
W11 . . . . .81 CZ72
Bexleyheath DA7 . . . . .106 EZ82
Southall UB2 . . . . .96 BX76
Weybridge KT13 . . . . .152 BN108
Lonsdale Sq, N1 . . . . .83 DN66
Loobert Rd, N15 . . . . .66 DS55
Looe Gdns, Ilf. IG6 . . . . .69 EP55
Loom Ct, E1 . . . . .197 N5
Loom La, Rad. WD7 . . . . .25 CG37
Loom Pl, Rad. WD7 . . . . .25 CG36
Loop Rd, Chis. BR7 . . . . .125 EQ93
Epsom KT18
off Woodcote Side 172 CQ116
Waltham Abbey EN9 . . . . . . .15 EB32
Woking GU22 . . . . .167 AZ121
Lopen Rd, N18 . . . . .46 DS49
Loraine Cl, Enf. EN3 . . . . .30 DW43
Loraine Gdns, Ashtd. KT21 . .172 CL117
Loraine Rd, N7 . . . . .65 DM63
W4 .98 CP79
Lorane Ct, Wat. WD17 . . . . . . .23 BU40
Lord Amory Way, E14 . . . . . . .204 D4
Lord Av, Ilf. IG5 . . . . .69 EM56
Lord Chancellor Wk, Kings.T.
KT2 . . . . .138 CQ95
Lord Chatham's Ride, Sev.
TN14 . . . . .180 EX117
Lordell Pl, SW19 . . . . .119 CW93
Lorden Wk, E2 . . . . .84 DU69
Lord Gdns, Ilf. IG5 . . . . .68 EL56
Lord Hills Br, W2
off Porchester Rd 82 DB71
Lord Hills Rd, W2 . . . . .82 DB71
Lord Holland La, SW9
off St. Lawrence Way 101 DN81
Lord Knyvett Cl, Stai. (Stanw.)
TW19 . . . . .114 BK86
Lord Napier Pl, W6
off Upper Mall 99 CU78
Lord N St, SW1 . . . . .199 P7
Lord Roberts Ms, SW6
off Moore Pk Rd 100 DB80
Lord Roberts Ter, SE18 . . . . .105 EN78
★ Lord's, Middlesex County
Cricket Club & Mus, NW8 .194 A2
Lordsbury Fld, Wall. SM6 . . . .159 DJ110
Lord's Cl, SE21 . . . . .122 DQ89
Lords Cl, Felt. TW13 . . . . . . .116 BY89
Radlett (Shenley) WD7 . . . . .10 CL32
Lordsgrove Cl, Tad. KT20
off Whitegate Way 173 CV120
Lordship Cl, Brwd. CM13 . . . .55 GD46
Lordship Gro, N16 . . . . .66 DR61
Lordship La, N17 . . . . .46 DQ53
N22 . . . . .45 DN54
SE22 . . . . .122 DT86
Lordship La Est, SE22 . . . . . .122 DU88
Lordship Pk, N16 . . . . .66 DQ61
Lordship Pk Ms, N16
off Allerton Rd 66 DQ61
Lordship Pl, SW3
off Cheyne Row 100 DE79
Lordship Rd, N16 . . . . .66 DR61
Northolt UB5 . . . . .78 BY66
Waltham Cross (Chsht.)
EN7 . . . . .14 DV30
Lordship Ter, N16 . . . . .66 DR61
Lordsmead Rd, N17 . . . . .46 DS53
Lord St, E16 . . . . .86 EL74
Gravesend DA12 . . . . .131 GH87
Watford WD17 . . . . .24 BW41
Lord's Vw, NW8 . . . . .194 A3
Lordswood Cl, Dart. (Lane End)
DA2 . . . . .129 FS91
Lords Wd Ho, Couls. CR5 . . .175 DK122
Lord Warwick St, SE18 . . . . .105 EM76
Lorenzo St, WC1 . . . . .196 B2
Loretto Gdns, Har. HA3 . . . . . .62 CL56
Lorian Cl, N12 . . . . .44 DB49
Lorian Dr, Reig. RH2 . . . . . . .184 DC133
Loriners Cl, Cob. KT11
off Between Sts 153 BU114
Loring Rd, N20 . . . . .44 DE47
Isleworth TW7 . . . . .97 CF82
Loris Rd, W6 . . . . .99 CW76
Lorn Ct, SW9 . . . . .101 DN82
Lorne Av, Croy. CR0 . . . . . . .143 DX101
Lorne Cl, NW8 . . . . .194 C3
Lorne Gdns, E11 . . . . .68 EJ56
W11 . . . . .99 CX75
Croydon CR0 . . . . .143 DX101
Lorne Rd, E7 . . . . .68 EH63
E17 . . . . .67 EA57
N4 .65 DM60
Brentwood CM14 . . . . .54 FW49
Harrow HA3 . . . . .41 CF54
Richmond TW10
off Albert Rd 118 CM85
Lorn Rd, SW9 . . . . .101 DM82
Lorraine Chase, S.Ock. RM15 .108 FM75
Lorraine Pk, Har. HA3 . . . . . . .41 CE52
Lorrimore Rd, SE17 . . . . .101 DP79
Lorrimore Sq, SE17 . . . . .101 DP79
Lorton Cl, Grav. DA12 . . . . . .131 GL89
Loseberry Rd, Esher (Clay.)
KT10 . . . . .155 CD106
Lossie Dr, Iver SL0 . . . . .75 BB73
Lothair Rd, W5 . . . . .97 CK75
Lothair Rd N, N4 . . . . .65 DP58
Lothair Rd S, N4 . . . . .65 DN59
Lothbury, EC2 . . . . .197 K8
Lothian Av, Hayes UB4 . . . . . .77 BV71
Lothian Cl, Wem. HA0 . . . . . . .61 CG63
Lothian Rd, SW9 . . . . .101 DP81
Lothian Wd, Tad. KT20 . . . . .173 CV122
Lothrop St, W10 . . . . .81 CY69
Lots Rd, SW10 . . . . .100 DC80

Lot - Lyn

Lotus Cl, SE21 122 DQ90
Lotus Rd, West. (Bigg.H.) TN16 179 EM118
Loubet St, SW17 120 DF93
Loudhams Rd, Amer. HP7 20 AW39
Loudhams Wd La, Ch.St.G. HP8 20 AX40
Loudoun Av, Ilf. IG6 69 EP57
Loudoun Rd, NW8 82 DC66
Loudoun Rd Ms, NW8
off Loudoun Rd 82 DC67
LOUDWATER, Rick. 22 BK41
Loudwater Cl, Sun. TW16 135 BU98
Loudwater Dr, Rick. (Loud.) WD3 22 BJ42
Loudwater Hts, Rick. (Loud.) WD3 22 BH41
Loudwater La, Rick. WD3 22 BK42
Loudwater Ridge, Rick. (Loud.) WD3 22 BJ42
Loudwater Rd, Sun. TW16 135 BU98
Loughborough Est, SW9
off Loughborough Rd 101 DP82
⇌ Loughborough Junction 101 DP83
Loughborough Pk, SW9 101 DP84
Loughborough Rd, SW9 101 DN82
Loughborough St, SE11 200 C10
Lough Rd, N7 83 DM65
LOUGHTON 33 EM43
⊖ Loughton 32 EL43
Loughton Cl, Wal.Abb. EN9 16 EH33
Loughton La, Epp. (They.B.) CM16 33 ER38
Loughton Way, Buck.H. IG9 48 EK46
Louisa Gdns, E1
off Louisa St 85 DX70
Louisa Ho, SW15 98 CS84
Louisa St, E1 85 DX70
Louise Aumonier Wk, N19
off Hillrise Rd 65 DL59
Louise Bennett Cl, SE24
off Shakespeare Rd 101 DP84
Louise Ct, E11
off Grosvenor Rd 68 EH57
Louise Gdns, Rain. RM13 89 FE69
Louise Rd, E15 86 EE65
Louise Wk, Hem.H. (Bov.) HP3 5 BA28
Louis Ms, N10 45 DH53
Louisville Rd, SW17 120 DG90
Louvaine Rd, SW11 100 DD84
Louvain Rd, Green. DA9 129 FS87
Louvain Way, Wat. WD25 7 BV32
Lovage App, E6 86 EL71
Lovat Cl, NW2 63 CT62
Lovat La, EC3 201 M1
Lovatt Cl, Edg. HA8 42 CP51
Lovatt Dr, Ruis. HA4 59 BU57
Lovatts, Rick. (Crox.Grn.) WD3 22 BN42
Lovat Wk, Houns. TW5
off Cranford La 96 BY80
Loveday Rd, W13 79 CH74
Love Grn La, Iver SL0 75 BD71
Lovegrove St, SE1 102 DU78
Lovegrove Wk, E14 204 D3
Love Hill La, Slou. SL3 75 BA73
Lovekyn Cl, Kings.T. KT2
off Queen Elizabeth Rd 138 CM96
Lovelace Av, Brom. BR2 145 EN100
Lovelace Cl, Lthd. (Eff.Junct.) KT24 169 BU123
Lovelace Dr, Wok. GU22 167 BF115
Lovelace Gdns, Bark. IG11 70 EU63
Surbiton KT6 137 CK101
Walton-on-Thames KT12 154 BW106
Lovelace Grn, SE9 105 EM83
Lovelace Rd, SE21 122 DQ89
Barnet EN4 44 DE45
Surbiton KT6 137 CJ101
Lovelands La, Tad. KT20 184 DB127
Love La, EC2 197 J8
N17 46 DT52
SE18 105 EP77
SE25 142 DV97
Abbots Langley WD5 7 BT30
Bexley DA5 126 EZ86
Godstone RH9 186 DW132
Gravesend DA12 131 GJ87
Iver SL0 75 BD72
Kings Langley WD4 6 BL29
Mitcham CR4 140 DE97
Morden SM4 140 DA101
Pinner HA5 60 BY55
South Ockendon (Aveley) RM15 108 FQ75
Surbiton KT6 137 CK103
Sutton SM3 157 CY106
Tadworth KT20 183 CT126
Woodford Green IG8 49 EM51
Lovel Av, Well. DA16 106 EU82
Lovel End, Ger.Cr. (Chal.St.P.) SL9 36 AW52
Lovelinch Cl, SE15 102 DW79
Lovell Ho, E8 84 DU67
Lovell Pl, SE16 203 L6
Lovell Rd, Enf. EN1 30 DV35
Richmond TW10 117 CJ90
Southall UB1 78 CB72
Lovell Wk, Rain. RM13 89 FG65
Lovel Mead, Ger.Cr. (Chal.St.P.) SL9 36 AW52
Lovelock Cl, Ken. CR8 176 DQ117
Lovel Rd, Ger.Cr. (Chal.St.P.) SL9 36 AW52
Loveridge Ms, NW6
off Loveridge Rd 81 CZ65
Loveridge Rd, NW6 81 CZ65
Lovering Rd, Wal.Cr. (Chsht.) EN7 14 DQ26
Lovers La, Green. DA9 109 FX84
Lovers Wk, N3 44 DA52
NW7 43 CZ51
SE10 104 EE79
Lover's Wk, W1 198 F2
Lovett Dr, Cars. SM5 140 DC101
Lovett Rd, Stai. TW18 113 BB91
Uxbridge (Hare.) UB9 58 BJ55
Lovett's Pl, SW18
off Old York Rd 100 DB84
Lovett Way, NW10 62 CQ64
Love Wk, SE5 102 DR82
Lovibonds Av, Orp. BR6 163 EP105
West Drayton UB7 76 BM72
Lowbell La, St.Alb. (Lon.Col.) AL2 10 CL27
Lowbrook Rd, Ilf. IG1 69 EP64
Low Cl, Green. DA9 129 FU85
Low Cross Wd La, SE21 122 DT90
Lowdell Cl, West Dr. UB7 76 BL72
Lowden Rd, N9 46 DV46
SE24 101 DP84
Southall UB1 78 BY73
Lowe, The, Chig. IG7 50 EU50
Lowe Av, E16 86 EG71
Lowe Cl, Chig. IG7 50 EU50
Lowell St, E14 85 DY72
Lowen Rd, Rain. RM13 89 FD68
Lower Addiscombe Rd, Croy. CR0 142 DS102
Lower Addison Gdns, W14 99 CY75
Lower Alderton Hall La, Loug. IG10 33 EN43
LOWER ASHTEAD, Ashtd. 171 CJ119
Lower Barn Rd, Pur. CR8 160 DR112
Lower Bedfords Rd, Rom. RM1 51 FE51
Lower Belgrave St, SW1 199 H7
Lower Boston Rd, W7 79 CE74
Lower Br Rd, Red. RH1 184 DF134
Lower Broad St, Dag. RM10 88 FA67
Lower Bury La, Epp. CM16 17 ES31
Lower Camden, Chis. BR7 125 EM94
Lower Ch Hill, Green. DA9 129 FS85
Lower Ch St, Croy. CR0
off Waddon New Rd 141 DP103
LOWER CLAPTON, E5 67 DX63
Lower Clapton Rd, E5 66 DV64
Lower Clarendon Wk, W11
off Lancaster Rd 81 CY72
Lower Common S, SW15 99 CV83
Lower Coombe St, Croy. CR0 160 DQ105
Lower Ct Rd, Epsom KT19 156 CQ111
Lower Cft, Swan. BR8 147 FF98
Lower Downs Rd, SW20 139 CX95
Lower Drayton Pl, Croy. CR0
off Drayton Rd 141 DP103
Lower Dunnymans, Bans. SM7
off Basing Rd 157 CZ114
LOWER EDMONTON, N9 46 DT46
Lower Fm Rd, Lthd. (Eff.) KT24 169 BV124
LOWER FELTHAM, Felt. 115 BS90
Lower George St, Rich. TW9
off George St 117 CK85
Lower Gravel Rd, Brom. BR2 144 EL102
LOWER GREEN, Esher 136 CA103
Lower Grn Rd, Esher KT10 136 CB103
Lower Grn W, Mitch. CR4 140 DE97
Lower Grosvenor Pl, SW1 199 H6
Lower Gro Rd, Rich. TW10 118 CM86
Lower Guild Hall, Green. (Bluewater) DA9
off Bluewater Parkway 129 FU88
Lower Hall La, E4 47 DY50
Lower Hampton Rd, Sun. TW16 136 BW97
Lower Ham Rd, Kings.T. KT2 117 CK93
Lower Higham Rd, Grav. DA12 131 GM88
Lower High St, Wat. WD17 24 BX44
Lower Hill Rd, Epsom KT19 156 CP112
LOWER HOLLOWAY, N7 65 DM64
Lower James St, W1 195 L10
Lower John St, W1 195 L10
Lower Kenwood Av, Enf. EN2 29 DK43
LOWER KINGSWOOD, Tad. 184 DA127
Lower Lea Crossing, E14 86 EE73
E16 86 EE73
Lower Maidstone Rd, N11
off Telford Rd 45 DJ51
Lower Mall, W6 99 CV78
Lower Mardyke Av, Rain. RM13 89 FC68
Lower Marsh, SE1 200 D5
Lower Marsh La, Kings.T. KT1 138 CM98
Lower Mead, Iver SL0 75 BD69
Lower Meadow, Wal.Cr. EN8 15 DX27
Lower Merton Ri, NW3 82 DE66
Lower Morden La, Mord. SM4 139 CW100
Lower Mortlake Rd, Rich. TW9 98 CL84
Lower Noke Cl, Brwd. CM14 52 FL47
Lower Northfield, Bans. SM7 157 CZ114
Lower Paddock Rd, Wat. WD19 24 BY44
Lower Pk Rd, N11 45 DJ50
Belvedere DA17 106 FA76
Coulsdon CR5 174 DE118
Loughton IG10 32 EK43
Lower Pillory Down, Cars. SM5 158 DG113
Lower Plantation, Rick. (Loud.) WD3 22 BJ41
Lower Queens Rd, Buck.H. IG9 48 EK47
Lower Range Rd, Grav. DA12 131 GL87
Lower Richmond Rd, SW14 98 CP83
SW15 99 CW83
Richmond TW9 98 CN83
Lower Rd, SE8 202 F6
SE16 203 H8
Belvedere DA17 106 FA76
Brentwood (Mtnsg.) CM13, CM15 55 GD41
Erith DA8 107 FD77
Gerrards Cross SL9 36 AY53
Gravesend (Nthflt.) DA11 110 FY84
Lower Rd, Har. HA2 61 CD61
Hemel Hempstead HP3 6 BN25
Kenley CR8 159 DP113
Leatherhead (Fetch.) KT22 171 CD123
Loughton IG10 33 EN40
Orpington BR5 146 EV101
Rickmansworth (Chorl.) WD3 21 BC42
Sutton SM1 158 DC105
Swanley BR8 127 FF94
Tilbury RM18 111 GG84
Uxbridge (Denh.) UB9 57 BC59
Lower Robert St, WC2
off John Adam St 83 DL73
Lower Rose Gallery, Green. (Bluewater) DA9
off Bluewater Parkway 129 FU88
Lower Sandfields, Wok. (Send) GU23 167 BD124
Lower Sand Hills, T.Ditt. KT7 137 CJ101
Lower Sawley Wd, Bans. SM7
off Upper Sawley Wd 157 CZ114
Lower Shott, Wal.Cr. (Chsht.) EN7 14 DT26
Lower Sloane St, SW1 198 F9
Lower Sq, Islw. TW7 97 CH83
Lower Sta Rd, Dart. (Cray.) DA1 127 FE86
Lower Strand, NW9 43 CT54
Lower Sunbury Rd, Hmptn. TW12 136 BZ96
Lower Swaines, Epp. CM16 17 ES30
LOWER SYDENHAM, SE26 123 DX91
⇌ Lower Sydenham 123 DZ92
Lower Sydenham Ind Est, SE26 123 DZ92
Lower Tail, Wat. WD19 40 BY48
Lower Talbot Wk, W11
off Lancaster Rd 81 CY72
Lower Teddington Rd, Kings.T. KT1 137 CK95
Lower Ter, NW3 64 DC62
Lower Thames St, EC3 201 L1
Lower Thames Wk, Green. (Bluewater) DA9
off Bluewater Parkway 129 FU88
Lower Tub, Bushey WD23 41 CD45
Lower Wd Rd, Esher (Clay.) KT10 155 CG107
Lowestoft Cl, E5
off Theydon Rd 66 DW61
Lowestoft Ms, E16 105 EP75
Lowestoft Rd, Wat. WD24 23 BV39
Loweswater Cl, Wat. WD25 8 BW33
Wembley HA9 61 CK61
Lowfield Rd, NW6 82 DA66
W3 80 CQ72
Lowfield St, Dart. DA1 128 FL89
Low Hall Cl, E4 47 EA45
Low Hall La, E17 67 DY58
Lowick Rd, Har. HA1 61 CE56
Lowlands Dr, Stai. (Stanw.) TW19 114 BK85
Lowlands Gdns, Rom. RM7 71 FB58
Lowlands Rd, Har. HA1 61 CE59
Pinner HA5 60 BW59
South Ockendon (Aveley) RM15 90 FP74
Lowman Rd, N7 65 DM63
Lowndes Cl, SW1 198 G7
Lowndes Ct, W1 195 K9
Bromley BR1
off Queens Rd 144 EG96
Lowndes Pl, SW1 198 F7
Lowndes Sq, SW1 198 E5
Lowndes St, SW1 198 E6
Lowood Ct, SE19 122 DT92
Lowood St, E1 off Dellow St 84 DV73
Lowry Cl, Erith DA8 107 FD77
Lowry Cres, Mitch. CR4 140 DE96
Lowry Rd, Dag. RM8 70 EV63
Lowshoe La, Rom. RM5 51 FB53
Lowson Gro, Wat. WD19 40 BY45
LOW STREET, Til. 111 GM79
Low St La, Til. (E.Til.) RM18 111 GM78
Lowswood Cl, Nthwd. HA6 39 BQ53
Lowther Cl, Borwd. (Elstree) WD6 26 CM43
Lowther Dr, Enf. EN2 29 DL42
Lowther Gdns, SW7 198 A5
Lowther Hill, SE23 123 DY87
Lowther Rd, E17 47 DY54
N7 off Mackenzie Rd 65 DN64
SW13 99 CT81
Kingston upon Thames KT2 138 CM95
Stanmore HA7 62 CM55
Lowthorpe, Wok. GU21
off Shilburn Way 166 AU118
Lowth Rd, SE5 102 DQ82
LOXFORD, Ilf. 69 EQ64
Loxford Av, E6 86 EK68
Loxford La, Ilf. IG1, IG3 69 EQ64
Loxford Rd, Bark. IG11 87 EP65
Caterham CR3 186 DT125
Loxford Ter, Bark. IG11
off Fanshawe Av 87 EQ65
Loxford Way, Cat. CR3 186 DT125
Loxham Rd, E4 47 EA52
Loxham St, WC1 196 A3
Loxley Cl, SE26 123 DX92
Loxley Rd, SW18 120 DD88
Hampton TW12 116 BZ91
Loxton Rd, SE23 123 DX88
Loxwood Cl, Felt. TW14 115 BR88
Orpington BR5 146 EX103
Loxwood Rd, N17 66 DS55
Lubbock Rd, Chis. BR7 125 EM94
Lubbock St, SE14 102 DW80
Lucan Dr, Stai. TW18 114 BK94
Lucan Pl, SW3 198 B9
Lucan Rd, Barn. EN5 27 CY41
Lucas Av, E13 86 EH67
Harrow HA2 60 CA61
Lucas Cl, NW10 off Pound La 81 CU66
Lucas Ct, Har. HA2 60 CA60
Waltham Abbey EN9 16 EF33
Lucas Gdns, N2 44 DC54
Lucas Rd, SE20 122 DW93
Grays RM17 110 GA76
Lucas Sq, NW11
off Hampstead Way 64 DA58
Lucas St, SE8 103 EA81
Lucerne Cl, Wal.Cr. (Chsht.) EN7 14 DS27
Lucerne Cl, N13 45 DL49
Woking GU22
off Claremont Av 166 AY119
Lucerne Ct, Erith DA18
off Middle Way 106 EY76
Lucerne Gro, E17 67 ED56
Lucerne Ms, W8
off Kensington Mall 82 DA74
Lucerne Rd, N5 65 DP63
Orpington BR6 145 ET102
Thornton Heath CR7 141 DP99
Lucerne Way, Rom. RM3 52 FK51
Lucey Rd, SE16 202 B7
Lucey Way, SE16 202 C7
Lucie Av, Ashf. TW15 115 BP93
Lucien Rd, SW17 120 DG91
SW19 120 DB89
Lucknow St, SE18 105 ES80
Lucorn Cl, SE12 124 EF86
Lucton Ms, Loug. IG10 33 EP42
Luctons Av, Buck.H. IG9 48 EJ46
Lucy Cres, W3 80 CQ71
Lucy Gdns, Dag. RM8
off Grafton Rd 70 EY62
Luddesdon Rd, Erith DA8 106 FA80
Luddington Av, Vir.W. GU25 133 AZ96
Ludford Cl, NW9 42 CS54
Croydon CR0
off Warrington Rd 159 DP105
Ludgate Bdy, EC4 196 F9
Ludgate Circ, EC4 196 F9
Ludgate Hill, EC4 196 F9
Ludgate Sq, EC4 196 G9
Ludham Cl, SE28
off Rollesby Way 88 EW72
Ludlow Cl, Brom. BR2
off Aylesbury Rd 144 EG97
Harrow HA2 60 BZ63
Ludlow Mead, Wat. WD19 39 BV48
Ludlow Pl, Grays RM17 110 GB76
Ludlow Rd, W5 79 CJ70
Feltham TW13 115 BU91
Ludlow St, EC1 197 H4
Ludlow Way, N2 64 DC56
Rickmansworth (Crox.Grn.) WD3 23 BQ42
Ludovick Wk, SW15 98 CS84
Ludwick Ms, SE14 103 DY80
Luffield Rd, SE2 106 EV76
Luffman Rd, SE12 124 EH90
Lugard Rd, SE15 102 DV82
Lugg App, E12 69 EN62
Luke Ho, E1 84 DV72
Luke St, EC2 197 M4
Lukin Cres, E4 47 ED48
Lukin St, E1 84 DW72
Lukintone Cl, Loug. IG10 32 EL44
Lullarook Cl, West. (Bigg.H.) TN16 178 EJ116
Lullingstone Av, Swan. BR8 147 FF97
Lullingstone Cl, Orp. BR5
off Lullingstone Cres 126 EV94
Lullingstone Cres, Orp. BR5 126 EU94
Lullingstone La, SE13 123 ED87
Dartford (Eyns.) DA4 148 FJ104
★ Lullingstone Park Visitor Cen, Dart. (Eyns.) DA4 165 FG107
Lullingstone Rd, Belv. DA17 106 EZ79
★ Lullingstone Roman Villa, Dart. DA4 147 FH104
Lullington Garth, N12 43 CZ50
Borehamwood WD6 26 CP43
Bromley BR1 124 EE94
Lullington Rd, SE20 122 DU94
Dagenham RM9 88 EY66
Lulot Gdns, N19 65 DH61
Lulworth, SE17 201 K10
Lulworth Av, Houns. TW5 96 CB80
Waltham Cross (Chsht.) EN7 13 DP29
Wembley HA9 61 CJ59
Lulworth Cl, Har. HA2 60 BZ62
Lulworth Cres, Mitch. CR4 140 DE96
Lulworth Dr, Pnr. HA5 60 BX59
Romford RM5 51 FB50
Lulworth Gdns, Har. HA2 60 BY61
Lulworth Rd, SE9 124 EL89
SE15 102 DV82
Welling DA16 105 ET82
Lulworth Waye, Hayes UB4 78 BW72
Lumen Rd, Wem. HA9 61 CK61
Lumley Cl, Belv. DA17 106 FA79
Lumley Ct, WC2 200 A1
Lumley Gdns, Sutt. SM3 157 CY106
Lumley Rd, Sutt. SM3 157 CY107
Lumley St, W1 194 G9
Lunar Cl, West. (Bigg.H.) TN16 178 EK116
Luna Rd, Th.Hth. CR7 142 DQ97
Lundin Wk, Wat. WD19
off Woodhall La 40 BX49
Lundy Dr, Hayes UB3 95 BS77
Lundy Wk, N1
off Clephane Rd 84 DQ65
Lunedale Rd, Dart. DA2 128 FQ88
Lunedale Wk, Dart. DA2
off Lunedale Rd 128 FP88
Lunghurst Rd, Cat. (Wold.) CR3 177 DZ120
Lunham Rd, SE19 122 DS93
Lupin Cl, SW2 off Palace Rd 121 DP89
Croydon CR0
off Primrose La 143 DX102
Romford (Rush Grn.) RM7 71 FD61
West Drayton UB7
off Magnolia St 94 BK78
Lupin Cres, Ilf. IG1
off Bluebell Way 69 EP64
Luppit Cl, Brwd. CM13 55 GA46
Lupton Cl, SE12 124 EH90
Lupton St, NW5 65 DJ63
Lupus St, SW1 101 DH79
Luralda Gdns, E14 204 E10
Lurgan Av, W6 99 CX79
Lurline Gdns, SW11 100 DG81
Luscombe Ct, Brom. BR2 144 EE96
Luscombe Way, SW8 101 DL80
Lushes Ct, Loug. IG10
off Lushes Rd 33 EP43
Lushes Rd, Loug. IG10 33 EP43
Lushington Dr, Cob. KT11 153 BV114
Lushington Rd, NW10 81 CV68
SE6 123 EB92
Lushington Ter, E8
off Wayland Av 66 DU64
Lusted Hall La, West. (Tats.) TN16 178 EJ120
Lusted Rd, Sev. TN13 181 FE120
Luther Cl, Edg. HA8 42 CQ47
Luther King Cl, E17 67 DY58
Luther Rd, Tedd. TW11 117 CF92
Luton Pl, SE10 103 EC80
Luton Rd, E17 67 DZ55
Sidcup DA14 126 EW90
Luton St, NW8 194 A5
Lutton Ter, NW3 off Flask Wk 64 DD63
Luttrell Av, SW15 119 CV85
Lutwyche Rd, SE6 123 DZ89
Luxborough La, Chig. IG7 48 EL48
Luxborough St, W1 194 F6
Luxemburg Gdns, W6 99 CX77
Luxfield Rd, SE9 124 EL88
Luxford St, SE16 203 H9
Luxmore St, SE4 103 DZ81
Luxor St, SE5 102 DQ83
Luxted Rd, Orp. BR6 163 EN112
Lyall Av, SE21 122 DS90
Lyall Ms, SW1 198 F7
Lyall Ms W, SW1 198 F7
Lyall St, SW1 198 F7
Lyal Rd, E3 85 DY68
Lycett Pl, W12 off Becklow Rd 99 CU75
Lych Gate, Wat. WD25 8 BX33
Lych Gate Rd, Orp. BR6 146 EU102
Lych Gate Wk, Hayes UB3 77 BT73
Lych Way, Wok. GU21 166 AX116
Lyconby Gdns, Croy. CR0 143 DY101
Lycrome Rd, Chesh. HP5 4 AS28
Lydd Cl, Sid. DA14 125 ES90
Lydden Ct, SE9 125 ES86
Lydden Gro, SW18 120 DB87
Lydden Rd, SW18 120 DB87
Lydd Rd, Bexh. DA7 106 EZ80
Lydeard Rd, E6 87 EM66
Lydele Cl, Wok. GU21 167 AZ115
Lydford Cl, N16
off Pellerin Rd 66 DS64
Lydford Rd, N15 66 DR57
NW2 81 CX65
W9 81 CZ70
Lydhurst Av, SW2 121 DM89
Lydia Rd, Erith DA8 107 FF79
Lydney Cl, SE15 102 DS80
SW19 off Princes Way 119 CY89
Lydon Rd, SW4 101 DJ83
Lydstep Rd, Chis. BR7 125 EN91
Lye, The, Tad. KT20 173 CW122
LYE GREEN, Chesh. 4 AT27
Lye La, St.Alb. (Brick.Wd.) AL2 8 CA30
Lyfield, Lthd. (Oxshott) KT22 154 CB114
Lyford Rd, SW18 120 DD87
Lygon Pl, SW1 199 H7
Lyham Cl, SW2 121 DL86
Lyham Rd, SW2 121 DL85
Lyle Cl, Mitch. CR4 140 DG101
Lyle Pk, Sev. TN13 191 FH123
Lymbourne Cl, Sutt. SM2 158 DA110
Lyme Fm Rd, SE12 104 EG84
Lyme Gro, E9
off St. Thomas's Sq 84 DW66
Lymer Av, SE19 122 DT92
Lyme Regis Rd, Bans. SM7 173 CZ117
Lyme Rd, Well. DA16 106 EV81
Lymescote Gdns, Sutt. SM1 140 DA103
Lyme St, NW1 83 DJ66
Lyme Ter, NW1
off Royal Coll St 83 DJ66
Lyminge Cl, Sid. DA14 125 ET91
Lyminge Gdns, SW18 120 DE88
Lymington Av, N22 45 DN54
Lymington Cl, E6
off Valiant Way 87 EM71
SW16 141 DK96
Lymington Dr, Ruis. HA4 59 BR61
Lymington Gdns, Epsom KT19 157 CT106
Lymington Rd, NW6 82 DB65
Dagenham RM8 70 EX60
Lympstone Gdns, SE15 102 DU80
Lynbridge Gdns, N13 45 DP49
Lynbrook Cl, SE15
off Blakes Rd 102 DS80
Rainham RM13 89 FD68
Lynceley Gra, Epp. CM16 18 EU29
Lynch, The, Uxb. UB8
off New Windsor St 76 BJ67
Lynch Cl, Uxb. UB8
off New Windsor St 76 BJ66
Lynchen Cl, Houns. TW5
off The Avenue 95 BU81
Lynch Wk, SE8 off Prince St 103 DZ79
Lyncott Cres, SW4 101 DH84
Lyncroft Av, Pnr. HA5 60 BY57
Lyncroft Gdns, NW6 64 DA64
W13 97 CJ75
Epsom KT17 157 CT109
Hounslow TW3 96 CC84
Lyndale, NW2 63 CZ63
Lyndale Av, NW2 63 CZ62
Lyndale Cl, SE3 104 EF79
Lyndale Ct, W.Byf. KT14
off Parvis Rd 152 BG113
Lyndale Est, Grays RM20 109 FV79
Lyndale Rd, Red. RH1 184 DF131
Lynden Way, Swan. BR8 147 FC97
Lyndhurst Av, N12 44 DF51

★ Place of interest ⇌ Railway station ⊖ London Underground station DLR Docklands Light Railway station Tramlink station H Hospital

289

Lyn - Mal

Lyndhurst Av, NW7 **42** CS51
SW16 **141** DK96
Pinner HA5 **39** BV53
Southall UB1 **78** CB74
Sunbury-on-Thames TW16 **135** BU97
Surbiton KT5 **138** CP102
Twickenham TW2 **116** BZ88
Lyndhurst Cl, NW10 **62** CR62
Bexleyheath DA7 **107** FB83
Croydon CR0 **142** DT104
Orpington BR6 **163** EP105
Woking GU21 **166** AX115
Lyndhurst Ct, E18
off Churchfields **48** EG53
Sutton SM2
off Overton Rd **158** DA108
Lyndhurst Dr, E10 **67** EC59
Hornchurch RM11 **72** FJ60
New Malden KT3 **138** CS100
Sevenoaks TN13 **190** FE124
Lyndhurst Gdns, N3 **43** CY53
NW3 **64** DD64
Barking IG11 **87** ES65
Enfield EN1 **30** DS42
Ilford IG2 **69** ER58
Pinner HA5 **39** BV53
Lyndhurst Gro, SE15 **102** DS82
Lyndhurst Ho, SW15
off Ellisfield Dr **119** CU87
Lyndhurst Ri, Chig. IG7 **49** EN49
Lyndhurst Rd, E4 **47** EC52
N18 **46** DU49
N22 **45** DM51
NW3 **64** DD64
Bexleyheath DA7 **107** FB83
Coulsdon CR5 **174** DG116
Greenford UB6 **78** CB70
Thornton Heath CR7 **141** DN98
Lyndhurst Sq, SE15 **102** DT81
Lyndhurst Ter, NW3 **64** DD64
Lyndhurst Way, SE15 **102** DT81
Brentwood CM13 **55** GC45
Chertsey KT16 **133** BE104
Sutton SM2 **158** DA108
Lyndon Av, Pnr. HA5 **40** BY51
Sidcup DA15 **125** ET85
Wallington SM6 **140** DG104
Lyndon Rd, Belv. DA17 **106** FA77
Lyndwood Dr, Wind. (Old Wind.) SL4 **112** AU86
LYNE, Cher. **133** BA102
Lyne Cl, Vir.W. GU25 **133** AZ100
Lyne Cres, E17 **47** DZ53
Lyne Crossing Rd, Cher. (Lyne) KT16 **133** BA100
Lynegrove Av, Ashf. TW15 **115** BQ92
Lyneham Wk, E5 **67** DY64
Pinner HA5 **59** BT55
Lyne La, Cher. (Lyne) KT16 **133** BA100
Egham TW20 **133** BA99
Virginia Water GU25 **133** BA100
Lyne Rd, Vir.W. GU25 **132** AX100
Lynette Av, SW4 **121** DH86
Lynett Rd, Dag. RM8 **70** EX61
Lynford Cl, Barn. EN5
off Rowley La **27** CT43
Edgware HA8 **42** CQ52
Lynford Gdns, Edg. HA8 **42** CP48
Ilford IG3 **69** ET61
Lynhurst Cres, Uxb. UB10 **77** BQ66
Lynhurst Rd, Uxb. UB10 **77** BQ66
Lynmere Rd, Well. DA16 **106** EV82
Lyn Ms, E3 *off Tredegar Sq* **85** DZ69
N16 **66** DS63
Lynmouth Av, Enf. EN1 **30** DT44
Morden SM4 **139** CX101
Lynmouth Dr, Ruis. HA4 **59** BV61
Lynmouth Gdns, Grnf. UB6 **79** CH67
Hounslow TW5 **96** BX81
Lynmouth Ri, Orp. BR5 **146** EV98
Lynmouth Rd, E17 **67** DY58
N2 **64** DF55
N16 **66** DT60
Greenford UB6 **79** CH67
Lynn Cl, Ashf. TW15
off Goffs Rd **115** BR92
Harrow HA3 **41** CD54
Lynne Cl, Orp. BR6 **163** ET107
South Croydon CR2 **160** DW111
Lynne Wk, Esher KT10 **154** CC106
Lynne Way, NW10 **80** CS65
Northolt UB5 **78** BX68
Lynn Ms, E11 *off Lynn Rd* **68** EE61
Lynn Rd, E11 **68** EE61
SW12 **121** DH87
Ilford IG2 **69** ER59
Lynn St, Enf. EN2 **30** DR39
Lynross Cl, Rom. RM3 **52** FM54
Lynscott Way, S.Croy. CR2 **159** DP109
Lynsted Cl, Bexh. DA6 **127** FB85
Bromley BR1 **144** EJ96
Lynsted Ct, Beck. BR3
off Churchfields Rd **143** DY96
Lynsted Gdns, SE9 **104** EK83
Lynton Av, N12 **44** DD49
NW9 **63** CT56
W13 **79** CG72
Orpington BR5 **146** EV98
Romford RM7 **50** FA53
Lynton Cl, NW10 **62** CS64
Chessington KT9 **156** CL105
Isleworth TW7 **97** CF84
Lynton Cres, Ilf. IG2 **69** EP58
Lynton Crest, Pot.B. EN6
off Strafford Gate **12** DA32
Lynton Est, SE1 **202** B9
Lynton Gdns, N11 **45** DK51
Enfield EN1 **46** DS45
Lynton Mead, N20 **44** DA48
Lynton Par, Wal.Cr. EN8
off Turners Hill **15** DX30
Lynton Rd, E4 **47** EB50
N8 **65** DK57
NW6 **81** CZ67
SE1 **202** A9
W3 **80** CN73
Lynton Rd, Croy. CR0 **141** DN100
Gravesend DA11 **131** GG88
Harrow HA2 **60** BY61
New Malden KT3 **138** CR99
Lynton Rd S, Grav. DA11 **131** GG88
Lynton Ter, W3
off Lynton Rd **80** CQ72
Lynton Wk, Hayes UB4 **77** BS69
Lynwood Av, Couls. CR5 **175** DH115
Egham TW20 **112** AY93
Epsom KT17 **157** CT114
Slough SL3 **92** AX76
Lynwood Cl, E18 **48** EJ53
Harrow HA2 **60** BY62
Romford RM5 **51** FB51
Woking GU21 **151** BD113
Lynwood Dr, Nthwd. HA6 **39** BT53
Romford RM5 **51** FB51
Worcester Park KT4 **139** CU103
Lynwood Gdns, Croy. CR0 **159** DM105
Southall UB1 **78** BZ72
Lynwood Gro, N21 **45** DN46
Orpington BR6 **145** ES101
Lynwood Hts, Rick. WD3 **22** BH43
Lynwood Rd, SW17 **120** DF90
W5 **80** CL70
Epsom KT17 **157** CT114
Redhill RH1 **184** DG132
Thames Ditton KT7 **137** CF103
Lyon Business Pk, Bark. IG11 **87** ES68
Lyon Meade, Stan. HA7 **41** CJ53
Lyon Pk Av, Wem. HA0 **80** CL65
Lyon Rd, SW19 **140** DC95
Harrow HA1 **61** CF58
Romford RM1 **71** FF59
Walton-on-Thames KT12 **136** BY103
Lyonsdene, Tad. KT20 **183** CZ127
Lyonsdown Av, Barn. EN5 **28** DC44
Lyonsdown Rd, Barn. EN5 **28** DC44
Lyons Pl, NW8 **82** DD70
Lyon St, N1
off Caledonian Rd **83** DM66
Lyons Wk, W14 **99** CY77
Lyon Way, Grnf. UB6 **79** CE67
Lyoth Rd, Orp. BR5 **145** EQ103
Lyric Dr, Grnf. UB6 **78** CB70
Lyric Ms, SE26 **122** DW91
Lyric Rd, SW13 **99** CT81
Lysander Cl, Hem.H. (Bov.) HP3 **5** AZ27
Lysander Gdns, Surb. KT6
off Ewell Rd **138** CM100
Lysander Gro, N19 **65** DK60
Lysander Ms, N19
off Lysander Gro **65** DJ60
Lysander Rd, Croy. CR0 **159** DM107
Ruislip HA4 **59** BR61
Lysander Way, Abb.L. WD5 **7** BU32
Orpington BR6 **145** EQ104
Lysias Rd, SW12 **120** DG86
Lysia St, SW6 **99** CX80
Lysley Pl, Hat. AL9 **12** DC27
Lysons Wk, SW15
off Swinburne Rd **119** CU85
Lyster Ms, Cob. KT11 **153** BV113
Lytchet Rd, Brom. BR1 **124** EH94
Lytchet Way, Enf. EN3 **30** DW39
Lytchgate Cl, S.Croy. CR2 **160** DS108
Lytcott Dr, W.Mol. KT8
off Freeman Dr **136** BZ97
Lytcott Gro, SE22 **122** DT85
Lyte St, E2 *off Bishops Way* **84** DW68
Lytham Av, Wat. WD19 **40** BX50
Lytham Cl, SE28 **88** EY72
Lytham Gro, W5 **80** CL69
Lytham St, SE17 **102** DR78
Lyttelton Cl, NW3 **82** DE66
Lyttelton Rd, E10 **67** EB62
N2 **64** DC57
Lyttleton Rd, N8 **65** DN55
Lytton Av, N13 **45** DN47
Enfield EN3 **31** DY38
Lytton Cl, N2 **64** DD57
Loughton IG10 **33** ER41
Northolt UB5 **78** BZ66
Lytton Gdns, Wall. SM6 **159** DK105
Lytton Gro, SW15 **119** CX85
Lytton Pk, Cob. KT11 **154** BZ112
Lytton Rd, E11 **68** EE59
Barnet EN5 **28** DC42
Grays RM16 **111** GG77
Pinner HA5 **40** BY52
Romford RM2 **71** FH57
Woking GU22 **167** BB116
Lytton Strachey Path, SE28
off Titmuss Av **88** EV73
Lyveden Rd, SE3 **104** EH80
SW17 **120** DE93
Lywood Cl, Tad. KT20 **173** CW122

M

Mabbotts, Tad. KT20 **173** CX121
Mabbutt Cl, St.Alb. (Brick.Wd.) AL2 **8** BY30
Mabel Rd, Swan. BR8 **127** FG93
Mabel St, Wok. GU21 **166** AX117
Maberley Cres, SE19 **122** DU94
Maberley Rd, SE19 **142** DT95
Beckenham BR3 **143** DX97
Mabledon Pl, WC1 **195** N3
Mablethorpe Rd, SW6 **99** CY80
Mabley St, E9 **85** DY65
McAdam Dr, Enf. EN2
off Rowantree Rd **29** DP40
Macaret Cl, N20 **44** DB45
MacArthur Cl, E7 **86** EG65
MacArthur Ter, SE7 **104** EL79
Macaulay Av, Esher KT10 **137** CE103
Macaulay Ct, SW4 **101** DH83
Macaulay Rd, E6 **86** EK68
SW4 **101** DH83
Caterham CR3 **176** DS122
Macaulay Sq, SW4 **101** DH84
Macaulay Way, SE28
off Booth Cl **88** EV73
McAuley Cl, SE1 **200** D6
SE9 **125** EP85
Macauley Ms, SE13 **103** EC82
Macbean St, SE18 **105** EN76
Macbeth St, W6 **99** CV78
McCall Cl, SW4
off Jeffreys Rd **101** DL82
McCall Cres, SE7 **104** EL78
McCarthy Rd, Felt. TW13 **116** BX92
Macclesfield Br, NW1 **82** DE68
Macclesfield Rd, EC1 **197** H2
SE25 **142** DV99
Macclesfield St, W1 **195** N10
McClintock Pl, Enf. EN3
off Government Row **31** EA37
McCoid Way, SE1 **201** H5
McCrone Ms, NW3
off Belsize La **82** DD65
McCudden Rd, Dart. DA1
off Cornwall Rd **108** FM83
McCullum Rd, E3 **85** DZ67
McDermott Cl, SW11 **100** DE83
McDermott Rd, SE15 **102** DU83
Macdonald Av, Dag. RM10 **71** FB62
Hornchurch RM11 **72** FL56
Macdonald Rd, E7 **68** EG63
E17 **47** EC54
N11 **44** DF50
N19 **65** DJ61
Macdonald Way, Horn. RM11 **72** FL56
Macdonnell Gdns, Wat. WD25
off High Rd **23** BT35
McDonough Cl, Chess. KT9 **156** CL105
McDowall Cl, E16 **86** EF71
McDowall Rd, SE5 **102** DQ81
Macduff Rd, SW11 **100** DG81
Mace Cl, E1 **202** D2
Mace Ct, Grays RM17 **110** GE79
Mace Gateway, E16 **205** M1
Mace La, Sev. (Cudham) TN14 **163** ER113
McEntee Av, E17 **47** DY53
Mace St, E2 **85** DX68
McEwen Way, E15 **85** ED67
MacFarlane La, Islw. TW7 **97** CF79
Macfarlane Rd, W12 **81** CW74
Macfarren Pl, NW1 **194** G5
McGrath Rd, E15 **68** EF64
McGredy, Wal.Cr. (Chsht.) EN7 **14** DV29
Macgregor Rd, E16 **86** EJ71
McGregor Rd, W11 **81** CZ72
Machell Rd, SE15 **102** DW83
McIntosh Cl, Rom. RM1 **71** FE55
Wallington SM6 **159** DL108
Macintosh Cl, Wal.Cr. EN7 **14** DR26
McIntosh Rd, Rom. RM1 **71** FE55
Mackay Rd, SW4 **101** DH83
McKay Rd, SW20 **119** CV94
McKay Trd Est, Slou. (Colnbr.) SL3 **93** BE82
McKellar Cl, Bushey (Bushey Hth.) WD23 **40** CC47
Mackennal St, NW8 **194** C1
Mackenzie Mall, Slou. SL1
off High St **92** AT75
Mackenzie Rd, N7 **83** DM65
Beckenham BR3 **142** DW96
Mackenzie St, Slou. SL1 **74** AT74
Mackenzie Wk, E14 **204** A3
Mackenzie Way, Grav. DA12 **131** GK93
McKerrell Rd, SE15 **102** DU81
Mackeson Rd, NW3 **64** DF63
Mackie Rd, SW2 **121** DN87
Mackintosh La, E9
off Homerton High St **67** DX64
Macklin St, WC2 **196** A8
Mackrow Wk, E14
off Robin Hood La **85** EC73
Macks Rd, SE16 **202** C8
Mackworth St, NW1 **195** K2
Maclaren Ms, SW15
off Clarendon Dr **99** CW84
Maclean Rd, SE23 **123** DY86
Maclennan Av, Rain. RM13 **90** FK69
Macleod Cl, Grays RM17 **110** GD77
Macleod Rd, N21 **29** DL43
McLeod Rd, SE2 **106** EV77
McLeod's Ms, SW7
off Emperor's Gate **100** DB76
Macleod St, SE17 **102** DQ78
Maclise Rd, W14 **99** CY76
McMillan Cl, Grav. DA12 **131** GJ91
Macmillan Gdns, Dart. DA1 **108** FN84
McMillan St, SE8 **103** EA79
Macmillan Way, SW17
off Church La **121** DH91
McNair Rd, Sthl. UB2 **96** CB75
McNeil Rd, SE5 **102** DS82
McNicol Dr, NW10 **80** CQ68
Macoma Rd, SE18 **105** ER79
Macoma Ter, SE18 **105** ER79
Maconochies Rd, E14 **204** B10
Macon Way, Upmin. RM14 **73** FT59
Macquarie Way, E14 **204** C9
McRae La, Mitch. CR4 **140** DF101
Macroom Rd, W9 **81** CZ69
Mac's Pl, EC4 *off Norwich St* **83** DN72
★ **Madame Tussaud's**, NW1 **194** F5
Madan Rd, West. TN16 **189** ER125
Madans Wk, Epsom KT18 **156** CR114
Mada Rd, Orp. BR6 **145** EP104
Maddams St, E3 **85** EB70
Madden Cl, Swans. DA10 **129** FX86
Maddison Cl, Tedd. TW11 **117** CF93
Maddocks Cl, Sid. DA14 **126** EY92
Maddock Way, SE17 **101** DP79
Maddox La, Lthd. (Bkhm.) KT23 **170** BY123
Maddox Pk, Lthd. (Bkhm.) KT23 **170** BY123
Maddox St, W1 **195** J10
Madeira Av, Brom. BR1 **124** EE94
Madeira Cl, W.Byf. KT14
off Brantwood Gdns **152** BG113
Madeira Cres, W.Byf. KT14
off Brantwood Gdns **152** BG113
Madeira Gro, Wdf.Grn. IG8 **48** EJ51
Madeira Rd, E11 **67** ED60
N13 **45** DP49
SW16 **121** DL92
Mitcham CR4 **140** DF98
West Byfleet KT14 **151** BF113
Madeira Wk, Brwd. CM15 **54** FY48
Reigate RH2 **184** DD133
Madeley Rd, W5 **80** CL72
Madeline Gro, Ilf. IG1 **69** ER64
Madeline Rd, SE20 **142** DU95
Madells, Epp. CM16 **17** ET31
Madge Gill Way, E6
off Ron Leighton Way **86** EL67
Madinah Rd, E8 **84** DU65
Madingley, Kings.T. KT1
off St. Peters Rd **138** CN96
Madison Cres, Bexh. DA7 **106** EW80
Madison Gdns, Bexh. DA7 **106** EW80
Bromley BR2 **144** EF97
Madison Way, Sev. TN13 **190** FF123
Madras Pl, N7 **83** DN65
Madras Rd, Ilf. IG1 **69** EP63
Madresfield Ct, Rad. (Shenley) WD7 *off Russet Dr* **10** CL32
Madrid Rd, SW13 **99** CU81
Madrigal La, SE5 **101** DP80
Madron St, SE17 **201** N10
Maesmaur Rd, West. (Tats.) TN16 **178** EK121
Mafeking Av, E6 **86** EK68
Brentford TW8 **98** CL79
Ilford IG2 **69** ER59
Mafeking Rd, E16 **86** EF70
N17 **46** DU54
Enfield EN1 **30** DT41
Staines (Wrays.) TW19 **113** BB89
Magazine Pl, Lthd. KT22 **171** CH122
Magazine Rd, Cat. CR3 **175** DP122
Magdala Av, N19 **65** DH61
Magdala Rd, Islw. TW7 **97** CG83
South Croydon CR2
off Napier Rd **160** DR108
Magdalen Cl, W.Byf. (Byfleet) KT14 **152** BL114
Magdalen Cres, W.Byf. (Byfleet) KT14 **152** BL114
Magdalene Cl, SE15
off Heaton Rd **102** DV82
Magdalene Gdns, E6 **87** EN70
Magdalene Rd, Shep. TW17 **134** BM98
Magdalen Gdns, Brwd. CM13 **55** GE44
Magdalen Gro, Orp. BR6 **164** EV105
Magdalen Pas, E1
off Prescot St **84** DT73
Magdalen Rd, SW18 **120** DC88
Magdalen St, SE1 **201** M3
Magee St, SE11 **101** DN79
Magellan Pl, E14
off Maritime Quay **103** EA78
Magna Carta La, Stai. (Wrays.) TW19 **112** AX88
★ **Magna Carta Monument**, Egh. (Runny.) TW20 **112** AX89
Magna Rd, Egh. (Eng.Grn.) TW20 **112** AV93
Magnaville Rd, Bushey (Bushey Hth.) WD23 **41** CE45
Magnet Est, Grays RM20 **109** FW78
Magnet Rd, Grays RM20 **109** FW79
Wembley HA9 **61** CK61
Magnin Cl, E8 *off Wilde Cl* **84** DU67
Magnolia Av, Abb.L. WD5 **7** BU32
Magnolia Cl, E10 **67** EA61
Kingston upon Thames KT2 **118** CQ93
St. Albans (Park St.) AL2 **9** CD27
Magnolia Ct, Har. HA3 **62** CM59
Richmond TW9
off West Hall Rd **98** CP81
Wallington SM6
off Parkgate Rd **159** DH106
Magnolia Dr, West. (Bigg.H.) TN16 **178** EK116
Magnolia Gdns, Edg. HA8 **42** CQ49
Slough SL3 **92** AW76
Magnolia Pl, SW4 **121** DL85
W5 *off Montpelier Rd* **80** CL71
Magnolia Rd, W4 **98** CP79
Magnolia St, West Dr. UB7 **94** BK77
Magnolia Way, Brwd. CM15 **54** FV43
Epsom KT19 **156** CQ106
Magnum Cl, Rain. RM13 **90** FJ70
Magpie All, EC4 **196** E9
Magpie Cl, E7 **68** EF64
NW9 *off Eagle Dr* **42** CS54
Coulsdon CR5
off Ashbourne Cl **175** DJ118
Enfield EN1 **30** DU39
Magpie Hall Cl, Brom. BR2 **144** EL100
Magpie Hall La, Brom. BR2 **145** EM99
Magpie Hall Rd, Bushey (Bushey Hth.) WD23 **41** CE47
Magpie La, Brwd. CM13 **53** FW54
Magpie Pl, SE14
off Milton Ct Rd **103** DY79
Magri Wk, E1 *off Ashfield St* **84** DW71
Maguire Dr, Rich. TW10 **117** CJ91
Maguire St, SE1 **202** A4
Mahatma Gandhi Ho, Wem. HA9 **62** CN64
Mahlon Av, Ruis. HA4 **59** BV64
Mahogany Cl, SE16 **203** L3
Mahon Cl, Enf. EN1 **30** DT39
Maida Av, E4 **47** EB45
W2 **82** DC71
MAIDA HILL, W9 **81** CZ70
Maida Rd, Belv. DA17 **106** FA76
MAIDA VALE, W9 **82** DB70
⊖ **Maida Vale** **82** DC69
Maida Vale, W9 **82** DB68
Maida Vale Rd, Dart. DA1 **127** FG85
Maida Way, E4 **47** EB45
Maiden Erlegh Av, Bex. DA5 **126** EY88
Maiden La, NW1 **83** DK66
Maiden La, SE1 **201** J2
WC2 **200** A1
Dartford DA1 **107** FG83
Maiden Rd, E15 **86** EE66
Maidenshaw Rd, Epsom KT19 **156** CR112
Maidenstone Hill, SE10 **103** EC81
Maids of Honour Row, Rich. TW9
off The Green **117** CK85
Maidstone Av, Rom. RM5 **51** FC54
Maidstone Bldgs, SE1 **201** J3
Maidstone Ho, E14
off Carmen St **85** EB72
Maidstone Rd, N11 **45** DJ51
Grays RM17 **110** GA79
Sevenoaks TN13 **190** FE122
Sevenoaks (Seal) TN15 **191** FN121
Sidcup DA14 **126** EX93
Swanley BR8 **147** FB95
Maidstone St, E2
off Audrey St **84** DU68
Main Av, Enf. EN1 **30** DT43
Northwood HA6 **39** BQ48
Main Dr, Ger.Cr. SL9 **56** AW57
Iver SL0 **93** BE77
Wembley HA9 **61** CK62
Main Par, Rick. (Chorl.) WD3
off Whitelands Av **21** BC42
Main Par Flats, Rick. (Chorl.) WD3
off Whitelands Av **21** BC42
Main Ride, Egh. TW20 **112** AS93
Mainridge Rd, Chis. BR7 **125** EN91
Main Rd, Dart. (Fnghm.) DA4 **148** FL100
Dartford (Sutt.H.) DA4 **128** FP93
Edenbridge (Crock.H.) TN8 **189** EQ134
Longfield DA3 **149** FX96
Orpington BR5 **146** EW95
Romford RM1, RM2 **71** FF56
Sevenoaks (Knock.) TN14 **179** ET119
Sevenoaks (Sund.) TN14 **180** EX124
Sidcup DA14 **125** ES90
Swanley (Crock.) BR8 **147** FD100
Swanley (Hext.) BR8 **127** FF94
Westerham TN16 **162** EJ113
Main St, Felt. TW13 **116** BX92
Maisemore St, SE15
off Peckham Pk Rd **102** DU80
Maisie Webster Cl, Stai. (Stanw.) TW19 *off Lauser Rd* **114** BK87
Maitland Cl, SE10 **103** EB80
Hounslow TW4 **96** BZ83
Walton-on-Thames KT12 **136** BY103
West Byfleet KT14 **152** BG113
Maitland Pk Est, NW3 **82** DF65
Maitland Pk Rd, NW3 **82** DF65
Maitland Pk Vil, NW3 **82** DF65
Maitland Pl, E5
off Clarence Rd **66** DV63
Maitland Rd, E15 **86** EF65
SE26 **123** DX93
Maizey Ct, Brwd. CM15
off Danes Way **54** FU43
Majendie Rd, SE18 **105** ER78
Majestic Way, Mitch. CR4 **140** DF96
Major Rd, E15 **67** EC64
SE16 **202** C6
Majors Fm Rd, Slou. SL3 **92** AX80
Makepeace Av, N6 **64** DG61
Makepeace Rd, E11 **68** EG56
Northolt UB5 **78** BY68
Makins St, SW3 **198** C9
Malabar St, E14 **203** P5
Malam Gdns, E14
off Wades Pl **85** EB73
Malan Cl, West. (Bigg.H.) TN16 **178** EL117
Malan Sq, Rain. RM13 **89** FH65
Malbrook Rd, SW15 **99** CV84
Malcolm Ct, Stan. HA7 **41** CJ50
Malcolm Cres, NW4 **63** CU58
Malcolm Dr, Surb. KT6 **138** CL102
Malcolm Pl, E2 **84** DW70
Malcolm Rd, E1 **84** DW70
SE20 **122** DW94
SE25 **142** DU100
SW19 **119** CY93
Coulsdon CR5 **175** DK115
Uxbridge UB10 **58** BM63
Malcolms Way, N14 **29** DJ43
Malcolm Way, E11 **68** EG57
Malden Av, SE25 **142** DV98
Greenford UB6 **61** CE64
Malden Cl, Amer. HP6 **20** AT38
Malden Cres, NW1 **82** DG65
Malden Grn Av, Wor.Pk. KT4 **139** CT102
Malden Hill, N.Mal. KT3 **139** CT97
Malden Hill Gdns, N.Mal. KT3 **139** CT97
⇌ **Malden Manor** **138** CS101
Malden Pk, N.Mal. KT3 **139** CT100
Malden Pl, NW5
off Grafton Ter **64** DG64
Malden Rd, NW5 **64** DG64
Borehamwood WD6 **26** CN41
New Malden KT3 **138** CS99
Sutton SM3 **157** CX105
Watford WD17 **23** BU40
Worcester Park KT4 **139** CT101
MALDEN RUSHETT, Chess. **155** CH111
Malden Way, N.Mal. KT3 **139** CT99
Maldon Cl, E15 *off David St* **67** ED64
N1 *off Popham Rd* **84** DQ67
SE5 **102** DS83
Maldon Ct, Wall. SM6
off Maldon Rd **159** DJ106
Maldon Rd, N9 **46** DT48
W3 **80** CQ73
Romford RM7 **71** FC59
Wallington SM6 **159** DH106
Maldon Wk, Wdf.Grn. IG8 **48** EJ51
Malet Cl, Egh. TW20 **113** BD93
Malet Pl, WC1 **195** M5
Malet St, WC1 **195** M5
Maley Av, SE27 **121** DP89

Mal - Man

Malford Ct, E18 48 EG54
Malford Gro, E18 68 EF56
Malfort Rd, SE5 102 DS83
Malham Cl, N11
off Catterick Cl 44 DG51
Malham Rd, SE23 123 DX88
Malins Cl, Barn. EN5 27 CV43
Mall, The, E15 85 ED66
N14 45 DL48
SW1 199 L4
SW14 118 CQ85
W5 80 CL73
Croydon CR0 142 DQ103
Harrow HA3 62 CM58
Hornchurch RM11 71 FH60
St. Albans (Park St.) AL2 8 CC27
Surbiton KT6 137 CK99
Mallams Ms, SW9
off St. James's Cres 101 DP83
Mallard Cl, E9
off Berkshire Rd 85 DZ65
NW6 82 DA68
W7 97 CE75
Barnet EN5 off The Hook 28 DD44
Dartford DA1 128 FM85
Redhill RH1 184 DG131
Twickenham TW2
off Stephenson Rd 116 CA87
Upminster RM14 73 FT59
Mallard Path, SE28 105 ER76
Mallard Pl, Twick. TW1 117 CG90
Mallard Pt, E3
off Rainhill Way 85 EB69
Mallard Rd, Abb.L. WD5 7 BU31
South Croydon CR2 161 DX110
Mallards, The, Hem.H. HP3
off Belswains La 6 BM25
Staines TW18
off Thames Side 134 BH96
Mallards Reach, Wey. KT13 135 BR103
Mallards Rd, Bark. IG11 88 EU70
Woodford Green IG8 48 EH52
Mallard Wk, Beck. BR3 143 DX99
Sidcup DA14 126 EW92
Mallard Way, NW9 62 CQ59
Brentwood CM13 55 GB45
Northwood HA6 39 BQ52
Wallington SM6 159 DJ109
Watford WD25 24 BY37
Mallet Dr, Nthlt. UB5 60 BZ64
Mallet Rd, SE13 123 ED86
★ Mall Galleries, SW1 199 N2
Malling, SE13 123 EC85
Malling Cl, Croy. CR0 142 DW100
Malling Gdns, Mord. SM4 140 DC100
Malling Way, Brom. BR2 144 EF101
Mallinson Cl, Horn. RM12 72 FJ64
Mallinson Rd, SW11 120 DE85
Croydon CR0 141 DK104
Mallion Ct, Wal.Abb. EN9 16 EF33
Mallord St, SW3 100 DD79
Mallory Cl, SE4 103 DY84
Mallory Gdns, Barn. EN4 44 DG45
Mallory St, NW8 194 C4
Mallow Cl, Croy. CR0
off Marigold Way 143 DX102
Gravesend (Nthflt.) DA11 130 GE91
Tadworth KT20 173 CV119
Mallow Ct, Grays RM17 110 GD79
Mallow Mead, NW7 43 CY52
Mallows, The, Uxb. UB10 59 BP62
Mallow St, EC1 197 K4
Mallow Wk, Wal.Cr. EN7 14 DR28
Mall Rd, W6 99 CV78
Mallys Pl, Dart. (S.Darenth)
DA4 148 FQ95
Malmains Cl, Beck. BR3 143 ED99
Malmains Way, Beck. BR3 143 EC98
Malm Cl, Rick. WD3 38 BK47
Malmesbury Cl, Pnr. HA5 59 BT56
Malmesbury Rd, E3 85 DZ69
E16 86 EE71
E18 48 EF53
Morden SM4 140 DC101
Malmesbury Ter, E16 86 EF71
Malmstone Av, Red. RH1 185 DJ128
Malpas Dr, Pnr. HA5 60 BX57
Malpas Rd, E8 84 DV65
SE4 103 DZ82
Dagenham RM9 88 EX65
Grays RM16 111 GJ76
Slough SL2 74 AV73
Malta Rd, E10 67 EA60
Tilbury RM18 111 GF82
Malta St, EC1 196 G4
Maltby Cl, Orp. BR6
off Vinson Cl 146 EU102
Maltby Dr, Enf. EN1 30 DV38
Maltby Rd, Chess. KT9 156 CN107
Maltby St, SE1 201 P5
Malt Hill, Egh. TW20 112 AY92
Malt Ho Cl, Wind. (Old Wind.)
SL4 112 AV87
Malthouse Dr, W4 98 CS79
Feltham TW13 116 BX92
Malthouse Pas, SW13
off The Terrace 98 CS82
Malthouse Pl, Rad. WD7 9 CG34
Malthus Path, SE28
off Owen Cl 88 EW74
Malting Ho, E14 85 DZ73
Maltings, The, Kings L. WD4 7 BQ33
Orpington BR6 145 ET102
Oxted RH8 188 EF131
Romford RM1 71 FF59
Staines TW18
off Church St 113 BE91
West Byfleet (Byfleet)
KT14 152 BM113
Maltings Cl, SW13
off Cleveland Gdns 98 CS82
Maltings Dr, Epp. CM16
off Palmers Hill 18 EU29
Maltings La, Epp. CM16 18 EU29
Maltings Ms, Sid. DA15
off Station Rd 126 EU90
Maltings Pl, SW6 100 DB81
Malting Way, Islw. TW7 97 CF83
Malt La, Rad. WD7 25 CG35
Maltmans La, Ger.Cr. (Chal.St.P.)
SL9 56 AW55
Malton Ms, SE18
off Malton St 105 ES79
W10 off Cambridge Gdns 81 CY72
Malton Rd, W10
off St. Marks Rd 81 CY72
Malton St, SE18 105 ES79
Maltravers St, WC2 196 C10
Malt St, SE1 102 DU79
Malus Cl, Add. KT15 151 BF108
Malus Dr, Add. KT15 151 BF107
Malva Cl, SW18
off St. Ann's Hill 120 DB85
Malvern Av, E4 47 ED52
Bexleyheath DA7 106 EY80
Harrow HA2 60 BY62
Malvern Cl, SE20
off Derwent Rd 142 DU96
W10 81 CZ71
Bushey WD23 24 CC44
Chertsey (Ott.) KT16 151 BC107
Mitcham CR4 141 DJ97
Surbiton KT6 138 CL102
Uxbridge UB10 59 BP61
Malvern Ct, SE14
off Avonley Rd 102 DW80
SW7 198 A9
Slough SL3 off Hill Ri 93 BA79
Sutton SM2
off Overton Rd 158 DA108
Malvern Dr, Felt. TW13 116 BX92
Ilford IG3 69 ET63
Woodford Green IG8 48 EJ50
Malvern Gdns, NW2 63 CY61
NW6 off Carlton Vale 81 CZ68
Harrow HA3 62 CL55
Loughton IG10 33 EM44
Malvern Ms, NW6
off Malvern Rd 82 DA69
Malvern Pl, NW6 81 CZ69
Malvern Rd, E6 86 EL67
E8 84 DU66
E11 68 EE61
N8 65 DM55
N17 66 DU55
NW6 82 DA69
Enfield EN3 31 DY37
Grays RM17 110 GD77
Hampton TW12 116 CA94
Hayes UB3 95 BS80
Hornchurch RM11 71 FG58
Orpington BR6 164 EV105
Surbiton KT6 138 CL103
Thornton Heath CR7 141 DN98
Malvern Ter, N1 83 DN67
N9 off Latymer Rd 46 DT46
Malvern Way, W13
off Templewood 79 CH71
Rickmansworth (Crox.Grn.)
WD3 23 BP43
Malvina Av, Grav. DA12 131 GH89
Malwood Rd, SW12 121 DH86
Malyons, The, Shep. TW17
off Gordon Rd 135 BR100
Malyons Rd, SE13 123 EB85
Swanley BR8 127 FF94
Malyons Ter, SE13 123 EB85
Managers St, E14 204 E3
Manatee Pl, Wall. SM6
off Croydon Rd 141 DK104
Manaton Cl, SE15 102 DV83
Manaton Cres, Sthl. UB1 78 CA72
Manbey Gro, E15 86 EE65
Manbey Pk Rd, E15 86 EE65
Manbey Rd, E15 86 EE65
Manbey St, E15 86 EE65
Manbre Rd, W6 99 CW79
Manbrough Av, E6 87 EM69
Manchester Ct, E16 86 EH72
Manchester Dr, W10 81 CY70
Manchester Gro, E14 204 D10
Manchester Ms, W1 194 F7
Manchester Rd, E14 204 D10
N15 66 DR58
Thornton Heath CR7 142 DQ97
Manchester Sq, W1 194 F8
Manchester St, W1 194 F7
Manchester Way, Dag. RM10 71 FB63
Manchuria Rd, SW11 120 DG86
Manciple St, SE1 201 K5
Mandalay Rd, SW4 121 DJ85
Mandarin St, E14 off Salter St 85 EA73
Mandarin Way, Hayes UB4 78 BX71
Mandela Cl, NW10 80 CQ66
Mandela Rd, E16 86 EG72
Mandela St, NW1 83 DJ67
SW9 101 DN80
Mandela Way, SE1 201 N8
Mandeville Cl, SE3
off Vanbrugh Pk 104 EF80
SW20 139 CY95
Watford WD17 23 BT38
Mandeville Ct, E4 47 DY49
Egham TW20 113 BA91
Mandeville Dr, Surb. KT6 137 CK102
Mandeville Ms, SW4
off Clapham Pk Rd 101 DL84
Mandeville Pl, W1 194 G8
Mandeville Rd, N14 45 DH47
Enfield EN3 31 DX36
Isleworth TW7 97 CG82
Northolt UB5 78 CA66
Potters Bar EN6 12 DC32
Shepperton TW17 134 BN99
Mandeville St, E5 67 DY62
Mandeville Wk, Brwd. CM13 55 GE44
Mandrake Rd, SW17 120 DF90
Mandrake Way, E15 86 EE66
Mandrell Rd, SW2 121 DL85
Manette St, W1 195 N9
Manford Cl, Chig. IG7 50 EU49
Manford Cross, Chig. IG7 50 EU50
Manford Ind Est, Erith DA8 107 FG79
Manford Way, Chig. IG7 49 ES49
Manfred Rd, SW15 119 CZ85
Manger Rd, N7 83 DL65
Mangold Way, Erith DA18 106 EY76
Manhattan Wf, E16 205 M4
Manilla St, E14 203 P4
Manister Rd, SE2 106 EU76
Manitoba Ct, SE16
off Renforth St 102 DW75
Manitoba Gdns, Orp. BR6
off Superior Dr 163 ET107
Manley Ct, N16 off Stoke
Newington High St 66 DT62
Manley St, NW1 82 DG67
Manly Dixon Dr, Enf. EN3 31 DY37
Mannamead, Epsom KT18 172 CS119
Mannamead Cl, Epsom KT18
off Mannamead 172 CS119
Mann Cl, Croy. CR0
off Salem Pl 142 DQ104
Manningford Cl, EC1 196 F2
Manning Gdns, Har. HA3 61 CK59
Manning Pl, Rich. TW10
off Grove Rd 118 CM86
Manning Rd, E17
off Southcote Rd 67 DY57
Dagenham RM10 88 FA65
Orpington BR5 146 EX99
Manning St, S.Ock. (Aveley)
RM15 90 FQ74
Manningtree Cl, SW19 119 CY88
Manningtree Rd, Ruis. HA4 59 BV63
Manningtree St, E1
off White Ch La 84 DU72
Mannin Rd, Rom. RM6 70 EV59
Mannock Dr, Loug. IG10 33 EQ40
Mannock Rd, N22 65 DP55
Dartford DA1
off Barnwell Rd 108 FM83
Manns Cl, Islw. TW7 117 CF85
Manns Rd, Edg. HA8 42 CN51
Manoel Rd, Twick. TW2 116 CC89
Manor Av, SE4 103 DZ82
Caterham CR3 176 DS124
Hornchurch RM11 72 FJ57
Hounslow TW4 96 BX83
Northolt UB5 78 BZ66
Manorbrook, SE3 104 EG84
Manor Chase, Wey. KT13 153 BP106
Manor Cl, E17
off Manor Rd 47 DY54
NW7 off Manor Dr 42 CR50
NW9 62 CP57
SE28 88 EW72
Barnet EN5 27 CY42
Dagenham RM10 89 FD65
Dartford (Cray.) DA1 107 FD84
Dartford (Wilm.) DA2 127 FG90
Romford RM1
off Manor Rd 71 FG57
Ruislip HA4 59 BT60
South Ockendon (Aveley)
RM15 90 FQ74
Warlingham CR6 177 DY117
Woking GU22 167 BF116
Worcester Park KT4 138 CS102
Manor Cl S, S.Ock. (Aveley)
RM15 off Manor Cl 90 FQ74
Manor Cotts, Nthwd. HA6 39 BT53
Manor Cotts App, N2 44 DC54
Manor Ct, E10
off Grange Pk Rd 67 EB60
N2 64 DF57
SW6 off Bagley's La 100 DB81
Enfield EN1 30 DV36
Radlett WD7 25 CF38
Twickenham TW2 116 CC89
Wembley HA9 62 CL64
Weybridge KT13 153 BP105
Manor Ct Rd, W7 79 CE73
Manor Cres, Epsom KT19
off Abbots Av 156 CN112
Hornchurch RM11 72 FJ57
Surbiton KT5 138 CN100
West Byfleet (Byfleet)
KT14 152 BM113
Manorcrofts Rd, Egh. TW20 113 BA93
Manordene Cl, T.Ditt. KT7 137 CG102
Manordene Rd, SE28 88 EW72
Manor Dr, N14 45 DH45
N20 44 DE48
NW7 42 CR50
Addlestone (New Haw)
KT15 152 BG110
Epsom KT19 156 CS107
Esher KT10 137 CF103
Feltham TW13
off Lebanon Av 116 BX92
St. Albans AL2 8 CA27
Sunbury-on-Thames
TW16 135 BU96
Surbiton KT5 138 CM100
Wembley HA9 62 CM63
Manor Dr, The, Wor.Pk. KT4 138 CS102
Manor Dr N, N.Mal. KT3 138 CR101
Worcester Park KT4 138 CS102
Manor Est, SE16 202 D9
Manor Fm, Dart. (Fnghm.)
DA4 148 FM101
Manor Fm Av, Shep. TW17 135 BP100
Manor Fm Cl, Wor.Pk. KT4 138 CS102
Manor Fm Dr, E4 48 EE48
Manor Fm Est, Stai. (Wrays.)
TW19 112 AX86
Manor Fm La, Egh. TW20 113 BA92
Manor Fm Rd, Enf. EN1 30 DV35
Thornton Heath CR7 141 DN96
Wembley HA0 79 CK68
Manorfield Cl, N19
off Junction Rd 65 DJ63
Manor Flds, SW15 119 CX86
Manorfields Cl, Chis. BR7 145 ET97
Manor Gdns, N7 65 DL62
SW20 139 CZ96
W3 98 CN77
Manor Gdns, W4
off Devonshire Rd 98 CS78
Hampton TW12 116 CB94
Richmond TW9 98 CM84
Ruislip HA4 60 BW64
South Croydon CR2 160 DT107
Sunbury-on-Thames
TW16 135 BU96
Manor Gate, Nthlt. UB5 78 BY66
Manorgate Rd, Kings.T. KT2 138 CN95
Manor Grn Rd, Epsom KT19 156 CP113
Manor Gro, SE15 102 DW79
Beckenham BR3 143 EB96
Richmond TW9 98 CN84
Manor Hall Av, NW4 43 CW54
Manor Hall Dr, NW4 43 CX54
Manorhall Gdns, E10 67 EA60
⊖ Manor House 65 DP59
Manor Ho Ct, Epsom KT18 156 CQ113
Shepperton TW17 135 BP101
Manor Ho Dr, NW6 81 CX66
Northwood HA6 39 BP52
Walton-on-Thames KT12 153 BT107
Manor Ho Est, Stan. HA7
off Old Ch La 41 CH51
Manor Ho Gdns, Abb.L. WD5 7 BR31
Manor Ho La, Slou. (Datchet)
SL3 92 AV80
Manor Ho Way, Islw. TW7 97 CH83
Manor La, SE12 124 EE86
SE13 104 EE84
Feltham TW13 115 BU89
Gerrards Cross SL9 56 AX59
Hayes UB3 95 BR79
Longfield (Fawk.Grn.) DA3 149 FW101
Sevenoaks TN15 149 FW103
Sunbury-on-Thames
TW16 135 BU96
Sutton SM1 158 DC106
Tadworth KT20 184 DA129
Manor La Ter, SE13 104 EE84
Manor Leaze, Egh. TW20 113 BB92
Manor Ms, NW6
off Cambridge Av 82 DA68
SE4 103 DZ82
Manor Mt, SE23 122 DW88
Manor Par, NW10
off Station Rd 81 CT68
MANOR PARK, E12 68 EL63
⇌ Manor Park 68 EK63
Manor Pk, SE13 103 ED84
Chislehurst BR7 145 ER96
Richmond TW9 98 CM84
Staines TW18 113 BD90
Manor Pk Cl, W.Wick. BR4 143 EB102
Manor Pk Cres, Edg. HA8 42 CN51
Manor Pk Dr, Har. HA2 60 CB55
Manor Pk Gdns, Edg. HA8 42 CN50
Manor Pk Par, SE13
off Lee High Rd 103 ED84
Manor Pk Rd, E12 68 EK63
N2 64 DD55
NW10 81 CT67
Chislehurst BR7 145 EQ95
Sutton SM1 158 DC106
West Wickham BR4 143 EB102
Manor Pl, SE17 101 DP78
Chislehurst BR7 145 ER95
Dartford DA1
off Highfield Rd S 128 FL88
Feltham TW14 115 BU88
Mitcham CR4 141 DJ97
Staines TW18 114 BH92
Sutton SM1 158 DB105
Walton-on-Thames KT12
off Manor Rd 135 BT101
Manor Rd, E10 67 EA59
E15 86 EE69
E16 86 EE69
E17 47 DY54
N16 66 DR61
N17 46 DU53
N22 45 DL51
SE25 142 DU98
SW20 139 CZ96
W13 79 CG73
Ashford TW15 114 BM92
Barking IG11 87 ET65
Barnet EN5 27 CY43
Beckenham BR3 143 EB96
Bexley DA5 127 FB88
Chigwell IG7 49 EP50
Dagenham RM10 89 FC65
Dartford DA1 107 FE84
East Molesey KT8 137 CD98
Enfield EN2 30 DR40
Erith DA8 107 FF79
Gravesend DA12 131 GH86
Grays RM17 110 GC79
Grays (W.Thur.) RM20 109 FW79
Harrow HA1 61 CG58
Hayes UB3 77 BU72
Loughton IG10 32 EH44
Loughton (High Beach)
IG10 32 EH38
Mitcham CR4 141 DJ98
Potters Bar EN6 11 CZ31
Redhill RH1 185 DJ129
Reigate RH2 183 CZ132
Richmond TW9 98 CM83
Romford RM1 71 FG57
Romford (Chad.Hth.) RM6 70 EX58
Romford (Lamb.End) RM4 50 EW47
Ruislip HA4 59 BR60
St. Albans (Lon.Col.) AL2 9 CJ26
Sevenoaks (Sund.) TN14 180 EX124
Sidcup DA15 125 ET90
Sutton SM2 157 CZ108
Swanscombe DA10 129 FX86
Teddington TW11 117 CH92
Tilbury RM18 111 GG82
Twickenham TW2 116 CC89
Wallington SM6 159 DH105
Waltham Abbey EN9 15 ED33
Walton-on-Thames KT12 135 BT101
Watford WD17 23 BV39
West Wickham BR4 143 EB103
Manor Rd, West. (Tats.) TN16 178 EL120
Woking GU21 166 AW116
Woking (Send M.) GU23 167 BF123
Woodford Green IG8 49 EM51
Manor Rd N, Esher KT10 137 CF104
Thames Ditton KT7 137 CG103
Wallington SM6 159 DH105
Manor Rd S, Esher KT10 155 CE105
Manorside, Barn. EN5 27 CY42
Manorside Cl, SE2 106 EW77
Manor Sq, Dag. RM8 70 EX61
Manor Vale, Brent. TW8 97 CJ78
Manor Vw, N3 44 DB54
Manor Wk, Wey. KT13 153 BP106
Manor Way, E4 47 ED49
NW9 62 CS55
SE3 104 EF84
SE28 88 EW74
Banstead SM7 174 DF116
Beckenham BR3 143 EA96
Bexley DA5 126 FA88
Bexleyheath DA7 107 FD83
Borehamwood WD6 26 CQ42
Brentwood CM14 54 FU48
Bromley BR2 144 EL100
Egham TW20 113 AZ93
Manorway, Enf. EN1 46 DS45
Manor Way, Grays RM17 110 GB80
Harrow HA2 60 CB56
Leatherhead (Oxshott)
KT22 170 CC115
Mitcham CR4 141 DJ97
Orpington BR5 145 EQ98
Potters Bar EN6 12 DA30
Purley CR8 159 DL112
Rainham RM13 89 FE71
Rickmansworth (Crox.Grn.)
WD3 22 BN42
Ruislip HA4 59 BS59
South Croydon CR2 160 DS107
Southall UB2 96 BX77
Swanscombe DA10 109 FX84
Waltham Cross (Chsht.) EN8
off Russells Ride 15 DY31
Woking GU22 167 BB121
Manorway, Wdf.Grn. IG8 48 EJ50
Manor Way, Wor.Pk. KT4 138 CS102
Manor Way, The, Wall. SM6 159 DH105
Manor Waye, Uxb. UB8 76 BK67
Manor Way Ind Est, Grays
RM17 110 GC80
Manor Wd Rd, Pur. CR8 159 DL113
Manpreet Ct, E12
off Morris Av 69 EM64
Manresa Rd, SW3 100 DE78
Mansard Beeches, SW17 120 DG92
Mansard Cl, Horn. RM12 71 FG61
Pinner HA5 60 BX55
Mansbridge Way, NW7
off Bittacy Hill 43 CY52
Manse Cl, Hayes UB3 95 BR79
Mansel Cl, Slou. SL2 74 AV71
Mansel Gro, E17 47 EA53
Mansell Rd, W3 98 CR75
Greenford UB6 78 CB71
Mansell St, E1 202 A1
Mansell Way, Cat. CR3 176 DR122
Mansel Rd, SW19 119 CY93
Mansergh Cl, SE18 104 EL80
Manse Rd, N16 66 DT62
Manser Rd, Rain. RM13 89 FE69
Manse Way, Swan. BR8 147 FG98
Mansfield Av, N15 66 DR56
Barnet EN4 28 DF44
Ruislip HA4 59 BV60
Mansfield Cl, N9 30 DU44
Orpington BR5 146 EX101
Weybridge KT13 153 BP106
Mansfield Dr, Hayes UB4 77 BS70
Redhill RH1 185 DK128
Mansfield Gdns, Horn.
RM12 72 FK61
Mansfield Hill, E4 47 EB46
Mansfield Ms, W1 195 H7
Mansfield Pl, NW3
off New End 64 DC63
Mansfield Rd, E11 68 EH58
E17 67 DZ56
NW3 64 DF64
W3 80 CP70
Chessington KT9 155 CJ106
Ilford IG1 69 EN61
South Croydon CR2 160 DR107
Swanley BR8 127 FE93
Mansfield St, W1 195 H7
Mansford St, E2 84 DU68
Manship Rd, Mitch. CR4 120 DG94
Mansion Cl, SW9
off Cowley Rd 101 DN81
Mansion Gdns, NW3 64 DB62
★ Mansion Ho, EC4 197 K9
⊖ Mansion House 197 J10
Mansion Ho, EC4 197 K9
Mansion Ho Pl, EC4 197 K9
Mansion Ho St, EC4 197 K9
Mansion La, Iver SL0 75 BC74
Manson Ms, SW7 100 DC77
Manson Pl, SW7 100 DD77
Manstead Gdns, Rain. RM13 89 FH72
Mansted Gdns, Rom. RM6 70 EW59
Manston Av, Sthl. UB2 96 CA77
Manston Cl, SE20
off Garden Rd 142 DW95
Waltham Cross (Chsht.)
EN8 14 DW30
Manstone Rd, NW2 63 CY64
Manston Gro, Kings.T. KT2 117 CK92
Manston Way, Horn. RM12 89 FH65
Manthorp Rd, SE18 105 EQ78
Mantilla Rd, SW17 120 DG91
Mantle Rd, SE4 103 DY83
Mantlet Cl, SW16 121 DJ94
Mantle Way, E15
off Romford Rd 86 EE66
Manton Av, W7 97 CF75
Manton Cl, Hayes UB3 77 BS73
Manton Rd, SE2 106 EU77

Manton Rd, Enf. EN3
off Government Row 31 EA37
Mantua St, SW11 100 DD83
Mantus Cl, E1 off Mantus Rd 84 DW70
Mantus Rd, E1 84 DW70
Manus Way, N20
off Blakeney Cl 44 DC47
Manville Gdns, SW17 121 DH89
Manville Rd, SW17 120 DG89
Manwood Rd, SE4 123 DZ85
Manwood St, E16 87 EM74
Manygate La, Shep. TW17 135 BQ101
Manygates, SW12 121 DH89
Mapesbury Rd, NW2 81 CY65
Mapeshill Pl, NW2 81 CW65
Mape St, E2 84 DV70
Maple Av, E4 47 DZ50
W3 80 CS74
Harrow HA2 60 CB61
Upminster RM14 72 FP62
West Drayton UB7 76 BL73
Maple Cl, N3 44 DA51
N16 66 DU58
SW4 121 DK86
Brentwood CM13
off Cherry Av 55 FZ48
Buckhurst Hill IG9 48 EK48
Bushey WD23 24 BY40
Epping (They.B.) CM16
off Loughton La 33 ER37
Hampton TW12 116 BZ93
Hayes UB4 78 BX69
Hornchurch RM12 71 FH62
Ilford IG6 49 ES50
Mitcham CR4 141 DH95
Orpington BR5 145 ER99
Ruislip HA4 59 BV58
Swanley BR8 147 FE96
Whyteleafe CR3 176 DT117
Maple Ct, Egh. (Eng.Grn.) TW20
off Ashwood Rd 112 AV93
New Malden KT3 138 CS97
Maple Cres, Sid. DA15 126 EU86
Slough SL2 74 AV73
Maplecroft Cl, E6
off Allhallows Rd 86 EL72
MAPLE CROSS, Rick. 37 BD49
Maple Cross Ind Est, Rick.
(Map.Cr.) WD3 37 BF49
Mapledale Av, Croy. CR0 142 DU103
Mapledene, Chis. BR7
off Kemnal Rd 125 EQ92
Mapledene Rd, E8 84 DT66
Maple Dr, S.Ock. RM15 91 FX70
Maplefield, St.Alb. (Park St.)
AL2 8 CB29
Maplefield La, Ch.St.G. HP8 20 AV41
Maple Gdns, Edg. HA8 42 CS52
Staines TW19 114 BL89
Maple Gate, Loug. IG10 33 EN40
Maple Gro, NW9 62 CQ59
W5 97 CK76
Brentford TW8 97 CH80
Southall UB1 78 BZ71
Watford WD17 23 BU39
Woking GU22 166 AY121
Maple Hill, Hem.H. (Bov.) HP3
off Ley Hill Rd 4 AX30
Maplehurst, Lthd. KT22 171 CD123
Maplehurst Cl, Kings.T. KT1 138 CL98
Maple Ind Est, Felt. TW13
off Maple Way 115 BU90
Maple Leaf Cl, Abb.L. WD5 7 BU32
Mapleleaf Cl, S.Croy. CR2 161 DX111
Maple Leaf Cl, West. (Bigg.H.)
TN16 off Main Rd 178 EK116
Maple Leaf Dr, Sid. DA15 125 ET88
Mapleleafe Gdns, Ilf. IG6 69 EP55
Maple Leaf Sq, SE16 203 J4
Maple Lo Cl, Rick. (Map.Cr.)
WD3 37 BE49
Maple Ms, NW6
off Kilburn Pk Rd 82 DB68
SW16 121 DM92
Maple Pl, W1 195 L5
Banstead SM7 157 CX114
West Drayton UB7
off Maple Av 76 BM73
Maple Rd, E11 68 EE58
SE20 142 DV95
Ashtead KT21 171 CK119
Dartford DA1 128 FJ88
Gravesend DA12 131 GJ91
Grays RM17 110 GC79
Hayes UB4 78 BW69
Surbiton KT6 138 CL99
Whyteleafe CR3 176 DT117
Woking (Ripley) GU23 168 BG124
Maples, The, Bans. SM7 158 DB114
Chertsey (Ott.) KT16 151 BB107
Esher (Clay.) KT10 155 CG108
Waltham Cross (Goffs Oak)
EN7 14 DS28
Maplescombe La, Dart. (Fnghm.)
DA4 148 FN104
Maples Pl, E1
off Raven Row 84 DV71
Maple Springs, Wal.Abb.
EN9 16 EG33
Maplestead Rd, SW2 121 DM87
Dagenham RM9 88 EV67
Maple St, W1 195 K6
Romford RM7 71 FC56
Maplethorpe Rd, Th.Hth.
CR7 141 DP98
Mapleton Cl, Brom. BR2 144 EG100
Mapleton Cres, SW18 120 DB86
Enfield EN3 30 DW38
Mapleton Rd, E4 47 EC48
SW18 120 DB86
Edenbridge TN8 189 ET133
Enfield EN1 30 DV40
Westerham TN16 189 ES130
Maple Wk, W10 off Droop St 81 CX70
Sutton SM2 158 DB110
Maple Way, Couls. CR5 175 DH121
Feltham TW13 115 BU90
Maple Way, Wal.Abb. EN9 off Breach
Barn Mobile Home Pk 16 EH30
Maplin Cl, N21 29 DM44
Maplin Ho, SE2
off Wolvercote Rd 106 EX75
Maplin Pk, Slou. SL3 93 BC75
Maplin Rd, E16 86 EG72
Maplin St, E3 85 DZ69
Mapperley Dr, Wdf.Grn. IG8
off Forest Dr 48 EE52
Maran Way, Erith DA18 106 EX75
Marban Rd, W9 81 CZ69
★ Marble Arch, W1 194 E10
⊖ Marble Arch 194 E10
Marble Arch, W1 194 E10
Marble Cl, W3 80 CP74
Marble Dr, NW2 63 CX60
Marble Hill Cl, Twick. TW1 117 CH87
Marble Hill Gdns, Twick. TW1 117 CH87
★ Marble Hill Ho, Twick.
TW1 117 CJ87
Marble Ho, SE18
off Felspar Cl 105 ET78
Marble Quay, E1 202 B2
Marbles Way, Tad. KT20 173 CX119
Marbrook Ct, SE12 124 EJ90
Marcella Rd, SW9 101 DN82
Marcellina Way, Orp. BR6 145 ES104
Marcet Rd, Dart. DA1 128 FJ85
Marchant Rd, E11 67 ED61
Marchant St, SE14
off Sanford St 103 DY79
Marchbank Rd, W14 99 CZ79
Marchmant Cl, Horn. RM12 72 FJ62
Marchmont Gdns, Rich. TW10
off Marchmont Rd 118 CM85
Marchmont Rd, Rich. TW10 118 CM85
Wallington SM6 159 DJ108
Marchmont St, WC1 195 P4
March Rd, Twick. TW1 117 CG87
Weybridge KT13 152 BN106
Marchside Cl, Houns. TW5
off Springwell Rd 96 BX81
Marchwood Cl, SE5 102 DS80
Marchwood Cres, W5 79 CJ72
Marcia Rd, SE1 201 N9
Marcilly Rd, SW18 120 DD85
Marconi Rd, E10 67 EA60
Gravesend (Nthflt.) DA11 130 GD90
Marconi Way, Sthl. UB1 78 CB72
Marcon Pl, E8 84 DV65
Marco Rd, W6 99 CW76
Marcourt Lawns, W5 80 CL70
Marcus Ct, E15 86 EE67
Marcuse Rd, Cat. CR3 176 DR123
Marcus Garvey Ms, SE22
off St. Aidan's Rd 122 DV85
Marcus Garvey Way, SE24 101 DN84
Marcus Rd, Dart. DA1 127 FG87
Marcus St, E15 86 EF67
SW18 120 DB86
Marcus Ter, SW18 120 DB86
Mardale Dr, NW9 62 CR57
Mardell Rd, Croy. CR0 143 DX99
Marden Av, Brom. BR2 144 EG100
Marden Cl, Chig. IG7 50 EV47
Marden Cres, Bex. DA5 127 FC85
Croydon CR0 141 DM100
Marden Pk, Cat. (Wold.) CR3 187 DZ125
Marden Rd, N17 66 DS55
Croydon CR0 141 DM100
Romford RM1 71 FE58
Marden Sq, SE16 202 D7
Marder Rd, W13 97 CG75
Mardyke Cl, Rain. RM13
off Lower Mardyke Av 89 FC68
Mardyke Ho, Rain. RM13
off Lower Mardyke Av 89 FD68
Marechal Niel Av, Sid. DA15 125 ER90
Maresfield, Croy. CR0 142 DS104
Maresfield Gdns, NW3 64 DC64
Mare St, E8 84 DV67
Marfleet Cl, Cars. SM5 140 DE103
Margaret Av, E4 31 EB44
Brentwood CM15 55 FZ45
Margaret Bondfield Av, Bark.
IG11 88 EU66
Margaret Bldgs, N16
off Margaret Rd 66 DT60
Margaret Cl, Abb.L. WD5 7 BT32
Epping CM16
off Margaret Rd 18 EU29
Potters Bar EN6 12 DC33
Romford RM2
off Margaret Rd 71 FH57
Staines TW18
off Charles Rd 114 BK93
Waltham Abbey EN9 15 ED33
Margaret Ct, W1 195 K8
Margaret Dr, Horn. RM11 72 FM60
Margaret Gardner Dr, SE9 125 EM89
Margaret Ingram Cl, SW6
off John Smith Av 99 CZ80
Margaret Lockwood Cl, Kings.T.
KT1 138 CM98
Margaret Rd, N16 66 DT60
Barnet EN4 28 DD42
Bexley DA5 126 EX86
Epping CM16 18 EU29
Romford RM2 71 FH57
Margaret Sq, Uxb. UB8 76 BJ67
Margaret St, W1 195 J8
Margaretta Ter, SW3 100 DE79
Margaretting Rd, E12 68 EJ61
Margaret Way, Couls. CR5 175 DP118
Ilford IG4 68 EL58
Margate Rd, SW2 121 DL85
Margeholes, Wat. WD19 40 BY47
MARGERY, Tad. 184 DA129
Margery Gro, Tad. KT20 183 CY129
Margery La, Tad. KT20 183 CZ129
Margery Pk Rd, E7 86 EG65
Margery Rd, Dag. RM8 70 EX62
Margery St, WC1 196 D3
Margery Wd La, Tad. KT20 183 CZ129
Margherita Pl, Wal.Abb. EN9 16 EF34
Margherita Rd, Wal.Abb. EN9 16 EG34
Margin Dr, SW19 119 CX92
Margravine Gdns, W6 99 CX78
Margravine Rd, W6 99 CX78
Marham Gdns, SW18 120 DE88
Morden SM4 140 DC100
Maria Cl, SE1 202 D8
Mariam Gdns, Horn. RM12 72 FM61
Marian Cl, Hayes UB4 78 BX70
Marian Ct, Sutt. SM1 158 DB106
Marian Pl, E2 84 DV68
Marian Rd, SW16 141 DJ95
Marian Sq, E2
off Pritchard's Rd 84 DU68
Marian St, E2 off Hackney Rd 84 DV68
Marian Way, NW10 81 CT66
Maria Ter, E1 85 DX70
Maria Theresa Cl, N.Mal.
KT3 138 CR99
Maricas Av, Har. HA3 41 CD53
H Marie Curie Cen, Cat.
CR3 186 DT125
Marie Lloyd Gdns, N19
off Hornsey Ri Gdns 65 DL59
Marie Lloyd Wk, E8
off Forest Rd 84 DU65
Mariette Way, Wall. SM6 159 DL109
Marigold All, SE1 200 F1
Marigold Cl, Sthl. UB1
off Lancaster Rd 78 BY73
Marigold Rd, N17 46 DW52
Marigold St, SE16 202 D5
Marigold Way, E4
off Silver Birch Av 47 DZ51
Croydon CR0 143 DX102
H Marillac Hosp, Brwd.
CM13 53 FX51
Marina App, Hayes UB4 78 BY71
Marina Av, N.Mal. KT3 139 CV99
Marina Cl, Brom. BR2 144 EG97
Chertsey KT16 134 BH102
Marina Dr, Dart. DA1 128 FN88
Gravesend (Nthflt.) DA11 131 GF87
Welling DA16 105 ES82
Marina Gdns, Rom. RM7 71 FC58
Waltham Cross (Chsht.)
EN8 14 DW30
Marina Way, Iver SL0 75 BF73
Teddington TW11
off Fairways 117 CK94
Marine Dr, SE18 105 EM77
Barking IG11 88 EV70
Marinefield Rd, SW6 100 DB82
Mariner Gdns, Rich. TW10 117 CJ90
Mariner Rd, E12
off Dersingham Av 69 EM63
Mariners Ct, Green. DA9
off High St 109 FV84
Mariners Ms, E14 204 F8
Mariners Wk, Erith DA8
off Frobisher Rd 107 FF79
Mariners Way, Grav. DA11
off Rosherville Way 130 GE87
Marine St, SE16 202 B6
Marine Twr, SE8
off Abinger Gro 103 DZ79
Marion Av, Shep. TW17 135 BP99
Marion Cl, Bushey WD23 24 BZ39
Ilford IG6 49 ER52
Marion Cres, Orp. BR5 146 EU99
Marion Gro, Wdf.Grn. IG8 48 EE50
Marion Rd, NW7 43 CU50
Thornton Heath CR7 142 DQ99
Marischal Rd, SE13 103 ED83
Marisco Cl, Grays RM16 111 GH77
Marish La, Uxb. (Denh.) UB9 57 BC56
Marish Wf, Slou. (Mdgrn.)
SL3 92 AY75
Maritime Cl, Green. DA9 129 FV85
Maritime Gate, Grav. DA11
off Rosherville Way 130 GE87
Maritime Ho, Bark. IG11
off Linton Rd 87 EQ66
Maritime Quay, E14 204 A10
Maritime St, E3 85 DZ70
Marius Pas, SW17
off Marius Rd 120 DG89
Marius Rd, SW17 120 DG89
Marjorams Av, Loug. IG10 33 EM40
Marjorie Gro, SW11 100 DF84
Marjorie Ms, E1
off Arbour Sq 85 DX72
Markab Rd, Nthwd. HA6 39 BT50
Mark Av, E4 31 EB44
Mark Cl, Bexh. DA7 106 EY81
Southall UB1
off Longford Av 78 CB74
Mark Dr, Ger.Cr. (Chal.St.P.)
SL9 36 AX49
Marke Cl, Kes. BR2 162 EL105
Markedge La, Couls. CR5 174 DE124
Redhill RH1 184 DF126
Markeston Grn, Wat. WD19 40 BX49
Market Ct, W1 195 K8
Market Est, N7 83 DL65
Marketfield Rd, Red. RH1 184 DF134
Marketfield Way, Red. RH1 184 DF134
Market Hill, SE18 105 EN76
Market La, Edg. HA8 42 CQ53
Iver SL0 93 BC75
Slough SL3 93 BC75
Market Link, Rom. RM1 71 FE56
Market Meadow, Orp. BR5 146 EW98
Market Ms, W1 199 H3
Market Pl, N2 64 DE55
NW11 64 DC56
SE16 202 C8
W1 195 K8
W3 80 CQ74
Bexleyheath DA6 106 FA84
Brentford TW8 97 CJ80
Dartford DA1
off Market St 128 FL87
Enfield EN2 off The Town 30 DR41
Gerrards Cross (Chal.St.P.)
SL9 36 AX53
Kingston upon Thames
KT1 137 CK96
Market Pl, Rom. RM1 71 FE57
Romford (Abridge) RM4 34 EV41
Tilbury RM18 111 GF82
Market Rd, N7 83 DL65
Richmond TW9 98 CN83
Market Row, SW9
off Atlantic Rd 101 DN84
Market Sq, E2 197 P2
E14 off Chrisp St 85 EB72
N9 off New Rd 46 DU47
Bromley BR1 144 EG96
Staines TW18
off Clarence St 113 BE91
Uxbridge UB8 off High St 76 BJ66
Waltham Abbey EN9
off Leverton Way 15 EC33
Westerham TN16 189 EQ127
Woking GU21
off Cawsey Way 166 AY117
Market St, E6 87 EM68
SE18 105 EN77
Dartford DA1 128 FL87
Watford WD18 23 BV42
Market Way, E14
off Kerbey St 85 EB72
Wembley HA0
off Turton Rd 62 CL64
Westerham TN16
off Costell's Meadow 189 ER126
Markfield, Croy. CR0 161 DZ110
Markfield Gdns, E4 47 EB45
Markfield Rd, N15 66 DU56
Caterham CR3 186 DV126
Markham Pl, SW3 198 D10
Markham Rd, Wal.Cr. (Chsht.)
EN7 14 DQ26
Markham Sq, SW3 198 D10
Markham St, SW3 198 C10
Markhole Cl, Hmptn. TW12
off Priory Rd 116 BZ94
Markhouse Av, E17 67 DY58
Markhouse Rd, E17 67 DZ57
Markland Ho, W10 81 CX73
Mark La, EC3 201 N1
Gravesend DA12 131 GL86
Markmanor Av, E17 67 DY59
Mark Oak La, Lthd. KT22 170 CA122
Mark Rd, N22 45 DP54
Marksbury Av, Rich. TW9 98 CN83
MARK'S GATE, Rom. 50 EY54
Mark Sq, EC2 197 M4
Marks Rd, Rom. RM7 71 FC57
Warlingham CR6 177 DY118
Marks Sq, Grav. (Nthflt.)
DA11 131 GF91
Mark St, E15 86 EE66
EC2 197 M4
Reigate RH2 184 DB133
Markville Gdns, Cat. CR3 186 DU125
Markway, Sun. TW16 136 BW96
Mark Way, Swan. BR8 147 FG99
Markwell Cl, SE26
off Longton Gro 122 DV91
Markyate Rd, Dag. RM8 70 EV64
Marlands Rd, Ilf. IG5 68 EL55
Marlborough, SW3 198 C8
Marlborough Av, E8 84 DU67
N14 45 DJ48
Edgware HA8 42 CP48
Ruislip HA4 59 BQ58
Marlborough Cl, N20
off Marlborough Gdns 44 DF48
SE17 200 G9
SW19 120 DE93
Grays RM16 110 GC75
Orpington BR6
off Aylesham Rd 145 ET101
Upminster RM14 73 FS60
Walton-on-Thames KT12
off Arch Rd 136 BX104
Marlborough Ct, W1 195 K9
W8 100 DA77
Wallington SM6
off Cranley Gdns 159 DJ108
Marlborough Cres, W4 98 CR76
Sevenoaks TN13 190 FE124
Marlborough Dr, Ilf. IG5 68 EL55
Weybridge KT13 135 BQ104
Marlborough Gdns, N20 44 DF48
Upminster RM14 73 FR60
Marlborough Gate Ho, W2
off Elms Ms 82 DD73
Marlborough Gro, SE1 102 DU78
Marlborough Hill, NW8 82 DC67
Harrow HA1 61 CF56
★ Marlborough Ho, SW1 199 L3
Marlborough La, SE7 104 EJ79
Marlborough Ms, Bans. SM7
off Court Rd 174 DA115
Marlborough Pk Av, Sid.
DA15 126 EU87
Marlborough Pl, NW8 82 DC68
Marlborough Rd, E4 47 EA51
E7 86 EJ66
E15 off Borthwick Rd 68 EE63
E18 68 EG55
N9 46 DT46
N19 65 DK61
N22 45 DL52
SW1 199 L3
SW19 120 DD93
W4 98 CQ78
W5 97 CK75
Ashford TW15 114 BK92
Bexleyheath DA7 106 EX83
Brentwood (Pilg.Hat.)
CM15 54 FU44
Bromley BR2 144 EJ98
Dagenham RM8 70 EV63
Dartford DA1 128 FJ86
Feltham TW13 116 BX89
Hampton TW12 116 CA93
Isleworth TW7 97 CH81
Richmond TW10 118 CL86
Romford RM7 70 FA56
Slough SL3 92 AX77
South Croydon CR2 160 DQ108
Marlborough Rd, Sthl. UB2 96 BW76
Sutton SM1 140 DA104
Uxbridge UB10 77 BP70
Watford WD18 23 BV42
Woking GU21 167 BA116
Marlborough St, SW3 198 B9
Marlborough Yd, N19 65 DK61
Marld, The, Ashtd. KT21 172 CM118
Marle Gdns, Wal.Abb. EN9 15 EC32
Marler Rd, SE23 123 DY88
Marlescroft Way, Loug. IG10 33 EP43
Marley Av, Bexh. DA7 106 EX79
Marley Cl, N15
off Stanmore Rd 65 DP56
Addlestone KT15 151 BF107
Greenford UB6 78 CA69
Marley Wk, NW2
off Lennon Rd 63 CW64
Marlin Cl, Sun. TW16 115 BT93
Marlingdene Cl, Hmptn.
TW12 116 CA93
Marlings Cl, Chis. BR7 145 ES98
Whyteleafe CR3 176 DS117
Marlings Pk Av, Chis. BR7 145 ES98
Marling Way, Grav. DA12 131 GL92
Marlins, The, Nthwd. HA6 39 BT51
Marlins Cl, Rick. (Chorl.) WD3 21 BE40
Sutton SM1
off Turnpike La 158 DC106
Marlins Meadow, Wat. WD18 23 BR44
Marlin Sq, Abb.L. WD5 7 BT31
Marloes Cl, Wem. HA0 61 CK63
Marloes Rd, W8 100 DB76
Marlow Av, Purf. RM19 108 FN77
Marlow Cl, SE20 142 DV97
Marlow Ct, NW6 81 CX66
NW9 63 CT55
Marlow Cres, Twick. TW1 117 CF86
Marlow Dr, Sutt. SM3 139 CX103
Marlowe Cl, Chis. BR7 125 ER93
Ilford IG6 49 EQ53
Marlowe Ct, SE19
off Lymer Av 122 DT92
Marlowe Gdns, SE9 125 EN86
Romford RM3
off Shenstone Gdns 52 FJ53
Marlowe Rd, E17 67 EC56
Marlowes, The, NW8 82 DD67
Dartford DA1 107 FD84
Marlowe Sq, Mitch. CR4 141 DJ98
Marlowe Way, Croy. CR0 141 DL103
Marlow Gdns, Hayes UB3 95 BR76
Marlow Rd, E6 87 EM69
SE20 142 DV97
Southall UB2 96 BZ76
Marlow Way, SE16 203 H4
Marlpit Av, Couls. CR5 175 DL117
Marlpit La, Couls. CR5 175 DK116
Marl Rd, SW18 100 DB84
Marl St, SW18 off Marl Rd 100 DC84
Marlton St, SE10 205 L10
Marlwood Cl, Sid. DA15 125 ES89
Marlyon Rd, Ilf. IG6 50 EV50
Marmadon Rd, SE18 105 ET77
Marmion App, E4 47 EA49
Marmion Av, E4 47 DZ49
Marmion Cl, E4 47 DZ49
Marmion Ms, SW11
off Taybridge Rd 100 DG83
Marmion Rd, SW11 100 DG84
Marmont Rd, SE15 102 DU81
Marmora Rd, SE22 122 DW86
Marmot Rd, Houns. TW4 96 BX83
Marne Av, N11 45 DH49
Welling DA16 106 EU83
Marnell Way, Houns. TW4 96 BX83
Marne St, W10 81 CY69
Marney Rd, SW11 100 DG84
Marneys Cl, Epsom KT18 172 CN115
Marnfield Cres, SW2 121 DM88
Marnham Av, NW2 63 CY63
Marnham Cres, Grnf. UB6 78 CB69
Marnock Rd, SE4 123 DY85
Maroon St, E14 85 DY71
Maroons Way, SE6 123 EA92
Marquess Rd, N1 84 DR65
Marquis Cl, Wem. HA0 80 CM66
Marquis Rd, N4 65 DM60
N22 45 DM51
NW1 83 DK65
Marrabon Cl, Sid. DA15 126 EU88
Marram Ct, Grays RM17
off Medlar Rd 110 GE79
Marrick Cl, SW15 99 CU84
Marrilyne Av, Enf. EN3 31 DZ38
Marriots Cl, NW9 63 CT58
Marriott Cl, Felt. TW14 115 BR86
Marriot Ter, Rick. (Chorl.) WD3 21 BF42
Marriott Lo Cl, Add. KT15 152 BJ105
Marriott Rd, E15 86 EE67
N4 65 DM60
N10 44 DF53
Barnet EN5 27 CX41
Dartford DA1 128 FN87
Mar Rd, S.Ock. RM15 91 FW70
Marrowells, Wey. KT13 135 BS104
Marryat Pl, SW19 119 CY91
Marryat Rd, SW19 119 CX92
Enfield EN1 30 DV35
Marryat Sq, SW6 99 CY81
Marsala Rd, SE13 103 EB84
Marsden Rd, N9 46 DV47
SE15 102 DT83
Marsden St, NW5 82 DG65
Marsden Way, Orp. BR6 163 ET105
Marshall Cl, SW18
off Allfarthing La 120 DC86
Harrow HA1
off Bowen Rd 61 CD59
Hounslow TW4 116 BZ85
South Croydon CR2 160 DU113
Marshall Dr, Hayes UB4 77 BT71
Marshall Path, SE28
off Attlee Rd 88 EV73

Mar - May

Marshall Pl, Add. (New Haw)
KT15 152 BJ109
Marshall Rd, E10 67 EB62
N17 46 DR53
Marshalls Cl, N11 45 DH49
Epsom KT19 156 CQ113
Marshalls Dr, Rom. RM1 71 FE55
Marshall's Gro, SE18 104 EL77
Marshalls Pl, SE16 202 A7
Marshalls Rd, Rom. RM7 71 FD56
Marshall's Rd, Sutt. SM1 158 DB105
Marshall St, W1 195 L9
Marshalsea Rd, SE1 201 J4
Marsham Cl, Chis. BR7 125 EP92
Marsham La, Ger.Cr. SL9 56 AY58
Marsham Lo, Ger.Cr. SL9 56 AY58
Marsham St, SW1 199 N7
Marsham Way, Ger.Cr. SL9 56 AY57
Marsh Av, Epsom KT19 156 CS110
Mitcham CR4 140 DG96
Marshbrook Cl, SE3 104 EK83
Marsh Cl, NW7 43 CT48
Waltham Cross EN8 15 DZ33
Marsh Ct, SW19 140 DC95
Marshcroft Dr, Wal.Cr. (Chsht.)
EN8 15 DY30
Marsh Dr, NW9 63 CT58
Marshe Cl, Pot.B. EN6 12 DD32
Marsh Fm Rd, Twick. TW2 117 CF88
Marshfield, Slou. (Datchet)
SL3 92 AW81
Marshfield St, E14 204 D6
Marshfoot Rd, Grays RM16,
RM17 110 GE78
Marshgate La, E15 85 EB67
Marshgate Path, SE28
off Tom Cribb Rd 105 EQ77
Marshgate Sidings, E15
off Marshgate La 85 EB66
Marsh Grn Rd, Dag. RM10 88 FA67
Marsh Hill, E9 67 DY64
Marsh La, E10 67 EA61
N17 46 DV52
NW7 42 CS49
Addlestone KT15 152 BH105
Stanmore HA7 41 CJ50
Marsh Rd, Pnr. HA5 60 BY56
Wembley HA0 79 CK68
Marshside Cl, N9 46 DW46
Marsh St, E14 204 B9
Dartford DA1 108 FN82
Marsh Ter, Orp. BR5
off Buttermere Rd 146 EX98
Marsh Vw, Grav. DA12
off Damigos Rd 131 GM88
Marsh Wall, E14 203 P3
Marsh Way, Rain. RM13 89 FD70
Marsland Cl, SE17 101 DP78
Marston, Epsom KT19 156 CQ111
Marston Av, Chess. KT9 156 CL107
Dagenham RM10 70 FA61
Marston Cl, NW6
off Fairfax Rd 82 DC66
Dagenham RM10 70 FA62
Marston Ct, Walt. KT12
off St. Johns Dr 136 BW102
Marston Dr, Warl. CR6 177 DY118
Marston Ho, Grays RM17 110 GA79
Marston Rd, Ilf. IG5 48 EL53
Teddington TW11 117 CH92
Woking GU21 166 AV117
Marston Way, SE19 121 DP94
Marsworth Av, Pnr. HA5 40 BX53
Marsworth Cl, Hayes UB4 78 BY71
Watford WD18 23 BS44
Martaban Rd, N16 66 DS61
Martello St, E8 84 DV66
Martello Ter, E8 84 DV66
Martell Rd, SE21 122 DR90
Martel Pl, E8 *off Dalston La* 84 DT65
Marten Rd, E17 47 EA54
Martens Av, Bexh. DA7 107 FC84
Martens Cl, Bexh. DA7 107 FC84
Martha Ct, E2 84 DV68
Martham Cl, SE28 88 EX73
Martha Rd, E4 47 DZ51
E15 86 EE65
Martha's Bldgs, EC1 197 K4
Martha St, E1 84 DV72
Marthorne Cres, Har. HA3 41 CD54
Martina Ter, Chig. IG7
off Manford Way 49 ET50
Martin Bowes Rd, SE9 105 EM83
Martinbridge Trd Est, Enf.
EN1 30 DU43
Martin Cl, N9 47 DX46
South Croydon CR2 161 DX111
Uxbridge UB10
off Valley Rd 76 BL68
Warlingham CR6 176 DV116
Martin Cres, Croy. CR0 141 DN102
Martindale, SW14 118 CQ85
Iver SL0 75 BD70
Martindale Av, E16 86 EG73
Orpington BR6 164 EU106
Martindale Rd, SW12 121 DH87
Hounslow TW4 96 BY83
Woking GU21 166 AT118
Martin Dene, Bexh. DA6 126 EZ85
Martin Dr, Dart. (Stone) DA2 128 FQ86
Northolt UB5 60 BZ64
Rainham RM13 89 FH70
Martineau Cl, Esher KT10 155 CD105
Martineau Ms, N5
off Martineau Rd 65 DP63
Martineau Rd, N5 65 DP63
Martineau St, E1 84 DW73
Martingale Cl, Sun. TW16 135 BU98
Martingales Cl, Rich. TW10 117 CK90
Martin Gdns, Dag. RM8 70 EW63
Martin Gro, Mord. SM4 140 DA97
Martini Dr, Enf. EN3
off Government Row 31 EA37
Martin La, EC4 197 L10
Martin Ri, Bexh. DA6 126 EZ85
Martin Rd, Dag. RM8 70 EW63
Dartford DA2 128 FJ90
Slough SL1 92 AS76
South Ockendon (Aveley)
RM15 91 FR73
Martins Cl, Orp. BR5 146 EX97
Radlett WD7 25 CE36
West Wickham BR4 143 ED102
Martins Dr, Wal.Cr. (Chsht.)
EN8 15 DY28
Martinsfield Cl, Chig. IG7 49 ES49
Martins Mt, Barn. EN5 28 DA42
Martin's Plain, Slou. (Stoke P.)
SL2 74 AS69
Martins Rd, Brom. BR2 144 EE96
Martins Shaw, Sev. (Chipstead)
TN13 190 FC122
Martinstown Cl, Horn. RM11 72 FN58
Martin St, SE28 87 ES74
Martins Wk, N10 44 DG53
Borehamwood WD6
off Siskin Cl 26 CN42
Martinsyde, Wok. GU22 167 BC117
Martin Way, SW20 139 CY97
Morden SM4 139 CY97
Woking GU21 166 AU118
Martlesham Cl, Horn. RM12 72 FJ64
Martlet Gro, Nthlt. UB5
off Javelin Way 78 BX69
Martlett Ct, WC2 196 A9
Martley Dr, Ilf. IG2 69 EP57
Martock Cl, Har. HA3 61 CG56
Martock Gdns, N11 44 DF50
Marton Cl, SE6 123 EA90
Marton Rd, N16 66 DS61
MARTYR'S GREEN, Wok. 169 BR120
Martyrs La, Wok. GU21 151 BB112
Martys Yd, NW3
off Hampstead High St 64 DD63
Marvell Av, Hayes UB4 77 BU71
Marvels Cl, SE12 124 EH89
Marvels La, SE12 124 EH89
Marville Rd, SW6 99 CZ80
Marvin St, E8
off Sylvester Rd 84 DV65
Marwell, West. TN16 189 EP126
Marwell Cl, Rom. RM1 71 FG57
West Wickham BR4
off Deer Pk Way 144 EF103
Marwood Cl, Kings L. WD4 6 BN29
Welling DA16 106 EV83
Marwood Dr, NW7
off Bittacy Hill 43 CY52
Mary Adelaide Cl, SW15 118 CS91
Mary Ann Gdns, SE8 103 EA79
Maryatt Av, Har. HA2 60 CB61
Marybank, SE18 105 EM77
Mary Cl, Stan. HA7 62 CM56
Mary Datchelor Cl, SE5 102 DR81
Maryfield Cl, Bex. DA5 127 FE90
Marygold Wk, Amer. HP6 20 AV39
Mary Grn, NW8 82 DB67
Maryhill Cl, Ken. CR8 176 DQ117
≠ **Maryland** 86 EE65
Maryland Ind Est, E15
off Maryland Rd 67 ED64
Maryland Pk, E15 68 EE64
Maryland Pt, E15
off Leytonstone Rd 86 EE65
Maryland Rd, E15 67 ED64
N22 45 DM51
Thornton Heath CR7 141 DP95
Maryland Sq, E15 68 EE64
Marylands Rd, W9 82 DA70
Maryland St, E15 67 ED64
Maryland Wk, N1
off Popham St 84 DQ67
Maryland Way, Sun. TW16 135 BU96
Mary Lawrenson Pl, SE3 104 EF80
MARYLEBONE, NW1 194 D8
≠ **Marylebone** 194 D5
⊖ **Marylebone** 194 D5
Marylebone Flyover, NW1 194 A7
W2 194 A7
Marylebone High St, W1 194 G6
Marylebone La, W1 195 H9
Marylebone Ms, W1 195 H7
Marylebone Pas, W1 195 L8
Marylebone Rd, NW1 194 C6
Marylebone St, W1 194 G7
Marylee Way, SE11 200 C10
Mary Macarthur Ho, W6
off Field Rd 99 CY79
Maryon Gro, SE7 104 EL77
Maryon Ms, NW3
off South End Rd 64 DE63
Maryon Rd, SE7 104 EL77
SE18 104 EL77
Mary Peters Dr, Grnf. UB6 61 CD64
Mary Pl, W11 81 CY73
Mary Rose Cl, Grays (Chaff.Hun.)
RM16 109 FW77
Hampton TW12
off Ashley Rd 136 CA95
Mary Rose Mall, E6
off Frobisher Rd 87 EN71
Maryrose Way, N20 44 DD46
Mary Seacole Cl, E8
off Clarissa St 84 DT67
Maryside, Slou. SL3 92 AY75
Mary's Ter, Twick. TW1 117 CG87
Mary St, E16 *off Barking Rd* 86 EF71
N1 84 DQ67
Mary Ter, NW1 83 DH67
Masbro Rd, W14 99 CX76
Mascalls Ct, SE7
off Victoria Way 104 EJ79
Mascalls Gdns, Brwd. CM14 54 FT49
Mascalls La, Brwd. CM14 54 FT49
Mascalls Rd, SE7 104 EJ79
Mascotte Rd, SW15 99 CX84
Mascotts Cl, NW2 63 CV62
Masefield Av, Borwd. WD6 26 CP43
Southall UB1 78 CA73
Stanmore HA7 41 CF50
Masefield Cl, Erith DA8 107 FF81
Masefield Cl, Rom. RM3 52 FJ53
Masefield Ct, Brwd. CM14 54 FW49
Masefield Cres, N14 29 DJ44
Romford RM3 52 FJ53
Masefield Dr, Upmin. RM14 72 FQ59
Masefield Gdns, E6 87 EN70
Masefield La, Hayes UB4 77 BV70
Masefield Rd, Dart. DA1 128 FP85
Gravesend (Nthflt.) DA11 130 GD90
Grays RM16 110 GE75
Hampton TW12
off Wordsworth Rd 116 BZ91
Masefield Vw, Orp. BR6 145 EQ104
Masefield Way, Stai. TW19 114 BM88
Masham Ho, Erith DA18
off Kale Rd 106 EX75
Mashie Rd, W3 80 CS72
Mashiters Hill, Rom. RM1 51 FD53
Mashiters Wk, Rom. RM1 71 FE55
Maskall Cl, SW2 121 DN88
Maskani Wk, SW16
off Bates Cres 121 DJ94
Maskell Rd, SW17 120 DC90
Maskelyne Cl, SW11 100 DE81
Mason Bradbear Ct, N1
off St. Paul's Rd 84 DR65
Mason Cl, E16 86 EG73
SE16 202 C10
SW20 139 CX95
Bexleyheath DA7 107 FB83
Borehamwood WD6 26 CQ40
Hampton TW12 136 BZ95
Mason Dr, Rom. (Harold Wd.) RM3
off Whitmore Av 52 FL54
Masonic Hall Rd, Cher. KT16 133 BF100
Mason Rd, Sutt. SM1
off Manor Pl 158 DB106
Woodford Green IG8 48 EE49
Masons Arms Ms, W1 195 J9
Masons Av, EC2 197 K8
Croydon CR0 142 DQ104
Harrow HA3 61 CF56
Masons Ct, Wem. HA9
off Mayfields 62 CN61
Masons Grn La, W3 80 CN71
Masons Hill, SE18 105 EP77
Bromley BR1, BR2 144 EG97
Mason's Pl, EC1 196 G2
Masons Pl, Mitch. CR4 140 DF95
Masons Rd, Enf. EN1 30 DW36
Mason St, SE17 201 L8
Mason's Yd, SW1 199 L2
SW19
off High St Wimbledon 119 CX92
Mason Way, Wal.Abb. EN9 16 EF34
Massey Cl, N11 *off Grove Rd* 45 DH50
Massey Ct, E6 86 EJ67
Massie Rd, E8 *off Graham Rd* 84 DU65
Massingberd Way, SW17 121 DH91
Massinger St, SE17 201 M9
Massingham St, E1 85 DX70
Masson Av, Ruis. HA4 78 BW65
Master Cl, Oxt. RH8
off Church La 188 EE129
Master Gunner Pl, SE18 104 EL80
Masterman Ho, SE5 102 DR80
Masterman Rd, E6 86 EL69
Masters Cl, SW16
off Blegborough Rd 121 DJ93
Masters Dr, SE16 102 DV78
Masters St, E1 85 DX71
Masthead Cl, Dart. DA2 108 FQ84
Mast Ho Ter, E14 204 A9
Mast Leisure Pk, SE16 203 J7
Mastmaker Rd, E14 204 A5
Maswell Pk Cres, Houns.
TW3 116 CC85
Maswell Pk Rd, Houns. TW3 116 CB85
Matcham Rd, E11 68 EE62
Matchless Dr, SE18 105 EN80
Matfield Cl, Brom. BR2 144 EG99
Matfield Rd, Belv. DA17 106 FA79
Matham Gro, SE22 102 DT84
Matham Rd, E.Mol. KT8 137 CD99
Matheson Rd, W14 99 CZ77
Mathews Av, E6 87 EN68
Mathews Pk Av, E15 86 EF65
Mathias Cl, Epsom KT18 156 CQ113
Mathisen Way, Slou. (Colnbr.)
SL3 93 BE81
Matilda Cl, SE19
off Elizabeth Way 122 DR94
Matilda St, N1 83 DM67
Matlock Cl, SE24 102 DQ84
Barnet EN5 27 CX43
Matlock Ct, SE5
off Denmark Hill Est 102 DR84
Matlock Cres, Sutt. SM3 157 CY105
Watford WD19 40 BW48
Matlock Gdns, Horn. RM12 72 FL62
Sutton SM3 157 CY105
Matlock Pl, Sutt. SM3 157 CY105
Matlock Rd, E10 67 EC58
Caterham CR3 176 DS121
Matlock St, E14 85 DY72
Matlock Way, N.Mal. KT3 138 CR95
Matrimony Pl, SW8 101 DJ82
Matson Ct, Wdf.Grn. IG8
off The Bridle Path 48 EE52
Matthew Arnold Cl, Cob.
KT11 153 BU114
Staines TW18
off Elizabeth Av 114 BJ93
Matthew Cl, W10 81 CX70
Matthew Ct, Mitch. CR4 141 DK99
Matthew Parker St, SW1 199 N5
Matthews Cl, Rom. (Hav.at.Bow.)
RM3 *off Oak Rd* 52 FM53
Matthews Gdns, Croy.
(New Adgtn.) CR0 161 ED111
Matthews Rd, Grnf. UB6 61 CD64
Matthews St, SW11 100 DF82
Matthews Yd, WC2 195 P9
Matthias Rd, N16 66 DR64
Mattingley Way, SE15
off Daniel Gdns 102 DT80
Mattison Rd, N4 65 DN58
Mattock La, W5 79 CH74
W13 79 CH74
Maud Cashmore Way, SE18 105 EM76
Maude Cres, Wat. WD24 23 BV37
Maude Rd, E17 67 DY57
SE5 102 DS81
Swanley BR8 127 FG93
Maudesville Cotts, W7
off The Broadway 79 CE74
Maude Ter, E17 67 DY56
Maud Gdns, E13 86 EF67
Barking IG11 87 ET68
Maudlin's Grn, E1 202 B2
Maud Rd, E10 67 EC62
E13 86 EF68
Maudslay Rd, SE9 105 EM83
H **Maudsley Hosp, The**, SE5 102 DR82
Maudsley Ho, Brent. TW8
off Green Dragon La 98 CL78
Maud St, E16 86 EF71
Maud Wilkes Cl, NW5 65 DJ64
Mauleverer Rd, SW2 121 DL85
Maundeby Wk, NW10
off Neasden La 80 CS65
Maunder Rd, W7 79 CF74
Maunsel St, SW1 199 M8
Maurice Av, N22 45 DP54
Caterham CR3 176 DR122
Maurice Brown Cl, NW7 43 CX50
Maurice St, W12 81 CV72
Maurice Wk, NW11 64 DC56
Maurier Cl, Nthlt. UB5 78 BW67
Mauritius Rd, SE10 205 J9
Maury Rd, N16 66 DU61
Mavelstone Cl, Brom. BR1 144 EL95
Mavelstone Rd, Brom. BR1 144 EL95
Maverton Rd, E3 85 EA67
Mavis Av, Epsom KT19 156 CS106
Mavis Cl, Epsom KT19 156 CS106
Mavis Gro, Horn. RM12 72 FL61
Mavis Wk, E6 86 EL71
Mawbey Est, SE1 102 DU78
Mawbey Pl, SE1 102 DT78
Mawbey Rd, SE1
off Old Kent Rd 102 DT78
Chertsey (Ott.) KT16 151 BD107
Mawbey St, SW8 101 DL80
Mawney Cl, Rom. RM7 51 FB54
Mawney Rd, Rom. RM7 71 FC56
Mawson Cl, SW20 139 CY96
Mawson La, W4
off Great W Rd 99 CT79
Maxey Gdns, Dag. RM9 70 EY63
Maxey Rd, SE18 105 EQ77
Dagenham RM9 70 EY63
Maxfield Cl, N20 44 DC45
Maxilla Gdns, W10
off Cambridge Gdns 81 CX72
Maxilla Wk, W10
off Kingsdown Cl 81 CX72
Maximfeldt Rd, Erith DA8 107 FE78
Maxim Rd, N21 29 DN44
Dartford DA1 127 FE85
Erith DA8 107 FE77
Maxted Pk, Har. HA1 61 CE59
Maxted Rd, SE15 102 DT83
Maxwell Cl, Croy. CR0 141 DL102
Hayes UB3 77 BU73
Rickmansworth (Mill End)
WD3 38 BG47
Maxwell Dr, W.Byf. KT14 152 BJ111
Maxwell Gdns, Orp. BR6 145 ET104
Maxwell Ri, Wat. WD19 40 BY45
Maxwell Rd, SW6 100 DB80
Ashford TW15 115 BQ93
Borehamwood WD6 26 CP41
Northwood HA6 39 BR52
Welling DA16 106 EU83
West Drayton UB7 94 BM77
Maxwelton Av, NW7 42 CR50
Maxwelton Cl, NW7 42 CR50
Maya Angelou Ct, E4
off Bailey Cl 47 EC49
Maya Cl, SE15
off Gordon Rd 102 DV82
Mayall Rd, SE24 121 DP85
Maya Rd, N2 64 DC56
May Av, Grav. (Nthflt.) DA11
off Lansdown Pl 131 GF88
Orpington BR5 146 EV99
May Av Ind Est, Grav. DA11
off Lansdown Pl 131 GF88
Maybank Av, E18 48 EH54
Hornchurch RM12 71 FH64
Wembley HA0 61 CF64
Maybank Gdns, Pnr. HA5 59 BU57
Maybank Lo, Horn. RM12 72 FJ64
Maybank Rd, E18 48 EH53
May Bate Av, Kings.T. KT2 137 CK95
Maybells Commercial Est, Bark.
IG11 88 EX68
Mayberry Pl, Surb. KT5 138 CM101
Maybourne Cl, SE26 122 DV92
Maybourne Ri, Wok. GU22 166 AX124
Maybrick Rd, Horn. RM11 72 FJ58
Maybrook Meadow Est, Bark.
IG11 88 EU66
MAYBURY, Wok. 167 BB117
Maybury Av, Dart. DA2 128 FQ88
Waltham Cross (Chsht.)
EN8 14 DV28
Maybury Cl, Enf. EN1 30 DV38
Loughton IG10 33 EP42
Orpington BR5 145 EP99
Tadworth KT20
off Ballards Grn 173 CY119
Maybury Gdns, NW10 81 CV65
Maybury Hill, Wok. GU22 167 BB116
Maybury Ms, N6 65 DJ59
Maybury Rd, E13 86 EJ70
Barking IG11 87 ET68
Woking GU21 167 AZ117
Maybury St, SW17 120 DE92
Maybush Rd, Horn. RM11 72 FL59
Maychurch Cl, Stan. HA7 41 CK52
May Cl, Chess. KT9 156 CM107
Maycock Gro, Nthwd. HA6 39 BT51
May Cotts, Wat. WD18 24 BW43
May Ct, SW19 140 DC95
Grays RM17 *off Medlar Rd* 110 GE79
Maycroft, Pnr. HA5 39 BV54
Maycroft Av, Grays RM17 110 GD78
Maycroft Gdns, Grays RM17 110 GD78
Maycroft Rd, Wal.Cr. (Chsht.)
EN7 14 DS26
Maycross Av, Mord. SM4 139 CZ97
Mayday Gdns, SE3 104 EL82
H **Mayday Hosp**, Th.Hth.
CR7 141 DP100
Mayday Rd, Th.Hth. CR7 141 DP100
Maydwell Lo, Borwd. WD6 26 CM40
Mayell Cl, Lthd. KT22 171 CJ123
Mayerne Rd, SE9 124 EK85
Mayer Rd, Wal.Abb. EN9
off Deer Pk Way 31 EB36
Mayesbrook Rd, Bark. IG11 87 ET67
Dagenham RM8 70 EU62
Ilford IG3 70 EU62
Mayes Cl, Swan. BR8 147 FG98
Warlingham CR6 177 DX118
Mayesford Rd, Rom. RM6 70 EW59
Mayes Rd, N22 45 DN54
Mayeswood Rd, SE12 124 EJ90
MAYFAIR, W1 199 H1
Mayfair Av, Bexh. DA7 106 EX81
Ilford IG1 69 EM61
Romford RM6 70 EX58
Twickenham TW2 116 CC87
Worcester Park KT4 139 CU102
Mayfair Cl, Beck. BR3 143 EB95
Surbiton KT6 138 CL102
Mayfair Gdns, N17 46 DR51
Woodford Green IG8 48 EG52
Mayfair Ms, NW1
off Regents Pk Rd 82 DF66
Mayfair Pl, W1 199 J2
Mayfair Rd, Dart. DA1 128 FK85
Mayfair Ter, N14 45 DK45
Mayfare, Rick. (Crox.Grn.)
WD3 23 BR43
Mayfield, Bexh. DA7 106 EZ83
Leatherhead KT22 171 CJ121
Waltham Abbey EN9 15 ED34
Mayfield Av, N12 44 DC49
N14 45 DK47
W4 98 CS77
W13 97 CH76
Addlestone (New Haw)
KT15 152 BH110
Gerrards Cross SL9 56 AX56
Harrow HA3 61 CH57
Orpington BR6 145 ET102
Woodford Green IG8 48 EG52
Mayfield Cl, E8 *off Forest Rd* 84 DT65
SW4 121 DK85
Addlestone (New Haw)
KT15 152 BJ110
Ashford TW15 115 BP93
Thames Ditton KT7 137 CH102
Uxbridge UB10 77 BP69
Walton-on-Thames KT12 153 BU105
Mayfield Cres, N9 30 DV44
Thornton Heath CR7 141 DM98
Mayfield Dr, Pnr. HA5 60 BZ56
Mayfield Gdns, NW4 63 CX58
W7 79 CD72
Brentwood CM14 54 FV46
Staines TW18 113 BF93
Walton-on-Thames KT12 153 BU105
Mayfield Mans, SW15
off West Hill 119 CX87
Mayfield Pk, West Dr. UB7 94 BJ76
Mayfield Rd, E4 47 EC47
E8 84 DT66
E13 86 EF70
E17 47 DY54
N8 65 DM58
SW19 139 CZ95
W3 80 CP73
W12 98 CS75
Belvedere DA17 107 FC77
Bromley BR1 144 EL99
Dagenham RM8 70 EW60
Enfield EN3 31 DX40
Gravesend DA11 131 GF87
South Croydon CR2 160 DR109
Sutton SM2 158 DD107
Thornton Heath CR7 141 DM98
Walton-on-Thames KT12 153 BU105
Weybridge KT13 152 BM106
Mayfields, Grays RM16 110 GC75
Swanscombe DA10
off Madden Cl 130 FY86
Wembley HA9 62 CN61
Mayfields Cl, Wem. HA9 62 CN61
Mayflower Cl, SE16 203 J8
Ruislip HA4
off Leaholme Way 59 BQ58
South Ockendon RM15 91 FW70
Mayflower Ct, SE16
off St. Marychurch St 102 DW75
Mayflower Rd, SW9 101 DL83
Grays (Chaff.Hun.) RM16 109 FW78
St. Albans (Park St.) AL2 8 CB27
Mayflower St, SE16 202 F5
Mayfly Cl, Orp. BR5 146 EX98
Pinner HA5 60 BW59
Mayfly Gdns, Nthlt. UB5
off Ruislip Rd 78 BX69
MAYFORD, Wok. 166 AW122
Mayford Cl, SW12 120 DF87
Beckenham BR3 143 DX97
Woking GU22 166 AX122
Mayford Grn, Wok. GU22
off Smarts Heath Rd 166 AW122
Mayford Rd, SW12 120 DF87
May Gdns, Borwd. (Elstree)
WD6 25 CK44
Wembley HA0 79 CJ68
Maygoods Cl, Uxb. UB8 76 BK71
Maygoods Grn, Uxb. UB8
off Worcester Rd 76 BK71
Maygoods La, Uxb. UB8 76 BK71
Maygood St, N1 83 DM68

Maygoods Vw, Uxb. UB8
off Benbow Waye 76 BJ71
Maygreen Cres, Horn. RM11 71 FG59
Maygrove Rd, NW6 81 CZ65
Mayhew Cl, E4 47 EA48
Mayhill Rd, SE7 104 EH79
Barnet EN5 27 CY44
Mayhurst Av, Wok. GU22 167 BC116
Mayhurst Cl, Wok. GU22 167 BC116
Mayhurst Cres, Wok. GU22 167 BC116
Maylands Av, Horn. RM12 71 FH63
Maylands Dr, Sid. DA14 126 EX90
Uxbridge UB8 76 BK65
Maylands Rd, Wat. WD19 40 BW49
Maylands Way, Rom. RM3 52 FQ51
Maynard Cl, N15
off Brunswick Rd 66 DS56
SW6 *off Cambria St* 100 DB80
Erith DA8 107 FF80
Maynard Ct, Wal.Abb. EN9 16 EF34
Maynard Path, E17 67 EC57
Maynard Pl, Pot.B. EN6 13 DL29
Maynard Rd, E17 67 EC57
Maynards, Horn. RM11 72 FL59
Maynards Quay, E1 202 F1
Maynooth Gdns, Cars. SM5 140 DF101
Mayo Cl, Wal.Cr. (Chsht.)
EN8 14 DW28
Mayola Rd, E5 66 DW63
Mayo Rd, NW10 80 CS65
Croydon CR0 142 DR99
Walton-on-Thames KT12 135 BT101
Mayor's La, Dart. DA2 128 FJ92
Mayow Rd, SE23 123 DX90
SE26 123 DX91
Mayplace Av, Dart. DA1 107 FG84
Mayplace Cl, Bexh. DA7 107 FB83
Mayplace La, SE18 105 EP80
Mayplace Rd E, Bexh. DA7 107 FB83
Dartford DA1 107 FC83
Mayplace Rd W, Bexh. DA7 106 FA84
MAYPOLE, Orp. 164 EZ106
Maypole Cres, Erith DA8 108 FK79
Ilford IG6 49 ER52
Maypole Dr, Chig. IG7 50 EU48
Maypole Rd, Grav. DA12 131 GM88
Orpington BR6 164 EZ106
May Rd, E4 47 EA51
E13 86 EG68
Dartford (Hawley) DA2 128 FM91
Twickenham TW2 117 CE88
Mayroyd Av, Surb. KT6 138 CN103
Mays Cl, Wey. KT13 152 BM110
Mays Ct, WC2 199 P1
Maysfield Rd, Wok. (Send)
GU23 167 BD123
MAY'S GREEN, Cob. 169 BT120
Mays Gro, Wok. (Send)
GU23 167 BD123
Mays Hill Rd, Brom. BR2 144 EE96
Mays La, E4 47 ED47
Barnet EN5 27 CY43
Maysoule Rd, SW11 100 DD84
Mays Rd, Tedd. TW11 117 CD92
Mayston Ms, SE10
off Westcombe Hill 104 EG78
May St, W14
off North End Rd 99 CZ78
Mayswood Gdns, Dag. RM10 89 FC65
Maythorne Cl, Wat. WD18 23 BS42
Mayton St, N7 65 DM62
Maytree Cl, Edg. HA8 42 CQ48
Rainham RM13 89 FE68
Maytree Cres, Wat. WD24 23 BT35
Maytree Gdns, W5
off South Ealing Rd 97 CK75
May Tree La, Stan. HA7 41 CF52
Maytrees, Rad. WD7 25 CG37
Maytree Wk, SW2 121 DN89
Mayville Est, N16
off King Henry St 66 DS64
Mayville Rd, E11 68 EE61
Ilford IG1 69 EP64
May Wk, E13 86 EH68
Maywater Cl, S.Croy. CR2 160 DR111
Maywin Dr, Horn. RM11 72 FM60
Maywood Cl, Beck. BR3 123 EB94
⇌ **Maze Hill** 104 EE79
Maze Hill, SE3 104 EE79
SE10 104 EE79
Mazenod Av, NW6 82 DA66
Maze Rd, Rich. TW9 98 CN80
Mead, The, N2 44 DC54
W13 79 CH71
Ashtead KT21 172 CL119
Beckenham BR3 143 EC95
Uxbridge UB10 58 BN61
Wallington SM6 159 DK107
Waltham Cross (Chsht.)
EN8 14 DW29
Watford WD19 40 BY48
West Wickham BR4 143 ED102
Mead Av, Slou. SL3 93 BB75
Mead Cl, Egh. TW20 113 BB93
Grays RM16 110 GB75
Harrow HA3 41 CD53
Loughton IG10 33 EP40
Redhill RH1 184 DG131
Romford RM2 51 FG54
Slough SL3 93 BB75
Swanley BR8 147 FG99
Uxbridge (Denh.) UB9 58 BG61
Mead Ct, NW9 62 CQ57
Egham TW20
off Holbrook Meadow 113 BC93
Waltham Abbey EN9 15 EB34
Woking (Knap.) GU21 166 AS116
Mead Cres, E4 47 EC49
Dartford DA1
off Beech Rd 128 FK88
Sutton SM1 158 DE105
Meadcroft Rd, SE11 101 DP79
Meade Cl, W4 98 CN79
Meade Ct, Tad. KT20 173 CU124
Mead End, Ashtd. KT21 172 CM116
Meades, The, Wey. KT13 153 BQ107
Meadfield, Edg. HA8 42 CP47
Mead Fld, Har. HA2
off Kings Rd 60 BZ62
Meadfield Av, Slou. SL3 93 BA76
Meadfield Grn, Edg. HA8 42 CP47
Meadfield Rd, Slou. SL3 93 BA76
Meadfoot Rd, SW16 121 DJ94
Meadgate Av, Wdf.Grn. IG8 48 EL50
Mead Gro, Rom. RM6 70 EY55
Mead Ho La, Hayes UB4 77 BR70
Meadhurst Rd, Cher. KT16 134 BH102
Meadlands Dr, Rich. TW10 117 CK89
Mead La, Cher. KT16 134 BH102
Mead La Caravan Pk, Cher.
KT16 134 BJ102
Meadow, The, Chis. BR7 125 EQ93
Meadow Av, Croy. CR0 143 DX100
Meadow Bk, N21 29 DM44
Meadowbank, NW3 82 DF66
SE3 104 EF83
Kings Langley WD4 6 BN30
Surbiton KT5 138 CM100
Watford WD19 40 BW45
Meadowbank Cl, SW6 99 CW80
Meadowbank Gdns, Houns.
TW5 95 BU82
Meadowbank Rd, NW9 62 CR59
Meadowbanks, Barn. EN5 27 CT43
Meadowbrook, Oxt. RH8 187 EC130
Meadowbrook Cl, Slou. (Colnbr.)
SL3 93 BF82
Meadow Cl, E4
off Mount Echo Av 47 EB46
E9 67 DZ64
SE6 123 EA92
SW20 139 CW98
Barnet EN5 27 CZ44
Bexleyheath DA6 126 EZ85
Chislehurst BR7 125 EP92
Enfield EN3 31 DY38
Esher KT10 137 CF104
Hounslow TW4 116 CA86
Northolt UB5 78 CA68
Purley CR8 159 DK113
Richmond TW10 118 CL88
Ruislip HA4 59 BT58
St. Albans (Brick.Wd.) AL2 8 CA29
St. Albans (Lon.Col.) AL2 9 CK27
Sevenoaks TN13 190 FG123
Sutton SM1
off Aultone Way 140 DB103
Walton-on-Thames KT12 154 BZ105
Windsor (Old Wind.) SL4 112 AV86
Meadow Ct, Epsom KT18 156 CQ113
Redhill RH1 185 DK130
Staines TW18 113 BE90
Meadowcourt Rd, SE3 104 EF84
Meadowcroft, Brom. BR1 145 EM97
Bushey WD23 24 CB44
Gerrards Cross (Chal.St.P.)
SL9 36 AX54
Meadowcroft Rd, N13 45 DN47
Meadowcross, Wal.Abb. EN9 16 EE34
Meadow Dr, N10 65 DH55
NW4 43 CW54
Amersham HP6 20 AS37
Woking (Ripley) GU23 167 BF123
Meadow Gdns, Edg. HA8 42 CP51
Staines TW18 113 BD92
Meadow Garth, NW10 80 CQ65
Meadow Hill, Couls. CR5 159 DJ113
New Malden KT3 138 CS100
Purley CR8 159 DJ113
Meadowlands, Cob. KT11 153 BU113
Hornchurch RM11 72 FL59
Oxted RH8 188 EG134
Meadowlands Pk, Add. KT15 134 BL104
Meadow La, SE12 124 EH90
Leatherhead (Fetch.) KT22 170 CC121
Meadowlea Cl, West Dr. UB7 94 BK79
Meadow Ms, SW8 101 DM79
Meadow Pl, SW8 101 DL80
W4 *off Edensor Rd* 98 CS80
Meadow Ri, Couls. CR5 159 DK113
Meadow Rd, SW8 101 DM79
SW19 120 DC94
Ashford TW15 115 BR92
Ashtead KT21 172 CL117
Barking IG11 87 ET66
Borehamwood WD6 26 CP40
Bromley BR2 144 EE95
Bushey WD23 24 CB43
Dagenham RM9 88 EZ65
Epping CM16 17 ET29
Esher (Clay.) KT10 155 CE107
Feltham TW13 116 BY89
Gravesend DA11 131 GG89
Loughton IG10 32 EL43
Pinner HA5 60 BX57
Romford RM7 71 FC60
Slough SL3 92 AY77
Southall UB1 78 BZ73
Sutton SM1 158 DE106
Virginia Water GU25 132 AS99
Watford WD25 7 BU34
Meadow Row, SE1 201 H7
Meadows, The, Amer. HP7 20 AS39
Orpington BR6 164 EW107
Sevenoaks (Halst.) TN14 164 EZ113
Warlingham CR6 177 DX117
Meadows Cl, E10 67 EA61
Meadows End, Sun. TW16 135 BU95
Meadowside, SE9 104 EJ84
Beaconsfield (Jordans) HP9 36 AT52
Dartford DA1 128 FK88
Leatherhead (Bkhm.)
KT23 170 CA123
Walton-on-Thames KT12 136 BW103
Meadow Side, Wat. WD25 7 BV31
Meadowside Rd, Sutt. SM2 157 CY109
Upminster RM14 72 FQ64
Meadows Leigh Cl, Wey.
KT13 135 BQ104
Meadow Stile, Croy. CR0
off High St 142 DQ104
Meadowsweet Cl, E16
off Monarch Dr 86 EK71
Meadow Vw, Ch.St.G. HP8 36 AU48
Meadow Vw, Har. HA1 61 CE60
Meadowview, Orp. BR5 146 EW97
Meadow Vw, Sid. DA15 126 EV87
Staines TW19 113 BF85
Meadowview Rd, SE6 123 DZ92
Bexley DA5 126 EY86
Epsom KT19 156 CS109
Meadow Vw Rd, Hayes UB4 77 BQ70
Thornton Heath CR7 141 DP99
Meadow Wk, E18 68 EG56
Dagenham RM9 88 EZ65
Dartford DA2 128 FJ91
Epsom KT17, KT19 156 CS107
Tadworth KT20 173 CV124
Wallington SM6 141 DH104
Meadow Way, NW9 62 CR57
Abbots Langley (Bedmond)
WD5 7 BT27
Addlestone KT15 152 BH105
Chessington KT9 156 CL106
Chigwell IG7 49 EQ48
Dartford DA2 128 FQ87
Kings Langley WD4 6 BN30
Leatherhead (Bkhm.)
KT23 170 CB123
Orpington BR6 145 EN104
Potters Bar EN6 12 DA34
Rickmansworth WD3 38 BJ45
Ruislip HA4 59 BV58
Tadworth KT20 173 CY118
Upminster RM14 72 FQ62
Wembley HA9 61 CK63
Windsor (Old Wind.) SL4 112 AV86
Meadow Way, The, Har. HA3 41 CE53
Meadow Waye, Houns. TW5 96 BY79
Mead Path, SW17 120 DC92
Mead Pl, E9 84 DW65
Croydon CR0 141 DP102
Rickmansworth WD3 38 BH46
Mead Plat, NW10 80 CQ65
Mead Rd, Cat. CR3 176 DT123
Chislehurst BR7 125 EQ93
Dartford DA1 128 FK88
Edgware HA8 42 CN51
Gravesend DA11 131 GH89
Radlett (Shenley) WD7 10 CM33
Richmond TW10 117 CJ90
Uxbridge UB8 76 BK66
Walton-on-Thames KT12 154 BY105
Mead Row, SE1 200 D6
Meads, The, Edg. HA8 42 CR51
St. Albans (Brick.Wd.) AL2 8 BZ29
Sutton SM3 139 CY104
Upminster RM14 73 FS61
Uxbridge UB8 76 BL70
Meads La, Ilf. IG3 69 ES59
Meads Rd, N22 45 DP54
Enfield EN3 31 DY39
Meadsway, Brwd. CM13 53 FV51
Mead Ter, Wem. HA9
off Meadow Way 61 CK63
Meadvale Rd, W5 79 CH70
Croydon CR0 142 DT101
Mead Wk, Slou. SL3 93 BB75
Meadway, N14 45 DK47
NW11 64 DB58
SW20 139 CW98
Ashford TW15 114 BN91
Barnet EN5 28 DA42
Beckenham BR3 143 EC95
Mead Way, Brom. BR2 144 EF100
Bushey WD23 24 BY40
Coulsdon CR5 175 DL118
Croydon CR0 143 DY103
Meadway, Enf. EN3 30 DW36
Epsom KT19 156 CQ112
Esher KT10 154 CB109
Grays RM17 110 GD77
Ilford IG3 69 ES63
Leatherhead (Oxshott)
KT22 155 CD114
Romford RM2 51 FG54
Ruislip HA4 59 BR58
Sevenoaks (Halst.) TN14 164 EZ113
Staines TW18 114 BG94
Surbiton KT5 138 CQ102
Twickenham TW2 117 CD88
Warlingham CR6 176 DW115
Woodford Green IG8 48 EJ50
Meadway, The, SE3
off Heath La 103 ED82
Buckhurst Hill IG9 48 EK46
Loughton IG10 33 EM44
Orpington BR6 164 EV106
Potters Bar (Cuffley) EN6 13 DM28
Sevenoaks TN13 190 FF122
Meadway Cl, NW11 64 DB58
Barnet EN5 28 DA42
Pinner HA5
off Highbanks Rd 40 CB51
Staines TW18 113 BF94
Meadway Ct, NW11 64 DB58
Meadway Dr, Add. KT15 152 BJ108
Woking GU21 166 AW116
Meadway Gdns, Ruis. HA4 59 BR58
Meadway Gate, NW11 64 DA58
Meadway Pk, Ger.Cr. SL9 56 AX60
Meaford Way, SE20 122 DV94
Meakin Est, SE1 201 M6
Meanley Rd, E12 68 EL63
Meard St, W1 195 M9
Meare Cl, Tad. KT20 173 CW123
Meath Cl, Orp. BR5 146 EV99
Meath Rd, E15 86 EF68
Ilford IG1 69 EQ62
Meath St, SW11 101 DH81
Mecklenburgh Pl, WC1 196 B4
Mecklenburgh Sq, WC1 196 B4
Mecklenburgh St, WC1 196 B4
Medburn St, NW1 83 DK68
Medbury Rd, Grav. DA12 131 GM88
Medcalf Rd, Enf. EN3 31 DZ37
Medcroft Gdns, SW14 98 CQ84
Medebourne Cl, SE3 104 EG83
Mede Cl, Stai. (Wrays.) TW19 112 AX88
Mede Fld, Lthd. KT22 171 CD124
Medesenge Way, N13 45 DP51
Medfield St, SW15 119 CV87
Medhurst Cl, E3
off Arbery Rd 85 DY68
Woking (Chobham) GU24 150 AT109
Medhurst Cres, Grav. DA12 131 GM90
Medhurst Gdns, Grav. DA12 131 GM90
Medhurst Rd, E3
off Arbery Rd 85 DY68
Median Rd, E5 66 DW64
★ **Medici Gall**, W1
off Grafton St 199 J1
Medick Ct, Grays RM17 110 GE79
Medina Av, Esher KT10 137 CE104
Medina Gro, N7
off Medina Rd 65 DN62
Medina Rd, N7 65 DN62
Grays RM17 110 GD77
Medlake Rd, Egh. TW20 113 BC93
Medland Cl, Wall. SM6 140 DG102
Medland Ho, E14
off Branch Rd 85 DY73
Medlar Cl, Nthlt. UB5
off Parkfield Av 78 BY68
Medlar Ct, Slou. SL2 74 AW74
Medlar Rd, Grays RM17 110 GD79
Medlar St, SE5 102 DQ81
Medley Rd, NW6 82 DA65
Medman Cl, Uxb. UB8
off Chiltern Vw Rd 76 BJ68
Medora Rd, SW2 121 DM87
Romford RM7 71 FD56
Medow Mead, Rad. WD7 9 CF33
Medusa Rd, SE6 123 EB86
Medway Bldgs, E3
off Medway Rd 85 DY68
Medway Cl, Croy. CR0 142 DW100
Ilford IG1 69 EQ64
Watford WD25 8 BW34
Medway Dr, Grnf. UB6 79 CF68
Medway Gdns, Wem. HA0 61 CG63
Medway Ms, E3
off Medway Rd 85 DY68
Medway Par, Grnf. UB6 79 CF68
Medway Rd, E3 85 DY68
Dartford DA1 107 FG83
Medway St, SW1 199 N7
Medwin St, SW4 101 DM84
Meerbrook Rd, SE3 104 EJ83
Meeson Rd, E15 86 EF67
Meesons La, Grays RM17 110 FZ77
Meeson St, E5 67 DY63
Meeting Flds Path, E9
off Morning La 84 DW65
Meeting Ho All, E1 202 E2
Meeting Ho La, SE15 102 DV81
Megg La, Kings L. (Chipper.)
WD4 6 BH29
Mehetabel Rd, E9 84 DW65
Meister Cl, Ilf. IG1 69 ER60
Melancholy Wk, Rich. TW10 117 CJ89
Melanda Cl, Chis. BR7 125 EM92
Melanie Cl, Bexh. DA7 106 EY81
Melba Gdns, Til. RM18 111 GG80
Melba Way, SE13 103 EB81
Melbourne Av, N13 45 DM51
W13 79 CG74
Pinner HA5 60 CB55
Melbourne Cl, Orp. BR6 145 ES101
Uxbridge UB10 58 BN63
Wallington SM6
off Melbourne Rd 159 DJ106
Melbourne Ct, E5
off Daubeney Rd 67 DY63
N10 *off Sydney Rd* 45 DH52
SE20 122 DU94
Melbourne Gdns, Rom. RM6 70 EY57
Melbourne Gro, SE22 102 DS84
Melbourne Ho, Hayes UB4 78 BW70
Melbourne Ms, SE6 123 EC87
SW9 101 DN81
Melbourne Pl, WC2 196 C10
Melbourne Rd, E6 87 EM67
E10 67 EB59
E17 67 DY56
SW19 140 DA95
Bushey WD23 24 CB44
Ilford IG1 69 EP60
Teddington TW11 117 CJ93
Tilbury RM18 110 GE81
Wallington SM6 159 DH106
Melbourne Sq, SW9
off Melbourne Ms 101 DN81
Melbourne Ter, SW6
off Waterford Rd 100 DB80
Melbourne Way, Enf. EN1 30 DT44
Melbury Av, Sthl. UB2 96 CB76
Melbury Cl, Cher. KT16 134 BG101
Chislehurst BR7 125 EM93
Esher (Clay.) KT10 155 CH107
West Byfleet KT14 152 BG114
Melbury Ct, W8 99 CZ76
Melbury Dr, SE5
off Sedgmoor Pl 102 DS80
Melbury Gdns, SW20 139 CV95
Melbury Rd, W14 99 CZ76
Harrow HA3 62 CM57
Melcombe Gdns, Har. HA3 62 CM58
Melcombe Pl, NW1 194 D6
Melcombe St, NW1 194 E5
Meldex Cl, NW7 43 CW51
Meldon Cl, SW6
off Bagley's La 100 DB81
Meldone Cl, Surb. KT5 138 CP100
Meldrum Cl, Orp. BR5
off Killewarren Way 146 EW100
Oxted RH8 188 EF132
Meldrum Rd, Ilf. IG3 70 EU61
Melfield Gdns, SE6 123 EB91
Melford Av, Bark. IG11 87 ES65
Melford Cl, Chess. KT9 156 CM106
Melford Rd, E6 87 EM70
E11 68 EE61
E17 67 DY56
SE22 122 DU87
Ilford IG1 69 ER61
Melfort Av, Th.Hth. CR7 141 DP97
Melfort Rd, Th.Hth. CR7 141 DP97
Melgund Rd, N5 65 DN64
Melina Cl, Hayes UB3
off Middleton Rd 77 BR71
Melina Pl, NW8 82 DD69
Melina Rd, W12 99 CV75
Melior Pl, SE1 201 M4
Melior St, SE1 201 L4
Meliot Rd, SE6 123 ED89
Melksham Cl, Rom. RM3 52 FL52
Melksham Dr, Rom. RM3
off Melksham Gdns 52 FM52
Melksham Gdns, Rom. RM3 52 FL52
Melksham Grn, Rom. RM3
off Melksham Gdns 52 FM52
Meller Cl, Croy. CR0 141 DL104
Melling Dr, Enf. EN1 30 DU39
Melling St, SE18 105 ES79
Mellish Cl, Bark. IG11 87 ET67
Mellish Gdns, Wdf.Grn. IG8 48 EG50
Mellish Ind Est, SE18 104 EL76
Mellish St, E14 203 P6
Mellison Rd, SW17 120 DE92
Melliss Av, Rich. TW9 98 CP81
Mellitus St, W12 81 CT72
Mellor Cl, Walt. KT12 136 BZ101
Mellow Cl, Bans. SM7 158 DB114
Mellow La E, Hayes UB4 77 BQ69
Mellow La W, Uxb. UB10 77 BQ69
Mellows Rd, Ilf. IG5 69 EM55
Wallington SM6 159 DK106
Mells Cres, SE9 125 EM91
Mell St, SE10
off Trafalgar Rd 104 EE78
Melody La, N5 65 DP64
Melody Rd, SW18 120 DC85
Westerham (Bigg.H.) TN16 178 EJ118
Melon Pl, W8
off Kensington Ch St 100 DA75
Melon Rd, E11 68 EE62
SE15 102 DU81
Melrose Av, N22 45 DP53
NW2 63 CV64
SW16 141 DM97
SW19 120 DA89
Borehamwood WD6 26 CP43
Dartford DA1
off Lower Sta Rd 127 FE86
Greenford UB6 78 CB68
Mitcham CR4 121 DH94
Potters Bar EN6 12 DB32
Twickenham TW2 116 CB87
Melrose Cl, SE12 124 EG88
Greenford UB6 78 CB68
Hayes UB4 77 BU71
Melrose Cres, Orp. BR6 163 ER105
Melrose Dr, Sthl. UB1 78 CA74
Melrose Gdns, W6 99 CW76
Edgware HA8 42 CP54
New Malden KT3 138 CR97
Walton-on-Thames KT12 154 BW106
Melrose Pl, Wat. WD17
off Wentworth Cl 23 BT38
Melrose Rd, SW13 99 CT82
SW18 119 CZ86
SW19 140 DA96
W3 *off Stanley Rd* 98 CQ76
Coulsdon CR5 175 DH115
Pinner HA5 60 BZ56
Westerham (Bigg.H.) TN16 178 EJ116
Weybridge KT13 152 BN106
Melrose Ter, W6 99 CW75
Melsa Rd, Mord. SM4 140 DC100
Melstock Av, Upmin. RM14 72 FQ63
Melthorne Dr, Ruis. HA4 60 BW62
Melthorpe Gdns, SE3 104 EL81
Melton Cl, Ruis. HA4 60 BW60
Melton Ct, SW7 198 A9
Sutton SM2 158 DC108
Melton Flds, Epsom KT19 156 CR109
Melton Gdns, Rom. RM1 71 FF59
Melton Pl, Epsom KT19 156 CR109
Melton Rd, Red. RH1 185 DJ130
Melton St, NW1 195 L3
Melville Av, SW20 119 CU94
Greenford UB6 61 CF64
South Croydon CR2 160 DT106
Melville Cl, Uxb. UB10 59 BR62
Melville Gdns, N13 45 DP50
Melville Pl, N1 *off Essex Rd* 83 DP67
Melville Rd, E17 67 DZ55
NW10 80 CR66
SW13 99 CU81
Rainham RM13 89 FG70
Romford RM5 51 FB52
Sidcup DA14 126 EW89
Melville Vil Rd, W3
off High St 80 CR74
Melvin Rd, SE20 142 DW95
Melvinshaw, Lthd. KT22 171 CJ121
Melvyn Cl, Wal.Cr. (Chsht.)
EN7 13 DP28
Melyn Cl, N7 *off Anson Rd* 65 DJ63
Memel Ct, EC1 197 H5
Memel St, EC1 197 H5
Memess Path, SE18 105 EN79
Memorial Av, E15 86 EE69
Memorial Cl, Houns. TW5 96 BZ79
H **Memorial Hosp**, SE18 105 EN82
Mendip Cl, SE26 122 DW91
Hayes UB3 95 BR80
Slough SL3 93 BA78
Worcester Park KT4 139 CW102
Mendip Dr, NW2 63 CX61
Mendip Ho, N9
off New Rd 46 DU48
Mendip Rd, SW11 100 DC83
Bexleyheath DA7 107 FE81
Bushey WD23 24 CC44
Hornchurch RM11 71 FG59
Ilford IG2 69 ES57
Mendora Rd, SW6 99 CY80
Mendoza Cl, Horn. RM11 72 FL57
Menelik Rd, NW2 63 CY63
Menlo Gdns, SE19 122 DR94

Men - Mil

Menon Dr, N9 *off Plevna Rd* .46 DV48
Menotti St, E2
off Dunbridge St .84 DU70
Menthone Pl, Horn. RM11 .72 FK59
Mentmore Cl, Har. HA3 .61 CJ58
Mentmore Ter, E8 .84 DV66
Meon Cl, Tad. KT20 .173 CV122
Meon Ct, Islw. TW7 .97 CE82
Meon Rd, W3 .98 CQ75
Meopham Rd, Mitch. CR4 .141 DJ95
Mepham Cres, Har. HA3 .40 CC52
Mepham Gdns, Har. HA3 .40 CC52
Mepham St, SE1 .200 C3
Mera Dr, Bexh. DA7 .106 FA84
Merantun Way, SW19 .140 DC95
Merbury Cl, SE13 .123 EC85
Merbury Rd, SE28 .105 ES75
Mercator Pl, E14 .204 A10
Mercator Rd, SE13 .103 ED84
Mercer Cl, T.Ditt. KT7 .137 CF101
Merceron St, E1 .84 DV70
Mercer Pl, Pnr. HA5
off Crossway .40 BW54
Mercers Cl, SE10 .205 K9
Mercers Pl, W6 .99 CW77
Mercers Rd, N19 .65 DK62
Mercer St, WC2 .195 P9
Mercer Wk, Uxb. UB8
off High St .76 BJ66
Merchant St, E3 .85 DZ69
Merchiston Rd, SE6 .123 ED89
Merchland Rd, SE9 .125 EQ88
Mercia Gro, SE13 .103 EC84
Mercia Wk, Wok. GU21
off Church St W .167 AZ117
Mercier Rd, SW15 .119 CY85
Mercury Cen, Felt. TW14 .115 BV85
Mercury Gdns, Rom. RM1 .71 FE56
Mercury Way, SE14 .103 DX79
Mercy Ter, SE13 .103 EB84
Merebank La, Croy. CR0 .159 DM106
Mere Cl, SW15 .119 CX87
Orpington BR6 .145 EP103
Meredith Av, NW2 .63 CW64
Meredith Cl, Pnr. HA5 .40 BX52
Meredith Rd, Grays RM16 .111 GG77
Meredith St, E13 .86 EG69
EC1 .196 F3
Meredyth Rd, SW13 .99 CU82
Mere End, Croy. CR0 .143 DX101
Merefield Gdns, Tad. KT20 .173 CX119
Mere Rd, Shep. TW17 .135 BP100
Slough SL1 .92 AT76
Tadworth KT20 .173 CV124
Weybridge KT13 .135 BR104
Mere Side, Orp. BR6 .145 EN103
Mereside Pl, Vir.W. GU25 .132 AX100
Meretone Cl, SE4 .103 DY84
Merevale Cres, Mord. SM4 .140 DC100
Mereway Rd, Twick. TW2 .117 CD88
Merewood Cl, Brom. BR1 .145 EN96
Merewood Rd, Bexh. DA7 .107 FC82
Mereworth Cl, Brom. BR2 .144 EF99
Mereworth Dr, SE18 .105 EP80
Merganser Gdns, SE28
off Avocet Ms .105 ER76
MERIDEN, Wat. .24 BY35
Meriden Cl, Brom. BR1 .124 EK94
Ilford IG6 .49 EQ53
Meriden Way, Wat. WD25 .24 BY36
Meridian Gate, E14 .204 D4
Meridian Pl, E14 .204 D4
Meridian Rd, SE7 .104 EK80
Meridian Sq, E15 .85 ED66
Meridian Trd Est, SE7 .104 EH77
Meridian Wk, N17
off Commercial Rd .46 DS51
Meridian Way, N9 .46 DW50
N18 .46 DW51
Enfield EN3 .31 DX44
Merifield Rd, SE9 .104 EJ84
Merino Cl, E11 .68 EJ56
Merino Pl, Sid. DA15
off Blackfen Rd .126 EU86
Merivale Rd, SW15 .99 CY84
Harrow HA1 .60 CC59
Merland Cl, Tad. KT20 .173 CW120
Merland Grn, Tad. KT20
off Merland Ri .173 CW120
Merland Ri, Epsom KT18 .173 CW119
Tadworth KT20 .173 CW119
Merle Av, Uxb. (Hare.)
UB9 .38 BH54
Merlewood, Sev. TN13 .191 FH123
Merlewood Cl, Cat. CR3 .176 DR120
Merlewood Dr, Chis. BR7 .145 EM95
Merley Ct, NW9 .62 CQ60
Merlin Cl, Croy. CR0
off Minster Dr .160 DS105
Grays (Chaff.Hun.) RM16 .110 FY76
Ilford IG6 .50 EW50
Mitcham CR4 .140 DE97
Northolt UB5 .78 BW69
Romford RM5 .51 FD51
Slough SL3 .93 BB79
Wallington SM6 .159 DM107
Waltham Abbey EN9 .16 EG34
Merlin Ct, Wok. GU21
off Blackmore Cres .151 BC114
Merlin Cres, Edg. HA8 .42 CM53
Merlin Gdns, Brom. BR1 .124 EG90
Romford RM5 .51 FD51
Merling Cl, Chess. KT9
off Coppard Gdns .155 CK106
Merlin Gro, Beck. BR3 .143 DZ98
Ilford IG6 .49 EP52
Merlin Ho, Enf. EN3
off Allington Ct .31 DX43
Merlin Rd, E12 .68 EJ61
Romford RM5 .51 FD51
Welling DA16 .106 EU84
Merlin Rd N, Well. DA16 .106 EU84
Merlins Av, Har. HA2 .60 BZ62
Merlin St, WC1 .196 D3
Merlin Way, Epp. (N.Wld.Bas.)
CM16 .18 FA27
Watford WD25 *off Ashfields* .7 BT34
Mermagen Dr, Rain. RM13 .89 FH66
Mermaid Cl, Grav. DA11
off Rosherville Way .130 GE87
Mermaid Ct, SE1 .201 K4
SE16 .203 M3
Mermaid Twr, SE8
off Abinger Gro .103 DZ79
Mermerus Gdns, Grav.
DA12 .131 GM91
Merredene St, SW2 .121 DM86
Merriam Cl, E4 .47 EC50
E9 .85 DZ65
Merrick Rd, Sthl. UB2 .96 BZ75
Merrick Sq, SE1 .201 J6
Merridale, SE12 .124 EG85
Merridene, N21 .29 DP44
Merrielands Cres, Dag. RM9 .88 EZ67
Merrilands Rd, Wor.Pk. KT4 .139 CW102
Merrilees Rd, Sid. DA15 .125 ES88
Merrilyn Cl, Esher (Clay.)
KT10 .155 CG107
Merriman Rd, SE3 .104 EJ81
Merrington Rd, SW6 .100 DA79
Merrion Av, Stan. HA7 .41 CK50
Merrion Wk, SE17
off Dawes St .102 DR78
Merritt Gdns, Chess. KT9 .155 CJ107
Merritt Rd, SE4 .123 DZ85
Merrivale, N14 .29 DK44
Merrivale Av, Ilf. IG4 .68 EK56
Merrivale Gdns, Wok. GU21 .166 AW117
Merrow Rd, Sutt. SM2 .157 CX109
Merrows Cl, Nthwd. HA6
off Rickmansworth Rd .39 BQ51
Merrow St, SE17 .102 DQ79
Merrow Wk, SE17 .201 L10
Merrow Way, Croy. (New Adgtn.)
CR0 .161 EC107
Merrydown Way, Chis. BR7 .144 EL95
Merryfield, SE3 .104 EF82
Merryfield Gdns, Stan. HA7 .41 CJ50
Merryfield Ho, SE9
off Grove Pk Rd .124 EJ90
Merryfields, Uxb. UB8
off The Greenway .76 BL68
Merryfields Way, SE6 .123 EB87
MERRY HILL, Bushey .40 CA46
Merryhill Cl, E4 .47 EB45
Merry Hill Mt, Bushey WD23 .40 CB46
Merry Hill Rd, Bushey WD23 .40 CB46
Merryhills Cl, West. (Bigg.H.)
TN16 .178 EK116
Merryhills Ct, N14 .29 DJ43
Merryhills Dr, Enf. EN2 .29 DK42
Merrylands, Cher. KT16 .133 BE104
Merrylands Rd, Lthd. (Bkhm.)
KT23 .170 BZ123
Merrymeet, Bans. SM7 .158 DF114
Merryweather Cl, Dart. DA1 .128 FM86
Merrywood Gro, Tad. KT20 .183 CX130
Merrywood Pk, Reig. RH2 .184 DB132
Tadworth KT20 .182 CP130
Mersea Ho, Bark. IG11 .87 EP65
Mersey Av, Upmin. RM14 .73 FR58
Mersey Rd, E17 .67 DZ55
Mersey Wk, Nthlt. UB5
off Brabazon Rd .78 CA68
Mersham Dr, NW9 .62 CN57
Mersham Pl, SE20 .142 DV95
Mersham Rd, Th.Hth. CR7 .142 DR97
MERSTHAM, Red. .184 DG128
⇌ **Merstham** .185 DJ128
Merstham Rd, Red. RH1 .185 DN129
Merten Rd, Rom. RM6 .70 EY59
Merthyr Ter, SW13 .99 CV79
MERTON, SW19 .140 DA95
Merton Av, W4 .99 CT77
Northolt UB5 .60 CC64
Uxbridge UB10 .77 BP66
Merton Gdns, Orp. BR5 .145 EP99
Tadworth KT20
off Marbles Way .173 CX120
Merton Hall Gdns, SW20 .139 CY95
Merton Hall Rd, SW19 .139 CY95
Merton High St, SW19 .120 DB94
Merton Ind Pk, SW19 .140 DC95
Merton La, N6 .64 DF61
Merton Mans, SW20 .139 CX96
MERTON PARK, SW19 .140 DA96
◆ **Merton Park** .140 DA95
Merton Pk Par, SW19
off Kingston Rd .139 CZ95
Merton Pl, Grays RM16 .111 GG77
Merton Ri, NW3 .82 DE66
Merton Rd, E17 .67 EC57
SE25 .142 DU99
SW18 .120 DA85
SW19 .120 DB94
Barking IG11 .87 ET66
Enfield EN2 .30 DR38
Harrow HA2 .60 CC60
Ilford IG3 .69 ET59
Slough SL1 .92 AU76
Watford WD18 .23 BV42
Merton Wk, Lthd. KT22
off Merton Way .171 CG118
Merton Way, Lthd. KT22 .171 CG119
Uxbridge UB10 .77 BP66
West Molesey KT8 .136 CB98
Merttins Rd, SE15 .123 DX85
Meru Cl, NW5 .64 DG63
Mervan Rd, SW2 .101 DN84
Mervyn Av, SE9 .125 EQ90
Mervyn Rd, W13 .97 CG76
Shepperton TW17 .135 BQ101
Meryfield Cl, Borwd. WD6 .26 CM40
Mesne Way, Sev. (Shore.)
TN14 .165 FF112
Messaline Av, W3 .80 CQ72
Messant Cl, Rom. (Harold Wd.)
RM3 .52 FK54
Messent Rd, SE9 .124 EJ85
Messeter Pl, SE9 .125 EN86
Messina Av, NW6 .82 DA66
Metcalf Rd, Ashf. TW15 .115 BP92
Metcalf Wk, Felt. TW13
off Gabriel Cl .116 BY91
Meteor St, SW11 .100 DG84
Meteor Way, Wall. SM6 .159 DL108
Metford Cres, Enf. EN3 .31 EA38
Metheringham Way, NW9 .42 CS53
Methley St, SE11 .101 DN78
★ **Methodist Cen Hall**,
SW1 .199 N5
Methuen Cl, Edg. HA8 .42 CN52
Methuen Pk, N10 .45 DH54
Methuen Rd, Belv. DA17 .107 FB77
Bexleyheath DA6 .106 EZ84
Edgware HA8 .42 CN52
Methwold Rd, W10 .81 CX71
Metro Cen, The, Islw. TW7 .97 CE82
Metropolis Cen, Borwd. WD6 .26 CN41
Metropolitan Cen, The, Grnf.
UB6 .78 CB67
Metropolitan Cl, E14
off Broomfield St .85 EA71
Metropolitan Ho, Pot.B. EN6 .12 DA32
Meux Cl, Wal.Cr. (Chsht.) EN7 .14 DU31
Mews, The, N1 *off St. Paul St* .84 DQ67
Grays RM17 .110 GC77
Ilford IG4 .68 EK57
Romford RM1
off Market Link .71 FE56
Sevenoaks TN13 .190 FG123
Twickenham TW1
off Bridge Rd .117 CH86
Mews Deck, E1 .202 E1
Mews End, West. (Bigg.H.)
TN16 .178 EK118
Mews Pl, Wdf.Grn. IG8 .48 EG49
Mews St, E1 .202 B2
Mexfield Rd, SW15 .119 CZ85
Meyer Grn, Enf. EN1 .30 DU38
Meyer Rd, Erith DA8 .107 FC79
Meymott St, SE1 .200 F3
Meynell Cres, E9 .85 DX66
Meynell Gdns, E9 .85 DX66
Meynell Rd, E9 .85 DX66
Romford RM3 .51 FH52
Meyrick Cl, Wok. (Knap.)
GU21 .166 AS116
Meyrick Rd, NW10 .81 CU65
SW11 .100 DD83
Mezen Cl, Nthwd. HA6 .39 BR50
Miah Ter, E1
off Wapping High St .84 DU74
Miall Wk, SE26 .123 DY91
Micawber Av, Uxb. UB8 .76 BN70
Micawber St, N1 .197 J2
Michael Faraday Ho, SE17
off Beaconsfield Rd .102 DS78
Michael Gdns, Grav. DA12 .131 GL92
Hornchurch RM11 .72 FK56
Michael Gaynor Cl, W7 .79 CF74
Michaelmas Cl, SW20 .139 CW97
Michael Rd, E11 .68 EE60
SE25 .142 DS97
SW6 .100 DB81
Michaels Cl, SE13 .104 EE84
Michaels La, Long. (Fawk.Grn.)
DA3 .149 FV103
Sevenoaks TN15 .149 FV103
Micheldever Rd, SE12 .124 EE86
Michelham Gdns, Tad. KT20
off Waterfield .173 CW121
Twickenham TW1 .117 CF90
Michels Row, Rich. TW9
off Kew Foot Rd .98 CL84
Michigan Av, E12 .68 EL63
Michleham Down, N12 .43 CZ49
Micholls Av, Ger.Cr. SL9 .36 AY49
Micklefield Way, Borwd. WD6 .26 CL38
Mickleham Cl, Orp. BR5 .145 ET96
Mickleham Gdns, Sutt. SM3 .157 CY107
Mickleham Rd, Orp. BR5 .145 ET95
Mickleham Way, Croy.
(New Adgtn.) CR0 .161 ED108
Micklethwaite Rd, SW6 .100 DA79
Midas Ind Est, Uxb. UB8 .76 BH68
Midas Metropolitan Ind Est, The,
Mord. SM4 *off Garth Rd* .139 CX102
Midcroft, Ruis. HA4 .59 BS60
Mid Cross La, Ger.Cr. (Chal.St.P.)
SL9 .36 AY50
Middle Boy, Rom. (Abridge)
RM4 .34 EW41
Middle Cl, Amer. HP6 .20 AT37
Coulsdon CR5 .175 DN120
Epsom KT17 *off Middle La* .156 CS112
Middle Cres, Uxb. (Denh.)
UB9 .57 BD59
Middle Dene, NW7 .42 CR48
Middle Fld, NW8 .82 DD67
Middlefielde, W13 .79 CH71
Middlefield Gdns, Ilf. IG2 .69 EP58
Middlefields, Croy. CR0 .161 DY109
Middle Furlong, Bushey
WD23 .24 CB42
Middle Gorse, Croy. CR0 .161 DY112
MIDDLE GREEN, Slou. .74 AY73
Middle Grn, Slou. SL3 .74 AY74
Staines TW18 .114 BK94
Middle Grn Cl, Surb. KT5
off Alpha Rd .138 CM100
Middlegreen Rd, Slou. SL3 .74 AX74
Middleham Gdns, N18 .46 DU51
Middleham Rd, N18 .46 DU51
Middle Hill, Egh. TW20 .112 AW91
Middle La, N8 .65 DL57
Epsom KT17 .156 CS112
Hemel Hempstead (Bov.)
HP3 .5 BA29
Sevenoaks (Seal) TN15
off Church Rd .191 FM121
Teddington TW11 .117 CF93
Middle La Ms, N8
off Middle La .65 DL57
Middle Meadow, Ch.St.G.
HP8 .36 AW48
Middle Ope, Wat. WD24 .23 BV37
Middle Pk Av, SE9 .124 EK86
Middle Path, Har. HA2
off Middle Rd .61 CD60
Middle Rd, E13
off London Rd .86 EG68
SW16 .141 DK96
Barnet EN4 .28 DE44
Brentwood CM13 .55 GC50
Harrow HA2 .61 CD61
Leatherhead KT22 .171 CH121
Uxbridge (Denh.) UB9 .57 BC59
Waltham Abbey EN9 .15 EB32
Middle Row, W10 .81 CY70
Middlesborough Rd, N18 .46 DU51
Middlesex Business Cen, Sthl.
UB2 .96 CA75
Middlesex Ct, W4
off British Gro .99 CT77
★ **Middlesex Guildhall**,
SW1 .199 P5
H **Middlesex Hosp**, W1 .195 L7
Middlesex Ho, Wem. HA0 .79 CK67
Middlesex Pas, EC1 .196 G7
Middlesex Rd, Mitch. CR4 .141 DL99
Middlesex St, E1 .197 N7
Middlesex Wf, E5 .66 DW61
Middle St, EC1 .197 H6
Croydon CR0
off Surrey St .142 DQ104
Middle Temple, EC4 .196 D10
Middle Temple La, EC4 .196 D9
Middleton Av, E4 .47 DZ49
Greenford UB6 .79 CD68
Sidcup DA14 .126 EW93
Middleton Cl, E4 .47 DZ48
Middleton Dr, SE16 .203 J5
Pinner HA5 .59 BU55
Middleton Gdns, Ilf. IG2 .69 EP58
Middleton Gro, N7 .65 DL64
Middleton Hall La, Brwd.
CM15 .54 FY47
Middleton Ms, N7
off Middleton Gro .65 DL64
Middleton Pl, W1 .195 K7
Middleton Rd, E8 .84 DT66
NW11 .64 DA59
Brentwood CM15 .54 FY46
Carshalton SM5 .140 DE101
Cobham (Down.) KT11 .169 BV119
Epsom KT19 .156 CR110
Hayes UB3 .77 BR71
Morden SM4 .140 DC100
Rickmansworth (Mill End)
WD3 .38 BG46
Middleton St, E2 .84 DV69
Middleton Way, SE13 .103 ED84
Middle Wk, Wok. GU21
off Commercial Way .166 AY117
Middleway, NW11 .64 DB57
Middle Way, SW16 .141 DK96
Erith DA18 .106 EY76
Hayes UB4 .78 BW70
Watford WD24 .23 BV37
Middle Way, The, Har. HA3 .41 CF54
Middle Yd, SE1 .201 L2
Middlings, The, Sev. TN13 .190 FF125
Middlings Ri, Sev. TN13 .190 FF126
Middlings Wd, Sev. TN13 .190 FF125
Midfield Av, Bexh. DA7 .107 FC83
Swanley BR8 .127 FH93
Midfield Par, Bexh. DA7 .107 FC83
Midfield Way, Orp. BR5 .146 EU95
Midford Pl, W1 .195 L5
Midgarth Cl, Lthd. (Oxshott)
KT22 .154 CC114
Midholm, NW11 .64 DB56
Wembley HA9 .62 CN60
Midholm Cl, NW11 .64 DB56
Midholm Rd, Croy. CR0 .143 DY103
Midhope Cl, Wok. GU22 .166 AY119
Midhope Gdns, Wok. GU22
off Midhope Rd .166 AY119
Midhope Rd, Wok. GU22 .166 AY119
Midhope St, WC1 .196 A3
Midhurst Av, N10 .64 DG55
Croydon CR0 .141 DN101
Midhurst Cl, Horn. RM12 .71 FG63
Midhurst Gdns, Uxb. UB10 .77 BQ66
Midhurst Hill, Bexh. DA6 .126 FA86
Midhurst Rd, W13 .97 CG75
Midland Cres, NW3
off Finchley Rd .82 DC65
Midland Pl, E14 .204 D10
Midland Rd, E10 .67 EC59
NW1 .195 N1
Midland Ter, NW2 .63 CX62
NW10 .80 CS70
Midleton Rd, N.Mal. KT3 .138 CQ97
Midlothian Rd, E3 .85 DZ71
Midmoor Rd, SW12 .121 DJ88
SW19 .139 CX95
Midship Cl, SE16 .203 J3
Midship Pt, E14 .203 P5
Midstrath Rd, NW10 .62 CS63
Mid St, Red. (S.Nutfld.) RH1 .185 DM134
Midsummer Av, Houns. TW4 .96 BZ84
Midway, Sutt. SM3 .139 CZ101
Walton-on-Thames KT12 .135 BV103
Midway Av, Cher. KT16 .134 BG97
Egham TW20 .133 BB97
Midway Cl, Stai. TW18 .114 BH90
Midwinter Cl, Well. DA16
off Hook La .106 EU83
Midwood Cl, NW2 .63 CV62
Miena Way, Ashtd. KT21 .171 CK117
Miers Cl, E6 .87 EN67
Mighell Av, Ilf. IG4 .68 EK57
Mike Spring Ct, Grav. DA12 .131 GK91
Milan Rd, Sthl. UB1 .96 BZ75
Milborne Gro, SW10 .100 DC78
Milborne St, E9 .84 DW65
Milborough Cres, SE12 .124 EE86
Milbourne La, Esher KT10 .154 CC107
Milbrook, Esher KT10 .154 CC107
Milburn Dr, West Dr. UB7 .76 BL73
Milburn Wk, Epsom KT18 .172 CS115
Milcombe Cl, Wok. GU21
off Inglewood .166 AV118
Milcote St, SE1 .200 F5
Mildenhall Rd, E5 .66 DW63
Slough SL1 .74 AS72
Mildmay Av, N1 .84 DR65
Mildmay Gro N, N1 .66 DR64
Mildmay Gro S, N1 .66 DR64
Mildmay Pk, N1 .66 DR64
Mildmay Pl, N16
off Boleyn Rd .66 DS64
Sevenoaks (Shore.) TN14 .165 FF111
Mildmay Rd, N1 .66 DS64
Ilford IG1
off Winston Way .69 EP62
Romford RM7 .71 FC57
Mildmay St, N1 .84 DR65
Mildred Av, Borwd. WD6 .26 CN42
Hayes UB3 .95 BR77
Northolt UB5 .60 CB64
Watford WD18 .23 BT42
Mildred Cl, Dart. DA1 .128 FN86
Mildred Rd, Erith DA8 .107 FE78
Mile Cl, Wal.Abb. EN9 .15 EC33
MILE END, E1 .85 DX69
⊖ **Mile End** .85 DY69
Mile End, The, E17 .47 DX53
MILE END GREEN, Dart. .149 FW96
Mile End Pl, E1 .85 DX70
Mile End Rd, E1 .84 DW71
E3 .84 DW71
Mile Path, Wok. GU22 .166 AV120
Mile Rd, Wall. SM6 .141 DJ102
Miles Dr, SE28 .87 ER74
Miles La, Cob. KT11 .154 BY113
Milespit Hill, NW7 .43 CV50
Miles Pl, NW1 .194 A6
Surbiton KT5
off Villiers Av .138 CM98
Miles Rd, N8 .65 DL55
Epsom KT19 .156 CR112
Mitcham CR4 .140 DE97
Miles St, SW8 .101 DL79
Milestone Cl, N9
off Chichester Rd .46 DU47
Sutton SM2 .158 DD107
Woking (Ripley) GU23 .168 BG122
Milestone Rd, SE19 .122 DT93
Dartford DA2 .128 FP86
Miles Way, N20 .44 DE47
Milfoil St, W12 .81 CU73
Milford Cl, SE2 .106 EY79
Milford Gdns, Croy. CR0
off Tannery Cl .143 DX99
Edgware HA8 .42 CN52
Wembley HA0 .61 CK64
Milford Gro, Sutt. SM1 .158 DC105
Milford La, WC2 .196 C10
Milford Ms, SW16 .121 DM90
Milford Rd, W13 .79 CH74
Southall UB1 .78 CA73
Milking La, Kes. BR2 .162 EK111
Orpington BR6 .162 EL112
Milk St, E16 .87 EP74
EC2 .197 J9
Bromley BR1 .124 EH93
Milkwell Gdns, Wdf.Grn.
IG8 .48 EH52
Milkwell Yd, SE5 .102 DQ81
Milkwood Rd, SE24 .121 DP85
Milk Yd, E1 .202 F1
Millais Av, E12 .69 EN64
Millais Gdns, Edg. HA8 .42 CN54
Millais Pl, Til. RM18 .111 GG80
Millais Rd, E11 .67 EC63
Enfield EN1 .30 DT43
New Malden KT3 .138 CS100
Millais Way, Epsom KT19 .156 CQ105
Millan Cl, Add. (New Haw)
KT15 .152 BH110
Milland Ct, Borwd. WD6 .26 CR39
Millard Cl, N16
off Boleyn Rd .66 DS64
Millard Ter, Dag. RM10
off Church Elm La .88 FA65
Mill Av, Uxb. UB8 .76 BJ68
Millbank, SW1 .199 P7
Staines TW18 .114 BH92
Millbank Twr, SW1 .199 P9
Millbank Way, SE12 .124 EG85
Millbourne Rd, Felt. TW13 .116 BY91
Mill Br Pl, Uxb. UB8 .76 BH68
Millbro, Swan. BR8 .127 FG94
Millbrook, Wey. KT13 .153 BS105
Millbrook Av, Well. DA16 .105 ER84
Millbrook Gdns, Rom. (Chad.Hth.)
RM6 .70 EZ58
Romford (Gidea Pk.) RM2 .51 FE54
Millbrook Pl, NW1
off Hampstead Rd .83 DJ68
Millbrook Rd, N9 .46 DV46
SW9 .101 DP83
Bushey WD23 .24 BZ39
Mill Brook Rd, Orp. BR5 .146 EW98
Millbrook Way, Slou. (Colnbr.)
SL3 .93 BE82
Mill Cl, Cars. SM5 .140 DG103
Chesham HP5 .4 AS34
Hemel Hempstead HP3 .6 BN25
Leatherhead (Bkhm.)
KT23 .170 CA124
West Drayton UB7 .94 BK76
Mill Cor, Barn. EN5 .27 CZ39
Mill Ct, E10 .67 EC62
Millcrest Rd, Wal.Cr. (Chsht.)
EN7 .13 DP28
Millcroft Ho, SE6 .123 EC91
MILL END, Rick. .37 BF46
Millender Wk, SE16 .202 G9
Millennium Br, EC4 .84 DQ73
SE1 .84 DQ73
Millennium Cl, E16
off Russell Rd .86 EG72
Uxbridge UB8 .76 BH68
Millennium Dr, E14 .204 F8
Millennium Harbour, E14 .103 DZ75
Millennium Pl, E2 .84 DV68
Millennium Sq, SE1 .202 A4
Millennium Way, SE10 .205 H4

★ Place of interest ⇌ Railway station ⊖ London Underground station DLR Docklands Light Railway station ◆ Tramlink station H Hospital

295
Mil - Mol

Millennium Wf, Rick. WD3
off Wharf La .38 BL45
Miller Av, Enf. EN3
off Government Row .31 EA37
Miller Cl, Mitch. CR4 .140 DF101
Pinner HA5 .40 BW54
Miller Pl, Ger.Cr. SL9 .56 AX57
Miller Rd, SW19 .120 DD93
Croydon CR0 .141 DM102
Miller's Av, E8 .66 DT64
Millers Cl, NW7 .43 CU49
Chigwell IG7 .50 EV47
Rickmansworth (Chorl.)
WD3 .21 BE41
Staines TW18 .114 BH92
Millers Copse, Epsom KT18 .172 CR119
Millers Ct, W4
off Chiswick Mall .99 CT78
Millers Grn Cl, Enf. EN2 .29 DP41
Miller's La, Chig. IG7 .50 EV46
Millers La, Wind. SL4 .112 AT86
Millers Meadow Cl, SE3
off Meadowcourt Rd .124 EF85
Miller's Ter, E8 .66 DT64
Miller St, NW1 .83 DJ68
Millers Way, W6 .99 CW75
Miller Wk, SE1 .200 E3
Millet Rd, Grnf. UB6 .78 CB69
Mill Fm Av, Sun. TW16 .115 BS94
Mill Fm Cl, Pnr. HA5 .40 BW54
Mill Fm Cres, Houns. TW4 .116 BY88
Millfield, Sun. TW16 .135 BR95
Millfield Av, E17 .47 DY53
Millfield Dr, Grav. (Nthflt.)
DA11 .130 GE89
Millfield La, N6 .64 DF61
Tadworth KT20 .183 CZ125
Millfield Pl, N6 .64 DG61
Millfield Rd, Edg. HA8 .42 CQ54
Hounslow TW4 .116 BY88
Millfields Cl, Orp. BR5 .146 EV97
Millfields Cotts, Orp. BR5
off Millfields Cl .146 EV98
Millfields Est, E5
off Denton Way .67 DX62
Millfields Rd, E5 .66 DW63
Millford, Wok. GU21 .166 AV117
Mill Gdns, SE26 .122 DV91
Mill Grn, Mitch. CR4
off London Rd .140 DG101
Mill Grn Business Pk, Mitch. CR4
off Mill Grn Rd .140 DG101
Mill Grn Rd, Mitch. CR4 .140 DF101
Millgrove St, SW11 .100 DG82
Millharbour, E14 .204 B5
Millhaven Cl, Rom. RM6 .70 EV58
Millhedge Cl, Cob. KT11 .170 BY116
MILL HILL, NW7 .43 CU50
Mill Hill, SW13
off Mill Hill Rd .99 CU82
Brentwood CM15 .54 FY45
⇌ Mill Hill Broadway .42 CS51
Mill Hill Circ, NW7
off Watford Way .43 CT50
⊖ Mill Hill East .43 CX52
Mill Hill Gro, W3
off Mill Hill Rd .80 CP74
Mill Hill La, Bet. (Brock.) RH3 .182 CP134
Mill Hill Rd, SW13 .99 CU82
W3 .98 CP75
Millhoo Ct, Wal.Abb. EN9 .16 EF34
Mill Ho Cl, Dart. (Eyns.) DA4
off Mill La .148 FL102
Millhouse La, Abb.L. (Bedmond)
WD5 .7 BT27
Mill Ho La, Cher. KT16 .133 BB98
Egham TW20 .133 BB98
Millhouse Pl, SE27 .121 DP91
Millicent Rd, E10 .67 DZ60
Milligan St, E14 .203 N1
Milliners Ct, Loug. IG10
off The Croft .33 EN40
Milling Rd, Edg. HA8 .42 CR52
Millington Rd, Hayes UB3 .95 BS76
Mill La, E4 .31 EB41
NW6 .63 CZ64
SE18 .105 EN78
Carshalton SM5 .158 DF105
Chalfont St. Giles HP8 .36 AU47
Croydon CR0 .141 DM104
Dartford (Eyns.) DA4 .148 FL102
Egham TW20 .133 BC98
Epsom KT17 .157 CT109
Gerrards Cross SL9 .57 AZ58
Grays RM20 .109 FX78
Kings Langley WD4 .6 BN29
Leatherhead (Fetch.) KT22 .171 CG122
Ongar (Toot Hill) CM5 .19 FE29
Orpington (Downe) BR6 .163 EN110
Oxted RH8 .188 EF132
Oxted (Lmpfld.Ch.) RH8 .189 EM131
Redhill RH1 .185 DJ131
Rickmansworth (Crox.Grn.)
WD3 .23 BQ44
Romford (Chad.Hth.) RM6 .70 EY58
Romford (Nave.) RM6 .35 FH40
Sevenoaks TN14 .191 FJ121
Sevenoaks (Shore.) TN14 .165 FF110
Slough (Horton) SL3 .93 BB83
Waltham Cross EN8 .15 DY28
West Byfleet (Byfleet)
KT14 .152 BM113
Westerham TN16 .189 EQ127
Woking (Ripley) GU23 .168 BK119
Woodford Green IG8 .48 EF50
Mill La Trd Est, Croy. CR0 .141 DM104
Millman Ms, WC1 .196 B5
Millman Pl, WC1
off Millman St .83 DM70
Millman St, WC1 .196 B5
Millmark Gro, SE14 .103 DY82
Millmarsh La, Enf. EN3 .31 DY40
Mill Mead, Stai. TW18 .113 BF91
Millmead, W.Byf. (Byfleet)
KT14 .152 BM112
Mill Mead Rd, N17 .66 DV56
Mill Pk Av, Horn. RM12 .72 FL61
Mill Pl, E14
off East India Dock Rd .85 DZ72
Chislehurst BR7 .145 EP95
Dartford DA1 .107 FG84
Kingston upon Thames
KT1 .138 CM97
Slough (Datchet) SL3 .92 AX82
Mill Pl Caravan Pk, Slou. (Datchet)
SL3 .92 AW82
Mill Plat, Islw. TW7 .97 CG82
Mill Plat Av, Islw. TW7 .97 CG82
Mill Pond Cl, SW8
off Crimsworth Rd .101 DK80
Sevenoaks TN14 .191 FK121
Millpond Ct, Add. KT15 .152 BL106
Millpond Est, SE16 .202 D5
Mill Pond Rd, Dart. DA1 .128 FL86
Mill Ridge, Edg. HA8 .42 CM50
Mill Rd, E16 .86 EH74
SW19 .120 DC94
Cobham KT11 .170 BW115
Dartford (Hawley) DA2 .128 FM91
Epsom KT17 .157 CT112
Erith DA8 .107 FC80
Esher KT10 .136 CA103
Gravesend (Nthflt.) DA11 .130 GE87
Ilford IG1 .69 EN62
Purfleet RM19 .108 FP79
Sevenoaks (Dunt.Grn.)
TN13 .190 FE121
South Ockendon (Aveley)
RM15 .90 FQ73
Tadworth KT20 .173 CX123
Twickenham TW2 .116 CC89
West Drayton UB7 .94 BJ76
Mill Row, N1 .84 DS67
Mills Cl, Uxb. UB10 .76 BN68
Mills Ct, EC2 .197 N3
Mills Gro, E14
off Dewberry St .85 EC71
NW4 .63 CX55
Mill Shaw, Oxt. RH8 .188 EF132
Mill Shot Cl, SW6 .99 CW80
Millside, Cars. SM5 .140 DF103
Millside Ct, Iver SL0 .94 BH75
Millside Ind Est, Dart. DA1 .108 FK84
Millside Pl, Islw. TW7 .97 CH82
Millsmead Way, Loug. IG10 .33 EM40
Millson Cl, N20 .44 DD47
Mills Rd, Walt. KT12 .154 BW106
Mills Row, W4 .98 CR77
Mills Spur, Wind. (Old Wind.)
SL4 .112 AV87
Millstead Cl, Tad. KT20 .173 CV122
Millstone Cl, Dart. (S.Darenth)
DA4 .148 FQ96
Millstone Ms, Dart. (S.Darenth)
DA4 .148 FQ95
Millstream Cl, N13 .45 DN50
Millstream Rd, SE1 .201 P5
Mill St, SE1 .202 A5
W1 .195 J10
Kingston upon Thames
KT1 .138 CL97
Slough SL2 .74 AT74
Slough (Colnbr.) SL3 .93 BD80
Westerham TN16 .189 ER127
Mills Way, Brwd. CM13 .55 GC46
Millthorne Cl, Rick. (Crox.Grn.)
WD3 .22 BM43
Mill Vale, Brom. BR2 .144 EF96
Mill Vw, St.Alb. (Park St.) AL2
off Park St .9 CD27
Mill Vw Cl, Epsom (Ewell)
KT17 .157 CT108
Millview Cl, Reig. RH2 .184 DD132
Mill Vw Gdns, Croy. CR0 .143 DX104
MILLWALL, E14 .204 B8
Millwall Dock Rd, E14 .203 P6
★ Millwall FC, SE16 .102 DW78
Millway, NW7 .42 CS50
Mill Way, Bushey WD23 .24 BY40
Feltham TW14 .115 BV85
Leatherhead KT22 .172 CM124
Millway, Reig. RH2 .184 DD134
Mill Way, Rick. (Mill End) WD3 .37 BF46
Millway Gdns, Nthlt. UB5 .78 BZ65
Millwell Cres, Chig. IG7 .49 ER50
Millwood Rd, Houns. TW3 .116 CC85
Orpington BR5 .146 EW97
Millwood St, W10
off St. Charles Sq .81 CY71
Mill Yd, E1
off Cable St .84 DU73
Milman Cl, Pnr. HA5 .60 BX55
Milman Rd, NW6 .81 CY68
Milman's St, SW10 .100 DD79
Milmead Ind Cen, N17 .46 DV54
Milne Ct, E18
off Churchfields .48 EG53
Milne Feild, Pnr. HA5 .40 CA52
Milne Gdns, SE9 .124 EL85
Milne Pk E, Croy. (New Adgtn.)
CR0 .161 ED111
Milne Pk W, Croy. (New Adgtn.)
CR0 .161 ED111
Milner App, Cat. CR3 .176 DU121
Milner Cl, Cat. CR3 .176 DT121
Watford WD25 .7 BV34
Milner Ct, Bushey WD23 .24 CB44
Milner Dr, Cob. KT11 .154 BZ112
Twickenham TW2 .117 CD87
Milner Pl, N1 .83 DN67
Carshalton SM5
off High St .158 DG105
Milner Rd, E15 .86 EE69
SW19 .140 DB95
Caterham CR3 .176 DU122
Dagenham RM8 .70 EW61
Kingston upon Thames
KT1 .137 CK97
Morden SM4 .140 DD99
Thornton Heath CR7 .142 DR97
Milner Sq, N1 .83 DP66
Milner St, SW3 .198 D8
Milner Wk, SE9 .125 ER89
Milne Way, Uxb. (Hare.) UB9 .38 BH53
Milnthorpe Rd, W4 .98 CR79
Milo Rd, SE22 .122 DT86
Milroy Av, Grav. (Nthflt.)
DA11 .130 GE89
Milroy Wk, SE1 .200 F2
Milson Rd, W14 .99 CY76
MILTON, Grav. .131 GK86
Milton Av, E6 .86 EK66
N6 .65 DJ59
NW9 .62 CQ55
NW10 .80 CQ67
Barnet EN5 .27 CZ43
Croydon CR0 .142 DR101
Gerrards Cross (Chal.St.P.)
SL9 .56 AX56
Gravesend DA12 .131 GJ88
Hornchurch RM12 .71 FF61
Sevenoaks (Bad.Mt.) TN14 .165 FB110
Sutton SM1 .140 DD104
Milton Cl, N2 .64 DC57
SE1 .201 P9
Hayes UB4 .77 BU72
Slough (Horton) SL3 .93 BA83
Sutton SM1 .140 DD104
Milton Ct, EC2 .197 K6
Romford (Chad.Hth.) RM6
off Cross Rd .70 EW59
Uxbridge UB10 .59 BP62
Waltham Abbey EN9 .15 EC34
Milton Ct Rd, SE14 .103 DY79
Milton Cres, Ilf. IG2 .69 EQ59
Milton Dr, Borwd. WD6 .26 CP43
Shepperton TW17 .134 BL98
Milton Flds, Ch.St.G. HP8 .36 AV48
Milton Gdn Est, N16
off Milton Gro .66 DS63
Milton Gdns, Epsom KT18 .156 CS114
Staines TW19
off Chesterton Dr .114 BM88
Tilbury RM18 .111 GH81
Milton Gro, N11 .45 DJ50
N16 .66 DR63
Milton Hall Rd, Grav. DA12 .131 GK88
Milton Hill, Ch.St.G. HP8 .36 AV48
Milton Pk, N6 .65 DJ59
Milton Pl, N7 off George's Rd .65 DN64
Gravesend DA12 .131 GJ86
Milton Rd, E17 .67 EA56
N6 .65 DJ59
N15 .65 DP56
NW7 .43 CU50
NW9 off West Hendon Bdy .63 CU59
SE24 .121 DP86
SW14 .98 CR83
SW19 .120 DC93
W3 .80 CR74
W7 .79 CF73
Addlestone KT15 .152 BG107
Belvedere DA17 .106 FA77
Brentwood CM14 .54 FV49
Caterham CR3 .176 DR121
Croydon CR0 .142 DR102
Egham TW20 .113 AZ92
Gravesend DA12 .131 GJ86
Grays RM17 .110 GB78
Hampton TW12 .116 CA94
Harrow HA1 .61 CE56
Mitcham CR4 .120 DG94
Romford RM1 .71 FG58
Sevenoaks (Dunt.Grn.)
TN13 .190 FE121
Sutton SM1 .140 DA104
Swanscombe DA10 .130 FY86
Uxbridge UB10 .58 BN63
Wallington SM6 .159 DJ107
Walton-on-Thames KT12 .136 BX104
Welling DA16 .105 ET81
★ Milton's Cottage, Ch.St.G.
HP8 .36 AV48
Milton St, EC2 .197 K6
Swanscombe DA10 .129 FX86
Waltham Abbey EN9 .15 EC34
Watford WD24 .23 BV38
Milton Way, West Dr. UB7 .94 BM77
Milverton Dr, Uxb. UB10 .59 BQ63
Milverton Gdns, Ilf. IG3 .69 ET61
Milverton Ho, SE23 .123 DY90
Milverton Rd, NW6 .81 CW66
Milverton St, SE11 .101 DN78
Milverton Way, SE9 .125 EN91
Milward St, E1
off Stepney Way .84 DV71
Milward Wk, SE18
off Spearman St .105 EN79
MIMBRIDGE, Wok. .150 AV113
Mimms Hall Rd, Pot.B. EN6 .11 CX31
Mimms La, Pot.B. (S.Mimms)
EN6 .10 CQ33
Radlett (Shenley) WD7 .10 CN33
Mimosa Cl, Brwd. CM15 .54 FV43
Orpington BR6
off Berrylands .146 EW104
Romford RM3 .52 FJ52
Mimosa Rd, Hayes UB4 .78 BW71
Mimosa St, SW6 .99 CZ81
Mina Av, Slou. SL3 .92 AX75
Minard Rd, SE6 .124 EE87
Mina Rd, SE17 .102 DS78
SW19 .140 DA95
Minchenden Cres, N14 .45 DJ48
Minchin Cl, Lthd. KT22 .171 CG122
Mincing La, EC3 .197 M10
Woking (Chobham) GU24 .150 AT108
Minden Rd, SE20 .142 DV95
Sutton SM3 .139 CZ103
Minehead Rd, SW16 .121 DM92
Harrow HA2 .60 CA62
Mineral St, SE18 .105 ES77
Minera Ms, SW1 .198 G8
Minerva Cl, SW9 .101 DN80
Sidcup DA14 .125 ES90
Staines TW19 .114 BG85
Minerva Dr, Wat. WD24 .23 BS36
Minerva Rd, E4 .47 EB52
NW10 .80 CQ70
Kingston upon Thames
KT1 .138 CM96
Minerva St, E2 .84 DV68
Minet Av, NW10 .80 CS68
Minet Dr, Hayes UB3 .77 BU74
Minet Gdns, NW10 .80 CS68
Hayes UB3 .77 BU74
Minet Rd, SW9 .101 DP82
Minford Gdns, W14 .99 CX75
Mingard Wk, N7
off Hornsey Rd .65 DM61
Ming St, E14 .85 EA73
Ministers Gdns, St.Alb. AL2
off Frogmore .9 CE28
★ Ministry of Defence, SW1 .199 P3
Ministry Way, SE9 .125 EM89
Miniver Pl, EC4
off Garlick Hill .84 DQ73
Mink Ct, Houns. TW4 .96 BW83
Minniedale, Surb. KT5 .138 CM99
Minnow St, SE17
off East St .102 DS77
Minnow Wk, SE17 .201 N9
Minorca Rd, Wey. KT13 .152 BN105
Minories, EC3 .197 P10
Minshull Pl, Beck. BR3 .123 EA94
Minshull St, SW8
off Wandsworth Rd .101 DK81
Minson Rd, E9 .85 DX67
Minstead Gdns, SW15 .119 CT87
Minstead Way, N.Mal. KT3 .138 CS100
Minster Av, Sutt. SM1
off Leafield Rd .140 DA103
Minster Ct, EC3
off Mincing La .84 DR73
Hornchurch RM11 .72 FN61
St. Albans (Frog.) AL2 .9 CE28
Minster Dr, Croy. CR0 .160 DS105
Minster Gdns, W.Mol. KT8
off Molesey Av .136 BZ99
Minsterley Av, Shep. TW17 .135 BS98
Minster Pavement, EC3
off Mincing La .84 DR73
Minster Rd, NW2 .63 CY64
Bromley BR1 .124 EH94
Minster Wk, N8
off Lightfoot Rd .65 DL56
Minster Way, Horn. RM11 .72 FM60
Slough SL3 .93 AZ75
Minstrel Gdns, Surb. KT5 .138 CM98
Mint Business Pk, E16 .86 EG71
Mint Cl, Uxb. (Hlgdn.) UB10 .77 BP69
Mintern Cl, N13 .45 DP48
Minterne Av, Sthl. UB2 .96 CA77
Minterne Rd, Har. HA3 .62 CM57
Minterne Waye, Hayes UB4 .78 BW72
Mintern St, N1 .84 DR68
Mint La, Tad. (Lwr.Kgswd.)
KT20 .184 DA129
Minton Ms, NW6
off Lymington Rd .82 DB65
Mint Rd, Bans. SM7 .174 DC116
Wallington SM6 .159 DH105
Mint St, SE1 .201 H4
Mint Wk, Croy. CR0
off High St .142 DQ104
Warlingham CR6 .177 DX118
Woking (Knap.) GU21 .166 AS117
Mirabel Rd, SW6 .99 CZ80
Mirador Cres, Slou. SL2 .74 AV73
Miramar Way, Horn. RM12 .72 FK64
Miranda Cl, E1 off Sidney St .84 DW71
Miranda Ct, W3
off Queens Dr .80 CM72
Miranda Rd, N19 .65 DJ60
Mirfield St, SE7 .104 EK77
Miriam Rd, SE18 .105 ES78
Mirravale Trd Est, Dag. RM8 .70 EZ59
Mirren Cl, Har. HA2 .60 BZ63
Mirrie La, Uxb. (Denh.) UB9 .57 BC57
Mirror Path, SE9
off Lambscroft Av .124 EJ90
Misbourne Av, Ger.Cr. (Chal.St.P.)
SL9 .36 AY50
Misbourne Cl, Ger.Cr. (Chal.St.P.)
SL9 .36 AY50
Misbourne Ct, Slou. SL3
off High St .93 BA77
Misbourne Meadows, Uxb. (Denh.)
UB9 .57 BC60
Misbourne Rd, Uxb. UB10 .76 BN67
Misbourne Vale, Ger.Cr. (Chal.St.P.)
SL9 .36 AX50
Miskin Rd, Dart. DA1 .128 FJ87
Miskin Way, Grav. DA12 .131 GK93
Missenden Cl, Felt. TW14 .115 BT88
Missenden Gdns, Mord.
SM4 .140 DC100
Mission Gro, E17 .67 DY57
Mission Pl, SE15 .102 DU81
Mission Sq, Brent. TW8 .98 CL79
Mistletoe Cl, Croy. CR0
off Marigold Way .143 DX102
Misty's Fld, Walt. KT12 .136 BW102
Mitali Pas, E1
off Back Ch La .84 DU72
MITCHAM .140 DG97
⊖ Mitcham .140 DE98
Mitcham Gdn Village, Mitch.
CR4 .140 DG99
Mitcham Ind Est, Mitch. CR4 .140 DG95
⇌ Mitcham Junction .140 DG99
⊖ Mitcham Junction .140 DG99
Mitcham La, SW16 .121 DJ93
Mitcham Pk, Mitch. CR4 .140 DF98
Mitcham Rd, E6 .86 EL69
SW17 .120 DF92
Croydon CR0 .141 DL100
Ilford IG3 .69 ET59
Mitchell Av, Grav. (Nthflt.)
DA11 .130 GD89
Mitchellbrook Way, NW10 .80 CR65
Mitchell Cl, SE2 .106 EW77
Abbots Langley WD5 .7 BU32
Belvedere DA17 .107 FC76
Dartford DA1 .128 FL89
Hemel Hempstead (Bov.)
HP3 .5 AZ27
Rainham RM13 .90 FJ68
Mitchell Rd, N13 .45 DP50
Orpington BR6 .163 ET105
Mitchell's Pl, SE21
off Dulwich Village .122 DS87
Mitchell St, EC1 .197 H4
Mitchell Wk, E6 .86 EL71
Amersham HP6 .20 AS38
Swanscombe DA10 .130 FY87
Mitchell Way, NW10 .80 CQ65
Bromley BR1 .144 EG95
Mitchison Rd, N1 .84 DR65
Mitchley Av, Pur. CR8 .160 DQ113
South Croydon CR2 .160 DQ113
Mitchley Gro, S.Croy. CR2 .160 DU113
Mitchley Hill, S.Croy. CR2 .160 DT113
Mitchley Rd, N17 .66 DU55
Mitchley Vw, S.Croy. CR2 .160 DU113
Mitford Cl, Chess. KT9
off Merritt Gdns .155 CJ107
Mitford Rd, N19 .65 DL61
Mitre, The, E14
off Three Colt St .85 DZ73
Mitre Av, E17
off Greenleaf Rd .67 DZ55
Mitre Cl, Brom. BR2
off Beckenham La .144 EF96
Shepperton TW17
off Gordon Dr .135 BR100
Sutton SM2 .158 DC108
Mitre Ct, EC2 .197 J8
EC4 .196 E9
Mitre Rd, E15 .86 EE68
SE1 .200 E4
Mitre Sq, EC3 .197 N9
Mitre St, EC3 .197 N9
Mitre Way, W10 .81 CV70
Mixbury Gro, Wey. KT13 .153 BR107
Mixnams La, Cher. KT16 .134 BG97
Mizen Cl, Cob. KT11 .154 BX114
Mizen Way, Cob. KT11 .170 BW115
Moat, The, N.Mal. KT3 .138 CS95
Ongar CM5 .19 FF29
Moat Cl, Bushey WD23 .24 CB43
Orpington BR6 .163 ET107
Sevenoaks (Chipstead)
TN13 .190 FB123
Moat Ct, Ashtd. KT21 .172 CL117
Moat Cres, N3 .64 DB55
Moat Cft, Well. DA16 .106 EW83
Moat Dr, E13
off Boundary Rd .86 EJ68
Harrow HA1 .60 CC56
Ruislip HA4 .59 BS59
Slough SL2 .74 AW71
Moated Fm Dr, Add. KT15 .152 BJ108
Moat Fm Rd, Nthlt. UB5 .78 BZ65
Moatfield Rd, Bushey WD23 .24 CB43
Moat La, Erith DA8 .107 FG81
Moat Pl, SW9 .101 DM83
W3 .80 CP72
Uxbridge (Denh.) UB9 .58 BH63
Moatside, Enf. EN3 .31 DX42
Feltham TW13 .116 BW91
Moatview Ct, Bushey WD23 .24 CB43
Moberley Rd, SW4 .121 DK87
Modbury Gdns, NW5
off Queen's Cres .82 DG65
Modder Pl, SW15 .99 CX84
Model Cotts, SW14
off Upper Richmond Rd W .98 CQ84
Model Fm Cl, SE9 .124 EL90
Modling Ho, E2 .85 DX68
Moelwyn Hughes Ct, N7
off Hilldrop Cres .65 DK64
Moelyn Ms, Har. HA1 .61 CG57
Moffat Rd, N13 .45 DL51
SW17 .120 DE91
Thornton Heath CR7 .142 DQ96
Moffats Cl, Hat. AL9 .12 DA26
Moffats La, Hat. AL9 .11 CZ26
MOGADOR, Tad. .183 CY129
Mogador Cotts, Tad. KT20
off Mogador Rd .183 CX128
Mogador Rd, Tad. (Lwr.Kgswd.)
KT20 .183 CX128
Mogden La, Islw. TW7 .117 CE85
Mohmmad Khan Rd, E11
off Harvey Rd .68 EF60
Moira Cl, N17 .46 DS54
Moira Rd, SE9 .105 EM84
Moir Cl, S.Croy. CR2 .160 DU109
Moland Mead, SE16 .203 H10
Molash Rd, Orp. BR5 .146 EX98
Molasses Row, SW11
off Cinnamon Row .100 DC83
Mole Abbey Gdns, W.Mol. KT8
off New Rd .136 CA97
Mole Business Pk, Lthd.
KT22 .171 CG121
Mole Ct, Epsom KT19 .156 CQ105
Molember Ct, E.Mol. KT8 .137 CE99
Molember Rd, E.Mol. KT8 .137 CE99
Mole Rd, Lthd. (Fetch.) KT22 .171 CD121
Walton-on-Thames KT12 .154 BX106
Molescroft, SE9 .125 EQ90
Molesey Av, W.Mol. KT8 .136 BZ98
Molesey Cl, Walt. KT12 .154 BY105
Molesey Dr, Sutt. SM3 .139 CY103
H Molesey Hosp, W.Mol.
KT8 .136 CA99
Molesey Pk Av, W.Mol. KT8 .136 CB99
Molesey Pk Cl, E.Mol. KT8 .136 CC99
Molesey Pk Rd, E.Mol. KT8 .137 CD99
West Molesey KT8 .136 CB99
Molesey Rd, Walt. KT12 .154 BX106
West Molesey KT8 .136 BY99
Molesford Rd, SW6 .100 DA81
Molesham Cl, W.Mol. KT8 .136 CB97
Molesham Way, W.Mol. KT8 .136 CB97
Moles Hill, Lthd. (Oxshott)
KT22 .155 CD111
Molesworth Rd, Cob. KT11 .153 BU113
Molesworth St, SE13 .103 EC83
Mole Valley Pl, Ashtd. KT21 .171 CK119

★ Place of interest ⇌ Railway station ⊖ London Underground station DLR Docklands Light Railway station ⊖ Tramlink station H Hospital

Mol - Mor

Mollands La, S.Ock. RM15 91 FW70
Mollison Av, Enf. EN3 31 DY43
Mollison Dr, Wall. SM6 159 DL107
Mollison Ri, Grav. DA12 131 GL92
Mollison Way, Edg. HA8 42 CN54
Molloy Ct, Wok. GU21
 off Courtenay Rd 167 BA116
Molly Huggins Cl, SW12 121 DJ87
Molteno Rd, Wat. WD17 23 BU39
Molyneaux Av, Hem.H. (Bov.)
 HP3 5 AZ27
Molyneux Dr, SW17 121 DH91
Molyneux Rd, Wey. KT13 152 BN106
Molyneux St, W1 194 C7
Monahan Av, Pur. CR8 159 DM112
Monarch Cl, Felt. TW14 115 BS87
 Tilbury RM18 111 GH82
 West Wickham BR4 162 EF105
Monarch Dr, E16 86 EK71
Monarch Ms, E17 67 EB57
 SW16 121 DN92
Monarch Par, Mitch. CR4
 off London Rd 140 DF96
Monarch Pl, Buck.H. IG9 48 EJ47
Monarch Rd, Belv. DA17 106 FA76
Monarchs Ct, NW7
 off Grenville Pl 42 CR50
Monarchs Way, Ruis. HA4 59 BR60
 Waltham Cross EN8 15 DY34
Mona Rd, SE15 102 DW82
Monastery Gdns, Enf. EN2 30 DR40
Mona St, E16 86 EF71
Monaveen Gdns, W.Mol.
 KT8 136 CA97
Monck St, SW1 199 N7
Monclar Rd, SE5 102 DR84
Moncorvo Cl, SW7 198 B5
Moncrieff Cl, E6
 off Linton Gdns 86 EL72
Moncrieff Pl, SE15 off Rye La 102 DU82
Moncrieff St, SE15 102 DU82
Mondial Way, Hayes UB3 95 BQ80
Monega Rd, E7 86 EJ65
 E12 86 EK65
Money Av, Cat. CR3 176 DR122
MONEYHILL, Rick. 38 BH46
Moneyhill Par, Rick. WD3
 off Uxbridge Rd 38 BH46
Money Hill Rd, Rick. WD3 38 BJ46
Money La, West Dr. UB7 94 BK76
Money Rd, Cat. CR3 176 DR122
Mongers La, Epsom KT17 157 CT110
Monica Cl, Wat. WD24 24 BW40
Monier Rd, E3 85 EA66
Monivea Rd, Beck. BR3 123 DZ94
Monkchester Cl, Loug. IG10 33 EN39
Monk Dr, E16 86 EG72
MONKEN HADLEY, Barn. 27 CZ39
Monkfrith Av, N14 29 DH44
Monkfrith Cl, N14 45 DH45
Monkfrith Way, N14 44 DG45
Monkhams Av, Wdf.Grn. IG8 48 EG50
Monkhams Dr, Wdf.Grn. IG8 48 EH49
Monkhams La, Buck.H. IG9 48 EH48
 Woodford Green IG8 48 EG50
Monkleigh Rd, Mord. SM4 139 CY97
Monk Pas, E16 off Monk Dr 86 EG73
Monks Av, Barn. EN5 28 DC44
 West Molesey KT8 136 BZ99
Monks Chase, Brwd. CM13 55 GC50
Monks Cl, SE2 106 EX77
 Enfield EN2 30 DQ40
 Harrow HA2 60 CB61
 Ruislip HA4 60 BX63
Monks Cres, Add. KT15 152 BH106
 Walton-on-Thames KT12 135 BV102
Monksdene Gdns, Sutt. SM1 140 DB104
Monks Dr, W3 80 CN71
Monks Grn, Lthd. (Fetch.)
 KT22 170 CC121
Monksgrove, Loug. IG10 33 EN43
Monksmead, Borwd. WD6 26 CQ42
MONKS ORCHARD, Croy. 143 DZ101
Monks Orchard, Dart. DA1 128 FJ89
Monks Orchard Rd, Beck.
 BR3 143 EA102
Monks Pk, Wem. HA9 80 CQ65
Monks Pk Gdns, Wem. HA9 80 CP65
Monks Pl, Cat. CR3
 off Tillingdown Hill 176 DU122
Monk's Ridge, N20 43 CV46
Monks Rd, Bans. SM7 174 DA116
 Enfield EN2 30 DQ40
 Virginia Water GU25 132 AX98
Monk St, SE18 105 EN77
Monks Wk, Cher. KT16 133 BE98
 Gravesend (Sthflt.)
 DA13 130 GA93
Monk's Wk, Reig. RH2 184 DB134
Monks Way, NW11
 off Hurstwood Rd 63 CZ56
 Beckenham BR3 143 EA99
 Orpington BR5 145 EQ102
 Staines TW18 114 BK94
 West Drayton UB7
 off Harmondsworth La 94 BL79
Monkswell Ct, N10
 off Pembroke Rd 44 DG53
Monkswell La, Couls. CR5 174 DB124
Monkswood Av, Wal.Abb.
 EN9 15 ED33
Monkswood Gdns, Borwd.
 WD6 26 CR42
 Ilford IG5 69 EN55
Monkton Rd, Well. DA16 105 ET82
Monkton St, SE11 200 E8
Monkville Av, NW11 63 CZ56
Monkwell Sq, EC2 197 J7
Monkwood Cl, Rom. RM1 71 FG57
Monmouth Av, E18 68 EH56
 Kingston upon Thames
 KT1 117 CJ94
Monmouth Cl, W4
 off Beaumont Rd 98 CR76
Monmouth Cl, Mitch. CR4
 off Recreation Way 141 DL98
 Welling DA16 106 EU84
Monmouth Gro, Brent. TW8
 off Sterling Pl 98 CL77
Monmouth Pl, W2
 off Monmouth Rd 82 DA72
Monmouth Rd, E6 87 EM69
 N9 46 DV47
 W2 82 DB72
 Dagenham RM9 70 EZ64
 Hayes UB3 95 BS77
 Watford WD17 23 BV41
Monmouth St, WC2 195 P9
Monnery Rd, N19 65 DJ62
Monnow Grn, S.Ock. (Aveley)
 RM15 off Monnow Rd 90 FQ73
Monnow Rd, SE1 202 B10
 South Ockendon (Aveley)
 RM15 90 FQ73
Mono La, Felt. TW13 115 BV89
Monoux Gro, E17 47 EA53
Monroe Cres, Enf. EN1 30 DV39
Monroe Dr, SW14 118 CP85
Monro Gdns, Har. HA3 41 CE52
Monro Way, E5 off Downs Rd 66 DU62
Monsal Ct, E5
 off Redwald Rd 67 DX63
Monsell Ct, N4
 off Monsell Rd 65 DP62
Monsell Gdns, Stai. TW18 113 BE92
Monsell Rd, N4 65 DP62
Monson Rd, NW10 81 CU68
 SE14 103 DX80
 Redhill RH1 184 DF130
Mons Wk, Egh. TW20 113 BC92
Mons Way, Brom. BR2 144 EL100
Montacute Rd, SE6 123 DZ87
 Bushey (Bushey Hth.)
 WD23 41 CE45
 Croydon (New Adgtn.)
 CR0 161 EC109
 Morden SM4 140 DD100
Montagu Cres, N18 46 DV49
Montague Av, SE4 103 DZ84
 W7 79 CF74
 South Croydon CR2 160 DS112
Montague Cl, SE1 201 K2
 Walton-on-Thames KT12 135 BU101
Montague Dr, Cat. CR3
 off Drake Av 176 DQ122
Montague Gdns, W3 80 CN73
Montague Hall Pl, Bushey
 WD23 24 CA44
Montague Pl, WC1 195 N6
Montague Rd, E8 66 DU64
 E11 68 EF61
 N8 65 DM57
 N15 66 DU56
 SW19 120 DB94
 W7 79 CF74
 W13 79 CH72
 Croydon CR0 141 DP102
 Hounslow TW3 96 CB83
 Richmond TW10 118 CL86
 Slough SL1 74 AT73
 Slough (Datchet) SL3 92 AV81
 Southall UB2 96 BY77
 Uxbridge UB8 76 BK66
Montague Sq, SE15
 off Clifton Way 102 DW80
Montague St, EC1 197 H7
 WC1 195 P6
Montague Waye, Sthl. UB2 96 BY76
Montagu Gdns, N18 46 DV49
 Wallington SM6 159 DJ105
Montagu Mans, W1 194 E6
Montagu Ms N, W1 194 E7
Montagu Ms S, W1 194 E8
Montagu Ms W, W1 194 E8
Montagu Pl, W1 194 D7
Montagu Rd, N9 46 DW49
 N18 46 DV50
 NW4 63 CU58
Montagu Rd Ind Est, N18 46 DW49
Montagu Row, W1 194 E7
Montagu Sq, W1 194 E7
Montagu St, W1 194 E8
Montalt Rd, Wdf.Grn. IG8 48 EF50
Montana Cl, S.Croy. CR2 160 DR110
Montana Gdns, SE26 123 DZ92
 Sutton SM1 off Lind Rd 158 DC106
Montana Rd, SW17 120 DG91
 SW20 139 CW95
Montayne Rd, Wal.Cr. (Chsht.)
 EN8 15 DX32
Montbelle Rd, SE9 125 EP90
Montbretia Cl, Orp. BR5 146 EW98
Montcalm Cl, Brom. BR2 144 EG100
 Hayes UB4 off Ayles Rd 77 BV69
Montcalm Rd, SE7 104 EK80
Montclare St, E2 197 P3
Monteagle Av, Bark. IG11 87 EQ65
Monteagle Way, E5
 off Rendlesham Rd 66 DU62
 SE15 102 DV83
Montefiore St, SW8 101 DH82
Montego Cl, SE24
 off Railton Rd 101 DN84
Montem Rd, SE23 123 DZ87
 New Malden KT3 138 CS98
Montem St, N4
 off Thorpedale Rd 65 DM60
Montenotte Rd, N8 65 DJ57
Monterey Cl, Bex. DA5 127 FC89
Montesole Ct, Pnr. HA5 40 BW54
Montevetro, SW11 100 DD81
Montford Pl, SE11 101 DN78
Montford Rd, Sun. TW16 135 BU98
Montfort Gdns, Ilf. IG6 49 EQ51
Montfort Pl, SW19 119 CX88
Montgolfier Wk, Nthlt. UB5
 off Jetstar Way 78 BY69
Montgomery Av, Esher KT10 137 CE104
Montgomery Cl, Grays
 RM16 110 GC75
 Mitcham CR4 141 DL98
Montgomery Cl, Sid. DA15 125 ET86
Montgomery Cres, Rom. RM3 52 FJ50
Montgomery Dr, Wal.Cr. (Chsht.)
 EN8 15 DY28
Montgomery Pl, Slou. SL2 74 AW72
Montgomery Rd, W4 98 CQ77
 Dartford (S.Darenth) DA4 149 FR95
 Edgware HA8 42 CM51
 Woking GU22 166 AY118
Montgomery St, E14 204 C3
Montholme Rd, SW11 120 DF86
Monthope Rd, E1
 off Casson St 84 DU71
Montolieu Gdns, SW15 119 CV85
Montpelier Av, W5 79 CJ71
 Bexley DA5 126 EX87
Montpelier Cl, Uxb. UB10 76 BN67
Montpelier Gdns, E6 86 EK69
 Romford RM6 70 EW59
Montpelier Gro, NW5 65 DJ64
Montpelier Ms, SW7 198 C6
Montpelier Pl, E1 84 DW72
 SW7 198 C6
Montpelier Ri, NW11 63 CY59
 Wembley HA9 61 CK60
Montpelier Rd, N3 44 DC53
 SE15 102 DV81
 W5 79 CK71
 Purley CR8 159 DP110
 Sutton SM1 158 DC105
Montpelier Row, SE3 104 EF82
 Twickenham TW1 117 CH87
Montpelier Sq, SW7 198 C5
Montpelier St, SW7 198 C5
Montpelier Ter, SW7 198 C5
Montpelier Vale, SE3 104 EF82
Montpelier Wk, SW7 198 C6
Montpelier Way, NW11 63 CY59
Montrave Rd, SE20 122 DW93
Montreal Pl, WC2 196 B10
Montreal Rd, Ilf. IG1 69 EQ59
 Sevenoaks TN13 190 FE123
 Tilbury RM18 111 GG82
Montrell Rd, SW2 121 DL88
Montrose Av, NW6 81 CY68
 Edgware HA8 42 CQ54
 Romford RM2 52 FJ54
 Sidcup DA15 126 EU87
 Slough (Datchet) SL3 92 AW80
 Twickenham TW2 116 CB87
 Welling DA16 105 ER83
Montrose Cl, Ashf. TW15 115 BQ93
 Welling DA16 105 ET83
 Woodford Green IG8 48 EG49
Montrose Ct, SW7 198 A5
Montrose Cres, N12 44 DC51
 Wembley HA0 80 CL65
Montrose Gdns, Lthd. (Oxshott)
 KT22 155 CD112
 Mitcham CR4 140 DF97
 Sutton SM1 140 DB103
Montrose Pl, SW1 198 G5
Montrose Rd, Felt. TW14 115 BR86
 Harrow HA3 41 CE54
Montrose Wk, Wey. KT13 135 BP104
Montrose Way, SE23 123 DX88
 Slough (Datchet) SL3 92 AX81
Montrouge Cres, Epsom
 KT17 173 CW116
Montserrat Av, Wdf.Grn. IG8 47 ED52
Montserrat Cl, SE19 122 DR92
Montserrat Rd, SW15 99 CY84
★ Monument, The, EC3 201 L1
⊖ Monument 197 L10
Monument Gdns, SE13 123 EC85
Monument Grn, Wey. KT13 135 BP104
Monument Hill, Wey. KT13 135 BP105
Monument La, Ger.Cr. (Chal.St.P.)
 SL9 36 AY51
Monument Rd, Wey. KT13 153 BP105
 Woking GU21 151 BA114
Monument St, EC3 197 L10
Monument Way, N17 66 DT55
Monument Way E, Wok.
 GU21 167 BB115
Monument Way W, Wok.
 GU21 167 BA115
Monza St, E1 202 F1
Moodkee St, SE16 202 G6
Moody Rd, SE15 102 DT80
Moody St, E1 85 DX69
Moon La, Barn. EN5 27 CZ41
Moon St, N1 83 DP67
Moorcroft Gdns, Brom. BR2
 off Southborough Rd 144 EL99
Moorcroft La, Uxb. UB8 76 BN71
Moorcroft Rd, SW16 121 DL90
Moorcroft Way, Pnr. HA5 60 BY57
Moordown, SE18 105 EN81
Moore Av, Grays RM20 110 FY78
 Tilbury RM18 111 GH82
Moore Cl, SW14
 off Little St. Leonards 98 CQ83
 Addlestone KT15 152 BH106
 Dartford DA2 129 FR89
 Mitcham CR4 141 DH96
 Wallington SM6
 off Brabazon Av 159 DL109
Moore Cres, Dag. RM9 88 EV67
Moorefield Rd, N17 46 DT54
Moore Gro Cres, Egh. TW20 112 AY94
Moorehead Way, SE3 104 EH83
Mooreland Rd, Brom. BR1 124 EF94
Moore Pk Rd, SW6 100 DB80
Moore Rd, SE19 122 DQ93
 Swanscombe DA10 130 FY86
Moores Pl, Brwd. CM14 54 FX47
Moore St, SW3 198 D8
Moore Wk, E7 off Stracey Rd 68 EG63
Moore Way, SE22
 off Lordship La 122 DU88
 Sutton SM2 158 DA109
Moorey Cl, E15
 off Stephen's Rd 86 EF67
Moorfield Av, W5 79 CK70
Moorfield Rd, Chess. KT9 156 CL106
 Enfield EN3 30 DW39
Montgomery Cl, Orp. BR6 146 EU101
 Uxbridge UB8 76 BK72
 Uxbridge (Hare.) UB9 58 BG59
Moorfields, EC2 197 K7
Moorfields Cl, Stai. TW18 133 BE95
H Moorfields Eye Hosp,
 EC1 197 K3
Moorfields Highwalk, EC2
 off Fore St 84 DR71
⇌ Moorgate 197 K7
⊖ Moorgate 197 K7
Moorgate, EC2 197 K8
Moorgate Pl, EC2 197 K8
Moorhall Rd, Uxb. (Hare.)
 UB9 58 BH58
Moorhayes Dr, Stai. TW18 134 BJ97
Moorhen Cl, Erith DA8 107 FH80
Moorholme, Wok. GU22
 off Oakbank 166 AY119
MOORHOUSE BANK, West. 189 EM128
Moorhouse Rd, W2 82 DA72
 Harrow HA3 61 CK55
 Oxted RH8 189 EM131
 Westerham TN16 189 EM128
Moorhurst Av, Wal.Cr. (Chsht.)
 EN7 13 DN29
Moorings, SE28 88 EV73
Moorings, The, Wind. SL4
 off Straight Rd 112 AW87
Moorland Cl, Rom. RM5 51 FB52
 Twickenham TW2
 off Telford Rd 116 CA87
Moorland Rd, SW9 101 DP84
 West Drayton UB7 94 BJ79
Moorlands, St.Alb. (Frog.) AL2
 off Frogmore 9 CE28
Moorlands, The, Wok. GU22 167 AZ121
Moorlands Av, NW7 43 CV51
Moorlands Est, SW9 101 DN84
Moor La, EC2 197 K7
 Chessington KT9 156 CL105
 Rickmansworth WD3 38 BM47
 Rickmansworth (Sarratt)
 WD3 21 BE36
 Staines TW18, TW19 113 BE90
 Upminster RM14 73 FS60
 West Drayton UB7 94 BJ79
 Woking GU22 166 AY122
Moor La Crossing, Wat. WD18 39 BQ46
Moormead Dr, Epsom KT19 156 CS106
Moor Mead Rd, Twick. TW1 117 CG86
Moormede Cres, Stai. TW18 113 BF91
Moor Mill La, St.Alb. (Coln.St.)
 AL2 9 CE29
MOOR PARK, Nthwd. 39 BQ49
⊖ Moor Park 39 BR48
Moor Pk Est, Nthwd. HA6 39 BQ49
Moor Pk Gdns, Kings.T. KT2 118 CS94
Moor Pk Ind Est, Wat. WD18 39 BQ45
★ Moor Park Mansion, Rick.
 WD3 38 BN48
Moor Pk Mansion, Rick. WD3 38 BN48
Moor Pk Rd, Nthwd. HA6 39 BR50
Moor Pl, EC2 197 K7
Moor Rd, The, Sev. TN14 181 FH120
Moorside Rd, Brom. BR1 124 EE90
Moorsom Way, Couls. CR5 175 DK117
Moorstown Ct, Slou. SL1 92 AS75
Moor St, W1 195 N9
Moortown Rd, Wat. WD19 40 BW49
Moor Vw, Wat. WD18 39 BU45
Moot Ct, NW9 62 CN57
Moran Cl, St.Alb. (Brick.Wd.)
 AL2 8 BZ31
Morant Gdns, Rom. RM5 51 FB50
Morant Pl, N22
 off Commerce Rd 45 DM53
Morant Rd, Grays RM16 111 GH76
Morants Ct Cross, Sev. (Dunt.Grn.)
 TN14 181 FC118
Morants Ct Rd, Sev. (Dunt.Grn.)
 TN13 181 FC118
Morant St, E14 85 EA73
Mora Rd, NW2 63 CW63
Mora St, EC1 197 J3
Morat St, SW9 101 DM81
Moravian Pl, SW10
 off Milman's St 100 DD79
Moravian St, E2 84 DW69
Moray Av, Hayes UB3 77 BT74
Moray Cl, Edg. HA8
 off Pentland Av 42 CP47
 Romford RM1 51 FE52
Moray Dr, Slou. SL2 74 AU72
Moray Ms, N7 off Durham Rd 65 DM61
Moray Rd, N4 65 DM61
Moray Way, Rom. RM1 51 FD52
Mordaunt Gdns, Dag. RM9 88 EY66
Mordaunt Ho, NW10 80 CR67
Mordaunt Rd, NW10 80 CR67
Mordaunt St, SW9 101 DM83
MORDEN, Mord. 140 DA97
⊖ Morden 140 DB97
Morden Cl, SE13 103 EC82
 Tadworth KT20
 off Marbles Way 173 CX120
Morden Ct, Mord. SM4 140 DB98
Morden Gdns, Grnf. UB6 61 CF64
 Mitcham CR4 140 DD98
★ Morden Hall Park NT, Mord.
 SM4 140 DB97
Morden Hall Rd, Mord. SM4 140 DB97
Morden Hill, SE13 103 EC82
Morden La, SE13 103 EC81
MORDEN PARK, Mord. 139 CY99
⊸ Morden Road 140 DB96
Morden Rd, SE3 104 EG82
 SW19 140 DB95
 Mitcham CR4 140 DC98
 Romford RM6 70 EY59
Morden Rd Ms, SE3 104 EG82
⇌ Morden South 140 DA99
Morden St, SE13 103 EB81
Morden Way, Sutt. SM3 140 DA101
Morden Wf Rd, SE10 205 H7
Mordon Rd, Ilf. IG3 69 ET59
Mordred Rd, SE6 124 EE89
Moreau Wk, Slou. (Geo.Grn.) SL3
 off Alan Way 74 AY72
Morecambe Cl, E1 85 DX71
 Hornchurch RM12 71 FH64
Morecambe Gdns, Stan. HA7 41 CK49
Morecambe St, SE17 201 J9
Morecambe Ter, N18 46 DR49
More Cl, E16 86 EF72
 W14 99 CY77
 Purley CR8 159 DN111
Morecoombe Cl, Kings.T.
 KT2 118 CP94
Moree Way, N18 46 DU49
Moreland Av, Grays RM16 110 GC75
 Slough (Colnbr.) SL3 93 BC80
Moreland Cl, Slou. (Colnbr.) SL3
 off Moreland Av 93 BC80
Moreland Dr, Ger.Cr. SL9 57 AZ59
Moreland St, EC1 196 G2
Moreland Way, E4 47 EB48
More La, Esher KT10 136 CB103
Morel Ct, Sev. TN13 191 FH122
Morella Cl, Vir.W. GU25 132 AW98
Morella Rd, SW12 120 DF87
Morell Cl, Barn. EN5
 off Galdana Av 28 DC41
Morello Av, Uxb. UB8 77 BP71
Morello Cl, Swan. BR8 147 FD98
Morello Dr, Slou. SL3 75 AZ74
Moremead, Wal.Abb. EN9 15 ED33
Moremead Rd, SE6 123 DZ91
Morena St, SE6 123 EB87
Moresby Av, Surb. KT5 138 CP101
Moresby Rd, E5 66 DV60
Moresby Wk, SW8 101 DJ82
Moretaine Rd, Ashf. TW15
 off Hengrove Cres 114 BK90
Moreton Av, Islw. TW7 97 CE81
Moreton Cl, E5 66 DW61
 N15 66 DR58
 NW7 43 CW51
 SW1 199 L10
 Swanley BR8
 off Bonney Way 147 FE96
 Waltham Cross (Chsht.)
 EN7 14 DV27
Moreton Gdns, Wdf.Grn. IG8 48 EL50
Moreton Ind Est, Swan. BR8 147 FH98
Moreton Pl, SW1 199 L10
Moreton Rd, N15 66 DR58
 South Croydon CR2 160 DR106
 Worcester Park KT4 139 CU103
Moreton St, SW1 199 L10
Moreton Ter, SW1 199 L10
Moreton Ter Ms N, SW1 199 L10
Moreton Ter Ms S, SW1 199 L10
Moreton Twr, W3 80 CP74
Morewood Cl, Sev. TN13 190 FF123
Morewood Cl Ind Pk, Sev. TN13
 off Morewood Cl 190 FF123
Morford Cl, Ruis. HA4 59 BV59
Morford Way, Ruis. HA4 59 BV59
Morgan Av, E17 67 ED56
Morgan Cl, Dag. RM10 88 FA66
 Northwood HA6 39 BT51
Morgan Cres, Epp. (They.B.)
 CM16 33 ER36
Morgan Dr, Green. DA9 129 FS87
Morgan Gdns, Wat. (Ald.)
 WD25 24 CB38
Morgan Rd, N7 65 DN64
 W10 81 CZ71
 Bromley BR1 124 EG94
Morgans La, SE1 201 M3
 Hayes UB3 77 BR71
Morgan St, E3 85 DY69
 E16 86 EF71
Morgan Way, Rain. RM13 90 FJ69
 Woodford Green IG8 48 EL51
Moriatry Cl, N7 65 DL63
Morie St, SW18 120 DB85
Morieux Rd, E10 67 DZ60
Moring Rd, SW17 120 DG91
Morkyns Wk, SE21 122 DS90
Morland Av, Croy. CR0 142 DS102
 Dartford DA1 127 FH85
Morland Cl, NW11 64 DB60
 Hampton TW12 116 BZ92
 Mitcham CR4 140 DE97
Morland Gdns, NW10 80 CR66
 Southall UB1 78 CB74
Morland Ms, N1
 off Lofting Rd 83 DN66
Morland Rd, E17 67 DX57
 SE20 123 DX93
 Croydon CR0 142 DS102
 Dagenham RM10 88 FA66
 Harrow HA3 62 CL57
 Ilford IG1 69 EP61
 Sutton SM1 158 DC106
H Morland Rd Day Hosp, Dag.
 RM10 88 FA66
Morland Way, Wal.Cr. (Chsht.)
 EN8 15 DY28
Morley Av, E4 47 ED52
 N18 46 DU49
 N22 45 DN54
Morley Cl, Orp. BR6 145 EP103
 Slough SL3 93 AZ75
Morley Cres, Edg. HA8 42 CQ47
 Ruislip HA4 60 BW61
Morley Cres E, Stan. HA7 41 CJ54
Morley Cres W, Stan. HA7 41 CJ54
Morley Hill, Enf. EN2 30 DR38
Morley Rd, E10 67 EC60
 E15 86 EF68
 SE13 103 EC84
 Barking IG11 87 ER67
 Chislehurst BR7 145 EQ95
 Romford RM6 70 EY57
 South Croydon CR2 160 DT110
 Sutton SM3 139 CZ102
 Twickenham TW1 117 CK86
Morley Sq, Grays RM16 111 GG77
Morley St, SE1 200 E6
Morna Rd, SE5 102 DQ82
Morning La, E9 84 DW65

★ Place of interest ⇌ Railway station ⊖ London Underground station DLR Docklands Light Railway station ⊸ Tramlink station H Hospital

Morning Ri, Rick. (Loud.) WD3 22 BK41
Morningside Rd, Wor.Pk.
KT4 139 CV103
Mornington Av, W14 99 CZ77
Bromley BR1 144 EJ97
Ilford IG1 69 EN59
Mornington Cl, West. (Bigg.H.)
TN16 178 EK117
Woodford Green IG8 48 EG49
Mornington Ct, Bex. DA5 127 FC88
⊖ Mornington Crescent 83 DH68
Mornington Cres, NW1 83 DJ68
Hounslow TW5 95 BV81
Mornington Gro, E3 85 EA69
Mornington Ms, SE5 102 DQ81
Mornington Pl, NW1
off Mornington Ter 83 DH68
Mornington Rd, E4 47 ED45
E11 68 EF60
SE8 103 DZ80
Ashford TW15 115 BQ92
Greenford UB6 78 CB71
Loughton IG10 33 EQ41
Radlett WD7 9 CG34
Woodford Green IG8 48 EF49
Mornington St, NW1 83 DH68
Mornington Ter, NW1 83 DH67
Mornington Wk, Rich. TW10 117 CK91
Morocco St, SE1 201 M5
Morpeth Av, Borwd. WD6 26 CM38
Morpeth Gro, E9 85 DX67
Morpeth Rd, E9 84 DW67
Morpeth St, E2 85 DX69
Morpeth Ter, SW1 199 K7
Morpeth Wk, N17 off West Rd 46 DV52
Morrab Gdns, Ilf. IG3 69 ET62
Morrice Cl, Slou. SL3 93 AZ77
Morris Av, E12 69 EM64
Morris Cl, Croy. CR0 143 DY100
Gerrards Cross (Chal.St.P.)
SL9 37 AZ53
Orpington BR6 145 ES104
Morris Ct, E4 off Flaxen Rd 47 EB48
Waltham Abbey EN9 16 EF34
Morris Gdns, SW18 120 DA87
Dartford DA1 128 FN85
Morrish Rd, SW2 121 DL87
Morrison Av, N17 66 DS55
Morrison Rd, Bark. IG11 88 EY68
Hayes UB4 77 BV69
Morrison St, SW11 100 DG83
Morris Pl, N4 65 DN61
Morris Rd, E14 85 EB71
E15 68 EE63
Dagenham RM8 70 EZ61
Isleworth TW7 97 CF83
Romford RM3 51 FH52
Morris St, E1 84 DV72
Morriston Cl, Wat. WD19 40 BW50
Morris Way, St.Alb. (Lon.Col.)
AL2 10 CL26
Morse Cl, E13 86 EG69
Uxbridge (Hare.) UB9 38 BJ54
Morshead Rd, W9 82 DA69
Morson Rd, Enf. EN3 31 DY44
Morston Cl, Tad. KT20
off Waterfield 173 CV120
Morston Gdns, SE9 125 EM91
Morten Cl, SW4 121 DK86
Morten Gdns, Uxb. (Denh.)
UB9 58 BG59
Mortens Wd, Amer. HP7 20 AS40
Morteyne Rd, N17 46 DR53
Mortgramit Sq, SE18
off Powis St 105 EN76
Mortham St, E15 85 EE67
Mortimer Cl, NW2 63 CZ62
SW16 121 DK89
Bushey WD23 24 CB44
Mortimer Cres, NW6 82 DB67
Worcester Park KT4 138 CR104
Mortimer Dr, Enf. EN1 30 DR43
Mortimer Est, NW6 82 DB67
Mortimer Gate, Wal.Cr. EN8 15 DZ27
Mortimer Ho, W11
off St. Anns Rd 81 CX74
Mortimer Mkt, WC1 195 L5
Mortimer Pl, NW6 82 DB67
Mortimer Rd, E6 87 EM69
N1 84 DS66
NW10 81 CW69
W13 79 CJ72
Erith DA8 107 FD79
Mitcham CR4 140 DF95
Orpington BR6 146 EU103
Slough SL3 92 AX76
Westerham (Bigg.H.) TN16 162 EJ112
Mortimer Sq, W11
off St. Anns Rd 81 CX73
Mortimer St, W1 195 K7
Mortimer Ter, NW5
off Gordon Ho Rd 65 DH63
MORTLAKE, SW14 98 CQ83
⇌ Mortlake 98 CQ83
Mortlake Cl, Croy. CR0
off Richmond Rd 141 DL104
Mortlake Dr, Mitch. CR4 140 DE95
Mortlake High St, SW14 98 CR83
Mortlake Rd, E16 86 EH72
Ilford IG1 69 EQ63
Richmond TW9 98 CN80
Mortlake Ter, Rich. TW9
off Kew Rd 98 CN80
Mortlock Cl, SE15
off Cossall Wk 102 DV81
Morton, Tad. KT20
off Hudsons 173 CX121
Morton Cl, Wall. SM6
off Lancastrian Rd 159 DM108
Woking GU21 166 AW115
Morton Ct, Nthlt. UB5 60 CC64
Morton Cres, N14 45 DK49
Morton Gdns, Wall. SM6 159 DJ106
Morton Ms, SW5
off Earls Ct Gdns 100 DB77
Morton Pl, SE1 200 D7
Morton Rd, E15 86 EF66
Morton Rd, N1 84 DQ66
Morden SM4 140 DD99
Woking GU21 166 AW115
Morton Way, N14 45 DJ48
Morvale Cl, Belv. DA17 106 EZ77
Morval Rd, SW2 121 DN85
Morven Cl, Pot.B. EN6 12 DC31
Morven Rd, SW17 120 DF90
Morville Ho, SW18
off Fitzhugh Gro 120 DD86
Morville St, E3 85 EA68
Morwell St, WC1 195 N7
Mosbach Gdns, Brwd. CM13 55 GB47
Moscow Pl, W2
off Moscow Rd 82 DB73
Moscow Rd, W2 82 DA73
Moseley Row, SE10 205 L8
Moselle Av, N22 45 DN54
Moselle Cl, N8 off Miles Rd 65 DM55
Moselle Ho, N17
off William St 46 DT52
Moselle Pl, N17 off High Rd 46 DT52
Moselle Rd, West. (Bigg.H.)
TN16 178 EL118
Moselle St, N17 46 DT52
Mospey Cres, Epsom KT17 173 CT115
Moss Bk, Grays RM17 110 FZ78
Mossborough Cl, N12 44 DB51
Mossbury Rd, SW11 100 DE83
Moss Cl, E1
off Old Montague St 84 DU71
Pinner HA5 40 BZ54
Rickmansworth WD3 38 BK47
Mossdown Cl, Belv. DA17 106 FA77
Mossendew Cl, Uxb. (Hare.)
UB9 38 BK53
Mossfield, Cob. KT11 153 BU113
Mossford Ct, Ilf. IG6 69 EP55
Mossford Grn, Ilf. IG6 69 EP55
Mossford La, Ilf. IG6 49 EP54
Mossford St, E3 85 DZ70
Moss Gdns, Felt. TW13 115 BU89
South Croydon CR2
off Warren Av 161 DX108
Moss Hall Ct, N12 44 DB51
Moss Hall Cres, N12 44 DB51
Moss Hall Gro, N12 44 DB51
Mossington Gdns, SE16 202 F9
Moss La, Pnr. HA5 60 BZ55
Romford RM1
off Wheatsheaf Rd 71 FF58
Mosslea Rd, SE20 122 DW93
Bromley BR2 144 EK99
Orpington BR6 145 EQ104
Whyteleafe CR3 176 DT116
Mossop St, SW3 198 C8
Moss Rd, Dag. RM10 88 FA66
South Ockendon RM15 91 FW71
Watford WD25 7 BV34
Moss Side, St.Alb. (Brick.Wd.)
AL2 8 BZ30
Mossville Gdns, Mord. SM4 139 CZ97
Moss Way, Dart. (Lane End)
DA2 129 FR91
Moston Cl, Hayes UB3
off Fuller Way 95 BT78
Mostyn Av, Wem. HA9 62 CM64
Mostyn Gdns, NW10 81 CX68
Mostyn Gro, E3 85 DZ68
Mostyn Rd, SW9 101 DN81
SW19 139 CZ95
Bushey WD23 24 CC43
Edgware HA8 42 CR52
Mosul Way, Brom. BR2 144 EL100
Mosyer Dr, Orp. BR5 146 EX103
Motcomb St, SW1 198 E6
Moth Cl, Wall. SM6
off Lancastrian Rd 159 DL108
Mothers' Sq, E5 66 DV63
Motherwell Way, Grays
RM20 109 FU78
Motley Av, EC2
off Scrutton St 84 DS70
Motley St, SW8
off St. Rule St 101 DJ82
MOTSPUR PARK, N.Mal. 139 CU100
⇌ Motspur Park 139 CV99
Motspur Pk, N.Mal. KT3 139 CT100
MOTTINGHAM, SE9 124 EJ89
⇌ Mottingham 124 EL88
Mottingham Gdns, SE9 124 EK88
Mottingham La, SE9 124 EJ88
SE12 124 EJ88
Mottingham Rd, N9 31 DX44
SE9 124 EL89
Mottisfont Rd, SE2 106 EU76
Motts Hill La, Tad. KT20 173 CU123
Mott St, E4 31 ED38
Loughton (High Beach)
IG10 32 EF39
Mouchotte Cl, West. (Bigg.H.)
TN16 162 EH112
Moulins Rd, E9 84 DW67
Moulsford Ho, N7 65 DK64
Moultain Hill, Swan. BR8 147 FG98
Moulton Av, Houns. TW3 96 BY82
Moultrie Way, Upmin. RM14 73 FS59
Mound, The, SE9 125 EN90
Moundfield Rd, N16 66 DU58
Mount, The, N20 44 DC47
NW3 off Heath St 64 DC63
W3 80 CP74
Brentwood CM14 54 FW48
Coulsdon CR5 174 DG115
Epsom (Ewell) KT17 157 CT110
Esher KT10 154 CA107
Leatherhead (Fetch.) KT22 171 CE123
New Malden KT3 139 CT97
Potters Bar EN6 12 DB30
Rickmansworth WD3 22 BJ44
Romford RM3 52 FJ48
Tadworth KT20 183 CZ126
Virginia Water GU25 132 AX100
Waltham Cross (Chsht.)
EN7 14 DR26
Warlingham CR6 176 DU119
Wembley HA9 62 CP61
Mount, The, Wey. KT13 135 BS103
Woking GU21 166 AX118
Woking (St. John's) GU21 166 AU119
Worcester Park KT4 157 CV105
Mountacre Cl, SE26 122 DT91
Mount Adon Pk, SE22 122 DU87
Mountague Pl, E14 85 EC73
Mountain Ct, Dart. (Eyns.) DA4
off Pollyhaugh 148 FL103
Mount Angelus Rd, SW15 119 CT87
Mount Ararat Rd, Rich. TW10 118 CL85
Mount Ash Rd, SE26 122 DV90
Mount Av, E4 47 EA48
W5 79 CK71
Brentwood CM13 55 GA44
Caterham CR3 176 DQ124
Romford RM3 52 FQ51
Southall UB1 78 CA72
Mountbatten Cl, SE18 105 ES79
SE19 122 DS92
Slough SL1 92 AU76
Mountbatten Ct, SE16
off Rotherhithe St 84 DW74
Buckhurst Hill IG9 48 EK47
Mountbatten Gdns, Beck. BR3
off Balmoral Av 143 DY98
Mountbatten Ms, SW18
off Inman Rd 120 DC88
Mountbel Rd, Stan. HA7 41 CG53
Mount Cl, W5 79 CJ71
Barnet EN4 28 DG42
Bromley BR1 144 EL95
Carshalton SM5 158 DG109
Kenley CR8 176 DQ116
Leatherhead (Fetch.) KT22 171 CE123
Sevenoaks TN13 190 FF123
Woking GU22 166 AV121
Mount Cl, The, Vir.W. GU25 132 AX100
Mountcombe Cl, Surb. KT6 138 CL101
Mount Cor, Felt. TW13 116 BX89
Mount Ct, SW15
off Weimar St 99 CY83
West Wickham BR4 144 EE103
Mount Cres, Brwd. CM14 54 FX49
Mount Culver Av, Sid. DA14 126 EX93
Mount Dr, Bexh. DA6 126 EY85
Harrow HA2 60 BZ57
St. Albans (Park St.) AL2 9 CD25
Wembley HA9 62 CQ61
Mount Dr, The, Reig. RH2 184 DC132
Mountearl Gdns, SW16 121 DM90
Mount Echo Av, E4 47 EB47
Mount Echo Dr, E4 47 EB46
MOUNT END, Epp. 18 EZ32
Mount Ephraim La, SW16 121 DK90
Mount Ephraim Rd, SW16 121 DK90
Mount Est, The, E5
off Mount Pleasant La 66 DV61
Mount Felix, Walt. KT12 135 BT102
Mountfield Cl, SE6 123 ED87
Mountfield Rd, E6 87 EN68
N3 64 DA55
W5 79 CK72
Mountfield Way, Orp. BR5 146 EW98
Mountford St, E1 off Adler St 84 DU72
Mountfort Cres, N1
off Barnsbury Sq 83 DN66
Mountfort Ter, N1
off Barnsbury Sq 83 DN66
Mount Gdns, SE26 122 DV90
Mount Grace Rd, Pot.B. EN6 12 DA31
Mount Gro, Edg. HA8 42 CQ48
Mountgrove Rd, N5 65 DP62
Mount Harry Rd, Sev. TN13 190 FG123
MOUNT HERMON, Wok. 166 AX118
Mount Hermon Cl, Wok.
GU22 166 AX118
Mount Hermon Rd, Wok.
GU22 166 AX119
Mount Hill La, Ger.Cr. SL9 56 AV60
Mounthurst Rd, Brom. BR2 144 EF101
Mountington Pk Cl, Har. HA3 61 CK58
Mountjoy Cl, SE2 106 EV75
Mountjoy Ho, EC2
off The Barbican 84 DQ71
Mount La, Uxb. (Denh.) UB9 57 BD61
Mount Lee, Egh. TW20 112 AY92
Mount Ms, Hmptn. TW12 136 CB95
Mount Mills, EC1 196 G3
Mountnessing Bypass, Brwd.
CM15 55 GD41
Mount Nod Rd, SW16 121 DM90
Mount Pk, Cars. SM5 158 DG109
Mount Pk Av, Har. HA1 61 CD61
South Croydon CR2 159 DP109
Mount Pk Cres, W5 79 CK72
Mount Pk Rd, W5 79 CK71
Harrow HA1 61 CD62
Pinner HA5 59 BU57
Mount Pl, W3 off High St 80 CP74
Mount Pleasant, SE27 122 DQ91
WC1 196 C5
Barnet EN4 28 DE42
Epsom KT17 157 CT110
Ruislip HA4 60 BW61
Uxbridge (Hare.) UB9 38 BG53
Wembley HA0 80 CL67
Westerham (Bigg.H.) TN16 178 EK117
Weybridge KT13 134 BN104
Mount Pleasant Av, Brwd.
CM13 55 GE44
Mount Pleasant Cres, N4 65 DM59
Mount Pleasant Hill, E5 66 DV61
Mount Pleasant La, E5 66 DV61
St. Albans (Brick.Wd.) AL2 8 BY30
Mount Pleasant Pl, SE18
off Orchard Rd 105 ER77
Mount Pleasant Rd, E17 47 DY54
N17 46 DS54
NW10 81 CW66
SE13 123 EB86
W5 79 CJ70
Caterham CR3 176 DU123
Chigwell IG7 49 ER49
Dartford DA1 128 FM86
New Malden KT3 138 CQ97
Romford RM5 51 FD51
Mount Pleasant Vil, N4 65 DM59
Mount Pleasant Wk, Bex.
DA5 127 FC85
Mount Rd, NW2 63 CV62
NW4 63 CU58
SE19 122 DR93
SW19 120 DA89
Barnet EN4 28 DE43
Bexleyheath DA6 126 EX85
Chessington KT9 156 CM106
Dagenham RM8 70 EZ60
Dartford DA1 127 FF86
Epping CM16 18 EW32
Feltham TW13 116 BY90
Hayes UB3 95 BT75
Ilford IG1 69 EP64
Mitcham CR4 140 DE96
New Malden KT3 138 CR97
Woking GU22 166 AV121
Woking (Chobham)
GU24 150 AV112
Mount Row, W1 199 H1
Mountsfield Cl, Stai. TW19 114 BG86
Mountsfield Ct, SE13 123 ED86
Mountside, Felt. TW13 116 BY90
Stanmore HA7 41 CF53
Mounts Pond Rd, SE3 103 ED82
Mount Sq, The, NW3
off Heath St 64 DC62
Mounts Rd, Green. DA9 129 FV85
Mount Stewart Av, Har. HA3 61 CK58
Mount St, W1 198 G1
Mount Ter, E1 off New Rd 84 DV71
Mount Vernon, NW3 64 DC63
H Mount Vernon Hosp, Nthwd.
HA6 39 BP51
Mount Vw, NW7 42 CR48
W5 79 CK70
Enfield EN2 29 DM38
Mountview, Nthwd. HA6 39 BT51
Mount Vw, Rick. WD3 38 BH46
St. Albans (Lon.Col.) AL2 10 CL27
Mountview Ct, N8
off Green Las 65 DP56
Mount Vw Rd, E4 47 EC45
N4 65 DL59
NW9 62 CR56
Mountview Rd, Esher (Clay.)
KT10 155 CH108
Orpington BR6 146 EU101
Waltham Cross (Chsht.)
EN7 14 DS26
Mount Vil, SE27 121 DP90
Mount Way, Cars. SM5 158 DG109
Mountway, Pot.B. EN6 12 DA30
Mountwood, W.Mol. KT8 136 CA97
Mountwood Cl, S.Croy. CR2 160 DV110
Movers La, Bark. IG11 87 ES68
Mowat Ind Est, Wat. WD24 24 BW38
Mowatt Cl, N19 65 DK60
Mowbray Av, W.Byf. (Byfleet)
KT14 152 BL113
Mowbray Cres, Egh. TW20 113 BA92
Mowbray Rd, NW6 81 CY66
SE19 142 DT95
Barnet EN5 28 DC42
Edgware HA8 42 CN49
Richmond TW10 117 CJ90
Mowbrays Cl, Rom. RM5 51 FC53
Mowbrays Rd, Rom. RM5 51 FC54
Mowbrey Gdns, Loug. IG10 33 EQ40
Mowlem St, E2 84 DV68
Mowlem Trd Est, N17 46 DW52
Mowll St, SW9 101 DN80
Moxom Av, Wal.Cr. (Chsht.)
EN8 15 DY30
Moxon Cl, E13
off Whitelegg Rd 86 EF68
Moxon St, W1 194 F7
Barnet EN5 27 CZ41
Moye Cl, E2 off Dove Row 84 DU67
Moyers Rd, E10 67 EC59
Moylan Rd, W6 99 CY79
Moyne Ct, Wok. GU21
off Iveagh Rd 166 AT118
Moyne Pl, NW10 80 CN68
Moynihan Dr, N21 29 DL43
Moys Cl, Croy. CR0 141 DL100
Moyser Rd, SW16 121 DH92
Mozart St, W10 81 CZ69
Mozart Ter, SW1 198 G9
Muchelney Rd, Mord. SM4 140 DC100
Muckhatch La, Egh. TW20 133 BB97
MUCKINGFORD, S.le H. 111 GM76
Muckingford Rd, S.le H. (Linford)
SS17 111 GM77
Tilbury (W.Til.) RM18 111 GL77
DLR Mudchute 204 C8
Muddy La, Slou. SL2 74 AS71
Mud La, W5 79 CK71
Muggeridge Cl, S.Croy.
CR2 160 DR106
Muggeridge Rd, Dag. RM10 71 FB63
MUGSWELL, Couls. 184 DB125
Muirdown Av, SW14 98 CQ84
Muir Dr, SW18 120 DD86
Muirfield, W3 80 CS72
Muirfield Cl, SE16
off Ryder Dr 102 DV78
Watford WD19 40 BW49
Muirfield Cres, E14 204 B6
Muirfield Grn, Wat. WD19 40 BW49
Muirfield Rd, Wat. WD19 40 BX49
Woking GU21 166 AU118
Muirkirk Rd, SE6 123 EC88
Muir Rd, E5 66 DU63
Muir St, E16 off Newland St 87 EM74
Mulberry Av, Stai. TW19 114 BL88
Windsor SL4 92 AT83
Mulberry Business Cen,
SE16 203 J5
Mulberry Cl, E4 47 EA47
N8 65 DL57
NW3 off Hampstead High St 64 DD63
NW4 63 CW55
SE7 off Charlton Pk Rd 104 EK79
SE22 122 DU85
Mulberry Cl, SW3
off Beaufort St 100 DD79
SW16 121 DJ91
Amersham HP7 20 AT39
Barnet EN4 28 DD42
Northolt UB5
off Parkfield Av 78 BY68
Romford RM2 71 FH56
St. Albans (Park St.) AL2 8 CB28
Weybridge KT13 135 BP104
Woking GU21 150 AY114
Mulberry Ct, Bark. IG11
off Westrow Dr 87 ET66
Mulberry Cres, Brent. TW8 97 CH80
West Drayton UB7 94 BN75
Mulberry Dr, Purf. RM19 108 FM77
Slough SL3 92 AY78
Mulberry Gdns, Rad. (Shenley)
WD7 10 CL33
Mulberry Gate, Bans. SM7 173 CZ116
Mulberry Hill, Brwd. CM15 55 FZ45
Mulberry La, Croy. CR0 142 DT102
Mulberry Ms, SE14
off Lewisham Way 103 DZ81
Wallington SM6
off Ross Rd 159 DJ107
Mulberry Par, West Dr. UB7 94 BN76
Mulberry Pl, W6
off Chiswick Mall 99 CU78
Mulberry Rd, E8 84 DT66
Gravesend (Nthflt.) DA11 130 GE90
Mulberry St, E1 off Adler St 84 DU72
Mulberry Trees, Shep. TW17 135 BQ101
Mulberry Wk, SW3 100 DD79
Mulberry Way, E18 48 EH54
Belvedere DA17 107 FC75
Ilford IG6 69 EQ56
Mulgrave Rd, NW10 63 CT63
SE18 105 EM77
SW6 99 CZ79
W5 79 CK69
Croydon CR0 142 DR104
Harrow HA1 61 CG61
Sutton SM2 158 DA107
Mulgrave Way, Wok. (Knap.)
GU21 166 AS118
Mulholland Cl, Mitch. CR4 141 DH96
Mulkern Rd, N19 65 DK60
Mullards Cl, Mitch. CR4 140 DF102
Mullein Ct, Grays RM17 110 GD79
Mullens Rd, Egh. TW20 113 BB92
Muller Rd, SW4 121 DK86
Mullet Gdns, E2
off St. Peter's Cl 84 DU68
Mullins Path, SW14 98 CR83
Mullion Cl, Har. HA3 40 CB53
Mullion Wk, Wat. WD19
off Ormskirk Rd 40 BX49
Mull Wk, N1 off Clephane Rd 84 DQ65
Mulready St, NW8 194 B5
Multi-way, W3 off Valetta Rd 98 CS75
Multon Rd, SW18 120 DD87
Mulvaney Way, SE1 201 L5
Mumford Ct, EC2 197 J8
Mumford Rd, SE24
off Railton Rd 121 DP85
Mumfords La, Ger.Cr. (Chal.St.P.)
SL9 56 AU55
Muncaster Cl, Ashf. TW15 114 BN91
Muncaster Rd, SW11 120 DF85
Ashford TW15 115 BP92
Muncies Ms, SE6 123 EC89
Mundania Rd, SE22 122 DV86
Munday Rd, E16 86 EG72
Mundells, Wal.Cr. EN7 14 DU27
Munden Dr, Wat. WD25 24 BY37
Munden Gro, Wat. WD24 24 BW38
Munden St, W14 99 CY77
Munden Vw, Wat. WD25 24 BX36
Mundesley Cl, Wat. WD19 40 BW49
Mundesley Spur, Slou. SL1 74 AS72
Mundford Rd, E5 66 DW61
Mundon Gdns, Ilf. IG1 69 ER60
Mund St, W14 99 CZ78
Mundy St, N1 197 M2
Munford Dr, Swans. DA10 130 FY87
Mungo Pk Cl, Bushey (Bushey Hth.)
WD23 40 CC47
Mungo Pk Rd, Grav. DA12 131 GK92
Rainham RM13 89 FG65
Mungo Pk Way, Orp. BR5 146 EW101
Munnery Way, Orp. BR6 145 EN104
Munnings Gdns, Islw. TW7 117 CD85
Munro Dr, N11 45 DJ51
Munro Ms, W10 81 CY71
Munro Rd, Bushey WD23 24 CB43
Munro Ter, SW10 100 DD80
Munslow Gdns, Sutt. SM1 158 DD105
Munster Av, Houns. TW4 96 BZ84
Munster Ct, Tedd. TW11 117 CJ93
Munster Gdns, N13 45 DP49
Munster Ms, SW6
off Munster Rd 99 CY80
Munster Rd, SW6 99 CZ81
Teddington TW11 117 CH93
Munster Sq, NW1 195 J3
Munton Rd, SE17 201 J8
Murchison Av, Bex. DA5 126 EX88
Murchison Rd, E10 67 EC61
Murdoch Cl, Stai. TW18 114 BG92
Murdock Cl, E16
off Rogers Rd 86 EF72
Murdock St, SE15 102 DV79
Murfett Cl, SW19 119 CY89
Murfitt Way, Upmin. RM14 72 FN63
Muriel Av, Wat. WD18 24 BW43
Muriel St, N1 83 DM68
Murillo Rd, SE13 103 ED84
Murphy St, SE1 200 D5
Murray Av, Brom. BR1 144 EH96
Hounslow TW3 116 CB85
Murray Business Cen, Orp.
BR5 146 EV97
Murray Cres, Pnr. HA5 40 BX53

★ Place of interest ⇌ Railway station ⊖ London Underground station DLR Docklands Light Railway station Tramlink station H Hospital

Murray Grn, Wok. GU21
off Bunyard Dr 151 BC114
Murray Gro, N1 197 J1
Murray Ms, NW1 83 DK66
Murray Rd, SW19 119 CX93
W5 97 CJ77
Chertsey (Ott.) KT16 151 BC107
Northwood HA6 39 BS53
Orpington BR5 146 EV97
Richmond TW10 117 CH89
Murrays La, W.Byf. (Byfleet)
KT14 152 BK114
Murray Sq, E16 86 EG72
Murray St, NW1 83 DK66
Murray Ter, NW3 off Flask Wk 64 DD63
W5 off Murray Rd 97 CK77
Murrells Wk, Lthd. (Bkhm.)
KT23 170 CA123
Murreys, The, Ashtd. KT21 171 CK118
Mursell Est, SW8 101 DM81
Murthering La, Rom. RM4 35 FG43
Murtwell Dr, Chig. IG7 49 EQ51
Musard Rd, W6 99 CY79
W14 99 CY79
Musbury St, E1 84 DW72
Muscal, W6 99 CY79
Muscatel Pl, SE5
off Dalwood St 102 DS81
Muschamp Rd, SE15 102 DT83
Carshalton SM5 140 DE103
Muscovy Ho, Erith DA18
off Kale Rd 106 EY75
Muscovy St, EC3 201 N1
★ Museum Interpretative Cen, E6
off Norman Rd 87 EM70
Museum La, SW7
off Exhibition Rd 100 DD76
★ Museum of Artillery,
The Rotunda, SE18 105 EM78
★ Museum of Docklands,
E14 204 A1
★ Museum of Garden History,
SE1 200 B7
★ Museum of Instruments,
Royal Coll of Music, SW7 100 DD76
★ Museum of London, EC2 197 H7
★ Museum of Richmond, Rich.
TW9 117 CK85
Museum Pas, E2
off Victoria Pk Sq 84 DV69
Museum St, WC1 195 P7
Musgrave Cl, Barn. EN4 28 DC39
Waltham Cross EN7
off Allwood Rd 14 DT27
Musgrave Cres, SW6 100 DA81
Musgrave Rd, Islw. TW7 97 CF81
Musgrove Rd, SE14 103 DX81
★ Musical Mus, Brent. TW8
off High St 98 CL79
Musjid Rd, SW11
off Kambala Rd 100 DD82
Muskalls Cl, Wal.Cr. (Chsht.)
EN7 14 DU27
Musket Cl, Barn. EN4
off East Barnet Rd 28 DD43
Musquash Way, Houns. TW4 96 BW82
Mussenden La, Dart. (Hort.Kir.)
DA4 148 FQ99
Longfield (Fawk.Grn.) DA3 149 FS101
Muston Rd, E5 66 DV61
Mustow Pl, SW6
off Munster Rd 99 CZ82
Muswell Av, N10 45 DH54
MUSWELL HILL, N10 65 DH55
Muswell Hill, N10 65 DH55
Muswell Hill Bdy, N10 65 DH55
Muswell Hill Pl, N10 65 DH56
Muswell Hill Rd, N6 64 DG58
N10 64 DG56
Muswell Ms, N10
off Muswell Rd 65 DH55
Muswell Rd, N10 65 DH55
Mutchetts Cl, Wat. WD25 8 BY33
Mutrix Rd, NW6 82 DA67
Mutton La, Pot.B. EN6 11 CY31
Mutton Pl, NW1
off Harmood St 83 DH65
Muybridge Rd, N.Mal. KT3 138 CQ96
Myatt Rd, SW9 101 DP81
Myatt's Flds N, SW9
off Eythorne Rd 101 DN81
Myatt's Flds S, SW9
off Loughborough Rd 101 DN82
Mycenae Rd, SE3 104 EG80
Myddelton Av, Enf. EN1 30 DS38
Myddelton Cl, Enf. EN1 30 DT39
Myddelton Gdns, N21 45 DP45
Myddelton Pk, N20 44 DD48
Myddelton Pas, EC1 196 E2
Myddelton Rd, N8 65 DL56
Myddelton Sq, EC1 196 E2
Myddelton St, EC1 196 E3
Myddleton Av, N4 66 DQ61
Myddleton Ms, N22 45 DL52
Myddleton Path, Wal.Cr. (Chsht.)
EN7 14 DV31
Myddleton Rd, N22 45 DL52
Uxbridge UB8 76 BJ67
Myers La, SE14 103 DX79
Mygrove Cl, Rain. RM13 90 FK68
Mygrove Gdns, Rain. RM13 90 FK68
Mygrove Rd, Rain. RM13 90 FK68
Myles Ct, Wal.Cr. EN7 14 DQ29
Mylis Cl, SE26 122 DV91
Mylius Cl, SE14
off Kender St 102 DW81
Mylne Cl, Wal.Cr. EN8 14 DW27
Mylne St, EC1 196 D1
Mylor Cl, Wok. GU21 150 AY114
Mymms Dr, Hat. AL9 12 DA26
Mynns Cl, Epsom KT18 156 CP114
Mynterne Ct, SW19
off Swanton Gdns 119 CX88
Myra St, SE2 106 EU78
Myrdle St, E1 84 DU71
Myrke, The, Slou. (Datchet)
SL3 92 AT77
Myrna Cl, SW19 120 DE94
Myron Pl, SE13 103 EC83
Myrtle Av, Felt. TW14 95 BS84
Ruislip HA4 59 BU59
Myrtleberry Cl, E8
off Beechwood Rd 84 DT65
Myrtle Cl, Barn. EN4 44 DF46
Erith DA8 107 FE81
Slough (Colnbr.) SL3 93 BE81
Uxbridge UB8 off Violet Av 76 BM71
West Drayton UB7 94 BM76
Myrtle Cres, Slou. SL2 74 AT73
Myrtledene Rd, SE2 106 EU78
Myrtle Gdns, W7 79 CE74
Myrtle Gro, Enf. EN2 30 DR38
New Malden KT3 138 CQ96
South Ockendon (Aveley)
RM15 108 FQ75
Myrtle Pl, Dart. DA2 129 FR87
Myrtle Rd, E6 86 EL67
E17 67 DY58
N13 46 DQ48
W3 80 CQ74
Brentwood CM14 54 FW49
Croydon CR0 143 EA104
Dartford DA1 128 FK88
Hampton (Hmptn.H.)
TW12 116 CC93
Hounslow TW3 96 CC82
Ilford IG1 69 EP61
Romford RM3 52 FJ51
Sutton SM1 158 DC106
Myrtleside Cl, Nthwd. HA6 39 BR52
Myrtle Wk, N1 197 M1
Mysore Rd, SW11 100 DF83
Myton Rd, SE21 122 DR90

N

N1 Shop Cen, N1 83 DN68
Nadine Ct, Wall. SM6
off Woodcote Rd 159 DJ109
Nadine St, SE7 104 EJ78
Nafferton Ri, Loug. IG10 32 EK43
Nagle Cl, E17 47 ED54
Nag's Head Ct, EC1 197 H5
Nags Head La, Brwd. CM14 53 FR51
Upminster RM14 52 FQ53
Welling DA16 106 EV83
Nags Head Rd, Enf. EN3 30 DW42
Nags Head Shop Cen, N7 65 DM63
Nailsworth Cres, Red. RH1 185 DK129
Nailzee Cl, Ger.Cr. SL9 56 AY59
Nairn Ct, Til. RM18
off Dock Rd 111 GF82
Nairne Gro, SE24 122 DR85
Nairn Grn, Wat. WD19 39 BU48
Nairn Rd, Ruis. HA4 78 BW65
Nairn St, E14 85 EC71
Naish Ct, N1 83 DL67
Nallhead Rd, Felt. TW13 116 BW92
Namba Roy Cl, SW16 121 DM91
Namton Dr, Th.Hth. CR7 141 DM98
Nan Clark's La, NW7 43 CT47
Nancy Downs, Wat. WD19 40 BW45
Nankin St, E14 85 EA72
Nansen Rd, SW11 100 DG84
Gravesend DA12 131 GK91
Nansen Village, N12 44 DB49
Nantes Cl, SW18 100 DC84
Nantes Pas, E1 197 P6
Nant Rd, NW2 63 CZ61
Nant St, E2
off Cambridge Heath Rd 84 DV69
Naoroji St, WC1 196 D3
Nap, The, Kings L. WD4 6 BN29
Napier Av, E14 204 A10
SW6 99 CZ83
Napier Cl, SE8
off Amersham Vale 103 DZ80
W14 off Napier Rd 99 CZ76
Hornchurch RM11 71 FH60
St. Albans (Lon.Col.) AL2 9 CK25
West Drayton UB7 94 BM76
Napier Ct, SW6
off Ranelagh Gdns 99 CZ83
Waltham Cross (Chsht.) EN8
off Flamstead End Rd 14 DV28
Napier Dr, Bushey WD23 24 BY42
Napier Gro, N1 197 J1
Napier Ho, Rain. RM13 89 FF69
Napier Pl, W14 99 CZ76
Napier Rd, E6 87 EN67
E11 68 EE63
E15 86 EE68
N17 66 DS55
NW10 81 CV69
SE25 142 DV98
W14 99 CY76
Ashford TW15 115 BR94
Belvedere DA17 106 EZ77
Bromley BR2 144 EH98
Enfield EN3 31 DX43
Gravesend (Nthflt.) DA11 131 GF88
Hounslow (Hthrw.Air.) TW6 94 BK81
Isleworth TW7 97 CG84
South Croydon CR2 160 DR108
Wembley HA0 61 CK64
Napier Ter, N1 83 DP66
Napoleon Rd, E5 66 DV62
Twickenham TW1 117 CH87
Napsbury Av, St.Alb. (Lon.Col.)
AL2 9 CJ26
Napton Cl, Hayes UB4
off Kingsash Dr 78 BY70
Narbonne Av, SW4 121 DJ85
Narboro Ct, Rom. RM1
off Manor Rd 71 FG57
Narborough Cl, Uxb. UB10
off Aylsham Dr 59 BQ61
Narborough St, SW6 100 DB82
Narcissus Rd, NW6 64 DA64
Narcot La, Ch.St.G. HP8 36 AU48
Gerrards Cross (Chal.St.P.)
SL9 36 AV52
Narcot Rd, Ch.St.G. HP8 36 AU48
Narcot Way, Ch.St.G. HP8 36 AU49
Nare Rd, S.Ock. (Aveley)
RM15 90 FQ73
Naresby Fold, Stan. HA7
off Bernays Cl 41 CJ51
Narford Rd, E5 66 DU62
Narrow Boat Cl, SE28
off Ridge Cl 105 ER75
Narrow La, Warl. CR6 176 DV119
Narrow St, E14 85 DY73
Narrow Way, Brom. BR2 144 EL100
Nascot Pl, Wat. WD17 23 BV39
Nascot Rd, Wat. WD17 23 BV40
Nascot St, W12 81 CW72
Watford WD17 23 BV40
Nascot Wd Rd, Wat. WD17 23 BT37
Naseberry Ct, E4
off Merriam Cl 47 EC50
Naseby Cl, NW6
off Fairfax Rd 82 DC66
Isleworth TW7 97 CE81
Naseby Ct, Walt. KT12
off Clements Rd 136 BW103
Naseby Rd, SE19 122 DR93
Dagenham RM10 70 FA62
Ilford IG5 49 EM53
Nash Cl, Borwd. (Elstree)
WD6 26 CM42
Sutton SM1 140 DD104
Nash Ct, E14 204 B3
Nash Cft, Grav. (Nthflt.)
DA11 130 GE91
Nash Dr, Red. RH1 184 DF132
Nash Gdns, Red. RH1 184 DF132
Nash Grn, Brom. BR1 124 EG93
Hemel Hempstead HP3 6 BM25
Nash La, Kes. BR2 162 EG106
Nash Mills La, Hem.H. HP3 6 BM26
Nash Rd, N9 46 DW47
SE4 103 DY84
Romford RM6 70 EX56
Slough SL3 93 AZ77
Nash St, NW1 195 J3
Nash's Yd, Uxb. UB8
off Bakers Rd 76 BK66
Nash Way, Har. HA3 61 CH58
Nasmyth St, W6 99 CV76
Nassau Path, SE28
off Disraeli Cl 88 EW74
Nassau Rd, SW13 99 CT81
Nassau St, W1 195 K7
Nassington Rd, NW3 64 DE63
Natalie Cl, Felt. TW14 115 BR87
Natalie Ms, Twick. TW2
off Sixth Cross Rd 117 CD90
Natal Rd, N11 45 DL51
SW16 121 DK93
Ilford IG1 69 EP63
Thornton Heath CR7 142 DR97
Nathan Cl, Upmin. RM14 73 FS60
Nathaniel Cl, E1
off Thrawl St 84 DT71
Nathans Rd, Wem. HA0 61 CJ60
Nathan Way, SE28 105 ES77
★ National Army Mus,
SW3 100 DF79
H National Blood Service/
Brentwood Tranfusion
Service, Brwd. CM15 55 FZ46
★ National Gall, WC2 199 N1
H National Hosp for Neurology
& Neurosurgery, N2 64 DE56
H National Hosp for Neurology
& Neurosurgery, The, WC1 196 A5
★ National Maritime Mus,
SE10 103 ED79
★ National Portrait Gall,
WC2 199 N1
National Ter, SE16
off Bermondsey Wall E 102 DV75
Nation Way, E4 47 EC46
★ Natural History Mus,
SW7 100 DD76
Naunton Way, Horn. RM12 72 FK62
Naval Row, E14 85 EC73
Naval Wk, Brom. BR1
off High St 144 EG97
Navarino Gro, E8 84 DU65
Navarino Rd, E8 84 DU65
Navarre Gdns, Rom. RM5 51 FB51
Navarre Rd, E6 86 EL68
Navarre St, E2 197 P4
Navenby Wk, E3
off Rounton Rd 85 EA70
Navestock Cl, E4
off Mapleton Rd 47 EC48
Navestock Cres, Wdf.Grn. IG8 48 EJ53
Navestock Ho, Bark. IG11 88 EV68
Navigator Dr, Sthl. UB2 96 CC75
Navy St, SW4 101 DK83
Naylor Gro, Enf. EN3
off South St 31 DX43
Naylor Rd, N20 44 DC47
SE15 102 DV80
Naylor Ter, Slou. (Colnbr.) SL3
off Vicarage Way 93 BC80
Nazareth Gdns, SE15 102 DV82
NAZEING GATE, Wal.Abb. 16 EJ25
Nazeing Wk, Rain. RM13
off Ongar Way 89 FE67
Nazrul St, E2 197 P2
Neagle Cl, Borwd. WD6
off Balcon Way 26 CQ39
Neal Av, Sthl. UB1 78 BZ70
Neal Cl, Ger.Cr. SL9 57 BB60
Northwood HA6 39 BU53
Neal Ct, Wal.Abb. EN9 16 EF33
Nealden St, SW9 101 DM83
Neale Cl, N2 64 DC55
Neal St, WC2 195 P9
Watford WD18 24 BW43
Neal's Yd, WC2 195 P9
Near Acre, NW9 43 CT53
NEASDEN, NW2 62 CS62
⊖ Neasden 62 CS64
Neasden Cl, NW10 62 CS64
Neasden La, NW10 62 CS63
Neasden La N, NW10 62 CR62
Neasham Rd, Dag. RM8 70 EV64
Neate St, SE5 102 DT79
Neath Gdns, Mord. SM4 140 DC100
Neathouse Pl, SW1 199 K8
Neats Acre, Ruis. HA4 59 BR59
Neatscourt Rd, E6 86 EK71
Neave Cres, Rom. RM3 52 FJ53
Neb La, Oxt. RH8 187 EC131
Nebraska St, SE1 201 K5
Neckinger, SE16 202 A6
Neckinger Est, SE16 202 A6
Neckinger St, SE1 202 A5
Nectarine Way, SE13 103 EB82
Needham Rd, W11
off Westbourne Gro 82 DA72
Needham Ter, NW2
off Kara Way 63 CX62
Needleman St, SE16 203 H5
Needles Bk, Gdse. RH9 186 DV131
Neela Cl, Uxb. UB10 59 BP63
Neeld Cres, NW4 63 CV57
Wembley HA9 62 CN64
Neeld Par, Wem. HA9
off Harrow Rd 62 CN64
Neil Cl, Ashf. TW15 115 BQ92
Neil Wates Cres, SW2 121 DN88
Nelgarde Rd, SE6 123 EA87
Nella Rd, W6 99 CX79
Nelldale Rd, SE16 202 F8
Nellgrove Rd, Uxb. UB10 77 BP70
Nell Gwynn Cl, Rad. (Shenley)
WD7 10 CL32
Nell Gwynne Av, Shep.
TW17 135 BR100
Nell Gwynne Cl, Epsom KT19
off Ripley Way 156 CN111
Nello James Gdns, SE27 122 DR91
Nelmes Cl, Horn. RM11 72 FM57
Nelmes Cres, Horn. RM11 72 FL57
Nelmes Rd, Horn. RM11 72 FL59
Nelmes Way, Horn. RM11 72 FL56
Nelson Cl, NW6 82 DA68
Brentwood CM14 54 FX50
Croydon CR0 141 DP102
Feltham TW14 115 BT88
Romford RM7 51 FB53
Slough SL3 92 AX77
Uxbridge UB10 77 BP69
Walton-on-Thames KT12 135 BV102
Westerham (Bigg.H.) TN16 178 EL117
Nelson Ct, SE16
off Brunel Rd 84 DW74
Nelson Gdns, E2 84 DU69
Hounslow TW3 116 CA86
Nelson Gro Rd, SW19 140 DB95
H Nelson Hosp, SW20 139 CZ96
Nelson La, Uxb. UB10
off Nelson Rd 77 BP69
Nelson Mandela Cl, N10 44 DG54
Nelson Mandela Rd, SE3 104 EJ83
Nelson Pas, EC1 197 J3
Nelson Pl, N1 196 G1
Sidcup DA14 126 EU91
Nelson Rd, E4 47 EB51
E11 68 EG56
N8 65 DM57
N9 46 DV47
N15 66 DS56
SE10 103 EC79
SW19 120 DB94
Ashford TW15 114 BL92
Belvedere DA17 106 EZ78
Bromley BR2 144 EJ98
Caterham CR3 176 DR123
Dartford DA1 128 FJ86
Enfield EN3 31 DX44
Gravesend (Nthflt.) DA11 131 GF89
Harrow HA1 61 CD60
Hounslow TW3 116 CC87
Hounslow (Hthrw.Air.) TW6 94 BM81
New Malden KT3 138 CR99
Rainham RM13 89 FF68
Sidcup DA14 126 EU91
South Ockendon RM15 91 FW68
Stanmore HA7 41 CJ51
Twickenham TW2 116 CC86
Uxbridge UB10 77 BP69
★ Nelson's Column, WC2 199 P2
Nelson Sq, SE1 200 F4
Nelson's Row, SW4 101 DK84
Nelson St, E1 84 DV72
E6 87 EM68
E16 off Huntingdon St 86 EF73
Nelsons Yd, NW1
off Mornington Cres 83 DJ68
Nelson Ter, N1 196 G1
Nelson Trd Est, SW19 140 DB95
Nelson Wk, SE16 203 L3
Nelwyn Av, Horn. RM11 72 FM57
Nemoure Rd, W3 80 CQ73
Nene Gdns, Felt. TW13 116 BZ89
Nene Rd, Houns. (Hthrw.Air.)
TW6 95 BP81
Nepaul Rd, SW11 100 DE82
Nepean St, SW15 119 CU86
Neptune Ct, Borwd. WD6
off Clarendon Rd 26 CN41
Neptune Rd, Har. HA1 61 CD58
Hounslow (Hthrw.Air.) TW6 95 BR81
Neptune St, SE16 202 F6
Neptune Wk, Erith DA8 107 FD77
Nesbit Rd, SE9 104 EK84
Nesbitt Cl, SE3 off Hurren Cl 104 EE83
Nesbitts All, Barn. EN5
off Bath Pl 27 CZ41
Nesbitt Sq, SE19
off Coxwell Rd 122 DS94
Nesham St, E1 202 B2
Ness Rd, Erith DA8 108 FK79
Ness St, SE16 202 B6
Nesta Rd, Wdf.Grn. IG8 48 EE51
Nestles Av, Hayes UB3 95 BT76
Neston Rd, Wat. WD24 24 BW37
Nestor Av, N21 29 DP44
Nethan Dr, S.Ock. (Aveley)
RM15 90 FQ73
Netheravon Rd, W4 99 CT77
W7 79 CF74
Netheravon Rd S, W4 99 CT78
Netherbury Rd, W5 97 CK76
Netherby Gdns, Enf. EN2 29 DL42
Netherby Pk, Wey. KT13 153 BS106
Netherby Rd, SE23 122 DW87
Nether Cl, N3 44 DA52
Nethercote Av, Wok. GU21 166 AT117
Nethercourt Av, N3 44 DA51
Netherfield Gdns, Bark. IG11 87 ER65
Netherfield Rd, N12 44 DB50
SW17 120 DG90
Netherford Rd, SW4 101 DJ82
Netherhall Gdns, NW3 82 DC65
Netherhall Way, NW3
off Netherhall Gdns 64 DC64
Netherlands, The, Couls.
CR5 175 DJ119
Netherlands Rd, Barn. EN5 28 DD44
Netherleigh Cl, N6 65 DH60
Nethern Ct Rd, Cat. (Wold.)
CR3 177 EA123
Netherne Dr, Couls. CR5 175 DH121
Netherne La, Couls. CR5 175 DK121
Redhill RH1 175 DJ123
Netherpark Dr, Rom. RM2 51 FF54
Nether St, N3 44 DA53
N12 44 DA52
Netherton Gro, SW10 100 DC79
Netherton Rd, N15 66 DR58
Twickenham TW1 117 CH85
Netherwood, N2 44 DD54
Netherwood Pl, W14
off Netherwood Rd 99 CX76
Netherwood Rd, W14 99 CX76
Netherwood St, NW6 81 CZ66
Netherwood St Est, NW6 81 CZ66
Netley Cl, Croy. (New Adgtn.)
CR0 161 EC108
Sutton SM3 157 CX106
Netley Dr, Walt. KT12 136 BZ101
Netley Gdns, Mord. SM4 140 DC101
Netley Rd, E17 67 DZ57
Brentford TW8 98 CL79
Hounslow (Hthrw.Air.) TW6 95 BR81
Ilford IG2 69 ER57
Morden SM4 140 DC101
Netley St, NW1 195 K3
Nettlecombe Cl, Sutt. SM2 158 DB109
Nettleden Av, Wem. HA9 80 CN65
Nettlefold Pl, SE27 121 DP90
Nettlestead Cl, Beck. BR3
off Copers Cope Rd 123 DZ94
Nettleton Rd, SE14 103 DX81
Hounslow (Hthrw.Air.)
TW6 95 BP81
Uxbridge UB10 58 BM63
Nettlewood Rd, SW16 121 DK94
Neuchatel Rd, SE6 123 DZ89
Nevada Cl, N.Mal. KT3
off Georgia Rd 138 CQ98
Nevada St, SE10 103 EC79
Nevell Rd, Grays RM16 111 GH76
Nevern Pl, SW5 100 DA77
Nevern Rd, SW5 100 DA77
Nevern Sq, SW5 100 DA77
Nevil Cl, Nthwd. HA6 39 BQ50
Neville Av, N.Mal. KT3 138 CR95
Neville Cl, E11 68 EF62
NW1 195 N1
NW6 81 CZ68
SE15 102 DU80
W3 off Acton La 98 CQ75
Banstead SM7 158 DB114
Esher KT10 154 BZ107
Hounslow TW3 96 CB82
Potters Bar EN6 11 CZ31
Sidcup DA15 125 ET91
Slough (Stoke P.) SL2 74 AT65
Neville Dr, N2 64 DC58
Neville Gdns, Dag. RM8 70 EX62
Neville Gill Cl, SW18 120 DA86
Neville Pl, N22 45 DM53
Neville Rd, E7 86 EG66
NW6 81 CZ68
W5 79 CK70
Croydon CR0 142 DR101
Dagenham RM8 70 EX61
Ilford IG6 49 EQ53
Kingston upon Thames
KT1 138 CN96
Richmond TW10 117 CJ90
Nevilles Ct, NW2 63 CU62
Neville St, SW7 100 DD78
Neville Ter, SW7 100 DD78
Neville Wk, Cars. SM5
off Green Wrythe La 140 DE101
Nevill Gro, Wat. WD24 23 BV39
Nevill Rd, N16 66 DS63
Nevill Way, Loug. IG10
off Valley Hill 48 EL45
Nevin Dr, E4 47 EB46
Nevinson Cl, SW18 120 DD86
Nevis Cl, Rom. RM1 51 FE51
Nevis Rd, SW17 120 DG89
Newacres Rd, SE28 87 ES74
NEW ADDINGTON, Croy. 161 ED109
New Addington 161 EC110
Newall Rd, Houns. (Hthrw.Air.)
TW6 95 BQ81
New Arc, Uxb. UB8
off High St 76 BK67
Newark Cl, Wok. (Ripley)
GU23 168 BG121
Newark Cotts, Wok. (Ripley)
GU23 168 BG121
Newark Ct, Walt. KT12
off St. Johns Dr 136 BW102
Newark Cres, NW10 80 CR69
Newark Grn, Borwd. WD6 26 CR41
Newark Knok, E6 87 EN72

299

New - Nig

Newark La, Wok. (Ripley) GU23 .... 167 BF118
Newark Par, NW4
off Greyhound Hill 63 CU55
Newark Rd, S.Croy. CR2 .... 160 DR107
Newark St, E1 .... 84 DV71
Newark Way, NW4 .... 63 CU56
New Ash Cl, N2
off Oakridge Dr 64 DD55
NEW ASH GREEN, Long. 149 FX103
New Atlas Wf, E14 .... 203 N7
New Barn Cl, Wall. SM6
off Merlin Cl 159 DM107
NEW BARNET, Barn. 28 DB42
⇌ New Barnet 28 DD43
New Barn La, Beac. HP9 .... 36 AS49
Sevenoaks (Cudham) TN14 .... 179 EQ116
Westerham TN16 .... 179 EQ118
Whyteleafe CR3 .... 176 DS117
New Barn Rd, Grav. (Sthflt.) DA13 .... 130 GC90
Swanley BR8 .... 147 FE95
New Barns Av, Mitch. CR4 .... 141 DK98
New Barn St, E13 .... 86 EG70
New Barns Way, Chig. IG7 .... 49 EP48
New Battlebridge La, Red. RH1 .... 185 DH130
NEW BECKENHAM, Beck. 123 DZ93
⇌ New Beckenham 123 DZ94
Newberries Av, Rad. WD7 .... 25 CJ35
New Berry La, Walt. KT12 .... 154 BX106
Newbery Rd, Erith DA8 .... 107 FF81
Newbiggin Path, Wat. WD19 .... 40 BW49
Newbolt Av, Sutt. SM3 .... 157 CW106
Newbolt Rd, Stan. HA7 .... 41 CF51
New Bond St, W1 .... 195 H9
Newborough Grn, N.Mal. KT3 .... 138 CR98
New Brent St, NW4 .... 63 CW57
Newbridge Pt, SE23
off Windrush La 123 DX90
New Br St, EC4 .... 196 F9
New Broad St, EC2 .... 197 M7
New Bdy, W5 .... 79 CJ73
Hampton (Hmptn.H.) TW12
off Hampton Rd 117 CD92
Newburgh Rd, W3 .... 80 CQ74
Grays RM17 .... 110 GD78
Newburgh St, W1 .... 195 K9
New Burlington Ms, W1 .... 195 K10
New Burlington Pl, W1 .... 195 K10
New Burlington St, W1 .... 195 K10
Newburn St, SE11 .... 200 C10
Newbury Av, Enf. EN3 .... 31 DZ38
Newbury Cl, Nthlt. UB5 .... 78 BZ65
Romford RM3 .... 52 FK51
Newbury Gdns, Epsom KT19 .... 157 CT105
Romford RM3 .... 52 FK51
Upminster RM14 .... 72 FM62
Newbury Ho, N22 .... 45 DL53
Newbury Ms, NW5
off Malden Rd 82 DG65
NEWBURY PARK, Ilf. 69 ER57
⊖ Newbury Park 69 ER58
Newbury Rd, E4 .... 47 EC51
Bromley BR2 .... 144 EG97
Hounslow (Hthrw.Air.) TW6 .... 94 BM81
Ilford IG2 .... 69 ER58
Romford RM3 .... 52 FK50
Newbury St, EC1 .... 197 H7
Newbury Wk, Rom. RM3 .... 52 FK50
Newbury Way, Nthlt. UB5 .... 78 BY65
New Butt La, SE8 .... 103 EA80
New Butt La N, SE8
off Reginald Rd 103 EA80
Newby Cl, Enf. EN1 .... 30 DS40
Newby Pl, E14 .... 85 EC73
Newby St, SW8 .... 101 DH83
New Caledonian Wf, SE16 .... 203 M6
Newcastle Av, Ilf. IG6 .... 50 EU51
Newcastle Cl, EC4 .... 196 F8
Newcastle Pl, W2 .... 194 A7
Newcastle Row, EC1 .... 196 E4
New Cavendish St, W1 .... 195 J6
New Change, EC4 .... 197 H9
New Chapel Sq, Felt. TW13 .... 115 BV88
New Charles St, EC1 .... 196 G2
NEW CHARLTON, SE7 .... 104 EJ77
New Ch Ct, SE19
off Waldegrave Rd 122 DU94
New Ch Rd, SE5 .... 102 DQ80
New City Rd, E13 .... 86 EJ69
New Cl, SW19 .... 140 DC97
Feltham TW13 .... 116 BY92
New Coll Ct, NW3
off College Cres 82 DC66
New Coll Ms, N1
off Islington Pk St 83 DN66
New Coll Par, NW3
off College Cres 82 DD65
Newcombe Gdns, SW16 .... 121 DL91
Newcombe Pk, NW7 .... 42 CS50
Wembley HA0 .... 80 CM67
Newcombe Ri, West Dr. UB7 .... 76 BL72
Newcombe St, W8
off Kensington Pl 82 DA74
Newcomen Rd, E11 .... 68 EF62
SW11 .... 100 DD83
Newcomen St, SE1 .... 201 K4
Newcome Path, Rad. (Shenley) WD7 off Newcome Rd 10 CN34
Newcome Rd, Rad. (Shenley) WD7 .... 10 CN34
New Compton St, WC2 .... 195 N9
New Concordia Wf, SE1 .... 202 B4
New Coppice, Wok. GU21 .... 166 AS119
New Cotts, Rain. (Wenn.) RM13 .... 90 FJ72
New Ct, EC4 .... 196 D10
Addlestone KT15 .... 134 BJ104
Newcourt, Uxb. UB8 .... 76 BJ71
Newcourt St, NW8 .... 194 B1
★ New Covent Garden Mkt, SW8 .... 101 DK80
New Covent Gdn Mkt, SW8 .... 101 DK80
New Crane Pl, E1 .... 202 F2
Newcroft Cl, Uxb. UB8 .... 76 BM71
NEW CROSS, SE14 .... 103 DY81
⇌ New Cross 103 DZ80
⊖ New Cross 103 DZ80
NEW CROSS GATE, SE14 .... 103 DX81
⇌ New Cross Gate 103 DY80
⊖ New Cross Gate 103 DY80
New Cross Rd, SE14 .... 102 DW80
Newdales Cl, N9
off Balham Rd 46 DU47
Newdene Av, Nthlt. UB5 .... 78 BX68
Newdigate Grn, Uxb. (Hare.) UB9 .... 38 BK53
Newdigate Rd, Uxb. (Hare.) UB9 .... 38 BJ53
Newdigate Rd E, Uxb. (Hare.) UB9 .... 38 BK53
Newell St, E14 .... 85 DZ72
NEW ELTHAM, SE9 .... 125 EN89
⇌ New Eltham 125 EP88
New End, NW3 .... 64 DC63
New End Sq, NW3 .... 64 DD63
Newent Cl, SE15 .... 102 DS80
Carshalton SM5 .... 140 DF102
New Era Est, N1
off Phillipp St 84 DS67
New Fm Av, Brom. BR2 .... 144 EG98
New Fm Dr, Rom. (Abridge) RM4 .... 34 EV41
New Fm La, Nthwd. HA6 .... 39 BS53
New Ferry App, SE18 .... 105 EN76
New Fetter La, EC4 .... 196 E8
Newfield Cl, Hmptn. TW12
off Percy Rd 136 CA95
Newfield Ri, NW2 .... 63 CV62
New Ford Rd, Wal.Cr. EN8 .... 15 DZ34
New Forest La, Chig. IG7 .... 49 EN51
Newgale Gdns, Edg. HA8 .... 42 CM53
New Gdn Dr, West Dr. UB7
off Drayton Gdns 94 BL75
Newgate, Croy. CR0 .... 142 DQ102
Newgate Cl, Felt. TW13 .... 116 BY89
Newgate St, E4 .... 48 EF48
EC1 .... 196 G8
Newgatestreet Rd, Wal.Cr. (Chsht.) EN7 .... 13 DP27
Newgate St Village, Hert. SG13 .... 13 DL25
New Globe Wk, SE1 .... 201 H2
New Goulston St, E1 .... 197 P8
New Grn Pl, SE19
off Hawke Rd 122 DS93
New Hall Cl, Hem.H. (Bov.) HP3 .... 5 BA27
Newhall Ct, Wal.Abb. EN9 .... 16 EF33
New Hall Dr, Rom. RM3 .... 52 FL53
Newhall Gdns, Walt. KT12
off Rodney Rd 136 BW103
H Newham Gen Hosp, E13 .... 86 EJ70
Newhams Row, SE1 .... 201 N5
Newham Way, E6 .... 86 EJ71
E16 .... 86 EF71
Newhaven Cl, Hayes UB3 .... 95 BT77
Newhaven Cres, Ashf. TW15 .... 115 BR92
Newhaven Gdns, SE9 .... 104 EK84
Newhaven La, E16 .... 86 EF70
Newhaven Rd, SE25 .... 142 DR99
NEW HAW, Add. 152 BK108
New Haw Rd, Add. KT15 .... 152 BJ106
New Heston Rd, Houns. TW5 .... 96 BZ80
New Horizons Ct, Brent. TW8
off Shield Dr 97 CG79
Newhouse Av, Rom. RM6 .... 70 EX55
Newhouse Cl, N.Mal. KT3 .... 138 CS101
Newhouse Cres, Wat. WD25 .... 7 BV32
New Ho La, Epp. (N.Wld.Bas.) CM16 .... 19 FC25
Gravesend DA11 .... 131 GF90
Newhouse Rd, Hem.H. (Bov.) HP3 .... 5 BA26
Newhouse Wk, Mord. SM4 .... 140 DC101
Newick Cl, Bex. DA5 .... 127 FB86
Newick Rd, E5 .... 66 DV62
Newing Grn, Brom. BR1 .... 124 EK94
NEWINGTON, SE1 .... 201 H8
Newington Barrow Way, N7 .... 65 DM62
Newington Butts, SE1 .... 200 G9
SE11 .... 200 G9
Newington Causeway, SE1 .... 200 G7
Newington Grn, N1 .... 66 DR64
N16 .... 66 DR64
Newington Grn Rd, N1 .... 84 DR65
New Inn Bdy, EC2 .... 197 N4
New Inn Pas, WC2 .... 196 C9
New Inn St, EC2 .... 197 N4
New Inn Yd, EC2 .... 197 N4
New James Ct, SE15
off Nunhead La 102 DV83
New Jersey Ter, SE15
off Nunhead La 102 DV83
New Jubilee Ct, Wdf.Grn. IG8
off Grange Av 48 EG52
New Kent Rd, SE1 .... 201 H7
New Kings Rd, SW6 .... 99 CZ82
New King St, SE8 .... 103 EA79
Newland Cl, Pnr. HA5 .... 40 BY51
Newland Ct, Wem. HA9
off Forty Av 62 CN61
Newland Dr, Enf. EN1 .... 30 DV39
Newland Gdns, W13 .... 97 CG75
Newland Rd, N8 .... 65 DL55
Newlands, Abb.L. (Bedmond) WD5 .... 7 BT26
Newlands, The, Wall. SM6 .... 159 DJ108
Newlands Av, Rad. WD7 .... 9 CF34
Thames Ditton KT7 .... 137 CE102
Woking GU22 .... 167 AZ121
Newlands Cl, Brwd. CM13 .... 55 GD45
Edgware HA8 .... 42 CL48
Southall UB2 .... 96 BY78
Walton-on-Thames KT12 .... 154 BY105
Wembley HA0 .... 79 CJ65
Newlands Ct, SE9 .... 125 EN86
Newlands Dr, Slou. (Colnbr.) SL3 .... 93 BE83
Newlands Pk, SE26 .... 123 DX92
Newlands Pl, Barn. EN5 .... 27 CX43
Newlands Quay, E1 .... 202 F1
Newlands Rd, SW16 .... 141 DL96
Woodford Green IG8 .... 48 EF47
Newland St, E16 .... 86 EL74
Newlands Wk, Wat. WD25
off Trevellance Way 8 BX33
Newlands Way, Chess. KT9 .... 155 CJ106
Potters Bar EN6 .... 12 DB30
Newlands Wd, Croy. CR0 .... 161 DZ109
New La, Guil. (Sutt.Grn.) GU4 .... 166 AY122
Newling Cl, E6 off Porter Rd 87 EM72
New Lo Dr, Oxt. RH8 .... 188 EF128
New London St, EC3 .... 197 N10
New Lydenburg St, SE7 .... 104 EJ76
Newlyn Cl, Orp. BR6 .... 163 ET105
St. Albans (Brick.Wd.) AL2 .... 8 BY30
Uxbridge UB8 .... 76 BN71
Newlyn Gdns, Har. HA2 .... 60 BZ59
Newlyn Rd, N17 .... 46 DT53
NW2 off Tilling Rd 63 CW60
Barnet EN5 .... 27 CZ42
Welling DA16 .... 105 ET82
NEW MALDEN 138 CR97
⇌ New Malden 138 CS97
Newman Cl, Horn. RM11 .... 72 FL57
Newman Pas, W1 .... 195 L7
Newman Rd, E13 .... 86 EH69
E17 off Southcote Rd 67 DX57
Bromley BR1 .... 144 EG95
Croydon CR0 .... 141 DM102
Hayes UB3 .... 77 BV73
Newmans Cl, Loug. IG10 .... 33 EP41
Newman's Ct, EC3 .... 197 L9
Newmans Dr, Brwd. CM13 .... 55 GC45
Newmans La, Loug. IG10 .... 33 EN41
Surbiton KT6 .... 137 CK100
Newmans Rd, Grav. (Nthflt.) DA11 .... 131 GF89
Newman's Row, WC2 .... 196 C7
Newman St, W1 .... 195 L7
Newmans Way, Barn. EN4 .... 28 DC39
Newman Yd, W1 .... 195 M8
Newmarket Av, Nthlt. UB5 .... 60 CA64
Newmarket Grn, SE9
off Middle Pk Av 124 EK87
Newmarket Way, Horn. RM12 .... 72 FL63
Newmarsh Rd, SE28 .... 87 ET74
New Mill Rd, Orp. BR5 .... 146 EW95
Newminster Rd, Mord. SM4 .... 140 DC100
New Mt St, E15 .... 85 ED66
Newnes Path, SW15
off Putney Pk La 99 CV84
Newnham Av, Ruis. HA4 .... 60 BW60
Newnham Cl, Loug. IG10 .... 32 EK44
Northolt UB5 .... 60 CC64
Slough SL2 .... 74 AU74
Thornton Heath CR7 .... 142 DQ96
Newnham Gdns, Nthlt. UB5 .... 60 CC64
Newnham Ms, N22
off Newnham Rd 45 DM53
Newnham Pl, Grays RM16 .... 111 GG77
Newnham Rd, N22 .... 45 DM53
Newnhams Cl, Brom. BR1 .... 145 EM97
Newnham Ter, SE1 .... 200 D6
Newnham Way, Har. HA3 .... 62 CL57
New N Pl, EC2 .... 197 M5
New N Rd, N1 .... 197 L1
Ilford IG6 .... 49 ER52
Reigate RH2 .... 183 CZ134
New N St, WC1 .... 196 B6
Newnton Cl, N4 .... 66 DR59
New Oak Rd, N2 .... 44 DC54
New Orleans Wk, N19 .... 65 DK59
New Oxford St, WC1 .... 195 N8
New Par, Ashf. TW15
off Church Rd 114 BM91
Rickmansworth (Chorl.) WD3
off Whitelands Av 21 BC42
New Par Flats, Rick. (Chorl.) WD3
off Whitelands Av 21 BC42
New Pk Av, N13 .... 46 DQ48
New Pk Cl, Nthlt. UB5 .... 78 BY65
New Pk Ct, SW2 .... 121 DL87
New Pk Par, SW2
off Doverfield Rd 121 DL86
New Pk Rd, SW2 .... 121 DK88
Ashford TW15 .... 115 BQ92
Uxbridge (Hare.) UB9 .... 38 BJ53
New Peachey La, Uxb. UB8 .... 76 BK72
Newpiece, Loug. IG10 .... 33 EP41
New Pl Gdns, Upmin. RM14 .... 73 FR61
New Pl Sq, SE16 .... 202 D6
New Plaistow Rd, E15 .... 86 EE67
Newport Av, E13 .... 86 EH70
E14 .... 85 ED73
Newport Cl, Enf. EN3 .... 31 DY37
Newport Ct, WC2 .... 195 N10
Newport Mead, Wat. WD19
off Kilmarnock Rd 40 BX49
Newport Pl, WC2 .... 195 N10
Newport Rd, E10 .... 67 EC61
E17 .... 67 DY56
SW13 .... 99 CU81
Hayes UB4 .... 77 BR71
Hounslow (Hthrw.Air.) TW6 .... 94 BN81
Newports, Swan. BR8 .... 147 FD101
Newport St, SE11 .... 200 B9
New Printing Ho Sq, WC1
off Gray's Inn Rd 83 DM70
New Priory Ct, NW6
off Mazenod Av 82 DA66
Newquay Cres, Har. HA2 .... 60 BY61
Newquay Gdns, Wat. WD19
off Fulford Gro 39 BV47
Newquay Rd, SE6 .... 123 EB89
New Quebec St, W1 .... 194 E9
New Ride, SW7 .... 198 D4
New River Ct, Wal.Cr. (Chsht.) EN7
off Pengelly Cl 14 DV30
New River Cres, N13 .... 45 DP49
New River Head, EC1 .... 196 E2
New River Trd Est, Wal.Cr. (Chsht.) EN8 .... 15 DX26
New River Wk, N1 .... 84 DQ65
New River Way, N4 .... 66 DR59
New Rd, E1 .... 84 DV71
E4 .... 47 EB49
N8 .... 65 DL57
N9 .... 46 DU48
N17 .... 46 DT53
N22 .... 46 DQ53
NW7 .... 43 CY52
NW7 (Barnet Gate) 43 CT45
SE2 .... 106 EX77
Amersham HP6 .... 20 AS37
Borehamwood (Elstree) WD6 .... 25 CK44
Brentford TW8 .... 97 CK79
Brentwood CM14 .... 54 FX47
Chalfont St. Giles HP8 .... 20 AY41
Chertsey KT16 .... 133 BF101
Dagenham RM9, RM10 .... 88 FA67
Dartford (S.Darenth) DA4 .... 148 FQ96
Epping CM16 .... 18 FA32
Esher KT10 .... 136 CC104
Esher (Clay.) KT10 .... 155 CF110
Feltham TW14 .... 115 BR86
Feltham (E.Bed.) TW14 .... 115 BV88
Feltham (Han.) TW13 .... 116 BY92
Gravesend DA11 .... 131 GH86
Grays RM17 .... 110 GA79
Grays (Manor Way) RM17 .... 110 GB79
Harrow HA1 .... 61 CF63
Hayes UB3 .... 95 BQ80
Hounslow TW3
off Station Rd 96 CB84
Ilford IG3 .... 69 ES61
Kings Langley (Chipper.) WD4 .... 5 BF30
Kingston upon Thames KT2 .... 118 CN94
Leatherhead KT22 .... 155 CF110
Mitcham CR4 .... 140 DF102
Orpington BR6 .... 146 EU101
Oxted (Lmpfld.) RH8 .... 188 EH130
Potters Bar (S.Mimms) EN6 .... 11 CU33
Radlett WD7 .... 25 CE36
Radlett (Shenley) WD7 .... 10 CN39
Rainham RM13 .... 89 FG69
Richmond TW10 .... 117 CJ91
Rickmansworth (Ch.End) WD3 .... 21 BF39
Rickmansworth (Crox.Grn.) WD3 .... 22 BN43
Romford (Abridge) RM4 .... 34 EX44
Sevenoaks (Sund.) TN14 .... 180 EX124
Shepperton TW17 .... 135 BP97
Slough (Datchet) SL3 .... 92 AX81
Slough (Langley) SL3 .... 93 BA76
Staines TW18 .... 113 BC92
Swanley BR8 .... 147 FF97
Swanley (Hext.) BR8 .... 127 FF94
Tadworth KT20 .... 173 CW123
Uxbridge UB8 .... 77 BQ70
Watford WD17 .... 24 BW42
Watford (Let.Hth.) WD25 .... 25 CE39
Welling DA16 .... 106 EV82
West Molesey KT8 .... 136 CA97
Weybridge KT13 .... 153 BQ106
New Rd Hill, Kes. BR2 .... 162 EL109
Orpington BR6 .... 162 EL109
New Row, WC2 .... 195 P10
Newry Rd, Twick. TW1 .... 97 CG84
Newsam Av, N15 .... 66 DR57
★ New Scotland Yd, SW1 .... 199 M6
Newsham Rd, Wok. GU21 .... 166 AT117
Newsholme Dr, N21 .... 29 DM43
NEW SOUTHGATE, N11 .... 45 DK49
⇌ New Southgate 45 DH50
New Spring Gdns Wk, SE11
off Goding St 101 DL78
New Sq, WC2 .... 196 C8
Feltham TW14 .... 115 BQ88
Slough SL1 .... 92 AT75
New Sq Pas, WC2
off New Sq 83 DM72
Newstead Av, Orp. BR6 .... 145 ER104
Newstead Ri, Cat. CR3 .... 186 DV126
Newstead Rd, SE12 .... 124 EE87
Newstead Wk, Cars. SM5 .... 140 DC101
Newstead Way, SW19 .... 119 CX91
New St, EC2 .... 197 N7
Staines TW18 .... 114 BG91
Watford WD18 .... 24 BW42
Westerham TN16 .... 189 EQ127
New St Hill, Brom. BR1 .... 124 EH92
New St Sq, EC4 .... 196 E8
New Swan Yd, Grav. DA12
off Bank St 131 GH86
Newteswell Dr, Wal.Abb. EN9 .... 15 ED32
Newton Abbot Rd, Grav. (Nthflt.) DA11 .... 131 GF89
Newton Av, N10 .... 44 DG53
W3 .... 98 CQ75
Newton Cl, E17 .... 67 DY58
Harrow HA2 .... 60 CA61
Slough SL3 .... 93 AZ75
Newton Ct, Wind. (Old Wind.) SL4 .... 112 AU86
Newton Cres, Borwd. WD6 .... 26 CQ42
Newton Gro, W4 .... 98 CS77
Newton La, Wind. (Old Wind.) SL4 .... 112 AV86
Newton Pl, E14 .... 203 P8
Newton Rd, E15 .... 67 ED64
N15 .... 66 DT57
NW2 .... 63 CW62
SW19 .... 119 CY94
W2 .... 82 DA72
Chigwell IG7 .... 50 EV50
Harrow HA3 .... 41 CE54
Isleworth TW7 .... 97 CF82
Purley CR8 .... 159 DJ112
Tilbury RM18 .... 111 GG82
Welling DA16 .... 106 EU83
Wembley HA0 .... 80 CM66
Newtons Cl, Rain. RM13 .... 89 FF66
Newtons Ct, Dart. DA2 .... 109 FR84
Newtonside Orchard, Wind. SL4 .... 112 AU86
Newton St, WC2 .... 196 A8
Newtons Yd, SW18
off Wandsworth High St 120 DB85
Newton Wk, Edg. HA8
off North Rd 42 CP53
Newton Way, N18 .... 46 DQ50
Newton Wd, Ashtd. KT21 .... 156 CL114
Newton Wd Rd, Ashtd. KT21 .... 172 CM116
NEW TOWN, Dart. 128 FN86
Newtown Rd, Uxb. (Denh.) UB9 .... 76 BH65
Newtown St, SW11
off Strasburg Rd 101 DH81
New Trinity Rd, N2 .... 64 DD55
New Turnstile, WC1 .... 196 B7
New Union Cl, E14 .... 204 E6
New Union St, EC2 .... 197 K7
H New Victoria Hosp, Kings.T. KT2 .... 138 CS95
New Wanstead, E11 .... 68 EF58
New Way Rd, NW9 .... 62 CS56
New Wf Rd, N1 .... 83 DL68
New Wickham La, Egh. TW20 .... 113 BA94
New Windsor St, Uxb. UB8 .... 76 BJ67
NEWYEARS GREEN, Uxb. 58 BN59
New Years Grn La, Uxb. (Hare.) UB9 .... 58 BL58
New Years La, Orp. BR6 .... 164 EU114
Sevenoaks (Knock.) TN14 .... 179 ET116
New Zealand Av, Walt. KT12 .... 135 BT102
New Zealand Way, W12 .... 81 CV73
Rainham RM13 .... 89 FF69
Niagara Av, W5 .... 97 CJ77
Niagara Cl, N1 off Cropley St 84 DR68
Waltham Cross (Chsht.) EN8 .... 15 DX29
Nibthwaite Rd, Har. HA1 .... 61 CE57
Nicholas Cl, Grnf. UB6 .... 78 CB68
South Ockendon RM15 .... 91 FW69
Watford WD24 .... 23 BV37
Nicholas Ct, E13
off Tunmarsh La 86 EH69
Nicholas Gdns, W5 .... 97 CK75
Woking GU22 .... 167 BE116
Nicholas La, EC4 .... 197 L10
Nicholas Ms, W4 off Short Rd 98 CS79
Nicholas Pas, EC4 .... 197 L10
Nicholas Rd, E1 .... 84 DW70
Borehamwood (Elstree) WD6 .... 26 CM44
Croydon CR0 .... 159 DL105
Dagenham RM8 .... 70 EZ61
Nicholas Wk, Grays RM16
off Godman Rd 111 GH75
Nicholas Way, Nthwd. HA6 .... 39 BQ53
Nicholay Rd, N19 .... 65 DK60
Nichol Cl, N14 .... 45 DK46
Nicholes Rd, Houns. TW3 .... 96 CA84
Nichol La, Brom. BR1 .... 124 EG94
Nicholl Rd, Epp. CM16 .... 17 ET31
Nicholls Av, Uxb. UB8 .... 76 BN70
Nichollsfield Wk, N7
off Hillmarton Rd 65 DM64
Nicholls Pt, E15 off Park Gro 86 EG67
Nicholl St, E2 .... 84 DU67
Nichols Cl, N4
off Osborne Rd 65 DN60
Chessington KT9
off Merritt Gdns 155 CJ107
Nichols Grn, W5
off Montpelier Rd 80 CL71
Nicholson Ms, Egh. TW20
off Nicholson Wk 113 BA92
Nicholson Rd, Croy. CR0 .... 142 DT102
Nicholson St, SE1 .... 200 F3
Nicholson Wk, Egh. TW20 .... 113 BA92
Nicholson Way, Sev. TN13 .... 191 FK122
Nickelby Cl, SE28 .... 88 EW72
Uxbridge UB8
off Dickens Av 77 BP72
Nicola Cl, Har. HA3 .... 41 CD54
South Croydon CR2 .... 160 DQ107
Nicola Ms, Ilf. IG6 .... 49 EP52
Nicol Cl, Ger.Cr. (Chal.St.P.) SL9 .... 36 AX53
Twickenham TW1
off Cassilis Rd 117 CH86
Nicol End, Ger.Cr. (Chal.St.P.) SL9 .... 36 AW53
Nicoll Pl, NW4 .... 63 CV58
Nicoll Rd, NW10 .... 80 CS67
Nicoll Way, Borwd. WD6 .... 26 CR43
Nicol Rd, Ger.Cr. (Chal.St.P.) SL9 .... 36 AW53
Nicolson Dr, Bushey (Bushey Hth.) WD23 .... 40 CC46
Nicolson Rd, Orp. BR5 .... 146 EX101
Nicosia Rd, SW18 .... 120 DE87
Niederwald Rd, SE26 .... 123 DY91
Nield Rd, Hayes UB3 .... 95 BT75
Nield Way, Rick. WD3
off Thellusson Way 37 BF45
Nigel Cl, Nthlt. UB5
off Church Rd 78 BY67
Nigel Fisher Way, Chess. KT9 .... 155 CJ108
Nigel Ms, Ilf. IG1 .... 69 EP63
Nigel Playfair Av, W6
off King St 99 CV77
Nigel Rd, E7 .... 68 EJ64
SE15 .... 102 DU83
Nigeria Rd, SE7 .... 104 EJ80
Nightingale Av, E4 .... 48 EE50
Harrow HA1 .... 61 CH59
Leatherhead (W.Hors.) KT24 .... 169 BR124
Upminster RM14 .... 73 FT60
Nightingale Cl, E4 .... 48 EE49
W4 off Grove Pk Ter 98 CQ79
Abbots Langley WD5 .... 7 BU31
Carshalton SM5 .... 140 DG103
Cobham KT11 .... 154 BX111
Epsom KT19 .... 156 CN112
Gravesend (Nthflt.) DA11 .... 130 GE91

Nig - Nor

Nightingale Cl, Pin. HA5 . . . . . .60 BW57
Radlett WD7 . . . . .25 CF36
Nightingale Ct, E11
off Nightingale La 68 EH57
Slough SL1
off St. Laurence Way 92 AU76
Nightingale Cres, Lthd. (W.Hors.)
KT24 . . . . .169 BQ124
Nightingale Dr, Epsom KT19 .156 CP107
Nightingale Est, E5 . . . . .66 DU62
Nightingale Gro, SE13 . . . . . .123 ED85
Dartford DA1 . . . . .108 FN84
Nightingale La, E11 . . . . .68 EG57
N6 . . . . .64 DE60
N8 . . . . .65 DL56
SW4 . . . . .120 DF87
SW12 . . . . .120 DF87
Bromley BR1 . . . . .144 EJ96
Richmond TW10 . . . . .118 CL87
Sevenoaks (Ide Hill) TN14 .190 FB130
Nightingale Ms, E3
off Chisenhale Rd 85 DY68
E11 . . . . .68 EG57
SE11 . . . . .200 E8
Kingston upon Thames KT1
off South La 137 CK97
Nightingale Pl, SE18 . . . . . . .105 EN79
SW10 *off Fulham Rd* 100 DC79
Rickmansworth WD3
off Nightingale Rd 38 BK45
Nightingale Rd, E5 . . . . .66 DV62
N9 . . . . .30 DW44
N22 . . . . .45 DL53
NW10 . . . . .81 CT68
W7 . . . . .79 CF74
Bushey WD23 . . . . .24 CA43
Carshalton SM5 . . . . .140 DF104
Esher KT10 . . . . .154 BZ106
Hampton TW12 . . . . .116 CA92
Orpington BR5 . . . . .145 EQ100
Rickmansworth WD3 . . . . . . .38 BJ46
South Croydon CR2 . . . . . .161 DX111
Waltham Cross (Chsht.)
EN7 . . . . .14 DQ25
Walton-on-Thames KT12 . . .135 BV101
West Molesey KT8 . . . . . . .136 CB99
Nightingales, Wal.Abb. EN9
off Roundhills 16 EE34
Nightingales, The, Stai. TW19 .114 BM87
Nightingales Cor, Amer. HP7
off Chalfont Sta Rd 20 AW40
Nightingale Shott, Egh.
TW20 . . . . .113 AZ93
Nightingales La, Ch.St.G. HP8 .36 AX46
Nightingale Sq, SW12 . . . . . .120 DG87
Nightingale Vale, SE18 . . . . . .105 EN79
Nightingale Wk, SW4 . . . . . . .121 DH86
Nightingale Way, E6 . . . . .86 EL71
Redhill (Bletch.) RH1 . . . . .186 DS134
Swanley BR8 . . . . .147 FE97
Uxbridge (Denh.) UB9 . . . . . .57 BF59
Nile Path, SE18
off Jackson St 105 EN79
Nile Rd, E13 . . . . .86 EJ68
Nile St, N1 . . . . .197 J2
Nile Ter, SE15 . . . . .102 DT78
Nimbus Rd, Epsom KT19 . . . .156 CR110
Nimegen Way, SE22 . . . . . . .122 DS85
Nimmo Dr, Bushey (Bushey Hth.)
WD23 . . . . .41 CD45
Nimrod Cl, Nthlt. UB5
off Britannia Cl 78 BX69
Nimrod Pas, N1
off Tottenham Rd 84 DS65
Nimrod Rd, SW16 . . . . .121 DH93
Nina Mackay Cl, E15
off Arthingworth St 86 EE67
Nine Acres Cl, E12 . . . . .68 EL64
Nineacres Way, Couls. CR5 . .175 DL116
NINE ELMS, SW8 . . . . .101 DH80
Nine Elms Cl, Felt. TW14 . . . .115 BT88
Uxbridge UB8 . . . . .76 BK72
Nine Elms Gro, Grav. DA11 . .131 GG87
Nine Elms La, SW8 . . . . .101 DJ79
Ninefields, Wal.Abb. EN9 . . . .16 EF33
Ninehams Cl, Cat. CR3 . . . . .176 DR120
Ninehams Gdns, Cat. CR3 . . .176 DR120
Ninehams Rd, Cat. CR3 . . . . .176 DR121
Westerham (Tats.) TN16 . . .178 EJ121
Nine Stiles Cl, Uxb. (Denh.)
UB9 . . . . .58 BH65
Nineteenth Rd, Mitch. CR4 . .141 DL98
Ninhams Wd, Orp. BR6 . . . . .163 EN105
Ninnings Rd, Ger.Cr. (Chal.St.P.)
SL9 . . . . .37 AZ52
Ninnings Way, Ger.Cr. (Chal.St.P.)
SL9 . . . . .37 AZ52
Ninth Av, Hayes UB3 . . . . .77 BU73
Nisbet Ho, E9
off Homerton High St 67 DX64
Nita Rd, Brwd. CM14 . . . . . . .54 FW50
Nithdale Rd, SE18 . . . . .105 EP80
Nithsdale Gro, Uxb. UB10
off Tweeddale Gro 59 BQ62
Niton Cl, Barn. EN5 . . . . .27 CX44
Niton Rd, Rich. TW9 . . . . .98 CN83
Niton St, SW6 . . . . .99 CX80
Niven Cl, Borwd. WD6 . . . . . . .26 CQ39
Nixey Cl, Slou. SL1 . . . . .92 AU75
N.L.A. Twr, Croy. CR0 . . . . . .142 DR103
NOAK HILL, Rom. RM3 . . . . . .52 FK47
Noak Hill Rd, Rom. RM3 . . . . .52 FJ49
Nobel Dr, Hayes UB3 . . . . .95 BR80
Nobel Rd, N18 . . . . .46 DW50
Noble St, EC2 . . . . .197 H8
Walton-on-Thames KT12 . . .135 BV103
Nobles Way, Egh. TW20 . . . . .112 AY93
NOEL PARK, N22 . . . . .45 DN54
Noel Pk Rd, N22 . . . . .45 DN54
Noel Rd, E6 . . . . .86 EL70
N1 . . . . .83 DP68
W3 . . . . .80 CP72
Noel Sq, Dag. RM8 . . . . .70 EW63

Noel St, W1 . . . . .195 L9
Noel Ter, SE23
off Dartmouth Rd 122 DW89
Noke Dr, Red. RH1 . . . . .184 DG133
Noke Fm Barns, Couls. CR5 . .174 DF122
Noke La, St.Alb. AL2 . . . . .8 BY26
Noke Side, St.Alb. AL2 . . . . .8 CA27
Nolan Way, E5 . . . . .66 DU63
Nolton Pl, Edg. HA8 . . . . .42 CM51
Nonsuch Cl, Ilf. IG6 . . . . .49 EP51
Nonsuch Ct Av, Epsom KT17 .157 CV110
Nonsuch Ind Est, Epsom
KT17 . . . . .156 CS111
★ Nonsuch Mansion Ho, Sutt.
SM3 . . . . .157 CW107
Nonsuch Wk, Sutt. SM2 . . . .157 CW110
Nora Gdns, NW4 . . . . .63 CX56
NORBITON, Kings.T. 138 CP96
≠ Norbiton 138 CN95
Norbiton Av, Kings.T. KT1 . . .138 CN96
Norbiton Common Rd, Kings.T.
KT1 . . . . .138 CP97
Norbiton Rd, E14 . . . . .85 DZ72
Norbreck Gdns, NW10
off Lytham Gro 80 CM69
Norbreck Par, NW10
off Lytham Gro 80 CM69
Norburn St, W10
off Chesterton Rd 81 CY71
NORBURY, SW16 . . . . .141 DN95
≠ Norbury 141 DM95
Norbury Av, SW16 . . . . .141 DM95
Hounslow TW3 . . . . .117 CD85
Thornton Heath CR7 . . . . .141 DN96
Watford WD24 . . . . .24 BW39
Norbury Cl, SW16 . . . . .141 DN95
Norbury Ct Rd, SW16 . . . . . .141 DL97
Norbury Cres, SW16 . . . . . . .141 DM95
Norbury Cross, SW16 . . . . . .141 DL97
Norbury Gdns, Rom. RM6 . . . .70 EX57
Norbury Gro, NW7 . . . . .42 CS48
Norbury Hill, SW16 . . . . .121 DN94
Norbury Ri, SW16 . . . . .141 DL97
Norbury Rd, E4 . . . . .47 EA50
Reigate RH2 . . . . .184 CZ134
Thornton Heath CR7 . . . . .142 DQ96
Norcombe Gdns, Har. HA3 . . . .61 CJ58
Norcott Cl, Hayes UB4
off Willow Tree La 78 BW70
Norcott Rd, N16 . . . . .66 DU61
Norcroft Gdns, SE22 . . . . . . .122 DU87
Norcutt Rd, Twick. TW2 . . . . .117 CE88
Nordenfeldt Rd, Erith DA8 . . .107 FD78
Nordmann Pl, S.Ock. RM15 . . .91 FX70
Norfield Rd, Dart. DA2 . . . . . .127 FC91
Norfolk Av, N13 . . . . .45 DP51
N15 . . . . .66 DT58
South Croydon CR2 . . . . . .160 DU110
Watford WD24 . . . . .24 BW38
Norfolk Cl, N2 *off Park Rd* . . .64 DE55
N13 . . . . .45 DP51
Barnet EN4 . . . . .28 DG42
Dartford DA1 . . . . .128 FN86
Twickenham TW1
off Cassilis Rd 117 CH86
Norfolk Cres, W2 . . . . .194 C8
Sidcup DA15 . . . . .125 ES87
Norfolk Fm Cl, Wok. GU22 . .167 BD116
Norfolk Fm Rd, Wok. GU22 . .167 BD115
Norfolk Gdns, Bexh. DA7 . . . .106 EZ81
Borehamwood WD6 . . . . . . .26 CR42
Norfolk Ho, SE3 . . . . .104 EE79
Norfolk Ho Rd, SW16 . . . . . .121 DK90
Norfolk Ms, W10
off Blagrove Rd 81 CZ71
Norfolk Pl, W2 . . . . .194 A8
Welling DA16 . . . . .106 EU82
Norfolk Rd, E6 . . . . .87 EM67
E17 . . . . .47 DX54
NW8 . . . . .82 DD67
NW10 . . . . .80 CS66
SW19 . . . . .120 DE94
Barking IG11 . . . . .87 ES66
Barnet EN5 . . . . .28 DA41
Dagenham RM10 . . . . .71 FB64
Enfield EN3 . . . . .30 DV44
Esher (Clay.) KT10 . . . . . .155 CE106
Feltham TW13 . . . . .116 BW88
Gravesend DA12 . . . . .131 GK86
Harrow HA1 . . . . .60 CB57
Ilford IG3 . . . . .69 ES60
Rickmansworth WD3 . . . . . .38 BL46
Romford RM7 . . . . .71 FC58
Thornton Heath CR7 . . . . .142 DQ97
Upminster RM14 . . . . .72 FN62
Uxbridge UB8 . . . . .76 BK65
Norfolk Row, SE1 . . . . .200 B8
Norfolk Sq, W2 . . . . .194 A9
Norfolk Sq Ms, W2 . . . . .194 A9
Norfolk St, E7 . . . . .68 EG63
Norfolk Ter, W6 *off Field Rd* . .99 CY78
Norgrove Pk, Ger.Cr. SL9 . . . .56 AY56
Norgrove St, SW12 . . . . .120 DG87
Norheads La, Warl. CR6 . . . . .178 EG119
Westerham (Bigg.H.) TN16 .178 EJ116
Norhyrst Av, SE25 . . . . .142 DT97
NORK, Bans. 173 CY115
Nork Gdns, Bans. SM7 . . . . . .157 CY114
Nork Ri, Bans. SM7 . . . . .173 CX116
Nork Way, Bans. SM7 . . . . . .173 CY115
Norland Ho, W11 . . . . .81 CX74
Norland Pl, W11 . . . . .81 CY74
Norland Rd, W11 . . . . .81 CX74
Norlands Cres, Chis. BR7 . . . .145 EP95
Norlands Gate, Chis. BR7 . . . .145 EP95
Norlands La, Egh. TW20 . . . . .133 BE97
Norley Vale, SW15 . . . . .119 CU88
Norlington Rd, E10 . . . . .67 EC60
E11 . . . . .68 EC60
Norman Av, N22 . . . . .45 DP53
Epsom KT17 . . . . .157 CT112
Feltham TW13 . . . . .116 BY89
South Croydon CR2 . . . . . .160 DQ110
Southall UB1 . . . . .78 BY73
Twickenham TW1 . . . . .117 CH87

Normanby Cl, SW15
off Manfred Rd 119 CZ85
Normanby Rd, NW10 . . . . . . .63 CT63
Norman Cl, Epsom KT18 . . . .173 CV119
Orpington BR6 . . . . .145 EQ104
Romford RM5 . . . . .51 FB54
Waltham Abbey EN9 . . . . . .15 ED33
Norman Ct, Ilf. IG2 . . . . .69 ER59
Potters Bar EN6 . . . . .12 DC30
Woodford Green IG8
off Monkhams Av 48 EH50
Norman Cres, Brwd. CM13 . . .55 GA48
Hounslow TW5 . . . . .96 BX81
Pinner HA5 . . . . .40 BW53
Normand Gdns, W14
off Greyhound Rd 99 CY79
Normand Ms, W14
off Normand Rd 99 CY79
Normand Rd, W14 . . . . .99 CZ79
Normandy Av, Barn. EN5 . . . . .27 CZ43
Normandy Dr, Hayes UB3 . . . .77 BQ72
Normandy Rd, SW9 . . . . .101 DN81
Normandy Ter, E16 . . . . .86 EH72
Normandy Wk, Egh. TW20
off Mullens Rd 113 BC92
Norman Gro, E3 . . . . .85 DY68
Normanhurst, Ashf. TW15 . . . .114 BN92
Brentwood CM13 . . . . .55 GC44
Normanhurst Av, Bexh. DA7 .106 EX81
Normanhurst Dr, Twick. TW1
off St. Margarets Rd 117 CH85
Normanhurst Rd, SW2 . . . . . .121 DM89
Orpington BR5 . . . . .146 EV96
Walton-on-Thames KT12 . . .136 BX103
Norman Rd, E6 . . . . .87 EM70
E11 . . . . .67 ED61
N15 . . . . .66 DT57
SE10 . . . . .103 EB80
SW19 . . . . .120 DC94
Ashford TW15 . . . . .115 BR93
Belvedere DA17 . . . . .107 FB76
Dartford DA1 . . . . .128 FL88
Hornchurch RM11 . . . . .71 FG59
Ilford IG1 . . . . .69 EP64
Sutton SM1 . . . . .158 DA106
Thornton Heath CR7 . . . . .141 DP99
Normans, The, Slou. SL2 . . . . .74 AV72
Norman's Bldgs, EC1
off Ironmonger Row 84 DQ69
Normans Cl, NW10 . . . . .80 CR65
Gravesend DA11 . . . . .131 GG87
Uxbridge UB8 . . . . .76 BL71
Normansfield Av, Tedd. TW11 .117 CJ94
Normansfield Cl, Bushey
WD23 . . . . .40 CB45
Normanshire Dr, E4 . . . . .47 EA49
Normanshire Dr, E4 . . . . .47 EA49
Normans Mead, NW10 . . . . . .80 CR65
Norman St, EC1 . . . . .197 H3
Normanton Av, SW19 . . . . . .120 DA89
Normanton Pk, E4 . . . . .48 EE48
Normanton Rd, S.Croy. CR2 .160 DS107
Normanton St, SE23 . . . . . . .123 DX88
Norman Way, N14 . . . . .45 DL47
W3 . . . . .80 CP71
Normington Cl, SW16 . . . . . .121 DN92
Norrice Lea, N2 . . . . .64 DD57
Norris Rd, Stai. TW18 . . . . . .113 BF91
Norris St, SW1 . . . . .199 M1
Norris Way, Dart. DA1 . . . . . .107 FF83
Norroy Rd, SW15 . . . . .99 CX84
Norrys Cl, Barn. EN4 . . . . .28 DF43
Norrys Rd, Barn. EN4 . . . . . . .28 DF43
Norseman Cl, Ilf. IG3 . . . . .70 EV60
Norseman Way, Grnf. UB6
off Olympic Way 78 CB67
Norstead Pl, SW15 . . . . .119 CU89
Norsted La, Orp. BR6 . . . . . . .164 EU110
North Access Rd, E17 . . . . . . .67 DX58
North Acre, NW9 . . . . .42 CS53
Banstead SM7 . . . . .173 CZ116
NORTH ACTON, W3 . . . . .80 CR70
⊖ North Acton 80 CR70
North Acton Rd, NW10 . . . . . .80 CR69
Northallerton Way, Rom. RM3 .52 FK50
Northall Rd, Bexh. DA7 . . . . .107 FC82
Northampton Gro, N1 . . . . . . .66 DR64
Northampton Pk, N1 . . . . .84 DQ65
Northampton Rd, EC1 . . . . . .196 E4
Croydon CR0 . . . . .142 DU103
Enfield EN3 . . . . .31 DY42
Northampton Sq, EC1 . . . . . .196 F3
Northampton St, N1 . . . . .84 DQ66
Northanger Rd, SW16 . . . . . .121 DL93
North App, Nthwd. HA6 . . . . . .39 BQ47
Watford WD25 . . . . .23 BT35
North Arc, Croy. CR0
off North End 142 DQ103
North Audley St, W1 . . . . . . .194 F9
North Av, N18 . . . . .46 DU49
W13 . . . . .79 CH72
Brentwood CM14 . . . . .53 FR45
Carshalton SM5 . . . . .158 DF108
Harrow HA2 . . . . .60 CB58
Hayes UB3 . . . . .77 BU73
Radlett (Shenley) WD7 . . . .10 CL32
Richmond TW9
off Sandycombe Rd 98 CN81
Southall UB1 . . . . .78 BZ73
Walton-on-Thames KT12 . . .153 BS109
NORTHAW, Pot.B. 12 DF30
Northaw Pl, Pot.B. EN6 . . . . . .12 DD30
Northaw Rd E, Pot.B. (Cuffley)
EN6 . . . . .13 DK31
Northaw Rd W, Pot.B. EN6 . . . .12 DG30
Northbank Rd, E17 . . . . .47 EC54
NORTH BECKTON, E6 . . . . . . .86 EL70
North Birkbeck Rd, E11 . . . . . .67 ED62
Northborough Rd, SW16 . . . . .141 DK97
Northbourne, Brom. BR2 . . . .144 EG101
Northbourne Rd, SW4 . . . . . .101 DK84
North Branch Av, W10
off Harrow Rd 81 CW69
Northbrook Dr, Nthwd. HA6 . . .39 BS53

Northbrook Rd, N22 . . . . .45 DL52
SE13 . . . . .123 ED85
Barnet EN5 . . . . .27 CY44
Croydon CR0 . . . . .142 DR99
Ilford IG1 . . . . .69 EN61
Northburgh St, EC1 . . . . .196 G4
North Carriage Dr, W2 . . . . . .194 B10
NORTH CHEAM, Sutt. 139 CW104
Northchurch, SE17 . . . . .201 L10
Northchurch Rd, N1 . . . . .84 DR66
Wembley HA9 . . . . .80 CM65
Northchurch Ter, N1 . . . . .84 DS66
North Circular Rd, E4 . . . . . . .47 DZ52
E18 . . . . .47 DZ52
N3 . . . . .64 DB55
N12 . . . . .44 DD53
N13 . . . . .45 DN50
NW2 . . . . .62 CS62
NW10 . . . . .80 CP66
NW11 . . . . .62 CS56
Northcliffe Cl, Wor.Pk. KT4 . .138 CS104
Northcliffe Dr, N20 . . . . .43 CZ46
North Cl, Barn. EN5 . . . . .27 CW43
Bexleyheath DA6 . . . . .106 EX84
Chigwell IG7 . . . . .50 EU50
Dagenham RM10 . . . . .88 FA67
Feltham TW14
off North Rd 115 BR86
Morden SM4 . . . . .139 CY98
St. Albans AL2 . . . . .8 CB25
North Colonnade, E14 . . . . . .204 A2
North Common, Wey. KT13 . .153 BP105
North Common Rd, W5 . . . . . .80 CL73
Uxbridge UB8 . . . . .58 BK64
Northcote, Add. KT15 . . . . . .152 BK105
Leatherhead (Oxshott)
KT22 . . . . .154 CC114
Pinner HA5 . . . . .40 BW54
Northcote Av, W5 . . . . .80 CL73
Isleworth TW7 . . . . .117 CG85
Southall UB1 . . . . .78 BY73
Surbiton KT5 . . . . .138 CN101
Northcote Ms, SW11
off Northcote Rd 100 DE84
Northcote Rd, E17 . . . . .67 DY56
NW10 . . . . .80 CS66
SW11 . . . . .100 DE84
Croydon CR0 . . . . .142 DR100
Gravesend DA11 . . . . .131 GF88
New Malden KT3 . . . . .138 CQ97
Sidcup DA14 . . . . .125 ES91
Twickenham TW1 . . . . .117 CG85
North Cotts, St.Alb. (Lon.Col.)
AL2 . . . . .9 CG25
Northcott Av, N22 . . . . .45 DL53
Northcotts, Abb.L. WD5
off Long Elms 7 BR33
North Countess Rd, E17 . . . . .47 DZ54
North Ct, W1 . . . . .195 L6
Northcourt, Rick. (Mill End) WD3
off Springwell Av 38 BG46
NORTH CRAY, Sid. 126 FA90
North Cray Rd, Bex. DA5 . . . .126 EZ90
Sidcup DA14 . . . . .126 EY93
North Cres, E16 . . . . .85 EE70
N3 . . . . .43 CZ54
WC1 . . . . .195 M6
Northcroft Cl, Egh. (Eng.Grn.)
TW20 . . . . .112 AV92
Northcroft Gdns, Egh. (Eng.Grn.)
TW20 . . . . .112 AV92
Northcroft Rd, W13 . . . . .97 CH75
Egham (Eng.Grn.) TW20 . . .112 AV92
Epsom KT19 . . . . .156 CR108
Northcroft Ter, W13
off Northcroft Rd 97 CH75
Northcroft Vil, Egh. (Eng.Grn.)
TW20 . . . . .112 AV92
North Cross Rd, SE22 . . . . . .122 DT85
Ilford IG6 . . . . .69 EQ56
North Dene, NW7 . . . . .42 CR48
Hounslow TW3 . . . . .96 CB81
Northdene, Chig. IG7 . . . . . . .49 ER50
North Dene, Hours. TW3 . . . . .96 CB81
Northdene Gdns, N15 . . . . . . .66 DT58
North Down, S.Croy. CR2 . . . .160 DS111
Northdown Cl, Ruis. HA4 . . . . .59 BT62
Northdown Gdns, Ilf. IG2 . . . .69 ES57
Northdown Rd, Cat. (Wold.)
CR3 . . . . .177 EA123
Gerrards Cross (Chal.St.P.)
SL9 . . . . .36 AY51
Hornchurch RM11 . . . . .71 FH59
Longfield DA3 . . . . .149 FX96
Sutton SM2 . . . . .158 DA110
Welling DA16 . . . . .106 EV82
North Downs Cres, Croy.
(New Adgtn.) CR0 . . . . . .161 EB110
H North Downs Private Hosp,
The, Cat. CR3 . . . . .186 DT125
North Downs Rd, Croy.
(New Adgtn.) CR0 . . . . . .161 EB110
Northdown St, N1 . . . . .83 DM68
North Downs Way, Bet. RH3 .183 CU130
Caterham CR3 . . . . .185 DN126
Godstone RH9 . . . . .187 DY128
Oxted RH8 . . . . .188 EE126
Redhill RH1 . . . . .184 DG128
Sevenoaks TN13, TN14 . . .181 FD118
Tadworth KT20 . . . . .183 CX130
Westerham TN16 . . . . .179 EQ121
North Dr, SW16 . . . . .121 DJ91
Hounslow TW3 . . . . .96 CC82
Orpington BR6 . . . . .163 ES105
Romford RM2 . . . . .71 FJ55
Ruislip HA4 . . . . .59 BS59
Slough SL2 . . . . .74 AS70
Virginia Water GU25 . . . . . .132 AS100
≠ North Dulwich 122 DR85
North Ealing 80 CL71
North End, NW3 . . . . .64 DC61
Northend, Brwd. CM14 . . . . . .54 FW49
North End, Buck.H. IG9 . . . . . .48 EJ45
Croydon CR0 . . . . .142 DQ103
Romford (Noak Hill) RM3 . . .52 FJ47
North End Av, NW3 . . . . .64 DC61
North End Cres, W14 . . . . .99 CZ77

North End Ho, W14 . . . . .99 CY77
North End La, Orp. BR6 . . . . . .163 EN110
North End Par, W14
off North End Rd 99 CY77
North End Rd, NW11 . . . . .64 DA60
SW6 . . . . .99 CZ79
W14 . . . . .99 CY77
Wembley HA9 . . . . .62 CN62
Northend Trd Est, Erith DA8 .107 FE81
North End Way, NW3 . . . . .64 DC61
Northern Av, N9 . . . . .46 DT47
Northernhay Wk, Mord. SM4 .139 CY98
Northern Perimeter Rd, Houns.
(Hthrw.Air.) TW6 . . . . .95 BQ81
Northern Perimeter Rd W, Houns.
(Hthrw.Air.) TW6 . . . . .94 BK81
Northern Relief Rd, Bark. IG11 .87 EP66
Northern Rd, E13 . . . . .86 EH67
Northern Service Rd, Barn.
EN5 . . . . .27 CY41
Northey Av, Sutt. SM2 . . . . . .157 CZ110
North Eyot Gdns, W6 . . . . . . .99 CU78
Northey St, E14 . . . . .85 DY73
Northfield, Loug. IG10 . . . . . .32 EK42
Northfield Av, W5 . . . . .97 CH75
W13 . . . . .97 CH75
Orpington BR5 . . . . .146 EW100
Pinner HA5 . . . . .60 BX56
Northfield Cl, Brom. BR1 . . . .144 EL95
Hayes UB3 . . . . .95 BT76
Northfield Ct, Stai. TW18 . . . .134 BH95
Northfield Cres, Sutt. SM3 . . .157 CY105
Northfield Gdns, Dag. RM9
off Northfield Rd 70 EZ63
Watford WD24 . . . . .24 BW37
Northfield Ind Est, NW10 . . . . .80 CN66
Northfield Pk, Hayes UB3 . . . .95 BT76
Northfield Path, Dag. RM9 . . . .70 EZ62
Northfield Pl, Wey. KT13 . . . .153 BP108
Northfield Rd, E6 . . . . .87 EM66
N16 . . . . .66 DS59
W13 . . . . .97 CH75
Barnet EN4 . . . . .28 DE41
Borehamwood WD6 . . . . . . .26 CP39
Cobham KT11 . . . . .153 BU113
Dagenham RM9 . . . . .70 EZ63
Enfield EN3 . . . . .30 DV43
Hounslow TW5 . . . . .96 BX79
Staines TW18 . . . . .134 BH95
Waltham Cross EN8 . . . . . .15 DY32
⊖ Northfields 97 CH76
Northfields, SW18 . . . . .100 DA84
Ashtead KT21 . . . . .172 CL119
Grays RM17 . . . . .110 GC77
Northfields Ind Est, Wem.
HA0 . . . . .80 CN67
Northfields Rd, W3 . . . . .80 CP71
NORTH FINCHLEY, N12 . . . . .44 DD50
NORTHFLEET, Grav. 130 GD86
≠ Northfleet 130 GA86
NORTHFLEET GREEN, Grav. .130 GC92
Northfleet Gm Rd, Grav.
DA13 . . . . .130 GC93
Northfleet Ind Est, Grav.
DA11 . . . . .110 FZ84
North Flockton St, SE16 . . . . .202 B4
North Gdn, E14
off Westferry Circ 85 DZ74
North Gdns, SW19 . . . . .120 DD94
Northgate, Nthwd. HA6 . . . . . .39 BQ52
Northgate Dr, NW9 . . . . .62 CS58
Northgate Ind Pk, Rom. RM5 . .50 EZ54
Northgate Path, Borwd. WD6 . .26 CM39
North Glade, The, Bex. DA5 . .126 EZ87
North Gower St, NW1 . . . . . . .195 L3
North Grn, NW9
off Clayton Fld 42 CS52
Slough SL1 . . . . .74 AS73
⊖ North Greenwich 205 H4
North Gro, N6 . . . . .64 DG59
N15 . . . . .66 DR57
Chertsey KT16 . . . . .133 BF100
NORTH HARROW, Har. 60 CA58
⊖ North Harrow 60 CA57
North Hatton Rd, Houns.
(Hthrw.Air.) TW6 . . . . .95 BR81
North Hill, N6 . . . . .64 DF58
Rickmansworth WD3 . . . . . .21 BE40
North Hill Av, N6 . . . . .64 DG58
North Hill Dr, Rom. RM3 . . . . .52 FK48
North Hill Grn, Rom. RM3 . . . .52 FK49
NORTH HILLINGDON, Uxb. . . .77 BQ66
NORTH HYDE, Sthl. 96 BY77
North Hyde Gdns, Hayes UB3 .95 BU77
Southall UB2 . . . . .96 BY78
North Hyde Rd, Hayes UB3 . . .95 BT76
Northiam, N12 . . . . .44 DA48
Northiam St, E9 . . . . .84 DV67
Northington St, WC1 . . . . . . .196 C5
NORTH KENSINGTON, W10 . . .81 CW72
North Kent Av, Grav. (Nthflt.)
DA11 . . . . .130 GC88
Northlands, Pot.B. EN6 . . . . . .12 DD31
Northlands Av, Orp. BR6 . . . .163 ES105
Northlands St, SE5 . . . . .102 DQ82
North La, Tedd. TW11 . . . . . .117 CF93
North Lo Cl, SW15
off Westleigh Av 119 CX85
H North London Blood
Transfusion Cen, NW9 . . . .42 CR54
H North London Nuffield Hosp,
Enf. EN2 . . . . .29 DN40
NORTH LOOE, Epsom 157 CW113
North Mall, N9
off St. Martins Rd 46 DV47
North Mead, Red. RH1 . . . . . .184 DF131
North Ms, WC1 . . . . .196 C5
H North Middlesex Hosp,
N18 . . . . .46 DS50
North Mymms Pk, Hat. AL9 . . .11 CT25
NORTH OCKENDON, Upmin. . .73 FV64
Northolm, Edg. HA8 . . . . .42 CR49
Northolme Cl, Grays RM16
off Premier Av 110 GC76

Northolme Gdns, Edg. HA8 . . .42 CN53
Northolme Ri, Orp. BR6 . . . . .145 ES103
Northolme Rd, N5 . . . . .66 DQ63
NORTHOLT 78 BZ66
⊖ Northolt 78 CA66
★ Northolt Aerodrome, Ruis.
HA4 . . . . .77 BT65
Northolt Av, Ruis. HA4 . . . . . .59 BV64
Northolt Gdns, Grnf. UB6 . . . .61 CF64
⇌ Northolt Park 60 CB63
Northolt Rd, Har. HA2 . . . . . . .60 CB63
Hounslow (Hthrw.Air.) TW6 .94 BK81
Northolt Way, Horn. RM12 . . .90 FJ65
North Orbital Rd, Rick. WD3 . .37 BE50
St. Albans AL1, AL2, AL4 . . . .9 CK25
Uxbridge (Denh.) UB9 . . . . .57 BF55
Watford WD25 . . . . .7 BU34
Northover, Brom. BR1 . . . . . .124 EF90
North Par, Chess. KT9 . . . . . .156 CL106
North Pk, SE9 . . . . .125 EM86
Gerrards Cross SL9 . . . . . . .56 AY56
Iver SL0 . . . . .93 BC76
North Pk La, Gdse. RH9 . . . . .186 DU129
North Pas, SW18 . . . . .100 DA84
North Peckham Est, SE15 . . .102 DT80
North Perimeter Rd, Uxb. UB8
off Kingston La 76 BL69
North Pl, Mitch. CR4 . . . . .120 DF94
Teddington TW11 . . . . .117 CF93
Waltham Abbey EN9
off Highbridge St 15 EB33
North Pole La, Kes. BR2 . . . . .162 EF107
North Pole Rd, W10 . . . . .81 CW71
Northport St, N1 . . . . .84 DR67
North Ride, W2 . . . . .198 B1
Northridge Rd, Grav. DA12 . . .131 GJ90
North Riding, St.Alb. (Brick.Wd.)
AL2 .8 CA30
North Rd, N6 . . . . .64 DG59
N7 .83 DL65
N9 .46 DV46
SE18 . . . . .105 ES77
SW19 . . . . .120 DC93
W5 .97 CK76
Belvedere DA17 . . . . .107 FB76
Brentford TW8 . . . . .98 CL79
Brentwood CM14 . . . . .54 FW46
Bromley BR1 . . . . .144 EH95
Dartford DA1 . . . . .127 FF86
Edgware HA8 . . . . .42 CP53
Feltham TW14 . . . . .115 BR86
Hayes UB3 . . . . .77 BR71
Ilford IG3 . . . . .69 ES61
Purfleet RM19 . . . . .109 FR77
Richmond TW9 . . . . .98 CN83
Rickmansworth (Chorl.)
WD3 . . . . .21 BD43
Romford (Chad.Hth.) RM6 . .70 EY57
Romford (Hav.at.Bow.)
RM4 . . . . .51 FE48
South Ockendon RM15 . . . .91 FW68
Southall UB1 . . . . .78 CA73
Surbiton KT6 . . . . .137 CK100
Waltham Cross EN8 . . . . . . .15 DY33
Walton-on-Thames KT12 . .154 BW106
West Drayton UB7 . . . . .94 BM76
West Wickham BR4 . . . . . .143 EB102
Woking GU21 . . . . .167 BA116
North Rd Av, Brwd. CM14 . . . .54 FW46
Northrop Rd, Houns. (Hthrw.Air.)
TW6 . . . . .95 BS81
North Row, W1 . . . . .194 E10
North Service Rd, Brwd.
CM14 . . . . .54 FW47
North Several, SE3
off Orchard Rd 103 ED82
NORTH SHEEN, Rich. 98 CN82
⇌ North Sheen 98 CN84
Northside Rd, Brom. BR1
off Mitchell Way 144 EG95
North Side Wandsworth
Common, SW18 . . . . .120 DD85
Northspur Rd, Sutt. SM1 . . . .140 DA104
North Sq, N9
off St. Martins Rd 46 DV47
NW11 . . . . .64 DA57
Northstead Rd, SW2 . . . . . . .121 DN89
North St, E13 . . . . .86 EG68
NW4 . . . . .63 CW57
SW4 . . . . .101 DJ83
Barking IG11 . . . . .87 EP65
Bexleyheath DA7 . . . . .106 FA84
Bromley BR1 . . . . .144 EG95
Carshalton SM5 . . . . .140 DF104
Dartford DA1 . . . . .128 FK87
Egham TW20 . . . . .113 AZ92
Gravesend DA12
off South St 131 GH87
Hornchurch RM11 . . . . .72 FK59
Isleworth TW7 . . . . .97 CG83
Leatherhead KT22 . . . . . . .171 CG121
Redhill RH1 . . . . .184 DF133
Romford RM1, RM5 . . . . .71 FD55
North St Pas, E13 . . . . .86 EH68
North Tenter St, E1 . . . . .84 DT72
North Ter, SW3 . . . . .198 B7
Northumberland All, EC3 . . . .197 N9
Northumberland Av, E12 . . . . .68 EJ60
WC2 . . . . .199 P2
Enfield EN1 . . . . .30 DV39
Hornchurch RM11 . . . . .72 FJ57
Isleworth TW7 . . . . .97 CF81
Welling DA16 . . . . .105 ER84
Northumberland Cl, Erith
DA8 . . . . .107 FC80
Staines (Stanw.) TW19 . . . .114 BL86
Northumberland Cres, Felt.
TW14 . . . . .115 BS86
Northumberland Gdns, N9 . . .46 DT48
Bromley BR1 . . . . .145 EN98
Isleworth TW7 . . . . .97 CG80
Mitcham CR4 . . . . .141 DK99
Northumberland Gro, N17 . . . .46 DV52
NORTHUMBERLAND HEATH,
Erith 107 FC80
⇌ Northumberland Park 46 DV53
Northumberland Pk, N17 . . . .46 DT52
Northumberland Pk, Erith
DA8 . . . . .107 FC80
Northumberland Pl, W2 . . . . . .82 DA72
Richmond TW10 . . . . .117 CK85
Northumberland Rd, E6 . . . . . .86 EL72
E17 .67 EA59
Barnet EN5 . . . . .28 DC44
Gravesend (Istead Rise)
DA13 . . . . .131 GF94
Harrow HA2 . . . . .60 BZ57
Northumberland Row, Twick. TW2
off Colne Rd 117 CE88
Northumberland St, WC2 . . .199 P2
Northumberland Way, Erith
DA8 . . . . .107 FC81
Northumbria St, E14 . . . . .85 EA72
North Verbena Gdns, W6
off St. Peter's Sq 99 CU78
Northview, N7 . . . . .65 DL62
North Vw, SW19 . . . . .119 CV92
W5 .79 CJ70
Ilford IG6 . . . . .50 EU52
Pinner HA5 . . . . .60 BW59
Northview, Swan. BR8 . . . . .147 FE96
North Vw Av, Til. RM18 . . . . .111 GG81
Northview Cres, NW10 . . . . . .63 CT63
North Vw Cres, Epsom
KT18 . . . . .173 CV117
North Vw Dr, Wdf.Grn. IG8 . . .48 EK54
North Vw Rd, N8 . . . . .65 DK55
Sevenoaks TN14
off Seal Rd 191 FJ121
North Vil, NW1 . . . . .83 DK65
North Wk, W2
off Bayswater Rd 82 DC73
Croydon (New Adgtn.)
CR0 . . . . .161 EB106
NORTH WATFORD, Wat. 23 BV37
North Way, N9 . . . . .46 DW47
N11 .45 DJ51
NW9 . . . . .62 CP55
Northway, NW11 . . . . .64 DB57
Morden SM4 . . . . .139 CY97
North Way, Pnr. HA5 . . . . .60 BW55
Northway, Rick. WD3 . . . . .38 BK45
North Way, Uxb. UB10 . . . . . . .76 BL66
Northway, Wall. SM6 . . . . . . .159 DJ105
Northway Circ, NW7 . . . . .42 CR49
Northway Cres, NW7 . . . . .42 CR49
Northway Ho, N20 . . . . .44 DC46
Northway Rd, SE5 . . . . .102 DQ83
Croydon CR0 . . . . .142 DT100
Northways Par, NW3
off College Cres 82 DD66
North Weald Airfield, Epp.
(N.Wld.Bas.) CM16 . . . . . . .18 EZ26
NORTH WEALD BASSETT, Epp.19 FB27
Northweald La, Kings.T. KT2 .117 CK92
NORTH WEMBLEY, Wem. 61 CH61
⇌ North Wembley 61 CK62
⊖ North Wembley 61 CK62
North Western Av, Wat.
WD24, WD25 . . . . .24 BW36
Northwest Pl, N1
off Chapel Mkt 83 DN68
North Wf Rd, W2 . . . . .82 DD71
Northwick Av, Har. HA3 . . . . . .61 CG58
Northwick Circle, Har. HA3 . . .61 CJ58
Northwick Cl, NW8
off Northwick Ter 82 DD70
Harrow HA1
off Nightingale Av 61 CH59
⊖ Northwick Park 61 CG59
H Northwick Park Hosp, Har.
HA1 . . . . .61 CH59
Northwick Pk Rd, Har. HA1 . . .61 CF58
Northwick Rd, Wat. WD19 . . . .40 BW49
Wembley HA0 . . . . .79 CK67
Northwick Ter, NW8 . . . . .82 DD70
Northwick Wk, Har. HA1 . . . . .61 CF59
Northwold Dr, Pnr. HA5
off Cuckoo Hill 60 BW55
Northwold Est, E5 . . . . .66 DU61
Northwold Rd, E5 . . . . .66 DT61
N16 .66 DT61
NORTHWOOD 39 BR51
⊖ Northwood 39 BS52
Northwood, Grays RM16 . . . .111 GH75
H Northwood & Pinner Comm
Hosp, Nthwd. HA6 . . . . . . .39 BU53
Northwood Av, Horn. RM12 . . .71 FG63
Purley CR8 . . . . .159 DN113
Northwood Cl, Wal.Cr. EN7 . . .14 DT27
North Wd Ct, SE25
off Regina Rd 142 DU97
Northwood Gdns, N12 . . . . . . .44 DD50
Greenford UB6 . . . . .61 CF64
Ilford IG5 . . . . .69 EN56
Northwood Hall, N6 . . . . .65 DJ59
NORTHWOOD HILLS, Nthwd. .39 BT54
⊖ Northwood Hills 39 BU54
Northwood Ho, SE27 . . . . . . .122 DR91
Northwood Pl, Erith DA18 . . .106 EZ76
Northwood Rd, N6 . . . . .65 DH59
SE23 . . . . .123 DZ88
Carshalton SM5 . . . . .158 DG107
Hounslow (Hthrw.Air.) TW6 .94 BK81
Thornton Heath CR7 . . . . . .141 DP96
Uxbridge (Hare.) UB9 . . . . . .38 BJ53
Northwood Twr, E17 . . . . .67 EC56
Northwood Way, SE19
off Roman Ri 122 DR93
Northwood HA6 . . . . .39 BU52
Uxbridge (Hare.) UB9 . . . . . .38 BK53
NORTH WOOLWICH, E16 . . . .104 EL75
⇌ North Woolwich 105 EN75
North Woolwich Rd, E16 . . . .205 L2
North Woolwich Roundabout, E16
off North Woolwich Rd 86 EK74
★ North Woolwich Station Mus,
E16 . . . . .105 EN75
North Worple Way, SW14 . . . .98 CR83
Nortoft Rd, Ger.Cr. (Chal.St.P.)
SL9 .37 AZ51
Norton Av, Surb. KT5 . . . . . .138 CP101
Norton Cl, E4 . . . . .47 EA50
Borehamwood WD6 . . . . .26 CN39
Norton Cl, Enf. EN1
off Brick La 30 DV40
Norton Folgate, E1 . . . . .197 N6
Norton Gdns, SW16 . . . . .141 DL96
Norton La, Cob. KT11 . . . . . . .169 BT119
Norton Rd, E10 . . . . .67 DZ60
Dagenham RM10 . . . . .89 FD65
Uxbridge UB8 . . . . .76 BK69
Wembley HA0 . . . . .79 CK65
Norval Rd, Wem. HA0 . . . . . . .61 CH61
Norway Dr, Slou. SL2 . . . . . . .74 AV71
Norway Gate, SE16 . . . . .203 L6
Norway Pl, E14
off East India Dock Rd 85 DZ72
Norway St, SE10 . . . . .103 EB79
Norway Wk, Rain. RM13
off The Glen 90 FJ70
Norwich Ho, E14
off Cordelia St 85 EB72
Norwich Ms, Ilf. IG3
off Ashgrove Rd 70 EU60
Norwich Pl, Bexh. DA6 . . . . .106 FA84
Norwich Rd, E7 . . . . .68 EG64
Dagenham RM9 . . . . .88 FA68
Greenford UB6 . . . . .78 CB67
Northwood HA6 . . . . .59 BT55
Thornton Heath CR7 . . . . . .142 DQ97
Norwich St, EC4 . . . . .196 D8
Norwich Wk, Edg. HA8 . . . . . .42 CQ52
Norwich Way, Rick. (Crox.Grn.)
WD3 . . . . .23 BP41
NORWOOD, SE19 . . . . .122 DS93
Norwood Av, Rom. RM7 . . . . . .71 FE59
Wembley HA0 . . . . .80 CM67
Norwood Cl, NW2 . . . . .63 CY62
Southall UB2 . . . . .96 CA77
Twickenham TW2
off Fourth Cross Rd 117 CD89
Norwood Cres, Houns. (Hthrw.Air.)
TW6 . . . . .95 BQ81
Norwood Dr, Har. HA2 . . . . . . .60 BZ58
Norwood Fm La, Cob. KT11 . .153 BU111
Norwood Gdns, Hayes UB4 . .78 BW70
Southall UB2 . . . . .96 BZ77
NORWOOD GREEN, Sthl. 96 CA77
Norwood Grn Rd, Sthl. UB2 . .96 CA77
Norwood High St, SE27 . . . . .121 DP90
⇌ Norwood Junction 142 DT98
Norwood La, Iver SL0 . . . . . . .75 BD70
NORWOOD NEW TOWN,
SE19 . . . . .122 DQ93
Norwood Pk Rd, SE27 . . . . . .122 DQ92
Norwood Rd, SE24 . . . . .121 DP88
SE27 . . . . .121 DP89
Southall UB2 . . . . .96 BZ77
Waltham Cross (Chsht.)
EN8 . . . . .15 DY30
Norwood Ter, Sthl. UB2
off Tentelow La 96 CB77
Notley End, Egh. (Eng.Grn.)
TW20 . . . . .112 AW93
Notley St, SE5 . . . . .102 DR80
Notre Dame Est, SW4 . . . . . .101 DJ84
Notson Rd, SE25 . . . . .142 DV98
Notting Barn Rd, W10 . . . . . . .81 CX70
Nottingdale Sq, W11
off Wilsham St 81 CY74
Nottingham Av, E16 . . . . .86 EJ71
Nottingham Cl, Wat. WD25 . . .7 BU33
Woking GU21 . . . . .166 AT118
Nottingham Ct, WC2 . . . . . . .195 P9
Woking GU21
off Nottingham Cl 166 AT118
Nottingham Pl, W1 . . . . .194 F5
Nottingham Rd, E10 . . . . .67 EC58
SW17 . . . . .120 DF88
Isleworth TW7 . . . . .97 CF82
Rickmansworth (Herons.)
WD3 . . . . .37 BC45
South Croydon CR2 . . . . . .160 DQ105
Nottingham St, W1 . . . . .194 F6
Nottingham Ter, NW1 . . . . . .194 F5
NOTTING HILL, W11 . . . . .81 CY73
⊖ Notting Hill Gate 82 DA73
Notting Hill Gate, W11 . . . . . .82 DA74
Nova Ms, Sutt. SM3 . . . . . . .139 CY102
Novar Cl, Orp. BR6 . . . . .145 ET101
Nova Rd, Croy. CR0 . . . . . . .141 DP101
Novar Rd, SE9 . . . . .125 EQ88
Novello St, SW6 . . . . .100 DA81
Novello Way, Borwd. WD6 . . . .26 CR39
Nowell Rd, SW13 . . . . .99 CU79
Nower, The, Sev. TN14 . . . . . .179 ET119
Nower Hill, Pnr. HA5 . . . . .60 BZ56
Noyna Rd, SW17 . . . . .120 DF90
Nuding Cl, SE13 . . . . .103 EA83
Nuffield Rd, Swan. BR8 . . . . .127 FG93
Nugent Ind Pk, Orp. BR5 . . . .146 EW99
Nugent Rd, N19 . . . . .65 DL60
SE25 . . . . .142 DT97
Nugents Ct, Pnr. HA5
off St. Thomas' Dr 40 BY53
Nugents Pk, Pnr. HA5 . . . . . . .40 BY53
Nugent Ter, NW8 . . . . .82 DC68
★ No. 2 Willow Rd, NW3 . . . . .64 DE63
Nunappleton Way, Oxt. RH8 .188 EG132
Nun Ct, EC2 . . . . .197 K8
Nuneaton Rd, Dag. RM9 . . . . .88 EX66
Nunfield, Kings L. (Chipper.)
WD4 .6 BH31
NUNHEAD, SE15 . . . . .102 DW83
⇌ Nunhead 102 DW82
Nunhead Cres, SE15 . . . . . . .102 DV83
Nunhead Est, SE15 . . . . .102 DV84
Nunhead Grn, SE15 . . . . .102 DV83
Nunhead Gro, SE15 . . . . .102 DV83
Nunhead La, SE15 . . . . .102 DV83
Nunhead Pas, SE15
off Peckham Rye 102 DU83
Nunnington Cl, SE9 . . . . .124 EL90
Nunns Rd, Enf. EN2 . . . . .30 DQ40
Nunns Way, Grays RM17 . . . .110 GD77
Nunsbury Dr, Brox. EN10 . . . . .15 DY25
Nuns Wk, Vir.W. GU25 . . . . . .132 AX99
NUPER'S HATCH, Rom. 51 FE45
Nupton Dr, Barn. EN5 . . . . . . .27 CW44
Nursery, The, Erith DA8 . . . . .107 FF80
Nursery Av, N3 . . . . .44 DC54
Bexleyheath DA7 . . . . .106 EZ83
Croydon CR0 . . . . .143 DX103
Nursery Cl, SE4 . . . . .103 DZ82
SW15 . . . . .99 CX84
Addlestone (Woodham)
KT15 . . . . .151 BF110
Amersham HP7 . . . . .20 AS39
Croydon CR0 . . . . .143 DX103
Dartford DA2 . . . . .128 FQ87
Enfield EN3 . . . . .31 DX39
Epsom KT17 . . . . .156 CS110
Feltham TW14 . . . . .115 BV87
Orpington BR6 . . . . .146 EU101
Romford RM6 . . . . .70 EX58
Sevenoaks TN13 . . . . .191 FJ122
South Ockendon RM15 . . . .91 FW70
Swanley BR8 . . . . .147 FC96
Tadworth KT20 . . . . .183 CU125
Woking GU21 . . . . .166 AW116
Woodford Green IG8 . . . . . .48 EH50
Nursery Ct, N17
off Nursery St 46 DT52
Nursery Gdns, Chis. BR7 . . . .125 EP93
Enfield EN3 . . . . .31 DX39
Hounslow TW4 . . . . .116 BZ85
Staines TW18 . . . . .114 BH94
Sunbury-on-Thames
TW16 . . . . .135 BT96
Waltham Cross EN7 . . . . . . .14 DR28
Nursery La, E2 . . . . .84 DT67
E7 . . . . .86 EG65
W10 . . . . .81 CW71
Slough SL3 . . . . .74 AW74
Uxbridge UB8 . . . . .76 BK70
Nurserymans Rd, N11 . . . . . . .44 DG47
Nursery Pl, Sev. TN13 . . . . . .190 FD122
Nursery Rd, E9
off Morning La 84 DW65
N2 .44 DD53
N14 .45 DJ45
SW9 . . . . .101 DM84
Broxbourne EN10 . . . . .15 DY25
Loughton IG10 . . . . .32 EJ43
Loughton (High Beach)
IG10 . . . . .32 EH39
Pinner HA5 . . . . .60 BW55
Sunbury-on-Thames
TW16 . . . . .135 BS96
Sutton SM1 . . . . .158 DC105
Tadworth KT20 . . . . .183 CU125
Thornton Heath CR7 . . . . . .142 DR98
Nursery Rd Merton, SW19 . . .140 DB96
Nursery Rd Mitcham, Mitch.
CR4 . . . . .140 DE97
Nursery Rd Wimbledon, SW19
off Worple Rd 119 CY94
Nursery Row, SE17 . . . . .201 K9
Barnet EN5
off St. Albans Rd 27 CY41
Nursery St, N17 . . . . .46 DT52
Nursery Wk, NW4 . . . . .63 CV55
Romford RM7 . . . . .71 FD59
Nursery Way, Stai. (Wrays.)
TW19 . . . . .112 AX86
Nursery Waye, Uxb. UB8 . . . . .76 BK67
Nurstead Rd, Erith DA8 . . . . .106 FA80
Nutberry Av, Grays RM16 . . .110 GA75
Nutberry Cl, Grays RM16
off Long La 110 GA75
Nutbourne St, W10 . . . . .81 CY69
Nutbrook St, SE15 . . . . .102 DU83
Nutbrowne Rd, Dag. RM9 . . . .88 EZ67
Nutcroft Gro, Lthd. (Fetch.)
KT22 . . . . .171 CE121
Nutcroft Rd, SE15 . . . . .102 DV80
NUTFIELD, Red. 185 DM133
Nutfield Cl, N18 . . . . .46 DU51
Carshalton SM5 . . . . .140 DE104
Nutfield Gdns, Ilf. IG3 . . . . . . .69 ET61
Northolt UB5 . . . . .78 BW68
Nutfield Marsh Rd, Red. (Nutfld.)
RH1 . . . . .185 DJ130
Nutfield Rd, E15 . . . . .67 EC63
NW2 . . . . .63 CU61
SE22 . . . . .122 DT85
Coulsdon CR5 . . . . .174 DG116
Redhill RH1 . . . . .184 DG134
Redhill (S.Merst.) RH1 . . . .185 DJ129
Thornton Heath CR7 . . . . . .141 DP98
Nutfield Way, Orp. BR6 . . . . .145 EN103
Nutford Pl, W1 . . . . .194 C8
Nuthatch Cl, Stai. TW19 . . . .114 BM88
Nuthatch Gdns, SE28 . . . . . .105 ER75
Nuthurst Av, SW2 . . . . .121 DM89
Nutkin Wk, Uxb. UB8
off Park Rd 76 BL66
Nutley Cl, Swan. BR8 . . . . . .147 FF95
Nutley Ct, Reig. RH2
off Nutley La 183 CZ134
Nutley La, Reig. RH2 . . . . . . .183 CZ133
Nutley Ter, NW3 . . . . .82 DC65
Nutmead Cl, Bex. DA5 . . . . . .127 FC88
Nutmeg Cl, E16
off Cranberry La 86 EE70
Nutmeg La, E14 . . . . .85 ED72
Nuttall St, N1 . . . . .84 DS68
Nutter La, E11 . . . . .68 EJ58
Nuttfield Cl, Rick. (Crox.Grn.)
WD3 . . . . .23 BP44
Nutt Gro, Edg. HA8 . . . . .41 CK47
Nut Tree Cl, Orp. BR6 . . . . . .146 EX104
Nutt St, SE15 . . . . .102 DT80
Nutty La, Shep. TW17 . . . . . .135 BQ98
Nutwell St, SW17 . . . . .120 DE92
Nutwood Gdns, Wal.Cr. (Chsht.)
EN7 off Gt. Stockwood Rd .14 DS26
Nuxley Rd, Belv. DA17 . . . . . .106 EZ79
Nyanza St, SE18 . . . . .105 ER79
Nye Bevan Est, E5 . . . . .67 DX62
Nyefield Pk, Tad. KT20 . . . . . .183 CU126
Nye Way, Hem.H. (Bov.) HP3 . . .5 BA28
Nylands Av, Rich. TW9 . . . . . . .98 CN81
Nymans Gdns, SW20
off Hidcote Gdns 139 CV97
Nynehead St, SE14 . . . . .103 DY80
Nyon Gro, SE6 . . . . .123 DZ89
Nyssa Cl, Wdf.Grn. IG8
off Gwynne Pk Av 49 EM51
Nyth Cl, Upmin. RM14 . . . . . . .73 FR58
Nyton Cl, N19
off Courtauld Rd 65 DL60

O

Oakapple Cl, S.Croy. CR2 . . .160 DV114
Oak Apple Ct, SE12 . . . . .124 EG89
Oak Av, N8 . . . . .65 DL56
N10 .45 DH52
N17 .46 DR52
Croydon CR0 . . . . .143 EA103
Egham TW20 . . . . .113 BC94
Enfield EN2 . . . . .29 DM38
Hampton TW12 . . . . .116 BY92
Hounslow TW5 . . . . .96 BX80
St. Albans (Brick.Wd.) AL2 . . .8 CA30
Sevenoaks TN13 . . . . .191 FH128
Upminster RM14 . . . . .72 FP62
Uxbridge UB10 . . . . .59 BP61
West Drayton UB7 . . . . .94 BN76
Oakbank, Brwd. CM13 . . . . . . .55 GE43
Oak Bk, Croy. (New Adgtn.)
CR0 . . . . .161 EC107
Oakbank, Lthd. (Fetch.) KT22 .170 CC123
Woking GU22 . . . . .166 AY119
Oakbank Av, Walt. KT12 . . . . .136 BZ101
Oakbank Gro, SE24 . . . . .102 DQ84
Oakbrook Cl, Brom. BR1 . . . .124 EH91
Oakbury Rd, SW6 . . . . .100 DB82
Oak Cl, N14 . . . . .45 DH45
Dartford DA1 . . . . .107 FE84
Sutton SM1 . . . . .140 DC103
Tadworth KT20 . . . . .182 CP130
Waltham Abbey EN9 . . . . . . .15 ED34
Oakcombe Cl, N.Mal. KT3
off Traps La 138 CS95
Oak Cottage Cl, SE6 . . . . . . .124 EF88
Oak Cres, E16 . . . . .86 EE71
Oakcroft Cl, Pnr. HA5 . . . . . . .39 BV54
West Byfleet KT14 . . . . . . .151 BF114
Oakcroft Rd, SE13 . . . . .103 ED82
Chessington KT9 . . . . .156 CM105
West Byfleet KT14 . . . . . . .151 BF114
Oakcroft Vil, Chess. KT9 . . . .156 CM105
Oakdale, N14 . . . . .45 DH46
Oakdale Av, Har. HA3 . . . . . . .62 CL57
Northwood HA6 . . . . .39 BU54
Oakdale Cl, Wat. WD19 . . . . . .40 BW49
Oakdale Gdns, E4 . . . . .47 EC50
Oakdale La, Eden. (Crock.H.)
TN8 . . . . .189 EP133
Oakdale Rd, E7 . . . . .86 EH66
E11 .67 ED61
E18 .48 EH54
N4 .66 DQ58
SE15 . . . . .102 DW83
SW16 . . . . .121 DL92
Epsom KT19 . . . . .156 CR109
Watford WD19 . . . . .40 BW48
Weybridge KT13 . . . . .134 BN104
Oakdale Way, Mitch. CR4
off Wolseley Rd 140 DG101
Oakdene, SE15
off Carlton Gro 102 DV81
Oak Dene, W13 off The Dene . .79 CH71
Oakdene, Rom. RM3 . . . . .52 FM54
Tadworth KT20 . . . . .173 CY120
Waltham Cross (Chsht.)
EN8 . . . . .15 DY30
Woking (Chobham) GU24 .150 AT110
Oakdene Av, Chis. BR7 . . . . .125 EN92
Erith DA8 . . . . .107 FC79
Thames Ditton KT7 . . . . . . .137 CG102
Oakdene Cl, Horn. RM11 . . . . .71 FH58
Pinner HA5 . . . . .40 BZ52
Oakdene Dr, Surb. KT5 . . . . .138 CQ101
Oakdene Ms, Sutt. SM3 . . . . .139 CZ102
Oakdene Par, Cob. KT11
off Anyards Rd 153 BV114
Oakdene Pk, N3 . . . . .43 CZ52
Oakdene Rd, Cob. KT11 . . . . .153 BV114
Leatherhead (Bkhm.)
KT23 . . . . .170 BZ124
Orpington BR5 . . . . .145 ET99
Redhill RH1 . . . . .184 DE134
Sevenoaks TN13 . . . . .190 FG122
Uxbridge UB10 . . . . .77 BP68
Watford WD24 . . . . .23 BV36
Oakden St, SE11 . . . . .200 E8
Oak Dr, Tad. KT20 . . . . .182 CP130
Oake Ct, SW15 . . . . .119 CY85
Oaken Coppice, Ashtd. KT21 .172 CN119
Oak End Dr, Iver SL0 . . . . .75 BC68
Oaken Dr, Esher (Clay.) KT10 .155 CF107
Oak End Way, Add. (Woodham)
KT15 . . . . .151 BE112
Gerrards Cross SL9 . . . . . . .56 AY57
Oakenholt Ho, SE2
off Hartslock Dr 106 EX75
Oaken La, Esher (Clay.) KT10 .155 CE106
Oakenshaw Cl, Surb. KT6 . . .138 CL101
Oakes Cl, E6 off Savage Gdns .87 EM72
Oakeshott Av, N6 . . . . .64 DG61
Oakey La, SE1 . . . . .200 D6
Oak Fm, Borwd. WD6 . . . . .26 CQ43
Oakfield, E4 . . . . .47 EB50
Rickmansworth (Mill End)
WD3 . . . . .37 BF45
Woking GU21 . . . . .166 AS116
Oakfield Av, Har. HA3 . . . . . . .61 CH55
Oakfield Cl, N.Mal. KT3
off Blakes La 139 CT99
Potters Bar EN6 . . . . .11 CZ31
Ruislip HA4 . . . . .59 BT58
Weybridge KT13 . . . . .153 BQ105
Oakfield Ct, N8 . . . . .65 DL59
NW2 off Hendon Way 63 CX59

Oak - Old

Oakfield Ct, Borwd. WD6 . . . . .26 CP41
Oakfield Dr, Reig. RH2 . . . . . .184 DA132
Oakfield Gdns, N18 . . . . .46 DS49
SE19 . . . . .122 DS92
Beckenham BR3 . . . . .143 EA99
Carshalton SM5 . . . . .140 DE102
Greenford UB6 . . . . .79 CD70
Oakfield Glade, Wey. KT13 . . .153 BQ105
Oakfield La, Bex. DA5 . . . . . . .127 FE89
Dartford DA1, DA2 . . . . .127 FG89
Keston BR2 . . . . .162 EJ105
Oakfield Pk Rd, Dart. DA1 . . .128 FK89
Oakfield Pl, Dart. DA1 . . . . . .128 FK89
Oakfield Rd, E6 . . . . .86 EL67
E17 .47 DY54
N3 . . . . .44 DB53
N4 . . . . .65 DN58
N14 .45 DL48
SE20 . . . . .122 DV94
SW19 . . . . .119 CX90
Ashford TW15 . . . . .115 BP92
Ashtead KT21 . . . . .171 CK117
Cobham KT11 . . . . .153 BV113
Croydon CR0 . . . . .142 DQ102
Ilford IG1 . . . . .69 EP61
Orpington BR6
off Goodmead Rd 146 EU101
Oakfields, Sev. TN13 . . . . . . .191 FH126
Walton-on-Thames KT12 . .135 BU102
West Byfleet KT14 . . . . . . .152 BH114
Oakfields Rd, NW11 . . . . .63 CY58
Oakfield St, SW10 . . . . .100 DC79
Oakford Rd, NW5 . . . . .65 DJ63
Oak Gdns, Croy. CR0 . . . . . . .143 EA103
Edgware HA8 . . . . .42 CQ54
Oak Glade, Epp. CM16
off Coopersale Common . .18 EX29
Epsom KT19
off Christ Ch Rd 156 CN112
Northwood HA6 . . . . .39 BP53
Oak Glen, Horn. RM11 . . . . . . .72 FL55
Oak Grn, Abb.L. WD5 . . . . .7 BS32
Oak Grn Way, Abb.L. WD5 . . . . .7 BS32
Oak Gro, NW2 . . . . .63 CY63
Ruislip HA4 . . . . .59 BV59
Sunbury-on-Thames TW16 .115 BV94
West Wickham BR4 . . . . . . .143 EC103
Oak Gro Rd, SE20 . . . . .142 DW95
Oakhall Ct, E11 . . . . .68 EH58
Oakhall Dr, Sun. TW16 . . . . . .115 BT92
Oak Hall Rd, E11 . . . . .68 EH58
Oakham Cl, SE6
off Rutland Wk 123 DZ89
Barnet EN4 . . . . .28 DF41
Oakham Dr, Brom. BR2 . . . . .144 EF98
Oakhampton Rd, NW7 . . . . . .43 CX52
Oak Hill, Epsom KT18 . . . . . .172 CR116
Oakhill, Esher (Clay.) KT10 . . .155 CG107
Oak Hill, Surb. KT6 . . . . .138 CL101
Woodford Green IG8 . . . . . .47 ED52
Oakhill Av, NW3 . . . . .64 DB63
Pinner HA5 . . . . .40 BY54
Oakhill Cl, Ashtd. KT21 . . . . .171 CJ118
Rickmansworth (Map.Cr.)
WD3 . . . . .37 BE49
Oak Hill Cl, Wdf.Grn. IG8 . . . .47 ED52
Oakhill Ct, SW19 . . . . .119 CX94
Oak Hill Cres, Surb. KT6 . . . .138 CL101
Woodford Green IG8 . . . . . .47 ED52
Oakhill Dr, Surb. KT6 . . . . . . .138 CL101
Oakhill Gdns, Wey. KT13 . . . .135 BS103
Oak Hill Gdns, Wdf.Grn. IG8 . .48 EE53
Oakhill Gro, Surb. KT6 . . . . . .138 CL100
Oak Hill Pk, NW3 . . . . .64 DB63
Oak Hill Pk Ms, NW3 . . . . .64 DC63
Oakhill Path, Surb. KT6 . . . . .138 CL100
Oakhill Pl, SW15
off Oakhill Rd 120 DA85
Oakhill Rd, SW15 . . . . .119 CZ85
SW16 . . . . .141 DL95
Addlestone KT15 . . . . .151 BF107
Ashtead KT21 . . . . .171 CJ118
Beckenham BR3 . . . . .143 EC96
Orpington BR6 . . . . .145 ET102
Purfleet RM19 . . . . .108 FP78
Rickmansworth (Map.Cr.)
WD3 . . . . .37 BD49
Oak Hill Rd, Rom. (Stap.Abb.)
RM4 . . . . .51 FD45
Sevenoaks TN13 . . . . .190 FG124
Surbiton KT6 . . . . .138 CL100
Oakhill Rd, Sutt. SM1 . . . . . .140 DB104
Oak Hill Way, NW3 . . . . .64 DC63
Oakhouse Rd, Bexh. DA6 . . . .126 FA85
Oakhurst, Wok. (Chobham)
GU24 . . . . .150 AS109
Oakhurst Av, Barn. EN4 . . . . .44 DE45
Bexleyheath DA7 . . . . .106 EY80
Oakhurst Cl, E17 . . . . .68 EE56
Chislehurst BR7 . . . . .145 EM95
Ilford IG6 . . . . .49 EQ53
Teddington TW11 . . . . .117 CE92
Oakhurst Gdns, E4 . . . . .48 EF46
E17 .68 EE56
Bexleyheath DA7 . . . . .106 EY80
Oakhurst Gro, SE22 . . . . . . .102 DU84
Oakhurst Pl, Wat. WD18
off Cherrydale 23 BT42
Oakhurst Ri, Cars. SM5 . . . . .158 DE110
Oakhurst Rd, Enf. EN3 . . . . . . .31 DX36
Epsom KT19 . . . . .156 CQ107
Oakington Av, Amer. HP6 . . . .20 AY39
Harrow HA2 . . . . .60 CA59
Hayes UB3 . . . . .95 BR77
Wembley HA9 . . . . .62 CM62
Oakington Dr, Sun. TW16 . . .136 BW96
Oakington Manor Dr, Wem.
HA9 . . . . .62 CN64
Oakington Rd, W9 . . . . .82 DA70
Oakington Way, N8 . . . . .65 DL58
Oakland Gdns, Brwd. CM13 . . .55 GC43
Oakland Pl, Buck.H. IG9 . . . . .48 EG47
Oakland Rd, E15 . . . . .67 ED63
Oaklands, N21 . . . . .45 DM47
Oaklands, Ken. CR8 . . . . .160 DQ114
Leatherhead (Fetch.) KT22 .171 CD124
Twickenham TW2 . . . . .116 CC87
Oaklands Av, N9 . . . . .30 DV44
Esher KT10 . . . . .137 CD102
Hatfield AL9 . . . . .11 CY27
Isleworth TW7 . . . . .97 CF79
Romford RM1 . . . . .71 FE55
Sidcup DA15 . . . . .125 ET87
Thornton Heath CR7 . . . . .141 DN98
Watford WD19 . . . . .39 BV46
West Wickham BR4 . . . . . . .143 EB104
Oaklands Cl, Bexh. DA6 . . . . .126 EZ85
Chessington KT9 . . . . .155 CJ105
Orpington BR5 . . . . .145 ES100
Oaklands Ct, Add. KT15 . . . . .134 BH104
Watford WD17 . . . . .23 BU39
Wembley HA0 . . . . .61 CK64
Oaklands Dr, S.Ock. RM15 . . . .91 FW71
Oaklands Est, SW4 . . . . .121 DJ86
Oaklands Gdns, Ken. CR8 . . .160 DQ114
Oaklands Gate, Nthwd. HA6
off Green La 39 BS51
Oaklands Gro, W12 . . . . .81 CU74
Oaklands La, Barn. EN5 . . . . . .27 CV42
Westerham (Bigg.H.) TN16 .162 EH113
Oaklands Pk Av, Ilf. IG1
off High Rd 69 ER61
Oaklands Pl, SW4
off St. Alphonsus Rd 101 DJ84
Oaklands Rd, N20 . . . . .43 CZ45
NW2 . . . . .63 CX63
SW14 . . . . .98 CR83
W7 .97 CF75
Bexleyheath DA6 . . . . .106 EZ84
Bromley BR1 . . . . .124 EE94
Dartford DA2 . . . . .128 FP88
Gravesend (Nthflt.) DA11 . .131 GF91
Waltham Cross (Chsht.)
EN7 . . . . .14 DS26
Oaklands Way, Tad. KT20 . . .173 CW122
Wallington SM6 . . . . .159 DK108
Oakland Way, Epsom KT19 . .156 CR107
Oak La, E14 . . . . .85 DZ73
N2 . . . . .44 DD54
N11 .45 DK51
Egham (Eng.Grn.) TW20 . .112 AW90
Isleworth TW7 . . . . .97 CE84
Potters Bar (Cuffley) EN6 . . .13 DM28
Sevenoaks TN13 . . . . .190 FG127
Twickenham TW1 . . . . .117 CG87
Woking GU22
off Beaufort Rd 167 BC116
Woodford Green IG8 . . . . . .48 EF49
Oaklawn Rd, Lthd. KT22 . . . .171 CE118
Oak Leaf Cl, Epsom KT19 . . .156 CQ112
Oakleafe Gdns, Ilf. IG6 . . . . . .69 EP55
Oaklea Pas, Kings.T. KT1 . . . .137 CK97
Oakleigh Av, N20 . . . . .44 DD47
Edgware HA8 . . . . .42 CP54
Surbiton KT6 . . . . .138 CN102
Oakleigh Cl, N20 . . . . .44 DF48
Swanley BR8 . . . . .147 FE97
Oakleigh Ct, Barn. EN4
off Church Hill Rd 28 DE44
Edgware HA8 . . . . .42 CQ54
Oakleigh Cres, N20 . . . . .44 DE47
Oakleigh Dr, Rick. (Crox.Grn.)
WD3 . . . . .23 BQ44
Oakleigh Gdns, N20 . . . . .44 DC46
Edgware HA8 . . . . .42 CM50
Orpington BR6 . . . . .163 ES105
Oakleigh Ms, N20
off Oakleigh Rd N 44 DC47
OAKLEIGH PARK, N20 . . . . . . .44 DD46
⇌ **Oakleigh Park** 44 DD45
Oakleigh Pk Av, Chis. BR7 . . .145 EN95
Oakleigh Pk N, N20 . . . . .44 DD46
Oakleigh Pk S, N20 . . . . .44 DE47
Oakleigh Ri, Epp. CM16
off Bower Hill 18 EU32
Oakleigh Rd, Pnr. HA5 . . . . . . .40 BZ51
Uxbridge UB10 . . . . .77 BQ66
Oakleigh Rd N, N20 . . . . .44 DD47
Oakleigh Rd S, N11 . . . . .44 DG48
Oakleigh Way, Mitch. CR4 . . .141 DH95
Surbiton KT6 . . . . .138 CN102
Oakley Av, W5 . . . . .80 CN73
Barking IG11 . . . . .87 ET66
Croydon CR0 . . . . .159 DL105
Oakley Cl, E4 . . . . .47 EC48
E6 *off Northumberland Rd* . .86 EL72
W7 .79 CE73
Addlestone KT15 . . . . .152 BK105
Grays RM20 . . . . .109 FW79
Isleworth TW7 . . . . .97 CD81
Oakley Ct, Loug. IG10
off Hillyfields 33 EN40
Mitcham CR4
off London Rd 140 DG102
Oakley Cres, EC1 . . . . .196 G1
Slough SL1 . . . . .74 AS73
Oakley Dr, SE9 . . . . .125 ER88
SE13 *off Hither Grn La* 123 EC85
Bromley BR2 . . . . .144 EL104
Romford RM3 . . . . .52 FN50
Oakley Gdns, N8 . . . . .65 DM57
SW3 . . . . .100 DE79
Banstead SM7 . . . . .174 DB115
Oakley Pk, Bex. DA5 . . . . . . .126 EW87
Oakley Pl, SE1 . . . . .102 DT78
Oakley Rd, N1 . . . . .84 DR66
SE25 . . . . .142 DV99
Bromley BR2 . . . . .144 EL104
Harrow HA1 . . . . .61 CE58
Warlingham CR6 . . . . .176 DU118
Oakley Sq, NW1 . . . . .83 DJ68
Oakley St, SW3 . . . . .100 DE79
Oakley Wk, W6 . . . . .99 CX79
Oakley Yd, E2
off Bacon St 84 DT70
Oak Lo Av, Chig. IG7 . . . . .49 ER50
Oak Lo Cl, Stan. HA7
off Dennis La 41 CJ50
Walton-on-Thames KT12 . .154 BW106
Oak Lo Dr, W.Wick. BR4 . . . . .143 EB101
Oak Lo La, West. TN16 . . . . .189 ER125
Oak Manor Dr, Wem. HA9
off Oakington Manor Dr . . .62 CM64
Oakmead Av, Brom. BR2 . . . .144 EG100
Oakmeade, Pnr. HA5 . . . . .40 CA51
Oakmead Gdns, Edg. HA8 . . . .42 CR49
Oakmead Grn, Epsom KT18 . .172 CP115
Oakmead Pl, Mitch. CR4 . . . .140 DE95
Oakmead Rd, SW12 . . . . . . .120 DG88
Croydon CR0 . . . . .141 DK100
Oakmere Av, Pot.B. EN6 . . . . .12 DC33
Oakmere Cl, Pot.B. EN6 . . . . .12 DD31
Oakmere La, Pot.B. EN6 . . . . .12 DC32
Oakmere Rd, SE2 . . . . .106 EU79
Oakmoor Way, Chig. IG7 . . . . .49 ES50
Oakmount Pl, Orp. BR6 . . . . .145 ER102
Oak Pk, W.Byf. KT14 . . . . . . .151 BE113
Oak Pk Gdns, SW19 . . . . .119 CX87
Oak Path, Bushey WD23
off Ashfield Av 24 CB44
Oak Piece, Epp. (N.Wld.Bas.)
CM16 . . . . .19 FC25
Oak Pl, SW18 *off East Hill* . . .120 DB85
Oakridge, St.Alb. (Brick.Wd.)
AL2 .8 BZ29
Oakridge Av, Rad. WD7 . . . . . . .9 CF34
Oakridge Dr, N2 . . . . .64 DD55
Oakridge La, Brom. BR1
off Downham Way 123 ED92
Radlett WD7 . . . . .9 CF33
Watford (Ald.) WD25 . . . . . .25 CD35
Oakridge Rd, Brom. BR1 . . . .123 ED91
Oak Ri, Buck.H. IG9 . . . . .48 EK48
Oak Rd, W5 *off The Broadway* .79 CK73
Caterham CR3 . . . . .176 DS122
Cobham KT11 . . . . .170 BX115
Epping CM16 . . . . .17 ET30
Erith (Northumb.Hth.)
DA8 . . . . .107 FC80
Erith (Slade Grn.) DA8 . . . .107 FG81
Gravesend DA12 . . . . .131 GJ90
Grays RM17 . . . . .110 GC79
Greenhithe DA9 . . . . .129 FS86
Leatherhead KT22 . . . . . . .171 CG118
New Malden KT3 . . . . .138 CR96
Orpington BR6 . . . . .164 EU108
Reigate RH2 . . . . .184 DB133
Romford RM3 . . . . .52 FM53
Westerham TN16 . . . . .189 ER125
Oak Row, SW16 . . . . .141 DJ96
Oakroyd Av, Pot.B. EN6 . . . . . .11 CZ33
Oakroyd Cl, Pot.B. EN6 . . . . . .11 CZ34
Oaks, The, N12 . . . . .44 DB49
SE18 . . . . .105 EQ78
Epsom KT18 . . . . .157 CT114
Hayes UB4 *off Charville La* . .77 BQ68
Ruislip HA4 . . . . .59 BS59
Staines TW18
off Moormede Cres 113 BF91
Swanley BR8 . . . . .147 FE96
Tadworth KT20 . . . . .173 CW123
Watford WD19 . . . . .40 BW46
West Byfleet KT14 . . . . . . .152 BG113
Woodford Green IG8 . . . . . .48 EE51
Oaks Av, SE19 . . . . .122 DS92
Feltham TW13 . . . . .116 BY89
Romford RM5 . . . . .51 FC54
Worcester Park KT4 . . . . . .139 CV104
Oaks Cl, Lthd. KT22 . . . . . . .171 CG121
Radlett WD7 . . . . .25 CF35
Oaksford Av, SE26 . . . . .122 DV90
Oaks Gro, E4 . . . . .48 EE47
Oakshade Rd, Brom. BR1 . . . .123 ED91
Leatherhead (Oxshott)
KT22 . . . . .154 CC114
Oakshaw, Oxt. RH8 . . . . .187 ED127
Oakshaw Rd, SW18 . . . . .120 DB87
Oakside, Uxb. (Denh.) UB9 . . .76 BH65
Oaks La, Croy. CR0 . . . . .142 DW104
Ilford IG2 . . . . .69 ES57
Oak Sq, Sev. TN13
off High St 191 FJ126
Oaks Rd, Croy. CR0 . . . . .160 DV106
Kenley CR8 . . . . .159 DP114
Reigate RH2 . . . . .184 DC133
Staines (Stanw.) TW19 . . . .114 BK86
Woking GU21 . . . . .166 AY117
Oaks Track, Cars. SM5 . . . . . .158 DF111
Wallington SM6 . . . . .159 DH110
Oak St, Rom. RM7 . . . . .71 FC57
Oaks Way, Cars. SM5 . . . . . .158 DF108
Epsom KT18
off Epsom La N 173 CV119
Kenley CR8 . . . . .160 DQ114
Surbiton KT6 . . . . .137 CK103
Oakthorpe Rd, N13 . . . . .45 DN50
Oaktree Av, N13 . . . . .45 DP48
Oak Tree Av, Green. (Bluewater)
DA9 . . . . .129 FT87
Oak Tree Cl, W5
off Pinewood Gro 79 CJ72
Abbots Langley WD5 . . . . . . .7 BR32
Oaktree Cl, Brwd. CM13
off Hawthorn Av 55 FZ49
Oak Tree Cl, Loug. IG10 . . . . .33 EQ39
Stanmore HA7 . . . . .41 CJ52
Virginia Water GU25 . . . . .132 AX101
Oaktree Cl, Wal.Cr. EN7 . . . . . .13 DP28
Oak Tree Ct, Borwd. (Elstree) WD6
off Barnet La 25 CK44
Oak Tree Dell, NW9 . . . . .62 CQ57
Oak Tree Dr, N20 . . . . .44 DB46
Egham (Eng.Grn.) TW20 . . .112 AW92
Oak Tree Gdns, Brom. BR1 . . .124 EH92
Oaktree Gro, Ilf. IG1 . . . . .69 ER64
Oak Tree Rd, NW8 . . . . .194 A3
Oakview Cl, Wal.Cr. EN7 . . . . .14 DV28
Oakview Gdns, N2 . . . . .64 DD56
Oakview Gro, Croy. CR0 . . . . .143 DY102
Oakview Rd, SE6 . . . . .123 EB92
Oak Village, NW5 . . . . .64 DG63
Oak Wk, Wall. SM6
off London Rd 140 DG102
Oak Way, N14 . . . . .45 DH45
Oakway, SW20 . . . . .139 CW98
Oak Way, W3 . . . . .80 CS74
Ashtead KT21 . . . . .172 CN116
Oakway, Brom. BR2 . . . . .143 ED96
Oak Way, Croy. CR0 . . . . .143 DX100
Feltham TW14 . . . . .115 BS88
Oakway, Wok. GU21 . . . . . . .166 AS119
Oakway Cl, Bex. DA5 . . . . . . .126 EY86
Oakway Pl, Rad. WD7
off Watling St 9 CG34
Oakways, SE9 . . . . .125 EP86
Oakwell Dr, Pot.B. EN6 . . . . . .13 DH32
OAKWOOD, N14 . . . . .29 DK44
⊖ **Oakwood** 29 DJ43
Oakwood, Wall. SM6 . . . . . . .159 DH109
Waltham Abbey EN9
off Roundhills 31 ED35
Oakwood Av, N14 . . . . .45 DK45
Beckenham BR3 . . . . .143 EC96
Borehamwood WD6 . . . . . . .26 CP42
Brentwood CM13 . . . . .55 GE44
Bromley BR2 . . . . .144 EH97
Mitcham CR4 . . . . .140 DD96
Purley CR8 . . . . .159 DP112
Southall UB1 . . . . .78 CA73
Oakwood Chase, Horn. RM11 .72 FM58
Oakwood Cl, N14 . . . . .29 DJ44
Chislehurst BR7 . . . . .125 EM93
Dartford DA1 . . . . .128 FP88
Redhill RH1 . . . . .184 DG134
Woodford Green IG8
off Green Wk 48 EL51
Oakwood Ct, W14 . . . . .99 CZ76
Oakwood Cres, N21 . . . . .29 DL44
Greenford UB6 . . . . .79 CG65
Oakwood Dr, SE19 . . . . .122 DR93
Bexleyheath DA7 . . . . .107 FD84
Edgware HA8 . . . . .42 CQ51
Sevenoaks TN13 . . . . .191 FH123
Oakwood Gdns, Ilf. IG3 . . . . . .69 ET61
Orpington BR6 . . . . .145 EQ103
Sutton SM1 . . . . .140 DA103
Oakwood Hill, Loug. IG10 . . . .33 EM44
Oakwood Hill Ind Est, Loug.
IG10 . . . . .33 EQ43
Oakwood La, W14 . . . . .99 CZ76
Oakwood Pk Rd, N14 . . . . .45 DK45
Oakwood Pl, Croy. CR0 . . . . .141 DN100
Oakwood Ri, Cat. CR3 . . . . . .186 DS125
Oakwood Rd, NW11 . . . . .64 DB57
SW20 . . . . .139 CU95
Croydon CR0 . . . . .141 DN100
Orpington BR6 . . . . .145 EQ103
Pinner HA5 . . . . .39 BV54
Redhill (Merst.) RH1 . . . . .185 DN129
St. Albans (Brick.Wd.) AL2 . . .8 BY29
Virginia Water GU25 . . . . .132 AW99
Woking GU21 . . . . .166 AS119
Oakwood Vw, N14 . . . . .29 DK44
Oakworth Rd, W10 . . . . .81 CW71
Oarsman Pl, E.Mol. KT8 . . . . .137 CE98
Oast Ho Cl, Stai. (Wrays.)
TW19 . . . . .112 AY87
Oasthouse Way, Orp. BR5 . . .146 EV98
Oast Rd, Oxt. RH8 . . . . .188 EF131
Oates Cl, Brom. BR2 . . . . . . .143 ED97
Oates Rd, Rom. RM5 . . . . .51 FB50
Oatfield Ho, N15
off Bushey Rd 66 DS58
Oatfield Rd, Orp. BR6 . . . . . .145 ET102
Tadworth KT20 . . . . .173 CV120
Oatland Ri, E17 . . . . .47 DY54
Oatlands Av, Wey. KT13 . . . . .153 BR106
Oatlands Chase, Wey. KT13 . .135 BS104
Oatlands Cl, Wey. KT13 . . . . .153 BQ105
Oatlands Dr, Wey. KT13 . . . . .135 BR104
Oatlands Grn, Wey. KT13
off Oatlands Dr 135 BR104
Oatlands Mere, Wey. KT13 . . .135 BR104
OATLANDS PARK, Wey. 153 BR105
Oatlands Rd, Enf. EN3 . . . . . . .30 DW39
Tadworth KT20 . . . . .173 CY119
Oat La, EC2 . . . . .197 H8
Oban Cl, E13 . . . . .86 EJ70
Oban Ho, Bark. IG11
off Wheelers Cross 87 ER68
Oban Rd, E13 . . . . .86 EJ69
SE25 . . . . .142 DR98
Oban St, E14 . . . . .85 ED72
Obelisk Ride, Egh. TW20 . . . .112 AS93
Oberon Cl, Borwd. WD6 . . . . . .26 CQ39
Oberon Way, Shep. TW17 . . . .134 BL97
Oberstein Rd, SW11 . . . . . . .100 DD84
Oborne Cl, SE24 . . . . .121 DP85
Observatory Gdns, W8 . . . . . .100 DA75
Observatory Ms, E14 . . . . . . .204 F8
Observatory Rd, SW14 . . . . . . .98 CQ84
Observatory Shop Cen, Slou.
SL1 . . . . .92 AU75
Observatory Wk, Red. RH1
off Lower Br Rd 184 DF134
Occupation La, SE18 . . . . . . .105 EP81
W5 .97 CK77
Occupation Rd, SE17 . . . . . . .201 H10
W13 . . . . .97 CH75
Watford WD18 . . . . .23 BV43
Ocean Est, E1 . . . . .85 DX70
Ocean St, E1 . . . . .85 DX71
Ocean Wf, E14 . . . . .203 P5
Ockenden Cl, Wok. GU22
off Ockenden Rd 167 AZ118
Ockenden Gdns, Wok. GU22
off Ockenden Rd 167 AZ118
Ockenden Rd, Wok. GU22 . . .167 AZ118
⇌ **Ockendon** 91 FX69
Ockendon Ms, N1
off Ockendon Rd 84 DR65
Ockendon Rd, N1 . . . . .84 DR65
Upminster RM14 . . . . .72 FQ64
OCKHAM, Wok. 168 BN121
Ockham Dr, Lthd. (W.Hors.)
KT24 . . . . .169 BR124
Orpington BR5 . . . . .126 EU94
Ockham La, Cob. KT11 . . . . . .169 BT118
Woking (Ockham) GU23 . . .169 BP120
Ockham Rd N, Lthd. KT24 . . .169 BQ124
Woking (Ockham) GU23 . . .168 BN121
Ockley Ct, Sutt. SM1
off Oakhill Rd 158 DC105
Ockley Rd, SW16 . . . . .121 DL90
Croydon CR0 . . . . .141 DM101
Ockleys Mead, Gdse. RH9 . . .186 DW129
Octagon Arc, EC2 . . . . .197 M7
Octagon Rd, Walt. KT12 . . . . .153 BS109
Octavia Cl, Mitch. CR4 . . . . .140 DE99
Octavia Rd, Islw. TW7 . . . . . . .97 CF82
Octavia St, SW11 . . . . .100 DE81
Octavia Way, SE28
off Booth Cl 88 EV73
Staines TW18 . . . . .114 BG93
Octavius St, SE8 . . . . .103 EA80
Odard Rd, W.Mol. KT8
off Down St 136 CA98
Oddesey Rd, Borwd. WD6 . . . .26 CP39
Odell Cl, Bark. IG11 . . . . .87 ET66
Odessa Rd, E7 . . . . .68 EF62
NW10 . . . . .81 CU68
Odessa St, SE16 . . . . .203 M5
Odger St, SW11 . . . . .100 DF82
Odhams Wk, WC2 . . . . .195 P9
Odyssey Business Pk, Ruis.
HA4 . . . . .59 BV64
Offa's Mead, E9
off Lindisfarne Way 67 DY63
Offenbach Ho, E2 . . . . .85 DX68
Offenham Rd, SE9 . . . . .125 EM91
Offers Ct, Kings.T. KT1
off Winery La 138 CM97
Offerton Rd, SW4 . . . . .101 DJ83
Offham Slope, N12 . . . . .43 CZ50
Offley Pl, Islw. TW7 . . . . .97 CD82
Offley Rd, SW9 . . . . .101 DN80
Offord Cl, N17 . . . . .46 DU52
Offord Rd, N1 . . . . .83 DM66
Offord St, N1 . . . . .83 DM66
Ogilby St, SE18 . . . . .105 EM77
Oglander Rd, SE15 . . . . .102 DT84
Ogle St, W1 . . . . .195 K6
Oglethorpe Rd, Dag. RM10 . . . .70 EZ62
Ohio Rd, E13 . . . . .86 EF70
Oil Mill La, W6 . . . . .99 CU78
Okeburn Rd, SW17 . . . . .120 DG92
Okehampton Cl, N12 . . . . .44 DD50
Okehampton Cres, Well.
DA16 . . . . .106 EV81
Okehampton Rd, NW10 . . . . . .81 CW67
Romford RM3 . . . . .52 FJ51
Okehampton Sq, Rom. RM3 . . .52 FJ51
Okemore Gdns, Orp. BR5 . . . .146 EW98
Olaf St, W11 . . . . .81 CX73
Old Acre, Wok. GU22 . . . . . . .152 BG114
Oldacre Ms, SW12
off Balham Gro 121 DH87
★ **Old Admiralty Bldgs (MoD)**,
SW1 . . . . .199 N3
Old Amersham Rd, Ger.Cr.
SL9 . . . . .57 BB60
Old Av, W.Byf. KT14 . . . . . . .151 BE113
Weybridge KT13 . . . . .153 BR107
Old Av Cl, W.Byf. KT14 . . . . . .151 BE113
Old Bailey, EC4 . . . . .196 G9
Old Barge Ho All, SE1
off Upper Grd 83 DN74
Old Barn Cl, Sutt. SM2 . . . . . .157 CY108
Old Barn La, Ken. CR8 . . . . . .176 DT116
Rickmansworth (Crox.Grn.)
WD3 . . . . .22 BM43
Old Barn Rd, Epsom KT18 . . .172 CQ117
Old Barn Way, Bexh. DA7 . . . .107 FD83
Old Barrack Yd, SW1 . . . . . . .198 F5
Old Barrowfield, E15
off New Plaistow Rd 86 EE67
Old Bath Rd, Slou. (Colnbr.)
SL3 . . . . .93 BE81
Old Bellgate Pl, E14 . . . . . . .203 P7
Oldberry Rd, Edg. HA8 . . . . . .42 CR51
Old Bethnal Grn Rd, E2 . . . . . .84 DU69
OLD BEXLEY, Bex. 127 FB87
Old Bexley La, Bex. DA5 . . . . .127 FD89
Dartford DA1 . . . . .127 FF88
Old Billingsgate Wk, EC3
off Lower Thames St 84 DS72
Old Bond St, W1 . . . . .199 K1
Oldborough Rd, Wem. HA0 . . .61 CJ61
Old Brewers Yd, WC2 . . . . . . .195 P9
Old Brewery Ms, NW3
off Hampstead High St . . .64 DD63
Old Br Cl, Nthlt. UB5 . . . . .78 CA68
Old Br St, Kings.T. KT1 . . . . .137 CK96
Old Broad St, EC2 . . . . .197 L9
Old Bromley Rd, Brom. BR1 . .123 ED92
Old Brompton Rd, SW5 . . . . .100 DA78
SW7 . . . . .100 DA78
Old Bldgs, WC2 . . . . .196 D8
Old Burlington St, W1 . . . . . .195 K10
Oldbury Cl, Cher. KT16
off Oldbury Rd 133 BE101
Orpington BR5 . . . . .146 EX98
Oldbury Pl, W1 . . . . .194 G6
Oldbury Rd, Cher. KT16 . . . . .133 BE101
Enfield EN1 . . . . .30 DU40
Old Canal Ms, SE15
off Nile Ter 102 DT78
Old Carriageway, The, Sev.
TN13 . . . . .190 FC123
Old Castle St, E1 . . . . .197 P8
Old Cavendish St, W1 . . . . . .195 H8
Old Change Ct, EC4
off Carter La 84 DQ72
Old Chapel Rd, Swan. BR8 . . .147 FC101
Old Charlton Rd, Shep.
TW17 . . . . .135 BQ99
Old Chelsea Ms, SW3
off Danvers St 100 DD79
Old Chertsey Rd, Wok. (Chobham)
GU24 . . . . .150 AV110
Old Chestnut Av, Esher
KT10 . . . . .154 CA107
Old Chorleywood Rd, Rick. WD3
off Chorleywood Rd 22 BK44
Oldchurch Gdns, Rom. RM7 . . .71 FD59
H **Oldchurch Hosp**, Rom.
RM7 . . . . .71 FE58
Old Ch La, NW9 . . . . .62 CQ61
Brentwood CM13 . . . . .55 GE42
Greenford UB6
off Perivale La 79 CG69
Stanmore HA7 . . . . .41 CJ52

★ Place of interest ⇌ Railway station ⊖ London Underground station DLR Docklands Light Railway station Tramlink station H Hospital

Old Ch Path, Esher KT10
off High St 154 CB105
Oldchurch Ri, Rom. RM7 .... 71 FD59
Old Ch Rd, E1 .... 85 DX72
E4 .... 47 EA49
Oldchurch Rd, Rom. RM7 .... 71 FD59
Old Ch St, SW3 .... 100 DD78
Old Claygate La, Esher (Clay.)
KT10 .... 155 CG107
Old Clem Sq, SE18
off Kempt St 105 EN79
Old Coach Rd, Cher. KT16 .... 133 BD99
Old Coal Yd, SE28
off Pettman Cres 105 ER77
Old Common Rd, Cob. KT11 .... 153 BU112
Old Compton St, W1 .... 195 M10
Old Cote Dr, Houns. TW5 .... 96 CA79
OLD COULSDON, Couls. 175 DN119
Old Ct, Ashtd. KT21 .... 172 CL119
Old Ct Pl, W8 .... 100 DB75
★ **Old Curiosity Shop**, WC2 .... 196 B8
Old Dairy Ms, SW12
off Chestnut Gro 120 DG87
Old Dartford Rd, Dart. (Fnghm.)
DA4 .... 148 FM100
Old Dean, Hem.H. (Bov.) HP3 .... 5 BA27
Old Deer Pk Gdns, Rich. TW9 .... 98 CL83
Old Devonshire Rd, SW12 .... 121 DH87
Old Dock App Rd, Grays
RM17 .... 110 GE77
Old Dock Cl, Rich. TW9
off Watcombe Cotts 98 CN79
Old Dover Rd, SE3 .... 104 EG80
Olden La, Pur. CR8 .... 159 DN112
Old Esher Cl, Walt. KT12
off Old Esher Rd 154 BX106
Old Esher Rd, Walt. KT12 .... 154 BX106
Old Farleigh Rd, S.Croy. CR2 .... 160 DW110
Warlingham CR6 .... 161 DY113
Old Fm Av, N14 .... 45 DJ45
Sidcup DA15 .... 125 ER88
Old Fm Cl, Houns. TW4 .... 96 BZ84
Old Fm Gdns, Swan. BR8 .... 147 FF97
Old Farmhouse Dr, Lthd. (Oxshott)
KT22 .... 171 CD115
Old Fm Pas, Hmptn. TW12 .... 136 CC95
Old Fm Rd, N2 .... 44 DD53
Hampton TW12 .... 116 BZ93
West Drayton UB7 .... 94 BK75
Old Fm Rd E, Sid. DA15 .... 126 EU89
Old Fm Rd W, Sid. DA15 .... 125 ET89
Old Ferry Dr, Stai. (Wrays.)
TW19 .... 112 AW86
Old Fld Cl, Amer. HP6 .... 20 AY39
Oldfield Cl, Brom. BR1 .... 145 EM98
Greenford UB6 .... 61 CE64
Stanmore HA7 .... 41 CG50
Waltham Cross (Chsht.)
EN8 .... 15 DY28
Oldfield Dr, Wal.Cr. (Chsht.)
EN8 .... 15 DY28
Oldfield Fm Gdns, Grnf. UB6 .... 79 CD67
Oldfield Gdns, Ashtd. KT21 .... 171 CK119
Oldfield Gro, SE16 .... 203 H9
Oldfield La N, Grnf. UB6 .... 79 CE65
Oldfield La S, Grnf. UB6 .... 78 CC70
Oldfield Ms, N6 .... 65 DJ59
Oldfield Rd, N16 .... 66 DS62
NW10 .... 81 CT66
SW19 .... 119 CY93
W3 off Valetta Rd 99 CT75
Bexleyheath DA7 .... 106 EY82
Bromley BR1 .... 145 EM98
Hampton TW12 .... 136 BZ95
St. Albans (Lon.Col.) AL2 .... 9 CK25
Oldfields Circ, Nthlt. UB5 .... 78 CC65
Oldfields Rd, Sutt. SM1 .... 139 CZ104
Oldfields Trd Est, Sutt. SM1 .... 140 DA104
Oldfield Wd, Wok. GU22
off Maybury Hill 167 BB117
Old Fish St Hill, EC4 .... 197 H10
Old Fleet La, EC4 .... 196 F8
Old Fold Cl, Barn. EN5
off Old Fold La 27 CZ39
Old Fold La, Barn. EN5 .... 27 CZ39
Old Fold Vw, Barn. EN5 .... 27 CW41
OLD FORD, E3 .... 85 DZ66
Old Ford Rd, E2 .... 84 DW68
E3 .... 85 DY68
Old Forge Cl, Stan. HA7 .... 41 CG49
Watford WD25 .... 7 BU33
Old Forge Cres, Shep. TW17 .... 135 BP100
Old Forge Ms, W12
off Goodwin Rd 99 CV75
Old Forge Rd, Enf. EN1 .... 30 DT38
Old Forge Way, Sid. DA14 .... 126 EV91
Old Fox Cl, Cat. CR3 .... 175 DP121
Old Fox Footpath, S.Croy. CR2
off Essenden Rd 160 DS108
Old Gannon Cl, Nthwd. HA6 .... 39 BQ50
Old Gdn, The, Sev. TN13 .... 190 FD123
Old Gloucester St, WC1 .... 196 A6
Old Gro Cl, Wal.Cr. (Chsht.)
EN7 .... 14 DR26
Old Hall Cl, Pnr. HA5 .... 40 BY53
Old Hall Dr, Pnr. HA5 .... 40 BY53
Oldham Ter, W3 .... 80 CQ74
Old Harrow La, West. TN16 .... 179 EQ119
Old Hatch Manor, Ruis. HA4 .... 59 BT59
Old Hill, Chis. BR7 .... 145 EN95
Orpington BR6 .... 163 ER107
Woking GU22 .... 166 AX120
Oldhill St, N16 .... 66 DU60
Old Homesdale Rd, Brom.
BR2 .... 144 EJ98
Old Hosp Cl, SW12 .... 120 DF88
Old Ho Cl, SW19 .... 119 CY92
Epsom KT17 .... 157 CT110
Old Ho Gdns, Twick. TW1 .... 117 CJ85
Old Ho La, Kings L. WD4 .... 22 BL35
Old Howlett's La, Ruis. HA4 .... 59 BQ58
Old Jamaica Rd, SE16 .... 202 B6
Old James St, SE15 .... 102 DV83
Old Jewry, EC2 .... 197 K9
Old Kenton La, NW9 .... 62 CP57
Old Kent Rd, SE1 .... 201 M8
SE15 .... 102 DS77
Old Kingston Rd, Wor.Pk.
KT4 .... 138 CQ104
Old La, Cob. KT11 .... 169 BP117
Westerham (Tats.) TN16 .... 178 EK121
Old La Gdns, Cob. KT11 .... 169 BT122
Old Lo La, Ken. CR8 .... 175 DN115
Purley CR8 .... 159 DM114
Old Lo Pl, Twick. TW1
off St. Margarets Rd 117 CH86
Old Lo Way, Stan. HA7 .... 41 CG50
Old London Rd, Epsom
KT18 .... 173 CU118
Sevenoaks (Bad.Mt.) TN14 .... 164 FA110
Sevenoaks (Knock.P.) TN14 .... 180 EY115
Old Maidstone Rd, Sid.
DA14 .... 126 EZ94
OLD MALDEN, Wor.Pk. 138 CR102
Old Malden La, Wor.Pk. KT4 .... 138 CR103
Old Malt Way, Wok. GU21 .... 166 AX117
Old Manor Dr, Grav. DA12 .... 131 GJ88
Isleworth TW7 .... 116 CC86
Old Manor Ho Ms, Shep. TW17
off Squires Br Rd 134 BN97
Old Manor Rd, Sthl. UB2 .... 96 BX77
Old Manor Way, Bexh. DA7 .... 107 FD82
Chislehurst BR7 .... 125 EM92
Old Manor Yd, SW5
off Earls Ct Rd 100 DB77
Old Marylebone Rd, NW1 .... 194 C7
Old Mead, Ger.Cr. (Chal.St.P.)
SL9 .... 36 AY51
Old Ms, Har. HA1
off Hindes Rd 61 CE57
Old Mill Cl, Dart. (Eyns.)
DA4 .... 148 FL102
Old Mill Ct, E18 .... 68 EJ55
Old Mill La, Red. RH1 .... 185 DH128
Uxbridge UB8 .... 76 BH72
Old Mill Pl, Rom. RM7 .... 71 FD58
Old Mill Rd, SE18 .... 105 ER79
Kings Langley WD4 .... 7 BQ33
Uxbridge (Denh.) UB9 .... 58 BG62
Old Mitre Ct, EC4
off Fleet St 83 DN72
Old Montague St, E1 .... 84 DU71
Old Nichol St, E2 .... 197 P4
Old N St, WC1 .... 196 B6
Old Oak Av, Couls. CR5 .... 174 DE119
Old Oak Cl, Chess. KT9 .... 156 CM105
OLD OAK COMMON, NW10 .... 81 CT71
Old Oak Common La, NW10 .... 80 CS70
W3 .... 80 CS71
Old Oak La, NW10 .... 80 CS69
Old Oak Rd, W3 .... 81 CT73
Old Oaks, Wal.Abb. EN9 .... 16 EE32
★ **Old Operating Thea Mus**
& Herb Garret, SE1 .... 201 L3
Old Orchard, St.Alb. (Park St.)
AL2 .... 8 CC26
Sunbury-on-Thames
TW16 .... 136 BW96
West Byfleet (Byfleet)
KT14 .... 152 BM112
Old Orchard, The, NW3
off Nassington Rd 64 DF63
Old Orchard Cl, Barn. EN4 .... 28 DD38
Uxbridge UB8 .... 76 BN72
Old Otford Rd, Sev. TN14 .... 181 FH117
Old Palace La, Rich. TW9 .... 117 CJ85
Old Palace Rd, Croy. CR0 .... 141 DP104
Weybridge KT13 .... 135 BP104
Old Palace Ter, Rich. TW9
off King St 117 CK85
Old Palace Yd, SW1 .... 199 P6
Richmond TW9 .... 117 CJ85
Old Paradise St, SE11 .... 200 B8
Old Pk Av, SW12 .... 120 DG86
Enfield EN2 .... 30 DQ42
Old Parkbury La, St.Alb. (Coln.St.)
AL2 .... 9 CF30
Old Pk Gro, Enf. EN2 .... 30 DQ42
Old Pk La, W1 .... 198 G3
Old Pk Ms, Houns. TW5 .... 96 BZ80
Old Pk Ride, Wal.Cr. EN7 .... 14 DT33
Old Pk Ridings, N21 .... 29 DP44
Old Pk Rd, N13 .... 45 DM49
SE2 .... 106 EU78
Enfield EN2 .... 29 DP41
Old Pk Rd S, Enf. EN2 .... 29 DP42
Old Pk Vw, Enf. EN2 .... 29 DN41
Old Parvis Rd, W.Byf. KT14 .... 152 BK112
Old Perry St, Chis. BR7 .... 125 ES94
Gravesend (Nthflt.) DA11 .... 130 GE89
Old Polhill, Sev. TN14 .... 181 FD115
Old Pound Cl, Islw. TW7 .... 97 CG81
Old Priory, Uxb. (Hare.) UB9 .... 59 BP59
Old Pye St, SW1 .... 199 M6
Old Quebec St, W1 .... 194 E9
Old Queen St, SW1 .... 199 N5
Old Rectory Cl, Tad. KT20 .... 173 CU124
Old Rectory Gdns, Edg. HA8 .... 42 CN51
Old Rectory La, Uxb. (Denh.)
UB9 .... 57 BE59
Old Rectory Rd, Ong. CM5 .... 19 FH34
Old Redding, Har. HA3 .... 40 CC49
Old Reigate Rd, Bet. RH3 .... 182 CP134
Dorking RH4 .... 182 CL134
Oldridge Rd, SW12 .... 120 DG87
Old Rd, SE13 .... 104 EE84
Addlestone KT15 .... 151 BF108
Betchworth (Buckland)
RH3 .... 182 CR134
Dartford DA1 .... 107 FD84
Enfield EN3 .... 30 DW39
Old Rd E, Grav. DA12 .... 131 GH88
Old Rd W, Grav. DA11 .... 131 GF88
Old Rope Wk, Sun. TW16
off The Avenue 135 BV97
Old Royal Free Pl, N1
off Liverpool Rd 83 DN67
Old Royal Free Sq, N1 .... 83 DN67
Old Ruislip Rd, Nthlt. UB5 .... 78 BX68
Olds App, Wat. WD18 .... 39 BP46
Old Savill's Cotts, Chig. IG7
off The Chase 49 EQ49
Old Sch Cl, SE10 .... 205 J7
SW19 .... 140 DA96
Old Sch Cl, Beck. BR3 .... 143 DX96
Old Sch Ct, Stai. (Wrays.)
TW19 .... 112 AY87
Old Sch Cres, E7 .... 86 EF65
Old Sch Ms, Egh. TW20 .... 113 BD92
Weybridge KT13 .... 153 BR105
Old Sch Pl, Wok. GU22 .... 166 AY121
Old Sch Rd, Uxb. UB8 .... 76 BM70
Old Schools La, Epsom
KT17 .... 157 CT109
Old Sch Sq, E14
off Pelling St 85 EA72
Thames Ditton KT7 .... 137 CF100
Olds Cl, Wat. WD18 .... 39 BP46
Old Seacoal La, EC4 .... 196 F8
Old Shire La, Ger.Cr. SL9 .... 37 BA46
Rickmansworth (Chorl.)
WD3 .... 21 BB44
Waltham Abbey EN9 .... 32 EG35
Old Slade La, Iver SL0 .... 93 BE76
Old Solesbridge La, Rick. (Chorl.)
WD3 .... 22 BG41
Old S Cl, Pnr. HA5 .... 40 BX53
Old S Lambeth Rd, SW8 .... 101 DL80
★ **Old Spitalfields Mkt**, E1 .... 197 P6
Old Spitalfields Mkt, E1 .... 197 P6
Old Sq, WC2 .... 196 C8
Old Sta App, Lthd. KT22 .... 171 CG121
Old Sta Rd, Hayes UB3 .... 95 BT76
Loughton IG10 .... 32 EL43
Old Sta Yd, Brom. BR2
off Bourne Way 144 EF102
Oldstead Rd, Brom. BR1 .... 123 ED91
Old Stockley Rd, West Dr.
UB7 .... 95 BP75
⇌ **Old Street** 197 K3
⊖ **Old Street** 197 K3
Old St, E13 .... 86 EH68
EC1 .... 197 H4
Old Swan Yd, Cars. SM5 .... 158 DF105
Old Tilburstow Rd, Gdse.
RH9 .... 186 DW134
Old Town, SW4 .... 101 DJ83
Croydon CR0 .... 141 DP104
Old Tram Yd, SE18
off Lakedale Rd 105 ES77
Old Tye Av, West. (Bigg.H.)
TN16 .... 178 EL116
Old Uxbridge Rd, Rick. (Map.Cr.)
WD3 .... 37 BE53
Old Wk, The, Sev. (Otford)
TN14 .... 181 FH117
Old Watford Rd, St.Alb. (Brick.Wd.)
AL2 .... 8 BY30
Old Watling St, Grav. DA11 .... 131 GG92
Old Westhall Cl, Warl. CR6 .... 177 DW119
Old Wf Way, Wey. KT13
off Weybridge Rd 152 BM105
OLD WINDSOR, Wind. 112 AU86
Old Windsor Lock, Wind.
(Old Wind.) SL4 .... 112 AW85
OLD WOKING, Wok. 167 BA121
Old Woking Rd, W.Byf. KT14 .... 151 BF113
Woking GU22 .... 167 BE116
Old Woolwich Rd, SE10 .... 103 ED79
Old Yd, The, West. TN16 .... 180 EW124
Old York Rd, SW18 .... 120 DB85
Oleander Cl, Orp. BR6 .... 163 ER106
O'Leary Sq, E1 .... 84 DW71
Olga St, E3 .... 85 DY68
Olinda Rd, N16 .... 66 DT58
Oliphant St, W10 .... 81 CX69
Oliver Av, SE25 .... 142 DT97
Oliver Cl, W4 .... 98 CP79
Addlestone KT15 .... 152 BG105
Grays RM20 .... 109 FT80
St. Albans (Park St.) AL2 .... 9 CD27
Oliver Cres, Dart. (Fnghm.)
DA4 .... 148 FM101
Oliver Gdns, E6 .... 86 EL72
Oliver-Goldsmith Est, SE15 .... 102 DU81
Oliver Gro, SE25 .... 142 DT98
Olive Rd, E13 .... 86 EJ69
NW2 .... 63 CW63
SW19 off Norman Rd 120 DC94
W5 .... 97 CK76
Dartford DA1 .... 128 FK88
Oliver Rd, E10 .... 67 EB61
E17 .... 67 EC57
NW10 .... 80 CQ68
Brentwood CM15 .... 55 GA43
Grays RM20 .... 109 FT81
New Malden KT3 .... 138 CQ96
Rainham RM13 .... 89 FF67
Sutton SM1 .... 158 DD105
Swanley BR8 .... 147 FD97
Olivers Yd, EC1 .... 197 L4
Olive St, Rom. RM7 .... 71 FD57
Olivette St, SW15 .... 99 CX83
Olivia Gdns, Uxb. (Hare.) UB9 .... 38 BJ53
Ollards Gro, Loug. IG10 .... 32 EK42
Olleberrie La, Rick. (Sarratt)
WD3 .... 5 BD32
Ollerton Grn, E3 .... 85 DZ67
Ollerton Rd, N11 .... 45 DK50
Olley Cl, Wall. SM6 .... 159 DL108
Ollgar Cl, W12 .... 81 CT74
Olliffe St, E14 .... 204 E7
Olmar St, SE1 .... 102 DU79
Olney Rd, SE17 .... 101 DP79
Olron Cres, Bexh. DA6 .... 126 EX85
Olven Rd, SE18 .... 105 EQ80
Olveston Wk, Cars. SM5 .... 140 DD100
Olwen Ms, Pnr. HA5 .... 40 BX54
Olyffe Av, Well. DA16 .... 106 EU82
Olyffe Dr, Beck. BR3 .... 143 EC95
★ **Olympia**, W14 .... 99 CY76
Olympia Ms, W2
off Queensway 82 DB73
Olympia Way, W14 .... 99 CY76
Olympic Way, Grnf. UB6 .... 78 CB67
Wembley HA9 .... 62 CN63
Olympus Sq, E5
off Nolan Way 66 DU63
Oman Av, NW2 .... 63 CW63
O'Meara St, SE1 .... 201 J3
Omega Cl, E14 .... 204 B6
Omega Pl, N1 .... 196 A1
Omega Rd, Wok. GU21 .... 167 BA115
Omega St, SE14 .... 103 EA81
Ommaney Rd, SE14 .... 103 DX81
Omnibus Way, E17 .... 47 EA54
Ondine Rd, SE15 .... 102 DT84
Onega Gate, SE16 .... 203 K6
O'Neill Path, SE18
off Kempt St 105 EN79
One Tree Cl, SE23 .... 122 DW86
Ongar Cl, Add. KT15 .... 151 BF107
Romford RM6 .... 70 EW57
Ongar Hill, Add. KT15 .... 152 BG107
Ongar Pl, Add. KT15 .... 152 BG107
Ongar Rd, SW6 .... 100 DA79
Addlestone KT15 .... 152 BG106
Brentwood CM15 .... 54 FV45
Romford RM4 .... 34 EW40
Ongar Way, Rain. RM13 .... 89 FE67
Onra Rd, E17 .... 67 EA59
Onslow Av, Rich. TW10 .... 118 CL85
Sutton SM2 .... 157 CZ110
Onslow Cl, E4 .... 47 EC47
Thames Ditton KT7 .... 137 CE102
Woking GU22 .... 167 BA117
Onslow Cres, Chis. BR7 .... 145 EP95
Woking GU22 .... 167 BA117
Onslow Dr, Sid. DA14 .... 126 EX89
Onslow Gdns, E18 .... 68 EH55
N10 .... 65 DH57
N21 .... 29 DN43
SW7 .... 100 DD78
South Croydon CR2 .... 160 DU112
Thames Ditton KT7 .... 137 CE102
Wallington SM6 .... 159 DJ107
Onslow Ms, Cher. KT16 .... 134 BG100
Onslow Ms E, SW7
off Cranley Pl 100 DD77
Onslow Ms W, SW7
off Cranley Pl 100 DD77
Onslow Rd, Croy. CR0 .... 141 DM101
New Malden KT3 .... 139 CU98
Richmond TW10 .... 118 CL85
Walton-on-Thames KT12 .... 153 BT105
Onslow Sq, SW7 .... 198 A8
Onslow St, EC1 .... 196 E5
Onslow Way, T.Ditt. KT7 .... 137 CE102
Woking GU22 .... 167 BF115
Ontario St, SE1 .... 200 G7
Ontario Way, E14 .... 203 P1
On The Hill, Wat. WD19 .... 40 BY47
Opal Cl, E16 .... 86 EK72
Opal Ct, Slou. (Wexham) SL3
off Wexham St 74 AV70
Opal Ms, NW6
off Priory Pk Rd 81 CZ67
Ilford IG1 off Ley St 69 EP61
Opal St, SE11 .... 200 F9
Openshaw Rd, SE2 .... 106 EV77
Openview, SW18 .... 120 DC88
Ophelia Gdns, NW2
off Hamlet Sq 63 CY62
Ophir Ter, SE15 .... 102 DU81
Opossum Way, Houns. TW4 .... 96 BW82
Oppenheim Rd, SE13 .... 103 EC82
Oppidans Ms, NW3
off Meadowbank 82 DF66
Oppidans Rd, NW3 .... 82 DF66
Orange Ct, E1 .... 202 C3
Orange Ct La, Orp. BR6 .... 163 EN109
Orange Gro, E11 .... 68 EE62
Chigwell IG7 .... 49 EQ51
Orange Hill Rd, Edg. HA8 .... 42 CQ52
Orange Pl, SE16 .... 202 G7
Orangery, The, Rich. TW10 .... 117 CJ89
Orangery La, SE9 .... 125 EM85
Orange Sq, SW1
off Ebury St 100 DG78
Orange St, WC2 .... 199 M1
Orange Tree Hill, Rom.
(Hav.at.Bow.) RM4 .... 51 FD50
Orange Yd, W1 .... 195 N9
Oratory La, SW3 .... 198 A10
Orbain Rd, SW6 .... 99 CY80
Orbel St, SW11 .... 100 DE81
Orbital Cres, Wat. WD25 .... 23 BT35
Orbital One, Dart. DA1 .... 128 FP89
Orb St, SE17 .... 201 K9
Orchard, The, N14 .... 29 DH43
N21 .... 30 DR44
NW11 .... 64 DA57
SE3 .... 103 ED82
W4 .... 98 CR77
W5 .... 79 CK71
Banstead SM7 .... 174 DA115
Epsom KT17 .... 157 CT108
Epsom (Ewell) KT17
off Tayles Hill Dr 157 CT110
Hounslow TW3 .... 96 CC82
Kings Langley WD4 .... 6 BN29
Rickmansworth (Crox.Grn.) WD3
off Green La 22 BM43
Sevenoaks (Dunt.Grn.)
TN13 .... 181 FE120
Swanley BR8 .... 147 FD96
Virginia Water GU25 .... 132 AY99
Weybridge KT13 .... 153 BP105
Woking GU22 .... 166 AY122
Orchard Av, N3 .... 64 DA55
N14 .... 29 DJ44
N20 .... 44 DD47
Addlestone (Woodham)
KT15 .... 151 BF111
Ashford TW15 .... 115 BQ93
Belvedere DA17 .... 106 EY79
Brentwood CM13 .... 55 FZ48
Croydon CR0 .... 143 DY101
Dartford DA1 .... 127 FH87
Feltham TW14 .... 115 BR85
Gravesend DA11 .... 131 GH92
Hounslow TW5 .... 96 BY80
Mitcham CR4 .... 140 DG102
New Malden KT3 .... 138 CS96
Rainham RM13 .... 90 FJ70
Southall UB1 .... 78 BY74
Thames Ditton KT7 .... 137 CG102
Watford WD25 .... 7 BV32
Orchard Cl, E4
off Chingford Mt Rd 47 EA49
E11 .... 68 EH56
N1 off Morton Rd 84 DQ66
NW2 .... 63 CU62
SE23 off Brenchley Gdns 122 DW86
SW20 off Grand Dr 139 CW98
W10 .... 81 CY71
Ashford TW15 .... 115 BQ93
Banstead SM7 .... 158 DB114
Bexleyheath DA7 .... 106 EY81
Borehamwood (Elstree)
WD6 .... 26 CM42
Bushey (Bushey Hth.)
WD23 .... 41 CD46
Edgware HA8 .... 42 CL51
Egham TW20 .... 113 BB92
Epsom (W.Ewell) KT19 .... 156 CP107
Leatherhead KT22 .... 171 CF119
Leatherhead (E.Hors.)
KT24 .... 169 BT124
Leatherhead (Fetch.) KT22 .... 171 CD122
Northolt UB5 .... 60 CC64
Potters Bar (Cuffley) EN6 .... 13 DL28
Radlett WD7 .... 25 CE37
Rickmansworth (Chorl.)
WD3 .... 21 BD42
Ruislip HA4 .... 59 BQ59
South Ockendon RM15 .... 91 FW70
Surbiton KT6 .... 137 CH101
Uxbridge (Denh.) UB9 .... 76 BH65
Walton-on-Thames KT12
off Garden Rd 135 BV101
Watford WD17 .... 23 BT40
Wembley HA0 .... 80 CL67
Woking GU22 .... 167 BB116
Orchard Ct, Hem.H. (Bov.) HP3 .... 5 BA27
Isleworth TW7
off Thornbury Av 97 CD81
Twickenham TW2 .... 117 CD89
Wallington SM6
off Parkgate Rd 159 DH106
Worcester Park KT4
off The Avenue 139 CU102
Orchard Cres, Edg. HA8 .... 42 CQ50
Enfield EN1 .... 30 DT39
Orchard Dr, SE3
off Orchard Rd 104 EE82
Ashtead KT21 .... 171 CK120
Edgware HA8 .... 42 CM50
Epping (They.B.) CM16 .... 33 ES36
Grays RM17 .... 110 GA75
Rickmansworth (Chorl.)
WD3 .... 21 BC41
St. Albans (Park St.) AL2 .... 8 CB27
Uxbridge UB8 .... 76 BK70
Watford WD17 .... 23 BT39
Woking GU21 .... 167 AZ115
Orchard End, Cat. CR3 .... 176 DS122
Leatherhead (Fetch.) KT22 .... 170 CC124
Weybridge KT13 .... 135 BS103
Orchard End Av, Amer. HP7 .... 20 AT39
Orchard Gdns, Chess. KT9 .... 156 CL105
Epsom KT18 .... 156 CQ114
Sutton SM1 .... 158 DA106
Waltham Abbey EN9 .... 15 EC34
Orchard Gate, NW9 .... 62 CS56
Esher KT10 .... 137 CD102
Greenford UB6 .... 79 CH65
Orchard Grn, Orp. BR6 .... 145 ES103
Orchard Gro, SE20 .... 122 DU94
Croydon CR0 .... 143 DY101
Edgware HA8 .... 42 CN53
Gerrards Cross (Chal.St.P.)
SL9 .... 36 AW53
Harrow HA3 .... 62 CM57
Orpington BR6 .... 145 ET103
Orchard Hill, SE13
off Coldbath St 103 EB82
Carshalton SM5 .... 158 DF106
Dartford DA1 .... 127 FE85
Orchard Ho, Erith DA8
off Northend Rd 107 FF81
Orchard La, SW20 .... 139 CV95
Brentwood CM15 .... 54 FT43
East Molesey KT8 .... 137 CD100
Woodford Green IG8 .... 48 EJ49
Orchard Lea Cl, Wok. GU22 .... 167 BE115
ORCHARD LEIGH, Chesh. 4 AV28
Orchard Leigh, Chesh. HP5 .... 4 AU28
Orchardleigh, Lthd. KT22 .... 171 CH122
Orchardleigh Av, Enf. EN3 .... 30 DW40
Orchard Mains, Wok. GU22 .... 166 AW119
Orchardmede, N21 .... 30 DR44
Orchard Ms, N1
off Southgate Gro 84 DR66
Orchard Path, Slou. SL3 .... 75 BA72
Orchard Pl, E14 .... 86 EE73
N17 .... 46 DT52
Keston BR2 .... 162 EJ109
Sevenoaks (Sund.) TN14 .... 180 EY124
Waltham Cross (Chsht.) EN8
off Turners Hill 15 DX30
Orchard Ri, Croy. CR0 .... 143 DY102
Kingston upon Thames
KT2 .... 138 CQ95
Pinner HA5 .... 59 BT55
Richmond TW10 .... 98 CP84
Orchard Ri E, Sid. DA15 .... 125 ET85
Orchard Ri W, Sid. DA15 .... 125 ES85
Orchard Rd, N6 .... 65 DH59
SE3 .... 104 EE82
SE18 .... 105 ER77
Barnet EN5 .... 27 CZ42
Belvedere DA17 .... 106 FA77
Brentford TW8 .... 97 CJ79
Bromley BR1 .... 144 EJ95
Chalfont St. Giles HP8 .... 36 AW47
Chessington KT9 .... 156 CL105
Dagenham RM10 .... 88 FA67
Enfield EN3 .... 30 DW43
Gravesend (Nthflt.) DA11 .... 130 GC89
Hampton TW12 .... 116 BZ94
Hayes UB3 .... 77 BT73

Orc - Oxf

Orchard Rd, Houns. TW4 116 BZ85
Kingston upon Thames KT1 138 CL96
Mitcham CR4 140 DG102
Orpington (Farnboro.) BR6 163 EP106
Orpington (Pr.Bot.) BR6 164 EW110
Reigate RH2 184 DB134
Richmond TW9 98 CN83
Romford RM7 51 FB53
Sevenoaks (Otford) TN14 181 FF116
Sevenoaks (Rvrhd.) TN13 190 FE122
Sidcup DA14 125 ES91
South Croydon CR2 160 DV114
South Ockendon RM15 91 FW70
Sunbury-on-Thames TW16 off Hanworth Rd 115 BV94
Sutton SM1 158 DA106
Swanscombe DA10 130 FY85
Twickenham TW1 117 CG85
Welling DA16 106 EV83
Windsor (Old Wind.) SL4 112 AV86
Orchards, The, Epp. CM16 18 EU32
Orchards Cl, W.Byf. KT14 152 BG114
Orchardson St, NW8 82 DD70
Orchard Sq, W14 off Sun Rd 99 CZ78
Orchards Residential Pk, The, Slou. SL3 75 AZ74
Orchards Shop Cen, Dart. DA1 128 FL86
Orchard St, E17 67 DY56
W1 194 F9
Dartford DA1 128 FL86
Orchard Ter, Enf. EN1 off Great Cambridge Rd 30 DU44
Orchard Vw, Uxb. UB8 76 BK70
Orchard Vil, Sid. DA14 off Haven Cl 126 EW93
Orchard Way, Add. KT15 152 BH106
Ashford TW15 114 BM89
Beckenham BR3 143 DY99
Chigwell IG7 50 EU48
Croydon CR0 143 DY102
Dartford DA2 128 FK90
Enfield EN1 30 DS41
Esher KT10 154 CC107
Hemel Hempstead (Bov.) HP3 5 BA28
Oxted RH8 188 EG133
Potters Bar EN6 12 DB28
Rickmansworth (Mill End) WD3 38 BG45
Slough SL3 74 AY74
Sutton SM1 158 DD105
Tadworth KT20 183 CZ126
Waltham Cross (Chsht.) EN7 13 DP27
Orchard Waye, Uxb. UB8 76 BK68
Orchehill Av, Ger.Cr. SL9 56 AX56
Orchehill Ct, Ger.Cr. SL9 56 AY56
Orchehill Ri, Ger.Cr. SL9 56 AY57
Orchid Cl, E6 86 EL71
Chessington KT9 155 CJ108
Romford (Abridge) RM4 34 EV41
Southall UB1 78 BY72
Waltham Cross EN7 off Silver St 14 DQ30
Orchid Ct, Egh. TW20 113 BB91
Romford RM7 71 FE61
Orchid Rd, N14 45 DJ45
Orchid St, W12 81 CU73
Orchis Gro, Grays (Bad.Dene) RM17 110 FZ78
Orchis Way, Rom. RM3 52 FM51
Orde Hall St, WC1 196 B5
Ordell Rd, E3 85 DZ68
Ordnance Cl, Felt. TW13 115 BU90
Ordnance Cres, SE10 204 G4
Ordnance Hill, NW8 82 DD67
Ordnance Ms, NW8 off St. Ann's Ter 82 DD68
Ordnance Rd, E16 86 EF71
SE18 105 EN79
Enfield EN3 31 DX37
Gravesend DA12 131 GJ86
Oregano Cl, West Dr. UB7 off Camomile Way 76 BM72
Oregano Dr, E14 85 ED72
Oregon Av, E12 69 EM63
Oregon Cl, N.Mal. KT3 off Georgia Rd 138 CQ98
Oregon Sq, Orp. BR6 145 ER102
Orestes Ms, NW6 off Aldred Rd 64 DA64
Oreston Rd, Rain. RM13 90 FK69
Orford Ct, SE27 121 DP89
Orford Gdns, Twick. TW1 117 CF89
Orford Rd, E17 67 EA57
E18 68 EH55
SE6 123 EB90
Organ Hall Rd, Borwd. WD6 26 CL39
Organ La, E4 47 EC47
Oriel Cl, Mitch. CR4 141 DK98
Oriel Ct, NW3 off Heath St 64 DC63
Oriel Dr, SW13 99 CV79
Oriel Gdns, Ilf. IG5 69 EM55
Oriel Pl, NW3 off Heath St 64 DC63
Oriel Rd, E9 85 DX65
Oriel Way, Nthlt. UB5 78 CB66
Oriental Cl, Wok. GU22 off Oriental Rd 167 BA117
Oriental Rd, E16 86 EK74
Woking GU22 167 BA117
Oriental St, E14 off Morant St 85 EA73
Orient Ind Pk, E10 67 EA61
Orient St, SE11 200 F8
Orient Way, E5 67 DX62
E10 67 DY61
Oriole Cl, Abb.L. WD5 7 BU31
Oriole Way, SE28 88 EV73
Orion Rd, N11 45 DH51
Orion Way, Nthwd. HA6 39 BT49
Orissa Rd, SE18 105 ES78
Orkney St, SW11 100 DG82
Orlando Gdns, Epsom KT19 156 CR110
Orlando Rd, SW4 101 DJ83
Orleans Cl, Esher KT10 137 CD103
★ **Orleans Ho Gall**, Twick. TW1 117 CH88
Orleans Rd, SE19 122 DR93
Twickenham TW1 117 CH87
Orlestone Gdns, Orp. BR6 164 EY106
Orleston Ms, N7 83 DN65
Orleston Rd, N7 83 DN65
Orley Fm Rd, Har. HA1 61 CE62
Orlop St, SE10 104 EE78
Ormanton Rd, SE26 122 DU91
Orme Ct, W2 82 DB73
Orme Ct Ms, W2 off Orme La 82 DB73
Orme La, W2 82 DB73
Ormeley Rd, SW12 121 DH88
Orme Rd, Kings.T. KT1 138 CP96
Sutton SM1 off Grove Rd 158 DB107
Ormerod Gdns, Mitch. CR4 140 DG96
Ormesby Cl, SE28 off Wroxham Rd 88 EX73
Ormesby Dr, Pot.B. EN6 11 CX32
Ormesby Way, Har. HA3 62 CM58
Orme Sq, W2 off Bayswater Rd 82 DB73
Ormiston Gro, W12 81 CV74
Ormiston Rd, SE10 104 EG78
Ormond Av, Hmptn. TW12 136 CB95
Richmond TW10 off Ormond Rd 117 CK85
Ormond Cl, WC1 196 A6
Romford (Harold Wd.) RM3 off Chadwick Dr 52 FK54
Ormond Cres, Hmptn. TW12 136 CB95
Ormond Dr, Hmptn. TW12 116 CB94
Ormonde Av, Epsom KT19 156 CR109
Orpington BR6 145 EQ103
Ormonde Gate, SW3 100 DF78
Ormonde Pl, SW1 198 F9
Ormonde Ri, Buck.H. IG9 48 EJ46
Ormonde Rd, SW14 98 CP83
Northwood HA6 39 BR49
Woking GU21 166 AW116
Ormonde Ter, NW8 82 DF67
Ormond Ms, WC1 196 A5
Ormond Rd, N19 65 DL60
Richmond TW10 117 CK85
Ormond Yd, SW1 199 L2
Ormsby, Sutt. SM2 off Grange Rd 158 DB108
Ormsby Gdns, Grnf. UB6 78 CC68
Ormsby Pl, N16 off Victorian Gro 66 DT62
Ormsby Pt, SE18 off Troy Ct 105 EP77
Ormsby St, E2 84 DT68
Ormside St, SE15 102 DW79
Ormside Way, Red. RH1 185 DH130
Ormskirk Rd, Wat. WD19 40 BX49
Ornan Rd, NW3 64 DE64
Oronsay Wk, N1 off Clephane Rd 84 DQ65
Orpen Wk, N16 66 DS62
Orphanage Rd, Wat. WD17, WD24 24 BW40
Orpheus St, SE5 102 DR81
ORPINGTON 145 ES102
⇌ **Orpington** 145 ET103
Orpington Bypass, Orp. BR6 146 EV103
Sevenoaks TN14 164 FA109
Orpington Gdns, N18 46 DS48
H **Orpington Hosp**, Orp. BR6 163 ET105
Orpington Rd, N21 45 DP46
Chislehurst BR7 145 ES97
Orpin Rd, Red. RH1 185 DH130
Orpwood Cl, Hmptn. TW12 116 BZ92
ORSETT HEATH, Grays 111 GG75
Orsett Heath Cres, Grays RM16 111 GG76
Orsett Rd, Grays RM17 110 GA78
Orsett St, SE11 200 C10
Orsett Ter, W2 82 DC72
Woodford Green IG8 48 EJ53
Orsman Rd, N1 84 DS67
Orton St, E1 202 B3
Orville Rd, SW11 100 DD82
Orwell Cl, Hayes UB3 77 BS73
Rainham RM13 89 FD71
Orwell Ct, N5 66 DQ63
Orwell Rd, E13 86 EJ68
Osbaldeston Rd, N16 66 DU61
Osberton Rd, SE12 124 EG85
Osbert St, SW1 199 M9
Osborn Cl, E8 84 DU67
Osborne Av, Stai. TW19 114 BL88
Osborne Cl, Barn. EN4 28 DF41
Beckenham BR3 143 DY98
Feltham TW13 116 BX92
Hornchurch RM11 71 FH58
Osborne Ct, Pot.B. EN6 12 DB29
Osborne Gdns, Pot.B. EN6 12 DB30
Thornton Heath CR7 142 DQ96
Osborne Gro, E17 67 DZ56
N4 65 DN60
Osborne Ms, E17 off Osborne Gro 67 DZ56
Osborne Pl, Sutt. SM1 158 DD106
Osborne Rd, E7 68 EH64
E9 85 DZ65
E10 67 EB62
N4 65 DN60
N13 45 DN48
NW2 81 CV65
W3 98 CP76
Belvedere DA17 106 EZ78
Brentwood (Pilg.Hat.) CM15 54 FU44
Buckhurst Hill IG9 48 EH46
Dagenham RM9 70 EZ64
Egham TW20 113 AZ93
Enfield EN3 31 DY40
Hornchurch RM11 71 FH58
Hounslow TW3 96 BZ83
Osborne Rd, Kings.T. KT2 118 CL94
Potters Bar EN6 12 DB30
Redhill RH1 184 DG131
Southall UB1 78 CC72
Thornton Heath CR7 142 DQ96
Uxbridge UB8 off Oxford Rd 76 BJ66
Waltham Cross (Chsht.) EN8 15 DY27
Walton-on-Thames KT12 135 BU102
Watford WD24 24 BW38
Osborne Sq, Dag. RM9 70 EZ63
Osborne St, Slou. SL1 92 AT75
Osborne Ter, SW17 off Church La 120 DG92
Osborn Gdns, NW7 43 CX52
Osborn La, SE23 123 DY87
Osborn St, E1 84 DT71
Osborn Ter, SE3 off Lee Rd 104 EF84
Osbourne Av, NW7 off Bittacy Hill 43 CY52
Kings Langley WD4 6 BM28
Osbourne Rd, Dart. DA2 128 FP86
Oscar St, SE8 103 EA81
Oseney Cres, NW5 83 DJ65
Osgood Av, Orp. BR6 163 ET106
Osgood Gdns, Orp. BR6 163 ET106
OSIDGE, N14 45 DH46
Osidge La, N14 44 DG46
Osier Cres, N10 44 DF53
Osier La, SE10 205 L7
Osier Ms, W4 99 CT79
Osier Pl, Egh. TW20 113 BC93
Osiers Rd, SW18 100 DA84
Osier St, E1 84 DW70
Osier Way, E10 67 EB62
Banstead SM7 157 CY114
Mitcham CR4 140 DE99
Oslac Rd, SE6 123 EB92
Oslo Ct, NW8 194 B1
Oslo Sq, SE16 203 L6
Osman Cl, N15 off Tewkesbury Rd 66 DR58
Osman Rd, N9 46 DU48
W6 off Batoum Gdns 99 CW76
Osmond Cl, Har. HA2 60 CC61
Osmond Gdns, Wall. SM6 159 DJ106
Osmund St, W12 off Braybrook St 81 CT72
Osnaburgh St, NW1 195 J5
NW1 (north section) off Robert St 83 DH69
Osnaburgh Ter, NW1 195 J4
Osney Ho, SE2 off Hartslock Dr 106 EX75
Osney Wk, Cars. SM5 140 DD100
Osney Way, Grav. DA12 131 GM89
Osprey Cl, E6 off Dove App 86 EL71
E11 68 EG56
E17 47 DY52
Leatherhead (Fetch.) KT22 170 CC122
Sutton SM1 off Sandpiper Rd 157 CZ106
Watford WD25 8 BY34
West Drayton UB7 94 BK75
Osprey Ct, Wal.Abb. EN9 16 EG34
Osprey Gdns, S.Croy. CR2 161 DX110
Osprey Ms, Enf. EN3 30 DV43
Osprey Rd, Wal.Abb. EN9 16 EG34
Ospringe Cl, SE20 122 DW94
Ospringe Ct, SE9 off Alderwood Rd 125 ER86
Ospringe Rd, NW5 65 DJ63
Osram Ct, W6 off Lena Gdns 99 CW76
Osram Rd, Wem. HA9 61 CK62
Osric Path, N1 197 M1
Ossian Ms, N4 65 DM59
Ossian Rd, N4 65 DM59
Ossington Bldgs, W1 194 F6
Ossington Cl, W2 off Ossington St 82 DB73
Ossington St, W2 82 DB73
Ossory Rd, SE1 102 DU78
Ossulston St, NW1 195 M1
Ossulton Pl, N2 off East End Rd 64 DC55
Ossulton Way, N2 64 DC56
Ostade Rd, SW2 121 DM87
Ostell Cres, Enf. EN3 off Government Row 31 EA37
Osten Ms, SW7 off Emperor's Gate 100 DB76
Osterberg Rd, Dart. DA1 108 FM84
OSTERLEY, Islw. 96 CC80
⊖ **Osterley** 97 CD80
Osterley Av, Islw. TW7 97 CD80
Osterley Cl, Orp. BR5 off Leith Hill 146 EU95
Osterley Ct, Islw. TW7 97 CD81
Osterley Cres, Islw. TW7 97 CE81
Osterley Gdns, Th.Hth. CR7 142 DQ96
Osterley Ho, E14 off Giraud St 85 EB72
Osterley La, Islw. TW7 97 CE78
Southall UB2 96 CA78
Osterley Pk, Islw. TW7 97 CD78
★ **Osterley Park Ho**, Islw. TW7 96 CC78
Osterley Pk Rd, Sthl. UB2 96 BZ76
Osterley Pk Vw Rd, W7 97 CE75
Osterley Rd, N16 66 DS63
Isleworth TW7 97 CE80
Osterley Views, Sthl. UB2 off West Pk Rd 78 CC74
Oster Ter, E17 off Southcote Rd 67 DX57
Ostliffe Rd, N13 46 DQ50
Oswald Cl, Lthd. (Fetch.) KT22 170 CC122
Oswald Rd, Lthd. (Fetch.) KT22 170 CC122
Southall UB1 78 BY74
Oswald's Mead, E9 off Lindisfarne Way 67 DY63
Oswald St, E5 67 DX62
Oswald Ter, NW2 off Temple Rd 63 CW62
Osward, Croy. CR0 161 DZ109
Osward Pl, N9 46 DV47
Osward Rd, SW17 120 DF89
Oswell Ho, E1 202 E2
Oswin St, SE11 200 G8
Oswyth Rd, SE5 102 DS82
OTFORD, Sev. 181 FG116
Otford Cl, SE20 142 DW95
Bexley DA5 off Southwold Rd 127 FB86
Bromley BR1 145 EN97
Otford Cres, SE4 123 DZ86
Otford La, Sev. (Halst.) TN14 164 EZ112
Otford Rd, Sev. TN14 181 FH118
Othello Cl, SE11 200 F10
Otis St, E3 85 EC69
Otley App, Ilf. IG2 69 EP58
Otley Dr, Ilf. IG2 69 EP57
Otley Rd, E16 86 EJ72
Otley Ter, E5 67 DX61
Otley Way, Wat. WD19 40 BW48
Otlinge Cl, Orp. BR5 146 EX98
Ottawa Gdns, Dag. RM10 89 FD66
Ottawa Rd, Til. RM18 111 GG82
Ottaway St, E5 off Stellman Cl 66 DU62
Ottenden Cl, Orp. BR6 off Southfleet Rd 163 ES105
Otterbourne Rd, E4 47 ED48
Croydon CR0 142 DQ103
Otterburn Gdns, Islw. TW7 97 CG80
Otterburn Ho, SE5 102 DQ80
Otterburn St, SW17 120 DF93
Otter Cl, E15 85 EC67
Chertsey (Ott.) KT16 151 BB107
Otterden St, SE6 123 EA91
Otterfield Rd, West Dr. UB7 76 BL73
Ottermead La, Cher. (Ott.) KT16 151 BC107
Otter Meadow, Lthd. KT22 171 CF119
Otter Rd, Grnf. UB6 78 CC70
Otters Cl, Orp. BR5 146 EX98
OTTERSHAW, Cher. 151 BC106
Otterspool La, Wat. WD25 24 BY38
Otterspool Service Rd, Wat. WD25 24 BZ39
Otterspool Way, Wat. WD25 24 BY37
Otto Cl, SE26 122 DV90
Ottoman Ter, Wat. WD17 off Ebury Rd 24 BW41
Otto St, SE17 101 DP79
Ottways Av, Ashtd. KT21 171 CK119
Ottways La, Ashtd. KT21 171 CK120
Otway Gdns, Bushey WD23 41 CE45
Otways Cl, Pot.B. EN6 12 DB32
Oulton Cl, E5 off Mundford Rd 66 DW61
SE28 off Rollesby Way 88 EW72
Oulton Cres, Bark. IG11 87 ET65
Potters Bar EN6 11 CX32
Oulton Rd, N15 66 DR57
Oulton Way, Wat. WD19 40 BY49
Oundle Av, Bushey WD23 24 CC44
Ousden Cl, Wal.Cr. (Chsht.) EN8 15 DY30
Ousden Dr, Wal.Cr. (Chsht.) EN8 15 DY30
Ouseley Rd, SW12 120 DF88
Staines (Wrays.) TW19 112 AW87
Windsor (Old Wind.) SL4 112 AW87
Outer Circle, NW1 194 F5
Outfield Rd, Ger.Cr. (Chal.St.P.) SL9 36 AX52
Outgate Rd, NW10 81 CT66
Outlook Dr, Ch.St.G. HP8 36 AX48
Outram Pl, N1 83 DL67
Weybridge KT13 153 BQ106
Outram Rd, E6 86 EL67
N22 45 DK53
Croydon CR0 142 DT102
Outwich St, EC3 197 N8
Outwood La, Couls. CR5 174 DF118
Tadworth (Kgswd.) KT20 174 DB122
★ **Oval, The, Surrey County Cricket Club**, SE11 101 DM79
⊖ **Oval** 101 DN79
Oval, The, E2 84 DV68
Banstead SM7 158 DA114
Broxbourne EN10 15 DY25
Sidcup DA15 126 EU87
Oval Gdns, Grays RM17 110 GC76
Oval Pl, SW8 101 DM80
Oval Rd, NW1 83 DH67
Croydon CR0 142 DS102
Oval Rd N, Dag. RM10 89 FB67
Oval Rd S, Dag. RM10 89 FB68
Oval Way, SE11 101 DM78
Gerrards Cross SL9 56 AY56
Ovenden Rd, Sev. (Sund.) TN14 180 EX120
Overbrae, Beck. BR3 123 EA93
Overbrook Wk, Edg. HA8 42 CN52
Overbury Av, Beck. BR3 143 EB97
Overbury Cres, Croy. (New Adgtn.) CR0 161 EC110
Overbury Rd, N15 66 DR58
Overbury St, E5 67 DX63
Overcliffe, Grav. DA11 131 GG86
Overcliff Rd, SE13 103 EA83
Grays RM17 110 GD78
Overcourt Cl, Sid. DA15 126 EV86
Overdale, Ashtd. KT21 172 CL115
Redhill (Bletch.) RH1 186 DQ133
Overdale Av, N.Mal. KT3 138 CQ96
Overdale Rd, W5 97 CJ76
Overdown Rd, SE6 123 EA91
Overhill, Warl. CR6 176 DW119
Overhill Rd, SE22 122 DU87
Purley CR8 159 DN109
Overhill Way, Beck. BR3 143 ED99
Overlea Rd, E5 66 DU59
Overmead, Sid. DA15 125 ER87
Swanley BR8 147 FE99
Oversley Ho, W2 82 DA71
Overstand Cl, Beck. BR3 143 EA99
Overstone Gdns, Croy. CR0 143 DZ101
Overstone Rd, W6 99 CW76
Overstream, Rick. (Loud.) WD3 22 BH42
Over The Misbourne, Ger.Cr. SL9 57 BA58
Uxbridge (Denh.) UB9 57 BC58
Overthorpe Cl, Wok. (Knap.) GU21 166 AS117
Overton Cl, NW10 80 CQ65
Isleworth TW7 off Avenue Rd 97 CF81
Overton Ct, E11 68 EG59
Overton Dr, E11 68 EH59
Romford RM6 70 EW59
Overton Ho, SW15 off Tangley Gro 119 CT87
Overton Rd, E10 67 DY60
N14 29 DL43
SE2 106 EW76
SW9 101 DN82
Sutton SM2 158 DA107
Overton Rd E, SE2 106 EX76
Overtons Yd, Croy. CR0 142 DQ104
Overy St, Dart. DA1 128 FL86
Ovesdon Av, Har. HA2 60 BZ60
Ovett Cl, SE19 122 DS93
Ovex Cl, E14 204 E5
Ovington Ct, Wok. GU21 off Roundthorn Way 166 AT116
Ovington Gdns, SW3 198 C7
Ovington Ms, SW3 198 C7
Ovington Sq, SW3 198 C7
Ovington St, SW3 198 C7
Owen Cl, SE28 88 EW74
Croydon CR0 142 DR100
Hayes UB4 77 BV69
Romford RM5 51 FB51
Owen Gdns, Wdf.Grn. IG8 48 EL51
Owenite St, SE2 106 EV77
Owen Pl, Lthd. KT22 off Church Rd 171 CH122
Owen Rd, N13 46 DQ50
Hayes UB4 77 BV69
Owen's Ct, EC1 196 F2
Owen's Row, EC1 196 F2
Owen St, EC1 196 F1
Owens Way, SE23 123 DY87
Rickmansworth (Crox.Grn.) WD3 22 BN43
Owen Wk, SE20 off Sycamore Gro 122 DU94
Owen Waters Ho, Ilf. IG5 49 EM53
Owen Way, NW10 80 CQ65
Owgan Cl, SE5 off Benhill Rd 102 DR80
Owl Cl, S.Croy. CR2 161 DX110
Owlets Hall Cl, Horn. RM11 off Prospect Rd 72 FM55
Owl Pk, Loug. (High Beach) IG10 32 EF40
Ownstead Gdns, S.Croy. CR2 160 DT111
Ownsted Hill, Croy. (New Adgtn.) CR0 161 EC110
Oxberry Av, SW6 99 CY82
Oxdowne Cl, Cob. (Stoke D'Ab.) KT11 154 CB114
Oxenden Wd Rd, Orp. BR6 164 EV107
Oxendon St, SW1 199 M1
Oxenford St, SE15 102 DT83
Oxenholme, NW1 195 L1
Oxenpark Av, Wem. HA9 62 CL59
Oxestalls Rd, SE8 203 L10
Oxford Av, SW20 139 CY96
Grays RM16 111 GG77
Hayes UB3 95 BT80
Hornchurch RM11 72 FN56
Hounslow TW5 96 CA78
★ **Oxford Circus**, W1 195 K8
⊖ **Oxford Circus** 195 K8
Oxford Circ Av, W1 195 K9
Oxford Cl, N9 46 DV47
Ashford TW15 115 BQ94
Gravesend DA12 131 GM89
Mitcham CR4 141 DJ97
Northwood HA6 39 BQ49
Waltham Cross (Chsht.) EN8 15 DX29
Oxford Ct, EC4 197 K10
W3 80 CN72
Brentwood (Warley) CM14 54 FX49
Feltham TW13 off Oxford Way 116 BX91
Oxford Cres, N.Mal. KT3 138 CR100
Oxford Dr, SE1 201 M3
Ruislip HA4 60 BW61
Oxford Gdns, N20 44 DD46
N21 46 DQ45
W4 98 CN78
W10 81 CY72
Uxbridge (Denh.) UB9 57 BF62
Oxford Gate, W6 99 CX77
Oxford Ms, Bex. DA5 off Bexley High St 126 FA87
Oxford Pl, NW10 off Neasden La N 62 CR62
Oxford Rd, E15 85 ED65
N4 65 DN60
N9 46 DV47
NW6 82 DA68
SE19 122 DR93
SW15 99 CY84
W5 79 CK73
Carshalton SM5 158 DE107
Enfield EN3 30 DV43
Gerrards Cross SL9 57 BA60
Harrow HA1 60 CC58
Harrow (Wldste.) HA3 61 CF55
Ilford IG1 69 EQ63
Redhill RH1 184 DE133
Romford RM3 52 FM51
Sidcup DA14 126 EV92
Teddington TW11 117 CD92
Uxbridge UB8, UB9 76 BJ65
Wallington SM6 159 DJ106
Woodford Green IG8 48 EJ50

★ Place of interest ⇌ Railway station ⊖ London Underground station DLR Docklands Light Railway station Tramlink station H Hospital

Oxford Rd N, W4 98 CP78
Oxford Rd S, W4 98 CN78
Oxford Sq, W2 194 C9
Oxford St, W1 194 F9
Watford WD18 23 BV43
Oxford Wk, Sthl. UB1 78 BZ74
Oxford Way, Felt. TW13 116 BX91
Oxgate Gdns, NW2 63 CV62
Oxgate La, NW2 63 CV61
Oxhawth Cres, Brom. BR2 145 EN99
OXHEY, Wat. 24 BW44
Oxhey Av, Wat. WD19 40 BX45
Oxhey Dr, Nthwd. HA6 39 BV50
Watford WD19 40 BW48
Oxhey Dr S, Nthwd. HA6 39 BV50
Oxhey La, Har. HA3 40 CA50
Pinner HA5 40 CA50
Watford WD19 40 BZ47
Oxhey Ridge Cl, Nthwd. HA6 39 BU50
Oxhey Rd, Wat. WD19 24 BW44
Ox La, Epsom KT17
off Church St 157 CU109
Oxleas, E6 87 EP72
Oxleas Cl, Well. DA16 105 ER82
Oxleay Ct, Har. HA2 60 CA60
Oxleay Rd, Har. HA2 60 CA60
Oxleigh Cl, N.Mal. KT3 138 CS99
Oxley Cl, SE1 202 A10
Romford RM2 52 FJ54
Oxleys Rd, NW2 63 CV62
Waltham Abbey EN9 16 EG32
Oxlip Cl, Croy. CR0
off Marigold Way 143 DX102
Oxlow La, Dag. RM9, RM10 70 FA63
Oxonian St, SE22 102 DT84
Oxo Twr Wf, SE1 200 E1
OXSHOTT, Lthd. 155 CD113
⇌ Oxshott 154 CC113
Oxshott Ri, Cob. KT11 154 BX113
Oxshott Rd, Lthd. KT22 171 CE115
Oxshott Way, Cob. KT11 170 BY115
OXTED 187 ED129
⇌ Oxted 188 EE129
Oxted Cl, Mitch. CR4 140 DD97
Oxted Rd, Gdse. RH9 186 DW130
Oxtoby Way, SW16 141 DK96
Oyster Catchers Cl, E16
off Freemasons Rd 86 EH72
Oyster Catcher Ter, Ilf. IG5
off Tiptree Cres 69 EN55
Oyster La, W.Byf. (Byfleet)
KT14 152 BK110
Oyster Row, E1 off Lukin St 84 DW72
Ozolins Way, E16 86 EG72

P

Pablo Neruda Cl, SE24
off Shakespeare Rd 101 DP84
Paceheath Cl, Rom. RM5 51 FD51
Pace Pl, E1
off Bigland St 84 DV72
PACHESHAM PARK, Lthd. 171 CG116
Pachesham Pk, Lthd. KT22 171 CG117
Pacific Cl, Felt. TW14 115 BT88
Pacific Rd, E16 86 EG72
Packet Boat La, Uxb. UB8 76 BH72
Packham Cl, Orp. BR6
off Berrylands 146 EW104
Packham Ct, Wor.Pk. KT4
off Lavender Av 139 CW104
Packham Rd, Grav. (Nthflt.)
DA11 131 GF90
Packhorse La, Borwd. WD6 26 CS37
Potters Bar EN6 10 CR31
Packhorse Rd, Ger.Cr. (Chal.St.P.)
SL9 56 AY58
Sevenoaks TN13 190 FC123
Packington Rd, W3 98 CQ76
Packington Sq, N1 84 DQ67
Packington St, N1 83 DP67
Packmores Rd, SE9 125 ER85
Padbrook, Oxt. RH8 188 EG129
Padbrook Cl, Oxt. RH8 188 EH128
Padbury, SE17 102 DS78
Padbury Cl, Felt. TW14 115 BR88
Padbury Ct, E2 84 DT69
Padcroft Rd, West Dr. UB7 76 BK74
Padden Ct, NW7
off Bittacy Hill 43 CY52
Paddenswick Rd, W6 99 CU76
PADDINGTON, W2 82 DB71
⇌ Paddington 82 DC72
⊖ Paddington 82 DC72
Paddington Cl, Hayes UB4 78 BX70
Paddington Grn, W2 194 A6
Paddington St, W1 194 F6
Paddock, The, Ger.Cr. (Chal.St.P.)
SL9 36 AY50
Slough (Datchet) SL3 92 AV81
Uxbridge (Ickhm.) UB10 59 BP63
Westerham TN16 189 EQ126
Paddock Cl, SE3 104 EG82
SE26 123 DX91
Dartford (S.Darenth) DA4 148 FQ95
Northolt UB5 78 CA68
Orpington BR6
off State Fm Av 163 EP105
Oxted RH8 188 EF131
Watford WD19 24 BY44
Worcester Park KT4 138 CS102
Paddock Gdns, SE19
off Westow St 122 DS93
Paddock Rd, NW2 63 CU62
Bexleyheath DA6 106 EY84
Ruislip HA4 60 BX62
Paddocks, The, NW7 43 CY51
Addlestone (New Haw)
KT15 152 BH110
Barnet EN4 28 DF41
Rickmansworth (Chorl.)
WD3 21 BF42
Romford (Stap.Abb.) RM4 35 FF44
Sevenoaks TN13 191 FK124
Paddocks, The, Vir.W. GU25 132 AY100
Wembley HA9 62 CP61
Weybridge KT13 135 BS104
Paddocks Cl, Ashtd. KT21 172 CL118
Cobham KT11 154 BW114
Harrow HA2 60 CB63
Orpington BR5 146 EX103
Paddocks Mead, Wok. GU21 166 AS116
Paddocks Retail Pk, Wey.
KT13 152 BL111
Paddocks Way, Ashtd. KT21 172 CL118
Chertsey KT16 134 BH102
Paddock Wk, Warl. CR6 176 DV119
Paddock Way, Chis. BR7 125 ER94
Oxted RH8 188 EF131
Woking GU21 151 BB114
Padfield Rd, SE5 102 DQ83
Padgets, The, Wal.Abb. EN9 15 ED34
Padley Cl, Chess. KT9
off Moor La 156 CM106
Padnall Ct, Rom. RM6
off Padnall Rd 70 EX55
Padnall Rd, Rom. RM6 70 EX56
Padstow Cl, Orp. BR6 163 ET105
Slough SL3 92 AY76
Padstow Rd, Enf. EN2 29 DP40
Padstow Wk, Felt. TW14 115 BT88
Padua Rd, SE20 142 DW95
Pagden St, SW8 101 DH81
Pageant Av, NW9 42 CR53
Pageant Cl, Til. RM18 111 GJ81
Pageant Cres, SE16 203 L2
Pageantmaster Ct, EC4 196 F9
Pageant Wk, Croy. CR0 142 DS104
Page Av, Wem. HA9 62 CQ62
Page Cl, Dag. RM9 70 EY64
Dartford (Bean) DA2 129 FW90
Hampton TW12 116 BY93
Harrow HA3 62 CM58
Page Cres, Croy. CR0 159 DN106
Erith DA8 107 FF80
Page Grn Rd, N15 66 DU57
Page Grn Ter, N15 66 DT57
Page Heath La, Brom. BR1 144 EK97
Page Heath Vil, Brom. BR1 144 EK97
Pagehurst Rd, Croy. CR0 142 DV101
Page Meadow, NW7 43 CU52
Page Rd, Felt. TW14 115 BR86
Pages Hill, N10 44 DG54
Pages La, N10 44 DG54
Romford RM3 52 FP54
Uxbridge UB8 76 BJ65
Page St, NW7 43 CU53
SW1 199 N8
Pages Wk, SE1 201 M8
Pages Yd, W4 off Church St 98 CS79
Paget Av, Sutt. SM1 140 DD104
Paget Cl, Hmptn. TW12 117 CD91
Paget Gdns, Chis. BR7 145 EP95
Paget La, Islw. TW7 97 CD83
Paget Pl, Kings.T. KT2 118 CQ93
Thames Ditton KT7
off Brooklands Rd 137 CG102
Paget Ri, SE18 105 EN80
Paget Rd, N16 66 DR60
Ilford IG1 69 EP63
Slough SL3 93 AZ77
Uxbridge UB10 77 BQ70
Paget St, EC1 196 F2
Paget Ter, SE18 105 EN79
Pagette Way, Grays (Bad.Dene)
RM17 110 GA77
Pagitts Gro, Barn. EN4 28 DB39
Paglesfield, Brwd. CM13 55 GC44
Pagnell St, SE14 103 DZ80
Pagoda Av, Rich. TW9 98 CM83
Pagoda Gdns, SE3 103 ED82
Pagoda Vista, Rich. TW9 98 CM82
Paignton Rd, N15 66 DS58
Ruislip HA4 59 BU62
Paines Brook Rd, Rom. RM3
off Paines Brook Way 52 FM51
Paines Brook Way, Rom. RM3 52 FM51
Paines Cl, Pnr. HA5 60 BY55
Paines La, Pnr. HA5 40 BY53
Pains Cl, Mitch. CR4 141 DH96
Pains Hill, Oxt. RH8 188 EJ132
★ Painshill Park, Cob. KT11 153 BS114
Painsthorpe Rd, N16
off Oldfield Rd 66 DS62
Painters Ash La, Grav. (Nthflt.)
DA11 130 GD90
Painters La, Enf. EN3 31 DY35
Painters Ms, SE16
off Macks Rd 102 DU77
Painters Rd, Ilf. IG2 69 ET55
Paisley Rd, N22 45 DP53
Carshalton SM5 140 DD102
Pakeman St, N7 65 DM62
Pakenham Cl, SW12
off Balham Pk Rd 120 DG88
Pakenham St, WC1 196 C4
Pakes Way, Epp. (They.B.)
CM16 33 ES37
Palace Av, W8 82 DB74
Palace Cl, Kings L. WD4 6 BM30
Palace Ct, NW3 64 DB64
W2 82 DB73
Bromley BR1
off Palace Gro 144 EH95
Harrow HA3 62 CL58
Palace Ct Gdns, N10 65 DJ55
Palace Dr, Wey. KT13 135 BP104
Palace Gdns, Buck.H. IG9 48 EK46
Palace Gdns Ms, W8 82 DA74
Palace Gdns Prec, Enf. EN2
off Sydney Rd 30 DR41
Palace Gdns Ter, W8 82 DA74
Palace Gate, W8 100 DC75
Palace Gates Rd, N22 45 DK53
Palace Grn, W8 100 DB75
Croydon CR0 161 DZ108
Palace Gro, SE19 122 DT94
Bromley BR1 144 EH95
Palace Ms, E17 67 DZ56
SW1 198 G9
SW6 off Hartismere Rd 99 CZ80
Palace of Industry, Wem. HA9 62 CN63
Palace Par, E17 67 EA56
Palace Pl, SW1 199 K6
Palace Rd, N8 65 DK57
N11 45 DL52
SE19 122 DT94
SW2 121 DM88
Bromley BR1 144 EH95
East Molesey KT8 137 CD97
Kingston upon Thames
KT1 137 CK98
Ruislip HA4 60 BY63
Westerham TN16 179 EN121
Palace Rd Est, SW2 121 DM88
Palace Sq, SE19 122 DT94
Palace St, SW1 199 K6
Palace Vw, SE12 124 EG89
Bromley BR1 144 EG97
Croydon CR0 161 DZ105
Palace Vw Rd, E4 47 EB50
Palace Way, Wey. KT13
off Palace Dr 135 BP104
Palamos Rd, E10 67 EA60
Palatine Av, N16
off Stoke Newington Rd 66 DT63
Palatine Rd, N16 66 DS63
Palermo Rd, NW10 81 CU68
Palestine Gro, SW19 140 DD95
Palewell Cl, Orp. BR5 146 EV96
Palewell Common Dr, SW14 118 CR85
Palewell Pk, SW14 118 CR85
Paley Gdns, Loug. IG10 33 EP41
Palfrey Pl, SW8 101 DM80
Palgrave Av, Sthl. UB1 78 CA73
Palgrave Gdns, NW1 194 C4
Palgrave Rd, W12 99 CT76
Palissy St, E2 197 P3
Palladino Ho, SW17
off Laurel Cl 120 DE92
Pallant Way, Orp. BR6 145 EN104
Pallet Way, SE18 104 EL81
Palliser Dr, Rain. RM13 89 FG71
Palliser Rd, W14 99 CY78
Chalfont St. Giles HP8 36 AU48
Pall Mall, SW1 199 L3
Pall Mall E, SW1 199 N2
Palmar Cres, Bexh. DA7 106 FA83
Palmar Rd, Bexh. DA7 106 FA82
Palmarsh Cl, Orp. BR5
off Wotton Grn 146 EX98
Palm Av, Sid. DA14 126 EX93
Palm Cl, E10 67 EB62
Palmeira Rd, Bexh. DA7 106 EX83
Palmer Av, Bushey WD23 24 CB43
Gravesend DA12 131 GK91
Sutton SM3 157 CW105
Palmer Cl, Houns. TW5 96 CA81
West Wickham BR4 143 ED104
Palmer Cres, Cher. (Ott.)
KT16 151 BD107
Kingston upon Thames
KT1 138 CL97
Palmer Gdns, Barn. EN5 27 CX43
Palmer Pl, N7 65 DN64
Palmer Rd, E13 86 EH70
Dagenham RM8 70 EX60
Palmers Av, Grays RM17 110 GC78
Palmers Dr, Grays RM17 110 GC77
Palmersfield Rd, Bans. SM7 158 DA114
PALMERS GREEN, N13 45 DN48
⇌ Palmers Green 45 DM49
Palmers Gro, W.Mol. KT8 136 CA98
Palmers Hill, Epp. CM16 18 EU29
Palmers La, Enf. EN1, EN3 30 DV39
Palmers Moor La, Iver SL0 76 BG70
Palmers Orchard, Sev. (Shore.)
TN14 165 FF111
Palmers Pas, SW14
off Palmers Rd 98 CQ83
Palmers Rd, E2 85 DX68
N11 45 DJ50
SW14 98 CQ83
SW16 141 DM96
Borehamwood WD6 26 CP39
Palmerston Av, Slou. SL3 92 AV76
Palmerston Cl, Wok. GU21 151 AZ114
Palmerston Cres, N13 45 DM50
SE18 105 EQ79
Palmerstone Ct, Vir.W. GU25
off Sandhills La 132 AY99
Palmerston Gdns, Grays
RM20 109 FX78
Palmerston Gro, SW19 120 DA94
Palmerston Rd, E7 68 EH64
E17 67 DZ56
N22 45 DM52
NW6 82 DA66
SW14 98 CQ84
SW19 120 DA94
W3 98 CQ76
Buckhurst Hill IG9 48 EH47
Carshalton SM5 158 DF105
Croydon CR0 142 DR99
Grays RM20 109 FX78
Harrow HA3 61 CF55
Hounslow TW3 96 CC81
Orpington BR6 163 EQ105
Rainham RM13 90 FJ68
Sutton SM1 off Vernon Rd 158 DC106
Twickenham TW2 117 CF86
Palmerston Way, SW8
off Bradmead 101 DH80
Palmer St, SW1 199 M5
Palmers Way, Wal.Cr. (Chsht.)
EN8 15 DY29
Palm Gro, W5 98 CL76
Palm Rd, Rom. RM7 71 FC57
Pamela Gdns, Pnr. HA5 59 BV57
Pamela Wk, E8
off Marlborough Av 84 DU67
Pampisford Rd, Pur. CR8 159 DN111
South Croydon CR2 159 DP108
Pams Way, Epsom KT19 156 CR106
Pancras La, EC4 197 J9
Pancras Rd, NW1 83 DK68
Pancroft, Rom. (Abridge)
RM4 34 EV41
Pandora Rd, NW6 82 DA65
Panfield Ms, Ilf. IG2
off Cranbrook Rd 69 EN58
Panfield Rd, SE2 106 EU76
Pangbourne Av, W10 81 CW71
Pangbourne Dr, Stan. HA7 41 CK50
Pangbourne Ho, N7 65 DL64
Panhard Pl, Sthl. UB1 78 CB73
Pank Av, Barn. EN5 28 DC43
Pankhurst Cl, SE14
off Briant St 103 DX80
Isleworth TW7 97 CF83
Pankhurst Rd, Walt. KT12 136 BW101
Panmuir Rd, SW20 139 CV95
Panmure Cl, N5 65 DP63
Panmure Rd, SE26 122 DV90
Pannells Cl, Cher. KT16 133 BF102
Pansy Gdns, W12 81 CU73
Panters, Swan. BR8 127 FF94
Panther Dr, NW10 62 CR64
Pantile Rd, Wey. KT13 153 BR105
Pantile Row, Slou. SL3 93 BA77
Pantiles, The, NW11
off Willifield Way 63 CZ57
Bexleyheath DA7 106 EZ80
Bromley BR1 144 EL97
Bushey (Bushey Hth.)
WD23 41 CD45
Pantiles Cl, N13 45 DP50
Woking GU21 166 AV118
Pantile Wk, Uxb. UB8
off High St 76 BJ66
Panton St, SW1 199 M1
Panyer All, EC4 197 H8
Papercourt La, Wok. (Ripley)
GU23 167 BF122
Papermill Cl, Cars. SM5 158 DG105
Papillons Wk, SE3 104 EG82
Papworth Gdns, N7
off Liverpool Rd 65 DM64
Papworth Way, SW2 121 DN87
Parade, The, SW11 100 DF80
Brentwood CM14
off Kings Rd 54 FW48
Dartford DA1
off Crayford Way 127 FF85
Epsom KT18 156 CR113
Esher (Clay.) KT10 155 CE107
Hampton TW12
off Hampton Rd 117 CD92
Romford RM3 52 FP51
South Ockendon (Aveley)
RM15 108 FQ75
Sunbury-on-Thames TW16 115 BT94
Virginia Water GU25 132 AX100
Watford WD17 23 BV41
Watford (Carp.Pk.) WD19 40 BY48
Watford (S.Oxhey) WD19
off Prestwick Rd 40 BX48
Parade Ms, SE27
off Norwood Rd 121 DP89
Paradise Cl, Wal.Cr. (Chsht.)
EN7 14 DV28
Paradise Pas, N7 65 DN64
Paradise Pl, SE18
off Woodhill 104 EL77
Paradise Rd, SW4 101 DL82
Richmond TW9 117 CK85
Waltham Abbey EN9 15 EC34
Paradise Row, E2
off Bethnal Grn Rd 84 DV69
Paradise St, SE16 202 D5
Paradise Wk, SW3 100 DF79
Paragon, The, SE3 104 EF82
Paragon Cl, E16 86 EG72
Paragon Gro, Surb. KT5 138 CM100
Paragon Ms, SE1 201 L8
Paragon Pl, SE3 104 EF82
Surbiton KT5
off Berrylands Rd 138 CM100
Paragon Rd, E9 84 DW65
Parbury Ri, Chess. KT9 156 CL107
Parbury Rd, SE23 123 DY86
Parchment Cl, Amer. HP6 20 AS37
Parchmore Rd, Th.Hth. CR7 141 DP96
Parchmore Way, Th.Hth. CR7 141 DP96
Pardoner St, SE1 201 L6
Pardon St, EC1 196 G4
Pares Cl, Wok. GU21 166 AX116
Parfett St, E1 84 DU71
Parfitt Cl, NW3
off North End 64 DC61
Parfour Dr, Ken. CR8 176 DQ116
Parfrey St, W6 99 CW79
Parham Dr, Ilf. IG2 69 EP58
Parham Way, N10 45 DJ54
Paris Gdn, SE1 200 F2
Parish Cl, Horn. RM11 71 FH61
Watford WD25 off Crown Ri 8 BX34
Parish Gate Dr, Sid. DA15 125 ES86
Parish La, SE20 123 DX93
Parish Ms, SE20 123 DX94
Parish Wf Pl, SE1
off Woodhill 104 EL77
Park, The, N6 64 DG58
NW11 64 DB60
SE19 122 DS94
SE23 off Park Hill 122 DV88
W5 79 CK74
Carshalton SM5 158 DF106
Leatherhead (Bkhm.)
KT23 170 CA123
Sidcup DA14 125 ET92
Park App, Well. DA16 106 EV84
Park Av, E6 87 EN67
E15 86 EE65
N3 44 DB53
N13 45 DN48
N18 46 DU49
N22 45 DL54
NW2 81 CV65
NW10 80 CM69
NW11 64 DB60
SW14 98 CR84
Barking IG11 87 EQ65
Brentwood CM13 55 GC46
Bromley BR1 124 EF93
Park Av, Bushey WD23 24 BZ40
Carshalton SM5 158 DG107
Caterham CR3 176 DS124
Egham TW20 113 BC93
Enfield EN1 30 DS44
Gravesend DA12 131 GJ88
Gravesend (Perry St.) DA11 130 GE88
Grays RM20 109 FU79
Hounslow TW3 116 CB86
Ilford IG1 69 EN61
Mitcham CR4 121 DH94
Orpington BR6 146 EU103
Orpington (Farnboro.)
BR6 145 EM104
Potters Bar EN6 12 DC34
Radlett WD7 9 CH33
Rickmansworth (Chorl.)
WD3 22 BG43
Ruislip HA4 59 BR58
Southall UB1 78 CA74
Staines TW18 113 BF93
Staines (Wrays.) TW19 112 AX85
Upminster RM14 73 FS59
Watford WD18 23 BU42
West Wickham BR4 143 EC103
Woodford Green IG8 48 EH50
Park Av E, Epsom KT17 157 CU107
Park Av Ms, Mitch. CR4
off Park Av 121 DH94
Park Av N, N8 65 DK55
NW10 63 CV64
Park Av Rd, N17 46 DV52
Park Av S, N8 65 DK56
Park Av W, Epsom KT17 157 CU107
Park Boul, Rom. RM2 51 FF53
Park Chase, Wem. HA9 62 CM63
Park Cl, E9 84 DW67
NW2 63 CV62
NW10 80 CM69
SW1 198 D5
W4 98 CR78
W14 99 CZ76
Addlestone (New Haw)
KT15 152 BH110
Bushey WD23 24 BX41
Carshalton SM5 158 DF107
Epping (N.Wld.Bas.) CM16 18 FA27
Esher KT10 154 BZ107
Hampton TW12 136 CC95
Harrow HA3 41 CE53
Hatfield (Brook.Pk.) AL9 11 CZ26
Hounslow TW3 116 CC85
Kingston upon Thames
KT2 138 CN95
Leatherhead (Fetch.)
KT22 171 CD124
Oxted RH8 188 EF128
Rickmansworth WD3 39 BP49
Walton-on-Thames KT12 135 BT103
Park Cor Rd, Grav. (Sthflt.)
DA13 130 FZ91
Park Ct, SE26 122 DV93
Kingston upon Thames
KT1 137 CJ95
New Malden KT3 138 CR98
Wembley HA9 62 CL64
West Byfleet KT14 152 BG113
Woking GU22 off Park Dr 167 AZ118
Park Cres, N3 44 DB52
W1 195 H5
Borehamwood (Elstree)
WD6 26 CM41
Enfield EN2 30 DR42
Erith DA8 107 FC79
Harrow HA3 41 CE53
Hornchurch RM11 71 FG59
Twickenham TW2 117 CD88
Park Cres Ms E, W1 195 J5
Park Cres Ms W, W1 195 H6
Park Cres Rd, Erith DA8 107 FD79
Park Cft, Edg. HA8 42 CQ53
Parkcroft Rd, SE12 124 EF87
Park Dale, N11 45 DK51
Parkdale Cres, Wor.Pk. KT4 138 CR104
Parkdale Rd, SE18 105 ES78
Park Dr, N21 30 DQ44
NW11 64 DB60
SE7 104 EL79
SW14 98 CR84
W3 98 CN76
Ashtead KT21 172 CN118
Dagenham RM10 71 FC62
Harrow (Har.Wld.) HA3 41 CE51
Harrow (N.Har.) HA2 60 CA59
Potters Bar EN6 12 DA31
Romford RM1 71 FD56
Upminster RM14 72 FQ63
Weybridge KT13 153 BP106
Woking GU22 167 AZ118
Park Dr Cl, SE7 104 EL78
Park End, NW3
off South Hill Pk 64 DE63
Bromley BR1 144 EF95
Park End Rd, Rom. RM1 71 FE56
Parker Av, Til. RM18 111 GJ81
Parker Cl, E16 86 EL74
Parker Ms, WC2 196 A8
Parke Rd, SW13 99 CU81
Sunbury-on-Thames
TW16 135 BU98
Parker Rd, Croy. CR0 160 DQ105
Grays RM17 110 FZ78
Parkers Cl, Ashtd. KT21 172 CL119
Parkers Hill, Ashtd. KT21 172 CL119
Parkers La, Ashtd. KT21 172 CL119
Parkers Row, SE1 202 A5
Parker St, E16 86 EL74
WC2 196 A8
Watford WD24 23 BV39
Parkes Rd, Chig. IG7 49 ES50
Park Fm Cl, N2 64 DC55
Pinner HA5
off Field End Rd 59 BV57
Park Fm Rd, Brom. BR1 144 EK95

★ Place of interest ⇌ Railway station ⊖ London Underground station DLR Docklands Light Railway station Tramlink station H Hospital

Par - Pat

Park Fm Rd, Kings.T. KT2 118 CL94
Upminster RM14 72 FM64
Parkfield, Rick. (Chorl.) WD3 21 BF42
SevenoaksTN15 191 FM123
Parkfield Av, SW14 98 CS84
FelthamTW13 115 BU90
Harrow HA2 40 CC54
Northolt UB5 78 BX68
Uxbridge (Hlgdn.) UB10 77 BP69
Parkfield Cl, Edg. HA8 42 CP51
Northolt UB5 78 BY68
Parkfield Cres, Felt. TW13 115 BU90
Harrow HA2 40 CC54
Ruislip HA4 60 BY62
Parkfield Dr, Nthlt. UB5 78 BX68
Parkfield Gdns, Har. HA2 60 CB55
Parkfield Rd, NW10 81 CU66
SE14 103 DZ81
FelthamTW13 115 BU90
Harrow HA2 60 CC62
Northolt UB5 78 BY68
Uxbridge (Ickhm.) UB10 59 BP61
Parkfields, SW15 99 CW84
Croydon CR0 143 DZ102
Leatherhead (Oxshott)
KT22 155 CD111
Parkfields Av, NW9 62 CR60
SW20 139 CV95
Parkfields Cl, Cars. SM5
off Devonshire Rd 158 DG105
Parkfields Rd, Kings.T. KT2 118 CM92
Parkfield St, N1
off Berners Rd 83 DN68
Parkfield Vw, Pot.B. EN6 12 DB32
Parkfield Way, Brom. BR2 145 EM100
Park Gdns, NW9 62 CP55
Erith DA8 *off Valley Rd* 107 FD77
Kingston upon Thames
KT2 118 CM92
Park Gate, N2 64 DD55
N21 45 DM45
Parkgate, SE3 104 EF83
Park Gate, W5 *off Mount Av* 79 CK71
Parkgate Av, Barn. EN4 28 DC39
Parkgate Cl, Kings.T. KT2
off Warboys App 118 CP93
Parkgate Cres, Barn. EN4 28 DC40
Parkgate Gdns, SW14 118 CR85
Parkgate Ms, N6
off Stanhope Rd 65 DJ59
Parkgate Rd, SW11 100 DE80
Orpington BR6 165 FB105
Wallington SM6 158 DG106
Watford WD24 24 BW37
Park Gates, Har. HA2 60 CA63
Park Gra Gdns, Sev. TN13
off Solefields Rd 191 FJ127
Park Grn, Lthd. (Bkhm.)
KT23 170 CA124
Park Gro, E15 86 EG67
N11 45 DK52
Bexleyheath DA7 107 FC84
Bromley BR1 144 EH95
Chalfont St. Giles HP8 20 AX41
Edgware HA8 42 CM50
Park Gro Rd, E11 68 EE61
Park Hall Rd, N2 64 DE56
SE21 122 DQ90
Reigate RH2 184 DA132
Parkham Ct, Brom. BR2 144 EE96
Parkham St, SW11 100 DE81
Park Hill, SE23 122 DV89
SW4 121 DK85
W5 79 CK71
Bromley BR1 144 EL98
Carshalton SM5 158 DE107
Loughton IG10 32 EK43
RichmondTW10 118 CM86
Park Hill Cl, Cars. SM5 158 DE106
Parkhill Cl, Horn. RM12 72 FJ62
Park Hill Ct, SW17
off Beeches Rd 120 DF90
Park Hill Ri, Croy. CR0 142 DS103
Parkhill Rd, E4 47 EC46
NW3 64 DF64
Bexley DA5 126 EZ87
Park Hill Rd, Brom. BR2 144 EE96
Croydon CR0 142 DS103
Epsom KT17 157 CT111
Parkhill Rd, Sid. DA15 125 ER90
Park Hill Rd, Wall. SM6 159 DH108
Parkhill Wk, NW3 64 DF64
Parkholme Rd, E8 84 DT65
Park Ho, N21 45 DM45
Park Ho Gdns, Twick. TW1 117 CJ86
Parkhouse St, SE5 102 DR80
Parkhurst, Epsom KT19 156 CQ110
Parkhurst Av, E16
off Wesley Av 86 EH74
Parkhurst Gdns, Bex. DA5 126 FA87
Parkhurst Rd, E12 69 EN63
E17 67 DY56
N7 65 DL63
N11 44 DG49
N17 46 DU54
N22 45 DM52
Bexley DA5 126 FA87
Sutton SM1 158 DD105
Park Ind Est, St.Alb. (Frog.)
AL2 9 CE27
Parkland Av, Rom. RM1 71 FE55
Slough SL3 92 AX77
Upminster RM14 72 FP64
Parkland Cl, Chig. IG7 49 EQ48
SevenoaksTN13 191 FJ129
Parkland Gdns, SW19 119 CX88
Parkland Gro, Ashf. TW15 114 BN91
Parkland Rd, N22 45 DM54
AshfordTW15 114 BN91
Woodford Green IG8 48 EG52
Parklands, N6 65 DH59
Addlestone KT15 152 BJ106
Chigwell IG7 49 EQ48
Epping (Cooper.) CM16 18 EX29
Parklands, Lthd. (Bkhm.)
KT23 170 CA123
Oxted RH8 188 EE131
Surbiton KT5 138 CM99
Waltham Abbey EN9 15 ED32
Parklands Cl, SW14 118 CQ85
Barnet EN4 28 DD38
Ilford IG2 69 EQ59
Parklands Ct, Houns. TW5 96 BX82
Parklands Dr, N3 63 CY55
Parklands Rd, SW16 121 DH92
Parklands Way, Wor.Pk. KT4 138 CS104
Parkland Wk, N4 65 DM59
N6 65 DK59
N10 65 DH56
Park La, E15 *off High St* 85 ED67
N9 46 DT48
N17 46 DU52
W1 198 G3
Ashtead KT21 172 CM118
Banstead SM7 174 DD118
Carshalton SM5 158 DG105
Coulsdon CR5 175 DK121
Croydon CR0 142 DR104
Harrow HA2 60 CB62
Hayes UB4 77 BS71
Hornchurch RM11 71 FG58
Hornchurch (Elm Pk.) RM12 89 FH65
HounslowTW5 95 BU80
RichmondTW9 97 CK84
Romford (Chad.Hth.) RM6 70 EX58
SevenoaksTN13 191 FJ124
Sevenoaks (Seal) TN15 191 FN121
Slough SL3 92 AV76
Slough (Horton) SL3 93 BA83
South Ockendon (Aveley)
RM15 91 FR74
Stanmore HA7 41 CG48
Sutton SM3 157 CY107
Swanley BR8 148 FJ96
TeddingtonTW11 117 CF93
Uxbridge (Hare.) UB9 38 BG53
Wallington SM6 158 DG105
Waltham Cross EN8 14 DW33
Waltham Cross (Chsht.)
EN7 14 DU26
Wembley HA9 62 CL64
Park La Cl, N17 46 DU52
PARK LANGLEY, Beck. 143 EC99
Parklawn Av, Epsom KT18 156 CP113
Park Lawn Rd, Wey. KT13 153 BQ105
Park Lawns, Wem. HA9 62 CM63
Parklea Cl, NW9 42 CS53
Parkleigh Rd, SW19 140 DB96
Park Ley Rd, Cat. (Wold.)
CR3 177 DX120
Parkleys, Rich. TW10 117 CK91
Parkmead, SW15 119 CV86
Park Mead, Har. HA2 60 CB62
Parkmead, Loug. IG10 33 EN43
Park Mead, Sid. DA15 126 EV85
Parkmead Gdns, NW7 43 CT51
Park Ms, SE24
off Croxted Rd 122 DQ86
Chislehurst BR7 125 EP93
East Molesey KT8 136 CC98
Hampton (Hmptn.H.) TW12
off Park Rd 116 CC92
Rainham RM13
off Sowrey Av 89 FG65
Parkmore Cl, Wdf.Grn. IG8 48 EG49
Park Nook Gdns, Enf. EN2 30 DR37
Park Par, NW10 81 CT68
Park Pl, E14 203 P2
SW1 199 K3
W3 98 CN77
W5 79 CK74
Amersham HP6 20 AT38
Gravesend DA12 131 GJ86
Hampton (Hmptn.H.)
TW12 116 CC93
St. Albans (Park St.) AL2 9 CD27
SevenoaksTN13 190 FD123
Wembley HA9 62 CM63
Woking GU22
off Park Dr 167 AZ118
Park Pl Vil, W2 82 DC71
Park Ridings, N8 65 DN55
Park Ri, SE23 123 DY88
Harrow HA3 41 CE53
Leatherhead KT22 171 CH121
Park Ri Cl, Lthd. KT22 171 CH121
Park Ri Rd, SE23 123 DY88
Park Rd, E6 86 EJ67
E10 67 EA60
E12 68 EH60
E15 86 EG67
E17 67 DZ57
N2 64 DD55
N8 65 DJ56
N11 45 DK52
N14 45 DK45
N15 65 DP56
N18 46 DT49
NW1 194 B2
NW4 63 CU59
NW8 194 B2
NW9 62 CR59
NW10 80 CS67
SE25 142 DS98
SW19 120 DD93
W4 98 CQ80
W7 79 CF73
Amersham HP6 20 AT37
AshfordTW15 115 BP92
Ashtead KT21 172 CL118
Banstead SM7 174 DB115
Barnet EN5 27 CZ42
Barnet (New Barn.) EN4 28 DE42
Beckenham BR3 123 DZ94
Brentwood CM14 54 FV46
Bromley BR1 144 EH95
Bushey WD23 24 CA44
Caterham CR3 176 DS123
Chislehurst BR7 125 EP93
Dartford DA1 128 FN87
East Molesey KT8 136 CC98
Park Rd, EghamTW20 113 BA91
Enfield EN3 31 DY36
Esher KT10 154 CB105
FelthamTW13 116 BX91
Gravesend DA11 131 GH88
Grays RM17 110 GB78
Hampton (Hmptn.H.)
TW12 116 CB91
Hayes UB4 77 BS71
HounslowTW3 96 CC84
Ilford IG1 69 ER62
IsleworthTW7 97 CH81
Kenley CR8 175 DP115
Kingston upon Thames
KT2 118 CM92
Kingston upon Thames
(Hmptn.W.) KT1 117 CF93
New Malden KT3 138 CR98
Orpington BR5 146 EW99
Oxted RH8 188 EF128
Potters Bar EN6 12 DG30
Radlett WD7 25 CG35
Redhill RH1 184 DF132
RichmondTW10 118 CM86
Rickmansworth WD3 38 BK45
SheppertonTW17 134 BN102
Staines (Stanw.) TW19 114 BH86
Sunbury-on-Thames
TW16 115 BV94
Surbiton KT5 138 CM99
Sutton SM3 157 CY107
Swanley BR8 147 FF97
Swanscombe DA10 130 FY86
TeddingtonTW11 137 CJ95
TwickenhamTW1 117 CJ86
Uxbridge UB8 76 BL66
Wallington SM6 159 DH106
Wallington (Hackbr.) SM6 141 DH103
Waltham Cross EN8 15 DX33
Warlingham CR6 162 EE114
Watford WD17 23 BU39
Wembley HA0 80 CL65
Woking GU22 167 BA117
Park Rd E, W3 98 CP75
Uxbridge UB10
off Hillingdon Rd 76 BK68
Park Rd N, W3 98 CP75
W4 98 CR78
Park Row, SE10 103 ED79
PARK ROYAL, NW10 80 CN69
⊖ **Park Royal** 80 CN70
Park Royal Rd, NW10 80 CQ69
W3 80 CQ69
Parkshot, Rich. TW9 98 CL84
Parkside, N3 44 DB53
NW2 63 CU62
NW7 43 CU51
SE3 104 EF80
SW19 119 CX91
Addlestone (New Haw)
KT15 152 BH110
Buckhurst Hill IG9 48 EH47
Gerrards Cross (Chal.St.P.) SL9
off Lower Rd 57 AZ56
Grays RM16 110 GE76
Hampton (Hmptn.H.) TW12 117 CD92
Potters Bar EN6
off High St 12 DC32
Sevenoaks (Halst.) TN14 164 EZ113
Sidcup DA14 126 EV89
Sutton SM3 157 CY107
Waltham Cross EN8 15 DY34
Watford WD19 24 BW44
Parkside Av, SW19 119 CX92
Bexleyheath DA7 107 FD82
Bromley BR1 144 EL98
Romford RM1 71 FD55
Tilbury RM18 111 GH82
Parkside Business Est, SE8
off Rolt St 103 DY79
Parkside Cl, SE20 122 DW94
Parkside Ct, Wey. KT13 152 BN105
Parkside Cres, N7 65 DN62
Surbiton KT5 138 CQ100
Parkside Cross, Bexh. DA7 107 FE82
Parkside Dr, Edg. HA8 42 CN48
Watford WD17 23 BS40
Parkside Est, E9
off Rutland Rd 84 DW67
Parkside Gdns, SW19 119 CX91
Barnet EN4 44 DF46
Coulsdon CR5 175 DH117
H **Parkside Hosp**, SW19 119 CX90
Parkside Ho, Dag. RM10 71 FC62
Parkside Rd, SW11 100 DG81
Belvedere DA17 107 FC77
HounslowTW3 116 CB85
Northwood HA6 39 BT50
Warlingham CR6 177 EA116
Parkside Ter, N18
off Great Cambridge Rd 46 DR49
Parkside Wk, SE10 205 H7
Slough SL1 92 AU76
Parkside Way, Har. HA2 60 CB56
Park S, SW11 *off Austin Rd* 100 DG81
Park Sq, Esher KT10
off Park Rd 154 CB105
Park Sq E, NW1 195 H4
Park Sq Ms, NW1 195 H5
Park Sq W, NW1 195 H4
Parkstead Rd, SW15 119 CU85
Parkstone Av, N18 46 DT50
Hornchurch RM11 72 FK58
Parkstone Rd, E17 67 EC55
SE15 *off Rye La* 102 DU82
PARK STREET, St.Alb. 9 CD26
⇌ **Park Street** 9 CD26
Park St, SE1 201 H2
W1 194 F10
Croydon CR0 142 DQ103
St. Albans AL2 9 CD26
Slough SL1 92 AT76
Slough (Colnbr.) SL3 93 BD80
TeddingtonTW11 117 CE93
Park St La, St.Alb. (Park St.)
AL2 8 CB30
Park Ter, Green. DA9 129 FV85
Park Ter, Sev. (Sund.) TN14
off Main Rd 180 EX124
Worcester Park KT4 139 CU102
Parkthorne Cl, Har. HA2 60 CB58
Parkthorne Dr, Har. HA2 60 CA58
Parkthorne Rd, SW12 121 DK87
Park Vw, N21 45 DM45
W3 80 CQ71
New Malden KT3 139 CT97
Pinner HA5 40 BZ53
Potters Bar EN6 12 DC33
South Ockendon (Aveley)
RM15 91 FR74
Wembley HA9 62 CP64
Parkview Ct, SW18
off Broomhill Rd 120 DA86
Park Vw Ct, Ilf. IG2
off Brancaster Rd 69 ES58
Woking GU22 166 AY119
Park Vw Cres, N11 45 DH49
Parkview Dr, Mitch. CR4 140 DD96
Park Vw Est, E2 85 DX68
Park Vw Gdns, NW4 63 CW57
Grays RM17 110 GB78
Ilford IG4 69 EM56
Park Vw Ho, SE24
off Hurst St 121 DP86
Park Vw Rd, N3 44 DB53
N17 66 DU55
NW10 63 CT63
Parkview Rd, SE9 125 EP89
Park Vw Rd, W5 80 CL71
Caterham (Wold.) CR3 177 DY122
Parkview Rd, Croy. CR0 142 DU102
Park Vw Rd, Pnr. HA5 39 BV52
Southall UB1 78 CA74
Uxbridge UB8 76 BN72
Welling DA16 106 EW83
Park Village E, NW1 83 DH68
Park Village W, NW1 83 DH68
Park Vil, Rom. RM6 70 EX58
Parkville Rd, SW6 99 CZ80
Park Vista, SE10 103 ED79
Park Wk, N6 *off North Rd* 64 DG59
SE10 *off Crooms Hill* 103 ED80
SW10 100 DC79
Ashtead KT21
off Rectory La 172 CM119
Parkway, N14 45 DL47
Park Way, N20 44 DF49
Parkway, NW1 83 DH67
Park Way, NW11 63 CY57
Parkway, SW20 139 CX98
Park Way, Bex. DA5 127 FE90
Brentwood CM15 55 FZ46
Parkway, Croy. (New Adgtn.)
CR0 161 EC109
Park Way, Edg. HA8 42 CP53
Enfield EN2 29 DN40
Parkway, Erith DA18 106 EY76
Park Way, Felt. TW14 115 BV87
Parkway, Ilf. IG3 69 ET62
Park Way, Lthd. (Bkhm.)
KT23 170 CA123
Parkway, Rain. RM13
off Upminster Rd S 89 FG70
Park Way, Rick. WD3 38 BJ46
Parkway, Rom. RM2 71 FF55
Park Way, Ruis. HA4 59 BU60
Parkway, Uxb. UB10 76 BN66
Park Way, W.Mol. KT8 136 CB97
Parkway, Wey. KT13 153 BR105
Woodford Green IG8 48 EJ50
Parkway, The, Hayes
UB3, UB4 78 BW72
Hounslow (Cran.)
TW4, TW5 95 BV82
Iver SL0 75 BC68
Northolt UB5 78 BX69
Southall UB2 95 BU78
Parkway Trd Est, Houns. TW5 96 BW79
Park W, W2 194 C9
Park W Pl, W2 194 C8
Parkwood, N20 44 DF48
Beckenham BR3 143 EA95
Parkwood Av, Esher KT10 136 CC102
Parkwood Cl, Bans. SM7 173 CX115
Parkwood Gro, Sun. TW16 135 BU97
Parkwood Ms, N6 65 DH58
Parkwood Rd, SW19 119 CZ92
Banstead SM7 173 CX115
Bexley DA5 126 EZ87
IsleworthTW7 97 CF81
Redhill (Nutfld.) RH1 185 DL133
Westerham (Tats.) TN16 178 EL121
Parkwood Vw, Bans. SM7 173 CW116
Park Wks Rd, Red. RH1 185 DM133
Parlaunt Rd, Slou. SL3 93 BA77
Parley Dr, Wok. GU21 166 AW117
Parliament Ct, E1
off Sandy's Row 84 DS71
Parliament Hill, NW3 64 DE63
Parliament Ms, SW14
off Thames Bk 98 CQ82
Parliament Sq, SW1 199 P5
Parliament St, SW1 199 P5
Parliament Vw Apartments,
SE1 200 B8
Parma Cres, SW11 100 DF84
Parmiter St, E2 84 DV68
Parmoor Ct, EC1 197 H4
Parnell Cl, Abb.L. WD5 7 BT30
Edgware HA8 42 CP49
Grays (Chaff.Hun.) RM16 109 FW78
Parnell Gdns, Wey. KT13 152 BN111
Parnell Rd, E3 85 DZ67
Parnham St, E1 *off Blount St* 85 DY72
Parolles Rd, N19 65 DJ60
Paroma Rd, Belv. DA17 106 FA76
Parr Av, Epsom KT17 157 CV109
Parr Cl, N9 46 DV49
N18 46 DV49
Grays (Chaff.Hun.) RM16 109 FW77
Leatherhead KT22 171 CF120
Parr Ct, N1 *off New N Rd* 84 DR68
FelthamTW13 116 BW91
Parrock, The, Grav. DA12 131 GJ88
Parrock Av, Grav. DA12 131 GJ88
PARROCK FARM, Grav. 131 GK91
Parrock Rd, Grav. DA12 131 GJ88
Parrock St, Grav. DA12 131 GH87
Parrotts Cl, Rick. (Crox.Grn.)
WD3 22 BN42
Parr Pl, W4
off Chiswick High Rd 99 CT77
Parr Rd, E6 86 EK67
Stanmore HA7 41 CK53
Parrs Cl, S.Croy. CR2
off Florence Rd 160 DR109
Parrs Pl, Hmptn. TW12 116 CA94
Parr St, N1 84 DR68
Parry Av, E6 87 EM72
Parry Cl, Epsom KT17 157 CU108
Parry Dr, Wey. KT13 152 BN110
Parry Grn N, Slou. SL3 93 AZ77
Parry Grn S, Slou. SL3 93 BA77
Parry Pl, SE18 105 EP77
Parry Rd, SE25 142 DS97
W10 81 CY69
Parry St, SW8 101 DL79
Parsifal Rd, NW6 64 DA64
Parsley Gdns, Croy. CR0
off Primrose La 143 DX102
Parsloes Av, Dag. RM9 70 EX63
Parsonage Cl, Abb.L. WD5 7 BS30
Hayes UB3 77 BT72
Warlingham CR6 177 DY116
Parsonage Gdns, Enf. EN2 30 DQ40
Parsonage La, Dart. (Sutt.H.)
DA4 128 FP93
Enfield EN1, EN2 30 DR40
Sidcup DA14 126 EZ91
Parsonage Manorway, Belv.
DA17 106 FA79
Parsonage Rd, Ch.St.G. HP8 36 AV48
Egham (Eng.Grn.) TW20 112 AX92
Grays RM20 109 FW79
Rainham RM13 90 FJ69
Rickmansworth WD3 38 BK45
Parsonage St, E14 204 E9
Parsons Cres, Edg. HA8 42 CN48
Parsonsfield Cl, Bans. SM7 173 CX115
Parsonsfield Rd, Bans. SM7 173 CX116
PARSONS GREEN, SW6 100 DA81
⊖ **Parsons Green** 99 CZ81
Parsons Grn, SW6 100 DA81
Parsons Grn La, SW6 100 DA81
Parsons Gro, Edg. HA8 42 CN48
Parsons Hill, SE18
off Powis St 105 EN76
Parsons Ho, SW2
off New Pk Rd 121 DL87
Parson's Ho, W2 82 DD70
Parsons La, Dart. DA2 127 FH90
Parson's Mead, Croy. CR0 141 DP102
Parsons Mead, E.Mol. KT8 136 CC97
Parsons Pightle, Couls. CR5 175 DN120
Parsons Rd, E13 *off Old St* 86 EJ68
Parson St, NW4 63 CW56
Parthenia Rd, SW6 100 DA81
Parthia Cl, Tad. KT20 173 CV119
Partingdale La, NW7 43 CX50
Partington Cl, N19 65 DK60
Partridge Cl, E16
off Fulmer Rd 86 EK71
Barnet EN5 27 CW44
Bushey WD23 40 CB46
Chesham HP5 4 AS28
Stanmore HA7 42 CL49
Partridge Ct, EC1
off Percival St 83 DP70
Partridge Dr, Orp. BR6 145 EQ104
Partridge Grn, SE9 125 EN90
Partridge Knoll, Pur. CR8 159 DP112
Partridge Mead, Bans. SM7 173 CW116
Partridge Rd, Hmptn. TW12 116 BZ93
Sidcup DA14 125 ES90
Partridge Sq, E6
off Nightingale Way 86 EL71
Partridge Way, N22 45 DL53
Parvills, Wal.Abb. EN9 15 ED32
Parvin St, SW8 101 DK81
Parvis Rd, W.Byf. KT14 152 BG113
Pasadena Cl, Hayes UB3 95 BV75
Pasadena Cl Trd Est, Hayes UB3
off Pasadena Cl 95 BV75
Pascal St, SW8 101 DK80
Pascoe Rd, SE13 123 ED85
Pasfield, Wal.Abb. EN9 15 ED33
Pasley Cl, SE17
off Penrose St 102 DQ78
Pasquier Rd, E17 67 DY55
Passey Pl, SE9 125 EM86
Passfield Dr, E14
off Uamvar St 85 EB71
Passfield Path, SE28
off Booth Cl 88 EV73
Passing All, EC1 196 G5
Passmore Gdns, N11 45 DK51
Passmore St, SW1 198 F9
★ **Passport Office**, SW1 199 L6
Pastens Rd, Oxt. RH8 188 EJ131
Pasteur Cl, NW9 42 CS54
Pasteur Dr, Rom. (Harold Wd.)
RM3 52 FK54
Pasteur Gdns, N18 45 DP50
Paston Cl, E5
off Caldecott Way 67 DX62
Wallington SM6 141 DJ104
Paston Cres, SE12 124 EH87
Pastor St, SE11 200 G8
Pasture Cl, Bushey WD23 40 CC45
Wembley HA0 61 CH62
Pasture Rd, SE6 124 EE88
Dagenham RM9 70 EZ63
Wembley HA0 61 CH61
Pastures, The, N20 43 CZ46
Watford WD19 40 BW45
Pastures Mead, Uxb. UB10 76 BN65
Patch, The, Sev. TN13 190 FE122
Patcham Ct, Sutt. SM2 158 DC109
Patcham Ter, SW8 101 DH81
Patch Cl, Uxb. UB10 76 BM67
PATCHETTS GREEN, Wat. 24 CC39

★ Place of interest ⇌ Railway station ⊖ London Underground station DLR Docklands Light Railway station Tramlink station H Hospital

307

Pat - Pen

Paternoster Cl, Wal.Abb. EN9 .16 EF33
Paternoster Hill, Wal.Abb.
EN9 .16 EF32
Paternoster Row, EC4 .197 H9
Romford (Noak Hill) RM4 .52 FJ47
Paternoster Sq, EC4 .196 G8
Paterson Rd, Ashf.TW15 .114 BK92
Pater St, W8 .100 DA76
Pates Manor Dr, Felt.TW14 .115 BR87
Path,The, SW19 .140 DB95
Pathfield Rd, SW16 .121 DK93
Pathway,The, Rad. WD7 .25 CF36
Watford WD19
off Anthony Cl .40 BX46
Patience Rd, SW11 .100 DE82
Patio Cl, SW4 .121 DK86
Patmore Est, SW8 .101 DJ81
Patmore La, Walt. KT12 .153 BT107
Patmore Rd, Wal.Abb. EN9 .16 EE34
Patmore St, SW8 .101 DJ81
Patmore Way, Rom. RM5 .51 FB50
Patmos Rd, SW9 .101 DP80
Paton Cl, E3 .85 EA69
Paton St, EC1 .197 H3
Patricia Ct, Chis. BR7
off Manor Pk Rd .145 ER95
Welling DA16 .106 EV80
Patricia Dr, Horn. RM11 .72 FL60
Patricia Gdns, Sutt. SM2
off The Crescent .158 DA111
Patrick Connolly Gdns, E3
off Talwin St .85 EB69
Patrick Gro, Wal.Abb. EN9
off Beaulieu Dr .15 EB33
Patrick Rd, E13 .86 EJ69
Patrington Cl, Uxb. UB8
off Boulmer Rd .76 BJ69
Patriot Sq, E2 .84 DV68
Patrol Pl, SE6 .123 EB86
Patrons Dr, Uxb. (Denh.) UB9 .57 BF58
Patshull Pl, NW5
off Patshull Rd .83 DJ65
Patshull Rd, NW5 .83 DJ65
Patten All, Rich.TW10
off The Hermitage .117 CK85
Pattenden Rd, SE6 .123 DZ88
Patten Rd, SW18 .120 DE87
Patterdale Cl, Brom. BR1 .124 EF93
Patterdale Rd, SE15 .102 DW80
Dartford DA2 .129 FR88
Patterson Ct, SE19 .122 DT94
Dartford DA1 .128 FN85
Patterson Rd, SE19 .122 DT93
Pattina Wk, SE16 .85 DZ74
Pattison Pt, E1 *off Fife Rd* .86 EG71
Pattison Rd, NW2 .64 DA62
Pattison Wk, SE18 .105 EQ78
Paul Cl, E15 .86 EE66
Paulet Rd, SE5 .101 DP82
Paul Gdns, Croy. CR0 .142 DT103
Paulhan Rd, Har. HA3 .61 CK56
Paulin Dr, N21 .45 DN45
Pauline Cres, Twick.TW2 .116 CC88
Paulinus Cl, Orp. BR5 .146 EW96
Paul Julius Cl, E14 .204 F1
Paul Robeson Cl, E6
off Eastbourne Rd .87 EN69
Pauls Grn, Wal.Cr. EN8
off Eleanor Rd .15 DY33
Paul's Pl, Ashtd. KT21 .172 CP119
Paul St, E15 .85 ED67
EC2 .197 L5
Paul's Wk, EC4 .196 G10
Paultons Sq, SW3 .100 DD79
Paultons St, SW3 .100 DD79
Pauntley St, N19 .65 DJ60
Paved Ct, Rich.TW9 .117 CK85
Paveley Dr, SW11 .100 DE80
Paveley St, NW8 .194 C4
Pavement,The, SW4 .101 DJ84
W5 *off Popes La* .98 CL76
Pavement Ms, Rom. RM6
off Clarissa Rd .70 EX59
Pavement Sq, Croy. CR0 .142 DU102
Pavet Cl, Dag. RM10 .89 FB65
Pavilion Gdns, Stai.TW18 .114 BH94
Pavilion La, Beck. BR3
off Lennard Rd .123 DZ93
Pavilion Ms, N3
off Windermere Av .44 DA54
Pavilion Rd, SW1 .198 E7
Ilford IG1 .69 EM59
Pavilions,The, Epp. (N.Wld.Bas.)
CM16 .19 FC25
Uxbridge UB8 .76 BJ66
Pavilion Shop Cen,The, Wal.Cr.
EN8 .15 DX34
Pavilion St, SW1 .198 E7
Pavilion Ter, E.Mol. KT8 .137 CF98
Ilford IG2
off Southdown Cres .69 ES57
Pavilion Way, Amer. HP6 .20 AW39
Edgware HA8 .42 CP52
Ruislip HA4 .60 BW61
Pawleyne Cl, SE20 .122 DW94
Pawsey Cl, E13 *off Plashet Rd* .86 EG67
Pawson's Rd, Croy. CR0 .142 DQ100
Paxford Rd, Wem. HA0 .61 CH61
Paxton Cl, Rich.TW9 .98 CM82
Walton-on-Thames KT12 .136 BW101
Paxton Gdns, Wok. GU21 .151 BE112
Paxton Pl, SE27 .122 DS91
Paxton Rd, N17 .46 DT52
SE23 .123 DY90
W4 .98 CS79
Bromley BR1 .124 EG94
Paxton Ter, SW1 .101 DH79
Payne Cl, Bark. IG11 .87 ES66
Paynell Ct, SE3
off Lawn Ter .104 EE83
Payne Rd, E3 .85 EB68
Paynesfield Av, SW14 .98 CR83
Paynesfield Rd, Bushey
(Bushey Hth.) WD23 .41 CF45
Westerham (Tats.) TN16 .178 EJ121
Payne St, SE8 .103 DZ79
Paynes Wk, W6 .99 CY79
Peabody Av, SW1 .199 H10
Peabody Cl, SE10
off Devonshire Dr .103 EB81
SW1 *off Lupus St* .101 DH79
Croydon CR0
off Shirley Rd .142 DW102
Peabody Ct, Enf. EN3
off Government Row .31 EA37
Peabody Dws, WC1 .195 P4
Peabody Est, EC1 .197 J5
N17 .46 DS53
SE1 .200 E3
SE24 .122 DQ87
SW3 *off Margaretta Ter* .100 DE79
W6 *off The Square* .99 CW78
W10 .81 CW71
Peabody Hill, SE21 .121 DP88
Peabody Hill Est, SE21 .121 DP87
Peabody Sq, N1 *off Essex Rd* .83 DP67
SE1 .200 F5
Peabody Twr, EC1
off Golden La .84 DQ70
Peabody Trust, SE1 .201 H3
Peabody Yd, N1
off Greenman St .84 DQ67
Peace Cl, N14 .29 DH43
SE25 .142 DS98
Waltham Cross EN7
off Goffs La .14 DU29
Peace Dr, Wat. WD17 .23 BU41
Peace Gro, Wem. HA9 .62 CP62
Peace Prospect, Wat. WD17 .23 BU41
Peace Rd, Iver SL0 .75 BA68
Slough SL3 .75 BA68
Peace St, SE18
off Nightingale Vale .105 EP79
Peach Cft, Grav. (Nthflt.)
DA11 .130 GE90
Peaches Cl, Sutt. SM2 .157 CY108
Peachey Cl, Uxb. UB8 .76 BK72
Peachey La, Uxb. UB8 .76 BK71
Peach Rd, W10 .81 CX69
Peach Tree Av, West Dr. UB7
off Pear Tree Av .76 BM72
Peachum Rd, SE3 .104 EF79
Peachwalk Ms, E3
off Grove Rd .85 DX68
Peacock Av, Felt.TW14 .115 BR88
Peacock Cl, Horn. RM11 .72 FL56
Peacock Gdns, S.Croy. CR2 .161 DY110
Peacocks Cen, The, Wok.
GU21 .166 AY117
Peacock St, SE17 .200 G9
Gravesend DA12 .131 GJ87
Peacock Wk, E16 .86 EH72
Abbots Langley WD5 .7 BU31
Peacock Yd, SE17 .200 G9
Peak, The, SE26 .122 DW90
Peakes La, Wal.Cr. (Chsht.)
EN7 .14 DT27
Peakes Way, Wal.Cr. (Chsht.)
EN7 .14 DT27
Peaketon Av, Ilf. IG4 .68 EK56
Peak Hill, SE26 .122 DW91
Peak Hill Av, SE26 .122 DW91
Peak Hill Gdns, SE26 .122 DW91
Peaks Hill, Pur. CR8 .159 DK110
Peaks Hill Ri, Pur. CR8 .159 DL110
Pea La, Upmin. RM14 .91 FU66
Peal Gdns, W13
off Ruislip Rd E .79 CG70
Peall Rd, Croy. CR0 .141 DM100
Pearce Cl, Mitch. CR4 .140 DG96
Pearcefield Av, SE23 .122 DW88
Pearce Rd, W.Mol. KT8 .136 CB97
Pear Cl, NW9 .62 CR56
SE14
off Southerngate Way .103 DY80
Pearcroft Rd, E11 .67 ED61
Pearcy Cl, Rom. (Harold Hill)
RM3 .52 FL52
Peardon St, SW8 .101 DH82
Peareswood Gdns, Stan. HA7 .41 CK53
Peareswood Rd, Erith DA8 .107 FF81
Pearfield Rd, SE23 .123 DY90
Pearl Cl, E6 .87 EN72
NW2 *off Marble Dr* .63 CX59
Pearl Ct, Wok. GU21
off Langmans Way .166 AS116
Pearl Rd, E17 .67 EA55
Pearl St, E1 .202 E2
Pearmain Cl, Shep.TW17 .135 BP99
Pearman St, SE1 .200 E6
Pear Pl, SE1 .200 D4
Pear Rd, E11 .67 ED62
Pearscroft Ct, SW6 .100 DB81
Pearscroft Rd, SW6 .100 DB81
Pearse St, SE15
off Dragon Rd .102 DS79
Pearson Ms, SW4
off Edgeley Rd .101 DK83
Pearsons Av, SE14
off Tanners Hill .103 EA81
Pearson St, E2 .84 DS68
Pearson Way, Dart. DA1 .128 FM89
Pears Rd, Houns.TW3 .96 CC83
Peartree Av, SW17 .120 DC90
Pear Tree Av, West Dr. UB7 .76 BM72
Pear Tree Cl, E2 .84 DT67
Addlestone KT15
off Pear Tree Rd .152 BG106
Amersham HP7
off Orchard End Av .20 AT39
Chessington KT9 .156 CN106
Peartree Cl, Erith DA8 .107 FD81
Pear Tree Cl, Mitch. CR4 .140 DE96
Peartree Cl, S.Croy. CR2 .160 DV114
South Ockendon RM15 .91 FW68
Pear Tree Cl, Swan. BR8 .147 FD96
Peartree Ct, E18
off Churchfields .48 EH53
Pear Tree Ct, EC1 .196 E5
Peartree Gdns, Dag. RM8 .70 EV63
Romford RM7 .51 FB54
Peartree La, E1 .202 G1
Pear Tree Rd, Add. KT15 .152 BG106
Ashford TW15 .115 BQ92
Peartree Rd, Enf. EN1 .30 DS41
Pear Tree St, EC1 .196 G4
Pear Tree Wk, Wal.Cr. (Chsht.)
EN7 .14 DR26
Peartree Way, SE10 .205 M8
Peary Pl, E2 *off Kirkwall Pl* .84 DW69
Pease Cl, Horn. RM12
off Dowding Way .89 FH66
Peatfield Cl, Sid. DA15
off Woodside Rd .125 ES90
Peatmore Av, Wok. GU22 .168 BG116
Peatmore Cl, Wok. GU22 .168 BG116
Pebble Cl, Tad. KT20 .182 CS128
PEBBLE COOMBE, Tad. .182 CS128
Pebble Hill Rd, Bet. RH3 .182 CS131
Tadworth KT20 .182 CS131
Pebble La, Epsom KT18 .172 CN121
Leatherhead KT22 .182 CL125
Pebble Way, W3 .80 CP74
Pebworth Rd, Har. HA1 .61 CG61
Peckarmans Wd, SE26 .122 DU90
Peckett Sq, N5
off Highbury Gra .66 DQ63
Peckford Pl, SW9 .101 DN82
PECKHAM, SE15 .102 DU81
Peckham Gro, SE15 .102 DS80
Peckham High St, SE15 .102 DU81
Peckham Hill St, SE15 .102 DU80
Peckham Pk Rd, SE15 .102 DU80
Peckham Rd, SE5 .102 DS81
SE15 .102 DS81
⇌ **Peckham Rye** .102 DU82
Peckham Rye, SE15 .102 DU83
SE22 .102 DU84
Pecks Yd, E1 .197 P6
Peckwater St, NW5 .65 DJ64
Pedham Pl Ind Est, Swan.
BR8 .147 FG99
Pedlars Wk, N7 .83 DL65
Pedley Rd, Dag. RM8 .70 EW60
Pedley St, E1 .84 DT70
Pedro St, E5 .67 DX62
Pedworth Gdns, SE16 .202 F9
Peek Cres, SW19 .119 CX92
Peel Cl, E4 .47 EB47
N9 *off Plevna Rd* .46 DU48
Peel Dr, NW9 .63 CT55
Ilford IG5 .68 EL55
Peel Gro, E2 .84 DW68
Peel Pas, W8 *off Peel St* .82 DA74
Peel Pl, Ilf. IG5 .48 EL54
Peel Prec, NW6 .82 DA68
Peel Rd, E18 .48 EF53
NW6 .81 CZ69
Harrow (Wldste.) HA3 .61 CF55
Orpington BR6 .163 EQ106
Wembley HA9 .61 CK62
Peel St, W8 .82 DA74
Peel Way, Rom. RM3 .52 FM54
Uxbridge UB8 .76 BL71
Peerage Way, Horn. RM11 .72 FL59
Peerless Dr, Uxb. (Hare.) UB9 .58 BJ57
Peerless St, EC1 .197 K3
Pegamoid Rd, N18 .46 DW48
Pegasus Cl, N16
off Green Las .66 DR63
Pegasus Ct, Abb.L. WD5
off Furtherfield .7 BT32
Gravesend DA12 .131 GJ90
Pegasus Pl, SE11
off Clayton St .101 DN79
SW6 *off Ackmar Rd* .100 DA81
Pegasus Rd, Croy. CR0 .159 DN107
Pegasus Way, N11 .45 DH51
Pegelm Gdns, Horn. RM11 .72 FM59
Peggotty Way, Uxb. UB8
off Dickens Av .77 BP72
Pegg Rd, Houns.TW5 .96 BX80
Pegley Gdns, SE12 .124 EG89
Pegmire La, Wat. (Ald.) WD25 .24 CC39
Pegwell St, SE18 .105 ES80
Peket Cl, Stai.TW18 .133 BE95
Pekin Cl, E14
off Pekin St .85 EA72
Pekin St, E14 .85 EA72
Peldon Ct, Rich.TW9 .98 CM84
Peldon Pas, Rich.TW10
off Worple Way .98 CM84
Peldon Wk, N1
off Britannia Row .83 DP67
Pelham Av, Bark. IG11 .87 ET67
Pelham Cl, SE5 .102 DS82
Pelham Cres, SW7 .198 B9
Pelham Pl, SW7 .198 B9
W13 *off Ruislip Rd E* .79 CF70
Pelham Rd, E18 .68 EH55
N15 .66 DT56
N22 .45 DN54
SW19 .120 DA94
Beckenham BR3 .142 DW96
Bexleyheath DA7 .106 FA83
Gravesend DA11 .131 GF87
Ilford IG1 .69 ER61
Pelham Rd S, Grav. DA11 .131 GF88
Pelhams, The, Wat. WD25 .24 BX35
Pelhams Cl, Esher KT10 .154 CA105
Pelham St, SW7 .198 A8
Pelhams Wk, Esher KT10 .136 CA104
Pelham Ter, Grav. DA11
off Campbell Rd .131 GF87
Pelican Est, SE15 .102 DT81
Pelican Pas, E1
off Cambridge Heath Rd .84 DW70
Pelican Wk, SW9
off Loughborough Pk .101 DP84
Pelier St, SE17
off Langdale Cl .102 DQ79
Pelinore Rd, SE6 .124 EE89
Pellant Rd, SW6 .99 CY80
Pellatt Gro, N22 .45 DN53
Pellatt Rd, SE22 .122 DT85
Wembley HA9 .61 CK61
Pellerin Rd, N16 .66 DS64
Pelling Hill, Wind. (Old Wind.)
SL4 .112 AV87
Pelling St, E14 .85 EA72
Pellipar Cl, N13 .45 DN48
Pellipar Gdns, SE18 .105 EM78
Pelly Ct, Epp. CM16 .17 ET31
Pelly Rd, E13 .86 EG68
Pelter St, E2 .197 P2
Pelton Av, Sutt. SM2 .158 DB110
Pelton Rd, SE10 .205 H10
Pembar Av, E17 .67 DY55
Pemberley Chase, Epsom
(W.Ewell) KT19 .156 CP106
Pemberley Cl, Epsom (W.Ewell)
KT19 .156 CP106
Pember Rd, NW10 .81 CX69
Pemberton Av, Rom. RM2 .71 FH55
Pemberton Gdns, N19 .65 DJ62
Romford RM6 .70 EY57
Swanley BR8 .147 FE97
Pemberton Ho, SE26
off High Level Dr .122 DU91
Pemberton Pl, E8
off Mare St .84 DV66
Esher KT10
off Carrick Gate .136 CC104
Pemberton Rd, N4 .65 DN57
East Molesey KT8 .136 CC98
Pemberton Row, EC4 .196 E8
Pemberton Ter, N19 .65 DJ62
Pembrey Way, Horn. RM12 .90 FJ65
Pembridge Av, Twick.TW2 .116 BZ88
Pembridge Chase, Hem.H. (Bov.)
HP3 *off Pembridge Cl* .5 BA28
Pembridge Cl, Hem.H. (Bov.)
HP3 .5 AZ28
Pembridge Cres, W11 .82 DA73
Pembridge Gdns, W2 .82 DA73
Pembridge Ms, W11 .82 DA73
Pembridge Pl, SW15 .120 DA85
W2 .82 DA73
Pembridge Rd, W11 .82 DA73
Hemel Hempstead (Bov.)
HP3 .5 BA28
Pembridge Sq, W2 .82 DA73
Pembridge Vil, W2 .82 DA73
W11 .82 DA73
Pembroke Av, N1
off Bingfield St .83 DL67
Enfield EN1 .30 DV38
Harrow HA3 .61 CG55
Pinner HA5 .60 BX60
Surbiton KT5 .138 CP99
Walton-on-Thames KT12 .154 BX105
Pembroke Cl, SW1 .198 G5
Banstead SM7 .174 DB117
Erith DA8
off Pembroke Rd .107 FD77
Hornchurch RM11 .72 FM56
Pembroke Cotts, W8
off Pembroke Sq .100 DA76
Pembroke Dr, Wal.Cr. (Chsht.)
EN7 .13 DP29
Pembroke Gdns, W8 .99 CZ77
Dagenham RM10 .71 FB62
Woking GU22 .167 BA118
Pembroke Gdns Cl, W8 .100 DA76
Pembroke Ms, E3
off Morgan St .85 DY69
N10 *off Pembroke Rd* .44 DG53
W8 *off Earls Wk* .100 DA76
Sevenoaks TN13
off Pembroke Rd .191 FH125
Pembroke Pl, W8 .100 DA76
Dartford (Sutt.H.) DA4 .148 FP95
Edgware HA8 .42 CN52
Isleworth TW7
off Thornbury Rd .97 CE82
Pembroke Rd, E6 .87 EM71
E17 .67 EB57
N8 .65 DL56
N10 .44 DG53
N13 .46 DQ48
N15 .66 DT57
SE25 .142 DS98
W8 .100 DA77
Bromley BR1 .144 EJ96
Erith DA8 .107 FC78
Greenford UB6 .78 CB70
Ilford IG3 .69 ET60
Mitcham CR4 .140 DG96
Northwood HA6 .39 BQ48
Ruislip HA4 .59 BS60
Sevenoaks TN13 .191 FH125
Wembley HA9 .61 CK62
Woking GU22 .167 BA118
Pembroke Sq, W8 .100 DA76
Pembroke St, N1 .83 DL66
Pembroke Studios, W8 .99 CZ76
Pembroke Vil, W8 .100 DA77
Richmond TW9 .97 CK84
Pembroke Wk, W8 .100 DA77
Pembroke Way, Hayes UB3 .95 BQ76
Pembry Cl, SW9 .101 DN81
Pembury Av, Wor.Pk. KT4 .139 CU101
Pembury Cl, Brom. BR2 .144 EF101
Coulsdon CR5 .158 DG114
Pembury Ct, Hayes UB3 .95 BR79
Pembury Cres, Sid. DA14 .126 EY89
Pembury Pl, E5 .66 DV64
Pembury Rd, E5 .66 DV64
N17 .46 DT54
SE25 .142 DU98
Bexleyheath DA7 .106 EY80
Pemdevon Rd, Croy. CR0 .141 DN101
Pemell Cl, E1 *off Colebert Av* .84 DW70
Pemerich Cl, Hayes UB3 .95 BT78
Pempath Pl, Wem. HA9 .61 CK61
Penally Pl, N1
off Shepperton Rd .84 DR67
Penang St, E1 .202 E2
Penard Rd, Sthl. UB2 .96 CA76
Penarth St, SE15 .102 DW79
Penates, Esher KT10 .155 CD105
Penberth Rd, SE6 .123 EC89
Penbury Rd, Sthl. UB2 .96 BZ77
Pencombe Ms, W11
off Denbigh Rd .81 CZ73
Pencraig Way, SE15 .102 DV79
Pencroft Dr, Dart. DA1
off Shepherds La .128 FJ87
Pendall Cl, Barn. EN4 .28 DE42
Penda Rd, Erith DA8 .107 FB80
Pendarves Rd, SW20 .139 CW95
Penda's Mead, E9
off Lindisfarne Way .67 DY63
Pendell Av, Hayes UB3 .95 BT80
Pendell Ct, Red. (Bletch.)
RH1 .185 DP131
Pendell Rd, Red. (Bletch.)
RH1 .185 DP131
Pendennis Cl, W.Byf. KT14 .152 BG114
Pendennis Rd, N17 .66 DR55
SW16 .121 DL91
Orpington BR6 .146 EW103
Sevenoaks TN13 .191 FH123
Penderel Rd, Houns.TW3 .116 CA85
Penderry Ri, SE6 .123 ED89
Penderyn Way, N7 .65 DK63
Pendle Rd, SW16 .121 DH93
Pendlestone Rd, E17 .67 EA57
Pendragon Ho, N9
off Salisbury Rd .46 DU48
Pendragon Rd, Brom. BR1 .124 EF90
Pendragon Wk, NW9 .62 CS58
Pendrell Rd, SE4 .103 DY82
Pendrell St, SE18 .105 ER80
Pendula Dr, Hayes UB4 .78 BX70
Pendulum Ms, E8
off Birkbeck Rd .66 DT64
Penerley Rd, SE6 .123 EB88
Rainham RM13 .89 FH71
Penfold Cl, Croy. CR0
off Epsom Rd .141 DN104
Penfold La, Bex. DA5 .126 EX89
Penfold Pl, NW1 .194 B6
Penfold Rd, N9 .47 DX46
Penfold St, NW1 .194 A5
NW8 .194 A5
Penford Gdns, SE9 .104 EK83
Penford St, SE5 .101 DP82
Pengarth Rd, Bex. DA5 .126 EX85
PENGE, SE20 .122 DW94
⇌ **Penge East** .122 DW93
Penge Ho, SW11 *off Wye St* .100 DD83
Penge La, SE20 .122 DW94
Pengelly Cl, Wal.Cr. (Chsht.)
EN7 .14 DV30
Penge Rd, E13 .86 EJ66
SE20 .142 DU97
SE25 .142 DU97
⇌ **Penge West** .122 DV93
Penhale Cl, Orp. BR6 .164 EU105
Penhall Rd, SE7 .104 EK77
Penhill Rd, Bex. DA5 .126 EW87
Penhurst, Wok. GU21 .151 AZ114
Penhurst Rd, Ilf. IG6 .49 EP52
Penifather La, Grnf. UB6 .79 CD69
Peninsular Cl, Felt.TW14 .115 BR86
Peninsular Pk Rd, SE7 .205 N9
Penistone Rd, SW16 .121 DL94
Penistone Wk, Rom. RM3
off Okehampton Rd .52 FJ51
Penketh Dr, Har. HA1 .61 CD62
Penman Cl, St.Alb. AL2 .8 CA27
Penman's Grn, Kings L. WD4 .5 BF32
Penmon Rd, SE2 .106 EU76
Pennack Rd, SE15 .102 DT79
Pennant Ms, W8 .100 DB77
Pennant Ter, E17 .47 DZ54
Pennard Rd, W12 .99 CW75
Pennards, The, Sun.TW16 .136 BW96
Penn Cl, Grnf. UB6 .78 CB68
Harrow HA3 .61 CJ56
Rickmansworth (Chorl.)
WD3 .21 BD44
Uxbridge UB8 .76 BK70
Penn Dr, Uxb. (Denh.) UB9 .57 BF58
Penne Cl, Rad. WD7 .9 CF34
Penner Cl, SW19
off Victoria Dr .119 CY89
Penners Gdns, Surb. KT6 .138 CL101
Pennethorne Cl, E9
off Victoria Pk Rd .84 DW67
Pennethorne Rd, SE15 .102 DV80
Penney Cl, Dart. DA1 .128 FK87
Penn Gdns, Chis. BR7 .145 EP96
Romford RM5 .50 FA52
Penn Gaskell La, Ger.Cr.
(Chal.St.P.) SL9 .37 AZ50
Pennine Dr, NW2 .63 CY61
Pennine Ho, N9
off Plevna Rd .46 DU48
Pennine La, NW2
off Pennine Dr .63 CY61
Pennine Way, Bexh. DA7 .107 FE81
Gravesend (Nthflt.) DA11 .130 GE90
Hayes UB3 .95 BR80
Pennington Cl, SE27
off Hamilton Rd .122 DR91
Romford RM5 .50 FA50
Pennington Dr, N21 .29 DL43
Weybridge KT13 .135 BS104
Pennington Rd, Ger.Cr. (Chal.St.P.)
SL9 .36 AX52
Penningtons, The, Amer. HP6 .20 AS37
Pennington St, E1 .202 C1
Pennington Way, SE12 .124 EH89
Pennis La, Long. (Fawk.Grn.)
DA3 .149 FX100
Penniston Cl, N17 .46 DQ54
Penn La, Bex. DA5 .126 EX85
Penn Meadow, Slou. (Stoke P.)
SL2 .74 AT67
Penn Pl, Rick. WD3
off Northway .38 BK45
Penn Rd, N7 .65 DL64
Gerrards Cross (Chal.St.P.)
SL9 .36 AX53
Rickmansworth (Mill End)
WD3 .37 BF46
St. Albans (Park St.) AL2 .8 CC27
Slough (Datchet) SL3 .92 AX81
Watford WD24 .23 BV39
Penn St, N1 .84 DR67

Pen - Pie

Penn Way, Rick. (Chorl.) WD3 .21 BD44
Penny Cl, Rain. RM13 .89 FH69
Pennycroft, Croy. CR0 .161 DY109
Pennyfather La, Enf. EN2 .30 DQ40
Pennyfield, Cob. KT11 .153 BU113
Pennyfields, E14 .85 EA73
Brentwood CM14 .54 FW49
Penny La, Shep. TW17 .135 BS101
Pennylets Grn, Slou. (Stoke P.)
SL2 .74 AT66
Penny Ms, SW12
off Caistor Rd .121 DH87
Pennymoor Wk, W9
off Ashmore Rd .81 CZ69
Penny Rd, NW10 .80 CP69
Pennyroyal Av, E6 .87 EN72
Penpoll Rd, E8 .84 DV65
Penpool La, Well. DA16 .106 EV83
Penrhyn Av, E17 .47 DZ53
Penrhyn Cres, E17 .47 EA53
SW14 .98 CQ84
Penrhyn Gdns, Kings.T. KT1
off Surbiton Rd .137 CK98
Penrhyn Gro, E17 .47 EA53
Penrhyn Rd, Kings.T. KT1 .138 CL97
Penrith Cl, SW15 .119 CY85
Beckenham BR3
off Albemarle Rd .143 EB95
Reigate RH2 .184 DE133
Uxbridge UB8
off Chippendale Waye .76 BK66
Penrith Cres, Rain. RM13 .71 FG64
Penrith Pl, SE27
off Harpenden Rd .121 DP89
Penrith Rd, N15 .66 DR57
Ilford IG6 .49 ET51
New Malden KT3 .138 CR98
Romford RM3 .52 FN51
Thornton Heath CR7 .142 DQ96
Penrith St, SW16 .121 DJ93
Penrose Av, Wat. WD19 .40 BX47
Penrose Dr, Epsom KT19
off Churchill Rd .156 CN111
Penrose Gro, SE17 .102 DQ78
Penrose Ho, SE17 .102 DQ78
Penrose Rd, Lthd. (Fetch.)
KT22 .170 CC122
Penrose St, SE17 .102 DQ78
Penryn St, NW1 .83 DK68
Penry St, SE1 .201 N9
Pensbury Pl, SW8 .101 DJ82
Pensbury St, SW8 .101 DJ82
Penscroft Gdns, Borwd. WD6 .26 CR42
Pensford Av, Rich. TW9 .98 CN82
Penshurst Av, Sid. DA15 .126 EU86
Penshurst Cl, Ger.Cr. (Chal.St.P.)
SL9 .36 AX54
Penshurst Gdns, Edg. HA8 .42 CP50
Penshurst Grn, Brom. BR2 .144 EF99
Penshurst Rd, E9 .85 DX66
N17 .46 DT52
Bexleyheath DA7 .106 EZ81
Potters Bar EN6 .12 DD31
Thornton Heath CR7 .141 DP99
Penshurst Wk, Brom. BR2
off Hayesford Pk Dr .144 EF99
Penshurst Way, Orp. BR5
off Star La .146 EW98
Sutton SM2 .158 DA108
Pensilver Cl, Barn. EN4 .28 DE42
Pensons La, Ong. CM5 .19 FG28
Penstemon Cl, N3 .44 DA52
Penstock Footpath, N22 .65 DL55
Pentavia Retail Pk, NW7
off Bunns La .43 CT52
Pentelow Gdns, Felt. TW14 .115 BU86
Pentire Cl, Upmin. RM14 .73 FS58
Pentire Rd, E17 .47 ED53
Pentland Av, Edg. HA8 .42 CP47
Shepperton TW17 .134 BN99
Pentland Cl, NW11 .63 CY61
Pentland Gdns, SW18
off St. Ann's Hill .120 DC86
Pentland Pl, Nthlt. UB5 .78 BY67
Pentland Rd, Bushey WD23 .24 CC44
Pentlands Cl, Mitch. CR4 .141 DH97
Pentland St, SW18 .120 DC86
Pentland Way, Uxb. UB10 .59 BQ62
Pentlow St, SW15 .99 CW83
Pentlow Way, Buck.H. IG9 .48 EL45
Pentney Rd, E4 .47 ED46
SW12 .121 DJ88
SW19 off Midmoor Rd .139 CY95
Penton Av, Stai. TW18 .113 BF94
Penton Dr, Wal.Cr. (Chsht.)
EN8 .15 DX29
Penton Gro, N1 .196 D1
Penton Hall Dr, Stai. TW18 .134 BG95
Penton Hook Rd, Stai. TW18 .114 BG94
Penton Ho, SE2
off Hartslock Dr .106 EX75
Penton Pk, Cher. KT16 .134 BG97
Penton Pl, SE17 .200 G10
Penton Ri, WC1 .196 C2
Penton Rd, Stai. TW18 .113 BF94
Penton St, N1 .83 DN68
PENTONVILLE, N1 .196 D1
Pentonville Rd, N1 .196 B1
Pentrich Av, Enf. EN1 .30 DU38
Pentridge St, SE15 .102 DT80
Pentyre Av, N18 .46 DR50
Penwerris Av, Islw. TW7 .96 CC80
Penwith Rd, SW18 .120 DB89
Penwith Wk, Wok. GU22
off Wych Hill Pk .166 AX119
Penwood End, Wok. GU22 .166 AV121
Penwood Ho, SW15
off Tunworth Cres .119 CT86
Penwortham Rd, SW16 .121 DH93
South Croydon CR2 .160 DQ110
Penylan Pl, Edg. HA8 .42 CN52
Penywern Rd, SW5 .100 DA78
Penzance Cl, Uxb. (Hare.)
UB9 .38 BK53
Penzance Gdns, Rom. RM3 .52 FN51
Penzance Pl, W11 .81 CY74
Penzance Rd, Rom. RM3 .52 FN51
Penzance St, W11 .81 CY74
Peony Cl, Brwd. CM15 .54 FV44
Peony Ct, Wdf.Grn. IG8
off The Bridle Path .48 EE52
Peony Gdns, W12 .81 CU73
Pepler Ms, SE5
off Cobourg Rd .102 DT79
Peplins Cl, Hat. AL9 .11 CY26
Peplins Way, Hat. AL9 .11 CY25
Peploe Rd, NW6 .81 CX68
Peplow Cl, West Dr. UB7
off Tavistock Rd .76 BK74
Pepper All, Loug. (High Beach)
IG10 .32 EG39
Pepper Cl, E6 .87 EM71
Caterham CR3 .186 DS125
Peppercorn Cl, Th.Hth. CR7 .142 DR96
Pepper Hill, Grav. (Nthflt.)
DA11 .130 GC90
Pepperhill La, Grav. (Nthflt.)
DA11 .130 GC90
Peppermead Sq, SE13 .123 EA85
Peppermint Cl, Croy. CR0 .141 DL101
Peppermint Pl, E11
off Birch Gro .68 EE62
Pepper St, E14 .204 B6
SE1 .201 H4
Peppie Cl, N16
off Bouverie Rd .66 DS61
Pepys Cl, Ashtd. KT21 .172 CN117
Dartford DA1 .108 FN84
Gravesend (Nthflt.) DA11 .130 GD90
Slough SL3 .93 BB79
Tilbury RM18 .111 GJ81
Uxbridge UB10 .59 BP63
Pepys Cres, E16 .205 N2
Barnet EN5 .27 CW43
Pepys Ri, Orp. BR6 .145 ET102
Pepys Rd, SE14 .103 DX81
SW20 .139 CW95
Pepys St, EC3 .197 N10
Perceval Av, NW3 .64 DE64
Percheron Cl, Islw. TW7 .97 CG83
Percheron Rd, Borwd. WD6 .26 CR44
Perch St, E8 .66 DT63
Percival Cl, Lthd. KT22 .154 CB111
Percival Ct, N17 off High Rd .46 DT52
Northolt UB5 .60 CA64
★ Percival David Foundation
of Chinese Art, WC1
off Gordon Square .195 N4
Percival Gdns, Rom. RM6 .70 EW58
Percival Rd, SW14 .98 CQ84
Enfield EN1 .30 DT42
Feltham TW13 .115 BT89
Hornchurch RM11 .72 FJ58
Orpington BR6 .145 EP103
Percival St, EC1 .196 F4
Percival Way, Epsom KT19 .156 CQ105
Percy Av, Ashf. TW15 .114 BN92
Percy Bryant Rd, Sun. TW16 .115 BS94
Percy Bush Rd, West Dr. UB7 .94 BM76
Percy Circ, WC1 .196 C2
Percy Gdns, Enf. EN3 .31 DX43
Hayes UB4 .77 BS69
Isleworth TW7 .97 CG82
Worcester Park KT4 .138 CR102
Percy Ms, W1 .195 M7
Percy Pas, W1 .195 L7
Percy Pl, Slou. (Datchet) SL3 .92 AV81
Percy Rd, E11 .68 EE59
E16 .86 EE71
N12 .44 DC50
N21 .46 DQ45
SE20 .143 DX95
SE25 .142 DU99
W12 .99 CU75
Bexleyheath DA7 .106 EY82
Hampton TW12 .116 CA94
Ilford IG3 .70 EU59
Isleworth TW7 .97 CG84
Mitcham CR4 .140 DG101
Romford RM7 .71 FB55
Twickenham TW2 .116 CB88
Watford WD18 .23 BV42
Percy St, W1 .195 M7
Grays RM17 .110 GC79
Percy Way, Twick. TW2 .116 CC88
Percy Yd, WC1 .196 C2
Peregrine Cl, NW10 .62 CR64
Watford WD25 .8 BY34
Peregrine Ct, SW16
off Leithcote Gdns .121 DM91
Welling DA16 .105 ET81
Peregrine Gdns, Croy. CR0 .143 DY103
Peregrine Ho, EC1 .196 G2
Peregrine Rd, Ilf. IG6 .50 EV50
Sunbury-on-Thames
TW16 .135 BT96
Waltham Abbey EN9 .16 EG34
Peregrine Wk, Horn. RM12
off Heron Flight Av .89 FH65
Peregrine Way, SW19 .119 CW94
Perham Rd, W14 .99 CY78
Perham Way, St.Alb. (Lon.Col.)
AL2 .9 CK26
Peridot St, E6 .86 EL71
Perifield, SE21 .122 DQ88
Perimeade Rd, Grnf. UB6 .79 CJ68
Periton Rd, SE9 .104 EK84
PERIVALE, Grnf. .79 CJ67
⊖ Perivale .79 CG68
Perivale Gdns, W13
off Bellevue Rd .79 CH70
Watford WD25 .7 BV34
Perivale Gra, Grnf. UB6 .79 CG69
Perivale Ind Pk, Grnf. UB6 .79 CH68
Perivale La, Grnf. UB6 .79 CG69
Perivale New Business Cen, Grnf.
UB6 .79 CH68
Perkin Cl, Wem. HA0 .61 CH64
Perkins Cl, Green. DA9 .129 FT85
Perkins Ct, Ashf. TW15 .114 BM92
Perkin's Rents, SW1 .199 M6
Perkins Rd, Ilf. IG2 .69 ER57
Perkins Sq, SE1 .201 J2
Perks Cl, SE3 off Hurren Cl .104 EE83
Perleybrooke La, Wok. GU21
off Bampton Way .166 AU117
Permain Cl, Rad. (Shenley)
WD7 .9 CK33
Perpins Rd, SE9 .125 ES86
Perram Cl, Brox. EN10 .15 DY26
Perran Rd, SW2
off Christchurch Rd .121 DP89
Perran Wk, Brent. TW8 .98 CL78
Perren St, NW5
off Ryland Rd .83 DH65
Perrers Rd, W6 .99 CV77
Perrin Cl, Ashf. TW15
off Fordbridge Rd .114 BM92
Perrin Ct, Wok. GU21
off Blackmore Cres .167 BB115
Perrin Rd, Wem. HA0 .61 CG63
Perrins Ct, NW3
off Hampstead High St .64 DC63
Perrins La, NW3 .64 DC63
Perrin's Wk, NW3 .64 DC63
Perriors Cl, Wal.Cr. (Chsht.)
EN7 .14 DU27
Perrott St, SE18 .105 EQ77
Perry Av, W3 .80 CR72
Perry Cl, Rain. RM13
off Lowen Rd .89 FD68
Uxbridge UB8
off Harlington Rd .77 BQ72
Perry Ct, E14
off Napier Av .103 EA78
N15 off Albert Rd .66 DS58
Perryfield Way, NW9 .63 CT58
Richmond TW10 .117 CH89
Perry Gdns, N9
off Deansway .46 DS48
Perry Garth, Nthlt. UB5 .78 BW67
Perry Gro, Dart. DA1 .108 FN84
Perry Hall Cl, Orp. BR6 .146 EU101
Perry Hall Rd, Orp. BR6 .145 ET100
Perry Hill, SE6 .123 DZ90
Perry Ho, SW2
off Tierney Rd .121 DL87
Rainham RM13
off Lowen Rd .89 FD68
Perry How, Wor.Pk. KT4 .139 CT102
Perryman Ho, Bark. IG11 .87 EQ67
Perrymans Fm Rd, Ilf. IG2 .69 ER58
Perry Mead, Bushey WD23 .40 CB45
Enfield EN2 .29 DP40
Perrymead St, SW6 .100 DA81
Perryn Rd, SE16 .202 D6
W3 .80 CR73
Perry Oaks Dr, Houns. (Hthrw.Air.)
TW6 .94 BH82
Perry Ri, SE23 .123 DY90
Perry Rd, Dag. RM9 .88 EZ70
Perrysfield Rd, Wal.Cr. (Chsht.)
EN8 .15 DY27
Perrys La, Sev. (Knock.) TN14 .164 EV113
Perrys Pl, W1 .195 M8
PERRY STREET, Grav. .130 GE88
Perry St, Chis. BR7 .125 ER93
Dartford DA1 .107 FE84
Gravesend (Nthflt.) DA11 .130 GE88
Perry St Gdns, Chis. BR7
off Old Perry St .125 ES93
Perry Vale, SE23 .122 DW89
Perry Way, S.Ock. (Aveley)
RM15 .90 FQ73
Persant Rd, SE6 .124 EE89
Perseverance Cotts, Wok. (Ripley)
GU23 .168 BJ121
Perseverance Pl, SW9 .101 DN80
Richmond TW9
off Shaftesbury Rd .98 CL83
Persfield Cl, Epsom KT17 .157 CU110
Pershore Cl, Ilf. IG2 .69 EP57
Pershore Gro, Cars. SM5 .140 DD100
Pert Cl, N10 .45 DH52
Perth Av, NW9 .62 CR59
Hayes UB4 .78 BW70
Perth Cl, SW20
off Huntley Way .139 CU96
Perth Rd, E10 .67 DY60
E13 .86 EH68
N4 .65 DN60
N22 .45 DP53
Barking IG11 .87 ER68
Beckenham BR3 .143 EC96
Ilford IG2 .69 EN58
Perth Ter, Ilf. IG2 .69 EQ59
Perwell Av, Har. HA2 .60 BZ60
Perwell Ct, Har. HA2 .60 BZ60
Peter Av, NW10 .81 CV66
Oxted RH8 .187 ED129
Peterboat Cl, SE10 .205 J8
Peterborough Av, Upmin.
RM14 .73 FS60
Peterborough Gdns, Ilf. IG1 .68 EL59
Peterborough Ms, SW6 .100 DA82
Peterborough Rd, E10 .67 EC57
SW6 .100 DA82
Carshalton SM5 .140 DE100
Harrow HA1 .61 CE60
Peterborough Vil, SW6 .100 DB81
Peterchurch Ho, SE15
off Commercial Way .102 DV79
Petergate, SW11 .100 DC84
Peterhead Ms, Slou. SL3
off Grampian Way .93 BA78
Peterhill Cl, Ger.Cr. (Chal.St.P.)
SL9 .36 AY50
Peterhouse Gdns, SW6
off Bagley's La .100 DB81
Peter James Business Cen,
Hayes UB3 .95 BU75
Peterley Business Cen, E2
off Hackney Rd .84 DV68
★ Peter Pan Statue, W2 .82 DD74
Peters Av, St.Alb. (Lon.Col.)
AL2 .9 CJ26
Peters Cl, Dag. RM8 .70 EX60
Stanmore HA7 .41 CK51
Peters Cl, Well. DA16 .105 ES82
Petersfield Av, Rom. RM3 .52 FL51
Slough SL2 .74 AU74
Staines TW18 .114 BJ92
Petersfield Cl, N18 .46 DQ50
Romford RM3 .52 FN51
Petersfield Cres, Couls. CR5 .175 DL115
Petersfield Ri, SW15 .119 CV88
Petersfield Rd, W3 .98 CQ75
Staines TW18 .114 BJ92
PETERSHAM, Rich. .118 CL88
Petersham Av, W.Byf. (Byfleet)
KT14 .152 BL112
Petersham Cl, Rich. TW10 .117 CK89
Sutton SM1 .158 DA106
West Byfleet (Byfleet)
KT14 .152 BL112
Petersham Dr, Orp. BR5 .145 ET96
Petersham Gdns, Orp. BR5 .145 ET96
Petersham La, SW7 .100 DC76
Petersham Ms, SW7 .100 DC76
Petersham Pl, SW7 .100 DC76
Petersham Rd, Rich. TW10 .118 CL86
Petersham Ter, Croy. CR0
off Richmond Grn .141 DL104
Peters Hill, EC4 .197 H10
Peter's La, EC1 .196 G6
Peterslea, Kings L. WD4 .7 BP29
Petersmead Cl, Tad. KT20 .173 CW123
Peters Path, SE26 .122 DV91
Peterstone Rd, SE2 .106 EV76
Peterstow Cl, SW19 .119 CY89
Peter St, W1 .195 L10
Gravesend DA12 .131 GH87
Peterwood Way, Croy. CR0 .141 DM103
Petherton Rd, N5 .66 DQ64
Petley Rd, W6 .99 CW79
Peto Pl, NW1 .195 J4
Peto St N, E16
off Victoria Dock Rd .86 EF73
Petrie Cl, NW2 .81 CY65
★ Petrie Mus of Egyptian
Archaeology, WC1
off Malet Pl .195 M5
Pett Cl, Horn. RM11 .71 FH61
Petten Cl, Orp. BR5 .146 EX102
Petten Gro, Orp. BR5 .146 EW102
Petters Rd, Ashtd. KT21 .172 CM116
Petticoat La, E1 .197 N7
★ Petticoat La (Mkt), E1 .197 N7
Petticoat Sq, E1 .197 P8
Pettits Boul, Rom. RM1 .51 FE53
Pettits Cl, Rom. RM1 .51 FE54
Pettits La, Rom. RM1 .51 FE54
Pettits La N, Rom. RM1 .51 FD53
Pettits Pl, Dag. RM10 .70 FA64
Pettits Rd, Dag. RM10 .70 FA64
Pettiward Cl, SW15 .99 CW84
Pettley Gdns, Rom. RM7 .71 FD57
Pettman Cres, SE28 .105 ER76
Pettsgrove Av, Wem. HA0 .61 CJ64
Petts Hill, Nthlt. UB5 .60 CB64
Petts La, Shep. TW17 .134 BN98
Pett St, SE18 .104 EL77
PETTS WOOD, Orp. .145 ER99
⇌ Petts Wood .145 EQ99
Petts Wd Rd, Orp. BR5 .145 EQ99
Petty France, SW1 .199 L6
Pettys Cl, Wal.Cr. (Chsht.)
EN8 .15 DX28
Petworth Cl, Couls. CR5 .175 DJ119
Northolt UB5 .78 BZ66
Petworth Gdns, SW20
off Hidcote Gdns .139 CV97
Uxbridge UB10 .77 BQ67
Petworth Rd, N12 .44 DE50
Bexleyheath DA6 .126 FA85
Petworth St, SW11 .100 DE81
Petworth Way, Horn. RM12 .71 FF63
Petyt Pl, SW3 off Old Ch St .100 DE79
Petyward, SW3 .198 C9
Pevensey Av, N11 .45 DK50
Enfield EN1 .30 DR40
Pevensey Cl, Islw. TW7 .96 CC80
Pevensey Rd, E7 .68 EF63
SW17 .120 DD91
Feltham TW13 .116 BY88
Peverel, E6 off Downings .87 EN72
Peverel Ho, Dag. RM10 .70 FA61
Peveret Cl, N11
off Woodland Rd .45 DH50
Peveril Dr, Tedd. TW11 .117 CD92
Pewsey Cl, E4 .47 EA50
Peyton Pl, SE10 .103 EC80
Peyton's Cotts, Red. RH1 .185 DM132
Pharaoh Cl, Mitch. CR4 .140 DF101
Pharaoh's Island, Shep.
TW17 .134 BM103
Pheasant Cl, E16
off Maplin Rd .86 EG72
Purley CR8
off Partridge Knoll .159 DP113
Pheasant Hill, Ch.St.G. HP8 .36 AW47
Pheasants Way, Rick. WD3 .38 BH45
Pheasant Wk, Ger.Cr. (Chal.St.P.)
SL9 .36 AX49
Phelp St, SE17 .102 DR79
Phelps Way, Hayes UB3 .95 BT77
Phene St, SW3 .100 DE79
Philan Way, Rom. RM5 .51 FD51
Philbeach Gdns, SW5 .100 DA78
Phil Brown Pl, SW8
off Heath Rd .101 DH82
Philchurch Pl, E1
off Ellen St .84 DU72
Philimore Cl, SE18 .105 ES78
Philip Av, Rom. RM7 .71 FD60
Swanley BR8 .147 FD98
Philip Cl, Brwd. CM15 .54 FV44
Romford RM7
off Philip Av .71 FD60
Philip Gdns, Croy. CR0 .143 DZ103
Philip La, N15 .66 DR56
Philipot Path, SE9 .125 EM86
Philippa Gdns, SE9 .124 EK85
Philippa Way, Grays RM16 .111 GH77
Philip Rd, Rain. RM13 .89 FE69
Philip Rd, Stai. TW18 .114 BK93
Philips Cl, Cars. SM5 .140 DG102
Philip St, E13 .86 EG70
Philip Sydney Rd, Grays
RM16 .109 FX78
Philip Wk, SE15 .102 DU83
Phillida Rd, Rom. RM3 .52 FN54
Phillimore Gdns, NW10 .81 CW67
W8 .100 DA75
Phillimore Gdns Cl, W8
off Phillimore Gdns .100 DA76
Phillimore Pl, W8 .100 DA75
Radlett WD7 .25 CE36
Phillimore Wk, W8 .100 DA76
Phillipers, Wat. WD25 .24 BY35
Phillipp St, N1 .84 DS67
Phillips Cl, Dart. DA1 .127 FH86
Philpot La, EC3 .197 M10
Woking (Chobham) GU24 .150 AV113
Philpot Path, Ilf. IG1
off Sunnyside Rd .69 EQ62
Philpots Cl, West Dr. UB7 .76 BK73
Philpot Sq, SW6
off Peterborough Rd .100 DB83
Philpot St, E1 .84 DV72
Phineas Pett Rd, SE9 .104 EL83
Phipps Bridge .140 DC97
Phipps Br Rd, SW19 .140 DC96
Mitcham CR4 .140 DC96
Phipps Hatch La, Enf. EN2 .30 DQ38
Phipp's Ms, SW1 .199 H7
Phipp St, EC2 .197 M4
Phoebeth Rd, SE4 .123 EA85
Phoenix Cl, E8 off Stean St .84 DT67
E17 .47 DZ54
Epsom KT19 off Queen
Alexandra's Way .156 CN112
Northwood HA6 .39 BT49
West Wickham BR4 .144 EE103
Phoenix Dr, Kes. BR2 .144 EK104
Phoenix Pk, Brent. TW8 .97 CK78
Phoenix Pl, WC1 .196 C4
Dartford DA1 .128 FK87
Phoenix Rd, NW1 .195 M2
SE20 .122 DW93
Phoenix St, WC2 .195 N9
Phoenix Way, Houns. TW5 .96 BW79
Phoenix Wf, SE10 .205 K4
Phoenix Wf Rd, SE1 .202 A5
Phoenix Yd, WC1
off King's Cross Rd .83 DM69
★ Photographers' Gall, WC2
off Great Newport St .195 N10
Phygtle, The, Ger.Cr. (Chal.St.P.)
SL9 .36 AY51
Phyllis Av, N.Mal. KT3 .139 CV99
★ Physical Energy Statue,
W2 .82 DC74
Physic Pl, SW3
off Royal Hosp Rd .100 DF79
Piazza, The, WC2
off Covent Gdn .83 DL73
Picardy Manorway, Belv.
DA17 .107 FB76
Picardy Rd, Belv. DA17 .106 FA77
Picardy St, Belv. DA17 .106 FA76
Piccadilly, W1 .199 J3
Piccadilly Arc, SW1 .199 K2
⊖ Piccadilly Circus .199 L1
Piccadilly Circ, W1 .199 M1
Piccadilly Pl, W1 .199 L1
Pickard St, EC1 .196 G2
Pickering Av, E6 .87 EN68
Pickering Cl, E9
off Cassland Rd .85 DX66
Pickering Gdns, N11 .44 DG51
Croydon CR0 .142 DT100
Pickering Ms, W2
off Bishops Br Rd .82 DB72
Pickering Pl, SW1 .199 L3
Pickering St, N1 off Essex Rd .83 DP67
Pickets Cl, Bushey (Bushey Hth.)
WD23 .41 CD46
Pickets St, SW12 .121 DH87
Pickett Cft, Stan. HA7 .41 CK53
Picketts Lock La, N9 .46 DW47
Pickford Cl, Bexh. DA7 .106 EY82
Pickford Dr, Slou. SL3 .75 AZ74
Pickford Gdn, Slou. SL1
off Stoke Poges La .74 AS74
Pickford La, Bexh. DA7 .106 EY82
Pickford Rd, Bexh. DA7 .106 EY83
Pickfords Wf, N1 .197 H1
Pick Hill, Wal.Abb. EN9 .16 EF32
Pickhurst Grn, Brom. BR2 .144 EF101
Pickhurst La, Brom. BR2 .144 EF102
West Wickham BR4 .144 EE100
Pickhurst Mead, Brom. BR2 .144 EF101
Pickhurst Pk, Brom. BR2 .144 EE99
Pickhurst Ri, W.Wick. BR4 .143 EC101
Pickins Piece, Slou. (Horton)
SL3 .93 BA82
Pickle Herring St, SE1
off Tooley St .84 DS74
Pickmoss La, Sev. (Otford)
TN14 .181 FH116
Pickwick Cl, Houns. TW4
off Dorney Way .116 BY85
Pickwick Ct, SE9
off West Pk .124 EL88
Pickwick Gdns, Grav. (Nthflt.)
DA11 .130 GD90
Pickwick Ms, N18 .46 DS50
Pickwick Pl, Har. HA1 .61 CE59
Pickwick Rd, SE21 .122 DR87
Pickwick St, SE1 .201 H5
Pickwick Ter, Slou. SL2
off Maple Cres .74 AV73
Pickwick Way, Chis. BR7 .125 EQ93
Pickworth Cl, SW8
off Kenchester Cl .101 DL80
Picquets Way, Bans. SM7 .173 CY116
Picton Pl, W1 .194 G9
Surbiton KT6 .138 CN102
Picton St, SE5 .102 DR80
Piedmont Rd, SE18 .105 ER78
Pield Heath Av, Uxb. UB8 .76 BN70

★ Place of interest ⇌ Railway station ⊖ London Underground station DLR Docklands Light Railway station Tramlink station H Hospital

Pield Heath Rd, Uxb. UB8 ....76 BM71
Piercing Hill, Epp. (They.B.)
CM16 ....33 ER35
Pier Head, E1 ....202 D3
Piermont Grn, SE22 ....122 DV85
Piermont Pl, Brom. BR1 ....144 EL96
Piermont Rd, SE22 ....122 DV85
Pier Par, E16 off Pier Rd 105 EN75
Pierrepoint Arc, N1
off Islington High St 83 DP68
Pierrepoint Rd, W3 ....80 CP73
Pierrepoint Row, N1
off Islington High St 83 DP68
Pier Rd, E16 ....105 EM75
Erith DA8 ....107 FE79
Feltham TW14 ....115 BV85
Gravesend (Nthflt.) DA11 ..131 GF86
Greenhithe DA9 ....109 FV84
Pier St, E14 ....204 E8
Pier Ter, SW18
off Jew's Row 100 DC84
Pier Wk, Grays RM17 ....110 GA80
Pier Way, SE28 ....105 ER76
Pigeonhouse La, Couls. CR5 .184 DC125
Pigeon La, Hmptn. TW12 ....116 CA91
Piggs Cor, Grays RM17 ....110 GC76
Piggy La, Rick. (Chorl.) WD3 ..21 BB44
Pigott St, E14 ....85 EA72
Pike Cl, Brom. BR1 ....124 EH92
Uxbridge UB10 ....76 BM67
Pike La, Upmin. RM14 ....73 FT64
Pike Rd, NW7
off Ellesmere Av 42 CR49
Pikes End, Pnr. HA5 ....59 BV56
Pikes Hill, Epsom KT17 ....156 CS113
Pikestone Cl, Hayes UB4
off Berrydale Rd 78 BY70
Pike Way, Epp. (N.Wld.Bas.)
CM16 ....18 FA27
Pilgrimage St, SE1 ....201 K5
Pilgrim Cl, Mord. SM4 ....140 DB101
St. Albans (Park St.) AL2 ....8 CC27
Pilgrim Hill, SE27 ....122 DQ91
Orpington BR5 ....146 EY96
Pilgrims Cl, N13 ....45 DM49
Brentwood CM15 ....54 FT43
Northolt UB5 ....60 CC64
Watford WD25 off Kytes Dr ..8 BX33
Pilgrims Ct, SE3 ....104 EG81
Dartford DA1 ....128 FN85
PILGRIM'S HATCH, Brwd. 54 FU42
Pilgrim's La, NW3 ....64 DD63
Pilgrims La, Cat. CR3 ....185 DM125
Grays (N.Stfd.) RM16 ....91 FW74
Oxted (Titsey) RH8 ....188 EH125
Westerham TN16 ....178 EL123
Pilgrims Ms, E14
off Blackwall Way 85 EC73
Pilgrims Pl, NW3
off Hampstead High St 64 DD63
Reigate RH2 ....184 DA132
Pilgrims Ri, Barn. EN4 ....28 DE43
Pilgrims Rd, Swans. DA10 ....110 FY84
Pilgrim St, EC4 ....196 F9
Pilgrims Vw, Green. DA9 ....129 FW86
Pilgrims Way, E6
off High St N 86 EL67
N19 ....65 DK60
Pilgrims' Way, Bet. RH3 ....183 CY131
Caterham CR3 ....185 DN126
Pilgrims Way, Dart. DA1 ....128 FN88
Pilgrims' Way, Red. RH1 ....185 DJ127
Pilgrims Way, Reig. RH2 ....184 DA131
Sevenoaks (Chev.) TN14 ..180 EV121
South Croydon CR2 ....160 DT106
Pilgrim's Way, Wem. HA9 ....62 CP60
Pilgrims Way, West. TN16 ..179 EM123
Pilgrims Way W, Sev. (Otford)
TN14 ....181 FD116
Pilkington Rd, SE15 ....102 DV82
Orpington BR6 ....145 EQ103
Pillions La, Hayes UB4 ....77 BR70
Pilot Cl, SE8 ....103 DZ79
Pilots Pl, Grav. DA12 ....131 GJ86
Pilsdon Cl, SW19
off Inner Pk Rd 119 CX88
Piltdown Rd, Wat. WD19 ....40 BX49
Pilton Est, The, Croy. (Pitlake) CR0
off Pitlake 141 DP103
Pilton Pl, SE17 ....201 J10
Pimento Ct, W5 off Olive Rd ..97 CK76
PIMLICO, SW1 ....199 K10
⊖ Pimlico 199 M10
Pimlico Rd, SW1 ....198 F10
Pimlico Wk, N1 ....197 M2
Pimpernel Way, Rom. RM3 ..52 FK51
Pinchbeck Rd, Orp. BR6 ....163 ET107
Pinchfield, Rick. (Map.Cr.)
WD3 ....37 BE50
Pinchin St, E1 ....84 DU73
Pincott Pl, SE4 ....103 DX84
Pincott Rd, SW19 ....120 DC94
Bexleyheath DA6 ....126 FA85
Pindar St, EC2 ....197 M6
PINDEN, Dart. 149 FW96
Pindock Ms, W9
off Warwick Av 82 DB70
Pineapple Ct, SW1 ....199 K6
Pineapple Rd, Amer. HP7 ....20 AT39
Pine Av, E15 ....67 EE64
Gravesend DA12 ....131 GK88
West Wickham BR4 ....143 EB102
Pine Cl, E10 off Walnut Rd 67 EB61
N14 ....45 DJ45
N19 off Hargrave Pk 65 DJ61
SE20 ....142 DW95
Addlestone (New Haw)
KT15 ....152 BH111
Kenley CR8 ....176 DR117
Stanmore HA7 ....41 CH49
Swanley BR8 ....147 FF98
Waltham Cross (Chsht.)
EN8 ....15 DX28
Woking GU21 ....166 AW117
Pine Coombe, Croy. CR0 ....161 DX105
Pine Ct, Upmin. RM14 ....72 FN63
Pine Cres, Brwd. CM13 ....55 GD43
Pine Cres, Cars. SM5 ....158 DD111
Pinecrest Gdns, Orp. BR6 ....163 EP105
Pinecroft, Brwd. CM13 ....55 GB45
Romford (Gidea Pk.) RM2 ..72 FJ56
Pinecroft Cres, Barn. EN5
off Hillside Gdns 27 CY42
Pinedene, SE15
off Meeting Ho La 102 DV81
Pinefield Cl, E14 ....85 EA73
Pine Gdns, Ruis. HA4 ....59 BV60
Surbiton KT5 ....138 CN100
Pine Glade, Orp. BR6 ....163 EM105
Pine Gro, N4 ....65 DL61
N20 ....43 CZ46
SW19 ....119 CZ92
Bushey WD23 ....24 BZ40
Hatfield AL9 ....12 DB25
St. Albans (Brick.Wd.) AL2 ...8 BZ30
Weybridge KT13 ....153 BP106
Pine Gro Ms, Wey. KT13 ....153 BQ106
Pine Hill, Epsom KT18 ....172 CR115
Pinehurst, Sev. TN14 ....191 FL121
Pinehurst Cl, Abb.L. WD5 ....7 BS32
Tadworth (Kgswd.) KT20 ..174 DA122
Pinehurst Wk, Orp. BR6 ....145 ES102
Pinelands Cl, SE3
off St. John's Pk 104 EF80
Pinel Cl, Vir.W. GU25 ....132 AY98
Pinemartin Cl, NW2 ....63 CW62
Pine Ms, NW10
off Clifford Gdns 81 CX68
Pineneedle La, Sev. TN13 ....191 FH123
Pine Pl, Bans. SM7 ....157 CX114
Hayes UB4 ....77 BT70
Pine Ridge, Cars. SM5 ....158 DG109
Pine Rd, N11 ....44 DG47
NW2 ....63 CW63
Woking GU22 ....166 AW120
Pines, The, N14 ....29 DJ43
Borehamwood WD6
off Anthony Rd 26 CM40
Coulsdon CR5 ....175 DH118
Purley CR8 ....159 DP113
Sunbury-on-Thames
TW16 ....135 BU97
Woking GU21 ....151 AZ114
Woodford Green IG8 ....48 EG48
Pines Av, Enf. EN1 ....30 DV36
Pines Cl, Nthwd. HA6 ....39 BS51
Pines Rd, Brom. BR1 ....144 EL96
Pine St, EC1 ....196 D4
Pinetree Cl, Ger.Cr. (Chal.St.P.)
SL9 ....36 AW52
Pine Tree Cl, Houns. TW5 ....95 BV81
Pine Tree Hill, Wok. GU22 ....167 BD116
Pine Trees Dr, Uxb. UB10 ....58 BL63
Pine Vw Manor, Epp. CM16 ..18 EU30
Pine Wk, Bans. SM7 ....174 DF117
Bromley BR1 ....144 EJ95
Carshalton SM5 ....158 DD110
Caterham CR3 ....176 DT122
Cobham KT11 ....154 BX114
Surbiton KT5 ....138 CN100
Pine Way, Egh. (Eng.Grn.) TW20
off Ashwood Rd 112 AV93
Pine Wd, Sun. TW16 ....135 BU95
Pinewood Av, Add. (New Haw)
KT15 ....152 BJ109
Pinner HA5 ....40 CB51
Rainham RM13 ....89 FH70
Sevenoaks TN14 ....191 FK121
Sidcup DA15 ....125 ES88
Uxbridge UB8 ....76 BM72
Pinewood Cl, Borwd. WD6 ....26 CR39
Croydon CR0 ....143 DY104
Gerrards Cross SL9
off Dukes Wd Av 56 AY59
Iver SL0 ....75 BC66
Northwood HA6 ....39 BV50
Orpington BR6 ....145 ER102
Pinner HA5 ....40 CB51
Watford WD17 ....23 BU39
Woking GU21 ....151 BA114
Pinewood Dr, Orp. BR6 ....163 ES106
Potters Bar EN6 ....11 CZ31
Staines TW18
off Cotswold Cl 114 BG92
Pinewood Grn, Iver SL0 ....75 BC66
Pinewood Gro, W5 ....79 CJ72
Addlestone (New Haw)
KT15 ....152 BH110
Pinewood Ms, Stai. (Stanw.) TW19
off Oaks Rd 114 BK86
Pinewood Pk, Add. (New Haw)
KT15 ....152 BH111
Pinewood Ride, Iver SL0 ....75 BA68
Slough SL3
off Fulmer Common Rd 75 BA65
Pinewood Rd, SE2 ....106 EX79
Bromley BR2 ....144 EG98
Feltham TW13 ....115 BV90
Iver SL0 ....75 BB65
Romford (Hav.at.Bow.)
RM4 ....51 FC49
Virginia Water GU25 ....132 AU98
Pinewood Way, Brwd. CM13 ..55 GD43
Pinfold Rd, SW16 ....121 DL91
Bushey WD23 ....24 BZ40
Pinglestone Cl, West Dr. UB7 .94 BL80
Pinkcoat Cl, Felt. TW13
off Tanglewood Way 115 BV90
Pinkerton Pl, SW16
off Riggindale Rd 121 DK91
Pinkham Way, N11 ....44 DG52
Pinks Hill, Swan. BR8 ....147 FE99
Pinkwell Av, Hayes UB3 ....95 BR77
Pinkwell La, Hayes UB3 ....95 BQ77
Pinley Gdns, Dag. RM9
off Stamford Rd 88 EV67
Pinnacle Hill, Bexh. DA7 ....107 FB84
Pinnacle Hill N, Bexh. DA7 ..107 FB83
Pinnacles, Wal.Abb. EN9 ....16 EE34
Pinn Cl, Uxb. UB8
off High Rd 76 BK72
Pinnell Rd, SE9 ....104 EK84
PINNER 60 BY56
⊖ Pinner 60 BY56
Pinner Ct, Pnr. HA5 ....60 CA56
PINNER GREEN, Pnr. 40 BW53
Pinner Grn, Pnr. HA5 ....40 BW54
Pinner Gro, Pnr. HA5 ....60 BY56
Pinner Hill, Pnr. HA5 ....40 BW53
Pinner Hill Rd, Pnr. HA5 ....40 BW54
Pinner Pk, Pnr. HA5 ....40 CA53
Pinner Pk Av, Har. HA2 ....60 CB55
Pinner Pk Gdns, Har. HA2 ....60 CC54
Pinner Rd, Har. HA1, HA2 ....60 CB57
Northwood HA6 ....39 BT53
Pinner HA5 ....60 BZ56
Watford WD19 ....24 BX44
Pinner Vw, Har. HA1, HA2 ....60 CC58
PINNERWOOD PARK, Pnr. 40 BW52
Pinnocks Av, Grav. DA11 ....131 GH88
Pinn Way, Ruis. HA4 ....59 BS59
Pinstone Way, Ger.Cr. SL9 ....57 BB61
Pintail Cl, E6 off Swan App ..86 EL71
Pintail Rd, Wdf.Grn. IG8 ....48 EH52
Pintail Way, Hayes UB4 ....78 BX71
Pinter Ho, SW9
off Grantham Rd 101 DL82
Pinto Cl, Borwd. WD6
off Percheron Rd 26 CR44
Pinto Way, SE3 ....104 EH84
Pioneer Pl, Croy. CR0 ....161 EA109
Pioneers Ind Pk, Croy. CR0 ..141 DL102
Pioneer St, SE15 ....102 DU81
Pioneer Way, W12
off Du Cane Rd 81 CV72
Swanley BR8 ....147 FE97
Watford WD18 ....23 BT44
Piper Cl, N7 ....65 DM64
Piper Rd, Kings.T. KT1 ....138 CN97
Pipers Cl, Cob. KT11 ....170 BX115
Pipers End, Vir.W. GU25 ....132 AX97
Piper's Gdns, Croy. CR0 ....143 DY101
Pipers Grn, NW9 ....62 CQ57
Pipers Grn La, Edg. HA8 ....42 CL48
Pipewell Rd, Cars. SM5 ....140 DE100
Pippin Cl, NW2 ....63 CV62
Croydon CR0 ....143 DZ102
Radlett (Shenley) WD7 ....9 CK33
Pippins, The, Slou. SL3
off Pickford Dr 75 AZ74
Watford WD25
off Garston Dr 8 BW34
Pippins Cl, West Dr. UB7 ....94 BK76
Pippins Ct, Ashf. TW15 ....115 BP93
Piquet Rd, SE20 ....142 DW96
Pirbright Cres, Croy. (New Adgtn.)
CR0 ....161 EC107
Pirbright Rd, SW18 ....119 CZ88
Pirie Cl, SE5 off Denmark Hill .102 DR83
Pirie St, E16 ....86 EH74
Pirrip Cl, Grav. DA12 ....131 GM89
Pitcairn Cl, Rom. RM7 ....70 FA56
Pitcairn Rd, Mitch. CR4 ....120 DF94
Pitcairn's Path, Har. HA2
off Eastcote Rd 60 CC62
Pitchfont La, Oxt. RH8 ....178 EF124
Pitchford St, E15 ....85 ED66
Pitfield Cres, SE28 ....88 EU74
Pitfield Est, N1 ....197 L2
Pitfield St, N1 ....197 M3
Pitfield Way, NW10 ....80 CQ65
Enfield EN3 ....30 DW39
Pitfold Cl, SE12 ....124 EG86
Pitfold Rd, SE12 ....124 EG86
Pitlake, Croy. CR0 ....141 DP103
Pitman St, SE5 ....102 DQ80
Pitmaston Ho, SE13
off Lewisham Rd 103 EC82
Pitsea Pl, E1 off Pitsea St 85 DX72
Pitsea St, E1 ....85 DX72
Pitshanger La, W5 ....79 CH70
★ Pitshanger Manor & Gall,
W5 (Ealing) 79 CJ74
Pitshanger Pk, W13 ....79 CJ69
Pitson Cl, Add. KT15 ....152 BK105
Pitt Cres, SW19 ....120 DB91
Pittman Cl, Brwd. CM13 ....55 GC50
Pittman Gdns, Ilf. IG1 ....69 EQ64
Pitt Pl, Epsom KT17 ....156 CS114
Pitt Rd, Croy. CR0 ....142 DQ99
Epsom KT17 ....156 CS114
Orpington BR6 ....163 EQ105
Thornton Heath CR7 ....142 DQ99
Pitt's Head Ms, W1 ....198 G3
Pittsmead Av, Brom. BR2 ....144 EG101
Pitt St, W8 ....100 DA75
Pittville Gdns, SE25 ....142 DU97
Pittwood, Brwd. CM15 ....55 GA46
Pitwood Grn, Tad. KT20 ....173 CW120
Pitwood Pk Ind Est, Tad. KT20
off Waterfield 173 CV120
Pixfield Ct, Brom. BR2
off Beckenham La 144 EF96
Pixley St, E14 ....85 DZ72
Pixton Way, Croy. CR0 ....161 DY109
Place Fm Av, Orp. BR6 ....145 ER102
Place Fm Rd, Red. (Bletch.)
RH1 ....186 DR130
Placehouse La, Couls. CR5 ..175 DM119
Plain, The, Epp. CM16 ....18 EV29
PLAISTOW, E13 ....86 EF69
PLAISTOW, Brom. 124 EF93
⊖ Plaistow 86 EF68
Plaistow Gro, E15 ....86 EF67
Bromley BR1 ....124 EH94
H Plaistow Hosp, E13 ....86 EJ68
Plaistow La, Brom. BR1 ....124 EH94
Plaistow Pk Rd, E13 ....86 EH68
Plaistow Rd, E13 ....86 EF67
E15 ....86 EF67
Plaitford Cl, Rick. WD3 ....38 BL47
Plane Av, Grav. (Nthflt.)
DA11 ....130 GD87
Planes, The, Cher. KT16 ....134 BJ101
Plane St, SE26 ....122 DV90
★ Planetarium, NW1 ....194 E5
Plane Tree Cres, Felt. TW13 ....115 BV90
Plane Tree Wk, N2 ....64 DD55
SE19 off Central Hill 122 DS93
Plantaganet Pl, Wal.Abb. EN9 .15 EB33
Plantagenet Cl, Wor.Pk. KT4 .156 CR105
Plantagenet Gdns, Rom.
RM6 ....70 EX59
Plantagenet Pl, Rom. RM6
off Broomfield Rd 70 EX59
Plantagenet Rd, Barn. EN5 ..28 DC42
Plantain Gdns, E11
off Hollydown Way 67 ED62
Plantain Pl, SE1 ....201 K4
Plantation, The, SE3 ....104 EG82
Plantation Cl, Green. DA9 ....129 FT86
Plantation Dr, Orp. BR5 ....146 EX102
Plantation La, Warl. CR6 ....177 DY119
Plantation Rd, Amer. HP6 ....20 AS37
Erith DA8 ....107 FG81
Swanley BR8 ....127 FG94
Plantation Way, Amer. HP6 ....20 AS37
Plantation Wf, SW11 ....100 DC83
Plasel Ct, E13 off Plashet Rd ..86 EG67
Plashet Gdns, Brwd. CM13 ....55 GA49
Plashet Gro, E6 ....86 EJ67
Plashet Rd, E13 ....86 EG67
Plassy Rd, SE6 ....123 EB87
Platford Grn, Horn. RM11 ....72 FL56
Platina St, EC2 ....197 L4
Plato Rd, SW2 ....101 DL84
Platt, The, SW15 ....99 CX83
Platts Av, Wat. WD17 ....23 BV41
Platt's Eyot, Hmptn. TW12 ....136 CA96
Platt's La, NW3 ....64 DA63
Platts Rd, Enf. EN3 ....30 DW39
Platt St, NW1 ....83 DK68
Plawsfield Rd, Beck. BR3 ....143 DX95
Plaxtol Cl, Brom. BR1 ....144 EJ95
Plaxtol Rd, Erith DA8 ....106 FA80
Plaxton Ct, E11
off Woodhouse Rd 68 EF62
Playfair St, W6
off Winslow Rd 99 CW78
Playfield Av, Rom. RM5 ....51 FC53
Playfield Cres, SE22 ....122 DT85
Playfield Rd, Edg. HA8 ....42 CQ54
Playford Rd, N4 ....65 DM61
Playgreen Way, SE6 ....123 EA91
Playground Cl, Beck. BR3
off Churchfields Rd 143 DX96
Playhouse Yd, EC4 ....196 F9
Plaza Par, NW6
off Kilburn High Rd 82 DB68
Plaza Shop Cen, The, W1 ....83 DJ72
Plaza W, Houns. TW3 ....96 CB81
Pleasance, The, SW15 ....99 CV84
Pleasance Rd, SW15 ....119 CV85
Orpington BR5 ....146 EV96
Pleasant Gro, Croy. CR0 ....143 DZ104
Pleasant Pl, N1 ....83 DP66
Rickmansworth (Map.Cr.)
WD3 ....37 BE52
Walton-on-Thames KT12 ..154 BW107
Pleasant Row, NW1 ....83 DH67
Pleasant Vw, Erith DA8 ....107 FE78
Pleasant Vw Pl, Orp. BR6
off High St 163 EP106
Pleasant Way, Wem. HA0 ....79 CJ68
Pleasure Pit Rd, Ashtd. KT21 .172 CP118
Plender St, NW1 ....83 DJ67
Pleshey Rd, N7 ....65 DK63
Plesman Way, Wall. SM6 ....159 DL109
Plevna Cres, N15 ....66 DS58
Plevna Rd, N9 ....46 DU48
Hampton TW12 ....136 CB95
Plevna Rd Shop Cen, N9
off Plevna Rd 46 DV47
Plevna St, E14 ....204 D6
Pleydell Av, SE19 ....122 DT94
W6 ....99 CT77
Pleydell Ct, EC4 ....196 E9
Pleydell Est, EC1
off Radnor St 84 DQ69
Pleydell St, EC4 ....196 E9
Plimsoll Cl, E14
off Grundy St 85 EB72
Plimsoll Rd, N4 ....65 DN62
Plough Ct, EC3 ....197 L10
Plough Fm Cl, Ruis. HA4 ....59 BR58
Plough Hill, Pot.B. (Cuffley)
EN6 ....13 DL28
Plough Ind Est, Lthd. KT22 ..171 CH119
Plough La, SE22 ....122 DT86
SW17 ....120 DB92
SW19 ....120 DB92
Cobham (Down.) KT11 ....169 BU116
Purley CR8 ....159 DL109
Rickmansworth (Sarratt)
WD3 ....5 BF33
Slough (Stoke P.) SL2 ....74 AV67
Teddington TW11 ....117 CG92
Uxbridge (Hare.) UB9 ....38 BJ51
Wallington SM6 ....159 DL105
Plough La Cl, Wall. SM6 ....159 DL106
Ploughlees La, Slou. SL1 ....74 AS73
Ploughmans Cl, NW1
off Crofters Way 83 DK67
Ploughmans End, Islw. TW7 ..117 CD85
Ploughmans Wk, N2
off Long La 44 DC54
Plough Ms, SW11
off Plough Ter 100 DD84
Plough Pl, EC4 ....196 E8
Plough Ri, Upmin. RM14 ....73 FS59
Plough Rd, SW11 ....100 DD83
Epsom KT19 ....156 CR109
Plough St, E1 off Leman St ..84 DT72
Plough Ter, SW11 ....100 DD84
Plough Way, SE16 ....203 J8
Plough Yd, EC2 ....197 N5
Plover Cl, Stai. TW18
off Waters Dr 113 BF90
Plover Gdns, Upmin. RM14 ....73 FT60
Plover Way, SE16 ....203 K6
Hayes UB4 ....78 BX72
Plowden Bldgs, EC4
off Middle Temple La 83 DN72
Plowman Cl, N18 ....46 DR50
Plowman Way, Dag. RM8 ....70 EW60
Plumbers Row, E1 ....84 DU71
Plumbridge St, SE10
off Blackheath Hill 103 EC81
Plum Cl, Felt. TW13
off Highfield Rd 115 BU88
Plum Garth, Brent. TW8 ....97 CK77
Plum La, SE18 ....105 EP80
Plummer La, Mitch. CR4 ....140 DF96
Plummer Rd, SW4 ....121 DK87
Plummers Cft, Sev. (Dunt.Grn.)
TN13 ....190 FE121
Plumpton Av, Horn. RM12 ....72 FL63
Plumpton Cl, Nthlt. UB5 ....78 CA65
Plumpton Way, Cars. SM5 ....140 DE104
PLUMSTEAD, SE18 ....105 ES78
⇌ Plumstead 105 ER77
Plumstead Common Rd,
SE18 ....105 EP79
Plumstead High St, SE18 ....105 ES77
Plumstead Rd, SE18 ....105 EP77
Plumtree Cl, Dag. RM10 ....89 FB65
Wallington SM6 ....159 DK108
Plumtree Ct, EC4 ....196 E8
Plumtree Mead, Loug. IG10 ....33 EN41
Plymouth Dr, Sev. TN13 ....191 FJ124
Plymouth Ho, Rain. RM13 ....89 FF69
Plymouth Pk, Sev. TN13 ....191 FJ124
Plymouth Rd, E16 ....86 EG71
Bromley BR1 ....144 EH95
Grays (Chaff.Hun.) RM16 ..109 FW77
Plymouth Wf, E14 ....204 F8
Plympton Av, NW6 ....81 CZ66
Plympton Cl, Belv. DA17
off Halifield Dr 106 EY76
Plympton Pl, NW8 ....194 B5
Plympton Rd, NW6 ....81 CZ66
Plympton St, NW8 ....194 B5
Plymstock Rd, Well. DA16 ....106 EW80
Pocketsdell La, Hem.H. (Bov.)
HP3 ....4 AX28
Pocklington Cl, NW9 ....42 CS54
Pocock Av, West Dr. UB7 ....94 BM76
Pococks La, Wind. (Eton) SL4 .92 AS78
Pocock St, SE1 ....200 F4
Podmore Rd, SW18 ....100 DC84
Poets Gate, Wal.Cr. EN7 ....14 DS28
Poets Rd, N5 ....66 DR64
Poets Way, Har. HA1
off Blawith Rd 61 CE56
Point, The, Ruis. HA4
off Bedford Rd 59 BU63
Pointalls Cl, N3 ....44 DC54
Point Cl, SE10 off Point Hill ..103 EC81
Pointer Cl, SE28 ....88 EX72
Pointers, The, Ashtd. KT21 ..172 CL120
Pointers Cl, E14 ....204 B10
Pointers Rd, Cob. KT11 ....169 BQ116
Point Hill, SE10 ....103 EC80
Point of Thomas Path, E1 ....202 G1
Point Pl, Wem. HA9 ....80 CP66
Point Pleasant, SW18 ....100 DA84
Poland Ho, E15 ....85 ED67
Poland St, W1 ....195 L9
Polebrook Rd, SE3 ....104 EJ83
Pole Cat All, Brom. BR2 ....144 EF103
Polecroft La, SE6 ....123 DZ89
Polehamptons, The, Hmptn. TW12
off High St 116 CC94
Pole Hill Rd, E4 ....47 EC45
Hayes UB4 ....77 BQ69
Uxbridge UB10 ....77 BQ69
Polesden Gdns, SW20 ....139 CV96
Polesden La, Wok. (Send M.)
GU23 ....167 BF122
Poles Hill, Rick. (Sarratt) WD3 ..5 BE33
Polesteeple Hill, West. (Bigg.H.)
TN16 ....178 EK117
Polesworth Ho, W2 ....82 DA71
Polesworth Rd, Dag. RM9 ....88 EX66
Polhill, Sev. (Halst.) TN14 ....181 FC115
Police Sta La, Bushey WD23
off Sparrows Herne 40 CB45
Police Sta Rd, Walt. KT12 ....154 BW107
★ Polish Institute & Sikorski
Mus, SW7
off Princes Gate 198 A5
Pollard Av, Uxb. (Denh.) UB9 ..57 BF58
Pollard Cl, E16 ....86 EG73
N7 ....65 DM63
Chigwell IG7 ....50 EU50
Windsor (Old Wind.) SL4 ..112 AV85
Pollard Rd, N20 ....44 DE47
Morden SM4 ....140 DD99
Woking GU22 ....167 BB116
Pollard Row, E2 ....84 DU69
Pollards, Rick. (Map.Cr.) WD3 .37 BD50
Pollards Cl, Loug. IG10 ....32 EJ43
Waltham Cross (Chsht.)
EN7 ....14 DQ29
Pollards Cres, SW16 ....141 DL97
Pollards Hill E, SW16 ....141 DM97
Pollards Hill N, SW16 ....141 DL97
Pollards Hill S, SW16 ....141 DL97
Pollards Hill W, SW16 ....141 DL97
Pollards Oak Cres, Oxt. RH8 .188 EG132
Pollards Oak Rd, Oxt. RH8 ..188 EG132
Pollard St, E2 ....84 DU69
Pollards Wd Hill, Oxt. RH8 ..188 EH130
Pollards Wd Rd, SW16 ....141 DL96
Oxted RH8 ....188 EH131
Pollard Wk, Sid. DA14 ....126 EW93
Pollen St, W1 ....195 J9
Pollitt Dr, NW8
off Cunningham Pl 82 DD70
★ Pollock's Toy Mus, W1
off Scala St 195 L6
Pollyhaugh, Dart. (Eyns.)
DA4 ....148 FL104
Polperro Cl, Orp. BR6
off Cotswold Ri 145 ET100
Polperro Ms, SE11 ....200 E8
Polsted Rd, SE6 ....123 DZ87
Polsten Ms, Enf. EN3
off Government Row 31 EA37
Polthorne Est, SE18 ....105 ER77
Polthorne Gro, SE18 ....105 EQ77
Polworth Rd, SW16 ....121 DL92

310

Pol - Pre

Polygon, The, SW4
off Old Town 101 DJ84
Polygon Rd, NW1 ....195 M1
Polytechnic St, SE18 ....105 EN77
Pomell Way, E1
off Commercial St 84 DT72
Pomeroy Cres, Wat. WD24 ....23 BV36
Pomeroy St, SE14 ....102 DW81
Pomfret Rd, SE5
off Flaxman Rd 101 DP83
Pomoja La, N19 ....65 DL61
Pompadour Cl, Brwd. CM14
off Queen St 54 FW50
Pond Cl, N12
off Summerfields Av 44 DE51
SE3 ....104 EF82
Ashtead KT21 ....172 CL117
Uxbridge (Hare.) UB9 ....38 BJ54
Walton-on-Thames KT12 ....153 BU107
Pond Cottage La, W.Wick. BR4 ....143 EA102
Pond Cotts, SE21 ....122 DS88
PONDERS END, Enf. 30 DW43
⇌ Ponders End 31 DX43
Ponders End Ind Est, Enf. EN3 ....31 DZ42
Ponder St, N7 ....83 DM66
Pond Fm Cl, Tad. KT20 ....173 CU124
Pond Fld End, Loug. IG10 ....48 EJ45
Pondfield La, Brwd. CM13 ....55 GA49
Pondfield Rd, Brom. BR2 ....144 EE102
Dagenham RM10 ....71 FB64
Kenley CR8 ....175 DP116
Orpington BR6 ....145 EP104
Pond Grn, Ruis. HA4 ....59 BS61
Pond Hill Gdns, Sutt. SM3 ....157 CY107
Pond La, Ger.Cr. (Chal.St.P.) SL9 ....36 AV53
Pond Lees Cl, Dag. RM10
off Leys Av 89 FD66
Pond Mead, SE21 ....122 DR86
Pond Path, Chis. BR7
off Heathfield La 125 EP93
Pond Piece, Lthd. (Oxshott) KT22 ....154 CB114
Pond Pl, SW3 ....198 B9
Pond Rd, E15 ....86 EE68
SE3 ....104 EF82
Egham TW20 ....113 BC93
Hemel Hempstead HP3 ....6 BN25
Woking GU22 ....166 AU120
Ponds, The, Wey. KT13
off Ellesmere Rd 153 BS107
Pondside Cl, Hayes UB3
off Providence La 95 BR80
Pond Sq, N6 off South Gro 64 DG60
Pond St, NW3 ....64 DE64
Pond Wk, Upmin. RM14 ....73 FS61
Pond Way, Tedd. TW11
off Holmesdale Rd 117 CJ93
Pondwood Ri, Orp. BR6 ....145 ES101
Ponler St, E1 ....84 DV72
Ponsard Rd, NW10 ....81 CV69
Ponsford St, E9 ....84 DW65
Ponsonby Pl, SW1 ....199 N10
Ponsonby Rd, SW15 ....119 CV87
Ponsonby Ter, SW1 ....199 N10
Pontefract Rd, Brom. BR1 ....124 EF92
Pontoise Cl, Sev. TN13 ....190 FF122
Ponton Rd, SW8 ....101 DK79
Pont St, SW1 ....198 D7
Pont St Ms, SW1 ....198 D7
Pontypool Pl, SE1 ....200 F4
Pontypool Wk, Rom. RM3
off Saddleworth Rd 52 FJ51
Pony Chase, Cob. KT11 ....154 BZ113
Pool Cl, Beck. BR3 ....123 EA92
West Molesey KT8 ....136 BZ99
Pool Ct, SE6 ....123 EA89
Poole Cl, Ruis. HA4
off Chichester Av 59 BS61
Poole Ct Rd, Houns. TW4
off Vicarage Fm Rd 96 BY82
Poole Ho, Grays RM16 ....111 GJ75
Pool End Cl, Shep. TW17 ....134 BN99
Poole Rd, E9 ....85 DX65
Epsom KT19 ....156 CR107
Hornchurch RM11 ....72 FM59
Woking GU21 ....166 AY117
Pooles Bldgs, EC1 ....196 D5
Pooles La, SW10 off Lots Rd 100 DC80
Dagenham RM9 ....88 EY68
Pooles Pk, N4
off Seven Sisters Rd 65 DN61
Poole St, N1 ....84 DR67
Poole Way, Hayes UB4 ....77 BR69
Pooley Av, Egh. TW20 ....113 BB92
POOLEY GREEN, Egh. 113 BC92
Pooley Grn Cl, Egh. TW20 ....113 BB92
Pooley Grn Rd, Egh. TW20 ....113 BB92
Pool Gro, Croy. CR0 ....161 DY112
Pool La, Slou. SL1 ....74 AS73
Poolmans St, SE16 ....203 H4
Pool Rd, Har. HA1 ....61 CD59
West Molesey KT8 ....136 BZ100
Poolsford Rd, NW9 ....62 CS56
Poonah St, E1
off Hardinge St 84 DW72
Pootings Rd, Eden. (Crock.H.) TN8 ....189 ER134
Pope Cl, SW19 ....120 DD93
Feltham TW14 ....115 BT88
Pope Rd, Brom. BR2 ....144 EK99
Popes Av, Twick. TW2 ....117 CE89
Popes Cl, Amer. HP6 ....20 AT37
Slough (Colnbr.) SL3 ....93 BB80
Popes Dr, N3 ....44 DA53
Popes Gro, Croy. CR0 ....143 DZ104
Twickenham TW1, TW2 ....117 CF89
Pope's Head All, EC3
off Cornhill 84 DR72
Popes La, W5 ....97 CK76
Oxted RH8 ....188 EE134
Watford WD24 ....23 BV37
Popes Rd, SW9 ....101 DN83
Abbots Langley WD5 ....7 BS31
Pope St, SE1 ....201 N5
Popham Cl, Felt. TW13 ....116 BZ90
Popham Gdns, Rich. TW9
off Lower Richmond Rd 98 CN83
Popham Rd, N1 ....84 DQ67
Popham St, N1 ....83 DP67
POPLAR, E14 ....204 B2
DLR Poplar 204 B1
Poplar Av, Amer. HP7 ....20 AT39
Gravesend DA12 ....131 GJ91
Leatherhead KT22 ....171 CH122
Mitcham CR4 ....140 DF95
Orpington BR6 ....145 EP103
Southall UB2 ....96 CB76
West Drayton UB7 ....76 BM73
Poplar Bath St, E14
off Lawless St 85 EB73
Poplar Business Pk, E14 ....204 D1
Poplar Cl, E9
off Lee Conservancy Rd 67 DZ64
Pinner HA5 ....40 BX53
Slough (Colnbr.) SL3 ....93 BE81
South Ockendon RM15 ....91 FX70
Poplar Ct, SW19 ....120 DA92
Poplar Cres, Epsom KT19 ....156 CQ107
Poplar Dr, Bans. SM7 ....157 CX114
Brentwood CM13 ....55 GC44
Poplar Fm Cl, Epsom KT19 ....156 CQ107
Poplar Gdns, N.Mal. KT3 ....138 CR96
Poplar Gro, N11 ....44 DG51
W6 ....99 CW75
New Malden KT3 ....138 CR97
Wembley HA9 ....62 CQ62
Woking GU22 ....166 AY119
Poplar High St, E14 ....85 EA73
Poplar Mt, Belv. DA17 ....107 FB77
Poplar Pl, SE28 ....88 EW73
W2 ....82 DB73
Hayes UB3 off Central Av 77 BU73
Poplar Rd, SE24 ....102 DQ84
SW19 ....140 DA96
Ashford TW15 ....115 BQ92
Leatherhead KT22 ....171 CH122
Sutton SM3 ....139 CZ102
Uxbridge (Denh.) UB9 ....58 BJ64
Poplar Rd S, SW19 ....140 DA97
Poplar Row, Epp. (They.B.) CM16 ....33 ES37
Poplars, The, N14 ....29 DH43
Gravesend DA12 ....131 GL87
Romford (Abridge) RM4
off Hoe La 34 EV41
Waltham Cross (Chsht.) EN7 ....14 DS26
Poplars Av, NW10 ....81 CW65
Poplars Cl, Ruis. HA4 ....59 BS60
Watford WD25 ....7 BV32
Poplar Shaw, Wal.Abb. EN9 ....16 EF33
Poplars Rd, E17 ....67 EB58
Poplar St, Rom. RM7 ....71 FC56
Poplar Vw, Wem. HA9
off Magnet Rd 61 CK61
Poplar Wk, SE24 ....102 DQ84
Caterham CR3 ....176 DS123
Croydon CR0 ....142 DQ103
Poplar Way, Felt. TW13 ....115 BU90
Ilford IG6 ....69 EQ56
Poppins Ct, EC4 ....196 F9
Poppleton Rd, E11 ....68 EE58
Poppy Cl, Brwd. CM15 ....54 FV43
Wallington SM6 ....140 DG102
★ Poppy Factory Mus, The, Rich. TW10 ....117 CK86
Poppy La, Croy. CR0 ....142 DW101
Poppy Wk, Wal.Cr. EN7 ....14 DR28
Porchester Cl, SE5 ....102 DQ84
Hornchurch RM11 ....72 FL58
Porchester Gdns, W2 ....82 DB73
Porchester Gdns Ms, W2
off Porchester Gdns 82 DB72
Porchester Mead, Beck. BR3 ....123 EB93
Porchester Ms, W2 ....82 DB72
Porchester Pl, W2 ....194 C9
Porchester Rd, W2 ....82 DB71
Kingston upon Thames KT1 ....138 CP96
Porchester Sq, W2 ....82 DB72
Porchester Ter, W2 ....82 DC73
Porchester Ter N, W2 ....82 DB72
Porchfield Cl, Grav. DA12 ....131 GJ89
Sutton SM2 ....158 DB110
Porch Way, N20 ....44 DF48
Porcupine Cl, SE9 ....124 EL89
Porden Rd, SW2 ....101 DM84
Porlock Av, Har. HA2 ....60 CC60
Porlock Rd, W10
off Ladbroke Gro 81 CX70
Enfield EN1 ....46 DT45
Porlock St, SE1 ....201 K4
Porrington Cl, Chis. BR7 ....145 EM95
Portal Cl, SE27 ....121 DN90
Ruislip HA4 ....59 BU63
Uxbridge UB10 ....76 BL66
Port Av, Green. DA9 ....129 FV86
Portbury Cl, SE15
off Clayton Rd 102 DU81
Port Cres, E13
off Jenkins Rd 86 EH70
★ Portcullis House - New Parliamentary Building, SW1 ....199 P4
Portcullis Lo Rd, Enf. EN2 ....30 DR41
Portelet Ct, N1
off De Beauvoir Est 84 DS67
Portelet Rd, E1 ....85 DX69
Porten Rd, W14 ....99 CY76
Porter Cl, Grays RM20 ....109 FW79
Porter Rd, E6 ....87 EM72
Porters Av, Dag. RM8, RM9 ....88 EV65
Porters Cl, Brwd. CM14 ....54 FU46
Portersfield Rd, Enf. EN1 ....30 DS42
Porters Pk Dr, Rad. (Shenley) WD7 ....9 CK33
Porter Sq, N19
off Hornsey Rd 65 DL60
Porter St, SE1 ....201 J2
W1 ....194 E6
Porters Wk, E1 ....202 E1
Porters Way, West Dr. UB7 ....94 BM76
Porteus Rd, W2 ....82 DC71
Portgate Cl, W9 ....81 CZ70
Porthallow Cl, Orp. BR6
off Sevenoaks Rd 163 ET105
Porthcawe Rd, SE26 ....123 DY91
Port Hill, Orp. BR6 ....164 EV112
Porthkerry Av, Well. DA16 ....106 EU84
Portia Way, E3 ....85 DZ70
Portinscale Rd, SW15 ....119 CY85
Portland Av, N16 ....66 DT59
Gravesend DA12 ....131 GH89
New Malden KT3 ....139 CT101
Sidcup DA15 ....126 EU86
Portland Cl, Rom. RM6 ....70 EY57
Portland Cres, SE9 ....124 EL89
Feltham TW13 ....115 BR91
Greenford UB6 ....78 CB70
Stanmore HA7 ....41 CK54
Portland Dr, Enf. EN2 ....30 DS38
Redhill RH1 ....185 DK129
Waltham Cross (Chsht.) EN7 ....14 DU31
Portland Gdns, N4 ....65 DP58
Romford RM6 ....70 EX57
Portland Gro, SW8 ....101 DM81
Portland Hts, Nthwd. HA6 ....39 BT49
H Portland Hosp for Women & Children, The, W1 ....195 J5
Portland Ho, Red. RH1 ....185 DK129
Portland Ms, W1 ....195 L9
Portland Pk, Ger.Cr. SL9 ....56 AX58
Portland Pl, W1 ....195 J7
Epsom KT17 ....156 CS112
Portland Ri, N4 ....65 DP60
Portland Ri Est, N4 ....66 DQ60
Portland Rd, N15 ....66 DT56
SE9 ....124 EL89
SE25 ....142 DU98
W11 ....81 CY73
Ashford TW15 ....114 BL90
Bromley BR1 ....124 EJ91
Gravesend DA12 ....131 GH88
Hayes UB4 ....77 BS69
Kingston upon Thames KT1 ....138 CL97
Mitcham CR4 ....140 DE96
Southall UB2 ....96 BZ76
Portland Sq, E1 ....202 D2
Portland St, SE17 ....201 K10
Portland Ter, Rich. TW9 ....97 CK84
Portland Wk, SE17
off Portland St 102 DR79
Portley La, Cat. CR3 ....176 DS121
Portley Wd Rd, Whyt. CR3 ....176 DT120
Portman Av, SW14 ....98 CR83
Portman Cl, W1 ....194 E8
Bexley DA5 ....127 FE88
Bexleyheath DA7
off Queen Anne's Gate 106 EX83
Portman Dr, Wdf.Grn. IG8 ....48 EK54
Portman Gdns, NW9 ....62 CR54
Uxbridge UB10 ....76 BN66
Portman Gate, NW1 ....194 C5
Portman Ms S, W1 ....194 F9
Portman Pl, E2 ....84 DW69
Portman Rd, Kings.T. KT1 ....138 CM96
Portman Sq, W1 ....194 E8
Portman St, W1 ....194 F9
Portmeadow Wk, SE2 ....106 EX75
Portmeers Cl, E17
off Lennox Rd 67 DZ58
Portmore Gdns, Rom. RM5 ....50 FA50
Portmore Pk Rd, Wey. KT13 ....152 BN105
Portmore Quays, Wey. KT13
off Weybridge Rd 152 BM105
Portmore Way, Wey. KT13 ....134 BN104
Portnall Dr, Vir.W. GU25 ....132 AT99
Portnall Ri, Vir.W. GU25 ....132 AT99
Portnall Rd, W9 ....81 CZ68
Virginia Water GU25 ....132 AT99
Portnalls Cl, Couls. CR5 ....175 DH116
Portnalls Ri, Couls. CR5 ....175 DH116
Portnalls Rd, Couls. CR5 ....175 DH118
Portnoi Cl, Rom. RM1 ....51 FD54
Portobello Ct, W11
off Westbourne Gro 81 CZ73
Portobello Ms, W11
off Portobello Rd 82 DA73
Portobello Rd, W10 ....81 CZ72
W11 ....81 CZ72
Porton Ct, Surb. KT6 ....137 CJ100
Portpool La, EC1 ....196 D6
Portree Cl, N22
off Nightingale Rd 45 DM52
Portree St, E14 ....85 ED72
Portsdown, Edg. HA8
off Rectory La 42 CN50
Portsdown Av, NW11 ....63 CZ58
Portsdown Ms, NW11 ....63 CZ58
Portsea Ms, W2 ....194 C9
Portsea Pl, W2 ....194 C9
Portsea Rd, Til. RM18 ....111 GJ81
Portslade Rd, SW8 ....101 DJ82
Portsmouth Av, T.Ditt. KT7 ....137 CG101
Portsmouth Ct, Slou. SL1 ....74 AS73
Portsmouth Ms, E16
off Wesley Av 86 EH74
Portsmouth Rd, SW15 ....119 CV87
Cobham KT11 ....153 BU114
Esher KT10 ....154 CC105
Kingston upon Thames KT1 ....137 CJ99
Surbiton KT6 ....137 CJ99
Thames Ditton KT7 ....137 CE103
Woking (Ripley) GU23 ....168 BM119
Portsmouth St, WC2 ....196 B9
Portsoken St, E1 ....197 P10
Portugal Gdns, Twick. TW2
off Fulwell Pk Av 116 CC89
Portugal Rd, Wok. GU21 ....167 BA116
Portugal St, WC2 ....196 B9
Portway, E15 ....86 EF67
Epsom KT17 ....157 CU110
Portway Cres, Epsom KT17 ....157 CU109
Portway Gdns, SE18
off Shooter's Hill Rd 104 EK80
Postern Grn, Enf. EN2 ....29 DN40
Post La, Twick. TW2 ....117 CD88
Post Meadow, Iver SL0 ....75 BD69
Postmill Cl, Croy. CR0 ....143 DX104
Post Office App, E7 ....68 EH64
Post Office Ct, EC3 ....197 L9
Post Office La, Slou. (Geo.Grn.) SL3 ....74 AX72
Post Office Row, Oxt. RH8 ....188 EL131
Post Office Way, SW8 ....101 DK80
Post Rd, Sthl. UB2 ....96 CB76
Postway Ms, Ilf. IG1
off Clements Rd 69 EP62
Potier St, SE1 ....201 L7
Potter Cl, Mitch. CR4 ....141 DH96
Potterells, Hat. (N.Mymms) AL9 ....11 CX25
Potteries, The, Cher. KT16 ....151 BE107
Potterne Cl, SW19 ....119 CX87
POTTERS BAR 12 DA32
⇌ Potters Bar 12 DA32
H Potters Bar Comm Hosp, Pot.B. EN6 ....12 DC34
★ Potters Bar Mus, The Wyllyotts Cen, Pot.B. EN6 ....11 CZ32
Potters Cl, Croy. CR0 ....143 DY102
Loughton IG10 ....32 EL40
Potters Ct, Pot.B. EN6
off Darkes La 12 DA32
Potters Cross, Iver SL0 ....75 BD69
POTTERS CROUCH, St.Alb. 8 BX25
Potters Flds, SE1 off Tooley St 84 DS74
Potters Gro, N.Mal. KT3 ....138 CQ98
Potters Hts Cl, Pnr. HA5 ....39 BV52
Potters La, SW16 ....121 DK93
Barnet EN5 ....28 DA42
Borehamwood WD6 ....26 CQ39
Woking (Send) GU23 ....167 BB123
Potters Ms, Borwd. (Elstree) WD6
off Elstree Hill N 25 CK44
Potters Rd, SW6 ....100 DC82
Barnet EN5 ....28 DB42
Potter St, Nthwd. HA6 ....39 BU53
Pinner HA5 ....39 BV53
Potter St Hill, Pnr. HA5 ....39 BV51
Pottery La, W11
off Portland Rd 81 CY73
Pottery Rd, Bex. DA5 ....127 FC89
Brentford TW8 ....98 CL79
Pottery St, SE16 ....202 D5
Pott St, E2 ....84 DV69
Poulcott, Stai. (Wrays.) TW19 ....112 AY86
Poulett Gdns, Twick. TW1 ....117 CG88
Poulett Rd, E6 ....87 EM68
Poulner Way, SE15
off Daniel Gdns 102 DT80
Poulters Wd, Kes. BR2 ....162 EK106
Poultney Cl, Rad. (Shenley) WD7 ....10 CM32
Poulton Av, Sutt. SM1 ....140 DD104
Poulton Cl, E8
off Spurstowe Ter 66 DV64
Poultry, EC2 ....197 K9
Pound Cl, Orp. BR6 ....145 ER103
Surbiton KT6 ....137 CJ102
Pound Ct, Ashtd. KT21 ....172 CM118
Pound Ct Dr, Orp. BR6 ....145 ER103
Pound Cres, Lthd. (Fetch.) KT22 ....171 CD121
Pound Fm Cl, Esher KT10 ....137 CD102
Poundfield, Wat. WD25
off Ashfields 23 BT35
Poundfield Ct, Wok. GU22
off High St 167 BC121
Poundfield Gdns, Wok. GU22 ....167 BC120
Poundfield Rd, Loug. IG10 ....33 EN43
Pound La, NW10 ....81 CU65
Epsom KT19 ....156 CR112
Radlett (Shenley) WD7 ....10 CM33
Sevenoaks TN13 ....180 EX115
Sevenoaks (Knock.P.) TN14 ....191 FH124
Pound Pk Rd, SE7 ....104 EK77
Pound Pl, SE9 ....125 EN86
Pound Rd, Bans. SM7 ....173 CZ117
Chertsey KT16 ....134 BH101
Pound St, Cars. SM5 ....158 DF106
Pound Way, Chis. BR7
off Royal Par 125 EQ94
Pounsley Rd, Sev. (Dunt.Grn.) TN13 ....190 FE121
Pountney Rd, SW11 ....100 DG83
POVEREST, Orp. 145 ET99
Poverest Rd, Orp. BR5 ....145 ET99
Powder Mill La, Dart. DA1 ....128 FL89
Twickenham TW2 ....116 BZ88
Powdermill La, Wal.Abb. EN9 ....15 EB33
Powdermill Ms, Wal.Abb. EN9
off Powdermill La 15 EB33
Powdermill Way, Wal.Abb. EN9 ....15 EB32
Powell Cl, Chess. KT9
off Coppard Gdns 155 CK106
Dartford DA2 ....129 FS89
Edgware HA8 ....42 CM51
Wallington SM6 ....159 DK108
Powell Gdns, Dag. RM10 ....70 FA63
Powell Rd, E5 ....66 DV62
Buckhurst Hill IG9 ....48 EJ45
Powell's Wk, W4 ....98 CS79
Power Dr, Enf. EN3 ....31 DZ36
Powergate Business Pk, NW10 ....80 CR69
Power Ind Est, Erith DA8 ....107 FG81
Power Rd, W4 ....98 CN77
Powers Ct, Twick. TW1 ....117 CK87
Powerscroft Rd, E5 ....66 DW63
Sidcup DA14 ....126 EW93
Powis Ct, Pot.B. EN6 ....12 DC34
Powis Gdns, NW11 ....63 CZ59
W11 ....81 CZ72
Powis Ms, W11
off Westbourne Pk Rd 81 CZ72
Powis Pl, WC1 ....196 A5
Powis Rd, E3 ....85 EB69
Powis Sq, W11 ....81 CZ72
Powis St, SE18 ....105 EN76
Powis Ter, W11 ....81 CZ72
Powle Ter, Ilf. IG1
off Oaktree Gro 69 EQ64
Powlett Pl, NW1
off Harmood St 83 DH65
Pownall Gdns, Houns. TW3 ....96 CB84
Pownall Rd, E8 ....84 DT67
Hounslow TW3 ....96 CB84
Pownsett Ter, Ilf. IG1
off Buttsbury Rd 69 EQ64
Powster Rd, Brom. BR1 ....124 EH92
Powys Cl, Bexh. DA7 ....106 EX79
Powys Ct, Borwd. WD6
off Kensington Way 26 CR41
Powys La, N13 ....45 DL50
N14 ....45 DL49
POYLE, Slou. 93 BE81
Poyle Pk, Slou. (Colnbr.) SL3 ....93 BE83
Poyle Rd, Slou. (Colnbr.) SL3 ....93 BE83
Poyle Technical Cen, Slou. SL3 ....93 BE82
Poynder Rd, Til. RM18 ....111 GH81
Poynders Ct, SW4
off Poynders Rd 121 DJ86
Poynders Gdns, SW4 ....121 DJ87
Poynders Rd, SW4 ....121 DJ86
Poynings, The, Iver SL0 ....93 BF77
Poynings Cl, Orp. BR6 ....146 EW103
Poynings Rd, N19 ....65 DJ62
Poynings Way, N12 ....44 DA50
Romford RM3
off Arlington Gdns 52 FL53
Poyntell Cres, Chis. BR7 ....145 ER95
Poynter Ho, W11 ....81 CX74
Poynter Rd, Enf. EN1 ....30 DU43
Poynton Rd, N17 ....46 DU54
Poyntz Rd, SW11 ....100 DF82
Poyser St, E2 ....84 DV68
Prae, The, Wok. GU22 ....167 BF118
Praed Ms, W2 ....194 A8
Praed St, W2 ....194 B7
Pragel St, E13 ....86 EH68
Pragnell Rd, SE12 ....124 EH89
Prague Pl, SW2 ....121 DL85
Prah Rd, N4 ....65 DN61
Prairie Cl, Add. KT15 ....134 BH104
Prairie Rd, Add. KT15 ....134 BH104
Prairie St, SW8 ....100 DG82
Pratt Ms, NW1 off Pratt St 83 DJ67
PRATT'S BOTTOM, Orp. 164 EV110
Pratts La, Walt. KT12
off Molesey Rd 154 BX105
Pratts Pas, Kings.T. KT1
off Eden St 138 CL96
Pratt St, NW1 ....83 DJ67
Pratt Wk, SE11 ....200 C8
Prayle Gro, NW2 ....63 CX60
Prebend Gdns, W4 ....99 CT76
W6 ....99 CT76
Prebend St, N1 ....84 DQ67
Precinct, The, W.Mol. KT8
off Victoria Av 136 CB97
Precinct Rd, Hayes UB3 ....77 BU73
Precincts, The, Mord. SM4
off Green La 140 DB100
Precinct, The, Egh. TW20
off High St 113 BA92
Premier Av, Grays RM16 ....110 GC75
Premier Cor, W9
off Kilburn La 81 CZ68
Premiere Pl, E14 ....203 P1
Premier Pk, NW10 ....80 CP67
Premier Pk Rd, NW10 ....80 CP68
Premier Pl, SW15
off Putney High St 99 CY84
Prendergast Rd, SE3 ....104 EE83
Prentis Rd, SW16 ....121 DK91
Prentiss Ct, SE7 ....104 EK77
Presburg Rd, N.Mal. KT3 ....138 CS99
Presburg St, E5 off Glyn Rd 67 DX62
Prescelly Pl, Edg. HA8 ....42 CM53
Prescot St, E1 ....84 DT73
Prescott Av, Orp. BR5 ....145 EP100
Prescott Cl, SW16 ....121 DL94
Hornchurch RM11 ....71 FH60
Prescott Grn, Loug. IG10 ....33 EQ41
Prescott Ho, SE17
off Hillingdon St 101 DP79
Prescott Pl, SW4 ....101 DK83
Prescott Rd, Slou. (Colnbr.) SL3 ....93 BE82
Waltham Cross (Chsht.) EN8 ....15 DY27
Presentation Ms, SW2
off Palace Rd 121 DM88
President Dr, E1 ....202 D2
President St, EC1 ....197 H2
Press Rd, NW10 ....62 CR62
Uxbridge UB8 ....76 BK65
Prestage Way, E14 ....85 EC73
Prestbury Ct, Wok. GU21
off Muirfield Rd 166 AU118
Prestbury Cres, Bans. SM7 ....174 DF116
Prestbury Rd, E7 ....86 EJ66
Prestbury Sq, SE9 ....125 EM91
Prested Rd, SW11
off St. John's Hill 100 DE84
Prestige Way, NW4
off Heriot Rd 63 CW57
PRESTON, Wem. 61 CK59
Preston Av, E4 ....47 ED51
Preston Cl, SE1 ....201 M8
Twickenham TW2 ....117 CE90
Preston Ct, Walt. KT12
off St. Johns Dr 136 BW102
Preston Dr, E11 ....68 EJ57
Bexleyheath DA7 ....106 EX81
Epsom KT19 ....156 CS107
Preston Gdns, NW10
off Church Rd 80 CS65
Enfield EN3 ....31 DY37
Ilford IG1 ....68 EL58
Preston Gro, Ashtd. KT21 ....171 CJ117
Preston Hill, Har. HA3 ....62 CM58

★ Place of interest ⇌ Railway station ⊖ London Underground station DLR Docklands Light Railway station Tramlink station H Hospital

Preston La, Tad. KT20 . . . 173 CV121
Preston Pl, NW2 . . . 81 CU65
Richmond TW10 . . . 118 CL85
⊖ Preston Road . . . 62 CL60
Preston Rd, E11 . . . 68 EE58
SE19 . . . 121 DP93
SW20 . . . 119 CT94
Gravesend (Nthflt.) DA11 . . . 130 GE88
Harrow HA3 . . . 62 CL59
Romford RM3 . . . 52 FK49
Shepperton TW17 . . . 134 BN99
Slough SL2 . . . 74 AW73
Wembley HA9 . . . 62 CL61
Prestons Rd, E14 . . . 204 E3
Bromley BR2 . . . 144 EG104
Preston Waye, Har. HA3 . . . 62 CL60
Prestwick Cl, Sthl. UB2
off Ringway . . . 96 BY78
Prestwick Rd, Wat. WD19 . . . 40 BX50
Prestwood, Slou. SL2 . . . 74 AV72
Prestwood Av, Har. HA3 . . . 61 CH56
Prestwood Cl, SE18 . . . 106 EU80
Harrow HA3 . . . 61 CJ56
Prestwood Dr, Rom. RM5 . . . 51 FC50
Prestwood Gdns, Croy. CR0 . . . 142 DQ101
Prestwood St, N1 . . . 197 J1
Pretoria Av, E17 . . . 67 DY56
Pretoria Cl, N17
off Pretoria Rd . . . 46 DT52
Pretoria Cres, E4 . . . 47 EC46
Pretoria Rd, E4 . . . 47 EC46
E11 . . . 67 ED60
E16 . . . 86 EF69
N17 . . . 46 DT52
SW16 . . . 121 DH93
Chertsey KT16 . . . 133 BF102
Ilford IG1 . . . 69 EP64
Romford RM7 . . . 71 FC56
Watford WD18 . . . 23 BU42
Pretoria Rd N, N18 . . . 46 DT51
Pretty La, Couls. CR5 . . . 175 DJ121
Prevost Rd, N11 . . . 44 DG47
Prey Heath, Wok. GU22 . . . 166 AV123
Prey Heath Cl, Wok. GU22 . . . 166 AW124
Prey Heath Rd, Wok. GU22 . . . 166 AV124
Price Cl, NW7 . . . 43 CY51
SW17 . . . 120 DF90
Price Rd, Croy. CR0 . . . 159 DP106
Price's Ct, SW11 . . . 100 DD83
Price's St, SE1 off Bear La . . . 83 DP74
Price's Yd, N1 . . . 83 DM67
Price Way, Hmptn. TW12
off Victors Dr . . . 116 BY93
Pricklers Hill, Barn. EN5 . . . 28 DB44
Prickley Wd, Brom. BR2 . . . 144 EF102
Priddy's Yd, Croy. CR0
off Church St . . . 142 DQ103
Prideaux Pl, W3
off Friars Pl La . . . 80 CR73
WC1 . . . 196 C2
Prideaux Rd, SW9 . . . 101 DL83
Pridham Rd, Th.Hth. CR7 . . . 142 DR98
Priest Ct, EC2 . . . 197 H8
Priestfield Rd, SE23 . . . 123 DY90
Priest Hill, Egh. TW20 . . . 112 AW90
Windsor (Old Wind.) SL4 . . . 112 AW90
Priestlands Pk Rd, Sid. DA15 . . . 125 ET90
Priestley Cl, N16
off Ravensdale Rd . . . 66 DT59
Priestley Gdns, Rom. RM6 . . . 70 EV58
Priestley Rd, Mitch. CR4 . . . 140 DG96
Priestley Way, E17 . . . 67 DX55
NW2 . . . 63 CU60
Priestly Gdns, Wok. GU22 . . . 167 BA120
Priestman Pt, E3
off Rainhill Way . . . 85 EB69
Priest Pk Av, Har. HA2 . . . 60 CA61
Priests Av, Rom. RM1 . . . 51 FD54
Priests Br, SW14 . . . 98 CS83
SW15 . . . 98 CS83
Priests Fld, Brwd. CM13 . . . 55 GC50
Priests La, Brwd. CM15 . . . 54 FY47
Prima Rd, SW9 . . . 101 DN80
Primrose Av, Enf. EN2 . . . 30 DR39
Romford RM6 . . . 70 EV59
Primrose Cl, SE6 . . . 123 EC92
Harrow HA2 . . . 60 BZ63
Wallington SM6 . . . 141 DH102
Primrose Dr, West Dr. UB7 . . . 94 BK77
Primrose Gdns, NW3 . . . 82 DE65
Bushey WD23 . . . 40 CB45
Ruislip HA4 . . . 60 BW64
Primrose Glen, Horn. RM11 . . . 72 FL56
PRIMROSE HILL, NW8 . . . 82 DF67
Primrose Hill, EC4 . . . 196 E9
Brentwood CM14 . . . 54 FW48
Kings Langley WD4 . . . 7 BP28
Primrose Hill Ct, NW3 . . . 82 DF66
Primrose Hill Rd, NW3 . . . 82 DE66
Primrose Hill Studios, NW1
off Fitzroy Rd . . . 82 DG67
Primrose La, Croy. CR0 . . . 143 DX102
Primrose Ms, NW1
off Sharpleshall St . . . 82 DF66
SE3 . . . 104 EH80
W5 off St. Mary's Rd . . . 97 CK75
Primrose Path, Wal.Cr. (Chsht.)
EN7 . . . 14 DU31
Primrose Rd, E10 . . . 67 EB60
E18 . . . 48 EH54
Walton-on-Thames KT12 . . . 154 BW106
Primrose Sq, E9 . . . 84 DW66
Primrose St, EC2 . . . 197 M6
Primrose Wk, SE14
off Alexandra St . . . 103 DY80
Epsom KT17 . . . 157 CT108
Primrose Way, Wem. HA0 . . . 79 CK68
Primula St, W12 . . . 81 CU72
Prince Albert Rd, NW1 . . . 194 C1
NW8 . . . 194 C1
Prince Alberts Wk, Wind. SL4 . . . 92 AU81
Prince Arthur Ms, NW3
off Perrins La . . . 64 DC63
Prince Arthur Rd, NW3 . . . 64 DC64
Prince Charles Av, Dart.
(S.Darenth) DA4 . . . 149 FR96
Prince Charles Dr, NW4 . . . 63 CW59
Prince Charles Rd, SE3 . . . 104 EF81
Prince Charles Way, Wall.
SM6 . . . 141 DH104
Prince Consort Dr, Chis. BR7 . . . 145 ER95
Prince Consort Rd, SW7 . . . 100 DC76
Princedale Rd, W11 . . . 81 CY74
Prince Edward Rd, E9 . . . 85 DZ65
Prince George Av, N14 . . . 29 DJ42
Prince George Duke of Kent Ct,
Chis. BR7 off Holbrook La . . . 125 ER94
Prince George Rd, N16 . . . 66 DS63
Prince George's Av, SW20 . . . 139 CW96
Prince George's Rd, SW19 . . . 140 DD95
Prince Henry Rd, SE7 . . . 104 EK80
★ Prince Henry's Room,
EC4 . . . 196 D9
Prince Imperial Rd, SE18 . . . 105 EM81
Chislehurst BR7 . . . 125 EP94
Prince John Rd, SE9 . . . 124 EL85
Princelet St, E1 . . . 84 DT71
Prince of Orange La, SE10
off Greenwich High Rd . . . 103 EC80
Prince of Wales Cl, NW4
off Church Ter . . . 63 CV56
Prince of Wales Dr, SW8 . . . 101 DH80
SW11 . . . 100 DF81
Prince of Wales Footpath, Enf.
EN3 . . . 31 DY38
Prince of Wales Gate, SW7 . . . 198 B4
Prince of Wales Pas, NW1 . . . 195 K3
Prince of Wales Rd, NW5 . . . 82 DG65
SE3 . . . 104 EF81
Sutton SM1 . . . 140 DD103
Prince of Wales Ter, W4 . . . 98 CS78
W8 off Kensington Rd . . . 100 DB75
DLR Prince Regent . . . 86 EJ73
Prince Regent La, E13 . . . 86 EH69
E16 . . . 86 EJ71
Prince Regent Ms, NW1
off Hampstead Rd . . . 83 DJ69
Prince Regent Rd, Houns.
TW3 . . . 96 CC83
Prince Rd, SE25 . . . 142 DS99
Prince Rupert Rd, SE9 . . . 105 EM84
Prince's Arc, SW1 . . . 199 L2
Princes Av, N3 . . . 44 DA53
N10 . . . 64 DG55
N13 . . . 45 DN50
N22 . . . 45 DK53
NW9 . . . 62 CP56
W3 . . . 98 CN76
Carshalton SM5 . . . 158 DF108
Dartford DA2 . . . 128 FP88
Enfield EN3 . . . 31 DY36
Greenford UB6 . . . 78 CB72
Orpington BR5 . . . 145 ES99
South Croydon CR2 . . . 176 DV115
Surbiton KT6 . . . 138 CN102
Watford WD18 . . . 23 BT43
Woodford Green IG8 . . . 48 EH49
Princes Cl, N4 . . . 65 DP60
NW9 . . . 62 CN56
SW4 off Old Town . . . 101 DJ83
Edgware HA8 . . . 42 CN50
Epping (N.Wld.) CM16 . . . 19 FC25
Sidcup DA14 . . . 126 EX90
South Croydon CR2 . . . 176 DV115
Teddington TW11 . . . 117 CD91
Princes Ct, E1 . . . 202 E1
SE16 . . . 203 M7
Wembley HA9 . . . 62 CL64
Princes Dr, Har. HA1 . . . 61 CE55
Prince's Dr, Lthd. (Oxshott)
KT22 . . . 155 CE112
Princesfield Rd, Wal.Abb. EN9 . . . 16 EH33
Princes Gdns, SW7 . . . 198 A6
W3 . . . 80 CN71
W5 . . . 79 CJ70
Princes Gate, SW7 . . . 198 B5
Princes Gate Ct, SW7 . . . 198 A5
Princes Gate Ms, SW7 . . . 198 A6
Princes La, N10 . . . 65 DH55
Princes Ms, W2
off Hereford Rd . . . 82 DA73
Princes Par, Pot.B. EN6
off High St . . . 12 DC32
Princes Pk, Rain. RM13 . . . 89 FG66
Princes Pk Av, NW11 . . . 63 CY58
Hayes UB3 . . . 77 BR73
Princes Pk Circle, Hayes UB3 . . . 77 BR73
Princes Pk Cl, Hayes UB3 . . . 77 BR73
Princes Pk La, Hayes UB3 . . . 77 BR73
Princes Pk Par, Hayes UB3 . . . 77 BR73
Princes Pl, SW1 . . . 199 L2
W11 . . . 81 CY74
Princes Plain, Brom. BR2 . . . 144 EL101
Princes Ri, SE13 . . . 103 EC82
Princes Riverside Rd, SE16 . . . 203 H2
Princes Rd, N18 . . . 46 DW49
SE20 . . . 123 DX93
SW14 . . . 98 CR83
SW19 . . . 120 DA93
W13 off Broomfield Rd . . . 79 CH74
Ashford TW15 . . . 114 BM92
Buckhurst Hill IG9 . . . 48 EJ47
Dartford DA1, DA2 . . . 127 FG86
Egham TW20 . . . 113 AZ93
Feltham TW13 . . . 115 BT89
Gravesend DA12 . . . 131 GJ90
Ilford IG6 . . . 69 ER56
Kingston upon Thames
KT2 . . . 118 CN94
Richmond TW10 . . . 118 CM85
Richmond (Kew) TW9 . . . 98 CM80
Romford RM1 . . . 71 FG57
Swanley BR8 . . . 127 FG93
Teddington TW11 . . . 117 CD91
Weybridge KT13 . . . 153 BP106
Princess Alice Way, SE28 . . . 105 ER75
Princess Av, Wem. HA9 . . . 62 CL61
Princess Cres, N4 . . . 65 DP61
Princesses Wk, Rich. TW9
off Kew Rd . . . 98 CL80
Princess Gdns, Wok. GU22 . . . 167 BB116
H Princess Grace Hosp, The,
W1 . . . 194 F5
Princess La, Ruis. HA4 . . . 59 BS60
Princess Louise Cl, W2 . . . 194 A6
H Princess Louise Hosp,
W10 . . . 81 CX71
Princess Mary's Rd, Add.
KT15 . . . 152 BJ105
Princess May Rd, N16 . . . 66 DS63
Princess Ms, NW3
off Belsize Cres . . . 82 DD65
Princess Par, Orp. BR6
off Crofton Rd . . . 145 EN104
Princess Pk Manor, N11 . . . 44 DG50
Princes Sq, W2 . . . 82 DB73
Princess Rd, NW1 . . . 82 DG67
NW6 . . . 82 DA68
Croydon CR0 . . . 142 DQ100
Woking GU22 . . . 167 BB116
Princess St, SE1 . . . 200 G7
Princes St, EC2 . . . 197 K9
N17 off Queen St . . . 46 DS51
W1 . . . 195 J9
Bexleyheath DA7 . . . 106 EZ84
Gravesend DA11 . . . 131 GH86
Richmond TW9
off Sheen Rd . . . 118 CL85
Slough SL1 . . . 92 AV75
Sutton SM1 . . . 158 DD105
Princess Way, Red. RH1 . . . 184 DG133
Princes Ter, E13 . . . 86 EH67
Prince St, SE8 . . . 103 DZ79
Watford WD17 . . . 24 BW41
Princes Vw, Dart. DA1 . . . 128 FN88
Princes Way, SW19 . . . 119 CX87
Brentwood CM13 . . . 55 GA46
Buckhurst Hill IG9 . . . 48 EJ47
Croydon CR0 . . . 159 DM106
Ruislip HA4 . . . 60 BY63
West Wickham BR4 . . . 162 EF105
Princes Yd, W11
off Princedale Rd . . . 81 CY74
Princethorpe Ho, W2 . . . 82 DB71
Princethorpe Rd, SE26 . . . 123 DX91
Princeton Ct, SW15
off Felsham Rd . . . 99 CX83
Princeton St, WC1 . . . 196 B6
Pringle Gdns, SW16 . . . 121 DJ91
Purley CR8 . . . 159 DM110
Printers Inn Ct, EC4 . . . 196 D8
Printers Ms, E3 . . . 85 DY67
Printer St, EC4 . . . 196 E8
Printing Ho La, Hayes UB3 . . . 95 BS75
Printing Ho Yd, E2 . . . 197 N2
Print Village, SE15
off Chadwick Rd . . . 102 DT82
Priolo Rd, SE7 . . . 104 EJ78
Prior Av, Sutt. SM2 . . . 158 DE108
Prior Bolton St, N1 . . . 83 DP65
Prior Chase, Grays (Bad.Dene)
RM17 . . . 110 FZ77
Prioress Rd, SE27 . . . 121 DP90
Prioress St, SE1 . . . 201 L7
Prior Rd, Ilf. IG1 . . . 69 EN62
Priors, The, Ashtd. KT21 . . . 171 CK119
Priors Cl, Slou. SL1 . . . 92 AU76
Priors Ct, Wok. GU21 . . . 166 AU118
Priors Cft, E17 . . . 47 DY54
Woking GU22 . . . 167 BA120
Priors Fld, Nthlt. UB5
off Arnold Rd . . . 78 BY65
Priorsford Av, Orp. BR5 . . . 146 EU98
Priors Gdns, Ruis. HA4 . . . 60 BW64
Priors Mead, Enf. EN1 . . . 30 DS39
Priors Pk, Horn. RM12 . . . 72 FJ62
Priors Shop Cen, The, N12
off High Rd . . . 44 DC50
Prior St, SE10 . . . 103 EC80
Priory, The, SE3 . . . 104 EF84
Godstone RH9 . . . 186 DV131
Priory Av, E4 . . . 47 DZ48
E17 . . . 67 EA57
N8 . . . 65 DK56
W4 . . . 98 CS77
Orpington BR5 . . . 145 ER100
Sutton SM3 . . . 157 CX105
Uxbridge (Hare.) UB9 . . . 58 BJ56
Wembley HA0 . . . 61 CF63
Priory Cl, E4 . . . 47 DZ48
E18 . . . 48 EG53
N3 off Church Cres . . . 43 CZ53
N14 . . . 29 DH43
N20 . . . 43 CZ45
SW19 off High Path . . . 140 DB95
Beckenham BR3 . . . 143 DY97
Brentwood CM15 . . . 54 FU43
Chislehurst BR7 . . . 145 EM95
Dartford DA1 . . . 128 FJ85
Hampton TW12
off Priory Gdns . . . 136 BZ95
Hayes UB3 . . . 77 BV73
Ruislip HA4 . . . 59 BT60
Stanmore HA7 . . . 41 CF48
Sunbury-on-Thames TW16
off Staines Rd E . . . 115 BU94
Uxbridge (Denh.) UB9 . . . 58 BG62
Uxbridge (Hare.) UB9 . . . 58 BH56
Walton-on-Thames KT12 . . . 135 BU104
Wembley (Sudbury) HA0 . . . 61 CF63
Woking GU21 . . . 151 BD113
Priory Ct, E17 . . . 67 DZ55
EC4 off Ludgate Hill . . . 83 DP72
SW8 . . . 101 DK81
Bushey WD23
off Sparrows Herne . . . 40 CC46
Epsom KT17
off Old Schools La . . . 157 CT109
Priory Ct Est, E17
off Priory Ct . . . 47 DZ54
Priory Cres, SE19 . . . 122 DQ94
Sutton SM3 . . . 157 CX105
Wembley HA0 . . . 61 CG62
Priory Dr, SE2 . . . 106 EX78
Stanmore HA7 . . . 41 CF48
Priory Fld Dr, Edg. HA8 . . . 42 CP49
Priory Flds, Dart. (Fnghm.)
DA4 . . . 148 FM103
Priory Gdns, N6 . . . 65 DH58
SE25 . . . 142 DT98
SW13 . . . 99 CT83
Priory Gdns, W4 . . . 98 CS77
W5 off Hanger La . . . 80 CL69
Ashford TW15 . . . 115 BR92
Dartford DA1 . . . 128 FK85
Hampton TW12 . . . 116 BZ94
Uxbridge (Hare.) UB9 . . . 58 BJ56
Wembley HA0 . . . 61 CG63
Priory Gate, Wal.Cr. EN8 . . . 15 DZ27
Priory Grn, Stai. TW18 . . . 114 BH92
Priory Grn Est, N1 . . . 83 DM68
Priory Gro, SW8 . . . 101 DL81
Barnet EN5 . . . 28 DA43
Romford RM3 . . . 52 FL48
Priory Hill, Dart. DA1 . . . 128 FK85
Wembley HA0 . . . 61 CG63
Priory La, SW15 . . . 118 CS86
Dartford (Fnghm.) DA4 . . . 148 FM102
Richmond TW9
off Forest Rd . . . 98 CN80
West Molesey KT8 . . . 136 CA98
Priory Ms, SW8 . . . 101 DK81
Hornchurch RM11 . . . 71 FH60
Staines TW18
off Chestnut Manor Cl . . . 114 BH92
Priory Pk, SE3 . . . 104 EF83
Priory Pk Rd, NW6 . . . 81 CZ67
Wembley HA0 . . . 61 CG63
Priory Path, Rom. RM3 . . . 52 FL48
Priory Pl, Dart. DA1 . . . 128 FK86
Walton-on-Thames KT12 . . . 135 BU104
Priory Rd, E6 . . . 86 EK67
N8 . . . 65 DK56
NW6 . . . 82 DB67
SW19 . . . 120 DD94
W4 . . . 98 CR76
Barking IG11 . . . 87 ER66
Chessington KT9 . . . 138 CL104
Croydon CR0 . . . 141 DN101
Gerrards Cross (Chal.St.P.)
SL9 . . . 56 AW55
Hampton TW12 . . . 116 BZ94
Hounslow TW3 . . . 116 CC85
Loughton IG10 . . . 32 EL42
Richmond TW9 . . . 98 CN79
Romford RM3 . . . 52 FL48
Sutton SM3 . . . 157 CX105
Priory Rd N, Dart. DA1 . . . 108 FK84
Priory Rd S, Dart. DA1 . . . 128 FK85
Priory Shop Cen, Dart. DA1 . . . 128 FL86
Priory St, E3
off St. Leonards St . . . 85 EB69
Priory Ter, NW6 . . . 82 DB67
Sunbury-on-Thames TW16
off Staines Rd E . . . 115 BU94
Priory Vw, Bushey (Bushey Hth.)
WD23 . . . 41 CE45
Priory Wk, SW10 . . . 100 DC78
Priory Way, Ger.Cr. (Chal.St.P.)
SL9 . . . 56 AX55
Harrow HA2 . . . 60 CB56
Slough (Datchet) SL3 . . . 92 AV80
Southall UB2 . . . 96 BX76
West Drayton UB7 . . . 94 BL79
Pritchard's Rd, E2 . . . 84 DU67
Pritchett Cl, Enf. EN3
off Government Row . . . 31 EA37
Priter Rd, SE16 . . . 202 C7
Priter Way, SE16
off Dockley Rd . . . 102 DU76
Private Rd, Enf. EN1 . . . 30 DS43
Probert Rd, SW2 . . . 121 DN85
Probyn Rd, SW2 . . . 121 DP89
Procter St, WC1 . . . 196 B7
Proctor Cl, Mitch. CR4 . . . 140 DG95
Proctors Cl, Felt. TW14 . . . 115 BU88
Profumo Rd, Walt. KT12 . . . 154 BX106
Progress Business Pk, Croy.
CR0 . . . 141 DM103
Progress Way, N22 . . . 45 DN53
Croydon CR0 . . . 141 DM103
Enfield EN1 . . . 30 DU43
Promenade, The, W4 . . . 98 CS81
Promenade App Rd, W4 . . . 98 CS80
Promenade de Verdun, Pur.
CR8 . . . 159 DK111
Promenade Mans, Edg. HA8
off Hale La . . . 42 CP50
Prospect Business Pk, Loug.
IG10 . . . 33 EQ42
Prospect Cl, SE26 . . . 122 DV91
Belvedere DA17 . . . 106 FA77
Hounslow TW3 . . . 96 BZ81
Ruislip HA4 . . . 60 BX59
Prospect Cotts, SW18
off Point Pleasant . . . 100 DA84
Prospect Cres, Twick. TW2 . . . 116 CC86
Prospect Gro, Grav. DA12 . . . 131 GK87
Prospect Hill, E17 . . . 67 EB56
Prospect La, Egh. (Eng.Grn.)
TW20 . . . 112 AT92
Prospect Pl, E1 . . . 202 F2
N2 . . . 64 DD56
N7 off Parkhurst Rd . . . 65 DL63
N17 . . . 46 DS53
NW2 off Ridge Rd . . . 63 CZ62
NW3 off Holly Wk . . . 64 DC63
Bromley BR2 . . . 144 EH97
Dartford DA1 . . . 128 FL86
Epsom KT17
off Clayton Rd . . . 156 CS113
Gravesend DA12 . . . 131 GK87
Grays RM17 . . . 110 GB79
Romford RM5 . . . 51 FC54
Staines TW18 . . . 113 BF92
Prospect Quay, SW18 . . . 100 DA84
Prospect Ring, N2 . . . 64 DD55
Prospect Rd, NW2 . . . 63 CZ62
Barnet EN5 . . . 28 DA43
Hornchurch RM11 . . . 72 FM55
Sevenoaks TN13 . . . 191 FJ123
Surbiton KT6 . . . 137 CJ100
Waltham Cross (Chsht.)
EN8 . . . 14 DW29
Woodford Green IG8 . . . 48 EJ50
Prospect St, SE16 . . . 202 E6
Prospect Vale, SE18 . . . 104 EL77
Prospect Way, Brwd. CM13 . . . 55 GE42
Prospero Rd, N19 . . . 65 DJ60
Prossers, Tad. KT20
off Croffets . . . 173 CX121
Protea Cl, E16 off Hermit Rd . . . 86 EF70
Prothero Gdns, NW4 . . . 63 CV57
Prothero Ho, NW10 . . . 80 CR66
Prothero Rd, SW6 . . . 99 CY80
Prout Gro, NW10 . . . 62 CS63
Prout Rd, E5 . . . 66 DV62
Provence St, N1
off St. Peters St . . . 84 DQ68
Providence Ct, W1 . . . 194 G10
Providence La, Hayes UB3 . . . 95 BR80
Providence Pl, N1
off Upper St . . . 83 DP67
Epsom KT17 . . . 156 CS112
Romford RM5 . . . 50 EZ54
Woking GU22 . . . 152 BG114
Providence Rd, West Dr. UB7 . . . 76 BL74
Providence Row, N1
off Pentonville Rd . . . 83 DM68
Providence Row Cl, E2
off Ainsley St . . . 84 DV69
Providence Sq, SE1
off Jacob St . . . 102 DT75
Providence St, N1
off St. Peters St . . . 84 DQ68
Greenhithe DA9 . . . 129 FU85
Providence Yd, E2
off Ezra St . . . 84 DU69
Provident Ind Est, Hayes UB3 . . . 95 BU75
Provost Est, N1 . . . 197 K2
Provost Rd, NW3 . . . 82 DF66
Provost St, N1 . . . 197 K3
Prowse Av, Bushey (Bushey Hth.)
WD23 . . . 40 CC47
Prowse Pl, NW1 off Bonny St . . . 83 DH66
Pruden Cl, N14 . . . 45 DJ47
Prudent Pas, EC2 . . . 197 J8
Prune Hill, Egh. (Eng.Grn.)
TW20 . . . 112 AX94
Prusom St, E1 . . . 202 E3
Pryor Cl, Abb.L. WD5 . . . 7 BT32
Pryors, The, NW3 . . . 64 DD62
★ PS Tattershall Castle,
SW1 . . . 200 A3
★ Public Record Office, Rich.
TW9 . . . 98 CP80
Puck La, Wal.Abb. EN9 . . . 15 ED29
Puddenhole Cotts, Bet. RH3 . . . 182 CN133
Pudding La, EC3 . . . 201 L1
Chigwell IG7 . . . 49 ET46
Sevenoaks (Seal) TN15
off Church St . . . 191 FN121
DLR Pudding Mill Lane . . . 85 EB67
Pudding Mill La, E15 . . . 85 EB67
Puddle Dock, EC4 . . . 196 G10
Puddledock La, Dart. DA2 . . . 127 FE92
Westerham TN16 . . . 189 ET133
Puers La, Beac. (Jordans)
HP9 . . . 36 AS51
Puffin Cl, Bark. IG11 . . . 88 EV69
Beckenham BR3 . . . 143 DX99
Puffin Ter, Ilf. IG5
off Tiptree Cres . . . 69 EN55
Pulborough Rd, SW18 . . . 119 CZ87
Pulborough Way, Houns. TW4 . . . 96 BW84
Pulford Rd, N15 . . . 66 DR58
Pulham Av, N2 . . . 64 DC56
Puller Rd, Barn. EN5 . . . 27 CY40
Pulleyns Av, E6 . . . 86 EL69
Pullman Ct, SW2 . . . 121 DL88
Pullman Gdns, SW15 . . . 119 CW86
Pullman Pl, SE9 . . . 124 EL85
Pullmans Pl, Stai. TW18 . . . 114 BG92
Pulross Rd, SW9 . . . 101 DM83
Pulteney Cl, E3 . . . 85 DZ67
Pulteney Gdns, E18
off Pulteney Rd . . . 68 EH55
Pulteney Rd, E18 . . . 68 EH55
Pulteney Ter, N1 . . . 83 DM67
Pulton Pl, SW6 . . . 100 DA80
Puma Ct, E1 . . . 197 P6
Pump All, Brent. TW8 . . . 97 CK80
Pump Cl, Nthlt. UB5
off Union Rd . . . 78 CA68
Pump Ct, EC4 . . . 196 D9
Pumphandle Path, N2
off Tarling Rd . . . 44 DC54
Pump Hill, Loug. IG10 . . . 33 EM40
Pump Ho Cl, SE16 . . . 202 G5
Bromley BR2 . . . 144 EF96
Pumping Sta Rd, W4 . . . 98 CS80
Pump La, SE14 . . . 102 DW80
Chesham HP5 . . . 4 AS32
Hayes UB3 . . . 95 BV75
Orpington BR6 . . . 165 FB106
Pump Pail N, Croy. CR0
off Old Town . . . 142 DQ104
Pump Pail S, Croy. CR0
off Southbridge Rd . . . 142 DQ104
Pundersons Gdns, E2 . . . 84 DV69
Punjab La, Sthl. UB1
off Herbert Rd . . . 78 BZ74
Purbeck Av, N.Mal. KT3 . . . 139 CT100
Purbeck Cl, Red. RH1 . . . 185 DK128
Purbeck Dr, NW2 . . . 63 CY61
Woking GU21 . . . 151 AZ114
Purbeck Rd, Horn. RM11 . . . 71 FG60
Purberry Gro, Epsom KT17 . . . 157 CT110
Purbrock Av, Wat. WD25 . . . 24 BW36
Purbrook Est, SE1 . . . 201 N5
Purbrook St, SE1 . . . 201 N6
Purcell Cl, Borwd. WD6 . . . 25 CK39
Kenley CR8 . . . 160 DR114
Purcell Cres, SW6 . . . 99 CY80
Purcell Ms, NW10
off Suffolk Rd . . . 80 CS66
Purcell Rd, Grnf. UB6 . . . 78 CB71
Purcells Av, Edg. HA8 . . . 42 CN50
Purcells Cl, Ashtd. KT21
off Albert Rd . . . 172 CM118
Purcell St, N1 . . . 84 DS68
Purchese St, NW1 . . . 83 DK68

Pur - Que

Purdy St, E3 85 EB70
Purelake Ms, SE13 103 ED83
PURFLEET 108 FP77
⇌ Purfleet 108 FN78
Purfleet Bypass, Purf. RM19 108 FP77
Purfleet Ind Pk, S.Ock. (Aveley) RM15 108 FM75
Purfleet Rd, S.Ock. (Aveley) RM15 108 FN75
Purfleet Thames Terminal, Purf. RM19 108 FQ8
Purland Cl, Dag. RM8 70 EZ60
Purland Rd, SE28 105 ET75
Purleigh Av, Wdf.Grn. IG8 48 EL51
PURLEY 159 DM111
⇌ Purley 159 DP112
H Purley & District War Mem Hosp, Pur. CR8 159 DN111
Purley Av, NW2 63 CY62
Purley Bury Av, Pur. CR8 160 DQ110
Purley Bury Cl, Pur. CR8 160 DQ111
Purley Cl, Ilf. IG5 49 EN54
Purley Downs Rd, Pur. CR8 160 DQ110
South Croydon CR2 160 DR111
Purley Hill, Pur. CR8 159 DP112
Purley Knoll, Pur. CR8 159 DM111
⇌ Purley Oaks 160 DQ109
Purley Oaks Rd, S.Croy. CR2 160 DR109
Purley Par, Pur. CR8 off High St 159 DN111
Purley Pk Rd, Pur. CR8 159 DP110
Purley Pl, N1 off Islington Pk St 83 DP66
Purley Ri, Pur. CR8 159 DM112
Purley Rd, N9 46 DR48
Purley CR8 159 DN111
South Croydon CR2 160 DR108
Purley Vale, Pur. CR8 159 DP113
Purley Way, Croy. CR0 141 DM101
Purley CR8 159 DN108
Purley Way Cres, Croy. CR0 off Purley Way 141 DM101
Purlieu Way, Epp. (They.B.) CM16 33 ES35
Purlings Rd, Bushey WD23 24 CB43
Purneys Rd, SE9 104 EK84
Purrett Rd, SE18 105 ET78
Purser's Cross Rd, SW6 99 CZ81
Pursewardens Cl, W13 79 CJ74
Pursley Gdns, Borwd. WD6 26 CN38
Pursley Rd, NW7 43 CV52
Purves Rd, NW10 81 CW68
Puteaux Ho, E2 85 DX68
PUTNEY, SW15 99 CY84
⇌ Putney 99 CY84
⊖ Putney Bridge 99 CY83
Putney Br, SW6 99 CY83
SW15 99 CY83
Putney Br App, SW6 99 CY83
Putney Br Rd, SW15 99 CY84
SW18 120 DA85
Putney Common, SW15 99 CW83
Putney Ex Shop Cen, SW15 99 CX84
Putney Gdns, Rom. (Chad.Hth.) RM6 off Heathfield Pk Dr 70 EV58
PUTNEY HEATH, SW15 119 CW86
Putney Heath, SW15 119 CW86
Putney Heath La, SW15 119 CX86
Putney High St, SW15 99 CX84
Putney Hill, SW15 119 CX86
H Putney Hosp, SW15 99 CW82
Putney Pk Av, SW15 99 CU84
Putney Pk La, SW15 99 CV84
Putney Rd, Enf. EN3 31 DX36
PUTNEY VALE, SW15 119 CT90
Puttenham Cl, Wat. WD19 40 BW48
Pycroft Way, N9 46 DU49
Pye Cl, Cat. CR3 off St. Lawrence Way 176 DR123
Pyecombe Cor, N12 43 CZ49
Pyghtle, The, Uxb. (Denh.) UB9 58 BG60
Pylbrook Rd, Sutt. SM1 140 DA104
Pyle Hill, Wok. GU22 166 AX124
Pylon Way, Croy. CR0 141 DL102
Pym Cl, Barn. EN4 28 DD43
Pymers Mead, SE21 122 DQ88
Pymmes Cl, N13 45 DM50
N17 46 DV53
Pymmes Gdns N, N9 46 DT48
Pymmes Gdns S, N9 46 DT48
Pymmes Grn Rd, N11 45 DH49
Pymmes Rd, N13 45 DL51
Pymms Brook Dr, Barn. EN4 28 DE42
Pym Orchard, West. (Brasted) TN16 180 EW124
Pym Pl, Grays RM17 110 GA77
Pynchester Cl, Uxb. UB10 58 BN61
Pyne Rd, Surb. KT6 138 CN102
Pynest Grn La, Wal.Abb. EN9 32 EG38
Pyne Ter, SW19 off Windlesham Gro 119 CX88
Pynfolds, SE16 202 E5
Pynham Cl, SE2 106 EU76
Pynnacles Cl, Stan. HA7 41 CH50
Pyrcroft La, Wey. KT13 153 BP106
Pyrcroft Rd, Cher. KT16 133 BF101
PYRFORD, Wok. 167 BE115
Pyrford Common Rd, Wok. GU22 167 BD116
★ Pyrford Ct, Wok. GU22 167 BE117
Pyrford Ct, Wok. GU22 167 BE117
PYRFORD GREEN, Wok. 168 BH117
Pyrford Heath, Wok. GU22 167 BF116
Pyrford Lock, Wok. (Wisley) GU23 168 BJ116
Pyrford Rd, W.Byf. KT14 152 BG113
Woking GU22 152 BG114
PYRFORD VILLAGE, Wok. 168 BG118
Pyrford Wds Cl, Wok. GU22 167 BF115
Pyrford Wds Rd, Wok. GU22 167 BE115
Pyrland Rd, N5 66 DR64
Richmond TW10 118 CM86
Pyrles Grn, Loug. IG10 33 EP39
Pyrles La, Loug. IG10 33 EP40
Pyrmont Gro, SE27 121 DP90
Pyrmont Rd, W4 98 CN79
Ilford IG1 off High Rd 69 EQ61
Pytchley Cres, SE19 122 DQ93
Pytchley Rd, SE22 102 DS8

Q

Quadrangle, The, W2 194 B8
Quadrangle Ms, Stan. HA7 41 CJ52
Quadrant, The, SE24 off Herne Hill 122 DQ85
SW20 139 CY95
Bexleyheath DA7 106 EX80
Epsom KT17 156 CS113
Purfleet RM19 108 FQ77
Richmond TW9 98 CL84
Sutton SM2 158 DC107
Quadrant Arc, W1 199 L1
Romford RM1 71 FE57
Quadrant Cl, NW4 off The Burroughs 63 CV57
Quadrant Gro, NW5 64 DF64
Quadrant Ho, Sutt. SM2 158 DC107
Quadrant Rd, Rich. TW9 97 CK84
Thornton Heath CR7 141 DP98
Quadrant Way, Wey. KT13 off Weybridge Rd 152 BM105
Quad Rd, Wem. HA9 off Courtenay Rd 61 CK62
Quaggy Wk, SE3 104 EG84
Quail Gdns, S.Croy. CR2 161 DY110
Quainton St, NW10 62 CR62
Quaker Cl, Sev. TN13 191 FK123
Quaker Ct, E1 197 P5
Quaker La, Sthl. UB2 96 CA76
Waltham Abbey EN9 15 EC34
Quakers Course, NW9 43 CT53
Quakers Hall La, Sev. TN13 191 FJ122
Quakers La, Islw. TW7 97 CG81
Potters Bar EN6 12 DB30
Quaker's Pl, E7 68 EK64
Quaker St, E1 197 P5
Quakers Wk, N21 30 DR44
Quality Ct, WC2 196 D8
Quality St, Red. RH1 185 DH128
Quantock Cl, Hayes UB3 95 BR80
Slough SL3 93 BA78
Quantock Dr, Wor.Pk. KT4 139 CW103
Quantock Gdns, NW2 63 CX61
Quantock Rd, Bexh. DA7 off Cumbrian Av 107 FE82
Quarles Cl, Rom. RM5 50 FA52
Quarley Way, SE15 off Daniel Gdns 102 DT80
Quarrendon St, SW6 100 DA82
Quarr Rd, Cars. SM5 140 DD100
Quarry, The, Bet. RH3 off Station Rd 182 CS132
Quarry Cl, Lthd. KT22 171 CK121
Oxted RH8 188 EE130
Quarry Cotts, Sev. TN13 190 FG123
Quarry Gdns, Lthd. KT22 171 CK121
Quarry Hill, Grays RM17 110 GA78
Sevenoaks TN15 191 FK123
Quarry Hill Pk, Reig. RH2 184 DC131
Quarry Ms, Purf. RM19 off Fanns Ri 108 FN77
Quarry Pk Rd, Sutt. SM1 157 CZ107
Quarry Ri, Sutt. SM1 157 CZ107
Quarry Rd, SW18 120 DC86
Godstone RH9 186 DW128
Oxted RH8 188 EE130
Quarryside Business Pk, Red. RH1 185 DH130
Quarterdeck, The, E14 203 P5
Quartermaine Av, Wok. GU22 167 AZ122
Quarter Mile La, E10 67 EB63
Quaves Rd, Slou. SL3 92 AV76
Quay La, Green. DA9 109 FV84
Quayside Wk, Kings.T. KT1 off Bishop's Hall 137 CK96
Quay W, Tedd. TW11 117 CH92
Quebec Av, West. TN16 189 ER126
★ Quebec Ho (Wolfe's Ho), West. TN16 189 ER126
Quebec Ms, W1 194 E9
Quebec Rd, Hayes UB4 78 BW73
Ilford IG1, IG2 69 EP59
Tilbury RM18 111 GG82
Quebec Sq, West. TN16 189 ER126
Quebec Way, SE16 203 J5
Queen Adelaide Rd, SE20 122 DW93
Queen Alexandra's Ct, SW19 119 CZ92
Queen Alexandra's Way, Epsom KT19 156 CN112
Queen Anne Av, N15 off Suffield Rd 66 DT57
Bromley BR2 144 EF97
Queen Anne Dr, Esher (Clay.) KT10 155 CE108
Queen Anne Ms, W1 195 J7
Queen Anne Rd, E9 85 DX65
Queen Anne's Cl, Twick. TW2 117 CD90
Queen Anne's Gdns, W4 98 CS76
Queen Annes Gdns, W5 98 CL75
Enfield EN1 30 DS44
Leatherhead KT22 off Upper Fairfield Rd 171 CH121
Queen Anne's Gdns, Mitch. CR4 140 DF97
Queen Anne's Gate, SW1 199 M5
Bexleyheath DA7 106 EX83
Queen Anne's Gro, W4 98 CS76
Queen Annes Gro, W5 98 CL75
Enfield EN1 46 DR45
Queen Anne's Ms, Lthd. KT22 off Fairfield Rd 171 CH121
Queen Annes Pl, Enf. EN1 30 DS44
Queen Annes Ter, Lthd. KT22 off Upper Fairfield Rd 171 CH121
Queen Anne St, W1 195 H8
Queen Anne's Wk, WC1 off Guilford St 83 DL70
Queen Anne Ter, E1 202 E1
Queenborough Gdns, Chis. BR7 125 ER93
Ilford IG2 69 EN56
Queen Caroline Est, W6 99 CW78
Queen Caroline St, W6 99 CW77
H Queen Charlotte & Chelsea Hosp, W12 81 CU72
Queendale Ct, Wok. GU21 off Roundthorn Way 166 AT116
Queen Elizabeth Ct, Brox. EN10 off Groom Rd 15 DZ26
Waltham Abbey EN9 off Greenwich Way 31 EC36
Queen Elizabeth Gdns, Mord. SM4 140 DA98
★ Queen Elizabeth Hall & Purcell Room, SE1 200 B2
H Queen Elizabeth Hosp, SE18 104 EL80
Queen Elizabeth Pl, Til. RM18 111 GG84
Queen Elizabeth Rd, E17 67 DY55
Kingston upon Thames KT2 138 CM95
Queen Elizabeths Cl, N16 66 DR61
Queen Elizabeths Dr, N14 45 DL46
Queen Elizabeth's Dr, Croy. (New Adgtn.) CR0 161 ED110
Queen Elizabeth II Br, Dart. DA1 109 FR82
Purfleet RM19 109 FR82
★ Queen Elizabeth II Conf Cen, SW1 199 N5
Queen Elizabeth's Gdns, Croy. (New Adgtn.) CR0 off Queen Elizabeth's Dr 161 ED110
★ Queen Elizabeth's Hunting Lodge, Epping Forest, E4 48 EF45
Queen Elizabeth St, SE1 201 N4
Queen Elizabeths Wk, N16 66 DR61
Queen Elizabeth's Wk, Wall. SM6 159 DK105
Queen Elizabeth Wk, SW13 99 CV81
Windsor SL4 92 AS82
Queen Elizabeth Way, Wok. GU22 167 AZ119
Queenhill Rd, S.Croy. CR2 160 DV110
Queenhithe, EC4 197 J10
Queen Margaret's Gro, N1 66 DS64
Queen Mary Av, Mord. SM4 139 CX99
Queen Mary Cl, Rom. RM1 71 FF58
Surbiton KT6 138 CN104
Woking GU22 167 BC116
Queen Mary Rd, SE19 121 DP93
Shepperton TW17 135 BQ96
Queen Mary's Av, Cars. SM5 158 DF108
Queen Marys Av, Wat. WD18 23 BS42
Queen Marys Ct, Wal.Abb. EN9 off Greenwich Way 31 EC35
Queen Marys Dr, Add. (New Haw) KT15 151 BF110
★ Queen Mary's Gdns, NW1 off Regent's Pk 194 F3
H Queen Mary's Hosp, NW3 64 DC62
H Queen Mary's Hosp, Sid. DA14 126 EU93
H Queen Mary's Hosp for Children, Cars. SM5 140 DC102
H Queen Mary's Uni Hosp (Roehampton), SW15 119 CU86
Queen Mother's Dr, Uxb. (Denh.) UB9 57 BF58
Queen of Denmark Ct, SE16 203 M6
Queens Acre, Sutt. SM3 157 CX108
Queens All, Epp. CM16 17 ET31
Queens Av, N3 44 DC52
N10 64 DG55
N20 44 DD47
Queen's Av, N21 45 DP46
Queens Av, Felt. TW13 116 BW91
Greenford UB6 78 CB72
Stanmore HA7 61 CJ55
Watford WD18 23 BT42
West Byfleet (Byfleet) KT14 152 BK112
Woodford Green IG8 48 EH50
Queensberry Ms W, SW7 off Queen's Gate 100 DD77
Queensberry Pl, E12 68 EK64
SW7 100 DD77
Richmond TW9 off Friars La 117 CK85
Queensberry Way, SW7 off Harrington Rd 100 DD77
Queensborough Ms, W2 off Porchester Ter 82 DC73
Queensborough Pas, W2 off Porchester Ter 82 DC73
Queensborough S Bldgs, W2 off Porchester Ter 82 DC73
Queensborough Studios, W2 off Porchester Ter 82 DC73
Queensborough Ter, W2 82 DB73
Queensbridge Pk, Islw. TW7 117 CE85
Queensbridge Rd, E2 84 DT67
E8 84 DT66
QUEENSBURY, Har. 61 CK55
⊖ Queensbury 62 CM55
Queensbury Circle Par, Har. HA3 off Streatfield Rd 62 CL55
Stanmore HA7 off Streatfield Rd 62 CL55
Queensbury Rd, NW9 62 CR59
Wembley HA0 80 CM68
Queensbury Sta Par, Edg. HA8 62 CM55
Queensbury St, N1 84 DQ66
Queen's Circ, SW8 off Queenstown Rd 101 DH80
SW11 off Queenstown Rd 101 DH80
Queens Cl, Edg. HA8 42 CN50
Tadworth KT20 173 CU124
Wallington SM6 off Queens Rd 159 DH106
Queens Cl, Wind. (Old Wind.) SL4 112 AU85
★ Queens Club (Tennis Cen), W14 99 CY78
Queens Club Gdns, W14 99 CY79
Queens Ct, SE23 122 DW88
Richmond TW10 118 CM86
Slough SL1 74 AT73
Queenscourt, Wem. HA9 62 CL63
Queens Ct, Wey. KT13 153 BR106
Woking GU22 off Hill Vw Rd 167 AZ118
Queens Ct Ride, Cob. KT11 153 BU113
Queen's Cres, NW5 82 DG65
Queens Cres, Rich. TW10 118 CM85
Queenscroft Rd, SE9 124 EK85
Queensdale Cres, W11 81 CX74
Queensdale Pl, W11 81 CY74
Queensdale Rd, W11 81 CX74
Queensdale Wk, W11 81 CY74
Queensdown Rd, E5 66 DV63
Queens Dr, E10 67 EA59
N4 65 DP61
W3 80 CM72
W5 80 CM72
Abbots Langley WD5 7 BT32
Leatherhead (Oxshott) KT22 154 CC111
Queen's Dr, Slou. SL3 75 AZ66
Queens Dr, Surb. KT5 138 CN101
Thames Ditton KT7 137 CG101
Waltham Cross EN8 15 EA34
Queens Dr, The, Rick. (Mill End) WD3 37 BF45
Queens Elm Par, SW3 off Old Ch St 100 DD78
Queen's Elm Sq, SW3 off Old Ch St 100 DD78
Queensferry Wk, N17 off Jarrow Rd 66 DV56
★ Queen's Gall, The, SW1 199 J5
Queens Gdns, NW4 63 CW57
W2 82 DC73
W5 79 CJ70
Dartford DA2 128 FP88
Queen's Gdns, Houns. TW5 96 BY81
Queens Gdns, Rain. RM13 89 FD68
Upminster RM14 73 FT58
Queen's Gate, SW7 100 DD77
Queensgate, Cob. KT11 154 BX112
Waltham Cross EN8 15 DZ34
Queen's Gate Gdns, SW7 100 DC76
Queens Gate Gdns, SW15 off Upper Richmond Rd 99 CV84
Queensgate Gdns, Chis. BR7 145 ER95
Queen's Gate Ms, SW7 100 DC75
Queensgate Pl, NW6 82 DA66
Queen's Gate Pl, SW7 100 DC76
Queen's Gate Pl Ms, SW7 100 DC76
Queen's Gate Ter, SW7 100 DC76
Queen's Gro, NW8 82 DD67
Queen's Gro Ms, NW8 82 DD67
Queens Gro Rd, E4 47 ED46
Queen's Head St, N1 83 DP67
Queens Head Yd, SE1 201 K3
Queens Ho, Tedd. TW11 117 CF93
★ Queen's Ice Rink, W2 off Queensway 82 DB73
Queensland Av, N18 46 DQ51
SW19 140 DB95
Queensland Cl, E17 47 DZ54
Queensland Ho, E16 off Rymill St 87 EN74
Queensland Pl, N7 off Queensland Rd 65 DN63
Queensland Rd, N7 65 DN63
Queens La, N10 65 DH55
Ashford TW15 off Clarendon Rd 114 BM91
Queens Mkt, E13 off Green St 86 EJ67
Queensmead, NW8 82 DD67
Leatherhead KT22 154 CC111
Slough (Datchet) SL3 92 AV81
Queensmead Av, Epsom KT17 157 CV110
Queensmead Rd, Brom. BR2 144 EF96
Queensmere Cl, SW19 119 CX89
Queensmere Rd, SW19 119 CX89
Slough SL1 off Wellington St 92 AU75
Queensmere Shop Cen, Slou. SL1 92 AT75
Queens Ms, W2 82 DB73
Queensmill Rd, SW6 99 CX80
Queens Par, N11 off Colney Hatch La 44 DF50
W5 80 CM72
Queens Par Cl, N11 off Colney Hatch La 44 DF50
⇌ Queen's Park 81 CY68
⊖ Queen's Park 81 CY68
Queens Pk Ct, W10 81 CX69
Queens Pk Gdns, Felt. TW13 off Vernon Rd 115 BU90
★ Queens Park Rangers FC, W12 81 CV74
Queens Pk Rd, Cat. CR3 176 DS123
Romford RM3 52 FM53
Queens Pas, Chis. BR7 off High St 125 EP93
Queens Pl, Mord. SM4 140 DA98
Watford WD17 24 BW41
Queen's Prom, Kings.T. KT1 off Portsmouth Rd 137 CK97
Queen Sq, WC1 196 A5
Queen Sq Pl, WC1 196 A5
Queens Reach, E.Mol. KT8 137 CE98
Queens Ride, SW13 99 CU83
SW15 99 CU83
Queen's Ride, Rich. TW10 118 CP88
Queens Ri, Rich. TW10 118 CM86
Queens Rd, E11 67 ED59
E13 86 EH67
Queen's Rd, E17 67 DZ58
Queens Rd, N3 44 DC53
N9 46 DV48
Queen's Rd, N11 45 DL52
Queens Rd, NW4 63 CW57
SE14 102 DV81
SE15 102 DV81
SW14 98 CR83
SW19 119 CZ93
W5 80 CL72
Barking IG11 87 EQ66
Barnet EN5 27 CX41
Beckenham BR3 143 DY96
Brentwood CM14 54 FW48
Bromley BR1 144 EG96
Buckhurst Hill IG9 48 EH47
Chislehurst BR7 125 EP93
Queen's Rd, Croy. CR0 141 DP100
Queens Rd, Egh. TW20 113 AZ93
Enfield EN1 30 DS42
Epping (N.Wld.Bas.) CM16 19 FB26
Queen's Rd, Erith DA8 107 FE79
Queens Rd, Felt. TW13 115 BV88
Gravesend DA12 131 GJ90
Hampton (Hmptn.H.) TW12 116 CB91
Hayes UB3 77 BS72
Queen's Rd, Houns. TW3 96 CB83
Queens Rd, Kings.T. KT2 118 CN94
Loughton IG10 32 EL41
Mitcham CR4 140 DD97
Morden SM4 140 DA98
New Malden KT3 139 CT98
Richmond TW10 118 CL87
Queen's Rd, Slou. SL1 74 AT73
Queens Rd, Slou. (Datchet) SL3 92 AU81
Southall UB2 96 BX75
Sutton SM2 158 DA110
Queen's Rd, Tedd. TW11 117 CE93
Thames Ditton KT7 137 CF99
Queens Rd, Twick. TW1 117 CF88
Queen's Rd, Uxb. UB8 76 BJ69
Queens Rd, Wall. SM6 159 DH106
Waltham Cross EN8 15 DY34
Walton-on-Thames KT12 153 BV106
Watford WD17 24 BW42
Queen's Rd, Well. DA16 106 EV82
Queens Rd, West Dr. UB7 94 BM75
Weybridge KT13 153 BQ105
⇌ Queens Road Peckham 102 DW81
Queens Rd W, E13 86 EG68
Queen's Row, SE17 102 DR79
Queens Ter, E13 86 EH67
Queen's Ter, NW8 82 DD68
Queens Ter, Islw. TW7 97 CG84
Queens Ter Cotts, W7 off Boston Rd 97 CE75
Queensthorpe Rd, SE26 123 DX91
★ Queen's Twr, SW7 100 DD76
Queenstown Gdns, Rain. RM13 89 FF69
Queenstown Ms, SW8 off Queenstown Rd 101 DH82
Queenstown Rd, SW8 101 DH79
⇌ Queenstown Road (Battersea) 101 DH81
Queen St, EC4 197 J10
N17 46 DS51
W1 199 H2
Bexleyheath DA7 106 EZ83
Brentwood CM14 54 FW50
Chertsey KT16 134 BG102
Croydon CR0 off Church Rd 142 DQ104
Erith DA8 107 FE79
Gravesend DA12 131 GH86
Kings Langley (Chipper.) WD4 6 BG32
Romford RM7 71 FD58
Queen St Pl, EC4 201 J1
Queensville Rd, SW12 121 DK87
Queens Wk, E4 off The Green Wk 47 ED46
NW9 62 CQ61
Queen's Wk, SE1 200 B3
SW1 199 K3
Queens Wk, W5 79 CJ70
Ashford TW15 114 BK91
Queen's Wk, Har. HA1 61 CE56
Queens Wk, Ruis. HA4 60 BX62
⊖ Queensway 82 DB73
Queens Way, NW4 63 CW57
Queensway, W2 82 DB72
Queensway, Croy. CR0 159 DM107
Queensway, Enf. EN3 30 DV42
Queens Way, Felt. TW13 116 BW91
Queensway, Orp. BR5 145 EQ99
Queens Way, Rad. (Shenley) WD7 10 CL32
Queensway, Red. RH1 184 DF133
Sunbury-on-Thames TW16 135 BV96
Queens Way, Wal.Cr. EN8 15 DZ34
Queensway, W.Wick. BR4 144 EE104
Queensway, The, Ger.Cr. (Chal.St.P.) SL9 56 AX55
Queensway N, Walt. KT12 off Robinsway 154 BW105
Queensway S, Walt. KT12 off Trenchard Cl 154 BW106
Queens Well Av, N20 44 DE48
Queenswood Av, E17 47 EC53
Brentwood CM13 55 GD43
Hampton TW12 116 CB93
Hounslow TW3 96 BZ82
Thornton Heath CR7 141 DN99
Wallington SM6 159 DK105
Queenswood Cres, Wat. WD25 7 BU33
Queenswood Gdns, E11 68 EG60
Queenswood Pk, N3 43 CY54
Queen's Wd Rd, N10 65 DH58
Queenswood Rd, SE23 123 DX90
Sidcup DA15 125 ET85
Queens Yd, WC1 195 L5
Queen Victoria Av, Wem. HA0 79 CK66
★ Queen Victoria Mem, SW1 199 K4
Queen Victoria St, EC4 196 G10
Queen Victoria's Wk, Wind. SL4 92 AS81

313

Que - Rav

Queen Victoria Ter, E1 ...202 E1
Quemerford Rd, N7 ...65 DM64
Quendon Dr, Wal.Abb. EN9 ...15 ED33
Quennell Cl, Ashtd. KT21
off Parkers La ...172 CL119
Quennel Way, Brwd. CM13 ...55 GC45
Quentin Pl, SE13 ...104 EE83
Quentin Rd, SE13 ...104 EE83
Quentins Dr, West. (Berry's Grn.) TN16 ...179 EP116
Quentins Wk, West. (Berry's Grn.) TN16
off St. Anns Way ...179 EP116
Quentin Way, Vir.W. GU25 ...132 AV98
Quernmore Cl, Brom. BR1 ...124 EG93
Quernmore Rd, N4 ...65 DN58
Bromley BR1 ...124 EG93
Querrin St, SW6 ...100 DC82
Quex Ms, NW6
off Quex Rd ...82 DA67
Quex Rd, NW6 ...82 DA67
Quickley La, Rick. (Chorl.) WD3 ...21 BB44
Quickley Ri, Rick. (Chorl.) WD3 ...21 BC44
Quickmoor La, Kings L. WD4 ...6 BH33
Quick Pl, N1 ...83 DP67
Quick Rd, W4 ...98 CS78
Quicks Rd, SW19 ...120 DB94
Quick St, N1 ...196 G1
Quick St Ms, N1 ...196 F1
Quickswood, NW3
off King Henry's Rd ...82 DE66
Quickwood Cl, Rick. WD3 ...22 BG44
Quiet Cl, Add. KT15 ...152 BG105
Quiet Nook, Brom. BR2
off Croydon Rd ...144 EK104
Quill Hall La, Amer. HP6 ...20 AT37
Quill La, SW15 ...99 CX84
Quillot, The, Walt. KT12 ...153 BT106
Quill St, N4 ...65 DN62
W5 ...80 CL69
Quilp St, SE1 ...201 H4
Quilter Gdns, Orp. BR5 ...146 EW102
Quilter Rd, Orp. BR5 ...146 EW102
Quilter St, E2 ...84 DU69
SE18 ...105 ET78
Quilting Ct, SE16
off Poolmans St ...103 DX75
Quinbrookes, Slou. SL2 ...74 AW72
Quince Tree Cl, S.Ock. RM15 ...91 FW70
Quincy Rd, Egh. TW20 ...113 BA92
Quinta Dr, Barn. EN5 ...27 CV43
Quintin Av, SW20 ...139 CZ95
Quintin Cl, Pnr. HA5
off High Rd ...59 BV57
Quinton Cl, Beck. BR3 ...143 EC97
Hounslow TW5 ...95 BV80
Wallington SM6 ...159 DH105
Quinton Rd, T.Ditt. KT7 ...137 CG102
Quinton St, SW18 ...120 DC89
Quintrell Cl, Wok. GU21 ...166 AV117
Quixley St, E14 ...85 ED73
Quorn Rd, SE22 ...102 DS84

R

Raans Rd, Amer. HP6 ...20 AT38
Rabbit La, Walt. KT12 ...153 BU108
Rabbit Row, W8
off Kensington Mall ...82 DA74
Rabbits Rd, E12 ...68 EL63
Dartford (S.Darenth) DA4 ...149 FR96
Rabbs Mill Ho, Uxb. UB8 ...76 BK68
Rabies Heath Rd, Gdse. RH9 ...186 DU134
Redhill (Bletch.) RH1 ...186 DS133
Rabournmead Dr, Nthlt. UB5 ...60 BY64
Raby Rd, N.Mal. KT3 ...138 CR98
Raby St, E14 off Salmon La ...85 DY72
Raccoon Way, Houns. TW4 ...96 BW82
Rachel Cl, Ilf. IG6 ...69 ER55
Rachel Pt, E5 off Muir Rd ...66 DU63
Rackham Cl, Well. DA16 ...106 EV82
Rackham Ms, SW16
off Westcote Rd ...121 DJ93
Racton Rd, SW6 ...100 DA79
Radbourne Av, W5 ...97 CJ77
Radbourne Cl, E5
off Overbury St ...67 DX63
Radbourne Cres, E17 ...47 ED54
Radbourne Rd, SW12 ...121 DJ87
Radcliffe Av, NW10 ...81 CU68
Enfield EN2 ...30 DQ39
Radcliffe Gdns, Cars. SM5 ...158 DE108
Radcliffe Ms, Hmptn. (Hmptn.H.) TW12 off Taylor Cl ...116 CC92
Radcliffe Path, SW8
off St. Rule St ...101 DJ82
Radcliffe Rd, N21 ...45 DP46
SE1 ...201 N6
Croydon CR0 ...142 DT103
Harrow HA3 ...41 CG54
Radcliffe Sq, SW15 ...119 CX86
Radcliffe Way, Nthlt. UB5 ...78 BX69
Radcot Av, Slou. SL3 ...93 BB76
Radcot Pt, SE23 ...123 DX90
Radcot St, SE11 ...101 DN78
Raddington Rd, W10 ...81 CY71
Radfield Way, Sid. DA15 ...125 ER87
Radford Rd, SE13 ...123 EC86
Radford Way, Bark. IG11 ...87 ET69
Radipole Rd, SW6 ...99 CZ81
Radius Pk, Felt. TW14 ...95 BT84
Radland Rd, E16 ...86 EF72
Radlet Av, SE26 ...122 DV90
RADLETT ...25 CH35
⇌ Radlett ...25 CG35
Radlett Cl, E7 ...86 EF65
Radlett La, Rad. (Shenley) WD7 ...25 CK35
Radlett Pk Rd, Rad. WD7 ...9 CG34
Radlett Pl, NW8 ...82 DE67
Radlett Rd, St.Alb. AL2 ...9 CE28
Watford WD17, WD24 ...24 BW41
Radlett Rd, Wat. (Ald.) WD25 ...24 CB39
Radley Av, Ilf. IG3 ...69 ET63
Radley Cl, Felt. TW14 ...115 BT88
Radley Ct, SE16 ...203 J4
Radley Gdns, Har. HA3 ...62 CL56
Radley Ho, SE2
off Wolvercote Rd ...106 EX75
Radley Ms, W8 ...100 DA76
Radley Rd, N17 ...46 DS54
Radley's La, E18 ...48 EG54
Radleys Mead, Dag. RM10 ...89 FB65
Radlix Rd, E10 ...67 EA60
Radnor Av, Har. HA1 ...61 CE57
Welling DA16 ...126 EV85
Radnor Cl, Chis. BR7
off Homewood Cres ...125 ES93
Mitcham CR4 ...141 DL98
Radnor Cres, SE18 ...106 EU79
Ilford IG4 ...69 EM57
Radnor Gdns, Enf. EN1 ...30 DS39
Twickenham TW1 ...117 CF89
Radnor Gro, Uxb. UB10
off Charnwood Rd ...76 BN68
Radnor Ms, W2 ...194 A9
Radnor Pl, W2 ...194 B9
Radnor Rd, NW6 ...81 CY67
SE15 ...102 DU80
Harrow HA1 ...61 CD57
Twickenham TW1 ...117 CF89
Weybridge KT13 ...134 BN104
Radnor St, EC1 ...197 J3
Radnor Ter, W14 ...99 CZ77
Radnor Wk, E14 ...204 A8
SW3 ...100 DE78
Croydon CR0 ...143 DZ100
Radnor Way, NW10 ...80 CP70
Slough SL3 ...92 AY77
Radolphs, Tad. KT20
off Heathcote ...173 CX122
Radstock Av, Har. HA3 ...61 CG55
Radstock Cl, N11
off Martock Gdns ...44 DG51
Radstock St, SW11 ...100 DE80
Radstock Way, Red. RH1 ...185 DK128
Radstone Ct, Wok. GU22 ...167 AZ118
Radwell Path, Borwd. WD6
off Cromwell Rd ...26 CL39
Raeburn Gdns, Barn. EN5 ...27 CV43
Raeburn Av, Dart. DA1 ...127 FH85
Surbiton KT5 ...138 CP100
Raeburn Cl, NW11 ...64 DC58
Kingston upon Thames KT1 ...117 CK94
Raeburn Ct, Wok. GU21
off Martin Way ...166 AU118
Raeburn Rd, Edg. HA8 ...42 CN54
Hayes UB4 ...77 BR68
Sidcup DA15 ...125 ES86
Raeburn St, SW2 ...101 DL84
Rafford Way, Brom. BR1 ...144 EH96
H RAF Rehabilitation Cen (Headley Ct), Epsom KT18 ...172 CP123
Raft Rd, SW18 off North Pas ...100 DA84
★ Ragged Sch Mus, E3
off Copperfield Rd ...85 DY71
Raggleswood, Chis. BR7 ...145 EN95
Rag Hill Cl, West. (Tats.) TN16 ...178 EL121
Rag Hill Rd, West. (Tats.) TN16 ...178 EK121
Raglan Av, Wal.Cr. EN8 ...15 DX34
Raglan Cl, Houns. TW4
off Vickers Way ...116 BY85
Reigate RH2 ...184 DC132
Raglan Ct, SE12 ...124 EG85
South Croydon CR2 ...159 DP106
Wembley HA9 ...62 CM63
Raglan Gdns, Wat. WD19 ...39 BV46
Raglan Prec, Cat. CR3 ...176 DS122
Raglan Rd, E17 ...67 EC57
SE18 ...105 EQ78
Belvedere DA17 ...106 EZ77
Bromley BR2 ...144 EJ98
Enfield EN1 ...46 DS45
Reigate RH2 ...184 DB131
Woking (Knap.) GU21 ...166 AS118
Raglan St, NW5 ...83 DH65
Raglan Ter, Har. HA2 ...60 CB63
Raglan Way, Nthlt. UB5 ...78 CC65
Ragley Cl, W3 off Church Rd ...98 CQ75
Rags La, Wal.Cr. (Chsht.) EN7 ...14 DS27
Ragwort Ct, SE26
off Lawrie Pk Gdns ...122 DV92
Rahn Rd, Epp. CM16 ...18 EU31
Raider Cl, Rom. RM7 ...50 FA53
Railey Ms, NW5 ...65 DJ64
Railpit La, Warl. CR6 ...178 EE115
Railshead Rd, Islw. TW7 ...97 CH84
Railton Rd, SE24 ...101 DN84
Railway App, N4
off Wightman Rd ...65 DN58
SE1 ...201 L2
Harrow HA3 ...61 CF56
Twickenham TW1 ...117 CG87
Wallington SM6 ...159 DH107
Railway Av, SE16 ...202 G4
Railway Cotts, Rad. WD7
off Shenley Hill ...25 CH35
Watford WD24 ...23 BV39
Railway Ms, E3
off Wellington Way ...85 EA69
W10 off Ladbroke Gro ...81 CY72
Railway Pas, Tedd. TW11
off Victoria Rd ...117 CG93
Railway Pl, SW19
off Hartfield Rd ...119 CZ93
Belvedere DA17 ...106 FA76
Gravesend DA12
off Windmill St ...131 GH87
Railway Ri, SE22
off Grove Vale ...102 DS84
Railway Rd, Tedd. TW11 ...117 CF91
Waltham Cross EN8 ...15 DY33
Railway Side, SW13 ...98 CS83
Railway Sq, Brwd. CM14
off Fairfield Rd ...54 FW48
Railway St, N1 ...196 A1
Railway St, Grav. (Nthflt.) DA11 ...130 GA85
Romford RM6 ...70 EW60
Railway Ter, SE13
off Ladywell Rd ...123 EB85
Feltham TW13 ...115 BU88
Kings Langley WD4 ...6 BN27
Slough SL2 ...74 AT74
Staines TW18 ...113 BD92
Westerham TN16 ...189 ER125
Rainborough Cl, NW10 ...80 CQ65
Rainbow Av, E14 ...204 B10
Rainbow Ct, Wat. WD19
off Oxhey Rd ...24 BW44
Woking GU21
off Langmans Way ...166 AS116
Rainbow Ind Est, West Dr. UB7 ...76 BK73
Rainbow Quay, SE16 ...203 L7
Rainbow Rd, Grays (Chaff.Hun.) RM16 ...109 FW77
Rainbow St, SE5 ...102 DS80
Rainer Cl, Wal.Cr. (Chsht.) EN8 ...15 DX29
Raine St, E1 ...202 E2
RAINHAM ...89 FG69
⇌ Rainham ...89 FF70
Rainham Cl, SE9 ...125 ER86
SW11 ...120 DE86
★ Rainham Hall, Rain. RM13 ...89 FG70
Rainham Rd, NW10 ...81 CW69
Rainham RM13 ...89 FE66
Rainham Rd N, Dag. RM10 ...71 FB61
Rainham Rd S, Dag. RM10 ...71 FB63
Rainhill Way, E3 ...85 EA69
Rainsborough Av, SE8 ...203 K9
Rainsford Cl, Stan. HA7
off Coverdale Cl ...41 CJ50
Rainsford Rd, NW10 ...80 CP69
Rainsford St, W2 ...194 B8
Rainsford Way, Horn. RM12 ...71 FG60
Rainton Rd, SE7 ...205 N10
Rainville Rd, W6 ...99 CW79
Raisins Hill, Pnr. HA5 ...60 BW55
Raith Av, N14 ...45 DK48
Raleana Rd, E14 ...204 E2
Raleigh Av, Hayes UB4 ...77 BV71
Wallington SM6 ...159 DK105
Raleigh Cl, NW4 ...63 CW57
Erith DA8 ...107 FF79
Pinner HA5 ...60 BX59
Ruislip HA4 ...59 BT61
Raleigh Ct, SE16
off Rotherhithe St ...85 DX74
SE19 off Lymer Av ...122 DT92
Beckenham BR3 ...143 EB95
Staines TW18 ...114 BG91
Wallington SM6 ...159 DH107
Raleigh Dr, N20 ...44 DE48
Esher (Clay.) KT10 ...155 CD106
Surbiton KT5 ...138 CQ102
Raleigh Gdns, SW2
off Brixton Hill ...121 DM86
Mitcham CR4 ...140 DF96
Raleigh Ms, N1
off Queen's Head St ...83 DP67
Orpington BR6
off Osgood Av ...163 ET106
Raleigh Rd, N8 ...65 DN56
SE20 ...123 DX94
Enfield EN2 ...30 DR42
Feltham TW13 ...115 BT90
Richmond TW9 ...98 CM83
Southall UB2 ...96 BY78
Raleigh St, N1 ...83 DP67
Raleigh Way, N14 ...45 DK46
Feltham TW13 ...116 BW92
Ralliwood Rd, Ashtd. KT21 ...172 CN119
Ralph Ct, W2 off Queensway ...82 DB72
Ralph Perring Ct, Beck. BR3 ...143 EA98
Ralston St, SW3
off Tedworth Sq ...100 DF78
Ralston Way, Wat. WD19 ...40 BX47
Rama Cl, SW16 ...121 DK94
Rama Ct, Har. HA1 ...61 CE61
Ramac Way, SE7 ...205 P9
Rama La, SE19 ...122 DT94
Rambler Cl, SW16 ...121 DJ91
Rambler La, Slou. SL3 ...92 AW76
Rame Cl, SW17 ...120 DG92
Ramilles Cl, SW2 ...121 DL86
Ramillies Pl, W1 ...195 K9
Ramillies Rd, NW7 ...42 CS47
W4 ...98 CR77
Sidcup DA15 ...126 EV86
Ramillies St, W1 ...195 K9
Ramney Dr, Enf. EN3 ...31 DY37
Ramornie Cl, Walt. KT12 ...154 BZ106
Rampart St, E1
off Commercial Rd ...84 DV72
Ram Pas, Kings.T. KT1
off High St ...137 CK96
Rampayne St, SW1 ...199 M10
Ram Pl, E9 off Chatham Pl ...84 DW65
Rampton Cl, E4 ...47 EA48
Ramsay Gdns, Rom. RM3 ...52 FJ53
Ramsay Ms, SW3
off King's Rd ...100 DE79
Ramsay Pl, Har. HA1 ...61 CE60
Ramsay Rd, E7 ...68 EE63
W3 ...98 CQ76
Ramscroft Cl, N9 ...46 DS45
Ramsdale Rd, SW17 ...120 DG92
RAMSDEN, Orp. ...146 EW102
Ramsden Cl, Orp. BR5 ...146 EW102
Ramsden Dr, Rom. RM5 ...50 FA52
Ramsden Rd, N11 ...44 DF50
SW12 ...120 DG86
Erith DA8 ...107 FD80
Orpington BR5, BR6 ...146 EV101
Ramsey Cl, NW9 ...63 CT58
Greenford UB6 ...60 CC64
Hatfield AL9 ...12 DD27
Ramsey Ho, Wem. HA9 ...80 CL65
Ramsey Ms, N4
off Monsell Rd ...65 DP62
Ramsey Rd, Th.Hth. CR7 ...141 DM100
Ramsey St, E2 ...84 DU70
Ramsey Wk, N1
off Clephane Rd ...84 DR65
Ramsey Way, N14 ...45 DJ45
Ramsgate Cl, E16 ...205 P3
Ramsgate St, E8
off Dalston La ...84 DT65
Ramsgill App, Ilf. IG2 ...69 ET56
Ramsgill Dr, Ilf. IG2 ...69 ET57
Rams Gro, Rom. RM6 ...70 EY56
Ram St, SW18 ...120 DB85
Ramulis Dr, Hayes UB4 ...78 BX70
Ramus Wd Av, Orp. BR6 ...163 ES106
Rancliffe Gdns, SE9 ...104 EL84
Rancliffe Rd, E6 ...86 EL68
Randall Av, NW2 ...63 CT62
Randall Cl, SW11 ...100 DE81
Erith DA8 ...107 FC79
Slough SL3 ...93 AZ78
Randall Ct, NW7 off Page St ...43 CU52
Randall Dr, Horn. RM12 ...72 FJ63
Randall Pl, SE10 ...103 EC80
Randall Rd, SE11 ...200 B10
Randall Row, SE11 ...200 B9
Randalls Cres, Lthd. KT22 ...171 CG120
Randalls Dr, Brwd. CM13 ...55 GE44
Randalls Pk Av, Lthd. KT22 ...171 CG120
Randalls Pk Dr, Lthd. KT22
off Randalls Rd ...171 CG121
Randalls Rd, Lthd. KT22 ...171 CE119
Randall's Wk, St.Alb. AL2 ...8 BZ30
Randalls Way, Lthd. KT22 ...171 CG121
Randell's Rd, N1 ...83 DL67
Randle Rd, Rich. TW10 ...117 CJ91
Randlesdown Rd, SE6 ...123 EA91
Randles La, Sev. (Knock.) TN14 ...180 EX115
Randolph App, E16 ...86 EK72
Randolph Av, W9 ...82 DC70
Randolph Cl, Bexh. DA7 ...107 FC83
Cobham (Stoke D'Ab.) KT11 ...170 CA115
Kingston upon Thames KT2 ...118 CQ92
Woking (Knap.) GU21
off Creston Av ...166 AS117
Randolph Cres, W9 ...82 DC70
Randolph Gdns, NW6 ...82 DB68
Randolph Gro, Rom. RM6
off Donald Dr ...70 EW57
Randolph Ho, Croy. CR0 ...142 DQ102
Randolph Ms, W9 ...82 DC70
Randolph Rd, E17 ...67 EB57
W9 ...82 DC70
Bromley BR2 ...145 EM102
Epsom KT17 ...157 CT114
Slough SL3 ...92 AY76
Southall UB1 ...96 BZ75
Randolph's La, West. TN16 ...189 EP126
Randolph St, NW1 ...83 DJ66
Randon Cl, Har. HA2 ...40 CB54
Ranelagh Av, SW6 ...99 CZ83
SW13 ...99 CU82
Ranelagh Br, W2
off Gloucester Ter ...82 DB71
Ranelagh Cl, Edg. HA8 ...42 CN49
Ranelagh Dr, Edg. HA8 ...42 CN49
Twickenham TW1 ...117 CH85
★ Ranelagh Gdns, SW3 ...100 DG78
Ranelagh Gdns, E11 ...68 EJ57
SW6 ...99 CZ83
W4 off Grove Pk Gdns ...98 CQ80
W6 ...99 CT76
Gravesend (Nthflt.) DA11 ...131 GF87
Ilford IG1 ...69 EN60
Ranelagh Gro, SW1 ...198 G10
Ranelagh Ms, W5
off Ranelagh Rd ...97 CK75
Ranelagh Pl, N.Mal. KT3
off Rodney Rd ...138 CS99
Ranelagh Rd, E6 ...87 EN67
E11 ...68 EE63
E15 ...86 EE67
N17 ...66 DS55
N22 ...45 DM53
NW10 ...81 CT68
SW1 off Lupus St ...101 DJ78
W5 ...97 CK75
Redhill RH1 ...184 DE134
Southall UB1 ...78 BX74
Wembley HA0 ...61 CK64
Ranfurly Rd, Sutt. SM1 ...140 DA103
Rangefield Rd, Brom. BR1 ...124 EE92
Rangemoor Rd, N15 ...66 DT57
Range Rd, Grav. DA12 ...131 GL87
Rangers Rd, E4 ...48 EE45
Loughton IG10 ...48 EE45
Rangers Sq, SE10 ...103 ED81
Ranger Wk, Add. KT15
off Monks Cres ...152 BH106
Range Way, Shep. TW17 ...134 BN101
Rangeworth Pl, Sid. DA15
off Priestlands Pk Rd ...125 ET90
Rangoon St, EC3
off Northumberland All ...84 DT72
Rankin Cl, NW9 ...62 CS55
Ranleigh Gdns, Bexh. DA7 ...106 EZ80
Ranmere St, SW12
off Ormeley Rd ...121 DH88
Ranmoor Cl, Har. HA1 ...61 CD56
Ranmoor Gdns, Har. HA1 ...61 CD56
Ranmore Av, Croy. CR0 ...142 DT104
Ranmore Cl, Red. RH1 ...184 DG131
Ranmore Path, Orp. BR5 ...146 EU98
Ranmore Rd, Sutt. SM2 ...157 CX109
Rannoch Cl, Edg. HA8 ...42 CP47
Rannoch Rd, W6 ...99 CW79
Rannock Av, NW9 ...62 CS59
Ranskill Rd, Borwd. WD6 ...26 CN39
Ransom Cl, Wat. WD19 ...40 BW45
Ransom Rd, SE7
off Harvey Gdns ...104 EJ78
Ransom Wk, SE7
off Woolwich Rd ...104 EJ78
Ranston Cl, Uxb. (Denh.) UB9
off Nightingale Way ...57 BF58
Ranston St, NW1 ...194 B6
Ranulf Rd, NW2 ...63 CZ63
Ranwell Cl, E3 off Beale Rd ...85 DZ67
Ranwell St, E3 ...85 DZ67
Ranworth Cl, Erith DA8 ...107 FE82
Ranworth Rd, N9 ...46 DW47
Ranyard Cl, Chess. KT9 ...138 CM104
Raphael Av, Rom. RM1 ...71 FF55
Tilbury RM18 ...111 GG80
Raphael Cl, Rad. (Shenley) WD7 ...10 CL32
Raphael Dr, T.Ditt. KT7 ...137 CF101
Watford WD24 ...24 BX40
Raphael Rd, Grav. DA12 ...131 GK87
Raphael St, SW7 ...198 D5
Rapier Cl, Purf. RM19 ...108 FN77
Rasehill Cl, Rick. WD3 ...22 BJ43
Rashleigh St, SW8
off Peardon St ...101 DH82
Rashleigh Way, Dart. (Hort.Kir.) DA4 ...148 FQ98
Rasper Rd, N20 ...44 DC47
Rastell Av, SW2 ...121 DK89
Ratcliffe Cl, SE12 ...124 EG87
Uxbridge UB8 ...76 BK69
Ratcliffe Cross St, E1 ...85 DX72
Ratcliffe La, E14 ...85 DY72
Ratcliffe Orchard, E1 ...85 DX73
Ratcliff Rd, E7 ...68 EJ64
Rathbone Mkt, E16
off Barking Rd ...86 EF71
Rathbone Pl, W1 ...195 M8
Rathbone Pt, E5
off Nolan Way ...66 DU63
Rathbone St, E16 ...86 EF71
W1 ...195 L7
Rathcoole Av, N8 ...65 DM56
Rathcoole Gdns, N8 ...65 DM57
Rathfern Rd, SE6 ...123 DZ88
Rathgar Av, W13 ...79 CH74
Rathgar Cl, N3 ...43 CZ54
Rathgar Rd, SW9
off Coldharbour La ...101 DP83
Rathlin Wk, N1
off Clephane Rd ...84 DQ65
Rathmell Dr, SW4 ...121 DK86
Rathmore Rd, SE7 ...104 EH78
Gravesend DA11 ...131 GH87
Rathwell Path, Borwd. WD6 ...26 CL39
Rats La, Loug. (High Beach) IG10 ...32 EH38
Rattray Rd, SW2 ...101 DN84
Raul Rd, SE15 ...102 DU81
Raveley St, NW5 ...65 DJ63
Ravel Gdns, S.Ock. (Aveley) RM15 ...90 FQ72
Ravel Rd, S.Ock. (Aveley) RM15 ...90 FQ72
Raven Cl, NW9 off Eagle Dr ...42 CS54
Rickmansworth WD3 ...38 BJ45
Raven Ct, E5
off Stellman Cl ...66 DU62
Ravencroft, Grays RM16
off Alexandra Cl ...111 GH75
Ravendale Rd, Sun. TW16 ...135 BT96
Ravenet St, SW11
off Strasburg Rd ...101 DH81
Ravenfield, Egh. (Eng.Grn.) TW20 ...112 AW93
Ravenfield Rd, SW17 ...120 DF90
Ravenhill Rd, E13 ...86 EJ68
Ravenna Rd, SW15 ...119 CX85
Ravenoak Way, Chig. IG7 ...49 ES50
Ravenor Pk Rd, Grnf. UB6 ...78 CB69
Raven Rd, E18 ...48 EJ54
Raven Row, E1 ...84 DV71
⇌ Ravensbourne ...123 ED94
Ravensbourne Av, Beck. BR3 ...123 ED94
Bromley BR2 ...123 ED94
Staines TW19 ...114 BL88
Ravensbourne Cres, Rom. RM3 ...72 FM55
Ravensbourne Gdns, W13 ...79 CH71
Ilford IG5 ...49 EN53
Ravensbourne Pk, SE6 ...123 EA87
Ravensbourne Pk Cres, SE6 ...123 DZ87
Ravensbourne Pl, SE13 ...103 EB82
Ravensbourne Rd, SE6 ...123 DZ87
Bromley BR1 ...144 EG97
Dartford DA1 ...107 FG83
Twickenham TW1 ...117 CJ86
Ravensbury Av, Mord. SM4 ...140 DC99
Ravensbury Ct, Mitch. CR4
off Ravensbury Gro ...140 DD98
Ravensbury Gro, Mitch. CR4 ...140 DD98
Ravensbury La, Mitch. CR4 ...140 DD98
Ravensbury Path, Mitch. CR4 ...140 DD98
Ravensbury Rd, SW18 ...120 DA89
Orpington BR5 ...145 ET98
Ravensbury Ter, SW18 ...120 DB89
Ravenscar Rd, Brom. BR1 ...124 EE91
Surbiton KT6 ...138 CM103
Ravens Cl, Brom. BR2 ...144 EF96
Chessington KT9 ...137 CK100
Enfield EN1 ...30 DS40
Redhill RH1 ...184 DF132
Ravenscourt, Sun. TW16 ...135 BT95
Ravenscourt Av, W6 ...99 CU77
Ravenscourt Cl, Horn. RM12
off Ravenscourt Dr ...72 FL62
Ruislip HA4 ...59 BQ59
Ravenscourt Dr, Horn. RM12 ...72 FL62
Ravenscourt Gdns, W6 ...99 CU77
Ravenscourt Gro, Horn. RM12 ...72 FL61
⊖ Ravenscourt Park ...99 CU77
Ravenscourt Pk, W6 ...99 CU76
Ravenscourt Pl, W6 ...99 CV77
Ravenscourt Rd, W6 ...99 CV77
Orpington BR5 ...146 EU97
Ravenscourt Sq, W6 ...99 CU76
Ravenscraig Rd, N11 ...45 DH49
Ravenscroft, Wat. WD25 ...8 BY34
Ravenscroft Av, NW11 ...63 CZ59
Wembley HA9 ...62 CM60

★ Place of interest ⇌ Railway station ⊖ London Underground station DLR Docklands Light Railway station Tramlink station H Hospital

Rav - Reg

Ravenscroft Cl, E16 86 EG71
Ravenscroft Cres, SE9 125 EM90
Ravenscroft Pk, Barn. EN5 27 CX42
Ravenscroft Pt, E9
off Kenton Rd 85 DX65
Ravenscroft Rd, E16 86 EG71
W4 98 CQ77
Beckenham BR3 142 DW96
Weybridge KT13 153 BQ111
Ravenscroft St, E2 84 DT68
Ravensdale Av, N12 44 DC49
Ravensdale Gdns, SE19 122 DR94
Hounslow TW4 96 BY83
Ravensdale Ms, Stai. TW18
off Worple Rd 114 BH93
Ravensdale Rd, N16 66 DT59
Hounslow TW4 96 BY83
Ravensdon St, SE11 101 DN78
Ravensfield, Slou. SL3 92 AX75
Ravensfield Cl, Dag. RM9 70 EX63
Ravensfield Gdns, Epsom
KT19 156 CS106
Ravenshaw St, NW6 63 CZ64
Ravenshead Cl, S.Croy. CR2 160 DW111
Ravenshill, Chis. BR7 145 EP95
Ravenshurst Av, NW4 63 CW56
Ravenside Cl, N18 47 DX51
Ravenside Retail Pk, N18 47 DX50
Ravenslea Rd, SW12 120 DF87
Ravensmead, Ger.Cr. (Chal.St.P.)
SL9 37 AZ50
Ravensmead Rd, Brom. BR2 123 ED94
Ravensmede Way, W4 99 CT77
Ravensmere, Epp. CM16 18 EU31
Ravens Ms, SE12
off Ravens Way 124 EG85
Ravenstone, SE17 102 DS78
Ravenstone Rd, N8 65 DN55
NW9
off West Hendon Bdy 63 CT58
Ravenstone St, SW12 120 DG88
Ravens Way, SE12 124 EG85
Ravenswold, Ken. CR8 176 DQ115
Ravenswood, Bex. DA5 126 EY88
Ravenswood Av, Surb. KT6 138 CM103
West Wickham BR4 143 EC102
Ravenswood Cl, Cob. KT11 170 BX115
Romford RM5 51 FB50
Ravenswood Ct, Kings.T.
KT2 118 CP93
Woking GU22 167 AZ118
Ravenswood Cres, Har. HA2 60 BZ61
West Wickham BR4 143 EC102
Ravenswood Gdns, Islw.
TW7 97 CE81
Ravenswood Pk, Nthwd. HA6 39 BU51
Ravenswood Rd, E17 67 EB56
SW12 121 DH87
Croydon CR0 141 DP104
Ravensworth Rd, NW10 81 CV69
SE9 125 EM91
Ravent Rd, SE11 200 C9
Ravey St, EC2 197 M4
Ravine Gro, SE18 105 ES79
Rawlings Cl, Orp. BR6 163 ET106
Rawlings Cres, Wem. HA9 62 CP62
Rawlings St, SW3 198 D8
Rawlins Cl, N3 63 CY55
South Croydon CR2 161 DY108
Rawnsley Av, Mitch. CR4 140 DD99
Rawreth Wk, N1 off Basire St 84 DQ67
Rawson St, SW11
off Strasburg Rd 100 DG81
Rawsthorne Cl, E16
off Kennard St 87 EM74
Rawstone Wk, E13 86 EG68
Rawstorne Pl, EC1 196 F2
Rawstorne St, EC1 196 F2
Rayburn Rd, Horn. RM11 72 FN59
Ray Cl, Chess. KT9
off Merritt Gdns 155 CJ107
Raydean Rd, Barn. EN5 28 DB43
Raydon Rd, Wal.Cr. (Chsht.)
EN8 15 DX32
Raydons Gdns, Dag. RM9 70 EY64
Raydons Rd, Dag. RM9 70 EY64
Raydon St, N19 65 DH61
Rayfield, Epp. CM16 18 EU30
Rayfield Cl, Brom. BR2 144 EL100
Rayford Av, SE12 124 EF87
Rayford Cl, Dart. DA1 128 FJ85
Ray Gdns, Bark. IG11 88 EU68
Stanmore HA7 41 CH50
Ray Lamb Way, Erith DA8 107 FH79
Raylands Mead, Ger.Cr. SL9
off Bull La 56 AW57
Rayleas Cl, SE18 105 EP81
Rayleigh Av, Tedd. TW11 117 CE93
Rayleigh Cl, N13
off Rayleigh Rd 46 DR48
Brentwood CM13 55 GC44
Rayleigh Ct, Kings.T. KT1 138 CM96
Rayleigh Ri, S.Croy. CR2 160 DS107
Rayleigh Rd, E16 86 EH74
N13 46 DQ48
SW19 139 CZ95
Brentwood CM13 55 GB44
Woodford Green IG8 48 EJ51
Ray Lo Rd, Wdf.Grn. IG8 48 EJ51
Ray Massey Way, E6
off Ron Leighton Way 86 EL67
Raymead, NW4
off Tenterden Gro 63 CW56
Raymead Av, Th.Hth. CR7 141 DN99
Raymead Cl, Lthd. (Fetch.)
KT22 171 CE122
Raymead Way, Lthd. (Fetch.)
KT22 171 CE122
Raymere Gdns, SE18 105 ER80
Raymond Av, E18 68 EF55
W13 97 CG76
Raymond Bldgs, WC1 196 C6
Raymond Cl, SE26 122 DW92
Abbots Langley WD5 7 BR32
Raymond Cl, Slou. (Colnbr.)
SL3 93 BE81
Raymond Ct, N10
off Pembroke Rd 44 DG52
Potters Bar EN6
off St. Francis Cl 12 DC34
Sutton SM2
off Mulgrave Rd 158 DB107
Raymond Gdns, Chig. IG7 50 EV48
Raymond Rd, E13 86 EJ66
SW19 119 CY93
Beckenham BR3 143 DY98
Ilford IG2 69 ER59
Slough SL3 93 BA76
Raymond Way, Esher (Clay.)
KT10 155 CG107
Raymouth Rd, SE16 202 E8
Rayne Ct, E18 68 EF56
Rayners Cl, Slou. (Colnbr.)
SL3 93 BC80
Wembley HA0 61 CK64
Rayners Ct, Grav. DA11 130 GB86
Harrow HA2 60 CA60
Rayners Cres, Nthlt. UB5 77 BV69
Rayners Gdns, Nthlt. UB5 77 BV68
RAYNERS LANE, Har. 60 BZ60
⊖ Rayners Lane 60 BZ59
Rayners La, Har. HA2 60 CB61
Pinner HA5 60 BZ58
Rayners Rd, SW15 119 CY85
Rayner Twr, E10 67 EA59
Raynes Av, E11 68 EJ59
RAYNES PARK, SW20 139 CV97
⇌ Raynes Park 139 CW96
Raynham Av, N18 46 DU51
Raynham Rd, N18 46 DU50
W6 99 CV77
Raynham Ter, N18 46 DU50
Raynor Cl, Sthl. UB1 78 BZ74
Raynor Pl, N1 off Elizabeth Av 84 DQ67
Raynton Cl, Har. HA2 60 BY60
Hayes UB4 77 BT70
Raynton Dr, Hayes UB4 77 BT70
Raynton Rd, Enf. EN3 31 DX37
Ray Rd, Rom. RM5 51 FB50
West Molesey KT8 136 CB99
Rays Av, N18 46 DW49
Rays Hill, Dart. (Hort.Kir.)
DA4 148 FQ98
Rays Rd, N18 46 DW49
West Wickham BR4 143 EC101
Ray St, EC1 196 E5
Ray St Br, EC1 196 E5
Ray Wk, N7 off Andover Rd 65 DM61
Raywood Cl, Hayes UB3 95 BQ80
Reachview Cl, NW1
off Baynes St 83 DJ66
Read Cl, T.Ditt. KT7 137 CG101
Read Ct, Wal.Abb. EN9 16 EG33
Reade Ct, Slou. SL2
off Victoria Rd 74 AV72
Readens, The, Bans. SM7 174 DF116
Reade Wk, NW10
off Denbigh Cl 80 CS66
Reading Arch Rd, Red. RH1 184 DF134
Reading La, E8 84 DV65
Reading Rd, Nthlt. UB5 60 CB64
Sutton SM1 158 DC106
Readings, The, Rick. (Chorl.)
WD3 21 BF41
Reading Way, NW7 43 CX50
Read Rd, Ashtd. KT21 171 CK117
Reads Cl, Ilf. IG1
off Chapel Rd 69 EP62
Reads Rest La, Tad. KT20 173 CZ119
Read Way, Grav. DA12 131 GK92
Reapers Cl, NW1
off Crofters Way 83 DK67
Reapers Way, Islw. TW7
off Hall Rd 117 CD85
Reardon Ct, N21
off Cosgrove Cl 46 DQ47
Reardon Path, E1 202 E3
Reardon St, E1 202 D2
Reaston St, SE14 102 DW80
Reckitt Rd, W4 98 CS78
Record St, SE15 102 DW79
Recovery St, SW17 120 DE92
Recreation Av, Rom. RM7 71 FC57
Romford (Harold Wd.) RM3 52 FM54
Recreation Rd, SE26 123 DX91
Bromley BR2 144 EF96
Sidcup DA15
off Woodside Rd 125 ES90
Southall UB2 96 BY77
Recreation Way, Mitch. CR4 141 DK97
Rector St, N1 84 DQ67
Rectory Chase, Brwd. (Lt.Warley)
CM13 73 FX56
Rectory Cl, E4 47 EA48
N3 43 CZ53
SW20 139 CW97
Ashtead KT21 172 CM119
Dartford DA1 107 FE84
Shepperton TW17 134 BN97
Sidcup DA14 126 EV91
Stanmore HA7 41 CH51
Surbiton KT6 137 CJ102
West Byfleet (Byfleet)
KT14 152 BL113
Rectory Cres, E11 68 EJ58
Rectory Fm Rd, Enf. EN2 29 DM38
Rectory Fld Cres, SE7 104 EJ80
Rectory Gdns, N8 65 DL56
SW4 off Fitzwilliam Rd 101 DJ83
Chalfont St. Giles HP8 36 AV48
Northolt UB5 78 BZ67
Upminster RM14 73 FR61
Rectory Grn, Beck. BR3 143 DZ95
Rectory Gro, SW4 101 DJ83
Croydon CR0 141 DP103
Hampton TW12 116 BZ91
Rectory La, SW17 120 DG93
Ashtead KT21 172 CM118
Banstead SM7 158 DF114
Betchworth (Buckland)
RH3 183 CT131
Rectory La, Edg. HA8 42 CN51
Kings Langley WD4 6 BN28
Loughton IG10 33 EN40
Radlett (Shenley) WD7 10 CN33
Rickmansworth WD3 38 BK46
Sevenoaks TN13 191 FJ126
Sidcup DA14 126 EV91
Stanmore HA7 41 CH50
Surbiton KT6 137 CH102
Wallington SM6 159 DJ105
West Byfleet (Byfleet)
KT14 152 BL113
Westerham TN16 178 EL123
Westerham (Brasted)
TN16 180 EW123
Rectory Meadow, Grav. (Sthflt.)
DA13 130 GA93
Rectory Orchard, SW19 119 CY91
Rectory Pk, S.Croy. CR2 160 DS113
Rectory Pk Av, Nthlt. UB5 78 BZ69
Rectory Pl, SE18 105 EN77
⇌ Rectory Road 66 DT62
Rectory Rd, E12 69 EM64
E17 67 EB55
N16 66 DT62
SW13 99 CU82
W3 80 CP74
Beckenham BR3 143 EA95
Coulsdon CR5 184 DD125
Dagenham RM10 88 FA66
Grays RM17 110 GD76
Hayes UB3 77 BU72
Hounslow TW4 95 BV81
Keston BR2 162 EK108
Rickmansworth WD3 38 BK46
Southall UB2 96 BZ76
Sutton SM1 140 DA104
Swanscombe DA10 130 FY87
Tilbury (W.Til.) RM18 111 GK79
Rectory Sq, E1 85 DX71
Rectory Way, Uxb. UB10 59 BP62
Reculver Ms, N18
off Lyndhurst Rd 46 DU49
Reculver Rd, SE16 203 H10
Red Anchor Cl, SW3
off Old Ch St 100 DE79
Redan Pl, W2 82 DB72
Redan St, W14 99 CX76
Redan Ter, SE5
off Flaxman Rd 102 DQ82
Redbarn Cl, Pur. CR8
off Whytecliffe Rd S 159 DP111
Red Barracks Rd, SE18 105 EM77
Redberry Gro, SE26 122 DW90
Redbourne Av, N3 44 DA53
Redbourne Dr, SE28 88 EX72
REDBRIDGE, Ilf. 69 EM58
⊖ Redbridge 68 EK58
Redbridge Enterprise Cen, Ilf.
IG1 69 EQ61
Redbridge Gdns, SE5 102 DS80
Redbridge La E, Ilf. IG4 68 EK58
Redbridge La W, E11 68 EH58
Redburn St, SW3 100 DF79
Redbury Cl, Rain. RM13
off Deri Av 89 FH70
Redcar Cl, Nthlt. UB5 60 CB64
Redcar Rd, Rom. RM3 52 FM50
Redcar St, SE5 102 DQ80
Redcastle Cl, E1 84 DW73
Red Cedars Rd, Orp. BR6 145 ES101
Redchurch St, E2 197 P4
Redcliffe Cl, SW5
off Warwick Rd 100 DB78
Redcliffe Gdns, SW5 100 DB78
SW10 100 DB78
W4 98 CP80
Ilford IG1 69 EN60
Redcliffe Ms, SW10 100 DB78
Redcliffe Pl, SW10 100 DC79
Redcliffe Rd, SW10 100 DC78
Redcliffe Sq, SW10 100 DB78
Redcliffe St, SW10 100 DB79
Redclose Av, Mord. SM4
off Chalgrove Av 140 DA99
Redclyffe Rd, E6 86 EJ67
Red Cottage Ms, Slou. SL3 92 AW76
Red Ct, Slou. SL1 74 AS74
Redcourt, Wok. GU22 167 BD115
Redcroft Rd, Sthl. UB1 78 CC73
Redcross Way, SE1 201 J4
Redden Ct Rd, Rom. RM3 72 FL55
Redding Cl, Dart. DA2 129 FS89
Reddings, The, NW7 43 CT48
Borehamwood WD6 26 CM41
Reddings Av, Bushey WD23 24 CB43
Reddings Cl, NW7 43 CT49
Reddington Cl, S.Croy. CR2 160 DR109
Reddington Dr, Slou. SL3 92 AY76
Reddins Rd, SE15 102 DU79
Reddons Rd, Beck. BR3 123 DY94
Reddown Rd, Couls. CR5 175 DK118
Reddy Rd, Erith DA8 107 FF79
Rede Ct, Wey. KT13
off Old Palace Rd 135 BP104
Redenham Ho, SW15
off Tangley Gro 119 CT87
Rede Pl, W2
off Chepstow Pl 82 DA72
Redesdale Gdns, Islw. TW7 97 CG80
Redesdale St, SW3 100 DF79
Redfern Av, Houns. TW4 116 CA87
Redfern Cl, Uxb. UB8 76 BJ67
Redfern Gdns, Rom. RM2 52 FK54
Redfern Rd, NW10 80 CS66
SE6 123 EC87
Redfield La, SW5 100 DA77
Redfield Ms, SW5
off Redfield La 100 DA77
Redford Av, Couls. CR5 159 DH114
Thornton Heath CR7 141 DM98
Wallington SM6 159 DL107
Redford Cl, Felt. TW13 115 BT89
Redford Wk, N1
off Britannia Row 83 DP67
Redford Way, Uxb. UB8 76 BJ66
Redgate Dr, Brom. BR2 144 EH103
Redgate Ter, SW15
off Lytton Gro 119 CX86
Redgrave Cl, Croy. CR0 142 DT100
Redgrave Rd, SW15 99 CX83
Redhall Ct, Cat. CR3 176 DR123
Redhall La, Rick. WD3 22 BL39
Redheath Cl, Wat. WD25 23 BT35
REDHILL 184 DG134
⇌ Redhill 184 DG133
Red Hill, Chis. BR7 125 EN92
Uxbridge (Denh.) UB9 57 BD61
Redhill Dr, Edg. HA8 42 CQ54
Redhill Rd, Cob. KT11 153 BP113
Redhill St, NW1 195 J2
★ Red Ho, The (William Morris
Ho), Bexh. DA6 106 EY84
Red Ho La, Bexh. DA6 106 EX84
Walton-on-Thames KT12 135 BU103
Redhouse Rd, Croy. CR0 141 DK100
Westerham (Tats.) TN16 178 EJ120
Red Ho Sq, N1
off Clephane Rd 84 DQ65
Redington Gdns, NW3 64 DB63
Redington Rd, NW3 64 DB63
Redland Gdns, W.Mol. KT8
off Dunstable Rd 136 BZ98
Redlands, Couls. CR5 175 DL116
Redlands Ct, Brom. BR1 124 EF94
Redlands Rd, Enf. EN3 31 DY39
Sevenoaks TN13 190 FF124
Redlands Way, SW2 121 DM87
Red La, Esher (Clay.) KT10 155 CG107
Oxted RH8 188 EH133
Redleaf Cl, Belv. DA17 106 FA79
Red Leaf Cl, Slou. SL3
off Pickford Dr 75 AZ74
Redleaves Av, Ashf. TW15 115 BP93
Redlees Cl, Islw. TW7 97 CG84
Red Leys, Uxb. UB8
off Park Rd 76 BL66
Red Lion Cl, SE17
off Red Lion Row 102 DQ79
Orpington BR5 146 EW100
Red Lion Ct, EC4 196 E8
Red Lion Hill, N2 44 DD54
Red Lion La, SE18 105 EN80
Hemel Hempstead HP3 6 BM26
Rickmansworth (Sarratt)
WD3 22 BG35
Woking (Chobham) GU24 150 AS109
Red Lion Pl, SE18
off Shooter's Hill Rd 105 EN81
Red Lion Rd, Surb. KT6 138 CM103
Woking (Chobham) GU24 150 AS109
Red Lion Row, SE17 102 DQ79
Red Lion Sq, SW18
off Wandsworth High St 120 DA85
WC1 196 B7
Red Lion St, WC1 196 B6
Richmond TW9 117 CK85
Red Lion Yd, W1 198 G2
Watford WD17 off High St 24 BW42
Red Lo Cres, Bex. DA5 127 FD90
Red Lo Rd, Bex. DA5 127 FD90
West Wickham BR4 143 ED100
Redman Cl, Nthlt. UB5 78 BW68
Redmans La, Sev. (Shore.)
TN14 165 FE107
Redman's Rd, E1 84 DW71
Redmead La, E1 202 B3
Redmead Rd, Hayes UB3 95 BS77
Redmore Rd, W6 99 CV77
Red Oak Cl, Orp. BR6 145 EP104
Red Oaks Mead, Epp. (They.B.)
CM16 33 ER37
Red Path, E9 85 DZ65
Red Pl, W1 194 F10
Redpoll Way, Erith DA18 106 EX76
Red Post Hill, SE21 122 DR85
SE24 102 DR84
Redriffe Rd, E13 86 EF67
Redriff Est, SE16 203 M6
Redriff Rd, SE16 203 J7
Romford RM7 51 FB54
Red Rd, Borwd. WD6 26 CM41
Brentwood CM14 54 FV49
Redroofs Cl, Beck. BR3 143 EB95
Redruth Cl, N22
off Palmerston Rd 45 DM52
Redruth Gdns, Rom. RM3 52 FM50
Redruth Rd, E9 85 DX67
Romford RM3 52 FM50
Redruth Wk, Rom. RM3 52 FN50
Redstart Cl, E6
off Columbine Av 86 EL71
SE14
off Southerngate Way 103 DY80
Croydon (New Adgtn.)
CR0 161 ED110
Redstone Hill, Red. RH1 184 DG134
Redstone Manor, Red. RH1 184 DG134
Redstone Pk, Red. RH1 184 DG134
Redston Rd, N8 65 DK56
REDSTREET, Grav. 130 GB93
Red St, Grav. (Sthflt.) DA13 130 GA93
Redvers Rd, N22 45 DN54
Warlingham CR6 176 DW118
Redvers St, N1 197 N2
Redwald Rd, E5 67 DX63
Redway Dr, Twick. TW2 116 CC87
Redwing Cl, S.Croy. CR2 161 DX111
Redwing Gdns, W.Byf. KT14 152 BH112
Redwing Gro, Abb.L. WD5 7 BU31
Redwing Path, SE28 105 ER75
Redwing Rd, Wall. SM6 159 DM108
Redwood, Egh. TW20 133 BE96
Redwood Chase, S.Ock.
RM15 91 FW70
Redwood Cl, N14 off The Vale 45 DK45
SE16 203 L3
Buckhurst Hill IG9
off Beech La 48 EH47
Kenley CR8 160 DQ114
Sidcup DA15 126 EU87
Uxbridge UB10
off The Larches 77 BP68
Watford WD19 40 BW49
Redwood Ct, NW6
off The Avenue 81 CY66
Redwood Est, Houns. TW5 95 BV79
Redwood Gdns, E4 31 EB44
Chigwell IG7 50 EU50
Redwood Ms, SW4
off Hannington Rd 101 DH83
Redwood Mt, Reig. RH2 184 DA131
Redwood Ri, Borwd. WD6 26 CN37
Redwoods, SW15 119 CU88
Addlestone KT15 152 BG107
Redwood Wk, Surb. KT6 137 CK102
Redwood Way, Barn. EN5 27 CX43
Reece Ms, SW7 100 DD77
Reed Av, Orp. BR6 145 ES104
Reed Cl, E16 86 EG71
SE12 124 EG85
Iver SL0 75 BE72
St. Albans (Lon.Col.) AL2 9 CK27
Reede Gdns, Dag. RM10 71 FB64
Reede Rd, Dag. RM10 88 FA65
Reede Way, Dag. RM10 89 FB65
⇌ Reedham 159 DM113
Reedham Cl, N17 66 DV56
St. Albans (Brick.Wd.) AL2 8 CA29
Reedham Dr, Pur. CR8 159 DN113
Reedham Pk Av, Pur. CR8 175 DN116
Reedham St, SE15 102 DU82
Reedholm Vil, N16
off Winston Rd 66 DR63
Reed Pl, Shep. TW17 134 BM102
West Byfleet KT14 151 BE113
Reed Pond Wk, Rom. RM2 51 FF54
Reed Rd, N17 46 DT54
Reeds Cres, Wat. WD24 24 BW40
Reedsfield Cl, Ashf. TW15
off The Yews 115 BP91
Reedsfield Rd, Ashf. TW15 115 BP91
Reeds Pl, NW1
off Royal Coll St 83 DJ66
Reeds Wk, Wat. WD24 24 BW40
Reedworth St, SE11 200 E9
Ree La Cotts, Loug. IG10
off Englands La 33 EN40
Reenglass Rd, Stan. HA7 41 CK49
Rees Dr, Stan. HA7 42 CL49
Rees Gdns, Croy. CR0 142 DT100
Reesland Cl, E12 87 EN65
Rees St, N1 84 DQ67
Reets Fm Cl, NW9 62 CS58
Reeves Av, NW9 62 CR59
⊸ Reeves Corner 141 DP103
Reeves Cor, Croy. CR0
off Roman Way 141 DP103
Reeves Cres, Swan. BR8 147 FD97
Reeves Ms, W1 198 F1
Reeves Rd, E3 85 EB70
SE18 105 EP79
Reflection, The, E16
off Woolwich Manor Way 105 EP75
Reform Row, N17 46 DT54
Reform St, SW11 100 DF82
Regal Cl, E1
off Old Montague St 84 DU71
W5 79 CK71
Regal Ct, N18
off College Cl 46 DT50
Regal Cres, Wall. SM6 141 DH104
Regal Dr, N11 45 DH50
Regal La, NW1
off Regents Pk Rd 82 DG67
Regal Pl, E3 off Coborn St 85 DZ69
SW6 off Maxwell Rd 100 DB80
Regal Row, SE15
off Queens Rd 102 DW81
Regal Way, Har. HA3 62 CL58
Watford WD24 24 BW38
Regan Way, N1 197 M1
Regarder Rd, Chig. IG7 50 EU50
Regarth Av, Rom. RM1 71 FE58
Regatta Ho, Tedd. TW11
off Twickenham Rd 117 CG91
Regency Cl, W5 80 CL72
Chigwell IG7 49 EQ50
Hampton TW12 116 BZ92
Regency Ct, Brwd. CM14 54 FW47
Sutton SM1
off Brunswick Rd 158 DB105
Regency Cres, NW4 43 CX54
Regency Dr, Ruis. HA4 59 BS60
West Byfleet KT14 151 BF113
Regency Gdns, Horn. RM11 72 FJ59
Walton-on-Thames KT12 136 BW102
Regency Lo, Buck.H. IG9 48 EK47
Regency Ms, NW10
off High Rd 81 CU65
Beckenham BR3 143 EC95
Isleworth TW7
off Queensbridge Pk 117 CE85
Regency Pl, SW1 199 N8
Woodford Green IG8 49 EN52
Regency St, SW1 199 N8
Regency Ter, SW7
off Fulham Rd 100 DD78
Regency Wk, Croy. CR0 143 DY100
Richmond TW10
off Friars Stile Rd 118 CL86
Regency Way, Bexh. DA6 106 EX83
Woking GU22 167 BD115
Regent Av, Uxb. UB10 77 BP66
Regent Cl, N12 off Nether St 44 DC50
Addlestone (New Haw)
KT15 152 BK109
Grays RM16 110 GC75
Harrow HA3 62 CL58
Hounslow TW4 95 BV81
Redhill RH1 185 DJ129
Regent Ct, Slou. SL1
off Stoke Poges La 74 AS72
Regent Cres, Red. RH1 184 DF132
Regent Gdns, Ilf. IG3 70 EU58
Regent Gate, Wal.Cr. EN8 15 DY34
Regent Pk, Lthd. KT22 171 CG118
Regent Pl, SW19
off Haydons Rd 120 DB92
W1 195 L10
Croydon CR0 off Grant Rd 142 DT102

Regent Rd, SE24 121 DP86
Epping CM16 17 ET30
Surbiton KT5 138 CM99
Regents Av, N13 45 DM50
Regents Br Gdns, SW8 101 DL80
Regents Cl, Hayes UB4
off Park Rd 77 BS71
Radlett WD7 9 CG34
South Croydon CR2 160 DS107
Whyteleafe CR3 176 DS118
Regents Dr, Kes. BR2 162 EK106
Regents Ms, NW8
off Langford Pl 82 DC68
REGENT'S PARK, NW1 194 G1
★ Regent's Park, NW1 194 D1
⊖ Regent's Park 195 H5
Regent's Pk, NW1 194 E1
Regent's Pk Est, NW1 195 K3
Regents Pk Rd, N3 63 CZ55
NW1 82 DF67
Regents Pk Ter, NW1
off Oval Rd 83 DH67
Regent's Pl, NW1 195 K4
SE3 104 EG82
Regents Pl, Loug. IG10 48 EK45
Regent Sq, E3 85 EB69
WC1 196 A3
Belvedere DA17 107 FB77
Regents Row, E8 84 DU67
Regent St, NW10
off Wellington Rd 81 CX69
SW1 199 M1
W1 195 J8
W4 98 CN78
Watford WD24 23 BV38
Regents Wf, N1
off All Saints St 83 DM68
Regina Cl, Barn. EN5 27 CX41
Reginald Rd, E7 86 EG66
SE8 103 EA80
Northwood HA6 39 BT53
Romford RM3 52 FN53
Reginald Sq, SE8 103 EA80
Regina Pt, SE16 202 G6
Regina Rd, N4 65 DM60
SE25 142 DU97
W13 79 CG74
Southall UB2 96 BY77
Regina Ter, W13 79 CG74
Regis Pl, SW2 101 DM84
Regis Rd, NW5 65 DH64
Regnart Bldgs, NW1 195 L4
Reid Av, Cat. CR3 176 DR121
Reid Cl, Couls. CR5 175 DH116
Pinner HA5 59 BU56
Reidhaven Rd, SE18 105 ES77
REIGATE 184 DA134
⇌ Reigate 184 DA133
Reigate Av, Sutt. SM1 140 DA102
Reigate Business Ms, Reig. RH2
off Albert Rd N 183 CZ133
Reigate Hill, Reig. RH2 184 DB130
Reigate Hill Cl, Reig. RH2 184 DA131
Reigate Rd, Bet. RH3 182 CS132
Bromley BR1 124 EF90
Epsom KT17, KT18 157 CT110
Ilford IG3 69 ET61
Leatherhead KT22 171 CJ122
Redhill RH1 184 DB134
Reigate RH2 184 DB134
Tadworth KT20 173 CX117
Reigate Way, Wall. SM6 159 DL106
Reighton Rd, E5 66 DU62
Relay Rd, W12 81 CW73
Relf Rd, SE15 102 DU83
Relko Ct, Epsom KT19 156 CR110
Relko Gdns, Sutt. SM1 158 DD106
Relton Ms, SW7 198 C6
Rembrandt Cl, E14 204 F7
SW1 198 F9
Rembrandt Ct, Epsom KT19 157 CT107
Rembrandt Dr, Grav. (Nthflt.)
DA11 130 GD90
Rembrandt Rd, SE13 104 EE84
Edgware HA8 42 CN54
Rembrandt Way, Walt. KT12 135 BV104
Remington Rd, E6 86 EL72
N15 66 DR58
Remington St, N1 196 G1
Remnant St, WC2 196 B8
Rempstone Ms, N1
off Mintern St 84 DR68
Remus Rd, E3 off Monier Rd 85 EA66
Renaissance Wk, SE10 205 L6
Rendle Cl, Croy. CR0 142 DT99
Rendlesham Av, Rad. WD7 25 CF37
Rendlesham Rd, E5 66 DU63
Enfield EN2 29 DP39
Rendlesham Way, Rick. (Chorl.)
WD3 21 BC44
Renforth St, SE16 202 G5
Renfree Way, Shep. TW17 134 BM101
Renfrew Cl, E6 87 EN73
Renfrew Rd, SE11 200 F8
Hounslow TW4 96 BX82
Kingston upon Thames
KT2 118 CP94
Renmans, The, Ashtd. KT21 172 CM116
Renmuir St, SW17 120 DF93
Rennell St, SE13 103 EC83
Rennels Way, Islw. TW7
off St. John's Rd 97 CE82
Renness Rd, E17 67 DY55
Rennets Cl, SE9 125 ES85
Rennets Wd Rd, SE9 125 ER85
Rennie Cl, Ashf. TW15 114 BK90
Rennie Est, SE16 202 E9
Rennie St, SE1 200 F2
Rennison Cl, Wal.Cr. EN7
off Allwood Rd 14 DT27
Renovation, The, E16
off Woolwich Manor Way 105 EP75
Renown Cl, Croy. CR0 141 DP102
Romford RM7 50 FA53
Rensburg Rd, E17 67 DX57
Renshaw Cl, Belv. DA17
off Grove Rd 106 EZ79
Renters Av, NW4 63 CW58
Renton Dr, Orp. BR5 146 EX101
Renwick Ind Est, Bark. IG11 88 EV67
Renwick Rd, Bark. IG11 88 EV70
Repens Way, Hayes UB4
off Stipularis Dr 78 BX70
Rephidim St, SE1 201 M7
Replingham Rd, SW18 119 CZ88
Reporton Rd, SW6 99 CY81
Repository Rd, SE18 105 EM79
Repton Av, Hayes UB3 95 BR77
Romford RM2 71 FG55
Wembley HA0 61 CJ63
Repton Cl, Cars. SM5 158 DE106
Repton Ct, Beck. BR3 143 EB95
Ilford IG5 off Repton Gro 49 EM53
Repton Dr, Rom. RM2 71 FG56
Repton Gdns, Rom. RM2 71 FG55
Repton Gro, Ilf. IG5 49 EM53
Repton Pl, Amer. HP7 20 AU39
Repton Rd, Har. HA3 62 CM56
Orpington BR6 146 EU104
Repton St, E14 85 DY72
Repton Way, Rick. (Crox.Grn.)
WD3 22 BN43
Repulse Cl, Rom. RM5 51 FB53
Reservoir Cl, Th.Hth. CR7 142 DR98
Reservoir Rd, N14 29 DJ43
SE4 103 DY82
Ruislip HA4 59 BQ57
Resolution Wk, SE18 105 EM76
Resolution Way, SE8
off Deptford High St 103 EA80
Restavon Pk, West. (Berry's Grn.)
TN16 179 EP116
Restell Cl, SE3 104 EE79
Restmor Way, Wall. SM6 140 DG103
Reston Cl, Borwd. WD6 26 CN38
Reston Path, Borwd. WD6 26 CN38
Reston Pl, SW7
off Hyde Pk Gate 100 DC75
Restons Cres, SE9 125 ER86
Restormel Cl, Houns. TW3 116 CA85
Retcar Cl, N19
off Dartmouth Pk Hill 65 DH61
Retcar Pl, N19 65 DH61
Retford Cl, Borwd. WD6
off The Campions 26 CN38
Romford RM3 52 FN51
Retford Path, Rom. RM3 52 FN51
Retford Rd, Rom. RM3 52 FM51
Retford St, N1 197 N1
Retingham Way, E4 47 EB47
Retreat, The, NW9 62 CR57
SW14
off South Worple Way 98 CS83
Addlestone KT15 152 BK106
Amersham HP6 20 AY39
Brentwood CM14
off Costead Manor Rd 54 FV46
Brentwood (Hutton) CM13 55 GB44
Egham TW20 112 AX92
Grays RM17 110 GB79
Harrow HA2 60 CA59
Kings Langley WD4 7 BQ31
Orpington BR6 164 EV107
Surbiton KT5 138 CM100
Thornton Heath CR7 142 DR98
Worcester Park KT4 139 CV103
Retreat Cl, Har. HA3 61 CJ57
Retreat Pl, E9 84 DW65
Retreat Rd, Rich. TW9 117 CK85
Retreat Way, Chig. IG7 50 EV48
Reubens Rd, Brwd. CM13 55 GB44
Reunion Row, E1 202 E1
Reveley Sq, SE16 203 L5
Revell Cl, Lthd. (Fetch.) KT22 170 CB122
Revell Dr, Lthd. (Fetch.)
KT22 170 CB122
Revell Ri, SE18 105 ET79
Revell Rd, Kings.T. KT1 138 CP95
Sutton SM1 157 CZ107
Revelon Rd, SE4 103 DY84
Revelstoke Rd, SW18 119 CZ89
Reventlow Rd, SE9 125 EQ88
Reverdy Rd, SE1 202 B9
Reverend Cl, Har. HA2 60 CB62
Revesby Rd, Cars. SM5 140 DD100
Review Rd, NW2 63 CT61
Dagenham RM10 89 FB67
Rewell St, SW6 100 DC80
Rewley Rd, Cars. SM5 140 DD100
Rex Av, Ashf. TW15 114 BN93
Rex Cl, Rom. RM5 51 FB52
Rex Pl, W1 198 G1
Reydon Av, E11 68 EJ58
Reynard Cl, SE4
off Foxwell St 103 DY83
Bromley BR1 145 EM97
Reynard Dr, SE19 122 DT94
Reynard Pl, SE14
off Milton Ct Rd 103 DY79
Reynardson Rd, N17 46 DQ52
Reynards Way, St.Alb. (Brick.Wd.)
AL2 8 BZ29
Reynolah Gdns, SE7
off Rathmore Rd 104 EH78
Reynolds Av, E12 69 EN64
Chessington KT9 156 CL108
Romford RM6 70 EW59
Reynolds Cl, NW11 64 DB59
SW19 140 DD95
Carshalton SM5 140 DF102
Reynolds Ct, E11
off Cobbold Rd 68 EF62
Romford RM6 70 EX55
Reynolds Dr, Edg. HA8 62 CM55
Reynolds Pl, SE3 104 EH80
Richmond TW10
off Cambrian Rd 118 CM86
Reynolds Rd, SE15 122 DW85
W4 98 CQ76
Hayes UB4 78 BW70
New Malden KT3 138 CR101
Reynolds Way, Croy. CR0 160 DS105
Rheidol Ms, N1
off Rheidol Ter 84 DQ68
Rheidol Ter, N1 83 DP68
Rheingold Way, Wall. SM6 159 DL109
Rheola Cl, N17 46 DT53
Rhoda St, E2 off Brick La 84 DT70
Rhodes Av, N22 45 DJ53
Rhodes Cl, Egh. TW20
off Mullens Rd 113 BC92
Rhodesia Rd, E11 67 ED61
SW9 101 DL82
Rhodes Moorhouse Ct, Mord.
SM4 140 DA100
Rhodes St, N7
off Mackenzie Rd 65 DM64
Rhodes Way, Wat. WD24 24 BX40
Rhodeswell Rd, E14 85 DZ72
Rhododendron Ride, Egh.
TW20 112 AT94
Slough SL3 75 AZ69
Rhodrons Av, Chess. KT9 156 CL106
Rhondda Gro, E3 85 DY69
Rhyl Rd, Grnf. UB6 79 CF68
Rhyl St, NW5 82 DG65
Rhys Av, N11 45 DK52
Rialto Rd, Mitch. CR4 140 DG96
Ribble Cl, Wdf.Grn. IG8
off Prospect Rd 48 EJ51
Ribbledale, St.Alb. (Lon.Col.)
AL2 10 CM27
Ribblesdale Av, N11 44 DG51
Northolt UB5 78 CB65
Ribblesdale Rd, N8 65 DM56
SW16 121 DH93
Dartford DA2 128 FQ88
Ribchester Av, Grnf. UB6 79 CF69
Ribston Cl, Brom. BR2 145 EM102
Radlett (Shenley) WD7
off Wayside 9 CK33
Ricardo Path, SE28
off Byron Cl 88 EW74
Ricardo Rd, Wind. (Old Wind.)
SL4 112 AV86
Ricardo St, E14 85 EB72
Ricards Rd, SW19 119 CZ92
Richard Cl, SE18 104 EL77
Richard Fell Ho, E12
off Walton Rd 69 EN63
Richard Foster Cl, E17 67 DZ59
Richard Ho Dr, E16 86 EK72
Richards Av, Rom. RM7 71 FC57
Richards Cl, Bushey WD23 41 CD45
Harrow HA1 61 CG57
Hayes UB3 95 BR79
Uxbridge UB10 76 BN67
Richards Fld, Epsom KT19 156 CR109
Richardson Cl, E8
off Clarissa St 84 DT67
Greenhithe DA9
off Steele Av 129 FU85
St. Albans (Lon.Col.) AL2 10 CL27
Richardson Cres, Wal.Cr. (Chsht.)
EN7 13 DP25
Richardson Rd, E15 86 EE68
Richardson's Ms, W1 195 K5
Richards Pl, E17 67 EA55
SW3 198 C8
Richards Rd, Cob. (Stoke D'Ab.)
KT11 154 CB114
Richard St, E1
off Commercial Rd 84 DV72
Richbell Cl, Ashtd. KT21 171 CK118
Richbell Pl, WC1 196 B6
Richborne Ter, SW8 101 DM80
Richborough Cl, Orp. BR5 146 EX98
Richborough Rd, NW2 63 CX63
Richens Cl, Houns. TW3 97 CD82
Riches Rd, Ilf. IG1 69 EQ61
Richfield Rd, Bushey WD23 40 CC45
Richford Rd, E15 86 EF67
Richford St, W6 99 CW75
RICHINGS PARK, Iver 93 BE75
Richings Way, Iver SL0 93 BF76
Richland Av, Couls. CR5 158 DG114
Richlands Av, Epsom KT17 157 CU105
Rich La, SW5 off Warwick Rd 100 DB78
Richmer Rd, Erith DA8 107 FG80
RICHMOND 118 CL86
⇌ Richmond 98 CL84
⊖ Richmond 98 CL84
Richmond Av, E4 47 ED50
N1 83 DM67
NW10 81 CW65
SW20 139 CY95
Feltham TW14 115 BS86
Uxbridge UB10 77 BP65
Richmond Br, Rich. TW9 117 CK86
Twickenham TW1 117 CK86
Richmond Bldgs, W1 195 M9
Richmond Cl, E17 67 DZ58
Amersham HP6 20 AT38
Borehamwood WD6 26 CR43
Epsom KT18 156 CS114
Leatherhead (Fetch.) KT22 170 CC124
Waltham Cross (Chsht.)
EN8 14 DW29
Westerham (Bigg.H.) TN16 178 EH119
Richmond Ct, Pot.B. EN6 12 DC31
Richmond Cres, E4 47 ED50
N1 83 DM67
N9 46 DU46
Slough SL1 74 AU74
Staines TW18 113 BF92
Richmond Dr, Grav. DA12 131 GL89
Shepperton TW17 135 BQ100
Watford WD17 23 BS39
Richmond Gdns, NW4 63 CU57
Harrow HA3 41 CF51
Richmond Grn, Croy. CR0 141 DL104
Richmond Gro, N1 83 DP66
Surbiton KT5 138 CM100
Richmond Hill, Rich. TW10 118 CL86
Richmond Hill Ct, Rich.
TW10 118 CL86
Richmond Ms, W1 195 M9
Teddington TW11
off Broad St 117 CF93
★ Richmond Palace (remains),
Rich. TW9 117 CJ85
★ Richmond Park, Rich.
TW10 118 CN88
Richmond Pk, Kings.T. KT2 118 CP88
Loughton IG10
off Fallow Flds 48 EJ45
Richmond TW10 118 CP88
Richmond Pk Rd, SW14 118 CQ85
Kingston upon Thames
KT2 118 CL94
Richmond Pl, SE18 105 EQ77
Richmond Rd, E4 47 EE46
E7 68 EH64
E8 84 DT66
E11 67 ED61
N2 44 DC54
N11 45 DL51
N15 66 DS58
SW20 139 CV95
W5 98 CL75
Barnet EN5 28 DB43
Coulsdon CR5 175 DH115
Croydon CR0 141 DL104
Grays RM17 110 GC79
Ilford IG1 69 EQ62
Isleworth TW7 97 CG83
Kingston upon Thames
KT2 117 CK92
Potters Bar EN6 12 DC31
Romford RM1 71 FF58
Staines TW18 113 BF92
Thornton Heath CR7 141 DP97
Twickenham TW1 117 CJ86
Richmond St, E13 86 EG68
Richmond Ter, SW1 199 P4
Richmond Ter Ms, SW1
off Parliament St 101 DL75
Richmond Way, E11 68 EG61
W12 99 CX75
W14 99 CX76
Leatherhead (Fetch.) KT22 170 CB123
Rickmansworth (Crox.Grn.)
WD3 23 BQ42
Richmount Gdns, SE3 104 EG83
Rich St, E14 85 DZ73
Rickard Cl, NW4 63 CV56
SW2 121 DM88
West Drayton UB7 94 BK76
Rickards Cl, Surb. KT6 138 CL102
Ricketts Hill Rd, West. (Tats.)
TN16 178 EK118
Rickett St, SW6 100 DA79
Rickman Cres, Add. KT15 134 BH104
Rickman Hill, Couls. CR5 175 DH118
Rickman Hill Rd, Couls. CR5 175 DH118
Rickmans La, Slou. (Stoke P.)
SL2 56 AS64
Rickman St, E1
off Mantus Rd 84 DW69
RICKMANSWORTH 38 BL45
⇌ Rickmansworth 38 BK45
⊖ Rickmansworth 38 BK45
Rickmansworth La, Ger.Cr.
(Chal.St.P.) SL9 37 AZ50
Rickmansworth Pk, Rick. WD3 38 BK45
Rickmansworth Rd, Nthwd.
HA6 39 BR52
Pinner HA5 39 BV54
Rickmansworth (Chorl.)
WD3 21 BE41
Uxbridge (Hare.) UB9 38 BJ53
Watford WD17, WD18 23 BS42
Rick Roberts Way, E15 85 EC67
Rickthorne Rd, N19
off Landseer Rd 65 DL61
Rickyard Path, SE9 104 EL84
Ridding La, Grnf. UB6 61 CF64
Riddings, The, Cat. CR3 186 DT125
⇌ Riddlesdown 160 DR113
Riddlesdown Av, Pur. CR8 160 DQ112
Riddlesdown Rd, Pur. CR8 160 DQ111
Riddons Rd, SE12 124 EJ90
Ride, The, Brent. TW8 97 CH78
Enfield EN3 30 DW41
Rideout St, SE18 105 EM77
Rider Cl, Sid. DA15 125 ES86
Riders Way, Gdse. RH9 186 DW131
Ridgdale St, E3 85 EB68
RIDGE, Pot.B. 10 CS34
Ridge, The, Bex. DA5 126 EZ87
Caterham (Wold.) CR3 187 EB126
Coulsdon CR5 159 DL114
Epsom KT18 172 CP117
Leatherhead (Fetch.) KT22 171 CD124
Orpington BR6 145 ER103
Purley CR8 159 DJ110
Surbiton KT5 138 CN99
Twickenham TW2 117 CD87
Woking GU22 167 BB117
Ridge Av, N21 46 DQ45
Dartford DA1 127 FF86
Ridgebrook Rd, SE3 104 EJ83
Ridge Cl, NW4 43 CX54
NW9 62 CR56
SE28 105 ER75
Woking GU22 166 AV121
Ridge Crest, Enf. EN2 29 DM39
Ridgecroft Cl, Bex. DA5 127 FC88
Ridgefield, Wat. WD17 23 BS37
Ridgegate Cl, Reig. RH2 184 DD132
RIDGEHILL, Rad. 10 CQ30
Ridge Hill, NW11 63 CY60
Ridgehurst Av, Wat. WD25 7 BT34
Ridgelands, Lthd. (Fetch.)
KT22 171 CD124
Ridge La, Wat. WD17 23 BS38
Ridge Langley, S.Croy. CR2 160 DU109
Ridgemead Rd, Egh. (Eng.Grn.)
TW20 112 AU90
Ridgemont Gdns, Edg. HA8 42 CQ49
Ridgemount, Wey. KT13
off Oatlands Dr 135 BS103
Ridgemount Av, Couls. CR5 175 DH117
Croydon CR0 143 DX102
Ridgemount Cl, SE20
off Anerley Pk 122 DV94
Ridgemount End, Ger.Cr.
(Chal.St.P.) SL9 36 AY50
Ridgemount Gdns, Enf. EN2 29 DP40
Ridge Pk, Pur. CR8 159 DK110
Ridge Rd, N8 65 DM58
N21 46 DQ46
NW2 63 CZ62
Mitcham CR4 121 DH94
Sutton SM3 139 CY102
Ridge St, Wat. WD24 23 BV38
Ridgeview Cl, Barn. EN5 27 CX44
Ridgeview Lo, St.Alb. (Lon.Col.)
AL2 10 CM28
Ridgeview Rd, N20 44 DB48
Ridge Way, SE19
off Central Hill 122 DS93
Ridgeway, SE28
off Pettman Cres 105 ER77
Brentwood CM13 55 GB46
Bromley BR2 144 EG103
Ridge Way, Dart. (Cray.) DA1 127 FF86
Ridgeway, Dart. (Lane End)
DA2 129 FS92
Epsom KT19 156 CQ112
Ridge Way, Felt. TW13 116 BY90
Ridgeway, Grays RM17 110 GE77
Ridge Way, Iver SL0 75 BE74
Ridgeway, Rick. WD3 38 BH45
Virginia Water GU25 132 AY99
Woking (Horsell) GU21 166 AX115
Woodford Green IG8 48 EJ49
Ridgeway, The, E4 47 EB47
N3 44 DB52
N11 44 DF49
N14 45 DL47
NW7 43 CU49
NW9 62 CS56
NW11 63 CZ60
W3 98 CN76
Croydon CR0 141 DM104
Enfield EN2 29 DN39
Gerrards Cross (Chal.St.P.)
SL9 56 AX55
Harrow (Kenton) HA3 61 CJ58
Harrow (N.Har.) HA2 60 BZ57
Leatherhead (Fetch.) KT22 171 CD123
Leatherhead (Oxshott)
KT22 154 CC114
Potters Bar EN6 12 DD34
Potters Bar (Cuffley) EN6 12 DE28
Radlett WD7 25 CF37
Romford (Gidea Pk.) RM2 71 FG56
Romford (Harold Wd.) RM3 52 FL53
Ruislip HA4 60 CA58
South Croydon CR2 160 DS110
Stanmore HA7 41 CJ51
Walton-on-Thames KT12 135 BT102
Watford WD17 23 BS37
Ridgeway Av, Barn. EN4 28 DF44
Gravesend DA12 131 GH90
Ridgeway Cl, Lthd. (Oxshott)
KT22 154 CC114
Woking GU21 166 AX116
Ridgeway Ct, Red. RH1 184 DE134
Ridgeway Cres, Orp. BR6 145 ES104
Ridgeway Cres Gdns, Orp.
BR6 145 ES103
Ridgeway Dr, Brom. BR1 124 EH91
Ridgeway E, Sid. DA15 125 ET85
Ridgeway Est, The, Iver SL0 75 BF74
Ridgeway Gdns, N6 65 DJ59
Ilford IG4 68 EL57
Woking GU21 166 AX115
Ridgeway Rd, SW9 101 DP83
Isleworth TW7 97 CE80
Redhill RH1 184 DE134
Ridgeway Rd N, Islw. TW7 97 CE79
Ridgeway Wk, Nthlt. UB5
off Fortunes Mead 78 BY65
Ridgeway W, Sid. DA15 125 ES85
Ridgewell Cl, N1 off Basire St 84 DQ67
SE26 123 DZ91
Dagenham RM10 89 FB67
Ridgmount Gdns, WC1 195 M5
Ridgmount Pl, WC1 195 M6
Ridgmount Rd, SW18 120 DB85
Ridgmount St, WC1 195 M6
Ridgway, SW19 119 CX93
Woking (Pyrford) GU22 167 BF115
Ridgway, The, Sutt. SM2 158 DD108
Ridgway Gdns, SW19 119 CX94
Ridgway Pl, SW19 119 CY93
Ridgway Rd, Wok. (Pyrford)
GU22 167 BF115
Ridgwell Rd, E16 86 EJ71
Riding, The, NW11
off Golders Grn Rd 63 CZ59
Woking GU21 151 BB114
Riding Ct Rd, Slou. (Datchet)
SL3 92 AW80
Riding Hill, S.Croy. CR2 160 DU113
Riding Ho St, W1 195 K7
Ridings, The, E11
off Malcolm Way 68 EG57
W5 80 CM70
Addlestone KT15 151 BF107
Ashtead KT21 171 CK117
Chesham HP5 20 AX36
Chigwell IG7
off Manford Way 50 EV49
Cobham KT11 154 CA112
Epsom KT18 172 CS115
Epsom (Ewell) KT17 157 CT109
Iver SL0 93 BF77
Reigate RH2 184 DD131
Sunbury-on-Thames
TW16 135 BU95
Surbiton KT5 138 CN99
Tadworth KT20 173 CZ120
Westerham (Bigg.H.) TN16 178 EL117
Woking (Ripley) GU23 168 BG123
Ridings Av, N21 29 DP42
Ridings Cl, N6
off Hornsey La Gdns 65 DJ59
Ridings La, Wok. GU23 168 BN123
Ridlands Gro, Oxt. RH8 188 EL130

Rid - Rod

Ridlands La, Oxt. RH8 188 EK130
Ridlands Ri, Oxt. RH8 188 EL130
Ridler Rd, Enf. EN1 30 DS38
Ridley Av, W13 97 CH76
Ridley Cl, Bark. IG11 87 ET66
Romford RM3 51 FH53
Ridley Rd, E7 68 EJ63
E8 66 DT64
NW10 81 CU68
SW19 120 DB94
Bromley BR2 144 EF97
Warlingham CR6 176 DW118
Welling DA16 106 EV81
Ridsdale Rd, SE20 142 DV95
Woking GU21 166 AV117
Riefield Rd, SE9 105 EQ84
Riesco Dr, Croy. CR0 160 DW107
Riffel Rd, NW2 63 CW64
Riffhams, Brwd. CM13 55 GB48
Rifle Butts All, Epsom KT18 173 CT115
Rifle Pl, SE11 101 DN79
Rifle St, E14 85 EB71
Rigault Rd, SW6 99 CY82
Rigby Cl, Croy. CR0 141 DN104
Rigby Gdns, Grays RM16 111 GH77
Rigby La, Hayes UB3 95 BR75
Rigby Ms, Ilf. IG1
off Cranbrook Rd 69 EP61
Rigby Pl, Enf. EN3
off Government Row 31 EA38
Rigden St, E14 85 EB72
Rigeley Rd, NW10 81 CU69
Rigg App, E10 67 DX60
Rigge Pl, SW4 101 DK84
Riggindale Rd, SW16 121 DK92
Riley Rd, SE1 201 N6
Enfield EN3 30 DW38
Riley St, SW10 100 DD79
Rinaldo Rd, SW12 121 DH87
Ring, The, W2 194 B10
Ring Cl, Brom. BR1
off Garden Rd 124 EH94
Ringcroft St, N7 65 DN64
Ringers Rd, Brom. BR1 144 EG97
Ringford Rd, SW18 119 CZ85
Ringlet Cl, E16 86 EH71
Ringlewell Cl, Enf. EN1
off Central Av 30 DV40
Ringley Pk Rd, Reig. RH2 184 DC134
Ringmer Av, SW6 99 CY81
Ringmer Gdns, N19
off Sussex Way 65 DL61
Ringmer Pl, N21 30 DR43
Ringmer Way, Brom. BR1 145 EM99
Ringmore Ri, SE23 122 DV87
Ringmore Rd, Walt. KT12 136 BW104
Ring Rd, W12 81 CW73
Ringshall Rd, Orp. BR5 146 EU97
Ringslade Rd, N22 45 DM54
Ringstead Rd, SE6 123 EB87
Sutton SM1 158 DD105
Ringway, N11 45 DJ51
Southall UB2 96 BY78
Ringway Rd, St.Alb. (Park St.)
AL2 8 CB27
Ringwold Cl, Beck. BR3 123 DY94
Ringwood Av, N2 44 DF54
Croydon CR0 141 DL101
Hornchurch RM12 72 FK61
Orpington BR6 164 EW110
Redhill RH1 184 DF131
Ringwood Cl, Pnr. HA5 60 BW55
Ringwood Gdns, E14 204 A8
SW15 119 CU89
Ringwood Rd, E17 67 DZ58
Ringwood Way, N21 45 DP46
Hampton (Hmptn.H.)
TW12 116 CA91
RIPLEY, Wok. 168 BJ122
Ripley Av, Egh. TW20 112 AY93
Ripley Bypass, Wok. GU23 168 BK122
Ripley Cl, Brom. BR1
off Ringmer Way 145 EM99
Croydon (New Adgtn.)
CR0 161 EC107
Slough SL3 92 AY77
Ripley Gdns, SW14 98 CR83
Sutton SM1 158 DC105
Ripley La, Wok. GU23 168 BL123
Ripley Ms, E11 off Wadley Rd 68 EE59
Ripley Rd, E16 86 EJ72
Belvedere DA17 106 FA77
Enfield EN2 30 DQ39
Hampton TW12 116 CA94
Ilford IG3 69 ET61
RIPLEY SPRINGS, Egh. 112 AY93
Ripley Vw, Loug. IG10 33 EP38
Ripley Vil, W5
off Castlebar Rd 79 CJ72
Ripley Way, Epsom KT19 156 CN111
Waltham Cross (Chsht.)
EN7 14 DV30
Riplington Ct, SW15
off Longwood Dr 119 CU87
Ripon Cl, Nthlt. UB5 60 CA64
Ripon Gdns, Chess. KT9 155 CK106
Ilford IG1 68 EL58
Ripon Rd, N9 46 DV45
N17 66 DR55
SE18 105 EP79
Ripon Way, Borwd. WD6 26 CQ43
Rippersley Rd, Well. DA16 106 EU81
Ripple Rd, Bark. IG11 87 EQ66
Dagenham RM9 88 EV67
Rippleside Commercial Est, Bark.
IG11 88 EW68
Ripplevale Gro, N1 83 DM66
Rippolson Rd, SE18 105 ET78
Ripston Rd, Ashf. TW15 115 BR92
Risborough Dr, Wor.Pk. KT4 139 CU101
Risborough St, SE1 200 G4
Risdon St, SE16 202 G5
Rise, The, E11 68 EG57
N13 45 DN49
Rise, The, NW7 43 CT51
NW10 62 CR63
Bexley DA5 126 EW87
Borehamwood (Elstree)
WD6 26 CM43
Buckhurst Hill IG9 48 EK45
Dartford DA1 107 FF84
Edgware HA8 42 CP50
Epsom KT17 157 CT110
Gravesend DA12 131 GL91
Greenford UB6 61 CG64
St. Albans (Park St.) AL2 9 CD25
Sevenoaks TN13 191 FJ129
South Croydon CR2 160 DW109
Tadworth KT20 173 CW121
Uxbridge UB10 76 BM68
Waltham Abbey EN9 off Breach
Barn Mobile Home Pk 16 EH30
Risebridge Chase, Rom. RM1 51 FF52
Risebridge Rd, Rom. RM2 51 FF54
Risedale Rd, Bexh. DA7 107 FB83
Riseldine Rd, SE23 123 DY86
Rise Pk Boul, Rom. RM1 51 FF53
Rise Pk Par, Rom. RM1 51 FE54
Riseway, Brwd. CM15 54 FY48
Rising Hill Cl, Nthwd. HA6
off Ducks Hill Rd 39 BQ51
Risinghill St, N1 83 DM68
Risingholme Cl, Bushey WD23 40 CB45
Harrow HA3 41 CE53
Risingholme Rd, Har. HA3 41 CE54
Risings, The, E17 67 ED56
Rising Sun Ct, EC1 196 G7
Risley Av, N17 46 DQ53
Rita Rd, SW8 101 DM80
Ritches Rd, N15 66 DQ57
Ritchie Rd, Croy. CR0 142 DV100
Ritchie St, N1 83 DN68
Ritchings Av, E17 67 DY56
Ritherdon Rd, SW17 120 DG89
Ritson Rd, E8 84 DU65
Ritter St, SE18 105 EN79
Ritz Ct, Pot.B. EN6 12 DA31
Ritz Par, W5 off Connell Cres 80 CM70
Rivaz Pl, E9 84 DW65
Rivenhall Gdns, E18 68 EF56
River Ash Est, Shep. TW17 135 BT101
River Av, N13 45 DP48
Thames Ditton KT7 137 CG101
River Bk, N21 46 DQ45
East Molesey KT8 137 CE97
Riverbank, Stai. TW18 113 BF93
River Bk, T.Ditt. KT7 137 CF99
West Molesey KT8 136 BZ97
Riverbank Way, Brent. TW8 97 CJ79
River Barge Cl, E14 204 E5
River Brent Business Pk, W7 97 CE76
River Cl, E11 68 EJ58
Rainham RM13 89 FH71
Ruislip HA4 59 BT58
Southall UB2 96 CC75
Surbiton KT6
off Catherine Rd 137 CK99
Waltham Cross EN8 15 EA34
River Ct, Wok. GU21 151 BC114
Rivercourt Rd, W6 99 CV77
River Crane Wk, Felt. TW13 116 BX88
Hounslow TW4 116 BX88
River Crane Way, Felt. TW13
off Watermill Way 116 BZ89
Riverdale, SE13
off Lewisham High St 103 EC83
Riverdale Cl, Bark. IG11 88 EV70
Riverdale Dr, SW18
off Strathville Rd 120 DB88
Woking GU22 167 AZ121
Riverdale Gdns, Twick. TW1 117 CJ86
Riverdale Rd, SE18 105 ET78
Bexley DA5 126 EZ87
Erith DA8 107 FB78
Feltham TW13 116 BY91
Twickenham TW1 117 CJ86
Riverdene, Edg. HA8 42 CQ48
Riverdene Rd, Ilf. IG1 69 EN62
River Dr, Upmin. RM14 72 FQ58
Riverfield Rd, Stai. TW18 113 BF93
River Front, Enf. EN1 30 DR41
River Gdns, Cars. SM5 140 DG103
Feltham TW14 115 BV85
River Gro Pk, Beck. BR3 143 DZ95
RIVERHEAD, Sev. 190 FD122
Riverhead Cl, E17 47 DX54
Riverhead Dr, Sutt. SM2 158 DA110
River Hill, Cob. KT11 169 BV115
Riverhill, Sev. TN15 191 FL130
Riverholme Dr, Epsom KT19 156 CR109
River Island Cl, Lthd. (Fetch.)
KT22 171 CD121
River La, Lthd. KT22 171 CD120
Richmond TW10 117 CK88
Rivermead, E.Mol. KT8 136 CC97
West Byfleet (Byfleet) KT14 152 BM113
Rivermead Cl, Add. KT15 152 BJ108
Teddington TW11 117 CH92
Rivermead Ct, SW6 99 CZ83
Rivermeads Av, Twick. TW2 116 CA90
Rivermount, Walt. KT12 135 BT101
Rivernook Cl, Walt. KT12 136 BW99
River Pk Av, Stai. TW18 113 BD91
River Pk Gdns, Brom. BR2 123 ED94
River Pk Rd, N22 45 DM54
River Pl, N1 84 DQ66
River Reach, Tedd. TW11 117 CJ92
River Rd, Bark. IG11 87 ES68
Brentwood CM14 54 FS49
Buckhurst Hill IG9 48 EL46
Staines TW18 133 BF95
River Rd Business Pk, Bark.
IG11 87 ET69
Riversdale, Grav. (Nthflt.)
DA11 130 GE89
Riversdale Rd, N5 65 DP62
Romford RM5 51 FB52
Thames Ditton KT7 137 CG99
Riversdell Cl, Cher. KT16 133 BF101
Riversfield Rd, Enf. EN1 30 DS41
Riverside, NW4 63 CV59
Riverside, SE7 205 P7
Chertsey KT16 134 BG97
Dartford (Eyns.) DA4 148 FK103
Egham (Runny.) TW20
off Windsor Rd 113 AZ90
St. Albans (Lon.Col.) AL2 10 CL27
Shepperton TW17 135 BS101
Staines TW18 133 BF95
Staines (Wrays.) TW19 112 AW87
Twickenham TW1 117 CH88
Riverside, The, E.Mol. KT8 137 CD97
Riverside Av, E.Mol. KT8 137 CD99
Riverside Business Cen,
SW18 120 DB88
Riverside Cl, E5 66 DW60
W7 79 CE70
Kings Langley WD4 7 BP29
Kingston upon Thames KT1 137 CK98
Orpington BR5 146 EW96
Staines TW18 133 BF95
Wallington SM6 141 DH104
Riverside Ct, E4
off Chelwood Cl 31 EB44
SW8 101 DK79
Riverside Dr, NW11 63 CY58
W4 98 CR80
Esher KT10 154 CA105
Mitcham CR4 140 DE99
Richmond TW10 117 CH89
Rickmansworth WD3 38 BK46
Staines TW18 133 BF95
Staines (Egh.H.) TW18 113 BE92
Riverside Gdns, N3 63 CY55
W6 99 CV78
Enfield EN2 30 DQ40
Wembley HA0 80 CL68
Woking (Old Wok.) GU22 167 BB121
Riverside Ind Est, Bark. IG11 88 EU69
Dartford DA1 128 FL85
Enfield EN3 31 DY44
Riverside Mans, E1 202 F2
Riverside Ms, Croy. CR0
off Wandle Rd 141 DL104
Riverside Path, Wal.Cr. (Chsht.)
EN8 off Dewhurst Rd 15 DY29
Riverside Pl, Stai. (Stanw.)
TW19 114 BK86
Riverside Retail Pk, Sev. TN14 181 FH119
Riverside Rd, E15 85 EC68
N15 66 DU58
SW17 120 DB91
Sidcup DA14 126 EY90
Staines TW18 113 BF94
Staines (Stanw.) TW19 114 BK85
Walton-on-Thames KT12 154 BX105
Watford WD19 23 BV44
Riverside Twr, SW6 100 DC82
Riverside Wk, Bex. DA5 126 EW87
Isleworth TW7 97 CE83
Kingston upon Thames KT1
off High St 137 CK96
Loughton IG10 33 EP44
West Wickham BR4
off The Alders 143 EB102
Riverside Way, Dart. DA1 128 FL85
St. Albans AL2 9 CD32
Uxbridge UB8 76 BH67
Riverside W, SW18
off Smugglers Way 100 DB84
River St, EC1 196 D2
River Ter, W6
off Crisp Rd 99 CW78
Riverton Cl, W9 81 CZ69
River Vw, Enf. EN2
off Chase Side 30 DQ41
Grays RM16 111 GG77
Riverview Gdns, SW13 99 CV79
Cobham KT11 153 BU113
Twickenham TW1 117 CF89
Riverview Gro, W4 98 CP79
River Vw Hts, SE16 202 B4
RIVERVIEW PARK, Grav. 131 GK92
Riverview Pk, SE6 123 EA89
Riverview Rd, W4 98 CP79
Epsom KT19 156 CQ105
Greenhithe DA9 129 FU85
River Wk, Uxb. (Denh.) UB9 58 BJ64
Walton-on-Thames KT12 135 BU100
Riverway, N13 45 DN50
River Way, Epsom KT19 156 CR106
Loughton IG10 33 EN44
Riverway, Stai. TW18 134 BH95
River Way, Twick. TW2 116 CB89
River Wey Navigation, Wok.
GU23 167 BB122
Riverwood La, Chis. BR7 145 ER95
Rivey Cl, W.Byf. KT14 151 BF114
Rivington Av, Wdf.Grn. IG8 48 EK54
Rivington Ct, NW10 81 CU67
Rivington Cres, NW7 43 CT52
Rivington Pl, EC2 197 N3
Rivington St, EC2 197 M3
Rivington Wk, E8 off Wilde Cl 84 DU67
Rivulet Rd, N17 46 DQ52
Rixon Cl, Slou. (Geo.Grn.) SL3 74 AY72
Rixon Ho, SE18
off Barnfield Rd 105 EP79
Rixon St, N7 65 DN62
Rixsen Rd, E12 68 EL64
Roach Rd, E3 85 EA66
Roads Pl, N19 off Hornsey Rd 65 DL61
Roakes Av, Add. KT15 134 BH103
Roan St, SE10 103 EC79
Robarts Cl, Pnr. HA5
off Field End Rd 59 BV57
Robb Rd, Stan. HA7 41 CG51
Robert Adam St, W1 194 F8
Roberta St, E2 84 DU69
Robert Cl, W9 off Randolph Av 82 DC70
Chigwell IG7 49 ET50
Potters Bar EN6 11 CY33
Walton-on-Thames KT12 153 BV106
Robert Dashwood Way, SE17 201 H9
Robert Keen Cl, SE15
off Cicely Rd 102 DU81
Robert Lowe Cl, SE14 103 DX80
Roberton Dr, Brom. BR1 144 EJ95
Robert Owen Ho, SW6 99 CX81
Robertsbridge Rd, Cars. SM5 140 DC102
Roberts Cl, SE9 125 ER88
SE16 203 J5
Orpington BR5 146 EW99
Romford RM3 51 FH53
Staines (Stanw.) TW19 114 BJ86
Sutton SM3 157 CX108
Thornton Heath CR7
off Kitchener Rd 142 DR97
Waltham Cross (Chsht.) EN8
off Norwood Rd 15 DY30
West Drayton UB7 76 BL74
Roberts La, Ger.Cr. (Chal.St.P.)
SL9 37 BA50
Roberts Ms, SW1 198 F7
Orpington BR6 146 EU102
Robertson Cl, Brox. EN10 15 DY26
Robertson Ct, Wok. GU21
off Raglan Rd 166 AS118
Robertson Rd, E15 85 EC67
Robertson St, SW8 101 DH83
Robert's Pl, EC1 196 E4
Roberts Rd, E17 47 EB53
NW7 43 CY51
Belvedere DA17 106 FA78
Watford WD18 off Tucker St 24 BW43
Robert St, E16 87 EP74
NW1 195 J3
SE18 105 ER77
WC2 200 A1
Croydon CR0 off High St 142 DQ104
Roberts Way, Egh. (Eng.Grn.)
TW20 112 AW94
Roberts Wd Dr, Ger.Cr. (Chal.St.P.)
SL9 37 AZ50
Robeson St, E3 off Ackroyd Dr 85 DZ71
Robeson Way, Borwd. WD6 26 CQ39
Robina Cl, Bexh. DA6 106 EX84
Northwood HA6 39 BT53
Robin Cl, NW7 42 CS48
Addlestone KT15 152 BK106
Hampton TW12 116 BY92
Romford RM5 51 FD52
Robin Ct, SE16 202 B8
Wallington SM6
off Carew Rd 159 DJ107
Robin Cres, E6 86 EK71
Robin Gdns, Red. RH1 184 DG131
Robin Gro, N6 64 DG61
Brentford TW8 97 CJ79
Harrow HA3 62 CM58
Robin Hill Dr, Chis. BR7 124 EL93
Robinhood Cl, Mitch. CR4 141 DJ97
Robin Hood Cl, Wok. GU21 166 AT118
Robin Hood Cres, Wok. (Knap.)
GU21 166 AS117
Robin Hood Dr, Bushey WD23 24 BZ39
Harrow HA3 41 CF52
Robin Hood Gdns, E14
off Woolmore St 85 EC73
Robin Hood Grn, Orp. BR5 146 EU99
Robin Hood La, E14 85 EC73
SW15 118 CS91
Bexleyheath DA6 126 EY85
Guildford (Sutt.Grn.) GU4 167 AZ124
Robinhood La, Mitch. CR4 141 DJ97
Robin Hood La, Sutt. SM1 158 DA106
Robin Hood Rd, SW19 119 CV92
Brentwood CM15 54 FV45
Woking GU21 166 AT118
Robin Hood Way, SW15 118 CS91
SW20 118 CS91
Greenford UB6 79 CF65
Robinia Av, Grav. (Nthflt.)
DA11 130 GD87
Robinia Cl, SE20
off Sycamore Gro 142 DU95
Ilford IG6 49 ES51
Robinia Cres, E10 67 EB61
Robins Cl, St.Alb. (Lon.Col.) AL2
off High St 10 CL27
Uxbridge UB8 off Newcourt 76 BJ71
Robins Ct, SE12 124 EJ90
Robinscroft Ms, SE10
off Sparta St 103 EB81
Robins Gro, W.Wick. BR4 144 EG104
Robins La, Epp. (They.B.)
CM16 33 EQ36
Robinson Av, Wal.Cr. (Chsht.)
EN7 13 DP28
Robinson Cl, E11 68 EE62
Hornchurch RM12 89 FH66
Robinson Cres, Bushey
(Bushey Hth.) WD23 40 CC46
Robinson Rd, E2 84 DW68
SW17 120 DE93
Dagenham RM10 70 FA63
Robinsons Cl, W13 79 CG71
Robinson St, SW3
off Christchurch St 100 DF79
Robins Orchard, Ger.Cr.
(Chal.St.P.) SL9 36 AY51
Robinsway, Wal.Abb. EN9
off Roundhills 16 EE34
Walton-on-Thames KT12 154 BW105
Robin Way, Orp. BR5 146 EV97
Potters Bar (Cuffley) EN6 13 DL28
Staines TW18 113 BF90
Robin Willis Way, Wind.
(Old Wind.) SL4 112 AU86
Robinwood Gro, Uxb. UB8 76 BM70
Robinwood Pl, SW15 118 CR91
Roborough Wk, Horn. RM12 90 FJ65
Robsart St, SW9 101 DM82
Robson Av, NW10 81 CU67
Robson Cl, E6
off Linton Gdns 86 EL72
Enfield EN2 29 DP40
Gerrards Cross (Chal.St.P.)
SL9 36 AY50
Robson Rd, SE27 121 DP90
Robsons Cl, Wal.Cr. EN8 14 DW29
Robyns Cft, Grav. (Nthflt.)
DA11 130 GE90
Robyns Way, Sev. TN13 190 FF122
Roch Av, Edg. HA8 42 CM54
Rochdale Rd, E17 67 EA59
SE2 106 EV78
Rochdale Way, SE8
off Octavius St 103 EA80
Rochelle Cl, SW11 100 DD84
Rochelle St, E2 197 P3
Rochemont Wk, E8
off Pownall Rd 84 DT67
Roche Rd, SW16 141 DM95
Rochester Av, E13 86 EJ67
Bromley BR1 144 EH96
Feltham TW13 115 BT89
Rochester Cl, SW16 121 DL94
Enfield EN1 30 DS39
Sidcup DA15 126 EV86
Rochester Dr, Bex. DA5 126 EZ86
Pinner HA5 60 BX57
Watford WD25 8 BW34
Rochester Gdns, Cat. CR3 176 DS122
Croydon CR0 142 DS104
Ilford IG1 69 EM59
Rochester Ms, NW1 83 DJ66
Rochester Pl, NW1 83 DJ65
Rochester Rd, NW1 83 DJ65
Carshalton SM5 158 DF105
Dartford DA1 128 FN87
Gravesend DA12 131 GL87
Northwood HA6 59 BT55
Staines TW18 113 BD92
Rochester Row, SW1 199 L8
Rochester Sq, NW1 83 DJ66
Rochester St, SW1 199 M7
Rochester Ter, NW1 83 DJ65
Rochester Wk, SE1 201 K2
Rochester Way, SE3 104 EH81
SE9 105 EM83
Dartford DA1 127 FD87
Rickmansworth (Crox.Grn.)
WD3 23 BP42
Rochester Way Relief Rd, SE3 104 EH81
SE9 104 EL84
Roche Wk, Cars. SM5 140 DD100
Rochford Av, Brwd. CM15 55 GA43
Loughton IG10 33 EQ41
Romford RM6 70 EW57
Waltham Abbey EN9 15 ED33
Rochford Cl, E6 off Boleyn Rd 86 EK68
Broxbourne EN10 15 DY26
Hornchurch RM12 89 FH65
Rochford Grn, Loug. IG10 33 EQ41
Rochfords Gdns, Slou. SL2 74 AW74
Rochford St, NW5 64 DF64
Rochford Wk, E8
off Wilman Gro 84 DU66
Rochford Way, Croy. CR0 141 DL100
Rockall Ct, Slou. SL3 93 BB76
Rock Av, SW14
off South Worple Way 98 CR83
Rockbourne Rd, SE23 123 DX88
Rockchase Gdns, Horn. RM11 72 FL58
★ Rock Circus, W1 199 M1
Rockdale Rd, Sev. TN13 191 FH125
Rockells Pl, SE22 122 DV86
Rockfield Cl, Oxt. RH8 188 EF131
Rockfield Rd, Oxt. RH8 188 EF129
Rockford Av, Grnf. UB6 79 CG68
Rock Gdns, Dag. RM10 71 FB64
Rock Gro Way, SE16 202 C8
Rockhall Rd, NW2 63 CX63
Rockhall Way, NW2
off Midland Ter 63 CX62
Rockhampton Cl, SE27
off Rockhampton Rd 121 DN91
Rockhampton Rd, SE27 121 DN91
South Croydon CR2 160 DS107
Rock Hill, SE26 122 DT91
Orpington BR6 164 FA107
Rockingham Av, Horn. RM11 71 FH58
Rockingham Cl, SW15 99 CT84
Uxbridge UB8 76 BJ67
Rockingham Est, SE1 201 H7
Rockingham Par, Uxb. UB8 76 BJ66
Rockingham Rd, Uxb. UB8 76 BH67
Rockingham St, SE1 201 H7
Rockland Rd, SW15 99 CY84
Rocklands Dr, Stan. HA7 41 CH54
Rockleigh Ct, Brwd. CM15
off Hutton Rd 55 GA45
Rockley Rd, W14 99 CX75
Rockliffe Av, Kings L. WD4 6 BN30
Rockmount Rd, SE18 105 ET78
SE19 122 DR93
Rockshaw Rd, Red. RH1 185 DM127
Rocks La, SW13 99 CU81
Rock St, N4 65 DN61
Rockware Av, Grnf. UB6 79 CD67
Rockways, Barn. EN5 27 CT44
Rockwell Gdns, SE19 122 DS92
Rockwell Rd, Dag. RM10 71 FB64
Rockwood Pl, W12 99 CW75
Rocky La, Reig. RH2 184 DF128
Rocliffe St, N1 196 G1
Rocombe Cres, SE23 122 DW87
Rocque La, SE3 104 EF83
Rodborough Rd, NW11 64 DA60
Roden Ct, N6 off Hornsey La 65 DK59
Roden Gdns, Croy. CR0 142 DS100
Rodenhurst Rd, SW4 121 DJ86
Roden St, N7 65 DM62
Ilford IG1 69 EN62
Rodeo Cl, Erith DA8 107 FH81
Roderick Rd, NW3 64 DF63
Rodgers Cl, Borwd. (Elstree)
WD6 25 CK44
Roding Av, Wdf.Grn. IG8 48 EL51
Roding Gdns, Loug. IG10 32 EL44
H Roding Hosp, Ilf. IG4 68 EK55
Roding La, Buck.H. IG9 48 EL46
Chigwell IG7 49 EN46
Roding La N, Wdf.Grn. IG8 48 EK54
Roding La S, Ilf. IG4 68 EK56
Woodford Green IG8 68 EK56
Roding Ms, E1 202 C2
Roding Rd, E5 67 DX63
E6 87 EP71
Loughton IG10 32 EL43
Rodings, The, Upmin. RM14 73 FR58

★ Place of interest | Railway station | London Underground station | DLR Docklands Light Railway station | Tramlink station | H Hospital

317

Rod - Ros

Rodings, The, Wdf.Grn IG8 48 EJ51
Rodings Row, Barn. EN5
off Leecroft Rd 27 CY43
Roding Trd Est, Bark. IG11 87 EP66
⊖ **Roding Valley** 48 EK49
Roding Vw, Buck.H. IG9 48 EK46
Roding Way, Rain. RM13 90 FK68
Rodmarton St, W1 194 E7
Rodmell Cl, Hayes UB4 78 BY70
Rodmell Slope, N12 43 CZ50
Rodmere St, SE10
off Trafalgar Rd 104 EE78
Rodmill La, SW2 121 DL87
Rodney Cl, Croy. CR0 141 DP102
New Malden KT3 138 CS99
Pinner HA5 60 BY59
Walton-on-Thames KT12
off Rodney Rd 136 BW102
Rodney Ct, W9 *off Maida Vale* 82 DC70
Rodney Gdns, Pnr. HA5 59 BV57
West Wickham BR4 162 EG105
Rodney Grn, Walt. KT12 136 BW103
Rodney Pl, E17 47 DY54
SE17 201 J8
SW19 140 DC95
Rodney Rd, E11 68 EH56
SE17 201 J8
Mitcham CR4 140 DE96
New Malden KT3 138 CS99
Twickenham TW2 116 CA86
Walton-on-Thames KT12 136 BW103
Rodney St, N1 83 DM68
Rodney Way, Rom. RM7 50 FA53
Slough (Colnbr.) SL3 93 BE81
Rodona Rd, Wey. KT13 153 BR111
Rodway Rd, SW15 119 CU87
Bromley BR1 144 EH95
Rodwell Cl, Ruis. HA4 60 BW60
Rodwell Ct, Add. KT15
off Garfield Rd 152 BJ105
Rodwell Pl, Edg. HA8
off Whitchurch La 42 CN51
Rodwell Rd, SE22 122 DT86
Roebourne Way, E16 105 EN75
Roebuck Cl, Ashtd. KT21 172 CL120
Feltham TW13 115 BV91
Reigate RH2 184 DB134
Roebuck La, N17 *off High Rd* 46 DT51
Buckhurst Hill IG9 48 EJ45
Roebuck Rd, Chess. KT9 156 CN106
Ilford IG6 50 EV50
Roedean Av, Enf. EN3 30 DW39
Roedean Cl, Enf. EN3 30 DW39
Orpington BR6 164 EV105
Roedean Cres, SW15 118 CS86
Roedean Dr, Rom. RM1 71 FE56
Roe End, NW9 62 CQ56
Roe Grn, NW9 62 CQ57
ROEHAMPTON, SW15 119 CU85
Roehampton Cl, SW15 99 CU84
Gravesend DA12 131 GL87
Roehampton Dr, Chis. BR7 125 EQ93
Roehampton Gate, SW15 118 CS86
Roehampton High St, SW15 119 CV87
Roehampton La, SW15 99 CU84
H **Roehampton Priory Hosp**,
SW15 99 CT84
Roehampton Vale, SW15 118 CS90
Roe La, NW9 62 CP56
Roe Way, Wall. SM6 159 DL107
Rofant Rd, Nthwd. HA6 39 BS51
Roffes La, Cat. CR3 176 DR124
Roffey Cl, Pur. CR8 175 DP116
Roffey St, E14 204 D5
Roffords, Wok. GU21 166 AV117
Rogate Ho, E5 *off Muir Rd* 66 DU62
Roger Dowley Ct, E2 84 DW68
Rogers Cl, Cat. CR3
off Tillingdown Hill 176 DV122
Coulsdon CR5 175 DP118
Waltham Cross (Chsht.)
EN7 14 DR26
Rogers Ct, Swan. BR8 147 FG98
Rogers Gdns, Dag. RM10 70 FA64
Rogers La, Slou. (Stoke P.) SL2 74 AT67
Warlingham CR6 177 DZ118
Rogers Mead, Gdse. RH9
off Ivy Mill La 186 DV132
Rogers Rd, E16 86 EF72
SW17 120 DD91
Dagenham RM10 70 FA64
Grays RM17 110 GC77
Rogers Ruff, Nthwd. HA6 39 BQ53
Roger St, WC1 196 C5
Rogers Wk, N12
off Brook Meadow 44 DB48
Rojack Rd, SE23 123 DX88
Rokeby Ct, Wok. GU21 166 AT117
Rokeby Gdns, Wdf.Grn. IG8 48 EG53
Rokeby Pl, SW20 119 CV94
Rokeby Rd, SE4 103 DZ82
Rokeby St, E15 86 EE67
Roke Cl, Ken. CR8 160 DQ114
Roke Lo Rd, Ken. CR8 159 DP113
Roke Rd, Ken. CR8 176 DQ115
Roker Pk Av, Uxb. UB10 58 BL63
Rokesby Cl, Well. DA16 105 ER82
Rokesby Pl, Wem. HA0 61 CK64
Rokesly Av, N8 65 DL57
Roland Gdns, SW7 100 DC78
Feltham TW13 116 BY90
Roland Ms, E1 *off Stepney Grn* 85 DX71
Roland Rd, E17 67 ED56
Roland Way, SE17 102 DR78
SW7 *off Roland Gdns* 100 DC78
Worcester Park KT4 139 CT103
Roles Gro, Rom. RM6 70 EX56
Rolfe Cl, Barn. EN4 28 DE42
Rolinsden Way, Kes. BR2 162 EK105
Rollesby Rd, Chess. KT9 156 CN107
Rollesby Way, SE28 88 EW73
Rolleston Av, Orp. BR5 145 EP100
Rolleston Cl, Orp. BR5 145 EP101
Rolleston Rd, S.Croy. CR2 160 DR108
Roll Gdns, Ilf. IG2 69 EN57
Rollins St, SE15 102 DW79
Rollit Cres, Houns. TW3 116 CA85
Rollit St, N7
off Hornsey Rd 65 DM64
Rollo Rd, Swan. BR8 127 FF94
Rolls Bldgs, EC4 196 D8
Rollscourt Av, SE24 122 DQ85
Rolls Pk Av, E4 47 EA51
Rolls Pk Rd, E4 47 EB50
Rolls Pas, EC4 196 D8
Rolls Rd, SE1 202 A10
Rolt St, SE8 103 DY79
Rolvenden Gdns, Brom. BR1 124 EK94
Rolvenden Pl, N17
off Manor Rd 46 DU53
★ **Roman Bath**, WC2
off Strand La 196 C10
Roman Cl, W3
off Avenue Gdns 98 CP75
Feltham TW14 116 BW85
Rainham RM13 89 FD68
Uxbridge (Hare.) UB9 38 BH53
Romanfield Rd, SW2 121 DM87
Roman Gdns, Kings L. WD4 7 BP30
Roman Ho, Rain. RM13
off Roman Cl 89 FD68
Romanhurst Av, Brom. BR2 144 EE98
Romanhurst Gdns, Brom.
BR2 144 EE98
Roman Ind Est, Croy. CR0 142 DS101
Roman Ri, SE19 122 DR93
Roman Rd, E2 84 DW69
E3 85 DY68
E6 86 EL70
N10 45 DH52
NW2 63 CW62
W4 99 CT77
Brentwood CM15 55 GC41
Gravesend (Nthflt.) DA11 130 GC90
Ilford IG1 87 EP65
Roman Sq, SE28 88 EU74
Romans Way, Wok. GU22 168 BG115
Roman Vil Rd, Dart. (S.Darenth)
DA2, DA4 128 FQ92
Roman Way, N7 83 DM65
SE15 *off Clifton Way* 102 DW80
Carshalton SM5 158 DF109
Croydon CR0 141 DP103
Dartford DA1 127 FE85
Enfield EN1 30 DT43
Waltham Abbey EN9 31 EB35
Roman Way Ind Est, N1
off Offord St 83 DM66
Romany Gdns, E17
off McEntee Av 47 DY53
Sutton SM3 140 DA101
Romany Ri, Orp. BR5 145 EQ102
Roma Read Cl, SW15
off Bessborough Rd 119 CV87
Roma Rd, E17 67 DY55
Romberg Rd, SW17 120 DG90
Romborough Gdns, SE13 123 EC85
Romborough Way, SE13 123 EC85
Rom Cres, Rom. RM7 71 FF59
Romeland, Borwd. (Elstree)
WD6 25 CK44
Waltham Abbey EN9 15 EC33
Romero Cl, SW9
off Stockwell Rd 101 DM83
Romero Sq, SE3 104 EJ84
Romeyn Rd, SW16 121 DM90
ROMFORD 71 FF57
⇌ **Romford** 71 FE58
Romford Rd, E7 68 EH64
E12 68 EL63
E15 86 EE66
Chigwell IG7 50 EU48
Romford RM5 50 EY52
South Ockendon (Aveley)
RM15 90 FQ73
Romford St, E1 84 DU71
Romilly Dr, Wat. WD19 40 BY49
Romilly Rd, N4 65 DP61
Romilly St, W1 195 M10
Rommany Rd, SE27 122 DR91
Romney Chase, Horn. RM11 72 FM58
Romney Cl, N17 46 DV53
NW11 64 DC60
SE14 *off Kender St* 102 DW80
Ashford TW15 115 BQ92
Chessington KT9 156 CL105
Harrow HA2 60 CA59
Romney Dr, Brom. BR1 124 EK94
Harrow HA2 60 CA59
Romney Gdns, Bexh. DA7 106 EZ81
Romney Lock, Wind. SL4 92 AS79
Romney Ms, W1 194 F6
Romney Par, Hayes UB4
off Romney Rd 77 BR68
Romney Rd, SE10 103 EC79
Gravesend (Nthflt.) DA11 130 GE90
Hayes UB4 77 BR68
New Malden KT3 138 CR100
Romney Row, NW2
off Brent Ter 63 CX61
Romney St, SW1 199 N7
Romola Rd, SE24 121 DP88
Romsey Cl, Orp. BR6 163 EP105
Slough SL3 93 AZ76
Romsey Gdns, Dag. RM9 88 EX67
Romsey Rd, W13 79 CG73
Dagenham RM9 88 EX67
Rom Valley Way, Rom. RM7 71 FE59
Ronald Av, E15 86 EE69
Ronald Cl, Beck. BR3 143 DZ98
Ronald Ct, St.Alb. AL2 8 BY29
Ronald Ho, SE3
off Cambert Way 104 EJ84
Ronald Rd, Rom. RM3 52 FN53
Ronaldsay Spur, Slou. SL1 74 AS71
Ronalds Rd, N5 65 DN64
Bromley BR1 144 EG95
Ronaldstone Rd, Sid. DA15 125 ES86
Ronald St, E1 *off Devonport St* 84 DW72
Rona Rd, NW3 64 DG63
Ronart St, Har. (Wldste.) HA3
off Stuart Rd 61 CF55
Rona Wk, N1 *off Clephane Rd* 84 DR65
Rondu Rd, NW2 63 CY64
Ronelean Rd, Surb. KT6 138 CM104
Roneo Cor, Horn. RM12 71 FF60
Roneo Link, Horn. RM12 71 FF60
Ronfearn Av, Orp. BR5 146 EX99
Ron Leighton Way, E6 86 EL67
Ronneby Cl, Wey. KT13 135 BS104
Ronson Way, Lthd. KT22 171 CF121
Ronver Rd, SE12 124 EF87
Rood La, EC3 197 M10
Roof of the World Caravan Pk,
Tad. KT20 182 CP131
Rookby Ct, N21
off Carpenter Gdns 45 DP47
Rook Cl, Horn. RM12 89 FG66
Wembley HA9 62 CP62
Rookdean, Sev. (Chipstead)
TN13 190 FC122
Rookeries Cl, Felt. TW13 115 BV90
Rookery, The, Grays RM20 109 FU79
Rookery Cl, NW9 63 CT57
Leatherhead (Fetch.) KT22 171 CE124
Rookery Ct, Grays RM20 109 FU79
Rookery Cres, Dag. RM10 89 FB66
Rookery Dr, Chis. BR7 145 EN95
Rookery Gdns, Orp. BR5 146 EW99
Rookery Hill, Ashtd. KT21 172 CN118
Rookery La, Brom. BR2 144 EK100
Grays RM17 110 GD78
Rookery Rd, SW4 101 DJ84
Orpington BR6 163 EM110
Staines TW18 114 BH92
Rookery Vw, Grays RM17 110 GD78
Rookery Way, NW9 63 CT57
Tadworth (Lwr.Kgswd.)
KT20 183 CZ127
Rookesley Rd, Orp. BR5 146 EX101
Rooke Way, SE10 205 K10
Rookfield Av, N10 65 DJ56
Rookfield Cl, N10
off Cranmore Way 65 DJ56
Rook La, Cat. CR3 175 DM124
Rookley Cl, Sutt. SM2 158 DB110
Rooks Hill, Rick. (Loud.) WD3 22 BK42
Rooksmead Rd, Sun. TW16 135 BT96
Rookstone Rd, SW17 120 DF92
Rook Wk, E6
off Allhallows Rd 86 EL72
Rookwood Av, Loug. IG10 33 EQ41
New Malden KT3 139 CU98
Wallington SM6 159 DK105
Rookwood Cl, Grays RM17 110 GB77
Redhill RH1 185 DH129
Rookwood Gdns, E4
off Whitehall Rd 48 EF46
Loughton IG10 33 EQ41
Rookwood Ho, Bark. IG11
off St. Marys 87 ER68
Rookwood Rd, N16 66 DT59
★ **Roosevelt Mem**, W1
off Grosvenor Sq 194 G10
Roosevelt Way, Dag. RM10 89 FD65
Rootes Dr, W10 81 CX70
Ropemaker Rd, SE16 203 K5
Ropemakers Flds, E14 203 M1
Ropemaker St, EC2 197 K6
Roper La, SE1 201 N5
Ropers Av, E4 47 EC50
Ropers Orchard, SW3
off Danvers St 100 DE79
Roper St, SE9 125 EM86
Ropers Wk, SW2
off Brockwell Pk Gdns 121 DN87
Roper Way, Mitch. CR4 140 DG96
Ropery St, E3 85 DZ70
Rope St, SE16 203 L7
Rope Wk, Sun. TW16 136 BW97
Rope Wk Gdns, E1
off Commercial Rd 84 DU72
Ropewalk Ms, E8
off Middleton Rd 84 DT66
Rope Yd Rails, SE18 105 EP76
Ropley St, E2 84 DU68
Rosa Alba Ms, N5
off Kelross Rd 66 DQ63
Rosa Av, Ashf. TW15 114 BN91
Rosaline Rd, SW6 99 CY80
Rosamond St, SE26 122 DV90
Rosamund Cl, S.Croy. CR2 160 DR105
Rosamun St, Sthl. UB2 96 BY77
Rosary, The, Egh. TW20 133 BD96
Rosary Cl, Houns. TW3 96 BY82
Rosary Ct, Pot.B. EN6 12 DB30
Rosary Gdns, SW7 100 DC77
Ashford TW15 115 BP91
Bushey WD23 41 CE45
Rosaville Rd, SW6 99 CZ80
Roscoe St, EC1 197 J5
Roscoff Cl, Edg. HA8 42 CQ53
Roseacre, Oxt. RH8 188 EG134
Roseacre Cl, W13
off Middlefielde 79 CH71
Hornchurch RM11 72 FM60
Shepperton TW17 134 BN99
Roseacre Rd, Well. DA16 106 EV83
Rose All, SE1 201 J2
Rose & Crown Ct, EC2 197 H8
Rose & Crown Yd, SW1 199 L2
Roseary Cl, West Dr. UB7 94 BK77
Rose Av, E18 48 EH54
Gravesend DA12 131 GL88
Mitcham CR4 140 DF95
Morden SM4 140 DC99
Rosebank, SE20 122 DV94
Rose Bk, Brwd. CM14 54 FX48
Rosebank, Epsom KT18 156 CQ114
Waltham Abbey EN9 16 EE33
Rosebank Av, Horn. RM12 72 FJ64
Wembley HA0 61 CF63
Rosebank Cl, N12 44 DE50
Teddington TW11 117 CG93
Rose Bk Cotts, Wok. GU22 166 AY122
Rosebank Gdns, E3 85 DZ68
Gravesend (Nthflt.) DA11 130 GE88
Rosebank Gro, E17 67 DZ55
Rosebank Rd, E17 67 EB58
W7 97 CE75
Rosebank Vil, E17 67 EA56
Rosebank Wk, NW1
off Maiden La 83 DK66
SE18 *off Woodhill* 104 EL77
Rosebank Way, W3 80 CR72
Rose Bates Dr, NW9 62 CN56
Roseberry Cl, Upmin. RM14 73 FT58
Roseberry Ct, Wat. WD17
off Grandfield Av 23 BU39
Roseberry Gdns, N4 65 DP58
Dartford DA1 128 FJ87
Orpington BR6 145 ES104
Upminster RM14 73 FT59
Roseberry Pl, E8 84 DT65
Roseberry St, SE16 202 D9
Rosebery Av, E12 86 EL65
EC1 196 D5
N17 46 DU54
Epsom KT17 156 CS114
Harrow HA2 60 BZ63
New Malden KT3 139 CT96
Sidcup DA15 125 ES87
Thornton Heath CR7 142 DQ96
Rosebery Cl, Mord. SM4 139 CX100
Rosebery Ct, EC1
off Rosebery Av 83 DN70
Gravesend (Nthflt.) DA11 131 GF88
Rosebery Cres, Wok. GU22 167 AZ121
Rosebery Gdns, N8 65 DL57
W13 79 CG72
Sutton SM1 158 DB105
Rosebery Ms, N10 45 DJ54
SW2 *off Rosebery Rd* 121 DL86
Rosebery Rd, N9 46 DU48
N10 45 DJ54
SW2 121 DL86
Bushey WD23 40 CB45
Epsom KT18 172 CR119
Grays RM17 110 FY79
Hounslow TW3 116 CC85
Kingston upon Thames KT1 138 CP96
Sutton SM1 157 CZ107
Rosebery Sq, EC1 196 D5
Kingston upon Thames KT1 138 CN96
Rosebine Av, Twick. TW2 117 CD87
Rosebriar Cl, Wok. GU22 168 BG116
Rosebriars, Cat. CR3 176 DS120
Esher KT10 154 CC106
Rosebriar Wk, Wat. WD24 23 BT36
Rosebury Rd, SW6 100 DB82
Rosebury Sq, Wdf.Grn. IG8 49 EN52
Rosebury Vale, Ruis. HA4 59 BT60
Rose Bushes, Epsom KT17 173 CV116
Rose Ct, E1 *off Sandy's Row* 84 DS71
SE26 122 DV89
Pinner HA5 *off Nursery Rd* 60 BW55
Waltham Cross EN7 14 DU27
Rosecourt Rd, Croy. CR0 141 DM100
Rosecroft Av, NW3 64 DA62
Rosecroft Cl, Orp. BR5 146 EW100
Westerham (Bigg.H.) TN16
off Lotus Rd 179 EM118
Rosecroft Dr, Wat. WD17 23 BS36
Rosecroft Gdns, NW2 63 CU62
Twickenham TW2 117 CD88
Rosecroft Rd, Sthl. UB1 78 CA70
Rosecroft Wk, Pnr. HA5 60 BX57
Wembley HA0 61 CK64
Rosedale, Ashtd. KT21 171 CJ118
Caterham CR3 176 DS123
Rose Dale, Orp. BR6 145 EP103
Rosedale Av, Hayes UB3 77 BR71
Waltham Cross (Chsht.) EN7 14 DT29
Rosedale Cl, SE2
off Finchale Rd 106 EV76
W7 *off Boston Rd* 97 CF75
Dartford DA2 128 FP87
St. Albans (Brick.Wd.) AL2 8 BY30
Stanmore HA7 41 CH51
Rosedale Ct, N5 65 DP63
Rosedale Gdns, Dag. RM9 88 EV66
Rosedale Pl, Croy. CR0 143 DX101
Rosedale Rd, E7 68 EJ64
Dagenham RM9 88 EV66
Epsom KT17 157 CU106
Grays RM17 110 GD78
Richmond TW9 98 CL84
Romford RM1 51 FC54
Rosedale Ter, W6
off Dalling Rd 99 CV76
Rosedale Way, Wal.Cr. (Chsht.)
EN7 14 DU29
Rosedene, NW6 81 CX67
Rosedene Av, SW16 121 DM90
Croydon CR0 141 DM101
Greenford UB6 78 CA69
Morden SM4 140 DA99
Rosedene Ct, Dart. DA1
off Shepherds La 128 FJ87
Ruislip HA4 59 BS60
Rosedene Gdns, Ilf. IG2 69 EN56
Rosedene Ter, E10 67 EB61
Rosedew Rd, W6 99 CX79
Rose Dr, Chesh. HP5 4 AS32
Rose End, Wor.Pk. KT4 139 CX102
Rosefield, Sev. TN13 190 FG124
Rosefield Cl, Cars. SM5 158 DE106
Rosefield Gdns, E14 85 EA73
Chertsey (Ott.) KT16 151 BD107
Rosefield Rd, Stai. TW18 114 BG91
Roseford Ct, W12 99 CX75
Rose Gdn Cl, Edg. HA8 42 CL51
Rose Gdns, W5 97 CK76
Feltham TW13 115 BU89
Southall UB1 78 CA70
Staines (Stanw.) TW19
off Diamedes Av 114 BK87
Watford WD18 23 BU43
Rose Glen, NW9 62 CR56
Romford RM7 71 FE60
Rosehart Ms, W11
off Westbourne Gro 82 DA72
Rosehatch Av, Rom. RM6 70 EX55
Roseheath Rd, Houns. TW4 116 BZ85
ROSEHILL, Sutt. 140 DB102
Rosehill, Esher (Clay.) KT10 155 CG107
Hampton TW12 136 CA95
Rose Hill, Sutt. SM1 140 DB104
Rosehill Av, Sutt. SM1 140 DC102
Woking GU21 166 AW116
Rosehill Ct, Slou. SL1
off Yew Tree Rd 92 AU76
Rosehill Fm Meadow, Bans. SM7
off The Tracery 174 DB115
Rosehill Gdns, Abb.L. WD5 7 BQ32
Greenford UB6 61 CF64
Sutton SM1 140 DB103
Rosehill Pk W, Sutt. SM1 140 DC102
Rosehill Rd, SW18 120 DC86
Westerham (Bigg.H.) TN16 178 EJ117
Roseland Cl, N17
off Cavell Rd 46 DR52
Rose La, Rom. RM6 70 EX55
Woking (Ripley) GU23 168 BJ121
Rose Lawn, Bushey (Bushey Hth.)
WD23 40 CC46
Roseleigh Av, N5 65 DP63
Roseleigh Cl, Twick. TW1 117 CK86
Rosemary Av, N3 44 DB54
N9 46 DV46
Enfield EN2 30 DR39
Hounslow TW4 96 BX82
Romford RM1 71 FF55
West Molesey KT8 136 CA97
Rosemary Cl, Croy. CR0 141 DL100
Oxted RH8 188 EG133
South Ockendon RM15 91 FW69
Uxbridge UB8 76 BN71
Rosemary Dr, E14 85 ED72
Ilford IG4 68 EK57
Rosemary Gdns, SW14
off Rosemary La 98 CQ83
Chessington KT9 156 CL105
Dagenham RM8 70 EZ60
Rosemary La, SW14 98 CQ83
Egham TW20 133 BB97
Rosemary Rd, SE15 102 DT80
SW17 120 DC90
Welling DA16 105 ET81
Rosemary St, N1
off Shepperton Rd 84 DR67
Rosemead, NW9 63 CT59
Chertsey KT16 134 BH101
Potters Bar EN6 12 DC30
Rosemead Av, Felt. TW13 115 BT89
Mitcham CR4 141 DJ96
Wembley HA9 62 CL64
Rosemead Gdns, Brwd. CM13 55 GD42
Rosemont Av, N12 44 DC51
Rosemont Rd, NW3 82 DC65
W3 80 CP73
New Malden KT3 138 CQ97
Richmond TW10 118 CL86
Wembley HA0 80 CL67
Rosemoor St, SW3 198 D9
Rosemount Av, W.Byf. KT14 152 BG113
Rosemount Cl, Wdf.Grn. IG8
off Chapelmount Rd 49 EM51
Rosemount Dr, Brom. BR1 145 EM98
Rosemount Pt, SE23
off Dacres Rd 123 DX90
Rosemount Rd, W13 79 CG72
Rosenau Cres, SW11 100 DE81
Rosenau Rd, SW11 100 DE81
Rosendale Rd, SE21 122 DQ87
SE24 122 DQ87
Roseneath Av, N21 45 DP46
Roseneath Cl, Orp. BR6 164 EW108
Roseneath Rd, SW11 120 DG86
Roseneath Wk, Enf. EN1 30 DS42
Rosens Wk, Edg. HA8 42 CP48
Rosenthal Rd, SE6 123 EB86
Rosenthorpe Rd, SE15 123 DX85
Rose Pk Cl, Hayes UB4 78 BW70
Rosepark Ct, Ilf. IG5 49 EM54
Roserton St, E14 204 D5
Rosery, The, Croy. CR0 143 DX100
Roses, The, Wdf.Grn. IG8 48 EF52
Rose Sq, SW3 198 A10
Rose St, WC2 195 P10
Gravesend (Nthflt.) DA11 130 GB86
★ **Rose Thea**, SE1
off Park St 201 J2
Rosethorn Cl, SW12 121 DJ87
Rosetta Cl, SW8 101 DL80
Rosetti Ter, Dag. RM8
off Marlborough Rd 70 EV63
Rose Valley, Brwd. CM14 54 FW48
Roseveare Rd, SE12 124 EJ91
Rose Vil, Dart. DA1 128 FP87
Roseville Av, Houns. TW3 116 CA85
Roseville Rd, Hayes UB3 95 BU78
Rosevine Rd, SW20 139 CW95
Rose Wk, Pur. CR8 159 DK111
Surbiton KT5 138 CP99
West Wickham BR4 143 ED103
Rose Wk, The, Rad. WD7 25 CH37
Rosewarne Cl, Wok. GU21
off Muirfield Rd 166 AU118
Rose Way, SE12 124 EG85
Roseway, SE21 122 DR86
Rose Way, Edg. HA8 42 CQ49
Rosewell Cl, SE20 122 DV94
Rosewood, Dart. DA2 127 FE91
Esher KT10 137 CG103
Sutton SM2 158 DC110
Woking GU22 167 BA119
Rosewood Av, Grnf. UB6 61 CG64
Hornchurch RM12 71 FG64
Rosewood Cl, Sid. DA14 126 EW90
Rosewood Ct, Brom. BR1 144 EJ95
Romford RM6 70 EW57
Rosewood Dr, Enf. EN2 29 DN35
Shepperton TW17 134 BM99
Rosewood Gdns, SE13
off Lewisham Rd 103 EC82
Rosewood Gro, Sutt. SM1 140 DC103
Rosewood Sq, W12
off Primula St 81 CU72
Rosewood Ter, SE20
off Laurel Gro 122 DW94
Rosher Cl, E15 85 ED66

Ros - Rug

ROSHERVILLE, Grav. 131 GF85
Rosherville Way, Grav. DA11 .130 GE87
Rosina St, E9 ....67 DX64
Roskell Rd, SW15 ....99 CX83
Roslin Rd, W3 ....98 CP76
Roslin Way, Brom. BR1 ....124 EG92
Roslyn Cl, Mitch. CR4 ....140 DD96
Roslyn Ct, Wok. GU21
off St. John's Rd 166 AU118
Roslyn Gdns, Rom. RM2 ....51 FF54
Roslyn Rd, N15 ....66 DR57
Rosmead Rd, W11 ....81 CY73
Rosoman Pl, EC1 ....196 E4
Rosoman St, EC1 ....196 E3
Rossall Cl, Horn. RM11 ....71 FG58
Rossall Cres, NW10 ....80 CM69
Ross Av, NW7 ....43 CY50
Dagenham RM8 ....70 EZ61
Ross Cl, Har. HA3 ....40 CC52
Hayes UB3 ....95 BR77
Ross Ct, SW15 ....119 CX87
Ross Cres, Wat. WD25 ....23 BU35
Rossdale, Sutt. SM1 ....158 DE106
Rossdale Dr, N9 ....30 DW44
NW9 ....62 CQ60
Rossdale Rd, SW15 ....99 CW84
Rosse Ms, SE3 ....104 EH81
Rossendale St, E5 ....66 DV61
Rossendale Way, NW1 ....83 DJ66
Rossetti Gdns, Couls. CR5 ...175 DM118
Rossetti Rd, SE16 ....202 D10
Rossignol Gdns, Cars. SM5 ..140 DG103
Rossindel Rd, Houns. TW3 ...116 CA85
Rossington Av, Borwd. WD6 ..26 CL38
Rossington Cl, Enf. EN1 ....30 DV38
Rossington St, E5 ....66 DU61
Rossiter Cl, Slou. SL3 ....92 AY77
Rossiter Flds, Barn. EN5 ....27 CY44
Rossiter Rd, SW12 ....121 DH88
Rossland Cl, Bexh. DA6 ....127 FB85
Rosslare Cl, West. TN16 ....189 ER125
Rosslyn Av, E4 ....48 EF47
SW13 ....98 CS83
Barnet EN4 ....28 DE44
Dagenham RM8 ....70 EZ59
Feltham TW14 ....115 BU86
Romford RM3 ....52 FM54
Rosslyn Cl, Hayes UB3
off Morgans La 77 BR71
Sunbury-on-Thames TW16
off Cadbury Rd 115 BS93
West Wickham BR4 ....144 EF104
Rosslyn Cres, Har. HA1 ....61 CF57
Wembley HA9 ....62 CL63
Rosslyn Gdns, Wem. HA9
off Rosslyn Cres 62 CL62
Rosslyn Hill, NW3 ....64 DD63
Rosslyn Ms, NW3
off Rosslyn Hill 64 DD63
Rosslyn Pk, Wey. KT13 ....153 BR105
Rosslyn Pk Ms, NW3
off Lyndhurst Rd 64 DD64
Rosslyn Rd, E17 ....67 EC56
Barking IG11 ....87 ER66
Twickenham TW1 ....117 CJ86
Watford WD18 ....23 BV41
Rossmore Ct, NW1 ....194 D4
Rossmore Rd, NW1 ....194 C5
Ross Par, Wall. SM6 ....159 DH107
Ross Rd, SE25 ....142 DR97
Cobham KT11 ....154 BW113
Dartford DA1 ....127 FG86
Twickenham TW2 ....116 CB88
Wallington SM6 ....159 DJ106
Ross Way, SE9 ....104 EL83
Northwood HA6 ....39 BT49
Rossway Dr, Bushey WD23 ...24 CC43
Rosswood Gdns, Wall. SM6 .159 DJ107
Rostella Rd, SW17 ....120 DD91
Rostrevor Av, N15 ....66 DT58
Rostrevor Gdns, Hayes UB3 ..77 BS74
Iver SL0 ....75 BD68
Southall UB2 ....96 BY78
Rostrevor Ms, SW6 ....99 CZ81
Rostrevor Rd, SW6 ....99 CZ81
SW19 ....120 DA92
Roswell Cl, Wal.Cr. (Chsht.)
EN8 ....15 DY30
Rotary St, SE1 ....200 F6
Rothbury Av, Rain. RM13 ....89 FH71
Rothbury Gdns, Islw. TW7 ....97 CG80
Rothbury Rd, E9 ....85 DZ66
Rothbury Wk, N17 ....46 DU52
Roth Dr, Brwd. CM13 ....55 GB47
Rother Cl, Wat. WD25 ....8 BW34
Rotherfield Rd, Cars. SM5 ...158 DG105
Enfield EN3 ....31 DX37
Rotherfield St, N1 ....84 DQ66
Rotherham Wk, SE1 ....200 F3
Rotherhill Av, SW16 ....121 DK93
ROTHERHITHE, SE16 ....203 H6
⊖ **Rotherhithe** 202 G4
★ **Rotherhithe Heritage Mus**,
SE16 ....203 L2
Rotherhithe New Rd, SE16 ..102 DU78
Rotherhithe Old Rd, SE16 ...203 H7
Rotherhithe St, SE16 ....202 G4
Rotherhithe Tunnel, E1 ....203 H2
Rotherhithe Tunnel App, E14 ..85 DY73
SE16 ....202 F5
Rothermere Rd, Croy. CR0 ...159 DM106
Rotherwick Hill, W5 ....80 CM70
Rotherwick Rd, NW11 ....64 DA59
Rotherwood Cl, SW20 ....139 CY95
Rotherwood Rd, SW15 ....99 CX83
Rothery St, N1 *off Gaskin St* ..83 DP67
Rothery Ter, SW9 ....101 DP80
Rothesay Av, SW20 ....139 CY96
Greenford UB6 ....79 CD65
Richmond TW10 ....98 CP84
Rothesay Rd, SE25 ....142 DS98
Rothsay Rd, E7 ....86 EJ65
Rothsay St, SE1 ....201 M6
Rothsay Wk, E14 ....204 A8
Rothschild Rd, W4 ....98 CQ77
Rothschild St, SE27 ....121 DP91
Roth Wk, N7 *off Durham Rd* ..65 DM62
Rothwell Gdns, Dag. RM9 ....88 EW66
Rothwell Rd, Dag. RM9 ....88 EW67
Rothwell St, NW1 ....82 DF67
Rotten Row, SW1 ....198 F4
SW7 ....198 B4
Rotterdam Dr, E14 ....204 E7
Rouel Rd, SE16 ....202 B7
Rouge La, Grav. DA12 ....131 GH88
Rougemont Av, Mord. SM4 ..140 DA100
Roughetts La, Gdse. RH9 ...186 DS129
Redhill RH1 ....186 DS129
Roughlands, Wok. GU22 ....167 BE115
Roughs, The, Nthwd. HA6 ....39 BT48
Roughtallys, Epp. (N.Wld.Bas.)
CM16 ....18 EZ27
Roughwood Cl, Wat. WD17 ...23 BS38
Roughwood La, Ch.St.G. HP8 .36 AY45
Roundacre, SW19
off Inner Pk Rd 119 CX89
Roundaway Rd, Ilf. IG5 ....49 EM54
ROUND BUSH, Wat. 24 CC38
Roundcroft, Wal.Cr. (Chsht.)
EN7 ....14 DT26
Roundel Cl, SE4
off Adelaide Av 103 DZ84
Round Gro, Croy. CR0 ....143 DX101
Roundhay Cl, SE23 ....123 DX89
Roundhedge Way, Enf. EN2 ...29 DM38
Round Hill, SE26 ....122 DW89
Roundhill, Wok. GU22 ....167 BB119
Roundhill Dr, Enf. EN2 ....29 DM42
Woking GU22 ....167 BB118
Roundhills, Wal.Abb. EN9 ....16 EE34
Roundhill Way, Cob. KT11 ...154 CB111
Roundlyn Gdns, Orp. (St.M.Cray)
BR5 *off Lynmouth Ri* 146 EV98
Roundmead Av, Loug. IG10 ...33 EN41
Roundmead Cl, Loug. IG10 ...33 EN41
Roundmoor Dr, Wal.Cr. (Chsht.)
EN8 ....15 DX29
Round Oak Rd, Wey. KT13 ...152 BM105
Roundshaw Cen, Wall. SM6
off Meteor Way 159 DL108
Roundtable Rd, Brom. BR1 ..124 EF90
Roundthorn Way, Wok. GU21 .166 AT116
Roundtree Rd, Wem. HA0 ....61 CH64
Roundway, Egh. TW20 ....113 BC92
Westerham (Bigg.H.) TN16
off Norheads La 178 EK116
Roundway, The, N17 ....46 DQ53
Esher (Clay.) KT10 ....155 CF106
Watford WD18 ....23 BT44
Roundways, Ruis. HA4 ....59 BT62
Roundwood, Chis. BR7 ....145 EP96
Kings Langley WD4 ....6 BL26
Roundwood Av, Brwd. CM13 .55 GA46
Uxbridge UB11 ....77 BQ74
Roundwood Cl, Ruis. HA4 ....59 BR59
Roundwood Gro, Brwd.
CM13 ....55 GB45
Roundwood Lake, Brwd. (Hutton)
CM13 ....55 GB46
Roundwood Rd, NW10 ....81 CT65
Amersham HP6 ....20 AS38
Roundwood Vw, Bans. SM7 ..173 CX115
Roundwood Way, Bans. SM7 .173 CX115
Rounton Rd, E3 ....85 EA70
Waltham Abbey EN9 ....16 EE33
Roupell Rd, SW2 ....121 DM88
Roupell St, SE1 ....200 E3
Rousden St, NW1 ....83 DJ66
Rousebarn La, Rick. WD3 ....23 BQ41
Rouse Gdns, SE21 ....122 DS91
Rous Rd, Buck.H. IG9 ....48 EL46
Routemaster Cl, E13 ....86 EH69
Routh Ct, Felt. TW14
off Loxwood Cl 115 BS88
Routh Rd, SW18 ....120 DE87
Routh St, E6 ....87 EM71
Routledge Cl, N19 ....65 DK60
Rover Av, Ilf. IG6 ....49 ET51
Rowallan Rd, SW6 ....99 CY80
Rowan Av, E4 ....47 DZ51
Egham TW20 ....113 BC92
Rowan Cl, SW16 ....141 DJ95
W5 ....98 CL75
Ilford IG1 ....69 ER64
New Malden KT3 ....138 CS96
Radlett (Shenley) WD7
off Juniper Gdns 10 CL33
St. Albans (Brick.Wd.) AL2 ...8 CA31
Stanmore HA7
off Woodlands Dr 41 CF51
Wembley HA0 ....61 CG62
Rowan Ct, Borwd. WD6
off Theobald St 26 CL39
Rowan Cres, SW16 ....141 DJ95
Dartford DA1 ....128 FJ88
Rowan Dr, NW9 ....63 CU56
Broxbourne EN10 ....15 DZ25
Rowan Gdns, Croy. CR0
off Radcliffe Rd 142 DT104
Iver SL0 ....75 BD68
Rowan Grn, Wey. KT13 ....153 BR105
Rowan Grn E, Brwd. CM13 ...55 FZ48
Rowan Grn W, Brwd. CM13 ...55 FZ49
Rowan Gro, Couls. CR5 ....175 DH121
Rowan Pl, Amer. HP6 ....20 AT38
Hayes UB3 *off West Av* 77 BT73
Rowan Rd, SW16 ....141 DJ96
W6 ....99 CX77
Bexleyheath DA7 ....106 EY83
Brentford TW8 ....97 CH80
Swanley BR8 ....147 FD97
West Drayton UB7 ....94 BK77
Rowans, The, N13 ....45 DP48
Gerrards Cross (Chal.St.P.)
SL9 ....56 AW55
South Ockendon (Aveley)
RM15 *off Purfleet Rd* 90 FQ74
Sunbury-on-Thames TW16 .115 BT92
Woking GU22 ....166 AY118
Rowans Cl, Long. DA3 ....149 FX96
Rowans Way, Loug. IG10 ....33 EM42
Rowan Ter, SE20
off Sycamore Gro 142 DU95
W6 *off Bute Gdns* 99 CX77
Rowantree Cl, N21 ....46 DR46
Rowantree Rd, N21 ....46 DR46
Enfield EN2 ....29 DP40
Rowan Wk, N2 ....64 DC58
N19 *off Bredgar Rd* 65 DJ61
W10 *off Droop St* 81 CY70
Barnet EN5 *off Station Rd* ..28 DB43
Bromley BR2 ....145 EM104
Hornchurch RM11 ....72 FK56
Rowan Way, Rom. RM6 ....70 EW55
South Ockendon RM15 ....91 FX70
Rowanwood Av, Sid. DA15 ..126 EU88
Rowanwood Ms, Enf. EN2
off Rowantree Rd 29 DP40
Rowben Cl, N20 ....44 DB46
Rowberry Cl, SW6 ....99 CW80
Rowcross St, SE1 ....201 P10
Rowdell Rd, Nthlt. UB5 ....78 CA67
Rowden Pk Gdns, E4
off Rowden Rd 47 EA51
Rowden Rd, E4 ....47 EA51
Beckenham BR3 ....143 DY95
Epsom KT19 ....156 CP105
Rowditch La, SW11 ....100 DG82
Rowdon Av, NW10 ....81 CV66
Rowdown Cres, Croy.
(New Adgtn.) CR0 ....161 ED109
Rowdowns Rd, Dag. RM9 ....88 EZ67
Rowe Gdns, Bark. IG11 ....87 ET68
Rowe La, E9 ....66 DW64
Rowena Cres, SW11 ....100 DE82
Rowe Wk, Har. HA2 ....60 CA62
Rowfant Rd, SW17 ....120 DG88
Rowhedge, Brwd. CM13 ....55 GA48
Row Hill, Add. KT15 ....151 BF107
Rowhill Rd, E5 ....66 DV63
Dartford DA2 ....127 FF93
Swanley BR8 ....127 FF93
Rowhurst Av, Add. KT15 ....152 BH107
Leatherhead KT22 ....171 CF117
Rowington Cl, W2 ....82 DB71
Rowland Av, Har. HA3 ....61 CJ56
Rowland Ct, E16 ....86 EF70
Rowland Cres, Chig. IG7 ....49 ES49
Rowland Gro, SE26
off Dallas Rd 122 DV90
Rowland Hill Av, N17 ....46 DQ52
Rowland Hill St, NW3 ....64 DE64
Rowlands Av, Pnr. HA5 ....40 CA51
Rowlands Cl, N6 *off North Hill* .64 DG58
NW7 ....43 CU52
Waltham Cross (Chsht.) EN8 .15 DX30
Rowlands Flds, Wal.Cr. (Chsht.)
EN8 ....15 DX29
Rowlands Rd, Dag. RM8 ....70 EZ61
Rowland Wk, Rom. (Hav.at.Bow.)
RM4 ....51 FE48
Rowland Way, SW19
off Hayward Cl 140 DB95
Ashford TW15
off Littleton Rd 115 BQ94
Rowlatt Cl, Dart. DA2 ....128 FJ91
Rowlatt Rd, Dart. DA2
off Whitehead Cl 128 FJ91
Rowley Av, Sid. DA15 ....126 EV87
Rowley Cl, Wat. WD19
off Lower Paddock Rd 24 BY44
Wembley HA0 ....80 CM66
Woking (Pyrford) GU22 ...168 BG116
Rowley Ct, Cat. CR3 ....176 DQ122
Rowley Gdns, N4 ....66 DQ59
Waltham Cross (Chsht.) EN8
off Warwick Dr 15 DX28
ROWLEY GREEN, Barn. 27 CT42
Rowley Grn Rd, Barn. EN5 ...27 CT43
Rowley Ind Pk, W3 ....98 CP76
Rowley La, Barn. EN5 ....27 CT43
Borehamwood WD6 ....26 CR39
Slough (Wexham) SL3 ....74 AW67
Rowley Mead, Epp. (Thnwd.)
CM16 ....18 EW25
Rowley Rd, N15 ....66 DQ57
Rowley Way, NW8 ....82 DB67
Rowlheys Pl, West Dr. UB7 ...94 BL76
Rowlls Rd, Kings.T. KT1 ....138 CM97
Rowmarsh Cl, Grav. (Nthflt.)
DA11 ....130 GD91
Rowney Gdns, Dag. RM9 ....88 EW65
Rowney Rd, Dag. RM9 ....88 EV65
Rowntree Clifford Cl, E13
off Liddon Rd 86 EH69
Rowntree Path, SE28
off Booth Cl 88 EV73
Rowntree Rd, Twick. TW2 ....117 CE88
Rowse Cl, E15 ....85 EC66
Rowsley Av, NW4 ....63 CW55
Rowstock Gdns, N7 ....65 DK64
Rowton Rd, SE18 ....105 EQ80
ROW TOWN, Add. 151 BF108
Rowtown, Add. KT15 ....151 BF108
Rowzill Rd, Swan. BR8 ....127 FF93
Roxborough Av, Har. HA1 ....61 CD59
Isleworth TW7 ....97 CF80
Roxborough Pk, Har. HA1 ....61 CE59
Roxborough Rd, Har. HA1 ....61 CD57
Roxbourne Cl, Nthlt. UB5 ....78 BX65
Roxburgh Av, Upmin. RM14 ..72 FQ62
Roxburgh Rd, SE27 ....121 DP92
Roxburn Way, Ruis. HA4 ....59 BT62
Roxby Pl, SW6 ....100 DA79
ROXETH, Har. 61 CD61
Roxeth Ct, Ashf. TW15 ....114 BN92
Roxeth Grn Av, Har. HA2 ....60 CB62
Roxeth Gro, Har. HA2 ....60 CB63
Roxeth Hill, Har. HA2 ....61 CD61
Roxford Cl, Shep. TW17 ....135 BS99
Roxley Rd, SE13 ....123 EB86
Roxton Gdns, Croy. CR0 ....161 EA106
Roxwell Gdns, Brwd. CM13 ...55 GC43
Roxwell Rd, W12 ....99 CU75
Barking IG11 ....88 EU68
Roxwell Trd Pk, E10 ....67 DY59
Roxwell Way, Wdf.Grn. IG8 ...48 EJ52
Roxy Av, Rom. RM6 ....70 EW59
★ **Royal Academy of Arts**, W1 .199 K1
★ **Royal Academy of Dramatic
Art (RADA)**, WC1 ....195 M6
★ **Royal Academy of Music**,
NW1 ....194 G5
★ **Royal Air Force Museums**,
NW9 (Hendon) 43 CU54
DLR **Royal Albert** 86 EL73
Royal Albert Dock, E16 ....87 EM73
★ **Royal Albert Hall**, SW7 ...100 DD75
Royal Albert Roundabout, E16
off Royal Albert Way 86 EL73
Royal Albert Way, E16 ....86 EK73
Royal Arc, W1 ....199 K1
Royal Artillery Barracks, SE18
off Repository Rd 105 EN78
Royal Av, SW3 ....198 D10
Waltham Cross EN8 ....15 DY33
Worcester Park KT4 ....138 CS103
★ **Royal Botanic Gardens, Kew**,
Rich. TW9 ....98 CL80
H **Royal Brompton Hosp**,
SW3 ....198 B10
Royal Circ, SE27 ....121 DN90
Royal Cl, N16 *off Manor Rd* ...66 DS60
SE8 ....103 DZ79
SW19 *off Queensmere Rd* .119 CX89
Ilford IG3 ....70 EU59
Orpington BR6 ....163 EP105
Uxbridge UB8 ....76 BM72
Worcester Park KT4 ....138 CS103
★ **Royal Coll of Art**, SW7 ...100 DC75
★ **Royal Coll of Music**, SW7 .100 DD76
★ **Royal Coll of Surgeons**,
WC2 ....196 C8
Royal Coll St, NW1 ....83 DJ66
Royal Ct, EC3 *off Cornhill* 84 DR72
SE16 ....203 M6
★ **Royal Courts of Justice**,
WC2 ....196 C9
Royal Cres, W11 ....81 CX74
Ruislip HA4 ....60 BY63
Royal Cres Ms, W11
off Queensdale Rd 81 CX74
Royal Docks Rd, E6 ....87 EP72
Royal Dr, N11 ....44 DG50
Epsom KT18 ....173 CV118
Royal Duchess Ms, SW12
off Dinsmore Rd 121 DH87
Royale Leisure Pk, W3 ....80 CN70
★ **Royal Exchange**, EC3 ....197 L9
Royal Ex, EC3 ....197 L9
Royal Ex Av, EC3 ....197 L9
Royal Ex Bldgs, EC3 ....197 L9
Royal Ex Steps, EC3
off Cornhill 84 DR72
★ **Royal Festival Hall**, SE1 ..200 B2
H **Royal Free Hosp, The**, NW3 .64 DE64
Royal Gdns, W7 ....97 CG76
★ **Royal Geographical Society**,
SW7 ....100 DD75
Royal Herbert Pavilions, SE18 ..105 EM81
Royal Hill, SE10 ....103 EC80
Royal Horticultural Society Cotts,
Wok. (Wisley) GU23
off Wisley La 168 BL116
★ **Royal Horticultural Society
Gdns, Wisley**, Wok. GU22 .168 BL118
★ **Royal Horticultural Society
(Lawrence Hall)**, SW1 ....199 M7
★ **Royal Horticultural Society
(Lindley Hall)**, SW1 ....199 M8
★ **Royal Hosp Chelsea & Mus**,
SW3 ....100 DG78
H **Royal Hosp for Neuro-
Disability**, SW15 ....119 CY86
H **Royal Hosp Richmond**, Rich.
TW9 ....98 CL83
Royal Hosp Rd, SW3 ....100 DF79
Royal La, Uxb. UB8 ....76 BM69
West Drayton UB7 ....76 BM72
Royal London Est, The, N17 ...46 DV51
H **Royal London Homeopathic
Hosp**, WC1 ....196 A6
H **Royal London Hosp
(Mile End)**, E1 ....85 DX70
H **Royal London Hosp
(St. Clements)**, E3 ....85 DZ69
H **Royal London Hosp
(Whitechapel)**, E1 ....84 DV71
H **Royal Marsden Hosp**, Sutt.
SM2 ....158 DC110
H **Royal Marsden Hosp
(Fulham)**, SW3 ....198 A10
★ **Royal Mews, The**, SW1 ..199 J6
Royal Ms, The, SW1 ....199 J6
★ **Royal Military Academy**,
SE18 ....105 EM80
Royal Mint Ct, EC3 ....202 A1
Royal Mint Pl, E1
off Blue Anchor Yd 84 DT73
Royal Mint St, E1 ....84 DT73
Royal Mt Ct, Twick. TW2 ....117 CE90
H **Royal National Orthopaedic
Hosp**, W1 ....195 J5
H **Royal National Orthopaedic
Hosp**, Stan. HA7 ....41 CJ47
★ **Royal National Thea**, SE1 .200 C2
H **Royal National Throat, Nose
& Ear Hosp**, WC1 ....196 B2
Royal Naval Pl, SE14 ....103 DZ80
⊖ **Royal Oak** 82 DB71
Royal Oak Ct, N1
off Pitfield St 84 DS69
Royal Oak Pl, SE22 ....122 DV86
Royal Oak Rd, E8 ....84 DV65
Bexleyheath DA6 ....126 EZ85
Woking GU21 ....166 AW118
Royal Opera Arc, SW1 ....199 M2
★ **Royal Opera Ho**, WC2 ....196 A9
Royal Orchard Cl, SW18 ....119 CY87
Royal Par, SE3 ....104 EE82
SW6 *off Dawes Rd* 99 CY80
W5 *off Western Av* 80 CL69
Chislehurst BR7 ....125 EQ94
Richmond TW9
off Station App 98 CN81
Royal Par Ms, SE3
off Royal Par 104 EF82
Chislehurst BR7 ....125 EQ94
Royal Pier Ms, Grav. DA12
off Royal Pier Rd 131 GH86
Royal Pier Rd, Grav. DA12 ...131 GH86
Royal Pl, SE10 ....103 EC80
Royal Rd, E16 ....86 EK72
SE17 ....101 DP79
Dartford (Darenth) DA2 ...128 FN92
Sidcup DA14 ....126 EX90
Teddington TW11 ....117 CD92
Royal Route, Wem. HA9 ....62 CM63
Royal St, SE1 ....200 C6
Royalty Ms, W1 ....195 M9
DLR **Royal Victoria** 86 EG73
Royal Victoria Dock, E16 ....86 EH73
Royal Victoria Patriotic Building,
SW18 *off Fitzhugh Gro* ..120 DD86
Royal Victoria Pl, E16
off Wesley Av 86 EH74
Royal Victoria Sq, E16 ....205 P1
Royal Victor Pl, E3 ....85 DX68
Royal Wk, Wall. SM6
off Prince Charles Way ...141 DH104
Royce Gro, Wat. WD25
off Ashfields 7 BT34
Roycraft Av, Bark. IG11 ....87 ET68
Roycraft Cl, Bark. IG11 ....87 ET68
Roycroft Cl, E18 ....48 EH53
SW2 ....121 DN88
Roydene Rd, SE18 ....105 ES79
Roydon Cl, SW11 *off Reform St* .100 DF82
Loughton IG10 ....48 EL45
Roydon Ct, Walt. KT12 ....153 BU105
Roydon St, SW11
off Southolm St 101 DH81
Roy Gdns, Ilf. IG2 ....69 ES56
Roy Gro, Hmptn. TW12 ....116 CB93
Royle Cl, Ger.Cr. (Chal.St.P.)
SL9 ....37 AZ52
Romford RM2 ....71 FH57
Royle Cres, W13 ....79 CG70
Roy Rd, Nthwd. HA6 ....39 BT52
Roy Sq, E14 *off Narrow St* 85 DY73
Royston Av, E4 ....47 EA50
Sutton SM1 ....140 DD104
Wallington SM6 ....159 DK105
West Byfleet (Byfleet) KT14 .152 BL112
Royston Cl, Houns. TW5 ....95 BV81
Walton-on-Thames KT12 ..135 BU102
Royston Ct, SE24
off Burbage Rd 122 DQ86
Richmond TW9
off Lichfield Rd 98 CM81
Surbiton KT6 *off Hook Ri N* .138 CN104
Royston Gdns, Ilf. IG1 ....68 EK58
Royston Gro, Pnr. HA5 ....40 BZ51
Royston Par, Ilf. IG1 ....68 EK58
Royston Pk Rd, Pnr. HA5 ....40 BZ51
Royston Rd, SE20 ....143 DX95
Dartford DA1 ....127 FF86
Richmond TW10 ....118 CL85
Romford RM3 ....52 FN52
West Byfleet (Byfleet) KT14 .152 BL112
Roystons, The, Surb. KT5 ....138 CP99
Royston St, E2 ....84 DW68
Rozel Ct, N1 ....84 DS67
Rozel Rd, SW4 ....101 DJ82
Rubastic Rd, Sthl. UB2 ....95 BV76
Rubens Rd, Nthlt. UB5 ....78 BW68
Rubens St, SE6 ....123 DZ89
Rubeus Pl, SW4
off Dolman St 101 DL84
Rubin Pl, Enf. EN3
off Government Row 31 EA37
Ruby Ms, E17 *off Ruby Rd* 67 EA55
Ruby Rd, E17 ....67 EA55
Ruby St, NW10 *off Fawood Av* .80 CR66
SE15 ....102 DV79
Ruby Triangle, SE15
off Sandgate St 102 DV79
Ruckholt Cl, E10 ....67 EB62
Ruckholt Rd, E10 ....67 EA63
Rucklers La, Kings L. WD4 ....6 BK27
Rucklidge Av, NW10 ....81 CT68
Rudall Cres, NW3
off Willoughby Rd 64 DD63
Ruddington Cl, E5 ....67 DY63
Ruddock Cl, Edg. HA8 ....42 CQ52
Ruddstreet Cl, SE18 ....105 EP77
Ruden Way, Epsom KT17 ....173 CV116
Rudge Ri, Add. KT15 ....151 BF106
Rudgwick Ter, NW8
off St. Stephens Cl 82 DE67
Rudland Rd, Bexh. DA7 ....107 FB83
Rudloe Rd, SW12 ....121 DJ87
Rudolf Pl, SW8 *off Miles St* ..101 DL79
Rudolph Ct, SE22 ....122 DU87
Rudolph Rd, E13 ....86 EF68
NW6 ....82 DA68
Bushey WD23 ....24 CA44
Rudsworth Cl, Slou. (Colnbr.)
SL3 ....93 BD80
Rudyard Gro, NW7 ....42 CQ51
Rue de St. Lawrence, Wal.Abb.
EN9 *off Quaker La* 15 EC34
Ruffets Wd, Grav. DA12 ....131 GJ93
Ruffetts, The, S.Croy. CR2 ...160 DV108
Ruffetts Cl, S.Croy. CR2 ....160 DV108
Ruffetts Way, Tad. KT20 ....173 CY118
Ruffle Cl, West Dr. UB7 ....94 BL75
Rufford Cl, Har. HA3 ....61 CG58
Watford WD17 ....23 BT37
Rufford St, N1 ....83 DL67
Rufford Twr, W3 ....80 CP74
Rufus Cl, Ruis. HA4 ....60 BY62
Rufus St, N1 ....197 M3
Rugby Av, N9 ....46 DT46
Greenford UB6 ....79 CD65
Wembley HA0 ....61 CH64
Rugby Cl, Har. HA1 ....61 CE57
★ **Rugby Football Union
Twickenham**, Twick. TW2 ..117 CE86
Rugby Gdns, Dag. RM9 ....88 EW65
Rugby La, Sutt. SM2
off Nonsuch Wk 157 CX109

★ Place of interest ⇌ Railway station ⊖ London Underground station DLR Docklands Light Railway station Tramlink station H Hospital

Rugby Rd, NW9 62 CP56
W4 98 CS75
Dagenham RM9 88 EV66
Twickenham TW1 117 CE86
Rugby St, WC1 196 B5
Rugby Way, Rick. (Crox.Grn.)
WD3 23 BP43
Rugged La, Wal.Abb. EN9 16 EK33
Ruggles-Brise Rd, Ashf.TW15 114 BK92
Rugg St, E14 85 EA73
RUISLIP 59 BS59
⊖ Ruislip 59 BS60
Ruislip Cl, Grnf. UB6 78 CB70
RUISLIP COMMON, Ruis. 59 BR57
Ruislip Ct, Ruis. HA4
off Courtfield Gdns 59 BT61
RUISLIP GARDENS, Ruis. 59 BS63
⊖ Ruislip Gardens 59 BU63
RUISLIP MANOR, Ruis. 59 BU61
⊖ Ruislip Manor 59 BU60
Ruislip Rd, Grnf. UB6 78 CA69
Northolt UB5 78 BX68
Southall UB1 78 CA69
Ruislip Rd E, W7 79 CD70
W13 79 CD70
Greenford UB6 79 CD70
Ruislip St, SW17 120 DF91
Rumania Wk, Grav. DA12 131 GM90
Rumbold Rd, SW6 100 DB80
Rum Cl, E1 202 F1
Rumsey Cl, Hmptn. TW12 116 BZ93
Rumsey Ms, N4 off Monsell Rd 65 DP62
Rumsey Rd, SW9 101 DM83
Rumsley, Wal.Cr. EN7 14 DU27
Runbury Circle, NW9 62 CR61
Runciman Cl, Orp. BR6 164 EW110
Runcorn Cl, N17 66 DV56
Runcorn Pl, W11 81 CY73
Rundell Cres, NW4 63 CV57
Runes Cl, Mitch. CR4 140 DD98
Runnel Fld, Har. HA1 61 CE62
Runnemede Rd, Egh. TW20 113 BA91
Running Horse Yd, Brent. TW8
off Pottery Rd 98 CL79
Running Waters, Brwd. CM13 55 GA49
Runnymede, SW19 140 DD95
Runnymede Cl, Twick. TW2 116 CB86
Runnymede Ct, Croy. CR0 142 DT103
Egham TW20 113 BA91
Runnymede Cres, SW16 141 DK95
Runnymede Gdns, Grnf. UB6 79 CD68
Twickenham TW2 116 CB86
H Runnymede Hosp, Cher.
KT16 133 BD104
Runnymede Rd, Twick. TW2 116 CB86
Runrig Hill, Amer. HP6 20 AS35
Runway, The, Ruis. HA4 59 BV64
Rupack St, SE16 202 F5
Rupert Av, Wem. HA9 62 CL64
Rupert Ct, W1 195 M10
West Molesey KT8
off St. Peter's Rd 136 CA98
Rupert Gdns, SW9 101 DP82
Rupert Rd, N19
off Holloway Rd 65 DK62
NW6 81 CZ68
W4 98 CS76
Rupert St, W1 195 M10
Rural Cl, Horn. RM11 71 FH60
Rural Vale, Grav. (Nthflt.) DA11 130 GE87
Rural Way, SW16 121 DH94
Redhill RH1 184 DG134
Ruscoe Dr, Wok. GU22
off Pembroke Rd 167 BA117
Ruscoe Rd, E16 86 EF72
Ruscombe Dr, St.Alb. (Park St.)
AL2 8 CB26
Ruscombe Gdns, Slou. (Datchet)
SL3 92 AU80
Ruscombe Way, Felt. TW14 115 BT87
Rush, The, SW19
off Kingston Rd 139 CZ95
Rusham Pk Av, Egh. TW20 113 AZ93
Rusham Rd, SW12 120 DF86
Egham TW20 113 AZ93
Rushbrook Cres, E17 47 DZ53
Rushbrook Rd, SE9 125 EQ89
Rush Common Ms, SW2 121 DM87
Rushcroft Rd, E4 47 EA52
SW2 101 DN84
Rushden Cl, SE19 122 DR94
Rushdene, SE2 106 EX76
Rushdene Av, Barn. EN4 44 DE45
Rushdene Cl, Nthlt. UB5 78 BW69
Rushdene Cres, Nthlt. UB5 78 BW68
Rushdene Rd, Brwd. CM15 54 FW45
Pinner HA5 60 BX58
Rushdene Wk, West. (Bigg.H.)
TN16 178 EK117
Rushden Gdns, NW7 43 CW51
Ilford IG5 69 EN55
Rushdon Cl, Grays RM17 110 GA76
Romford RM1 71 FG57
Rush Dr, Wal.Abb. EN9 31 EC36
Rushen Wk, Cars. SM5
off Paisley Rd 140 DD102
Rushes Mead, Uxb. UB8
off Frays Waye 76 BJ67
Rushet Rd, Orp. BR5 146 EU96
Rushett Cl, T.Ditt. KT7 137 CH102
Rushett La, Chess. KT9 155 CJ111
Epsom KT18 155 CJ111
Rushett Rd, T.Ditt. KT7 137 CH101
Rushey Cl, N.Mal. KT3 138 CR98
Rushey Grn, SE6 123 EB87
Rushey Hill, Enf. EN2 29 DM42
Rushey Mead, SE4 123 EA85
Rushfield, Pot.B. EN6 11 CX33
Rushford Rd, SE4 123 DZ86
RUSH GREEN, Rom. 71 FC59
Rush Grn Gdns, Rom. RM7 71 FC60
Rush Grn Rd, Rom. RM7 71 FC60
Rushgrove Av, NW9 63 CT57
Rush Gro St, SE18 105 EM77
Rush Hill Ms, SW11
off Rush Hill Rd 100 DG83
Rush Hill Rd, SW11 100 DG83
Rushleigh Av, Wal.Cr. (Chsht.)
EN8 15 DX31
Rushley Cl, Kes. BR2 162 EK105
Rushmead, E2 off Florida St 84 DV69
Richmond TW10 117 CH90
Rushmead Cl, Croy. CR0 160 DT105
Rushmere Av, Upmin. RM14 72 FQ62
Rushmere Ct, Wor.Pk. KT4
off The Avenue 139 CU103
Rushmere Ho, SW15
off Fontley Way 119 CU88
Rushmere La, Chesh. (Orch.L.)
HP5 4 AU28
Rushmere Pl, SW19 119 CX92
Egham TW20 112 AY92
Rushmoor Cl, Pnr. HA5 59 BV56
Rickmansworth WD3 38 BK47
Rushmore Cl, Brom. BR1 144 EL97
Rushmore Cres, E5
off Rushmore Rd 67 DX63
Rushmore Hill, Orp. BR6 164 EW110
Sevenoaks (Knock.) TN14 164 EX112
Rushmore Rd, E5 66 DW63
Rusholme Av, Dag. RM10 70 FA62
Rusholme Gro, SE19 122 DS92
Rusholme Rd, SW15 119 CX86
Rushout Av, Har. HA3 61 CH58
Rushton Av, Wat. WD25 23 BU35
Rushton St, N1 84 DR68
Rushworth Av, NW4
off Rushworth Gdns 63 CU55
Rushworth Gdns, NW4 63 CU56
Rushworth Rd, Reig. RH2 184 DA133
Rushworth St, SE1 200 G4
Rushy Meadow La, Cars. SM5 140 DE103
Ruskin Av, E12 86 EL65
Feltham TW14 115 BT86
Richmond TW9 98 CN80
Upminster RM14 72 FQ59
Waltham Abbey EN9 16 EE34
Welling DA16 106 EU83
Ruskin Cl, NW11 64 DB58
Waltham Cross (Chsht.) EN7 14 DS26
Ruskin Dr, Orp. BR6 145 ES104
Welling DA16 106 EU83
Worcester Park KT4 139 CV103
Ruskin Gdns, W5 79 CK70
Harrow HA3 62 CM56
Romford RM3 51 FH52
Ruskin Gro, Dart. DA1 128 FN85
Welling DA16 106 EU82
Ruskin Pk Ho, SE5 102 DR83
Ruskin Rd, N17 46 DT53
Belvedere DA17 106 FA77
Carshalton SM5 158 DF106
Croydon CR0 141 DP103
Grays RM16 111 GG77
Isleworth TW7 97 CF83
Southall UB1 78 BY73
Staines TW18 113 BF94
Ruskin Wk, N9 off Durham Rd 46 DU47
SE24 122 DQ85
Bromley BR2 145 EM100
Ruskin Way, SW19 140 DD95
Rusland Av, Orp. BR6 145 ER104
Rusland Hts, Har. HA1
off Rusland Pk Rd 61 CE56
Rusland Pk Rd, Har. HA1 61 CE56
Rusper Cl, NW2 63 CW62
Stanmore HA7 41 CJ49
Rusper Rd, N22 46 DQ54
Dagenham RM9 88 EW65
Russell Av, N22 45 DP54
Russell Cl, NW10 80 CQ66
SE7 104 EJ80
W4 99 CT79
Amersham HP6 20 AX39
Beckenham BR3 143 EB97
Bexleyheath DA7 106 FA84
Brentwood CM15 54 FV45
Dartford DA1 107 FG83
Northwood HA6 39 BQ50
Ruislip HA4 60 BW61
Tadworth KT20 183 CU125
Woking GU21 166 AW115
Russell Ct, SW1 199 L3
Leatherhead KT22 171 CH122
St. Albans AL2 8 CA30
Russell Cres, Wat. WD25
off High Rd 23 BT35
Russell Dr, Stai. (Stanw.)
TW19 114 BK86
Russell Gdns, N20 44 DE47
NW11 63 CY58
W14 99 CY76
Richmond TW10 117 CJ89
West Drayton UB7 94 BN78
Russell Gdns Ms, W14 99 CY76
Russell Grn Cl, Pur. CR8 159 DN110
Russell Gro, NW7 42 CS50
SW9 101 DN80
Russell Hill, Pur. CR8 159 DM110
Russell Hill Pl, Pur. CR8 159 DN111
Russell Hill Rd, Pur. CR8 159 DN110
Russell Kerr Cl, W4
off Burlington La 98 CQ80
Russell La, N20 44 DE47
Watford WD17 23 BR36
Russell Mead, Har. (Har.Wld.)
HA3 41 CF53
Russell Par, NW11
off Golders Grn Rd 63 CY58
Russell Pl, NW3 off Aspern Gro 64 DE64
SE16 203 K7
Dartford (Sutt.H.) DA4 148 FN95
Russell Rd, E4 47 DZ49
E10 67 EB58
E16 86 EG72
E17 67 DZ55
N8 65 DK58
N13 45 DM51
N15 66 DS57
N20 44 DE47
NW9 63 CT58
SW19 120 DA94
W14 99 CY76
Buckhurst Hill IG9 48 EH46
Russell Rd, Enf. EN1 30 DT38
Gravesend DA12 131 GK86
Grays RM17 110 GA77
Mitcham CR4 140 DE97
Northolt UB5 60 CC64
Northwood HA6 39 BQ49
Shepperton TW17 135 BQ101
Tilbury RM18 110 GE81
Twickenham TW2 117 CF86
Walton-on-Thames KT12 135 BU100
Woking GU21 166 AW115
Russells, Tad. KT20 173 CX122
Russell's Footpath, SW16 121 DL92
⊖ Russell Square 195 P5
Russell Sq, WC1 195 P5
Longfield DA3
off Cavendish Sq 149 FX97
Russells Ride, Wal.Cr. (Chsht.)
EN8 15 DX31
Russell St, WC2 196 A10
Russell Wk, Rich. TW10
off Park Hill 118 CM86
Russell Way, Sutt. SM1 158 DA106
Watford WD19 39 BV45
Russet Cl, Stai. TW19 113 BF86
Uxbridge UB10
off Uxbridge Rd 77 BQ70
Walton-on-Thames KT12 136 BX104
Russet Cres, N7
off Stock Orchard Cres 65 DM64
Russet Dr, Croy. CR0 143 DY102
Radlett (Shenley) WD7 10 CL32
Russets, The, Ger.Cr. (Chal.St.P.)
SL9 off Austenwood Cl 36 AX54
Russets Cl, E4 off Larkshall Rd 47 ED49
Russett Cl, Orp. BR6 164 EV106
Waltham Cross EN7 14 DS26
Russett Ct, Cat. CR3 186 DU125
Russett Hill, Ger.Cr. (Chal.St.P.)
SL9 56 AY55
Russetts, Horn. RM11 72 FL56
Russetts Cl, Wok. GU21 167 AZ115
Russett Way, SE13
off Conington Rd 103 EB82
Swanley BR8 147 FD96
Russia Ct, EC2 197 J8
Russia Dock Rd, SE16 203 L3
Russia La, E2 84 DW68
Russia Row, EC2 197 J9
Russia Wk, SE16 203 K5
Russington Rd, Shep. TW17 135 BR100
Rusthall Av, W4 98 CR77
Rusthall Cl, Croy. CR0 142 DW100
Rustic Av, SW16 121 DH94
Rustic Cl, Upmin. RM14 73 FS60
Rustic Pl, Wem. HA0 61 CK63
Rustic Wk, E16 off Lambert Rd 86 EH72
Rustington Wk, Mord. SM4 139 CZ101
Ruston Av, Surb. KT5 138 CP101
Ruston Gdns, N14 off Farm La 28 DG44
Ruston Ms, W11
off St. Marks Rd 81 CY72
Ruston Rd, SE18 104 EL76
Ruston St, E3 85 DZ67
Rust Sq, SE5 102 DR80
Rutford Rd, SW16 121 DL92
Ruth Cl, Stan. HA7 62 CM56
Ruthen Cl, Epsom KT18 156 CP114
Rutherford Cl, Borwd. WD6 26 CQ40
Sutton SM2 158 DD107
Uxbridge UB8 76 BM70
Rutherford St, SW1 199 M8
Rutherford Twr, Sthl. UB1 78 CB72
Rutherford Way, Bushey
(Bushey Hth.) WD23 41 CD46
Wembley HA9 62 CN63
Rutherglen Rd, SE2 106 EU79
Rutherwick Ri, Couls. CR5 175 DL117
Rutherwyke Cl, Epsom KT17 157 CU107
Rutherwyk Rd, Cher. KT16 133 BE101
Ruthin Cl, NW9 62 CS58
Ruthin Rd, SE3 104 EG79
Ruthven Av, Wal.Cr. EN8 15 DX33
Ruthven St, E9
off Lauriston Rd 85 DX67
Rutland App, Horn. RM11 72 FN57
Rutland Av, Sid. DA15 126 EU87
Rutland Cl, SW14 98 CQ83
SW19 off Rutland Rd 120 DE94
Ashtead KT21 172 CL117
Bexley DA5 126 EX88
Chessington KT9 156 CM107
Dartford DA1 128 FK87
Epsom KT19 156 CR110
Redhill RH1 184 DF133
Rutland Ct, Enf. EN3 30 DW43
Rutland Dr, Horn. RM11 72 FN57
Morden SM4 139 CZ100
Richmond TW10 117 CK88
Rutland Gdns, N4 65 DP58
SW7 198 C5
W13 79 CG71
Croydon CR0 160 DS105
Dagenham RM8 70 EW64
Rutland Gdns Ms, SW7 198 C5
Rutland Gate, SW7 198 C5
Belvedere DA17 107 FB78
Bromley BR2 144 EF98
Rutland Gate Ms, SW7 198 B5
Rutland Gro, W6 99 CV78
Rutland Ms, NW8
off Boundary Rd 82 DB67
Rutland Ms E, SW7 198 B6
Rutland Ms S, SW7 198 B6
Rutland Ms W, SW7
off Ennismore St 100 DE76
Rutland Pk, NW2 81 CW65
SE6 123 DZ89
Rutland Pk Gdns, NW2
off Rutland Pk 81 CW65
Rutland Pk Mans, NW2
off Walm La 81 CW65
Rutland Pl, EC1 197 H5
Bushey (Bushey Hth.) WD23
off The Rutts 41 CD46
Rutland Rd, E7 86 EK66
E9 84 DW67
Rutland Rd, E11 68 EH57
E17 67 EA58
SW19 120 DE94
Harrow HA1 60 CC58
Hayes UB3 95 BR77
Ilford IG1 69 EP63
Southall UB1 78 CA71
Twickenham TW2 117 CD89
Rutland St, SW7 198 C6
Rutland Wk, SE6 123 DZ89
Rutland Way, Orp. BR5 146 EW100
Rutley Cl, SE17 off Royal Rd 101 DP79
Romford (Harold Wd.) RM3
off Pasteur Dr 52 FK54
Rutlish Rd, SW19 140 DA95
Rutson Rd, W.Byf. (Byfleet)
KT14 152 BM114
Rutter Gdns, Mitch. CR4 140 DC98
Rutters Cl, West Dr. UB7 94 BN75
Rutts, The, Bushey (Bushey Hth.)
WD23 41 CD46
Rutts Ter, SE14 103 DX81
Ruvigny Gdns, SW15 99 CX83
Ruxbury Rd, Cher. KT16 133 BC100
Ruxley Cl, Epsom KT19 156 CP106
Sidcup DA14 126 EX93
Ruxley Cor Ind Est, Sid. DA14 126 EX93
Ruxley Cres, Esher (Clay.)
KT10 155 CH107
Ruxley Gdns, Shep. TW17 135 BQ99
Ruxley La, Epsom KT19 156 CR106
Ruxley Ms, Epsom KT19 156 CP106
Ruxley Ridge, Esher (Clay.)
KT10 155 CG108
Ruxton Cl, Swan. BR8 147 FE97
Ryall Cl, St.Alb. (Brick.Wd.) AL2 8 BY29
Ryalls Ct, N20 44 DF48
Ryan Cl, SE3 104 EJ84
Ruislip HA4 59 BV60
Ryan Dr, Brent. TW8 97 CG79
Ryan Way, Wat. WD24 24 BW39
Ryarsh Cres, Orp. BR6 163 ES105
Rycott Path, SE22
off Lordship La 122 DU87
Rycroft La, Sev. TN14 190 FE130
Rycroft Way, N17 66 DT55
Ryculff Sq, SE3 104 EF82
Rydal Cl, NW4 43 CY53
Purley CR8 160 DR113
Rydal Ct, Wat. WD25
off Grasmere Cl 7 BV32
Rydal Cres, Grnf. UB6 79 CH69
Rydal Dr, Bexh. DA7 106 FA81
West Wickham BR4 144 EE103
Rydal Gdns, NW9 62 CS57
SW15 118 CS92
Hounslow TW3 116 CB86
Wembley HA9 61 CJ60
Rydal Rd, SW16 121 DK91
Rydal Way, Egh. TW20 113 BB94
Enfield EN3 30 DW44
Ruislip HA4 60 BW63
Ryde, The, Stai. TW18 134 BH95
Ryde Cl, Wok. (Ripley) GU23 168 BJ121
Ryde Heron, Wok. (Knap.) GU21
off Robin Hood Rd 166 AS117
RYDENS, Walt. 136 BW103
Rydens Av, Walt. KT12 135 BV103
Rydens Cl, Walt. KT12 136 BW103
Rydens Gro, Walt. KT12 154 BX105
Rydens Pk, Walt. KT12
off Rydens Rd 136 BX103
Rydens Rd, Walt. KT12 136 BX103
Rydens Way, Wok. GU22 167 BA120
Ryde Pl, Twick. TW1 117 CJ86
Ryder Cl, Brom. BR1 124 EH92
Bushey WD23 24 CB44
Hemel Hempstead (Bov.) HP3 5 BA28
Ryder Ct, SW1 199 L2
Ryder Dr, SE16 102 DV78
Ryder Gdns, Rain. RM13 89 FF65
Ryder Ms, E9
off Homerton High St 66 DW64
Ryders Ter, NW8
off Blenheim Ter 82 DC68
Ryder St, SW1 199 L2
Ryder Yd, SW1 199 L2
Rydes Cl, Wok. GU22 167 BC120
Ryde Vale Rd, SW12 121 DH89
Rydon Business Cen, Lthd.
KT22 171 CH119
Rydons Cl, SE9 104 EL83
Rydon's La, Couls. CR5 176 DQ120
Rydon St, N1 off St. Paul St 84 DQ67
Rydon's Wd Cl, Couls. CR5 176 DQ120
Rydston Cl, N7
off Sutterton St 83 DM66
Rye, The, N14 45 DJ45
Ryebridge Cl, Lthd. KT22 171 CG118
Ryebrook Rd, Lthd. KT22 171 CG118
Rye Cl, Bex. DA5 127 FB86
Hornchurch RM12 72 FJ64
Ryecotes Mead, SE21 122 DS88
Rye Ct, Slou. SL1
off Alpha St S 92 AU76
Rye Cres, Orp. BR5 146 EW102
Ryecroft, Grav. DA12 131 GL92
Ryecroft Av, Ilf. IG5 49 EP54
Twickenham TW2 116 CB87
Ryecroft Cres, Barn. EN5 27 CV43
Ryecroft Rd, SE13 123 EC85
SW16 121 DN93
Orpington BR5 145 ER100
Sevenoaks (Otford) TN14 181 FG116
Ryecroft St, SW6 100 DB81
Ryedale, SE22 122 DV86
Ryedale Ct, Sev. TN13
off London Rd 190 FE121
Rye Fld, Ashtd. KT21 171 CK117
Orpington BR5 146 EX102
Ryefield Av, Uxb. UB10 77 BP66
Ryefield Ct, Nthwd. HA6
off Ryefield Cres 39 BU54
Ryefield Cres, Nthwd. HA6 39 BU54
Ryefield Par, Nthwd. HA6
off Ryefield Cres 39 BU54
Ryefield Path, SW15 119 CU88
Ryefield Rd, SE19 122 DQ93
Ryegates, SE15
off Caulfield Rd 102 DV82
Rye Hill Pk, SE15 102 DW84
Ryeland Cl, West Dr. UB7 76 BL72
Ryelands Cl, Cat. CR3 176 DS121
Ryelands Ct, Lthd. KT22 171 CG118
Ryelands Cres, SE12 124 EJ86
Ryelands Pl, Wey. KT13 135 BS104
Rye La, SE15 102 DU81
Sevenoaks (Dunt.Grn.) TN14 181 FG117
Rye Pas, SE15 102 DU83
Rye Rd, SE15 103 DX84
Rye Wk, SW15
off Chartfield Av 119 CX85
Rye Way, Edg. HA8
off Canons Dr 42 CM51
Ryfold Rd, SW19 120 DA90
Ryhope Rd, N11 45 DH49
Rykhill, Grays RM16 111 GH76
Ryland Cl, Felt. TW13 115 BT91
Rylandes Rd, NW2 63 CU62
South Croydon CR2 160 DV109
Ryland Ho, Croy. CR0 142 DQ104
Ryland Rd, NW5 83 DH65
Rylett Cres, W12 99 CT76
Rylett Rd, W12 99 CT75
Rylston Rd, N13 46 DR48
SW6 99 CZ79
Rymer Rd, Croy. CR0 142 DS101
Rymer St, SE24 121 DP86
Rymill Cl, Hem.H. (Bov.) HP3 5 BA28
Rymill St, E16 87 EN74
Rysbrack St, SW3 198 D6
Rysted La, West. TN16 189 EQ126
Rythe Cl, Chess. KT9
off Nigel Fisher Way 155 CJ108
Rythe Ct, T.Ditt. KT7 137 CG101
Rythe Rd, Esher (Clay.) KT10 155 CD106
Ryvers Rd, Slou. SL3 93 AZ76

S

★ Saatchi Gall, NW8 82 DB67
Sabah Ct, Ashf. TW15 114 BN91
Sabbarton St, E16
off Victoria Dock Rd 86 EF72
Sabella Ct, E3 85 DZ68
Sabina Rd, Grays RM16 111 GJ77
Sabine Rd, SW11 100 DF83
Sable Cl, Houns. TW4 96 BW83
Sable St, N1 off Canonbury Rd 83 DP66
Sach Rd, E5 66 DV61
Sackville Av, Brom. BR2 144 EG102
Sackville Cl, Har. HA2 61 CD62
Sevenoaks TN13 191 FH122
Sackville Ct, Rom. RM3
off Sackville Cres 52 FL53
Sackville Cres, Rom. RM3 52 FL53
Sackville Est, SW16 121 DL90
Sackville Gdns, Ilf. IG1 69 EM60
Sackville Rd, Dart. DA2 128 FK89
Sutton SM2 158 DA108
Sackville St, W1 199 L1
Sackville Way, SE22
off Dulwich Common 122 DU88
Saddington St, Grav. DA12 131 GH87
Saddlebrook Pk, Sun. TW16 115 BS94
Saddlers Cl, Barn. (Arkley) EN5 27 CV43
Borehamwood WD6
off Farriers Way 26 CR44
Pinner HA5 40 CA51
Saddlers Ms, SW8
off Portland Gro 101 DM81
Kingston upon Thames KT1 137 CJ95
Wembley HA0
off The Boltons 61 CF63
Saddler's Pk, Dart. (Eyns.)
DA4 148 FK104
Saddlers Path, Borwd. WD6 26 CR43
Saddlers Way, Epsom KT18 172 CR119
Saddlescombe Way, N12 44 DA50
Saddleworth Rd, Rom. RM3 52 FJ51
Saddleworth Sq, Rom. RM3 52 FJ51
Saddle Yd, W1 199 H2
Sadler Cl, Mitch. CR4 140 DF96
Waltham Cross (Chsht.) EN7
off Markham Rd 14 DQ25
Sadlers Ride, W.Mol. KT8 136 CC96
★ Sadler's Wells Thea, EC1 196 F2
Saffron Av, E14 85 ED73
Saffron Cl, NW11 63 CZ57
Croydon CR0 141 DL100
Slough (Datchet) SL3 92 AV81
Saffron Ct, Felt. TW14
off Staines Rd 115 BQ87
Saffron Hill, EC1 196 E5
Saffron Rd, Grays (Chaff.Hun.)
RM16 109 FW77
Romford RM5 51 FC54
Saffron St, EC1 196 E6
Saffron Way, Surb. KT6 137 CK102
Sage Cl, E6
off Bradley Stone Rd 87 EM71
Sage St, E1 off Cable St 84 DW73
Sage Way, WC1 196 B3
Saigasso Cl, E16 off Royal Rd 86 EK72
Sailmakers Ct, SW6
off William Morris Way 100 DC83
Sail St, SE11 200 C8
Sainfoin Rd, SW17 120 DG89
Sainsbury Rd, SE19 122 DS92
St. Agatha's Dr, Kings.T. KT2 118 CM93
St. Agathas Gro, Cars. SM5 140 DF102
St. Agnes Cl, E9 off Gore Rd 84 DW67
St. Agnes Pl, SE11 101 DN79
St. Agnes Well, EC1 off Old St 84 DR70
St. Aidans Ct, W13
off St. Aidans Rd 97 CH75
Barking IG11
off Choats Rd 88 EV69

A B C D E F G H I J K L M N O P Q R S T U V W X Y Z

St. A- St. J

St. Aidan's Rd, SE22 ... 122 DV86
St. Aidans Rd, W13 ... 97 CH75
St. Aidan's Way, Grav. DA12 . 131 GL90
St. Albans Av, E6 ... 87 EM69
St. Alban's Av, W4 ... 98 CR77
St. Albans Av, Felt. TW13 ... 116 BX92
Upminster RM14 ... 73 FS60
Weybridge KT13 ... 134 BN104
St. Albans Cl, NW11 ... 64 DA60
Gravesend DA12 ... 131 GK90
St. Albans Cres, N22 ... 45 DN53
St. Alban's Cres, Wdf.Grn. IG8 . 48 EG52
St. Albans Gdns, Grav. DA12 . 131 GK90
St. Alban's Gdns, Tedd. TW11 . 117 CG92
St. Albans Gro, W8 ... 100 DB76
St. Alban's Gro, Cars. SM5 .. 140 DE101
St. Albans La, NW11
off West Heath Dr ... 64 DA60
Abbots Langley (Bedmond)
WD5 ... 7 BT26
St. Alban's Pl, N1 ... 83 DP67
St. Albans Rd, NW5 ... 64 DG62
NW10 ... 80 CS67
Barnet EN5 ... 27 CZ39
Dartford DA1 ... 128 FM87
Epping CM16 ... 18 EX29
Ilford IG3 ... 69 ET60
St. Alban's Rd, Kings.T. KT2 .. 118 CL93
St. Albans Rd, Pot.B. (Dance.H.)
EN6 ... 27 CV35
Potters Bar (S.Mimms) EN6 . 11 CV34
Radlett (Shenley) WD7 ... 10 CQ30
Reigate RH2 ... 184 DA133
St. Albans (Lon.Col.) AL2 ... 10 CN28
St. Alban's Rd, Sutt. SM1 ... 157 CZ105
St. Albans Rd, Wat. WD17,
WD24, WD25 ... 23 BV40
St. Alban's Rd, Wdf.Grn. IG8 . 48 EG52
St. Albans St, SW1 ... 199 M1
St. Albans Ter, W6
off Margravine Rd ... 99 CY79
St. Alban's Vil, NW5
off Highgate Rd ... 64 DG62
St. Alfege Pas, SE10 ... 103 EC79
St. Alfege Rd, SE7 ... 104 EK79
St. Alphage Gdns, EC2 ... 197 J7
St. Alphage Highwalk, EC2
off London Wall ... 84 DR71
St. Alphage Wk, Edg. HA8 ... 42 CQ54
St. Alphege Rd, N9 ... 46 DW45
St. Alphonsus Rd, SW4 ... 101 DJ84
St. Amunds Cl, SE6 ... 123 EA91
H St. Andrew's at Harrow (Bowden
Ho Hosp), Har. HA1 ... 61 CE61
St. Andrews Av, Horn. RM12 .. 71 FG64
Wembley HA0 ... 61 CG63
St. Andrew's Cl, N12
off Woodside Av ... 44 DC49
St. Andrews Cl, NW2 ... 63 CV62
SE16 *off Ryder Dr* ... 102 DV78
SE28 ... 88 EX72
St. Andrew's Cl, Islw. TW7 ... 97 CD81
St. Andrews Cl, Ruis. HA4 ... 60 BX61
St. Andrew's Cl, Shep. TW17 . 135 BR98
Staines (Wrays.) TW19 ... 112 AY87
St. Andrews Cl, Stan. HA7 ... 41 CJ54
St. Andrew's Cl, Wind. (Old Wind.)
SL4 ... 112 AU86
St. Andrews Cl, Wok. GU21
off St. Mary's Rd ... 166 AW117
St. Andrew's Ct, SW18
off Waynflete St ... 120 DC89
St. Andrews Ct, Slou. (Colnbr.)
SL3 *off High St* ... 93 BD80
Watford WD17 ... 23 BV39
St. Andrews Dr, Orp. BR5 .. 146 EV100
Stanmore HA7 ... 41 CJ53
St. Andrews Gdns, Cob. KT11 . 154 BW113
St. Andrew's Gro, N16 ... 66 DR60
St. Andrew's Hill, EC4 ... 196 G10
H St. Andrew's Hosp, E3 ... 85 EB70
St. Andrew's Ms, N16 ... 66 DS60
St. Andrews Ms, SE3
off Mycenae Rd ... 104 EG80
St. Andrews Pl, NW1 ... 195 J4
Brentwood CM15 ... 55 FZ47
St. Andrews Rd, E11 ... 68 EE58
E13 ... 86 EH69
E17 ... 47 DX54
N9 ... 46 DW45
NW9 ... 62 CR60
NW10 ... 81 CV65
NW11 ... 63 CZ58
W3 ... 80 CS73
W7 *off Church Rd* ... 97 CE75
W14 ... 99 CY79
Carshalton SM5 ... 140 DE104
Coulsdon CR5 ... 174 DG116
Croydon CR0
off Lower Coombe St ... 160 DQ105
Enfield EN1 ... 30 DR41
St. Andrew's Rd, Grav. DA12 . 131 GJ87
St. Andrews Rd, Ilf. IG1 ... 69 EM59
Romford RM7 ... 71 FD58
Sidcup DA14 ... 126 EX90
St. Andrew's Rd, Surb. KT6 . 137 CK100
St. Andrews Rd, Til. RM18 ... 110 GE81
Uxbridge UB10 ... 76 BM66
Watford WD19 ... 40 BX48
St. Andrews Sq, W11
off St. Marks Rd ... 81 CY72
St. Andrew's Sq, Surb. KT6 . 137 CK100
St. Andrews Twr, Sthl. UB1 ... 78 CC73
St. Andrew St, EC4 ... 196 E7
St. Andrews Wk, Cob. KT11 .. 169 BV115
St. Andrews Way, E3 ... 85 EB70
Oxted RH8 ... 188 EL130
St. Anna Rd, Barn. EN5
off Sampson Av ... 27 CX43
St. Annes Av, Stai. (Stanw.)
TW19 ... 114 BK87
St. Annes Boul, Red. RH1 .. 185 DH132
St. Anne's Cl, N6
off Highgate W Hill ... 64 DG62
St. Annes Cl, Wal.Cr. (Chsht.)
EN7 ... 14 DU28
St. Anne's Cl, Wat. WD19 ... 40 BW49
St. Anne's Ct, W1 ... 195 M9
St. Anne's Dr, Red. RH1 ... 184 DG133
St. Annes Dr N, Red. RH1 ... 184 DG132
St. Annes Gdns, NW10 ... 80 CM69
St. Anne's Mt, Red. RH1 ... 184 DG133
St. Annes Pas, E14
off Newell St ... 85 DZ72
St. Annes Ri, Red. RH1 ... 184 DG133
St. Annes Rd, E11 ... 67 ED61
St. Anne's Rd, St.Alb. (Lon.Col.)
AL2 ... 9 CK27
Uxbridge (Hare.) UB9 ... 58 BJ55
Wembley HA0 ... 61 CK64
St. Anne's Row, E14
off Commercial Rd ... 85 DZ72
St. Anne St, E14
off Commercial Rd ... 85 DZ72
St. Anne's Way, Red. RH1
off St. Anne's Dr ... 184 DG133
St. Ann's, Bark. IG11 ... 87 EQ67
St. Anns Cl, Cher. KT16 ... 133 BF100
St. Ann's Cres, SW18 ... 120 DC86
St. Ann's Gdns, NW5
off Queen's Cres ... 82 DG65
St. Ann's Hill, SW18 ... 120 DB85
St. Anns Hill Rd, Cher. KT16 . 133 BC100
H St. Ann's Hosp, N15 ... 66 DQ57
St. Ann's La, SW1 ... 199 N6
St. Ann's Pk Rd, SW18 ... 120 DC86
St. Ann's Pas, SW13 ... 98 CS83
St. Anns Rd, N9 ... 46 DT47
St. Ann's Rd, N15 ... 65 DP57
SW13 ... 99 CT82
St. Anns Rd, W11 ... 81 CX73
St. Ann's Rd, Bark. IG11
off Axe St ... 87 EQ67
St. Anns Rd, Cher. KT16 ... 133 BF100
St. Ann's Rd, Har. HA1 ... 61 CE58
St. Ann's Shop Cen, Har. HA1 . 61 CE58
St. Ann's St, SW1 ... 199 N6
St. Ann's Ter, NW8 ... 82 DD68
St. Anns Vil, W11 ... 81 CX74
St. Anns Way, S.Croy. CR2 .. 159 DP107
Westerham (Berry's Grn.)
TN16 ... 179 EP116
St. Anselm's Pl, W1 ... 195 H9
St. Anselms Rd, Hayes UB3 ... 95 BT75
St. Anthonys Av, Wdf.Grn. IG8 . 48 EJ51
St. Anthonys Cl, E1 ... 202 B2
SW17 *off College Gdns* ... 120 DE89
H St. Anthony's Hosp, Sutt.
SM3 ... 139 CX102
St. Anthony's Way, Felt. TW14 . 95 BT84
St. Antony's Rd, E7 ... 86 EH66
St. Arvans Cl, Croy. CR0 ... 142 DS104
St. Asaph Rd, SE4 ... 103 DX83
St. Aubyn's Av, SW19 ... 119 CZ92
St. Aubyns Av, Houns. TW3 .. 116 CA85
St. Aubyns Cl, Orp. BR6 ... 145 ET104
St. Aubyns Gdns, Orp. BR6 .. 145 ET103
St. Aubyn's Rd, SE19 ... 122 DT93
St. Audrey Av, Bexh. DA7 ... 106 FA82
St. Augustine Rd, Grays RM16 . 111 GH77
St. Augustine's Av, W5 ... 80 CL68
St. Augustines Av, Brom. BR2 . 144 EL99
St. Augustine's Av, S.Croy.
CR2 ... 160 DQ107
St. Augustines Av, Wem. HA9 . 62 CL62
St. Augustine's Path, N5 ... 65 DP64
St. Augustines Rd, NW1 ... 83 DK66
St. Augustine's Rd, Belv.
DA17 ... 106 EZ77
St. Austell Cl, Edg. HA8 ... 42 CM54
St. Austell Rd, SE13 ... 103 EC82
St. Awdry's Rd, Bark. IG11 ... 87 ER66
St. Awdry's Wk, Bark. IG11
off Station Par ... 87 EQ66
St. Barnabas Cl, SE22
off East Dulwich Gro ... 122 DS85
Beckenham BR3 ... 143 EC96
St. Barnabas Ct, Har. HA3 ... 40 CC53
St. Barnabas Gdns, W.Mol.
KT8 ... 136 CA99
St. Barnabas Rd, E17 ... 67 EA58
Mitcham CR4 ... 120 DG94
Sutton SM1 ... 158 DD106
Woodford Green IG8 ... 48 EH53
St. Barnabas St, SW1 ... 198 G10
St. Barnabas Ter, E9 ... 67 DX64
St. Barnabas Vil, SW8 ... 101 DL81
St. Bartholomews Cl, SE26 .. 122 DW91
H St. Bartholomew's Hosp,
EC1 ... 196 G7
St. Bartholomew's Rd, E6 ... 86 EL67
★ St. Bartholomew-the-Great
Church, EC1 *off Cloth Fair* . 196 G7
St. Benedict's Av, Grav. DA12 131 GK89
St. Benedict's Cl, SW17
off Church La ... 120 DG92
St. Benet's Cl, SW17
off College Gdns ... 120 DE89
St. Benet's Gro, Cars. SM5 .. 140 DC101
St. Benet's Pl, EC3 ... 197 L10
St. Benjamins Dr, Orp. BR6 .. 164 EW109
St. Bernards, Croy. CR0 ... 142 DS104
St. Bernard's Cl, SE27
off St. Gothard Rd ... 122 DR91
H St. Bernard's Hosp, Sthl.
UB1 ... 97 CD75
St. Bernard's Rd, E6 ... 86 EK67
St. Bernards Rd, Slou. SL3 ... 92 AW76
St. Blaise Av, Brom. BR1 ... 144 EH96
St. Botolph Rd, Grav. DA11 .. 130 GC90
St. Botolph Row, EC3 ... 197 P9
St. Botolph's Av, Sev. TN13 .. 190 FG124
St. Botolph's Rd, Sev. TN13 .. 190 FG124
St. Botolph St, EC3 ... 197 P9
St. Bride's Av, EC4
off New Br St ... 83 DP72
St. Brides Av, Edg. HA8 ... 42 CM53
★ St. Bride's Church & Crypt
Mus, EC4 ... 196 F9
St. Brides Cl, Erith DA18
off St. Katherines Rd ... 106 EX75
St. Bride's Pas, EC4 ... 196 F9
★ St. Bride's Printing Lib, EC4
off Bride La ... 196 F9
St. Bride St, EC4 ... 196 F8
St. Catherines, Wok. GU22 .. 166 AW119
St. Catherines Cl, SW17
off College Gdns ... 120 DE89
St. Catherines Cross, Red.
(Bletch.) RH1 ... 186 DS134
St. Catherines Dr, SE14
off Kitto Rd ... 103 DX82
St. Catherines Fm Ct, Ruis.
HA4 ... 59 BQ58
St. Catherine's Ms, SW3 ... 198 D8
St. Catherines Rd, E4 ... 47 EA47
Ruislip HA4 ... 59 BR57
St. Catherines Twr, E10
off Kings Cl ... 67 EB59
St. Cecilia Rd, Grays RM16 .. 111 GH77
St. Cecilia's Cl, Sutt. SM3 ... 139 CY102
St. Chads Cl, Surb. KT6 ... 137 CJ101
St. Chad's Dr, Grav. DA12 ... 131 GL90
St. Chad's Gdns, Rom. RM6 ... 70 EY59
St. Chad's Pl, WC1 ... 196 A2
St. Chad's Rd, Rom. RM6 ... 70 EY58
Tilbury RM18 ... 111 GG80
St. Chad's St, WC1 ... 196 A2
St. Charles Ct, Wey. KT13 ... 152 BN106
H St. Charles Hosp, W10 ... 81 CX71
St. Charles Pl, W10
off Chesterton Rd ... 81 CY71
Weybridge KT13 ... 152 BN106
St. Charles Rd, Brwd. CM14 ... 54 FV46
St. Charles Sq, W10 ... 81 CY71
St. Christopher Rd, Uxb. UB8 . 76 BK71
St. Christopher's Cl, Islw. TW7 . 97 CE81
St. Christopher's Dr, Hayes
UB3 ... 77 BV73
St. Christophers Gdns, Th.Hth.
CR7 ... 141 DN97
St. Christophers Ms, Wall.
SM6 ... 159 DJ106
St. Christopher's Pl, W1 ... 194 G8
St. Clair Cl, Oxt. RH8 ... 187 EC130
Reigate RH2 ... 184 DC134
St. Clair Dr, Wor.Pk. KT4 ... 139 CV104
St. Clair Rd, E13 ... 86 EH68
St. Clair's Rd, Croy. CR0 ... 142 DS103
St. Clare Business Pk, Hmptn.
TW12 ... 116 CC93
St. Clare Cl, Ilf. IG5 ... 49 EM54
St. Clare St, EC3 ... 197 P9
St. Clement Cl, Uxb. UB8 ... 76 BK72
★ St. Clement Danes Church,
WC2 *off Strand* ... 196 C9
St. Clements Av, Grays RM20 . 109 FU79
St. Clement's Cl, Grav. (Nthflt.)
DA11 *off Coldharbour Rd* . 131 GF90
St. Clements Ct, EC4
off Clements La ... 84 DR73
N7 *off Arundel Sq* ... 83 DN65
Purfleet RM19 *off Thamley* . 108 FN77
St. Clements Hts, SE26 ... 122 DU90
St. Clement's La, WC2 ... 196 C9
St. Clements Rd, Grays
RM20 ... 109 FW80
St. Clements St, N7 ... 83 DN65
St. Cloud Rd, SE27 ... 122 DQ91
St. Columba's Cl, Grav. DA12 . 131 GL90
St. Crispins Cl, NW3 ... 64 DE63
Southall UB1 ... 78 BZ72
St. Crispins Way, Cher. (Ott.)
KT16 ... 151 BC109
St. Cross St, EC1 ... 196 E6
St. Cuthberts Cl, Egh. TW20 .. 112 AX92
St. Cuthberts Gdns, Pnr. HA5
off Westfield Pk ... 40 BZ52
St. Cuthberts Rd, N13 ... 45 DN51
NW2 ... 81 CZ65
St. Cyprian's St, SW17 ... 120 DF91
St. David Cl, Uxb. UB8 ... 76 BK71
St. Davids, Couls. CR5 ... 175 DM117
St. Davids Cl, SE16
off Masters Dr ... 102 DV78
Iver SL0 ... 75 BD67
St. David's Cl, Reig. RH2 ... 184 DC133
St. Davids Cl, Wem. HA9 ... 62 CQ62
St. David's Cl, W.Wick. BR4 .. 143 EB101
St. David's Ct, E17 ... 67 EC55
St. David's Cres, Grav. DA12 . 131 GK91
St. Davids Dr, Edg. HA8 ... 42 CM53
St. David's Dr, Egh. (Eng.Grn.)
TW20 ... 112 AW94
St. Davids Ms, E3
off Morgan St ... 85 DY69
St. Davids Pl, NW4 ... 63 CV59
St. Davids Rd, Swan. BR8 ... 127 FF93
St. Davids Sq, E14 ... 204 C10
St. Denis Rd, SE27 ... 122 DR91
St. Dionis Rd, SW6 ... 99 CZ82
St. Donatts Rd, SE14 ... 103 DZ81
St. Dunstan's All, EC3 ... 197 M10
St. Dunstans Av, W3 ... 80 CR73
St. Dunstans Cl, Hayes UB3 ... 95 BT77
St. Dunstan's Ct, EC4
off Fleet St ... 83 DN72
St. Dunstan's Dr, Grav. DA12 . 131 GL91
St. Dunstans Gdns, W3
off St. Dunstans Av ... 80 CR73
St. Dunstan's Hill, EC3 ... 201 M1
Sutton SM1 ... 157 CY106
St. Dunstan's La, EC3 ... 201 M1
Beckenham BR3 ... 143 EC100
St. Dunstan's Rd, E7 ... 86 EJ65
St. Dunstans Rd, SE25 ... 142 DT98
W6 ... 99 CX78
W7 ... 97 CE75
St. Dunstan's Rd, Felt. TW13 . 115 BT90
St. Dunstans Rd, Houns. TW4 . 96 BW82
H St. Ebba's Hosp, Epsom
KT19 ... 156 CQ109
St. Edith Cl, Epsom KT18
off St. Elizabeth Dr ... 156 CQ114
St. Edmunds Av, Ruis. HA4 ... 59 BR58
St. Edmunds Cl, NW8
off St. Edmunds Ter ... 82 DF67
SW17 *off College Gdns* ... 120 DE89
St. Edmunds Cl, Erith DA18
off St. Katherines Rd ... 106 EX75
St. Edmunds Dr, Stan. HA7 ... 41 CG53
St. Edmund's La, Twick. TW2 . 116 CB87
St. Edmunds Rd, N9 ... 46 DU45
Dartford DA1 ... 108 FM84
Ilford IG1 ... 69 EM58
St. Edmunds Sq, SW13 ... 99 CW79
St. Edmunds Ter, NW8 ... 82 DE67
St. Edwards Cl, NW11 ... 64 DA58
Croydon (New Adgtn.) CR0 . 161 ED111
St. Edwards Way, Rom. RM1 .. 71 FD57
St. Egberts Way, E4 ... 47 EC46
St. Elizabeth Dr, Epsom KT18 . 156 CQ114
St. Elmo Rd, W12 ... 81 CT74
St. Elmos Rd, SE16 ... 203 K4
St. Erkenwald Ms, Bark. IG11
off St. Erkenwald Rd ... 87 ER67
St. Erkenwald Rd, Bark. IG11 .. 87 ER67
St. Ermin's Hill, SW1 ... 199 M6
St. Ervans Rd, W10 ... 81 CY71
St. Fabian Twr, E4 *off Iris Way* . 47 DZ51
St. Faiths Cl, Enf. EN2 ... 30 DQ39
St. Faith's Rd, SE21 ... 121 DP88
St. Fidelis Rd, Erith DA8 ... 107 FD77
St. Fillans Rd, SE6 ... 123 EC88
St. Francis Av, Grav. DA12 ... 131 GL91
St. Francis Cl, Orp. BR5 ... 145 ES100
Potters Bar EN6 ... 12 DC33
Watford WD19 ... 39 BV46
St. Francis Rd, SE22 ... 102 DS84
Erith DA8 *off West St* ... 107 FD77
Uxbridge (Denh.) UB9 ... 57 BF58
St. Francis Way, Grays RM16 . 111 GJ77
Ilford IG1 ... 69 ES63
St. Frideswides Ms, E14
off Lodore St ... 85 EC72
St. Gabriel's Cl, E11 ... 68 EH61
St. Gabriels Rd, NW2 ... 63 CX64
St. Georges Av, E7 ... 86 EH66
N7 ... 65 DK63
NW9 ... 62 CQ56
St. George's Av, W5 ... 97 CK75
St. Georges Av, Grays RM17 . 110 GC77
Hornchurch RM11 ... 72 FM59
Southall UB1 ... 78 BZ73
St. George's Av, Wey. KT13 .. 153 BP107
St. Georges Cen, Har. HA1
off St. Ann's Rd ... 61 CE58
St. Georges Circ, SE1 ... 200 F6
St. Georges Cl, NW11 ... 63 CZ58
SE28 *off Redbourne Dr* ... 88 EX72
St. George's Cl, SW8
off Patmore Est ... 101 DJ81
St. Georges Cl, Wem. HA0 ... 61 CG62
St. George's Cl, Wey. KT13 .. 153 BQ106
St. Georges Ct, E6 ... 87 EM70
EC4 ... 196 F8
SW7 *off Gloucester Rd* ... 100 DC76
St. Georges Cres, Grav. DA12 . 131 GK91
St. George's Dr, SW1 ... 199 K10
St. Georges Dr, Uxb. UB10 ... 58 BM62
Watford WD19 ... 40 BY48
St. Georges Flds, W2 ... 194 C9
St. Georges Gdns, Epsom KT17
off Lynwood Rd ... 157 CT114
St. George's Gdns, Surb. KT6
off Hamilton Av ... 138 CP103
St. Georges Gro, SW17 ... 120 DD90
St. Georges Gro Est, SW17 .. 120 DD90
ST. GEORGE'S HILL, Wey. ... 153 BQ110
H St. George's Hosp, SW17 . 120 DD92
H St. Georges Hosp, Horn.
RM12 ... 72 FK63
St. Georges Ind Est, Kings.T. KT2
off Richmond Rd ... 117 CK92
St. Georges La, EC3 ... 197 M10
St. George's Lo, Wey. KT13 .. 153 BR106
St. Georges Ms, NW1
off Regents Pk Rd ... 82 DF66
St. Georges Pl, Twick. TW1
off Church St ... 117 CG88
St. Georges Rd, E7 ... 86 EH65
E10 ... 67 EC62
N9 ... 46 DU48
N13 ... 45 DM48
NW11 ... 63 CZ58
SE1 ... 200 E6
St. George's Rd, SW19 ... 119 CZ93
St. Georges Rd, W4 ... 98 CS75
W7 ... 79 CF74
Addlestone KT15 ... 152 BJ105
St. George's Rd, Beck. BR3 .. 143 EB95
St. Georges Rd, Brom. BR1 .. 145 EM96
Dagenham RM9 ... 70 EY64
Enfield EN1 ... 30 DT38
St. George's Rd, Felt. TW13 .. 116 BX91
St. Georges Rd, Ilf. IG1 ... 69 EM59
St. George's Rd, Kings.T. KT2 . 118 CN94
Mitcham CR4 ... 141 DH97
Orpington BR5 ... 145 ER100
St. Georges Rd, Rich. TW9 ... 98 CM83
St. George's Rd, Sev. TN13 .. 191 FH122
Sidcup DA14 ... 126 EX93
St. Georges Rd, Swan. BR8 .. 147 FF98
Twickenham TW1 ... 117 CH85
Wallington SM6 ... 159 DH106
Watford WD24 ... 23 BV38
St. George's Rd, Wey. KT13 .. 153 BR107
St. Georges Rd W, Brom. BR1 144 EL95
St. Georges Shop Cen, Grav.
DA11 ... 131 GH86
St. Georges Sq, E7 ... 86 EH66
E14 *off Narrow St* ... 85 DY73
SE8 ... 203 M8
St. George's Sq, SW1 ... 199 M10
New Malden KT3
off High St ... 138 CS97
St. George's Sq Ms, SW1 ... 101 DK78
St. Georges Ter, NW1
off Regents Pk Rd ... 82 DF66
St. George St, W1 ... 195 J9
St. Georges Wk, Croy. CR0 .. 142 DQ104
St. Georges Way, SE15 ... 102 DS79
St. George Wf, SW8 ... 101 DL78
St. Gerards Cl, SW4 ... 121 DJ85
St. German's Pl, SE3 ... 104 EG81
St. Germans Rd, SE23 ... 123 DY88
St. Giles Av, Dag. RM10 ... 89 FB66
Potters Bar EN6 ... 11 CV32
Uxbridge UB10 ... 59 BQ63
St. Giles Cl, Dag. RM10
off St. Giles Av ... 89 FB66
Orpington BR6 ... 163 ER106
St. Giles Ct, WC2
off St. Giles High St ... 83 DL72
St. Giles High St, WC2 ... 195 N8
St. Giles Pas, WC2 ... 195 N9
St. Giles Rd, SE5 ... 102 DS80
St. Gilles Ho, E2 ... 85 DX68
St. Gothard Rd, SE27 ... 122 DR91
St. Gregory Cl, Ruis. HA4 ... 60 BW63
St. Gregorys Cres, Grav.
DA12 ... 131 GL89
St. Helena Rd, SE16 ... 203 H9
St. Helena St, WC1 ... 196 D3
St. Helens Cl, Uxb. UB8 ... 76 BK72
St. Helens Ct, Epp. CM16
off Hemnall St ... 18 EU30
Rainham RM13 ... 89 FG70
St. Helens Cres, SW16
off St. Helens Rd ... 141 DM95
St. Helens Gdns, W10 ... 81 CX72
St. Helens Pl, EC3 ... 197 M8
St. Helens Rd, SW16 ... 141 DM95
St. Helen's Rd, W13
off Dane Rd ... 79 CH74
St. Helens Rd, Erith DA18 ... 106 EX75
Ilford IG1 ... 69 EM58
ST. HELIER, Cars. ... 140 DD101
⇌ St. Helier ... 140 DA100
St. Helier Av, Mord. SM4 ... 140 DC101
H St. Helier Hosp, Cars.
SM5 ... 140 DC102
St. Heliers Av, Houns. TW3 .. 116 CA85
St. Heliers Rd, E10 ... 67 EC58
St. Hildas Av, Ashf. TW15 ... 114 BL92
St. Hildas Cl, NW6 ... 81 CX66
SW17 ... 120 DE89
St. Hilda's Rd, SW13 ... 99 CV79
St. Hilda's Way, Grav. DA12 .. 131 GK91
St. Huberts Cl, Ger.Cr. SL9 ... 56 AY60
St. Huberts La, Ger.Cr. SL9 ... 57 AZ61
St. Hughe's Cl, SW17
off College Gdns ... 120 DE89
St. Hughs Rd, SE20
off Ridsdale Rd ... 142 DV95
St. Ives Cl, Rom. RM3 ... 52 FM52
St. Ivians Dr, Rom. RM2 ... 71 FG55
St. James Av, N20 ... 44 DE48
W13 ... 79 CG74
Epsom KT17 ... 157 CT111
Sutton SM1 ... 158 DA106
St. James Cl, N20 ... 44 DE48
SE18 *off Congleton Gro* ... 105 EQ78
Barnet EN4 ... 28 DD42
Epsom KT18 ... 156 CS114
New Malden KT3 ... 139 CT99
Ruislip HA4 ... 60 BW61
Woking GU21 ... 166 AU118
St. James Ct, Green. DA9 ... 129 FT86
St. James Gdns, Rom. (Lt.Hth.)
RM6 ... 70 EV56
Wembley HA0 ... 79 CK66
St. James Gate, NW1
off St. Paul's Cres ... 83 DK66
St. James Gro, SW11
off Reform St ... 100 DF82
St. James La, Green. DA9 ... 129 FS88
St. James Ms, E14 ... 204 E7
E17 *off St. James's St* ... 67 DY57
Weybridge KT13 ... 153 BP105
St. James Oaks, Grav. DA11
off Trafalgar Rd ... 131 GG87
St. James Pl, Dart. DA1
off Spital St ... 128 FK86
St. James Rd, E15 ... 68 EF64
N9 *off Queens Rd* ... 46 DV47
Brentwood CM14 ... 54 FW48
Carshalton SM5 ... 140 DE104
Kingston upon Thames
KT1 ... 138 CL96
Mitcham CR4 ... 120 DG94
Purley CR8 ... 159 DP113
Sevenoaks TN13 ... 191 FH122
Surbiton KT6 ... 137 CK100
Sutton SM1 ... 158 DA106
Waltham Cross (Chsht.) EN7 . 14 DQ28
Watford WD18 ... 23 BV43
ST. JAMES'S, SW1 ... 199 L3
St. James's, SE14 ... 103 DY81
St. James's Av, E2 ... 84 DW68
Beckenham BR3 ... 143 DY97
Gravesend DA11 ... 131 GG87
Hampton (Hmptn.H.) TW12 . 116 CC92
St. James's Cl, SW17
off St. James's Dr ... 120 DF89
St. James's Cotts, Rich. TW9
off Paradise Rd ... 117 CK85
St. James's Ct, SW1 ... 199 L6
St. James's Cres, SW9 ... 101 DN83
St. James's Dr, SW12 ... 120 DF88
SW17 ... 120 DF88
St. James's Gdns, W11 ... 81 CY74
St. James's La, N10 ... 65 DH56
St. James's Mkt, SW1 ... 199 M1
★ St. James's Palace, SW1 . 199 L4
St. James's Palace, SW1 ... 199 L4
★ St. James's Park, SW1 ... 199 M4
⊖ St. James's Park ... 199 M5
St. James's Pk, SW1 ... 199 M4
Croydon CR0 ... 142 DQ101
St. James's Pas, EC3 ... 197 N9
St. James's Pl, SW1 ... 199 K3
St. James's Rd, SE1 ... 202 C10
SE16 ... 202 C6
Croydon CR0 ... 141 DP101
Gravesend DA11 ... 131 GG86
Hampton (Hmptn.H.) TW12 . 116 CB92
St. James's Row, EC1 ... 196 E4
St. James's Sq, SW1 ... 199 L2
St. James's St, E17 ... 67 DY57
SW1 ... 199 K2
Gravesend DA11 ... 131 GG86

★ Place of interest · ⇌ Railway station · ⊖ London Underground station · DLR Docklands Light Railway station · Tramlink station · H Hospital

321

St. J - St. P

St. James's Ter, NW8
off Prince Albert Rd 82 DF68
St. James's Ter Ms, NW8 .....82 DF67
⇌ St. James Street 67 DY57
St. James St, W6 ....99 CW78
St. James's Wk, EC1 ....196 F4
St. James Wk, Iver SL0 ......93 BE75
St. James Way, Sid. DA14 ...126 EY92
St. Jeromes Gro, Hayes UB3 ..77 BQ72
St. Joans Rd, N9 ....46 DT46
St. John Fisher Rd, Erith
DA18 ....106 EX76
ST. JOHN'S, SE8 ....103 EA82
ST. JOHN'S, Wok. 166 AV118
⇌ St. John's 103 EA82
St. Johns Av, N11 ....44 DF50
St. John's Av, NW10 ....81 CT67
SW15 ....119 CX85
St. Johns Av, Brwd. CM14 ....54 FX49
St. John's Av, Epsom KT17 ..157 CT112
St. Johns Av, Lthd. KT22 ....171 CH121
St. John's Ch Rd, E9 ....66 DW64
St. Johns Cl, N14
off Chase Rd 29 DJ44
St. John's Cl, SW6
off Dawes Rd 100 DA80
St. Johns Cl, Lthd. KT22 ....171 CJ120
St. John's Cl, Pot.B. EN6 ....12 DC33
St. Johns Cl, Rain. RM13 .....89 FG66
St. John's Cl, Uxb. UB8 .....76 BH67
Wembley HA9 ....62 CL64
St. Johns Cl, West. (Berry's Grn.)
TN16 off St. Johns Ri ...179 EP116
St. John's Cotts, SE20
off Maple Rd 122 DW94
St. Johns Cotts, Rich. TW9
off Kew Foot Rd 98 CL84
St. Johns Ct, Buck.H. IG9 ....48 EH46
St. John's Ct, Egh. TW20 ....113 BA92
Isleworth TW7 ....97 CF82
St. Johns Ct, Nthwd. HA6
off Murray Rd 39 BS53
St. John's Ct, Wok. GU21
off St. Johns Hill Rd 166 AU119
St. John's Cres, SW9 ....101 DN83
St. Johns Dr, SW18 ....120 DB88
Walton-on-Thames KT12 ..136 BW102
St. John's Est, N1 ....197 L1
SE1 ....201 P4
St. John's Gdns, W11 ....81 CZ73
★ St. John's Gate & Mus of
the Order of St. John, EC1 .196 F5
St. Johns Gro, N19 ....65 DJ61
SW13 off Terrace Gdns 99 CT82
Richmond TW9
off Kew Foot Rd 98 CL84
St. John's Hill, SW11 ....100 DD84
Coulsdon CR5 ....175 DN117
Purley CR8 ....175 DN116
Sevenoaks TN13 ....191 FJ123
St. John's Hill Gro, SW11 ....100 DD84
St. Johns Hill Rd, Wok. GU21 .166 AU119
★ St. John's Jerusalem, Dart.
(Sutt.H.) DA4 ....128 FP94
St. John's La, EC1 ....196 F5
St. John's Lye, Wok. GU21 ...166 AT119
St. John's Ms, W11
off Ledbury Rd 82 DA72
Woking GU21 ....166 AU119
St. Johns Par, Sid. DA14 ....126 EU91
St. John's Pk, SE3 ....104 EF80
St. John's Pas, SW19
off Ridgway Pl 119 CY93
St. John's Path, EC1 ....196 F5
St. Johns Pathway, SE23
off Devonshire Rd 122 DW88
St. John's Pl, EC1 ....196 F5
St. Johns Ri, West. (Berry's Grn.)
TN16 ....179 EP116
Woking GU21 ....166 AV119
St. John's Rd, E4 ....47 EB48
E6 off Ron Leighton Way ...86 EL67
St. Johns Rd, E16 ....86 EG72
St. John's Rd, E17 ....47 EB54
N15 ....66 DS58
St. Johns Rd, NW11 ....63 CZ58
St. John's Rd, SE20 ....122 DW94
SW11 ....100 DE84
SW19 ....119 CY94
Barking IG11 ....87 ES67
Carshalton SM5 ....140 DE104
St. Johns Rd, Croy. CR0
off Sylverdale Rd 141 DP104
St. John's Rd, Dart. DA2 ....128 FQ87
St. Johns Rd, E.Mol. KT8 ....137 CD98
St. John's Rd, Epp. CM16 ....17 ET30
St. Johns Rd, Erith DA8 .....107 FD78
St. John's Rd, Felt. TW13 ....116 BY91
St. Johns Rd, Grav. DA12 ...131 GK87
Grays RM16 ....111 GH78
St. John's Rd, Har. HA1 ......61 CF58
St. Johns Rd, Ilf. IG2 ....69 ER59
St. John's Rd, Islw. TW7 .....97 CE82
Kingston upon Thames KT1 .137 CJ96
St. Johns Rd, Lthd. KT22 ....171 CJ121
Loughton IG10 ....33 EM40
New Malden KT3 ....138 CQ97
St. John's Rd, Orp. BR5 .....145 ER100
Richmond TW9 ....98 CL84
St. Johns Rd, Rom. RM5 ......51 FC50
St. John's Rd, Sev. TN13 ....191 FH121
St. Johns Rd, Sid. DA14 .....126 EV91
Slough SL2 ....74 AU74
Southall UB2 ....96 BY76
Sutton SM1 ....140 DA103
Uxbridge UB8 ....76 BH67
Watford WD17 ....23 BV40
St. John's Rd, Well. DA16 ...106 EV83
Wembley HA9 ....61 CK63
Woking GU21 ....166 AV118
St. John's Sq, EC1 ....196 F5
St. Johns Ter, E7 ....86 EH65
SE18 ....105 EQ79
SW15 off Kingston Vale ...118 CR91
W10 off Harrow Rd 81 CX70
Enfield EN2 ....30 DR37
St. John St, EC1 ....196 G5
St. Johns Vale, SE8 ....103 EA82
St. Johns Vil, N19 ....65 DK61
St. John's Vil, W8
off St. Mary's Pl 100 DB76
St. John's Waterside, Wok. GU21
off Copse Rd 166 AU118
St. Johns Way, N19 ....65 DK60
ST. JOHN'S WOOD, NW8 .....82 DC69
⊖ St. John's Wood 82 DD68
St. John's Wd Ct, NW8 .....194 A3
St. John's Wd High St, NW8 .194 A1
St. John's Wd Pk, NW8 ......82 DD67
St. John's Wd Rd, NW8 ......82 DD70
St. John's Wd Ter, NW8 .....82 DD68
St. Josephs Cl, W10
off Bevington Rd 81 CY71
St. Joseph's Cl, Orp. BR6 ...163 ET105
St. Joseph's Ct, SE7 ....104 EH79
St. Josephs Dr, Sthl. UB1 ....78 BY74
St. Joseph's Gro, NW4 ....63 CV56
St. Josephs Rd, N9 ....46 DV45
St. Joseph's Rd, Wal.Cr. EN8 ..15 DY33
St. Josephs St, SW8
off Battersea Pk Rd 101 DH81
St. Joseph's Vale, SE3 ......103 ED82
St. Judes Cl, Egh. TW20 .....112 AW92
St. Jude's Rd, E2 ....84 DV68
Egham TW20 ....112 AW90
St. Jude St, N16 ....66 DS64
St. Julians, Sev. TN15 ......191 FN128
St. Julian's Cl, SW16 ....121 DN91
St. Julian's Fm Rd, SE27 ....121 DN91
St. Julian's Rd, NW6 ....81 CZ66
St. Justin Cl, Orp. BR5 ......146 EX97
★ St. Katharine's Dock, E1 .202 A1
St. Katharines Prec, NW1
off Outer Circle 83 DH68
St. Katharine's Way, E1 .....202 A2
St. Katherines Rd, Cat. CR3 ..186 DU125
Erith DA18 ....106 EX75
St. Katherine's Row, EC3 ....197 N9
St. Katherine's Wk, W11
off Freston Rd 81 CX73
St. Keverne Rd, SE9 ....124 EL91
St. Kilda Rd, W13 ....79 CG74
Orpington BR6 ....145 ET102
St. Kilda's Rd, N16 ....66 DR60
Brentwood CM15 ....54 FV45
Harrow HA1 ....61 CE58
St. Kitts Ter, SE19 ....122 DS92
St. Laurence Cl, NW6 ....81 CX67
Orpington BR5 ....146 EX97
Uxbridge UB8 ....76 BJ71
St. Laurence Way, Slou. SL1 ..92 AU76
St. Lawrence Cl, Abb.L. WD5 ...7 BS30
Edgware HA8 ....42 CM52
Hemel Hempstead (Bov.) HP3 .5 BA27
St. Lawrence Dr, Pnr. HA5 ....59 BV58
★ St. Lawrence Jewry Church,
EC2 off Gresham St 197 J8
St. Lawrence Rd, Upmin.
RM14 ....72 FQ61
St. Lawrence St, E14 ....204 E2
St. Lawrence's Way, Reig. RH2
off Church St 184 DA134
St. Lawrence Ter, W10 ....81 CY71
St. Lawrence Way, SW9 .....101 DN81
Caterham CR3 ....176 DQ123
St. Albans (Brick.Wd.) AL2 ...8 BZ30
St. Leonards Av, E4 ....47 ED51
Harrow HA3 ....61 CJ56
St. Leonards Cl, Bushey WD23 .24 BY42
Grays RM17 ....110 FZ79
St. Leonard's Cl, Well. DA16
off Hook La 106 EU83
St. Leonards Ct, N1 ....197 J2
St. Leonard's Gdns, Houns.
TW5 ....96 BY80
St. Leonards Gdns, Ilf. IG1 ...69 EQ64
St. Leonards Ri, Orp. BR6 ...163 ES105
St. Leonards Rd, E14 ....85 EB71
NW10 ....80 CR70
St. Leonard's Rd, SW14 ....98 CP83
St. Leonards Rd, W13 ....79 CJ73
Amersham HP6 ....20 AS35
Croydon CR0 ....141 DP104
Epsom KT18 ....173 CW119
Esher (Clay.) KT10 ....155 CF107
St. Leonard's Rd, Surb. KT6 .137 CK99
St. Leonards Rd, T.Ditt. KT7 ..137 CG100
Waltham Abbey EN9 ....16 EE25
St. Leonards Sq, NW5 ....82 DG65
St. Leonard's Sq, Surb. KT6
off St. Leonard's Rd 137 CK99
St. Leonards St, E3 ....85 EB69
St. Leonard's Ter, SW3 .....100 DF78
St. Leonards Wk, SW16 .....121 DM94
Iver SL0 ....93 BF76
St. Leonards Way, Horn. RM11 .71 FH61
St. Loo Av, SW3 ....100 DE79
St. Louis Rd, SE27 ....122 DQ91
St. Loy's Rd, N17 ....46 DS54
St. Lucia Dr, E15 ....86 EF67
St. Luke Cl, Uxb. UB8 ....76 BK72
ST. LUKE'S, EC1 ....197 J4
St. Luke's Av, SW4 ....101 DK84
St. Lukes Av, Enf. EN2 ....30 DR38
St. Luke's Av, Ilf. IG1 ....69 EP64
St. Lukes Cl, EC1 off Old St ..84 DQ70
St. Luke's Cl, SE25 ....142 DV100
St. Lukes Cl, Dart. (Lane End)
DA2 ....129 FS92
Swanley BR8 ....147 FD96
St. Luke's Est, EC1 ....197 K3
H St. Lukes Hosp for the Clergy,
W1 ....195 K5
St. Lukes Ms, W11 off Basing St .81 CZ72
St. Lukes Pas, Kings.T. KT2 ..138 CM95
St. Lukes Rd, W11 ....81 CZ71
Uxbridge UB10 ....76 BL66
Whyteleafe CR3
off Whyteleafe Hill 176 DT118
Windsor (Old Wind.) SL4 ..112 AU86
St. Lukes Sq, E16 ....86 EF72
St. Luke's St, SW3 ....198 B10
H St. Luke's Woodside Hosp,
N10 ....64 DG56
St. Luke's Yd, W9 ....81 CZ68
St. Malo Av, N9 ....46 DW48
St. Margaret Dr, Epsom KT18 .156 CR114
ST. MARGARETS, Twick. 117 CG85
⇌ St. Margarets, Twick. 117 CH86
St. Margarets, Bark. IG11 .....87 ER67
St. Margarets Av, N15 ....65 DP56
N20 ....44 DC47
Ashford TW15 ....115 BP92
Harrow HA2 ....60 CC62
Sidcup DA15 ....125 ER90
St. Margaret's Av, Sutt. SM3 .139 CY104
St. Margarets Av, Uxb. UB8 ...76 BN70
Westerham (Berry's Grn.) TN16
off Berry's Grn Rd 179 EP116
St. Margarets Cl, Dart. DA2 ..129 FR89
Iver SL0
off St. Margarets Gate 75 BD68
Orpington BR6 ....164 EV105
St. Margaret's Ct, SE1 ......201 J3
St. Margaret's Cres, SW15 ...119 CV85
St. Margaret's Cres, Grav.
DA12 ....131 GL90
St. Margaret's Dr, Twick. TW1 .117 CH85
St. Margarets Gate, Iver SL0 ..75 BD68
St. Margaret's Gro, E11 ......68 EF62
SE18 ....105 EQ79
St. Margarets Gro, Twick. TW1 .117 CG86
H St. Margaret's Hosp, Epp.
CM16 ....18 EV29
St. Margarets La, W8 ....100 DB76
St. Margarets Pas, SE13
off Church Ter 104 EE83
St. Margarets Path, SE18 ....105 EQ78
St. Margarets Rd, E12 ....68 EJ61
St. Margaret's Rd, N17 ....66 DS55
NW10 ....81 CW69
St. Margarets Rd, SE4 ....103 DZ84
W7 ....97 CE75
Coulsdon CR5 ....175 DH121
Dartford (S.Darenth) DA2,
DA4 ....129 FS93
Edgware HA8 ....42 CP50
St. Margaret's Rd, Grav. (Nthflt.)
DA11 ....130 GE89
St. Margarets Rd, Islw. TW7 ...97 CH84
St. Margarets Rd, Ruis. HA4 ..59 BR58
St. Margarets Rd, Twick. TW1 ..97 CH84
St. Margarets Sq, SE4
off Adelaide Av 103 DZ84
St. Margaret's St, SW1 ......199 P5
St. Margaret's Ter, SE18 .....105 EQ78
St. Marks Av, Grav. (Nthflt.)
DA11 ....131 GF87
St. Marks Cl, SE10
off Ashburnham Gro 103 EC80
SW6 off Ackmar Rd 100 DA81
W11 off Lancaster Rd 81 CY72
St. Mark's Cl, Barn. EN5 .....28 DB41
St. Marks Cl, Har. HA1
off Nightingale Av 61 CH59
St. Marks Cres, NW1 ....82 DG67
St. Mark's Gate, E9
off Cadogan Ter 85 DZ66
St. Mark's Gro, SW10 ....100 DB79
St. Mark's Hill, Surb. KT6 ....138 CL100
St. Mark's Pl, SW19
off Wimbledon Hill Rd ...119 CZ93
St. Marks Pl, W11 ....81 CY72
St. Marks Ri, E8 ....66 DT64
St. Marks Rd, SE25
off Coventry Rd 142 DU98
St. Mark's Rd, W5
off The Common 80 CL74
St. Marks Rd, W7 ....97 CE75
W10 ....81 CX72
W11 ....81 CY72
Bromley BR2 ....144 EH97
Enfield EN1 ....30 DT44
St. Mark's Rd, Epsom KT18 ..173 CW118
St. Marks Rd, Mitch. CR4 ....140 DF96
St. Mark's Rd, Tedd. TW11 ....117 CH94
St. Marks Sq, NW1 ....82 DG67
St. Mark St, E1 ....84 DT72
St. Martha's Av, Wok. GU22 ..167 AZ121
St. Martin Cl, Uxb. UB8 ......76 BK72
★ St. Martin-in-the-Fields Church,
WC2 off Trafalgar Sq 199 P1
St. Martins App, Ruis. HA4 ....59 BS59
St. Martins Av, E6 ....86 EK68
Epsom KT18 ....156 CS114
St. Martins Cl, NW1 ....83 DJ67
Enfield EN1 ....30 DV39
Epsom KT17 off Church Rd .156 CS113
Erith DA18
off St. Helens Rd 106 EX75
St. Martin's Cl, Wat. WD19
off Muirfield Rd 40 BW49
West Drayton UB7
off St. Martin's Rd 94 BK76
St. Martin's Ct, WC2
off St. Martin's La 83 DK73
Ashford TW15 ....114 BJ92
St. Martins Dr, Walt. KT12 ..136 BW104
St. Martins Est, SW2 ....121 DN88
St. Martin's La, WC2 ....195 P10
St. Martins La, Beck. BR3 ...143 EB99
St. Martin's-le-Grand, EC1 ..197 H8
St. Martins Meadow, West.
(Brasted) TN16 ....180 EW123
St. Martin's Ms, WC2 ....199 P1
St. Martins Ms, Wok. (Pyrford)
GU22 ....168 BG116
St. Martin's Pl, WC2 ....199 P1
St. Martins Rd, N9 ....46 DV47
St. Martin's Rd, SW9 ....101 DM82
St. Martins Rd, Dart. DA1 ....128 FM86
St. Martin's Rd, West Dr. UB7 .94 BJ76
St. Martin's St, WC2 ....199 N1
St. Martins Way, SW17 ......120 DC90
St. Mary Abbots Pl, W8 ....99 CZ76
St. Mary Abbots Ter, W14 .....99 CZ76
St. Mary at Hill, EC3 ....201 M1
★ St. Mary at Hill Church, EC3
off Lovat La 201 M1
St. Mary Av, Wall. SM6 .....140 DG104
St. Mary Axe, EC3 ....197 M9
St. Marychurch St, SE16 ....202 F5
ST. MARY CRAY, Orp. 146 EW99
⇌ St. Mary Cray 146 EU98
★ St. Mary-le-Bow Church,
EC2 ....197 J9
St. Mary Rd, E17 ....67 EA56
St. Marys, Bark. IG11 ....87 ER67
St. Marys App, E12 ....69 EM64
St. Marys Av, E11 ....68 EH58
St. Mary's Av, N3 ....43 CY54
St. Marys Av, Brwd. CM15 ....55 GA43
St. Mary's Av, Brom. BR2 ....144 EE97
Northwood HA6 ....39 BS50
Staines (Stanw.) TW19 ....114 BK87
Teddington TW11 ....117 CF93
St. Mary's Av Cen, Sthl. UB2 ..96 CB77
St. Mary's Av N, Sthl. UB2 ....96 CB77
St. Mary's Av S, Sthl. UB2 ....96 CB77
St. Mary's Cl, N17
off Kemble Rd 46 DT53
St. Marys Cl, Chess. KT9 ....156 CM108
Epsom KT17 ....157 CU108
St. Mary's Cl, Grav. DA12 ...131 GJ89
St. Marys Cl, Grays RM17
off Dock Rd 110 GD79
St. Mary's Cl, Lthd. (Fetch.)
KT22 ....171 CD123
St. Marys Cl, Orp. BR5 ......146 EV96
St. Mary's Cl, Oxt. RH8 .....188 EE129
Staines (Stanw.) TW19 ....114 BK87
Sunbury-on-Thames TW16
off Green Way 135 BU98
Uxbridge (Hare.) UB9 ......58 BH55
St. Marys Ct, E6 ....87 EM70
St. Mary's Ct, SE7 ....104 EK80
W5 off St. Mary's Rd 97 CK75
St. Mary's Cres, NW4 ....63 CV55
Hayes UB3 ....77 BT73
St. Marys Cres, Islw. TW7 ....97 CD80
St. Mary's Cres, Stai. (Stanw.)
TW19 ....114 BK87
St. Marys Dr, Felt. TW14 .....115 BQ87
St. Mary's Dr, Sev. TN13 .....190 FE123
St. Mary's Gdns, SE11 ....200 E8
St. Mary's Gate, W8 ....100 DB76
St. Marys Grn, N2
off Thomas More Way 64 DC55
Westerham (Bigg.H.) TN16 .178 EJ118
St. Mary's Gro, N1 ....83 DP65
SW13 ....99 CV83
W4 ....98 CP79
Richmond TW9 ....98 CM84
St. Marys Gro, West. (Bigg.H.)
TN16 ....178 EJ118
H St. Mary's Hosp, W2 ....194 A8
St. Mary's La, Upmin. RM14 ..72 FN61
St. Marys Mans, W2 ....82 DC71
St. Mary's Ms, NW6
off Priory Rd 82 DB66
Richmond TW10 ....117 CJ89
St. Mary's Mt, Cat. CR3 .....176 DT124
St. Marys Path, N1 ....83 DP67
St. Mary's Pl, SE9
off Eltham High St 125 EN86
W5 off St. Mary's Rd 97 CK75
W8 ....100 DB76
St. Marys Rd, E10 ....67 EC62
E13 ....86 EH68
N8 off High St 65 DL56
N9 ....46 DW46
St. Mary's Rd, NW10 ....80 CS67
St. Marys Rd, NW11 ....63 CY59
St. Mary's Rd, SE15 ....102 DW81
SE25 ....142 DS97
SW19 (Wimbledon) 119 CY92
W5 ....97 CK75
Barnet EN4 ....44 DF45
Bexley DA5 ....127 FC88
St. Marys Rd, E.Mol. KT8 ....137 CD99
St. Mary's Rd, Grays RM16 ...111 GH77
Greenhithe DA9 ....129 FS85
Hayes UB3 ....77 BT73
St. Marys Rd, Ilf. IG1 ....69 EQ61
Leatherhead KT22 ....171 CH122
St. Mary's Rd, Slou. SL3 ......74 AY74
South Croydon CR2 ......160 DR110
St. Marys Rd, Surb. KT6 ....137 CK100
Surbiton (Long Dit.) KT6 ..137 CJ101
Swanley BR8 ....147 FD98
St. Mary's Rd, Uxb. (Denh.)
UB9 ....57 BF58
Uxbridge (Hare.) UB9 ......58 BH56
Waltham Cross (Chsht.)
EN8 ....14 DW29
Watford WD18 ....23 BV42
St. Marys Rd, Wey. KT13 ....153 BR105
St. Mary's Rd, Wok. GU21 ...166 AW117
Worcester Park KT4 ......138 CS103
St. Marys Sq, W2 ....82 DD71
St. Mary's Sq, W5
off St. Mary's Rd 97 CK75
St. Marys Ter, W2 ....82 DD71
St. Mary's Twr, EC1
off Fortune St 84 DQ70
St. Mary St, SE18 ....105 EM77
St. Marys Vw, Har. HA3 ......61 CJ57
St. Mary's Vw, Wat. WD18
off King St 24 BW42
St. Mary's Wk, SE11 ....200 E8
Hayes UB3 off St. Mary's Rd .77 BT73
Redhill (Bletch.) RH1 ......186 DR133
St. Mary's Way, Chig. IG7 ....49 EN50
Gerrards Cross (Chal.St.P.)
SL9 ....36 AX54
St. Matthew Cl, Uxb. UB8 .....76 BK72
St. Matthew's Av, Surb. KT6 ..138 CL102
St. Matthews Cl, Rain. RM13 ..89 FG66
Watford WD19 ....24 BX44
St. Matthew's Dr, Brom. BR1 .145 EM97
St. Matthew's Rd, SW2 ......101 DM84
St. Matthews Rd, W5
off The Common 80 CL74
St. Matthew's Rd, Red. RH1 ..184 DF133
St. Matthew's Row, E2 ....84 DU69
St. Matthew St, SW1 ....199 M7
St. Matthias Cl, NW9 ....63 CT57
St. Maur Rd, SW6 ....99 CZ81
St. Mellion Cl, SE28
off Redbourne Dr 88 EX72
St. Merryn Cl, SE18 ....105 ER80
St. Michael's All, EC3 ....197 L9
St. Michaels Av, N9 ....46 DW45
St. Michael's Av, Wem. HA9 ...80 CN65
St. Michaels Cl, E16
off Fulmer Rd 86 EK71
St. Michael's Cl, N3 ....43 CZ54
St. Michaels Cl, N12 ....44 DE50
Bromley BR1 ....144 EL97
Erith DA18
off St. Helens Rd 106 EX75
South Ockendon (Aveley)
RM15 ....90 FQ73
Walton-on-Thames KT12 ..136 BW103
Worcester Park KT4 ......139 CT103
St. Michaels Cres, Pnr. HA5 ...60 BY58
St. Michaels Dr, Wat. WD25 ....7 BV33
St. Michaels Gdns, W10
off St. Lawrence Ter 81 CY71
St. Michaels Rd, NW2 ....63 CW63
St. Michael's Rd, SW9 ....101 DM82
Ashford TW15 ....114 BN92
St. Michaels Rd, Cat. CR3 ...176 DR122
Croydon CR0 ....142 DQ102
Grays RM16 ....111 GH78
Wallington SM6 ....159 DJ107
Welling DA16 ....106 EV83
St. Michael's Rd, Wok. GU21 .151 BD114
St. Michaels St, W2 ....194 A8
St. Michaels Ter, N22 ....45 DL54
St. Michaels Way, Pot.B. EN6 .12 DB30
St. Mildred's Ct, EC2
off Poultry 84 DR72
St. Mildreds Rd, SE12 ....124 EE87
St. Monica's Rd, Tad. KT20 ...173 CZ121
St. Nazaire Cl, Egh. TW20
off Mullens Rd 113 BC92
St. Neots Cl, Borwd. WD6 ....26 CN38
St. Neots Rd, Rom. RM3 ......52 FM52
St. Nicholas Av, Horn. RM12 ..71 FG62
St. Nicholas Cl, Amer. HP7 ...20 AV39
Borehamwood (Elstree) WD6 .25 CK44
Uxbridge UB8 ....76 BK72
St. Nicholas Cres, Wok. (Pyrford)
GU22 ....168 BG116
St. Nicholas Dr, Sev. TN13 ...191 FH126
Shepperton TW17 ....134 BN101
St. Nicholas Glebe, SW17 ...120 DG93
St. Nicholas Gro, Brwd. CM13 .55 GC50
St. Nicholas Hill, Lthd. KT22 .171 CH122
St. Nicholas Rd, SE18 ....105 ET78
Sutton SM1 ....158 DB106
Thames Ditton KT7 ....137 CF100
St. Nicholas St, SE8
off Lucas St 103 EA81
St. Nicholas Way, Sutt. SM1 .158 DB105
St. Nicolas La, Chis. BR7 ....144 EL95
St. Ninian's Ct, N20 ....44 DF48
St. Norbert Grn, SE4 ....103 DY84
St. Norbert Rd, SE4 ....103 DY84
St. Normans Way, Epsom
KT17 ....157 CU110
St. Olaf's Rd, SW6 ....99 CY80
St. Olaves Cl, Stai. TW18 ....113 BF94
St. Olaves Ct, EC2 ....197 K9
St. Olave's Est, SE1 ....201 N4
St. Olaves Gdns, SE11 ....200 D8
St. Olaves Rd, E6 ....87 EN67
St. Olave's Wk, SW16 ....141 DJ96
St. Olav's Sq, SE16 ....202 F6
St. Oswald's Pl, SE11 ....101 DM78
St. Oswald's Rd, SW16 ......141 DP95
St. Oswulf St, SW1 ....199 N9
ST. PANCRAS, WC1 ....195 P3
⇌ St. Pancras 195 P2
H St. Pancras Hosp & Hosp
for Tropical Diseases, NW1 ..83 DK67
St. Pancras Way, NW1 ....83 DJ66
St. Patrick's Ct, Wdf.Grn. IG8 ..48 EE52
St. Patrick's Gdns, Grav. DA12 .131 GK90
St. Patricks Pl, Grays RM16 ..111 GJ77
St. Paul Cl, Uxb. UB8 ....76 BK71
⊖ St. Paul's 197 H8
St. Paul's All, EC4
off St. Paul's Chyd 83 DP72
St. Paul's Av, NW2 ....81 CV65
SE16 ....203 J2
St. Pauls Av, Har. HA3 ....62 CM57
Slough SL2 ....74 AT73
★ St. Paul's Cathedral, EC4 .197 H9
St. Paul's Chyd, EC4 ....196 G9
St. Paul's Cl, SE7 ....104 EK78
W5 ....98 CM75
St. Pauls Cl, Add. KT15 ......152 BG106
St. Paul's Cl, Ashf. TW15 ....115 BQ92
Carshalton SM5 ....140 DE102
St. Pauls Cl, Chess. KT9 ....155 CK105
Hayes UB3 ....95 BR78
St. Paul's Cl, Houns. TW3 ....96 BY82
St. Pauls Cl, S.Ock. (Aveley)
RM15 ....90 FQ73
Swanscombe DA10
off Swanscombe St 130 FY87
St. Paul's Ct, W14
off Colet Gdns 99 CX77
St. Pauls Ctyd, SE8
off Deptford High St 103 EA80
ST. PAUL'S CRAY, Orp. 146 EU96
St. Pauls Cray Rd, Chis. BR7 .145 ER95
St. Paul's Cres, NW1 ....83 DK66
St. Pauls Dr, E15 ....67 ED64
St. Paul's Ms, NW1
off St. Paul's Cres 83 DK66
St. Paul's Pl, N1 ....84 DR65
St. Pauls Pl, S.Ock. (Aveley)
RM15 ....90 FQ73
St. Pauls Ri, N13 ....45 DP51
St. Paul's Rd, N1 ....83 DP65
N17 ....46 DU52
Barking IG11 ....87 EQ67
Brentford TW8 ....97 CK79
Erith DA8 ....107 FC80

★ Place of interest ⇌ Railway station ⊖ London Underground station DLR Docklands Light Railway station Tramlink station H Hospital

St. P - San

St. Paul's Rd, Rich. TW9 98 CM83
Staines TW18 113 BD92
Thornton Heath CR7 142 DQ97
St. Pauls Rd, Wok. GU22 167 BA117
St. Paul's Shrubbery, N1 84 DR65
St. Pauls Sq, Brom. BR2 144 EG96
St. Paul's Ter, SE17
off Westcott Rd 101 DP79
St. Pauls Twr, E10 67 EB59
St. Paul St, N1 84 DQ67
St. Pauls Wk, Kings.T. KT2
off Alexandra Rd 118 CN94
St. Pauls Way, E3 85 DZ71
E14 85 DZ71
St. Paul's Way, N3 44 DB52
St. Pauls Way, Wal.Abb. EN9
off Rochford Av 15 ED33
Watford WD24 24 BW40
St. Pauls Wd Hill, Orp. BR5 145 ES96
St. Peter's All, EC3 197 L9
St. Peter's Av, E2
off St. Peter's Cl 84 DU68
E17 68 EE56
St. Peters Av, N18 46 DU49
Westerham (Berry's Grn.)
TN16 179 EP116
St. Petersburgh Ms, W2 82 DB73
St. Petersburgh Pl, W2 82 DB73
St. Peter's Cl, E2 84 DU68
St. Peters Cl, SW17
off College Gdns 120 DE89
St. Peter's Cl, Barn. EN5 27 CV43
St. Peters Cl, Bushey
(Bushey Hth.) WD23 41 CD46
Chislehurst BR7 125 ER94
Gerrards Cross (Chal.St.P.) SL9
off Lewis La 36 AY53
Ilford IG2 69 ES56
Rickmansworth (Mill End)
WD3 38 BH46
St. Peter's Cl, Ruis. HA4 60 BX61
St. Peters Cl, Stai. TW18 113 BF93
Swanscombe DA10 130 FZ87
Windsor (Old Wind.) SL4
off Church Rd 112 AU85
Woking GU22 167 BC120
St. Peter's Ct, NW4 63 CW57
St. Peters Ct, SE3
off Eltham Rd 104 EF84
SE4 off Wickham Rd 103 DZ82
Gerrards Cross (Chal.St.P.) SL9
off High St 36 AY53
West Molesey KT8 136 CA98
St. Peter's Gdns, SE27 121 DN90
St. Peter's Gro, W6 99 CU77
H St. Peter's Hosp, Cher.
KT16 133 BD104
St. Peters La, Orp. BR5 146 EU96
St. Peter's Pl, W9
off Shirland Rd 82 DB70
St. Peters Rd, N9 46 DW46
St. Peter's Rd, W6 99 CU78
St. Peters Rd, Brwd. CM14
off Crescent Rd 54 FV49
St. Peter's Rd, Croy. CR0 160 DR105
Grays RM16 111 GH77
St. Peters Rd, Kings.T. KT1 138 CN96
Southall UB1 78 CA71
Twickenham TW1 117 CH85
Uxbridge UB8 76 BK71
St. Peter's Rd, W.Mol. KT8 136 CA98
St. Peters Rd, Wok. GU22 167 BB121
St. Peter's Sq, E2
off St. Peter's Cl 84 DU68
W6 99 CU78
St. Peters St, N1 83 DP67
St. Peter's St, S.Croy. CR2 160 DR106
St. Peters Ter, SW6 99 CY80
St. Peter's Vil, W6 99 CU77
St. Peter's Way, N1 84 DS66
St. Peters Way, W5 79 CK71
St. Peter's Way, Add. KT15 134 BG104
Chertsey KT16 151 BD105
St. Peters Way, Hayes UB3 95 BR78
Rickmansworth (Chorl.) WD3 21 BB43
St. Philip's Av, Wor.Pk. KT4 139 CV103
St. Philips Gate, Wor.Pk. KT4 139 CV103
St. Philip Sq, SW8 101 DH82
St. Philip's Rd, E8 84 DU65
St. Philips Rd, Surb. KT6 137 CK100
St. Philip St, SW8 101 DH82
St. Philip's Way, N1
off Linton St 84 DQ67
St. Pinnock Av, Stai. TW18 134 BG95
St. Quentin Ho, SW18
off Fitzhugh Gro 120 DD86
St. Quentin Rd, Well. DA16 105 ET83
St. Quintin Av, W10 81 CW71
St. Quintin Gdns, W10 81 CW71
St. Quintin Rd, E13 86 EH68
St. Raphael's Way, NW10 62 CQ64
St. Regis Cl, N10 45 DH54
St. Ronan's Cl, Barn. EN4 28 DD38
St. Ronans Cres, Wdf.Grn. IG8 48 EG52
St. Rule St, SW8 101 DJ82
St. Saviour's Est, SE1 201 P6
St. Saviour's Rd, SW2 121 DM85
St. Saviours Rd, Croy. CR0 142 DQ100
Saints Cl, SE27
off Wolfington Rd 121 DP91
Saints Dr, E7 68 EK64
St. Silas Pl, NW5 82 DG65
St. Silas St Est, NW5 82 DG65
St. Simon's Av, SW15 119 CW85
St. Stephens Av, E17 67 EC57
W12 99 CV75
W13 79 CH72
St. Stephen's Av, Ashtd. KT21 172 CL116
St. Stephens Cl, E17 67 EB57
NW8 82 DE67
Southall UB1 78 CA71
St. Stephens Cres, W2 82 DA72
Brentwood CM13 55 GA49
Thornton Heath CR7 141 DN97
St. Stephens Gdn Est, W2
off Shrewsbury Rd 82 DA72
St. Stephens Gdns, SW15
off Manfred Rd 119 CZ85
W2 82 DA72
Twickenham TW1 117 CJ86
St. Stephens Gro, SE13 103 EC83
St. Stephens Ms, W2
off Chepstow Rd 82 DA71
St. Stephen's Par, E7
off Green St 86 EJ66
St. Stephen's Pas, Twick. TW1
off Richmond Rd 117 CJ86
St. Stephen's Rd, E3 85 DZ68
St. Stephens Rd, E6 86 EJ66
St. Stephen's Rd, E17
off Grove Rd 67 EB57
St. Stephens Rd, W13 79 CH72
St. Stephen's Rd, Barn. EN5 27 CX43
St. Stephens Rd, Enf. EN3 31 DX37
Hounslow TW3 116 CA86
St. Stephen's Rd, West Dr. UB7 76 BK74
St. Stephens Row, EC4 197 K9
St. Stephens Ter, SW8 101 DM80
St. Stephen's Wk, SW7 100 DC77
Saints Wk, Grays RM16 111 GJ77
St. Swithin's La, EC4 197 K10
St. Swithun's Rd, SE13 123 ED85
St. Teresa Wk, Grays RM16 111 GH76
St. Theresa Cl, Epsom KT18 156 CQ114
St. Theresa's Rd, Felt. TW14 95 BT84
St. Thomas' Cl, Surb. KT6 138 CM102
St. Thomas Cl, Wok. GU21
off St. Mary's Rd 166 AW117
St. Thomas Ct, Bex. DA5 126 FA87
St. Thomas Dr, Orp. BR5 145 EQ102
St. Thomas' Dr, Pnr. HA5 40 BY53
St. Thomas Gdns, Ilf. IG1 87 EQ65
H St. Thomas' Hosp, SE1 200 B6
St. Thomas Pl, NW1
off Maiden La 83 DK66
St. Thomas Rd, E16 86 EG72
N14 45 DK45
St. Thomas' Rd, W4 98 CQ79
St. Thomas Rd, Belv. DA17 107 FC75
Brentwood CM14 54 FX47
Gravesend (Nthflt.) DA11
off St. Margaret's Rd 130 GE89
St. Thomas's Av, Grav. DA11 131 GH88
St. Thomas's Cl, Wal.Abb. EN9 16 EH33
St. Thomas's Gdns, NW5
off Queen's Cres 82 DG65
St. Thomas's Pl, E9 84 DW66
St. Thomas's Rd, N4 65 DN61
NW10 80 CS67
St. Thomas's Sq, E9 84 DV66
St. Thomas St, SE1 201 K3
St. Thomas's Way, SW6 99 CZ80
St. Thomas Wk, Slou. (Colnbr.)
SL3 93 BD80
St. Timothy's Ms, Brom. BR1
off Wharton Rd 144 EH95
St. Ursula Gro, Pnr. HA5 60 BX57
St. Ursula Rd, Sthl. UB1 78 CA72
St. Vincent Cl, SE27 121 DP92
St. Vincent Rd, Twick. TW2 116 CC86
Walton-on-Thames KT12 135 BV104
St. Vincents Av, Dart. DA1 128 FN85
ST. VINCENT'S HAMLET, Brwd. 52 FP46
St. Vincents Rd, Dart. DA1 128 FN86
St. Vincent St, W1 194 G7
St. Vincents Way, Pot.B. EN6 12 DC33
St. Wilfrids Cl, Barn. EN4 28 DE43
St. Wilfrids Rd, Barn. EN4 28 DD43
St. Winefride's Av, E12 69 EM64
St. Winifreds, Ken. CR8 176 DQ115
St. Winifreds Cl, Chig. IG7 49 EQ50
St. Winifred's Rd, Tedd. TW11 117 CH93
Westerham (Bigg.H.) TN16 179 EM118
Saladin Dr, Purf. RM19 108 FN77
Sala Ho, SE3 off Pinto Way 104 EH84
Salamanca Pl, SE1 200 B9
Salamanca St, SE1 200 A9
Salamander Cl, Kings.T. KT2 117 CJ92
Salamander Quay, Uxb. (Hare.)
UB9 off Coppermill La 38 BG52
Salamons Way, Rain. RM13 89 FE72
Salcombe Dr, Mord. SM4 139 CX102
Romford RM6 70 EZ58
Salcombe Gdns, NW7 43 CW51
Salcombe Pk, Loug. IG10 32 EK43
Salcombe Rd, E17 67 DZ59
N16 66 DS64
Ashford TW15 114 BL91
Salcombe Way, Hayes UB4
off Portland Rd 77 BS69
Ruislip HA4 59 BU61
Salcot Cres, Croy. (New Adgtn.)
CR0 161 EC110
Salcote Rd, Grav. DA12 131 GL92
Salcott Rd, SW11 120 DE85
Croydon CR0 141 DL104
Salehurst Cl, Har. HA3 62 CL57
Salehurst Rd, SE4 123 DZ86
Salem Pl, Croy. CR0 142 DQ104
Gravesend (Nthflt.) DA11 130 GD87
Salem Rd, W2 82 DB73
Sale Pl, W2 194 B7
Salesian Gdns, Cher. KT16 134 BG102
Sale St, E2 off Hereford St 84 DU70
Salford Rd, SW2 121 DK88
Salhouse Cl, SE28
off Rollesby Way 88 EW72
Salisbury Av, N3 63 CZ55
Barking IG11 87 ES66
Sutton SM1 157 CZ107
Swanley BR8 147 FG98
Salisbury Cl, SE17 201 K8
Amersham HP7 20 AS39
Potters Bar EN6 12 DC32
Upminster RM14
off Canterbury Av 73 FT61
Worcester Park KT4 139 CT104
Salisbury Ct, EC4 196 F9
Salisbury Cres, Wal.Cr. (Chsht.)
EN8 15 DX32
Salisbury Gdns, SW19 119 CY94
Salisbury Gdns, Buck.H. IG9 48 EK47
Salisbury Hall Gdns, E4 47 EA51
Salisbury Ho, E14
off Hobday St 85 EB72
Salisbury Ms, SW6
off Dawes Rd 99 CZ80
Bromley BR2
off Salisbury Rd 144 EL99
Salisbury Pl, SW9 101 DP80
W1 194 D6
West Byfleet KT14 152 BJ111
Salisbury Rd, E4 47 EA48
E7 86 EG65
E10 67 EC61
E12 68 EK64
E17 67 EC57
N4 65 DP57
N9 46 DU48
N22 45 DP53
SE25 142 DU100
SW19 119 CY94
W13 97 CG75
Banstead SM7 158 DB114
Barnet EN5 27 CY41
Bexley DA5 126 FA88
Bromley BR2 144 EL99
Carshalton SM5 158 DF107
Dagenham RM10 89 FB65
Dartford DA2 128 FQ88
Enfield EN3 31 DZ37
Feltham TW13 116 BW88
Godstone RH9 186 DW131
Gravesend DA11 131 GF88
Grays RM17 110 GC79
Harrow HA1 61 CD57
Hounslow TW4 96 BW83
Hounslow (Hthrw.Air.) TW6 115 BQ85
Ilford IG3 69 ES61
New Malden KT3 138 CR97
Pinner HA5 59 BU56
Richmond TW9 98 CL84
Romford RM2 71 FH57
Southall UB2 96 BY77
Uxbridge UB8 76 BH68
Watford WD24 23 BV38
Woking GU22 166 AY119
Worcester Park KT4 139 CT104
Salisbury Sq, EC4 196 E9
Salisbury St, NW8 194 B5
W3 98 CQ75
Salisbury Ter, SE15 102 DW83
Salisbury Wk, N19 65 DJ61
Salix Cl, Lthd. (Fetch.) KT22 170 CB123
Sunbury-on-Thames TW16
off Oak Gro 115 BV94
Salix Rd, Grays RM17 110 GD79
Salliesfield, Twick. TW2 117 CD86
Sally Murrey Cl, E12
off Grantham Rd 69 EN63
Salmen Rd, E13 86 EF68
Salmond Cl, Stan. HA7
off Robb Rd 41 CG51
Salmonds Gro, Brwd. CM13 55 GC50
Salmon La, E14 85 DY72
Salmon Rd, Belv. DA17 106 FA78
Dartford DA1 108 FM83
Salmons La, Whyt. CR3 176 DU119
Salmons La W, Cat. CR3 176 DS120
Salmons Rd, N9 46 DU46
Chessington KT9 155 CK107
Salmon St, E14 off Salmon La 85 DZ72
NW9 62 CP60
Salomons Rd, E13 off Chalk Rd 86 EJ71
Salop Rd, E17 67 DX58
Saltash Cl, Sutt. SM1 157 CZ105
Saltash Rd, Ilf. IG6 49 ER52
Welling DA16 106 EW81
Salt Box Hill, West. TN16 162 EH113
Saltcoats Rd, W4 98 CS75
Saltcote Cl, Dart. DA1
off Lower Sta Rd 127 FE86
Saltcroft Cl, Wem. HA9 62 CP60
Salter Cl, Har. HA2 60 BZ62
Salterford Rd, SW17 120 DG93
Salter Rd, SE16 203 H3
Salters Cl, Rick. WD3 38 BL46
Salters Gdns, Wat. WD17 23 BU39
Salters Hall Ct, EC4 197 K10
Salters Hill, SE19 122 DR92
Salters Rd, E17 67 ED56
W10 81 CX70
Salter St, E14 85 EA73
NW10 81 CU69
Salterton Rd, N7 65 DL62
Saltford Cl, Erith DA8 107 FE78
Salthill Cl, Uxb. UB8 58 BL64
Saltley Cl, E6
off Dunnock Rd 86 EL72
Saltoun Rd, SW2 101 DN84
Saltram Cl, N15 66 DT56
Saltram Cres, W9 81 CZ69
Saltwell St, E14 85 EA73
Saltwood Cl, Orp. BR6 164 EW105
Saltwood Gro, SE17
off Merrow St 102 DR78
Salusbury Rd, NW6 81 CY67
Salutation Rd, SE10 205 J8
Salvia Gdns, Grnf. UB6
off Selborne Gdns 79 CG68
Salvin Rd, SW15 99 CX83
Salway Cl, Wdf.Grn. IG8 48 EF52
Salway Pl, E15 off Broadway 86 EE65
Salway Rd, E15
off Great Eastern Rd 85 ED65
Samantha Cl, E17 67 DZ59
Samantha Ms, Rom. (Hav.at.Bow.)
RM4 51 FE48
Sam Bartram Cl, SE7 104 EJ78
Sambruck Ms, SE6 123 EB88
Samels Ct, W6
off South Black Lion La 99 CU78
Samford St, NW8 194 A5
Samira Cl, E17
off Colchester Rd 67 EA58
Samos Rd, SE20 142 DV96
Samphire Ct, Grays RM17
off Salix Rd 110 GE80
Sampson Av, Barn. EN5 27 CX43
Sampson Cl, Belv. DA17
off Carrill Way 106 EX76
Sampsons Ct, Shep. TW17
off Linden Way 135 BQ99
Sampson St, E1 202 C3
Samson St, E13 86 EJ68
Samuel Cl, E8 off Pownall Rd 84 DT67
SE14 103 DX79
SE18 104 EL77
Samuel Gray Gdns, Kings.T.
KT2 137 CK95
Samuel Johnson Cl, SW16
off Curtis Fld Rd 121 DN91
Samuel Lewis Trust Dws, E8
off Amhurst Rd 66 DU63
N1 off Liverpool Rd 83 DN66
SW3 198 B9
SW6 100 DA80
Samuels Cl, W6
off South Black Lion La 99 CU78
Samuel St, SE15 102 DT80
SE18 105 EM77
Sancroft Cl, NW2 63 CV62
Sancroft Rd, Har. HA3 41 CF54
Sancroft St, SE11 200 C10
Sanctuary, The, SW1 199 N5
Bexley DA5 126 EX86
Morden SM4 140 DA100
Sanctuary Cl, Dart. DA1 128 FJ86
Uxbridge (Hare.) UB9 38 BJ52
Sanctuary Rd, Houns. (Hthrw.Air.)
TW6 114 BN86
Sanctuary St, SE1 201 J5
Sandale Cl, N16 off Stoke
Newington Ch St 66 DR62
Sandall Cl, W5 80 CL70
Sandall Rd, NW5 83 DJ65
W5 80 CL70
Sandal Rd, N18 46 DU50
New Malden KT3 138 CR99
Sandal St, E15 86 EE67
Sandalwood Av, Cher. KT16 133 BD104
Sandalwood Cl, E1
off Solebay St 85 DY70
Sandalwood Dr, Ruis. HA4 59 BQ59
Sandalwood Rd, Felt. TW13 115 BV90
Sandbach Pl, SE18 105 EQ77
Sandbanks, Felt. TW14 115 BT88
Sandbanks Hill, Dart. (Bean)
DA2 129 FV93
Sandbourne Av, SW19 140 DB97
Sandbourne Rd, SE4 103 DY82
Sandbrook Cl, NW7 42 CR51
Sandbrook Rd, N16 66 DS62
Sandby Grn, SE9 104 EL83
Sandcliff Rd, Erith DA8 107 FD77
Sandcroft Cl, N13 45 DP51
Sandells Av, Ashf. TW15 115 BQ91
Sandell St, SE1 200 D4
Sanders Cl, Hmptn. (Hmptn.H.)
TW12 116 CC92
St. Albans (Lon.Col.) AL2 9 CK27
Sandersfield Gdns, Bans.
SM7 174 DA115
Sandersfield Rd, Bans. SM7 174 DB115
Sanders La, NW7 43 CX52
Sanderson Av, Sev. (Bad.Mt.)
TN14 164 FA110
Sanderson Cl, NW5 65 DH63
Sanderson Rd, Uxb. UB8 76 BJ65
SANDERSTEAD, S.Croy. 160 DT111
⇌ Sanderstead 160 DR109
Sanderstead Av, NW2 63 CY61
Sanderstead Cl, SW12
off Atkins Rd 121 DJ87
Sanderstead Ct Av, S.Croy.
CR2 160 DU113
Sanderstead Hill, S.Croy. CR2 160 DS111
Sanderstead Rd, E10 67 DY60
Orpington BR5 146 EV100
South Croydon CR2 160 DR108
Sanders Way, N19
off Sussex Way 65 DK60
Sandes Pl, Lthd. KT22 171 CG118
Sandfield Gdns, Th.Hth. CR7 141 DP97
Sandfield Pas, Th.Hth. CR7 142 DQ97
Sandfield Rd, Th.Hth. CR7 141 DP97
Sandfields, Wok. (Send) GU23 167 BD124
Sandford Av, N22 46 DQ52
Loughton IG10 33 EQ41
Sandford Cl, E6 87 EM70
Sandford Ct, N16 66 DS60
Sandford Rd, E6 86 EL70
Bexleyheath DA7 106 EY84
Bromley BR2 144 EG98
Sandford St, SW6
off King's Rd 100 DB80
Sandgate Cl, Rom. RM7 71 FD59
Sandgate La, SW18 120 DE88
Sandgate Rd, Well. DA16 106 EW80
Sandgate St, SE15 102 DV79
Sandham Pt, SE18 off Troy Ct 105 EP77
Sandhills, Wall. SM6 159 DK105
Sandhills La, Vir.W. GU25 132 AY99
Sandhills Meadow, Shep.
TW17 135 BQ101
Sandhurst Av, Har. HA2 60 CB58
Surbiton KT5 138 CP101
Sandhurst Cl, NW9 62 CN55
South Croydon CR2 160 DS109
Sandhurst Dr, Ilf. IG3 69 ET63
Sandhurst Rd, N9 30 DW44
NW9 62 CN55
SE6 123 ED88
Bexley DA5 126 EX85
Orpington BR6 146 EU104
Sidcup DA15 125 ET90
Tilbury RM18 111 GJ82
Sandhurst Way, S.Croy. CR2 160 DS108
Sandifer Dr, NW2 63 CX62
Sandiford Rd, Sutt. SM3 139 CZ103
Sandiland Cres, Brom. BR2 144 EF103
Sandilands 142 DT103
Sandilands, Croy. CR0 142 DU103
Sevenoaks TN13 190 FD122
Sandilands Rd, SW6 100 DB81
Sandison St, SE15 102 DT83
Sandlands Gro, Tad. KT20 173 CU123
Sandlands Rd, Tad. KT20 173 CU123
Sandland St, WC1 196 C7
Sandling Ri, SE9 125 EN90
Sandlings, The, N22 45 DN54
Sandlings Cl, SE15
off Pilkington Rd 102 DV82
Sandmartin Way, Wall. SM6
off London Rd 140 DG102
Sandmere Rd, SW4 101 DL84
Sandon Cl, Esher KT10 137 CD101
Sandon Rd, Wal.Cr. (Chsht.)
EN8 14 DW30
Sandow Cres, Hayes UB3 95 BT76
Sandown Av, Dag. RM10 89 FC65
Esher KT10 154 CC106
Hornchurch RM12 72 FK61
Sandown Cl, Houns. TW5 95 BU81
Sandown Ct, Sutt. SM2
off Grange Rd 158 DB108
Sandown Dr, Cars. SM5 158 DG109
Sandown Gate, Esher KT10 136 CC104
Sandown Ind Pk, Esher KT10 136 CA103
★ Sandown Park Racecourse,
Esher KT10 136 CB104
Sandown Rd, SE25 142 DV99
Coulsdon CR5 174 DG116
Esher KT10 154 CC105
Gravesend DA12 131 GJ93
Watford WD24 24 BW38
Sandown Way, Nthlt. UB5 78 BY65
Sandpiper Cl, E17 47 DX53
SE16 203 M4
Sandpiper Dr, Erith DA8 107 FH80
Sandpiper Rd, S.Croy. CR2 161 DX111
Sutton SM1 157 CZ106
Sandpipers, The, Grav. DA12 131 GK89
Sandpiper Way, Orp. BR5 146 EX98
Sandpit Hall Rd, Wok. (Chobham)
GU24 150 AU112
Sandpit La, Brwd. (Pilg.Hat.)
CM14, CM15 54 FT46
Sandpit Pl, SE7 104 EL78
Sandpit Rd, Brom. BR1 124 EE92
Dartford DA1 108 FJ84
Sandpits Rd, Croy. CR0 161 DX105
Richmond TW10 117 CK89
Sandra Cl, N22 off New Rd 46 DQ53
Hounslow TW3 116 CB85
Sandridge Cl, Har. HA1 61 CE56
Sandridge St, N19 65 DJ61
Sandringham Av, SW20 139 CY96
Sandringham Cl, SW19 119 CX88
Enfield EN1 30 DS40
Ilford IG6 69 EQ55
Woking GU22 168 BG116
Sandringham Ct, W9
off Maida Vale 82 DC69
Sandringham Cres, Har. HA2 60 CA61
Sandringham Dr, Ashf. TW15 114 BK91
Welling DA16 105 ES82
Sandringham Gdns, N8 65 DL58
N12 44 DC51
Hounslow TW5 95 BU81
Ilford IG6 69 EQ55
Sandringham Ms, W5
off High St 79 CK73
Sandringham Pk, Cob. KT11 154 BZ112
Sandringham Rd, E7 68 EJ64
E8 66 DT64
E10 67 ED58
N22 66 DQ55
NW2 81 CV65
NW11 63 CY59
Barking IG11 87 ET65
Brentwood CM15 54 FV43
Bromley BR1 124 EG92
Hounslow (Hthrw.Air.) TW6 114 BL85
Northolt UB5 78 CA66
Potters Bar EN6 12 DB30
Thornton Heath CR7 142 DQ99
Watford WD24 24 BW37
Worcester Park KT4 139 CU104
Sandringham Way, Wal.Cr.
EN8 15 DX34
Sandrock Pl, Croy. CR0 161 DX105
Sandrock Rd, SE13 103 EA83
Sandroyd Way, Cob. KT11 154 CA113
SANDS END, SW6 100 DC81
Sand's End La, SW6 100 DB81
Sandstone Pl, N19 65 DH61
Sandstone Rd, SE12 124 EH89
Sands Way, Wdf.Grn. IG8 48 EL51
Sandtoft Rd, SE7 104 EH79
Sandway Path, Orp. BR5
off Okemore Gdns 146 EW98
Sandway Rd, Orp. BR5 146 EW98
Sandwell Cres, NW6 82 DA65
Sandwich St, WC1 195 P3
Sandwick Cl, NW7
off Sebergham Gro 43 CU52
Sandy Bk Rd, Grav. DA12 131 GH88
Sandy Bury, Orp. BR6 145 ER104
Sandy Cl, Wok. GU22
off Sandy La 167 BB117
Sandycombe Rd, Felt. TW14 115 BU88
Richmond TW9 98 CN83
Sandycoombe Rd, Twick. TW1 117 CJ86
Sandycroft, SE2 106 EU79
Epsom KT17 157 CW110
Sandycroft Rd, Amer. HP6 20 AV39
Sandy Dr, Cob. KT11 154 CA111
Feltham TW14 115 BS88
Sandy Hill Av, SE18 105 EP78
Sandy Hill Rd, SE18 105 EP78
Sandyhill Rd, Ilf. IG1 69 EP63
Sandy Hill Rd, Wall. SM6 159 DJ109
Sandy La, Bushey WD23 24 CC41
Cobham KT11 154 CA112
Dartford (Bean) DA2 129 FW89
Grays (Chad.St.M) RM16 111 GH79
Grays (W.Thur.) RM20
off London Rd W Thurrock 109 FV79
Harrow HA3 62 CM58
Kingston upon Thames KT1 117 CG94
Leatherhead KT22 154 CA112

San - See

Sandy La, Mitch. CR4 140 DG95
Northwood HA6 39 BU50
Orpington BR6 146 EU101
Orpington (St.P.Cray) BR5 146 EX95
Oxted RH8 187 EC129
Oxted (Lmpfld.) RH8 188 EH127
Redhill (Bletch.) RH1 185 DP132
Richmond TW10 117 CJ89
Sevenoaks TN13 191 FJ123
Sidcup DA14 126 EX94
South Ockendon (Aveley)
RM15 90 FM73
Sutton SM2 157 CY108
Tadworth (Kgswd.) KT20 173 CZ124
Teddington TW11 117 CG94
Virginia Water GU25 132 AY98
Walton-on-Thames KT12 135 BV100
Watford WD25 24 CC41
Westerham TN16 189 ER125
Woking GU22 167 BC116
Woking (Chobham) GU24 150 AS109
Woking (Pyrford) GU22 167 BF117
Woking (Send) GU23 167 BC123
Sandy La Est, Rich. TW10 117 CK89
Sandy La N, Wall. SM6 159 DK107
Sandy La S, Wall. SM6 159 DK107
Sandy Lo La, Nthwd. HA6 39 BR47
Sandy Lo Rd, Rick. WD3 39 BP47
Sandy Lo Way, Nthwd. HA6 39 BS50
Sandymount Av, Stan. HA7 41 CJ50
Sandy Ridge, Chis. BR7 125 EN93
Sandy Ri, Ger.Cr. (Chal.St.P.)
SL9 36 AY53
Sandy Rd, NW3 64 DB62
Addlestone KT15 152 BG107
Sandy's Row, E1 197 N7
Sandy Way, Cob. KT11 154 CA112
Croydon CR0 143 DZ104
Walton-on-Thames KT12 135 BT102
Woking GU22 167 BC117
Sanford La, N16
off Lawrence Bldgs 66 DT61
Sanford St, SE14 103 DY79
Sanford Ter, N16 66 DT62
Sanford Wk, N16
off Sanford Ter 66 DT61
SE14 off Cold Blow La 103 DY79
Sanger Av, Chess. KT9 156 CL106
Sanger Dr, Wok. (Send) GU23 167 BC123
Sangley Rd, SE6 123 EB87
SE25 142 DS98
Sangora Rd, SW11 100 DD84
Sansom Rd, E11 68 EE61
Sansom St, SE5 102 DR80
Sans Wk, EC1 196 E4
Santers La, Pot.B. EN6 11 CY33
Santley St, SW4 101 DM84
Santos Rd, SW18 120 DA85
Santway, The, Stan. HA7 41 CE50
Sanway Cl, W.Byf. (Byfleet)
KT14 152 BL114
Sanway Rd, W.Byf. (Byfleet)
KT14 152 BL114
Sapcote Trd Cen, NW10 63 CT64
Saperton Wk, SE11 200 C8
Sapho Pk, Grav. DA12 131 GM91
Saphora Cl, Orp. BR6
off Oleander Cl 163 ER106
Sapperton Ct, EC1 197 H4
Sapphire Cl, E6 87 EN72
Dagenham RM8 70 EW60
Sapphire Rd, SE8 203 L9
Sappho Ct, Wok. GU21
off Langmans Way 166 AS116
Saracen Cl, Croy. CR0 142 DR100
Saracen's Head Yd, EC3 197 P9
★ Saracens RFC (share
Vicarage Rd with Watford
FC), Wat. WD18 23 BV43
Saracen St, E14 85 EA72
Sara Ct, Beck. BR3
off Albemarle Rd 143 EB95
Sara Cres, Green. DA9 109 FU84
Sarah Ho, SW15 99 CT84
Sara Pk, Grav. DA12 131 GL91
Saratoga Rd, E5 66 DW63
Sardinia St, WC2 196 B9
Sargeant Cl, Uxb. UB8
off Ratcliffe Cl 76 BK69
Sarita Cl, Har. HA3 41 CD54
Sarjant Path, SW19
off Queensmere Rd 119 CX89
Sark Cl, Houns. TW5 96 CA80
Sark Ho, Enf. EN3
off Eastfield Rd 31 DX38
Sark Wk, E16 86 EH72
Sarnesfield Ho, SE15
off Pencraig Way 102 DV79
Sarnesfield Rd, Enf. EN2
off Church St 30 DR41
SARRATT, Rick. 22 BG35
Sarratt Bottom, Rick. (Sarratt)
WD3 21 BE36
Sarratt La, Rick. WD3 22 BH40
Sarratt Rd, Rick. WD3 22 BM41
Sarre Av, Horn. RM12 90 FJ65
Sarre Rd, NW2 63 CZ64
Orpington BR5 146 EW99
Sarsby Dr, Stai. TW19 113 BA89
Sarsen Av, Houns. TW3 96 BZ82
Sarsfeld Rd, SW12 120 DF88
Sarsfield Rd, Grnf. UB6 79 CH68
Sartor Rd, SE15 103 DX84
Sarum Complex, Uxb. UB8 76 BH68
Sarum Grn, Wey. KT13 135 BS104
Sarum Ter, E3 85 DZ70
Satanita Cl, E16
off Fulmer Rd 86 EK72
Satchell Mead, NW9 43 CT53
Satchwell Rd, E2 84 DU69
Satis Ct, Epsom KT17
off Windmill Av 157 CT111
Sattar Ms, N16 off Clissold Rd 66 DR62
Sauls Grn, E11 off Napier Rd 68 EE62
Saunder Cl, Wal.Cr. EN8
off Welsummer Way 15 DX27
Saunders Cl, E14 203 N1
Saunders Cl, Grav. (Nthflt.)
DA11 130 GE89
Saunders Copse, Wok. GU22 166 AV122
Saunders La, Wok. GU22 166 AS122
Saunders Ness Rd, E14 204 E10
Saunders Rd, SE18 105 ET78
Uxbridge UB10 76 BM66
Saunders St, SE11 200 D8
Saunders Way, SE28
off Oriole Way 88 EV73
Dartford DA1 128 FM89
Saunderton Rd, Wem. HA0 61 CH64
Saunton Av, Hayes UB3 95 BT80
Saunton Rd, Horn. RM12 71 FG61
Savage Gdns, E6 87 EM72
EC3 197 N10
Savay Cl, Uxb. (Denh.) UB9 58 BG59
Savay La, Uxb. (Denh.) UB9 58 BG58
Savernake Rd, N9 30 DU44
NW3 64 DF63
Savery Dr, Surb. KT6 137 CJ101
Savile Cl, N.Mal. KT3 138 CS99
Thames Ditton KT7 137 CF102
Savile Gdns, Croy. CR0 142 DT103
Savile Row, W1 195 K10
Savill Cl, Wal.Cr. (Chsht.) EN7
off Markham Rd 14 DQ25
Saville Cres, Ashf. TW15 115 BR93
Saville Rd, E16 86 EL74
W4 98 CR76
Romford RM6 70 EZ58
Twickenham TW1 117 CF88
Saville Row, Brom. BR2 144 EF102
Enfield EN3 31 DX40
Savill Gdns, SW20
off Bodnant Gdns 139 CU97
Savill Row, Wdf.Grn. IG8 48 EF51
Savona Cl, SW19 119 CY94
Savona Est, SW8 101 DJ80
Savona St, SW8 101 DJ80
Savoy Av, Hayes UB3 95 BS78
Savoy Bldgs, WC2 200 B1
Savoy Cl, E15
off Arthingworth St 86 EE67
Edgware HA8 42 CN50
Uxbridge (Hare.) UB9 38 BK54
Savoy Ct, WC2 200 A1
Savoy Hill, WC2 200 B1
Savoy Pl, WC2 200 A1
Savoy Rd, Dart. DA1 128 FK85
Savoy Row, WC2 196 B10
Savoy Steps, WC2
off Savoy St 83 DM73
Savoy St, WC2 196 B10
Savoy Way, WC2 200 B1
Sawbill Cl, Hayes UB4 78 BX71
Sawkins Cl, SW19 119 CY89
Sawley Rd, W12 81 CT74
Sawmill Yd, E3 85 DY67
Sawtry Cl, Cars. SM5 140 DE101
Sawtry Way, Borwd. WD6 26 CN38
Sawyer Cl, N9
off Lion Rd 46 DU47
Sawyers Chase, Rom. (Abridge)
RM4 34 EV41
Sawyers Cl, Dag. RM10 89 FC65
Sawyers Hall La, Brwd. CM15 54 FW45
Sawyer's Hill, Rich. TW10 118 CP87
Sawyers La, Borwd. (Elstree)
WD6 25 CH40
Potters Bar EN6 11 CX34
Sawyers Lawn, W13 79 CF72
Sawyer St, SE1 201 H4
Saxby Rd, SW2 121 DL87
Saxham Rd, Bark. IG11 87 ES68
Saxlingham Rd, E4 47 ED48
Saxon Av, Felt. TW13 116 BZ89
Saxonbury Av, Sun. TW16 135 BV97
Saxonbury Cl, Mitch. CR4 140 DD97
Saxonbury Gdns, Surb. KT6 137 CJ102
Saxon Cl, E17 67 EA59
Brentwood CM13 55 GA48
Gravesend (Nthflt.) DA11 130 GC90
Romford RM3 52 FM54
Sevenoaks (Otford) TN14 181 FF117
Slough SL3 93 AZ75
Surbiton KT6 137 CK100
Uxbridge UB8 76 BM71
Saxon Ct, Borwd. WD6 26 CL40
Saxon Dr, W3 80 CP72
Saxonfield Cl, SW2 121 DM87
Saxon Gdns, Sthl. UB1
off Saxon Rd 78 BY73
Saxon Pl, Dart. (Hort.Kir.) DA4 148 FQ99
Saxon Rd, E3 85 DZ68
E6 87 EM70
N22 45 DP53
SE25 142 DR99
Ashford TW15 115 BR93
Bromley BR1 124 EF94
Dartford (Hawley) DA2 128 FL91
Ilford IG1 87 EP65
Southall UB1 78 BY74
Walton-on-Thames KT12 136 BX104
Wembley HA9 62 CQ62
Saxons, Tad. KT20 173 CX121
Saxon Shore Way, Grav.
DA12 131 GM86
Saxon Wk, Sid. DA14 126 EW93
Saxon Way, N14 29 DK44
Reigate RH2 183 CZ133
Waltham Abbey EN9 15 EC33
West Drayton UB7 94 BJ79
Windsor (Old Wind.) SL4 112 AV86
Saxony Par, Hayes UB3 77 BQ71
Saxton Cl, SE13 103 ED83
Saxton Ms, Wat. WD17
off Dellfield Cl 23 BU40
Saxville Rd, Orp. BR5 146 EV97
Sayer Cl, Green. DA9 129 FU85
Sayers Cl, Lthd. (Fetch.) KT22 170 CC124
Sayers Wk, Rich. TW10
off Stafford Pl 118 CM87
Sayesbury La, N18 46 DU50
Sayes Ct, SE8
off Sayes Ct St 103 DZ78
Addlestone KT15 152 BJ106
Sayes Ct Fm Dr, Add. KT15 152 BH106
Sayes Ct Rd, Orp. BR5 146 EU98
Sayes Ct St, SE8 103 DZ79
Scadbury Pk, Chis. BR7 125 ET93
Scads Hill Cl, Orp. BR6 145 ET100
Scala St, W1 195 L6
Scales Rd, N17 66 DT55
Scammel Way, Wat. WD18 23 BT44
Scampston Ms, W10 81 CX72
Scampton Rd, Houns. (Hthrw.Air.)
TW6 off Southampton Rd 114 BM86
Scandrett St, E1 202 D3
Scarba Wk, N1
off Marquess Rd 84 DR65
Scarborough Cl, Sutt. SM2 157 CZ111
Westerham (Bigg.H.) TN16 178 EJ118
Scarborough Rd, E11 67 ED60
N4 65 DN59
N9 46 DW45
Hounslow (Hthrw.Air.) TW6
off Southern Perimeter Rd 115 BQ86
Scarborough St, E1
off West Tenter St 84 DT72
Scarbrook Rd, Croy. CR0 142 DQ104
Scarle Rd, Wem. HA0 79 CK65
Scarlet Cl, Orp. BR5 146 EV98
Scarlet Rd, SE6 124 EE90
Scarlett Cl, Wok. GU21
off Bingham Dr 166 AT118
Scarlette Manor Way, SW2
off Papworth Way 121 DN87
Scarsbrook Rd, SE3 104 EK83
Scarsdale Pl, W8
off Wrights La 100 DB76
Scarsdale Rd, Har. HA2 60 CC62
Scarsdale Vil, W8 100 DA76
Scarth Rd, SW13 99 CT83
Scatterdells La, Kings L. (Chipper.)
WD4 5 BF30
Scawen Cl, Cars. SM5 158 DG105
Scawen Rd, SE8 103 DY78
Scawfell St, E2 84 DT68
Scaynes Link, N12 44 DA50
Sceaux Est, SE5 102 DS81
Sceptre Rd, E2 84 DW69
Schofield Wk, SE3
off Dornberg Cl 104 EH80
Scholars Rd, E4 47 EC46
SW12 121 DJ88
Scholars Wk, Ger.Cr. (Chal.St.P.)
SL9 36 AY51
Scholars Way, Amer. HP6 20 AT38
Scholefield Rd, N19 65 DK60
Schonfeld Sq, N16 66 DR61
Schoolbank Rd, SE10 205 K8
Schoolbell Ms, E3
off Arbery Rd 85 DY68
School Cres, Dart. (Cray.) DA1 107 FF84
Schoolfield Rd, Grays RM20 109 FU79
School Grn La, Epp. (N.Wld.Bas.)
CM16 19 FC25
School Hill, Red. RH1 185 DJ128
Schoolhouse Gdns, Loug. IG10 33 EP42
Schoolhouse La, E1 85 DX73
School Ho La, Tedd. TW11 117 CH94
School La, SE23 122 DV89
Addlestone KT15 152 BG105
Bushey WD23 40 CB45
Caterham CR3 186 DT126
Chalfont St. Giles HP8 36 AW47
Chigwell IG7 49 ET49
Dartford (Bean) DA2 129 FW90
Dartford (Hort.Kir.) DA4 148 FQ98
Egham TW20 113 BA92
Gerrards Cross (Chal.St.P.)
SL9 36 AX54
Kingston upon Thames KT1
off School Rd 137 CJ95
Leatherhead (Fetch.) KT22 171 CD122
Longfield DA3 149 FT100
Pinner HA5 60 BY56
St. Albans (Brick.Wd.) AL2 8 CA31
Sevenoaks (Seal) TN15 191 FM121
Shepperton TW17 135 BP100
Slough SL2 74 AT73
Slough (Stoke P.) SL2 74 AV67
Surbiton KT6 138 CN102
Swanley BR8 147 FH95
Tadworth KT20
off Chequers La 183 CU125
Welling DA16 106 EV83
Woking (Ockham) GU23 169 BP122
School Mead, Abb.L. WD5 7 BS32
School Pas, Kings.T. KT1 138 CM96
Southall UB1 78 BZ74
School Rd, E12 off Sixth Av 69 EM63
NW10 80 CR70
Ashford TW15 115 BP93
Chislehurst BR7 145 EQ95
Dagenham RM10 88 FA67
East Molesey KT8 137 CD98
Hampton (Hmptn.H.) TW12 116 CC93
Hounslow TW3 96 CC83
Kingston upon Thames KT1 137 CJ95
Ongar CM5 19 FG32
Potters Bar EN6 12 DC30
West Drayton UB7 94 BK79
School Rd Av, Hmptn. (Hmptn.H.)
TW12 116 CC93
School Wk, Slou. SL2
off Grasmere Av 74 AV73
Sunbury-on-Thames TW16 135 BT98
Schoolway, N12 44 DD51
School Way, N12 off High Rd 44 DC49
Dagenham RM8 70 EW62
Schooner Cl, E14 204 F7
SE16 203 H4
Barking IG11 88 EV69
Schooner Ct, Dart. DA2 108 FQ84
Schroder Ct, Egh. (Eng.Grn.)
TW20 112 AV92
Schubert Rd, SW15 119 CZ85
Borehamwood (Elstree)
WD6 25 CK44
★ Science Mus, SW7 198 A7
Scilla Ct, Grays RM17 110 GD79
Sclater St, E1 197 P4
Scoble Pl, N16 off Amhurst Rd 66 DT63
Scoles Cres, SW2 121 DN88
Scope Way, Kings.T. KT1 138 CL98
Scoresby St, SE1 200 F3
Scorton Av, Grnf. UB6 79 CG68
Scotch Common, W13 79 CG71
Scoter Cl, Wdf.Grn. IG8
off Mallards Rd 48 EH52
Scot Gro, Pnr. HA5 40 BX52
Scotia Rd, SW2 121 DN87
Scotland Br Rd, Add. (New Haw)
KT15 152 BG111
Scotland Grn, N17 46 DT54
Scotland Grn Rd, Enf. EN3 31 DX43
Scotland Grn Rd N, Enf. EN3 31 DX42
Scotland Pl, SW1 199 P2
Scotland Rd, Buck.H. IG9 48 EJ46
Scotney Cl, Orp. BR6 163 EN105
Scotney Wk, Horn. RM12
off Bonington Rd 72 FK64
Scotscraig, Rad. WD7 25 CF35
Scotsdale Cl, Orp. BR5 145 ES98
Sutton SM3 157 CY108
Scotsdale Rd, SE12 124 EH85
Scotshall La, Warl. CR6 161 EC114
Scots Hill, Rick. (Crox.Grn.)
WD3 22 BM44
Scots Hill Cl, Rick. WD3
off Scots Hill 22 BM44
Scotsmill La, Rick. (Crox.Grn.)
WD3 22 BM44
Scotswood St, EC1 196 E4
Scotswood Wk, N17 46 DU52
Scott Cl, SW16 141 DM95
Epsom KT19 156 CQ106
West Drayton UB7 94 BM77
Scott Ct, W3
off Petersfield Rd 98 CQ75
Scott Cres, Erith DA8
off Cloudesley Rd 107 FF81
Harrow HA2 60 CB60
Scott Ellis Gdns, NW8 82 DD69
Scottes La, Dag. RM8
off Valence Av 70 EX60
Scott Fm Cl, T.Ditt. KT7 137 CH102
Scott Gdns, Houns. TW5 96 BX80
Scott Ho, N18 46 DU50
Scott Lidgett Cres, SE16 202 B5
Scott Rd, Grav. DA12 131 GK92
Grays RM16 111 GG77
Scott Russell Pl, E14 204 B10
Scotts Av, Brom. BR2 143 ED96
Sunbury-on-Thames TW16 115 BS94
Scotts Cl, Horn. RM12
off Rye Cl 72 FJ64
Staines TW19 114 BK88
Scotts Dr, Hmptn. TW12 116 CB94
Scotts Fm Rd, Epsom KT19 156 CQ107
Scotts La, Brom. BR2 143 ED97
Walton-on-Thames KT12 154 BX105
Scotts Rd, E10 67 EC60
W12 99 CV75
Bromley BR1 124 EG94
Southall UB2 96 BW76
Scott St, E1 84 DV70
Scotts Way, Sev. TN13 190 FE122
Sunbury-on-Thames TW16 115 BS93
Scottswood Cl, Bushey WD23
off Scottswood Rd 24 BY40
Scottswood Rd, Bushey WD23 24 BY40
Scott's Yd, EC4 197 K10
Scott Trimmer Way, Houns.
TW3 96 BY82
Scottwell Dr, NW9 63 CT57
Scoulding Rd, E16 86 EF72
Scouler St, E14 204 F1
Scout App, NW10 62 CS63
Scout La, SW4 off Old Town 101 DJ83
Scout Way, NW7 42 CR49
Scovell Cres, SE1 201 H5
Scovell Rd, SE1 201 H5
Scratchers La, Long. (Fawk.Grn.)
DA3 149 FR103
Scrattons Ter, Bark. IG11 88 EX68
Scriven St, E8 84 DT67
Scrooby St, SE6 123 EB86
Scrubbitts Pk Rd, Rad. WD7 25 CG35
Scrubbitts Sq, Rad. WD7
off The Dell 25 CG36
Scrubs La, NW10 81 CU69
W10 81 CU69
Scrutton Cl, SW12 121 DK87
Scrutton St, EC2 197 M5
Scudamore La, NW9 62 CQ55
Scudders Hill, Long. (Fawk.Grn.)
DA3 149 FV100
Scutari Rd, SE22 122 DW85
Scylla Cres, Houns. (Hthrw.Air.)
TW6 115 BP87
Scylla Pl, Wok. (St. John's) GU21
off Church Rd 166 AU119
Scylla Rd, SE15 102 DV83
Hounslow (Hthrw.Air.) TW6 115 BP86
Seaborough Rd, Grays RM16 111 GJ76
Seabright St, E2
off Bethnal Grn Rd 84 DV69
Seabrook Dr, W.Wick. BR4 144 EE103
Seabrooke Ri, Grays RM17 110 GB79
Seabrook Gdns, Rom. RM7 70 FA59
Seabrook Rd, Dag. RM8 70 EX62
Kings Langley WD4 7 BR27
Seaburn Cl, Rain. RM13 89 FE68
Seacole Cl, W3 80 CR71
Seacourt Rd, SE2 106 EX75
Slough SL3 93 BB77
Seacroft Gdns, Wat. WD19 40 BX48
Seafield Rd, N11 45 DK49
Seaford Cl, Ruis. HA4 59 BR61
Seaford Rd, E17 67 EB55
N15 66 DR57
W13 79 CH74
Enfield EN1 30 DS42
Hounslow (Hthrw.Air.) TW6 114 BK85
Seaford St, WC1 196 A3
Seaforth Av, N.Mal. KT3 139 CV99
Seaforth Cl, Rom. RM1 51 FE52
Seaforth Cres, N5 66 DQ64
Seaforth Dr, Wal.Cr. EN8 15 DX34
Seaforth Gdns, N21 45 DM45
Epsom KT19 157 CT105
Woodford Green IG8 48 EJ50
Seaforth Pl, SW1
off Buckingham Gate 101 DJ76
Seagrave Rd, SW6 100 DA79
Seagry Rd, E11 68 EG58
Seagull Cl, Bark. IG11 88 EU69
SEAL, Sev. 191 FN121
Sealand Rd, Houns. (Hthrw.Air.)
TW6 114 BN86
Sealand Wk, Nthlt. UB5
off Wayfarer Rd 78 BY69
Seal Dr, Sev. (Seal) TN15 191 FM121
Seal Hollow Rd, Sev. TN13,
TN15 191 FJ124
Seal Rd, Sev. TN14, TN15 191 FJ121
Seal St, E8 66 DT63
Seaman Cl, St.Alb. (Park St.)
AL2 9 CD25
Searches La, Abb.L. (Bedmond)
WD5 7 BV28
Searchwood Rd, Warl. CR6 176 DV118
Searle Pl, N4 off Evershot Rd 65 DM60
Searles Cl, SW11 100 DE80
Searles Dr, E6 87 EP71
Searles Rd, SE1 201 L8
Sears St, SE5 102 DR80
Seasprite Cl, Nthlt. UB5 78 BX69
Seaton Av, Ilf. IG3 69 ES64
Seaton Cl, E13
off New Barn St 86 EH70
SE11 200 E10
SW15 119 CV88
Twickenham TW2 117 CD86
Seaton Dr, Ashf. TW15 114 BL89
Seaton Gdns, Ruis. HA4 59 BU62
Seaton Pt, E5 66 DV63
Seaton Rd, Dart. DA1 127 FG87
Hayes UB3 95 BR77
Mitcham CR4 140 DE96
St. Albans (Lon.Col.) AL2 9 CK26
Twickenham TW2 116 CC86
Welling DA16 106 EW80
Wembley HA0 80 CL68
Seaton Sq, NW7
off Bittacy Hill 43 CY52
Seaton St, N18 46 DU50
Sebastian Av, Brwd. CM15 55 GA44
Sebastian St, EC1 196 G3
Sebastopol Rd, N9 46 DU49
Sebbon St, N1 83 DP66
Sebergham Gro, NW7 43 CU52
Sebert Rd, E7 68 EH64
Sebright Pas, E2
off Hackney Rd 84 DU68
Sebright Rd, Barn. EN5 27 CX40
Secker Cres, Har. HA3 40 CC53
Secker St, SE1 200 D3
Second Av, E12 68 EL63
E13 86 EG69
E17 67 EA57
N18 46 DW49
NW4 63 CX56
SW14 98 CS83
W3 81 CT74
W10 81 CY70
Dagenham RM10 89 FB67
Enfield EN1 30 DT43
Grays RM20 109 FU79
Hayes UB3 77 BT74
Romford RM6 70 EW57
Waltham Abbey EN9 off Breach
Barn Mobile Home Pk 16 EH30
Walton-on-Thames KT12 135 BV100
Watford WD25 24 BX35
Wembley HA9 61 CK61
Second Cl, W.Mol. KT8 136 CC98
Second Cross Rd, Twick. TW2 117 CE89
Second Way, Wem. HA9 62 CP63
Sedan Way, SE17 201 M10
Sedcombe Cl, Sid. DA14
off Knoll Rd 126 EV91
Sedcote Rd, Enf. EN3 30 DW43
Sedding St, SW1 198 F8
Seddon Highwalk, EC2
off Beech St 84 DQ71
Seddon Ho, EC2
off The Barbican 84 DQ71
Seddon Rd, Mord. SM4 140 DD99
Seddon St, WC1 196 C3
Sedgebrook Rd, SE3 104 EK82
Sedgecombe Av, Har. HA3 61 CJ57
Sedge Ct, Grays RM17 110 GE80
Sedgefield Cl, Rom. RM3 52 FM49
Sedgefield Cres, Rom. RM3 52 FM49
Sedgeford Rd, W12 81 CT74
Sedgehill Rd, SE6 123 EA91
Sedgemere Av, N2 64 DC55
Sedgemere Rd, SE2 106 EW76
Sedgemoor Dr, Dag. RM10 70 FA63
Sedge Rd, N17 46 DW52
Sedgeway, SE6 124 EF88
Sedgewick Av, Uxb. UB10 77 BP66
Sedgewood Cl, Brom. BR2 144 EF101
Sedgmoor Pl, SE5 102 DS80
Sedgwick Rd, E10 67 EC61
Sedgwick St, E9 67 DX64
Sedleigh Rd, SW18 119 CZ86
Sedlescombe Rd, SW6 99 CZ79
Sedley, Grav. (Sthflt.) DA13 130 GA93
Sedley Cl, Enf. EN1 30 DV38
Sedley Gro, Uxb. (Hare.) UB9 58 BJ56
Sedley Pl, W1 195 H9
Sedley Ri, Loug. IG10 33 EM40
Sedum Cl, NW9 62 CP57
Seeley Dr, SE21 122 DS91
Seelig Av, NW9 63 CU59
Seely Rd, SW17 120 DG93
Seer Grn La, Beac. (Jordans)
HP9 36 AS52
Seething La, EC3 201 N1
Seething Wells La, Surb. KT6 137 CJ100

Sef - She

Sefton Av, NW7 . . . . .42 CR50
Harrow HA3 . . . . .41 CD53
Sefton Cl, Orp. BR5 . . . . . . .145 ET98
Slough (Stoke P.) SL2 . . . . . .74 AT66
Sefton Paddock, Slou. (Stoke P.)
SL2 . . . . .74 AU66
Sefton Pk, Slou. (Stoke P.) SL2 .74 AU66
Sefton Rd, Croy. CR0 . . . . . . .142 DU102
Epsom KT19 . . . . .156 CR110
Orpington BR5 . . . . .145 ET98
Sefton St, SW15 . . . . .99 CW82
Sefton Way, Uxb. UB8 . . . . . .76 BJ72
Segal Cl, SE23 . . . . .123 DY87
Segrave Cl, Wey. KT13 . . . . . .152 BN108
Sekforde St, EC1 . . . . .196 F5
Sekhon Ter, Felt. TW13 . . . . . .116 CA90
Selah Dr, Swan. BR8 . . . . . . .147 FC95
Selan Gdns, Hayes UB4 . . . . . .77 BV71
Selbie Av, NW10 . . . . .63 CT64
Selborne Av, E12 *off Walton Rd* .69 EN63
Bexley DA5 . . . . .126 EY88
Selborne Gdns, NW4 . . . . .63 CU56
Greenford UB6 . . . . .79 CG67
Selborne Rd, E17 . . . . .67 DZ57
N14 . . . . .45 DL48
N22 . . . . .45 DM53
SE5 *off Denmark Hill* 102 DR82
Croydon CR0 . . . . .142 DS104
Ilford IG1 . . . . .69 EN61
New Malden KT3 . . . . .138 CS96
Sidcup DA14 . . . . .126 EV91
Selbourne Av, E17 . . . . .67 DZ56
Addlestone (New Haw)
KT15 . . . . .152 BH110
Surbiton KT6 . . . . .138 CM103
Selbourne Cl, Add. (New Haw)
KT15 . . . . .152 BH109
Selbourne Sq, Gdse. RH9 . . .186 DW130
Selbourne Wk, E17 *off Selbourne Wk Shop Cen* 67 DZ56
Selbourne Wk Shop Cen, E17 .67 DZ56
Selby Chase, Ruis. HA4 . . . . . .59 BV61
Selby Cl, E6 *off Linton Gdns* . .86 EL71
Chessington KT9 . . . . .156 CL108
Chislehurst BR7 . . . . .125 EN93
Selby Gdns, Sthl. UB1 . . . . . .78 CA70
Selby Grn, Cars. SM5 . . . . . .140 DE101
Selby Rd, E11 . . . . .68 EE62
E13 . . . . .86 EH71
N17 . . . . .46 DS51
SE20 . . . . .142 DU96
W5 . . . . .79 CH70
Ashford TW15 . . . . .115 BQ93
Carshalton SM5 . . . . .140 DE101
Selby St, E1 . . . . .84 DU70
Selby Wk, Wok. GU21
off Wyndham Rd 166 AV118
Selcroft Rd, Pur. CR8 . . . . . .159 DP112
Selden Rd, SE15 . . . . .102 DW82
Selden Wk, N7 *off Durham Rd* .65 DM61
★ **Selfridges**, W1 . . . . .194 G9
SELHURST, SE25 . . . . .142 DS100
⇌ **Selhurst** 142 DS99
Selhurst Cl, SW19 . . . . .119 CX88
Woking GU21 . . . . .167 AZ115
Selhurst New Rd, SE25 . . . . .142 DS100
Selhurst Pl, SE25 . . . . .142 DS100
Selhurst Rd, N9 . . . . .46 DR48
SE25 . . . . .142 DS99
Selinas La, Dag. RM8 . . . . . . .70 EY59
Selkirk Dr, Erith DA8 . . . . . . .107 FE81
Selkirk Rd, SW17 . . . . .120 DE91
Twickenham TW2 . . . . .116 CC89
Sell Cl, Wal.Cr. (Chsht.) EN7
off Gladding Rd 13 DP26
Sellers Cl, Borwd. WD6 . . . . . .26 CQ39
Sellers Hall Cl, N3 . . . . .44 DA52
Sellincourt Rd, SW17 . . . . . . .120 DE92
Sellindge Cl, Beck. BR3 . . . . .123 DZ94
Sellon Ms, SE11 . . . . .200 C9
Sellons Av, NW10 . . . . .81 CT67
Sellwood Dr, Barn. EN5 . . . . . .27 CX43
Sellwood St, SW2
off Tulse Hill 121 DN87
SELSDON, S.Croy. 160 DW110
Selsdon Av, S.Croy. CR2
off Selsdon Rd 160 DR107
Selsdon Cl, Rom. RM5 . . . . . . .51 FC53
Surbiton KT6 . . . . .138 CL99
Selsdon Cres, S.Croy. CR2 . . .160 DW109
Selsdon Pk Rd, S.Croy. CR2 . .161 DX109
Selsdon Rd, E11 . . . . .68 EG59
E13 . . . . .86 EJ67
NW2 . . . . .63 CT61
SE27 . . . . .121 DP90
Addlestone (New Haw)
KT15 . . . . .152 BG111
South Croydon CR2 . . . . . .160 DR106
Selsdon Rd Ind Est, S.Croy. CR2
off Selsdon Rd 160 DR107
Selsdon Way, E14 . . . . .204 C7
Selsea Pl, N16
off Crossway 66 DS64
Selsey Cres, Well. DA16 . . . . .106 EX81
Selsey St, E14 . . . . .85 EA71
Selvage La, NW7 . . . . .42 CR50
Selway Cl, Pnr. HA5 . . . . .59 BV56
Selwood Cl, Stai. (Stanw.)
TW19 . . . . .114 BJ86
Selwood Gdns, Stai. (Stanw.)
TW19 . . . . .114 BJ86
Selwood Pl, SW7 . . . . .100 DD78
Selwood Rd, Brwd. CM14 . . . . .54 FT48
Chessington KT9 . . . . .155 CK105
Croydon CR0 . . . . .142 DV103
Sutton SM3 . . . . .139 CZ102
Woking GU22 . . . . .167 BB120
Selwood Ter, SW7
off Onslow Gdns 100 DD78
Selworthy Cl, E11 . . . . .68 EG57
Selworthy Ho, SW11 . . . . . . .100 DD81
Selworthy Rd, SE6 . . . . .123 DZ90
Selwyn Av, E4 . . . . .47 EC51
Ilford IG3 . . . . .69 ES58
Selwyn Av, Rich. TW9 . . . . . . .98 CL83
Selwyn Cl, Houns. TW4 . . . . . .96 BY84
Selwyn Ct, SE3 . . . . .104 EE83
Edgware HA8
off Camrose Av 42 CP52
Selwyn Cres, Well. DA16 . . . . .106 EV84
Selwyn Pl, Orp. BR5 . . . . .146 EV97
Selwyn Rd, E3 . . . . .85 DZ68
E13 . . . . .86 EH67
NW10 . . . . .80 CR66
New Malden KT3 . . . . .138 CR99
Tilbury RM18 *off Dock Rd* . .111 GF82
Semley Pl, SW1 . . . . .198 G9
Semley Rd, SW16 . . . . .141 DL96
Semper Cl, Wok. (Knap.)
GU21 . . . . .166 AS117
Semper Rd, Grays RM16 . . . . .111 GJ75
Senate St, SE15 . . . . .102 DW82
Senator Wk, SE28
off Broadwater Rd 105 ER76
SEND, Wok. 167 BC124
Sendall Ct, SW11 . . . . .100 DD83
Send Barns La, Wok. (Send)
GU23 . . . . .167 BD124
Send Cl, Wok. (Send) GU23 . .167 BC123
SEND MARSH, Wok. 167 BF124
Send Marsh Rd, Wok. (Ripley)
GU23 . . . . .167 BF123
Send Par Cl, Wok. (Send) GU23
off Send Rd 167 BC123
Send Rd, Wok. (Send) GU23 .167 BB122
Seneca Rd, Th.Hth. CR7 . . . . .142 DQ98
Senga Rd, Wall. SM6 . . . . . . .140 DG102
Senhouse Rd, Sutt. SM3 . . . . .139 CX104
Senior St, W2 . . . . .82 DB71
Senlac Rd, SE12 . . . . .124 EH88
Sennen Rd, Enf. EN1 . . . . .46 DT45
Sennen Wk, SE9 . . . . .124 EL90
Senrab St, E1 . . . . .85 DX72
Sentinel Cl, Nthlt. UB5 . . . . . .78 BY70
Sentinel Sq, NW4 . . . . .63 CW56
Sentis Ct, Nthwd. HA6
off Carew Rd 39 BS51
September Way, Stan. HA7 . . .41 CH51
Sequoia Cl, Bushey (Bushey Hth.)
WD23 *off Giant Tree Hill* . . .41 CD46
Sequoia Gdns, Orp. BR6 . . . . .145 ET101
Sequoia Pk, Pnr. HA5 . . . . . . .40 CB51
Serbin Cl, E10 . . . . .67 EC59
Serenaders Rd, SW9 . . . . . . .101 DN82
Sergeants Grn La, Wal.Abb.
EN9 . . . . .16 EJ33
Sergeants Pl, Cat. CR3
off Coulsdon Rd 176 DQ122
Sergehill La, Abb.L. (Bedmond)
WD5 . . . . .7 BT27
Serjeants Inn, EC4 . . . . .196 E9
Serle St, WC2 . . . . .196 C8
Sermed Ct, Slou. SL2 . . . . . . .74 AW74
Sermon Dr, Swan. BR8 . . . . . .147 FC97
Sermon La, EC4 . . . . .197 H9
★ **Serpentine, The**, W2 . . . . . .198 B3
Serpentine Ct, Sev. TN13 . . . .191 FK122
★ **Serpentine Gall**, W2 . . . . . .198 A3
Serpentine Grn, Red. RH1
off Malmstone Av 185 DK129
Serpentine Rd, W2 . . . . .198 D3
Sevenoaks TN13 . . . . .191 FJ123
Service Rd, The, Pot.B. EN6 . . .12 DA32
Servidén Dr, Brom. BR1 . . . . .144 EK95
Setchell Rd, SE1 . . . . .201 P8
Setchell Way, SE1 . . . . .201 P8
Seth St, SE16 . . . . .202 G5
Seton Gdns, Dag. RM9 . . . . . . .88 EW66
Settle Pt, E13 *off London Rd* . .86 EG68
Settle Rd, E13 *off London Rd* . .86 EG68
Romford RM3 . . . . .52 FN49
Settles St, E1 . . . . .84 DU71
Settrington Rd, SW6 . . . . . . .100 DB82
Seven Acres, Cars. SM5 . . . . .140 DE103
Northwood HA6 . . . . .39 BU51
Swanley BR8 . . . . .147 FD100
Seven Arches App, Wey. KT13 .152 BM108
Seven Arches Rd, Brwd. CM14 .54 FX48
Seven Hills Cl, Walt. KT12 . . .153 BS109
Seven Hills Rd, Cob. KT11 . . .153 BS111
Iver SL0 . . . . .75 BC65
Walton-on-Thames KT12 . . .153 BS109
Seven Hills Rd S, Cob. KT11 .153 BS113
SEVEN KINGS, Ilf. 69 ES59
⇌ **Seven Kings** 69 ES60
Seven Kings Rd, Ilf. IG3 . . . . . .69 ET61
SEVENOAKS 191 FJ125
⇌ **Sevenoaks** 190 FG124
Sevenoaks Business Cen, Sev.
TN14 . . . . .191 FJ121
Sevenoaks Bypass, Sev. TN14 .190 FC123
Sevenoaks Cl, Bexh. DA7 . . . .107 FC84
Romford RM3 . . . . .52 FJ49
Sutton SM2 . . . . .158 DA110
SEVENOAKS COMMON, Sev. 191 FH129
Sevenoaks Ct, Nthwd. HA6 . . .39 BQ52
🅷 **Sevenoaks Hosp**, Sev.
TN13 . . . . .191 FJ121
Sevenoaks Ho, SE25 . . . . . . .142 DU97
★ **Sevenoaks Mus**, Sev.
TN13 . . . . .191 FJ125
Sevenoaks Rd, SE4 . . . . .123 DY86
Orpington BR6 . . . . .163 ET106
Orpington (Grn.St.Grn.)
BR6 . . . . .163 ET108
Sevenoaks (Otford) TN14 . .181 FH116
Sevenoaks Way, Orp. BR5 . . .126 EW94
Sidcup DA14 . . . . .126 EW94
⇌ **Seven Sisters** 66 DS57
⊖ **Seven Sisters** 66 DS57
Seven Sisters Rd, N4 . . . . . . .65 DM62
N7 . . . . .65 DM62
N15 . . . . .66 DQ59
Seven Stars Cor, W12
off Goldhawk Rd 99 CU76
Seventh Av, E12 . . . . .69 EM63
Hayes UB3 . . . . .77 BU74
Severnake Cl, E14 . . . . .204 A8
Severn Av, Rom. RM2 . . . . . . .71 FH55
Severn Cres, Slou. SL3 . . . . . .93 BB78
Severn Dr, Enf. EN1 . . . . .30 DU38
Severn Dr, Esher KT10 . . . . . .137 CG103
Upminster RM14 . . . . .73 FR58
Walton-on-Thames KT12 . .136 BX103
Severn Rd, S.Ock. (Aveley)
RM15 . . . . .90 FQ72
Severns Fld, Epp. CM16 . . . . . .18 EU29
Severnvale, St.Alb. (Lon.Col.)
AL2 *off Thamesdale* 10 CM27
Severn Way, NW10 . . . . .63 CT64
Watford WD25 . . . . .8 BW34
Severus Rd, SW11 . . . . .100 DE84
Seville Ms, N1 . . . . .84 DS66
Seville St, SW1 . . . . .198 E5
Sevington Rd, NW4 . . . . .63 CV58
Sevington St, W9 . . . . .82 DB70
Seward Rd, W7 . . . . .97 CG75
Beckenham BR3 . . . . .143 DX96
SEWARDSTONE, E4 . . . . .31 EC39
SEWARDSTONEBURY, E4 . . . . .32 EE42
Sewardstone Gdns, E4 . . . . . .31 EB43
Sewardstone Grn, E4 . . . . .32 EE42
Sewardstone Rd, E2 . . . . .84 DW68
E4 . . . . .47 EB45
Waltham Abbey EN9 . . . . . . .31 EC38
Sewardstone Roundabout,
Wal.Abb. EN9 . . . . .31 EC35
Sewardstone St, Wal.Abb. EN9 .15 EC34
Seward St, EC1 . . . . .196 G4
Sewdley St, E5 . . . . .67 DX62
Sewell Cl, Grays (Chaff.Hun.)
RM16 . . . . .109 FW78
Sewell Rd, SE2 . . . . .106 EU76
Sewell St, E13 . . . . .86 EG69
Sextant Av, E14 . . . . .204 F8
Sexton Cl, Rain. RM13
off Blake Cl 89 FF67
Waltham Cross (Chsht.) EN7
off Shambrook Rd 14 DQ25
Sexton Rd, Til. RM18 . . . . . . .111 GF81
Seymer Rd, Rom. RM1 . . . . . . .71 FD55
Seymour Av, N17 . . . . .46 DU54
Caterham CR3 . . . . .176 DQ123
Epsom KT17 . . . . .157 CV109
Morden SM4 . . . . .139 CX101
Seymour Cl, E.Mol. KT8 . . . . .136 CC99
Loughton IG10 . . . . .32 EL44
Pinner HA5 . . . . .40 BZ53
Seymour Ct, E4 . . . . .48 EF47
Seymour Dr, Brom. BR2 . . . . .145 EM102
Seymour Gdns, SE4 . . . . .103 DY83
Feltham TW13 . . . . .116 BW91
Ilford IG1 . . . . .69 EM60
Ruislip HA4 . . . . .60 BX60
Surbiton KT5 . . . . .138 CM99
Twickenham TW1 . . . . .117 CH87
Seymour Ms, W1 . . . . .194 F8
Seymour Pl, SE25 . . . . .142 DV98
W1 . . . . .194 D7
Seymour Rd, E4 . . . . .47 EB46
E6 . . . . .86 EK68
E10 . . . . .67 DZ60
N3 . . . . .44 DB52
N8 . . . . .65 DN57
N9 . . . . .46 DV47
SW18 . . . . .119 CZ87
SW19 . . . . .119 CX89
W4 . . . . .98 CQ77
Carshalton SM5 . . . . .158 DG106
Chalfont St. Giles HP8 . . . . .36 AW49
East Molesey KT8 . . . . .136 CC99
Gravesend (Nthflt.) DA11 . . .131 GF88
Hampton (Hmptn.H.) TW12 . .116 CC92
Kingston upon Thames KT1 .137 CK95
Mitcham CR4 . . . . .140 DG101
Tilbury RM18 . . . . .111 GF81
Seymours, The, Loug. IG10 . . .33 EN39
Seymour St, W1 . . . . .194 D9
W2 . . . . .194 D9
Seymour Ter, SE20 . . . . .142 DV95
Seymour Vil, SE20 . . . . .142 DV95
Seymour Wk, SW10 . . . . .100 DC79
Swanscombe DA10 . . . . . . .130 FY87
Seymour Way, Sun. TW16 . . . .115 BS93
Seyssel St, E14 . . . . .204 E8
Shaa Rd, W3 . . . . .80 CR73
Shacklands Rd, Sev. (Bad.Mt.)
TN14 . . . . .165 FB111
Shackleford Rd, Wok. GU22 . .167 BA121
Shacklegate La, Tedd. TW11 . .117 CE91
Shackleton Cl, SE23
off Featherstone Av 122 DV89
Shackleton Ct, E14
off Maritime Quay 103 EA78
W12 . . . . .99 CV75
Shackleton Rd, Slou. SL1 . . . . .74 AT73
Southall UB1 . . . . .78 BZ73
Shackleton Way, Abb.L. WD5
off Lysander Way 7 BU32
SHACKLEWELL, N16 . . . . .66 DT63
Shacklewell Grn, E8 . . . . .66 DT63
Shacklewell La, E8 . . . . .66 DT64
Shacklewell Rd, N16 . . . . .66 DT63
Shacklewell Row, E8 . . . . .66 DT63
Shacklewell St, E2 . . . . .84 DT70
Shadbolt Av, E4 . . . . .47 DY50
Shadbolt Cl, Wor.Pk. KT4 . . . .139 CT103
Shad Thames, SE1 . . . . .201 P3
SHADWELL, E1 . . . . .202 F1
⊖ **Shadwell** 84 DW73
DLR **Shadwell** 84 DW73
Shadwell Ct, Nthlt. UB5
off Shadwell Dr 78 BZ68
Shadwell Dr, Nthlt. UB5 . . . . .78 BZ69
Shadwell Gdns Est, E1
off Martha St 84 DW72
Shadwell Pierhead, E1 . . . . . .202 G1
Shadwell Pl, E1 *off Sutton St* .84 DW73
Shady Bush Cl, Bushey WD23
off Richfield Rd 40 CC45
Shady La, Wat. WD17 . . . . .23 BV40
Shaef Way, Tedd. TW11 . . . . .117 CG94
Shafter Rd, Dag. RM10 . . . . . . .89 FC65
Shaftesbury, Loug. IG10 . . . . . .32 EK41
Shaftesbury Av, W1 . . . . .195 M10
WC2 . . . . .195 M10
Barnet EN5 . . . . .28 DC42
Enfield EN3 . . . . .31 DX40
Shaftesbury Av, Felt. TW14 . .115 BU86
Harrow HA2 . . . . .60 CB60
Harrow (Kenton) HA3 . . . . . .61 CK58
Southall UB2 . . . . .96 CA77
Shaftesbury Circle, Har. HA2
off Shaftesbury Av 60 CC60
Shaftesbury Ct, N1
off Shaftesbury St 84 DR68
Shaftesbury Cres, Stai. TW18 .114 BK94
Shaftesbury Gdns, NW10 . . . .80 CS70
Shaftesbury La, Dart. DA1 . . .108 FP84
Shaftesbury Ms, SW4 *off Clapham Common S Side* 121 DJ85
W8 *off Stratford Rd* 100 DA76
Shaftesbury Pl, W14
off Warwick Rd 99 CZ77
Shaftesbury Pt, E13 *off High St* .86 EH68
Shaftesbury Rd, E4 . . . . .47 ED46
E7 . . . . .86 EJ66
E10 . . . . .67 EA60
E17 . . . . .67 EB58
N18 . . . . .46 DS51
N19 . . . . .65 DL60
Beckenham BR3 . . . . .143 DZ96
Carshalton SM5 . . . . .140 DD101
Epping CM16 . . . . .17 ET29
Richmond TW9 . . . . .98 CL83
Romford RM1 . . . . .71 FF58
Watford WD17 . . . . .24 BW41
Woking GU22 . . . . .167 BA117
Shaftesburys, The, Bark. IG11 .87 EQ67
Shaftesbury St, N1 . . . . .197 J1
Shaftesbury Way, Kings L. WD4 .7 BQ28
Twickenham TW2 . . . . .117 CD90
Shaftesbury Waye, Hayes UB4 .77 BV71
Shafto Ms, SW1 . . . . .198 D7
Shafton Rd, E9 . . . . .85 DX67
Shaggy Calf La, Slou. SL2 . . . .74 AU73
Shakespeare Av, N11 . . . . .45 DJ50
NW10 . . . . .80 CR67
Feltham TW14 . . . . .115 BU86
Hayes UB4 . . . . .77 BV70
Tilbury RM18 . . . . .111 GH82
Shakespeare Cres, E12 . . . . . .87 EM65
NW10 . . . . .80 CR67
Shakespeare Dr, Har. HA3 . . . .62 CM58
Shakespeare Gdns, N2 . . . . . .64 DF56
Shakespeare Ho, N14
off High St 45 DK47
Shakespeare Rd, E17 . . . . . . .47 DX54
N3 *off Popes Dr* 44 DA53
NW7 . . . . .43 CT49
SE24 . . . . .121 DP85
W3 . . . . .80 CQ74
W7 . . . . .79 CF73
Addlestone KT15 . . . . .152 BK105
Bexleyheath DA7 . . . . .106 EY81
Dartford DA1 . . . . .108 FN84
Romford RM1 . . . . .71 FF58
★ **Shakespeare's Globe Thea**,
SE1 . . . . .201 H1
Shakespeare Sq, Ilf. IG6 . . . . .49 EQ51
Shakespeare St, Wat. WD24 . . .23 BV38
Shakespeare Twr, EC2 . . . . . .197 J6
Shakespeare Way, Felt. TW13 .116 BW91
Shakspeare Ms, N16
off Shakspeare Wk 66 DS63
Shakspeare Wk, N16 . . . . .66 DS63
Shalbourne Sq, E9 . . . . .85 DZ65
Shalcomb St, SW10 . . . . .100 DC79
Shalcross Dr, Wal.Cr. (Chsht.)
EN8 . . . . .15 DZ30
Shalden Ho, SW15
off Tunworth Cres 119 CT86
Shaldon Dr, Mord. SM4 . . . . .139 CY99
Ruislip HA4 . . . . .60 BW62
Shaldon Rd, Edg. HA8 . . . . . . .42 CM53
Shaldon Way, Walt. KT12 . . .136 BW104
Shale Grn, Red. RH1
off Bletchingley Rd 185 DK129
Shalfleet Dr, W10 . . . . .81 CX73
Shalford Cl, Orp. BR6 . . . . . .163 EQ105
Shalimar Gdns, W3 . . . . .80 CQ73
Shalimar Rd, W3
off Hereford Rd 80 CQ73
Shallons Rd, SE9 . . . . .125 EP91
Shalstone Rd, SW14 . . . . .98 CP83
Shalston Vil, Surb. KT6 . . . . .138 CM100
Shambrook Rd, Wal.Cr. (Chsht.)
EN7 . . . . .13 DP25
Shamrock Cl, Lthd. (Fetch.)
KT22 . . . . .171 CD121
Shamrock Ho, SE26
off Talisman Sq 122 DU91
Shamrock Rd, Croy. CR0 . . . .141 DM100
Gravesend DA12 . . . . .131 GL87
Shamrock St, SW4 . . . . .101 DK83
Shamrock Way, N14 . . . . .45 DH46
Shandon Rd, SW4 . . . . .121 DJ86
Shand St, SE1 . . . . .201 M4
Shandy St, E1 . . . . .85 DX71
Shanklin Cl, Wal.Cr. EN7
off Hornbeam Way 14 DT29
Shanklin Gdns, Wat. WD19 . . . .40 BW49
Shanklin Rd, N8 . . . . .65 DK57
N15 . . . . .66 DU56
Shanklin Way, SE15
off Pentridge St 102 DT80
Shannon Cl, NW2 . . . . .63 CX62
Southall UB2 . . . . .96 BX78
Shannon Gro, SW9 . . . . .101 DM84
Shannon Pl, NW8
off Allitsen Rd 82 DE68
Shannon Way, Beck. BR3 . . . . .123 EB93
South Ockendon (Aveley)
RM15 . . . . .90 FQ73
Shantock Hall La, Hem.H. (Bov.)
HP3 . . . . .4 AY29
Shantock La, Hem.H. (Bov.) HP3 .4 AX30
Shap Cres, Cars. SM5 . . . . . .140 DF102
Shapland Way, N13 . . . . .45 DM50
Shapwick Cl, N11
off Friern Barnet Rd 44 DF50
Shardcroft Av, SE24 . . . . .121 DP85
Shardeloes Rd, SE14 . . . . . . .103 DZ83
Sharland Cl, Th.Hth. CR7
off Dunheved Rd N 141 DN100
Sharland Rd, Grav. DA12 . . . . .131 GJ89
Sharman Ct, Sid. DA14 . . . . . .126 EU91
Sharnbrooke Cl, Well. DA16 . .106 EW83
Sharney Av, Slou. SL3 . . . . . . .93 BB76
Sharon Cl, Epsom KT19 . . . . .156 CQ113
Leatherhead (Bkhm.) KT23 . .170 CA124
Surbiton KT6 . . . . .137 CK102
Sharon Gdns, E9 . . . . .84 DW67
Sharon Rd, W4 . . . . .98 CR78
Enfield EN3 . . . . .31 DY40
Sharpe Cl, W7
off Templeman Rd 79 CF71
Sharpleshall St, NW1 . . . . . . .82 DF66
Sharpness Cl, Hayes UB4 . . . .78 BY71
Sharps La, Ruis. HA4 . . . . .59 BR60
Sharp Way, Dart. DA1 . . . . . .108 FM83
Sharratt St, SE15 . . . . .102 DW79
Sharsted St, SE17 . . . . .101 DP78
Sharvel La, Nthlt. UB5 . . . . . . .77 BU67
Shavers Pl, SW1 . . . . .199 M1
Shaw Av, Bark. IG11 . . . . .88 EY68
Shawbrooke Rd, SE9 . . . . . . .124 EJ85
Shawbury Rd, SE22 . . . . .122 DT85
Shaw Cl, SE28 . . . . .88 EV74
Bushey (Bushey Hth.) WD23 . .41 CE47
Chertsey (Ott.) KT16 . . . . . .151 BC107
Epsom KT17 . . . . .157 CT111
Hornchurch RM11 . . . . .71 FH60
South Croydon CR2 . . . . . .160 DT112
Waltham Cross (Chsht.) EN8 .14 DW28
Shaw Ct, SW11 . . . . .100 DD83
Windsor SL4 . . . . .112 AU85
Shaw Cres, Brwd. CM13 . . . . . .55 GD43
South Croydon CR2 . . . . . .160 DT112
Tilbury RM18 . . . . .111 GH81
Shaw Dr, Walt. KT12 . . . . . . .136 BW101
Shawfield Ct, West Dr. UB7 . . .94 BL76
Shawfield Pk, Brom. BR1 . . .144 EK96
Shawfield St, SW3 . . . . .100 DE78
Shawford Ct, SW15 . . . . .119 CU87
Shawford Rd, Epsom KT19 . .156 CR107
Shaw Gdns, Bark. IG11 . . . . . .88 EY68
Shawley Cres, Epsom KT18 . .173 CW118
Shawley Way, Epsom KT18 . .173 CV118
Shaw Rd, SE22 . . . . .102 DS84
Bromley BR1 . . . . .124 EF90
Enfield EN3 . . . . .31 DX39
Westerham (Tats.) TN16 . . .178 EJ120
Shaws Cotts, SE23 . . . . .123 DY90
Shaw Sq, E17 . . . . .47 DY53
Shaw Way, Wall. SM6 . . . . . .159 DL108
Shaxton Cres, Croy. (New Adgtn.)
CR0 . . . . .161 EC109
Shearing Dr, Cars. SM5
off Stavordale Rd 140 DC101
Shearling Way, N7 . . . . .83 DL65
Shearman Rd, SE3 . . . . .104 EF84
Shears Ct, Sun. TW16
off Staines Rd W 115 BS94
Shearsmith Ho, E1
off Cable St 84 DU73
Shearwater Cl, Bark. IG11 . . . .88 EU69
Shearwater Rd, Sutt. SM1 . . .157 CZ106
Shearwater Way, Hayes UB4 . .78 BX72
Shearwood Cres, Dart. DA1 . .107 FF83
Sheath's La, Lthd. KT22 . . . . .154 CB113
Sheaveshill Av, NW9 . . . . .62 CS56
Sheehy Way, Slou. SL2 . . . . . .74 AV73
Sheen Common Dr, Rich.
TW10 . . . . .98 CN84
Sheen Ct, Rich. TW10 . . . . .98 CN84
Sheen Ct Rd, Rich. TW10 . . . . .98 CN84
Sheendale Rd, Rich. TW9 . . . . .98 CM84
Sheenewood, SE26 . . . . .122 DV92
Sheen Gate Gdns, SW14 . . . . .98 CQ84
Sheen Gro, N1
off Richmond Av 83 DN67
Sheen La, SW14 . . . . .98 CQ83
Sheen Pk, Rich. TW9 . . . . .98 CM84
Sheen Rd, Orp. BR5 . . . . .145 ET98
Richmond TW9, TW10 . . . . .118 CL85
Sheen Way, Wall. SM6 . . . . . .159 DM106
Sheen Wd, SW14 . . . . .118 CQ85
Sheepbarn La, Warl. CR6 . . . .162 EF112
Sheepcot Dr, Wat. WD25 . . . . . .8 BW34
Sheepcote Cl, Houns. TW5 . . . .95 BU80
Sheepcote Gdns, Uxb. (Denh.)
UB9 . . . . .58 BG58
Sheepcote La, SW11 . . . . . . .100 DF82
Orpington BR5 . . . . .146 EZ99
Swanley BR8 . . . . .146 EZ98
Sheepcote Rd, Har. HA1 . . . . . .61 CF58
Sheepcotes Rd, Rom. RM6 . . . .70 EX56
Sheepcot La, Wat. WD25 . . . . . .7 BV34
Sheephouse Way, N.Mal. KT3 .138 CS101
Sheep La, E8 . . . . .84 DV67
Sheep Wk, Epsom KT17 . . . . .172 CR122
Reigate RH2 . . . . .183 CY131
Shepperton TW17 . . . . .134 BM101
Sheep Wk, The, Wok. GU22 . .167 BE118
Sheep Wk Ms, SW19 . . . . . . .119 CX93
Sheerness Ms, E16 . . . . .105 EP75
SHEERWATER, Wok. 151 BC113
Sheerwater Av, Add. (Woodham)
KT15 . . . . .151 BE112
Sheerwater Rd, E16 . . . . .86 EK71
Addlestone (Woodham)
KT15 . . . . .151 BE112
West Byfleet KT14 . . . . . . .151 BE112
Sheffield Dr, Rom. RM3 . . . . . .52 FN50
Sheffield Gdns, Rom. RM3 . . . .52 FN50
Sheffield Rd, Houns. (Hthrw.Air.)
TW6 *off Southern Perimeter Rd* 115 BR85
Sheffield Sq, E3
off Malmesbury Rd 85 DZ69
Sheffield St, WC2 . . . . .196 B9
Sheffield Ter, W8 . . . . .82 DA74
Shefton Ri, Nthwd. HA6 . . . . . .39 BU52
Sheila Cl, Rom. RM5 . . . . .51 FB52
Sheila Rd, Rom. RM5 . . . . .51 FB52
Sheilings, The, Horn. RM11 . . .72 FM57
Shelbourne Cl, Pnr. HA5 . . . . .60 BZ55
Shelbourne Pl, Beck. BR3 . . . .123 DZ94
Shelbourne Rd, N17 . . . . .46 DV54
Shelburne Dr, Houns. TW4
off Hanworth Rd 116 CA86

325

She - Shu

Shelburne Rd, N7 ... 65 DM63
Shelbury Cl, Sid. DA14 ... 126 EU90
Shelbury Rd, SE22 ... 122 DV85
Sheldon Av, N6 ... 64 DE59
  Ilford IG5 ... 49 EP54
Sheldon Cl, SE12 ... 124 EH85
  SE20 ... 142 DV95
  Waltham Cross (Chsht.) EN7 ... 14 DS26
Sheldon Rd, N18 ... 46 DS49
  NW2 ... 63 CX63
  Bexleyheath DA7 ... 106 EZ81
  Dagenham RM9 ... 88 EY66
Sheldon St, Croy. CR0 *off Wandle Rd* ... 142 DQ104
Sheldrake Cl, E16 ... 87 EM74
Sheldrake Pl, W8 ... 99 CZ75
Sheldrick Cl, SW19 ... 140 DD96
Shelduck Cl, E15 ... 68 EF64
Sheldwich Ter, Brom. BR2 ... 144 EL100
Shelford Pl, N16 *off Stoke Newington Ch St* ... 66 DR62
Shelford Ri, SE19 ... 122 DT94
Shelford Rd, Barn. EN5 ... 27 CW44
Shelgate Rd, SW11 ... 120 DE85
Shellbank La, Dart. (Bean) DA2 ... 129 FU93
★ Shell Cen, SE1 ... 200 C3
Shell Cl, Brom. BR2 ... 145 EM100
Shellduck Cl, NW9 *off Swan Dr* ... 42 CS54
Shell Est, N16 ... 66 DS64
Shelley Av, E12 ... 86 EL65
  Greenford UB6 ... 79 CD69
  Hornchurch RM12 ... 71 FF61
Shelley Cl, SE15 ... 102 DV82
  Banstead SM7 ... 173 CX115
  Coulsdon CR5 ... 175 DM117
  Edgware HA8 ... 42 CN49
  Greenford UB6 ... 79 CD69
  Hayes UB4 ... 77 BU71
  Northwood HA6 ... 39 BT50
  Orpington BR6 ... 145 ES104
  Slough SL3 ... 93 AZ78
Shelley Cres, Houns. TW5 ... 96 BX82
  Southall UB1 ... 78 BZ72
Shelley Dr, Well. DA16 ... 105 ES81
Shelley Gdns, Wem. HA0 ... 61 CJ61
Shelley Gro, Loug. IG10 ... 33 EM42
Shelley La, Uxb. (Hare.) UB9 ... 38 BG53
Shelley Pl, Til. RM18 *off Kipling Av* ... 111 GH81
Shelley Rd, NW10 ... 80 CR67
  Brentwood CM13 ... 55 GD45
Shelleys La, Sev. (Knock.) TN14 ... 179 ET116
Shelley Way, SW19 ... 120 DD93
Shellfield Cl, Stai. TW19 ... 114 BG85
Shellness Rd, E5 ... 66 DV64
Shell Rd, SE13 ... 103 EB83
Shellwood Rd, SW11 ... 100 DF82
Shelmerdine Cl, E3 ... 85 EA71
Shelson Av, Felt. TW13 ... 115 BT90
Shelton Av, Warl. CR6 ... 176 DW117
Shelton Cl, Warl. CR6 ... 176 DW117
Shelton Ct, Slou. SL3 *off London Rd* ... 92 AW76
Shelton Rd, SW19 ... 140 DA95
Shelton St, WC2 ... 195 P9
Shelvers Grn, Tad. KT20 ... 173 CW121
Shelvers Hill, Tad. KT20 *off Ashurst Rd* ... 173 CW121
Shelvers Spur, Tad. KT20 ... 173 CW121
Shelvers Way, Tad. KT20 ... 173 CW121
Shenden Cl, Sev. TN13 ... 191 FJ128
Shenden Way, Sev. TN13 ... 191 FJ128
SHENFIELD, Brwd. ... 55 GA45
⇌ Shenfield ... 55 GA45
Shenfield Cl, Couls. CR5 *off Woodfield Cl* ... 175 DJ119
Shenfield Common, Brwd. CM15 ... 54 FY48
Shenfield Cres, Brwd. CM15 ... 54 FY47
Shenfield Gdns, Brwd. CM13 ... 55 GB44
Shenfield Grn, Brwd. CM15 *off Hutton Rd* ... 55 GA45
Shenfield Ho, SE18 *off Shooter's Hill Rd* ... 104 EK80
Shenfield Pl, Brwd. CM15 ... 54 FY45
Shenfield Rd, Brwd. CM15 ... 54 FX46
  Woodford Green IG8 ... 48 EH52
Shenfield St, N1 ... 197 N1
SHENLEY, Rad. ... 10 CN33
Shenley Av, Ruis. HA4 ... 59 BT61
Shenleybury, Rad. (Shenley) WD7 ... 10 CL30
Shenleybury Cotts, Rad. (Shenley) WD7 ... 10 CL31
Shenley Hill, Rad. WD7 ... 25 CG35
Shenley La, St.Alb. (Lon.Col.) AL2 ... 9 CJ27
Shenley Manor, Rad. (Shenley) WD7 ... 9 CK33
Shenley Rd, SE5 ... 102 DS81
  Borehamwood WD6 ... 26 CN42
  Dartford DA1 ... 128 FN86
  Hounslow TW5 ... 96 BY81
  Radlett WD7 ... 9 CH34
Shenstone Cl, Dart. DA1 ... 107 FD84
Shenstone Gdns, Rom. RM3 ... 52 FJ53
Shepcot Ho, N14 ... 29 DJ44
Shepherd Cl, W1 *off Lees Pl* ... 82 DG73
  Abbots Langley WD5 ... 7 BT30
Shepherdess Pl, N1 ... 197 J2
Shepherdess Wk, N1 ... 84 DQ68
Shepherd Mkt, W1 ... 199 H2
SHEPHERD'S BUSH, W12 ... 81 CW74
⊖ Shepherd's Bush ... 99 CW75
Shepherds Bush Grn, W12 ... 99 CW75
Shepherds Bush Mkt, W12 ... 99 CW75
Shepherds Bush Pl, W12 ... 99 CX75
Shepherds Bush Rd, W6 ... 99 CW77
Shepherds Cl, N6 ... 65 DH58
  Leatherhead KT22 ... 172 CL124
  Orpington BR6 *off Stapleton Rd* ... 145 ET104
  Romford RM6 ... 70 EX57
  Shepperton TW17 ... 135 BP100
Shepherds Cl, Uxb. (Cowley) UB8 *off High St* ... 76 BJ70
Shepherds Ct, W12 *off Shepherds Bush Grn* ... 99 CX75
Shepherds Grn, Chis. BR7 ... 125 ER94
Shepherds Hill, N6 ... 65 DH58
  Redhill RH1 ... 185 DJ126
  Romford RM3 ... 52 FN54
Shepherds La, E9 ... 67 DX64
Shepherd's La, Brwd. CM14 ... 54 FS45
Shepherds La, Dart. DA1 ... 127 FG88
  Rickmansworth WD3 ... 37 BF45
Shepherds Path, Nthlt. UB5 *off Fortunes Mead* ... 78 BY65
Shepherd's Pl, W1 ... 194 F10
Shepherds Rd, Wat. WD18 ... 23 BT41
Shepherd St, W1 ... 199 H3
  Gravesend (Nthflt.) DA11 ... 130 GD87
Shepherds Wk, NW2 ... 63 CU61
  NW3 ... 64 DD64
  Bushey (Bushey Hth.) WD23 ... 41 CD47
Shepherds' Wk, Epsom KT18 ... 172 CP121
Shepherds Way, Hat. (Brook.Pk.) AL9 ... 12 DC27
  Rickmansworth WD3 ... 38 BH45
  South Croydon CR2 ... 161 DX108
Shepiston La, Hayes UB3 ... 95 BR77
  West Drayton UB7 ... 95 BQ77
Shepley Cl, Cars. SM5 ... 140 DG104
  Hornchurch RM12 *off Chevington Way* ... 72 FK64
Shepley Ms, Enf. EN3 ... 31 EA37
Sheppard Cl, Enf. EN1 ... 30 DV39
  Kingston upon Thames KT1 *off Beaufort Rd* ... 138 CL98
Sheppard Dr, SE16 ... 202 D10
Sheppard St, E16 ... 86 EF70
SHEPPERTON ... 134 BN101
⇌ Shepperton ... 135 BQ99
Shepperton Business Pk, Shep. TW17 ... 135 BQ99
Shepperton Cl, Borwd. WD6 ... 26 CR39
Shepperton Ct, Shep. TW17 ... 135 BP100
Shepperton Ct Dr, Shep. TW17 ... 135 BP99
Shepperton Rd, N1 ... 84 DQ67
  Orpington BR5 ... 145 EQ100
  Staines TW18 ... 134 BJ97
Sheppey Cl, Erith DA8 ... 107 FH80
Sheppey Gdns, Dag. RM9 *off Sheppey Rd* ... 88 EW66
Sheppey Rd, Dag. RM9 ... 88 EV66
Sheppeys La, Abb.L. (Bedmond) WD5 ... 7 BS28
Sheppey Wk, N1 *off Clephane Rd* ... 84 DQ66
Sheppy Pl, Grav. DA12 ... 131 GH87
Sherard Ct, N7 *off Manor Gdns* ... 65 DL62
Sherard Rd, SE9 ... 124 EL85
Sheraton Business Cen, Grnf. UB6 ... 79 CH68
Sheraton Cl, Borwd. (Elstree) WD6 ... 26 CM43
Sheraton Dr, Epsom KT19 ... 156 CQ113
Sheraton Ms, Wat. WD18 ... 23 BS42
Sheraton St, W1 ... 195 M9
Sherborne Av, Enf. EN3 ... 30 DW40
  Southall UB2 ... 96 CA77
Sherborne Cl, Epsom KT18 ... 173 CW117
  Hayes UB4 ... 78 BW72
  Slough (Colnbr.) SL3 ... 93 BE81
Sherborne Cres, Cars. SM5 ... 140 DE101
Sherborne Gdns, NW9 ... 62 CN55
  W13 ... 79 CH72
  Romford RM5 ... 50 FA50
Sherborne La, EC4 ... 197 K10
Sherborne Pl, Nthwd. HA6 ... 39 BR51
Sherborne Rd, Chess. KT9 ... 156 CL106
  Feltham TW14 ... 115 BR87
  Orpington BR5 ... 145 ET98
  Sutton SM3 ... 140 DA103
Sherborne St, N1 ... 84 DR67
Sherborne Wk, Lthd. KT22 *off Windfield* ... 171 CJ121
Sherborne Way, Rick. (Crox.Grn.) WD3 ... 23 BP42
Sherboro Rd, N15 *off Ermine Rd* ... 66 DT58
Sherbourne Cotts, Wat. WD18 *off Watford Fld Rd* ... 24 BW43
Sherbourne Gdns, Shep. TW17 ... 135 BS101
Sherbourne Pl, Stan. HA7 ... 41 CG51
Sherbrooke Cl, Bexh. DA6 ... 106 FA84
Sherbrooke Rd, SW6 ... 99 CZ80
Sherbrook Gdns, N21 ... 45 DP45
Shere Av, Sutt. SM2 ... 157 CW110
Shere Cl, Chess. KT9 ... 155 CK106
Sheredan Rd, E4 ... 47 ED50
Shere Rd, Ilf. IG2 ... 69 EN57
Sherfield Av, Rick. WD3 ... 38 BK47
Sherfield Cl, N.Mal. KT3 ... 138 CP98
Sherfield Gdns, SW15 ... 119 CT86
Sherfield Rd, Grays RM17 ... 110 GB79
Sheridan Cl, Rom. RM3 ... 51 FH52
  Swanley BR8 *off Willow Av* ... 147 FF97
  Uxbridge UB10 *off Alpha Rd* ... 77 BQ70
Sheridan Ct, Houns. TW4 *off Vickers Way* ... 116 BZ85
  Northolt UB5 ... 60 CB64
Sheridan Cres, Chis. BR7 ... 145 EP96
Sheridan Dr, Reig. RH2 ... 184 DB132
Sheridan Gdns, Har. HA3 ... 61 CK58
Sheridan Ms, E11 *off Woodbine Pl* ... 68 EG58
Sheridan Pl, SW13 *off Brookwood Av* ... 99 CT82
  Hampton TW12 ... 136 CB95
Sheridan Rd, E7 ... 68 EF62
  E12 ... 68 EL64
  SW19 ... 139 CZ95
  Belvedere DA17 ... 106 FA77
  Bexleyheath DA7 ... 106 EY83
  Richmond TW10 ... 117 CJ90
  Watford WD19 ... 40 BX45
Sheridan St, E1 *off Watney St* ... 84 DV72
Sheridan Ter, Nthlt. UB5 *off Whitton Av W* ... 60 CB64
Sheridan Wk, NW11 ... 64 DA58
  Carshalton SM5 *off Carshalton Pk Rd* ... 158 DF106
Sheridan Way, Beck. BR3 *off Turners Meadow Way* ... 143 DZ95
Sheriff Way, Wat. WD25 ... 7 BU33
Sheringham Av, E12 ... 69 EM63
  N14 ... 29 DK43
  Feltham TW13 ... 115 BU90
  Romford RM7 ... 71 FC58
  Twickenham TW2 ... 116 BZ88
Sheringham Dr, Bark. IG11 ... 69 ET64
Sheringham Rd, N7 ... 83 DM65
  SE20 ... 142 DV97
Sheringham Twr, Sthl. UB1 ... 78 CB73
Sherington Av, Pnr. HA5 ... 40 CA52
Sherington Rd, SE7 ... 104 EH79
Sherland Rd, Twick. TW1 ... 117 CF88
Sherlies Av, Orp. BR6 ... 145 ES103
★ Sherlock Holmes Mus, NW1 ... 194 E5
Sherlock Ms, W1 ... 194 F6
Sherman Rd, Brom. BR1 ... 144 EG95
  Slough SL1 ... 74 AS71
Shernbroke Rd, Wal.Abb. EN9 ... 16 EF34
Shernhall St, E17 ... 67 EC57
Sherrard Rd, E7 ... 86 EJ65
  E12 ... 86 EK65
Sherrards Way, Barn. EN5 ... 28 DA43
Sherrick Grn Rd, NW10 ... 63 CV64
Sherriff Rd, NW6 ... 82 DA65
Sherringham Av, N17 ... 46 DU54
Sherrin Rd, E10 ... 67 EA63
Sherrock Gdns, NW4 ... 63 CU56
Sherry Ms, Bark. IG11 *off Cecil Av* ... 87 ER66
Sherwin Rd, SE14 ... 103 DX81
Sherwood Av, E18 ... 68 EH55
  SW16 ... 121 DK94
  Greenford UB6 ... 79 CE65
  Hayes UB4 ... 77 BV70
  Potters Bar EN6 ... 11 CY32
  Ruislip HA4 ... 59 BS58
Sherwood Cl, SW13 *off Lower Common S* ... 99 CV83
  W13 ... 79 CH74
  Bexley DA5 ... 126 EW86
  Leatherhead (Fetch.) KT22 ... 170 CC122
  Slough SL3 ... 92 AY76
Sherwood Ct, Slou. (Colnbr.) SL3 *off High St* ... 93 BD80
Sherwood Gdns, E14 ... 204 A8
  SE16 ... 102 DU78
  Barking IG11 ... 87 ER66
Sherwood Pk Av, Sid. DA15 ... 126 EU87
Sherwood Pk Rd, Mitch. CR4 ... 141 DJ98
  Sutton SM1 ... 158 DA106
Sherwood Rd, NW4 ... 63 CW55
  SW19 ... 119 CZ94
  Coulsdon CR5 ... 175 DJ116
  Croydon CR0 ... 142 DV101
  Hampton (Hmptn.H.) TW12 ... 116 CC92
  Harrow HA2 ... 60 CC61
  Ilford IG6 ... 69 ER56
  Welling DA16 ... 105 ES82
  Woking (Knap.) GU21 ... 166 AS117
Sherwoods Rd, Wat. WD19 ... 40 BY45
Sherwood St, N20 ... 44 DD48
  W1 ... 195 L10
Sherwood Ter, N20 *off Green Rd* ... 44 DD48
Sherwood Way, W.Wick. BR4 ... 143 EB103
Shetland Cl, Borwd. WD6 *off Percheron Rd* ... 26 CR44
Shetland Rd, E3 ... 85 DZ68
Shevon Way, Brwd. CM14 ... 54 FT49
Shewens Rd, Wey. KT13 ... 153 BR105
Shey Copse, Wok. GU22 ... 167 BC117
Shield Dr, Brent. TW8 ... 97 CG79
Shieldhall St, SE2 ... 106 EW77
Shield Rd, Ashf. TW15 ... 115 BQ91
Shifford Path, SE23 ... 123 DX90
Shilburn Way, Wok. GU21 ... 166 AU118
Shillibeer Pl, W1 ... 194 C6
Shillibeer Wk, Chig. IG7 ... 49 ET48
Shillingford Cl, NW7 *off Bittacy Hill* ... 43 CY52
Shillingford St, N1 *off Cross St* ... 83 DP66
Shillitoe Av, Pot.B. EN6 ... 11 CX32
Shinfield St, W12 ... 81 CW72
Shingle Ct, Wal.Abb. EN9 ... 16 EG33
Shinglewell Rd, Erith DA8 ... 106 FA80
Shinners Cl, SE25 ... 142 DU99
Ship All, W4 *off Thames Rd* ... 98 CN79
Ship & Mermaid Row, SE1 ... 201 L4
Shipfield Cl, West. (Tats.) TN16 ... 178 EJ121
Ship Hill, West. (Tats.) TN16 ... 178 EJ121
Shipka Rd, SW12 ... 121 DH88
Ship La, SW14 ... 98 CQ82
  Brentwood CM13 ... 55 GF41
  Dartford (Sutt.H.) DA4 ... 148 FK95
  Purfleet RM19 ... 109 FS76
  South Ockendon (Aveley) RM15 ... 109 FR75
  Swanley BR8 ... 148 FK95
Ship La Caravan Site, S.Ock. RM15 ... 109 FR76
Shipman Rd, E16 ... 86 EH72
  SE23 ... 123 DX89
Ship St, SE8 ... 103 EA81
Ship Tavern Pas, EC3 ... 197 M10
Shipton Cl, Dag. RM8 ... 70 EX62
Shipton St, E2 ... 84 DT69
Shipwright Rd, SE16 ... 203 K5
Ship Yd, E14 ... 204 B10
  Weybridge KT13 *off High St* ... 153 BP105
Shirburn Cl, SE23 *off Tyson Rd* ... 122 DW87
Shirbutt St, E14 ... 85 EB73
Shirebrook Rd, SE3 ... 104 EK83
Shire Cl, Brox. EN10 *off Groom Rd* ... 15 DZ26
Shire Ct, Epsom KT17 ... 157 CT108
Shire Ct, Erith DA18 *off St. John Fisher Rd* ... 106 EX76
Shirehall Cl, NW4 ... 63 CX58
Shirehall Gdns, NW4 ... 63 CX58
Shirehall La, NW4 ... 63 CX58
Shirehall Pk, NW4 ... 63 CX58
Shirehall Rd, Dart. DA2 ... 128 FK92
Shire Horse Way, Islw. TW7 ... 97 CF83
Shire La, Ger.Cr. (Chal.St.P.) SL9 ... 37 BD54
  Keston BR2 ... 163 EM108
  Orpington BR6 ... 163 ER107
  Rickmansworth (Chorl.) WD3 ... 21 BB43
  Uxbridge (Denh.) UB9 ... 57 BE55
Shiremeade, Borwd. (Elstree) WD6 ... 26 CM43
Shire Pl, SW18 *off Whitehead Cl* ... 120 DC87
Shires, The, Rich. TW10 ... 118 CL91
  Watford WD25 *off High Elms La* ... 8 BW31
Shires Cl, Ashtd. KT21 ... 171 CK118
Shires Ho, W.Byf. (Byfleet) KT14 *off Eden Gro Rd* ... 152 BL113
Shirland Ms, W9 ... 81 CZ69
Shirland Rd, W9 ... 82 DA69
SHIRLEY, Croy. ... 143 DX104
Shirley Av, Bex. DA5 ... 126 EX87
  Coulsdon CR5 ... 175 DP119
  Croydon CR0 ... 142 DW102
  Sutton SM1 ... 158 DE105
  Sutton (Cheam) SM2 ... 157 CZ109
Shirley Ch Rd, Croy. CR0 ... 143 DX104
Shirley Cl, E17 *off Addison Rd* ... 67 EB57
  Dartford DA1 ... 108 FJ84
  Hounslow TW3 ... 116 CC85
  Waltham Cross (Chsht.) EN8 ... 14 DW29
Shirley Ct, Croy. CR0 ... 143 DX104
Shirley Cres, Beck. BR3 ... 143 DY98
Shirley Dr, Houns. TW3 ... 116 CC85
Shirley Gdns, W7 ... 79 CF74
  Barking IG11 ... 87 ES65
  Hornchurch RM12 ... 72 FJ61
Shirley Gro, N9 ... 46 DW45
  SW11 ... 100 DG83
Shirley Hts, Wall. SM6 ... 159 DJ109
Shirley Hills Rd, Croy. CR0 ... 161 DX106
Shirley Ho Dr, SE7 ... 104 EJ80
H Shirley Oaks Hosp, Croy. CR0 ... 142 DW101
Shirley Oaks Rd, Croy. CR0 ... 143 DX102
Shirley Pk Rd, Croy. CR0 ... 142 DV102
Shirley Rd, E15 ... 86 EE66
  W4 ... 98 CR75
  Abbots Langley WD5 ... 7 BT32
  Croydon CR0 ... 142 DV101
  Enfield EN2 ... 30 DQ41
  Sidcup DA15 ... 125 ES90
  Wallington SM6 ... 159 DJ109
Shirley St, E16 ... 86 EF72
Shirley Way, Croy. CR0 ... 143 DY104
Shirlock Rd, NW3 ... 64 DF63
Shirwell Cl, NW7 *off Bittacy Hill* ... 43 CY52
Shobden Rd, N17 ... 46 DR53
Shobroke Cl, NW2 ... 63 CW62
Shoebury Rd, E6 ... 87 EM66
Shoe La, EC4 ... 196 E8
Sholden Gdns, Orp. BR5 ... 146 EW99
Sholto Rd, Houns. (Hthrw.Air.) TW6 ... 114 BM85
Shonks Mill Rd, Rom. (Nave.) RM4 ... 35 FG37
Shooters Av, Har. HA3 ... 61 CJ56
SHOOTER'S HILL, SE18 ... 105 EQ81
Shooter's Hill, SE18 ... 105 EN81
  Welling DA16 ... 105 EN81
Shooter's Hill Rd, SE3 ... 104 EF81
  SE10 ... 103 ED81
  SE18 ... 104 EH80
Shooters Rd, Enf. EN2 ... 29 DP39
Shoot Up Hill, NW2 ... 63 CY64
Shord Hill, Ken. CR8 ... 176 DR116
Shore, The, Grav. (Nthflt.) DA11 ... 130 GC85
  Gravesend (Rosh.) DA11 ... 131 GF86
Shore Cl, Felt. TW14 ... 115 BU87
  Hampton TW12 *off Stewart Cl* ... 116 BY92
Shorediche Cl, Uxb. UB10 ... 58 BM62
SHOREDITCH, E1 ... 197 P5
⊖ Shoreditch ... 84 DT70
Shoreditch High St, E1 ... 197 N3
Shoreditch Ho, N1 ... 197 L3
Shore Gro, Felt. TW13 ... 116 CA89
SHOREHAM, Sev. ... 165 FG111
⇌ Shoreham ... 165 FG111
Shoreham Cl, SW18 *off Ram St* ... 120 DB85
  Bexley DA5 *off Stansted Cres* ... 126 EX88
  Croydon CR0 ... 142 DW100
Shoreham La, Orp. BR6 ... 164 FA107
  Sevenoaks TN13 ... 190 FF122
  Sevenoaks (Halst.) TN14 ... 164 EZ112
Shoreham Pl, Sev. (Shore.) TN14 ... 165 FG112
Shoreham Rd, Orp. BR5 ... 146 EV95
  Sevenoaks (Otford) TN14 ... 165 FH111
Shoreham Rd E, Houns. (Hthrw.Air.) TW6 ... 114 BL85
Shoreham Rd W, Houns. (Hthrw.Air.) TW6 ... 114 BL85
Shoreham Way, Brom. BR2 ... 144 EG100
Shore Pl, E9 ... 84 DW66
Shore Rd, E9 ... 84 DW66
Shores Rd, Wok. GU21 ... 150 AY114
Shorncliffe Rd, SE1 ... 201 P10
Shorndean St, SE6 ... 123 EC88
Shorne Cl, Orp. BR5 ... 146 EX98
  Sidcup DA15 ... 126 EW86
Shornefield Cl, Brom. BR1 ... 145 EN97
Shornells Way, SE2 *off Willrose Cres* ... 106 EW78
Shorrolds Rd, SW6 ... 99 CZ80
Shortacres, Red. RH1 ... 185 DM133
Shortcroft Rd, Epsom KT17 ... 157 CT108
Shortcrofts Rd, Dag. RM9 ... 88 EZ65
Shorter Av, Brwd. CM15 ... 55 FZ44
Shorter St, E1 ... 197 P10
Shortfern, Slou. SL2 ... 74 AW72
Shortgate, N12 ... 43 CZ49
Short Hedges, Houns. TW3, TW5 ... 96 CB81
Short Hill, Har. HA1 *off High St* ... 61 CE60
SHORTLANDS, Brom. ... 144 EE97
⇌ Shortlands ... 144 EE96
Shortlands, W6 ... 99 CX77
  Hayes UB3 ... 95 BR79
Shortlands Cl, N18 ... 46 DR48
  Belvedere DA17 ... 106 EZ76
Shortlands Gdns, Brom. BR2 ... 144 EE96
Shortlands Gro, Brom. BR2 ... 143 ED97
Shortlands Rd, E10 ... 67 EB59
  Bromley BR2 ... 143 ED97
  Kingston upon Thames KT2 ... 118 CM94
Short La, Oxt. RH8 ... 188 EH132
  St. Albans (Brick.Wd.) AL2 ... 8 BZ30
  Staines TW19 ... 114 BM88
Shortmead Dr, Wal.Cr. (Chsht.) EN8 ... 15 DY31
Short Path, SE18 *off Westdale Rd* ... 105 EP79
Short Rd, E11 ... 68 EE61
  E15 ... 85 ED67
  W4 ... 98 CS79
  Hounslow (Hthrw.Air.) TW6 ... 114 BL86
Shorts Cft, NW9 ... 62 CP56
Shorts Gdns, WC2 ... 195 P9
Shorts Rd, Cars. SM5 ... 158 DE105
Short St, NW4 *off New Brent St* ... 63 CW56
  SE1 ... 200 E4
Short Wall, E15 ... 85 EC69
Shortway, N12 ... 44 DE51
Short Way, SE9 ... 104 EL83
  Twickenham TW2 ... 116 CC87
Shortwood Av, Stai. TW18 ... 114 BH90
Shortwood Common, Stai. TW18 ... 114 BH91
Shotfield, Wall. SM6 ... 159 DH107
Shothanger Way, Hem.H. (Bov.) HP3 ... 5 BC26
Shott Cl, Sutt. SM1 *off Turnpike La* ... 158 DC106
Shottendane Rd, SW6 ... 100 DA81
Shottery Cl, SE9 ... 124 EL90
Shottfield Av, SW14 ... 98 CS84
Shoulder of Mutton All, E14 *off Narrow St* ... 85 DY73
Shouldham St, W1 ... 194 C7
Showers Way, Hayes UB3 ... 77 BU74
Shrapnel Cl, SE18 ... 104 EL80
Shrapnel Rd, SE9 ... 105 EM83
SHREDING GREEN, Iver ... 75 BB72
Shrewsbury Av, SW14 ... 98 CQ84
  Harrow HA3 ... 62 CL56
Shrewsbury Cl, Surb. KT6 ... 138 CL103
Shrewsbury Ct, EC1 *off Whitecross St* ... 84 DQ70
Shrewsbury Cres, NW10 ... 80 CR67
Shrewsbury La, SE18 ... 105 EP81
Shrewsbury Ms, W2 *off Chepstow Rd* ... 82 DA71
Shrewsbury Rd, E7 ... 68 EK64
  N11 ... 45 DJ51
  W2 ... 82 DA72
  Beckenham BR3 ... 143 DY97
  Carshalton SM5 ... 140 DE100
  Hounslow (Hthrw.Air.) TW6 ... 115 BQ86
  Redhill RH1 ... 184 DE134
Shrewsbury St, W10 ... 81 CW70
Shrewsbury Wk, Islw. TW7 *off South St* ... 97 CG83
Shrewton Rd, SW17 ... 120 DF94
Shroffold Rd, Brom. BR1 ... 124 EE91
Shropshire Cl, Mitch. CR4 ... 141 DL98
Shropshire Ho, N18 *off Cameron Cl* ... 46 DV50
Shropshire Pl, WC1 ... 195 L5
Shropshire Rd, N22 ... 45 DM52
Shroton St, NW1 ... 194 B6
Shrubberies, The, E18 ... 48 EG54
  Chigwell IG7 ... 49 EQ50
Shrubbery, The, E11 ... 68 EH57
  Upminster RM14 ... 72 FQ62
Shrubbery Cl, N1 *off St. Paul St* ... 84 DQ67
Shrubbery Gdns, N21 ... 45 DP45
Shrubbery Rd, N9 ... 46 DU48
  SW16 ... 121 DL91
  Dartford (S.Darenth) DA4 ... 149 FR95
  Gravesend DA12 ... 131 GH88
  Southall UB1 ... 78 BZ74
Shrubland Gro, Wor.Pk. KT4 ... 139 CW104
Shrubland Rd, E8 ... 84 DU67
  E10 ... 67 EA59
  E17 ... 67 EA57
  Banstead SM7 ... 173 CZ116
Shrublands, Hat. AL9 ... 12 DB26
Shrublands, The, Pot.B. EN6 ... 11 CY33
Shrublands Av, Croy. CR0 ... 161 EA105
Shrublands Cl, N20 ... 44 DD46
  SE26 ... 122 DW90
  Chigwell IG7 ... 49 EQ51
Shrubsall Cl, SE9 ... 124 EL88
Shrubs Rd, Rick. WD3 ... 38 BM51
Shuna Wk, N1 *off St. Paul's Rd* ... 84 DR65
Shurland Av, Barn. EN4 ... 28 DD44
Shurland Gdns, SE15 *off Rosemary Rd* ... 102 DT80
Shurlock Av, Swan. BR8 ... 147 FD96
Shurlock Dr, Orp. BR6 ... 163 EQ105
Shuters Sq, W14 *off Sun Rd* ... 99 CZ78
Shuttle Cl, Sid. DA15 ... 125 ET87
Shuttlemead, Bex. DA5 ... 126 EZ87
Shuttle Rd, Dart. DA1 ... 107 FG83

326

Shu - Som

Shuttle St, E1 off Buxton St ..84 DU70
Shuttleworth Rd, SW11 ..100 DE82
Siamese Ms, N3 off Station Rd .44 DA53
Sibella Rd, SW4 ..101 DK82
Sibley Cl, Bexh. DA6 ..126 EY85
Sibley Gro, E12 ..86 EL66
Sibthorpe Rd, SE12 ..124 EH86
Sibton Rd, Cars. SM5 ..140 DE101
Sicilian Av, WC1 ..196 A7
Sicklefield Cl, Wal.Cr. (Chsht.)
EN7 ..14 DT26
Sidbury St, SW6 ..99 CY81
SIDCUP ..125 ET91
⇌ Sidcup ..126 EU89
Sidcup Bypass, Chis. BR7 ..125 EP89
Orpington BR5 ..126 EX94
Sidcup DA14 ..125 ES91
Sidcup High St, Sid. DA14 ..126 EU91
Sidcup Hill, Sid. DA14 ..126 EV91
Sidcup Hill Gdns, Sid. DA14
off Sidcup Hill ..126 EW92
Sidcup Pl, Sid. DA14 ..126 EU92
Sidcup Rd, SE9 ..124 EK87
SE12 ..124 EH85
Sidcup Technology Cen, Sid.
DA14 ..126 EX92
Siddeley Dr, Houns. TW4 ..96 BY83
Siddons La, NW1 ..194 E5
Siddons Rd, N17 ..46 DU53
SE23 ..123 DY89
Croydon CR0 ..141 DN104
Side Rd, E17 ..67 DZ57
Uxbridge (Denh.) UB9 ..57 BD59
Sidewood Rd, SE9 ..125 ER88
Sidford Pl, SE1 ..200 C7
Sidings, The, E11 ..67 EC60
Loughton IG10 ..32 EL44
Staines TW18 off Leacroft ..114 BH91
Sidings Ms, N7 ..65 DN62
Sidmouth Av, Islw. TW7 ..97 CE82
Sidmouth Cl, Wat. WD19 ..39 BV47
Sidmouth Dr, Ruis. HA4 ..59 BU62
Sidmouth Par, NW2
off Sidmouth Rd ..81 CW66
Sidmouth Rd, E10 ..67 EC62
NW2 ..81 CW66
Orpington BR5 ..146 EV99
Welling DA16 ..106 EW80
Sidmouth St, WC1 ..196 A3
Sidney Av, N13 ..45 DM50
Sidney Elson Way, E6
off Edwin Av ..87 EN68
Sidney Gdns, Brent. TW8 ..97 CJ79
Sidney Gro, EC1 ..196 F1
Sidney Rd, E7 ..68 EG62
N22 ..45 DM52
SE25 ..142 DU99
SW9 ..101 DM82
Beckenham BR3 ..143 DY96
Epping (They.B.) CM16 ..33 ER36
Harrow HA2 ..60 CC55
Staines TW18 ..114 BG91
Twickenham TW1 ..117 CG86
Walton-on-Thames KT12 ..135 BU101
Sidney Sq, E1 ..84 DW72
Sidney St, E1 ..84 DV71
Sidworth St, E8 ..84 DV66
Siebert Rd, SE3 ..104 EG79
Siemens Rd, SE18 ..104 EK76
Sigdon Rd, E8 ..66 DU64
Sigers, The, Pnr. HA5 ..59 BV58
Signmakers Yd, NW1
off Delancey St ..83 DH67
Sigrist Sq, Kings.T. KT2 ..138 CL95
Silbury Av, Mitch. CR4 ..140 DE95
Silbury St, N1 ..197 K2
Silchester Rd, W10 ..81 CX72
Silecroft Rd, Bexh. DA7 ..106 FA81
Silesia Bldgs, E8 off London La .84 DV66
Silex St, SE1 ..200 G5
Silk Cl, SE12 ..124 EG85
Silkfield Rd, NW9 ..62 CS57
Silkham Rd, Oxt. RH8 ..187 ED127
Silkin Ho, Wat. WD19 ..40 BW48
Silk Mill Ct, Wat. WD19
off Silk Mill Rd ..39 BV45
Silk Mill Rd, Wat. WD19 ..39 BV45
Silk Mills Cl, Sev. TN14 ..191 FJ121
Silk Mills Path, SE13
off Lewisham Rd ..103 EC82
Silkmills Sq, E9 ..85 DZ65
Silkstream Rd, Edg. HA8 ..42 CQ53
Silk St, EC2 ..197 J6
Silsden Cres, Ch.St.G. HP8
off London Rd ..36 AX48
Silsoe Rd, N22 ..45 DM54
Silver Birch Av, E4 ..47 DZ51
Epping (N.Wld.Bas.) CM16 .18 EY27
Silver Birch Cl, N11 ..44 DG51
SE28 ..88 EU74
Addlestone (Woodham)
KT15 ..151 BE112
Dartford DA2 ..127 FE91
Uxbridge UB10 ..58 BL63
Silver Birches, Brwd. CM13 ..55 GA46
Silver Birch Gdns, E6 ..87 EM70
Silver Birch Ms, Ilf. IG6
off Fencepiece Rd ..49 EQ51
Silverbirch Wk, NW3
off Queen's Cres ..82 DG65
Silvercliffe Gdns, Barn. EN4 ..28 DE42
Silver Cl, SE14
off Southerngate Way ..103 DY80
Harrow HA3 ..41 CD52
Tadworth (Kgswd.) KT20 ..173 CY124
Silver Cres, W4 ..98 CP77
Silverdale, SE26 ..122 DW91
Enfield EN2 ..29 DL42
Silverdale Av, Ilf. IG3 ..69 ES57
Leatherhead (Oxshott) KT22 .154 CC114
Walton-on-Thames KT12 ..135 BT104
Silverdale Cl, W7 ..79 CE74
Northolt UB5 ..60 BZ64
Sutton SM1 ..157 CZ105
Silverdale Ct, Stai. TW18 ..114 BH92
Silverdale Dr, SE9 ..124 EL89
Hornchurch RM12 ..71 FH64
Sunbury-on-Thames TW16 ..135 BV96
Silverdale Gdns, Hayes UB3 ..95 BU75
Silverdale Rd, E4 ..47 ED51
Bexleyheath DA7 ..107 FB82
Bushey WD23 ..24 BY43
Hayes UB3 ..95 BU75
Orpington (Petts Wd) BR5 .145 EQ98
Orpington (St.P.Cray) BR5 .146 EU97
Silver Dell, Wat. WD24 ..23 BT35
Silverglade Business Pk, Chess.
KT9 ..155 CJ112
Silverhall St, Islw. TW7 ..97 CG83
Silver Hill, Ch.St.G. HP8 ..36 AV47
Silverholme Cl, Har. HA3 ..61 CK59
Silver Jubilee Way, Houns.
TW4 ..95 BV82
Silverland St, E16 ..87 EM74
Silver La, Pur. CR8 ..159 DK112
West Wickham BR4 ..143 ED103
Silverleigh Rd, Th.Hth. CR7 ..141 DM98
Silverlocke Rd, Grays RM17 ..110 GD79
Silvermead, E18
off Churchfields ..48 EG52
Silvermere Av, Rom. RM5 ..51 FB51
Silvermere Rd, SE6 ..123 EB86
Silver Pl, W1 ..195 L10
Silver Rd, SE13 off Elmira St .103 EB83
W12 ..81 CX73
Gravesend DA12 ..131 GL89
Silversmiths Way, Wok. GU21 .166 AW118
Silver Spring Cl, Erith DA8 ..107 FB79
Silverstead La, West. TN16 ..179 ER121
Silverstone Cl, Red. RH1
off Goodwood Rd ..184 DF132
Silverston Way, Stan. HA7 ..41 CJ51
⇌ Silver Street ..46 DT50
Silver St, N18 ..46 DS49
Enfield EN1 ..30 DR41
Romford (Abridge) RM4 ..34 EV41
Waltham Abbey EN9 ..15 EC34
Waltham Cross (Goffs Oak)
EN7 ..14 DR30
Silverthorne Rd, SW8 ..101 DH82
Silverthorn Gdns, E4 ..47 EA47
Silverton Rd, W6 ..99 CX79
SILVERTOWN, E16 ..104 EJ75
⇌ Silvertown & London City
Airport ..86 EK74
Silvertown Way, E16 ..86 EE72
Silver Tree Cl, Walt. KT12 ..135 BU104
Silvertree La, Grnf. UB6
off Cowgate Rd ..79 CD69
Silvertrees, St.Alb. (Brick.Wd.)
AL2 off West Riding ..8 BZ30
Silver Wk, SE16 ..203 M3
Silver Way, Rom. RM7 ..71 FB55
Uxbridge UB10
off Oakdene Rd ..77 BP68
Silverwood Cl, Beck. BR3 ..123 EA94
Croydon CR0 ..161 DZ109
Northwood HA6 ..39 BQ53
Silvester Rd, SE22 ..122 DT85
Silvester St, SE1 ..201 J5
Silvocea Way, E14 ..85 ED72
Silwood Est, SE16 ..202 G9
Silwood St, SE16 ..202 G9
Simla Cl, SE14 ..103 DY79
Simla Ho, SE1 ..201 L5
Simmil Rd, Esher (Clay.) KT10 .155 CE106
Simmons Cl, N20 ..44 DE46
Chessington KT9 ..155 CJ108
Slough SL3 off Common Rd .93 BA77
Simmons La, E4 ..47 ED47
Simmons Pl, Stai. TW18
off Chertsey La ..113 BE92
Simmons Rd, SE18 ..105 EP78
Simmons Way, N20 ..44 DE47
Simms Cl, Cars. SM5 ..140 DE103
Simms Gdns, N2 ..44 DC54
Simms Rd, SE1 ..202 B9
Simnel Rd, SE12 ..124 EH87
Simon Cl, W11
off Portobello Rd ..81 CZ73
Simon Dean, Hem.H. (Bov.) HP3 .5 BA27
Simonds Rd, E10 ..67 EA61
Simone Cl, Brom. BR1 ..144 EK95
Simone Dr, Ken. CR8 ..176 DQ116
Simons Cl, Cher. (Ott.) KT16 .151 BC107
Simons Wk, E15
off Waddington Rd ..67 ED64
Egham (Eng.Grn.) TW20 ..112 AW94
Simplemarsh Ct, Add. KT15
off Simplemarsh Rd ..152 BH105
Simplemarsh Rd, Add. KT15 .152 BG105
Simpson Cl, N21
off Macleod Rd ..29 DL43
Simpson Dr, W3 ..80 CR72
Simpson Rd, Houns. TW4 ..116 BZ86
Rainham RM13 ..89 FF65
Richmond TW10 ..117 CJ91
Simpsons Rd, E14 ..204 C1
Bromley BR2 ..144 EG97
Simpson St, SW11 ..100 DE82
Simrose Ct, SW18
off Wandsworth High St ..120 DA85
Sims Cl, Rom. RM1 ..71 FF56
Sims Wk, SE3 ..104 EF84
Sinclair Ct, Beck. BR3 ..123 EA94
Sinclair Dr, Sutt. SM2 ..158 DB109
Sinclair Gdns, W14 ..99 CX75
Sinclair Gro, NW11 ..63 CX58
Sinclair Rd, E4 ..47 DZ50
W14 ..99 CX75
Sinclair Way, Dart. (Lane End)
DA2 ..129 FR91
Sinclare Cl, Enf. EN1 ..30 DT39
Sincots Rd, Red. RH1
off Lower Br Rd ..184 DF134
Sinderby Cl, Borwd. WD6 ..26 CL39
Singapore Rd, W13 ..79 CG74
Singer St, EC2 ..197 L3
Singles Cross La, Sev. (Knock.)
TN14 ..164 EW114
SINGLE STREET, West. ..179 EN115
Single St, West. (Berry's Grn.)
TN16 ..179 EP115
Singleton Cl, SW17 ..120 DF94
Croydon CR0
off St. Saviours Rd ..142 DQ101
Hornchurch RM12
off Carfax Rd ..71 FF63
Singleton Rd, Dag. RM9 ..70 EZ64
Singleton Scarp, N12 ..44 DA50
SINGLEWELL, Grav. ..131 GK93
Singlewell Rd, Grav. DA11 ..131 GH89
Singret Pl, Uxb. (Cowley) UB8
off High St ..76 BJ70
Sinnott Rd, E17 ..47 DX53
Sion Rd, Twick. TW1 ..117 CH88
SIPSON, West Dr. ..94 BN79
Sipson Cl, West Dr. UB7 ..94 BN79
Sipson La, Hayes UB3 ..94 BN79
West Drayton UB7 ..94 BN79
Sipson Rd, West Dr. UB7 ..94 BN78
Sipson Way, West Dr. UB7 ..94 BN80
Sir Alexander Cl, W3 ..81 CT74
Sir Alexander Rd, W3 ..81 CT74
Sir Cyril Black Way, SW19 ..120 DA94
Sirdar Rd, N22 ..65 DP55
W11 ..81 CX73
Mitcham CR4
off Grenfell Rd ..120 DG93
Sirdar Strand, Grav. DA12 ..131 GM92
Sir Francis Way, Brwd. CM14 ..54 FV47
Sirinham Pt, SW8 ..101 DM79
Sirius Rd, Nthwd. HA6 ..39 BU50
★ Sir John Soane's Mus, WC2
off Lincoln's Inn Flds ..196 B8
Sir Thomas More Est, SW3
off Beaufort St ..100 DD79
Sise La, EC4 ..197 K9
Siskin Cl, Borwd. WD6 ..26 CN42
Bushey WD23 ..24 BY42
Sisley Rd, Bark. IG11 ..87 ES67
Sispara Gdns, SW18 ..119 CZ86
Sissinghurst Rd, Croy. CR0 ..142 DU101
Sissulu Ct, E6 ..86 EJ67
Sister Mabel's Way, SE15
off Radnor Rd ..102 DU80
Sisters Av, SW11 ..100 DF84
Sistova Rd, SW12 ..121 DH88
Sisulu Pl, SW9 ..101 DN83
Sittingbourne Av, Enf. EN1 ..30 DR44
Sitwell Gro, Stan. HA7 ..41 CF50
Siverst Cl, Nthlt. UB5 ..78 CB65
Sivill Ho, E2 ..84 DT69
Siviter Way, Dag. RM10 ..89 FB66
Siward Rd, N17 ..46 DR53
SW17 ..120 DC90
Bromley BR2 ..144 EH97
Six Acres Est, N4 ..65 DN61
Six Bells La, Sev. TN13 ..191 FJ126
Six Bridges Trd Est, SE1 ..102 DU78
Sixth Av, E12 ..69 EM63
W10 ..81 CY69
Hayes UB3 ..95 BT74
Watford WD25 ..24 BX35
Sixth Cross Rd, Twick. TW2 ..116 CC90
Skardu Rd, NW2 ..63 CY64
Skarnings Ct, Wal.Abb. EN9 ..16 EG33
Skeena Hill, SW18 ..119 CY87
Skeet Hill La, Orp. BR5, BR6 .146 EY103
Skeffington Rd, E6 ..86 EL67
Skelbrook St, SW18 ..120 DB89
Skelgill Rd, SW15 ..99 CZ84
Skelley Rd, E15 ..86 EF66
Skelton Cl, E8
off Buttermere Wk ..84 DT65
Skelton Rd, E7 ..86 EG65
Skeltons La, E10 ..67 EB59
Skelwith Rd, W6 ..99 CW79
Skenfrith Ho, SE15
off Commercial Way ..102 DV79
Skerne Rd, Kings.T. KT2 ..137 CK95
Skerries Ct, Slou. (Langley) SL3
off Blacksmith Row ..93 BA77
Sketchley Gdns, SE16 ..203 H10
Sketty Rd, Enf. EN1 ..30 DS41
Skibbs La, Orp. BR5, BR6 ..146 EZ103
Skid Hill La, Warl. CR6 ..162 EF113
Skidmore Way, Rick. WD3 ..38 BL46
Skiers St, E15 ..86 EE67
Skiffington Cl, SW2 ..121 DN88
Skillet Hill, Wal.Abb. EN9 ..32 EH35
Skinner Ct, E2 off Parmiter St .84 DV68
Skinner Pl, SW1 ..198 F9
★ Skinners' Hall, EC4
off Dowgate Hill ..197 K10
Skinners La, EC4 ..197 J10
Ashtead KT21 ..171 CK118
Hounslow TW5 ..96 CB81
Skinner St, EC1 ..196 E3
Skinney La, Dart. (Hort.Kir.)
DA4 ..148 FQ97
Skip La, Uxb. (Hare.) UB9 ..58 BL60
Skippers Cl, Green. DA9 ..129 FV85
Skips Cor, Epp. (N.Wld.Bas.)
CM16 ..19 FD25
Skipsea Ho, SW18
off Fitzhugh Gro ..120 DD86
Skipsey Av, E6 ..87 EM69
Skipton Cl, N11
off Ribblesdale Av ..44 DG51
Skipton Dr, Hayes UB3 ..95 BQ76
Skipworth Rd, E9 ..84 DW67
Skomer Wk, N1
off Clephane Rd ..84 DQ65
Skylark Rd, Uxb. (Denh.) UB9 .57 BC60
Skylines Village, E14 ..204 D5
Sky Peals Rd, Wdf.Grn. IG8 ..47 ED53
Skyport Dr, West Dr. UB7 ..94 BK80
Slade, The, SE18 ..105 ES79
Sladebrook Rd, SE3 ..104 EK83
Slade Ct, Cher. (Ott.) KT16 ..151 BD107
Radlett WD7 ..25 CG35
Sladedale Rd, SE18 ..105 ES78
Slade End, Epp. (They.B.)
CM16 ..33 ES36
Slade Gdns, Erith DA8 ..107 FF81
⇌ Slade Green ..107 FG81
Slade Grn Rd, Erith DA8 ..107 FG80
Slade Ho, Houns. TW4 ..116 BZ86
Slade Oak La, Ger.Cr. SL9 ..57 BB55
Uxbridge (Denh.) UB9 ..57 BD59
Slade Rd, Cher. (Ott.) KT16 ..151 BD107
Slades Cl, Enf. EN2 ..29 DN41
Slades Dr, Chis. BR7 ..125 EQ90
Slades Gdns, Enf. EN2 ..29 DN40
Slades Hill, Enf. EN2 ..29 DN41
Slades Ri, Enf. EN2 ..29 DN41
Slade Twr, E10 ..67 EB61
Slade Wk, SE17 off Heiron St .101 DP79
Slagrove Pl, SE13 ..123 EB85
Slaidburn St, SW10 ..100 DC79
Slaithwaite Rd, SE13 ..103 EC84
Slaney Pl, N7 off Hornsey Rd .65 DN64
Slaney Rd, Rom. RM1 ..71 FE57
Slapleys, Wok. GU22 ..166 AX120
Slater Cl, SE18
off Woolwich New Rd ..105 EN78
Slattery Rd, Felt. TW13 ..116 BW88
Sleaford Grn, Wat. WD19 ..40 BX48
Sleaford St, SW8 ..101 DJ80
Sledmere Ct, Felt. TW14
off Kilross Rd ..115 BS88
Sleepers Fm Rd, Grays RM16 .111 GH75
Slewins Cl, Horn. RM11 ..72 FJ57
Slewins La, Horn. RM11 ..72 FJ57
Slievemore Cl, SW4
off Voltaire Rd ..101 DK83
Slines Oak Rd, Cat. (Wold.)
CR3 ..177 EA123
Warlingham CR6 ..177 EA119
Slingsby Pl, WC2 ..195 P10
Slip, The, West. TN16 ..189 EQ126
Slippers Pl, SE16 ..202 E6
Slipshoe St, Reig. RH2
off West St ..183 CZ134
Sloane Av, SW3 ..198 B8
Sloane Ct E, SW3 ..198 F10
Sloane Ct W, SW3 ..198 F10
Sloane Gdns, SW1 ..198 F9
Orpington BR6 ..145 EQ104
H Sloane Hosp, The, Beck.
BR3 ..143 ED95
⊖ Sloane Square ..198 F9
Sloane Sq, SW1 ..198 F9
Sloane St, SW1 ..198 E6
Sloane Ter, SW1 ..198 E8
Sloane Wk, Croy. CR0 ..143 DZ100
Slocock Hill, Wok. GU21 ..166 AW117
Slocum Cl, SE28 ..88 EW73
SLOUGH ..74 AS74
⇌ Slough ..74 AT74
Slough La, NW9 ..62 CQ58
Betchworth (Buckland) RH3 .183 CU133
Epsom (Headley) KT18 ..182 CQ125
★ Slough Mus, Slou. SL1 ..92 AU75
Slough Rd, Iver SL0 ..75 BC69
Slough (Datchet) SL3 ..92 AU78
Slowmans Cl, St.Alb. (Park St.)
AL2 ..8 CC28
Sly St, E1 off Cannon St Rd ..84 DV72
Smaldon Cl, West Dr. UB7
off Walnut Av ..94 BN76
Smallberry Av, Islw. TW7 ..97 CF82
Smallbrook Ms, W2
off Craven Rd ..82 DD72
Smalley Cl, N16 ..66 DT62
Smalley Rd Est, N16
off Smalley Cl ..66 DT62
Small Grains, Long. (Fawk.Grn.)
DA3 ..149 FV104
Smallholdings Rd, Epsom
KT17 ..157 CW114
Smallwood Rd, SW17 ..120 DD91
Smardale Rd, SW18
off Alma Rd ..120 DC85
Smarden Cl, Belv. DA17
off Essenden Rd ..106 FA78
Smarden Gro, SE9 ..125 EM91
Smart Cl, Rom. RM3 ..51 FH53
Smarts Grn, Wal.Cr. (Chsht.)
EN7 ..14 DT27
Smarts Heath La, Wok. GU22 .166 AU123
Smarts Heath Rd, Wok. GU22 .166 AT123
Smarts La, Loug. IG10 ..32 EK42
Smarts Pl, N18 off Fore St ..46 DU50
Smart's Pl, WC2 ..196 A8
Smarts Rd, Grav. DA12 ..131 GH89
Smart St, E2 ..85 DX69
Smeaton Cl, Chess. KT9
off Merritt Gdns ..155 CK107
Waltham Abbey EN9 ..16 EE32
Smeaton Rd, SW18 ..120 DA87
Enfield EN3 ..31 EA37
Woodford Green IG8 ..49 EM50
Smeaton St, E1 ..202 D2
Smedley St, SW4 ..101 DK82
SW8 ..101 DK82
Smeed Rd, E3 ..85 EA66
Smiles Pl, SE13 ..103 EC82
⇌ Smitham ..175 DL115
Smitham Bottom La, Pur.
CR8 ..159 DJ111
Smitham Downs Rd, Pur.
CR8 ..159 DK113
Smith Cl, SE16 ..203 H3
★ Smithfield Cen Mkt, EC1 .196 G7
Smithfield St, EC1 ..196 F7
Smithies Ct, E15 ..67 EC64
Smithies Rd, SE2 ..106 EV77
Smiths Caravan Site, Iver SL0 .75 BC74
Smith's Ct, W1 ..195 L10
Smiths Fm Est, Nthlt. UB5 ..78 CA68
Smiths La, Eden. (Crock.H.)
TN8 ..189 EQ133
Waltham Cross (Chsht.) EN7 .14 DR26
Smithson Rd, N17 ..46 DR53
Smiths Pt, E13 off Brooks Rd .86 EG67
Smith Sq, SW1 ..199 P7
Smith St, SW3 ..198 D10
Surbiton KT5 ..138 CM100
Watford WD18 ..24 BW42
Smiths Yd, SW18
off Summerley St ..120 DC89
Smith's Yd, Croy. CR0
off St. Georges Wk ..142 DQ104
Smith Ter, SW3 ..100 DF78
Smithwood Cl, SW19 ..119 CY88
Smithy Cl, Tad. (Lwr.Kgswd.)
KT20 ..183 CZ126
Smithy La, Tad. (Lwr.Kgswd.)
KT20 ..183 CZ127
Smithy St, E1 ..84 DW71
Smock Wk, Croy. CR0 ..142 DQ100
Smokehouse Yd, EC1 ..196 G6
Smugglers Wk, Green. DA9 ..129 FV85
Smugglers Way, SW18 ..100 DB84
Smug Oak Grn Business Cen,
St.Alb. AL2 ..8 CB30
Smug Oak La, St.Alb. (Brick.Wd.)
AL2 ..8 CB30
Smyrks Rd, SE17 ..102 DS78
Smyrna Rd, NW6 ..82 DA66
Smythe Rd, Dart. (Sutt.H.)
DA4 ..148 FN95
Smythe St, E14 ..85 EB73
Snag La, Sev. (Cudham) TN14 .163 ES109
Snakes La, Barn. EN4 ..29 DH41
Snakes La E, Wdf.Grn. IG8 ..48 EJ51
Snakes La W, Wdf.Grn. IG8 ..48 EG51
Snape Spur, Slou. SL1 ..74 AS72
SNARESBROOK, E11 ..68 EE57
⊖ Snaresbrook ..68 EG57
Snaresbrook Dr, Stan. HA7 ..41 CK49
Snaresbrook Rd, E11 ..68 EE56
Snarsgate St, W10 ..81 CW71
Snatts Hill, Oxt. RH8 ..188 EF129
Sneath Av, NW11 ..63 CZ59
Snelling Av, Grav. (Nthflt.)
DA11 ..130 GE89
Snellings Rd, Walt. KT12 ..154 BW106
Snells La, Amer. HP7 ..20 AV39
Snells Pk, N18 ..46 DT51
Snells Wd Ct, Amer. HP7 ..20 AW40
Sneyd Rd, NW2 ..63 CW63
Snipe Cl, Erith DA8 ..107 FH80
Snodland Cl, Orp. BR6
off Mill La ..163 EN110
Snowberry Cl, E15 ..67 ED63
Snowbury Rd, SW6 ..100 DB82
Snowden Av, Uxb. UB10 ..77 BP68
Snowden St, EC2 ..197 M5
Snowdon Cres, Hayes UB3 ..95 BQ76
Snowdon Dr, NW9 ..62 CS58
Snowdon Rd, Houns. (Hthrw.Air.)
TW6 off Southern
Perimeter Rd ..115 BQ85
Snowdown Cl, SE20 ..143 DX95
Snowdrop Cl, Hmptn. TW12
off Gresham Rd ..116 CA93
Snowdrop Path, Rom. RM3 ..52 FK52
Snow Hill, EC1 ..196 F7
Snow Hill Ct, EC1 ..196 G8
Snowman Ho, NW6 ..82 DB67
Snowsfields, SE1 ..201 L4
Snowshill Rd, E12 ..68 EL64
Snowy Fielder Waye, Islw. TW7 .97 CH82
Soames St, SE15 ..102 DT83
Soames Wk, N.Mal. KT3 ..138 CS95
Soap Ho La, Brent. TW8 ..98 CL80
Socket La, Brom. BR2 ..144 EH100
SOCKETT'S HEATH, Grays ..110 GD76
Soham Rd, Enf. EN3 ..31 DZ37
SOHO, W1 ..195 M10
Soho Sq, W1 ..195 M8
Soho St, W1 ..195 M8
Sojourner Truth Cl, E8
off Richmond Rd ..84 DV65
Solander Gdns, E1
off Dellow St ..84 DV73
Solar Way, Enf. EN3 ..31 DZ36
Solebay St, E1 ..85 DY70
Sole Fm Cl, Lthd. (Bkhm.)
KT23 ..170 BZ124
Solefields Rd, Sev. TN13 ..191 FH128
Solent Ri, E13 ..86 EG69
Solent Rd, NW6 ..64 DA64
Hounslow (Hthrw.Air.) TW6 ..114 BM86
Soleoak Dr, Sev. TN13 ..191 FH127
Solesbridge Cl, Rick. (Chorl.) WD3
off Solesbridge La ..21 BF41
Solesbridge La, Rick. WD3 ..22 BG40
Soley Ms, WC1 ..196 D2
Solna Av, SW15 ..119 CW85
Solna Rd, N21 ..46 DR46
Solomon Av, N9 ..46 DU49
Solomons Hill, Rick. WD3
off Northway ..38 BK45
Solomon's Pas, SE15 ..102 DV84
Solom's Ct Rd, Bans. SM7 ..174 DE117
Solon New Rd, SW4 ..101 DL84
Solon New Rd Est, SW4
off Solon New Rd ..101 DL84
Solon Rd, SW2 ..101 DL84
Solway Cl, E8
off Buttermere Wk ..84 DT65
Hounslow TW4 ..96 BY83
Solway Rd, N22 ..45 DP53
SE22 ..102 DU84
Somaford Gro, Barn. EN4 ..28 DD44
Somali Rd, NW2 ..63 CZ63
Somborne Ho, SW15
off Fontley Way ..119 CU87
Somerby Rd, Bark. IG11 ..87 ER66
Somercoates Cl, Barn. EN4 ..28 DE41
Somerden Rd, Orp. BR5 ..146 EX101
Somerfield Cl, Tad. KT20 ..173 CY119
Somerfield Rd, N4 ..65 DP61
Somerford Cl, Pnr. HA5 ..59 BU56
Somerford Gro, N16 ..66 DT63
N17 ..46 DU52
Somerford Gro Est, N16
off Somerford Gro ..66 DT63
Somerford St, E1 ..84 DV70
Somerford Way, SE16 ..203 K5
Somerhill Av, Sid. DA15 ..126 EV87
Somerhill Rd, Well. DA16 ..106 EV82
Somerleyton Pas, SW9 ..101 DP84
Somerleyton Rd, SW9 ..101 DN84
Somersby Gdns, Ilf. IG4 ..69 EM57
Somers Cl, NW1 off Platt St ..83 DK68
Reigate RH2 ..184 DA133
Somers Cres, W2 ..194 B9

A B C D E F G H I J K L M N O P Q R S T U V W X Y Z

★ Place of interest ⇌ Railway station ⊖ London Underground station DLR Docklands Light Railway station Tramlink station H Hospital

Somerset Av, SW20 139 CV96
Chessington KT9 155 CK105
Welling DA16 125 ET85
Somerset Cl, N17 46 DR54
Epsom KT19 156 CS109
New Malden KT3 138 CS100
Walton-on-Thames KT12
off Queens Rd 153 BV106
Woodford Green IG8 48 EG53
Somerset Est, SW11 100 DD81
Somerset Gdns, N6 64 DG59
N17 46 DS52
SE13 103 EB82
SW16 141 DM97
Hornchurch RM11 72 FN60
Teddington TW11 117 CE92
★ Somerset Ho, WC2 196 B10
Somerset Ho, SW19 119 CX90
Somerset Rd, E17 67 EA57
N17 66 DT55
N18 46 DT50
NW4 63 CW56
SW19 119 CY91
W4 98 CR76
W13 79 CH74
Barnet EN5 28 DB43
Brentford TW8 97 CJ79
Dartford DA1 127 FH86
Enfield EN3 31 EA38
Harrow HA1 60 CC57
Kingston upon Thames KT1 138 CM96
Orpington BR6 146 EU101
Southall UB1 78 BZ71
Teddington TW11 117 CE92
Somerset Sq, W14 99 CY75
Somerset Way, Iver SL0 93 BF75
Somerset Waye, Houns. TW5 96 BY79
Somersham Rd, Bexh. DA7 106 EY82
Somers Ms, W2 194 B9
Somers Pl, SW2 121 DM87
Reigate RH2 184 DA133
Somers Rd, E17 67 DZ56
SW2 121 DM86
Reigate RH2 183 CZ133
SOMERS TOWN, NW1 195 M2
Somers Way, Bushey WD23 40 CC45
Somerton Av, Rich. TW9 98 CP83
Somerton Cl, Pur. CR8 175 DN115
Somerton Rd, NW2 63 CY62
SE15 102 DV84
Somertrees Av, SE12 124 EH89
Somervell Rd, Har. HA2 60 BZ64
Somerville Av, SW13 99 CV79
Somerville Rd, SE20 123 DX94
Cobham KT11 154 CA114
Dartford DA1 128 FM86
Romford RM6 70 EW58
Sonderburg Rd, N7 65 DM61
Sondes St, SE17 102 DR79
Sonia Cl, Wat. WD19 40 BW45
Sonia Ct, Har. HA1 61 CF58
Sonia Gdns, N12
off Woodside Av 44 DC49
NW10 63 CT63
Hounslow TW5 96 CA80
Sonnet Wk, West. (Bigg.H.) TN16
off Kings Rd 178 EH118
Sonning Gdns, Hmptn. TW12 116 BY93
Sonning Rd, SE25 142 DU100
Soper Cl, E4 47 DZ50
Soper Dr, Cat. CR3
off Hambledon Rd 176 DR123
Soper Ms, Enf. EN3
off Harston Dr 31 EA38
Sopers Rd, Pot.B. (Cuffley) EN6 13 DM29
Sophia Cl, N7
off Mackenzie Rd 83 DM65
Sophia Rd, E10 67 EB60
E16 86 EH72
Sophia Sq, SE16 203 K1
Sopwith Av, Chess. KT9 156 CL106
Sopwith Cl, Kings.T. KT2 118 CM92
Westerham (Bigg.H.) TN16 178 EK116
Sopwith Dr, W.Byf. KT14 152 BL111
Weybridge KT13 152 BL111
Sopwith Rd, Houns. TW5 96 BW80
Sopwith Way, SW8 101 DH80
Kingston upon Thames KT2 138 CL95
Sorbie Cl, Wey. KT13 153 BR107
Sorrel Bk, Croy. CR0 161 DY110
Sorrel Cl, SE28 88 EU74
Sorrel Ct, Grays RM17
off Salix Rd 110 GD79
Sorrel Gdns, E6 86 EL71
Sorrel La, E14 85 ED72
Sorrell Cl, SE14
off Southerngate Way 103 DY80
Sorrel Wk, Rom. RM1 71 FF55
Sorrel Way, Grav. (Nthflt.)
DA11 130 GE91
Sorrento Rd, Sutt. SM1 140 DB104
Sotheby Rd, N5 65 DP62
Sotheran Cl, E8 84 DU67
Sotheron Rd, SW6 100 DB80
Watford WD17 24 BW40
Soudan Rd, SW11 100 DF81
Souldern Rd, W14 99 CX76
Souldern St, Wat. WD18 23 BU43
Sounds Lo, Swan. BR8 147 FC100
South Access Rd, E17 67 DY59
Southacre Way, Pnr. HA5 40 BW53
SOUTH ACTON, W3 98 CN76
⇌ South Acton 98 CQ76
South Africa Rd, W12 81 CV74
South Albert Rd, Reig. RH2 183 CZ133
SOUTHALL 78 BX74
⇌ Southall 96 BZ75
Southall La, Houns. TW5 95 BV79
Southall UB2 95 BV79
Southall Pl, SE1 201 K5
Southall Way, Brwd. CM14 54 FT49
Southampton Bldgs, WC2 196 D8
Southampton Gdns, Mitch.
CR4 141 DL99
Southampton Ms, E16 205 P2
Southampton Pl, WC1 196 A7
Southampton Rd, NW5 64 DF64
Southampton Rd, Houns.
(Hthrw.Air.) TW6 114 BN86
Southampton Row, WC1 196 A6
Southampton St, WC2 196 A10
Southampton Way, SE5 102 DR80
Southam St, W10 81 CY70
South App, Nthwd. HA6 39 BR48
South Audley St, W1 198 G1
South Av, E4 47 EB45
Carshalton SM5 158 DF108
Egham TW20 113 BC93
Richmond TW9
off Sandycombe Rd 98 CN82
Southall UB1 78 BZ73
Walton-on-Thames KT12 153 BS110
South Av Gdns, Sthl. UB1 78 BZ73
South Bk, Chis. BR7 125 EQ91
Surbiton KT6 138 CL100
Southbank, T.Ditt. KT7 137 CH101
South Bk, West. TN16 189 ER126
South Bk Ter, Surb. KT6 138 CL100
SOUTH BEDDINGTON, Wall. 159 DK107
⇌ South Bermondsey 202 F10
South Birkbeck Rd, E11 67 ED62
South Black Lion La, W6 99 CU78
South Bolton Gdns, SW5 100 DB78
South Border, The, Pur. CR8 159 DK111
SOUTHBOROUGH, Brom. 145 EM100
Southborough Cl, Surb. KT6 137 CK102
Southborough La, Brom. BR2 144 EL99
Southborough Rd, E9 84 DW67
Bromley BR1 144 EL97
Surbiton KT6 138 CL102
Southbourne, Brom. BR2 144 EG101
Southbourne Av, NW9 42 CQ54
Southbourne Cl, Pnr. HA5 60 BY59
Southbourne Cres, NW4 63 CY56
Southbourne Gdns, SE12 124 EH85
Ilford IG1 69 EQ64
Ruislip HA4 59 BV60
Southbridge Pl, Croy. CR0 160 DQ105
Southbridge Rd, Croy. CR0 160 DQ105
Southbridge Way, Sthl. UB2 96 BY75
Southbrook Dr, Wal.Cr. (Chsht.)
EN8 15 DX28
Southbrook Ms, SE12 124 EF86
Southbrook Rd, SE12 124 EF86
SW16 141 DL95
⇌ Southbury 30 DV42
Southbury Av, Enf. EN1 30 DU43
Southbury Cl, Horn. RM12 72 FK64
Southbury Rd, Enf. EN1, EN3 30 DR41
South Carriage Dr, SW1 198 D4
SW7 198 A5
SOUTH CHINGFORD, E4 47 DZ50
Southchurch Rd, E6 87 EM68
Southcliffe Dr, Ger.Cr. (Chal.St.P.)
SL9 36 AY50
South Cl, N6 65 DH58
Barnet EN5 27 CZ41
Bexleyheath DA6 106 EX84
Dagenham RM10 88 FA67
Morden SM4 *off Green La* 140 DB100
Pinner HA5 60 BZ59
St. Albans AL2 8 CB25
Twickenham TW2 116 CA90
West Drayton UB7 94 BM76
Woking GU21 166 AW116
South Cl Grn, Red. RH1 185 DH129
South Colonnade, E14 204 A2
Southcombe St, W14 99 CY77
South Common Rd, Uxb. UB8 76 BL65
Southcote, Wok. GU21 166 AX115
Southcote Av, Felt. TW13 115 BT89
Surbiton KT5 138 CP101
Southcote Ri, Ruis. HA4 59 BR59
Southcote Rd, E17 67 DX57
N19 65 DJ63
SE25 142 DV100
Redhill RH1 185 DJ129
South Croydon CR2 160 DS110
South Cottage Dr, Rick. (Chorl.)
WD3 21 BF43
South Cottage Gdns, Rick. (Chorl.)
WD3 21 BF43
South Countess Rd, E17 67 DZ55
South Cres, E16 85 ED70
WC1 195 M7
South Cft, Egh. (Eng.Grn.)
TW20 112 AV92
Southcroft Av, Well. DA16 105 ES83
West Wickham BR4 143 EC103
Southcroft Rd, SW16 120 DG93
SW17 120 DG93
Orpington BR6 145 ES104
South Cross Rd, Ilf. IG6 69 EQ57
South Croxted Rd, SE21 122 DR90
SOUTH CROYDON 160 DQ107
⇌ South Croydon 160 DR106
Southdale, Chig. IG7 49 ER51
SOUTH DARENTH, Dart. 149 FR95
Southdean Gdns, SW19 119 CZ89
South Dene, NW7 42 CR48
Southdene, Sev. (Halst.) TN14 164 EY113
Southdown Av, W7 97 CG76
Southdown Cres, Har. HA2 60 CB60
Ilford IG2 69 ES57
Southdown Dr, SW20
off Crescent Rd 119 CX94
Southdown Rd, SW20 139 CX95
Carshalton SM5 158 DG109
Caterham (Wold.) CR3 177 DZ122
Hornchurch RM11 71 FH59
Walton-on-Thames KT12 154 BY105
Southdowns, Dart. (S.Darenth)
DA4 149 FR96
South Dr, Bans. SM7 158 DE113
Brentwood CM14 54 FX49
Coulsdon CR5 175 DK115
Orpington BR6 163 ES106
Potters Bar (Cuffley) EN6 13 DL30
Romford RM2 72 FJ55
Ruislip HA4 59 BS60
Sutton SM2 157 CY110
Virginia Water GU25 132 AU102
⊖ South Ealing 97 CJ76
South Ealing Rd, W5 97 CK75
South Eastern Av, N9 46 DT48
South Eaton Pl, SW1 198 G8
South Eden Pk Rd, Beck. BR3 143 EB100
South Edwardes Sq, W8 99 CZ76
SOUTHEND, SE6 123 EB91
South End, W8
off St. Albans Gro 100 DB76
Croydon CR0 160 DQ105
Southend Arterial Rd, Brwd.
CM13 73 FV57
Hornchurch RM11 52 FK54
Romford RM2, RM3 52 FK54
Upminster RM14 73 FR57
South End Cl, NW3 64 DE63
Southend Cl, SE9 125 EP86
Southend Cres, SE9 125 EN86
South End Grn, NW3
off South End Rd 64 DE63
Southend La, SE6 123 DZ91
SE26 123 DZ91
Waltham Abbey EN9 16 EH34
Southend Rd, E4 47 DY50
E6 87 EM66
E17 47 EB53
E18 48 EG53
South End Rd, NW3 64 DE63
Southend Rd, Beck. BR3 123 EA94
Grays RM17 110 GC77
South End Rd, Horn. RM12 89 FH65
Rainham RM13 89 FG67
Southend Rd, Wdf.Grn. IG8 48 EJ54
South End Row, W8 100 DB76
Southerland Cl, Wey. KT13 153 BQ105
Southern Av, SE25 142 DT97
Feltham TW14 115 BU88
Southern Dr, Loug. IG10 33 EM44
Southerngate Way, SE14 103 DY80
Southern Gro, E3 85 DZ69
Southernhay, Loug. IG10 32 EK43
Southern Perimeter Rd, Houns.
(Hthrw.Air.) TW6 115 BR85
Southern Pl, Swan. BR8 147 FD98
Southern Rd, E13 86 EH68
N2 64 DF56
Southern Row, W10 81 CY70
Southerns La, Couls. CR5 184 DC125
Southern St, N1 83 DM68
Southern Way, SE10 205 L8
Romford RM7 70 FA58
Southerton Rd, W6 99 CW76
Southerton Way, Rad. (Shenley)
WD7 10 CL33
South Esk Rd, E7 86 EJ65
Southey Ms, E16 205 N2
Southey Rd, N15 66 DS57
SW9 101 DN81
SW19 120 DA94
Southey St, SE20 123 DX94
Southey Wk, Til. RM18 111 GH81
Southfield, Barn. EN5 27 CX44
Southfield Av, Wat. WD24 24 BW38
Southfield Cl, Uxb. UB8 76 BN69
Southfield Cotts, W7
off Oaklands Rd 97 CF75
Southfield Gdns, Twick. TW1 117 CF91
Southfield Pk, Har. HA2 60 CB56
Southfield Pl, Wey. KT13 153 BP108
Southfield Rd, N17
off The Avenue 46 DS54
W4 98 CS76
Chislehurst BR7 145 ET97
Enfield EN3 30 DV44
Waltham Cross EN8 15 DY32
SOUTHFIELDS, SW18 120 DA88
⊖ Southfields 119 CZ88
Southfields, NW4 63 CU55
East Molesey KT8 137 CE100
Swanley BR8 127 FE94
Southfields Av, Ashf. TW15 115 BP93
Southfields Ct, SW19 119 CY88
Sutton SM1
off Sutton Common Rd 140 DA103
Southfields Pas, SW18 120 DA86
Southfields Rd, SW18 120 DA86
Caterham (Wold.) CR3 177 EB123
SOUTHFLEET, Grav. 130 GB93
Southfleet Rd, Dart. (Bean)
DA2 129 FW91
Gravesend (Nthflt.) DA11 131 GF89
Orpington BR6 145 ES104
Swanscombe DA10 130 FZ87
South Gdns, SW19 120 DD94
SOUTHGATE, N14 45 DJ47
⊖ Southgate 45 DJ46
Southgate, Purf. RM19 108 FQ77
Southgate Av, Felt. TW13 115 BR91
Southgate Circ, N14
off The Bourne 45 DK46
Southgate Gro, N1 84 DR66
Southgate Rd, N1 84 DR67
Potters Bar EN6 12 DC33
South Gipsy Rd, Well. DA16 106 EX83
South Glade, The, Bex. DA5 126 EZ88
South Grn, NW9
off Clayton Fld 42 CS53
Slough SL1 74 AS73
⇌ South Greenford 79 CE69
South Gro, E17 67 DZ57
N6 64 DG60
N15 66 DR57
Chertsey KT16 133 BF100
South Gro Ho, N6
off Highgate W Hill 64 DG60
SOUTH HACKNEY, E9 84 DW66
South Hall Cl, Dart. (Fnghm.)
DA4 148 FM101
South Hall Dr, Rain. RM13 89 FH71
SOUTH HAMPSTEAD, NW6 82 DB66
⇌ South Hampstead 82 DC66
SOUTH HAREFIELD, Uxb. 58 BJ56
SOUTH HARROW, Har. 60 CB62
⊖ South Harrow 60 CC62
South Hill, Chis. BR7 125 EM93
South Hill Av, Har. HA1, HA2 60 CC62
South Hill Gro, Har. HA1 61 CE63
South Hill Pk, NW3 64 DE63
South Hill Pk Gdns, NW3 64 DE63
South Hill Rd, Brom. BR2 144 EE97
Gravesend DA12 131 GH88
Southholme Cl, SE19 142 DS95
SOUTH HORNCHURCH, Rain. 89 FE67
South Huxley, N18 46 DR50
Southill La, Pnr. HA5 59 BU56
Southill Rd, Chis. BR7 124 EL94
Southill St, E14 *off Chrisp St* 85 EB72
South Island Pl, SW9 101 DM80
SOUTH KENSINGTON, SW7 100 DB76
⊖ South Kensington 198 A8
South Kensington Sta Arc, SW7
off Pelham St 100 DD77
South Kent Av, Grav. (Nthflt.)
DA11 130 GC86
⇌ South Kenton 61 CJ60
⊖ South Kenton 61 CJ60
SOUTH LAMBETH, SW8 101 DL81
South Lambeth Pl, SW8 101 DL79
South Lambeth Rd, SW8 101 DL79
Southland Rd, SE18 105 ET80
Southlands Av, Orp. BR6 163 ER105
Southlands Cl, Couls. CR5 175 DM117
Southlands Dr, SW19 119 CX89
Southlands Gro, Brom. BR1 144 EL97
Southlands La, Oxt. (Tand.)
RH8 187 EB134
Southlands Rd, Brom.
BR1, BR2 144 EJ99
Iver SL0 57 BF64
Uxbridge (Denh.) UB9 57 BF63
Southland Way, Houns. TW3 117 CD85
South La, Kings.T. KT1 137 CK97
New Malden KT3 138 CR98
South La W, N.Mal. KT3 138 CR98
SOUTHLEA, Slou. 92 AV82
Southlea Rd, Slou. (Datchet)
SL3 92 AV81
Windsor SL4 92 AU84
South Lo Av, Mitch. CR4 141 DL98
South Lo Cres, Enf. EN2 29 DK42
South Lo Dr, N14 29 DL43
South Lo Rd, Walt. KT12 153 BU109
★ South London Art Gall,
SE5 102 DS81
Southly Cl, Sutt. SM1 140 DA104
South Mall, N9 *off Plevna Rd* 46 DU48
South Mead, NW9 43 CT53
Epsom KT19 156 CS108
Redhill RH1 184 DF131
Southmead Cres, Wal.Cr. (Chsht.)
EN8 15 DY30
South Meadows, Wem. HA9 62 CM64
Southmead Rd, SW19 119 CY88
SOUTH MERSTHAM, Red. 185 DJ130
⇌ South Merton 139 CZ97
SOUTH MIMMS, Pot.B. 11 CT32
South Molton La, W1 195 H9
South Molton Rd, E16 86 EG72
South Molton St, W1 195 H9
Southmont Rd, Esher KT10 137 CE103
Southmoor Way, E9 85 DZ65
SOUTH NORWOOD, SE25 142 DT97
South Norwood Hill, SE25 142 DS96
South Oak Rd, SW16 121 DM91
SOUTH OCKENDON 91 FW70
Southold Ri, SE9 125 EM90
Southolm St, SW11 101 DH81
South Ordnance Rd, Enf. EN3 31 EA37
Southover, N12 44 DA49
Bromley BR1 124 EG92
SOUTH OXHEY, Wat. 40 BW48
South Par, SW3 198 A10
W4 98 CR77
Waltham Abbey EN9
off Sun St 15 EC33
South Pk, SW6 100 DA82
Gerrards Cross SL9 57 AZ57
Sevenoaks TN13 191 FH125
South Pk Av, Rick. (Chorl.)
WD3 21 BF43
South Pk Cres, SE6 124 EF88
Gerrards Cross SL9 56 AY56
Ilford IG1 69 ER62
South Pk Dr, Bark. IG11 69 ES63
Gerrards Cross SL9 56 AY56
Ilford IG3 69 ES63
South Pk Gro, N.Mal. KT3 138 CQ98
South Pk Hill Rd, S.Croy. CR2 160 DR106
South Pk Ms, SW6 100 DB83
South Pk Rd, SW19 120 DA93
Ilford IG1 69 ER62
South Pk Ter, Ilf. IG1 69 ER62
South Pk Vw, Ger.Cr. SL9 57 AZ56
South Pk Way, Ruis. HA4 78 BW65
South Penge Pk Est, SE20 142 DV96
South Perimeter Rd, Uxb. UB8
off Kingston La 76 BL69
South Pl, EC2 197 L6
Enfield EN3 30 DW43
Surbiton KT5 138 CM101
South Pl Ms, EC2 197 L7
South Pt, Sutt. SM1 158 DC107
Southport Rd, SE18 105 ER77
DLR South Quay 204 B4
South Ridge, Wey. KT13 153 BP110
Southridge Pl, SW20 119 CX94
South Riding, St.Alb. (Brick.Wd.)
AL2 8 CA30
South Ri, Cars. SM5 158 DE109
South Ri Way, SE18 105 ER78
South Rd, N9 46 DU46
SE23 123 DX89
SW19 120 DC93
W5 97 CK77
Edgware HA8 42 CP53
Egham (Eng.Grn.) TW20 112 AW93
Erith DA8 107 FF79
Feltham TW13 116 BX92
Hampton TW12 116 BY93
Rickmansworth (Chorl.) WD3 21 BC43
Romford (Chad.Hth.) RM6 70 EY58
Romford (Lt.Hth.) RM6 70 EW57
South Ockendon RM15 91 FW72
Southall UB1 96 BZ75
Twickenham TW2 117 CD90
West Drayton UB7 94 BM76
South Rd, Wey. KT13 153 BQ106
Weybridge (St.Geo.H.)
KT13 153 BP109
Woking GU21 150 AX114
South Row, SE3 104 EF82
SOUTH RUISLIP, Ruis. 60 BW63
⇌ South Ruislip 60 BW63
⊖ South Ruislip 60 BW63
Southsea Av, Wat. WD18 23 BU42
Southsea Rd, Kings.T. KT1 138 CL98
South Sea St, SE16 203 M6
South Side, W6 99 CT76
Southside, Ger.Cr. (Chal.St.P.)
SL9 56 AX55
Southside Common, SW19 119 CW93
Southspring, Sid. DA15 125 ER87
South Sq, NW11 64 DB58
WC1 196 D7
SOUTH STIFFORD, Grays 109 FW78
SOUTH STREET, West. 179 EM119
South St, W1 198 G2
Brentwood CM14 54 FW47
Bromley BR1 144 EG96
Enfield EN3 31 DX43
Epsom KT18 156 CR113
Gravesend DA12 131 GH87
Isleworth TW7 97 CG83
Rainham RM13 89 FC68
Romford RM1 71 FF58
Staines TW18 113 BF92
South Tenter St, E1 84 DT73
South Ter, SW7 198 B8
Surbiton KT6 138 CL100
SOUTH TOTTENHAM, N15 66 DS57
⇌ South Tottenham 66 DT57
South Vale, SE19 122 DS93
Harrow HA1 61 CE63
Southvale Rd, SE3 104 EE82
South Vw, Brom. BR1 144 EH96
Southview Av, NW10 63 CT64
South Vw Av, Til. RM18 111 GG81
Southview Cl, SW17 120 DG92
Bexley DA5 126 EZ86
Swanley BR8 147 FF98
Waltham Cross (Chsht.) EN7 14 DS26
South Vw Ct, Wok. GU22
off Constitution Hill 166 AY118
Southview Cres, Ilf. IG2 69 EP58
South Vw Dr, E18 68 EH55
Upminster RM14 72 FN62
Southview Gdns, Wall. SM6 159 DJ108
South Vw Rd, N8 65 DK55
Ashtead KT21 171 CK119
Southview Rd, Brom. BR1 123 ED91
Caterham (Wold.) CR3 177 EB124
South Vw Rd, Dart. DA2 128 FK90
Gerrards Cross SL9 56 AX56
Grays RM20 109 FW79
Loughton IG10 33 EM44
Pinner HA5 39 BV51
Southview Rd, Warl. CR6 176 DU119
Southviews, S.Croy. CR2 161 DX109
South Vil, NW1 83 DK65
Southville, SW8 101 DK81
Southville Cl, Epsom KT19 156 CR109
Feltham TW14 115 BS88
Southville Cres, Felt. TW14 115 BS88
Southville Rd, Felt. TW14 115 BS88
Thames Ditton KT7 137 CH101
South Wk, Hayes UB3
off Middleton Rd 77 BR71
Reigate RH2 *off Church St* 184 DB134
West Wickham BR4 144 EE104
SOUTHWARK, SE1 200 G3
⊖ Southwark 200 F3
Southwark Br, EC4 201 J2
SE1 201 J2
Southwark Br Rd, SE1 200 G6
★ Southwark Cathedral,
SE1 201 K2
Southwark Gro, SE1 201 H3
Southwark Pk Est, SE16 202 D8
Southwark Pk Rd, SE16 202 A8
Southwark Pl, Brom. BR1
off St. Georges Rd 145 EM97
Southwark St, SE1 200 G2
Southwater Cl, E14 85 DZ72
Beckenham BR3 123 EB94
South Way, N9 46 DW47
N11 *off Ringway* 45 DJ51
Southway, N20 44 DA47
NW11 64 DB58
SW20 139 CW98
South Way, Abb.L. WD5 7 BT33
Bromley BR2 144 EG101
Southway, Cars. SM5 158 DD110
South Way, Croy. CR0 143 DY104
Harrow HA2 60 CA56
Purfleet RM19 109 FS76
Southway, Wall. SM6 159 DJ105
South Way, Wem. HA9 62 CN64
SOUTH WEALD, Brwd. 54 FS47
South Weald Dr, Wal.Abb. EN9 15 ED33
South Weald Rd, Brwd. CM14 54 FU48
Southwell Av, Nthlt. UB5 78 CA65
Southwell Gdns, SW7 100 DC77
Southwell Gro Rd, E11 68 EE61
Southwell Rd, SE5 102 DQ83
Croydon CR0 141 DN100
Harrow HA3 61 CK58
Southwest Rd, E11 67 ED60
South Western Rd, Twick. TW1 117 CG86
South Wf Rd, W2 82 DD72
Southwick Ms, W2 194 A8
Southwick Pl, W2 194 B9
Southwick St, W2 194 B8
SOUTH WIMBLEDON, SW19 120 DB94
⊖ South Wimbledon 120 DB94
Southwold Dr, Bark. IG11 70 EU64
Southwold Rd, E5 66 DV61
Bexley DA5 127 FB86
Watford WD24 24 BW38
Southwold Spur, Slou. SL3 93 BC75
Southwood Av, N6 65 DH59

★ Place of interest ⇌ Railway station ⊖ London Underground station DLR Docklands Light Railway station Tramlink station H Hospital

Sou - Sta

Southwood Av, Cher. (Ott.)
KT16 ...151 BC108
Coulsdon CR5 ...175 DJ115
Kingston upon Thames KT2 .138 CQ95
Southwood Cl, Brom. BR1 ..145 EM98
Worcester Park KT4 ...139 CX102
Southwood Dr, Surb. KT5 ..138 CQ101
SOUTH WOODFORD, E18 ...48 EF54
⊖ **South Woodford** ...48 EG54
South Woodford to Barking Relief Rd, E11 ...68 EJ56
E12 ...69 EN62
E18 ...68 EJ56
Barking IG11 ...69 EN62
Ilford IG1, IG4 ...69 EN62
Southwood Gdns, Esher
KT10 ...137 CG104
Ilford IG2 ...69 EP56
H **Southwood Hosp**, N6 ...64 DG59
Southwood La, N6 ...64 DG59
Southwood Lawn Rd, N6 ...64 DG59
Southwood Rd, SE9 ...125 EP89
SE28 ...88 EV74
Southwood Smith St, N1
off Old Royal Free Sq ...83 DN67
South Worple Av, SW14 ...98 CS83
South Worple Way, SW14 ...98 CR83
Soval Ct, Nthwd. HA6
off Maxwell Rd ...39 BR52
Sovereign Cl, E1 ...202 E1
W5 ...79 CJ71
Purley CR8 ...159 DM110
Ruislip HA4 ...59 BS60
Sovereign Ct, Brom. BR2 ...145 EM99
West Molesey KT8 ...136 BZ98
Sovereign Cres, SE16 ...203 K1
Sovereign Gro, Wem. HA0 ...61 CK62
Sovereign Ms, E2
off Pearson St ...84 DT68
Barnet EN4
off Bournwell Cl ...28 DF41
Sovereign Pk, NW10 ...80 CP70
Sovereign Pl, Kings L.WD4 ...6 BN29
Sovereign Rd, Bark. IG11 ...88 EW69
Sowerby Cl, SE9 ...124 EL85
Sowrey Av, Rain. RM13 ...89 FF65
Soyer Ct, Wok. GU21
off Raglan Rd ...166 AS118
Space Waye, Felt.TW14 ...115 BU85
Spa Cl, SE25 ...142 DS95
Spa Dr, Epsom KT18 ...156 CN114
Spafield St, EC1 ...196 D4
Spa Grn Est, EC1 ...196 E2
Spa Hill, SE19 ...142 DR95
Spalding Cl, Edg. HA8
off Blundell Rd ...42 CS52
Spalding Rd, NW4 ...63 CW58
SW17 ...121 DH92
Spalt Cl, Brwd. CM13 ...55 GB47
Spanby Rd, E3 ...85 EA70
Spaniards Cl, NW11 ...64 DD60
Spaniards End, NW3 ...64 DC60
Spaniards Rd, NW3 ...64 DC61
Spanish Pl, W1 ...194 G8
Spanish Rd, SW18 ...120 DC85
Spareleaze Hill, Loug. IG10 ...33 EM43
Sparepenny La, Dart. (Eyns.)
DA4 ...148 FL102
Sparkbridge Rd, Har. HA1 ...61 CE56
Sparkford Gdns, N11
off Friern Barnet Rd ...44 DG50
Sparkford Ho, SW11 ...100 DD81
Sparks Cl, W3 *off Joseph Av* ..80 CR72
Dagenham RM8 ...70 EX61
Hampton TW12
off Victors Dr ...116 BY93
Spa Rd, SE16 ...201 P7
Sparrow Cl, Hmptn.TW12 ...116 BY93
Sparrow Dr, Orp. BR5 ...145 EQ102
Sparrow Fm Dr, Felt.TW14 ...116 BX87
Sparrow Fm Rd, Epsom KT17 .157 CU105
Sparrow Grn, Dag. RM10 ...71 FB62
Sparrows Herne, Bushey
WD23 ...40 CB45
Sparrows La, SE9 ...125 EQ87
Sparrows Mead, Red. RH1 ...184 DG131
Sparrows Way, Bushey WD23
off Sparrows Herne ...40 CC46
Sparsholt Rd, N19 ...65 DM60
Barking IG11 ...87 ES67
Sparta St, SE10 ...103 EB81
★ **Speaker's Cor**, W2 ...194 E10
Speaker's Ct, Croy. CR0
off St. James's Rd ...142 DR102
Spearman St, SE18 ...105 EN79
Spear Ms, SW5 ...100 DA77
Spearpoint Gdns, Ilf. IG2 ...69 ET56
Spears Rd, N19 ...65 DL60
Speart La, Houns.TW5 ...96 BY80
Spedan Cl, NW3 ...64 DB62
Speechly Ms, E8
off Alvington Cres ...66 DT64
Speedbird Way, West Dr. UB7 .94 BH80
Speedgate Hill, Long. (Fawk.Grn.)
DA3 ...149 FU103
Speed Highwalk, EC2
off Beech St ...84 DQ71
Speed Ho, EC2 ...197 K6
Speedwell Ct, Grays RM17 ..110 GE80
Speedwell St, SE8
off Comet St ...103 EA80
Speedy Pl, WC1 ...195 P3
Speer Rd, T.Ditt. KT7 ...137 CF99
Speirs Cl, N.Mal. KT3 ...139 CT100
Spekehill, SE9 ...125 EM90
Speke Ho, SE5 ...102 DQ80
Speke Rd, Th.Hth. CR7 ...142 DR96
Speldhurst Cl, Brom. BR2 ...144 EF99
Speldhurst Rd, E9 ...85 DX66
W4 ...98 CR76
Spellbrook Wk, N1
off Basire St ...84 DQ67
Spelman St, E1 ...84 DU71
Spelthorne Gro, Sun.TW16 ...115 BT94
Spelthorne La, Ashf.TW15 ...135 BQ95
★ **Spelthorne Mus**, Stai.
TW18 ...113 BE92
Spence Av, W.Byf. (Byfleet)
KT14 ...152 BL114
Spence Cl, SE16 ...203 M5
Spencer Av, N13 ...45 DM51
Hayes UB4 ...77 BU71
Waltham Cross (Chsht.) EN7 .14 DS26
Spencer Cl, N3 ...43 CZ54
NW10 ...80 CM69
Epsom KT18 ...172 CS119
Orpington BR6 ...145 ES103
Uxbridge UB8 ...76 BJ69
Woking GU21 ...151 BC113
Woodford Green IG8 ...48 EJ50
H **Spencer Close Mental Hosp**,
Epp. CM16 ...18 EV29
Spencer Ct, NW8
off Marlborough Pl ...82 DC68
Spencer Dr, N2 ...64 DC58
Spencer Gdns, SE9 ...125 EM85
SW14 ...118 CQ85
Egham (Eng.Grn.) TW20 ...112 AX92
Spencer Hill, SW19 ...119 CY93
Spencer Hill Rd, SW19 ...119 CY94
★ **Spencer Ho**, SW1 ...199 K3
Spencer Ms, SW8
off Lansdowne Way ...101 DM81
W6 *off Greyhound Rd* ...99 CY79
Spencer Pk, SW18 ...120 DD85
Spencer Pas, E2
off Pritchard's Rd ...84 DV68
Spencer Pl, N1
off Canonbury La ...83 DP66
Croydon CR0
off Gloucester Rd ...142 DR101
Spencer Ri, NW5 ...65 DH63
Spencer Rd, E6 ...86 EK67
E17 ...47 EC53
N8 ...65 DM57
N11 ...45 DH49
N17 ...46 DU53
SW18 ...100 DD84
SW20 ...139 CV95
W3 ...80 CQ74
W4 ...98 CQ80
Bromley BR1 ...124 EE94
Caterham CR3 ...176 DR121
Cobham KT11 ...169 BV115
East Molesey KT8 ...136 CC99
Harrow HA3 ...41 CE54
Ilford IG3 ...69 ET60
Isleworth TW7 ...97 CD81
Mitcham CR4 ...140 DG97
Mitcham (Bedd.Cor.) CR4 ..140 DG101
Rainham RM13 ...89 FD69
Slough SL3 ...93 AZ76
South Croydon CR2 ...160 DS106
Twickenham TW2 ...117 CE90
Wembley HA0 ...61 CJ61
Spencer St, EC1 ...196 F3
Gravesend DA11 ...131 GG87
Southall UB2 ...96 BX75
Spencer Wk, NW3
off Hampstead High St ...64 DC63
SW15 ...99 CX84
Rickmansworth WD3 ...22 BJ43
Tilbury RM18 ...111 GG82
Spencer Yd, SE3
off Blackheath Village ...104 EF82
Spenser Av, Wey. KT13 ...152 BN108
Spenser Cres, Upmin. RM14 ..72 FQ59
Spenser Gro, N16 ...66 DS63
Spenser Ms, SE21
off Croxted Rd ...122 DR88
Spenser Rd, SE24 ...121 DN85
Spenser St, SW1 ...199 L6
Spensley Wk, N16
off Clissold Rd ...66 DR62
Speranza St, SE18 ...105 ET78
Sperling Rd, N17 ...46 DS54
Spert St, E14 ...85 DY73
Speyhawk Pl, Pot.B. EN6 ...12 DB30
Speyside, N14 ...29 DJ44
Spey St, E14 ...85 EC71
Spey Way, Rom. RM1 ...51 FE52
Spezia Rd, NW10 ...81 CU68
Spice Quay Hts, SE1 ...202 A3
Spicer Cl, SW9 ...101 DP82
Walton-on-Thames KT12 ..136 BW100
Spicers Fld, Lthd. (Oxshott)
KT22 ...155 CD113
Spicersfield, Wal.Cr. (Chsht.)
EN7 ...14 DU27
Spice's Yd, Croy. CR0 ...160 DQ105
Spielman Rd, Dart. DA1 ...108 FM84
Spigurnell Rd, N17 ...46 DR53
Spikes Br Rd, Sthl. UB1 ...78 BY72
Spilsby Cl, NW9
off Kenley Av ...42 CS54
Spilsby Rd, Rom. RM3 ...52 FK52
Spindle Cl, SE18 ...104 EL76
Spindles, Til. RM18 ...111 GG80
Spindlewood Gdns, Croy.
CR0 ...160 DS105
Spindlewoods, Tad. KT20 ...173 CV122
Spindrift Av, E14 ...204 B8
Spinel Cl, SE18 ...105 ET78
Spingate Cl, Horn. RM12 ...72 FK64
Spinnaker Cl, Bark. IG11 ...88 EV69
Spinnells Rd, Har. HA2 ...60 BZ60
Spinney, The, N21 ...45 DN45
SW16 ...121 DK90
Barnet EN5 ...28 DB40
Brentwood (Hutton) CM13 ..55 GC44
Epsom KT18 ...173 CV119
Leatherhead (Bkhm.) KT23 ..170 CB124
Leatherhead (Oxshott) KT22 .154 CC112
Potters Bar EN6 ...12 DD31
Purley CR8 ...159 DP111
Sidcup DA14 ...126 EY92
Stanmore HA7 ...42 CL49
Sunbury-on-Thames TW16 ..135 BU95
Sutton SM3 ...157 CW105
Swanley BR8 ...147 FE96
Watford WD17 ...23 BU39
Spinney, The, Wem. HA0 ...61 CG62
Spinney Cl, Beck. BR3 ...143 EB98
Cobham KT11 ...154 CA111
New Malden KT3 ...138 CS99
Rainham RM13 ...89 FE68
West Drayton UB7
off Yew Av ...76 BL73
Worcester Park KT4 ...139 CT104
Spinneycroft, Lthd. KT22 ...171 CD115
Spinney Dr, Felt.TW14 ...115 BQ87
Spinney Gdns, SE19 ...122 DT92
Dagenham RM9 ...70 EY64
Spinney Hill, Add. KT15 ...151 BE106
Spinney Oak, Brom. BR1 ...144 EL96
Chertsey (Ott.) KT16 ...151 BD107
Spinneys, The, Brom. BR1 ...145 EM96
Spinney Way, Sev. (Cudham)
TN14 ...163 ER111
Spire Cl, Grav. DA12 ...131 GH88
Spires, The, Dart. DA1 ...128 FK89
Spires Shop Cen, The, Barn.
EN5 ...27 CY41
Spirit Quay, E1 ...202 C2
★ **Spitalfields Comm Fm**, E1 .84 DU70
Spital La, Brwd. CM14 ...54 FT48
Spital Sq, E1 ...197 N6
Spital St, E1 ...84 DU70
Dartford DA1 ...128 FK86
Spital Yd, E1 ...197 N6
Spitfire Est, Houns.TW5 ...96 BW78
Spitfire Rd, Wall. SM6
off Lancastrian Rd ...159 DM108
Spitfire Way, Houns.TW5 ...96 BW78
Spode Wk, NW6
off Lymington Rd ...82 DB65
Spondon Rd, N15 ...66 DU56
Spoonbill Way, Hayes UB4 ...78 BX71
Spooners Dr, St.Alb. (Park St.)
AL2 ...8 CC27
Spooners Ms, W3
off Churchfield Rd ...80 CR74
Spooner Wk, Wall. SM6 ...159 DK106
Sporle Ct, SW11 ...100 DD83
Sportsbank St, SE6 ...123 EC87
Spotted Dog Path, E7
off Upton La ...86 EG65
Spottons Gro, N17
off Gospatrick Rd ...46 DQ53
Spout Hill, Croy. CR0 ...161 EA106
Spout La, Eden. (Crock.H.)
TN8 ...189 EQ134
Staines TW19 ...114 BG85
Spout La N, Stai.TW19 ...94 BH84
Spratt Hall Rd, E11 ...68 EG58
Spratts All, Cher. (Ott.) KT16 .151 BE107
Spratts La, Cher. (Ott.) KT16 .151 BE107
Spray La, Twick.TW2 ...117 CE86
Spray St, SE18 ...105 EP77
Spreighton Rd, W.Mol. KT8 ..136 CB98
Spriggs Oak, Epp. CM16
off Palmers Hill ...18 EU29
Sprimont Pl, SW3 ...198 D10
Springall St, SE15 ...102 DV80
Springate Fld, Slou. SL3 ...92 AY75
Spring Av, Egh.TW20 ...112 AY93
Springbank, N21 ...29 DM44
Springbank Av, Horn. RM12 ..72 FJ64
Springbank Rd, SE13 ...123 ED86
Springbank Wk, NW1
off St. Paul's Cres ...83 DK66
Spring Bottom La, Red. RH1 .185 DN127
Springbourne Ct, Beck. BR3 .143 EC95
Spring Br Ms, W5
off Spring Br Rd ...79 CK73
Spring Br Rd, W5 ...79 CK73
Spring Cl, Barn. EN5 ...27 CX43
Borehamwood WD6 ...26 CN39
Chesham (Latimer) HP5 ...20 AX36
Dagenham RM8 ...70 EX60
Uxbridge (Hare.) UB9 ...38 BK53
Springclose La, Sutt. SM3 ...157 CY107
Spring Cotts, Surb. KT6
off St. Leonard's Rd ...137 CK99
Spring Ct, Sid. DA15
off Station Rd ...126 EU90
Spring Ct Rd, Enf. EN2 ...29 DN38
Springcroft Av, N2 ...64 DF56
Spring Cfts, Bushey WD23 ...24 CA43
Springdale Ms, N16
off Springdale Rd ...66 DR63
Springdale Rd, N16 ...66 DR63
Spring Dr, Pnr. HA5
off Eastcote Rd ...59 BU58
Spring Fm Cl, Rain. RM13 ...90 FK69
Springfield, E5 ...66 DV60
Bushey (Bushey Hth.) WD23 ..41 CD46
Epping CM16 ...17 ET32
Oxted RH8 ...187 ED130
Springfield Av, N10 ...65 DJ55
SW20 ...139 CZ97
Brentwood CM13 ...55 GE45
Hampton TW12 ...116 CB93
Swanley BR8 ...147 FF98
Springfield Cl, N12 ...44 DB50
Potters Bar EN6 ...12 DD31
Rickmansworth (Crox.Grn.)
WD3 ...23 BP43
Stanmore HA7 ...41 CG48
Woking (Knap.) GU21 ...166 AS118
Springfield Ct, Wall. SM6
off Springfield Rd ...159 DH106
Springfield Dr, Ilf. IG2 ...69 EQ58
Leatherhead KT22 ...171 CE119
Springfield Gdns, E5 ...66 DV60
NW9 ...62 CR57
Bromley BR1 ...145 EM98
Ruislip HA4 ...59 BV60
Upminster RM14 ...72 FQ62
West Wickham BR4 ...143 EB103
Woodford Green IG8 ...48 EJ52
Springfield Gro, SE7 ...104 EJ79
Sunbury-on-Thames
TW16 ...135 BT95
H **Springfield Hosp (London)**,
SW17 ...120 DE89
Springfield La, NW6 ...82 DB67
Weybridge KT13 ...153 BP105
Springfield Meadows, Wey.
KT13 ...153 BP105
Springfield Mt, NW9 ...62 CS57
Springfield Pl, N.Mal. KT3 ...138 CQ98
Springfield Ri, SE26 ...122 DV90
Springfield Rd, E4 ...48 EE46
E6 ...87 EM66
E15 ...86 EE69
E17 ...67 DZ58
N11 ...45 DH50
N15 ...66 DU56
NW8 ...82 DC67
SE26 ...122 DV92
SW19 ...119 CZ92
W7 ...79 CE74
Ashford TW15 ...114 BM92
Bexleyheath DA7 ...107 FB83
Bromley BR1 ...145 EM98
Epsom KT17 ...157 CW110
Grays RM16 ...110 GD75
Harrow HA1 ...61 CE58
Hayes UB4 ...78 BW74
Kingston upon Thames KT1 .138 CL97
Slough SL3 ...93 BB80
Teddington TW11 ...117 CG92
Thornton Heath CR7 ...142 DQ95
Twickenham TW2 ...116 CA88
Wallington SM6 ...159 DH106
Waltham Cross (Chsht.) EN8 .15 DY32
Watford WD25
off Haines Way ...7 BV33
Welling DA16 ...106 EV83
Springfields, Wal.Abb. EN9 ...16 EE34
Springfields Cl, Cher. KT16 ..134 BH102
Springfield Wk, NW6 ...82 DB67
Orpington BR6
off Place Fm Av ...145 ER102
Spring Gdns, N5
off Grosvenor Av ...66 DQ64
SE11 ...200 B10
SW1 ...199 N2
Hornchurch RM12 ...71 FH63
Orpington BR6 ...164 EV107
Romford RM7 ...71 FC57
Wallington SM6 ...159 DJ106
Watford WD25 ...24 BW35
West Molesey KT8 ...136 CC99
Westerham (Bigg.H.) TN16 .178 EJ118
Woodford Green IG8 ...48 EJ52
Spring Gdns Ind Est, Rom.
RM7 ...71 FC57
SPRING GROVE, Islw. ...97 CF81
Spring Gro, SE19 *off Alma Pl* .122 DT94
W4 ...98 CN78
Gravesend DA12 ...131 GH88
Hampton TW12
off Plevna Rd ...136 CB95
Leatherhead (Fetch.) KT22 .170 CB123
Loughton IG10 ...32 EK44
Mitcham CR4 ...140 DG95
Spring Gro Cres, Houns.TW3 .96 CC81
Spring Gro Rd, Houns.TW3 ...96 CB81
Isleworth TW7 ...96 CB81
Richmond TW10 ...118 CM85
Springhead Enterprise Pk, Grav.
DA11 ...130 GC88
Springhead Rd, Erith DA8 ...107 FF79
Gravesend (Nthflt.) DA11 ..130 GC87
Spring Hill, E5 ...66 DU59
SE26 ...122 DW91
Springhill Cl, SE5 ...102 DR83
Springholm Cl, West. (Bigg.H.)
TN16 ...178 EJ118
Springhurst Cl, Croy. CR0 ...161 DZ105
Spring Lake, Stan. HA7 ...41 CH49
Spring La, E5 ...66 DV60
N10 ...64 DG55
SE25 ...142 DV100
Oxted RH8 ...187 ED131
Spring Ms, W1 ...194 E6
Epsom KT17
off Old Schools La ...157 CT109
Richmond TW9
off Rosedale Rd ...98 CL84
Spring Pk Av, Croy. CR0 ...143 DX103
Spring Pk Dr, N4 ...66 DQ60
Springpark Dr, Beck. BR3 ...143 EC97
Spring Pk Rd, Croy. CR0 ...143 DX103
Spring Pas, SW15
off Embankment ...99 CX83
Spring Path, NW3 ...64 DD64
Spring Pl, N3
off Windermere Av ...44 DA54
NW5 ...65 DH64
Springpond Rd, Dag. RM9 ...70 EY64
Springrice Rd, SE13 ...123 EC86
Spring Ri, Egh.TW20 ...112 AY93
Spring Rd, Felt.TW13 ...115 BT90
Springs, The, Brox. EN10 ...15 DY25
Springshaw Cl, Sev. TN13 ...190 FD123
Spring Shaw Rd, Orp. BR5 ...146 EU95
Spring St, W2 ...82 DD72
Epsom KT17 ...157 CT109
Spring Ter, Rich. TW9 ...118 CL85
Spring Vale, Bexh. DA7 ...107 FB84
Greenhithe DA9 ...129 FW86
Springvale Av, Brent.TW8 ...97 CK78
Spring Vale Cl, Swan. BR8 ...147 FF95
Springvale Est, W14
off Blythe Rd ...99 CY76
Spring Vale N, Dart. DA1 ...128 FK87
Springvale Retail Pk, Orp.
BR5 ...146 EW97
Spring Vale S, Dart. DA1 ...128 FK87
Springvale Ter, W14 ...99 CX76
Springvale Way, Orp. BR5 ...146 EW97
Spring Vil Rd, Edg. HA8 ...42 CN52
Spring Wk, E1
off Old Montague St ...84 DU71
Springwater Cl, SE18 ...105 EN81
Springway, Har. HA1 ...61 CD59
Springwell Av, NW10 ...81 CT67
Rickmansworth (Mill End)
WD3 ...38 BG47
Springwell Cl, SW16
off Etherstone Rd ...121 DN91
Springwell Ct, Houns.TW4 ...96 BX82
Springwell Hill, Uxb. (Hare.)
UB9 ...38 BH51
Springwell La, Rick. WD3 ...38 BG49
Uxbridge (Hare.) UB9 ...38 BG49
Springwell Rd, SW16 ...121 DN91
Hounslow TW4, TW5 ...96 BX81
Springwood, Wal.Cr. (Chsht.)
EN7 ...14 DU26
Springwood Cl, Uxb. (Hare.)
UB9 ...38 BK53
Springwood Cres, Edg. HA8 ..42 CP47
Spring Wds, Vir.W. GU25 ...132 AV98
Springwood Way, Rom. RM1 ..71 FG57
Sprowston Ms, E7 ...86 EG65
Sprowston Rd, E7 ...68 EG64
Spruce Cl, Red. RH1 ...184 DF133
Spruce Ct, W5
off Elderberry Rd ...98 CL76
Sprucedale Cl, Swan. BR8 ...147 FE96
Sprucedale Gdns, Croy. CR0 .161 DX105
Wallington SM6 ...159 DK109
Spruce Hills Rd, E17 ...47 EC54
Spruce Pk, Brom. BR2
off Cumberland Rd ...144 EF98
Spruce Rd, West. (Bigg.H.)
TN16 ...178 EK116
Spruce Way, St.Alb. (Park St.)
AL2 ...8 CB27
Sprules Rd, SE4 ...103 DY82
Spur, The, Wal.Cr. (Chsht.) EN8
off Welsummer Way ...15 DX28
Spur Cl, Abb.L. WD5 ...7 BR33
Romford (Abridge) RM4 ...34 EV41
Spurfield, W.Mol. KT8 ...136 CB97
Spurgate, Brwd. CM13 ...55 GA47
Spurgeon Av, SE19 ...142 DR95
Spurgeon Rd, SE19 ...142 DR95
Spurgeon St, SE1 ...201 K7
Spurling Rd, SE22 ...102 DT84
Dagenham RM9 ...88 EZ65
Spurrell Av, Bex. DA5 ...127 FD91
Spur Rd, N15 *off Philip La* ...66 DR56
SE1 ...200 D4
SW1 ...199 K5
Barking IG11 ...87 EQ69
Edgware HA8 ...42 CL49
Feltham TW14 ...115 BV85
Isleworth TW7 ...97 CH80
Orpington BR6 ...146 EU103
Spur Rd Est, Edg. HA8 ...42 CM49
Spurstowe Rd, E8
off Marcon Pl ...84 DV65
Spurstowe Ter, E8 ...66 DV64
Squadrons App, Horn. RM12 ..90 FJ65
Square, The, W6 ...99 CW78
Carshalton SM5 ...158 DG106
Hayes UB3 ...77 BR74
Ilford IG1 ...69 EN59
Richmond TW9 ...117 CK85
Sevenoaks TN13
off Amherst Hill ...190 FE122
Swanley BR8 ...147 FD97
Watford WD24
off The Harebreaks ...23 BV37
West Drayton UB7 ...94 BH81
Westerham (Tats.) TN16 ...178 EJ120
Weybridge KT13 ...153 BQ105
Woking (Wisley) GU23 ...168 BL116
Woodford Green IG8 ...48 EG50
Square Rigger Row, SW11
off York Pl ...100 DC83
Squarey St, SW17 ...120 DC90
★ **Squerryes Ct**, West. TN16 .189 EQ128
Squerryes Mede, West. TN16 .189 EQ127
Squire Gdns, NW8
off St. John's Wd Rd ...82 DD69
Squires, The, Rom. RM7 ...71 FC58
Squires Br Rd, Shep. TW17 ...134 BM98
Squires Ct, SW19 ...120 DA91
Chertsey KT16
off Springfields Cl ...134 BH102
Squires Fld, Swan. BR8 ...147 FF95
Squires La, N3 ...44 DB54
Squires Mt, NW3
off East Heath Rd ...64 DD62
Squires Rd, Shep.TW17 ...134 BM98
Squires Wk, Ashf.TW15
off Napier Rd ...115 BR94
Squires Way, Dart. DA2 ...127 FD91
Squires Wd Dr, Chis. BR7 ...124 EL94
Squirrel Cl, Houns.TW4 ...96 BW82
Squirrel Keep, W.Byf. KT14 ..152 BH112
Squirrel Ms, W13 ...79 CG73
Squirrels, The, SE13
off Belmont Hill ...103 ED83
Bushey WD23 ...25 CD44
Pinner HA5 ...60 BZ55
Squirrels Chase, Grays (Orsett)
RM16 *off Hornsby La* ...111 GG75
Squirrels Cl, N12
off Woodside Av ...44 DC49
Uxbridge UB10 ...76 BN66
Squirrels Grn, Lthd. (Bkhm.)
KT23 ...170 CA123
Worcester Park KT4 ...139 CT102
Squirrels Heath Av, Rom. RM2 .71 FH55
Squirrels Heath La, Horn.
RM11 ...72 FJ56
Romford RM2 ...72 FJ56
Squirrels Heath Rd, Rom. RM3 .72 FL55
Squirrels La, Buck.H. IG9 ...48 EK48
Squirrels Trd Est, The, Hayes
UB3 ...95 BU76
Squirrels Way, Epsom KT18 ..172 CR115
Squirrel Wd, W.Byf. KT14 ...152 BH112
Squirries St, E2 ...84 DU69
Stable Cl, Nthlt. UB5 ...78 CA68
Stables, The, Buck.H. IG9 ...48 EJ45
Cobham KT11 ...154 BZ114
Swanley BR8 ...147 FH95
Stables End, Orp. BR6 ...145 EQ104
Stables Ms, SE27 ...122 DQ92
Stables Way, SE11 ...200 D10
Stable Wk, N2 *off Old Fm Rd* ..44 DD53
Stable Way, W10
off Latimer Rd ...81 CW72
Stable Yd, SW1 ...199 K4

★ Place of interest · ⇄ Railway station · ⊖ London Underground station · DLR Docklands Light Railway station · Tramlink station · H Hospital

329

Sta - Sta

Stable Yd, SW9
off Broomgrove Rd 101 DM82
SW15 off Danemere St 99 CW83
Stable Yd Rd, SW1 199 K3
Stacey Av, N18 46 DW49
Stacey Cl, E10 off Halford Rd 67 ED57
Gravesend DA12 131 GL92
Stacey St, N7 65 DN62
WC2 195 N9
Stackhouse St, SW3 198 D6
Stack Rd, Dart. (Hort.Kir.) DA4 149 FR97
Stacy Path, SE5 off Harris St 102 DS80
Stadium Business Cen, Wem. HA9 62 CP62
Stadium Retail Pk, Wem. HA9 off Wembley Pk Dr 62 CN62
Stadium Rd, NW2 63 CW59
SE18 104 EL80
Stadium St, SW10 100 DC80
Stadium Way, Dart. DA1 127 FE85
Wembley HA9 62 CM63
Staffa Rd, E10 67 DY60
Stafford Av, Horn. RM11 72 FK55
Stafford Cl, E17 67 DZ58
N14 29 DJ43
NW6 82 DA69
Caterham CR3 176 DT123
Grays (Chaff.Hun.) RM16 109 FW77
Greenhithe DA9 129 FT85
Sutton SM3 157 CY107
Waltham Cross (Chsht.) EN8 14 DV29
Stafford Ct, W8 100 DA76
Stafford Cross, Croy. CR0 159 DM106
Stafford Gdns, Croy. CR0 159 DM106
Stafford Pl, SW1 199 K6
Richmond TW10 118 CM87
Stafford Rd, E3 85 DZ68
E7 86 EJ66
NW6 82 DA69
Caterham CR3 176 DT122
Croydon CR0 159 DN105
Harrow HA3 40 CC52
New Malden KT3 138 CQ97
Ruislip HA4 59 BT63
Sidcup DA14 125 ES91
Wallington SM6 159 DJ107
Staffordshire St, SE15 102 DU81
Stafford Sq, Wey. KT13 off Rosslyn Pk 153 BR105
Stafford St, W1 199 K2
Stafford Ter, W8 100 DA76
Stafford Way, Sev. TN13 191 FJ127
Staff St, EC1 197 L3
Stagbury Av, Couls. CR5 174 DE118
Stagbury Cl, Couls. CR5 174 DE119
Stag Cl, Edg. HA8 42 CP54
Staggart Grn, Chig. IG7 49 ET51
Stagg Hill, Barn. EN4 28 DD35
Potters Bar EN6 28 DD35
Stag La, NW9 62 CQ55
SW15 119 CT89
Buckhurst Hill IG9 48 EH47
Edgware HA8 42 CP54
Rickmansworth (Chorl.) WD3 21 BC44
Stag Leys, Ashtd. KT21 172 CL120
Stag Leys Cl, Bans. SM7 174 DD115
Stag Pl, SW1 199 K6
Stag Ride, SW19 119 CT90
Stags Way, Islw. TW7 97 CF79
Stainash Cres, Stai. TW18 114 BH92
Stainash Par, Stai. TW18 off Kingston Rd 114 BH92
Stainbank Rd, Mitch. CR4 141 DH97
Stainby Cl, West Dr. UB7 94 BL76
Stainby Rd, N15 66 DT56
Stainer Ho, SE3 off Ryan Cl 104 EJ84
Stainer Rd, Borwd. WD6 25 CK39
Stainer St, SE1 201 L3
STAINES 114 BG91
⇌ Staines 114 BG92
Staines Av, Sutt. SM3 139 CX103
Staines Br, Stai. TW18 113 BE92
Staines Bypass, Ashf. TW15 114 BH91
Staines TW18, TW19 114 BH91
Staines La, Cher. KT16 133 BF99
Staines La Cl, Cher. KT16 133 BF100
Staines Rd, Cher. KT16 133 BF97
Feltham TW14 115 BR87
Hounslow TW3, TW4 96 CB83
Ilford IG1 69 EQ63
Staines TW18 134 BH95
Staines (Wrays.) TW19 112 AY87
Twickenham TW2 116 CA90
Staines Rd E, Sun. TW16 115 BU94
Staines Rd W, Ashf. TW15 115 BP93
Sunbury-on-Thames TW16 115 BP93
Staines Wk, Sid. DA14 off Evry Rd 126 EW93
Stainford Cl, Ashf. TW15 115 BR92
Stainforth Rd, E17 67 EA56
Ilford IG2 69 ER59
Staining La, EC2 197 J8
Stainmore Cl, Chis. BR7 145 ER95
Stainsbury St, E2 off Royston St 84 DW68
Stainsby Pl, E14 off Stainsby Rd 85 EA72
Stainsby Rd, E14 85 EA72
Stains Cl, Wal.Cr. (Chsht.) EN8 15 DY28
Stainton Rd, SE6 123 ED86
Enfield EN3 30 DW39
Stainton Wk, Wok. GU21 off Inglewood 166 AW118
Stairfoot La, Sev. (Chipstead) TN13 190 FC122
Staithes Way, Tad. KT20 173 CV120
Stalbridge St, NW1 194 C6
Stalham St, SE16 202 E7
Stalisfield Pl, Orp. BR6 off Mill La 163 EN110
Stambourne Way, SE19 122 DS94
West Wickham BR4 143 EC104
H Stamford, The, W6 99 CU77
⊖ Stamford Brook 99 CT77
Stamford Brook Av, W6 99 CT76
Stamford Brook Rd, W6 99 CT76
Stamford Cl, N15 66 DU56
Stamford Cl, NW3 off Heath St 64 DC63
Harrow HA3 41 CE52
Potters Bar EN6 12 DD32
Southall UB1 78 CA73
Stamford Cotts, SW10 off Billing St 100 DB80
Stamford Ct, W6 off Goldhawk Rd 99 CT77
Stamford Dr, Brom. BR2 144 EF98
Stamford Gdns, Dag. RM9 88 EW66
Stamford Grn Rd, Epsom KT18 156 CP113
Stamford Gro E, N16 off Oldhill St 66 DU60
Stamford Gro W, N16 off Oldhill St 66 DU60
STAMFORD HILL, N16 66 DS60
⇌ Stamford Hill 66 DS59
Stamford Hill, N16 66 DT61
Stamford Hill Est, N16 66 DT60
Stamford Rd, E6 86 EL67
N1 84 DS66
N15 66 DU57
Dagenham RM9 88 EV67
Walton-on-Thames KT12 off Kenilworth Dr 136 BX104
Watford WD17 23 BV40
Stamford St, SE1 200 D3
Stamp Pl, E2 197 P2
Stanard Cl, N16 66 DS59
Stanborough Av, Borwd. WD6 26 CN37
Stanborough Cl, Borwd. WD6 26 CN38
Hampton TW12 116 BZ93
Stanborough Pk, Wat. WD25 23 BV35
Stanborough Pas, E8 off Abbot St 84 DT65
Stanborough Rd, Houns. TW3 97 CD83
Stanbridge Pl, N21 45 DP47
Stanbridge Rd, SW15 99 CW83
Stanbrook Rd, SE2 106 EV75
Gravesend DA11 131 GF88
Stanbury Av, Wat. WD17 23 BS37
Stanbury Rd, SE15 102 DV81
Stancroft, NW9 62 CS56
Standale Gro, Ruis. HA4 59 BQ57
Standard Ind Est, E16 105 EM75
Standard Pl, EC2 197 N3
Standard Rd, NW10 80 CQ70
Belvedere DA17 106 FA78
Bexleyheath DA6 106 EY84
Enfield EN3 31 DY38
Hounslow TW4 96 BY83
Orpington BR6 163 EN110
Standen Av, Horn. RM12 72 FK62
Standen Rd, SW18 119 CZ87
Standfield, Abb.L. WD5 7 BS31
Standfield Gdns, Dag. RM10 off Standfield Rd 88 FA65
Standfield Rd, Dag. RM10 70 FA64
Standish Ho, SE3 off Elford Cl 104 EJ84
Standish Rd, W6 99 CU77
Standlake Pt, SE23 123 DX90
Stane Cl, SW19 off Hayward Cl 140 DB95
Stane St, Lthd. KT22 182 CL126
Stane Way, SE18 104 EK80
Epsom KT17 157 CU110
Stanfield Rd, E3 85 DY68
Stanford Cl, Hmptn. TW12 116 BZ93
Romford RM7 71 FB58
Ruislip HA4 59 BQ58
Woodford Green IG8 48 EL50
Stanford Ct, SW6 off Bagley's La 100 DB81
Waltham Abbey EN9 16 EG33
Stanford Gdns, S.Ock. (Aveley) RM15 91 FR74
Stanford Ho, Bark. IG11 88 EV68
Stanford Pl, SE17 201 M9
Stanford Rd, N11 44 DF50
SW16 141 DK96
W8 100 DB76
Grays RM16 110 GD76
Stanford St, SW1 199 M9
Stanford Way, SW16 141 DK96
Stangate Cres, Borwd. WD6 26 CS43
Stangate Gdns, Stan. HA7 41 CH49
Stanger Rd, SE25 142 DU98
Stanham Pl, Dart. DA1 off Crayford Way 107 FG84
Stanham Rd, Dart. DA1 128 FJ85
Stanhope Av, N3 63 CZ55
Bromley BR2 144 EF102
Harrow HA3 41 CD53
Stanhope Cl, SE16 203 J4
Stanhope Gdns, N4 65 DP58
N6 65 DH58
NW7 43 CT50
SW7 100 DC77
Dagenham RM8 70 EZ62
Ilford IG1 69 EM60
Stanhope Gate, W1 198 G2
Stanhope Gro, Beck. BR3 143 DZ99
Stanhope Heath, Stai. (Stanw.) TW19 114 BJ86
Stanhope Ms E, SW7 100 DC77
Stanhope Ms S, SW7 off Gloucester Rd 100 DC77
Stanhope Ms W, SW7 100 DC77
Stanhope Par, NW1 195 K2
Stanhope Pk Rd, Grnf. UB6 78 CC70
Stanhope Pl, W2 194 D9
Stanhope Rd, E17 67 EB57
N6 65 DJ58
N12 44 DC50
Barnet EN5 27 CW44
Bexleyheath DA7 106 EY82
Carshalton SM5 158 DG108
Croydon CR0 142 DS104
Dagenham RM8 70 EZ61
Greenford UB6 78 CC71
Rainham RM13 89 FG68
Sidcup DA15 126 EU91
Swanscombe DA10 130 FZ85
Waltham Cross EN8 15 DY33
Stanhope Row, W1 199 H3
Stanhopes, Oxt. RH8 188 EH128
Stanhope St, NW1 195 K3
Stanhope Ter, W2 194 A10
Stanhope Way, Sev. TN13 190 FD122
Staines (Stanw.) TW19 114 BJ86
Stanier Cl, W14 off Aisgill Av 99 CZ78
Staniland Dr, Wey. KT13 152 BM110
Stanlake Ms, W12 81 CW74
Stanlake Rd, W12 81 CV74
Stanlake Vil, W12 81 CV74
Stanley Av, Bark. IG11 87 ET68
Beckenham BR3 143 EC96
Dagenham RM8 70 EZ60
Greenford UB6 78 CC67
New Malden KT3 139 CU99
Romford RM2 71 FG56
St. Albans AL2 8 CA25
Wembley HA0 80 CL66
Stanley Cl, SW8 101 DM79
Coulsdon CR5 175 DM117
Greenhithe DA9 129 FS85
Hornchurch RM12 off Stanley Rd 72 FJ61
Romford RM2 71 FG56
Uxbridge UB8 76 BK67
Wembley HA0 80 CL66
Stanley Cotts, Slou. SL2 74 AT74
Stanley Ct, Cars. SM5 off Stanley Pk Rd 158 DG108
Stanley Cres, W11 81 CZ73
Gravesend DA12 131 GK92
Stanleycroft Cl, Islw. TW7 97 CE81
Stanley Gdns, NW2 63 CW64
W3 80 CS74
W11 81 CZ73
Borehamwood WD6 26 CL39
Mitcham CR4 off Ashbourne Rd 120 DG93
South Croydon CR2 160 DU112
Wallington SM6 159 DJ107
Walton-on-Thames KT12 154 BW107
Stanley Gdns Ms, W11 off Stanley Cres 81 CZ73
Stanley Gdns Rd, Tedd. TW11 117 CE92
Stanley Grn E, Slou. SL3 93 AZ77
Stanley Grn W, Slou. SL3 93 AZ77
Stanley Gro, SW8 100 DG82
Croydon CR0 141 DN100
Stanley Pk Dr, Wem. HA0 80 CM66
Stanley Pk Rd, Cars. SM5 158 DF108
Wallington SM6 159 DH107
Stanley Pas, NW1 195 P1
Stanley Rd, E4 47 ED46
E10 67 EB58
E12 68 EL64
E15 85 ED67
E18 48 EF53
N2 64 DD55
N9 46 DT46
N10 45 DH52
N11 45 DK51
N15 65 DP56
NW9 off West Hendon Bdy 63 CU59
SW14 98 CP84
SW19 120 DA94
W3 98 CQ76
Ashford TW15 114 BL92
Bromley BR2 144 EH98
Carshalton SM5 158 DG108
Croydon CR0 141 DN101
Enfield EN1 30 DS41
Gravesend (Nthflt.) DA11 130 GE88
Grays RM17 110 GB78
Harrow HA2 60 CC61
Hornchurch RM12 72 FJ61
Hounslow TW3 96 CC84
Ilford IG1 69 ER61
Mitcham CR4 120 DG94
Morden SM4 140 DA98
Northwood HA6 39 BU53
Orpington BR6 146 EU102
Sidcup DA14 126 EU90
Southall UB1 78 BY73
Sutton SM2 158 DB107
Swanscombe DA10 130 FZ86
Teddington TW11 117 CE91
Twickenham TW2 117 CD90
Watford WD17 24 BW41
Wembley HA9 80 CM65
Woking GU21 167 AZ116
Stanley Rd N, Rain. RM13 89 FE67
Stanley Rd S, Rain. RM13 89 FF68
Stanley Sq, Cars. SM5 158 DF109
Stanley St, SE8 103 DZ80
Caterham CR3 off Coulsdon Rd 176 DQ122
Stanley Ter, N19 65 DL61
Stanley Way, Orp. BR5 146 EV99
Stanmer St, SW11 100 DE81
STANMORE 41 CG50
⊖ Stanmore 41 CK50
Stanmore Gdns, Rich. TW9 98 CM83
Sutton SM1 140 DC104
Stanmore Hall, Stan. HA7 41 CH48
Stanmore Hill, Stan. HA7 41 CG48
Stanmore Pk, Stan. HA7 41 CH50
Stanmore Pl, NW1 off Arlington Rd 83 DH67
Stanmore Rd, E11 68 EF60
N15 65 DP56
Belvedere DA17 107 FC77
Richmond TW9 98 CM83
Watford WD24 23 BV39
Stanmore St, N1 off Caledonian Rd 83 DM67
Stanmore Ter, Beck. BR3 143 EA96
Stanmore Way, Loug. IG10 33 EN39
Stanmount Rd, St.Alb. AL2 8 CA25
Stannard Ms, E8 84 DU65
Stannard Rd, E8 84 DU65
Stannary Pl, SE11 101 DN78
Stannary St, SE11 101 DN79
Stannet Way, Wall. SM6 159 DJ105
Stannington Path, Borwd. WD6 26 CN39
Stansfield Rd, E6 86 EK71
Stansfield Rd, SW9 101 DM83
Stansfield Rd, Houns. TW4 95 BV82
Stansgate Rd, Dag. RM10 70 FA61
Stanstead Cl, Brom. BR2 144 EF99
Stanstead Gro, SE6 off Catford Hill 123 DZ88
Stanstead Manor, Sutt. SM1 158 DA107
Stanstead Rd, E11 68 EH57
SE6 123 DX88
SE23 123 DX88
Caterham CR3 186 DR125
Hounslow (Hthrw.Air.) TW6 114 BM86
Stansted Cl, Horn. RM12 89 FH65
Stansted Cres, Bex. DA5 126 EX88
Stanswood Gdns, SE5 off Sedgmoor Pl 102 DS80
Stanthorpe Cl, SW16 121 DL92
Stanthorpe Rd, SW16 121 DL92
Stanton Av, Tedd. TW11 117 CE92
Stanton Cl, Epsom KT19 156 CP106
Orpington BR5 146 EW101
Worcester Park KT4 139 CX102
Stanton Ho, SE16 203 M4
Stanton Rd, SE26 off Stanton Way 123 DZ91
SW13 99 CT82
SW20 139 CX96
Croydon CR0 142 DQ101
Stanton Sq, SE26 off Stanton Way 123 DZ91
Stanton Way, SE26 123 DZ91
Slough SL3 92 AY77
Stanway Cl, Chig. IG7 49 ES50
Stanway Ct, N1 197 N1
Stanway Gdns, W3 80 CN74
Edgware HA8 42 CQ50
Stanway Rd, Wal.Abb. EN9 16 EG33
Stanway St, N1 84 DS68
STANWELL, Stai. 114 BL87
Stanwell Cl, Stai. (Stanw.) TW19 114 BK86
Stanwell Gdns, Stai. (Stanw.) TW19 114 BK86
STANWELL MOOR, Stai. 114 BG85
Stanwell Moor Rd, Stai. TW19 114 BH85
West Drayton UB7 94 BH81
Stanwell New Rd, Stai. TW18 114 BH90
Stanwell Rd, Ashf. TW15 114 BL89
Feltham TW14 115 BQ87
Slough (Horton) SL3 93 BA83
Stanwick Rd, W14 99 CZ77
Stanworth St, SE1 201 P5
Stanwyck Dr, Chig. IG7 49 EQ50
Stanwyck Gdns, Rom. RM3 51 FH50
Stapenhill Rd, Wem. HA0 61 CH62
Staple Cl, Bex. DA5 127 FD90
Staplefield Cl, SW2 121 DL88
Pinner HA5 40 BY52
STAPLEFORD ABBOTTS, Rom. 35 FC43
★ Stapleford Airfield, Rom. RM4 34 EZ40
Stapleford Av, Ilf. IG2 69 ES57
Stapleford Cl, E4 47 EC48
SW19 119 CY87
Kingston upon Thames KT1 138 CN97
Stapleford Ct, Sev. TN13 190 FF123
Stapleford Gdns, Rom. RM5 50 FA51
Stapleford Rd, Rom. RM4 35 FB42
Wembley HA0 79 CK66
STAPLEFORD TAWNEY, Rom. 35 FC37
Stapleford Tawney, Ong. CM5 19 FC32
Romford RM4 35 FD35
Stapleford Way, Bark. IG11 88 EV69
Staple Hill Rd, Wok. (Chob.Com.) GU24 150 AS105
Staplehurst Rd, SE13 124 EE85
Carshalton SM5 158 DE108
Staple Inn, WC1 196 D7
Staple Inn Bldgs, WC1 196 D7
Staples Cl, SE16 203 K2
Staples Cor, NW2 63 CV60
Staples Cor Business Pk, NW2 63 CV60
Staples Rd, Loug. IG10 32 EL41
Staple St, SE1 201 L5
Stapleton Cl, Pot.B. EN6 12 DD31
Stapleton Cres, Rain. RM13 89 FG65
Stapleton Gdns, Croy. CR0 159 DN106
Stapleton Hall Rd, N4 65 DM59
Stapleton Rd, SW17 120 DG90
Bexleyheath DA7 106 EZ80
Borehamwood WD6 26 CN38
Orpington BR6 145 ET104
Stapley Rd, Belv. DA17 106 FA78
Stapylton Rd, Barn. EN5 27 CY41
Star All, EC3 197 N10
Star & Garter Hill, Rich. TW10 118 CL88
Starboard Av, Green. DA9 129 FV86
Starboard Way, E14 204 A6
Starch Ho La, Ilf. IG6 49 ER54
Starcross St, NW1 195 L3
Starfield Rd, W12 99 CU75
Star Hill, Dart. DA1 127 FE85
Woking GU22 166 AW119
Star Hill Rd, Sev. (Dunt.Grn.) TN14 180 EZ116
Starkey Cl, Wal.Cr. (Chsht.) EN7 off Shambrook Rd 14 DQ25
Star La, E16 86 EE70
Coulsdon CR5 174 DG122
Epping CM16 18 EU30
Orpington BR5 146 EW98
Starling Cl, Buck.H. IG9 48 EG46
Pinner HA5 60 BW55
Starling La, Pot.B. (Cuffley) EN6 13 DM28
Starling Ms, SE28 off Whinchat Rd 105 ER75
Starlings, The, Lthd. (Oxshott) KT22 154 CC113
Starling Wk, Hmptn. TW12 off Oak Av 116 BY93
Starmans Cl, Dag. RM9 88 EY67
Star Path, Nthlt. UB5 off Brabazon Rd 78 CA68
Star Pl, E1 202 A1
Star Rd, W14 99 CZ79
Isleworth TW7 97 CD82
Uxbridge UB10 77 BQ70
Starrock La, Couls. (Chipstead) CR5 174 DF120
Starrock Rd, Couls. CR5 175 DH119
Star St, E16 86 EF71
W2 194 A8
Starts Cl, Orp. BR6 145 EN104
Starts Hill Av, Orp. BR6 163 EP105
Starts Hill Rd, Orp. BR6 145 EN104
Starveall Cl, West Dr. UB7 94 BM76
Starwood Cl, W.Byf. KT14 152 BJ111
Starwood Ct, Slou. SL3 off London Rd 92 AW76
Star Yd, WC2 196 D8
State Fm Av, Orp. BR6 163 EP105
Staten Gdns, Twick. TW1 117 CF88
Statham Gro, N16 off Green Las 66 DQ63
N18 46 DS50
Station App, E4 (Highams Pk.) off The Avenue 47 ED51
E7 off Woodford Rd 68 EH63
E11 (Snaresbrook) off High St 68 EG57
N11 off Friern Barnet Rd 45 DH50
N12 (Woodside Pk.) 44 DB49
N16 (Stoke Newington) off Stamford Hill 66 DT61
NW10 off Station Rd 81 CT69
SE1 200 C5
SE3 off Kidbrooke Pk Rd 104 EH83
SE9 (Mottingham) 125 EM88
SE26 (Lwr.Sydenham) off Worsley Br Rd 123 DZ92
SE26 (Sydenham) off Sydenham Rd 122 DW91
SW6 99 CY83
SW16 121 DK92
W7 79 CE74
Amersham (Lt.Chal.) HP7 off Chalfont Sta Rd 20 AX39
Ashford TW15 114 BL91
Barnet EN5 28 DC42
Bexley DA5 off Bexley High St 126 FA87
Bexleyheath DA7 off Avenue Rd 106 EY82
Bexleyheath (Barne.) DA7 107 FC82
Bromley (Hayes) BR2 144 EG102
Buckhurst Hill IG9 off Cherry Tree Ri 48 EK49
Chislehurst BR7 145 EN95
Chislehurst (Elm.Wds.) BR7 124 EL93
Coulsdon CR5 175 DK116
Coulsdon (Chipstead) CR5 174 DF118
Dartford DA1 128 FL86
Dartford (Cray.) DA1 127 FF86
Epping (They.B.) CM16 off Coppice Row 33 ES36
Epsom KT18 156 CR113
Epsom (Ewell E.) KT17 157 CV110
Epsom (Ewell W.) KT19 off Chessington Rd 157 CT109
Epsom (Stoneleigh) KT19 157 CU106
Esher (Hinch.Wd.) KT10 137 CF104
Gerrards Cross SL9 56 AY57
Grays RM17 110 GA79
Greenford UB6 79 CD66
Hampton TW12 off Milton Rd 136 CA95
Harrow HA1 61 CE59
Hayes UB3 95 BT75
Kenley CR8 off Hayes La 160 DQ114
Kingston upon Thames KT1 138 CN95
Leatherhead KT22 171 CG121
Leatherhead (Oxshott) KT22 154 CC113
Loughton IG10 32 EL43
Loughton (Debden) IG10 33 EQ42
Northwood HA6 39 BS52
Orpington BR6 145 ET103
Orpington (Chels.) BR6 164 EV106
Orpington (St.M.Cray) BR5 146 EV98
Oxted RH8 188 EE128
Pinner HA5 60 BY55
Pinner (Hatch End) HA5 off Uxbridge Rd 40 CA52
Purley CR8 off Whytecliffe Rd S 159 DN111
Radlett WD7 off Shenley Hill 25 CG35
Richmond TW9 98 CN81
Rickmansworth (Chorl.) WD3 21 BC42
Ruislip (S.Ruis.) HA4 59 BV64
Shepperton TW17 135 BQ100
South Croydon CR2 off Sanderstead Rd 160 DR109
Staines TW18 114 BG92
Sunbury-on-Thames TW16 135 BU95
Sutton (Belmont) SM2 off Brighton Rd 158 DB110
Sutton (Cheam) SM2 157 CY108
Swanley BR8 147 FE98
Upminster RM14 72 FQ61
Uxbridge (Denh.) UB9 off Middle Rd 57 BD59
Virginia Water GU25 132 AX98
Waltham Cross EN8 15 DY34
Waltham Cross (Chsht.) EN8 15 DZ30
Watford WD18 off Cassiobury Pk Av 23 BT41
Watford (Carp.Pk.) WD19 off Prestwick Rd 40 BX48
Welling DA16 105 ET82
Wembley HA0 79 CH65
West Byfleet KT14 152 BG112
West Drayton UB7 76 BL74
Weybridge KT13 152 BN107
Whyteleafe CR3 176 DU117
Woking GU22 167 AZ117
Station App N, Sid. DA15 126 EU89
Station App Rd, W4 98 CQ80
Coulsdon CR5 175 DK115
Tadworth KT20 173 CW122
Tilbury RM18 111 GG84

★ Place of interest ⇌ Railway station ⊖ London Underground station DLR Docklands Light Railway station Tramlink station H Hospital

Sta - Sto

Station Av, SW9
off Coldharbour La 101 DP83
Caterham CR3 176 DU124
Epsom KT19 156 CS109
New Malden KT3 138 CS97
Richmond TW9 98 CN81
Walton-on-Thames KT12 153 BU105
Station Cl, N3 44 DA53
N12 (Woodside Pk.) 44 DB49
Hampton TW12 136 CB95
Hatfield AL9 *off Station Rd* 11 CY26
Potters Bar EN6 11 CZ31
Station Cres, N15 66 DR56
SE3 104 EG78
Ashford TW15 114 BK90
Wembley HA0 79 CH65
Stationers Hall Ct, EC4
off Ludgate Hill 83 DP72
Station Est, Beck. BR3
off Elmers End Rd 143 DX98
Station Est Rd, Felt. TW14 115 BV88
Station Footpath, Kings L.
WD4 7 BP31
Station Garage Ms, SW16
off Estreham Rd 121 DK93
Station Gdns, W4 98 CQ80
Station Gro, Wem. HA0 80 CL65
Station Hill, Brom. BR2 144 EG103
Station Ho Ms, N9 *off Fore St* 46 DU49
Station La, Horn. RM12 72 FK62
Station Par, E11 68 EG57
N14 *off High St* 45 DK46
NW2 81 CW65
SW12 *off Balham High Rd* 120 DG88
W3 80 CN72
Ashford TW15
off Woodthorpe Rd 114 BM91
Barking IG11 87 EQ66
Feltham TW14 115 BV87
Hornchurch RM12
off Rosewood Av 71 FH63
Richmond TW9 98 CN81
Sevenoaks TN13
off London Rd 190 FG124
Uxbridge (Denh.) UB9 58 BG59
Virginia Water GU25 132 AX98
Station Pas, E18
off Maybank Rd 48 EH54
Station Path, E8
off Amhurst Rd 84 DV65
Staines TW18 113 BF91
Station Pl, N4
off Seven Sisters Rd 65 DN61
Station Ri, SE27
off Norwood Rd 121 DP89
Station Rd, E4 (Chingford) 47 ED46
E7 68 EG63
E12 68 EK63
E17 67 DY58
N3 44 DA53
N11 45 DH50
N17 66 DU55
N19 65 DJ62
N21 45 DP46
N22 45 DM54
NW4 63 CU58
NW7 42 CS50
NW10 81 CT68
SE13 103 EC83
SE20 122 DW93
SE25 (Norwood Junct.) 142 DT98
SW13 99 CU83
SW19 140 DC95
W5 80 CM72
W7 (Hanwell) 79 CE74
Addlestone KT15 152 BJ105
Ashford TW15 114 BM91
Barnet EN5 28 DB43
Belvedere DA17 106 FA76
Betchworth RH3 182 CS131
Bexleyheath DA7 106 EY83
Borehamwood WD6 26 CN42
Brentford TW8 97 CJ79
Bromley BR1 144 EG95
Bromley (Short.) BR2 144 EE96
Carshalton SM5 158 DF105
Caterham CR3 177 DZ123
Chertsey KT16 133 BF102
Chessington KT9 156 CL106
Chigwell IG7 49 EP48
Cobham (Stoke D'Ab.) KT11 170 BY117
Croydon (E.Croy.) CR0 142 DR103
Croydon (W.Croy.) CR0 142 DQ102
Dartford (Cray.) DA1 127 FF86
Dartford (Eyns.) DA4 148 FK104
Dartford (S.Darenth) DA4 148 FP96
Edgware HA8 42 CN51
Egham TW20 113 BA92
Epping CM16 18 EU31
Epping (N.Wld.Bas.) CM16 19 FB27
Esher KT10 137 CD103
Esher (Clay.) KT10 155 CD106
Gerrards Cross SL9 56 AY57
Gravesend (Betsham) DA13 130 GA91
Gravesend (Nthflt.) DA11 130 GB86
Greenhithe DA9 129 FU85
Hampton TW12 136 CA95
Harrow HA1 61 CF59
Harrow (N.Har.) HA2 60 CB57
Hatfield (Brook.Pk.) AL9 11 CX25
Hayes UB3 95 BT76
Hounslow TW3 96 CB84
Ilford IG1 69 EP62
Ilford (Barkingside) IG6 69 ER55
Kenley CR8 160 DQ114
Kings Langley WD4 7 BP29
Kingston upon Thames KT2 138 CN95
Kingston upon Thames
(Hmptn.W.) KT1 137 CJ95
Leatherhead KT22 171 CG121
Loughton IG10 32 EL42
New Malden (Mots.Pk.) KT3 139 CV99
Orpington BR6 145 ET103
Orpington (St.P.Cray) BR5 146 EW98
Station Rd, Pot.B. (Cuffley)
EN6 13 DM29
Radlett WD7 25 CG35
Redhill RH1 184 DG133
Redhill (Merst.) RH1 185 DJ128
Rickmansworth WD3 38 BK45
Romford (Chad.Hth.) RM6 70 EX59
Romford (Gidea Pk.) RM2 71 FH56
Romford (Harold Wd.) RM3 52 FM53
St. Albans (Brick.Wd.) AL2 8 CA31
Sevenoaks (Dunt.Grn.) TN13 181 FE120
Sevenoaks (Halst.) TN14 164 EZ111
Sevenoaks (Otford) TN14 181 FH116
Sevenoaks (Shore.) TN14 165 FG111
Shepperton TW17 135 BQ99
Sidcup DA15 126 EU91
Slough (Langley) SL3 93 BA76
Staines (Wrays.) TW19 113 AZ86
Sunbury-on-Thames TW16 115 BU94
Sutton (Belmont) SM2 158 DA110
Swanley BR8 147 FE98
Teddington TW11 117 CF92
Thames Ditton KT7 137 CF101
Twickenham TW1 117 CF88
Upminster RM14 72 FQ61
Uxbridge UB8 76 BJ70
Waltham Cross EN8 15 EA34
Watford WD17 23 BV40
West Byfleet KT14 152 BG112
West Drayton UB7 76 BK74
West Wickham BR4 143 EC102
Westerham (Brasted) TN16 180 EV123
Whyteleafe CR3 176 DT118
Woking (Chobham) GU24 150 AT111
Station Rd E, Oxt. RH8 188 EE128
Station Rd N, Belv. DA17 107 FB76
Egham TW20 113 BA92
Redhill (Merst.) RH1 185 DJ128
Station Rd S, Red. (Merst.)
RH1 185 DJ128
Station Rd W, Oxt. RH8 188 EE129
Station Sq, Orp. (Petts Wd)
BR5 145 EQ99
Romford RM2 71 FH56
Station St, E15 85 ED66
E16 87 EP74
Station Ter, NW10 81 CX68
SE5 102 DQ81
St. Albans (Park St.) AL2
off Park St 9 CD26
Station Vw, Grnf. UB6 79 CD67
Station Way, Buck.H. (Rod.Val.)
IG9 48 EJ49
Epsom (Epsom) KT19 156 CR113
Esher (Clay.) KT10 155 CE107
Sutton (Cheam) SM3 157 CY107
Station Yd, Twick. TW1 117 CG87
Staunton Rd, Kings.T. KT2 118 CL93
Staunton St, SE8 103 DZ79
★ **Stave Hill Ecological Pk**,
SE16 103 DY75
Staveley Cl, E9
off Churchill Wk 66 DW64
N7 *off Penn Rd* 65 DL63
SE15 *off Asylum Rd* 102 DV81
Staveley Gdns, W4 98 CR81
Staveley Rd, W4 98 CR80
Ashford TW15 115 BR93
Staveley Way, Wok. (Knap.)
GU21 166 AS117
Staverton Rd, NW2 81 CW66
Hornchurch RM11 72 FK58
Stave Yd Rd, SE16 203 K3
Stavordale Rd, N5 65 DP63
Carshalton SM5 140 DC101
Stayne End, Vir.W. GU25 132 AU98
Stayner's Rd, E1 85 DX70
Stayton Rd, Sutt. SM1 140 DA104
Steadfast Rd, Kings.T. KT1 137 CK95
Stead St, SE17 201 K9
Steam Fm La, Felt. TW14 95 BT84
Stean St, E8 84 DT67
Stebbing Ho, W11 81 CX74
Stebbing Way, Bark. IG11 88 EU68
Stebondale St, E14 204 E9
Stedham Pl, WC1 195 P8
Stedman Cl, Bex. DA5 127 FE90
Uxbridge UB10 58 BN62
Steed Cl, Horn. RM11 71 FH61
Steedman St, SE17 201 H9
Steeds Rd, N10 44 DF53
Steeds Way, Loug. IG10 32 EL41
Steele Av, Green. DA9 129 FT85
Steele Rd, E11 68 EE63
N17 66 DS55
NW10 80 CQ68
W4 98 CQ76
Isleworth TW7 97 CG84
Steeles Ms N, NW3
off Steeles Rd 82 DF65
Steeles Ms S, NW3
off Steeles Rd 82 DF65
Steeles Rd, NW3 82 DF65
Steele Wk, Erith DA8 107 FB79
Steel's La, E1 *off Devonport St* 84 DW72
Steels La, Lthd. (Oxshott)
KT22 154 CB114
Steelyard Pas, EC4
off Upper Thames St 84 DR73
Steen Way, SE22
off East Dulwich Gro 122 DS85
Steep Cl, Orp. BR6 163 ET107
Steep Hill, SW16 121 DK90
Croydon CR0 160 DS105
Steeplands, Bushey WD23 40 CB45
Steeple Cl, SW6 99 CY82
SW19 119 CY92
Steeple Ct, E1 *off Coventry Rd* 84 DV70
Steeple Gdns, Add. KT15
off Weatherall Cl 152 BH106
Steeple Hts Dr, West. (Bigg.H.)
TN16 178 EK117
Steeplestone Cl, N18 46 DQ50
Steeple Wk, N1 *off Basire St* 84 DQ67
Steerforth St, SW18 120 DB89
Steers Mead, Mitch. CR4 140 DF95
Steers Way, SE16 203 L5
Stellar Ho, N17 46 DT51
Stella Rd, SW17 120 DF93
Stelling Rd, Erith DA8 107 FD80
Stellman Cl, E5 66 DU62
Stembridge Rd, SE20 142 DV96
Sten Cl, Enf. EN3
off Government Row 31 EA38
Stents La, Cob. KT11 170 BZ120
Stepbridge Path, Wok. GU21
off Goldsworth Rd 166 AX117
Stepgates, Cher. KT16 134 BH101
Stepgates Cl, Cher. KT16 134 BH101
Stephan Cl, E8 84 DU67
Stephen Av, Rain. RM13 89 FG65
Stephen Cl, Egh. TW20 113 BC93
Orpington BR6 145 ET104
Stephendale Rd, SW6 100 DB82
Stephen Ms, W1 195 M7
Stephen Pl, SW4
off Rectory Gro 101 DJ83
Stephen Rd, Bexh. DA7 107 FC83
Stephens Cl, Rom. RM3 52 FJ50
Stephenson Av, Til. RM18 111 GG81
Stephenson Rd, E17 67 DY57
W7 79 CF72
Twickenham TW2 116 CA87
Stephenson St, E16 86 EE70
NW10 80 CS69
Stephenson Way, NW1 195 L4
Watford WD24 24 BX41
Stephen's Rd, E15 86 EE67
Stephen St, W1 195 M7
Stephens Way, Hem.H. HP3
off Belswains La 6 BM25
STEPNEY, E1 84 DW71
Stepney Causeway, E1 85 DX72
H **Stepney Day Hosp**, E1 84 DW72
⊖ **Stepney Green** 85 DX70
Stepney Grn, E1 84 DW71
Stepney High St, E1 85 DX71
Stepney Way, E1 84 DV71
Sterling Av, Edg. HA8 42 CM49
Pinner HA5 60 BY59
Waltham Cross EN8 15 DX34
Sterling Cl, NW10 81 CU65
Pinner HA5 60 BX60
Sterling Gdns, SE14 103 DY79
Sterling Ho, SE3
off Cambert Way 104 EH84
Sterling Ind Est, Dag. RM10 71 FB63
Sterling Pl, W5 98 CL77
Sterling Rd, Enf. EN2 30 DR38
Sterling St, SW7 198 C6
Sterling Way, N18 46 DR50
★ **Sternberg Cen**,
N3 (Finchley) 44 DB54
Stern Cl, Bark. IG11 88 EW68
Sterndale Rd, W14 99 CX76
Dartford DA1 128 FM87
Sterne St, W12 99 CX75
Sternhall La, SE15 102 DU83
Sternhold Av, SW2 121 DK89
Sterry Cres, Dag. RM10
off Alibon Rd 70 FA64
Sterry Dr, Epsom KT19 156 CS105
Thames Ditton KT7 137 CE100
Sterry Gdns, Dag. RM10 88 FA65
Sterry Rd, Bark. IG11 87 ET67
Dagenham RM10 70 FA63
Sterry St, SE1 201 K5
Steucers La, SE23 123 DY87
Steve Biko La, SE6 123 EA91
Steve Biko Rd, N7 65 DN62
Steve Biko Way, Houns. TW3 96 CA83
Stevedale Rd, Well. DA16 106 EW82
Stevedore St, E1 202 D2
Stevenage Cres, Borwd. WD6 26 CL39
Stevenage Rd, E6 87 EN65
SW6 99 CX80
Stevens Av, E9 84 DW65
Stevens Cl, Beck. BR3 123 EA93
Bexley DA5 127 FD91
Steven's Cl, Dart. (Lane End)
DA2 129 FS92
Stevens Cl, Epsom KT17
off Upper High St 156 CS113
Hampton TW12 116 BY93
Pinner HA5
off Bridle Rd 60 BW57
Stevens Grn, Bushey
(Bushey Hth.) WD23 40 CC46
Stevens La, Esher (Clay.)
KT10 155 CG108
Stevenson Cl, Barn. EN5 28 DD44
Erith DA8 107 FH80
Stevenson Cres, SE16 202 C10
Stevens Pl, Pur. CR8 159 DP113
Stevens Rd, Dag. RM8 70 EV62
Stevens St, SE1 201 N6
Steven's Wk, Croy. CR0 161 DY111
Stevens Way, Chig. IG7 49 ES49
Steventon Rd, W12 81 CT73
Steward Cl, Wal.Cr. (Chsht.)
EN8 15 DY30
Stewards Cl, Epp. CM16 18 EU33
Stewards Grn La, Epp. CM16 18 EV32
Stewards Grn Rd, Epp. CM16 18 EU33
Stewards Holte Wk, N11
off Coppies Gro 45 DH49
Steward St, E1 197 N7
Stewards Wk, Rom. RM1 71 FE57
Stewart, Tad. KT20 173 CX121
Stewart Av, Shep. TW17 134 BN98
Slough SL1 74 AT71
Upminster RM14 72 FP62
Stewart Cl, NW9 62 CQ58
Abbots Langley WD5 7 BT32
Chislehurst BR7 125 EP92
Hampton TW12 116 BY92
Woking GU21
off Nethercote Av 166 AT117
Stewart Rainbird Ho, E12 69 EN64
Stewart Rd, E15 67 EC63
Stewartsby Cl, N18 46 DQ50
Stewart's Gro, SW3 198 A10
Stewart's Rd, SW8 101 DJ80
Stewart St, E14 204 E5
Stew La, EC4 197 H10
Steyne Rd, W3 80 CQ74
Steyning Cl, Ken. CR8 175 DP116
Steyning Gro, SE9 125 EM91
Steynings Way, N12 44 DA50
Steyning Way, Houns. TW4 96 BW84
Steynton Av, Bex. DA5 126 EX89
Stickland Rd, Belv. DA17
off Picardy Rd 106 FA77
Stickleton Cl, Grnf. UB6 78 CB69
Stifford Hill, Grays (N.Stfd.)
RM16 91 FX74
South Ockendon RM15 91 FW73
Stifford Rd, S.Ock. RM15 91 FR74
Stilecroft Gdns, Wem. HA0 61 CH62
Stile Hall Gdns, W4 98 CN78
Stile Hall Par, W4
off Chiswick High Rd 98 CN78
Stile Path, Sun. TW16 135 BU98
Stile Rd, Slou. SL3 92 AX76
Stiles Cl, Brom. BR2 145 EM100
Erith DA8 *off Riverdale Rd* 107 FB78
Stillingfleet Rd, SW13 99 CU79
Stillington St, SW1 199 L8
Stillness Rd, SE23 123 DY86
Stilton Cres, NW10 80 CQ66
Stilton Path, Borwd. WD6 26 CN38
Stilwell Dr, Uxb. UB8 76 BM70
Stilwell Roundabout, Uxb.
UB8 76 BN73
Stipularis Dr, Hayes UB4 78 BX70
Stirling Cl, SW16 141 DJ95
Banstead SM7 173 CZ117
Rainham RM13 89 FH69
Uxbridge UB8
off Ferndale Cres 76 BJ69
Stirling Cor, Barn. EN5 26 CR44
Borehamwood WD6 26 CR44
Stirling Dr, Orp. BR6 164 EV106
Stirling Gro, Houns. TW3 96 CC82
Stirling Rd, E13 86 EH68
E17 67 DY55
N17 46 DU53
N22 45 DP53
SW9 101 DL82
W3 98 CP76
Harrow HA3 61 CF55
Hayes UB3 77 BV73
Hounslow (Hthrw.Air.) TW6 114 BM86
Twickenham TW2 116 CA87
Stirling Rd Path, E17 67 DY55
Stirling Wk, N.Mal. KT3 138 CQ99
Surbiton KT5 138 CP100
Stirling Way, Abb.L. WD5 7 BU32
Borehamwood WD6 26 CR44
Croydon CR0 141 DL101
Stites Hill Rd, Couls. CR5 175 DP120
Stiven Cres, Har. HA2 60 BZ62
Stoats Nest Rd, Couls. CR5 159 DL114
Stoats Nest Village, Couls.
CR5 175 DL115
Stockbury Rd, Croy. CR0 142 DW100
Stockdale Rd, Dag. RM8 70 EZ61
Stockdove Way, Grnf. UB6 79 CF69
Stocker Gdns, Dag. RM9 88 EW66
Stockers Fm Rd, Rick. WD3 38 BK48
Stockers La, Wok. GU22 167 AZ120
★ **Stock Exchange**, EC2 197 L9
Stockfield Rd, SW16 121 DM90
Esher (Clay.) KT10 155 CE106
Stockham's Cl, S.Croy. CR2 160 DR111
Stock Hill, West. (Bigg.H.)
TN16 178 EK116
Stockholm Ho, E1 84 DU73
Stockholm Rd, SE16 102 DW78
Stockholm Way, E1 202 B2
Stockhurst Cl, SW15 99 CW82
Stockingswater La, Enf. EN3 31 DY41
Stockland Rd, Rom. RM7 71 FD58
Stock La, Dart. DA2 128 FJ91
Stockley Cl, West Dr. UB7 95 BP75
Stockley Fm Rd, West Dr. UB7
off Stockley Rd 95 BP76
Stockley Pk, Uxb. UB11 77 BP74
Stockley Pk Roundabout, Uxb.
UB11 77 BP74
Stockley Rd, Uxb. UB8 77 BP73
West Drayton UB7 95 BP77
Stock Orchard Cres, N7 65 DM64
Stock Orchard St, N7 65 DM64
Stockport Rd, SW16 141 DK95
Rickmansworth (Herons.)
WD3 37 BC45
Stocksfield Rd, E17 67 EC55
Stocks Pl, E14 *off Grenade St* 85 DZ73
Stock St, E13 86 EG68
Stockton Cl, Barn. EN5 28 DC42
Stockton Gdns, N17
off Stockton Rd 46 DQ52
NW7 42 CS48
Stockton Rd, N17 46 DQ52
N18 46 DU51
STOCKWELL, SW9 101 DK83
⊖ **Stockwell** 101 DL81
Stockwell Av, SW9 101 DM83
Stockwell Cl, Brom. BR1 144 EH96
Waltham Cross (Chsht.) EN7 14 DU28
Stockwell Gdns, SW9 101 DM82
Stockwell Gdns Est, SW9 101 DL82
Stockwell Grn, SW9 101 DM82
Stockwell La, SW9 101 DM82
Waltham Cross (Chsht.)
EN7 14 DU28
Stockwell Ms, SW9
off Stockwell Rd 101 DM82
Stockwell Pk Cres, SW9 101 DM81
Stockwell Pk Est, SW9 101 DN82
Stockwell Pk Rd, SW9 101 DM81
Stockwell Pk Wk, SW9 101 DM83
Stockwell Rd, SW9 101 DM82
Stockwell St, SE10 103 EC79
Stockwell Ter, SW9 101 DM81
Stodart Rd, SE20 142 DW95
Stofield Gdns, SE9
off Aldersgrove Av 124 EK90
Stoford Cl, SW19 119 CY87
Stoke Av, Ilf. IG6 50 EU51
Stoke Cl, Cob. (Stoke D'Ab.)
KT11 170 BZ116
Stoke Common Rd, Slou.
(Fulmer) SL3 56 AU63
Stoke Ct Dr, Slou. (Stoke P.)
SL2 74 AS67
STOKE D'ABERNON, Cob. 170 BZ116
Stoke Gdns, Slou. SL1 74 AS74
STOKE GREEN, Slou. 74 AU70
Stoke Grn, Slou. (Stoke P.) SL2 74 AU70
Stokenchurch St, SW6 100 DB81
STOKE NEWINGTON, N16 66 DS61
≠ **Stoke Newington** 66 DT61
Stoke Newington Ch St, N16 66 DR62
Stoke Newington Common,
N16 66 DT62
Stoke Newington High St,
N16 66 DT62
Stoke Newington Rd, N16 66 DT64
Stoke Pl, NW10 81 CT69
STOKE POGES, Slou. 74 AT66
Stoke Poges La, Slou.
SL1, SL2 74 AS72
Stoke Rd, Cob. KT11 170 BW115
Kingston upon Thames KT2 118 CQ94
Rainham RM13 90 FK68
Slough SL2 74 AT71
Walton-on-Thames KT12 136 BW104
Stokesay, Slou. SL2 74 AT73
Stokesby Rd, Chess. KT9 156 CM107
Stokesheath Rd, Lthd. (Oxshott)
KT22 154 CC111
Stokesley St, W12 81 CT72
Stokes Ridings, Tad. KT20 173 CX123
Stokes Rd, E6 86 EL70
Croydon CR0 143 DX100
Stoke Wd, Slou. (Stoke P.) SL2 56 AT63
Stoll Cl, NW2 63 CW62
Stompond La, Walt. KT12 135 BU103
Stonard Rd, N13 45 DN48
Dagenham RM8 70 EV64
Stonards Hill, Epp. CM16 18 EW31
Loughton IG10 33 EM44
Stondon Pk, SE23 123 DY87
Stondon Wk, E6 86 EK68
STONE, Green. 129 FT85
Stonebanks, Walt. KT12 135 BU101
STONEBRIDGE, NW10 80 CP67
Stonebridge Common, E8
off Mayfield Rd 84 DT66
≠ **Stonebridge Park** 80 CN66
⊖ **Stonebridge Park** 80 CN66
Stonebridge Pk, NW10 80 CR66
Stonebridge Rd, N15 66 DS57
Gravesend (Nthflt.) DA11 130 GA85
Stonebridge Way, Wem. HA9 80 CP65
Stone Bldgs, WC2 196 C7
Stonechat Sq, E6
off Peridot St 86 EL71
Stone Cl, SW4 *off Larkhall Ri* 101 DJ82
Dagenham RM8 70 EZ61
West Drayton UB7 76 BM74
Stonecot Cl, Sutt. SM3 139 CY102
Stonecot Hill, Sutt. SM3 139 CY102
Stone Cres, Felt. TW14 115 BT87
Stonecroft Av, Iver SL0 75 BE72
Stonecroft Cl, Barn. EN5 27 CV42
Stonecroft Rd, Erith DA8 107 FC80
Stonecroft Way, Croy. CR0 141 DL101
Stonecrop Cl, NW9 62 CR55
≠ **Stone Crossing** 129 FS85
Stonecutter Ct, EC4
off Stonecutter St 83 DP72
Stonecutter St, EC4 196 F8
Stonefield Cl, Bexh. DA7 106 FA83
Ruislip HA4 60 BY64
Stonefield St, N1 83 DN67
Stonefield Way, SE7
off Greenbay Rd 104 EK80
Ruislip HA4 60 BY63
Stonegate Cl, Orp. BR5
off Main Rd 146 EW97
Stonegrove, Edg. HA8 42 CL49
Stonegrove Est, Edg. HA8 42 CM49
Stonegrove Gdns, Edg. HA8 42 CM50
Stonehall Av, Ilf. IG1 68 EL58
Stone Hall Gdns, W8
off St. Mary's Gate 100 DB76
Stone Hall Pl, W8
off St. Mary's Gate 100 DB76
Stone Hall Rd, N21 45 DM45
Stoneham Rd, N11 45 DJ51
STONEHILL, Cher. 150 AY107
Stonehill Cl, SW14 118 CR85
Stonehill Cres, Cher. (Ott.)
KT16 150 AY107
Stonehill Grn, Dart. DA2 127 FC94
Stonehill Rd, SW14 118 CQ85
W4 *off Wellesley Rd* 98 CN78
Chertsey (Ott.) KT16 151 BA105
Woking (Chobham) GU24 150 AW108
Stonehills Ct, SE21 122 DS90
Stonehill Wds Pk, Sid. DA14 127 FB93
Stonehorse Rd, Enf. EN3 30 DW43
Stone Ho Ct, EC3 197 M8
Stonehouse Gdns, Cat. CR3 186 DS125
H **Stone House Hosp**, Dart.
DA2 128 FQ86
Stonehouse La, Purf. RM19 109 FS79
Sevenoaks (Halst.) TN14 164 EX109
Stonehouse Rd, Sev. (Halst.)
TN14 164 EW110
Stoneings La, Sev. (Knock.)
TN14 179 ET118
Stone Lake Retail Pk, SE7 104 EH77
STONELEIGH, Epsom 157 CU106
≠ **Stoneleigh** 157 CU106
Stoneleigh Av, Enf. EN1 30 DV39
Worcester Park KT4 157 CU105
Stoneleigh Bdy, Epsom KT17 157 CU106
Stoneleigh Cl, Wal.Cr. EN8 15 DX33
Stoneleigh Cres, Epsom KT19 157 CT106
Stoneleigh Pk, Wey. KT13 153 BQ106
Stoneleigh Pk Av, Croy. CR0 143 DX100
Stoneleigh Pk Rd, Epsom
KT19 157 CT107
Stoneleigh Pl, W11 81 CX73

Stoneleigh Rd, N17 66 DT55
Carshalton SM5 140 DE101
Ilford IG5 68 EL55
Oxted RH8 188 EL130
Stoneleigh St, W11 81 CX73
Stoneleigh Ter, N19 65 DH61
Stonells Rd, SW11
off Chatham Rd 120 DF85
Stonemasons Cl, N15 66 DR56
Stone Ness Rd, Grays RM20 109 FV79
Stonenest St, N4 65 DM60
Stone Pk Av, Beck. BR3 143 EA98
Stone Pl, Wor.Pk. KT4 139 CU103
Stone Pl Rd, Green. DA9 129 FS85
Stone Rd, Brom. BR2 144 EF99
Stones All, Wat. WD18 23 BV42
Stones Cross Rd, Swan. BR8 147 FC99
Stones End St, SE1 201 H5
Stones Rd, Epsom KT17 156 CS112
Stone St, Croy. CR0 159 DN106
Gravesend DA11 131 GH86
Stoneswood Rd, Oxt. RH8 188 EH130
Stonewall, E6 87 EN71
Stonewood, Dart. (Bean) DA2 129 FW90
Stonewood Rd, Erith DA8 107 FE78
Stoney All, SE18 105 EN82
Stoneyard La, E14 204 B1
Stoney Cft, Couls. CR5 175 DJ122
Stoneycroft Cl, SE12 124 EF87
Stoneycroft Rd, Wdf.Grn. IG8 48 EL51
Stoneydeep, Tedd. TW11
off Twickenham Rd 117 CG91
Stoneydown, E17 67 DY56
Stoneydown Av, E17 67 DY56
Stoneyfield Rd, Couls. CR5 175 DM117
Stoneyfields Gdns, Edg. HA8 42 CQ49
Stoneyfields La, Edg. HA8 42 CQ50
Stoneylands Ct, Egh. TW20 113 AZ92
Stoneylands Rd, Egh. TW20 113 AZ92
Stoney La, E1 197 N8
SE19 *off Church Rd* 122 DT93
Hemel Hempstead (Bov.) HP3 5 BB27
Kings Langley (Chipper.) WD4 5 BE30
Stoney St, SE1 201 K2
Stonhouse St, SW4 101 DK83
Stonny Cft, Ashtd. KT21 172 CM117
Stonor Rd, W14 99 CZ77
Stonycroft Cl, Enf. EN3
off Brimsdown Av 31 DY40
Stony La, Amer. HP6 20 AY38
Stony Path, Loug. IG10 33 EM40
Stonyshotts, Wal.Abb. EN9 16 EE34
Stoop Ct, W.Byf. KT14 152 BH112
Stopes St, SE15 102 DT80
Stopford Rd, E13 86 EG67
SE17 101 DP78
Store Rd, E16 105 EN75
Storers Quay, E14 204 F9
Store St, E15 67 ED64
WC1 195 M7
Storey Rd, E17 67 DZ56
N6 64 DF58
Storey's Gate, SW1 199 N5
Storey St, E16 87 EN74
Stories Ms, SE5 102 DS82
Stories Rd, SE5 102 DS83
Stork Rd, E7 86 EF65
Storksmead Rd, Edg. HA8 42 CS52
Storks Rd, SE16 202 C7
Stormont Rd, N6 64 DF59
SW11 100 DG83
Stormont Way, Chess. KT9 155 CJ106
Stormount Dr, Hayes UB3 95 BQ75
Stornaway Rd, Slou. SL3 93 BC77
Stornaway Strand, Grav.
DA12 131 GM91
Storr Gdns, Brwd. CM13 55 GD43
Storrington Rd, Croy. CR0 142 DT102
Story St, N1 *off Carnoustie Dr* 83 DM66
Stothard Pl, EC2
off Bishopsgate 84 DS71
Stothard St, E *off Colebert Av* 84 DW70
Stott Cl, SW18 120 DD86
Stoughton Av, Sutt. SM3 157 CX106
Stoughton Cl, SE11 200 C9
SW15 *off Bessborough Rd* 119 CU88
Stour Av, Sthl. UB2 96 CA76
Stourcliffe St, W1 194 D9
Stour Cl, Kes. BR2 162 EJ105
Stourhead Cl, SW19
off Castlecombe Dr 119 CX87
Stourhead Gdns, SW20 139 CU97
Stour Rd, E3 85 EA66
Dagenham RM10 70 FA61
Dartford DA1 107 FG83
Grays RM16 111 GG78
Stourton Av, Felt. TW13 116 BZ91
Stour Way, Upmin. RM14 73 FS58
Stowage, SE8 103 EA79
Stow Cres, E17 47 DY52
Stowe Ct, Dart. DA2 128 FQ87
Stowe Cres, Ruis. HA4 59 BP58
Stowe Gdns, N9 46 DT46
Stowell Av, Croy. (New Adgtn.)
CR0 161 ED110
Stowe Pl, N15 66 DS55
Stowe Rd, W12 99 CV75
Orpington BR6 164 EV105
Stowting Rd, Orp. BR6 163 ES105
Stox Mead, Har. HA3 41 CD53
Stracey Rd, E7 68 EG63
NW10 80 CR67
Strachan Pl, SW19
off Woodhayes Rd 119 CW93
Stradbroke Dr, Chig. IG7 49 EN51
Stradbroke Gro, Buck.H. IG9 48 EK46
Ilford IG5 68 EL55
Stradbroke Pk, Chig. IG7 49 EP51
Stradbroke Rd, N5 66 DQ63
Stradbrook Cl, Har. HA2
off Stiven Cres 60 BZ62
Stradella Rd, SE24 122 DQ86
Strafford Av, Ilf. IG5 49 EN54
Strafford Cl, Pot.B. EN6
off Strafford Gate 12 DA32
Strafford Gate, Pot.B. EN6 12 DA32
Strafford Rd, W3 98 CQ75
Strafford Rd, Bar. EN5 27 CY41
Hounslow TW3 96 BZ83
Twickenham TW1 117 CG87
Strafford St, E14 203 P4
Strahan Rd, E3 85 DY69
Straight, The, Sthl. UB1 96 BX75
Straight Rd, Rom. RM3 52 FJ52
Windsor (Old Wind.) SL4 112 AU85
Straightsmouth, SE10 103 EC80
Strait Rd, E6 86 EL73
Straker's Rd, SE22 102 DV84
STRAND, WC2 195 P10
Strand, WC2 199 P1
Strand Cl, Epsom KT18 172 CR119
Strand Ct, SE18
off Strandfield Cl 105 ES78
Strandfield Cl, SE18 105 ES78
Strand La, WC2 196 C10
Strand on the Grn, W4 98 CN79
Strand Pl, N18 46 DR49
Strand Sch App, W4
off Thames Rd 98 CN79
Strangeways, Wat. WD17 23 BS36
Strangways Ter, W14
off Melbury Rd 99 CZ76
Stranraer Gdns, Slou. SL1 74 AS74
Stranraer Rd, Houns. (Hthrw.Air.)
TW6 114 BL86
Stranraer Way, N1 83 DL66
Strasburg Rd, SW11 101 DH81
Stratfield Pk Cl, N21 45 DP45
Stratfield Rd, Borwd. WD6 26 CN41
Slough SL1 92 AU75
STRATFORD, E15 85 EC65
⇌ **Stratford** 85 EC65
⊖ **Stratford** 85 EC66
DLR **Stratford** 85 EC66
Stratford Av, W8
off Stratford Rd 100 DA76
Uxbridge UB10 76 BM68
Stratford Cen, The, E15 85 ED66
Stratford Cl, Bark. IG11 88 EU66
Dagenham RM10 89 FC66
Stratford Ct, N.Mal. KT3
off Kingston Rd 138 CR98
Stratford Gro, SW15 99 CX84
Stratford Ho Av, Brom. BR1 144 EL97
Stratford Pl, W1 195 H9
Stratford Rd, E13 86 EF67
NW4 63 CX56
W8 100 DA76
Hayes UB4 77 BV70
Hounslow (Hthrw.Air.) TW6 115 BP86
Southall UB2 96 BY77
Thornton Heath CR7 141 DN98
Watford WD17 23 BU40
Stratford Vil, NW1 83 DJ66
Stratford Way, St.Alb. (Brick.Wd.)
AL2 8 BZ29
Watford WD17 23 BT40
Strathan Cl, SW18 119 CY86
Strathaven Rd, SE12 124 EH86
Strathblaine Rd, SW11 100 DD84
Strathbrook Rd, SW16 121 DM94
Strathcona Rd, Wem. HA9 61 CK61
Strathdale, SW16 121 DM92
Strathdon Dr, SW17 120 DD90
Strathearn Av, Hayes UB3 95 BT80
Twickenham TW2 116 CB88
Strathearn Pl, W2 194 A10
Strathearn Rd, SW19 120 DA92
Sutton SM1 158 DA106
Stratheden Par, SE3
off Stratheden Rd 104 EG80
Stratheden Rd, SE3 104 EG81
Strathfield Gdns, Bark. IG11 87 ER65
Strathleven Rd, SW2 121 DL85
Strathmore Cl, Cat. CR3 176 DS121
Strathmore Gdns, N3 44 DB53
W8 *off Palace Gdns Ter* 82 DA74
Edgware HA8 42 CP54
Hornchurch RM12 71 FF60
Strathmore Rd, SW19 120 DA90
Croydon CR0 142 DQ101
Teddington TW11 117 CE91
Strathnairn St, SE1 202 C9
Strathray Gdns, NW3 82 DE65
Strath Ter, SW11 100 DE84
Strathville Rd, SW18 120 DB89
Strathyre Av, SW16 141 DN97
Stratton Av, Enf. EN2 30 DR37
Wallington SM6 159 DK109
Stratton Chase Dr, Ch.St.G.
HP8 36 AU47
Stratton Cl, SW19 140 DA96
Bexleyheath DA7 106 EY83
Edgware HA8 42 CM51
Hounslow TW3 96 BZ81
Walton-on-Thames KT12
off St. Johns Dr 136 BW102
Strattondale St, E14 204 D6
Stratton Dr, Bark. IG11 69 ET64
Stratton Gdns, Sthl. UB1 78 BZ72
Stratton Rd, SW19 140 DA96
Bexleyheath DA7 106 EY83
Romford RM3 52 FN50
Sunbury-on-Thames TW16 135 BT96
Stratton St, W1 199 J2
Stratton Ter, West. TN16
off High St 189 EQ127
Stratton Wk, Rom. RM3 52 FN50
Strauss Rd, W4 98 CR75
Strawberry Flds, Swan. BR8 147 FE95
STRAWBERRY HILL, Twick. 117 CE90
⇌ **Strawberry Hill** 117 CE90
Strawberry Hill, Twick. TW1 117 CF90
Strawberry Hill Cl, Twick. TW1 117 CF90
Strawberry Hill Rd, Twick.
TW1 117 CF90
Strawberry La, Cars. SM5 140 DF104
Strawberry Vale, N2 44 DD53
Twickenham TW1 117 CG90
Straw Cl, Cat. CR3 176 DQ123
Strayfield Rd, Enf. EN2 29 DP37
Streakes Fld Rd, NW2 63 CU61
Stream Cl, W.Byf. (Byfleet)
KT14 152 BK112
Streamdale, SE2 106 EU79
Stream La, Edg. HA8 42 CP50
Streamside Cl, N9 46 DT46
Bromley BR2 144 EG98
Streamway, Belv. DA17 106 FA79
Streatfield Av, E6 87 EM67
Streatfield Rd, Har. HA3 61 CK55
STREATHAM, SW16 121 DL91
⇌ **Streatham** 121 DL92
Streatham Cl, SW16 121 DL89
⇌ **Streatham Common** 121 DK94
Streatham Common N,
SW16 121 DL92
Streatham Common S,
SW16 121 DL93
Streatham Ct, SW16 121 DL90
Streatham High Rd, SW16 121 DL92
STREATHAM HILL, SW2 121 DM87
⇌ **Streatham Hill** 121 DL89
Streatham Hill, SW2 121 DL89
STREATHAM PARK, SW16 121 DJ91
Streatham Pl, SW2 121 DL87
Streatham Rd, SW16 140 DG95
Mitcham CR4 140 DG95
Streatham St, WC1 195 N8
STREATHAM VALE, SW16 121 DK94
Streatham Vale, SW16 121 DJ94
Streathbourne Rd, SW17 120 DG89
Streatley Pl, NW3
off New End Sq 64 DC63
Streatley Rd, NW6 81 CZ66
Street, The, Ashtd. KT21 172 CL119
Betchworth RH3 182 CS134
Dartford (Hort.Kir.) DA4 148 FP98
Kings Langley (Chipper.) WD4 6 BG31
Leatherhead (Fetch.) KT22 171 CD122
Streeters La, Wall. SM6 141 DK104
Streetfield Ms, SE3 104 EG83
Streimer Rd, E15 85 EC68
Strelley Way, W3 80 CS73
Stretton Pl, Amer. HP6 20 AT38
Stretton Rd, Croy. CR0 142 DS101
Richmond TW10 117 CJ89
Stretton Way, Borwd. WD6 26 CL38
Strickland Av, Dart. DA1 108 FL83
Strickland Row, SW18 120 DD87
Strickland St, SE8 103 EA82
Strickland Way, Orp. BR6 163 ET105
Stride Rd, E13 86 EF68
Strides Ct, Cher. KT16
off Brox Rd 151 BC107
Stringhams Copse, Wok. (Ripley)
GU23 167 BF124
Stripling Way, Wat. WD18 23 BU44
Strode Cl, N10
off Pembroke Rd 44 DG52
Strode Rd, E7 68 EG63
N17 46 DS54
NW10 81 CU65
SW6 99 CX80
Strodes Coll La, Egh. TW20 113 AZ92
Strodes Cres, Stai. TW18 114 BJ92
Strode St, Egh. TW20 113 BA91
Strone Rd, E7 86 EJ65
E12 86 EK65
Strone Way, Hayes UB4 78 BY70
Strongbow Cres, SE9 125 EM85
Strongbow Rd, SE9 125 EM85
Strongbridge Cl, Har. HA2 60 CA60
Stronsa Rd, W12 99 CT75
Strood Av, Rom. RM7 71 FD60
Stroud Cres, SW15 119 CU90
STROUDE, Vir.W. 133 AZ96
Stroude Rd, Egh. TW20 113 BA93
Virginia Water GU25 132 AY98
Stroudes Cl, Wor.Pk. KT4 138 CS101
Stroud Fld, Nthlt. UB5 78 BY65
Stroud Gate, Har. HA2 60 CB63
STROUD GREEN, N4 65 DM58
Stroud Grn Gdns, Croy. CR0 142 DW101
Stroud Grn Rd, N4 65 DM60
Stroud Grn Way, Croy. CR0 142 DV101
Stroudley Wk, E3 85 EB69
Stroud Rd, SE25 142 DU100
SW19 120 DA90
Strouds Cl, Rom. (Chad.Hth.)
RM6 70 EV57
Stroudwater Pk, Wey. KT13 153 BP107
Stroud Way, Ashf. TW15
off Courtfield Rd 115 BP93
Strouts Pl, E2 197 P2
Struan Gdns, Wok. GU21 166 AY115
Strutton Grd, SW1 199 M6
Struttons Av, Grav. (Nthflt.)
DA11 131 GF89
Strype St, E1 197 P7
Stuart Av, NW9 63 CU59
W5 80 CM74
Bromley BR2 144 EG102
Harrow HA2 60 BZ62
Walton-on-Thames KT12 135 BV102
Stuart Cl, Brwd. CM15 54 FV43
Swanley BR8 127 FF94
Uxbridge UB10 76 BN65
Stuart Ct, Borwd. (Elstree) WD6
off High St 25 CK44
Stuart Cres, N22 45 DM53
Croydon CR0 143 DZ104
Hayes UB3 77 BQ72
Stuart Evans Cl, Well. DA16 106 EW83
Stuart Gro, Tedd. TW11 117 CE92
Stuart Mantle Way, Erith DA8 107 FD80
Stuart Pl, Mitch. CR4 140 DF95
Stuart Rd, NW6 82 DA69
SE15 102 DW84
SW19 120 DA90
W3 80 CQ74
Barking IG11 87 ET66
Barnet EN4 44 DE45
Gravesend DA11 131 GG86
Grays RM17 110 GB78
Harrow HA3 41 CF54
Richmond TW10 117 CH89
Thornton Heath CR7 142 DQ98
Warlingham CR6 176 DV120
Welling DA16 106 EV81
Stuart Twr, W9 82 DC69
Stuart Way, Stai. TW18 114 BH93
Virginia Water GU25 132 AU97
Waltham Cross (Chsht.)
EN7 14 DV31
Stubbers La, Upmin. RM14 91 FR65
Stubbins Hall La, Wal.Abb.
EN9 15 EB28
Stubbs Cl, NW9 62 CQ57
Stubbs Dr, SE16 202 D10
Stubbs End Cl, Amer. HP6 20 AS37
Stubbs Hill, Sev. (Knock.)
TN14 164 EW113
Stubbs La, Tad. (Lwr.Kgswd.)
KT20 183 CZ128
Stubbs Ms, Dag. RM8
off Marlborough Rd 70 EV63
Stubbs Pt, E13 86 EH70
Stubbs Way, SW19
off Brangwyn Cres 140 DD95
Stubbs Wd, Amer. HP6 20 AS36
Stucley Pl, NW1
off Hawley Cres 83 DH66
Stucley Rd, Houns. TW5 96 CC80
Studdridge St, SW6 100 DA82
Studd St, N1 83 DP67
Stud Grn, Wat. WD25 7 BV32
Studholme Ct, NW3 64 DA63
Studholme St, SE15 102 DV80
Studio Pl, SW1 198 E5
Studios, The, Bushey WD23 24 CA44
Studios Rd, Shep. TW17 134 BM97
Studio Way, Borwd. WD6 26 CQ40
Studland, SE17 201 K10
Studland Cl, Sid. DA15 125 ET90
Studland Rd, SE26 123 DX92
W7 79 CD72
Kingston upon Thames KT2 118 CL93
West Byfleet (Byfleet) KT14 152 BM113
Studland St, W6 99 CV77
Studley Av, E4 47 ED52
Studley Cl, E5 67 DY64
Studley Ct, Sid. DA14 126 EV92
Studley Dr, Ilf. IG4 68 EK58
Studley Est, SW4 101 DL81
Studley Gra Rd, W7 97 CE75
Studley Rd, E7 86 EH65
SW4 101 DL81
Dagenham RM9 88 EX66
Stukeley Rd, E7 86 EH66
Stukeley St, WC2 196 A8
Stump Rd, Epp. CM16 18 EW27
Stumps Hill La, Beck. BR3 123 EA93
Stumps La, Whyt. CR3 176 DS117
Sturdy Rd, SE15 102 DV82
Sturge Av, E17 47 EB54
Sturgeon Rd, SE17 102 DQ78
Sturges Fld, Chis. BR7 125 ER93
Sturgess Av, NW4 63 CV59
Sturge St, SE1 201 H4
Sturlas Way, Wal.Cr. EN8 15 DX33
Sturmer Way, N7 65 DM64
Sturminster Cl, Hayes UB4 78 BW72
Sturrock Cl, N15 66 DR56
Sturry St, E14 85 EB72
Sturts La, Tad. KT20 183 CT127
Sturt St, N1 197 J1
Stutfield St, E1 84 DU72
Stychens Cl, Red. (Bletch.)
RH1 186 DQ133
Stychens La, Red. (Bletch.)
RH1 186 DQ132
Stylecroft Rd, Ch.St.G. HP8 36 AX47
Styles Gdns, SW9 101 DP83
Styles Way, Beck. BR3 143 EC98
Styventon Pl, Cher. KT16 133 BF101
Subrosa Dr, Red. RH1 185 DH130
Succombs Hill, Warl. CR6 176 DV120
Whyteleafe CR3 176 DV120
Succombs Pl, Warl. CR6 176 DV120
Sudbourne Rd, SW2 121 DL85
Sudbrooke Rd, SW12 120 DF86
Sudbrook Gdns, Rich. TW10 117 CK90
Sudbrook La, Rich. TW10 118 CL88
SUDBURY, Wem. 61 CG64
Sudbury, E6 *off Newark Knok* 87 EN72
⇌ **Sudbury & Harrow Road** 61 CH64
Sudbury Av, Wem. HA0 61 CK62
Sudbury Ct, E5 67 DY63
Sudbury Ct Dr, Har. HA1 61 CF62
Sudbury Ct Rd, Har. HA1 61 CF62
Sudbury Cres, Brom. BR1 124 EG93
Wembley HA0 61 CH64
Sudbury Cft, Wem. HA0 61 CF63
Sudbury Gdns, Croy. CR0
off Langton Way 160 DS105
Sudbury Hts Av, Grnf. UB6 61 CF64
⊖ **Sudbury Hill** 61 CE63
Sudbury Hill, Har. HA1 61 CE61
Sudbury Hill Cl, Wem. HA0 61 CF63
⇌ **Sudbury Hill Harrow** 61 CE63
Sudbury Rd, Bark. IG11 69 ET64
⊖ **Sudbury Town** 79 CH65
Sudeley St, N1 196 G1
Sudicamps Ct, Wal.Abb. EN9 16 EG33
Sudlow Rd, SW18 100 DA84
Sudrey St, SE1 201 H5
Suez Av, Grnf. UB6 79 CF68
Suez Rd, Enf. EN3 31 DY42
Suffield Cl, S.Croy. CR2 161 DX112
Suffield Rd, E4 47 EB48
N15 66 DT57
SE20 142 DW96
Suffolk Cl, Borwd. WD6
off Clydesdale Cl 26 CR43
St. Albans (Lon.Col.) AL2 9 CJ25
Suffolk Ct, E10 67 EA59
Ilford IG3 69 ES58
Suffolk La, EC4 197 K10
Suffolk Pk Rd, E17 67 DY56
Suffolk Pl, SW1 199 N2
Suffolk Rd, E13 86 EF69
N15 66 DR58
NW10 80 CS66
SE25 142 DT98
SW13 99 CT80
Barking IG11 87 ER66
Dagenham RM10 71 FC64
Suffolk Rd, Dart. DA1 128 FL86
Enfield EN3 30 DV43
Gravesend DA12 131 GK86
Harrow HA2 60 BZ58
Ilford IG3 69 ES58
Potters Bar EN6 11 CY32
Sidcup DA14 126 EW93
Worcester Park KT4 139 CT103
Suffolk St, E7 68 EG64
SW1 199 N2
Suffolk Way, Horn. RM11 72 FN56
Sevenoaks TN13 191 FJ125
Sugar Bakers Ct, EC3
off Creechurch La 84 DS72
Sugar Ho La, E15 85 EC68
Sugar Loaf Wk, E2
off Victoria Pk Sq 84 DW69
Sugar Quay Wk, EC3 201 N1
Sugden Rd, SW11 100 DG83
Thames Ditton KT7 137 CH102
Sugden Way, Bark. IG11 87 ET68
Sulgrave Gdns, W6
off Sulgrave Rd 99 CW75
Sulgrave Rd, W6 99 CW75
Sulina Rd, SW2 121 DL87
Sulivan Ct, SW6 100 DA83
Sulivan Rd, SW6 100 DA83
Sullivan Av, E16 86 EK71
Sullivan Cl, SW11 100 DE83
Dartford DA1 127 FH86
Hayes UB4 78 BW71
West Molesey KT8
off Victoria Av 136 CA97
Sullivan Cres, Uxb. (Hare.)
UB9 38 BK54
Sullivan Rd, SE11 200 E8
Tilbury RM18 111 GG81
Sullivans Reach, Walt. KT12 135 BT101
Sullivan Way, Borwd. (Elstree)
WD6 25 CJ44
Sultan Rd, E11 68 EH56
Sultan St, SE5 102 DQ80
Beckenham BR3 143 DX96
Sumatra Rd, NW6 64 DA64
Sumburgh Rd, SW12 120 DG86
Sumburgh Way, Slou. SL1 74 AS71
Summer Av, E.Mol. KT8 137 CE99
Summercourt Rd, E1 84 DW72
Summerene Cl, SW16 121 DJ94
Summerfield, Ashtd. KT21 171 CK119
Summerfield Av, NW6 81 CY68
Summerfield Cl, Add. KT15
off Spinney Hill 151 BF106
St. Albans (Lon.Col.) AL2 9 CJ26
Summerfield La, Surb. KT6 137 CK103
Summerfield Pl, Cher. (Ott.) KT16
off Crawshaw Rd 151 BD107
Summerfield Rd, W5 79 CH70
Loughton IG10 32 EK44
Watford WD25 23 BU35
Summerfields Av, N12 44 DE51
Summerfield St, SE12 124 EF87
Summer Gdns, E.Mol. KT8 137 CE99
Summer Gro, Borwd. (Elstree)
WD6 25 CK44
Summerhayes Cl, Wok. GU21 150 AY114
Summerhays, Cob. KT11 154 BX113
Summer Hill, Borwd. (Elstree)
WD6 26 CN43
Chislehurst BR7 145 EN96
Summerhill Cl, Orp. BR6 145 ES104
Summerhill Gro, Enf. EN1 30 DS44
Summerhill Rd, N15 66 DR56
Dartford DA1 128 FK87
Summer Hill Vil, Chis. BR7 145 EN95
Summerhill Way, Mitch. CR4 140 DG95
Summerhouse Av, Houns.
TW5 96 BY81
Summerhouse Dr, Bex. DA5 127 FD91
Dartford DA2 127 FD91
Summerhouse La, Uxb. (Hare.)
UB9 38 BG52
Watford (Ald.) WD25 24 CC40
West Drayton UB7 94 BK79
Summerhouse Rd, N16 66 DS61
Summerhouse Way, Abb.L.
WD5 7 BT30
Summerland Gdns, N10 65 DH55
Summerlands Av, W3 80 CQ73
Summerlay Cl, Tad. KT20 173 CY120
Summerlee Av, N2 64 DF56
Summerlee Gdns, N2 64 DF56
Summerley St, SW18 120 DB89
Summerly Av, Reig. RH2
off Burnham Dr 184 DA133
Summer Rd, E.Mol. KT8 137 CE99
Thames Ditton KT7 137 CF99
Summersby Rd, N6 65 DH58
Summers Cl, Sutt. SM2
off Overton Rd 158 DA108
Wembley HA9 62 CP60
Weybridge KT13 152 BN111
Summers La, N12 44 DD52
Summers Row, N12 44 DE51
SUMMERSTOWN, SW17 120 DB90
Summerstown, SW17 120 DC90
Summer St, EC1 196 D5
Summerswood Cl, Ken. CR8
off Longwood Rd 176 DR116
Summerswood La, Borwd.
WD6 10 CS34
Summerton Way, SE28 88 EX72
Summer Trees, Sun. TW16
off The Avenue 135 BV95
Summerville Gdns, Sutt. SM1 157 CZ107
Summerwood Rd, Islw. TW7 117 CF85
Summit, The, Loug. IG10 33 EM39
Summit Av, NW9 62 CR57
Summit Cl, N14 45 DJ47
NW9 62 CR56
Edgware HA8 42 CN52
Summit Ct, NW2 63 CY64
Summit Dr, Wdf.Grn. IG8 48 EK54
Summit Est, N16 66 DU59

★ Place of interest ⇌ Railway station ⊖ London Underground station DLR Docklands Light Railway station Tramlink station H Hospital

Sum - Swi

Summit Pl, Wey. KT13
off Caenshill Rd ... 152 BN108
Summit Rd, E17 ... 67 EB56
Northolt UB5 ... 78 CA66
Potters Bar EN6 ... 11 CY30
Summit Way, N14 ... 45 DH47
SE19 ... 122 DS94
Sumner Av, SE15
off Sumner Rd ... 102 DT81
Sumner Cl, Lthd. (Fetch.)
KT22 ... 171 CD124
Orpington BR6 ... 163 EQ105
Sumner Est, SE15 ... 102 DT80
Sumner Gdns, Croy. CR0 ... 141 DN102
Sumner Pl, SW7 ... 198 A9
Addlestone KT15 ... 152 BG106
Sumner Pl Ms, SW7 ... 198 A9
Sumner Rd, SE15 ... 102 DT80
Croydon CR0 ... 141 DN102
Harrow HA1 ... 60 CC59
Sumner Rd S, Croy. CR0 ... 141 DN102
Sumner St, SE1 ... 200 G2
Sumpter Cl, NW3 ... 82 DC65
Sun All, Rich. TW9 off Kew Rd ... 98 CL84
Sunbeam Cres, W10 ... 81 CW70
Sunbeam Rd, NW10 ... 80 CQ70
SUNBURY, Sun. ... 153 BV107
⇌ Sunbury ... 135 BT95
Sunbury Av, NW7 ... 42 CR50
SW14 ... 98 CR84
Sunbury Ct, Sun. TW16 ... 136 BX96
Sunbury Ct Island, Sun.
TW16 ... 136 BX97
Sunbury Ct Ms, Sun. TW16
off Lower Hampton Rd ... 136 BX96
Sunbury Ct Rd, Sun. TW16 ... 136 BW96
Sunbury Cres, Felt. TW13
off Ryland Cl ... 115 BT91
Sunbury Cross Cen, Sun.
TW16 ... 115 BT94
Sunbury Gdns, NW7 ... 42 CR50
Sunbury La, SW11 ... 100 DD81
Walton-on-Thames KT12 ... 135 BU100
Sunbury Lock Ait, Walt. KT12 ... 135 BV98
Sunbury Rd, Felt. TW13 ... 115 BT90
Sutton SM3 ... 139 CX104
Sunbury St, SE18 ... 105 EM76
Sunbury Way, Felt. TW13 ... 116 BW92
Sun Ct, EC3 ... 197 L9
Erith DA8 ... 107 FF82
Suncroft Pl, SE26 ... 122 DW90
Sundale Av, S.Croy. CR2 ... 160 DW110
Sunderland Ct, SE22 ... 122 DU87
Sunderland Gro, Wat. WD25
off Ashfields ... 7 BT34
Sunderland Mt, SE23
off Sunderland Rd ... 123 DX89
Sunderland Rd, SE23 ... 123 DX88
W5 ... 97 CK76
Sunderland Ter, W2 ... 82 DB72
Sunderland Way, E12 ... 68 EK61
Sundew Av, W12 ... 81 CU73
Sundew Ct, Grays RM17
off Salix Rd ... 110 GD79
Sundial Av, SE25 ... 142 DT97
Sundon Cres, Vir.W. GU25 ... 132 AV99
Sundorne Rd, SE7 ... 104 EH78
Sundown Av, S.Croy. CR2 ... 160 DT111
Sundown Rd, Ashf. TW15 ... 115 BQ92
Sundra Wk, E1
off Beaumont Gro ... 85 DX70
SUNDRIDGE, Brom. ... 124 EJ93
SUNDRIDGE, Sev. ... 180 EZ124
Sundridge Av, Brom. BR1 ... 144 EK95
Chislehurst BR7 ... 124 EK94
Welling DA16 ... 105 ER82
Sundridge Cl, Dart. DA1 ... 128 FN86
Sundridge Ho, Brom. BR1
off Burnt Ash La ... 124 EH92
Sundridge La, Sev. (Knock.)
TN14 ... 180 EV117
⇌ Sundridge Park ... 124 EH94
Sundridge Pl, Croy. CR0
off Inglis Rd ... 142 DU102
Sundridge Rd, Croy. CR0 ... 142 DT101
Sevenoaks (Dunt.Grn.)
TN14 ... 180 FA120
Woking GU22 ... 167 BA119
Sunfields Pl, SE3 ... 104 EH80
Sunflower Way, Rom. RM3 ... 52 FK53
Sun Hill, Long. (Fawk.Grn.)
DA3 ... 149 FU104
Woking GU22 ... 166 AU121
Sunken Rd, Croy. CR0
off Coombe La ... 160 DW106
Sunkist Way, Wall. SM6 ... 159 DL109
Sunland Av, Bexh. DA6 ... 106 EY84
Sun La, SE3 ... 104 EH80
Gravesend DA12 ... 131 GJ89
Sunleigh Rd, Wem. HA0 ... 80 CL67
Sunley Gdns, Grnf. UB6 ... 79 CG67
Sunlight Cl, SW19 ... 120 DC93
Sunlight Sq, E2 ... 84 DV69
Sunmead Cl, Lthd. (Fetch.)
KT22 ... 171 CF122
Sunmead Rd, Sun. TW16 ... 135 BU97
Sunna Gdns, Sun. TW16 ... 135 BV96
Sunningdale, N14
off Wilmer Way ... 45 DK50
Sunningdale Av, W3 ... 80 CS73
Barking IG11 ... 87 ER67
Feltham TW13 ... 116 BY89
Rainham RM13 ... 89 FH70
Ruislip HA4 ... 60 BW60
Sunningdale Cl, E6 ... 87 EM69
SE16 off Ryder Dr ... 102 DV78
SE28 ... 88 EY72
Stanmore HA7 ... 41 CG52
Surbiton KT6
off Culsac Rd ... 138 CL103
Sunningdale Gdns, NW9 ... 62 CQ57
W8 off Lexham Ms ... 100 DA76
Sunningdale Rd, Brom. BR1 ... 144 EL98
Rainham RM13 ... 89 FG66
Sunningdale Rd, Sutt. SM1 ... 157 CZ105
Sunningfields Cres, NW4 ... 43 CV54
Sunningfields Rd, NW4 ... 43 CV54
Sunning Hill, Grav. (Nthflt.)
DA11 ... 130 GE89
Sunninghill Rd, SE13 ... 103 EB82
Sunnings La, Upmin. RM14 ... 90 FQ65
Sunningvale Av, West. (Bigg.H.)
TN16 ... 178 EJ115
Sunningvale Cl, West. (Bigg.H.)
TN16 ... 178 EK116
Sunny Bk, SE25 ... 142 DU97
Sunnybank, Epsom KT18 ... 172 CQ116
Sunny Bk, Warl. CR6 ... 177 DY117
Sunnybank Rd, Pot.B. EN6 ... 12 DA33
Sunnybank Vil, Red. RH1 ... 186 DT132
Sunny Cres, NW10 ... 80 CQ66
Sunnycroft Gdns, Upmin.
RM14 ... 73 FT59
Sunnycroft Rd, SE25 ... 142 DU97
Hounslow TW3 ... 96 CB82
Southall UB1 ... 78 CA71
Sunnydale, Orp. BR6 ... 145 EN103
Sunnydale Gdns, NW7 ... 42 CR51
Sunnydale Rd, SE12 ... 124 EH85
Sunnydell, St.Alb. AL2 ... 8 CB26
Sunnydene Av, E4 ... 47 ED50
Ruislip HA4 ... 59 BU61
Sunnydene Cl, Rom. RM3 ... 52 FM52
Sunnydene Gdns, Wem. HA0 ... 79 CJ65
Sunnydene Rd, Pur. CR8 ... 159 DP113
Sunnydene St, SE26 ... 123 DY91
Sunnyfield, NW7 ... 43 CT49
Sunnyfield Rd, Chis. BR7 ... 146 EU97
Sunny Gdns Par, NW4
off Great N Way ... 43 CW54
Sunny Gdns Rd, NW4 ... 43 CV54
Sunny Hill, NW4 ... 63 CV55
Sunnyhill Cl, E5 ... 67 DY63
Sunnyhill Rd, SW16 ... 121 DL91
Rickmansworth (Map.Cr.)
WD3 ... 37 BD51
Sunnyhurst Cl, Sutt. SM1 ... 140 DA104
Sunnymead Av, Mitch. CR4 ... 141 DJ97
Sunnymead Rd, NW9 ... 62 CR59
SW15 ... 119 CV85
SUNNYMEADS, Stai. ... 92 AY84
⇌ Sunnymeads ... 92 AY83
Sunnymede, Chig. IG7 ... 50 EV48
Sunnymede Av, Cars. SM5 ... 158 DD111
Chesham HP5 ... 4 AS28
Epsom KT19 ... 156 CS109
Sunnymede Dr, Ilf. IG6 ... 69 EP56
Sunny Nook Gdns, S.Croy. CR2
off Selsdon Rd ... 160 DR107
Sunny Ri, Cat. CR3 ... 176 DR124
Sunny Rd, The, Enf. EN3 ... 31 DX39
Sunnyside, NW2 ... 63 CZ62
SW19 ... 119 CY93
Walton-on-Thames KT12 ... 136 BW99
Sunnyside Cotts, Chesh. HP5 ... 4 AU26
Sunnyside Dr, E4 ... 47 EC45
Sunnyside Gdns, Upmin.
RM14 ... 72 FQ61
Sunnyside Pas, SW19 ... 119 CY93
Sunnyside Pl, SW19
off Sunnyside ... 119 CY93
Sunnyside Rd, E10 ... 67 EA60
N19 ... 65 DK59
W5 ... 79 CK74
Epping CM16 ... 17 ET32
Ilford IG1 ... 69 EQ62
Teddington TW11 ... 117 CD91
Sunnyside Rd E, N9 ... 46 DU48
Sunnyside Rd N, N9 ... 46 DT48
Sunnyside Rd S, N9 ... 46 DT48
Sunnyside Ter, NW9
off Edgware Rd ... 62 CR55
Sunny Vw, NW9 ... 62 CR57
Sunny Way, N12 ... 44 DE52
Sun Pas, SE16 ... 202 B6
Sunray Av, SE24 ... 102 DR84
Brentwood CM13 ... 55 GE44
Bromley BR2 ... 144 EL100
Surbiton KT5 ... 138 CP103
West Drayton UB7 ... 94 BK75
Sunrise Av, Horn. RM12 ... 72 FJ62
Sunrise Cl, Felt. TW13
off Exeter Rd ... 116 BZ90
Sun Rd, W14 ... 99 CZ78
Swanscombe DA10 ... 130 FZ86
Sunset Av, E4 ... 47 EB46
Woodford Green IG8 ... 48 EF49
Sunset Ct, Erith DA8 ... 107 FH81
Sunset Ct, Wdf.Grn. IG8
off Navestock Cres ... 48 EJ52
Sunset Dr, Rom. (Hav.at.Bow.)
RM4 ... 51 FH50
Sunset Gdns, SE25 ... 142 DT96
Sunset Rd, SE5 ... 102 DQ84
SE28 ... 106 EU75
Sunset Vw, Barn. EN5 ... 27 CY40
Sunshine Way, Mitch. CR4 ... 140 DF96
Sunstone Gro, Red. RH1 ... 185 DL129
Sun St, EC2 ... 197 M7
Waltham Abbey EN9 ... 15 EC33
Sun St Pas, EC2 ... 197 M7
Sun Wk, E1 ... 202 B1
Sunwell Cl, SE15
off Cossall Wk ... 102 DV81
Superior Dr, Orp. BR6 ... 163 ET107
SURBITON ... 138 CM101
⇌ Surbiton ... 137 CK100
Surbiton Ct, Surb. KT6 ... 137 CJ100
Surbiton Cres, Kings.T. KT1 ... 138 CL98
H Surbiton Gen Hosp, Surb.
KT6 ... 138 CL100
Surbiton Hall Cl, Kings.T.
KT1 ... 138 CL98
Surbiton Hill Pk, Surb. KT5 ... 138 CN99
Surbiton Hill Rd, Surb. KT6 ... 138 CL98
Surbiton Par, Surb. KT6
off St. Mark's Hill ... 138 CL100
Surbiton Rd, Kings.T. KT1 ... 138 CL98
Surlingham Cl, SE28 ... 88 EX73
Surma Cl, E1 ... 84 DV70
Surman Cres, Brwd. CM13 ... 55 GC45
Surmans Cl, Dag. RM9
off Goresbrook Rd ... 88 EV67
Surrendale Pl, W9 ... 82 DA70
Surrey Canal Rd, SE14 ... 102 DW79
SE15 ... 102 DW79
Surrey Cres, W4 ... 98 CN78
★ Surrey Docks Fm, SE16 ... 203 M5
Surrey Dr, Horn. RM11 ... 72 FN56
Surrey Gdns, N4
off Finsbury Pk Av ... 66 DQ58
Leatherhead (Eff.Junct.)
KT24 ... 169 BT123
Surrey Gro, SE17
off Surrey Sq ... 102 DS78
Sutton SM1 ... 140 DD104
Surrey Hills, Tad. KT20 ... 182 CP130
Surrey Hills Av, Tad. KT20 ... 182 CQ130
Surrey La, SW11 ... 100 DE81
Surrey La Est, SW11 ... 100 DE81
Surrey Lo, SE1 ... 200 D7
Surrey Ms, SE27
off Hamilton Rd ... 122 DS91
Surrey Mt, SE23 ... 122 DV88
⊖ Surrey Quays ... 203 H8
Surrey Quays Retail Cen,
SE16 ... 103 DX76
Surrey Quays Rd, SE16 ... 202 G6
Surrey Rd, SE15 ... 123 DX85
Barking IG11 ... 87 ES67
Dagenham RM10 ... 71 FB64
Harrow HA1 ... 60 CC57
West Wickham BR4 ... 143 EB102
Surrey Row, SE1 ... 200 F4
Surrey Sq, SE17 ... 201 M10
Surrey St, E13 ... 86 EH69
WC2 ... 196 C10
Croydon CR0 ... 142 DQ104
Surrey Ter, SE17 ... 201 N10
Surrey Twr, SE20 ... 122 DW94
Surrey Twrs, Add. KT15
off Garfield Rd ... 152 BJ106
Surrey Water Rd, SE16 ... 203 J3
Surridge Cl, Rain. RM13 ... 90 FJ69
Surridge Gdns, SE19
off Hancock Rd ... 122 DR93
Surr St, N7 ... 65 DL64
Susan Cl, Rom. RM7 ... 71 FC55
Susannah St, E14 ... 85 EB72
Susan Rd, SE3 ... 104 EH82
Susan Wd, Chis. BR7 ... 145 EN95
Sussex Av, Islw. TW7 ... 97 CE83
Romford RM3 ... 52 FM52
Sussex Cl, N19
off Cornwallis Rd ... 65 DL61
Chalfont St. Giles HP8 ... 36 AV47
Ilford IG4 ... 69 EM58
New Malden KT3 ... 138 CS98
Slough SL1 ... 92 AV75
Twickenham TW1
off Westmorland Cl ... 117 CH86
Sussex Cres, Nthlt. UB5 ... 78 CA65
Sussex Gdns, N4 ... 66 DQ57
N6 off Great N Rd ... 64 DF57
W2 ... 82 DD72
Chessington KT9 ... 155 CK107
Sussex Keep, Slou. SL1
off Sussex Cl ... 92 AV75
Sussex Ms, SE6
off Ravensbourne Pk ... 123 EA87
Sussex Ms E, W2 ... 194 A9
Sussex Ms W, W2 ... 194 A10
Sussex Pl, NW1 ... 194 D3
W2 ... 194 A9
W6 ... 99 CW78
Erith DA8 ... 107 FB80
New Malden KT3 ... 138 CS98
Slough SL1 ... 92 AV75
Sussex Ring, N12 ... 44 DA50
Sussex Rd, E6 ... 87 EN67
Brentwood CM14 ... 54 FV49
Carshalton SM5 ... 158 DF107
Dartford DA1 ... 128 FN87
Erith DA8 ... 107 FB80
Harrow HA1 ... 60 CC57
Mitcham CR4 off Lincoln Rd ... 141 DL99
New Malden KT3 ... 138 CS98
Orpington BR5 ... 146 EW100
Sidcup DA14 ... 126 EV92
South Croydon CR2 ... 160 DR107
Southall UB2 ... 96 BX76
Uxbridge UB10 ... 59 BQ63
Watford WD24 ... 23 BU38
West Wickham BR4 ... 143 EB102
Sussex Sq, W2 ... 194 A10
Sussex St, E13 ... 86 EH69
SW1 ... 101 DH78
Sussex Wk, SW9 ... 101 DP84
Sussex Way, N7 ... 65 DL61
N19 ... 65 DL60
Barnet EN4 ... 28 DG43
Uxbridge (Denh.) UB9 ... 57 BF57
Sutcliffe Cl, NW11 ... 64 DB57
Bushey WD23 ... 24 CC42
Sutcliffe Ho, Hayes UB3 ... 77 BU72
Sutcliffe Rd, SE18 ... 105 ES79
Welling DA16 ... 106 EW82
Sutherland Av, W9 ... 82 DC69
W13 ... 79 CH72
Hayes UB3 ... 95 BU77
Orpington BR5 ... 145 ET100
Potters Bar (Cuffley) EN6 ... 13 DK28
Sunbury-on-Thames TW16 ... 135 BT96
Welling DA16 ... 105 ES84
Westerham (Bigg.H.) TN16 ... 178 EK117
Sutherland Cl, Barn. EN5 ... 27 CY42
Greenhithe DA9 ... 129 FT85
Sutherland Ct, NW9 ... 62 CP57
Sutherland Dr, SW19 ... 140 DD95
Sutherland Gdns, SW14 ... 98 CS83
Sunbury-on-Thames TW16
off Sutherland Av ... 135 BT96
Worcester Park KT4 ... 139 CV102
Sutherland Gro, SW18 ... 119 CY86
Teddington TW11 ... 117 CE92
Sutherland Pl, W2 ... 82 DA72
Sutherland Rd, E17 ... 47 DX54
N9 ... 46 DU46
Sutherland Rd, N17 ... 46 DU52
W4 ... 98 CS79
W13 ... 79 CG72
Belvedere DA17 ... 106 FA76
Croydon CR0 ... 141 DN101
Enfield EN3 ... 31 DX43
Southall UB1 ... 78 BZ72
Sutherland Rd Path, E17 ... 67 DX55
Sutherland Row, SW1 ... 199 J10
Sutherland Sq, SE17 ... 102 DQ78
Sutherland St, SW1 ... 199 H10
Sutherland Wk, SE17 ... 102 DQ78
Sutherland Way, Pot.B. (Cuffley)
EN6 ... 13 DK28
Sutlej Rd, SE7 ... 104 EJ80
Sutterton St, N7 ... 83 DM65
SUTTON ... 158 DB107
⇌ Sutton ... 158 DC107
SUTTON AT HONE, Dart. ... 148 FN95
Sutton Av, Slou. SL3 ... 92 AW75
Woking GU21 ... 166 AS119
Sutton Cl, Beck. BR3
off Albemarle Rd ... 143 EB95
Loughton IG10 ... 48 EL45
Pinner HA5 ... 59 BU57
⇌ Sutton Common ... 140 DB103
Sutton Common Rd, Sutt.
SM1, SM3 ... 139 CZ101
Sutton Ct, W4 ... 98 CQ79
Sutton Ct Rd, E13 ... 86 EJ69
W4 ... 98 CQ80
Sutton SM1 ... 158 DC107
Uxbridge UB10 ... 77 BP67
Sutton Cres, Barn. EN5 ... 27 CX43
Sutton Dene, Houns. TW3 ... 96 CB81
Sutton Est, SW3 ... 198 C10
W10 ... 81 CW71
Sutton Est, The, N1 ... 83 DP66
Sutton Gdns, Bark. IG11
off Sutton Rd ... 87 ES67
Croydon CR0 ... 142 DT99
Redhill RH1 ... 185 DK129
Sutton Grn, Bark. IG11
off Sutton Rd ... 87 ES67
Sutton Gro, Sutt. SM1 ... 158 DD105
Sutton Hall Rd, Houns. TW5 ... 96 CA80
★ Sutton Heritage Cen, Cars.
SM5 ... 158 DF105
H Sutton Hosp, Sutt. SM2 ... 158 DB110
★ Sutton Ho, E9 ... 66 DW64
Sutton La, Bans. SM7 ... 174 DB115
Hounslow TW3 ... 96 BZ83
Slough SL3 ... 93 BC78
Sutton SM2 ... 158 DB111
Sutton La N, W4 ... 98 CQ78
Sutton La S, W4 ... 98 CQ79
Sutton Par, NW4
off Church Rd ... 63 CW56
Sutton Pk Rd, Sutt. SM1 ... 158 DB107
Sutton Path, Borwd. WD6
off Stratfield Rd ... 26 CN40
Sutton Pl, E9 ... 66 DW64
Dartford DA4 ... 128 FP92
Slough SL3 ... 93 BB79
Sutton Rd, E13 ... 86 EF70
E17 ... 47 DX53
N10 ... 64 DG54
Barking IG11 ... 87 ES68
Hounslow TW5 ... 96 CA81
Watford WD17 ... 24 BW41
Sutton Row, W1 ... 195 N8
Suttons Av, Horn. RM12 ... 72 FJ62
Suttons Gdns, Horn. RM12 ... 72 FK62
Suttons La, Horn. RM12 ... 72 FK64
Sutton Sq, E9 off Urswick Rd ... 66 DW64
Hounslow TW5 ... 96 BZ81
Sutton St, E1 ... 84 DW72
Sutton's Way, EC1 ... 197 J5
Sutton Wk, SE1 off York Rd ... 83 DM74
Sutton Way, W10 ... 81 CW71
Hounslow TW5 ... 96 BZ81
Swabey Rd, Slou. SL3 ... 93 BA77
Swaby Rd, SW18 ... 120 DC88
Swaffham Way, N22
off White Hart La ... 45 DP52
Swaffield Rd, SW18 ... 120 DB87
Sevenoaks TN13 ... 191 FJ122
Swain Cl, SW16 ... 121 DH93
Swain Rd, Th.Hth. CR7 ... 142 DQ99
Swains Cl, West Dr. UB7 ... 94 BL75
Swains La, N6 ... 64 DG62
Swainson Rd, W3 ... 99 CT75
Swains Rd, SW17 ... 120 DF94
Swain St, NW8 ... 194 B4
Swaisland Dr, Dart. (Cray.)
DA1 ... 127 FF85
Swaisland Rd, Dart. DA1 ... 127 FH85
Swakeleys Dr, Uxb. UB10 ... 58 BM63
Swakeleys Rd, Uxb. (Ickhm.)
UB10 ... 58 BM62
Swale Cl, S.Ock. (Aveley) RM15 ... 90 FQ72
Swaledale Cl, N11
off Ribblesdale Av ... 44 DG51
Swaledale Rd, Dart. DA2 ... 128 FQ88
Swale Rd, Dart. DA1 ... 107 FG83
Swallands Rd, SE6 ... 123 EA90
Swallow Cl, SE14 ... 102 DW81
Bushey WD23 ... 40 CC46
Erith DA8 ... 107 FE81
Grays (Chaff.Hun.) RM16 ... 109 FW77
Greenhithe DA9 ... 129 FT85
Rickmansworth WD3 ... 38 BJ45
Staines TW18 ... 113 BF91
Swallowdale, Iver SL0 ... 75 BD69
South Croydon CR2 ... 161 DX109
Swallow Dr, NW10
off Kingfisher Way ... 80 CR65
Northolt UB5 ... 78 CA68
Swallowfield, Egh. (Eng.Grn.)
TW20 off Heronfield ... 112 AV93
Swallowfield Rd, SE7 ... 104 EH78
Swallowfields, Grav. (Nthflt.)
DA11 off Hillary Av ... 130 GE90
Swallowfield Way, Hayes UB3 ... 95 BR75
Swallow Gdns, SW16 ... 121 DK92
Swallow Oaks, Abb.L. WD5 ... 7 BT31
Swallow Pas, W1 ... 195 J9
Swallow Pl, W1 ... 195 J9
Swallow St, E6 ... 86 EL71
W1 ... 199 L1
Iver SL0 ... 75 BD69
Swallowtail Cl, Orp. BR5 ... 146 EX98
Swallow Wk, Horn. RM12
off Heron Flight Av ... 89 FH65
Swanage Rd, E4 ... 47 EC52
SW18 ... 120 DC86
Swanage Way, Hayes UB4 ... 78 BW72
Swan & Pike Rd, Enf. EN3 ... 31 EA38
Swan App, E6 ... 86 EL71
Swan Av, Upmin. RM14 ... 73 FT60
Swanbourne Dr, Horn. RM12 ... 72 FJ64
Swanbridge Rd, Bexh. DA7 ... 106 FA81
Swan Business Pk, Dart. DA1 ... 108 FK84
Swan Cl, E17 ... 47 DY53
Croydon CR0 ... 142 DS101
Feltham TW13 ... 116 BY91
Orpington BR5 ... 146 EU97
Rickmansworth WD3
off Parsonage Rd ... 38 BK45
Swan Ct, SW3
off Flood St ... 100 DE78
Swandon Way, SW18 ... 100 DB84
Swan Dr, NW9 ... 42 CS54
Swanfield Rd, Wal.Cr. EN8 ... 15 DY33
Swanfield St, E2 ... 197 P3
Swanland Rd, Hat. AL9 ... 11 CV31
Potters Bar EN6 ... 11 CV33
Swan La, EC4 ... 201 K1
N20 ... 44 DC48
Dartford DA1 ... 127 FF87
Loughton IG10 ... 48 EJ45
SWANLEY ... 147 FE98
⇌ Swanley ... 147 FD98
Swanley Bar La, Pot.B. EN6 ... 12 DB28
Swanley Bypass, Sid. DA14 ... 147 FC97
Swanley BR8 ... 147 FC97
Swanley Cen, Swan. BR8 ... 147 FE97
Swanley Cres, Pot.B. EN6 ... 12 DB29
Swanley La, Swan. BR8 ... 147 FF97
Swanley Rd, Well. DA16 ... 106 EW81
SWANLEY VILLAGE, Swan. ... 148 FJ95
Swanley Village Rd, Swan.
BR8 ... 147 FH95
Swan Mead, SE1 ... 201 M7
Hemel Hempstead HP3
off Belswains La ... 6 BM25
Swan Pas, E1 off Cartwright St ... 84 DT73
Swan Path, E10 off Jesse Rd ... 67 EC60
Swan Pl, SW13 ... 99 CT82
Swan Rd, SE16 ... 202 G4
SE18 ... 104 EK76
Feltham TW13 ... 116 BY92
Iver SL0 ... 75 BF72
Southall UB1 ... 78 CB72
West Drayton UB7 ... 94 BK75
SWANSCOMBE ... 130 FZ86
⇌ Swanscombe ... 130 FZ85
Swanscombe Ho, W11
off St. Anns Rd ... 81 CX74
Swanscombe Rd, W4 ... 98 CS78
W11 ... 81 CX74
Swanscombe St, Swans.
DA10 ... 130 FY87
Swansea Ct, E16
off Fishguard Way ... 87 EP74
Swansea Rd, Enf. EN3 ... 30 DW42
Hounslow (Hthrw.Air.) TW6
off Southern Perimeter Rd ... 115 BQ86
Swanshope, Loug. IG10 ... 33 EP40
Swansland Gdns, E17
off McEntee Av ... 47 DY53
Swanston Path, Wat. WD19 ... 40 BW48
Swan St, SE1 ... 201 J6
Isleworth TW7 ... 97 CH83
Swanton Gdns, SW19 ... 119 CX88
Swanton Rd, Erith DA8 ... 107 FB80
Swan Wk, SW3 ... 100 DF79
Romford RM1 ... 71 FE57
Shepperton TW17 ... 135 BS101
Swan Way, Enf. EN3 ... 31 DX40
Swanwick Cl, SW15 ... 119 CT87
Swan Yd, N1
off Highbury Sta Rd ... 83 DP65
Sward Rd, Orp. BR5 ... 146 EU100
Swaton Rd, E3 ... 85 EA70
Swaylands Rd, Belv. DA17 ... 106 FA79
Swaynesland Rd, Eden. (Crock.H.)
TN8 ... 189 EM134
Swaythling Cl, N18 ... 46 DV49
Swaythling Ho, SW15
off Tunworth Cres ... 119 CT86
Swedenborg Gdns, E1 ... 84 DU73
Sweden Gate, SE16 ... 203 K7
Sweeney Cres, SE1 ... 202 A5
Sweeps Ditch Cl, Stai. TW18 ... 134 BG95
Sweeps La, Egh. TW20 ... 113 AZ92
Orpington BR5 ... 146 EX99
Sweet Briar Grn, N9 ... 46 DT48
Sweet Briar Gro, N9 ... 46 DT48
Sweet Briar La, Epsom KT18 ... 156 CR114
Sweet Briar Wk, N18 ... 46 DT49
Sweetcroft La, Uxb. UB10 ... 76 BN66
Sweetmans Av, Pnr. HA5 ... 60 BX55
Sweets Way, N20 ... 44 DD47
Swetenham Wk, SE18
off Sandbach Pl ... 105 EQ78
Swete St, E13 ... 86 EG68
Sweyne Rd, Swans. DA10 ... 130 FY86
Sweyn Pl, SE3 ... 104 EG82
Swievelands Rd, West. (Bigg.H.)
TN16 ... 178 EH119
Swift Cl, E17 ... 47 DY52
Harrow HA2 ... 60 CB61
Hayes UB3
off Church Rd ... 77 BT72
Upminster RM14 ... 73 FS60
Swift Rd, Felt. TW13 ... 116 BY90
Southall UB2 ... 96 BZ76
Swiftsden Way, Brom. BR1 ... 124 EE93
Swift St, SW6 ... 99 CZ81
Swiftsure Rd, Grays (Chaff.Hun.)
RM16 ... 109 FW77
SWILLET, THE, Rick. ... 21 BB44
Swinbrook Rd, W10 ... 81 CY71

Swinburne Ct, SE5
off Basingdon Way ... 102 DR84
Swinburne Cres, Croy. CR0 ... 142 DW100
Swinburne Gdns, Til. RM18 ... 111 GH82
Swinburne Rd, SW15 ... 99 CU84
Swinderby Rd, Wem. HA0 ... 80 CL65
Swindon Cl, Ilf. IG3
off Salisbury Rd ... 69 ES61
Romford RM3 ... 52 FM50
Swindon Gdns, Rom. RM3 ... 52 FM50
Swindon La, Rom. RM3 ... 52 FM50
Swindon Rd, Houns. (Hthrw.Air.)
TW6 ... 115 BQ85
Swindon St, W12 ... 81 CV74
Swinfield Cl, Felt. TW13 ... 116 BY91
Swinford Gdns, SW9 ... 101 DP83
Swingate La, SE18 ... 105 ES79
Swinnerton St, E9 ... 67 DY64
Swinton Cl, Wem. HA9 ... 62 CP60
Swinton Pl, WC1 ... 196 B2
Swinton St, WC1 ... 196 B2
Swires Shaw, Kes. BR2 ... 162 EK105
Swiss Av, Wat. WD18 ... 23 BS42
Swiss Cl, Wat. WD18 ... 23 BS41
⊖ Swiss Cottage ... 82 DD66
Swiss Ct, W1 ... 199 N1
Swiss Ter, NW6 ... 82 DD66
Swithland Gdns, SE9 ... 125 EN91
Swyncombe Av, W5 ... 97 CH77
Swynford Gdns, NW4
off Handowe Cl ... 63 CU56
Sybil Ms, N4 off Lothair Rd N ... 65 DP58
Sybil Phoenix Cl, SE8 ... 203 J10
Sybil Thorndike Ho, N1
off Clephane Rd ... 84 DQ65
Sybourn St, E17 ... 67 DZ59
Sycamore App, Rick. (Crox.Grn.)
WD3 ... 23 BQ43
Sycamore Av, E3 ... 85 DZ67
W5 ... 97 CK76
Hayes UB3 ... 77 BS73
Sidcup DA15 ... 125 ET86
Upminster RM14 ... 72 FN62
Sycamore Cl, E16
off Clarence Rd ... 86 EE70
N9 off Pycroft Way ... 46 DU49
SE9 ... 124 EL89
W3 off Bromyard Av ... 80 CS74
Barnet EN4 ... 28 DD44
Bushey WD23 ... 24 BY40
Carshalton SM5 ... 158 DF105
Chalfont St. Giles HP8 ... 36 AU48
Edgware HA8 off Ash Cl ... 42 CQ49
Feltham TW13 ... 115 BU90
Gravesend DA12 ... 131 GK87
Leatherhead (Fetch.) KT22 ... 171 CE123
Loughton IG10 off Cedar Dr ... 33 EP40
Northolt UB5 ... 78 BY67
Waltham Cross EN7 ... 14 DT27
Watford WD25 ... 23 BV35
West Drayton UB7
off Whitethorn Av ... 76 BM73
Sycamore Ct, Surb. KT6
off Penners Gdns ... 138 CL101
Sycamore Dr, Brwd. CM14
off Copperfield Gdns ... 54 FW46
St. Albans (Park St.) AL2 ... 9 CD27
Swanley BR8 ... 147 FE97
Sycamore Gdns, W6 ... 99 CV75
Mitcham CR4 ... 140 DD96
Sycamore Gro, NW9 ... 62 CQ59
SE6 ... 123 EC86
SE20 ... 122 DU94
New Malden KT3 ... 138 CR97
Sycamore Hill, N11 ... 44 DG51
Sycamore Ms, SW4 ... 101 DJ83
Sycamore Ri, Bans. SM7 ... 157 CX114
Chalfont St. Giles HP8 ... 36 AU48
Sycamore Rd, SW19 ... 119 CW93
Chalfont St. Giles HP8 ... 36 AU48
Dartford DA1 ... 128 FK88
Rickmansworth (Crox.Grn.)
WD3 ... 23 BQ43
Sycamores, The, Rad. WD7
off The Avenue ... 9 CH34
South Ockendon (Aveley) RM15
off Dacre Av ... 91 FR74
Sycamore St, EC1 ... 197 H5
Sycamore Wk, W10 off Fifth Av ... 81 CY70
Egham (Eng.Grn.) TW20 ... 112 AV93
Ilford IG6 off Civic Way ... 69 EQ56
Slough (Geo.Grn.) SL3 ... 74 AY72
Sycamore Way, S.Ock. RM15 ... 91 FX70
Teddington TW11 ... 117 CJ93
Thornton Heath CR7 ... 141 DN99
SYDENHAM, SE26 ... 122 DW92
⇌ Sydenham ... 122 DW91
Sydenham Av, N21
off Chadwick Av ... 29 DM43
SE26 ... 122 DV92
Sydenham Cl, Rom. RM1 ... 71 FF56
Sydenham Cotts, SE12 ... 124 EJ89
⇌ Sydenham Hill ... 122 DT90
Sydenham Hill, SE23 ... 122 DV88
SE26 ... 122 DU90
Sydenham Hill Est, SE26 ... 122 DU90
Sydenham Pk, SE26 ... 122 DW90
Sydenham Pk Rd, SE26 ... 122 DW90
Sydenham Ri, SE23 ... 122 DV89
Sydenham Rd, SE26 ... 122 DW92
Croydon CR0 ... 142 DR101
Sydmons Ct, SE23 ... 122 DW87
Sydner Ms, N16 off Sydner Rd ... 66 DT63
Sydner Rd, N16 ... 66 DT63
Sydney Av, Pur. CR8 ... 159 DM112
Sydney Cl, SW3 ... 198 A9
Sydney Cres, Ashf. TW15 ... 115 BP93
Sydney Gro, NW4 ... 63 CW57
Sydney Ms, SW3 ... 198 A9
Sydney Pl, SW7 ... 198 A9
Sydney Rd, E11
off Mansfield Rd ... 68 EH58
N8 ... 65 DN56
N10 ... 44 DG53
SE2 ... 106 EW76
SW20 ... 139 CX96
W13 ... 79 CG74
Sydney Rd, Bex. DA6 ... 106 EX84
Enfield EN2 ... 30 DR42
Feltham TW14 ... 115 BU88
Ilford IG6 ... 49 EQ54
Richmond TW9 ... 98 CL84
Sidcup DA14 ... 125 ES91
Sutton SM1 ... 158 DA105
Teddington TW11 ... 117 CF92
Tilbury RM18 ... 111 GG82
Watford WD18 ... 23 BS43
Woodford Green IG8 ... 48 EG49
Sydney St, SW3 ... 198 B10
Syke Cluan, Iver SL0 ... 93 BE75
Syke Ings, Iver SL0 ... 93 BE76
Sykes Dr, Stai. TW18 ... 114 BH92
Sylvana Cl, Uxb. UB10 ... 76 BM67
Sylvan Av, N3 ... 44 DA54
N22 ... 45 DM52
NW7 ... 43 CT51
Hornchurch RM11 ... 72 FL58
Romford RM6 ... 70 EZ58
Sylvan Cl, Grays (Chaff.Hun.)
RM16 off Warren La ... 110 FY77
Oxted RH8 ... 188 EH129
South Croydon CR2 ... 160 DV110
Woking GU22 ... 167 BB117
Sylvan Ct, N12 off Holden Rd ... 44 DB49
Sylvan Est, SE19 ... 142 DT95
Sylvan Gdns, Surb. KT6 ... 137 CK101
Sylvan Gro, NW2 ... 63 CX63
SE15 ... 102 DV80
Sylvan Hill, SE19 ... 142 DS95
Sylvan Rd, E7 ... 86 EG65
E11 ... 68 EG57
E17 ... 67 EA57
SE19 ... 142 DT95
Ilford IG1 off Hainault St ... 69 EQ61
Sylvan Wk, Brom. BR1 ... 145 EM97
Sylvan Way, Chig. IG7 ... 50 EV48
Dagenham RM8 ... 70 EV62
West Wickham BR4 ... 162 EE105
Sylverdale Rd, Croy. CR0 ... 141 DP104
Purley CR8 ... 159 DP113
Sylvester Av, Chis. BR7 ... 125 EM93
Sylvester Gdns, Ilf. IG6 ... 50 EV50
Sylvester Path, E8
off Sylvester Rd ... 84 DV65
Sylvester Rd, E8 ... 84 DV65
E17 ... 67 DZ59
N2 ... 44 DC54
Wembley HA0 ... 61 CJ64
Sylvestres, Sev. (Rvrhd.) TN13 ... 190 FD121
Sylvestrus Cl, Kings.T. KT1 ... 138 CN95
Sylvia Av, Brwd. CM13 ... 55 GC47
Pinner HA5 ... 40 BZ51
Sylvia Ct, Wem. HA9
off Harrow Rd ... 80 CP66
Sylvia Gdns, Wem. HA9 ... 80 CP66
Symes Ms, NW1
off Camden High St ... 83 DJ68
Symonds Ct, Wal.Cr. (Chsht.) EN8
off High St ... 15 DX28
Symons St, SW3 ... 198 E9
Symphony Ms, W10
off Third Av ... 81 CY69
Syon Gate Way, Brent. TW8 ... 97 CG80
★ Syon Ho & Pk, Brent. TW8 ... 97 CJ81
⇌ Syon Lane ... 97 CG80
Syon La, Islw. TW7 ... 97 CH80
Syon Pk Gdns, Islw. TW7 ... 97 CF80
Syon Vista, Rich. TW9 ... 97 CK81
Syracuse Av, Rain. RM13 ... 90 FL69
Syringa Ct, Grays RM17 ... 110 GD80
Sythwood, Wok. GU21 ... 166 AV117

T

Tabard Cen, SE1
off Prioress St ... 102 DR76
Tabard Gdn Est, SE1 ... 201 L5
Tabard St, SE1 ... 201 K5
Tabarin Way, Epsom KT17 ... 173 CW116
Tabernacle Av, E13
off Barking Rd ... 86 EG70
Tabernacle St, EC2 ... 197 L5
Tableer Av, SW4 ... 121 DK85
Tabley Rd, N7 ... 65 DL63
Tabor Gdns, Sutt. SM3 ... 157 CZ107
Tabor Gro, SW19 ... 119 CY94
Tabor Rd, W6 ... 99 CV76
Tabors Ct, Brwd. (Shenf.) CM15
off Shenfield Rd ... 55 FZ45
Tabrums Way, Upmin. RM14 ... 73 FS59
Tachbrook Est, SW1 ... 101 DK78
Tachbrook Ms, SW1 ... 199 K8
Tachbrook Rd, Felt. TW14 ... 115 BT87
Southall UB2 ... 96 BX77
Uxbridge UB8 ... 76 BJ68
Tachbrook St, SW1 ... 199 L9
Tack Ms, SE4 ... 103 EA83
Tadema Rd, SW10 ... 100 DC80
Tadlows Cl, Upmin. RM14 ... 72 FP64
Tadmor Cl, Sun. TW16 ... 135 BT98
Tadmor St, W12 ... 81 CX74
Tadorne Rd, Tad. KT20 ... 173 CW121
TADWORTH ... 173 CV121
⇌ Tadworth ... 173 CW122
Tadworth Av, N.Mal. KT3 ... 139 CT99
Tadworth Cl, Tad. KT20 ... 173 CX122
Tadworth Par, Horn. RM12
off Maylands Av ... 71 FH63
Tadworth Rd, NW2 ... 63 CU61
Tadworth St, Tad. KT20 ... 173 CW123
Taeping St, E14 ... 204 B8
Taffy's How, Mitch. CR4 ... 140 DE97
Taft Way, E3
off St. Leonards St ... 85 EB69
Tagalie Pl, Rad. (Shenley) WD7
off Porters Pk Dr ... 10 CL32
Tagg's Island, Hmptn. TW12 ... 137 CD96
Tailworth St, E1
off Chicksand St ... 84 DU71
Tait Rd, Croy. CR0 ... 142 DS101
Takeley Cl, Rom. RM5 ... 51 FD54
Takeley Cl, Wal.Abb. EN9 ... 15 ED33
Takhar Ms, SW11
off Cabul Rd ... 100 DE82
Talacre Rd, NW5 ... 82 DG65
Talbot Av, N2 ... 64 DD55
Slough SL3 ... 93 AZ76
Watford WD19 ... 40 BY45
Talbot Cl, N15 ... 66 DT56
Talbot Ct, EC3 ... 197 L10
Talbot Cres, NW4 ... 63 CU57
Talbot Gdns, Ilf. IG3 ... 70 EU61
Talbot Ho, E14 off Giraud St ... 85 EB72
N7 off Harvist Est ... 65 DN62
Talbot Pl, SE3 ... 104 EE82
Slough (Datchet) SL3 ... 92 AW81
Talbot Rd, E6 ... 87 EN68
E7 ... 68 EG63
N6 ... 64 DG58
N15 ... 66 DT56
N22 ... 45 DJ54
SE22 ... 102 DS84
W2 ... 81 CZ72
W11 ... 81 CZ72
W13 ... 79 CG73
Ashford TW15 ... 114 BK92
Bromley BR2
off Masons Hill ... 144 EH98
Carshalton SM5 ... 158 DG106
Dagenham RM9 ... 88 EZ65
Harrow HA3 ... 41 CF54
Isleworth TW7 ... 97 CG84
Rickmansworth WD3 ... 38 BL46
Southall UB2 ... 96 BY77
Thornton Heath CR7 ... 142 DR98
Twickenham TW2 ... 117 CE88
Wembley HA0 ... 61 CK64
Talbot Roundabout, Epp. (N.Wld.)
CM16 ... 19 FD25
Talbot Sq, W2 ... 194 A9
Talbot Wk, NW10 off Garnet Rd ... 80 CS65
W11 ... 81 CY72
Talbot Yd, SE1 ... 201 K3
Talbrook, Brwd. CM14 ... 54 FT48
Taleworth Cl, Ashtd. KT21 ... 171 CK120
Taleworth Pk, Ashtd. KT21 ... 171 CK120
Taleworth Rd, Ashtd. KT21 ... 171 CK119
Talfourd Pl, SE15 ... 102 DT81
Talfourd Rd, SE15 ... 102 DT81
Talgarth Rd, W6 ... 99 CY78
W14 ... 99 CY78
Talgarth Wk, NW9 ... 62 CS57
Talisman Cl, Ilf. IG3 ... 70 EV60
Talisman Sq, SE26 ... 122 DU91
Talisman Way, Epsom KT17 ... 173 CW116
Wembley HA9 ... 62 CM62
Tallack Cl, Har. HA3
off College Hill Rd ... 41 CE52
Tallack Rd, E10 ... 67 DZ60
Tall Elms Cl, Brom. BR2 ... 144 EF99
Tallents Cl, Dart. (Sutt.H.) DA4 ... 128 FP94
Tallis Cl, E16 ... 86 EH72
Tallis Gro, SE7 ... 104 EH79
Tallis St, EC4 ... 196 E10
Tallis Vw, NW10 ... 80 CR65
Tallis Way, Borwd. WD6 ... 25 CK39
Tallon Rd, Brwd. CM13 ... 55 GE43
Tall Trees, SW16 ... 141 DM97
Slough (Colnbr.) SL3 ... 93 BE81
Tall Trees Cl, Horn. RM11 ... 72 FK58
Tally Ho Cor, N12 ... 44 DC50
Tally Rd, Oxt. RH8 ... 188 EL131
Talma Gdns, Twick. TW2 ... 117 CE86
Talmage Cl, SE23
off Tyson Rd ... 122 DW87
Talman Gro, Stan. HA7 ... 41 CK51
Talma Rd, SW2 ... 101 DN84
Talus Cl, Purf. RM19
off Brimfield Rd ... 109 FR77
Talwin St, E3 ... 85 EB69
Tamar Cl, E3 off Lefevre Wk ... 85 DZ67
Upminster RM14 ... 73 FS58
Tamar Dr, S.Ock. (Aveley)
RM15 ... 90 FQ72
Tamarind Yd, E1 ... 202 C2
Tamarisk Cl, S.Ock. RM15 ... 91 FW70
Tamarisk Rd, S.Ock. RM15 ... 91 FW69
Tamarisk Sq, W12 ... 81 CT73
Tamar Sq, Wdf.Grn. IG8 ... 48 EH51
Tamar St, SE7
off Woolwich Rd ... 104 EL76
Tamar Way, N17 ... 66 DU55
Slough SL3 ... 93 BB78
Tamerton Sq, Wok. GU22 ... 166 AY119
Tamesis Gdns, Wor.Pk. KT4 ... 138 CS102
Tamesis Strand, Grav. DA12 ... 131 GL92
Tamian Way, Houns. TW4 ... 96 BW84
Tamworth Av, Wdf.Grn. IG8 ... 48 EE51
Tamworth La, Mitch. CR4 ... 141 DH96
Tamworth Pk, Mitch. CR4 ... 141 DH98
Tamworth Pl, Croy. CR0 ... 142 DQ103
Tamworth Rd, Croy. CR0 ... 141 DP103
Tamworth St, SW6 ... 100 DA79
Tancred Rd, N4 ... 65 DP58
Tandem Cen, SW19
off Prince George's Rd ... 140 DD95
Tandem Way, SW19 ... 140 DD95
TANDRIDGE, Oxt. ... 187 EA133
Tandridge Ct, Cat. CR3 ... 176 DU122
Tandridge Dr, Orp. BR6 ... 145 ER102
Tandridge Gdns, S.Croy. CR2 ... 160 DT113
Tandridge Hill La, Gdse. RH9 ... 187 DZ128
Tandridge La, Oxt. (Tand.)
RH8 ... 187 EA131
Tandridge Pl, Orp. BR6
off Tandridge Dr ... 145 ER101
Tandridge Rd, Warl. CR6 ... 177 DX119
Tanfield Av, NW2 ... 63 CT63
Tanfield Cl, Wal.Cr. EN7 ... 14 DU27
Tanfield Rd, Croy. CR0 ... 160 DQ105
Tangent Link, Rom. (Harold Hill)
RM3 ... 52 FK53
Tangent Rd, Rom. RM3
off Ashton Rd ... 52 FK53
Tangier Rd, Rich. TW10 ... 98 CP83
Tangier Way, Tad. KT20 ... 173 CY117
Tangier Wd, Tad. KT20 ... 173 CY118
Tanglebury Cl, Brom. BR1 ... 145 EM98
Tangle Tree Cl, N3 ... 44 DB54
Tanglewood Cl, Cher. (Longcr.)
KT16 ... 132 AV104
Croydon CR0 ... 142 DW104
Stanmore HA7 ... 41 CE47
Uxbridge UB10 ... 76 BN69
Woking GU22 ... 167 BD116
Tanglewood Way, Felt. TW13 ... 115 BV90
Tangley Gro, SW15 ... 119 CT86
Tangley Pk Rd, Hmptn. TW12 ... 116 BZ93
Tanglyn Av, Shep. TW17 ... 135 BP99
Tangmere Cres, Horn. RM12 ... 89 FH65
Tangmere Gdns, Nthlt. UB5 ... 78 BW68
Tangmere Gro, Kings.T. KT2 ... 117 CK92
Tangmere Way, NW9 ... 42 CS54
Tanhouse Rd, Oxt. RH8 ... 187 ED132
Tanhurst Wk, SE2
off Alsike Rd ... 106 EX76
Tankerton Rd, Surb. KT6 ... 138 CM103
Tankerton St, WC1 ... 196 A3
Tankerville Rd, SW16 ... 121 DK93
Tank Hill Rd, Purf. RM19 ... 108 FN78
Tank La, Purf. RM19 ... 108 FN77
Tankridge Rd, NW2 ... 63 CV61
Tanner Pt, E13 off Pelly Rd ... 86 EG67
Tanners Cl, Walt. KT12 ... 135 BV100
Tanners Dean, Lthd. KT22 ... 171 CJ122
Tanners End La, N18 ... 46 DS49
Tanners Hill, SE8 ... 103 DZ81
Abbots Langley WD5 ... 7 BT31
Tanners La, Ilf. IG6 ... 69 EQ55
Tanner St, SE1 ... 201 N5
Barking IG11 ... 87 EQ65
Tanners Wd Cl, Abb.L. WD5
off Tanners Wd La ... 7 BS32
Tanners Wd La, Abb.L. WD5 ... 7 BS32
Tannery, The, Red. RH1
off Oakdene Rd ... 184 DE134
Tannery Cl, Beck. BR3 ... 143 DX99
Dagenham RM10 ... 71 FB62
Tannery La, Wok. (Send)
GU23 ... 167 BF122
Tannington Ter, N5 ... 65 DN62
Tannsfeld Rd, SE26 ... 123 DX92
Tansley Cl, N7 off Hilldrop Rd ... 65 DK64
Tanswell Est, SE1 ... 200 E5
Tanswell St, SE1 ... 200 D5
Tansy Cl, E6 ... 87 EN72
Romford RM3 ... 52 FL51
Tantallon Rd, SW12 ... 120 DG88
Tant Av, E16 ... 86 EF72
Tantony Gro, Rom. RM6 ... 70 EX55
Tanworth Cl, Nthwd. HA6 ... 39 BQ51
Tanworth Gdns, Pnr. HA5 ... 39 BV54
Tanyard La, Bex. DA5
off Bexley High St ... 126 FA87
Tanza Rd, NW3 ... 64 DF63
Tapestry Cl, Sutt. SM2 ... 158 DB108
Taplow, NW3 ... 82 DD66
SE17 off Thurlow St ... 102 DS78
Taplow Rd, N13 ... 46 DQ49
Taplow St, N1 ... 197 J1
Tappesfield Rd, SE15 ... 102 DW83
Tapp St, E1 ... 84 DV70
Tapster St, Barn. EN5 ... 27 CZ42
Tara Ms, N8 off Edison Rd ... 65 DK58
Taransay Wk, N1
off Marquess Rd ... 84 DR65
Tarbert Rd, SE22 ... 122 DS85
Tarbert Wk, E1 off Juniper St ... 84 DW73
Target Cl, Felt. TW14 ... 115 BS86
Tariff Cres, SE8 ... 203 M8
Tariff Rd, N17 ... 46 DU51
Tarleton Gdns, SE23 ... 122 DV88
Tarling Cl, Sid. DA14 ... 126 EV90
Tarling Rd, E16 ... 86 EF72
N2 ... 44 DC54
Tarling St, E1 ... 84 DV72
Tarling St Est, E1 ... 84 DW72
Tarmac Way, West Dr. UB7 ... 94 BH80
Tarnbank, Enf. EN2 ... 29 DL43
Tarn St, SE1 ... 201 H7
Tarnwood Pk, SE9 ... 125 EM88
Tarnworth Rd, Rom. RM3 ... 52 FN50
Tarpan Way, Brox. EN10 ... 15 DZ26
Tarquin Ho, SE26 ... 122 DU91
Tarragon Cl, SE14 ... 103 DY80
Tarragon Gro, SE26 ... 123 DX93
Tarrant Pl, W1 ... 194 D7
Tarrington Cl, SW16 ... 121 DK90
Tarry La, SE8 ... 203 K8
Tartar Rd, Cob. KT11 ... 154 BW113
Tarver Rd, SE17 ... 101 DP78
Tarves Way, SE10 ... 103 EB80
Tash Pl, N11 off Woodland Rd ... 45 DH50
Tasker Cl, Hayes UB3 ... 95 BQ80
Tasker Ho, Bark. IG11
off Dovehouse Mead ... 87 ER68
Tasker Rd, NW3 ... 64 DF64
Grays RM16 ... 111 GH76
Tasman Ct, E14
off Westferry Rd ... 103 EB77
Sunbury-on-Thames TW16 ... 115 BS94
Tasmania Ho, Til. RM18
off Hobart Rd ... 111 GG81
Tasmania Ter, N18 ... 46 DQ51
Tasman Rd, SW9 ... 101 DL83
Tasman Wk, E16 off Royal Rd ... 86 EK72
Tasso Rd, W6 ... 99 CY79
Tatam Rd, NW10 ... 80 CQ66
Tatchbury Ho, SW15
off Tunworth Cres ... 119 CT86
Tate & Lyle Jetty, E16 ... 104 EL75
★ Tate Britain, SW1 ... 199 P9
Tate Cl, Lthd. KT22 ... 171 CJ123
★ Tate Modern, SE1 ... 200 G2
Tate Rd, E16 off Newland St ... 87 EM74
Gerrards Cross (Chal.St.P.)
SL9 ... 37 AZ50
Sutton SM1 ... 158 DA106
TATLING END, Ger.Cr. ... 57 BB61
Tatnell Rd, SE23 ... 123 DY86
TATSFIELD, West. ... 178 EL120
Tatsfield App Rd, West. (Tats.)
TN16 ... 178 EH123
Tatsfield La, West. (Tats.)
TN16 ... 179 EM121
TATTENHAM CORNER,
Epsom ... 173 CV118
⇌ Tattenham Corner ... 173 CV118
Tattenham Cor Rd, Epsom
KT18 ... 173 CT117
Tattenham Cres, Epsom KT18 ... 173 CU118
Tattenham Gro, Epsom KT18 ... 173 CV118
Tattenham Way, Tad. KT20 ... 173 CX118
Tattersall Cl, SE9 ... 124 EL85
Tatton Cres, N16
off Clapton Common ... 66 DT59
Tatum St, SE17 ... 201 L9
Tauber Cl, Borwd. (Elstree)
WD6 ... 26 CM42
Tauheed Cl, N4 ... 66 DQ61
Taunton Av, SW20 ... 139 CV96
Caterham CR3 ... 176 DT123
Hounslow TW3 ... 96 CC82
Taunton Cl, Bexh. DA7 ... 107 FD82
Ilford IG6 ... 49 ET51
Sutton SM3 ... 140 DA102
Taunton Dr, N2 ... 44 DC54
Enfield EN2 ... 29 DN41
Taunton La, Couls. CR5 ... 175 DN119
Taunton Ms, NW1 ... 194 D5
Taunton Pl, NW1 ... 194 D4
Taunton Rd, SE12 ... 124 EE85
Gravesend (Nthflt.) DA11 ... 130 GA85
Greenford UB6 ... 78 CB67
Romford RM3 ... 52 FJ49
Taunton Vale, Grav. DA12 ... 131 GK90
Taunton Way, Stan. HA7 ... 62 CL55
Tavern Cl, Cars. SM5 ... 140 DE101
Taverners Cl, W11
off Addison Av ... 81 CY74
Taverner Sq, N5
off Highbury Gra ... 66 DQ63
Taverners Way, E4
off Douglas Rd ... 48 EE46
Tavern La, SW9 ... 101 DN82
Tavistock Av, E17 ... 67 DY55
NW7 off Bittacy Hill ... 43 CY52
Greenford UB6 ... 79 CG68
Tavistock Cl, N16 off Crossway ... 66 DS64
Potters Bar EN6 ... 12 DD31
Romford RM3 ... 52 FK53
Staines TW18 ... 114 BK94
Tavistock Ct, WC2
off Tavistock St ... 83 DL73
Tavistock Cres, W11 ... 81 CZ71
Mitcham CR4 ... 141 DL98
Tavistock Gdns, Ilf. IG3 ... 69 ES63
Tavistock Gate, Croy. CR0 ... 142 DR102
Tavistock Gro, Croy. CR0 ... 142 DR101
Tavistock Ms, E18
off Avon Way ... 68 EG56
W11 off Lancaster Rd ... 81 CZ72
Tavistock Pl, E18 off Avon Way ... 68 EG55
N14 off Chase Side ... 45 DH45
WC1 ... 195 N4
Tavistock Rd, E7 ... 68 EF63
E15 ... 86 EF65
E18 ... 68 EG55
N4 ... 66 DR58
NW10 ... 81 CT68
W11 ... 81 CZ72
Bromley BR2 ... 144 EF98
Carshalton SM5 ... 140 DD102
Croydon CR0 ... 142 DR102
Edgware HA8 ... 42 CN53
Uxbridge UB10 ... 59 BQ64
Watford WD24 ... 24 BX39
Welling DA16 ... 106 EW81
West Drayton UB7 ... 76 BK74
Tavistock Sq, WC1 ... 195 N4
Tavistock St, WC2 ... 196 A10
Tavistock Ter, N19 ... 65 DK62
Tavistock Twr, SE16 ... 203 K7
Tavistock Wk, Cars. SM5
off Tavistock Rd ... 140 DD102
Taviton St, WC1 ... 195 M4
Tavy Cl, SE11 ... 200 E10
Tawney Common, Epp. CM16 ... 18 FA32
Tawney Rd, SE28 ... 88 EV73
Tawny Av, Upmin. RM14 ... 72 FP64
Tawny Cl, W13 ... 79 CH74
Feltham TW13 off Chervil Cl ... 115 BU90
Tawny Way, SE16 ... 203 J8
Tayben Av, Twick. TW2 ... 117 CE86
Taybridge Rd, SW11 ... 100 DG83
Tayburn Cl, E14 ... 85 EC72
Tayfield Cl, Uxb. UB10 ... 59 BQ62
Tayler Cotts, Pot.B. EN6
off Crossoaks La ... 11 CT34
Tayles Hill, Epsom KT17
off Tayles Hill Dr ... 157 CT110
Tayles Hill Dr, Epsom KT17 ... 157 CT110
Taylor Av, Rich. TW9 ... 98 CP82
Taylor Cl, N17 ... 46 DU52
SE8 ... 103 DZ79
Epsom KT19
off Williams Evans Rd ... 156 CN111
Hampton (Hmptn.H.) TW12 ... 116 CC92
Hounslow TW3 ... 96 CC81
Orpington BR6 ... 163 ET105
Romford RM5 ... 50 FA52
Uxbridge (Hare.) UB9
off High St ... 38 BJ53
Taylor Ct, E15 off Clays La ... 67 EC64
Taylor Rd, Ashtd. KT21 ... 171 CK117
Mitcham CR4 ... 120 DE94
Wallington SM6 ... 159 DH106
Taylor Row, Dart. DA2 ... 128 FJ90
Romford (Noak Hill) RM3
off Cummings Hall La ... 52 FJ48
Taylors Bldgs, SE18
off Spray St ... 105 EP77
Taylors Cl, Sid. DA14 ... 125 ET91
Taylors Grn, W3 off Long Dr ... 80 CS72
Taylors La, NW10 ... 80 CS66
SE26 ... 122 DV91
Barnet EN5 ... 27 CZ39
Taymount Ri, SE23 ... 122 DW89
Taynton Dr, Red. RH1 ... 185 DK129

Tay - Thi

Tayport Cl, N1 .83 DL66
Tayside Dr, Edg. HA8 .42 CP48
Tay Way, Rom. RM1 .51 FF53
Taywood Rd, Nthlt. UB5 .78 BZ69
Teak Cl, SE16 .203 L3
Teal Av, Orp. BR5 .146 EX98
Teal Cl, E16 off Fulmer Rd .86 EK71
South Croydon CR2 .161 DX111
Teal Ct, Wall. SM6
off Carew Rd .159 DJ107
Teal Dr, Nthwd. HA6 .39 BQ52
Teale St, E2 .84 DU68
Tealing Dr, Epsom KT19 .156 CR105
Teal Pl, Sutt. SM1
off Sandpiper Rd .157 CZ106
Teal St, SE10 .205 L6
Teal Way, Hem.H. HP3
off Belswains La .6 BM25
Teardrop Ind Est, Swan. BR8 .147 FH99
Teasel Cl, Croy. CR0 .143 DX102
Teasel Way, E15 .86 EE69
Teazle Meade, Epp. (Thnwd.) CM16
off Carpenters Arms La .18 EV25
Teazle Wd Hill, Lthd. KT22 .171 CE117
Teazlewood Pk, Lthd. KT22 .171 CG117
Tebworth Rd, N17 .46 DT52
Teck Cl, Islw. TW7 .97 CG82
Tedder Cl, Chess. KT9 .155 CJ106
Ruislip HA4 off West End Rd .59 BV64
Uxbridge UB10 .76 BM66
Tedder Rd, S.Croy. CR2 .160 DW108
TEDDINGTON .117 CG93
⇌ Teddington .117 CG93
Teddington Cl, Epsom KT19 .156 CR110
Teddington Lock, Tedd. TW11 .117 CH91
H Teddington Mem Hosp, Tedd.
TW11 .117 CE93
Teddington Pk, Tedd. TW11 .117 CF92
Teddington Pk Rd, Tedd. TW11 .117 CF91
Tedworth Gdns, SW3
off Tedworth Sq .100 DF78
Tedworth Sq, SW3 .100 DF78
Tee, The, W3 .80 CS72
Tees Av, Grnf. UB6 .79 CE68
Tees Cl, Upmin. RM14 .73 FR59
Teesdale Av, Islw. TW7 .97 CG81
Teesdale Cl, E2 .84 DV68
Teesdale Gdns, SE25 .142 DS96
Isleworth TW7 .97 CG81
Teesdale Rd, E11 .68 EF58
Dartford DA2 .128 FQ88
Teesdale St, E2 .84 DV68
Teesdale Yd, E2 off Teesdale St .84 DV68
Tees Dr, Rom. RM3 .52 FK48
Teeswater Ct, Erith DA18
off Middle Way .106 EX76
Teevan Cl, Croy. CR0 .142 DU101
Teevan Rd, Croy. CR0 .142 DU101
Teggs La, Wok. GU22 .167 BF116
Teignmouth Cl, SW4 .101 DK84
Edgware HA8 .42 CM54
Teignmouth Gdns, Grnf. UB6 .79 CF68
Teignmouth Rd, NW2 .63 CX64
Welling DA16 .106 EW82
Telcote Way, Ruis. HA4
off Woodlands Av .60 BW59
★ Telecom Twr, W1 .195 K6
Telegraph Hill, NW3 .64 DB62
Telegraph La, Esher (Clay.)
KT10 .155 CF107
Telegraph Ms, Ilf. IG3 .70 EU60
Telegraph Path, Chis. BR7 .125 EP92
Telegraph Pl, E14 .204 B8
Telegraph Rd, SW15 .119 CV87
Telegraph St, EC2 .197 K8
Telegraph Track, Cars. SM5 .158 DG110
Telemann Sq, SE3 .104 EH83
Telephone Pl, SW6
off Lillie Rd .99 CZ79
Telfer Cl, W3 off Church Rd .98 CQ75
Telferscot Rd, SW12 .121 DK88
Telford Av, SW2 .121 DL88
Telford Cl, E17 .67 DY59
SE19 off St. Aubyn's Rd .122 DT93
Watford WD25 .24 BX35
Telford Dr, Walt. KT12 .136 BW101
Telford Rd, N11 .45 DJ51
NW9 off West Hendon Bdy .63 CU58
SE9 .125 ER89
W10 .81 CY71
St. Albans (Lon.Col.) AL2 .9 CJ27
Southall UB1 .78 CB73
Twickenham TW2 .116 CA87
Telfords Yd, E1 .202 C1
Telford Ter, SW1 .101 DJ79
Telford Way, W3 .80 CS71
Hayes UB4 .78 BY71
Telham Rd, E6 .87 EN68
Tell Gro, SE22 .102 DT84
Tellisford, Esher KT10 .154 CB105
Tellson Av, SE18 .104 EL81
Telscombe Cl, Orp. BR6 .145 ES103
Telston La, Sev. (Otford) TN14 .181 FF117
Temeraire St, SE16 .202 G5
Temperley Rd, SW12 .120 DG87
Tempest Av, Pot.B. EN6 .12 DC32
Tempest Mead, Epp. (N.Wld.Bas.)
CM16 .19 FB27
Tempest Rd, Egh. TW20 .113 BC93
Tempest Way, Rain. RM13 .89 FG65
Templar Dr, SE28 .88 EX72
Gravesend DA11 .131 GG92
Templar Ho, NW2
off Shoot Up Hill .81 CZ65
Rainham RM13
off Chantry Way .89 FD68
Templar Pl, Hmptn. TW12 .116 CA94
Templars Av, NW11 .63 CZ58
Templars Cres, N3 .44 DA54
Templars Dr, Har. HA3 .41 CD51
Templar St, SE5 .101 DP82
★ Temple, The, EC4 .196 D10
⊖ Temple .196 C10
Temple, EC4 .83 DN73
Temple Av, EC4 .196 E10
N20 .44 DD45
Croydon CR0 .143 DZ103
Dagenham RM8 .70 FA60
★ Temple Bar, EC4 .196 D9
Temple Bar Rd, Wok. GU21 .166 AT119
Temple Cl, E11 off Wadley Rd .68 EE59
N3 off Cyprus Rd .43 CZ54
SE28 .105 EQ76
Epsom KT19 .156 CR112
Waltham Cross (Chsht.)
EN7 .14 DU31
Watford WD17 .23 BT40
Templecombe Ms, Wok. GU22
off Dorchester Ct .167 BA116
Templecombe Rd, E9 .84 DW67
Templecombe Way, Mord.
SM4 .139 CY99
Temple Ct, E1 off Rectory Sq .85 DX71
Potters Bar EN6 .11 CY31
Templecroft, Ashf. TW15 .115 BR93
Templedene Av, Stai. TW18 .114 BH94
Templefield Cl, Add. KT15 .152 BH107
Temple Fortune Hill, NW11 .64 DA57
Temple Fortune La, NW11 .64 DA58
Temple Fortune Par, NW11
off Finchley Rd .63 CZ57
Temple Gdns, N21
off Barrowell Grn .45 DP47
NW11 .63 CZ58
Dagenham RM8 .70 EX62
Rickmansworth WD3 .39 BP49
Staines TW18 .133 BF95
Temple Gro, NW11 .64 DA58
Enfield EN2 .29 DP41
Temple Hill, Dart. DA1 .128 FM86
Temple Hill Sq, Dart. DA1 .128 FM85
Templehof Av, NW2 .63 CW59
Temple La, EC4 .196 E9
Templeman Cl, Pur. CR8
off Croftleigh Av .175 DP116
Templeman Rd, W7 .79 CF71
Templemead Cl, W3 .80 CS72
Temple Mead Cl, Stan. HA7 .41 CH51
Templemere, Wey. KT13 .135 BR104
Temple Mill La, E15 .67 EB63
★ Temple of Mithras, EC4
off Queen Victoria St .197 J9
Templepan La, Rick. WD3 .22 BL37
Temple Pk, Uxb. UB8 .76 BN69
Temple Pl, WC2 .196 C10
Templer Av, Grays RM16 .111 GG77
Temple Rd, E6 .86 EL67
N8 .65 DM56
NW2 .63 CW63
W4 .98 CQ76
W5 .97 CK76
Croydon CR0 .160 DR105
Epsom KT19 .156 CR112
Hounslow TW3 .96 CB84
Richmond TW9 .98 CM83
Westerham (Bigg.H.) TN16 .178 EK117
Temple Sheen, SW14 .118 CQ85
Temple Sheen Rd, SW14 .98 CP84
Temple St, E2 .84 DV68
Templeton Av, E4 .47 EA49
Templeton Cl, N16
off Truman's Rd .66 DS64
SE19 .142 DR95
Templeton Ct, NW7
off Bittacy Hill .43 CY52
Templeton Pl, SW5 .100 DA77
Templeton Rd, N15 .66 DR58
Temple Way, Sutt. SM1 .140 DD104
Temple W Ms, SE11 .200 F7
Templewood, W13 .79 CH71
Templewood Av, NW3 .64 DB62
Temple Wd Dr, Red. RH1 .184 DF130
Templewood Gdns, NW3 .64 DB62
Templewood La, Slou. SL2 .56 AS63
Templewood Pk, Slou. SL2 .56 AT63
Templewood Pt, NW2
off Granville Rd .63 CZ61
Tempsford Av, Borwd. WD6 .26 CR42
Tempsford Cl, Enf. EN2
off Gladbeck Way .30 DQ41
Temsford Cl, Har. HA2 .40 CC54
Ten Acre, Wok. GU21
off Abercorn Way .166 AU118
Ten Acre La, Egh. TW20 .133 BC96
Ten Acres, Lthd. (Fetch.) KT22 .171 CD124
Ten Acres Cl, Lthd. (Fetch.)
KT22 .171 CD124
Tenbury Cl, E7
off Romford Rd .68 EK64
Tenbury Ct, SW2 .121 DK88
Tenby Av, Har. HA3 .41 CH54
Tenby Cl, N15
off Hanover Rd .66 DT56
Romford RM6 .70 EY58
Tenby Gdns, Nthlt. UB5 .78 CA65
Tenby Rd, E17 .67 DY57
Edgware HA8 .42 CM53
Enfield EN3 .30 DW41
Romford RM6 .70 EY58
Welling DA16 .106 EX81
Tenchleys La, Oxt. RH8 .188 EK131
Tench St, E1 .202 D3
Tenda Rd, SE16 .202 D9
Tendring Way, Rom. RM6 .70 EW57
Tenham Av, SW2 .121 DK88
Tenison Ct, W1 .195 K10
Tenison Way, SE1 .200 D3
Tennand Cl, Wal.Cr. (Chsht.)
EN7 .14 DT26
Tenniel Cl, W2
off Porchester Gdns .82 DC72
Tennis Ct La, E.Mol. KT8
off Hampton Ct Way .137 CF97
Tennison Av, Borwd. WD6 .26 CP43
Tennison Cl, Couls. CR5 .175 DP120
Tennison Rd, SE25 .142 DT98
Tennis St, SE1 .201 K4
Tenniswood Rd, Enf. EN1 .30 DT39
Tennyson Av, E11 .68 EG59
E12 .86 EL66
NW9 .62 CQ55
Tennyson Av, Grays RM17 .110 GB76
New Malden KT3 .139 CV99
Twickenham TW1 .117 CF88
Waltham Abbey EN9 .16 EE34
Tennyson Cl, Enf. EN3 .31 DX43
Feltham TW14 .115 BT86
Welling DA16 .105 ES81
Tennyson Rd, E10 .67 EB61
E15 .86 EE66
E17 .67 DZ58
NW6 .81 CZ67
NW7 .43 CU50
SE20 .123 DX94
SW19 .120 DC93
W7 .79 CF73
Addlestone KT15 .152 BL105
Ashford TW15 .114 BL92
Brentwood CM13 .55 GC45
Dartford DA1 .128 FN85
Hounslow TW3 .96 CC82
Romford RM3 .52 FJ52
St. Albans AL2 .8 CA26
Tennyson St, SW8 .101 DH82
Tennyson Wk, Grav. (Nthflt.)
DA11 .130 GD90
Tilbury RM18 .111 GH82
Tennyson Way, Horn. RM12 .71 FF61
Tensing Av, Grav. (Nthflt.)
DA11 .130 GE90
Tensing Rd, Sthl. UB2 .96 CA76
Tentelow La, Sthl. UB2 .96 CA78
Tenterden Cl, NW4 .63 CX55
SE9 .125 EM91
Tenterden Dr, NW4 .63 CX55
Tenterden Gdns, NW4 .63 CX55
Croydon CR0 .142 DU101
Tenterden Gro, NW4 .63 CX56
Tenterden Rd, N17 .46 DT52
Croydon CR0 .142 DU101
Dagenham RM8 .70 EZ61
Tenterden St, W1 .195 J9
Tenter Grd, E1 .197 P7
Tenter Pas, E1 off Mansell St .84 DT72
Tent Peg La, Orp. BR5 .145 EQ99
Tent St, E1 .84 DV70
Terborch Way, SE22
off East Dulwich Gro .122 DS85
Tercel Path, Chig. IG7 .50 EV49
Teredo St, SE16 .203 J7
Terence Cl, Grav. DA12 .131 GM88
Terence Ct, Belv. DA17
off Nuxley Rd .106 EZ79
Teresa Gdns, Wal.Cr. EN8 .14 DW34
Teresa Ms, E17 .67 EA56
Teresa Wk, N10
off Connaught Gdns .65 DH57
Terling Cl, E11 .68 EF62
Terling Rd, Dag. RM8 .70 FA61
Terlings, The, Brwd. CM14 .54 FU48
Terling Wk, N1
off Britannia Row .84 DQ67
Terminus Pl, SW1 .199 J7
Tern Gdns, Upmin. RM14 .73 FS60
Tern Way, Brwd. CM14 .54 FS49
Terrace, The, E4
off Chingdale Rd .48 EE48
N3 off Hendon La .43 CZ54
NW6 .82 DA67
SW13 .98 CS82
Addlestone KT15 .152 BL106
Gravesend DA12 .131 GH86
Sevenoaks TN13 .190 FD122
Woodford Green IG8
off Broadmead Rd .48 EG51
Terrace Gdns, SW13 .99 CT82
Watford WD17 .23 BV40
Terrace La, Rich. TW10 .118 CL86
Terrace Rd, E9 .84 DW66
E13 .86 EG67
Walton-on-Thames KT12 .135 BU101
Terraces, The, Dart. DA2 .128 FQ87
Terrace St, Grav. DA12 .131 GH86
Terrace Wk, Dag. RM9 .70 EY64
Terrapin Rd, SW17 .121 DH90
Terretts Pl, N1 off Upper St .83 DP66
Terrick Rd, N22 .45 DL53
Terrick St, W12 .81 CV72
Terrilands, Pnr. HA5 .60 BZ55
Terront Rd, N15 .66 DQ57
Tersha St, Rich. TW9 .98 CM84
Tessa Sanderson Pl, SW8 .101 DH83
Tessa Sanderson Way, Grnf. UB6
off Lilian Board Way .61 CD64
Testers Cl, Oxt. RH8 .188 EH131
Testerton Wk, W11 .81 CX73
Tetbury Pl, N1 off Upper St .83 DP67
Tetcott Rd, SW10 .100 DC80
Tetherdown, N10 .64 DG55
Tetty Way, Brom. BR2 .144 EG96
Teversham La, SW8 .101 DL81
Teviot Av, S.Ock. (Aveley)
RM15 .90 FQ72
Teviot Cl, Well. DA16 .106 EV81
Teviot St, E14 .85 EC71
Tewkesbury Av, SE23 .122 DV88
Pinner HA5 .60 BY57
Tewkesbury Cl, N15
off Tewkesbury Rd .66 DR58
Loughton IG10 .32 EL44
West Byfleet (Byfleet) KT14 .152 BK111
Tewkesbury Gdns, NW9 .62 CP55
Tewkesbury Rd, N15 .66 DR58
W13 .79 CG73
Carshalton SM5 .140 DD102
Tewkesbury Ter, N11 .45 DJ51
Tewson Rd, SE18 .105 ES78
Teynham Av, Enf. EN1 .30 DR44
Teynham Grn, Brom. BR2 .144 EG99
Teynton Ter, N17 .46 DQ53
Thackeray Av, N17 .46 DU54
Tilbury RM18 .111 GH81
Thackeray Cl, SW19 .119 CX94
Harrow HA2 .60 CA60
Isleworth TW7 .97 CG82
Uxbridge UB8
off Dickens Av .77 BP72
Thackeray Dr, Rom. RM6 .70 EU59
Thackeray Rd, E6 .86 EK68
SW8 .101 DH82
Thackeray St, W8 .100 DB75
Thakeham Cl, SE26 .122 DV92
Thalia Cl, SE10 .103 ED79
Thalmassing Cl, Brwd. CM13 .55 GB47
Thame Rd, SE16 .203 J4
Thames Av, SW10 .100 DC81
Chertsey KT16 .134 BG97
Dagenham RM9 .89 FB70
Greenford UB6 .79 CF68
Thames Bk, SW14 .98 CQ82
Thamesbank Pl, SE28 .88 EW72
Thames Circle, E14 .204 A8
Thames Cl, Cher. KT16 .134 BH101
Hampton TW12 .136 CB96
Rainham RM13 .89 FH72
Thames Ct, W.Mol. KT8 .136 CB96
Thames Cres, W4
off Corney Rd .98 CS80
Thamesdale, St.Alb. (Lon.Col.)
AL2 .10 CM27
THAMES DITTON .137 CF100
⇌ Thames Ditton .137 CF101
Thames Ditton Island, T.Ditt.
KT7 .137 CG99
Thames Dr, Grays RM16 .111 GG78
Ruislip HA4 .59 BQ58
Thames Europort, Dart. DA2 .109 FS84
Thamesfield Ct, Shep. TW17 .135 BQ101
★ Thames Flood Barrier &
Visitors Cen, SE18 .104 EK76
Thames Gate, Dart. DA1
off St. Edmunds Rd .108 FN84
Thamesgate Cl, Rich. TW10
off Locksmeade Rd .117 CH91
Thames Gateway, Dag. RM9 .88 EZ68
Rainham RM13 .89 FG72
South Ockendon RM15 .108 FP75
Thameshill Av, Rom. RM5 .51 FC54
★ Thames Ho, SW1 .199 P8
Thameside, Tedd. TW11 .117 CK94
Thameside Ind Est, E16 .104 EL75
Thameside Wk, SE28 .87 ET72
THAMESMEAD, SE28 .87 ET74
Thamesmead, Walt. KT12 .135 BU101
THAMESMEAD NORTH, SE28 .88 EW72
Thames Meadow, Shep.
TW17 .135 BR102
West Molesey KT8 .136 CA96
Thamesmead Spine Rd, Belv.
DA17 .107 FB75
THAMESMEAD WEST, SE18 .105 EQ76
Thamesmere Dr, SE28 .88 EU73
Thames Path, SE1 .200 E1
SE7 .205 N7
SE10 .205 N7
W6 .99 CW79
Thames Pl, SW15 .99 CX83
Thames Quay, SW10
off Harbour Av .100 DC81
Thames Rd, E16 .86 EK74
W4 .98 CN79
Barking IG11 .87 ET69
Dartford DA1 .107 FF82
Grays RM17 .110 GB80
Slough SL3 .93 BA77
Thames Side, Cher. KT16 .134 BJ100
Kingston upon Thames KT1 .137 CK95
Staines TW18 .134 BH96
Thames St, SE10 .103 EB79
Hampton TW12 .136 CB95
Kingston upon Thames KT1 .137 CK96
Staines TW18 .113 BE91
Sunbury-on-Thames
TW16 .135 BV98
Walton-on-Thames KT12 .135 BT101
Weybridge KT13 .135 BP103
Thamesvale Cl, Houns. TW3 .96 CA83
H Thames Valley Nuffield
Hosp, Slou. SL2 .74 AW67
Thames Vw, Grays RM16 .111 GG78
Thames Village, W4 .98 CQ81
Thames Way, Grav. DA11 .130 GD88
Thames Wf, E16 .205 K2
Thamley, Purf. RM19 .108 FN77
Thanescroft Gdns, Croy. CR0 .142 DS104
Thanet Dr, Kes. BR2
off Phoenix Dr .144 EK104
Thanet Pl, Croy. CR0 .160 DQ105
Thanet Rd, Bex. DA5 .126 FA87
Erith DA8 .107 FE80
Thanet St, WC1 .195 P3
Thane Vil, N7 .65 DM62
Thane Wks, N7 .65 DM62
Thanington Ct, SE9 .125 ES86
Thant Cl, E10 .67 EB62
Tharp Rd, Wall. SM6 .159 DK106
Thatcham Gdns, N20 .44 DC45
Thatcher Cl, West Dr. UB7
off Classon Cl .94 BL75
Thatcher Ct, Dart. DA1
off Heath St .128 FK87
Thatchers Cl, Loug. IG10 .33 EQ40
Thatchers Way, Islw. TW7 .117 CD85
Thatches Gro, Rom. RM6 .70 EY56
Thavies Inn, EC1 .196 E8
Thaxted Ct, N1 .197 K1
Thaxted Grn, Brwd. CM13 .55 GC43
Thaxted Ho, Dag. RM10 .89 FB66
Thaxted Pl, SW20 .119 CX94
Thaxted Rd, SE9 .125 EQ89
Buckhurst Hill IG9 .48 EL45
Thaxted Wk, Rain. RM13
off Ongar Way .89 FF67
Thaxted Way, Wal.Abb. EN9 .15 ED33
Thaxton Rd, W14 .99 CZ79
Thayers Fm Rd, Beck. BR3 .143 DY95
Thayer St, W1 .194 G7
Thaynesfield, Pot.B. EN6 .12 DD31
★ Theatre Royal, WC2 .196 A9
Theatre Sq, E15
off Great Eastern Rd .85 ED65
Theatre St, SW11 .100 DF83
Theberton St, N1 .83 DN67
Theed St, SE1 .200 D3
Thellusson Way, Rick. WD3 .37 BF45
Thelma Cl, Grav. DA12 .131 GM92
Thelma Gdns, SE3 .104 EK81
Feltham TW13 .116 BY90
Thelma Gro, Tedd. TW11 .117 CG93
Theobald Cres, Har. HA3 .40 CB53
Theobald Rd, E17 .67 DZ59
Croydon CR0 .141 DP103
Theobalds Av, N12 .44 DC49
Grays RM17 .110 GC78
Theobalds Cl, Pot.B. (Cuffley)
EN6 .13 DM30
Theobalds Ct, N4
off Queens Dr .66 DQ61
⇌ Theobalds Grove .15 DX32
Theobalds La, Wal.Cr. (Chsht.)
EN8 .14 DV32
Theobalds Pk Rd, Enf. EN2 .29 DP35
Theobald's Rd, WC1 .196 B6
Theobalds Rd, Pot.B. (Cuffley)
EN6 .13 DL30
Theobald St, SE1 .201 K7
Borehamwood WD6 .26 CM40
Radlett WD7 .25 CH36
Theodora Way, Pnr. HA5 .59 BT55
Theodore Rd, SE13 .123 EC86
⊸ Therapia Lane .141 DL101
Therapia La, Croy. CR0 .141 DL100
Therapia Rd, SE22 .122 DW86
Theresa Rd, W6 .99 CU77
Theresas Wk, S.Croy. CR2
off Sanderstead Rd .160 DR110
Therfield Ct, N4
off Brownswood Rd .66 DQ61
Thermopylae Gate, E14 .204 C9
Theseus Wk, N1 .196 G1
Thesiger Rd, SE20 .123 DX94
Thessaly Rd, SW8 .101 DJ80
Thetford Cl, N13 .45 DP51
Thetford Gdns, Dag. RM9 .88 EX66
Thetford Rd, Ashf. TW15 .114 BL91
Dagenham RM9 .88 EX67
New Malden KT3 .138 CR100
Thetis Ter, Rich. TW9
off Kew Grn .98 CN79
THEYDON BOIS, Epp. .33 ET37
⊖ Theydon Bois .33 ET36
Theydon Bower, Epp. CM16 .18 EU31
Theydon Ct, Wal.Abb. EN9 .16 EG33
Theydon Gdns, Rain. RM13 .89 FE66
THEYDON GARNON, Epp. .34 EW35
Theydon Gate, Epp. (They.B.)
CM16 off Coppice Row .33 ES37
Theydon Gro, Epp. CM16 .18 EU30
Woodford Green IG8 .48 EJ51
THEYDON MOUNT, Epp. .18 FA34
Theydon Pk Rd, Epp. (They.B.)
CM16 .33 ES39
Theydon Pl, Epp. CM16 .17 ET31
Theydon Rd, E5 .66 DW61
Epping CM16 .17 ER34
Theydon St, E17 .67 DZ59
Thicket, The, West Dr. UB7 .76 BL72
Thicket Cres, Sutt. SM1 .158 DC105
Thicket Gro, SE20
off Anerley Rd .122 DU94
Dagenham RM9 .88 EW65
Thicket Rd, SE20 .122 DU94
Sutton SM1 .158 DC105
Thicketts, Sev. TN13 .191 FJ123
Thickthorne La, Stai. TW18 .114 BJ94
Third Av, E12 .68 EL63
E13 .86 EG69
E17 .67 EA57
W3 .81 CT74
W10 .81 CY69
Dagenham RM10 .89 FB67
Enfield EN1 .30 DT43
Grays RM20 .109 FU79
Hayes UB3 .77 BT74
Romford RM6 .70 EW58
Waltham Abbey EN9 off Breach
Barn Mobile Home Pk .16 EH30
Watford WD25 .24 BX35
Wembley HA9 .61 CK61
Third Cl, W.Mol. KT8 .136 CB98
Third Cross Rd, Twick. TW2 .117 CD89
Third Way, Wem. HA9 .62 CP63
Thirleby Rd, SW1 .199 L7
Edgware HA8 .42 CR53
Thirlmere Av, Grnf. UB6 .79 CJ69
Thirlmere Cl, Egh. TW20
off Keswick Rd .113 BB94
Thirlmere Gdns, Nthwd. HA6 .39 BQ51
Wembley HA9 .61 CJ60
Thirlmere Ho, Islw. TW7
off Summerwood Rd .117 CF85
Thirlmere Ri, Brom. BR1 .124 EF93
Thirlmere Rd, N10 .45 DH53
SW16 .121 DK91
Bexleyheath DA7 .107 FC82
Thirsk Cl, Nthlt. UB5 .78 CA65
Thirsk Rd, SE25 .142 DR98
SW11 .100 DG83
Borehamwood WD6 .26 CN37
Mitcham CR4 .120 DG94
Thirston Path, Borwd. WD6 .26 CN40
Thirza Rd, Dart. DA1 .128 FM86
Thistlebrook, SE2 .106 EW76
Thistlebrook Ind Est, SE2 .106 EW75
Thistlecroft Gdns, Stan. HA7 .41 CK53
Thistlecroft Rd, Walt. KT12 .154 BW105
Thistledene, T.Ditt. KT7 .137 CE100
West Byfleet KT14 .151 BF113
Thistledene Av, Har. HA2 .60 BY62
Romford RM5 .51 FB50
Thistledown, Grav. DA12 .131 GK93
Thistle Gro, SW10 .100 DC78
Thistlemead, Chis. BR7 .145 EP96
Thistle Mead, Loug. IG10 .33 EN41
Thistle Rd, Grav. DA12 .131 GL87
Thistlewaite Rd, E5 .66 DV62
Thistlewood Cl, N7 .65 DM61
Thistlewood Cres, Croy.
(New Adgtn.) CR0 .161 ED112
Thistleworth Cl, Islw. TW7 .97 CD80
Thistley Cl, N12
off Summerfields Av .44 DE51

Thomas a'Beckett Cl, Wem. HA0 61 CF63
Thomas Av, Cat. CR3 176 DQ121
Thomas Baines Rd, SW11 100 DD83
Thomas Cl, Brwd. CM15 54 FY48
Thomas Cribb Ms, E6 87 EM72
Thomas Darby Ct, W11 81 CY72
Thomas Dean Rd, SE26
off Kangley Br Rd 123 DZ91
Thomas Dinwiddy Rd, SE12 124 EH89
Thomas Doyle St, SE1 200 F6
Thomas Dr, Grav. DA12 131 GK89
Thomas Hardy Ho, N22 45 DM52
Thomas La, SE6 123 EA87
Thomas More Ho, EC2
off The Barbican 84 DQ71
Thomas More St, E1 202 B1
Thomas More Way, N2 64 DC55
Thomas Pl, W8
off St. Mary's Pl 100 DB76
Thomas Rd, E14 85 DZ72
Thomas Rochford Way, Wal.Cr. EN8 15 DZ27
Thomas Sims Ct, Horn. RM12 71 FH64
Thomas St, SE18 105 EP77
Thomas Wall Cl, Sutt. SM1
off Clarence Rd 158 DB106
Thompson Av, Rich. TW9 98 CN83
Thompson Cl, Ilf. IG1
off High Rd 69 EQ61
Slough SL3 93 BA77
Sutton SM3
off Barrington Rd 140 DA102
Thompson Rd, SE22 122 DT86
Dagenham RM9 70 EZ62
Hounslow TW3 96 CB84
Uxbridge UB10 76 BL66
Thompson's Av, SE5 102 DQ80
Thompsons Cl, Wal.Cr. EN7 14 DT29
Thompson's La, Loug. (High Beach) IG10 32 EF39
Thompson Way, Rick. WD3 38 BG45
Thomson Cres, Croy. CR0 141 DN102
Thomson Rd, Har. HA3 61 CE55
Thong La, Grav. DA12 131 GM90
Thorburn Sq, SE1 202 B9
Thorburn Way, SW19 140 DC95
Thoresby St, N1 197 J2
Thorkhill Gdns, T.Ditt. KT7 137 CG102
Thorkhill Rd, T.Ditt. KT7 137 CH101
Thorley Cl, W.Byf. KT14 152 BG114
Thorley Gdns, Wok. GU22 152 BG114
Thornaby Gdns, N18 46 DU51
Thornash Cl, Wok. GU21 166 AW115
Thornash Rd, Wok. GU21 166 AW115
Thornash Way, Wok. GU21 166 AW115
Thorn Av, Bushey (Bushey Hth.) WD23 40 CC46
Thornbank Cl, Stai. TW19 114 BG85
Thornbridge Rd, Iver SL0 75 BC67
Thornbrook, Epp. (Thnwd.) CM16 18 EX25
Thornbury Av, Islw. TW7 97 CD80
Thornbury Cl, N16
off Truman's Rd 66 DS64
NW7 off Bittacy Hill 43 CY52
Thornbury Gdns, Borwd. WD6 26 CQ42
Thornbury Rd, SW2 121 DL86
Isleworth TW7 97 CD81
Thornbury Sq, N6 65 DJ60
Thornby Rd, E5 66 DW62
Thorncliffe Rd, SW2 121 DL86
Southall UB2 96 BZ78
Thorn Cl, Brom. BR2 145 EN100
Northolt UB5 78 BZ69
Thorncombe Rd, SE22 122 DS85
Thorncroft, Egh. (Eng.Grn.) TW20 112 AW94
Hornchurch RM11 71 FH58
Thorncroft Cl, Couls. CR5
off Waddington Av 175 DN120
Thorncroft Dr, Lthd. KT22 171 CH123
Thorncroft Rd, Sutt. SM1 158 DB105
Thorncroft St, SW8 101 DL80
Thorndales, Brwd. CM14 54 FX49
Thorndean St, SW18 120 DC89
Thorndene Av, N11 44 DG46
Thorndike Av, Nthlt. UB5 78 BX67
Thorndike Cl, SW10 100 DC80
Thorndike St, SW1 199 M10
Thorndon Cl, Orp. BR5 145 ET96
Thorndon Ct, Brwd. CM13 53 FW51
Thorndon Gdns, Epsom KT19 156 CS105
Thorndon Gate, Brwd. CM13 55 GC50
Thorndon Rd, Orp. BR5 145 ET96
Thorn Dr, Slou. (Geo.Grn.) SL3 74 AY72
Thorndyke Ct, Pnr. HA5
off Westfield Pk 40 BZ52
Thorne Cl, E11 68 EE63
E16 86 EG72
Ashford TW15 115 BQ94
Erith DA8 107 FC79
Thorneloe Gdns, Croy. CR0 159 DN106
Thorne Pas, SW13 98 CS82
Thorne Rd, SW8 101 DL80
Thornes Cl, Beck. BR3 143 EC97
Thorne St, E16 86 EF72
SW13 98 CS83
Thornet Wd Rd, Brom. BR1 145 EN97
THORNEY, Iver 94 BH76
Thorney Cres, SW11 100 DD80
Thorneycroft Cl, Walt. KT12 136 BW100
Thorneycroft Dr, Enf. EN3
off Government Row 31 EA38
Thorney Hedge Rd, W4 98 CP77
Thorney La N, Iver SL0 75 BF74
Thorney La S, Iver SL0 93 BF75
Thorney Mill Rd, Iver SL0 94 BG76
West Drayton UB7 94 BG76
Thorney St, SW1 199 P8
Thornfield Av, NW7 43 CY53
Thornfield Rd, W12 99 CV75
Banstead SM7 174 DA117
Thornford Rd, SE13 123 EC85
Thorngate Rd, W9 82 DA70
Thorngrove Rd, E13 86 EH67
Thornham Gro, E15 67 ED64
Thornham St, SE10 103 EB79
Thornhaugh Ms, WC1 195 N5
Thornhaugh St, WC1 195 N6
Thornhill, Epp. (N.Wld.Bas.) CM16 19 FC26
Thornhill Av, SE18 105 ES80
Surbiton KT6 138 CL103
Thornhill Br Wf, N1
off Caledonian Rd 83 DM67
Thornhill Cres, N1 83 DM66
Thornhill Gdns, E10 67 EB61
Barking IG11 87 ES66
Thornhill Gro, N1
off Lofting Rd 83 DM66
Thornhill Rd, E10 67 EB61
N1 83 DN66
Croydon CR0 142 DQ101
Northwood HA6 39 BQ49
Surbiton KT6 138 CL103
Uxbridge UB10 58 BM63
Thornhill Sq, N1 83 DM66
Thornhill Way, Shep. TW17 134 BN99
Thorn Ho, Beck. BR3 143 DY95
Thorn La, Rain. RM13 90 FK68
Thornlaw Rd, SE27 121 DN91
Thornley Cl, N17 46 DU52
Thornley Dr, Har. HA2 60 CB61
Thornley Pl, SE10
off Caradoc St 104 EE78
Thornridge, Brwd. CM14 54 FV45
Thornsbeach Rd, SE6 123 EC88
Thornsett Pl, SE20 142 DV96
Thornsett Rd, SE20 142 DV96
SW18 120 DB89
Thornside, Edg. HA8
off High St 42 CN51
Thorns Meadow, West. (Brasted) TN16 180 EW123
Thorn Ter, SE15
off Nunhead Gro 102 DW83
Thornton Av, SW2 121 DK88
W4 98 CS77
Croydon CR0 141 DM100
West Drayton UB7 94 BM76
Thornton Cl, West Dr. UB7 94 BM76
Thornton Ct, SW20 139 CX99
Thornton Cres, Couls. CR5 175 DN119
Thornton Dene, Beck. BR3 143 EA96
Thornton Gdns, SW12 121 DK88
Thornton Gro, Pnr. HA5 40 CA51
THORNTON HEATH 141 DP98
≑ Thornton Heath 142 DQ98
Thornton Hill, SW19 119 CY94
Thornton Pl, W1 194 E6
Thornton Rd, E11 67 ED61
N18 46 DW48
SW12 121 DK87
SW14 98 CR83
SW19 119 CX93
Barnet EN5 27 CY41
Belvedere DA17 107 FB77
Bromley BR1 124 EG92
Carshalton SM5 140 DD102
Croydon CR0 141 DM101
Ilford IG1 69 EP63
Potters Bar EN6 12 DC30
Thornton Heath CR7 141 DM101
Thornton Rd E, SW19
off Thornton Rd 119 CX93
Thornton Rd Retail Pk, Croy. CR0 141 DM100
Thornton Row, Th.Hth. CR7
off London Rd 141 DN99
Thorntons Fm Av, Rom. RM7 71 FD60
Thornton St, SW9 101 DN82
Thornton Way, NW11 64 DB57
Thorntree Rd, SE7 104 EK78
Thornville Gro, Mitch. CR4 140 DC96
Thornville St, SE8 103 EA81
THORNWOOD, Epp. 18 EW25
Thornwood Cl, E18 48 EH54
Thornwood Rd, SE13 124 EE85
Epping CM16 18 EV29
Thorogood Gdns, E15 68 EE64
Thorogood Way, Rain. RM13 89 FE67
Thorold Cl, S.Croy. CR2 161 DX110
Thorold Rd, N22 45 DL52
Ilford IG1 69 EP61
Thoroughfare, The, Tad. KT20 183 CU125
Thorparch Rd, SW8 101 DK81
THORPE, Egh. 133 BC97
Thorpebank Rd, W12 81 CU74
Thorpe Bypass, Egh. TW20 133 BB96
Thorpe Cl, W10
off Cambridge Gdns 81 CY72
Croydon (New Adgtn.) CR0 161 EC111
Orpington BR6 145 ES103
H Thorpe Coombe Hosp, E17 67 EC55
Thorpe Cres, E17 47 DZ54
Watford WD19 40 BW45
Thorpedale Gdns, Ilf. IG2, IG6 69 EN56
Thorpedale Rd, N4 65 DL60
THORPE GREEN, Egh. 133 BA98
Thorpe Hall Rd, E17 47 EC53
Thorpe Ind Est, Egh. TW20 133 BC96
THORPE LEA, Egh. 113 BB93
Thorpe Lea Rd, Egh. TW20 113 BB93
Thorpe Lo, Horn. RM11 72 FL59
★ Thorpe Park, Cher. KT16 133 BE98
Thorpe Rd, E6 87 EM67
E7 68 EF63
E17 47 EC54
N15 66 DS58
Barking IG11 87 ER66
Chertsey KT16 133 BD99
Kingston upon Thames KT2 118 CL94
Staines TW18 113 BD93
Thorpeside Cl, Stai. TW18 133 BE96
Thorpewood Av, SE26 122 DV89
Thorpland Av, Uxb. UB10 59 BQ62
Thorsden Cl, Wok. GU22 166 AY118
Thorsden Ct, Wok. GU22
off Guildford Rd 166 AY118
Thorsden Way, SE19
off Oaks Av 122 DS91
Thorverton Rd, NW2 63 CY62
Thoydon Rd, E3 85 DY68
Thrale Rd, SW16 121 DJ92
Thrale St, SE1 201 J3
Thrasher Cl, E8 off Stean St 84 DT67
Thrawl St, E1 84 DT71
Threadneedle St, EC2 197 L9
Three Barrels Wk, EC4 197 J10
Three Colts Cor, E2
off Weaver St 84 DU70
Three Colts La, E2 84 DV70
Three Colt St, E14 85 DZ73
Three Cors, Bexh. DA7 107 FB82
Three Cups Yd, WC1 196 C7
Three Forests Way, Chig. IG7 50 EW48
Loughton IG10
off The Clay Rd 32 EK38
Romford RM4 50 EW48
Waltham Abbey EN9 32 EK36
Three Gates Rd, Long. (Fawk.Grn.) DA3 149 FU102
Three Households, Ch.St.G. HP8 36 AT49
Three Kings Rd, Mitch. CR4 140 DG97
Three Kings Yd, W1 195 H10
Three Mill La, E3 85 EC69
Three Oak La, SE1 201 P4
Three Oaks Cl, Uxb. UB10 58 BM62
Three Quays Wk, EC3 201 N1
Threshers Pl, W11 81 CY73
Thriffwood, SE26 122 DW90
Thrift, The, Dart. (Bean) DA2 129 FW90
Thrift Fm La, Borwd. WD6 26 CP40
Thrift Grn, Brwd. CM13
off Knight's Way 55 GA48
Thrift La, Sev. (Cudham) TN14 179 ER117
Thrifts Hall Fm Ms, Epp. (They.B.)
CM16 off Abridge Rd 33 ET37
Thrifts Mead, Epp. (They.B.) CM16 33 ES37
Thrigby Rd, Chess. KT9 156 CM107
Throckmorten Rd, E16 86 EH72
Throgmorton Av, EC2 197 L8
Throgmorton St, EC2 197 L8
Throwley Cl, SE2 106 EW76
Throwley Rd, Sutt. SM1 158 DB106
Throwley Way, Sutt. SM1 158 DB105
Thrums, The, Wat. WD24 23 BV37
Thrupp Cl, Mitch. CR4 141 DH96
Thrupps Av, Walt. KT12 154 BX106
Thrupps La, Walt. KT12 154 BX106
Thrush Grn, Har. HA2 60 CA56
Rickmansworth WD3 38 BJ45
Thrush La, Pot.B. (Cuffley) EN6 13 DL28
Thrush St, SE17 200 H10
Thruxton Way, SE15
off Daniel Gdns 102 DT80
Thunderer Rd, Dag. RM9 88 EY70
Thurbarn Rd, SE6 123 EB92
Thurland Rd, SE16 202 B6
Thurlby Cl, Har. HA1
off Gayton Rd 61 CG58
Woodford Green IG8 49 EM50
Thurlby Rd, SE27 121 DN91
Wembley HA0 79 CK65
Thurleigh Av, SW12 120 DG86
Thurleigh Rd, SW12 120 DG86
Thurleston Av, Mord. SM4 139 CY99
Thurlestone Av, N12 44 DF51
Ilford IG3 69 ET63
Thurlestone Cl, Shep. TW17 135 BQ100
Thurlestone Rd, SE27 121 DN90
Thurloe Cl, SW7 198 B8
Thurloe Gdns, Rom. RM1 71 FF58
Thurloe Pl, SW7 198 A8
Thurloe Pl Ms, SW7 198 A8
Thurloe Sq, SW7 198 B8
Thurloe St, SW7 198 A8
Thurloe Wk, Grays RM17 110 GA76
Thurlow Cl, E4
off Higham Sta Av 47 EB51
Thurlow Gdns, Ilf. IG6 49 ER51
Wembley HA0 61 CK64
Thurlow Hill, SE21 122 DQ88
Thurlow Pk Rd, SE21 121 DP88
Thurlow Rd, NW3 64 DD64
W7 97 CG75
Thurlow St, SE17 201 L10
Thurlow Ter, NW5 64 DG64
Thurlstone Rd, Ruis. HA4 59 BU62
Thurlton Ct, Wok. GU21
off Chobham Rd 166 AY116
Thurnby Ct, Twick. TW2 117 CE90
Thurnham Way, Tad. KT20 173 CW120
Thurrock Lakeside, Grays RM20 109 FV77
★ Thurrock Local History Mus, Grays RM17 110 GB78
Thurrock Pk Way, Til. RM18 110 GD80
Thursby Rd, Wok. GU21 166 AU118
Thursland Rd, Sid. DA14 126 EY92
Thursley Cres, Croy. (New Adgtn.) CR0 161 ED108
Thursley Gdns, SW19 119 CX89
Thursley Rd, SE9 125 EM90
Thurso Cl, Rom. RM3 52 FP51
Thurso St, SW17 120 DD91
Thurstan Rd, SW20 119 CV94
Thurston Rd, SE13 103 EB82
Slough SL1 74 AS72
Southall UB1 78 BZ72
Thurston Rd Ind Est, SE13
off Jerrard St 103 EB83
Thurtle Rd, E2 84 DT67
Thwaite Cl, Erith DA8 107 FC79
Thyer Cl, Orp. BR6
off Isabella Dr 163 EQ105
Thyra Gro, N12 44 DB51
Tibbatts Rd, E3 85 EB70
Tibbenham Wk, E13 86 EF68
Tibberton Sq, N1
off Popham Rd 84 DQ66
Tibbets Cl, SW19 119 CX88
Tibbet's Cor, SW15 119 CX87
Tibbet's Cor Underpass, SW15
off West Hill 119 CX87
Tibbet's Ride, SW15 119 CX87
Tibbles Cl, Wat. WD25 24 BY35
Tibbs Hill Rd, Abb.L. WD5 7 BT30
Tiber Gdns, N1 off Treaty St 83 DM67
Ticehurst Cl, Orp. BR5
off Grovelands Rd 126 EU94
Ticehurst Rd, SE23 123 DY89
Tichborne, Rick. (Map.Cr.) WD3 37 BD50
Tichmarsh, Epsom KT19 156 CQ110
Tickford Cl, SE2
off Ampleforth Rd 106 EW75
Tidal Basin Rd, E16 205 L1
Tidenham Gdns, Croy. CR0 142 DS104
Tideswell Rd, SW15 119 CW85
Croydon CR0 143 EA104
Tideway Cl, Rich. TW10
off Locksmeade Rd 117 CH91
Tidey St, E3 85 EA71
Tidford Rd, Well. DA16 105 ET82
Tidworth Rd, E3 85 EA70
Tidy's La, Epp. CM16 18 EV29
Tiepigs La, Brom. BR2 144 EE103
West Wickham BR4 144 EE103
Tierney Rd, SW2 121 DL88
Tiger La, Brom. BR2 144 EH98
Tiger Way, E5 66 DV63
Tilbrook Rd, SE3 104 EJ83
Tilburstow Hill Rd, Gdse. RH9 186 DW132
TILBURY 111 GG81
Tilbury Cl, SE15
off Willowbrook Rd 102 DT80
Orpington BR5 146 EV96
Tilbury Docks, Til. RM18 110 GE84
★ Tilbury Energy & Environmental Cen, Til. RM18 111 GK83
★ Tilbury Fort, Til. RM18 111 GJ84
Tilbury Gdns, Til. RM18 111 GG84
Tilbury Hotel Rd, Til. RM18 111 GG84
Tilbury Rd, E6 87 EM68
E10 67 EC59
≑ Tilbury Town 110 GE82
Tilbury Wk, Slou. SL3 93 BB76
Tildesley Rd, SW15 119 CW86
Tile Fm Rd, Orp. BR6 145 ER104
Tilehouse Cl, Borwd. WD6 26 CM41
Tilehouse La, Ger.Cr. SL9 37 BE53
Rickmansworth (Map.Cr.) WD3 37 BE53
Uxbridge (Denh.) UB9 57 BE58
Tilehouse Way, Uxb. (Denh.) UB9 57 BF59
Tilehurst Pt, SE2
off Yarnton Way 106 EW75
Tilehurst Rd, SW18 120 DD88
Sutton SM3 157 CY106
Tilekiln Cl, Wal.Cr. EN7 14 DT29
Tile Kiln La, N6
off Winchester Rd 65 DH60
N13 46 DQ50
Bexley DA5 127 FC89
Uxbridge (Hare.) UB9 59 BP59
Tile Yd, E14 off Commercial Rd 85 DZ72
Tileyard Rd, N7 83 DL66
Tilford Av, Croy. (New Adgtn.) CR0 161 EC109
Tilford Gdns, SW19 119 CX89
Tilia Cl, Sutt. SM1 157 CZ106
Tilia Rd, E5 off Clarence Rd 66 DV63
Tilia Wk, SW9
off Moorland Rd 101 DP84
Till Av, Dart. (Fnghm.) DA4 148 FM102
Tiller Rd, E14 203 P6
Tillett Cl, NW10 80 CQ65
Tillett Sq, SE16 203 L5
Tillett Way, E2
off Gosset St 84 DU69
Tilley La, Epsom (Headley) KT18 172 CQ123
Tillgate Common, Red. RH1 186 DQ133
Tillingbourne Gdns, N3 63 CZ55
Tillingbourne Grn, Orp. BR5 146 EU98
Tillingbourne Way, N3
off Tillingbourne Gdns 63 CZ55
Tillingdown Hill, Cat. CR3 176 DU122
Tillingdown La, Cat. CR3 176 DV124
Tillingham Ct, Wal.Abb. EN9 16 EG33
Tillingham Way, N12 44 DA49
Tilling Rd, NW2 63 CW60
Tilling Way, Wem. HA9 61 CK61
Tillman St, E1 off Bigland St 84 DV72
Tilloch St, N1
off Carnoustie Dr 83 DM66
Tillotson Rd, N9 46 DT47
Harrow HA3 40 CB52
Ilford IG1 69 EN59
Tilly's La, Stai. TW18 113 BF91
Tilmans Mead, Dart. (Fnghm.) DA4 148 FM101
Tilney Ct, EC1 197 J4
Tilney Dr, Buck.H. IG9 48 EG47
Tilney Gdns, N1 84 DR65
Tilney Rd, Dag. RM9 88 EZ65
Southall UB2 96 BW77
Tilney St, W1 198 G2
Tilson Gdns, SW2 121 DL87
Tilson Ho, SW2
off Tilson Gdns 121 DL87
Tilson Rd, N17 46 DU53
Tilston Cl, E11 off Matcham Rd 68 EF62
Tilt Cl, Cob. KT11 170 BY116
Tilt Meadow, Cob. KT11 170 BY116
Tilton St, SW6 99 CY79
Tilt Rd, Cob. KT11 170 BW115
Tiltwood, The, W3
off Acacia Rd 80 CQ73
Tilt Yd App, SE9 125 EM86
Timber Cl, Chis. BR7 145 EN96
Woking GU22
off Hacketts La 151 BF114
Timber Ct, Grays RM17
off Columbia Wf Rd 110 GA79
Timbercroft, Epsom KT19 156 CS105
Timbercroft La, SE18 105 ES79
Timberdene, NW4 43 CX54
Timberdene Av, Ilf. IG6 49 EP53
Timberhill, Ashtd. KT21
off Ottways La 172 CL119
Timber Hill Cl, Cher. KT16 151 BC108
Timber Hill Rd, Cat. CR3 176 DU124
Timberland Rd, E1 84 DV72
Timber La, Cat. CR3
off Timber Hill Rd 176 DU124
Timberling Gdns, S.Croy. CR2
off Sanderstead Rd 160 DR109
Timber Mill Way, SW4 101 DK83
Timber Pond Rd, SE16 203 J3
Timber Ridge, Rick. (Loud.) WD3 22 BK42
Timberslip Dr, Wall. SM6 159 DK109
Timber St, EC1 197 H4
Timbertop Rd, West. (Bigg.H.) TN16 178 EJ118
Timberwharf Rd, N16 66 DU58
Timbrell Pl, SE16 203 M3
Time Sq, E8 66 DT64
Times Sq, Sutt. SM1 158 DB106
Timothy Cl, SW4 off Elms Rd 121 DJ85
Bexleyheath DA6 126 EY85
Timothy Ho, Erith DA18
off Kale Rd 106 EY75
Timothy Rd, E3 85 DZ71
Timperley Gdns, Red. RH1 184 DE132
Timsbury Wk, SW15 119 CU88
Timsway, Stai. TW18 113 BF92
Tindale Cl, S.Croy. CR2 160 DR111
Tindall Cl, Rom. RM3 52 FM54
Tindal St, SW9 101 DP81
Tinderbox All, SW14 98 CR83
Tine Rd, Chig. IG7 49 ES50
Tingeys Top La, Enf. EN2 29 DN36
Tinniswood Cl, N5
off Drayton Pk 65 DN64
Tinsey Cl, Egh. TW20 113 BB92
Tinsley Rd, E1 84 DW71
Tintagel Cl, Epsom KT17 157 CT114
Tintagel Cres, SE22 102 DT84
Tintagel Dr, Stan. HA7 41 CK49
Tintagel Gdns, SE22
off Oxonian St 102 DT84
Tintagel Ho, N9
off Salisbury Rd 46 DU48
Tintagel Rd, Orp. BR5 146 EW103
Tintagel Way, Wok. GU22 167 BA116
Tintern Av, NW9 62 CP55
Tintern Cl, SW15 119 CY85
SW19 120 DC94
Tintern Gdns, N14 45 DL45
Tintern Path, NW9
off Ruthin Cl 62 CS58
Tintern Rd, N22 46 DQ53
Carshalton SM5 140 DD102
Tintern St, SW4 101 DL84
Tintern Way, Har. HA2 60 CB60
Tinto Rd, E16 86 EG70
Tinwell Ms, Borwd. WD6
off Cranes Way 26 CQ43
Tinworth St, SE11 200 A10
Tippendell La, St.Alb. (Park St.) AL2 8 CB26
Tippetts Cl, Enf. EN2 30 DQ39
Tipthorpe Rd, SW11 100 DG83
Tipton Cotts, Add. KT15
off Oliver Cl 152 BG105
Tipton Dr, Croy. CR0 160 DS105
Tiptree Cl, E4 off Mapleton Rd 47 EC48
Hornchurch RM11 72 FN60
Tiptree Cres, Ilf. IG5 69 EN55
Tiptree Dr, Enf. EN2 30 DR42
Tiptree Est, Ilf. IG5 69 EN55
Tiptree Rd, Ruis. HA4 59 BV63
Tirlemont Rd, S.Croy. CR2 160 DQ108
Tirrell Rd, Croy. CR0 142 DQ100
Tisbury Ct, W1 off Rupert St 83 DK73
Tisbury Rd, SW16 141 DL96
Tisdall Pl, SE17 201 L9
Titan Rd, Grays RM17 110 GA78
Titchborne Row, W2 194 C9
Titchfield Rd, NW8 82 DF67
Carshalton SM5 140 DD102
Enfield EN3 31 DY37
Titchfield Wk, Cars. SM5
off Titchfield Rd 140 DD101
Titchwell Rd, SW18 120 DD87
Tite Hill, Egh. TW20 112 AX92
Tite St, SW3 100 DF78
★ Tithe Barn Agricultural & Folk Mus, The, Upmin. RM14 73 FR59
Tithe Barn Cl, Kings.T. KT2 138 CM95
Tithe Barn Ct, Abb.L. WD5
off Dairy Way 7 BT29
Tithe Barn Way, Nthlt. UB5 77 BV69
Tithe Cl, NW7 43 CU53
Hayes UB4
off Gledwood Dr 77 BT71
Virginia Water GU25 132 AX100
Walton-on-Thames KT12 135 BV100
Tithe Ct, Slou. SL3 93 BA77
Tithe Fm Av, Har. HA2 60 CA62
Tithe Fm Cl, Har. HA2 60 CA62
Tithe La, Stai. (Wrays.) TW19 113 BA86
Tithe Meadow, Wat. WD18 23 BR44
Tithe Meadows, Vir.W. GU25 132 AX100
Tithepit Shaw La, Warl. CR6 176 DV115
Tithe Wk, NW7 43 CU53
Titian Av, Bushey (Bushey Hth.) WD23 41 CE45
Titley Cl, E4 47 EA50
Titmus Cl, Uxb. UB8 77 BQ72
Titmuss Av, SE28 88 EV73
Titmuss St, W12
off Goldhawk Rd 99 CW75
TITSEY, Oxt. 188 EH125
Titsey Hill, Oxt. (Titsey) RH8 178 EF123
Titsey Rd, Oxt. RH8 188 EH125
Tiverton Av, Ilf. IG5 69 EN55
Tiverton Dr, SE9 125 EQ88
Tiverton Gro, Rom. RM3 52 FN50
Tiverton Ho, Enf. EN3 31 DX41

Tiv - Tre

Tiverton Rd, N15 66 DR58
N18 46 DS50
NW10 81 CX67
Edgware HA8 42 CM54
Hounslow TW3 96 CC82
Potters Bar EN6 12 DD31
Ruislip HA4 59 BU62
Thornton Heath CR7
off Willett Rd 141 DN99
Wembley HA0 80 CL68
Tiverton St, SE1 201 H7
Tiverton Way, NW7
off Bittacy Hill 43 CY52
Chessington KT9 155 CJ106
Tivoli Ct, SE16 203 M4
Tivoli Gdns, SE18 104 EL77
Tivoli Rd, N8 65 DK57
SE27 122 DQ92
Hounslow TW4 96 BY84
Toad La, Houns. TW4 96 BZ84
Tobacco Dock, E1 202 D1
Tobacco Quay, E1 202 D1
Tobago St, E14 203 P4
Tobin Cl, NW3 82 DE66
Toby La, E1 85 DY70
Toby Way, Surb. KT5 138 CP103
Todd Cl, Rain. RM13 90 FK70
Todds Wk, N7 off Andover Rd 65 DM61
Toft Av, Grays RM17 110 GD77
Tokenhouse Yd, EC2 197 K8
Token Yd, SW15
off Montserrat Rd 99 CY84
TOKYNGTON, Wem. 80 CP65
Tokyngton Av, Wem. HA9 80 CN65
Toland Sq, SW15 119 CU85
Tolcarne Dr, Pnr. HA5 59 BV55
Toldene Ct, Couls. CR5 175 DM120
Toley Av, Wem. HA9 62 CL59
Toll Bar Ct, Sutt. SM2 158 DB109
Tollbridge Cl, W10
off Kensal Rd 81 CY70
Tolldene Cl, Wok. (Knap.) GU21
off Robin Hood Rd 166 AS117
Tollers La, Couls. CR5 175 DM119
Tollesbury Gdns, Ilf. IG6 69 ER55
Tollet St, E1 85 DX70
Tollgate Cl, Rick. (Chorl.) WD3 21 BF41
Tollgate Dr, SE21 122 DS89
Hayes UB4 78 BX73
Tollgate Gdns, NW6 82 DB68
Tollgate Rd, E6 86 EK71
E16 86 EJ71
Dartford DA2 129 FR87
Waltham Cross EN8 31 DX35
Tollhouse La, Wall. SM6 159 DJ109
Tollhouse Way, N19 65 DJ61
Tollington Pk, N4 65 DM61
Tollington Pl, N4 65 DM61
Tollington Rd, N7 65 DM63
Tollington Way, N7 65 DL62
Tolmers Av, Pot.B. (Cuffley)
EN6 13 DL28
Tolmers Gdns, Pot.B. (Cuffley)
EN6 13 DL29
Tolmers Ms, Hert. (Newgate St.)
SG13 13 DL25
Tolmers Pk, Hert. (Newgate St.)
SG13 13 DL25
Tolmers Rd, Pot.B. (Cuffley)
EN6 13 DL27
Tolmers Sq, NW1 195 L4
Tolpits Cl, Wat. WD18 23 BT43
Tolpits La, Wat. WD18 23 BT44
Tolpuddle Av, E13
off Rochester Av 86 EJ67
Tolpuddle St, N1 196 DN68
Tolsford Rd, E5 66 DV64
Tolson Rd, Islw. TW7 97 CG83
Tolvaddon, Wok. GU21
off Cardingham 166 AU117
Tolverne Rd, SW20 139 CW95
TOLWORTH, Surb. 138 CN103
⇌ Tolworth 138 CP103
Tolworth Cl, Surb. KT6 138 CP102
Tolworth Gdns, Rom. RM6 70 EX57
H Tolworth Hosp, Surb. KT6 138 CN103
Tolworth Pk Rd, Surb. KT6 138 CM103
Tolworth Ri N, Surb. KT5
off Elmbridge Av 138 CQ101
Tolworth Ri S, Surb. KT5
off Warren Dr S 138 CQ102
Tolworth Rd, Surb. KT6 138 CL103
Tolworth Twr, Surb. KT6 138 CP103
Tomahawk Gdns, Nthlt. UB5
off Javelin Way 78 BX69
Tom Coombs Cl, SE9
off Well Hall Rd 104 EL84
Tom Cribb Rd, SE28 105 EQ76
Tom Gros Cl, E15
off Maryland St 67 ED64
Tom Hood Cl, E15
off Maryland St 67 ED64
Tom Jenkinson Rd, E16 205 N2
Tomkins Cl, Borwd. WD6
off Tallis Way 26 CL39
Tomkyns La, Upmin. RM14 73 FR56
Tomlin Cl, Epsom KT19 156 CR111
Tomlins Gro, E3 85 EA69
Tomlinson Cl, E2 84 DT69
W4 off Oxford Rd N 98 CP78
Tomlins Orchard, Bark. IG11 87 EQ67
Tomlins Ter, E14
off Rhodeswell Rd 85 DZ71
Tomlins Wk, N7 off Briset Way 65 DM61
Tomlyns Cl, Brwd. CM13 55 GE44
Tom Mann Cl, Bark. IG11 87 ES67
Tom Nolan Cl, E15 86 EE68
Tomo Ind Est, Uxb. UB8 76 BJ72
Tompion St, EC1 196 F3
Toms Hill, Kings L. WD4
off Bucks Hill 6 BJ33
Rickmansworth WD3 22 BL36
Toms La, Abb.L. (Bedmond)
WD5 7 BR28
Toms La, Kings L. WD4 7 BP29
Tom Smith Cl, SE10
off Maze Hill 104 EE79
Tomswood Ct, Ilf. IG6 49 EQ53
Tomswood Hill, Ilf. IG6 49 EP52
Tomswood Rd, Chig. IG7 49 EN51
Tom Thumbs Arch, E3
off Malmesbury Rd 85 EA68
Tom Williams Ho, SW6
off Clem Attlee Ct 99 CZ79
Tonbridge Cl, Bans. SM7 158 DF114
Tonbridge Cres, Har. HA3 62 CL56
Tonbridge Ho, SE25 142 DU97
Tonbridge Rd, Rom. RM3 52 FK52
Sevenoaks TN13 191 FJ127
West Molesey KT8 136 BY98
Tonbridge St, WC1 195 P2
Tonbridge Wk, WC1
off Tonbridge St 83 DL69
Tonfield Rd, Sutt. SM3 139 CZ102
Tonge Cl, Beck. BR3 143 EA99
Tonsley Hill, SW18 120 DB85
Tonsley Pl, SW18 120 DB85
Tonsley Rd, SW18 120 DB85
Tonsley St, SW18 120 DB85
Tonstall Rd, Epsom KT19 156 CR110
Mitcham CR4 140 DG96
Tony Cannell Ms, E3
off Maplin St 85 DZ69
Tooke Cl, Pnr. HA5 40 BY53
Tookey Cl, Har. HA3 62 CM59
Took's Ct, EC4 196 D8
Tooley St, SE1 201 L2
Gravesend (Nthflt.) DA11 130 GD87
Toorack Rd, Har. HA3 41 CD54
TOOT HILL, Ong. 19 FF30
Toot Hill Rd, Ong. CM5 19 FF29
⇌ Tooting 120 DG93
⊖ Tooting Bec 120 DF90
Tooting Bec Gdns, SW16 121 DK91
Tooting Bec Rd, SW16 120 DG90
SW17 120 DG90
⊖ Tooting Broadway 120 DE92
TOOTING GRAVENEY, SW17 120 DE93
Tooting Gro, SW17 120 DE92
Tooting High St, SW17 120 DE93
Tootswood Rd, Brom. BR2 144 EE99
Tooveys Mill Cl, Kings L. WD4 6 BN28
Topaz Wk, NW2 off Marble Dr 63 CX59
Topcliffe Dr, Orp. BR6 163 ER105
Top Dartford Rd, Dart. DA2 127 FF94
Swanley BR8 127 FF94
Topham Sq, N17 46 DQ53
Topham St, EC1 196 D4
Top Ho Ri, E4 off Parkhill Rd 47 EC45
Topiary, The, Ashtd. KT21 171 CL120
Topiary Sq, Rich. TW9 98 CM83
Topland Rd, Ger.Cr. (Chal.St.P.)
SL9 36 AX52
Toplands Av, S.Ock. (Aveley)
RM15 90 FP74
Topley St, SE9 104 EK84
Topmast Pt, E14 203 P5
Top Pk, Beck. BR3 144 EE99
Gerrards Cross SL9 56 AW58
Topping La, Uxb. UB8 76 BK69
Topp Wk, NW2 63 CW61
Topsfield Cl, N8
off Wolseley Rd 65 DK57
Topsfield Par, N8
off Tottenham La 65 DL57
Topsfield Rd, N8 65 DL57
Topsham Rd, SW17 120 DF90
Torbay Rd, NW6 81 CZ66
Harrow HA2 60 BY61
Torbay St, NW1 off Hawley Rd 83 DH66
Torbitt Way, Ilf. IG2 69 ET57
Torbridge Cl, Edg. HA8 42 CL52
Torbrook Cl, Bex. DA5 126 EY86
Torcross Dr, SE23 122 DW89
Torcross Rd, Ruis. HA4 59 BV62
Tor Gdns, W8 100 DA75
Torin Ct, Egh. (Eng.Grn.) TW20 112 AW92
Torland Dr, Lthd. (Oxshott)
KT22 155 CD114
Tor La, Wey. KT13 153 BQ111
Tormead Cl, Sutt. SM1 158 DA107
Tormount Rd, SE18 105 ES79
Toronto Av, E12 69 EM63
Toronto Rd, E11 67 ED63
Ilford IG1 69 EP60
Tilbury RM18 111 GG82
Torquay Gdns, Ilf. IG4 68 EK56
Torquay St, W2 off Harrow Rd 82 DB71
Torrance Cl, SE7 104 EK79
Hornchurch RM11 71 FH60
Torrens Rd, E15 86 EF65
SW2 121 DM85
Torrens Sq, E15 86 EE65
Torrens St, EC1 196 E1
Torrens Wk, Grav. DA12 131 GL92
Torres Sq, E14
off Maritime Quay 103 EA78
Torre Wk, Cars. SM5 140 DE102
Torriano Av, NW5 65 DK64
Torriano Cotts, NW5
off Torriano Av 65 DJ64
Torriano Ms, NW5
off Torriano Av 65 DK64
Torridge Gdns, SE15 102 DW84
Torridge Rd, Slou. SL3 93 BB79
Thornton Heath CR7 141 DP99
Torridon Cl, Wok. GU21 166 AV117
Torridon Rd, SE6 123 ED88
SE13 123 ED87
Torrington Av, N12 44 DD50
Torrington Cl, N12 44 DD49
Esher (Clay.) KT10 155 CE107
Torrington Dr, Har. HA2 60 CB63
Loughton IG10 33 EQ42
Potters Bar EN6 12 DD32
Torrington Gdns, N11 45 DJ51
Greenford UB6 79 CJ66
Loughton IG10 33 EQ42
Torrington Gro, N12 44 DE50
Torrington Pk, N12 44 DC50
Torrington Pl, E1 202 C2
Torrington Pl, WC1 195 L6
Torrington Rd, E18 68 EG55
Dagenham RM8 70 EZ60
Esher (Clay.) KT10 155 CE107
Greenford UB6 79 CJ67
Ruislip HA4 59 BT62
Torrington Sq, WC1 195 N5
Croydon CR0
off Tavistock Gro 142 DR101
Torrington Way, Mord. SM4 140 DA100
Tor Rd, Well. DA16 106 EW81
Torr Rd, SE20 123 DX94
Torver Rd, Har. HA1 61 CE56
Torver Way, Orp. BR6 145 ER104
Torwood La, Whyt. CR3 176 DT120
Torwood Rd, SW15 119 CU85
Torworth Rd, Borwd. WD6 26 CM39
Tothill St, SW1 199 M5
Totnes Rd, Well. DA16 106 EV80
Totnes Wk, N2 64 DD56
Tottan Ter, E1 85 DX72
Tottenhall Rd, N13 45 DN51
TOTTENHAM, N17 46 DS53
⊖ Tottenham Court Road 195 M8
Tottenham Ct Rd, W1 195 L5
Tottenham Grn E, N15 66 DT56
TOTTENHAM HALE, N17 66 DV55
⇌ Tottenham Hale 66 DV55
⊖ Tottenham Hale 66 DV55
★ Tottenham Hotspur FC,
N17 46 DT52
Tottenham La, N8 65 DL57
Tottenham Ms, W1 195 L6
Tottenham Rd, N1 84 DS65
Tottenham St, W1 195 L7
Totterdown St, SW17 120 DF91
TOTTERIDGE, N20 43 CY46
⊖ Totteridge & Whetstone 44 DB47
Totteridge Common, N20 43 CU47
Totteridge Grn, N20 44 DA47
Totteridge Ho, SW11 100 DD82
Totteridge La, N20 44 DA47
Totteridge Rd, Enf. EN3 31 DX37
Totteridge Village, N20 43 CY46
Totternhoe Cl, Har. HA3 61 CJ57
Totton Rd, Th.Hth. CR7 141 DN97
Toulmin St, SE1 201 H5
Toulon St, SE5 102 DQ80
Tournay Rd, SW6 99 CZ80
Tours Pas, SW11 100 DC84
Toussaint Wk, SE16 202 C6
Tovey Cl, St.Alb. (Lon.Col.)
AL2 9 CK26
Tovil Cl, SE20 142 DU96
Towcester Rd, E3 85 EB70
Tower, The, Couls. CR5 175 DK122
★ Tower 42, EC2 84 DS72
Tower 42, EC2 197 M8
Tower Br, E1 201 P3
SE1 201 P3
Tower Br App, E1 201 P2
★ Tower Bridge Experience,
SE1 201 P3
Tower Br Piazza, SE1 201 P3
Tower Br Rd, SE1 201 M7
Tower Br Wf, E1 202 B3
Tower Cl, NW3
off Lyndhurst Rd 64 DD64
SE20 122 DV94
Gravesend DA12 131 GL92
Ilford IG6 49 EP51
Orpington BR6 145 ET103
Woking GU21 166 AX117
Tower Ct, WC2 195 P9
Brentwood CM14 54 FV47
Tower Cft, Dart. (Eyns.) DA4
off High St 148 FL103
Tower Gdns, Esher (Clay.)
KT10 155 CG108
Tower Gdns Rd, N17 46 DQ53
DLR Tower Gateway 84 DT73
Tower Gro, Wey. KT13 135 BS103
Tower Hamlets Rd, E7 68 EF63
E17 67 EA55
⊖ Tower Hill 197 P10
Tower Hill, EC3 201 N1
Brentwood CM14 54 FW47
Kings Langley (Chipper.) WD4 5 BE29
Tower Hill Ter, EC3
off Tower Hill 84 DS73
Tower La, Wem. HA9
off Main Dr 61 CK62
Tower Ms, E17 67 EA56
Tower Mill Rd, SE15
off Wells Way 102 DS79
★ Tower of London, EC3 201 P1
Tower Pk Rd, Dart. DA1 127 FF85
★ Tower Pier, EC3 201 N2
Tower Pier, EC3 201 N2
Tower Pl, Warl. CR6 177 EA115
Tower Pt, Enf. EN2 30 DR42
Tower Retail Pk, Dart. DA1 127 FF85
Tower Ri, Rich. TW9
off Jocelyn Rd 98 CL83
Tower Rd, NW10 81 CU66
Belvedere DA17 107 FC77
Bexleyheath DA7 107 FB84
Dartford DA1 128 FJ86
Epping CM16 17 ES30
Orpington BR6 145 ET103
Tadworth KT20 173 CW123
Twickenham TW1 117 CF90
Tower Royal, EC4 197 J10
Towers, The, Ken. CR8 176 DQ115
Towers Av, Uxb. (Hlgdn.) UB10 77 BQ69
Towers Pl, Rich. TW9
off Eton St 118 CL85
Towers Rd, Grays RM17 110 GC78
Pinner HA5 40 BY53
Southall UB1 78 CA70
Tower St, WC2 195 N9
Towers Wk, Wey. KT13 153 BP107
Towers Wd, Dart. (S.Darenth)
DA4 149 FR95
Tower Ter, N22 off Mayes Rd 45 DM54
Tower Vw, Croy. CR0 143 DX101
Towfield Rd, Felt. TW13 116 BZ89
Towing Path Wk, N1
off York Way 83 DL67
Town, The, Enf. EN2 30 DR41
Towncourt Cres, Orp. BR5 145 EQ99
Towncourt La, Orp. BR5 145 ER100
Town Ct Path, N4 66 DQ60
Town End, Cat. CR3 176 DS122
Town End Cl, Cat. CR3 176 DS122
Towney Mead, Nthlt. UB5 78 BZ68
Towney Mead Ct, Nthlt. UB5
off Towney Mead 78 BZ68
Town Fm Way, Stai. (Stanw.)
TW19 off Town La 114 BK87
Townfield, Rick. WD3 38 BJ45
Townfield Cor, Grav. DA12 131 GJ88
Town Fld La, Ch.St.G. HP8 36 AW48
Townfield Rd, Hayes UB3 77 BT74
Townfield Sq, Hayes UB3 77 BT74
Town Fld Way, Islw. TW7 97 CG82
Towngate, Cob. KT11 170 BY115
Town Hall App, N16
off Milton Gro 66 DS63
Town Hall App Rd, N15 66 DT56
Town Hall Av, W4 98 CR78
Town Hall Rd, SW11 100 DF83
Townholm Cres, W7 97 CF76
Town La, Stai. (Stanw.) TW19 114 BK86
Townley Ct, E15 86 EF65
Townley Rd, SE22 122 DS85
Bexleyheath DA6 126 EZ85
Townley St, SE17 201 K10
Townmead, Red. RH1 186 DR133
Town Meadow, Brent. TW8 97 CK80
Townmead Rd, SW6 100 DC82
Richmond TW9 98 CP82
Waltham Abbey EN9 15 EC34
Town Path, Egh. TW20 113 BA92
Town Pier, Grav. DA11
off West St 131 GH86
Town Quay, Bark. IG11 87 EP67
Town Rd, N9 46 DV47
Townsend Av, N14 45 DK49
Townsend Ind Est, NW10 80 CR68
Townsend La, NW9 62 CR59
Woking GU22
off St. Peters Rd 167 BB121
Townsend Rd, N15 66 DT57
Ashford TW15 114 BL92
Southall UB1 78 BY74
Townsend St, SE17 201 L9
Townsend Way, Nthwd. HA6 39 BT52
Townsend Yd, N6 65 DH60
Townshend Cl, Sid. DA14 126 EV93
Townshend Est, NW8 82 DE68
Townshend Rd, NW8 82 DE67
Chislehurst BR7 125 EP92
Richmond TW9 98 CM84
Townshend Ter, Rich. TW9 98 CM84
Townslow La, Wok. (Wisley)
GU23 168 BJ116
Townson Av, Nthlt. UB5 77 BU69
Townson Way, Nthlt. UB5
off Townson Av 77 BU68
Town Sq, Erith DA8
off Pier Rd 107 FE79
Woking GU21
off Church St E 167 AZ117
Town Sq Cres, Green. (Bluewater)
DA9 129 FT87
Town Tree Rd, Ashf. TW15 114 BN92
Towpath, Shep. TW17 134 BM103
Towpath Wk, E9 67 DZ64
Towpath Way, Croy. CR0 142 DT100
Towton Rd, SE27 122 DQ89
Toynbec Cl, Chis. BR7
off Beechwood Ri 125 EP91
★ Toynbee Hall, E1 84 DT71
Toynbee Rd, SW20 139 CY95
Toynbee St, E1 197 P7
Toyne Way, N6
off Gaskell Rd 64 DF58
Tracery, The, Bans. SM7 174 DB115
Tracey Av, NW2 63 CW64
Tracious Cl, Wok. GU21
off Sythwood 166 AV116
Tracious La, Wok. GU21 166 AV116
Tracy Ct, Stan. HA7 41 CJ52
Trade Cl, N13 45 DN49
Trader Rd, E6 87 EP72
Tradescant Rd, SW8 101 DL80
Trading Est Rd, NW10 80 CQ70
Trafalgar Av, N17 46 DS51
SE15 102 DT78
Worcester Park KT4 139 CX102
Trafalgar Business Cen, Bark.
IG11 87 ET70
Trafalgar Cl, SE16 203 K8
Trafalgar Ct, E1 202 G1
Cobham KT11 153 BU113
Trafalgar Dr, Walt. KT12 135 BU104
Trafalgar Gdns, E1 85 DX71
W8 off South End Row 100 DB76
Trafalgar Gro, SE10 103 ED79
Trafalgar Pl, E11 68 EG56
N18 46 DU50
Trafalgar Rd, SE10 103 ED79
SW19 120 DB94
Dartford DA1 128 FL89
Gravesend DA11 131 GG87
Rainham RM13 89 FF68
Twickenham TW2 117 CD89
Trafalgar Sq, SW1 199 N2
WC2 199 N2
Trafalgar St, SE17 201 K10
Trafalgar Ter, Har. HA1
off Nelson Rd 61 CE60
Trafalgar Way, E14 204 D2
Croydon CR0 141 DM103
Trafford Cl, E15 67 EB64
Ilford IG6 49 ET51
Radlett (Shenley) WD7 10 CL32
Trafford Rd, Th.Hth. CR7 141 DM99
Tralee Ct, SE16 202 E10
Tramsheds Ind Est, Croy. CR0
off Coomber Way 141 DK101
Tramway Av, E15 86 EE66
N9 46 DV45
Tramway Cl, SE20
off Oak Gro Rd 142 DW96
Tramway Path, Mitch. CR4 140 DF99
Tranby Pl, E9
off Homerton High St 67 DX64
Tranley Ms, NW3
off Fleet Rd 64 DE64
Tranmere Rd, N9 46 DT45
SW18 120 DC89
Twickenham TW2 116 CB87
Tranquil Dale, Bet. (Buckland)
RH3 183 CT132
Tranquil Pas, SE3
off Tranquil Vale 104 EF82
Tranquil Ri, Erith DA8
off West St 107 FE78
Tranquil Vale, SE3 104 EE82
Transay Wk, N1
off Marquess Rd 84 DR65
Transept St, NW1 194 B7
Transmere Cl, Orp. BR5 145 EQ100
Transmere Rd, Orp. BR5 145 EQ100
Transom Cl, SE16 203 L8
Transom Sq, E14 204 B9
Transport Av, Brent. TW8 97 CG78
Tranton Rd, SE16 202 C6
Traps Hill, Loug. IG10 33 EM41
Traps La, N.Mal. KT3 138 CS95
Travellers Way, Houns. TW4 96 BW82
Travers Cl, E17 47 DX53
Travers Rd, N7 65 DN62
Treacy Cl, Bushey (Bushey Hth.)
WD23 40 CC47
Treadgold St, W11 81 CX73
Treadway St, E2 84 DV68
Treadwell Rd, Epsom KT18 172 CS115
Treaty Cen, Houns. TW3 96 CB83
Treaty Rd, Houns. TW3
off Hanworth Rd 96 CB83
Treaty St, N1 83 DM67
Trebble Rd, Swans. DA10 130 FY86
Trebeck St, W1 199 H2
Trebovir Rd, SW5 100 DA78
Treby St, E3 85 DZ70
Trecastle Way, N7
off Carleton Rd 65 DK63
Tredegar Ms, E3
off Tredegar Ter 85 DZ69
Tredegar Rd, E3 85 DZ68
N11 45 DK52
Dartford DA2 127 FG89
Tredegar Sq, E3 85 DZ69
Tredegar Ter, E3 85 DZ69
Trederwen Rd, E8 84 DU67
Tredown Rd, SE26 122 DW92
Tredwell Cl, SW2
off Hillside Rd 121 DM89
Bromley BR2 144 EL98
Tredwell Rd, SE27 121 DP91
Treebourne Rd, West. (Bigg.H.)
TN16 178 EJ117
Tree Cl, Rich. TW10 117 CK88
Treen Av, SW13 99 CT83
Tree Rd, E16 86 EJ72
Treeside Cl, West Dr. UB7 94 BK77
Tree Tops, Brwd. CM15 54 FW46
Treetops, Grav. DA12 131 GH92
Whyteleafe CR3 176 DU118
Treetops Cl, SE2 106 EY78
Northwood HA6 39 BR50
Treetops Vw, Loug. IG10 48 EK45
Treeview Cl, SE19 142 DS95
Treewall Gdns, Brom. BR1 124 EH91
Tree Way, Reig. RH2 184 DB131
Trefgarne Rd, Dag. RM10 70 FA61
Trefil Wk, N7 65 DL63
Trefoil Ho, Erith DA18
off Kale Rd 106 EY75
Trefoil Rd, SW18 120 DC85
Trefusis Wk, Wat. WD17 23 BS39
Tregaron Av, N8 65 DL58
Tregaron Gdns, N.Mal. KT3
off Avenue Rd 138 CS98
Tregarthen Pl, Lthd. KT22 171 CJ121
Tregarth Pl, Wok. GU21 166 AT117
Tregarvon Rd, SW11 100 DG84
Tregenna Av, Har. HA2 60 BZ63
Tregenna Cl, N14 29 DJ43
Tregenna Ct, Har. HA2 60 CA63
Tregony Rd, Orp. BR6 163 ET105
Trego Rd, E9 85 EA66
Tregothnan Rd, SW9 101 DL83
Tregunter Rd, SW10 100 DC79
Trehearn Rd, Ilf. IG6 49 ER52
Treherne Ct, SW9
off Eythorne Rd 101 DN81
SW17 120 DG91
Trehern Rd, SW14 98 CR83
Trehurst St, E5 67 DY64
Trelawn Cl, Cher. (Ott.) KT16 151 BC108
Trelawney Av, Slou. SL3 92 AX76
Trelawney Cl, E17
off Orford Rd 67 EB56
Trelawney Est, E9 84 DW65
Trelawney Gro, Wey. KT13 152 BN107
Trelawney Rd, Ilf. IG6 49 ER52
Trelawn Rd, E10 67 EC62
SW2 121 DN85
Trellick Twr, W10 81 CZ70
Trellis Sq, E3
off Malmesbury Rd 85 DZ69
Treloar Gdns, SE19
off Hancock Rd 122 DR93
Tremadoc Rd, SW4 101 DK84
Tremaine Cl, SE4 103 EA82
Tremaine Rd, SE20 142 DV96
Trematon Pl, Tedd. TW11 117 CJ94
Tremlett Gro, N19 65 DJ62
Tremlett Ms, N19 65 DJ62
Trenance, Wok. GU21
off Cardingham 166 AU117
Trenance Gdns, Ilf. IG3 70 EU62
Trenchard Av, Ruis. HA4 59 BV63
Trenchard Cl, NW9
off Fulbeck Dr 42 CS53
Stanmore HA7 41 CG51
Walton-on-Thames KT12 154 BW106

Trenchard Ct, Mord. SM4
off Green La 140 DB100
Trenchard St, SE10 ....103 EE78
Trenches La, Slou. SL3 ....75 BA73
Trenchold St, SW8 ....101 DL79
Trench Yd Ct, Mord. SM4
off Green La 140 DB100
Trenear Cl, Orp. BR6 ....164 EU105
Trenham Dr, Warl. CR6 ....176 DW116
Trenholme Cl, SE20 ....122 DV94
Trenholme Ct, Cat. CR3 ....176 DU122
Trenholme Rd, SE20 ....122 DV94
Trenholme Ter, SE20 ....122 DV94
Trenmar Gdns, NW10 ....81 CV69
Trent Av, W5 ....97 CJ76
Upminster RM14 ....73 FR58
Trentbridge Cl, Ilf. IG6 ....49 ET51
Trent Cl, Rad. (Shenley) WD7
off Edgbaston Dr 10 CL32
Trent Gdns, N14 ....29 DH44
Trentham Cres, Wok. GU22 ....167 BA121
Trentham Dr, Orp. BR5 ....146 EU98
Trentham St, SW18 ....120 DA88
★ Trent Park Country Pk, Barn.
EN4 ....29 DH40
Trent Rd, SW2 ....121 DM85
Buckhurst Hill IG9 ....48 EH46
Slough SL3 ....93 BB79
Trent Way, Hayes UB4 ....77 BS68
Worcester Park KT4 ....139 CW104
Trentwood Side, Enf. EN2 ....29 DM41
Treport St, SW18 ....120 DB87
Tresco Cl, Brom. BR1 ....124 EE93
Trescoe Gdns, Har. HA2 ....60 BY59
Romford RM5 ....51 FC50
Tresco Gdns, Ilf. IG3 ....70 EU61
Tresco Rd, SE15 ....102 DV84
Tresham Cres, NW8 ....194 B4
Tresham Rd, Bark. IG11 ....87 ET66
Tresham Wk, E9
off Churchill Wk 66 DW64
Tresilian Av, N21 ....29 DM43
Tresillian Way, Wok. GU21 ....166 AU116
Tressell Cl, N1 off Sebbon St 83 DP66
Tressillian Cres, SE4 ....103 EA83
Tressillian Rd, SE4 ....103 DZ84
Tresta Wk, Wok. GU21 ....166 AU115
Trestis Cl, Hayes UB4
off Jollys La 78 BY71
Treston Ct, Stai. TW18 ....113 BF92
Treswell Rd, Dag. RM9 ....88 EY67
Tretawn Gdns, NW7 ....42 CS49
Tretawn Pk, NW7 ....42 CS49
Trevanion Rd, W14 ....99 CY78
Treve Av, Har. HA1 ....60 CC59
Trevellance Way, Wat. WD25 ....8 BW33
Trevelyan Av, E12 ....69 EM63
Trevelyan Cl, Dart. DA1 ....108 FM84
Trevelyan Cres, Har. HA3 ....61 CK59
Trevelyan Gdns, NW10 ....81 CW67
Trevelyan Rd, E15 ....68 EF63
SW17 ....120 DE92
Trevera Ct, Wal.Cr. EN8
off Eleanor Rd 15 DY33
Trevereux Hill, Oxt. RH8 ....189 EM131
Treveris St, SE1 ....200 F3
Treverton St, W10 ....81 CX70
Treves Cl, N21 ....29 DM43
Treville St, SW15 ....119 CV87
Treviso Rd, SE23
off Farren Rd 123 DX89
Trevithick Cl, Felt. TW14 ....115 BT88
Trevithick Dr, Dart. DA1 ....108 FM84
Trevithick St, SE8 ....103 EA78
Trevone Gdns, Pnr. HA5 ....60 BY58
Trevor Cl, Barn. EN4 ....28 DD43
Bromley BR2 ....144 EF101
Harrow HA3 off Kenton La 41 CF52
Isleworth TW7 ....117 CF85
Northolt UB5 ....78 BW68
Trevor Cres, Ruis. HA4 ....59 BT63
Trevor Gdns, Edg. HA8 ....42 CR53
Northolt UB5 ....78 BW68
Ruislip HA4 off Clyfford Rd 59 BU63
Trevor Pl, SW7 ....198 C5
Trevor Rd, SW19 ....119 CY94
Edgware HA8 ....42 CR53
Hayes UB3 ....95 BS75
Woodford Green IG8 ....48 EG52
Trevor Sq, SW7 ....198 D5
Trevor St, SW7 ....198 C5
Trevor Wk, SW7
off Trevor Sq 100 DF75
Trevose Av, W.Byf. KT14 ....151 BF114
Trevose Rd, E17 ....47 ED53
Trevose Way, Wat. WD19 ....40 BW48
Trewarden Av, Iver SL0 ....75 BD68
Trewenna Dr, Chess. KT9 ....155 CK106
Potters Bar EN6 ....12 DD32
Trewince Rd, SW20 ....139 CW95
Trewint St, SW18 ....120 DC89
Trewsbury Ho, SE2
off Hartslock Dr 106 EX75
Trewsbury Rd, SE26 ....123 DX92
Triandra Way, Hayes UB4 ....78 BX71
Triangle, The, EC1
off Goswell Rd 83 DP70
N13 off Lodge Dr 45 DN49
Barking IG11 off Tanner St 87 EQ65
Hampton TW12 off High St 136 CC95
Kingston upon Thames KT1
off Kenley Rd 138 CQ96
Woking GU21 ....166 AW118
Triangle Business Cen, NW10
off Enterprise Way 81 CU69
Triangle Ct, E16 off Tollgate Rd 86 EK71
Triangle Est, SE11
off Kennington La 101 DM78
Triangle Pas, Barn. EN4
off Station App 28 DC42
Triangle Pl, SW4 ....101 DK84
Triangle Rd, E8 ....84 DV67
Trident Cen, Wat. WD24 ....24 BW39
Trident Gdns, Nthlt. UB5
off Jetstar Way 78 BX69
Trident Ind Est, Slou. (Colnbr.)
SL3 ....93 BE83
Trident Rd, Wat. WD25 ....7 BT34
Trident St, SE16 ....203 J8
Trident Way, Sthl. UB2 ....95 BV76
Trigg's Cl, Wok. GU22 ....166 AX119
Trigg's La, Wok. GU21, GU22 ....166 AW118
Trig La, EC4 ....197 H10
Trigo Ct, Epsom KT19
off Blakeney Cl 156 CR111
Trigon Rd, SW8 ....101 DM80
Trilby Rd, SE23 ....123 DX89
Trimmer Wk, Brent. TW8 ....98 CL79
Trim St, SE14 ....103 DZ79
Trinder Gdns, N19
off Trinder Rd 65 DL60
Trinder Rd, N19 ....65 DL60
Barnet EN5 ....27 CW43
Tring Av, W5 ....80 CM74
Southall UB1 ....78 BZ72
Wembley HA9 ....80 CN65
Tring Cl, Ilf. IG2 ....69 EQ57
Romford RM3 ....52 FM49
Tring Gdns, Rom. RM3 ....52 FL49
Tring Grn, Rom. RM3 ....52 FM49
Tringham Cl, Cher. (Ott.) KT16 ....151 BC107
Tring Wk, Rom. RM3
off Tring Gdns 52 FL49
Trinidad Gdns, Dag. RM10 ....89 FD66
Trinidad St, E14 ....85 DZ73
Trinity Av, N2 ....64 DD55
Enfield EN1 ....30 DT44
Trinity Buoy Wf, E14 ....205 K1
Trinity Ch Pas, SW13 ....99 CV79
Trinity Ch Rd, SW13 ....99 CV79
Trinity Ch Sq, SE1 ....201 J6
Trinity Cl, E8 ....84 DT65
E11 ....68 EE61
NW3 off Hampstead High St 64 DD63
SE13 off Wisteria Rd 103 ED84
SW4 off The Pavement 101 DJ84
Bromley BR2 ....144 EL102
Hounslow TW4 ....96 BY84
Northwood HA6 ....39 BS51
South Croydon CR2 ....160 DS109
Staines (Stanw.) TW19 ....114 BJ86
Trinity Cotts, Rich. TW9
off Trinity Rd 98 CM83
Trinity Ct, N1 off Downham Rd 84 DS66
NW2 off Anson Rd 63 CW64
SE7 off Charlton La 104 EK77
Trinity Cres, SW17 ....120 DF89
Trinity Gdns, E16 off Cliff Wk 86 EF70
SW9 ....101 DM84
Dartford DA1
off Summerhill Rd 128 FK86
Trinity Gro, SE10 ....103 EC81
Trinity Hall Cl, Wat. WD24 ....24 BW41
★ Trinity Ho, EC3 ....197 N10
Trinity La, Wal.Cr. EN8 ....15 DY32
Trinity Ms, SE20 ....142 DV95
W10 off Cambridge Gdns 81 CX72
Trinity Path, SE26 ....122 DW90
Trinity Pl, Bexh. DA6 ....106 EZ84
Trinity Ri, SW2 ....121 DN88
Trinity Rd, N2 ....64 DD55
N22 ....45 DL53
SW17 ....120 DF89
SW18 ....120 DD85
SW19 ....120 DA93
Gravesend DA12 ....131 GJ87
Ilford IG6 ....69 EQ55
Richmond TW9 ....98 CM83
Southall UB1 ....78 BY74
Trinity Sq, EC3 ....201 N1
Trinity St, E16 off Vincent St 86 EG71
SE1 ....201 J5
Enfield EN2 ....30 DQ40
Trinity Wk, NW3 ....82 DC65
Trinity Way, E4 ....47 DZ51
W3 ....80 CS73
Trio Pl, SE1 ....201 J5
Tripps Hill, Ch.St.G. HP8 ....36 AU48
Tripps Hill Cl, Ch.St.G. HP8 ....36 AU48
Tristan Sq, SE3 ....104 EE83
Tristram Cl, E17 ....67 ED55
Tristram Rd, Brom. BR1 ....124 EF91
Triton Sq, NW1 ....195 K4
Tritton Av, Croy. CR0 ....159 DL105
Tritton Rd, SE21 ....122 DR90
Trittons, Tad. KT20 ....173 CW121
Triumph Cl, Grays (Chaff.Hun.)
RM16 ....109 FW77
Hayes UB3 ....95 BQ80
Triumph Ho, Bark. IG11 ....88 EV69
Triumph Rd, E6 ....87 EM72
Trivett Cl, Green. DA9 ....129 FU85
★ Trocadero Cen, W1 ....199 M1
Trocadero Shop Cen, W1 ....83 DK73
Trojan Ct, NW6
off Willesden La 81 CY66
Trojan Way, Croy. CR0 ....141 DM104
Trolling Down Hill, Dart. DA2 ....128 FP89
Troon Cl, SE16 ....202 E10
SE28 off Fairway Dr 88 EX72
Troon St, E1 ....85 DY72
Troopers Dr, Rom. RM3 ....52 FK49
Trosley Av, Grav. DA11 ....131 GH89
Trosley Rd, Belv. DA17 ....106 FA79
Trossachs Rd, SE22 ....122 DS85
Trothy Rd, SE1 ....202 C8
Trotsworth Av, Vir.W. GU25 ....132 AX98
Trotsworth Ct, Vir.W. GU25 ....132 AY98
Trotters Bottom, Barn. EN5 ....27 CU37
Trotters La, Wok. (Mimbr.)
GU24 ....150 AV112
Trotter Way, Epsom KT19
off Abbots Av 156 CN112
Trott Rd, N10 ....44 DF52
Trotts La, West. TN16 ....189 EQ127
Trott St, SW11 ....100 DE81
Trotwood, Chig. IG7 ....49 ER51
Trotwood Cl, Brwd. CM15
off Middleton Rd 54 FY46
Troughton Rd, SE7 ....205 P10
Troutbeck Cl, Slou. SL2 ....74 AU73
Troutbeck Rd, SE14 ....103 DY81
Trout La, West Dr. UB7 ....76 BJ73
Trout Ri, Rick. (Loud.) WD3 ....22 BH41
Trout Rd, West Dr. UB7 ....76 BK74
Troutstream Way, Rick. (Loud.)
WD3 ....22 BH42
Trouville Rd, SW4 ....121 DJ86
Trowbridge Est, E9
off Osborne Rd 85 DZ65
Trowbridge Rd, E9 ....85 DZ65
Romford RM3 ....52 FK51
Trowers Way, Red. RH1 ....185 DH131
Trowley Ri, Abb.L. WD5 ....7 BS31
Trowlock Av, Tedd. TW11 ....117 CJ93
Trowlock Island, Tedd. TW11 ....117 CK92
Trowlock Way, Tedd. TW11 ....117 CK93
Troy Cl, Tad. KT20 ....173 CV120
Troy Ct, SE18 ....105 EP77
Troy Rd, SE19 ....122 DR93
Troy Town, SE15 ....102 DU83
Trubshaw Rd, Sthl. UB2
off Havelock Rd 96 CB76
Truesdale Dr, Uxb. (Hare.)
UB9 ....58 BJ57
Truesdale Rd, E6 ....87 EM72
Trulock Ct, N17 ....46 DU52
Trulock Rd, N17 ....46 DU52
Truman Cl, Edg. HA8
off Pavilion Way 42 CP52
Truman's Rd, N16 ....66 DS64
Trumpers Way, W7 ....97 CE76
Trumper Way, Uxb. UB8 ....76 BJ67
Trumpington Rd, E7 ....68 EF63
Trumps Grn Av, Vir.W. GU25 ....132 AX100
Trumps Grn Cl, Vir.W. GU25
off Trumps Grn Rd 132 AY99
Trumps Grn Rd, Vir.W. GU25 ....132 AX100
Trumps Mill La, Vir.W. GU25 ....133 AZ100
Trump St, EC2 ....197 J9
Trundlers Way, Bushey
(Bushey Hth.) WD23 ....41 CE46
Trundle St, SE1 ....201 H4
Trundleys Rd, SE8 ....203 J10
Trundleys Ter, SE8 ....203 J9
Trunks All, Swan. BR8 ....147 FB96
Truro Gdns, Ilf. IG1 ....68 EL59
Truro Rd, E17 ....67 DZ56
N22 ....45 DL52
Gravesend DA12 ....131 GK90
Truro St, NW5 ....82 DG65
Truro Wk, Rom. RM3
off Saddleworth Rd 52 FJ51
Truro Way, Hayes UB4
off Portland Rd 77 BS69
Truslove Rd, SE27 ....121 DN92
Trussley Rd, W6 ....99 CW76
Trustees Way, Uxb. (Denh.)
UB9 ....57 BF57
Trustons Gdns, Horn. RM11 ....71 FG59
Trust Rd, Wal.Cr. EN8 ....15 DY34
Trust Wk, SE21
off Peabody Hill 121 DP88
Tryfan Cl, Ilf. IG4 ....68 EK57
Tryon Cres, E9 ....84 DW67
Tryon St, SW3 ....198 D10
Trys Hill, Cher. (Lyne) KT16 ....133 AZ103
Trystings Cl, Esher (Clay.)
KT10 ....155 CG107
Tuam Rd, SE18 ....105 ER79
Tubbenden Cl, Orp. BR6 ....145 ES103
Tubbenden Dr, Orp. BR6 ....163 ER105
Tubbenden La, Orp. BR6 ....145 ES104
Tubbenden La S, Orp. BR6 ....163 ER106
Tubbs Rd, NW10 ....81 CT68
Tubs Hill Par, Sev. TN13 ....190 FG124
Tubwell Rd, Slou. (Stoke P.)
SL2 ....74 AV67
Tucker Rd, Cher. (Ott.) KT16 ....151 BD107
Tucker St, Wat. WD18 ....24 BW43
Tuckey Gro, Wok. (Ripley)
GU23 ....167 BF124
Tuck Rd, Rain. RM13 ....89 FG65
Tudor Av, Hmptn. TW12 ....116 CA93
Romford RM2 ....71 FG55
Waltham Cross (Chsht.) EN7 ....14 DU31
Watford WD24 ....24 BX38
Worcester Park KT4 ....139 CV104
Tudor Cl, N6 ....65 DJ59
NW3 ....64 DE64
NW7 ....43 CU51
NW9 ....62 CQ61
SW2 off Elm Pk 121 DM86
Ashford TW15 ....114 BL91
Banstead SM7 ....173 CY115
Brentwood CM15 ....55 FZ44
Chessington KT9 ....156 CL106
Chigwell IG7 ....49 EN49
Chislehurst BR7 ....145 EM95
Cobham KT11 ....154 BZ113
Coulsdon CR5 ....175 DN118
Dartford DA1 ....127 FH86
Epsom KT17 ....157 CT110
Gravesend (Nthflt.) DA11 ....130 GE88
Leatherhead (Bkhm.) KT23 ....170 CA124
Pinner HA5 ....59 BU57
South Croydon CR2 ....176 DV115
Sutton SM3 ....157 CX106
Wallington SM6 ....159 DJ108
Waltham Cross (Chsht.) EN7 ....14 DV31
Woking GU22 ....167 BA117
Woodford Green IG8 ....48 EH50
Tudor Ct, E17 ....67 DY59
Borehamwood WD6 ....26 CL40
Feltham TW13 ....116 BW91
Swanley BR8 ....147 FC101
Tudor Ct N, Wem. HA9 ....62 CN64
Tudor Ct S, Wem. HA9 ....62 CN64
Tudor Cres, Enf. EN2 ....29 DP39
Ilford IG6 ....49 EP51
Tudor Dr, Kings.T. KT2 ....118 CL92
Morden SM4 ....139 CX100
Romford RM2 ....71 FG56
Walton-on-Thames KT12 ....136 BX102
Watford WD24 ....24 BX38
Tudor Est, NW10 ....80 CP68
Tudor Gdns, NW9 ....62 CQ61
SW13 off Treen Av 98 CS83
W3 ....80 CN72
Harrow HA3 off Tudor Rd 41 CD54
Romford RM2 ....71 FG56
Tudor Gdns, Twick. TW1 ....117 CF88
Upminster RM14 ....72 FQ61
West Wickham BR4 ....143 EC104
Tudor Gro, E9 ....84 DW66
N20 off Church Cres 44 DE48
Tudor Ho, Surb. KT6
off Lenelby Rd 138 CN102
Tudor La, Wind. (Old Wind.)
SL4 ....112 AW87
Tudor Manor Gdns, Wat.
WD25 ....8 BX32
Tudor Ms, Rom. RM1
off Eastern Rd 71 FF57
Tudor Par, Rick. WD3
off Berry La 38 BG45
Tudor Pl, W1 ....195 M8
Mitcham CR4 ....120 DE94
Tudor Rd, E4 ....47 EB51
E6 ....86 EJ67
E9 ....84 DV67
N9 ....46 DV45
SE19 ....122 DT94
SE25 ....142 DV99
Ashford TW15 ....115 BR93
Barking IG11 ....87 ET67
Barnet EN5 ....28 DA41
Beckenham BR3 ....143 EB97
Hampton TW12 ....116 CA94
Harrow HA3 ....41 CD54
Hayes UB3 ....77 BR72
Hounslow TW3 ....97 CD84
Kingston upon Thames KT2 ....118 CN94
Pinner HA5 ....40 BW54
Southall UB1 ....78 BY73
Tudors, The, Reig. RH2 ....184 DC131
Tudor Sq, Hayes UB3 ....77 BR71
Tudor St, EC4 ....196 E10
Tudor Wk, Bex. DA5 ....126 EY86
Tudorwalk, Grays RM17
off Thurloe Wk 110 GA76
Tudor Wk, Lthd. KT22 ....171 CF120
Watford WD24 ....24 BX37
Weybridge KT13
off West Palace Gdns 135 BP104
Tudor Way, N14 ....45 DK46
W3 ....98 CN75
Orpington BR5 ....145 ER100
Rickmansworth (Mill End)
WD3 ....38 BG46
Uxbridge UB10 ....76 BN65
Waltham Abbey EN9 ....15 ED33
Tudor Well Cl, Stan. HA7 ....41 CH50
Tudway Rd, SE3 ....104 EH83
Tufnail Rd, Dart. DA1 ....128 FM86
TUFNELL PARK, N7 ....65 DK63
⊖ Tufnell Park 65 DJ63
Tufnell Pk Rd, N7 ....65 DJ63
N19 ....65 DJ63
Tufter Rd, Chig. IG7 ....49 ET50
Tufton Gdns, W.Mol. KT8 ....136 CB96
Tufton Rd, E4 ....47 EA49
Tufton St, SW1 ....199 N6
Tugboat St, SE28 ....105 ES75
Tugela Rd, Croy. CR0 ....142 DR100
Tugela St, SE6 ....123 DZ89
Tugmutton Cl, Orp. BR6
off Acorn Way 163 EP105
Tuilerie St, E2 ....84 DU68
Tulip Cl, E6
off Bradley Stone Rd 87 EM71
Brentwood CM15
off Poppy Cl 54 FV43
Croydon CR0 ....143 DX102
Hampton TW12
off Partridge Rd 116 BZ93
Romford RM3
off Cloudberry Rd 52 FK51
Southall UB2 off Chevy Rd 96 CC75
Tulip Ct, Pnr. HA5 ....60 BW55
Tulip Gdns, Ilf. IG1 ....87 EP65
Tulip Tree Ct, Sutt. SM2
off The Crescent 158 DA111
Tulip Way, West Dr. UB7 ....94 BK77
Tull St, Mitch. CR4 ....140 DF101
Tulse Cl, Beck. BR3 ....143 EC97
TULSE HILL, SE21 ....122 DQ88
⇌ Tulse Hill 121 DP89
Tulse Hill, SW2 ....121 DN86
Tulse Hill Est, SW2 ....121 DN86
Tulsemere Rd, SE27 ....122 DQ89
Tulyar Cl, Tad. KT20 ....173 CV120
Tumber St, Epsom (Headley)
KT18 ....182 CQ125
Tumblewood Rd, Bans. SM7 ....173 CY116
Tumbling Bay, Walt. KT12 ....135 BU100
Tummons Gdns, SE25 ....142 DS96
Tuncombe Rd, N18 ....46 DS49
Tunis Rd, W12 ....81 CV74
Tunley Grn, E14 off Burdett Rd 85 DZ71
Tunley Rd, NW10 ....80 CS67
SW17 ....120 DG88
Tunmarsh La, E13 ....86 EJ69
Tunmers End, Ger.Cr. (Chal.St.P.)
SL9 ....36 AW53
Tunnan Leys, E6 ....87 EN72
Tunnel Av, SE10 ....204 G4
Tunnel Est, Grays RM20 ....109 FT77
Tunnel Gdns, N11 ....45 DJ52
Tunnel Rd, SE16 ....202 F4
Reigate RH2 off Church St 184 DA133
Tunnel Wd Cl, Wat. WD17 ....23 BT37
Tunnel Wd Rd, Wat. WD17 ....23 BT37
Tunstall Av, Ilf. IG6 ....50 EU51
Tunstall Cl, Orp. BR6 ....163 ES105
Tunstall Rd, SW9 ....101 DM84
Croydon CR0 ....142 DS102
Tunstall Wk, Brent. TW8 ....98 CL79
Tunstock Way, Belv. DA17 ....106 EY76
Tunworth Cl, NW9 ....62 CQ58
Tunworth Cres, SW15 ....119 CT86
Tun Yd, SW8 off Peardon St 101 DH82
Tupelo Rd, E10 ....67 EB61
Tupwood Ct, Cat. CR3 ....186 DU125
Tupwood La, Cat. CR3 ....186 DU125
Tupwood Scrubbs Rd, Cat.
CR3 ....186 DU128
Turenne Cl, SW18 ....100 DC84
Turfhouse La, Wok. (Chobham)
GU24 ....150 AS109
Turin Rd, N9 ....46 DW45
Turin St, E2 ....84 DU69
Turkey Oak Cl, SE19 ....142 DS95
⇌ Turkey Street 30 DW37
Turkey St, Enf. EN1, EN3 ....30 DV37
Turks Cl, Uxb. UB8
off Harlington Rd 76 BN69
Turk's Head Yd, EC1 ....196 F6
Turks Row, SW3 ....198 E10
Turle Rd, N4 ....65 DM60
SW16 ....141 DL96
Turlewray Cl, N4 ....65 DM60
Turley Cl, E15 ....86 EE67
Turnagain La, EC4 ....196 F8
Dartford DA2 ....127 FG90
Turnage Rd, Dag. RM8 ....70 EY60
Turnberry Cl, NW4 ....43 CX54
SE16 off Ryder Dr 102 DV78
Turnberry Ct, Wat. WD19 ....40 BW48
Turnberry Dr, St.Alb. (Brick.Wd.)
AL2 ....8 BY30
Turnberry Quay, E14 ....204 C6
Turnberry Way, Orp. BR6 ....145 ER102
Turnbull Cl, Green. DA9 ....129 FS87
Turnbury Cl, SE28 ....88 EX72
Turnchapel Ms, SW4
off Cedars Rd 101 DH83
Turner Av, N15 ....66 DS56
Mitcham CR4 ....140 DF95
Twickenham TW2 ....116 CC90
Turner Cl, NW11 ....64 DB58
SW9 ....101 DP81
Hayes UB4 off Charville La 77 BQ68
Hornchurch RM12
off Upper Rainham Rd 71 FF61
Wembley HA0 ....61 CK64
Turner Ct, Dart. DA1 ....128 FJ85
Turner Dr, NW11 ....64 DB58
Turner Pl, SW11 off Cairns Rd 120 DE85
Turner Rd, E17 ....67 EC55
Bushey WD23 ....24 CC42
Dartford (Bean) DA2 ....129 FV90
Edgware HA8 ....62 CM55
New Malden KT3 ....138 CR101
Slough SL3 ....92 AW75
Westerham (Bigg.H.) TN16 ....162 EJ112
Turners Cl, Stai. TW18 ....114 BH92
Turners Ct, Rom. (Abridge) RM4
off Ongar Rd 34 EV41
Turners Gdns, Sev. TN13 ....191 FJ128
Turners Hill, Wal.Cr. (Chsht.)
EN8 ....15 DX30
Turners La, Walt. KT12 ....153 BV107
Turners Meadow Way, Beck.
BR3 ....143 DZ95
Turners Rd, E3 ....85 DZ71
Turner St, E1 ....84 DV71
E16 ....86 EF72
Turners Way, Croy. CR0 ....141 DN103
Turners Wd, NW11 ....64 DC59
Turners Wd Dr, Ch.St.G. HP8 ....36 AX48
Turneville Rd, W14 ....99 CZ79
Turney Grn, E14
off Wallwood St 85 DZ71
Turney Rd, SE21 ....122 DR87
Turneys Orchard, Rick. (Chorl.)
WD3 ....21 BD43
TURNFORD, Brox. 15 DZ26
⊖ Turnham Green 98 CS77
Turnham Grn Ter, W4 ....98 CS77
Turnham Grn Ter Ms, W4
off Turnham Grn Ter 98 CS77
Turnham Rd, SE4 ....123 DY85
Turnmill St, EC1 ....196 E5
Turnoak Av, Wok. GU22 ....166 AY120
Turnoak La, Wok. GU22
off Wych Hill La 166 AY119
Turnpike Cl, SE8
off Amersham Vale 103 DZ80
Turnpike Dr, Orp. BR6 ....164 EW109
Turnpike Ho, EC1 ....196 G3
⊖ Turnpike Lane 65 DN55
Turnpike La, N8 ....65 DM56
Sutton SM1 ....158 DC106
Tilbury (W.Til.) RM18 ....111 GK78
Uxbridge UB10 ....76 BL69
Turnpike Link, Croy. CR0 ....142 DS103
Turnpike Way, Islw. TW7 ....97 CG81
Turnpin La, SE10 ....103 EC79
Turnstone Cl, E13 ....86 EG69
NW9 off Kestrel Cl 42 CS54
South Croydon CR2 ....161 DY110
Uxbridge (Ickhm.) UB10 ....59 BP64
Turnstones, The, Grav. DA12 ....131 GK89
Watford WD25 ....24 BY36
Turp Av, Grays RM16 ....110 GC75
Turpentine La, SW1 ....199 J10
Turpin Av, Rom. RM5 ....50 FA52
Turpin Cl, Enf. EN3
off Government Row 31 EA38
Turpington Cl, Brom. BR2 ....144 EL100
Turpington La, Brom. BR2 ....144 EL101
Turpin La, Erith DA8 ....107 FG80
Turpin Rd, Felt. TW14
off Staines Rd 115 BT86
Turpins La, Wdf.Grn. IG8 ....49 EM50
Turpin Way, N19
off Elthorne Rd 65 DK61
Wallington SM6 ....159 DH108
Turquand St, SE17 ....201 J9
Turret Gro, SW4 ....101 DJ83
Turton Rd, Wem. HA0 ....62 CL64
Turville St, E2 ....197 P4
Tuscan Rd, SE18 ....105 ER78
Tuskar St, SE10 ....104 EE78
Tustin Est, SE15 ....102 DW79
Tuttlebee La, Buck.H. IG9 ....48 EG47
Tuxford Cl, Borwd. WD6 ....26 CL38
Twankhams All, Epp. CM16
off Hemnall St 18 EU30
Tweedale Ct, E15 ....67 EC64
Tweeddale Gro, Uxb. UB10 ....59 BQ62

Twe - Uve

Tweeddale Rd, Cars. SM5 ...140 DD102
Tweed Glen, Rom. RM1 ...51 FD52
Tweed Grn, Rom. RM1 ...51 FE52
Tweedmouth Rd, E13 ...86 EH68
Tweed Rd, Slou. SL3 ...93 BA79
Tweed Way, Rom. RM1 ...51 FD52
Tweedy Cl, Enf. EN1 ...30 DT43
Tweedy Rd, Brom. BR1 ...144 EF95
Tweezer's All, WC2 ...196 D10
Twelve Acre Cl, Lthd. (Bkhm.) KT23 ...170 BZ124
Twelvetrees Cres, E3 ...85 EC70
Twentyman Cl, Wdf.Grn. IG8 ...48 EG50
TWICKENHAM ...117 CG89
⇌ Twickenham ...117 CF87
Twickenham Br, Rich. TW9 ...117 CJ85
Twickenham TW1 ...117 CJ85
Twickenham Cl, Croy. CR0 ...141 DM104
Twickenham Gdns, Grnf. UB6 .61 CG64
Harrow HA3 ...41 CE52
Twickenham Rd, E11 ...67 ED61
Feltham TW13 ...116 BZ90
Isleworth TW7 ...97 CG83
Richmond TW9 ...97 CJ84
Teddington TW11 ...117 CG92
Twickenham Trd Est, Twick. TW1 ...117 CF86
Twig Folly Cl, E2
off Roman Rd ...85 DX68
Twigg Cl, Erith DA8 ...107 FE80
Twilley St, SW18 ...120 DB87
Twine Cl, Bark. IG11
off Thames Rd ...88 EV69
Twine Ct, E1 ...84 DW73
Twineham Grn, N12
off Tillingham Way ...44 DA49
Twine Ter, E3 off Ropery St ...85 DZ70
Twining Av, Twick. TW2 ...116 CC90
Twinn Rd, NW7 ...43 CY51
Twinoaks, Cob. KT11 ...154 CA113
Twin Tumps Way, SE28 ...88 EU73
Twisden Rd, NW5 ...65 DH63
Twisleton Ct, Dart. DA1
off Priory Hill ...128 FK86
Twitchells La, Beac. (Jordans) HP9 ...36 AT51
TWITTON, Sev. ...181 FF116
Twitton La, Sev. (Otford) TN14 .181 FD115
Twitton Meadows, Sev. (Otford) TN14 ...181 FE116
Two Rivers Retail Pk, Stai. TW18 ...113 BE91
Twybridge Way, NW10 ...80 CQ66
Twycross Ms, SE10 ...205 J9
Twyford Abbey Rd, NW10 ...80 CM69
Twyford Av, N2 ...64 DF55
W3 ...80 CN73
Twyford Cres, W3 ...80 CN74
Twyford Ho, N15
off Chisley Rd ...66 DS58
Twyford Pl, WC2 ...196 B8
Twyford Rd, Cars. SM5 ...140 DD102
Harrow HA2 ...60 CB60
Ilford IG1 ...69 EQ64
Twyford St, N1 ...83 DM67
Tyas Rd, E16 ...86 EF70
Tybenham Rd, SW19 ...140 DA97
Tyberry Rd, Enf. EN3 ...30 DV41
Tyburn La, Har. HA1 ...61 CE59
Tyburns, The, Brwd. CM13 ...55 GC47
Tyburn Way, W1 ...194 E10
Tycehurst Hill, Loug. IG10 ...33 EM42
Tydcombe Rd, Warl. CR6 ...176 DW119
Tye La, Epsom KT18 ...182 CR127
Orpington BR6 ...163 EQ106
Tadworth KT20
off Dorking Rd ...183 CT128
Tyers Est, SE1 ...201 M4
Tyers Gate, SE1 ...201 M4
Tyers St, SE11 ...200 B10
Tyers Ter, SE11 ...101 DM78
Tyeshurst Cl, SE2 ...106 EY78
Tyfield Cl, Wal.Cr. (Chsht.) EN8 .14 DW30
Tykeswater La, Borwd. (Elstree) WD6 ...25 CJ39
Tylecroft Rd, SW16 ...141 DL96
Tyle Grn, Horn. RM11 ...72 FL56
Tylehurst Gdns, Ilf. IG1 ...69 EQ64
Tyle Pl, Wind. (Old Wind.) SL4 .112 AU85
Tyler Cl, E2 ...84 DT68
Tyler Gdns, Add. KT15 ...152 BJ105
Tyler Gro, Dart. DA1
off Spielman Rd ...108 FM84
Tyler Rd, Sthl. UB2
off McNair Rd ...96 CB76
Tylers Cl, Gdse. RH9 ...186 DV130
Kings Langley WD4 ...6 BL28
Loughton IG10 ...48 EL45
Tyler's Ct, W1 ...195 M9
Tylers Cres, Horn. RM12 ...72 FJ64
Tylersfield, Abb.L. WD5 ...7 BT31
Tylers Gate, Har. HA3 ...62 CL58
TYLER'S GREEN, Gdse. ...186 DV129
Tylers Grn Rd, Swan. BR8 ...147 FC100
Tylers Hill Rd, Chesh. HP5 ...4 AT30
Tylers Path, Cars. SM5
off Rochester Rd ...158 DF105
Tyler St, SE10 ...104 EE78
Tylers Way, Wat. WD25 ...25 CD42
Tyler Way, Brwd. CM14 ...54 FV46
Tylney Av, SE19 ...122 DT92
Tylney Rd, E7 ...68 EJ63
Bromley BR1 ...144 EK96
Tymperley Ct, SW19
off Windlesham Gro ...119 CY88
Tynan Cl, Felt. TW14
off Sandycombe Rd ...115 BU88
Tyndale Ct, E14 ...204 B10
Tyndale La, N1 off Upper St ...83 DP66
Tyndale Ter, N1
off Canonbury La ...83 DP66
Tyndall Rd, E10 ...67 EC61
Welling DA16 ...105 ET83
Tyne Cl, Upmin. RM14 ...73 FR58
Tynedale, St.Alb. (Lon.Col.) AL2
off Thamesdale ...10 CM27
Tynedale Cl, Dart. DA2 ...129 FR88
Tyne Gdns, S.Ock. (Aveley) RM15 ...90 FQ73
Tyneham Cl, SW11
off Shirley Gro ...100 DG83
Tyneham Rd, SW11 ...100 DG82
Tynemouth Cl, E6
off Covelees Wall ...87 EP72
Tynemouth Dr, Enf. EN1 ...30 DU38
Tynemouth Rd, N15 ...66 DT56
SE18 ...105 ET78
Mitcham CR4 ...120 DG94
Tynemouth St, SW6 ...100 DC82
Tyne St, E1 off Old Castle St ...84 DT72
Type St, E2 ...85 DX68
Tyrawley Rd, SW6 ...100 DB81
Tyre La, NW9
off Sheaveshill Av ...62 CS56
Tyrell Cl, Har. HA1 ...61 CE63
Tyrell Ct, Cars. SM5 ...158 DF105
Tyrell Ri, Brwd. CM14 ...54 FW50
Tyrells Cl, Upmin. RM14 ...72 FN61
Tyrols Rd, SE23
off Wastdale Rd ...123 DX88
Tyrone Rd, E6 ...87 EM68
Tyron Way, Sid. DA14 ...125 ES91
Tyrrell Av, Well. DA16 ...126 EU85
Tyrrell Rd, SE22 ...102 DU84
Tyrrells Hall Cl, Grays RM17 ...110 GD79
Tyrrell Sq, Mitch. CR4 ...140 DE95
TYRRELL'S WOOD, Lthd. ...172 CM123
Tyrrel Way, NW9 ...63 CT59
Tyrwhitt Rd, SE4 ...103 EA83
Tysea Hill, Rom. (Stap.Abb.) RM4 ...51 FF45
Tysoe Av, Enf. EN3 ...31 DZ36
Tysoe St, EC1 ...196 D3
Tyson Rd, SE23 ...122 DW87
Tyssen Pas, E8 ...84 DT65
Tyssen Pl, S.Ock. RM15 ...91 FW69
Tyssen Rd, N16 ...66 DT62
Tyssen St, E8 ...84 DT65
N1 off Hoxton St ...84 DS68
Tytherton Rd, N19 ...65 DK62

U

Uamvar St, E14 ...85 EB71
Uckfield Gro, Mitch. CR4 ...140 DG95
Uckfield Rd, Enf. EN3 ...31 DX37
Udall Gdns, Rom. RM5 ...50 FA51
Udall St, SW1 ...199 L9
Udney Pk Rd, Tedd. TW11 ...117 CG92
Uffington Rd, NW10 ...81 CU67
SE27 ...121 DN91
Ufford Cl, Har. HA3
off Ufford Rd ...40 CB52
Ufford Rd, Har. HA3 ...40 CB52
Ufford St, SE1 ...200 E4
Ufton Gro, N1 ...84 DR66
Ufton Rd, N1 ...84 DR66
Uhura Sq, N16 ...66 DS62
Ujima Ct, SW16
off Sunnyhill Rd ...121 DL91
Ullathorne Rd, SW16 ...121 DJ91
Ulleswater Rd, N14 ...45 DL49
Ullin St, E14
off St. Leonards Rd ...85 EC71
Ullswater Business Pk, Couls. CR5 ...175 DL116
Ullswater Cl, SW15 ...118 CR91
Bromley BR1 ...124 EE93
Hayes UB4 ...77 BS68
Ullswater Ct, Har. HA2
off Oakington Av ...60 CA59
Ullswater Cres, SW15 ...118 CR91
Coulsdon CR5 ...175 DL116
Ullswater Rd, SE27 ...121 DP89
SW13 ...99 CU80
Ullswater Way, Horn. RM12 ...71 FG64
Ulstan Cl, Cat. (Wold.) CR3 ...177 EA123
Ulster Gdns, N13 ...46 DQ49
Ulster Pl, NW1 ...195 H5
Ulster Ter, NW1 ...195 H4
Ulundi Rd, SE3 ...104 EE79
Ulva Rd, SW15
off Ravenna Rd ...119 CX85
Ulverscroft Rd, SE22 ...122 DT85
Ulverstone Rd, SE27 ...121 DP89
Ulverston Rd, E17 ...47 ED54
Ulwin Av, W.Byf. (Byfleet) KT14 ...152 BL113
Ulysses Rd, NW6 ...63 CZ64
Umberston St, E1
off Hessel St ...84 DV72
Umbria St, SW15 ...119 CU86
Umfreville Rd, N4 ...65 DP58
Undercliff Rd, SE13 ...103 EA83
UNDERHILL, Barn. ...28 DA43
Underhill, Barn. EN5 ...28 DA43
Underhill Pk Rd, Reig. RH2 ...184 DA131
Underhill Pas, NW1
off Camden High St ...83 DH67
Underhill Rd, SE22 ...122 DV86
Underhill St, NW1
off Camden High St ...83 DH67
Underne Av, N14 ...45 DH47
UNDERRIVER, Sev. ...191 FN130
Underriver Ho Rd, Sev. (Undrvr.) TN15 ...191 FP130
Undershaft, EC3 ...197 M9
Undershaw Rd, Brom. BR1 ...124 EE90
Underwood, Croy. (New Adgtn.) CR0 ...161 EC106
Underwood, The, SE9 ...125 EM89
Underwood Rd, E1 ...84 DU70
E4 ...47 EB50
Caterham CR3 ...186 DS126
Woodford Green IG8 ...48 EK52
Underwood Row, N1 ...197 J2
Underwood St, N1 ...197 J2
Undine Rd, E14 ...204 C8
Undine St, SW17 ...120 DF92
Uneeda Dr, Grnf. UB6 ...79 CD67
Unicorn Ho, Brom. BR1
off Elmfield Rd ...144 EG97
Unicorn Wk, Green. DA9 ...129 FT85
Union Cl, E11 ...67 ED63
Union Cotts, E15
off Welfare Rd ...86 EE66
Union Ct, EC2 ...197 M8
Richmond TW9 off Eton St ...118 CL85
Union Dr, E1 off Canal Cl ...85 DY70
Union Gro, SW8 ...101 DK82
Union Rd, N11 ...45 DK51
SW4 ...101 DK82
SW8 ...101 DK82
Bromley BR2 ...144 EK99
Croydon CR0 ...142 DQ101
Northolt UB5 ...78 CA68
Wembley HA0 ...80 CL65
Union Sq, N1 ...84 DQ67
Union St, E15 ...85 EC67
SE1 ...200 G3
Barnet EN5 ...27 CY42
Kingston upon Thames KT1 ...137 CK96
Union Wk, E2 ...197 N2
H United Elizabeth Garrett Anderson Hosp & Soho Hosp for Women, NW1 ...195 N3
Unity Cl, NW10 ...81 CU65
SE19 off Crown Dale ...122 DQ92
Croydon (New Adgtn.) CR0 ...161 EB109
Unity Rd, Enf. EN3 ...30 DW37
Unity Trd Est, Wdf.Grn. IG8 ...68 EK55
Unity Way, SE18 ...104 EK76
Unity Wf, SE1 ...202 A4
University Cl, NW7 ...43 CT52
Bushey WD23 ...24 CA42
★ University Coll London, WC1 ...195 M4
University Gdns, Bex. DA5 ...126 EZ87
H University Hosp Lewisham, SE13 ...123 EB85
★ University of London, WC1 ...195 N5
★ University of London - Royal Holloway Coll, Egh. TW20 ...112 AX93
H University of London - UCL - Uni Coll Hosp, WC1 ...195 L5
University Pl, Erith DA8
off Belmont Rd ...107 FB80
University Rd, SW19 ...120 DD93
University St, WC1 ...195 L5
University Way, E16 ...87 EN73
Dartford DA1 ...108 FJ84
Unwin Av, Felt. TW14 ...115 BS85
Unwin Cl, SE15 ...102 DU79
Unwin Rd, SW7 ...198 A6
Isleworth TW7 ...97 CE83
Upbrook Ms, W2
off Chilworth St ...82 DC72
Upcerne Rd, SW10 ...100 DC80
Upchurch Cl, SE20 ...122 DV94
Up Cor, Ch.St.G. HP8 ...36 AW47
Up Cor Cl, Ch.St.G. HP8 ...36 AV47
Upcroft Av, Edg. HA8 ...42 CQ50
Updale Cl, Pot.B. EN6 ...11 CY33
Updale Rd, Sid. DA14 ...125 ET91
Upfield, Croy. CR0 ...142 DV103
Upfield Rd, W7 ...79 CF70
Upgrove Manor Way, SW2
off Trinity Ri ...121 DN87
Uphall Rd, Ilf. IG1 ...69 EP64
Upham Pk Rd, W4 ...98 CS77
Uphill Dr, NW7 ...42 CS50
NW9 ...62 CQ57
Uphill Gro, NW7 ...42 CS49
Uphill Rd, NW7 ...42 CS49
Upland Ct Rd, Rom. RM3 ...52 FM54
Upland Dr, Hat. AL9 ...12 DB25
Upland Ms, SE22
off Upland Rd ...122 DU85
Upland Rd, E13 off Sutton Rd ...86 EF70
SE22 ...122 DU85
Bexleyheath DA7 ...106 EZ83
Caterham CR3 ...177 EB120
Epping CM16 ...17 ET25
South Croydon CR2 ...160 DR106
Sutton SM2 ...158 DD108
Uplands, Ashtd. KT21 ...171 CK120
Beckenham BR3 ...143 EA96
Rickmansworth (Crox.Grn.) WD3 ...22 BM44
Uplands, The, Ger.Cr. SL9 ...56 AY60
Loughton IG10 ...33 EM41
Ruislip HA4 ...59 BU60
St. Albans (Brick.Wd.) AL2 ...8 BY30
Uplands Av, E17
off Blackhorse La ...47 DX54
Uplands Business Pk, E17 ...47 DX54
Uplands Cl, SW14
off Monroe Dr ...118 CP85
Gerrards Cross SL9 ...56 AY60
Sevenoaks TN13 ...190 FF123
Uplands Dr, Lthd. (Oxshott) KT22 ...155 CD113
Uplands End, Wdf.Grn. IG8 ...48 EL52
Uplands Pk Rd, Enf. EN2 ...29 DN41
Uplands Rd, N8 ...65 DM57
Barnet EN4 ...44 DG46
Brentwood CM14 ...54 FY50
Kenley CR8 ...176 DQ116
Orpington BR6 ...146 EV102
Romford RM6 ...70 EX55
Woodford Green IG8 ...48 EL52
Uplands Way, N21 ...29 DN43
Sevenoaks TN13 ...190 FF123
Upland Way, Epsom KT18 ...173 CW118
UPMINSTER ...72 FQ62
⇌ Upminster ...72 FQ61
⊖ Upminster ...72 FQ61
⊖ Upminster Bridge ...72 FN61
Upminster Rd, Horn. RM11, RM12 ...72 FM61
Upminster RM14 ...72 FM61
Upminster Rd N, Rain. RM13 ...90 FJ69
Upminster Rd S, Rain. RM13 ...89 FG70
Upminster Trd Pk, Upmin. RM14 ...73 FX59
⊖ Upney ...87 ET66
Upney Cl, Horn. RM12
off Tylers Cres ...72 FJ64
Upney La, Bark. IG11 ...87 ES65
Upnor Way, SE17 ...201 N10
Uppark Dr, Ilf. IG2 ...69 EQ58
Upper Abbey Rd, Belv. DA17 ...106 EZ77
Upper Addison Gdns, W14 ...99 CY75
Upper Bk St, E14 ...204 B3
Upper Bardsey Wk, N1
off Clephane Rd ...84 DQ65
Upper Belgrave St, SW1 ...198 G6
Upper Berkeley St, W1 ...194 D9
Upper Beulah Hill, SE19 ...142 DS95
Upper Bourne End La, Hem.H. HP1 ...5 BA25
Upper Brentwood Rd, Rom. RM2 ...72 FJ56
Upper Br Rd, Red. RH1 ...184 DE134
Upper Brighton Rd, Surb. KT6 ...137 CK100
Upper Brockley Rd, SE4 ...103 DZ82
Upper Brook St, W1 ...198 F1
Upper Butts, Brent. TW8 ...97 CJ79
Upper Caldy Wk, N1
off Clephane Rd ...84 DQ65
Upper Camelford Wk, W11
off Lancaster Rd ...81 CY72
Upper Cavendish Av, N3 ...64 DA55
Upper Cheyne Row, SW3 ...100 DE79
Upper Ch Hill, Green. DA9 ...129 FS85
UPPER CLAPTON, E5 ...66 DV60
Upper Clapton Rd, E5 ...66 DV60
Upper Clarendon Wk, W11
off Lancaster Rd ...81 CY72
Upper Cornsland, Brwd. CM14 ...54 FX48
Upper Ct Rd, Cat. (Wold.) CR3 ...177 EA123
Epsom KT19 ...156 CQ111
Upper Dengie Wk, N1
off Popham Rd ...84 DQ67
Upper Dr, West. (Bigg.H.) TN16 ...178 EJ118
Upper Dunnymans, Bans. SM7
off Basing Rd ...157 CZ114
UPPER EDMONTON, N18 ...46 DU51
UPPER ELMERS END, Beck. ...143 DZ100
Upper Elmers End Rd, Beck. BR3 ...143 DY98
Upper Fairfield Rd, Lthd. KT22 ...171 CH121
Upper Fm Rd, W.Mol. KT8 ...136 BZ98
Upper Fosters, NW4
off New Brent St ...63 CW57
Upper Grn E, Mitch. CR4 ...140 DF97
Upper Grn W, Mitch. CR4
off London Rd ...140 DF97
Upper Grenfell Wk, W11
off Whitchurch Rd ...81 CX73
Upper Grosvenor St, W1 ...198 F1
Upper Grotto Rd, Twick. TW1 ...117 CF89
Upper Grd, SE1 ...200 D2
Upper Gro, SE25 ...142 DS98
Upper Gro Rd, Belv. DA17 ...106 EZ79
Upper Guild Hall, Green. (Bluewater) DA9
off Bluewater Parkway ...129 FU88
Upper Gulland Wk, N1
off Clephane Rd ...84 DQ65
UPPER HALLIFORD, Shep. ...135 BS97
⇌ Upper Halliford ...135 BS96
Upper Halliford Bypass, Shep. TW17 ...135 BS99
Upper Halliford Grn, Shep. TW17
off Holmbank Dr ...135 BS98
Upper Halliford Rd, Shep. TW17 ...135 BS96
Upper Ham Rd, Kings.T. KT2 ...117 CK91
Richmond TW10 ...117 CK91
Upper Handa Wk, N1
off Clephane Rd ...84 DR65
Upper Hawkwell Wk, N1
off Popham Rd ...84 DQ67
Upper High St, Epsom KT17 ...156 CS113
Upper Highway, Abb.L. WD5 ...7 BR33
Kings Langley WD4 ...7 BQ32
Upper Hill Ri, Rick. WD3 ...22 BH44
Upper Hitch, Wat. WD19 ...40 BY46
UPPER HOLLOWAY, N19 ...65 DJ62
⇌ Upper Holloway ...65 DK61
Upper Holly Hill Rd, Belv. DA17 ...107 FB78
Upper James St, W1 ...195 L10
Upper John St, W1 ...195 L10
Upper Lismore Wk, N1
off Clephane Rd ...84 DQ65
Upper Mall, W6 ...99 CU78
Upper Marsh, SE1 ...200 C6
Upper Montagu St, W1 ...194 D6
Upper Mulgrave Rd, Sutt. SM2 ...157 CY108
Upper N St, E14 ...85 EA71
UPPER NORWOOD, SE19 ...122 DR94
Upper Paddock Rd, Wat. WD19 ...24 BY44
Upper Palace Rd, E.Mol. KT8 ...136 CC97
Upper Pk, Loug. IG10 ...32 EK42
Upper Pk Rd, N11 ...45 DH50
NW3 ...64 DF64
Belvedere DA17 ...107 FB77
Bromley BR1 ...144 EH95
Kingston upon Thames KT2 ...118 CN93
Upper Phillimore Gdns, W8 ...100 DA75
Upper Pillory Down, Cars. SM5 ...158 DG113
Upper Pines, Bans. SM7 ...174 DF117
Upper Rainham Rd, Horn. RM12 ...71 FF63
Upper Ramsey Wk, N1
off Clephane Rd ...84 DR65
Upper Rawreth Wk, N1
off Popham Rd ...84 DQ67
Upper Richmond Rd, SW15 ...99 CY84
Upper Richmond Rd W, SW14 ...98 CP84
Richmond TW10 ...98 CN84
Upper Rd, E13 ...86 EG69
Uxbridge (Denh.) UB9 ...57 BD59
Wallington SM6 ...159 DK106
Upper Rose Gallery, Green. (Bluewater) DA9
off Bluewater Parkway ...129 FU88
Upper Ryle, Brwd. CM14 ...54 FV45
Upper St. Martin's La, WC2 ...195 P10
Upper Sawley Wd, Bans. SM7 ...157 CZ114
Upper Selsdon Rd, S.Croy. CR2 ...160 DT108
Upper Sheppey Wk, N1
off Clephane Rd ...84 DQ66
Upper Sheridan Rd, Belv. DA17
off Coleman Rd ...106 FA77
Upper Shirley Rd, Croy. CR0 ...142 DW103
Upper Shott, Wal.Cr. (Chsht.) EN7 ...14 DT26
Upper Sq, Islw. TW7 ...97 CG83
Upper Sta Rd, Rad. WD7 ...25 CG35
Upper St, N1 ...83 DN68
Upper Sunbury Rd, Hmptn. TW12 ...136 BY95
Upper Sutton La, Houns. TW5 ...96 CA80
Upper Swaines, Epp. CM16 ...17 ET30
UPPER SYDENHAM, SE26 ...122 DU91
Upper Tachbrook St, SW1 ...199 K8
Upper Tail, Wat. WD19 ...40 BY48
Upper Talbot Wk, W11
off Lancaster Rd ...81 CY72
Upper Teddington Rd, Kings.T. KT1 ...137 CJ95
Upper Ter, NW3 ...64 DC62
Upper Thames St, EC4 ...196 G10
Upper Thames Wk, Green. (Bluewater) DA9
off Bluewater Parkway ...129 FU88
Upper Tollington Pk, N4 ...65 DN60
Upperton Rd, Sid. DA14 ...125 ET92
Upperton Rd E, E13
off Inniskilling Rd ...86 EJ69
Upperton Rd W, E13 ...86 EJ69
UPPER TOOTING, SW17 ...120 DE90
Upper Tooting Pk, SW17 ...120 DF89
Upper Tooting Rd, SW17 ...120 DF91
Upper Town Rd, Grnf. UB6 ...78 CB70
Upper Tulse Hill, SW2 ...121 DM87
Upper Vernon Rd, Sutt. SM1 ...158 DD106
Upper Wk, Vir.W. GU25 ...132 AY98
UPPER WALTHAMSTOW, E17 ...67 EB56
Upper Walthamstow Rd, E17 ...67 ED56
⇌ Upper Warlingham ...176 DU118
Upper W St, Reig. RH2 ...183 CZ134
Upper Wickham La, Well. DA16 ...106 EV80
Upper Wimpole St, W1 ...195 H6
Upper Woburn Pl, WC1 ...195 N3
Upper Woodcote Village, Pur. CR8 ...159 DK112
Uppingham Av, Stan. HA7 ...41 CH53
Upsdell Av, N13 ...45 DN51
UPSHIRE, Wal.Abb. ...16 EJ32
Upshirebury Grn, Wal.Abb. EN9
off Horseshoe Hill ...16 EK33
Upshire Rd, Wal.Abb. EN9 ...16 EF32
Upshott La, Wok. GU22 ...167 BF117
Upstall St, SE5 ...101 DP81
UPTON, E7 ...86 EH66
UPTON, Slou. ...92 AU76
Upton, Wok. GU21 ...166 AV117
Upton Av, E7 ...86 EG66
Upton Cl, NW2
off Somerton Rd ...63 CY62
Bexley DA5 ...126 EZ86
St. Albans (Park St.) AL2 ...9 CD25
Slough SL1 ...92 AT76
Upton Ct, SE20
off Blean Gro ...122 DW94
Upton Ct Rd, Slou. SL3 ...92 AU76
Upton Dene, Sutt. SM2 ...158 DB108
Upton Gdns, Har. HA3 ...61 CH57
H Upton Hosp, Slou. SL1 ...92 AT76
Upton La, E7 ...86 EG66
Upton Lo Cl, Bushey WD23 ...40 CC45
UPTON PARK, E6 ...86 EJ67
UPTON PARK, Slou. ...92 AT76
⊖ Upton Park ...86 EH67
Upton Pk, Slou. SL1 ...92 AT76
Upton Pk Rd, E7 ...86 EH66
Upton Rd, N18 ...46 DU50
SE18 ...105 EQ79
Bexley DA5 ...126 EZ86
Bexleyheath DA6 ...106 EY84
Hounslow TW3 ...96 CA83
Slough SL1 ...92 AU76
Thornton Heath CR7 ...142 DR96
Watford WD18 ...23 BV42
Upton Rd S, Bex. DA5 ...126 EZ86
Upway, N12 ...44 DE52
Gerrards Cross (Chal.St.P.) SL9 ...37 AZ53
Upwood Rd, SE12 ...124 EG86
SW16 ...141 DL95
Urban Av, Horn. RM12 ...72 FJ62
Urlwin St, SE5 ...102 DQ79
Urlwin Wk, SW9 ...101 DN82
Urmston Dr, SW19 ...119 CY88
Ursula Ms, N4 off Portland Ri ...66 DQ60
Ursula St, SW11 ...100 DE81
Urswick Gdns, Dag. RM9
off Urswick Rd ...88 EY66
Urswick Rd, E9 ...66 DW64
Dagenham RM9 ...88 EX66
Usborne Ms, SW8 ...101 DM80
Usher Rd, E3 ...85 DZ68
Usherwood Cl, Tad. KT20 ...182 CP131
Usk Rd, SW11 ...100 DC84
South Ockendon (Aveley) RM15 ...90 FQ72
Usk St, E2 ...85 DX69
Utopia Village, NW1
off Chalcot Rd ...82 DG67
Uvedale Cl, Croy. (New Adgtn.) CR0 off Uvedale Cres ...161 ED111
Uvedale Cres, Croy. (New Adgtn.) CR0 ...161 ED111
Uvedale Rd, Dag. RM10 ...70 FA62
Enfield EN2 ...30 DR43
Oxted RH8 ...188 EF129

Uverdale Rd, SW10 ... 100 DC80
UXBRIDGE ... 76 BK66
⊖ **Uxbridge** ... 76 BK66
Uxbridge Gdns, Felt. TW13
off Marlborough Rd ... 116 BX89
UXBRIDGE MOOR, Iver ... 76 BG67
UXBRIDGE MOOR, Uxb. ... 76 BG67
Uxbridge Rd, W3 ... 80 CL73
W5 ... 80 CL73
W7 ... 79 CF74
W12 ... 81 CU74
W13 ... 79 CF74
Feltham TW13 ... 116 BW89
Hampton (Hmptn.H.) TW12 ... 116 CA91
Harrow HA3 ... 40 CC52
Hayes UB4 ... 78 BW73
Iver SL0 ... 74 AY71
Kingston upon Thames KT1 ... 137 CK98
Pinner HA5 ... 40 CB52
Rickmansworth WD3 ... 37 BF47
Slough SL1, SL2, SL3 ... 92 AU75
Southall UB1 ... 78 CA74
Stanmore HA7 ... 41 CF51
Uxbridge UB10 ... 76 BN69
Uxbridge St, W8 ... 82 DA74
Uxendon Cres, Wem. HA9 ... 62 CL60
Uxendon Hill, Wem. HA9 ... 62 CM60

V

Vache La, Ch.St.G. HP8 ... 36 AW47
Vache Ms, Ch.St.G. HP8 ... 36 AX46
Vaillant Rd, Wey. KT13 ... 153 BQ105
Valance Av, E4 ... 48 EF46
Valan Leas, Brom. BR2 ... 144 EE97
Vale, The, N10 ... 44 DG53
N14 ... 45 DK45
NW11 ... 63 CX62
SW3 ... 100 DD79
W3 ... 80 CR74
Brentwood CM14 ... 54 FW46
Coulsdon CR5 ... 159 DK114
Croydon CR0 ... 143 DX103
Feltham TW14 ... 115 BV86
Gerrards Cross (Chal.St.P.)
SL9 ... 36 AX53
Hounslow TW5 ... 96 BY79
Ruislip HA4 ... 60 BW63
Sunbury-on-Thames TW16
off Ashridge Way ... 115 BU93
Woodford Green IG8 ... 48 EG52
Vale Av, Borwd. WD6 ... 26 CP43
Vale Border, Croy. CR0 ... 161 DX111
Vale Cl, N2 *off Church Vale* ... 64 DF55
W9 *off Maida Vale* ... 82 DC69
Brentwood CM15 ... 54 FT43
Gerrards Cross (Chal.St.P.)
SL9 ... 36 AX53
Orpington BR6 ... 163 EN105
Weybridge KT13 ... 135 BR104
Woking GU21 ... 166 AY116
Vale Cotts, SW15
off Kingston Vale ... 118 CR91
Vale Ct, W9 *off Maida Vale* ... 82 DC69
Weybridge KT13 ... 135 BR104
Vale Cres, SW15 ... 118 CS90
Vale Cft, Esher (Clay.) KT10 ... 155 CE108
Pinner HA5 ... 60 BY57
Vale Dr, Barn. EN5 ... 27 CZ42
Vale End, SE22 *off Grove Vale* ... 102 DS84
Vale Fm Rd, Wok. GU21 ... 166 AX117
Vale Gro, N4 ... 66 DQ59
W3 *off The Vale* ... 80 CR74
Slough SL1 ... 92 AS76
Vale Ind Est, Wat. WD18 ... 39 BQ46
Vale La, W3 ... 80 CN71
Valence Av, Dag. RM8 ... 70 EX62
Valence Circ, Dag. RM8 ... 70 EX62
Valence Dr, Wal.Cr. (Chsht.)
EN7 ... 14 DU28
★ **Valence Ho Mus**, Dag.
RM8 ... 70 EY61
Valence Rd, Erith DA8 ... 107 FD80
Valence Wd Rd, Dag. RM8 ... 70 EX62
Valencia Rd, Stan. HA7 ... 41 CJ49
Valency Cl, Nthwd. HA6 ... 39 BT49
Valentia Pl, SW9
off Brixton Sta Rd ... 101 DN84
Valentine Av, Bex. DA5 ... 126 EY89
Valentine Ct, SE23 ... 123 DX89
Valentine Pl, SE1 ... 200 F4
Valentine Rd, E9 ... 85 DX65
Harrow HA2 ... 60 CC62
Valentine Row, SE1 ... 200 F5
Valentines Rd, Ilf. IG1 ... 69 EP60
Valentines Way, Rom. RM7 ... 71 FE61
Valentine Way, Ch.St.G. HP8 ... 36 AX48
Valentyne Cl, Croy. (New Adgtn.)
CR0 ... 162 EE111
Vale of Health, NW3
off East Heath Rd ... 64 DD62
Vale Par, SW15
off Kingston Vale ... 118 CR91
Valerian Way, E15 ... 86 EE69
Valerie Ct, Bushey WD23 ... 40 CC45
Sutton SM2 *off Stanley Rd* ... 158 DB108
Vale Ri, NW11 ... 63 CZ60
Vale Rd, E7 ... 86 EH65
N4 ... 66 DQ59
Bromley BR1 ... 145 EN96
Bushey WD23 ... 24 BY43
Dartford DA1 ... 127 FH88
Epsom KT19 ... 157 CT105
Esher (Clay.) KT10 ... 155 CE109
Gravesend (Nthflt.) DA11 ... 130 GD87
Mitcham CR4 ... 141 DK97
Sutton SM1 ... 158 DB105
Weybridge KT13 ... 135 BR104
Worcester Park KT4 ... 157 CT105
Vale Rd N, Surb. KT6 ... 138 CL103
Vale Rd S, Surb. KT6 ... 138 CL103
Vale Row, N5 *off Gillespie Rd* ... 65 DP62
Vale Royal, N7 ... 83 DL66
Vale St, SE27 ... 122 DR90
Valeswood Rd, Brom. BR1 ... 124 EF92
Vale Ter, N4 ... 66 DQ58
Valetta Gro, E13 ... 86 EG68
Valetta Rd, W3 ... 98 CS75
Valette St, E9 ... 84 DV65
Valiant Cl, Nthlt. UB5
off Ruislip Rd ... 78 BX69
Romford RM7 ... 50 FA54
Valiant Ho, SE7 ... 104 EJ78
Valiant Path, NW9
off Blundell Rd ... 42 CS52
Valiant Way, E6 ... 87 EM71
Vallance Rd, E1 ... 84 DU70
E2 ... 84 DU69
N22 ... 45 DJ54
Vallentin Rd, E17 ... 67 EC56
Valley Av, N12 ... 44 DD49
Valley Cl, Dart. DA1 ... 127 FF86
Loughton IG10 ... 33 EM44
Pinner HA5 *off Alandale Dr* ... 39 BV54
Waltham Abbey EN9 ... 15 EC32
Valley Ct, Cat. CR3
off Beechwood Gdns ... 176 DU122
Kenley CR8 *off Hayes La* ... 160 DQ114
Valley Dr, NW9 ... 62 CN58
Gravesend DA12 ... 131 GK91
Sevenoaks TN13 ... 191 FH125
Valleyfield Rd, SW16 ... 121 DM92
Valley Flds Cres, Enf. EN2 ... 29 DN40
★ **Valley Gdns, The**, Egh.
TW20 ... 132 AS96
Valley Gdns, SW19 ... 120 DD94
Wembley HA0 ... 80 CM66
Valley Gro, SE7 ... 104 EJ78
Valley Hill, Loug. IG10 ... 48 EL45
Valley Link Ind Est, Enf. EN3 ... 31 DY44
Valley Ms, Twick. TW1
off Cross Deep ... 117 CG89
Valley Ri, Wat. WD25 ... 7 BV33
Valley Rd, SW16 ... 121 DM91
Belvedere DA17 ... 107 FB77
Bromley BR2 ... 144 EE96
Dartford DA1 ... 127 FF86
Erith DA8 ... 107 FD77
Kenley CR8 ... 176 DR115
Longfield (Fawk.Grn.) DA3 ... 149 FV102
Orpington BR5 ... 146 EV95
Rickmansworth WD3 ... 22 BG43
Uxbridge UB10 ... 76 BL68
Valley Side, E4 ... 47 EA47
Valley Side Par, E4
off Valley Side ... 47 EA47
Valley Vw, Barn. EN5 ... 27 CY44
Greenhithe DA9 ... 129 FV86
Waltham Cross (Chsht.) EN7 ... 14 DQ28
Westerham (Bigg.H.) TN16 ... 178 EJ118
Valley Vw Gdns, Ken. CR8
off Godstone Rd ... 176 DS115
Valley Wk, Croy. CR0 ... 142 DW103
Rickmansworth (Crox.Grn.)
WD3 ... 23 BQ43
Valley Way, Ger.Cr. SL9 ... 56 AW58
Valliere Rd, NW10 ... 81 CV69
Valliers Wd Rd, Sid. DA15 ... 125 ER88
Vallis Way, W13 ... 79 CG71
Chessington KT9 ... 155 CK105
Valmar Rd, SE5 ... 102 DQ81
Val McKenzie Av, N7
off Parkside Cres ... 65 DN62
Valnay St, SW17 ... 120 DF92
Valognes Av, E17 ... 47 DY53
Valonia Gdns, SW18 ... 119 CZ86
Vambery Rd, SE18 ... 105 EQ79
Vanbrough Cres, Nthlt. UB5 ... 78 BW67
Vanbrugh Cl, E16
off Fulmer Rd ... 86 EK71
Vanbrugh Dr, Walt. KT12 ... 136 BW101
Vanbrugh Flds, SE3 ... 104 EF80
Vanbrugh Hill, SE3 ... 104 EF78
SE10 ... 104 EF78
Vanbrugh Pk, SE3 ... 104 EF80
Vanbrugh Pk Rd, SE3 ... 104 EF80
Vanbrugh Pk Rd W, SE3 ... 104 EF80
Vanbrugh Rd, W4 ... 98 CR76
Vanbrugh Ter, SE3 ... 104 EF81
Vanburgh Cl, Orp. BR6 ... 145 ES102
Vancouver Cl, Epsom KT19 ... 156 CQ111
Orpington BR6 ... 163 ET105
Vancouver Rd, SE23 ... 123 DY89
Edgware HA8 ... 42 CP53
Hayes UB4 ... 77 BV70
Richmond TW10 ... 117 CJ91
Vanderbilt Rd, SW18 ... 120 DC88
Vanderville Gdns, N2
off Tarling Rd ... 44 DC54
Vandome Cl, E16 ... 86 EH72
Vandon Pas, SW1 ... 199 L6
Vandon St, SW1 ... 199 L6
Van Dyck Av, N.Mal. KT3 ... 138 CR101
Vandyke Cl, SW15 ... 119 CX87
Redhill RH1 ... 184 DF131
Vandyke Cross, SE9 ... 124 EL85
Vandy St, EC2 ... 197 M5
Vane Cl, NW3 ... 64 DD63
Harrow HA3 ... 62 CM58
Vanessa Cl, Belv. DA17 ... 106 FA78
Vanessa Wk, Grav. DA12 ... 131 GM92
Vanessa Way, Bex. DA5 ... 127 FD90
Vane St, SW1 ... 199 L8
Vanguard Cl, E16 ... 86 EG71
Croydon CR0 ... 141 DP102
Romford RM7 ... 51 FB54
Vanguard St, SE8 ... 103 EA81
Vanguard Way, Cat. CR3
off Slines Oak Rd ... 177 EB121
Wallington SM6 ... 159 DL108
Warlingham CR6 ... 177 EB121
Vanneck Sq, SW15 ... 119 CU85
Vanner Pt, E9 *off Wick Rd* ... 85 DX65
Vanners Par, W.Byf. (Byfleet)
KT14 *off Brewery La* ... 152 BL113
Vanoc Gdns, Brom. BR1 ... 124 EG90
Vanquisher Wk, Grav. DA12 ... 131 GM90
Vansittart Rd, E7 ... 68 EF63
Vansittart St, SE14 ... 103 DY80
Vanston Pl, SW6 ... 100 DA80
Vantage Ms, E14 ... 204 E3
Vantage Pl, W8
off Abingdon Rd ... 100 DA76
Vant Rd, SW17 ... 120 DF92
Varcoe Rd, SE16 ... 102 DV78
Vardens Rd, SW11 ... 100 DD84
Varden St, E1 ... 84 DV72
Vardon Cl, W3 ... 80 CR72
Varley Par, NW9 ... 62 CS56
Varley Rd, E16 ... 86 EH72
Varley Way, Mitch. CR4 ... 140 DD96
Varna Rd, SW6 ... 99 CY80
Hampton TW12 ... 136 CB95
Varndell St, NW1 ... 195 K2
Varney Cl, Wal.Cr. (Chsht.) EN7 ... 14 DU27
Varsity Dr, Twick. TW1 ... 117 CE85
Varsity Row, SW14
off William's La ... 98 CQ82
Vartry Rd, N15 ... 66 DR58
Vassall Rd, SW9 ... 101 DN80
Vauban Est, SE16 ... 202 A7
Vauban St, SE16 ... 202 A7
Vaughan Av, NW4 ... 63 CU57
W6 ... 99 CT77
Hornchurch RM12 ... 72 FK63
Vaughan Cl, Hmptn. TW12
off Oak Av ... 116 BY93
Vaughan Gdns, Ilf. IG1 ... 69 EM59
Vaughan Rd, E15 ... 86 EF65
SE5 ... 102 DQ83
Harrow HA1 ... 60 CC59
Thames Ditton KT7 ... 137 CH101
Welling DA16 ... 105 ET82
Vaughan St, SE16 ... 203 M5
Vaughan Way, E1 ... 202 B1
Vaughan Williams Cl, SE8
off Watson's St ... 103 EA80
Vaux Cres, Walt. KT12 ... 153 BV107
VAUXHALL, SE11 ... 101 DL78
⇌ **Vauxhall** ... 101 DL79
⊖ **Vauxhall** ... 101 DL79
Vauxhall Br, SE1 ... 101 DL78
SW1 ... 101 DL78
Vauxhall Br Rd, SW1 ... 199 L8
Vauxhall Cl, Grav. (Nthflt.)
DA11 ... 131 GF87
Vauxhall Gdns, S.Croy. CR2 ... 160 DQ107
Vauxhall Gdns Est, SE11 ... 101 DM78
Vauxhall Gro, SW8 ... 101 DL79
Vauxhall Pl, Dart. DA1 ... 128 FL87
Vauxhall St, SE11 ... 101 DM78
Vauxhall Wk, SE11 ... 200 B10
Vawdrey Cl, E1 ... 84 DW70
Veals Mead, Mitch. CR4 ... 140 DE95
Vectis Gdns, SW17
off Vectis Rd ... 121 DH93
Vectis Rd, SW17 ... 121 DH93
Veda Rd, SE13 ... 103 EA84
Vega Cres, Nthwd. HA6 ... 39 BT50
Vegal Cres, Egh. (Eng.Grn.)
TW20 ... 112 AW92
Vega Rd, Bushey WD23 ... 40 CC45
Veldene Way, Har. HA2 ... 60 BZ62
Velde Way, SE22
off East Dulwich Gro ... 122 DS85
Velletri Ho, E2 ... 85 DX68
Vellum Dr, Cars. SM5 ... 140 DG104
Venables Cl, Dag. RM10 ... 71 FB63
Venables St, NW8 ... 194 A6
Vencourt Pl, W6 ... 99 CU78
Venetian Rd, SE5 ... 102 DQ82
Venetia Rd, N4 ... 65 DP58
W5 ... 97 CK75
Venette Cl, Rain. RM13 ... 89 FH71
Venner Rd, SE26 ... 122 DW93
Venners Cl, Bexh. DA7 ... 107 FE82
Venn St, SW4 ... 101 DJ84
Ventnor Av, Stan. HA7 ... 41 CH53
Ventnor Dr, N20 ... 44 DB48
Ventnor Gdns, Bark. IG11 ... 87 ES65
Ventnor Rd, SE14 ... 103 DX80
Sutton SM2 ... 158 DB108
Venton Cl, Wok. GU21 ... 166 AV117
Ventura Pk, St.Alb. AL2 ... 9 CF29
Venture Cl, Bex. DA5 ... 126 EY87
Venue St, E14 ... 85 EC71
Venus Hill, Hem.H. (Bov.) HP3 ... 5 BA31
Venus Rd, SE18 ... 105 EM76
Veny Cres, Horn. RM12 ... 72 FK64
Vera Av, N21 ... 29 DN43
Vera Ct, Wat. WD19 ... 40 BX45
Vera Lynn Cl, E7
off Dames Rd ... 68 EG63
Vera Rd, SW6 ... 99 CY81
Verbena Cl, E16
off Pretoria Rd ... 86 EF70
South Ockendon RM15 ... 91 FW72
West Drayton UB7
off Magnolia St ... 94 BK78
Verbena Gdns, W6 ... 99 CU78
Verdant La, SE6 ... 124 EE88
Verdayne Av, Croy. CR0 ... 143 DX102
Verdayne Gdns, Warl. CR6 ... 176 DW116
Verderers Rd, Chig. IG7 ... 50 EU50
Verdun Rd, SE18 ... 106 EU79
SW13 ... 99 CU79
Verdure Cl, Wat. WD25 ... 8 BY32
Vereker Dr, Sun. TW16 ... 135 BU97
Vereker Rd, W14 ... 99 CY78
Vere Rd, Loug. IG10 ... 33 EQ42
Vere St, W1 ... 195 H9
Verity Cl, W11 ... 81 CY72
Vermeer Gdns, SE15
off Elland Rd ... 102 DW84
Vermont Cl, Enf. EN2 ... 29 DP42
Vermont Rd, SE19 ... 122 DR93
SW18 ... 120 DB86
Sutton SM1 ... 140 DB104
Verney Gdns, Dag. RM9 ... 70 EY63
Verney Rd, SE16 ... 102 DU79
Dagenham RM9 ... 70 EY64
Slough SL3 ... 93 BA77
Verney St, NW10 ... 62 CR62
Verney Way, SE16 ... 102 DV78
Vernham Rd, SE18 ... 105 EQ79
Vernon Av, E12 ... 69 EM63
SW20 ... 139 CX96
Enfield EN3 ... 31 DY36
Vernon Av, Wdf.Grn IG8 ... 48 EH52
Vernon Cl, Cher. (Ott.) KT16 ... 151 BD107
Epsom KT19 ... 156 CQ107
Orpington BR5 ... 146 EV97
Vernon Ct, Stan. HA7
off Vernon Dr ... 41 CH53
Vernon Cres, Barn. EN4 ... 28 DG44
Brentwood CM13 ... 55 GA48
Vernon Dr, Cat. CR3 ... 176 DQ122
Stanmore HA7 ... 41 CG53
Uxbridge (Hare.) UB9 ... 38 BJ53
Vernon Ms, E17 *off Vernon Rd* ... 67 DZ56
W14 *off Vernon St* ... 99 CY77
Vernon Pl, WC1 ... 196 A7
Vernon Ri, WC1 ... 196 C2
Greenford UB6 ... 61 CD64
Vernon Rd, E3 ... 85 DZ68
E11 ... 68 EE60
E15 ... 86 EE66
E17 ... 67 DZ57
N8 ... 65 DN55
SW14 ... 98 CR83
Bushey WD23 ... 24 BY43
Feltham TW13 ... 115 BT89
Ilford IG3 ... 69 ET60
Romford RM5 ... 51 FC50
Sutton SM1 ... 158 DC106
Swanscombe DA10 ... 130 FZ86
Vernon Sq, WC1 ... 196 C2
Vernon St, W14 ... 99 CY77
Vernon Wk, Tad. KT20 ... 173 CX120
Vernon Yd, W11
off Portobello Rd ... 81 CZ73
Veroan Rd, Bexh. DA7 ... 106 EY82
Verona Cl, Uxb. UB8 ... 76 BJ72
Verona Dr, Surb. KT6 ... 138 CL103
Verona Gdns, Grav. DA12 ... 131 GL91
Verona Rd, E7 *off Upton La* ... 86 EG66
Veronica Cl, Rom. RM3 ... 52 FJ52
Veronica Gdns, SW16 ... 141 DJ95
Veronica Rd, SW17 ... 121 DH90
Veronique Gdns, Ilf. IG6 ... 69 EP57
Verralls, Wok. GU22 ... 167 BB117
Verran Rd, SW12
off Balham Gro ... 121 DH87
Versailles Rd, SE20 ... 122 DU94
Verulam Av, E17 ... 67 DZ58
Purley CR8 ... 159 DJ112
Verulam Bldgs, WC1 ... 196 C6
Verulam Pas, Wat. WD17 ... 23 BV40
Verulam Rd, Grnf. UB6 ... 78 CA70
Verulam St, WC1 ... 196 D6
Verwood Dr, Barn. EN4 ... 28 DF41
Verwood Rd, Har. HA2 ... 40 CC54
Veryan, Wok. GU21 ... 166 AU117
Veryan Cl, Orp. BR5 ... 146 EW98
Vesey Path, E14
off East India Dock Rd ... 85 EB72
Vespan Rd, W12 ... 99 CU75
Vesta Rd, SE4 ... 103 DY82
Vestris Rd, SE23 ... 123 DX89
Vestry Ms, SE5 ... 102 DS81
Vestry Rd, E17 ... 67 EB56
SE5 ... 102 DS81
Vestry St, N1 ... 197 K2
Vetch Cl, Felt. TW14 ... 115 BT88
Vevey St, SE6 ... 123 DZ89
Vexil Cl, Purf. RM19 ... 109 FR77
Veysey Gdns, Dag. RM10 ... 70 FA62
Viaduct Pl, E2 *off Viaduct St* ... 84 DV69
Viaduct St, E2 ... 84 DV69
Vian Av, Enf. EN3 ... 31 DY35
Vian St, SE13 ... 103 EB83
Vibart Gdns, SW2 ... 121 DM87
Vibart Wk, N1 *off Outram Pl* ... 83 DL67
Vicarage Av, SE3 ... 104 EG81
Egham TW20 ... 113 BB93
Vicarage Cl, Brwd. CM14 ... 54 FS49
Erith DA8 ... 107 FC79
Northolt UB5 ... 78 BZ66
Potters Bar EN6 ... 12 DF30
Ruislip HA4 ... 59 BR59
Tadworth KT20 ... 173 CY124
Worcester Park KT4 ... 138 CS102
Vicarage Ct, W8
off Vicarage Gate ... 100 DB75
Egham TW20 ... 113 BB93
Feltham TW14 ... 115 BQ87
Vicarage Cres, SW11 ... 100 DD81
Egham TW20 ... 113 BB92
Vicarage Dr, SW14 ... 118 CR85
Barking IG11 ... 87 EQ66
Beckenham BR3 ... 143 EA95
Gravesend (Nthflt.) DA11 ... 130 GC86
Vicarage Fm Rd, Houns.
TW3, TW5 ... 96 BY82
Vicarage Flds, Walt. KT12 ... 136 BW100
Vicarage Fld Shop Cen, Bark.
IG11 ... 87 EQ66
Vicarage Gdns, SW14
off Vicarage Rd ... 118 CQ85
W8 ... 82 DA74
Mitcham CR4 ... 140 DE97
Vicarage Gate, W8 ... 100 DB75
Vicarage Gate Ms, Tad. KT20 ... 173 CY124
Vicarage Gro, SE5 ... 102 DR81
Vicarage Hill, West. TN16 ... 189 ER126
Vicarage La, E6 ... 87 EM69
E15 ... 86 EE66
Chigwell IG7 ... 49 EQ47
Epsom KT17 ... 157 CU109
Hemel Hempstead (Bov.) HP3 ... 5 BB26
Ilford IG1 ... 69 ER60
Kings Langley WD4 ... 6 BM29
Leatherhead KT22 ... 171 CH122
Sevenoaks (Dunt.Grn.) TN13
off London Rd ... 181 FD119
Staines (Laleham) TW18 ... 134 BH97
Staines (Wrays.) TW19 ... 112 AY88
Vicarage Pk, SE18 ... 105 EQ78
Vicarage Path, N8 ... 65 DL59
Vicarage Pl, Slou. SL1 ... 92 AU76
Vicarage Rd, E10 ... 67 EB60
E15 ... 86 EF66
N17 ... 46 DU52
NW4 ... 63 CU58
SE18 ... 105 EQ78
Vicarage Rd, SW14 ... 118 CQ85
Bexley DA5 ... 127 FB88
Croydon CR0 ... 141 DN104
Dagenham RM10 ... 89 FB65
Egham TW20 ... 113 BB93
Epping CM16 ... 18 EW29
Hornchurch RM12 ... 71 FG60
Kingston upon Thames KT1 ... 137 CK96
Kingston upon Thames
(Hmptn.W.) KT1 ... 137 CJ95
Staines TW18 ... 113 BE91
Sunbury-on-Thames TW16 ... 115 BT92
Sutton SM1 ... 158 DB105
Teddington TW11 ... 117 CG92
Twickenham TW2 ... 117 CE89
Twickenham (Whitton) TW2 ... 116 CC86
Watford WD18 ... 23 BU44
Woking GU22 ... 167 AZ121
Woodford Green IG8 ... 48 EL52
Vicarage Sq, Grays RM17 ... 110 GA79
Vicarage Wk, Reig. RH2
off Chartway ... 184 DB134
Vicarage Way, NW10 ... 62 CR62
Gerrards Cross SL9 ... 57 AZ58
Harrow HA2 ... 60 CA59
Slough (Colnbr.) SL3 ... 93 BC80
Vicars Br Cl, Wem. HA0 ... 80 CL68
Vicars Cl, E9 *off Northiam St* ... 84 DW67
E15 ... 86 EG67
Enfield EN1 ... 30 DS40
Vicars Hill, SE13 ... 103 EB84
Vicars Moor La, N21 ... 45 DN45
Vicars Oak Rd, SE19 ... 122 DS93
Vicars Rd, NW5 ... 64 DG64
Vicars Wk, Dag. RM8 ... 70 EV62
Viceroy Cl, N2 *off Market Pl* ... 64 DE56
Viceroy Ct, NW8
off Prince Albert Rd ... 82 DE68
Viceroy Par, N2 *off High Rd* ... 64 DE55
Viceroy Rd, SW8 ... 101 DL81
Vickers Cl, Wall. SM6
off Hurricane Rd ... 159 DM108
Vickers Dr N, Wey. KT13 ... 152 BL110
Vickers Dr S, Wey. KT13 ... 152 BL111
Vickers Rd, Erith DA8 ... 107 FD78
Vickers Way, Houns. TW4 ... 116 BY85
Victor App, Horn. RM12
off Abbs Cross Gdns ... 72 FK60
Victor Cl, Horn. RM12 ... 72 FK60
Victor Ct, Horn. RM12 ... 72 FK60
Rainham RM13
off Askwith Rd ... 89 FD68
Victor Gdns, Horn. RM12 ... 72 FK60
Victor Gro, Wem. HA0 ... 80 CL66
⇌ **Victoria** ... 199 J8
⊖ **Victoria** ... 199 J7
★ **Victoria & Albert Mus**,
SW7 ... 198 A7
Victoria Arc, SW1
off Terminus Pl ... 101 DH76
Victoria Av, E6 ... 86 EK67
EC2 ... 197 N7
N3 ... 43 CZ53
Barnet EN4 ... 28 DD42
Gravesend DA12
off Sheppy Pl ... 131 GH87
Grays RM16 ... 110 GC75
Hounslow TW3 ... 116 BZ85
Romford RM5 ... 51 FB51
South Croydon CR2 ... 160 DQ110
Surbiton KT6 ... 137 CK101
Uxbridge UB10 ... 77 BP66
Wallington SM6 ... 140 DG104
Wembley HA9 ... 80 CP65
West Molesey KT8 ... 136 CA97
Victoria Cl, Barn. EN4 ... 28 DD42
Grays RM16 ... 110 GC75
Hayes UB3
off Commonwealth Av ... 77 BR72
Rickmansworth WD3
off Nightingale Rd ... 38 BK45
Waltham Cross EN8 ... 15 DX30
West Molesey KT8
off Victoria Av ... 136 CA97
Weybridge KT13 ... 135 BR104
★ **Victoria Coach Sta**, SW1 ... 199 H9
Victoria Cotts, Rich. TW9 ... 98 CM81
Victoria Ct, Wem. HA9 ... 80 CN65
Victoria Cres, N15 ... 66 DS57
SE19 ... 122 DS93
SW19 ... 119 CZ94
Iver SL0 ... 76 BG73
Victoria Dock Rd, E16 ... 86 EE72
Victoria Dr, SW19 ... 119 CX87
Dartford (S.Darenth) DA4 ... 149 FR96
Victoria Embk, EC4 ... 200 B1
SW1 ... 200 A4
WC2 ... 200 B1
★ **Victoria Embankment Gdns**,
WC2 ... 200 A1
Victoria Gdns, W11 ... 82 DA74
Hounslow TW5 ... 96 BY81
Westerham (Bigg.H.) TN16 ... 178 EJ115
Victoria Gro, N12 ... 44 DC50
W8 ... 100 DC76
Victoria Gro Ms, W2
off Ossington St ... 82 DB73
Victoria Hill Rd, Swan. BR8 ... 147 FF95
H **Victoria Hosp**, Rom. RM1 ... 71 FF56
Victoria Ind Est, NW10 ... 80 CS69
Victoria Ind Pk, Dart. DA1 ... 128 FL85
Victoria La, Barn. EN5 ... 27 CZ42
Hayes UB3 ... 95 BQ78
Victoria Ms, NW6 ... 82 DA67
SW4 *off Victoria Ri* ... 101 DH84
SW18 ... 120 DC88
Victorian Gro, N16 ... 66 DS62
Victorian Rd, N16 ... 66 DS62
★ **Victoria Park**, E9 ... 85 DY66
Victoria Pk, E9 ... 85 DY66
Victoria Pk Rd, E9 ... 84 DW67
Victoria Pk Sq, E2 ... 84 DW69
Victoria Pas, NW8
off Cunningham Pl ... 82 DD70

Vic - Wal

Victoria Pas, Wat. WD18 23 BV42
Victoria Pl, SW1 199 J8
Epsom KT17 156 CS112
Richmond TW9 117 CK85
Victoria Pt, E13
off Victoria Rd 86 EG68
Victoria Retail Pk, Ruis. HA4 60 BY64
Victoria Ri, SW4 101 DH83
Victoria Rd, E4 48 EE46
E11 68 EE63
E13 86 EG68
E17 47 EC54
E18 48 EH54
N4 65 DM59
N9 46 DT49
N15 66 DU56
N18 46 DT49
N22 45 DJ53
NW4 63 CW56
NW6 81 CZ67
NW7 43 CT50
NW10 80 CR71
SW14 98 CR83
W3 80 CR71
W5 79 CH71
W8 100 DC76
Addlestone KT15 152 BK105
Barking IG11 87 EP65
Barnet EN4 28 DD42
Bexleyheath DA6 106 FA84
Brentwood CM14 54 FW49
Bromley BR2 144 EK99
Buckhurst Hill IG9 48 EK47
Bushey WD23 40 CB46
Chislehurst BR7 125 EN92
Coulsdon CR5 175 DK115
Dagenham RM10 71 FB64
Dartford DA1 128 FK85
Erith DA8 107 FE79
Feltham TW13 115 BV88
Gravesend (Nthflt.) DA11 131 GF88
Kingston upon Thames KT1 138 CM96
Mitcham CR4 120 DE94
Romford RM1 71 FE58
Ruislip HA4 60 BW64
Sevenoaks TN13 191 FH125
Sidcup DA15 125 ET90
Slough SL2 74 AV74
Southall UB2 96 BZ76
Staines TW18 113 BE90
Surbiton KT6 137 CK100
Sutton SM1 158 DD106
Teddington TW11 117 CG93
Twickenham TW1 117 CG87
Uxbridge UB8
off New Windsor St 76 BJ66
Waltham Abbey EN9 15 EC34
Watford WD24 23 BV38
Weybridge KT13 135 BR104
Woking GU22 166 AY117
Victoria Scott Ct, Dart. DA1 107 FE83
Victoria Sq, SW1 199 J6
Victoria Sta, SW1 199 J8
Victoria Steps, Brent. TW8
off Kew Br Rd 98 CM79
Victoria St, E15 86 EE66
SW1 199 K7
Belvedere DA17 106 EZ78
Egham (Eng.Grn.) TW20 112 AW93
Slough SL1 92 AT75
Victoria Ter, N4 65 DN60
NW10 *off Old Oak La* 80 CS69
Harrow HA1 61 CE60
★ **Victoria Twr**, SW1 199 P6
Victoria Vil, Rich. TW9 98 CM83
Victoria Way, SE7 205 P10
Weybridge KT13 135 BR104
Woking GU21 166 AY117
Victoria Wf, E14 203 L1
Victoria Yd, E1
off Fairclough St 84 DU72
Victor Rd, NW10 81 CV69
SE20 123 DX94
Harrow HA2 60 CC55
Teddington TW11 117 CE91
Victors Cres, Brwd. CM13 55 GB47
Victors Dr, Hmptn. TW12 116 BY93
Victor Smith Ct, St.Alb. AL2 8 CA31
Victors Way, Barn. EN5 27 CZ41
Victor Vil, N9 46 DR48
Victor Wk, NW9 42 CS53
Hornchurch RM12
off Abbs Cross Gdns 72 FK60
Victory Av, Mord. SM4 140 DC99
Victory Business Cen, Islw.
TW7 97 CF83
Victory Cl, Grays (Chaff.Hun.)
RM16 109 FW77
Victory Pk Rd, Add. KT15 152 BJ105
Victory Pl, E14 *off Northey St* 85 DY73
SE17 201 J8
SE19 *off Westow St* 122 DS93
Victory Rd, E11 68 EH56
SW19 120 DC94
Chertsey KT16 134 BG102
Rainham RM13 89 FG68
Victory Rd Ms, SW19
off Victory Rd 120 DC94
Victory Wk, SE8 *off Ship St* 103 EA81
Victory Way, SE16 203 L5
Dartford DA2 108 FQ84
Hounslow TW5 96 BW78
Romford RM7 51 FB54
Vidler Cl, Chess. KT9
off Merritt Gdns 155 CJ107
Vienna Cl, Ilf. IG5 68 EK55
View, The, SE2 106 EY78
View Cl, N6 64 DF59
Chigwell IG7 49 ER50
Harrow HA1 61 CD56
Westerham (Bigg.H.) TN16 178 EJ116
Viewfield Cl, Har. HA3 62 CL59
Viewfield Rd, SW18 119 CZ86
Bexley DA5 126 EW88
Viewland Rd, SE18 105 ET78
Viewlands Av, West. TN16 179 ES120
View Rd, N6 64 DF59
Potters Bar EN6 12 DC32
Viga Rd, N21 29 DN44
Vigerons Way, Grays RM16 111 GH77
Viggory La, Wok. GU21 166 AW115
Vigilant Cl, SE26 122 DU91
Vigilant Way, Grav. DA12 131 GL92
Vignoles Rd, Rom. RM7 70 FA59
Vigo St, W1 199 K1
Viking Cl, E3 *off Selwyn Rd* 85 DY68
Viking Ct, SW6 100 DA79
Viking Gdns, E6
off Jack Dash Way 86 EL70
Viking Pl, E10 67 DZ60
Viking Rd, Grav. (Nthflt.)
DA11 130 GC90
Southall UB1 78 BY73
Viking Way, Brwd. CM15 54 FV45
Erith DA8 107 FC76
Rainham RM13 89 FG70
Villa Ct, Dart. DA1
off Greenbanks 128 FL89
Villacourt Rd, SE18 106 EU80
Village, The, SE7 104 EJ79
Greenhithe (Bluewater)
DA9 129 FT87
Village Arc, E4 *off Station Rd* 47 ED46
Village Cl, E4 47 EC50
NW3 *off Ornan Rd* 64 DE64
Weybridge KT13
off Oatlands Dr 135 BR104
Village Ct, E17
off Eden Rd 67 EB57
Village Gdns, Epsom KT17 157 CT110
Village Grn Av, West. (Bigg.H.)
TN16 178 EL117
Village Grn Rd, Dart. DA1 107 FG84
Village Grn Way, West. (Bigg.H.)
TN16 *off Main Rd* 178 EL117
Village Hts, Wdf.Grn. IG8 48 EF50
Village Ms, NW9 62 CR61
Village Pk Cl, Enf. EN1 30 DS44
Village Rd, N3 43 CY53
Egham TW20 133 BC97
Enfield EN1 30 DS44
Uxbridge (Denh.) UB9 57 BF61
Village Row, Sutt. SM2 158 DA108
Village Way, NW10 62 CR63
SE21 122 DR86
Amersham HP7 20 AX40
Ashford TW15 114 BM91
Beckenham BR3 143 EA96
Pinner HA5 60 BY59
South Croydon CR2 160 DU113
Village Way E, Har. HA2 60 BZ59
Villa Rd, SW9 101 DN83
Villas Rd, SE18 105 EQ77
Villa St, SE17 102 DR78
Villier Ct, Uxb. UB8
off Villier St 76 BK68
Villiers, The, Wey. KT13 153 BR107
Villiers Av, Surb. KT5 138 CM99
Twickenham TW2 116 BZ88
Villiers Cl, E10 67 EA61
Surbiton KT5 138 CM98
Villiers Ct, N20
off Buckingham Av 44 DC45
Villiers Gro, Sutt. SM2 157 CX109
Villiers Path, Surb. KT5 138 CL99
Villiers Rd, NW2 81 CU65
Beckenham BR3 143 DX96
Isleworth TW7 97 CE82
Kingston upon Thames KT1 138 CM97
Southall UB1 78 BZ74
Watford WD19 24 BY44
Villiers St, WC2 199 P1
Villier St, Uxb. UB8 76 BK68
Vincam Cl, Twick. TW2 116 CA87
Vincent Av, Cars. SM5 158 DD111
Croydon CR0 161 DY111
Surbiton KT5 138 CP102
Vincent Cl, SE16 203 K5
Barnet EN5 28 DA41
Bromley BR2 144 EH98
Chertsey KT16 133 BE101
Esher KT10 136 CB104
Ilford IG6 49 EQ51
Leatherhead (Fetch.) KT22 170 CB123
Sidcup DA15 125 ES88
Waltham Cross (Chsht.) EN8 15 DY28
West Drayton UB7 94 BN79
Vincent Dr, Shep. TW17 135 BS97
Uxbridge UB10
off Birch Cres 76 BM67
Vincent Gdns, NW2 63 CT62
Vincent Grn, Couls. CR5
off High Rd 174 DF120
Vincent Ms, E3 85 EA68
Vincent Rd, E4 47 ED51
N15 66 DQ56
N22 45 DN54
SE18 105 EP77
W3 98 CQ76
Chertsey KT16 133 BE101
Cobham (Stoke D'Ab.) KT11 170 BY116
Coulsdon CR5 175 DJ116
Croydon CR0 142 DS101
Dagenham RM9 88 EY66
Hounslow TW4 96 BX82
Isleworth TW7 97 CD81
Kingston upon Thames KT1 138 CN97
Rainham RM13 90 FJ70
Wembley HA0 80 CM66
Vincent Row, Hmptn. (Hmptn.H.)
TW12 116 CC93
Vincent's Cl, Couls. CR5 174 DF120
Vincents Path, Nthlt. UB5
off Arnold Rd 78 BY65
Vincent Sq, SW1 199 L8
Westerham (Bigg.H.) TN16 162 EJ113
Vincent St, E16 86 EF71
SW1 199 M8
Vincent Ter, N1 83 DP68
Vince St, EC1 197 L3
Vine, The, Sev. TN13 191 FH124
Vine Av, Sev. TN13 191 FH124
Vine Cl, Stai. TW19 114 BG85
Surbiton KT5 138 CM100
Sutton SM1 140 DC104
West Drayton UB7 94 BN77
Vine Ct, E1
off Whitechapel Rd 84 DU71
Harrow HA3 62 CL58
Vine Ct Rd, Sev. TN13 191 FJ124
Vinegar All, E17 67 EB56
Vine Gdns, Ilf. IG1 69 EQ64
Vinegar St, E1 202 D2
Vinegar Yd, SE1 201 M4
Vine Gro, Uxb. UB10 76 BN66
Vine Hill, EC1 196 D5
Vine La, SE1 201 N3
Uxbridge UB10 76 BM67
Vine Pl, W5 *off The Common* 80 CL74
Hounslow TW3 96 CB84
Viner Cl, Walt. KT12 136 BW100
Vineries, The, N14 29 DJ44
Enfield EN1 30 DS41
Vineries Bk, NW7 43 CV50
Vineries Cl, Dag. RM9
off Heathway 88 FA65
West Drayton UB7 94 BN79
Vine Rd, E15 86 EF66
SW13 99 CT83
East Molesey KT8 136 CC98
Orpington BR6 163 ET107
Slough (Stoke P.) SL2 74 AT65
Vines Av, N3 44 DB53
Vine Sq, W14 99 CZ78
Vine St, EC3 197 P10
W1 199 L1
Romford RM7 71 FC57
Uxbridge UB8 76 BK67
Vine St Br, EC1 196 E5
Vine Way, Brwd. CM14 54 FW46
Vine Yd, SE1 201 J4
Vineyard, The, Rich. TW10 118 CL85
Vineyard Av, NW7 43 CY52
Vineyard Cl, SE6 123 EA88
Kingston upon Thames
KT1 138 CM97
Vineyard Gro, N3 44 DB53
Vineyard Hill, Pot.B. (Northaw)
EN6 12 DG29
Vineyard Hill Rd, SW19 120 DA91
Vineyard Pas, Rich. TW9
off Paradise Rd 118 CL85
Vineyard Path, SW14 98 CR83
Vineyard Rd, Felt. TW13 115 BU90
Vineyard Row, Kings.T. KT1 137 CJ95
Vineyards Rd, Pot.B. EN6 12 DF30
Vineyard Wk, EC1 196 D4
Viney Bk, Croy. CR0 161 DZ109
Viney Rd, SE13 103 EB83
Vining St, SW9 101 DN84
Vinlake Av, Uxb. UB10 58 BM62
★ **Vinopolis**, SE1 201 J2
Vinson Cl, Orp. BR6 146 EU102
Vintners Pl, EC4
off Upper Thames St 84 DQ73
Vintry Ms, E17
off Cleveland Pk Cres 67 EA56
Viola Av, SE2 106 EV77
Feltham TW14 116 BW86
Staines TW19 114 BK88
Viola Cl, S.Ock. RM15 91 FW69
Viola Sq, W12 81 CT73
Violet Av, Enf. EN2 30 DR38
Uxbridge UB8 76 BM71
Violet Cl, E16 86 EE70
SE8 *off Dorking Cl* 103 DZ79
Wallington SM6 141 DH102
Violet Gdns, Croy. CR0 159 DP106
Violet Hill, NW8 82 DC68
Violet La, Croy. CR0 159 DP106
Violet Rd, E3 85 EB70
E17 67 EA58
E18 48 EH54
Violet St, E2
off Three Colts La 84 DV70
Violet Way, Rick. (Loud.) WD3 22 BJ42
Virgil Pl, W1 194 D7
Virgil St, SE1 200 C6
Virginia Av, Vir.W. GU25 132 AW99
Virginia Beeches, Vir.W.
GU25 132 AW97
Virginia Cl, Ashtd. KT21
off Skinners La 171 CK118
New Malden KT3
off Willow Rd 138 CQ98
Romford RM5 51 FC52
Staines TW18
off Blacksmiths La 134 BJ97
Weybridge KT13 153 BQ107
Virginia Dr, Vir.W. GU25 132 AW99
Virginia Gdns, Ilf. IG6 49 EQ54
Virginia Pl, Cob. KT11 153 BU114
Virginia Rd, E2 197 P3
Thornton Heath CR7 141 DP95
Virginia St, E1 202 C1
Virginia Wk, SW2 121 DM86
Gravesend DA12 131 GK93
VIRGINIA WATER 132 AX99
⇌ **Virginia Water** 132 AY99
Viscount Cl, N11 45 DH50
Viscount Dr, E6 87 EM71
Viscount Gdns, W.Byf. KT14 152 BL112
Viscount Gro, Nthlt. UB5
off Wayfarer Rd 78 BX69
Viscount Rd, Stai. (Stanw.)
TW19 114 BK88
Viscount St, EC1 197 H5
Viscount Way, Houns. (Hthrw.Air.)
TW6 95 BS84
Vista, The, SE9 124 EK86
Sidcup DA14
off Langdon Shaw 125 ET92
Vista Av, Enf. EN3 31 DX40
Vista Dr, Ilf. IG4 68 EK57
Vista Way, Har. HA3 62 CL58
Viveash Cl, Hayes UB3 95 BT76
Vivian Av, NW4 63 CV57
Wembley HA9 62 CN64
Vivian Cl, Wat. WD19 39 BU46
Vivian Comma Cl, N4
off Blackstock Rd 65 DP62
Vivian Gdns, Wat. WD19 39 BU46
Wembley HA9 62 CN64
Vivian Rd, E3 85 DY68
Vivian Sq, SE15
off Scylla Rd 102 DV83
Vivian Way, N2 64 DD57
Vivien Cl, Chess. KT9 156 CL108
Vivienne Cl, Twick. TW1 117 CJ86
Voce Rd, SE18 105 ER80
Voewood Cl, N.Mal. KT3 139 CT100
Voltaire Rd, SW4 101 DK83
Voltaire Way, Hayes UB3
off Judge Heath La 77 BS73
Volt Av, NW10 80 CR69
Volta Way, Croy. CR0 141 DM102
Voluntary Pl, E11 68 EG58
Vorley Rd, N19 65 DJ61
Voss Ct, SW16 121 DL93
Voss St, E2 84 DU69
Voyagers Cl, SE28 88 EW72
Voysey Cl, N3 63 CY55
Vulcan Cl, E6 87 EN72
Wallington SM6
off De Havilland Rd 159 DM108
Vulcan Gate, Enf. EN2 29 DN40
Vulcan Rd, SE4 103 DZ82
Vulcan Sq, E14 204 A9
Vulcan Ter, SE4 103 DZ82
Vulcan Way, N7 83 DM65
Croydon (New Adgtn.)
CR0 162 EE110
Vyne, The, Bexh. DA7 107 FB83
Vyner Rd, W3 80 CR73
Vyner St, E2 84 DV67
Vyners Way, Uxb. UB10 58 BN64
Vyse Cl, Barn. EN5 27 CW42

W

Wacketts, Wal.Cr. (Chsht.) EN7
off Spicersfield 14 DU27
Wadbrook St, Kings.T. KT1 137 CK96
Wadding St, SE17 201 K9
Waddington Av, Couls. CR5 175 DN120
Waddington Cl, Couls. CR5 175 DP119
Enfield EN1 30 DS42
Waddington Rd, E15 67 ED64
Waddington St, E15 85 ED65
Waddington Way, SE19 122 DQ94
WADDON, Croy. 141 DN103
⇌ **Waddon** 159 DN105
Waddon Cl, Croy. CR0 141 DN104
Waddon Ct Rd, Croy. CR0 159 DN105
Waddon Marsh 141 DM102
Waddon Marsh Way, Croy.
CR0 141 DM102
Waddon New Rd, Croy. CR0 141 DP104
Waddon Pk Av, Croy. CR0 159 DN105
Waddon Rd, Croy. CR0 141 DN104
Waddon Way, Croy. CR0 159 DP107
Wade Av, Orp. BR5 146 EX101
Wades Gro, N21 45 DN45
Wades Hill, N21 29 DN44
Wades La, Tedd. TW11
off High St 117 CG92
Wades Ms, N21 *off Wades Hill* 45 DN45
Wadeson St, E2 84 DV68
Wades Pl, E14 85 EB73
Wadeville Av, Rom. RM6 70 EZ59
Wadeville Cl, Belv. DA17 106 FA79
Wadham Av, E17 47 EB52
Wadham Cl, Shep. TW17 135 BQ101
Wadham Gdns, NW3 82 DE67
Greenford UB6 79 CD65
Wadham Rd, E17 47 EB53
SW15 99 CY84
Abbots Langley WD5 7 BT31
Wadhurst Cl, SE20 142 DV96
Wadhurst Rd, SW8 101 DJ81
W4 98 CR76
Wadley Rd, E11 68 EE59
Wadsworth Business Cen, Grnf.
UB6 79 CJ68
Wadsworth Cl, Enf. EN3 31 DX43
Greenford UB6 79 CJ68
Wadsworth Rd, Grnf. UB6 79 CH68
Wager St, E3 85 DZ70
Waggon Ms, N14
off Chase Side 45 DJ46
Waggon Rd, Barn. EN4 28 DC37
Waghorn Rd, E13 86 EJ67
Harrow HA3 61 CK55
Waghorn St, SE15 102 DU83
Wagner St, SE15 102 DW80
Wagon Rd, Barn. EN4 28 DB36
Wagon Way, Rick. (Loud.)
WD3 22 BJ41
Wagstaff Gdns, Dag. RM9 88 EW66
Wagtail Cl, NW9
off Swan Dr 42 CS54
Wagtail Gdns, S.Croy. CR2 161 DY110
Wagtail Wk, Beck. BR3 143 EC99
Wagtail Way, Orp. BR5 146 EX98
Waid Cl, Dart. DA1 128 FM86
Waights Ct, Kings.T. KT2 138 CL95
Wain Cl, Pot.B. EN6 12 DB29
Wainfleet Av, Rom. RM5 51 FC54
Wainford Cl, SW19
off Windlesham Gro 119 CX88
Wainwright Av, Brwd. CM13 55 GD44
Wainwright Gro, Islw. TW7 97 CD84
Waite Davies Rd, SE12 124 EF87
Waite St, SE15 102 DT79
Waithman St, EC4 196 F9
Wakefield Cl, W.Byf. (Byfleet)
KT14 152 BL112
Wakefield Cres, Slou. (Stoke P.)
SL2 74 AT66
Wakefield Gdns, SE19 122 DS94
Ilford IG1 68 EL58
Wakefield Ms, WC1 196 A3
Wakefield Rd, N11 45 DK50
N15 66 DT57
Greenhithe DA9 129 FW85
Richmond TW10 117 CK85
Wakefield St, E6 86 EK67
N18 46 DU50
WC1 196 A4
Wakefield Wk, Wal.Cr. (Chsht.)
EN8 15 DY31
Wakehams Hill, Pnr. HA5 60 BZ55
Wakeham St, N1 84 DR65
Wakehurst Path, Wok. GU21 151 BC114
Wakehurst Rd, SW11 120 DE85
Wakeling Rd, W7 79 CF71
Wakeling St, E14 85 DY72
Wakelin Rd, E15 86 EE68
Wakely Cl, West. (Bigg.H.)
TN16 178 EJ118
Wakeman Rd, NW10 81 CW69
Wakemans Hill Av, NW9 62 CR57
Wakerfield Cl, Horn. RM11 72 FM57
Wakering Rd, Bark. IG11 87 EQ65
Wakerley Cl, E6
off Truesdale Rd 87 EM72
Wake Rd, Loug. (High Beach)
IG10 32 EJ38
Wakley St, EC1 196 F2
Walberswick St, SW8 101 DL80
Walbrook, EC4 197 K10
Walbrook Ho, N9 46 DW46
Walbrook Wf, EC4
off Upper Thames St 84 DQ73
Walburgh St, E1
off Bigland St 84 DV72
Walburton Rd, Pur. CR8 159 DJ113
Walcorde Av, SE17 201 J9
Walcot Rd, Enf. EN3 31 DZ40
Walcot Sq, SE11 200 E8
Walcott St, SW1 199 L8
Waldair Ct, E16
off Barge Ho Rd 105 EP75
Waldair Wf, E16 105 EP75
Waldeck Gro, SE27 121 DP90
Waldeck Rd, N15 65 DP56
SW14
off Lower Richmond Rd 98 CQ83
W4 98 CN79
W13 79 CH72
Dartford DA1 128 FM86
Waldeck Ter, SW14
off Lower Richmond Rd 98 CQ83
Waldegrave Av, Tedd. TW11
off Waldegrave Rd 117 CF92
Waldegrave Ct, Upmin. RM14 72 FP60
Waldegrave Gdns, Twick. TW1 117 CF89
Upminster RM14 72 FP60
Waldegrave Pk, Twick. TW1 117 CF91
Waldegrave Rd, N8 65 DN55
SE19 122 DT94
W5 80 CM72
Bromley BR1 144 EL98
Dagenham RM8 70 EW61
Teddington TW11 117 CF91
Twickenham TW1 117 CF91
Waldegrove, Croy. CR0 142 DT104
Waldemar Av, SW6 99 CY81
W13 79 CJ74
Waldemar Rd, SW19 120 DA92
Walden Av, N13 46 DQ49
Chislehurst BR7 125 EM91
Rainham RM13 89 FD68
Walden Cl, Belv. DA17 106 EZ78
Walden Gdns, Th.Hth. CR7 141 DM97
Waldenhurst Rd, Orp. BR5 146 EX101
Walden Par, Chis. BR7
off Walden Rd 125 EM93
Walden Rd, N17 46 DR53
Chislehurst BR7 125 EM93
Hornchurch RM11 72 FK58
Waldens Cl, Orp. BR5 146 EX101
Waldenshaw Rd, SE23 122 DW88
Waldens Pk Rd, Wok. GU21 166 AW116
Waldens Rd, Orp. BR5 146 EY101
Woking GU21 166 AX117
Walden St, E1 84 DV72
Walden Way, NW7 43 CX51
Hornchurch RM11 72 FK58
Ilford IG6 49 ES52
Waldo Cl, SW4 121 DJ85
Waldo Pl, Mitch. CR4 120 DE94
Waldorf Cl, S.Croy. CR2 159 DP109
Waldo Rd, NW10 81 CU69
Bromley BR1 144 EK97
Waldram Cres, SE23 122 DW88
Waldram Pk Rd, SE23 123 DX88
Waldram Pl, SE23
off Waldram Cres 122 DW88
Waldrist Way, Erith DA18 106 EZ75
Waldron Gdns, Brom. BR2 143 ED97
Waldronhyrst, S.Croy. CR2 159 DP105
Waldron Ms, SW3
off Old Ch St 100 DD79
Waldron Rd, SW18 120 DC90
Harrow HA1, HA2 61 CE60
Waldrons, The, Croy. CR0 159 DP105
Oxted RH8 188 EF131
Waldrons Path, S.Croy. CR2 160 DQ105
Waldstock Rd, SE28 88 EU73
Waleran Cl, Stan. HA7
off Chenduit Way 41 CF51
Walerand Rd, SE13 103 EC82
Waleran Flats, SE1
off Old Kent Rd 102 DS77
Wales Av, Cars. SM5 158 DF106
Wales Cl, SE15 102 DV80
Wales Fm Rd, W3 80 CR71
Waleton Acres, Wall. SM6 159 DJ107
Waley St, E1 85 DX71
Walfield Av, N20 44 DB45
Walford Rd, N16 66 DS63
Uxbridge UB8 76 BJ68
Walfrey Gdns, Dag. RM9 88 EY66
WALHAM GREEN, SW6 100 DB80
Walham Grn Ct, SW6
off Waterford Rd 100 DB80
Walham Gro, SW6 100 DB80
Walham Ri, SW19 119 CY93

★ Place of interest ⇌ Railway station London Underground station DLR Docklands Light Railway station Tramlink station H Hospital

Walham Yd, SW6
off Walham Gro 100 DA80
Walk, The, Horn. RM11 ....72 FM61
Oxted (Tand.) RH8 ....187 EA133
Potters Bar EN6 ....12 DA32
Sunbury-on-Thames TW16 .115 BT94
Walkden Rd, Chis. BR7 .....125 EN92
Walker Cl, N11 ....45 DJ49
SE18 ....105 EQ77
W7 ....79 CE74
Dartford DA1 ....107 FF83
Feltham TW14
off Westmacott Dr 115 BT87
Hampton TW12
off Fearnley Cres 116 BZ93
Walker Ms, SW2 off Effra Rd .121 DN85
Walkers Ct, E8 off Wilton Way .84 DU65
W1 ....195 M10
Walkerscroft Mead, SE21 ....122 DQ88
Walkers Pl, SW15
off Felsham Rd 99 CY83
Walkfield Dr, Epsom KT18 ...173 CV117
Walkford Way, SE15
off Daniel Gdns 102 DT80
Walkley Rd, Dart. DA1 ......127 FH85
Walks, The, N2 ....64 DD55
Walkynscroft, SE15
off Firbank Rd 102 DV82
Wallace Cl, SE28
off Haldane Rd 88 EX73
Shepperton TW17 ....135 BR98
Uxbridge UB10
off Grays Rd 76 BL68
★ Wallace Collection, W1 ..194 F8
Wallace Cres, Cars. SM5 ....158 DF106
Wallace Flds, Epsom KT17 ...157 CT112
Wallace Gdns, Swans. DA10
off Milton St 130 FY86
Wallace Rd, N1 ....84 DQ65
Grays RM17 ....110 GA76
Wallace Sq, Couls. CR5
off Cayton Rd 175 DK122
Wallace Wk, Add. KT15 .....152 BJ105
Wallace Way, N19
off Giesbach Rd 65 DK61
Wallasey Cres, Uxb. UB10 ....58 BN61
Wallbutton Rd, SE4 ....103 DY82
Wallcote Av, NW2 ....63 CX60
Walled Gdn, The, Tad. KT20
off Heathcote 173 CX122
Wall End Rd, E6 ....87 EN66
Wallenger Av, Rom. RM2 ......71 FH55
Waller Dr, Nthwd. HA6 ....39 BU54
Waller La, Cat. CR3 ....176 DT123
Waller Rd, SE14 ....103 DX81
Wallers Cl, Dag. RM9 ....88 EY67
Woodford Green IG8 ......49 EM51
Wallers Hoppit, Loug. IG10 ...32 EL40
Waller Way, SE10
off Greenwich High Rd ...103 EB80
Wallflower St, W12 ....81 CT73
Wallgrave Rd, SW5 ....100 DB77
Wallhouse Rd, Erith DA8 ....107 FH80
Wallingford Av, W10 ....81 CX71
Wallingford Rd, Uxb. UB8 ....76 BH68
WALLINGTON 159 DJ106
⇌ Wallington 159 DH107
Wallington Cl, Ruis. HA4 .....59 BQ58
Wallington Cor, Wall. SM6
off Manor Rd N 159 DH105
Wallington Rd, Ilf. IG3 ....69 ET59
Wallington Sq, Wall. SM6
off Woodcote Rd 159 DH107
Wallis All, SE1 ....201 J4
Wallis Cl, SW11 ....100 DD83
Dartford DA2 ....127 FF90
Hornchurch RM11 ....71 FH60
Wallis Ct, Slou. SL1
off Nixey Cl 92 AU76
Wallis Ms, N22
off Brampton Pk Rd 65 DN55
Leatherhead (Fetch.) KT22 .171 CG122
Wallis Pk, Grav. (Nthflt.) DA11 .130 GB85
Wallis Rd, E9 ....85 DZ65
Southall UB1 ....78 CB72
Wallis's Cotts, SW2 ....121 DL87
Wallman Pl, N22
off Bounds Grn Rd 45 DM53
Wallorton Gdns, SW14 ....98 CR84
Wallside, EC2 ....197 J7
Wall St, N1 ....84 DR65
Wallwood Rd, E11 ....67 ED60
Wallwood St, E14 ....85 DZ71
Walmar Cl, Barn. EN4 ....28 DD39
Walmer Cl, E4 ....47 EB47
Orpington BR6
off Tubbenden La S 163 ER105
Romford RM7 ....51 FB54
Walmer Gdns, W13 ....97 CG75
Walmer Ho, N9 ....46 DT45
Walmer Pl, W1 ....194 D6
Walmer Rd, W10
off Latimer Rd 81 CW72
W11 ....81 CY73
Walmer St, W1 ....194 D6
Walmer Ter, SE18 ....105 EQ77
Walmgate Rd, Grnf. UB6 ......79 CH67
Walmington Fold, N12 ....44 DA51
Walm La, NW2 ....63 CX64
Walmsley Ho, SW16
off Colson Way 121 DJ91
Walney Wk, N1
off St. Paul's Rd 84 DQ65
Walnut Av, West Dr. UB7 .....94 BN76
Walnut Cl, SE8 off Clyde St ..103 DZ79
Carshalton SM5 ....158 DF106
Dartford (Eyns.) DA4 .....148 FK104
Epsom KT18 ....173 CT115
Hayes UB3 ....77 BS73
Ilford IG6 off Civic Way ...69 EQ56
St. Albans (Park St.) AL2 ....8 CB27
Walnut Ct, W5 ....98 CL75
Walnut Dr, Tad. (Kgswd.) KT20
off Warren Lo Dr 173 CY124
Walnut Flds, Epsom KT17 ...157 CT109
Walnut Gdns, E15
off Burgess Rd 68 EE63
Walnut Grn, Bushey WD23 ...24 BZ40
Walnut Gro, Bans. SM7 .....157 CX114
Enfield EN1 ....30 DR43
Walnut Ms, Sutt. SM2 ....158 DC108
Walnut Rd, E10 ....67 EA61
Walnuts, The, Orp. BR6
off High St 146 EU102
Walnut Shop Cen, Orp. BR6 .146 EU102
Walnuts Rd, Orp. BR6 ......146 EU102
Walnut Tree Av, Dart. DA1 ...128 FL89
Mitcham CR4
off De'Arn Gdns 140 DE97
Walnut Tree Cl, SW13 ....99 CT81
Banstead SM7 ....157 CY112
Chislehurst BR7 ....145 EQ95
Waltham Cross (Chsht.)
EN8 ....15 DX31
Walnut Tree Cotts, SW19
off Church Rd 119 CY91
Walnut Tree La, W.Byf. (Byfleet)
KT14 ....152 BK112
Walnut Tree Rd, SE10 ....104 EE78
Brentford TW8 ....98 CL79
Dagenham RM8 ....70 EX61
Erith DA8 ....107 FE78
Hounslow TW5 ....96 BZ79
Shepperton TW17 ....135 BQ96
Walnut Tree Wk, SE11 ......200 D8
Walnut Way, Buck.H. IG9 .....48 EK48
Ruislip HA4 ....78 BW65
Swanley BR8 ....147 FD96
Walpole Av, Couls. CR5 .....174 DF118
Richmond TW9 ....98 CM82
Walpole Cl, W13 ....97 CJ75
Grays RM17
off Palmers Dr 110 GC77
Pinner HA5 ....40 CA51
Walpole Cres, Tedd. TW11 ...117 CF92
Walpole Gdns, W4 ....98 CQ78
Twickenham TW2 ....117 CE89
Walpole Ms, NW8
off Queen's Gro 82 DD67
SW19 off Walpole Rd 120 DD93
Walpole Pk, W5 ....79 CJ74
Weybridge KT13 ....152 BN108
Walpole Pl, SE18
off Anglesea Rd 105 EP77
Teddington TW11 ....117 CF92
Walpole Rd, E6 ....86 EJ66
E17 ....67 DY56
E18 ....48 EF53
N17 (Downhills Way) 66 DQ55
N17 (Lordship La) 46 DQ54
SW19 ....120 DD93
Bromley BR2 ....144 EK99
Croydon CR0 ....142 DR103
Surbiton KT6 ....138 CL100
Teddington TW11 ....117 CF92
Twickenham TW2 ....117 CE89
Windsor (Old Wind.) SL4 ..112 AV87
Walpole St, SW3 ....198 D10
Walrond Av, Wem. HA9 ....62 CL64
Walsham Cl, N16
off Braydon Rd 66 DU59
SE28 ....88 EX73
Walsham Rd, SE14 ....103 DX82
Feltham TW14 ....115 BV87
Walsh Cres, Croy. (New Adgtn.)
CR0 ....162 EE112
Walshford Way, Borwd. WD6 ..26 CN38
Walsingham Gdns, Epsom
KT19 ....156 CS105
Walsingham Pk, Chis. BR7 ...145 ER96
Walsingham Pl, SW4 off Clapham
Common W Side 100 DF84
SW11 ....120 DG86
Walsingham Rd, E5 ....66 DU62
W13 ....79 CG74
Croydon (New Adgtn.) CR0 .161 EC110
Enfield EN2 ....30 DR42
Mitcham CR4 ....140 DF99
Orpington BR5 ....146 EV95
Walsingham Wk, Belv. DA17 .106 FA79
Walsingham Way, St.Alb.
(Lon.Col.) AL2 ....9 CJ27
Walter Rodney Cl, E6
off Stevenage Rd 87 EM65
Walters Cl, Wal.Cr. (Chsht.)
EN7 ....13 DP25
Walters Ho, SE17 off Otto St .101 DP79
Walters Mead, Ashtd. KT21 ..172 CL117
Walters Rd, SE25 ....142 DS98
Enfield EN3 ....30 DW43
Walter St, E2 ....85 DX69
Kingston upon Thames KT2
off Sopwith Way 138 CL95
Walters Way, SE23 ....123 DX86
Walters Yd, Brom. BR1 .....144 EG96
Walter Ter, E1 ....85 DX72
Walterton Rd, W9 ....81 CZ70
Walter Wk, Edg. HA8 ....42 CQ51
WALTHAM ABBEY 32 EF35
★ Waltham Abbey (ruins),
Wal.Abb. EN9 ....15 EC33
Waltham Av, NW9 ....62 CN58
Hayes UB3 ....95 BQ76
Waltham Cl, Brwd. (Hutton)
CM13 off Bannister Dr 55 GC44
Dartford DA1 ....127 FG86
Orpington BR5 ....146 EX102
WALTHAM CROSS 15 DZ33
⇌ Waltham Cross 15 DY34
Waltham Dr, Edg. HA8 ....42 CN54
Waltham Gdns, Enf. EN3 .....30 DW36
Waltham Gate, Wal.Cr. EN8 ...15 DZ26
Waltham Pk Way, E17 ....47 EA53
Waltham Rd, Cars. SM5 .....140 DD101
Caterham CR3 ....176 DV122
Southall UB2 ....96 BY76
Waltham Abbey EN9 ......16 EF26
Woodford Green IG8 ......48 EL51
WALTHAMSTOW, E17 ....47 EB54
Walthamstow Av, E4 ....47 EA52
Walthamstow Business Cen,
E17 ....47 EC54
⇌ Walthamstow Central 67 EA56
⊖ Walthamstow Central 67 EA56
⇌ Walthamstow Queens
Road 67 DZ57
Waltham Way, E4 ....47 DZ49
Waltheof Av, N17 ....46 DR53
Waltheof Gdns, N17 ....46 DR53
Walton Av, Har. HA2 ....60 BZ64
New Malden KT3 ....139 CT98
Sutton SM3 ....139 CZ104
Wembley HA9 ....62 CP62
Walton Br, Shep. TW17 .....135 BS101
Walton-on-Thames KT12
off Bridge St 135 BS101
Walton Br Rd, Shep. TW17 ...135 BS101
Walton Cl, E5
off Orient Way 67 DX62
NW2 ....63 CV61
SW8 ....101 DL80
Harrow HA1 ....61 CD56
🅷 Walton Comm Hosp, Walt.
KT12 ....135 BV103
Walton Ct, Wok. GU21 ......167 BA116
Walton Cres, Har. HA2 ....60 BZ63
Walton Dr, NW10
off Mitchellbrook Way 80 CR65
Harrow HA1 ....61 CD56
Walton Gdns, W3 ....80 CP71
Brentwood CM13 ....55 GC43
Feltham TW13 ....115 BT91
Waltham Abbey EN9 ......15 EB33
Wembley HA9 ....62 CL61
Walton Grn, Croy. (New Adgtn.)
CR0 ....161 EC108
Walton La, Shep. TW17 .....135 BR101
Walton-on-Thames KT12 ..135 BQ102
Weybridge KT13 ....135 BP103
WALTON-ON-THAMES 135 BT103
⇌ Walton-on-Thames 153 BU105
WALTON ON THE HILL, Tad. ..183 CT125
Walton Pk, Walt. KT12 ......136 BX103
Walton Pk La, Walt. KT12 ....136 BX103
Walton Pl, SW3 ....198 D6
Walton Rd, E12 ....69 EN63
E13 ....86 EJ68
N15 ....66 DT57
Bushey WD23 ....24 BX42
East Molesey KT8 ....136 CA98
Epsom (Epsom Downs)
KT18 ....173 CT117
Epsom (Headley) KT18 ...172 CQ121
Harrow HA1 ....61 CD56
Romford RM5 ....50 EZ52
Sidcup DA14 ....126 EW89
Walton-on-Thames KT12 ..136 BW99
West Molesey KT8 ....136 BY99
Woking GU21 ....167 AZ116
Walton St, SW3 ....198 C8
Enfield EN2 ....30 DR39
Tadworth KT20 ....173 CU124
Walton Ter, Wok. GU21 ......167 BB115
Walton Way, W3 ....80 CP71
Mitcham CR4 ....141 DJ98
Walt Whitman Cl, SE24
off Shakespeare Rd 101 DP84
Walverns Cl, Wat. WD19 ......24 BW44
WALWORTH, SE17 ....201 H10
★ Walworth Garden Fm -
Horticultural Training Cen,
SE17 ....101 DP78
Walworth Pl, SE17 ....102 DQ78
Walworth Rd, SE1 ....201 H8
SE17 ....201 H8
Walwyn Av, Brom. BR1 ......144 EK97
Wambrook Cl, Brwd. CM13 ...55 GC46
Wanborough Dr, SW15 ......119 CV88
Wanderer Dr, Bark. IG11 .....88 EV69
Wandle Bk, SW19 ....120 DD93
Croydon CR0 ....141 DL104
Wandle Ct, Epsom KT19 .....156 CQ105
Wandle Ct Gdns, Croy. CR0 ..159 DL105
Wandle Park 141 DN103
Wandle Rd, SW17 ....120 DE89
Croydon CR0 ....142 DQ104
Croydon (Waddon) CR0 ...141 DL104
Morden SM4 ....140 DC98
Wallington SM6 ....141 DH103
Wandle Side, Croy. CR0 .....141 DM104
Wallington SM6 ....141 DH104
Wandle Technology Pk, Mitch.
CR4 off Goat Rd 140 DF101
Wandle Trd Est, Mitch. CR4
off Budge La 140 DF101
Wandle Way, SW18 ....120 DB88
Mitcham CR4 ....140 DF99
Wandon Rd, SW6 ....100 DB80
WANDSWORTH, SW18 ....119 CZ85
Wandsworth Br, SW6 ....100 DB83
SW18 ....100 DB83
Wandsworth Br Rd, SW6 .....100 DB81
⇌ Wandsworth Common 120 DF88
Wandsworth Common,
SW12 ....120 DE86
Wandsworth Common W Side,
SW18 ....120 DC85
Wandsworth High St, SW18 .120 DA85
★ Wandsworth Mus, SW18
off Garratt La 120 DB85
Wandsworth Plain, SW18 ....120 DB85
⇌ Wandsworth Road 101 DJ82
Wandsworth Rd, SW8 ....101 DK80
Wandsworth Shop Cen,
SW18 ....120 DB86
⇌ Wandsworth Town 100 DB84
Wangey Rd, Rom. RM6 ....70 EX59
Wang Ho, Brent. TW8 ....97 CJ78
Wanless Rd, SE24 ....102 DQ83
Wanley Rd, SE5 ....102 DR84
Wanlip Rd, E13 ....86 EH70
Wanmer Ct, Reig. RH2
off Birkheads Rd 184 DA133
Wannions Cl, Chesh. HP5 .....4 AU30
Wannock Gdns, Ilf. IG6 ....49 EP52
Wansbeck Rd, E9 ....85 DZ66
Wansbury Way, Swan. BR8 ...147 FG99
Wansdown Pl, SW6
off Fulham Rd 100 DB80
Wansey St, SE17 ....201 H9
Wansford Cl, Brwd. CM14 .....54 FT48
Wansford Grn, Wok. GU21
off Kenton Way 166 AT117
Wansford Pk, Borwd. WD6 ...26 CS42
Wansford Rd, Wdf.Grn. IG8 ...48 EJ53
WANSTEAD, E11 ....68 EH59
⊖ Wanstead 68 EH58
Wanstead Cl, Brom. BR1 ....144 EJ96
Wanstead La, Ilf. IG1 ....68 EK58
⇌ Wanstead Park 68 EH63
Wanstead Pk, E11 ....68 EK59
Wanstead Pk Av, E12 ....68 EK61
Wanstead Pk Rd, Ilf. IG1 .....69 EM60
Wanstead Pl, E11 ....68 EG58
Wanstead Rd, Brom. BR1 ....144 EJ96
Wansunt Rd, Bex. DA5 ......127 FC88
Wantage Rd, SE12 ....124 EF85
Wantz La, Rain. RM13 ....89 FH70
Wantz Rd, Dag. RM10 ....71 FB63
Waplings, The, Tad. KT20 ....173 CV124
WAPPING, E1 ....202 C2
⊖ Wapping 202 F3
Wapping Dock St, E1 ....202 E3
Wapping High St, E1 ....202 B3
Wapping La, E1 ....202 E1
Wapping Wall, E1 ....202 F2
Wapseys La, Slou. (Hedg.)
SL2 ....56 AS58
Wapshott Rd, Stai. TW18 ....113 BE93
Warbank Cl, Croy. (New Adgtn.)
CR0 ....162 EE111
Warbank Cres, Croy. (New Adgtn.)
CR0 ....162 EE110
Warbank La, Kings.T. KT2 ...119 CT94
Warbeck Rd, W12 ....81 CV74
Warberry Rd, N22 ....45 DM54
Warblers Grn, Cob. KT11 ....154 BZ114
Warboys App, Kings.T. KT2 ..118 CP93
Warboys Cres, E4 ....47 EC50
Warboys Rd, Kings.T. KT2 ...118 CP93
Warburton Cl, N1
off Culford Rd 84 DS65
Harrow HA3 ....41 CD51
Warburton Rd, E8 ....84 DV66
Twickenham TW2 ....116 CB88
Warburton St, E8
off Warburton Rd 84 DV67
Warburton Ter, E17 ....47 EB54
War Coppice Rd, Cat. CR3 ...186 DR127
Wardalls Gro, SE14 ....102 DW80
Ward Av, Grays RM17 ....110 GA77
Ward Cl, Erith DA8 ....107 FD79
Iver SL0 ....75 BF72
South Croydon CR2 ......160 DS106
Waltham Cross (Chsht.) EN7
off Spicersfield 14 DU27
Wardell Cl, NW7 ....42 CS52
Wardell Fld, NW9 ....42 CS53
Warden Av, Har. HA2 ....60 BZ60
Romford RM5 ....51 FC50
Warden Rd, NW5 ....82 DG65
Wardens Fld Cl, Orp. BR6 ...163 ES107
Wardens Gro, SE1 ....201 H3
Ward Gdns, Rom. (Harold Wd.)
RM3 off Whitmore Av 52 FK54
Ward La, Warl. CR6 ....176 DW116
Wardle St, E9 ....67 DX64
Wardley St, SW18
off Garratt La 120 DB87
Wardo Av, SW6 ....99 CY81
Wardour Ms, W1 ....195 L9
Wardour St, W1 ....195 M10
Ward Rd, E15 ....85 ED67
N19 ....65 DJ62
Wardrobe Pl, EC4 ....196 G10
Wardrobe Ter, EC4 ....196 G10
Wards La, Borwd. (Elstree)
WD6 ....25 CG40
Ward's Pl, Egh. TW20 ......113 BC93
Wards Rd, Ilf. IG2 ....69 ER59
Wareham Cl, Houns. TW3 ....96 CB84
Waremead Rd, Ilf. IG2 ....69 EP57
Warenford Way, Borwd. WD6 .26 CN39
Warenne Rd, Lthd. (Fetch.)
KT22 ....170 CC122
Ware Pt Dr, SE28 ....105 ER75
Warescot Cl, Brwd. CM15 ....54 FV45
Warescot Rd, Brwd. CM15 ....54 FV45
Warfield Rd, NW10 ....81 CX69
Feltham TW14 ....115 BS87
Hampton TW12 ....136 CB95
Warfield Yd, NW10
off Warfield Rd 81 CX69
Wargrave Av, N15 ....66 DT58
Wargrave Rd, Har. HA2 ......60 CC62
Warham Rd, N4 ....65 DN57
Harrow HA3 ....41 CF54
Sevenoaks (Otford) TN14 ..181 FH116
South Croydon CR2 .....160 DQ106
Warham St, SE5 ....101 DP80
Waring Cl, Orp. BR6 ....163 ET107
Waring Dr, Orp. BR6 ....163 ET107
Waring Rd, Sid. DA14 ......126 EW93
Waring St, SE27 ....122 DQ91
Warkworth Gdns, Islw. TW7 ..97 CG80
Warkworth Rd, N17 ....46 DR52
Warland Rd, SE18 ....105 ER80
WARLEY, Brwd. 54 FV50
Warley Av, Dag. RM8 ....70 EZ59
Hayes UB4 ....77 BU71
Warley Cl, E10 off Millicent Rd .67 DZ60
Warley Gap, Brwd. CM13 .....53 FV52
Warley Hill, Brwd. CM13,
CM14 ....53 FV51
🅷 Warley Hosp, Brwd. CM14 .54 FV50
Warley Mt, Brwd. CM14 ......54 FW49
Warley Rd, N9 ....46 DW47
Brentwood CM13 ....53 FT54
Hayes UB4 ....77 BU72
Ilford IG5 ....49 EN53
Upminster RM14 ....52 FQ54
Woodford Green IG8 ......48 EH52
Warley St, E2 ....85 DX69
Brentwood CM13 ....73 FW58
Upminster RM14 ....73 FW58
Warley St Flyover, Brwd.
CM13 ....73 FX57
Warley Wds Cres, Brwd. CM14 .54 FV49
WARLINGHAM 177 DX118
Warlingham Rd, Th.Hth. CR7 .141 DP98
Warlock Rd, W9 ....82 DA70
Warlow Cl, Enf. EN3
off Government Row 31 EA37
Warlters Cl, N7
off Warlters Rd 65 DL63
Warlters Rd, N7 ....65 DL63
Warltersville Rd, N19 ....65 DL59
Warmington Cl, E5
off Orient Way 67 DX62
Warmington Rd, SE24 ......122 DQ86
Warmington St, E13
off Barking Rd 86 EG70
Warminster Gdns, SE25 .....142 DU96
Warminster Rd, SE25 ....142 DT96
Warminster Sq, SE25 ....142 DU96
Warminster Way, Mitch. CR4 .141 DH95
Warndon St, SE16 ....202 G9
Warneford Pl, Wat. WD19 .....24 BY44
Warneford Rd, Har. HA3 ......61 CK55
Warneford St, E9 ....84 DV67
Warne Pl, Sid. DA15
off Westerham Dr 126 EV86
Warner Av, Sutt. SM3 ......139 CY103
Warner Cl, E15 ....68 EE64
NW9 ....63 CT59
Hampton TW12
off Tangley Pk Rd 116 BZ92
Hayes UB3 ....95 BR80
Warner Ho, SE13
off Conington Rd 103 EB82
Warner Par, Hayes UB3 ......95 BR80
Warner Pl, E2 ....84 DU68
Warner Rd, E17 ....67 DY56
N8 ....65 DK56
SE5 ....102 DQ81
Bromley BR1 ....124 EF94
Warners Cl, Wdf.Grn. IG8 ....48 EG50
Warners La, Kings.T. KT2 ....117 CK91
Warners Path, Wdf.Grn. IG8 ...48 EG50
Warner St, EC1 ....196 D5
Warner Ter, E14
off Broomfield St 85 EA71
Warner Yd, EC1 ....196 D5
Warnford Ho, SW15
off Tunworth Cres 119 CT86
Warnford Ind Est, Hayes UB3 .95 BS75
Warnford Rd, Orp. BR6 .....163 ET106
Warnham Ct Rd, Cars. SM5 ..158 DF108
Warnham Rd, N12 ....44 DE50
Warple Ms, W3
off Warple Way 98 CS75
Warple Way, W3 ....80 CS74
Warren, The, E12 ....68 EL63
Ashtead KT21 ....172 CL119
Carshalton SM5 ....158 DD109
Gerrards Cross (Chal.St.P.)
SL9 ....37 AZ52
Gravesend DA12 ....131 GK91
Hayes UB4 ....77 BU72
Hounslow TW5 ....96 BZ80
Leatherhead (Oxshott) KT22 .154 CC112
Radlett WD7 ....9 CG33
Tadworth (Kgswd.) KT20 ..173 CY123
Worcester Park KT4 .....156 CR105
Warren Av, E10 ....67 EC62
Bromley BR1 ....124 EE94
Orpington BR6 ....163 ET106
Richmond TW10 ....98 CP84
South Croydon CR2 .....161 DX108
Sutton SM2 ....157 CZ110
Warren Cl, N9 ....47 DX45
SE21 off Lairdale Cl 122 DQ87
Bexleyheath DA6 ....126 FA85
Esher KT10 ....154 CB105
Hayes UB4 ....78 BW71
Slough SL3 ....92 AY76
Wembley HA9 ....61 CK61
Warren Ct, Chig. IG7 ....49 ER49
Sevenoaks TN13 ....191 FJ125
Weybridge KT13 ....152 BN106
Warren Cres, N9 ....46 DT45
Warren Cutting, Kings.T. KT2 .118 CR94
Warrender Rd, N19 ....65 DJ62
Chesham HP5 ....4 AS29
Warrender Way, Ruis. HA4 ....59 BU59
Warren Dr, Grnf. UB6 ....78 CB70
Hornchurch RM12 ....71 FG62
Orpington BR6 ....164 EV106
Ruislip HA4 ....60 BX59
Tadworth (Kgswd.) KT20 ..173 CZ122
Warren Dr, The, E11 ....68 EJ59
Warren Dr N, Surb. KT5 .....138 CP102
Warren Dr S, Surb. KT5 .....138 CQ102
Warreners La, Wey. KT13 ....153 BR109
Warren Fld, Epp. CM16 ....18 EU32
Iver SL0 ....75 BC68
Warrenfield Cl, Wal.Cr. (Chsht.)
EN7 off Portland Dr 14 DU31
Warren Flds, Stan. HA7
off Valencia Rd 41 CJ49
Warren Footpath, Twick. TW1 .117 CJ88
Warren Gdns, E15
off Ashton Rd 67 ED64
Orpington BR6 ....164 EU106
Warrengate La, Pot.B. EN6 ....11 CW31
Warrengate Rd, Hat. AL9 .....11 CW28
Warren Gro, Borwd. WD6 .....26 CR42
Warren Hastings Ct, Grav. DA11
off Pier Rd 131 GF86
Warren Hts, Grays (Chaff.Hun.)
RM16 ....110 FY77
Loughton IG10
off Warren Hill 32 EJ43
Warren Hill, Epsom KT18 ....172 CR116
Loughton IG10 ....32 EJ44
Warren Ho, E3
off Bromley High St 85 EB69
Warren La, SE18 ....105 EP76
Grays RM16 ....109 FW77
Leatherhead (Oxshott) KT22 .154 CC111
Oxted RH8 ....188 EF134
Stanmore HA7 ....41 CF48

★ Place of interest ⇌ Railway station ⊖ London Underground station DLR Docklands Light Railway station Tramlink station 🅷 Hospital

War - Wea

Warren La, Wok. GU22 168 BH118
Warren Lo Dr, Tad. (Kgswd.) KT20 173 CY124
Warren Mead, Bans. SM7 173 CW115
Warren Ms, W1 195 K5
Warrenne Way, Reig. RH2 184 DA134
Warren Pk, Kings.T. KT2 118 CQ93
Tadworth KT20 182 CQ131
Warlingham CR6 177 DX118
Warren Pk Rd, Sutt. SM1 158 DD107
Warren Pl, E1
off Pitsea St 85 DX72
Warren Pond Rd, E4 48 EF46
Warren Ri, N.Mal. KT3 138 CR95
Warren Rd, E4 47 EC47
E10 67 EC62
E11 68 EJ60
NW2 63 CT61
SW19 120 DE93
Addlestone (New Haw) KT15 152 BG110
Ashford TW15 115 BS94
Banstead SM7 157 CW114
Bexleyheath DA6 126 FA85
Bromley BR2 144 EG103
Bushey (Bushey Hth.) WD23 40 CC46
Croydon CR0 142 DS102
Dartford DA1 128 FK90
Gravesend (Sthflt.) DA13 130 GB92
Ilford IG6 69 ER57
Kingston upon Thames KT2 118 CQ93
Orpington BR6 163 ET106
Purley CR8 159 DP112
Reigate RH2 184 DB133
Sidcup DA14 126 EW90
Twickenham TW2 116 CC86
Uxbridge UB10 58 BL63
Warrens Shawe La, Edg. HA8 42 CP46
⊖ Warren Street 195 L4
Warren St, W1 195 J5
Warren Ter, Grays RM16
off Arterial Rd W Thurrock 109 FX75
Romford RM6 70 EX56
Warren Wk, SE7 104 EJ79
Warren Way, NW7 43 CY51
Weybridge KT13 153 BQ106
Warren Wd Cl, Brom. BR2 144 EF103
Warriner Av, Horn. RM12 72 FK61
Warriner Dr, N9 46 DU48
Warriner Gdns, SW11 100 DF81
Warrington Cres, W9 82 DC70
Warrington Gdns, W9
off Warwick Av 82 DC70
Hornchurch RM11 72 FJ58
Warrington Pl, E14 204 E2
Warrington Rd, Croy. CR0 141 DP104
Dagenham RM8 70 EX61
Harrow HA1 61 CE57
Richmond TW10 117 CK85
Warrington Spur, Wind. (Old Wind.) SL4 112 AV87
Warrington Sq, Dag. RM8 70 EX61
Warrior Av, Grav. DA12 131 GJ91
Warrior Sq, E12 69 EN63
Warsaw Cl, Ruis. HA4
off Glebe Av 77 BV65
Warsdale Dr, NW9
off Mardale Dr 62 CR57
Warspite Rd, SE18 104 EL76
Warton Rd, E15 85 EC66
Warwall, E6 87 EP72
⊖ Warwick Avenue 82 DC70
Warwick Av, W2 82 DC70
W9 82 DC70
Edgware HA8 42 CP48
Egham TW20 133 BC95
Harrow HA2 60 BZ63
Potters Bar (Cuffley) EN6 13 DK27
Staines TW18 114 BJ93
Warwick Cl, Barn. EN4 28 DD43
Bexley DA5 126 EZ87
Bushey (Bushey Hth.) WD23
off Magnaville Rd 41 CE45
Hampton TW12 116 CC94
Orpington BR6 146 EU104
Potters Bar (Cuffley) EN6 13 DK27
Warwick Ct, SE15 102 DU82
WC1 196 C7
Rickmansworth (Chorl.) WD3 21 BF41
Surbiton KT6 off Hook Rd 138 CL103
Warwick Cres, W2 82 DC71
Hayes UB4 77 BT70
Warwick Deeping, Cher. (Ott.) KT16 151 BC106
Warwick Dene, W5 80 CL74
Warwick Dr, SW15 99 CV83
Waltham Cross (Chsht.) EN8 15 DX28
Warwick Est, W2 82 DB71
Warwick Gdns, N4 66 DQ57
W14 99 CZ76
Ashtead KT21 171 CJ117
Barnet EN5 off Great N Rd 27 CZ38
Ilford IG1 69 EP60
Romford RM2 72 FJ55
Thames Ditton KT7 137 CF99
Warwick Gro, E5 66 DV60
Surbiton KT5 138 CM101
Warwick Ho St, SW1 199 N2
Warwick La, EC4 196 G9
Rainham RM13 90 FM68
Upminster RM14 90 FP68
Woking GU21 166 AU119
Warwick Pas, EC4 196 G8
Warwick Pl, W5 off Warwick Rd 97 CK75
W9 82 DC71
Gravesend (Nthflt.) DA11 130 GB85
Uxbridge UB8 76 BJ66
Warwick Pl N, SW1 199 K9
Warwick Quad Shop Mall, Red. RH1 off London Rd 184 DG133
Warwick Rd, E4 47 EA50
E11 68 EH57
E12 68 EL64
Warwick Rd, E15 86 EF65
E17 47 DZ53
N11 45 DK51
N18 46 DS49
SE20 142 DV97
SW5 99 CZ77
W5 97 CK75
W14 99 CZ77
Ashford TW15 114 BL92
Barnet EN5 28 DB42
Borehamwood WD6 26 CR41
Coulsdon CR5 159 DJ114
Enfield EN3 31 DZ37
Hounslow TW4 95 BV83
Kingston upon Thames KT1 137 CJ95
New Malden KT3 138 CQ97
Rainham RM13 90 FJ70
Redhill RH1 184 DF133
Sidcup DA14 126 EV92
Southall UB2 96 BZ76
Sutton SM1 158 DC105
Thames Ditton KT7 137 CF99
Thornton Heath CR7 141 DN97
Twickenham TW2 117 CE88
Welling DA16 106 EW83
West Drayton UB7 94 BL75
Warwick Row, SW1 199 J6
Warwickshire Path, SE8 103 DZ80
Warwick Sq, EC4 196 G8
SW1 199 K10
Warwick Sq Ms, SW1 199 K9
Warwick St, W1 195 L10
Warwick Ter, SE18 105 ER79
Warwick Way, SW1 199 K9
Rickmansworth (Crox.Grn.) WD3 23 BQ42
WARWICK WOLD, Red. 185 DN129
Warwick Wold Rd, Red. RH1 185 DN128
Warwick Yd, EC1 197 J5
Washington Av, E12 68 EL63
Washington Cl, Reig. RH2 184 DA131
Washington Rd, E6
off St. Stephens Rd 86 EJ66
E18 48 EF54
SW13 99 CU80
Kingston upon Thames KT1 138 CN96
Worcester Park KT4 139 CV103
Wash La, Pot.B. EN6 11 CV33
Washneys Rd, Orp. BR6 164 EV113
Washpond La, Warl. CR6 177 EC118
Wash Rd, Brwd. CM13 55 GD44
Wastdale Rd, SE23 123 DX88
Watchfield Ct, W4 98 CQ78
Watchgate, Dart. (Lane End) DA2 129 FR91
Watcombe Cotts, Rich. TW9 98 CN79
Watcombe Pl, SE25
off Albert Rd 142 DV99
Watcombe Rd, SE25 142 DV99
Waterbank Rd, SE6 123 EB90
Waterbeach Rd, Dag. RM9 88 EW65
Waterbrook La, NW4 63 CW57
Water Circ, Green. (Bluewater) DA9 129 FT88
Watercress Pl, N1
off Hertford Rd 84 DS66
Watercress Rd, Wal.Cr. (Chsht.) EN7 14 DR26
Watercress Way, Wok. GU21 166 AV117
Watercroft Rd, Sev. (Halst.) TN14 164 EZ110
Waterdale Rd, SE2 106 EU79
Waterdales, Grav. (Nthflt.) DA11 130 GD88
Waterdell Pl, Rick. WD3
off Uxbridge Rd 38 BG47
Waterden Rd, E15 67 EA64
WATER END, Hat. 11 CV26
Waterer Gdns, Tad. KT20 173 CX118
Waterer Ri, Wall. SM6 159 DK107
Waterfall Cl, N14 45 DJ48
Virginia Water GU25 132 AU97
Waterfall Cotts, SW19 120 DD93
Waterfall Rd, N11 45 DH49
N14 45 DJ48
SW19 120 DD93
Waterfall Ter, SW17 120 DE93
Waterfield, Rick. (Herons.) WD3 37 BC45
Tadworth KT20 173 CV119
Waterfield Cl, SE28 88 EV74
Belvedere DA17 106 FA76
Waterfield Dr, Warl. CR6 176 DW119
Waterfield Gdns, SE25 142 DS99
Waterfield Grn, Tad. KT20 173 CW120
Waterfields, Lthd. KT22 171 CH119
Waterfields Way, Wat. WD17 24 BX42
Waterford Cl, Cob. KT11 154 BY111
Waterford Rd, SW6 100 DB81
Water Gdns, Stan. HA7 41 CH51
Water Gdns, The, W2 194 C8
Watergardens, The, Kings.T. KT2 118 CQ93
Watergate, EC4 196 F10
Watergate, The, Wat. WD19 40 BX47
Watergate St, SE8 103 EA79
Watergate Wk, WC2 200 A2
Waterglade Ind Pk, Grays RM20 109 FT78
Waterhall Av, E4 48 EE49
Waterhall Cl, E17 47 DX53
Waterhead Cl, Erith DA8 107 FE80
Waterhouse Cl, E16 86 EK71
NW3 off Lyndhurst Rd 64 DD64
W6 off Great Ch La 99 CX77
Waterhouse La, Ken. CR8 176 DQ119
Redhill (Bletch.) RH1 186 DT132
Tadworth (Kgswd.) KT20 173 CY121
Waterhouse Sq, EC1 196 D7
Wateridge Cl, E14 203 P7
Wateringbury Cl, Orp. BR5 146 EV97
Water La, E15 86 EE65
EC3 201 M1
N9 46 DV46
NW1 off Kentish Town Rd 83 DH66
SE14 102 DW80
Cobham KT11 170 BY115
Water La, Hem.H. (Bov.) HP3 5 BA29
Ilford IG3 69 ES62
Kings Langley WD4 7 BP29
Kingston upon Thames KT1 137 CK95
Oxted (Titsey) RH8 188 EG126
Purfleet RM19 108 FN77
Redhill RH1 186 DP130
Richmond TW9 117 CK85
Sevenoaks (Shore.) TN14 165 FF112
Sidcup DA14 126 EZ89
Twickenham TW1
off The Embankment 117 CG88
Watford WD17 24 BW42
Westerham TN16 189 ER127
Water Lily Cl, Sthl. UB2
off Navigator Dr 96 CC75
⇌ Waterloo 200 D4
⊖ Waterloo 200 D4
Waterloo Br, SE1 200 B1
WC2 200 B1
Waterloo Cl, E9
off Churchill Wk 66 DW64
Feltham TW14 115 BT88
⇌ Waterloo East 200 D3
Waterloo Est, E2 84 DW68
Waterloo Gdns, E2 84 DW68
N1 off Barnsbury St 83 DP66
Romford RM7 71 FD58
⇌ Waterloo International 200 C4
Waterloo Pas, NW6 81 CZ66
Waterloo Pl, SW1 199 M2
Richmond TW9
off Sheen Rd 118 CL85
Richmond (Kew) TW9 98 CN79
Waterloo Rd, E6 86 EJ66
E7 off Wellington Rd 68 EF64
E10 67 EA59
NW2 63 CU60
SE1 200 D4
Brentwood CM14 54 FW46
Epsom KT19 156 CR112
Ilford IG6 49 EQ54
Romford RM7 71 FE57
Sutton SM1 158 DD106
Uxbridge UB8 76 BJ67
Waterloo St, Grav. DA12 131 GJ87
Waterloo Ter, N1 83 DP66
Waterlow Ct, NW11
off Heath Cl 64 DB59
Waterlow Rd, N19 65 DJ60
Waterman Cl, Wat. WD19 23 BV44
★ Watermans Art Cen, Brent. TW8 98 CL79
Waterman's Cl, Kings.T. KT2
off Woodside Rd 118 CL94
Waterman St, SW15 99 CX83
Watermans Wk, SE16 203 K6
Watermans Way, Epp. (N.Wld.Bas.) CM16 18 FA27
Waterman Way, E1 202 D2
Watermead, Felt. TW14 115 BS88
Tadworth KT20 173 CV120
Woking GU21 166 AT116
Watermead La, Cars. SM5
off Middleton Rd 140 DF101
Watermeadow Cl, Erith DA8 107 FH81
Watermeadow La, SW6 100 DC82
Watermead Rd, SE6 123 EC91
Watermead Twr, SW6 100 DC81
Watermead Way, N17 66 DV55
Watermen's Sq, SE20 122 DW94
Water Ms, SE15 102 DW84
Watermill Cl, Rich. TW10 117 CJ90
Watermill La, N18 46 DS50
Watermill Way, SW19 140 DC95
Water Mill Way, Dart. (S.Darenth) DA4 148 FP96
Watermill Way, Felt. TW13 116 BZ89
Watermint Cl, Orp. BR5
off Wagtail Way 146 EX98
Watermint Quay, N16 66 DU59
Waterperry La, Wok. (Chobham) GU24 150 AT110
Water Rd, Wem. HA0 80 CM67
Waters Dr, Rick. WD3 38 BL46
Staines TW18 113 BF90
Watersedge, Epsom KT19 156 CQ105
Watersfield Way, Edg. HA8 41 CK52
Waters Gdns, Dag. RM10 70 FA64
Waterside, Beck. BR3
off Rectory Rd 143 EA95
Dartford DA1 127 FE85
Water Side, Kings L. WD4 6 BN29
Waterside, Rad. WD7 9 CH34
St. Albans (Lon.Col.) AL2 10 CL27
Uxbridge UB8 76 BJ71
Waterside Cl, E3 85 DZ67
SE16 202 C5
Barking IG11 70 EU63
Northolt UB5 78 BZ69
Romford (Harold Wd.) RM3 52 FN52
Surbiton KT6
off Culsac Rd 138 CL103
Waterside Ct, SE13
off Weardale Rd 103 ED84
Kings Langley WD4
off Water Side 7 BP29
Waterside Dr, Slou. (Langley) SL3 93 AZ75
Walton-on-Thames KT12 135 BU99
Waterside Pl, NW1
off Princess Rd 82 DG67
Waterside Pt, SW11 100 DE80
Waterside Rd, Sthl. UB2 96 CA76
Waterside Trd Cen, W7 97 CE76
Waterside Way, SW17 120 DC91
Woking GU21
off Winnington Way 166 AV118
Watersmeet Way, SE28 88 EW72
Waterson Rd, Grays RM16 111 GH77
Waterson St, E2 197 N2
Waters Pl, SW15
off Danemere St 99 CW82
Watersplash Cl, Kings.T. KT1 138 CL97
Watersplash La, Hayes UB3 95 BU77
Hounslow TW5 95 BV78
Watersplash Rd, Shep. TW17 134 BN98
Waters Rd, SE6 124 EE90
Kingston upon Thames KT1 138 CP96
Waters Sq, Kings.T. KT1 138 CP97
Water St, WC2 196 C10
Waterton Av, Grav. DA12 131 GL87
Water Twr Cl, Uxb. UB8 58 BL64
Water Twr Hill, Croy. CR0 160 DR105
Water Twr Pl, N1
off Old Royal Free Sq 83 DN67
Waterview Ho, E14 85 DY71
Waterway Rd, Lthd. KT22 171 CG122
Waterworks La, E5 67 DX61
Waterworks Rd, SW2 121 DM86
Waterworks Yd, Croy. CR0
off Surrey St 142 DQ104
Watery La, SW20 139 CZ96
Chertsey (Lyne) KT16 133 BD102
Northolt UB5 78 BW68
St. Albans (Flam.) AL3 9 CK28
Sidcup DA14 126 EV93
Wates Way, Brwd. CM15 54 FX46
Mitcham CR4 140 DF100
Wates Way Ind Est, Mitch. CR4
off Wates Way 140 DF100
Wateville Rd, N17 46 DQ53
WATFORD 23 BT41
⊖ Watford 23 BT41
Watford Arches Retail Pk, Wat. WD17 off Lower High St 24 BX43
Watford Business Pk, Wat. WD18 23 BS44
Watford Bypass, Borwd. WD6 41 CG45
Watford Cl, SW11
off Petworth St 100 DE81
Watford Fld Rd, Wat. WD18 24 BW43
★ Watford FC, Wat. WD18 23 BV43
H Watford Gen Hosp, Wat. WD18 23 BV43
WATFORD HEATH, Wat. 40 BY46
Watford Heath, Wat. WD19 40 BX45
⇌ Watford High Street 24 BW42
⇌ Watford Junction 24 BW40
★ Watford Mus, Wat. WD17 24 BW43
⇌ Watford North 24 BW37
Watford Rd, E16 86 EG71
Borehamwood (Elstree) WD6 25 CJ44
Harrow HA1 61 CG61
Kings Langley WD4 7 BP32
Northwood HA6 39 BT52
Radlett WD7 25 CE36
Rickmansworth (Crox.Grn.) WD3 23 BQ43
St. Albans AL2 8 CA27
Wembley HA0 61 CG61
⇌ Watford Stadium Halt (closed) 23 BU44
Watford Way, NW4 63 CU56
NW7 63 CU56
⇌ Watford West (closed) 23 BT43
Watkin Rd, Wem. HA9 62 CP62
Watkinson Rd, N7 83 DM65
Watkins Ri, Pot.B. EN6
off The Walk 12 DB32
Watling Av, Edg. HA8 42 CR52
Watling Ct, EC4 197 J9
Borehamwood WD6 25 CK44
Watling Fm Cl, Stan. HA7 41 CJ46
Watling Gdns, NW2 81 CY65
Watling Knoll, Rad. WD7 9 CF33
Watlings Cl, Croy. CR0 143 DY100
Watling St, EC4 197 H9
SE15 off Dragon Rd 102 DS79
Bexleyheath DA6 107 FB84
Borehamwood (Elstree) WD6 25 CJ40
Dartford DA1, DA2 128 FP87
Gravesend DA11, DA12, DA13 130 GC90
Radlett WD7 9 CF32
St. Albans AL2 8 CC25
Watling St Caravan Site (Travellers), St.Alb. AL2 8 CC25
Watlington Gro, SE26 123 DY92
Watney Mkt, E1
off Commercial Rd 84 DV72
Watney Rd, SW14 98 CQ83
Watneys Rd, Mitch. CR4 141 DK99
Watney St, E1 84 DV72
Watson Av, E6 87 EN66
Sutton SM3 139 CY103
Watson Cl, N16
off Matthias Rd 66 DR64
SW19 120 DE93
Grays RM20 109 FU81
Watson Gdns, Rom. (Harold Wd.) RM3 52 FK54
Watson's Ms, W1 194 C7
Watsons Rd, N22 45 DM53
Watson's St, SE8 103 EA80
Watson St, E13 86 EH68
Watsons Yd, NW2
off North Circular Rd 63 CT61
Wattendon Rd, Ken. CR8 175 DP116
Wattisfield Rd, E5 66 DW62
Watts Cl, N15 off Seaford Rd 66 DS57
Tadworth KT20 173 CX122
Watts Cres, Purf. RM19 108 FQ77
Watts Fm Par, Wok. (Chobham) GU24 off Barnmead 150 AT110
Watts Gro, E3 85 EB71
Watts La, Chis. BR7 145 EP95
Tadworth KT20 173 CX122
Teddington TW11 117 CG92
Watts Mead, Tad. KT20 173 CX122
Watts Pt, E13 off Brooks Rd 86 EG67
Watts Rd, T.Ditt. KT7 137 CG101
Watts St, E1 202 E2
SE15 102 DT81
Watts Way, SW7 198 A6
Wat Tyler Rd, SE3 103 EC82
SE10 103 EC82
Wauthier Cl, N13 45 DP50
Wavell Cl, Wal.Cr. (Chsht.) EN8 15 DY27
Wavell Dr, Sid. DA15 125 ES86
Wavel Ms, N8 65 DK56
Wavel Ms, NW6 off Acol Rd 82 DB66
Wavel Pl, SE26
off Sydenham Hill 122 DT91
Wavendene Av, Egh. TW20 113 BB94
Wavendon Av, W4 98 CR78
Waveney Av, SE15 102 DV84
Waveney Cl, E1 202 C2
Waverley Av, E4 47 DZ49
E17 67 ED55
Kenley CR8 176 DS116
Surbiton KT5 138 CP100
Sutton SM1 140 DB103
Twickenham TW2 116 BZ88
Wembley HA9 62 CM64
Waverley Cl, E18 48 EJ53
Bromley BR2 144 EK99
Hayes UB3 95 BR77
West Molesey KT8 136 CA99
Waverley Ct, Wok. GU22 166 AY118
Waverley Cres, SE18 105 ER78
Romford RM3 52 FJ52
Waverley Dr, Cher. KT16 133 BD104
Virginia Water GU25 132 AU97
Waverley Gdns, E6
off Oliver Gdns 86 EL71
NW10 80 CM69
Barking IG11 87 ES68
Grays RM16 110 GA75
Ilford IG6 49 EQ54
Northwood HA6 39 BU53
Waverley Gro, N3 63 CY55
Waverley Ind Est, Har. HA1 61 CD55
Waverley Pl, N4
off Adolphus Rd 65 DP61
NW8 82 DD68
Leatherhead KT22
off Church Rd 171 CH122
Waverley Rd, E17 67 EC55
E18 48 EJ53
N8 65 DK58
N17 46 DV52
SE18 105 EQ78
SE25 142 DV98
Cobham (Stoke D'Ab.) KT11 154 CB114
Enfield EN2 29 DP42
Epsom KT17 157 CV106
Harrow HA2 60 BZ60
Leatherhead (Oxshott) KT22 154 CB114
Rainham RM13 89 FH69
Southall UB1 78 CA73
Weybridge KT13 152 BN106
Waverley Vil, N17 46 DT54
Waverley Wk, W2 82 DA71
Waverley Way, Cars. SM5 158 DE107
Waverton Ho, E3 85 DZ67
Waverton Rd, SW18 120 DC87
Waverton St, W1 198 G2
Wavertree Ct, SW2
off Streatham Hill 121 DM88
Wavertree Rd, E18 48 EG54
SW2 121 DL88
Waxlow Cres, Sthl. UB1 78 CA72
Waxlow Rd, NW10 80 CQ68
Waxwell Cl, Pnr. HA5 40 BX54
Waxwell La, Pnr. HA5 40 BX54
Waxwell Ter, SE1 200 C5
Way, The, Reig. RH2 184 DD133
Wayborne Gro, Ruis. HA4 59 BQ58
Waycross Rd, Upmin. RM14 73 FS58
Waye Av, Houns. TW5 95 BU81
Wayfarer Rd, Nthlt. UB5 78 BX70
Wayfaring Grn, Grays (Bad.Dene) RM17 off Curling La 110 FZ78
Wayfield Link, SE9 125 ER86
Wayford St, SW11 100 DE82
Wayland Av, E8 66 DU64
Waylands, Hayes UB3 77 BR71
Staines (Wrays.) TW19 112 AY86
Swanley BR8 147 FF98
Waylands Cl, Sev. (Knock.) TN14 180 EY115
Waylands Mead, Beck. BR3 143 EB95
Wayleave, The, SE28 88 EV73
Waylett Pl, SE27 121 DP90
Wembley HA0 61 CK63
Wayman Ct, E8 84 DV65
Wayne Cl, Orp. BR6 145 ET104
Wayneflete Twr Av, Esher KT10 136 CA104
Waynflete Av, Croy. CR0 141 DP104
Waynflete Sq, W10 81 CX73
Waynflete St, SW18 120 DC89
Wayside, NW11 63 CY60
SW14 118 CQ85
Croydon CR0 off Field Way 161 EB107
Kings Langley (Chipper.) WD4 6 BH30
Potters Bar EN6 12 DD33
Radlett (Shenley) WD7 9 CK33
Wayside Av, Bushey WD23 25 CD44
Hornchurch RM12 72 FK61
Wayside Cl, N14 29 DJ44
Romford RM1 71 FF55
Wayside Commercial Est, Bark. IG11 88 EU67
Wayside Ct, Twick. TW1 117 CJ86
Wembley HA9
off Oakington Av 62 CN62
Woking GU21
off Langmans Way 166 AS116
Wayside Gdns, SE9
off Wayside Gro 125 EM91
Dagenham RM10 70 FA64
Gerrards Cross SL9 56 AX59
Wayside Gro, SE9 125 EM91
Wayside Ms, Ilf. IG2
off Gaysham Av 69 EN57
Wayville Rd, Dart. DA1 128 FP87
Way Volante, Grav. DA12 131 GL91
Weald, The, Chis. BR7 125 EM93
Weald Cl, SE16 202 D10
Brentwood CM14 54 FU48
Bromley BR2 144 EL103
Gravesend (Istead Rise) DA13 130 GE94
★ Weald Country Pk, Brwd. CM14 54 FS45

Weald Hall La, Epp. (Thnwd.)
CM16 . . . 18 EW25
Weald La, Har. HA3 . . . 41 CD54
Weald Pk Way, Brwd. CM14 . . 54 FS48
Weald Ri, Har. HA3 . . . 41 CF52
Weald Rd, Brwd. CM14 . . . 53 FR46
SevenoaksTN13 . . . 191 FH129
Uxbridge UB10 . . . 76 BN68
Weald Sq, E5
off Rossington St . . . 66 DV61
WEALDSTONE, Har. . . . 61 CF55
Wealdstone Rd, Sutt. SM3 . . 139 CZ103
Weald Way, Cat. CR3 . . . 186 DS128
Wealdway, Grav. DA13 . . . 131 GH93
Weald Way, Hayes UB4 . . . 77 BS69
Romford RM7 . . . 71 FB58
Wealdwood Gdns, Pnr. HA5
off Highbanks Rd . . . 40 CB51
Weale Rd, E4 . . . 47 ED48
Weall Cl, Pur. CR8 . . . 159 DM112
Weall Grn, Wat. WD25 . . . 7 BV32
Weardale Av, Dart. DA2 . . . 128 FQ89
Weardale Gdns, Enf. EN2 . . . 30 DR39
Weardale Rd, SE13 . . . 103 ED84
Wear Pl, E2 . . . 84 DV69
Wearside Rd, SE13 . . . 103 EB84
Weasdale Ct, Wok. GU21
off Roundthorn Way . . . 166 AT116
Weatherall Cl, Add. KT15 . . . 152 BH106
Weatherley Cl, E3 . . . 85 DZ71
Weaver Cl, E6 off Trader Rd . . 87 EP73
Croydon CR0 . . . 160 DT105
Weavers Cl, Grav. DA11 . . . 131 GG88
IsleworthTW7 . . . 97 CE84
Weavers La, Sev. TN14 . . . 191 FJ121
Weavers Orchard, Grav. (Sthflt.)
DA13 . . . 130 GA93
Weavers Ter, SW6 . . . 100 DA79
Weaver St, E1 . . . 84 DU70
Weavers Way, NW1 . . . 83 DK67
Weaver Wk, SE27 . . . 121 DP91
Webb Cl, W10 . . . 81 CW70
Slough SL3 . . . 92 AX77
Webber Cl, Borwd. (Elstree)
WD6 off Rodgers Cl . . . 25 CK44
Erith DA8 . . . 107 FH80
Webber Row, SE1 . . . 200 E6
Webber St, SE1 . . . 200 E4
Webb Est, E5 . . . 66 DU59
Webb Gdns, E13
off Kelland Rd . . . 86 EG70
Webb Pl, NW10
off Old Oak La . . . 81 CT69
Webb Rd, SE3 . . . 104 EF79
Webb's All, Sev. TN13, TN15 . . 191 FJ125
Webbscroft Rd, Dag. RM10 . . 71 FB63
Webbs Rd, SW11 . . . 120 DF85
Hayes UB4 . . . 77 BV69
Webb St, SE1 . . . 201 M7
Webster Cl, Horn. RM12 . . . 72 FK62
Leatherhead (Oxshott)
KT22 . . . 154 CB114
Waltham Abbey EN9 . . . 16 EG33
Webster Gdns, W5 . . . 79 CK74
Webster Rd, E11 . . . 67 EC62
SE16 . . . 202 C7
Websters Cl, Wok. GU22 . . . 166 AU120
Wedderburn Rd, NW3 . . . 64 DD64
Barking IG11 . . . 87 ER67
Wedgewood Cl, Epp. CM16
off Theydon Gro . . . 18 EU30
Northwood HA6 . . . 39 BQ51
Wedgewoods, West. (Tats.) TN16
off Westmore Rd . . . 178 EJ121
Wedgewood Wk, NW6
off Lymington Rd . . . 64 DB64
Wedgwood Ms, W1 . . . 195 N9
Wedgwood Pl, Cob. KT11
off Portsmouth Rd . . . 153 BU114
Wedgwood Way, SE19 . . . 122 DQ94
Wedlake Cl, Horn. RM11 . . . 72 FL60
Wedlake St, W10
off Kensal Rd . . . 81 CY70
Wedmore Av, Ilf. IG5 . . . 49 EN53
Wedmore Gdns, N19 . . . 65 DK61
Wedmore Ms, N19
off Wedmore St . . . 65 DK62
Wedmore Rd, Grnf. UB6 . . . 79 CD69
Wedmore St, N19 . . . 65 DK62
Wednesbury Gdns, Rom. RM3 . 52 FM52
Wednesbury Grn, Rom. RM3
off Wednesbury Gdns . . . 52 FM52
Wednesbury Rd, Rom. RM3 . 52 FM52
Weech Rd, NW6 . . . 64 DA63
Weedington Rd, NW5 . . . 64 DG64
Weedon Cl, Ger.Cr. (Chal.St.P.)
SL9 . . . 36 AV53
Weekley Sq, SW11
off Thomas Baines Rd . . . 100 DD83
Weigall Rd, SE12 . . . 104 EG84
Weighhouse St, W1 . . . 194 G9
Weighton Rd, SE20 . . . 142 DV96
Harrow HA3 . . . 41 CD53
Weihurst Gdns, Sutt. SM1 . . 158 DD106
Weimar St, SW15 . . . 99 CY83
Weind, The, Epp. (They.B.)
CM16 . . . 33 ES36
Weirdale Av, N20 . . . 44 DF47
Weir Est, SW12 . . . 121 DJ87
Weir Hall Av, N18 . . . 46 DR51
Weir Hall Gdns, N18 . . . 46 DR50
Weir Hall Rd, N17 . . . 46 DR50
N18 . . . 46 DR50
Weir Pl, Stai. TW18 . . . 133 BE95
Weir Rd, SW12 . . . 121 DJ87
SW19 . . . 120 DB90
Bexley DA5 . . . 127 FB87
Chertsey KT16 . . . 134 BH101
Walton-on-Thames KT12 . . 135 BU100
Weirside Gdns, West Dr. UB7 . 76 BK74
Weir's Pas, NW1 . . . 195 N2
Weiss Rd, SW15 . . . 99 CX83
Welbeck Av, Brom. BR1 . . . 124 EG91
Hayes UB4 . . . 77 BV70
Sidcup DA15 . . . 126 EU88
Welbeck Cl, N12
off Torrington Pk . . . 44 DD50
Welbeck Cl, Borwd. WD6 . . . 26 CN41
Epsom KT17 . . . 157 CU108
New Malden KT3 . . . 139 CT99
Welbeck Rd, E6 . . . 86 EK69
Barnet EN4 . . . 28 DD44
Carshalton SM5 . . . 140 DE102
Harrow HA2 . . . 60 CB60
Sutton SM1 . . . 140 DD103
Welbeck St, W1 . . . 195 H8
Welbeck Wk, Cars. SM5
off Welbeck Rd . . . 140 DE102
Welbeck Way, W1 . . . 195 H8
Welby St, SE5 . . . 101 DP81
Welch Ho, Enf. EN3
off Beaconsfield Rd . . . 31 DX37
Welch Pl, Pnr. HA5 . . . 40 BW53
Welcomes Rd, Ken. CR8 . . . 176 DQ116
Welcote Dr, Nthwd. HA6 . . . 39 BR51
Welden, Slou. SL2 . . . 74 AW72
Welders La, Beac. (Jordans)
HP9 . . . 36 AT52
Gerrards Cross (Chal.St.P.)
SL9 . . . 36 AT52
Weldon Cl, Ruis. HA4 . . . 77 BV65
Weldon Dr, W.Mol. KT8 . . . 136 BZ98
Weldon Way, Red. RH1 . . . 185 DK129
Weld Pl, N11 . . . 45 DH50
Welfare Rd, E15 . . . 86 EE66
Welford Cl, E5 off Denton Way . 67 DX62
Welford Pl, SW19 . . . 119 CY91
Welham Rd, SW16 . . . 120 DG92
SW17 . . . 120 DG92
Welhouse Rd, Cars. SM5 . . . 140 DE102
Wellacre Rd, Har. HA3 . . . 61 CH58
Wellan Cl, Sid. DA15 . . . 126 EV85
Welland Cl, Slou. SL3 . . . 93 BA79
Welland Gdns, Grnf. UB6 . . . 79 CF68
Welland Ms, E1 . . . 202 C2
Wellands Cl, Brom. BR1 . . . 145 EM96
Welland St, SE10 . . . 103 EC79
Well App, Barn. EN5 . . . 27 CW43
Wellbrook Rd, Orp. BR6 . . . 163 EN105
Well Cl, SW16 . . . 121 DM91
Ruislip HA4
off Parkfield Cres . . . 60 BY62
Woking GU21 . . . 166 AW117
Wellclose Sq, E1 . . . 84 DU73
Wellclose St, E1 . . . 202 C1
Wellcome Av, Dart. DA1 . . . 108 FM84
★ Wellcome Trust, NW1 . . . 83 DK70
Well Cottage Cl, E11 . . . 68 EJ59
Well Ct, EC4 . . . 197 J9
SW16 . . . 121 DM91
Welldon Cres, Har. HA1 . . . 61 CE58
WELL END, Borwd. . . . 26 CR38
Well End Rd, Borwd. WD6 . . . 26 CQ37
Weller Cl, Amer. HP6 . . . 20 AS37
Weller Rd, Amer. HP6 . . . 20 AS37
Wellers Cl, West. TN16 . . . 189 EQ127
Weller's Ct, NW1 . . . 195 P1
Wellers Gro, Wal.Cr. (Chsht.)
EN7 . . . 14 DU28
Weller St, SE1 . . . 201 H4
Wellesford Cl, Bans. SM7 . . . 173 CZ117
Wellesley Av, W6 . . . 99 CV76
Iver SL0 . . . 93 BF76
Northwood HA6 . . . 39 BT50
Wellesley Ct, W9
off Maida Vale . . . 82 DC69
Wellesley Ct Rd, Croy. CR0 . . 142 DR103
Wellesley Cres, Pot.B. EN6 . . . 11 CY33
Twickenham TW2 . . . 117 CE89
Wellesley Gro, Croy. CR0 . . . 142 DR103
Wellesley Pk Ms, Enf. EN2 . . . 29 DP40
Wellesley Pas, Croy. CR0
off Wellesley Rd . . . 142 DQ103
Wellesley Path, Slou. SL1
off Wellesley Rd . . . 92 AU75
Wellesley Pl, NW1 . . . 195 M3
Tramlink Wellesley Road . . . 142 DQ103
Wellesley Rd, E11 . . . 68 EG57
E17 . . . 67 EA58
N22 . . . 45 DN54
NW5 . . . 64 DG64
W4 . . . 98 CN78
Brentwood CM14 . . . 54 FW46
Croydon CR0 . . . 142 DQ102
Harrow HA1 . . . 61 CE57
Ilford IG1 . . . 69 EP61
Slough SL1 . . . 92 AU75
Sutton SM2 . . . 158 DC107
Twickenham TW2 . . . 117 CD90
Wellesley St, E1 . . . 85 DX71
Wellesley Ter, N1 . . . 197 J2
Welley Av, Stai. (Wrays.) TW19 . 92 AY84
Welley Rd, Slou. (Horton) SL3 . 92 AY84
Staines (Wrays.) TW19 . . . 92 AY84
Well Fm Rd, Warl. CR6 . . . 176 DU119
Wellfield Av, N10 . . . 65 DH55
Wellfield Gdns, Cars. SM5 . . . 158 DE109
Wellfield Rd, SW16 . . . 121 DL91
Wellfields, Loug. IG10 . . . 33 EN41
Wellfield Wk, SW16 . . . 121 DM92
Wellfit St, SE24 off Hinton Rd . 101 DP83
Wellgarth, Grnf. UB6 . . . 79 CH65
Wellgarth Rd, NW11 . . . 64 DB60
Well Gro, N20 . . . 44 DC45
Well Hall Par, SE9
off Well Hall Rd . . . 105 EM84
Well Hall Rd, SE9 . . . 105 EM83
WELL HILL, Orp. . . . 165 FB107
Well Hill, Orp. BR6 . . . 165 FB107
Well Hill La, Orp. BR6 . . . 165 FB108
Well Hill Rd, Sev. TN14 . . . 165 FC107
Wellhouse La, Barn. EN5 . . . 27 CW42
Wellhouse Rd, Beck. BR3 . . . 143 DZ98
WELLING . . . 106 EU83
Rail Welling . . . 106 EU82
Welling High St, Well. DA16 . 106 EV83
Wellings Ho, Hayes UB3 . . . 77 BV74
★ Wellington Arch, W1 . . . 198 G4
Wellington Av, E4 . . . 47 EA47
N9 . . . 46 DV48
N15 . . . 66 DT58
Hounslow TW3 . . . 116 CA85
Pinner HA5 . . . 40 BZ53
Sidcup DA15 . . . 126 EU86
Wellington Av, Vir.W. GU25 . . 132 AV99
Worcester Park KT4 . . . 157 CW105
Wellington Bldgs, SW1
off Ebury Br Rd . . . 101 DH78
Wellington Cl, SE14
off Rutts Ter . . . 103 DX81
W11 off Ledbury Rd . . . 82 DA72
Dagenham RM10 . . . 89 FC66
Walton-on-Thames KT12
off Hepworth Way . . . 135 BT102
Watford WD19
off Highfield . . . 40 BZ48
Wellington Ct, NW8
off Wellington Rd . . . 82 DD68
Ashford TW15
off Wellington Rd . . . 114 BL92
Staines TW19 off Clare Rd . 114 BL87
Wellington Cres, N.Mal. KT3 . 138 CQ97
Wellington Dr, Dag. RM10 . . . 89 FC66
Purley CR8 . . . 159 DM110
Wellington Gdns, SE7 . . . 104 EJ79
Twickenham TW2 . . . 117 CD91
Wellington Gro, SE10
off Crooms Hill . . . 103 ED80
Wellington Hill, Loug.
(High Beach) IG10 . . . 32 EG37
H Wellington Hosp North,
NW8 . . . 194 A1
H Wellington Hosp South,
NW8 . . . 194 A1
Wellingtonia Av, Rom.
(Hav.at.Bow.) RM4 . . . 51 FE48
Wellington Ms, SE7 . . . 104 EJ79
SE22 off Peckham Rye . . . 102 DU84
SW16 off Woodbourne Av . 121 DK90
Wellington Pk Est, NW2 . . . 63 CU61
Wellington Pas, E11
off Wellington Rd . . . 68 EG57
Wellington Pl, N2
off Great N Rd . . . 64 DE57
NW8 . . . 194 A2
Brentwood CM14 . . . 54 FW50
Cobham KT11 . . . 154 BZ112
Wellington Rd, E6 . . . 87 EM68
E7 . . . 68 EF63
E10 . . . 67 DY60
E11 . . . 68 EG57
E17 . . . 67 DY55
NW8 . . . 82 DD68
NW10 . . . 81 CX69
SW19 . . . 120 DA89
W5 . . . 97 CJ76
Ashford TW15 . . . 114 BL92
Belvedere DA17 . . . 106 EZ78
Bexley DA5 . . . 126 EX85
Bromley BR2 . . . 144 EJ98
Caterham CR3 . . . 176 DQ122
Croydon CR0 . . . 141 DP101
Dartford DA1 . . . 128 FJ86
Enfield EN1 . . . 30 DS42
Epping (N.Wld.Bas.) CM16 . 18 FA27
Feltham TW14 . . . 115 BS85
Hampton TW12 . . . 117 CD92
Harrow HA3 . . . 61 CE55
Orpington BR5 . . . 146 EV100
Pinner HA5 . . . 40 BZ53
St. Albans (Lon.Col.) AL2 . . . 9 CK26
Tilbury RM18 . . . 111 GG83
Twickenham TW2 . . . 117 CD92
Uxbridge UB8 . . . 76 BJ67
Watford WD17 . . . 23 BV40
Wellington Rd N, Houns. TW4 . 96 BZ83
Wellington Rd S, Houns. TW4 . 96 BZ84
Wellington Row, E2 . . . 84 DT69
Wellington Sq, SW3 . . . 198 D10
Wellington St, SE18 . . . 105 EN77
WC2 . . . 196 A10
Barking IG11 off Axe St . . . 87 EQ67
Gravesend DA12 . . . 131 GJ87
Slough SL1 . . . 92 AT75
Wellington Ter, E1 . . . 202 D2
W2 off Notting Hill Gate . . 82 DB73
Harrow HA1 off West St . . . 61 CD60
Woking (Knap.) GU21
off Victoria Rd . . . 166 AS118
Wellington Way, E3 . . . 85 EA69
Weybridge KT13 . . . 152 BN110
Welling Way, SE9 . . . 105 ER83
Welling DA16 . . . 105 ER83
Well La, SW14 . . . 118 CQ85
Brentwood CM15 . . . 54 FT41
Woking GU21 . . . 166 AW117
Wellmeade Dr, Sev. TN13 . . . 191 FH127
Wellmeadow Rd, SE6 . . . 124 EE87
SE13 . . . 124 EE86
W7 . . . 97 CG77
Wellow Wk, Cars. SM5 . . . 140 DD102
Well Pas, NW3 . . . 64 DD62
Well Path, Wok. GU21
off Well La . . . 166 AW117
Well Rd, NW3 . . . 64 DD62
Barnet EN5 . . . 27 CW43
Potters Bar EN6 . . . 12 DE28
Wells, The, N14 . . . 45 DK45
Wells Cl, Lthd. KT23 . . . 170 CB124
Northolt UB5 off Yeading La . 78 BW69
South Croydon CR2 . . . 160 DS106
Waltham Cross (Chsht.) EN7
off Bloomfield Rd . . . 14 DQ25
Wells Dr, NW9 . . . 62 CR60
Wells Gdns, Dag. RM10 . . . 71 FB64
Ilford IG1 . . . 68 EL59
Rainham RM13 . . . 89 FF65
Wells Ho Rd, NW10 . . . 80 CS71
Wellside Cl, Barn. EN5 . . . 27 CW42
Wellside Gdns, SW14
off Well La . . . 118 CQ85
Wells Ms, W1 . . . 195 L7
Wellsmoor Gdns, Brom. BR1 . 145 EN97
Wells Pk Rd, SE26 . . . 122 DU90
Wells Path, Hayes UB4 . . . 77 BS69
Wells Pl, Red. RH1 . . . 185 DH130
Wells Ri, NW8 . . . 82 DF67
Wells Rd, W12 . . . 99 CW75
Bromley BR1 . . . 145 EM96
Epsom KT18 . . . 156 CN114
Wells Sq, WC1 . . . 196 B3
Wells St, W1 . . . 195 K7
Wellstead Av, N9 . . . 46 DW45
Wellstead Rd, E6 . . . 87 EN68
Wells Ter, N4 . . . 65 DN61
Wellstones, Wat. WD17 . . . 23 BV41
Wellstones Yd, Wat. WD17
off Wellstones . . . 23 BV41
Well St, E9 . . . 84 DV66
E15 . . . 86 EE65
Wells Way, SE5 . . . 102 DS79
SW7 . . . 100 DD76
Wells Yd S, N7 off George's Rd . 65 DN64
Well Wk, NW3 . . . 64 DD63
Well Way, Epsom KT18 . . . 172 CN115
Wellwood Cl, Couls. CR5
off The Vale . . . 159 DL114
Wellwood Rd, Ilf. IG3 . . . 70 EU60
Welsford St, SE1 . . . 202 B10
Welsh Cl, E13 . . . 86 EG69
Welshpool Ho, E8
off Benjamin Cl . . . 84 DU67
Welshpool St, E8
off Broadway Mkt . . . 84 DV67
Welshside Wk, NW9
off Fryent Gro . . . 62 CS58
Welstead Way, W4 . . . 99 CT77
Welsummer Way, Wal.Cr. EN8 . 15 DX27
Weltje Rd, W6 . . . 99 CU78
Welton Rd, SE18 . . . 105 ES80
Welwyn Av, Felt. TW14 . . . 115 BT86
Welwyn St, E2 off Globe Rd . . 84 DW69
Welwyn Way, Hayes UB4 . . . 77 BS70
WEMBLEY . . . 62 CL64
Rail Wembley Central . . . 62 CL64
Underground Wembley Central . . . 62 CL64
Wembley Commercial Cen,
Wem. HA9 . . . 61 CK61
★ Wembley Conf Cen, Wem.
HA9 . . . 62 CM63
Wembley Hill Rd, Wem. HA9 . . 62 CM64
WEMBLEY PARK, Wem. . . . 62 CM61
Underground Wembley Park . . . 62 CN62
Wembley Pk Business Cen,
Wem. HA9 . . . 62 CP62
Wembley Pk Dr, Wem. HA9 . . 62 CM62
Wembley Pt, Wem. HA9 . . . 80 CP66
Wembley Rd, Hmptn. TW12 . . 116 CA94
★ Wembley Stadium
(under redevelopment),
Wem. HA9 . . . 62 CN63
Rail Wembley Stadium . . . 62 CM64
Wembley Way, Wem. HA9 . . . 80 CP65
Wemborough Rd, Stan. HA7 . . 41 CJ52
Wembury Ms, N6
off Wembury Rd . . . 65 DH59
Wembury Rd, N6 . . . 65 DH59
Wemyss Rd, SE3 . . . 104 EF82
Wend, The, Couls. CR5 . . . 159 DK114
Croydon CR0 . . . 161 DZ111
Wendela Cl, Wok. GU22 . . . 167 AZ118
Wendela Ct, Har. HA1 . . . 61 CE62
Wendell Rd, W12 . . . 99 CT75
Wendle Ct, SW8 . . . 101 DL79
Wendley Dr, Add. (New Haw)
KT15 . . . 151 BF110
Wendling Rd, Sutt. SM1 . . . 140 DD102
Wendon St, E3 . . . 85 DZ67
Wendover, SE17 . . . 102 DS78
Wendover Cl, Hayes UB4
off Kingsash Dr . . . 78 BY70
Wendover Dr, N.Mal. KT3 . . . 139 CT100
Wendover Gdns, Brwd. CM13 . 55 GB47
Wendover Pl, Stai. TW18 . . . 113 BD92
Wendover Rd, NW10 . . . 81 CT68
SE9 . . . 104 EK83
Bromley BR2 . . . 144 EH97
Staines TW18 . . . 113 BC92
Wendover Way, Bushey WD23 . 24 CC44
Hornchurch RM12 . . . 72 FJ64
Orpington BR6
off Glendower Cres . . . 146 EU100
Welling DA16 . . . 126 EU85
Wendron Cl, Wok. GU21
off Shilburn Way . . . 166 AU118
Wendy Cl, Enf. EN1 . . . 30 DT44
Wendy Way, Wem. HA0 . . . 80 CL67
Wenham Gdns, Brwd. CM13
off Bannister Dr . . . 55 GC44
Wenlack Cl, Uxb. (Denh.) UB9
off Lindsey Rd . . . 58 BG62
Wenlock Ct, N1 . . . 197 L1
Wenlock Gdns, NW4
off Rickard Cl . . . 63 CU56
Wenlock Rd, N1 . . . 197 H1
Edgware HA8 . . . 42 CP52
Wenlock St, N1 . . . 197 J1
WENNINGTON, Rain. . . . 90 FK73
Wennington Rd, E3 . . . 85 DX68
Rainham RM13 . . . 89 FG70
Wensley Av, Wdf.Grn. IG8 . . . 48 EF52
Wensley Cl, N11
off Pickering Gdns . . . 44 DG51
SE9 . . . 125 EM86
Romford RM5 . . . 50 FA50
Wensleydale Av, Ilf. IG5 . . . 48 EL54
Wensleydale Gdns, Hmptn.
TW12 . . . 116 CB94
Wensleydale Pas, Hmptn.
TW12 . . . 136 CA95
Wensleydale Rd, Hmptn.
TW12 . . . 116 CA93
Wensley Rd, N18 . . . 46 DV51
Wensum Way, Rick. WD3 . . . 38 BK46
Wentbridge Path, Borwd. WD6 . 26 CN38
Wentland Cl, SE6 . . . 123 ED89
Wentland Rd, SE6 . . . 123 ED89
WENTWORTH, Vir.W. . . . 132 AS100
Wentworth Av, N3 . . . 44 DA52
Borehamwood (Elstree) WD6 . 26 CM43
Wentworth Cl, N3 . . . 44 DB52
SE28 . . . 88 EX72
Ashford TW15
off Reedsfield Rd . . . 115 BP91
Bromley BR2
off Hillside La . . . 144 EG103
Gravesend DA11 . . . 131 GG92
Morden SM4 . . . 140 DA101
Wentworth Cl, Orp. BR6 . . . 163 ES106
Potters Bar EN6
off Strafford Gate . . . 12 DA31
Surbiton KT6 . . . 137 CK103
Watford WD17 . . . 23 BT38
Woking (Ripley) GU23 . . . 168 BH121
Wentworth Ct, Surb. KT6
off Culsac Rd . . . 138 CL103
Wentworth Cres, SE15 . . . 102 DU80
Hayes UB3 . . . 95 BR76
Wentworth Dr, Dart. DA1 . . . 127 FG86
Pinner HA5 . . . 59 BU57
Virginia Water GU25 . . . 132 AT98
Wentworth Gdns, N13 . . . 45 DP49
★ Wentworth Golf Course,
Vir.W. GU25 . . . 132 AT100
Wentworth Hill, Wem. HA9 . . 62 CM60
Wentworth Ms, E3
off Eric St . . . 85 DZ70
Wentworth Pk, N3 . . . 44 DA52
Wentworth Pl, Grays RM16 . . 110 GD76
Stanmore HA7
off Greenacres Dr . . . 41 CH51
Wentworth Rd, E12 . . . 68 EK63
NW11 . . . 63 CZ58
Barnet EN5 . . . 27 CX41
Croydon CR0 . . . 141 DN101
Southall UB2 . . . 96 BW77
Wentworth St, E1 . . . 197 P8
Wentworth Way, Pnr. HA5 . . . 60 BX56
Rainham RM13 . . . 89 FH69
South Croydon CR2 . . . 160 DU114
Wenvoe Av, Bexh. DA7 . . . 107 FB82
Wernbrook St, SE18 . . . 105 EQ79
Werndee Rd, SE25 . . . 142 DU98
Werneth Hall Rd, Ilf. IG5 . . . 69 EM55
Werrington St, NW1 . . . 195 L1
Werter Rd, SW15 . . . 99 CY84
Wescott Way, Uxb. UB8 . . . 76 BJ68
Wesleyan Pl, NW5
off Gordon Ho Rd . . . 65 DH63
Wesley Av, E16 . . . 205 P2
NW10 . . . 80 CR69
Hounslow TW3 . . . 96 BY82
Wesley Cl, N7 . . . 65 DM61
SE17 . . . 200 G9
Harrow HA2 . . . 60 CC61
Orpington BR5 . . . 146 EW97
Waltham Cross (Chsht.) EN7 . 14 DQ28
Wesley Dr, Egh. TW20 . . . 113 BA93
Wesley Rd, E10 . . . 67 EC59
NW10 . . . 80 CQ67
Hayes UB3 . . . 77 BU73
★ Wesley's Ho, EC1 . . . 197 L4
Wesley Sq, W11 off Bartle Rd . 81 CY72
Wesley St, W1 . . . 194 G7
Wessels, Tad. KT20 . . . 173 CX121
Wessex Av, SW19 . . . 140 DA96
Wessex Cl, Ilf. IG3 . . . 69 ES58
Kingston upon Thames KT1
off Gloucester Rd . . . 138 CP95
Thames Ditton KT7 . . . 137 CF103
Wessex Dr, Erith DA8 . . . 107 FE81
Pinner HA5 . . . 40 BY52
Wessex Gdns, NW11 . . . 63 CY60
Wessex La, Grnf. UB6 . . . 79 CD68
Wessex Rd, Houns. (Hthrw.Air.)
TW6 . . . 94 BK82
Wessex St, E2 . . . 84 DW69
Wessex Way, NW11 . . . 63 CY60
West 12 Shop Cen, W12
off Shepherds Bush Grn . . 99 CX75
Westacott, Hayes UB4 . . . 77 BS71
Westacott Cl, N19 . . . 65 DK60
Westacres, Esher KT10 . . . 154 BZ108
WEST ACTON, W3 . . . 80 CN72
Underground West Acton . . . 80 CN72
Westall Rd, Loug. IG10 . . . 33 EP41
West App, Orp. BR5 . . . 145 EQ99
West Arbour St, E1 . . . 85 DX72
West Av, E17 . . . 67 EB56
N3 . . . 44 DA51
NW4 . . . 63 CX57
Hayes UB3 . . . 77 BT73
Pinner HA5 . . . 60 BZ58
St. Albans AL2 . . . 8 CB25
Southall UB1 . . . 78 BZ73
Wallington SM6 . . . 159 DL106
Walton-on-Thames KT12 . . 153 BS109
West Av Rd, E17 . . . 67 EA56
West Bk, N16 . . . 66 DS59
Barking IG11
off Highbridge Rd . . . 87 EP67
Enfield EN2 . . . 30 DQ40
Westbank Rd, Hmptn. (Hmptn.H.)
TW12 . . . 116 CC93
WEST BARNES, N.Mal. . . . 139 CU99
West Barnes La, SW20 . . . 139 CV97
New Malden KT3 . . . 139 CV97
Westbeech Rd, N22 . . . 65 DN55
Westbere Dr, Stan. HA7 . . . 41 CK49
Westbere Rd, NW2 . . . 63 CY63
Westbourne Av, W3 . . . 80 CR72
Sutton SM3 . . . 139 CY103
Westbourne Br, W2 . . . 82 DC71
Westbourne Cl, Hayes UB4 . . 77 BV70
Westbourne Cres, W2 . . . 82 DD73
Westbourne Cres Ms, W2
off Westbourne Cres . . . 82 DD73
Westbourne Dr, SE23 . . . 123 DX89
Brentwood CM14 . . . 54 FT49
Westbourne Gdns, W2 . . . 82 DB72
WESTBOURNE GREEN, W2 . . 82 DA71
Westbourne Gro, W2 . . . 82 DA72
W11 . . . 81 CZ73
Westbourne Gro Ms, W11
off Westbourne Gro . . . 82 DA72
Westbourne Gro Ter, W2 . . . 82 DB72
Underground Westbourne Park . . . 81 CZ71
Westbourne Pk Ms, W2
off Westbourne Gdns . . . 82 DB72
Westbourne Pk Pas, W2
off Westbourne Pk Vil . . . 82 DA71
Westbourne Pk Rd, W2 . . . 82 DA71

★ Place of interest | Railway station | London Underground station | DLR Docklands Light Railway station | Tramlink station | H Hospital

Wes - Wes

Westbourne Pk Rd, W11 81 CY72
Westbourne Pk Vil, W2 82 DA71
Westbourne Pl, N9
off Eastbournia Av 46 DV48
Westbourne Rd, N7 83 DN65
SE26 123 DX93
Bexleyheath DA7 106 EY80
Croydon CR0 142 DT100
Feltham TW13 115 BT90
Staines TW18 114 BH94
Uxbridge UB8 77 BP70
Westbourne St, W2 82 DD73
Westbourne Ter, SE23
off Westbourne Dr 123 DX89
W2 82 DD72
Westbourne Ter Ms, W2 82 DC72
Westbourne Ter Rd, W2 82 DC71
Westbridge Rd, SW11 100 DD81
WEST BROMPTON, SW10 100 DB79
⇌ West Brompton 100 DA78
⊖ West Brompton 100 DA78
Westbrook Av, Hmptn. TW12 116 BZ94
Westbrook Cl, Barn. EN4 28 DD41
Westbrook Cres, Barn. EN4 28 DD41
Westbrook Dr, Orp. BR5 146 EW102
Westbrooke Cres, Well. DA16 106 EW83
Westbrooke Rd, Sid. DA15 125 ER89
Welling DA16 106 EV83
Westbrook Rd, SE3 104 EH81
Hounslow TW5 96 BZ80
Staines TW18 *off South St* 113 BF92
Thornton Heath CR7 142 DR95
Westbrook Sq, Barn. EN4
off Westbrook Cres 28 DD41
Westbury Av, N22 65 DP55
Esher (Clay.) KT10 155 CF107
Southall UB1 78 CA70
Wembley HA0 80 CL66
Westbury Cl, Ruis. HA4 59 BU59
Shepperton TW17
off Burchetts Way 135 BP100
Whyteleafe CR3
off Beverley Rd 176 DS116
Westbury Dr, Brwd. CM14 54 FV47
Westbury Gro, N12 44 DA51
Westbury La, Buck.H. IG9 48 EJ47
Westbury Lo Cl, Pnr. HA5 60 BX55
Westbury Par, SW12
off Balham Hill 121 DH86
Westbury Pl, Brent. TW8 97 CK79
Westbury Rd, E7 68 EH64
E17 67 EA56
N11 45 DL51
N12 44 DA51
SE20 143 DX95
W5 80 CL72
Barking IG11 87 ER67
Beckenham BR3 143 DY97
Brentwood CM14 54 FW47
Bromley BR1 144 EK95
Buckhurst Hill IG9 48 EJ47
Croydon CR0 142 DR100
Feltham TW13 116 BX88
Ilford IG1 69 EM61
New Malden KT3 138 CR98
Northwood HA6 39 BS49
Waltham Cross (Chsht.) EN8
off Turners Hill 15 DX30
Watford WD18 23 BV43
Wembley HA0 80 CL66
Westbury St, SW8 101 DJ82
Westbury Ter, E7 86 EH65
Upminster RM14 73 FS61
Westerham TN16 189 EQ127
WEST BYFLEET 152 BH113
⇌ West Byfleet 152 BG112
Westcar La, Walt. KT12 153 BV107
West Carriage Dr, W2 198 A3
West Cen St, WC1 195 P8
West Cen Av, W10
off Harrow Rd 81 CV69
West Chantry, Har. HA3
off Chantry Rd 40 CB53
Westchester Dr, NW4 63 CX55
West Cl, N9 46 DT48
Ashford TW15 114 BL91
Barnet EN5 27 CV43
Barnet (Cockfos.) EN4 28 DG42
Greenford UB6 78 CC68
Hampton TW12
off Oak Av 116 BY93
Rainham RM13 89 FH70
Wembley HA9 62 CM60
Westcombe Av, Croy. CR0 141 DL100
Westcombe Ct, SE3
off Westcombe Pk Rd 104 EF80
Westcombe Dr, Barn. EN5 28 DA43
Westcombe Hill, SE3 104 EG78
SE10 104 EG78
Westcombe Lo Dr, Hayes
UB4 77 BR71
⇌ Westcombe Park 104 EG78
Westcombe Pk Rd, SE3 104 EE79
West Common, Ger.Cr. SL9 56 AX57
West Common Cl, Ger.Cr.
SL9 56 AY57
West Common Rd, Brom.
BR2 144 EG103
Keston BR2 162 EH105
Uxbridge UB8 58 BK64
Westcoombe Av, SW20 139 CT95
Westcote Ri, Ruis. HA4 59 BQ59
Westcote Rd, SW16 121 DJ92
West Cotts, NW6 64 DA64
Westcott Av, Grav. (Nthflt.)
DA11 131 GG90
Westcott Cl, N15
off Ermine Rd 66 DT58
Bromley BR1
off Ringmer Way 144 EL99
Croydon (New Adgtn.) CR0
off Castle Hill Av 161 EB109
Westcott Cres, W7 79 CE72
Westcott Rd, SE17 101 DP79
Westcott Way, Sutt. SM2 157 CW110
WESTCOURT, Grav. 131 GL89
West Ct, SE18
off Prince Imperial Rd 105 EM81
Westcourt, Sun. TW16 135 BV96
West Ct, Wem. HA0 61 CJ61
West Cres Rd, Grav. DA12 131 GH86
Westcroft Cl, NW2 63 CY63
Enfield EN3 30 DW38
Westcroft Gdns, Mord. SM4 139 CZ97
Westcroft Rd, Cars. SM5 158 DG105
Wallington SM6 158 DG105
Westcroft Sq, W6 99 CU77
Westcroft Way, NW2 63 CY63
West Cromwell Rd, SW5 99 CZ77
W14 99 CZ77
West Cross Cen, Brent. TW8 97 CG79
West Cross Route, W10 81 CX73
W11 81 CX73
West Cross Way, Brent. TW8 97 CH79
⇌ West Croydon 142 DQ102
⯁ West Croydon 142 DQ102
Westdale Pas, SE18 105 EP79
Westdale Rd, SE18 105 EP79
Westdean Av, SE12 124 EH88
Westdean Cl, SW18 120 DB86
West Dene, Sutt. SM3
off Park La 157 CY107
West Dene Dr, Rom. RM3 52 FK50
Westdene Way, Wey. KT13 135 BS104
Westdown Rd, E15 67 EC63
SE6 123 EA87
WEST DRAYTON 94 BK76
⇌ West Drayton 76 BL74
West Drayton Pk Av, West Dr.
UB7 94 BL76
West Drayton Rd, Uxb. UB8 77 BP71
West Dr, SW16 121 DJ91
Carshalton SM5 158 DD110
Harrow HA3 41 CD51
Sutton (Cheam) SM2 157 CX109
Tadworth KT20 173 CX118
Virginia Water GU25 132 AT101
Watford WD25 23 BV36
West Dr Gdns, Har. HA3 41 CD51
WEST DULWICH, SE21 122 DR90
⇌ West Dulwich 122 DR88
⇌ West Ealing 79 CH73
West Eaton Pl, SW1 198 F8
West Eaton Pl Ms, SW1 198 F8
Wested La, Swan. BR8 147 FG101
West Ella Rd, NW10 80 CS66
WEST END, Esher 154 BZ107
West End Av, E10 67 EC57
Pinner HA5 60 BX56
West End Cl, NW10 80 CQ66
West End Ct, Pnr. HA5 60 BX56
Slough (Stoke P.) SL2 74 AT67
West End Gdns, Esher KT10 154 BZ106
Northolt UB5 *off Edward Cl* 78 BW68
West End La, NW6 82 DA67
Barnet EN5 27 CX42
Esher KT10 154 BZ107
Hayes UB3 95 BQ80
Pinner HA5 60 BX55
Slough (Stoke P.) SL2 74 AS67
West End Rd, Nthlt. UB5 78 BW66
Ruislip HA4 59 BV64
Southall UB1 78 BY74
Westerdale Rd, SE10 104 EG78
Westerfield Rd, N15 66 DT57
Westerfolds Cl, Wok. GU22 167 BC116
Westergate Rd, SE2 106 EY78
WESTERHAM 189 EQ126
Westerham Av, N9 46 DR48
Westerham Cl, Add. KT15 152 BJ107
Sutton SM2 158 DA110
Westerham Dr, Sid. DA15 126 EV86
Westerham Hill, West. TN16 179 EN121
Westerham Rd, E10 67 EB59
Keston BR2 162 EK107
Oxted RH8 188 EF129
Sevenoaks TN13 190 FC123
Westerham TN16 189 EM128
Westerham (Brasted)
TN16 189 ET125
Westerley Cres, SE26 123 DZ92
Westerley Ware, Rich. TW9
off Kew Grn 98 CN79
Westermain, Add. (New Haw)
KT15 152 BJ110
Western Av, NW11 63 CX58
W3 80 CR71
W5 80 CM70
Brentwood CM14 54 FW46
Chertsey KT16 134 BG97
Dagenham RM10 89 FC65
Egham TW20 133 BB97
Epping CM16 17 ET32
Grays RM20 109 FT78
Greenford UB6 79 CK69
Northolt UB5 78 BZ67
Romford RM2 52 FJ54
Ruislip HA4 77 BP65
Uxbridge (Denh.) UB9 58 BJ63
Uxbridge (Ickhm.) UB10 77 BP65
Western Av Business Pk, W3
off Mansfield Rd 80 CP70
Western Av Underpass, W5
off Western Av 80 CM69
Western Beach Apartments,
E16 205 M2
Western Cl, Cher. KT16
off Western Av 134 BG97
Western Ct, N3 *off Huntley Dr* 44 DA51
Western Cross Cl, Green. DA9
off Johnsons Way 129 FW86
Western Dr, Shep. TW17 135 BR100
Western Gdns, W5 80 CN73
Brentwood CM14 54 FW47
Western La, SW12 120 DG87
Western Ms, W9
off Great Western Rd 81 CZ70
Western Par, Barn. EN5
off Great N Rd 28 DA43
Western Pathway, Horn.
RM12 90 FJ65
Western Perimeter Rd, Houns.
(Hthrw.Air.) TW6 94 BH83
Western Pl, SE16 202 G4
Western Rd, E13 86 EJ67
E17 67 EC57
N2 64 DF56
N22 45 DM54
NW10 80 CQ70
SW9 101 DN83
SW19 140 DD95
W5 79 CK73
Brentwood CM14 54 FW47
Epping CM16 17 ET32
Mitcham CR4 140 DD95
Romford RM1 71 FE57
Southall UB2 96 BX76
Sutton SM1 158 DA106
Western Ter, W6
off Chiswick Mall 99 CU78
Western Trd Est, NW10 80 CQ70
Western Vw, Hayes UB3 95 BT75
Westernville Gdns, Ilf. IG2 69 EQ59
Western Way, SE28 105 ER76
Barnet EN5 28 DA44
WEST EWELL, Epsom 156 CS108
West Fm Av, Ashtd. KT21 171 CJ118
West Fm Cl, Ashtd. KT21 171 CJ119
West Fm Dr, Ashtd. KT21 171 CK119
DLR Westferry 85 EA73
Westferry Circ, E14 203 P2
Westferry Rd, E14 203 N2
WESTFIELD, Wok. 167 AZ122
Westfield, Ashtd. KT21 172 CM118
Loughton IG10 32 EJ43
Reigate RH2 184 DB131
Sevenoaks TN13 191 FJ122
Westfield Av, S.Croy. CR2 160 DR113
Watford WD24 24 BW37
Woking GU22 166 AY121
Westfield Cl, NW9 62 CQ55
SW10 100 DC80
Enfield EN3 31 DY41
Gravesend DA12 131 GJ93
Sutton SM1 157 CZ105
Waltham Cross EN8 15 DZ31
Westfield Common, Wok.
GU22 166 AY122
Westfield Dr, Har. HA3 61 CK57
Leatherhead (Bkhm.)
KT23 170 CA122
Westfield Gdns, Har. HA3 61 CK56
Westfield Gro, Wok. GU22 167 AZ120
Westfield La, Har. HA3 61 CK56
Slough (Geo.Grn.) SL3 74 AX73
Westfield Par, Add. (New Haw)
KT15 152 BK110
Westfield Pk, Pnr. HA5 40 BZ52
Westfield Pk Dr, Wdf.Grn. IG8 48 EL51
Westfield Rd, NW7 42 CR48
W13 79 CG74
Beckenham BR3 143 DZ96
Bexleyheath DA7 107 FC82
Croydon CR0 141 DP103
Dagenham RM9 70 EY63
Mitcham CR4 140 DF96
Surbiton KT6 137 CK99
Sutton SM1 157 CZ105
Walton-on-Thames KT12 136 BY101
Woking GU22 166 AX122
Westfields, SW13 99 CT83
Westfields Av, SW13 98 CS83
Westfields Rd, W3 80 CP71
Westfield St, SE18 104 EK76
Westfield Wk, Wal.Cr. EN8
off Westfield Cl 15 DZ31
Westfield Way, E1 85 DY69
Ruislip HA4 59 BS62
Woking GU22 166 AY122
⊖ West Finchley 44 DB51
West Gdn Pl, W2 194 C9
West Gdns, E1 202 E1
SW17 120 DE93
Epsom KT17 156 CS110
West Gate, W5 80 CL69
Westgate Cl, Epsom KT18
off Chalk La 172 CR115
Westgate Ct, Wal.Cr. EN8
off Holmesdale 31 DX35
Westgate Ho, Brent. TW8 97 CK78
Westgate Rd, SE25 142 DV98
Beckenham BR3 143 EB96
Dartford DA1 128 FK86
Westgate St, E8 84 DV67
Westgate Ter, SW10 100 DB78
Westglade Ct, Har. HA3 61 CK57
West Gorse, Croy. CR0 161 DY112
WEST GREEN, N15 66 DQ55
West Grn Pl, Grnf. UB6
off Uneeda Dr 79 CD67
West Grn Rd, N15 65 DP56
West Gro, SE10 103 EC81
Walton-on-Thames KT12 153 BV105
Woodford Green IG8 48 EJ51
Westgrove La, SE10 103 EC81
West Halkin St, SW1 198 F6
West Hallowes, SE9 124 EK88
Westhall Pk, Warl. CR6 176 DW119
West Hall Rd, Rich. TW9 98 CP81
Westhall Rd, Warl. CR6 176 DV119
WEST HAM, E15 86 EF66
⇌ West Ham 86 EE69
⊖ West Ham 86 EE69
West Ham La, E15 86 EE66
West Ham Pk, E7 86 EG66
WEST HAMPSTEAD, NW6 64 DB64
⇌ West Hampstead 82 DA65
⊖ West Hampstead 82 DA65
West Hampstead Ms, NW6 82 DB65
⇌ West Hampstead
(Thameslink) 82 DA65
★ West Ham United FC, E13 86 EJ68
West Harding St, EC4 196 E8
West Harold, Swan. BR8 147 FD97
WEST HARROW, Har. 60 CC59
⊖ West Harrow 60 CC58
West Hatch Manor, Ruis. HA4 59 BT60
Westhay Gdns, SW14 118 CP85
WEST HEATH, SE2 106 EX79
West Heath, Oxt. RH8 188 EG130
West Heath Av, NW11 64 DA60
West Heath Cl, NW3 64 DA62
Dartford DA1
off West Heath Rd 127 FF86
West Heath Dr, NW11 64 DA60
West Heath Gdns, NW3 64 DA62
West Heath La, Sev. TN13 191 FH128
West Heath Rd, NW3 64 DA61
SE2 106 EX79
Dartford DA1 127 FF86
WEST HENDON, NW9 62 CS59
West Hendon Bdy, NW9 63 CT58
West Hill, SW15 119 CX87
SW18 120 DA85
Dartford DA1 128 FK86
Epsom KT19 156 CQ113
Harrow HA2 61 CE61
Orpington BR6 163 EM112
Oxted RH8 187 ED130
South Croydon CR2 160 DS110
Wembley HA9 62 CM60
West Hill Av, Epsom KT19 156 CQ112
West Hill Bk, Oxt. RH8 187 ED130
Westhill Cl, Grav. DA12
off Leith Pk Rd 131 GH88
West Hill Ct, N6 64 DG62
West Hill Dr, Dart. DA1 128 FJ86
West Hill Pk, N6
off Merton La 64 DF61
West Hill Ri, Dart. DA1 128 FK86
West Hill Rd, SW18 120 DA86
Woking GU22 166 AX119
West Hill Way, N20 44 DB46
Westholm, NW11 64 DB56
West Holme, Erith DA8 107 FC81
Westholme, Orp. BR6 145 ES101
Westholme Gdns, Ruis. HA4 59 BU60
Westhorne Av, SE9 124 EJ86
SE12 124 EG87
Westhorpe Gdns, NW4 63 CW55
Westhorpe Rd, SW15 99 CW83
West Ho Cl, SW19 119 CY88
Westhurst Dr, Chis. BR7 125 EP92
West Hyde La, Ger.Cr. (Chal.St.P.)
SL9 37 AZ52
West India Av, E14 203 P2
West India Dock Rd, E14 85 DZ72
DLR West India Quay 204 B1
⊖ West Kensington 99 CZ78
West Kent Av, Grav. (Nthflt.)
DA11 130 GC86
West Kent Cold Storage, Sev.
(Dunt.Grn.) TN14 181 FF120
West Kentish Town Est, NW5 64 DG64
WEST KILBURN, W9 81 CZ69
Westlake Cl, N13 45 DN48
Hayes UB4 *off Lochan Cl* 78 BY70
Westlake Rd, Wem. HA9 61 CK61
Westland Av, Horn. RM11 72 FL60
Westland Cl, Stai. (Stanw.)
TW19 114 BL86
Watford WD25 *off Ashfields* 7 BT34
Westland Dr, Brom. BR2 144 EF103
Hatfield AL9 11 CY27
Westland Ho, E16
off Rymill St 87 EN74
Westland Pl, N1 197 K2
Westland Rd, Wat. WD17 23 BV40
Westlands Cl, Hayes UB3
off Granville Rd 95 BU77
Westlands Ct, Epsom KT18 172 CQ115
Westlands Ter, SW12
off Gaskarth Rd 121 DJ86
Westlands Way, Oxt. RH8 187 ED127
West La, SE16 202 D5
Westlea Av, Wat. WD25 24 BY37
Westlea Rd, W7 97 CG76
Westleigh Av, SW15 119 CV85
Coulsdon CR5 174 DG116
Westleigh Dr, Brom. BR1 144 EL95
Westleigh Gdns, Edg. HA8 42 CN53
Westlinks, Wem. HA0
off Alperton La 79 CK69
Westlinton Cl, NW7 43 CY51
West Lo Av, W3 80 CN74
Westlyn Cl, Rain. RM13 90 FJ69
Westmacott Dr, Felt. TW14 115 BT88
West Mall, W8
off Palace Gdns Ter 82 DA74
West Malling Way, Horn.
RM12 72 FJ64
Westmark Pt, SW15
off Norley Vale 119 CV88
Westmead, SW15 119 CV86
West Mead, Epsom KT19 156 CS107
Ruislip HA4 60 BW63
Westmead, Wok. GU21 166 AV117
Westmead Cor, Cars. SM5
off Colston Av 158 DE105
Westmeade Cl, Wal.Cr. (Chsht.)
EN7 14 DV29
Westmead Rd, Sutt. SM1 158 DD105
Westmede, Chig. IG7 49 EQ51
Westmere Dr, NW7 42 CR48
West Mersea Cl, E16 205 P3
West Ms, N17 46 DV51
SW1 199 J9
H West Middlesex Uni Hosp,
Islw. TW7 97 CG82
West Mill, Grav. DA11 131 GF86
Westmill Ct, N4
off Brownswood Rd 66 DQ61
WESTMINSTER, SW1 199 K6
⊖ Westminster 200 A5
★ Westminster Abbey,
SW1 199 P6
★ Westminster Abbey Mus,
SW1 199 P6
Westminster Av, Th.Hth.
CR7 141 DP96
Westminster Br, SE1 200 A5
SW1 200 A5
Westminster Br Rd, SE1 200 C5
★ Westminster Cathedral,
SW1 199 K7
★ Westminster City Hall,
SW1 199 L6
Westminster Cl, Felt. TW14 115 BU88
Ilford IG6 49 ER54
Teddington TW11 117 CG92
Westminster Dr, N13 45 DL50
Westminster Gdns, E4 48 EE46
SW1 199 P8
Barking IG11 87 ES68
Ilford IG6 49 EQ54
★ Westminster Pier, SW1 200 A4
Westminster Rd, N9 46 DV46
W7 79 CE74
Sutton SM1 140 DD103
Westmoat Cl, Beck. BR3 123 EC94
WEST MOLESEY 136 BZ99
Westmont Rd, Esher KT10 137 CE103
Westmoor Gdns, Enf. EN3 31 DX40
Westmoor Rd, Enf. EN3 31 DX40
Westmoor St, SE7 104 EJ76
Westmore Grn, West. (Tats.)
TN16 178 EJ121
Westmoreland Av, Horn.
RM11 72 FJ57
Welling DA16 105 ES83
Westmoreland Bldgs, EC1
off Bartholomew Cl 84 DQ71
Westmoreland Dr, Sutt. SM2 158 DB109
Westmoreland Pl, SW1 101 DH78
W5 *off Mount Av* 79 CK71
Bromley BR1 144 EG97
Westmoreland Rd, NW9 62 CN56
SE17 102 DQ79
SW13 99 CT81
Bromley BR1, BR2 144 EE99
Westmoreland St, W1 194 G7
Westmoreland Ter, SW1 101 DH78
Westmoreland Wk, SE17 102 DR79
Westmore Rd, West. (Tats.)
TN16 178 EJ121
Westmorland Cl, E12 68 EK61
Epsom KT19 156 CS110
Twickenham TW1 117 CH86
Westmorland Rd, E17 67 EA58
Harrow HA1 60 CB57
Westmorland Sq, Mitch. CR4
off Westmorland Way 141 DL99
Westmorland Ter, SE20 122 DV94
Westmorland Way, Mitch.
CR4 141 DK98
Westmount Rd, SE9 105 EM82
WEST NORWOOD, SE27 122 DQ90
⇌ West Norwood 121 DP90
West Oak, Beck. BR3 143 ED95
Westoe Rd, N9 46 DV47
Weston Av, Add. KT15 152 BG105
Grays RM20 109 FT77
Thames Ditton KT7 137 CE101
West Molesey KT8 136 BY97
Weston Cl, Brwd. CM13 55 GC45
Coulsdon CR5 175 DM120
Potters Bar EN6 11 CZ32
Weston Ct, N4 *off Queens Dr* 66 DQ62
N20 *off Farnham Cl* 44 DC45
Weston Dr, Cat. CR3
off Coulsdon Rd 176 DQ122
Stanmore HA7 41 CH53
West One Shop Cen, W1
off Oxford St 83 DH72
Weston Gdns, Islw. TW7 97 CD81
Woking GU22 167 BE116
WESTON GREEN, T.Ditt. 137 CF102
Weston Grn, Dag. RM9 70 EZ63
Thames Ditton KT7 137 CE102
Weston Grn Rd, Esher KT10 137 CD102
Thames Ditton KT7 137 CE102
Weston Gro, Brom. BR1 144 EF95
Weston Pk, N8 65 DL58
Kingston upon Thames KT1
off Fairfield W 138 CL96
Thames Ditton KT7 137 CE102
Weston Pk Cl, T.Ditt. KT7
off Weston Pk 137 CE102
Weston Ri, WC1 196 C1
Weston Rd, W4 98 CQ76
Bromley BR1 124 EF94
Dagenham RM9 70 EY63
Enfield EN2 30 DR39
Epsom KT17 156 CS111
Thames Ditton KT7 137 CE102
Weston St, SE1 201 L6
Weston Wk, E8 *off Mare St* 84 DV66
Weston Way, Wok. GU22 167 BE116
Westover Cl, Sutt. SM2 158 DB109
Westover Hill, NW3 64 DA61
Westover Rd, SW18 120 DC86
Westow Hill, SE19 122 DS93
Westow St, SE19 122 DS93
West Palace Gdns, Wey.
KT13 135 BP104
West Pk, SE9 124 EL89
West Pk Av, Rich. TW9 98 CN81
West Pk Cl, Houns. TW5
off Heston Gra La 96 BZ79
Romford RM6 70 EX57
West Pk Hill, Brwd. CM14 54 FU48
H West Park Hosp, Epsom
KT19 156 CM112
West Pk Rd, Epsom KT19 156 CM112
Richmond TW9 98 CN81
Southall UB2 78 CC74
West Parkside, SE10 205 L7
Warlingham CR6 177 EA115
West Pier, E1 202 D3
West Pl, SW19 119 CW92
Westpoint Trd Est, W3 80 CP71
Westpole Av, Barn. EN4 28 DG42
Westport Rd, E13 86 EH70
Westport St, E1 85 DX72
West Poultry Av, EC1 196 F7
West Quarters, W12 81 CU72
West Quay Dr, Hayes UB4 78 BY71
West Ramp, Houns. (Hthrw.Air.)
TW6 94 BN81
West Ridge Gdns, Grnf. UB6 78 CC68
West Riding, St.Alb. (Brick.Wd.)
AL2 8 BZ30

★ Place of interest ⇌ Railway station ⊖ London Underground station DLR Docklands Light Railway station ⯁ Tramlink station H Hospital

345

Wes- Whi

West Rd, E15 86 EF67
N17 46 DV51
SW3 100 DF79
SW4 121 DK85
W5 80 CL71
Barnet EN4 44 DG46
Chessington KT9 155 CJ112
Feltham TW14 115 BR86
Kingston upon Thames KT2 138 CQ95
Romford (Chad.Hth.) RM6 70 EX58
Romford (Rush Grn.) RM7 71 FD59
South Ockendon RM15 91 FV69
West Drayton UB7 94 BM76
Weybridge KT13 153 BP109
Westrow, SW15 119 CW85
West Row, W10 81 CY70
Westrow Dr, Bark. IG11 87 ET65
Westrow Gdns, Ilf. IG3 69 ET61
⇌ **West Ruislip** 59 BQ61
⊖ **West Ruislip** 59 BQ61
West Shaw, Long. DA3 149 FX96
West Sheen Vale, Rich. TW9 98 CM84
Westside, NW4 43 CV54
West Side, Brox. EN10
off High Rd Turnford 15 DY25
West Side Common, SW19 119 CW92
West Smithfield, EC1 196 F7
West Spur Rd, Uxb. UB8 76 BK69
West Sq, SE11 200 F7
Iver SL0 *off High St* 75 BF72
West St, E2 84 DV68
E11 68 EE62
E17 *off Grove Rd* 67 EB57
WC2 195 N9
Bexleyheath DA7 106 EZ84
Brentford TW8 97 CJ79
Bromley BR1 144 EG95
Carshalton SM5 140 DF104
Croydon CR0 160 DQ105
Epsom KT18 156 CR113
Epsom (Ewell) KT17 156 CS110
Erith DA8 107 FD77
Gravesend DA11 131 GG86
Grays RM17 110 GA79
Harrow HA1 61 CD60
Reigate RH2 183 CY133
Sutton SM1 158 DB106
Watford WD17 23 BV40
Woking GU21
off Church St E 167 AZ117
West St La, Cars. SM5 158 DF105
⇌ **West Sutton** 158 DA105
West Temple Sheen, SW14 98 CP84
West Tenter St, E1 84 DT72
West Thamesmead Business Pk,
SE28 105 ET76
WEST THURROCK, Grays 109 FU78
West Thurrock Way, Grays
RM20 109 FT77
WEST TILBURY, Til. 111 GL79
West Twrs, Pnr. HA5 60 BX58
Westvale Ms, W3 80 CS74
West Valley Rd, Hem.H. HP3 6 BJ25
West Vw, NW4 63 CW56
Feltham TW14 115 BQ87
Loughton IG10 33 EM41
West Vw Av, Whyt. CR3
off Station Rd 176 DU118
Westview Cl, NW10 63 CT64
W7 79 CE72
W10 81 CW72
Rainham RM13 90 FJ69
West Vw Ct, Borwd. (Elstree)
WD6 *off High St* 25 CK44
Westview Cres, N9 46 DS45
Westview Dr, Wdf.Grn. IG8 48 EK54
West Vw Gdns, Borwd. (Elstree)
WD6 *off High St* 25 CK44
West Vw Rd, Dart. DA1 128 FM86
Swanley BR8 147 FG98
Swanley (Crock.) BR8 147 FD100
Westview Rd, Warl. CR6 176 DV119
Westville Rd, W12 99 CU75
Thames Ditton KT7 137 CG102
West Wk, W5 80 CL71
Barnet EN4 44 DG45
Hayes UB3 77 BU74
West Walkway, The, Sutt. SM1
off Cheam Rd 158 DB106
Westward Rd, E4 47 DZ50
Westward Way, Har. HA3 62 CL58
West Warwick Pl, SW1 199 J9
WEST WATFORD, Wat. 23 BU42
West Way, N18 46 DR49
NW10 62 CR62
Westway, SW20 139 CV97
W2 82 DA71
W9 82 DA71
W10 81 CY72
W12 81 CU73
West Way, Brwd. CM14 54 FU48
Carshalton SM5 158 DD110
Westway, Cat. CR3 176 DR122
West Way, Croy. CR0 143 DY103
Edgware HA8 42 CP51
Hounslow TW5 96 BZ81
Westway, Orp. BR5 145 ER99
West Way, Pnr. HA5 60 BX56
Rickmansworth WD3 38 BH46
Ruislip HA4 59 BT60
Shepperton TW17 135 BR100
West Wickham BR4 143 ED100
Westway Cl, SW20 139 CV97
Westway Cross Shop Pk, Grnf.
UB6 79 CE67
West Way Gdns, Croy. CR0 143 DX103
Westway Gdns, Red. RH1 184 DG131
Westways, Epsom KT19 157 CT105
Westerham TN16 189 EQ126
Westwell Cl, Orp. BR5 146 EX102
Westwell Rd, SW16 121 DL93
Westwell Rd App, SW16
off Westwell Rd 121 DL93
Westwick Gdns, W14 99 CX75
Hounslow TW4 95 BV82
WEST WICKHAM 143 EC103
⇌ **West Wickham** 143 EC101
Westwick Pl, Wat. WD25 8 BW34
Westwood Av, SE19 142 DQ95
Addlestone (Woodham)
KT15 151 BF112
Brentwood CM14 54 FU49
Harrow HA2 60 CB63
Westwood Cl, Amer. HP6 20 AX39
Bromley BR1 144 EK97
Esher KT10 136 CC104
Potters Bar EN6 12 DA30
Ruislip HA4 59 BP58
Westwood Dr, Amer. HP6 20 AX39
Westwood Gdns, SW13 99 CT83
Westwood Hill, SE26 122 DU92
Westwood La, Sid. DA15 126 EU85
Welling DA16 105 ET83
Westwood Pk, SE23 122 DV87
Westwood Pl, SE26 122 DU91
Westwood Rd, E16 205 P3
SW13 99 CT83
Coulsdon CR5 175 DK118
Gravesend (Sthflt.) DA13 130 FY93
Ilford IG3 69 ET60
West Woodside, Bex. DA5 126 EY87
Westwood Way, Sev. TN13 190 FF122
West World, W5 80 CL69
West Yoke, Sev. (Ash) TN15 149 FX103
Wetheral Dr, Stan. HA7 41 CH53
Wetherby Cl, Nthlt. UB5 78 CB65
Wetherby Gdns, SW5 100 DC77
Wetherby Ms, SW5
off Bolton Gdns 100 DB78
Wetherby Pl, SW7 100 DC77
Wetherby Rd, Borwd. WD6 26 CL39
Enfield EN2 30 DQ39
Wetherby Way, Chess. KT9 156 CL108
Wetherden St, E17 67 DZ59
Wetherell Rd, E9 85 DX67
Wetherill Rd, N10 44 DG53
★ **Wetlands Cen, The**, SW13 99 CV80
Wettern Cl, S.Croy. CR2
off Purley Oaks Rd 160 DS110
Wetton Pl, Egh. TW20 113 AZ92
Wexfenne Gdns, Wok. GU22 168 BH116
Wexford Rd, SW12 120 DF87
H **Wexham Park Hosp**, Slou.
SL2 74 AW70
Wexham Pk La, Slou. (Wexham)
SL3 74 AX70
Wexham Pl, Slou. (Wexham)
SL2 74 AX65
Wexham Rd, Slou. SL1, SL2 74 AV71
WEXHAM STREET, Slou. 74 AW67
Wexham St, Slou. (Wexham)
SL2, SL3 74 AW67
Wexham Wds, Slou. (Wexham)
SL3 74 AW71
Wey Av, Cher. KT16 134 BG97
Weybank, Wok. (Wisley)
GU23 168 BL116
Wey Barton, W.Byf. (Byfleet)
KT14 152 BM113
Weybourne Pl, S.Croy. CR2 160 DR110
Weybourne St, SW18 120 DC89
WEYBRIDGE 152 BN105
⇌ **Weybridge** 152 BN107
Weybridge Business Pk, Add.
KT15 152 BL105
Weybridge Ct, SE16
off Argyle Way 102 DU78
H **Weybridge Hosp**, Wey.
KT13 152 BN105
Weybridge Pk, Wey. KT13 153 BP106
Weybridge Pt, SW11 100 DG82
Weybridge Rd, Add. KT15 134 BK104
Thornton Heath CR7 141 DN98
Weybridge KT13 134 BL104
Weybridge Trd Est, Add.
KT15 152 BL105
Wey Cl, W.Byf. KT14
off Broadoaks Cres 152 BH113
Wey Ct, Add. (New Haw)
KT15 152 BK109
Epsom KT19 156 CQ105
Weydown Cl, SW19 119 CY88
Weyhill Rd, E1
off Commercial Rd 84 DU72
Weylands Cl, Walt. KT12 136 BZ102
Weylands Pk, Wey. KT13 153 BR107
Weylond Rd, Dag. RM8 70 EZ62
Wey Manor Rd, Add. (New Haw)
KT15 152 BK109
Weyman Rd, SE3 104 EJ81
Weymead Cl, Cher. KT16 134 BJ102
Wey Meadows, Wey. KT13 152 BL106
Weymede, W.Byf. (Byfleet)
KT14 152 BM112
Weymouth Av, NW7 42 CS50
W5 97 CJ76
Weymouth Cl, E6
off Covelees Wall 87 EP72
Weymouth Ct, Sutt. SM2 158 DA108
Weymouth Ms, W1 195 H6
Weymouth Rd, Hayes UB4 77 BS69
Weymouth St, W1 194 G7
Weymouth Ter, E2 84 DT68
Weymouth Wk, Stan. HA7 41 CG51
Wey Rd, Wey. KT13 134 BM104
Weyside Cl, W.Byf. (Byfleet)
KT14 152 BM112
Weystone Rd, Add. KT15
off Weybridge Rd 152 BM105
Whadcote St, N4
off Seven Sisters Rd 65 DN61
Whalebone Av, Rom. RM6 70 EZ58
Whalebone Ct, EC2 197 L8
Whalebone Gro, Rom. RM6 70 EZ58
Whalebone La, E15
off West Ham La 86 EE66
Whalebone La N, Rom. RM6 70 EY57
Whalebone La S, Dag. RM8 70 EZ59
Romford RM6 70 EZ59
Whaley Rd, Pot.B. EN6 12 DC33
Wharfdale Cl, N11
off Ribblesdale Av 44 DG51
Wharfdale Ct, E5
off Rushmore Rd 67 DX63
Wharfdale Rd, N1 83 DL68
Wharfedale Gdns, Th.Hth.
CR7 141 DM98
Wharfedale Rd, Dart. DA2 128 FQ88
Wharfedale St, SW10 100 DB78
Wharf La, Rick. WD3 38 BL46
Twickenham TW1 117 CG88
Woking (Ripley) GU23 168 BJ118
Woking (Send) GU23 167 BC123
Wharf Pl, E2 84 DU67
Wharf Rd, E15 85 ED67
N1 84 DQ68
Brentwood CM14 54 FW48
Enfield EN3 31 DY44
Gravesend DA12 131 GL86
Grays RM17 110 FZ79
Staines (Wrays.) TW19 112 AW87
Wharf Rd S, Grays RM17 110 FZ79
Wharfside Rd, E16 86 EE71
Wharf St, E16 86 EE71
Wharncliffe Dr, Sthl. UB1 79 CD74
Wharncliffe Gdns, SE25 142 DS96
Wharncliffe Rd, SE25 142 DS96
Wharton Cl, NW10 80 CS65
Wharton Cotts, WC1
off Wharton St 83 DM69
Wharton Rd, Brom. BR1 144 EH95
Wharton St, WC1 196 C3
Whateley Rd, SE20 123 DX94
SE22 122 DT85
Whatley Av, SW20 139 CY97
Whatman Rd, SE23 123 DX87
Whatmore Cl, Stai. TW19 114 BG86
Wheatash Rd, Add. KT15 134 BH103
Wheatcroft, Wal.Cr. (Chsht.)
EN7 14 DV28
Wheatfields, E6 *off Oxleas* 87 EP72
Enfield EN3 31 DY40
Wheatfield Way, Kings.T.
KT1 138 CL96
Wheathill Rd, SE20 142 DV97
Wheat Knoll, Ken. CR8 176 DQ116
Wheatlands, Houns. TW5 96 CA79
Wheatlands Rd, SW17
off Stapleton Rd 120 DG90
Slough SL3 92 AW76
Wheatley Cl, NW4 43 CU54
Greenhithe DA9
off Steele Av 129 FU85
Hornchurch RM11 72 FK57
Wheatley Cres, Hayes UB3 77 BU73
Wheatley Gdns, N9 46 DS47
Wheatley Ho, SW15
off Tangley Gro 119 CU87
Wheatley Rd, Islw. TW7 97 CF83
Wheatley's Ait, Sun. TW16 135 BU99
Wheatley St, W1 194 G7
Wheatley Ter Rd, Erith DA8 107 FF79
Wheatley Way, Ger.Cr. (Chal.St.P.)
SL9 36 AY51
Wheat Sheaf Cl, E14 204 B8
Wheatsheaf Cl, Cher. (Ott.)
KT16 151 BD107
Northolt UB5 60 BY64
Woking GU21 166 AY116
Wheatsheaf Hill, Sev. (Halst.)
TN14 164 EZ109
Wheatsheaf La, SW6 99 CW80
SW8 101 DL80
Staines TW18 113 BF94
Wheatsheaf Rd, Rom. RM1 71 FF58
Wheatsheaf Ter, SW6 99 CZ80
Wheatstone Cl, Mitch. CR4 140 DE95
Wheatstone Rd, W10 81 CY71
Wheeler Av, Oxt. RH8 187 ED129
Wheeler Cl, Wdf.Grn. IG8
off Chigwell Rd 49 EM50
Wheeler Gdns, N1
off Outram Pl 83 DL67
Wheelers, Epp. CM16 17 ET29
Wheelers Cross, Bark. IG11 87 ER68
Wheelers Dr, Ruis. HA4
off Wallington Cl 59 BQ58
Wheelers Fm Gdns, Epp.
(N.Wld.Bas.) CM16 19 FB26
Wheelers La, Epsom KT18 156 CP113
Wheelers Orchard, Ger.Cr.
(Chal.St.P.) SL9 36 AY51
Wheel Fm Dr, Dag. RM10 71 FC62
Wheelock Cl, Erith DA8 107 FB80
Wheelwright Cl, Bushey WD23
off Ashfield Av 24 CB44
Wheelwright St, N7 83 DM66
Whelan Way, Wall. SM6 141 DK104
Wheler St, E1 197 P5
Whellock Rd, W4 98 CS76
WHELPLEY HILL, Chesh. 4 AX26
Whelpley Hill Pk, Chesh.
(Whel.Hill) HP5 4 AX26
Whenman Av, Bex. DA5 127 FC89
Whernside Cl, SE28 88 EW73
WHETSTONE, N20 44 DB47
Whetstone Cl, N20
off Oakleigh Rd N 44 DD47
Whetstone Pk, WC2 196 B8
Whetstone Rd, SE3 104 EJ82
Whewell Rd, N19 65 DL61
Whichcote St, SE1 200 D3
Whidborne Cl, SE8
off Cliff Ter 103 EA82
Whidborne St, WC1 196 A3
Whiffins Orchard, Epp. CM16 18 EX29
Whimbrel Cl, SE28 88 EW73
South Croydon CR2 160 DR111
Whimbrel Way, Hayes UB4 78 BX72
Whinchat Rd, SE28 105 ER76
Whinfell Cl, SW16 121 DK92
Whinfell Way, Grav. DA12 131 GM91
Whinyates Rd, SE9 104 EL83
Whippendell Cl, Orp. BR5 146 EV95
Whippendell Hill, Kings L.
WD4 6 BJ30
Whippendell Rd, Wat. WD18 23 BU43
Whippendell Way, Orp. BR5 146 EV95
H **Whipps Cross Hosp**, E11 67 ED58
Whipps Cross Rd, E11 67 ED57
Whiskin St, EC1 196 F3
Whisperwood, Rick. (Loud.)
WD3 22 BH41
Whisperwood Cl, Har. HA3 41 CE52
Whistler Gdns, Edg. HA8 42 CM54
Whistler Ms, SE15
off Commercial Way 102 DT80
Dagenham RM8
off Fitzstephen Rd 70 EV64
Whistlers Av, SW11 100 DD80
Whistler St, N5 65 DP63
Whistler Wk, SW10
off World's End Est 100 DD80
Whiston Rd, E2 84 DT68
Whitakers Way, Loug. IG10 33 EM39
Whitbread Cl, N17 46 DU53
Whitbread Rd, SE4 103 DY84
★ **Whitbread Shire Horse Stables**,
EC1 *off Garrett St* 197 J4
Whitburn Rd, SE13 103 EB84
Whitby Av, NW10 80 CP69
Whitby Cl, Green. DA9 129 FU85
Westerham (Bigg.H.) TN16 178 EH119
Whitby Gdns, NW9 62 CN55
Sutton SM1 140 DD103
Whitby Rd, SE18 105 EM77
Harrow HA2 60 CC62
Ruislip HA4 60 BV62
Sutton SM1 140 DD103
Whitby St, E1 197 P4
Whitcher Cl, SE14 103 DY79
Whitcher Pl, NW1
off Rochester Rd 83 DJ66
Whitchurch Av, Edg. HA8 42 CM52
Whitchurch Cl, Edg. HA8 42 CM51
Whitchurch Gdns, Edg. HA8 42 CM51
Whitchurch La, Edg. HA8 41 CK52
Whitchurch Rd, W11 81 CX73
Romford RM3 52 FK49
Whitcomb Ct, WC2
off Whitcomb St 83 DK73
Whitcombe Ms, Rich. TW9 98 CP81
Whitcomb St, WC2 199 N1
White Acre, NW9 42 CS54
Whiteadder Way, E14 204 C8
Whitear Wk, E15 85 ED65
White Av, Grav. (Nthflt.)
DA11 131 GF90
Whitebarn La, Dag. RM10 88 FA67
Whitebeam Av, Brom. BR2 145 EN100
Whitebeam Cl, SW9
off Clapham Rd 101 DM80
Radlett (Shenley) WD7
off Mulberry Gdns 10 CM33
Waltham Cross EN7
off The Laurels 14 DS26
Whitebeam Dr, S.Ock. RM15 91 FW69
White Beams, St.Alb. (Park St.)
AL2 8 CC28
Whitebeam Twr, E17
off Hillyfield 67 DY55
White Beam Way, Tad. KT20 173 CU121
White Bear Pl, NW3
off New End Sq 64 DD63
White Br Av, Mitch. CR4 140 DD98
Whitebridge Cl, Felt. TW14 115 BT86
White Butts Rd, Ruis. HA4 60 BX62
WHITECHAPEL, E1 84 DU72
⊖ **Whitechapel** 84 DV71
★ **Whitechapel Art Gall**, E1 84 DT72
Whitechapel High St, E1 84 DT72
Whitechapel Rd, E1 84 DU72
White Ch La, E1 84 DU72
White Ch Pas, E1
off White Ch La 84 DU72
⊖ **White City** 81 CW73
White City Cl, W12 81 CW73
White City Est, W12 81 CV73
White City Rd, W12 81 CV73
White Conduit St, N1
off Chapel Mkt 83 DN68
Whitecote Rd, Sthl. UB1 78 CB72
White Craig Cl, Pnr. HA5 40 CA50
Whitecroft, Swan. BR8 147 FE96
Whitecroft Cl, Beck. BR3 143 ED98
Whitecroft Way, Beck. BR3 143 EC99
Whitecross Pl, EC2 197 L6
Whitecross St, EC1 197 J4
Whitefield Av, NW2 63 CW59
Purley CR8 175 DN116
Whitefield Cl, SW15 119 CY86
Orpington BR5 146 EW97
Whitefields Rd, Wal.Cr. (Chsht.)
EN8 14 DW28
Whitefoot La, Brom. BR1 123 EC91
Whitefoot Ter, Brom. BR1 124 EE90
Whiteford Rd, Slou. SL2 74 AS71
White Friars, Sev. TN13 190 FG127
Whitefriars Av, Har. HA3 41 CE54
Whitefriars Dr, Har. HA3 41 CD54
Whitefriars St, EC4 196 E9
White Gdns, Dag. RM10 88 FA65
Whitegate Gdns, Har. HA3 41 CF52
White Gates, Horn. RM12 72 FJ61
Whitegates, Whyt. CR3
off Court Bushes Rd 176 DU119
Woking GU22 *off Loop Rd* 167 AZ120
Whitegates Cl, Rick. (Crox.Grn.)
WD3 22 BN42
Whitegate Way, Tad. KT20 173 CV120
Whitehall, SW1 199 P2
White Hall, Rom. (Abridge) RM4
off Market Pl 34 EV41
Whitehall Cl, Chig. IG7 50 EU48
Uxbridge UB8 76 BJ67
Whitehall Ct, SW1 199 P3
Whitehall Cres, Chess. KT9 155 CK106
Whitehall Fm La, Vir.W.
GU25 132 AY96
Whitehall Gdns, E4 48 EE46
SW1 199 P3
W3 80 CN74
W4 98 CP79
Whitehall La, Buck.H. IG9 48 EG47
Egham TW20 113 AZ94
Erith DA8 107 FF82
Grays RM17 110 GC78
Staines (Wrays.) TW19 113 BA86
Whitehall Pk, N19 65 DJ60
Whitehall Pk Rd, W4 98 CP79
Whitehall Pl, E7 *off Station Rd* 68 EG64
SW1 199 P3
Wallington SM6
off Bernard Rd 159 DH105
Whitehall Rd, E4 48 EE47
W7 97 CG75
Bromley BR2 144 EK99
Grays RM17 110 GC77
Harrow HA1 61 CE59
Thornton Heath CR7 141 DN99
Uxbridge UB8 76 BK67
Woodford Green IG8 48 EE47
Whitehall St, N17 46 DT52
White Hart Cl, Ch.St.G. HP8 36 AU48
Sevenoaks TN13 191 FJ128
White Hart Ct, EC2
off Bishopsgate 84 DS72
Woking (Ripley) GU23 168 BJ121
⇌ **White Hart Lane** 46 DT52
White Hart La, N17 46 DR52
N22 45 DN53
NW10 *off Church Rd* 81 CT65
SW13 98 CS83
Romford RM7 50 FA53
White Hart Meadows, Wok.
(Ripley) GU23 168 BJ121
White Hart Rd, SE18 105 ES77
Orpington BR6 146 EU101
White Hart Row, Cher. KT16
off Heriot Rd 134 BG101
White Hart Slip, Brom. BR1
off Market Sq 144 EG96
White Hart St, SE11 200 E10
White Hart Wd, Sev. TN13 191 FJ129
White Hart Yd, SE1 201 K3
Whitehaven, Slou. SL1 74 AT73
Whitehaven Cl, Brom. BR2 144 EG98
Whitehaven St, NW8 194 B5
Whitehead Cl, N18 46 DR50
SW18 120 DC87
Dartford DA2 128 FJ90
Whitehead's Gro, SW3 198 C10
Whiteheart Av, Uxb. UB8 77 BQ71
Whiteheath Av, Ruis. HA4 59 BQ59
White Heron Ms, Tedd. TW11 117 CF93
White Hill, Couls. (Chipstead)
CR5 174 DC124
Northwood HA6 38 BN51
Rickmansworth WD3 38 BN51
South Croydon CR2
off St. Mary's Rd 160 DR109
Whitehill La, Grav. DA12 131 GK90
Redhill RH1 186 DR127
Woking GU23 169 BQ123
Whitehill Par, Grav. DA12 131 GJ90
Whitehill Pl, Vir.W. GU25 132 AY99
White Hill Rd, Chesh. HP5 4 AX26
Whitehill Rd, Dart. DA1 127 FG85
Gravesend DA12 131 GJ89
Gravesend (Hook Grn.)
DA13 149 FX96
Longfield DA3 149 FX96
Whitehills Rd, Loug. IG10 33 EN41
White Horse All, EC1
off Cowcross St 83 DP71
White Horse Dr, Epsom
KT18 156 CQ114
Whitehorse Hill, Chis. BR7 125 EN91
White Horse La, E1 85 DX70
Whitehorse La, SE25 142 DR98
White Horse La, St.Alb. (Lon.Col.)
AL2 10 CL25
Woking (Ripley) GU23 168 BJ121
White Horse Ms, SE1 200 E6
White Horse Rd, E1 85 DY72
E6 87 EM69
Whitehorse Rd, Croy. CR0 142 DR100
Thornton Heath CR7 142 DR100
White Horse St, W1 199 H3
White Horse Yd, EC2 197 K8
Whitehouse Av, Borwd. WD6 26 CP41
White Ho Cl, Ger.Cr. (Chal.St.P.)
SL9 36 AY52
White Ho Dr, Stan. HA7 41 CJ49
Whitehouse La, Abb.L.
(Bedmond) WD5 7 BV26
Enfield EN2
off Brigadier Hill 30 DQ39
White Ho La, Sev. TN14 190 FF130
White Ho Rd, Sev. TN14 190 FF130
Whitehouse Way, N14 45 DH47
Iver SL0 75 BD69
Slough SL3 92 AW76
White Kennett St, E1 197 N8
White Knights Rd, Wey.
KT13 153 BQ108
White Knobs Way, Cat. CR3 186 DU125
Whitelands Av, Rick. (Chorl.)
WD3 21 BC42
Whitelands Way, Rom. RM3 52 FK54
White La, Oxt. RH8 178 EH123
Warlingham CR6 178 EH123
Whiteledges, W13 79 CJ72
Whitelegg Rd, E13 86 EF68
Whiteley Rd, SE19 122 DR92
Whiteleys Cotts, W14 99 CZ77
Whiteleys Shop Cen, W2 82 DB72
Whiteleys Way, Felt. TW13 116 CA90
WHITELEY VILLAGE, Walt. 153 BS110
White Lion Cl, Amer. HP7 20 AU39
White Lion Ct, EC3 197 M9
White Lion Hill, EC4 196 G10
White Lion Rd, Amer. HP7 20 AT38
White Lion St, N1 196 D1
White Lo, SE19 121 DP94
White Lo Cl, N2 64 DD58
Sevenoaks TN13 191 FH123
Sutton SM2 158 DC108
White Lyon Ct, EC2
off Fann St 84 DQ70
White Lyons Rd, Brwd.
CM14 54 FW47

★ Place of interest ⇌ Railway station ⊖ London Underground station DLR Docklands Light Railway station Tramlink station H Hospital

Whi - Wil

White Oak Business Pk, Swan. BR8 *off London Rd* 147 FE97
White Oak Dr, Beck. BR3 143 EC96
White Oak Gdns, Sid. DA15 125 ET87
Whiteoaks, Bans. SM7 158 DB113
Whiteoaks La, Grnf. UB6 79 CD68
White Orchards, N20 43 CZ45
Stanmore HA7 41 CG50
White Post Hill, Dart. (Fnghm.) DA4 148 FN101
Whitepost Hill, Red. RH1 184 DE134
White Post La, E9 85 DZ66
SE13 103 EA83
White Post St, SE15 102 DW80
White Rd, E15 86 EE66
Betchworth RH3 182 CN133
Tadworth KT20 182 CN133
White Rose La, Wok. GU22 167 AZ117
Whites Av, Ilf. IG2 69 ES58
Whites Cl, Green. DA9 129 FW86
Whites Grds, SE1 201 N5
Whites Grds Est, SE1 201 N4
White Shack La, Rick. WD3 22 BM37
Whites La, Slou. (Datchet) SL3 92 AV79
White's Row, E1 197 P7
White's Sq, SW4 *off Nelson's Row* 101 DK84
Whitestile Rd, Brent. TW8 97 CJ78
Whitestone La, NW3 *off Heath St* 64 DC62
Whitestone Wk, NW3 *off North End Way* 64 DC62
White St, Sthl. UB1 96 BX75
White Swan Ms, W4 *off Bennett St* 98 CS79
Whitethorn Av, Couls. CR5 174 DG115
West Drayton UB7 76 BL73
Whitethorn Gdns, Croy. CR0 142 DV103
Enfield EN2 30 DR43
Hornchurch RM11 72 FJ58
Whitethorn Pl, West Dr. UB7 *off Whitethorn Av* 76 BM74
Whitethorn St, E3 85 EA70
Whiteways Ct, Stai. TW18 *off Pavilion Gdns* 114 BH94
Whitewebbs La, Enf. EN2 30 DS35
Whitewebbs Pk, Enf. EN2 30 DQ35
Whitewebbs Rd, Enf. EN2 29 DP35
Whitewebbs Way, Orp. BR5 145 ET95
Whitewood Cotts, West. (Tats.) TN16 178 EJ120
Whitfield Pl, W1 195 K5
Whitfield Rd, E6 86 EJ66
SE3 103 ED81
Bexleyheath DA7 106 EZ80
Whitfield St, W1 195 M7
Whitfield Way, Rick. (Mill End) WD3 37 BF46
Whitford Gdns, Mitch. CR4 140 DF97
Whitgift Av, S.Croy. CR2 160 DQ106
Whitgift Cen, Croy. CR0 142 DQ103
Whitgift St, SE11 200 B8
Croydon CR0 142 DQ104
Whit Hern Ct, Wal.Cr. EN8 *off College Rd* 14 DW30
Whiting Av, Bark. IG11 87 EP66
Whitings, Ilf. IG2 69 ER57
Whitings Rd, Barn. EN5 27 CW43
Whitings Way, E6 87 EN71
Whitland Rd, Cars. SM5 140 DD102
Whitlars Dr, Kings L. WD4 6 BM28
Whitley Cl, Abb.L. WD5 7 BU32
Staines (Stanw.) TW19 114 BL86
Whitley Rd, N17 46 DS54
Whitlock Dr, SW19 119 CY87
Whitman Rd, E3 *off Mile End Rd* 85 DY70
Whitmead Cl, S.Croy. CR2 160 DS107
Whitmore Av, Rom. (Harold Wd.) RM3 52 FL54
Whitmore Cl, N11 45 DH50
Whitmore Est, N1 84 DS67
Whitmore Gdns, NW10 81 CW68
Whitmore Rd, N1 84 DS67
Beckenham BR3 143 DZ97
Harrow HA1 60 CC59
Whitmores Cl, Epsom KT18 172 CQ115
Whitnell Way, SW15 119 CX85
Whitney Av, Ilf. IG4 68 EK56
Whitney Rd, E10 67 EB59
Whitney Wk, Sid. DA14 126 EY93
Whitstable Cl, Beck. BR3 143 DZ95
Ruislip HA4 *off Chichester Av* 59 BS61
Whitstable Ho, W10 81 CX72
Whitstable Pl, Croy. CR0 160 DQ105
Whittaker Av, Rich. TW9 *off Hill St* 117 CK85
Whittaker Rd, E6 86 EJ66
Sutton SM3 139 CZ104
Whittaker St, SW1 198 F9
Whittaker Way, SE1 202 C9
Whitta Rd, E12 68 EK63
Whittell Gdns, SE26 122 DW90
Whittenham Cl, Slou. SL2 74 AU74
Whittingstall Rd, SW6 99 CZ81
Whittington Av, EC3 197 M9
Hayes UB4 77 BT71
Whittington Ct, N2 64 DF57
H **Whittington Hosp**, N19 65 DJ61
Whittington Ms, N12 *off Fredericks Pl* 44 DC49
Whittington Rd, N22 45 DL52
Brentwood CM13 55 GC44
Whittington Way, Pnr. HA5 60 BY57
Whittlebury Cl, Cars. SM5 158 DF108
Whittle Cl, E17 67 DY58
Southall UB1 78 CB72
Whittle Rd, Houns. TW5 96 BW80
Southall UB2 *off Post Rd* 96 CB75
Whittlesea Cl, Har. HA3 40 CC52
Whittlesea Path, Har. HA3 40 CC53
Whittlesea Rd, Har. HA3 40 CC53
Whittlesey St, SE1 200 D3
WHITTON, Twick. 116 CB87
⇌ **Whitton** 116 CC87
Whitton Av E, Grnf. UB6 61 CE64
Whitton Av W, Grnf. UB6 60 CC64
Northolt UB5 60 CC64
Whitton Cl, Grnf. UB6 79 CH65
Whitton Dene, Houns. TW3 116 CB85
Isleworth TW7 117 CD85
Whitton Dr, Grnf. UB6 79 CG65
Whitton Manor Rd, Islw. TW7 116 CC85
Whitton Rd, Houns. TW3 96 CB84
Twickenham TW1, TW2 117 CF86
Whitton Wk, E3 85 EA68
Whitton Waye, Houns. TW3 116 CA86
Whitwell Rd, E13 86 EG69
Watford WD25 24 BX35
Whitworth Pl, SE18 105 EP77
Whitworth Rd, SE18 105 EN80
SE25 142 DS97
Whitworth St, SE10 205 J10
Whopshott Av, Wok. GU21 166 AW116
Whopshott Cl, Wok. GU21 166 AW116
Whopshott Dr, Wok. GU21 166 AW116
Whorlton Rd, SE15 102 DV83
Whybridge Cl, Rain. RM13 89 FE67
Whychcote Pt, NW2 *off Claremont Rd* 63 CW59
Whymark Av, N22 65 DN55
Whytebeam Vw, Whyt. CR3 176 DT118
Whytecliffe Rd N, Pur. CR8 159 DP111
Whytecliffe Rd S, Pur. CR8 159 DN111
Whytecroft, Houns. TW5 96 BX80
WHYTELEAFE, Cat. 176 DS118
⇌ **Whyteleafe** 176 DT117
Whyteleafe Business Village, Whyt. CR3 *off Whyteleafe Hill* 176 DT118
Whyteleafe Hill, Whyt. CR3 176 DT118
Whyteleafe Rd, Cat. CR3 176 DS120
⇌ **Whyteleafe South** 176 DU119
Whyteville Rd, E7 86 EH65
Wichling Cl, Orp. BR5 146 EX102
Wickenden Rd, Sev. TN13 191 FJ122
Wicken's Meadow, Sev. (Dunt.Grn.) TN14 181 FF119
Wickersley Rd, SW11 100 DG82
Wickers Oake, SE19 122 DT91
Wicker St, E1 *off Burslem St* 84 DV72
Wicket, The, Croy. CR0 161 EA106
Wicket Rd, Grnf. UB6 79 CG69
Wickets, The, Ashf. TW15 114 BL91
Wickets End, Rad. (Shenley) WD7 10 CL33
Wickets Way, Ilf. IG6 49 ET51
Wickford Cl, Rom. RM3 *off Wickford Dr* 52 FM50
Wickford Dr, Rom. RM3 52 FM50
Wickford St, E1 84 DW70
Wickford Way, E17 67 DX56
Wickham Av, Croy. CR0 143 DY103
Sutton SM3 157 CW106
Wickham Chase, W.Wick. BR4 143 ED101
Wickham Cl, E1 84 DW71
Enfield EN3 30 DV41
New Malden KT3 139 CT99
Uxbridge (Hare.) UB9 38 BK53
Wickham Ct Rd, W.Wick. BR4 143 EC103
Wickham Cres, W.Wick. BR4 143 EC103
Wickham Fld, Sev. (Otford) TN14 181 FF116
Wickham Gdns, SE4 103 DZ83
Wickham La, SE2 106 EU78
Egham TW20 113 BA94
Welling DA16 106 EU78
Wickham Ms, SE4 103 DZ82
Wickham Rd, E4 47 EC52
SE4 103 DZ84
Beckenham BR3 143 EB96
Croydon CR0 143 DX103
Grays RM16 111 GJ75
Harrow HA3 41 CD54
Wickham St, SE11 200 B10
Welling DA16 105 ES82
Wickham Way, Beck. BR3 143 EC98
Wick La, E3 85 EA68
Egham (Eng.Grn.) TW20 112 AT92
Wickliffe Av, N3 43 CY54
Wickliffe Gdns, Wem. HA9 62 CP61
Wicklow St, WC1 196 B2
Wick Rd, E9 85 DX65
Egham (Eng.Grn.) TW20 112 AV94
Teddington TW11 117 CH94
Wicks Cl, SE9 124 EK91
Wick Sq, E9 *off Eastway* 85 DZ65
Wicksteed Cl, Bex. DA5 127 FD90
Wicksteed Ho, Brent. TW8 *off Green Dragon La* 98 CM78
Wickwood St, SE5 101 DP82
Wid Cl, Brwd. CM13 55 GD43
Widdecombe Av, Har. HA2 60 BY61
Widdenham Rd, N7 65 DM63
Widdin St, E15 85 ED66
Widecombe Cl, Rom. RM3 52 FK53
Widecombe Gdns, Ilf. IG4 68 EL56
Widecombe Rd, SE9 124 EL90
Widecombe Way, N2 64 DD57
Widecroft Rd, Iver SL0 75 BE72
Widegate St, E1 197 N7
Widenham Cl, Pnr. HA5 *off Bridle Rd* 60 BW57
Wide Way, Mitch. CR4 141 DK97
Widewing Cl, Tedd. TW11 117 CH94
Widgeon Cl, E16 *off Maplin Rd* 86 EH72
Widgeon Rd, Erith DA8 107 FH80
Widgeon Way, Wat. WD25 24 BY36
Widley Rd, W9 82 DA69
WIDMORE, Brom. 144 EH97
WIDMORE GREEN, Brom. 144 EJ95
Widmore Lo Rd, Brom. BR1 144 EK96
Widmore Rd, Brom. BR1 144 EG96
Uxbridge UB8 77 BP70
Widworthy Hayes, Brwd. CM13 55 GB46
Wieland Rd, Nthwd. HA6 39 BU52
Wigan Ho, E5 *off Warwick Gro* 66 DV60
Wigeon Path, SE28 105 ER76
Wigeon Way, Hayes UB4 78 BX72
Wiggenhall Rd, Wat. WD18 23 BV43
Wiggie La, Red. RH1 184 DG132
Wiggins La, Rich. TW10 117 CJ89
Wiggins Mead, NW9 43 CT52
Wigginton Av, Wem. HA9 80 CP65
Wigham Ho, Bark. IG11 87 EQ66
Wightman Rd, N4 65 DN57
N8 65 DN56
Wigley Bush La, Brwd. CM14 54 FS47
Wigley Rd, Felt. TW13 116 BX88
Wigmore Pl, W1 195 H8
Wigmore Rd, Cars. SM5 140 DD103
Wigmore St, W1 194 F9
Wigmore Wk, Cars. SM5 140 DD103
Wigram Rd, E11 68 EJ58
Wigram Sq, E17 47 EC54
Wigston Cl, N18 46 DS50
Wigston Rd, E13 86 EH70
Wigton Gdns, Stan. HA7 42 CL53
Wigton Pl, SE11 *off Milverton St* 101 DN78
Wigton Rd, E17 47 DZ53
Romford RM3 52 FL49
Wigton Way, Rom. RM3 52 FL49
Wilberforce Rd, N4 65 DP61
NW9 63 CU58
Wilberforce Way, SW19 119 CX93
Gravesend DA12 131 GK92
Wilbraham Pl, SW1 198 E8
Wilbury Av, Sutt. SM2 157 CZ110
Wilbury Rd, Wok. GU21 166 AX117
Wilbury Way, N18 46 DR50
Wilby Ms, W11 81 CZ74
Wilcon Way, Wat. WD25 8 BX34
Wilcot Av, Wat. WD19 40 BY45
Wilcot Cl, Wat. WD19 *off Wilcot Av* 40 BY45
Wilcox Cl, SW8 101 DL80
Borehamwood WD6 26 CQ39
Wilcox Gdns, Shep. TW17 134 BM97
Wilcox Pl, SW1 199 L7
Wilcox Rd, SW8 101 DL80
Sutton SM1 158 DB105
Teddington TW11 117 CD91
Wildacres, Nthwd. HA6 39 BT49
West Byfleet KT14 152 BJ111
Wildbank Ct, Wok. GU22 *off White Rose La* 167 AZ118
Wild Ct, WC2 196 B8
Wildcroft Gdns, Edg. HA8 41 CK51
Wildcroft Rd, SW15 119 CW87
Wilde Cl, E8 84 DU67
Tilbury RM18 *off Coleridge Rd* 111 GJ82
Wilde Pl, N13 *off Medesenge Way* 45 DP51
SW18 *off Heathfield Rd* 120 DD87
Wilder Cl, Ruis. HA4 59 BV60
Wilderness, The, E.Mol. KT8 136 CC99
Hampton (Hmptn.H.) TW12 *off Park Rd* 116 CB91
WILDERNESSE, Sev. 191 FL122
Wildernesse Av, Sev. (Seal) TN15 191 FL122
Wildernesse Mt, Sev. TN13 191 FK122
Wilderness Rd, Chis. BR7 125 EP94
Oxted RH8 188 EE130
Wilde Rd, Erith DA8 107 FB80
Wilders Cl, Wok. GU21 166 AW118
Wilderton Rd, N16 66 DS59
Wildfell Rd, SE6 123 EB87
Wild Goose Dr, SE14 102 DW81
Wild Grn N, Slou. SL3 *off Verney Rd* 93 BA77
Wild Grn S, Slou. SL3 *off Swabey Rd* 93 BA77
Wild Hatch, NW11 64 DA58
Wild Oaks Cl, Nthwd. HA6 39 BT51
Wild's Rents, SE1 201 M6
Wild St, WC2 196 A9
Wildwood, Nthwd. HA6 39 BR51
Wildwood Av, St.Alb. (Brick.Wd.) AL2 8 BZ30
Wildwood Cl, SE12 124 EF87
Woking GU22 167 BF115
Wildwood Ct, Ken. CR8 176 DR115
Wildwood Gro, NW3 *off North End Way* 64 DC60
Wildwood Ri, NW11 64 DC60
Wildwood Rd, NW11 64 DC59
Wildwood Ter, NW3 64 DC60
Wilford Cl, Enf. EN2 30 DR41
Northwood HA6 39 BR52
Wilford Rd, Slou. SL3 93 AZ77
Wilfred Av, Rain. RM13 89 FG71
Wilfred Owen Cl, SW19 *off Tennyson Rd* 120 DC93
Wilfred St, SW1 199 K6
Gravesend DA12 131 GH86
Woking GU21 166 AX118
Wilfred Turney Est, W6 *off Hammersmith Gro* 99 CW76
Wilfrid Gdns, W3 80 CQ71
Wilhelmina Av, Couls. CR5 175 DJ119
Wilkes Rd, Brent. TW8 98 CL79
Brentwood CM13 55 GD43
Wilkes St, E1 84 DT71
Wilkie Way, SE22 *off Lordship La* 122 DU88
Wilkins Cl, Hayes UB3 95 BT78
Mitcham CR4 140 DE95
Wilkinson Cl, Dart. DA1 108 FM84
Uxbridge UB10 77 BP67
Waltham Cross (Chsht.) EN7 14 DQ26
Wilkinson Rd, E16 86 EJ72
Wilkinson St, SW8 101 DM80
Wilkinson Way, W4 98 CR75
Wilkin St, NW5 83 DH65
Wilkin St Ms, NW5 *off Wilkin St* 83 DH65
Wilkins Way, West. (Brasted) TN16 180 EV124
Wilks Av, Dart. DA1 128 FM89
Wilks Gdns, Croy. CR0 143 DY102
Wilks Pl, N1 197 N1
Willan Rd, N17 46 DR54
Willan Wall, E16 *off Victoria Dock Rd* 86 EF73
Willard St, SW8 101 DH83
Willats Cl, Cher. KT16 *off Alwyns La* 133 BF100
Willcocks Cl, Chess. KT9 138 CL104
Willcott Rd, W3 80 CP74
Will Crooks Gdns, SE9 104 EJ84
Willen Fld Rd, NW10 80 CQ68
Willenhall Av, Barn. EN5 28 DC44
Willenhall Dr, Hayes UB3 77 BS73
Willenhall Rd, SE18 105 EP78
Willersley Av, Orp. BR6 145 ER104
Sidcup DA15 125 ET88
Willersley Cl, Sid. DA15 125 ET88
WILLESDEN, NW10 81 CT65
H **Willesden Comm Hosp**, NW10 81 CU66
WILLESDEN GREEN, NW10 81 CV66
⊖ **Willesden Green** 81 CW65
⇌ **Willesden Junction** 81 CT69
⊖ **Willesden Junction** 81 CT69
Willesden La, NW2 81 CX65
NW6 81 CX65
Willes Rd, NW5 83 DH65
Willett Cl, Nthlt. UB5 *off Broomcroft Av* 78 BW69
Orpington BR5 145 ES100
Willett Pl, Th.Hth. CR7 *off Willett Rd* 141 DN99
Willett Rd, Th.Hth. CR7 141 DN99
Willetts La, Uxb. (Denh.) UB9 57 BF63
Willett Way, Orp. BR5 145 ER99
Willey Broom La, Cat. CR3 185 DN125
Willey Fm La, Cat. CR3 186 DQ126
Willey La, Cat. CR3 186 DR125
William Barefoot Dr, SE9 125 EN91
William Bonney Est, SW4 101 DK84
William Booth Rd, SE20 142 DU95
William Carey Way, Har. HA1 61 CE59
William Cl, N2 *off King St* 64 DD55
Romford RM5 51 FC53
Southall UB2 *off Windmill Av* 96 CC75
William Cory Prom, Erith DA8 107 FE78
William Covell Cl, Enf. EN2 29 DM38
William Dunbar Ho, NW6 81 CZ68
William Dyce Ms, SW16 *off Babington Rd* 121 DK91
William Ellis Cl, Wind. (Old Wind.) SL4 112 AU85
William Ellis Way, SE16 202 C7
William IV St, WC2 199 P1
William Gdns, SW15 119 CV85
William Guy Gdns, E3 *off Talwin St* 85 EB69
William Harvey Ho, SW19 *off Whitlock Dr* 119 CY88
William Margrie Cl, SE15 *off Moncrieff St* 102 DU82
William Ms, SW1 198 E5
William Morley Cl, E6 86 EK67
William Morris Cl, E17 67 DZ55
★ **William Morris Gall, Lloyd Pk**, E17 67 EA55
William Morris Way, SW6 100 DC83
William Nash Ct, Orp. BR5 *off Brantwood Way* 146 EW97
William Pl, E3 *off Roman Rd* 85 DZ68
William Rd, NW1 195 J3
SW19 119 CY94
Caterham CR3 176 DR122
Sutton SM1 158 DC106
William Russell Ct, Wok. GU21 *off Raglan Rd* 166 AS118
Williams Av, E17 47 DZ53
William Saville Ho, NW6 81 CZ68
Williams Bldgs, E2 84 DW70
Williams Cl, N8 *off Coolhurst Rd* 65 DK58
Addlestone KT15 *off Monks Cres* 152 BH106
Williams Evans Rd, Epsom KT19 156 CN111
Williams Gro, N22 45 DN53
Surbiton KT6 137 CJ100
William's La, SW14 98 CQ83
Williams La, Mord. SM4 140 DC99
Williamson Cl, SE10 205 K10
Williamson Rd, N4 65 DP58
Williamson St, N7 65 DL63
Williamson Way, NW7 43 CY51
Rickmansworth WD3 38 BG46
William Sq, SE16 203 L1
Williams Rd, W13 79 CG73
Southall UB2 96 BY77
Williams Ter, Croy. CR0 159 DN107
William St, E10 67 EB58
N17 46 DT52
SW1 198 E5
Barking IG11 87 EQ66
Bushey WD23 24 BX41
Carshalton SM5 140 DE104
Gravesend DA12 131 GH87
Grays RM17 110 GB79
Slough SL1 74 AT74
Williams Way, Rad. WD7 25 CJ35
Willifield Way, NW11 63 CZ56
Willingale Cl, Brwd. CM13 *off Fairview Av* 55 GE44
Loughton IG10 *off Willingale Rd* 33 EQ40
Woodford Green IG8 48 EK51
Willingale Rd, Loug. IG10 33 EQ41
Willingdon Rd, N22 45 DP54
Willinghall Cl, Wal.Abb. EN9 15 ED32
Willingham Cl, NW5 *off Leighton Rd* 65 DJ64
Willingham Ter, NW5 *off Leighton Rd* 65 DJ64
Willingham Way, Kings.T. KT1 138 CN97
Willington Ct, E5 *off Mandeville St* 67 DY62
Willington Rd, SW9 101 DL83
Willis Av, Sutt. SM2 158 DE107
Willis Cl, Epsom KT18 156 CP113
Willis Rd, E15 86 EF67
Croydon CR0 142 DQ101
Erith DA8 107 FC77
Willis St, E14 85 EB72
Willmore End, SW19 140 DB95
Willoughby Av, Croy. CR0 159 DM105
Willoughby Ct, St.Alb. (Lon.Col.) AL2 9 CK26
Willoughby Dr, Rain. RM13 89 FE66
Willoughby Gro, N17 46 DV52
Willoughby Ho, EC2 *off The Barbican* 84 DQ71
Willoughby La, N17 46 DV52
Willoughby Ms, SW4 *off Wixs La* 101 DH84
Willoughby Pk Rd, N17 46 DV52
Willoughby Pas, E14 203 P2
Willoughby Rd, N8 65 DN55
NW3 64 DD63
Kingston upon Thames KT2 138 CM95
Slough SL3 93 BA76
Twickenham TW1 117 CK86
Willoughbys, The, SW14 *off Upper Richmond Rd W* 98 CS84
Willoughby St, WC1 195 P7
Willoughby Way, SE7 205 P8
Willow Av, SW13 99 CT82
Sidcup DA15 126 EU86
Swanley BR8 147 FF97
Uxbridge (Denh.) UB9 58 BJ64
West Drayton UB7 76 BM73
Willow Bk, SW6 99 CY83
Richmond TW10 117 CH90
Woking GU22 166 AY122
Willowbank Gdns, Tad. KT20 173 CV122
Willowbank Pl, Pur. CR8 *off Kingsdown Av* 159 DP109
Willow Br Rd, N1 84 DQ65
Willowbrook Est, SE15 *off Sumner Rd* 102 DT80
Willowbrook Rd, SE15 102 DT79
Southall UB2 96 CA76
Staines TW19 114 BL89
Willow Business Cen, Mitch. CR4 *off Willow La* 140 DF99
Willow Cl, Add. (Woodham) KT15 151 BF111
Bexley DA5 126 EZ86
Brentford TW8 97 CJ79
Brentwood CM13 55 GB44
Bromley BR2 145 EM99
Buckhurst Hill IG9 48 EK48
Erith DA8 *off Willow Rd* 107 FG81
Hornchurch RM12 71 FH62
Orpington BR5 146 EV101
Slough (Colnbr.) SL3 93 BC80
Thornton Heath CR7 141 DP100
Waltham Cross (Chsht.) EN7 14 DS26
Willow Cotts, Mitch. CR4 141 DJ97
Richmond TW9 *off Kew Grn* 98 CN79
Willow Ct, EC2 197 M4
Edgware HA8 42 CL49
Willowcourt Av, Har. HA3 61 CH57
Willow Cres E, Uxb. (Denh.) UB9 58 BJ64
Willow Cres W, Uxb. (Denh.) UB9 58 BJ64
Willowdene, N6 *off Denewood Rd* 64 DF59
Brentwood CM15 54 FT43
Willow Dene, Bushey (Bushey Hth.) WD23 41 CE45
Pinner HA5 40 BX54
Willowdene, Wal.Cr. EN8 15 DY27
Willowdene Cl, Twick. TW2 116 CC87
Willowdene Ct, Brwd. CM14 54 FW49
Willow Dr, Barn. EN5 27 CY42
Woking (Ripley) GU23 168 BG124
Willow Edge, Kings L. WD4 6 BN29
Willow End, N20 44 DA47
Northwood HA6 39 BU51
Surbiton KT6 138 CL102
Willow Fm La, SW15 *off Queens Ride* 99 CV83
Willowfield Cl, SE18 105 ES78
Willow Gdns, Houns. TW3 96 CA81
Ruislip HA4 59 BT61
Willow Grn, NW9 *off Clayton Fld* 42 CS53
Borehamwood WD6 26 CR43
Willow Gro, E13 *off Libra Rd* 86 EG68
Chislehurst BR7 125 EN93
Ruislip HA4 59 BT61
Willowhayne Dr, Walt. KT12 135 BV101
Willowhayne Gdns, Wor.Pk. KT4 139 CW104
Willowherb Wk, Rom. RM3 *off Clematis Cl* 52 FJ52
Willow La, SE18 105 EM77
Amersham HP7 20 AT41
Mitcham CR4 140 DF99
Watford WD18 23 BU43
Willow Mead, Chig. IG7 50 EU48
Willowmead, Stai. TW18 *off Northfield Rd* 134 BH95
Willowmead Cl, W5 79 CK71
Woking GU21 166 AU116
Willowmere, Esher KT10 154 CC105
Willow Mt, Croy. CR0 *off Langton Way* 142 DS104
Willow Pk, Sev. (Otford) TN14 181 FF117
Slough (Stoke P.) SL2 74 AU66
Willow Path, Wal.Abb. EN9 16 EE34
Willow Pl, SW1 199 L8
Willow Rd, NW3 64 DD63
W5 98 CL75
Dartford DA1 128 FJ88
Enfield EN1 30 DS41

Willow Rd, Erith DA8 107 FG81
New Malden KT3 138 CQ98
Romford RM6 70 EY58
Slough (Colnbr.) SL3 93 BE82
Wallington SM6 159 DH108
Willows, The, Buck.H. IG9 48 EK48
Esher (Clay.) KT10
off Albany Cres 155 CE107
Grays RM17 110 GE79
Rickmansworth (Mill End) WD3
off Uxbridge Rd 38 BG47
Watford WD19
off Brookside Rd 39 BV45
West Byfleet (Byfleet)
KT14 152 BL113
Weybridge KT13 134 BN104
Willows Av, Mord. SM4 140 DB99
Willows Cl, Pnr. HA5 40 BW54
Willowside, St.Alb. (Lon.Col.)
AL2 10 CL27
Willows Path, Epsom KT18 156 CP114
Willow St, E4 47 ED45
EC2 197 M4
Romford RM7 71 FC56
Willow Tree Cl, E3
off Birdsfield La 85 DZ67
SW18 *off Cargill Rd* 120 DB88
Hayes UB4 78 BW70
Romford (Abridge) RM4 34 EV41
Uxbridge UB10 59 BQ62
Willow Tree La, Hayes UB4 78 BW70
Willowtree Marina, Hayes
UB4 78 BY72
Willow Tree Wk, Brom. BR1 144 EH95
Willowtree Way, Th.Hth. CR7
off Kensington Av 141 DN95
Willow Vale, W12 81 CU74
Chislehurst BR7 125 EP93
Leatherhead (Fetch.) KT22 170 CB123
Willow Vw, SW19 140 DD95
Willow Wk, E17 67 DZ57
N2 44 DD54
N15 65 DP56
N21 29 DM44
SE1 201 N8
Chertsey KT16 134 BG101
Dartford DA1 128 FJ85
Egham (Eng.Grn.) TW20 112 AW92
Orpington BR6 145 EP104
Sutton SM3 139 CZ104
Tadworth KT20 *off Oak Dr* 182 CQ130
Upminster RM14 73 FS60
Willow Way, N3 44 DB52
SE26 122 DV90
W11 *off Freston Rd* 81 CX74
Epsom KT19 156 CR107
Godstone RH9 186 DV132
Potters Bar EN6 12 DB33
Radlett WD7 25 CE36
Romford RM3 52 FP51
St. Albans AL2 8 CA27
Sunbury-on-Thames
TW16 135 BU98
Tadworth KT20 *off Oak Dr* 182 CP130
Twickenham TW2 116 CB89
Wembley HA0 61 CG62
West Byfleet KT14 152 BJ111
Woking GU22 166 AX121
Willow Wd Cres, SE25 142 DS100
Willrose Cres, SE2 106 EW78
Wills Cres, Houns. TW3 116 CB86
Wills Gro, NW7 43 CU50
Willson Rd, Egh. (Eng.Grn.)
TW20 112 AV92
Wilman Gro, E8 84 DU66
Wilmar Cl, Hayes UB4 77 BR70
Uxbridge UB8 76 BK66
Wilmar Gdns, W.Wick. BR4 143 EB102
Wilmcote Ho, W2 82 DB71
Wilmer Cl, Kings.T. KT2 118 CM92
Wilmer Cres, Kings.T. KT2 118 CM92
Wilmer Gdns, N1 84 DS67
Wilmerhatch La, Epsom
KT18 172 CP118
Wilmer Lea Cl, E15 85 EC66
Wilmer Pl, N16 *off Stoke Newington Ch St* 66 DT61
Wilmer Way, N14 45 DK50
WILMINGTON, Dart. 128 FK91
Wilmington Av, W4 98 CR80
Orpington BR6 146 EW103
Wilmington Ct Rd, Dart.
DA2 127 FG90
Wilmington Gdns, Bark. IG11 87 ER65
Wilmington Sq, WC1 196 D3
Wilmington St, WC1 196 D3
Wilmot Cl, N2 44 DC54
SE15 102 DU80
Wilmot Grn, Brwd. CM13 53 FW51
Wilmot Pl, NW1 83 DJ66
W7 *off Boston Rd* 79 CE74
Wilmot Rd, E10 67 EB61
N17 66 DR55
Carshalton SM5 158 DF106
Dartford DA1 127 FH85
Purley CR8 159 DN112
Wilmots Cl, Reig. RH2 184 DC133
Wilmot St, E2 84 DV70
Wilmot Way, Bans. SM7 158 DA114
Wilmount St, SE18 105 EP77
Wilna Rd, SW18 120 DC87
Wilsham St, W11 81 CX74
Wilshaw Cl, NW4 63 CU55
Wilshaw St, SE14 103 EA81
Wilsman Rd, S.Ock. RM15 91 FW68
Wilsmere Dr, Har. HA3 41 CF52
Northolt UB5 78 BY65
Wilson Av, Mitch. CR4 120 DE94
Wilson Cl, S.Croy. CR2
off Bartlett St 160 DR106
Wembley HA9 62 CM59
Wilson Dr, Cher. (Ott.) KT16 151 BB106
Wembley HA9 62 CM59
Wilson Gdns, Har. HA1 60 CC59
Wilson Gro, SE16 202 D5
Wilson La, Dart. DA4 149 FT96
Wilson Rd, E6 86 EK69
Wilson Rd, SE5 102 DS81
Chessington KT9 156 CM107
Ilford IG1 69 EM59
Wilsons, Tad. KT20
off Heathcote 173 CX121
Wilsons Pl, E14 *off Salmon La* 85 DZ72
Wilsons Rd, W6 99 CX78
Wilson St, E17 67 EC57
EC2 197 L6
N21 45 DN45
Wilson Way, Wok. GU21 166 AX116
Wilstone Cl, Hayes UB4
off Kingsash Dr 78 BY70
Wilthorne Gdns, Dag. RM10
off Acre Rd 89 FB66
Wilton Av, W4 98 CS78
Wilton Cl, West Dr. UB7 94 BK79
Wilton Cres, SW1 198 F5
SW19 139 CZ95
Wilton Dr, Rom. RM5 51 FC52
Wilton Gdns, Walt. KT12 136 BX102
West Molesey KT8 136 CA97
Wilton Gro, SW19 139 CZ95
New Malden KT3 139 CT100
Wilton Ms, SW1 198 G6
Wilton Par, Felt. TW13
off Highfield Rd 115 BU89
Wilton Pk Ct, SE18
off Prince Imperial Rd 105 EN81
Wilton Pl, SW1 198 F5
Addlestone (New Haw)
KT15 152 BK109
Wilton Rd, N10 44 DG54
SE2 106 EW76
SW1 199 J7
SW19 120 DE94
Barnet (Cockfos.) EN4 28 DF42
Hounslow TW4 96 BX83
Ilford IG1 *off Ilford La* 69 EP62
Wilton Row, SW1 198 F5
Wilton Sq, N1 84 DR67
Wilton St, SW1 199 H6
Wilton Ter, SW1 198 F6
Wilton Vil, N1 84 DR67
Wilton Way, E8 84 DU65
Wiltshire Av, Horn. RM11 72 FM56
Wiltshire Cl, NW7 43 CT50
SW3 198 D8
Dartford DA2 129 FR87
Wiltshire Gdns, N4 66 DQ58
Twickenham TW2 116 CC88
Wiltshire La, Pnr. HA5 59 BT55
Wiltshire Rd, SW9 101 DN83
Orpington BR6 146 EU101
Thornton Heath CR7 141 DN97
Wiltshire Row, N1 84 DR67
Wilverley Cres, N.Mal. KT3 138 CS100
Wimbart Rd, SW2 121 DM87
WIMBLEDON, SW19 119 CY93
⇌ **Wimbledon** 119 CZ93
⊖ **Wimbledon** 119 CZ93
Tramlink **Wimbledon** 119 CZ93
★ **Wimbledon (All England Tennis & Croquet Club)**, SW19 119 CY91
Wimbledon Br, SW19 119 CZ93
⇌ **Wimbledon Chase** 139 CY96
★ **Wimbledon Common**,
SW19 119 CT91
Wimbledon Common, SW19 119 CU91
★ **Wimbledon FC (share Selhurst Pk with Crystal Palace FC)**, SE25 142 DS98
Wimbledon Hill Rd, SW19 119 CY93
WIMBLEDON PARK, SW19 119 CZ90
⊖ **Wimbledon Park** 120 DA90
Wimbledon Pk, SW19 119 CZ89
Wimbledon Pk Est, SW19 119 CY88
Wimbledon Pk Rd, SW18 119 CZ87
SW19 119 CZ88
Wimbledon Pk Side, SW19 119 CX89
Wimbledon Rd, SW17 120 DC91
Wimbledon Sta, SW19 119 CZ93
★ **Wimbledon Windmill Mus**,
SW19 119 CV89
Wimbolt St, E2 84 DU69
Wimborne Av, Hayes UB4 77 BV72
Southall UB2 96 CA77
Wimborne Cl, SE12 124 EF85
Buckhurst Hill IG9 48 EH47
Epsom KT17 156 CS113
Worcester Park KT4 139 CW102
Wimborne Dr, NW9 62 CN55
Pinner HA5 60 BX59
Wimborne Gdns, W13 79 CH72
Wimborne Gro, Wat. WD17 23 BS37
Wimborne Rd, N9 46 DU47
N17 46 DS54
Wimborne Way, Beck. BR3 143 DX97
Wimbourne Av, Chis. BR7 145 ET98
Orpington BR5 145 ET98
Wimbourne Ct, N1
off Wimbourne St 84 DR68
Wimbourne St, N1 84 DR68
Wimpole Cl, Brom. BR2 144 EJ98
Kingston upon Thames
KT1 138 CM96
Wimpole Ms, W1 195 H6
Wimpole Rd, West Dr. UB7 76 BK74
Wimpole St, W1 195 H8
Wimshurst Cl, Croy. CR0 141 DL102
Winans Wk, SW9 101 DN82
Wincanton Cres, Nthlt. UB5 60 CA64
Wincanton Gdns, Ilf. IG6 69 EP55
Wincanton Rd, SW18 119 CZ87
Romford RM3 52 FK48
Winchcombe Rd, Cars. SM5 140 DD101
Winchcomb Gdns, SE9 104 EK83
Winchelsea Av, Bexh. DA7 106 EZ80
Winchelsea Cl, SW15 119 CX85
Winchelsea Rd, E7 68 EG62
N17 66 DS55
NW10 80 CR67
Winchelsey Ri, S.Croy. CR2 160 DT107
Winchendon Rd, SW6 99 CZ80
Teddington TW11 117 CD91
Winchester Av, NW6 81 CY67
NW9 62 CN55
Winchester Av, Houns. TW5 96 BZ79
Upminster RM14 73 FT60
Winchester Cl, E6
off Boultwood Rd 86 EL72
SE17 200 G9
Amersham HP7 20 AS39
Bromley BR2 144 EF97
Enfield EN1 30 DS43
Esher KT10 154 CA105
Kingston upon Thames
KT2 118 CP94
Slough (Colnbr.) SL3 93 BE81
Winchester Ct, E17
off Billet Rd 47 DY53
Winchester Cres, Grav.
DA12 131 GK90
Winchester Dr, Pnr. HA5 60 BX57
Winchester Gro, Sev. TN13 191 FH123
Winchester Ho, SE18
off Shooter's Hill Rd 104 EK80
Winchester Ms, NW3
off Winchester Rd 82 DD66
Winchester Pk, Brom. BR2 144 EF97
Winchester Pl, E8
off Kingsland High St 66 DT64
N6 65 DH60
W3 *off Avenue Rd* 98 CQ75
Winchester Rd, E4 47 EC52
N6 65 DH59
N9 46 DU46
NW3 82 DD66
Bexleyheath DA7 106 EX82
Bromley BR2 144 EF97
Feltham TW13 116 BZ90
Harrow HA3 62 CL56
Hayes UB3 95 BS80
Ilford IG1 69 ER62
Northwood HA6 59 BT55
Orpington BR6 164 EW105
Twickenham TW1 117 CH86
Walton-on-Thames KT12 135 BU102
Winchester Sq, SE1 201 K2
Winchester St, SW1 199 J10
W3 80 CQ74
Winchester Wk, SE1 201 K2
Winchester Way, Rick. (Crox.Grn.)
WD3 23 BP43
Winchet Wk, Croy. CR0 142 DW100
Winchfield Cl, Har. HA3 61 CJ58
Winchfield Ho, SW15
off Highcliffe Dr 119 CT86
Winchfield Rd, SE26 123 DY92
Winchfield Way, Rick. WD3 38 BJ45
Winchilsea Cres, W.Mol. KT8 136 CC96
WINCHMORE HILL, N21 45 DM45
⇌ **Winchmore Hill** 45 DN46
Winchmore Hill Rd, N14 45 DK46
N21 45 DK46
Winchstone Cl, Shep. TW17 134 BM98
Winckley Cl, Har. HA3 62 CM57
Wincott St, SE11 200 E8
Wincrofts Dr, SE9 105 ER84
Windall Cl, SE19 142 DU95
Windborough Rd, Cars. SM5 158 DG108
Windermere Av, N3 64 DA55
NW6 81 CY67
SW19 140 DB97
Harrow HA3 61 CJ59
Hornchurch RM12 71 FG64
Ruislip HA4 60 BW59
Wembley HA9 61 CJ59
Windermere Cl, Dart. DA1 127 FH88
Egham TW20
off Derwent Rd 113 BB94
Feltham TW14 115 BT88
Orpington BR6 145 EP104
Rickmansworth (Chorl.)
WD3 21 BC43
Staines TW19 *off Viola Av* 114 BL88
Windermere Ct, SW13 99 CT79
Kenley CR8 175 DP115
Wembley HA9
off Windermere Av 61 CJ59
Windermere Gdns, Ilf. IG4 68 EL57
Windermere Gro, Wem. HA9
off Windermere Av 61 CJ60
Windermere Ho, Islw. TW7
off Summerwood Rd 117 CF85
Windermere Pt, SE15
off Ilderton Rd 102 DW80
Windermere Rd, N10 45 DH53
N19 *off Holloway Rd* 65 DJ61
SW15 118 CS91
SW16 141 DJ95
W5 97 CJ76
Bexleyheath DA7 107 FC82
Coulsdon CR5 175 DL115
Croydon CR0 142 DT102
Southall UB1 78 BZ71
West Wickham BR4 144 EE103
Windermere Way, Reig. RH2 184 DD133
West Drayton UB7
off Providence Rd 76 BM74
Winders Rd, SW11 100 DE82
Windfield, Lthd. KT22 171 CH121
Windfield Cl, SE26 123 DX91
Windham Av, Croy. (New Adgtn.)
CR0 161 ED110
Windham Rd, Rich. TW9 98 CM83
Windhover Way, Grav. DA12 131 GL91
Windings, The, S.Croy. CR2 160 DT111
Winding Way, Dag. RM8 70 EW62
Harrow HA1 61 CE63
Windlass Pl, SE8 203 L9
Windlesham Gro, SW19 119 CX88
Windley Cl, SE23 122 DW89
Windmill All, W4
off Windmill Rd 98 CS77
Windmill Av, Epsom KT17 157 CT111
Southall UB2 96 CC75
Windmill Br Ho, Croy. CR0 142 DS102
Windmill Cl, SE1 202 C8
SE13 103 EC82
Caterham CR3 176 DQ121
Epsom KT17 157 CT112
Sunbury-on-Thames TW16 115 BS94
Surbiton KT6 137 CH102
Windmill Cl, Upmin. RM14 72 FN61
Waltham Abbey EN9 16 EE34
Windmill Ct, NW2 81 CY65
Windmill Dr, NW2 63 CY62
SW4 121 DJ85
Keston BR2 162 EJ105
Leatherhead KT22 171 CJ123
Reigate RH2 184 DD132
Rickmansworth (Crox.Grn.)
WD3 22 BM44
Windmill End, Epsom KT17 157 CT112
Windmill Gdns, Enf. EN2 29 DN41
Windmill Grn, Shep. TW17 135 BS101
Windmill Gro, Croy. CR0 142 DQ101
WINDMILL HILL, Grav. 131 GG88
Windmill Hill, NW3 64 DC62
Enfield EN2 29 DP41
Kings Langley WD4 5 BF32
Ruislip HA4 59 BT59
Windmill Ho, E14 203 P8
Windmill La, E15 85 ED65
Barnet EN5 27 CT44
Bushey (Bushey Hth.)
WD23 41 CE46
Epsom KT17 157 CT112
Greenford UB6 78 CC71
Isleworth TW7 97 CE77
Southall UB2 96 CC76
Surbiton KT6 137 CH100
Waltham Cross (Chsht.)
EN8 15 DX30
Windmill Ms, W4
off Windmill Rd 98 CS77
Windmill Pas, W4 98 CS77
Windmill Ri, Kings.T. KT2 118 CP94
Windmill Rd, N18 46 DR49
SW18 120 DD86
SW19 119 CV88
W4 98 CS77
W5 97 CJ77
Brentford TW8 97 CK78
Croydon CR0 142 DQ101
Gerrards Cross (Chal.St.P.)
SL9 36 AX52
Hampton (Hmptn.H.) TW12 116 CB92
Mitcham CR4 141 DJ99
Sevenoaks TN13 191 FH130
Slough (Fulmer) SL3 56 AX64
Sunbury-on-Thames TW16 135 BS95
Windmill Rd W, Sun. TW16 135 BS96
Windmill Row, SE11 101 DN78
Windmill Shott, Egh. TW20
off Rusham Rd 113 AZ93
Windmill St, W1 195 M7
Bushey (Bushey Hth.) WD23 41 CE46
Gravesend DA12 131 GH86
Windmill Wk, SE1 200 E3
Windmill Way, Reig. RH2 184 DD132
Ruislip HA4 59 BT60
Windmore Av, Pot.B. EN6 11 CW31
Windover Av, NW9 62 CR56
Windrose Cl, SE16 203 H4
Windrush, N.Mal. KT3 138 CP98
Windrush Av, Slou. SL3 93 BB77
Windrush Cl, SW11
off Maysoule Rd 100 DD84
W4 98 CQ81
Uxbridge UB10 58 BM63
Windrush La, SE23 123 DX90
Windrush Rd, NW10
off Milton Av 80 CR67
Windrush Sq, SW2
off Rushcroft Rd 101 DN84
Windsock Cl, SE16 203 M8
WINDSOR 92 AS82
Windsor Av, E17 47 DY54
SW19 140 DC95
Edgware HA8 42 CP49
Grays RM16 110 GB75
New Malden KT3 138 CQ99
Sutton SM3 139 CY104
Uxbridge UB10 77 BP67
West Molesey KT8 136 CA97
★ **Windsor Castle**, Wind.
SL4 92 AS81
Windsor Castle, Wind. SL4 92 AS80
Windsor Cen, The, SE27
off Advance Rd 122 DQ91
Windsor Cl, N3 43 CY54
SE27 122 DQ91
Borehamwood WD6 26 CN39
Brentford TW8 97 CH79
Chislehurst BR7 125 EP92
Harrow HA2 60 CA62
Hemel Hempstead (Bov.)
HP3 5 BA28
Northwood HA6 39 BU54
Waltham Cross (Chsht.) EN7 14 DU30
Windsor Ct, N14 45 DJ45
Sunbury-on-Thames TW16
off Windsor Rd 115 BU93
Windsor Ct Rd, Wok. (Chobham)
GU24 150 AS109
Windsor Cres, Har. HA2 60 CA63
Wembley HA9 62 CP62
Windsor Dr, Ashf. TW15 114 BK91
Barnet EN4 28 DF44
Dartford DA1 127 FG86
Orpington BR6 164 EU107
Windsor Gdns, W9 82 DA71
Croydon CR0
off Richmond Rd 141 DL104
Hayes UB3 95 BR76
★ **Windsor Great Pk**,
Egh. & Wind. 112 AS93
Windsor Gro, SE27 122 DQ91
Windsor Pk Rd, Hayes UB3 95 BT80
Windsor Pl, SW1 199 L7
Chertsey KT16
off Windsor St 134 BG100
Windsor Rd, E4 *off Chivers Rd* 47 EB49
E7 68 EH64
E10 67 EB61
E11 68 EG60
N3 43 CY54
N7 65 DL62
N13 45 DN48
Windsor Rd, N17 46 DU54
NW2 81 CV65
W5 80 CL73
Barnet EN5 27 CY44
Bexleyheath DA6 106 EY84
Brentwood (Pilg.Hat.) CM15 54 FV44
Dagenham RM8 70 EY62
Egham (Eng.Grn.) TW20 113 AZ90
Enfield EN3 31 DX36
Gerrards Cross SL9 56 AW60
Gravesend DA12 131 GH90
Harrow HA3 41 CD53
Hornchurch RM11 72 FJ59
Hounslow TW4 95 BV82
Ilford IG1 69 EP63
Kingston upon Thames KT2 118 CL94
Richmond TW9 98 CM82
Slough SL1 92 AS76
Slough (Datchet) SL3 92 AT80
Slough (Stoke P.) SL2 56 AU63
Southall UB2 96 BZ76
Staines (Wrays.) TW19 112 AY86
Sunbury-on-Thames TW16 115 BU93
Teddington TW11 117 CD92
Thornton Heath CR7 141 DP96
Watford WD24 24 BW38
Woking (Chobham) GU24 150 AS109
Worcester Park KT4 139 CU103
Windsors, The, Buck.H. IG9 48 EL47
Windsor St, N1 83 DP67
Chertsey KT16 134 BG100
Uxbridge UB8 76 BJ66
Windsor Ter, N1 197 J2
Windsor Wk, SE5 102 DR82
Walton-on-Thames KT12
off King George Av 136 BX102
Weybridge KT13 153 BP106
Windsor Way, W14 99 CX77
Rickmansworth WD3 38 BG46
Woking GU22 167 BC116
Windsor Wf, E9 67 DZ64
Windsor Wd, Wal.Abb. EN9
off Monkswood Av 16 EE33
Windspoint Dr, SE15
off Ethnard Rd 102 DV79
Windus Rd, N16 66 DT60
Windus Wk, N16 66 DT60
Windward Cl, Enf. EN3
off Bullsmoor La 31 DX35
Windycroft Cl, Pur. CR8 159 DK113
Windy Hill, Brwd. CM13 55 GC46
Windy Ridge, Brom. BR1 144 EL95
Windyridge Cl, SW19 119 CX92
Wine Cl, E1 202 F1
Wine Office Ct, EC4 196 E8
Winern Glebe, W.Byf. (Byfleet)
KT14 152 BK113
Winery La, Kings.T. KT1 138 CM97
Winey Cl, Chess. KT9
off Nigel Fisher Way 155 CJ108
Winfield Mobile Home Pk, Wat.
WD25 24 CB39
Winford Ho, E3 85 DZ66
Winford Par, Sthl. UB1
off Telford Rd 78 CB72
Winforton St, SE10 103 EC81
Winfrith Rd, SW18 120 DC87
Wingate Cres, Croy. CR0 141 DK100
Wingate Rd, W6 99 CV76
Ilford IG1 69 EP64
Sidcup DA14 126 EW92
Wingate Trd Est, N17 46 DU52
Wing Cl, Epp. (N.Wld.Bas.) CM16
off Epping Rd 18 FA27
Wingfield, Grays (Bad.Dene)
RM17 110 FZ78
Wingfield Bk, Grav. (Nthflt.)
DA11 130 GC89
Wingfield Cl, Add. (New Haw)
KT15 152 BH110
Brentwood CM13
off Pondfield La 55 GA48
Wingfield Gdns, Upmin. RM14 73 FT58
Wingfield Ms, SE15
off Wingfield St 102 DU83
Wingfield Rd, E15 68 EE64
E17 67 EB57
Gravesend DA12 131 GH87
Kingston upon Thames KT2 118 CN93
Wingfield St, SE15 102 DU83
Wingfield Way, Ruis. HA4 77 BV65
Wingford Rd, SW2 121 DL86
Wingletye La, Horn. RM11 72 FM60
Wingmore Rd, SE24 102 DQ83
Wingrave Cres, Brwd. CM14 54 FS49
Wingrave Rd, W6 99 CW79
Wingrove Dr, Purf. RM19 108 FP78
Wingrove Rd, SE6 124 EE89
Wings Cl, Sutt. SM1 158 DA105
Wing Way, Brwd. CM14
off Geary Dr 54 FW46
Winifred Av, Horn. RM12 72 FK63
Winifred Gro, SW11 100 DF84
Winifred Pl, N12 *off High Rd* 44 DC50
Winifred Rd, SW19 140 DA95
Coulsdon CR5 174 DG116
Dagenham RM8 70 EY61
Dartford DA1 127 FH85
Erith DA8 107 FE78
Hampton (Hmptn.H.) TW12 116 CA91
Winifred St, E16 87 EM74
Winifred Ter, E13
off Victoria Rd 86 EG68
Enfield EN1
off Great Cambridge Rd 46 DT45
Winkers Cl, Ger.Cr. (Chal.St.P.)
SL9 37 AZ53
Winkers La, Ger.Cr. (Chal.St.P.)
SL9 37 AZ53
Winkfield Rd, E13 86 EH68
N22 45 DN53
Winkley St, E2 84 DV68
Winkworth Pl, Bans. SM7
off Bolters La 157 CZ114

★ Place of interest ⇌ Railway station ⊖ London Underground station DLR Docklands Light Railway station Tramlink station H Hospital

Win - Woo

Winkworth Rd, Bans. SM7 ...157 CZ114
Winlaton Rd, Brom. BR1 ...123 ED91
Winmill Rd, Dag. RM8 ...70 EZ62
Winnards, Wok. GU21
off Abercorn Way ...166 AV118
Winn Common Rd, SE18 ...105 ES79
Winnett St, W1 ...195 M10
Winningales Ct, Ilf. IG5
off Vienna Cl ...68 EL55
Winnings Wk, Nthlt. UB5
off Arnold Rd ...78 BY65
Winnington Cl, N2 ...64 DD58
Winnington Rd, N2 ...64 DD59
Enfield EN3 ...30 DW38
Winnington Way, Wok. GU21 .166 AV118
Winnipeg Dr, Orp. BR6 ...163 ET107
Winnock Rd, West Dr. UB7 ...76 BK74
Winn Rd, SE12 ...124 EG88
Winns Av, E17 ...67 DY55
Winns Ms, N15
off Grove Pk Rd ...66 DS56
Winns Ter, E17 ...47 EA54
Winsbeach, E17 ...67 ED55
Winscombe Cres, W5 ...79 CK70
Winscombe St, N19 ...65 DH61
Winscombe Way, Stan. HA7 ...41 CG50
Winsford Rd, SE6 ...123 DZ90
Winsford Ter, N18 ...46 DR50
Winsham Gro, SW11 ...120 DG85
Winslade Rd, SW2 ...121 DL85
Winslade Way, SE6
off Rushey Grn ...123 EB87
Winsland Ms, W2
off London St ...82 DD72
Winsland St, W2 ...82 DD72
Winsley St, W1 ...195 K8
Winslow, SE17 ...102 DS78
Winslow Cl, NW10
off Neasden La N ...62 CS62
Pinner HA5 ...59 BV58
Winslow Gro, E4 ...48 EE47
Winslow Rd, W6 ...99 CW79
Winslow Way, Felt. TW13 ...116 BX90
Walton-on-Thames KT12 ..136 BW104
Winsor Ter, E6 ...87 EN71
Winsor Ter Roundabout, E6
off Royal Docks Rd ...87 EP71
Winstanley Cl, Cob. KT11 ...153 BV114
Winstanley Est, SW11 ...100 DD83
Winstanley Rd, SW11 ...100 DD83
Winstanley Wk, Cob. KT11
off Winstanley Cl ...153 BU114
Winstead Gdns, Dag. RM10 ...71 FC64
Winston Av, NW9 ...62 CS59
Winston Cl, Green. DA9 ...129 FT85
Harrow HA3 ...41 CF51
Romford RM7 ...71 FB56
Winston Ct, Har. HA3 ...40 CB52
Winston Dr, Cob. (Stoke D'Ab.)
KT11 ...170 BY116
Winston Rd, N16 ...66 DR63
Winston Wk, W4
off Beaconsfield Rd ...98 CR77
Winston Way, Ilf. IG1 ...69 EP62
Potters Bar EN6 ...12 DA34
Woking (Old Wok.) GU22 ..167 BB120
Winstre Rd, Borwd. WD6 ...26 CN39
Winter Av, E6 ...86 EL67
Winterborne Av, Orp. BR6 ...145 ER104
Winterbourne Gro, Wey.
KT13 ...153 BQ107
Winterbourne Rd, SE6 ...123 DZ88
Dagenham RM8 ...70 EW61
Thornton Heath CR7 ...141 DN97
Winter Box Wk, Rich. TW10 ...98 CM84
Winterbrook Rd, SE24 ...122 DQ86
Winterburn Cl, N11 ...44 DG51
Winterdown Gdns, Esher
KT10 ...154 BZ107
Winterdown Rd, Esher KT10 .154 BZ107
Winterfold Cl, SW19 ...119 CY89
Wintergarden, Green. (Bluewater)
DA9 off Bluewater Parkway .129 FU88
Winter Gdn Cres, Green.
(Bluewater) DA9 ...129 FU87
Wintergreen Cl, E6
off Yarrow Cres ...86 EL71
Winters Cft, Grav. DA12 ...131 GK93
Wintersells Rd, W.Byf. (Byfleet)
KT14 ...152 BK110
Winters Rd, T.Ditt. KT7 ...137 CH101
Winterstoke Gdns, NW7 ...43 CU50
Winterstoke Rd, SE6 ...123 DZ88
Winters Way, Wal.Abb. EN9 ...16 EG33
Winterton Ho, E1 ...84 DV72
Winterton Pl, SW10
off Park Wk ...100 DC79
Winterwell Rd, SW2 ...121 DL85
Winthorpe Rd, SW15 ...99 CY84
Winthrop St, E1 ...84 DV71
Winthrop Wk, Wem. HA9
off Everard Way ...62 CL62
Winton App, Rick. (Crox.Grn.)
WD3 ...23 BQ43
Winton Av, N11 ...45 DJ52
Winton Cl, N9 ...47 DX45
Winton Cres, Rick. (Crox.Grn.)
WD3 ...23 BP43
Winton Dr, Rick. (Crox.Grn.)
WD3 ...23 BP44
Waltham Cross (Chsht.)
EN8 ...15 DY29
Winton Gdns, Edg. HA8 ...42 CM52
Winton Rd, Orp. BR6 ...163 EP105
Winton Way, SW16 ...121 DN92
Winvale, Slou. SL1 ...92 AS76
Winwood, Slou. SL2 ...74 AW72
Wireless Rd, West. (Bigg.H.)
TN16 ...178 EK115
Wisbeach Rd, Croy. CR0 ...142 DR99
Wisborough Rd, S.Croy. CR2 .160 DT109
Wisdons Cl, Dag. RM10 ...71 FB60
Wise La, NW7 ...43 CV51
West Drayton UB7 ...94 BK77
Wiseman Ct, SE19 ...122 DS92
Wiseman Rd, E10 ...67 EA61
Wise Rd, E15 ...85 ED67
Wise's La, Hat. AL9 ...11 CW27
Wiseton Rd, SW17 ...120 DE88
Wishart Rd, SE3 ...104 EK81
Wishbone Way, Wok. GU21 ..166 AT116
Wishford Ct, Ashtd. KT21
off The Marld ...172 CM118
WISLEY, Wok. ...168 BL116
Wisley Common, Wok. GU23 .168 BN117
Wisley Ct, S.Croy. CR2
off Sanderstead Rd ...160 DS110
Wisley La, Wok. (Wisley)
GU23 ...168 BJ116
Wisley Rd, SW11 ...120 DG85
Orpington BR5 ...126 EU94
Wistaria Cl, Brwd. CM15 ...54 FW43
Wisteria Cl, NW7 ...43 CT51
Ilford IG1 ...69 EP64
Orpington BR6 ...145 EP103
Wisteria Gdns, Swan. BR8 ...147 FD96
Wisteria Rd, SE13 ...103 ED84
Witan St, E2 ...84 DV69
Witches La, Sev. TN13 ...190 FD122
Witham Cl, Loug. IG10 ...32 EL44
Witham Rd, SE20 ...142 DW97
W13 ...79 CG74
Dagenham RM10 ...70 FA64
Isleworth TW7 ...97 CD81
Romford RM2 ...71 FH57
Withens Cl, Orp. BR5 ...146 EW98
Witherby Cl, Croy. CR0 ...160 DS106
Witherings, The, Horn. RM11 ..72 FL57
Witherington Rd, N5 ...65 DN64
Withers Cl, Chess. KT9
off Coppard Gdns ...155 CJ107
Withers Mead, NW9 ...43 CT53
Witherston Way, SE9 ...125 EN89
Witheygate Av, Stai. TW18 ...114 BH93
Withies, The, Lthd. KT22 ...171 CH120
Woking (Knap.) GU21 ...166 AS117
Withybed Cor, Tad. KT20 ...173 CV123
Withycombe Rd, SW19 ...119 CX87
Withycroft, Slou. (Geo.Grn.)
SL3 ...74 AY72
Withy La, Ruis. HA4 ...59 BQ57
Withy Mead, E4 ...47 ED48
Withy Pl, St.Alb. (Park St.) AL2 .8 CC28
Witley Cres, Croy. (New Adgtn.)
CR0 ...161 EC107
Witley Gdns, Sthl. UB2 ...96 BZ77
Witley Pt, SW15
off Wanborough Dr ...119 CV88
Witley Rd, N19
off Holloway Rd ...65 DJ61
Witney Cl, Pnr. HA5 ...40 BZ51
Uxbridge UB10 ...58 BM63
Witney Path, SE23 ...123 DX90
Wittenham Way, E4 ...47 ED48
Wittering Cl, Kings.T. KT2 ...117 CK92
Wittering Wk, Horn. RM12 ...90 FJ65
Wittersham Rd, Brom. BR1 ...124 EF92
Wivenhoe Cl, SE15 ...102 DV83
Wivenhoe Ct, Houns. TW3 ...96 BZ84
Wivenhoe Rd, Bark. IG11 ...88 EU68
Wiverton Rd, SE26 ...122 DW93
Wixom Ho, SE3
off Romero Sq ...104 EJ84
Wix Rd, Dag. RM9 ...88 EX67
Wixs La, SW4 ...101 DH84
Woburn Av, Epp. (They.B.)
CM16 ...33 ES37
Hornchurch RM12 ...71 FG63
Purley CR8 off High St ...159 DN111
Woburn Cl, SE28
off Summerton Way ...88 EX72
SW19 off Tintern Cl ...120 DC93
Bushey WD23 ...24 CC43
Woburn Ct, SE16
off Masters Dr ...102 DV78
Woburn Hill, Add. KT15 ...134 BJ103
Woburn Pl, WC1 ...195 N4
Woburn Rd, Cars. SM5 ...140 DE102
Croydon CR0 ...142 DQ102
Woburn Sq, WC1 ...195 N5
Woburn Wk, WC1 ...195 N3
Wodehouse Av, SE5 ...102 DT81
Wodehouse Rd, Dart. DA1 ...108 FN84
Woffington Cl, Kings.T. KT1 ..137 CJ95
Wokindon Rd, Grays RM16 ...111 GH76
WOKING ...167 AZ118
⇌ Woking ...167 AZ117
Woking Business Pk, Wok.
GU21 ...167 BB115
Woking Cl, SW15 ...99 CT84
H Woking Comm Hosp, Wok.
GU22 ...167 AZ118
H Woking Nuffield Hosp, Wok.
GU21 ...150 AY114
Wold, The, Cat. (Wold.) CR3 ..177 EA122
Woldham Pl, Brom. BR2 ...144 EJ98
Woldham Rd, Brom. BR2 ...144 EJ98
WOLDINGHAM, Cat. ...177 EB122
⇌ Woldingham ...177 DX122
WOLDINGHAM GARDEN
VILLAGE, Cat. ...177 DY121
Woldingham Rd, Cat. (Wold.)
CR3 ...176 DV120
Wolds Dr, Orp. BR6 ...163 EN105
Wolfe Cl, Brom. BR2 ...144 EG100
Hayes UB4 off Ayles Rd ...77 BV69
Wolfe Cres, SE7 ...104 EK78
SE16 ...203 H5
Wolferton Rd, E12 ...69 EM63
Wolffe Gdns, E15 ...86 EF65
Wolfram Cl, SE13 ...124 EE85
Wolfington Rd, SE27 ...121 DP91
Wolfs Hill, Oxt. RH8 ...188 EG131
H Wolfson Medical Rehabilitation
Cen, SW20 ...119 CV94
Wolf's Row, Oxt. RH8 ...188 EH130
Wolfs Wd, Oxt. RH8 ...188 EG132
Wolftencroft Cl, SW11 ...100 DD83
Wollaston Cl, SE1 ...201 H8
Wolmer Cl, Edg. HA8 ...42 CP49
Wolmer Gdns, Edg. HA8 ...42 CN48
Wolseley Av, SW19 ...120 DA89
Wolseley Gdns, W4 ...98 CP79
Wolseley Rd, E7 ...86 EH66
N8 ...65 DK58
N22 ...45 DM53
W4 ...98 CQ77
Harrow HA3 ...61 CE55
Mitcham CR4 ...140 DG101
Romford RM7 ...71 FD59
Wolseley St, SE1 ...202 A5
Wolsey Av, E6 ...87 EN69
E17 ...67 DZ55
Thames Ditton KT7 ...137 CF99
Waltham Cross (Chsht.)
EN7 ...14 DT29
Wolsey Business Pk, Wat.
WD18 ...39 BR45
Wolsey Cl, SW20 ...119 CV94
Hounslow TW3 ...96 CC84
Kingston upon Thames KT2 .138 CP95
Southall UB2 ...96 CC76
Worcester Park KT4 ...157 CU105
Wolsey Cres, Croy. (New Adgtn.)
CR0 ...161 EC109
Morden SM4 ...139 CY101
Wolsey Dr, Kings.T. KT2 ...118 CL92
Walton-on-Thames KT12 ..136 BX102
Wolsey Gdns, Ilf. IG6 ...49 EQ51
Wolsey Gro, Edg. HA8 ...42 CR52
Esher KT10 ...154 CB105
Wolsey Ms, NW5 ...83 DJ65
Orpington BR6
off Osgood Av ...163 ET106
Wolsey Pl Shop Cen, Wok. GU21
off Commercial Way ...166 AY117
Wolsey Rd, N1 ...66 DR64
Ashford TW15 ...114 BL91
East Molesey KT8 ...137 CD98
Enfield EN1 ...30 DV40
Esher KT10 ...154 CB105
Hampton (Hmptn.H.) TW12 .116 CB93
Northwood HA6 ...39 BQ47
Sunbury-on-Thames TW16 .115 BT94
Wolsey St, E1
off Sidney St ...84 DW71
Wolsey Wk, Wok. GU21 ...166 AY117
Wolsey Way, Chess. KT9 ...156 CN106
Wolsley Cl, Dart. DA1 ...127 FE85
Wolstan Cl, Uxb. (Denh.) UB9
off Lindsey Rd ...58 BG62
Wolstonbury, N12 ...44 DA50
Wolvercote Rd, SE2 ...106 EX75
Wolverley St, E2
off Bethnal Grn Rd ...84 DV69
Wolverton, SE17 ...201 L10
Wolverton Av, Kings.T. KT2 ..138 CN95
Wolverton Gdns, W5 ...80 CM73
W6 ...99 CX77
Wolverton Rd, Stan. HA7 ...41 CH51
Wolverton Way, N14 ...29 DJ43
Wolves La, N13 ...45 DN52
N22 ...45 DN52
Wombwell Gdns, Grav. (Nthflt.)
DA11 ...130 GE89
WOMBWELL PARK, Grav. ...130 GD89
Womersley Rd, N8 ...65 DM58
Wonersh Way, Sutt. SM2 ...157 CX109
Wonford Cl, Kings.T. KT2 ...138 CS95
Tadworth KT20 ...183 CU126
Wontford Rd, Pur. CR8 ...175 DN115
Wontner Cl, N1
off Greenman St ...84 DQ66
Wontner Rd, SW17 ...120 DF89
Wooburn Cl, Uxb. UB8
off Aldenham Dr ...77 BP70
Woodall Cl, E14
off Lawless St ...85 EB73
Woodall Rd, Enf. EN3 ...31 DX44
Wood Av, Purf. RM19 ...108 FQ77
Woodbank, Rick. WD3 ...22 BJ44
Woodbank Av, Ger.Cr. SL9 ...56 AX58
Woodbank Dr, Ch.St.G. HP8 ..36 AX48
Woodbank Rd, Brom. BR1 ...124 EF90
Woodbastwick Rd, SE26 ...123 DX92
Woodberry Av, N21 ...45 DN47
Harrow HA2 ...60 CB56
Woodberry Cl, NW7
off Bittacy Hill ...43 CY52
Sunbury-on-Thames TW16
off Ashridge Way ...115 BU93
Woodberry Cres, N10 ...65 DH55
Woodberry Down, N4 ...66 DQ59
Epping CM16 ...18 EU29
Woodberry Down Est, N4 ...66 DQ59
Woodberry Gdns, N12 ...44 DC51
Woodberry Gro, N4 ...66 DQ59
N12 ...44 DC51
Bexley DA5 ...127 FD90
Woodberry Way, E4 ...47 EC46
N12 ...44 DC51
Woodbine Cl, Twick. TW2 ...117 CD89
Waltham Abbey EN9 ...32 EJ35
Woodbine Gro, SE20 ...122 DV94
Enfield EN2 ...30 DR38
Woodbine La, Wor.Pk. KT4 ..139 CW104
Woodbine Pl, E11 ...68 EG58
Woodbine Rd, Sid. DA15 ...125 ES88
Woodbines Av, Kings.T. KT1 .137 CK97
Woodbine Ter, E9
off Morning La ...84 DW65
Woodborough Rd, SW15 ...99 CV84
Woodbourne Av, SW16 ...121 DK90
Woodbourne Cl, SW16
off Woodbourne Av ...121 DL90
Woodbourne Dr, Esher (Clay.)
KT10 ...155 CF107
Woodbourne Gdns, Wall.
SM6 ...159 DH108
Woodbridge Av, Lthd. KT22 ..171 CG118
Woodbridge Cl, N7 ...65 DM61
NW2 ...63 CU62
Romford RM3 ...52 FK49
Woodbridge Ct, Wdf.Grn. IG8 .48 EL52
Woodbridge Gro, Lthd. KT22 .171 CG118
Woodbridge La, Rom. RM3 ...52 FK48
Woodbridge Rd, Bark. IG11 ...69 ET64
Woodbridge St, EC1 ...196 F4
Woodbrook Gdns, Wal.Abb.
EN9 ...16 EE33
Woodbrook Rd, SE2 ...106 EU79
Woodburn Cl, NW4 ...63 CX57
Woodbury Cl, E11 ...68 EH56
Croydon CR0 ...142 DT103
Westerham (Bigg.H.) TN16 .179 EM118
Woodbury Dr, Sutt. SM2 ...158 DC110
Woodbury Hill, Loug. IG10 ...32 EL41
Woodbury Hollow, Loug. IG10 .32 EL40
Woodbury Pk Rd, W13 ...79 CH70
Woodbury Rd, E17 ...67 EB56
Westerham (Bigg.H.) TN16 .179 EM118
Woodbury St, SW17 ...120 DE92
Woodchester Sq, W2 ...82 DB71
Woodchurch Cl, Sid. DA14 ...125 ER90
Woodchurch Dr, Brom. BR1 ..124 EK94
Woodchurch Rd, NW6 ...82 DA66
Wood Cl, E2 ...84 DU70
NW9 ...62 CR59
Bexley DA5 ...127 FE90
Harrow HA1 ...61 CD59
Woodclyffe Dr, Chis. BR7 ...145 EN96
Woodcock Ct, Har. HA3 ...62 CL59
Woodcock Dell Av, Har. HA3 ..61 CK59
Woodcock Hill, Har. HA3 ...61 CK59
Rickmansworth WD3 ...38 BL50
Woodcocks, E16 ...86 EJ71
Woodcombe Cres, SE23 ...122 DW88
WOODCOTE, Epsom ...172 CQ116
WOODCOTE, Pur. ...159 DK111
Woodcote Av, NW7 ...43 CW51
Hornchurch RM12 ...71 FG63
Thornton Heath CR7 ...141 DP98
Wallington SM6 ...159 DH108
Woodcote Cl, Enf. EN3 ...30 DW44
Epsom KT18 ...156 CR114
Kingston upon Thames KT2 .118 CM92
Waltham Cross (Chsht.) EN8 .14 DW30
Woodcote Dr, Orp. BR6 ...145 ER102
Purley CR8 ...159 DK110
Woodcote End, Epsom KT18 .172 CR115
Woodcote Grn, Wall. SM6 ...159 DJ109
Woodcote Grn Rd, Epsom
KT18 ...172 CQ116
Woodcote Gro, Couls. CR5 ..159 DH112
Woodcote Gro Rd, Couls.
CR5 ...175 DK115
Woodcote Hurst, Epsom
KT18 ...172 CQ116
Woodcote La, Pur. CR8 ...159 DK111
Woodcote Ms, Loug. IG10 ...48 EK45
Wallington SM6 ...159 DH107
Woodcote Pk Av, Pur. CR8 ..159 DJ112
Woodcote Pk Rd, Epsom
KT18 ...172 CQ116
Woodcote Pl, SE27 ...121 DP92
Woodcote Rd, E11 ...68 EG59
Epsom KT18 ...156 CR114
Purley CR8 ...159 DJ109
Wallington SM6 ...159 DH107
Woodcote Side, Epsom KT18 .172 CP115
Woodcote Valley Rd, Pur.
CR8 ...159 DK113
Woodcott Ho, SW15
off Ellisfield Dr ...119 CU87
Woodcrest Rd, Pur. CR8 ...159 DL113
Woodcrest Wk, Reig. RH2 ...184 DE132
Woodcroft, N21 ...45 DM46
SE9 ...125 EM90
Greenford UB6 ...79 CG65
Woodcroft Av, NW7 ...42 CS52
Stanmore HA7 ...41 CF53
Woodcroft Cres, Uxb. UB10 ...77 BP67
Woodcroft Ms, SE8 ...203 K9
Woodcroft Rd, Th.Hth. CR7 ...141 DP99
Woodcutters Av, Grays RM16 .110 GC75
Wood Dr, Chis. BR7 ...124 EL93
Sevenoaks TN13 ...190 FF126
Woodedge Cl, E4 ...48 EF46
Woodend, SE19 ...122 DQ93
Esher KT10 ...136 CC103
Wood End, Hayes UB3 ...77 BS72
St. Albans (Park St.) AL2 ...8 CC28
Woodend, Sutt. SM1 ...140 DC103
Woodend, The, Wall. SM6 ...159 DH109
Wood End Av, Har. HA2 ...60 CB63
Wood End Cl, Nthlt. UB5 ...61 CD64
Woodend Cl, Wok. GU21 ...166 AU119
Woodend Gdns, Enf. EN2 ...29 DL42
Wood End Gdns, Nthlt. UB5 ...60 CC64
Wood End Grn Rd, Hayes UB3 .77 BR71
Wood End La, Nthlt. UB5 ...78 CB65
Woodend Pk, Cob. KT11 ...170 BX115
Woodend Rd, E17 ...47 EC54
Wood End Rd, Har. HA1 ...61 CD63
Wood End Way, Nthlt. UB5 ...60 CC64
Wooder Gdns, E7 ...68 EF63
Wooderson Cl, SE25 ...142 DS98
Woodfall Av, Barn. EN5 ...27 CZ43
Woodfall Dr, Dart. DA1 ...107 FE84
Woodfall Rd, N4 ...65 DN60
Woodfall St, SW3 ...100 DF78
Woodfarrs, SE5 ...102 DR84
Woodfield, Ashtd. KT21 ...171 CK117
Woodfield Av, NW9 ...62 CS56
SW16 ...121 DK90
W5 ...79 CJ70
Carshalton SM5 ...158 DG107
Gravesend DA11 ...131 GH88
Northwood HA6 ...39 BS49
Wembley HA0 ...61 CJ62
Woodfield Cl, SE19 ...122 DQ94
Ashtead KT21 ...171 CK117
Coulsdon CR5 ...175 DJ119
Enfield EN1 ...30 DS42
Redhill RH1 ...184 DE133
Woodfield Cres, W5 ...79 CJ70
Woodfield Dr, Barn. EN4 ...44 DG46
Romford RM2 ...71 FG56
Woodfield Gdns, W9
off Woodfield Rd ...81 CZ71
New Malden KT3 ...139 CT99
Woodfield Gro, SW16 ...121 DK90
Woodfield Hill, Couls. CR5 ..175 DH119
Woodfield La, SW16 ...121 DK90
Ashtead KT21 ...172 CL116
Woodfield Pl, W9 ...81 CZ70
Woodfield Ri, Bushey WD23 ..41 CD45
Woodfield Rd, W5 ...79 CJ70
W9 ...81 CZ71
Ashtead KT21 ...171 CK117
Hounslow TW4 ...95 BV82
Radlett WD7 ...25 CG36
Thames Ditton KT7 ...137 CF103
Woodfields, Sev. TN13 ...190 FD122
Woodfields, The, S.Croy. CR2 .160 DT111
Woodfield Ter, Epp. (Thnwd.)
CM16 off High Rd ...18 EW25
Uxbridge (Hare.) UB9 ...38 BH54
Woodfield Way, N11 ...45 DK52
Hornchurch RM12 ...72 FK60
Redhill RH1 ...184 DE132
Woodfines, The, Horn. RM11 ..72 FK58
WOODFORD, Wdf.Grn. ...48 EH51
⊖ Woodford ...48 EH51
Woodford Av, Ilf. IG2, IG4 ...69 EM57
Woodford Green IG8 ...68 EK55
WOODFORD BRIDGE, Wdf.Grn.49 EM52
Woodford Br Rd, Ilf. IG4 ...68 EK55
Woodford Ct, W12
off Shepherds Bush Grn ...99 CX75
Waltham Abbey EN9 ...16 EG33
Woodford Cres, Pnr. HA5 ...39 BV54
WOODFORD GREEN ...48 EF49
Woodford New Rd, E17 ...68 EE56
E18 ...48 EE53
Woodford Green IG8 ...48 EE53
Woodford Pl, Wem. HA9 ...62 CL60
Woodford Rd, E7 ...68 EH63
E18 ...68 EG56
Watford WD17 ...23 BV40
WOODFORD WELLS, Wdf.Grn. .48 EH49
Woodgate, Wat. WD25 ...7 BV33
Woodgate Av, Chess. KT9 ...155 CK106
Potters Bar EN6 ...13 DH33
Woodgate Cres, Nthwd. HA6 ..39 BU51
Woodgate Dr, SW16 ...121 DK94
Woodgavil, Bans. SM7 ...173 CZ116
Woodger Rd, W12
off Goldhawk Rd ...99 CW75
Woodgers Gro, Swan. BR8 ...147 FF96
Woodget Cl, E6
off Remington Rd ...86 EL72
Woodgrange Av, N12 ...44 DD51
W5 ...80 CN74
Enfield EN1 ...30 DU44
Harrow HA3 ...61 CJ57
Woodgrange Cl, Har. HA3 ...61 CK57
Woodgrange Gdns, Enf. EN1 ..30 DU44
⇌ Woodgrange Park ...68 EK64
Woodgrange Rd, E7 ...68 EH63
Woodgrange Ter, Enf. EN1
off Great Cambridge Rd ...30 DU44
WOOD GREEN, N22 ...45 DL53
⊖ Wood Green ...45 DM54
Woodgreen Rd, Wal.Abb. EN9 .32 EJ35
Wood Grn Shop City, N22
off High Rd ...45 DN54
Wood Grn Way, Wal.Cr. (Chsht.)
EN8 ...15 DY31
Woodhall Av, SE21 ...122 DT90
Pinner HA5 ...40 BY54
Woodhall Cl, Chess. KT9
off Ashlyns Way ...155 CK107
Uxbridge UB8 ...58 BK64
Woodhall Cres, Horn. RM11 ...72 FM59
Woodhall Dr, SE21 ...122 DT90
Pinner HA5 ...40 BX53
Woodhall Gate, Pnr. HA5 ...40 BX52
Woodhall Ho, SW18
off Fitzhugh Gro ...120 DD86
Woodhall La, Rad. (Shenley)
WD7 ...26 CL35
Watford WD19 ...40 BX49
Woodhall Rd, Pnr. HA5 ...40 BX52
WOODHAM, Add. ...151 BF111
Woodham Ct, E18 ...68 EF56
Woodham La, Add. (New Haw)
KT15 ...152 BG110
Woking GU21 ...151 BB114
Woodham Pk Rd, Add.
(Woodham) KT15 ...151 BF109
Woodham Pk Way, Add.
(Woodham) KT15 ...151 BF111
Woodham Ri, Wok. GU21 ...151 AZ114
Woodham Rd, SE6 ...123 EC90
Woking GU21 ...166 AY115
Woodham Waye, Wok. GU21 .151 BB113
Woodhatch Cl, E6
off Remington Rd ...86 EL72
Woodhatch Spinney, Couls.
CR5 ...175 DL116
Woodhaven Gdns, Ilf. IG6
off Brandville Gdns ...69 EQ55
Woodhaw, Egh. TW20 ...113 BB91
Woodhayes Rd, SW19 ...119 CW94
Woodhead Dr, Orp. BR6
off Sherlies Av ...145 ES103
Woodheyes Rd, NW10 ...62 CR64
Woodhill, SE18 ...104 EL77
Woodhill Av, Ger.Cr. SL9 ...57 BA58
Woodhill Cres, Har. HA3 ...61 CK58
Wood Ho, SW17 off Laurel Cl .120 DE92
Woodhouse Av, Grnf. UB6 ...79 CF68
Woodhouse Cl, Grnf. UB6 ...79 CF68
Hayes UB3 ...95 BS76
Woodhouse Eaves, Nthwd.
HA6 ...39 BU50
Woodhouse Gro, E12 ...86 EL65
Woodhouse Rd, E11 ...68 EF62
N12 ...44 DD51
Woodhurst Av, Orp. BR5 ...145 EQ100
Watford WD25 ...24 BX35
Woodhurst Dr, Uxb. (Denh.)
UB9 ...57 BF57
Woodhurst La, Oxt. RH8 ...188 EE130
Woodhurst Pk, Oxt. RH8 ...188 EE130
Woodhurst Rd, SE2 ...106 EU78
W3 ...80 CQ73
Woodhyrst Gdns, Ken. CR8
off Firs Rd ...175 DP115
Woodington Cl, SE9 ...125 EN86
Woodknoll Dr, Chis. BR7 ...145 EM95

349

Woo - Wor

Woodland App, Grnf. UB6 79 CG65
Woodland Av, Brwd. CM13 55 GC43
Woodland Cl, NW9 62 CQ58
SE19
off Woodland Hill 122 DS93
Brentwood CM13 55 GC43
Epsom KT19 156 CS107
Uxbridge (Ickhm.) UB10 59 BP61
Weybridge KT13
off Woodland Gro 153 BR105
Woodford Green IG8 48 EH48
Woodland Ct, Oxt. RH8 187 ED128
Woodland Cres, SE10 104 EE79
SE16 203 H5
Woodland Dr, Wat. WD17 23 BT39
Woodland Gdns, N10 65 DH57
Epsom KT18 173 CW117
Isleworth TW7 97 CE82
South Croydon CR2 160 DW111
Woodland Gro, SE10 104 EE78
Epping CM16 18 EU31
Weybridge KT13 153 BR105
Woodland Hill, SE19 122 DS93
Woodland La, Rick. (Chorl.)
WD3 21 BD41
Woodland Pl, Rick. (Chorl.)
WD3 21 BF42
Woodland Ri, N10 65 DH56
Greenford UB6 79 CG65
Oxted RH8 188 EE130
Sevenoaks TN15 191 FL123
Woodland Rd, E4 47 EC46
N11 45 DH50
SE19 122 DS92
Loughton IG10 32 EL41
Rickmansworth (Map.Cr.)
WD3 37 BD50
Thornton Heath CR7 141 DN98
WOODLANDS, Islw. 97 CE82
Woodlands, NW11 63 CY58
SW20 139 CW98
Gerrards Cross SL9 57 AZ57
Harrow HA2 60 CA56
Hatfield AL9 12 DB26
Radlett WD7 9 CG34
St. Albans (Park St.) AL2 8 CC27
Woking GU22
off Constitution Hill 166 AY118
Woodlands, The, N14 45 DH46
SE13 123 ED87
SE19 122 DQ94
Beckenham BR3 143 EC95
Esher KT10 136 CC103
Isleworth TW7 97 CF82
Orpington BR6 164 EV107
Wallington SM6 159 DH109
Woodlands Av, E11 68 EH60
N3 44 DC52
W3 80 CP74
Hornchurch RM11 72 FK57
New Malden KT3 138 CQ95
Romford RM6 70 EY58
Ruislip HA4 60 BW60
Sidcup DA15 125 ES88
West Byfleet KT14 151 BF113
Worcester Park KT4 139 CT103
Woodlands Cl, NW11 63 CY57
Borehamwood WD6 26 CP42
Bromley BR1 145 EM96
Chertsey (Ott.) KT16 151 BB110
Esher (Clay.) KT10 155 CF108
Gerrards Cross SL9 57 BA58
Grays RM16 110 GE76
Swanley BR8 147 FF97
Woodlands Copse, Ashtd.
KT21 171 CK116
Woodlands Ct, Wok. GU22
off Constitution Hill 166 AY119
Woodlands Dr, Kings L. WD4 7 BQ28
Stanmore HA7 41 CF51
Sunbury-on-Thames TW16 136 BW96
Woodlands Gro, Couls. CR5 174 DG117
Isleworth TW7 97 CE82
Woodlands La, Cob. (Stoke D'Ab.)
KT11 170 CA117
Woodlands Par, Ashf. TW15 115 BQ93
Woodlands Pk, Add. KT15 151 BF106
Bexley DA5 127 FC91
Tadworth KT20 182 CP131
Woking GU21
off Blackmore Cres 151 BC114
Woodlands Pk Rd, N15 65 DP57
SE10 104 EE79
Woodlands Ri, Swan. BR8 147 FF96
Woodlands Rd, E11 68 EE61
E17 67 EC55
N9 46 DW46
SW13 99 CT83
Bexleyheath DA7 106 EY83
Bromley BR1 144 EL96
Bushey WD23 24 BY43
Enfield EN2 30 DR39
Epsom KT18 172 CN115
Harrow HA1 61 CF57
Hemel Hempstead HP3 6 BN27
Ilford IG1 69 EQ62
Isleworth TW7 97 CE82
Leatherhead KT22 171 CD117
Orpington BR6 164 EU107
Romford RM1 71 FF55
Romford (Harold Wd.) RM3 52 FN53
Southall UB1 78 BX74
Surbiton KT6 137 CK101
Virginia Water GU25 132 AW98
West Byfleet KT14 151 BF114
Woodlands Rd E, Vir.W.
GU25 132 AW98
Woodlands Rd W, Vir.W.
GU25 132 AW97
Woodlands St, SE13 123 ED87
Woodland St, E8
off Dalston La 84 DT65
Woodlands Vw, Sev. (Bad.Mt.)
TN14 164 FA110
Woodlands Way, SW15
off Oakhill Rd 119 CZ85
Ashtead KT21 172 CN116
Woodlands Way, Tad. KT20 182 CQ130
Woodland Ter, SE7 104 EL77
Woodland Wk, NW3 64 DE64
SE10 off Woodland Gro 104 EE78
Bromley BR1 124 EE91
Woodland Way, N21 45 DN47
NW7 42 CS51
SE2 106 EX77
Abbots Langley (Bedmond)
WD5 7 BT27
Caterham CR3 186 DS128
Croydon CR0 143 DY102
Epping (They.B.) CM16 33 ER35
Greenhithe DA9 109 FU84
Mitcham CR4 120 DG94
Morden SM4 139 CZ98
Orpington BR5 145 EQ98
Purley CR8 159 DN113
Surbiton KT5 138 CP103
Tadworth (Kgswd.) KT20 173 CY122
Waltham Cross (Chsht.)
EN7 13 DP28
West Wickham BR4 161 EB105
Weybridge KT13 153 BR106
Woodford Green IG8 48 EH48
Wood La, N6 65 DH58
NW9 62 CS59
W12 81 CW72
Caterham CR3 176 DR124
Dagenham RM8, RM9,
RM10 70 EW63
Dartford (Lane End) DA2 129 FR91
Hornchurch RM12 71 FG64
Isleworth TW7 97 CF80
Iver SL0 75 BC71
Ruislip HA4 59 BR60
Stanmore HA7 41 CG48
Tadworth KT20 173 CZ116
Weybridge KT13 153 BQ109
Woodford Green IG8 48 EF50
Wood La Cl, Iver SL0 75 BB69
Woodlawn Cl, SW15 119 CZ85
Woodlawn Cres, Twick. TW2 116 CB89
Woodlawn Dr, Felt. TW13 116 BX89
Woodlawn Gro, Wok. GU21 167 AZ115
Woodlawn Rd, SW6 99 CX80
Woodlea Dr, Brom. BR2 144 EE99
Woodlea Gro, Nthwd. HA6 39 BQ51
Woodlea Rd, N16 66 DS62
Woodlee Cl, Vir.W. GU25 132 AW96
Woodleigh, E18
off Churchfields 48 EG53
Woodleigh Av, N12 44 DE51
Woodleigh Gdns, SW16 121 DL90
Woodley Cl, SW17
off Arnold Rd 120 DF94
Woodley La, Cars. SM5 140 DD104
Woodley Rd, Orp. BR6 146 EW103
Wood Lo Gdns, Brom. BR1 124 EL94
Wood Lo La, W.Wick. BR4 143 EC104
Woodmancote Gdns, W.Byf.
KT14 152 BG113
Woodman La, E4 32 EE43
Woodman Path, Ilf. IG6 49 ES51
Woodman Rd, Brwd. CM14 54 FW50
Coulsdon CR5 175 DJ115
Woodmans Gro, NW10 63 CT64
Woodmans Ms, W12 81 CV71
WOODMANSTERNE, Bans. 174 DD115
⇌ Woodmansterne 175 DH116
Woodmansterne La, Bans.
SM7 174 DB115
Carshalton SM5 158 DF112
Wallington SM6 159 DH111
Woodmansterne Rd, SW16 141 DK95
Carshalton SM5 158 DE109
Coulsdon CR5 175 DJ115
Woodmansterne St, Bans.
SM7 174 DE115
Woodman St, E16 87 EN74
Wood Meads, Epp. CM16 18 EU29
Woodmere, SE9 125 EM88
Woodmere Av, Croy. CR0 143 DX101
Watford WD24 24 BX38
Woodmere Cl, SW11
off Lavender Hill 100 DG83
Croydon CR0 143 DX101
Woodmere Gdns, Croy. CR0 143 DX101
Woodmere Way, Beck. BR3 143 ED99
Woodmount, Swan. BR8 147 FC101
Woodnook Rd, SW16 121 DH92
Woodpecker Cl, N9 30 DV44
Bushey WD23 40 CC46
Cobham KT11 154 BY112
Harrow HA3 41 CF53
Woodpecker Mt, Croy. CR0 161 DY109
Woodpecker Rd, SE14 103 DY79
SE28 88 EW73
Woodpecker Way, Wok.
GU22 166 AX123
Woodplace Cl, Couls. CR5 175 DJ119
Woodplace La, Couls. CR5 175 DJ118
Wood Pt, E16 off Fife Rd 86 EG71
Woodquest Av, SE24 122 DQ85
Woodredon Fm La, Wal.Abb.
EN9 32 EK35
Wood Retreat, SE18 105 ER80
Woodridden Hill, Wal.Abb.
EN9 32 EK35
Wood Ride, Barn. EN4 28 DD39
Orpington BR5 145 ER98
Woodridge Cl, Enf. EN2 29 DN39
Woodridge Way, Nthwd. HA6 39 BS51
Wood Riding, Wok. GU22
off Pyrford Wds Rd 167 BF115
Woodridings Av, Pnr. HA5 40 BZ53
Woodridings Cl, Pnr. HA5 40 BY52
Woodriffe Rd, E11 67 ED59
Wood Ri, Pnr. HA5 59 BU57
Wood Rd, NW10
off Fawood Av 80 CR66
Shepperton TW17 134 BN98
Westerham (Bigg.H.)
TN16 178 EJ118
Woodrow, SE18 105 EM77
Woodrow Av, Hayes UB4 77 BT71
Woodrow Cl, Grnf. UB6 79 CH66
Woodrow Ct, N17
off Heybourne Rd 46 DV52
Woodrush Cl, SE14
off Southerngate Way 103 DY80
Woodrush Way, Rom. RM6 70 EX56
Woods, The, Nthwd. HA6 39 BU50
Radlett WD7 9 CH34
Uxbridge UB10 59 BP63
Wood's Bldgs, E1
off Whitechapel Rd 84 DV71
Woodseer St, E1 84 DT71
Woodsford, SE17
off Portland St 102 DR78
Woodsford Sq, W14 99 CY75
Woodshire Rd, Dag. RM10 71 FB62
Woodshore Cl, Vir.W. GU25 132 AV100
WOODSIDE, Croy. 142 DU100
WOODSIDE, Wat. 7 BU33
◆ Woodside 142 DV100
Woodside, NW11 64 DA57
SW19 119 CZ93
Borehamwood (Elstree)
WD6 26 CM42
Buckhurst Hill IG9 48 EJ47
Epping (Thnwd.) CM16 18 EX27
Leatherhead (Fetch.) KT22 170 CB122
Orpington BR6 164 EU106
Tadworth (Lwr.Kgswd.)
KT20 183 CZ128
Waltham Cross (Chsht.)
EN7 14 DU31
Walton-on-Thames KT12
off Ashley Rd 135 BU102
Watford WD24 23 BU36
Woodside Av, N6 64 DF57
N10 64 DF57
N12 44 DC49
SE25 142 DV100
Chislehurst BR7 125 EQ92
Esher KT10 137 CE101
Walton-on-Thames KT12 153 BV105
Wembley HA0 80 CL67
Woodside Cl, Bexh. DA7 107 FD84
Brentwood CM13 55 GD43
Caterham CR3 176 DS124
Gerrards Cross (Chal.St.P.)
SL9 36 AY54
Rainham RM13 90 FJ70
Stanmore HA7 41 CH50
Surbiton KT5 138 CQ101
Wembley HA0 80 CL67
Woodside Commercial Est,
Epp. (Thnwd.) CM16 18 EX26
Woodside Ct, N12
off Woodside Av 44 DC49
Woodside Ct Rd, Croy. CR0 142 DU101
Woodside Cres, Sid. DA15 125 ES90
Woodside Dr, Dart. DA2 127 FE91
Woodside End, Wem. HA0 80 CL67
Woodside Gdns, E4 47 EB50
N17 46 DS54
Woodside Gra Rd, N12 44 DB49
Woodside Grn, SE25 142 DV100
Woodside Gro, N12 44 DC48
Woodside Hill, Ger.Cr. (Chal.St.P.)
SL9 36 AY54
Woodside La, N12 44 DB48
Bexley DA5 126 EX86
Woodside Ms, SE22
off Heber Rd 122 DT86
⊖ Woodside Park 44 DB49
Woodside Pk, SE25 142 DU99
Woodside Pk Av, E17 67 ED56
Woodside Pk Rd, N12 44 DB49
Woodside Pl, Wem. HA0 80 CL67
Woodside Rd, E13 86 EJ70
N22 45 DM52
SE25 142 DV100
Abbots Langley WD5 7 BV31
Bexleyheath DA7 107 FD84
Bromley BR1 144 EL99
Cobham KT11 154 CA113
Kingston upon Thames KT2 118 CL94
New Malden KT3 138 CR96
Northwood HA6 39 BT52
Purley CR8 159 DK113
St. Albans (Brick.Wd.) AL2 8 BZ30
Sevenoaks TN13 190 FG123
Sevenoaks (Sund.) TN14 180 EX124
Sidcup DA15 125 ES90
Sutton SM1 140 DC104
Watford WD25 7 BV31
Woodford Green IG8 48 EG49
Woodside Way, Croy. CR0 142 DV100
Mitcham CR4 141 DH95
Virginia Water GU25 132 AV97
Woods Ms, W1 194 E10
Woodsome Lo, Wey. KT13 153 BQ107
Woodsome Rd, NW5 64 DG62
Woods Pl, SE1 201 N7
Woodspring Rd, SW19 119 CY89
Woods Rd, SE15 102 DV81
Woodstead Gro, Edg. HA8 42 CL51
Woodstock Av, NW11 63 CY59
W13 97 CG76
Isleworth TW7 117 CG85
Romford RM3 52 FP50
Slough SL3 92 AX77
Southall UB1 78 BZ69
Sutton SM3 139 CZ101
Woodstock Cl, Bex. DA5 126 EZ88
Stanmore HA7 42 CL54
Woking GU21 166 AY116
Woodstock Ct, SE12 124 EG86
Woodstock Cres, N9 30 DV44
Woodstock Dr, Uxb. UB10 58 BL63
Woodstock Gdns, Beck. BR3 143 EB95
Hayes UB4 77 BT71
Ilford IG3 70 EU61
Woodstock Gro, W12 99 CX75
Woodstock La N, Surb. KT6 137 CJ103
Woodstock La S, Chess. KT9 155 CJ105
Esher (Clay.) KT10 155 CH106
Woodstock Ms, W1 194 G7
Woodstock Ri, Sutt. SM3 139 CZ101
Woodstock Rd, E7 86 EJ66
E17 47 ED54
Woodstock Rd, N4 65 DN60
NW11 63 CZ59
W4 98 CS76
Bushey (Bushey Hth.) WD23 41 CE45
Carshalton SM5 158 DG106
Coulsdon CR5
off Chipstead Valley Rd 175 DH116
Croydon CR0 142 DR104
Wembley HA0 80 CM66
Woodstock St, E16
off Victoria Dock Rd 86 EE72
W1 195 H9
Woodstock Ter, E14 85 EB73
Woodstock Way, Mitch. CR4 141 DH96
Woodstone Av, Epsom KT17 157 CU106
⇌ Wood Street 67 EC56
Wood St, E17 67 EC55
EC2 197 J9
W4 98 CS78
Barnet EN5 27 CW42
Grays RM17 110 GC79
Kingston upon Thames KT1 137 CK95
Mitcham CR4 140 DG101
Redhill RH1 185 DJ129
Swanley BR8 148 FJ96
Woodsway, Lthd. (Oxshott)
KT22 155 CE114
Woodsyre, SE26 122 DT91
Woodthorpe Rd, SW15 99 CV84
Ashford TW15 114 BL91
Woodtree Cl, NW4
off Ashley La 43 CW54
Wood Vale, N10 65 DJ57
SE23 122 DV88
Woodvale Av, SE25 142 DT97
Wood Vale Est, SE23 122 DW86
Woodvale Wk, SE27
off Elder Rd 122 DQ92
Woodvale Way, NW11
off The Vale 63 CX62
Woodview, Chess. KT9 155 CJ111
Grays RM16, RM17 110 GE76
Wood Vw, Pot.B. (Cuffley) EN6 13 DL27
Woodview Av, E4 47 EC49
Woodview Cl, N4 65 DP59
SW15 118 CR91
Orpington BR6
off Crofton Rd 145 EQ103
South Croydon CR2 160 DV114
Woodview Rd, Swan. BR8 147 FC96
Woodville, SE3 104 EH81
Woodville Cl, SE12 124 EG85
Teddington TW11 117 CG91
Woodville Ct, Wat. WD17 23 BU40
Woodville Gdns, NW11 63 CX59
W5 80 CL72
Ilford IG6 69 EP55
Ruislip HA4 59 BQ59
Woodville Gro, Well. DA16 106 EU83
Woodville Pl, Cat. CR3 176 DQ121
Gravesend DA12 131 GH87
Woodville Rd, E11 68 EF60
E17 67 DY56
E18 48 EH54
N16 66 DS64
NW6 81 CZ68
NW11 63 CX59
W5 79 CK72
Barnet EN5 28 DB41
Leatherhead KT22 171 CH120
Morden SM4 140 DA98
Richmond TW10 117 CH90
Thornton Heath CR7 142 DQ98
Woodville St, SE18
off Woodhill 104 EL77
Wood Wk, Rick. (Chorl.) WD3 21 BE40
Woodward Av, NW4 63 CU57
Woodward Cl, Esher (Clay.)
KT10 155 CF107
Grays RM17 110 GB77
Woodwarde Rd, SE22 122 DS86
Woodward Gdns, Dag. RM9
off Woodward Rd 88 EW66
Stanmore HA7 41 CF52
Woodward Hts, Grays RM17 110 GB77
Woodward Rd, Dag. RM9 88 EV66
Woodward Ter, Green. DA9 129 FS86
Woodway, Brwd. CM13,
CM15 55 GA46
Wood Way, Orp. BR6 145 EN103
Woodway Cres, Har. HA1 61 CG58
Woodwaye, Wat. WD19 40 BW45
Woodwell St, SW18
off Huguenot Pl 120 DC85
Wood Wf, SE10 103 EB79
Woodwicks, Rick. (Map.Cr.)
WD3 37 BD50
Woodyard, The, Epp. CM16 18 EW28
Woodyard Cl, NW5
off Gillies St 64 DG64
Woodyard La, SE21 122 DS87
Woodyates Rd, SE12 124 EG86
Woolacombe Rd, SE3 104 EJ81
Woolacombe Way, Hayes UB3 95 BS77
Woolbrook Rd, Dart. DA1
off Lower Sta Rd 127 FE86
Wooler St, SE17 102 DR78
Woolf Cl, SE28 88 EV74
Woolf Ms, WC1 off Burton St 83 DK70
Woolf Wk, Til. RM18
off Coleridge Rd 111 GJ82
Woolhampton Way, Chig. IG7 50 EV48
Woolhams, Cat. CR3 186 DT126
Woollard St, Wal.Abb. EN9 15 EC34
Woollaston Rd, N4 65 DP58
Woollett Cl, Dart. (Cray.) DA1 107 FG84
Woolmead Av, NW9 63 CU59
Woolmer Cl, Borwd. WD6 26 CN38
Woolmerdine Ct, Bushey
WD23 24 BX41
Woolmer Gdns, N18 46 DU50
Woolmer Rd, N18 46 DU50
Woolmore St, E14 85 EC73
Woolneigh St, SW6 100 DB83
Woolpack Ho, Enf. EN3 31 DX37
Wool Rd, SW20 119 CV93
Woolstaplers Way, SE16 202 B7
Woolston Cl, E17
off Riverhead Cl 47 DX54
Woolstone Rd, SE23 123 DY89
WOOLWICH, SE18 105 EN78
⇌ Woolwich Arsenal 105 EP77
Woolwich Ch St, SE18 104 EL76
★ Woolwich Common,
SE18 105 EM80
Woolwich Common, SE18 105 EN79
⇌ Woolwich Dockyard 105 EM77
Woolwich Ferry Pier, E16 105 EN75
Woolwich Foot Tunnel, E16 105 EN75
SE18 105 EN75
Woolwich Garrison, SE18 105 EM79
Woolwich High St, SE18 105 EN76
Woolwich Ind Est, SE28
off Hadden Rd 105 ES76
Woolwich Manor Way, E6 87 EM70
E16 105 EP75
Woolwich Mkt, SE18 105 EP77
Woolwich New Rd, SE18 105 EN78
Woolwich Rd, SE2 106 EX79
SE7 104 EG78
SE10 205 K10
Belvedere DA17 106 EX79
Bexleyheath DA7 106 FA84
Wooster Gdns, E14 85 ED72
Wooster Ms, Har. HA2
off Fairfield Dr 60 CC55
Wooster Pl, SE1 201 L8
Wootton Cl, Epsom KT18 173 CT115
Hornchurch RM11 72 FK57
Wootton Gro, N3 44 DA53
Wootton St, SE1 200 E4
Worbeck Rd, SE20 142 DV96
Worcester Av, N17 46 DU52
Upminster RM14 73 FT61
Worcester Cl, NW2
off Newfield Ri 63 CV62
Croydon CR0 143 DZ103
Gravesend (Istead Rise)
DA13 131 GF94
Greenhithe DA9 109 FV84
Mitcham CR4 141 DH97
Worcester Ct, Walt. KT12
off Rodney Rd 136 BW102
Worcester Cres, NW7 42 CS48
Woodford Green IG8 48 EH50
Worcester Dr, W4 98 CS75
Ashford TW15 115 BP93
Worcester Gdns, SW11
off Grandison Rd 120 DF85
Greenford UB6 78 CC65
Ilford IG1 68 EL59
Worcester Park KT4 138 CS104
Worcester Ms, NW6
off Lymington Rd 82 DB65
WORCESTER PARK 139 CT103
⇌ Worcester Park 139 CU102
Worcester Pk Rd, Wor.Pk.
KT4 138 CQ104
Worcester Rd, E12 69 EM63
E17 47 DX54
SW19 119 CZ92
Reigate RH2 184 DA133
Sutton SM2 158 DB107
Uxbridge UB8 76 BJ71
Worcesters Av, Enf. EN1 30 DU38
Wordsworth Av, E12 86 EL65
E18 68 EF55
Greenford UB6 79 CD68
Kenley CR8 off Valley Rd 176 DR115
Wordsworth Cl, Rom. RM3 52 FJ53
Tilbury RM18 111 GJ82
Wordsworth Dr, Sutt. SM3 157 CW105
Wordsworth Mead, Red. RH1 184 DG132
Wordsworth Rd, N16 66 DS63
SE1 201 P9
SE20 123 DX94
Addlestone KT15 152 BK105
Hampton TW12 116 BZ91
Wallington SM6 159 DJ107
Welling DA16 105 ES81
Wordsworth Wk, NW11 64 DA56
Wordsworth Way, Dart. DA1 108 FN84
West Drayton UB7 94 BL77
Worfield St, SW11 100 DE80
Worgan St, SE11 200 B10
SE16 203 J7
Worland Rd, E15 86 EE66
WORLD'S END, Enf. 29 DN41
World's End, Cob. KT11 153 BU114
World's End Est, SW10 100 DD80
Worlds End La, N21 29 DM43
Enfield EN2 29 DM43
Orpington BR6 163 ET107
World's End Pas, SW10
off Riley St 100 DD80
World's End Pl, SW10
off King's Rd 100 DC80
Worlidge St, W6 99 CW78
Worlingham Rd, SE22 102 DT84
Wormholt Rd, W12 81 CU73
Wormley Ct, Wal.Abb. EN9
off Winters Way 16 EG33
Wormwood St, EC2 197 M8
Wormyngford Ct, Wal.Abb. EN9
off Ninefields 16 EG33
Wornington Rd, W10 81 CY71
Woronzow Rd, NW8 82 DD67
Worple, The, Stai. (Wrays.)
TW19 113 AZ86
Worple Av, SW19 119 CX94
Isleworth TW7 117 CG85
Staines TW18 114 BH93
Worple Cl, Har. HA2 60 BZ60
Worple Rd, SW19 119 CY94
SW20 139 CW96
Epsom KT18 156 CS114
Isleworth TW7 97 CG84
Leatherhead KT22 171 CH123
Staines TW18 114 BH94
Worple Rd Ms, SW19 119 CZ93
⇌ Worplesdon 166 AV124

Worple St, SW14 98 CR83
Worple Way, Har. HA2 60 BZ60
Richmond TW10 118 CL85
Worrin Cl, Brwd. CM15 55 FZ46
Worrin Rd, Brwd. CM15 55 FZ47
Worsfold Cl, Wok. (Send) GU23 167 BB123
Worships Hill, Sev. TN13 190 FE123
Worship St, EC2 197 L5
Worslade Rd, SW17 120 DD91
Worsley Br Rd, SE26 123 DZ91
Beckenham BR3 123 DZ92
Worsley Gro, E5 66 DU63
Worsley Rd, E11 68 EE63
Worsopp Dr, SW4 121 DJ85
Worsted Grn, Red. RH1 185 DJ129
Worth Cl, Orp. BR6 163 ES105
Worthfield Cl, Epsom KT19 156 CR108
Worth Gro, SE17
off Merrow St 102 DR78
Worthing Cl, E15 off Mitre Rd 86 EE68
Grays RM20 110 FY79
Worthing Rd, Houns. TW5 96 BZ79
Worthington Cl, Mitch. CR4 141 DH97
Worthington Rd, Surb. KT6 138 CM102
Worthy Down Ct, SE18
off Prince Imperial Rd 105 EN81
Wortley Rd, E6 86 EK66
Croydon CR0 141 DN101
Worton Gdns, Islw. TW7 97 CD82
Worton Hall Ind Est, Islw. TW7 97 CE84
Worton Rd, Islw. TW7 97 CE83
Worton Way, Houns. TW3 97 CD82
Isleworth TW7 96 CC81
Wotton Grn, Orp. BR5 146 EX98
Wotton Rd, NW2 63 CW63
SE8 103 DZ79
Wotton Way, Sutt. SM2 157 CW110
Wouldham Rd, E16 86 EF72
Grays RM20 110 FY79
Wrabness Way, Stai. TW18 134 BH95
Wragby Rd, E11 68 EE62
Wrampling Pl, N9 46 DU46
Wrangley Ct, Wal.Abb. EN9 16 EG33
Wrangthorn Wk, Croy. CR0
off Epsom Rd 159 DN105
Wray Av, Ilf. IG5 69 EN55
Wray Cl, Horn. RM11 72 FJ59
Wray Common, Reig. RH2 184 DD132
Wray Common Rd, Reig. RH2 184 DC133
Wray Cres, N4 65 DL61
Wrayfield Av, Reig. RH2 184 DC133
Wrayfield Rd, Sutt. SM3 139 CX104
Wraylands Dr, Reig. RH2 184 DD132
Wray La, Reig. RH2 184 DC130
Wray Mill Pk, Reig. RH2 184 DD132
Wray Pk Rd, Reig. RH2 184 DB133
Wray Rd, Sutt. SM2 157 CZ109
WRAYSBURY, Stai. 113 AZ86
⇌ Wraysbury 113 BA86
Wraysbury Cl, Houns. TW4
off Dorney Way 116 BY85
Wraysbury Gdns, Stai. TW19 113 BE91
Wraysbury Rd, Stai. TW18, TW19 113 BC90
Wrays Way, Hayes UB4
off Balmoral Dr 77 BS70
Wrekin Rd, SE18 105 EQ80
Wren Av, NW2 63 CW64
Southall UB2 96 BZ77
Wren Cl, E16 off Ibbotson Av 86 EF72
N9 off Chaffinch Cl 47 DX46
Orpington BR5 146 EX97
South Croydon CR2 161 DX109
Wren Ct, Slou. SL3
off New Rd 93 BA76
Wren Cres, Add. KT15 152 BK106
Bushey WD23 40 CC46
Wren Dr, Wal.Abb. EN9 16 EG34
West Drayton UB7 94 BK76
Wren Gdns, Dag. RM9 70 EX64
Hornchurch RM12 71 FF60
Wren Landing, E14 204 A2
Wren Ms, SE13
off Lee High Rd 104 EE84
Wren Path, SE28 105 ER76
Wren Pl, Brwd. CM14 54 FX48
Wren Rd, SE5 102 DR81
Dagenham RM9 70 EX64
Sidcup DA14 126 EW91
Wrens Av, Ashf. TW15 115 BQ92
Wrens Cft, Grav. (Nthflt.) DA11 130 GE91
Wrens Hill, Lthd. (Oxshott) KT22 170 CC115
Wren St, WC1 196 C4
Wren Ter, Ilf. IG5
off Tiptree Cres 69 EN55
Wrentham Av, NW10 81 CX68
Wrenthorpe Rd, Brom. BR1 124 EE91
Wren Wk, Til. RM18 111 GH80
Wrenwood Way, Pnr. HA5 59 BV56
Wrestlers Ct, EC3
off Camomile St 84 DS72
Wrexham Rd, E3 85 EA68
Romford RM3 52 FK48
Wricklemarsh Rd, SE3 104 EH81
Wrigglesworth St, SE14 103 DX80
Wright Cl, Swans. DA10
off Milton St 129 FX86
Wright Gdns, Shep. TW17
off Laleham Rd 134 BN99
Wright Rd, N1 off Burder Cl 84 DS65
Hounslow TW5 96 BW80
Wrights All, SW19 119 CW93
Wrightsbridge Rd, Brwd. CM14 52 FN46
Wrights Cl, SE13
off Wisteria Rd 103 ED84
Dagenham RM10 71 FB62
Wrights Grn, SW4
off Nelson's Row 101 DK84
Wrights La, W8 100 DB75
Wrights Pl, NW10
off Mitchell Way 80 CQ65
Wrights Rd, E3 85 DZ68
SE25 142 DS97
Wrights Row, Wall. SM6 159 DH105
Wrights Wk, SW14 98 CR83
Wrigley Cl, E4 47 ED50
Wriotsley Way, Add. KT15
off Coombelands La 152 BG107
Writtle Wk, Rain. RM13 89 FF67
★ Wrotham Park, Barn. EN5 27 CZ36
Wrotham Pk, Barn. EN5 27 CZ36
Wrotham Rd, NW1
off Agar Pl 83 DJ66
W13 off Mattock La 79 CH74
Barnet EN5 27 CY40
Gravesend DA11, DA13 131 GG88
Welling DA16 106 EW81
Wroths Path, Loug. IG10 33 EM39
Wrottesley Rd, NW10 81 CU68
SE18 105 EQ79
Wroughton Rd, SW11 120 DF86
Wroughton Ter, NW4 63 CW56
Wroxall Rd, Dag. RM9 88 EW65
Wroxham Gdns, N11 45 DJ52
Enfield EN2 29 DN35
Potters Bar EN6 11 CX31
Wroxham Rd, SE28 88 EX73
Wroxton Rd, SE15 102 DV82
WRYTHE, THE, Cars. 140 DE103
Wrythe Grn, Cars. SM5
off Wrythe Grn Rd 140 DF104
Wrythe Grn Rd, Cars. SM5 140 DF104
Wrythe La, Cars. SM5 140 DC102
Wulfstan St, W12 81 CT72
Wulstan Pk, Pot.B. EN6
off Tempest Av 12 DD32
Wyatt Cl, SE16 203 M5
Bushey (Bushey Hth.) WD23 41 CE45
Feltham TW13 116 BW88
Hayes UB4 77 BU71
Wyatt Dr, SW13 99 CW80
Wyatt Pk Rd, SW2 121 DL89
Wyatt Rd, E7 86 EG65
N5 66 DQ62
Dartford DA1 107 FF83
Staines TW18 114 BG92
Wyatts Cl, Rick. (Chorl.) WD3 22 BG41
Wyatt's Covert Caravan Site, Uxb. (Denh.) UB9 57 BF56
Wyatts La, E17 67 EC55
Wyatts Rd, Rick. (Chorl.) WD3 21 BF42
Wybert St, NW1 195 J4
Wyborne Way, NW10 80 CQ66
Wyburn Av, Barn. EN5 27 CZ41
Wyche Gro, S.Croy. CR2 160 DQ108
Wych Elm Cl, Horn. RM11 72 FN59
Wych Elm Dr, Brom. BR1
off London La 124 EF94
Wych Elm Pas, Kings.T. KT2 118 CM94
Wych Elm Rd, Horn. RM11 72 FN58
Wych Elms, St.Alb. (Park St.) AL2 8 CB28
Wycherley Cl, SE3 104 EF80
Wycherley Cres, Barn. EN5 28 DB44
Wych Hill, Wok. GU22 166 AW119
Wych Hill La, Wok. GU22 166 AY119
Wych Hill Pk, Wok. GU22 166 AX119
Wych Hill Ri, Wok. GU22 166 AW119
Wych Hill Way, Wok. GU22 166 AX120
Wychwood Av, Edg. HA8 41 CK51
Thornton Heath CR7 142 DQ97
Wychwood Cl, Edg. HA8 41 CK51
Sunbury-on-Thames TW16 115 BU93
Wychwood End, N6 65 DJ59
Wychwood Gdns, Ilf. IG5 69 EM56
Wychwood Way, SE19
off Roman Ri 122 DR93
Northwood HA6 39 BT52
Wycliffe Cl, Well. DA16 105 ET81
Wycliffe Ct, Abb.L. WD5 7 BS32
Wycliffe Rd, SW11 100 DG82
SW19 120 DB93
Wycliffe Row, Grav. (Nthflt.) DA11 131 GF88
Wyclif St, EC1 196 F3
Wycombe Gdns, NW11 64 DA61
Wycombe Pl, SW18 120 DC86
Wycombe Rd, N17 46 DU53
Ilford IG2 69 EM57
Wembley HA0 80 CN67
Wydehurst Rd, Croy. CR0 142 DU101
Wydell Cl, Mord. SM4 139 CW100
Wydeville Manor Rd, SE12 124 EH91
Wyecliffe Gdns, Red. RH1 185 DJ130
Wye Cl, Ashf. TW15 115 BP91
Orpington BR6 145 ET101
Ruislip HA4 59 BQ58
Wyedale, St.Alb. (Lon.Col.) AL2 10 CM27
Wyemead Cres, E4 48 EE47
Wye Rd, Grav. DA12 131 GK89
Wye St, SW11 100 DD82
Wyeth's Ms, Epsom KT17 157 CT113
Wyeths Rd, Epsom KT17 157 CT113
Wyevale Cl, Pnr. HA5 59 BU55
Wyfields, Ilf. IG5
off Ravensbourne Gdns 49 EP53
Wyfold Ho, SE2
off Wolvercote Rd 106 EX75
Wyfold Rd, SW6 99 CY80
Wyhill Wk, Dag. RM10 89 FC65
Wyke Cl, Islw. TW7 97 CF79
Wyke Gdns, W7 97 CG76
Wykeham Av, Dag. RM9 88 EW65
Hornchurch RM11 72 FK58
Wykeham Cl, Grav. DA12 131 GL93
West Drayton UB7 94 BN78
Wykeham Grn, Dag. RM9 88 EW65
Wykeham Hill, Wem. HA9 62 CM60
Wykeham Ri, N20 43 CY46
Wykeham Rd, NW4 63 CW57
Harrow HA3 61 CH56
Wyke Rd, E3 85 EA66
SW20 139 CW96
Wylands Rd, Slou. SL3 93 BA77
Wylchin Cl, Pnr. HA5 59 BT56
Wyldes Cl, NW11
off Wildwood Rd 64 DC60
Wyldfield Gdns, N9 46 DT47
Wyld Way, Wem. HA9 80 CP65
Wyleu St, SE23 123 DY87
Wylie Rd, Sthl. UB2 96 CA76
Wyllen Cl, E1 84 DW70
Wyllyotts Cl, Pot.B. EN6 11 CZ32
Wyllyotts La, Pot.B. EN6 11 CZ32
Wyllyotts Pl, Pot.B. EN6 11 CZ32
Wylo Dr, Barn. EN5 27 CU44
Wymering Rd, W9 82 DA69
Wymond St, SW15 99 CW83
Wynan Rd, E14 204 B10
Wynash Gdns, Cars. SM5 158 DE106
Wynaud Ct, N22
off Palmerston Rd 45 DM51
Wyncham Av, Sid. DA15 125 ES88
Wynchgate, N14 45 DK46
N21 45 DL46
Harrow HA3 41 CE52
Wyncote Way, S.Croy. CR2 161 DX109
Wyncroft Cl, Brom. BR1 145 EM97
Wyndale Av, NW9 62 CN58
Wyndcliff Rd, SE7 104 EH79
Wyndcroft Cl, Enf. EN2 29 DP41
Wyndham Av, Cob. KT11 153 BU113
Wyndham Cl, Orp. BR6 145 EQ102
Sutton SM2 158 DA108
Wyndham Cres, N19 65 DJ62
Hounslow TW4 116 CA86
Wyndham Est, SE5 102 DQ80
Wyndham Ms, W1 194 D7
Wyndham Pl, W1 194 D7
Wyndham Rd, E6 86 EK66
SE5 101 DP80
W13 97 CH76
Barnet EN4 44 DF46
Kingston upon Thames KT2 118 CM94
Woking GU21 166 AV118
Wyndham St, W1 194 D6
Wyndham Yd, W1 194 D7
Wyneham Rd, SE24 122 DR85
Wynell Rd, SE23 123 DX90
Wynford Gro, Orp. BR5 146 EV97
Wynford Pl, Belv. DA17 106 FA79
Wynford Rd, N1 83 DM68
Wynford Way, SE9 125 EM90
Wynlie Gdns, Pnr. HA5 39 BV54
Wynn Br Cl, Wdf.Grn. IG8
off Chigwell Rd 48 EJ53
Wynndale Rd, E18 48 EH53
Wynne Rd, SW9 101 DN82
Wynns Av, Sid. DA15 126 EU85
Wynnstay Gdns, W8 100 DA76
Wynnstow Pk, Oxt. RH8 188 EF131
Wynter St, SW11 100 DC84
Wynton Gdns, SE25 142 DT99
Wynton Gro, Walt. KT12 135 BU104
Wynton Pl, W3 80 CP72
Wynyard Cl, Rick. (Sarratt) WD3 22 BG36
Wynyard Ter, SE11 200 C10
Wynyatt St, EC1 196 F3
Wyre Gro, Edg. HA8 42 CP48
Hayes UB3 95 BU77
Wyresdale Cres, Grnf. UB6 79 CF69
Wyteleaf Cl, Ruis. HA4 59 BQ58
Wythburn Pl, W1 194 D9
Wythenshawe Rd, Dag. RM10 70 FA62
Wythens Wk, SE9 125 EP86
Wythes Cl, Brom. BR1 145 EM96
Wythes Rd, E16 86 EL74
Wythfield Rd, SE9 125 EM86
Wyvenhoe Rd, Har. HA2 60 CC62
Wyvern Cl, Dart. DA1 128 FJ87
Orpington BR6 146 EV104
Wyvern Est, N.Mal. KT3 139 CU98
Wyvern Gro, Hayes UB3 95 BP80
Wyvern Pl, Add. KT15
off Green La 152 BH105
Wyvern Rd, Pur. CR8 159 DP110
Wyvern Way, Uxb. UB8 76 BH66
Wyvil Est, SW8
off Luscombe Way 101 DL80
Wyvil Rd, SW8 101 DL79
Wyvis St, E14 85 EB71

Y

Yabsley St, E14 204 E2
Yaffle Rd, Wey. KT13 153 BQ110
Yalding Cl, Orp. BR5 146 EX98
Yalding Rd, SE16 202 B7
Yale Cl, Houns. TW4
off Bramley Way 116 BZ85
Yale Way, Horn. RM12 71 FG63
Yaohan Plaza, NW9 62 CR55
Yarborough Rd, SW19 140 DD95
Yarbridge Cl, Sutt. SM2 158 DB110
Yardley Cl, E4 31 EB43
Reigate RH2 184 DB132
Yardley Ct, Sutt. SM3
off Hemingford Rd 157 CW105
Yardley La, E4 31 EB43
Yardley St, WC1 196 D3
Yard Mead, Egh. TW20 113 BA90
Yarm Cl, Lthd. KT22 171 CJ123
Yarm Ct Rd, Lthd. KT22 171 CJ123
Yarmouth Cres, N17 66 DV57
Yarmouth Pl, W1 199 H3
Yarmouth Rd, Wat. WD24 24 BW38
Yarm Way, Lthd. KT22 171 CJ123
Yarnfield Sq, SE15
off Clayton Rd 102 DU81
Yarnton Way, SE2 106 EX75
Erith DA18 106 EZ76
Yarrow Cres, E6 86 EL71
Yarrowfield, Wok. GU22 166 AX123
Yarrowside, Amer. HP7 20 AV41
Yateley St, SE18 104 EK76
Yates Ct, NW2 81 CX65
YEADING, Hayes 77 BV69
Yeading Av, Har. HA2 60 BY61
Yeading Fork, Hayes UB4 78 BW71
Yeading Gdns, Hayes UB4 77 BV71
Yeading La, Hayes UB4 77 BV72
Northolt UB5 78 BW69
Yeames Cl, W13 79 CG72
Yeate St, N1 84 DR66
Yeatman Rd, N6 64 DF58
Yeats Cl, NW10 80 CS65
SE13 off Eliot Pk 103 ED82
Yeats Ct, N15
off Tynemouth Rd 66 DT56
Ye Cor, Wat. WD19 24 BY44
Yeend Cl, W.Mol. KT8 136 CA98
Yeldham Rd, W6 99 CX78
Yellow Hammer Ct, NW9
off Eagle Dr 42 CS54
Yellowpine Way, Chig. IG7 50 EV49
Yelverton Cl, Rom. RM3 52 FK53
Yelverton Rd, SW11 100 DD82
Yenston Cl, Mord. SM4 140 DA100
Yeoman Cl, E6 off Ferndale St 87 EP73
SE27 121 DP90
Yeoman Rd, Nthlt. UB5 78 BY66
Yeomanry Cl, Epsom KT17
off Dirdene Gdns 157 CT112
Yeomans Acre, Ruis. HA4 59 BU58
Yeomans Keep, Rick. (Chorl.) WD3
off Rickmansworth Rd 21 BF41
Yeomans Meadow, Sev. TN13 190 FG126
Yeoman's Ms, Islw. TW7
off Queensbridge Pk 117 CE85
Yeoman's Row, SW3 198 C7
Yeoman St, SE8 203 K8
Yeomans Way, Enf. EN3 30 DW40
Yeomans Yd, E1
off Chamber St 84 DT73
Yeomen Way, Ilf. IG6 49 EQ51
Yeo St, E3 85 EB71
Yeoveney Cl, Stai. TW19 113 BD89
Yeovil Cl, Orp. BR6 145 ES103
Yeovilton Pl, Kings.T. KT2 117 CJ92
Yerbury Rd, N19 65 DK62
Yester Dr, Chis. BR7 124 EL94
Yester Pk, Chis. BR7 125 EM94
Yester Rd, Chis. BR7 125 EM94
Yevele Way, Horn. RM11 72 FL59
Yew Av, West Dr. UB7 76 BL73
Yewbank Cl, Ken. CR8 176 DR115
Yew Cl, Buck.H. IG9 48 EK47
Waltham Cross EN7 14 DS27
Yewdale Cl, Brom. BR1 124 EE93
Yewdells Cl, Bet. (Buckland) RH3 183 CU133
Yewfield Rd, NW10 81 CT66
Yew Gro, NW2 63 CX63
Yewlands Cl, Bans. SM7 174 DC115
Yew Pl, Wey. KT13 135 BT104
Yews, The, Ashf. TW15 115 BP91
Gravesend DA12 131 GK88
Yews Av, Enf. EN1 30 DV36
Yew Tree Bottom Rd, Epsom KT17, KT18 173 CV116
Yew Tree Cl, N21 45 DN45
Yewtree Cl, N22 45 DJ53
Yew Tree Cl, Brwd. CM13 55 GB44
Chesham (Ley Hill) HP5
off Botley Rd 4 AU30
Coulsdon CR5 174 DF119
Yewtree Cl, Har. HA2 60 CB56
Yew Tree Cl, Sev. TN13 190 FD123
Welling DA16 106 EU81
Worcester Park KT4 138 CS102
Yew Tree Ct, Borwd. (Elstree)
WD6 off Barnet La 25 CK44
Yew Tree Dr, Cat. CR3 186 DT125
Hemel Hempstead (Bov.) HP3 5 BB28
Yewtree End, St.Alb. (Park St.) AL2 8 CB27
Yew Tree Gdns, Epsom KT18 172 CP115
Romford RM7 71 FD57
Romford (Chad.Hth.) RM6 70 EY57
Yew Tree La, Reig. RH2 184 DB131
Yew Tree Rd, W12 81 CT73
Yewtree Rd, Beck. BR3 143 DZ97
Yew Tree Rd, Slou. SL1 92 AU76
Uxbridge UB10 76 BM67
Yew Trees, Egh. TW20 133 BC97
Shepperton TW17
off Laleham Rd 134 BM98
Yew Tree Wk, Houns. TW4 116 BZ85
Purley CR8 160 DQ110
Yew Tree Way, Croy. CR0 161 DY110
Yew Wk, Har. HA1 61 CE60
YIEWSLEY, West Dr. 76 BL74
Yoakley Rd, N16 66 DS61
Yoke Cl, N7 off Ewe Cl 83 DL65
Yolande Gdns, SE9 124 EL85
Yonge Pk, N4 65 DN62
York Av, SW14 118 CQ85
W7 79 CE74
Hayes UB3 77 BQ71
Sidcup DA15 125 ES89
Stanmore HA7 41 CH53
York Br, NW1 194 F4
York Bldgs, WC2 200 A1
York Cl, E6 off Boultwood Rd 87 EM72
W7 off York Av 79 CE74
Amersham HP7 20 AT39
Brentwood CM15 55 FZ45
Kings Langley WD4 6 BN29
Morden SM4 140 DB98
West Byfleet (Byfleet) KT14 152 BL112
York Cres, Borwd. WD6 26 CR40
Loughton IG10 32 EL41
Yorke Gdns, Reig. RH2 184 DA133
Yorke Gate Rd, Cat. CR3 176 DR122
Yorke Rd, Reig. RH2 183 CZ133
Rickmansworth (Crox.Grn.) WD3 22 BN44
York Gdns, Walt. KT12 136 BX103
York Gate, N14 45 DL45
NW1 194 F5
York Gro, SE15 102 DW81
York Hill, SE27 121 DP90
Loughton IG10 32 EL41
York Hill Est, SE27 121 DP90
York Ho, Wem. HA9 62 CM63
York Ho Pl, W8 100 DB75
Yorkland Av, Well. DA16 105 ET83
York Ms, NW5
off Kentish Town Rd 65 DH64
Ilford IG1
off York Rd 69 EN62
York Par, Brent. TW8 97 CK78
York Pl, SW11 100 DD83
WC2 200 A1
Dagenham RM10 89 FC65
Grays RM17 110 GA79
Ilford IG1
off York Rd 69 EN61
York Ri, NW5 65 DH62
Orpington BR6 145 ES102
York Rd, E4 47 EA50
E7 86 EG65
E10 67 EC62
E17 67 DX57
N11 45 DK51
N18 46 DV51
N21 46 DR45
SE1 200 C4
SW11 100 DC83
SW18 100 DC83
SW19 120 DC93
W3 80 CQ72
W5 97 CJ76
Barnet EN5 28 DD43
Brentford TW8 97 CK78
Brentwood CM15 55 FZ45
Croydon CR0 141 DN101
Dartford DA1 128 FM87
Epping (N.Wld.Bas.) CM16 18 FA27
Gravesend DA12 131 GJ90
Gravesend (Nthflt.) DA11 130 GD87
Hounslow TW3 96 CB83
Ilford IG1 69 EN62
Kingston upon Thames KT2 118 CM94
Northwood HA6 39 BU54
Rainham RM13 89 FD66
Richmond TW10
off Albert Rd 118 CM85
South Croydon CR2 161 DX110
Sutton SM2 158 DA107
Teddington TW11 117 CE91
Uxbridge UB8 76 BK66
Waltham Cross EN8 15 DY34
Watford WD18 24 BW43
West Byfleet (Byfleet) KT14 152 BK112
Westerham (Bigg.H.) TN16 178 EH119
Weybridge KT13 153 BQ105
Woking GU22 166 AY118
Yorkshire Cl, N16 66 DS62
Yorkshire Gdns, N18 46 DV50
Yorkshire Grey Pl, NW3
off Heath St 64 DC63
Yorkshire Grey Yd, WC1 196 B7
Yorkshire Rd, E14 85 DY72
Mitcham CR4 141 DL99
York Sq, E14 85 DY72
York St, W1 194 E6
Barking IG11 off Abbey Rd 87 EQ67
Mitcham CR4 140 DG101
Twickenham TW1 117 CG88
York Ter, Enf. EN2 30 DQ38
Erith DA8 107 FC81
York Ter E, NW1 194 G5
York Ter W, NW1 194 F5
Yorkton St, E2 84 DU68
York Way, N1 83 DL67
N7 83 DK65
N20 44 DF48
Borehamwood WD6 26 CR40
Chessington KT9 156 CL108
Feltham TW13 116 BZ90
Watford WD25 24 BX36
York Way Ct, N1 83 DL67
York Way Est, N7 off York Way 83 DL65
Youngmans Cl, Enf. EN2 30 DQ39
Young Rd, E16 86 EJ72
Young's Bldgs, EC1 197 J4
★ Young's Ram Brewery, SW18 120 DB85
Youngs Rd, Ilf. IG2 69 ER57
Young St, W8 100 DB75
Youngstroat La, Wok. GU21, GU24 150 AY110
Yoxley App, Ilf. IG2 69 EQ58
Yoxley Dr, Ilf. IG2 69 EQ58
Yukon Rd, SW12 121 DH87
Yule Cl, St.Alb. (Brick.Wd.) AL2 8 BZ30
Yuletide Cl, NW10 80 CS66
Yunus Khan Cl, E17 67 EA57

Z

Zampa Rd, SE16 102 DW78
Zander Ct, E2
off St. Peter's Cl 84 DU68
Zangwill Rd, SE3 104 EK81
Zealand Av, West Dr. UB7 94 BK80
Zealand Rd, E3 85 DY68
Zelah Rd, Orp. BR5 146 EV101
Zeland Cl, NW2 63 CW60
Zennor Rd, SW12 121 DJ88
Zenoria St, SE22 102 DT84
Zermatt Rd, Th.Hth. CR7 142 DQ98
Zetland St, E14 85 EB71
Zig Zag Rd, Ken. CR8 176 DQ116
Zion Pl, Grav. DA12 131 GH87
Thornton Heath CR7 142 DR98
Zion Rd, Th.Hth. CR7 142 DR98
Zion St, Sev. (Seal) TN15
off Church Rd 191 FM121
Zoar St, SE1 201 H2
Zoffany St, N19 65 DK61

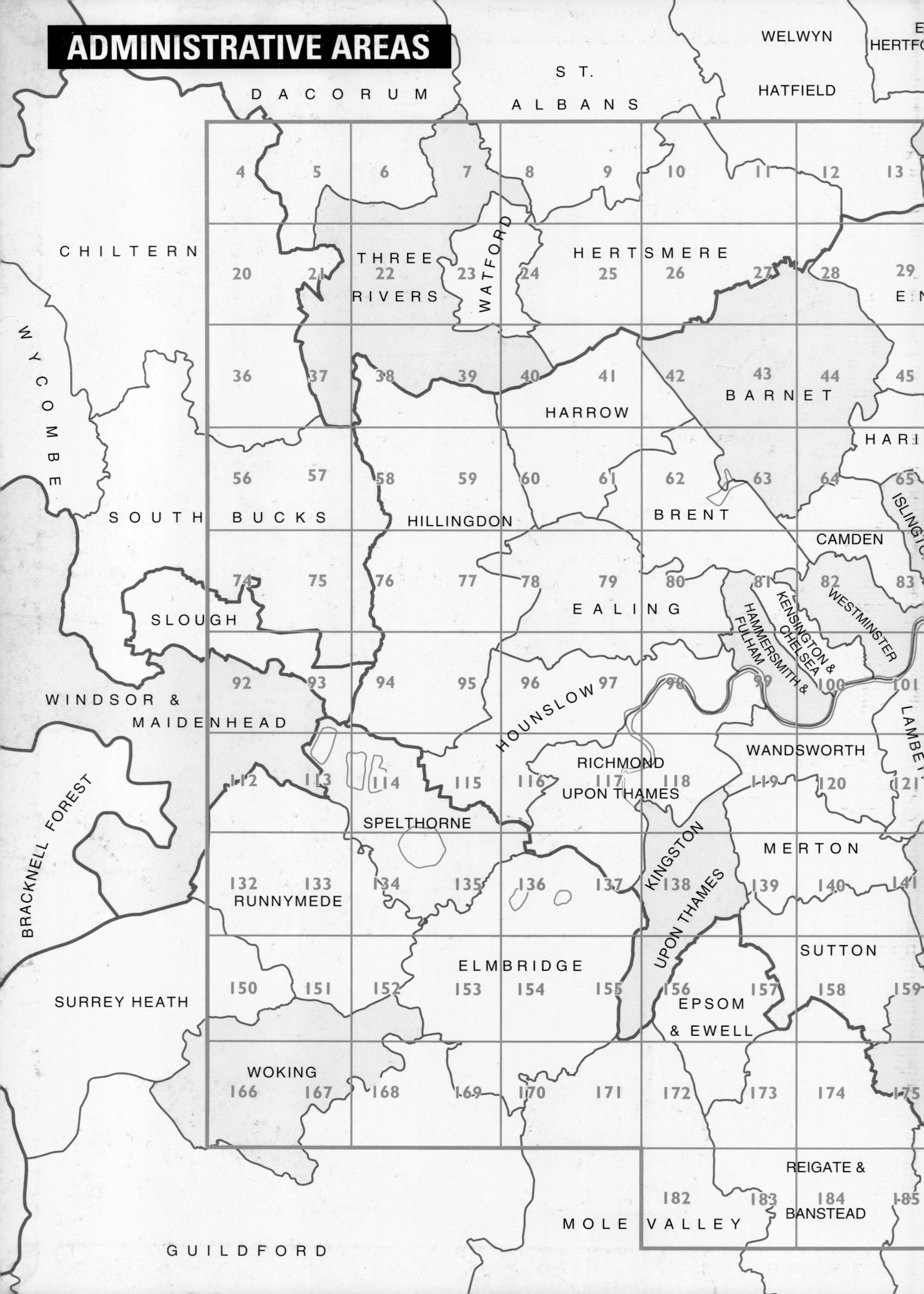